The Facts On File

STUDENT'S DICTIONARY
OF AMERICAN ENGLISH

Cynthia A. Barnhart

An imprint of Infobase Publishing

Facts On File, Inc.
An imprint of Infobase Publishing
132 West 31st Street
New York NY 10001

Library of Congress Cataloging-in-Publication Data
Barnhart, Cynthia A.
The Facts on File student's dictionary of American English / Cynthia Barnhart.
p. cm.
ISBN-13: 978-0-8160-6379-6 (alk. paper)
1. English language—Dictionaries, Juvenile.   2. English language—Dictionaries.
I. Facts on File, Inc.   II. Title.   III. Title: Student's dictionary of American English.
PE1628.5.B38   2007
423—dc22   2007023460

Facts On File books are available at special discounts when purchased in bulk quantities for businesses, associations, institutions, or sales promotions. Please call our Special Sales Department in New York at (212) 967-8800 or (800) 322-8755.

You can find Facts On File on the World Wide Web at http://www.factsonfile.com

Text design by Erika Arroyo
Cover design by Salvatore Luongo

Printed in the United States of America

VB CGI 10 9 8 7 6 5 4 3 2 1

This book is printed on acid-free paper.

CONTENTS

PREFACE

The first purpose of any student's dictionary is to provide the basic information necessary to be able to understand a meaning, decipher a pronunciation, make a correct syllable break, and employ vocabulary appropriate to a particular situation. *The Facts On File Student's Dictionary of American English* is designed to provide such information as accurately, concisely, and clearly as possible. Its modest entry list of about 90,000 words includes the vocabulary most of us use every day in ordinary writing and encounter in reading a newspaper, novel, magazine, or online article. It also includes a selection of widely used new terms in English from science and technology and contemporary American culture.

Each entry of the standard vocabulary has been evaluated and revised according to current usage. The English language often adds new meanings to "old words," which have been pressed into service to describe changing times, perceptions, and attitudes. In order to call attention to extended and new meanings for older words, the editor of this dictionary has made free use of the label *Fig.* (Figurative) to mark usages that have strayed from the bounds of a term's core meaning. Such adaptability is surely what makes English a lively and inventive language.

Along with abundant use of the figurative label, this *Student's Dictionary of American English* radically differs from more expansive dictionaries, and even collegiate dictionaries, in its concise treatment of function words—*come, have, go, for, open,* etc. These are the words so essential to the basic formulations of English that traditional dictionaries often identify scores of meanings for them. Except for the language specialist, most of these meanings are separated

by so little difference that the ordinary student or general user is hard pressed to understand the distinction. In this dictionary, such entries have been trimmed to *core* meanings; *shades* of meaning are illustrated by phrases or sentences that follow a definition, not by different definitions entirely.

The editor has eschewed overreliance on usage labels (*Slang, Informal*) as well, using them only where the user should be alerted to the level of use, so that an informed decision can be made as to whether a particular word is appropriate to a particular context. Likewise, archaic vocabulary has been systematically reduced to those poetic archaisms and other vestiges of ancient vocabulary that students are most likely to encounter. The argument that a student might encounter a particular archaic term does not outweigh the necessity of using available space in the dictionary to cover more completely current usage of words whose definitions have expanded in recent years. While a glossary in a literary text will most likely define an archaism, it will not do the same for the expanded meanings of terms such as *marriage* or *partner,* which today have new and different meanings in addition to their core meanings.

Any dictionary is a reflection of the work of many people who have contributed their ideas and knowledge of language to the long line of dictionaries compiled over the years, and any new dictionary draws heavily on works that have preceded it. The editor has drawn on the experience, expertise, and traditions of the people and tools of the dictionary trade. One such tool, without which the dictionary would descend into a personal account of today's English, is a citation file, the editor's primary source. It is a collection of examples of vocabulary and usage taken from contemporary newspapers, magazines, journals, novels—and including, transcripts of television and radio broadcasts, newsletters, and other casual written materials. This editor had unrestricted access to one of the word's largest citation files of American English.

This editor has benefited greatly from the advice and assistance of many people, includ-ing Robert K. Barnhart, an especially gifted and experienced dictionary maker whose insights and balanced views have been of great value. And without the help of Albert Crocco and Vivien Gentile, individuals willing to number, check, copy, and keep pages in order, the project would surely have foundered.

Cynthia A. Barnhart
Garrison, New York, 2007

EXPLANATORY NOTES

The Facts On File Student's Dictionary of American English is a dictionary for the general user who has questions about contemporary English vocabulary. The following notes explain how the dictionary is organized to make it easier for the user to find information.

ORGANIZATION

The **entries** in the dictionary are arranged in one alphabetical list.

Guide words at the top of the page indicate the alphabetic span of each two-page spread.

Entry words that have the same spelling (**homographs**) but are different words altogether are listed separately and marked by a superscript homograph number. For example,

bit[1] . . . part of a bridle . . .
bit[2] . . . small piece . . .
bit[3] . . . unit of information . . .

PARTS OF AN ENTRY

The sample entries below show the order of information in this dictionary.

ac·tion (ak′shən), *n.* **1** process of acting: *a machine in action.* **2** thing done; act. **3** way of moving or working; movement. **4** a minor battle or combat between military forces. **5** a lawsuit. **actions,** conduct; behavior.
take action, a become active. **b** start working. **c** Also, **bring action,** start a lawsuit. [< F < L *actio.* See ACT.] —**ac′tion·less,** *adj.*

ar·rest (ə rest′), *v.* **1** seize by legal authority; apprehend. **2** catch and hold; capture. **3** stop; check; halt. —*n.* **1** a seizing by legal authority. **2** a stopping; checking. **3** any device for arresting motion in a mechanism.

under arrest, held by the authorities; in custody. [< OF < VL, < L *ad–* + *re–* back + *stare* stand] —**ar·rest′er,** *n.* —**ar·rest′ment,** *n.*

The **entry word**, in **boldface**, is broken into syllables.

The **pronunciation** is a phonetic respelling of the entry word, including accents indicating stress in pronunciation. Variant pronunciations, including those for foreign words, are also provided. A pronunciation key is provided on page viii.

ar·tic·u·late (*adj.* är tik′yə lit; *v.* är tik′yə lāt) . . .
bi·va·lent (bī vā′lənt; biv′ə–) . . .

Inflected forms follow the pronunciation. They are given for all entry words where the spelling for different parts of speech differs from the form of the entry word, as in the following example: **blab** (blab), v., **blabbed, blab·bing** . . .

Inflected forms are also individually pronounced where there might be a question about their pronunciation: **for·mu·la** . . . *n., pl.* **–las, –lae** (–le) . . .

The **part of speech** indicates the grammatical function of a word. In the case of words that have more than one part of speech, each is labeled and defined separately within an entry.

Labels provide various kinds of information, and most of them are self-explanatory, such as part of speech or a language (French, Latin, etc.). For example,

ex li·bris . . . *Latin* . . .
a ri·ve·der·ci, ar·ri·ve·der·ci . . . *Italian* . . .

or, sometimes, a regionalism,

ar·roy·o . . . *SW U.S.*

A label also shows the level of usage, for example, *Informal* or *Slang*. (See also Special Features, below.) The label *Archaic* indicates that a term is not considered part of the modern vocabulary; writers will sometimes deliberately use an archaism for effect.

Numbered definitions distinguish between different meanings for an entry word. In general, the most common meaning is given first. Figurative meanings are often given after the core or concrete meaning to highlight semantic development.

Idioms associated with an entry word are listed separately and defined after the last definition. The full idiom (and any variant forms) is printed in boldface type followed by the definition or definitions for it.

The **etymology**, a brief language history of a word, comes at the end of all definitions, including the idioms. A complete list of abbreviations and symbols used in the etymologies is provided below.

The last part of the entry contains **derived** forms for the entry word. They are printed in boldface type and broken into syllables, followed by a part of speech, as at the entry **ex·haust** . . . —**ex·haust′i·ble,** *adj.* —**ex·haust ′i·bil′i·ty,** *n.*

SPECIAL FEATURES

The **equal sign** (=) is used in the dictionary for exactly equivalent terms and cross-refer to the preferred or more widely used term that has the same meaning (for example, **ben·zol** . . . **1** =benzene . . .).

Words added to a definition following a semicolon can be used as substitutes for the entry word (for example, **bit·ing** . . . *adj.* . . . **2** sarcastic; sneering). They are not, however, exact equivalents of the entry word.

The **figurative label (Fig.)** generally indicates that a particular meaning for a word has been broadened to encompass more than a word's core or literal meaning. For example,

Ar·ca·di·a . . . **1** a mountain district in the S part of ancient Greece, famous for the simple, contented life of its people. **2** *Fig.* a place of contentment.

Many usages marked ***Informal*** are widely used in conversation and can be freely used in writing except when a more formal tone may be required, as, for example, in applying for a job, writing a term paper, etc. We have used the label *Informal* very liberally because of the widespread use among writers of many words and usages that entered English as slang but have become integral parts of the common vocabulary. By contrast, the ***Slang*** label has been used very sparingly. The writer should be aware that slang is generally not used in formal writing but is usually acceptable to use in emails and other writing among friends and contemporaries.

The dictionary also distinguishes between ***combining forms,*** which are abstracted from whole words and which combine with other words to make new ones (**bio–**, as in *biodegradable*), and ***prefixes*** (**arch–**, as in *archduke, archliberal, archencephalon*).

COMPLETE PRONUNCIATION KEY

The pronunciation of each word is shown just after the word, in this way: **ab·bre·vi·ate** (ə brē′vi āt). The letters and signs used are pronounced as in the words on page viii. The mark ′ is placed after a syllable with primary, or strong, accent, as in the example above. The mark ′ after a syllable shows a secondary, or lighter, accent, as in **ab·bre·vi·a·tion** (ə brē ′vi ā′shən).

Some words, taken from foreign languages, are spoken with sounds that otherwise do not occur in English. Symbols for these sounds are given as "Foreign Sounds."

a	hat, cap	i	it, pin, antimatter;	p	pet, cup
ā	age, face		final syllable as in	r	run, try
ã	care, air		*city*	s	say, yes
ä	father, far	ī	ice, five	sh	she, rush
				t	tell, it
b	bad, rob	j	jam, enjoy	th	thin, both
ch	child, much	k	kind, seek	th̶	then, smooth
d	did, red	l	land, coal		
		m	me, am	u	cup, son
e	let, best	n	no, in	u̇	put, book
ē	equal, see	ng	long, bring	ü	rule, move
ėr	term, learn			ū	use, music
		o	hot, rock		
f	fat, if	ō	open, go	v	very, save
g	go, bag	ô	order, all	w	will, woman
h	he, how	oi	oil, toy	y	you, yet
		ou	out, now	z	zero, breeze
				zh	measure, seizure

ə   occurs only in unaccented syllables and represents the sound of *a* in *a*bout, *e* in tak*e*n, *i* in penc*i*l, *o* in lem*o*n, and *u* in circ*u*s.

FOREIGN SOUNDS

Y   as in French *lune,* German *süss.* Pronouce ē as in *equal* with the lips rounded for ü as in *rule.*

œ   as in French *peu,* German *könig.* Pronounce ā as in *age* with the lips rounded for ō as in *open.*

N   as in French *bon.* The N is not pronounced, but shows that the vowel before it is nasalized.

H   as in German *ach,* Scottish *loch.* Pronounce k without closing the breath passage.

ETYMOLOGY KEY

abl.	ablative	*lit.*	literally
accus.	accusative	*masc.*	masculine
alter.	alteration	*neut.*	neuter
appar.	apparently	*orig.*	origin, original, originally
assoc.	associated, association	*pp.*	past participle
compar.	comparative	*ppr.*	present participle
dial.	dialect, dialectal	*(prob.)*	probably
dim.	diminutive	*ref.*	reference
fem.	feminine	*superl.*	superlative
gen.	genitive	*trans.*	translation
imit.	imitative	*ult.*	ultimately
inf.	infinitive	*uncert.*	uncertain
infl.	influenced	*var.*	variant
irreg.	irregular, irregularly	*?*	possibly
lang.	language	*<*	from, derived from, taken from

LANGUAGE ABBREVIATIONS

AF	Anglo-French	Med.Gk.	Medieval Greek (700–1500)
Am. Ind.	American Indian	Med.L	Medieval Latin (700–1500)
Ar.	Arabic	Mex.	Mexican indigenous languages
Aram.	Aramaic	MFr	Middle French (1400–1600)
Dan.	Danish	MHG	Middle High German (1100–1450)
Du.	Dutch	MLG	Middle Low German (1100–1450)
E	English	NL	New Latin (after 1500)
Egypt.	Egyptian	Norw.	Norwegian
F	French	O	Old
Flem.	Flemish	OE	Old English (before 1100)
Fris.	Frisian	OF	Old French (before 1400)
G	German	OHG	Old High German (before 1100)
Gk.	Greek	OS	Old Saxon
Gmc.	Germanic	Pers.	Persian
Heb.	Hebrew	Pg.	Portuguese
HG	High German	Pol.	Polish
Hind.	Hindustani	Pr.	Provençal
Hung.	Hungarian	Rom.	Romanic
Ital.	Italian	Rum.	Romanian
Jap.	Japanese	Russ.	Russian
L	Latin	Scand.	Scandinavian
LG	Low German	Scot.	Scottish
LGk.	Late Greek (300–700)	Skt.	Sanskrit
LL	Late Latin (300–700)	Sp.	Spanish
M	Middle	Sw.	Swedish
ME	Middle English (1100–1500)	Turk.	Turkish
Med.	Medieval	VL	Vulgar Latin

ABBREVIATIONS FREQUENTLY USED IN THIS BOOK

(NOTE: Certain abbreviations used chiefly in the etymologies will be found in the complete etymology key on the previous page.)

ab.	about	*Bacteriol.*	Bacteriology
abbrev.	abbreviation	B.C.	before Christ; before the birth of Christ
A.D.	anno Domini; in the year of the Lord; since the birth of Christ	*Biochem.*	Biochemistry
		Biol.	Biology
adj.	adjective	*Bot.*	Botany
adv.	adverb	*Brit.*	British
Am.	Americanism (applied to words or meanings that originated in the United States)	*C*	central
		Chem.	Chemistry
		Class. Myth.	Classical Mythology (Greek and Roman Mythology)
Anat.	Anatomy	*Colloq.*	Colloquial
Ant.	Antonym	*Com.*	Commerce
Archit.	Architecture	*compar.*	comparative
Astron.	Astronomy	*conj.*	conjunction
		def.	definition
		Deut.	Deuteronomy

Dial.	Dialect		*nom.*	nominative
E	east; eastern		*NW*	northwest; northwestern
Econ.	Economics		*Obs.*	Obsolete (applied to words and meanings not used now)
Educ.	Education			
Elect.	Electricity		*Pathol.*	Pathology
Embryol.	Embryology		*pers.*	person
esp.	especially		*Philos.*	Philosophy
etc.	et cetera; and others; and the rest; and so forth; and so on; and the like		*Phonet.*	Phonetics
			Photog.	Photography
			Physiol.	Physiology
fem.	feminine		*pl.*	plural
Fig.	figurative		*poss.*	possessive
Fr.	French		*pp.*	past participle
ft.	foot; feet		*ppr.*	present participle
Gen.	Genesis		*prep.*	preposition
gen.	genitive		*pres.*	present
Geol.	Geology		*pron.*	pronoun
Geom.	Geometry		*Psychol.*	Psychology
Ger.	German		*pt.*	past tense
Gk. Myth.	Greek Mythology		*Rom. Cath.*	Roman Catholic
Gram.	Grammar		*S*	south; southern
Hist.	History		*Scot.*	Scotch; Scottish
in.	inch; inches		*SE*	southeast; southeastern
interj.	interjection		*sing.*	singular
Mach.	Machinery		*SW*	southwest; southwestern
masc.	masculine		*Theol.*	Theology
Math.	Mathematics		*Trigon.*	Trigonometry
Matt.	Matthew		*U.S.*	United States (applied to words or meanings that are used chiefly in the United States but originated elsewhere)
Med.	Medicine			
Mil.	Military			
Myth.	Mythology			
N	north; northern		*v.*	verb
n.	noun		*W*	west; western
Naut.	Nautical		*Zool.*	Zoology
NE	northeast; northeastern		=	synonym of

A, a (ā), *n., pl.,* **A's; a's.**
1 the first letter of the alphabet. **2** first in a series: *questions A through L.* **3** best; first: *grade A; all A's in history.* **4** one of four main blood groups **5** the sixth note in the scale of C major.

a (ə; *stressed* ā), *adj. or indefinite article.* **1** any: *a tree.* **2** one: *a pound of butter.* **3** to or for each: *ten dollars a day.* [var. of *an*[1]]

a-[1], *prefix.* not; without, as in *atonal.* [< Gk.; *a-* becomes *an-* before a vowel or *h*]

a-[2], *prefix.* **1** in; on; to, as in *abed.* **2** in the act of ___ing, as in *a-fishing.* [OE *an, on*]

A, 1 *Physics.* angstrom unit. **2** *Chem.* argon.

a., 1 about. **2** acre; acres. **3** adjective.

A 1 *Colloq.* A one.

AA, 1 Alcoholics Anonymous. **2** anti-aircraft.

A.A., Associate in Arts.

AAA, American Automobile Association.

AAAS American Association for the Advancement of Science.

Aa·chen (ä'Hən), *n.* city in W Germany, French, **Aix-la-Chapelle.**

aard·vark (ärd'värk'), *n.* a burrowing African mammal that eats ants and termites. [< Afrikaans < Dutch *aarde* earth + *vark* pig]

Aar·on (ãr'ən), *n.* the brother of Moses and first high priest of the Jews.

AARP, American Association of Retired Persons.

ab-, *prefix.* from; away from; off, as in *abnormal, abduct, abjure.* [< L *ab,* prep.; *ab-* appears as *a-* before *m* and *v,* and *abs-* before *c* and *t.* Akin to Greek *apo-* from, and English *of* and *off.*]

AB, one of the four main blood groups.

A.B., Bachelor of Arts. Also, **B.A.**

a·ba (ä'bə), *n.* **1** loose, sleeveless outer garment worn by Arabs. **2** woolen fabric, usually striped, woven in Arab countries.

a·ba·cá (ä'bə kä'), *n.* **1** hemp made from the fibers of a Philippine banana plant; Manila hemp. **2** the plant itself. [< Malay]

a·back (ə bak'), *adv.* **taken aback,** suddenly surprised.

ab·a·cus (ab'ə kəs), *n., pl.* **-cu·ses, -ci** (-sī). frame with rows of counters or beads that slide back and forth, used for calculating. [< L < Gk. *abax*]

a·baft (ə baft'; ə bäft'), *prep.* back of a boat or ship; behind. —*adv.* toward or at the stern.

ab·a·lo·ne (ab'ə lō'nē), *n.* an edible mollusk, with a large, rather flat shell lined with mother-of-pearl. [< Am. Sp. *abulón* < Am. Ind. *aulun*]

a·ban·don (ə ban'dən), *v.* **1** give up entirely; renounce; relinquish: *abandon a career.* **2** leave without intending to return; desert; forsake: *abandon one's*

home. **3** yield (oneself) completely (to a feeling, impulse, etc.); succumb; surrender: *abandon oneself to grief.* —*n.* freedom from conventional restraint. [< OF *a bandon* at liberty] —**a·ban'don·er,** *n.* —**a·ban'don·ment,** *n.*

a·ban·doned (ə ban'dənd), *adj.* **1** deserted; forsaken. **2** wicked; immoral. **3** unrestrained. —**a·ban'don·ed·ly,** *adv.*

a·base (ə bās'), *v.,* **a·based, a·bas·ing.** make lower in rank, condition, or character; degrade: *a traitor abases himself.* [< OF < LL, *ad-* + L *bassus* low] —**a·base'ment,** *n.*

a·bash (ə bash'), *v.* embarrass and confuse; disconcert. [<OF *esbaïr* be astonished] —**a·bashed',** *adj.* —**a·bash'ment,** *n.*

a·bate (ə bāt'), *v.,* **a·bat·ed, a·bat·ing.** **1** make less; decrease: *the medicine abated his pain.* **2** become less; diminish: *the storm has abated.* [< OF *abatre* beat down] —**a·bat'a·ble,** *adj.* —**a·bate'ment,** *n.* —**a·bat'er,** *n.*

ab·at·toir (ab'ə twär; -twôr), *n.* slaughterhouse. [< F]

ab·ba·cy (ab'ə si), *n., pl.* **-cies. 1** position, term of office, or district of an abbot. **2** an abbey. [< LL *abbatia.* See ABBOT.]

ab·bé (ab'ā; a bā'), *n.* in France: **1** an abbot. **2** any clergyman, esp. a priest. [< F]

ab·bess (ab'is), *n.* woman at the head of a community of nuns. [< OF < LL *abbatissa*]

ab·bey (ab'i), *n., pl.* **-beys. 1** building or buildings where monks or nuns live a religious life ruled by an abbot or abbess; a monastery or convent. **2** the monks or nuns living there. **3** building that was once an abbey or a part of an abbey. [< OF < LL *abbatia*]

ab·bot (ab'ət), *n.* man at the head of an abbey of monks. [OE < LL < LGk. < Aramaic *abbā* father] —**ab'bot·ship,** *n.*

abbrev., abbr., abbreviation.

ab·bre·vi·ate (ə brē'vi āt), *v.,* **-at·ed, -at·ing. 1** make (a word or phrase) shorter so that a part stands for the whole: *abbreviate "hour" to "hr."* **2** make briefer; condense. [< L, < *ad-* + *brevis* short. Doublet of ABRIDGE.] —**ab·bre'vi·a'tor,** *n.*

ab·bre·vi·a·tion (ə brē'vi ā'shən), *n.* **1** shortened form of a word or phrase standing for the whole: *"in." is an abbreviation of "inch."* **2** act of shortening; abridgment.

ABC (ā'bē'sē'), *n., pl.* **ABC's. 1** elementary principles. **2** ABC's, the alphabet.

ab·di·cate (ab'də kāt), *v.,* **-cat·ed, -cat·ing. 1** give up or renounce formally; relinquish: *the king abdicated his throne.* **2** renounce office or power: *why did the king abdicate?* **3** ignore an obligation or duty: *abdicated her responsibility for the children's welfare.* [< L, < *ab-* away + *dicare* proclaim] —**ab'di·ca'tion,** *n.* —**ab'di·ca'tor,** *n.*

ab·do·men (ab'də mən; ab dō'mən), *n.* **1** the part of the body containing the

stomach and other digestive organs; belly. **2** the last of the three parts of the body of an insect or crustacean. [< L]

ab·dom·i·nal (ab dom'ə nəl), *adj.* of, in, or for the abdomen. —**ab·dom'i·nal·ly,** *adv.*

ab·duce (ab dūs'; -dūs'), *v.,* **-duced, -ducing.** lead away; abduct.

ab·duct (ab dukt'), *v.* **1** carry away (a person) unlawfully and by force; kidnap. **2** pull (a part of the body) away from its usual position. [< L, < *ab-* away + *ducere* lead] —**ab·duc'tion,** *n.* —**ab·duc'tor,** *n.*

a·beam (ə bēm'), *adv.* directly opposite to the middle part of a ship's side.

a·bed (ə bed'), *adj., adv.* in bed.

A·bel (ā'bəl), *n.* in the Bible, second son of Adam and Eve, killed by his older brother Cain.

Ab·er·deen (ab'ər dēn'), *n.* city in E Scotland.

ab·er·rant (ab er'ənt), *adj.* deviating from what is regular, normal, or right. [< L, < *ab-* away + *errare* wander] —**ab·er'rance, ab·er'ran·cy,** *n.*

ab·er·ra·tion (ab'ər ā'shən), *n.* **1** deviation from the right path or usual course of action. **2** deviation from a standard or type. **3** temporary mental disorder. **4** failure of rays of light coming from one point to converge to one focus. **5** apparent change in the position of a celestial body when viewed from earth. —**ab'er·ra'tion·al,** *adj.*

a·bet (ə bet'), *v.,* **a·bet·ted, a·bet·ting.** encourage or help, esp. in something wrong; support; assist. [< OF *abeter* arouse < L *ad-* + Frankish *bētan* cause to bite] —**a·bet'ment,** *n.* —**a·bet'tor, a·bet'ter,** *n.*

a·bey·ance (ə bā'əns), *n.* temporary inactivity: *hold the question in abeyance.* [< AF < OF *abeance* expectation < L *ad-* at + VL *batare* gape] —**a·bey'ant,** *adj.*

ab·hor (ab hôr'), *v.,* **-horred, -hor·ring.** feel disgust or hate for; detest; loathe. [< L, < *ab-* from + *horrere* shrink] —**ab·hor'rer,** *n.*

ab·hor·rence (ab hôr'əns; -hor'-), *n.* **1** feeling of very great dislike. **2** something detested.

ab·hor·rent (ab hôr'ənt; -hor'-), *adj.* **1** causing horror; disgusting; repugnant (*to*). **2** feeling disgust or hate (*of*). **3** having dislike of. —**ab·hor'rent·ly,** *adv.*

a·bide (ə bīd'), *v.,* **a·bode** or **a·bid·ed, a·bid·ing. 1** continue to stay. **2** dwell. **3** put up with; stand: *she cannot abide dirt.* **4** endure bravely, defiantly.

abide by, a accept and follow out. **b** remain faithful to. [OE *ābīdan* stay on, and *onbīdan* wait for] —**a·bid'er,** *n.*

a·bid·ing (ə bīd'ing), *adj.* continuing; lasting. —**a·bid'ing·ly,** *adv.*

Ab·i·djan (ab'i jän'), *n.* capital of Ivory Coast (Côle d'Ivoire).

a·bil·i·ty (ə bil'ə ti), *n., pl.* **-ties. 1** power to do or act in any relation; cleverness: *give according to your ability.* **2** skill; capacity: *mechanical ability.* **3** power to do some special thing; talent: *musical ability, natural abilities.* [< F < L. See ABLE.]

ab·ject (ab′jekt; ab jekt′), *adj.* **1** wretched; miserable. **2** deserving contempt; contemptible; despicable. [<L, < *ab–* down + *jacere* throw] —**ab·jec′tion,** *n.* —**abject′ly,** *adv.* —**ab·ject′ness,** *n.*

ab·jure (ab jŭr′), *v.,* **–jured, –jur·ing. 1** renounce on oath; repudiate; forswear. **2** refrain from. [< L, < *ab–* away + *jurare* swear] —**ab′ju·ra′tion,** *n.* —**ab·jur′a·to·ry** (ab jŭr′ə tô′ri;–tō′–), *adj.* —**ab·jur′er,** *n.*

abl., ablative.

ab·late (ab lāt′), *v.,* **–lat·ed, –lat·ing. 1** remove or be removed by burning. **2** melt away or vaporize.

ab·la·tion (ab lā′shən), *n.* **1** melting or burning away of the nosecone of a spacecraft or missile on reentry into the atmosphere. **2** removal or wearing away.

ab·la·tive (ab′lə tiv), *n.* **1** the case in Latin expressing removal or separation. **2** a word or construction in this case. [< L *ablativus* < *ab–* away + *ferre* carry]

a·blaze (ə blāz′), *adv., adj.* **1** burning; blazing. **2** brilliantly lit. **3** showing great excitement or anger.

a·ble (ā′bəl), *adj.* **a·bler, a·blest. 1** having ordinary capacity, power, or means to do; capable: *a man able to work.* **2** having more power or skill than most others have; talented; clever; expert: *a supreme court justice should be an able lawyer.* **3** competently done; effective: *an able speech.* **4** qualified, especially legally. [< OF < L *habilis* easily held or handled < *habere* hold]

–able, *suffix.* **1** that can be ___ed; able to be ___ed: *obtainable = that can be obtained.* **2** likely to or suitable for: *comfortable = suitable for comfort.* **3** inclined to: *peaceable = inclined to peace.* **4** deserving to be —ed: *lovable = deserving to be loved.* **5** likely to be —ed: *chargeable = likely to be charged.* See **–ible.** [< OF < L *-abilis*]

a·ble-bod·ied (ā′bəl bod′id), *adj.* physically fit and competent; strong and healthy.

a·bloom (ə blüm′), *adv., adj.* in bloom.

ab·lu·tion (ab lü′shən), *n.* **1** washing of one's person. **2** washing or cleansing as a religious ceremony of purification. **3** the liquid used. [< L, < *ab–* away + *luere* wash]

a·bly (ā′bli), *adv.* with skill or ability.

ab·ne·gate (ab′nə gāt), *v.,* **–gat·ed, –gat·ing.** deny (anything) to oneself; renounce; give up. [<L, *ab–* off, away + *negare* deny] —**ab′ne·ga′tion,** *n.* —**ab′ne·ga′tor,** *n.*

ab·nor·mal (ab nôr′məl), *adj.* deviating from the normal, the standard, or a type; markedly irregular; unusual; exceptional. [< AB– from + NORMAL] —**ab·nor′mal·ly,** *adv.* —**ab·nor′mal·ness,** *n.*

ab·nor·mal·ity (ab′nôr mal′ə ti), *n., pl.* **–ties. 1** abnormal thing. **2** abnormal condition.

abnormal psychology, the study of abnormal behavior in people, including the causes and treatment of mental disorders.

a·board (ə bôrd′; ə bōrd′), *adv.* **1** in or on a ship. **2** in or on a train, bus, airplane, etc. **3** alongside. —*prep.* on board of.

a·bode (ə bōd′), *n.* place to live in; dwelling. —*v.* pt. and pp. of **abide.** [OE ābād]

a·bol·ish (ə bol′ish), *v.* do away with (a law, institution, or custom) completely; suppress: *abolish slavery.* [<F abolir <L *abolere* destroy] —**a·bol′ish·a·ble,** *adj.* —**a·bol′ish·er,** *n.* —**a·bol′ish·ment,** *n.*

ab·o·li·tion (ab′ə lish′ən), *n.* **1** act or fact of abolishing. **2** suppression of black slavery. —**ab′o·li′tion·ism,** *n.* —**ab′o·li′tion·ist,** *n.*

ab·o·ma·sum (ab′ə mā′səm), **ab·o·ma·sus** (–səs), *n.* the fourth stomach of cows, sheep, and other cud-chewing animals. [< L]

A-bomb (ā′bom′), *n.* the atomic bomb. —*v.* bomb with an atomic bomb.

a·bom·i·na·ble (ə bom′nə bəl; ə bom′ə nə–), *adj.* **1** causing disgust; loathsome; detestable; odious. **2** unpleasant. —**a·bom′i·na·ble·ness,** *n.* —**a·bom′i·na·bly,** *adv.*

a·bom·i·nate (ə bom′ə nāt), *v.,* **–nat·ed, –nat·ing. 1** feel disgust for; abhor; detest; loathe. **2** dislike. [< L, deplore as an ill omen, < *ab–* off + *ominari* prophesy < *omen* omen] —**a·bom′i·na′tor,** *n.*

a·bom·i·na·tion (ə bom′ə nā′shən), *n.* **1** a disgusting thing. **2** a shamefully wicked action or custom. **3** a feeling of disgust.

ab·o·rig·i·nal (ab′ə rij′ə nəl), *adj.* **1** existing from the beginning; first; original; native: *aboriginal inhabitants.* **2** of the earliest known inhabitants. —*n.* =aborigine. —**ab′o·rig′i·nal·ly,** *adv.*

ab·o·rig·i·ne (ab′ə rij′ə nēz), *n.* **1** the earliest known inhabitant of a country. **2 aborigines,** the native animals and plants of a region. [< L, < *ab origine* from the beginning]

a·bort (ə bôrt′), *v.* **1** miscarry. **2** fail to develop. **3** check the development of. [< L, < *ab–* amiss + *oriri* be born]

a·bor·tion (ə bôr′shən), *n.* **1** birth that occurs before the embryo has developed enough to live; miscarriage. **2** failure to develop properly. **3** something that has failed to develop properly. —**a·bor′tion·al,** *adj.*

a·bor·tion·ist (ə bôr′shən ist), *n.* person who produces abortions, especially illegal abortions.

a·bor·tive (ə bôr′tiv), *adj.* **1** coming to nothing; unsuccessful. **2** born or begun before the right time. —**a·bor′tive·ly,** *adv.* —**a·bor′tive·ness,** *n.*

a·bound (ə bound′), *v.* **1** be plentiful: *fish abound in the ocean.* **2** be rich (*in*): *America abounds in many natural resources.* **3** be well supplied (*with*): *the*

ocean abounds with fish. [< OF < L, < *ab–* off + *undare* rise in waves < *unda* a wave] —**a·bound′ing,** *adj.* —**a·bound′ing·ly,** *adv.*

a·bout (ə bout′), *prep.* **1** of; concerned with: *a book about bridges.* **2** near: *he was about five miles from home.* **3** around: *a fence about the garden; scatter papers about the room.* **4** ready: *a plane about to take off.* —*adv.* **1** nearly; almost: *about full.* **2** somewhere near: *loiter about.* **3** all around: *the boy looked about.* [OE *onbūtan* on the outside of]

a·bout-face (*n.* ə bout′fās′; *v.* ə bout′fās′), *n., v.,* **–faced, –fac·ing.** —*n.* **1** a turning or going in the opposite direction. **2** a turning to the opposite opinion or point of view. —*v.* turn or go in the opposite direction.

a·bove (ə buv′), *adv.* **1** in or at a higher place: *the sky is above.* **2** higher in rank or power: *the courts above.* **3** earlier, in a book or article. —*prep.* **1** in or to a higher place than: *birds fly above the earth.* **2** higher than; over: *a captain is above a sergeant.* **3** more than: *the weight is above a ton.* —*adj.* written above. —*n.* **the above,** something that is written above. [OE *abufan*]

a·bove-board (ə buv′bôrd′; –bōrd′), *adv., adj.* without tricks or concealment.

ab·ra·ca·dab·ra (ab′rə kə dab′rə), *n.* **1** word supposed to have magical powers, used in incantations, or as a charm to ward off diseases. **2** gibberish. [< L]

a·brade (ə brād′), *v.,* **a·brad·ed, a·brad·ing.** wear away by rubbing; scrape off. [< L, < *ab–* off + *radere* scrape] —**a·brad′er,** *n.*

A·bra·ham (ā′brə ham; –həm), *n.* in the Bible, the ancestor of the Hebrews. Gen. 12–25.

a·bra·sion (ə brā′zhən), *n.* **1** place scraped or worn by rubbing. **2** act of abrading.

a·bra·sive (ə brā′siv; –ziv), *n.* substance used for grinding, smoothing, or polishing, as sandpaper. —*adj.* tending to abrade.

a·breast (ə brest′), *adv., adj.* side by side. **abreast of** or **with,** up with; alongside of: *keep abreast of what is going on.*

a·bridge (ə brij′), *v.,* **a·bridged, a·bridg·ing. 1** make shorter by using fewer words. **2** make less: *abridge the rights of citizens.* **3** deprive (*of*): *abridge citizens of their rights.* [< OF *abregier* < L, < *ad–* + *brevis* short. Doublet of ABBREVIATE.] —**a·bridg′a·ble, a·bridge′a·ble,** *adj.* —**a·bridged′,** *adj.* —**a·bridg′er,** *n.*

a·bridg·ment, a·bridge·ment (ə brij′mənt), *n.* **1** condensed form of a book, long article, etc. **2** an abridging. **3** a cutting back or reduction: *abridgment of the right to privacy.*

a·broad (ə brôd′), *adv.* **1** in or to a foreign land or lands: *go abroad.* **2** out in the open air. **3** going around; current: *a rumor is abroad.* **4** far and wide.

ab·ro·gate (ab′rə gāt), *v.,* **–gat·ed, –gat·ing. 1** abolish or annul (a law or custom) by an authoritative act; repeal. **2** do away with. [< L, < *ab-* away + *rogare* demand] —**ab·ro·ga'tion,** *n.* —**ab'ro·ga·tor,** *n.*

a·brupt (ə brupt'), *adj.* **1** sudden; unexpected: *an abrupt turn.* **2** very steep. **3** (of speech or manners) short or sudden; blunt; brusque. **4** (of style) disconnected. [< L *abruptus* < *ab-* off + *rumpere* break] —**a·brupt'ly,** *adv.* —**a·brupt'ness,** *n.*

Ab·sa·lom (ab'sə ləm), *n.* in the Bible, David's favorite son, who rebelled against him.

ab·scess (ab'ses; –sis), *n.* a collection of pus in the tissues of some part of the body. [< L *abscessus* < *ab-* away + *cedere* go] —**ab'scessed,** *adj.*

ab·scis·sa (ab sis'ə), *n., pl.* **–scis·sas, –scis·sae** (–sis'ē). *Math.* line running from left to right on a graph that defines a point in a system of coordinates. [< L (*linea*) *abscissa* (line) cut off]

ab·scond (ab skond'), *v.* go away suddenly and secretly; go off and hide; flee. [< L, < *ab-* away + *condere* store] —**ab·scond'er,** *n.*

ab·sence (ab'səns), *n.* **1** a being away: *absence from work.* **2** time of being away: *an absence of two weeks.* **3** a being without; lack: *absence of light.* **4** absent-mindedness.

absence of mind, inattentiveness.

ab·sent (*adj.* ab'sənt; *v.* ab sent'), *adj.* **1** not present (at a place); away: *John is absent today.* **2** not existing; lacking: *snow is absent in some countries.* **3** absent-minded. —*v.* take or keep (oneself) away: *absent oneself from class.* [< L *absens* < *ab-* away + *esse* to be] —**ab·sent'er,** *n.* —**ab'sent·ness,** *n.*

ab·sen·tee (ab'sən tē'), *n.* person who is absent or remains absent. —*adj.* of or for a voter or voters permitted to vote by mail. —**ab'sen·tee'ism,** *n.*

ab·sent·ly (ab'sənt li), *adv.* absent-mindedly.

ab·sent-mind·ed (ab'sənt mīn'did), *adj.* inattentive; forgetful. —**ab'sent-mind'ed·ly,** *adv.* —**ab'sent-mind'ed·ness.** *n.*

ab·sinthe, ab·sinth (ab'sinth), *n.* a bitter, green liqueur flavored with herbs, wormwood, and anise. [< F < L < Gk. *apsinthion* wormwood]

ab·so·lute (ab'sə lüt), *adj.* **1** complete; entire: *absolute ignorance.* **2** free from imperfection; perfect: *absolute purity.* **3** free from control or restrictions: *absolute liberty.* **4** not compared with anything else: *absolute velocity, absolute zero.* **5** certain; infallible: *absolute proof.* **6** forming a part of a sentence, but not connected with it grammatically. In "The train being late, we missed the boat," *the train being late* is an absolute construction. —*n.* **the absolute,** that which is absolute. [< L *absolutus,* pp. See ABSOLVE.] —**ab'so·lute'ness,** *n.*

ab·so·lute·ly (ab'sə lüt'li), *adv.* **1** completely. **2** positively. **3** yes.

absolute majority, more than one-half the total votes cast.

absolute monarchy, monarchy which has no limits to its power.

absolute pitch, pitch of a tone according to the frequency of its vibrations per second.

absolute value, value of a real number regardless of any signs attached to it.

absolute zero, temperature at which substances would have no heat whatever; –273.13° centigrade or –459.72° Fahrenheit.

ab·so·lu·tion (ab'sə lü'shən), *n.* **1** remission of guilt and punishment for sin by a priest after the sinner confesses and does penance. **2** act of declaring such remission. **3** formula declaring remission of sin. **4** release from consequences or penalties.

ab·so·lut·ism (ab'sə lüt iz'əm), *n.* government whose rule has unrestricted power; despotism. —**ab'so·lut·ist,** *n., adj.* —**ab'so·lut·is'tic,** *adj.*

ab·solve (ab solv'; –zolv'), *v.,* **–solved, –solv·ing. 1** declare free from sin, guilt, or blame; exonerate; acquit; forgive. **2** set free (from a promise or duty); release; exempt. [< L, < *ab-* from + *solvere* loosen] —**ab·solv'a·ble,** *adj.* —**ab·sol'vent,** *adj., n.* —**ab·solv'er,** *n.*

ab·sorb (ab sôrb'; –zôrb'), *v.* **1** take in or suck up (liquids): *a towel absorbs water.* **2** swallow up and make a part of itself; assimilate. **3** take in and hold: *absorb noise.* **4** interest very much: *the circus absorbed the boys.* **5** take up by chemical or molecular action: *charcoal absorbs gases.* **6** take (digested food, oxygen, etc.) into the bloodstream by osmosis. [< L, < *ab-* from + *sorbere* suck in] —**ab·sorb'a·ble,** *adj.* —**ab·sorb'a·bil'i·ty,** *n.* —**ab·sorb'er,** *n.*

ab·sorbed (ab sôrbd'; –zôrbd'), *adj.* very much interested. —**ab·sorb'ed·ly,** *adv.* —**ab·sorb'ed·ness,** *n.*

ab·sorb·ent (ab sôr'bənt; –zôr'–), *adj.* absorbing or capable of absorbing. —*n.* any thing or substance that absorbs.

ab·sorb·ing (ab sôr'bing; –zôr'–), *adj.* extremely interesting. —**ab·sorb'ing·ly,** *adv.*

ab·sorp·tion (ab sôrp'shən; –zôrp'–), *n.* **1** an absorbing. **2** great interest (in something). **3** process of taking digested food, oxygen, etc., into the bloodstream by osmosis. **4** in plants, process of taking in nutrients through the roots. —**ab·sorp'tive,** *adj.* —**ab·sorp'tive·ness,** *n.*

ab·stain (ab stān'), *v.* do without something voluntarily; refrain (*from*); forbear; cease: *abstain from smoking.* [< F < L, < *ab-* off *tenere* hold] —**ab·stain'er,** *n.*

ab·ste·mi·ous (ab stē'mi əs), *adj.* moderate in eating and drinking; temperate. [< L, < *ab-* off + unrecorded *temum* intoxicating drink] —**ab·ste'mi·ous·ly,** *adv.* —**ab·ste'mi·ous·ness,** *n.*

ab·sten·tion (ab sten'shən), *n.* act of abstaining; abstinence. —**ab·sten'tious,** *adj.*

ab·sti·nence (ab'stə nəns), *n.* **1** partly or entirely giving up certain pleasures, food, drink, etc.; abstention. **2** act or practice of refraining (*from*); abstention: *abstinence from smoking, sexual abstinence.*

total abstinence, a refraining from the use of any alcoholic liquor. —**ab'stinent,** *adj.* —**ab'sti·nent·ly,** *adv.*

ab·stract (*adj.* ab'strakt, ab strakt'; *v.* ab strakt' *for 1, 3, 4,* ab'strakt *for 2; n.* ab'strakt), *adj.* **1** thought of apart from any particular object or real thing; not concrete: *an abstract number.* **2** expressing a quality that is thought of apart from any particular object or real thing: *"goodness" is an abstract noun.* **3** ideal; theoretical. **4** hard to understand; difficult. **5** not representing anything material or concrete: *abstract paintings.* —*v.* **1** think of (a quality) apart from a particular object or real thing having that quality. **2** make an abstract of; summarize. **3** remove, esp. dishonestly. **4** withdraw attention; preoccupy; disengage. —*n.* a short statement giving the main ideas of an article, book, etc.; summary.

in the abstract, in theory rather than in practice. [< L *abstractus* < *ab-* away + *trahere* draw] —**ab'stract'er,** *n.* —**ab'stract·ly,** *adv.* —**ab'stract·ness,** *n.*

ab·stract·ed (ab strak'tid), *adj.* absent-minded; preoccupied; inattentive. —**ab·stract'ed·ly,** *adv.* —**ab·stract'ed·ness,** *n.*

abstract expressionism, style of painting that expresses emotions rather than the concrete. —**abstract expressionist,** *n.*

ab·strac·tion (ab strak'shən), *n.* **1** idea of a quality thought of apart from any particular object or real thing having that quality. **2** formation of such an idea. **3** removal. **4** absent-mindedness. **5** a work of abstract art.

ab·struse (ab strüs'), *adj.* hard to understand; profound; recondite. [< L *abstrusus* < *ab-* away + *trudere* thrust] —**ab·struse'ly,** *adv.* —**ab·struse'ness,** *n.*

ab·surd (ab sėrd'; –zėrd'), *adj.* plainly not true or sensible; foolish; ridiculous. [< L *absurdus* out of tune, senseless] —**ab·surd'ly,** *adv.* —**ab·surd'ness,** *n.*

ab·surd·i·ty (ab sėr'də ti; –zėr'–), *n., pl.* **–ties. 1** something absurd. **2** an absurd quality or condition; folly.

a·bun·dance (ə bun'dəns), *n.* great plenty; full supply; profusion. [< OF < L. See ABOUND.]

a·bun·dant (ə bun'dənt), *adj.* more than enough; very plentiful. —**a·bun'dant·ly,** *adv.*

a·buse (*v.* ə būz'; *n.* əbūs'), *v.,* **a·bused, a·bus·ing,** *n.* —*v.* **1** put to a wrong or bad use; misuse: *abuse a privilege.* **2** treat badly; mistreat; maltreat: *abuse a child.* **3** use harsh and insulting language to; revile. —*n.* **1** a wrong or improper use. **2** harsh or severe treatment of a person.

3 harsh and insulting language. **4** a corrupt practice or custom. [< F < L *abusus* < *ab-* away + *uti* use] —a·bus′er, *n.*

a·bu·sive (ə bū′siv; –ziv), *adj.* **1** using harsh or insulting language. **2** containing abuse. —a·bu′sive·ly, *adv.* —a·bu′sive·ness, *n.*

a·but (ə but′), *v.*, a·but·ted, a·but·ting. **1** touch at one end or edge; end (*on* or *against*): *our house abuts on the street.* **2** join at a boundary; border (*on* or *upon*): *his land abuts upon mine.* [< OF]

a·but·ment (ə but′mənt), *n.* **1** a support for an arch or bridge. **2** the point or place where the support joins the thing supported.

a·but·ting (ə but′ing), *adj.* adjacent.

a·buzz (ə buz′), *adj., adv.* **1** filled with sounds of buzzing. **2** active; busy.

a·bysm (ə biz′əm), *n.* an abyss. [< OF *abisme*]

a·bys·mal (ə biz′məl), *adj.* **1** too deep to be measured; bottomless. **2** of very bad quality. **3** of or pertaining to the deepest parts of the ocean. —a·bys′mal·ly, *adv.*

a·byss (ə bis′), *n.* **1** a bottomless or immeasurably deep space; chasm. **2** the lowest depths of anything, esp. the ocean. **3** *fig.* anything too great to be measured. [< L < Gk., < *a-* without + *byssos* bottom]

Ab·ys·sin·i·a (ab′ə sin′i ə), *n.* Ethiopia. —Ab′ys·sin′i·an, *adj., n.*

ac- prefix. form of **ad-**.

Ac, actinium.

A.C., a.c., alternating current.

a·ca·cia (ə kā′shə), *n.* **1** any of a genus of trees native to warm regions, several species of which yield gum arabic. **2** the locust tree of North America. [< L <Gk. *akakia* a thorny Egyptian tree]

ac·a·dem·ic (ak′ə dem′ik), *adj.* **1** of or having to do with schools, colleges, and their studies. **2** concerned with general rather than commercial, technical, or professional education. **3** scholarly. **4** theoretical. **5** following rules and traditions; formal. —*n.* student or teacher; scholar. —ac′a·dem′i·cal, *adj.* —ac′a·dem′i·cal·ly, *adv.*

academic freedom, **1** freedom of a teacher to teach and explore controversial subjects without fear of interference or loss of position or standing. **2** freedom of an educational institution to set academic standards and curriculum without interference, esp. from a government.

a·cad·e·mi·cian (ə kad′ə mish′ən; ak′ə də-), *n.* **1** member of a society for encouraging literature, science, or art. **2** student or teacher.

a·cad·e·my (ə kad′ə mi), *n., pl.* -mies. **1** high school, esp. a private high school. **2** school for instruction in a particular art or science: *a military academy.* **3** society of authors, scholars, scientists, artists, etc., for encouraging literature, science, or art. [< L < Gk. *Akademeia* the grove where Plato taught]

A·ca·di·a (ə kā′di ə), *n.* a former French territory in SE Canada. —A·ca′di·an, *n., adj.*

a·can·thus (ə kan′thəs), *n., pl.* -thus·es, -thi (-thī). **1** a prickly plant with large, toothed leaves that grows in Mediterranean regions. **2** an architectural ornament imitating these leaves. [< L < Gk., < *ake* thorn]

a cap·pel·la (ä′ kə pel′ə), without instrumental accompaniment. [< Ital., in the manner of chapel (music)]

acc., **1** account. **2** accusative.

ac·cede (ak sēd′), *v.*, -ced·ed, -ced·ing. **1** give consent (*to*); agree: *please accede to my request.* **2** become a party (*to*): *our government acceded to the treaty.* **3** attain (to an office or dignity); come (*to*): *the king's oldest son acceded to the throne.* [< L, < *ad-* to + *cedere* come] —ac·ced′ence, *n.* —ac·ced′er, *n.*

ac·cel·er·an·do (ak sel′ər an′dō), *adv., adj. Music.* gradually increasing in speed. [< Ital.]

ac·cel·er·ate (ak sel′ər āt), *v.*, -at·ed, -at·ing. **1** go or cause to go faster. **2** cause to happen sooner; hasten. **3** change the speed or velocity of (a moving object). [< L, < *ad-* + *celer* swift] —ac·cel′er·a′tive, *adj.*

ac·cel·er·a·tion (ak sel′ər ā′shən), *n.* **1** an accelerating or being accelerated. **2** change in velocity, either a gradual increase (**positive acceleration**) or decrease (**negative acceleration**). **3** rate of change in the velocity of a moving body.

ac·cel·er·a·tor (ak sel′ər ā′tər), *n.* **1** thing that accelerates. **2** device or pedal that controls the speed of the engine in a vehicle. **3** cyclotron.

ac·cent (*n.* ak′sent; *v.* ak′sent, ak sent′), *n.* **1** special force or emphasis given to a syllable or a word in pronouncing it. **2** mark to indicate special force or emphasis of pronunciation. **3** characteristic manner of pronunciation: *a foreign accent.* **4 accents,** tone of voice: *in soothing accents.* **5** distinctive character or quality: *accent on grammar.* **6** emphasis on or approval of: *an accent on good taste.* **7** mark to indicate vowel quality in foreign languages, as acute (′), grave (`), or circumflex (^). **8** emphasis on certain words or syllables in a line of poetry to give them rhythm. **9** emphasis on certain notes or chords. **10** mark used with numbers showing: **a** minutes or seconds of a degree. **b** feet, inches, or lines. **c** prime, double prime, etc. **11** light or color used to emphasize something in a picture, photograph, etc. —*v.* **1** pronounce or mark with an accent. **2** emphasize; accentuate. [< L *accentus* < *ad-* to + *canere* sing]

ac·cen·tu·al (ak sen′chú əl), *adj.* **1** of or formed by accent. **2** (of poetry) using stress instead of quantity. —ac·cen′tu·al·ly, *adv.*

ac·cen·tu·ate (ak sen′chú āt), *v.*, -at·ed, -at·ing. **1** emphasize. **2** pronounce

or mark with an accent. —ac·cen′tu·a′tion, *n.*

ac·cept (ak sept′), *v.* **1** take or receive (something offered): *accept a gift.* **2** agree to; consent to; accede: *accept a proposal.* **3** take as true or satisfactory; believe; acknowledge: *accept an excuse.* **4** receive with favor; approve: *Einstein's theory was widely accepted.* **5** undertake as a responsibility; assume: *accept a position as cashier.* **6** sign and promise to pay: *accept a note.* [< L *acceptare* < *ad-* to + *capere* take] —ac·cept′er, *esp. in Com.,* ac·cep′tor, *n.*

ac·cept·a·ble (ak sep′tə bəl), *adj.* worth accepting; satisfactory; agreeable; welcome. —ac·cept′a·bil′i·ty, ac·cept′a·ble·ness, *n.* —ac·cept′a·bly, *adv.*

ac·cept·ance (ak sep′təns), *n.* **1** act of accepting. **2** state of being accepted; favorable reception; approval. **3 a** agreement as to terms, esp. to pay a draft or bill of exchange when it is due. **b** the draft or bill itself.

ac·cep·ta·tion (ak′sep tā′shən), *n.* **1** usual meaning; generally accepted meaning. **2** acceptance.

ac·cess (ak′ses), *n.* **1** right to approach, enter, or use; admission: *access to the library.* **2** condition of being easy or hard to reach: *access to the mountain town was difficult.* **3** way or means of approach: *access to powerful men.* **4** an attack (of disease). **5** outburst (of anger). **6** increase. —*v.* reach or gain access to: *easy to access your data files.* [< L *accessus* < *ad-* to + *cedere* come]

ac·ces·sa·ry (ak ses′ə ri), *n., pl.* -ries, *adj. Esp. Law.* accessory. —ac·ces′sa·ri·ly, *adv.* —ac·ces′sa·ri·ness, *n.*

ac·ces·si·ble (ak ses′ə bəl), *adj.* **1** that can be entered or reached; approachable. **2** easy to get at; easy to reach. **3** that can be obtained; available.

accessible to, capable of being influenced by; susceptible.; susceptible. —ac·ces′si·bil′i·ty, *n.* —ac·ces′si·bly, *adv.*

ac·ces·sion (ak sesh′ən), *n.* **1** act of attaining to a right, office, etc.; attainment. **2** a yielding or agreeing (to a plan, opinion, demand, etc.); consent; assent. **3** an increase; addition. **4** thing added. —ac·ces′sion·al, *adj.*

ac·ces·so·ry (ak ses′ə ri), *n., pl.* -ries, *adj.* —*n.* **1** an extra thing added to help something of more importance; subordinate part or detail. **2** person who encourages or helps someone commit an offense against the law, without being present at the time of the offense; accomplice. —*adj.* **1** helping something more important; subsidiary. **2** *Law.* giving aid as an accessory. Also, *esp. Law,* **accessary.**

accessory after the fact, person who shields the offender after the commission of an offense.

accessory before the fact, person who encourages someone to commit an offense. —ac·ces′so·ri·ly, *adv.* —ac·ces′so·ri·ness, *n.*

ac·ci·dence (ak′sə dəns), *n.* part of grammar dealing with word order and those changes in words that show case, number, tense, etc.

ac·ci·dent (ak′sə dənt), *n.* 1 an undesirable or unfortunate chance happening: *an automobile accident.* 2 an unexpected or unintentional happening: *their meeting was an accident.* 3 a nonessential. **by accident,** by chance; without being planned or anticipated. [< L *accidens* < *ad-* to + *cadere* fall]

ac·ci·den·tal (ak′sə den′təl), *adj.* 1 happening by chance; unexpected; fortuitous; unintentional. 2 nonessential; incidental. 3 *Music.* of or having to do with an accidental. —*n. Music.* a sign used to show a change of pitch after the key signature and before the note to be changed. —**ac′ci·den′tal·ly,** *adv.* —**ac′ci·den′tal·ness,** *n.*

ac·ci·dent-prone (ak′sə dənt prōn′), *adj.* tending to have accidents.

ac·claim (ə klām′), *v.* 1 show satisfaction and approval of by words or sounds; applaud. 2 announce with signs of approval; hail. —*n.* shout or show of approval; applause [< L, < *ad-* to + *clamare* cry out] —**ac·claim′er,** *n.*

ac·cla·ma·tion (ak′lə mā′shən), *n.* 1 shout of approval by a crowd; applause. 2 oral vote.

ac·cli·mate (ə klī′mit; ak′lə māt), *v.,* **-mated, -mat·ing.** accustom or become accustomed to a new climate or to new conditions. [< F *acclimater.* See CLIMATE.] **ac·cli′ma·ta·ble** *adj.* **ac′cli-ma′tion** *n.*

ac·cli·ma·tize (ə klī′mə tīz), *v.,* **-tized, -tizing.** acclimate. —**ac·cli′ma·tiz′a·ble,** *adj.* —**ac·cli′ma·ti·za′tion,** *n.*

ac·cliv·i·ty (ə kliv′ə ti), *n., pl.* **-ties.** an upward slope, as of ground. [< L, < *ad-* toward + *clivus* rising ground]

ac·co·lade (ak′ə lād′; -läd′), *n.* 1 honor; praise. 2 a ceremony used in making a man a knight. [< F < Pg. *acolada* an embrace about the neck < L *ad-* to + *collum* neck]

ac·com·mo·date (ə kom′ə dāt), *v.,* **-dated, -dat·ing.** 1 have room for; hold comfortably. 2 do a kindness or favor to; oblige. 3 furnish with lodging and sometimes with food as well. 4 supply; furnish; equip. 5 provide (a person) with (a loan of) money. 6 make fit; make suitable. 7 reconcile; adjust. [< L, < *ad-* + *com-* with + *modus* measure] —**ac·com′mo·da′tor,** *n.*

ac·com·mo·dat·ing (ə kom′ə dāt′ing), *adj.* obliging. —**ac·com′mo·dat′ingly,** *adv.*

ac·com·mo·da·tion (ə kom′ə dā′shən), *n.* 1 anything that helps; favor; convenience. 2 **accomodations,** *pl.* lodging and sometimes food as well: *the hotel has accommodations for one hundred.* 3 loan. 4 willingness to help out. 5 adjustment; adaptation. 6 settlement of differences; reconciliation.

ac·com·mo·da·tive (ə kom′ə dā′tiv), *adj.* obliging. —**ac·com′mo·da′tive·ness,** *n.*

ac·com·pa·ni·ment (ə kum′pə ni mənt), *n.* 1 something incidental that goes along with something else. 2 supplementary instrumental or vocal music that supports or enriches a vocal or instrumental solo.

ac·com·pa·nist (ə kum′pə nist), *n.* person who plays an instrumental accompaniment.

ac·com·pa·ny (ə kum′pə ni), *v.,* **-nied, -ny·ing.** 1 go along with; escort: *accompany a friend on a walk.* 2 be or happen in connection with: *fire is accompanied by heat.* 3 cause to be attended by; supplement (*with*) : *accompany a speech with gestures.* 4 play or sing a musical accompaniment. [< F *accompagner* < *à* to + *compagne* COMPANION] —**ac·com′pa·ni·er,** *n.*

ac·com·plice (ə kom′plis), *n.* person who aids another in committing an unlawful act. [earlier *a complice* a confederate < F *complice* < L, < *com-* together with + *plicare* fold]

ac·com·plish (ə kom′plish), *v.* 1 succeed in completing; carry out; fulfill: *accomplish a purpose.* 2 finish; actually do; achieve: *accomplish nothing.* [< OF < LL, < *ad-* + *complere* fill up] —**ac·com′plish-a·ble,** *adj.* —**ac·com′plish·er,** *n.*

ac·com·plished (ə kom′plisht), *adj.* 1 done; carried out; completed. 2 expert; skilled. 3 skilled in social arts and graces.

ac·com·plish·ment (ə kom′plish mənt), *n.* 1 an accomplishing or being accomplished; completion. 2 thing accomplished; achievement; attainment. 3 skill in some social art or grace: *good manners are a desirable accomplishment.*

ac·cord (ə kôrd′), *v.* 1 be in harmony; agree; correspond: *his report accords with yours.* 2 grant; award: *accord the boy praise for good work.* —*n.* 1 agreement; harmony: *opinions in accord.* 2 an informal agreement between nations. 3 harmony of color, pitch, or tone. **of one's own accord,** without being asked. **with one accord,** all together. [< OF < VL *acchordare* bring into harmony < L *ad-* to + *chorda* string] —**ac·cord′a·ble,** *adj.* —**ac·cord′er,** *n.*

ac·cord·ance (ə kôr′dəns), *n.* agreement; harmony: *in accordance with the plan.*

ac·cord·ant (ə kôr′dənt), *adj.* agreeing; in harmony. —**ac·cord′ant·ly,** *adv.*

ac·cord·ing (ə kôr′ding), *adv.* accordingly. **according as,** in proportion as; accordingly. —*adj.* in harmony. **according to, a** in agreement with: *according to his promise.* **b** in proportion to: *spend according to your income.* **c** on the authority of: *according to this book.*

ac·cord·ing·ly (ə kôr′ding li), *adv.* 1 in agreement with something that has been stated; suitably. 2 for this reason; therefore.

ac·cor·di·on (ə kôr′di ən), *n.* a portable musical wind instrument with a bellows, metallic reeds, and keys. —*adj.* having folds like the bellows of an accordion. [< G < Ital. *accordare* harmonize] —**ac·cor′di·on·ist,** *n.*

ac·cost (ə kôst′; ə kost′), *v.* approach and speak to first; address; greet. [< F < Ital. < LL, < L *ad-* to + *costa* side, rib]

ac·couche·ment (ə küsh′mənt; *Fr.* ä küsh män′), *n.* confinement for childbirth; lying-in. [< F]

ac·count (ə kount′), *n.* 1 detailed or explanatory statement; report; description: *please give an account of your trip; I need an account of your actions.* 2 worth; significance: *a report of little account.* 3 statement of money received and paid out. 4 a record of business dealings between a bank and a depositor. 5 a periodic record of purchases for which a customer is billed. —*v.* 1 give a statement of money received or paid out. 2 hold to be; consider: *Solomon was accounted wise.* **account for, a** give a reason for; explain. **b** answer for. **call to account, a** demand an explanation. **b** scold; reprimand. **for one's account,** for one's sake; on one's account. **of no account,** of no importance or value. **on account,** as part payment. **on account of, a** because of. **b** for the sake of. **on any account,** for any reason. **on one's account,** for one's sake. **on one's own account,** for one's own purpose; at one's own risk. **take account of, a** make allowance for; consider. **b** make a note of note. **turn to account,** get profit or advantage from. [< OF *aconter* count up < LL, <L *ad-* + *computare* compute]

ac·count·a·ble (ə koun′tə bəl), *adj.* 1 responsible. 2 explainable. —**ac·count′a·bil′i·ty, ac·count′a·ble·ness,** *n.* —**account′a·bly,** *adv.*

ac·count·an·cy (ə koun′tən si), *n.* the examining or keeping of business accounts.

ac·count·ant (ə koun′tənt), *n.* person who examines or manages business accounts.

ac·count·ing (ə koun′ting), *n.* theory or system of keeping, analyzing, and interpreting business accounts.

ac·cou·ter, *esp. Brit.* **ac·cou·tre** (ə kü′tər), *v.,* **-tered, -ter·ing; -tred, -tring.** outfit or equip; array. [< F *accoutrer*]

ac·cou·ter·ments (ə kü′tər mənts), *n. pl.* 1 personal equipment; outfit. 2 a soldier's equipment with the exception of his weapons and clothing.

Ac·cra (ə krä′), *n.* seaport in W Africa, capital of Ghana.

ac·cred·it (ə kred′it), *v.* **1** give (a person) credit (for something); credit; attribute: *accredit her with kindness.* **2** send or provide with credentials: *accredited to be our ambassador to the UN.* **3** recognize as meeting an official standard: *an accredited high school.* **4** consider (a thing) as belonging or due (to a person): *we accredit the invention of the telephone to Bell.* **5** accept as worth believing; trust: *accredited as an authority in mathematics.* **6** give authority to; authorize. [< F *accréditer*]

ac·cre·tion (ə krē′shən), *n.* **1** growth in size. **2** a growing together of separate things. **3** an increase in size by natural growth or gradual external addition. **4** thing added; addition. **5** a whole that results from such growths or additions. —**ac·cre′tive,** *adj.*

ac·cru·al (ə krü′əl), *n.* **1** an accruing. **2** amount accrued or accruing.

ac·crue (ə krü′), *v.,* **-crued, -cru·ing. 1** grow or come about as a result of investment. **2** come as a natural product or result. [< F < L, < *ad-* to + *crescere* grow] —**ac·crue′ment,** *n.*

acct., 1 account. **2** accountant.

ac·cu·mu·late (ə kū′myə lāt), *v.,* **-lat·ed, -lat·ing. 1** collect or heap up little by little; amass: *accumulate a fortune.* **2** grow into a heap or mass; accrue. [< L, < *ad-* up + *cumulus* heap] —**ac·cu′mu·la′tor,** *n.*

ac·cu·mu·la·tion (ə kū′myə lā′shən), *n.* **1** gradual collection. **2** material collected; mass.

ac·cu·mu·la·tive (ə kū′myə lā′tiv; -lə tiv), *adj.* tending to accumulate; collective. —**ac·cu′mu·la′tive·ly,** *adv.* —**ac·cu′mu·la′tive·ness,** *n.*

ac·cu·ra·cy (ak′yə rə si), *n.* condition of being without errors or mistakes; correctness.

ac·cu·rate (ak′yə rit), *adj.* **1** making few or no errors; precise: *an accurate observer.* **2** without errors or mistakes; exact: *accurate measure.* [< L, < *ad-* to + *cura* care] —**ac′cu·rate·ly,** *adv.* —**ac′cu·rate·ness,** *n.*

ac·curs·ed (ə kėr′sid; ə kerst′), **ac·curst** (ə kėrst′), *adj.* **1** annoying and detestable; abominable. **2** under a curse. —**ac·curs′ed·ly** *adv.*

accus., accusative.

ac·cu·sa·tion (ak′yù zā′shən), *n.* **1** a charge of wrongdoing. **2** the offense charged. **3** act of accusing.

ac·cu·sa·tive (ə kū′zə tiv), *n.* **1** the objective case. **2** word used as an object of a verb or preposition. —*adj.* showing the direct object; objective. —**ac·cu′sa·tive·ly,** *adv.*

ac·cu·sa·to·ry (ə kū′zə tô′ri; -tō′-), *adj.* containing an accusation; accusing.

ac·cuse (ə kūz′), *v.,* **-cused, -cus·ing. 1** charge with some crime, offense, etc.; arraign. **2** find fault with; blame. [< OF < L *accusare* < *ad-* to + *causa* cause] —**ac·cus′er,** *n.* —**ac·cus′ing·ly,** *adv.*

ac·cus·tom (ə kus′təm), *v.* make familiar by use or habit; get used; habituate. [< OF *acostumer*]

ac·cus·tomed (ə kus′təmd), *adj.* usual; customary. —**ac·cus′tomed·ness,** *n.*

ace (ās), *n.* **1** a playing card, domino, or side of a die having a single spot. **2** a single spot. **3** a point won by a single stroke in tennis and certain other games. **4** an expert. **5** a combat pilot who has shot down five or more enemy planes. —*adj.* of great skill; expert. —*v.* **aced, acing. 1** serve an ace to an opponent, esp. in tennis. **2** do extremely well on a test, in a class, etc. [< OF *as* < L, smallest unit (of coinage, measure, etc.)]

a·cer·bi·ty (ə sėr′bə ti), *n., pl.* **-ties. 1** sharpness of taste; sourness. **2** harshness of manner; severity. [<F <L, < *acerbus* bitter]

ac·e·tab·u·lum (as′ə tab′yə ləm), *n., pl.* **-la** (-lə). **1** the hip socket. **2** any cup-shaped structure. [<L, cup-shaped holder for vinegar, < *acetum* vinegar] —**ac′e·tab′u·lar,** *adj.*

ac·et·an·i·lide, ac·et·an·i·lid, (as′ət an′-ə lid; -ə lĭd), *n.* a white, crystalline drug, C_8H_9NO, used in medicines to relieve pain and lessen fever.

ac·e·tate (as′ə tāt), *n.* **1** any salt or ester of acetic acid. **2** any synthetic resins or fibers made from cellulose acetate. —**ac′e·tat′ed,** *adj.*

a·ce·tic (ə sē′tik; ə set′ik), *adj.* of or derived from vinegar or acetic acid. [< L *acetum* vinegar]

acetic acid, a very sour, colorless acid, CH_3COOH, present in vinegar.

a·cet·i·fy (ə set′ə fī), *v.,* **-fied, -fy·ing.** turn into vinegar. —*n.* **a·cet′i·fi·ca′tion,** *n.*

ac·e·tone (as′ə tōn), *n.* a colorless, volatile, inflammable liquid, CH_3CO-, used as a solvent and in making varnishes, etc.

a·ce·tyl·cho·line (as′ə til kō′lēn; -lin), *n.* chemical compound that transmits nerve impulses.

a·cet·y·lene (ə set′ə lēn; -lin), *n.* a colorless gas, C_2H_2, that burns with a bright light and very hot flame, used for lighting and, combined with oxygen, for welding metals.

ac·e·tyl·sal·i·cyl·ic acid (as′ə til sal′-ə sil′ik; ə sē′təl-), aspirin.

A·chae·a (ə kē′ə), *n.* country in ancient Greece, in the S part. —**A·chae′an,** *adj., n.*

ache (āk), *v.,* **ached, ach·ing,** *n.* —*v.* **1** be in continued pain; hurt. **2** *Colloq.* wish very much; long; yearn. —*n.* a dull, steady pain. [OE *acan*] —**ach′ing·ly,** *adv.*

a·chene (ā kēn′), *n.* any small, dry, hard fruit consisting of one seed with a thin outer covering that does not burst when ripe. Also, **akene.** [< NL < Gk., < *a-* not + *chainein* gape; because it ripens without bursting]

Ach·er·on (ak′ər on), *n.* **1** river in Hades. **2** the lower world; Hades.

a·chieve (ə chēv′), *v.,* **a·chieved, a·chiev·ing. 1** bring to a successful end; accom-

plish; finish; complete: *achieve one's purpose.* **2** get by effort; gain; attain: *achieve distinction.* [< OF, < (*venir*) a chief (come) to a head] —**a·chiev′a·ble,** *adj.* —**a·chiev′er,** *n.*

a·chieve·ment (ə chēv′mənt), *n.* **1** thing achieved; accomplishment. **2** act of achieving.

A·chil·les (ə kil′ēz), *n.* legendary hero of the Greeks at the siege of Troy. No weapon could injure Achilles anywhere, except in the heel. —**Ach·il′le·an,** *adj.*

Achilles heel, weak or vulnerable point.

Achilles tendon, tendon at the back of the leg.

ach·ro·mat·ic (ak′rə mat′ik), *adj.* **1** transmitting white light without breaking it up into the colors of the spectrum. **2** colorless. [< Gk., < *a-* without + *chroma* color] —**ach′ro·mat′i·cal·ly,** *adv.*

ac·id (as′id), *n.* **1** compound that yields hydrogen ions when dissolved in water, usually reacts with a base to form salt and water, and turns blue litmus paper red. **2** substance having a sour taste. **3** = LSD. —*adj.* **1** of or having the properties of an acid. **2** sour; sharp; biting in taste or manner. [< L *acidus* sour] —**ac′id·ly,** *adv.* —**ac′id·ness.** *n.*

a·cid·ic (ə sid′ik), *adj.* forming acid.

a·cid·i·fy (ə sid′ə fī), *v.,* **-fied, -fy·ing. 1** make or become sour. **2** change into an acid. —**a·cid′i·fi·ca′tion,** *n.* —**a·cid′i·fi′er,** *n.*

a·cid·i·ty (ə sid′ə ti), *n., pl.* **-ties.** acid quality or condition; sourness.

ac·i·do·sis (as′ə dō′sis), *n.* a harmful condition in which the blood and tissues are less alkaline than is normal.

acid rain, rain that contains acidic pollutants.

acid rock, rock music with a beat and words that suggest drug-induced experiences.

acid test, a thorough test.

a·cid·u·late (ə sij′ə lāt), *v.,* **-lat·ed, -lat·ing.** make slightly acid or sour. —**a·cid′u·la′tion,** *n.*

a·cid·u·lous (ə sij′ə ləs), *adj.* slightly acid or sour. —**a·cid′u·lous·ly,** *adv.* —**a·cid′u·lous·ness,** *n.*

ack-ack (ak′ak′), *n.* anti-aircraft fire. [British radio operator's code word for AA (anti-aircraft)]

ac·knowl·edge (ak nol′ij), *v.* **-edged, -edg·ing. 1** admit to be true; concede. **2** recognize the authority or claims of; accept. **3** express appreciation of (a gift, favor, etc.). **4** make known the receipt of: *acknowledge a letter.* **5** recognize or certify in legal form: *acknowledge a deed.* [blend of obs. *acknow* admit + *knowledge,* v., admit] —**ac·knowl′edge·a·ble,** *adj.* —**ac·knowl′edged·ly,** *adv.* —**ac·knowl′edg·er,** *n.*

ac·knowl·edg·ment, ac·knowl·edge·ment (ak nol′ij mənt), *n.* **1** thing given or done to show that one has received a gift, favor, message, etc. **2** act of admitting the existence or truth of anything;

admission. **3** recognition of authority or claims; acceptance. **4** expression of thanks. **5** official certificate in legal form.

ac·me (ak′mē), *n.* the highest point; apex. [< Gk. *akme* point]

ac·ne (ak′nē), *n.* a skin disease in which the oil glands in the skin become clogged and inflamed, often causing pimples. [?< Gk. *akme* point]

ac·o·lyte (ak′ə līt), *n.* **1** altar boy. **2** person ordained to a minor order in the Roman Catholic Church. **3** attendant; assistant; follower. [< Med.L < Gk. *akolouthos* follower]

ac·o·nite (ak′ə nīt), *n.* **1** any of a genus of poisonous plants, with blue, purple, or yellow flowers shaped like hoods, including wolf's-bane and monkshood. **2** drug used to relieve inflammation and pain, obtained from one of these plants. [< F < L < Gk. *akoniton*]

a·corn (ā′kôrn; ā′kərn), *n.* the nut, or fruit, of an oak tree. [OE *æcern*]

a·cous·tic (ə küs′tik), **a·cous·ti·cal** (-tə kəl), *adj.* **1** having to do with the sense or the organs of hearing. **2** having to do with the science of sound. **3** acted on or directed by sound waves: *an acoustic mine.* **4** produced on a musical instrument without amplification. [< F < Gk. *akoustikos* having to do with hearing < *akouein* hear] —**a·cous′ti·cal·ly,** *adv.*

a·cous·tics (əküs′tiks), *n.* **1** (*pl. in use*) the qualities of a room, hall, auditorium, etc., that determine how well sounds can be heard in it; acoustic qualities. **2** (*sing. in use*) science of sound.

ac·quaint (ə kwānt′), *v.* **1** inform; tell: *acquaint him with your intention.* **2** make more or less familiar; familiarize: *acquaint oneself with the facts.*

be acquainted with, have personal knowledge of: *he is acquainted with my father.* [< OF *acointer* < LL, < L *ad-* to + *cognitus* known < *com* with + *gnoscere* come to know]

ac·quaint·ance (ə kwān′təns), *n.* **1** person known to one, but not a close friend. **2** knowledge of persons or things gained from experience with them. —**ac·quaint′ance·ship,** *n.*

ac·qui·esce (ak′wi es′), *v.,* **-esced, -escing.** give consent by keeping silent; submit quietly: *we acquiesced in their plan.* [< F < L, < *ad-* to + *quiescere* to rest] —**ac′qui·esc′ing·ly,** *adv.*

ac·qui·es·cence (ak′wi es′əns), *n.* consent without making objections; submitting quietly.

ac·qui·es·cent (ak′wi es′ənt), *adj.* submitting with apparent consent. —**ac′qui·es′cent·ly,** *adv.*

ac·quire (ə kwīr′), *v.,* **-quired, -quiring.** **1** receive or get as one's own; obtain: *acquire land.* **2** get by one's own efforts or actions; gain: *acquire an education.* [< L, < *ad-* to + *quaerere* seek] —**ac·quir′a·ble,** *adj.* —**ac·quir′er,** *n.*

ac·quire·ment (ə kwīr′mənt), *n.* **1** act of acquiring. **2** something acquired; attainment.

ac·qui·si·tion (ak′wə zish′ən), *n.* **1** act of acquiring. **2** thing acquired.

ac·quis·i·tive (ə kwiz′ə tiv), *adj.* fond of acquiring; likely to get and keep. —**ac·quis′i·tive·ly,** *adv.* —**ac·quis′i·tive·ness,** *n.*

ac·quit (ə kwit′), *v.,* **-quit·ted, -quit·ting.** **1** declare (a person) not guilty (of an offense); exonerate. **2** set free (from a duty, an obligation, etc.); release. **3** pay off or settle (a debt, claim, etc.).

acquit oneself, conduct oneself; behave: *the soldiers acquitted themselves well in battle.* [< OF, < *a-* + *quitte* free < L *quietus* quiet] —**ac·quit′ter,** *n.*

ac·quit·tal (ə kwit′əl), *n.* **1** a setting free by declaring not guilty; discharge; release. **2** performance (of a duty, obligation, etc.).

ac·quit·tance (ə kwit′əns), *n.* **1** release from a debt or obligation. **2** payment of a debt. **3** a written acknowledgment.

a·cre (ā′kər), *n.* **1** a measure of land, 160 square rods or 43,560 square feet. **2 acres,** lands; property. [OE *æcer* field]

A·cre (ä′kər; ā′kər), *n.* seaport in NW Israel, important during the Crusades.

a·cre·age (ā′kər ij), *n.* **1** number of acres. **2** piece of land sold by the acre.

ac·rid (ak′rid), *adj.* **1** sharp or stinging to the nose, mouth, or skin. **2** sharp or irritating in manner. [< L *acer* sharp] —**a·crid′i·ty, ac′rid·ness,** *n.* —**ac′rid·ly,** *adv.*

ac·ri·mo·ni·ous (ak′rə mō′ni əs), *adj.* caustic and stinging; bitter. —**ac′ri·mo′ni·ous·ly,** *adv.* —**ac′ri·mo′ni·ous·ness,** *n.*

ac·ri·mo·ny (ak′rə mō′ni), *n., pl.* **-nies.** sharpness or bitterness in temper, language, or manner. [< L *acrimonia* < *acer* sharp]

ac·ro·bat (ak′rə bat), *n.* **1** person who can perform on a trapeze, a tightrope, etc. **2** skillful, daring, nimble performer. [< F < Gk., < *akros* tip (of the toes) + *-batos* going] —**ac′ro·bat′ic,** *adj.* —**ac′ro·bat′i·cal·ly,** *adv.*

ac·ro·bat·ics (ak′rə bat′iks), *n. pl.* **1** gymnastic feats. **2** feats like those of an acrobat.

ac·ro·gen (ak′rə jən), *n. Bot.* plant growing only at the apex, such as the ferns and mosses. [< Gk. *akros* tip + *-genes* born] —**ac′ro·gen′ic, a·crog′e·nous,** *adj.* —**a·crog′e·nous·ly,** *adv.*

ac·ro·meg·a·ly (ak′rō meg′ə li), *n.* a disease in which the head, hands, and feet become permanently enlarged. [<F, < Gk. *akros* tip + *megas* big] —**ac′ro·me·gal′ic,** *adj.*

ac·ro·nym (ak′rə nim), *n.* word formed from the first letters or syllables of other words, as NAFTA. [< Gk. *akros* tip + *onyma* name]

a·crop·o·lis (ə krop′ə lis), *n.* the high, fortified part of an ancient Greek city, esp.

the Acropolis of Athens. [< Gk., < *akros* highest part of + *polis* city]

a·cross (ə krôs′; ə kros′), *prep.* **1** from side to side of; over: *across a river.* **2** beyond: *across the sea.* **3** into contact with: *come across a new word.* —*adv.* from one side to the other: *the distance across?*

across the board, without any exceptions.

come across, a pay up; hand over. **b** own up; admit.

a·cros·tic (ə krôs′tik; ə kros′-), *n.* **1** composition in verse or an arrangement of words in which the first, last, or certain other letters of each line, taken in order, spell a word or phrase. **2** puzzle having acrostic clues to its solution. —*adj.* of or forming an acrostic. [< L < Gk., < *akros* tip + *stichos* row] —**a·cros′ti·cal·ly,** *adv.*

a·cryl·ic (ə kril′ik), *n.* **1** acrylic resin. **2** acrylic paint. **3** painting done with acrylic paint. —*adj.* of acrylic.

ac·ry·lo·ni·trile (ak′rə lō nī′trəl), *n.* a colorless inflammable, poisonous liquid, C_3H_3N, used in synthetic rubber, fabrics, plastics, etc.

act (akt), *n.* **1** thing done; deed: *an act of kindness.* **2** process of doing: *in the act of stealing.* **3** a main division of a play or opera. **4** one of several performances on a program. **5** a law: *an act of Congress.* —*v.* **1** put forth effort: *act at once.* **2** perform specific duties. **3** behave: *act tired.* **4** have an effect: *yeast acts on dough.* **5** play a part; perform in a theater. **act as or for,** take the place of.

act up, a behave badly. **b** make mischief.

get one's act together, get oneself organized. [< L *actus* a doing and *actum* (thing) done < *agere* do] —**act′a·ble,** *adj.*

ACT, American College Testing Program.

ACTH, *n.* a hormone of the pituitary gland, used in treating arthritis, rheumatic fever, etc.

ac·tin (ak′tən), *n.* hormone involved in muscle contraction.

act·ing (ak′ting), *adj.* **1** temporarily taking another's place; substitute. **2** that acts or functions. **3** arranged for the use of actors.

ac·tin·ic (ak tin′ik), *adj.* **1** of actinism. **2** producing chemical changes by radiation. [< Gk. *aktis* ray]

ac·tin·ism (ak′tən iz əm), *n.* property in light that causes chemical changes.

ac·tin·i·um (ak tin′i əm), *n.* a radioactive chemical element, Ac, somewhat like radium, found in pitchblende.

ac·ti·no·zo·an (ak′tə nə zō′ən), *n.* = anthozoan.

ac·tion (ak′shən), *n.* **1** process of acting: *a machine in action.* **2** thing done; act. **3** way of moving or working; movement. **4** a minor battle or combat between military forces. **5** a lawsuit.

actions, conduct; behavior.

take action, a become active. **b** start working. **c** *Also,* **bring action,** start a lawsuit. [< F < L *actio*. See ACT.] —ac′tion·less, *adj.*

ac·tion·a·ble (ak′shən ə bəl), *adj.* justifying a lawsuit. —ac′tion·a·bly, *adv.*

ac·ti·vate (ak′tə vāt), *v.,* –vat·ed, –vat·ing. 1 make active. 2 make radioactive. 3 make capable of reacting or of speeding up a chemical reaction. 4 purify (sewage) by treating it with air and bacteria. —ac′ti·va′tion, *n.* —ac′ti·va′tor, *n.*

ac·tive (ak′tiv), *adj.* 1 acting; working: *an active volcano.* 2 moving rather quickly; lively; nimble. 3 showing much or constant action; vigorous: *an active market.* 4 real; effective: *take an active part.* 5 causing action or change. 6 showing the subject of a verb as acting. In "He broke the window," *broke* is in the active voice. —*n.* the active voice. [< F < L *activus.* See ACT.] —ac′tive·ly, *adv.* —ac′tive·ness, *n.*

active duty or service, 1 military service with full pay and regular duties. 2 service in the armed forces in time of war.

ac·tiv·ism (ak tə viz′əm), *n.* policy or practice of personal involvement in activities that advance one's own political or philosophical beliefs. —ac′tiv·ist, *n., adj.*

ac·tiv·i·ty (ak tiv′ə ti), *n., pl.* –ties. 1 state of being active: *mental activity.* 2 action; doing: *the activities of enemy spies.* 3 vigorous action; liveliness: *no activity in the market.* 4 thing to do; sphere of action: *outside activities.* 5 anything active; active force.

act of God, a sudden, unforeseeable, and uncontrollable action of natural forces, such as flood, storm, or earthquake.

ac·tor (ak′tər), *n.* 1 person who acts on the stage, in moving pictures, or in a broadcast. 2 person who acts; doer.

ac·tress (ak′tris), *n.* a female actor.

Acts (akts), or Acts of the Apostles, *n.* the fifth book of the New Testament.

ac·tu·al (ak′chü əl), *adj.* 1 existing as a fact; real; true; genuine: *the actual as opposed to the imaginary.* 2 now existing; present; current: *the actual state of affairs.* [< F < LL < L *actus* a doing. See ACT.] —ac′tu·al·ness, *n.*

ac·tu·al·i·ty (ak′chü al′ə ti), *n., pl.* –ties. 1 actual existence. 2 actual thing; fact.

ac·tu·al·ize (ak′chü əl īz), *v.,* –ized, –iz·ing. make actual. —ac′tu·al·i·za′tion, *n.*

ac·tu·al·ly (ak′chü əl i), *adv.* really; in fact.

ac·tu·ar·y (ak′chü er′i), *n., pl.* –ar·ies. person whose work is figuring risks, rates, etc., for insurance companies. [< L *actuarius* account keeper. See ACT.] —ac′tu·ar′i·al, *adj.* —ac′tu·ar′i·al·ly, *adv.*

ac·tu·ate (ak′chü āt), *v.,* –at·ed, –at·ing. 1 put into action. 2 influence to act. [< LL, < L *actus* action] —ac′tu·a′tion, *n.* —ac′tu·a′tor, *n.*

a·cu·i·ty (ə kū′ə ti), *n.* sharpness; acuteness. [< Med.L < OF *agüeté* < *agu* sharp < L *acutus*]

a·cu·men (ə kū′mən), *n.* sharpness and quickness in seeing and understanding; keen insight. [< L, < *acuere* sharpen]

a·cute (ə kūt′), *adj.* 1 having a sharp point. 2 sharp and severe: *an acute fuel shortage.* 3 brief and severe: *an acute attack of appendicitis.* 4 keen: *an acute sense of smell.* 5 intense; poignant: *acute jealousy.* 6 (of sounds) high in pitch; shrill. 7 having the mark (′) over it. —*n.* acute accent. [< L, < *acuere* sharpen] —a·cute′ly, *adv.* —a·cute′ness, *n.*

acute accent, mark (′) used to show the quality of a vowel, as in French *abbé,* or to show stress, as in Spanish *adiós.*

acute angle, angle less than a right angle.

ad (ad), *n.* advertisement.

ad–, *prefix.* to; toward, as in *admit, administer, adverb, advert.* [< L *ad,* prep.; appears also, by assimilation to the following consonant, as *ac–, af–, ag–, al–, an–, ap–, ar–, as–, at–,* and, by reduction before *sc, sp, st,* as *a–*]

A.D., in the year of the Lord; since Christ was born. [for LL *anno domini*]

ad·age (ad′ij), *n.* a brief, familiar proverb; an old saying. [< F < L *adagium*]

a·da·gio (ə dä′jō; –zhi ō), *adv., adj., n., pl.* –gios. *Music.* —*adv.* slowly. —*adj.* slow. —*n.* a slow part in a piece of music. [< Ital. *ad agio* at ease]

Ad·am (ad′əm), *n.* in the Bible, the first man.

ad·a·mant (ad′ə mant), *adj.,* 1 unyielding; firm; immovable. 2 too hard to be cut or broken. —*n.* substance too hard to be cut or broken. [< OF *adamaunt* the hardest stone (= diamond) < L < Gk., < *a–* not + *damaein* subdue]

ad·a·man·tine (ad′ə man′tin; –tēn; –tīn), *adj.* adamant; impenetrable; unyielding.

Ad·ams (ad′əmz), *n.* 1 John, 1735–1826, second president of the United States, 1797–1801. 2 John Quincy, 1767–1848, sixth president of the United States, 1825–29, son of John Adams.

Adam's apple, the lump in the front of the throat formed by the thyroid cartilage.

a·dapt (ə dapt′), *v.* 1 make fit or suitable; adjust; accommodate: *adapt oneself to a new job.* 2 modify or alter for a different use: *adapt a novel for the stage.* [< L, < *ad–* to + *aptare* fit] —a·dapt′er, *n.*

a·dapt·a·ble (ə dap′tə bəl), *adj.* 1 easily changed to fit different conditions. 2 changing easily to fit different conditions. —a·dapt′a·bil′i·ty, a·dapt′a·ble·ness, *n.*

ad·ap·ta·tion (ad′əp tā′shən), *n.* 1 adjustment to new or different circumstances. 2 result of altering for a different use. 3 change in structure, form, or habits to fit different conditions. —ad′ap·ta′tion·al, *adj.*

a·dap·tive (ə dap′tiv), *adj.* 1 that can adapt. 2 showing adaptation. —a·dap′tive·ly, *adv.* —a·dap′tive·ness, *n.*

add (ad), *v.* 1 join (one thing to another): *add another stone to the pile.* 2 find the sum of. 3 increase: *add to our pleasure.*

4 say further. [<L, < *ad–* to + *dare* put] —add′a·ble, add′i·ble, *adj.* —add′er, *n.*

ad·dax (ad′aks), *n.* a large antelope of Arabia and N Africa. [< L < an African word]

ad·dend (ad′end), *n.* number or quantity to be added.

ad·den·dum (ə den′dəm), *n., pl.* –da (–də). 1 thing to be added. 2 things added; appendix.

ad·der (ad′ər), *n.* 1 a small, poisonous snake of Europe. 2 a small, harmless snake of North America. 3 =puff adder. [OE *nædre*; in ME *a nadder* was taken as *an adder*]

ad·der's-tongue (ad′ərz tung′), *n.* 1 a variety of small fern with a fruiting spike. 2 the dogtooth violet.

ad·dict (*n.* ad′ikt; *v.* ə dikt′), *n.* a person who is a slave or devotee to a habit. —*v.* give (oneself) over, as to a habit. [< L, < *ad–* to + *dicere* say] —ad·dic′tion, *n.*

ad·dict·ed (ə dik′tid), *adj.* slavishly following (a habit, practice); strongly inclined.

Ad·dis Ab·a·ba (ad′is ab′ə bə), the capital of Ethiopia.

ad·di·tion (ə dish′ən), *n.* 1 act or process of adding. 2 result of adding; thing added. 3 part added to a building. 4 a land added that is next to existing holdings. b in a city, an area that extends existing development.

in addition to, besides; also. [< F < L. See ADD.]

ad·di·tion·al (ə dish′ən əl), *adj.* added; supplementary. —ad·di′tion·al·ly, *adv.*

ad·di·tive (ad′ə tiv), *adj.* to be added; involving addition. —*n.* something added to improve flavor, effectiveness, etc.: *food additives; ethylene is now a common additive in gasoline.*

ad·dle (ad′əl), *v.,* –dled, –dling, *adj.* —*v.* 1 make or become confused. 2 make or become rotten. —*adj.* 1 muddled; confused: *addlebrained.* 2 rotten: *addle eggs.* [OE *adela* liquid filth]

ad·dress (ə dres′; *esp. for n. def. 2,* ad′res), *n., v.,* –dressed or –drest, –dress·ing. —*n.* 1 a speech: *the President's inaugural address.* 2 place at which a person, business, etc., receives mail. 3 skill; adroitness. 4 symbol that shows location of a data file in a computer. —*v.* 1 direct speech or writing to: *the President addressed the nation on TV.* 2 write on (a letter, package, etc.) where it is to be sent. 3 apply or devote (oneself); direct one's energies.

addresses, attention paid in courtship. [< F *adresser* direct to < OF < L, < *ad–* to + *directus* straight] —ad·dress′er, ad·dres′sor, *n.*

address book, location in a computer where email addreses are stored.

ad·dress·ee (ə dres ē′; ad′res ē′), *n.* person to whom a letter, etc., is addressed.

ad·duce (ə dūs′; ə dūs′), *v.,* –duced, –duc·ing. offer as a reason; give as proof or evidence. [< L, < *ad–* to + *ducere* lead]

ad·duct (ə dukt′), v. pull (a part of the body) inward toward the main axis. [< L adductus, pp. See ADDUCE.] —**ad·duc′tive**, adj. —**ad·duc′tor**, n.

ad·duc·tion (ə duk′shən), n. 1 an adducing. 2 an adducting.

ad·e·noid (ad′ə noid), **ad·e·noi·dal** (ad′ə noi′dəl), adj. 1 of the lymphatic glands. 2 glandular.

ad·e·noids (ad′ə noidz), n. pl. growths of glandular tissue in the part of the throat behind the nose, that often interfere with natural breathing and speaking. [< Gk., < aden gland]

a·den·o·sine (ə den′ə sēn′), n. compound of adenine and ribose and formed in living cells.

ad·ept (n. ad′ept, ə dept′; adj. ə dept′), n. a thoroughly skilled person; expert. —adj. thoroughly skilled. [< L adeptus < ad– to + apisci get] —**a·dept′ly**, adv. —**a·dept′ness**, n.

ad·e·qua·cy (ad′ə kwə si), n. as much as is needed for a particular purpose; sufficiency.

ad·e·quate (ad′ə kwit), adj. 1 as much as is needed; fully sufficient; enough: means adequate to the object. 2 suitable; competent: an adequate person for the job. [< L, < ad– to + aequus equal] —**ad′e·quate·ly**, adv. —**ad′e·quate·ness**, n.

ad·here (ad hir′), v., –hered, –her·ing. 1 stick fast (to): mud adheres to your shoes. 2 hold closely or firmly (to): adhere to a plan. 3 be devoted (to): most people adhere to the church of their parents. [< L, < ad to + haerere stick]

ad·her·ence (ad hir′əns), n. 1 steady attachment or loyalty (to a person, group, belief, etc.). 2 a holding to and following closely.

ad·her·ent (ad hir′ənt), n. faithful supporter. —adj. adhering. —**ad·her′ent·ly**, adv.

ad·he·sion (ad hē′zhən), n. 1 act or state of adhering; a sticking fast. 2 following and supporting; faithfulness. 3 agreement; assent. 4 the attraction that holds molecules together. 5 the growing together of tissues that should be separate.

ad·he·sive (ad hē′siv; –ziv), adj. 1 holding fast; adhering easily; sticky. 2 smeared with a sticky substance for holding (something) fast: adhesive tape. —n. gummed tape used to hold bandages in place. —**ad·he′sive·ly**, adv. —**ad·he′sive·ness**, n.

ad hoc (ad hok′), for a certain purpose; special. [< L, for this]

ad·i·a·bat·ic (ad′i ə bat′ik; ā′dī–), adj. Physics. without transmission as a gain or loss of heat. —**ad′i·a·bat′i·cal·ly**, adv.

a·dieu (ə dü′; ə dū′), interj., **a·dieux** (ə düz′; ə dūz′). good-by; farewell. —n., pl. **a·dieus**, a farewell. [< F à dieu to God]

ad in·fi·ni·tum (ad in′fə nī′təm), Latin. without limit; forever.

ad in·te·rim (ad in′tə rim), Latin. 1 in the meantime. 2 temporary.

a·di·os (ä′di ōs′; ad′i–), interj. good-by. —n. a farewell. [< Sp. a dios to God]

ad·i·pose (ad′ə pōs), adj. fatty. —n. animal fat. [< NL < L adeps fat] —**ad′i·pose·ness**, **ad′i·pos′i·ty**, n.

Ad·i·ron·dacks (ad′ə ron′daks), n. pl. a mountain range in NE New York.

adj., 1 adjective. 2 adjunct. 3 adjustment.

ad·ja·cen·cy (ə jā′sən si), n., pl. –cies. 1 nearness. 2 that which is adjacent.

ad·ja·cent (ə jā′sənt), adj. lying near or close; adjoining; bordering: the garage is adjacent to our house. [< L, < ad– near + jacere to lie] —**ad·ja′cent·ly**, adv.

adjacent angles, two angles that have the same vertex and the same line as one of their sides.

ad·jec·ti·val (aj′ik tī′vəl; aj′ik ti vəl), adj. of or used as an adjective. —n. word or words used as an adjective. —**ad′jec·ti′val·ly**, adv.

ad·jec·tive (aj′ik tiv), n. a word used to qualify or limit a noun or pronoun. —adj. 1 of an adjective. 2 used as an adjective. [< L adjectivus that is added to < ad– to + jacere throw] —**ad′jec·tive·ly**, adv.

ad·join (ə join′), v. 1 be next to; be in contact with: Canada adjoins the United States. 2 be next or close to each other; be in contact. [< OF ajoindre < L, < ad– to + jungere join] —**ad·join′ing**, adj.

ad·journ (ə jėrn′), v. 1 put off until a later time: the club adjourned consideration of the question. 2 suspend a meeting to a future time or to another place: the judge adjourned the court for two hours. 3 stop business or proceedings for a time: the court adjourned from Friday until Monday. 4 go to another place, esp. for privacy. [< OF ajorner < a– for (< L ad–) + jorn day < LL diurnum, ult. < L dies day]

ad·journ·ment (ə jėrn′mənt), n. 1 act of adjourning. 2 time during which a court, lawmaking body, etc., is adjourned.

Adjt., Adjutant.

ad·judge (ə juj′), v., –judged, –judg·ing. 1 decree or declare by law: the accused man was adjudged guilty. 2 condemn or sentence by law: the thief was adjudged to prison for two years. 3 decide or settle by law; judge. 4 award or assign by law. [< OF ajugier < L, < ad– to + judicare judge. Doublet of ADJUDICATE.] —**ad·judge′a·ble**, adj.

ad·ju·di·cate (ə jü′də kāt), v., –cat·ed, –cat·ing. 1 decide or settle by law. 2 act as judge. [< L adjudicatus, pp. Doublet of ADJUDGE.] —**ad·ju′di·ca′tion**, n. —**ad·ju′di·ca′tive**, adj. —**ad·ju′di·ca′tor**, n.

ad·junct (aj′ungkt), n. 1 something added that is less important or not necessary, but helpful. 2 a subordinate colleague. 3 word or phrase qualifying or modifying another word or phrase. [< L adjunctus, pp. of adjungere join to. See ADJOIN.] —**ad·junc′tive**, adj. —**ad·junc′tive·ly**, **ad′junct·ly**, adv.

ad·jure (ə jūr′), v., –jured, –jur·ing. 1 command or charge (a person) on oath or under some penalty (to do something). 2 ask earnestly or solemnly. [< L, < ad– to + jurare swear] —**ad·ju·ra′tion**, n. —**ad·jur′a·to′ry**, adj. —**ad·jur′er**, **ad·ju′ror**, n.

ad·just (ə just′), v. 1 fit or adapt (one thing to another): adjust a seat to the height of a child. 2 regulate for use: adjust a radio dial. 3 arrange satisfactorily; settle: adjust a difference of opinion. 4 accommodate oneself; get used: adjust well to army life. [< F ajuster < a– (< L ad–) + juste right < L justus] —**ad·just′a·ble**, adj. —**ad·just′a·bly**, adv. —**ad·just′ed**, adj. —**ad·just′er**, **ad·jus′tor**, n.

ad·just·ment (ə just′mənt), n. 1 act or process of adjusting. 2 orderly arrangement of parts or elements. 3 means of adjusting. 4 settlement of a dispute, a claim, etc.

ad·ju·tan·cy (aj′ə tən si), n., pl. –cies. rank or position of an adjutant in the army.

ad·ju·tant (aj′ə tənt), n. 1 army officer who assists a commanding officer by sending out orders, writing letters, giving messages, etc. 2 helper; assistant. 3 a very large species of stork of India and Africa. —adj. helping. [< L adjutans, ult. < ad– to + juvare help]

adjutant general, pl. **adjutants general**. adjutant of a division or a larger military unit.

ad lib. or **ad libit**, Music. ad libitum.

ad·lib (ad lib′), v., –libbed, –lib·bing. make up as one speaks, performs, or acts; extemporize freely. —adj. extemporized. —adv. at the moment. [< L ad libitum at pleasure]

ad lib·i·tum (ad lib′ə təm), Music. a direction to change, omit, or expand a passage as much as the player wishes. [< NL, at pleasure]

Adm., Admiral; Admiralty.

ad·min·is·ter (ad min′əs tər), v. 1 manage the affairs of (a business, city, etc.); control on behalf of others: administer a government department. 2 give out; dispense: administer relief. 3 deliver or apply: administer punishment to a person. 4 offer formally (an oath). 5 take charge of (an estate) as administrator. 6 be helpful; add something; contribute. [< L, ad– + ministrare serve < minister servant] —**ad·min′is·tra·ble**, —adj. —**ad·min′is·trant**, n.

ad·min·is·trate (ad min′əs trāt), v., –trat·ed, –trat·ing. administer.

ad·min·is·tra·tion (ad min′əs trā′shən), n. 1 management (of a business, town, etc.). 2 the management of public affairs by executive government officials. 3 a public officials as a group. b the President of the United States, the Cabinet, and officials appointed by the President. 4 a the period of office of these officials. b the term or terms during which a government holds office, esp. the U.S. President. **5** a giving out, applying, or dispensing (medicine, justice, etc.).

ad·min·is·tra·tive (ad min′əs trā′tiv), *adj.* **1** executive. **2** of the administration. —**ad·min′is·tra′tive·ly,** *adv.*

ad·min·is·tra·tor (ad min′əs trā′tər), *n.* **1** person who administers; manager; director. **2** *Law.* person appointed by a court to take charge of or settle an estate or manage the affairs of person judged incompetent. —**ad·min′is·tra′-tor·ship,** *n.*

ad·min·is·tra·trix (ad min′əs trā′triks), *n. Law.* female administrator.

ad·mi·ra·ble (ad′mə rə bəl), *adj.* **1** worth admiring. **2** excellent; very good. —**ad′mi·ra·ble·ness,** *n.* —**ad′mi·ra·bly,** *adv.*

ad·mi·ral (ad′mə rəl), *n.* **1** admiral, vice-admiral, or rear admiral. **2** in the U.S. Navy, a commander of a navy or fleet. **3** naval officer having the highest rank next below a fleet admiral. **4** flagship. **5** any of several species of colorful butterflies. [earlier *amiral* < OF < Ar. *amīr al* chief of the; akin to AMIR]

ad·mi·ral·ty (ad′mə rəl ti), *n., pl.* **–ties. 1** law or court dealing with affairs of the sea and ships. **2 the Admiralty,** in England (until 1963), the government department in charge of naval affairs.

ad·mi·ra·tion (ad′mə rā′shən), *n.* **1** a feeling of wonder, pleasure, and approval. **2** the act of regarding with delight something fine or beautiful. **3** someone or something so admired. **4** *Archaic.* wonder.

ad·mire (ad mīr′), *v.,* **–mired, –mir·ing. 1** regard with wonder, approval, and pleasure. **2** feel or express admiration for. **3** wonder at. [< L, < *ad–* at + *mirari* wonder] —**ad·mir′er,** *n.*

ad·mir·ing (ad mīr′ing), *adj.* full of admiration. —**ad·mir′ing·ly,** *adv.*

ad·mis·si·ble (ad mis′ə bəl), *adj.* **1** capable or worthy of being admitted. **2** permitted according to an authority or rules; permissible. **3** allowable as evidence or proof. —**ad·mis′si·bil′i·ty, ad·mis′si·ble·ness,** *n.* —**ad·mis′si·bly,** *adv.*

ad·mis·sion (ad mish′ən), *n.* **1** act of allowing (a person, animal, etc.) to enter: *admission of aliens.* **2** power or right to enter. **3** price paid for the right to enter. **4** acceptance into an office or position. **5** confession of an error or a crime. **6** an acknowledging; accepting as true or valid. **7** fact or point acknowledged; something accepted as true or valid.

ad·mis·sive (ad mis′iv), *adj.* tending to admit.

ad·mit (ad mit′), *v.,* **–mit·ted, –mit·ting. 1** acknowledge: *admit a mistake.* **2** accept as true or valid; recognize. **3** allow to enter or use; let in. **4** give the right to enter to. **5** allow; permit. **6** allow or have space for: *the harbor admits three ships.*
admit of, have room for; be capable of: *his answer admits of no reply.* [<L, < *ad–* to + *mittere* let go] —**ad·mit′ter,** *n.*

ad·mit·tance (ad mit′əns), *n.* **1** right to go in. **2** act of admitting. **3** actual entrance.

ad·mit·ted·ly (ad mit′id li), *adv.* without denial; by general consent.

ad·mix (ad miks′), *v.* add in mixing; mix in.

ad·mix·ture (ad miks′chər), *n.* **1** act of mixing. **2** mixture. **3** anything added in mixing. [< L *admixtus* < *ad–* in addition + *miscere* mix]

ad·mon·ish (ad mon′ish), *v.* **1** advise against something; warn: *the police officer admonished him not to drive too fast.* **2** reprove gently: *admonish a student for careless work.* **3** urge strongly; advise. **4** recall to a duty overlooked or forgotten; remind. [< *admonition*] —**ad·mon′ish-er,** *n.* —**ad·mon′ish·ing·ly,** *adv.* —**ad·mon′ish·ment,** *n.*

ad·mo·ni·tion (ad′mə nish′ən), *n.* an admonishing; warning. [< L, < *ad–* to + *monere* warn]

ad·mon·i·to·ry (ad mon′ə tô′ri; –tō′–), *adj.* admonishing; warning.

ad nau·se·am (ad nô′shē am, –sē–; –əm), *Latin.* to a disgusting extent.

a·do (ə dü′), *n.* **1** stir; bustle. **2** trouble; difficulty. [ME *at do* to do]

a·do·be (ə dō′bē), —*n.* **1** a brick of sun-dried clay or mud. **2** a brick or bricklike piece of such bricks or sun-dried clay. —*adj.* built or made of sun-dried bricks: *an adobe house.* [< Sp., < *adobar* to daub < Gmc.]

a·do·bo (ə dō′bo), *n.* a spicy sauce for chicken and pork made of chilis, vinegar, and cloves. [< Spanish *adobo* (pickle sauce)]

ad·o·lesce (ad′ə les′), *v.,* **–lesced, –lesc-ing. 1** be or become an adolescent. **2** act like an adolescent. [< *adolescent*]

ad·o·les·cence (ad′ə les′əns), *n.* **1** growth from childhood to adulthood. **2** period or time of this growth; youth.

ad·o·les·cent (ad′ə les′ənt), *n.* person from about 12 to about 20 years of age. —*adj.* **1** growing up from childhood to maturity. **2** of or characteristic of adolescents. **3** *Fig.* immature. [< L *adolescens* < *ad–* to + *alescere* grow]

A·don·is (ə don′is; ə dō′nis), *n.* **1** *Class. Myth.* a handsome young man loved by Aphrodite (Venus). **2** any handsome young man. **3** any vain young man; dandy.

a·dopt (ə dopt′), *v.* **1** take or use as one's own; embrace. **2** accept formally: *the committee adopted the report.* **3** take (a child of other parents) and bring up as one's own. **4** take (a person) into close relationship. **5** take a word from another language without changing its form: *English adopted "déja vu" from French.* [< L, < *ad–* to + *optare* choose] —**a·dopt′a·ble,** *adj.* —**a·dopt′a·bil′i·ty,** *n.* —**a·dopt′er,** *n.* —**a·dop′tion,** *n.*

a·dop·tive (ə dop′tiv), *adj.* **1** related by adoption; adopted. **2** tending to adopt. —**a·dop′tive·ly,** *adv.*

a·dor·a·ble (ə dôr′ə bəl; ə dōr′–), *adj.* **1** lovely; delightful. **2** worthy of being

adored; revered; worshipful. —**a·dor′a-ble·ness, a·dor′a·bil′i·ty,** *n.* —**a·dor′a-bly,** *adv.*

ad·o·ra·tion (ad′ə rā′shən), *n.* **1** worship; reverence. **2** highest respect; devoted love.

a·dore (ə dôr′; ə dōr′), *v.* **a·dored, a·dor-ing. 1** respect very highly; love very greatly; revere; idolize. **2** admire very much. **3** worship; venerate. [< OF < L, < *ad–* to + *orare* pray] —**a·dor′er,** *n.* —**a-dor′ing,** *adj.* —**a·dor′ing·ly,** *adv.*

a·dorn (ə dôrn′), *v.* **1** add beauty to; beautify. **2** put ornaments on; decorate; grace. **3** make greater the splendor or honor of. [< OF < L, < *ad–* + *ornare* fit out] —**a-dorn′er,** *n.* —**a·dorn′ing·ly,** *adv.*

a·dorn·ment (ə dôrn′mənt), *n.* **1** something that adds beauty; decoration. **2** act of adorning; ornamentation.

ADP, 1 automatic data processing. **2** adenosinediphosphate, compound formed in the muscles.

ad·re·nal (ə drē′nəl), *adj.* **1** near or on the kidney. **2** of or from the adrenal glands. —*n.* an adrenal gland. [< L *ad–* near + *renes* kidneys]

adrenal gland, one of the two endocrine glands above the kidneys; suprarenal gland.

ad·ren·al·in (ə dren′əl in), **ad·ren·al·ine** (–in; –ēn), *n.* **1** hormone secreted by the adrenal glands, which stimulates the heartbeat, increasing available energy. **2 Adrenalin,** *Trademark.* artificial adrenalin; epinephrine.

A·dri·at·ic Sea (ā′dri at′ik), arm of the Mediterranean between Italy and the Balkan Peninsula.

a·drift (ə drift′), *adv., adj.* **1** drifting. **2** *fig.* without direction; at a loss.

a·droit (ə droit′), *adj.* **1** intellectually resourceful; clever; ingenious: *an adroit diplomat.* **2** skilled in the use of the hands or body; skillful: *an adroit climber.* [< F *à droit* rightly < L *ad–* to + *directus* straight] —**a·droit′ly,** *adv.* —**a-droit′ness,** *n.*

ad·sorb (ad sôrb′; –zôrb′), *v.* gather (a gas, liquid, or dissolved substance) in a thin layer on a solid substance. [< L *ad–* to + *sorbere* suck in] —**ad·sorb′ent,** *adj., n.*

ad·sorp·tion (ad sôrp′shən; –zôrp′–), *n.* **1** process of adsorbing; condensation of a gas, liquid, or dissolved substance on the surface of solids. **2** condition of being adsorbed. —**ad·sorp′tive,** *adj.*

ad·u·late (aj′ə lāt), *v.,* **–lat·ed, –lat·ing.** praise excessively; slavishly flatter. [< L *adulatus*] —**ad′u·la′tion,** *n.* —**ad′u·la′tor,** *n.* —**ad′u·la·to′ry,** *adj.*

a·dult (ə dult′; ad′ult), *adj.* **1** having full size and strength; grown-up. **2** of or for adults. **3** for adults only: *adult videos.* —*n.* **1** grown-up person. **2** a full-grown plant or animal. [< L *adultus* < *ad–* to + *alescere* grow up] —**a·dult′hood,** *n.* —**a-dult′ly,** *adv.* —**a·dult′ness,** *n.*

a·dul·ter·ant (ə dul′tər ənt), *n.* substance used to adulterate. —*adj.* adulterating.

a·dul·ter·ate (ə dul′tər āt), v., **-at·ed, -at·ing.** make lower in quality or purity by adding inferior improper, or impure materials; debase: *adulterate milk with water.* [< L *adulteratus,* ult. < *ad-* + *alter* other, different] —**a·dul′ter·a′tion,** n. —**a·dul′ter·a′tor,** n.

a·dul·ter·er (ə dul′tər ər), n. person, esp. a man, who commits adultery.

a·dul·ter·ess (ə dul′tər is; -tris), n. female who commits adultery.

a·dul·ter·y (ə dul′tər i), n., pl. **-ter·ies.** voluntary sexual relations of a married person with any person other than the lawful mate. —**a·dul′ter·ous,** adj. —**a·dul′ter·ous·ly,** adv.

ad·um·brate (ad um′brāt; ad′əm brāt), v., **-brat·ed, -brat·ing. 1** indicate faintly; sketch. **2** indicate beforehand; foreshadow. **3** partially conceal; overshadow. [<L, < *ad-* + *umbra* shade] —**ad′um·bra′tion,** n.

adv., 1 adverb. **2** adverbial. **3** advertisement.

ad va·lo·rem (ad və lô′rəm; -lō′-), assessed in proportion to the value esp. of a tax on merchandise. [< Med.L]

ad·vance (ad vans′; -väns′), v. **-vanced, -vanc·ing,** n., adj. —v. **1** move forward; progress: *the troops advanced.* **2** bring forward: *advance a theory.* **3** make progress; improve: *we advance in understanding.* **4** help forward; further: *advance a cause.* **5** raise to a higher rank; promote: *advance him from lieutenant to captain.* **6** rise in rank; be promoted: *advance the profession.* **7** raise (prices): *advance gas prices.* **8** rise in price: *the stock advanced three points.* **9** make earlier; hasten: *advance the time to meet.* **10** move a timepiece ahead: *advance clocks one hour.* **11** supply beforehand: *advance funds for expenses.* **12** lend (money), esp. on security: *advance a loan.* **13** put forward; suggest; offer: *advance an opinion.* —n. **1** movement forward. **2** a step forward; progress. **3** a rise in price; increase. **4** the furnishing of money or goods before they are due or as a loan. **5** the money or goods furnished. **6** a forward position.

advances, approach or offer to another or others to settle a difference, to make an acquaintance, etc.

in advance, a in front; ahead. **b** ahead of time. —adj. **1** going before. **2** ahead of time. [< OF *avancier* < LL, < L *ab-* from + *ante* before] —**ad·vanc′er,** n.

ad·vanced (ad vanst′; -vänst′), adj. **1** in front of others; forward. **2** beyond most others. **3** far along in life; old.

ad·vance·ment (ad vans′mənt; -väns′-), n. **1** movement forward; advance. **2** progress; improvement. **3** promotion.

ad·van·tage (ad van′tij; -vän′-), n., v., **-taged, -tag·ing.** —n. **1** any favorable condition, circumstance, or opportunity; means helpful in getting something desired. **2** better or superior position; superiority. **3** the result of a better posi-tion; benefit; gain. **4** the first point scored in a tennis game after deuce. —v. give an advantage to; help; benefit.

take advantage of, a use to help or benefit oneself. **b** impose upon.

to advantage, to a good effect; with a useful effect.

to one's advantage, to benefit oneself. [<OF, < *avant* before < LL. See ADVANCE.]

ad·van·ta·geous (ad′vən tā′jəs), adj. giving advantage; profitable. —**ad′van·ta′geous·ly,** adv. —**ad′van·ta′geous·ness,** n.

ad·vent (ad′vent), n. **1** coming; arrival. **2 Advent, a** the season of devotion including the four Sundays before Christmas. **b** the birth of Christ. **3 Second Advent,** the coming of Christ at the Last Judgment. [< L, < *ad-* to + *venire* come]

Ad·vent·ism (ad′ven tiz əm; ad ven′-), n. belief that the second coming of Christ is near at hand. —**Ad′vent·ist,** n.

ad·ven·ti·tious (ad′ven tish′əs), adj. **1** coming from outside. **2** *Bot., Zool.* appearing in an unusual position or place. —**ad′ven·ti′tious·ly,** adv. —**ad′ven·ti′tious·ness,** n.

ad·ven·tive (ad ven′tiv), adj. *Bot., Zool.* introduced into a new environment; not native, though growing with cultivation. —n. a nonnative plant or animal.

ad·ven·ture (ad ven′chər), n., v., **-tured, -tur·ing.** —n. **1** an exciting or unusual experience. **2** a bold undertaking, usually exciting and somewhat dangerous. **3** seeking excitement or danger: *spirit of adventure.* **4** business undertaking; commercial speculation. —v. venture; dare. [< OF < L. See ADVENT.]

ad·ven·tur·er (ad ven′chər ər), n. **1** person who seeks or has adventures. **2** soldier who is available for hire to any army. **3** person who schemes to get money, social position, etc. **4** speculator.

ad·ven·ture·some (ad ven′chər səm), adj. bold and daring; adventurous.

ad·ven·tur·ess (ad ven′chər is), n. **1** female who schemes to get money, social position, etc. **2** female adventurer.

ad·ven·tur·ous (ad ven′chər əs), adj. **1** fond of adventures; ready to take risks; daring. **2** full of risk; dangerous. —**ad·ven′tur·ous·ly,** adv. —**ad·ven′tur·ous·ness,** n.

ad·verb (ad′vėrb), n. word that extends or limits the meaning of verbs and qualifies adjectives or other adverbs, clauses, and phrases esp. as to how, when, or where. *Soon, here, very, gladly,* and *not* are adverbs. Adverbs are freely formed by the addition of *-ly* to adjectives and participles. [< L, < *ad-* to + *verbum* verb] —**ad·ver′bi·al,** adj. —**ad·ver′bi·al·ly,** adv.

ad·ver·sar·y (ad′vər ser′i), n., pl. **-sar·ies. 1** unfriendly opponent; enemy; foe. **2** person or group on the other side in a contest; opponent; antagonist.

ad·ver·sa·tive (ad vėr′sə tiv), adj. (of words, etc.) expressing contrast or opposition. *But* and *yet* are adversative conjunctions.

ad·verse (ad vėrs′; ad′vėrs), adj. **1** unfriendly in purpose; inimical; hostile: *adverse criticism.* **2** unfavorable; harmful. **3** acting in a contrary direction; opposing: *adverse winds.* **4** opposite in position. [< L *adversus.* See ADVERT.] —**ad·verse′ly,** adv. —**ad·verse′ness,** n.

ad·ver·si·ty (ad vėr′sə ti), n., pl. **-ties. 1** condition of unhappiness, misfortune, or distress, esp. financial. **2** instance of misfortune.

ad·vert (ad vėrt′), v. direct attention; refer (*to*); allude: *advert to the need for more parks.* [< L, *ad-* to + *vertere* turn]

ad·vert·ent (ad vėr′tənt), adj. attentive; heedful. —**ad·vert′ence, ad·vert′en·cy,** n.

ad·ver·tise, (ad′vər tīz; ad′vər tīz′), v., **-tised, -tis·ing. 1** give public notice of; publicize: *advertise a house for sale.* **2** ask by public notice (*for*): *advertise for a job.* **3** make generally known. **4** inform. **5** publicly praise the good qualities of (a product, etc.) in order to promote sales. **6** issue advertising: *it pays to advertise.* **7** call attention to (oneself); announce. [< obs. F *advertir* < L. See ADVERT.] —**ad′ver·tis′er,** n.

ad·ver·tise·ment, n. a public notice or announcement in the media.

ad·ver·tis·ing, (ad′vər tīz′ing), n. **1** business of preparing, publishing, or circulating advertisements. **2** advertisements. **3** bringing to public notice through advertisements.

ad·vice (ad vīs′) n. opinion about what should be done; suggestion; counsel. **advices,** information; news: *financial advices.* [< obs. F *advis.* var. of *avis* < L *ad-* + *visum* thing seen]

ad·vis·a·ble (ad vīz′ə bəl), adj. to be recommended; wise; sensible. —**ad·vis′a·bil′i·ty, ad·vis′a·ble·ness,** n. —**ad·vis′a·bly,** adv.

ad·vise (ad vīz′), v., **-vised, -vis·ing. 1** give advice to; counsel; caution: *advise care.* **2** give advice; recommend: *I shall act as you advise.* **3** give notice; inform; notify; acquaint: *we were advised of the dangers.* **4** talk over plans; consult; confer: *he advised with friends.* [< OF *aviser* < *avis* opinion. See ADVICE.]

ad·vised (ad vīzd′), adj. **1** planned, considered. **2** informed: *kept me advised.* —**ad·vis′ed·ness,** n.

ad·vis·ed·ly (ad vīz′id li), adv. after careful consideration; deliberately.

ad·vise·ment (ad vīz′mənt), n. careful consideration: *take a case under advisement.*

ad·vis·er, ad·vi·sor (ad vīz′ər), n. **1** person who gives advice. **2** teacher who is appointed to advise students.

ad·vi·so·ry (ad vī′zə ri), adj. **1** having power to advise. **2** containing advice. —n. bulletin or report to advise of developments, as of the movement and direction of a hurricane.

ad·vo·ca·cy (ad′və kə si), *n.* **1** speaking in favor; public recommendation; support. **2** profession of pleading a case in court. **3** the pleading of a case.

ad·vo·cate (*v.* ad′və kāt; *n.* ad′və kit, –kāt), *v.*, **-cat·ed, -cat·ing,** *n.* —*v.* speak in favor of; recommend publicly: *he advocates building more schools.* —*n.* **1** person who pleads or argues for: *an advocate of peace.* **2** lawyer who pleads in a law court. [< L, < *ad–* to + *vocare* call] —**ad′·vo·ca′tion,** *n.* —**ad′vo·ca′tor,** *n.*

advt., advertisement.

adz, adze (adz), *n.* tool somewhat like an ax but with a blade set across the end of the handle and curving inward. [OE *adesa*]

A.E.F., Allied Expeditionary Forces (World War II). **2** American Expeditionary Forces.

Ae·ge·an (i jē′ən), *n.* arm of the Mediterranean between Greece and Turkey. —*adj.* of or in the Aegean.

ae·gis (ē′jis), *n.* **1** *Gk. Myth.* the shield of Zeus, used also by Athena. **2** protection. **3** patronage. Also, **egis.** [< L. < Gk. *aigis*]

Ae·ne·as (i nē′əs), *n. Class. Legend.* Trojan hero who escaped from Troy and settled in Italy.

ae·o·li·an harp or **lyre** (ē ō′li ən), a boxlike stringed instrument that produces musical sounds when currents of air blow across it.

Ae·o·lus (ē′ə ləs), *n. Gk. Myth.* god of the winds. —**Ae·o·li·an** (ē ō′li ən), *adj.*

ae·on (ē′ən; ē′on), *n.* =eon.

aer·ate (ār′āt; ā′ər āt), *v.*, **-at·ed, -at·ing.** **1** expose to air. **2** expose to and mix with air. **3** fill with a gas, esp. carbon dioxide. **4** expose to chemical action with oxygen. [< L *aer* < Gk., air] —**aer·a′tion,** *n.* —**aer′a·tor,** *n.*

aer·i·al (*adj.* ār′i əl, ā ir′i əl; *n.* ār′i əl), *adj.* **1** in the air. **2** of or pertaining to the air. **3** like air; thin and light as air. **4** ideal; imaginary. **5** growing in the air. **6** relating to aircraft. —*n.* wire or wires used in radio, television, or radar for sending out or receiving electromagnetic waves. [< L *aerius* < Gk., *aer* air] —**aer′i·al·ly,** *adv.*

aer·i·al·ist (ār′i əl ist), *n.* performer on a trapeze or high wire; aerial acrobat.

aer·ie, aer·y (ār′ij ir′i), *n.*, *pl.* **aer·ies.** **1** the lofty nest of an eagle or other bird of prey. **2** young eagles or other birds of prey. **3** house, castle, etc., built in a high place. Also, **eyrie, eyry.** [< Med.L. *aeria* < OF < L *area* AREA or *atrium* ATRIUM]

aer·i·fy (ār′ə fī; ā ir′–), *v.*, **-fied, -fy·ing.** **1** convert into vapor. **2** =aerate. —**aer′i·fi·ca′tion,** *n.*

aer·o (ār′ō), *adj.* of or for aircraft.

aero-, *combining form.* **1** air; of the air. **2** atmosphere; atmospheric. **3** gas; of gas or gases. **4** of or for aircraft. [< Gk. *aer* air]

aer·obe (ār′ōb; ā′ər ōb), *n.* any microorganism that requires oxygen to live or grow. [< NL < Gk. *aer* air + *bios* life] —**aer·o′bic,** *adj.* —**aer·o′bi·cal·ly,** *adv.*

aer·o·brak·ing (ār′ō brā′king) *n.* use of friction to slow or stop a spacecraft.

aer·o·dy·nam·ics (ār′ō dī nam′iks; –di–), *n.* the branch of physics that deals with the forces exerted by air or other gases in motion. —**aer′o·dy·nam′ic,** *adj.*

aer·o·me·chan·ics (ār′ō mə kan′iks), *n.* science of the motion and equilibrium of air and other gases; aerodynamics and aerostatics. —**aer′o·me·chan′ic, aer′o·me·chan′i·cal,** *adj.*

aer·o·naut (ār′ə nôt), *n.* **1** pilot of an aircraft or balloon; balloonist. **2** person who travels in an airship or balloon. [< F, < Gk. *aer* air + *nautes* sailor]

aer·o·nau·tics (ār′ə nô′tiks), *n.* science or art having to do with the design, manufacture, and operation of aircraft. —**aer′o·nau′tic, aer′o·nau′ti·cal,** *adj.* —**aer′o·nau′ti·cal·ly,** *adv.*

aer·o·plane (ār′ə plān), *n. Esp. Brit.* airplane.

aer·o·sol (ār′ə sol), *n.* fine particles of a liquid or solid suspended in a gas: *Fog is an aerolsol; an aerosol spray.*

aer·o·space (ār′ə spās), *n.* **1** science, technology, and industry dealing with the flight of rockets, missiles, vehicles, etc., through the atmosphere or through space: *studies in aerospace.* **2** earth's envelope of air and the space enclosing it.

aer·o·stat (ār′ə stat), *n.* any lighter-than-air aircraft, as a balloon or dirigible. [< AERO- + Gk. *statos* standing]

aer·o·stat·ics (ār′ə stat′iks), *n.* branch of physics that deals with the equilibrium of air and other gases, and with the equilibrium of solid objects floating in air and other gases. —**aer′o·stat′ic, aer′o·stat′i·cal,** *adj.*

Aes·chy·lus (es′kə ləs), *n.* 525–456 B.C., Greek tragic poet and dramatist.

Ae·sop (ē′səp; ē′sop), *n.* 620?–650? B.C., Greek writer of fables. —**Ae·so′pi·an,** *adj.*

aes·thete (es′thēt), *n.* **1** person who pretends to care a great deal about beauty. **2** person who is sensitive to or loves beauty. Also, **esthete.** [< Gk. *aisthetes* one who perceives]

aes·thet·ic (es thet′ik), *adj.* **1** Also, **aesthet′i·cal.** having to do with the beautiful, as distinguished from the useful, scientific, etc. **2** (of persons) sensitive to beauty. **3** (of things) pleasing; artistic. —*n.* aesthetic philosophy or point of view. Also, **esthetic.** —**aes·thet′i·cal·ly,** *adv.*

aes·thet·ics (es thet′iks), *n.* study of beauty in art and nature; philosophy of beauty; theory of the fine arts. Also, **esthetics.** —**aes·thet′i·cism,** *n.*

aet., aetat., at the age of.

ae·ther (ē′thər), *n.* =ether.

ae·the·re·al (i thir′i əl), *adj.* =ethereal.

ae·ti·ol·o·gy (ē′ti ol′ə ji), *n.* =etiology. —**ae′ti·o·log′i·cal,** *adj.*

Aet·na (et′nə), *n.* **Mount.** See **Etna, Mount.**

AF, 1 Air Force. **2** Anglo-French.

A.F., af., *Physics, Electronics.* audio frequency.

a·far (ə fär′), *adv.* **1** from a distance: *see from afar.* **2** far away: *stand afar off.*

a·feard, a·feared (ə fird′), *adj. Archaic* frightened; afraid.

af·fa·ble (af′ə bəl), *adj.* **1** easy to speak to or approach; courteous, friendly, and pleasant. **2** gracious; mild; benign. [< F < L *affabilis* easy to speak to < *ad–* to + *fari* speak] —**af′fa·bil′i·ty, af′fa·ble·ness,** *n.* —**af′fa·bly,** *adv.*

af·fair (ə fãr′), *n.* **1** anything done or to be done; activity. **2** **affairs,** matters of interest, esp. business matters. **3** particular action or event (referred to in vague terms); happening: *a jolly affair.* **4** private concern: *that's my affair.* **5** thing: *this machine is a complicated affair.* **6** romance; love affair. [< OF *a faire* to do < L *ad–* to + *facere* do]

af·fect¹ (ə fekt′), *v.* **1** have an effect on; influence, esp. injuriously: *disease affects the body.* **2** stir the emotions of; touch. [< L *affectus* < *ad–* to + *facere* do] **affect, effect.** *Affect* is nearly always a verb, meaning "to influence"; *this will affect the lives of thousands. Effect* is most commonly a noun, meaning "result": *long-lasting effects of the storm. Effect* is also a verb in formal English, meaning to "bring about": *the change was effected peaceably.*

af·fect² (ə fekt′), *v.* **1** pretend to have or feel; feign; simulate: *affect ignorance.* **2** assume, use, or frequent by preference: *he affects carelessness in dress.* **3** seem to be fond of; like: *she affects anything antique.* **4** (of animals and plants) inhabit naturally. [< F < L *affectare* strive for < *ad–* to + *facere* do] —**af·fect′er,** *n.*

af·fec·ta·tion (af′ek tā′shən; –ik–), *n.* **1** behavior that is not natural; peculiarity. **2** outward appearance; pretense.

af·fect·ed¹ (ə fek′tid), *adj.* **1** influenced. **2** influenced injuriously. **3** moved emotionally.

af·fect·ed² (ə fek′tid), *adj.* **1** put on for effect; not natural; artificial. **2** behaving, speaking, writing, etc., unnaturally for effect. —**af·fect′ed·ly,** *adv.* —**af·fect′ed·ness,** *n.*

af·fect·ing (ə fek′ting), *adj.* stirring the emotions —**af·fect′ing·ly,** *adv.*

af·fec·tion (ə fek′shən), *n.* **1** friendly feeling; fondness; tenderness; love. 2. feeling; inclination. **3** disease; unhealthy condition.

af·fec·tion·ate (ə fek′shən it), *adj.* **1** having affection; devoted; tender. **2** showing affection. —**af·fec′tion·ate·ly,** *adv.* —**af·fec′tion·ate·ness,** *n.*

af·fec·tive (ə fek′tiv), *adj.* of the feelings; emotional.

af·fer·ent (af′ər ənt), *adj.* (of nerves or blood vessels) carrying inward to a central organ or point. [< L, < *ad-* to + *ferre* bring]

af·fi·ance (ə fī′əns), *v.,* **-anced, -anc·ing.** pledge solemnly, esp. in marriage; engage; betroth. [< OF *afiancer* ult. < L *ad-* to + *fidus* faithful] —**af·fi′anced,** *adj.*

af·fi·da·vit (af′ə dā′vit), *n.* statement written down and sworn to be true. An affidavit is usually made before a judge or notary public. [< Med.L, he has stated on oath]

af·fil·i·ate (*v.* ə fil′i āt; *n.* ə fil′i it, -āt), *v.* **-at·ed, -at·ing,** *v., n.* —*v.* **1** connect in close association: *affiliated clubs.* **2** associate oneself (*with*): *affiliate with a political party.* **3** bring into relationship; adopt. —*n.* organization or group associated with other similar bodies. [< LL, < L *ad-* + *filius* son]

af·fil·i·a·tion (ə fil′i ā′shən), *n.* association; relation.

af·fin·i·ty (ə fin′ə ti), *n., pl.* **-ties. 1** natural attraction to a person or liking for a thing: *an affinity for dancing.* **2** relation; connection. **3** relationship by marriage. **4** person to whom one is especially attracted. **5** resemblance; likeness. **6** force that attracts certain chemical elements to others and keeps them combined. [< F < L, < *ad-* on + *finis* boundary]

af·firm (ə fėrm′), *v.* **1** declare to be true; assert. **2** confirm; ratify: *the higher court affirmed the lower court's decision.* **3** declare solemnly, but without taking an oath. [< OF < L, < *ad-* + *firmus* strong] —**af·firm′a·ble,** *adj.* —**af·firm′a·bly,** *adv.* —**af·firm′er,** *n.*

af·fir·ma·tion (af′ər mā′shən), *n.* **1** a positive statement; assertion. **2** solemn declaration, equivalent to taking an oath, made by a person whose conscience forbids his taking an oath. **3** act of confirming.

af·firm·a·tive (ə fėr′mə tiv), *adj.* asserting that a statement is a fact. —*n.* **1** word or statement that gives assent or agrees. **2 the affirmative,** the side arguing in favor of a question being debated. —**af·firm′a·tive·ly,** *adv.*

affirmative action, plan or program designed to improve employment or educational opportunities for women or minorities.

af·fix (*v.* ə fiks′; *n.* af′iks), *v.* **1** make firm or fix (one thing to or on another); fasten. **2** add at the end. **3** make an impression of (a seal, etc.). **4** connect with; attach: *affix blame.* —*n.* **1** thing affixed. **2** a prefix, suffix, or infix. *Un-* and *-ly* are affixes. [< Med.L *affixare,* ult. < L *ad-* to + *figere* fix] —**af·fix′er,** *n.*

af·fla·tus (ə flā′təs), *n.* inspiration, esp. divinely imparted. [< L, < *ad-* on + *flare* blow]

af·flict (ə flikt′), *v.* cause pain to; trouble greatly; distress; torment. [< L *afflictus* < *ad-* upon + *fligere* dash] —**af·flict′er,** *n.*

af·flic·tion (ə flik′shən), *n.* **1** state of pain or distress; misery; wretchedness. **2** cause of pain, trouble, or distress; misfortune.

af·flu·ence (af′lù əns), *n.* **1** wealth. **2** abundant supply; profusion. [< F < L, < *ad-* to + *fluere* flow]

af·flu·ent (af′lù ənt), *adj.* **1** very wealthy. **2** abundant; plentiful. —*n.* stream flowing into a larger stream, river, etc. —**af′flu·ent·ly,** *adv.*

af·ford (ə fôrd′; ə fōrd′), *v.* **1** spare the money for: *we can't afford a new car.* **2** spare: *can you afford the time?* **3** manage; bear: *I can't afford to take the chance.* **4** yield or give as an effect or a result; provide: *reading affords pleasure.* **5** furnish from natural resources; yield: *some trees afford resin.* [OE *geforthian* further, accomplish] —**af·ford′a·ble,** *adj.*

af·fray (ə frā′), *n.* a noisy quarrel; fight in public; brawl. [< OF *affrei,* ult. < L *ex-* out of + unrecorded Frankish *frithu* peace]

af·front (ə frunt′), *n.* **1** a word or act expressing openly intentional disrespect; insult. **2** a slight or injury to one's dignity. —*v.* **1** insult openly; offend purposely. **2** confront. [< OF < VL < L *ad frontem* on the forehead] —**af·front′er,** *n.*

Af·ghan (af′gən; -gan), *n.* **1** native or person living in Afghanistan. **2 afghan,** blanket or shawl often made of knitted or crocheted wool. —*adj.* of Afghanistan or its people.

Af·ghan·i·stan (af gan′ə stan), *n.* country in SW Asia.

a·fi·cio·na·do (ə fē′syə na′dō), *n., pl.* **-dos. 1** person who is very enthusiastic about anything; enthusiast; devotee. **2** person who takes a very great interest in bullfighting, but who is not a bullfighter. [< Sp., lit., fond of < *afición* affection < L *affectio* < *affectus,* pp. See AFFECT².]

a·field (ə fēld′), *adv.* **1** on or in the field; to the field. **2** away from home; away. **3** out of the way; astray.

a·fire (ə fīr′), *adv., adj.* on fire; burning.

a·flame (ə flām′), *adv., adj.* **1** on fire. **2** excited; eager; enthusiastic.

AFL-CIO or **A.F.L.-C.I.O.** union formed by the merger of the American Federation of Labor and the Congress of Industrial Organizations.

a·float (ə flōt′), *adv., adj.* **1** floating. **2** on shipboard; at sea. **3** adrift. **4** flooded. **5** going around: *rumors of an outbreak were afloat.* **6** in operation, esp. business, financially secure.

a·flut·ter (ə flut′ər), *adv., adj.* fluttering.

a·foot (ə fùt′), *adv., adj.* **1** on foot; walking. **2** going on; in progress: *mischief afoot.*

a·fore (ə fôr′; ə fōr′), *adv., prep., conj.* before.

a·fore·men·tioned (ə fôr′men′shənd; ə fōr′-), *adj.* spoken of before; mentioned above.

a·fore·said (ə fôr′sed′; ə fōr′-), *adj.* spoken of before; mentioned above.

a·fore·thought (ə fôr′thôt′; ə fōr′-), *adj.* thought of beforehand; deliberately planned.

a for·ti·o·ri (ā fôr′shi ô′rī; -ō′-; -ri), *Latin.* for a still stronger reason; all the more.

a·foul (ə foul′), *adv., adj.* in a tangle, in collision; entangled.

run afoul of, get into difficulties with.

Afr., 1 Africa. **2** African.

a·fraid (ə frād′), *adj.* feeling fear; frightened. [orig. pp. of archaic v. *affray* frighten]

af·reet, af·rit (af′rēt; ə frēt′), *n.* in Arabian myths, a powerful evil demon or giant. [< Ar. *'ifrīt*]

a·fresh (ə fresh′), *adv.* once more; again.

Af·ri·ca (af′rə kə), *n.* continent south of Europe; the second largest continent.

Af·ri·can (af′rə kən), *adj.* **1** of or from Africa. **2** of or belonging to the people of Africa. —*n.* **1** a native of Africa. **2** a black.

African-American (af′rə kən ə mer′ə kən) *n., adj.* —*n.* American black; Afro-American. —*adj.* of or pertaining to American blacks.

Af·ri·kaans (af′rə käns′; -känz′), *n.* variety of Dutch spoken in South Africa; South African Dutch.

Af·ri·kan·er (af′rə kan′ər), *n.* person born in South Africa, usually of Dutch or Huguenot descent.

Afro-American (af′rō ə mər′ə kən), *n., adj* = African-American.

aft (aft; äft), *adv.* at, near, or toward the stern of a boat, aircraft, etc.; abaft. [OE *œftan* from behind]

af·ter (af′tər; äf′-), *prep.* **1** behind in place: *in line one after another.* **2** in search of: *run after him.* **3** later in time than: *after supper.* **4** because of: *after the selfish way she acted, who could like her?* **5** lower in rank or importance: *a captain comes after a general.* —*adv.* **1** behind: *follow after.* **2** later: *three hours after.* —*adj.* **1** later; subsequent: *in after years he regretted the mistakes of his boyhood.* **2** nearer or toward the stern of a boat, aircraft, etc.: *after sails.* —*conj.* later than the time that: *after he goes, we shall eat.* [OE *œfter* more to the rear, later]

af·ter·birth (af′tər bėrth′; äf′-), *n.* **1** placenta and membranes expelled from the uterus after birth.

af·ter·burn·er (af′tər bėr′nər; äf′-), *n.* (in the engine of a jet plane) a device which supplies additional fuel to the exhaust and reignites it to increase the thrust of the plane.

af·ter·deck (af′tər dek′; äf′-), *n.* deck toward or at the stern of a ship.

af·ter·ef·fect (af′tər i fekt′; äf′-), *n.* result or effect that follows later.

af·ter·glow (af′tər glō′; äf′-), *n.* **1** glow after something bright has gone. **2** glow in the sky after sunset. **3** intense feeling of pleasure that remains after an experience.

af·ter·im·age (af′tər im′ij; äf′-), *n.* visual sensation that persists or recurs after the stimulus that caused it is gone.

af·ter·math (af′tər math; äf′–), *n.* result; consequence. [< *after* + dial. *math* a mowing]

af·ter·most (af′tər mōst; äf′–), *adj.* **1** nearest the stern of a boat, aircraft, etc. **2** hindmost; last.

af·ter·noon (*n.* af′tər nün′, äf′–; adj. af′tər nün′, äf′–), *n.* the part of the day between noon and evening. —*adj.* of, in, or suitable for the afternoon.

af·ter·thought (af′tər thôt′; äf′–), *n.* **1** thought that comes after the time when it could have been used. **2** later thought or explanation.

af·ter·ward (af′tər wərd; äf′–), **af·ter·wards** (–wərdz), *adv.* later.

Ag, silver.

A.G., 1 Adjutant General. **2** Attorney General.

a·gain (ə gen′; *esp. Brit.,* ə gān′), *adv.* **1** once more; another time: *try again.* **2** moreover; besides: *again, I must say.*
   again and again, often; frequently.
   as much again, twice as much. [OE *ongegn* < *on–* on + *gegn* direct]

a·gainst (ə genst′; *esp. Brit.* ə gänst′), *prep.* **1** in opposition to: *against reason.* **2** in preparation for: *against a rainy day.* [See AGAIN]

Ag·a·mem·non (ag′ə mem′non; –nən), *n. Gk. Legend.* king of Mycenae and leader of the Greeks in the Trojan War.

A·ga·ña (ä gän′yə), *n.* capital of Guam.

a·gape (ə gāp′; ə gap′), *adv., adj.* with the mouth wide open in wonder or surprise.

a·gar (ä′gər; ag′ər), *n.* a gelatinlike extract obtained from certain seaweeds, used in making cultures for bacteria, fungi, etc. [< Malay]

a·gar·a·gar (ä′gər ä′gər; ag′ər ag′ər), *n.* agar.

ag·a·ric (ag′ə rik; ə gar′ik), *n.* any of several fungi, including mushrooms and toadstools. [< L < Gk., < *Agaria,* place name]

ag·ate (ag′it), *n.* a variety of quartz with variously colored stripes or clouded colors. [< F < L < Gk. *achates*] —**ag′ate·like′,** *adj.*

a·ga·ve (ə gä′vē), *n.* any of several North American desert plants, including the century plant, sisal, etc. Soap, alcoholic drinks, and rope are made from some kinds of agave. [< NL < Gk. *Agaue,* fem. proper name, noble]

age (āj), *n., v.,* **aged, ag·ing** or **age·ing.** —*v.* **1** length of life: *he died at the age of eighty.* **2** a period in life: *middle age.* **3** a period of history: *the golden age.* **4** a long time: *I haven't seen you for an age.* —*v.* **1** grow old: *he aged rapidly.* **2** make old: *age with makeup.* **3** make mature: *age wine.*
   of age, 18 or 21 years old, and having full legal rights.
   come of age, reach legal adulthood. [< OF *aage* < VL *aeticum* < L *aetas* age]

-age, *suffix.* **1** act of, as in *breakage.* **2** collection of; group of, as in *baggage.*

3 condition of; rank of, as in *peerage.* **4** cost of, as in *postage.* **5** home of, as in *orphanage.* [< OF < L *-aticum* < Gk.]

a·ged (ā′jid *for 1 and 3;* ājd *for 2), adj.* **1** having lived a long time; old. **2** of the age of. **3** characteristic of old age. —**a′ged·ly,** *adv.*

age·ism (ā′jiz əm) *n.* discrimination against older people. —**age′ist,** *n.*

age·less (āj′lis), *adj.* never growing old, out of date, or coming to an end.

age·long (āj′lông′; -long′), *adj.* lasting a long time.

a·gen·cy (ā′jən si), *n., pl.* **-cies. 1** person or company that has the authority to act for another. **2** office of such a person or company. **3** department of government. **4** organization or bureau that provides a public service: *adoption agencies.* **5** means of producing an effect; action.

a·gen·da (ə jen′də), *n. pl., sing.* **-dum** (-dəm). **1** things to be done. **2** list of items of business to be considered, as at a meeting. [< L, things to be done]

a·gent (ā′jənt), *n.* **1** person or company that has the authority to act for another; representative; intermediary. **2** law enforcement officer or member of the secret service. **3** active power or cause that produces an effect. **4** means; instrument: *a drying agent.* **5** traveling salesman. **6** substance that is capable of causing a chemical reaction. [< L, < *agere* do] —**a·gen′tial,** *adj.*

age-old (āj′ōld′), *adj.* very old; ancient.

ag·er·a·tum (aj′ər ā′təm; ə jer′ə–), *n.* any of several plants of the aster family with small, dense flower heads, usually blue. [< NL < Gk., < *a–* without + *geras* old age]

ag·glom·er·ate (*v.* ə glom′ər āt; *n., adj.* ə glom′ər it, –āt), *v.,* **-at·ed, -at·ing,** *n., adj.* —*v.* gather together in a mass. —*n.* mass; collection; cluster. —*adj.* **1** packed together in a mass. **2** volcanic rock formed by heat. [< L, < *ad–* + *glomus* ball] —**ag·glom′er·a′tive,** *adj.*

ag·glom·er·a·tion (ə glom′ər ā′shən), *n.* **1** mass of things gathered together. **2** agglomerated condition. **3** an agglomerating.

ag·glu·ti·nate (*v.* ə glü′tə nāt; *adj.* ə glü′tə nit, –nāt), *v.,* **-nat·ed, -nat·ing,** *adj.* —*v.* **1** stick or join together, as with glue. **2** form (words) by joining words, or words and affixes. —*adj.* stuck together or joined: *"never-to-be-forgotten" is an agglutinate word.* [< L, < *ad–* to + *gluten* glue] —**ag·glu′ti·na′tion,** *n.* —**ag·glu′ti·na′tive,** *adj.*

ag·glu·ti·nin (ə glüt′in ən), *n.* antibody that causes bacteria or blood cells to agglutinate.

ag·gran·dize (ə gran′dīz; ag′rən dīz), *v.,* **-dized, -diz·ing.** increase, as in power, wealth, rank, etc.; make greater. [< F *agrandir,* ult, < L *ad–* + *grandis* great] —**ag·gran′dize·ment,** *n.* —**ag·gran′diz·er,** *n.*

ag·gra·vate (ag′rə vāt), *v.,* **-vat·ed, -vat·ing, 1** make worse or more severe;

intensify; increase. **2** annoy; irritate; provoke. [< L. < *ad–* on, to + *gravis* heavy. Doublet of AGGRIEVE.] —**ag′gra·vat′ing,** *adj.* —**ag′gra·vat′ing·ly,** *adv.* —**ag′gra·va′tion,** *n.* —**ag′gra·va′tive·ly,** *adv.* —**ag′gra·va′tor,** *n.*

ag·gre·gate (*v.* ag′rə gāt; *n., adj.* ag′rə git, –gāt), *v.,* **-gat·ed, -gat·ing,** *n., adj.* —*v.* **1** gather into a mass or group; collect; unite. **2** amount to. —*n.* **1** mass of separate things joined together; collection. **2** whole amount; total. —*adj.* **1** gathered together in one mass or group. **2** total. [< L *aggregatus* < *ad–* + *grex* flock]
   in the aggregate, together; as a whole. —**ag′gre·ga′tive,** *adj.*

aggregate fruit, fruit made up of clusters of ripened ovaries, as the blackberry or raspberry.

ag·gre·ga·tion (ag′rə gā′shən), *n.* collection of separate things into one mass or whole.

ag·gres·sion (ə gresh′ən), *n.* **1** first step in an attack or quarrel; an unprovoked attack. **2** practice of making assaults or attacks. **3** hostility toward others. [< L *aggressio* < *ad–* to + *gradi* to step]

ag·gres·sive (ə gres′iv), *adj.* **1** beginning an attack or quarrel. **2** having the quality of aggression. **3** active; energetic. **4** too confident or assertive; pushy. —**ag·gres′sive·ly,** *adv.* —**ag·gres′sive·ness,** *n.*

ag·gres·sor (ə gres′ər), *n.* one that begins an attack or quarrel, esp. a country.

ag·grieved (ə grēvd′), *adj.* **1** injured; wronged. **2** troubled; shocked. [< OF *agrever* < L. Doublet of AGGRAVATE.]

a·ghast (ə gast′; ə gäst′), *adj.* filled with horror; terrified. [pp. of obs. *agast* terrify; akin to GHOST]

ag·ile (aj′əl), *adj.* **1** moving quickly and easily; active; lively; nimble. **2** mentally quick or inventive. [< L *agilis* < *agere* move] —**ag′ile·ly,** *adv.* —**ag′ile·ness,** *n.*

a·gil·i·ty (ə jil′ə ti), *n.* **1** ability to move quickly and easily; nimbleness. **2** ability to think nimbly.

ag·i·tate (aj′ə tāt), *v.,* **-tat·ed, -tat·ing. 1** move or shake violently. **2** disturb; excite feelings or thoughts. **3** argue about; discuss vigorously. **4** keep arguing and discussing to arouse public interest: *agitate for a shorter working day.* [< L *agitatus* < *agere* drive, move] —**ag′i·tat′ed·ly,** *adv.*

ag·i·ta·tion (aj′ə tā′shən), *n.* **1** a violent moving or shaking. **2** disturbed, upset, or troubled state. **3** argument or discussion to arouse public interest; debate.

ag·i·ta·tor (aj′ə tā′tər), *n.* **1** person who stirs discontent among others, esp. for a cause. **2** device for shaking or stirring.

a·glow (ə glō′), *adv., adj.* glowing.

ag·nos·tic (ag nos′tik), *n.* person who believes that nothing is known or can be known about the existence of God or about things outside of human experience. —*adj.* of agnostics or their beliefs. [< Gk., < *a–* not + *gnostos* (to be) known] —**ag·nos′ti·cal·ly,** *adv.*

ag·nos·ti·cism (ag nos′tə siz əm), *n.* the belief or intellectual attitude of agnostics.

a·go (ə gō′), *adj.* gone by; past (always after the noun): *a year ago.* —*adv.* in the past: *he went long ago.* [OE *āgān* gone by]

a·gog (ə gog′), *adj.* eager, curious; excited. —*adv.* with eagerness, curiosity, or excitement. [? < F *en gogues* in happy mood]

a·gon·ic (ā gon′ik; ə gon′-), *adj.* not forming an angle. [< Gk., < *a-* without + *gonia* angle]

ag·o·nize (ag′ə nīz), *v.,* **-nized, -niz·ing.** 1 feel very great pain. 2 pain very much; torture. 3 strive painfully; struggle. —**ag′o·niz′ing,** *adj.* —**ag′o·niz′ing·ly,** *adv.*

ag·o·ny (ag′ə ni), *n., pl.* **-nies.** 1 great pain or suffering; anguish; torment. 2 intense mental suffering. 3 the struggle often preceding death. [< LL < Gk. *agonia* struggle]

ag·o·ra (ag′ə rə), *n., pl.* **-rae** (-rē). market place in an ancient Greek city. [< Gk.]

ag·o·ra·pho·bi·a (ag′ə rə fō′bi ə), *n.* irrational fear of open spaces.

a·gou·ti (ə gü′ti), *n., pl.* **-tis, -ties.** a rodent of tropical America related to the guinea pig, but having longer legs. [< F < Sp. < native Indian name]

A·gra (ä′grə), *n.* city in N India; site of the Taj Mahal.

a·grar·i·an (ə grãr′i ən), *adj.* 1 having to do with land, its use, or its ownership. 2 for the support and advancement of the interests of farmers. 3 agricultural. —*n.* person who favors a redistribution of land. [< L *agrarius* < *ager* field] —**a·grar′i·an·ism,** *n.*

a·gree (ə grē′), *v.* **a·greed, a·gree·ing.** 1 have the same opinion or opinions: *I agree with you.* 2 be in harmony; correspond (*with*); match; coincide (*with*): *your story agrees with mine.* 3 get along well together. 4 consent (*to*): *he agreed to accompany us.* 5 come to an understanding, esp. in settling a dispute. 6 have a good effect on; suit (*with*): *this food does not agree with me.* 7 *Gram.* have the same number, case, gender, person, etc. (*with*): *that verb agrees with its subject.* [< OF, < *a gre* to (one's) liking < L *ad-* to + *gratus* pleasing]

a·gree·a·ble (ə grē′ə bəl), *adj.* 1 to one's liking; pleasing: *agreeable manners.* 2 ready to agree; willing to agree: *agreeable to a suggestion.* 3 in agreement; suitable (*to*): *music agreeable to the occasion.* —**a·gree′a·bil′i·ty, a·gree′a·ble·ness,** *n.* —**a·gree′a·bly,** *adv.*

a·greed (ə grēd′), *adj.* 1 fixed by common consent. 2 of like mind; agreeing.

a·gree·ment (ə grē′mənt), *n.* 1 consent. 2 sameness of opinion. 3 harmony: correspondence. 4 an agreeing; an understanding reached by two or more nations, persons, or groups of persons among themselves. 5 document that sets forth

an understanding. 6 *Gram.* correspondence of words with respect to number, case, gender, person, etc.

ag·ri·busi·ness (ag′rə biz′ness), *n.* business of producing agricultural products. [blend of *agriculture* + *business*]

ag·ri·cul·tur·al (ag′rə kul′chər əl), *adj.* 1 having to do with farming; of agriculture. 2 promoting the interests or the study of agriculture. —**ag′ri·cul′tur·al·ly,** *adv.*

ag·ri·cul·tur·al·ist (ag′rə kul′chər əl ist), *n.* =agriculturist.

ag·ri·cul·ture (ag′rə kul′chər), *n.* farming; the raising of crops and livestock; science or art of cultivating the ground. [< L, < *ager* field + *cultura* cultivation]

ag·ri·cul·tur·ist (ag′rə kul′chər ist), *n.* 1 farmer. 2 an expert in farming.

ag·ri·mo·ny (ag′rə mō′ni), *n., pl.* **-nies.** plant with slender stalks of feathery leaves and yellow flowers, whose roots are used as an astringent. [< L < Gk. *argemone*]

ag·ro-, *combining form.* 1 field; soil: *agrochemical.* 2 agriculture: *agroclimatology.* 3 agricultural plus ____: *agro-industrial.*

ag·ro·bi·ol·o·gy (ag′ro bī ol′əjē), *n.* study of plant nutrition and soil composition. —**ag′ro·bi′o·log′i·cal,** *adj.* —**ag′ro·bi′o·log′i·cal·ly,** *adv.* —**ag′ro·bi·ol′o gist,** *n.*

a·gron·o·my (ə gron′ə mi), *n.* study of crop production and farm management; husbandry. [< Gk., < *agros* land + *nemein* manage] —**ag′ro·nom′ic, —ag′ro·nom′i·cal,** *adj.* —**a·gron′o·mist,** *n.*

a·ground (ə ground′), *adv., adj.* on the ground; on the bottom in shallow water.

agt., agent.

a·gue (ā′gū), *n.* 1 malarial fever characterized by intermittent incidents of sweating and shivering. 2 fit of shivering; chill. [< OF < L *acuta* (*febris*) severe (fever)] —**a′gu·ish,** *adj.*

ah (ä), *interj.* exclamation of pain, surprise, pity, joy, etc.

a·ha (ä hä′), *interj.* exclamation of triumph, satisfaction, surprise, etc.

A·hab (ā′hab), *n.* in the Bible, king of Israel who was led into idolatry by his wife Jezebel.

a·head (ə hed′), *adv.* 1 in front; before: *walk ahead of me.* 2 forward; onward: *go ahead with this work.* 3 in an advanced or successful position or state. 4 in advance: *ahead of his times.*

be ahead, to the good.

get ahead, succeed.

get ahead of, surpass.

a·hem (ə hem′). *interj.* sound made to attract attention, express doubt, gain time, etc.

a·hold (ə hōld′), *n.* **get ahold of,** obtain.

-aholic, *combining form.* compulsively addicted to: *workaholic; chocaholic.* [taken from alc*oholic*]

a·hoy (ə hoi′), *interj.* a call used by sailors to hail persons at a distance.

ai (ī), *n., pl.* **ais** (īz). a three-toed sloth of South America.

AI, artificial intelligence.

aid (ād), *v.* 1 give support to; help; assist: *aid flood victims.* 2 help to accomplish or achieve something: *exercise aids recovery.* —*n.* 1 help; support. 2 helper; assistant. 3 *U.S.* aide-de-camp. [< OF *aidier* < L, < *ad-* to + *juvare* help] —**aid′er,** *n.* —**aid′less,** *adj.*

aid-de-camp (ād′də kamp′), *n., pl.* **aids-de-camp.** *U.S.* an aide-de-camp.

aide (ād), *n.* 1 assistant, especially to a person of high rank. 2 aide-de-camp.

aide-de-camp (ād′də kamp′), *n., pl.* **aides-de-camp.** army or navy officer who acts as an assistant to a superior officer. [< F]

AIDS (ādz), *n.* acquired immunodeficiency syndrome, a disease that attacks and suppresses the body's immune system and leaves it vulnerable to other infections or disease.

ai·grette (ā′gret; ā gret′), *n.* 1 tuft of feathers worn as an ornament on the head. 2 anything shaped or used like this. 3 egret. [< F. See EGRET.]

ai·ki·do (ī kē′dō), *n.* Japanese method of self-defense without weapons.

ail (āl), *v.* 1 be the matter with; trouble: *what ails the man?* 2 be ill; feel sick: *he is ailing.* [OE *eglan*]

ai·lan·thus (ā lan′thəs), *n.* an Asiatic tree with many leaflets and clusters of small, bad-smelling, greenish flowers. [< NL < Amboinan (language of Amboina in the Dutch East Indies) *aylanto* tree of heaven; form infl. by Gk. *anthos* flower]

ai·ler·on (ā′lər on), *n.* a movable part of an airplane wing, usually part of the trailing edge, used primarily to maintain lateral balance while flying. [< F, dim. of *aile* < L *ala* wing]

ail·ment (āl′mənt), *n.* a slight sickness.

AIM, American Indian Movement.

aim (ām), *v.* 1 point or direct (a gun, blow, etc.) in order to hit a target: *aim a gun.* 2 direct one's efforts: *man aims at happiness.* 3 intend: *I aim to go.* 4 try: *he aims to be helpful.* —*n.* 1 act of aiming. 2 direction aimed in; line of sighting. 3 mark aimed at; target. 4 purpose; intention; intent; object. [< OF *esmer* < L *aestimare* appraise, and OF *aesmer* < VL *adaestimare*] —**aim′er,** *n.*

aim·less (ām′lis), *adj.* without purpose. —**aim′less·ly,** *adv.* —**aim′less·ness,** *n.*

ain't (ānt), *Dial.* contraction of the phrases: **a** am not. **b** are not; is not. **c** have not; has not. ➔ **Ain't** is not acceptable in formal English.

Ai·nu (ī′nü), *n.* 1 member of an aboriginal, light-skinned race in N Japan, now becoming extinct. 2 the language of these people.

air (ãr), *n.* 1 the mixture of gases that surrounds the earth; atmosphere. 2 a light wind; breeze. 3 melody; tune. 4 public mention: *he gave air to his feelings.* 5 general character or appearance

of anything: *an air of mystery; an air of importance.*
—*v.* **1** put out in the air: *air clothes.* **2** make known; mention publicly: *do not air your troubles.* —*adj.* **1** conducting or supplying air: *air duct.* **2** using or worked by compressed air: *air drill.* **3** done by means of aircraft: *air photography.*

airs, unnatural or affected manners: *put on airs to impress us.*

by air, on an airplane or airline.

clear the air, express views, emotions, etc. to reduce tension or misunderstanding.

in the air, a going around: *wild rumors were in the air.* **b** uncertain.

on the air, broadcasting.

up in the air, a uncertain. **b** very angry or excited. [< OF < L < Gk. *aer*]

air bag, bag that fills with air automatically to protect passengers in an automobile from serious injury in a collision.

air base, headquarters and airport for military aircraft.

air bladder, sac in most fishes and various animals and plants, filled with air.

air boat, small boat with a flat bottom and driven by a large propeller fastened above the back of the boat, esp. for use in shallow water.

air-borne (ār′bôrn′; –bōrn′), *adj.* **1** carried in aircraft or gliders. **2** carried by air.

air brake, brake operated by a piston or pistons worked by compressed air.

air-brush, *n.* device operated by compressed air that is used to spray paint on a surface. —*v.* to use an airbrush.

air-burst (ār′bėrst′), *n.* exploding of a bomb in the air.

air castle, daydream.

air chamber, any compartment filled with air, esp. one in a hydraulic engine.

air coach, 1 low-cost class of air travel. **2** aircraft with low passenger rates.

air-con-di-tion (ār′kən dish′ən), *v.* **1** supply with the equipment for air conditioning. **2** treat (air) by means of air conditioning.

air-con-di-tioned (ār′kən dish′ənd), *adj.* having air conditioning.

air conditioner, a machine for air-conditioning buildings, rooms, trains, etc.

air conditioning, a means of treating air in buildings to regulate its humidity and temperature and to free it from dust, etc.

air-cool (ār′kül′), *v.* **1** remove heat produced in a motor by blowing air on it. **2** remove heat in a room by blowing cool air in. —**air′-cooled′,** *adj.* —**air′-cool′er,** *n.*

air-craft (ār′kraft′; –kräft′), *n., pl.* –**craft.** **1** machine for air navigation that is supported in air by buoyancy (such as a balloon) or by dynamic action (such as an airplane). **2** such machines collectively or as a class.

aircraft carrier, warship designed as a base for aircraft.

air-crew (ār′krü′), *n.* group that flies an aircraft.

air-drome (ār′drōm′), *n.* =airport. Also, *Brit.* **aerodrome.** [< AIR- + Gk. *dromos* race course]

air drop, delivery of food, supplies, etc., from aircraft, esp. as relief to victims of a disaster or to supply troops, etc. —**air′drop′,** *v.*

Aire-dale (ār′dāl), *n.* large terrier having a wiry brown or tan coat with dark markings. [< *Airedale* in Yorkshire, England]

air-express (ār′ik spres′), *v.* ship packages, etc. by air.

air express, shipment of letters, packages, and goods by air.

air field, landing field of an airport.

air-foil (ār′foil′), *n.* any surface, such as a wing, rudder, etc., designed to help lift or control an aircraft.

air force, 1 branch of the military or naval forces that uses aircraft. **2 Air Force,** a separate branch of the armed forces of the U.S. that includes aviation personnel, equipment, etc. **3** group of fliers for military aircraft.

air-frame (ār′frām′), *n.* the structural part of an airplane, ballistic missile, etc., apart from propulsion and guidance components.

air-head (ār′hed′), *n.* a frivolous, empty-headed person; ditz.

air hole, 1 opening through which air can pass, esp. a space in the ice on a river, pond, etc. **2** air pocket.

air-i-ly (ār′ə li), *adv.* in an airy manner.

air-i-ness (ār′i nis), *n.* airy quality.

air-ing (ār′ing), *n.* **1** exposure to air for drying, etc. **2** a walk, ride, etc. in the open air. **3** exposure to public discussion, criticism, etc.: *the proposed ordinance is due for an airing.*

air kiss, *v.* embrace and kiss, but to the side so that the kiss does not touch the cheek. —**air kisser.**

air lane, a regular route used by aircraft.

air-less (ār′lis), *adj.* **1** without fresh air; stuffy. **2** without a breeze.

air letter, 1 thin sheet of paper for writing a short letter and folding to form an envelope. **2** letter sent by air.

air-lift (ār′lift′), *n.* **1** system of using aircraft for transporting people and freight to a place when land approaches are closed. **2** aircraft used in such an operation. **3** goods and people transported. —*v.* transport by airlift.

air-line (ār′līn), *n.* **1** system of transportation of people and things by aircraft. **2** company operating such a system. **3** route for aircraft. —**air′line′,** *adj.*

air-liner (ār′līn ər), *n.* large aircraft for carrying many passengers.

air lock, an airtight compartment between places where there is a difference in air pressure.

air-mail, 1 system of sending mail by aircraft. **2** mail so sent. —*v.* send mail by air. —*adj.* sent or to be sent by air.

air-man (ār′mən), *n., pl.* –**men. 1** enlisted man in the air force. **2** pilot of an aircraft. **3** one of the crew of an aircraft.

air mass, large body of air that moves through the atmosphere over long distances without great change in temperature, etc.

air mattress, inflatable bag used as a mattress.

air mile, measure of distance of aircraft; nautical mile.

air-mind-ed (ār′mīn′did), *adj.* **1** interested in aviation. **2** fond of traveling by air. —**air′-mind′ed-ness,** *n.*

air piracy, hijacking of an aircraft.

air-plane (ār′plān′), *n.* a mechanically driven heavier-than-air aircraft supported in flight by the action of the air flowing past or thrusting upward on its fixed wings. Also, *esp. Brit.* **aeroplane.**

air pocket, a vertical current in the air that causes a sudden drop of an airplane.

air pollution, contamination of the air, esp. by exhaust from burning fossil fuels and from waste products produced by industrial processes.

air-port (ār′pôrt′; –pōrt′), *n.* tract of land or water where aircraft can land or take off, with facilities for catering to passengers, refueling, and servicing aircraft.

air pressure, pressure of the atmosphere.

air pump, apparatus for forcing air in or drawing air out of something.

air raid, attack by aircraft, esp. with bombs.

air rifle, gun worked by compressed air.

air sac, 1 small sac in the lung; alveolus. **2** air-filled space in the body of a bird, connected with the lungs.

air service, 1 transportation of people or things by aircraft. **2** air force (def. 1).

air-ship (ār′ship′), *n.* dirigible.

air-sick (ār′sik′), *adj.* sick as a result of traveling by air. —**air′sick′ness,** *n.*

air-space (ār′spās′), *n.* the atmosphere as used by aircraft, esp. that part of it regarded as under the control of a particular country, etc.

air-speed, speed of an aircraft measured by its greater movement than that of the air.

air-stream (ār′strēm′), *n.* flow of air around a flying object, related to its speed.

air strike, attack from aircraft on a particular target.

air-strip (ār′strip′), *n.* a paved or cleared strip on which aircraft land and take off.

air-tight (ār′tīt′), *adj.* **1** so tight that no air or gas can get in or out. **2** having no weak points open to an opponent's attack.

air time, 1 start of a radio or television broadcast. **2** length of time a show is broadcast, esp. as a measure for pricing advertisements.

air-to-air (ār′tŭ ār′), *adj.* **1** launched from one flying aircraft, to another: *air-to-air rockets.* **2** between two flying aircraft: *air-to-air refueling.*

air waves, =broadcasting.

air·way (ār′wā′), *n.* **1** route for aircraft. **2** passage for air.

air·wor·thy (ār′wẽr′thī), *adj.* fit or safe for service in the air. —**air′wor′thi·ness,** *n.*

air·y (ār′i), *adj.* **air·i·er, air·i·est. 1** like air; not solid or substantial. **2** light as air; graceful; delicate. **3** light in manner; light-hearted. **4** open to the air; breezy. **5** reaching high into the air; lofty. **6** of air; in the air. **7** unnatural; affected.

aisle (īl), *n.* **1** passage between rows of seats in a hall, theater, school, etc. **2** any long or narrow passageway, as in a store. **3** part of a church along the side of the nave, separated from it by columns or piers. [< OF < L *ala* wing; infl. in form by *isle* and in meaning by *alley*] —**aisled** (īld), *adj.*

Aix-la-Cha·pelle (āks′lä shä pel′), *n.* French name of Aachen.

a·jar[1] (ə jär′), *adj., adv.* partly opened. [ME *on char* on the turn; OE *cerr* turn]

a·jar[2] (ə jär′), *adv., adj.* not in harmony. [< *a-* in + *jar* discord]

A·jax (ā′jaks), *n. Gk. Legend.* Greek hero at the siege of Troy.

AK, (*zip code*) Alaska.

aka or **a.k.a.,** also known as.

AKC, American Kennel Club.

a·kene (a ken′), *n.* achene.

A·ki·hi·to (ä′kē hē′tō), *n.* emperor of Japan (1989–).

a·kim·bo (ə kim′bō), *adj., adv.* with the hand on the hip and the elbow bent outward. [ME *in kene bowe,* appar., in keen bow, at a sharp angle]

a·kin (ə kin′), *adj.* **1** related by blood; *your cousins are akin to you.* **2** alike; similar. [for *of kin*]

al- *prefix.* to or toward, form of *ad-* before *-l-.*

-al[1], *suffix.* of; like; having the nature of, as in *ornamental.* [< L *-alis, -ale* pertaining to]

-al[2], *suffix.* act of ____ing, as in *refusal.* [< L *-ale,* neut. of *-alis*]

AL, (*zip code*) Alabama.

Al, aluminum.

a la (ä′lə), *French* **à la** (ä lä), after; according to: *a la Roman.*

Ala., Alabama.

Al·a·bam·a (al′ə bam′ə), *n.* southern state of the United States. —**Al′a·bam′an, Al′a·bam′i·an** *adj.*

al·a·bam·ine (al′ə bam′ēn; -in), *n.* =astatine.

al·a·bas·ter (al′ə bas′tər; -bäs′-), *n.* **1** a smooth white, translucent variety of gypsum. **2** a variety of calcite, often banded like marble. —*adj.* Also, **al·a·bas·trine,** of or like alabaster. [< L < Gk. *alabast(r)os* an alabaster box]

à la carte (ä′ lə kärt′), with a state price for each dish. [< F]

a·lack (ə lak′), *interj. Archaic.* exclamation of sorrow or regret; alas.

a·lac·ri·ty (ə lak′rə ti), *n.* **1** brisk and eager action; liveliness. **2** cheerful willingness. [< L, < *alacer* brisk] —**a·lac′ri·tous,** *adj.*

A·lad·din (ə lad′ən), *n.* a youth in *The Arabian Nights,* who found a magic lamp and a magic ring.

à la king (ä′ lə king′), creamed with pimiento or green pepper: *chicken à la king.*

al·a·me·da (al′ə mā′də), *n. SW U.S.* promenade with trees, esp. poplars, on each side. [< Sp., < *álamo* poplar]

Al·a·mo (al′ə mō), *n.* a mission in San Antonio, Texas. After a siege, Mexicans captured it from Americans on March 6, 1836.

à la mode, a la mode, or **a·la·mode** (ä′ lə mōd′; al′ə-), *adv.* **1** according to the prevailing fashion; in style. **2** *Cookery.* **a** (of desserts) served with ice cream. **b** (of meat) cooked with vegetables. [< F]

Al·a·ric (al′ə rik), *n.* 370?–410 A.D., king of the Visigoths who captured Rome in 410 A.D.

a·larm (ə lärm′), *n.* **1** sudden fear or fright. **2** a warning of approaching danger. **3** thing that gives such a warning. **4** call to arms or action. **5** a device that makes noise to warn or awaken people. —*v.* **1** fill with sudden fear. **2** warn (anyone) of approaching danger. [< OF < Ital., < *all'arme!* to arms!]

alarm clock, clock that can be set to make a noise at any desired time.

a·larm·ing (ə lär′ming), *adj.* that alarms; frightening. —**a·larm′ing·ly,** *adv.*

a·larm·ist (ə lär′mist), *n.* person who is easily alarmed or alarms others needlessly or on very slight grounds. —**a·larm′ism,** *n.*

a·lar·um (ə lar′əm; ə lär′-), *n. Archaic.* alarm.

a·las (ə las′; ə läs′), *interj.* exclamation of sorrow, grief, regret, pity, or dread. [< OF *a* ah + *las* miserable < L *lassus* weary]

Alas., Alaska.

A·las·ka (ə las′kə), *n.* the largest state of the United States, in NW North America. —**A·las′kan,** *adj., n.*

Alaska Highway, a highway that extends from Dawson Creek, British Columbia, Canada, to Fairbanks, Alaska.

a·late (ā′lāt), **a·lat·ed** (-id), *adj.* having wings or winglike parts. [< L, < *ala* wing]

alb (alb), *n.* a white linen robe worn by Roman Catholic and some Anglican priests at the Eucharist. [< L (*vestis*) *alba* white (robe)]

al·ba·core (al′bə kôr; -kôr), *n., pl.* **-cores** or (*esp. collectively*) **-core.** a long-finned, edible fish related to the tuna, found in the Atlantic. [< Pg. < Ar. *al-bakūra*]

Al·ba·ni·a (al bā′ni ə; -bān′yə), *n.* country in Europe, between the former Yugoslavia and Greece. —**Al·ba′ni·an,** *adj., n.*

Al·ba·ny (ôl′bə ni), *n.* capital of New York State.

al·ba·tross (al′bə trôs; -tros), *n.* **1** any of various web-footed sea birds related to the petrel. **2** *Fig.* burden, hindrance. [var. of obs. *alcatras* frigate bird < Sp. < Pg. < Ar. *al-qādus* the bucket < Gk. *kados* < Phoenician]

Al·bee (ôl′bē), *n.* **Edward,** 1928– , American playwright.

al·be·it (ôl bē′it), *conj.* although; even though. [ME *al be it* although it be]

Al·ber·ta (al bẽr′tə), *n.* province in W Canada.

al·bi·no (al bī′nō), *n., pl.* **-nos. 1** person lacking pigmentation. Albinos have pale skin, light hair, and pink eyes. **2** any animal or plant that has pale, defective coloring. [< Pg., < *albo* < L *albus* white] —**al·bin′ic,** *adj.* —**al′bi·nism,** *n.*

Al·bi·on (al′bi ən), *n. Poetic.* England.

al·bum (al′bəm), *n.* **1** book with blank pages for pictures, stamps, etc. **2** collection of recordings, as on a CD. [< L, tablet, neut. of *albus* white]

al·bu·men (al bū′mən, *n.* **1** white of an egg, consisting mostly of albumin dissolved in water. **2** *Chem.* albumin. **3** *Bot.* endosperm. [< L *albumen* < *albus* white]

al·bu·min (al bū′mən), *n. Chem.* any of a class of proteins soluble in water and found in the white of egg and in many other animal and plant tissues and juices, esp. $C_{77}H_{117}N_{18}O_{77}S$. [< L. See ALBUMEN.]

Al·bu·quer·que (al′bə kẽr′kē), *n.* city in central New Mexico.

Al·ca·traz (al′kə traz), *n.* **1** island in San Francisco Bay. **2** former U.S. penitentiary there.

al·ca·zar (al′kə zär; al kaz′ər), *n.* palace of the Spanish Moors. [< Ar. *al-qaṣr* the castle < L *castrum* fort]

al·che·mist (al′kə mist), *n.* person who studied alchemy. —**al′che·mis′tic, al′·che·mis′ti·cal,** *adj.*

al·che·my (al′kə mi), *n.* **1** medieval chemistry, esp. the search for a process by which baser metals could be turned into gold. **2** *Fig.* magic power or process for changing one thing into another. [< OF < Med.L < Ar. *al-kīmiyā′,* < LGk. *chymeia* < Gk. *chyma* molten metal] —**al·chem′ic,** —**al·chem′i·cal,** *adj.* —**al·chem′i·cal·ly,** *adv.*

al·co·hol (al′kə hôl; -hol), *n.* **1** colorless liquid, C_2H_5OH, in wine, beer, whiskey, gin, etc., that makes them intoxicating; grain alcohol; ethyl alcohol. Alcohol is used in medicine, in manufacturing, and as a fuel. **2** any intoxicating liquor containing this liquid. **3** any of a group of similar organic compounds. Alcohols contain a hydroxyl group and react with organic acids to form esters. [< Med. L (orig., "fine powder," then "essence") < Ar. *al-kuhl* powdered antimony]

al·co·hol·ic (al′kə hôl′ik; –hol′–), *adj.* **1** of alcohol. **2** containing alcohol. **3** suffering from the excessive use of alcoholic liquors. —*n.* person suffering from alcoholism.

al·co·hol·ism (al′kə hôl iz′əm; –hol–), *n.* **1** a disease having as its chief symptom the inability to drink alcoholic liquors in moderation. **2** a diseased condition caused by drinking too much alcoholic liquor.

Al·co·ran (al′kō rän′; –ran′), *n.* the Koran.

al·cove (al′kōv), *n.* **1** small room opening out of a larger room. **2** part in a wall set back from the rest. **3** summerhouse. [< F < Sp. < Ar. *al-qubba* the vaulted chamber]

Ald., Aldm., Alderman.

al·de·hyde (al′də hīd), *n.* **1** a transparent, colorless liquid, CH_3CHO, with a suffocating smell, produced by the partial oxidation of ordinary alcohol. **2** any similar organic compound. —**al′de·hy′dic,** *adj.*

Al·den (ôl′dən), *n.* **John,** 1599?–1687, one of the Pilgrims who settled at Plymouth, Massachusetts.

al·der (ôl′dər), *n.* any of several trees and shrubs that usually grow in wet land and have clusters of catkins. [OE *alor*]

al·der·man (ôl′dər mən), *n., pl.* –men. **1** *U.S.* member of a council that governs a city. **2** in English and Irish cities, a member of a city or county council next in rank to the mayor. [see ELDER¹] —**al′der·man·cy, al′der·man·ship′,** *n.* —**al·der·man′ic,** *adj.*

Al·der·ney (äl′dər ni), *n., pl.* –neys. **1** one of a group of British islands in the English Channel. **2** one of a breed of dairy cattle.

ale (āl), *n.* a heavy, bitter beer, fermented from hops and malt. [OE *alu*]

a·lee (ə lē′), *adv., adj.* on or toward the side of a ship that is away from the wind. [< Scand., < *ā* on + *hlē* shelter, lee]

ale·house (āl′hous′), *n.* place where ale or beer is sold; pub.

a·lem·bic (ə lem′bik), *n.* **1** a glass or metal container formerly used in distilling. **2** *Fig.* something that transforms or refines. [< Med.L < Ar. *al anbīq* the still < Gk. *ambix* cup]

A·lençon (ä län-sôn′ *for 1;* ə len′sən, –son *for 2*), *n.* **1** city in NW France. **2** lace made there.

A·lep·po (ə lep′ō), *n.* city in NW Syria.

a·lert (ə lèrt′), *adj.* **1** watchful; wide-awake. **2** brisk; active; nimble. —*n.* **1** a signal warning of an air attack. **2** a signal to troops, etc., to be ready for action. —*v.* **1** warn against and prepare for an approaching air attack. **2** notify; arouse. **on the alert,** on the lookout; watchful; wide-awake. [< F < Ital. *all' erta* on the watch, ult. < L *erigere* raise up] —**a·lert′ly,** *adv.* —**a·lert′ness,** *n.*

Al·e·ut (al′i üt), *n.* **1** native of the Aleutian Islands. **2** language of these people. —**A·leu′tian,** *adj.*

A·leu·tians (ə lü′shənz), *or* **Aleutian Islands,** *n.pl.* chain of many small islands SW of Alaska, belonging to the United States.

ale·wife (āl′wīf′), *n., pl.* –wives. *Am.* a sea fish related to the herring and the shad.

Al·ex·an·der the Great (al′ig zan′dər; –zän′–), *n.* 356–323 B.C., king of Macedonia from 336 to 323 B.C.

Al·ex·an·dri·a (al′ig zan′dri ə; –zän′–), *n.* seaport in N Egypt, on the Mediterranean.

Al·ex·an·dri·an (al′ig zan′dri ən; –zän′–), *adj.* **1** of Alexandria. **2** of Alexander the Great. **3** of Alexandrine verse.

Al·ex·an·drine (al′ig zan′drin; –drēn; –zän′–), *n.* line of poetry having six iambic feet, with a caesura (pause) after the third foot.

al·fal·fa (al fal′fə), *n.* a plant of the pea family, grown for pasture and forage; lucerne. [< Sp. < Ar. *al-faṣ faṣah* the best kind of fodder]

Al·fred (al′frid), *n.* (*"Alfred the Great"*) 849–899 A.D., king of the West Saxons, 871–899 A.D.

al·fres·co, al fres·co (al fres′kō), *adv., adj.* in the open air; outdoors. [< Ital.]

alg., algebra.

al·ga (al′gə), *n., pl.* –gae (-jē). one of the algae. —**al′gal,** *adj.*

al·gae (al′jē), *n.pl.* group of plants that have chlorophyll but do not have true stems, roots, or leaves. Some algae are single-celled and form scum on rocks; others, such as the seaweeds, are very large. [< L, seaweed]

al·ge·bra (al′jə brə), *n.* branch of mathematics in which quantities are denoted by letters, negative numbers as well as ordinary numbers are used, and problems are solved in the form of equations. [<Med.L < Ar. *al-jebr* the bone setting; hence, reduction] —**al·ge·bra′ic, al′ge·bra′i·cal,** *adj.* —**al′ge·bra′i·cal·ly,** *adv.*

al·ge·bra·ist (al′jə brā′ist), *n.* expert in algebra.

Al·ge·ri·a (al jir′i ə), *n.* country in N Africa. —**Al′geari·an, Al′ge·rine,** *adj., n.*

Al·giers (al jirz′), *n.* **1** capital of Algeria. **2** Algeria.

AL·GOL (al′gol), *n.* computer language.

Al·gon·ki·an (al gong′kē ən), *n.* **1** the most widespread linguistic stock of American Indians. **2** an Indian belonging to an Algonkian tribe. —*adj.* of or belonging to this linguistic stock.

Al·gon·quin (al gong′kin; -kwin), *n.* **1** member of a family of North American Indian tribes living in eastern Canada. **2** the language of any of these tribes. **3** any Algonkian.

al·go·rithm (al go rith′əm), *n.* procedure for solving a mathematical problem. —**al′go·rith′mic,** *adj.*

Al·ham·bra (al ham′brə), *n.* palace of the Moorish kings at Granada, Spain.

al·ien·ate (āl′yən āt; ā′li ən–), *v.,* –at·ed, –at·ing. **1** turn away in feeling or affection; make unfriendly. **2** transfer the

ownership of (property) to another. —**al′ien·a′tion,** *n.*

al·ien·ist (āl′yən ist; ā′li ən–), *n.* psychiatrist, esp. one who testifies in court. [< F < L *alienus* insane]

a·light¹ (ə līt′), *v.,* **a·light·ed** or **a·lit, a·light·ing. 1** get down; get off, as from horseback; dismount. **2** come down from the air and settle: *a bird alights on a tree.* **3** come upon by chance; happen to find. [OE *ālīhtan*]

a·light² (ə līt′), *adv., adj.* **1** lighted up: *her face was alight with joy.* **2** on fire. [OE *ālīht* illuminated]

a·lign (ə līn′), *v.* **1** bring into line; adjust to a line: *align the sights of a gun.* **2** form in line: *the troops aligned.* **3** join with others in or against a cause: *Britain aligned with the U.S. in the Iraq War.* Also, **aline.** [< F, < *a-* to + *ligner* < L, < *linea* line] —**a·lign′er,** *n.* —**a·lign′ment,** *n.*

a·like (ə līk′), *adv.* **1** in the same way. **2** similarly; equally. —*adj.* like one another; similar. [OE *gelīc, onlīc*]

al·i·ment (al′ə mənt), *n.* nourishment; food. [< L *alimentum* < *alere* nourish] —**al′i·men′tal** *adj.* —**al′i·men′tal·ly,** *adv.*

al·i·men·ta·ry (al′ə men′tə ri; –men′tri), *adj.* **1** having to do with food and nutrition. **2** nourishing; nutritious. **3** providing support.

alimentary canal, the digestive tract of any animal, extending from the mouth to the anus.

al·i·men·ta·tion (al′ə men tā′shən), *n.* **1** nutrition. **2** support. —**al′i·men′ta·tive,** *adj.*

al·i·mo·ny (al′ə mō′ni), *n.* regular payment of money that a person must make to a spouse after a legal separation or divorce. [< L *alimonia* < *alere* nourish]

a·line (ə līn′), *v.,* **a·lined, a·lin·ing.** =align. —**a·line′ment,** *n.* —**a·lin′er,** *n.*

al·i·quant (al′ə kwənt), *adj.* not dividing a number without a remainder: *5 is an aliquant part of 14.* [< L, < *alius* other + *quantus* how much]

al·i·quot (al′ə kwət), *adj.* dividing a number without a remainder: *3 is an aliquot part of 12.* [< L, < *alius* some + *quot* how many]

a·lit (ə līt′), *v.* pt. and pp. of **alight¹.**

a·live (ə līv′), *adj.* **1** living; not dead: *the man is alive.* **2** in continued activity or operation: *keep the principles of liberty alive.* **3** of all living: *happiest man alive.* **4** active; sprightly; lively. **5** connected to an electric source; live. **6** connected for broadcast or recording.
alive to, awake to; sensitive to.
alive with, full of; swarming with.
look alive, hurry up! [OE *on līfe* in life] —**a·live′ness,** *n.*

al·ka·li (al′kə lī), *n., pl.* –lis, –lies. **1** any base or hydroxide that is soluble in water, neutralizes acids and forms salts with them, and turns red litmus blue. **2** any salt or mixture of salts that neutralizes acids. [< MF < Ar. *al-qalī* the ashes of saltwort (a genus of plants)]

al·ka·line (al′kə līn; –lin), *adj.* **1** of or like an alkali. **2** impregnated with alkali. —**al′ka·lin′i·ty,** *n.*

alkaline-earth metals, group of elements including calcium, strontium, barium, magnesium, and radium.

alkaline earths, oxides of the alkaline-earth metals.

al·ka·lize (al′kə līz), *v.,* –**lized, –liz·ing.** make alkaline. —**al′ka·li·za′tion,** *n.*

al·ka·loid (al′kə loid), *n.* any organic base containing nitrogen. Many alkaloids from plants are drugs, such as strychnine, morphine, and quinine.

al·ka·loi·dal (al′kə loi′dəl), *adj.* of or having to do with an alkaloid or alkaloids.

all (ôl), *adj.* **1** the whole of: *all Europe.* **2** every one of: *all men.* **3** the greatest possible: *with all speed.* —*pron.* **1** (*pl. in use*) the whole number: *all of us are going.* **2** (*sing. in use*) everything: *all that glitters is not gold.* —*adv.* **1** entirely: *the cake is all gone.* **2** each: *the score was one all.* **above all,** before everything else.
after all, nevertheless.
all but, nearly.
all in, weary.
all in all, a everything. **b** completely.
at all, a under any conditions. **b** in any way.
in all, altogether. [OE *eall*]

Al·lah (al′ə; ä′lä), *n.* the Muslim name of the Supreme Being.

all-A·mer·i·can (ôl′ ə mer′ə kən), *adj.* **1** representing the whole United States. **2** made up entirely of Americans or American elements. **3** selected as the best in the United States. **4** characteristic of America or Americans. —*n.* an all-American person, esp. a player on a team.

all-a·round (ôl′ə round′), *adj.* **1** able to do many things; useful in many ways. **2** including all. —**all′-a·round′er,** *n.* —**all′-a·round′ness,** *n.*

al·lay (ə lā′), *v.,* –**layed, –lay·ing. 1** put at rest; quiet; calm: *his fears were allayed.* **2** relieve; check: *fever allayed by medicine.* **3** make less. [OE *ālecgan*] —**al·lay′er,** *n.* —**al·lay′ment,** *n.*

all clear, signal indicating the end of danger. —**all′-clear′,** *adj.*

al·le·ga·tion (al′ə gā′shən), *n.* **1** assertion without proof. **2** act of alleging; assertion: *the lawyer's allegation was proved.* **3** assertion made as a plea or excuse.

al·lege (ə lej′), *v.,* –**leged, –leg·ing. 1** assert without proof; *the alleged theft never happened.* **2** state positively; affirm: *this man alleges that his watch has been stolen.* **3** give or bring forward as a reason, etc.; produce; cite. [< AF *alegier* < L *ex-* + *litigare* strive, sue; with sense of L *allegare* charge] —**al·lege′a·ble,** *adj.* —**al·leg′er,** *n.*

al·leg·ed·ly (ə lej′id li), *adv.* according to what is or has been alleged.

Al·le·ghe·nies (al′ə gā′niz; al′ə gā ′niz), or **Allegheny Mountains,** *n.pl.* a moun-

tain range in Pennsylvania, Maryland, Virginia, and West Virginia. —**Al′le·ghe′ni·an,** *n., adj.*

al·le·giance (ə lē′jəns), *n.* **1** the loyalty owed by a citizen to his country or by a subject to his ruler. **2** loyalty; faithfulness; devotion. [ME *ligeaunce* < OF, < *lige* liege]

al·le·gor·i·cal (al′ə gôr′ə kəl; –gor′–), **al·le·gor·ic** (-ik), *adj.* using allegory. —**al′le·gor′i·cal·ly,** *adv.* —**al′le·gor′i·cal·ness,** *n.*

al·le·go·rist (al′ə gô′rist; –gō ′–; al′ə gə rist), *n.* one who uses allegories.

al·le·go·rize (al′ə gə rīz), *v.,* –**rized, –riz·ing. 1** make into allegory. **2** treat or interpret as an allegory. **3** use allegory. —**al′le·gor′i·za′tion,** *n.* —**al′le·go·riz′er,** *n.*

al·le·go·ry (al′ə gô′ri; -gō′-), *n., pl.* –**ries.** story which is told to explain or teach something: *Many nursery rhymes are allegories.* [< L < Gk., < *allos* other + *agoreuein* speak]

al·le·gret·to (al′ə gret′ō), *adj., adv., n., pl.* –**tos.** —*adj.* moderately fast. —*adv.,* in a moderately fast tempo. —*n.* a moderately fast musical passage or piece.

al·le·gro (ə lā′grō; ə leg′rō), *adj., adv., n., pl.* –**gros.** —*adj.* quick; lively. —*adv.* in a quick, lively tempo. —*n.* a quick, lively musical passage or piece. [< Ital. < L *alacer* brisk]

al·le·lu·ia (al′ə lü′yə), liturgical form of **hallelujah,** meaning "praise ye the Lord." —*n.* hymn of praise to the Lord. [< L < Gk. < Heb. *hallēlūjāh* praise ye Jehovah]

al·ler·gen (al′ər jən), *n.* thing that causes or reveals an allergy in a person or animal. —**al·ler·gen′ic,** *adj.*

al·ler·gic (ə lėr′jik), *adj.* **1** of allergy. **2** having an allergy. —**al·ler′gi·cal·ly,** *adv.*

al·ler·gy (al′ər ji), *n., pl.* –**gies.** unusual sensitiveness to a particular substance, as certain pollens and dusts. [< NL < Gk. *allos* different, strange + *ergon* action]

al·le·vi·ate (ə lē′vi āt), *v.,* –**at·ed, –at·ing. 1** make easier to endure (suffering of the body or mind); allay; mitigate. **2** lessen; diminish. [< LL, < L *ad-* up + *levis* light] —**al·le′vi·a′tion,** *n.* —**al·le′vi·a′tive,** *adj., n.* —**al·le′vi·a′tor,** *n.*

al·ley (al′i), *n., pl.* –**leys. 1** a narrow back street, especially one that is behind a row of buildings in a city or town. **2** *Brit.* a narrow street. **3** path in a park or garden, bordered by trees. **4** a long, narrow enclosed place for bowling. [< OF *alee* a going]

al·ley·way (al′i wā′), *n.* **1** a narrow lane in a city or town, especially one that is behind buildings. **2** a narrow passageway.

All Fools' Day, April 1, April Fools' Day.

all fours, 1 all four legs of an animal. **2** arms and legs of a person; hands and knees.

All·hal·lows (ôl′hal′ōz), *n.* Nov. 1, All Saints' Day.

al·li·ance (ə lī′əns), *n.* **1** union formed by agreement; joining of interests. An alliance may be a joining of family interests by marriage, a joining of national interests by treaty, etc. **2** nations, persons, etc., who belong to such a union. **3** association; connection. **4** similarity in structure or descent. [< OF, < *alier* unite < L, < *ad-* to + *ligare* bind]

al·lied (ə līd′; al′īd), *adj.* **1** united by agreement or treaty: *allied nations.* **2** associated: *allied banks.* **3** connected by nature; akin: *allied animals.* **4 Allied,** of the Allies of World War I and II.

Al·lies (al′īz; ə līz′), *n.pl.* **1** nations that fought against Germany and Austria in World War I. **2** nations that fought against Germany, Italy, and Japan in World War II.

al·li·ga·tor (al′ə gā′tər), *n., v.* **1** American reptile, similar to the crocodile but having a shorter and flatter head. **2** leather prepared from its skin. —*v.* become cracked or blistered on the surface. [< Sp. *el lagarto* the lizard < L *lacertus* lizard]

alligator pear, =avocado.

al·lit·er·ate (ə lit′ər āt), *v.,* –**at·ed, –at·ing. 1** begin with the same letter or sound. **2** use alliteration. [< L *ad-* to + *litera* letter] —**al·lit′er·a′tor,** *n.*

al·lit·er·a·tion (ə lit′ər ā′shən), *n.* repetition of the same first letter or sound in a group of words or line of poetry; initial rhyme. *Example:* the sun sank slowly. —**al·lit′er·a′tive,** *adj.* —**al·lit′er·a′tive·ly,** *adv.* —**al·lit′er·a′tive·ness,** *n.*

al·lo·cate (al′ə kāt), *v.,* –**cat·ed, –cat·ing. 1** assign or allot, as a share, portion, etc.; distribute. **2** locate. [< Med.L, < L *ad-* to, at + *locare* to place] —**al′lo·ca′tion.** *n.*

al·lo·path (al′ə path), **al·lop·a·thist** (ə lop′ə thist), *n.* **1** doctor who uses allopathy. **2** person who favors allopathy.

al·lop·a·thy (ə lop′ə thi), *n.* method of treating a disease by using remedies to produce effects different from those caused by the disease treated (opposite of *homeopathy*). [< G < Gk. *allos* other + -PATHY] —**al′lo·path′ic,** *adj.* —**al′lo·path′i·cal·ly,** *adv.*

al·lo·phone (al′ə fōn), *n.* one of the several individual sounds belonging to a single phoneme. The *t* in *take* and the *t* in *try* are allophones of the phoneme *t*. [< Gk. *allos* other + *phone* sound]

al·lot (ə lot′), *v.,* –**lot·ted, –lot·ting. 1** divide and distribute in parts or shares: *profits allotted to the partners.* **2** appropriate to a special purpose. [< OF *aloter.* See LOT.] —**al·lot′ta·ble,** *adj.* —**al·lot′ter,** *n.*

al·lot·ment (ə lot′mənt), *n.* **1** division and distribution in parts or shares. **2** share.

al·lo·trope (al′ə trōp), *n.* an allotropic form.

al·lo·trop·ic (al′ə trop′ik), *adj.* occurring in two or more forms that differ in physical and chemical properties but not in the kind of atoms of which they are composed, as oxygen and ozone. —al′lo·trop′i·cal, *adj.* —al′lo·trop′i·cal·ly, *adv.*

al·lot·ro·py (ə lot′rə pi), **al·lot·ro·pism** (-piz əm), *n.* the property or fact of being allotropic. [< Gk., < *allos* other + *tropos* way]

all-out (ôl′out′), *adj.* greatest possible. —*adv.* to the greatest possible extent.

al·low (ə lou′), *v.* 1 permit: *smoking is not allowed.* 2 let have; give; grant: *allow $10 a week for lunch.* 3 admit; acknowledge; recognize: *allow a claim.* 4 add or subtract to make up for something: *allow an extra hour for traveling time.* 5 say or think.

allow for, take into consideration; provide for. [< OF *alouer* < L *allaudare* (< *ad-* + *laudare* praise) and *allocare* ALLOCATE] —al·low′er, *n.*

al·low·a·ble (ə lou′ə bəl), *adj.* 1 allowed by law or by a person in authority. 2 permitted by the rules of the game; not forbidden. —al·low′a·ble·ness, *n.* —al·low′a·bly, *adv.*

al·low·ance (ə lou′əns), *n., v.,* -anced, -anc·ing. —*n.* 1 definite portion or amount given out: *a weekly allowance.* 2 subtraction or addition to make up for something: *an allowance on a used car.* 3 an allowing: *allowance of a claim.* 4 tolerance: *no allowance of smoking.* —*v.* put upon an allowance; to limit (supplies, food, etc.) to a fixed, regular amount.

make allowance for or **make allowances,** take into consideration: *make allowance for their inexperience.*

al·low·ed·ly (ə lou′id li), *adv.* admittedly.

al·loy (*n.* al′oi, ə loi′; *v.* ə loi′), *n.* 1 an inferior metal mixed with a more valuable one. 2 metal made by the fusion of two or more metals, or a metal and a nonmetal. 3 any injurious addition: *no happiness is without alloy.* —*v.* 1 make into an alloy. 2 lower in value by mixing with an inferior metal: *alloy gold with copper.* 3 make worse; debase: *happiness alloyed by misfortune.* [< OF *alei* < L, < *ad-* to + *ligare* bind. Doublet of ALLY.]

all-pur·pose (ôl′pèr′pəs), *adj.* that can be used for any end: *all-purpose thread.*

all right, 1 without error; correct. 2 yes. 3 certainly. 4 in good health. 5 satisfactory.

all-round (ôl′round′), *adj.* 1 =all-around. 2 extending everywhere around.

All Saints' Day, Nov. 1, a church festival honoring all the saints; Allhallows.

all·spice (ôl′spīs′), *n.* 1 a spice having a flavor like a mixture of cinnamon, nutmeg, and cloves. 2 the berry of the West Indian pimento tree that it is made from.

all-star (ôl′stär′), *adj.* composed of the best players or performers. —*n.* member of an all-star team or group.

al·lude (ə lüd′), *v.,* -lud·ed, -lud·ing. refer indirectly; mention slightly (*to*): *do not mention or even allude to his deformity.* [< L, < *ad-* with + *ludere* play]

al·lure (ə lür′), *v.,* -lured, -lur·ing, *n.* —*v.* 1 fascinate; charm. 2 tempt by some advantage. —*n.* attractiveness. [< OF *alurer* LURE] —al·lure′ment, *n.* —al·lur′er, *n.*

al·lur·ing (ə lür′ing), *adj.* 1 tempting. 2 attractive. —al·lur′ing·ly, *adv.* —al·lur′ing·ness, *n.*

al·lu·sion (ə lü′zhən), *n.* 1 an indirect or casual reference; slight mention. 2 reference to a well-known quotation or fact to give emphasis.

al·lu·sive (ə lü′siv), *adj.* containing allusions. —al·lu′sive·ly, *adv.* —al·lu′sive·ness, *n.*

al·lu·vi·al (ə lü′vi əl), *adj.* consisting of or forming alluvium. —*n.* alluvial soil.

al·lu·vi·um (ə lü′vi əm), *n., pl.* -vi·ums, -vi·a (-vi ə). sand, mud, etc., left by flowing water. [< L, < *ad-* up + *luere* wash]

al·ly (*v.* ə lī′; *n.* al′ī, ə lī′), *v.,* -lied, -ly·ing, *n., pl.* -lies. —*v.* 1 unite by formal agreement, as by marriage, treaty, or league (*to* or *with*): *France allied itself with England.* 2 connect by some relation, as of likeness, kinship, or friendship. 3 enter into an alliance. —*n.* 1 person or nation united with another for some special purpose. 2 a related animal, plant, or thing. 3 helper; supporter. See also **Allies.** [< OF *alier* < L, < *ad-* to + *ligare* bind. Doublet of ALLOY.]

-ally, *suffix, forming adverbs.* in a manner: *frantically = in a frantic manner.*

al·ma ma·ter, Al·ma Ma·ter (al′mə mä′tər; äl–; al′mə mā′tər), person's school, college, or university. [< L, nourishing mother]

al·ma·nac (ôl′mə nak), *n.* 1 table or book of tables containing a calendar, astronomical data, etc. 2 book published yearly that gives summaries of world events and other information. [< Med.L < Sp. < Ar. *almanākh*, appar. < LGk. *almenichiakon* calendar]

al·might·y (ôl mīt′i), *adj.* 1 having supreme power; all-powerful; omnipotent. 2 great; very. —*adv.* exceedingly. —*n.* the Almighty, God. —al·might′i·ly, *adv.* —al·might′i·ness, *n.*

al·mond (ä′mənd); am′ənd), *n.* 1 the nut, or seed, of a peachlike fruit growing in warm regions. 2 tree that it grows on. [< OF *almande* < L < Gk. *amygdale*] —al′mond·like′, *adj.*

al·mon·er (al′mən ər; ä′mən–), *n.* person who distributes alms for a king, monastery, etc. [< OF *almosnier* < VL *alemosynarius* of ALMS]

al·mon·ry (al′mən ri; ä′mən–), *n., pl.* -ries. place where alms are distributed.

al·most (ôl′mōst; ôl mōst′), *adv.* nearly. [OE *eal māst* nearly]

alms (ämz), *n.pl.* (*sometimes sing. in use*) money or gifts to help the poor. [< VL < L < Gk. *eleemosyne* compassion < *eleos* mercy]

alms·giv·ing (ämz′giv′ing), *n., adj.* giving help to the poor. —alms′giv′er, *n.*

alms·house (ämz′hous′), *n.* Brit. house endowed by private charity for the poor to live in.

al·oe (al′ō), *n., pl.* -oes. 1 plant having a long spike of flowers and thick, narrow leaves, that grows in South Africa and other warm, dry climates. 2 **aloes** (*sing. in use*), a bitter drug made from the leaves of this plant. 3 the century plant. See **agave.** [< L < Gk.]

a·loft (ə lôft′; ə loft′), *adv., adj.* 1 far above the earth; high up. 2 high above the deck of a ship in the rigging. [< Scand. *ā lopti* in the air]

a·lo·ha (ə lō′ə; ä lō′hä), *n., interj.* 1 hello; welcome. 2 good-by. [< Hawaiian]

a·lone (ə lōn′), *adj.* 1 apart from other persons or things: *he was alone.* 2 only: *he alone remained.* 3 without anything more. 4 unique.

leave alone, not bother.

let alone, a not bother. **b** not to mention. —*adv.* only; merely. [ME *al one* all (completely) one] —a·lone′ness, *n.*

a·long (ə lông′; ə long′), *prep.* on or by the length of; lengthwise of: *walk along a river.* —*adv.* 1 lengthwise: *cars parked along by the stadium.* 2 onward: *let us walk along.* 3 together (*with*): *I'll go along with you.*

all along, all the time. [OE *andlang*]

a·long·shore (ə lông′shôr′; ə long′–; –shōr′), *adv.* near or along the shore.

a·long·side (ə lông′sīd′; ə long′–), *adv.* side by side: *anchor alongside.* —*prep.* beside: *alongside the wharf.*

a·loof (ə lüf′), *adv.* withdrawn; apart: *aloof from the others.* —*adj.* unsympathetic; indifferent. [< *a-* on + *loof* windward, prob. < Du. *loef*] —a·loof′ly, *adv.* —a·loof′ness, *n.*

a·loud (ə loud′), *adv.* 1 loud enough to be heard: *read aloud.* 2 in a loud voice; loudly.

al·pac·a (al pak′ə), *n.* 1 a variety of llama with long, soft, silky hair or wool. 2 its wool. 3 cloth made from this wool. [< Sp. < Ar. *al* the + Peruvian *paco* alpaca]

al·pen·horn (al′pən hôrn′), **alp·horn** (alp′hôrn′), *n.* long, powerful horn used in Switzerland for calling sheep, signals, etc. [< G]

al·pen·stock (al′pən stok′), *n.* a strong staff with an iron point, used in climbing mountains. [< G]

al·pha (al′fə), *n.* 1 the first letter of the Greek alphabet (A, α). 2 the first; beginning. 3 first; best; strongest: *alpha female; Rufus is the alpha of the pack.*

al·pha·bet (al′fə bet), *n.* 1 series of characters or signs representing sounds, used in writing a language. 2 letters of a language arranged in the customary order. 3 elementary principles. [< LL < Gk., < *alpha* A + *beta* B]

al·pha·bet·i·cal (al′fə bet′ə kəl), **al·pha·bet·ic** (–bet′ik), *adj.* 1 arranged in the order of the alphabet. 2 of the alphabet. 3 using an alphabet. —al′pha·bet′i·cal·ly, *adv.*

al·pha·bet·ize (al′fə bə tīz), v., **–ized, –iz-ing. 1** arrange in alphabetical order. **2** express by an alphabet. —**al′pha·bet·i·za′tion,** n. —**al′pha·bet·iz′er,** n.

alpha decay, disintegration of a radioactive substance by emission of alpha particles.

alpha particle, positively charged particle consisting of two protons and two neutrons, released in the disintegration of radioactive substances, as radium.

alpha ray, stream of alpha particles.

Al·pine (al′pīn; –pin), adj. **1** of the Alps. **2 alpine, a** of high mountains. **b** very high.

Alps (alps), n.pl. mountain system in S Europe, famous for its beautiful scenery.

al Qaida (al kī′də, –kā′–), loosely connected Muslim organization that follows Islamist principles. [< Ar. the base, a name bestowed by the Central Intelligence Agency]

al·read·y (ôl red′i), adv. before this time; by this time; even now: the house is already full.

al·right (ôl rīt′), adv. =all right.

Al·sace (al′sās; –sas; al sās′), n. region in NE France. —**Al·sa′tian,** adj., n.

Al·sace-Lor·raine (al′sās lə rān′; al′sas–), n. Alsace and Lorraine, region in NE France.

al·so (ôl′sō), adv. in addition; too. [< OE ealswā all so, quite so]

al·so ran (ôl′sō ran′), person who is roundly defeated in a contest, as an election.

alt., 1 alternate. **2** altitude.

al·tar (ôl′tər), n. **1** table or stand in the most sacred part of a church, synagogue, or temple. **2** an elevated structure on which sacrifices are offered to a deity. **3** Fig. focus of something, as an ideal: the altar of ambition. [< LL, <L altus high]

altar boy, person who helps a priest during certain religious services, esp. Mass; acolyte.

al·tar·piece (ôl′tər pēs′), n. a decorated panel or wall behind or above an altar.

al·ter (ôl′tər), v. **1** make different in some respect without changing into something else: alter a dress. **2** become different: her whole outlook has altered. **3** castrate or spay (an animal); neuter. [< OF < LL, < alter other]

alter., alteration.

al·ter·a·ble (ôl′tər ə bəl), adj. that can be altered. —**al′ter·a·bil′i·ty, al′ter·a·ble-ness,** n. —**al′ter·a·bly,** adv.

al·ter·a·tion (ôl′tər ā′shən), n. **1** result of altering; change. **2** act of altering.

al·ter·a·tive (ôl′tər ā′tiv), adj. causing change.

al·ter·cate (ôl′tər kāt; al′–), v., **–cat·ed, –cat·ing.** dispute angrily; quarrel. [<L, < alter other]

al·ter·ca·tion (ôl′tər kā′shən; al′–), n. angry dispute; quarrel.

al·ter e·go (ôl′tər ē′gō; al′tər; eg′ō), **1** another aspect of one's nature. **2** a very intimate or close friend. [< L, trans. of Gk. heteros ego]

al·ter·nate (v. ôl′tər nāt, al′–; adj., n. ôl′tər nit, al′–), v., **–nat·ed, –nat·ing,** adj., n. —v. **1** happen or be arranged by turns. **2** arrange by turns: alternate work and pleasure. **3** take turns: the sisters will alternate setting the table. **4** interchange regularly. **5** reverse direction of electric current at regular intervals. —adj. **1** by turns; first one and then the other. **2** every other. **3** placed singly at different heights along a stem, as leaves. —n. person appointed to take the place of another if necessary; substitute. [< L, < alternus every second < alter other] —**al′ter·nate·ly,** adv. —**al′ter-nate·ness,** n.

alternating current, electric current that reverses its direction at regular intervals.

al·ter·na·tion (ôl′tər nā′shən; al′–), n. act of alternating; occurring by turns.

al·ter·na·tive (ôl tėr′nə tiv; al–), adj. giving or requiring a choice between two or more things; choice; selection: alternative results of two different actions; several alternative suggestions. —n. **1** choice between two or more things: he had the alternative of going home or staying all night. **2** one of the things to be chosen: we have no alternative but to leave. —**al·ter′na·tive·ly,** adv. —**al·ter′na·tive·ness,** n.

alternative medicine, use of nontraditional treatments, as acupuncture and herbal remedies.

al·ter·na·tor (ôl′tər nā′tər; al′–), n. dynamo or generator for producing an alternating electric current.

al·the·a, al·thae·a (al thē′ə), n. rose of Sharon, a shrub like the mallow. [< L < Gk. althaia wild mallow, ? < althainein heal]

alt·horn (alt′hôrn′), n. a brass musical instrument similar to the French horn. Also, **alto horn.**

al·though (ôl thō′), conj. though; despite; albeit. [ME al thogh even though]

al·tim·e·ter (al tim′ə tər; al′tə mē tər), n. any instrument for measuring altitudes, as a quadrant, sextant, or device for aircraft navigation (an aneroid barometer, radar, etc.).

al·tim·e·try (al tim′ə trē), n. practice or art of measuring altitudes.

al·ti·tude (al′tə tüd; –tūd), n. **1** the vertical height above sea level, the earth's surface, or some other reference plane. **2** elevation or high place: mountain altitude. **3** high position, power, etc. **4** the vertical distance from the base of a geometrical figure to its highest point. **5** the angular distance of a star, etc., above the horizon. **6** distance of a spacecraft from the surface of some reference body, as the moon. [< L, < altus high] —**al′ti-tu′di·nal,** adj.

al·to (al′tō), n., pl. **-tos,** adj. —n. **1 a** the lowest female voice; contralto. **b** the highest male voice. **2** singer with such a voice. **3** an alto part. **4** instrument playing such a part. —adj. of, sung by, or composed for an alto. [< Ital. < L altus high]

al·to·geth·er (ôl′tə geth′ər), adv. **1** wholly; entirely; completely: altogether wicked. **2** on the whole: altogether, I'm sorry it happened. **3** all included: altogether there were 14 books. —n. a whole; general effect. [ME altogeder]

alto horn, =althorn.

al·tru·ism (al′trù iz əm), n. unselfish devotion to the interests and welfare of others, esp. as a principle of action. [< F altruisme < Ital. altrui of or for others < L alter other] —**al′tru·ist,** n.

al·tru·is·tic (al′trù is′tik), adj. having regard for the well-being and best interests of others; unselfish. —**al′tru·is′ti-cal·ly,** adv.

al·um (al′əm), n. **1** astringent crystalline substance, $KAl(SO_4)_2 \cdot 12H_2O$, a double sulfate of aluminum and potassium, used in dyeing, medicine, etc. **2** one of a class of double sulfates analogous to the potassium alum. **3** aluminum sulfate, $Al_2(SO_4)_3 \cdot 18H_2O$. [< OF < L alumen]

a·lu·mi·na (ə lü′mə nə), n. aluminum oxide, Al_2O_3, occurring in clay. [< NL < L alumen alum]

a·lu·mi·nous (ə lü′mə nəs), adj. **1** of or containing alum. **2.** of or containing aluminum.

a·lu·mi·num (ə lü′mə nəm), n., adj. —n a silver-white, very light, ductile metal that resists tarnish and is used for making utensils, instruments, etc. It is a metallic element that occurs in nature only in combination. —adj. of or containing aluminum [< ALUMINA]

a·lum·na (ə lum′nə), n., pl. **-nae** (-nē). a woman graduate or former student of a school, college, or university. See **alumnus.**

a·lum·nus (ə lum′nəs), n., pl. **-ni** (-nī). **1** graduate or former student of a school, college, or university. **2** a former member, as of a baseball team. [< L, foster child, < alere nourish]

al·ve·o·lar (al vē′ə lər), adj. **1 a** of or pertaining to a socket, as of a tooth. **b** of or pertaining to the air cells of the lungs. **2** formed by touching the tip of the tongue to or bringing it near the alveoli. English t and d are alveolar sounds.

al·ve·o·late (al vē′ə lit; –lāt), adj. deeply pitted. —**al·ve′o·la′tion,** n.

al·ve·o·li (al vē′ə lī), n.pl. **1** Phonet. ridge behind and above the upper front teeth. **2** pl. of **alveolus.**

al·ve·o·lus (al vē′ə ləs), n., pl. **-li** (-lī). **1** a little cell or cavity, as the air cells of the lungs, etc. **2** socket of a tooth. [< L, dim. of alveus cavity]

al·ways (ôl′wiz; –wāz), adv. **1** all the time; continually: she is always cheerful. **2** at all times: he always comes home on Saturday. [all + way]

a·lys·sum (ə lis′əm), *n.* **1** a plant of the mustard family, having small white or yellow flowers. **2** =sweet alyssum. [< NL < Gk. *alysson,* name of a plant thought to cure rabies]

am (am; *unstressed* əm), *v.* the first person singular, present indicative of **be.** [OE *eom*]

Am, americium.

AM, A.M., amplitude modulation.

Am., **1** America; American. **2** Americanism.

a.m., A.M., 1 before noon. **2** time from midnight to noon. [for L *ante meridiem*]

A.M.A., AMA, American Medical Association.

a·mal·gam (ə mal′gəm), *n.* **1** an alloy of mercury with some other metal or metals, formerly used for filling teeth, silvering mirrors, etc. **2** mixture; blend. [< Med.L, appar. < L < Gk. *malagma* emollient < *malassein* soften]

a·mal·gam·ate (ə mal′gə māt), *v.,* **-at·ed, -at·ing. 1** unite together; combine. **2** alloy (one or more metals) with mercury. —**a·mal′gam·a·ble,** *adj.* —**a·mal′gam·a′tive.** *adj.* —**a·mal′gam·a′tor,** *n.*

a·mal·gam·a·tion (ə mal′gə mā′shən), *n.* mixture; combination; blend; union.

a·man·u·en·sis (ə man′yū en′sis), *n., pl.* **-ses** (-sēz). person who writes what another says, or copies what another has written. [< L, < (*servus*) *a manu* secretary]

am·a·ranth (am′ə ranth), *n.* **1** any of a large genus of plants, esp. some with colorful red or purple flowers. **2** purple or purplish red. **3** imaginary flower that never fades. [< L < Gk. *amarantos* everlasting < *a-* not + *marainein* wither; infl. by Gk. *anthos* flower]

am·a·ran·thine (am′ə ran′thin; -thīn), *adj.* **1** of the amaranth. **2** never-fading; undying. **3** purplish-red.

am·a·ryl·lis (am′ə ril′is), *n.* a bulbous plant related to the lily, with large red, white, or purple flowers. [< L < Gk., typical name of a country girl]

a·mass (ə mas′), *v.* **1** collect or accumulate for oneself: *amass a fortune.* **2** collect into a mass or heap. [< OF, < *a-* to + *masse* MASS] —**a·mass′a·ble,** *adj.* —**a·mass′er,** *n.* —**a·mass′ment,** *n.*

am·a·teur (am′ə chùr; -chər; -tyùr; am′ə tėr′), *n.* **1** person who does something for pleasure, not for money or as a profession. **2** person who does something rather poorly. **3** superficial student or worker; dilettante; dabbler. **4** athlete who is not a professional. —*adj.* **1** of amateurs; made or done by amateurs. **2** being an amateur; *amateur pianist.* [< F < L *amator* < *amare* love] —**am′a·teur′ish,** *adj.* —**am′a·teur′ish·ly,** *adv.* —**am′a·teur′ish·ness,** *n.* —**am′a·teur·ship′,** *n.*

am·a·teur·ism (am′ə chùr iz′əm; -chər-; -tyùr-; am′ə tėr′iz əm), *n.* **1** amateur-

ish way of doing things. **2** position of an amateur.

am·a·to·ry (am′ə tô′ri; -tō′-), *adj.* of love; causing love; having to do with making love or with lovers. [< L *amatorius* < *amare* love]

a·maze (ə māz′), *v.,* **a·mazed, a·maz·ing,** *n.* —*v.* surprise greatly; strike with sudden wonder; astonish; astound. [OE *āmasian*]

a·mazed (ə māzd′), *adj.* greatly surprised. —**a·maz′ed·ly,** *adv.* —**a·maz′ed·ness,** *n.*

a·maze·ment (ə māz′mənt), *n.* great surprise; sudden wonder; astonishment.

a·maz·ing (ə māz′ing), *adj.* very surprising; wonderful; astonishing. —*adv.* wonderfully. —**a·maz′ing·ly,** *adv.*

Am·a·zon (am′ə zon; -zən), *n.* **1** largest river in the world, flowing from the Andes Mountains in NW South America across Brazil to the Atlantic. **2** *Gk. Legend.* one of a race of women warriors living near the Black Sea. **3** **amazon,** a warlike or masculine woman. —**Am′a·zo′ni·an** *adj.*

am·bas·sa·dor (am bas′ə dər; -dôr), *n.* **1** highest representative sent by one government or ruler to another who speaks and acts in behalf of his government. **2** person thought to represent special characteristics or qualities: *the violinist was America's ambassador of music.* **3** official messenger with a special errand. Also, **embassador.** [< F < Ital. *ambasciatore*] —**am·bas′sa·do′ri·al,** *adj.* —**am·bas′sa·dor·ship′,** *n.*

am·ber (am′bər), *n.* **1** a hard, translucent, yellow or yellowish-brown fossil resin of pine trees, used for jewelry, etc. **2** color of amber. —*adj.* **1** made of amber. **2** yellow; yellowish-brown. [< OF < Ar. *'anbar* ambergris]

am·ber·gris (am′bər grēs; -gris), *n.* a waxy intestinal concretion of the sperm whale, used esp. in perfumes. [< F *ambre gris* gray amber]

ambi-, *prefix.* around; round about; on both sides, as in *ambidexterity.* [< L; also (before vowels) *amb-*; (before *p*) *am-*]

am·bi·dex·ter·i·ty (am′bə deks ter′ə ti), *n.* **1** ability to use both hands equally well. **2** unusual skillfulness.

am·bi·dex·trous (am′bə dek′strəs), *adj.* **1** able to use both hands equally well. **2** very skillful. [< LL < L *ambi-* both + *dexter* right] —**am′bi·dex′trous·ly,** *adv.* —**am′bi·dex′trous·ness,** *n.*

am·bi·ent (am′bi ənt), *adj.* surrounding. [< L *ambiens* < *ambi-* around + *ire* go]

am·bi·gu·i·ty (am′bə gū′ə ti), *n., pl.* **-ties. 1** possibility of two or more meanings. **2** an ambiguous word or expression.

am·big·u·ous (am big′yù əs), *adj.* **1** having more than one possible meaning; equivocal. **2** of uncertain meaning or nature; puzzling. **3** obscure; vague. [< L *ambiguus* < *ambi-* in two ways + *agere* drive] —**am·big′u·ous·ly,** *adv.* —**am·big′u·ous·ness,** *n.*

am·bi·tion (am bish′ən), *n.* **1** strong desire for fame or honor; seeking after a high position or great power; aspiration. **2** thing strongly desired or sought after. [< L *ambitio* a canvassing for votes < *ambi-* around + *ire* go] —**am·bi′tion·less,** *adj.*

am·bi·tious (am bish′əs), *adj.* **1** having or guided by ambition. **2** arising from or showing ambition. **3** strongly desirous; eager (*of*): *ambitious of power.* **4** showy; pretentious. —**am·bi′tious·ly,** *adv.* —**am·bi′tious·ness,** *n.*

am·biv·a·lence (am biv′ə ləns), *n.* coexistence of contrary tendencies or feelings, as in the mind. —**am·biv′a·lent,** *adj.*

am·ble (am′bəl), *n., v.,* **-bled, -bling.** —*n.* **1** gait of a horse in which both legs on one side are moved at the same time. **2** easy, slow pace in walking. —*v.* **1** walk at a slow, easy pace. **2** (of a horse) move at an amble. [< OF < L *ambulare* walk] —**am′bler,** *n.* —**am′bling·ly,** *adv.*

am·bro·sia (am brō′zhə), *n.* **1** *Class. Myth.* food of the ancient Greek and Roman gods. **2** something especially pleasing to taste or smell. **3** dessert of orange and banana slices with shredded coconut. [< L < Gk., < *a-* not + *brotos* mortal] —**am·bro′sial, am·bro′sian,** *adj.* —**am·bro′sial·ly,** *adv.*

am·bu·lance (am′byə ləns), *n.* a vehicle, boat, or aircraft equipped to carry sick or wounded persons. [< F, < (*hôpital*) *ambulant* walking (hospital)]

am·bu·lant (am′byə lənt), *adj.* walking.

am·bu·late (am′byə lāt), *v.,* **-lat·ed, -lat·ing.** walk; move about. —**am′bu·la′tion,** *n.*

am·bu·la·to·ry (am′byə lə tô′ri; -tō′-), *adj., n., pl.* **-ries.** —*adj.* **1** of or fitted for walking. **2** moving from place to place. **3** able to walk; not confined to bed. **4** not permanent; changeable. —*n.* covered place for walking; cloister.

am·bus·cade (am′bəs kād′), *n., v.,* **-cad·ed, -cad·ing.** ambush. [< F < Ital. *imboscata* < *imboscare* AMBUSH] —**am′bus·cad′er,** *n. Am.*

am·bush (am′bùsh), *n.* **1** soldiers or other enemies hidden to make a surprise attack. **2** place where they are hidden. **3** act or condition of lying in wait. —*v.* **1** attack from an ambush. **2** wait in hiding to make a surprise attack. **3** put (soldiers or other persons) in hiding for a surprise attack. [< OF *embusche,* ult. < *en-* in + *busche* bush¹] —**am′bush·er,** *n.* —**am′bush·like′,** *adj.* —**am′bush·ment,** *n.*

a·me·ba (ə mē′bə), *n., pl.* **-bas, -bae** (-bē). any of a group of microorganisms found in fresh and salt water that moves by forming temporary projections that are constantly changing. Also, **amoeba.** [< Gk. *amoibe* change] —**a·me′ba·like′,** *adj.* —**a·me′ban, a·me′bic,** *adj.*

a·me·boid (ə mē′boid), *adj.* of or like an ameba. Also, **amoeboid.**

a·meer (ə mir′), *n.* =amir.

a·mel·io·ra·ble (ə mēl′yə rə bəl; ə mē′-li ə-), *adj.* that can be improved.

a·mel·io·rate (ə mēl′yə rāt; ə mē′li ə-), *v.,* **-rat·ed, -rat·ing.** make or become better; improve: *new housing ameliorated living conditions in the slums.* [< F *améliorer,* ult. < LL, < L *melior* better] —**a·mel′io·ra′tion,** *n.* —**a·mel′io·ra′-tive,** *adj.* —**a·mel′io·ra′tor,** *n.*

a·men (ā′men′; ä′men′), *interj.* **1** be it so; said after a prayer or wish and used as an expression of assent. **2** an expression of approval. —*n.* the word *amen.* [< L < Gk. < Heb., truth, certainly < *āman* strengthen]

a·me·na·ble (ə mē′nə bəl; ə men′ə-), *adj.* **1** open to suggestion or advice: *amenable to persuasion.* **2** accountable; answerable: *amenable to the law.* [< AF, < *a-* to + *mener* lead < L *minare* drive] —**a·me′na·bil′i·ty, a·me′na·ble·ness,** *n.* —**a·me′na·bly,** *adv.*

a·mend (ə mend′), *v.* **1** change the form of (a law, bill, or motion, etc.) by addition, omission, etc. **2** change for the better; improve: *amend one's conduct.* **3** free from faults; correct: *amend the spelling of a word.* **4** become better, as by reform or by regaining health. [< OF < L, < *ex-* out of + *mendum* fault] —**a·mend′a·ble,** *adj.* —**a·mend′er,** *n.*

a·mend·a·to·ry (ə men′də tôr′ē), *adj.* that amends or corrects.

a·mend·ment (ə mend′mənt), *n.* **1** change made in a law, bill, motion, etc.: *a constitutional amendment.* **2** change for the better; improvement. **3** change made to remove an error; correction.

a·mends (ə mendz′), *n.pl.* (*sometimes sing. in use*) compensation for a loss or injury.

a·men·i·ty (ə men′ə ti; ə mē′nə-), *n., pl.* **-ties. 1 amenities,** pleasing manners or courteous acts that lead to agreeable social relations. **2** pleasant feature. **3** pleasantness; agreeableness. [< L, < *amoenus* pleasant]

am·ent (am′ənt; ā′mənt), *n.* a long, slender spike covered with rows of bracts having flowers of one sex and no petals; catkin. [< L *amentum* thong]

Amer., **1** America. **2** American.

a·merce (ə mèrs′), *v.,* **a·merced, a·merc·ing. 1** punish by an arbitrary or discretionary fine. **2** punish by any penalty. [< AF, < *a merci* at the mercy (of)] —**a·merce′a·ble,** *adj.* —**a·merce′ment,** *n.* —**a·merc′er,** *n.*

A·mer·i·ca (ə mer′ə kə), *n.* **1** the United States of America. **2** North America. **3** North America and South America; the Western Hemisphere. **4** South America.

A·mer·i·can (ə mer′ə kən), *adj.* **1** of, having to do with, or in the United States: *an American citizen.* **2** of or in the Western Hemisphere: *the Amazon and other American rivers.* **3** native only or specific to the United States: *American eagle, American aloe.* —*n.* **1** citizen of the United States. **2** native or inhabitant

of the Western Hemisphere. **3** = American English.

A·mer·i·ca·na (ə mer′ə kä′nə; -kan′ə; -kä′nə), *n.pl.* collection of objects or documents about America, esp. its history.

American Dream, idea of success and achievement as being available or possible in the United States.

American English, English as written and spoken in the United States.

American Indian, one of the people who were already living in America long before Europeans arrived.

A·mer·i·can·ism (ə mer′ə kən iz′əm), *n.* **1** devotion or loyalty to the United States, its customs, traditions, etc. **2** a word, phrase, or idiom originating in the United States, as *raccoon.* **3** custom or trait peculiar to the United States. **4** thing considered typically American.

A·mer·i·can·ize (ə mer′ə kən īz), *v.,* **-ized, -iz·ing.** make or become American in habits, customs, or character. —**A·mer′i·can·i·za′tion, A·mer′i·can·iz′-ing,** *n.* —**A·mer′i·can·ized,** *adj.*

American language, = American English.
American Revolution, 1 war fought by the American colonies from 1775 to 1783 to win their independence from England. **2** series of protests and acts of the American colonists from 1763 to 1783 against England's attempts to increase its power over them.

am·er·i·ci·um (am′ər ish′i əm), *n.* artificial, radioactive metallic element, Am.

Am·er·ind (am′ər ind), *n.* the American Indian. —**Am′er·in′di·an,** *adj., n.* —**Am′er·in′dic,** *adj.*

am·e·thyst (am′ə thist), *n.* **1** a purple or violet variety of quartz, used as a precious stone. **2** violet-colored corundum, used for jewelry. [< OF < L < Gk. *amethystos* < *a-* not + *methy* wine; thought to prevent intoxication] —**am′e·thyst·like′,** *adj.*

a·mi·a·ble (ā′mi ə bəl), *adj.* good-natured and friendly; pleasant and agreeable: *an amiable disposition.* [< OF < LL *amicabilis* < L *amicus* friend. Doublet of AMICABLE.] —**a′mi·a·bil′i·ty, a′mi·a·ble·ness,** *n.* —**a′mi·a·bly,** *adv.*

am·i·ca·ble (am′ə kə bəl), *adj.* peaceable; friendly. [< LL *amicabilis* < L *amicus* friend. Doublet of AMIABLE.] —**am′i·ca·bil′i·ty, am′i·ca·ble·ness,** *n.* —**am′i·ca·bly,** *adv.*

am·ice (am′is), *n.* an oblong piece of linen covering the shoulders, worn by priests at Mass. [< OF < L *amictus* cloak]

a·mi·cus cu·ri·ae (ə mī′kəs kyùr′i ē; ə mē′kəs kyùr′i ī), person with no interest in a legal case who is called in to advise the judge. [< NL, friend of the court]

a·mid (ə mid′), **a·midst** (ə midst′), *prep.* in the midst or middle of; among.

am·ide (am′īd; -id) **amid** (-id), *n.* a compound produced by replacing one or more of the hydrogen atoms of

ammonia by univalent acid radicals. —**a·mid′ic,** *adj.*

a·mid·ships (ə mid′ships), **a·mid·ship** (-ship), *adv.* in or toward the middle of a ship; halfway between the bow and stern.

a·mi·go (ə mē′gō), *n.* friend. [< Sp. < L *amicus,*]

a·mine (ə mēn′; am′in), **am·in** (am′in), *n.* a compound produced by replacing one or more of the hydrogen atoms of ammonia by univalent hydrocarbon radicals.

a·mi·no acids (ə mē′nō; am′ə nō), complex organic compounds of nitrogen that combine in various ways to form proteins.

a·mir (ə mir′), *n.* in Muslim countries, a commander, ruler, or prince. Also, **ameer.** [< Ar., commander. See ADMIRAL.]

Am·ish (am′ish; ä′mish), *n., pl.* **Am·ish,** *adj.* —*n.* member of a strict Mennonite sect, founded in the 17th century. —*adj.* of this sect or its members. —**Am′ish·man′,** *n. Am.*

a·miss (ə mis′), *adv.* in a faulty manner; wrongly. —*adj.* improper; wrong: *it is not amiss to ask advice.*
take amiss, be offended at. [< ME *a mis* by (way of) fault. See MISS[1].]

am·i·to·sis (am′ə tō′sis), *n.* simple cell division without exact division of chromosomes. —**am′i·tot′ic,** *adj.* —**am′i·tot′i·cal·ly,** *adv.*

am·i·ty (am′ə ti), *n., pl.* **-ties.** peace and friendship; friendly relations: *treaty of amity.* [< MF *amitié,* ult. < L *amicus* friend]

am·me·ter (am′mē′tər; am′ē′tər), *n.* instrument for measuring in amperes the strength of an electric current. [< *am(pere)* + -METER]

am·mo (am′ō) *n., pl.* **-mos.** = ammunition.

am·mo·nia (ə mō′nyə; ə mo′ni ə), *n.* **1** a colorless, pungent gas, NH_3, consisting of nitrogen and hydrogen. **2** this gas dissolved in water, NH_4OH. [< NL; so named because obtained from sal *ammoniac*]

am·mo·ni·ac (ə mō′ni ak), *adj.* Also, **am·mo·ni·a·cal** (am′ə nī′ə kəl). of or like ammonia. —*n.* gum ammoniac. [< L < Gk. *ammoniakon;* applied to a salt obtained near the shrine of Ammon in Libya]

am·mo·nite (am′ə nīt), *n.* one of the spiraled fossil shells of an extinct mollusk. [< NL *ammonites* < Med.L *cornu Ammonis* horn of Ammon (Egyptian god)]

am·mo·ni·um (ə mō′ni əm), *n.* the radical NH_4, which never appears in a free state by itself, but acts as a unit in chemical reactions.

ammonium chloride, NH_4Cl, colorless crystals or white powder used in medicine, in printing cloth, etc.; sal ammoniac.

ammonium hydroxide, = ammonia (def. 2).

am·mu·ni·tion (am′yə nish′ən), *n*. **1** bullets, shells, gunpowder, etc., for guns or other weapons. **2** thing or things that can be shot or thrown. **3** means of attack or defense, as information that can be used against someone. [< obs. F *amunition*, used for *munition*]

am·ne·sia (am nē′zhə), *n*. loss of memory caused by injury to the brain, by disease, or by shock. [< NL < Gk., < *a*- not + *mnasthai* remember] —**am·ne′sic, am·nes′tic,** *adj*.

am·nes·ty (am′nəs ti), *n*., *pl*. **-ties,** *v*., **-tied, -ty·ing.** —*n*. a general pardon for past offenses against a government. —*v*. give amnesty to; pardon. [< L < Gk. *amnestia* < *a*- not + *mnasthai* remember]

am·ni·on (am′ni ən), *n*., *pl*. **-ni·ons, -ni·a** (-ni ə). membrane lining the sac which encloses a fetus. [< Gk., dim. of *amnos* lamb] —**am′ni·ot′ic,** *adj*.

a·moe·ba (ə mē′bə), *n*., *pl*. **-bas, -bae** (-bē). =ameba. —**a·moe′ba·like′,** *adj*. —**a·moe′ban, a·moe′bio,** *adj*.

a·moe·boid (ə mē′boid), *adj*. =ameboid.

a·mok (ə muk′; ə mok′), *adv*., *n*. —*adv*. =amuck. —*n*. nervous disturbance of the Malays, characterized by a period of depression followed by a murderous frenzy. [See AMUCK.]

a·mong (ə mung′), *prep*. **1** in the number or class of: *the best among modern novels*. **2** by, with, or through the whole of: *political unrest among the people*. **3** surrounded by: *a house among the trees*. **4** to each of: *divide the money among them*. **5** by the combined action of: *settle it among yourselves*. [OE *amang* < *on* (*ge*)*mang* in a crowd]

a·mongst (ə mungst′), *prep*. =among.

a·mor·al (ā môr′əl; ā mor′–; a–), *adj*. **1** not involving any question of morality; nonmoral. **2** unable to distinguish right from wrong. [< *a*- not + *moral*] —**a′mo·ral′i·ty** *n*. —**a·mor′al·ly,** *adv*.

am·o·rous (am′ə rəs), *adj*. **1** inclined to love: *an amorous disposition*. **2** in love; enamored. **3** showing love; loving; fond; devoted. **4** having to do with love or courtship: *amorous poems*. [< OF, < *amour* love < L *amor*] —**am′o·rous·ly,** *adv*. —**am′o·rous·ness,** *n*.

a·mor·phism (ə môr′fiz əm), *n*. amorphous condition.

a·mor·phous (ə môr′fəs), *adj*. **1** of no particular kind or type. **2** having no definite form; shapeless. **3** not crystallized. Glass is amorphous; sugar is crystalline. [< Gk., < *a*- without + *morphe* shape] —**a·mor′phous·ly,** *adv*. —**a·mor′phous·ness,** *n*.

am·or·tize, (am′ər tīz; ə môr′tīz), *v*., **-tized, -tiz·ing.** set aside money regularly for future payment of (a debt, etc.). [< OF *amortir* deaden < *a*- to + *mort* death < L *mors*] —**am′or·tiz′a·ble,** *adj*. —**am′or·ti·za′tion, a·mor′tize·ment,** *n*.

A·mos (ā′məs), *n*. **1** a Hebrew prophet who lived about 760 B.C. **2** book of the Old Testament.

a·mount (ə mount′), *n*. **1** sum; total: *amount of the day's sales*. **2** the full effect, value, or extent: *the amount of evidence against him is this*. **3** quantity viewed as a whole: *a great amount of intelligence*. **4** principal plus interest. —*v*. **1** be equal; reach (*to*): *the debt amounted to $50*. **2** be equivalent in quantity, value, force, effect, etc. (*to*): *his answer amounted to a threat*. [< OF, < *a mont* up; lit. to the mountain. See MOUNT².]

a·mour (ə mùr′), *n*. **1** a love affair. **2** an illicit love affair. [< OF, prob. < Pr. < L *amor* love]

amp (amp), *n*. =amplifier.

amp or **amp.,** **1** amperage. **2** ampere.

am·per·age (am′pər ij; am pir′-), *n*. strength of a current measured in amperes.

am·pere (am′pir; am pir′), *n*. unit for measuring the strength of an electric current. It is the current one volt can send through a resistance of one ohm. [for A. M. *Ampère*, French physicist]

am·per·sand (am′pər sand), *n*. the character &, meaning "and." [alter. of *and per se = and*, & by itself = and]

am·phet·a·mine (am fet′ə mēn; –min), *n*. **1** drug that relieves congestion. **2** stimulant drug; methamphetamine

amphi–, *combining form*. **1** around; on both sides, as in *amphitheater*. **2** in two ways; of two kinds, as in *amphibious*. [< Gk.]

Am·phib·i·a (am fib′i ə), *n.pl*. class of cold-blooded vertebrates with moist, scaleless skin, including frogs, toads, newts, salamanders, etc. Their young usually develop as tadpoles that have gills and live in water.

am·phib·i·an (am fib′i ən), *n*. **1** animal that lives on land and in water. **2** one of the Amphibia. **3** plant that grows on land or in water. **4** aircraft that can take off from and alight on land or water. **5** tank or other vehicle for use both on land and in water. —*adj*. **1** able to live both on land and in water. **2** able to take off and alight on either land or water.

am·phib·i·ous (am fib′i əs), *adj*. **1** able to live both on land and in water. **2** suited for use on land or water: *an amphibious tank*. **3** having two qualities, kinds, natures, or parts. **4** by the combined action of land, water, and air forces: *amphibious attack*. [< L < Gk., < *amphi*- both + *bios* life] —**am·phib′i·ous·ly,** *adv*. —**am·phib′i·ous·ness,** *n*.

am·phi·the·a·ter, am·phi·the·a·tre (am′fə thē′ə tər), *n*. **1** a circular or oval building with rows of seats rising around a central open space. **2** something resembling an amphitheater in shape. [< L < Gk., < *amphi*- on all sides + *theatron* theater] —**am′phi·the·at′ric, am′phi·the·at′ri·cal,** *adj*. —**am′phi·the·at′ri·cal·ly,** *adv*.

am·pho·ra (am′fə rə), *n*., *pl*. **-rae** (-rē). tall two-handled jar, used by the ancient Greeks and Romans. [< L < Gk., < *amphi*- on both sides + *phoreus* bearer; with ref. to handles]

am·ple (am′pəl), *adj*., **-pler, -plest. 1** fully sufficient for any purpose; abundant; plentiful: *ample food for the table, ample praise*. **2** large; big; roomy: *an ample room*. [< F < L *amplus*] —**am′ple·ness,** *n*.

am·plex·i·caul (am plek′sə kôl), *adj*. clasping the stem, as some leaves do at their bases. [< NL, < L *amplexus* an embrace + *caulis* stem]

am·pli·fi·ca·tion (am′plə fə kā′shən), *n*. **1** act of amplifying; expansion. **2** detail, example, etc., that amplifies a statement, narrative, etc. **3** an expanded statement, etc. **4** increase in the strength of an electric current. —**am′pli·fi·ca′tive, am·plif′i·ca·to′ry,** *adj*.

am·pli·fi·er (am′plə fī′ər), *n*. **1** person or thing that amplifies. **2** device for strengthening electrical impulses, as a transistor, vacuum tube, etc.

am·pli·fy (am′plə fī), *v*., **-fied, -fy·ing. 1** make fuller and more extensive; expand; enlarge. **2** expand by giving details, examples, comparisons, etc.; develop fully: *amplify a theory*. **3** increase the strength of (a sound or an electrical impulse). [< F < L, < *amplus* ample + *facere* make]

am·pli·tude (am′plə tüd; –tūd), *n*. **1** width; breadth; size. **2** abundance; fullness, as of intelligence, understanding, etc. **3** one half the range of symmetric vibrations. **4** the peak strength of an alternating current in a given cycle. [< L *amplitudo*. See AMPLE.]

amplitude modulation, purposeful alteration of the amplitude of radio waves. Much ordinary broadcasting uses amplitude modulation. Compare **frequency modulation.**

am·ply (am′pli), *adv*. in an ample manner; to an ample degree; liberally; sufficiently.

am·poule (am′pül; –pūl), **am·pule** (am′-pül), *n*. small glass tube or bulb filled with a drug and hermetically sealed. [< F < L *ampulla* jar, dim. of *amphora*. See AMPHORA.]

am·pu·tate (am′pyə tāt), *v*., **-tat·ed, -tat·ing. 1** cut off part of a leg, hand, etc., usually by surgery. **2** *Fig*. lop off something; prune. [< L, < *ambi*- about + *putare* prune] —**am′pu·ta′tion,** *n*. —**am′pu·ta′tor,** *n*.

am·pu·tee (am′pyə tē′), *n*. **1** person who has undergone an amputation by surgery, as of an arm or leg. **2** a lopping off.

Am·ster·dam (am′stər dam), *n*. important seaport and capital of the Netherlands.

amt., amount.

a·muck (ə muk′), *adv*. **run amuck,** run about in a murderous frenzy. Also, **amok.** [< Malay *amoq*]

am·u·let (am′yə lit), *n.* some object worn as a magic charm against evil or harm. [< L *amuletum*]

A·mur (ä mûr′), *n.* river in NE Asia.

a·muse (ə mūz′), *v.*, **a·mused, a·mus·ing. 1** cause to laugh or smile: *amuse an audience.* **2** keep pleasantly interested; entertain: *new toys amuse children.* [< OF *amuser* divert, < *a–* + *muser* stare] **—a·mus′a·ble,** *adj.* **—a·mus′er,** *n.*

a·mused (ə mūzd′), *adj.* pleasantly entertained. **—a·mus′ed·ly,** *adv.*

a·muse·ment (ə mūz′mənt), *n.* **1** condition of being amused. **2** thing that amuses.

amusement park, place outdoors offering games, rides, on rollercoasters, etc.

a·mus·ing (ə mūz′ing), *adj.* **1** entertaining. **2** causing laughter, smiles, etc. **—a·mus′ing·ly,** *adv.* **—a·mus′ing·ness,** *n.*

am·yl (am′il), *n.* group of carbon and hydrogen atoms, $-C_5H_{11}$, that acts as a unit in forming compounds. [< L < Gk. *amylon* starch, orig., unground < *a–* not + *myle* mill] **—a·myl′ic,** *adj.*

am·yl·ase (am′ə lās), *n.* enzyme in saliva, pancreatic juice, etc., or in parts of plants, that helps to change starch into sugar. [< *amyl*]

an¹ (an; *unstressed* ən), *adj. or indefinite article.* **1** one; any: *an apple.* **2** each; every: *twice an hour.* See **a.** [OE (unstressed) *ān* (before vowels)]

an², **an′** (an; *unstressed* ən), *conj.* **1** *Dial.* and. **2** *Dial.* if. [var. of *and*]

an–, *prefix.* not; without, as in *anhydrous.* [var. of *a–¹* before vowels and *h*]

–an, *suffix.* **1** of or having to do with, as in *republican.* **2** native or inhabitant of, as in *American.* [< L *–ānus*]

An·a·bap·tist (an′ə bap′tist), *n.* member of a Protestant sect opposing infant baptism. **—An′a·bap′tism,** *n.*

a·nab·o·lism (ə nab′ ə liz əm), *n.* constructive metabolism in which matter is changed into the tissues of a living animal or plant (opposite of *catabolism*). [coined from *metabolism* by substitution of Gk. *ana–* up] **—an′a·bol′ic** *adj.*

a·nach·ro·nism (ə nak′rə niz əm), *n.* **1** placement of a person, thing, or event in a period of time where it does not belong. It would be an anachronism to speak of Julius Caesar using a telephone. **2** something placed or occurring out of its proper time or era. [< F < Gk., < *ana–* backwards + *chronos* time]

a·nach·ro·nis·tic (ə nak′rə nis′tik), *adj.* having or involving an anachronism.

a·nach·ro·nous (ə nak′rə nəs), *adj.* placed or occurring out of the proper time. **—a·nach′ro·nous·ly,** *adv.*

an·a·con·da (an′ə kon′də), *n.* **1** a very large tropical snake that crushes its prey in its coils; water boa. **2** any large snake that crushes its prey in its folds, such as the python.

a·nad·ro·mous (ə nad′rə məs), *adj.* going up rivers from the sea to spawn. [<LGk., < *ana–* up + *dromos* a running]

a·nae·mi·a (ə nē′mi ə), *n.* =anemia. **—a·nae′mic,** *adj.*

an·aer·obe (an ār′ōb; an ā′ər ōb), *n.* **1** organism that cannot live in the presence of free oxygen. **2** organism that can live without free oxygen. **—an′aer·o′bic,** *adj.* **—an′aer·o′bi·cal·ly,** *adv.*

an·aes·the·sia (an′əs thē′zhə), *n.* =anesthesia.

an·aes·thet·ic (an′əs thet′ik), *adj., n.* =anesthetic.

an·aes·the·tist (ə nes′thə tist), *n.* =anesthetist.

an·aes·the·tize (ə nes′thə tīz), *v.*, **-tized, -tiz·ing.** =anesthetize. **—an·aes′the·ti·za′tion,** *n.*

an·a·gram (an′ə gram), *n.* **1** word or phrase formed from another by transposing the letters. *Example:* lived—devil. **2 anagrams** (*sing. in use*), game in which players make words by changing and adding letters. [< NL < Gk. *anagrammatizein* transpose letters < *ana–* up or back + *gramma* letter]

a·nal (ā′nəl), *adj.* **1** of or near the anus. **2** having personality traits such as obsessive neatness, control, etc.

anal. 1 analogous. **2** analogy. **3** analysis. **4** analytic.

an·al·ge·si·a (an′əl jē′zi ə; –si ə; –zha; –shə), *n.* insensibility to pain without losing consciousness. [< NL < Gk., < *an–* not + *algeein* feel pain]

an·al·ge·sic (an′əl jē′zik; –sik), *adj.* of or causing analgesia. **—n.** drug or other agent causes analgesia.

an·a·log (an′ə lôg), *n., adj.* =analogue.

analog computer, calculating machine or automatic control which deals directly with physical quantities (weights, lengths, etc.) rather than a numerical code.

an·a·log·i·cal (an′ə loj′ə kəl), **an·a·log·ic** (–loj′ik), *adj.* using analogy; having to do with analogy. **—an′a·log′i·cal·ly,** *adv.*

a·nal·o·gize (ə nal′ə jīz), *v.* **-gized, -giz·ing. 1** explain by analogy. **2** use analogy. **—a·nal′o·gist**

a·nal·o·gous (ə nal′ə gəs), *adj.* **1** corresponding in some way; similar; comparable. **2** corresponding in function, but not in structure and origin, as the wing of an insect and a bird. **—a·nal′o·gous·ly,** *adv.* **—a·nal′o·gous·ness,** *n.*

an·a·logue (an′ə lôg; –log), *n.* **1** something analogous; parallel. **2** organ or body part that is analogous to another organ or part. **—adj.** of or having to do with analog computers.

a·nal·o·gy (ə nal′ə ji), *n., pl.* **-gies. 1** likeness in some ways between things that are otherwise unlike; similarity. **2** comparison of such things: *it is risky to argue by analogy.* **3** of organs, etc., correspondence in function but not in structure and origin. [< L < Gk. *analogia*]

a·nal·y·sis (ə nal′ə sis), *n., pl.* **-ses** (–sēz). **1** separation of a thing into parts; examination of a thing's parts to find out their

essential features: *analysis of a book.* **2 a** intentional separation of a substance into its ingredients or elements to determine their amount and nature. **b** determination of the kind or amount of one or more of the constituents of a substance, whether actually obtained in separate form or not. **3** statement of the results of an analysis. [< Med.L < Gk., a breaking up, < *ana–* up + *lyein* loose]

an·a·lyst (an′ə list), *n.* **1** one who analyzes. **2** one who practices psychoanalysis.

an·a·lyt·ic (an′ə lit′ik), **an·a·lyt·i·cal** (–ə kəl), *adj.* of or using analysis. **—an′a·lyt′i·cal·ly,** *adv.*

an·a·lyt·ics (an′ə lit′iks), *n.* mathematical or algebraic analysis.

an·a·lyze (an′ə līz), *v.*, **-lyzed, -lyz·ing. 1** separate into its parts. **2** examine the parts or elements critically: *analyze an argument.* **3** subject to chemical analysis. **—an′a·lyz′a·ble,** *adj.* **—an′a·ly·za′tion,** *n.* **—an′a·lyz′er,** *n.*

An·a·ni·as (an′ə nī′əs), *n.* **1** liar who was struck dead for this fault. Acts 5:1–10. **2** any liar.

an·a·pest, an·a·paest (an′ə pest), *n.* measure or foot in poetry consisting of two unaccented syllables followed by an accented syllable. [< L < Gk. *anapaistos* < *ana–* back + *paiein* strike] **—an′a·pes′tic, an′a·paes′tic,** *adj., n.*

a·naph·o·ra (ə naf′ər ə), *n.* repetition of a word or phrase at the beginning of a series of clauses or sentences, used for rhetorical effect.

an·a·phy·lax·is (an′ə fə lak′sis), *n.* increased sensitivity to a usually nontoxic substance, sometimes causing severe or fatal shock. **—an′a·phy·lac′tic,** *adj.*

an·ar·chism (an′ər kiz əm), *n.* **1** political theory that all systems of government and law are harmful and prevent individuals from reaching their greatest development. **2** practice or support of this doctrine. **3** terrorism; lawlessness.

an·ar·chist (an′ər kist), *n.* person who wants to overthrow established governments and have a world without rulers and laws. **—an′ar·chis′tic,** *adj.*

an·ar·chy (an′ər ki), *n.* **1** absence of a system of government and law. **2** confusion; lawlessness. [< Gk., < *an–* without + *archos* ruler] **—an·ar′chic, an·ar′chi·cal,** *adj.* **—an·ar′chi·cal·ly,** *adv.*

anat., 1 anatomical. **2** anatomy.

a·nath·e·ma (ə nath′ə mə), *n., pl.* **-mas. 1** person or thing that is detested and condemned. **2** person or thing accursed. **3** solemn curse by church authorities excommunicating some person from the church. **4** denouncing and condemning some person or thing as evil; curse. [< L < Gk., thing devoted, esp. to evil, < *ana–* up + *tithenai* set]

a·nath·e·ma·tize (ə nath′ə mə tīz), *v.*, **-tized, -tiz·ing.** denounce; curse. **—a·nath′e·ma·ti·za′tion,** *n.* **—a·nath′e·ma·tiz′er,** *n.*

An·a·to·li·a (an´ə tō´li ə), *n.* =Asia Minor. —**An´a·to´li·an,** *adj., n.*

an·a·tom·i·cal (an´ə tom´ə kəl), **an·a·tom·ic** (-tom´ik), *adj.* of or having to do with anatomy. —**an´a·tom´i·cal·ly,** *adv.*

a·nat·o·mist (ə nat´ə mist), *n.* **1** an expert in anatomy. **2** person who dissects or analyzes.

a·nat·o·mize (ə nat´ə mīz), *v.,* —**mized,** —**miz·ing. 1** divide into parts to study the structure; dissect. **2** examine the parts of; analyze. —**a·nat´o·mi·za´tion,** *n.*

a·nat·o·my (ə nat´ə mi), *n., pl.* —**mies. 1** structure of an animal or plant. **2** science of the structure of animals and plants. **3** dissecting of animals or plants to study their structure. [< LL < Gk., < *ana-* up + *tomos* cutting]

anc., ancient.

-ance, *suffix.* **1** act or fact of ____ing, as in *avoidance.* **2** quality or state of being ____ed, as in *annoyance.* **3** quality or state of being ____ant, as in *importance.* **4** thing that ____s, as in *conveyance.* **5** what is ____ed, as in *contrivance.* [< F < L *-antia, -entia*]

an·ces·tor (an´ses tər), *n.* **1** person from whom one is descended; forefather. **2** early form from which the species or group in question has descended. **3** the precursor of a later type. [< OF *ancestre* < L *antecessor* < *ante* before + *cedere* go]

an·ces·tral (an ses´trəl), *adj.* **1** of or pertaining to ancestors: *the ancestral home of the Pilgrims was England.* **2** inherited from ancestors. —**an·ces´tral·ly,** *adv.*

an·ces·try (an´ses tri), *n., pl.* —**tries. 1** line of descent from ancestors; lineage. **2** honorable descent. **3** parents, grandparents, and other ancestors.

an·chor (ang´kər), *n.* **1** shaped piece of iron attached to a chain or rope and used to hold a boat or ship in place. **2** thing for holding something else in place. **3** something that makes a person feel safe and secure. **4** =anchorman. —*v.* **1** hold in place by an anchor: *anchor a ship.* **2** hold in place; fix firmly.

at anchor, held by an anchor.

cast or **drop anchor,** let down the anchor to hold in place.

ride at anchor, stay anchored in a place.

weigh anchor, raise the anchor to sail on. [< L < Gk. *ankyra*] —**an´chor·less,** *adj.* —**an´chor·like´,** *adj.*

an·chor·age (ang´kər ij), *n.* **1** place to anchor. **2** money paid for the right to anchor. **3** an anchoring or being anchored. **4** something to hold on to or depend on.

an·cho·rite (ang´kə rīt), **an·cho·ret** (ang´-kə rit; -ret), *n.* **1** person who lives alone in a solitary place for religious meditation. **2** hermit. [< Med.L < LL < Gk. *anachoretes,* < *ana-* back + *choreein* withdraw] —**an´cho·rit´ic,** an´cho·ret´ic, *adj.*

an·chor·man (ang´kər man´), *n.* **1** last person to compete on a relay team. **2** last person on line in a tug of war. **3** last team member to bowl a frame in a bowling match. **4** person who introduces various reports on a television or radio newscast.

an·cho·vy (an´chō vi; -chə vi; an chō´vi), *n., pl.* —**vies.** very small fish that looks somewhat like a herring. Anchovies are pickled or made into a paste. [< Sp. and Pg. *anchova* < VL *apiuva* < Gk. *aphye*]

an·cien ré·gime (äN syaN´ rā zhēm´), *French.* **1** social and political structure of France before the Revolution of 1789. **2** *Fig.* way things used to be done; old order of things.

an·cient (ān´shənt), *adj.* **1** of great age; very old: *an ancient city.* **2** existing or occurring in time long past: *ancient records.* **3** pertaining to the period of history before the fall of the Western Roman Empire (476 A.D.). **4** having to do with the ancients. —*n.* **1** a very old person. **2** the ancients, **a** Greeks and Romans and other civilized people of antiquity. **b** the classical authors of ancient times. [< OF *ancien* < LL, < L *ante* before] —**an´cient·ness,** *n.*

an·cient·ly (ān´shənt li), *adv.* in ancient times.

an·cil·lar·y (an´sə ler´i), *adj.* **1** subordinate. **2** assisting. [< L, < *ancilla* handmaid]

an·con (ang´kon), *n., pl.* **an·co·nes** (ang kō´nēz). **1** elbow. **2** projection like a bracket, used to support a cornice. [< L < Gk. *ankon* bend] —**an´co·nal,** **an·co´ne·al** *adj.*

-ancy, *suffix.* variant of **-ance,** as in *infancy.*

and (and; *unstressed* ənd, ən), *conj.* **1** as well as: *nice and cold.* **2** added to; with: *ham and eggs.* **3** as a result: *the sun came out and the grass dried.* **4** to: *try and come.* [OE]

An·da·lu·sia (an´də lü´zhə; -shə), *n.* region in S Spain. —**An´da·lu´sian,** *adj., n.*

an·dan·te (an dan´tē; än dän´tā), —*adj.* of musical tempo, moderately slow. —*adv.* in andante time. —*n.* musical piece in andante time. [< Ital., < *andare* walk]

An·der·sen (an´dər sən), *n.* **Hans Christian,** 1805-1875, Danish writer of fairy tales.

An·des (an´dēz), *n.pl.* mountain system in W South America. —**An·de´an,** *adj., n.*

and·i·ron (and´ī´ərn), *n.* one of a pair of metal supports for wood burned in a fireplace. [< OF *andier; -iron* by association with *iron*]

and/or, both or either.

An·dor·ra (an dôr´ə; -dor´ə), *n.* **1** a small country between France and Spain. **2** its capital.

An·drew (an´drü), *n.* one of Jesus' apostles.

an·dro·gen (an´drə jən), *n.* any substance that induces or strengthens masculine characteristics, as a male sex hormone. [< Gk. *aner* (*andr-*) male + *-genes* born, produced] —**an´dro·gen´ic,** *adj.*

an·drog·y·nous (an droj´ə nəs), *adj.* **1** having male and female flowers in the same cluster. **2** =hermaphroditic. [< L < Gk., < *aner* (*andr-*) man + *gyne* woman] —**an·drog´y·ny,** *n.*

an·droid (an´droid), *n.* robot that resembles a person.

An·drom·a·che (an drom´ə kē), *n.* Gk. Legend. **1** the loyal wife of Hector. **2** northern constellation.

an·ec·dot·age (an´ik dōt´ij), *n.* **1** anecdotes. **2** talkative old age.

an·ec·do·tal (an´ik dō´təl; an´ik dō´təl), *adj.* of anecdotes; containing anecdotes. —**an´ec·do´tal·ist,** *n.*

an·ec·dote (an´ik dōt), *n.* short account of some interesting incident or event. [< Med.L < Gk. *anekdota* (things) unpublished < *an-* not + *ek-* out + *didonai* give] —**an´ec·dot´ic,** an´ec·dot´i·cal, *adj.*

a·ne·mi·a (ə nē´mi ə), *n.* **1** deficiency of the blood; insufficiency of red corpuscles or hemoglobin in the blood. **2** general weakness. Also, **anaemia.** [< NL < Gk. *anaimia* lack of blood < *an-* not + *haima* blood] —**a·ne´mic,** *adj.*

an·e·mom·e·ter (an´ə mom´ə tər), *n.* instrument for measuring the velocity or pressure of the wind. [< Gk. *anemos* wind + **-METER** —**an´e·mo·met´ric,** an´e·mo·met´ri·cal,** *adj.*

a·nem·o·ne (ə nem´ə nē), *n.* **1** plant with small white flowers that blossoms early in the spring. **2** plant of the same genus with much larger, bright-red, blue, or white flowers. **3** sea anemone. [< L < Gk., wind flower, *anemos* wind]

a·nent (ə nent´), *prep.* **1** concerning. **2** beside. [OE *on emn, on efn* on even (ground with)]

an·er·oid (an´ər oid), *adj.* using no fluid. —*n.* an aneroid barometer. [< F *anéroïde* < Gk. *a-* without + LGk. *neros* water]

aneroid barometer, barometer that works by the pressure of air on the elastic lid of a box containing no air.

an·es·the·sia (an´əs thē´zhə), *n.* loss of sensation produced by ether, chloroform, hypnotism, etc., or as the result of hysteria, paralysis, or disease. [< NL < Gk., < *an-* without + *aisthesis* sensation]

an·es·thet·ic (an´əs thet´ik), *n.* substance that causes anesthesia, as ether. —*adj.* **1** causing anesthesia. **2** of or with anesthesia: *anesthetic effects.* —**an´es·thet´i·cal·ly,** *adv.*

an·es·the·tist (ə nes´thə tist), *n.* person who administers anesthetics during operations, etc.

an·es·the·tize (ə nes´thə tīz), *v.,* —**tized,** —**tiz·ing.** make unable to feel pain, touch, cold, etc.; make insensible. —**an·es´the·ti·za´tion,** *n.* —**an·es´the·tiz´er,** *n.*

an·eu·rysm, an·eu·rism (an´yə riz əm), *n.* permanent swelling of an artery, due to pressure of the blood on a part weakened by disease or injury. [< Gk. *aneurysma* dilatation, < *ana-* up + *eurys* wide] —an′eu·rys′mal, an′eu·ris′mal, *adj.*

a·new (ə nü′; ə nū′), *adv.* 1 once more; again: *try anew.* 2 in a new form or way. [OE *ofniowe.* See NEW.]

an·gel (ān′jəl), *n.* 1 one of an order of spiritual beings that are attendants and messengers of God. 2 conventional representation of such a being, usually with a halo and wings. 3 *Fig.* person as good or lovely as an angel. 4 *Fig.* any guardian or guiding spirit. 5 person who pays for producing a play. [< L < Gk. *angelos* messenger]

angel cake, or angel food cake, delicate, white, spongy cake made of the whites of eggs, sugar, and a little flour.

angel dust, hallucenogenic drug, PCP.

An·ge·le·no (an′jə lē′nō), *n.* person who lives in Los Angeles.

an·gel·fish (ān′jəl fish′), *n., pl.* -fish·es or (*esp. collectively*) -fish. 1 any of several showy tropical fish. 2 small silver fish with wing-like fins and black bars on its body.

an·gel·ic (an jel′ik), *adj.* 1 of angels; heavenly. 2 like an angel; pure; innocent; good and lovely. —an·gel′i·cal, *adj.* —an·gel′i·cal·ly, *adv.*

an·gel·i·ca (an jel′ə kə), *n.* perennial plant of the same family as the carrot, used in cooking, in medicine, etc. [< Med.L; named from its use as an antidote]

An·ge·li·co (an jel′ə kō), *n.* Fra, 1387–1455, Italian painter.

An·ge·lus (an′jə ləs), *n.* 1 prayer said by Roman Catholics in memory of Christ's assuming human form. 2 bell rung at morning, noon, and night as a signal for Roman Catholics to say this prayer. [from first word in service]

an·ger (ang′gər), *n.* the feeling one has toward something that hurts, opposes, offends, or annoys; wrath; fury; rage. —*v.* 1 make angry. 2 become angry: *he angers easily.* [< Scand. *angr* grief]

an·gi·na (an jī′nə; in *Med. often* an′jə nə), *n.* 1 any inflammatory disease of the throat, such as croup or mumps. 2 any sudden and sharp pain. 3 =angina pectoris. [< L, quinsy, < *angere* choke]

angina pec·to·ris (pek′tə ris), serious disease of the heart that causes sharp chest pains and a feeling of being suffocated.

an·gi·o·gen·e·sis (an′ji o jen′ə sis), *n.* formation of blood vessels.

an·gi·o·sperm (an′ji ō spėrm′), *n.* plant having its seeds enclosed in an ovary; flowering plant. [< NL, < Gk. *angeion* vessel + *sperma* seed] —an′gi·o·sper′mous, *adj.*

an·gle¹ (ang′gəl), *n., v.,* -gled, -gling. —*n.* 1 a space between two lines or surfaces that meet. b figure formed by two such lines or surfaces. c difference in direction between two such lines or surfaces. 2 corner. 3 point of view. 4 one aspect of something; phase. —*v.* 1 move at an angle. 2 turn or bend at an angle. 3 present with bias or prejudice. [< F < L *angulus*] —an′gled, *adj.*

an·gle² (ang′gəl), *v.,* -gled, -gling. 1 fish with a hook and line. 2 scheme to get: *she angled for an invitation to his party by flattering him.* [OE *angel* fishhook] —an′gler, *n.*

angle iron, strip of iron or steel bent at an angle.

angle of incidence. See incidence, def. 3.

angle of reflection. See reflection, def. 8.

An·gles (ang′gəlz), *n.pl.* a Germanic tribe that settled in England in the fifth century A.D. —An′gli·an, *adj., n.*

an·gle·worm ang′gəl·wėrm′), *n.* earthworm.

An·gli·can (ang′glə kən), *adj.* 1 of or having to do with the Church of England or other churches of the same faith elsewhere. 2 *Esp. U.S.* English. —*n.* member of an Anglican church. —An′gli·can·ism, *n.*

An·gli·cism (ang′glə siz əm), *n.* 1 *U.S.* a Briticism. 2 custom or trait peculiar to the English.

An·gli·cize, an·gli·cize (ang′glə sīz), *v.,* -cized, -ciz·ing. make or become English in form, pronunciation, habits, customs, or character. *Chauffeur* and *garage* are French words that have been Anglicized. —An′gli·ci·za′tion, an′gli·ci·za′tion, *n.*

an·gling (ang′gling), *n.* act or art of fishing with a rod and line.

An·glo (ang′glō), *n., pl.* -glos. white American not of Spanish or Mexican descent.

Anglo–, *word element.* 1 English, as in *Anglo-Catholic church.* 2 English and, as in *the Anglo-American alliance.*

An·glo-A·mer·i·can (ang′glō ə mer′ə kən), Am. —*adj.* 1 English and American. 2 of Anglo-Americans. —*n.* an American, esp. a U.S. citizen of English descent.

An·glo-French (ang′glō french′), *adj.* of or having to do with England and France together. —*n.* the dialect of French spoken by the Normans in England (esp. 1066–c1154); Anglo-Norman; Norman-French.

An·glo-Nor·man (ang′glō nôr′mən), *n.* 1 one of the Normans who lived in England after its conquest in 1066. 2 descendant of an English Norman. 3 Anglo-French. —*adj.* English and Norman.

An·glo·phile (ang′glə fīl), An·glo·phil (-fil), *n.* person who greatly likes or admires England or the English.

An·glo-Sax·on (ang′glō sak′sən), *n.* 1 Englishman of the fifth to twelfth centuries. 2 his speech. 3 member of the English-speaking world. 4 person of English descent. 5 plain English. —*adj.* 1 of the Anglo-Saxons. 2 of Anglo-Saxon.

An·go·ra (ang gô′rə, -gō′-), *n.* 1 variety of long-haired cat. 2 variety of goat with long, silky hair. 3 variety of rabbit with long, silky hair.

an·go·ra (ang gô′rə), *n.* 1 =mohair. 2 yarn made from the hair of Angora goats or rabbits.

an·gry (ang′gri), *adj.* -gri·er, -gri·est. 1 feeling or showing anger; furious; infuriated: *an angry reply.* 2 raging or stormy: *angry sky.* 3 inflamed and sore: *an infected cut looks angry.* —an′gri·ly, *adv.* —an′gri·ness, *n.*

angst (ängst), *n.* anxiety. [< G]

ang·strom (ang′strəm), or angstrom unit, *n.* one ten-millionth of a millimeter, a unit of measurement of the wave lengths of various radiations, as of light.

an·guish (ang′gwish), *n.* very great pain or grief; torment. [< OF < L *angustia* tightness < *angustus* narrow]

an·guished (ang′gwisht), *adj.* 1 suffering anguish. 2 full of anguish; showing anguish.

an·gu·lar (ang′gyə lər), *adj.* 1 having angles; sharp-cornered. 2 measured by an angle. 3 not plump; thin and bony; gaunt. 4 stiff and awkward. —an′gu·lar·ly, *adv.* —an′gu·lar·ness, *n.*

an·gu·lar·i·ty (ang′gyə lar′ə ti), *n., pl.* -ties. 1 angular quality or form. 2 an angular part; an angle.

an·hy·dride (an hī′drīd; –drid), an·hy·drid (–drid), *n.* 1 any oxide that unites with water to form an acid or base. 2 any compound formed by removing water.

an·hy·drous (an hī′drəs), *adj.* 1 without water. 2 containing no water of crystallization. [< Gk., < *an-* without + *hydor* water]

an·i·line (an′ə lin; –līn), an·i·lin (–lin), *n.* a colorless liquid, $C_6H_5NH_2$, obtained from coal tar and esp. from nitrobenzene, used in making dyes, plastics, etc. —*adj.* made from aniline.

an·i·mal (an′ə məl), *n.* 1 any living thing that is not a plant. Most animals can move about, while most plants cannot; most animals cannot make their own food from carbon dioxide, water, nitrogen, etc., while most plants can. 2 an inferior living being, as distinguished from human; brute; beast. 3 person like a brute or beast. —*adj.* 1 of animals. 2 like an animal. 3 of a person, sensual. [< L, < *anima* life, breath]

an·i·mal·cule (an′ə mal′kūl), *n.* a minute or microscopic animal. [< NL *animalculum,* dim. of L *animal*] —an′i·mal′cu·lar, *adj.*

an·i·mal·ism (an′ə məl iz′əm), *n.* 1 doctrine that human beings are mere animals without souls. 2 animal existence, nature, or enjoyment. —an′i·mal·ist, *n.* —an′i·mal·is′tic, *adj.*

an·i·mal·i·ty (an′ə mal′ə ti), *n.* 1 animal nature or character in humans. 2 animal life.

animal spirits, natural liveliness.

an·i·mate (*v.* an′ə māt; *adj.* an′ə mit), *v.,* -mat·ed, -mat·ing, *adj.* —*v.* 1 make lively, gay, or vigorous. 2 inspire; encourage. 3 put into action; cause to act or work. 4 give life to; make alive. —*adj.* 1. living; alive: *all plants and animals are animate.* 2 lively; vigorous. [< L, < *anima* life, breath] —an′i·mate·ly, *adv.*

—**an'i·mat'er, an'i·ma'tor,** *n.* —**an'i·ma'tion,** *n.*

an·i·mat·ed (an'ə māt'id), *adj.* **1** lively. **2** living. —**an'i·mat'ed·ly,** *adv.*

animated cartoon, series of drawings arranged to be photographed and shown like a motion picture. Each drawing shows a slight change from the one before it creating the illusion of movement.

an·i·mat·ing (an'ə māt'ing), *adj.* giving life to; making lively; inspiring; encouraging. —**an'i·mat'ing·ly,** *adv.*

an·i·ma·tron·ic (an'ə mə trôn'ik), *adj.* animated electronically: *the versatile animatronic process.* [< *anima*ted-elec*tronic* robotic]

an·i·mism (an'ə miz əm), *n.* the belief that animals, trees, rocks, and other natural objects have souls. [< L *anima* life] —**an'i·mist,** *n.* —**an'i·mis'tic,** *adj.*

an·i·mos·i·ty (an'ə mos'ə ti), *n., pl.* **–ties.** violent hatred; active enmity.

an·i·mus (an'ə məs), *n.* **1** violent hatred; ill will; active dislike or enmity. **2** moving spirit; intention. [< L, spirit]

an·i·on (an'ī ən), *n.* **1** a negatively charged ion that moves toward the positive pole in electrolysis. **2** atom or group of atoms having a negative charge. [< Gk., (thing) going up, < *ana*– up + *ienai* go]

an·ise (an'is), *n.* **1** plant of the carrot family grown for its fragrant seeds. **2** the seed. [< OF < L < Gk, *anison*]

an·i·seed (an'ə sēd; an'is sēd), *n.* seed of anise, used as a flavoring or in medicine.

An·jou (an'jü), *n.* a former duchy in W France.

An·ka·ra (ang'kə rə; äng'–), *n.* capital of Turkey.

ankh (ängk), *n.* cross with a loop at the top, rather than a straight upper part, symbol of life in ancient Egypt.

an·kle (ang'kəl), *n.* **1** joint that connects the foot and the leg. **2** part of the leg between this joint and the calf. [< Scand. Cf. Dan. *ankel.*]

an·kle·bone (ang'kəl bōn'), *n.* talus.

an·klet (ang'klit), *n.* **1** a short sock. **2** band, often ornamental, worn around the ankle.

an·ky·lo·sis (ang'kə lō'sis), *n.* **1** *Anat.* a growing together of bones as a result of disease or injury. **2** *Pathol.* stiffness of a joint caused by this. [< NL < Gk., < *ankyloein* stiffen < *ankylos* crooked] —**an'ky·lot'ic,** *adj.*

ann., **1** annals. **2** annuals. **3** annuity. **4** years.

an·na (an'ə), *n.* in India and Pakistan: **a** one-sixteenth of a rupee. **b** a coin having this value.

an·nal·ist (an'əl ist), *n.* writer of annals. —**an'nal·is'tic,** *adj.*

an·nals (an'əlz), *n.pl.* **1** a written account of events year by year. **2** historical records; history. [< L, < *annus* year]

An·nap·o·lis (ə nap'ə lis), *n.* seaport and capital of Maryland, site of the U.S. Naval Academy.

Anne (an), *n.* 1665–1714, queen of Great Britain and Ireland, 1702–14.

an·neal (ə nēl'), *v.* toughen (glass, metals, etc.) by heating and then cooling; temper. [OE *anǣlan* < *an*– on +*ǣlan* burn] —**an·neal'er,** *n.*

an·ne·lid (an'ə lid), —*n.* any one of the segmented worms, as the earthworms and leeches. —*adj.* of or having to do with annelids. [< F < OF *annel* ring < L *anellus,* double dim. of *anus* ring] —**an·nel'i·dan,** *adj., n.*

an·nex (*v.* ə neks'; *n.* an'eks), *v., n.* —*v.* **1** join or add to a larger thing: *the United States annexed Texas in 1845.* **2** attach as a limitation or consequence. **3** add to a book, document, etc. **4** take as one's own; appropriate. —*n.* **1** something annexed; an added part. **2** a supplementary building. [< Med.L, < L *annexus* < *ad*– to + *nectere* bind] —**an·nex'a·ble,** *adj.* —**an·nex'ment,** *n.*

an·nex·a·tion (an'ik sā'shən; –ek–), *n.* **1** an annexing or being annexed. **2** something annexed. —**an'nex·a'tion·ist,** *n.*

an·ni·hi·la·ble (ə nī'ə lə bəl), *n.* that can be annihilated. —**an·ni'hi·la·bil'i·ty,** *n.*

an·ni·hi·late (ə nī'ə lāt), *v.* **–lat·ed, –lat·ing.** **1** destroy completely; wipe out of existence. **2** bring to ruin or confusion. [< LL, < L *ad*– + *nihil* nothing] —**an·ni'hi·la'tion,** *n.* —**an·ni'hi·la'tive,** *adj.* —**an·ni'hi·la'tor,** *n.*

an·ni·ver·sa·ry (an'ə vėr'sə ri), *n., pl.* **–ries,** *adj.* —*n.* **1** the yearly return of a date: *a birthday is an anniversary.* **2** celebration of the yearly return of a date. —*adj.* **1** celebrated each year at the same date. **2** having to do with an anniversary: *an anniversary gift.* [< L, returning annually, < *annus* year + *vertere* turn]

an·no Dom·i·ni (an'ō dom'ə nī), in the year of our Lord; any year of the Christian Era. *Abbrev.:* A.D.

annointing of the sick, =extreme unction.

an·no·tate (an'ō tāt), *v.,* **–tat·ed, –tat·ing.** **1** provide with explanatory notes or comments. **2** make explanatory notes or comments. [< L, < *ad*– + *nota* note] —**an'no·ta'tor,** *n.*

an·no·ta·tion (an'ō tā'shən), *n.* **1** act of annotating. **2** note of explanation.

an·nounce (ə nouns'), *v.,* **–nounced, –nounc·ing.** **1** give formal or public notice of: *announce a wedding in the papers.* **2** make known; make evident. **3** be an announcer; introduce broadcasts; read news, etc. **4** make known the presence or arrival of: *a flurry of activity announced their arrival.* [< OF < L, < *ad*– + *nuntius* messenger] —**an·nounce'ment,** *n.*

an·nounc·er (ə noun'sər), *n.* **1** someone or some thing that announces. **2** person who announces, esp. on a radio or television broadcast.

an·noy (ə noi'), *v.* **1** make angry; disturb; trouble; irritate; bother: *annoy by teasing.* **2** hurt; harm; molest: *annoy the*

enemy by raids. [< OF *anuier* < LL, < L *in odio* in hatred] —**an·noy'er,** *n.*

an·noy·ance (ə noi'əns), *n.* **1** an annoying. **2** a being annoyed. **3** thing that annoys; bother; pest.

an·noy·ing (ə noi'ing), *adj.* disturbing. —**an·noy'ing·ly,** *adv.* —**an·noy'ing·ness,** *n.*

an·nu·al (an'yü əl), *adj.* **1** coming once a year: *annual celebration.* **2** of or for a year; yearly: *an annual salary of $30,000.* **3** accomplished during a year: *the earth's annual course around the sun.* **4** living but one year or season: *annual plants.* *n.* **1** an annual publication. **2** plant that lives one year or season. [< OF < LL, < L *annus* year] —**an'nu·al·ly,** *adv.*

an·nu·i·tant (ə nü'ə tənt; –nü'–), *n.* person who receives an annuity.

an·nu·i·ty (ə nü'ə ti; –nü'–), *n., pl.* **–ties.** **1** sum of money paid every year. **2** right to receive or duty to pay such a yearly sum. **3** investment that provides a fixed yearly income. [< F < Med. L, < L *annus* year]

an·nul (ə nul'), *v.,* **–nulled, –nul·ling.** destroy the force of; make void: *annul a marriage.* [< LL, < L *ad*– + *nullus* none] —**an·nul'la·ble,** *adj.* —**an·nul'ler,** *n.* —**an·nul'ment,** *n.*

an·nu·lar (an'yə lər), *adj.* ringlike; ring-shaped; ringed. [< L, < *annulus* ring] —**an'nu·lar'i·ty,** *n.* —**an'nu·lar·ly** *adv.*

an·nu·lus (an'yə ləs), *n., pl.* **–li** (–lī) **, –lus·es.** a ringlike part, band, or space. [< L *annulus,* dim. of *anus* ring]

an·nun·ci·ate (ə nun'shi āt; –si–), *v.,* **–at·ed, –at·ing.** make known; announce. [< Med.L < L, *ad*– to + *nuntius* messenger]

an·nun·ci·a·tion (ə nun'si ā'shən; –shi–), *n.* **1** announcement. **2 the Annunciation, a** the angel Gabriel's announcement to the Virgin Mary that she was to be the mother of Christ. Luke 1:26–33. **b** Annunciation Day; Lady Day.

A No. 1, A one.

an·ode (an'ōd), *n.* **1** positive electrode. **2** negative terminal on a battery. [< Gk., < *ana*– up + *hodos* way] —**an·od'ic,** *adj.*

an·o·dyne (an'ə dīn), *n.* anything that relieves pain or soothes. —*adj.* soothing. [< L < Gk., < *an*– without + *odyne* pain]

a·noint (ə noint'), *v.* **1** put oil on; rub with ointment; smear. **2** consecrate by applying oil. [< OF *enoint* < L, < *in*– on + *unguere* smear] —**a·noint'er,** *n.* —**a·noint'ment,** *n.*

a·nom·a·lous (ə nom'ə ləs), *adj.* departing from the common rule; irregular; abnormal. [< LL < Gk., *an*– not + *homalos* even] —**a·nom'a·lous·ly,** *adv.* —**a·nom'a·lous·ness,** *n.*

a·nom·a·ly (ə nom'ə li), *n., pl.* **–lies.** **1** departure from a common rule; irregularity. **2** something abnormal. —**a·nom'a·lism** *n.*

a·non (ə non'), *adv.* **1** in a little while; soon. **2** at another time; again. **3** ever

and anon, now and then. [OE *on ān* into one, *on āne* in one, at once]

anon., anonymous.

an·o·nym·i·ty (an´ə nim´ə ti), *n.* state of being anonymous.

a·non·y·mous (ə non´ə məs), *adj.* **1** of unknown or unacknowledged authorship: *an anonymous letter, pamphlet, etc.* **2** having no name; nameless. [< Gk., < *an-* without + dial. *onyma* name] —**a·non´y·mous·ly,** *adv.*

a·noph·e·les (ə nof´ə lēz), *n., pl.* **-les.** mosquito that can transmit malaria.

an·o·rec·tic (an´ə rek´tik), *adj.* **1** having little appetite. **2** =anorexic.

an·o·rex·i·a (an´ə rek´sē ə), *n.* **1** aversion to or avoidance of food. **2** *also* **anorexia nervosa,** condition marked by avoidance of food so extreme that it sometimes leads to death by starvation. —**an´o·rex´ic,** *adj.*

an·oth·er (ə nuth´ər), *adj.* **1** one more: *another glass of milk.* **2** different: *another matter.* —*pron.* **1** one more: *have another.* **2** a different one. **3** one of the same kind. [for *an other*]

ans., answer; answered.

an·ser·ine (an´sər īn; –in), **an·ser·ous** (–əs), *adj.* **1** of, like, or pertaining to a goose or geese. **2** stupid; foolish. [< L, < *anser* goose]

an·swer (an´sər; än´–), *n.* **1** words spoken or written in reply to a question: *a quick answer.* **2** solution to a problem. —*v.* **1** reply to: *he answered my question.* **2** reply: *he would not answer.* **3** serve: *a poor excuse will not answer.* **4** be responsible: *answer for your mistakes.* **5** correspond (*to*): *this house answers to his description.* [OE *andswaru* < *and*– against + *swerian* swear] —**an´swer·er,** *n.*

an·swer·a·ble (an´sər ə bəl; än´–), *adj.* **1** responsible. **2** that can be answered. —**an´swer·a·ble·ness,** *n.* —**an´swer·a·bly,** *adv.*

answering machine, device that records messages from telephone callers in the absence of a person to respond to a call.

answering service, an agency that cuts in on the telephone circuits of its clients to answer calls, etc. in their absence.

ant (ant), *n.* any member of a family of small hymenopterus insects that live with others in colonies. [OE *æmete*] —**ant´like´,** *adj.*

ant- *prefix.* form of **anti-** before vowels.

-ant, *suffix.* **1** ____ing, as in *buoyant, compliant, triumphant.* **2** one that ____s, as in *assistant.* See also **-ent.** [< F < L *-ans, -ens*]

ant., **1** antonym. **2** antiquary.

ant·ac·id (ant as´id), *adj.* neutralizing acids; counteracting acidity. —*n.* substance that neutralizes acids, such as baking soda.

an·tag·o·nism (an tag´ə niz əm), *n.* active opposition; hostility.

an·tag·o·nist (an tag´ə nist), *n.* **1** person who fights, struggles or contends with another; opponent; adversary. **2** muscle that contracts when another muscle relaxes. **3** drug that counteracts another drug.

an·tag·o·nis·tic (an tag´ə nis´tik), *adj.* acting against each other; opposing; conflicting. —**an·tag´o·nis´ti·cal·ly,** *adv.*

an·tag·o·nize (an tag´ nīz), *v.,* **-nized, -niz·ing.** **1** make an enemy of; arouse dislike in. **2** oppose. **3** counteract. [< Gk., < *anti-* against + *agon* contest] —**an·tag´o·niz´er,** *n.*

ant·arc·tic (ant ärk´tik; –är´tik), *adj.* of or near the South Pole or the south polar region. —*n.* the south polar region.

Ant·arc·ti·ca (ant ärk´tə kə; –är´tə–), or **Antarctic Continent,** *n.* continent around or near the South Pole.

Antarctic Circle or **antarctic circle,** imaginary boundary of the south polar region, running parallel to the equator at 23°30´ north of the South Pole.

Antarctic Ocean, ocean of the south polar region.

Antarctic Zone, region between the Antarctic Circle and the South Pole.

ant bear, **1** a large, shaggy, gray anteater of South America. **2** =aardvark.

an·te (an´tē), *n., v.,* **-ted** or **-teed, -te·ing.** *n.* **1** stake in the game of poker that every player must put up before receiving a hand or drawing new cards. **2** amount required; cost. —*v. Colloq.* **1** put (one's stake) into the pool. **2** pay (one's share).

ante up, a put (one's stake) into the pool. **b** pay (one's shares). [See ANTE–]

ante-, *prefix.* before, as in *antenatal, anteroom.* [< L]

ant·eat·er (ant´ēt´ər), *n.* mammal with a long, slender, sticky tongue, such as the pangolin or ant bear, that feeds on ants.

an·te·bel·lum (an´ti bel´əm), *adj.* **1** before the war. **2** before the Civil War. [< L, before the war]

an·te·ced·ence (an´tə sēd´əns), *n.* **1** a going before; precedence; priority. **2** apparent motion of a planet from east to west.

an·te·ced·ent (an´tə sēd´ənt), *adj.* coming or happening before; preceding; previous; prior: *an event antecedent to this one.* —*n.* **1** a previous thing or event. **2** **antecedents, a** the past life or history. **b** ancestors. **3** word, phrase, or clause that is referred to by a pronoun. **4** the first term in any ratio; the first or third term in a proportion. [< L, *ante-* before + *cedere* go] —**an´te·ced´ent·ly,** *adv.*

an·te·cham·ber (an´ti chām´bər), *n.* =anteroom.

an·te·date (an´ti dāt; an´ti dāt´), *v.,* **-dat·ed, -dat·ing,** *n.* —*v.* **1** be or happen before. **2** give too early a date to, esp. to a document. —*n.* **1** a prior date. **2** date earlier than the true date.

an·te·di·lu·vi·an (an´ti di lü´vi ən), *adj.* **1** very old; old-fashioned. **2** before the Flood. —*n.* **1** old-fashioned person. **2** very old person. **3** person who lived before the Flood. [< ANTE– + L *diluvium* deluge]

an·te·lope (an´tə lōp), *n., pl.* **-lope, -lopes.** **1** a cud-chewing, deerlike animal related to cattle, sheep, and goats. **2** pronghorn. **3** leather from the hide of any of these animals. [< OF < Med.L < LGk. *antholops*]

an·te me·rid·i·em (an´tē mə rid´i əm), before noon. *Abbrev.:* a.m., A.M. [< L, before midday]

an·te·na·tal (an´ti nā´təl), *adj.* before birth; prenatal.

an·ten·na (an ten´ə), *n., pl.* **-ten·nae** (–ten´ē) *for 1;* **-ten·nas** *for 2.* **1** one of two feelers on the head of an insect, lobster, etc. **2** aerial. **3** *Fig.* insight; perceptiveness. [< L, orig., sail yard]

an·te·pe·nult (an´ti pē´nult; –pi nult´), *n.* the third syllable, counting back from the end of a word. In *an te ri or, te* is the antepenult.

an·te·pe·nul·ti·mate (an´ti pi nul´tə mit), *adj.* third from the end. —*n.* =antepenult.

an·te·ri·or (an tir´i ər), *adj.* **1** toward the front; fore. **2** going before; earlier; previous. [< L, comparative of *ante* before] —**an·te´ri·or´i·ty, an·te´ri·or·ness,** *n.*

an·te·room (an´ti rüm´; –rùm´), *n.* a small room leading to a larger one; a waiting room.

an·them (an´thəm), *n.* **1** song of praise, devotion, or patriotism: *the national anthem.* **2** piece of sacred music, usually with words from some passage in the Bible. **3** hymn sung in two alternating parts. [< VL < LL < Gk. *antiphona* antiphon. Doublet of ANTIPHON.]

an·ther (an´thər), *n.* part of the stamen of a flower that bears the pollen. [< NL < Gk., < *anthos* flower]

an·ther·id·i·um (an´thər id´i əm), *n., pl.* **-id·i·a** (–id´i ə). part of a fern, moss, etc., that produces male reproductive cells. —**an´ther·id´i·al,** *adj.*

an·thol·o·gy (an thol´ə ji), *n., pl.* **-gies.** **1** collection of poems or prose selections from various authors. **2** collection of paintings, films, etc. [< L < Gk., < *anthos* flower + *legein* gather] —**an´tho·log´i·cal,** *adj.* —**an·thol´o·gist,** *n.*

an·tho·zo·an (an´thə zō´ən), *n.* any sea anemone, coral, or other polyp with radial segments. —*adj.* of such polyps.

an·thra·cene (an´thrə sēn), *n.* a colorless, crystalline compount, $C_{14}H_{10}$, used in making alizarin dyes.

an·thra·cite (an´thrə sīt), *n.* coal that burns with very little smoke or flame; hard coal. [< L < Gk., name of a gem, < *anthrax* charcoal] —**an´thra·cit´ic,** *adj.*

an·thrax (an´thraks), *n., pl.* **-thra·ces** (–thrə sēz). an infectious, often fatal, disease of cattle, sheep, etc., that may be transmitted to human beings. [< LL < Gk., carbuncle, live coal]

anthrop- or **anthropo-,** *combining form.* man; human being; human, as in *anthropology, anthropometry*. [< Gk. *anthropos*]

an·thro·po·gen·ic (an´thrə pə jen´ik), *adj*. caused by humans. [< *anthropo–* + *–genic* producing]

an·thro·poid (an´thrə poid), *adj*. **1** humanlike; resembling man. **2** of people, resembling an ape. —*n*. a man-like ape. Chimpanzees and gorillas are anthropoids. —**an´thro·poi´dal**, *adj*.

an·thro·pol·o·gy (an´thrə pol´ə ji), *n*. science that deals with the origin, development, groups, customs, and beliefs of humankind.—**an´thro·po·log´i·cal, an´-thro·po·log´ic**, *adj*. —**an´thro·po·log´i·cal·ly**, *adv*. —**an´thro·pol´o·gist**, *n*.

an·thro·pom·e·try (an´thrə pom´ə tri), *n*. branch of anthropology that deals with the measurement of the human body. —**an´thro·po·met´ric, an´thro·po·met´ri·cal**, *adj*. —**an´thro·pom´e·trist**, *n*.

an·thro·po·mor·phic (an´thrə pə môr´fik), *adj*. attributing human form or qualities to gods or things. —**an´thro·po·mor´phi·cal·ly**, *adv*.

an·thro·po·mor·phism (an´thrə pə môr´fiz əm), *n*. an attributing of human form or qualities to animals, gods, or things. —**an´thro·po·mor´phist**, *n*.

an·ti (an´tī; –ti), *n., pl*. **-tis**. person opposed to some plan, idea, party, etc.

anti–, *prefix*. **1** against; opposed to, as in *anti-British*. **2** not; the opposite of, as in *antisocial*. **3** rival, as in *antipope*. **4** preventing or counteracting, as in *antitrust*. **5** preventing, curing, or alleviating, as in *antituberculosis*. **6** placed in opposition or moving in opposition to, as in *anticyclonic*. [< Gk.; also (before vowels and *h*), *ant–*]

an·ti-air·craft (an´ti är´kraft´; –kräft´), *adj*. used in defense against enemy aircraft.

an·ti·bi·ot·ic (an´ti bī ot´ik), *n*. product of an organism, as penicillin, that works against harmful microorganisms.

an·ti·bod·y (an´ti bod´i), *n., pl*. **-bod·ies**. protein produced in the blood or tissues that destroys or weakens bacteria or neutralizes toxins.

an·tic (an´tik), *n., adj., v.*, **-ticked, -ticking**. —*n*. **antics**. silly gesture or action; playful trick; caper. —*adj*. silly; grotesque. —*v*. perform antics; caper. [< Ital. *antico* old (with sense of *grottesco* grotesque) < L *antiquus* ancient]

an·ti·christ (an´ti krīst´), *n*. **1** person who opposes or denies Christ. **2 Antichrist.** great enemy and last opponent of Christ, as told in the Bible.

an·tic·i·pate (an tis´ə pāt), *v.*, **-pat·ed, -pat·ing**. **1** look forward to; expect: *anticipate a good vacation*. **2** use or realize in advance: *anticipate the disaster*. **3** take care of ahead of time: *anticipate a person's wishes*. **4** be before (another) in thinking, acting, etc. [< L *anticipatus* < *ante* before + *capere* take] —**an·tic´i·pa´tor**, *n*.

an·tic·i·pa·tion (an tis´ə pā´shən), *n*. **1** act of anticipating. **2** expectation.

an·tic·i·pa·tive (an tis´ə pā´tiv), *adj*. tending to anticipate; having anticipation (*of*).

an·tic·i·pa·to·ry (an tis´ə pə tô´ri; –tō´–), *adj*. anticipating. —**an·tic·i·pa·to´ri·ly**, *adv*.

an·ti·cler·i·cal (an´ti kler´ə kəl), *adj*. opposed to the influence of the church and clergy, esp. in public affairs. —**an´ti·cler´i·cal·ism**, *n*.

an·ti·cli·max (an´ti klī´maks), *n*. **1** an abrupt descent from the important to the trivial. **2** descent (in importance, interest, etc.) contrasting with a previous rise or peak. —**an´ti·cli·mac´tic**, *adj*.

an·ti·co·ag·u·lant (an´ti kō ag´yə lənt), *n*. substance that slows the process of blood clotting.

an·ti·co·lo·ni·al (an´ti kə lō´ni əl), *adj*. opposed to colonialism. —**an´ti·co·lo´ni·al·ism**, *n*.

an·ti·co·lo·ni·al·ist (an´ti kə lō´ni ə list), *n*. an opponent of colonialism. —*adj*. anticolonial.

an·ti·cy·clone (an´ti sī´klōn), *n*. winds moving around and away from a center of high pressure, which also moves. —**an´ti·cy·clon´ic** *adj*.

an·ti·de·pres·sant (an´ti dē pres´ənt), drug used to reduce mental depression.

an·ti·dote (an´ti dōt), *n*. **1** medicine or remedy that counteracts a poison. **2** remedy for any evil. [< L < Gk. *antidoton* (thing) given against < *anti–* against + *didonai* give] —**an´ti·dot´al**, *adj*. —**an´ti·dot´al·ly**, *adv*.

An·tie·tam (an tē´təm), *n*. small creek in Maryland near which a major battle of the Civil War was fought in 1862.

an·ti·freeze (an´ti frēz´), *n*. substance added to a liquid to prevent it from freezing.

an·ti·fric·tion (an´ti frik´shən), *n*. prevention or reduction of friction.

an·ti·gen (an´tə jən), *n*. any substance that stimulates the production of antibodies. —**an´ti·gen´ic**, *adj*.

An·ti·gua (an tē´gə; –gwə), *n*. island SE of Puerto Rico, in the West Indies.

an·ti·her·o (an´ti hir´ō), *n*. central character in a novel, play, etc., who has none of the usual qualities of a hero.

an·ti·his·ta·mine (an´ti his´tə mēn; –min), *n*. chemical compound used esp. against allergies.

An·til·les (an til´ēz), *n.pl*. chain of islands in the West Indies.

antilock brakes or **antilock disk brakes,** computer-regulated brakes on a vehicle that prevent skids on icy or very wet pavement.

an·ti·log·a·rithm (an´ti lôg´ə riŧħ əm; –log´–), *n*. number corresponding to a given logarithm.

an·ti·ma·cas·sar (an´ti mə kas´ər), *n*. a small covering to protect the back or arms of a chair, sofa, etc. [< *anti–* against + *macassar* a hair oil from Macassar]

an·ti·mat·ter or **an·ti-mat·ter** (an´ti mat´ər), *n*. physical matter identical to normal matter except for having reversed electric charges of its particles.

an·ti·mis·sile (an´ti mis´əl), *adj*. used in defense against ballistic missiles, rockets, etc.

an·ti·mo·ny (an´tə mō´ni), *n*. a metallic, crystalline element, Sb, with a bluish-white luster, used chiefly in alloys and medicinal compounds. [< Med.L *antimonium*]

an·ti·pas·to (än´tē päs´tō), *n., pl*. **-tos**. *Italian*. an appetizer consisting of fish, meats, etc.

an·tip·a·thet·ic (an tip´ə thet´ik; an´ti pə–), **an·tip·a·thet·i·cal** (–ə kəl), *adj*. contrary or opposed in nature or disposition. —**an·tip´a·thet´i·cal·ly**, *adv*.

an·tip·a·thy (an tip´ə thi), *n., pl*. **-thies**. **1** intense or fixed dislike; a feeling against. **2** object of intense dislike. [< L < Gk., < *anti–* against + *pathos* feeling]

an·ti·phon (an´tə fon), *n*. verses sung or chanted by two groups alternately in a church service. [< LL < Gk. *antiphona* sounding in response < *anti–* opposed to + *phone* sound. Doublet of ANTHEM.] —**an·tiph´o·nal**, *adj*. —**an·tiph´o·nal·ly**, *adv*.

an·tip·o·dal (an tip´ə dəl), *adj*. **1** on the opposite side of the earth. **2** directly opposite; exactly contrary: *antipodal ideas*.

an·ti·pode (an´tə pōd), *n*. the direct opposite.

an·tip·o·des (an tip´ə dēz), *n.pl*. **1** two places on directly opposite sides of the earth. **2** (*sometimes sing. in use*) a place on the opposite side of the earth. **3** (*sometimes sing. in use*) the direct opposite. [< L < Gk., < *anti–* opposite to + *pous* foot] —**an·tip´o·de´an**, *adj., n*.

an·ti·pro·ton (an´ti prō´ton), *n*. a particle of the same mass as a proton, but negatively charged, created when a proton hits a neutron.

an·ti·py·ret·ic (an´ti pī ret´ik), *Med*. —*adj*. checking or preventing fever. —*n*. any medicine or remedy for checking or preventing fever.

an·ti·quar·i·an (an´tə kwār´i ən), *adj*. having to do with antiques or antiquaries. —*n*. antiquary. —**an´ti·quar´i·an·ism**, *n*.

an·ti·quark (an´tə kwark´), *n*. hypothetical elementary particle of antimatter analogous to the quark.

an·ti·quar·y (an´tə kwer´i), *n., pl*. **-quaries**. student or collector of antiques.

an·ti·quate (an´tə kwāt), *v.*, **-quat·ed, -quat·ing**. make old-fashioned or out-of-date.

an·ti·quat·ed (an´tə kwāt´id), *adj*. **1** old-fashioned; out-of-date. **2** old. —**an´ti·quat´ed·ness**, *n*.

an·tique (an tēk´), *adj*. **1** old-fashioned; out-of-date. **2** in the style of times long ago. **3** of or from times long ago; ancient. **4** of or belonging to ancient Greece or Rome. —*n.* **1** something made long ago. **2** antique style, usually of Greek or Roman art. [< L *antiquus* < *ante* before] —**an·tique′ly,** *adv.* —**an·tique′ness,** *n.*

an·tiq·ui·ty (an tik′wə ti), *n., pl.* **-ties. 1** great age. **2** times long ago; early ages of history; the period from 5000 B.C. to A.D. 476. **3** people of long ago. **4 antiquities, a** things from ancient times. **b** customs and life of ancient times.

an·ti·scor·bu·tic (an′ti skôr bū′tik), *adj.* preventing or curing scurvy. —*n.* remedy for scurvy.

an·ti·Sem·i·tism (an′ti sem′ə tiz əm), *n.* dislike or hatred for Jews; prejudice against Jews. —**an′ti·Sem′ite,** *n.* —**an′ti·Se·mit′ic,** *adj.*

an·ti·sep·sis (an′tə sep′sis), *n.* **1** prevention of infection. **2** method or medicine that prevents infection.

an·ti·sep·tic (an′tə sep′tik), *adj.* preventing infection. —*n.* substance, as iodine, that prevents infection. —**an′ti·sep′ti·cal·ly,** *adv.*

an·ti·slav·er·y (an′ti slāv′ər i), *adj.* opposed to slavery; against slavery.

an·ti·so·cial (an′ti sō′shəl), *adj.* **1** harmful to the public welfare; against the common good. **2** averse to social relations; unsociable.

an·tis·tro·phe (an tis′trə fē), *n.* **1** part of an ancient Greek ode sung by the chorus when moving from left to right. **2** stanza following a strophe and usually in the same meter. [< LL < Gk., < *anti-* against + *strephein* turn] —**an′ti·stroph′ic,** *adj.*

an·ti·tank (an′ti tangk′), *adj.* designed for use against armored vehicles, esp. tanks.

an·tith·e·sis (an tith′ə sis), *n., pl.* **-ses** (-sēz). **1** the direct opposite: *hate is the antithesis of love.* **2** contrast of ideas. **3** opposition; contrast (*of* or *between*): *antithesis of theory and fact.* [< L < Gk., < *anti-* against + *tithenai* set]

an·ti·thet·ic (an′tə thet′ik), **an·ti·thet·i·cal** (-ə kəl), *adj.* **1** of or using antithesis. **2** contrasted; opposite. —**an′ti·thet′i·cal·ly,** *adv.*

an·ti·tox·ic (an′ti tok′sik), *adj.* **1** counteracting diseases or poisonings caused by toxins. **2** having to do with or like an antitoxin.

an·ti·tox·in (an′ti tok′sən), **an·ti·tox·ine** (-sən; -sēn) *n.* **1** substance formed in the body to counteract a disease or poison. **2** a serum containing antitoxin.

an·ti·trades (an′ti trādz′), *n.pl.* winds that blow in a direction opposite to the trade winds on a level above them and descend beyond the trade-wind belt.

an·ti·trust (an′ti trust′), *adj.* opposed to large corporations that control the trade practices of certain kinds of business.

ant·ler (ant′ler), *n.* **1** a branched horn of a deer or similar animal. **2** branch of such a horn. [< OF *antoillier* < L *ante* before + *oculus* eye]

ant lion, 1 insect whose larva digs a pit, where it lies in wait to catch ants, etc. **2** its larva.

An·to·ni·us (an tō′ni əs), *n.* **Marcus** (*Mark Antony*), 83?–30 B.C., Roman general, friend of Julius Caesar, and rival of Augustus.

an·to·nym (an′tə nim), *n.* word that means the opposite of another word (contrasted with *synonym*) : *"hot" is the antonym of "cold."* [< Gk., < *anti-* opposite to + dial. *onyma* word]

ants·y (an′tsi), *adj.* **ants·i·er, ants·i·est.** jumpy; nervous.

a·nus (ā′nəs), *n.* opening at the lower end of the alimentary canal where waste is eliminated from the body. [< L, orig., ring]

an·vil (an′vəl), *n., v.,* **-viled, -vil·ing.** —*n.* **1** an iron or steel block on which metals are hammered and shaped. **2** incus. —*v.* form or shape on or as on an anvil. [OE *anfilt*]

anx·i·e·ty (ang zī′ə ti), *n., pl.* **-ties. 1** anxious state or feeling; troubled, worried, or uneasy feeling; apprehension; dread. **2** eager desire: *anxiety to succeed.*

anx·ious (angk′shəs; ang′–), *adj.* **1** uneasy because of thoughts or fears of what may happen; troubled; worried; concerned; apprehensive. **2** eagerly desiring; wishing very much. **3** attended by uneasiness or anxiety. [< L *anxius* troubled < *angere* choke, cause distress] —**anx′ious·ly,** *adv.* —**anx′ious·ness,** *n.*

an·y (en′i), *adj.* **1** one out of many: *any book.* **2** some: *any fresh fruit?* **3** every: *any child knows.* —*pron.* **1** any person or thing: *I don't want any.* **2** some: *have you any?* —*adv.* at all: *has the sick child improved any?* [OE *ǣnig*]

an·y·bod·y (en′i bod′i), *pron., n., pl.* **-bod·ies. 1** any person; anyone: *has anybody been here?* **2** important person: *is he anybody?*

an·y·how (en′i hou), *adv.* **1** in any way whatever. **2** in any case. **3** at least. **4** carelessly.

an·y·one (en′i wun; -wən), *pron.* any person; anybody.

an·y·place (en′i plās), *adv.* anywhere.

an·y·thing (en′i thing), *pron.* any thing. —*n.* a thing of any kind whatever. —*adv.* at all.

an·y·way (en′i wā), *adv.* **1** in any way whatever. **2** in any case. **3** carelessly.

an·y·where (en′i hwâr), *adv.* in, at, or to any place.

an·y·wise (en′i wīz), *adv.* in any way; at all.

A-OK or **A-O.K.** (ā′ō kā′), *adj., adv., interj.* OK.

A one (ā′ wun′), first-rate; first-class; excellent. Also, **A 1.**

a·or·ta (ā ôr′tə), *n., pl.* **-tas, -tae** (-tē). the main artery that conveys blood from the left side of the heart to all parts of the body except the lungs. [< NL or Med.L < Gk. *aorte*] —**a·or′tic,** *adj.*

a·ou·dad (ä′ū dad), *n.* a wild sheep of N Africa; barbary sheep. [< F < Berber *audad*]

A.P., AP, Associated Press.

a·pace (ə pās′), *adv.* swiftly; quickly; fast.

A·pach·e (ə pach′ē), *n., pl.* **A·pach·es, A·pach·e. 1** member of a tribe of nomadic Indians living in the SW United States. **2** their language.

ap·a·nage (ap′ə nij), *n.* =appanage.

a·part (ə pärt′), *adv.* **1** to pieces; in pieces; in separate parts: *take the watch apart.* **2** away from each other: *keep the dogs apart.* **3** to one side; aside: *he stood apart from the others.* [< F *à part* to the side. See PART.] —**a·part′ness,** *n.*

a·part·heid (ä pärt′hāt), *n.* racial segregation, esp. as formerly enforced in the Republic of South Africa. [Afrikaans, separateness < *apart* separate < F *à part*]

a·part·ment (ə pärt′mənt), *n.* **1** a set of rooms in a building for a single household. **2** a single room.

ap·a·thet·ic (ap′ə thet′ik), *adj.* **1** with little interest or desire for action; indifferent. **2** lacking in feeling. —**ap′a·thet′i·cal·ly,** *adv.*

ap·a·thy (ap′ə thi), *n., pl.* **-thies. 1** lack of interest or desire for activity; indifference. **2** lack of feeling. [< L < Gk., < *a-* without + *pathos* feeling]

ape (āp), *n., v.,* **aped, ap·ing.** —*n.* **1** any of various large, tailless monkeys that can stand almost erect and walk on two feet. Chimpanzees, gorillas, orangutans, and gibbons are apes. **2** any monkey. **3** person who imitates or mimics. —*v.* imitate; mimic. [OE *apa*] —**ape′like′,** *adj.*

Ap·en·nines (ap′ə nīnz), *n.pl.* mountain system extending north and south in Italy.

a·pe·ri·ent (ə pir′i ənt), *Med.* —*adj.* laxative. —*n.* a mild laxative. [< L, < *aperire* open]

a·pe·ri·tif, a·pé·ri·tif (ə per′ə tēf′; *Fr.* ä pā rē tēf′), *n.* French. **1** alcoholic drink taken as an appetizer. **2** appetizer.

ap·er·ture (ap′ər chùr; -chər), *n.* **1** opening; gap; hole. **2** in a telescope, camera, etc., the diameter of the exposed part of a lens. [< L *apertura* < *aperire* open. Doublet of OVERTURE.] —**ap′er·tured,** *adj.*

a·pet·al·ous (ā pet′əl əs), *adj.* having no petals.

a·pex (ā′peks), *n., pl.* **a·pex·es, ap·i·ces. 1** the highest point; tip. **2** climax. [< L]

a·pha·sia (ə fā′zhə), *n.* loss of the ability to use or understand words. [< NL < Gk., < *a-* not + *phanai* speak] —**a·pha′si·ac,** *adj., n.* —**a·pha′sic,** *adj., n.*

a·phe·li·on (ə fē′li ən; a–), *n., pl.* **-li·a** (-li ə). point most distant from the sun, in the orbit of a planet or comet. [< NL < Gk. *apo-* away from + *helios* sun]

a·pher·e·sis (ə fer′ə sis), *n.* omission, especially of a vowel, from the beginning of a word. Also **aphaeresis.**

a·phid (ā′fid; af′id), **a·phis** (ā′fis; af′is), *n., pl.* **a·phids; aph·i·des** (af′ə dēz). very small insect that lives by sucking juices from plants; plant louse. [< NL *aphis*] —**a·phid′i·an**, *adj., n.*

aph·o·rism (af′ə riz əm), *n.* a short sentence stating a general truth; maxim; proverb. [< Med.L < Gk. *aphorismos* definition < *apo*– off + *horizein* to limit < *horos* boundary] —**aph′o·rist**, *n.* —**aph′o·ris′tic**, *adj.* —**aph′o·ris′ti·cal·ly**, *adv.*

aph·ro·dis·i·ac (af′rə diz′i ak), *adj.* exciting sexual desire; erotic. —*n.* an aphrodisiac drug or food.

Aph·ro·di·te (af′rə dī′tē), *n.* Greek goddess of love and beauty, identified by the Romans with Venus.

a·pi·ar·y (ā′pi er′i), *n., pl.* **-ar·ies.** place where bees are kept. [< L, < *apis* bee] —**a′pi·a·rist**, *n.*

ap·i·cal (ap′ə kəl; ā′pə–), *adj.* of or at the apex; forming the apex. —**ap′i·cal·ly**, *adv.*

ap·i·ces (ap′ə sēz; ā′pə–), *n.* pl. of **apex.**

a·pi·cul·ture (ā′pə kul′chər), *n.* the raising and caring for bees; beekeeping. [< L *apis* bee + E *culture*] —**a′pi·cul′tur·al**, *adj.* —**a′pi·cul′tur·ist**, *n.*

a·piece (ə pēs′), *adv.* for each one; each.

ap·ish (āp′ish), *adj.* **1** like an ape. **2** senselessly imitative. **3** foolish; silly. —**ap′ish·ly**, *adv.* —**ap′ish·ness**, *n.*

a·plen·ty (ə plen′ti), *adv.* in plenty.

a·plomb (ə plom′), *n.* self-possession; poise. [< F, < *à plomb* according to the plummet. See PLUMB.]

a·poc·a·lypse (ə pok′ə lips), *n.* **1** revelation, esp. of great turmoil and upheaval. **2 the Apocalypse,** last book of the New Testament. [< L < Gk., < *apo*– off, un– + *kalyptein* cover]

a·poc·a·lyp·tic (ə pok′ə lip′tik), **a·poc·a·lyp·ti·cal** (–tə kəl), *adj.* **1** of the Apocalypse. **2** like a revelation; giving a revelation. —**a·poc′a·lyp′ti·cal·ly**, *adv.*

a·poc·o·pe (ə pok′ə pē), *n.* the dropping out of the last sound, syllable, or letter in a word. *Th′* for *the* is an example of apocope. [< L < Gk., < *apo*– off + *koptein* cut]

A·poc·ry·pha (ə pok′rə fə), *n.pl.* **1** fourteen books included in the Roman Catholic Bible, but not accepted as genuine by Jews and Protestants. **2** *apocrypha,* writings or statements of doubtful authorship or authority.

a·poc·ry·phal (ə pok′rə fəl), *adj.* **1** of doubtful authorship or authority. **2** false; counterfeit; sham. **3 Apocryphal,** of the Apocrypha. —**a·poc′ry·phal·ly**, *adv.* —**a·poc′ry·phal·ness**, *n.*

ap·o·gee (ap′ə jē), *n.* **1** furthermost point; highest point. **2** point most distant from the earth in the orbit of a planet, comet, etc. [< F < Gk., < *apo*– away from + *ge* or *gaia* earth] —**ap′o·ge′al**, **ap′o·ge′an**, *adj.*

A·pol·lo (ə pol′ō), *n., pl.* **-los. 1** Greek and Roman god of the sun, poetry, music,

prophecy, and healing. **2** an extremely handsome young man.

A·pol·lyon (ə pol′yən), *n.* in the Bible, the Devil.

a·pol·o·get·ic (ə pol′ə jet′ik), **a·pol·o·get·i·cal** (–ə kəl), *adj.* **1** making an apology; expressing regret; acknowledging a fault; excusing failure. **2** defending by speech or writing. —**a·pol′o·get′i·cal·ly**, *adv.*

a·pol·o·get·ics (ə pol′ə jet′iks), *n.* branch of theology that deals with the defense of Christianity on the basis of reason.

ap·o·lo·gi·a (ap′ə lō′ji ə), *n.* statement in defense or justification; apology.

a·pol·o·gist (ə pol′ə jist), *n.* person who defends an idea, belief, religion, etc., in speech or writing; a defender.

a·pol·o·gize (ə pol′ə jīz), *v.* **-gized, -giz·ing. 1** make an apology; express regret. **2** make a defense in speech or writing. —**a·pol′o·giz′er**, *n.*

ap·o·logue (ap′ə lôg; –log), *n.* fable with a moral: *Aesop's fables are apologues.*

a·pol·o·gy (ə pol′ə ji), *n., pl.* **-gies. 1** words of regret for an offense or accident. **2** defense in speech or writing; justification: *an apology for the Christian religion.* **3** a poor substitute; makeshift. [< LL < Gk. *apologia* a speech in defense, ult. < *apo*– off + *legein* speak]

ap·o·phthegm (ap′ə them), *n.* apothegm. —**ap′o·phtheg′mat·ic**, **ap′o·phtheg·mat′i·cal**, *adj.*

ap·o·plec·tic (ap′ə plek′tik), *adj.* Also, **ap′o·plec′ti·cal. 1** of or causing apoplexy. **2** suffering from apoplexy. **3** showing symptoms of a tendency to apoplexy. **4** *Fig.* extremely excited or angry. —*n.* person who has or is likely to have apoplexy. —**ap′o·plec′ti·cal·ly**, *adv.*

ap·o·plex·y (ap′ə plek′si), *n.* **1** =stroke. **2** *Fig.* sudden loss or impairment of the power to feel or think rationally, caused by shock or surprise. [< LL < Gk. *apoplexia,* < *apo*– off, from + *plessein* strike]

a·port (ə pôrt′; ə pōrt′), *adv.* to the port side of a ship or boat; to the left.

a·pos·ta·sy (ə pos′tə si), *n., pl.* **-sies.** complete forsaking of one's religion, faith, principles, or political party. [< LL < Gk., < *apo*– away from + *stenai* stand]

a·pos·tate (ə pos′tāt; –tit), *n.* person guilty of apostasy. —*adj.* guilty of apostasy; unfaithful.

a·pos·ta·tize (əpos′tə tīz), *v.,* **-tized, -tiz·ing.** forsake completely one's religion, faith, principles, or political party.

a pos·te·ri·o·ri (ā pos tir′i ô′rī; –ri; –ō′–), **1** from particular cases to a general rule. **2** based on actual observation or experience. [< Med.L, from what comes after]

a·pos·tle (ə pos′əl), *n.* **1 Apostle,** one of the twelve disciples chosen by Christ to go forth and preach the gospel to all the world. **2** any early Christian leader or missionary. **3** the first Christian missionary to any country or region. **4** leader of any reform movement or belief. **5** one

of the council of twelve officials of the Mormon Church who help administer the affairs of the church. [< L < Gk. *apostolos* messenger < *apo*– off + *stellein* send] —**a·pos′tle·ship**, *n.*

Apostles' Creed, statement of belief that contains the fundamental doctrines of Christianity.

ap·os·tol·ic (ap′əs tol′ik), **ap·os·tol·i·cal** (–ə kəl), *adj.* **1** of or having to do with apostles, esp. the twelve Apostles. **2** according to the beliefs and teachings of the Apostles. **3** of the Pope; papal. —**ap′os·tol′i·cal·ly**, *adv.* —**ap′ostol′i·cism**, *n.* —**a·pos′to·lic′i·ty**, *n.*

Apostolic See, bishopric of the Pope.

a·pos·tro·phe[1] (ə pos′trə fē), *n.* sign (′) used to show: **a** omission of one or more letters, as in *o'er* for *over, thro'* for *through.* **b** the possessive forms of nouns, as in *John's book, the lions' den.* **c** certain plurals, as in *two o's, four 9's* in 9,999. [< F < LL < Gk. *apostrophos* (*prosodia*) omission (mark) < *apostrephein* avert, get rid of. See APOSTROPHE[2].]

a·pos·tro·phe[2] (ə·pos′trə fē), *n.* words addressed to an absent person as if he or she were present or to a thing or idea as if it could appreciate them. [< LL < Gk., < *apo*– away from + *strephein* turn] —**ap′os·troph′ic**, *adj.*

a·pos·tro·phize (ə pos′trə fīz), *v.,* **-phized, –phiz·ing. 1** stop in a speech, poem, etc., and address some person or thing, usually with emotion. **2** address an apostrophe to. **3** mark with an apostrophe.

apothecaries' measure, system of units used in the U.S. in compounding and dispensing liquid drugs.

apothecaries' weight, system of weights used in mixing drugs and filling prescriptions.

a·poth·e·car·y (ə poth′ə ker′i), *n., pl.* **-car·ies.** pharmacist; druggist. [< LL *apothecarius* warehouseman, < L *apotheca* storehouse < Gk., < *apo*– away + *tithenai* put]

ap·o·thegm (ap′ə them), *n.* a short, forceful saying; maxim. Also, **apophthegm.** [< Gk. *apophthegma* < *apo*– forth + *phthengesthai* utter] —**ap′o·theg·mat′ic**, **ap′o·theg·mat′i·cal**, *adj.* —**ap′o·theg·mat′i·cal·ly**, *adv.*

a·poth·e·o·sis (ə poth′i ō′sis; ap′ə thē′ə sis), *n., pl.* **-ses** (–sēz). **1** a glorified ideal. **2** raising of a human being to the rank of a god; deification. **3** glorification; exaltation. [< L < Gk., ult. < *apo*– + *theos* god]

a·poth·e·o·size (ə poth′i ə sīz; ap′ə thē′ə sīz), *v.,* **-sized, –siz·ing. 1** glorify; exalt. **2** make a god of; deify.

app., 1 apparent; apparently. **2** appendix.

Ap·pa·la·chia (ap′ə lā′chə), *n.* rural region of the southeastern U.S., marked by great poverty and the survival of folk culture.

Ap·pa·la·chi·ans (ap′ə lā′chi ənz, –lach′i ənz; –lā′chənz, –lach′ənz), *n.pl.* chief mountain system of E North America, extending from Quebec to Alabama.

ap·pall, ap·pal (ə pôl′), v. **-palled, -pall-ing.** fill with horror; dismay; terrify. [< OF *apallir* become or make pale < *a-* (< L *ad-*) + *pale* PALE¹]

ap·pall·ing (ə pôl′ing), adj. dismaying; terrifying. —**ap·pall′ing·ly,** adv.

ap·pa·nage (ap′ə nij), n. **1** land, property, or money set aside to support the younger children of kings, princes, etc. **2** person's assigned portion; rightful property. **3** something that is a natural accompaniment; adjunct. **4** territory under the control of another country. Also, **apanage.** [< F, < *apaner* give bread to, ult. < L *ad-* to + *panis* bread]

ap·pa·rat·chik (ä′pä rät′chik), n. official of a political party or a bureaucrat, originally of the former Soviet Union. [< Russian]

ap·pa·ra·tus (ap′ə rā′təs; -rat′əs), n., pl. **-tus, -tus·es. 1** things necessary to carry out a purpose or for a particular use: *chemical apparatus.* **2** any complex appliance or piece of machinery for a particular purpose. **3** an administrative organization, as a political party. [< L, preparation, < *ad-* + *parare* make ready]

ap·par·el (ə par′əl), n., v., **-eled, -el·ing.** —n. **1** clothing; dress; attire. **2** *Fig.* something that clothes or hides: *the apparel of deception.* —v. clothe; dress up. [< OF, < *apareiller* clothe, ult. < L *ad-* + *par* equal]

ap·par·ent (ə par′ənt; ə pār′-), adj. **1** plain to see; so plain that one cannot help seeing it; easily understood; obvious; unmistakable; evident. **2** according to appearances; seeming: *the apparent truth was really a lie.* **3** entitled to inherit a throne, title, etc.: *heir apparent.* [< OF < L, < *ad-* to + *parere* come in sight] —**ap·par′ent·ness,** n.

ap·par·ent·ly (ə par′ənt li; ə pār′-), adv. **1** seemingly. **2** clearly; plainly; obviously.

ap·pa·ri·tion (ap′ə rish′ən), n. **1** ghost; phantom. **2** appearance of something strange, remarkable, or unexpected. **3** act of appearing; appearance. —**ap′pa·ri′tion·al,** adj.

ap·peal (ə pēl′), n. **1** attraction; interest. **2** earnest request; call for help, favor, mercy, etc. **3** a request to have a case heard again before a higher court or judge. —v. **1** be attractive, interesting, or enjoyable. **2** make an earnest request; apply for help, sympathy, etc.; plea; petition. **3** ask that a case be taken to a higher court or judge to be heard again. [< OF < L, *ad-* up + *pellare* call] —**ap·peal′a·ble,** adj. —**ap·peal′er,** n. —**ap·peal′ing,** adj. —**ap·peal′ing·ly,** adv. —**ap·peal′ing·ness,** n.

ap·pear (ə pir′), v. **1** be seen; come in sight: *the sun appeared on the horizon.* **2** seem; look: *he appears very old.* **3** be published. **4** present oneself publicly or formally: *appear on stage; appear in court.* **5** become known to the mind: *it appears*

that we must go. [< OF < L, < *ad-* + *parere* come in sight] —**ap·pear′er,** n.

ap·pear·ance (ə pir′əns), n. **1** act of appearing. **2** the coming into court of a party to a law suit. **3** outward look; aspect; air; mien. **4** outward show or seeming; semblance; guise. **5** apparition.

ap·pease (ə pēz′), v., **-peased, -peas·ing. 1** satisfy, as an appetite or desire: *appease one's hunger.* **2** make calm; quiet. **3** give in to the demands of (esp. a potential enemy): *No one could appease Hitler and prevent war.* [< OF, < *a* to (< L *ad-*) + *pais* peace < L *pax*] —**ap·peas′·a·ble,** adj. —**ap·pease′ment,** n. —**ap·peas′er,** n. —**ap·peas·ing·ly,** adv.

ap·pel·lant (ə pel′ənt), n. person who appeals. —adj. appellate.

ap·pel·late (ə pel′it), adj. **1** appealed to. **2** having the power to examine again and reverse the decisions of a lower court. [< *appellatus,* pp. See APPEAL.]

ap·pel·la·tion (ap′ə lā′shən), n. **1** name; title. **2** act or mode of naming.

ap·pel·la·tive (ə pel′ə tiv), n. name; title. —adj. that names. —**ap·pel′la·tive·ly,** adv.

ap·pend (ə pend′), v. add; attach. [< L, < *ad-* on + *pendere* hang]

ap·pend·age (ə pen′dij), n. **1** thing attached; addition. **2** any of various external or subordinate parts, such as a leg, fin, tail, etc. —**ap·pend′aged,** adj.

ap·pend·ant, ap·pend·ent (ə pen′dənt), adj. added; attached. —n. appendage; addition.

ap·pen·dec·to·my (ap′ən dek′tə mi), n., pl. **-mies.** removal of the vermiform appendix by surgical operation.

ap·pen·di·ci·tis (ə pen′də sī′tis), n. inflammation of the vermiform appendix.

ap·pen·dix (ə pen′diks), n., pl. **-dix·es, -di·ces** (-də sēz). **1** addition at the end of a book or document. **2** outgrowth of some part of the body, esp. the vermiform appendix. [< L. See APPEND.]

ap·per·cep·tion (ap′ər sep′shən), n. **1** clear perception; full understanding. **2** assimilation of a new perception by means of a mass of ideas already in the mind. [< F < NL. See PERCEPTION.] —**ap′per·cep′tive,** adj. —**ap′per·cep′tive·ly,** adv.

ap·per·tain (ap′ər tān′), v. belong as a part; pertain; relate. [< OF < LL, < L *ad-* to + *pertinere* PERTAIN]

ap·pe·tite (ap′ə tīt), n. **1** desire for food; hunger. **2** desire to satisfy a need; craving; longing. [< OF < L *appetitus* < *ad-* + *petere* seek]

ap·pe·tiz·er (ap′ə tīz′ər), n. something that arouses the appetite or gives relish to food.

ap·pe·tiz·ing (ap′ə tīz′ing), adj. exciting the appetite. —**ap′pe·tiz′ing·ly,** adv.

ap·plaud (ə plôd′), v. **1** express approval by clapping hands, shouting, etc. **2** express approval of in this way; acclaim. **3** approve; praise. [< L, < *ad-* + *plaudere* clap] —**ap·plaud′er,** n.

ap·plause (ə plôz′), n. **1** approval expressed by clapping the hands, shouting, etc. **2** approval; praise; commendation.

ap·ple (ap′əl), n. **1** the firm, fleshy fruit of a tree of the rose family widely grown in temperate regions. **2** the tree. **3** any of various other fruits or fruitlike products, as the oak apple. [OE *æppel*]

ap·ple·jack (ap′əl jak′), n. alcoholic liquor distilled from apple cider.

ap·ple·sauce (ap′əl sôs′), n. **1** apples cut in pieces and cooked with sugar and water until soft. **2** nonsense.

ap·pli·ance (ə plī′əns), n. **1** thing like a tool, small machine, etc., used in doing something; device. **2** an applying.

ap·pli·ca·ble (ap′lə kə bəl; ə plik′ə-), adj. capable of being applied; suitable; fitting. —**ap′pli·ca·bil′i·ty, ap′pli·ca·ble-ness,** n. —**ap′pli·ca·bly,** adv.

ap·pli·cant (ap′lə kənt), n. person who applies (for loan, job, etc.).

ap·pli·ca·tion (ap′lə kā′shən), n. **1** act of putting to use; use. **2** applying or putting on. **3** thing applied. **4** a request. **5** close attention. —**ap′pli·ca′tive, ap′pli·ca·to′ry,** adj.

ap·pli·ca·tor (ap′lə kā′tər), n. brush, pad, or other device for applying a substance, as paint, makeup, medicine, etc.

ap·plied (ə plīd′), adj. put to practical use.

ap·pli·qué (ap′lə kā′), n., v., **-quéd, -qué·ing.** —n. ornaments made of one material sewed or otherwise fastened on another. —v. trim or ornament with appliqué. —adj. trimmed in this way. [< F, < *appliquer* APPLY]

ap·ply (ə plī′), v., **-plicd, -ply·ing. 1** put. *apply paint.* **2** put to practical use. **3** be useful or suitable; fit: *when does this rule apply?* **4** make a request; petition; solicit: *apply for a job.* **5** use (a word or words) appropriately: *apply a nickname.* **6** set to work and stick to it: *he applied himself to learning French.* [< OF *aplier* < L, < *ad-* on + *plicare* fold, lay] —**ap·pli′er,** n.

ap·pog·gia·tu·ra (ə poj′ə tür′ə; -tyůr′ə), n. grace note. [< Ital., < *appoggiare* lean, ult. < L *ad-* on + < *podium* PODIUM]

ap·point (ə point′), v. **1** name for an office or position; choose; designate: *appointed postmaster.* **2** decide on; set: *appoint a time.* **3** fix; prescribe: *appointed death as punishment for murder.* **4** furnish; equip; supply: *a well-appointed office.* [< OF *apointer,* ult. < L *ad-* to + *punctum* a POINT] —**ap·point′a·ble,** adj. —**ap·point′er,** n.

ap·point·ee (ə poin tē′; ap′oin tē′; ə poin′ tē), n. person appointed.

ap·poin·tive (ə poin′tiv), adj. filled by appointment. —**ap·poin′tive·ly,** adv.

ap·point·ment (ə point′mənt), n. **1** act of naming for an office or position; choosing. **2** office or position; post. **3** act of ordaining. **4** engagement to be somewhere or to meet someone. **5 appointments,** furniture; equipment.

Ap·po·mat·tox (ap′ə mat′əks), n. village in C Virginia where the Civil War ended with Lee's surrender to Grant, April 9, 1865.

ap·por·tion (ə pôr'shən; ə pōr'–), *v.* divide and give out in fair shares; distribute according to some rule. [< obs. F, ult. < L *ad–* to + *portio* portion] —**ap·por'tion·er,** *n.*

ap·por·tion·ment (ə pôr'shən mənt), *n.* 1 a dividing and distribution in fair shares. 2 a determining of representation in a legislature, as in the House of Representatives.

ap·pose (ə pōz'), *v.,* –**posed, –pos·ing.** 1 put next; place side by side. 2 put (one thing to another). [< F, < *a–* to + *poser* put, POSE] —**ap·pos'a·ble,** *adj.*

ap·po·site (ap'ə zit), *adj.* appropriate; suitable; apt. [< L *appositus* < *ad–* + *ponere* place] —**ap'po·site·ly,** *adv.* —**ap'po·site·ness,** *n.*

ap·po·si·tion (ap'ə zish'ən), *n.* 1 act of putting side by side. 2 a a placing together in the same grammatical relation. b relation of two words or phrases when the second is added to the first as an explanation. In "Mr. Brown, our neighbor, has a new car," *Mr. Brown* and *neighbor* are in apposition. 3 position side by side. —**ap'po·si'tion·al,** *adj.* —**ap'po·si'tion·al·ly,** *adj.*

ap·pos·i·tive (ə poz'ə tiv), *n.* noun added to another noun as an explanation; phrase or clause in apposition. —*adj.* placed in apposition. —**ap·pos'i·tive·ly,** *adv.*

ap·prais·al (ə prāz'əl), *n.* 1 an appraising. 2 estimate of the value.

ap·praise (ə prāz'), *v.,* –**praised, –prais·ing.** 1 estimate the value, amount, quality, etc., of. 2 set a price on; fix the value of. [< *praise,* ? after *prize*[3], *apprize*[2]] —**ap·prais'a·ble,** *adj.* —**ap·praise'ment,** *n.* —**ap·prais'er,** *n.* —**ap·prais'ing·ly,** *adv.*

ap·pre·ci·a·ble (ə prē'shi ə bəl; –shə bəl), *adj.* enough to be felt or estimated. —**ap·pre'ci·a·bly,** *adv.*

ap·pre·ci·ate (ə prē'shi āt), *v.,* –**at·ed, –at·ing.** 1 think highly of; esteem; prize: *appreciate good food.* 2 be thankful for. 3 be sensitive to: *a blind man cannot appreciate color.* 4 estimate the value or worth of; appraise: *appreciate knowledge.* 5 estimate correctly. 6 raise (property, etc.) in value. 7 rise in value. [< L *apretiatus* appraised < *ad–* + *pretium* price. Doublet of APPRIZE[2].] —**ap·pre'ci·a'tor,** *n.* —**ap·pre'ci·a·to'ry** *adj.*

ap·pre·ci·a·tion (ə prē'shi ā'shən), *n.* 1 a valuing. 2 sympathetic understanding. 3 favorable criticism. 4 a rise in value.

ap·pre·ci·a·tive (ə prē'shi ā'tiv; –shə tiv), *adj.* having or showing appreciation. —**ap·pre'ci·a'tive·ly,** *adv.* —**ap·pre'ci·a'tive·ness,** *n.*

ap·pre·hend (ap'ri hend'), *v.* 1 anticipate with fear; dread. 2 arrest. 3 become aware of; notice. 4 understand. [< L, < *ad–* upon + *prehendere* seize]

ap·pre·hen·si·ble (ap'ri hen'sə bəl), *adj.* capable of being apprehended. —**ap'pre·hen'si·bil'i·ty,** *n.*

ap·pre·hen·sion (ap'ri hen'shən), *n.* 1 fear; dread. 2 arrest. 3 understanding. 4 awareness.

ap·pre·hen·sive (ap'ri hen'siv), *adj.* 1 afraid; anxious; worried. 2 quick to understand; able to learn. —**ap'pre·hen'sive·ly,** *adv.* —**ap'pre·hen'sive·ness,** *n.*

ap·pren·tice (ə pren'tis), *n., v.,* –**ticed, –tic·ing.** —*n.* 1 person learning a trade or art. 2 beginner; learner. —*v.* bind or take as an apprentice. [< OF *aprentis* < *aprendre* learn. See APPREHEND.] —**ap·pren'tice·ment,** *n.* —**ap·pren'tice·ship,** *n.*

ap·prise[1], **ap·prize**[1] (əprīz'), *v.,* –**prised, –pris·ing;** –**prized, –priz·ing.** inform; notify; advise. [< F *appris,* pp. of *apprendre* learn. See APPREHEND.]

ap·prize[2], **ap·prise**[2] (ə prīz'), *v.,* –**prized, –priz·ing; –prised, –pris·ing.** appraise. [< OF < L *appretiare.* Doublet of APPRECIATE.] —**ap·prize'ment, ap·prise'ment,** *n.* —**ap·priz'er, ap·pris'er,** *n.*

ap·proach (ə prōch'), *v.* 1 come near or nearer to: *approach the gate.* 2 come near: *winter approaches; approach manhood.* 3 make advances or overtures to. 4 begin to work on something, esp. a new or difficult task. 5 bring near to something. —*n.* 1 act of coming near. 2 way by which a place or a person can be reached; access. 3 approximation. [< OF *aprochier* < LL, < L *ad–* to + *prope* near] —**ap·proach'a·ble,** *adj.* —**ap·proach'a·bil'i·ty, ap·proach'a·ble·ness,** *n.*

ap·pro·ba·tion (ap'rə bā'shən), *n.* 1 approval. 2 sanction. [< L, < *approbare* APPROVE]

ap·pro·pri·ate (*adj.* ə prō'pri it; *v.* ə prō'pri āt), *adj., v.,* –**at·ed, –at·ing.** —*adj.* suitable; proper fitting: *clothes appropriate for school.* —*v.* 1 set apart for some special use; allot: *appropriate money for roads.* 2 take for oneself. [LL, < *ad–* to + *proprius* one's own] —**ap·pro'pri·ate·ly,** *adv.* —**ap·pro'pri·ate·ness,** *n.* —**ap·pro'pri·a'tive,** *adj.* —**ap·pro'pri·a'tor,** *n.*

ap·pro·pri·a·tion (ə prō'pri ā'shən), *n.* 1 sum of money or other thing appropriated. 2 an appropriating. 3 a being appropriated.

ap·prov·al (ə prüv'əl), *n.* 1 approving; favorable opinion; commendation. 2 consent; sanction. 3 **on approval,** with permission to return (an article purchased).

ap·prove (ə prüv'), *v.,* –**proved, –prov·ing.** 1 think or speak well of; be pleased with; praise; laud. 2 speak or think favorably (*of*); commend. 3 sanction; consent to; authorize; endorse: *Congress approved the bill.* [< OF < L, < *ad–* to + *probus* good] —**ap·prov'a·ble,** *adj.* —**ap·prov'er,** *n.* —**ap·prov'ing·ly,** *adv.*

approx., approximately.

ap·prox·i·mate (*adj.* ə prok'sə mit; *v.* ə prok'sə māt), *adj., v.,* –**mat·ed, –mat**–

ing. —*adj.* 1 nearly correct. 2 very like. —*v.* 1 come near to; approach: *the crowd approximated a thousand people.* 2 come near; be almost equal: *approximate the truth.* [< L, < *ad–* to + *proximus* nearest < *prope* near] —**ap·prox'i·mate·ly,** *adv.*

ap·prox·i·ma·tion (ə prok'sə mā'shən), *n.* 1 an approximating; approach. 2 nearly correct amount; close estimate.

ap·pur·te·nance (ə pèr'tə nəns), *n.* 1 added thing; accessory. 2 minor right or privilege. **appurtenances,** a accessories. b special equipment. [< AF. See APPERTAIN.]

ap·pur·te·nant (ə pèr'tə nənt), *adj.* pertaining; belonging (*to*).

Apr., April.

a·pri·cot (ā'prə kot; ap'rə–), *n.* 1 a roundish, orange-colored fruit somewhat like both a peach and a plum. 2 tree that it grows on. 3 pale orange-yellow color. —*adj.* orange-yellow. [earlier *apricock* (< Pg., *albricoque*), later infl. by F *abricot* < Pg. < Sp. < Ar. < Gk. < L, < *prae* before + *coquere* cook, ripen]

A·pril (ā'prəl), *n.* the fourth month of the year; containing 30 days. [< L *aprilis*]

April fool, person who gets fooled on April 1.

April Fools' Day, April 1, a day observed by fooling people with tricks and jokes; All Fools' Day.

a pri·o·ri (ā prī ô'rī; ā prī ō'rī; –ô'–), 1 from a general rule to a particular case. 2 based on opinion or theory rather than on actual observation or experience. [< Med.L, from (something) previous]

a·pron a·pron (ā'prən), *n.* 1 garment worn over the front part of the body to cover or protect clothes. 2 a an area in front of an opening in a wall, as at the front of a stage or a garage. b an area at an airport in front of a hangar or terminal. [< OF *naperon,* dim. of *nape* < L *nappa* napkin; ME *a napron* taken as *an apron*]

ap·ro·pos (ap'rə pō'), *adv.* 1 fittingly; opportunely. 2 **apropos of,** concerning; with regard to. —*adj.* fitting; suitable. [< F *à propos* to the purpose]

apse (aps), *n.* a semicircular or many-sided arched or vaulted recess in a church, usually at the east end. [< L < Gk. *hapsis* loop, arch < *haptein* fasten]

apt (apt), *adj.* 1 fitted by nature; likely; prone; inclined: *apt to make mistakes.* 2 suitable; fitting; appropriate: *an apt reply.* 3 quick to learn; clever; bright: *an apt pupil.* [< L *aptus* joined, fitted] —**apt'ly,** *adv.* —**apt'ness,** *n.*

apt., *pl.* **apts.** apartment.

ap·ter·ous (ap'tər əs), *adj.* wingless.

ap·ter·yx (ap'tər iks), *n., pl.* –**ter·yx·es** (–tər ik siz). kiwi. [< NL, < *a–* without + Gk. *pteryx* wing]

ap·ti·tude (ap'tə tüd; –tūd), *n.* 1 natural tendency; ability; capacity. 2 readiness in learning; quickness to understand. 3 special fitness. [< LL *aptitudo.* See APT.]

aq·ua (ak′wə), *n.* 1 =water. 2 light bluish-green color. —*adj.* light bluish-green. [< Latin]

aq·ua·cul·ture (ak′wə kul′chər), *n.* raising of fish or cultivation of plants in water; mariculture.

aq·ua for·tis (ak′wə fôr′tis; ā′kwə), nitric acid. [< L, strong water]

aq·ua·lung (ak′wə lung′), *n.* 1 a diving device consisting of cylinders of compressed air strapped to the diver's back and a clear mask placed over the eyes and nose. The supply of air to the diver is regulated automatically by a valve. 2 **Aqua-Lung,** trademark for the device.

aq·ua·ma·rine (ak′wə mə rēn′), *n.* 1 a transparent, bluish-green precious stone, a variety of beryl. 2 bluish green. [< F < L *aqua marina* sea water]

aq·ua·plane (ak′wə plān′), *n., v.,* –planed, –plan·ing. —*n.* wide board on which a person rides for sport as he is towed by a speeding motorboat. —*v.* ride on such a board for sport. [< L *aqua* water + E *plane*[1]]

aq·ua re·gi·a (ak′wə rē′ji ə; ā′kwə), mixture of nitric acid and hydrochloric acid. [< NL, royal water; because it dissolves gold]

a·quar·i·um (ə kwãr′i əm), *n., pl.* **a·quar·i·ums, a·quar·i·a** (ə kwãr′i ə). 1 pond, tank, or glass bowl in which living fish, water animals, and water plants are kept. 2 place where collections of living fish, etc., are exhibited. [< L, of water, < *aqua* water]

A·quar·i·us (ə kwãr′i əs), *n.* 1 a northern constellation supposed to represent a man pouring water out of a vase. 2 the 11th sign of the zodiac.

a·quat·ic (ə kwat′ik; ə kwot′–), *adj.* 1 growing or living in water. 2 taking place in or on water: *aquatic sports.* —*n.* 1 plant or animal that lives in water. 2 **aquatics,** sports that take place in or on water. —**a·quat′i·cal·ly,** *adv.*

aq·ua·tint (ak′wə tint′), *n.* 1 process in which tones, not lines, are etched by acid. 2 etching made by this process. —*v.* etch by the aquatint process.

aq·ua vi·tae (ak′wə vī′tē; ā′kwə), 1 =alcohol. 2 brandy; whiskey, etc. [< NL, water of life]

aq·ue·duct (ak′wə dukt), *n.* 1 an artificial channel or large pipe for bringing water from a distance. 2 structure that supports such a channel or pipe. 3 canal or passage in the body. [< L, < *aqua* water + *ducere* lead, convey]

a·que·ous (ā′kwi əs; ak′wi–), *adj.* 1 of water; like water; watery. 2 containing water.

aqueous humor, watery liquid that fills the space in the eye between the cornea and the lens.

aq·ui·line (ak′wə līn; –lin), *adj.* 1 of or like an eagle. 2 curved like an eagle's beak; hooked. [< L, < *aquila* eagle]

A·qui·nas (ə kwī′nəs), *n.* **Saint Thomas,** 1225?–74, Roman Catholic theologian and philosopher.

Aq·ui·taine (ak′wə tān; ak′wə tān′), *n.* region in SW France.

Ar, argon.

Ar., 1 Arabic. 2 Arabian. 3 Aramaic. 4 argentum.

AR, (*zip code*) Arkansas.

ar. or **ar,** 1 arrival. 2 arrive.

Ar·ab (ar′əb), *n.* 1 native or inhabitant of Arabia; member of a Semitic race now widely scattered over SW and S Asia and N, E, and C Africa. 2 one of a breed of swift, graceful horses. —*adj.* of the Arabs or Arabia.

Arab. or **Arab,** 1 Arabia. 2 Arabian. 3 Arabic.

ar·a·besque (ar′ə besk′), *n.* an elaborate and fanciful design of flowers, leaves, geometrical figures, etc. —*adj.* 1 carved or painted in arabesque. 2 elaborate; fanciful. 3 position in ballet. [< F < Ital. *arabesco* < *Arabo* Arab]

A·ra·bi·a (ə rā′bi ə), *n.* a large peninsula in SW Asia. —**A·ra′bi·an,** *adj., n.*

Arabian Sea, part of the Indian Ocean between Arabia and India.

Ar·a·bic (ar′ə bik), *adj.* of or coming from the Arabs; belonging to Arabia. —*n.* the Semitic language of the Arabs.

Arabic numerals figures 1, 2, 3, 4, 5, 6, 7, 8, 9, 0.

ar·a·ble (ar′ə bəl), *adj.* fit for plowing and producing crops: *arable land.* [< L, < *arare* plow]

Arab League, a loose confederation, since 1945, of Egypt, Iraq, Lebanon, Saudi Arabia, Syria, Jordan, Yemen, and other Arab states.

a·rach·nid (ə rak′nid), *n.* any of a large group of small arthropods including spiders, scorpions, mites, etc. [< Gk. *arachne* spider, web] —**a·rach′ni·dan,** *adj., n.*

Ar·a·gon (ar′ə gon), *n.* region in NE Spain, formerly a kingdom.

Ar·al Sea (ar′əl), inland sea between the republics of Kazakhstan and Kyrgyzstan.

Aram., Aramaic.

Ar·a·ma·ic (ar′ə mā′ik), *n.* a Semitic language or group of dialects, including Syriac and the language spoken in Palestine at the time of Christ. —*adj.* of or in Aramaic.

A·rap·a·ho (ə rap′əhō), *n., pl.* –ho or –hos. member of an Algonkian tribe.

Ar·a·rat (ar′ə rat), *n.* mountain in E Turkey.

ar·ba·lest, ar·ba·list (är′bə list), *n.* powerful crossbow with a steel bow. [< OF *arbaleste* < LL, < L *arcus* bow + *ballista* military engine, ult. < Gk. *ballein* throw] —**ar′ba·lest·er, ar′ba·list·er,** *n.*

ar·bi·ter (är′bə tər), *n.* 1 person chosen to decide a dispute; arbitrator; judge; umpire. 2 person with full power to decide. [< L, orig., one who approaches (two disputants) < *ad*– up to + *baetere* go]

ar·bi·tra·ble (är′bə trə bəl), *adj.* capable of being decided by arbitration.

ar·bit·ra·ment (äar bit′rə mənt), *n.* decision by an arbitrator or arbiter.

ar·bi·trar·y (är′bə trer′i), *adj.* 1 based on one's own wishes, notions, or will; not going by rule or law. 2 capricious; willful; unreasonable. 3 tyrannical; despotic. 4 set or determined by chance: *an arbitrary date to begin the process.* —**ar′bi·trar′i·ly,** *adv.* —**ar′bi·trar′i·ness,** *n.*

ar·bi·trate (är′bə trāt), *v.* –trat·ed, –trat·ing. 1 give a decision in a dispute; act as arbiter. 2 settle by arbitration. 3 submit to arbitration. [< L, < *arbiter* ARBITER] —**ar′bi·tra′tive,** *adj.*

ar·bi·tra·tion (är′bə trā′shən), *n.* settlement of a dispute by the decision of somebody chosen to be a judge, umpire, or arbiter. —**ar′bi·tra′tion·al,** *adj.*

ar·bi·tra·tor (är′bə trā′tər), *n.* person chosen to decide a dispute; judge; umpire. —**ar′bi·tra′tor·ship,** *n.*

ar·bor[1] (är′bər), *n.* a shady place formed by trees or shrubs or by vines growing on latticework. [< AF *erber* < L, < *herba* plant]

ar·bor[2] (är′bər), *n.* the main shaft or axle of a machine. [< F *arbre*]

Arbor Day, day observed in many states of the United States by planting trees.

ar·bo·re·al (är bô′ri əl; –bō′–), *adj.* 1 of or like trees. 2 living in or among trees: *an arboreal animal.*

ar·bo·res·cent (är′bə res′ənt), *adj.* like a tree in structure or growth; branching.

ar·bo·re·tum (är′bə rē′təm), *n., pl.* –tums, –ta (–tə). botanical garden of trees and shrubs. [< L]

ar·bor vi·tae (är′bər vī′tē), an evergreen tree of the pine family often planted for hedges. [< L, tree of life]

ar·bo·vi·rus (är′bə vī′res), *n.* virus transmitted chiefly by ticks and fleas the cause of some hemorrhagic fevers.

ar·bu·tus (är bū′təs), *n.* 1 plant that has clusters of fragrant pink or white flowers and grows in patches on the ground; Mayflower; trailing arbutus. 2 shrub or tree of the heath family, that has clusters of large white flowers and scarlet berries. [< L]

arc (ärk), *n., v.,* **arced** (ärkt), **arc·ing** (är′king), or **arked, arck·ing.** —*n.* 1 any part of a circle or other curved line. 2 a curved stream of brilliant light or sparks formed as a current jumps from one conductor to another. —*v.* form an electric arc. [< L *arcus* bow]

ARC[1] or **A.R.C.,** American Red Cross.

ARC[2], AIDS-related complex.

Arc (ärk), *n.* **Jeanne d′.** See **Joan of Arc.**

ar·cade (är kād′), *n.* 1 passageway with an arched roof. 2 any covered passageway. 3 row of arches supported by columns. [< F < Pr. *arcado* < OPr. *arca* ARCH[1]] —**ar·cad′ed,** *adj.*

Ar·ca·di·a (är kā′di ə), *n.* 1 a mountain district in the S part of ancient Greece, famous for the simple, contented life of its people. 2 *Fig.* a place of contentment. —**Ar·ca′di·an,** *adj., n.*

Ar·ca·dy (är′kə di), *n. Poetic.* Arcadia.

ar·cane (är kān′), *adj.* secret; mysterious.

ar·ca·num (är kā′nəm), *n., pl.* **–nums, –na** (-nə). a secret; mystery. [< L, (thing) hidden, < *arca* chest]

arch[1] (ärch), *n.* **1** a curved structure that bears the weight of the material above it. **2** monument forming an arch or arches. **3** archway. **4** instep. **5** something like an arch. —*v.* **1** bend into an arch; curve. **2** furnish with an arch. **3** form an arch over; span. [< OF, < VL *arca*, irreg. var. of L *arcus* bow] —**arched**, *adj.*

arch[2] (ärch), *adj.* **1** chief. **2** playfully mischievous. [< *arch-*] —**arch′ly**, *adv.* —**arch′ness**, *n.*

arch-, *prefix.* **1** chief; principal, as in *archbishop, archduke, archfiend.* **2** extreme, as in *archliberal.* **3** primitive, as in *archencephalon.* [< L < Gk. *arch(e)-, archi- < archein* be first, lead]

arch., **1** archaic; archaism. **2** Arch., Archbishop. **3** Also, **archit.** architecture.

ar·chae·ol·o·gy (är′ki ol′ə ji), *n.* study of the people, customs, and life of the remote past by excavating and classifying the remains of ancient cities, tools, monuments, etc. Also, **archeology.** [< Gk., < *archaios* ancient + *logos* discourse] —**ar′chae·o·log′i·cal, ar′chae·o·log′ic,** *adj.* —**ar′chae·o·log′i·cal·ly,** *adv.* —**ar′chae·ol′o·gist,** *n.*

ar·chae·op·ter·yx (är′kē op′tər iks), *n.* oldest fossil bird.

ar·cha·ic (är kā′ik), *adj.* **1** no longer in general use. **2** old-fashioned; out-of-date. **3** ancient. [< Gk. *archaikos,* ult. < *arche* beginning] —**ar·cha′i·cal·ly,** *adv.*

ar·cha·ism (är′ki iz əm; -kā-), *n.* **1** word or expression no longer in general use. *In sooth* is an archaism meaning *in truth.* **2** use of something out of date in language or art. —**ar′cha·is′ti·cal·ly,** *adv.* —**ar′cha·is′tic,** *adj.*

arch·an·gel (ärk′ān′jəl), *n.* angel of highest rank. [< L < Gk. See ARCH-, ANGEL.]

Arch·an·gel (ärk′ān′jəl), *n.* seaport in N Russia, on the White Sea.

arch·bish·op (ärch′bish′əp), *n.* bishop of the highest rank.

arch·bish·op·ric (ärch′bish′əp rik), *n.* **1** =archdiocese. **2** position, rank, or dignity of an archbishop.

arch·con·serv·a·tive (ärch′kən sėr′və tiv), *n.* person who is a reactionary. —*adj.* reactionary, esp. of politics.

arch·dea·con (ärch′dē′kən), *n.* assistant to a bishop in the Church of England. —**arch′dea′con·ate,** *n.* —**arch′dea′con·ship,** *n.*

arch·dea·con·ry (ärch′dē′kən ri), *n., pl.* **–ries.** position, rank, or residence of an archdeacon.

arch·di·o·cese (ärch′dī′ə sis; -sēs), *n.* church district governed by an archbishop.

arch·du·cal (ärch′dü′kəl; -dū′-), *adj.* of an archduke or an archduchy.

arch·duch·ess (ärch′duch′is), *n.* **1** wife or widow of an archduke. **2** princess of the former ruling house of Austria.

arch·duch·y (ärch′duch′i), *n., pl.* **–duchies.** territory under the rule of an archduke or archduchess.

arch·duke (ärch′dük′; -dūk′), *n.* prince of the former ruling house of Austria.

arch·e·go·ni·um (är′kə gō′ni əm), *n., pl.* **–ni·a** (-ni ə). the female reproductive organ in ferns, mosses, etc. [< NL, ult. < Gk. *arche* beginning + *gonos* race] —**ar′che·go′ni·al,** *adj.* —**ar′che·go′ni·ate,** *adj.*

arch·en·ceph·a·lon (ärk′en sef′ə lon), *n.* primitive part of the brain.

ar·che·ol·o·gy (är′ki ol′ə ji), *n.* archaeology. —**ar′che·o·log′i·cal, ar′che·o·log′ic,** *adj.* —**ar′che·ol′o·gist,** *n.*

Ar·che·o·zo·ic (är′kē ə zō′ik), *n.* **1** oldest geological period. **2** rocks from this period.

arch·er (är′chər), *n.* **1** person who shoots with a bow and arrows. **2 Archer,** Sagittarius. [< AF < L, < *arcus* bow]

arch·er·y (är′chər i), *n.* **1** practice or art of shooting with bows and arrows. **2** archers. **3** weapons of an archer.

ar·che·type (är′kə tīp), *n.* an original model or pattern from which copies are made, or out of which later forms develop. [< L < Gk.] —**ar′che·typ′al,** *adj.* —**ar′che·typ′i·cal,** *adj.*

arch·fiend (ärch′fēnd′), *n.* **1** chief fiend. **2** Satan.

ar·chi·e·pis·co·pal (är′ki i pis′kə pəl), *adj.* of an archbishop or archbishopric.

ar·chi·e·pis·co·pate (är′ki i pis′kə pit; -pāt), *n.* archbishopric.

Ar·chi·me·des (är′kə mē′dēz), *n.* 287?–212 B.C., Greek mathematician, physicist, and inventor. —**Ar′chi·me′de·an,** *adj.*

ar·chi·pel·a·go (är′kə pel′ə gō), *n., pl.* **–gos, –goes. 1** sea having many islands in it. **2** group of many islands. [< Ital., < *arci-* chief (ult. < Gk. *archi-*) + *pelago* sea (ult. < Gk. *pelagos*); orig., the Aegean] —**ar′chi·pel′a·gic,** *adj.*

archit., architecture.

ar·chi·tect (är′kə tekt), *n.* **1** person whose profession is to design buildings and superintend their construction. **2** person skilled in architecture. **3** maker; creator. [< L < Gk., < *archi-* chief + *tekton* builder]

ar·chi·tec·ton·ic (är′kə tek ton′ik), *adj.* **1** having to do with architecture, construction, or design. **2** showing skill in construction or design. **3** directive. —**ar·chi·tec·ton′i·cal·ly,** *adv.*

ar·chi·tec·ture (är′kə tek′chər), *n.* **1** science or art of building, including design, construction, and decorative treatment. **2** style or special manner of building: *Greek architecture made much use of columns.* **3** construction. **4** a building; structure; edifice. —**ar′chi·tec′tur·al,** *adj.* —**ar′chi·tec′tur·al·ly,** *adv.*

ar·chi·trave (är′kə trāv), *n.* **1** the main beam resting on the top of a column. **2** the molding around a door, window, etc. [< Ital., < *archi-* chief (ult. < Gk.) + *trave* beam (< L *trabs*)]

ar·chives (är′kīvz), *n.pl.* **1** place where public records or historical documents are kept. **2** public records or historical documents. [< F < L < Gk. *archeia* < *arche* government] —**ar·chi′val,** *adj.* —**ar′chi·vist,** *n.*

ar·chon (är′kon), *n.* chief magistrate in ancient Athens. —**ar′chon·ship,** *n.*

arch·priest (ärch′prēst′), *n.* **1** chief priest. **2** chief assistant to a bishop and dean of a cathedral chapter. —**arch′priest′hood,** *n.*

arch·way (ärch′wā′), *n.* **1** passageway with an arch above it. **2** an arch covering a passageway.

arc·tic (ärk′tik; är′tik), *adj.* **1** of or near the North Pole or the north polar region. **2** extremely cold; frigid. —*n.* **1** the north polar region. **2 arctics,** warm, waterproof overshoes. [< L < Gk. *arktikos* of the Bear (constellation) < *arktos* bear]

Arctic Circle or **arctic circle, 1** imaginary boundary of the north polar region running parallel to the equator at 23°30′ south of the North Pole. **2** the polar region surrounded by this parallel.

Arctic Ocean, ocean of the north polar region.

Arctic Zone, region between the Arctic Circle and the North Pole; Frigid Zone.

Arc·tu·rus (ärk tür′əs; -tyür′-), *n.* a very bright star in the northern sky.

ar·den·cy (är′dən si), *n.* being ardent.

ar·dent (är′dənt), *adj.* **1** full of zeal; very enthusiastic; eager; fervent; keen. **2** burning; fiery; hot. **3** glowing. [< F < L, < *ardere* burn] —**ar′dent·ly,** *adv.* —**ar′dent·ness,** *n.*

ar·dor (är′dər), *n.* **1** warmth of emotion; great enthusiasm, fervor; zeal. **2** burning heat. [< L, < *ardere* burn]

ar·du·ous (är′jü əs), *adj.* **1** hard to do; requiring much effort; difficult. **2** using up much energy; strenuous. **3** hard to climb; steep. [< L *arduus* steep] —**ar′du·ous·ly,** *adv.* —**ar′du·ous·ness,** *n.*

are[1] (är; *unstressed* ər), *v.* plural of the present indicative of **be:** *we are, you are, they are.* [OE (Northumbrian) *aron*]

are[2] (âr; är), *n.* in the metric system, a surface measure equal to 100 square meters, or 119.6 square yards. [< F < L *area* AREA]

ar·e·a (âr′i ə), *n.* **1** amount of surface; extent of surface: *an area of 600 square feet.* **2** extent of knowledge or expertise. **3** region; tract: *the Rocky Mountain area.* **4** level space. [< L, piece of level ground] —**ar′e·al,** *adj.*

area code, group of three numbers used to call another region by telephone.

ar·e·a·way (âr′i ə wā′), *n.* area serving as a passageway between buildings.

a·re·na (ə rē′nə), *n.* **1** space where contests or shows take place. **2** building where such events take place: *sports arena.* **3** any place of conflict and trial or effort: *in the public arena.* [< later var. of

L *harena* sand; because floor of Roman arenas was sand]

ar·e·na·ceous (ar′ə nā′shəs), *adj.* sandy.

aren't (ärnt), are not.

a·re·o·la (ə rē′ə lə), *n., pl.* **–lae** (–lē), **–las.** colored area surrounding something.

Ar·es (ār′ēz), *n.* the Greek god of war, identified with the Roman god Mars.

ar·ga·li (är′gə li), *n., pl.* **–li.** 1 a large wild sheep of Asia with big curved horns. 2 the bighorn, or other wild sheep.

ar·gent (är′jənt), *n. Archaic or Poetic.* silver. —*adj.* silvery. [< F < L *argentum*]

Ar·gen·ti·na (är′jən tē′nə), *n.* country in S South America. —**Ar′gen·tine,** *adj., n.* —**Ar′gen·tin′e·an, Ar′gen·tin′i·an,** *n., adj.*

ar·gil (är′jil), *n.* clay, esp. potter's clay. [< F < L < Gk., < *argos* shining]

Ar·give (är′jīv; –gīv), *n., adj.* Greek.

Ar·go (är′gō), *n. Gk. Legend.* 1 ship in which Jason and his companions sailed in search of the Golden Fleece. 2 large southern constellation.

ar·gon (är′gon), *n.* a colorless, odorless, inert gas, an element that forms a very small part of the air. [< NL < Gk. *argos* idle < *a–* without + *ergon* work]

Ar·go·naut (är′gə nôt), *n. Gk. Legend.* one of the men who sailed with Jason in search of the Golden Fleece. —**Ar′go·nau′tic,** *adj.*

Ar·gonne (är′gon), *n.* forest in NE France; site of battles in World War I.

ar·go·sy (är′gə si), *n., pl* **–sies.** 1 large merchant ship. 2 fleet of such ships. [< Ital. *Ragusea* ship of Ragusa, Italian port formerly trading extensively with England]

ar·got (är′gō; –gət), *n.* jargon or slang used by a group of persons: *argot of thieves.* [< F]

ar·gue (är′güu), *v.,* **–gued, –gu·ing.** 1 discuss with someone who disagrees; debate. 2 bring forward reasons for or against: *argue a question.* 3 persuade by giving reasons: *he argued me into going.* 4 try to prove by reasoning; maintain: *Columbus argued that the world was round.* 5 indicate; show; prove; demonstrate; imply: *her rich clothes argue her to be wealthy.* [< OF < L, < *arguere* make clear] —**ar′gu·a·ble,** *adj.* —**ar′gu·er,** *n.*

ar·gu·ment (är′gyə ment), *n.* 1 discussion by persons who disagree; debate. 2 process of reasoning. 3 reason or statement intended to persuade or convince. 4 short statement of what is in a book, poem, etc.

ar·gu·men·ta·tion (är′gyə men tā′shən), *n.* 1 process of arguing. 2 discussion.

ar·gu·men·ta·tive (är′gyə men′tə tiv), *adj.* 1 fond of arguing. 2 controversial. —**ar′gu·men′ta·tive·ly,** *adv.* —**ar′gu·men′ta·tive·ness,** *n.*

Ar·gus (är′gəs), *n.* 1 *Gk. Legend.* giant with a hundred eyes, killed by Hermes. 2 watchful guardian.

a·ri·a (ä′ri ə), *n.* air or melody; melody for a single voice with instrumental or vocal accompaniment. [< Ital. < L *aer* air < Gk.]

Ar·i·ad·ne (ar′i ad′nē), *n. Gk. Legend.* daughter of a king of Crete, who gave Theseus a ball of thread to help him find his way out of the Labyrinth of the Minotaur.

Ar·i·an[1] (ār′i ən; ar′–), *adj.* of or pertaining to Arius or his doctrines. —*n.* believer in the doctrines of Arius. —**Ar′i·an·ism,** *n.*

Ar·i·an[2] (ār′i ən; ar′–), *adj., n.* Aryan.

ar·id (ar′id), *adj.* 1 dry; barren: *desert lands are arid.* 2 dull; uninteresting; lifeless. [< L, < *arere* be dry] —**a·rid′i·ty, ar′id·ness,** *n.* —**ar′id·ly,** *adv.*

Ar·ies (ār′ēz; –i ēz), *n., gen.* **A·ri·e·tis** (ə rī′ ətis). 1 a northern constellation that was thought of as arranged in the shape of a ram. 2 the first sign of the zodiac; the Ram.

a·right (ə rīt′), *adv.* correctly; rightly.

ar·il (ar′il), *n.* accessory covering of certain seeds. [< NL < Med.L *arilli* raisins] —**ar′il·ate,** *adj.*

a·rise (ə rīz′), *v.,* **a·rose, a·ris·en, a·ris·ing.** 1 rise up; get up: *the audience arose.* 2 move upward ascend; mount: *vapors arose from the swamp.* 3 come into being or action; come about; appear; begin: *a great wind arose, accidents arise from carelessness.* 4 originate. 5 rebel. [OE *ārīsan*]

Ar·is·ti·des (ar′əs tī′dēz), *n.* 530?–468? B.C., Athenian statesman and general.

ar·is·toc·ra·cy (ar′əs tok′rə si), *n., pl.* **–cies.** 1 a ruling body of nobles; nobility. 2 any class that is superior because of birth, intelligence, culture, or wealth; upper class. 3 government in which a privileged upper class rules. 4 country or state having such a government. 5 government by the best citizens. [< LL < Gk., < *aristos* best + *krateein* rule]

a·ris·to·crat (ə ris′tə krat; ar′is–), *n.* 1 person who belongs to the aristocracy; noble. 2 person who has the tastes, opinions, manners, etc., of the upper classes. 3 person who favors government by an aristocracy.

a·ris·to·crat·ic (ə ris′tə krat′ik; ar′is–), *adj.* 1 belonging to the upper classes. 2 like an aristocrat in manners; proud; noble. 3 having to do with an aristocracy. 4 dignified. 5 snobbish. —**a·ris′to·crat′i·cal·ly,** *adv.*

Ar·is·toph·a·nes (ar′əs tof′ə nēz), *n.* 448?–385? B.C., Greek writer of comedies.

Ar·is·tot·le (ar′əs tot′əl), *n.* 384–322 B.C., Greek philosopher. —**Ar′is·to·te′lian,** *adj., n.* —**Ar′is·to·te′lian·ism,** *n.*

arith., arithmetic; arithmetical.

a·rith·me·tic (ə rith′mə tik), *n.* 1 science of positive, real numbers; art of computing by figures. 2 textbook or handbook of arithmetic. 3 calculation of the possible outcome of something, such as a political strategy. [< L < Gk. *arithmetike* < *arithmos* number] —**ar′ith·met′i·cal,** *adj.* —**ar′ith·met′i·cal·ly,** *adv.*

arithmetical progression. See **progression** (def. 2).

a·rith·me·ti·cian (ə rith′mə tish′ən; ar′ith–), *n.* expert in arithmetic.

Ar·i·us (ār′i əs; ə rī′əs), *n.* d. A.D. 336, Alexandrian priest who asserted that Christ the Son was subordinate to God the Father.

a ri·ve·der·ci, ar·ri·ve·der·ci (ä rē′va der′chē), *Italian.* until we meet again; goodby.

Ariz., Arizona.

Ar·i·zo·na (ar′ə zō′nə), *n.* southwestern state of the United States. *Abbrev.:* Ariz. —**Ar′i·zo′nan, Ar′i·zo′ni·an,** *adj., n.*

ark (ärk), *n.* 1 large boat in which Noah saved himself, his family, and a pair of each kind of animal from the Flood. 2 any large, clumsy boat or vehicle. 3 the repository of the Jewish tables of the law in a synagogue. [< L *arca* chest]

Ark., Arkansas.

Ar·kan·sas (är′kən sô *for 1;* är kan′zəs *for 2*), *n.* 1 southern state of the United States. *Abbrev.:* Ark. 2. river flowing from C Colorado SE into the Mississippi. —**Ar·kan′san,** *n., adj.*

Ar·ling·ton (är′ling tən), *n.* the largest national cemetery in the United States, in NE Virginia.

arm[1] (ärm), *n.* 1 part of the human body between the shoulder and the hand. 2 forelimb of an animal. 3 anything resembling an arm in shape or use: *the arm of a chair, an arm of the sea.* 4 *Fig.* power; authority. 5 in baseball, ability to throw powerful pitches.

arm in arm, with arms linked.

at arm's length, distant; detached.

twist one's arm, put pressure on.

with open arms, cordially. [OE *earm*] —**arm′less,** *adj.*

arm[2] (ärm), *n.* 1 weapon. See **arms.** 2 branch of the military. —*v.* 1 supply with weapons. 2 prepare for war. 3 provide with a means of defense or attack. [< F < L *arma,* pl.] —**arm′er,** *n.*

ar·ma·da (är mä′də; –mā′–), *n.* 1 fleet of warships. 2 fleet of military aircraft. 3 **the Armada,** the Spanish fleet sent to attack England in 1588. [< Sp. < L *armata armare* to arm. Doublet of ARMY.]

ar·ma·dil·lo (är′mə dil′ō), *n., pl.* **–los.** any of several small burrowing animals of South America and S North America, with an armorlike shell of bony plates. [< Sp., dim. of *armado* armed (one) < L, < *armare* arm]

Ar·ma·ged·don (är′mə ged′ən), *n.* 1 place of a great and final conflict between the forces of good and evil in the book of Revelations. 2 any great and final conflict.

ar·ma·ment (är′mə mənt), *n.* 1 war equipment and supplies. 2 army, navy, and other military forces of a nation. 3 process of equipping or arming for war.

ar·ma·ture (är′mə chûr; –chər), *n.* 1 a piece of soft iron placed in contact with the poles of a magnet. **b** revolving part of an electric motor or dynamo. **c** a movable part of an electric relay, buzzer, etc. **2** wire wound round and round a cable. **3** protective covering. **4** =armor. **5** metal frame to support a clay sculpture. [< L *armatura* < *armare* arm. Doublet of ARMOR.]

arm·chair (ärm′chãr′), *n.* chair with side pieces to support a person's arms or elbows. —*adj.* **1** expressing opinions about something without having experience or actual involvement in it. **2** interested or informed about something but not directly involved.

Ar·me·ni·a (är mē′ni ə; –mēn′yə), *n.* a former country of W Asia, now divided among Turkey, Iran, and Russia. —**Ar·me′ni·an,** *adj., n.*

arm·ful (ärm′fùl), *n., pl.* –**fuls.** as much as one arm or both arms can hold.

arm·hole (ärm′hōl′), *n.* hole for the arm in a garment.

ar·mi·stice (är′mə stis), *n.* temporary stop in fighting; truce. [< NL *armistitium* < L *arma* arms + *sistere* stop, stand]

arm·let (ärm′lit), *n.* **1** an ornamental band for the upper arm. **2** a small inlet.

ar·mor (är′mər), *n.* **1** covering worn to protect the body in fighting. **2** any kind of protective covering. **3** steel or iron plates or other protective covering of a warship or fortification. —*v.* cover or protect with armor. [< OF *armeüre* < L *armatura* < *armare* arm. Doublet of ARMATURE.]

ar·mor·bear·er (är′mər bãr′ər), *n.* attendant who carried the armor or weapons of a warrior.

ar·mored (är′mərd), *adj.* **1** covered or protected with armor. **2** composed of or using armored vehicles.

ar·mor·er (är′mər ər), *n.* **1** person in charge of firearms on a ship, aircraft, etc. **2** manufacturer of firearms. **3** person who made or repaired armor.

ar·mo·ri·al (är mô′ri əl; –mō′-), *adj.* of coats of arms or heraldry.

armorial bearings, the design of a coat of arms.

armor plate, steel or iron plating to protect warships, tanks, etc. —**ar′mor·plat′ed,** *adj.*

ar·mor·y, (är′mər i), *n., pl.* –**mor·ies; 1** place where weapons are kept. **2** place where weapons are made. **3** building with a drill hall, offices, etc., for militia.

arm·pit (ärm′pit′), *n.* the hollow under the arm at the shoulder.

arm·rest (ärm′rest′), *n.* support for the arm while seated in a chair, automobile, airplane, etc.

arms (ärmz), *n. pl.* **1** weapons. **2** fighting; war. **3** symbols and designs used in heraldry or by governments.

bear arms, serve as a soldier.

take up arms, arm to attack or defend.

up in arms, angry; upset.

arms race 1 competition between countries to build and maintain supremacy in military might. **2** *Fig.* competition to add strength to a team, organization, etc.

ar·my (är′mi), *n., pl.* –**mies. 1** large, organized group of soldiers trained and armed for war; troops. **2** Often, **Army.** military organization of a nation, exclusive of its navy. **3** any organized group of people: *the Salvation Army.* **4** very large number; multitude; throng; host. [< OF < L *armata.* Doublet of ARMADA.]

army worm, caterpillar that travels in large numbers and is destructive to crops.

ar·ni·ca (är′nə kə), *n.* **1** a healing liquid used on bruises, sprains, etc., prepared, from the dried flowers, leaves, or roots of a plant of the aster family. **2** the plant itself. [< NL]

Ar·nold (är′nəld), *n.* **Benedict,** 1741–1801, American general in the Revolutionary War who turned traitor.

a·ro·ma (ə rō′mə), *n.* **1** fragrance; spicy odor. **2** distinctive fragrance or flavor; subtle quality. [< L < Gk., spice]

ar·o·mat·ic (ar′ə mat′ik), *adj.* fragrant. —*n.* fragrant plant or substance. —**ar′o·mat′i·cal·ly,** *adv.*

a·rose (ə rōz′), *v.* pt. of **arise.**

a·round (ə round′), *prep.* **1** in a circle about: *travel around the world.* **2** closely surrounding: *she had a coat around her shoulders.* **3** somewhere near: *play around the house.* —*adv.* **1** in a circle: *the tree measures four feet around.* **2** on all sides: *a dense fog lay around.*

around the clock, without stopping, closing, etc.: *work around the clock.*

a·rouse (ə rouz′), *v.,* **a·roused, a·rous·ing. 1** awaken. **2** stir to action; excite; stimulate. —**a·rous′al,** *n.* —**a·rous′er,** *n.*

ar·peg·gi·o (är pej′i ō), *n., pl.* –**gi·os.** *Music.* **1** the sounding of the notes of a chord in rapid succession instead of together. **2** chord sounded in this way. [< Ital., < *arpa* harp < Gmc.]

ar·que·bus (är′kwə bəs), *n.* =harquebus.

ar·raign (ə rān′), *v.* **1** bring before a court for trial. **2** call in question; find fault with; accuse. [< AF *arainer* < VL, < L *ad–* to + *ratio* account] —**ar·raign′er,** *n.* —**ar·raign′ment,** *n.*

ar·range (ə rānj′), *v.,* –**ranged, –rang·ing. 1** put in the proper order; group; organize. **2** settle (a dispute). **3** come to an agreement. **4** plan; prepare; devise. **5** adapt (a piece of music) to voices or instruments for which it was not written. [< OF, < *a* to + *rang* rank[1] < Gmc.] —**ar·range′a·ble,** *adj.* —**arrang′er,** *n.*

ar·range·ment (ə rānj′mənt), *n.* **1** a putting or being put in proper. **2** way or order in which things or persons are put. **3** adjustment; settlement. **4** Usually, **arrangements.** plan; preparation. **5** something arranged in a particular way, as a piece of music.

ar·rant (ar′ənt), *adj.* thoroughgoing; downright. [var. of *errant*] —**ar′rant·ly,** *adv.*

ar·ras (ar′əs), *n.* **1** kind of tapestry. **2** tapestry screen or hangings. [named for *Arras,* a city in France]

ar·ray (ə rā′), *n.* **1** order; formation: *in battle array.* **2** display of persons or things. **3** military force; soldiers; troops. **4** clothes; dress; attire: *bridal array.* —*v.* **1** arrange in order; marshal. **2** dress in fine clothes; adorn. [< OF *a* to + *rei* order < Gmc.] —**ar·ray′er, ar·ray′ment,** *n.*

ar·rear·age (ə rir′ij), *n.* debts; arrears.

ar·rears (ə rirz′), *n. pl.* **1** debts. **2** unfinished work.

in arrears, behind in payments, work, etc. [< OF *arere* < LL *ad retro* to the rear]

ar·rest (ə rest′), *v.* **1** seize by legal authority; apprehend. **2** catch and hold; capture. **3** stop; check; halt. —*n.* **1** a seizing by legal authority. **2** a stopping; checking. **3** any device for arresting motion in a mechanism.

under arrest, held by the authorities; in custody. [< OF < VL, < L *ad–* + *re–* back + *stare* stand] —**ar·rest′er,** *n.* —**ar·rest′ment,** *n.*

ar·rest·ing (ə res′ting) *adj.* capturing and holding attention.

ar·riv·al (ə rīv′əl), *n.* **1** act of arriving; coming. **2** person or thing that arrives.

ar·rive (ə rīv′), *v.,* –**rived, –riv·ing. 1** reach the end of a journey; come to a place. **2** reach a point in any course of action: *arrive at a decision.* **3** be successful. **4** come, as a time, opportunity, etc.; occur. [< OF *ar(r)iver* < VL, < L *ad ripam* to the shore]

ar·ro·gance (ar′ə gəns), *n.* overbearing pride; haughtiness.

ar·ro·gant (ar′ə gənt), *adj.* too proud; haughty; overbearing. [< L, < *ad–* to + *rogare* ask] —**ar′rogant·ly,** *adv.*

ar·ro·gate (ar′ə gāt), *v.,* –**gat·ed, –gat·ing. 1** claim or take without right. **2** attribute or assign without good reasons. [< L, < *ad–* + *rogare* ask] —**ar′ro·ga′tion,** *n.* —**ar′ro·ga′tor,** *n.*

ar·ron·disse·ment (ä rôn dēs mäN′), *n., pl.* –**ments** (-mäN′). **1** in France, the largest administrative subdivision of a department. **2** administrative district of Paris.

ar·row (ar′ō), *n.* **1** a slender, pointed shaft or stick for shooting from a bow. **2** anything resembling an arrow in shape or speed. **3** a sign (→) used to show direction or position. [OE *arwe*]

ar·row·head (ar′ō hed′), *n.* **1** head or tip of an arrow. **2** plant with leaves shaped like arrowheads.

ar·row·root (ar′ō rüt′; –rùt′), *n.* **1** easily digested starch made from the roots of a tropical American plant. **2** the plant itself.

ar·row·wood (ar′ō wùd′), *n.* viburnum or other shrub with a tough, straight stem.

ar·roy·o (ə roi′ō), *n., pl.* **-roy·os.** *SW U.S.* 1 the dry bed of a stream; gully. 2 a small river. [< Sp. < L *arrugia* mine shaft]

ar·se·nal (är′sə nəl), *n.* a place for storing or manufacturing weapons and ammunition for the military. 2 supply of weapons. 3 *Fig.* store or supply of something; *an arsenal of facts.* [< Ital. < Ar. *dār aṣ-ṣinā'a* house (of) the manufacturing]

ar·se·nate (är′sə nāt; -nit), *n.* a salt of arsenic acid.

ar·se·nic (*n.* är′sə nik; *adj.* är sen′ik), *n.* 1 a grayish-white chemical element, As, having a metallic luster and volatilizing when heated. 2 a violent poison that is a compound of this element, As_2O_3, a white, tasteless powder. —*adj.* Also, **ar·sen′i·cal.** of or containing arsenic. [< L < Gk. *arsenikon* < Heb. < OPers., golden]

ar·son (är′sən), *n.* the crime of intentionally setting fire to a building or other property. [< OF < LL *arsio* a burning < L *ardere* burn]

art[1] (ärt), *n.* 1 drawing, painting, and sculpture. 2 drawings, paintings, sculptures; works of art. 3 branch of learning that depends more on special practice than on general principles: *writing compositions is an art; grammar is a science.* 4 **the arts,** *pl.,* branches or divisions of learning as a group: *literature is one of the liberal arts.* 5 skill. 6 human skill; ingenuity. 7 some kind of skill or practical application of skill: *cooking is a household art.* 8 principles; methods. 9 skillfull act. 10 trick. [< OF < L *ars*]

art[2] (ärt), *v. Archaic or Poetic.* are. "Thou art" means "You are." [OE *eart*]

art., 1 article. 2 artillery. 3 artist.

Art De·co or **art de·co** (de′kō), decorative style of the 1920s and 1930s, distinguished by bold use of color and geometric forms.

Ar·te·mis (är′tə mis), *n. Gk. Myth.* the goddess of the hunt, of the forests, of wild animals, and of the moon, identified by the Romans with Diana.

ar·te·ri·al (är tir′i əl), *adj.* 1 pertaining to or resembling the arteries. 2 pertaining to the bright-red blood of the arteries. 3 serving as a main transportation and supply route. —**ar·te′ri·al·ly,** *adv.*

ar·te·ri·o·scle·ro·sis (är tir′i ō sklə rō′sis), *n.* a hardening of the walls of the arteries that makes circulation of the blood difficult. —**ar·te·ri′o·scle·rot′ic** *adj.*

ar·ter·y (är′tər i), *n., pl.* **-ter·ies.** 1 any of the blood vessels or tubes that carry blood from the heart to all parts of the body. 2 a main road; important channel. [< L < Gk. *arteria*]

ar·te·sian well (är tē′zhən), a deep-drilled well. [< F *artésien* of Artois, province where such wells first existed]

art·ful (ärt′fəl), *adj.* 1 crafty; deceitful. 2 skillful; clever. 3 artificial. —**art′ful·ly,** *adv.* —**art′ful·ness,** *n.*

ar·thri·tis (är thrī′tis), *n.* inflammation of a joint or joints. —**ar·thrit′ic,** *adj.*

ar·thro·pod (är′thrə pod), *n.* any of a phylum of invertebrate animals having segmented legs, such as the insects, arachnids, and crustaceans. —**ar·throp′o·dous,** *adj.*

Ar·thur (är′thər), *n.* 1 a legendary king of ancient Britain who gathered about him a famous group of knights. 2 **Chester A.,** 1830–86, the 21st president of the U.S., 1881–85.

Ar·thu·ri·an (är thür′i ən; -thyûr′-), *adj.* of King Arthur and his knights.

ar·ti·choke (är′ti chōk), *n.* 1 thistlelike plant whose flowering head is cooked and eaten. 2 the flowering head. 3 =Jerusalem artichoke. [< Ital. < Provençal < Ar. *al-kharshūf*]

ar·ti·cle (är′tə kəl), *n., v.,* **-cled, -cling.** —*n.* 1 literary composition, complete in itself, but forming part of a magazine, newspaper, or book. 2 clause in a contract, treaty, statute, etc. 3 particular thing; item: *bread is a main article of food.* 4 one of the words *a, an,* or *the* or the corresponding words in certain other languages. —*v.* 1 bind by contract: *an apprentice articled to serve for seven years.* 2 bring charges; accuse. [< F < L *articulus,* dim. of *artus* joint]

article of faith, conviction that does not change.

ar·tic·u·lar (är tik′yə lər), *adj.* of the joints: *arthritis is an articular disease.*

ar·tic·u·late (*adj.* är tik′yə lit; *v.* är tik′yə lāt), *adj., v.,* **-lat·ed. -lat·ing.** —*adj.* 1 uttered in distinct syllables or words. 2 capable of expressing thoughts clearly. 3 made up of distinct parts; distinct. 4 jointed; segmented. —*v.* 1 speak distinctly; express clearly. 2 fit together in a joint. 3 connect by joints. [< L *articulatus* divided into single joints. See ARTICLE.] —**ar·tic′u·late·ly,** *adv.* —**ar·tic′u·late·ness,** *n.* —**ar·tic′u·la′tive,** *adj.* **ar·tic′u·la′tor,** *n.*

ar·tic·u·la·tion (är tik′yə lā′shən), *n.* 1 way of speaking; enunciation. 2 an articulate sound. 3 joint. 4 act or manner of connecting by a joint or joints.

ar·ti·fact, ar·te·fact (är′tə fakt), *n.* anything made by human skill or work. [< L *ars* art + *factus* made]

ar·ti·fice (är′tə fis), *n.* 1 a clever stratagem or trick. 2 trickery; craft. 3 skill. [< F < L *artificium* < *arti*- art + *facere* make]

ar·tif·i·cer (är tif′ə sər), *n.* 1 skilled workman; craftsman. 2 maker.

ar·ti·fi·cial (är′tə fish′əl), *adj.* 1 made by human skill or labor; not natural. 2 made as a substitute for or in imitation of; not real. 3 assumed; false; affected. —**ar′ti·fi′cial·ly,** *adv.* —**ar′ti·fi′cial·ness,** *n.*

artificial insemination, fertilization of an ovum by injection of sperm, especially in breeding livestock.

artificial intelligence, 1 ability through programming of a computer to perform tasks requiring thought when done by a person. 2 branch of computer science concerned with the use and development of computer intelligence.

ar·ti·fi·ci·al·i·ty (är′tə fish′i al′ə ti), *n., pl.* **-ties.** 1 artificial quality or condition. 2 something unnatural or unreal.

ar·til·ler·y (är til′ər i), *n.* 1 rocket launchers and mounted guns; cannon, as distinguished from small arms. 2 part of an army that uses and manages such weapons. 3 science of ballistics and firing of large weapons. [< OF, < *artiller* equip, ult. < *a-* + *tire* order]

ar·til·ler·y·man (är til′ər i mən), **ar·til·ler·ist** (-ər ist), *n., pl.* **-men; -ists.** soldier who belongs to the artillery.

ar·ti·san (är′tə zən), *n.* workman skilled in some industry or trade; craftsman; mechanic. [< F < Ital. *artigiano* < L *ars* art] —**ar′ti·san·al,** *adj.*

art·ist (är′tist), *n.* 1 person who paints pictures. 2 person who is skilled in any of the fine arts, such as sculpture, music, or literature. 3 performer or actor. 4 person who does work with skill and good taste. [< F < Ital. *artista* < VL, < L *ars* art]

ar·tiste (är tēst′), *n.* very skillful performer or worker, especially one who regards work as art. [< French]

ar·tis·tic (är tis′tik), **ar·tis·ti·cal** (-tə kəl), *adj.* 1 of art or artists. 2 done with skill and good taste. 3 having pleasing color and design. 4 having or showing appreciation of beauty. —**artis′ti·cal·ly,** *adv.*

art·ist·ry (är′tis tri), *n., pl.* **-ries.** artistic work; workmanship of an artist.

art·less (ärt′lis), *adj.* 1 without any trickery or deceit; simple. 2 natural. 3 without art; unskilled; unaffected; naive. —**art′less·ly,** *adv.* —**art′less·ness,** *n.*

art nou·veau (nü vō′), *n.* decorative style of the early 20th century distinguished by its use of natural and flowing forms. [< F new art]

art·sy (ärt′sē), *adj.,* **art·si·er, art·si·est.** =arty.

art·y (är′ti), *adj.,* **art·i·er, art·i·est.** trying to be artistic. —**art′i·ness,** *n.*

ar·um (ar′əm), *n.* 1 a plant having heart-shaped or sword-shaped leaves and a partly hooded flower cluster. 2 calla lily. [< L < Gk. *aron*]

-ary, *suffix.* 1 place for ____, as in *library.* 2 collection of ____, as in *statuary.* 3 person or thing that is, does, belongs to, etc., ____, as in *commentary.* 4 of or pertaining to ____, as in *legendary.* 5 being; having the nature of ____, as in *supplementary.* 6 characterized by ____, as in *honorary.* [< L *-arius* or (neut.) *-arium*]

Ar·y·an (ar′i ən; är′-), *n.* 1 the assumed prehistoric language from which the Indo-European languages are derived. 2 person who spoke this language. 3 descendant of this assumed prehistoric group of people. 4 in Nazi use, a non-Jew. —*adj.* 1 Indo-European. 2 of the Aryans. Also, **Arian.**

as[1] (az; *unstressed* əz), *adv.* 1 equally: *as black as coal.* 2 for example: *animals, as dogs, eat meat.* —*conj.* 1 to the same degree or extent that: *she worked as she was told to.* 2 in the same way that: *run as I do.* 3 when; while: *she sang as she worked.* 4 because: *as he came early, we left sooner.* 5 though: *brave as they were, the danger made them afraid.* —*prep.* doing the work of: *who will act as teacher?* —*pron.* 1 a condition or fact that: *she is very careful, as her work shows.* 2 that: *do the same as I do.*

as for, about; concerning; referring to.

as if, as it would be if.

as yet, so far. [OE (unstressed) *ealswā* quite so. See ALSO.]

as² (as), *n., pl.* **as·ses** (as'iz). 1 ancient Roman pound, equal to twelve ounces. 2 ancient Roman coin, worth a few cents. [< L]

as– *prefix. ad–* before *s.*

As, arsenic.

AS, A.S., Anglo-Saxon.

ASAP, as soon as possible.

as·a·fet·i·da, as·a·foet·i·da (as´ə fet'ə də), *n.* gum resin with a garliclike odor, once used in medicine to prevent spasms. Also, **assafetida, assafoetida.** [< Med.L, < *asa* (< Pers. *azā*) mastic + L *fetidus* stinking]

as·bes·tos, as·bes·tus (as bes'təs; az–), *n.* 1 a mineral, a silicate of calcium and magnesium, that does not burn or conduct heat, usually occurring in fibers. 2 a fireproof fabric made of these fibers. [< OF < L < Gk. *asbestos* unquenchable (orig., of quicklime), < *a–* not + *sbennunai* quench]

as·bes·to·sis (as bes tō'sis), *n.* diseased condition of the lungs caused by inhaling asbestos particles.

as·cend (ə send'), *v.* 1 go up; rise; move upward. 2 climb; go to or toward the top of; scale. 3 go toward the source or beginning. 4 go back in time. 5 slope upward. 6 go up in pitch. [< L *ascendere* < *ad–* up + *scandere* climb] —**as·cend'a·ble, as·cend'i·ble,** *adj.* —**as·cend'er,** *n.*

as·cend·ance, as·cend·ence (ə sen'dəns), *n.* ascendancy.

as·cend·an·cy, as·cend·en·cy (ə sen'dən si), *n.* controlling influence.

as·cend·ant, as·cend·ent (ə sen'dənt), *adj.* 1 ascending; rising. 2 superior; dominant; ruling; controlling. —*n.* position of power; controlling influence.

in the ascendant, a in control. **b** increasing in power or influence.

as·cen·sion (ə sen'shən), *n.* 1 act of ascending; ascent. 2 **Ascension, a** the bodily passing of Christ from earth to heaven. **b** Also, **Ascension Day.** a church festival in honor of this on the fortieth day after Easter. —**as·cen'sion·al,** *adj.*

as·cent (ə sent'), *n.* 1 act of going up; a rising. 2 a climbing; upward movement. 3 a going back toward a source or beginning. 4 place or way that slopes up.

as·cer·tain (as´ər tān'), *v.* find out with certainty; determine. [< OF, < *a–* + *certain* CERTAIN] —**as´cer·tain'a·ble,** *adj.*

—**as´cer·tain´a·ble·ness, as´cer·tain´a·bil´i·ty,** *n.* —**as´cer·tain´a·bly,** *adv.* —**as·cer·tain'ment,** *n.*

as·cet·ic (ə set'ik), *n.* 1 person who practices unusual self-denial and devotion, or severe self-discipline for religious reasons. 2 person who refrains from pleasures and comforts. —*adj.* Also, **as·cetical.** refraining from pleasures and comforts; self-denying. [< Gk., < *askeein* exercise; hence, discipline] —**as·cet'i·cal·ly,** *adv.*

as·cet·i·cism (ə set'ə siz əm), *n.* 1 life or habits of an ascetic. 2 doctrine that abstinence and self-denial will train a person to live in conformity with God's will.

as·cid·i·an (ə sid'i ən), *n.* sea animal with a tough saclike covering.

as·cid·i·um (ə sid'i um), *n., pl.* **-cid·i·a** (–sid'i ə). baglike or pitcherlike part of a plant. [< NL < Gk. *askidion,* dim. of *askos* bag]

a·scor·bic acid (ā skôr'bik; ə–), vitamin C, $C_6H_8O_6$.

as·cot (as'kət; –kot), *n.* necktie with broad ends, tied so that the ends may be laid flat, one across the other.

as·cribe (əs krīb'), *v.,* **-cribed, -crib·ing.** 1 assign; attribute: *the police ascribed the automobile accident to fast driving.* 2 consider as belonging: *she ascribed her talent to her mother.* [< OF < L, < *ad–* to + *scribere* write] —**as·crib'a·ble,** *adj.*

as·crip·tion (əs krip'shən), *n.* 1 act of ascribing. 2 statement or words ascribing something.

a·sep·sis (ə sep'sis; ā–), *n.* 1 aseptic condition. 2 aseptic methods or treatment.

a·sep·tic (ə sep'tik; ā–), *adj.* free from germs causing infection. —**a·sep'ti·cal·ly,** *adv.*

a·sex·u·al (ā sek'shù əl), *adj.* 1 having no sex. 2 independent of sexual processes: *reproduction by spore formation is asexual.* —**a·sex´u·al'i·ty,** *n.* —**a·sex'u·al·ly,** *adv.*

ash¹ (ash), *n.* 1 what remains of a thing after it has been thoroughly burned. 2 powdered lava. [OE *æsce* ashes]

ash² (ash), *n.* 1 timber or shade tree that has straight-grained wood. 2 its tough, springy wood. [OE *æsc* the tree]

a·shamed (ə shāmd'), *adj.* 1 feeling shame. 2 unwilling because of shame. —**a·sham'ed·ly,** *adv.* —**a·sham'ed·ness,** *n.*

ash·en¹ (ash'ən), *adj.* 1 like ashes; pale as ashes. 2 of ashes.

ash·en² (ash'ən), *adj.* 1 of the ash tree. 2 made from the wood of the ash tree.

ash·es (ash'iz), *n. pl.* 1 what remains of a thing after it has been burned. 2 what remains of a body after cremation. 3 remains; dead body.

ash·lar, ash·ler (ash'lər), *n.* 1 square stone used in building. 2 masonry made of ashlars. [< OF < VL *axillarium* < *axis* plank]

a·shore (ə shôr'; ə shōr'), *adv., adj.* 1 to the shore. 2 on the shore.

a·shram (ä'shram), *n.* 1 rural retreat or religious community in India. 2 any similar retreat or community.

Ash Wednesday, the first day of Lent.

ash·y (ash'i), *adj.,* **ash·i·er, ash·i·est.** 1 like ashes; pale as ashes. 2 of ashes. 3 covered with ashes.

A·sia (ā'zhə; ā'shə), *n.* the largest continent. China and India are in Asia.

Asia Minor, peninsula of W Asia, between the Black Sea and the Mediterranean.

A·sian (ā'zhən), *n.* native or inhabitant of Asia. —*adj.* of or having to do with Asia or its people.

Asian flu or **Asiatic flu,** kind of influenza caused by a strain of virus first identified in Hong Kong in early 1957.

A·si·at·ic (ā´zhi at'ik; ā´shi-), =Asian.

a·side (ə sīd'), *adv.* 1 on one side; to one side; away: *move the table aside.* 2 out of one's thoughts, consideration, etc.: *put one's troubles aside.* —*n.* actor's remark that the other actors are not supposed to hear.

aside from, a apart from. **b** except for.

as·i·nine (as'ə nīn), *adj.* 1 of or like an ass. 2 stupid; silly. [< L, < *asinus* ass] —**as'i·nine·ly,** *adv.*

as·i·nin·i·ty (as´ə nin'ə ti), *n., pl.* **-ties.** stupidity; silliness.

ask (ask; äsk), *v.* 1 try to find out by words: *why don't you ask?* 2 put a question to; inquire of. 3 claim; demand: *ask too high a price.* 4 invite. 5 need; require. [OE *āscian*] —**ask'er,** *n.*

a·skance (ə skans'), **a·skant** (ə skant'), *adv.* 1 with suspicion. 2 sideways.

a·skew (ə skū'), *adv., adj.* to one side; turned or twisted the wrong way.

a·slant (ə slant'; ə slänt'), *adv.* in a slanting direction. —*prep.* slantingly across. —*adj.* slanting.

a·sleep (ə slēp'), *adj.* 1 sleeping. 2 dull; inactive. 3 numb: *my foot is asleep.* 4 dead. —*adv.* into a condition of sleep.

a·slope (ə slōp'), *adv., adj.* at a slant.

a·so·cial (ā sō'shəl), *adj.* 1 not interested in observing social customs. 2 not interested in associating with other people; unsociable.

asp (asp), *n.* 1 any of several small, poisonous snakes of Africa, esp. the Egyptian cobra. 2 small, poisonous snake of Europe; adder. [< L < Gk. *aspis*]

as·par·a·gus (əs par'ə gəs), *n.* 1 perennial plant of the lily family having scalelike leaves and stems with many branches. 2 green tender shoots of one species, used as a vegetable. [< L < Gk. *asparagos*]

as·par·tame (ə spär'tām), *n.* artificial sweetener.

A.S.P.C.A., American Society for the Prevention of Cruelty to Animals.

as·pect (as'pekt), *n.* 1 look; appearance: *aspect of the countryside.* 2 countenance; expression: *the solemn aspect of a judge.* 3 one side or part or view (of a subject): *various aspects of a plan.* 4 side fronting in a given direction: *the southern aspect of a house.* 5 relative position of planets as determining their supposed influence upon human affairs. [< L, < *ad-* at + *specere* look]

as·pen (as′pən), *n.* poplar tree whose leaves tremble and rustle in the slightest breeze. —*adj.* 1 of this tree. 2 quivering; trembling.

as·per·i·ty (as per′ə ti), *n., pl.* **-ties.** roughness; harshness; severity. [< OF < L, < *asper* rough]

as·per·sion (əs pėr′zhən; –shən), *n.* damaging or false report; slander.

as·phalt (as′fôlt; –falt), *n.* 1 dark-colored substances, much like tar, found in various parts of the world or obtained by evaporating petroleum. 2 mixture of this substance with crushed rock, used for pavements, roofs, etc. —*v.* cover a surface with asphalt. [< LL < Gk. *asphaltos* < Semitic] —**as·phal′tic,** *adj.*

as·pho·del (as′fə del), *n.* 1 plant of the lily family with spikes of white or yellow flowers. 2 *Gk. Myth.* flower of the Greek paradise. 3 daffodil. [< L < Gk. *asphodelos*]

as·phyx·i·a (as fik′si ə), *n.* suffocation or unconscious condition caused by lack of oxygen and excess of carbon dioxide in the blood. [< NL < Gk., < *a-* without + *sphyxis* pulse < *sphyzein* throb]

as·phyx·i·ate (as fik′si āt), *v.,* **-at·ed, -at·ing.** suffocate because of lack of oxygen. —**as·phyx′i·a′tion,** *n.* **as·phyx′i·a′tor,** *n.*

as·pic (as′pik), *n.* kind of jelly made from meat, tomato juice, etc. [< F]

as·pi·dis·tra (as′pə dis′trə), *n.* plant with large, green leaves and very small flowers, used as a house plant. [< NL < Gk. *aspis* shield + *astron* star]

as·pi·rant (əs pīr′ənt; as′pə rənt), *n.* person who aspires; person who seeks a position of honor. —*adj.* aspiring.

as·pi·rate (*v.* as′pə rāt; *adj., n.* as′pə rit), *v.,* **-rat·ed, -rat·ing,** *adj., n. Phonet.* —*v.* 1 pronounce with a breathing or *h*-sound. The *h* in *hot* is aspirated. 2 withdraw by suction. —*adj.* pronounced with a breathing or *h*-sound. —*n.* aspirated sound. [< L *aspiratus.* See ASPIRE.]

as·pi·ra·tion (as′pə rā′shən), *n.* 1 earnest desire; longing. 2 act of drawing air into the lungs; breathing. 3 *Phonet.* **a** an aspirating (of sounds). **b** an aspirated sound. 4 withdrawal by suction.

as·pi·ra·tor (as′pə rā′tər), *n.* apparatus or device employing suction.

as·pire (əs pīr′), *v.,* **-pired, -pir·ing.** 1 have an ambition for something; desire earnestly. 2 rise. [< L, < *ad-* toward + *spirare* breathe] —**as·pir′er,** *n.* —**as·pir′ing·ly,** *adv.*

as·pi·rin (as′pə rin), *n.* drug for headaches, colds, etc., $C_9H_8O_4$. It is the acetate of salicylic acid. [from trademark]

ass (as), *n.* 1 a long-eared mammal of the horse family, serving as a patient, sure-footed beast of burden when domesticated; donkey. 2 stupid fool; silly

person. [OE *assa* < OWelsh < L *asinus*] —**ass′like′,** *adj.*

as·sail (ə sāl′), *v.* 1 set upon with violence; attack. 2 set upon vigorously with arguments, abuse, etc. [< OF < VL < L *ad-* at + *salire* leap] —**as·sail′a·ble,** *adj.* —**as·sail′er,** *n.* —**as·sail′ment,** *n.*

as·sail·ant (ə sāl′ənt), *n.* person who attacks. —*adj.* assailing.

as·sas·sin (ə sas′ən), *n.* murderer, esp. one hired to murder. [< F < Ital. < Ar. *hashshāshīn* HASHISH eaters; with ref. to fanatics who murdered while under the influence of hashish]

as·sas·si·nate (ə sas′ə nāt), *v.,* **-nat·ed, -nat·ing.** kill by a sudden or secret attack; murder. —**as·sas′si·na′tion,** *n.* —**as·sas′si·na′tor,** *n.*

as·sault (ə sôlt′), *n.* 1 sudden, vigorous attack; onslaught; charge. 2 vigorous attack made on traditions, institutions, opinions, etc. 3 *Law.* an attempt or offer to do violence to another. 4 final phase of an attack; close hand-to-hand fighting. —*v.* make an assault on. [< OF, < L *ad-* + *saltare* leap] —**as·sault′a·ble,** *adj.* —**as·sault′er,** *n.*

as·say (*v.* ə sā′; *n.* ə sā′, as′ā), *v.* 1 analyze (an ore, alloy, etc.) to find out the quantity of gold, silver, or other metal in it. 2 try; test; examine. 3 (of ore) contain, as shown by analysis, a certain proportion of metal. —*n.* 1 analysis of an ore, alloy, etc., to find out the amount of metal in it. 2 trial; test; examination. 3 the substance analyzed or tested. 4 list of the results of assaying an ore, drug, etc. [< OF *a(s)sayer,* ult. < LL, < VL *exagere* weigh] —**as·say′a·ble,** *adj.* —**as·say′er,** *n.*

as·sem·blage (ə sem′blij), *n.* 1 group of persons gathered together; assembly. 2 collection; group. 3 a bringing or coming together; meeting. 4 a putting or fitting together, as parts of a machine. 5 work of art made from miscellaneous things.

as·sem·ble (ə sem′bəl), *v.,* **-bled, -bling.** 1 gather or bring together. 2 come together; meet; congregate. 3 put or fit together. [< OF *as(s)embler* < VL *assimulare* bring together < L, compare, ult. < *ad-* to + *similis* like, or *simul* together] —**as·sem′bler,** *n.*

as·sem·bly (ə sem′bli), *n., pl.* **-blies.** 1 group of people gathered together for some purpose; meeting; convention. 2 lawmaking group; legislature. 3 an assembling; gathering: *unlawful assembly.* 4 the act or process of putting or fitting together. 5 parts put together to form a unit. 6 **Assembly,** in some states, the lower branch of the state legislature.

assembly line, row of workers and machines along which work is successively passed until the final product is made.

as·sem·bly·man, As·sem·bly·man (ə sem′bli mən), *n., pl.* **-men.** member of a lawmaking group.

as·sent (ə sent′), *v.* express agreement; agree. —*n.* acceptance of a proposal, statement, etc.; agreement. [< OF < L, *ad-* along with + *sentire* feel, think] —**as·sent′er,** *n.* —**as·sent′ing·ly,** *adv.*

as·sert (ə sėrt′), *v.* 1 state positively; declare; affirm; maintain. 2 insist on (a right, a claim, etc.); defend.

assert oneself, put oneself forward; refuse to be ignored. [< L, < *ad-* to + *serere* join] —**as·sert′a·ble, as·sert′i·ble,** *adj.* —**as·sert′er, as·ser′tor,** *n.*

as·ser·tion (ə sėr′shən), *n.* 1 positive statement; declaration. 2 act of asserting.

as·ser·tive (ə sėr′tiv), *adj.* too confident and certain; positive. —**as·ser′tive·ly,** *adv.* —**as·ser′tive·ness,** *n.*

as·sess (ə ses′), *v.* 1 estimate the value of (property or income) for taxation. 2 fix the amount of (a tax, fine, damages, etc.). 3 put a tax or fine on (a person, property, etc.). 4 portion out as a tax; apportion. 5 consider the importance or value of. [< OF < VL *assessare* fix a tax < L *assidere* < *ad-* by + *sedere* sit] —**as·sess′a·ble,** *adj.*

as·sess·ment (ə ses′mənt), *n.* 1 act of assessing. 2 amount assessed. 3 appraisal of the value or importance of something.

as·ses·sor (ə ses′ər), *n.* person who assesses taxes. —**as·ses′sor·ship,** *n.*

as·set (as′et), *n.* 1 something having value. 2 a single item of property.

as·sets (as′ets), *n. pl.* 1 things of value; property. 2 property that can be used to pay debts. [< OF *asez* enough < L *ad* to + *satis* enough]

as·sev·er·ate (ə sev′ər āt), *v.,* **-at·ed, -at·ing.** declare solemnly; state positively. [< L, < *ad-* + *severus* serious] —**as·sev′er·a′tion,** *n.*

as·si·du·i·ty (as′ə dü′ə ti; –dū′ə–), *n., pl.* **-ties.** careful and steady attention; diligence.

as·sid·u·ous (ə sij′ù əs), *adj.* careful and attentive; diligent. [< L, < *assidere* sit at. See ASSESS.] —**as·sid′u·ous·ly,** *adv.* —**as·sid′u·ousness,** *n.*

as·sign (ə sīn′), *v.* 1 give as a share; allot. 2 appoint, as to a post or duty. 3 name definitely; fix; set; designate. 4 refer; ascribe; attribute. 5 transfer or hand over (property, a right, etc.) legally. —*n.* person to whom property, a right, etc., is legally transferred. [< OF < L, *ad-* to, for + *signum* mark] —**as·sign′a·ble,** *adj.* —**as·sign′a·bil′i·ty,** *n.* —**as·sign′a·bly,** *adv.* —**as·sign′er,** *n.*

as·sig·na·tion (as′ig nā′shən), *n.* 1 illicit meeting of lovers. 2 appointment for a meeting. 3 legal transfer of property, a right, etc. 4 an allotting.

as·sign·ee (ə sī nē′; as′ə nē′), *n.* person to whom some property, right, etc., is legally transferred.

as·sign·ment (ə sīn′mənt), *n.* 1 something assigned. 2 duty, task, position, etc., given to one to perform or fill. 3

an assigning. **4** legal transfer of some property, right, etc.

as·sign·or (ə sī nôr′; as′ə nôr′), *n.* person who legally transfers to another some property, right, etc.

as·sim·i·la·ble (ə sim′ə lə bəl), *adj.* that can be assimilated. **—as·sim′i·la·bil′i·ty,** *n.*

as·sim·i·late (ə sim′ə lāt), *v.,* **-lat·ed, -lat·ing. 1** absorb; digest; incorporate. **2** be absorbed. **3** make like or cause to be like in language, customs, etc. **4** absorb a consonant sound into the sound before or after it. [< L, < *ad-* to + *similis* like] **—as·sim′i·la′tion,** *n.* **—as·sim′ila′tor,** *n.*

as·sim·i·la·tive (ə sim′ə lā′tiv), *adj.* assimilating. **—as·sim′i·la′tive·ness,** *n.*

as·sist (ə sist′), *v.* **1** help; aid. **2** be an assistant. **3** in sports, help a teammate score or complete a play. **—n.** in sports, help given to put a runner out, complete a play, etc. [< F < L, < *ad-* by + *sistere* take a stand] **—as·sist′er,** *Law* **assis′tor,** *n.*

as·sist·ance (ə sis′təns), *n.* help; aid.

as·sist·ant (ə sis′tənt), *n.* helper; aid. **—adj.** helping; assisting. **—as·sist′ant·ship,** *n.*

assisted living, type of housing for people who need some assistance in daily life but are not infirm.

as·size (ə sīz′), *n.* **1** session of a law court. **2** verdict; judgment. **3 assizes,** periodical sessions of court held in each county of England. [< OF]

assn., ass′n., or **Assn.** association.

association football, *esp. Brit.,* soccer.

as·so·ci·a·tive (ə sō′shi ā′tiv), *adj.* **1** tending to associate. **2** pertaining to association. **3** of or having to do with the associative law of numbers. **—asso′ci·a′tive·ly,** *adv.*

associative law, law of numbers that the product or sum of two or more numbers will not change regardless of their order in combination. (4 + 3) +5 and (5 + 3) + 4 both yield 12.

associative memory or **storage,** type of computer data memory.

as·so·nance (as′ə nəns), *n.* **1** resemblance in sound. **2** a substitute for rhyme in which the vowels are alike but the consonants are different, as in *brave—vain, lone—show.* [< F < L, < *ad-* to + *sonare* sound] **—as′so·nant,** *adj., n.* **—as′so·nan′tal,** *adj.*

as·sort (ə sôrt′), *v.* **1** sort out; classify; arrange in sorts. **2** furnish with various sorts. **3** agree; suit; match. **4** associate. [< F, < *a-* to (< L *ad-*) + *sorte* SORT] **—as·sort′er,** *n.* **—as·sort′ment,** *n.*

as·sort·ed (ə sôr′tid), *adj.* **1** selected so as to be of different kinds; various. **2** arranged by kinds; classified.

as·ter (as′tər), *n.* **1** any plant of a widespread genus with colorful, daisylike blossoms. **2** plant of some allied genus, as the China aster. [< L < Gk., star] **—as′ter·like′,** *adj.*

as·ter·isk (as′tər isk), *n.* a star-shaped mark (*) used in printing and writing to call attention to a footnote, indicate an omission, etc. **—v.** mark with an asterisk. [< LL < Gk., dim. of *aster* star]

a·stern (ə stėrn′), *adv.* **1** at or toward the rear of a ship. **2** backward. **3** behind.

as·ter·oid (as′tər oid), *n.* **1** any of the very numerous small planets revolving about the sun between the orbit of Mars and the orbit of Jupiter. **2** any starfish. **—as′ter·oi′dal,** *adj.*

asth·ma (az′mə; as′-), *n.* a chronic disease that causes difficulty in breathing, a feeling of suffocation, and coughing. [< Gk., panting, < *azein* breathe hard]

asth·mat·ic (az mat′ik; as-), *adj.* **1** of or pertaining to asthma. **2** suffering from asthma. **—n.** person suffering from asthma. **—asth·mat′i·cal·ly,** *adv.*

as·tig·mat·ic (as′tig mat′ik), *adj.* **1** having astigmatism. **2** pertaining to astigmatism. **3** correcting astigmatism. **—as′tig·mat′i·cal·ly,** *adv.*

a·stig·ma·tism (ə stig′mə tiz əm), *n.* defect of the eye or of a lens whereby rays of light fail to converge to a focus, thus making objects look indistinct or imperfect. [< *a-* without + Gk. *stigma* point]

a·stir (ə stėr′), *adv., adj.* in motion.

as·ton·ish (əs ton′ish), *v.* surprise greatly; amaze; astound. [var. of *astoun* < OF *estoner* < VL *extonare.* Cf. L *attonare.*] **—as·ton′ished·ly,** *adv.* **—as·ton′ish·er,** *n.*

as·ton·ish·ing (əs ton′ish ing), *adj.* very surprising; amazing. **—as·ton′ish·ing·ly,** *adv.*

as·ton·ish·ment (əs ton′ish mənt), *n.* **1** great surprise; amazement; sudden wonder. **2** anything that causes great surprise.

as·tound (əs tound′), *v.* surprise very greatly; amaze. [earlier *astoun,* var. of *astony* ASTONISH] **—as·tound′ing,** *adj.* **—as·tound′ing·ly,** *adv.*

a·strad·dle (ə strad′əl), *adv., adj.* astride.

as·tra·gal (as′trə gəl), *n. Archit.* a small, convex molding cut into the form of a string of beads.

as·trag·a·lus (as trag′ə ləs), *n., pl.* **-li** (-lī). *Anat.* the uppermost bone of the tarsus; anklebone; talus. [< L < Gk. *astragalos*]

as·tra·khan, as·tra·chan (as′trə kən), *n.* **1** the curly furlike wool on the skin of young lambs from Astrakhan, a district in SW Russia. **2** a woolen cloth resembling it. [named for *Astrakhan*]

as·tral (as′trəl), *adj.* of the stars; starry. [< LL, < *astrum* star < Gk. *astron*]

a·stray (ə strā′), *adj., adv.* out of the right way; straying.

a·stride (ə strīd′), *adj., adv.* **1** with one leg on each side. **2** with legs far apart. **—prep.** with one leg on each side of (something).

as·trin·gent (əs trin′jənt), *adj.* **1** having the property of shrinking or contracting. **2** severe. **—n.** substance that shrinks tissues and checks the flow of blood by

contracting blood vessels, as alum. [< L, < *ad-* to + *stringere* bind] **—astrin′gen·cy,** *n.* **—as·trin′gently,** *adv.*

astrol., astrologer; astrology.

as·tro·labe (as′trə lāb), *n.* an astronomical instrument formerly used for measuring the altitude of the sun or stars. [< OF < Med.L < Gk. *astrolabon,* orig., star-taking < *astron* star + *lambanein* take]

as·trol·o·ger (əs trol′ə jər), *n.* person who claims to interpret the influence of the stars and planets on persons, events, etc.

as·trol·o·gy (əs trol′ə ji), *n.* **1** study of the supposed influence of the stars and planets on persons, events, etc. **2** *Archaic.* practical astronomy. **—as′tro·log′i·cal, as′tro·log′ic,** *adj.* **—as′tro·log′i·cally,** *adv.*

astron., astronomer; astronomical; astronomy.

as·tro·naut (as′trə nôt), *n.* a pilot or member of a crew of a spacecraft.

as·tro·nau·tics (as′trə nô′tiks), *n.* science that deals with spacecraft and space travel. **—as′tronau′ti·cal, as′tro·nau′tic,** *adj.*

as·tron·o·mer (əs tron′ə mər), *n.* expert in astronomy.

as·tro·nom·i·cal (as′trə nom′ə kəl), **as·tronom·ic** (-nom′ik), *adj.* **1** of astronomy; having to do with astronomy. **2** extremely large. **—as′tro·nom′i·cal·ly,** *adv.*

astronomical year, period of the earth's revolution around the sun; solar year.

as·tron·o·my (əs tron′ə mi), *n.* science of the sun, moon, planets, stars, and other celestial bodies, their composition, motions, positions, distances, sizes, etc. [< L < Gk., < *astron* star + *nomos* distribution]

as·tro·phys·ics (as′trō fiz′iks), *n.* branch of astronomy that deals with the physical and chemical characteristics of celestial bodies. **—as′tro·phys′i·cal,** *adj.* **—as′tro·phys′i·cist,** *n.*

As·tro Turf (as′trō tėrf′), *Trademark.* artificial grass.

as·tro·turf (as′trō tėrf′), *n. Fig.* phoney grassroots movement or support for a position, project, candidate, etc., esp. that is government-sponsored.

as·tute (əs tüt′; -tūt′), *adj.* sagacious; shrewd; crafty. [< L, < *astus* sagacity] **—as·tute′ly,** *adv.* **—as·tute′ness,** *n.*

A·sun·ción (ä sün syôn′), *n.* capital of Paraguay.

a·sun·der (ə sun′dər), *adj.* apart; separate. **—adv.** in pieces; into separate parts.

a·sy·lum (ə sī′ləm), *n.* **1** institution for the support and care of people who cannot care for themselves. **2** refuge, as a church for a fugitive or country of sanctuary. [< L < Gk. *asylon* refuge < *a-* without + *syle* right of seizure]

a·sym·me·try (ā sim′ə tri; a–), *n.* lack of symmetry. **—a′sym·met′ric, a′symmet′ri·cal,** *adj.* **—a′sym·met′ri·cal·ly,** *adv.*

as·ymp·tote (as′im tōt), *n. Math.* a straight line that continually approaches a curve, but does not meet it within a finite distance. —**as′ymp·tot′ic, as′ymp·tot′i·cal,** *adj.* —**as′ymp·tot′i·cal·ly,** *adv.*

at (at; *unstressed* ət, it), *prep.* **1** in; on; by; near: *at school.* **2** to; toward: *look at me.* **3** in a condition of: *at war.* **4** on or near the time of: *at midnight.* **5** because of. [OE *æt*]

at., **1** atmosphere. **2** atomic.

At·a·lan·ta (at′ə lan′tə), *n. Gk. Legend.* a maiden famous for her beauty and her speed in running.

at·a·vism (at′ə viz əm), *n.* **1** resemblance to a remote ancestor. **2** reversion to a primitive type. [< L *atavus* ancestor] —**at′a·vist,** *n.* —**at′a·vis′tic,** *adj.* —**at′a·vis′ti·cal·ly,** *adv.*

a·tax·i·a (ə tak′si ə), *n.* inability to coordinate voluntary movements; irregularity in bodily functions or muscular movements. [< NL, Gk., < *a–* without + *taxis* order] —**a·tax′ic,** *adj.*

ate (āt), *v.* pt. of **eat.**

A·te (ā′tē), *n.* the Greek goddess of blind recklessness, later regarded as an avenging goddess.

–ate[1], *suffix.* **1** of or having to do with, as in *collegiate.* **2** having; containing, as in *compassionate.* **3** having the form of; like, as in *stellate.* **4** become, as in *maturate.* **5** cause to be, as in *alienate.* **6** produce, as in *ulcerate.* **7** supply or treat with, as in *aerate.* **8** combine with, as in *oxygenate.* [< L *-atus, -atum,* pp. endings]

ate[2], *suffix. Chem.* a salt formed by the action of an ____ic acid on a base, as in *sulfate.* [special use of *-ate*[1]]

–ate[3], *suffix.* office, rule, or condition of, as in *caliphate, magistrate.* [< L *-atus,* from 4th declension nouns]

A team, the best, most qualified group available for a usually difficult task.

at·el·ier (at′əl yā), *n.* workshop; studio. [< F, orig., pile of chips, < OF *astele* chip, ult. < L *astula*]

a·the·ism (ā′thi iz əm), *n.* **1** belief that there is no God. **2** godless living. [< F, < Gk. *atheos* denying the gods < *a–* without + *theos* a god] —**a′the·ist,** *n.*

a·the·is·tic (ā′thi is′tik), **a·the·is·ti·cal** (–tə kəl), *adj.* of atheism or atheists. —**a′the·is′tical·ly,** *adv.*

A·the·na (ə thē′nə), **A·the·ne** (–nē), *n.* Greek goddess of wisdom, arts, industries, and prudent warfare, identified with the Roman goddess Minerva. Also, **Pallas, Pallas Athena.**

ath·e·nae·um, ath·e·ne·um (ath′ə nē′əm), *n.* **1** scientific or literary club. **2** reading room; library.

Ath·ens (ath′ənz), *n.* capital of Greece, in the SE part. Athens was famous in ancient times for its art and literature. —**A·the′ni·an,** *adj., n.*

a·thirst (ə thėrst′), *adj.* **1** thirsty. **2** eager.

ath·lete (ath′lēt), *n.* person trained in exercises of physical strength, speed,

and skill, esp. one who competes. [< L < Gk., < *athlon* prize]

athlete's foot, *Am.* a contagious skin disease of the feet, caused by a fungus.

ath·let·ic (ath let′ik), *adj.* **1** active and strong. **2** of, like, or suited to an athlete. **3** for ahtletes. **4** having to do with active games and sports. —**ath·let′i·cal·ly,** *adv.*

ath·let·i·cism (ath let′ə siz əm), *n.* **1** the practice of athletics. **2** athletic quality.

ath·let·ics (ath let′iks), *n.* **1** (*usually pl.*) exercises of strength, speed, and skill; active games and sports: *athletics include baseball and basketball.* **2** (*usually as sing.*) the principles of athletic training: *athletics is recommended for every student.*

at-home (ət hōm′), *n.* an informal reception, usually in the afternoon.

–athon or **a-thon,** *combining form,* involving endurance, especially of a difficult or exhausting event: *a six-day sale-athon; a walkathon to raise money for the hospital.*

a·thwart (ə thwôrt′), *adv.* crosswise; across from side to side. —*prep.* **1** across. **2** across the line or course of. **3** in opposition to; against.

a·tilt (ə tilt′), *adj., adv.* tilted.

a·tin·gle (ə ting′gəl), *adj.* tingling.

–ation, *suffix.* **1** act or state of ____ing, as in *admiration.* **2** condition or state of being ____ed, as in *agitation.* **3** result of ____ing, as in *civilization.* [< L *-atio*]

-ative, *suffix.* **1** tending to, as in *talkative.* **2** having to do with, as in *qualitative.* [< L *-ativus*]

At·lan·ta (at lan′tə), *n.* the capital of Georgia, in the NW part.

At·lan·tic (at lan′tik), *n.* ocean east of North and South America, extending to Europe and Africa. —*adj.* **1** of, on, or near the Atlantic Ocean. **2** of or on the Atlantic coast of the U.S. **3** having to do with NATO and its member nations.

At·lan·tis (at lan′tis), *n.* legendary sunken island in the Atlantic.

at·las (at′ləs), *n.* **1** book of maps. **2** book of plates or tables illustrating any subject. **3 Atlas,** *Gk. Legend.* giant who supported the heavens on his shoulders.

Atlas Mountains, mountain range in NW Africa.

ATM, automatic teller machine

at·mos·phere (at′məs fir), *n.* **1** air that surrounds the earth; the air. **2** air in any given place: *a damp atmosphere.* **3** mass of gases that surrounds any celestial body. **4** unit of pressure equal to 14.69 pounds per square inch. **5** surrounding influence. [< NL < Gk. *atmos* vapor + *sphaira* sphere]

at·mos·pher·ic (at′məs fer′ik), *adj.* **1** of, in, or having to do with the atmosphere. **2** caused, produced, or worked by the atmosphere. —*n.* **atmospherics,** radio static. —**at′mos·pher′i·cal,** *adj.* —**at′mos·pher′i·cal·ly,** *adv.*

at. no., atomic number.

at·oll (at′ol; ə tol′), *n.* a ring-shaped coral island enclosing or partly enclosing a lagoon. [? < Malayalam *aḍal* uniting]

at·om (at′əm), *n.* **1** smallest particle of a chemical element that can take part in a chemical reaction without being permanently changed. **2** a very small particle; tiny bit. [< L < Gk. *atomos* indivisible < *a–* not + *tomos* a cutting]

a·tom·ic (ə tom′ik), *adj.* **1** of or having to do with atoms. **2** using atomic energy. **3** separated into atoms. **4** of or pertaining to atomic bombs. **5** *Fig.* extremely small; minute. —**a·tom′i·cal,** *adj.* —**a·tom′i·cal·ly,** *adv.*

atomic age, era marked by the first use of atomic energy.

atomic bomb, atom bomb, bomb that uses the splitting of atoms to cause an explosion of tremendous force. Also, **A-bomb.**

atomic clock, a highly accurate clock, that uses atomic vibrations as its standard of accuracy.

atomic energy, energy present in atoms and released either under control in a reactor or uncontrolled, as in a bomb.

atomic mass, mass of an atom; physical atomic weight.

atomic number, number used in describing an element and giving its relation to other elements. It is the number of positive charges on the nucleus of an atom of the element.

atomic pile or **reactor.** See **reactor.**

atomic submarine, submarine powered by a reactor.

atomic theory, theory that all matter is composed of atoms, esp. the modern theory that an atom is made of a nucleus of neutrons and protons around which electrons speed.

atomic weight, weight of an atom of a chemical element.

at·om·ize (at′əm īz), *v.,* **–ized, –iz·ing. 1** separate into atoms. **2** change (a liquid) into a fine spray. —**at′om·i·za′tion,** *n.* —**at′om·iz′er,** *n.*

a·ton·al (ā tōn′əl), *adj.* without tonality. —**a·ton′al·ism,** *n.* —**a·ton′al·is′tic,** *adj.* —**a′ton·al′i·ty,** *n.* —**a·ton′al·ly,** *adv.*

a·tone (ə tōn′), *v.,* **a·toned, a·ton·ing.** make up; make amends (*for*). [< *atonement*] —**a·ton′er,** *n.*

a·tone·ment (ə tōn′mənt), *n.* **1** giving satisfaction for a wrong, loss, or injury; amends. **2 the Atonement,** reconciliation of God with sinners through the sufferings and death of Christ. [< *at onement* a being at one, i.e., in accord]

a·top (ə top′), *adv.* on or at the top. —*prep.* on the top of.

a·tri·um (ā′tri əm), *n., pl.* **a·tri·a** (ā′tri ə). **1** the main room of an ancient Roman house. **2** hall; court. **3** any of various cavities or sacs in marine animals. [< L]

a·tro·cious (ə trō′shəs), *adj.* **1** very wicked or cruel; very savage or brutal. **2** very bad; abominable. —**a·tro′cious·ly,** *adv.* —**a·tro′ciousness,** *n.*

a·troc·i·ty (ə tros′ə ti), *n., pl.* **–ties. 1** very great wickedness or cruelty. **2** very cruel or brutal act. **3** very bad blunder as something inappropriate or in bad taste. [< L, < *atrox* fierce < *ater* dark]

at·ro·phy (at′rə fi), *n., v.,* **–phied, –phy-ing.** —*n.* a wasting away of a part or parts of the body. —*v.* waste away. [< LL < Gk., < *a–* without + *trophe* nourishment] —**a·troph′ic,** *adj.* —**at′ro·phied,** *adj.*

at·ro·pine (at′rə pēn; –pin), **at·ro·pin** (–pin), *n.* a poisonous drug, $C_{17}H_{23}NO_3$, obtained from belladonna and similar plants, that relaxes muscles and dilates the pupil of the eye. [< NL *Atropa* belladonna < Gk. *Atropos* one of the Fates]

at·tach (ə tach′), *v.* **1** fasten (to). **2** join. **3** assign; appoint: *a captain attached to a new ship.* **4** affix: *attach one's signature.* **5** fasten itself; belong: *the blame attaches to you.* **6** bind by affection: *attached to his dog.* **7** take (property) by legal authority. [< OF *atachier* < L *ad–* to + Gmc. ancestor of OF *tache* a fastening, a nail. See TACK.] —**at·tach′a·ble,** *adj.* —**attached′,** *adj.*

at·ta·ché (at′ə shā′; ə tash′ā), *n.* person belonging to the official staff of an ambassador or minister to a foreign country. [< F. See ATTACH.] —**at′ta-ché′ship,** *n.*

at·tach·ment (ə tach′mənt), *n.* **1** an attaching. **2** a being attached. **3** thing attached. **4** means of attaching; fastening. **5** bond of affection. **6** legal taking of a property.

at·tack (ə tak′), *v.* **1** use force or weapons on to hurt; assail; assault. **2** talk or write against; criticize: *the article attacked the mayor's record.* **3** begin to work vigorously on: *attack a problem.* **4** act harmfully on: *a virus that attacks both young and old.* **5** make an attack. —*n.* **1** sudden occurrence of illness, discomfort, etc. **2** act or fact of attacking. **3** offensive part of an action or proceeding. **4** start of vigorous work on something, as a problem or task. [< F < Ital. *attaccare.* See ATTACH.] —**at·tack′a·ble,** *adj.* —**at-tack′er,** *n.*

at·tain (ə tān′), *v.* **1.** arrive at in due course; reach, as by effort or progress. **2** gain; accomplish; achieve. **3** succeed in coming to or getting. [< OF *ataindre* < VL, < *ad–* to + *tangere* touch] —**at-tain′a·ble,** *adj.* —**at·tain′a·bil′i·ty, at-tain′a·ble·ness,** *n.* —**at·tain′er,** *n.*

at·tain·der (ə tān′dər), *n.* loss of property and civil rights as the result of being sentenced to death or being outlawed. [< OF *ataindre* attain; infl. by F *taindre* TAINT]

at·tain·ment (ə tān′mənt), *n.* **1** act or fact of attaining. **2** something attained. **3** accomplishment; ability.

at·taint (ə tānt′), *v.* **1** condemn to death and loss of property and civil rights. **2** disgrace. —*n.* disgrace. [< OF *ataint,* pp. of *ataindre* ATTAIN] —**at·taint′ment,** *n.*

at·tar (at′ər), *n.* perfume made from the petals of roses or other flowers. [< Pers. < Ar. *iṭr*]

at·tempt (ə tempt′), *v.* **1** make an effort at; try; endeavor. **2** try to take or destroy (life, etc.). —*n.* **1** a putting forth of effort to accomplish something, esp. something difficult. **2** an attack, as on one's life. [< L, < *ad–* + *temptare* try] —**at-tempt′a·ble,** *adj.* —**at·tempt′a·bil′i·ty,** *n.* —**attempt′er,** *n.*

at·tend (ə tend′), *v.* **1** be present at: *attend class.* **2** give care and thought; pay attention: *attend to directions.* **3** apply oneself. **4** go with; accompany: *attend the king.* **5** go with as a result: *disease attends filth.* **6** wait on; care for; tend: *a nurse attended the injured.* [< OF < L, < *ad–* toward + *tendere* stretch] —**at·tend′er,** *n.*

at·tend·ance (ə ten′dəns), *n.* **1** act of attending. **2** persons attending.

at·tend·ant (ə ten′dənt), *adj.* **1** waiting on another to help or serve. **2** going with as a result; accompanying. **3** present: *attendant hearers.* —*n.* **1** person who waits on another, such as a servant. **2** accompanying thing or event. **3** person who is present.

at·ten·tion (ə ten′shən), *n.* **1** act or fact of attending. **2** ability to give care and thought. **3** care and thought; application; concentration. **4** courtesy; deference; civility. **5** military attitude of readiness. —*interj.* command to soldiers to come to attention.

attentions, acts of devotion or courtesy, esp. of an admirer.

come to attention, take a straight and still position.

stand at attention, stand straight and still. [< L *attentio.* See ATTEND.]

at·ten·tive (ə ten′tiv), *adj.* **1** giving attention. **2** courteous; polite. —**at·ten′tive·ly,** *adv.* —**atten′tive·ness,** *n.*

at·ten·u·ate (ə ten′ú āt), *v.,* **–at·ed, –at-ing. 1** make or become thin or slender. **2** weaken; reduce. **3** make less dense; dilute. [< L, < *ad–* + *tenuis* thin] —**at-ten′u·a′tion,** *n.*

at·test (ə test′), *v.* **1** give proof or evidence of. **2** declare to be true or genuine; certify. **3** bear witness; testify. [< L, < *ad–* to + *testis* witness] —**at′tes·ta′tion,** *n.* —**at·test′er, at·tes′tor,** *n.*

at·tic (at′ik), *n.* **1** space just below the roof in a house. **2** a low story above an entablature or main cornice of a building. [< F < L *Atticus* Attic < Gk.]

At·tic (at′ik), *adj.* **1** of Attica; of Athens; Athenian. **2** simple; elegant; refined.

At·ti·ca (at′ə kə), *n.* district in ancient Greece which included Athens.

At·ti·la (at′ə lə), *n.* died A.D. 453, king of the Huns A.D. 433–453.

at·tire (ə tīr′), *v.,* **–tired, –tir·ing,** *n.* dress; array. [< OF *atirer* arrange < *a–* to (< L *ad–*) | *tire* row < Gmc.] —**at·tire′ment,** *n.* —**at·tir′er,** *n.*

at·ti·tude (at′ə tüd; –tūd), *n.* **1** disposition or manner toward a person or thing. **2**

position of the body appropriate to an action, purpose emotion, etc.; posture, pose. **3** position of an aircraft, spacecraft, etc. in flight in relation to some reference line or plane, as the horizon. [< F < Ital. < LL *aptitudo* APTITUDE]

at·ti·tu·di·nize (at′ə tü′də nīz; –tū′–), *v.,* **–nized, –niz·ing.** pose for effect. —**at′ti-tu′diniz′er,** *n.*

attn or **attn.,** attention.

at·tor·ney (ə tėr′ni), *n., pl.* **–neys. 1** lawyer. **2** person who has power to act for another; agent. [< OF *atourné,* pp. of *atourner* assign, appoint < *a–* to + *tourner* TURN] —**at·tor′ney·ship,** *n.*

attorney general, *n., pl.* **attorneys general, attorney generals. 1** the chief law officer of a country. **2 a** the chief law officer of the United States. **b** the chief law officer of a state of the United States.

at·tract (ə trakt′), *v.* **1** draw to oneself: *a magnet attracts iron.* **2** be pleasing to; win the attention and liking of; fascinate. [< L *attractus* < *ad–* to + *trahere* draw] —**at·tract′a·ble,** *adj.* —**at·tract′a·bil′i-ty,** *n.* —**at·trac′tor, at·tract′er,** *n.*

at·trac·tion (ə trak′shən), *n.* **1** act or power of attracting. **2** thing that delights or attracts people. **3** charm; fascination. **4** force exerted by molecules on one another, which holds them together.

at·trac·tive (ə trak′tiv), *adj.* **1** pleasing; winning attention and liking; alluring. **2** attracting; magnetic. **at·trac′tive·ly,** *adv.* —**at·trac′tive·ness,** *n.*

attrib., **1** attribute. **2** attributive.

at·trib·ute (*v.* ə trib′ūt; *n.* at′rə būt), *v.,* **–ut·ed, –ut·ing.** —*v.* **1** think of as caused by: *attributed her success to hard work.* **2** consider (something) as belonging or appropriate (to a person or thing); ascribe; credit: *attribute loyalty to a dog.* —*n.* **1** a quality considered as belonging to a person or thing; a characteristic; trait. **2** an object considered appropriate to a person, rank, or office; symbol. **3** adjective; word or phrase used as an adjective. [< L, < *ad–* to + *tribuere* assign, orig., divide among the tribes < *tribus* tribe] —**at·trib′ut·a·ble,** *adj.* —**at·trib′ut·er, at·trib′u·tor,** *n.*

at·tri·bu·tion (at′rə bū′shən), *n.* **1** act of attributing. **2** thing attributed.

at·trib·u·tive (ə trib′yə tiv), *adj.* **1** expressing a quality or attribute. **2** that attributes. **3** of or like an attribute. —*n.* an attributive word. In the phrase "big brown dog," *big* and *brown* are attributives. —**at·trib′u·tive·ly,** *adv.* —**attrib′u-tive·ness,** *n.*

at·tri·tion (ə trish′ən), *n.* **1** wearing away by friction. **2** any gradual process of wearing down: *war of attrition.* [< L *attritio* < *ad–* against + *terere* rub]

at·tune (ə tün′; ə tūn′), *v.,* **–tuned, –tun-ing.** put in tune or accord; tune. —**at-tune′ment,** *n.*

atty., attorney.

ATV, all-terrain vehicle.

at. wt., atomic weight.

a·typ·i·cal (atip′ə kəl), *adj.* not typical; abnormal.

Au, gold.

au·burn (ô′bǝrn), *n., adj.* reddish brown. [< OF *auborne* < L *alburnus* whitish < *albus* white; appar. confused with *brown*]

auc·tion (ôk′shǝn), *n.* a public sale in which each thing is sold to the highest bidder. —*v.* sell at an auction. [< L *auctio* < *augere* increase]

auc·tion·eer (ôk´shǝn ir′), *n.* person who conducts auctions. —*v.* sell at an auction.

au·da·cious (ô dā′shǝs), *adj.* **1** bold; daring. **2** too bold; impudent. [< F, < *audace* daring (n.) < L *audacia*, ult. < *audere* dare] —**au·da′cious·ly**, *adv.* —**au·da′cious·ness**, *n.*

au·dac·i·ty (ô das′ǝ ti), *n., pl.* –**ties. 1** boldness; reckless daring. **2** rude boldness.

au·di·ble (ô′dǝ dǝl), *adj.* capable of being heard. [< Med.L. < L *audire* hear] —**au′di·bil′i·ty, au′di·ble·ness**, *n.* —**au′di·bly**, *adv.*

au·di·ence (ô′di ǝns), *n.* **1** people gathered in a place to hear or see. **2** any person within hearing. **3** chance to be heard; hearing. **4** formal interview with a person of high rank. **5** act or fact of hearing. **6** readers of a book, newspaper, or magazine. [< OF < L *audientia* hearing < *audire* hear]

au·di·o (ô′di ō), *adj.* **1** having to do with electronic frequencies that are audible, as sound waves. **2** of or pertaining to the transmission or reception of sound in television, mobile telephones, etc. —*n.* reproduction of sound, especially electronically. [L, I hear]

audio-, *combining form.* **1** hearing, as in *audiometer = device that measures hearings.* **2** sound, as in *audiovisual = sound and sight.*

au·di·o·tape (ô′dē ō tāp′), *n.* tape recording of sound.

audio frequency, frequency of sound vibrations from about 20 to about 20,000 cycles per second.

au·di·o·phile (ô′di ǝ fīl′), *n.* person who is an enthusiast of high-fidelity sound reproduction.

au·dit (ô′dit), *n.* **1** an official examination and check of accounts. **2** statement of an account that has been examined and checked authoritatively. —*v.* **1** examine and check (accounts) officially. **2** attend (a course) as an auditor. [< L *auditus* a hearing < *audire* hear]

au·di·tion (ô dish′ǝn), *n.* **1** a hearing to test the voice of a singer, speaker, etc. **2** act of hearing. **3** power or sense of hearing. —*v.* give (a person) an audition.

au·di·tor (ô′dǝ tǝr), *n.* **1** person who audits accounts. **2** person who attends a course, but not for credit toward a degree. **3** hearer; listener. —**au′di·tor·ship′**, *n.*

au·di·to·ri·um (ô′dǝ tô′ri ǝm; –tō–), *n., pl.* –**to·ri·ums, –to·ri·a** (–tô′ri·ǝ, –tō′–).

1 a large room for an audience in a church, theater, school, etc. **2** building especially designed for the giving of lectures, concerts, etc.

au·di·to·ry (ô′dǝ tô′ri; –tō′–), *adj., n., pl.* –**ries.** —*adj.* of or having to do with hearing, the sense of hearing, or the organs of hearing. —*n.* **1** audience. **2** =auditorium.

Au·du·bon (ô′dǝ bon), *n.* **John James,** 1785–1851, American ornithologist and artist.

Aug., August.

au·ger (ô′gǝr), *n.* tool for boring holes in wood, rock, etc. [OE *nafugār*, orig., a nave borer < *nafu* nave of a wheel + *gār* spear; ME *a nauger* taken as *an auger*]

aught[1] (ôt), *n.* anything: *you may go for aught I care.* —*adv.* at all: *help came too late to avail aught.* Also, **ought.** [OE *āwiht* < *ā–* ever + *wiht* a thing]

aught[2] (ôt), *n.* zero; cipher; nothing. Also, **ought, nought.** [see NAUGHT; *a naught* taken as *an aught*]

aug·ment (ôg ment′), *v.* increase; enlarge. [< L, < *augere* increase] —**aug·ment′a·ble**, *adj.* —**aug′men·ta′tion**, *n.* —**aug·ment′a·tive**, *adj.* —**aug·ment′er**, *n.*

au grat·in (ō grat′ǝn; grä′tǝn; *Fr.* ō grä taN′), *French.* cooked with crumbs or cheese, or both.

au·gur (ô′gǝr), *n.* **1** priest in ancient Rome who made predictions and gave advice. **2** prophet; fortuneteller. —*v.* **1** predict; foretell. **2** be a sign. [< L, appar. increase, growth (of crops), personified in ritual service, < *augere* increase]

au·gu·ry (ô′gyǝ ri), *n., pl.* –**ries. 1** indication; sign; omen. **2** art or practice of foretelling the future.

Au·gust (ô′gǝst), *n.* the eighth month of the year, containing 31 days. [after *Augustus*]

au·gust (ô gust′), *adj.* inspiring reverence and admiration; majestic; venerable. [< L, < unrecorded *augus* increase, power < *augere* to increase] —**au·gust′ly**, *adv.* —**au·gust′ness**, *n.*

Au·gus·ta (ô gus′tǝ), *n.* capital of Maine, in the SW part.

Au·gus·tine (ô′gǝs tēn; ô gus′tin), *n.* **1 Saint,** A.D. 354–430, bishop of N Africa and one of the great leaders in the early Christian church. **2 Saint,** died A.D. 604, Roman monk sent to preach Christianity in England in A.D. 597. —**Au′gus·tin′i·an**, *adj., n.*

Au·gus·tus (ô gus′tǝs), *n.* (*Augustus Caesar*), 63 B.C.–A.D. 14, title of Gaius Octavianus (Octavian) as first emperor of Rome, 27 B.C.–A.D. 14. —**Au·gus′tan**, *adj.*

auk (ôk), *n.* northern sea bird with short wings used only as paddles. [< Scand. *ālka*]

auk·let (ôk′lit), *n.* small kind of auk.

au lait (ō lā′), *French.* with milk.

auld (ôld), *adj. Scot.* old.

auld lang syne (ôld′ lang sīn′; zīn′), *Scot.* old times; long ago in one's life.

aunt (ant; änt), *n.* **1** sister of one's father or mother. **2** uncle's wife. [< OF < L *amita* father's sister]

au·ra (ô′rǝ), *n., pl.* **au·ras, au·rae** (ô′rē). **1** something supposed to come from and surround a person or thing as an atmosphere. **2** something that comes from or is given off by a substance, as the scent of freshly mown hay. [< L < Gk.]

au·ral (ô′rǝl), *adj.* of the ear; having to do with hearing. —**au′ral·ly**, *adv.*

au·re·ate (ô′ri it; –āt), *adj.* **1** golden; gilded. **2** brilliant; glowing. [< L, < *aurum* gold]

au·re·ole (ô′ri ōl), **au·re·o·la** (ô rē′ǝ lǝ), *n.* **1** encircling radiance; halo. **2** a ring of light surrounding the sun. [< L *aureola* (*corona*) golden (crown) < *aurum* gold]

au re·voir (ō rǝ vwär′), good-by; till we see each other again. [< F; *revoir* < L, < *re–* again + *videre* see]

au·ri·cle (ô′rǝ kǝl), *n.* **1 a** chamber of the heart that receives the blood from the veins. **b** outer part of the ear. **2** earlike part. [< L *auricula*, dim. of *auris* ear] —**au′ri·cled**, *adj.*

au·ric·u·lar (ô rik′yǝ lǝr), *adj.* **1** of or near the ear. **2** said privately. **3** perceived by the sense of hearing. **4** shaped like an ear. **5** having to do with an auricle of the heart. —**au·ric′u·lar·ly**, *adv.*

au·rif·er·ous (ô rif′ǝr ǝs), *adj.* yielding gold. [< L, < *aurum* gold + *ferre* bear] —**au·rif′er·ous·ly**, *adv.*

au·rochs (ô′roks), *n., pl.* **–rochs. 1** European bison, now almost extinct. **2** extinct wild ox. [< G *auerochs*]

Au·ro·ra ô rô′rǝ, –rō′–), *n.* **1** Roman goddess of the dawn. **2 aurora,** streamers or bands of light appearing in the sky at night. —**au·ro′ral**, *adj.* —**au·ro′ral·ly**, *adv.*

aurora aus·tra·lis (ôs trā′lis), streamers or bands of light appearing in the southern sky at night.

aurora bo·re·a·lis (bō′ri al′is; –ā′lis; bō′–), streamers or bands of light appearing in the northern sky at night.

Aus. 1 Australia. **2** Austria.

Aus·sie (ô′sē), *n.* Australian.

aus·pice (ôs′pis). *n., pl.* **aus·pic·es** (ôs′pǝ siz). **1 auspices,** patronage. **2** favorable circumstance; indication of success. **3** divination or prophecy, esp. one made from the flight of birds. **4** omen; sign. [< F < L *auspicium* < *avis* bird + *specere* look at. See def. 3.]

aus·pi·cious (ôs pish′ǝs), *adj.* **1** with signs of success; favorable. **2** fortunate. —**aus·pi′cious·ly**, *adv.* —**aus·pi′cious·ness**, *n.*

Aust. 1 Australia. **2** Austria. **3** Austrian.

aus·tere (ôs tir′), *adj.* **1** harsh to the feelings; stern in manner. **2** strict in self-discipline or in self-restraint. **3** severely simple. **4** somber. [< L < Gk. *austeros* < *auein* dry] —**aus·tere′ly**, *adv.*

aus·ter·i·ty (ôs ter′ǝ ti), *n., pl.* –**ties. 1** sternness; severity. **2 austerities,** severe practices.

Aus·tin (ôs′tǝn), *n.* capital of Texas in the C part.

Austl. or **Austr.** Australia.

aus·tral (ôs´trəl), *adj.* 1 southern. 2 **Austral, a** Australian. **b** Australasian. [< L, < *auster* the south wind; akin to EAST]

Aus·tral·a·sia (ôs´trəl ā´zhə; –shə), *n.* Australia, Tasmania, New Zealand, and nearby islands. —**Aus´tral·a´sian,** *adj., n.*

Aus·tral·ia (ôs trāl´yə), *n.* 1 continent SE of Asia. 2 **Commonwealth of,** country that includes this continent and Tasmania. —**Aus·tral´ian,** *adj., n.*

Aus·tral·ian ballot (ôs trāl´yən), ballot with the names of all candidates on it, which is marked secretly.

Aus·tri·a (ôs´tri ə), *n.* country in C Europe. —**Aus´tri·an,** *adj., n.*

Aus·tri·a-Hun·ga·ry (ôs´tri ə hung´gə ri), *n.* a former monarchy in C Europe. —**Aus´tro-Hun·gar´i·an ,** *adj.*

Aus·tro·ne·sia (ô´strō nē´zhə), *n.* South and mid-Pacific islands. —**Aus´tro·ne´-sian,** *adj., n.*

au·tar·chy (ô´tär ki), *n., pl.* –**chies.** 1 autocracy. 2 autarky. —**au·tar´chic, au·tar´chi·cal,** *adj.*

au·tar·ky (ô´tär ki), *n., pl.* –**kies.** independence of imports from other nations. —**au·tar´ki·cal,** *adj.* —**au´tar·kist,** *n.*

au·teur (ô tœr´), *n. French.* 1 film director whose films have the distinctive personal style of an author. 2 author.

auth. 1 author. 2 authorized.

au·then·tic (ô then´tik), **au·then·ti·cal** (–tə kəl), *adj.* 1 reliable: *an authentic count.* 2 genuine: *an authentic signature.* 3 authoritative. [< L < Gk., < *auto–* by oneself + *hentes* one who acts] —**au·then´ti·cal·ly,** *adv.*

au·then·ti·cate (ô then´tə kāt), *v.,* –**cat·ed,** –**cat·ing.** 1 establish the truth of. 2 establish the authorship of. —**au·then´ti·ca´-tion,** *n.* —**au·then´ti·ca´tor,** *n.*

au·then·tic·i·ty (ô´then tis´ə ti), *n.* 1 reliability. 2 genuineness.

au·thor (ô´thər), *n.* 1 person who writes books, stories, or articles; writer. 2 an author's publications: *have you read this author?* 3 person who creates or begins anything; creator. [< OF < L *auctor* < *augere* increase]

au·thor·i·tar·i·an (ə thôr´ə tār´i ən; –thor´–), *adj.* favoring obedience to authority instead of individual freedom. —*n.* person who supports authoritarian principles. —**au·thor´i·tar´i·an·ism,** *n.*

au·thor·i·ta·tive (ə thôr´ə tā´tiv; ə thor´–), *adj.* 1 having authority; officially ordered. 2 commanding: *authoritative tones.* 3 that ought to be believed or obeyed. —**au·thor´i·ta´tive·ly,** *adv.* —**au·thor´i·ta´tive·ness,** *n.*

au·thor·i·ty (ə thôr´ə ti; ə thor´–), *n., pl.* –**ties.** 1 legal power to enforce obedience; control, jurisdiction. 2 influence that creates respect and confidence; prestige. 3 source of correct information or wise advice. 4 expert on some subject. 5 legal opinion that can serve as a precedent.

the authorities, a government officials. **b** persons in control. [< F < L *auctoritas*]

au·thor·ize (ô´thər īz), *v.,* –**ized, –iz·ing.** 1 give power or right to; empower. 2 make legal; sanction. 3 give authority for; justify. —**au´thor·i·za´tion,** *n.* —**au´thor·iz´er,** *n.*

au·thor·ized (ô´thər īzd), *adj.* 1 having authority. 2 supported by authority.

Authorized Version, the English translation of the Bible published in 1611; the King James Version.

au·thor·ship (ô´thər ship), *n.* 1 occupation of an author. 2 source; origin.

au·tism (ô´tiz´əm), *n.* disorder that appears in young children, characterized by an inability to relate to others. —**au·tis´tic,** *adj.*

au·to (ô´tō), *n., pl.* **au·tos.** automobile.

auto-, *combining form.* 1 self, as in *auto-biography, auto-intoxication.* 2 automobile, as in *autobus.* [< Gk.; also (before vowels and *h*), *aut*–]

Au·to·bahn (ou´tō bän´), *n., pl.* –**bahns.** in Germany, a four-lane highway with no speed limit.

au·to·bi·og·ra·phy (ô´tə bī og´rə fi; –bi–), *n., pl.* –**phies.** story of a person's life written by himself or herself. —**au´to-bi·og´ra·pher,** *n.* —**au´to·bi´o·graph´ic, au´to·bi´o·graph´i·cal,** *adj.* —**au´to-bi´o·graph´i·cal·ly,** *adv.*

au·to·clave (ô´tə klāv), *n.* a strong, closed vessel used for sterilizing, cooking, etc. —*v.* cook or sterilize using an autoclave. [< F, < *auto–* self + L *clavis* key]

au·toc·ra·cy (ô tok´rə si), *n., pl.* –**cies.** 1 government having absolute power over its citizens. 2 absolute authority; unlimited power over a group. —**au·to·crat´ic, au´to·crat´i·cal,** *adj.* —**au´to·crat´i·cal·ly,** *adv.*

au·to·crat (ô´tə krat), *n.* 1 ruler who has absolute power. 2 person having unlimited power over a group of persons. [< Gk., < *auto–* self + *kratos* strength]

au·to-da-fé (ô´tō dä fā´; ou´–), *n., pl.* **au·tos-da-fé** 1 public ceremony accompanying the passing of sentence by the Spanish Inquisition. 2 act of burning a heretic. [< Pg., act of the faith, < L *actus* and *fides*]

au·to·fo·cus (ô´tə fō´kəs), *n.* automatic focus of a camera lens.

au·to·graph (ô´tə graf; –gräf), *n.* 1 person's signature. 2 something written in a person's own handwriting. —*v.* 1 write one's signature in or on. 2 write with one's own hand.

au·to·im·mune (ô´tō i myün´), *adj.* attacking the body's own cells: *autoimmune response.*

au·tol·o·gous (ô tol´əg əs), *adj.* 1 transplanted from one's own body. 2 donated and preserved for one's own future use; self-donated: *an autologous blood transfusion.*

au·to·mate (ô´tə māt), *v.,* –**mat·ed, –mat·ing.** convert to or make use of automation. [< *automation*]

au·to·mat·ic (ô´tə mat´ik), *adj.* 1 moving or acting by itself: *automatic pump.* 2 **a** done unconsciously, as certain muscular reactions. **b** independent of external stimuli, as the beating of the heart. 3 of a firearm, pistol, etc., reloading itself. —*n.* automatic pistol or rifle. [see AUTOMATON] —**au´to·mat´i·cal·ly,** *adv.*

automatic pilot, mechanism in an aircraft or spacecraft that regulates its course, altitude, etc.; autopilot.

on automatic pilot, *Fig.* acting or behaving without thinking.

automatic teller machine, electronic banking machine that receives deposits, dispenses withdrawals, etc.

au·to·ma·tion (ô´tə mā´shən), *n.* 1 use of automatic controls and systems to operate machinery. 2. method of making a production line, etc., operate automatically by self-regulating controls. [< *autom(atic)* + *(oper)ation*]

au·tom·a·tism (ô tom´ə tiz əm), *n.* 1 action not controlled by the will. 2 automatic quality.

au·tom·a·ton (ô tom´ə ton; –tən), *n., pl.* –**tons, –ta** (–tə). 1 person or animal whose actions are purely mechanical. 2 machine that has its motive power concealed. 3 thing able to move itself. [< Gk., acting by one's self]

au·to·mo·bile (*n.* ô´tə mə bēl,ô´tə mə bēl´, –mō´bēl; *adj.* ô´tə mō´bil, –bēl; *v.* ô´tə mə bēl´, –mō´bēl),*n., adj., v.,* –**biled, –bil·ing.** —*n.* passenger vehicle with four wheels that is self-propelled. —*adj.* of or having to do with the automobile. —*v.* travel by automobile. [< F. See MOBILE.]

au·to·mo·tive (ô´tə mō´tiv), *adj.* 1 of automobiles. 2 self-moving.

au·to·nom·ic (ô´tə nom´ik), **au·to·nom·i·cal** (–ə kəl), *adj.* 1 of or having to do with the autonomic nervous system. 2 in plants, caused by internal stimuli; spontaneous. 3 =autonomous.

autonomic nervous system, the ganglia and nerves that control digestive and other involuntary reactions.

au·ton·o·mous (ô ton´ə məs), *adj.* 1 self-governing; independent. 2 reacting independently. 3 of plants, spontaneous. —**au·ton´o·mous·ly,** *adv.*

au·ton·o·my (ô ton´ə mi), *n., pl.* –**mies.** 1 power or right of self-government. 2 a self-governing community. [< Gk., < *auto–* of oneself + *nomos* law] —**au·ton´o·mist,** *n.*

au·to·pi·lot (ô´tə pī´lət), *n.* =automatic pilot.

au·top·sy (ô´top si; ô´təp–), *n., pl.* –**sies.** medical examination of a dead body to find the cause of death. [< NL < Gk., < *auto–* for oneself + *opsis* a seeing]

au·to·sug·ges·tion ô´tō səg jes´chən; –sə jes´–), *n.* suggestion to oneself of ideas that produce actual effects.

au·to·troph (ô´tə trof), *n.* organism capable of making its own food from inorganic substances. —**au´to·troph´ic,** *adj.*

au·tumn (ô′təm), *n*. **1** season of the year between summer and winter. **2** season of maturity. —*adj*. of autumn; coming in autumn. [< L *autumnus*] —**au·tum′nal**, *adj*.

autumnal equinox. See **equinox.**

aux or **aux.**, auxiliary.

aux·il·ia·ry (ôg zil′yə ri; –zil′ə–), *adj.*, *n.*, *pl*. **-ries.** —*adj*. **1** helping; assistant. **2** additional. *n*. **1** helper; aid. **2** auxiliary verb. **3 auxiliaries,** foreign or allied troops that help the army of a nation at war. [< L, < *auxilium* aid]

auxiliary verb, verb used to form the tenses, moods, or voices of other verbs, such as *be, can, do, have,* and *may*: I *am* going; he *will* go; they *are* lost; they *were* lost.

av., **1** avenue. **2** average. **3** avoirdupois.

A.V., Authorized Version.

a·vail (ə vāl′), *v*. be of use or value to; help; benefit. —*n*. **1** help; benefit. **2** efficacy for a purpose; use.

avail oneself of, take advantage of; make use of. [appar. < *a*- to (< OF < L *ad-* + *vail* < F < L *valere* be worth]

a·vail·a·ble (ə vāl′ə bəl), *adj*. **1** that can be used. **2** that can be had. —**a·vail′a·bil′i·ty, a·vail′a·ble·ness,** *n*. —**a·vail′a·bly,** *adv*.

av·a·lanche (av′ə lanch, –länch), *n.*, *v.*, **-lanched, -lanch·ing.** —*n*. **1** a large mass of snow and ice, or of dirt and rocks, sliding or falling down a mountainside. **2** anything like an avalanche. —*v*. slide down in or like an avalanche. [< F < Swiss F *lavenche,* infl. by F *avaler* go down < *à val* < L *ad vallem* to the valley]

a·vant garde (ä väN gärd′), *n*. in art, literature, music, etc., those who are most experimental and inventive in a particular period. —*adj*. experimental and inventive. [< F < *avant* forward + *garde* guard] —**a·vant′-gard′ist,** *n*.

av·a·rice (av′ə ris), *n*. greedy desire for money. [< OF < L, < *avarus* greedy] —**av′a·ri′cious,** *adj*. —**av′a·ri′cious·ly,** *adv*. —**av′a·ri′cious·ness,** *n*.

a·vast (ə vast′; ə väst′), *interj*. of ships or boots, stop! stay! [prob. < Du. *houd vast* hold fast]

a·vaunt (ə vônt′; ə vänt′), *interj*. *Archaic*. go away! [< F < L *ab ante* forward, in front]

a·ve (ä′vā; ä′vē), *interj*. hail! farewell! —*n*. **Ave,** the prayer Ave Maria. [< L]

Ave, ave, Avenue; avenue.

A·ve Ma·ri·a (ä′vä mə rē′ə; ä′vē), **A·ve Mar·y** (ä′vē mãr′i), **1** "Hail Mary!", the first words of the Latin form of a prayer of the Roman Catholic Church. **2** the prayer.

a·venge (ə venj′), *v.*, **a·venged, a·veng·ing. 1** get revenge for. **2** get revenge on behalf of. **3** get revenge. [< OF, < *a-* to (< L *ad-*) + *vengier* < L *vindicare* punish < *vindex* champion] —**a·venge′ment,** *n*. —**a·veng′er,** *n*.

av·e·nue (av′ə nü; –nü), *n*. **1** wide or main street. **2** road or walk bordered by

trees. **3** way of approach or departure; passage. **4** a city thoroughfare, running at right angles to others called "streets." [< F, fem. pp. of *avenir* < L, < *ad-* to + *venire* come]

a·ver (ə vėr′, *v.*, **a·verred, a·ver·ring.** state to be true; assert. [< OF, ult. < L *ad-* to + *verus* true] —**a·ver′ment,** *n*.

av·er·age (av′rij; av′ər ij), *n.*, *adj.*, *v.*, **-aged, -ag·ing.** —*n*. **1** quantity found by dividing the sum of all the quantities by the number of quantities: *the average of 3, 5, and 10 is 6.* **2** usual kind or quality; ordinary amount or rate. **3** ratio or percentage that indicates a record of achievement or success. —*adj*. **1** obtained by averaging; being an average: *an average price.* **2** usual; ordinary: *average intelligence.* —*v*. **1** find the average of. **2** have as an average. **3** do on an average: *he averages six hours work a day.* **4** divide among several proportionately. [< F *avarie* damage to ship or cargo < Ar. *ʾawārīya* damage from sea water. —**av′er·age·ly,** *adv*. —**av′er·ag·er,** *n*.

A·ver·nus (ə vėr′nəs), *n. Rom. Myth.* the lower world; Hades. —**A·ver′nal,** *adj*.

a·verse (ə vėrs′), *adj*. opposed; unwilling. [< L *aversus.* See AVERT.] —**a·verse′ly,** *adv*. —**a·verse′ness,** *n*.

a·ver·sion (ə vėr′zhən; –shən), *n*. **1** strong or fixed dislike; antipathy. **2** object of dislike. **3** unwillingness.

a·vert (ə vėrt′), *v*. **1** prevent; avoid. **2** turn away; turn aside. [< OF < LL, < L *ab-* from + *vertere* turn] —**a·vert′ed·ly,** *adv*. —**a·vert′i·ble, a·vert′a·ble,** *adj*. —**a·vert′er,** *n*.

A·ves (ā′vēz), *n. pl.* class of vertebrates comprising the birds. [< L]

A·ves·ta (ə ves′tə), *n*. the sacred writings of ancient Zoroastrianism. —**A·ves′tan,** *adj*.

a·vi·ar·y (ā′vi er′i), *n.*, *pl.* **-ar·ies.** place where many birds are kept. [< L, < *avis* bird]

a·vi·a·tion (ā′vi ā′shən; av′i–), *n*. **1** flying in aircraft; art or science of navigating aircraft. **2** design and manufacture of aircraft. **3** the aircraft industry, including employees and equipment. [< F, < L *avis* bird]

a·vi·a·tor (ā′vi ā′tər; av′i–), *n*. person who flies an aircraft; pilot.

av·id (av′id), *adj*. eager; greedy. [< L *avidus* < *avere* desire eagerly] —**a·vid′i·ty,** *n*. —**av′id·ly,** *adv*.

A·vi·gnon (ä vē nyôN′), *n*. city in SE France.

a·vi·on·ics (ā′vi on′iks), *n*. science of adapting electronic devices to aviation, rocketry, and astronautics. [< *avi*(ation) + (electr)*onics*]

av·o·ca·do (av′ə kä′dō; ä′və–), *n.*, *pl.* **-dos. 1** pear-shaped tropical fruit with a dark green skin; alligator pear. **2** tree that it grows on. [< Sp., var. of *aguacate* < Mexican *ahuacatl*]

av·o·ca·tion (av′ə kā′shən), *n*. minor occupation; hobby. [< L, < *ab-* away + *vocare* to call]

av·o·cet, av·o·set (av′ə set), *n*. a web-footed wading bird. [< F < Ital. *avosetta*]

a·void (ə void′), *v*. **1** keep away from. **2** keep out of the way of. **3** in law, make void; annul [< AF var. of OF *esvuidier* empty, quit < *es*- out (< L *ex-*) + *vuidier* < VL *vocitare* empty] —**a·void′a·ble,** *adj*. —**a·void′a·bly,** *adv*. —**a·void′ance,** *n*.

av·oir·du·pois (av′ər də poiz′), *n*. avoirdupois weight. [< OF *avoir de pois* (goods that) have weight < L *habere* have, *de* of, and *pensum* weight]

avoirdupois weight, system of weighing in which a pound containing sixteen ounces is used.

A·von (ā′vən; av′ən), *n*. river in C England.

a·vouch (ə vouch′), *v*. **1** declare to be true. **2** guarantee. **3** acknowledge; affirm. [< OF *avochier* < *a-* + *vochier.* See VOUCH.] —**a·vouch′ment** *n*.

a·vow (ə vou′), *v*. declare frankly or openly; confess; admit; acknowledge. [< OF, < *a-* (< L *ad-*) + *vouer* < VL *votare* vow] —**a·vow′er,** *n*.

a·vow·al (ə vou′əl), *n*. frank or open declaration; confession; admission.

a·vowed (ə voud′), *adj*. openly declared; admitted; acknowledged. —**a·vow′ed·ly,** *adv*. —**a·vow′ed·ness,** *n*.

a·vun·cu·lar (ə vung′kyə lər), *adj*. **1** of an uncle. **2** like an uncle. [< L *avunculus* mother's brother, dim. of *avus* grandfather]

a·wait (ə wāt′), *v*. **1** wait for; look forward to; expect. **2** be ready for; be in store for. **3** wait; be expectant. [< OF, < *a-* for (< L *ad-*) + *waitier* wait < Gmc.] —**a·wait′er,** *n*.

a·wake (ə wāk′), *v.*, **a·woke** or **a·waked, a·wak·ing,** *adj*. —*v*. wake up; arouse. —*adj*. not asleep; alert.

awake to, realize. [OE *āwacian* + OE *onwœcnan*]

a·wak·en (ə wāk′ən), *v*. wake up; arouse. **awaken to,** come to realize. —**a·wak′en·er,** *n*.

a·wak·en·ing (ə wāk′ən ing), *adj*. arousing. —*n*. act of awaking.

a·ward (ə wôrd′), *v*. **1** give after careful consideration; grant. **2** decide or settle by law; adjudge. —*n*. **1** something given after careful consideration; prize. **2** decision by a judge. [< AF var. of OF *esguarder* observe, decide < L *ex-* from + *wardare* guard < Gmc.] —**a·ward′a·ble,** *adj*. —**a·ward′er,** *n*.

a·ware (ə wãr′), *adj*. knowing; realizing; conscious. [OE *gewœr*] —**a·ware′ness,** *n*.

a·wash (ə wosh′; ə wôsh′), *adv.*, *adj*. **1** just covered with water; flooded. **2** washed over. **3** floating. **4** *Fig.* filled to overflowing.

a·way (ə wā′), *adv*. **1** from a place. **2** at a distance; far. **3** in another direction: *turn away.* **4** out of one's possession: *he* *gave his boat away.* **5** continuously: *she worked away at her job.* [OE *onweg*]

awe (ô), *n., v.,* **awed, aw·ing.** —*n.* **1** great fear and wonder. **2** fear and reverence. —*v.* **1** cause to feel awe; fill with awe. **2** influence or restrain by awe. [< Scand. *agi*] —**aw′less, awe′less,** *adj.*

a·weigh (ə wā′), *adj.* raised off the bottom: *anchors aweigh.*

awe·some (ô′səm), *adj.* **1** causing awe. **2** showing awe; awed. **3** *Informal.* wonderful; amazing; cool. —**awe′some·ly,** *adv.* —**awe′some·ness,** *n.*

awe-struck (ô′struk′), **awe-strick·en** (ô′strik′ən), *adj.* filled with awe.

aw·ful (ô′fəl), *adj.* **1** dreadful; terrible; fearful: *an awful storm.* **2** very bad, great, ugly, etc. **3** deserving great respect and reverence; sublime; grand. **4** filling with awe; impressive; imposing. —*adv.* very: *he was awful mad.* [< *awe* + *-ful*] —**aw′ful·ness,** *n.*

aw·ful·ly (ô′fli; ô′fəl i), *adv.* **1** dreadfully; terribly. **2** very.

a·while (ə hwīl′), *adv.* for a short time.

awk·ward (ôk′wərd), *adj.* **1** clumsy; not graceful or skillful. **2** not well-suited to use. **3** not easy to manage or deal with. **4** embarrassing; trying. [< obs. *awk* perversely, in the wrong way (< Scand. *öfugr* turned the wrong way) + *-ward*] —**awk′ward·ly,** *adv.* —**awk′ward·ness,** *n.*

awl (ôl), *n.* tool used for making small holes in leather or wood. [OE *æl*]

awn (ôn), *n.* one of the bristly hairs forming the beard on a head of barley, oats, etc. [< Scand. *ögn* chaff] —**awned,** *adj.* —**awn′less,** *adj.*

awn·ing ôn′ing), *n.* a rooflike shelter of canvas, etc., over a door, window, porch, etc.

a·woke (ə wōk′), *v.* pt. and pp. of **awake.**

AWOL (ā′wôl, *or pronounced as initials*), absent without leave or permission.

a·wry (ə rī′), *adv., adj.* **1** with a twist or turn to one side. **2** wrong. [< *a* on, in + *wry*]

ax, axe (aks), *n., pl.* **ax·es,** *v.,* **axed, ax·ing.** —*n.* **1** tool with a bladed head on a handle, used for chopping, etc. **2** battle-ax. —*v.* **1** cut or shape with an ax. **2** discharge an employee; fire. **3** reduce greatly.

get the ax, be fired.

have an ax to grind, have a personal reason or special purpose for doing something or having an interest in something. [OE *æx*] —**ax′like′,** *adj.*

ax·es[1] (ak′sēz), *n. pl.* of **axis.**

ax·es[2] (ak′siz), *n.* pl of **ax.**

ax·i·al (ak′si əl), **ax·ile** (ak′sil; -sō), *adj.* **1** of an axis; forming an axis. **2** on or around an axis. —**ax′i·al·ly,** *adv.*

ax·il (ak′sil), *n.* angle between the upper side of a leaf or stem and the supporting stem or branch. [< L *axilla* armpit]

ax·il·la (ak sil′ə), *n., pl.* **ax·il·lae** (ak sil′ē). **1** armpit. **2** axil. [< L]

ax·il·lar·y (ak′sə ler′i), *adj.* **1** of or near the armpit. **2** in or growing from an axil.

ax·i·om (ak′si əm), *n.* **1** statement seen to be true without proof; self-evident truth. **2** established principle. [< L < Gk., < *axios* worthy] —**ax′i·o·mat′ic, ax′i·o·mat′i·cal,** *adj.* —**ax′i·o·mat′i·cal·ly,** *adv.*

ax·is (ak′sis), *n., pl.* **ax·es** (ak′sēz). **1** imaginary or real line that passes through an object and about which the object turns or seems to turn. **2** central or principal line around which parts are arranged regularly. **3** central or principal structure extending lengthwise. **4 the Axis,** Germany, Italy, Japan, and their allies, during World War II. [< L]

ax·le (ak′səl), *n.* **1** bar on which or with which a wheel turns. **2** axletree. [OE *eaxl*

shoulder, *eax* axle; ? infl. by Scand. *öxl* axle] —**ax′led,** *adj.*

ax·le·tree (ak′səl trē′), *n.* crossbar that connects two opposite wheels.

Ax·min·ster (aks′min stər), *n.* a velvet-like carpet.

ay[1] (ā), *adv.* always; ever. Also, **aye.** [< Scand. *ei*]

ay[2] (ī), *adv., n.* yes. Also, **aye.**

a·ya·tol·lah (ä′ya tō′lə), *n.* Muslim religious leader; imam; mullah.

aye[1] (ā), *adv.* always; ever.

aye[2] (ī), *adv., n.* yes. [OE *gī* YEA]

aye-aye (ī′ī′), *n.* a squirrellike lemur of Madagascar.

AZ, (*zip code*) Arizona.

a·zal·ea (ə zāl′yə), *n.* **1** shrub with many showy flowers. **2** the flower. [< NL < Gk., dry, < *azein* parch]

az·i·muth (az′ə məth), *n.* the angular distance east or west from the north point. The azimuth of the North Star is 0 degrees. [< F < Ar. *as-sumūt* the ways < *samt* way] —**az′i·muth′al,** *adj.* —**az′i·muth·al·ly,** *adv.*

A·zores (ə zôrz′, ə zōrz′; ā′zôrz, ā′zōrz), *n. pl.* group of islands in the Atlantic west of and belonging to Portugal.

AZT, antiviral drug, azidothymidine, used in the treatment of AIDS.

Az·tec (az′tek), *n.* member of a highly civilized people who ruled Mexico before its conquest by the Spaniards in 1519. —*adj.* of the Aztecs. —**Az′tec·an,** *adj.*

az·ure (azh′ər; ā′zhər), *n.* **1** blue; sky blue. **2** the blue sky. **3** a blue pigment. —*adj.* blue; sky-blue. [< OF *l′azur* the azure < Ar. < Pers. *lajward* lapis lazuli]

az·u·rite (azh′ə rīt), *n.* **1** blue copper ore. It is a basic carbonate of copper, $2CuCo_3 \cdot Cu(OH)_2$ **2** form of azurite used in jewelry.

B, b (bē), *n., pl.* **B's; b's.**
1 second letter of the alphabet. **2** second best.
3 second highest grade in school or college. **4** seventh note in the scale of C major.

B, 1 boron. **2** one of the four main blood groups.

B., 1 Bay. **2** Bible. **3** British.

b., 1 base. **2** bass. **3** bay. **4** book. **5** born.

Ba, barium.

B.A., Bachelor of Arts. Also, **A.B.**

baa (bä), *n., v.,* **baaed, baa·ing.** bleat.

Ba·al (bā'əl; bāl), *n., pl.* **Ba·al·im** (bā'əl-im). **1** the chief god of the Canaanites and Phoenicians. **2** a false god. —**Ba'al·ism,** *n.* —**Ba'al·ist, Ba'al·ite,** *n.*

bab·bitt (bab'it), *n.* alloy of tin, antimony, and copper, used in bearings to lessen friction.

Bab·bitt (bab'it), *n.* a self-satisfied businessman who conforms to middle-class ideas of respectability and success. —**bab'bitt·ry,** *n.*

bab·ble (bab'əl), *v.,* **-bled, -bling,** *n.* —*v.* **1** make indistinct sounds like a baby. **2** talk or speak foolishly. **3** tell secrets. **4** murmur. —*n.* **1** talk that cannot be understood. **2** foolish talk. **3** murmur. [ME *babel;* imit.] —**bab'bler,** *n.* —**bab'bling·ly,** *adv.*

babe (bāb), *n.* **1** baby. **2** an innocent or inexperienced person. **3** girl or young woman.

Ba·bel (bā'bəl; bab'əl), *n.* **1** Babylon, where, according to the Bible, the building of a lofty tower intended to reach heaven was begun and a confusion of the language of the people took place. Gen. 11:1–9. **2** Also, **babel.** **a** confusion of sounds; noise. **b** place of noise and confusion. [< Heb.]

ba·bies'-breath, ba·by's-breath (bā'biz-breth'), *n.* tall herb bearing numerous small, fragrant, white or pink flowers.

ba·boo, ba·bu (bä'bü), *n., pl.* **-boos; -bus.** **1** Hindu title meaning "Mr." **2** Indian clerk who writes English. [< Hind. *babu*]

ba·boon (ba bün'), *n.* any of various (usually large, fierce monkeys of Arabia and Africa, with a doglike face and a short tail. [< OF *babouin* stupid person] —**ba·boon'ish, ba·boon'like,** *adj.*

ba·bush·ka (bə bùsh'kə), *n.* **1** woman's head scarf worn tied under the chin. **2** grandmother. [< Russian grandmother]

ba·by (bā'bi), *n., pl.* **-bies,** *adj., v.,* **-bied, -by·ing.** —*n.* **1** a very young child. **2** the youngest of a family or group. **3** person who acts like a baby. —*adj.* **1** of or for a baby. **2** young. **3** small. **4** childish. —*v.* treat as a baby; pamper. [ME *babi*] —**ba'by·ish,** *adj.* —**ba'by·ish·ly,** *adv.* —**ba'by·ish·ness,** *n.* —**ba'by·like',** *adj.*

Bab·y·lon (bab'ə lən; -lon), *n.* **1** capital of ancient Babylonia, noted for its wealth and wickedness. **2** any rich or wicked city.

Bab·y·lo·ni·a (bab'ə lō'ni ə), *n.* an ancient empire in SW Asia, from 2800 to 1000 B.C. —**Bab'y·lo'ni·an,** *adj., n.*

ba·by-sit (bā'bi sit'), *v.,* **-sat, -sit·ting.** take care of a child during the temporary absence of its parents. —**baby sitter.**

bac·ca·lau·re·ate (bak'ə lô'ri it), *n.* **1** degree of bachelor given by a college or university. **2** sermon or address delivered to a graduating class at commencement. [< Med. L, < *baccalarius*]

bac·ca·rat, bac·ca·ra (bak'ə rä; bak'ə rä'), *n.* card game in which the players bet against a banker. [< F]

bac·cha·nal (bak'ə nəl; -nal), *adj.* having to do with Bacchus or his worship. —*n.* **1** worshiper of Bacchus. **2** drunken reveler. **3** drunken revelry. **4** Bacchanals, the Bacchanalia. [< L, < *Bacchus* god of wine < Gk. *Bakchos*]

Bac·cha·na·li·a (bak'ə nā'li ə; -nāl'yə), *n. pl.* **1** wild, noisy Roman festival in honor of Bacchus. **2** bacchanalia, drunken revelry; orgy. —**bac'cha·na'li·an,** *adj., n.*

bac·chant (bak'ənt), *n., pl.* **bac·chants, bac·chan·tes** (bə kan'tēz). **1** priest or worshiper of Bacchus. **2** drunken reveler. —**bac·chan'tic,** *adj.*

bac·chan·te (bə kan'tē; bə kant'; bak'-ənt), *n.* priestess or female worshiper of Bacchus.

Bac·chic (bak'ik), *adj.* **1** of Bacchus or his worship. **2** Also, **bacchic.** drunken; riotous.

Bac·chus (bak'əs), *n. Class. Myth.* god of wine. The Greeks also called him Dionysus.

Bach (bäн), *n.* **Johann Sebastian,** 1685–1750, German composer and organist.

bach·e·lor (bach'ə lər; bach'lər), *n.* **1** man who has not married. **2** person who has the first degree of a college or university. **3** young knight who served under the banner of another. [< OF < Med. L *baccalārius,* appar., small landowner] —**bach'e·lor·dom** *n.* —**bach'e·lor·hood',** *n.* —**bach'e·lor·ship',** *n.*

bach·e·lor's-but·ton (bach'ə lərz but'ən; bach'lərz–), *n.* **1** =cornflower. **2** any of several button-shaped flowers or the plants that bear them.

ba·cil·lus (bə sil'əs), *n., pl.* **-cil·li** (-sil'ī). **1** any of the rod-shaped bacteria. **2** any of the bacteria. [< LL, dim of *baculus* rod] —**ba·cil'lar·y,** *adj.*

back¹ (bak), *n.* **1** part of a person's body opposite to the face or to the front part of the body. **2** the upper part of an animal's body **3** the backbone. **4** part opposite the front. **5** part of a chair, couch, etc., that supports the back of a person sitting down. **6** player whose position is behind the front line in certain games. —*v.* **1** support; help. **2** move backward. **3** make or be a back for. —*adj.* **1** opposite the front. **2** at, in, to, or toward an earlier place, position, etc. **3** belonging to the past. **4** overdue. **5** in distant or frontier regions.

back and fill, a move in a zigzag way. **b** *Fig.* keep changing one's mind.

back down, give up.

back up, a move backward. **b** help. [OE *bæc*] —**back'less,** *adj.*

back² (bak), *adv.* **1** behind. **2** in or toward the past. **3** in return. **4** in the place from which it (he, she, etc.) came: *put the books back.* **5** in reserve. **6** in check.

back of, a in the rear of; behind. **b** supporting; helping.

go back on, break a promise to. [var. of *aback*]

back·ache (bak'āk'), *n.* pain in the back.

back·bite (bak'bīt'), *v.,* **-bit, -bit·ten** or **-bit, -bit·ing.** slander (an absent person). —**back'bit'er,** *n.* —**back'bit'ing,** *n.*

back·bone (bak'bōn'), *n.* **1** main bone along the middle of the back in vertebrates; the spine. **2** anything resembling a backbone. **3** *Fig.* most important part; chief support. **4** *Fig.* strength of character. —**back'boned',** *adj.*

back·break·ing (bak'brā'king), *adj.* very hard, exhausting.

back·door (bak'dôr'; -dōr'), *adj.* secret; sly.

back·drop (bak'drop'), *n.* **1** curtain at the back of a stage. **2** background.

back·er (bak'ər), *n.* person who backs or supports another person, a plan or idea, etc.

back·field (bak'fēld'), *n.* **1** in football, players behind the front line quarterback, two halfbacks, and fullback. **2** in baseball, the outfield.

back·fire (bak'fīr'), *n., v.,* **-fired, -fir·ing.** —*n.* **1** explosion of gas occurring too soon or in the wrong place in a gasoline engine, etc. **2** fire set to check a forest or prairie fire by burning off the area in front of it. **3** an adverse reaction. —*v.* **1** explode prematurely. **2** set a backfire. **3** have adverse results.

back formation, a word formed on analogy with other words and usually needed to serve as a different part of speech. *Diagnose* is a back formation of *diagnosis.*

back·gam·mon (bak'gam'ən; bak'-gam'ən), *n.* game for two played on a special board, with pieces moved according to the throw of dice. [< *back¹,* adj. + *gammon* game; because the men are sometimes set back]

back·ground (bak'ground'), *n.* **1** part of a picture or scene toward the back. **2** surface against which things are seen or upon which things are made or placed. **3** earlier conditions or events that help to explain some later condition or event. **4** past experience, knowledge, and training of a person. **5** accompanying music or sound effects in a play, film, etc. **6** interference from radiation, as of radio signals.

in the background, out of sight; not apparent.

back·hand (bak'hand'), *n.* **1** stroke made with back of the hand turned outward. **2**

handwriting in which the letters slope to the left. —*adj.* backhanded.

back·hand·ed (bak′han′did), *adj.* **1** done or made with the back of the hand turned outward. **2** slanting to the left. **3** awkward; clumsy. **4** indirect; insincere. —**back′hand′ed·ly,** *adv.*

back·hoe (bak′hō), *n.* **1** shovel at the end of a mechanical arm, mounted on a tractor for digging trenches and small excavations. **2** tractor with such a mechanism.

back·ing (bak′ing), *n.* **1** support; help. **2** supporters; helpers. **3** back part supporting or strengthening something: *fabric backing.*

back·lash (bak′lash′), *n.* **1** the jarring reaction of a machine or mechanical device. **2** movement between worn or loosely fitting parts. **3** any sudden, unfavorable reaction.

back·log (bak′lôg′; –log′), *n.* **1** a reserve of orders, commitments, etc., that have not yet been filled. **2** a large log at the back of a wood fire.

back number, an old issue of a magazine or newspaper.

back seat, place of inferiority or insignificance.

back·side (bak′sīd′), *n.* **1** back. **2** rump.

back slash, =virgule.

back·slide (bak′slīd′), *v.,* **–slid, –slid-den** or **–slid, –slid·ing.** slide back into wrongdoing or former bad habits. —**back′slid′er,** *n.*

back·stage (bak′stāj′), *adv.* **1** in the dressing rooms of a theater. **2** toward the rear of a stage. —*adj.* happening, located, etc., backstage.

back·stay (bak′stā′), *n.* **1** rope extending from the top of the mast to the ship's side. **2** supporting or checking device on a mechanism.

back·stop (bak′stop′), *n.* **1** fence or screen used in various games to keep the ball from going too far away. **2** player who stops balls in various games, esp. the catcher in baseball.

back·stroke (bak′strōk′), *n.* **1** swimming stroke made with the swimmer lying on his back. **2** backhanded stroke in racquet sports.

back talk, talking back; impudent answers.

back-to-back (bak′tə bak′), *adj.* **1** placed or standing with backs near or against each other. **2** following closely one after another.

back·track (bak′trak′), *v.* **1** go back over a course or path; return. **2** withdraw from an undertaking, position, etc.

back·up (bak′up′), *n.* **1** someone or something kept in readiness to assist or substitute for. **2** accumulation, as of work or traffic. —*adj.* **1** ready to assist, support, or substitute for. **2** assisting; supporting.

back·ward (bak′wərd), *adv.* **1** toward the back: *walk backward.* **2** with the back first. **3** toward the starting point. **4** oppo-site to the usual way: *read backward.* **5** from better to worse. **6** toward the past. Also **backwards.** —*adj.* **1** directed toward the back: *a backward glance.* **2** with the back first. **3** reversed; returning. **4** done in reverse order. **5** from better to worse; retrogressive. **6** reaching back into the past. **7** slow in development; dull. **8** behind time; late. **9** shy; bashful. [ME *backward* < *bak* BACK[1] + –WARD) —**back′ward·ly,** *adv.* —**back′ward·ness,** *n.*

back·wash (bak′wosh′; –wôsh′), *n.* **1** water thrown back by oars, paddle wheels, the passing of a ship, etc. **2** backward current. **3** *Fig.* reaction after some significant or stressful event.

back·wa·ter (bak′wô′tər; –wot′ər), *n.* **1** water held or pushed back. **2** *Fig.* a sluggish, stagnant condition; backward place. **3** backwash.

back·woods (bak′wùdz′), *n. pl.* **1** uncleared regions far away from towns. **2** crude, uncivilized place. —*adj.* Also, **backwood. 1** of the backwoods. **2** crude; rough. —**back′woods′man,** *n.*

ba·con (bā′kən), *n.* salted and smoked meat from the back and sides of a hog. [< OF < Gmc.]

Ba·con (bā′kən), *n.* **Francis,** 1561–1626, English essayist, statesman, and philosopher. —**Ba·co′ni·an,** *adj., n.*

bac·te·ri·a (bak tir′i ə), *n. pl.* microscopic organisms, usually single-celled and having no chlorophyll, multiplying by fission and spore formation. Various species of bacteria cause disease while others perform useful functions, as aiding digestion. —**bac·te′ri·al,** *adj.* —**bac·te′ri·al·ly,** *adv.*

bac·te·ri·cide (bak tir′ə sīd), *n.* substance that destroys bacteria. [< *bacterium* + –*cide* < L –*cida* killer < *caedere* kill] —**bac·te′ri·cid′al,** *adj.*

bacteriol., bacteriology.

bac·te·ri·ol·o·gy (bak tir′i ol′ə ji), *n.* science that deals with bacteria. [< *bacterium* + –LOGY] —**bac·te′ri·o·log′i·cal,** *adj.* —**bac·te′ri·ol′o·gist,** *n.*

bac·te·ri·o·phage (bak tir′i ə fāj), *n.* bactericide produced within the body and normally present in the intestines, urine, blood, etc. [< *bacterium* + –*phage* eating < Gk. *phagein* eat]

bac·te·ri·um (bak tir′i əm), *n., pl.* **–te·ri·a** (–tir′i ə). one of the bacteria. [< NL < Gk. *baktērion,* dim. of *baktron*]

Bac·tri·an camel (bak′tri ən), camel with two humps.

bad[1] (bad), *adj.,* **worse, worst,** *n., adv.* —*adj.* **1** not as it ought to be; not good. **2** evil; wicked. **3** disagreeable; painful. **4** harmful. **5** sick; injured. **6** unfavorable: *he came at a bad time.* **7** worthless: *a bad check.* **8** incorrect; faulty. **9** not valid. **10** rotten; spoiled: *a bad apple.* **11** hostile; dangerous. —*n.* bad condition, quality, etc. —*adv.* badly. [orig. pp. of OE *bœdan* defile] —**bad′ness,** *n.*

bad[2] (bad), *v.,* pt. of **bid** (defs. 1, 2.)

bade (bad, bād), *v.* pt. of **bid.**

badge (baj), *n., v.,* **badged, badg·ing.** —*n.* **1** a token or device worn as a sign of occupation, authority, achievements, or membership. **2** symbol; sign. —*v.* furnish with a badge or as with a badge. [ME *bage*] —**badge′less,** *adj.*

badg·er (baj′ər), *n.* **1** any of various burrowing carnivorous mammals of Europe and America related to the weasels. **2** its fur. —*v.* keep on teasing or annoying; torment by nagging. [? < *badge;* with ref. to white spot on head]

bad·i·nage (bad′ə näzh′; bad′ə nij), *n.* joking; banter. [< F, < *badiner* banter < *badin* silly < VL *batāre* gape]

Bad Lands, 1 rugged, barren region in SW South Dakota and NW Nebraska. **2** *Fig.* barren, desolate place.

bad·ly (bad′li), *adv.* **1** in a bad manner. **2** greatly; much.

bad·min·ton (bad′min tən), *n.* game like tennis, but played with a feathered cork instead of a ball. [named for Duke of Beaufort's estate]

bad-tem·pered (bad′tem′pərd), *adj.* having a bad temper or disposition.

baf·fle (baf′əl), *v.,* **–fled, –fling,** *n.* —*v.* **1** be too hard for (a person) to understand or solve. **2** hinder; thwart. **3** struggle without success. —*n.* a wall or screen for hindering or changing the flow of air, water, sound, etc. —**baf′fle·ment,** *n.* —**baf′fler,** *n.* —**baf′fling,** *adj.*

bag (bag), *n., v.,* **bagged, bag·ging.** —*n.* **1** container made of paper, cloth, leather, etc., that can be closed at the top; sack; pouch. **2** sac in an animal's body. **3** something suggesting a bag by its use or shape, as a valise, suitcase, udder, etc. **4** game killed or caught by a hunter. **5** a base in baseball. —*v.* **1** put in a bag. **2** swell; bulge. **3** hang loosely. **4** kill or catch in hunting; capture. **5** catch; take; steal.

bag and baggage, with all one's belongings; entirely.

hold the bag, a be left to take the blame. **b** be left with nothing.

in the bag, sure; certain. [< Scand. *baggi* pack]

ba·gasse (bə gas′), *n.* pulp of sugar cane after the juice has been extracted [< F < Pr. *bagasso* husks]

bag·a·telle (bag′ə tel′), *n.* **1** a mere trifle. **2** game somewhat like billiards. [< F < Ital. *bagatella,* dim. of *baga* berry]

bag·gage (bag′ij), *n.* **1** trunks, bags, suitcases, etc., a person takes while traveling. **2** portable equipment of an army. **3** *Fig.* beliefs, opinions, experiences, etc. that are part of a person's character. [< OF, < *bagues* bundles]

bag·ging (bag′ging), *n.* material for making bags.

bag·gy (bag′i), *adj.,* **–gi·er, –gi·est. 1** swelling; bulging. **2** hanging loosely. —**bag′gi·ly,** *adv.* —**bag′gi·ness.** *n.*

Bagh·dad (bag′dad), *n.* capital of Iraq, on the Tigris River.

bagn·io (ban′yō; bän′–), *n., pl.* **bagn·ios. 1** prison. **2** house of prostitution; brothel. [< Ital. < L *balneum* < Gk. *balaneion* bath]

bag·pipe (bag pīp′), *n.* Often, **bagpipes.** shrill-toned musical instrument made of a windbag and pipes, often used in parades and funerals. —**bag′pip′er,** *n.*

ba·guette (ba get′), *n.* **1** Also **baguet.** gem that is cut in a narrow oblong shape. **2** long, thin loaf of French bread. [< F < Ital., ult. < L *baculum* staff]

Ba·ha·mas (bə hä′məz; –hā′–), *n. pl.* group of islands in the West Indies. —**Ba·ha′mi·an,** *n., adj.*

Bah·rain, Bah·rein (bä rān′), group of islands in the Persian Gulf.

bail[1] (bāl), *n.* **1** guarantee necessary to set a person free from arrest until he is to appear for trial. **2** amount guaranteed. **3** person or persons who stand ready to pay the money guaranteed. —*v.* obtain the freedom of (a person under arrest) by guaranteeing to pay bail.

bail out, a supply bail for. **b** *Fig.* help someone, especially out of a difficult situation. [< OF, custody, < *baillier* deliver < L *bajulāre.* —**bail′a·ble,** *adj.* —**bail′ment,** *n.*

bail[2] (bāl), *n.* **1** the arched handle of a kettle or pail. **2** a hooplike support. [prob. < Scand. *beygla*]

bail[3] (bāl), *n.* scoop or pail used to throw water out of a boat. —*v.* **1** throw (water) out of a boat with a pail, a dipper, or any other container. **2** dip water from.

bail out, drop from an airplane in a parachute. [< F *baille* < L *bajulus* carrier] —**bail′er,** *n.*

bail[4] (bāl), *n.* either of two small bars that form the top of a wicket in cricket. [< OF, barrier]

bail·iff (bāl′if), *n.* **1** assistant to a sheriff. **2** officer of a court who has charge of prisoners while they are in the courtroom. **3** overseer or steward of an estate. **4** in England, the chief magistrate in certain towns. [< OF *baillif* < *baillir* govern. See BAIL[1].]

bail·i·wick (bāl′i wik), *n.* **1** district over which a bailiff has authority. **2** person's field of knowledge, work, or authority. [< ME *bailie* bailiff + *wick* office < OE *wīce*]

bails·man (bālz′mən), *n., pl.* **-men.** person who gives bail.

bairn (bārn), *n. Scot.* child. [OE *bearn*]

bait (bāt), *n.* **1** anything, esp. food, used to attract fish or other animals so that they may be caught. **2** thing used to tempt or attract. —*v.* **1** put bait on (a hook) or in (a trap). **2** tempt; attract. **3** set dogs to attack and worry for sport. **4** torment or worry by unkind or annoying remarks. **5** stop and feed. [< Scand. *beita* cause to bite] —**bait′er,** *n.*

baize (bāz), *n.* a thick woolen cloth used for curtains, table covers, etc. [< F *baies,* pl. of *bai* chestnut-colored < L *badius*]

bake (bāk), *v.,* **baked, bak·ing,** *n.* —*v.* **1** cook (food) by dry heat without exposing it directly to the fire. **2** dry or harden by heat. **3** become baked: *cookies bake quickly.* —*n.* **1** a baking. **2** a social gathering at which a meal is served: *a New England clam bake.* [OE *bacan*]

Ba·ke·lite (bā′kə līt), *n.* trademark for an artificial material used to make beads, electric insulators, etc.

bak·er (bāk′ər), *n.* **1** person who makes or sells baked goods. **2** a small portable oven.

baker's dozen, thirteen.

bak·er·y (bāk′ər i), *n., pl.* **-er·ies.** a baker's shop.

bak·ing (bāk′ing), *n.* **1** act or process of baking. **2** amount baked at one time; batch.

baking powder, mixture of soda and cream of tartar, or of other substances, used to raise biscuits, cakes, etc.

baking soda, sodium bicarbonate.

bak·la·va or **bak·la·wa** (bäk lä vä′), *n.* dessert made of thin layers of pastry, honey, nuts, etc.

bak·sheesh, bak·shish (bak′shēsh), *n.* money given as a tip in Egypt, Turkey, India, etc. [< Pers. *bakhshīsh* < *bakhshīdan* give]

Ba·ku (bä kü′), *n.* capital of Azerbaijan on the Caspian Sea.

bal., balance.

Ba·laam (bā′ləm), *n.* in the Bible, prophet who was rebuked by the ass he rode.

bal·a·lai·ka (bal′ə lī′kə), *n.* a Russian musical instrument somewhat like a guitar, usually having three strings. [< Russ.]

bal·ance (bal′əns), *n., v.,* **-anced, -anc·ing.** —*n.* **1** instrument for weighing; scale. **2** equality in weight, amount, force, effect, etc. **3** comparison as to weight, amount, importance, etc.; estimate. **4** harmony; proportion. **5** steady condition or position; steadiness; poise. **6** anything that counteracts the effect, weight, etc., of something else. **7** difference between the debit and credit sides of an account. **8** part that is left over; remainder; surplus. **9** wheel that regulates the rate of movement of a clock or watch. **10** preponderant weight, amount, or power. **11** balancing movement in dancing. —*v.* **1** weigh in a balance. **2** make or be equal in weight, amount, force, effect, etc. **3** compare the value, importance, etc., of. **4** make or be proportionate to. **5** bring into or keep in a steady condition or position; steady. **6** counteract the effect, influence, etc., of; make up for; offset. **7** make the debit and credit sides of (an account) equal. **8** be equal in the debit and credit sides of an account. **9** hesitate; waver.

in the balance, undecided.

on balance, after considering everything. [< OF < LL *bilanx* two-scaled < *bi-* two + *lanx* scale[2]] —**bal′ance·a·ble,** *adj.* —**bal′anc·er,** *n.*

balanced diet, diet having the correct amounts of all kinds of foods necessary for health.

balance of power, even distribution of power among nations or groups of nations.

balance of trade, difference in value between the imports and the exports of a country.

balance sheet, a written statement showing the profits and losses, the assets and liabilities, and the net worth of a business.

bal·a·ta (bal′ə tə), *n.* **1** a tropical tree whose dried gumlike juice is used in making chewing gum, etc. **2** its juice. [< Sp.]

Bal·bo·a (bal bō′ə), *n.* **Vasco de,** 1475?–1517, Spanish adventurer, discovered the Pacific, 1513.

bal·co·ny (bal′kə ni), *n., pl.* **-nies. 1** projecting platform with an entrance from an upper floor of a building. **2** gallery in a theater or hall. [< Ital., < *balco* scaffold < OHG *balcho* beam] —**bal′co·nied,** *adj.*

bald (bôld), *adj.* **1** wholly or partly without hair on the head. **2** without its natural covering. **3** bare; plain. **4** undisguised. **5** having a white spot on the head. [ME *balled,* appar. < obs. *ball* white spot] —**bald′ly,** *adv.* —**bald′ness,** *n.*

bald eagle, a large, powerful eagle with white feathers on its head, neck, and tail.

bal·der·dash (bôl′dər dash), *n.* nonsense.

bald·pate (bôld′pat′), *n.* **1** person who has a bald head. **2** kind of duck. —**bald′pat′ed,** *adj.* —**bald′pat′ed·ness,** *n.*

bal·dric (bôl′drik), *n.* belt for a sword, horn, etc., hung from one shoulder to the opposite side of the body. [akin to MHG *balderich* girdle]

bale[1] (bāl), *n., v.,* **baled, bal·ing.** —*n.* a large bundle of merchandise wrapped or bound for shipping or storage: *a bale of cotton.* —*v.* make into bales. [prob. < Flem. < OF < OHG *balla* BALL[1]] —**bal′er,** *n.*

bale[2] (bāl), *n. Archaic.* **1** evil; harm. **2** sorrow; pain. [OE *bealu*]

Bal·e·ar·ic Islands (bal′i ar′ik; bə lir′ik), a group of Spanish islands in the W Mediterranean.

bale·ful (bāl′fəl), *adj.* evil; harmful. —**bale′ful·ly,** *adv.* —**bale′ful·ness,** *n.*

Ba·li (bä′li), *n.* island in SE Indonesia, south of Borneo. —**Ba′li·nese′,** *adj., n.*

balk (bôk), *v.* **1** stop short and stubbornly refuse to go on. **2** thwart; hinder; check. **3** fail to use; let slip; miss. **4** fail to complete a pitch in baseball. [< n.] —*n.* **1** hindrance; check; defeat. **2** blunder; mistake. **3** ridge between furrows; strip left unplowed. **4** a large beam or timber. **5** failure of a pitcher to complete a pitch. Also, **baulk.** (OE *balca* ridge) —**balk′er,** *n.* —**balk′ing,** *n., adj.*

Bal·kan (bôl′kən), *adj.* **1** having to do with the Balkan Peninsula. **2** having to do with the Balkan countries or people.

Balkan Mountains, mountain range in the Balkan Peninsula.

Balkan Peninsula, peninsula in SE Europe.

Bal·kans (bôl′kənz), *n.* countries of the Balkan Peninsula, including Slovenia, Croatia, Bosnia, Serbia, Macedonia, Romania, Bulgaria, Albania, Greece, and European Turkey.

balk·y (bôk′i), *adj.* **balk·i·er, balk·i·est. 1** stopping short and stubbornly refusing to go on. **2** likely to balk.

ball[1] (bül), *n.* **1** anything round or roundish: *ball of the foot.* **2** game in which some kind of ball is used. **3** baseball. **4** baseball pitched too high, too low, or not over the plate, that the batter does not strike at. **5** bullet. **6** roots of a plant gathered and tied into a ball, ready for planting. —*v.* make or form into a ball.
ball up, confuse.
keep the ball rolling, keep something moving ahead by doing one's part.
on the ball, alert; knowledgeable.
play ball, a begin or resume a game. **b** get busy; become active. **c** work together; cooperate. [< Scand. *böllr*]

ball[2] (bôl), *n.* large, formal dance party. [< F *bal* < *baler* dance < LL *ballāre*]

bal·lad (bal′əd), *n.* **1** a simple song. **2** a narrative poem, esp. one that tells a popular legend. [< OF < Pr. *balada* dancing song]

bal·last (bal′əst), *n.* **1** something heavy carried in a ship to steady it. **2** weight carried by a balloon or dirigible to control it. **3** *Fig.* anything that steadies a person or thing. **4** gravel or crushed rock used in making the bed for a road or railroad track. —*v.* **1** furnish with ballast. **2** give steadiness to. **3** load or weigh down. [appar. <Scand. (ODan.) *barlast* < *bar* bare + *last* load] —**bal′last·er,** *n.*

ball bearing, 1 bearing in which the shaft turns upon a channel filled with a number of loose metal balls to lessen friction. **2** one of the metal balls.

bal·le·ri·na (bal′ə rē′nə), *n., pl.* **-nas.** a female ballet dancer. [< Ital.]

bal·let (bal′ā; ba lā′), *n.* **1** an elaborate dance by a group on a stage. **2** steps and movements of this of dance. **3** the dancers. **4** music for this kind of dance. [< F, dim. of *bal* dance. See BALL[2].]

bal·lis·tic (bə lis′tik), *adj.* pertaining to the motion of projectiles.
go ballistic, *Informal.* become very angry and upset.

ballistic missile, projectile powered by a rocket engine or engines and aimed at its target when launched.

bal·lis·tics (bə lis′tiks), *n.* science that deals with the motion of projectiles, such as bullets and shells. —**bal·lis′ti·cal·ly,** *adv.* —**bal′lis·ti′cian,** *n.*

bal·loon (bə lün′), *n.* airtight bag filled with gas lighter than air, that allows it to rise and float in the air. —*v.* **1** ride in a

balloon. **2** swell out like a balloon. [< Ital. *ballone* < *balla* ball] —**bal·loon′ist,** *n.*

bal·lot (bal′ət), *n., v.,* **-lot·ed, -lot·ing.** —*n.* **1** piece of paper or other object used in voting. **2** the total number of votes cast. —*v.* vote by ballots. [< Ital. *ballotta,* dim. of *balla* BALL[1]]

ballot box, 1 box into which voters put their ballots after they have voted. **2** secret voting by ballot.

ball·play·er (bôl′plā′ər), *n.* **1** a baseball player. **2** person who plays ball.

ball·room (bôl′rüm′; -rùm′), *n.* a large room for dancing.

bal·ly·hoo (*n.* bal′i hü; *v.* bal′i hü, bal′-i hü′), *n., pl.* **-hoos,** *v.,* **-hooed, -hoo-ing.** —*n.* **1** noisy advertising. **2** uproar; outcry. —*v.* advertise noisily. —**bal′ly·hoo′er,** *n.*

balm (bäm), *n.* **1** fragrant ointment or oil used in anointing or for healing or soothing. **2** anything that heals or soothes. **3** aromatic fragrance; sweet odor. **4** fragrant, oily, sticky substance obtained from certain kinds of trees. **5** fragrant plant of the same family as mint. [< OF < L *balsamum* BALSAM]

balm·y[1] (bäm′i), *adj.,* **balm·i·er, balm·i·est. 1** mild and soothing; temperate; bland. **2** fragrant. —**balm′i·ly,** *adv.* —**balm′i·ness,** *n.*

balm·y[2] (bäm′i), *adj.,* **balm·i·er, balm·i·est.** *Brit. Slang.* silly; crazy. [var. of *barmy*] —**balm′i·ly,** *adv.* —**balm′i·ness,** *n.*

ba·lo·ney (bə lō′ni), *n.* nonsense. Also, **boloney.**

bal·sa (bôl′sə; bäl′-), *n.* **1** a tropical American tree with very lightweight wood. **2** the wood. **3** a raft or float. [< Sp., raft]

bal·sam (bôl′səm), *n.* **1** an ointment or preparation for healing or soothing. **2** a fragrant, oily, sticky substance obtained from certain kinds of trees. **3** tree that yields balsam; balsam fir. **4** any transparent liquid turpentine. **5** a garden plant with seed vessels that burst open violently when ripe. **6** anything that heals or soothes. [< L < Gk. *balsamon*] —**bal·sam′ic** *adj.* —**bal·sam′i·cal·ly,** *adv.*

balsam fir, 1 an evergreen tree of North America that yields turpentine. **2** its wood.

balsam poplar, a species of poplar grown as a shade tree.

Bal·tic (bôl′tik), *adj.* **1** of the Baltic Sea. **2** of the Baltic States.

Baltic Sea, sea in N Europe, north of Germany and southeast of Sweden.

Baltic States, Estonia, Latvia, Lithuania, and, sometimes, Finland.

Bal·ti·more (bôl′tə môr; -mōr), *n.* city in N Maryland, on Chesapeake Bay.

Baltimore oriole, North American bird with orange and black feathers.

Ba·lu·chi·stan (bə lü′chə stän′; bə lü′-chə stan), *n.* former country on the Arabian Sea, now partly in Pakistan.

bal·us·ter (bal′əs tər), *n.* a pillarlike support for a railing. [< F < Ital. < L < Gk.

balaustion pomegranate blossom; from the shape]

bal·us·trade (bal′əs trād′), *n.* row of balusters and the railing on top of them. [< F, < Ital. *balustro* BALUSTER] —**bal′us·trad′ed,** *adj.*

Bal·zac (bal′zak; bôl′-), *n.* **Honoré de,** 1799–1850, French novelist.

bam·bi·no (bam bē′nō), *n., pl.* **-ni** (-ni). baby; little child. [< Ital., dim. of *bambo* silly]

bam·boo (bam bü′), *n., pl.* **-boos.** any of various woody or treelike tropical or semitropical grasses whose stiff, hollow stems are used for making canes, furniture, and even houses. —*adj.* of bamboo. [< Du. *bamboes,* prob. < Malay]

bam·boo·zle (bam bü′zəl), *v.,* **-zled, -zling. 1** impose upon; cheat; trick. **2** puzzle. —**bam·boo′zle·ment,** *n.* —**bamboo′zler,** *n.*

ban (ban), *v.,* **banned, ban·ning,** *n.* —*v.* **1** prohibit; forbid. **2** place a ban on; pronounce a curse on. —*n.* **1** the forbidding of an act or speech by authority of the law, the church, or public opinion. **2** a solemn curse by the church. **3** sentence of outlawry. [< Scand. *banna* forbid]

ba·nal (bā′nəl; bə nal′; -näl′; ban′əl), *adj.* commonplace; trite; hackneyed. [< F, < *ban* proclamation < Gmc.; orig. sense, "of feudal service"; later, "open to the community"] —**ba·nal′i·ty,** *n.* —**ba′nal·ly,** *adv.*

ba·nan·a (bə nan′ə), *n.* **1** slightly curved, yellow or red fruit with firm, creamy flesh. **2** treelike tropical plant on which bananas grow in large clusters. —*adj.* **bananas.** crazy. [< Pg. or Sp.]

band[1] (band), *n.* **1** number of persons or animals joined or acting together; company; group. **2** group of musicians playing various instruments together. **3** drove or flock of animals; herd. **4** a thin, flat strip of material for binding, trimming, or some other purpose. **5** stripe. **6** collar with two strips hanging in front, worn by certain clergymen. **7** a particular range of wave lengths in broadcasting. —*v.* **1** unite in a group. **2** put a band on. **3** mark with stripes. [< F *bande,* ult. < Gmc.]

band[2] (band), *n.* anything that ties, binds, or unites. [< Scand. *band* + F *bande* < Gmc.]

band·age (ban′dij), *n., v.,* **-aged, -ag·ing.** —*n.* strip of cloth or other material used in binding up and dressing a wound or other injury. —*v.* bind, tie up, or dress with a bandage. [< F, < *bande* BAND[1]] —**band′ag·er,** *n.*

band-aid (ban′ād′), *n.* **1** sterile adhesive bandage for small cuts, etc. **2 Band-Aid,** trademark for this bandage. **3** *Fig.* temporary solution to a problem.

ban·dan·na, ban·dan·a (ban dan′ə), *n.* a large, colored handkerchief, usually worn on the head or neck. [prob. < Hind. *bāndhnū* tie-dyeing]

band·box (band′boks′), *n.* a light cardboard box to put hats, scarves, etc., in.

ban·deau (ban dō′; ban′dō), *n., pl.* **-deaux** (-dōz′; -dōz). **1** band worn about the head. **2** a narrow band. [< F *bandeau*, dim. of *bande* band², ult. < Gmc.]

ban·de·role, ban·de·rol (ban′də rōl), *n.* a small flag. [< F < Ital., < *bandiera* BANNER]

ban·di·coot (ban′də küt), *n.* **1** a very large rat of India, about two feet long. **2** a ratlike marsupial of Australia. [< Indian dial. *pandikokku* pig-rat]

ban·dit (ban′dit), *n., pl.* **ban·dits, ban·dit·ti** (ban dit′i). highwayman; robber; outlaw; brigand. [< Ital. *bandito*, pp. of *bandire* banish, proscribe, ult. < Gmc.; akin to BAN] **—ban′dit·ry,** *n.*

band·mas·ter (band′mas′tər; -mäs′-), *n.* leader of a band of musicians.

ban·do·leer, ban·do·lier (ban′də lir′), *n.* a shoulder belt having loops for carrying cartridges. [< F < Sp., < *banda* BAND¹]

band·stand (band′stand′), *n.* an outdoor platform, usually roofed, for band concerts.

band·wag·on (band′wag′ən), *n.* **1** wagon that carries a musical band in a parade. **2** popular, fashionable, or winning group, trend, etc.

climb or **jump on the bandwagon,** join the winning side or group.

ban·dy (ban′di), *v.,* **-died, -dy·ing,** *n., pl.* **-dies,** *adj.* **—v. 1** throw back and forth; toss about. **2** give and take; exchange: *bandy words.* **—n.** *Esp. Brit.* the game of hockey. **—adj.** curved outward. [cf. F *bander* bandy, *se bander* band together]

ban·dy-leg·ged (ban′di leg′id; -legd′), *adj.* having legs that curve outward; bowlegged.

bane (bān), *n.* **1** cause of death or harm. **2** thing that ruins or spoils. [OE *bana* murderer]

bane·ful (bān′fəl), *adj.* deadly; harmful. **—bane′ful·ly,** *adv.* **—bane′ful·ness,** *n.*

bang¹ (bang), *n.* **1** a sudden, loud noise. **2** a violent, noisy blow. **3** vigor; impetus. **4** kick; thrill. **—v. 1** make a sudden loud noise. **2** hit with violent and noisy blows; strike noisily. **3** shut with noise; slam. **4** handle roughly. **—adv. 1** suddenly and loudly. **2** violently and noisily. [? < Scand. *banga* to hammer]

bang² (bang), **—n. bangs,** hair cut straight over the forehead. **—v.** cut squarely across. [short for *bangtail* docked tail (of a horse)]

Bang·kok (bang′kok), *n.* capital of Thailand.

Ban·gla·desh (bäng′glə desh′), *n.,* country in S Asia. **—Ban′gla·desh′i,** *adj., n.*

ban·gle (bang′gəl), *n.* ring worn around the wrist, arm, or ankle. [< Hind. *bangri* glass bracelet]

ban·ian (ban′yən), *n.* **1** =banyan. **2** a Hindu merchant of a caste that eats no meat. [< Pg., prob. < Ar. *banyān* < Gujarati (a language of western India), ult. <Skt. *vanij* merchant]

ban·ish (ban′ish), *v.* **1** condemn to leave a country; exile; expel. **2** force to go away; send away; drive away. [< OF <LL *bannīre* ban < Gmc.] **—ban′ish·er,** *n.* **—ban′ish·ment,** *n.*

ban·is·ter (ban′is tər), *n.* **1** baluster, **2 banisters,** balustrade of a staircase. [var. of *baluster*]

ban·jo (ban′jō), *n., pl.* **-jos, -joes.** stringed musical instrument of the guitar class, played with the fingers or a plectrum. [alter. of *bandore* < Sp. < LL < Gk. *pandoura* 3-stringed instrument] **—ban′jo·ist,** *n.*

bank¹ (bangk), *n.* **1** a long pile or heap; ridge; mound. **2** ground bordering a river, lake, etc. **3** a shallow place in a body of water; shoal; bar. **4** slope of an airplane when making a turn. **—v. 1** pile or heap up. **2** make (an airplane) bank. **3** cover (a fire) with ashes or fresh fuel so that it will burn long and slowly. [prob. < Scand.] **—banked,** *adj.*

bank² (bangk), *n.* **1** an institution for keeping, lending, exchanging, and issuing money. **2** fund of money out of which the dealer in games pays losses or players draw. **3** any place where reserve supplies are kept, as of blood for transfusions. **—v. 1** keep a bank. **2** put (money) in a bank.

bank on, depend on; be sure of. [< F < Ital. *banca*, orig., bench < Gmc.] **—bank′a·ble,** *adj.*

bank³ (bangk), *n.* **1** row of things: *bank of relay switches.* **2** row of keys on an organ, typewriter, etc. **3** bench for rowers in a galley. **4** row or tier of oars. **—v.** arrange in rows. [< OF < LL *bancus* < Gmc.; akin to BENCH] **—banked,** *adj.*

bank account, money in a bank that can be withdrawn by a depositor.

bank·book (bangk′bůk′), *n.* book in which a record of a person's account is kept.

bank card, electronic card issued by a bank that allows a depositor to carry out electronic banking and make purchases.

bank·er (bangk′ər), *n.* **1** person or company that keeps a bank. **2** dealer in a game.

bank·ing (bangk′ing), *n.* business of a bank.

bank note, note issued by a bank that must be paid on demand.

bank·rupt (bangk′rupt), *n.* person declared by a law court unable to pay debts and whose property is distributed among creditors. **—adj. 1** declared legally unable to pay debts. **2** at the end of one's resources; destitute. **3** wanting; lacking. **4** of bankrupts. **—v.** make bankrupt. [< F < Ital. *bancarotta* bankruptcy < *banca* bank² + *rotta*, fem. pp. of *rompere* break < L *rumpere*]

bank·rupt·cy (bangk′rupt si; -rəp si), *n., pl.* **-cies.** bankrupt condition.

ban·ner (ban′ər), *n.* **1** flag; ensign; standard. **2** piece of cloth with some design or words on it, attached by its upper edge to a pole or staff. **—adj.** leading; foremost. [< OF *baniere* < LL *bandum* < Gmc.] **—ban′nered,** *adj.*

banns (banz), *n.pl.* public notice, given three times in church, that a certain man and woman are to be married. [var. of *bans* proclamations]

ban·quet (bang′kwit), *n., v.,* **-quet·ed, -quet·ing. —n. 1** feast. **2** a formal dinner with speeches. **—v. 1** give a banquet to. **2** enjoy a banquet. [< F < Ital. *banchetto*, dim. of *banco* bench < Gmc.] **—ban′quet·er,** *n.*

ban·quette (bang ket′), *n.* **1** platform along the inside of a parapet or trench for gunners. **2** upholstered bench, esp. along a wall in a restaurant. [< F]

ban·shee, ban·shie (ban′shē; ban shē′), *n.* spirit whose wails mean that there will soon be a death in the family, in Irish and Scottish folk belief. [< Irish *bean sidhe* woman of the fairies]

ban·tam (ban′təm), *n.* **1** Often, **Bantam.** a small-sized kind of fowl. **2** a small person who is fond of fighting. **—adj. 1** light in weight; small. **2** ridiculously cocky and agressive. [prob. named for *Bantam*, city in Java]

ban·tam·weight (ban′təm wāt′), *n.* boxer who weighs 118 pounds or less. **—adj.** very small or weighing little for its kind or type.

ban·ter (ban′tər), *n.* playful teasing; joking. **—v. 1** tease playfully. **2** talk in a joking way. **—ban′ter·er,** *n.* **—ban′ter·ing·ly,** *adv.*

Ban·tu (ban′tü), *n., pl.* **-tu, -tus,** *adj.* **—n. 1** member of a large group of peoples living in C and S Africa. **2** any of the languages of these peoples. **—adj.** of these peoples or their languages.

ban·yan (ban′yən), *n.* a fig tree of India whose branches have hanging roots that grow down to the ground and sprout. Also, **banian.**

ban·zai (bän′zī′), *interj.* a Japanese greeting or patriotic cheer. It means "May you live ten thousand years!"

Bap., Bapt., Baptist.

bap·tism (bap′tiz əm), *n.* **1** rite or sacrament in which a person is dipped into or sprinkled with water, as a sign of washing away of sin and admission into the Christian church. **2** experience that cleanses a person or introduces one into a new kind of life. **—bap·tis′mal,** *adj.* **—bap·tis′mal·ly,** *adv.*

Bap·tist (bap′tist), *n.* **1** member of a Christian church that believes in baptism by submerging a person in water. **2** person who baptizes, as **John the Baptist. —adj.** of or having to do with the Baptists.

bap·tis·ter·y (bap′tis tər i; -tis tri), **bap·tist·ry** (bap′tis tri), *n., pl.* **-ter·ies; -ries.** building, or a part of a church, in which baptism is administered.

bap·tize (bap tīz′; bap′tīz), *v.,* **-tized, -tiz·ing. 1** dip into water or sprinkle with water, in baptism. **2** purify; cleanse. **3**

christen. [< OF < LL < Gk., < *baptein* dip] —**bap·tiz′er,** *n.*

bar (bär), *n., v.,* **barred, bar·ring,** *prep.* —*n.* **1** an evenly shaped piece of some solid, longer than it is wide or thick: *bar of soap.* **2** pole or rod put across a door, gate, window, etc., **3** barrier; obstruction. **4** stripe. **5** unit of rhythm in music. **6** line between two such units on a musical staff. **7** counter where drinks are served to customers. **8** place containing such a counter. **9** railing around the place where lawyers sit in a court. **10** profession of a lawyer. **11** lawyers as a group. —*v.* **1** fasten or shut off with a bar. **2** block; obstruct. **3** exclude; forbid. —*prep.* except. [< OF < VL *barra* thick ends of bushes (collectively) < Celtic]

bar., **1** barometer; barometric. **2** barrel.

barb (bärb), *n.* **1** point projecting backward from the main point, as of a fishhook. **2** a beardlike growth or part of a plant or animal. **3** *Fig.* anything that wounds or strings, as a remark. —*v.* furnish with barbs. [< F < L *barba* beard] —**barbed,** *adj.* —**barb′less,** *adj.*

Bar·ba·dos (bär bā′dōz; bä′bə dōz), *n.* island country in the West Indies.

bar·bar·i·an (bär bär′i ən), *n.* **1** person who is not civilized. **2** foreigner differing from the speaker or writer in language and customs. **3** person without sympathy for culture or art. —*adj.* **1** not civilized; barbarous. **2** differing from the speaker or writer in language and customs. —**bar·bar′i·an·ism,** *n.*

bar·bar·ic (bär bar′ik), *adj.* **1** uncivilized; rough and rude. **2** of or like that of barbarians. **3** crudely rich or too splendid. [< L < Gk., < *barbaros* foreign] —**bar·bar′i·cal·ly,** *adv.*

bar·ba·rism (bär′bə riz əm), *n.* **1** condition of uncivilized people. **2** barbarous act, custom, or trait. **3** use of a word or expression not in accepted use. **4** word or expression not in accepted use, as "his'n" for *his.*

bar·bar·i·ty (bär bar′ə ti), *n., pl.* **-ties.** **1** brutal cruelty. **2** act of cruelty. **3** barbaric manner, taste, or style.

bar·ba·rize (bär′bə rīz), *v.,* **-rized, -riz·ing.** make or become barbarous. —**bar′ba·ri·za′tion,** *n.*

bar·ba·rous (bär′bə rəs), *adj.* **1** not civilized; barbarian. **2** rough; rude. **3** savagely cruel; brutal. **4** crude; harsh. **5** differing from the language and customs of the speaker or writer. **6** filled with words or expressions not in accepted use. [< L < Gk. *barbaros* foreign, appar. orig., stammering] —**bar′ba·rous·ly,** *adv.* —**bar′ba·rous·ness,** *n.*

Bar·ba·ry (bär′bə ri), *n.* the Muslim countries west of Egypt on the N coast of Africa.

Barbary ape, a tailless monkey that lives in N Africa and on the Rock of Gibraltar.

Barbary States, former name for the countries of Morocco, Algeria, Tunis,

and Tripoli, once famous havens for pirates.

bar·be·cue (bär′bə kū), *n., v.,* **-cued, -cu·ing.** —*n.* **1** meat roasted before an open fire or on a grill. **2 a** feast at which animals are roasted whole. **b** food at such a feast. **c** device on which the food is prepared. **3** animal roasted whole. —*v.* **1** roast (meat) before an open fire or on a grill. **2** roast (an animal) whole. **3** cook (meat or fish) in a highly flavored sauce. [< Sp. < Haitian *barboka* framework of sticks]

barbed wire or **barb·wire** (bärb′wīr′), *n.* wire with sharp points on it every few inches, used for fences, etc.

bar·bel (bär′bəl), *n.* **1** a long, thin growth hanging from the mouths of some fishes. **2** fish having such growths. [< OF < LL *barbellus,* dim. of *barbus* a kind of fish < L *barba* beard]

bar·ber (bär′bər), *n.* person whose business is cutting hair, shaving, and trimming beards. —*v.* cut the hair of; shave; trim the beard of. [< AF < L *barba* beard]

bar·ber·ry (bär′ber′i; -bər i), *n., pl.* **-ries.** **1** shrub with sour red berries. **2** the berry.

bar·ber·shop (bär′bər shop′), *n.* shop where barbers work.

bar·bi·can (bär′bə kən), *n.* tower for defense built over a gate or bridge to a city or castle. [< OF < Med.L *barbicana*]

bar·bi·tal (bär′bə tôl; -tal), *n.* drug containing barbituric acid, used as a sedative or to induce sleep.

bar·bi·tu·rate (bär bich′ə rāt, -rit; bär′bə tùr′āt, -it, -tyùr′-), *n.* **1** salt or ester of barbituric acid. **2** any one of a group of drugs derived from barbituric acid.

bar·bi·tu·ric acid (bär′bə tùr′ik; -tyùr′-), an acid, $C_4H_4O_3N_2$, used as the basis of sedatives and sleep-inducing drugs.

bar·ca·role, bar·ca·rolle (bär′kə rōl), *n.* **1** Venetian boat song. **2** music imitating such a song. [< F < Ital. *barcarola* boatman's song < *barca* BARK[3]]

Bar·ce·lo·na (bär′sə lā′nə), *n.* seaport in NE Spain.

bar code, electronically coded lines and numbers stamped on product packaging and used to monitor prices and inventory. —*v.* apply a bar code to.

bard (bärd), *n.* **1** ancient Celtic poet and singer. **2** poet. [< Scotch Gaelic and Irish] —**bard′ic,** *adj.*

bare¹ (bãr), *adj., v.,* **bar·er, bar·est,** *v.,* **bared, bar·ing.** *adj.* **1** not clothed; naked. **2** not concealed, open. **3** empty. **4** plain; unadorned. **5** just enough and no more. —*v.* uncover; reveal.

lay bare, uncover; expose; reveal. [OE *bær*] —**bare′ness,** *n.* —**bar′er,** *n.*

bare² (bãr), *v. Archaic.* pt. of **bear¹.**

bare·back (bãr′bak′), *adv., adj.* without a saddle; on a horse's bare back. —**bare′backed′,** *adj.*

bare bones, only the essentials of something.

bare·faced (bãr′fãst′), *adj.* **1** shameless; impudent. **2** with the face bare. **3** not disguised. —**bare′fac′ed·ly,** *adv.* —**bare′fac′ed·ness,** *n.*

bare·foot (bãr′fùt′), *adj., adv.* without shoes and stockings. —**bare′foot′ed,** *adj.*

bare·hand·ed (bãr′hand′did), *adj.* **1** without any covering on the hands. **2** *Fig.* with empty hands.

bare·head·ed (bãr′hed′id), *adj., adv.* wearing nothing on the head. —**bare′head′ed·ness,** *n.*

bare·leg·ged (bãr′leg′id; -legd′), *adj.* without stockings.

bare·ly (bãr′li), *adv.* **1** only just; scarcely: *barely enough.* **2** without any extra thing. **3** openly; plainly.

bar·gain (bär′gin), *n.* **1** agreement to trade or exchange; contract. **2** something offered for sale cheap or bought cheap. **3** any trade or exchange. —*v.* **1** try to get good terms. **2** make a bargain; come to terms. **3** trade.

bargain for, be ready for; expect.

into the bargain, besides; also.

strike a bargain, reach an agreement. [< OF *bargaigne*] —**bar′gain·er,** *n.*

barge (bärj), *n., v.,* **barged, barg·ing.** —*n.* **1** a large, flat-bottomed boat for carrying freight. **2** a large boat used for excursions, pageants, etc. **3** a large motorboat or rowboat used by the commanding officer of a flagship. **4** houseboat. —*v.* **1** carry by barge. **2** move clumsily like a barge. **3** push oneself rudely. [< OF < L < Gk. *baris* boat used on Nile] —**barge′man,** *n.*

bar·ite (bãr′īt; bar′-), *n.* barium sulfate in its natural, mineral form. Also, **barytes.**

bar·i·tone (bar′ə tōn), *n.* **1** a male voice between tenor and bass. **2** part to be sung by such a voice. **3** person who sings this part. **4** a musical instrument that has the quality or range of this voice. —*adj.* of or for a baritone. Also, **barytone.** [< Gk., < *barys* deep + *tonos* pitch]

bar·i·um (bãr′i əm; bar′-), *n.* soft, silvery-white metallic element, Ba. [< NL < Gk. *barytes* weight] —**bar′ic,** *adj.*

barium sulfate, a sulfate of barium, $BaSO_4$.

bark¹ (bärk), *n.* the tough outside covering of the trunk, branches, and roots of trees and plants —*v.* **1** strip the bark from (a tree, etc.). **2** cover with bark. **3** scrape the skin from (shins, knuckles. etc.). [< Scand. *börkr*] —**bark′er,** *n.* —**bark′less,** *adj.*

bark² (bärk), *n.* **1** the short, sharp sound that a dog makes; yelp. **2** a sound like this. —*v.* **1** make this sound or one like it. **2** *Fig.* shout sharply; speak gruffly. **3** cough. **4** act as barker. [OE *beorcan*]

bark³ (bärk), *n.* **1** ship with three masts, square-rigged on the first two masts and fore-and-aft-rigged on the other. **2** boat; ship. Also, **barque.** [< F < Ital. < LL *barca*]

bar·keep (bär′kēp′), *n.* =bar keeper. —*v.* tend a bar.

bar·keep·er (bär′kēp′ər), *n.* **1** person who owns or operates a bar where alcoholic drinks are sold. **2** =bartender.

bar·ken·tine, bar·kan·tine (bär′kən tēn), *n.* three-masted ship with the foremast square-rigged and the other masts fore-and-aft-rigged. Also, **barquentine.** [< *bark³*; modeled on *brigantine*]

bark·er (bär′kər), *n.* **1** one or that which barks. **2** person who stands in front of a store, show, etc., urging people to go in.

bar·ley (bär′li), *n.* **1** the seed or grain of a cereal grass used for food and for making malt. **2** plant yielding this grain. [OE *bærlīc*]

barm (bärm), *n.* a foamy yeast that forms on malt liquors while they are fermenting. [OE *beorma*]

bar·maid (bär′mād′), *n.* female bartender.

bar·man (bär′mən), *n., pl.* **-men.** =barkeeper.

barm·y (bär′mi), *adj.,* **barm·i·er, barm·i·est. 1** full of barm; fermenting. **2** silly.

barn (bärn), *n.* a building for storing hay grain, or and sheltering cows, horses, etc. [OE *bœrn* < *bere* barley + *œrn* place]

bar·na·cle (bär′nə kəl), *n.* a crustacean that attaches itself to rocks, the bottoms of ships, etc. [< OF *bernac*]

barn dance, 1 informal dance held in a barn. **2** a lively dance resembling a polka.

barn·storm (bärn′stôrm′), *v.* travel to small towns and rural areas to perform, give plays, make speeches, etc. —**barn′storm′er,** *n.* —**barn′storm′ing,** *adj., n.*

Bar·num (bär′nəm), *n.* **Phineas Taylor,** 1810–91, American showman.

barn·yard (bärn′yärd′), *n.* yard around a barn for livestock, etc.

bar·o·graph (bar′ə graf; –gräf), *n.* instrument that automatically records changes in air pressure. [< Gk. *baros* weight + –GRAPH] —**bar′o·graph′ic,** *adj.*

ba·rom·e·ter (bə rom′ə tər), *n.* **1** instrument for measuring the pressure of the atmosphere, and thus determining the height above sea level, probable changes in the weather, etc. **2** *Fig.* something that indicates changes: *barometer of public opinion.* [< Gk. *baros* weight + –METER] —**bar′o·met′ric, bar′o·met′ri·cal,** *adj.* —**bar′o·met′ri·cal·ly,** *adv.*

bar·on (bar′ən), *n.* **1** nobleman of the lowest rank in Great Britain and other countries. **2** powerful merchant or financier. [< OF < L *barō* man, fellow] —**ba·ro′ni·al,** *adj.*

bar·on·age (bar′ən ij), *n.* **1** all the barons. **2** the nobility. **3** rank or title of a baron.

bar·on·ess (bar′ən is), *n.* **1** wife or widow of a baron. **2** woman whose rank is equal to that of a baron.

bar·on·et (bar′ən it; –et), *n.* **1** member of a hereditary order of honor in Great Britain ranking next below a baron and next above a knight. **2** title indicating this rank. —**bar′on·et·cy,** *n.*

bar·o·ny (bar′ə ni), *n., pl.* **-nies. 1** lands of a baron. **2** rank or title of a baron.

ba·roque (bə rōk′; –rok′), *adj.* **1** artistically irregular; tastelessly odd; ornate; fantastic; grotesque. **2** irregular in shape. —*n.* **a** art in the baroque style. **b** something in a baroque style. [< F < Pg. *barroco* irregular]

bar·o·scope (bar′ə skōp), *n.* instrument for showing changes in the pressure or density of the air. [< Gk. *baros* weight + E –*scope* instrument for viewing < Gk. *skopein* look at] —**bar′o·scop′ic, bar′o·scop′i·cal,** *adj.*

ba·rouche (bə rüsh′), *n.* a four-wheeled carriage with two seats facing each other and a folding top. [< dial. G < Ital. < L *birotus* two-wheeled < *bi*– two + *rota* wheel]

barque (bärk), *n.* =bark³.

bar·quen·tine (bär′kən tēn), *n.* =barkentine.

bar·rack (bar′ək), *n.* Usually, **barracks. 1** building or group of buildings for soldiers to live in. **2** large, plain building in which many people live. —*v.* lodge in barracks. [< F < Ital. *baracca*]

bar·ra·cu·da (ba′ə kü′də), *n., pl.* **-da, -das.** a large, voracious fish of the seas near the West Indies. [< Sp. < West Indian name]

bar·rage (bə räsh′ *for n. 1 and 2 and v.;* bär′ij *for n. 3*), *n., v.,* **-raged, -rag·ing.** —*n.* **1** barrier of artillery fire to check the enemy or to protect one's own soldiers in advancing or retreating. **2** stream of questions, accusations, etc. directed at a person. **3** artificial bar in a river; dam. —*v.* fire at with artillery. [< F, < *barrier* BAR]

bar·ra·try (bar′ə tri), *n.* **1** fraud or gross negligence of a ship's officer or seaman against owners, insurers, etc. **2** act or practice of stirring up lawsuits or quarrels. [< OF, < *barater* exchange, cheat] —**bar′ra·trous,** *adj.*

barred (bärd), *adj.* **1** having bars: *a barred window.* **2** marked with stripes.

bar·rel (bar′əl), *n., v.,* **-reled, -rel·ing;** *esp. Brit.* **-relled, -rel·ling.** —*n.* **1** container with round, flat top and bottom and slightly curved sides, usually made of thick boards held together by hoops; cask. **2** amount that a barrel can hold. **3** something somewhat like a barrel: *the barrel of a drum.* **4** the metal tube or a gun. **5** great deal of something: *barrel of laughs.* —*v.* put in barrels.

over a barrel, in a defenseless position.

the bottom of the barrel, a the last of one's resources. **b** the least desirable; most unpromising: *applicants from the bottom of the barrel.* [< OF *baril*, prob. < VL *barra* bar, stave]

barrel organ, a hand organ.

bar·ren (bar′ən), *adj.* **1** not producing anything; unproductive. **2** not able to bear offspring; sterile. **3** fruitless; unprofitable. **4** without interest; dull. —*n.* Usually, **barrens.** barren stretch of land. [< OF *baraine*] —**bar′ren·ly,** *adv.* —**bar′ren·ness,** *n.*

bar·rette (bə ret′), *n.* a clasp to hold the hair in place.

bar·ri·cade (bar′ə kād′; bar′ə kād), *n., v.,* **-cad·ed, -cad·ing.** —*n.* **1** a rough, hastily made barrier for defense. **2** any barrier or obstruction. —*v.* block or obstruct with a barricade. [< F, appar. < Pr. *barricada* < *barrica* cask; orig., made of casks. See BARREL.] —**bar′ri·cad′er,** *n.*

bar·ri·er (bar′i ər), *n.* **1** something that stands in the way; something stopping progress or preventing approach. **2** something that keeps apart. [< AF < LL, < *barra* BAR]

bar·ring (bär′ing), *prep.* except; not including.

bar·ris·ter (bar′is tər), *n.* lawyer in England who can plead in any court. [< *bar* + *-ster*] —**bar′ris·te′ri·al,** *adj.*

bar·room (bär′rüm′; –rùm′), *n.* room with a bar for the sale of alcoholic drinks.

bar·row¹ (bar′ō), *n.* **1** wheelbarrow. **2** =handcart. **3** frame with two short shafts for handles at each end, used for carrying a load. [OE *bearwe;* akin to BEAR¹]

bar·row² (bar′ō), *n.* mound of earth or stones over an ancient grave. [OE *beorg*]

Bar·row (bar′ō), *n.* **Point,** northernmost point of land in Alaska.

bar sinister, supposed sign of illegitimacy.

Bart., Baronet.

bar·tend·er (bär′ten′dər), *n.* person who serves alcoholic drinks to customers at a bar.

bar·ter (bär′tər), *v.* **1** trade by exchanging one kind of goods for other goods without using money. **2** exchange. —*n.* **1** act of bartering. **2** exchange. **3** something bartered. [< OF *barater* exchange; akin to BARRATRY] —**bar′ter·er,** *n.*

bar·ti·zan (bär′tə zan; bär′tə zan′), *n.* a small overhanging turret on a wall or tower. [alter. of *bratticing* < *brattice* parapet < OF, prob. < OE *brittisc* British (type of fortification)]

Bar·ton (bär′tən), *n.* **Clara,** 1821–1912, American woman who organized the American Red Cross in 1881.

ba·ry·tes (bə rī′tēz), *n.* =barite.

bar·y·tone (bar′ə tōn), *n., adj.* =baritone.

bas·al (bās′əl), *adj.* **1** of or at the base; forming the base. **2** fundamental; basic. —**bas′al·ly,** *adv.*

basal metabolism, amount of energy used by an animal at rest.

ba·salt (bə sôlt′; bas′ôlt), *n.* a hard, dark-colored rock of volcanic origin. [< LL *basaltēs,* a manuscript corruption of L *basanītēs* < Gk., < *basanos* touchstone]

bas·cule (bas′kūl), *n.* device that works like a seesaw. In a **bascule bridge** the rising part is counterbalanced by a weight. [< F, seesaw, ult. < *battre* beat (infl. by *bas* low) + *cul* posterior]

base[1] (bās), *n.*, *v.*, **based, bas·ing.** —*n.* 1 bottom. 2 a fundamental principle; basis. 3 essential part. 4 chemical compound that reacts with an acid to form a salt. 5 goal in certain games, such as baseball. 6 starting place. 7 place from which an army, air force, or navy operates. 8 number that is a starting point for a system of numeration. 9 line or surface forming that part of a geometric figure on which it is supposed to stand. —*v.* 1 make or form a base or foundation for. 2 establish; found (on): *his large business was based on good service.* [< OF < L < Gk. *basis* base; lit., a step]

base[2] (bās), *adj.*, **bas·er, bas·est,** *n.* —*adj.* 1 mean; selfish; cowardly. 2 inferior. 3 coarse in quality. 4 menial; common. 5 *Archaic.* of humble origin. [< OF < LL *bessus* low] —**base′ly,** *adv.* —**base′ness,** *n.*

base·ball (bās′bôl′), *n.* 1 game played with bat and ball by two teams of nine players each on a field with four bases. 2 ball used in this game.

base·board (bās′bôrd′; –bōrd′), *n.* Am. 1 line of boards around the walls of a room, next to the floor. 2 board forming the base of anything.

base·born (bās′bôrn′), *adj.* 1 born of humble parents. 2 illegitimate.

base hit, successful hit of the baseball so that the batter reaches at least first base without the help of an error.

Ba·sel (bä′zəl), *n.* city in NW Switzerland.

base·less (bās′lis), *adj.* groundless. —**base′less·ness,** *n.*

base line, 1 line used as a base. 2 line between bases in baseball.

base·ment (bās′mənt), *n.* 1 story of a building partly or wholly below ground. 2 the lowest division of the wall of a building.

ba·ses[1] (bā′sēz), *n.* pl. of **basis.**

bas·es[2] (bās′iz), *n.* pl. of **base**[1].

bash (bash), *v.* strike with a smashing blow. —*n.* a smashing blow. [? imit.]

bash·ful (bash′fəl), *adj.* uneasy and awkward in the presence of strangers; shy; timid. [< *bash,* v. (var. of *abash*) + –*ful*] —**bash′ful·ly,** *adv.* —**bash′ful·ness,** *n.*

bas·ic (bās′ik), *adj.* 1 of or at the base; forming the base; fundamental. 2 a relating to, having the nature of, or containing a chemical base. b alkaline. —**bas′i·cal·ly,** *adv.*

BASIC (bā′sik), *n.* computer language based on English. Also **Basic.** [*B*(eginners) *A*(ll-purpose) *S*(ymbolic) *I*(nstruction) *C*(ode)]

Basic Law or **basic law,** written statement of the organization of a government.

bas·il (baz′əl), *n.* sweet-smelling plant of the same family as mint, used in cooking. [< OF < L < Gk. *basilikon* royal]

bas·i·lar (bas′ə lər), **bas·i·lar·y** (–lər′i), *adj.* at the base.

ba·sil·i·ca (bə sil′ə kə), *n.* 1 oblong building with a broad nave separated from side aisles by rows of columns, used in ancient Rome for law courts and public meetings. 2 an early Christian church built in this form. 3 title conferred by the Pope on a Roman Catholic church. [< L < Gk. *basilike* (*oikia*) royal (house) < *basileus* king] —**ba·sil′i·can,** *adj.*

bas·i·lisk (bas′ə lisk; baz′–), *n.* 1 *Class. Legend.* fabled reptile whose breath and look were thought to be fatal. 2 crested lizard of tropical America. [< L < Gk. *basiliskos,* dim. of *basileus* king]

ba·sin (bā′sən), *n.* 1 wide, shallow bowl; bowl. 2 amount that a basin can hold. 3 hollow place containing water. 4 all the land drained by a river and the streams that flow into it. [< OF *bacin* < LL *baccinum* < *bacca* water vessel] —**ba′sined,** *adj.* —**ba′sin·like′,** *adj.*

ba·sis (bā′sis), *n.*, *pl.* **-ses** (–sēz). 1 main part; base. 2 a fundamental principle or set of principles; foundation. 3 the principal ingredient. 4 a starting point. [< L < Gk. See BASE[1].]

bask (bask; bäsk), *v.* warm oneself pleasantly. [< Scand. *bathask* bathe oneself] —**bask′er,** *n.*

bas·ket (bas′kit; bäs′–), *n.* 1 container made of twigs, grasses, and other fibers woven together. 2 amount that a basket holds. 3 anything resembling or shaped like a basket. 4 the structure beneath a balloon for carrying passengers or ballast. 5 net shaped like a basket, used as a goal in basketball. 6 score made in basketball by tossing the ball through a ring and the basket. —**bas′ket·like′,** *adj.*

bas·ket·ball (bas′kit bôl′; bäs′–), *n.* 1 game played with a large ball by two teams of five players each who try to score by tossing the ball through the basket. 2 the ball used.

bas·ket·ry (bas′kit ri; bäs′–), *n.* 1 basketwork; baskets. 2 art of making baskets.

bas·ket·work (bas′kit wèrk′; bäs′–), *n.* work woven like a basket; wickerwork.

Basque (bask), *n.* 1 member of a people living in the Pyrenees in S France and in N Spain. 2 their language. —*adj.* having to do with the Basques or their language.

bas·re·lief (bä′ri lēf′, bas′–; bä′ri lēf, bas′–), *n.* carving or sculpture in which the figures project only slightly from the background. [< F < Ital. *basso-rilievo* low relief]

bass[1] (bās), *adj.* 1 low or deep in sound. 2 of or for the lowest part or voice. —*n.* 1 the lowest male voice. 2 singer with such a voice. 3 lowest part in harmonized music. 4 instrument for such a part. [var. of *base*[2]; after Ital. *basso*]

bass[2] (bas), *n.*, *pl.* **bass·es** or (*esp. collectively*) **bass.** any of various spiny-finned fish that live in fresh or salt water, as the black bass. [var. of *barse* perch; OE *bears*]

bass[3] (bas), *n.* 1 =basswood. 2 =bast. [alter. of *bast*]

bass drum (bās), large drum that makes a deep, low sound when struck.

bas·set (bas′it), or **basset hound,** *n* dog with short legs and a long body, like a dachshund, but larger and heavier. [< F, dim. of *bas* low]

bas·si·net (bas′ə net′; bas′ə net), *n.* 1 basketlike cradle with a hood. 2 baby carriage of similar shape. [< F, dim. of *bassin* BASIN]

bas·so (bas′ō; bäs′ō), *n.*, *pl.* **-sos, -si** (–si), *adj.* —*n.* singer with a bass voice. —*adj.* bass[1·] [< Ital. See BASE[1].]

bas·soon (bə sün′; ba–), *n.* a deep-toned wind instrument with a doubled wooden tube and a curved metal mouthpiece. [< F < Ital. *bassone* < *basso* basso] —**bas·soon′ist,** *n.*

bass viol (bās), a deep-toned stringed instrument like a very large violin.

bass·wood (bas′wùd′), *n.* 1 Also, **basswood tree. a** =linden tree. **b** =tulip tree. 2 wood of either of these trees. —*adj.* made of basswood.

bast (bast), *n.* 1 inner layer of bark that contains cells for carrying sap. 2 the tough fibers in this inner layer. [OE *bœst*]

bas·tard (bas′tərd), *n.* 1 child whose parents are not married to each other; illegitimate child. 2 anything inferior or spurious. —*adj.* 1 born of parents who are not married to each other. 2 spurious; inferior. 3 irregular or unusual in shape, size, style, etc. [< OF < (*fils de*) *bast* packsaddle (child)] —**bas′tar·dy,** *n.*

baste[1] (bāst), *v.*, **bast·ed, bast·ing.** drip or pour melted fat or butter on (meat, etc.) while roasting.

baste[2] (bāst), *v.*, **bast·ed, bast·ing.** sew with long stitches to hold the cloth until the final sewing. [< OF *bastir,* < Gmc. Cf. OHG *bestan* tie up, sew with bast.] —**bast′er,** *n.*

baste[3] (bāst), *v.*, **bast·ed, bast·ing,** beat; thrash [Scand. *beysta*]

Bas·tille (bas tēl′), *n.* 1 old fort in Paris used as a prison, destroyed by a mob on July 14, 1789, marking the start of the French Revolution. 2 **bastille, bastile.** =prison. [< F < LL *bastilia* < *bastire* build]

bas·ti·na·do (bas′tə nā′dō), *n.*, *pl.* **-does,** *v.*, **-doed, -do·ing.** —*n.* 1 a beating with a stick, esp. on the soles of the feet. 2 stick; cudgel. —*v.* beat or flog with a stick. [< Sp. *bastonada* < *bastón* cudgel, ult. < Gmc.]

bast·ings (bās′tingz), *n. pl.* long, loose stitches to hold the cloth in place until the final sewing.

bas·tion (bas′chən; –ti ən), *n.* **1** a projecting part of a fortification. **2** defense; fortification. [< F < Ital. *bastione* < *bastire* build. See BASTILLE.] —**bas′tioned,** *adj.*

bat[1] (bat), *n., v.,* **bat·ted, bat·ting.** —*n.* **1** a stout wooden stick or club, used to hit the ball in baseball, etc. **2** act of batting. **3** turn at batting. **4** stroke; blow. **5** wild, gay time; spree. —*v.* **1** hit with a bat; hit. **2** in baseball, hit safely balls served by the pitcher. [OE *batt*]

at bat, in the batter's position.

bat around, go from place to place without plan or purpose.

bat[2] (bat), *n.* a nocturnal flying mammal characterized by modified forelimbs which serve as wings. [< Scand. (Dan.) –*bakke*] —**bat′like**′, *adj.*

bat[3] (bat), *v.,* **bat·ted, bat·ting.** wink. [< OF < L *battuere* beat]

bat., batt., **1** battalion. **2** battery.

Ba·taan (bə tän′; –tan′), *n.* peninsula near Manila in the Philippines.

batch (bach), *n.* **1** quantity of bread made at one baking. **2** quantity of anything made as one lot. **3** number of persons or things taken together. [ME *bacche* < OE *bacan* bake]

bate (bāt), *v.,* **bat·ed, bat·ing.** abate; lessen.

with bated breath, holding the breath in great fear, awe, etc. [var. of *abate*]

ba·teau (ba tō′), *n., pl.* –**teaux** (–tōz′). a light boat with a flat bottom and tapering ends. [< F, ult. < OE *bāt* BOAT]

bath (bath; bäth), *n., pl.* **baths** (baτħz; bäτħz). **1** a washing of the body. **2** water, etc., for a bath. **3** a tub, room, or other place for bathing. **4** often, **baths.** especially in Roman times, an elaborate establishment for public bathing and exercise. **5** Often, **baths.** resort with baths for medical treatment. **6** liquid in which something is washed or dipped. **7** container holding the liquid. [OE *bæth*]

Bath (bath; bäth), *n.* city in SW England.

bathe (bāτħ), *v.,* **bathed, bath·ing.** **1** take a bath. **2** give a bath to. **3** apply water to; wash or moisten with any liquid. **4** go swimming. **5** cover; surround. [OE *bathian*] —**bath′er,** *n.*

bath·house (bath′hous′, bäth′–), *n.* **1** building fitted up for bathing. **2** building containing dressing rooms for swimmers.

ba·thos (bā′thos), *n.* **1** a ludicrous descent from the lofty or elevated to the commonplace in writing or speech; anticlimax. **2** excessive or insincere pathos. [< Gk., depth] —**ba·thet′ic,** *adj.*

bath·robe (bath′rōb′; bäth′–), *n.* a long, loose garment worn after bathing or while lounging.

bath·room (bath′rüm′; –rům′; bäth′–), *n.* **1** room fitted up for taking baths, etc. **2** toilet.

bath·tub (bath′tub′; bäth′–), *n.* tub to bathe in.

bath·y·scaph or **bath·y·scafe** (bath′-ə skaf), *n.* a round, deep-diving craft

that can be navigated underwater. [< Gk *bathys* + *skáphē* bowl, tub]

bath·y·sphere (bath′ə sfir), *n.* watertight chamber with glass windows, in which people descend to the ocean depths to study animal and plant life. [< Gk. *bathys* deep + E –*sphere* < Gk. *sphaira* sphere]

ba·tik (bə tēk′; bat′ik), *n.* **1** method of making designs on cloth by covering with wax the parts not to be dyed. **2** cloth dyed in this way. **3** design formed in this way. —*adj.* **1** made by batik; made of batik. **2** like batik; brightly or gaily colored. Also, **battik.** [< Malay]

ba·tiste (bə tēst′), *n.* a fine, thin, cotton cloth. [< F *Baptiste,* prob. from name of maker]

ba·ton (ba ton′; bə–), *n.* **1** stick used by the leader of an orchestra, chorus, etc., to indicate tempo and direct the performance. **2** staff or stick used as a symbol of office or authority. **3** hollow metal stick twirled by a drum major or majorette in a showy display, especially in a parade. **4** stick carried by a relay runner and passed to the next runner on the team. [< F]

Bat·on Rouge (bat′ən rüzh′), capital of Louisiana, in the SE part, on the Mississippi.

ba·tra·chi·an (bə trā′ki ən), *Zool.* —*adj.* **1** of or belonging to the division of vertebrates consisting of tailless amphibians, as frogs and toads. **2** like frogs and toads. —*n.* a tailless amphibian. [< Gk. *batrachos* frog]

bat·tal·ion (bə tal′yən), *n.* **1** *U.S.* tactical military unit made up of two or more companies, usually part of a regiment. **2** any large part of an army organized to act together. **3** army. **4** organized group. **batallions, a** armies. **b** large number. [< F < Ital. *battaglione,* dim. of *battaglia* BATTLE]

bat·ten[1] (bat′ən), *v.* **1** grow fat. **2** fatten. **3** feed greedily. [< Scand. *batna* < *bati* improvement] —**bat′ten·er,** *n.*

bat·ten[2] (bat′ən), *n.* **1** board used for flooring. **2** strip of wood nailed across parallel boards to strengthen them, cover cracks, etc. —*v.* fasten or strengthen with strips of wood. [var. of *baton*]

bat·ter[1] (bat′ər), *v.* **1** beat with repeated blows; pound. **2** damage by hard use. [< *bat*[1]]

bat·ter[2] (bat′ər), *n.* mixture of flour, milk, eggs, etc., beaten together for pancakes, cakes, etc. [prob. < OF, < *batre* BAT[3]]

bat·ter[3] (bat′ər), *n.* player whose turn it is to bat in baseball, cricket, etc.

battering ram, 1 military machine with a heavy horizontal beam used in ancient times for battering down walls, gates, etc. **2** any heavy object similarly used.

bat·ter·y (bat′ər i), *n., pl.* –**ter·ies. 1** set of similar or connected things. **2** set of one or more cells that produce electric current. **3** *Mil.* **a** set of big guns for

combined action in attack or defense. **b** these guns together with the soldiers and equipment for them. **4** in baseball, the pitcher and catcher together. **5** the unlawful beating of another person. **6** any act of beating or battering. [< F, < *battre* beat. See BAT[3], BATTLE.]

bat·tik (bat′ik), *n., adj.* =batik.

bat·ting (bat′ing), *n.* wool or other fibers pressed into thin layers used in quilts, coats, etc., for warmth.

bat·tle (bat′əl), *n., v.,* –**tled, –tling.** —*n.* **1** fight between armies or navies. **2** fighting; warfare. **3** any fight; contest. —*v.* **1** take part in a battle. **2** fight; struggle; contend.

do battle (*with* or *over*), struggle; contend; fight over.

join battle, begin to fight. [< OF < LL *battalia* < L *battuere* beat] —**bat′tler,** *n.*

bat·tle·ax, bat·tle·axe (bat′əl aks′), *n.* **1** ax formerly used as a weapon in war. **2** assertive, strong-willed woman.

battle cruiser, a large, fast warship, not as heavily armored as a battleship.

battle cry, 1 shout of soldiers in battle. **2** motto or slogan in any contest.

bat·tle·dore (bat′əl dôr′; –dōr′), *n.* **1** small racket used to hit a shuttlecock back and forth in the game of battledore and shuttlecock. **2** the game itself.

battle fatigue, neurosis from stress of combat.

bat·tle·field (bat′əl fēld′), **bat·tle·ground** (bat′əl ground′), *n.* place where a battle is fought or has been fought.

bat·tle·front (bat′əl frunt′), *n.* place where combat between armies takes place.

bat·tle·ment (bat′əl mənt), *n.* **1** wall with indentations for soldiers to shoot through. **2** wall built like this for ornament. [ult. < OF *bastiller* fortify]

bat·tle·ship (bat′əl ship′), *n.* largest and most heavily armored warship.

bat·ty (bat′i), *adj.,* –**ti·er, –ti·est. 1** batlike. **2** crazy; odd.

bau·ble (bô′bəl), *n.* a showy trifle having no real value. [< OF *babel* toy]

baulk (bôk), *v., n.* =balk.

baux·ite (bôk′sīt; bō′zīt), *n.* a claylike mineral from which aluminum is obtained. [from Les *Baux,* France]

Ba·var·i·a (bə vār′i ə), *n.* a state in SW Germany. —**Ba·var′i·an,** *n., adj.*

bawd (bôd), *n.* **1** person, especially a woman, who keeps a brothel. **2** prostitute. [< OF *baud* gay < Gmc.]

bawd·ry (bôd′ri), *n.* obscenity; lewdness.

bawd·y (bôd′i), *adj.,* **bawd·i·er, bawd·i·est.** lewd; obscene. —**bawd′i·ly,** *adv.* —**bawd′i·ness,** *n.*

bawl (bôl), *n.* **1** noisy shout at the top of one's voice. **2** a loud crying. —*v.* **1** shout or cry out in a noisy way. **2** weep loudly; cry hard.

bawl out, *Slang.* reprimand. [prob. < Med.L *baulare* bark] —**bawl′er,** *n.*

bay[1] (bā), *n.* part of a sea or lake, extending into the land. [< OF *baie* < Gmc.]

bay² (bā), *n.* **1** space or division of a wall or building between columns, pillars, etc. **2** space with a window or set of windows in it, projecting out from a wall. **3** =bay window. [< F *baie* opening < VL *batare* gape]

bay³ (bā), *n.* long, deep bark of a dog or similar animal. —*v.* bark; bark at. **hold** or **keep at bay,** hold off; resist successfully. [< OF *bayer,* prob. < VL *batare* gape] —**bay´er,** *n.*

bay⁴ (bā), *n.* **1** a small evergreen tree with smooth, shiny leaves; laurel tree. **2** bays. **a** laurel wreath worn by poets or victors. **b** honor; renown: fame. [< OF *baie* < L *baca* berry]

bay⁵ (bā), *n.* **1.**reddish brown. **2** reddish-brown horse. *adj.* reddish-brown. [< OF *bai* < L *badius*]

bay·ber·ry (bā´ber´i), *n., pl.* **-ries. 1 a** North American shrub with grayish-white berries coated with wax. **b** one of the berries. **2** West Indian tree whose leaves contain an oil used in bay rum.

bay·o·net (bā´ə nit; –net), *n., v.,* **-net-ed, –net-ing.** —*n.* blade for piercing or stabbing, attached to a gun. —*v.* pierce or stab with a bayonet. [< F *baïonnette;* named for *Bayonne,* France]

bay·ou (bī´ü), *n., pl.* **-ous.** marshy inlet or outlet of a lake, river, or gulf in the southern United States. [< Louisiana F < Choctaw *bayuk* small stream]

bay rum, a fragrant liquid made from the leaves of the bayberry tree, used as a lotion.

bay window, window or set of windows that projects from a wall.

ba·zaar, ba·zar (bə zär´), *n.* **1** street or streets full of shops. **2** place for the sale of many kinds of goods. **3** sale held to benefit a charity, a worthy cause, etc. [< F < Ar. < Pers. *bāzār*]

ba·zoo·ka (bə zü´kə), *n.* rocket gun used against tanks. [from resemblance to trombonelike instrument created and named by Bob Burns, American humorist]

BB, 1 standard size of shot. **2** shot of this size, especially shot used in an air rifle.

BBC, British Broadcasting Corporation.

bbl., *pl.* **bbls.** barrel.

B-bop (bē´bop´). *n. Slang.* bebop.

B.C., 1 before Christ; before the birth of Christ. 350 B.C. is 100 years earlier than 250 B.C. **2** British Columbia.

B cell or **B-cell** (bē´sel´), *n.* type of lymphocyte that produces antibodies.

bd., *pl.* **bds. 1** board. **2** bond. **3** bound.

be (bē), *v., pres. indic. sing.* **am, are, is,** *pl.* **are;** *pt. indic. sing.* **was, were, was,** *pl.* **were;** *pp.* **been;** *ppr.* **be·ing. 1** have reality; exist; live. **2** *Be* is used as a linking verb between a subject and a predicate modifier or to form infinitives and participial phrases: *you will be late, try to be just.* **3** *Be* is used as an auxiliary verb; with: **a** the present participle of another verb to form the progressive tense: *he is*

building a house. **b** the past participle of another verb to form the passive voice: *the date was fixed.* [OE *bēon*]

be-, *prefix.* **1** thoroughly; all around, as in *bespatter.* **2** at; on; to; for; about; against, as in *bewail.* **3** make, as in *belittle.* **4** provide with, as in *bespangle.* [OE, unstressed form of *bī* by]

Be, beryllium.

BE, B/E, b.e., bill of exchange.

beach (bēch), *n.* the almost flat shore of sand or little stones at the edge of the sea, a river, or a large lake; strand. —*v.* run or draw (a boat) ashore. —**beach´less,** *adj.*

beach·comb·er (bēch´kōm´ər), *n.* **1** vagrant or loafer on beaches. **2** long wave rolling in from the ocean onto a beach.

beach·head (bēch´hed´), *n.* the first position established by an invading army on an enemy beach or shore.

bea·con (bē´kən), *n.* **1** fire or light used as a signal to guide or warn. **2** signal to guide aircraft and ships through fogs, storms, etc. **3** a tall tower for a signal; lighthouse. —*v.* **1** give light to; guide; warn. **2** shine brightly. **3** supply with beacons. [OE *bēacn*] —**bea´con-less,** *adj.*

bead (bēd), *n.* **1** a small ball or bit of glass, metal, etc., with a hole through it, so that it can be strung on a thread with others like it. **2** any small, round object like a drop or bubble: *beads of sweat.* **3** front sight of a rifle. **4** narrow, semicircular molding. —*v.* **1** put beads on; ornament with beads. **2** form beads.

beads, a a string of beads as a necklace. **b** =rosary.

draw a bead on, take aim at.

say, tell, or **count one's beads,** say a prayer, esp. using a rosary. [OE *bedu* prayer. See def. 2b.] —**bead´ed,** *adj.*

bead·ing (bēd´ing), *n.* **1** trimming made of beads threaded into patterns. **2** narrow trimming. **3** pattern or edge on woodwork, silver, etc., made of small beads. **4** narrow, semicircular molding.

bea·dle (bē´dəl), *n.* a minor officer in the Church of England. [OE *bydel*]

bead·work (bēd´werk´), *n.* =beading.

bead·y (bēd´i), *adj.,* **bead·i·er, bead·i·est. 1** small, round, and shiny. **2** trimmed with beads. **3** covered with drops or bubbles.

bea·gle (bē´gəl), *n.* a small hunting dog with short legs and drooping ears. [ME *begle*]

beak (bēk), *n.* **1** bird's bill, esp. one that is strong and hooked and useful in striking or tearing. **2** similar part in other animals. **3** *Fig.* large, esp. pointed, nose on a person. **4** projecting bow of an ancient warship. **5** spout. [< OF < L *beccus* < Celtic] —**beaked,** *adj.* —**beak´less,** *adj.* —**beak´like,** *adj.*

beak·er (bēk´ər), *n.* **1** large cup or drinking glass. **2** contents of a beaker. **3** thin glass or metal cup used in laboratories. [< Scand. *bikarr*]

beam (bēm), *n.* **1** large, long piece of timber or metal ready for use in building. **2** main horizontal support of a building or ship. **3** crosswise bar of a balance, from the ends of which the scales or pans are suspended. **4** ray of light or heat. **5** bright look or smile. **6** radio signal used to guide aircraft, ships, etc. **7** side of a ship, or the direction at right angles to the keel, with reference to wind, sea, etc. **8** widest part of a ship. —*v.* **1** send out rays of light; shine. **2** smile radiantly. **3** direct (a broadcast): *beam* telecasts to a satellite.

beam down, appear suddenly, as if from space.

on the beam, a on the right course or track. **b** *Fig.* just right; exactly. [OE *bēam* tree, piece of wood, ray of light] —**beamed,** *adj.* —**beam´less,** *adj.* —**beam´like´,** *adj.*

beam·ing (bēm´ing), *adj.* **1** shining; bright. **2** smiling brightly. —**beam´ing-ly,** *adv.*

bean (bēn), *n.* **1** smooth, kidney-shaped seed used as a vegetable. **2** the long pod containing such seeds, esp. one eaten as a vegetable. **3** plant that beans grow on. **4** any seed shaped somewhat like a bean. **5** *Informal.* head. —*v.* hit on the head. [OE *bēan*]

bean·ball (bēn´bôl´), *n.* baseball thrown by the pitcher so as to hit or attempt to hit the batter's head. —**bean´ball´er,** *n.*

bear¹ (bãr), *v.,* **bore** or (*Archaic*) **bare, borne** or **born, bear·ing. 1** carry: *bear a burden.* **2** endure: *he can't bear the noise.* **3** yield: *bear fruit.* **4** give birth to; have (offspring): *bear a child.* **5** have an effect; on; relate to: *his story does not bear on the question.* **6** press: push. **7** move; go; tend in direction: *the ship bore north.* **8** allow; permit: *the accident bears two explanations.*

bear down, a put pressure on. **b** approach.

bear out, support; prove.

bear up, not lose hope or faith.

bear with, put up with. [OE *beran*]

bear² (bãr), *n., adj., v.,* **beared, bear·ing.** —*n.* **1** a large quadruped animal that has coarse hair and a very short tail. **2** a gruff or surly person. **3** person who tries to lower prices in the stock market, etc. **4** Bear, *Astron.* one of two northern groups of stars; the Little Bear or the Great Bear. —*adj.* having to do with lowering prices in the stock market, etc. —*v.* operate for a decline in stocks, etc. [OE *bera*]

bear·a·ble (bãr´ə bəl), *adj.* that can be borne; endurable. —**bear´a·ble·ness,** *n.* —**bear´a·bly,** *adv.*

beard (bird), *n.* **1** hair growing on a man's face. **2** something resembling or suggesting this, as the chin tuft of a goat. **3** hairs on the heads of plants like oats, barley, and wheat; awns. —*v.* face boldly; defy. [OE] —**beard´ed,** *adj.*

—**beard′less,** *adj.* —**beard′less·ness,** *n.* —**beard′like′,** *adj.*

bear·er (bâr′ər), *n.* **1** person or thing that carries. **2** person who holds or presents a check, draft, or note for payment. **3** tree or plant that produces fruit or flowers. **4** holder of a rank or office. **5** pallbearer.

bear·ing (bâr′ing), *n.* **1** way of standing, sitting, walking, etc.; carriage: *a dignified bearing.* **2** reference; relation: *the question has no bearing on the problem.* **3** act, power, or season of bearing or producing as offspring or fruit. **4** that which is produced. **5** act of a person or thing that bears; supporting; sustaining. **6** part of a machine on which another part turns or slides. **7** supporting part, as of a structure. **8** single device in a coat of arms. **bearings,** direction; position in relation to other things: *the hiker got his bearings from the sun.*

bear·ish (bâr′ish), *adj.* **1** like a bear; rough; surly. **2** aiming at or tending to lower prices in the stock market, etc. **3** *Fig.* not hopeful or confident; pessimistic. —**bear′ish·ly,** *adv.* —**bear′ish·ness,** *n.*

bear·skin (bâr′skin′), *n.* fur of a bear.

beast (bēst), *n.* **1** any animal except man, esp. a four-footed animal. **2** coarse, dirty, or brutal person. **3** beastly person, esp. one who lacks self-control. [< OF < LL *besta*] —**beast′like′,** *adj.*

beast·ly (bēst′li), *adj.* **-li·er, -li·est,** —*adj.* **1** like a beast; brutal; coarse. **2** annoying; irksome. *-adv.* unpleasantly annoying. —**beast′li·ness,** *n.*

beat (bēt), *v.,* **beat, beat·en** or **beat, beat·ing,** *n., adj.* —*v.* **1** strike again and again; **2** throb: *her heart beats fast with joy.* **3** defeat; overcome. **4** make flat: *beat gold into gold leaf.* **5** mix by stirring rapidly: *beat eggs.* **6** move up and down; flap: *the bird beat its wings.* **7** make a sound by being struck: *the drums beat loudly.* **8** mark (time). **9** go through in a hunt or search. **10** win; surpass: *we beat!* —*n.* **1** blow made again and again: *the beat of a drum.* **2** *Music.* unit of time. **3** a regular route of a policeman. —*adj.* exhausted. **beat a retreat,** hurry away. **beat it,** go away. **beat off,** drive away with blows. **beat up,** attack; thrash. [OE *bēatan*] —**beat′er,** *n.*

beat·en (bēt′ən), *v.* pp. of **beat.** —*adj.* **1** whipped; thrashed. **2** shaped by blows. **3** much walked on or traveled: *beaten path.* **4** defeated; overcome. **5** exhausted.

be·a·tif·ic (bē′ə tif′ik), *adj.* **1** showing great happiness. **2** making blessed; blissful. [< L *beatificus* < *beare* bless + *facere* make] —**be′a·tif′i·cal·ly,** *adv.*

be·at·i·fy (bi at′ə fī), *v.,* **-fied, -fy·ing. 1** make supremely happy; bless. **2** declare (a dead person) by a decree of the Pope to be among the blessed in heaven. —**be·at′i·fi·ca′tion,** *n.*

beat·ing (bēt′ing), *n.* **1** act of one that beats. **2** whipping; thrashing. **3** defeat. **4** throbbing. **take a beating, a** suffer physical punishment. **b** lose decisively.

be·at·i·tude (bi at′ə tüd; -tüd), *n.* **1** supreme happiness; bliss. **2** blessing. **3** **the Beatitudes,** verses in the Bible beginning "Blessed are the poor in spirit." Matt. 5:3–12. [< L *beatitudo* < *beare* bless]

beat·nik (bēt′nik), *n.* a person who lives in an unconventional way; Bohemian.

beat-up bāt′up′), *adj.* in very bad condition; showing evidence of hard use.

beau (bō), *n., pl.* **beaus, beaux** (bōz). **1** a suitor; lover. **2** dandy. [< F, handsome, < L *bellus* fine] —**beau′ish,** *adj.*

Beau·fort scale (bō′fərt), internationally used scale of wind velocities, ranging from 0 (calm) to 12 (hurricane).

beau geste (bō zhest′), *pl.* **beaux gestes** (bō zhest′), **1** a graceful or kindly act. **2** *French.* pretense of kindness merely for effect.

beaut (būt), *n. Informal.* something amazing or outstanding: *a beaut of an accident.*

beau·te·ous (bū′ti əs), *adj.* beautiful. —**beau′te·ous·ly,** *adv.* —**beau′te·ous·ness,** *n.*

beau·ti·ful (bū′tə fəl), *adj.* very pleasing to see or hear; delighting the mind or senses. —**beau′ti·ful·ly,** *adv.* —**beau′ti·ful·ness,** *n.*

beau·ti·fy (bū′tə fī), *v.,* **-fied, -fy·ing.** make or become beautiful or more beautiful. —**beau′ti·fi·ca′tion,** *n.* —**beau′ti·fi′er,** *n.*

beau·ty (bū′ti), *n., pl.* **-ties. 1** good looks. **2** quality that pleases in flowers, pictures, music. etc.; loveliness. **3** quality that pleases the intellect or moral sense. **4** beautiful person, animal, or thing, esp. a beautiful woman. **5** something remarkable or excellent. **6** in nuclear physics, property possessed by a bottom quark. See BEAU.]

beauty salon or **parlor** or **shop,** place where women have their hair, skin, and nails cared for.

beaux-arts (bō zär′), *n. pl. French.* fine arts; painting, sculpture, music, etc.

bea·ver (bē′vər), *n.* **1** amphibious rodent with a broad, flat tail, noted for its ingenuity in damming streams with mud, branches, etc. **2** its soft brown fur. **3** man's high silk hat. [OE *beofor*] —**bea′ver·like′,** *adj.*

be·bop (bē′bop′), *n.* form of jazz characterized by unusual rhythms, dissonance, and improvization. Also, **bop, B-bop.**

be·calm (bi käm′), *v.* **1** prevent from moving by lack of wind. **2** make calm.

be·came (bi kām′), *v.* pt. of **become.**

be·cause (bi kôz′), *conj.* for the reason that; since; inasmuch as. —*adv.* **because of,** by reason of; on account of: *we did not go because of the rain.* [ME *bicause* by cause]

be·chance (bi chans′; -chäns′), *v.,* **-chanced, -chanc·ing.** happen; happen to; befall.

beck (bek), *n.* motion of the head or hand meant as a call or command. —*v.* beckon to, as by nodding the head or waving the hand. **at one's beck and call, a** ready whenever wanted. **b** under one's complete control.

Beck·et (bek′it), *n.* **Saint Thomas à,** 1118?–70, archbishop of Canterbury, murdered on orders of Henry II.

beck·on (bek′ən), *v.* signal (to a person) by a motion of the head or hand. —*n.* a beckoning gesture. [OE *bēcnan*] —**beck′on·er,** *n.*

be·cloud (bi kloud′), *v.* obscure.

be·come (bi kum′), *v.* **be·came, be·come, be·com·ing. 1** come to be; grow to be. **2** be suitable for; suit. **3** become of, happen to: *what will become of her?* [OE *becuman*]

be·com·ing (bi kum′ing), *adj.* fitting; suitable; appropriate: *becoming conduct for a gentleman.* —**be·com′ing·ly,** *adv.* —**be·com′ing·ness,** *n.*

Becque·rel rays (bek′rel), invisible rays given off by radioactive substances.

bed (bed), *n., v.,* **bed·ded, bed·ding.** —*n.* **1** anything to sleep or rest on. **2** foundation. **3** ground under a body of water: *the bed of a river.* **4** piece of ground in which plants are grown. **5** layer; stratum: *a bed of coal.* —*v.* **1** put to bed. **2** fix or set in a permanent position; embed. **3** plant in a garden bcd. **4** form a compact layer. **5** lay flat, [OE *bedd*] —**bed′less,** *adj.* —**bed′like′,** *adj.*

be·daz·zle (bi daz′əl), *v.,* **-zled, -zling.** dazzle completely; confuse. —**be·daz′-zle·ment,** *n.*

bed·bug (bed′bug′), *n.* a small, flat blood-sucking hemipterous insect.

bed·cham·ber (bed′chām′bər), *n.* bedroom.

bed·clothes (bed′klōz′; -klōthz′), *n. pl.* =bedding.

bed·ding (bed′ing), *n.* **1** sheets, blankets, quilts, etc.; bedclothes. **2** material for beds. **3** foundation; bottom layer.

be·deck (bi dek′), *v.* adorn; decorate.

be·dev·il (bi dev′əl), *v.,* **-iled, -il·ing 1** trouble greatly; torment. **2** confuse completely; muddle. **3** put under a spell; bewitch. —**be·dev′il·ment,** *n.*

be·dew (bi dü′; -dū′), *v.* wet with dew or with drops like dew.

bed·fast (bed′fast′; -fäst′), *adj.* bedridden.

bed·fel·low (bed′fel′ō), *n.* **1** sharer of one's bed. **2** *Fig.* associate.

be·dim (bi dim′), *v.,* **-dimmed, -dim·ming.** make dim; darken; obscure.

be·di·zen (bi dī′zən; -diz′ən), *v.* ornament with showy finery. —**be·di′zen·ment,** *n.*

bed·lam (bed′ləm), *n.* **1** uproar; confusion. **2** insane asylum; madhouse. **3**

Bedlam, insane asylum in London. [alter. of *Bethlehem.*]

Bed·ou·in (bed′ů in), *n.* **1** a wandering Arab who lives in the deserts of Arabia, Syria, or N Africa. **2** wanderer; nomad.

bed·pan (bed′pan′), *n.* **1** *Am.* pan used as a toilet by sick people in bed. **2** pan filled with hot coals for warming a bed.

be·drag·gle (bi drag′əl), *v.,* **-gled, -gling.** make limp and soiled, as with dirt. —**be·drag′gle·ment.** *n.*

bed·rid·den (bed′rid ′ən), **bed·rid** (-rid ′), *adj.* confined to bed for a long time because of sickness or weakness.

bed·rock (bed′rok′), *n.* **1** solid rock beneath the soil and looser rocks. **2** *Fig.* firm foundation. **3** *Fig.* lowest level; bottom. **4** *Fig.* fundamental or essential principle.

bed·room (bed′rüm′; -rům), *n.* room to sleep in.

bedroom community, place where commuters live.

bed·side (bed′sīd′), *n.* side of a bed. —*adj.* **1** with or attending the sick: *a bedside vigil.* **2** for use while in bed: *bedside table.*

bed·spread (bed′spred′), *n.* cover for a bed, usually decorative.

bed·stead (bed′sted; -stid), *n.* the wooden or metal framework of a bed.

bed·time (bed′tīm′), *n.* time to go to bed.

bee (bē), *n.* **1** any of various hymenopterous insects, esp. the common honeybee, producing honey and wax, and forming highly organized colonies. **2** any of various similar insects. **3** gathering for work or amusement: *a quilting bee.*

have a bee in one's bonnet, be preoccupied by one idea or thing.

the bee's knees, something excellent; special. [OE *bēo*]

bee·bread (bē′bred′), *n.* a brownish, bitter substance consisting of pollen, or pollen mixed with honey, used by bees as food.

beech (bēch), *n.* a tree with smooth, gray bark and glossy leaves that bears a sweet edible nut. **2** its wood. [OE *bēce*] —**beech′en,** *adj.*

beech·nut (bēch′nut′), *n.* the small, triangular nut of the beech tree.

beef (bēf), *n., pl.* **beeves** (bēvz *for 2*) or **beefs** (*for 5*), *v.* —*n.* **1** meat from a steer, cow, or bull. **2** steer, cow, or bull when full-grown and fattened for food. **3** *Fig.* strength; muscle. **4** *Fig.* weight. **5** complaint; grievance. —*v.* complain loudly.

beef up, strengthen: *beef up defenses.* [< OF *boef* < L *bos* ox] —**beef′less,** *adj.*

beef·steak (bēf′stāk′), *n.* slice of beef for broiling or frying.

beef·y (bēf′i), *adj.,* **beef·i·er, beef·i·est.** stong; muscular; solid. —**beef′i·ness,** *n.*

bee·hive (bē′hīv′), *n.* **1** hive or house for bees. **2** a busy, swarming place.

bee·line (bē′lin′), *n.* straightest way or line between two places. —*v.* move or hurry someplace in the most direct way.

make a beeline for, hurry or race directly toward.

Be·el·ze·bub (bi el′zə bub), *n.* **1** the Devil. **2** a devil.

been (bin; *rarely* bēn), *v.* pp. of **be.**

beer (bir), *n.* **1** alcoholic drink made from malt and usually hops. **2** drink made from roots or plants, as root beer. [OE *bēor*]

beer·y (bir′i), *adj.,* **beer·i·er, beer·i·est.** **1** of or like beer. **2** caused by beer. —**beer′i·ness,** *n.*

beest·ings (bēs′tingz), *n.pl.* first milk from a cow after it has given birth to a calf. [OE *bôysting* < *bēost* beestings]

bees·wax (bēz′waks′), *n.* wax given out by bees, from which they make their honeycomb. —*v.* rub, polish, or treat with beeswax.

beet (bēt), *n.* **1** thick root of a plant. Red beets are eaten as vegetables. Sugar is made from white beets. **2** the plant. The leaves are sometimes eaten as greens. [< L *beta*]

Bee·tho·ven (bā′tō vən), *n.* **Ludwig van,** 1770–1837, German musical composer.

bee·tle¹ (bē′təl), *n.* **1** any of an order of insects with two hard, shiny cases to cover the wings when folded. **2** any similar insect. [OE *bitela* < *bītan* bite]

bee·tle² (bē′təl), *n., v.,* **-tled, -tling.** —*n.* **1** heavy wooden mallet. **2** a wooden household utensil for beating or mashing. —*v.* pound with a beetle. [OE *bîetel* < *bēatan* beat]

bee·tle³ (bē′təl), *v.,* **-tled, -tling,** *adj.* —*v.* project; overhang. —*adj.* projecting; overhanging. [< *beetle-browed*]

bee·tle-browed (bē′təl broud′), *adj.* **1** having overhanging eyebrows. **2** scowling; sullen. [ME *bitel* biting + *brow.* See BEETLE¹.]

beeves (bēvz), *n.* pl. of **beef** (def. 2).

be·fall (bi fôl′), *v.,* **-fell, -fall·en, -fall·ing. 1** happen to. **2** happen; occur.

be·fit (bi fit′), *v.,* **-fit·ted, -fit·ting.** be suitable for; be proper for; be suited to. —**be·fit′ting,** *adj.* —**be·fit′ting·ly,** *adv.*

be·fog (bi fog′; -fôg′), *v.,* **-fogged, -fog·ging. 1** surround with fog; make foggy. **2** *Fig.* obscure; confuse.

be·fore (bi fôr′; -fōr′), *prep.* **1** in front of: *walk before me.* **2** earlier; sooner than: *come before five o'clock; I will die before giving in.* **3** in the presence of: *stand before the king.* —*adv.* **1** in front: *go before.* **2** earlier: **3** until now: *I didn't know that before.* —*conj.* rather than. [OE *beforan*]

be·fore·hand (bi fôr′hand′; -fōr′-), *adv., adj.* ahead of time; in advance.

be·foul (bi foul′), *v.* **1** make dirty; cover with filth. **2** entangle.

be·friend (bi frend′), *v.* act as a friend to.

be·fud·dle (bi fud′əl), *v.,* **-dled, -dling.** stupefy; confuse, esp. with alcoholic drink.

beg (beg), *v.,* **begged, beg·ging. 1** ask for (food, money, clothes, etc.) as a charity. **2** ask help or charity. **3** ask earnestly or humbly; entreat; implore. **4** ask formally and courteously.

beg off, make an excuse for not doing something.

go begging, find no acceptance or support. [OE *bedecian*]

be·gan (bi gan′), *v.* pt. of **begin.**

be·get (bi get′), *v.,* **be·got** or (*Archaic*) **be·gat, be·got·ten** or **be·got, be·get·ting. 1** become the father of. **2** cause to be; produce. —**be·get′ter,** *n.*

beg·gar (beg′ər), *n.* **1** person who lives by begging. **2** a very poor person. **3** fellow. —*v.* **1** bring to poverty. **2** make seem poor. —**beg′gar·dom, beg′gar·hood,** *n.*

beg·gar·ly (beg′ər li), *adj.* fit for a beggar; poor. —**beg′gar·li·ness,** *n.*

beg·gar's-lice (beg′ərz lis′), **beg·gar-lice** (beg′ər lis′), *n.* **1** (*pl. in use*) burs or seeds of various plants that stick to clothes. **2** (*pl. or sing. in use*) weed on which such burs or seeds grow.

beg·gar's-ticks (beg′ərz tiks′), **beg·gar-ticks** (beg′ər tiks′), *n. sing. or pl.* =beggar's-lice.

beg·gar·y (beg′ər i), *n.* very great poverty.

be·gin (bi gin′), *v.c* **be·gan, be·gun, be·gin·ning. 1** start. **2** come into being; originate. **3** be near; come near: *that suit doesn't even begin to fit you.* [OE *beginnan*]

be·gin·ner (bi gin′ər), *n.* **1** person who is doing something for the first time; person who lacks skill and experience; amateur; novice. **2** person who begins anything.

be·gin·ning (bi gin′ing), *n.* **1** start; initiation. **2** time when anything begins. **3** first part. **4** origin. —*adj.* that begins.

be·gird (bi gèrd′), *v.,* **-girt** (-gèrt′) or **-gird·ed, -gird·ing.** surround; encircle.

be·gone (bi gôn′; -gon′), *interj., v.* be gone; go away; depart.

be·go·ni·a (bi gō′ni ə; -gōn′yə), *n.* a tropical plant with handsome leaves and waxy flowers. [from Michel *Bégon,* patron of botany]

be·got (bi got′), *v.* pt. and pp. of **beget.**

be·got·ten (bi got′ən), *v.* pp. of **beget.**

be·grime (bi grīm′), *v.,* **-grimed, -grim·ing.** make grimy; make dirty.

be·grudge (bi gruj′), *v.,* **-grudged, -grudg·ing. 1** be reluctant to give (something). **2** envy (someone) the possession of. —**be·grudg′ing·ly,** *adv.*

be·guile (bi gīl′), *v.,* **-guiled, -guil·ing. 1** deceive; cheat. **2** take away from deceitfully or cunningly. **3** entertain; amuse; charm. **4** while away (time) pleasantly. —**be·guil′er,** *n.* —**be·guil′ing·ly,** *adv.*

be·gun (bi gun′), *v.* pp. of **begin.**

be·half (bi haf′; -häf′), *n.* side; interest; favor: *his friends will act in his behalf.*

in behalf of, in the interest of; for. **on behalf of, a** as a representative of. **b** =in behalf of. [ME *behalve* beside, on the side of]

be·have (bi hāv′), *v.,* **-haved, -hav·ing. 1** act. **2** conduct (oneself or itself) in a certain way. **3** act well; do what is right.

be·hav·ior (bi hāv′yər), *n.* **1** way of acting; conduct; actions; acts. **2** manners; deportment; demeanor. —**be·hav′ior·al**, *adj.*

behavioral science, any of the social sciences that objectively deals with human behavior.

be·hav·ior·ism (bi hāv′yer iz əm), *n.* doctrine that the objective acts of persons and animals are the chief or only subject matter of scientific psychology. —**be·hav′ior·ist**, *n.* —**be·hav′ior·is′tic**, *adj.* —**be·hav′ior·is′ti·cal·ly**, *adv.*

be·head (bi hed′), *v.* cut off the head of.

be·held (bi held′), *v.* pt. and pp. of **behold.**

be·he·moth (bi hē′məth; bē′ə–), *n.* **1** huge animal mentioned in Job 40:15–24. **2** *Fig.* any very large, strong thing. [< Heb. *b′hēmōth*, pl. of *b′hēmah* beast]

be·hest (bi hest′), *n.* command; order. [OE *behǣs* promise]

be·hind (bi hīnd′), *prep.* **1** at the back or far side of: *behind the hill.* **2** concealed by: *treachery behind his smooth manner.* **3** inferior to. **4** later than; after: *behind time.* **5.**supporting: *friends behind him.* —*adv.* **1** at or toward the back. **2** farther back. **3** slow; late. [OE *behindan.* See BE–, HIND¹.]

be·hind·hand (bi hīnd′hand′), *adv., adj.* **1** late. **2** backward; slow. **3** in debt.

be·hold (bi hōld′), *v.,* **be·held, be·hold·ing,** *interj.* see; look at. [OE *beheaidan* —**be·hold′er**, *n.*

be·hold·en (bi hōl′dən), *adj.* indebted.

be·hoof (bi hüf′), *n.* use; advantage; benefit. [OE *behōf* need]

be·hoove (bi hüv′), *esp. Brit.* **be·hove** (bi hōv′), *v.,* **–hooved, –hoov·ing; –hoved, –hov·ing. 1** be necessary for. **2** be proper for. [OE *behōfian* to need]

beige (bāzh), *n., adj.* pale brown. [< F]

Bei·jing (bā′jing′), *n.* capital of China.

be·ing (bē′ing), *n.* **1** life; existence. **2** nature; constitution. **3** person; living creature. —*adj.* that is; present: *the time being.*

Bei·rut (bā′rüt), *n.* capital of Lebanon.

be·jew·el (bi jü′el), *v.,* **–eled, –el·ing.** adorn with jewels.

be·la·bor (bi lā′bər), *v.* **1** beat vigorously; thrash. **2** *Fig.* attack with too much criticism or advice.

be·lat·ed (bi lāt′id), *adj.* **1** delayed; too late. **2** overtaken by darkness. —**be·lat′ed·ly**, *adv.* —**be·lat′ed·ness**, *n.*

be·lay (bi lā′), *v.,* **be·layed, be·lay·ing. 1** fasten (a rope) by winding it around a pin or cleat. **2** stop. [OE *belecgan.* See BE–, LAY¹.]

belaying pin, pin on a rail of a ship or boat around which ropes can be wound and fastened.

belch (belch), *v.* **1** expel gas from the stomach through the mouth. **2** expel with force: *the volcano belched fire.* —*n.* act of belching. [cf. OE *bealcian*] —**belch′er**, *n.*

bel·dam (bel′dəm), **bel·dame** (–dəm; –dam′), *n.* **1** an old woman. **2** an ugly old woman; witch. [< *bel–* grand– [< OF, < *belle* fair) + *dam* DAME]

be·lea·guer (bi lē′gər), *v.* **1** besiege. **2** *Fig.* surround. [< Du. *belegeren* < *leger* camp] —**be·lea′guered**, *adj.* —**be·lea′guer·er**, *n.* —**be·lea′guer·ment**, *n.*

Bel·fast (bel′fast; –fäst), *n.* seaport and capital of Northern Ireland.

bel·fry (bel′fri), *n., pl.* **–fries. 1** tower for a bell or bells. **2** space for the bell in a tower. [< OF *berfrei* < Gmc.] —**bel′fried**, *adj.*

Belg., Belgium; Belgian.

Bel·gium (bel′jəm), *n.* a small country in W Europe. —**Bel′gian**, *adj., n.*

Bel·grade (bel′grād; bel grād′), *n.* capital of Serbia on the Danube River.

Be·li·al (bē′l əl; bēl′yəl), *n.* the devil.

be·lie (bi lī′), *v.,* **–lied, –ly·ing. 1** give a false idea of; misrepresent. **2** show to be false; prove to be mistaken. **3** be false to; disappoint. —**be·li′er**, *n.*

be·lief (bi lēf′), *n.* **1** what is held true; thing believed; conviction; opinion. **2** acceptance as true or real. **3** faith; trust: *he expressed his belief in the boy's honesty.* [ME *bileafe.* Cf. OE *gelēafa.*]

be·lieve (bi lēv′), *v.,* **–lieved, –liev·ing. 1** accept as true or real. **2** have faith in; trust. **3** think (somebody) tells the truth. **4** think; suppose. [ME *bileve(n).* Cf. OE *gellefan.*] —**be·liev′a·ble**, *adj.* —**be·liev′a·ble·ness**, *n.* —**be·liev′er**, *n.*

be·lit·tle (bi lit′əl), *v.,* **–lit·tled, –lit·tling.** *Am.* cause to seem little or unimportant; disparage. —**be·lit′tle·ment**, *n.* —**be·lit′tler**, *n. Am.*

bell (bel), *n.* **1** a hollow metal cup that makes a musical sound when struck by a clapper or hammer. **2** sound of a bell. **3** stroke of a bell every half hour to tell time on shipboard. —*v.* **1** put a bell on. **2** flare like a bell. [OE *belle*] —**bell′less**, *adj.* —**bell′-like′**, *adj.*

Bell, (bel), *n.* **Alexander Graham,** 1847–1922, American inventor of the telephone.

bel·la·don·na (bel′ə don′ə), *n.* **1** a poisonous plant with black berries and red flowers. **2** drug made from this plant. [< Ital., fair lady]

bell·boy (bel′boi′), *n.* man or boy whose work is carrying hand baggage and doing errands for the guests of a hotel or club.

bell buoy, buoy with a bell rung by the movement of the waves.

belle (bel), *n.* **1** a beautiful woman or girl. **2** the prettiest or most admired woman or girl. [< F, fem. of *beau.* See BEAU.]

belles-let·tres (bel′let′rə), *n.pl.* the finer forms of literature. [< F] —**bel′let′rist**, *n.* —**bel′le·tris′tic**, *adj.*

bell·hop (bel′hop′), *n.* =bellboy.

bel·li·cose (bel′ə kos), *adj.* warlike; fond of fighting. [< L *bellicosus* < *bellum* war] —**bel′li·cose′ly**, *adv.* —**bel′li·cos′i·ty**, *n.*

bel·lig·er·ence (bə lij′ər əns), *n.* **1** fondness for fighting. **2** fighting; war.

bel·lig·er·en·cy (bə lij′ər ən si), *n.* **1** state of being at war. **2** belligerence.

bel·lig·er·ent (bə lij′ər ənt), *adj.* **1** fond of fighting; warlike; pugnacious. **2** at war; engaged in war; fighting. **3** having to do with nations or persons at war. —*n.* nation or person at war. [< L, < *bellum* war + *gerere* wage] —**bel·lig′er·ent·ly**, *adv.*

bel·low (bel′ō), *v.* **1** make a loud, deep noise; roar as a bull does. **2** shout loudly or angrily. —*n.* **1** such a roar. **2** any noise made by bellowing. [OE *bylgan*] —**bel′low·er**, *n.*

bel·lows (bel′ōz; –əs), *n. sing. or pl.* **1** instrument for producing a strong current of air, used for blowing fires or sounding an organ. **2** folding part of a camera, behind the lens. [OE *belgas;* akin to BELLY]

bell·weth·er (bel′wetħ′ər), *n.* **1** a male sheep that wears a bell and leads the flock. **2** person or thing that sets a standard.

bel·ly (bel′i), *n., pl.* **–lies,** *v.,* **–lied, –ly·ing.** —*n.* **1** the lower part of the human body that contains the stomach and intestines; abdomen. **2** under part of an animal's body. **3** stomach. **4** the bulging part of anything; hollow space in a bulging part. —*v.* swell out; bulge. [OE *belg*]

bel·ly·ful (bel′ē fūl), *n.* **1** as much as fills the stomach or satisfies the appetite. **2** too much of something, esp. something unpleasant.

belly laugh, loud, deep, and unrestrained laugh.

be·long (bi lông′; –long′), *v.* have one's or its proper place: *that book belongs on this shelf.*

belong to, a be the property of. **b** be a part of. **c** be a member of. [ME *bilonge(n)* < *bi–* BE– + *longen* belong, ult. < OE *gelang* belonging to]

be·long·ing (bi lông′ing; –long′–), *n.* **1** being a part of a group. **2** something that belongs.

be·long·ings (bi long′ingz), *n.* things that belong to a person; possessions.

be·lov·ed (bi luv′id; –luvd′), *adj.* dearly loved; dear. —*n.* person who is loved; darling.

be·low (bi lō′), *adv.* **1** in or to a lower place. **2** in a lower rank. **3** on a lower floor or deck. **4** on earth. **5** in hell. **6** after, in a book or article. —*prep.* **1** lower than; under: *below the third floor.* **2** less than: *four degrees below freezing.* [ME *bilooghe* by low]

belt (belt), *n.* **1** strip of leather, cloth, etc., worn around the body. **2** any broad strip or band. **3** region having distinctive characteristics; zone: *the cotton belt.* **4** an endless band that moves the wheels and pulleys it passes over. —*v.* **1** put a belt around. **2** fasten on with a belt. **3** beat with a belt. **4** hit.

below the belt, a foul; unfair. **b** foully; unfairly.

belt out, sing or play forcefully.

tighten one's belt, be or become more thrifty. [OE, appar. ult. < L *balteus* girdle] —**belt´ed,** *adj.* —**belt´less,** *adj.*

belt·ing (bel´ting), *n.* **1** material for making belts. **2** belts.

belt·way (belt´wā´), *n.* **1** an express highway that goes around a city, congested area, etc. **2 the Beltway.** Washington, D.C. as the center of the U.S. government and all the people connected with it.

be·moan (bi mōn´), *v.* lament; bewail.

be·muse (bi mūz´), *v.* **-mused, -mus·ing.** confuse; bewilder; stupefy.

bench (bench), *n.* **1** a long seat, usually of wood or stone. **2** seat where judges sit in a law court. **3** judge or judges sitting in a law court. **4** law court. **5** work table of a carpenter or other person who uses tools; workbench. —*v.* take (a player) out of a game.

on the bench, a sitting in a law court, as a judge. **b** sitting among substitute players on a team, as a penalty. [OE *benc*] —**bench´less,** *adj.*

bench warrant, a written order from a judge or law court to arrest a person.

bend (bend), *v.,* **bent** or (*Archaic*) **bend·ed, bend·ing,** *n.* —*v.* curve; twist; warp. **2** stoop; bow. **3** force to submit. **4** submit. **5** direct (mind or effort). **6** fasten (a sail, rope, etc.). —*n.* **1** curve; turn. **2** stoop; bow. **3** knot for tying two ropes together or tying a rope to something else.

the bends, decompression sickness, esp. the painful cramps associated with it. [OE *bendan* bind, band] —**bend´a·ble,** *adj.*

bend·er (ben´dər), *n.* **1** person or thing that bends. **2** drinking spree.

be·neath (bi nēth´), *adv.* below; underneath. —*prep.* **1** below; under; lower than. **2** unworthy of; worthy not even of: *beneath contempt.* [OE *beneothan* < *be-* by + *neothan* below]

ben·e·dic·i·te (ben´ə dis´ə tē), *interj.* Latin word that means *Bless you!* or *Bless us!* or *Bless me!* —*n.* **1** invocation of a blessing. **2 Benedicite,** hymn of praise to God. [< L, < *bene* well + *dicere* say]

ben·e·dict (ben´ə dikt), *n.* **1** a recently married man, esp. one who was a bachelor for a long time. **2** a married man. [< *Benedick,* character in Shakespeare's *Much Ado About Nothing*]

Ben·e·dict (ben´ə dikt), *n.* **Saint,** 480?–543?, Italian founder of the Benedictine order.

Ben·e·dic·tine (ben´ə dik´tin, –tēn, –tīn for *n.* 1 *and adj.*; ben´ə dik´tēn for *n.* 2), *n.* **1** monk or nun following the rules of Saint Benedict or the order founded by him. **2** a kind of liqueur. —*adj.* of Saint Benedict or a religious order following his rules.

ben·e·dic·tion (ben´ə dik´shən), *n.* **1** the asking of God's blessings at the end of a church service. **2** blessing. [< L *benedictio.* See BENEDICITE.] —**ben´e·dic´tion·al,** *adj.* —**ben´e·dic´to·ry,** *adj.*

ben·e·fac·tion (ben´ə fak´shən), *n.* **1** a doing good; kind act. **2** help given for any good purpose; charitable gift.

ben·e·fac·tor (ben´ə fak´tər; ben´ə fak´–), *n.* person who has given money or kindly help. [< L, < *bene* well + *facere* do]

ben·e·fac·tress (ben´ə fak´tris; ben´ə fak´–), *n.* woman benefactor.

ben·e·fice (ben´ə fis), *n.* permanent ecclesiastical office or position consisting of a sacred duty and the income that goes with it. [< OF < L *beneficium* benefit. See BENEFACTOR.]

ben·e·fi·cence (bə nef´ə səns), *n.* **1** kindness; doing good. **2** a kindly act; gift.

ben·e·fi·cent (bə nef´ə sənt), *adj.* **1** kind; doing good. **2** beneficial. —**be·nef´i·cent·ly,** *adv.*

ben·e·fi·cial (ben´ə fish´əl), *adj.* helpful; productive of good: *sunshine and moisture are beneficial to plants.* —**ben´e·fi´cial·ly,** *adv.* —**ben´e·fi´cial·ness,** *n.*

ben·e·fi·ci·ar·y (ben´ə fish´i er´i; –fish´ər i), *n., pl.* **-ar·ies. 1** person who receives benefit. **2** person who receives money or property from an insurance policy, a will, etc.

ben·e·fit (ben´ə fit), *n., v.,* **-fit·ed, -fit·ing.** —*n.* **1** anything which is for the good of a person or thing; advantage; profit; help. **2** money paid to the sick, disabled, etc. by an insurance company, government agency, etc. **3** performance at the theater, a game, etc., to raise money which goes to a worthy cause. —*v.* **1** give benefit to; be good for. **2** receive good; profit.

benefit of the doubt, favorable opinion or judgment about someone or something despite lingering questions. [< AF *benfet* < L *benefactum.* See BENEFACTOR.] —**ben´e·fit·er,** *n.*

benefit of clergy, 1 former privilege of being tried in church courts instead of regular courts. **2** services or approval of the church.

be·nev·o·lence (bə nev´ə ləns), *n.* **1** good will; kindly feeling. **2** act of kindness; something good that is done; generous gift. [< OF < L, < *bene* well + *velle* wish]

be·nev·o·lent (bə nev´ə lənt), *adj.* kindly; charitable; generous. —**be·nev´o·lent·ly,** *adv.*

Ben·gal (ben gôl´; beng–), *n.* **1** former province of NE India now divided between India and the country of Bangladesh. **2 Bay of,** bay between India and Myanmar.

Ben·gha·zi (ben gä´zē), *n.* city in Libya, on the Mediterranean.

be·night·ed (bi nīt´id), *adj.* **1** not knowing right and wrong; ignorant. **2** overtaken by night. —**be·night´ed·ness,** *n.*

be·nign (bi nīn´), *adj.* **1** gentle: kindly: *a benign gentleman.* **2** favorable; mild: *a benign climate.* **3** doing no harm; not dangerous to health: *a benign tumor.* [< OF < L *benignus* < *bene* well + *–gnus* born] —**be·nign´ly,** *adv.*

be·nig·nant (bi nig´nənt), *adj.* **1** kindly; gracious. **2** favorable; beneficial. —**be·nig´nan·cy,** *n.* —**be·nig´nant·ly,** *adv.*

be·nig·ni·ty (bi nig´nə ti), *n., pl.* **-ties. 1** kindliness; graciousness. **2** a kind act; favor.

Ben·in (bə nēn´), republic in W Africa on the Atlantic ocean.

ben·i·son (ben´ə zən; –sən), *n.* blessing. [< OF *beneison* < L *benedictiō*]

Ben·ja·min (ben´jə mən), *n.* **1** in the Bible, youngest and favorite son of Jacob. **2** one of the twelve tribes of Israel.

bent[1] (bent), *v.* pt. and pp. of **bend.** —*adj.* **1** not straight; curved; crooked. **2** strongly inclined; determined; resolved. —*n.* **1** bent condition. **2** capacity of enduring. **3** inclination; tendency; bias.

bent[2] (bent), *n.* **1** Also, **bent grass.** stiff, wiry grass that grows on sandy or waste land. **2** *Archaic.* heath; moor. [OE *beonet*]

be·numb (bi num´), *v.* **1** make numb. **2** stupefy; deaden.

Ben·ze·drine (ben´zə drēn; –drin), *n.* trademark of amphetamine, a drug, $C_9H_{13}N$, that causes wakefulness.

ben·zene (ben´zēn; ben zēn´), *n.* a colorless, volatile, inflammable liquid, C_6H_6, obtained chiefly from coal tar and used for removing grease and in making dyes.

ben·zine (ben´zēn; ben zēn´), *n.* a colorless, volatile, inflammable liquid consisting of a mixture of hydrocarbons obtained in distilling petroleum, used in cleaning, dyeing, etc.

ben·zo·ate (ben´zō āt; –it), *n.* salt or ester of benzoic acid.

ben·zo·ic acid (ben zō´ik), an acid, C_6H_5COOH, occurring in benzoin, cranberries, etc., used as an antiseptic or as a food preservative.

ben·zo·in (ben´zō in: –zoin; ben zō´in), *n.* **1** a fragrant resin obtained from certain species of trees of Java, Sumatra, etc., used in perfume and medicine. **2** substance somewhat like camphor made from this resin. [< F < Sp. < Pg. < Ar. *lubān jāwī* incense of Java]

ben·zol (ben´zōl; –zol), *n.* **1** =benzene, C_6H_6. **2** liquid containing about 70 percent of benzene and 20 to 30 percent of toluene.

Be·o·wulf (bā´ə wùlf), *n.* **1** Old English epic poem, probably composed in England about A.D. 700. **2** hero of this poem.

be·queath (bi kwēth´; –kwēth´), *v.* **1** give or leave (property, etc.) by a will. **2** hand down to posterity. [OE *becwethan* < *be-* to, for + *cwethan* say] —**be·queath´ment,** *n.*

be·queath·al (bi kwēth´əl), *n.* a bequeathing.

be·quest (bi kwest´), *n.* **1** something bequeathed; legacy. **2** act of bequeathing.

be·rate (bi rāt´), *v.* **-rat·ed, -rat·ing.** scold sharply; upbraid; reprimand.

Ber·ber (bėr′bər), *n.* **1** member of a group of Muslim tribes living in N Africa. **2** their language. —*adj.* of the Berbers or their language.

be·reave (bi rēv′), *v.,* **be·reaved** or **be·reft** (bi reft′), **be·reav·ing. 1** leave desolate and alone. **2** deprive (of) ruthlessly; rob: *bereft of hope.* [OE *berēafian* < *be-* away + *rēafian* rob] —**be·reave′ment,** *n.* —**be·reav′er,** *n.*

be·ret (bə rā′; ber′ā), *n.* soft, round woolen cap. [< F. See BIRETTA.]

berg (bėrg), *n.* =iceberg.

ber·ga·mot (bėr′gə mot), *n.* **1** pear-shaped variety of orange. **2** tree on which it grows. **3** oil obtained from its rind, used in perfume. [< F < Ital., appar. < Turk. *begarmudi* prince's pear]

Ber·gen (bėr′gən), *n.* seaport in SW Norway.

Ber·ge·rac (bār′zhə räk), *n.* **Cyrano de,** 1619–55, French dramatist and poet, hero of a famous play by Rostand.

ber·i·ber·i (ber′i ber′i), *n.* disease affecting the nerves, accompanied by weakness, loss of weight, and wasting away. [< Singhalese (the lang. of Sri Lanka), reduplication of *beri* weakness]

Ber·ing Sea (bir′ing; bār′–), sea in the N Pacific, between Alaska and Siberia.

Bering Strait, strait between Bering Sea and the Arctic Ocean.

ber·ke·li·um (bėr kē′li əm), *n.* radioactive element, Bk, produced by the cyclotron at the University of California. [< *Berkeley,* California (site of the university)]

Berk·shires (berk′shirz; –shərz), *n.pl.* range of hills and mountains in W Massachusetts.

Ber·lin (bėr lin′), *n.* capital of Germany, in the N part.

berm (bėrm), *n.* **1** sand and stones deposited at the top of a beach. **2** the side of a road. [< F *berme* < MDu. and G]

Ber·mu·da (bər mū′də), *n.* group of British islands in the Atlantic, 580 miles east of North Carolina. —**Ber·mu′di·an,** *adj., n.*

Bermuda onion, a large, mild onion grown in Bermuda, Texas, and California.

Bermuda shorts, trousers that end about an inch above the knee.

Bern, Berne (bėrn; bern), *n.* capital of Switzerland, in the W part.

Ber·nard (bėr′nərd; bər närd′), *n.* **Saint,** 1090–1153, French abbot.

ber·ry (ber′i), *n., pl.* **-ries,** *v.,* **-ried, -ry·ing.** —*n.* **1** small, juicy fruit with many seeds, as the strawberry. **2** dry seed or kernel, as of wheat. **3** simple fruit with the seeds in the pulp and a skin or rind, as grapes or tomatoes. **4** single egg of a lobster or fish. —*v.* **1** gather or pick berries. **2** produce berries. [OE *berie*]

ber·serk (bėr′sėrk; bėr sėrk′), *adj., adv.* in a frenzy; unsound; mad. [< Scand. *berserkr* wild warrior]

berth (bėrth), *n.* **1** place to sleep on a ship, train, or airplane. **2** ship's place at a wharf. **3** place for a ship to anchor conveniently or safely. **4** appointment; position; job. —*v.* **1** put in a berth; provide with a berth. **2** have or occupy a berth.

give a wide berth to, keep well away from. [? < *bear*[1]]

ber·yl (ber′əl), *n.* very hard mineral, usually green or greenish-blue, a silicate of beryllium and aluminum. Emeralds and aquamarines are beryls. [< L < Gk. *beryllos*]

be·ryl·li·um (bə ril′i əm), *n.* rare metallic element, Be; glucinum.

be·seech (bi sēch′), *v.,* **-sought** or **-seeched, -seech·ing.** ask earnestly; beg; entreat. [ME *biseche(n)* < *be-* thoroughly + *seche(n)* seek] —**be·seech′er,** *n.* —**be·seech′ing·ly,** *adv.*

be·set (bi set′), *v.,* **-set, -set·ting. 1** attack on all sides; assail; besiege. **2** surround; hem in; encompass. **3** set with decorative bits of gems, glass, etc. [OE *besettan* < *be-* around + *settan* set]

be·set·ting (bi set′ing), *adj.* habitually attacking: *laziness is her besetting sin.*

be·side (bi sīd′), *prep.* **1** near; close to: *beside the fire.* **2** in addition to: *others beside ourselves.* **3** compared with. **4** aside from: *beside the point.* —*adv.* =besides.

beside oneself, out of one's senses; upset. [OE *be sīdan* by side]

be·sides (bi sīdz′), *adv.* **1** moreover. **2** in addition: *we tried two other ways besides.* —*prep.* **1** in addition to. **2** except: *we spoke of no one besides you.*

be·siege (bi sēj′), *v.,* **-sieged, -sieg·ing. 1** make a long-continued attempt to get possession of (a place) by armed force: *besiege a city.* **2** crowd around. **3** overwhelm with requests, questions, etc. —**be·siege′ment,** *n.* —**be·sieg′er,** *n.*

be·smear (bi smir′), *v.* smear over.

be·smirch (bi smėrch′), *v.* make dirty; soil; sully. —**be·smirch′er,** *n.* —**be·smirch′ment,** *n.*

be·som (bē′zəm), *n.* **1** broom made of twigs. **2** the broom plant. [OE *besma*]

be·sot (bi sot′), *v.,* **-sot·ted, -sot·ting. 1** make foolish. **2** intoxicate. —**be·sot′ted·ly,** *adv.* —**be·sot′tedness,** *n.*

be·sought (bi sôt′), *v.* pt. and pp. of **beseech.**

be·span·gle (bi spang′gəl), *v.,* **-gled, -gling.** adorn with or as with spangles.

be·spat·ter (bi spat′ər), *v.* **1** spatter all over; soil by spattering. **2** slander. —**be·spat′ter·er,** *n.* —**be·spat′ter·ment,** *n.*

be·speak (bi spēk′), *v.,* **-spoke, -spo·ken** or **-spoke, -speak·ing. 1** indicate: *a neat appearance bespeaks care.* **2** engage in advance; reserve: *bespeak tickets for a play.*

be·spec·ta·cled (bi spek′tə kəld), *adj.* wearing eyeglasses.

be·spread (bi spred′), *v.,* **-spread, -spread·ing.** spread over.

be·sprin·kle (bi spring′kəl), *v.,* **-kled, -kling.** sprinkle all over.

Bes·sa·ra·bi·a (bes′ə rā′bi ə), *n.* region in E Europe. —**Bes′sa·ra′bi·an,** *adj., n.*

Bes·se·mer process (bes′ə mər), method of making steel by burning out carbon and impurities in molten iron with a blast of air.

best (best), *adj.* (superlative of **good**). **1** the most desirable, valuable. **2** largest: *the best part of the day.* —*adv.* (superlative of **well**[1]). **1** in the most excellent way. **2** in the highest degree. —*n.* **1** the best thing or state. —*v.* outdo; defeat.

at best, under the most favorable circumstances.

get the best of, defeat.

make the best of, do as well as possible with. [OE *betst*]

be·stead (bi sted′), *v.,* **-stead·ed, -steaded** or **-stead, -stead·ing,** *adj.* —*v.* help; assist; serve. —*adj.* placed; situated. [< *be-* + *stead,* v., help]

bes·tial (bes′chəl; best′yəl), *adj.* beastly; brutal; vile. [< L, < *bestia*] —**bes·ti·al′i·ty,** *n.* —**bes′tial′ly,** *adv.*

be·stir (bi stėr′), *v.,* **-stirred, -stir·ring.** stir up; rouse to action; exert.

best man, chief attendant of the bridegroom at a wedding.

be·stow (bi stō′), *v.* **1** give as a gift; give; confer. **2** make use of; apply. —**be·stow′a·ble,** *adj.* —**be·stow′al,** *n.*

be·strad·dle (bi strad′əl), *v.,* **-dled, -dling.** bestride; straddle.

be·strew (bi strü′), *v.,* **-strewed, -strewed** or **-strewn, -strew·ing. 1** strew. **2** strew (things) around; scatter about.

be·stride (bi strīd′), *v.,* **-strode** or **-strid, -strid·den** or **-strid, -strid·ing. 1** get on, sit on, or stand over with one leg on each side. **2** stride across; step over.

best seller, 1 anything, esp. a book, that has a very large sale. **2** author of such a book.

bet (bet), *v.,* **bet** or **bet·ted, bet·ting,** *n.* —*v.* **1** promise (money or a certain thing) to another if he or she is right and you are wrong. **2** make a bet. —*n.* **1** act of betting; wager. **2** the money or thing promised. **3** thing to bet on.

be·ta (bā′tə; bē′–), *n.* **1** the second letter of the Greek alphabet (B, β). **2** the second of a series.

be·take (bi tāk′), *v.,* **-took, -tak·en, -tak·ing.** betake oneself, **a** go: *betake oneself to the mountains.* **b** apply oneself.

beta particle, an electron, esp. one in a stream of electrons.

beta rays, stream of electrons from radium and other radioactive substances.

be·ta·tron (bā′tə tron; bē′–), *n.* particle accelerator in which electrons are accelerated to high speeds.

be·tel (bē′təl), *n.* kind of pepper plant of the East Indies, the leaves of which are chewed with the nut. [< Pg. < Malayalam *veṭṭila*]

Be·tel·geuse (bē′təl jüz; bet′əl jœz), *n.* very large reddish star in the constellation Orion. [< F, ? < Ar. *bīt-al-jāuza* shoulder of the giant]

betel nut, orange-colored nut of a tropical Asiatic palm tree.

betel palm, Asiatic palm tree on which the betel nut grows.

bête noire (bāt′ nwär′), thing or person dreaded or detested. [< F, black beast]

beth·el (beth′əl), *n.* 1 holy place. 2 church or chapel for seamen. [< Heb., house of God]

be·think (bi thingk′), *v.,* **-thought, -think·ing.** 1 think about; consider. 2 remember.

Beth·le·hem (beth′li əm; -lə hem), *n.* birthplace of Jesus, six miles south of Jerusalem.

be·tide (bi tīd′), *v.,* **-tid·ed, -tid·ing.** 1 happen to. 2 happen. [ME *betide(n)* < *be-* + *tiden* happen]

be·times (bi tīmz′), *adv.* 1 early. 2 soon. [ME *bitime* by time]

be·to·ken (bi tō′kən), *v.* be a sign or token of; indicate; show. —**be·to′ken·er,** *n.*

be·took (bi tůk′), *v.* pt. of betake.

be·tray (bi trā′), *v.* 1 give away to the enemy. 2 be unfaithful to. 3 give away (a secret); disclose unintentionally. [ME *bitraien* < *be-* (intensive) + *traie(n)* betray < L *tradere* hand over] —**be·tray′al,** *n.* —**be·tray′er,** *n.*

be·troth (bi trōth′; -trôth′), *v.* promise in marriage; engage. [ME *betrouthe(n),* var. of *betreuthien* < *be-* + *treuthe,* OE *trēowth* pledge] —**be·troth′ment,** *n.*

be·troth·al (bi trōth′əl; -trôth′-), *n.* promise of marriage; engagement.

be·trothed (bi trōthd′; -trôtht′), *n.* person engaged to be married.

bet·ter¹ (bet′ər), *adj. comparative of* **good).** 1 more desirable, useful, etc. 2 of superior quality. 3 less sick. 4 larger: *the better part of a week.* —*adv.* (*comparative of* **well¹**). 1 in a superior manner. 2 in a higher degree; more. 3 **had better,** should. —*n.* better person, thing, or state. —*v.* 1 improve. 2 surpass.

better off, in better circumstances.

betters, one's superior.

get the better of, defeat. [OE *betera*] —**bet′ter·er,** *n.*

bet·ter², bet·tor (bet′ər), *n.* person who bets.

bet·ter·ment (bet′ər mənt), *n.* improvement.

be·tween (bi twēn′), *prep.* 1 in the range, space, or time separating: *between New York and Chicago.* 2 connecting. 3 involving: *war between two countries.* 4 in the combined possession of: *they caught twelve fish between them.* —*adv.* in the intervening space or time. [OE *betwēonum* < *be-* by + *twā* two]

be·twixt (bi twikst′), *prep., adv.* 1 =between. 2 **betwixt and between,** neither one nor the other. [OE *betweox*]

Bev (bev), *n.* billion electron volts.

bev·a·tron (bev′ə tron), *n.* a high-energy cyclotron.

bev·el (bev′əl), *n., v.,* **-eled, -el·ing,** *adj.* —*n.* 1 the angle that one line or surface makes with another when not at right angles. 2 instrument or tool for drawing angles, etc. —*v.* cut a square edge to a sloping edge; make slope. —*adj.* slanting; oblique.

bev·er·age (bev′ər ij; bev′ rij), *n.* liquid for drinking. Milk, tea, coffee, beer, and wine are beverages. [< OF *bevrage* < *bevre* drink < L *bibere*]

bev·y (bev′i), *n., pl.* **bev·ies.** 1 flock of birds. 2 small group.

be·wail (bi wāl′), *v.* mourn; lament. —**be·wail′er,** *n.* —**be·wail′ing·ly,** *adv.*

be·ware (bi wār′), *v.* be on one's guard against; be careful. [< phrase *be ware!* See WARY.]

be·wil·der (bi wil′dər), *v.* confuse completely; puzzle; perplex. —**be·wil′dered,** *adj.* —**be·wil′dered·ly,** *adv.* —**be·wil′der·ing,** *adj.* —**be·wil′der·ing·ly,** *adv.* —**be·wil′der·ment,** *n.*

be·witch (bi wich′), *v.* 1 put under a spell. 2 charm; fascinate. —**be·witch′er,** *n.* —**be·witch′er·y,** *n.* —**be·witch′ing,** *adj.* —**be·witch′ing·ly,** *adv.*

bey (bā), *n., pl.* **beys.** 1 governor of a Turkish province. 2 Turkish title of respect. [< Turk. *beg*]

be·yond (bi yond′), *prep.* 1 on or to the farther side of: *beyond the barn.* 2 later than. 3 out of the reach, range, or understanding of: *beyond help.* 4 more than; exceeding. —*adv.* farther away: *beyond were the hills.*

the great beyond, a life after death. **b** anything that lies on the other side or far away. [OE *begeonden* < *be-* at, near + *geondan* beyond]

be·zique (bə zēk′), *n.* card game somewhat like pinochle. [< F *bésigue*]

bg., *pl.* **bgs.,** bag.

Bhu·tan (bü tan′), *n.* small kingdom between Tibet and NE India.

bi-, *prefix.* 1 twice, as in *biannual.* 2 doubly, as in *bipinnate.* 3 two, as in *bicuspid.* 4 every two, as in *biweekly.* 5 having two parts, as in *bicarbonate.* [< L, < *bis*]

Bi, bismuth.

bi·an·nu·al (bī an′yü əl), *adj.* occurring twice a year. —**bi·an′nu·al·ly,** *adv.*

bi·as (bī′əs), *n., adj., adv., v.,* **bi·ased, bi·as·ing.** —*n.* 1 a slanting or oblique line. Cloth is cut on the bias when it is cut diagonally across the weave. 2 opinion before there is basis for it; prejudice; —*adj.* oblique; diagonal. —*adv.* obliquely. —*v.* influence, usually not fairly. [< F *biais* slant < VL *biaxius* having a double axis]

bi·ax·i·al (bī ak′si əl), *adj.* having two axes.

bib (bib), *n.* 1 cloth worn under the chin by babies and small children to protect their clothing. 2 part of an apron above the waist. [< *bib* drink, ? < L *bibere*]

bi·be·lot (bib′lō; *Fr.* bē blō′), *n.* a small object of curiosity, beauty, or rarity. [< F]

Bi·ble (bī′bəl), *n.* 1 the collection of sacred writings of the Christian religion, comprising the Old and New Testaments. 2 the Old Testament in the form received by the Jews. 3 the sacred writings of any religion. 4 **bible,** book accepted as an authority. [< Med.L < Gk. *biblia,* pl. dim. of *biblos* book]

Bib·li·cal, bib·li·cal (bib′lə kəl), *adj.* 1 of or in the Bible. 2 according to the Bible. —**Bib′li·cal·ly, bib′li·cal·ly,** *adv.*

bib·li·og·ra·phy (bib′li og′rə fi), *n., pl.* **-phies.** list of books, articles, etc., about a subject or person by a certain author. [< Gk., < *biblion* book + *graphein* write] —**bib′li·og′ra·pher,** *n.* —**bib′li·o·graph′ic, bib′li·o·graph′i·cal,** *adj.* —**bib′li·o·graph′i·cal·ly,** *adv.*

bib·li·o·ma·ni·a (bib′li ō mā′ni ə), *n.* craze for collecting books. —**bib′li·o·ma′ni·ac,** *n., adj.*

bib·li·o·hile (bib′li ə fīl), **bib·li·o·phil** (-fil), *n.* lover of books. [< F, < Gk. *biblion* book + *philos* loving]

bib·u·lous (bib′yə ləs), *adj.* 1 fond of drinking alcoholic liquor. 2 absorbent. [< L *bibulus* < *bibere* drink] —**bib′u·lous·ly,** *adv.*

bi·cam·er·al (bī kam′ər əl), *adj.* having or consisting of two legislative assemblies. [< *bi-* two + L *camera* chamber. See CAMERA.]

bi·car·bo·nate (bī kär′bə nit; -nāt), *n.* salt of carbonic acid that contains a base and hydrogen.

bicarbonate of soda, sodium bicarbonate.

bi·cen·te·nar·y (bī sen′tə ner′i; bī′sen·ten′ər i), *adj., n., pl.* **-nar·ies.** =bicentennial.

bi·cen·ten·ni·al (bī′sen ten′i əl), *adj.* 1 having to do with a period of 200 years. 2 recurring every 200 years. —*n.* 1 200th anniversary. 2 its celebration.

bi·ceps (bī′seps), *n.* any muscle having two heads or origins, esp.: **a** the large muscle in the front part of the upper arm. **b** the large muscle in the back of the thigh. [< L, two-headed, < *bi-* two + *caput* head]

bi·chlor·ride (bī klô′rīd; -rid; -klō-), **bi·chlo·rid** (-rid), *n.* 1 compound containing two atoms of chlorine combined with another element or radical. 2 =bichloride of mercury.

bichloride of mercury, an extremely poisonous, white substance, $HgCl_2$, used in solution as an antiseptic, in medicine, and in dyeing.

bick·er (bik′ər), *v., n.* quarrel. [ME *biker(en)*]

bi·cus·pid (bī kus′pid), *n.* a double-pointed tooth. —*adj.* having two points. [< *bi-* two + L *cuspis* point]

bi·cy·cle (bī′sə kəl; -sik′əl), *n., v.,* **-cled, -cling.** —*n.* a metal frame with two wheels, handles for steering, and a seat for the rider who pushes pedals with the feet. —*v.* ride a bicycle. [< F. See BI-, CYCLE.] —**bi′cy·cler, bi·cy·clist,** *n.*

bid (bid), *v.,* **bade** or **bad** (*for 1, 2*) or **bid** (*for 3, 4*), **bid·den** or **bid, bid·ding,** *n.* —*v.* **1** command. **2** say; tell: *bid farewell.* **3** proclaim; declare. **4** offer a price; state a price, esp. as to what one proposes to win in some card game. —*n.* **1** a bidding. **2** an offer. **3** amount offered. **4** amount bid in a card game. **5** appeal: *a bid for sympathy.*
bid up, raise the price of by bidding more. [OE *biddan* ask; meaning infl. by OE *bēodan* offer] —**bid′da·ble,** *adj.* —**bid′der,** *n.*

bid·ding (bid′ing), *n.* **1** command. **2** invitation. **3** offers at an auction. **4** in card games, bids collectively.

bid·dy (bid′i), *n., pl.* **-dies.** hen.

bide (bīd), *v.,* **bode** or **bid·ed, bid·ed, bid·ing.** **1** *Archaic or Dial.* dwell; abide. **2** *Archaic or Dial.* continue; wait.
bide one's time, wait for a good chance. [OE *bīdan*] —**bid′er,** *n.*

bi·en·ni·al (bī en′i əl), *adj.* **1** occurring every two years. **2** living two years, as some plants. —*n.* **1** event that occurs every two years. **2** plant that lives two years. [< L *biennium* < *bi-* two + *annus* year] —**bi·en′ni·al·ly,** *adv.*

bier (bir), *n.* movable stand on which a coffin or dead body is placed. [OE *bēr* < *beran* bear¹]

biff (bif), *n., v.* hit; slap.

bi·fo·cal (bī fō′kəl), *adj.* **1** having two focuses. **2** (used of glasses) having two parts, the upper for far vision, the lower for near vision. —*n.* **1** Usually, **bifocals,** pair of glasses having bifocal lenses. **2** bifocal lens.

bi·fur·cate (*v., adj.* bī′fər kāt, bī fėr′kāt; *adj. also* –kit), *v.,* **-cat·ed, -cat·ing,** *adj.* —*v.* divide into two branches. —*adj.* divided into two branches; forked. [< Med.L, < L *bi-* two + *furca* fork] —**bi′fur·cate·ly,** *adv.* —**bi′fur·ca′tion,** *n.*

big (big), *adj.,* **big·ger, big·gest.** —*adj.* **1** large. **2** grown up. **3** important; great. **4** loud: *a big voice.* **5** boastful: *big talk.* —*adv.* boastfully. [ME; orig. uncert.] —**big′ly,** *adv.* —**big′ness,** *n.*

big·a·my (big′ə mi), *n.* having two wives or two husbands at the same time. [< F, < *bigame* < Med.L, < *bi-* twice + Gk. *gamos* married] —**big′a·mist,** *n.* —**big′a·mous,** *adj.* —**big′a·mous·ly,** *adv.*

Big Dipper, group of stars in the constellation of Ursa Major.

big game, 1 large animals sought by hunters, such as elephants, tigers, or lions. **2** *Fig.* very important thing that is sought.

big-heart·ed (big′här′tid), *adj.* kindly; generous.

big·horn (big′hôrn′), *n., pl.* **-horn, -horns.** wild, grayish-brown sheep of the Rocky Mountains, with large, curved horns.

bight (bīt), *n.* **1** long curve in a coastline. **2** =bay¹. **3** slack of rope between the fastened ends. [OE *byht*]

big·mouth (big mouth), *n.* person who talks too much, esp. one who brags or gossips.

big·no·ni·a (big nō′ni ə), *n.* vine with showy, trumpet-shaped orange flowers. [< NL; named for Abbé *Bignon*]

big·ot (big′ət), *n.* a bigoted person. [< F]

big·ot·ed (big′ət id), *adj.* sticking to an opinion, belief, party, etc., without reason and not tolerating other views; intolerant. —**big′ot·ed·ly,** *adv.*

big·ot·ry (big′ət ri), *n., pl.* **-ries.** bigoted conduct or attitude; prejudice; intolerance.

big top, a circus.

big·wig (big′wig′), *n.* important person.

bi·jou (bē′zhü), *n., pl.* **-joux** (–zhüz). **1** a jewel. **2** something small and fine. [< F]

bi·ju·gate (bī′jü gāt; bī jü′gāt), **bi·ju·gous** (bī′jü gəs), *adj.* having two pairs of leaflets. [< *bi-* two + L *jugatus* yoked]

bike (bīk), *n., v.,* **biked, bik·ing.** —*n.* =bicycle. —*v.* **1** ride a bicycle. **2** ride a motorcycle.

biker (bī′kər), *n.* **1** person who rides a bicycle. **2** person who rides a motorcycle.

bike·path (bīk′ path′), *n.* paved path especially for bicycle riding. Also, **bikeway.**

bi·ki·ni (bi kē′ni), *n.* a woman's two-piece swimsuit.

bi·la·bi·al (bī lā′bi əl), *adj.* **1** having two lips, as some plants. **2** formed by both lips. —*n.* sound formed by both lips, as *b, p, m,* and *w.*

hi·la·bi·ate (bī lā′bi āt; –it), *adj.* having an upper and a lower lip, as some plants.

bi·lat·er·al (bī lat′ər əl), *adj.* **1** having two sides. **2** on two sides. **3** affecting or influencing two sides. **bi·lat′er·al·ism, bi·lat′er·al·ness,** *n.* —**bi·lat′er·al·ly,** *adv.*

bil·ber·ry (bil′ber′i), *n., pl.* **-ries. 1** an edible berry much like a blueberry. **2** shrub that it grows on. [appar. alter. of Scand. (Dan.) *böllebær* after *berry*]

bile (bīl), *n.* **1** a bitter, yellow or greenish liquid secreted by the liver and stored in the gall bladder to aid digestion. **2** ill humor; anger. [< F < L *bilis*]

bilge (bilj), *n., v.,* **bilged, bilg·ing.** —*n.* **1 a** lowest part of a ship's hold. **b** bottom of a ship's hull. **2** =bilge water. **3** the bulging part of a barrel. **4** nonsense. —*v.* **1** spring a leak. **2** bulge; swell out.

bilge water, dirty water that collects in the bottom of a ship.

bil·i·ar·y (bil′i er′i), *adj.* **1** of bile. **2** carrying bile. **3** bilious.

bi·lin·gual (bī ling′gwəl), *adj.* **1** able to speak one's own language and another equally well. **2** containing or written in two languages. —**bi·lin′gual·ism,** *n.* —**bi·lin′gual·ly,** *adv.*

bil·ious (bil′yəs), *adj.* **1** having to do with bile. **2** suffering from or caused by some

trouble with bile or the liver. **3** peevish; cross; bad-tempered. —**bil′ious·ly,** *adv.* —**bil′ious·ness,** *n.*

bilk (bilk), *v.* **1** avoid payment of. **2** defraud; cheat; deceive. —*n.* **1** fraud; deception. **2** person who avoids paying his bills. —**bilk′er,** *n.*

bill¹ (bil), *n.* **1** account of money owed for work done or things supplied; invoice. **2** piece of paper money: *a dollar bill.* **3** poster; handbill. **4** list of items. **5** theater program. **6** proposed law presented to a law-making body. **7** written request or complaint presented to a court. —*v.* **1** send a bill to. **2** announce by bills.
fill the bill, satisfy requirements.
foot the bill, pay or settle the bill. [< Anglo-L *billa,* alter. of Med.L *bulla* document, seal, BULL²] —**bill′a·ble,** *adj.* —**bill′er,** *n.*

bill² (bil), *n.* **1** beak. **2** anything shaped like a bird's bill. —*v.* **1** touch bills: *two birds billed and chirped.* **2** show affection. [OE *bile*]

bill³ (bil), *n.* tool for pruning or cutting. [OE *bil*]

bil·la·bong (bil′ə bong), *n.* in Australia, branch of a river flowing away from the main stream.

bill·board (bil′bôrd′; –bōrd′), *n.* signboard for posting advertisements or notices.

bil·let¹ (bil′it), *n., v.,* **-let·ed, -let·ing.** —*n.* **1** written letter to provide board and lodging for a soldier. **2** place where a soldier is lodged. **3** job; position. —*v.* assign to quarters by billet. [< OF *billette,* dim. of *bille* bill¹]

bil·let² (bil′it), *n.* **1** thick stick of wood. **2** bar of iron or steel. [< F *billette,* dim. of *bille* log, tree trunk]

bil·let-doux (bil′i dü′; bil′ā–), *n., pl.* **bil·lets-doux** (bil′i düz′; bil′ā–). love letter. [< F]

bill·fold (bil′fōld′), *n.* folding pocketbook for money; wallet.

bill·head (bil′hed′), *n.* name and business address printed at the top of a sheet of paper with space below for a bill.

bill·hook (bil′hůk′), *n.* =bill³ (def. 2).

bil·liard (bil′yərd), *adj.* of or for billiards. —*n.* point made by hitting the balls in billiards.

bil·liards (bil′yərdz), *n.* game played with balls on a special table. A long stick called a cue is used to hit the balls. [< F *billard(s),* dim. of *bille* log, tree trunk]

bil·lion (bil′yən), *n., adj.* **1** in the United States and France, one thousand millions. **2** in Great Britain and Germany, one million millions. [< F, < *bi-* two (i.e., to the second power) + (*mi*)*llion* million] —**bil′lionth,** *adj., n.*

bil·lion·aire (bil′yən ār′), *n.* **1** person who has a billion or more dollars, francs, marks, etc. **2** any very wealthy person.

bill of attainder, a legal act depriving a person of property and civil rights because of a sentence of death or outlawry.

bill of exchange, written order to pay a certain sum of money to a specified person.

bill of fare, =menu.

bill of health, certificate stating whether or not there are infectious diseases on a ship or in a port.

clean bill of health, a certification of the absence of infectious disease. **b** any favorable or good report, esp. of a person's qualifications.

bill of lading, receipt given by a carrier showing a list of goods delivered to it for transportation.

bill of rights, 1 statement of the fundamental rights of the people of the nation. **2 Bill of Rights,** the first ten amendments to the Constitution of the United States.

bill of sale, written statement transferring ownership of something from seller to buyer.

bil·low (bil′ō), *n.* **1** a great wave or surge of the sea. **2** any great wave. —*v.* **1** rise or roll in big waves. **2** any great wave. —*v.* **1** rise or roll in big waves. **2** swell out; bulge. [< Scand. *bylgja*]

bil·low·y (bil′ō i), *adj.,* **-low·i·er, -low·i·est. 1** rising or rolling in big waves. **2** swelling out; bulging. —**bil′low·i·ness,** *n.*

bil·ly (bil′i), *n., pl.* **-lies.** club; stick.

billy goat, male goat.

bi·me·tal·lic (bī′mə tal′ik), *adj.* **1** using two metals. **2** of or based on bimetallism.

bi·met·al·lism (bī met′əl iz əm), *n.* use of both gold and silver at a fixed relative value as the basis of the money system of a nation. —**bi·met′al·list,** *n.*

bi·month·ly (bī munth′li), *adj., n., pl.* **-lies,** *adv.* —*adj.* **1** happening once every two months. **2** happening twice a month. —*n.* magazine published bimonthly. —*adv.* **1** once every two months. **2** twice a month.

bin (bin), *n., v.,* **binned, bin·ning.** —*n.* box or enclosed place for holding grain, trash, etc. —*v.* store in a bin. [OE *binn*]

bi·na·ry (bī′nə ri), *adj., n., pl.* **-ries.** —*adj.* consisting of two; involving two; dual. —*n.* a whole composed of two. [< L *binarius* < *bini* two at a time]

binary digit, 1 either of the digits 0 or 1, used in binary notation. **2** =bit^3.

binary notation, system of counting using only the symbols 0 and 1.

binary star, pair of stars that revolve around a common center of gravity.

bi·nate (bī′nāt), *adj.* growing in pairs; double; *binate leaves.* —**bi′nate·ly,** *adv.*

bind (bīnd), *v.,* **bound, bind·ing,** *n.* —*v.* **1** tie together; attach. **2** stick together. **3** restrain. **4** oblige: *she was bound to help.* **5** put under legal obligation: *bound to keep the peace.* **6** put a bandage on. **7** fasten (sheets of paper) into a cover. **8** constipate. —*n.* anything that binds or ties. [OE *bindan*]

bind·er (bīn′dər), *n.* **1** person or thing that binds. **2** cover for holding loose

sheets of paper together. **3** machine that cuts grain and ties it in bundles.

bind·er·y (bīn′dər i), *n., pl.* **-er·ies.** place where books are bound.

bind·ing (bīn′ding), *n.* **1** covering of a book. **2** strip protecting or ornamenting an edge. **3** device that fastens a ski to a boot. —*adj.* **1** that binds, fastens, or connects. **2** having force or power to hold to some agreement, pledge, etc.; obligatory. —**bind′ing·ly,** *adv.* —**bind′ing·ness,** *n.*

binding energy, energy necessary to break a particular atomic nucleus into its smaller component parts.

bind·weed (bīnd′wēd′), *n.* plant that twines about the stems of other plants.

bin·go (bing′gō), *n.* game derived from lotto.

bin·na·cle (bin′ə kəl), *n.* box or stand that contains a ship's compass, placed near the helm. [alter. of *bittacle* < Sp. or Pg. < L *habitaculum* dwelling place < *habitare* dwell]

bi·noc·u·lar (bə nok′yə lər; bī–), *adj.* **1** using both eyes. **2** for both eyes. —*n.* Often, **binoculars.** field glass or opera glass for both eyes. [< L *bini* two at a time + *oculi* eyes] —**bi·noc′u·lar′i·ty,** *n.* —**bi·noc′u·lar·ly,** *adv.*

bi·no·mi·al (bī nō′mi əl), *adj.* consisting of two terms. —*n.* expression or name consisting of two terms. 8a + 2b is a binomial. [< LL *binomius* having two names < *bi–* two + *nomen* name] —**bi·no′mi·al·ly,** *adv.*

bi·o (bī′ō), *n., pl.* **bi·os.** =biography.

bio–, *combining form.* **1** life; living things: *biology = study of living things.* **2** biological: *biochemistry = biological chemistry.*

biochem., biochemistry.

bi·o·chem·is·try (bī′ō kem′is tri), *n.* chemistry of living animals and plants; biological chemistry. [< Gk. *bios* life + E *chemistry*] —**bi′o·chem′i·cal, bi′o·chem′ic,** *adj.* —**bi′o·chem′i·cal·ly,** *adv.* —**bi′o·chem′ist,** *n.*

bi·o·de·grad·a·ble (bī′ō di grā′də bəl), *adj.* that can be broken down, especially by the action of bacteria.

bi·o·di·ver·si·ty (bī′ō di vėr′sə tē), *n.* variety of different animals and plants living in a place.

biog., biographer; biographical; biography.

bi·o·gen·e·sis (bī′ō jen′ə sis), *n.* theory that living things can be produced only by other living things. Also **biogeny.** [< Gk. *bios* life + E *genesis*] —**bi′o·gen′ic,** *adj.* —**bi′o·ge·net′i·cal·ly,** *adv.*

bi·og·ra·phy (bī og′rə fi; bi–), *n., pl.* **-phies. 1** written story of a person's life. **2** part of literature that consists of biographies. [< L < Gk., < *bios* life + *graphein* write] —**bi·og′ra·pher,** *n.* —**bi′o·graph′i·cal, bi′o·graph′ic,** *adj.* —**bi′o·graph′i·cal·ly,** *adv.*

biol., biology.

bi·o·log·i·cal (bī′ə loj′ə kəl), **bi·o·log·ic** (–loj′ik), *adj.* **1** of plant and animal life. **2** having to do with biology. —**bi′o·log′i·cal·ly,** *adv.*

biological clock, 1 mechanism in plants and animals that regulates the rhythm of functions and activities, such as photosynthesis in plants. **2** *Fig.* time to settle down and have children.

biological warfare, a waging of war by using disease germs, etc., against an enemy.

bi·ol·o·gy (bī ol′ə ji), *n.* science of life or living matter in all its forms and phenomena; study of the origin, reproduction, structure, etc., of plant and animal life. [< Gk. *bios* life + –LOGY] —**bi·ol′o·gist,** *n.*

bi·om·e·try (bī om′ə tri), *n.* **1** measurement of life; calculation of the probable duration of human life. **2** Also, **bi·o·met·rics.** branch of biology that deals with living things by measurements and statistics. [< Gk. *bios* life + E *–metry* < Gk. *metron* measure] **bi′o·met′ric, bi′o·met′ri·cal,** *adj.* —**bi′o·met′ri·cal·ly,** *adv.*

bi·on·ics (bī on′iks), *n.* the study of the anatomy and physiology of animals as a basis for new or improved electronic devices or methods.

bi·o·pic (bī′ō pik′), *n.* biographical film. [< *bio–* + *pic*ture]

bi·o·sphere (bī ō′sfir), *n.* =ecosphere.

bi·par·ti·san (bī pär′tə zən), *adj.* of or representing two political parties. —**bi·par′ti·san·ship′,** *n.*

bi·par·tite (bī pär′tīt), *adj.* **1** having two parts. **2** of plants, divided into two parts nearly to the base. —**bi·par′tite·ly,** *adv.* —**bi′par′ti·tion,** *n.*

bi·par·ty (bī′pär′ti), *adj.* combining two different political groups, etc.

bi·ped (bī′ped), —*n.* animal having two feet. —*adj.* having two feet. [< L, < *bi–* two + *pes* foot]

bi·pet·al·ous (bī pet′əl əs), *adj.* having two petals.

bi·pin·nate (bī pin′āt), *adj.* doubly pinnate.

bi·plane (bī′plān′), *n.* airplane having two wings, one above the other.

birch (bėrch), *n.* **1** tree whose smooth bark peels off in thin layers. **2** its close-grained wood, often used in making furniture. **3** bundle of birch twigs or a birch stick, formerly used for whipping. —*v.* whip with a birch; flog. [OE *bierce*] —**birch′en,** *adj.*

birch·bark (berch′bärk′), *n.* **1** bark of a birch tree. **2** Also, **birchbark canoe.** canoe made of birchbark. —*adj.* made of or covered with birchbark.

bird (bėrd), *n.* **1** any of a class of warm-blooded vertebrates having a body covered with feathers and the forelimbs modified to form wings by means of which most species fly. **2** =shuttlecock. **3** fellow; guy. [OE *bridd, bird*]

bird dog, dog trained to find or bring back birds for hunters.

bird flu, a form of influenza transmitted by wildfowl, birds, and domesticated fowl.

bird·ie (bėr′di), *n.* **1** a little bird. **2** score of one stroke less than par for any hole on a golf course.

bird·lime (bėrd′līm′), *n.* a sticky substance smeared on twigs to catch small birds.

bird of paradise, bird of New Guinea noted for its magnificent plumage.

bird of passage, bird that flies from one region to another as the seasons change.

bird of prey, any of a group of flesh-eating birds, including eagles, hawks, vultures, etc.

bird's-eye (bėrdz′ī′), *adj.* 1 seen from above or from a distance; general: *a bird's-eye view.* 2 having markings somewhat like birds' eyes.

bi·ret·ta (bə ret′ə), *n.* a stiff, square cap with three upright projecting pieces, worn by Roman Catholic or Episcopal priests. [< Ital., ult. < LL *birretum* cap, dim. of *birrus* cloak]

birl (bėrl), *v.* among lumberjacks, to revolve a log in the water while standing on it.

Bir·ming·ham (bėr′ming ham), *n.* city in C Alabama.

birth (bėrth), *n.* 1 being born. 2 beginning; origin. 3 a bringing forth. 4 descent; family: *of humble birth.*

give birth to, a bear; bring forth. **b** be the origin or cause of. [ME *birthe*, prob. < Scand. *byrth*].

birth control, contraception; family planning.

birth·day (bėrth′dā′), *n.* 1 day on which a person was born. 2 anniversary of the day on which a person was born, or a thing began.

birth·mark (bėrth′märk′), *n.* spot or mark on the skin that was there at birth.

birth·place (bėrth′plās′), *n.* 1 place where a person was born. 2 place of origin.

birth rate, proportion of the number of births per year to the total population or to some other stated number.

birth·right (bėrth′rīt′), *n.* right belonging to a person because of any fact about his or her birth.

birth·stone (bėerth′stōn′), *n.* jewel associated with a certain month of the year.

Bis·cay (bis′kā; –ki), *n.* **Bay of,** bay N of Spain and W of France, part of the Atlantic.

bis·cuit (bis′kit), *n., pl.* **–cuits, –cuit.** 1 a kind of bread in small soft cakes, made with baking powder, soda, etc. 2 *Brit.* cracker. 3 a pale brown. [< OF *bescuit* < *bes* twice (< L *bis*) + *cuit,* pp. of *cuire* cook (< L *coquere*)]

bi·sect (bī sekt′), *v.* 1 divide into two parts. 2 divide into two equal parts. [< *bi-* two + L *sectus,* pp. of *secare* cut] —**bi·sec′tion,** *n.* —**bi·sec′tion·al,** *adj.* —**bi·sec′tion·al·ly,** *adv.* —**bi·sec′tor,** *n.*

bi·sex·u·al (bī sek′shü əl), *adj., n.* —*adj.* 1 of or having to do with both sexes. 2 having the reproductive organs of both sexes; hermaphroditic. 3 attracted to both sexes. —*n.* bisexual animal or plant.

bish·op (bish′əp), *n.* 1 clergyman of high rank who has certain spiritual duties and who administers the affairs of a church district. 2 one of the pieces in the game of chess. [< VL (*e*) *biscopus,* var. of L *episcopus* < Gk. *episkopos* overseer < *epi* on, over + *skopos* watcher] —**bish′op·less,** *adj.*

bish·op·ric (bish′əp rik), *n.* 1 position, office, or rank of bishop. 2 diocese.

Bis·marck (biz′märk), *n.* capital of North Dakota, in the S part.

Bismarck Archipelago, group of islands NE of New Guinea, governed by Australia.

bis·muth (biz′məth), *n.* brittle, reddish-white metallic element, Bi, used in medicine. [< G] —**bis′muth·al,** *adj.*

bi·son (bī′sən; –zən), *n., pl.* **–son.** 1 the American buffalo, a wild ox with a big, shaggy head and strong front legs. 2 the European buffalo, slightly larger than the American buffalo and now almost extinct. [< L < Gmc.]

bisque (bisk), *n.* smooth, creamy soup. [< F]

bis·sex·tile (bi seks′til), *n.* leap year. —*adj.* containing the extra day of leap year. [< L *bissextilis* (*annus*) leap (year) < *bis* twice + *sextus* sixth. The Julian calendar added an extra day after the *sixth* day before the calends of March.]

bis·ter, bis·tre (bis′tər), *n.* 1 a dark-brown coloring matter made from soot. 2 a dark brown. [< F *bistre*] —**bis′tered, bis′tred,** *adj.*

bi·sul·fate, bi·sul·phate (bī sul′fāt), *n.* salt of sulfuric acid in which half of the hydrogen is replaced by a metal.

bi·sul·fide, (bī sul′fīd; –fid), **bi·sul·fid,** (–fid), *n.* disulfide.

bit¹ (bit), *n., v.,* **bit·ted, bit·ting.** —*n.* 1 part of a bridle that goes in a horse's mouth. 2 anything that curbs or restrains. 3 tool for boring or drilling. —*v.* 1 put a bit in the mouth of; bridle. 2 curb; restrain.

champ at the bit, be restless or impatient. [OE *bite* < *bītan* bite]

bit² (bit), *n.* 1 a small piece; small amount. 2 somewhat; a little. 3 short time. 4 12½ cents. 5 a stage routine.

a bit much, more than is convenient or appropriate.

do one's bit, do one's share. [OE *bita* < *bītan* bite]

bit³ (bit), *n.* basic unit of information in a computer. [< *bi*(nary digi)*t*]

bitch (bich), *n.* 1 a female dog, wolf, or fox. 2 term of contempt for a woman. 3 =complaint. 4 something very difficult. —*v.* 1 spoil; bungle. 2 complain. [OE *bicce*]

bite (bīt), *n., v.,* **bit, bit·ten** (bit′ən) or **bit, bit·ing.** —*n.* 1 bit of food. 2 act of biting. 3 sharp, smarting pain. 4 amount of money, taken from a total: *the tax bite.* —*v.* 1 seize, cut into, or cut off with the teeth. 2 cut; pierce. 3 wound with teeth, fangs, etc. 4 cause a sharp, smarting

pain to. 5 take a tight hold on; grip. [OE *bītan*] —**bit′er,** *n.*

bit·ing (bīt′ing), *adj.* 1 sharp; cutting. 2 sarcastic; sneering. —**bit′ing·ly,** *adv.*

bitt (bit), *n.* a strong post on a ship's deck to which ropes, cables, etc., are fastened. —*v.* put (ropes, cables, etc.) around the bitts. [var. of *bit¹*]

bit·ter (bit′ər), *adj.* 1 having a sharp, harsh, unpleasant taste. 2 hard to admit or bear. 3 sharp; severe. 4 of weather, very cold. 5 expressing grief, pain, misery, etc. —*n.* that which is bitter; bitterness. —*v.* make or become bitter. [OE *biter;* akin to BITE] —**bit′ter·ish,** *adj.* —**bit′ter·ly,** *adv.* —**bit′ter·ness,** *n.*

bit·tern (bit′ərn), *n.* a small kind of heron that lives in marshes and has a peculiar booming cry. [< OF *butor*]

bit·ter·root (bit′ər rüt′; –rút′), *n.* a small plant with pink flowers, found in the northern Rocky Mountains.

bit·ters (bit′ərz), *n. pl.* a liquid, usually alcoholic, flavored with some bitter plant.

bit·ter·sweet (*n.* bit′ər swēt′; *adj.* bit′ər-swēt′), *n.* 1 a climbing plant with purple flowers and poisonous, scarlet berries. 2 a climbing shrub of North America, with greenish flowers, and scarlet arils growing from orange capsules. —*adj.* both bitter and sweet.

bi·tu·men (bi tü′mən; –tū′–; bich′ù–), *n.* mineral that will burn, such as asphalt, petroleum, naphtha, etc. [< L] —**bi·tu′mi·noid,** *adj.* —**bi·tu′mi·nous,** *adj.*

bituminous coal, coal that burns with much smoke and a yellow flame; soft coal.

bi·va·lent (bī vā′lənt; biv′ə), *adj.* having a valence of two. [< *bi-* two + L *valens,* ppr. of *valere* be worth] —**bi·va′lence, bi·va′len·cy,** *n.*

bi·valve (bī′valv′), *n.* any mollusk whose shell consists of two parts hinged together, as oysters and clams. —*adj.* having two parts hinged together. —**bi′valved′, bi·val′vu·lar,** *adj.*

biv·ou·ac (biv′ü ak; biv′wak), *n., v.,* **–acked, –ack·ing.** camp outdoors. [< F, prob. < Swiss G *bīwache* < *bī* by + *wache* watch]

bi·week·ly (bī wēk′li), *adj., n., pl.* **–lies,** *adv.* —*adj.* 1 happening once every two weeks. 2 happening twice a week; semiweekly. —*n.* newspaper or magazine published biweekly. —*adv.* 1 once every two weeks. 2 twice a week; semiweekly.

bi·zarre (bi zär′), *adj.* odd; fantastic; grotesque. [< F < Sp., brave, < Basque *bezar* beard] —**bi·zarre′ly,** *adv.* —**bizarre′ness,** *n.*

bk., 1 bank. 2 bark. 3 block. 4 book.

bl., *pl.* **bls.** 1 bale. 2 barrel.

blab (blab), *v.,* **blabbed, blab·bing,** *n.* —*v.* tell (secrets); talk too much. —*n.* 1 blabbing talk; chatter. 2 person who blabs. —**blab′ber,** *n.*

black (blak), *adj.* 1 opposite of white. 2 very dark. 3 Also, **Black.** having a dark skin. 4 dirty; filthy. 5 dismal; gloomy. 6 sullen. 7 evil. —*n.* 1 opposite of white. 2 black coloring matter. 3 black clothes; mourning. 4 Also, **Black.** person who has dark skin. —*v.* 1 make or become black. 2 put blacking on (shoes, etc.). [OE *blæc*] —**black′er,** *n.* —**black′ly,** *adv.* —**black′ness,** *n.*

black·a·moor (black′ə mür), *n.* a dark-skinned person. [var. of *black Moor*]

black art, evil magic.

black·ball (black′bôl′), *v.* 1 vote against. 2 ostracize. —*n.* a vote against a person or thing. —**black′ball′er,** *n.*

black bass, a North American game fish that lives in fresh water.

black bear, 1 a large American bear. 2 a large Asiatic bear.

black·ber·ry (black′ber′i), *n., pl.* –ries, *v.,* –ried, –ry·ing. —*n.* 1 small, black or dark-purple, edible fruit of certain bushes and vines. 2 thorny bush or vine that it grows on. —*v.* gather blackberries.

black·bird (black′bèrd′), *n.* 1 any American bird so named because the male is mostly black, as the red-winged blackbird. 2 any similar bird, as the European blackbird.

black·board (black′bôrd′; –bōrd′), *n.* smooth surface for writing or drawing on with chalk or crayon.

black box, 1 electronic device that monitors something, esp. the performance of various systems on an aircraft. 2 any device or system whose operation seems mysterious or is poorly understood.

Black Death, violent plague that spread through Asia and Europe in the 14th century.

black·en (black′ən), *v.,* –ened, –en·ing. 1 make or become black. 2 speak evil of. —**black′en·er,** *n.*

black eye, 1 bruise around an eye. 2 cause of disgrace or discredit.

black-eyed Su·san (black′īd′ sü′zən) yellow daisy with a black center.

black·face (black′fās′), *n.* 1 black minstrel. 2 theatrical entertainment given by blackfaces. 3 makeup for black parts in a show, etc. —*adj.* having a black face.

Black·foot (black′füt′), *n., pl.* –**feet** (–fēt′), –**foot,** *adj.* —*n.* 1 confederacy of Algonkian Indians of the northern plains and Canada. 2 their language. 3 an Algonkian Indian. —*adj.* of or having to do with the Blackfeet or their language.

Black Forest, mountains covered with forests in SW Germany.

black·guard (blag′ärd; –ərd), *n.* scoundrel. —*v.* abuse with vile language. [< *black* + *guard*] —**black′guard·ism,** *n.* —**black′guard·ly,** *adj.*

black·head (black′hed′), *n.* 1 a small, black-tipped lump in a pore of the skin. 2 any of various birds that have a black head. 3 disease that attacks turkeys.

black-heart·ed (black′här′tid), *adj.* evil.

Black Hills, mountains in W South Dakota and NE Wyoming.

black·ing (black′ing), *n.* black polish used on shoes.

black·ish (black′ish), *adj.* somewhat black.

black·jack (black′jak′), *n.* 1 club with a flexible handle, used as a weapon. 2 large drinking cup or jug. 3 black flag of a pirate. —*v.* 1 hit (a person) with a blackjack. 2 coerce. —**black′jack′,** *adj.*

black lead, = graphite.

black·leg (black′leg′), *n.* 1 swindler. 2 an infectious, usually fatal disease of cattle and sheep.

black list, list of persons who are believed to deserve punishment, blame, suspicion, etc.

black-list (black′list′), *v.* put on a black list.

black magic, evil magic.

black·mail (black′māl′), *v.* get or try to get blackmail from. —*n.* 1 money obtained from a person by threatening to tell something bad about him or her. 2 act of blackmailing. [< *black* + *mail* rent, tribute, coin < OF *maille* < *mail, medaille* coin, medal] —**black′mail′er,** *n.*

black mark, mark of criticism or punishment.

black market, the selling of goods at illegal prices or in illegal quantities.

black marketeer, one who deals on the black market.

black nightshade, plant with white flowers, poisonous black berries, and poisonous leaves.

black oak, 1 any of various American oaks, having dark bark and foliage. 2 its wood.

black·out (black′out′), *n.* 1 condition of having no electric power; power failure. 2 a turning out or concealing of all the lights of a city, district, etc., as a protection. 3 failure in radio reception. 4 withholding of a television broadcast in a particular area, esp. of a sports event. 5 withholding of information, esp. from newspapers, television broadcasts, etc. 6 temporary blindness or unconsciousness experienced by a pilot, resulting from loss of oxygen to the brain. 7 a turning off of all the lights on the stage of a theater.

black out, 1 darken completely. 2 experience a blackout.

black pepper, 1 seasoning with a hot taste. It is made by grinding the berries of a plant. 2 the plant itself.

Black Sea, sea between Turkey and S Russia.

black sheep, worthless member of a decent family; scoundrel.

black·smith (black′smith′), *n.* man who works with iron. Blacksmiths mend tools and used to shoe horses. [with ref. to black metals, e.g., iron]

black·snake (black′snāk′), *n.* a harmless, dark-colored snake of North America.

black spruce, 1 North American evergreen tree with dark-green foliage. 2 its light, soft wood.

black·thorn (black′thôrn′), *n.* a thorny European shrub of the peach family that has dark-purple, plumlike fruit called sloes.

black·top (black′top′), *n., v.* = asphalt.

black walnut, 1 oily nut that is good to eat. 2 the tall tree that it grows on. 3 its dark-brown wood, often used for furniture.

black widow, very poisonous spider, so called from its color and its habit of eating its mate.

blad·der (blad′ər), *n.* 1 a soft, thin bag in the body that collects urine from the kidneys. 2 anything like this. [OE *blædare*] —**blad′der·like′,** *adj.* —**blad′der·y,** *adj.*

blad·der·wort (blad′ər wèrt′), *n.* any of various plants with yellow flowers. Some varieties float on the water; others take root in mud.

blade (blād), *n.* 1 the cutting part of a knife or sword. 2 sword. 3 swordsman. 4 smart or dashing fellow. 5 the flat, wide part of a leaf. 6 a flat, wide part of anything: *blade of a paddle; shoulder blade.* [OE *blæd*] —**blad′ed,** *adj.* —**blade′less,** *adj.* —**blade′like′,** *adj.*

blah (blä), *adj.* dull; boring.

(case of) the blahs, feeling bored or depressed.

blain (blān), *n.* an inflamed swelling or sore; blister; pustule. [OE *blegen*]

blam·a·ble (blām′ə bəl), *adj.* deserving blame. —**blam′a·ble·ness,** *n.* —**blam′a·bly,** *adv.*

blame (blām), *v.,* blamed, blam·ing, *n.* —*v.* 1 hold responsible. 2 find fault with. —*n.* 1 responsibility. 2 finding fault. **be to blame,** deserve blame. [< OF < L Gk. *blasphemeein,* ? < *blapsis* harm + –*phemos* speaking] —**blame′ful,** *adj.* —**blame′ful·ly,** *adv.* —**blame′ful·ness,** *n.* —**blame′less,** *adj.* —**blame′less·ly,** *adv.* —**blame′less·ness,** *n.* —**blam′er,** *n.*

blame·wor·thy (blām′wèr′thi), *adj.* deserving blame. —**blame′wor′thi·ness,** *n.*

blanch (blanch; blänch), *v.* 1 bleach: *almonds are blanched.* 2 turn white or pale: *blanch with fear.* [< OF *blanchir* < *blanc* white, BLANK] —**blanch′er,** *n.*

blanc·mange (blə mänzh′), *n.* a sweet dessert made of milk thickened with gelatin, cornstarch, etc. [< OF *blanc-manger* white food]

bland (bland), *adj.* 1 mild; gentle: *a bland spring breeze.* 2 agreeable; polite. [< L *blandus* soft] —**bland′ly,** *adv.* —**bland′ness,** *n.*

blan·dish (blan′dish), *v.* coax; flatter. [< F < L *blandiri* flatter < *blandus* soft] —**blan′dish·er,** *n.* —**blan′dish·ment,** *n.*

blank (blangk), *n.* 1 space left empty or to be filled in. 2 paper with spaces to be filled in: *an application blank.* 3 piece of metal to be filed into a coin or key. —*adj.* 1 not written or printed on. 2 with spaces to be filled in: *a blank check.* 3 empty; dull. 4 lacking some usual feature: *a blank cartridge.* [< F *blanc* white, shining < Gmc.] —**blank′ly,** *adv.* —**blank′ness,** *n.*

blank check, a signed check that allows the bearer to fill in the amount.

blan·ket (blang′kit), *n.* **1** a soft, heavy covering of wool or cotton, used to keep people or animals warm. **2** anything like a blanket. —*v.* **1** cover with a blanket. **2** obscure. —*adj.* covering several or all: *blanket insurance policy.* [< OF *blankete* < *blanc* white] —**blan′ket·less,** *adj.*

blank verse, 1 unrhymed poetry having five iambic feet in each line. **2** unrhymed poetry.

blare (blãr), *v.,* **blared, blar·ing,** *n.* —*v.* **1** make a loud, harsh sound: *the trumpets blared.* **2** utter harshly or loudly. —*n.* **1** a loud, harsh sound. **2** brilliance of color; glare. [< MDu. *blaren*]

blar·ney (blär′ni), *n., v.,* **-neyed, -ney·ing.** —*n.* flattering, coaxing talk. —*v.* flatter; coax. [< *Blarney stone,* stone in a castle in Ireland, said to give skill in flattery to those who kiss it] —**blar′ney·er,** *n.*

bla·sé (blä zā′; blä′zā), *adj.* tired of pleasures; bored. [< F, pp. of *blaser* exhaust with pleasure]

blas·pheme (blas fēm′), *v.,* **-phemed, -phem·ing. 1** speak about (God or sacred things) with abuse or contempt; utter blasphemy. **2** speak evil of. [< OF < L *blasphemare.* See BLAME.] —**blas·phem′er,** *n.*

blas·phe·my (blas′fə mi), *n., pl.* **-mies.** abuse or contempt for God or sacred things.—**blas′phe·mous,***adj.*—**blas′phe·mous·ly,** *adv.* —**blas′phe·mous·ness,** *n.*

blast (blast; bläst), *n.* **1** a strong sudden rush of wind or air. **2** the blowing of a trumpet, horn, etc. **3** a blasting explosion. **4** cause of blight or ruin. —*v.* **1** blow up (rocks, earth, etc.) with dynamite, gunpowder, etc. **2** blight; ruin. **full blast,** in full operation; at highest speed or greatest capacity. [OE *blǣst*] —**blast′er,** *n.*

blast·ed (blas′tid; bläs′-), *adj.* **1** blighted; ruined. **2** damned; cursed.

blast furnace, furnace in which ores are smelted by blowing a strong current of air into the furnace to make a very great heat.

blas·tu·la (blas′chú lə), *n., pl.* **-lae** (-lē). embryo of an animal. [< NL, dim. of Gk. *blastos* sprout, germ] —**blas′tu·lar,** *adj.*

blat (blat), *v.,* **blat·ted, blat·ting. 1** cry like a calf or sheep; bleat. **2** say loudly and foolishly; blurt out. [imit.]

bla·tant (blā′tənt), *adj.* **1** noisy; loudmouthed. **2** showy in dress, manner, etc. [coined by Spenser < L *blatire* babble] —**bla′tan·cy,** *n.* —**bla′tant·ly,** *adv.*

blaze¹ (blāz), *n., v.,* **blazed, blaz·ing.** —*n.* **1** bright flame or fire. **2** glare. **3** bright display. **4** violent outburst: *a blaze of temper.* —*v.* **1** burn with a bright flame. **2** show bright colors or lights. **3** burst out in anger or excitement. [OE *blǣse*] —**blaz′ing·ly,** *adv.*

blaze² (blāz), *n., v.,* **blazed, blaz·ing.** —*n.* **1** mark made on a tree by chipping off a piece of bark. **2** a white spot on the face of a horse, cow, etc. —*v.* mark (a tree, trail, etc.) with a blaze. [< LG *bläse*]

blaze³ (blāz), *v.,* **blazed, blaz·ing.** make known; proclaim. [< MDu. *blasen*]

blaz·er (blāz′ər), *n.* a distinctively colored jacket.

bla·zon (blā′zən), *v.* **1** make known; proclaim. **2** decorate; adorn. **3** display; show. —*n.* **1** coat of arms. **2** display; show. [< OF *blason* shield] —**bla′zon·er,** *n.* —**bla′zon·ment, bla′zon·ry,** *n.*

bldg., *pl.* **bldgs.** building.

bleach (blēch), *v.* **1** whiten by exposing to sunlight or by using chemicals. **2** turn white. —*n.* **1** chemical used in bleaching. **2** act of bleaching. [OE *blǣcean;* akin to BLEAK]

bleach·er (blēch′ər), *n.* **1** person who bleaches. **2** thing that bleaches or is used in bleaching. **3 bleachers,** low-priced, often roofless seats at outdoor sports events.

bleak (blēk), *adj.* **1** swept by winds; bare; desolate. **2** chilly; cold. **3** dreary; dismal. [ME *bleke* pale. Cf. OE *blǣc, blāc.*] —**bleak′ly,** *adv.* —**bleak′ness,** *n.*

blear (blir), *adj.* dim; blurred. —*v.* make dim or blurred. [ME *blere(n)*]

blear·y (blir′i), *adj.,* **blear·i·er, blear·i·est.** dim; blurred. —**blear′i·ness,** *n.*

blear·y·eyed (blir′i īd′), *adj.* having eyes dim with tears, fatigue, etc. Also, **bleareyed.**

bleat (blēt), *n.* cry made by a sheep, goat, or calf, or a sound like it. —*v.* make such a cry. [OE *blǣtan*] —**bleat′er,** *n.* —**bleat′ing·ly,** *adv.*

bleed (blēd), *v.,* **bled** (bled), **bleed·ing. 1** lose blood. **2** shed one's blood; suffer wounds or death. **3** take blood from: *doctors used to bleed sick people.* **4** feel pity, sorrow, or grief (for). **5** lose sap, juice, etc. **6** take sap, juice, etc., from. **7** extend text or illustrations into the margins of a page. **8** drain slowly from, as fluid from hydraulic brakes. **9** get money from by extortion. [OE *blēdan* < *blōd* blood]

bleed·er (blēd′ər), *n.* person who bleeds excessively when injured because the blood fails to clot; hemophiliac.

bleeding heart, 1 garden plant that has drooping clusters of red or pinkish flowers. **2** person who expresses insincere or exaggerated pity, sympathy, etc.

blem·ish (blem′ish), *n.* stain; spot; scar: *a blemish on the skin.* —*v.* **1** stain; spot; scar. **2** injure; mar; tarnish: *blemish one's reputation.* [< OF *ble(s)mir* make livid] —**blem′ish·er,** *n.*

blench¹ (blench), *v.* draw back; shrink away. [appar. OE *blencan* deceive] —**blench′er,** *n.*

blench² (blench), *v.* **1** turn pale. **2** make white. [var. of *blanch*]

blend (blend), *v.,* **blend·ed** or **blent, blend·ing,** *n.* —*v.* **1** mix together thor-

oughly so that the things mixed cannot be distinguished. **2** make by mixing several kinds together. **3** shade into each other, little by little; merge. **4** go well together; harmonize. —*n.* **1** thorough mixture. **2** mixture of several kinds: *a blend of coffee.* **3** word made by fusing two words, often with a syllable in common, as *cinemactress. Blotch* is a blend of *blot* and *botch.* [pt. of OE *blandan*] —**blend′er,** *n.*

bless (bles), *v.,* **blessed** or **blest, bless·ing. 1** make holy or sacred. **2** ask God's favor for. **3** wish good to. **4** make happy or successful. **5** praise; glorify. **6** guard; protect. **7** make the sign of the cross over. [OE *blētsian* consecrate (i.e., with blood) < *blōd* blood] —**bless′er,** *n.*

bless·ed (bles′id; blest), *adj.* **1** holy; sacred. **2** beatified. **3** happy; successful. **4** in heaven. **5** annoying; cursed. —**bless′ed·ly,** *adv.* —**bless′ed·ness,** *n.*

bless·ing (bles′ing), *n.* **1** prayer asking God to show His favor. **2** giving of God's favor. **3** wish for happiness or success. **4** anything that makes one happy or contented.

blew (blü), *v.* pt. of **blow².**

blight (blīt), *n.* **1** any disease that causes plants to wither or decay. **2** insect or fungus that causes such a disease. **3** anything that causes destruction or ruin. —*v.* **1** cause to wither or decay. **2** destroy; ruin.

blimp (blimp), *n.* a small, nonrigid dirigible airship. [appar. from Type *B limp,* designation for "limp dirigible"]

blind (blīnd), *adj.* **1** not able to see; sightless. **2** lacking discernment, understanding, or judgment: *blind to the dangers ahead.* **3** not controlled by reason: *blind fury.* **4** made without thought or good sense: *a blind guess.* **5** covered; hidden: *a blind driveway.* **6** without an opening: *a blind wall.* **7** with only one opening: *a blind alley.* **8** of or for blind persons. —*v.* **1** make unable to see temporarily or permanently. **2** darken; dim; cover; conceal. **3** rob of power to understand or judge. —*n.* **1** something that keeps out light or hinders sight. **2** anything that conceals an action or purpose. **3** hiding place for a hunter. [OE] —**blind′ing,** *adj.* —**blind′ing·ly,** *adv.* —**blind′ly,** *adv.* —**blind′ness,** *n.*

blind·er (blīn′dər), *n.* blinker for a horse.

blind flying, directing an aircraft by instruments only.

blind·fold (blīnd′fōld′), *v.* cover the eyes of. —*adj.* with the eyes covered. —*n.* thing covering the eyes. [OE *blindfellian* < *blind* blind + *fell,* var. of *fiell* fall; infl. by *fold*]

blind spot, 1 a round spot on the retina of the eye that is not sensitive to light. **2** matter on which a person does not know that he or she is prejudiced or poorly informed. **3** an area of poor radio or television reception. **4** area of poor visibility.

blink (blingk), *v.* **1** look with the eyes opening and shutting: *blink at a sudden light.* **2** wink: *blink one's eyes.* **3** shine with an unsteady light: *a lantern blinked in the darkness.* **4** look with indifference at; ignore. —*n.* **1** a blinking. **2** glimpse. **on the blink,** not working or not working properly. [ME *blenken*] —**blink′ing-ly,** *adv.*

blink·er (blingk′ər), *n.* **1** a leather flap to keep a horse from seeing sidewise; blinder. **2** a warning signal with flashing lights.

blink·ered (bling′kərd), *adj.* restricted in outlook; narrow-minded.

blip (blip), *n.* **1** image on a radar screen. **2** *Fig.* something insignificant.

bliss (blis), *n.* **1** great happiness; perfect joy. **2** the joy of heaven; blessedness. [OE *blīths* < *blīthe* blithe] —**bliss′ful,** *adj.* —**bliss′ful·ly,** *adv.* —**bliss′ful·ness,** *n.*

blis·ter (blis′tər), *n.* **1** small baglike swelling under the skin filled with watery matter, often caused by burns or rubbing. **2** similar swelling on a surface. —*v.* **1** raise a blister on. **2** become covered with blisters. **3** attack with sharp words. [< OF *blestre* tumor, lump, prob. < Gmc.] —**blis′ter·y,** *adj.*

blithe (blīth; blīth), *adj.* happy; cheerful. [OE *blīthe*] —**blithe′ly,** *adv.* —**blithe′ness,** *n.*

blithe·some (blīth′səm; blīth′–), *adj.* happy; cheerful. —**blithe′some·ly,** *adv.* —**blithe′some·ness,** *n.*

blitz (blits), *n.* **1** sudden, violent attack using many airplanes and tanks. **2** any sudden violent attack: *endure a blitz of criticism.* —*v.* attack by a blitz. [< G *Blitzkrieg* lightning war]

bliz·zard (bliz′ərd), *n.* violent, blinding snowstorm with a very strong wind and very great cold. [var. of *blizzer* blow, shot; orig., flash, blaze, Cf. OE *blysian* burn.]

bloat (blōt), *v.* swell up; puff up. [< *bloat, adj.* soft < Scand. *blautr*]

blob (blob), *n.* small lump; bubble; drop.

bloc (blok), *n.* member or members of a group combined for a purpose, as a group of politicians or various nations: *the farm bloc.* [< F. See BLOCK.]

block (blok), *n.* **1** a solid piece of wood, stone, metal, etc. **2** obstruction; hindrance. **3** a hindering of an opponent's play. **4** space in a city enclosed by streets. **5** length of one side of a city block. **6** number of buildings close together. **7** group of things of the same kind: *a block of ten tickets for a play.* **8** short section of railroad track with signals for spacing trains. **9** support for the neck of a person condemned to be beheaded. **10** platform where things are put up for sale at an auction. **11** pulley in a casing. **12** mold on which things are shaped. **13** piece of wood, etc., engraved for printing. —*v.* **1** fill so as to prevent passage or progress. **2** put things in the way of; obstruct; hinder. **3** mount on a block.

block in or **out,** plan roughly; outline.
block off, close off.
block up, fill up to prevent passage.
on the block, for sale or auction. [< OF *bloc* < Gmc.] —**block′er,** *n.*

block·ade (blok ād′), *n., v.,* **–ad·ed, –ad·ing.** —*n.* **1** control of who or what goes into or out of a place by the use of an army or navy. **2** army or navy used to blockade a place. **3** anything that blocks up or obstructs. —*v.* **1** put under blockade. **2** obstruct. —**block·ad′er,** *n.*

block·ade-run·ner (blok ād′run ′ər), *n.* **1** ship that tries to sneak into or out of a port that is being blockaded. **2** person who is involved in doing this.

block and tackle, pulleys and ropes to lift or pull something.

block·bust·er (blok′bus ′tər), *n.* anything that is forceful or overwhelming.

block·head (blok′hed ′), *n.* a stupid person.

block·house (blok′hous ′), *n.* **1** *Am.* house of square logs, often with a jutting second story, having holes for guns. **2** *Mil.* any small fortified building with ports for gunfire.

block·ish (blok′ish), *adj.* stupid; dull. —**block′ish·ly,** *adv.* —**block′ish·ness,** *n.*

block·y (blok′i), *adj.,* **block·i·er, block·i·est. 1** like a block; chunky. **2** having patches of light and shade.

blond, blonde (blond), *adj.* **1** light-colored. **2** having yellow or light-brown hair, blue or gray eyes, and light skin; fair. —*n.* person having such hair, eyes, and skin. A man is a blond; a woman is a blonde. [< F < Gmc.] —**blond′ness, blonde′ness,** *n.*

blood (blud), *n.* **1** the red liquid in the veins, arteries, and capillaries of the vertebrates. **2** the corresponding liquid in invertebrate animals. **3** juice; sap. **4** family; birth; relationship; parentage; descent. **5** high lineage, esp. royal lineage. **6** bloodshed; slaughter. **7** temper; emotion; passion: *bad blood between them.* **8** man of dash and spirit.
curdle one's (or the) blood, frighten very much; terrify.
draw blood, inflict damage or pain.
in cold blood, a cruelly. **b** on purpose. [OE *blōd*] —**blood′like ′,** *adj.*

blood bank, 1 place for storage of blood. **2** the blood kept in storage.

blood brother, brother by birth.

blood count, a count of the number of red and white corpuscles and the amount of hemoglobin in a sample of a person's blood to see if it is normal.

blood·cur·dling (blud′kėrd ′ling), *adj.* terrifying; horrible.

blood·ed (blud′id), *adj.* **1** of good stock or breed. **2** having a certain kind of blood.

blood group, any one of the four groups into which blood is divided; blood type.

blood·hound (blud′hound ′), *n.* **1** one of a breed of large, powerful dogs with a keen sense of smell. **2** detective.

blood·less (blud′lis), *adj.* **1** without blood; pale. **2** without bloodshed. **3** without energy; spiritless. **4** cold-hearted; cruel. —**blood′less·ly,** *adv.* —**blood′less·ness,** *n.*

blood·let·ting (blud′let ′ing), *n.* **1** act of opening a vein to take out blood. **2** bloodshed; slaughter.

blood money, 1 money paid to have somebody killed. **2** money paid as compensation.

blood poisoning, a diseased condition of blood usually caused by bacteria; septicemia.

blood pressure, pressure of the blood against the inner walls of the blood vessels, varying with exertion, excitement, health, age, etc.

blood relation or **relative,** person related by birth.

blood·root (blud′rüt ′; –rùt ′), *n.* plant that has a red root, red sap, and a white flower.

blood·shed (blud′shed ′), *n.* the shedding of blood; slaughter.

blood·shot (blud′shot ′), *adj.* of eyes, red and sore; tinged with blood.

blood sport, sport that involves killing animals, as fox or boar hunting.

blood·stained (blud′stānd ′), *adj.* **1** stained with blood. **2** guilty of murder or bloodshed.

blood·stone (blud′stōn ′), *n.* a semiprecious green stone with specks of red jasper scattered through it.

blood·suck·er (blud′suk ′ər), *n.* **1** animal that sucks blood; leech. **2** person who gets all he or she can by any means; extortioner.

blood sugar, glucose in the blood, too much being an indication of diabetes.

blood·thirst·y (blud′thėrs ′ti), *adj.* eager for bloodshed; cruel; murderous. —**blood′thirst ′i·ly,** *adv.* —**blood′thirst ′i·ness,** *n.*

blood transfusion, injection of blood from one person or animal into another.

blood type, =blood group.

blood vessel, tube in the body through which the blood circulates, as an artery, vein, or capillary.

blood·y (blud′i), *adj.,* **blood·i·er, blood·i·est,** *v.,* **blood·ied, blood·y·ing.** —*adj.* **1** bleeding. **2** stained with blood. **3** with much bloodshed. **4** eager for bloodshed; cruel. **5** of the color of blood. **6** *Brit. Slang.* cursed; confounded. —*v.* **1** cause to bleed. **2** stain with blood. —**blood′i-ly,** *adv.* —**blood′i·ness,** *n.*

bloom (blüm), *n.* **1** flower; blossom. **2** condition or time of flowering. **3** condition or time of greatest health, vigor, or beauty. **4** glow of health and beauty. **5** powdery coating on some fruits and leaves. —*v.* **1** have flowers; open into flowers; blossom. **2** be in the condition or time of greatest health, vigor, or beauty. **3** glow with health and beauty. [< Scand. *blōm*] —**bloom′ing·ly,** *adv.*

bloom·ers (blüm′ərz), *n.pl.* **1** loose trousers, gathered at the knee, formerly worn by women and girls for physical training. **2** underwear made like these. [first referred to in magazine published by Amelia J. *Bloomer,* 1851]

bloop·er (blüp′ər), *n.* **1** very foolish mistake; blunder. **2** baseball hit high into the air.

blos·som (blos′əm), *n.* **1** flower, esp. of a plant that produces fruit. **2** condition or time of flowering. —*v.* **1** have flowers; open into flowers. **2** flourish; develop. [OE *blōstma*]

blot (blot), *v.,* **blot·ted, blot·ting,** *n.* —*v.* **1** spot with liquid; stain. **2** dry (liquid) with paper that soaks it up. **3** blemish; disgrace. —*n.* **1** spot; stain of any kind. **2** blemish; disgrace.

blot out, a hide; cover up. **b** wipe out; destroy. —**blot′less,** *adj.*

blotch (bloch), *n.* **1** a large, irregular spot or stain. **2** place where the skin is red or broken out. —*v.* cover or mark with blotches. [blend of *blot* and *botch*] —**blotch′y,** *adj.*

blot·ter (blot′ər), *n.* book for writing down happenings, transactions, arrests, etc.

blouse (blous; blouz), *n.* **1** a loose garment like a shirt for the upper body. **2** short loosely fitting coat, worn as part of a military uniform. [< F, Pr., short (wool)] —**blouse′like′,** *adj*

blow¹ (blō), *n.* **1** a hard hit; knock. **2** a severe shock; misfortune. **3** a sudden attack or assault. [ME *blaw*]

blow² (blō), *v.,* **blew, blown, blow·ing,** *n.* —*v.* **1** send forth a strong current of air. **2** move in a current. **3** drive by a current of air. **4** force a current of air into. **5** form or shape by air: *blow glass.* **6** make a sound by a current of air or steam. **7** puff up: *blown up with pride.* **8** break by an explosion. **9** pant; cause to pant. **10** *Slang.* spend (money, etc.) recklessly. **11** reveal; expose. **12** melt (a fuse) or cause (an electric light) to burn out. —*n.* **1** a blowing. **2** gale of wind.

blow in, appear unexpectedly; drop in. **blow up, a** explode. **b** fill with air. **c** become very angry. **d** scold; abuse. **e** arise; become stronger: *a storm suddenly blew up.* **f** *Informal.* go to pieces emotionally. [OE *blāwan*] —**blow′er,** *n.*

blow-dry (blō′drī′), *v.,* **-dried, -dry·ing,** *adj.* —*v.* **1** dry or style the hair with a blow dryer. **2** blow-dry the hair of. —*adj.* involving the use of a blow dryer.

blow dryer, portable electric blower for drying and styling the hair.

blow·fly (blō′flī′), *n., pl.* **-flies.** two-winged fly that deposits its eggs on meat or in wounds.

blow·gun (blō′gun′), *n.* tube through which a person blows arrows, darts, etc.

blow·hole (blō′hōl′), *n.* **1** hole where air or gas can escape. **2** hole for breathing, in the top of the head of whales and some other animals.

blown¹ (blōn), *adj.* **1** tainted by flies. **2** shaped by blowing. —*v.* pp. of **blow².**

blown² (blōn), *adj.* fully opened. [pp. of *blow* blossom, OE *blōwan*]

blow·out (blō′out′), *n.* **1** the bursting of an automobile tire. **2** a sudden or violent escape of air, steam, etc. **3** the melting of an electric fuse caused by too much current. **4** *Informal.* big party or meal.

blow·pipe (blō′pīp′), *n.* **1** tube for blowing air or gas into a flame to increase the heat. **2** =blowgun.

blow·torch (blō′tôrch′), *n.* a small torch that shoots out a very hot flame.

blow·up (blō′up′), *n.* **1** explosion. **2** outburst of anger. **3** quarrel.

blow·y (blō′i), *adj.,* **blow·i·er, blow·i·est.** windy. —**blow′i·ness,** *n.*

blowz·y (blouz′i), *adj.,* **blowz·i·er, blowz·i·est. 1** untidy; frowzy. **2** red-faced and coarse-looking. [< *blowze* wench, slattern]

blub·ber (blub′ər), *n.* **1** fat of whales and other sea animals. **2** noisy weeping. —*v.* weep noisily. —**blub′ber·er,** *n.* —**blub′ber·y,** *adj.*

bludg·eon (bluj′ən), *n.* short club with a heavy end. —*v.* **1** strike with a club. **2** bully; threaten. —**bludg′eon·er, bludg′con·ccr′,** *n.*

blue (blü), *n., adj.,* **blu·er, blu·est,** *v.,* **blued, blu·ing** or **blue·ing.** —*n.* **1** color of the clear sky in daylight. **2** blue coloring matter or pigment. —*adj.* **1** having the color of the clear sky in daylight. **2** sad; gloomy; discouraged. —*v.* make blue.

out of the blue, completely unexpected. **the blue, a** the sky. **b** the sea.

the blues. See **blues.** [< OF *bleu* < Gmc.] —**blue′ly,** *adv.* —**blue′ness,** *n.*

blue·bell (blü′bel′), *n.* any of various plants with blue flowers shaped like bells.

blue·ber·ry (blü′ber′i; -bər i), *n., pl.* **-ries. 1** a small, sweet, edible berry that has smaller seeds than the huckleberry. **2** the shrub that it grows on.

blue·bird (blü′bėrd′), *n.* a small songbird of North America whose prevailing color is blue.

blue blood, aristocratic descent. —**blue′blood′ed,** *adj.*

blue·bon·net (blü′bon′it), *n.* **1** plant with blue flowers resembling sweet peas. **2** =bachelor's button.

blue·bot·tle (blü′bot′əl), *n.* **1** large blowfly that has a blue abdomen and a hairy body. **2** any similar fly. **3** =cornflower.

blue chip, 1 a poker chip of high value. **2** stock issued by a well-established and profitable company. **3** *Fig.* anything of high value or quality. —**blue′-chip′,** *adj.*

blue·fish (blü′fish′), *n., pl.* **-fish·es** or (*esp. collectively*) **-fish.** a blue-and-silver saltwater edible fish of the Atlantic Coast.

blue·grass (blü′gras′; -gräs′), *n.* any of various American grasses with bluish-green stems, esp. **Kentucky bluegrass.**

blue gum, =eucalyptus.

blue·ish (blü′ish), *adj.* bluish. —**blue′ish·ness,** *n.*

blue·jay (blü′jā′), *n.* any of various North American jays, esp. a noisy, chattering bird with a crest and a blue back.

blue jeans, =jeans.

blue-pen·cil (blü′pen′səl), *v.,* **-ciled, -cil·ing.** edit, esp. with a blue pencil.

blue·print (blü′print′), *n.* **1** detailed plan or outline of a project. **2** photograph that shows blue or white outlines, esp. of a building plan.

blue ribbon, 1 blue ribbon awarded to the winner of a contest. **2** first prize.

blue-ribbon (blü′rib ən), *adj.* comprised of or selected as representative of the best.

Blue Ridge, range of the Appalachian Mountains, extending from E Pennsylvania to N Georgia.

blues (blüz), *n. pl.* **1** depression of spirits; despondency. **2** slow, melancholy jazz song. **2** bluefish.

blue·stock·ing (blü′stok′ing), *n.* woman who displays great interest in intellectual or literary subjects. [because blue stockings were affected by a group of such women in London c 1750] —**blue′stock′ing·ism,** *n.*

blue streak, with lightning speed: *talk a blue streak.*

blu·et (blü′it), *n.* small plant of the U.S., with pale bluish flowers.

bluff¹ (bluf), *n.* a high, steep bank or cliff. —*adj.* **1** rising with a straight, broad front. **2** abrupt, frank, and hearty in manner. [prob. <Du. *blaf* broad flat face] —**bluff′ly,** *adv.* —**bluff′ness,** *n.*

bluff² (bluf), *n.* **1** show of pretended confidence, used to deceive or mislead. **2** threat that cannot be carried out. **3** person who bluffs. —*v.* **1** deceive by a show of pretended confidence. **2** frighten with a threat that cannot be carried out. —**bluff′er,** *n.*

blu·ish (blü′ish), *adj.* somewhat blue. Also, **blueish.** —**blu′ish·ness,** *n.*

blun·der (blun′dər), *v.* **1** make a stupid mistake. **2** do clumsily or wrongly; bungle. **3** move clumsily or blindly; stumble. **4** blurt out. —*n.* stupid mistake. —**blun′der·er,** *n.* —**blun′der·ing·ly,** *adv.*

blun·der·buss (blun′dər bus), *n.* **1** short gun with a wide muzzle, now no longer used. **2** person who blunders. [alter. of Du. *donderbus* thunder box]

blunt (blunt), *adj.* **1** without a sharp edge or point; dull. **2** plain-spoken; outspoken; frank. **3** slow in perceiving or understanding. —*v.* make or become blunt. —**blunt′ly,** *adv.* —**blunt′ness,** *n.*

blur (blėr), *v.,* **blurred, blur·ring,** *n.* —*v.* **1** make confused in form or outline: *mist blurred the hills.* **2** dim: *tears blurred my eyes.* **3** become dim or indistinct. **4** smear; blot; stain. —*n.* **1** a blurred condition; dimness. **2** thing seen dimly or indistinctly. **3** smear; blot; stain. [? var. of *blear*] —**blur'ry,** *adj.*

blurb (blèrb), *n., v.,* **blurbed, blurb·ing.** —*n.* advertisement or announcement full of extremely high praise, esp. on a book jacket or cover. —*v.* call attention to by use of blurbs. [coined by Gelett Burgess, American humorist]

blurt (blèrt), *v.* say suddenly or without thinking: *blurt out a secret.* [imit.]

blush (blush), *n.* **1** a reddening of the skin caused by shame, confusion, or excitement. **2** rosy color. —*v.* **1** become red because of shame, confusion, or excitement. **2** be ashamed. **3** be or become rosy. [ME *blusche(n).* Cf. OE *blyscan* be red.] —**blush'ful,** *adj.* —**blush'ing·ly,** *adv.*

blush·er (blush'ər), *n.* **1** cosmetic that adds rosy color to the skin. **2** person who blushes easily.

blus·ter (blus'tər), *v.* **1** storm or blow noisily and violently. **2** talk noisily and violently. **3** do or say noisily and violently. **4** make or get by blustering. —*n.* **1** stormy noise and violence. **2** noisy and violent talk. —**blus'ter·er,** *n.* —**blus'ter·ing·ly,** *adv.* —**blus'ter·y, blus'ter·ous,** *adj.*

blvd., boulevard.

bo·a (bō'ə), *n., pl.* **bo·as. 1** any of various large nonpoisonous tropical American snakes that kill their prey by squeezing with their coils. **2** long scarf made of fur or feathers, worn around a woman's neck. [< L (def. 1)]

boa constrictor, large tropical American boa.

boar (bôr; bōr), *n.* **1** male pig or hog. **2** the wild boar. [OE *bār*]

board (bôrd; bōrd), *n.* **1** a broad, thin piece of wood ready for use in building, etc. **2** a flat piece of wood used for some special purpose: *an ironing board.* **3** pasteboard, esp. the covers of a hardcover book. **4** table to serve food on; table. **5** food served on a table. **6** meals provided for pay. **7** chalkboard. **8** stock exchange. **9** group of persons managing something; council. **10** side of a ship. **11** border; edge. —*v.* **1** cover with boards. **2** provide with regular meals, or room and meals, for pay. **3** get meals, or room and meals, for pay. **4** get on a plane, train, ship, etc. **5** go on or into a vehicle. **6** come alongside of or against (a ship). —*adj.* made of boards.

on board, a on a ship, train, etc. **b** *Fig.* in agreement.

the boards, the stage of a theater. [OE *bord*]

board·er (bôr'dər; bōr'–), *n.* **1** person who pays for meals, or for room and meals, at another's house. **2** one of the men assigned to board an enemy ship. **3** pupil living at a boarding school.

board foot, unit of measure equal to a board 1 foot square and 1 inch thick; 144 cu. in.

board·ing (bôr'ding; bōr'–), *n.* **1** boards. **2** structure made of boards.

boarding house, house where meals, or room and meals, are provided for pay.

boarding school, school where pupils live during the school year.

board measure, system for measuring logs and lumber. The unit is the board foot.

board·walk (bôrd'wôk'; bōrd'–), *n.* promenade made of boards, esp. along a beach.

boast (bōst), *v.* **1** praise oneself; brag. **2** brag about. **3** be proud. **4** have and be proud of: *our town boasts many fine parks.* —*n.* **1** praising oneself; bragging. **2** thing to be proud of. —**boast'er,** *n.* —**boast'ing·ly,** *adv.*

boast·ful (bōst'fəl), *adj.* **1** boasting. **2** fond of boasting. —**boast'ful·ly,** *adv.* —**boast'ful·ness,** *n.*

boat (bōt), *n.* **1** small, open vessel for traveling on water. **2** ship. **3** a boat-shaped dish for gravy, sauce, etc. —*v.* **1** go in a boat. **2** put or carry in a boat.

in the same boat, in the same condition or position.

miss the boat, miss an opportunity.

rock the boat, disturb or upset the way things are. [OE *bāt*]

boat·house (bōt'hous'), *n.* house or shed at the water's edge for sheltering a boat or boats.

boat·ing (bōt'ing), *n.* rowing; sailing.

boat·load (bōt'lōd'), *n.* **1** as much or as many as a boat can hold or carry. **2** load that a boat is carrying.

boat·man (bōt'mən), *n., pl.* **-men.** man who manages or works on a boat.

boat·swain (bō'sən; *less often* bōt'swān'), *n.* a ship's officer in charge of anchors, ropes, rigging, etc. Also, **bo's'n, bosun.**

Bo·az (bō'az), *n.* in the Bible, the husband of Ruth.

bob¹ (bob), *n., v.,* **bobbed, bob·bing.** —*n.* a short, quick motion up and down, or to and fro. —*v.* move with short, quick motions.

bob² (bob), *n., v.,* **bobbed, bob·bing.** —*n.* **1** short haircut. **2** horse's docked tail. **3** weight on the end of a pendulum or plumb line. **4** float for a fishing line. —*v.* **1** cut (hair) short. **2** fish with a bob.

bob³ (bob), *n., v.,* **bobbed, bob·bing.** —*n.* a light rap; tap. —*v.* rap lightly; tap.

bob⁴ (bob), *n., pl.* **bob.** *Brit.* shilling.

bob·bin (bob'ən), *n.* reel or spool on which thread, yarn, etc., is wound. [< F *bobine*]

bob·ble (bob'əl), *n., v.,* **-bled, -bling.** —*n.* **1** slight up and down movement, caused by rippling water. **2** blunder; error. —*v.* **1** move up and down slightly. **2** make a bobble.

bob·by (bob'i), *n., pl.* **-bies.** *Brit.* policeman. [for Sir *Robert* Peel, who improved the London police system]

bobby pin, metal hairpin whose prongs are close together.

bob·by·socks (bob'i soks'), *n.pl.* ankle-length socks, worn esp. by girls.

bob·by·sox·er (bob'i sok'sər), *n.* adolescent girl, esp. of the 1940s who followed every new fad.

bob·cat (bob'kat'), *n.* wildcat of N America; lynx.

bob·o·link (bob'ə lingk), *n.* American songbird that lives in fields. [imit.]

bob·sled (bob'sled'), **bob·sleigh** (bob'-slā'), *n., v.,* **-sled·ded, -sled·ding; -sleighed, -sleigh·ing.** —*n.* **1** sled for coasting made of two pairs of runners connected by a long board. **2** two short sleds fastened together by a plank. **3** either of the short sleds. —*v.* ride on a bobsled.

bob·stay (bob'stā'), *n.* rope or chain to hold a bowsprit down.

bob·tail (bob'tāl'), *n.* **1** a short tail; tail cut short. **2** animal having a bobtail. —*adj.* having a bobtail. —*v.* cut short the tail of.

bob·white (bob'hwīt'), *n.* **1** American quail that has a grayish body with brown and white markings. **2** its call.

bock beer (bok), strong, dark beer, usually brewed in the spring. [< G *Bockbier* for *Einbocker Bier* beer of Einbeck, city in Germany]

bode¹ (bōd), *v.,* **bod·ed, bod·ing.** be a sign of; portend. [OE *bodian* < *boda* messenger] —**bode'ment,** *n.*

bode² (bōd), *v.* pt. of **bide.**

bod·ice (bod'is), *n.* **1** the close-fitting upper part of a dress. **2** wide girdle worn over a dress and laced up the front. [var. of pl. of *body,* part of a dress]

-bodied, *combining form,* having a ___ body: *light-bodied =having body of a light-weight material.*

bod·i·ly (bod'ə li), *adj.* of or in the body. —*adv.* **1** in person. **2** all together; as one group.

bod·kin (bod'kin), *n.* **1** a large, blunt needle used for drawing tapes, ribbons, etc. through loops, hems, etc. **2** a long hairpin. **3** a pointed tool for making holes.

bod·y (bod'i), *n., pl.* **bod·ies,** *v.,* **bod·ied, bod·y·ing.** —*n.* **1** the whole material part of a human, animal, or plant. **2** the main part of anything. **3** a group of persons or things: *a body of troops.* **4** corpse. **5** portion of matter; mass: *a lake is a body of water.* **6** substance; substantial quality: *wine with an excellent body.* —*v.* provide with a body; give substance to; embody. [OE *bodig*] —**bod'ied,** *adj.*

body clock, natural rhythms of the body dictating when a person sleeps, etc.

bod·y·guard (bod'i gärd'), *n.* **1** person who guards another. **2** retinue; escort.

body language, unconscious movements of the body, gestures, etc. as a form of communication.

body politic, people forming a political group with an organized government.

Boer (bôr; bōr; bür), *n.* person of Dutch descent living in South Africa. [< Du., farmer]

bog (bog; bôg), *n.*, *v.*, **bogged, bog·ging.** —*n.* soft, wet, spongy ground; marsh; swamp. —*v.* **1** sink or get stuck in a bog. **2 bog down,** get stuck as if in mud. [< Irish or Scotch Gaelic *bogach* < *bog* soft] —**bog′gish,** *adj.* —**bog′gy,** *adj.* —**bog′gi·ness,** *n.*

bo·gey, bo·gie (bō′gi), *n.*, *pl.* **-geys; -gies. 1** =bogy. **2** in golf, **a** =par. **b** one stroke over par on a hole. **3** an unidentified aircraft. [from Colonel *Bogey,* imaginary partner]

bog·gle (bog′əl), *v.*, **-gled, -gling,** *n.* —*v.* **1** blunder; bungle. **2** hesitate. **3** shy. —*n.* a boggling. —**bog′gler,** *n.*

Bo·go·tá (bō′gə tä′), *n.* capital of Colombia.

bo·gus (bō′gəs), *adj.* counterfeit; sham.

bo·gy (bō′gi), *n.*, *pl.* **-gies. 1** goblin; specter. **2** =bugaboo. Also, **bogey, bogie.** [< obs. *bog,* var. of *bug* bugbear]

Bo·he·mi·a (bō hē′mi ə), *n.* a former country in C Europe, now part of the Czech Republic.

Bo·he·mi·an (bō hē′mi ən; -hēm′yən), *adj.* **1** of Bohemia or Bohemians. **2** free and easy; unconventional. —*n.* **1** native or inhabitant of Bohemia. **2.** Often, **bohemian.** artist, writer, etc., who lives in a free and easy, unconventional way. **3** =gypsy. —**Bo·he′mi·an·ism,** *n.*

boil[1] (boil), *v.* **1** bubble up and give off vapor. **2** cause to boil. **3** cook by boiling. **4** be very excited or angry. —*n.* **1** a boiling. **2** boiling condition.
boil down, a reduce by boiling. **b** reduce by getting rid of unimportant parts.
boil over, a come to the boiling point and overflow. **b** show excitement or anger. [< OF < L *bullire* form bubbles]

boil[2] (boil), *n.* a painful, red swelling on the skin, formed by pus around a hard core. [OE *bȳl(e)*]

boil·er (boil′ər), *n.* **1** container for heating liquids. **2** tank for making steam to heat buildings or drive engines. **3** tank for holding hot water.

boiling point, 1 temperature at which a liquid boils. **2** *Fig.* point at which a relationship will become hostile.

Boi·se (boi′zē; -sē), *n.* capital of Idaho, in the SW part.

bois·ter·ous (bois′tər əs; -trəs), *adj.* **1** abounding in rough and noisily cheerful activity. **2** violent; rough. —**bois′ter·ous·ly,** *adv.* —**bois′ter·ous·ness,** *n.*

bo·la (bō′lə), **bo·las** (bō′ləs), *n.* weapon consisting of stone or metal balls tied to cords. [< Sp. and Pg., ball, < L *bulla* bubble]

bold (bōld), *adj.* **1** without fear; daring: *a bold act.* **2** too free in manners; impudent. **3** striking; clear: *in bold outline.* **4** steep; abrupt.
make bold, take the liberty; dare. [OE *bald*] —**bold′ly,** *adv.* —**bold′ness.** *n.*

bold·face (bōld′fās′), *n.* heavy type that stands out clearly. **This line is in bold-face.**

bole (bōl), *n.* trunk of a tree. [< Scand. *bolr*]

bo·le·ro (bə lār′ō), *n.*, *pl.* **-ros. 1** a lively Spanish dance in ¾ time. **2** music for it. **3** a short, loose jacket. [< Sp.]

Bol·í·var (bol′ə vər; bo lē′vär), *n.* **Simón,** 1783–1830, Venezuelan general and statesman.

Bo·liv·i·a (bə liv′i ə), *n.* country in W South America. —**Bo·liv′i·an,** *adj., n.*

boll (bōl), *n.* a rounded seed pod or capsule, as of cotton or flax. [var. of *bowl*]

boll weevil, a long-billed beetle whose larva damages young cotton bolls.

boll·worm (bōl′wėrm′), *n.* larva that eats cotton bolls and the ears of corn.

bo·lo (bō′lō), *n.*, *pl.* **-los.** a long, heavy knife, used in the Philippine Islands. [< Sp. < Philippine dial.]

Bo·lo·gna (bə lōn′yə), *n.* city in N Italy.

bo·lo·gna (bə lō′ni; -nə), *n.* a large sausage made of beef, veal, and pork.

bo·lo·ney (bə lō′ni), *n.* **1** =bologna. **2** baloney.

Bol·she·vik (bōl′shə vik; bol′-), *n.*, *pl.* **-viks, -vi·ki** (-vē′ki), *adj.* —*n.* **1** member of a political party in Russia that seized power and formed the Communist Party in 1918. **2** an extreme radical. —*adj.* **1** of the Bolsheviks or Bolshevism. **2** extremely radical. [< Russ., < *bolshe* greater; with ref. to the majority of the party]

Bol·she·vism (bōl′shə viz əm; bol′-), *n.* **1** doctrines and methods of the Bolsheviks. **2** extreme radicalism.

Bol·she·vist, bol·she·vist (bōl′shə vist; bol′-), *n.*, *adj.* Bolshevik.

bol·ster (bōl′stər), *v.* **1** support with a bolster; support. **2** keep from falling; prop. —*n.* a long pillow for a bed. [OE] —**bol′ster·er,** *n.*

bolt[1] (bōlt), *n.* **1** rod with a head on one end and a screw thread for a nut on the other. **2** a sliding fastener for a door. **3** short arrow with a thick head. **4** discharge of lightning. **5** sudden start. **6** roll of cloth or wallpaper. —*v.* **1** fasten with a bolt. **2** run away. **3** break away from one's political party or its candidates. **4** swallow (one's food) without chewing.
bolt upright, stiff and straight. [OE, arrow] —**bolt′er,** *n.* —**bolt′less,** *adj.* —**bolt′like′,** *adj.*

bolt[2] (bōlt), *v.* **1** sift through a cloth or sieve. **2** examine carefully; separate. [< OF *bulter*]

bomb (bom), *n.* **1** container filled with an explosive charge or a chemical substance. **2** a sudden, unexpected happening. —*v.* attack with bombs. [< F < Ital. < L < Gk. *bombos* boom[1]]

bom·bard (bom bärd′), *v.* **1** attack with heavy fire of shells from big guns. **2** keep attacking vigorously. [< F *bombarder* < *bombarde* cannon. See BOMB.] —**bom·bard′er,** *n.* —**bombard′ment,** *n.*

bom·bar·dier (bom′bər dir′), *n.* member of an aircraft crew who operates

the bombsight and the bomb-release mechanism.

bom·bast (bom′bast), *n.* fine-sounding language that is unsuitable. [< F < LL *bombax* cotton, var. of L *bombyx* silk < Gk.] —**bom·bas′tic, bom·bas′ti·cal,** *adj.* —**bom·bas′ti·cal·ly,** *adv.*

Bom·bay (bom bā′), *n.* seaport in W India. Also, **Mumbai.**

bomb bay, space in an aircraft for bombs and from which they are dropped.

bomb·er (bom′ər), *n.* **1** a combat aircraft used for dropping bombs on the enemy. **2** person who throws or places bombs.

bomb·proof (bom′prüf′), *adj.* strong enough to be safe from bombs and shells.

bomb·shell (bom′shel′), *n.* **1** =bomb. **2** a sudden unexpected happening; disturbing surprise.

bomb·sight (bom′sīt′), *n.* instrument used by a bombardier to aim bombs.

bo·na fide (bō′nə fīd; fī′dē), in good faith; genuine; without make-believe or fraud. [< L]

bo·nan·za (bə nan′zə), *n.* **1** accidental discovery of a rich mass of ore in a mine. **2** the mass itself. **3** any rich source of profit. [< Sp., fair weather, prosperity, < L *bonus* good]

Bo·na·parte (bō′nə pärt), *n.* **Napoléon,** 1769–1821, French general and emperor of France, 1804–15. Also, **Napoléon I.**

bon·bon (bon′bon′), *n.* piece of candy, often one with a fancy shape. [< F, good-good]

bond[1] (bond), *n.* **1** anything that ties, binds, or unites. **2** certificate issued by a government or company promising to pay back with interest the money borrowed. **3** written agreement by which a person says he will pay a certain sum of money if he, or another specified, does not perform certain duties properly. **4** condition of goods placed in a warehouse until taxes are paid. —*v.* **1** issue bonds on; mortgage. **2** provide surety against financial loss by the act or default of. **3** put (goods) under bond. **4** bind or join firmly together.
bonds, chains; shackles. [var. of *band*[2]] —**bond′er,** *n.*

bond[2] (bond), *adj.* in slavery; captive; not free. [< Scand. *bōndi* peasant, orig., dweller]

bond·age (bon′dij), *n.* **1** lack of freedom; slavery. **2** condition of being under some power or influence.

bond·ed (bon′did), *adj.* **1** secured by bonds. **2** put in a warehouse until taxes are paid.

bond·hold·er (bond′hōl′dər), *n.* person who owns bonds issued by a government or company. —**bond′hold′ing,** *n., adj.*

bond·man (bond′mən), *n., pl.* **-men. 1** slave. **2** serf in the Middle Ages.

bonds·man (bondz′mən), *n., pl.* **-men.** person who becomes responsible for another by bond.

bond·wom·an (bond′wùm′ən), *n., pl.* -wom·en. woman slave.

bone (bōn), *n., v.,* **boned, bon·ing.** —*n.* **1 a** one of the pieces of the skeleton of an animal with a backbone. **b** the hard substance of which bones are made. **2** any of various similar substances, as ivory. —*v.* take bones out of.

bone up (on), study strenuously or diligently. [OE *bān*] —**bone′less,** *adj.* —**bone′like′,** *adj.*

bone-dry (bōn′drī′), *adj.* completely dry.

bone·head (bōn′hed′), *n.* very stupid person. —**bone′head′ed,** *adj.*

bon·er (bōn′ər), *n.* foolish mistake.

bon·fire (bon′fīr′), *n.* fire built outdoors. [for *bone fire*]

bong (bông, bong), *n.* water pipe for smoking marijuana.

bon·ho·mie (bon′ə mē′), *n.* good nature; pleasant ways. [< F, < *bonhomme* good fellow]

bo·ni·to (bə nē′tō), *n., pl.* -tos, -toes. type of saltwater mackerel with very red edible flesh. [< Sp., pretty, < L *bonus* good]

bon jour (bôn zhür′), *French.* good day.

bon mot (bôn mō′), *pl.* **bons mots** (bôn mōz′; *Fr.* mō′). *French.* clever saying; witty remark.

bon·net (bon′it), *n.* **1** a head covering usually tied under the chin, worn by women and children. **2** cap worn by men and boys in Scotland. **3** headdress of feathers worn by American Indians. **4** a covering that protects a machine or chimney. —*v.* put a bonnet on. [< OF, orig., fabric for hats]

bon·ny, bon·nie (bon′i), *adj.,* -ni·er, -ni·est. **1** rosy and pretty; handsome. **2** fine; excellent. **3** healthy-looking. [ME *bonie,* appar. < OF *bon, bonne* good < L *bonus*] —**bon′ni·ly,** *adv.* —**bon′ni·ness,** *n.*

bo·nus (bō′nəs), *n.* something extra; thing given in addition to what is due. [< L, good]

bon vo·yage (bôn vwä yäzh′), *French.* good-by; good luck; pleasant trip.

bon·y (bōn′i), *adj.,* **bon·i·er, bon·i·est. 1** of or like bone. **2** full of bones. **3** having big bones that stick out. **4** thin. —**bon′i·ness,** *n.*

boo (bü), *n., pl.* **boos,** *interj., v.,* **booed, boo·ing.** —*n., interj.* sound made to show dislike or contempt or to frighten. —*v.* **1** make such a sound. **2** cry "boo" at.

boob (büb), *n.* a stupid person; fool; dunce. [see BOOBY]

boo·by (bü′bi), *n., pl.* -bies. **1** stupid person; fool; dunce. **2** kind of large sea bird. [prob. < Sp. *bobo* fool < L *balbus* stammering] —**boo′by·ish,** *adj.*

booby trap, 1 bomb arranged to explode when an object is moved by an unwary person. **2** trick arranged to annoy some unsuspecting person.

boo·by-trap (bü′bi trap′), *v.,* -trapped, -trap·ping. —*v.* **1** set booby traps in

a place. **2** catch with a booby trap. —*n.* =booby trap.

boo·hoo (bü′hü′), *n., pl.* -hoos, *v.,* -hooed, -hoo·ing. —*n.* loud crying. —*v.* cry loudly.

book (bùk), *n.* **1** sheets of paper bound together, esp. of a written or printed work. **2** division of a literary work: *the books of the Bible.* **3** words of an opera, operetta, etc.; libretto. **4** record of bets. —*v.* **1** enter in a book or list. **2** engage (a place, passage, etc.). **3** make engagements for. [OE *bōc*] —**book′er,** *n.* —**book′less,** *adj.*

book·case (bùk′kās′), *n.* piece of furniture with shelves for holding books.

book club, a business that supplies certain books regularly to subscribers.

book end, something placed at the end of a row of books to hold them upright.

book·ie (bùk′i), *n.* =bookmaker (def. 2).

book·ish (bùk′ish), *adj.* **1** fond of reading or studying. **2** knowing books better than real life. **3** of books. **4** pedantic; formal. —**book′ish·ly,** *adv.* —**book′ish·ness,** *n.*

book·keep·er (bùk′kēp′ər), *n.* person who keeps a record of business accounts.

book·keep·ing (bùk′kēp′ing), *n.* work or skill of keeping a record of business accounts.

book learning, knowledge learned from books, not from real life.

book·let (bùk′lit), *n.* a little book; thin book.

book·lore (bùk′lôr′; -lōr′), *n.* book learning.

book·mak·er (bùk′māk′ər), *n.* **1** maker of books. **2** person who makes a business of betting other peoples' money on horse races or other sporting events. —**book′mak′ing,** *n.*

book·mark (bùk′märk′), *n.* something put between the pages of a book to mark the reader's place.

book review, article written about a book, discussing its merits, faults, etc.

book·sell·er (bùk′sel′ər), *n.* person whose business is selling books. —**book′sell′ing,** *n.*

book·stall (bùk′stôl′), *n.* place where books (usually secondhand) are sold.

book·stand (bùk′stand′), *n.* **1** =bookrack. **2** =bookstall.

book·store (bùk′stôr′; -stōr′), **book·shop** (-shop′), *n.* store where books are sold.

book·worm (bùk′wérm′), *n.* **1** insect larva that gnaws the bindings or leaves of books. **2** person very fond of reading and studying.

boom¹ (büm), *n.* **1** deep hollow sound. **2** sudden activity and increase in business, prices, or values of property. —*v.* **1** make a deep hollow sound: *the big guns boomed.* **2** increase suddenly in activity. —*adj.* produced by a boom. [imit.]

boom² (büm), *n.* **1** a long pole or beam, used to extend the bottom of a sail or as the lifting pole of a derrick. **2** chain,

cable, or line of timbers that keeps logs from floating away. [< Du., tree, pole]

boom·er·ang (büm′ər ang), *n.* **1** a curved piece of wood, used as a weapon by Australian natives, which can be so thrown that it returns to the thrower. **2** *Fig.* anything that recoils or reacts to harm the doer or user. [< dial. of New South Wales]

boom town, town that has grown up suddenly.

boon¹ (bün), *n.* **1** a blessing; great benefit. **2** *Archaic.* something asked or granted as a favor. [< Scand. *bōn* petition]

boon² (bün), *adj.* **1** jolly; merry. **2** *Poetic.* kindly. [< OF *bon* good < L *bonus*]

boon·docks (bün′doks), *n.pl.* a desolate place or area, as a swamp, scrub forest, etc.

boon·dog·gle (bün′dog′əl), *v.,* -gled, -gling. do useless work. —*n.* useless work or a worthless product. —**boon′dog′gler,** *n.* —**boon′dog′gling,** *n.*

Boone (bün), *n.* **Daniel,** 1735–1820, American pioneer in Kentucky.

boor (bùr), *n.* a rude, bad-mannered, or clumsy person. [< LG *bur* or Du. *boer* farmer] —**boor′ish,** *adj.* —**boor′ish·ly,** *adv.* —**boor′ish·ness,** *n.*

boost (büst), —*n.* a push or shove that helps a person in rising or advancing. —*v.* **1** to lift or push from below or behind. **2** speak favorably of. **3** raise; increase: *boost prices.* **4** cheer; hearten. [blend of *boom* and *hoist*]

boost·er (büs′tər), *n.* **1** person or thing which gives support to a person, cause, etc. **2** device that gives added power to an engine. **3** a powerful rocket engine that provides thrust for take-off. **4** =booster shot.

booster shot, additional inoculation of a vaccine or serum to continue the effectiveness of a previous inoculation.

boot¹ (büt), *n.* **1** a leather or rubber covering for the foot and leg. **2** shoe that reaches above the ankle. **3** kick. **4** discharge; dismissal. —*v.* **1** put boots on. **2** kick. **3** dismiss; discharge. [< OF *bote* < Gmc.]

boot² (büt), *n.* **to boot,** in addition; besides. [OE *bōt* advantage]

boot·ee (büt′ē), *n.* a baby's soft shoe.

booth (büth), *n., pl.* **booths** (büthz). **1** place where goods are sold or shown at a fair, market, etc. **2** a small, closed place for a telephone, motion-picture projector, etc. **3** small, closed place for voting at elections. **4** partly enclosed space in a restaurant with a table and places for people to sit. [< Scand. (ODan.) *bōth*]

boot·jack (büt′jak′), *n.* device to help in pulling off boots.

boot·leg (büt′leg′), *n., v.,* -legged, -legging, *adj.* —*n. Slang.* alcoholic liquor made or distributed illegally. —*v.* **1** sell or deal in illegally or secretly. **2** transport goods secretly for illicit disposal.

—*adj.* made, transported, or sold illegally. [modern use from practice of smuggling liquor in boot legs] —**boot′leg′ger,** *n.* —**boot′leg′ging,** *n.*

boot·lick (büt′lik′), *v.* *Slang.* curry favor with (a person); be a toady. —**boot′lick′er,** *n.* —**boot′lick′ing,** *n.*

boo·ty (bü′ti), *n., pl.* **-ties. 1** things taken from the enemy in war. **2** plunder. **3** any valuable thing or things obtained; prize. [akin to BOOT²]

booze (büz), *n., v.,* **boozed, booz·ing.** *Colloq.* —*n.* intoxicating liquor. —*v.* drink heavily. [prob. < MDu. *bûzen* drink to excess] —**booz′er,** *n.*

booz·y (bü′zi), *adj.,* **booz·i·er, booz·i·est.** drunk.

bop (bop), *n.* =bebop.

bo·rac·ic (bə ras′ik), *adj.* boric.

bor·age (bėr′ij; bôr′–; bor′–), *n.* plant, native to S Europe, with hairy leaves and blue or purplish flowers. [< AF *burage* < LL *burra* hair; with ref. to foliage]

bo·rate (*n.* bô′rāt, –rit, bô′–; *v.* bô′rāt, bô′–), *n., v.,* **–rat·ed, –rat·ing.** —*n.* salt or ester of boric acid. —*v.* treat with boric acid or borax.

bo·rax (bô′raks; –raks; bō′–), *n.* a white crystalline powder, $Na_2B_4O_7 \cdot 10H_2O$, used as an antiseptic, in washing clothes, etc. [< OF < Med.L < Ar. < Pers. *bōrah*]

Bor·deaux (bôr dō′), *n.* **1** seaport in SW France. **2** red or white wine made near Bordeaux.

bor·der (bôr′dər), *n.* **1** a side, edge, or boundary of anything, or the part near it. **2** frontier. **3** strip on the edge of anything for strength or ornament. —*v.* **1** form a border to; bound. **2** put a border on; edge.
border on, a be next to; adjoin. **b** be close to; resemble. [< OF, < *bord* side < Gmc.] —**bor′dered,** *adj.* —**bor′der·less,** *adj.*

bor·der·land (bôr′dər land′), *n.* **1** land forming, or next to, a border. **2** uncertain district or space.

bor·der·line (bôr′dər līn′), *adj.* **1** on a border or boundary. **2** uncertain; in between.

bore¹ (bôr; bōr), *v.,* **bored, bor·ing,** *n.* —*v.* **1** make a hole by a tool that keeps turning, or as a worm does in fruit. **2** make (a hole, passage, entrance, etc.) by pushing through or digging out. **3** bore a hole in; hollow out evenly. —*n.* **1** hole made by a revolving tool. **2** a hollow space inside a pipe, tube, or gun barrel. **3** distance across the inside of a hole or tube. [OE *borian*] —**bor′er,** *n.*

bore² (bôr; bōr), *v.,* **bored, bor·ing,** *n.* —*v.* make weary by being dull or tiresome. —*n.* dull, tiresome person or thing.

bore³ (bôr; bōr), *v.* pt. of **bear¹.**

bore⁴ (bôr; bōr), *n.* sudden tidal wave that rushes up a channel with force. [< Scand. *bāra* wave]

bo·re·al (bô′ri əl; bō′–), *adj.* **1** northern. **2** of Boreas.

Bo·re·as (bô′ri əs; bō′–), *n.* *Greek Mythol.* the north wind as a god. [< Gk.]

bore·dom (bôr′dəm; bōr′–), *n.* weariness caused by dull, tiresome people or events.

bore·some (bôr′səm; bōr′–), *adj.* dull; tiresome.

bo·ric (bô′rik; bō′–), *adj.* of or containing boron. Also, **boracic.**

boric acid, a white, crystalline substance, H_3BO_3, used as a mild antiseptic, to preserve food, etc.

born (bôrn), *adj.* **1** brought into life; brought forth. **2** by birth; by nature: *a born athlete.* —*v.* pp. of **bear¹.** [pp. of *bear¹*]

born-a·gain (bôrn′ ə gen′), *adj.* acknowledging Jesus Christ as the source of personal salvation; evangelical.

borne (bôrn; bōrn), *v.* pp. of **bear¹.**

Bor·ne·o (bôr′ni ō; bōr′–), *n.* island in the East Indies. Part of it is Malaysian, part is Indonesian.

bo·ron (bô′ron; bō′–), *n.* a nonmetallic element, B, found in borax. [blend of *borax* and *carbon*]

bor·ough (bėr′ō), *n.* **1** (in some states) an incorporated town smaller than a city. **2** one of the five divisions of New York City. **3** town in England with a municipal corporation and a charter that guarantees the right of local self-government. **4** town in England that sends representatives to Parliament. [OE *burg*]

bor·row (bôr′ō; bor′ō), *v.* **1** get (something) from another person with the understanding that it must be returned. **2** take and use as one's own; take. **3** in subtraction, to take from one denomination to add to the next lower. [OE *borgian* < *borg* pledge, surety] —**bor′row·er,** *n.*

borsch (bôrsch), **borscht** (bôrsht), *n.* a Russian soup containing beets.

bosh (bosh), *n., interj.* nonsense.

bosk·y (bos′ki), *adj.* **1** wooded. **2** shady. —**bosk′i·ness,** *n.*

bo's'n (bō′sən), *n.* =boatswain.

Bos·ni·a (boz′ni ə), *n.* region that forms part of the state of Bosnia and Herzegovina. —**Bos′ni·an,** *adj., n.*

Bosnia and Herzegovina, country in the Balkans.

bos·om (bùz′əm; bü′zəm), *n.* **1** the upper, front part of the human body; breast. **2** part of a garment covering this. **3** center or inmost part. **4** heart, thought, affections, desires, etc. —*adj.* close; trusted: *a bosom friend.* [OE *bōsm*]

Bos·po·rus (bos′pə rəs), *n.* strait connecting the Black Sea and the Sea of Marmara.

boss¹ (bôs; bos), *n.* **1** person who hires workers or watches over or directs them; foreman; manager. **2** person who controls a political organization. —*v.* **1** be the boss of; direct; control. **2** be too overbearing. —*adj.* master; chief. [< Du. *baas*]

boss² (bôs; bos), *n.* **1** a roundish protuberance on an animal or plant. **2** a raised ornament on a flat surface. —*v.* decorate with bosses. [< OF *boce*]

boss·ism (bôs′iz əm; bos′–), *n.* control by bosses, esp. political bosses.

boss·y¹ (bôs′i; bos′i), *adj.,* **boss·i·er, boss·i·est.** fond of telling others what to do and how to do it; domineering.

bos·sy² (bos′i; bôs′i), *n., pl.* **–sies.** calf or cow. [cf. L *bos* ox]

Bos·ton (bôs′tən; bos′–), *n.* seaport and capital of Massachusetts, in the E part. —**Bos·to′ni·an,** *adj., n.*

Boston terrier or **bull,** small, dark-brown dog with white markings and smooth, short hair.

bo·sun (bō′sən), *n.* =boatswain.

bot (bot), *n.* larva of a botfly. It is a parasite of horses, cattle, and sheep. Also, **bott.**

bot., botany.

bo·tan·i·cal (bə tan′ə kəl), **bo·tan·ic** (–tan′ik), *adj.* **1** having to do with plants. **2** having to do with botany. [< Med.L < Gk., < *botane* plant] —**bo·tan′i·cal·ly,** *adv.*

bot·a·nize (bot′ə nīz), *v.,* **–nized, –niz·ing.** study plants where they grow.

bot·a·ny (bot′ə ni), *n., pl.* **–nies. 1** science of plants; study of plants and plant life. **2** textbook or manual of this science. **3** botanical facts. [< *botanic*] —**bot′a·nist,** *n.*

Botany Bay, bay on the SE coast of Australia, near Sydney, site of a former penal colony.

botch (boch), *v.* **1** spoil by poor work; bungle. **2** patch or mend clumsily. —*n.* a clumsy patch. —**botch′er,** *n.* —**botch′er·y,** *n.* —**botch′y,** *adj.*

bot·fly (bot′flī′), *n., pl.* **–flies.** fly whose larvae are parasites of horses, cattle, etc.

both (bōth), *adj.* the two together: *both houses are whites.* —*pron.* the two together: *both belong to him.* —*adv.* together; alike; equally: *he can sing and dance both.* —*conj.* together; alike; equally: *he is both strong and healthy.* [appar. < Scand. *bāther*]

both·er (both′ər), *n.* **1** worry; fuss; trouble. **2** person or thing that causes worry, fuss, or trouble. —*v.* **1** worry; fuss; trouble. **2** trouble oneself, as in an effort to do something. [appar. < Irish *bodhar* deaf] —**both′er·er,** *n.*

both·er·a·tion (both′ər ā′shən), *n., interj.* bother.

both·er·some (both′ər səm), *adj.* causing worry or fuss; troublesome.

Bo·tswa·na (bō tswä′nä), *n.* country in S Africa.

bott (bot), *n.* bot.

bot·tle (bot′əl), *n., v.,* **–tled, –tling.** —*n.* **1** container for holding liquids that has a narrow neck that can be closed with a stopper, and is usually without handles. **2** contents of a bottle. **3** amount that a bottle can hold. —*v.* **1**

put into bottles. 2 hold in; keep back; control.

bottle up, hold in; control. [< OF < VL *butticula,* dim. of LL *buttis* butt³] —**bot′tler,** *n.*

the bottle, intoxicating liquor.

bot·tle·neck (bot′əl nek′), *n.* 1 a narrow thoroughfare. 2 **a** person or thing that hinders progress. **b** situation in which progress is hindered.

bot·tom (bot′əm), *n.* 1 the lowest part. 2 part on which anything rests. 3 ground under water. 4 seat. 5 basis; foundation; origin. 6 keel or hull of a ship; ship. —*adj.* lowest; last.

be at the bottom of, be the cause of. [OE *botm*] —**bot′tom·less,** *adj.*

bot·u·lism (boch′ə liz əm), *n.* poisoning caused by a toxin formed in food that has been infected by certain bacteria. [< L *botulus* sausage; orig. attributed esp. to sausages]

bou·doir (bü′dwär; –dwôr; bü dwär′; –dwôr′), *n.* a lady's private sitting room or dressing room. [< F, < *bouder* sulk]

bough (bou), *n.* 1 one of the main branches of a tree. 2 branch cut from a tree. [OE *bōg* bough, shoulder] —**bough′less,** *adj.*

bought (bôt), *v.* pt. and pp. of **buy.**

bouil·lon (bul′yon; –yən), *n.* a clear, thin soup. [< F. < *bouillir* boil < L *bullire*]

boul·der (bōl′dər), *n.* a large rock, rounded or worn by the action of water or weather. Also, **bowlder.** [for *boulderstone* < Scand. (Sw.) *bullersten* < *bullra* roar + *sten* stone]

boul·e·vard (bul′ə värd; bü′lə–), *n.* a broad street. [< F < Gmc. See BULWARK.]

bounce (bouns), *v.,* **bounced, bounc·ing.** *n.* —*v.* 1 bound like a ball. 2 cause to bounce. 3 spring suddenly. 4 throw out. 5 discharge from work or employment. —*n.* 1 a bound; a spring; a bouncing. 2 resilience. 3 liveliness. 4 discharge from work or employment. [Cf. Du. *bonzen* thump] —**bounc′er,** *n.*

bounc·ing (boun′sing), *adj.* 1 that bounces. 2 big; strong. 3 vigorous; healthy.

bound¹ (bound), *v.* pt. and pp. of **bind.** —*adj.* 1 put in covers: *a bound book.* 2 obliged. 3 certain; sure. 4 determined; resolved.

bound up in or **with, a** closely connected with. **b** very devoted to. [pp. of *bind*]

bound² (bound), *v.* 1 leap; jump: *bounding deer.* 2 spring back; bounce: *the ball bounded from the wall.* —*n.* 1 leap or spring. 2 spring back; bounce. [< F *bondir* leap, orig., resound, ? < L *bombus.* See BOMB.]

bound³ (bound), *n.* 1 Usually, **bounds.** boundary; limit. 2 **bounds,** area within boundaries. —*v.* 1 limit as by bounds. 2 form the boundary or limit of. 3 name the boundaries of. 4 have its boundary (on). [< OF < LL *butina*] —**bound′less,**

adj. —**bound′less·ly,** *adv.* —**bound′less-ness,** *n.*

bound⁴ (bound), *adj.* ready or intending to go: *I am bound for home.* [< Scand. *būinn,* pp. of *būa* get ready]

bound·a·ry (boun′də ri; –dri), *n., pl.* -ries. a limiting line; limit; border.

bound·en (boun′dən), *adj.* required. [pp. of *bind*]

bound·er (boun′dər), *n.* a rude, vulgar person; upstart; cad.

boun·te·ous (boun′ti əs), *adj.* 1 generous; giving freely. 2 plentiful; abundant. —**boun′te·ous·ly,** *adv.* —**boun′te·ous-ness,** *n.*

boun·ti·ful (boun′tə fəl), *adj.* =bounteous. —**boun′ti·ful·ly,** *adv.* —**boun′ti·ful-ness,** *n.*

boun·ty (boun′ti), *n., pl.* -ties. 1 generosity. 2 a generous gift. 3 a reward. [< OF < L *bonitas* < *bonus* good]

bou·quet (bō kā′, bü– for 1; bü kā′ for 2), *n.* 1 bunch of flowers. 2 characteristic fragrance; aroma. [< F, little wood, dim. of OF *bosc* wood. See BUSH¹.]

Bour·bon (bur′bən, *occas.* bėr′– for 1; bėr′bən for 2), *n.* 1 member of a former royal family of France, Spain, Naples, and Sicily. 2 Also, **bourbon.** kind of whiskey. —**Bour′bon·ism,** *n.* —**Bour′bon·ist,** *n.*

bour·geois (bur zhwä′; bùr′zhwä), *n., pl.* -geois, *adj.* —*n.* 1 person of the middle class. 2 any property owner. —*adj.* 1 of the middle class. 2 like the middle class; ordinary. [< F < LL *burgensis* < *burgus* fort < Gmc.]

bour·geoi·sie (bùr′zhwä zē′), *n.* 1 people of the middle class. 2 the opposite of the proletariat.

bourn¹, bourne¹ (bôrn; bōrn), *n.* =brook. [OE *burna*]

bourn², bourne² (bôrn; bōrn; bùrn), *n.* Archaic. 1 boundary; limit. 2 goal. [< F *borne.* Akin to BOUND³.]

bourse (bùrs), *n.* stock exchange in Paris and other European cities. [< F, orig., purse, < LL *bursa* < Gk. *byrsa* hide]

bout (bout), *n.* 1 trial of strength; contest. 2 spell or fit of anything: *a bout of sickness.* [var. of *bought* a bending, turn; akin to BOW¹]

bou·tique (bü tēk′), *n., adj.* —*n.* small specialty shop selling stylish clothes, accessories, etc. —*adj.* specialized: *boutique brewery; boutique farming.* [< F *boutique* small shop]

bou·ton·niere, bou·ton·nière (bü′tə nyär′), *n.* flower or flowers worn in a buttonhole. [< F, buttonhole. See BUTTON.]

bou·zou·ki (bü zü′kē), *n.* stringed instrument somewhat like a mandolin that produces sounds similar to the harpsichord.

bo·vine (bō′vīn; –vin), *adj.* 1 of an ox or cow; like an ox or cow. 2 slow; stupid. 3 without emotion; stolid. —*n.* ox, cow, etc. [< LL *bovinus* < L *bos* ox, cow]

bow¹ (bou), *v.* 1 bend the head or body in greeting, respect, worship, or submission. 2 show by bowing: *bow one's thanks.* 3 bend; stoop. 4 submit; yield. —*n.* act of bowing. [OE *būgan*] —**bow′er,** *n.*

bow² (bō), *n.* 1 weapon for shooting arrows, consisting of a strip of elastic wood bent by a string. 2 curve; bend. 3 a bowknot: *a bow of ribbon.* 4 a slender rod with horsehairs stretched on it, for playing a violin, etc. 5 something curved; curved part, as a rainbow. —*v.* 1 curve; bend. 2 play (a violin, etc.) with a bow. [OE *boga*] —**bow′less,** *adj.* —**bow′like′,** *adj.*

bow³ (bou), *n.* the forward part of a ship, boat, or airship. [prob. of LG or Scand. orig.; akin to BOUGH]

bowd·ler·ize (boud′lər īz), *v.,* -ized, -iz-ing. =expurgate. [for Dr. T. *Bowdler,* who published an expurgated Shakespeare in 1818] —**bowd′ler·ism,** *n.* —**bowd′ler-i·za′tion,** *n.*

bow·el (bou′əl), *n.* an intestine.

bowels, a tube in the body into which food passes from the stomach; intestines. **b** *Fig.* inner part: *the bowels of the earth.* [< OF < L *botellus,* dim. of *botulus* sausage]

bow·er¹ (bou′ər), *n.* 1 shelter of leafy branches. 2 summerhouse or arbor. [OE *būr* dwelling] —**bow′er·like′,** *adj.*

bow·er² (bou′ər), *n.* the high card in certain games. [< G *bauer* jack (in cards), peasant]

bow·er·y (bou′ər i), *adj.* leafy; shady.

bow·fin (bō′fin′), *n.* a North American freshwater ganoid fish.

bow·ie knife (bō′i; bü′i), a long, single-edged hunting knife carried in a sheath. [named for Col. J. Bowie, U.S. pioneer]

bow·knot (bō′not′), *n.* a looped slipknot, such as is made in tying shoelaces, usually with loops and two ends.

bowl¹ (bōl), *n.* 1 a hollow, rounded dish. 2 amount that a bowl can hold. 3 a hollow, rounded part: *the bowl of a spoon or a pipe.* 4 formation or structure shaped like a bowl, as an amphitheater. [OE *bolla*] —**bowl′like′,** *adj.*

bowl² (bōl), *n.* 1 a wooden ball used in games. 2 a turn in the game of bowls. —*v.* 1 play the game of bowls; roll a ball in the game of bowls. 2 throw (the ball) to the batsman in the game of cricket. 3 roll or move along rapidly and smoothly. **bowl over, a** knock over. **b** make helpless and confused. [< F < L *bulla* ball, bubble] —**bowl′er,** *n.*

bowl·der (bōl′dər), *n.* =boulder.

bow·leg (bō′leg′), *n.* an outward curve of the legs. —**bow′leg′ged,** *adj.*

bow·line (bō′lən; –līn), *n.* 1 Also, **bowline knot.** knot used in making a loop. 2 rope to hold a sail steady when sailing into the wind.

bowl·ing (bōl′ing), *n.* 1 game of bowls. 2 *U.S. and Canada.* =tenpins. 3 playing the game of bowls.

bowling alley, long, narrow, enclosed floor for bowling.

bowls (bōlz), *n.* **1** game played by rolling with a lopsided or weighted wooden ball toward a stationary ball. **2** =ninepins or tenpins. [pl. of *bowl²*]

bow·man (bō′mən), *n., pl.* **-men.** =archer.

bow·shot (bō′shot′), *n.* distance that a bow will shoot an arrow.

bow·sprit (bou′sprit; bō′-), *n.* pole or spar projecting forward from the bow of a ship. Ropes from it help to steady sails and masts. [prob. < LG or Du. See BOW³, SPRIT.]

bow·string (bō′string′), *n.* **1** a strong cord stretched from the ends of a bow. **2** cord like this.

box¹ (boks), *n.* **1** container made of wood, metal, paper, etc., **2** amount that a box can hold. **3** a space with chairs at a theater, etc. **4** an enclosed space for a jury, witnesses, etc. **5** a small shelter; *a sentry's box.* **6** the driver's seat on a coach, carriage, etc. **7** in baseball, place where the batter, or sometimes the pitcher or coach, stands. **8** an awkward situation. **9** receptacle in a post office for a subscriber's mail. —*v.* **1** pack in a box; put into a box. **2** provide with a box.

box up, shut in; keep from getting out. [specialization of meaning of *box³*] —**box′like′,** *adj.*

box² (boks), *n.* blow with the open hand or the fist, esp. on the ear. —*v.* **1** strike such a blow. **2** fight with the fists.

box³ (boks), *n.* **1** shrub or small, bushy tree that stays green all winter, much used for hedges, etc. **2** its hard, durable wood. [< L < Gk. *pyxos*]

box·car (boks′kär′), *n.* railroad freight car enclosed on all sides.

box elder, a maple tree of North America, often grown for shade or ornament.

box·er (bok′sər), *n.* **1** person who fights with the fists in padded gloves and according to special rules. **2** a dog with a smooth brown coat, related to the bulldog and terrier.

box·ing (bok′sing), *n.* sport or act of fighting with the fists.

boxing gloves, padded gloves worn when boxing.

box office, 1 place where tickets are sold in a theater, hall, etc. **2** money taken in at the box office.

box score, tabular record of the plays of a baseball game arranged by the players' names.

box seat, seat in a box of a theater, etc.

box·wood (boks′wüd′), *n.* =box³.

boy (boi), *n.* **1** a male child from birth to about eighteen. **2** guy; follow. **3** a term for a man, esp. a servant, sometimes used in an unfriendly way. [< OF *embuié* fettered < L *in* in + *boiae* fetters]

boy·cott (boi′kot), *v.* **1** combine against and have nothing to do with (a person, business, nation, etc.) as a means of

intimidation or coercion. **2** refuse to buy or use (a product, etc.). —*n.* a boycotting. [for Captain *Boycott,* first man so treated] —**boy′cott·er,** *n.*

boy·friend (boi′frend), *n.* **1** a girl's sweetheart or steady male companion. **2** male friend. Also, **boy friend.**

boy·hood (boi′hůd), *n.* **1** time or condition of being a boy. **2** boys as a group.

boy·ish (boi′ish), *adj.* **1** of a boy. **2** like a boy. **3** like a boy's. **4** fit for a boy. —**boy′ish·ly,** *adv.* —**boy′ish·ness,** *n.*

boy scout, member of the Boy Scouts.

Boy Scouts, organization for boys that develops manly qualities and usefulness to others.

boy·sen·ber·ry (boi′zən ber′i), *n., pl.* **-ries.** a purple berry like a blackberry in size and shape, and like a raspberry in flavor.

bp, bp., or **Bp,** bishop.

bp., 1 boiling point. **2** blood pressure

Br, bromine.

Br., Britain; British.

bra (brä), *n.* brassière.

brace (brās), *n., v.,* **braced, brac·ing.** —*n.* **1** thing that holds parts together or in place. **2** pair; couple: *a brace of ducks.* **3** handle for a tool or drill used for boring. **4** either of these signs { } used to enclose words, figures, etc. **5** Often, **braces.** a metal wire or other device used to straighten crooked teeth. [< v., but partly < OF *brace* the two arms] —*v.* **1** support. **2** hold or fix firmly in place.

brace up, summon one's strength or courage. [< OF *bracier* embrace < *brace* the two arms < L *bracchia,* pl. < Gk. *brachion*]

brace·let (brās′lit), *n.* band or chain worn for ornament around the wrist or arm. [< OF, dim. of *bracel* L *bracchium* arm < Gk. *brachion*] —**brace′let·ed,** *adj.*

brach·i·o·pod (brak′i ə pod′; brā′ki-), *n.* sea animal with upper and lower shells and a pair of armlike tentacles, one on each side of its mouth. [< NL < Gk. *brachion* arm + *pous* foot]

brach·y·ce·phal·ic (brak′i sə fal′ik), **brachy·ceph·a·lous** (brak′i sef′ə ləs), *adj.* having a short, broad head. [< Gk. *brachys* short + *kephale* head]

brac·ing (brās′ing), *adj.* giving strength and energy; refreshing. —*n.* brace or braces. —**brac′ing·ly,** *adv.*

brack·en (brak′ən), *n. Brit.* **1** a large fern. **2** growth of these ferns. [ME *braken,* appar. < Scand.]

brack·et (brak′it), *n.* **1** a flat piece of stone, etc., projecting from a wall as a support for a shelf, a statue, etc. **2** support in the shape of a right triangle. **3** either of these signs [ ], used to enclose words or figures. **4** group thought of together: *high income bracket.* —*v.* **1** support with brackets. **2** enclose within brackets. **3** think of together; group. [< F < Sp. *bragueta,* dim. of *braga* < L *bracae* breeches < Celtic]

brack·ish (brak′ish), *adj.* **1** somewhat salty. **2** distasteful; unpleasant. —**brack′ish·ness,** *n.*

bract (brakt), *n.* a small leaf at the base of a flower or flower stalk. [< L *bractea* thin metal plate] —**brac′te·al,** *adj.* —**bract′less,** *adj.*

brad (brad), *n.* a small, thin nail with a small head. [var. of *brod* < Scand. *broddr* spike]

brae (brā), *n. Scot.* slope; hillside.

brag (brag), *n., v.,* **bragged, brag·ging.** —*n.* **1** boast. **2** boasting. —*v.* boast. [cf. Scand. *bragga sig* recover heart] —**brag′ger,** *n.*

brag·ga·do·ci·o (brag′ə dō′shi ō), *n., pl.* **-cios. 1** boasting; bragging. **2** boaster; braggart. [coined by Spenser as name of character in his *Faerie Queene*]

brag·gart (brag′ərt), *n.* boaster. —*adj.* boastful. [< F *bragard* < *braguer* brag]

Brah·ma (brä′mə *for 1;* brä′mə, brä′mə *for 2*), *n.* **1** in Hindu theology: **a** the god of creation. **b** impersonal and absolute divinity. **2** species of cattle, originally imported from India.

Brah·man (brä′mən), *n., pl.* **-mans.** member of the priestly caste, in India. Also, **Brahmin.** —**Brah·man′ic, Brah·man′i·cal,** *adj.* —**Brah′manism,** *n.* —**Brah′man·ist,** *n.*

Brah·min (brä′mən), *n., pl.* **-min. 1** Brahman. **2** a cultured, highly intellectual person, often snobbish. —**Brah·min′ic, Brah·min′i·cal,** *adj.* —**Brah′min·ism,** *n.*

Brahms (brämz), *n.* **Johannes,** 1833–97, German composer of music.

braid (brād), *n.* **1** band formed by weaving together three or more strands of hair, ribbon, straw, etc. **2** a narrow band of fabric used to trim or bind clothing. —*v.* **1** form by weaving together three or more strands of hair, etc.; plait. **2** trim or bind with braid. [OE *bregdan*] —**braid′er,** *n.*

Braille, braille (brāl), *n.* system of writing and printing for blind people. The letters in Braille are made of raised dots and are read by touching them. [for Louis *Braille,* French teacher of the blind]

brain (brān), *n.* **1** mass of nerve tissue enclosed in the skull or head of vertebrate animals. The brain is used in feeling and thinking. **2** large electronic computer. **3** *Informal.* very intelligent person. **4** Usually, **brains.** mind; intelligence. —*v.* kill by smashing the skull of.

pick the brains of, extract useful information or ideas from (someone).

rack one's brains, try hard to remember or think of something. [OE *brægen*]

brain·less (brān′lis), *adj.* **1** stupid; foolish. **2** without a brain. —**brain′less·ly,** *adv.* —**brain′less·ness,** *n.*

brain bleed, hemorrhage in the brain.

brain dead or **brain-dead** (brān′ded′), *adj.* **1** showing no activity of the cerebral cortex. **2** *Fig.* showing little imagination or thought. —**brain death,** *n.*

brain·pan (brān'pan'), *n.* =cranium.

brain-storm, (brān'stôrm'), **1** sudden inspired idea. **2** episode of mental instability.

brain·wash·ing (brān'wosh'ing; –wôsh'–), *n.* the process of purging a person's mind of his or her political, economic, and social ideas, and causing willing acceptance of other views.

brain·y (brān'i), *adj.,* **brain·i·er, brain·i·est.** intelligent; clever. —**brain'i·ness,** *n.*

braise (brāz), *v.,* **braised, brais·ing.** brown (meat) quickly and then cook it long and slowly in a covered pan with very little water. [< F *braiser* < *braise* hot charcoal < Gmc.]

brake[1] (brāk), *n., v.,* **braked, brak·ing.** —*n.* **1** anything used to check by pressing or scraping or by rubbing against. **2** tool or machine for breaking up flax or hemp into fibers. —*v.* **1** slow up or stop by using a brake. **2** use a brake on. **3** break up (flax or hemp) into fibers. [< MLG or ODu. *braeke;* akin to BREAK]

brake[2] (brāk), *n.* a thick growth of bushes; thicket. [cf. MLG *brake*]

brake[3] (brāk), *n.* large, coarse fern. [prob. var. of *bracken*]

brake·man (brāk'mən), *n., pl.* **-men.** person who works brakes and helps the engineer or conductor of a railroad train.

bram·ble (bram'bəl), *n.* **1** a prickly shrub of the rose family, such as the blackberry or raspberry. **2** any rough, prickly shrub. [OE *brēmel* < *brōm* BROOM] —**bram'bly,** *adj.*

bran (bran), *n.* the broken covering of wheat, rye, etc., separated from the flour. [< OF]

branch (branch; bränch), *n.* **1** part of a tree growing out from the trunk; bough; twig. **2** any division that resembles a branch of a tree: *a branch of a river.* **3** division; part: *history is a branch of learning.* **4** a local office: *a branch of a bank.* **5** a line of family descent. —*v.* **1** put out branches; spread in branches. **2** divide into branches.

branch out, a put out branches. **b** extend business, interests, activities, etc. [< OF *branche* < LL *branca* paw]

brand (brand), *n.* **1** a certain kind, grade, or make as indicated by a stamp, trademark, etc.: *a brand of coffee.* **2** =trademark. **3** mark made by burning the skin with a hot iron, as on cattle and horses to show who owns them. **4** iron stamp for burning a mark. **5** mark of disgrace. **6** piece of wood that is burning or partly burned. **7** *Archaic and Poetic.* sword. —*v.* **1** mark by burning the skin with a hot iron. **2** put a mark of disgrace on. [OE] —**brand'er,** *n.*

bran·died (bran'did), *adj.* prepared, mixed, or flavored with brandy.

bran·dish (bran'dish), *v.* wave or shake threateningly; flourish: *brandish a sword.* —*n.* threatening shake; flourish.

[< OF *brandir* < *brand* sword < Gmc.] —**bran'dish·er,** *n.*

brand-new (brand'nü'; –nū'), *adj.* very new; entirely new.

bran·dy (bran'di), *n., pl.* **-dies,** *v.,* **-died, -dy·ing.** —*n.* **1** strong alcoholic liquor made from wine. **2** similar alcoholic liquor made from fruit juice. —*v.* mix, flavor, or preserve with brandy. [< Du. *brandewijn* burnt (i.e., distilled) wine]

brant (brant), *n., pl.* **brants** or (*esp.* collectively) **brant.** a small, dark, wild goose.

brash (brash), *adj.* **1** hasty; rash. **2** impudent; saucy. —*n.* a rush or dash. —**brash'y,** *adj.*

bra·sier (brā'zhər), *n.* =brazier.

Bra·sí·lia (brä sē'lyä), *n.* capital of Brazil in the C part.

brass (bras; bräs), *n.* **1** yellow metal that is an alloy of copper and zinc. **2** thing made of brass. **3** Also, **brasses.** the brass winds. **4** *Colloq.* shamelessness; impudence. **5** *Slang.* high-ranking military officers. —*adj.* made of brass. [OE *bræs*]

bras·sard (bras'ärd), *n.* **1** band worn above the elbow as a badge. **2** Also, **brassart** (bras'ərt). armor for the upper part of the arm. [< F, < *bras* arm]

brass·ie, brass·y (bras'i; bräs'i), *n., pl.* **brass·ies.** golf club with a wooden head on the bottom of which is a metal plate.

bras·sière (brə zir'), *n.* a bust support worn by women. [< F, bodice, < *bras* arm]

brass knuckles, a protective metal device for the knuckles, used in fighting.

brass winds, metal musical instruments that are played by blowing, such as trumpets or trombones. —**brass'wind',** *adj.*

brass·y (bras'i; bräs'i), *adj.* **brass·i·er, brass·i·est. 1** of or like brass. **2** loud and harsh. **3** *Colloq.* shameless; impudent. —**brass'i·ness,** *n.*

brat (brat), *n.* any child, esp. an unpleasant one. [cf. OE *bratt* cloak, covering]

bra·va·do (brə vä'dō), *n., pl.* **-does, -dos.** a boastful defiance without much real desire to fight. [< Sp. *bravada.* See BRAVE.]

brave (brāv), *adj.,* **brav·er, brav·est,** *n., v.,* **braved, brav·ing.** —*adj.* **1** without fear; having courage. **2** making a fine appearance; showy. **3** *Archaic.* fine; excellent. —*n.* **1** a brave person. **2** a North American Indian warrior. —*v.* **1** meet without fear. **2** dare; defy. [< F < Ital. *bravo* brave, bold < Sp., vicious (as applied to bulls), ? < L *pravus*] —**brave'ly,** *adv.* —**brave'ness,** *n.*

brav·er·y (brāv'ər i), *n., pl.* **-er·ies. 1** fearlessness; courage. **2** showy dress; finery.

bra·vo (brä'vō), *interj., n., pl.* **-vos.** —*interj.* well done! fine! —*n.* cry of "bravo!" [< Ital. See BRAVE.]

bra·vu·ra (brə vyūr'ə), *n.* **1** piece requiring skill and spirit in the performer. **2** display of daring; dash; spirit. [< Ital., bravery. See BRAVE.]

braw (brô; brä), *adj. Scot.* **1** making a fine appearance. **2** excellent; fine. [var. of *brave*]

brawl (brôl), *n.* noisy quarrel. —*v.* quarrel noisily. [ME *brallen* < *brawl* brawler]

brawn (brôn), *n.* muscle; firm, strong muscles; muscular strength. [< OF *braon* < Gmc.]

brawn·y (brôn'i), *adj.,* **brawn·i·er, brawn·i·est.** strong; muscular. —**brawn'i·ness,** *n.*

bray (brā), *n.* **1** the loud, harsh sound made by a donkey. **2** noise like it. —*v.* **1** make a loud, harsh sound. **2** utter in a loud, harsh voice. [< F *braire*] —**bray'er,** *n.*

Braz., Brazil; Brazilian.

braze[1] (brāz), *v.,* **brazed, braz·ing. 1** cover or decorate with brass. **2** make like brass. [OE *brasian* < *bræs* brass]

braze[2] (brāz), *v.,* **brazed, braz·ing.** solder with brass or other hard solder. [? < F *braser* < OF, burn]

bra·zen (brā'zən), *adj.* **1** made of brass. **2** like brass in color or strength. **3** loud and harsh. **4** shameless; impudent. —*v.* make shameless or impudent.

brazen out or **through,** face boldly or shamelessly. [OE *bræsen* < *bræs* brass] —**bra'zen·ly,** *adj.* —**bra'zen·ness,** *n.*

bra·zier[1] (brā'zhər), *n.* a metal container to hold burning charcoal or coal, used for heating rooms. Also, **brasier.** [< F *brasier* < *braise* hot coals]

bra·zier[2] (brā'zhər), *n.* person who works with brass. Also, **brasier.** [< *braze*[1]]

Bra·zil (brə zil'), *n.* largest country in South America. —**Bra·zil'ian,** *adj., n.*

Brazil nut, a large, triangular nut of a tree growing in Brazil.

Braz·za·ville (braz'ə vil), *n.* capital of the Republic of the Congo, in the S part.

breach (brēch), *n.* **1** opening made by breaking down something solid; gap. **2** breaking (of a law, promise, duty, etc.); neglect. **3** breaking of friendly relations; quarrel. —*v.* break through; make an opening in. [< OF *breche* < Gmc.]

breach of promise, breaking of a promise to marry.

breach of the peace, public disturbance.

bread (bred), *n.* **1** food made of flour or meal mixed with milk or water and baked. **2** food; livelihood. —*v.* cover with bread crumbs before cooking.

break bread, share a meal. [OE *brēad*] —**bread'less,** *adj.*

bread·board (bred'bôrd'; –bōrd'), *n.* **1** board on which dough is kneaded, pastry is rolled, etc. **2** board on which bread is cut.

bread·fruit (bred'früt'), *n.* a large, round, starchy, tropical fruit of the Pacific Islands, much used, baked or roasted, for food.

bread line, line of people waiting to get food given as charity or relief.

bread·stuff (bred'stuf'), *n.* **1** grain, flour, or meal for making bread. **2** bread.

breadth (bredth; bretth), *n.* **1** how broad a thing is; distance across; width. **2** piece of a certain width: *a breadth of cloth.* **3** freedom from narrowness; latitude; tolerance. **4** spaciousness; extent. [< OE *brēdu* < *brād* broad]

breadth·ways (bredth′wāz′; bretth′–), *adv.* in the direction of the breadth.

bread·win·ner (bred′win′ər), *n.* person who earns a living for those dependent on him or her.

break (brāk), *v.,* **broke** or (*Archaic*) **brake, bro·ken** or (*Archaic*) **broke, break·ing,** *n.* —*v.* **1** make come to pieces by a blow or pull; shatter; smash: *break a window; break a leg, break a blood vessel.* **2** come apart; crack; burst. **3** interrupt; disturb: *break silence.* **4** open (an electrical circuit). **5** destroy evenness, wholeness, etc.: *break a five-dollar bill.* **6** fail to keep; act against: *break a law.* **7** come suddenly: *a storm broke.* **8** change suddenly: *the drought broke.* **9** of stocks, bonds, etc., decline suddenly and sharply in price. **10** of a voice or wind instrument, change in register or tone. **11** of a baseball pitch, swerve or curve at or near the plate. **12** lessen the force of: *break a fall.* **13** of the heart, be overcome by grief. **14** stop; put an end to: *break a habit.* **15** reduce in rank. **16** train to obey; tame: *break a colt.* **17** go beyond; exceed: *break a record.* **18** dig or plow (ground). **19** make known; reveal: *break the bad news.* **20** make a rush toward; dash; run (*for, to*). —*n.* **1** act or fact of breaking. **2** a broken place; gap; crack. **3** interruption. **4** act of forcing one's way out. **5** an abrupt or marked change. **6** a sudden sharp decline in the prices of stocks, etc. **7** sharp change in direction of a pitched or bowled ball. **8** *Informal.* chance; opportunity. **9** opening in an electric circuit.

break down, a have an accident; fail to work. **b** collapse; become weak; lose one's health. **c** begin to cry.

break in, a prepare for work or use; train. **b** enter by force. **c** interrupt.

break out, a start; begin. **b** have pimples, rashes, etc. on the skin.

break up, a scatter. **b** stop; put an end to. **c** upset; disturb greatly. [OE *brecan*] —**break′a·ble,** *adj.*

break·age (brāk′ij), *n.* **1** act of breaking; break. **2** damage or loss caused by breaking. **3** allowance made for such damage or loss.

break·dancing (brāk′dan′sing), *n.* athletic, acrobatic dancing in which the dancer executes spins and turns, etc., esp. on pavement, floor, etc. —**break dance,** *v.*

break·down (brāk′doun′), *n.* **1** failure to work. **2** loss of health; collapse. **3** *Am.* a noisy, lively dance. **4** analysis, as of a total.

break·er (brāk′ər), *n.* **1** wave that breaks into foam on the shore, rocks, etc. **2** machine for breaking things into smaller pieces.

break·fast (brek′fəst), *n.* the first meal of the day. —*v.* eat breakfast. [< *break* + *fast²*] —**break′fast·er,** *n.* —**break′fast·less,** *adj.*

break·neck (brāk′nek′), *adj.* likely to cause a broken neck; very dangerous.

break·through (brāk′thrü′), *n.* **1** an offensive military operation that pierces a defensive system and reaches the area behind it. **2** a solving of the major problem or problems hindering some undertaking, esp. in science.

break·up (brāk′up′), *n.* **1** collapse; decay. **2** separation. **3** end.

break·wa·ter (brāk′wô′tər; –wot′ər), *n.* wall or barrier to break the force of waves.

bream (brēm), *n., pl.* **breams** or (*esp. collectively*) **bream. 1** carp of inland European waters. **2** any of various related fishes. **3** the common freshwater sunfish. [< F *brême* < Gmc.]

breast (brest), *n.* **1** the upper, front part of the human body; chest. **2** the corresponding part in animals. **3** the upper, front part of a coat, dress, etc. **4** a front or forward part. **5** gland that gives milk. **6** heart; feelings. —*v. U.S.* struggle with; advance against; oppose; face.

make a clean breast of, confess completely. [OE *brēost*]

breast·bone (brest′bōn′), *n.* the thin, flat bone in the front of the chest to which the ribs are attached; sternum.

breast-feed (brest′fēd′), *v.,* **-fed, -feeding.** feed at the mother's breast; nurse.

breast·plate (brest′plāt′), *n.* armor for the chest.

breast·stroke (brest′strōk′), *n.* swimming stroke made with the swimmer face down and with both arms extended forward under the water, then drawn to the sides and extended forward while the legs make a frog kick.

breast·work (brest′werk′), *n.* a low, hastily built wall for defense.

breath (breth), *n.* **1** air drawn into and forced out of the lungs. **2** act of breathing. **3** ability to breathe easily: *out of breath.* **4** pause; respite. **5** light breeze. **6** utterance; whisper. **7** life.

catch one's breath, a gasp; pant. **b** rest; stop or pause.

in the same breath, at the same time.

out of breath, breathless.

save one's breath, no comment; be silent.

take one's breath away, surprise; delight.

under or **below one's breath,** in a whisper. [OE *brǣth* odor]

breathe (brēth), *v.,* **breathed, breath·ing. 1** draw (air) into the lungs and force it out. **2** stop for breath; rest. **3** *Fig.* say softly; whisper; utter. **4** *Fig.* be alive; live. **5** *Fig.* utter with the breath and not with the voice. **6** send out; infuse: *breathe new life into tired ideas.* **7** *Fig.* send out an odor or scent.

breathe again or **freely,** be relieved; feel easy.

breathe easy or **easily,** be free from anxiety or pain. —**breath′a·ble,** *adj.*

breath·er (brēth′ər), *n.* **1** a short stop for breath; rest. **2** person or thing that breathes.

breath·ing (brēth′ing), *n.* respiration.

breath·less (breth′lis), *adj.* **1** out of breath. **2** unable to breathe freely because of fear, interest, or excitement. **3** without a breeze. —**breath′less·ly,** *adv.* —**breath′less·ness,** *n.*

breath-tak·ing (breth′tāk′ing), *adj.* thrilling; exciting: *a breath-taking view.*

bred (bred), *v.* pt. and pp. of **breed.**

breech (brēch), *n.* **1** the lower part; back part. **2** part of a gun behind the barrel. [OE *brēc,* gen. and dat. of *brōc*]

breech·cloth (brēch′klôth′; –kloth′), **breech-clout** (–klout′), *n.* cloth worn as a loincloth.

breech·es (brich′iz), *n.pl.* **1** short trousers reaching from the waist to the knees. **2** *Colloq.* trousers. [OE *brēc,* pl. of *brōc* BREECH]

breeches buoy, pair of short canvas trousers fastened to a belt or life preserver. A breeches buoy slides along a rope on a pulley and is used to rescue people or transfer them between ships.

breech·ing (brich′ing; brēch′–), *n.* part of a harness that passes around a horse's rump.

breech·load·ing (brēch′lōd′ing), *adj.* of guns, loading from behind the barrel instead of at the mouth,

breed (brēd), *v.,* **bred, breed·ing,** *n.* —*v.* **1** produce (young). **2** raise (livestock, etc.). **3** produce; cause: *careless driving breeds accidents.* **4** be the native place or source of. **5** bring up; train. —*n.* **1** race; stock: *Jerseys and Guernseys are breeds of cattle.* **2** kind; sort. [OE *brēdan*] —**breed′er,** *n.*

breeder reactor, nuclear reactor which produces fissionable material in excess of the amount required for the chain reaction.

breed·ing (brēd′ing), *n.* **1** producing offspring. **2** producing animals, esp. to get improved kinds. **3** bringing up; training; behavior.

breeze (brēz), *n., v.,* **breezed, breez·ing.** —*n.* a light wind. —*v. Colloq.* proceed easily or briskly. [< OSp. and Pg. *briza* northeast wind]

breez·y (brēz′i), *adj.,* **breez·i·er, breez·i·est. 1** with light winds blowing. **2** brisk; lively; jolly. —**breez′i·ly,** *adv.* —**breez′i·ness,** *n.*

Bren·ner Pass (bren′ər), a mountain pass in the Alps between Austria and Italy.

breth·ren (breth′rən), *n.pl.* **1** brothers. **2** the fellow members of a church or society.

Bret·on (bret′ən), *n.* **1** native or inhabitant of Brittany. **2** language of Brittany. **3 Cape,** the northeastern part of Nova Scotia. —*adj.* having to do with Brittany, its people, or their language.

breve (brēv), *n.* **1** curved mark (ˇ) put over a vowel or syllable to show that it is short. **2** musical note equal to two whole notes. [< Ital. < L *brevis* short]

bre·vet (brə vet′; *esp. Brit.* brev′it), *n., v.,* **–vet·ted, –vet·ting; –vet·ed, –vet·ing.** —*n.* commission promoting an army officer to a higher rank without an increase in pay. —*v.* give rank by a brevet. [< F, dim. of *bref* letter. See BRIEF.]

bre·vi·ar·y (brē′vi er′i; brev′i–), *n., pl.* **–ar·ies.** book of prescribed prayers to be said daily by certain clergymen and religious of the Roman Catholic Church. [< L *breviarium* summary < *brevis* short]

brev·i·ty (brev′ə ti), *n., pl.* **–ties.** shortness; briefness. [< L, < *brevis* short]

brew (brü), *v.* **1** make (beer, ale, etc.) by soaking, boiling, and fermenting. **2** make (a drink) by soaking, boiling, or mixing. **3** bring about; plan; plot: *boys brewing mischief.* **4** begin to form; gather: *a storm is brewing.* —*n.* **1** drink brewed. **2** quantity brewed at one time. [OE *brēowan*] —**brew′er,** *n.*

brew·er·y (brü′ər i; brür′i), *n., pl.* **–er·ies.** place where beer, ale, etc., are brewed.

brew·ing (brü′ing), *n.* **1** preparing a brew. **2** amount brewed at one time.

bri·ar (brī′ər), *n.* =brier. —**bri′ar·y,** *adj.*

bri·ar·wood (brī′ər wůd′), *n.* =brier-wood.

bribe (brīb), *n., v.,* **bribed, brib·ing.** —*n.* **1** anything given or offered to get a person to do something that he or she thinks is wrong. **2** reward for doing something that a person does not want to do. —*v.* **1** offer a bribe to. **2** influence by giving a bribe. **3** give bribes. [? < OF, bit of bread given to a beggar] —**brib′a·ble,** *adj.* —**brib′a·bil′i·ty,** *n.* —**brib′er,** *n.*

brib·er·y (brīb′ər i), *n., pl.* **–er·ies.** **1** giving or offering a bribe. **2** taking a bribe.

bric-a-brac, bric-à-brac (brik′ə brak′), *n.* interesting or curious knickknacks used as decorations. [< F]

brick (brik), *n.* **1** block of clay baked by sun or fire, used in building and paving. **2** bricks. **3** anything shaped like a brick. —*adj.* made of bricks. —*v.* build or pave with bricks; wall in with bricks. [< F < MDu. *bricke*] —**brick′like′,** *adj.*

brick·lay·ing (brik′lā′ing), *n.* act or work of building with bricks. —**brick′lay′er,** *n.*

brick·work (brik′wèrk′), *n.* **1** thing made of bricks. **2** building with bricks; bricklaying.

brid·al (brī′dəl), *adj.* of a bride or a wedding. —*n.* wedding. [OE *brȳdealo* bride ale] —**brid′al·ly,** *adv.*

bridal wreath, a kind of spiraea.

bride (brīd), *n.* woman just married or about to be married. [OE *brȳd*]

bride·groom (brīd′grüm′; –grům′), *n.* man just married or about to be married. [OE *brȳdguma* < *brȳd* bride + *guma* man; infl. by *groom*]

brides·maid (brīdz′mād′), *n.* young, usually unmarried woman who attends the bride at a wedding.

bridge[1] (brij), *n., v.,* **bridged, bridg·ing.** —*n.* **1** structure built over a river, road, etc., so that people, trains, etc., can get across. **2** platform above the deck of a ship for the officer in command. **3** the upper, bony part of the nose. **4** mounting for false teeth fastened to real teeth near by. **5** a movable piece over which the strings of a violin etc., are stretched. —*v.* **1** build a bridge over. **2** extend over; span. **3** make a way over: *politeness will bridge many difficulties.*

burn one's bridges, cut off all chance of retreat or of following a different course. [OE *brycg*] —**bridge′a·ble,** *adj.* —**bridge′less,** *adj.*

bridge[2] (brij), *n.* **1** a card game for four players resembling whist, in which the dealer or his partner (the dummy) declares the trump, and the dealer plays both his own and his partner's hand. **2** =auction bridge.

bridge·head (brij′hed′), *n.* **1** fortification protecting the end of a bridge toward the enemy. **2** position obtained and held within enemy territory, used as a starting point for further attack. **3** either end of a bridge.

bridge·work (brij′wèrk′), *n.* false teeth in a mounting fastened to real teeth near by.

bri·dle (brī′dəl), *n., v.,* **–dled, –dling.** —*n.* **1** head part of a horse's harness, used to hold back or control a horse. **2** anything that holds back or checks. —*v.* **1** put a bridle on. **2** hold back; check; control. **3** hold the head up high with the chin drawn back to express pride, vanity, scorn, or anger. [OE *brīdel, brigdels* < *bregdan* braid] —**bri′dle·less,** *adj.* —**bri′dler,** *n.*

brief (brēf), *adj.* **1** lasting only a short time. **2** using few words. —*n.* **1** short statement; summary. **2 a** a writ. **b** statement of the facts and the points of law of a case to be pleaded in court. —*v.* **1** make a brief of; summarize. **2** furnish with a brief. **3** *Brit. Law.* retain as a lawyer or counsel. **4** give a briefing to.

briefs, short underpants.

hold a brief for, argue for; support; defend.

in brief, in few words. [< OF < L *brevis* short] —**brief′ly,** *adv.* —**brief′ness,** *n.*

brief case, flat container for carrying loose papers, books, drawings, etc.

brief·ing (brēf′ing), *n.* **1** a short summary of the details of a flight mission, given to the crew of a combat aircraft just before it takes off. **2** any similar short, preparatory summary.

bri·er[1] (brī′ər), *n.* a thorny or prickly bush, esp. the wild rose. Also, **briar.** [OE *brēr*]

bri·er[2] (brī′ər), *n.* white heath bush. Its root is used in making tobacco pipes.

Also, **briar.** [< F *bruyère* heath < Celtic] —**bri′er·y,** *adj.*

bri·er·wood (brī′ər wůd′), *n.* roots of the brier tree. Also, **briarwood.**

brig (brig), *n.* **1** a square-rigged ship with two masts. **2** prison on a warship. **3** *Informal.* guardhouse. [short for *brigantine*]

bri·gade (bri gād′), *n., v.,* **–gad·ed, –gad·ing.** —*n.* **1** part of an army. It is usually made up of two or more regiments. **2** group of people organized for some purpose: *a fire brigade puts out fires.* —*v.* form into a brigade. [< F < Ital. *brigata,* ult. < *briga* strife]

brig·a·dier (brig′ə dir′), *n.* =brigadier general.

brigadier general, *pl.* **brigadier generals.** officer commanding a brigade, a wing of the Air Force, or an equivalent unit, ranking above a colonel and below a major general.

brig·and (brig′ənd), *n.* man who robs travelers on the road; robber; bandit. [< OF < Ital. *brigante.* See BRIGADE.] —**brig′and·ish,** *adj.*

brig·and·age (brig′ən dij), **brig·and·ism** (–diz əm), *n.* robbery; plundering.

brig·an·tine (brig′ən tēn; –tīn), *n.* brig with the mainmast fore-and-aft-rigged. [< F < Ital. *brigantino.* See BRIGAND, BRIGADE.]

bright (brīt), *adj.* **1** giving much light; shining. **2** quick-witted; clever; intelligent. **3** vivid; glowing. **4** lively; cheerful. **5** favorable. —*adv.* in a bright manner. [OE *briht, beorht*] —**bright′ly,** *adv.* —**bright′ness,** *n.*

bright·en (brīt′ən), *v.* **1** become bright or brighter. **2** make bright or brighter.

Bright's disease, *Pathol.* kidney disease characterized by albumin in the urine.

bril·liance (bril′yəns), **bril·lian·cy** (–yən si), *n.* **1** great brightness; radiance; sparkle. **2** splendor; magnificence. **3** great ability.

bril·liant (bril′yənt), *adj.* **1** shining brightly; sparkling. **2** splendid; magnificent. **3** having great ability. —*n.* diamond or other gem cut to sparkle brightly. [< F *brillant,* ppr. of *briller* shine, ? < L *beryllus* beryl] —**bril′liant·ly,** *adv.* —**bril′liant·ness,** *n.*

brim (brim), *n., v.,* **brimmed, brim·ming.** —*n.* **1** edge of a cup, bowl, etc.; rim. **2** the projecting edge of a hat. —*v.* fill to the brim; be full to the brim. [OE *brim* sea] —**brim′less,** *adj.*

brim·ful (brim′fůl′), *adj.* completely full.

brim·stone (brim′stōn′), *n.* =sulfur. [ME *brinston* < *brinn–* burn + *ston* stone]

brin·dle (brin′dəl), *adj.* =brindled. —*n.* **1** brindled color. **2** brindled animal. [< *brindled*]

brin·dled (brin′dəld), *adj.* gray, tan, or tawny with darker streaks and spots. [? akin to BRAND]

brine (brīn), *n.* **1** very salty water. **2** salt lake or sea; ocean. [OE *brȳne*] —**brin′ish,** *adj.*

bring (bring), *v.*, **brought, bring·ing. 1** come with (some thing or person) from another place. **2** cause to come. **3** influence; lead. **4** present (reasons, arguments, etc.); adduce.

bring about, cause to happen.

bring around, a restore to consciousness. **b** convince; persuade.

bring forth, a give birth to; bear. **b** reveal; show.

bring out, a reveal; show. **b** offer to the public.

bring to, a restore to consciousness. **b** stop; check.

bring up, a care for in childhood. **b** educate; train. **c** suggest for action or discussion. **d** stop suddenly. [OE *bringan*] —**bring′er,** *n.*

bring·ing-up (bring′ing up′), *n.* **1** care in childhood. **2** education; training.

brink (bringk), *n.* edge at the top of a steep place.

on the brink of, very near. [ME; prob. < Scand.]

brink·man·ship (bringk′mən ship), *n.* urging or pursuit of a policy even to the brink of disaster.

brin·y (brīn′i), *adj.,* **brin·i·er, brin·i·est.** of or like brine; salty. —**brin′i·ness,** *n.*

bri·quette, bri·quet (bri ket′), *n.* a molded block, esp. of charcoal used for broiling on a grill. [< F]

Bris·bane (briz′bān; –bən), *n.* seaport in E Australia.

brisk (brisk), *adj.* **1** quick and active; lively. **2** keen; sharp. [? akin to BRUSQUE] —**brisk′ly,** *adv.* —**brisk′ness,** *n.*

bris·ket (bris′kit), *n.* **1** meat from the breast of an animal. **2** breast of an animal. [< OF *bruschet* < Gmc.]

bris·tle (bris′əl), *n., v.,* **-tled, -tling.** —*n.* a short, stiff hair. —*v.* **1** stand up straight: *the angry dog's hair bristled.* **2** cause (hair) to stand up straight; ruffle. **3** have one's hair stand up straight: *the dog bristled.* **4** show that one is aroused and ready to fight. **5** be thickly set: *our path bristled with difficulties.* [ME *bristel*] —**bris′tly,** *adj.* —**bris′tli·ness,** *n.*

bris·tle·tail (bris′əl tāl′), *n.* a wingless insect having long, bristlelike appendages.

Bris·tol (bris′təl), *n.* seaport in SW England.

Brit., 1 Britain; British. **2** Briticism.

Brit·ain (brit′ən), *n.* England, Scotland, and Wales; Great Britain.

Bri·tan·nia (bri tan′i ə; –tan′yə), *n.* Britain; Great Britain.

Bri·tan·nic (bri tan′ik), *adj.* =British.

Brit·i·cism (brit′ə siz əm), *n.* word or phrase peculiar to the British. *Lift* meaning *elevator* is a Briticism. Also, **Britishism.**

Brit·ish (brit′ish), *adj.* **1** of Great Britain, or its people. **2** of or pertaining to the ancient Britons. —*n.* **1** (*pl. in use*) people of Great Britain collectively. **2** their language. [OE *brittisc* < *Brittas* Britons < Celtic]

British Columbia, province in W Canada.

British Commonwealth of Nations, =Commonwealth of Nations.

British Empire, originally, all the countries and colonies owing allegiance to the British crown.

British English, English language as spoken and written in Britain.

Brit·ish·er (brit′ish ər), *n.* =Englishman.

British Isles, Great Britain, Ireland, the Isle of Man, and other nearby islands.

Brit·ish·ism (brit′ish iz əm), *n.* =Briticism.

British thermal unit, amount of heat necessary to raise a pound of water one degree Fahrenheit at its maximum density.

British West Indies, British islands in the West Indies, including the Bahamas, Bermuda, and the British Virgin Islands.

Brit·on (brit′ən), *n.* **1** native or inhabitant of Great Britain. **2** member of a Celtic people who lived in S Britain long ago.

Brit·ta·ny (brit′ə ni), *n.* region in NW France.

brit·tle (brit′əl), *adj.* very easily broken; breaking with a snap; apt to break. [ME *britel* < OE *brēotan* break] —**brit′tle·ly,** *adv.* —**brit′tle·ness,** *n.*

bro., Bro., *pl.* **bros., Bros.** brother.

broach (brōch), *n.* **1** a pointed tool for making and shaping holes. **2** slender spit for roasting meat. **3** tool for opening casks. **4** =brooch. —*v.* **1** open by making a hole. **2** begin to talk about: *broach a subject.* [< OF < L *broccus* projecting] —**broach′er,** *n.*

broad (brôd), *adj.* **1** wide. **2** extensive: *a broad experience.* **3** liberal; tolerant: *broad ideas.* **4** main; general: *broad outlines.* **5** clear; full: *broad daylight.* **6** plain-spoken. **7** coarse; not refined: *broad jokes.* **8** pronounced with the vocal passage open wide. The *a* in *father* is broad. —*n. Informal.* a woman. [OE *brād*] —**broad′ish,** *adj.* —**broad′ly,** *adv.*

broad·ax, broad·axe (brôd′aks′), *n., pl.* **-axes.** ax with a broad blade.

broad·band (brôd′band′), *adj.* operating over a wide range of frequencies; *a broadband station.*

broad·cast (brôd′kast′; –käst′), *v.,* **-cast** or **-cast·ed, -cast·ing,** *n., adj., adv.* —*v.* **1** send out by radio or television. **2** scatter widely. —*n.* **1** a sending out by radio or television. **2** speech, music, etc., sent out by radio or television. **3** radio or television program. **4** scattering far and wide. —*adj.* **1** sent out by radio or television. **2** scattered widely. —*adv.* over a wide surface. —**broad′cast′er,** *n.*

broad·cloth (brôd′klôth′; –kloth′), *n.* **1** a smooth, cotton or silk cloth, used in making shirts and dresses. **2** a smooth, closely woven woolen cloth, used in making men's suits. [orig. 2 yards "broad"]

broad·en (brôd′ən), *v.* **1** make broad or broader. **2** become broad or broader.

broad jump, 1 a jump that covers as much ground as possible. **2** athletic contest for the longest broad jump. —**broad′jump′,** *v.*

broad·loom (brôd′lüm′), *adj.* woven on a wide loom in one color: *a broadloom carpet.*

broad·mind·ed (brôd′mīn′did), *adj.* liberal; tolerant; not prejudiced or bigoted. —**broad′-mind′ed·ly,** *adv.* —**broad′mind′ed·ness,** *n.*

broad·side (brôd′sīd′), *n.* **1** the whole side of a ship above the water line. **2** all the guns that can be fired from one side of a ship. **3** the firing of all these guns at the same time. **4** *Fig.* violent attack. —*adv.* with the side turned.

broad·sword (brôd′sôrd′; –sōrd′), *n.* sword with a broad, flat blade.

Broad·way (brôd′wā′), *n.* **1** street running NE and SW through New York City. **2** theater district of New York City: *the lights dimmed on Broadway.*

bro·cade (brō kād′), *n., v.,* **-cad·ed, -cad·ing.** —*n.* an expensive cloth woven with raised designs on it. —*v.* weave or decorate with raised designs. [< Sp., Pg. *brocado,* pp. of *brocar* embroider; akin to BROACH] —**bro·cad′ed,** *adj.*

broc·co·li (brok′ə li), *n.* variety of cauliflower whose green branching stems and flower heads are used as a vegetable. [< Ital. (pl.) sprouts < L *broccus* projecting]

bro·chure (brō shùr′), *n.* =pamphlet. [< F, < *brocher* stitch]

bro·gan (brō′gən), *n.* a coarse, strong shoe. [< Irish, Scotch Gaelic, dim. of *brōg* shoe]

brogue[1] (brōg), *n.* **1** Irish accent or pronunciation of English. **2** accent or pronunciation peculiar to any dialect. [? specialization of meaning of *brogue*[2]]

brogue[2] (brōg), *n.* **1** shoe made for comfort and long wear. **2** =brogan. [< Irish, Scotch Gaelic *brōg* shoe]

broil[1] (broil), *v.* **1** cook by putting or holding near the fire. **2** make very hot. **3** be very hot. —*n.* **1** a broiling. **2** broiled meat, etc. [? < OF *bruillir* burn]

broil[2] (broil), *v.* engage in a broil; quarrel; fight. —*n.* an angry quarrel or struggle; brawl. [< F *brouiller* disorder]

broil·er (broil′ər), *n.* **1** pan or rack for broiling. **2** device in a stove or small appliance for broiling. **3** a young chicken for broiling. **4** *Informal.* extremely hot day; scorcher.

broke (brōk), *v.* **1** pt. of **break. 2** *Archaic.* pp. of **break.** —*adj. Informal.* without money.

bro·ken (brō′kən), *v.* pp. of **break.** —*adj.* **1** crushed; in pieces. **2** destroyed. **3** weakened. **4** tamed. **5** imperfectly spoken. **6** interrupted. —**bro′ken·ly,** *adv.* —**bro′ken·ness,** *n.*

bro·ken-heart·ed (brō′kən här′tid), *adj.* crushed by sorrow or grief; heartbroken.

bro·ker (brō′kər), *n.* person who buys and sells stocks, bonds, grain, cotton, etc., for other people; agent. [< AF *brocour* tapster, retailer of wine; akin to BROACH]

bro·ker·age (brō′kər ij), *n.* **1** business of a broker. **2** money charge by a broker for his services.

bro·mide (brō′mīd; –mid), *n.* **1** compound of bromine with another element or radical. **2** potassium bromide, KBr, a drug used to calm nervousness, cause sleep, etc. **3** commonplace, unoriginal thought or remark: *the usual bromides were offered up in the speech.*

bro·mine (brō′mēn; –min), *n.* a nonmetallic element, Br, somewhat like chlorine and iodine. Bromine is a dark-brown liquid that gives off an irritating vapor.

bron·chi (brong′kī), *n. pl.* of **bronchus. 1** two main branches of the windpipe. **2** the smaller, branching tubes in the lungs.

bron·chi·a (brong′ki ə), *n.pl.* the bronchi, esp. their smaller branches.

bron·chi·al (brong′ki əl), *adj.* of the bronchi.

bron·chi·tis (brong kī′tis), *n.* inflammation of the lining of the bronchial tubes. —**bron·chit′ic,** *adj.*

bron·chus (brong′kəs), *n., pl.* –**chi** (–kī). one of the bronchi. [< NL < Gk. *bronchos*]

bron·co (brong′kō), *n., pl.* –**cos.** pony of the W United States. Broncos are often wild or only half tame. [< Sp., rough, rude]

bron·to·sau·rus (bron′tə sôr′əs), *n.* a huge, extinct dinosaur of America. [< NL < Gk. *bronte* thunder + *sauros* lizard]

Bronx (brongks), *n.* **The,** northern borough of New York City.

bronze (bronz), *n., adj., v.,* **bronzed, bronz·ing.** —*n.* **1** a brown alloy of copper and tin. **2** a similar alloy of copper with zinc or other metals. **3** statue, medal, disk, etc., made of bronze. **4** yellowish brown; reddish brown. —*adj.* **1** made of bronze. **2** yellowish-brown; reddish-brown. —*v.* make or become bronze in color. [< F < Ital. *bronzo* bell metal] —**bronz′y,** *adj.*

Bronze Age, period after the Stone Age when bronze tools, weapons, etc., were used.

brooch (brōch; brüch), *n.* an ornamental pin with the point secured by a catch. [var. of *broach, n.*]

brood (brüd), *n.* **1** young birds hatched at one time in the nest or cared for together. **2** young who are cared for. **3** breed; kind. —*v.* **1** sit on in order to hatch. **2** hover over; hang close over. **3** dwell on in thought: *for years he brooded vengeance.* [OE *brōd*] —**brood′ing·ly,** *adv.* —**brood′y,** *adj.*

brood·er (brüd′ər), *n.,* **1** a closed place that can be heated, used in raising chicks, etc. **2** one that broods.

brook¹ (brük), *n.* a small natural stream of water. [OE *brōc*]

brook² (brük), *v.* put up with; endure; tolerate: *her pride would not brook such insults.* [OE *brūcan* use]

brook·let (brük′lit), *n.* a little brook.

Brook·lyn (brük′lən), *n.* borough of New York City, on Long Island.

brook trout, a freshwater game fish of the E part of North America.

broom (brüm; brùm), *n.* **1** shrub with slender branches, small leaves, and yellow flowers. **2** a long-handled brush for sweeping. [OE *brōm*]

broom·corn (brüm′kôrn′; brüm′–), *n.* tall plant resembling corn, with flower clusters having long, stiff stems used for making brooms.

broom·stick (brüm′stik′; brùm′–), *n.* long handle of a broom.

broth (brôth; broth), *n.* water in which meat has been boiled; thin soup. [OE]

broth·el (broth′əl; brôth′–; brôth′–), *n.* house of prostitution. [ME, < OE *brēothan* go to ruin]

broth·er (bruth′ər), *n., pl.* **broth·ers, breth·ren,** *v.* —*n.* **1** son of the same parents. **2** a close friend; companion; countryman. **3** a fellow member of a group or association. **4** member of a religious order who is not a priest. [OE *brōthor*]

broth·er·hood (bruth′ər hùd), *n.* **1** bond between brothers. **2** persons joined as brothers in association.

broth·er-in-law (bruth′ər in lô′), *n., pl.* **broth·ers-in-law. 1** brother of one's husband or wife. **2** husband of one's sister. **3** husband of the sister of one's wife or husband.

broth·er·ly (bruth′ər li), *adj.* **1** of or like a brother. **2** friendly; kindly. —**broth′er·li·ness,** *n.*

brougham (brüm; brü′əm; brō′əm), *n.* a closed carriage or automobile having an outside seat for the driver. [for Lord H. P. *Brougham*]

brought (brôt), *v.* pt. and pp. of **bring.**

brow (brou), *n.* **1** =forehead. **2** =eyebrow. **3** edge of a steep place. [OE *brū*]

brow·beat (brou′bēt′), *v.,* –**beat,** –**beat·en,** –**beat·ing.** frighten into doing something by overbearing looks or words; bully. —**brow′beat′er,** *n.*

brown (broun), *n.* **1** color like that of toast, potato skins, and coffee. **2** paint or dye having this color. **3** something brown. —*adj.* **1** having this color. **2** dark-skinned; tanned. —*v.* make or become brown. [OE *brūn*] —**brown′ish,** *adj.* —**brown′ness,** *n.*

Brown (broun), *n.* **John,** 1800–59, American abolitionist.

brown bear, any bear that has brown fur and lives in Europe, Asia, and North America, esp. Alaska.

brown dwarf, celestial object smaller than a star.

Brown·i·an movement (broun′i ən), a rapid oscillatory motion often observed in very minute particles suspended in water or other liquids.

brown·ie (broun′i), *n.* **1** good-natured, helpful elf or fairy. **2** flat, sweet, chocolate cake with nuts, often in small squares. **3 Brownie,** member of the youngest division of the Girl Scouts.

Brown·ing (broun′ing), *n.* **1 Elizabeth Barrett,** 1806–61, English poet, wife of Robert Browning. **2 Robert,** 1812–89, English poet.

brown·stone (broun′stōn′), *n.* **1** reddish-brown sandstone, used as a building material. **2** house built of brownstone, esp. in a city.

brown sugar, sugar that is not refined or only partly refined.

browse (brouz), *v.,* **browsed, brows·ing,** *n.* —*v.* **1** feed; graze. **2** read here and there in a book, library, etc. [< n., or < F *brouster* feed on buds and shoots] —*n.* tender shoots of shrubs. [appar. < MF *broust* bud, shoot < Gmc.] —**brows′er,** *n.*

bru·in (brü′ən), *n.* =bear. [< MDu., brown]

bruise (brüz), *v.,* **bruised, bruis·ing,** *n.* —*v.* **1** injure the outside of. **2** injure; hurt: *harsh words bruised her feelings.* **3** become bruised. **4** pound; crush. —*n.* **1** injury to the body, caused by a fall or a blow, that changes the color of the skin without breaking it. **2** injury to the outside of a fruit, vegetable, plant, etc. [fusion of OE *brȳsan* crush and OF *bruisier* break, shatter]

bruis·er (brüz′ər), *n.* **1** prize fighter. **2** bully. **3** very muscular person.

bruit (brüt), *v.* spread a report or rumor of. [< OF, < *bruire* roar]

bru·nette, bru·net (brü net′), *adj.* **1** dark-colored; having an olive color. **2** having dark-brown or black hair, brown or black eyes, and a dark skin. —*n.* person having such hair, eyes, and skin. A man with this complexion is a brunet; a woman is a brunette. [< F, dim. of *brun* brown < Gmc.]

brunt (brunt), *n.* main force or violence.

brush¹ (brush), *n.* **1** tool for cleaning, rubbing, painting, etc., made of bristles set in a stiff back or handle. **2** a brushing. **3** a light touch in passing. **4** a short, brisk fight or quarrel. **5** brief encounter: *brush with the law.* **6** the bushy tail of a fox. **7** piece of carbon, copper, etc., used to connect the electricity from the revolving part of a motor or generator to the outside circuit. —*v.* **1** clean, rub, paint, etc., with a brush. **2** wipe away: *brush the tears away.* **3** touch lightly in passing.

brush aside or **away,** refuse to consider.

brush up (on), refresh one's knowledge. [< OF *broisse* < Gmc.] —**brush′er,** *n.* —**brush′y,** *adj.*

brush² (brush), *n.* **1 a** U.S. branches broken or cut off. **b** thick growth of shrubs, bushes, small trees, etc. **2**

SW U.S. backwoods. [< OF broche] —**brush′y,** adj.

brush·wood (brush′wüd′), n. brush[2] (def. 1).

brush·work (brush′werk′), n. an artist's distinctive technique and skill in applying paint with a brush.

brusque (brusk), adj. abrupt in manner or speech; blunt. [< F < Ital. brusco coarse < LL bruscus, blend of ruscum broom and Gaulish brucus broom] —**brusque′ly,** adv. —**brusque′ness,** n.

Brus·sels (brus′əlz), n. capital of Belgium, in the C part.

Brussels sprouts, 1 variety of cabbage that has many small heads growing along a stalk. **2** heads of this plant, used as a vegetable.

bru·tal (brü′təl), adj. coarse and savage; like a brute; cruel. —**bru′tal·ly,** adv.

bru·tal·i·ty (brü tal′ə ti), n., pl. –**ties. 1** cruelty; savageness; coarseness: whipping a tired horse is brutality. **2** cruel, savage, or coarse act.

bru·tal·ize (brü′təl īz), v., –**ized, –iz·ing. 1** make brutal: war brutalizes many men. **2** become brutal. —**bru′tal·i·za′tion,** n.

brute (brüt), n. **1** animal without power to reason. **2** a stupid, cruel, or coarse person. —adj. **1** without power to reason. **2** stupid; cruel; coarse. **3** unconscious: the brute forces of nature. [< F brut < L brutus heavy, dull]

brut·ish (brüt′ish), adj. stupid; coarse; savage; like a brute. —**brut′ish·ly,** adv. —**brut′ish·ness,** n.

Bru·tus (brü′təs), n. **Marcus Junius,** 85–42 B.C., Roman political leader and one of the men who killed Julius Caesar.

bry·ol·o·gy (brī ol′ə ji), n. branch of botany that deals with mosses and liverworts. [< Gk. bryon moss + –LOGY] —**bry′o·log′i·cal,** adj. —**bry·ol′o·gist,** n.

bry·o·phyte (brī′ə fīt), n. any mosses or liverworts. [< NL < Gk. bryon moss + phyton plant] —**bry′o·phyt′ic,** adj.

B.S., B.Sc., Bachelor of Science.

B.T.U., B.t.u., Btu, British thermal unit.

bu., bushel.

bub·ble (bub′əl), n., v., –**bled, –bling.** —n. **1** a thin film of liquid enclosing air or gas. **2** a small globule of air in a solid or in a liquid. **3** act or process of bubbling; sound of bubbling. **4** plan or idea that looks good, but soon goes to pieces. **5** speculation in stocks, housing, etc. that raises prices for above value and likely to lead to a sudden decline. —v. **1** have bubbles; make bubbles; look like water boiling. **2** make sounds like water boiling; gurgle.

bubble over, a boil over; overflow. **b** be very enthusiastic. [ME bobel] —**bub′bling·ly,** adv. —**bub′bly,** adj.

bubble gum, chewing gum which can be inflated to form a large bubble.

bu·bon·ic plague (bü bon′ik), a very dangerous contagious disease, accompanied by fever, chills, and swelling of the lymphatic glands. [< LL < Gk. boubon groin]

buc·cal (buk′əl), adj. **1** of the cheek. **2** of the mouth or the sides of the mouth. [< L bucca cheek, mouth]

buc·ca·neer (buk′ə nir′), n. pirate; sea robber. [< F boucanier < boucan frame for curing meat, as done by the French in Haiti]

Bu·chan·an (bü kan′ən; bə–), n. **James,** 1791–1868, 15th president of the United States, 1857–61.

Bu·cha·rest (bü′kə rest; bü′–), n. capital of Romania, in the S part.

buck[1] (buk), n. **1** a male deer, goat, hare, rabbit, antelope, or sheep. **2** dandy. **3** Colloq. man. [coalescence of OE buc male deer and OE bucca male goat]

buck[2] (buk), v. **1** Colloq. fight against; resist stubbornly. **b** rush at; charge against. **2** in football, charge into the opposing line with the ball. **3** (of horses) jump into the air with back curved and come down with the front legs stiff. —n. a throw or attempt to throw by bucking.

buck up, Informal. cheer up. [special use of buck[1]] —**buck′er,** n.

buck[3] (buk), n. **pass the buck,** Colloq. shift the responsibility, work, etc., to someone else.

buck[4] (buk), n., Slang. dollar.

buck·a·roo (buk′ə rü; buk′ə rü′), n., pl. –**roos.** Am., SW cowboy.

buck·board (buk′bôrd′; –bōrd′), n. an open, four-wheeled carriage having the seat fastened to a platform of long, springy boards instead of a body and springs.

buck·et (buk′it), n., v., –**et·ed, –et·ing.** —n. **1** pail made of wood or metal. **2** amount that a bucket can hold. **3** scoop of a dredging machine. —v. lift or carry in a bucket or buckets.

kick the bucket, Informal. die. [appar. < AF buket wash tub, milk pail < OE būc vessel, pitcher]

buck·et·ful (buk′it fûl), n., pl. –**fuls.** amount that a bucket can hold.

buck·eye (buk′ī′), n. tree or shrub of the same family as the horse chestnut with showy clusters of small flowers, large divided leaves, and large brown seeds. [< buck[1] + eye; with ref. to mark on the seed]

buck·le (buk′əl), n., v., –**led, –ling.** —n. **1** catch or clasp used to fasten together the ends of a belt, strap, etc. **2** metal ornament for a shoe. **3** bend; bulge; kink; wrinkle. —v. **1** fasten together with a buckle. **2** bend; bulge; kink; wrinkle.

buckle down to, work hard at. [< F < L buccula cheek strap on helmet, dim. of bucca cheek]

buck·ler (buk′lər), n. **1** a small, round shield. **2** protection; defense.

buck private, Slang. a common soldier below the rank of private first class.

buck·ram (buk′rəm), n. a coarse cloth made stiff with glue or something like glue. [? ult. named for Bukhāra in central Asia]

buck·saw (buk′sô′), n. saw set in a light frame and held with both hands.

buck·shot (buk′shot′), n. lead shot used for shooting large game such as deer.

buck·skin (buk′skin′), n. **1** a strong, soft leather, yellowish or grayish in color, made from the skins of deer or sheep. **2 buckskins,** breeches made of buckskin.

buck·thorn (buk′thôrn′), n. U.S. **1** a small thorny tree or shrub with clusters of black berries. **2** a low, thorny tree that grows in S United States.

buck·tooth (buk′tüth′), n., pl. –**teeth.** a large, protruding front tooth.

buck·wheat (buk′hwēt′), n. **1** plant with brown, triangular seeds and fragrant white flowers. **2** the seeds, used as food for animals or ground into flour.

bu·col·ic (bü kol′ik), adj. **1** of shepherds; pastoral. **2** rustic; rural. —n. poem about shepherds. [< L < Gk. boukolikos rustic < boukolos shepherd] —**bu·col′i·cal·ly,** adv.

bud (bud), n., v., **bud·ded, bud·ding.** —n. **1** a small swelling on a plant that develops into a flower, leaf, or branch. **2** beginning stage. **3** small organ or part, as a taste bud. —v. **1** put forth buds. **2** graft (a bud) from one kind of plant into the stem of a different kind. **3** begin to grow or develop.

in bud, in the time or condition of budding.

nip in the bud, stop at the very beginning. —**bud′der,** n. —**bud′less,** adj.

Bu·da·pest (bü′də pest), n. capital of Hungary, on the Danube River.

Bud·dha (bùd′ə; bü′də), n. 563? 483? B.C., a great religious teacher of Asia. Also, **Gautama.**

Bud·dhism (bùd′iz əm; bü′diz–), n. religion that originated in the sixth century B.C. in N India and spread widely over C, SE, and E Asia. —**Bud′dhist,** n. —**Bud·dhis′tic,** adj.

bud·dy (bud′i), n., pl. –**dies.** comrade; pal.

budge (buj), v., **budged, budg·ing.** move just slightly: he wouldn't budge from his chair. [< F bouger stir < VL bullicare boil furiously < L bullire boil]

budg·et (buj′it), n., v., –**et·ed, –et·ing.** —n. **1** estimate of the amount of money to be received and that can be spent, and the amounts to be spent for various purposes, in a given time. **2** detailed plan of expenditures, for a particular time period. **3** stock or collection: a budget of news. —v. **1** make a plan for spending. **2** put in a budget; allot: budget purchases; budget time. [< F bougette, dim. of bouge bag < L bulga < Celtic] —**budg′et·ar′y,** adj.

Bue·nos Ai·res (bwā′nəs ī′riz; bō′nəs ār′ēz), capital of Argentina, on the Plata River.

buff[1] (buf), n. **1** strong, soft, dull-yellow leather having a fuzzy surface. **2** soldier's coat made of buff. **3** dull yellow. **4** polishing wheel covered with leather. **5**

bare skin. —*adj.* 1 made of buff leather. 2 dull-yellow. —*v.* polish with a buff. [< F *buffle* BUFFALO]

buff² (buf), *n.* devotee; fan: *a model-train buff.*

buf·fa·lo (buf′ə lō), *n., pl.* **-loes, -los,** or (*esp. collectively*) **-lo,** *v.,* **-loed, -lo·ing.** —*n.* 1 the bison of America, a wild ox, with a big, shaggy head and strong front legs. 2 any of several kinds of oxen, as the water buffalo of India or the Cape buffalo of Africa. —*v.* 1 intimidate or overawe. 2 puzzle; mystify. [< Ital. < L *bubalus* < Gk. *boubalos* wild ox]

Buf·fa·lo (buf′ə lō), *n.* port in W New York State, on Lake Erie.

Buffalo Bill (*William F. Cody*), 1846–1917, American frontier scout and showman.

buffalo grass, short grass of central and western North America.

buff·er¹ (buf′ər), *n., v.* —*n.* 1 anything that softens the shock of a blow. 2 person or thing that serves as a balance between opposing forces: *a buffer zone between the brothers.* —*v.* act as a buffer. [< buff deaden force]

buff·er² (buf′ər), *n.* 1 person who polishes. 2 thing for polishing, covered with leather.

buffer state, a small country between two larger countries that are enemies or competitors.

buf·fet¹ (buf′it), *n., v.,* **-fet·ed, -fet·ing.** —*n.* 1 blow of the hand or fist. 2 knock; stroke; hurt. —*v.* 1 strike with the hand or fist. 2 knock about; strike; hurt. 3 fight; struggle. [< OF, dim. of *buffe* blow] —**buf′fet·er,** *n.*

buf·fet² (bù fā′; bu–; bə–), *n.* 1 piece of dining-room furniture for holding dishes, silver, and table linen; sideboard. 2 counter where food and drinks are served. 3 restaurant with such a counter where diners serve themselves. [< F]

buffet supper or **lunch,** meal where the food is arranged on tables and buffet, and the guests serve themselves.

buf·foon (bu fün′; bə–), *n.* person who amuses people with tricks, pranks, and jokes; clown. [< F < Ital. *buffone* < *buffa* jest] —**buf·foon′er·y,** *n.* —**buf·foon′ish,** *adj.*

bug (bug), *n., v.,* **bugged, bug·ging.** —*n.* 1 crawling insect. 2 any insect or insect-like animal. 3 bedbug. 4 disease germ: *intestinal bug.* 5 enthusiasm: *the racing bug.* 6 Often, **bugs,** defect, esp. mechanical; fault. 7 small microphone used in wire taps and electronic surveillance. —*v.* 1 place a hidden microphone in a house, telephone, etc. 2 irritate; pester. **bug off,** retreat; rush away. **bug out, a** of the eyes, bulge out. **b** retreat. [? < obs. Welsh *bwg* ghost]

bug·a·boo (bug′ə bü), *n., pl.* **-boos.** imaginary thing feared. [< bug bogy + boo, interj.]

bug·bear (bug′bãr′), *n.* =bugaboo. [< bug bogy + *bear²*]

bug·gy¹ (bug′i), *n., pl.* **-gies.** light carriage with one seat, drawn by a horse.

bug·gy² (bug′i), *adj.,* **-gi·er, -gi·est.** swarming with bugs.

bu·gle (bū′gəl), *n., v.,* **-gled, -gling.** —*n.* musical instrument like a small trumpet, made of brass or copper, used in the army and navy for sounding calls and orders. —*v.* 1 blow a bugle. 2 direct or summon by blowing on a bugle. [< OF < L *buculus,* dim. of *bos* ox; with ref. to early hunting horns] —**bu′gler,** *n.*

buhl (bül), *n.* 1 wood inlaid with metal, tortoise shell, ivory, etc., in elaborate patterns. 2 furniture decorated with this. [< G spelling of F *Boule,* name of a cabinetmaker]

build (bild), *v.,* **built, build·ing,** *n.* —*v.* 1 make by putting materials together; construct: *men build houses, dams, bridges, etc.* 2 establish; base: *build a business; build a case on facts.* 3 rely; depend: *build on honesty.* —*n.* form, style, or manner of construction: *an elephant has a heavy build.* [OE *byldan* < *bold* dwelling]

build·er (bil′dər), *n.* 1 person or animal who builds. 2 person whose business is building.

build·ing (bil′ding), *n.* 1 thing built, such as a house, factory, barn, etc.; structure. 2 business, art, or process of making houses, stores, ships, etc.

build-up, build·up (bild′up′), *n.* 1 a building up; formation; development: *build-up of military strength; build-up of pressure.* 2 promotion of a person or thing, esp. in advance of a performance or appearance.

built-in (bilt′in′), *adj.* 1 built as part of a room or wall, etc.: *a built-in bookcase.* 2 *Fig.* having as an integral part: *built-in optimism.*

built-up (bilt′up′), *adj.* (of an area or land) having many houses or other buildings; urban or suburban rather than rural.

bulb (bulb), *n.* 1 a round, underground bud from which certain plants grow, as onions, tulips, and lilies. b the thick part of an underground stem resembling a bulb; tuber: *a crocus bulb.* c plant growing from a bulb. 2 a the glass case of an incandescent lamp or the tube of a fluorescent lamp. b an incandescent lamp. 3 anything shaped like a bulb, as the rounded end of a thermometer. [< L < Gk. *bolbos* onion] —**bulb′ar,** *adj.* —**bulb′less,** *adj.*

bulb·ous (bul′bəs), *adj.* 1 having bulbs; growing from bulbs, as daffodils. 2 shaped like a bulb; rounded and swelling: *a bulbous nose.*

Bul·gar (bul′gär; bul′–; –gər), *n.* =Bulgarian.

Bul·gar·i·a (bul gãr′i ə; bùl–), *n.* country in SE Europe.

Bul·gar·i·an (bul gãr′i ən; bùl–), *adj.* of or having to do with Bulgaria, its people, or their language. —*n.* 1 a native or inhabitant of Bulgaria. 2 language of Bulgaria.

bulge (bulj), *v.,* **bulged, bulg·ing,** *n.* —*v.* 1 swell outward; protrude. 2 cause to swell outward. —*n.* 1 an outward swelling. 2 temporary increase. [< OF < L *bulga* bag] —**bulg′y,** *adj.*

bulk (bulk), *n.* 1 size; large size. 2 largest part; main mass. 3 a not in packages. b in large quantities. —*v.* 1 have size; be of importance. 2 grow large; swell. 3 cause to swell out. **in bulk, a** loose; not in packages. **b** in large quantities. [< Scand. *bulki* heap]

bulk·head (bulk′hed′), *n.* 1 one of the upright partitions dividing a ship into watertight compartments to prevent sinking. 2 wall or partition built to hold back water, earth, rocks, air, etc. 3 a flat or slanting door over a cellar entrance.

bulk·y (bul′ki), *adj.,* **bulk·i·er, bulk·i·est.** 1 taking up much space; large. 2 hard to handle; clumsy; unwieldy. —**bulk′i·ly,** *adv.* **bulk′i·ness,** *n.*

bull¹ (bùl), *n., adj., v.* —*n.* 1 the male of beef cattle. 2 male of the whale, elephant, seal, walrus, and other large animals. 3 a person who believes stock prices will rise. b person who speculates in the stock market, etc. 4 *Informal.* foolish talk. 5 =bulldog. 6 **Bull,** Taurus. —*adj.* 1 male. 2 having to do with rising prices in the stock market, etc. —*v.* push through or ahead: *you have to simply bull ahead to do it.* **take the bull by the horns,** deal decisively with something. [OE *bula;* akin to BULLOCK] —**bull′ish,** *adj.* —**bull′ish·ly,** *adv.* —**bull′ish·ness,** *n.*

bull² (bùl), *n.* formal announcement or official order from the Pope. [< Med.L *bulla* document, seal < L, bubble]

Bull (bùl), *n.* **John,** name for England or its people.

bull·dog (bùl′dôg; –dog′), *n., adj., v.,* **-dogged, -dog·ging.** —*n.* a heavily built dog with a large head and short hair, that is very muscular and courageous. —*adj.* like a bulldog's. —*v. W U.S.* 1 throw (a steer, etc.) by grasping its horns and twisting its neck. 2 act like a bulldog, esp. by being aggressive or persistent.

bull·doze (bùl′dōz′), *v.,* **-dozed, -doz·ing.** 1 frighten by violence or threats; bully. 2 level ground with a bulldozer.

bull·doz·er (bùl′dōz′ər), *n.* 1 very powerful scraper or pusher for grading, road-building, etc. 2 person who frightens or bullies.

bul·let (bùl′it), *n.* a shaped piece of lead, steel, or other metal to be shot from a gun. **bite the bullet,** be courageous, decisive. [< F *boulette,* dim. of *boule* ball]

bul·le·tin (bùl′ə tən), *n.* 1 short statement of news. Newspapers publish bulletins and television stations give bulletins of unfolding news events. 2 magazine or newspaper appearing regularly, esp. one published by a club or society for its members. [< F < Ital. *bullettino*, double dim. of *bulla* BULL²]

bulletin board, 1 board on which notices are posted. **2** place on a website where users can post notices and exchange messages.

bul·let·proof (bul'it prüf'), *adj., v.* —*adj.* made so that a bullet cannot go through. —*v.* make bulletproof.

bull·fight (bul'fīt'), *n.* fight between men and a bull in an enclosed arena. —**bull'fight'er,** *n.* **bull'fight'ing,** *n.*

bull·finch (bul'finch'), *n.* European songbird with handsome plumage and a short, stout bill.

bull·frog (bul'frog'; –frôg'), *n.* large frog of North America that makes a loud croaking noise.

bull·head (bul'hed'), *n.* any of several American freshwater catfishes.

bull·head·ed (bul'hed'id), *adj.* stupidly stubborn; obstinate. —**bull'head'ed·ness,** *n.*

bull·horn (bul'hôrn'), *n.* megaphone or loudspeaker.

bul·lion (bul'yən), *n.* **1** lumps, bars, etc., of gold or silver. **2** embroidery stitch. [< AF *bullion* < *bouillir* boil; infl. by OF *billon* debased metal]

bull·necked (bul'nekt'), *adj.* having a thick neck.

bull·ock (bul'ək), *n.* ox; steer.

bull pen, 1 enclosure where relief pitchers warm up during a game. **2** place to hold prisoners, suspects, etc. temporarily. **3** large, open office space, esp. for temporary workers. **4** pen for a bull or bulls.

bull ring, enclosed arena for bullfights.

bull's-eye (bulz'ī'), *n.* **1** center of a target. **2** shot that hits it. **3** *Fig.* any successful effort or initiative. **4** lens shaped like a half-sphere to concentrate light. **5** a small lantern with such a lens. **6** any round opening that lets in light and air.

bull terrier, a strong, active, white dog, a cross between a bulldog and a terrier.

bull·whip (bul'hwip'), *n.* whip made of rawhide, usually about 18 feet long.

bul·ly¹ (bul'i), *n., pl.* **–lies,** *v.,* **–lied, –ly·ing,** *interj.* —*n.* person who teases, frightens, or hurts smaller or weaker people. —*v.* **1** be a bully. **2** tease; frighten; hurt. —*adj.* fine; good. —*interj.* bravo! well done!

bul·ly² (bul'i), or **bully beef,** *n.* canned or pickled beef. [? < F *bouilli* boiled beef]

bul·rush (bul'rush'), *n.* **1** a tall, slender plant that grows in wet places. **2** any of various rushes. **3** *Brit.* cattail. **4** papyrus of Egypt, in the Bible. Also, **bullrush.**

bul·wark (bul'wərk), *n.* **1** defense; protection. **2** earthwork or other wall for defense against the enemy. **3** Usually, **bulwarks.** a ship's side above the deck. —*v.* **1** defend; protect. **2** provide with a

bulwark or bulwarks. [appar. < *bole* + *work*; akin to BOULEVARD]

bum (bum), *n., v.,* **bummed, bum·ming,** *adj.,* **bum·mer, bum·mest.** —*n.* **1 a** idle or good-for-nothing person; tramp. **b** a drunken loafer. **2** spree. —*v.* **1** loaf. **2** drink heavily. **3** sponge on others; beg. **4** get (something) by sponging on others. —*adj.* **1** of poor quality. **2** sore or injured. —**bum'mer,** *n.*

bum·ble (bum'bəl), *n., v.,* **–bled, –bling.** —*n.* a clumsy mistake. —*v.* do in a clumsy, awkward manner; bungle.

bum·ble·bee (bum'bəl bē'), *n.* a large bee with a thick, hairy body, usually banded with gold. Bumblebees live in colonies in nests in the ground. [< *bumble* buzz + *bee*]

bum·bling (bum'bling), *adj.* muddled; bungling. —**bum'bling·ly,** *adv.*

bum·mer (bum'ər), *n.* unpleasant, disappointing experience or event.

bum out, *v. Informal.* disgust; annoy.

bump (bump), *v.* **1** push, throw, or strike against something large or solid. **2** move along with bumps. **3** hit or come against with heavy blows. —*n.* **1** a heavy blow or knock. **2** swelling caused by a bump. **3** any swelling or lump.

bump off, kill; murder. [imit.]

bump·er (bump'ər), *n.* **1** a bar or bars at the front or rear of a car or truck to keep it from being damaged if the vehicle is bumped. **2** cup or glass filled to the brim. —*adj.* unusually large: *a bumper crop.*

bump·kin (bump'kin), *n.* awkward, unsophisticated person. [? < MDu. *bommekyn* little barrel]

bump·tious (bump'shəs), *adj.* unpleasantly assertive or conceited. [< *bump*] —**bump'tious·ly,** *adv.* —**bump'tious·ness,** *n.*

bump·y (bump'i), *adj.,* **bump·i·er, bump·i·est.** having bumps; causing bumps; rough. —**bump'i·ly,** *adv.* —**bump'i·ness,** *n.*

bun (bun), *n.* **1** slightly sweet roll. **2** coil or twist of hair like a bun, pinned at the back of the head.

bu·na (bü'nə; bü'–), *n.* artificial rubber made from butadiene.

bunch (bunch), *n.* **1** group of things of the same kind growing or fastened together, placed together, or thought of together: *a bunch of grapes, a bunch of sheep.* **2** a group of people. —*v.* **1** come together in one place. **2** bring together and make into a bunch.

bunch·y (bun'chi), *adj.,* **bunch·i·er, bunch·i·est. 1** having bunches. **2** growing in bunches. —**bunch'i·ness,** *n.*

bun·co (bung'kō), *n., pl.* **–cos,** *v.,* **–coed, –co·ing.** *Informal.* —*n.* **1** a dice game. **2** any swindling or confidence game. —*v.* swindle. Also, **bunko.** [short for *buncombe*]

bun·combe (bung'kəm), *n.* insincere talk; humbug. Also, **bunkum.** [after *Buncombe* Co., North Carolina, whose

congressman kept making pointless speeches "for Buncombe"]

Bun·des·rat (bun'dəs rät'), *n.* the upper house of the legislature of Germany or Austria.

Bun·des·tag (bun'dəs täk'), *n.* the lower, popularly elected house of the legislature of Germany.

bun·dle (bun'dəl), *n., v.,* **–dled, –dling.** —*n.* **1** number of things tied or wrapped together. **2** parcel; package. **3** group; bunch. —*v.* **1** wrap or tie together; make into a bundle. **2** send or go in a hurry; hustle.

bundle up, dress warmly. [cf. MDu. *bondel;* akin to BIND] —**bun'dler,** *n.*

bung (bung), *n.* **1** stopper for closing the hole in the side or end of a barrel, keg, or cask. **2** =bunghole. —*v.* **1** close with a stopper. **2** shut up in, or as in, a cask.

bung up, a close with a stopper. **b** choke up. **c** bruise. [prob. < MDu. *bonghe*]

bun·ga·low (bung'gə lō), *n.* one-story house. [< Hind. *banglā* of Bengal]

bung·hole (bung'hōl'), *n.* hole in the side or end of a barrel, keg, or cask through which it is filled and emptied.

bun·gle (bung'gəl), *v.,* **–gled, –gling,** *n.* —*v.* do or make (something) in a clumsy, unskillful way. —*n.* a clumsy, unskillful performance. —**bun'gler,** *n.* —**bun'gling·ly,** *adv.*

bun·ion (bun'yən), *n.* painful, inflamed swelling on the foot, esp. on the first joint of the big toe.

bunk¹ (bungk), *n.* **1** a narrow bed set against a wall like a shelf. **2** any place to sleep. —*v.* **1** occupy a bunk. **2** sleep in rough quarters. [? < Scand. (Dan.) *bunke* heap]

bunk² (bungk), *n. Informal.* humbug. [short for *buncombe*]

bunk·er (bungk'ər), *n.* **1.** place or bin for coal on a ship. **2** a sandy hollow or mound of earth on a golf course, used as an obstacle. **3** fortified shelter, usually underground.

Bunker Hill, hill in Charlestown, Massachusetts. An early battle of the American Revolution was fought near there on June 17, 1775.

bunk·house (bungk'hous'), *n.* rough building with sleeping quarters for laborers.

bun·kum (bung'kəm), *n. Informal.* buncombe.

bun·ny (bun'i), *n., pl.* **–nies. 1** rabbit. **2** squirrel.

Bun·sen burner (bun'sən), a gas burner with a very hot, blue flame, used in laboratories.

bunt (bunt), *v.* **1** strike with the head or horns, as a goat does. **2** push; shove. **3** hit a baseball lightly so that the ball goes to the ground and rolls only a short distance. —*n.* **a** act of bunting. **b** ball that is bunted. —**bunt'er,** *n.*

bun·ting¹ (bun'ting), *n.* **1** a thin cloth used for flags. **2** long pieces of cloth in flag colors and designs, used to decorate buildings and streets on holidays, etc.; flags.

bun·ting² (bun′ting), *n.* a small bird with a stout bill, somewhat like a sparrow.

Bun·yan (bun′yən), *n.* **Paul,** imaginary hero of northwestern lumber camps.

buoy (boi; bü′i), *n.* **1** a floating object anchored in water to warn of hidden dangers or guide through a channel. **2** =life buoy. —*v.* **1** furnish with buoys; mark with a buoy. **2** keep from sinking. **3** *Fig.* hold up; sustain; encourage. [< OF or MDu. < L *boia* fetter]

buoy·an·cy (boi′ən si; bü′yən–), *n.* **1** power to float: *wood has more buoyancy than iron.* **2** power to keep things afloat: *salt water has more buoyancy than fresh water.* **3.** tendency to rise. **4** *Fig.* cheerfulness; hopefulness.

buoy·ant (boi′ənt; bü′yənt), *adj.* **1** able to float. **2** able to keep things afloat: *air is buoyant.* **3** tending to rise. **4** *Fig.* lighthearted; cheerful; hopeful. —**buoy′ant·ly,** *adv.*

bur (bėr), *n., v.,* **burred, bur·ring.** —*n.* **1** prickly, clinging seed case or flower. **2** plant or weed bearing burs. **3** person or thing that clings like a bur. —*v.* remove burs from. Also, **burr.** [prob. < Scand. (Dan.) *borre* burdock]

bur·bot (bėr′bət), *n., pl.* **-bots** or (*esp. collectively*) **-bot.** a freshwater fish with a slender body, related to the cod. [< F *bourbotte* < L *barba* beard; infl. by F *bourbe* mud]

bur·den¹ (bėr′dən), *n.* **1** what is carried; a load (of things, care, work, duty, or sorrow). **2** thing hard to carry or bear; heavy load. **3** quantity of freight that a ship can carry; weight of a ship's cargo. —*v.* **1** put a burden on. **2** load too heavily; oppress. [OE *byrthen*; akin to BEAR¹]

bur·den² (bėr′dən), *n.* **1** main idea or message. **2** repeated verse in a song; chorus; refrain. [< OF *bourdon* humming, drone of bagpipe < LL *burda* pipe]

burden of proof, obligation of proving something to be true.

bur·den·some (bėr′dən səm), *adj.* hard to bear; very heavy; oppressive. —**bur′den·some·ly,** *adv.*

bur·dock (bėr′dok′), *n.* a coarse weed with prickly burs and broad leaves. [< *bur* + *dock*⁴]

bu·reau (byùr′ō), *n., pl.* **bu·reaus, bu·reaux** (byùr′ōz). **1** chest of drawers for clothes. **2** office: *a travel bureau.* **3** division of a government department: *the Weather Bureau.* [< F, desk (orig. cloth-covered) < OF *burel,* dim. of *bure* coarse woolen cloth < LL *burra*]

bu·reauc·ra·cy (byù rok′rə si), *n., pl.* **-cies.** **1** government by groups of officials. **2** officials administering the government. **3** concentration of power in any administrative bureau.

bu·reau·crat (byùr′ə krat), *n.* **1** official in a bureaucracy. **2** pretentious, rigid

government official. [blend of *bureau* + (*auto)crat*] —**bu′reau·crat′ic, bu′reau·crat′i·cal,** *adj.* —**bu′reau·crat′i·cal·ly,** *adv.*

bu·rette, bu·ret (byù ret′), *n.* a graduated glass tube with a valve at the bottom, for measuring out small amounts of a liquid or gas. [< F, dim. of *buire* vase]

burg (bėrg), *n. Informal.* town; city. [var. of *borough*]

bur·geon (bėr′jən), *v., n.* **1** bud; sprout. **2** flourish. [< OF *burjon,* appar. < Gmc.]

bur·ger (bėr′gər), *n.* =hamburger.

-burger, *combining form.* **1** roll with a cooked patty inside: *chickenburger* =*roll with a patty of chicken inside.* **2** hamburger with: *baconburger* =*hamburger with bacon on top.*

bur·gess (bėr′jis), *n.* **1** citizen of a borough. **2** member of the lower house of the colonial legislature in Virginia or Maryland. [< OF < LL *burgensis* citizen. See BOURGEOIS.]

burgh (bėrg), *n.* **1** chartered town in Scotland; borough. **2** =burg. [var. of *borough*] —**burgh′al,** *adj.*

burgh·er (bėr′gər), *n.* citizen of a burgh or town; citizen.

bur·glar (bėr′glər), *n.* person who breaks into a building at night to steal. [< Anglo-L *burglator,* ? partly < OE *burgbryce*]

bur·glar·ize (bėr′glər īz), *v.,* **-ized, -izing.** commit burglary in.

bur·glar·proof (bėr′glər prüf′), *adj.* so strong or safe that burglars cannot break in.

bur·glar·y (bėr′glər i), *n., pl.* **-glar·ies.** breaking into a house, building, etc., to steal or commit some other crime, usually at night.

bur·gle (bėr′gəl), *v.,* **-gled, -gling.** *Informal.* burglarize.

bur·go·mas·ter (bėr′gə mas′tər; –mäs′–), *n.* **1** mayor of a town in the Netherlands, Belgium, Austria, or Germany. **2** large arctic gull. [< Du. *burgemeester* < *burg* borough + *meester* master]

Bur·gun·dy (bėr′gən di), *n., pl.* **-dies.** **1** region in E France. **2** a red or white wine made there. —**Bur·gun′di·an,** *adj., n.*

bur·i·al (ber′i əl), *n.* a burying. —*adj.* having to do with burying: *a burial service.*

burial ground, graveyard; cemetery.

burl (bėrl), *n.* **1** knot in wool, cloth, or wood. **2** a hard, round growth on the trunks of certain trees. —*v.* remove knots from. [< OF < LL *burra* flock of wool] —**burled,** *adj.* —**burl′er,** *n.*

bur·lap (bėr′lap), *n.* a coarse fabric made from jute or hemp, used to make bags, curtains, etc.

bur·lesque (bėr lesk′), *n., v.,* **-lesqued, -les·quing,** *adj.* —*n.* **1** a literary or dramatic composition in which a serious subject is treated ridiculously, or with mock solemnity; parody. **2** *U.S.* a kind of vaudeville that is somewhat coarse and vulgar. —*v.* imitate so as to ridicule.

—*adj.* comical; making people laugh. [< F < Ital. *burlesco* < *burla* jest] —**burlesque′ly,** *adv.* —**bur·les′quer,** *n.*

bur·ley, Bur·ley (bėr′li), *n., pl.* **-leys.** kind of thin-leaved tobacco grown widely in Kentucky. [from a proper name]

bur·ly (bėr′li), *adj.,* **-li·er, -li·est. 1** strong; sturdy; big. **2** bluff; rough. [OE *borlice* excellently] —**bur′li·ly,** *adv.* —**bur′li·ness,** *n.*

Bur·ma (bėr′mə), *n.* former name of Myanmar.

Bur·mese (bėr mēz′; –mēs′), *n., pl.* **-mese,** *adj.* —*n.* **1** native of Burma (Myanmar). **2** language of the people of Myanmar. —*adj.* of Burma, the people, or their language.

burn¹ (bėrn), *v.,* **burned** or **burnt, burning,** *n.* —*v.* **1** be on fire. **2** set on fire. **3** destroy or be destroyed by fire. **4** injure or be injured by fire or heat. **5** make by fire: *sparks burned a hole in the rug.* **6** feel hot. **7** be very excited or inflamed with anger, etc. **8** give light: *lamps were burning in every room.* **9** sunburn; tan. **10** produce, harden, glaze, etc., by fire or heat: *burn bricks.* **11** *Chem.* oxidize. **12** cauterize. —*n.* **1** injury caused by fire or heat. **2** a burned place. [coalescence of OE *beornan* be on fire and OE *bœrnan* consume with fire] —**burn′a·ble,** *adj.*

burn² (bėrn), *n. Scot. and N. Eng.* a small stream; brook. [OE *burna*]

burn·er (bėr′nər), *n.* **1** part of a lamp, stove, etc., where flame is produced. **2** thing that burns or works by burning, as a stove or water heater. **3** person whose work is burning something.

on the back burner, not requiring immediate attention.

burn·ing (bėr′ning), *adj.* **1** glowing; hot. **2** *Fig.* vitally important: *a burning issue.* —**burn′ing·ly,** *adv.*

bur·nish (bėr′nish), *v., n.* polish; shine. [< OF *burnir* make brown, polish < *brun* BROWN]

bur·noose, bur·nous (bėr nüs′; bėr′nüs), *n.* cloak with a hood, worn by Moors and Arabs. [< F < Ar. *burnus*]

burn·out (bėrn′out′), *n.* **1** failure caused by burning or extreme heat. **2 a** extinguishing of the flame in a rocket engine. **b** time when burnout occurs. **3** *Fig.* loss of interest or energy, esp. from fatigue.

Burns (bėrnz), *n.* **Robert,** 1759–96, Scottish poet.

burn·sides, Burn·sides (bėrn′sīdz′), *n.pl.* growth of hair on cheeks but not on the chin. [for Gen. A. E. *Burnside,* American Civil War general]

burnt (bėrnt), *v.* pt. and pp. of **burn¹.**

burr¹ (bėr), *n.* **1** =bur. **2** rough ridge or edge left by a tool on metal, wood, etc., after cutting or drilling. **3** tool that resembles a burr: *dentists use tiny burrs.* **4** rounded growth, as on a tree. —*v.* =bur. [var. of *bur*]

burr² (bėr), *n.* **1** rough pronunciation of *r.* **2** rough pronunciation: *a Scotch burr.*

3 whirring sound. —v. 1 pronounce r roughly. 2 pronounce roughly. 3 make a whirring sound. [prob. imit.]

Burr (bėr), n. Aaron, 1756–1836, vice-president of the United States, 1801–05.

bur·ri·to (bėr rē′tō; bür–), n. rolled tortilla filled with meat, cheese, etc.

bur·ro (bėr′ō; bür′ō), n., pl. **–ros.** small donkey. [< Sp., < burrico small horse < LL burricus]

bur·row (bėr′ō), n. 1 hole dug in the ground by an animal for refuge or shelter. 2 similar dwelling or refuge. —v. 1 dig a hole in the ground. 2 live in burrows. 3 hide. 4 dig. 5 search: burrow in the library for a book. [cf. OE beorg; akin to BOROUGH, BURY] —**bur′row·er,** n.

bur·sa (bėr′sə), n., pl. **–sae** (–sē), **–sas.** sac, esp. one containing a lubricating fluid, as for a joint; pouch; cavity. [< LL < Gk. byrsa wineskin] —**bur′sal,** adj.

bur·sar (bėr′sər; –sär), n. treasurer of a college. [< Med.L bursarius < LL bursa purse]

bur·si·tis (bər sī′tis), n. inflammation of a bursa.

burst (bėrst), v., **burst, burst·ing,** n. —v. 1 fly apart suddenly with force; explode: the bomb burst. 2 be very full: barns bursting with hay. 3 go, come, do, etc., suddenly: burst into the room, burst into laughter. 4 open suddenly: trees burst into bloom. —n. 1 bursting; explosion. 2 sudden issuing forth. 3 sudden display of activity or energy: a burst of speed. [OE berstan] —**burst′er,** n.

bur·y (bėr′i), v., **bur·ied, bur·y·ing.** 1 put (a dead body) in the earth, tomb, etc. 2 perform a funeral service for. 3 cover up; hide. 4 plunge; sink. [OE byrgan] —**bur′i·er,** n.

bus (bus), n., pl. **bus·es, bus·ses,** v., **bused or bussed, bus·ing or bus·sing.** —n. 1 vehicle that carries many passengers along a certain route; omnibus. 2 Informal. any large vehicle. 3 common conductor for multiple electric circuits. 4 conductor for multiple devices on a computer. —v. 1 take or travel by bus. 2 work as a bus boy or girl. [short for omnibus]

bus boy or **girl,** waiter's assistant, who fills glasses, carries off dishes, etc.

bus·by (buz′bi), n., pl. **–bies.** a tall fur hat, worn by certain corps in the British army.

bush[1] (bush), n., v. —n. 1 a woody plant smaller than a tree, often with many separate branches starting from or near the ground. 2 something that resembles or suggests a bush. 3 open forest; uncleared land: take to the bush. —v. spread out like a bush; grow thickly. [ME busch, busk]

bush[2] (bush), n. a bushing. —v. put a bushing in. [< MDu. busse BOX[1]]

Bush (bush). 1 **George Herbert Walker** 1924–, 41st president of the United States, 1989–93. 2 **George Walker,** 1946–, 43rd president of the United States, 2001–.

bushed (busht), adj. worn-out

bush·el (bush′əl), n. 1 measure for grain, fruit, vegetables, and other dry things, equal to 4 pecks or 32 quarts. 2 container that holds a bushel. [< OF boissiel, dim. of boisse a measure]

bush·ing (bush′ing), n. 1 metal lining. 2 removable metal lining used as a bearing.

bush league, 1 minor baseball league. 2 any person or thing of minor importance.

bush·man (buush′mən), n., pl. **–men.** 1 settler in the Australian bush. 2 person who knows much about life in the bush. 3 **Bushman,** member of a South African tribe of roving hunters.

bush·mas·ter (bush′mas′tər; –mäs′–), n. a large, poisonous snake of tropical America.

bush pilot, pilot who flies a small plane over relatively unsettled country, as Alaska.

bush·whack (buush′hwak′), v. 1 live or work in the backwoods. 2 fight or attack as a guerrilla or bushwhacker.

bush·whack·er (buush′hwak′ər), n. 1 frontiersman. 2 guerrilla fighter. —**bush′whack′ing,** n.

bush·y (bush′i), adj., **bush·i·er, bush·i·est.** 1 spreading out like a bush; growing thickly. 2 overgrown with bushes. —**bush′i·ness,** n.

bus·i·ly (biz′ə li), adv. in a busy manner.

busi·ness (biz′nis), n. 1 thing that one is busy at, work. 2 matter; affair. 3 buying and selling; trade. 4 commercial enterprise: a bakery business. 5 concern: not your business.

business as usual, in the usual way, esp. by ignoring problems or difficulties.

get down to business, deal with important matters.

mean business, be serious.

mind one's own business, focus on one's own affairs. [< busy + –ness]

business college or **school,** school that gives training in computer programming, bookkeeping, and other business subjects.

busi·ness·like (biz′nis līk′), adj. systematic; well-managed; practical.

busi·ness·man (biz′nis man′), n., pl. **–men.** 1 man in business. 2 man who runs a business.

busi·ness·wom·an (biz′nis wum′ən), n., pl. **–wom·en.** 1 woman in business. 2 woman who runs a business.

bus·kin (bus′kin), n. 1 high shoe with a very thick sole, worn by Greek and Roman actors of tragedies. 2 tragedy; tragic drama. 3 high boot worn long ago. [cf. OF brouzequin] —**bus′kined,** adj.

bus·man's holiday (bus′mənz), holiday spent in doing what one does at one's daily work.

buss (bus), v., n. = kiss.

bus·ses (bus′iz), n. a pl. of bus.

bust[1] (bust), n. 1 statue of a person's head, shoulders, and chest. 2 the upper, front part of the body. 3 a woman's bosom. [< F < Ital. < L bustum funeral monument]

bust[2] (bust), n. Informal. 1 burst. 2 total failure; bankruptcy. 3 punch. 4 arrest. 5 spree. —v. 1 burst. 2 bankrupt; ruin. 3 fail financially; become bankrupt. 4 lower in rank, esp. to punish. 5 punch; hit. 6 train to obey; tame, as a wild colt. 7 break up (a trust) into smaller companies. 8 arrest; jail. [var. of burst]

bus·tard (bus′tərd), n. a large game bird of Africa, Europe, and Asia. [blend of OF bistarde and oustarde, both < L avis tarda slow bird]

bus·tle[1] (bus′əl), v., **–tled, –tling,** n. —v. 1 be noisily busy and in a hurry. 2 make (others) hurry or work hard. —n. noisy or excited activity; commotion. [? imit.] —**bus′tler,** n. —**bus′tling·ly,** adv.

bus·tle[2] (bus′əl), n. pad used to puff out the upper back part of a woman's skirt. [? special use of bustle[1]]

bus·y (biz′i), adj., **bus·i·er, bus·i·est,** v., **bus·ied, bus·y·ing.** adj. 1 working; active. 2 of a telephone line, in use. 3 full of work or activity. 4 prying into other people's affairs; meddling. —v. make busy; keep busy. [OE bisig] —**bus′y·ness,** n.

bus·y·bod·y (biz′i bod′i), n., pl. **–bod·ies.** person who pries into other people's affairs.

busy work, something unimportant done to keep busy; make-work.

but (but; unstressed bət), conj. 1 on the other hand; yet: it rained, but I went anyway. 2 if; except that: it never rains but it pours. 3 other than: we cannot choose but hear. 4 who not; which not: none sought his aid but were helped. —prep. except: every day but Sunday. —adv. only: he is but a boy. —n. objection: too many buts.

all but, nearly; almost. [OE būtan without, unless < be– + ūtan outside < ūt OUT]

bu·ta·di·ene (bū′tə dī′ēn; –dī ēn′), n. 1 a colorless gas, C_4H_6, used in making artificial rubber and as an anesthetic. 2 its isomeric hydrocarbon.

bu·tane (bū′tān; bū tān′), n. Chem. either of two isomeric hydrocarbons, C_4H_{10}, of the methane series. Both are inflammable gases.

butch·er (buch′ər), n. 1 person who cuts up and sells meat. 2 person whose work is killing animals for food. 3 brutal killer; murderer. 4 person who bungles or botches. —v. 1 kill (animals) for food. 2 kill wholesale; slaughter large numbers of people or animals. 3 kil brutally; murder. 4 spoil by poor work. [< OF bocher < boc he-goat, BUCK[1] < Gmc.] —**butch′er·er,** n.

butch·er·y (buch′ər i), n., pl. **–er·ies.** 1 brutal killing; wholesale murder. 2 slaughterhouse; butcher shop.

but·ler (but′lər), *n.* male servant in charge of the pantry and table service in a household; head servant. [< AF var. of OF *bouteillier* < *bouteille* BOTTLE] —**but′ler·ship,** *n.*

butler's pantry, a small room between the kitchen and dining room, for serving and clearing the table.

butt[1] (but), *n.* **1** the thicker end of anything, as a tool, weapon, ham, etc. **2** end that is left; stub; stump. [akin to BUTTOCKS]

butt[2] (but), *n.* **1** target. **2** object of ridicule or scorn. **3** embankment of earth on which targets are placed for shooting practice. —*v.* join end to end; abut. [< F *bout* end < Gmc.]

butt[3] (but), *v.* push or hit with the head or horns. —*n.* push or hit with the head. **butt in,** meddle; interfere. [< OF *bouter* thrust < *bout* end < Gmc.] —**butt′er,** *n.*

butt[4] (but), *n.* **1** a large barrel for wine or beer. **2** a liquid measure equal to 126 gallons. [< OF < LL *butta*]

butte (būt), *n. W U.S.* steep hill standing alone.

but·ter (but′ər), *n.* **1** the solid yellowish fat obtained from cream by churning. **2** something with the consistency of butter, as apple butter. **3** excessive flattery. —*v.* **1** put butter on. **2** flatter, excessively. **butter up,** flatter. [< L < Gk. *boutyron*] —**but′ter·less,** *adj.*

butter bean, 1 variety of lime bean. **2** yellow wax bean.

but·ter·cup (but′ər kup′), *n.* plant with bright-yellow flowers shaped like cups.

but·ter·fat (but′ər fat′), *n.* fat in milk.

but·ter·fin·gers (but′ər fing′gərz), *n. Informal.* careless or clumsy person. —**but′ter·fin′gered,** *adj.*

but·ter·fish (but′ər fish′), *n., pl.* **-fish·es** or (*esp. collectively*) **-fish.** a small, silvery fish, used for food.

but·ter·fly (but′ər flī), *n., pl.* **-flies. 1** insect with a slender body and four large, usually bright-colored, wings. **2** person who suggests a butterfly by delicate beauty, bright clothes, fickleness, etc. **3** =butterfly stroke.

butterflies (in the stomach), nervousness, esp. in anticipation of something. [OE *buterflēoge.* See BUTTER, FLY[1].]

butterfly stroke, overarm breaststroke, in swimming.

but·ter·milk (but′er milk′), *n.* liquid left when butter is churned from cream, used as a beverage and in baking.

but·ter·nut (but′ər nut′), *n.* **1** an oily kind of walnut. **2** tree that bears butternuts.

but·ter·scotch (but′ər skoch′), *n.* sauce or candy made from brown sugar and butter. —*adj.* flavored with brown sugar and butter.

but·ter·y[1] (but′ər i), *adj.* **1** like butter. **2** containing butter; spread with butter.

but·ter·y[2] (but′ər i; but′ri), *n., pl.* **-ter·ies. 1** storeroom, esp. for wines and liquors. **2** =pantry. [< OF, < *botte* BUTT[4]]

but·tocks (but′əks), *n.pl.* =rump. [ME *buttok.* Cf. OE *buttuc* end, small piece of land]

but·ton (but′ən), *n.* **1** knob or round, flat piece of metal, plastic, etc., sewn onto clothing, bags, etc. to hold them closed or decorate them. **2** anything that resembles or suggests a button, as the knob or disk pressed to ring an electric bell. **3** knob on a stringed instrument that holds the tailpiece. —*v.* fasten with buttons; close with buttons. [< OF *boton* < *bouter* thrust. See BUTT[3].] —**but′ton·er,** *n.* —**but′ton·less,** *adj.* —**but′ton·like′,** *adj.*

but·ton·hole (but′ən hōl′), *n., v.,* **-holed, -hol·ing.** —*n.* slit or loop through which a button is passed. —*v.* **1** make buttonholes in **2** hold in conversation; force to listen.

but·ton·wood (but′ən wùd′), *n.* **1** tall plane tree with button-shaped fruit. **2** its wood.

but·tress (but′ris), *n.* **1** support built against a wall or building to strengthen it. **2** support; prop. —*v.* **1** strengthen with a buttress. **2** support; prop. [< OF *bouterez* (pl.) < *bouter* thrust against. See BUTT[3].]

bu·tyl (bū′təl), *n.* univalent hydrocarbon radical obtained from butane and used in making inner tubes and electrical insulation.

bu·tyr·ic (bū tir′ik), *adj.* of or derived from butyric acid. [< L *butyrum* butter]

butyric acid, colorless liquid, $C_4H_8O_2$, that has an unpleasant odor. It is formed by fermentation in rancid butter, cheese, etc.

bux·om (buk′səm), *adj.* plump and good to look at; healthy and cheerful. [ME *buhsum,* ? < OE *būgan* bend] —**bux′om·ly,** *adv.* —**bux′om·ness,** *n.*

buy (bī), *v.,* **bought, buy·ing,** *n.* —*v.* **1** get by paying a price. **2** get by sacrifice: *buy peace by surrender.* **3** bribe. —*n. Informal.* **1** a purchase. **2** a bargain.

buy off, get rid of by paying money to.

buy out, buy all the shares, rights, etc., of.

buy up, buy all that one can of. [OE *bycgan*]

buy·er (bī′ər), *n.* **1** person who buys; customer. **2** person whose work is buying goods for a department store or other business.

buyer's strike, refusal of consumers as a group to buy in protest against high prices.

buzz (buz), *n.* **1** humming sound made by flies, mosquitoes, or bees. **2** a low, confused sound of many people talking quietly. **3** whisper; rumor. **4** stir, esp. talk about something new or interesting. **5** telephone call. —*v.* **1** hum loudly. **2** sound in a low, confused way. **3** talk excitedly. **4** whisper; rumor. **5** fly a plane low and fast over something.

buzz about, move about busily.

buzz off, *Informal.* go away; leave. [imit.]

buz·zard (buz′ərd), *n.* **1** any of various heavy and slow-moving hawks. **2** =turkey buzzard. **3** mean, stingy person, esp. an older person. [< OF *busart,* ult. < L *buteo* hawk]

buzz bomb, robot bomb developed by the Germans in World War II.

buzz·er (buz′ər), *n.* **1** thing that buzzes. **2** electrical device that makes a buzzing sound as a signal.

buzz saw, circular saw.

buzz word, popular, overused word.

bx., *pl.* **bxs.** box.

by (bī), *prep.* **1** near: *by the house.* **2.** along; over; through: *go by the bridge.* **3** through the act or use of: *travel by airplane.* **4** in dimensions: *a room ten by twenty feet.* **5** in the measure of: *eggs by the dozen.* **6** according to: *work by rule.* **7** during: *by day.* **8** not later than: *by six o'clock.* —*adv.* **1** at hand: *near by.* **2** past: *a car dashed by; days gone by.* **3** aside or away: *to put something by.* —*n.* bye.

by and by, after a while.

by and large, in every way. [OE *bī,* unstressed *be*]

by–, *prefix.* **1** secondary; minor; less important, as in *by-product.* **2** near by, as in *bystander.*

bye (bī), *n., adj.* —*n.* **1** odd man or condition of being the odd player esp. in a tournament where players are grouped in pairs. **2** in golf, holes not played after a player has won. —*adj.* **1** aside from the main point, subject, etc. **2** secondary. **3** incidental. Also **by.**

by the bye, incidentally. [var. of *by,* prep.]

bye-bye (bī′bī′), *interj.* =good-by.

by-e·lec·tion (bī′i lek′shən), *n.* a special election, not held at the time of regular elections.

by·gone (bī′gôn′; -gon′), *adj.* past; former. —*n.* **1** something in the past. **2** the past.

let bygones be bygones, forgive and forget.

by·law (bī′lô′), *n.* **1** law made by a city, company, club, etc., for the control of its own affairs. **2** a secondary law or rule; not one of the main rules. [< Scand. (Dan.) *bylov* < *by* town + *lov* LAW; meaning infl. by BY–]

by-line (bī′līn′), *n.* line at the beginning of a newspaper or magazine article giving the name of the writer.

by-name (bī′nām′), *n.* **1** second name. **2** =nickname.

by-pass (bī′pas′; -päs′), *n.* **1** road, channel, pipe, etc., providing a secondary passage to be used instead of the main passage. **2** =shunt (def. 3). —*v.* **1** provide a secondary passage for. **2** go around. **3** pass over the head of (a superior, etc.) to a higher authority. **4** set aside or ignore (regulations, etc.) in order to reach a desired objective. **5** get away from; avoid; escape: *by-pass a question.* **6** =flank (def. 4).

by-path (bī′path′; -päth′), *n.* side path.

by-play (bī′plā ′), *n.* action that is not part of the main action, esp. on the stage.

by-prod·uct (bī′prod ′əkt), *n.* something produced in making or doing something else; not the main product.

by-road (bī′rōd ′), *n.* a side road.

By·ron (bī′rən), *n.* **George Gordon, Lord,** 1788–1824, English poet. —**By·ron′ic,** *adj.* —**By·ron′i·cal·ly,** *adv.*

by·stand·er (bī′stan ′dər), *n.* person standing near or by; looker-on.

by-street (bī′strēt ′), *n.* a side street.

byte (bīt), *n.* unit of digital information, equal to eight bits, in a computer memory.

by·word (bī′wėrd ′), *n.* **1** object of contempt; thing scorned. **2** common saying; proverb.

Byz·an·tine (biz′ən tēn; –tīn; bi zan′tin), *adj.* **1** having to do with Byzantium or a style of architecture developed there that uses round arches, crosses, circles, domes, and mosaics. **2** of or having to do with the Eastern Church. **3** filled with intrigue and scheming, suggestive of the politics of Byzantium. —*n.* native or inhabitant of Byzantium.

Byzantine Empire, eastern part of the Roman Empire from A.D. 395 to 1453.

By·zan·ti·um (bi zan′shi əm; –ti əm), *n.* ancient city where Istanbul now is.

C

C, c (sē), *n., pl.* **C's; c's.**
1 the third letter of the alphabet. 2 the first note of the musical scale of C major. 3 Roman numeral for 100.

C, 1 carbon. 2 central. 3 copyright. 4 a hundred-dollar bill.

C., 1 Cape. 2 Catholic. 3 centigrade.

c., 1 carton; cartons. 2 case. 3 cent; cents. 4 center. 5 centimeter. 6 Also, **ca.** approximately. [L *circa* or *circum*] 7 cubic. 8 cup.

CA, *(zip code)* California.

Ca., calcium.

CAA, Civil Aeronautics Administration.

Caa·ba (kä′bə), *n.* Kaaba.

cab (kab), *n.* 1 =taxicab. 2 covered part of a locomotive where the engineer sits. 3 enclosed seat on a truck for the driver. [for *cabriolet*]

ca·bal (kə bal′), *n., v.,* **-balled, -bal·ling.** —*n.* 1 a small group of people working or plotting in secret. 2 a secret scheme of such a group. —*v.* form such a group; conspire. [see CABALA]

cab·a·la (kab′ə lə; kə bä′–), *n.* 1 a secret religious philosophy of the Jewish rabbis. 2 a mystical belief. Also, **cabbala.** [< Med.L < Heb. *qabbalah* tradition] —**cab′a·lism,** *n.* —**cab′a·list,** *n.*

cab·a·lis·tic (kab′ə lis′tik), **cab·a·lis·ti·cal** (–tə kəl), *adj.* having a mystical meaning; secret. —**cab′a·lis′ti·cal·ly,** *adv.*

cab·al·le·ro (kab′əl yär′ō), *n., pl.* **-ros.** 1 *SW U.S.* horseman or gallant. 2 in Spain, gentleman or knight. [< Sp. < L *caballarius* horseman < *caballus* horse]

ca·ba·ña (kə bä′nyə; –ban′ə), *n.* 1 bathhouse. 2 cabin (def. 1). [< Sp. < LL *capanna*. Doublet of CABIN.]

cab·a·ret (kab′ə rā′; kab′ə rā), *n.* 1 restaurant where an entertainment of singing and dancing is provided. 2 the entertainment. [< F]

cab·bage (kab′ij), *n.,* vegetable whose leaves are closely folded into a round head that grows from a short stem. [< F < Pr., ult. < L *caput* head]

cab·ba·la (kab′ə lə; kə bä′-), *n.* =cabala.

cab·by (kab′i), *n., pl.* **-bies.** cabdriver.

cab·in (kab′ən), *n.* 1 a small, roughly built house; hut. 2 room in a ship. 3 place for passengers in an aircraft. [< F < LL *capanna*. Doublet of CABANA.]

cabin boy, boy whose work was waiting on the officers and passengers in a ship.

cab·i·net (kab′ə nit), *n.* 1 piece of furniture with shelves or drawers for holding dishes, etc. 2 group of advisers chosen by the head of a nation to help with the administration of the government. 3 **the Cabinet,** the cabinet of the President of the United States. 4 a small, private room.—*adj.* 1 of or having to do with a political cabinet. 2 private. [< F < Ital. *gabinetto*, ult. < LL *cavea* CAGE]

cab·i·net·mak·er (kab′ə nit māk′ ər), *n.* person who makes fine furniture and woodwork. —**cab′i·net-mak′ing,** *n.*

cab·i·net·work (kab′ə nit wėrk′), *n.* 1 beautifully made furniture and woodwork. 2 the making of such furniture and woodwork.

ca·ble (kā′bəl), *n., v.,* **-bled, -bling.** —*n.* 1 a strong, thick rope, usually made of wires twisted together. 2 =cable's length. 3 a protected bundle of wires to carry current. 4 =cable television. 5 =cablegram. —*v.* 1 tie or fasten with a cable. 2 send a message by cable. [< F < Pr. < L *capulum* halter]

cable car, car pulled by a moving cable operated by a stationary engine.

ca·ble·cast (kā′bəl kast′), *n., v.* —*n.* a telecast by cable television. —*v.* telecast by cable television. —**ca′ble·cast′ing,** *n.*

ca·ble·gram (kā′bəl gram), *n.* telegram sent by cable.

cable's length, unit of measurement at sea, 720 ft.

cable stitch, knitting in a pattern that resembles a twisted cable.

ca·ble-stitch (kā′bəl stitch′), *v.,* knit using cable stitch.

cable television, transmission of television programs by cable to individual subscribers.

cable TV, =cable television.

cab·man (kab′mən), *n., pl.* **-men.** a cabdriver.

ca·boo·dle (kə bü′dəl), *n. Informal.* group of people or things.

ca·boose (kə büs′), *n.* 1 a small car formerly on a freight train in which the trainmen could rest and sleep. 2 kitchen on the deck of a ship. [< MLG *kabuse* cabin]

Cab·ot (kab′ət), *n.* **John,** 1450?–98, Italian navigator who explored for England, reaching the North American continent in 1497.

cab·ri·o·let (kab′ri ə lā′), *n.* a one-horse carriage with two wheels, and often with a folding top. [< F, < *cabrioler* leap < Ital. < L *caper* goat; from bouncing motion]

ca·ca·o (kə kā′ō; –kä′ō), *n., pl.* **-ca·os.** 1 seeds from which cocoa and chocolate are made. 2 the tropical American tree they grow on. [< Sp. < Mex. *caca-uatl*]

cach·a·lot (kash′ə lot; –lō), *n.* sperm whale. [< F < Pg. < L *caccabus* pot]

cache (kash), *n., v.,* **cached, cach·ing.** —*n.* 1 a hiding place to store food or supplies. 2 a hidden store of food or supplies. —*v.* put in a cache; hide. [< F, < *cacher* hide]

ca·chet (ka shā′; kash′ā), *n.* 1 a private seal or stamp. 2 a distinguishing mark. [< F, < *cacher* hide]

cach·in·nate (kak′ə nāt), *v.,* **-nat·ed, -nat·ing.** laugh loudly. [< L *cachinnatus*] —**cach′in·na′tion,** *n.*

ca·cique (kə sēk′), *n.* 1 a native chief in the West Indies, Mexico, etc. 2 pompous political leader. [< Sp. < Haitian]

cack·le (kak′əl), *v.,* **-led, -ling,** *n.* —*v.* 1 make a shrill, broken sound. 2 laugh shrilly, harshly, and brokenly. 3 chatter. —*n.* 1 the shrill, broken sound that a hen makes after laying an egg. 2 shrill, harsh, broken laughter. 3 noisy chatter; silly talk. [ME *cakelen*; imit.]

ca·coph·o·ny (kə kof′ə ni), *n., pl.* **-nies.** harsh, clashing sound; dissonance; discord. [< NL < Gk., < *kakos* bad + *phone* sound] —**ca·coph′o·nous,** *adj.* —**ca·coph′o·nous·ly,** *adv.*

cac·tus (kak′təs), *n., pl.* **-tus·es, -ti** (–tī). plant whose thick, fleshy stems have spines but usually have no leaves. Most cactuses grow in very hot, dry regions. [< L < Gk. *kaktos*]

cad (kad), *n.* an ill-bred person. [< *caddie*]

ca·dav·er (kə dav′ər; –dā′vər), *n.* dead body; corpse. [< L] —**ca·dav′er·ic,** *adj.*

ca·dav·er·ous (kə dav′ər əs), *adj.* 1 of or like a cadaver. 2 pale and ghastly. 3 thin and worn. —**ca·dav′er·ous·ly,** *adv.* —**ca·dav′er·ous·ness,** *n.*

cad·die (kad′i), *n., v.,* **-died, -dy·ing.** —*n.* person who carries a golf player's clubs, etc. —*v.* help a golf player in this way. Also, **caddy.** [< F *cadet* CADET]

cad·dis fly (kad′is), a mothlike insect whose larvae (**caddis worms**) live under water in cocoons that are coated with sand, gravel, etc.

cad·dish (kad′ish), *adj.* ungentlemanly; ill-bred. —**cad′dish·ly,** *adv.* —**cad′dish·ness,** *n.*

cad·dy[1] (kad′i), *n., pl.* **-dies.** a small box, can, or chest. [< Malay *kati* a small weight]

cad·dy[2] (kad′i), *n., pl.* **-dies,** *v.,* **-died, -dy·ing.** =caddie.

ca·dence (kā′dəns), **ca·den·cy** (–dən si), *n., pl.,* **-den·ces; -cies.** 1 rhythm. 2 measure or beat or any rhythmical movement. 3 fall of the voice. 4 rising and falling sound; modulation. 5 series of chords, a trill, etc., that brings part of a piece of music to an end. [< F < Ital. See CADENZA.] —**ca′denced,** *adj.*

ca·den·za (kə den′zə), *n.* an elaborate flourish or showy musical passage near the end of an aria, concerto, etc. [< Ital. < L *cadentia* < *cadere* fall]

ca·det (kə det′), *n.* 1 a young person training to be an officer in the military. 2 a younger son or brother. [< F < Gascon *capdet* < L *capitellum*, dim. of *caput* head] —**ca·det′ship, ca·det′cy,** *n.*

cadge (kaj), *v.,* **cadged, cadg·ing.** *Informal.* beg. —**cadg′er,** *n.*

ca·di (kä′di; kā′–), *n., pl.* **-dis.** a minor Muslim judge. Also, **kadi.** [< Ar. *qāḍī* judge]

Cá·diz (kə diz′; kā′diz), *n.* seaport in SW Spain.

cad·mi·um (kad′mi əm), *n.* a bluish-white, ductile metallic element, Cd, resembling tin, used in making certain alloys. [< NL < L *cadmia* zinc ore < Gk. *kadmeia*] —**cad′mic,** *adj.*

ca·dre (kä′dər; kad′r), *n.* 1 a small group of people who form the core of an organization or a military unit. 2 =framework. [< F < Ital. < L *quadrum* square]

ca·du·ce·us (kə dü′si əs; –dū′–), *n., pl.* **–ce·i** (–sī ī). staff carried by the god Hermes and by heralds in ancient Greece and Rome, now often used as an emblem of the medical profession. [< L < dial. Gk. *karykeion* herald's staff] —**ca·du′ce·an,** *adj.*

cae·cum (sē′kəm), *n., pl.* **–ca** (–kə). = cecum.

Cae·sar (sē′zər), *n.* **1 Gaius Julius,** 102?–44 B.C., Roman general, statesman, and historian, conqueror of Gaul. **2** a title of the Roman emperors from Augustus to Hadrian. **3** an emperor. **4** dictator; tyrant.

Cae·sar·e·an, Cae·sar·i·an (si zār′i ən), *adj.* of Julius Caesar or the Caesars. —*n.* =cesarean section. Also, **Cesarean, Cesarian.**

caesarean section, =cesarean section.

cae·si·um (sē′zi əm), *n.* =cesium.

cae·su·ra (si zhůr′ə; –zyůr′ə), *n., pl.* **–sur·as, –sur·ae** (–zhůr′ē; –zyůr′ē). a break, esp. a pause in a line of poetry. Also, **cesura.** [< L, cutting, < *caedere* cut] —**cae·sur′al,** *adj.*

ca·fe (ka fā′; kə–), *n.*, **1** restaurant. **2** barroom. [< F. See COFFEE.]

ca·fé (ka fē′; kə–, ká–), *n.* **1** =cafe. **2** *French.* coffee. **3** =coffeehouse.

caf·e·te·ri·a (kaf′ə tir′i ə), *n.* restaurant where people wait on themselves. [< Mex. Sp., coffee shop]

caf·feine, caf·fein (kaf′ēn; kaf′i in), *n.* a stimulating drug, $C_8H_{10}N_4O_2$, found in coffee and tea. [< F, < *café* coffee]

caf·tan (kaf′tən; kåf tän′), *n.* **1** a long tunic with a girdle, worn under the coat in Turkey, Egypt, etc. **2** woman's loose, long gown, worn as evening dress or for lounging. Also, **kaftan.** [< Turk.]

cage (kāj), *n., v.,* **caged, cag·ing.** —*n.* **1** frame or place closed in with wires, bars, etc., for confining birds, wild animals, etc. **2** thing shaped like a cage, as the closed platform of an elevator. **3** prison. —*v.* put or keep in a cage. [< F < L *cavea* cell < *cavus* hollow]

cag·ey (kāj′i), *adj.* **cag·i·er, cag·i·est.** *Informal.* shrewd; sharp. —**cag′i·ly,** *adv.* —**cag′i·ness,** *n.*

ca·hoot (kə hüt′), *n. Informal.* **in cahoots,** in company or league.

ca·ique or **ca·ïque** (kä ēk′), **1** long, narrow Turkish rowboat. **2** small Mediterranean sailing vessel.

cai·man (kā′mən), *n., pl.* **–mans.** large alligator of tropical America. Also, **cay·man.**

Cain (kān), *n.* **1** the oldest son of Adam and Eve, who killed his brother Abel. **2** murderer.
raise Cain, *Informal.* make a great disturbance.

cairn (kärn), *n.* **1** pile of stones heaped up as a memorial, tomb, or landmark. **2 cairn terrier,** small, wiry-haired terrier, originally from Scotland. [< Scotch Gaelic *carn* heap of stones] —**cairned,** *adj.*

Cai·ro (kī′rō), *n.* capital of Egypt, in the NE part.

cais·son (kā′sən; –son), *n.* **1** wagon to carry ammunition. **2** a watertight box or chamber in which people can work under water. **3** a watertight float used in raising sunken ships. [< F, < *caisse* chest < L *capsa* box]

caisson disease, =the bends.

ca·jole (kə jōl′), *v.,* **–joled, –jol·ing.** persuade by pleasant words, flattery, or false promises; coax. [< F *cajoler*] —**ca·jol′er,** *n.*

ca·jol·er·y (kə jōl′ər i), *n., pl.* **–er·ies.** persuasion by smooth, deceitful words; flattery; coaxing.

Ca·jun (kā′jən), *n.* descendant of the French who come to Louisiana from Acadia. [<altered pronunciation of *Acadian*]

cake (kāk), *n., v.,* **caked, cak·ing.** —*n.* **1** a baked mixture of flour, sugar, eggs, flavoring, and other things. **2** a flat, thin mass of dough baked or fried. **3** any small, flat mass of food fried on both sides: *a fish cake.* **4** a shaped mass: *a cake of soap.* —*v.* form into a solid mass.
piece of cake, *Informal.* something easy to do or obtain.
take the cake, *Informal.* **a** win first prize. **b** excel; surpass. [prob. < Scand. *kaka*]

cakes and ale, pleasures of life.

cake·walk (kāk′wôk′), *n.* **1** a march or dance to music of black American origin, to see who could do the most graceful or eccentric steps. **2** *Fig.* something sure and easy; cinch. —*v.* do a cakewalk. —**cake′walk·er,** *n.*

cal or **cal.** **1** calendar. **2** caliber. **3** calorie or calories.

Cal., California.

cal·a·bash (kal′ə bash), *n.* **1** gourd or fruit whose dried shell is used to make bottles, bowls, drums, rattles, etc. **2** a tropical plant or tree that it grows on. **3** bottle, bowl, etc., made from such a dried shell. [< F < Sp., prob. < Pers. *kharbuz* melon]

cal·a·boose (kal′ə büs; kal′ə büs′), *n. Esp. S U.S. Informal.* jail; prison. [< Sp. *calabozo* dungeon]

ca·la·di·um (kə lā′di əm), *n.* a tropical plant with large leaves. [< Malay *kelady*]

Cal·ais (ka lā′; kal′ā), *n.* seaport in N France that is nearest England.

cal·a·mine (kal′ə mīn; –min), *n.* native hydrous zinc silicate, $(ZnOH)_2SiO_3$. [< F < Med.L *calamina* < L *cadmia.* See CADMIUM.]

ca·lam·i·tous (kə lam′ə təs), *adj.* causing calamity; accompanied by calamity; disastrous. —**ca·lam′i·tous·ly,** *adv.* —**ca·lam′i·tous·ness,** *n.*

ca·lam·i·ty (kəlam′ə ti), *n., pl.* **–ties. 1** a great misfortune. **2** serious trouble; misery. [< L *calamitas*]

cal·a·mus (kal′ə məs), *n., pl.* **–mi** (–mī). **1** =sweet flag. **2** its fragrant root. [< L < Gk. *kalamos* reed]

cal·car·e·ous (kal kār′i əs), *adj.* **1** of or containing lime or limestone. **2** of or containing calcium. [< L, < *calx* lime]

cal·ces (kal′sēz), *n.* pl. of calx.

cal·cif·er·ous (kal sif′ər əs), *adj.* **1** containing calcite. **2** forming calcium salts.

cal·ci·fy (kal′sə fī), *v.,* **–fied, –fy·ing. 1** harden by the deposit of lime. **2** *Fig.* harden; become fixed, as an idea or opinion. [< L *calx* lime] —**cal′ci·fi·ca′tion,** *n.*

cal·ci·mine (kal′sə mīn; –min), *n., v.,* **–mined, –min·ing.** —*n.* a white or colored liquid consisting of a mixture of water, coloring matter, glue, etc., used as a wash on ceilings and walls. —*v.* cover with calcimine. Also, **kalsomine.**

cal·cine (kal′sīn; –sin), *v.,* **–cined, –cin·ing. 1** burn to ashes or powder. **2** change to lime by heating. —**cal′ci·na′tion,** *n.* —**cal·cin′a·to′ry** *adj., n.*

cal·cite (kal′sīt), *n.* mineral composed of calcium carbonate, $CaCO_3$. It occurs as limestone, chalk, marble, etc.

cal·ci·um (kal′si əm), *n.* a soft, silvery-white metallic element, Ca. It is a part of limestone, milk, bones, etc. [< L *calx* lime]

calcium carbide, a heavy gray substance, CaC_2, that reacts with water to form acetylene gas.

calcium carbonate, mineral, $CaCO_3$, occurring in rocks as marble and limestone and in animals as bones, shells, teeth, etc.

calcium chloride, compound of calcium and chlorine, $CaCl_2$, used in making artificial ice and chlorine.

cal·cu·la·ble (kal′kyə lə bəl), *adj.* **1** that can be calculated. **2** reliable. —**cal′cu·la·bil′i·ty,** *n.* —**cal′cu·la·bly,** *adv.*

cal·cu·late (kal′kyə lāt), *v.,* **–lat·ed, –lat·ing. 1** find out by adding, subtracting, multiplying, or dividing; figure; compute. **2** find out beforehand by any process of reasoning; estimate. **3** rely; depend; count. **4** plan; intend. [< L, < *calculus* stone, used in counting, dim. of *calx* stone] —**cal′cu·la′tor,** *n.*

calculated risk, venture or undertaking whose outcome can be estimated with some degree of confidence but not with certainty.

cal·cu·lat·ing (kal′kyə lāt′ing), *adj.* **1** that calculates. **2** shrewd; careful. **3** scheming; selfish.

cal·cu·la·tion (kal′kyə lā′shən), *n.* **1** act of calculating. **2** result found by calculating. **3** careful thinking; deliberate planning. —**cal′cu·la′tive,** *adj.*

cal·cu·lus (kal′kyə ləs), *n., pl.* **–li** (–lī), **–lus·es. 1** a method of calculation in higher mathematics. **2** *Fig.* analysis of various factors to predict the probable outcome of a particular undertaking or situation. **3** a stone that has formed in the body because of a diseased condition. Gallstones are calculi. [see CALCULATE]

Cal·cut·ta (kal kut′ə), *n.* seaport in E India.

cal·de·ra (kal dir′ə), *n.* dish-shaped depression at the top of a volcano's cone.

cal·dron (kôl′drən), *n.* a large kettle or boiler. Also, **cauldron.** [< OF < L *caldus* hot]

Cal·e·do·ni·a (kal′ə dō′ni ə), *n. Poetic.* Scotland. —**Cal′e·do′ni·an,** *adj.*

cal·en·dar (kal′ən dər), *n.* **1** table showing the months, weeks, and days of the year. **2** system by which the beginning, length, and divisions of the year are fixed. **3** list; record; schedule: *a court calendar.* —*v.* enter in a calendar or list. [< AF < L *calendarium* account book < *calendae* calends (day bills were due)]

calendar day, the 24 hours from one midnight to the next midnight.

calendar month, month.

calendar year, period of 365 days (or in leap year, 366 days) that begins on January 1 and ends on December 31.

cal·en·der (kal′ən dər), *n.* machine in which cloth, paper, etc., is smoothed and glazed by pressing between rollers. —*v.* make smooth and glossy by pressing in a calender. [< F < L < Gk. *kylindros* cylinder] —**cal′en·der·er,** *n.*

cal·ends (kal′əndz), *n.pl.* the first day of the month in the ancient Roman calendar. Also, **kalends.** [< L *calendae*]

ca·len·du·la (kə len′jə lə), *n.* kind of marigold with yellow or orange flowers. [< NL, dim. of *calendae* the calends]

calf¹ (kaf; käf), *n., pl.* **calves. 1** a young cow or bull. **2** a young elephant, whale, seal, etc. **3** leather made from the skin of a calf. [OE *calf*]

calf² (kaf; käf), *n., pl.* **calves.** the thick, fleshy part of the back of the leg below the knee. [< Scand. *kálfi*]

calf·skin (kaf′skin′; käf′–), *n.* **1** skin of a calf. **2** leather made from it.

cal·i·ber (kal′ə bər), *n.* **1** diameter, esp. inside diameter. A .45-caliber revolver has a barrel with an inside diameter of ⁴⁵/₁₀₀ of an inch. **2** *Fig.* amount of ability. **3** *Fig.* amount of merit or importance. [< F < Ar. *qālib* mold]

cal·i·brate (kal′ə brāt), *v.,* **–brat·ed, –brat·ing. 1** determine, check, or rectify the scale of (a thermometer, gauge, or other measuring instrument). **2** find the caliber of. —**cal′i·bra′tion,** *n.* —**cal′i·bra′tor,** *n.*

cal·i·co kal′ə kō), *n., pl.* **–coes, –cos,** *adj.* —*n.* cotton cloth, usually with colored patterns printed on one side. —*adj.* **1** made of calico. **2** spotted in colors: *a calico cat.* [after *Calicut,* India]

ca·lif (kā′lif; kal′if), *n.* =caliph.

Calif., California.

cal·if·ate (kal′ə fāt; –fit; kā′lə–), *n.* =caliphate.

Cal·i·for·nia (kal′ə fôr′nyə; –fôr′ni ə), *n.* a W state of the United States, on the Pacific coast. —**Cal′i·for′nian,** *adj., n.*

California condor or **vulture,** a vulture with a bold yellow head and long hooked beak. It is the largest land bird of North America.

California Current, cold ocean current that originates in the N Pacific Ocean and passes SW along the W coast of North America.

California poppy, 1 a small poppy with finely divided leaves and colorful flowers. **2** its flower.

cal·i·for·ni·um (kal′ə fôr′ni əm), *n.* a radioactive element, Cf, produced by the bombardment of curium. [< *California*]

cal·i·pers (kal′ə pərz), *n.pl.* instrument used to measure the diameter or thickness of something. Also, **callipers.** [var. of *caliber*]

ca·liph (kā′lif; kal′if), *n.* the head of a Muslim state. Also, **calif, khalif.** [< OF < Med.L < Ar. *khalīfa* successor, vicar]

cal·iph·ate (kal′ə fāt; –fit; kā′lə–), *n.* rank, reign, government, or territory of a caliph. Also, **califate.**

cal·is·then·ic (kal′əs then′ik), *adj.* of calisthenics. Also, **callisthenic.**

cal·is·then·ics (kal′əs then′iks), *n.* **1** (*sing. in use*) the practice or art of calisthenic exercises. **2** (*pl. in use*) exercises to develop a strong and graceful body. Also, **callisthenics.** [< Gk. *kallos* beauty + *sthenos* strength]

calk¹ (kôk), *v.* fill up (a seam, crack, or joint) so that it will not leak; make watertight, as with oakum and tar. Also, **caulk.** [< OF < L *calcare* tread, press in] —**calk′er,** *n.*

calk² (kôk), *n.* a projecting piece on a horseshoe to prevent slipping. —*v.* put calks on. [< L *calx* heel or *calcar* spur] —**calk′er,** *n.*

call (kôl), *v.* **1** speak loudly; cry; shout: *he called from downstairs.* **2** (of a bird or animal) utter its cry. **3** rouse; waken: *call me in the morning.* **4** command; summon: *obey when duty calls.* **5** cause to come: *call your dog.* **6** give a name to: *they called the baby John.* **7** consider: *called a big hit.* **8** make a stop: *they called on us.* **9** read over: *called the roll.* **10** telephone (to). **11** demand payment of. **12** *Baseball.* **a** declare (a game) ended: *called on account of rain.* **b** pronounce (a pitch) a strike or ball. —*n.* **1** a shout; a cry. **2** the characteristic sound of a bird or other animal. **3** command; summons. **4** demand: *on call at all hours.* **5** occasion: *no call to meddle.* **6** a short stop. **7** demand for payment.

call back, a ask (a person) to return. **b** telephone a person who has called earlier. **c** retract.

call down, scold.

call for, go and get.

call in, a summon for advice. **b** withdraw; make unavailable. **c** collect as debts.

call off, a cancel. **b** enumerate. **c** order to withdraw.

call on or **upon, a** pay a short visit to. **b** appeal to.

call out, a shout. **b** summon to serve. **c** *Fig.* evoke.

call up, a bring to mind. **b** telephone to. **c** draft into the military.

on call, a ready to respond to a call to duty. **b** subject to payment on demand.

within call, near enough to hear a call. [OE. Cf. West Saxon *ceallian.*] —**call′a·ble,** *adj.*

cal·la (kal′ə), *n.* **1** Also, **calla lily.** plant with a large, petallike, white leaf around a thick spike of yellow florets. **2** a marsh plant with heart-shaped leaves. [< NL]

call·er (kôl′ər), *n.* **1** person who makes a short visit. **2** person who calls.

cal·lig·ra·phy (kə lig′rə fi), *n.* **1** handwriting. **2** beautiful handwriting. [< Gk., < *kallos* beauty + *graphein* write] —**cal·lig′ra·pher,** *n.* —**cal·li·graph′ic,** *adj.*

call·ing (kôl′ing), *n.* **1** business; occupation. **2** command; summons.

calling card, 1 =phone card. **2** a small card with a person's name on it.

cal·li·o·pe (kə lī′ə pē; *for 1, also* kal′i ōp), *n.* **1** musical instrument having a series of steam whistles played by pushing keys. **2 Calliope,** the Muse of eloquence and heroic poetry. [< L < Gk. *kalliope* beautiful-voiced < *kallos* beauty + *ops* voice]

cal·li·pers (kal′ə pərz), *n.* =calipers.

cal·lis·then·ic (kal′əs then′ik), *adj.* =calisthenic.

cal·lis·then·ics (kal′əs then′iks), *n.* =calisthenics.

call letters, letters that identify a radio or television station.

cal·los·i·ty (kə los′ə ti), *n., pl.* **–ties. 1** =callus. **2** lack of feeling; hardness of heart.

cal·lous (kal′əs), *adj.* **1** hard; hardened, as portions of the skin exposed to friction. **2** unfeeling; not sensitive. [< L, < *callus* hard skin] —**cal′lous·ly,** *adv.* —**cal′lous·ness,** *n.*

cal·low (kal′ō), *adj.* **1** young and inexperienced. **2** (of birds) without feathers sufficiently developed for flight. [OE *calu* bald] —**cal′low·ness,** *n.*

cal·lus (kal′əs), *n., pl.* **–lus·es. 1** a hard, thickened place on the skin. **2** a new growth to unite the ends of a broken bone. [see CALLOUS]

call waiting, telephone service that signals an incoming call while another call is in progress.

calm (käm), *adj.* **1** not stormy or windy; quiet; still; not moving. **2** peaceful; not excited. —*n.* **1** absence of motion or wind; quietness; stillness. **2** absence of excitement; peacefulness. —*v.* make or become calm. [< OF < Ital. < VL < Gk. *kauma* heat of the day; hence, time for rest, stillness] —**calm′ly,** *adv.* —**calm′ness,** *n.*

cal·o·mel (kal′ə mel; –məl), *n.* mercurous chloride, Hg_2Cl_2, a white, tasteless, crystalline powder, used in medicine as a cathartic, etc.

ca·lor·ic (kə lôr′ik; –lor′–), *n.* heat.—*adj.* having to do with heat. —**cal′o·ric′i·ty,** *n.*

cal·o·rie, cal·o·ry (kal′ə ri), *n., pl.* **–ries. 1** unit of heat. The quantity of heat necessary to raise the temperature of a gram of water one degree centigrade is a **small calorie;** heat needed to raise a kilogram of water one degree centigrade is a **large calorie. 2 a** unit of the energy supplied by food. It corresponds to a large calorie. **b** quantity of food capable of producing such an amount of energy. [< F < L *calor* heat]

cal·o·rif·ic (kal′ə rif′ik), *adj.* **1** producing heat. **2** =caloric.

cal·u·met (kal′yə met; kal′yə met′), *n.* long, ornamented tobacco pipe smoked by the American Indians in ceremonies as a symbol of peace; peace pipe. [< F, ult. < L *calamus* < Gk. *kalamos* reed]

ca·lum·ni·ate (kə lum′ni āt), *v.,* **–at·ed, –at·ing.** say false and injurious things about; slander. —**ca·lum′ni·a′tor,** *n.*

ca·lum·ni·a·tion (kə lum′ni ā′shən), *n.* slander; calumny.

ca·lum·ni·ous (kə lum′ni əs), *adj.* slanderous. —**ca·lum′ni·ous·ly,** *adv.*

cal·um·ny (kal′əm ni), *n., pl.* **–nies.** false statement made to injure someone's reputation; slander. [< L *calumnia*]

Cal·va·ry (kal′və ri), *n.* place near Jerusalem where Jesus died on the cross. Luke 23:33. [< L *calvaria* skull, trans. of Aram. *Gogoltha* Golgotha]

calve (kav; käv), *v.,* **calved, calv·ing.** give birth to a calf. [OE *calfian* < *calf* calf[1]]

calves (kavz; kävz), *n.* pl. of **calf**[1] and **calf**[2].

Cal·vin (kal′vən), *n.* **John,** 1509–64, French Protestant religious leader at Geneva.

Cal·vin·ism (kal′vən iz əm), *n.* religious teachings of Calvin and his followers. —**Cal′vin·ist,** *n.* —**Cal′vin·is′tic,** *adj.*

calx (kalks), *n., pl.* **calx·es, cal·ces** (kal′sēz). an ashy substance left after a metal or a mineral has been thoroughly roasted, burned, etc. [< L *calx* lime]

Ca·lyp·so (kə lip′sō), *n.* Gk. Legend. sea nymph who detained Odysseus on her island for seven years.

ca·lyp·so (kə lip′sō), *n.* a type of improvised song that originated in the British West Indies.

ca·lyx (kā′liks; kal′iks), *n., pl.* **ca·lyx·es, caly·ces** (kal′ə sēz; kā′lə–). **1** the outer leaves that surround the bud of a flower; the sepals joined in a cup. **2** cuplike structure or organ. [< L < Gk. *kalyx* covering]

cam (kam), *n.* projection on a wheel or shaft that changes a regular circular motion into an irregular circular motion or into a back-and-forth motion. [< Du. *kam* cog, comb]

ca·ma·ra·de·rie (kä′mə rä′də ri), *n.* comradeship. [< F. See COMRADE.]

cam·a·ril·la (kam′ə ril′ə), *n.* cabal; clique. [< Sp., dim. of *cámara* chamber]

cam·ass, cam·as (kam′as), *n.* plant of the lily family growing in the W United States. [< Am. Ind.]

cam·ber (kam′bər), *v.* arch slightly. —*n.* **1** a slight arch. **2** a slightly arching piece of timber. **3** the rise and fall of the curve of an airfoil. [< F *cambre* bent < L *camur* crooked]

cam·bi·um (kam′bi əm), *n.* layer of soft, growing tissue between the bark and the wood of trees and shrubs. [< LL *cambium* exchange]

Cam·bo·di·a (kam bō′di ə), *n.* country in SE Asia.

Cam·bri·a (kam′bri ə), *n.* old name of Wales.

Cam·bri·an (kam′bri ən), *adj.* **1** =Welsh. **2** having to do with an early geological period or group of rocks. —*n.* **1** =Welshman. **2 a** the earliest geological period of the Paleozoic era. **b** rocks formed during this period.

cam·bric (kām′brik), *n.* a fine, thin linen or cotton cloth. [after *Cambrai*, France]

Cam·bridge (kām′brij), *n.* **1** city in SE England. **2** city in E Massachusetts, near Boston.

came (kām), *v.* pt. of **come.**

cam·el (kam′əl), *n.* large animal with one or two humps on its back, used in the desert as a beast of burden. The **Arabian camel,** or dromedary, has one hump; the **Bactrian camel** of S Asia has two humps. [< L < Gk. *kamelos* < Semitic]

ca·mel·lia (kə mēl′yə; –mē′li ə), *n.* **1** shrub or tree with glossy leaves and waxy white or red flowers shaped like roses. **2** the flower. [for G. J. *Kamel*, missionary in Luzon]

ca·mel·o·pard (kə mel′ə pärd), *n.* **1** =giraffe. **2 Camelopard,** northern constellation, the giraffe.

Cam·e·lot (kam′ə lot), *n.* a legendary place in England where King Arthur had his palace.

camel's hair, 1 hair of a camel, used in making cloth, paintbrushes, etc. **2** cloth made of this hair or something like it.

Cam·em·bert (kam′əm bār), *n.* a rich, soft cheese.

cam·e·o (kam′i ō), *n., pl.* **–e·os.** a precious or semiprecious stone carved so that there is a raised part on a background, usually of a different color. [< Ital.]

cam·er·a (kam′ər ə; kam′rə), *n., pl.* **–er·as** *for 1,* **–er·ae** (–ər ē) *for 2* **1** an apparatus in which photographic film or plates are exposed, the image being formed by means of a lens. **2** part of a television transmitter which converts images into electronic impulses for transmitting. **3** a judge's private office.

in camera, a in a judge's private office. **b** privately. [< L, arched chamber, arch < Gk. *kamara.* Doublet of CHAMBER.]

cam·er·a·man (kam′ər ə man′; kam′rə–), *n., pl.* **–men.** person who operates a camera, esp. a television or motion-picture camera.

Cam·er·oon or **Cam·er·oun** (kam′ər ün′), *n.* country in W Africa.

cam·i·sole (kam′ə sōl), *n.* **1 a** woman's undershirt, similar to the top of a slip. **b** woman's fitted shirt or blouse of similar design. **2** a loose jacket worn by women as a dressing gown. [< F < Sp., < *camisa* shirt; akin to CHEMISE]

cam·o·mile (kam′ə mīl), *n.* plant of the aster family with daisylike flowers. Also, **chamomile.** [< L < Gk. *chamaimēlon* earth apple]

cam·ou·flage (kam′ə fläzh), *n., v.,* **–flaged, –flag·ing.** —*n.* **1** disguise; deception. **2** in warfare, giving things a false appearance to deceive the enemy. **3** materials or means for achieving deception. —*v.* give a false appearance to in order to conceal; disguise. [< F, < *camoufler* disguise] —**cam′ou·flag′er,** *n.*

camp[1] (kamp), *n.* **1** group of tents, huts, or other shelters where people live for a time. **2** people living in a camp. **3** buildings, as near a lake or in woods, forming a residence, esp. in summer. **4** camping. **5** people working together. —*v.* **1** make a camp. **2** live in a camp.

break camp, pack up tents and equipment.

camp out, a spend the night outdoors. **b** live in camp. [< F < Ital. < L *campus* field]

camp[2] (kamp), something admired because it is tasteless, banal, outmoded, excessive, etc. —**camp′i·ness,** *n.* —**camp′y,** *adj.*

cam·paign (kam pān′), *n.* **1** series of related military operations for some special purpose. **2** planned course of action for some special purpose: *a campaign to raise money.* **3** organized action to influence voters in an election: *a political campaign.* —*v.* **1** take part in or serve in a campaign. **2** conduct a political campaign. [< F *campagne* open country, ult. < L *campus* field] —**campaign′er,** *n.*

cam·pa·ni·le (kam′pə nē′lē), *n., pl.* **–ni·les, –ni·li** (–nē′lē). a bell tower. [< Ital., ult. < LL *campana* bell]

cam·pan·u·la (kam pan′yə lə), *n.* bluebell, Canterbury bell, or other similar plant with bell-shaped flowers. [< LL, dim. of *campana* bell]

camp·er (kam′pər), *n.* **1** person who goes camping. **2** person who attends a camp. **3** vehicle fitted with bunks, etc. for camping.

camp·fire (kamp′fīr′), *n.* fire in a camp for warmth or cooking.

camp follower, 1 person who attaches him or herself to an army, traditionally as a peddler or prostitute. **2** *Fig.* person who attaches him or herself to a group, cause, or person for profit or gain.

camp·ground (kamp′ground′), *n.* **1** place for camping, esp. one with facilities for campers. **2** place where a camp meeting is held.

cam·phor (kam′fər), *n.* **1** a white, crystalline substance with a strong odor and a bitter taste, $C_{10}H_{16}O$, used in medicine, to protect clothes from moths, in the manufacture of celluloid, etc. **2** camphor in alcohol; spirits of camphor. [< Med.L < Ar.,ult.< Malay *kapur*] —**cam·phor′ic,** *adj.*

cam·phor·ate (kam′fər āt), *v.,* **-at·ed, -at·ing.** impregnate with camphor. —**cam′phor·at′ed,** *adj.*

camp·ing (kam′ping), *n.* practice or recreation of living outdoors in a tent or vehicle.

cam·pi·on (kam′pi ən), *n.* plant with red or white flowers of the same family as the pink. [< L *campus* field]

camp meeting, religious meeting held outdoors or in a tent.

camp·site (kamp′sīt), *n.* place suitable or used for camping.

cam·pus (kam′pəs), *n.* grounds of a college, university, or school. [< L, field, plain]

can¹ (kan; *unstressed* kən), *v., pres. sing.* **can;** *pt.* **could. 1** be able to. **2** know how to. **3** have the right to. **4** be allowed to. [OE *can(n)* know, know how, can]

can² (kan), *n., v.,* **canned, can·ning.** —*n.* **1** a metal container: *a milk can.* **2** contents of a can. **3** a glass jar for canning at home. —*v.* **1** preserve by putting in airtight cans or jars. **2** *Informal.* dismiss from a job. [OE *canne*]

Can., Canada; Canadian.

Ca·naan (kā′nən), *n.* **1** region in Palestine between the Jordan River and the Mediterranean. **2** *Fig.* land of promise.

Ca·naan·ite (kā′nən īt), *n.* inhabitant of Canaan before its conquest by the Hebrews.

Can·a·da (kan′ə də), *n.* a country north of the United States.

Canada goose, the common wild goose of North America.

Ca·na·di·an (kə nā′di ən), *adj.* of Canada or its people. —*n.* native or inhabitant of Canada.

ca·nal (kə nal′), *n., v.,* **-nalled, -nal·ling; -naled, -nal·ing.** —*n.* **1** waterway dug across land for navigation. **2** tube in the body or in a plant for carrying food, liquid, or air. —*v.* **1** make a canal through. **2** furnish with canals. [< L *canalis* trench, pipe. Doublet of CHANNEL.]

canal boat, a long, narrow boat used on canals.

can·a·lic·u·lus (kan′ə lik′yə ləs), *n., pl.* **-li** (-lī). small duct in the body, esp. that connect the small cavities in the bones. [< L dim. of *canālis* groove, canal] —**can′a·lic′u·lar,** *adj.*

Canal Zone, Panama Canal and the land five miles on each side, formerly governed by the U.S.

can·a·pé (kan′ə pā; -pē), *n.* a cracker, thin piece of bread, etc., spread with a seasoned mixture of fish, cheese, etc. [< F, orig., a couch covered with mosquito netting. See CANOPY.]

ca·nard (kə närd′), *n.* a false rumor; exaggerated report; hoax. [< F *canard* duck]

Canary Islands, group of Spanish islands in the Atlantic.

ca·nar·y (kə nãr′i), *n., pl.* **-nar·ies. 1** small, yellow songbird. Canaries are often kept in cages. **2** Also, **canary yellow.** light yellow. **3** wine from the Canary Islands. —*adj.* light-yellow. [after the islands]

ca·nas·ta (kə nas′tə), *n.* a card game.

Ca·nav·er·al (kə nav′ər əl), *n.* **Cape,** cape on the Atlantic coast of Florida, site of spacecraft launchings.

Can·ber·ra (kan′ber ə; -bər ə), *n.* capital of Australia, in the SE part.

can·can (kan′kan), *n.* a dance by women marked by extravagant kicking. [< F]

can·cel (kan′səl), *v.,* **-celed, -cel·ing,** *n.* —*v.* **1** cross out; mark (something) so that it cannot be used. **2** cross out the same factor from the numerator and denominator of a fraction, or from the two sides of an equation. **3** do away with; abolish: *he canceled his order.* **4** make up for; balance. —*n.* **1** a canceling. **2** a canceled part. [< L *cancellare* cross out with latticed lines < *cancelli* cross bars] —**can′cel·a·ble,** *adj.* —**can′cel·er,** *n.*

can·cel·la·tion (kan′sə lā′shən), *n.* **1** a canceling or being canceled. **2** marks made when something is canceled or crossed out.

can·cer (kan′sər), *n.* **1** very harmful growth in the body; malignant tumor. Cancer tends to spread and destroy the healthy tissues and organs of the body. **2** *Fig.* evil or harmful thing that tends to spread. **3 Cancer, a** tropic of Cancer. **b** a northern constellation that was thought of as arranged in the shape of a crab. **c** the fourth sign of the zodiac. [< L *cancer* crab, tumor] —**can′cer·ous,** *adj.*

can·de·la·bra (kan′də lä′brə; -lä′-), *n.* **1** pl. of **candelabrum. 2** (*pl. but taken as sing. with pl.* **-bras**) candelabrum.

can·de·la·brum (kan′də lä′brəm; -lä′-), *n., pl.* **-bra** (-brə) or **-brums.** an ornamental candlestick with several branches for candles. [< L, < *candela* candle]

can·des·cent (kan des′ənt), *adj.* glowing with heat; incandescent. [< L *candescens* beginning to glow] —**can·des′cence,** *n.* —**can·des′cent·ly,** *adv.*

can·did (kan′did), *adj.* **1** frank; sincere. **2** fair; impartial. **3** unposed; natural. [< L *candidus* white] —**can′did·ly,** *adv.* —**can′did·ness,** *n.*

can·di·da·cy (kan′də də si), *n.* being a candidate: *please support my candidacy for treasurer.*

can·di·date (kan′də dāt; -dit), *n.* **1** person who seeks, or is proposed for, some office or honor. **2** person studying for a degree. **3** applicant for a position. [< L *candidatus* clothed in white (toga)] —**can′di·date·ship′,** *n.*

can·died (kan′did), *adj.* **1** turned into sugar: *candied honey.* **2** cooked in sugar; covered with sugar. **3** made sweet or agreeable.

can·dle (kan′dəl), *n., v.,* **-dled, -dling.** —*n.* **1** stick of wax or tallow with a wick in it, burned to give light. **2** anything shaped or used like a candle. **3** unit for measuring the strength of a light. —*v.* test (eggs) for freshness by holding them in front of a light.

burn the candle at both ends, use up one's strength and resources rapidly.

not hold a candle to, not compare with. [< L *candela* < *candere* shine] —**can′dler,** *n.*

can·dle·ber·ry (kan′dəl ber′i), *n., pl.* **-ries. 1** wax myrtle or bayberry. **2** its fruit.

can·dle·fish (kan′dəl fish′), *n.* an edible fish of the NW coast of America.

can·dle·light (kan′dəl līt′), *n.* **1** light of a candle or candles. **2** time when candles are lighted; dusk; twilight; nightfall.

can·dle·lit (kan′dəl līt′), *adj.* lit by candlelight.

Can·dle·mas (kan′dəl məs), *n.* February 2, a church festival in honor of the purification of the Virgin Mary. [OE *candelmœsse*]

candle power, light given by a standard candle, used as a unit for measuring light.

can·dle·stick (kan′dəl stik′), **can·dle·hold·er** (-hōl′dər), *n.* holder for a candle, to make it stand up straight.

can-do (kan′dü′), *adj. Informal.* willing and able to get things done: *a can-do person.*

can·dor, (kan′dər), *n.* **1** speaking openly what one really thinks; honesty in giving one's view or opinion. **2** fairness; impartiality. [< L, whiteness, purity < *candere* shine]

can·dy (kan′di), *n., pl.* **-dies,** *v.,* **-died, -dy·ing.** —*n.* **1** sugar or syrup, cooked and flavored, then cooled and made into small pieces for eating. Chocolate, butter, milk, nuts, fruits, etc., are often added. **2** piece of this. —*v.* **1** turn into sugar. **2** cook in sugar; preserve by boiling in sugar. **3** make sweet or agreeable. [< F < Pers. *qand* sugar]

candy stripe, alternating narrow stripe of two colors, esp. red and white, resembling stripes on peppermint candy.

can·dy·tuft (kan′di tuft′), *n.* plant with clusters of white, purple, or pink flowers.

cane (kān), *n., v.,* **caned, can·ing.** —*n.* **1** stick to help a person in walking; walking stick. **2** stick used to beat with. **3** a long, jointed stem, such as that of the bamboo. **4** plant having such stems. Sugar cane and bamboo are canes. **5** material made of such stems, used for furniture, chair seats, etc. **6** a slender stalk or stem. —*v.* **1** beat with a cane. **2** make or provide with cane: *cane the chair seat.* [< F < L < Gk. *kanna* reed]

cane·brake (kān′brāk′), *n.* thicket or region of cane plants.

cane sugar, sugar made from sugar cane.

ca·nine (kā′nīn), *n.* **1** dog. **2** canine tooth. —*adj.* **1** of a dog; like a dog. **2** belonging to a group of meat-eating animals including dogs, foxes, and wolves. [< L, < *canis* dog]

canine tooth, one of the four pointed teeth next to the incisors.

Ca·nis Ma·jor (kā′nis mā′jər), group of stars SE of Orion that contains Sirius, the brightest of the stars.

Ca·nis Mi·nor (kā′nis mī′nər), group of stars SE of Orion, separated from Canis Major by the Milky Way.

can·is·ter (kan′is tər), *n.* **1** a small box or can. **2** can or cylinder filled with bullets that is shot from a cannon. [< L < Gk. *kanastron* basket]

can·ker (kang′kər), *n.* **1** a spreading sore, esp. one in the mouth. **2** disease of plants that causes slow decay. **3** anything that causes decay, rotting, or gradual eating away. **4** =cankerworm. —*v.* **1** infect or be infected with canker. **2** become malignant; decay. [< L *cancer* crab, gangrene]

can·ker·worm (kang′kər wėrm′), *n.* caterpillar that eats away the leaves of trees and plants.

can·na (kan′ə), *n.* **1** plant with large, pointed leaves and large, red, pink, or yellow flowers. **2** the flower. [< L, reed. See CANE.]

can·na·bis (kan′ə bis), *n.* **1** dried, flowering tops of hemp, from which hashish and marijuana are made. **2** =hemp (plant).

canned (kand), *adj.* **1** put up and sealed for preservation. **2** recorded, as music.

can·ner (kan′ər), *n.* person who cans food.

can·ner·y (kan′ər i), *n., pl.* **–ner·ies.** factory where meat, fish, fruit, vegetables, etc., are canned.

can·ni·bal (kan′ə bəl), *n.* **1** person who eats human flesh. **2** animal that eats others of its own kind. —*adj.* of or like cannibals. [< Sp. *Caníbal* < *Caribe* Carib]

can·ni·bal·ism (kan′ə bəl iz′əm), *n.* practice of eating the flesh of one's own kind. —**can′ni·bal·is′tic,** *adj.* —**can′ni·bal·is′ti·cal·ly,** *adv.*

can·ni·bal·ize (kan′ə bəl īz), *v.,* **–ized, –iz·ing. 1** take parts from nonworking machines, vehicles, etc. in order to repair another or others. **2** salvage usable parts from a vehicle, piece of machinery, etc. for repairs.

can·ni·kin (kan′ə kin), *n.* a small can; cup. [< *can*[2] + *–kin*],

can·ning (kan′ing), *n.* the process or business of preserving food by putting it in airtight cans or jars.

can·non (kan′ən), *n., pl.* **–nons** or (*esp. collectively*) **–non,** *v.* —*n.* **1** big mounted gun or guns. **2** cannon bone. **3** the part of a bit that goes inside a horse's mouth: a smooth round bit. —*v.* **1** discharge cannon. **2** strike and rebound. **3** collide violently. [< F *canon* < Ital. < L < Gk. *kanna* reed]

can·non·ade (kan′ən ād′), *n., v.,* **–ad·ed, –ad·ing.** —*n.* continued firing of cannons. —*v.* attack with cannons.

cannon ball, a large, iron or steel ball, formerly fired from cannons.

cannon bone, bone between the hock and fetlock.

can·non·eer (kan′ən ir′), *n.* gunner.

can·non·ry (kan′ən ri), *n., pl.* **–ries. 1** continuous firing of cannons. **2** artillery.

can·not (kan′ot; ka not′; kə–), *v.* can not.

can·ny (kan′i), *adj.,* **–ni·er, –ni·est.** shrewd; cautious. [< *can*[1]] —**can′ni·ly,** *adv.* —**can′ni·ness,** *n.*

ca·noe (kə nü′), *n., v.,* **ca·noed, ca·noe·ing.** —*n.* light boat moved with paddles. —*v.* paddle a canoe; go in a canoe. [< F < Sp. < Carib *kanoa*] —**ca·noe′ing,** *n.* —**ca·noe′ist,** *n.*

can·on[1] (kan′ən), *n.* **1** law of a church. **2** rule by which a thing is judged. **3** the official list of the books contained in the Bible. **4** list of saints. **5** an official list. **6** part of the Mass coming after the offertory. **7** a musical composition in which the different participants begin the same melody one after another. [< L < Gk. *kanon*]

can·on[2] (kan′ən), *n.* **1** member of a group of clergymen belonging to a cathedral or collegiate church. **2** member of a group of clergymen living according to a certain rule. [< OF < L *canonicus* canonical < *canon* canon[1]]

ca·ñon (kan′yən), *n.* =canyon.

ca·non·i·cal (kə non′ə kəl), *adj.* **1** according to or prescribed by the laws of a church. **2** in the canon of the Bible. **3** authorized; accepted. —*n.* canonicals, clothes worn by a clergyman at a church service. —**ca·non′i·cal·ly,** *adv.* —**ca·non′i·cal·ness,** *n.*

canonical hours, the seven periods of the day for prayer and worship.

can·on·ize (kan′ən īz), *v.,* **–ized, –iz·ing. 1** declare (a dead person) to be a saint; place in the official list of the saints. **2** treat as a saint; glorify. **3** make or recognize as canonical. **4** authorize. —**can′on·i·za′tion,** *n.*

canon law, laws of a church governing ecclesiastical affairs.

can·on·ry (kan′ən ri), *n., pl.* **–ries.** office or benefice of a canon.

can·o·py (kan′ə pi), *n., pl.* **–pies,** *v.,* **–pied, –py·ing.** —*n.* **1** a covering fixed over a bed, throne, entrance, etc., or held over a person. **2** a rooflike covering; shelter; shade. **3** *Fig.* sky. **4** the umbrella-like part of a parachute. **5** the sliding top of the cockpit of a small aircraft. —*v.* cover with a canopy. [< F < L < Gk. *konopeion* mosquito net < *konops* gnat]

canst (kanst), *v. Archaic.* 2nd pers. sing. present of **can.**

cant[1] (kant), *n.* **1** insincere talk; moral and religious statements that many people make, but few really believe or follow out. **2** whining or singsong speech like that of beggars. **3** peculiar language of a special group, using many strange words: *thieves' cant.* —*adj.* peculiar to a special group. —*v.* use cant. [< L *cantus* song]

cant[2] (kant), *n., v.* **1** slant; slope; bevel. **2** tip; tilt. **3** pitch; toss; throw with a sudden jerk. [prob. < MDu., MLG < OF < L *cant(h)us* corner, side < Celtic]

can't (kant; känt), cannot.

can·ta·bi·le (kän tä′bi lā), —*adj.* in a smooth and flowing style; songlike. —*n.* a cantabile style, passage, or piece. [< Ital. < L *cantare* sing]

can·ta·loupe (kan′tə lōp), *n.* a sweet, juicy melon with a hard, rough rind; muskmelon. [< F < Ital. *Cantalupo* place where first cultivated]

can·tan·ker·ous (kan tang′kər əs), *adj.* hard to get along with because ready to make trouble and oppose anything suggested; ill-natured. —**can·tan′ker·ous·ly,** *adv.* —**can·tan′ker·ous·ness ,** *n.*

can·ta·ta (kən tä′tə), *n.* story or play set to music to be sung by a chorus, but not acted. [< Ital. < L *cantare* sing]

can·teen (kan tēn′), *n.* **1** a small container for carrying water or other drinks. **2** a store in a business, school, etc., where food, drinks, and notions, are sold. **3** box of cooking utensils for use in camp. [< F < Ital. *cantina* cellar < LL *canthus* side]

can·ter (kan′tər), *n.* gentle gallop. —*v.* gallop gently. [for *Canterbury gallop,* pace of pilgrims to Canterbury]

Can·ter·bur·y (kan′tər ber ′i), *n.* city in SE England.

Canterbury bell, plant with tall stalks of bell-shaped flowers, usually purplish-blue or white.

cant hook, pole with a movable hook at one end, used to grip and turn over logs.

can·ti·cle (kan′tə kəl), *n.* a short song, hymn, or chant used in church services. [< L *canticulum* little song < *cantus* song]

can·ti·lev·er (kan′tə lev′ər; –lē′vər), *n.* a large, projecting bracket or beam that is fastened at one end only.

cantilever bridge, bridge made of two cantilevers whose projecting ends meet but do not support each other.

can·tle (kan′təl), *n.* part of a saddle that sticks up at the back. [< OF < Med.L *cantellus* little corner]

can·to (kan′tō), *n., pl.* **–tos.** one of the main divisions of a long poem. A canto of a poem corresponds to a chapter of a novel. [< Ital. < L *cantus* song]

can·ton (kan′tən, –ton, kan ton′ *for n. and v. 1;* kan ton′, –tōn′, *for v. 2*), *n.* small part or political division of a country. Switzerland is made up of 22 cantons. —*v.* **1** divide into cantons. **2** allot quarters to. [< OF *canton* corner, portion. See CANT[2].]

Can·ton (kan ton′ *for 1;* kan′tən *for 2*), *n.* **1** city in S China. **2** city in NE Ohio.

Can·ton·ese (kan′tən ēz′; –ēs′), *n., pl.* **–ese. 1** native or inhabitant of Canton, China. **2** Chinese dialect spoken in or near Canton, China. —*adj.* of Canton, China, its people, or their dialect.

Can·ton flannel (kan′tən), a strong cotton cloth that is soft and fleecy on one side.

can·ton·ment (kan ton′mənt; –tōn′–), *n.* place where soldiers live; quarters. [< F]

can·tor (kan′tər; –tôr), *n.* **1** person who leads the singing of a choir or congregation. **2** person who chants prayers and leads worship in a synagogue. [< L, singer, < *canere* sing]

Ca·nuck (kə nuk′), *n., adj. Slang.* **1** Canadian. **2** French-Canadian.

can·vas (kan′vəs), *n.* **1** a strong cloth made of cotton, flax, or hemp, used to make tents and sails. **2** something made of canvas. **3** sail or sails. **4** piece of canvas on which an oil painting is done. **5** an oil painting. —*adj.* made of canvas.

under canvas, a in tents. **b** with sails spread. [< OF < L *cannabis* hemp]

can·vas·back (kan′vəs bak′), *n.* a wild duck of North America with grayish feathers on its back.

can·vass (kan′vəs), *v.* **1** go through (a city, district, etc.) asking for votes, orders, etc. **2** examine carefully; study. **3** discuss; debate. **4** examine and count votes cast in an election. —*n.* **1** act, fact, or process of canvassing. **2** an official scrutiny of votes. **3** personal visiting of homes or stores to sell something. [< *canvas*, orig., toss (someone) in a sheet, later, shake out, discuss] —**can′vass·er,** *n.*

can·yon (kan′yən), *n.* narrow valley with high, steep sides, usually with a stream at the bottom. Also, **cañon.** [< Sp. *cañón* tube, ult. < L *canna* cane]

caou·tchouc (kü′chük; kou chük′), *n.* the gummy, coagulated juice of various tropical plants; rubber. [< F < Sp. < S Am.Ind.]

cap (kap), *n., v.,* **capped, cap·ping.** —*n.* **1** close-fitting covering for the head. **2** special head covering worn to show rank, occupation, etc.: *a nurse's cap.* **3** anything like a cap: *a bottle cap.* **4** the highest part; top. **5** a small quantity of explosive in a wrapper. —*v.* **1** put a cap on. **2** do or follow with something as good or better: *each clown capped the other's joke.* [< LL *cappa.* Cf. L *caput* head]

cap., **1** capacity. **2** capital. **3** capitalize. **4** *pl.* **caps.** capital letter. **5** chapter.

ca·pa·bil·i·ty (kā′pə bil′ə ti), *n., pl.* **–ties.** ability; power; fitness; capacity.

ca·pa·ble (kā′pə bəl), *adj.* having capacity or qualifications to meet ordinary requirements; competent: *a capable teacher.*

capable of, a having ability, power, or fitness for: *capable of criticizing music.* **b** open to; ready for: *a statement capable of many interpretations.* [< LL *capabilis* < L *capere* take] —**ca′pa·ble·ness,** *n.* —**ca′pa·bly,** *adv.*

ca·pa·cious (kə pā′shəs), *adj.* able to hold much; roomy; large. —**ca·pa′cious·ly,** *adv.* —**ca·pa′cious·ness,** *n.*

ca·pac·i·tance (kə pas′ə təns), *n.* property of a capacitor that determines the amount of electrical charge it can receive and store; capacity.

ca·pac·i·tate (kə pas′ə tāt), *v.,* **–tat·ed, –tat·ing.** make capable or fit; qualify.

ca·pac·i·tor (kə pas′ə tər), *n.* device for receiving and storing a charge of electricity. Also **capacitator.**

ca·pac·i·ty (kə pas′ə ti), *n., pl.* **–ties. 1** amount of room or space inside: *the theater has a capacity of 400.* **2** ability; power; fitness: *a great capacity for learning.* **3** position; relation: *he acted in the capacity of guardian.* **4** power of delivering electric current, power, etc. [< L *capacitas* < *capere* take]

ca·par·i·son (kə par′ə sən), *n.* **1** ornamental covering for a horse. **2** rich dress; outfit. —*v.* dress richly; fit out. [< F < Pr. *capa* cape]

cape¹ (kāp), *n.* an outer garment, or part of one, without sleeves, worn falling loosely from the shoulders. [< F < Sp. < LL *cappa* cap]

cape² (kāp), *n.* **1** point of land extending into the water. **2 the Cape,** the Cape of Good Hope. [< F < Pr. < L *caput* head]

Cape buffalo, a large, savage buffalo of southern Africa.

cap·e·lin (kap′ə lin), *n.* a small fish of the N Atlantic, used as bait for cod. [< F < Pr. *capelan* chaplain]

ca·per¹ (kā′pər), *n.* **1** a playful leap or jump. **2** prank; trick. —*v.* leap or jump about playfully; gambol. [< L *caper* he-goat] —**ca′per·er,** *n.*

ca·per² (kā′pər), *n.* **1** a prickly shrub of the Mediterranean region. **2 capers,** the green flower buds of this shrub, pickled and used for seasoning. [< L < Gk. *kapparis*]

Cape Town, (kāp′toun′), seaport near the S tip of Africa. The legislature for the Republic of South Africa meets there.

Cape Verde (kāp′ vèrd′), **1** cape in extreme W Africa. **2 Cape Verde Islands,** group of islands west of this cape, belonging to Portugal.

cap·ful (kap′fùl), *n., pl.* **–fuls.** as much as a cap will hold.

cap·il·lar·i·ty (kap′ə lar′ə ti), *n.* **1** capillary attraction or repulsion. **2** quality of having or causing capillary attraction or repulsion. Also **capillary action.**

cap·il·lar·y (kap′ə ler′i), *n., adj. pl.* **–lar·ies.** —*n.* tube with a very slender, hairlike opening or bore. Capillaries join the end of an artery to the beginning of a vein. —*adj.* **1** hairlike; very slender. **2** of, by means of, or in a tube of fine bore. [< L *capillaris* of hair, hairlike < *capillus* hair]

capillary attraction, 1 force that raises the part of the surface of a liquid that is in contact with a solid. **2** ability of a porous substance to soak up a liquid.

capillary repulsion, force that causes a liquid to be depressed when in contact with the sides of a narrow tube, as mercury in a glass tube.

cap·i·tal¹ (kap′ə təl), *n.* **1** city where the government of a country or state is located. **2** A, B, C, D, or any similar large letter. **3** amount of money or property that a company or person uses in carrying on a business. **4** source of power or advantage. —*adj.* **1** of or having to do with capital. **2** important; leading. **3** main; chief. **4** (of letters) of the large kind. **5** involving death; punishable by death.

make capital of, take advantage of. [< L *capitalis* chief, pertaining to the head < *caput* head]

cap·i·tal² (kap′ə təl), *n.* the top part of a column, pillar, etc. [< L *capitellum,* dim. of *caput* head]

capital asset, any asset held by a business, individual, foundation, government, including land, buildings, and certain types of investments.

capital gain, profit derived from the sale of investments.

cap·i·tal·ism (kap′ə təl iz′əm), *n.* **1** economic system based on private property, competition, and the production of goods for profit. **2** concentration of wealth with its power and influence in the hands of a few people. **3** possession of capital.

cap·i·tal·ist (kap′ə təl ist), *n.* **1** person whose money and property are used in carrying on business. **2** a wealthy person. **3** person who favors or supports capitalism. —*adj.* capitalistic.

cap·i·tal·is·tic (kap′ə təl is′tik), *adj.* **1** of or having to do with capitalism or capitalists. **2** favoring or supporting capitalism. —**cap′i·tal·is′ti·cal·ly,** *adv.*

cap·i·tal·ize (kap′ə təl īz), *v.,* **–ized, –iz·ing. 1** write or print with a capital letter. **2** invest in or provide with capital. **3** set the capital of (a company) at a certain amount. **4** turn into capital. **5** take advantage of. —**cap′i·tal·i·za′tion,** *n.*

cap·i·tal·ly (kap′ə təl i), *adv.* **1** very well; excellently. **2** chiefly.

capital punishment, the death penalty for a crime.

cap·i·ta·tion (kap′ə tā′shən), *n.* tax, fee, or charge of the same amount for every person.

Cap·i·tol (kap′ə təl), *n.* **1** the building at Washington, D.C., in which Congress meets. **2** Often, **capitol,** the building in which a state legislature meets. [< L *Capitolium* chief temple (of Jupiter) < *caput* head]

ca·pit·u·late (kə pich′ə lāt), *v.,* **–lat·ed, –lat·ing.** surrender on certain terms or conditions: *the strikers capitulated on condition that they keep their jobs.* [< Med.L, < *capitulare* draw up under separate heads, arrange in chapters < L *caput* head]

ca·pit·u·la·tion (kə pich′ə lā′shən), *n.* **1** a surrender on certain terms or conditions. **2** agreement; condition. **3** statement of the main facts of a subject; summary.

ca·pon (kā′pon; –pən), *n.* rooster specially raised to be eaten. It is castrated and fattened. [< OF < L *capo*]

Ca·pri (kä′pri; kə prē′), *n.* a small island in the Bay of Naples, Italy.

ca·pric·ci·o (kə prē′chi ō), *n., pl.* **–ci·os.** a lively piece of music in a free, irregular style. [< Ital., < *capro* goat < L *caper*]

ca·price (kə prēs′), *n.* **1** sudden change of mind without reason; unreasonable notion or desire. **2** =capriccio [< F < Ital. *capriccio.* See CAPRICCIO.]

ca·pri·cious (kə prish′əs; –prē′shəs), *adj.* guided by one's fancy; changeable; fickle. **—ca·pri′cious·ly,** *adv.* **—ca·pri′cious-ness,** *n.*

Cap·ri·corn (kap′rə kôrn), *n.* **1** tropic of Capricorn. **2** a southern constellation that was thought of as arranged in the shape of a goat. **3** the 10th sign of the zodiac.

cap·ri·ole (kap′ri ōl), *n., v.,* **–oled, –ol·ing.** —*n.* **1** high leap made by a horse without moving forward. **2** a leap; caper. —*v.* **1** of a horse, make a high leap. **2** to leap; caper. [< F < Ital. *capriola,* ult. < *capro* goat. See CAPRICCIO.]

caps., capital letters.

cap·si·cum (kap′sə kəm), *n.* **1** any of several plants with red or green pods containing seeds that usually have a hot, peppery taste. Green peppers, chilies, and pimientos are pods of different kinds of capsicum. **2** such pods prepared for seasoning or medicine. [< NL < L *capsa* box]

cap·size (kap sīz′; kap′sīz), *v.,* **–sized, –sizing.** turn bottom side up; upset; overturn.

cap·stan (kap′stən), *n.* machine for lifting or pulling that stands upright. [< Pr. < L *capistrum* halter, < *capere* take]

capstan bar, pole used to turn a capstan.

cap·stone (kap′stōn′), *n.* top stone of a wall or other structure.

cap·su·lar (kap′sə lər; –syə–), *adj.* **1** of or like, a capsule. **2** in a capsule.

cap·sule (kap′səl; –syùl), *n.* **1** a small gelatin container that holds a dose of medicine. **2** =space capsule. **3** a dry seedcase that opens when ripe. **4** a membrane enclosing an organ; membranous bag or sac. [< L *capsula,* dim. of *capsa* box]

Capt., Captain.

cap·tain, (kap′tən), *n.* **1** leader; chief. **2** an army officer ranking next below a major and next above a lieutenant. **3** a navy officer ranking next below a commodore and next above a commander. **4** commander of a ship. **5** leader of a team in sports. —*v.* lead or command as captain. [< OF < LL *capitaneus* chief < L *caput* head] **—cap′tain·cy,** *n.*

cap·tain·ship (kap′tən ship), *n.* **1** rank, position, or authority of a captain. **2** ability as a captain; leadership.

cap·tan (kap′tan), *n.* powder used in solution on plants as a fungicide.

cap·tion (kap′shən), *n.* **1** title or heading at the head of a page, article, chapter, etc., or under a picture. **2** subtitle on a film or television screen. —*v.* put a caption on. [< L *captio* a taking < *capere* take]

cap·tious (kap′shəs), *adj.* hard to please; faultfinding. [< L *captiosus,* ult. < *capere* take] **—cap′tious·ly,** *adv.* **—cap′tious-ness,** *n.*

cap·ti·vate (kap′tə vāt), *v.,* **–vat·ed, –vat·ing.** hold captive by beauty or interest; charm; fascinate. **—cap′ti·vat′-ing·ly,** *adv.* **—cap′ti·va′tion,** *n.* **—cap′ti-va′tor,** *n.*

cap·tive (kap′tiv), *n.* prisoner. —*adj.* **1** held as a prisoner; made a prisoner. **2** captivated. [< L *captivus,* ult. < *capere* take]

captive audience, group of persons who may be involuntarily subjected to an advertising appeal or other message, as passengers on a bus.

cap·tiv·i·ty (kap tiv′ə ti), *n., pl.* **–ties. 1** a being in prison. **2** a being held or detained anywhere against one's will.

cap·tor (kap′tər), *n.* person who captures.

cap·ture (kap′chər), *v.,* **–tured, –tur·ing,** *n.* —*v.* make a prisoner of; take by force, skill, or trick; seize. [< n.] —*n.* **1** person or thing taken in this way. **2** act of capturing; fact of capturing or being captured. [< F < L *captura* taking < *capere* take] **—cap′tur·a·ble,** *adj.* **—cap′tur·er,** *n.*

cap·u·chin (kap′yù chin; –shin), *n.* **1** a South American monkey with black hair on its head that looks like a hood. **2 Capuchin,** Franciscan monk belonging to an order that wears a long, pointed hood or cowl.

car (kär), *n.* **1** automobile. **2** vehicle moving on wheels. **3** railroad vehicle for freight or passengers. **4** closed platform of an elevator, balloon, etc., for carrying passengers. **5** *Poetic.* chariot. [< OF < L *carrus* two-wheeled cart]

ca·ra·ba·o (kä′rə bä′ō), *n., pl.* **–ba·os.** water buffalo of the Philippine Islands. [< Sp. < Malay *karbau*]

car·a·bi·neer, car·a·bi·nier (kar′ə bə nir′), *n.* cavalry soldier armed with a carbine. Also, **carbineer.**

ca·ra·ca·ra (kä′rə kä′rə), *n.* a vulturelike bird of South America.

Ca·rac·as (kə rak′əs; –rä′kəs), *n.* capital of Venezuela.

car·a·cole (kar′ə kōl), **car·a·col** (–kol), *n., v.,* **–coled, –col·ing; –colled, –col·ling.** —*n.* a half turn to the right or left, made by a horse and rider. —*v.* prance from side to side. [< F < Ital. < Sp. *caracol* spiral shell]

car·a·cul (kar′ə kəl), *n.* flat, loose, curly fur made from the skin of newborn lambs of a breed of Asian sheep. **2** any sheep of this breed. Also, **karakul.** [< *Kara Kul,* lake in Turkestan]

ca·rafe (kə raf′; –räf′), *n.* a glass water bottle. [< F < Ital. < Sp. < Ar. *gharrâf* drinking vessel]

car·a·mel (kar′ə məl; –ə mel; kär′məl; kär-mel′), *n.* **1** browned or burnt sugar used for coloring and flavoring. **2** a small block of chewy candy. **3** the brown color of caramel. [< F < Sp. *caramelo*]

car·a·pace (kar′ə pās), *n.* shell on the back of a turtle, lobster, crab, etc. [< F < Sp. *carapacho*]

car·at (kar′ət), *n.* **1** unit of weight for precious stones, equal to ⅙ gram. **2** one 24th part of gold in an alloy. Also, **karat.** [< F < Ital. < Ar. < Gk. *keration* small horn-shaped bean used as a weight, dim. of *keras* horn]

car·a·van (kar′ə van), *n.* **1 a** group of merchants, pilgrims, tourists, etc., traveling together for safety through a desert or a dangerous country. **b** transport used by such a group. **2** a large, covered truck or wagon for people or goods; van. **3** *Brit.* house on wheels. [< F < Pers. *kārwān*]

car·a·van·sa·ry (kar′ə van′sə ri), **car·a·van·se·rai** (–rī; –rā), *n., pl.* **–ries –rais. 1** inn or hotel where caravans rest in the East. **2** *Fig.* any large inn or hotel. [< Pers., < *kārwān* caravan + *serāī* inn]

car·a·vel (kar′ə vel), *n.* **1** a small, fast ship of the type used by Columbus and other navigators. **2** any small, fast ship of former times. Also, **carvel.** [< F *caravelle* < Ital. < LL *carabus* < Gk. *karabos* kind of light ship < ancient Macedonian]

car·a·way (kar′ə wā), *n.* **1** plant yielding fragrant, spicy seeds used to flavor bread, rolls, cakes, etc. **2** its seeds. [< Med.L < Ar. *karawyā*]

car·bide (kär′bīd; –bid), *n.* **1** compound of carbon with a more electropositive element or radical. **2** =calcium carbide.

car·bine (kär′bīn; –bēn), *n.* a short rifle. [< F]

car·bi·neer (kär′bə nir′), *n.* =carabineer.

car·bo·hy·drate (kär′bō hī′drāt), *n.* substance composed of carbon, hydrogen, and oxygen. Sugar and starch are carbohydrates. Carbohydrates are made from carbon dioxide and water by green plants in sunlight and are a major class of foods. [< *carbo(n)* + *hydrate*]

car·bo·lat·ed (kär′bə lāt′id), *adj.* containing carbolic acid.

car·bol·ic acid (kär bol′ik), *adj.* a very poisonous, corrosive, white, crystalline substance, C_6H_5OH, used in solution as a disinfectant and antiseptic; phenol.

car·bon (kär′bən), *n.* **1** a very common nonmetallic element, C. Diamonds and graphite are pure carbon; coal and charcoal are impure carbon. **2** piece of carbon used in batteries, arc lamps, etc. [< F < L *carbo* coal]

carbon 12, the most abundant isotope of carbon, a stable isotope having a mass number of 12, now recognized as the official standard for atomic weights.

carbon 14, a radioactive form of carbon. The extent of its decay in wood, bone, etc. is evidence of the age of archaeological finds or geological formations in which organic matter occurs.

car·bo·na·ceous (kär′bə nā′shəs), *adj.* of, like, or containing coal.

car·bon·ate (*n.* kär′bən āt, –it; *v.* kär′-bən āt), *n., v.,* **-at·ed, -at·ing.** *n.* a salt or ester of carbonic acid. —*v.* **1** change into a carbonate. **2** charge with carbon dioxide. Soda water is carbonated to make it fizz. —**car′bon·a′tion,** *n.*

carbon black, black pigment of pure carbon, used in manufacturing rubber and printing.

carbon copy, 1 copy made with carbon paper. **2** *Fig.* any person or thing that appears to duplicate someone or something else.

carbon cycle, 1 circulation of carbon in nature through photosynthesis and a part of the food chain. **2** the series of nuclear transformations in stars that begin and end with a carbon 12 atom.

carbon dating, method of determining the age of an artifact or specimen by measuring the amount of carbon 14 that is present. —**carbon-date,** *v.*

carbon dioxide, a heavy, colorless, odorless gas, CO_2, present in the atmosphere.

car·bon·ic acid (kär bon′ik), acid made when carbon dioxide is dissolved in water, H_2CO_3.

Car·bon·if·er·ous (kär′bən if′ər əs), *n.* **1** period when the warm, moist climate produced great forests, whose remains form the great coal beds. **2** rock and coal beds formed during this period. —*adj.* **carboniferous,** containing coal.

car·bon·ize (kär′bən īz), *v.,* **-ized, -iz·ing. 1** change into carbon by burning. **2** cover or combine with carbon. —**car′bon·i·za′tion,** *n.*

carbon monoxide, a colorless, odorless, very poisonous gas, CO, formed when carbon burns with an insufficient supply of air.

carbon paper, thin paper having a preparation of carbon or other inky substance on one surface, used for making copies of drawings, etc.

carbon tet·ra·chlo·ride (tet′rə klô′rīd; –rid; –klō′–), a colorless, noninflammable liquid, CCl_4, often used in cleaning fluids.

car·bo·run·dum (kär′bə run′dəm), *n.* an extremely hard compound of carbon and silicon, SiC, used for grinding, polishing, etc. **2 Carborundum,** trademark for this abrasive. [< *carbo(n)* + *(co)rundum*]

car·bun·cle (kär′bung kəl), *n.* **1** very painful, inflamed swelling under the skin. **2** smooth, round garnet or other deep-red jewel. [< L *carbunculus* < *carbo* coal] —**car′bun·cled,** *adj.* —**car·bun′cu·lar,** *adj.*

car·bu·ret (kär′bə rāt), *v.,* **-ret·ed, -ret·ing. 1** mix (air or gas) with carbon compounds, such as gasoline, etc. **2** combine with carbon. –**car′bu·re′tion,** *n.*

car·bu·re·tor (kär′bə rā′tər), *n.* device for mixing air with gasoline to make an explosive mixture in an internal combustion engine.

car·ca·jou (kär′kə jü; –zhü), *n.* **1** =wolverine. **2** =American badger. [< Canadian F < Algonkian]

car·cass, car·case (kär′kəs), *n.* **1** dead body of an animal or human being. **2** a living body. **3** an unfinished framework or skeleton. [< F < Ital. *carcassa*]

car·cin·o·gen (kär sin′ə jən), *n.* any substance or agent that produces cancer.

car·cin·o·gen·ic (kär sin′ə jen′ik), *adj.* **1** tending to cause cancer. **2** caused by cancer.

car·ci·no·ma (kär′sə nō′mə), *n., pl.* **-mas, -ma·ta** (–mə tə). =cancer. [< L < Gk. *karkinoma*]

card[1] (kärd), *n.* **1** piece of stiff paper or thin cardboard, usually small and rectangular. **2** one of a pack of cards used in playing games. **3** queer or amusing person. —*v.* **1** provide with a card. **2** put on a card.

cards, a game played with a deck of cards.

card up one's sleeve, a plan or extra help held in reserve.

in the cards, likely to happen; possible.

lay one's cards on the table, be completely frank and honest about something. [< F *carte* < L *charta*. Doublet of CHART.]

card[2] (kärd), *n.* a toothed tool or wire brush. —*v.* clean or comb with such a tool. [< F < Pr. < L *carrere* to card; infl. by L *carduus* thistle] —**card′er,** *n.*

car·da·mom, car·da·mum (kär′də məm), or **car·da·mon** (–mən), *n.* **1** a spicy seed used as seasoning and in medicine. **2** the Asiatic plant that it grows on. [< L < Gk. *kardamomon*]

card·board (kärd′bôrd′; –bōrd′), *n.* a stiff material made of paper, used to make cards and boxes.

car·di·ac (kär′di ak), *adj.* of or having to do with the heart. —*n.* medicine that stimulates the heart. [< L < Gk. *kardiakos* < *kardia* heart]

Car·diff (kär′dif), *n.* seaport in SE Wales.

car·di·gan (kär′də gən), *n.* a knitted woolen jacket or sweater, open at the front. [named for the Earl of *Cardigan* (1797–1868)]

car·di·nal (kär′də nəl), *adj.* **1** of first importance; main. **2** bright-red. —*n.* **1** bright red. **2** American songbird that has bright-red feathers marked with black. It is a kind of finch. **3** one of the princes, or high officials, of the Roman Catholic Church, appointed by the Pope. **4** =cardinal number. [< L *cardinalis* chief, pertaining to a hinge *cardo* hinge] —**car′di·nal·ly,** *adv.* —**car′di·nal·ship′,** *n.*

car·di·nal·ate (kär′də nəl āt), *n.* position or rank of cardinal.

cardinal flower, 1 the bright-red flower of a North American plant. **2** the plant it grows on; the scarlet lobelia.

cardinal number or **numeral,** number that shows how many are meant; 3, 10, 246, are numbers used in counting, contrasted with 1st, 2nd, 24th, etc., which are ordinal numbers.

cardinal points, the four main directions of the compass; north, south, east, and west.

card·ing (kär′ding), *n.* preparation of the fibers of wool, cotton, flax, etc., for spinning by combing them.

cardio-, *combining form.* **1** the heart: *cardiologist = expert in the diseases of the heart.* **2** the heart and: *cardiorespiratory = the heart and lungs.*

car·di·o·graph (kär′di ə graf′; –gräf′), *n.* =electrocardiograph.

car·di·ol·o·gy (kär′dē ol′ə jē), *n.* branch of medicine that deals with the heart and its diseases. —**car′di·ol′o·gist,** *n.*

car·di·o·pul·mo·nar·y (kär′dē ō pul′mə-nər′ē), *adj.* of or having to do with the heart and lungs.

car·di·o·vas·cu·lar (kär′dē ō vas′kyə lər), *adj.* of or having to do with the heart and blood vessels.

cards (kärdz), *n.pl.* See **card**[1]

card·sharp (kärd′shärp′), *n.* a dishonest professional cardplayer. —**card′-sharp′ing,** *n.*

care (kār), *n., v.,* **cared, car·ing.** —*n.* **1** worry. **2** attention; caution. **3** object of concern or attention. **4** watchful oversight. **5** food, shelter, and protection. —*v.* **1** be concerned; feel an interest. **2** like; want; wish.

care for, a be fond of; like. **b** want; wish: *I don't care for dessert.* **c** attend to; provide for.

have a care, be careful.

in care of, at the address of.

take care, be careful.

take care of, a attend to; provide for. **b** be careful of. **c** deal with. [OE *caru*] —**car′er,** *n.*

ca·reen (kə rēn′), *v.* **1** lean to one side; tilt; tip. **2** lay (a ship) over on one side for cleaning, painting, repairing, etc. [< F < L *carina* keel] —**ca·reen′er,** *n.*

ca·reer (kə rir′), *n.* **1** general course of action or progress through life. **2** way of living; occupation; profession. **3** speed; full speed. —*v.* rush along wildly; dash. —*adj.* having to do with someone who has seriously followed a profession: *a career diplomat.* [< F *carrière* race course < L *carrus* wagon] —**ca·reer′ist,** *n.*

care·free (kār′frē′), *adj.* without worry; happy.

care·ful (kār′fəl), *adj.* **1** thinking what one says; watching what one does; cautious. **2** done with thought or pains; exact; thorough. —**care′ful·ly,** *adv.* —**care′ful·ness,** *n.*

care·giv·er (kār′giv′ər), *n.* person who provides care for children and adults, esp. those who are disabled or ill.

care·less (kār′lis), *adj.* **1** not thinking what one says; not watching what one does. **2** done without enough thought or pains; not exact or thorough. **3** not troubling oneself. —**care′less·ly,** *adv.* —**care′less·ness,** *n.*

ca·ress (kə res′), *n.* a touch or stroke to show affection; embrace; kiss. —*v.* touch or stroke to show affection; embrace; kiss. [< F < Ital. *carezza,* ult. < L *carus* dear] —**ca·ress′a·ble,** *adj.* —**ca·ress′er,** *n.* —**ca·ress′ing·ly,** *adv.*

car·et (kar′ət), *n.* mark (∧) to show where something should be put in, in writing. [< L, there is wanting]

care·tak·er (kār′tāk′ər), *n.* person who takes care of a person, place, or thing.

care·worn (kār′wôrn′; –wōrn′), *adj.* showing signs of worry; tired; weary.

car·fare (kär′fār′), *n.* money to pay for riding on public transport.

car·go (kär′gō), *n., pl.* **–goes, –gos.** load of goods carried on a ship. [< Sp., < *cargar* load, ult. < L *carrus* wagon]

Car·ib (kar′ib), *n.* **1** member of an Indian tribe of NE South America. **2** a language family found primarily in NE South America, and to a lesser extent in Central America and the West Indies. —**Car′ib·an,** *adj.*

Car·ib·be·an (kar′ə bē′ən; kə rib′i–), *n.* sea between Central America, the West Indies, and South America. —*adj.* **1** of this sea or the islands in it. **2** of the Caribs.

car·i·bou (kar′ə bü), *n., pl.* **–bous** or (*esp, collectively*) **–bou.** North American reindeer. [< Canadian F < Algonkian *xalibu* pawer]

car·i·ca·ture (kar′i kə chùr; –chər), *n., v.,* **–tured, –tur·ing.** —*n,* **1** picture, cartoon, description, etc., that ridiculously exaggerates the peculiarities or defects of a person or thing. **2** art of making such pictures or descriptions. **3** a very inferior imitation. —*v.* make a caricature of. [< F < Ital., < *caricare* overload] —**car′i·ca·tur·al,** *adj.* —**car′i·ca·tur′ist,** *n.*

car·ies (kār′ēz; –i ēz), *n.* decay of teeth, bones, or tissues. [< L]

car·il·lon (kar′ə lon; –lən; kə ril′yən), *n., v.,* **–lonned, –lon·ning.** —*n.* **1** set of bells arranged for playing melodies. **2** melody played on such bells. **3** part of an organ imitating the sound of bells. —*v.* play a carillon. [< F, ult. < L *quattuor* four; orig. consisted of four bells]

car·il·lon·neur (kar′ə lə nèr′), *n.* person who plays a carillon. Also **carilloner.**

car·i·ole (kar′i ōl), *n.* **1** a small carriage drawn by one horse. **2** a covered cart. Also, **carriole** [< F < Ital. < L *carrus* wagon]

car·i·ous (kār′i əs), *adj.* having caries; decayed. [< L *cariosus* < *caries* decay] —**car·i·os·i·ty** (kār′i os′ə ti), **car′i·ous·ness,** *n.*

car·jack (kar′jak′), *v.* steal by force a car with a driver in it. —*n.* theft of a car and driver. [< *car* + hi*jack*]

car·load (kär′lōd′), *n.* as much as a car, esp. a railroad freight car, can hold or

carry. —*adj.* bought and sold by the carload.

Carls·bad Caverns (kärlz′bad), national park in SE New Mexico, famous for its huge limestone caverns.

Car·mel·ite (kär′məl īt), *n.* a mendicant friar or nun of a religious order founded in the 12th century. —*adj.* of this order.

car·min·a·tive (kär min′ə tiv; kär′mə nā′ tiv), *adj.* expelling gas from the stomach and intestines. —*n.* medicine that does this. [< L *carminatus* carded]

car·mine (kär′min; –mīn), *n.* **1** deep red with a tinge of purple. **2** light crimson. **3** crimson coloring matter found in cochineal. —*adj.* **1** deep-red with a tinge of purple. **2** light-crimson. [< Med.L < Sp. *carmesi* CRIMSON]

car·nage (kär′nij), *n.* slaughter of a great number of people. [< F < Ital. *carnaggio* < L *caro* flesh]

car·nal (kär′nəl), *adj.* **1** worldly; not spiritual. **2** bodily; sensual. [< L *carnalis* < *caro* flesh] —**car·nal′i·ty** *n.* —**car′nal·ly,** *adv.*

car·na·tion (kär nā′shən), *n.* **1** a red, white, or pink flower with a spicy fragrance. **2** the plant that it grows on. **3** rosy pink. —*adj.* rosy-pink. [< F < Ital. *carnagione* flesh color. See CARNAGE.]

car·nel·ian (kär nēl′yən), *n.* a red stone used in jewelry. Also, **cornelian.** [alter. of *cornelian;* infl. by L *caro* flesh]

car·ni·val (kär′nə vəl), *n.* **1** place of amusement or traveling show having merry-go-rounds, side shows, etc. **2** feasting and merrymaking. **3** time of feasting and merrymaking just before Lent. [< Ital. < Med.L < L *carnem levare* the putting away of flesh]

Car·niv·o·ra (kär niv′ə rə), *n.pl.* large group of flesh-eating animals, including cats, dogs, lions, tigers, and bears.

car·ni·vore (kär′nə vôr; –vōr), *n.* flesh-eating animal. —**car·niv′o·ral** *adj.*

car·niv·o·rous (kär niv′ə rəs), *adj.* **1** flesh-eating: *carnivorous animals.* **2** of or having to do with the Carnivora. [< L *carnivorus* < *caro* flesh + *vorare* devour] —**car·niv′o·rous·ly,** *adv.* —**car·niv′o·rous·ness,** *n.*

car·no·tite (kär′nə tīt), *n.* yellowish, radioactive element found in the W and SW United States and a source of uranium, radium, and vanadium.

car·ob (kar′əb), *n.* **1** evergreen tree of the Mediterranean region. **2** Also, **carob bean.** long, flat pod of the tree, used as fodder or food.

car·ol (kar′əl), *n., v.,* **–oled, –ol·ing.** —*n.* **1** song of joy. **2** hymn: *Christmas carols.* —*v.* sing; sing joyously; praise with carols. [< OF *carole,* ? < L < Gk. *choraules* flute player] —**car′ol·er,** *n.*

Car·o·li·na (kar′ə lī′nə), *n.* **1** an early American colony on the Atlantic coast. **2** either North Carolina or South Carolina. **3 the Carolinas,** North Carolina and South Carolina. —**Car·o·lin′i·an** *adj., n.*

car·om (kar′əm), *n.* **1** shot in which the billiard ball struck with the cue hits two balls, one after the other. **2** a hitting and bouncing off. —*v.* **1** make a carom. **2** hit and bounce off. Also, **carrom.** [< F < Sp. *carambola,* ? < Malay *carambil* name of fruit]

car·o·tene (kar′ə tēn), *n.* red or yellow crystalline pigment found in carrots and other plants and in animal tissues. Also **carotin.**

ca·rot·en·oid (kə rot′ə noid), *n.* any one of a group of pigments whose colors range from yellow to dark red, found in plants and animal tissues.

ca·rot·id (kə rot′id), —*n.* either of two large arteries, one on each side of the neck, that carry blood to the head. —*adj.* having to do with these arteries. [< Gk. *karotides* < *karos* stupor (state produced by compression of carotids)]

ca·rous·al (kə rouz′əl), *n.* **1** noisy revelry. **2** a drinking party.

ca·rouse (kə rouz′), *n., v.,* **–roused, –rous·ing.** —*n.* a noisy feast; drinking party. —*v.* drink heavily; take part in noisy feasts or revels. [< obs. adv. < G *gar aus*(*trinken*) (drink) all up] —**ca·rous′er,** *n.*

car·ou·sel (kar′ə sel′; –zel′), *n.* =carrousel.

carp¹ (kärp), *v.* find fault with; complain. [< Scand. *karpa* wrangle] —**carp′er,** *n.* —**carp′ing·ly,** *adv.*

carp² (kärp), *n., pl.* **carps** or (*esp. collectively*) **carp.** **1** a freshwater fish containing many bones that feeds mostly on plants. **2** any of a group of similar fishes, including goldfish, minnows, chub, and dace. [< OF < Pr. < LL *carpa* < Gmc.]

carp., carpenter; carpentry.

car·pal (kär′pəl), —*adj.* of the carpus. —*n.* bone of the carpus. [< NL < Gk. *karpos* wrist]

Car·pa·thi·an Mountains (kär pā′thi ən), mountain system in E and C Europe, chiefly in Slovakia, Romania, and Poland.

car·pe di·em (kär′pē dī′əm, di–), *Latin.* **1** make the most of today. **2** (literally) seize the day.

car·pel (kär′pəl), *n.* a modified leaf from which a pistil of a flower is formed. [< Gk. *karpos* fruit] —**car′pel·lar′y** *adj.*

car·pen·ter (kär′pən tər), *n.* person whose work is building with wood. —*v.* do such work. [< OF < LL *carpentarius* wagonmaker < L *carpentum* wagon]

car·pen·try (kär′pən tri), *n.* work of a carpenter.

car·pet (kär′pit), *n.* **1** a heavy, woven fabric for covering floors and stairs. **2** a covering made of this fabric. **3** anything like a carpet. —*v.* cover with a carpet. **on the carpet,** being scolded or rebuked. **sweep (shove** or **push) under the carpet,** conceal or ignore something difficult or unpleasant. [< Med.L *carpeta* < L *carpere* card (wool)] —**car′pet·less,** *adj.*

car·pet·bag (kär′pit bag′), *n.* formerly, traveling bag made of carpet.

car·pet·bag·ger (kär′pit bag′ər), *n.* Northerner who went to the South to get political or other advantages after the Civil War.

car·pet·ing (kär′pit ing), *n.* **1** fabric for carpets. **2** carpets.

car·port (kär′pôrt; –pōrt′), *n.* a roofed shelter for one or more automobiles, usually attached to a house and open on at least one side.

car·pus (kär′pəs), *n., pl.* **–pi** (–pī). **1** wrist. **2** bones of the wrist. [< NL < Gk. *karpos* wrist]

car·riage (kar′ij; *for 5, also* kar′i ij), *n.* **1** vehicle moving on wheels, for carrying persons. **2** moving part of a machine that supports some other part. **3** manner of holding the head and body; bearing. **4** act of transporting. **5** cost of carrying. [< OF *cariage* < *carier* CARRY]

carriage trade, wealthy people who patronize expensive shops, restaurants, etc., so called because at one time such patrons traveled in their own carriage.

car·ri·er (kar′i ər), *n.* **1** person or thing that carries something: *mail carrier.* **2** thing to carry something in or on. **3** person or thing that carries or transmits a disease. **4** radio wave whose intensity is decreased or increased and whose frequency is regulated in transmitting a signal. **5** aircraft carrier.

carrier pigeon, 1 homing pigeon. **2** one of a breed of large, heavy, domestic pigeons.

carrier wave, radio wave whose intensity and frequency are varied in order to transmit a signal, as in radio, and television broadcasts.

car·ri·ole (kar′i ōl), *n.* =cariole.

car·ri·on (kar′i ən), *n.* **1** dead and decaying flesh. **2** rottenness; filth. —*adj.* **1** dead and decaying. **2** feeding on dead and decaying flesh. **3** rotten. [< OF *caroigne* < VL < L *caries* decay]

Car·roll (kar′əl), *n.* Lewis, 1832–98, English writer and mathematician. His real name was Charles L. Dodgson.

car·rom (kar′əm), *n., v.* =carom.

car·rot (kar′ət), *n.* **1** plant that has a long, tapering, orange-red root eaten as a vegetable. **2** its root. [< F < L < Gk. *karoton*]

car·rot·y (kar′ət i), *adj.* **1** like a carrot in color; orange-red. **2** red-haired.

car·rou·sel (kar′ə sel′; –zel′), *n.* **1** merry-go-round. **2** circular conveyor, as for delivering luggage to passengers at an airport. **3** circular tray that holds slides for a projector. **4** kind of medieval tournament to which dances, etc., were sometimes added. Also, **carousel.** [< F < Ital. *carosello* < L *carrus* cart]

car·ry (kar′i), *v.,* **–ried, –ry·ing,** *n., pl.* **–ries.** —*v.* **1** take from one place to another: *carry goods in a ship.* **2** hold up; support; sustain: *those columns carry the roof.* **3** hold (one's body and head)

in a certain way. **4** capture; win. **5** get (a motion or bill) passed. **6** cover a certain distance: *his voice carries well.* **7** involve: *his judgment carries great weight.* **8** keep in stock. **9** extend credit to. **10** sustain or perform (a melody or musical part): *carry the tune.* **11** arouse; complete. —*n.* **1** distance covered. **2** a portage.

carry away, a influence strongly or unreasonably. **b** cause the death of.

carry off, a win a prize or honor. **b** succeed with; pass off. **c** be the death of; kill.

carry on, a manage; conduct. **b** go on with after being stopped. **c** continue. **d** *Informal.* behave foolishly or wildly.

carry out, do; complete.

carry through, a do; complete. **b** bring through trouble. [< OF < LL *carricare* < L *carrus* wagon, cart. Doublet of CHARGE.]

car·ry·o·ver (kar′i ō′vər), *n.* part left over.

car·sick (kär′sik′), *adj.* nauseated by traveling in a car, train, etc. —**car′sick′-ness,** *n.*

Car·son City (kär′sən), capital of Nevada.

cart (kärt), *n.* **1** vehicle with two wheels, for carrying heavy loads. **2** a light wagon, used to deliver goods, etc. **3** a small vehicle on wheels, moved by hand. —*v.* carry in a cart. [OE *cræt* or < Scand. *kartr*], —**cart′er,** *n.*

cart·age (kär′tij), *n.* **1** cost or price of carting. **2** act of carting.

carte blanche (kärt′ bläNsh′), *French,* full authority; freedom to use one's own judgment.

car·tel (kär tel′; kär′təl), *n.* large group of businesses that agree to fix prices and production to operate as a monopoly. [< F < Ital. *cartello* little CARD[1]]

Car·ter (kärt′ər), **James (Jimmy) Earl, Jr.** 1924–, 39th president of the United States, 1977–81.

Car·te·sian (kär tē′zhən), *adj.* having to do with Descartes, or with his doctrines or methods. [< NL, < *Cartesius,* Latinized form of *Descartes*]

Car·thage (kär′thij), *n.* a powerful ancient city and seaport in N Africa, founded by the Phoenicians, destroyed by the Romans in 146 B.C. —**Car′tha·gin′i-an,** *adj., n.*

Car·thu·sian (kär thü′zhən), *n.* member of an order of monks founded in 1086. —*adj.* of this order. [< *Chatrousse,* village where the first monastery of the order was]

car·ti·lage (kär′tə lij), *n.* **1** the firm, tough, elastic, flexible substance forming parts of a skeleton; gristle. **2** part formed of this substance. The nose is supported by cartilages. [< F < L *cartilago*]

car·ti·lag·i·nous (kär′tə laj′ə nəs), *adj.* **1** of or like cartilage; gristly. **2** having the skeleton formed mostly of cartilage.

cart·load (kärt′lōd′), *n.* as much as a cart can hold or carry.

car·tog·ra·phy (kär tog′rə fi), *n.* the making of maps or charts. [< Med.L *carta* chart, map + E *–graphy* drawing < Gk. *graphein* draw, write] —**car·tog′ra·pher,** *n.* —**car′to·graph′ic, car′to·graph′i·cal,** *adj.* —**car′to·graph′i·cal·ly,** *adv.*

car·ton (kär′tən), *n.* **1** box made of pasteboard. **2** as much as a carton can hold. [< F *carton* pasteboard < Ital., < *carta.* See CARD[1].]

car·toon (kär tün′), *n.* **1** sketch or drawing showing persons, things, political events, etc., in an exaggerated way. **2** a full-size drawing of a design or painting, for a fresco, mosaic, tapestry, etc. **3** =comic strip. **4** animated cartoon. —*v.* make a cartoon of. [var. of *carton;* because drawn on paper] —**car·toon′-ing,** *n.* —**car·toon′ist,** *n.*

car·tridge (kär′trij), *n.* **1** case made of metal or cardboard for holding gunpowder. **2** roll of camera film. **3** any of various containers to hold ink, charcoal for filters, etc. [alter. of *cartouche* (< F) a roll of paper]

cart·wheel (kärt′hwēl′), *n.* **1** wheel of a cart. **2** a sidewise handspring or somersault.

carve (kärv), *v.,* **carved, carv·ing. 1** cut into slices or pieces. **2** cut; make by cutting. **3** decorate with figures or designs cut on the surface.

carve up, divide into shares or pieces. [OE *ceorfan*] —**carv′er,** *n.*

car·vel (kär′vəl), *n.* =caravel.

carv·en (kär′vən), *adj. Poetic.* carved.

carv·ing (kär′ving), *n.* **1** act or art of one that carves. **2** carved work: *a wood carving.*

car wash, 1 business that washes automobiles automatically as the vehicle is passed through a series of water sprays, scrubbers, and rinses. **2** washing of an automobile.

car·y·at·id (kar′i at′id), *n., pl.* **–ids, –i-des** (–ə dēz). statue of a woman used as a column. [< L < Gk. *Karyatides* women of Caryae] —**car′y·at′i·dal,** *adj.*

car·y·op·sis (kar′i op′sis), *n.* small, dry seed fruit, esp. of grasses as a grain of wheat.

ca·sa·ba (kə sä′bə), or **casaba melon,** *n.* kind of muskmelon with a yellow rind. Also, **cassaba.** [after *Kasaba* near Smyrna, Asia Minor]

Cas·a·blan·ca (kas′ə blang′kə; kä′sə bläng′kə), *n.* seaport in NW Morocco.

Cas·bah (käz′bä), *n.* **1** old quarter of Algiers. **2** Also, **casbah.** similar section of various other esp. N African cities. **3** *Fig.* any place suggestive of the old, winding streets of the Casbah.

cas·cade (kas kād′), *n., v.,* **–cad·ed, –cad-ing.** —*n.* **1** a small waterfall. **2** anything like this. —*v.* fall in a cascade. [< F < Ital. *cascata* < L *cadere* fall]

Cascade Range, mountain range in NW United States, extending from N California to British Columbia.

cas·car·a (kas kär′ə), *n.* laxative made from the dried bark of a species of buckthorn. [< Sp., bark]

case¹ (kās), *n.* **1** instance; example: *a case of poor work.* **2** condition: *a case of poverty.* **3** instance of a disease or injury: *a case of measles.* **4** matter for a law court to decide. **5** a convincing argument. **6** one of the forms of a noun, pronoun, or adjective used to show its relation to other words.
in any case, under any circumstances; anyhow.
in case, if; supposing.
in case of, in the event of. [< OF < L *casus* a falling, chance < *cadere* fall]

case² (kās), *n., v.,* **cased, cas·ing.** —*n.* **1** covering. **2** box. **3** quantity in a box. **4** frame: *a window fits in a case.* —*v.* put in a case; cover with a case. [< OF < L *capsa* box < *capere* hold]

case·hard·en (kās′här′dən), *v.* **1** harden (iron or steel) on the surface. **2** render callous; make unfeeling.

case history, 1 all facts concerning a person or group that may be useful in deciding treatment or future action. **2** record of a particular case.

ca·se·in (kā′si in; –sēn), *n.* protein present in milk. Cheese is mostly casein. [< L *caseus* cheese]

case·load (kās′lōd′), *n.* number of cases handled by a court, social worker, etc.

case·ment (kās′mənt), *n.* **1** a window opening on hinges like a door. **2** *Poetic.* any window. **3** casing; covering; frame. —**case′ment·ed,** *adj.*

ca·se·ous (kā′si əs), *adj.* of or like cheese. [< L *caseus* cheese]

case·work (kās′werk′), *n.* **1** investigation and help by social workers of particular individuals, or families as units. **2** the occupation of doing this. —**case′work′er,** *n.*

cash (kash), *n.* **1** ready money; coins and bills. **2** money, or an equivalent, as a check, paid at the time of buying something. —*v.* **1** get cash for. **2** give cash for.
cash in, in poker, etc., change (chips, etc.) into cash.
cash in on, a make a profit from. **b** use to advantage. [< F *caisse* < Pr. < L *capsa* box, coffer]

cash-and-carry (kash′ən kar′i), *adj.* **1** with immediate payment and no delivery of goods purchased. **2** operated on this basis.

cash·book (kash′buk′), *n.* book in which a record is kept of money received and paid out.

cash cow, regular and reliable source of income, often with little investment of time or money involved.

cash crop, crop grown for sale on a farm.

cash·ew (kash′ü; kə shü′), *n.* **1** a small kidney-shaped nut. **2** the tropical American tree that it grows on. [< F < Brazilian Pg. *acajú* < Tupi]

cash·ier¹ (kash ir′), *n.* person who has charge of money in a bank or business. [< F *caissier* treasurer. See CASH¹.]

cash·ier² (kash ir′), *v.* dismiss from service; discharge in disgrace. [< Du. < F < L *quassare* shatter and LL *cassare* annul]

cash machine, =automatic teller machine.

cash·mere (kash′mir), *n.* **1** fine, soft wool from goats. **2** fine, soft wool from sheep. **3** a fine, soft woolen cloth. [after *Kashmir*]

Cash·mere (kash mir′; kash′mir), *n.* =Kashmir.

cash register, machine which records and shows the amount of a sale, usually with a drawer to hold money.

cas·ing (kās′ing), *n.* **1** thing put around something; covering; case. **2** the part of a sausage that encloses the meat. **3** framework around a door or window.

ca·si·no (kə sē′nō), *n., pl.* **-nos. 1** a building or room for dancing, gambling, etc. **2** a card game. Also, **cassino.** [< Ital., dim. of *casa* house < L *casa*]

cask (kask; käsk), *n.* **1** barrel. A cask may be large or small, and is usually made to hold liquids. **2** amount that a cask holds. [< Sp. *casco* skull, cask of wine, ult. < L *quassare* break]

cas·ket (kas′kit; käs′–), *n.* **1** coffin. **2** small box to hold jewels, letters, etc.

Cas·pi·an Sea (kas′pi ən), an inland salt sea between Europe and Asia.

cas·sa·ba (kə sä′bə), *n.* =casaba.

Cas·san·dra (kə san′drə), *n.* **1** *Gk. Legend.* a prophetess of ancient Troy, who was fated never to be believed. **2** person who prophesies misfortune, but is not believed.

cas·sa·va (kə sä′və), *n.* **1** a tropical plant with starchy roots. **2** a nutritious starch from its roots; manioc. Tapioca is made from cassava. [< F < Sp. < Haitian *cacábi*]

cas·se·role (kas′ə rōl), *n.* **1** a covered baking dish in which food can be both cooked and served. **2** food cooked and served in such a dish. [< F, < *casse* pan < VL *cattia* < Gk. *kyathion,* dim. of *kyathos* cup]

cas·sette (kä set′), *n.* **1** cartridge of photographic film, magnetic tape, or typewriter ribbon. **2** cartridge of videotape.

cas·sia (kash′ə; kas′i ə), *n.* **1** an inferior kind of cinnamon. **2** the tree that produces it. **3** plant from whose leaves and pods the drugs senna is obtained. **4** the pods or their pulp. [< L < Gk. < Heb. *q'tsīāh*]

cas·si·mere (kas′ə mir), *n.* soft, lightweight woolen cloth, used in men's suits. [variant of *cashmere*]

cas·si·no (kə sē′nō), *n.* =casino (def. 2).

Cas·si·o·pe·ia (kas′i ə pē′ə), *n.* **1** *Gk. Legend.* mother of an Ethiopian princess who was rescued from a sea monster by Perseus. **2** northern constellation fancied to resemble Cassiopeia sitting in a chair.

cas·sock (kas′ək), *n.* a long outer garment, usually black, worn by a clergyman. [< F < Ital. *casacca*] —**cas′socked,** *adj.*

cas·so·war·y (kas′ə wer′i), *n., pl.* **-war-ies.** a large bird of Australia and New Guinea, like an ostrich, but smaller. [< Malay *kasuari*]

cast (kast; käst), *v.,* **cast, cast·ing,** *n., adj.* —*v.* **1** throw: *cast a fishing line.* **2** throw off; let fall: *the snake cast its skin.* **3** direct; turn: *he cast me a look.* **4** shape by pouring or squeezing into a mold to harden. **5** arrange (actors and parts in a play). **6** lower. —*n.* **1** act of throwing. **2** thing made by casting. **3** mold. **4** actors in a play. **5** form; look; appearance. **6** kind; sort. **7** a slight amount of color. —*adj.* (of a play) having all the actors chosen.
cast about, a search; look. **b** lay plans; scheme.
cast aside, a throw or put aside. **b** discard.
cast away, a abandon. **b** shipwreck.
cast down, a turn downward; lower. **b** make sad or discouraged.
cast off, a let loose; untie. **b** abandon; discard. **c** make the last row in knitting.
cast on, make the first row of stitches in knitting.
cast out, banish; expel.
cast up, a arise. **b** add up. [< Scand. *kasta* throw]

cas·ta·net (kas′tə net′), *n.* a pair, or one of a pair, of instruments of hard wood or ivory like little cymbals, held in the hand and clicked together to beat time for dancing or music. [< Sp. *castaneta* < L *castanea* CHESTNUT]

cast·a·way (kast′ə wā′; käst′–), *adj.* **1** thrown away; cast adrift. **2** outcast. —*n.* **1** shipwrecked person. **2** outcast.

caste (kast; käst), *n.* **1** any of the hereditary social classes into which the Hindus are divided. **2** an exclusive social group; distinct class. **3** a social system having class distinctions based on rank, wealth, position, etc.
lose caste, lose social rank or position. [< Sp. < Pg. *casta* race < L *castus* pure]

cas·tel·lat·ed (kas′tə lāt′id), *adj.* having turrets and battlements. —**cas′tel·la′-tion,** *n.*

cast·er (kas′tər; käs′–), *n.* **1** person or thing that casts. **2** Also, **castor, a** a small wheel on a piece of furniture to make it easier to move. **b** bottle containing salt, mustard, vinegar, or other seasoning for table use. **c** stand or rack for such bottles.

cas·ti·gate (kas′tə gāt), *v.,* **-gat·ed, -gat·ing.** criticize severely; punish. [< L *castigatus,* ult. < *castus* pure] —**cas′ti·ga′-tion,** *n.* —**cas′ti·ga′tor,** *n.*

Cas·tile (kas tēl′), *n.* **1** region in N and C Spain, formerly a kingdom. **2** Castile soap.

Castile soap, a pure, hard soap made from olive oil.

Cas·til·ian (kas til′yən), *adj.* of Castile, its people, or their language. —*n.* **1 Castilian Spanish,** the accepted standard form of Spanish. **2** native or inhabitant of Castile.

cast·ing (kas′ting; käs′–), *n.* thing shaped by being poured into a mold to harden.

cast iron, a hard, brittle form of iron made by casting.

cast-i·ron (kast′ī′ərn; käst′–), *adj.* 1 made of cast iron. 2 hard; not yielding. 3 hardy; strong.

cas·tle (kas′əl; käs′–), *n., v.,* –tled, –tling. —*n.* 1 building or group of buildings with thick walls, towers, and other defenses against attack. 2 palace that once had defenses against attack. 3 large and imposing residence. 4 piece in the game of chess, shaped like a tower. —*v.* move the king two squares toward a castle and bring that castle to the square the king has passed over. [< L *castellum,* dim. of *castrum* fort. Doublet of CHA-TEAU.] —**cas′tled,** *adj.*

castle in the air, =daydream.

cast-off (kast′ôf′; –ôf′; käst′–), *adj.* thrown away; abandoned. —*n.* person or thing that has been cast off.

cas·tor¹ (kas′tər; käs′–), *n.* =caster (def. 2).

cas·tor² (kas′tər; käs′–), *n.* an oily substance with a strong odor, secreted by beavers. It is used in making perfume and in medicines. [< L < Gk. *kastor* beaver]

Cas·tor (kas′tər; käs′–), *n.* 1 *Class. Myth.* the mortal twin brother of Pollux. 2 the fainter star of the two bright stars in the constellation called Gemini.

castor bean, seed of the castor-oil plant.

castor oil, yellow oil obtained from castor beans, used as a cathartic, a lubricant, etc.

cas·tor-oil plant (kas′tər oil′; käs′–), a tall tropical plant from whose seeds castor oil is obtained.

cas·trate (kas′trāt), *v.,* –trat·ed, –trat·ing. 1 a remove the male glands of. b =spay. 2 *Fig.* mutilate; expurgate. —*n.* castrated person or animal. [< L *castratus*] —**cas·tra′tion,** *n.*

Cas·tro (kas′trō), *n.* **Fidel,** (1927–), premier of Cuba since 1959.

cas·u·al (kazh′ü əl), *adj.* 1 happening by chance; accidental. 2 careless; unconcerned; offhand. 3 occasional; irregular. A **casual laborer** does any kind of work that is available. [< L *casualis* < *casus* chance] —**cas′u·al·ly,** *adv.* —**cas′u·al·ness,** *n.*

cas·u·al·ty (kazh′ü əl ti), *n., pl.* –ties. 1 accident. 2 mishap. 3 soldier or sailor who has been wounded, killed, or lost. 4 person injured or killed in an accident.

cas·u·ist (kazh′ü ist), *n.* 1 person who reasons cleverly but falsely. 2 person who decides questions of right and wrong in regard to conduct, duty, etc. [< F *casuiste* < L *casus* case]

cas·u·is·tic (kazh′ü is′tik), **cas·u·is·ti·cal** (–tə kəl), *adj.* 1 of or like casuistry. 2 too subtle; sophistical. —**cas′u·is′ti·cal·ly,** *adv.*

cas·u·ist·ry (kazh′ü is tri), *n., pl.* –ries. 1 clever but false reasoning. 2 act or pro-

cess of deciding questions of right and wrong in regard to conduct, duty, etc.

ca·sus bel·li (kā′səs bel′ī), *Latin.* 1 occurrence on series of events considered to justify going to war. 2 (literally) a case of war.

cat¹ (kat), *n.,* 1 a small four-footed, furry animal often kept as a pet or for catching mice. 2 any animal of the group including cats, lions, tigers, leopards, etc. 3 a mean, spiteful woman. 4 =cat-o′-nine-tails.

bell the cat, undertake to do something dangerous.

let the cat out of the bag, reveal a secret.

rain cats and dogs, rain very hard. [OE *catt* (male), *catte* (fem.), prob. < LL *cattus, catta*] —**cat′like′,** *adj.*

cat² (kat), *n.* 1 =caterpillar (tractor). 2 **Cat** = *Trademark,* Caterpillar.

CAT, 1 computerized axial tomography. 2 clear air turbulence.

cat. 1 catalog. 2 catechism.

ca·tab·o·lism (kə tab′ə liz əm), *n.* process of breaking down living tissues into simpler substances or waste matter, thereby producing energy. [prob. < *metabolism,* by substitution of *cata-* down] —**cat′a·bol′ic,** *adj.* —**cat′a·bol′i·cal·ly,** *adv.*

cat·a·chre·sis (kat′ə krē′sis), *n., pl.* –ses (–sēz). misuse of words. [< L < Gk. *katachresis* misuse < *kata-* amiss + *chresthai* use] —**cat′a·chres′tic,** *adj.* —**cat′achres′ti·cal·ly,** *adv.*

cat·a·clysm (kat′ə kliz əm), *n.* 1 a flood, earthquake, or any sudden, violent change in the earth. 2 any violent change. [< L < Gk. *kataklysmos* flood < *kata-* down + *klyzein* wash]

cat·a·clys·mic (kat′ə kliz′mik), **cat·a·clys·mal** (–məl), *adj.* of or like a cataclysm; extremely sudden and violent. —**cat′a·clys′mi·cal·ly,** *adv.*

cat·a·comb (kat′ə kōm), *n.* Usually, **cata·combs.** an underground gallery forming a burial place. [< LL *catacumbae* < *cata* (< Gk.) *tumbas* among the tombs. See TOMB.]

cat·a·falque (kat′ə falk), *n.* stand or frame to support the coffin in which a dead person lies. [< F < Ital. *catafalco* < LL, < L *cata-* down + *fala* tower]

Cat·a·lan (kat′ə lan; –lən), *adj.* of Catalonia, its people, or their language. —*n.* 1 native or inhabitant of Catalonia. 2 language spoken in Catalonia.

cat·a·lep·sy (kat′ə lep′si), **cat·a·lep·sis** (kat′ə lep′sis), *n.* kind of fit during which a person loses consciousness and power to feel and his muscles become rigid. [< LL < Gk. *katalepsis* seizure < *kata-*down + *lambanein* seize] —**cat′a·lep′tic,** *adj., n.*

Cat·a·li·na (kat′ə lē′nə), *n.* Santa Catalina.

cat·a·log (katēə lôg; –log), *n., v.,* –loged, –log·ing. —*n.* 1 a list, esp. a list arranged in alphabetical or other methodical order, with brief particulars concerning

the names, articles, etc., listed. 2 volume or booklet issued by a college or university listing rules, courses to be given, etc. —*v.* make a catalog of; put in a catalog. Also **catalogue.** [< F < LL < Gk. *katalogos* list < *kata-* down + *legein* count] —**cat′a·log′er, cat′a·log′ist,** *n.*

Cat·a·lo·ni·a (kat′ə lō′ni ə), *n.* region in NE Spain.

ca·tal·pa (kə tal′pə), *n.* tree with large, heart-shaped leaves, bell-shaped flowers, and long pods. [< NL < Am.Ind. (Creek) *kutuhlpa*]

ca·tal·y·sis (kə tal′ə sis), *n., pl.* –ses (–sēz). the causing or speeding up of a chemical reaction by the presence of a substance that does not itself change. [< NL < Gk. *katalysis* dissolution < *kata-* down + *lyein* to loose] —**cat′a·lyt′ic,** *adj.* —**cat′a·lyt′i·cal·ly,** *adv.*

cat·a·lyst (kat′ə list), *n.* substance that causes catalysis.

catalytic converter, device in automobiles and chimneys that uses a chemical catalyst to convert exhaust gases into harmless products.

cat·a·lyze (kat′ə līz), *v.,* –lyzed, –lyz·ing. act upon by catalysis. —**cat′a·lyz′er,** *n.*

cat·a·ma·ran (kat′ə mə ran′), *n.* 1 boat with two hulls side by side. 2 raft made of pieces of wood lashed together. [< Tamil *katta-maram* tied tree]

cat·a·mount (kat′ə mount′), *n.* wildcat, such as a puma or lynx. [short for *cata-mountain* cat of (the) mountain]

cat·a·pult (kat′ə pult), *n.* 1 an ancient weapon for shooting stones, arrows, etc. 2 device for launching an airplane from the deck of a ship. —*v.* 1 shoot from a catapult; throw; hurl. 2 *Fig.* launch or hurl suddenly: *catapulted to success.* [< L < Gk. *katapeltes,* prob. < *kata-* down + *pallein* hurl]

cat·a·ract (kat′ə rakt), *n.* 1 a large, steep waterfall. 2 a violent rush or downpour of water; flood. 3 an opaque region in the lens or capsule of the eye that causes partial or total blindness. [< L < Gk. *kataraktes* < *kata-* down + *aras-sein* dash]

ca·tarrh (kə tär′), *n.* an inflamed condition of a mucous membrane, usually that of the nose or throat, causing a discharge of mucus. [< F < L < Gk. *katarrhous* < *kata-* down + *rheein* flow] —**ca·tarrh′al,** *adj.*

ca·tas·tro·phe (kə tas′trə fē), *n.* a sudden, widespread, or extraordinary disaster; great calamity or misfortune. [< Gk. *katastrophe* overturning < *kata-* down + *strophein* turn] —**cat′a·stroph′ic,** *adj.*

cat·a·to·ni·a (kat′ə tō′nē ə), *n.* condition characterized by mental stupor and rigidity. —**cat′a·ton′ic,** *adj., n.*

Ca·taw·ba (kə tô′bə), *n., pl.* –bas. 1 a light-red grape. 2 a light wine made from it.

cat·bird (kat′bérd′), *n.* a slate-gray, American songbird that makes a sound like a cat mewing.

catbird seat, *Informal.* position of advantage and power.

cat·boat (kat′bōt′), *n.* sailboat with one mast set far forward. It has no bowsprit or jib.

cat burglar, burglar who gains entry by means of skillful climbing.

cat·call (kat′kôl′), *n.* a shrill cry or whistle to express disapproval. —*v.* **1** make catcalls. **2** attack with catcalls.

catch (kach), *v.,* **caught, catch·ing,** *n., adj.* —*v.* **1** seize; capture. **2** take; get. **3** burn: *tinder catches easily.* **4** surprise. **5** act as catcher in baseball. —*n.* **1** act of catching. **2** thing that catches as a fastener for a door or window. **3** thing caught. **4** a good person to marry. **5** a hidden condition. —*adj.* **1** getting one's attention: *a catch phrase.* **2** tricky; deceptive: *a catch question.*

catch on, a understand; get the idea. **b** become popular; be widely used or accepted.

catch up, a overtake. **b** snatch; grab. **c** *Fig.* become involved. **d** held up in loops: *a long shirt caught up with ribbons.* **e** heckle. [< OF *cachier* < LL *captiare* < L *capere* take. Doublet of CHASE[1].] —**catch′a·ble,** *adj.*

Catch-22 or **catch-22** (kach′twen′ti tü), *n.* situation or condition that cannot be remedied regardless of all efforts made to fix it, usually because of a contrary rule or situation.

catch·all (kach′ôl′), *n.* container for odds and ends.

catch basin, 1 reservoir for catching and storing drainage over a large area. **2** receptacle in a storm drain that catches debris.

catch·er (kach′ər), *n.* **1** person or thing that catches. **2** a baseball player who stands behind the batter to catch the ball thrown by the pitcher.

catch·ing (kach′ing), *adj.* **1** contagious; infectious. **2** attractive; fascinating.

catch·ment (kach′mənt), *n.* **1** reservoir for catching water. **2** =drainage.

catch phrase, phrase that draws attention and is easily remembered.

catch·up (kech′əp; kach′–), *n.* =ketchup.

catch·word (kach′wėrd′), *n.* **1** word or phrase used again and again for effect; slogan. **2** word so placed as to catch attention.

catch·y (kach′i), *adj.,* **catch·i·er, catch·i·est.** **1** easy to remember; attractive. **2** tricky; misleading; deceptive.

cat·e·chism (kat′ə kiz əm), *n.* **1** book of questions and answers about religion, used for teaching religious doctrine. **2** set of questions and answers about any subject. **3** a long or formal set of questions. —**cat′e·chis′mal,** *adj.*

cat·e·chist (kat′ə kist), *n.* person who catechizes. —**cat′e·chis′tic, cat′e·chis′ti·cal,** *adj.* —**cat′e·chis′ti·cal·ly,** *adv.*

cat·e·chize, (kat′ə kīz), *v.,* **–chized, –chiz·ing.** **1** teach by questions and answers. **2** question closely. [< L < Gk. *kate-*

chizein teach orally < *kata–* thoroughly + *echeein* sound] —**cat′e·chi·za′tion,** *n.* —**cat′e·chiz′er** *n.*

cat·e·gor·ic (kat′ə gor′ik), *adj.* =categorical.

cat·e·gor·i·cal (kat′ə gôr′ə kəl; –gor′–), *adj.* **1** without conditions or qualifications; positive. **2** of or in a category. —**cat′e·gor′i·cal·ly,** *adv.* —**cat′e·gor′i·cal·ness,** *n.*

cat·e·go·rize (kat′ə gə rīz), *v.,* **–ized, –iz·ing.** put into a category or categories; classify. —**cat′e·go·ri·za′tion,** *n.*

cat·e·go·ry (kat′ə gô′ri; –gō′–), *n., pl.* **–ries.** group or division in a general system of classification; class. [< L < Gk. *kategoria* assertion < *kata–* down + *agoreuein* speak]

cat·e·nate (kat′ə nāt), *v.,* **–nat·ed, –nat·ing.** connect in a series. [< L, *catena* chain] —**cat′e·na′tion,** *n.*

ca·ter (kā′tər), *v.* **1** provide food or supplies. **2** *Fig.* supply what is needed or wanted. [verbal use of *cater,* n., ME *acatour* buyer of provisions < F, < *acater* < LL *accaptare* acquire]

cat·er-cor·nered (kat′ər kôr′nərd), *adj.* diagonal. —*adv.* diagonally. [< *cater* diagonally (< F *quatre* four) + *cornered*]

ca·ter·er (kā′tər ər), *n.* person who provides food or supplies for parties, etc.

cat·er·pil·lar (kat′ər pil′ər), *n.* **1** wormlike form or larva of a butterfly or moth. **2 Caterpillar.** *Trademark.* tractor and other machinery that can travel over very rough ground on its two endless belts. [cf. OF *chatepelose* hairy cat]

cat·er·waul (kat′ər wôl), *v.* howl like a cat; screech. —*n.* Also, **cat′er·waul′ing.** such a howl or screech. [ME *caterwrawe* < *cater,* appar., cat + *wrawe* wail, howl]

cat·fight (kat′fīt′), *n.* noisy, spiteful quarrel, esp. between women.

cat·fish (kat′fish′), *n., pl.* **–fish·es** or (*esp. collectively*) **–fish.** a scaleless fish with long, slender feelers around the mouth.

cat·gut (kat′gut′), *n.* a tough string made from the dried and twisted intestines of sheep or other animals, used for violin strings, etc.

Cath., 1 Also, **cath.** Cathedral. **2** Catholic.

ca·thar·sis (kə thär′sis), *n.* **1** a purging. **2** emotional purification or relief. [< NL < Gk. *katharsis,* ult. < *katharos* clean]

ca·thar·tic (kə thär′tik), *n.* strong laxative. Epsom salts and castor oil are cathartics. —*adj.* Also, **ca·thar′ti·cal.** strongly laxative.

Ca·thay (ka thā′), *n.* *Poetic or Archaic.* China.

ca·the·dral (kə thē′drəl), *n.* **1** official church of a bishop. **2** large or important church. —*adj.* **1** having a bishop's throne. **2** of or like a cathedral. **3** authoritative. [< Med.L < L Gk. *kathedra* seat]

Catherine the Great, 1729–96, empress of Russia from 1762 to 1796.

cath·e·ter (kath′ə tər), *n.* a slender tube to be inserted into a duct of the body.

[< LL < Gk. *katheter* < *kata–* down + *hienai* send]

cath·e·ter·ize (kath′ə tə rīz′), *v.,* **–ized, –iz·ing.** insert a catheter into.

cath·ode (kath′ōd), *n.* negative electrode. The zinc case of a dry cell is a cathodes. [< Gk. *kathodos* a way down < *kata–* down + *hodos* a way] —**ca·thod′ic, ca·thod′i·cal,** *adj.*

cathode rays, invisible streams of electrons from the cathode in a vacuum tube. When cathode rays strike a solid substance, they produce X rays.

cath·ode-ray tube (kath′ōd rā), vacuum tube in which high-speed electrons are formed into a beam to reproduce an image on television, computer, and radar screens.

cath·o·lic (kath′ə lik; kath′lik), *adj.* **1** of interest or use to all people; including all; universal. **2** having sympathies with all; broad-minded; liberal. **3** of the whole Christian church. [< L < Gk. *katholikos* < *kata–* in respect to + *holos* whole] —**ca·thol′i·cal·ly,** *adv.*

Cath·o·lic (kath′ə lik; kath′lik), *adj.* **1** of the Christian church governed by the Pope; Roman Catholic. **2** of the ancient undivided Christian church, or of its present representatives. —*n.* member of either of these churches.

Ca·thol·i·cism (kə thol′ə siz əm), **Cath·o·lic·i·ty** (kath′ə lis′ə ti), *n.* faith, doctrine, organization, and methods of the Roman Catholic Church.

cath·o·lic·i·ty (kath′ə lis′ə ti), **ca·thol·i·cism** (kə thol′ə siz əm), *n.* **1** universality; wide prevalence. **2** broad-mindedness, liberalness.

ca·thol·i·cize (kə thol′ə sīz), *v.,* **–cized, –ciz·ing.** make or become catholic; universalize.

cat·i·on (kat′ī′ən), *n.* **1** positive ion. During electrolysis, cations move toward the negative pole. **2** atom or group of atoms having a positive charge. Also, **kation.** [< Gk. *kation* going down < *kata–* down + *ienai* go]

cat·kin (kat′kin), *n.* the downy or scaly spike of flowers that grows on willows, birches, etc.; ament. [< Du. *katteken* little cat]

cat·nap (kat′nap′), *n., v.,* **–napped, –nap·ping.** —*n.* doze. —*v.* sleep or doze for a little while.

catnip (kat′nip), *n.* kind of mint of which cats are fond. [< *cat* + *nip,* var. of *nep* catnip < L *nepeta*]

Ca·to (kā′tō), *n.* **1 Marcus Porcius,** 234–149 B.C., Roman statesman and patriot. **2** his great-grandson, **Marcus Porcius,** 95–46 B.C., Roman statesman, soldier, and Stoic philosopher.

cat-o′-nine-tails (kat′ə nīn′tālz′), *n., pl.* **–tails.** whip consisting of nine pieces of knotted cord fastened to a handle.

CAT scan, 1 X-ray picture made by computerized axial tomography that shows cross-sections of any part of the body. **2** =CAT scanner. **3** =CAT scanning.

CAT scanner, machine that takes X-ray pictures by computerized axial tomography.

CAT scanning, act or process of taking X-ray pictures by means of computerized axial tomography.

cat's cradle, child's game played with string looped over both hands.

cat's-eye (kats'ī'), *n.* **1** semi-precious gem that has a streak of reflected light in its center, resembling the eye of a cat. **2** small reflector in a road, on a fence, etc.

Cats·kills (kats'kilz), *n.pl.* a low mountain range in SE New York State.

cat's-paw, cats·paw (kats'pô'), *n.* **1** person used by another to do something unpleasant or dangerous. **2** a light breeze that ruffles a small stretch of water.

cat·sup (kech'əp; kat'səp), *n.* =ketchup.

cat·tail (kat'tāl'), *n.,* **1** tall marsh plant with flowers in long, round, furry, brown spikes. **2** ament; catkin.

cat·tish (kat'ish), *adj.* **1** catlike. **2** catty. —**cat'tish·ly,** *adv.* —**cat'tish·ness,** *n.*

cat·tle (kat'əl), *n.* **1** cows, bulls, and steers; oxen. **2** farm animals; livestock. **3** low, worthless people. [< OF *catel* < L *capitale* property, CAPITAL[1]. Doublet of CHATTEL.]

cat·tle·man (kat'əl mən), *n., pl.* **-men.** person who raises or takes care of cattle.

cat·ty (kat'i), *adj.,* **-ti·er, -ti·est. 1** mean; spiteful. **2** catlike. **3** of cats. —**cat'ti·ly,** *adv.* —**cat'ti·ness,** *n.*

cat·walk (kat'wôk'), *n.* narrow place for walking on a bridge.

Cau·ca·sia (kô kā'zhə; -shə), *n.* region in S Russia, between the Black and Caspian Seas. Also, **Caucasus.**

Cau·ca·sian (kô kā'zhən; -shən; -kazh'ən; -kash'ən), *n.* **1** member of the so-called white race, including the chief peoples of Europe, SW Asia, and N Africa. **2** native of Caucasia. —*adj.* **1** of or having to do with the so-called white race. **2** of or having to do with Caucasia or its inhabitants.

Cau·ca·sus (kô'kə səs), *n.* **1** mountain range in S Russia, between the Black and Caspian Seas. **2** Caucasia.

cau·cus (kô'kəs), *n.* a meeting of members or leaders of a political party to make plans, choose candidates, decide how to vote, etc. —*v.* hold a caucus. [? < Med.L *caucus* < Med.Gk. *kaukos,* a drinking vessel; "in allusion to the convivial feature" of the Caucus Club, a political club of the 18th century]

cau·dal (kô'dəl), *adj.* **a** of, at, or near the tail of an animal: *a caudal fin.* **b** tail-like. [< NL *caudalis* < L *cauda* tail] —**cau'dal·ly,** *adv.*

cau·date (kô'dāt), **cau·dat·ed** (-dāt id), *adj.* having a tail.

caught (kôt), *v.* pt. and pp. of **catch.**

caul (kôl), *n.* membrane sometimes covering the head of a child at birth. [< OF *cale* a kind of little cap]

caul·dron (kôl'drən), *n.* =caldron.

cau·li·flow·er (kô'lə flou'ər; kol'i-), *n.* vegetable having a solid, white head with a few leaves around it. [half-trans. of NL *cauliflora* < *caulis* cabbage + *flos* flower]

caulk (kôk), *v.* =calk[1]. —**caulk'er,** *n.*

caus·al (kôz'əl), *adj.* **1** of a cause. **2** having to do with cause and effect. **3** showing a cause. —**caus'al·ly,** *adv.*

cau·sal·i·ty (kô zal'ə ti), *n., pl.* **-ties. 1** relation of cause and effect; principle that nothing can exist without a cause. **2** causal quality or agency.

cau·sa·tion (kô zā'shən), *n.* **1** a causing or being caused. **2** whatever produces an effect. **3** relation of cause and effect; principle that nothing can exist without a cause.

caus·a·tive (kôz'ə tiv), *adj.* **1** being a cause; productive. **2** expressing causation. —**caus'a·tive·ly,** *adv.* —**caus'a·tive·ness,** *n.*

cause (kôz), *n., v.,* **caused, caus·ing.** —*n.* **1** person or thing that makes something happen: *the earthquake was the cause of much damage.* **2** reason; motive: *cause for celebration.* **3** good reason: *he was angry without cause.* **4** movement in which many people are interested. —*v.* make happen; bring about.

make common cause with, join efforts with; help and support.

show cause, present reason or reasons why an order, judgment, etc. from a court should not be carried out. [< L *causa*] —**caus'a·ble,** *adj.* —**cause'less,** *adj.* —**caus'er,** *n.*

cause cé·lè·bre (kōz sā leb'rə), *French.* **1** famous case (in law). **2** situation or event attracting intense attention. **3** (literally) a celebrated cause.

cau·se·rie (kō'zə rē'), *n.* **1** an informal talk. **2** short written article. [< F, < *causer* talk]

cause·way (kôz'wā'), *n.* **1** a raised road or path, usually built across wet ground, shallow water, etc. **2** a highway. [var. of *causey(way)* < OF < LL *calciata* paved way < L *calx* limestone]

caus·tic (kôs'tik), *n.* substance that burns or destroys flesh; corrosive substance. —*adj.* **1** that burns or destroys flesh; corrosive. **2** sarcastic; stinging; biting. [< L < Gk. *kaustikos*] —**caus'ti·cal·ly,** *adv.*

caustic soda, sodium hydroxide, NaOH.

cau·ter·ize (kô'tər īz), *v.,* **-ized, -iz·ing.** burn with a hot iron or a caustic substance, esp. to prevent bleeding or infection. —**cau'ter·i·za'tion,** *n.*

cau·ter·y (kô'tər i), *n., pl.* **-ter·ies. 1** a cauterizing. **2** instrument or substance used in cauterizing. [< L < Gk. *kauterion,* dim. of *kauter* branding iron]

cau·tion (kô'shən), *n.* **1** cautious behavior. **2** a warning. **3** very unusual person or thing. —*v.* warn; urge to be careful. [< L *cautio* < *cavere* beware]

cau·tion·ar·y (kô'shən er'i), *adj.* warning; urging to be careful.

cau·tious (kô'shəs), *adj.* very careful; taking care to be safe; never taking chances. —**cau'tious·ly,** *adv.* —**cau'tious·ness,** *n.*

cav·al·cade (kav'əl kād'; kav'əl kād), *n.* procession of persons riding on horses or in carriages. [< F < Ital., < *cavalcare* ride horseback < LL, < L *caballus* horse]

cav·a·lier (kav'ə lir'), *n.* **1** a courteous gentleman. **2** a courteous escort for a lady. **3** horseman; mounted soldier; knight. **4 Cavalier,** person who supported Charles I of England in his struggle with Parliament from 1641 to 1649. —*adj.* **1** proud and scornful; haughty; arrogant. **2** free and easy; offhand. **3 Cavalier,** of the Cavaliers. [< F < Ital. *cavalliere* < *cavallo* horse < L *caballus*] —**cav'a·lier'ly,** *adv.*

cav·al·ry (kav'əl ri), *n., pl.* **-ries. 1** soldiers who fight on horseback. **2** horsemen, horses, etc., collectively. [< F < Ital. *cavalleria* knighthood. See CAVALIER.]

cave (kāv), *n., v.,* **caved, cav·ing.** —*n.* hollow space underground. —*v.* **cave in, a** sink. **b** smash. **c** yield; submit. [< F < L *cava* hollow (places)]

ca·ve·at (kā'vi at), *n.* **1** a warning. **2** legal notice given to a law officer or some legal authority not to do something until the person giving notice can be heard. [< L *caveat* let him beware]

ca·ve·at emp·tor (kā'vēat emp'tôr), *Latin.* let the buyer beware; buy at your own risk.

cave-in (kāv'in'), *n.* **1** a caving in. **2** place where something has caved in.

cave man, 1 Also, **cave dweller,** person who lived in caves in prehistoric times. **2** *Fig.* a rough, crude man.

cav·ern (kav'ərn), *n.* a large cave. [< F < L *caverna* < *cavus* hollow]

cav·ern·ous (kav'ər nəs), *adj.* **1** like a cavern; large and hollow. **2** full of caverns. —**cav'ern·ous·ly,** *adv.*

cav·i·ar, cav·i·are (kav'i är; kä'vi-), *n.* salty relish made from the eggs of sturgeon or other large fish. [< F < Ital. < Turk. *khaviar*]

cav·il (kav'əl), *v.,* **-iled, -il·ing,** *n.* —*v.* find fault unnecessarily; raise trivial objections. —*n.* a petty objection. [< F < L *cavillari* jeer] —**cav'il·er,** *n.*

cav·i·ty (kav'ə ti), *n., pl.* **-ties. 1** hole; hollow place: *a cavity in a tooth.* **2** enclosed space inside the body: *the abdominal cavity.* [< F < LL *cavitas* < L *cavus* hollow]

ca·vort (kə vôrt'), *v.* prance about; jump around. [orig. unknown] —**ca·vort'er,** *n.* —**ca·vort'ing,** *n., adj.*

ca·vy (kā'vi), *n., pl.* **-vies.** a South American rodent of the family which includes the guinea pig.

caw (kô), *n.* the harsh cry made by a crow or raven. —*v.* make this cry. [imit.]

Cax·ton (kak'stən), *n.* **William,** 1422?–91, first English printer.

cay (kā; kē), *n.* =key[2].

cay·enne (kī en'; kā-), or **cayenne pepper,** *n.* red pepper; very hot, biting powder made from seeds or fruit of a pepper plant. [after *Cayenne*, French Guiana]

cay·man (kā′mən), *n., pl.* **-mans.** a large alligator of tropical America. Also, **caiman.**

Ca·yu·ga (kā ū′gə; kī–), *n., pl.* **-ga, -gas.** 1 member of a tribe of Iroquois Indians formerly living in W New York State. 2 language of this tribe. —*adj.* of this tribe. [< Iroquoian tribal name]

cay·use (kī ūs′), *n.* W. 1 an Indian pony. 2 *Informal.* any horse. [for the *Cayuse* Indians]

Cb, columbium.

CB, 1 chemical and biological. 2 citizens band (radio).

C.B.er or **CBer** (sē′bē′ər), *n. Informal.* person who uses a citizens band radio.

cc, CC, Cc, copies to, in emails, letters, etc.

cc., c.c., cubic centimeter; cubic centimeters.

C clef, symbol in music that shows the position of middle C.

ccm, centimeters.

CCTV, closed-circuit television.

Cd, cadmium.

CD 1 compact disk. 2 certificate of deposit.

CD-ROM (sē dē′rom′), *n.* compact disk read-only memory, used for storage of electronic data.

Ce, cerium.

C.E. 1 Christian Era. 2 Common Era.

cease (ses), *v.*, **ceased, ceas·ing.** 1 come to an end. 2 put an end or stop to. [< F < L *cessare*]

cease-fire (ses′fīr′), *n.* a halt in military operations, esp. for the purpose of discussing peace.

cease·less (sēs′lis), *adj.* never stopping; going on all the time; continual. —**cease′less·ly,** *adv.*

Ce·cro·pi·a moth (si krō′pi ə), a large silkworm moth of the E United States.

ce·cum (sē′kəm), *n.* cavity closed at one end, esp. the first part of the large intestine. Also, **caecum.** [< L blind intestine]

ce·dar (sē′dər), *n.* 1 an evergreen tree with wide-spreading branches and fragrant, durable wood. 2 any of several trees with similar wood. 3 wood of any of these trees. —*adj.* made of cedar. [< L < Gk. *kedros*]

ce·dar·bird (sē′dər bėrd′), **cedar waxwing,** *n.* a small American bird with a crest and small, red markings on its wings; waxwing.

cede (sēd), *v.*, **ced·ed, ced·ing.** give up; surrender; hand over to another. [< L *cedere* yield, go]

ce·dil·la (si dil′ə), *n.* mark somewhat like a comma (ç) put under *c* in certain words to show that it has the sound of *s* before *a*, *o*, or *u*. *Example:* façade. [< Sp. < VL, dim. of L *zeta* < Gk., the letter *z*]

ceil·ing (sēl′ing), *n.* 1 the inside, top covering of a room; surface opposite to the floor. 2 a greatest height to which an air-

plane can go under certain conditions. **b** distance from the earth of the lowest clouds. 3 upper limit to which prices, wages, etc., are permitted to go. [< F *ciel* canopy, sky < L *caelum* heaven]

cel (sel), *n.* transparent sheet of celluloid on which drawings for animated cartoons are drawn.

cel·an·dine (sel′ən dīn), *n.* plant with yellow flowers. [< OF < L < Gk., < *chelidon* swallow[2]]

cel·e·brant (sel′ə brənt), *n.* 1 person who performs a ceremony or rite. 2 priest who performs Mass.

cel·e·brate (sel′ə brāt), *v.*, **-brat·ed, -brating.** 1 observe a festival or event with ceremonies or festivities. 2 observe with the proper ceremonies or festivities. 3 perform publicly with the proper ceremonies and rites: *a priest celebrates Mass in church.* 4 make known publicly; proclaim. 5 praise; honor. 6 have a joyous time. [< L *celebratus*] —**cel′e·bra′tor,** *n.*

cel·e·brat·ed (sel′ə brāt′id), *adj.* famous; well-known.

cel·e·bra·tion (sel′ə brā′shən), *n.* 1 act of celebrating. 2 whatever is done to celebrate something.

ce·leb·ri·ty (sə leb′rə ti), *n., pl.* **-ties.** 1 a famous person. 2 fame; being well known or much talked about.

ce·ler·i·ac (sə ler′ē ak), *n.* variety of celery having an edible root, used esp. in salads and soups; celery root.

ce·ler·i·ty (sə ler′ə ti), *n.* swiftness; speed. [< L, < *celer* swift]

cel·er·y (sel′ər ı; sel′rı), *n.* vegetable whose long, crisp stalks are eaten raw or cooked. [< F < dial. Ital. < L < Gk. *selinon* parsley]

ce·les·tial (sə les′chəl), *adj.* 1 of the sky; having to do with the heavens. The sun, moon, planets, and stars are celestial bodies. 2 heavenly; divine. 3 very beautiful. [< OF < L *caelestis* heavenly < *caelum* heaven] —**ce·les′tial·ly,** *adv.*

ce·li·ac (sē′li ak), *adj.* of or having to do with the abdominal cavity. Also, **coeliac.**

cel·i·ba·cy (sel′ə bə si), *n., pl.* **-cies.** unmarried state; single life.

cel·i·bate (sel′ə bit; –bāt), *n.* unmarried person; person who takes a vow to lead a single life, usually of sexual abstinence. —*adj.* 1 unmarried; single. 2 sexually abstinent. [< L *caelibatus* < *caelebs* unmarried]

cell (sel), *n.* 1 a small room in a prison, convent, etc. 2 a small, hollow place. Bees store honey in the cells of a honeycomb. 3 unit of living matter. Most cells have a nucleus near the center and are enclosed by a cell wall or membrane. 4 container holding materials for producing electricity by chemical action. 5 small group that acts as a political, social, or religious unit for a larger, sometimes revolutionary, organization. 6 =cell phone. [< L *cella* small room]

cel·lar (sel′ər), *n.* 1 an underground room or rooms, usually under a building. 2 cellar for wines. 3 supply of wines. [< F < L *cellarium* < *cella* small room]

cel·lar·age (sel′ər ij), *n.* 1 space in a cellar. 2 cellars. 3 charge for storage in a cellar.

cel·lar·er (sel′ər ər), *n.* person who takes care of a cellar and the food or wines in it.

Cel·li·ni (chə lē′ni), *n.* **Benvenuto,** 1500–71, Italian artist.

cel·list (chel′ist), *n.* person who plays the cello. Also, **violoncellist.**

cel·lo (chel′ō), *n., pl.* **-los.** instrument like a violin, but very much larger and held between the knees. Also, **violoncello.**

cel·lo·phane (sel′ə fān), *n.* a transparent substance made from cellulose, used as a wrapping to keep food, candy, etc., fresh and clean. [< *cell(ul)o(se)* + Gk. *phanein* appear]

cell phone, mobile telephone able to reach a wide area by means of low-power radio transmitters linking smaller areas called cells. Also, **cellular phone** or **telephone.**

cel·lu·lar (sel′yə lər), *adj.* 1 having to do with cells. 2 consisting of cells. —**cel′lu·lar′i·ty,** *n.*

cel·lu·lite (sel′yə līt; –ə lēt), *n.* fatty deposits beneath the skin. [< F *cellulite* < *cellule* cell]

cel·lu·li·tis (sel′yə lī′tis), *n.* inflammation of cellular tissue. [< L *cellula* cell + E –*itis*]

cel·lu·loid (sel′yə loid), *n.* a hard, transparent substance made from cellulose and camphor. —*adj.* pertaining to motion pictures.

cel·lu·lose (sel′yə lōs), *n.* substance that forms the walls of plant cells; woody part of trees and plants. Cellulose is used to make paper, artificial silk, explosives, etc. [L *cellula* small cell]

Celt (selt; kelt), *n.* member of a people to which the Irish, Highland Scotch, Welsh, and Bretons belong. The ancient Gauls and Britons were Celts. Also, **Kelt.**

Celt·ic (sel′tik; kel′tik), *adj.* of the Celts or their language. —*n.* the group of languages spoken by the Celts, including Irish, Gaelic, Welsh, and Breton. Also, **Keltic.**

ce·ment (si ment′), *n.* 1 substance made by burning clay and limestone. 2 this substance mixed with sand and water to make sidewalks, streets, floors, and walls and to hold stones or bricks together in building. 3 any soft substance that hardens and holds things together. 4 anything that joins together or unites. —*v.* 1 hold together with cement. 2 cover with cement. 3 join together; unite. [< OF < L *caementum* chippings of stone < *caedere* cut] —**ce·ment′er,** *n.*

ce·men·tum (sə men′təm), *n.* bony tissue that forms the outer crust of the root of a tooth.

cem·e·ter·y (sem′ə ter′i), *n., pl.* **-ter·ies.** place for burying the dead; graveyard. [< LL < Gk. *koimeterion* < *koimaein* lull to sleep]

ce·no·bite (sē′nə bīt; sen′ə-), *n.* member of a religious group living in a monastery or convent. [< LL *coenobita* < Gk., < *koinos* common + *bios* life] —**ce′no·bit′ic, ce′no·bit′i·cal,** *adj.*

cen·o·taph (sen′ə taf; -täf), *n.* monument erected in memory of a dead person whose body is elsewhere. [< L < Gk., < *kenos* empty + *taphos* tomb] —**cen′o·taph′ic,** *adj.*

Ce·no·zo·ic (sē′nə zō′ik; sen′ə-), *n.* **1** most recent and present geological era; Age of Mammals. **2** group of rocks formed during this period. —*adj.* of this era or its rocks.

cen·ser (sen′sər), *n.* container in which incense is burned. [< OF (*en*)*censier,* ult. < L *incensum* incense]

cen·sor (sen′sər), *n.* **1** person who examines and, if necessary, changes books, plays, motion pictures, etc., to make them satisfactory to the government or to the organization that employs him or her. **2** a Roman magistrate who took the census and told people how to behave. **3** person who tells others how they ought to behave. **4** person who likes to find fault. —*v.* act as censor; make changes in; take out part of (letters, etc.). [< L, < *censere* appraise] —**cen·so′ri·al,** *adj.*

cen·so·ri·ous (sen sô′ri əs; -sō′-), *adj.* too severely critical. —**cen·so′ri·ous·ly,** *adv.* —**cen·so′ri·ous·ness,** *n.*

cen·sor·ship (sen′sər ship), *n.* **1** act or system of censoring. **2** position or work of a censor.

cen·sur·a·ble (sen′shər ə bəl), *adj.* worthy of censure. —**cen′sur·a·ble·ness, cen′-sur·a·bil′i·ty,** *n.* —**cen′sur·a·bly,** *adv.*

cen·sure (sen′shər), *n., v.,* **-sured, -sur·ing.** —*n.* act or fact of blaming; expression of disapproval; criticism. —*v.* express disapproval of; blame; criticize. [< L *censura* < *censere* appraise] —**cen′sur·er,** *n.*

cen·sus (sen′səs), *n.* an official count of the people of a country, with details as to age, sex, occupation, etc. [< L, < *censere* appraise]

cent (sent), *n.* a coin, usually copper, of the United States and Canada, equal to the hundredth part of a dollar. [? < L *centesimus* hundredth]

cent., **1** centigrade. **2** central. **3** century.

cen·taur (sen′tôr), *n.* Gk. *Legend.* a monster that is half man and half horse. [< L < Gk. *kentauros*]

cen·ta·vo (sen tä′vō), *n., pl.* **-vos.** a small coin used in Mexico, Cuba, the Philippines, etc., equal to the hundredth part of a peso. [< Am.Sp. See CENT.]

cen·te·nar·i·an (sen′tə när′i ən), *n.* person who is 100 years old or more.

cen·te·nar·y (sen′tə ner′i; sen ten′ə ri), *n., pl.* **-nar·ies.** **1** period of 100 years. **2** 100th anniversary. [< L *centenarius* relating to a hundred < *centum* hundred]

cen·ten·ni·al (sen ten′i əl), *adj.* of or having to do with 100 years or the 100th anniversary. —*n.* 100th anniversary. [< L *centum* hundred + E (*bi*)*ennial*] —**cen·ten′ni·al·ly,** *adv.*

cen·ter (sen′tər), *n.* **1** a point within a circle or sphere equally distant from all of the circumference or surface. **2** the middle point, place, or part. **3** person, thing, or group in a middle position. **4** point toward which people or things go or come; main point. **5** player in the center of the line in football. **6** player who starts play in basketball. **7** the political groups of a legislature having moderate opinions. —*v.* **1** place in or at the center. **2** collect at a center.

center around (or **about**), *Informal.* focus on.

center on (or **upon**), focus on. [< OF < L < Gk. *kentron* sharp point.]

cen·ter·board (sen′tərbôrd), *n.* movable part of the keel of a sailboat, which is lowered to prevent drifting to the side.

center field, section of the baseball outfield behind second base. —**center fielder.**

cen·ter·fold (sen′tərfōld′), *n.* illustration in the middle of a magazine or book that fills both left- and right-hand pages or even a third page that has to be unfolded to be completely visible.

center of gravity, point in something around which its weight is evenly balanced.

cen·ter·piece (sen′tər pēs′), *n.* **1** ornamental piece for the center of a dining table. **2** any piece at the center of something. **3** principal feature of a policy or program.

cen·tes·i·mal (sen tes′ə məl), *adj.* **1** 100th. **2** divided into 100ths. [< L *centesimus* hundredth] —**cen·tes′i·mal·ly,** *adv.*

centi-, *combining form.* **1** 100: *centigrade* = *divided into 100 degrees.* **2** 100th part of: *centigram* = $^1/_{100}$ *of a gram.* [< L *centum* hundred]

cen·ti·grade (sen′tə grād), *adj.* **1** divided into 100 degrees. **2** of or according to a centigrade thermometer. [< F < L *centum* hundred + *gradus* degree]

centigrade thermometer, thermometer having 0 for the temperature at which ice melts and 100 for the temperature at which water boils.

cen·ti·gram (sen′tə gram), *n.* $^1/_{100}$ of a gram. [< F]

cen·ti·li·ter (sen′tə lē′tər), *n.* $^1/_{100}$ of a liter. [< F]

cen·time (sän′tēm), *n.* $^1/_{100}$ of a franc. [< F < L *centesimus* hundredth]

cen·ti·me·ter (sen′tə mē′tər), *n.* $^1/_{100}$ of a meter. [< F]

cen·ti·pede (sen′tə pēd), *n.* a small wormlike animal with many pairs of legs. [< L *centipeda* < *centum* hundred + *pes* foot]

cen·tral (sen′trəl), *adj.* **1** of or being the center. **2** at or near the center. **3** from the center. **4** equally distant from all points; easy to get to or from. **5** main; chief. [< L *centralis.* See CENTER.] —**cen′tral·ly,** *adv.* —**cen′tral·ness,** *n.*

Central African Republic, republic in C Africa, N of the Congo.

Central America, that part of North America between Mexico and South America. —**Central American.**

central heating, system for heating a building or buildings.

Central Intelligence Agency, agency of the United States government responsible for gathering intelligence from other countries, counterintelligence, etc. to promote American national security.

cen·tral·ize (sen′trəl īz), *v.,* **-ized, -iz·ing.** **1** collect at a center; gather together. **2** bring or come under one control. —**cen′tral·i·za′tion,** *n.* —**cen′tral·iz′er,** *n.*

central nervous system, the part of the nervous system in vertebrates that includes the brain and spinal cord.

central processing unit, part of a computer that carries out instructions and processes data.

cen·tre (sen′tər), *n., v.,* **-tred, -tring.** *Esp. Brit.* center.

cen·tric (sen′trik), **cen·tri·cal** (-trə kəl), *adj.* central. —**cen′tri·cal·ly,** *adv.* —**cen·tric′i·ty,** *n.*

cen·trif·u·gal (sen trif′yə gəl; -trif′ə-), *adj.* **1** moving away from the center. **2** making use of or acted upon by centrifugal force. [< NL, < E *centri-* center + L *fugere* flee] —**cen·trif′u·gal·ly,** *adv.*

centrifugal force or **action,** inertia of a body rotated around a center, tending to move it away from the center.

cen·tri·fuge (sen′trə fūj), *n.* machine for separating two substances of varying density, as cream from milk, bacteria from a fluid, etc., by means of centrifugal force. [< F]

cen·trip·e·tal (sen trip′ə təl), *adj.* **1** moving toward the center. **2** making use of or acted upon by centripetal force. [< NL, < E *centri-* center + L *petere* seek] —**cen·trip′e·tal·ly,** *adv.*

centripetal force or **action,** force that tends to move things toward the center around which they are turning.

cen·tu·ple (sen′tə pəl; -tyə-), *adj., v.,* **-pled, -pling.** —*adj.* 100 times as much or as many; hundredfold. —*v.* make 100 times as much or as many. [< F < LL *centuplus* hundredfold]

cen·tu·ri·on (sen tür′i ən; -tyûr′-), *n.* commander of a group of about 100 soldiers in the ancient Roman army. [< L, < *centuria* CENTURY]

cen·tu·ry (sen′chə ri), *n.,pl.* **-ries. 1** each 100 years, counting from some special time, such as the birth of Christ. **2** period of 100 years. **3** group of 100 people or things. **4** body of soldiers in the ancient Roman army. [< L *centuria* a division of a hundred units < *centum* hundred]

century plant, a large, thick-leaved plant growing in Mexico and SW United States.

ce·phal·ic (sə fal′ik), *adj.* **1** of the head. **2** near, on, or in the head. **3** toward the head. [< L < Gk., < *kephale* head]

ceph·a·lo·pod (sef′ə lə pod′), *n.* sea mollusk that has long, armlike tentacles around the mouth, a soft body, a pair of large eyes, and a sharp, birdlike beak. Cuttlefish and squids are cephalopods. —*adj.* of or belonging to the cephalopods. —**ceph′a·lop′o·dan,** *adj.*

ceph·a·lo·spo·rin (sef′ə lō spôr′ən), *n.* any of a group of antibiotics related to penicillin.

ceph·a·lo·tho·rax (sef′ə lō thôr′aks), *n.* combined head and thorax of animals such as crabs and spiders.

ce·ram·ic (sə ram′ik), *adj.* having to do with pottery, earthenware, porcelain, etc., or with making them. [< Gk., < *keramos* potter's clay]

ce·ram·ics (sə ram′iks), *n.* **1** (*sing. in use*) art of making pottery, earthenware, porcelain, etc. **2** (*pl. in use*) articles made of pottery, earthenware, porcelain, etc. —**ce·ram′i·cist, cer′a·mist,** *n.*

cer·a·tops (ser′ə tops), *n.* plant-eating dinosaur with a horn over each eye of the Cretaceous era.

cer·a·top·si·an (ser′ə top′sēən), *n.* any of a group of large, horned and plant-eating dinosaurs of the Cretaceous period. —*adj.* of or having to do with the ceratopsians or the ceratops.

Cer·ber·us (sèr′bər əs), *n.* **1** *Gk. and Roman Legend.* three-headed dog that guarded the entrance to Hades. **2** surly, watchful guard.

ce·re·al (sir′i əl), *n.* **1** any grass that produces a grain used as food, as wheat, rice, oats, etc. **2** the grain. **3** a food made from the grain, as oatmeal and corn meal. —*adj.* of or having to do with grain or the grasses producing it. [< L *Cerealis* pertaining to Ceres]

cer·e·bel·lum (ser′ə bel′əm), *n., pl.* **–bellums, –bel·la** (–bel′ə). part of the brain that controls the coordination of the muscles. [< L, dim. of *cerebrum* brain] —**cer′e·bel′lar,** *adj.*

cer·e·bral (ser′ə brəl; se rē′brəl), *adj.* **1** of the brain. **2** of the cerebrum. [< L *cerebrum* brain]

cerebral palsy, paralysis due to a lesion of the brain, usually occurring before or at birth.

cer·e·brate (ser′ə brāt), *v.,* **–brat·ed, –brat·ing.** use the brain; think. —**cer′e·bra′tion,** *n.*

cer·e·brum (ser′ə brəm), *n., pl.* **–brums, –bra** (–brə). **1** part of the human brain that controls thought and voluntary muscular movements. **2** the corresponding part (anatomically) of the brain of any vertebrate. [< L]

cere·ment (sir′mənt), *n.* Usually, **cerements.** cloth or garment in which a dead person is wrapped for burial.

cer·e·mo·ni·al (ser′ə mō′ni əl), *adj.* **1** formal. **2** of or having to do with ceremony. —*n.* formal actions proper to an occasion. —**cer′e·mo′ni·al·ism,** *n.* —**cer′e·mo′ni·al·ist,** *n.* —**cer′e·mo′ni·al·ly,** *adv.*

cer·e·mo·ni·ous (ser′ə mō′ni əs), *adj.* **1** full of ceremony. **2** very formal; extremely polite. —**cer′e·mo′ni·ous·ly,** *adv.* —**cer′e·mo′ni·ous·ness,** *n.*

cer·e·mo·ny (ser′ə mō′ni), *n., pl.* **–nies.** **1** a special form or set of acts to be done on special occasions. **2** very polite conduct. **3** a meaningless formality. **4** formality. [< L *caerimonia* rite]

Ce·res (sir′əz), *n.* Roman goddess of agriculture, identified with the Greek goddess Demeter.

ce·rise (sə raz′; –rēs′), *n., adj.* bright, pinkish red. [< F *cerise* cherry < VL < LGk. *kerasia* < Gk. *kerasos* cherry tree]

ce·ri·um (sir′i əm), *n.* a grayish metallic element, Ce. [< NL, from the asteroid *Ceres*]

CERN (sèrn), European Council for Nuclear Research (French, *Conseil Européen pour la Recherche Nucléaire*), an organization of 11 nations based in Geneva.

cer·tain (sèr′tən), *adj.* **1** sure: *certain to happen.* **2** settled; fixed: *at a certain hour.* **3** reliable; dependable. **4** some; one: *certain persons.* —*n.* **for certain,** without a doubt. [< OF, ult. < L *certus* sure] —**cer′tain·ness,** *n.*

cer·tain·ly (sèr′tən li), *adv.* surely; without a doubt. —*interj.* surely! of course!

cer·tain·ty (sèr′tən ti), *n., pl.* **–ties.** **1** freedom from doubt. **2** a sure fact.

cer·tif·i·cate (*n.* sər tif′ə kit; *v.* sər tif′ə kāt), *n., v.,* **–cat·ed, –cat·ing.** —*n.* a written or printed statement that declares something to be a fact. —*v.* give a certificate to. [< Med.L *certificatum.* See CERTIFY.] —**cer′ti·fi·ca′tion,** *n.*

certificate of deposit, written acknowledgement by a bank that it has received from the person named a certain sum of money as a deposit.

certified check, check whose value is guaranteed by the bank upon whose account it is drawn.

certified mail, piece of mail whose delivery is recorded and certified by the postal service.

cer·ti·fy (sèr′tə fī), *v.,* **–fied, –fy·ing.** **1** declare (something) true or correct by spoken, written, or printed statement. **2** guarantee. **3** make certain. [< Med.L *certificare* < L *certus* sure + *facere* make] —**cer′ti·fi′a·ble,** *adj.* —**cer′ti·fi′er,** *n.*

cer·ti·o·ra·ri (sèr′shi ə rār′i; –rär′i), *n.* order from a higher court to a lower one, calling for the record of a case for review. [< LL, be informed. See CERTAIN.]

cer·ti·tude (sèr′tə tüd; –tūd), *n.* certainty; sureness. [< LL *certitudo* < L. See CERTAIN.]

ce·ru·le·an (sə rü′li ən), *adj., n.* sky-blue. [< L *caeruleus* dark blue]

Cer·van·tes (sər van′tēz), *n.* **Miguel de,** 1547–1616, Spanish author of *Don Quixote.*

cer·vi·cal (sèr′və kəl), *adj.* **1** of the neck. **2** of a cervix or necklike part.

cer·vine (sèr′vīn; –vin), *adj.* of or like a deer. [< L, < *cervus* deer]

cer·vix (sèr′viks), *n., pl.* **cer·vix·es, cer·vi·ces** (sər vī′sēz). **1** the neck, esp. the back of the neck. **2** a necklike part, as the narrow end of the uterus. [< L]

Ce·sar·e·an, Ce·sar·i·an (si zār′i ən), *adj.,* =Caesarean. —*n.* =cesarean section.

cesarean section, surgical delivery of a baby from the uterus by cutting through the abdominal and uterine walls.

ce·si·um (sē′zi əm), *n.* a silvery metallic element, Cs. Also, **caesium.** [< NL, < L *caesius* bluish-gray]

ces·sa·tion (se sā′shən), *n.* a ceasing or stopping. [< L, < *cessare* cease]

ces·sion (sesh′ən), *n.* a handing over to another; ceding; giving up; surrendering. [< L *cessio* < *cedere* yield]

cess·pool (ses′pül), *n.* **1** pool or pit for house drains to empty into. **2** filthy place.

ce·su·ra (sə zhúr′ə; –zyúr′ə), *n.* =caesura. —**ce·su′ral,** *adj.*

Ce·ta·ce·a (sə tā′shə), *n.* order of mammals comprising the cetaceans.

ce·ta·cean (sə tā′shən), *adj.* Also, **ce·ta′ceous.** of or belonging to a group of mammals living in the water, including whales, dolphins, and porpoises. —*n.* animal that belongs to this group.

Cey·lon (si lon′), *n.* =Sri Lanka.

cf., compare.

cg., centigram; centigrams.

ch., Ch., 1 chapter. **2** church.

chad (chad), *n.* small piece punched out of a tape or card when indicating a choice on a ballot.

Chad (chad), *n.* republic in C Africa, S of Libya.

chafe (chāf), *v.,* **chafed, chaf·ing,** *n.* —*v.* **1** rub to make warm. **2** wear or be worn away by rubbing. **3** make or become sore by rubbing. **4** make irritated or angry. **5** become angry. —*n.* a chafing; irritation. [< OF *chaufer,* ult. < L, < *calere* be warm + *facere* make]

chaff[1] (chaf; chäf), *n.* **1** husks of wheat, oats, rye, etc., separated from grain by threshing. **2** hay or straw cut fine as cattle feed. **3** worthless stuff; rubbish. [OE *ceaf*] —**chaff′y,** *adj.*

chaff[2] (chaf; chäf), *v.* banter; tease. —*n.* banter. —**chaff′er,** *n.*

chaf·fer (chaf′ər), *v.* dispute about a price; bargain. —*n.* bargaining. [ME *chaffare* < OE *cēap* bargain + *faru* journey] —**chaf′fer·er,** *n.*

chaf·finch (chaf′inch), *n.* a European songbird with a pleasant, short song, often kept as a cage bird. [OE *ceaffinc.* See CHAFF[1], FINCH.]

chaf·ing dish (chāf′ing), pan with a heater under it, used to cook food at the table or to keep it warm.

cha·grin (shə grin′), *n.* a feeling of disappointment, failure, or humiliation. —*v.* cause to feel chagrin. [< F, < OF *graignier* < *graim* sad, sorrowful] chain (chān), *n.* 1 series of links joined together. 2 series of things joined or linked together: *a mountain chain.* 3 anything that binds or restrains. 4 a measuring instrument like a chain. A surveyor's chain is 66 feet long; an engineer's chain is 100 feet long. 5 number of similar restaurants, theaters, etc., owned and operated by one person or company. 6 a number of atoms of the same element linked together like a chain. —*v.* 1 join together or fasten with a chain. 2 bind; restrain. 3 keep in prison; make a slave of.

chains, a bonds; fetters. **b** imprisonment; bondage. [< OF *chaeine* < L *catena* chain]

chain drive, 1 mechanism for transmitting power by means of an endless chain. 2 system using this mechanism.

chain gang, gang of convicts, etc., chained together while at work outdoors.

chain letter, letter that each recipient is asked to copy and send to other recipients.

chain link fence, metal fence made of heavy wire woven into a lattice and fastened to steel posts.

chain mail, flexible armor made of metal rings linked together.

chain reaction, 1 process marked by an explosive release of nuclear energy, as in the bombardment of unstable uranium nuclei by plutonium neutrons in the explosion of an atomic bomb, each uranium nucleus releasing a number of plutonium neutrons, which in turn split other uranium nuclei. 2 any series of events or happenings, each caused by the preceding one or ones. —**chain′- re·act′ing,** *adj.*

chain saw, power saw that has an endless chain with a sharp tooth on each link, used on trees, etc.

chain stitch, kind of sewing or crocheting in which each stitch makes a loop through which the next stitch is taken.

chain store, one of a group of retail stores owned and operated by one company.

chair (chār), *n.* 1 seat for one person that has a back and, sometimes, arms. 2 seat of position, dignity, or authority. 3 chairperson. 4 electric chair. —*v.* 1 put or carry in a chair. 2 put in a position of authority. 3 act as chairperson of (a committee, etc.).

take the chair, a begin a meeting. **b** be in charge of or preside at a meeting. [< OF *chaiere* < L < Gk. *kathedra* seat]

chair lift, series of seats suspended from an endless cable to carry people between two points, esp. tourists or skiers to the top of a slope.

chair·man (chār′mən), *n., pl.* **-men.** 1 person who presides at or is in charge of a meeting. 2 head of a committee. —**chair′man·ship,** *n.*

chair·per·son (chār′pėr′sən), *n.* 1 person who is in charge of or presides at

a meeting. 2 person who is head of a committee.

chair·wom·an (chār′wům′ən), *n., pl.* **-wom·en.** a woman chairperson.

chaise (shāz), *n.* 1 lightweight carriage, often one with a folding top. =chaise longue. [< F *chaise* chair, var. of *chaire* CHAIR]

chaise longue (shāz′ lông′; long′), chair with a long seat and a back at one end, somewhat like a couch. Also, **chaise lounge.** [< F, long chair]

chal·ce·do·ny (kal sed′ə ni; kal′sə dō′ni), *n., pl.* **-nies.** variety of quartz that has a waxy luster and occurs in various colors and forms. [< L < Gk. *chalkedon*]

Chal·da·ic (kal dā′ik), *adj., n.* Chaldean.

Chal·de·a (kal dē′ə), *n.* ancient region in SW Asia, on the Tigris and Euphrates Rivers. —**Chal·de′an,** *adj., n.*

Chal·dee (kal dē′; kal′dē), *adj., n.* Chaldean.

cha·let (sha lā′; shal′ā), *n.* 1 a house or villa with wide, overhanging eaves. 2 a herdsman's hut or cabin in the Swiss mountains. [< Swiss F]

chal·ice (chal′is), *n.* 1 =cup. 2 cup that holds the wine used in the Communion service. 3 a cup-shaped flower. [< OF < L *calix* cup] —**chal′iced,** *adj.*

chalk (chôk), *n.* 1 soft limestone, made up mostly of very small fossil sea shells. 2 substance like chalk, used for writing or drawing on a board. 3 piece of this substance. —*v.* 1 mark, write, or draw with chalk. 2 mix or rub with chalk; whiten with chalk. 3 score; record.

chalk up, write down; record. [< L *calx* lime] —**chalk′like′,** *adj.* —**chalk′y,** *adj.* —**chalk′i·ness,** *n.*

chalk·board (chôk′bôrd′), *n.* smooth, hard surface for writing or drawing with chalk.

chal·lenge (chal′inj), *v.,* **-lenged, -leng- ing,** *n.* —*v.* 1 call to fight. 2 invite to a game or contest. 3 call on (a person, etc.) to answer and explain. 4 doubt; dispute. 5 object to (a juror, vote, etc.). 6 claim; demand: *a problem that challenges everyone's attention.* —*n.* 1 call to fight. 2 call to a game or contest. 3 a demand to answer and explain: *"Who goes there?" is the guard's challenge.* 4 objection made, as to a juror or a vote. [< OF < L *calumnia* CALUMNY] —**chal′lenge·a·ble,** *adj.* —**chal′leng·er,** *n.*

chal·lis, chal·lie (shal′i), *n.* a lightweight, fine plain or printed cloth, used for dresses.

cham·ber (chām′bər), *n.* 1 a room (in a house). 2 bedroom. 3 hall where a legislature body meets. 4 a legislative, or judicial body. 5 a cavity: *the heart has four chambers.* 6 that part of the barrel of a gun which receives the charge. —*v.* provide with chamber.

chambers, a *Brit.* set of rooms in a building to live in or use as offices. **b** office of a lawyer or judge. [< OF < L

< Gk. *kamara* vaulted place. Doublet of CAMERA.] —**cham′bered,** *adj.*

cham·ber·lain (chām′bər lin), *n.* 1 person who manages the household of a king or lord; steward. 2 a high official of a king's court. 3 treasurer: *city chamberlain.* [< OF < L *camera* vault + Gmc. *-ling*]

cham·ber·maid (chām′bər mād′), *n.* maid who makes the beds, cleans the bedrooms, etc.

chamber music, music suited to a room or small hall; music for a trio, quartet, etc.

chamber of commerce, group of people organized to protect and promote business interests of a city, state, etc.

chamber pot, small recepticle, used esp. in the bedroom for urine and slops.

cham·bray (sham′brā), *n.* a fine variety of gingham. [var. of *cambric*]

cha·me·le·on (kə mē′li ən; -mēl′yən), *n.* 1 lizard that can change the color of its skin. 2 a changeable or fickle person. [< L < Gk., lit., ground lion, < *chamai* on the ground, dwarf + *leon* lion] —**cha- me′le·on′ic,** *adj.*

cham·ois (sham′i), *n., pl.* **-ois.** 1 a small, goatlike antelope that lives in the high mountains of Europe and SW Asia. 2 Also, **cham′my.** a soft leather made from the skin of the sheep, goats, deer, etc. [< F < LL *camox*]

cham·o·mile (kam′ə mīl), *n.* =camomile.

champ[1] (champ), *v.* 1 bite and chew noisily. 2 bite on impatiently. [? akin to *chap* CHOP[2]]

champ[2] (champ), *n.* champion.

cham·pagne (sham pān′), *n.* 1 a sparkling, bubbling wine, originally produced in Champagne, France. 2 pale, brownish yellow. —*adj.* pale brownish yellow: *a champagne blouse.*

cham·paign (sham pān′), *n.* a wide plain; level, open country. —*adj.* level and open. [< OF *champaigne.* See CAMPAIGN.]

cham·pi·on (cham′pi ən), *n.* 1 person, animal, or thing that wins first place in a game or contest. 2 person who fights or speaks for another; defender; supporter. —*adj.* having won first place; ahead of all others. —*v.* fight or speak in behalf of; defend; support. [< OF < LL *campio* < *campus* field (i.e., of battle)] —**cham′pi- on·less,** *adj.*

cham·pi·on·ship (cham′pi ən ship′), *n.* 1 position of a champion; first place. 2 defense; support.

chance (chans; chäns), *n., v.,* **chanced, chanc·ing,** *adj.* —*n.* 1 opportunity: *the chance to go to college.* 2 possibility or probability: *the chances are that he will have enough money.* 3 fate; luck. 4 a risk. 5 ticket, as for a raffle or lottery. —*v.* 1 happen. 2 take the risk of: risk. —*adj.* not expected or planned; accidental; casual.

by any chance, possibly; perhaps.

by chance, accidentally.

chance upon (or **on**), happen to find or meet.

on the chance, depending on the possibility.

on the off chance, depending on luck.

stand a chance, have favorable prospects.

(the) chances are, it is likely. [< OF < L *cadentia* a falling < *cadere* fall]

chan·cel (chan′səl; chän′–), *n.* space around the altar of a church, usually enclosed, used by the clergy and the choir. [< F < L *cancelli* a grating]

chan·cel·ler·y (chan′sə lər i; –slə ri; chän′–), *n., pl.* **–ler·ies. 1** position of a chancellor. **2** office of a chancellor.

chan·cel·lor (chan′sə lər; –slər; chän′–), *n.* **1** the title, esp. in Great Britain, of various high officials: *Chancellor of the Exchequer.* **2** the chief judge of a court of chancery or equity in some states. **3** title of the president in certain universities. [< AF < L *cancellarius* officer stationed at tribunal. See CHANCEL.] **—chan′cel·lor·ship′,** *n.*

chan·cer·y (chan′sər i; chän′–), *n., pl.* **–cer·ies. 1** court of equity. **2** office where public records are kept. **3** office of a chancellor.

in chancery, a in a court of equity. **b** in a helpless position. [var. of CHANCEL·LERY]

chan·cre (shang′kər), *n.* ulcer or sore with a hard base. [< F. See CANKER.] **—chan′crous,** *adj.*

chan·de·lier (shan′də lir′), *n.* fixture with branches for lights, usually hanging from a ceiling. [< F < VL *candelarius* < L *candela* CANDLE] **—chan′de·liered′,** *adj.*

chan·dler (chan′dlər; chän′–), *n.* **1** maker or seller of candles. **2** dealer in groceries and supplies: *a ship chandler.* [< AF *chaundeler* < VL *candelarius* < L *candela* CANDLE]

change (chānj), *v.,* **changed, chang·ing,** *n.* —*v.* **1** make or become different. **2** substitute. **3** take in place of. **4** give or get (money of a different sort) for. **5** put other clothing or covering on: *change a bed.* —*n.* **1** act or fact of changing. **2** a changed condition or appearance. **3** variety; difference. **4** a second set of clothes. **5** money returned to a person when he or she has given an amount larger than the price of what is bought. **6** small coins.

change hands, a pass from one owner to another. **b** substitute one hand for the other.

changes, different ways in which a set of bells can be rung.

ring the changes, a ring a set of bells in all its different ways. **b** *Fig.* do a thing in many different ways. [< OF < LL *cambiare*] **—change′ful,** *adj.* **—change′ful·ly,** *adv.* **—change′ful·ness,** *n.* **—chang′er,** *n.*

change·a·ble (chān′jə bəl), *adj.* **1** likely to change: *a changeable person.* **2** likely to be changed. **—change′a·bil′i·ty, change′a·ble·ness,** *n.* **—change′a·bly,** *adv.*

change·less (chānj′lis), *adj.* not changing; constant. **—change′less·ly,** *adv.* **—change′less·ness,** *n.*

change·ling (chānj′ling), *n.* child secretly substituted for another.

change of life, =menopause.

change of pace, 1 sudden shift from one routine or activity to another, often to relieve boredom or fatigue. **2** in baseball, a change-up.

change of venue, change of the place of a trial.

change-up (chānj′up′), a slow pitch thrown in the same way as a fast pitch, to confuse a batter.

chan·nel (chan′əl), *n., v.,* **–neled, –nel·ing.** —*n.* **1** bed of a stream, river, etc. **2** body of water joining two larger bodies of water: *the English Channel.* **3** the deeper part of a waterway. **4** passage for liquids; groove. **5** means by which something is carried: *secret channels.* **6** person through whom spirits supposedly communicate. **7** narrow band of radio or television frequencies. **8** *Fig.* avenue or course of action: *useful channels.* —*v.* **1** form a channel in. **2** act as a channel. [< OF < L *canalis* CANAL. Doublet of CANAL.]

Channel Islands, British islands near the NW coast of France; Alderney, Guernsey, Jersey, and Sark.

chan·nel·ize (chan′ə līz), *v.,* **–ized, –iz·ing.** =channel.

chan·nel-surf (chan′əl sèrf′), *v.* switch from one television channel to another without watching any one channel for long. **—channel surfer.**

chant (chant; chänt), *n.* **1** a simple song in which several syllables or words are sung in one tone. **2** a singsong way of talking. —*v.* sing to, or in the manner of, a chant. [< OF < L *cantare* < *canere* sing] **—chant′er,** *n.*

chant·ey, chant·y (shan′ti; chan′–), *n., pl.* **–eys; –ies.** song sung by sailors, in rhythm with the motions made during their work. Also, **shanty,** [alter. of F *chanter* sing. See CHANT.]

chan·ti·cleer (chan′tə klir), *n.* =rooster. [< OF < *chanter* sing + *cler* clear]

chan·try (chan′trē), *n.* **1** chapel attached to a church. **2 a** endowment to pay for Masses for a person's soul. **b** chapel, altar, or part of a church similarly endowed. **c** endowed priests.

Cha·nu·kah (hä′nə kə), *n.* =Hanukkah.

cha·os (kā′os), *n.* **1** great confusion; complete disorder. **2** infinite space or formless matter before the universe existed. [< L < Gk.]

cha·ot·ic (kā ot′ik), *adj.* in great confusion; completely disordered. **—cha·ot′i·cal·ly,** *adv.*

chap¹ (chap), *v.,* **chapped, chap·ping,** *n.* —*v.* crack open; make or become rough. —*n.* crack in the skin; place where the skin is chapped. [ME *chappe(n)* cut]

chap² (chap), *n.* fellow; man; boy. [short for *chapman* a peddler; OE *cēapman* < *cēap* trade + *man* man]

chap³ (chap), *n.* =chop² (def. 2).

chap., 1 chapel. **2** chaplain. **3** chapter.

chap·ar·ral (chap′ə ral′), *n.* SW thicket of low shrubs, thorny bushes, etc. [< Sp., < *chaparro* evergreen oak]

chap·book (chap′bùk′), *n.* a small book or pamphlet of popular tales, ballads, etc., formerly sold on the streets.

cha·peau (sha pō′), *n., pl.* **–peaux** or **–peous.** *French.* hat.

chap·el (chap′əl), *n.* **1** a building for Christian worship, not so large as a church. **2** a small place for worship in a larger building. **3** room or building for worship in a palace, school, etc. **4** a religious service in a chapel. [< OF < LL *cappella* orig., a shrine in which was preserved the *cappa* or cape of St. Martin]

chap·er·on, chap·er·one (shap′ər ōn), *n., v.,* **–oned, –on·ing.** —*n.* a married woman or an older person who accompanies young people at a party or a young unmarried woman in public for the sake of good form and protection. —*v.* act as a chaperon to. [< F *chaperon* hood, protector. See CAPE¹.] **—chap′er·on′age,** *n.*

chap·fall·en (chop′fôl′ən; chap′–), *adj.* dejected; discouraged. Also, **chopfallen.**

chap·lain (chap′lin), *n.* clergyman officially authorized to perform religious functions for a family, court, society, public institution, regiment, or warship. [< OF < LL *capellanus* < *cappella* CHAPEL] **—chap′lain·cy, chap′lain·ship,** *n.*

chap·let (chap′lit), *n.* **1** wreath worn on the head. **2** string of beads. **3** string of beads for keeping count in saying prayers, one third as long as a rosary. **4** prayers said with such beads. [< OF *chapelet,* dim. of *chapel* headdress. See CAP.] **—chap′let·ed,** *adj.*

chaps (chaps; shaps), *n. pl.* SW strong leather trousers without a back, worn over other trousers, esp. by cowhands.

chap·ter (chap′tər), *n.* **1** a main division of a book or other writing. **2** part; section. **3** branch of a club, society, etc. **4** group of clergymen usually attached to a cathedral. —*v.* arrange in chapters. [< OF < L *capitulum,* dim. of *caput* head]

char¹ (chär), *v.,* **charred, char·ring. 1** burn to charcoal. **2** scorch. —*n.* **1** charred substance. **2** charcoal. [? < *charcoal*]

char² (chär), *n., v.,* **charred, char·ring.** *Brit.* —*n.* an odd job; chore. —*v.* do odd jobs or chores. Also, **chare.** [OE *cerr* turn, occasion]

char., 1 character. **2** charter.

char·ac·ter (kar′ik tər), *n.* **1** all qualities or features possessed by a person; kind; sort; nature. **2** moral strength or weakness. **3** good character. **4** reputation. **5** special thing or quality that makes one person, animal, thing, or group different from others. **6** person in a play or book. **7** person who attracts attention because he or she is different or odd. **8** letter, mark, or sign used in writing or printing.

in character, as expected; natural or usual.

out of character, not as expected; not natural or usual. [< F < L *charak-ter* instrument for marking < *charassein* engrave]

character actor, actor who commonly plays the role of a person with unusual or eccentric characteristics.

char·ac·ter·is·tic (kar´ik tər is´tik), *adj.* distinguishing from others; special. —*n.* a special quality or feature. —**char´ac·ter·is´ti·cal·ly,** *adv.*

char·ac·ter·ize (kar´ik tər īz), *v.,* **-ized, -iz·ing.** **1** describe. **2** be a characteristic of; distinguish. —**char´ac·ter·i·za´tion,** *n.* —**char´ac·ter·iz´er,** *n.*

char·ac·ter·less (kar´ik tər lis), *adj.* **1** without a character. **2** without distinction; uninteresting.

character witness, person called to give testimony in behalf of the character and reputation of one of the parties in a legal case.

cha·rade (shə rād´), *n.* **1** game of guessing a word from the dramatic representation of each syllable. **2** sham performance or behavior. [< F < Pr. *charrada* < *charra* chatter]

char·broil (chär´broil´), *v.* broil with charcoal. [< *char*(coal) + *broil*]

char·coal (chär´kōl´), *n.* **1** black substance made by partly burning wood or bones in a place from which the air is shut out. **2** pencil made of charcoal for drawing. **3** drawing made with such a pencil. [ME *charcole*]

chard (chärd), *n.* =Swiss chard.

charge (chärj), *v.,* **charged, charg·ing,** *n.* —*v.* **1** put on a price of. **2** put down as a debt to be paid. **3** give a task, duty, or responsibility to. **4** give an order or command to; direct. **5** accuse: *charged with speeding.* **6** load; fill: *a gun charged with powder and shot.* **7** restore the capacity of, as an electric battery. **8** make a violent final rush: *charge the enemy.* —*n.* **1** price put on something. **2** a debt to be paid. **3 a** task; duty; responsibility. **b** care; management: *nurses have charge of sick people.* **4** person, or thing under the care of someone. **5** order; direction. **6** formal instruction: *a judge's charge to the jury.* **7** formal statement accusing a person of having broken the law, etc. **8** quantity needed to load or fill something, esp. the explosive used in firing a gun. **9** the violent final rush in an attack or assault.

charge off, a subtract as a loss. **b** put down as belonging to or as part of: *charged off the loss to incompetence.* **c** dash away.

charge up, put down as belonging to: *charge up to boredom.*

get a charge from (out of, by, etc.), *Informal.* get pleasure, or thrill, or excitement from.

in charge (of), a having the care or management. **b** in command. [< F < LL *carricare* load < L *carrus* wagon. Doublet of CARRY.]

charge·a·ble (chär´jə bəl), *adj.* **1** that can be charged. **2** liable to become a public charge.

charged (chärjd), *adj.* **1** loaded; filled. **2** having an electrical charge: *charged ions.*

char·gé d'af·faires (shär zhä´ də fãr´), *pl.* **char·gés d'af·faires** (shär zhäz´ də fãr´). *French.* deputy of a diplomat.

charg·er¹ (chär´jər), *n.* **1** war horse. **2** person or thing that charges.

charg·er² (chär´jər), *n.* a large, flat dish; platter. [< OF, < *charger* CHARGE]

char·i·ly (chär´ə li), *adv.* carefully; warily.

char·i·ness (chär´i nis), *n.* chary quality.

char·i·ot (char´i ət), *n.* a two-wheeled car pulled by horses, used in ancient times in fighting, racing, and processions. [< OF, < *char* CAR]

char·i·ot·eer (chär´ i ət ir´) *n.* person who drives a chariot.

cha·ris·ma (kə riz´mə), *n.,* *pl.* **-ma·ta** (-mə tə). **1** personal appeal or power to fascinate; personal magnetism or glamour. **2** glamour or sex appeal. **3** spiritual gift giving a person the power to prophesy, heal, etc. —**cha´ris·mat´ic,** *adj., n.*

char·i·ta·ble (chär´ə tə bəl), *adj.* **1** of charity. **2** generous in giving help to poor or suffering people. **3** kindly in judging people and their actions. —**char´i·ta·ble·ness,** *n.* —**char´i·ta·bly,** *adv.*

char·i·ty (chär´ə ti), *n.,* *pl.* **-ties.** **1** help given to the poor or suffering. **2** act or work of charity. **3** fund, institution, or organization for helping the poor or suffering. **4** Christian love of one's fellow men. **5** kindness in judging people. [< OF < L *caritas* dearness < *carus* dear]

char·la·tan (shär´lə tən), *n.* person who pretends to have more knowledge or skill than he or she really has; quack. [< F < Ital. *ciarlatano,* ult. < Mongolian *dzar* proclaim, tell lies]

char·la·tan·ism (shär´lə tən iz´əm), **char·la·tan·ry** (-tən ri), *n.* =quackery.

Char·le·magne (shär´lə mān), *n.* A.D. 742?–814, king of the Franks from 768 to 814 and emperor of the Holy Roman Empire 800–814.

Charles·ton (chärlz´tən), *n.* capital of West Virginia, in the W part.

char·ley horse (chär´li), stiffness caused by straining a muscle.

char·lotte russe (shär´lət rüs´), dessert made of a mold of sponge cake filled with whipped cream or custard. [< F, Russian charlotte (a type of dessert)]

charm (chärm), *n,* **1** power of delighting or fascinating; attractiveness. **2** a very pleasing quality or feature. **3** a small

ornament or trinket. **4** word, verse, or thing supposed to have magic power. **5** in nuclear physics, a quantum unit of +1 for any quark and −1 for its antiquark. —*v.* **1** delight; attract. **2** act on as if by magic. **3** protect as by a charm. [< OF < L *carmen* song, enchantment < *canere* sing] —**charm´er,** *n.* —**charm´less,** *adj.*

charm·ing (chär´ming), *adj.* very pleasing; attractive. —**charm´ing·ly,** *adv.* —**charm´ing·ness,** *n.*

char·nel house (chär´nəl), place where dead bodies or bones are laid. [< OF < LL *carnale.* See CARNAL.]

Char·on (kãr´ən), *n.* Gk. Myth. boatman who ferried the spirits of the dead across the river Styx to Hades.

chart (chärt), *n.* **1** map, esp. a hydrographic or marine map. **2** an outline map showing special conditions or facts: *a weather chart.* **3** sheet giving information in lists, pictures, tables, or diagrams. **4** such a list, table, picture, or diagram. —*v.* make a chart of; show on a chart. [< F < L *charta* < Gk. *chartes* leaf of paper. Doublet of CARD.] —**chart´less,** *adj.*

char·ter (chär´tər), *n.* **1** a written grant of certain rights or privileges, esp. one by a ruler to his subjects, or by a legislature to a city or company, telling how it is to be organized and what it can do. **2** a written order from the authorities of a society, giving to a group of persons the right to organize a new chapter, branch, or lodge. —*v.* **1** give a charter to. **2** hire; rent. [< OF < L *chartula,* dim. of *charta.* See CHART.] —**char´ter·er,** *n.* —**char´ter·less,** *adj.*

charter member, one of the original members of an organization, club, etc.

Chart·ism (chär´tiz´əm), *n.* English reform movement of the first half of the 19th century whose members were chiefly working men. —**Chart´ist,** *n.*

char·treuse (shär trœz´; *for* 2, *also* shär trüz´, -trüs´), *n.* **1** a green, yellow, or white liqueur first made by Carthusian monks. **2** a light, yellowish green. [< F, Carthusian]

char·wom·an (chär´wùm´ən), *n.,* *pl.* **-wom·en.** woman whose work is doing odd jobs by the day, esp. cleaning. [see CHAR²]

char·y (chär´i), *adj.,* **char·i·er, char·i·est.** **1** careful. **2** shy. **3** sparing; stingy. [OE *cearig* < *caru* care]

Cha·ryb·dis (kə rib´dis), *n.* whirlpool in the strait between Sicily and Italy, opposite the rock Scylla. Charybdis sucked down ships.

chase¹ (chās), *v.,* **chased, chas·ing,** *n.* —*v.* **1** run after to catch or kill. **2** drive; drive away. **3** follow; pursue. **4** rush; hurry. —*n.* **1** chasing. **2** hunting as a sport. **3** a hunted animal.

give chase, run after; chase. [< OF *chacier* < LL *captiare.* Doublet of CATCH.] —**chas´er,** *n.*

chase² (chās), v., **chased, chas·ing.** engrave; emboss, [var. of *enchase*] —**chas′er,** n.

chase³ (chās), n. groove; furrow; trench. [< F < L *capsa* box]

chasm (kaz′əm), n. **1** a deep opening or crack in the earth; gap. **2** *Fig.* wide difference of feelings or interests between people or groups. [< L < Gk. *chasma*] —**chas′mal,** adj.

chas·sis (shas′i; chas′i), n., pl. **chas·sis** (shas′iz; chas′–). **1** frame, wheels, and machinery of a motor vehicle. **2** main landing gear of an aircraft. [< F < VL *capsiceum* < L *capsa*. See CHASE³.]

chaste (chāst), adj. **1** pure; virtuous. **2** decent; modest. **3** simple in taste or style. [< OF < L *castus* pure] —**chaste′ly,** adv. —**chaste′ness,** n.

chas·ten (chās′ən), v. **1** punish to improve. **2** restrain from excess or crudeness. [< obs. v. *chaste* < F < L *castigare* make pure < *castus* pure] —**chas′ten·er,** n.

chas·tise (chas tīz′), v., **–tised, –tis·ing.** punish by beating or thrashing. [< obs. *chaste* CHASTEN + *–ise*] —**chas′tise·ment,** n. —**chas·tis′er,** n.

chas·ti·ty (chas′tə ti), n. **1** purity; virtue. **2** decency; modesty. **3** simplicity of style or taste; absence of too much decoration.

chas·u·ble (chaz′yə bəl; chas′–), n. a sleeveless outer vestment covering all other vestments, worn by the priest at Mass. [< F < LL *casubula* < L *casa* house; akin to CASSOCK]

chat (chat), n., v., **chat·ted, chat·ting.** —n. **1** easy, familiar talk. **2** any of several birds with a chattering cry. —v. **1** talk in an easy, familiar way. **2** post electronic messages, comments, etc. online in response to similar messages from others.

chat up, a talk informally; have a chat with. **b** flatter, esp. to attract someone. [short for *chatter*]

châ·teau (sha tō′), n., pl. **–teaux** (–tōz′). in France: **1** a castle. **2** a large country house. —adj. **Chateau,** denoting wine from a particular estate. [< F < L *castellum* CASTLE. Doublet of CASTLE.]

chat·e·laine (shat′ə lān), n. **1** mistress or lady of a castle. **2** clasp to which keys, a purse, etc., may be attached. [< F, ult. < L *castellum* CASTLE]

chat room, location on a website where a person can post comments and information.

chat·tel (chat′əl), n. movable possession; piece of property that is not real estate. Furniture, automobiles, slaves, and animals are chattels. [< OF *chatel.* Doublet of CATTLE.]

chat·ter (chat′ər), v. **1** talk constantly, rapidly, and foolishly. **2** make quick, indistinct sounds: *monkeys chatter.* **3** utter rapidly or uselessly. **4** rattle together. —n. **1** quick, foolish talk. **2** quick, indistinct sounds. [imit.] —**chat′ter·er,** n.

chat·ter·box (chat′ər boks′), n. person who talks all the time.

chat·ty (chat′i), adj., **–ti·er, –ti·est. 1** fond of friendly, familiar talk. **2** conversational. —**chat′ti·ly,** adv. —**chat′ti·ness,** n.

Chau·cer (chô′sər), n. Geoffrey, 1340?–1400, English poet, author of *The Canterbury Tales.* —**Chau·ce′ri·an,** adj.

chauf·feur (shō′fər; shō fér′), n. person whose work is driving an automobile. —v. act as a chauffeur to. [< F, stoker < *chauffer* to heat; term from days of steam automobiles]

chaunt (chônt; chänt), n., v. *Archaic.* chant.

chau·vin·ism (shō′vən iz əm), n. **1** boastful, warlike patriotism. **2** *Fig.* excessive enthusiasm for one's sex, race, or group. [< F *chauvinisme;* after Nicolas *Chauvin,* overenthusiatic patriot] —**chau′vin·ist,** n., adj. —**chau′vin·is′tic,** adj. —**chau′vin·is·ti·cal·ly,** adv.

cheap (chēp), adj. **1** costing little. **2** costing less than it is worth. **3** charging low prices: *a cheap market.* **4** easily obtained. **5** of low value; common. —adv. at a low price; at small cost.

feel cheap, feel inferior and ashamed. **on the cheap,** in a cheap manner; cheaply. [short for *good cheap* a good bargain; OE *cēap* price, bargain] —**cheap′ly,** adv. —**cheap′ness,** n.

cheap·en (chēp′ən), v. make or become cheap. —**cheap′en·er,** n.

cheap·ie (chē′pē), n. *Informal.* anything made at little cost, esp. a film.

cheat (chēt), v. **1** deceive or trick. **2** beguile. **3** elude. —n. **1** person who is not honest. **2** fraud; trick.

cheat on, deceive or be unfaithful to someone. [var. of *escheat*] —**cheat′er,** n. —**cheat′ing·ly,** adv.

check (chek), v. **1** stop suddenly. **2** hold back; control; restrain. **3** rebuff; repulse; reverse. **4** compare to prove true or right. **5** put a check on. **6** write a check. **7** mark in a pattern of squares. **8** send (baggage) to a given destination. **9** in chess, have (an opponent's king) in check. —n. **1** a sudden stop. **2** means of preventing error, fraud, etc. **3** any person or thing that holds back action. **4** comparison to prove something true or right. **5** mark to show that something has been checked. **6** ticket given for a coat, hat, package, etc., to show ownership. **7** bill for a meal, etc. **8** written order directing a bank to pay money to the person named on it. **9** pattern of squares. **10** in chess, position of an opponent's king when it is in danger and must be moved. —adj. **1** used in checking. **2** marked in a pattern of squares. —interj. a call in chess warning that an opponent's king is in danger and must be moved.

check in, register at a hotel or motel.

check off, mark as checked and found true or right.

check out, a pay one's bill at a hotel or motel. **b** inspect or examine to see if (something) is in proper order or condition. **c** substantiate. **d** *Informal.* die.

check up, examine or compare to prove true or correct.

in check, a held back; controlled. **b** (of a king) attacked by an opposing chess piece. [< OF *eschec* a check at chess < Pers. *shāh* king, king at chess] —**check′a·ble,** adj. —**check′er,** n.

check·book (chek′bůk′), n. book of blank checks on a bank.

check·er (chek′ər), v. **1** mark in a pattern of squares of different colors. **2** mark off with patches different from one another. **3** have ups and downs; change; vary. —n. **1** pattern of squares. **2** one of the flat, round pieces used in the game of checkers. [< OF *escheker* chessboard]

check·er·board (chek′ər bôrd′; –bōrd′), n. board marked in a pattern of 64 squares of two alternating colors, used in playing checkers or chess.

check·ered (chek′ərd), adj. **1** marked in a pattern of many-colored squares. **2** marked in patches. **3** often changing; varied; unstable.

check·ers (chek′ərz), n. game played on a checkerboard by two people. Each player has 12 round, flat pieces to move.

checking account, bank account against which checks may be drawn.

check list or **check·list** (chek′list′), n. list of names, titles, jobs, etc. arranged to form a ready means of reference or checking.

check·mate (chek′māt′), v., **–mat·ed, –mat·ing,** n. —v. **1** make a move in chess that wins the game. **2** defeat completely. —n. **1** in chess, a move that ends the game by putting the opponent's king in inescapable check. **2** a complete defeat. [< OF *echec et mat* < Ar. *shāh māt* the king is dead]

check point, place on a border, road, etc. at which persons are stopped and passports, documents, baggage, etc. are inspected.

check·rein (chek′rān′), n. a short rein to keep a horse from lowering its head.

check·up (chek′up′), n. **1** a careful examination. **2** a thorough physical examination.

cheek (chēk), n. **1** side of the face below either eye. **2** anything suggesting the human cheek in form or position. **3** saucy talk or behavior; impudence. [OE *cēce*]

cheek·bone (chēk′bōn′), n. bone just below either eye.

cheek·y (chēk′i), adj., **cheek·i·er, cheek·i·est.** saucy; impudent. —**cheek′i·ly,** adv. —**cheek′i·ness,** n.

cheep (chēp), v. make a short, sharp sound like a young bird; chirp; peep. —n. such a sound. [imit.] —**cheep′er,** n.

cheer (chir), n. **1** joy; gladness. **2** shout of encouragement. **3** food. **4** state of mind; *"Be of good cheer."* —v. **1** fill with cheer; encourage. **2** shout encouragement.

cheer up, be or make glad. [< F < LL *cara* face < Gk. *kara* head, face] —**cheer′er,** *n.*

cheer·ful (chir′fəl), *adj.* **1** joyful; glad: *a cheerful person.* **2** pleasant; bright: *a cheerful room.* **3** willing: *a cheerful giver.* —**cheer′ful·ly,** *adv.* —**cheer′ful·ness,** *n.*

cheer·lead·er (chir′lē′dər), *n.* person who leads a group in organized cheering, esp. at high school and college athletic events.

cheer·less (chir′lis), *adj.* gloomy; dreary. —**cheer′less·ly,** *adv.* —**cheer′less·ness,** *n.*

cheer·y (chir′i), *adj.,* **cheer·i·er, cheer·i·est.** pleasant; bright. —**cheer′i·ly,** *adv.* —**cheer′i·ness,** *n.*

cheese (chēz), *n.* **1** solid food made from the thick part of milk. **2** mass of this pressed into shape. [< L *caseus*]

cheese·burg·er (chēz′bėr′gər), *n.* hamburger sandwich with melted cheese on top of the meat.

cheese cake, 1 dessert made of cheese, eggs, sugar, etc., baked together. **2** *Informal.* **a** the photographing of women to emphasize physical charms. **b** such photographs.

cheese·cloth (chēz′klôth′; –kloth′), *n.* a thin, loosely woven cotton cloth.

chees·y (chēz′i), *adj.,* **chees·i·er, chees·i·est. 1** of or like cheese. **2** *Informal.* poorly made; inferior. —**chees′i·ness,** *n.*

chee·tah (chē′tə), *n.* animal somewhat like a leopard, found in S Asia and Africa. Also, **chetah.** [< Hind. *chītā*]

chef (shef), *n.* **1** head cook. **2** any cook. [< F. Doublet of CHIEF.]

chef-d'oeu·vre (she dœ′vrə), *n., pl.* **chefs-d'oeu·vre** (she dœ′vrə). *French.* **1** masterpiece. **2** (literally) chief (piece of) work.

Che·khov (chek′ôf; –of), *n.* **Anton,** 1860–1904, Russian dramatist and novelist.

che·la (kē′lə), *n., pl.* **-lae** (–lē). claw of a lobster, crab, scorpion, etc. [< L < Gk. *chele* claw] —**che′late,** *adj.*

che·lo·ni·an (ki lō′nē ən), *adj.* of or having to do with turtles and tortoises. —*n.* a turtle or tortoise.

chem., chemical; chemist; chemistry.

chem·i·cal (kem′ə kəl), *adj.* **1** of chemistry. **2** made by or used in chemistry. —*n.* substance obtained by or used in a chemical process. Oxygen, sulfuric acid, borax, etc., are chemicals. —**chem′i·cal·ly,** *adv.*

che·mise (shə mēz′), *n.* a loose, shirt-like undergarment worn by women and girls. [< F < LL *camisia* shirt < Celtic]

chem·ist (kem′ist), *n.* **1** expert in chemistry. **2** *Brit.* druggist [var. of *alchemist*]

chem·is·try (kem′is tri), *n., pl.* **-tries. 1** science that deals with the characteristics of elements or simple substances, the changes that take place when they combine to form other substances, and the laws of their combination and behavior under various conditions. **2**

application of this to a certain subject. [< *chemist*]

chemo-, *combining form.* chemical; by chemical reaction: *chemotherapy =treatment by chemical reaction (of cells).*

che·mo·re·cept·or (kē′mō ri sep′tər), *n.* nerve ending or sense organ that reacts to chemical stimulation, as the taste buds.

che·mo·sphere (kē mə sfir; kem′ə–), *n.* region of predominant photochemical activity in the earth's atmosphere.

che·mo·syn·the·sis (kē′mō sin′thə sis; kem′ō–), *n.* formation in cells of carbohydrates with energy obtained from chemical reaction.

chem·o·ther·a·py (kē′mō ther′ə pē; kem′o–), *n.* treatment of infection and disease by chemicals toxic to specific cells.

chem·ur·gy (kem′ėr ji), *n.* branch of applied chemistry that deals with the use of organic raw materials, such as casein and cornstalks, otherwise than for food, and especially in manufacturing.

che·nille (shə nēl′), *n.* **1** a velvety cord, used in embroidery, fringe, etc. **2** fabric woven from this cord, used for rugs and curtains. [< F *chenille* caterpillar < L *canicula* little dog; from its furry look]

Che·ops (kē′ops), *n.* Egyptian king who lived about 2900 B.C., builder of a great pyramid. Also, **Khufu.**

Cher·bourg (shâr′būrg), *n.* seaport in NW France.

cher·ish (cher′ish), *v.* **1** hold dear; treat with affection. **2** care for tenderly. **3** keep in mind; cling to. [< F < *chérir* < *cher* dear < L *carus*] —**cher′ish·er,** *n.* —**cher′ish·ing·ly,** *adv.*

Cher·o·kee (cher′ə kē; cher′ə kē′), *n., pl.* **-kee, -kees. 1** member of a tribe of Iroquois Indians, originally of the S Appalachians, now living mostly in Oklahoma. **2** their language.

cher·ry (cher′i), *n., pl.* **-ries,** *adj.* —*n.* **1** a small, round, juicy fruit with a stone or pit in it. **2** tree that it grows on. **3** its wood. **4** bright red. —*adj.* **1** made of this wood. **2** bright-red. [OE *ciris* < VL *cerisia* < LGk. *kerasia* < Gk. *kerasos* cherry tree. See CERISE.]

cher·ry-pick (cher′ē pik′), *v.* select the best or most desirable elements of: *cherry-picked reporters' questions before the news conference.*

cher·ry picker, 1 movable crane with a bucket or platform to hold a worker making repairs, cutting trees, etc. **2** crane for picking up objects from a heap.

cher·ry·stone (cher′ē stōn′), *n.* **1** pit of a cherry. **2** =quahog.

cher·ub (cher′əb), *n., pl.* **cher·u·bim** (cher′ə bim; –yù bim) *for 1 and 2,* **cher·ubs** *for 3.* **1** one of the second highest order of angels. **2** picture or statue of a child with wings, or of a child's head with wings. **3** beautiful, innocent, or good child. [< Heb. *kerūb*] —**che·ru′bic,** *adj.* —**che·ru′bi·cal·ly,** *adv.*

Ches·a·peake Bay (ches′ə pēk), bay of the Atlantic, in Maryland and Virginia.

Chesh·ire (chesh′ər; –ir), *n.* county in W England. Also, **Chester.**

Cheshire cat, any person or creature that appears to have a wide, fixed grin.

chess (ches), *n.* game played on a chessboard by two people. Each player has 16 pieces to move in different ways. [< OF *esches* (pl.). See CHECK.]

chess·board (ches′bôrd′; –bōrd′), *n.* board marked in a pattern of 64 squares of two different colors, used in playing chess.

chess·man (ches′man′; –mən), *n., pl.* **-men** (–men′; –mən). one of the pieces used in playing chess.

chest (chest), *n.* **1 a** part of the human body enclosed by ribs; thorax. **b** corresponding part of the body in other animals. **2** a large box with a lid, used for holding things: *a linen chest.* **3** piece of furniture with drawers. **4** place where money is kept; treasury. **5** the money itself. [< L < Gk. *kiste* box]

Ches·ter·field (ches′tər fēld′), *n.* **4th Earl of,** 1694–1773, English statesman who wrote witty and instructive letters to his son.

chest·nut (ches′nut; –nət), *n.* **1** large tree belonging to the same family as the beech, that bears sweet edible nuts in prickly burs. **2** nut of this tree. **3** wood of this tree. **4** =horse chestnut. **5** reddish brown. **6** reddish-brown horse. —*adj.* reddish-brown. [< obs. *chesten* chestnut (< L < Gk. *kastanea* chestnut) + *nut*]

che·tah (chē′tə), *n.* =cheetah.

chev·a·lier (shev′ə lir′), *n.* **1** *Archaic.* knight. **2** member of the Legion of Honor of France. **3** in the old French nobility, a younger son. [< F, < *cheval* horse < L *caballus.* See CAVALIER.]

Chev·i·ot (chev′i ət, chē′vi– *for 1;* shev′-i ət *for 2),* *n.* **1** breed of sheep that originated in the Cheviot Hills. **2 cheviot, a** a rough, woolen cloth, **b** a cotton cloth like it.

Cheviot Hills, hills on the boundary between England and Scotland.

chev·ron (shev′rən), *n.* **1** a cloth design consisting of stripes meeting at an angle, worn on the sleeve as an indication of rank or of service or wounds in war. **2** design shaped like an inverted V, used in coats of arms and in architecture. [< F, rafter, < *chèvre* goat < L *capra*]

chew (chü), *v.* **1** crush or grind with the teeth. **2** think over; consider. —*n.* **1** chewing. **2** thing chewed; piece for chewing. [OE *cēowan*] —**chew′er,** *n.*

chewing gum, gum prepared for chewing, usually sweetened and flavored with chicle.

che·wink (chi wingk′), finch of E and C North America whose cry sounds somewhat like its name. [imit.]

Chey·enne (shī en′; –an′), *n.* capital of Wyoming, in the SE part.

Chey·enne (shī en′), *n., pl.* **–enne, –ennes,** *adj.* —*n.* **1** member of an Algonkian tribe of American Indians, now living in Montana and Oklahoma. **2** this tribe. —*adj.* of this tribe.

chez (shā), *prep. French.* at the home or establishment of.

chg., *pl.* **chgs.,** charge.

chi (kī), *n.* the 22nd letter of the Greek alphabet (X, χ), written as *ch* in English, but sounded like *k.*

Chi·an·ti (ki än′ti; –an′–), *n.* a dry, red Italian wine.

chic (shēk; shik), *n.* style. —*adj.* **1** stylish. **2** *Colloq.* clever; neat. [< F]

Chi·ca·go (shə kô′gō; –kä–), *n.* city in NE Illinois, on Lake Michigan. —**Chi·ca′go·an,** *n.*

Chi·ca·na (chi kä′nä), *n.* Mexican-American female.

chi·can·er·y (shi kān′ər i), *n., pl.* **–er·ies.** low trickery; unfair practice; quibbling.

Chi·ca·no (chi kä′nō), *n.* Mexican-American male.

chic·co·ry (chik′ə ri), *n., pl.* **–ries.** =chicory.

chi·chi (shē′shē′), *adj.* too elegant; too chic.

chick (chik), *n.* **1** young chicken. **2** young bird. **3** child. **4** *Informal.* attractive young woman. [var. of *chicken*]

chick·a·dee (chik′ə dē), *n.* a small bird with black, white, and gray feathers. [imit.]

Chick·a·saw (chik′ə sô), *n., pl.* **–saw** or **–saws. 1** member of a tribe of American Indians, formerly of Mississippi, now living in Oklahoma. **2** their Muskhogean language.

chick·en (chik′ən), *n.* **1** the young of domestic fowl. **2** domestic or barnyard fowl of any age. **3** flesh of a chicken used for food. **4** a young bird of certain other kinds. **5** *U.S. Slang.* young or immature woman. **6** *Informal.* person who is afraid, esp. one who is a coward. —*adj.* **1** young; small. **2** afraid; cowardly.

chicken out, refuse or fail to do something because of fear. [OE *cīcen*]

chicken feed, *U.S. Informal.* trifling amount; small undertaking.

chicken hawk, 1 any of certain hawks that raids poultry yards. **2** person who favors war but avoids military service.

chick·en-heart·ed (chik′ən här′tid), *adj.* timid; cowardly.

chicken pox, a mild contagious disease of children accompanied by a rash on the skin.

chick·pea (chik′pē′), *n.* **1** plant of the pea family that bears pealike seeds, used as food. **2** seed of this plant; garbanzo.

chick·weed (chik′wēd′), *n.* a common weed whose leaves and seeds are eaten by birds.

chic·le (chik′əl), or **chicle gum,** *n.* a tasteless, gumlike substance used in making chewing gum. It is the dried milky juice of a sapodilla tree of tropical America. [< Am.Sp. < Mex. *jiktli*]

chic lit, romance novels, esp. for young women. [< *chick* girl + *lit*erature]

chic·o·ry (chik′ə ri), *n., pl.* **–ries. 1** plant with bright-blue flowers whose leaves are used for salad. **2** its root, roasted and used as a substitute for coffee. Also, **chic·cory.** [< F < L < Gk. *kichoreion*]

chide (chīd), *v.,* **chid·ed** or **chid** (chid); **chid·ed, chid,** or **chid·den** (chid′ən); **chid·ing.** reproach; blame; scold. [OE *cīdan*] —**chid′er,** *n.* —**chid′ing·ly,** *adv.*

chief (chēf), *n.* person highest in rank or authority; head of a group; leader. —*adj.* **1** highest in rank or authority; at the head; leading. **2** most important; main.

in chief, at the head; of the highest rank or authority. [< OF < L *caput* head. Doublet of CHEF.] —**chief′less,** *adj.*

chief executive, 1 head of the executive branch of a government or corporation. **2 Chief Executive,** the President of the United States or the governor of a state.

chief justice, 1 judge who acts as chairman of a group of judges on a court. **2 Chief Justice,** presiding judge of the United States Supreme Court.

chief·ly (chēf′li), *adv.* **1** mainly; mostly. **2** first of all; above all.

chief·tain (chēf′tən), *n.* **1** chief of a tribe or clan. **2** leader. [< OF < LL *capitanus.* See CAPTAIN.] —**chief′tain·cy, chief′tain·ship,** *n.*

chif·fon (shi fon′; shif′on), *n.* a very thin silk or rayon cloth, used for dresses. [< F, < *chiffe* rag]

chif·fo·nier (shif′ə nir′), *n.* a high bureau or chest of drawers. [< F. See CHIFFON.]

chig·ger (chig′ər), *n.* **1** mite whose larvae stick to the skin and cause severe itching. **2** chigoe. [alter. of *chigoe*]

chig·oe, chig·o (chig′ō), *n.* flea of the West Indies and South America. [< WInd.]

Chi·hua·hua (chi wä′wä), *n.* **1** state in N Mexico. **2** Also, **chihuahua,** very small dog of ancient Mexican breed.

chil·blain (chil′blān′), *n.* Usually, **chilblains.** an itching sore or redness on the hands or feet caused by cold. [< *chill* + *blain*] —**chil′blained′,** *adj.*

child (chīld), *n., pl.* **chil·dren** (chil′drən). **1** baby; infant. **2** boy or girl. **3** son or daughter. **4** descendant. **5** *Fig.* result; product.

with child, pregnant. [OE *cild*] —**child′less,** *adj.*

child·bear·ing (chīld′bār′ing), *n.* giving birth to children.

child·bed (chīld′bed′), *n.* condition of a woman giving birth to a child.

child·birth (chīld′bėrth′), *n.* giving birth to a child.

child·hood (chīld′hùd), *n.* condition or time of being a child.

child·ish, (chīl′dish), *adj.* **1** of a child. **2** like a child. **3** silly; foolish. —**child′ish·ly,** *adv.* —**child′ish·ness,** *n.*

child labor, work done by children for hire, now legally restricted or, in many countries, outlawed.

child·like (chīld′līk′), *adj.* **1** innocent; frank; simple. **2** suitable for a child.

child·proof (chīld′prüf′), *adj.* safe for or around children: *a childproof lock.*

chil·dren (chil′drən), *n., pl.* of **child.**

child's play, something very easy to do.

Chil·e (chil′ē), *n.* country in SW South America. —**Chil′e·an,** *adj., n.*

Chile saltpeter, sodium nitrate, NaNO₃.

chil·i, chil·e, or **chil·li** (chil′ē), *n., pl.* **chil·ies; chil·es; chil·lies. 1** a hot-tasting pod of red pepper, used for seasoning. **2** plant that it grows on. **3** meat cooked with red peppers and beans. [< Sp. < Mex. *chilli*]

chili sauce, chilli sauce, sauce made of red peppers, tomatoes, and spices, used on meat, fish, etc.

chill (chil), *n.* **1** unpleasant coldness. **2** sudden coldness of the body with shivering. **3** unfriendliness. **4** feeling cold; shivering. —*adj.* **1** unpleasantly cold. **2** unfriendly. —*v.* **1** make cold. **2** feel cold [OE *ciele*] —**chill′er,** *n.* —**chill′ing·ly,** *adv.* —**chill′ness,** *n.*

chill·ing (chil′ing), *adj.* **1** very cold. **2** *Fig.* frightening; terrifying.

chill·y (chil′i), *adj.,* **chill·i·er, chill·i·est. 1** unpleasantly cool. **2** unfriendly. —**chill′i·ly,** *adv.* —**chill′i·ness,** *n.*

chime (chīm), *n., v.,* **chimed, chim·ing.** —*n.* **1** set of tuned bells to make musical sounds. **2** musical sound made by a set of tuned bells. **3** agreement. —*v.* **1** make musical sounds on (a set of tuned bells). **2** ring out musically: *the bells chimed midnight.* **3** agree.

chime in, join in. [< L < Gk. *kymbalon* CYMBAL]

chi·me·ra, chi·mae·ra (kə mir′ə; kī–), *n., pl.* **–ras. 1** Often, **Chimera.** *Gk. Legend.* monster with a lion's head, a goat's body, and a serpent's tail, supposed to breathe out fire. **2** a horrible creature of the imagination. **3** an absurd idea; wild fancy. [< F < L < Gk. *chimaira* she-goat]

chi·mer·i·cal (kə mer′ə kəl; –mir′–; kī–), **chi·mer·ic** (–ik), *adj.* **1** unreal; imaginary. **2** absurd; impossible. **3** wildly fanciful; visionary.

chim·ney (chim′ni), *n., pl.* **–neys. 1** an upright structure to make a draft and carry away smoke. **2** part of this that rises above a roof. **3** glass tube put around the flame of a lamp. **4** crack or opening in a rock, mountain, volcano, etc. [< OF < LL *caminata* < L *caminus* oven < Gk. *kaminos*] —**chim′ney·less,** *adj.*

chimney corner, corner or side of a fireplace; place near the fire.

chimney piece, mantelpiece.

chimney pot, earthenware or metal pipe fitted to the top of a chimney to carry off smoke.

chimney sweep or **sweeper,** person whose work is cleaning out chimneys.

chimney swift, bird of North America that often builds its nest in unused chimneys.

chimp (chimp), *n*. =chimpanzee.

chim·pan·zee (chim'pan zē'; chim pan'-zē), *n*. African ape, smaller than a gorilla. [from native West African name]

chin (chin), *n., v.*, **chinned, chin-ning**. —*n*. the front of the lower jaw below the mouth.

chin oneself, hang by the hands from a bar and pull oneself up until one's chin is even with the bar.

keep one's chin up, endure adversity without flinching or complaining.

take it on the chin, *Informal*. take a beating, esp. in the form of criticism. [OE *cin*]

Chi·na (chī'nə), **1** People's Republic of, large country in E Asia. **2** Republic of, =Taiwan.

chi·na (chī'nə), *n*. **1** fine, white pottery made of clay by a special process and baked at a high temperature, first used in China. **2** dishes, vases, ornaments, etc., made of china. **3** dishes of any kind. —*adj*. made of china.

chi·na·ber·ry (chī'nə ber'i), **china tree, 1** an ornamental tree with purple flowers and yellow fruit, esp. used as a shade tree in the South. **2** soapberry of the S United States, Mexico, and the West Indies.

China Sea, part of the Pacific E and SE of Asia. Taiwan divides it into **South China Sea** and **East China Sea.**

chi·na·ware (chī'nə wâr'), *n*. **1** dishes, vases, ornaments, etc., made of china. **2** dishes of any kind.

chin·ca·pin (ching'kə pin), *n*. =chinqua-pin.

chinch bug (chinch), a small, black-and-white bug that does much damage to grain in dry weather. [< Sp. < L *cimex* bedbug]

chin·chil·la (chin chil'ə), *n*. **1** a South American rodent that looks somewhat like a squirrel. **2** its very valuable soft, whitish-gray fur. **3** a thick woolen fabric woven in small, closely set tufts, used for overcoats. [< Sp., dim. of *chinche* CHINCH BUG]

chine (chīn), *n*. **1** backbone; spine. **2** piece of an animal's backbone with the meat on it, for cooking. [< OF *eschine* < Gmc.]

Chi·nese (chī nēz'; –nēs'), *n., pl*. **–nese,** *adj*. —*n*. **1** native or inhabitant of China. **2** person of Chinese descent. **3** language of China. —*adj*. of China, its people, or their language.

Chinese cabbage, plant of the mustard family with a lettucelike head and flavor somewhat like cabbage, used as a vegetable and in salads.

Chinese checkers, game resembling checkers, played by as many as six people using different colored marbles.

chink¹ (chingk), *n*. narrow opening; crack. —*v*. **1** fill up the chinks in. **2** make chinks in.

chink² (chingk), *n*. a short, sharp, ringing sound like coins or glasses hitting

together. —*v*. **1** make such a sound. **2** cause to make such a sound. [imit.]

chin·ka·pin (ching'kə pin), *n*. =chinqua-pin.

chino (chē'nō), *n*. cotton twill or duck fabric, used esp. in making trousers. **chinos,** trousers made of this fabric. [< Am.Sp. *chino* nonwhite half breed (referring to the light coffee color of the fabric)]

Chi·nook (chi nük'; –nūk'), *n., pl*. **–nook, –nooks. 1** member of a group of American Indian tribes living along the Columbia River in NW United States. **2** dialect of Indian, French, and English. **3 chinook, a** a warm, moist wind blowing from the sea to land in winter and spring in NW United States. **b** a warm, dry wind that comes down from the Rocky Mountains.

chin·qua·pin (ching'kə pin), **1** a dwarf chestnut tree, whose nuts are good to eat. **2** an evergreen tree of California and Oregon that has a similar nut. **3** nut of either tree. Also, **chincapin, chinkapin.** [< Am.Ind. (Algonkian)]

chintz (chints), *n*. a cotton cloth printed in patterns of various colors and often glazed. [orig. pl., < Hind. *chint* < Skt. *citra* variegated]

chip (chip), *n., v.*, **chipped, chip·ping.** —*n*. **1** small, thin piece cut or broken off. **2** place where a small, thin piece has been cut or broken off. **3** small piece of food, as a potato chip. **4** round, flat piece used for counting in games. **5 a** tiny piece of silicon with one or more microcircuits engraved or imprinted on it. **b** =micro-circuit. —*v*. **1** cut or break off in small, thin pieces. **2** shape by cutting as with an ax or chisel.

cash in one's chips, a change poker chips into cash. **b** close or sell a business. **c** *Informal*. die.

chip away at, a reduce by small amounts. **b** *Fig*. weaken; undermine.

chip in, a give a portion of (money or help). **b** put in (a remark) when others are talking. **c** add (one's stake or bet) to a pool.

chip on one's shoulder, readiness to quarrel or fight.

in the chips, wealthy; rich. [OE (*for*) *cippian*]

chip·munk (chip'mungk), *n*. a small, striped American squirrel. [< Ojibwa *achitamo* squirrel]

chip·per¹ (chip'ər), *adj*. *U.S.* lively; cheerful.

chip·per² (chip'ər), *n*. **1** person or thing that chips or cuts. **2** machine that reduces tree limbs and trunks to chips.

Chip·pe·wa (chip'ə wä; –wā; –wə), *n., pl*. **–wa, –was,** *adj*. =Ojibwa.

chipping sparrow, a small sparrow of E and C North America.

chi·rog·ra·phy (kī rog'rə fi), *n*. handwriting. [< Gk. *cheir* hand + E –*graphy* writing < Gk. *graphein* write] —**chi·rog'ra-**

pher, *n*. —**chi'ro·graph'ic, chi'ro-graph'i·cal,** *adj*.

chi·rop·o·dist (kə rop'ə dist; kī–), *n*. person who removes corns and treats other troubles of the feet.

chi·rop·o·dy (kə rop'ə di; kī–), *n*. work of a chiropodist. [< Gk. *cheir* hand + *pous* foot; orig. treatment of hands and feet]

chi·ro·prac·tic (kī'rə prak'tik), *n*. **1** treatment of diseases by manipulating the spine. **2** chiropractor. —*adj*. having to do with the treatment of diseases by manipulating the spine. [< Gk. *cheir* hand + *praktikos* practical]

chi·ro·prac·tor (kī'rə prak'tər), *n*. person who treats diseases by manipulating the spine.

chirp (chėrp), *v*. **1** make a short, sharp sound such as some small birds and insects make. **2** utter with a chirp. —*n*. such a sound. [? var. of *chirk*] —**chirp'er,** *n*.

chirr (chėr), *v*. make a shrill, trilling sound. —*n*. such a sound. Also, **churr.** [imit.]

chir·rup (chir'əp; chėr'–), *v.*, **–ruped, –rup·ing.** chirp; chirp again and again. [< *chirp*]

chis·el (chiz'əl), *n., v.*, **–eled, –el·ing.** —*n*. a tool with a sharp edge at the end of a strong blade, used to cut or shape wood, stone, or metal. —*v*. **1** cut or shape with a chisel. **2** *U.S.* unfair practices; swindle. [< OF, ult. < L *caesus* < *caedere* cut]

chit (chit), *n*. voucher of a debt, as for food. [< Hind. *chitthi*]

chit-chat (chit'chat'), *n*. **1** friendly, informal talk; chat. **2** gossip. [< *chat*]

chi·tin (kī'tin), *n*. a horny substance forming the hard outer covering of beetles, lobsters, crabs, etc. [< F < Gk. *chiton* tunic] —**chi'tin·ous,** *adj*.

chit·ter·ling (chit'ər ling), *n*. Usually, **chitterlings.** part of the small intestine of pigs, cooked as food. Also, **chitlins.**

chiv·al·ric (shiv'əl rik; shi val'rik), *adj*. **1** having to do with chivalry. **2** chivalrous.

chiv·al·rous (shiv'əl rəs), *adj*. **1** having the qualities of an ideal knight. **2** having to do with chivalry. —**chiv'al·rous·ly,** *adv*. —**chiv'al·rous·ness,** *n*.

chiv·al·ry (shiv'əl ri), *n*. **1** qualities of an ideal knight, including bravery, honor, courtesy, respect for women, protection of the weak, generosity, and fairness to enemies. **2** rules and customs of knights in the Middle Ages; system of knighthood. **3** knights as a group. **4** gallant warriors or gentlemen. [< OF. See CHEVALIER.]

chive (chīv), *n*. plant of the same family as the onion, with long, slender leaves used as seasoning. [< OF < L *caepa* onion]

chla·myd·i·a (klə mid'ē ə), **1** any one of a group of parasitic rickettsias that cause disease, including psittacosis. **2** sexually transmitted disease caused by a species of chlamydia that usually affects the lymph nodes in the groin.

chlo·ro·plast (klôr′ə plast; klōr′–), *n.* specialized body in green plants that contains chlorophyll. [< Gk. *chlōros* green + *plastos* formed]

chlo·ral (klô′rəl; klō′–), *n.* 1 a colorless liquid, CCl₃CHO, made from chlorine and alcohol. 2 chloral hydrate.

chloral hydrate, a white, crystalline drug, CCl₃CH (OH)₂, that causes sleep.

chlo·rate (klô′rāt; –rit; klō′–), *n.* salt of chloric acid.

chlo·ric (klô′rik; klō′–), *adj.* of or containing chlorine.

chloric acid, acid, HClO₃, existing only as salts and in solution.

chlo·ride (klô′rīd; –rid; klō′–), **chlo·rid** (–rid), *n.* compound of chlorine with another element or radical; salt of hydrochloric acid.

chlo·rin·ate (klô′rə nāt; klō′–), *v.,* **–at·ed, –at·ing.** 1 combine or treat with chlorine. 2 disinfect with chlorine. —**chlo′rin·a′tion,** *n.*

chlo·rine (klô′rēn; –rin; klō′–), **chlo·rin** (–rin), *n.* a poisonous, greenish-yellow, gaseous chemical element, Cl, used in bleaching and disinfecting. It is very irritating to the nose, throat, and lungs. [< Gk. *chloros* green]

chlo·ro·form (klô′rə fôrm; klō′–), *n.* CHCl₃, a colorless liquid with a sweetish smell, used as an anesthetic and to dissolve rubber, resin, wax, and many other substances. —*v.* 1 make unable to feel pain by giving chloroform. 2 kill with chloroform.

chlo·ro·phyll, chlo·ro·phyl (klô′rə fil; klō′–), *n.* the green coloring matter of plants. In the presence of light it makes carbohydrates, such as starch, from carbon dioxide and water. [< Gk. *chloros* green + E –*phyll* leaf < Gk. *phyllon*]

chm., 1 Also, **chmn.** chairman. 2 checkmate.

chock (chok), *n.* 1 block; wedge. 2 *Naut.* **a** block with two arms curving inward for a rope to pass through. **b** one of the pieces of wood on which a boat rests. —*v.* 1 provide or fasten with chocks. 2 *Naut.* put (a boat) on chocks. —*adv.* as close or as tight as can be; quite, [appar. < OF *choque* log]

chock-full (chok′fǔl′), *adj.* as full as can be. Also, **chuck-full, choke-full.**

choc·o·late (chôk′lit; chôk′–; chôk′ə lit; chok′ə–), *n.* 1 preparation made by roasting and grinding cacao seeds. 2 drink made of chocolate with hot milk or water and sugar. 3 candy made of chocolate. 4 dark brown. —*adj.* 1 made of chocolate. 2 dark-brown. [< Sp. < Mex. *chocolatl*]

Choc·taw (chok′tô), *n., pl.* **-taw, -taws,** *adj.* —*n.* member of a tribe of American Indians, now living mostly in Oklahoma. —*adj.* of this tribe.

choice (chois), *n., adj.,* **choic·er, choic·est.** —*n.* 1 act of choosing: *make your choice; his choice was to stay.* 2 person or thing chosen. 3 power or chance to choose. 4 quantity and variety to choose from. —*adj.* 1 carefully chosen. 2 excellent; superior. [< OF *chois* < Gmc.] —**choice′ly,** *adv.* —**choice′ness,** *n.*

choir (kwīr), *n.* 1 group of singers used in a church service. 2 part of a church set apart for such a group. 3 any group of singers. [< OF < L *chorus* CHORUS]

choke (chōk), *v.,* **choked, chok·ing,** *n.* —*v.* 1 keep from breathing by blocking up the throat. 2 be unable to breathe. 3 extinguish by cutting off the supply of air. 4 control; hold. 5 block; fill; clog. 6 stop. —*n.* 1 act or sound of choking. 2 valve that cuts off the supply of air in a gasoline engine.

choke back, control or suppress.
choke off, put an end to; stop.
choke up, a block up; fill up. **b** *Fig.* fill with emotion. [var. of OE *acēocian*]

choke·damp (chōk′damp′), *n.* a heavy, suffocating gas, mainly carbon dioxide, that gathers in mines, old wells, etc.

chok·er (chōk′ər), *n.* 1 one that chokes. 2 a necklace that closely fits the neck.

chol·er (kol′ər), *n.* irritable disposition; anger. [< L < Gk. *cholera* cholera, appar. < *chole* bile]

chol·er·a (kol′ər ə), *n.* an acute disease of the stomach and intestines, characterized by vomiting, cramps, and diarrhea. **Summer cholera** is not infectious. **Asiatic cholera** is infectious and often causes death. [< L < Gk. See CHOLER.]

chol·er·ic (kol′ər ik), *adj.* 1 easily made angry. 2 wrathful.

cho·les·ter·ol (kə les′tər ōl; –ol), *n.* a white, crystalline substance, C₂₇H₄₅OH, a constituent of all animal fats, bile, gallstones, egg yolk, etc. It is important in metabolism.

chomp (chomp), *v.* =champ¹.

choose (chüz), *v.,* **chose, cho·sen** or (*Obs.*) **chose, choos·ing.** 1 make a choice: *you must choose; chose a book from the library.* 2 prefer and decide: *choose not to go.*

choose up, pick opponents in a game or contest. [OE *cēosan*] —**choos′er,** *n.*

choos·y (chü′zi), *adj.,* **choos·i·er, choos·i·est.** *Informal.* particular; fussy. Also, **choosey.**

chop¹ (chop), *v.,* **chopped, chop·ping,** *n.* —*v.* 1 cut by hitting with something sharp. 2 cut into small pieces. 3 make quick, sharp movements. —*n.* 1 a cutting stroke. 2 slice of lamb, pork, veal, etc. 3 a short, irregular, motion of waves. [ME *choppe(n)*]

chop² (chop), *n.* 1 Usually, **chops.** jaw. 2 cheek. Also, **chap.** [< *chop¹*]

chop³ (chop), *v.,* **chopped, chop·ping.** change suddenly; shift quickly. [? akin to *cheap* change. See CHEAP.]

chop·house (chop′hous′), *n.* restaurant that makes a specialty of serving chops, steaks, etc.

Cho·pin (shō′pan), *n.* **Frédéric François,** 1809–49, Polish pianist and composer in France.

chop·per (chop′ər), *n.* 1 person who chops: *a good wood chopper.* 2 tool or machine for chopping up food, wood, etc. 3 *Informal.* =helicopter.

chop·py (chop′i), *adj.,* **–pi·er, –pi·est.** 1 making quick, sharp movements; jerky. 2 moving in short, irregular, broken waves. [< *chop¹*]

chop·sticks (chop′stiks′), *n.* pair of slender, tapered sticks used to raise food to the mouth by the Chinese. [< Chinese Pidgin English *chop* quick + E *stick¹*]

chop su·ey (chop′ sü′i), fried or stewed meat and vegetables cut up and cooked together in a sauce, [alter. of Chinese word meaning "mixed pieces"]

cho·ral (*adj.* kô′rəl, kō′–; *n.* kô ral′, –räl′, kō–, kô′rəl, kō′–), *adj.* 1 of a choir or chorus. 2 sung by a choir or chorus. —*n.* Also, **chorale, 1** a hymn tune. 2 a simple hymn tune sung by the choir and congregation together. —**cho′ral·ly,** *adv.*

cho·rale (kə ral′; kə räl′), *n.* 1 musical setting of a hymn. 2 simple hymn sung in unison.

chord¹ (kôrd), *n.* combination of three or more musical notes sounded together in harmony. [var. of *cord,* var. of *accord, n.*]

chord² (kôrd), *n.* 1 a straight line connecting two points on a circumference. 2 =cord (def. 4). 3 string of a harp or other musical instrument. 4 a feeling; emotion: *touch a sympathetic chord.* [< L < Gk. *chorde* gut, string of a musical instrument. Doublet of CORD.] —**chord′al,** *adj.*

chor·date (kôr′dāt), *n.* any animal of a phylum that has a notochord at some stage of development, including humans and all other vertebrates. —*adj.* 1 of or belonging to this phylum. 2 having a notochord. [< NL < L *chorda* chord²]

chore (chôr; chōr), *n. U.S.* 1 an odd job; small task. 2 a difficult or disagreeable thing to do. [OE *cyrr,* var. of *cierr, cerr* turn, business]

cho·re·a (kô rē′ə; kō–), *n.* a nervous disease characterized by involuntary twitching of the muscles; St. Vitus's dance. [< NL < Gk. *choreia* dance]

cho·re·og·ra·phy (kô′ri og′rə fi; kō′–) *n.* 1 art of planning the dances in a ballet. 2 dancing; ballet dancing. [< Gk. *choreia* dance + E –*graphy* writing < Gk. *graphein* write] —**cho′re·o·graph′ic,** *adj.* —**cho′re·og′ra·pher,** *n.*

cho·ric (kô′rik), *adj.* of or for a chorus.

cho·ri·on (kôr′ē on), *n.* outermost membrane, enclosing the amnion, of the sac which envelops the fetus or embryo of higher vertebrates. —**cho′ri·on′ic,** *adj.*

chor·is·ter (kôr′is tər; kor′–), *n.* 1 singer in a choir. 2 boy who sings in a choir. 3 leader of a choir. [< Med.L *chorista* chorister < L *chorus* CHORUS]

chor·tle (chôr′təl), *v.,* **–tled, –tling,** *n.* —*v.* chuckle or snort with glee. —*n.* a gleeful chuckle or snort, [blend of *chuckle*

and *snort;* coined by Lewis Carroll]
—**chor′tler,** *n.*

cho·rus (kô′rəs; kō′–), *n., pl.* **–rus·es,** *v.,* **–rused, –rus·ing.** —*n.* **1** group of singers who sing together. **2** song sung by many singers together. **3** the repeated part of a song coming after each stanza. **4** a saying by many at once: *a chorus of noes.* **5** group of singers and dancers. —*v.* sing or speak all at the same time. **in chorus,** all together at the same time. [< L < Gk. *choros* dance, band of dancers]

chose (chōz), *v.* pt. of **choose.**

cho·sen (chō′zən), *v.* pp. of **choose.** —*adj.* picked out; selected from a group.

chow (chou), *n.* **1** a medium-sized Chinese breed of dog with short, compact body, large head, and thick coat of one color, usually brown or black. **2** *Slang.* food. [short for Chinese Pidgin English *chow-chow*]

chow·der (chou′dər), *n.* a thick soup or stew usually made of clams or fish with potatoes, onions, etc. [appar. < F *chaudière* pot, ult. < L *calidus* hot]

chow mein (chou′ mān′), fried noodles served with a thickened stew of onions, celery, meat, etc. [< Chinese, fried flour]

chres·tom·a·thy (kres tom′ə thi), *n., pl.* **–thies.** collection of passages from literature or a foreign language. [< Gk., < *chrestos* useful + *–matheia* learning]

chrism (kriz′əm), *n.* **1** consecrated oil, used by some churches in baptism and other sacred rites. **2** sacramental anointing. Also, **chrisom.** [< L < Gk. *chrisma* < *chriein* anoint]

Christ (krīst), *n.* **1** Jesus, the founder of the Christian religion. **2** Also, **the Christ.** the Messiah. [< L < Gk. *christos* anointed]

chris·ten (kris′ən), *v.* **1** admit to a Christian church by baptism; baptize. **2** give a first name to at baptism. **3** give a name to. **4** make the first use of. [OE *christnian* make Christian < *cristen* Christian < L *christianus*]

Chris·ten·dom (kris′ən dəm), *n.* **1** the Christian part of the world. **2** all Christians.

chris·ten·ing (kris′ən ing; kris′ning), *n.* act or ceremony of baptizing and naming; baptism.

Chris·tian (kris′chən), *adj.* **1** of Christ or his teachings. **2** believing in Christ. **3** of Christians or Christianity. **4** showing a gentle, humble, helpful spirit: *Christian charity.* —*n.* believer in Christ. —**Chris′tian·ly,** *adj., adv.*

Christian Era, time since the birth of Christ. Also, **Common Era.**

Chris·ti·an·i·ty (kris′chi an′ə ti), *n., pl.* **–ties.** **1** religion taught by Christ. **2** Christian beliefs or faith.

Chris·tian·ize (kris′chən īz), *v.,* **–ized, –iz·ing.** make Christian; convert to Christianity. —**Chris′tian·i·za′tion,** *n.* —**Chris′tian·iz′er,** *n.*

Christian name, first name; given name.

Christian Science, religion and system of healing founded by Mary Baker Eddy in 1866. —**Christian Scientist.**

Christ·like (krīst′līk′), *adj.* like Christ; like that of Christ. —**Christ′like′ness,** *n.*

Christ·mas (kris′məs), *n.* the yearly celebration of the birth of Christ; December 25. [OE *Christes mœsse* Christ's MASS] —**Christ′mas·y, Christ′mas·sy,** *adj.*

Christmas Eve, the evening before Christmas.

Christ·mas·tide (kris′məs tīd′), *n.* Christmas time.

chro·mate (krō′māt), *n.* salt of chromic acid.

chro·mat·ic (krō mat′ik), *adj.* **1** of color or colors. **2** progressing by half tones instead of by the regular intervals of the scale. [< L < Gk., < *chroma* color (in musical sense)] —**chro·mat′i·cal·ly,** *adv.*

chro·mat·ics (krō mat′iks), **chro·ma·tol·o·gy** (krō′mə tol′ə ji), *n.* branch of science that deals with colors. —**chro′ma·tist,** *n.*

chromatic scale, scale divided equally into twelve half tones.

chro·ma·tid (krō′mə tid), *n.* one of the two identical halves into which a chromosome divides during cell division.

chro·ma·tin (krō′mə tin), *n.* that part of the nucleus of an animal or plant cell which absorbs stains readily and comprises the chromosomes.

chrome (krōm), *n.* chromium, esp. as the source of various pigments (chrome green, chrome red, chrome yellow, etc.). [< F < Gk. *chroma* color]

chro·mic (krō′mik), *adj.* of or containing chromium.

chromic acid, acid, H_2CrO_4, existing only as salts and in solution.

chro·mi·um (krō′mi əm), *n.* a shiny, hard, brittle metallic element, Cr, that does not rust or become dull easily when exposed to air. [< Gk. *chroma* color]

chro·mo·plast (krō′mə plast), *n.* yellow or red body in the cytoplasm of a plant cell, largely responsible for the colors of flowers and fruit.

chro·mo·some (krō′mə sōm), *n.* any of the microscopic filaments composed of chromatin that appear in an animal or plant cell during mitosis or division. Chromosomes are derived from the parents and carry the genes that determine heredity. [< Gk. *chroma* color + E *–some* body < Gk. *soma*] —**chro′mo·so′mal,** *adj.*

chro·mo·sphere (krō′mə sfir), *n.* a scarlet layer of gas around the sun.

Chron., Chronicles (in the Bible).

chron·ic (kron′ik), *adj.* **1** continuing a long time. **2** constant. **3** having had a disease, habit, etc., for a long time: *a chronic liar.* [< L < Gk., < *chronos* time] —**chron′i·cal·ly,** *adv.*

chron·i·cle (kron′ə kəl), *n., v.,* **–cled, –cling.** —*n.* record of happenings in the order in which they happened.

—*v.* record in a chronicle; write the history of; tell the story of. [< AF < L < Gk. *chronika* annals. See CHRONIC.] —**chron′i·cler,** *n.*

Chron·i·cles (kron′ə kəlz), *n.pl.* two books of the Old Testament, called I and II Chronicles.

chron·o·log·i·cal (kron′ə loj′ə kəl), *adj.* arranged in the order in which the events happened. —**chron′o·log′i·cal·ly,** *adv.*

chro·nol·o·gy (krə nol′ə ji), *n., pl.* **–gies.** **1** arrangement of time in periods; giving the exact dates of events arranged in the order in which they happened. **2** table or list that gives the exact dates of events arranged in the order in which they happened. —**chro·nol′o·gist, chro·nol′o·ger,** *n.*

chro·nom·e·ter (krə nom′ə tər), *n.* clock or watch that keeps very accurate time. —**chron′o·met′ric, chron′o·met′ri·cal,** *adj.* —**chron′o·met′ri·cal·ly,** *adv.*

chrys·a·lid (kris′ə lid), *n.* =chrysalis. —*adj.* of a chrysalis.

chrys·a·lis (kris′ə lis), *n., pl.* **chrys·a·lis·es, chry·sal·i·des** (kri sal′ə dēz). **1** form of an insect when it is in a case; pupa. **2** the case; cocoon. **3** stage of development or change. [< L < Gk. *chrysallis* golden sheath < *chrysos* gold]

chry·san·the·mum (kri san′thə məm), *n.* **1** any of several cultivated plants of the aster family, which have showy, ball-shaped flowers in the autumn. **2** one of these flowers. [< L < Gk., < *chrysos* gold + *anthemon* flower]

chrys·o·lite (kris′ə lit), *n.* a green or yellow semiprecious stone; peridot. [< L < Gk., < *chrysos* gold + *lithos* stone]

chub (chub), *n., pl.* **chubs** or (*esp. collectively*) **chub.** **1** a thick freshwater fish, related to the carp. **2** any of various American fishes, such as the tautog, black bass, etc. [ME *chubbe*]

chub·by (chub′i), *adj.,* **–bi·er, –bi·est.** round and plump. —**chub′bi·ness,** *n.*

chuck¹ (chuk), *n., v.* **1** pat; tap. **2** throw; toss. [prob. imit.]

chuck² (chuk), *n.* **1** clamp. A chuck holds a tool or piece of work in a lathe. **2** cut of beef between the neck and the shoulder. [var. of *chock*]

chuck-full (chuk′fůl′), *adj.* =chock-full.

chuck·le (chuk′əl), *v.,* **chuck·led, chuck·ling.** —*v.* **1** laugh to oneself. **2** cluck. —*n.* **1** a soft, quiet laugh. **2** cluck. [< *chuck* cluck, laugh; imit.] —**chuck′·ler,** *n.*

chuck wagon, *W U.S.* wagon carrying provisions and cooking equipment for cowboys.

chug (chug), *n., v.,* **chugged, chug·ging.** —*n.* a short, loud, explosive sound: *the chug of an engine's exhaust.* —*v.* **1** make such sounds. **2** *Colloq.* move with such sounds. [imit.]

chukka boot, ankle-high leather boot, similar to that worn for polo.

chuk·ker, chuk·kar (chuk′ər), *n.* one of the periods of play in polo. [< Hind. *chakar*]

chum (chum), *n.*, *v.*, **chummed, chum-ming.** —*n.* a very close friend. —*v.* be very close friends.

chum·my (chum'i), *adj.*, **-mi·er, -mi·est.** like a chum; very friendly. —**chum'mi·ly,** *adv.*

chump (chump), *n.* blockhead.

chunk (chungk), *n.* a thick piece or lump. [var. of *chuck*[2]]

chunk·y (chungk'i), *adj.*, **chunk·i·er, chunk·i·est.** 1 like a chunk; short and thick. 2 stocky. —**chunk'i·ly,** *adv.* —**chunk'i·ness,** *n.*

church (chèrch), *n.* 1 a building for public Christian worship. 2 public Christian worship in a church. 3 Usually, **the Church.** all Christians. 4 group of Christians with the same beliefs: *the Methodist Church.* 5 organization of a church; ecclesiastical authority or power. 6 profession of a clergyman. —*adj.* of a church. [< Gk. *kyriakon* (*doma*) (house) of the Lord < *kyrios* lord < *kyros* power] —**church'less,** *adj.* —**church'like',** *adj.*

church·go·er (chèrch'gō´ər), *n.* person who goes to church regularly. —**church'go´ing,** *n.*

Church·ill (chèrch'il; –əl), *n.* **Sir Winston,** 1874–1965, English statesman and writer, prime minister of England 1940–45 and 1951–55.

church·ly (chèrch'li), *adj.* 1 of a church. 2 suitable for a church. —**church'li·ness,** *n.*

church·man (chèrch'mən), *n.*, *pl.* **-men.** 1 clergyman. 2 member of a church. **church'man·ly.** *adv.* —**church'man·ship,** *n.*

Church of Christ Scientist, official name of the Christian Science Church.

Church of England, the Christian church in England that is recognized as a national institution by the government. Its head is the king or queen.

Church of Jesus Christ of Latter-day Saints, official name of the Mormon Church.

church·ward·en (chèrch'wôr´dən), *n.* 1 a lay official in the Church of England or the Episcopal Church who manages the business, property, and money of a church. 2 a clay tobacco pipe with a very long stem.

church·yard (chèrch'yärd´), *n.* ground around a church, sometimes used as a burial ground.

churl (chèrl), *n.* 1 a rude, surly person. 2 person of low birth; peasant. [OE *ceorl* freeman (of low rank)]

churl·ish (chèr'lish), *adj.* rude; surly. —**churl'ish·ly,** *adv.* —**churl'ish·ness,** *n.*

churn (chèrn), *n.* 1 container or machine in which cream or milk is made into butter by beating and shaking. 2 act or fact of stirring violently. —*v.* 1 stir or shake (cream or milk) in a churn. 2 make (butter) by using a churn. 3 stir violently. 4 move as if beaten and shaken.

churn out, produce (writing, music, etc.) in large amounts and without much thought. [OE *cyrn*] —**churn'er,** *n.*

churr (chèr), *v.*, *n.* =chirr.

chute (shüt), *n.* 1 an inclined trough, tube, etc., for sliding or dropping things down to a lower level. 2 rapids in a river. 3 a steep slope. 4 parachute. [appar. blend of F *chute* fall (of water) and E *shoot*]

chut·ney, (chut'ni), *n.*, *pl.* **-neys.** a spicy sauce or relish made of fruits, herbs, pepper, etc. [< Hind. *chatni*]

chutz·pah (hùts'pə; Hùts'pə), *n. Informal.* impudence; gall. [< Yiddish *khutspe*]

chyle (kīl), *n.* a milky liquid composed of digested fat and lymph, formed from the chyme in the small intestine and carried from there into the veins. [< Med.L < Gk. *chylos* < *cheein* pour]

chyme (kīm), *n.* a pulpy, semiliquid mass into which food is changed by the action of the stomach. [< Med.L < Gk. *chymos* < *cheein* pour]

CIA, C.I.A., Central Intelligence Agency.

ciao (chou), *interj. Italian.* 1 hello. 2 goodbye.

ci·bo·ri·um (si bô'ri əm; –bō'–), *n.*, *pl.* **-bo·ri·a** (–bô'ri ə; –bō'–). 1 vessel used to hold the consecrated bread of the Eucharist. 2 a dome-shaped canopy over an altar. [<Med.L, < L, drinking cup, < Gk. *kiborion* cuplike seed vessel]

ci·ca·da (si kā'də; –kä'–), *n.*, *pl.* **-das, -dae** (–dē). a large insect with transparent wings. The male makes a shrill sound in hot, dry weather. [< L]

cic·a·trix (sik'ə triks; si kā'–), **cic·a·trice** (sik'ə tris), *n.*, *pl.* **cic·a·tri·ces** (sik´ə trī'sēz). 1 scar left by a healed wound. 2 scar left on a tree or plant by a fallen leaf, seed, etc. [< L]

cic·a·trize (sik'ə trīz), *v.*, **-trized, -triz-ing.** heal by forming a scar.

Cic·e·ro (sis'ə rō), *n.* **Marcus Tullius,** 106–43 B.C., Roman orator, writer, and statesman. —**Cic'e·ro'ni·an,** *adj.*

–cide, *combining form.* 1 killer: *insecticide* = *insect killer.* 2 act of killing: *fratricide* = *killing (one's) brother.*

ci·der (sī'dər), *n.* 1 juice pressed out of apples, used as a drink and in making vinegar. 2 juice pressed from other fruits. [< OF < LL < Gk. < Heb. *shēkār* liquor]

ci·gar (si gär'), *n.* a tight roll of tobacco leaves for smoking. [< Sp. *cigarro*]

cig·a·rette, cig·a·ret (sig'ə ret´; sig'ə ret), *n.* a small roll of finely cut tobacco enclosed in a thin sheet of paper for smoking. [< F, dim. of *cigare* CIGAR]

ci·lan·tro (sə lan'trō), *n.* =coriander. [< Sp.]

cil·i·a (sil'i ə), *n.pl.*, *sing.* **cil·i·um** (sil'i əm). 1 eyelashes. 2 very small hairlike projections. Some microscopic animals use cilia to move themselves or to set up currents in the surrounding water. [< L]

cil·i·ar·y (sil'i er´i), *adj.* 1 of or resembling cilia. 2 of or having to do with certain delicate structures of the eyeball.

Cim·me·ri·an (si mir'i ən), *n.* one of a mythical people said to live in perpetual mists and darkness. —*adj.* very dark and gloomy.

cinch (sinch), *n.* 1 a strong girth for fastening a saddle or pack on a horse. 2 a firm hold or grip. 3 something sure and easy. —*v.* fasten on with a cinch; bind firmly. [< Sp. < L *cincta* girdle < *cingere* bind]

cin·cho·na (sin kō'nə), *n.* 1 a small tree that grows in South America, the East Indies, India, and Java. 2 its bitter bark, from which quinine is obtained; Peruvian bark. [< NL; named for Countess *Chinchón,* wife of a Spanish viceroy of Peru] —**cin·chon'ic,** *adj.*

cinc·ture (singk'chər), *n.* 1 belt; girdle. 2 border; enclosure. [< L *cinctura* < *cingere* bind, gird]

cin·der (sin'dər), *n.* 1 **cinders,** wood or coal partly burned and no longer flaming. 2 piece of burned-up wood or coal. [OE *sinder*]

cinder block, rectangular building block of cement and crushed cinders, usually hollow and used in walls.

Cin·der·el·la (sin'dər el'ə), *n.* 1 heroine of a famous fairy tale. 2 person whose real worth or beauty is not recognized.

cin·e·ma (sin'ə mə), *n.* 1 a motion picture. 2 a motion-picture theater. 3 **the cinema,** motion pictures. [short for *cinematograph*] —**cin'e·mat'ic,** *adj.* —**cin'e·mat'i·cal·ly,** *adv.*

cin·e·rar·i·um (sin'ə rãr'i əm), *n.*, *pl.* **-rar·i·a** (–rãr'i ə). place for keeping the ashes of cremated bodies. [< L]

cin·na·bar (sin'ə bär), *n.* 1 a reddish mineral that is the chief source of mercury; native mercuric sulfide. 2 artificial mercuric sulfide, used as a red pigment in making paints, dyes, etc. 3 bright red; vermilion. [<L < Gk. *kinnabari*; of Oriental orig.]

cin·na·mon (sin'ə mən), *n.* 1 spice made from the dried, reddish-brown inner bark of a laurel tree or shrub of the East Indies. 2 this bark. 3 tree or shrub yielding this bark. 4 a light, reddish brown. —*adj.* 1 flavored with cinnamon. 2 light reddish-brown. [< F < LL < Gk. *kinnamon*; of Semitic orig.]

cinque·foil (singk'foil´), *n.* 1 plant having small, yellow flowers and leaves divided into five parts. 2 ornament in architecture, made of five connected semicircles or part circles. [< OF < L, < *quinque* five + *folium* leaf]

CIO, Congress of Industrial Organizations. It was merged with the AFL in December 1955.

ci·on (sī'ən), *n.* =scion (def. 2).

Ci·pan·go (si pang'gō), *n. Poetic.* Japan.

ci·pher (sī'fər), *n.* 1 method of secret writing. 2 person or thing of no importance. 3 Arabic numeral. 4 zero; 0. —*v.* 1 do arithmetic. 2 work by arithmetic. Also, **cypher.** [< Med.L < Ar. *Ṣifr* empty. Doublet of ZERO.]

cir. or **circ.**, 1 circa. 2 circulation. 3 circumference.

cir·ca (sėr′kə), *adv., prep.* about: *Muhammad was born circa A.D. 570.* [< L]

cir·ca·di·an (sėr kā′dē ən), *adj.* of or having to do with a biological or behavioral process that recurs in a daily rhythm, as the 24-hour cycle of sleep and wakefulness in humans.

Cir·cas·sia (sər kash′ə), *n.* region in S Russia, on the Black Sea. —**Cir·cas′sian,** *adj., n.*

Cir·ce (sėr′sē), *n. Gk. Legend.* an enchantress who changed men into swine. —**Cir·ce′an,** *adj.*

cir·cle (sėr′kəl), *n., v.,* –**cled, –cling.** —*n.* 1 line every point of which is equally distant from a point within called the center. 2 anything shaped like a circle. 3 a complete series or course; period; cycle. 4 group of people held together by the same interests: *the family circle.* 5 sphere of influence, action, etc. —*v.* 1 revolve around. 2 surround; encircle. [< F < L *circulus,* dim. of *circus* ring] —**cir′cler,** *n.*

cir·clet (sėr′klit), *n.* a small circle.

cir·cuit (sėr′kit), *n.* 1 a going around. 2 way over which a person or group makes repeated journeys at certain times. 3 distance around any space. 4 path over which an electric current flows. —*v.* make a circuit of. [< L *circuitus* a going round < *circum* around + *ire* go]

circuit breaker, switch that automatically interrupts the flow of electricity in a circuit.

circuit court, court whose judges regularly hold court at certain places in a district.

cir·cu·i·tous (sər kū′ə təs), *adj.* not direct. —**cir·cu′i·tous·ly,** *adv.* —**cir·cu′i·tous·ness,** *n.*

cir·cuit·ry (sėr′kə tri), *n.* 1 science of electric or electronic circuits. 2 wiring, transistors, chips, etc. that make up a circuit.

cir·cu·lar (sėr′kyə lər), *adj.* 1 round like a circle. 2 moving in a circle. 3 sent to each of a number of people: *a circular letter.* 4 indirect. —*n.* letter, notice, or advertisement sent to each of a number of people. [< L *circularis.* See CIRCLE.] —**cir′cu·lar′i·ty,** *n.* —**cir′cu·lar·ly,** *adv.*

cir·cu·lar·ize (sėr′kyə lər īz), *v.,* –**ized, –iz·ing.** send circulars to. —**cir′cu·lar·i·za′tion,** *n.* —**cir′cu·lar·iz′er,** *n.*

circular saw, a thin disk with teeth in its edge, turned at high speed by a motor.

cir·cu·late (sėr′kyə lāt), *v.,* –**lat·ed, –lat·ing.** 1 go around: *money circulates.* 2 send around from person to person or place to place. [< L *circulatus.* See CIRCLE.] —**cir′cu·la′tive,** *adj.* —**cir′cu·la′tor,** *n.* —**cir′cu·la·to′ry,** *adj.*

cir·cu·la·tion (sėr′kyə lā′shən), *n.* 1 a going around. 2 movement of blood from the heart through the body and back to the heart. 3 a sending around of books, papers, news, etc. 4 number of copies of a book, newspaper, magazine, etc., that are sent out.

cir·cu·la·to·ry (sėr′kyə lə tôr′i; –tōr′–), *adj.,* having to do with circulation: *the body's circulatory system.*

circum–, *prefix.* 1 round about; on all sides, as in *circumstance.* 2 in a circle; around, as in *circumnavigate.* [< L]

cir·cum·am·bi·ent (sėr′kəm am′bi ənt), *adj.* surrounding; encircling. —**cir′cum·am′bi·ence, cir′cum·am′bi·en·cy,** *n.*

cir·cum·cise (sėr′kəm sīz), *v.,* –**cised, –cis·ing.** cut off the foreskin of. [< L *circumcisus* < *circum* around + *caedere* cut] —**cir′cum·cis′er,** *n.* —**cir′cum·ci′·sion,** *n.*

cir·cum·fer·ence (sər kum′fər əns), *n.* 1 the boundary line of a circle. 2 the distance around. [< L *circumferentia* < *circum* around + *ferre* bear] —**cir·cum′fer·en′tial,** *adj.*

cir·cum·flex (sėr′kəm fleks), *n.* a circumflex accent. —*adj.* of or having a circumflex accent. [< L *circumflexus* bent around < *circum* around + *flectere* bend] —**cir′cum·flex′ion,** *n.*

circumflex accent, mark (ˆ or ˆ) placed over a vowel to tell something about its pronunciation, as in the French words *fête* and *goût.*

cir·cum·flu·ent (sər kum′flù ənt), *adj.* flowing around; surrounding. Also, **cir·cumfluous.** [< L, < *circum* around + *fluere* flow]

cir·cum·fuse (sėr′kəm fūz′), *v.,* –**fused, –fus·ing.** 1 pour or spread around. 2 surround; suffuse. [< L *circumfusus* < *circum* around + *fundere* pour] —**cir′cum·fu′sion,** *n.*

cir·cum·lo·cu·tion (sėr′kəm lō kū′shən), *n.* a roundabout way of speaking. [< L *circumlocutio* < *circum* around + *loqui* speak] —**cir′cum·loc′u·to·ry,** *adj.*

cir·cum·nav·i·gate (sėr′kəm nav′ə gāt), *v.,* –**gat·ed, –gat·ing.** sail around. —**cir′cum·nav′i·ga′tion,** *n.* —**cir′cum·nav′i·ga′tor,** *n.*

cir·cum·po·lar (sėr′kəm pō′lər), *adj.* 1 around the North or South Pole. 2 revolving around either pole of the heavens without sinking below the horizon: *the circumpolar midnight sun.*

cir·cum·scribe (sėr′kəm skrīb′), *v.,* –**scribed, –scrib·ing.** 1 draw a line around. 2 limit; restrict. 3 a draw (a figure) around another figure so as to touch as many points as possible. b be so drawn around. [< L, < *circum* around + *scribere* write] —**cir′cum·scrib′er,** *n.*

cir·cum·scrip·tion (sėr′kəm skrip′shən), *n.* 1 a circumscribing. 2 thing that circumscribes. 3 outline; boundary. 4 limitation; restriction.

cir·cum·spect (sėr′kəm spekt), *adj.* careful; cautious; prudent. [< L, < *circum* around + *specere* look] —**cir′cum·spec′tion,** *n.* —**cir′cum·spec′tive,** *adj.* —**cir′cum·spect′ly,** *adv.* —**cir′cum·spect′ness,** *n.*

cir·cum·stance (sėr′kəm stans), *n.* 1 condition of an act or event. 2 fact or event. **circumstances,** condition or state of affairs.

under no circumstances, never.

under the circumstances, because of conditions. [< L *circumstantia* surrounding condition < *circum* around + *stare* stand] —**cir′cum·stanced,** *adj.*

cir·cum·stan·tial (sėr′kəm stan′shəl), *adj.* 1 depending on circumstances: *circumstantial evidence.* 2 not essential. 3 giving full and exact details: *a circumstantial report.* —**cir′cum·stan′ti·al′i·ty, cir′cum·stan′tial·ness,** *n.* —**cir′cum·stan′tial·ly,** *adv.*

cir·cum·stan·ti·ate (sėr′kəm stan′shi āt), *v.,* –**at·ed, –at·ing.** support or prove with details. —**cir′cum·stan′ti·a′tion,** *n.*

cir·cum·vent (sėr′kəm vent′), *v.* get the better of; defeat by trickery. [< L, < *circum* around + *venire* come] —**cir′cum·vent′er, cir′cum·ven′tor,** *n.* —**cir′cum·ven′tion,** *n.* —**cir′cum·ven′tive,** *adj.*

cir·cus (sėr′kəs), *n.* 1 a traveling show of acrobats, clowns, horses, riders, and wild animals. 2 *Colloq.* an amusing person, thing, or event. [< L, ring]

cirque (sėrk), *n.* 1 a circular space. b natural amphitheater encircled by heights, esp. one in the mountains formed by erosion at the head of a glacier. 2 circlet; ring. 3 =circus.

cir·rho·sis (si rō′sis), *n.* a diseased condition of the liver, kidneys, etc., due to excessive formation of connective tissue. [< NL < Gk. *kirrhos* orange-yellow] —**cir·rhot′ic,** *adj.*

cir·ro·cu·mu·lus or **cir·ro·cu·mu·lus** (sir′ō kyü′myə ləs), *n.* wavelike cloud formation of ice crystals occurring at 20,000 feet and alone.

cir·ro·stra·tus or **cir·ro·stra·tus** (sir′ō strā′təs), *n.* thin veil-like cloud formation of ice crystals occurring at 20,000 feet and alone.

cir·rus (sir′əs), *n., pl.* **cir·ri** (sir′ī). 1 a thin, fleecy cloud very high in the air. 2 a tendril. 3 a slender appendage. [< L *cirrus* curl]

cis·al·pine (sis al′pīn; –pin), *adj.* occurring on the S side of the Alps.

cis·co (sis′kō), *n., pl.* –**coes, –cos.** a whitefish or herring of the Great Lakes. [< Am.Ind.]

Cis·ter·cian (sis tėr′shən), *n.* member of a Benedictine order of monks and nuns founded in France in 1098. —*adj.* of this order.

cis·tern (sis′tərn), *n.* 1 reservoir or tank for storing water. 2 vessel or cavity of the body. [< L *cisterna* < *cista* box]

cit·a·del (sit′ə dəl; –del), *n.* 1 fortress commanding a city. 2 a strongly fortified place; stronghold. 3 a refuge. [< F < Ital. *cittadella,* dim. of *città* CITY]

ci·ta·tion (sī tā′shən), *n.* 1 quotation or reference, esp. given as an authority. 2 specific mention in an official dispatch. 3 public commendation or decoration. 4

summons to appear before a law court. —**ci′ta·to′ry,** *adj.*

cite (sīt), *v.,* **cit·ed, cit·ing. 1** quote (a passage, book, or author). **2** refer to. [< L *citare* summon < *ciere* set in motion]

cith·a·ra (sith′ə rə), *n.* an ancient musical instrument somewhat like a lyre. [< L < Gk. *kithara.* Doublet of GUITAR and ZITHER.]

cith·er (sith′ər), *n.* **1** =cithara. **2** =cithern.

cith·ern (sith′ərn), *n.* a musical instrument somewhat like a guitar, popular in the 16th and 17th centuries. Also, **cittern.** [see CITTERN]

cit·i·zen (sit′ə zən; –sən), *n.* **1** person who by birth or by choice is a member of a state or nation. **2** person who is not a soldier, policeman, etc.; civilian. **3** inhabitant of a city or town. [< AF *citisein* < OF *cite* CITY]

cit·i·zen·ry (sit′ə zən ri; –sən–), *n., pl.* **–ries.** citizens as a group.

citizens band, radio band designated by the federal government for use by private citizens.

cit·i·zen·ship (sit′ə zən ship′; –sən–), *n.* **1** condition of being a citizen. **2** duties, rights, and privileges of a citizen.

cit·rate (sit′rāt; sī′trāt), *n.* salt or ester of citric acid.

cit·ric (sit′rik), *adj.* of or from fruits such as lemons, limes, oranges, etc.

citric acid, acid, $C_6H_8O_7$, from such fruits as lemons, limes, etc., used as a flavoring, as a medicine, and in making dyes.

cit·rine (sit′rən), *adj.* lemon-colored. —*n.* a pale yellow.

cit·ron (sit′rən), *n.* **1** a pale-yellow fruit somewhat like a lemon but larger, less acid, and with a thicker rind. **2** the candied rind of this fruit, used in fruit cakes, plum pudding, candies, etc. **3** shrub or small tree that this citrus grows on. [< F < Ital. *citrone* < L *citrus* citrus tree]

cit·ron·el·la (sit′rən el′ə), *n.* oil used in making perfume, soap, liniment, etc., and for keeping mosquitoes away. [< NL]

cit·rous (sit′rəs), *adj.* pertaining to fruits such as lemons, grapefruit, limes, oranges, etc.

cit·rus (sit′rəs), *n.* **1** any tree bearing lemons, limes, oranges, or similar fruit. **2** Also, **citrus fruit.** fruit of such a tree. —*adj.* of such trees. [< L]

cit·tern (sit′ərn), *n.* =cithern. [blend of L *cithara* CITHARA + E *gittern*]

cit·y (sit′i), *n., pl.* **cit·ies,** *adj.* —*n.* **1** a large and important town. **2** division of local government having a charter from the state that fixes its boundaries and powers. **3** people living in a city. —*adj.* **1** of a city. **2** in a city. [< OF < L *civitas* citizenship, state, city < *civis* citizen]

city hall, a building containing offices for the officials, bureaus, etc., of a city government.

city manager, person appointed by a city council or commission to manage the government of a city. He or she is not elected by the people.

cit·y-state (sit′i stāt′), *n.* an independent state consisting of a city and the territories depending on it.

civ·et (siv′it), *n.* **1** a yellowish secretion of certain glands of the civet cat. It has a musky odor and is used in making perfume. **2** Also, **civet cat. a** a small, spotted animal of Africa, Europe, and Asia having glands that secrete a yellowish substance with a musky odor. **b** any of certain similar animals. [< F < Ital. < Ar. *zabād*]

civ·ic (siv′ik), *adj.* **1** of a city. **2** of or having to do with citizenship. **3** of citizens. [< L *civicus* < *civis* citizen] —**civ′i·cal·ly,** *adv.*

civ·ics (siv′iks), *n.* study of the duties, rights, and privileges of citizens.

civ·il (siv′əl), *adj.* **1** of a citizen or citizens; **2** of the government, state, or nation: *civil servants.* **3** not military, naval, or connected with the church. Post offices are part of the civil service of the government. **4** polite; courteous. [< L *civilis* < *civis* citizen]

civil disobedience, refusal to obey the laws of the state, as by not paying taxes.

civil engineering, the planning and directing of the construction of bridges, roads, harbors, etc. —**civil engineer.**

ci·vil·ian (sə vil′yən), *n.* person who is not in the military or part of a force, as the police or fire department. —*adj.* of civilians; not military or naval.

ci·vil·i·ty (sə vil′ə ti), *n., pl.* **–ties. 1** politeness; courtesy. **2** act of politeness or courtesy.

civ·i·li·za·tion (siv′ə lə zā′shən), *n.* **1** advanced stage in social development. **2** nations and peoples that have reached advanced stages in social development. **3** the culture and ways of living of a race, nation, etc.: *Chinese civilization.* **4** process of becoming civilized; improvement in culture. **5** act of civilizing.

civ·i·lize (siv′ə līz), *v.,* **–lized, –liz·ing.** bring out of a savage or barbarian condition; train in culture, science, and art; humanize. [< Med.L *civilizare.* See CIVIL, –IZE.] —**civ′i·liz′a·ble,** *adj.* —**civ′i·liz′er,** *n.*

civ·i·lized (siv′ə līzd), *adj.* **1** trained in culture, art, and science. **2** of civilized nations or persons.

civil law, law that regulates and protects private rights and is controlled and used by civil courts, not military courts.

civil liberty, right of a person to do and say what he pleases as long as he does not harm anyone else.

civ·il·ly (siv′ə li), *adv.* **1** politely; courteously. **2** according to the civil law.

civil rights, the rights of a citizen, esp. the rights guaranteed to citizens of the United States, irrespective of race or color, by the Thirteenth and Fourteenth Amendments to the Constitution.

civil service, public service concerned with affairs not military, naval, legislative, or judicial. —**civil servant.**

civil war, 1 war between two groups of citizens of one nation. **2 Civil War,** war between the N and S states of the United States from 1861 to 1865.

Cl, *Chem.* chlorine.

cl., 1 centiliter. **2** class. **3** clause.

clab·ber (klab′ər), *n.* thick, sour milk. —*v.* become thick in souring; curdle. [< Irish *clabar* curds, short for *bainne clabair* bonnyclabber (curdled milk)]

clack (klak), *v.* make or cause to make a short, sharp sound. —*n.* short, sharp sound. [imit.] —**clack′er,** *n.*

clad (klad), *v.* pt. and pp. of **clothe.**

claim (klām), *v.* **1** demand as one's own or one's right. **2** assert one's right to. **3** declare as a fact. **4** require; call for; deserve. —*n.* **1** demand for something due. **2** right or title to something. **3** something that is claimed. **4** piece of land that a settler or prospector marks out.

jump a claim, seize land already claimed by another.

lay claim to, assert one's right to. [< OF < L *clamare* call, proclaim] —**claim′a·ble,** *adj.* —**claim′er,** *n.*

claim·ant (klām′ənt), *n.* one who makes a claim.

clair·voy·ance (klār voi′əns), *n.* exceptional insight. [< F, < *clair* clear + *voyant* seeing] —**clair·voy′ant,** *adj., n.*

clam (klam), *n., v.,* **clammed, clam·ming.** —*n.* mollusk somewhat like an oyster, with a shell in two halves. **2** dull person. —*v.* dig for clams.

clam up, *Informal.* stop talking; refuse to speak.

happy as a clam, *Informal.* very happy. [appar. special use of *clam* pair of pincers; OE *clamm* fetter]

clam·bake (klam′bāk′), *n.* **1** picnic where clams are baked or steamed, esp. at a beach. **2** *Informal. Fig.* any meeting or lively get-together.

clam·ber (klam′bər), *v.* climb, using both hands and feet; scramble. [ME *clambre(n)*] —**clam′ber·er,** *n.*

clam·my (klam′i), *adj.,* **–mi·er, –mi·est.** cold and damp. —**clam′mi·ly,** *adv.* —**clam′mi·ness,** *n.*

clam·or (klam′ər), *n.* **1** continual uproar; shouting. **2** a noisy demand. —*v.* **1** shout. **2** demand or complain noisily. [< OF < L, < *clamare* cry out] —**clam′or·er,** *n.*

clam·or·ous (klam′ər əs), *adj.* **1** shouting. **2** making noisy demands. —**clam′or·ous·ly,** *adv.* —**clam′or·ous·ness,** *n.*

clamp (klamp), *n.* device for holding things tightly together. —*v.* fasten together with a clamp.

clamp down, *Informal.* become stricter. [< MDu. *klampe*]

clan (klan), *n.* **1** group of related families that claim to be descended from a common ancestor. **2** group of people closely joined together by some common interest. [< Scotch Gaelic *clann* family]

clan·des·tine (klan des′tən), *adj.* secret; concealed; underhand. [< L *clandestinus,* ult. < *clam* secretly] —**clan·des′tine·ly,** *adv.* —**clan·des′tine·ness,** *n.*

clang (klang), *n.* a loud, harsh, ringing sound. —*v.* make a clang. [imit.]

clan·gor (klang′gər; klang′ər), *n.* 1 continued clanging. 2 clang. —*v.* clang. [< L, < *clangere* clang] —**clan′gor·ous,** *adj.* —**clan′gor·ous·ly,** *adv.*

clank (klangk), *n.* a sharp, harsh sound like the rattle of a heavy chain. —*v.* make such a sound. [? < Du. *klank*]

clan·nish (klan′ish), *adj.* 1 pertaining to a clan. 2 closely united; not liking outsiders. —**clan′nish·ly,** *adv.* —**clan′nish·ness,** *n.*

clans·man (klanz′mən), *n.,* *pl.* -men. member of a clan.

clap (klap), *n.,* *v.,* **clapped, clap·ping.** —*n.* 1 a sudden noise, such as a burst of thunder, the sound of hands struck together, or the sound of a loud slap. 2 applause. —*v.* 1 strike together loudly. 2 applaud by striking the hands together. 3 put or place quickly and effectively. [OE *clæppan*]

clap·board (klab′ərd; klap′bôrd; –bōrd), *n.* a thin board, thicker along one edge than along the other, used to cover the outer walls of wooden buildings. —*v.* cover with clapboards.

clap·per (klap′ər), *n.* 1 one that claps. 2 part that strikes a bell. 3 device for making noise.

clap·trap (klap′trap′), *n.* empty talk; insincere remark. —*adj.* cheap and showy.

claque (klak), *n.* 1 group that applauds or follows another person for selfish reasons. 2 group of persons hired to applaud in a theater. [< F, < *claquer* clap]

clar·et (klar′ət), *n.* 1 kind of red wine. 2 a dark, purplish red. —*adj.* dark purplish-red. [< OF, light colored, < *cler* CLEAR]

clar·i·fy (klar′ə fī), *v.,* -fied, -fy·ing. 1 make or become clear; purify: *clarify fat by straining it.* 2 make clearer; explain. [< OF < LL *clarificare* < L *clarus* clear + *facere* make] —**clar′i·fi·ca′tion,** *n.* —**clar′i·fi′er,** *n.*

clar·i·net (klar′ə net′), *n.* a wooden wind instrument played by means of holes and keys. [< F *clarinette,* dim. of *clarine* bell < L *clarus* clear] —**clar′i·net′ist, clar′i·net′tist,** *n.*

clar·i·on (klar′i ən), *adj.* clear and shrill. —*n.* 1 a clear, shrill sound. 2 a kind of trumpet with clear, shrill tones. [< Med. L *clario* < L *clarus* clear]

clar·i·ty (klar′ə ti), *n.* clearness.

clash (klash), *n.* 1 a loud, harsh sound like that of striking metal. 2 conflict. —*v.* 1 strike with a clash. 2 disagree strongly; conflict. [imit.]

clasp (klasp; kläsp), *n.* 1 thing to fasten two parts or pieces together. 2 a firm grip with the hand. —*v.* 1 fasten together with a clasp. 2 hold closely with the arms

or hands. 3 grip firmly with the hand. [ME *claspe(n)*] —**clasp′er,** *n.*

class (klas; kläs), *n.* 1 group of persons or things alike in some way; kind; sort. 2 group of students taught together. 3 a meeting of such a group. 4 rank or division of society: *the middle class.* 5 high rank in society. 6 grade; quality: *first class is the best way to travel.* 7 group of animals or plants ranking below a phylum or subkingdom and above an order. —*v.* put or be in a class or group.

the classes, economic and social divisions of society. [< L *classis* class, collection, fleet] —**class′a·ble,** *adj.* —**class′er,** *n.*

class., 1 classic; classical. 2 classification. 3 classified.

clas·sic (klas′ik), *adj.* 1 of the highest grade or quality; excellent; first-class. 2 of the literature, art, and life of ancient Greece and Rome. 3 like this literature and art; simple, regular, and restrained. 4 famous in literature or history. —*n.* 1 work of literature or art of the highest quality. 2 author or artist of acknowledged excellence.

the classics, the literature of ancient Greece and Rome. [< L *classicus* < *classis* CLASS]

clas·si·cal (klas′ə kəl), *adj.* 1 =classic. 2 knowing the classics well. 3 devoted to the classics. 4 based on the classics. 5 orthodox and sound, but not quite up to date: *classical physics.* 6 *Music.* of high quality and enjoyed especially by serious students of music. —**clas′si·cal′i·ty,** *n.* —**clas′si·cal·ly,** *adv.* —**clas′si·cal·ness,** *n.*

clas·si·cism (klas′ə siz əm), **clas·si·cal·ism** (–kəl iz′əm), *n.* 1 principles of the literature and art of ancient Greece and Rome. 2 adherence to these principles. 3 knowledge of the literature of ancient Greece and Rome; classical scholarship. 4 idiom or form from Greek or Latin introduced into another language.

clas·si·cist (klas′ə sist), *n.* 1 follower of the principles of classicism in literature and art. 2 expert in the literature of ancient Greece and Rome. 3 person who urges the study of Greek and Latin. Also, **clas·si·cal·ist.**

clas·si·fi·ca·tion (klas′ə fə kā′shən), *n.* arrangement in classes or groups; a grouping according to some system. —**clas′si·fi·ca·to′ry,** *adj.*

clas·si·fied (klas′ə fīd), *adj.* 1 of certain public documents of the U.S., having a classification as secret, confidential, or restricted. 2 secret.

the classifieds, classified ads in a newspaper.

classified ad, want ad.

class·ism (klas′ iz əm), *n.* discrimination based on economic or social class. —**class′ist,** *n., adj.*

clas·si·fy (klas′ə fī), *v.,* -fied, -fy·ing. arrange in classes or groups; group according to some system. —**clas′si·fi′a·ble,** *adj.* —**clas′si·fi′er,** *n.*

class·less (klas′lis; kläs′–), *adj.* without classes, esp. social or economic: *the dream of a classless society.*

class·mate (klas′māt′; kläs′–), *n.* member of the same class in school.

class·room (klas′rüm′; –rum′; kläs′–), *n.* room where classes meet in school; schoolroom.

class·y (klas′ē), *adj.,* **class·i·er, class·i·est.** *Informal.* smart; stylish.

clat·ter (klat′ər), *n.* 1 a confused noise like that of many plates being struck together. 2 noisy talk. —*v.* 1 move or fall with confused noise; make a confused noise. 2 talk fast and noisily. 3 cause to clatter. [OE *clatrian*] —**clat′ter·er,** *n.* —**clat′ter·ing·ly,** *adv.*

clause (klôz), *n.* 1 part of a sentence having a subject and predicate. In "He came before we left," "He came" is a **main clause,** and "before we left" is a **subordinate clause.** 2 a single provision of a law, treaty, or any other written agreement. [< Med.L *clausa* for L *clausula* close of a period < *claudere* close] —**claus′al,** *adj.*

claus·tro·pho·bi·a (klôs′trə fō′bi ə), *n.* morbid fear of enclosed spaces. [< NL, < L *claustrum* closed place + E *–phobia* fear (< Gk.)]

clave (klāv), *v. Archaic.* pt. of **cleave**[2].

clav·i·chord (klav′ə kôrd), *n.* a stringed musical instrument with a keyboard. The piano developed from it. [< Med.L < L *clavis* key + *chorda* string]

clav·i·cle (klav′ə kəl), *n.* =collarbone. [< L *clavicula* bolt, dim. of *clavis* key] —**cla·vic′u·lar,** *adj.*

cla·vier (klə vir′), *n.* any musical instrument with a keyboard, as the harpsichord and clavichord. [< G < F < L *clavis* key]

claw (klô), *n.* 1 a sharp, hooked nail on a bird's or animal's foot. 2 foot with such sharp, hooked nails. 3 pincers of lobsters, crabs, etc. 4 anything like a claw. 5 act of clawing. —*v.* scratch, tear, seize, or pull with claws or hands.

get one's claws into, lay hold of; attack. [OE *clawu*]

clay (klā), *n.* 1 a stiff, sticky kind of earth, that can be easily shaped when wet and hardens after drying or baking. 2 earth. 3 human body. [OE *clæg*] —**clay′ey, clay′ish,** *adj.*

clay·more (klā′môr; –mōr), *n.* a heavy, two-edged sword, formerly used by Scottish Highlanders. [< Scotch Gaelic *claidheamh mor* great sword]

clay pigeon, 1 disk-shaped clay target thrown or shot into the air, used as a target in trap-shooting. 2 *Informal. Fig.* person in a vulnerable position.

clean (klēn), *adj.* 1 free from dirt or filth. 2 pure; innocent. 3 having clean habits. 4 even; regular: *a clean cut.* 5 free from anything that mars or impedes; clear: *clean copy.* 6 complete; entire; total. 7 of atomic weapons, causing little or no radioactive fallout. —*adv.* completely;

totally. —v. **1** make clean. **2** perform a process of cleaning.

clean out, a empty. **b** use up. **c** *Informal.* eject (undesirable people) from a place. **d** *Informal.* steal or take by cheating.

clean up, a make clean. **b** put in order. **c** *Informal.* finish; complete. **d** free of undesirable people. **e** *Informal.* make a great deal of money.

come clean, *Informal.* tell everything; confess fully. [OE *clǣne*] —**clean′a·ble,** *adj.* —**clean′ness,** *n.*

clean-cut (klēn′kut′), *adj.* **1** having clear, sharp outlines. **2** clear; definite; distinct.

clean·er (klēn′ər), *n.* **1** person whose work is cleaning. **2** anything that removes dirt, grease, or stains.

clean·ly (*adj.* klen′li; *adv.* klēn′li), *adj.,* –**li·er,** –**li·est,** *adv.* —*adj.* clean; habitually clean. —*adv.* in a clean manner. —**clean′li·ly,** *adv.* —**clean′li·ness,** *n.*

clean room, sterilized and pressurized room for laboratory work, making parts for electronics, spacecraft, etc.

cleanse (klenz), *v.,* **cleansed, cleansing. 1** make clean. **2** make pure. [OE *clǣnsian < clǣne* clean] —**cleans′a·ble,** *adj.* —**cleans′er,** *n.*

clean·up (klēn′up′), *n.* a cleaning up.

clear (klir), *adj.* **1** not cloudy; bright. **2** transparent: *clear glass.* **3** having a pure color: *a clear blue.* **4** that perceives distinctly: *a clear mind.* **5** easily seen, heard, or understood. **6** sure; certain. **7** not blocked; open. **8** innocent. **9** free from debts or charges. **10** complete. —*v.* **1** make or become clear. **2** remove to leave a space. **3** pass by or over without touching. **4** make free from blame or guilt. **5** make as profit. **6** get (a ship or cargo) free on entering or leaving a port. **7** exchange (checks and bills) between banks. —*adv.* **1** in a clear manner. **2** completely; entirely.

clear away, a remove to leave a space clear. **b** disappear. **c** clear dishes from a table.

clear off, a remove something. **b** be off; leave a place clear.

clear out, a make clear by throwing out or emptying. **b** *Informal.* go away.

clear up, a make clear. **b** become clear. **c** put in order by clearing. **d** *Fig.* make clear by explaining.

in the clear, free; innocent. [< OF < L *clarus* clear] —**clear′a·ble,** *adj.* —**clear′er,** *n.* —**clear′ly,** *adv.* —**clear′ness,** *n.*

clear·ance (klir′əns), *n.* **1** act of making clear. **2** a clear space between two objects. **3** permission of ship or aircraft to leave. **4** the settling of accounts between banks.

clear-cut (klir′kut′), *adj.* **1** having clear, sharp outlines. **2** clear; definite; distinct.

clear-head·ed (klir′hed′id), *adj.* having or showing a clear understanding. —**clear′-head′ed·ly,** *adv.* —**clear′-head′ed·ness,** *n.*

clear·ing (klir′ing), *n.* an open space of cleared land in a forest.

clearing house, central location for settling financial transactions.

clear-sight·ed (klir′sīt′id), *adj.* **1** able to see clearly. **2** able to understand or think clearly. —**clear′-sight′ed·ly,** *adv.* —**clear′-sight′ed·ness,** *n.*

clear·sto·ry (klir′stô′ri; –stō′–), *n., pl.* –**ries.** =clerestory.

cleat (klēt), *n.* **1** strip of wood or iron fastened across anything for support or for sure footing. **2** piece of wood or metal used for securing ropes or lines. —*v.* fasten to or with a cleat. [ME *cleete*]

cleav·age (klēv′ij), *n.* **1** split; division. **2** way in which something splits or divides. **3** any of the series of divisions by which a fertilized egg develops into an embryo.

cleave¹ (klēv), *v.,* **cleft** or **cleaved** or **clove, cleft** or **cleaved** or **clo·ven, cleav·ing. 1** split; divide. **2** pass through; pierce; penetrate. **3** make by cutting. [OE *clēofan*] —**cleav′a·ble,** *adj.*

cleave² (klēv), *v.,* **cleaved** or (*Archaic*) **clave, cleaved, cleav·ing.** stick; cling; be faithful. [OE *cleofian*]

cleav·er (klēv′ər), *n.* **1** one that cleaves. **2** cutting tool with a heavy blade and a short handle.

clef (klef), *n.* symbol indicating the pitch of the musical notes on a staff. [< F < L *clavis* key]

cleft (kleft), *v.* pt. and pp. of **cleave¹.** —*adj.* split; divided. —*n.* a space or opening made by splitting; crack. [OE *geclyft*]

clem·a·tis (klem′ə tis), *n.* vine with clusters of fragrant white or purple flowers. [< L < Gk., < *klema* vine branch]

clem·en·cy (klem′ən sē), *n.* **1** mercy or leniency in the use of power or authority. **2** mildness, as of weather.

clem·ent (klem′ənt), *adj.* **1** merciful. **2** mild. [< L *clemens*] —**clem′ent·ly,** *adv.*

clench (klench), *v.* **1** close tightly together: *clench one's fists in anger.* **2** grasp firmly; grip tightly. **3** clinch (a nail, etc.). —*n.* firm grasp; tight grip. [OE *(be)clencan* hold fast] —**clench′er,** *n.*

Cle·o·pat·ra (klē′ə pat′rə; –pā′trə; –pä′trə), *n.* 69?–30 B.C., last queen of ancient Egypt, 47–30 B.C.

clere·sto·ry (klir′stô′ri; –stō′–), *n., pl.* –**ries. 1** the upper part of the wall of a church, having windows in it above the roofs of the aisles. **2** a similar structure in any building. Also, **clearstory.** [appar. < *clere* clear + *story²*]

cler·gy (klėr′ji), *n., pl.* –**gies.** persons ordained for religious work; ministers, pastors, and priests. [< OF *clergie,* ult. < LL *clericus* CLERIC]

cler·gy·man (klėr′ji mən), *n., pl.* –**men.** member of the clergy; minister; pastor; priest.

cler·ic (kler′ik), *n.* clergyman. —*adj.* of a clergyman or the clergy. [< LL < Gk., < *kleros* clergy, orig., lot, allotment. Doublet of CLERK.]

cler·i·cal (kler′ə kəl), *adj.* **1** of a clerk or clerks; for clerks. **2** of a clergyman or the clergy. **3** supporting the power or influence of the clergy in politics. —**cler′i·cal·ly,** *adv.*

cler·i·cal·ism (kler′ə kəl iz′em), *n.* power or influence of the clergy in politics. —**cler′i·cal·ist,** *n.*

clerk (klėrk), *n.* **1** person whose work is waiting on customers and selling goods in a store. **2** person whose work is keeping records or accounts, in an office. **3** official who keeps records and takes care of regular business in a law court, legislature, etc. **4** layman who has minor church duties. —*v.* work as a clerk. [< LL *clericus.* Doublet of CLERIC.] —**clerk′ly,** *adv.* —**clerk′li·ness,** *n.* —**clerk′ship,** *n.*

Cleve·land (klēv′lənd), *n.* **1** city in NE Ohio, on Lake Erie. **2 (Stephen) Grover,** 1837–1908, the 22nd and 24th president of the United States 1885–89, 1893–97.

clev·er (klev′ər), *adj.* **1** bright; intelligent. **2** skillful or expert. [ME *cliver*] —**clev′er·ly,** *adv.* —**clev′er·ness,** *n.*

clev·is (klev′is), *n.* a U-shaped piece of metal with a bolt or pin through the ends. [akin to CLEAVE¹]

clew (klü), *n.* **1** =clue. **2** ball of thread or yarn. —*v.* coil into a ball. [OE *cleowen*]

cli·ché (klē shā′), *n.* a worn-out idea or trite expression. [< F, pp. of *clicher* stereotype] —**cli·chéd′,** *adj.*

click (klik), *n.* a light, sharp sound like that of a key turning in a lock. —*v.* **1** make a light, sharp sound. **2** activate an icon for a computer program, using a mouse. **3** be a success. [imit.] —**click′er,** *n.*

cli·ent (klī′ənt), *n.* **1** person for whom a lawyer acts. **2** customer. [< L *cliens;* akin to –*clinare* lean] —**cli·en′tal,** *adj.* —**cli′ent·less,** *adj.*

cli·en·tele (klī′ən tel′), *n.* **1** clients; customers. **2** number of clients. [< L *clientela*]

cliff (klif), *n.* a high, steep rock. [OE *clif*]

cliff dweller, 1 member of a group of prehistoric people in the SW United States who lived in a cave or house built into a cliff and were ancestors of the Pueblo Indians. **2** *Informal.* person who lives in a large apartment house. —**cliff dwelling.**

cliff·hang·er (klif′hang′ər), *n.* film, story, etc. that depends upon sustained suspense for dramatic interest. —*adj.* suspenseful.

cli·mac·ter·ic (klī mak′tər ik; klī′-mak ter′ik), *n.* time when some important event occurs; crucial period. —*adj.* Also, **climacterical.** of or like such a period; crucial. [< L < Gk., < *klimakter* rung of a ladder < *klimax* ladder]

cli·mac·tic (klī mak′tik), **cli·mac·ti·cal** (–tə kəl), *adj.* of or forming a climax.

cli·mate (klī′mit), *n.* **1** the kind of weather a place has. **2** intellectual and moral atmosphere. [< L < Gk. *klima* slope (of the earth) < *klinein* incline] —**cli·mat′ic,** *adj.* —**cli·mat′i·cal·ly,** *adv.*

cli·ma·tol·o·gy (klī′mə tol′ə ji), *n.* science that deals with climate. —**cli′ma·to·log′ic, cli′ma·to·log′i·cal,** *adj.* —**cli′ma·tol′o·gist,** *n.*

cli·max (klī′maks), *n.* **1** the highest point; most exciting part. **2** arrangement of ideas in a rising scale of interest. —*v.* bring or come to a climax. [< LL < Gk. *klimax* ladder]

climb (klīm), *v.,* **climbed, climb·ing,** *n.* —*v.* **1** go up by using the hands or feet; ascend: *climb a ladder.* **2** rise slowly: *climb from poverty to wealth.* **3** grow upward: *some vines climb.* —*n.* **1** a climbing; ascent. **2** place to be climbed.
climb down, a go down. **b** give in. [OE *climban*] —**climb′a·ble,** *adj.* —**climb′er,** *n.*

clime (klīm), *n. Poetic.* **1** country; region. **2** climate. [< L *clima.* See CLIMATE.]

clinch (klinch), *v.* **1** fasten (a driven nail, a bolt, etc.) firmly by bending over the part that projects. **2** settle decisively: *clinch a bargain.* **3** grasp tight. —*n.* **1** a clinching. **2** a tight grasp in fighting or wrestling, [var. of *clench*]

clinch·er (klin′chər), *n.* **1** nail or bolt that is clinched. **2** argument, statement, etc., that is decisive.

cling (kling), *v.,* **clung, cling·ing,** *n.* —*v.* **1** stick; hold fast. **2** keep near. —*n.* act of clinging. [OE *clingan*] —**cling′er,** *n.* —**cling′ing·ly,** *adv.* —**cling′y,** *adj.*

cling·stone (kling′stōn′), *n.* peach whose stone clings to the fleshy part.

clin·ic (klin′ik), *n.* **1** place, usually connected with a hospital or medical school, where out-patients can receive medical treatment. **2** instruction of medical students by treating patients in the students' presence. [< L < Gk. *klinikos* of a bed < *kline* bed]

clin·i·cal (klin′ə kəl), *adj.* **1** of or having to do with a clinic. **2** having to do with the study of disease by observation of the patient. **3** *Fig.* coldly analytical; impersonal. —**clin′i·cal·ly,** *adv.*

clinical medicine, study of disease by observation of the patient rather than by experiment or autopsy.

cli·ni·cian (kli nish′ən), *n.* physician who practices or teaches clinical medicine.

clink (klingk), *n.* a light, sharp, ringing sound. —*v.* **1** make a clink. **2** cause to clink. [ME *clinke(n),* ? < Du. *klinken*]

clink·er (klingk′ər), *n.* **1** a large, rough cinder. **2** *Informal. Fig.* stupid mistake or the result of one. [< Du. *klinker* brick < *klinken* ring]

cli·nom·e·ter (klī nom′ə tər; kli-), *n.* instrument for measuring deviation from the horizontal. [< L *-clinare* incline + -METER]

Clin·ton (klin′tən), **William (Bill) Jefferson,** 1946- . 42nd president of the United States, 1993–2001.

Cli·o (klī′ō), *n. Gk. Myth.* the Muse of history.

clip¹ (klip), *v.,* **clipped, clip·ping,** *n.* —*v.* **1** cut. **2** cut the hair or fleece of. **3** omit sounds in pronouncing. **4** curtail. **5** hit or punch sharply. —*n.* **1** act of clipping. **2** anything clipped off. **3** fast motion. **4** a sharp blow, etc. **5** one time: *at one clip.* [ME *clippe(n),* prob. < Scand. *klippa*]

clip² (klip), *v.,* **clipped, clip·ping,** *n.* —*v.* hold tight; fasten. —*n.* **1** thing used for clipping (things) together. **2** a metal holder for cartridges on some firearms. [OE *clyppan* embrace]

clip·board (klip′bôrd′; -bōrd′), *n.* small board with a strong spring clip on one end for holding paper while writing.

clipped word, a shortened form made by dropping a syllable or more, as *ad* for *advertisement.*

clip·per (klip′ər), *n.* **1** person who clips or cuts. **2** Often, *clippers.* tool for cutting. **3** a sailing ship built and rigged for speed.

clip·ping (klip′ing), *n.* piece cut out of a newspaper, magazine, etc.

clique (klēk; klik), *n.* a small, exclusive set or snobbish group of people. [< F, < *cliquer* click] —**cli′quish,** *adj.* —**cli′quish·ly,** *adv.* —**cli′quish·ness,** *n.*

cli·to·ris (klī′tə ris; klit′ə-), *n.* in most mammals, a small organ of the female homologous to the penis of the male. [< NL < Gk., < *kleiein* shut]

clo·a·ca (klō ā′kə), *n., pl.* **-cae** (-sē). **1** sewer. **2** cavity in the body of birds, reptiles, amphibians, etc., into which the intestinal, urinary, and generative canals open. [< L, prob. < *cluere* purge] —**clo·a′cal,** *adj.*

cloak (klōk), *n.* **1** a loose outer garment with or without sleeves. **2** anything that hides or conceals. —*v.* **1** cover with a cloak. **2** hide. [< OF < LL *clocca,* orig., bell, < OIrish *cloc*]

cloak-and-dag·ger (klōk′ənd dag′ər), *adj.* associated or done with secrecy and violence.

cloak·room (klōk′rüm′; -rüm′), *n.* room where coats, hats, etc., can be left for a time.

clob·ber (klob′ər), *v. Slang.* **1** attack violently. **2** *Fig.* defeat severely.

clock (klok), *n.* instrument for measuring and showing time, esp. one that is not carried around like a watch. —*v.* **1** measure the time of. **2** record the time of.
against the clock, so as to finish in a given amount of time.
around the clock, all day and night.
beat the clock, complete something in less time than expected or allotted. [< MDu. *clocke* < OF *cloque* or LL *clocca* < OIrish *cloc*] —**clock′er,** *n.*

clock·wise (klok′wīz′), *adv., adj.* in the direction in which the hands of a clock move.

clock·work (klok′wèrk′), *n.* **1** machinery used to run a clock. **2** machinery like this.
like clockwork, with great regularity.

clod (klod), *n.* **1** lump of earth; lump. **2** a stupid person; blockhead. [OE *clod*] —**clod′dy,** *adj.*

clod·hop·per (klod′hop′ər), *n.* **1** a clumsy boor. **2** a large, heavy shoe.

clog (klog), *v.,* **clogged, clog·ging,** *n.* —*v.* **1** fill up; choke up. **2** become filled or choked up. **3** hinder; interfere; hold back. —*n.* **1** thing that hinders or inter-

feres. **2** a heavy shoe with a wooden sole. **3** a lighter shoe [ME *clogge* block]

cloi·son·né (kloi′zə ne′), *n.* decorative enamel applied to a metal surface between thin metal strips that outline the design, which is then fired and polished.

clois·ter (klois′tər), *n.* **1** a covered walk along the wall of a building, with a row of pillars on the open side. **2** place of religious retirement; convent or monastery. **3** a quiet place shut away from the world. —*v.* shut away in a quiet place.
the cloister, the secluded monastic or conventual life [< OF < L *claustrum* closed place, lock < *claudere* close] —**clois′tral,** *adj.*

clois·tered (klois′tərd), *adj.* **1** secluded. **2** having a cloister.

clone (klōn), *n.* **1** any plant or animal produced asexually from a single parent or ancestor. **2** *Fig.* exact duplicate of another. —*v.* **1** reproduce asexually from a single parent or ancestor. **2** *Fig.* copy.

clonk (klongk), *n., v.* =clunk.

clop (klop), *n.* sharp sound such as made by a horse's hoof on a hard surface. —*v.* make such a sound.

close¹ (klōz), *v.,* **closed, clos·ing,** *n.* —*v.* **1** shut. **2** fill: *close a gap.* **3** bring or come together: *close the ranks of troops.* **4** come to terms; agree. **5** end; finish: *close a debate.* —*n.* end; finish.
close down, shut completely.
close in, come near and shut in on all sides.
close out, sell to get rid of.
close up, a shut completely. **b** bring or come nearer together. **c** heal. **d** finish off; wind up. [< OF *clore* < L *claudere* close]

close² (klōs), *adj.,* **clos·er, clos·est,** *adv.* —*adj.* **1** near together; near. **2** tight; narrow: *close quarters.* **3** compact. **4** intimate; dear. **5** exact: *a close translation.* **6** strict: *close attention.* **7** having little fresh air: *a close room.* **8** secret; hidden. **9** stingy. **10** nearly equal; almost even. —*adv.* in a close manner. [< OF *clos* < L *clausum* closed place < *claudere* close] —**close′ly,** *adv.* —**close′ness,** *n.*

close call (klōs), *Colloq.* narrow escape.

closed captioning, use of captions in television programming to assist viewers who cannot hear the sound. —**closed captioned.**

closed-cir·cuit (klōzd′sèr′kit), *adj.* denoting or having to do with television broadcasting that is limited to a certain audience, as in a group of classrooms, etc.

closed shop, factory or business that employs only members of labor unions.

close-fist·ed (klōs′fis′tid), *adj.* =stingy. —**close′fist′ed·ly,** *adv.* —**close′fist′ed·ness,** *n.*

close-hauled (klōs′hôld′), *adj.* having sails set for sailing as nearly as possible in the direction from which the wind is blowing.

close-knit (klōs′nit′), *adj.* firmly united by affection or common interest.

close-mouthed (klōs′mouthd′; -moutht′), *adj.* not fond of talking; reticent.

close shave (klōs), *Informal.* narrow escape from danger or an accident.

clos·et (kloz′it), *n.* 1 a small room used for storing clothes or household supplies. 2 a small, private room for prayer, study, or interviews. 3 a water closet; toilet. —*adj.* private; secluded. —*v.* shut up in a private room for a secret talk. [< OF, dim. of *clos* < L *clausum* closed place < *claudere* to close]

close-up (klōs′up′), *n.* 1 picture taken at close range. 2 a close view.

clo·sure (klō′zhər), *n.* 1 a closing. 2 a closed condition. 3 Also, **cloture.** way of ending a debate in a legislature and getting an immediate vote on the question being discussed. 4 in psychology, acceptance of a fact or situation, etc., as a loss or death. [< OF < LL *clausura* < L *claudere* close]

clot (klot), *n., v.,* **clot·ted, clot·ting.** —*n.* a half-solid lump; thickened mass, as of coagulated blood. —*v.* form into clots. [OE *clott*]

cloth (klôth; kloth), *n., pl.* **cloths** (klôt͟hz; klôt͟hs; klot͟hz; kloths), *adj.* —*n.* 1 material made from wool, cotton, silk, linen, hair, etc., by weaving, knitting, or rolling and pressing. 2 piece of this material for some purpose, as a tablecloth. —*adj.* made of cloth.

(made) out of whole cloth, entirely false or imaginary.

the cloth, clergymen; the clergy. [OE *clāth*]

clothe (klōt͟h), *v.,* **clothed** or **clad, clothing.** 1 put clothes on; cover with clothes; dress. 2 provide with clothes. 3 cover. 4 provide; furnish; equip: *clothed with authority.* [OE *clāthian* < *clāth* cloth]

clothes (klōz; klōt͟hz), *n.pl.* 1 covering for a person's body. 2 coverings for a bed.

clothes·horse (klōz′hôrs′; klōt͟hz′-), *n.* 1 frame to hang clothes on to dry or air them. 2 *Fig.* **a** person who models clothes. **b** person, usually a woman, who has an unusually strong interest in clothes.

clothes·line (klōz′līn′; klōt͟hz′-), *n.* rope or wire to hang clothes on to dry or air them.

clothes·pin (klōz′pin′; klōt͟hz′-), *n.* a wooden or plastic clip to hold clothes on a clothesline.

clothes tree, an upright pole with branches on which to hang coats and hats.

cloth·ier (klōt͟h′yər; -i ər), *n.* 1 seller or maker of clothing. 2 seller of cloth.

cloth·ing (klōt͟h′ing), *n.* 1 clothes. 2 covering.

Clo·tho (klō′thō), *n.* Gk. Myth. one of the three Fates. Clotho spins the thread of life.

clo·ture (klō′chər), *n. U.S.* =closure (def. 3.). [< F < VL *clausitura.* See CLOSURE.]

cloud (kloud), *n.* 1 a white, gray, or almost black mass in the sky, made up of tiny drops of water. 2 mass of smoke or dust. 3 a great number of things moving close together: *a cloud of arrows.* 4 streak; spot. 5 anything that darkens or dims; cause of gloom, trouble, suspicion, or disgrace. —*v.* 1 cover with a cloud or clouds. 2 grow cloudy. 3 streak; spot: *clouded marble.* 4 make or become gloomy, troubled, suspected, or disgraced.

in the clouds, a far above the earth. **b** fanciful; theoretical. **c** daydreaming; absent-minded.

under a cloud, a under suspicion; in disgrace. **b** in gloom or trouble. [OE *clūd* rock, hill] —**cloud′less,** *adj.*

cloud·burst (kloud′bėrst′), *n.* a sudden, violent rainfall.

cloud·y (kloud′i), *adj.,* **cloud·i·er, cloud·i·est.** 1 covered with clouds; having clouds in it. 2 of or like clouds. 3 not clear: *a cloudy liquid.* 4 streaked; spotted: *cloudy marble.* 5 confused; indistinct: *a cloudy notion.* 6 gloomy; frowning. —**cloud′i·ly,** *adv.* —**cloud′i·ness,** *n.*

clout (klout), *n.* 1 a blow, esp. with the hand. 2 *Fig.* importance; power or influence. —*v.* strike, esp. with the hand; cuff. [OE *clūt* small piece of cloth or metal]

clove[1] (klōv), *n.* 1 a strong, fragrant spice obtained from the dried flower buds of a tropical tree. 2 the dried flower bud. 3 the tree. [ME *cloue* < OF *clou* < L *clavus* nail]

clove[2] (klōv), *n.* a small, separate section of a bulb: *a clove of garlic.* [OE *clufu*]

clove[3] (klōv), *v.* pt. of **cleave**[1].

clo·ven (klō′vən), *v.* pp. of **cleave**[1]. —*adj.* split; divided.

clo·ven-hoofed (klō′vən huft′; -hüft′), *adj.* 1 having cloven hoofs. 2 devilish.

clo·ver (klō′vər), *n.* a low plant with leaves in three small parts and rounded heads of small red, white, or purple flowers, grown as food for horses and cattle. [OE *clāfre*]

clown (kloun), *n.* 1 person whose business is to amuse others by wearing funny costumes and makeup and performing tricks and jokes. 2 a bad-mannered, awkward person. —*v.* act like a clown; play tricks and jokes; act silly. —**clown′ish,** *adj.* —**clown′ish·ly,** *adv.* —**clown′ish·ness,** *n.*

cloy (kloi), *v.* 1 weary by too much, too sweet, or too rich food. 2 weary by too much of anything pleasant. [< MF *encloyer* < *clou* < L *clavus* nail] —**cloy′ing·ly,** *adv.* —**cloy′ing·ness,** *n.*

club (klub), *n., v.,* **clubbed, club·bing.** —*n.* 1 a heavy stick of wood, thicker at one end, used as a weapon. 2 stick or bat used to hit a ball in games. 3 group of people joined together for some special purpose: *a tennis club.* 4 a building or rooms used by a club. 5 =nightclub. 6 a playing card with one or more black, three-leafed designs on it shaped like this: ♣. —*v.* 1 beat or hit with a club. 2 join; unite; combine.

clubs, suit of cards marked with black, three-leafed figures. [< Scand. *klubba*]

club-foot (klub′füt′), *n., pl.* **-feet.** 1 a deformed foot. 2 deformity of the foot caused by faulty development before birth. —**club′foot′ed,** *adj.*

club·house (klub′hous′), *n.* a building used by a club.

club sandwich, sandwich, usually made in two layers of toast, with tomato, lettuce, bacon, and turkey or chicken.

club soda, =soda water.

cluck (kluk), *n.* 1 sound made by a hen calling her chickens. 2 *Slang. Informal.* =blockhead. —*v.* make such a sound. [imit.]

clue (klü), *n.* guide to the solving of a mystery or problem. Also, **clew.** [var. of *clew;* OE *cliwen*]

clue·less (klü′lis), *adj.* naive; unsophisticated.

clump (klump), *n.* 1 cluster: *a clump of trees.* 2 lump: *a clump of earth.* 3 sound of heavy, clumsy walking. —*v.* 1 form into a clump; form a clump. 2 walk heavily and clumsily. [var. of OE *clympre* lump of metal] —**clump′y, clump′ish,** *adj.*

clum·sy (klum′zi), *adj.,* **-si·er, -si·est.** 1 not graceful or skillful; awkward. 2 not well-shaped or well-made. [< *clumse* be numb with cold, prob. < Scand.] —**clum′si·ly,** *adv.* —**clum′si·ness,** *n.*

clung (klung), *v.* pt. and pp. of **cling.**

clus·ter (klus′tər), *n.* number of things of the same kind growing or grouped together. —*v.* form into a cluster; gather in clusters; group together closely. [OE] —**clus′ter·y,** *adj.*

cluster bomb, bomb that scatters small bombs upon impact.

clutch[1] (kluch), *n.* 1 a tight grasp. 2 a grasping claw, paw, hand, etc. 3 device in a machine for connecting or disconnecting the engine or motor that makes it go. 4 lever or pedal that operates this device. —*v.* 1 grasp tightly. 2 seize eagerly; snatch.

clutches, control; power. [var. of OE *clyccan* bend, clench]

clutch[2] (kluch), *n.* 1 nest of eggs. 2 brood of chickens. [var. of *cletch* < *cleck* hatch < Scand. *klekja*]

clut·ter (klut′ər), *n.* a litter; confusion; disorder. —*v.* litter with things. —**clut′ter·y,** *adj.*

Clydes·dale (klīdz′dāl), *n.* strong draft horse with distinctive long hair on the legs.

Cly·tem·nes·tra (klī′təm nes′trə), *n. Gk. Legend.* wife of Agamemnon. She killed her husband and was killed by her son, Orestes.

Cm, curium.

cm., cm, centimeter; centimeters.

co-, *prefix.* 1 with; together: *cooperate = act with or together.* 2 joint; fellow: *coauthor = joint or fellow author.* 3 equally:

coextensive = *equally extensive.* [< L, var. of *com*-]

Co, cobalt.

Co., co., 1 Company. **2** County.

CO, (*zip code*) Colorado.

C.O., Commanding Officer.

c.o., c/o, 1 in care of. **2** carried over.

coach (kōch), *n.* **1** a large, closed carriage with seats inside and often on top. **2** a railroad passenger car. **3** =motorcoach. **4** class of airfare that is less expensive than first class. **5** person who teaches or trains athletic teams, etc. **6** private teacher who helps a student prepare for a special test. —*v.* **1** teach; train. **2** help to prepare for a special test. [< Hung. *kocsi*]

coach-and-four (kōch'ən fôr'; –fōr'), *n.* coach pulled by four horses.

coach dog, =Dalmatian.

coach·man (kōch'mən), *n., pl.* **-men.** man whose work was driving a coach or carriage.

co·ad·ju·tor (kō aj'ə tər; kō'ə jü'tər), *n.* **1** assistant; helper. **2** bishop appointed to assist a bishop.

co·ag·u·late (kō ag'yə lāt), *v.,* **-lat·ed, -lat·ing.** change from a liquid into a thickened mass; thicken. [< L, < *coagulum* means of curdling < *co*– together + *agere* drive] —**co·ag'u·la'tion,** *n.* —**co·ag'u·la'tive,** *adj.* —**co·ag'u·la'tor,** *n.*

coal (kōl), *n.* **1** black mineral that burns and gives off heat, composed mostly of carbon. It is formed from partly decayed vegetable matter under great pressure in the earth. **2** piece of this mineral. **3** piece of wood, coal, etc., burning, partly burned, or all burned. **4** charcoal. —*v.* **1** supply with coal. **2** take in a supply of coal.

haul (or **rake**) **over the coals,** scold; blame. [OE *col* (def. 3)]

co·a·lesce (kō'ə les'), *v.,* **-lesced, -lesc·ing. 1** grow together. **2** unite into one body, mass, party, etc.; combine. [< L, < *co*– together + *alescere* grow] —**co'a·les'cence,** *n.* —**co'a·les'cent,** *adj.*

co·a·li·tion (kō'ə lish'ən), *n.* **1** union; combination. **2** a temporary alliance of statesmen, political parties, etc., for some special purpose. [< Med.L *coalitio* < L *coalescere.* See COALESCE.]

coal oil, 1 kerosene. **2** petroleum.

coal tar, a black, sticky residue left after soft coal has been distilled. Coal tar is distilled to make aniline dyes, flavorings, perfumes, benzene, etc.

coam·ing (kōm'ing), *n.* a raised edge around a hatch in the deck of a ship, a skylight, etc., to prevent water from running down below.

coarse (kôrs; kōrs), *adj.,* **coars·er, coars·est. 1** made up of fairly large parts; not fine: *coarse sand.* **2** rough: *coarse cloth.* **3** common; poor; inferior: *coarse food.* **4** not delicate or refined, crude; vulgar: *coarse manners.* [adjectival use of *course, n.,* meaning "ordinary"] —**coarse'ly,** *adv.* —**coarse'ness,** *n.*

coarse-grained (kôrs'grānd'; kōrs'–), *adj.* **1** having a coarse texture. **2** crude.

coars·en (kôr'sən; kōr'–), *v.* make or become coarse.

coast (kōst), *n.* **1** land along the sea; seashore. **2** region near a coast. **3** ride or slide down a hill without using power. —*v.* **1** go along or near the coast of. **2** ride or slide down a hill without using power.

from coast to coast, from the Atlantic to the Pacific coast.

the Coast, *U.S.* the region along the Pacific.

the coast is clear, no one is in the way; danger is past. [< OF < L *costa* side] —**coast'al,** *adj.*

coast·er (kōs'tər), *n.* **1** person or thing that coasts. **2** ship trading along a coast. **3** a little tray to hold a glass or bottle.

coast guard, 1 a group of people whose work is saving lives and preventing smuggling along the coast of a country. **b** member of this group. **2 Coast Guard,** U.S. government organization whose duty is to protect lives and property and prevent smuggling in coastal waters.

coast·guards·man (kōst'gärdz'mən), *n., pl.* **-men. 1** member of a coast guard. **2 Coast Guardsman,** member of the Coast Guard.

coast·land (kōst'land'), *n.* land along a coast.

coast·line (kōst'līn'), *n.* outline of a coast.

coast·ward (kōst'wərd), *adv., adj.* toward the coast.

coast·ways (kōst'wāz'), *adv.* =coastwise.

coast·wise (kōst'wīz'), *adv., adj.* along the coast.

coat (kōt), *n.* **1** an outer garment with sleeves. **2** an outer covering: *a dog's coat of hair.* **3** layer covering a surface: *a coat of paint.* —*v.* **1** provide with a coat. **2** cover with a layer. [< OF *cote* < Gmc.] —**coat'less,** *adj.*

co·a·ti (kō ä'ti), *n., pl.* **-tis.** a small animal somewhat like a raccoon, living in Central and South America. [< Brazilian (Tupi)]

coat·ing (kōt'ing), *n.* **1** layer covering a surface. **2** cloth for making coats.

coat of arms, *pl.* **coats of arms.** shield, or drawing of a shield, with pictures and designs on it. Each family of noble rank has its own special coat of arms.

coat of mail, *pl.* **coats of mail.** garment made of metal rings or plates, worn as armor.

coat·tail (kōt'tāl'), *n.* one of a pair of flaps or tails on the lower rear part of a coat.

coattails, tails of a man's formal coat or jacket.

ride on (**someone's**) **coattails,** advance by means of another's success, esp. in politics.

co·au·thor (kō ô'thər), *n.* a joint author.

coax (kōks), *v.* **1** persuade by soft words; influence by soft ways. **2** get by

coaxing. [< obs. *cokes* a fool] —**coax'er,** *n.* —**coax'ing·ly,** *adv.*

co·ax·i·al (kō ak'si əl), **co·ax·al** (–ak'səl), *adj.* having a common axis.

coaxial cable, an insulated connecting cable containing conducting materials surrounding a central conductor, used for transmitting telegraph, telephone, and television impulses.

cob (kob), *n.* **1** the center part of an ear of corn, on which the kernels grow. **2** a strong horse with short legs. [ME]

co·balt (kō'bôlt), *n.* **1** a silver-white metallic element, Co, with a pinkish tint, used in making steel, paints, etc. **2** dark-blue coloring matter made from cobalt. **3** dark blue. —*adj.* dark-blue. [< G *kobalt,* var. of *kobold* goblin] —**co·bal'tic,** *adj.* —**co·bal'tous,** *adj.*

cob·ble[1] (kob'əl), *v.,* **-bled, -bling. 1** mend (shoes, etc.). **2** put together clumsily.

cob·ble[2] (kob'əl), *n.* =cobblestone.

cob·bler (kob'lər), *n.* **1** person whose work is mending shoes. **2** a fruit pie baked in a deep dish.

cob·ble·stone (kob'əl stōn'), *n.* a rounded stone that was formerly much used in paving.

co·bel·lig·er·ent (kō'bə lij'ər ənt), *n.* nation that helps another nation carry on a war.

CO·BOL or **Co·bol** (kō'bôl), *n.* computer processing language.

co·bra (kō'brə), *n.* a very poisonous snake of S Asia and Africa. [short for Pg. *cobra de capello* snake with a hood]

cob·web (kob'web'), *n.* **1** a spider's web or the stuff it is made of. **2** anything thin and slight or entangling like a spider's web. [OE (*ātor*) *coppe* spider + *web*] —**cob'web'by,** *adj.*

co·ca (kō'kə), *n.* **1** a small tropical shrub growing in South America whose dried leaves are used to make cocaine and other alkaloids. **2** its dried leaves. [< Peruvian *cuca*]

co·caine, co·cain (kō kān'; kō'kān), *n.* drug used to deaden pain and as a stimulant.

coc·cus (kok'əs), *n., pl.* **coc·ci** (kok'sī). bacterium shaped like a sphere. [< NL < Gk. *kokkos* seed]

coc·cyx (kok'siks), *n., pl.* **coc·cy·ges** (kok sī'jēz). a small triangular bone at the lower end of the spinal column. [< L < Gk. *kokkyx,* orig., cuckoo; because shaped like cuckoo's bill]

coch·i·neal (koch'ə nēl'; koch'ə nēl'), *n.* a bright-red dye made from the dried bodies of the females of a scale insect that lives on cactus plants of tropical America. [< F < Sp. *cochinilla,* ult. < L *coccinus* scarlet < Gk.]

coch·le·a (kok'li ə), *n., pl.* **-le·ae** (–li ē). a spiral-shaped cavity of the inner ear, containing the sensory ends of the auditory nerve. [< L < Gk. *kochlias* snail] —**coch'le·ar,** *adj.*

cock[1] (kok), *n.* **1** a male chicken; rooster. **2** the male of other birds. **3** faucet used to turn the flow of a liquid or gas on or off. **4** hammer of a gun. **5** position of the hammer of a gun when it is pulled back, ready to fire. **6** =weathercock. —*v.* pull back the hammer of (a gun), ready to fire. [OE *cocc*]

cock² (kok), *v.* turn up jauntily; stick up defiantly. —*n.* an upward turn, as of the brim of a hat. [appar. < *cock¹*]

cock³ (kok), *n.* a small, cone-shaped pile of hay in a field. —*v.* pile in cocks. [ME]

cock·ade (kok ād′), *n.* knot of ribbon or a rosette worn on the hat as a badge. [alter, of *cockard* < F, < *cog* cock] —**cock·ad′ed,** *adj.*

cock·a·too (kok′ə tü′; kok′ə tü), *n., pl.* **-toos.** a large, brightly colored parrot of Australia, East Indies, etc. [< Du. < Malay *kakatua*]

cock·a·trice (kok′ə tris), *n.* a fabled serpent whose look was supposed to cause death. [< OF *cocatris* < L *calcare* tread]

cock·chaf·er (kok′chāf ər), *n.* a large European beetle that destroys plants.

cock·crow (kok′krō′), *n.* =dawn.

cocked hat, 1 hat with the brim turned up. **2** hat pointed in front and in back.

cock·er·el (kok′ər əl; kok′rəl), *n.* a young rooster, not more than one year old.

cock·er spaniel (kok′ər), or **cocker,** *n.* any of a breed of small dogs with long, silky hair and drooping ears.

cock·eyed (kok′īd′), *adj.* **1** cross-eyed. **2** *Slang.* tilted or twisted to one side. **3** *Slang.* foolish; silly.

cock·fight (kok′fīt′), *n.* fight between roosters or gamecocks armed with steel spurs. —**cock′fight′ing,** *n.*

cock·horse (kok′hôrs′), *n.* a child's hobbyhorse.

cock·le (kok′əl), *n., v.,* **-led, -ling.** —*n.* **1** a saltwater mollusk with two ridged shells that are somewhat heart-shaped. **2** =cockleshell. **3** bulge on the surface. —*v.* wrinkle; pucker.

cockles of one's heart, inmost part of one's heart or feelings. [< F *coquille,* blend of F *coque* shell and L *conchylium* < Gk. *konchylion,* dim. of *konche* conch]

cock·le·bur (kok′əl bėr′), *n.* any of several weeds with spiny burs.

cock·le·shell (kok′əl shel′), *n.* **1** shell of the cockle. **2** small, light, shallow boat.

cock·ney (kok′ni), *n., pl.* **-neys,** *adj.* —*n.* **1** native or inhabitant of the E section of London who speaks a particular dialect of English. **2** this dialect. —*adj.* **1** of or like this dialect. **2** of or like cockneys. [ME *cokeney*]

cock·pit (kok′pit′), *n.* **1** a place in an airplane where the pilot sits. **2** a small, open place in a boat where the pilot and passengers sit. **3** an enclosed place for cockfights.

cock·roach (kok′rōch′), *n.* any of a family of insects, esp. a small brownish or yellowish species found in kitchens, around water pipes, etc. [alter, of Sp. *cucaracha*]

cocks·comb (koks′kōm′), *n.* **1** the fleshy red part on the head of a rooster. **2** =coxcomb. **3** plant with crested or feathery clusters of red or yellow flowers.

cock·sure (kok′shùr′), *adj.* **1** perfectly sure; absolutely certain. **2** too sure. —*adv.* in a cocksure manner. —**cock′sure′ness,** *n.*

cock·swain (kok′sən; -swān′), *n.* =coxswain.

cock·tail (kok′tāl′), *n.* **1** an iced drink, often composed of gin or whiskey, mixed with bitters, vermouth, fruit juices, etc. **2** appetizer: *a tomato-juice cocktail.* **3** shellfish served in a small glass with a highly seasoned sauce. **4** mixed fruits served in a glass.

cock·y (kok′i), *adj.,* **cock·i·er, cock·i·est,** conceited; swaggering. —**cock′i·ly,** *adv.* —**cock′i·ness,** *n.*

co·co (kō′kō), *n., pl.* **co·cos. 1** =coconut palm. **2** its fruit or seed. Also, **cocoa, coco palm.** [< Pg. *coco* grinning face]

co·coa¹ (kō′kō), *n.* **1** powder made by roasting and grinding cacao seeds. **2** drink made of this powder with milk or water and sugar. **3** deep reddish brown. —*adj.* of or having to do with cocoa. [var. of *cacao*]

co·coa² (kō′kō), *n.* =coco.

cocoa butter, fat obtained from cacao seeds, used in soap and cosmetics.

co·co·nut, co·coa·nut (kō′kə nut′; -nət), *n.* a large, round, brown, hard-shelled fruit of the coconut palm. Coconuts have a white, edible lining and a white liquid called **coconut milk.**

coconut oil, oil obtained from the coconut, used in confections, baked goods, soap, etc.

coconut palm, tall, tropical palm tree on which coconuts grow.

co·coon (kə kün′), *n.* a silky case spun by the larva of an insect to live in while it is a pupa. [< F *cocon* < *coque* shell]

cod (kod), *n., pl.* **cods** or (*esp. collectively*) **cod.** food fish found in the cold parts of the N Atlantic. [ME]

Cod (kod), *n.* **Cape,** hook-shaped peninsula in SE Massachusetts.

c.o.d., C.O.D., cash on delivery; collect on delivery.

co·da (kō′də), *n.* **1** final passage of a musical composition. **2** *Fig.* an ending or conclusion.

cod·dle (kod′əl), *v.,* **-dled, -dling. 1** treat tenderly; pamper. **2** cook in hot water without boiling: *a coddled egg.* [var. of *caudle,* n., gruel < OF < L *calidus* hot]

code (kōd), *n., v.,* **cod·ed, cod·ing.** —*n.* **1** a collection of the laws of a country arranged in a clear way so that they can be understood and used. **2** any set of rules. **3** system of signals for sending messages by telegraph flags, etc. **4** arrangement of words, figures, etc., to keep a message short or secret. **5** genetic code. —*v.* **1** change or translate into a code. **2** arrange in a code. [< F < L *codex* CODEX]

co·deine (kō′dēn; -di ēn), **co·de·in** (kō′di in), *n.* a white, crystalline drug

obtained from opium, used to relieve pain and cause sleep. [< Gk. *kodeia* poppy head]

code word or **code·word** (kōd′werd′), *n.* **1** inoffensive word or expression that stands for something controversial. **2** =codon.

co·dex (kō′deks), *n., pl.* **co·di·ces** (kō′də sēz; kod′ə-). volume of manuscripts, esp. of the Scriptures. [< L, var. of *caudex* tree trunk, book]

cod·fish (kod′fish′), *n., pl.* **-fish·es** or (*esp. collectively*) **-fish.** =cod.

codg·er (koj′ər), *n. Colloq.* an odd person.

cod·i·cil (kod′ə səl), *n.* **1** something added to a will to change it, add to it, or explain it. **2** anything added to change or explain something. [< L *codicillus,* dim. of *codex* CODEX]

cod·i·fy (kod′ə fi; kō′də-), *v.,* **-fied, -fy·ing.** arrange (laws, etc.) according to a system. —**cod′i·fi·ca′tion,** *n.* —**cod′i·fi′er,** *n.*

cod·ling (kod′ling), **cod·lin** (-lin), *n.* an unripe apple.

codling moth, codlin moth, a small moth whose larvae destroy apples, pears, etc.

cod-liv·er oil (kod′liv′ər), oil extracted from the liver of cod, used as a medicine. It is rich in vitamins A and D.

co·don (kō′don), *n.* **1** sequence of three chemical units or bases represented in the genetic code by three letters. **2** the three-letter genetic code word.

co·ed, co-ed (kō′ed′), *n.* a girl or woman student at a coeducational college or school.

co·ed·u·ca·tion (kō′ej ù kā′shən), *n.* education of boys and girls or men and women together in the same school or classes. —**co′ed·u·ca′tion·al,** *adj.* —**co′ed·u·ca′tion·al·ly,** *adv.*

co·ef·fi·cient (kō′ə fish′ənt), *n.* **1** a number or symbol put before and multiplying another. In $3x$, 3 is the coefficient of x. **2** a ratio used as a multiplier to calculate the behavior of a substance under different conditions of heat, light, etc.

coe·la·canth (sē′lə kanth), *n.* any of a group of fishes having rounded scales and lobed fins, formerly considered extinct. A coelacanth is similar to the primitive sea vertebrates which gave rise to all land vertebrates. [< NL, < Gk. *koilos* hollow + *akantha* thorn, spine]

coe·len·ter·ate (si len′tər āt; -it), *n.* one of a group of saltwater animals with saclike bodies. —*adj.* belonging to this group. Hydras, jellyfish, corals, etc., are coelenterates. [< NL < Gk. *koilos* hollow + *enteron* intestine]

coe·li·ac (sē′li ak), *adj.* of or in the abdominal cavity. Also, **celiac.**

co·en·zyme (kō en′zīm), *n.* an organic substance, usually containing a mineral or vitamin, able to attach itself to a specific protein and supplement it to form an active enzyme system.

co·e·qual (kō ē′kwəl), *adj.* equal in rank, degree, etc. —*n.* one that is coequal. —**co′e·qual′i·ty,** *n.* —**co·e′qual·ly,** *adv.*

co·erce (kō ėrs′), *v.,* **co·erced, co·erc·ing.** 1 compel; force. 2 control or restrain by force. [< L *coercere* < *co*– together + *arcere* restrain] —**co·erc′er,** *n.* —**co·er′ci·ble,** *adj.* —**co·er′cive,** *adj.* —**co·er′cive·ly,** *adv.* —**co·er′cive·ness,** *n.*

co·er·cion (kō ėr′shən), *n.* 1 use of force; compulsion; constraint. 2 government by force. —**co·er′cion·ist,** *n.*

co·e·val (kō ē′vəl), *adj.* 1 of the same age, date, or duration. 2 contemporary. —*n.* a contemporary. [< LL, < *co*– equal + *aevum* age]

co·ex·ec·u·tor (kō′ig zek′yə tər), *n.* person who is an executor of a will along with another.

co·ex·ist (kō′ig zist′), *v.* exist together or at the same time. —**co′ex·ist′ence,** *n.* —**co′ex·ist′ent,** *adj.*

co·ex·tend (kō′iks tend′), *v.* extend equally or to the same limits. —**co′ex·ten′sion,** *n.* —**co′ex·ten′sive,** *adj.*

cof·fee (kôf′i; kof′i), *n.* 1 a dark-brown drink, first used in Europe about 1600. 2 the seeds from which the drink is made. 3 a tall, tropical shrub on which the seeds grow. 4 the color of coffee. [< Turk. *qahveh* < Ar. *qahwa*]

coffee break, a period during which employees may take time off to have coffee, rest, etc.

cof·fer (kôf′ər; kof′–), *n.* 1 box, chest, or trunk, esp. one used to hold money or other valuable things. 2 ornamental panel, esp. in a ceiling. 3 =cofferdam. 4 =caisson (def. 3).

coffers, treasury; funds. [< OF < L *cophinus* basket. See COFFIN.]

cof·fer·dam (kôf′ər dam′, kof′–), *n.* 1 temporary dam in a body of water that encloses an underwater area that can be pumped dry. 2 =caisson (def. 3).

cof·fin (kôf′in; kof′–), *n.* box into which a dead person is put to be buried. —*v.* put into a coffin. [< OF < L < Gk. *kophinos* basket]

cog (kog), *n.* 1 one of a series of teeth on the edge of a wheel that transfers motion by locking into the teeth of another wheel of the same kind. 2 wheel with such a row of teeth on it. [< Scand. (Sw.) *kugge*] —**cogged,** *adj.*

co·gent (kō′jənt), *adj.* forcible; convincing: *cogent arguments.* [< L *cogens,* ult. < *co*– together + *agere* drive] —**co′gen·cy,** *n.* —**co′gent·ly,** *adv.*

cog·i·tate (koj′ə tāt), *v.,* **–tat·ed, –tat·ing.** think over; consider with care; meditate; ponder. [< L, < *co*– (intensive) + *agitare* consider < *agere* discuss] —**cog′i·ta′tion,** *n.* —**cog′i·ta′tive,** *adj.* —**cog′i·ta′tive·ly,** *adv.* —**cog′i·ta′tor,** *n.*

co·gnac (kōn′yak; kon′–), *n.* kind of French brandy. [< F]

cog·nate (kog′nāt), *adj.* related by family, origin, nature, or quality: *English, Dutch, and German are cognate languages.*

—*n.* person, word, or thing so related to another. German *Wasser* and English *water* are cognates. [< L, < *co*– together + *gnatus* born]

cog·ni·tion (kog nish′ən), *n.* 1 act of knowing; perception; awareness. 2 thing known, perceived, or recognized. [< L *cognitio,* < *co*– (intensive) + *gnoscere* know] —**cog·ni′tion·al,** *adj.*

cog·ni·zance (kog′nə zəns; kon′ə–), *n.* 1 knowledge; perception; awareness. 2 a an official notice. b right or power to deal with judicially. [< OF *conoissance* < *conoistre* know < L *cognoscere.* See COGNITION.]

cog·ni·zant (kog′nə zənt; kon′ə–), *adj.* aware.

cog·no·men (kog nō′mən), *n.* 1 surname; family name; last name. 2 any name. 3 nickname. [< L, < *co*– with + *nomen* name; form. infl. by *cognoscere* recognize] —**cog·nom′i·nal,** *adj.*

cog·wheel (kog′hwēl′), *n.* wheel with teeth projecting from the rim for transmitting or receiving motion.

co·hab·it (kō hab′it), *v.* 1 live together as husband and wife do. 2 live together. —**co·hab′i·tant,** *n.* —**co·hab′i·ta′tion,** *n.*

co·here (kō hir′), *v.,* **–hered, –her·ing.** 1 stick together; hold together. 2 be connected logically; be consistent. [< L, < *co*– together + *haerere* cleave]

co·her·ence (kō hir′əns), **co·her·en·cy** (–ən si), *n.* 1 logical connection; consistency. 2 a sticking together; cohesion.

co·her·ent (kō hir′ənt), *adj.* 1 sticking together; holding together. 2 logically connected; consistent. —**co·her′ent·ly,** *adv.*

co·he·sion (kō hē′zhən), *n.* 1 a sticking together; tendency to hold together. 2 attraction between molecules of the same kind. —**co·he′sive,** *adj.* —**co·he′sive·ly,** *adv.* —**co·he′sive·ness,** *n.*

co·hort (kō′hôrt), *n.* 1 one of the ten infantry divisions of an ancient Roman legion. 2 group of soldiers. 3 any group or company. [< L *cohors* court, enclosure. Doublet of COURT.]

coif (koif), *n.* cap or hood that fits closely around the head. —*v.* cover with a coif or something like a coif. [< OF < LL *cofia* < Gmc.]

coif·fure (kwä fyúr′), *n.* 1 style of arranging the hair. 2 headdress. [< F < *coiffer* COIF, v.]

coil (koil), *v.* 1 wind around and around in circular or spiral shape. 2 move in a winding course. —*n.* 1 anything wound around and around in this way. 2 one wind or turn of a coil. 3 a spiral of wire for conducting electricity. [< OF < L *colligere* COLLECT] —**coil′er,** *n.*

coin (koin), *n.* 1 piece of metal stamped by the government for use as money. 2 metal money. —*v.* 1 make (money) by stamping metal. 2 make (metal) into money. 3 make up; invent: *the word "blurb" was coined by Gelett Burgess.*

coin money, become rich. [< F, corner, < L *cuneus* wedge] —**coin′er,** *n.*

coin·age (koin′ij), *n.* 1 the making of coins. 2 coins; metal money. 3 system of coins. 4 right of coining money. 5 act or process of making up; inventing. 6 word, phrase, etc., invented.

co·in·cide (kō′in sīd′), *v.,* **–cid·ed, –cid·ing.** 1 occupy the same place in space. 2 occupy the same time. 3 correspond exactly; agree. [< Med.L *coincidere* < L *co*– together + *in* upon + *cadere* fall]

co·in·ci·dence (kō in′sə dəns), *n.* 1 exact correspondence; agreement, esp. the chance occurrence of two things at such a time as to seem remarkable, fitting, etc. 2 a coinciding; act or fact of occupying the same time or place.

co·in·ci·dent (kō in′sə dənt), *adj.* 1 happening at the same time. 2 occupying the same place or position. —**co·in′ci·dent·ly,** *adv.*

co·in·ci·den·tal (kō in′sə den′təl), *adj.* 1 coincident. 2 showing coincidence. —**co·in′ci·den·tal·ly,** *adv.*

co·i·tus (kō′ə təs), *n.* sexual intercourse. Also, **coition.** [< L *co*– together + *ire* go] —**co′i·tal,** *adj.*

coke¹ (kōk), *n., v.,* **coked, cok·ing.** —*n.* fuel made from coal by heating it in a closed oven until the gases have been removed. Coke burns with much heat and little smoke, and is used in furnaces, for melting metal, etc. —*v.* change into coke. [? var. of *colk* core]

coke² (kōk), *n. Slang.* =cocaine.

Coke³ (kōk), *n. Trademark.* a dark-colored, carbonated soft drink. [short for *Coca-Cola,* a trademark]

coke·head (kōk′hed′), *n. Slang.* cocaine addict.

Col., 1 Colonel. 2 Colorado.

col., column.

co·la (kō′lə), *n.* 1 any dark-colored, carbonated soft drink. 2 =kola.

col·an·der (kul′ən dər; kol′–), *n.* vessel or dish full of small holes for draining off liquids. [alter. of VL *colator* < L *colare* strain]

cold (kōld), *adj.* 1 much less warm than the body. 2 not warm enough for comfort. 3 unconscious. 4 lacking in feeling; unfriendly: *a cold greeting.* 5 faint; weak: *a cold scent.* —*n.* 1 lack of heat or warmth. 2 cold weather. 3 sickness that causes running at the nose, sore throat, sneezing, etc.

catch cold, become sick with a cold.

in the cold, all alone; neglected. [OE *cald*] —**cold′ish,** *adj.* —**cold′ly,** *adv.* —**cold′ness,** *n.*

cold-blood·ed (kōld′blud′id), *adj.* 1 having blood whose temperature varies with that of the surroundings. 2 feeling the cold because of poor circulation. 3 lacking in feeling; cruel. —**cold′-blood′ed·ly,** *adv.* —**cold′-blood′ed·ness,** *n.*

cold cream, a creamy, soothing salve for the skin.

cold cuts, slices of prepared meat, such as corned beef, salami, etc., served cold.

cold-heart·ed (kōld'här'tid), *adj.* lacking in feeling; unsympathetic; unkind. —**cold'-heart'ed·ly**, *adv.* —**cold'-heart'ed·ness**, *n.*

cold shoulder, deliberately unfriendly or indifferent treatment; neglect.

cold-shoul·der (kōld'shōl'dər), *v.* treat in an unfriendly or indifferent way.

cold sore, blister in or on the mouth, often accompanying a cold or a fever.

cold turkey, sudden and complete withdraw from use of narcotics, cigarettes, etc.

cold war, 1 a prolonged contest for national advantage, conducted by diplomatic, economic, and psychological rather than military means. **2 Cold War,** contest for world leadership between Communist and Western nations following World War II.

cold wave, period of very cold weather.

cole (kōl), or **cole-wort** (kōl'wèrt'), *n.* any of various plants belonging to the same family as the cabbage, esp. rape. [< L *caulis* cabbage]

co·le·op·ter·ous (kō'li op'tər əs; kol'i–), *adj.* belonging to a group of insects including beetles and weevils. [< Gk., < *koleos* sheath + *pteron* wing]

cole·slaw (kōl'slô'), *n.* salad made of sliced raw cabbage. [<Du. *kool sla* cabbage salad]

col·ic (kol'ik), *n.* severe pains in the abdomen. —*adj.* of or pertaining to the colon. [< LL < Gk. *kolikos* of the COLON[2]] —**col'ick·y**, *adj.*

col·i·se·um (kol'ə sē'əm), *n.* a large building or stadium for games, contests, etc. [< Med.L var. of *colosseum*]

co·li·tis (kō li'tis; kə–), *n.* inflammation of the colon, often causing severe pain in the abdomen.

coll., 1 collect. **2** college; collegiate.

col·lab·o·rate (kə lab'ə rāt), *v.,* –**rat·ed,** –**rat·ing. 1** work together. **2** aid or cooperate traitorously. [< L, < *com-* with + *laborare* work] —**col·lab'o·ra'tion,** *n.* —**col·lab'o·ra'tive,** *adj.* —**col·lab'o·ra'tor, col·lab'o·ra'tion·ist,** *n.*

col·lage (kə läzh'), *n.* picture made by securing on a background portions of photographs and newspapers, fabric and string, etc. —*v.* make a collage. [< MF, a gluing < OF *colle* glue < VL < Gk. *kolla*]

col·la·gen (kol'ə jən), *n.* **1** protein substance in connective tissue, bone, and cartilage in vertebrates. **2** purified collagen extracted from calf's skin and injected under a person's skin to remove wrinkles and other flaws.

col·lapse (kə laps'), *v.,* –**lapsed,** –**laps·ing,** *n.* —*v.* **1** fall in; shrink together suddenly. **2** break down; fail suddenly. **3** fold or push together: *collapse a telescope.* **4** lose courage, strength, etc., suddenly. —*n.* **1** a falling in; a sudden shrinking together. **2** breakdown; failure. [< L *collapsus* < *com-* completely + *labi* fall] —**col·laps'i·ble, col·laps'a·ble,** *adj.*

col·lar (kol'ər), *n.* **1** a straight or turned-over neckband of a coat, a dress, or a shirt. **2** a separate band of linen, lace, or other material worn around the neck. **3** a leather or metal band for a dog's neck. **4** a leather roll for a horse's neck to bear the weight of the loads he pulls. —*v.* **1** put a collar on. **2** seize by the collar; capture. **3** seize; take. [< L *collare* < *collum* neck]

col·lar·bone (kol'ər bōn'), *n.* bone connecting the breastbone and the shoulder blade; clavicle.

col·late (kə lāt'; kol'āt), *v.,* –**lat·ed,** –**lat·ing. 1** compare carefully. **2** check (pages, sheets, etc.) for correct arrangement. [< L, < *com-* together + *latus,* pp. of *ferre* bring] —**col·la'tor,** *n.*

col·lat·er·al (kə lat'ər əl), *adj.* **1** situated at the side. **2** parallel; side by side. **3** related but less important; secondary; indirect. **4** descended from the same ancestors, but in a different line. **5** additional. **6** accompanying. **7** secured by stocks, bonds, etc. —*n.* **1** a collateral relative. **2** stocks, bonds, etc., pledged as security for a loan. [< Med.L, < *com-* + L *lateralis* lateral] —**col·lat'er·al·ly,** *adv.*

collateral damage, killing of civilians and destruction of nonmilitary structures as a result of military operations.

col·la·tion (kə lā'shən), *n.* **1** a light meal. **2** a collating. **3** a careful comparison.

col·league (kol'ēg), *n.* an associate; fellow worker. [< F < L *collega* < *com-* together + *legare* send or choose as deputy] —**col'league·ship,** *n.*

col·lect (*v., adj., adv.* kə lekt'; *n.* kol'ekt), *v.* **1** gather together: *collect stamps for a hobby.* **2** ask pay for (bills, taxes, etc.) **3** regain control of (oneself). —*n.* a short prayer used in certain church services. —*adj., adv.* to be paid for at the place of delivery: *telephone collect.* [< L *collectus* < *com-* together + *legere* gather] —**col·lect'a·ble, col·lect'i·ble,** *adj.*

col·lect·ed (kə lek'tid), *adj.* **1** gathered together. **2** under control; calm. —**col·lect'ed·ly,** *adv.* —**col·lect'ed·ness,** *n.*

col·lec·tion (kə lek'shən), *n.* **1** act or practice of collecting. **2** group of things gathered together. **3** money collected. **4** mass; heap.

col·lec·tive (kə lek'tiv), *adj.* **1** of a group; as a group. **2** singular in form, but plural in meaning. *Crowd* and *herd* are collective nouns. **3** formed by collecting. **4** forming a collection. —*n.* noun whose singular form names a group.

collective bargaining, negotiation about wages, hours, and other working conditions between workers organized as a group and their employer or employers.

col·lec·tive·ly (kə lek'tiv li), *adv.* **1** as a group; all together. **2** in a singular form, but with a plural meaning.

col·lec·tor (kə lek'tər), *n.* **1** person or thing that collects. **2** person hired to collect money owed. —**col·lec'tor·ship,** *n.*

col·leen (kol'ēn; kə lēn'), *n. Irish.* girl.

col·lege (kol'ij), *n.* **1** institution of higher learning that gives degrees. **2** the academic department of a university for general instruction, as distinguished from the special, professional, or graduate schools. **3** school for special or professional instruction, as in medicine, pharmacy, agriculture, or music. **4** an organized association of persons having certain powers, rights, duties, and purposes. **5** building or buildings used by a college. [< OF < L *collegium* < *collega* COLLEAGUE]

College Boards, *U.S.* group of tests measuring aptitude and achievement in various subjects given to students applying for entrance to college.

College of Cardinals, Sacred College.

col·le·gi·al (kə lē'jē əl) *adj.* **1** =collegiate. **2** associating or sharing as colleagues.

col·le·gian (kə lē'jən; –ji ən), *n.* a college student.

col·le·giate (kə lē'jit; –ji it), *adj.* of or like a college or college students.

col·lide (kə līd'), *v.,* –**lid·ed,** –**lid·ing. 1** come violently into contact; run into with force; crash. **2** clash; conflict. [< L *collidere* < *com-* together + *laedere,* orig., to strike]

col·lie (kol'i), *n.* a large, intelligent, long-haired breed of dog used for tending sheep and as a pet.

col·lier (kol'yər), *n.* **1** ship for carrying coal. **2** a coal miner. [ME *colier* < *col* COAL]

col·lier·y (kol'yər i), *n., pl.* –**lier·ies.** coal mine and its buildings and equipment.

col·li·mate (kol'ə māt), *v.,* –**mat·ed,** –**mat·ing. 1** bring into line; make parallel. **2** adjust accurately the line of sight of (a surveying instrument, telescope, etc.) [< L *collimatus,* misread for *collineatus,* ult. < *com-* together + *linea* line] —**col'li·ma'tion,** *n.*

col·lin·e·ar (kə lin'ē ər), *adj.* in geometry, lying along the same straight line.

col·li·sion (kə lizh'ən), *n.* **1** a violent rushing against; hitting or striking violently together. **2** clash; conflict.

col·lo·cate (kol'ō kāt), *v.,* –**cat·ed,** –**cat·ing. 1** place together. **2** arrange. [< L, < *com-* together + *locare* place] —**col'lo·ca'tion,** *n.*

col·lo·di·on (kə lō'di ən), *n.* a gluelike liquid that dries very rapidly and leaves a tough, waterproof, transparent film. [< Gk. *kollodes* gluey < *kolla* glue]

col·loid (kol'oid), *n.* substance composed of particles that are extremely small but larger than most molecules. Colloids do not actually dissolve, but remain suspended in a suitable gas, liquid, or solid. —*adj.* colloidal. [< Gk. *kolla* glue]

col·loi·dal (kə loi'dəl), *adj.* being, containing, or like a colloid. —**col'loid·al'i·ty,** *n.*

colloq., colloquial; colloquialism.

col·lo·qui·al (kə lō'kwi əl), *adj.* used in everyday, informal talk, but not in formal speech or writing. —**col·lo'qui·al·ly,** *adv.* —**col·lo'qui·al·ness,** *n.*

col·lo·qui·al·ism (kə lō′kwi əl iz′əm), *n.* 1 a colloquial word or phrase. 2 a colloquial style or usage.

col·lo·quist (kol′ə kwist), *n.* =interlocutor.

col·lo·quy (kol′ə kwi), *n., pl.* **–quies.** 1 a talking together; conversation. 2 conference. [< L, < *com–* with + *loqui* speak]

col·lude (kə lüd′), *v.,* **–lud·ed, –lud·ing.** act together through a secret understanding; conspire in a fraud. [< L, < *com–* with + *ludere* play]

col·lu·sion (kə lü′zhən), *n.* a secret agreement for some wrong purpose; conspiracy.—**col·lu′sive,***adj.*—**col·lu′sive·ly,** *adv.* —**col·lu′sive·ness,** *n.*

Colo., Colorado.

co·logne (kə lōn′), *n.* a fragrant liquid, not so strong as perfume. [for *eau de Cologne,* a trademark meaning water of Cologne]

Co·lom·bi·a (kə lum′bi ə), *n.* country in NW South America. —**Co·lom′bi·an,** *adj., n.*

Co·lom·bo (kə lum′bō), *n.* seaport and capital of Sri Lanka.

co·lon¹ (kō′lən), *n.* mark (:) of punctuation used before a series of items, explanations, long quotations, etc., to set them off from the rest of the sentence. [< L < Gk. *kolon* limb, clause]

co·lon² (kō′lən), *n., pl.* **co·lons, co·la** (kō′lə). the power part of the large intestine. [< L < Gk. *kolon*] —**co·lon′ic,** *adj.*

colo·nel (kėr′nəl), *n.* an army officer ranking next below a brigadier general and next above a lieutenant colonel. He usually commands a regiment. [earlier *coronel,* < F *coronel,* now *colonel* < Ital. *colonnello* < *colonna* COLUMN] —**colo·nel·cy, colo·nel·ship,** *n.*

co·lo·ni·al (kə lō′ni əl), *adj.* 1 of a colony; having to do with colonies. 2 of or having to do with the thirteen British colonies that became the United States. *n.* person living in a colony. —**co·lo′ni·al·ly,** *adv.*

co·lo·ni·al·ism (kə lō′nē ə liz′əm), *n.* policy of a nation to rule weaker states, often for economic reasons.

co·lo·ni·al·ist (kə lō′nē ə list), *n.* person or nation that favors or practices colonialism.

col·o·nist (kol′ə nist), *n.* 1 person who helps to found a colony; settler. 2 person living in a colony.

col·o·nize (kol′ə nīz), *v.,* **–nized, –niz·ing.** 1 establish a colony or colonies in. 2 establish (persons) in a colony; settle in a colony. 3 form a colony. —**col′o·ni·za′tion,** *n.* —**col′o·niz′er,** *n.*

col·on·nade (kol′ə nād′), *n.* series of columns set the same distance apart. [< F < Ital. *colonnata* < *colonna* COLUMN] —**col′on·nad′ed,** *adj.*

col·o·ny (kol′ə ni), *n., pl.* **–nies.** 1 group of people who settle in another land, but remain citizens of their own country. 2 settlement made by such a group of people. 3 group of people from the same country or with the same occupation,

living in a certain part of a city: *a colony of artists.* 4 group of animals or plants of the same kind, living or growing together: *a colony of ants.* 5 an aggregation of bacteria in a culture. 6 **the Colonies,** the thirteen British colonies that became the United States of America. [< L, < *colonus* cultivator, settler < *colere* cultivate]

col·o·phon (kol′ə fon; –fən), *n.* 1 design or device of a publisher. 2 words or inscription placed at the end of a book, telling the name of the publisher, etc. [< LL < Gk. *kolophon* summit, final touch]

col·or (kul′ər), *n.* 1 sensation produced by waves of light striking the retina. 2 red, yellow, green, blue, purple, etc. 3 paint; dye; pigment. 4 ruddy complexion. 5 an outward appearance; show: *some color of truth.* 6 distinguishing quality; vividness. 7 property of quarks by which they combine with larger particles. —*v.* 1 give color to. 2 blush. 3 change to give a wrong idea: *to color a report.*

change color, a turn pale. **b** blush.

colors, badge, ribbon, dress, etc., worn to show allegiance.

give (or **lend**) **color to,** cause to seem likely or true.

lose color, turn pale.

show one's colors, a show oneself as one really is. **b** declare one's opinions or plans.

the colors, flag of a nation, regiment, etc.: *salute the colors.*

with flying colors, successfully; victoriously. [< L] —**col′or·er,** *n.*

col·or·a·ble (kul′ər ə bəl), *adj.* capable of being colored. —**col′or·a·bil′i·ty, col′or·a·ble·ness,** *n.* —**col′or·a·bly,** *adv.*

Col·o·rad·o (kol′ə rad′ō; –rä′dō), *n.* a W state of the United States. —**Col′o·rad′an,** *adj., n.*

col·or·a·tion (kul′ər ā′shən), *n.* =coloring.

col·o·ra·tu·ra (kul′ə rə tùr′ə; –tyùr′ə), *n.* 1 ornamental passages in music, such as trills, runs, etc. 2 a soprano who sings such passages. —*adj.* fit for singing such passages: *a coloratura soprano.* [< Ital., < L *color* color]

col·or·blind (kul′ər blīnd′), *adj.* unable to tell certain colors apart; unable to see certain colors. —**color blindness.**

col·ored (kul′ərd), *adj.* 1 having color; not black or white. 2 having a certain kind of color. 3 of black people or other nonwhite people. 4 influenced; influenced unfairly.

col·or·fast (kul′ər fast′), *adj.* dyed so as not to lose color, esp. in washing.

col·or·ful (kul′ər fəl), *adj.* 1 abounding in color. 2 vivid. —**col′or·ful·ly,** *adv.* —**col′or·ful·ness,** *n.*

col·or·ing (kul′ər ing), *n.* 1 way in which a person or thing is colored. 2 substance used to color; pigment. 3 false appearance.

col·or·ist (kul′ər ist), *n.* 1 artist who is skillful in painting with colors. 2 user of color. —**col′or·is′tic,** *adj.*

col·or·ize (kul′ə rīz), *v.,* **–ized, –iz·ing.** 1 make the color of something visible. 2 color, esp. to add color to a black-and-white film. —**col′or·i·za′tion,** *n.*

col·or·less (kul′ər lis), *adj.* 1 without color. 2 without excitement or variety; uninteresting. —**col′or·less·ly,** *adv.* —**col′or·less·ness,** *n.*

co·los·sal (kə los′əl), *adj.* huge; gigantic; vast. —**co·los′sal·ly,** *adv.*

Col·os·se·um (kol′ə sē′əm), *n.* a large, outdoor theater at Rome, completed in A.D. 80. The Colosseum was used for games and contests. [< LL, neut. of L *colosseus* gigantic < *colossus* < Gk.]

Co·los·sians (kə losh′ənz), *n.* book of the New Testament, written by the apostle Paul to the Christian people of Colossae, an ancient city of Asia Minor.

co·los·sus (kə los′əs), *n., pl.* **–los·si** (–los′ī), **–los·sus·es.** 1 a huge statue. 2 anything huge; gigantic person or thing. [< L < Gk. *kolossos*]

Colossus of Rhodes, huge statue of Apollo made at Rhodes about 280 B.C. It was one of the seven wonders of the ancient world.

col·our (kul′ər), *n., v. Esp. Brit.* color.

colt (kōlt), *n.* 1 a young horse, donkey, etc. A male horse until it is four or five years old is a colt. 2 a young or inexperienced person. [OE]

col·ter (kōl′tər), *n.* a sharp blade or disk on a plow to cut the earth ahead of the plowshare. Also, **coulter.** [< L *culter* knife]

colt·ish (kōl′tish), *adj.* lively and frisky.

colts·foot (kōlts′fut′), *n.* plant of the aster family with yellow flowers and large, heart-shaped leaves which were formerly much used in medicine.

Co·lum·bi·a (kə lum′bi ə), *n.* 1 capital of South Carolina, in the C part. 2 a name for the United States of America. —**Co·lum′bi·an,** *adj., n.*

col·um·bine (kol′əm bīn), *n.* plant whose flowers have petals shaped like hollow spurs. [< LL *columbina* < L, fem., dove-like < *columba* dove]

Co·lum·bus (kə lum′bəs), *n.* 1 **Christopher,** 1446?–1506, Italian navigator in the service of Spain who discovered the Americas in 1492. 2 capital of Ohio, in the C part.

Columbus Day, October 12, the anniversary of Columbus's discovery of the Americas.

col·umn (kol′əm), *n.* 1 a slender, upright structure, usually used as support or ornament to a building; pillar. 2 anything like a column: *a column of figures.* 3 arrangement of soldiers or ships, one behind another. 4 a narrow division of a page reading from top to bottom. 5 part of a newspaper used for a special subject or written by a special writer. [< L *columna*] —**col′umned,** *adj.*

co·lum·nar (kə lum′nər), *adj.* **1** like a column. **2** made of columns. **3** written or printed in columns.

col·um·nist (kol′əm nist; –əm ist), *n.* journalist who comments on people, events, etc., in a special, regular column in a newspaper.

com-, *prefix.* with; together; altogether: *commingle = mingle with one another; compress = press together.* [< L; also (by assimilation to the following consonant) *col-, con-, cor-*]

Com., **1** Commander. **2** Committee. **3** Commission; Commissioner.

.com (dot′kom′), domain address for websites on the Internet.

com., commerce.

co·ma[1] (kō′mə), *n., pl.* **co·mas**, a prolonged unconsciousness caused by disease, injury, or poison; stupor. [< Gk. *koma*]

co·ma[2] (kō′mə), *n., pl.* **co·mae** (kō′mē). a cloudlike mass around the nucleus of a comet. [< L < Gk. *kome* hair] —**co′mal**, *adj.*

Co·man·che (kə man′chē), *n., pl.* **-ches. 1** member of a tribe of American Indians that formerly roamed from Wyoming to N Mexico, now living in Oklahoma. **2** their language.

com·a·tose (kom′ə tōs; kō′mə–), *adj.* **1** unconscious. **2** lethargic. —**com′a·tose·ly**, *adv.*

comb (kōm), *n.* **1** a narrow, short piece of metal, rubber, etc., with teeth, used to arrange the hair or hold it in place. **2** anything shaped or used like a comb. One kind of comb cleans and takes out the tangles in wool or flax. **3** =currycomb. **4** the red, fleshy piece on the top of the head in some fowls. **5** =honeycomb. **6** top of a wave rolling over or breaking. —*v.* **1** arrange, clean, or take out tangles in, with a comb. **2** search through; look everywhere in. **3** (of waves) roll over or break at the top. [OE]

comb., combination.

com·bat (*v., n.* kom′bat; *v.* also kəm bat′), *v.*, **-bat·ed, -bat·ing**, *n.* —*v.* **1** fight (*with* or *against*); battle; contend. **2** oppose vigorously. —*n.* **1** a fight, esp. between two. **2** a struggle; a conflict; a battle. [< F *combattre* < LL < L *com-* (intensive) + *battuere* beat] —**com′bat·a·ble**, *adj.* —**com′bat·er**, *n.*

com·bat·ant (kəm bat′ənt; kom′bə tənt), *n.* fighter. —*adj.* **1** fighting. **2** ready to fight.

combat fatigue, =battle fatigue.

com·bat·ive (kəm bat′iv; kom′bə tiv), *adj.* ready to fight or oppose; fond of fighting. —**com′bat′ive·ly**, *adv.* —**com′bat′ive·ness**, *n.*

comb·er (kōm′ər), *n.* **1** one that combs. **2** wave that rolls over or breaks at the top.

com·bi·na·tion (kom′bə nā′shən), *n.* **1** a combining or being combined. **2** thing made by combining. **3** group of persons or parties joined together for some common purpose. **4** series of numbers or letters used in opening or closing a certain kind of lock. **5** suit of underwear having the shirt and drawers in one piece. —**com′bi·na′tion·al**, *adj.*

com·bine (*v.* kēm bīn′; *n.* **1** kom′bīn, kəm bīn′; *n.* **2** kom′bīn), *v.*, **-bined, -bin·ing**, *n.* —*v.* **1** join together; unite. **2** unite to form a compound. —*n.* **1** *Colloq.* combination (def. 3). **2** machine for harvesting and threshing grain. [< LL *combinare* < *com-* together + *bini* two by two] —**com·bin′a·ble**, *adj.* —**com·bin′er**, *n.*

combining form, form of a word in English or other language used for combining with other words or other combining forms to make new words; word element. *Psychoanalysis* is composed of the combining form *psycho-* mind and *analysis* examination; *Francophile* is made up of the combining forms *Franco-* French and *-phile* person who is fond of.

com·bus·ti·ble (kəm bus′tə bəl), *adj.* **1** capable of taking fire and burning; easy to burn. **2** easily excited; fiery. —*n.* a combustible substance. —**com·bus′ti·bil′i·ty, com·bus′ti·ble·ness**, *n.* —**com·bus′ti·bly**, *adv.*

com·bus·tion (kəm bus′chən), *n.* **1** act or process of burning. **2** rapid oxidation accompanied by high temperature and usually by light. **3** slow oxidation not accompanied by high temperature and light. **4** violent excitement; tumult. [< L *combustio* < *com-* up + *urere* burn] —**com·bus′tive**, *adj.*

come (kum), *v.*, **came, come, com·ing. 1** move toward: *come this way.* **2** arrive: *came to town yesterday.* **3** appear: *light comes and goes.* **4** reach; extend. **5** happen: *what will come, let come.* **6** be caused; result. **7** be born. **8** get to be; become. **9** occur to the mind. **10** be available. **11** amount: *the total comes to $100.*

come about, a happen. **b** change direction.

come across, a meet by chance. **b** *Informal.* pay. **c** reach an audience or the public.

come around, come round, a return to consciousness. **b** give in; yield; agree. **c** change direction.

come at, rush toward; attack.

come back, a return. **b** come to mind. **c** retort. **d** return to a former position or condition.

come by, a obtain; acquire. **b** pass near.

come down, a lose position, rank, money, etc. **b** be handed down. **c** become ill (*with*). **d** *Informal.* scold; blame (*on*). **e** attack suddenly (*on*).

come out, a be shown. **b** be offered to the public. **c** leave an activity. **d** make a debut. **e** say; speak (*with*). **f** offer to the public (*with*).

come through, a be successful. **b** last through successfully.

come to, return to consciousness.

come up to, compare with; equal.

come up with, produce; improvise a solution. [OE *cuman*] —**com′er**, *n.*

come·back (kum′bak′), *n.* **1** return to a former condition or position. **2** *Slang.* clever answer. **3** cause for complaining.

co·me·di·an (kə mē′di ən), *n.* **1** actor in comedies. **2** writer of comedies. **3** person who amuses others with funny talk and actions.

co·me·di·enne (kə mē′di en′), *n.* actress in comedies; actress of comic parts.

come·down (kum′doun′), *n.* loss of position, rank, money, etc.

com·e·dy (kom′ə di), *n., pl.* **-dies. 1** amusing play or show having a happy ending. **2** branch of drama concerned with such plays. **3** the comic element of drama, literature, or life. **4** funny incident. [< L < Gk., < *komoidos* comedian < *komos* merrymaking + *aoidos* singer]

come·ly (kum′li), *adj.*, **-li·er, -li·est.** having a pleasant appearance; attractive. [OE *cymlic*] —**come·li·ness**, *n.*

come-on (kum′on′), *n. Informal.* something offered to attract or allure.

com·er (kum′ər), *n. Informal.* person who seems likely to succeed.

com·et (kom′it), *n.* a bright celestial body with a starlike center and often with a cloudy tail of light, moving around the sun in a long, oval course. [< L < Gk. *kometes* wearing long hair < *kome* hair] —**co·met′ic**, *adj.*

come·up·pance (kum′up′əns), *n.* one's just deserts.

com·fit (kum′fit; kom′–), *n.* piece of candy. [< OF < L *confectus* prepared < *com-* + *facere* make]

com·fort (kum′fərt), *v.* **1** ease the grief or sorrow of; cheer. **2** give ease to. —*n.* **1** anything that makes trouble or sorrow easier to bear. **2** freedom from pain or hardship; ease. **3** person or thing that makes life easier or takes away hardship. [< OF < LL *confortare* strengthen < *com-* + *fortis* strong] —**com′fort·ing**, *adj.* —**com′fort·ing·ly**, *adv.* —**com′fort·less**, *adj.*

com·fort·a·ble (kumf′tə bəl; kum′fər tə bəl), *adj.* **1** giving comfort. **2** in comfort. **3** at ease; contented. **4** enough for one's needs. —**com′fort·a·ble·ness**, *n.* —**com′fort·a·bly**, *adv.*

com·fort·er (kum′fər tər), *n.* **1** person or thing that gives comfort. **2** a padded or quilted covering for a bed.

com·fy (kum′fē), *adj.*, **-fi·er, -fi·est.** *Informal.* =comfortable.

com·ic (kom′ik), *adj.* **1** of comedy. **2** amusing; funny. —*n.* the amusing or funny side of literature, life, etc. [< L < Gk. *komikos.* See COMEDY.]

com·i·cal (kom′ə kəl), *adj.* amusing; funny. —**com′i·cal·ly**, *adv.* —**com′i·cal·ness**, *n.*

comic book, magazine with comic strips.

comic opera, amusing opera having a happy ending.

comic strip, series of drawings, sometimes humorous, presenting an adventure.

com·ing (kum′ing), *n.* arrival. —*adj.* **1** next. **2** on the way to importance or fame.

com·i·ty (kom′ə ti), *n., pl.* **–ties.** courtesy; civility. [< L, < *comis* friendly]

com·ma (kom′ə), *n.* mark (,) of punctuation, used to show the smallest interruptions in the thought or in the grammatical structure of a sentence. [< L < Gk. *komma* piece cut off < *koptein* to cut]

com·mand (kə mand′; –mänd′), *v.* **1** give an order to; direct. **2** be in control of. **3** overlook. **4** be able to have and use. **5** deserve and get: *command respect.* —*n.* **1** order; direction. **2** authority; control. **3** position of a person to command. **4** soldiers, ships, district, etc., under a person who commands them. **5** outlook over. **6** ability to use; mastery: *good command of French.* [< OF < LL, < L *com-* + *mandare* commit, command]

com·man·dant (kom′ən dant′; –dänt′), *n.* officer in command of a fort, navy yard, etc.

com·man·deer (kom′ən dir′), *v.* seize (private property) for military or public use. [< Afrikaans < F *commander*]

com·mand·er (kə man′dər; –män′–), *n.* **1** person who commands. **2** officer in charge of an army or a part of an army. **3** a navy officer ranking next below a captain and next above a lieutenant commander. —**com·mand′er·ship,** *n.*

commander in chief, *pl.* **commanders in chief. 1** person who has complete command of the army and navy of a country. **2** officer in command of part of an army or navy.

com·mand·ing (kə man′ding; –män′–), *adj.* **1** in command. **2** controlling; powerful. **3** impressive. —**com·mand′ing·ly,** *adv.*

com·mand·ment (kə mand′mənt; –mänd′–), *n.* **1** order; direction; law. **2** one of the ten laws that, according to the Bible, God gave to Moses. Exod. 20:2–17; Deut. 5:6–21.

com·man·do (kə man′do; –man′–), *n., pl.* **–dos, –does.** soldier who makes brief, daring raids upon enemy territory. [< Afrikaans < Pg.]

command performance, 1 stage performance, film, etc. given by request or order, esp. before royalty. **2** *Fig.* any appearance at a social function, meeting, etc. that is required.

com·mem·o·rate (kə mem′ə rāt), *v.,* **–rated, –rat·ing. 1** preserve the memory of. **2** honor the memory of. [< L, < *com-* + *memorare* relate] —**com·mem′o·ra·ble,** *adj.* —**com·mem′o·ra′tion,** *n.* —**com·mem′o·ra′tive,** *adj.* —**com·mem′o·ra′tive·ly,** *adv.* —**com·mem′o·ra·tor,** *n.* —**com·mem′o·ra·to′ry** *adj.*

com·mence (kə mens′), *v.,* **–menced, –menc·ing.** begin; start. [< OF *comencer* < VL < L *com-* + *initiare* begin. See INITIATE.] —**com·menc′er,** *n.*

com·mence·ment (kə mens′mənt), *n.* **1** a beginning; start. **2** day when a school or college gives diplomas or degrees to students. **3** ceremonies on this day.

com·mend (kə mend′), *v.* **1** praise. **2** mention favorably; recommend. **3** hand over for safekeeping. [< L *commendare.* See COMMAND.] —**com·mend′a·ble,** *adj.* —**com·mend′a·bly,** *adv.*

com·men·da·tion (kom′ən dā′shən) *n.* **1** praise; approval. **2** favorable mention. **3** a handing over to another for safekeeping; entrusting.

com·mend·a·to·ry (kə men′də tô′ri; –tō′–), *adj.* approving; mentioning favorably.

com·men·su·ra·ble (kə men′shə rə bəl; –sə rə–), *adj.* measurable by the same set of units. —**com·men′su·ra·bil′i·ty, com·men′su·ra·ble·ness,** *n.* —**com·men′su·ra·bly,** *adv.*

com·men·su·rate (kə men′shə rit; –sə–), *adj.* **1** in the proper proportion; proportionate. **2** of the same size, extent, etc.; equal. **3** measurable by the same set of units. [< LL *commensuratus.* See COM-, MENSURATION.] —**com·men′su·rate·ly,** *adv.* —**com·men′su·rate·ness,** *n.* —**com·men′su·ra′tion,** *n.*

com·ment (kom′ent), *n.* **1** remark that explains, praises, or criticizes something. **2** remark. **3** talk; gossip. —*v.* **1** make a comment or comments. **2** talk; gossip. [< L *commentum* < *commentus,* pp. of *comminisci* < *com-* up + *-minisci* think]

com·men·tar·y (kom′ən ter′i), *n., pl.* **–tar·ies. 1** explanation. **2** an explanatory essay or treatise.

com·men·ta·tor (kom ən tā′tər), *n.* person who makes comments, explaining or criticizing books, concerts, recent events, etc.

com·merce (kom′ərs; –ėrs), *n.* buying and selling in large amounts between different places; trade; business. [< F < L *commercium,* ult. < *com-* with + *merx* wares]

com·mer·cial (kə mėr′shəl), *adj.* **1** having to do with commerce. **2** made to be sold. **3** manufactured in sizable quantities. **4** supported subsidized by an advertiser: *a commercial TV program.* —*n.* a radio or television program, or the part of a program, that advertises something. —**com·mer′cial·ly,** *adv.*

com·mer·cial·ism (kə mėr′shəl iz əm), *n.* **1** methods and spirit of commerce. **2** business custom; expression used in business.

com·mer·cial·ize (kə mėr′shəl īz), *v.,* **–ized, –iz·ing.** make a matter of business or trade. —**com·mer′cial·i·za′tion,** *n.*

com·min·gle (kə ming′gəl), *v.,* **–gled, –gling.** mingle together; blend.

com·mi·nute (kom′ə nüt; –nūt), *v.,* **–nuted, –nut·ing.** pulverize. [< L, < *com-* + *minuere* make smaller < *minus* less] —**com′mi·nu′tion,** *n.*

com·mis·er·ate (kə miz′ər āt), *v.,* **–ated, –at·ing.** feel or express sorrow for;

sympathize with; pity. —**com·mis′er·a′tion,** *n.*

com·mis·sar·i·at (kom′ə sār′i ət; –at), *n.* department of an army that supplies food, etc. [< F, < Med.L *commissarius.* See COMMISSARY.]

com·mis·sar·y (kom′ə ser′i), *n., pl.* **–sar·ies. 1** store handling food and supplies in a mining camp, lumber camp, army camp, etc. **2** an army officer in charge of food and daily supplies for soldiers. **3** deputy; representative. [< Med.L *commissarius* < L *commissus,* pp., entrusted. See COMMIT.]

com·mis·sion (kə mish′ən), *n.* **1** a written paper giving certain powers, privileges, and duties. **2** a written order giving military or naval rank and authority. **3** authority, power, or right given. **4** thing for which authority is given; thing trusted to a person to do. **5** group of people with authority to do certain things. **6** doing; performance: *commission of a crime.* **7** pay based on a percentage of the amount of business done. —*v.* **1** give a commission to. **2** give authority, right or power (to do something). **3** put in service or use; make ready.

in commission, a in service; in use. **b** in working order.

out of commission, a not in service or use. **b** not in working order.

com·mis·sioned officer (ke mish′ənd), officer having the rank of second lieutenant or above in the U.S. Army, Air Force, or Marines, or an ensign or above in the U. S. Navy.

com·mis·sion·er (kə mish′ən ər), *n.* **1** member of a commission. **2** official in charge of some department of a government: *police commissioner.* —**com·mis′sion·er·ship′,** *n.*

com·mit (kə mit′), *v.,* **–mit·ted, –mit·ting. 1** hand over for safekeeping; deliver. **2** confine officially: *commit to prison.* **3** do or perform (usually something wrong). **4** involve; pledge.

commit to memory, learn by heart. [< L < *com-* with + *mittere,* send, put] —**com·mit′ta·ble,** *adj.*

com·mit·al (kə mit′əl), *n.* =commitment (defs. 2 and 3).

com·mit·ment (kə mit′mənt), *n.* **1** a committing or being committed. **2** a sending to prison. **3** order sending a person to prison or hospital. **4** pledge; promise.

com·mit·tee (kə mit′i), *n.* group of persons appointed or elected to do certain things. [< AF, committed. See COMMIT.]

com·mit·tee·man (kə mit′i mən; –man′), *n., pl.* **–men** (–mən; –men′). member of a committee.

com·mit·tee·wom·an (kə mit′i wùm′ən), *n., pl.* **–wom·en.** female member of a committee.

com·mode (kə mōd′), *n.* **1** chest of drawers. **2** =toilet. [< F < L *commodus* convenient < *com-* with + *modus* measure]

com·mo·di·ous (kə mō′di əs), *adj.* **1** roomy. **2** convenient; handy. [< Med.L *commodiosus.* See COMMODE.] —**com·mo′di·ous·ly,** *adv.*

com·mod·i·ty (kə mod′ə ti), *n., pl.* **-ties. 1** anything that is bought and sold. **2** useful thing.

com·mo·dore (kom′ə dôr; –dōr), *n.* **1** an officer in the U.S. Navy ranking next below a rear admiral and next above a captain. **2** title of honor given to the president or head of a yacht club. [earlier *commandore; ?* < Du. < F, < *commander* to command]

com·mon (kom′ən), *adj.* **1** belonging equally to all. **2** of all; general: *common knowledge.* **3** belonging to the community at large; public: *a common council.* **4** usual; familiar. **5** without rank. **6** inferior; low; vulgar. **7** belonging equally to two or more quantities: *a common factor.* —*n.* land owned or used by all the people of a town, village, etc.

in common, equally with another or others. [< OF <L < *communis* < *com-* together + *munia* duties] —**com′mon·ly,** *adv.* —**com′mon·ness,** *n.*

com·mon·al·i·ty (kom′ə nal′ə ti), *n.* **1** =commonalty. **2** common quality or condition.

com·mon·al·ty (kom′ən əl ti), *n., pl.* **-ties. 1** the common people. **2** people as a group.

common carrier, person or company whose business is conveying goods or people for pay.

com·mon·er (kom′ən ər), *n.* one of the common people; person who is not a nobleman.

Common Era, =Christian Era.

common law, the unwritten law based on custom and usage and confirmed by the decisions of judges, as distinct from statute law.

common noun, name for any one of a class. *Boy, city,* and *dog* are common nouns.

com·mon·place (kom′ən plās′), *n.* **1** everyday thing. **2** ordinary remark. —*adj.* not new or interesting; everyday; ordinary. —**com′mon·place′ness,** *n.*

com·mons (kom′ənz), *n.pl.* **1** the common people. **2** a dining hall. **3 the Commons,** House of Commons.

common sense, practical intelligence. —**com′mon·sense′, com′mon·sen′si·cal,** *adj.* —**com′mon·sen′si·cal·ly,** *adv.*

common time, musical meter of four quarter notes to the measure.

com·mon·weal (kom′ən wēl′), **common weal,** *n.* general welfare; public good.

com·mon·wealth (kom′ən welth′), *n.* **1** citizens of a state. **2** a democratic state; republic. **3** one of the states of the United States. **4** group of persons, nations, etc., united by some common interest.

Commonwealth of Nations, group of independent countries tied economically to the United Kingdom, formerly under British rule and called the British Commonwealth of Nations.

com·mo·tion (kə mō′shən), *n.* violent movement; confusion; disturbance; tumult.

com·mu·nal (kom′yə nəl; kə mū′nəl), *adj.* **1** of a community; public. **2** owned jointly by all. **3** of a commune. —**com′mu·nal·ly,** *adv.*

com·mune[1] (*v.* kə mūn′; *n.* kom′ūn), *v.,* **-muned, -mun·ing,** *n.* —*v.* talk intimately. —*n.* intimate talk; communion. [< OF, < *comun* COMMON]

com·mune[2] (kom′ūn), *n.* **1 a** place where people live communally. **b** group of people living together. **2** the smallest division for local government in France, Belgium, and several other European countries. [< F, fem. of *commun* COMMON]

com·mu·ni·ca·ble (kə mū′nə kə bəl), *adj.* that can be transferred or passed along to others. —**com·mu′ni·ca·bil′i·ty, com·mu′ni·ca·ble·ness,** *n.*

com·mu·ni·cant (kə mū′nə kənt), *n.* **1** person who receives Holy Communion. **2** person who gives information by talking, writing, etc.

com·mu·ni·cate (kə mū′nə kāt), *v.,* **-cat·ed, -cat·ing. 1** pass along; transfer: *a stove communicates heat to a room.* **2** give (information) by talking, writing, etc. **3** be connected. [< L *communicatus* < *communis* COMMON] —**com·mu′ni·ca′tor,** *n.*

com·mu·ni·ca·tion (kə mū′nə kā′shən), *n.* **1** act or fact of passing along; transfer. **2** a giving of information by talking, writing, etc. **3** information given in this way. **4** letter, message, etc., that gives information. **5** means of going from one place to the other; connection; passage.

communications, a system of communicating by Internet, computer, telephone, etc. **b** system of routes of transportation. **c** study of providing information or entertainment through talking or writing for various media.

com·mu·ni·ca·tive (kə mū′nə kā′tiv; –kə tiv), *adj.* **1** ready to give information; talkative. **2** pertaining to communication. —**com·mu′ni·ca′tive·ly,** *adv.* —**com·mu′ni·ca′tive·ness,** *n.*

com·mun·ion (kə mūn′yən), *n.* **1** a having in common. **2** intimate talk; fellowship. **3** close spiritual relationship. **4** group of people having the same religious beliefs. **Communion,** celebration of the Lord's Supper. [< L *communio.* See COMMON.]

com·mu·ni·qué (kə mū′nə kā′; kə mū′nə kā), *n.* an official bulletin, statement, etc.

com·mu·nism (kom′yə niz əm), *n.* **1** system by which the means of production and distribution are owned and managed by the government, and the goods produced are shared by all citizens. **2 Communism,** political principles and practices of a Communist Party. [< F *communisme* < *commun* COMMON]

com·mu·nist (kom′yə nist), *n.* **1** person who favors and supports communism. **2 Communist,** member of a political party advocating communism. —**com′mu·nis′tic, com′mu·nis′ti·cal,** *adj.*

com·mu·ni·ty (kə mū′nə ti), *n., pl.* **-ties. 1** a number of people living in the same locality. **2** group of people living together: *a community of monks.* **3** the public. **4** ownership together. **5** group of animals or plants living together. **6** likeness; similarity; identity. [< OF < L *communitas.* See COMMON.]

community college, college, often a two-year college, that offers courses to nonresident students from the local area.

com·mu·tate (kom′yə tāt), *v.,* **-tat·ed, -tat·ing.** reverse the direction of (an electric current). —**com′mu·ta′tor,** *n.*

com·mu·ta·tion (kom′yə tā′shən), *n.* **1** exchange; substitution. **2** reduction (of an obligation, penalty, etc.) to a less severe one. **3** regular, daily travel back and forth to work.

com·mute (kə mūt′), *v.,* **-mut·ed, -mut·ing. 1** exchange: substitute. **2** change (an obligation, penalty, etc.) to an easier one. **3** travel regularly back and forth to work. [< L, < *com–* + *mutare* change]

com·mut·er (kə mūt′ər), *n.* person who travels regularly back and forth to work.

comp (komp), *n.* =compensation (defs. 1 and 2).

com·pact[1] (kəm pakt′), *adj.* **1** firmly packed together; closely joined. **2** composed or made (*of*). **3** using few words; brief. —*v.* **1** pack firmly together; join closely. **2** make by putting together firmly. **3** condense. [< L *compactus* < *com–* together + *pangere* fasten] —**com·pact′ly,** *adv.* —**com·pact′ness,** *n.*

com·pact[2] (kom′pakt), *n.* agreement. [< L *compactum* < *com–* + *pacisci* contract]

compact disk or **disc, 1** digital disk whose encoded data or sounds are read by a laser. **2 Compact Disc.** trademark for such a disk.

com·pan·ion (kəm pan′yən), *n.* **1** person who goes along with another. **2** anything that matches or goes with another in kind, size, color, etc. **3** person paid to live or travel with another. —*v.* be a companion to. [< OF < LL *companio* < *com–* together + *panis* bread] —**com·pan′ion·less,** *adj.* —**com·pan′ion·ship,** *n.*

com·pan·ion·a·ble (kəm pan′yən ə bəl), *adj.* pleasant; agreeable; sociable. —**com·pan′ion·a·bil′i·ty, com·pan′ion·a·ble·ness,** *n.* —**com·pan′ion·a·bly,** *adv.*

com·pan·ion·ate (kəm pan′yən it), *adj.* of companions.

com·pan·ion·way (kəm pan′yən wā′), *n.* stairway from the deck of a ship down to the rooms below.

com·pa·ny (kum′pə ni), *n., pl.* **-nies,** *v.,* **-nied, -ny·ing.** —*n.* **1** group of people. **2** group of people joined together for some purpose: *a business company, a company of actors.* **3** companion or companions. **4** association as companions. **5** guest or guests; visitor or visitors. **6** part of an army commanded by a captain. **7** a ship's crew; officers and sailors of a ship. —*v.* associate.

keep company, a go with; remain with for companionship. **b** go together, as a couple.

keep company with, a associate with. **b** associate with, as a couple.

part company, a go separate ways. **b** end companionship. [< OF, < *compagne* COMPANION]

compar., comparative; comparison.

com·pa·ra·ble (kom′pə rə bəl), *adj.* **1** able to be compared. **2** fit to be compared. —**com′pa·ra·ble·ness,** *n.* —**com′pa·ra·bly,** *adv.*

com·par·a·tive (kəm par′ə tiv), *adj.* **1** that compares. **2** measured by comparison with something else. **3** showing the comparative form. —*n.* **1** the second degree of comparison of an adjective or adverb. **2** form or combination of words that shows this degree. *Fairer* is the comparative of *fair.* —**com·par′a·tive·ly,** *adv.*

com·pare (kəm pãr′), *v.,* **-pared, -paring,** *n.* —*v.* **1** find out or point out the likenesses or differences of. **2** consider as similar; liken. **3** be considered like or equal. **4** change the form of (an adjective or adverb) to show the comparative and superlative degree. —*n.* comparison. **beyond compare,** without an equal. [< F < L, < *com-* with + *par* equal] —**com·par′er,** *n.*

com·par·i·son (kəm par′ə sən), *n.* **1** act or process of comparing; finding the likenesses and differences. **2** likeness; similarity. **3** change in an adjective or adverb to show degrees. The three degrees of comparison are positive, comparative, and superlative. *Example:* good, better, best; cold, colder, coldest; helpful, more helpful, most helpful.

by comparison with, as compared with something else.

in comparison with, compared with.

com·part·ment (kəm pärt′mənt), *n.* a separate division or section; part of an enclosed space set off by walls or partitions. [< F < Ital. *compartimento* < *compartire* divide < LL, < L *com-* with + *partiri* share]

com·pass (kum′pəs), *n.* **1** instrument for showing directions, consisting of a needle that points to the N Magnetic Pole. **2** boundary; circumference. **3** extent; range. **4** circuit; going around. **5** instrument for drawing circles and measuring distances. —*v.* **1** make a circuit of; go around. **2** form a circle around; surround. **3** do; accomplish; get. [< OF, < *compasser* divide equally < VL < L *com-* with + *passus* step]

com·pas·sion (kəm pash′ən), *n.* feeling for another's sorrow or hardship; sym-

pathy; pity. [< L *compassio* < *com-* with + *pati* suffer]

com·pas·sion·ate (*adj.* kəm pash′ən it; *v.* kəm pash′ən āt), *adj., v.,* **-at·ed, -at·ing.** —*adj.* deeply sympathetic. —*v.* take pity on. —**com·pas′sion·ate·ly,** *adv.* —**com·pas′sion·ate·ness,** *n.*

com·pat·i·ble (kəm pat′ə bəl), *adj.* able to exist together; agreeing; in harmony. [< Med.L *compatibilis.* See COMPASSION.] —**com·pat′i·bil′i·ty, com·pat′i·ble·ness,** *n.* —**com·pat′i·bly,** *adv.*

com·pa·tri·ot (kəm pā′tri ət; *esp. Brit.* kəm pat′ri ət), *n.* a fellow countryman.

com·peer (kəm pir′; kom′pir), *n.* **1** equal. **2** comrade. [< OF < L, < *com-* with + *par* equal]

com·pel (kəm pel′), *v.,* **-pelled, -pel·ling. 1** force. **2** cause or get by force. [< L, < *com-* + *pellere* drive] —**com·pel′la·ble,** *adj.* —**com·pel′ler,** *n.*

com·pen·di·ous (kəm pen′di əs), *adj.* brief but comprehensive; concise. —**com·pen′di·ous·ly,** *adv.* —**com·pen′di·ous·ness,** *n.*

com·pen·di·um (kəm pen′di əm), *n., pl.* **-di·ums, -di·a** (-di ə). summary that gives much information in little space; concise treatise. Also, **compend.** [< L, a saving, shortening, < *com-* in addition + *pendere* weigh]

com·pen·sate (kom′pən sāt), *v.,* **-sat·ed, -sat·ing. 1** make an equal return to; give an equivalent to. **2** balance by equal weight, power, etc.; make up (*for*). **3** pay. [< L, < *com-* with + *pensare* weigh < *pendere*] —**com′pen·sa′tor,** *n.* —**com·pen′sa·to·ry,** *adj.*

com·pen·sa·tion (kom′pən sā′shən), *n.* **1** something given as an equivalent; something given to make up for a loss, injury, etc. **2** pay. **3** a balancing by equal power, weight, etc. **4** increased activity of one part to make up for loss or weakness of another. **5** any act or instance of compensating. —**com′pen·sa′tion·al,** *adj.*

com·pete (kəm pēt′), *v.,* **-pet·ed, -pet·ing. 1** try hard to obtain something wanted by others; be rivals; contend. **2** take part (in a contest). [< L, < *com-* together + *petere* seek]

com·pe·tence (kom′pə təns), **com·pe·ten·cy** (-tən si), *n.* **1** ability; fitness. **2** enough money or property to provide a comfortable living.

com·pe·tent (kom′pə tənt), *adj.* **1** able; fit. **2** legally qualified. [< L, being fit, < *competere* meet. See COMPETE.] —**com′pe·tent·ly,** *adv.*

com·pe·ti·tion (kom′pə tish′ən), *n.* **1** effort to obtain something wanted by others; rivalry. **2** contest.

com·pet·i·tive (kəm pet′ə tiv), *adj.* of or having competition; based on or decided by competition. —**com·pet′i·tive·ly,** *adv.* —**com·pet′i·tive·ness,** *n.*

com·pet·i·tor (kəm pet′ə tər), *n.* person who competes; rival.

com·pile (kəm pīl′), *v.,* **-piled, -pil·ing. 1** collect and bring together in one list

or account. **2** make (a book, report, etc.) out of various materials. [< F < L *compilare* steal, orig., pile up < *com-* together + *pilare* press] —**com′pi·la′tion,** *n.* —**com·pil′er,** *n.*

com·pla·cen·cy (kəm plā′sən si), **com·pla·cence** (-səns), *n., pl.* **-cies; -ces. 1** being pleased with oneself; self-satisfaction. **2** contentment.

com·pla·cent (kəm plā′sənt), *adj.* pleased with oneself; self-satisfied. [< L, < *com-* + *placere* please] —**com·pla′cent·ly,** *adv.*

com·plain (kəm plān′), *v.* **1** say that something is wrong; find fault. **2** talk about one's pains, troubles, etc. **3** make an accusation or charge. [< OF < VL, bewail, < L *com-* + *plangere* lament] —**com·plain′er,** *n.* —**com·plain′ing·ly,** *adv.*

com·plain·ant (kəm plān′ənt), *n.* **1** person who complains. **2** plaintiff.

com·plaint (kəm plānt′), *n.* **1** a complaining; a finding fault. **2** a cause for complaining. **3** accusation; charge. **4** sickness; ailment.

com·plai·sant (kəm plā′zənt; kom′plə zant), *adj.* **1** obliging; gracious; courteous. **2** compliant. [< F, < *complaire* acquiesce < L, < *com-* + *placere* please] —**com·plai′sance,** *n.* —**com·plai′sant·ly,** *adv.*

com·ple·ment (kom′plə mənt), *n.* **1** something that completes or makes perfect. **2** number required to fill. **3** either of two parts or things needed to complete each other. **4** full quantity. **5** word or group of words completing a predicate. In "The man is good" *good* is a complement. **6** amount needed to make an angle or an arc equal to 90 degrees. —*v.* supply a lack of any kind; complete. [< L *complementum* < *complere* to COMPLETE]

com·ple·men·tal (kom′plə men′təl), *adj.* complementary. —**com′ple·men′tal·ly,** *adv.*

com·ple·men·ta·ry (kom′plə men′tə ri; -tri), *adj.* forming a complement; completing.

complementary angle, either of two angles which together form an angle of 90 degrees.

complementary colors, two colors whose reflected light combine to produce white or gray. Red and green are complementary colors.

com·plete (kəm plēt′), *adj., v.,* **-plet·ed, -plet·ing.** —*adj.* **1** with all the parts; whole; entire. **2** perfect; thorough. **3** ended; finished; done. —*v.* **1** make up all the parts of; make whole or entire. **2** make perfect or thorough. **3** get done; end; finish. [< L *completus < com-* up + *-plere* fill] —**com·plete′ly,** *adv.* —**com·plete′ness,** *n.* —**com·plet′er,** *n.* —**com·ple′tive,** *adj.*

com·ple·tion (kəm plē′shən), *n.* **1** act of completing. **2** condition of being completed.

com·plex (*adj.* kəm pleks′, kom′pleks; *n.* kom′pleks), *adj.* **1** made up of a number of parts. **2** complicated. —*n.* **1** a complicated whole. **2** idea or group of ideas associated with emotional disturbance so as to influence a person's behavior to an abnormal degree. **3** an unreasonable prejudice; strong dislike. [< L *complexus* embracing < *com–* together + *plecti* twine] —**com·plex′ly,** *adv.* —**com·plex′-ness,** *n.*

complex fraction, fraction having a fraction or mixed number in the numerator, denominator, or both. Also, **compound fraction.**

com·plex·ion (kəm plek′shən), *n.* **1** color, quality, and general appearance of the skin, particularly of the face. **2** general appearance; nature; character. [< LL *complexio* constitution < L, combination. See COMPLEX.] —**com·plex′ion·al, com·plex′ion·ed,** *adj.*

com·plex·i·ty (kəm plek′sə ti), *n., pl.* **-ties.** **1** a complex quality, condition, or structure. **2** something complex; complication.

complex number, sum of a real number and an imaginary number.

com·pli·a·ble (kəm plī′ə bəl), *adj.* complying. —**com·pli′a·ble·ness,** *n.* —**com·pli′a·bly,** *adv.*

com·pli·ance (kəm plī′əns), **com·pli·an·cy** (–ən si), *n.* **1** act doing as another wishes or yielding to a request. **2** tendency to yield to others.

com·pli·ant (kəm plī′ənt), *adj.* complying; yielding; obliging. —**com·pli·ant·ly,** *adv.*

com·pli·cate (*v.* kom′plə kāt; *adj.* kom′plə kit), *v.,* **-cat·ed, -cat·ing,** *adj.* —*v.* **1** make hard to understand; confuse. **2** make worse or more mixed up. —*adj.* complex; involved. [< L, < *com–* together + *plicare* fold]

com·pli·cat·ed (kom′plə kāt′id), *adj.* made up of many parts; intricate. —**com′pli·cat′ed·ly,** *adv.* —**com′pli·cat′ed·ness,** *n.*

com·pli·ca·tion (kom′plə kā′shən), *n.* **1** a complex or confused state of affairs. **2** something causing such a state of affairs. **3** act or process of complicating.

com·plic·i·ty (kəm plis′ə ti), *n., pl.* **-ties.** partnership in wrongdoing. [< *complice* confederate < L *complex* < *com–* together + *plicare* fold]

com·pli·ment (kom′plə mənt), *n.* something good said about one; something said in praise of one's work. —*v.* pay a compliment to; congratulate. [< F < Ital. < Sp. *cumplimiento.* Var. of COMPLEMENT.]

com·pli·men·ta·ry (kom′plə men′tə ri; –tri), *adj.* **1** like or containing a compliment; praising. **2** *U.S.* given free. —**com′pli·men′ta·ri·ly,** *adv.*

com·ply (kəm plī′), *v.,* **-plied, -ply·ing.** act in agreement with a request or a command. [< Ital. < Sp. < L *complere* complete; infl. by *ply*[1]] —**com·pli′er,** *n.*

com·po·nent (kəm pō′nənt), *adj.* constituent. —*n.* an essential part; part. [< L, < *com–* together + *ponere* put]

com·port (kəm pôrt′; –pōrt′), *v.* **1** behave: *comport oneself with dignity.* **2** agree; suit. [< F < L, < *com–* together + *portare* carry] —**com·port′ment,** *n.*

com·pose (kəm pōz′), *v.,* **-posed, -pos·ing.** **1** make up. **2** be the parts of. **3** get (oneself) ready; make up one's mind. **4** make calm. **5** settle; arrange: *compose a dispute.* **6** write music, books, etc. [< OF, < *com–* (< L) together + *poser* place (see POSE)]

com·posed (kəm pōzd′), *adj.* calm; tranquil. —**com·pos′ed·ly,** *adv.*

com·pos·er (kəm pōz′ər), *n.* person who composes, esp. a writer of music.

com·pos·ite (kəm poz′it), *adj.* **1** made up of various parts; compound. **2** belonging to a group of plants, as the aster, daisy, etc., in which the florets are borne in dense heads. —*n.* **1** composite plant. **2** any composite thing. [< L *compositus* < *com–* together + *ponere* put] —**com·pos′ite·ly,** *adv.*

composite number, number exactly divisible by a whole number other than itself or one. Nine is a composite number.

com·po·si·tion (kom′pə zish′ən), *n.* **1** makeup of anything. **2** a putting together of a whole. **3** thing composed. **4** act or art of composing prose or verse or a musical work. **5** mixture of substances.

com·post (kom′pōst), *n.* mixture of leaves, manure, etc., for fertilizing land. [< OF. See COMPOSITE.]

com·po·sure (kəm pō′zhər), *n.* calmness; self-control.

com·pote (kom′pōt), *n.* **1** dish with a supporting stem for fruit, etc. **2** stewed fruit. [< F. See COMPOSITE.]

com·pound[1] (*adj.* kom′pound, kom-pound′; *n.* kom′pound; *v.* kom pound′, kəm–), *adj.* having more than one part. *Steamship* is a compound word; *5 ft. 2 in* is a compound number. [< v.] —*n.* **1** something made by combining parts. **2** compound word. **3** substance formed by chemical combination of two or more substances. [< adj.] —*v.* **1** mix; combine. **2** make by combining parts.

compound a felony, accept money not to prosecute a crime, etc. [< OF < L, < *com–* together + *ponere* put] —**compound′a·ble,** *adj.* —**com·pound′er,** *n.*

com·pound[2] (kom′pound), *n.* an enclosed yard with buildings in it. [prob. < Malay *kampong*]

compound eye, eye of certain arthropods composed of many visual units, such as the large lateral eyes of insects.

compound interest, interest paid on both the original sum of money borrowed and on the unpaid interest added to it.

compound sentence, sentence made up of coordinate independent clauses. *Example:* He went but she came.

com·pre·hend (kom′pri hend′), *v.* **1** understand. **2** include; contain. [< L, < *com–* + *prehendere* seize] —**com′pre·hend′i·ble,** *adj.* —**com′pre·hend′ing·ly,** *adv.*

com·pre·hen·si·ble (kom′pri hen′sə bəl), *adj.* understandable. —**com′pre·hen′si·bil′i·ty, com′pre·hen′si·ble·ness,** *n.* —**com′pre·hen′si·bly,** *adv.*

com·pre·hen·sion (kom′pri hen′shən), *n.* **1** act or power of understanding; ability to get the meaning. **2** act or fact of including. **3** comprehensiveness.

com·pre·hen·sive (kom′pri hen′siv), *adj.* **1** including; including much. **2** comprehending. —**com′pre·hen′sive·ly,** *adv.* —**com′pre·hen′sive·ness,** *n.*

com·press (*v.* kəm pres′; *n.* kom′pres), *v.* squeeze together; make smaller by pressure. —*n.* pad of wet cloth applied to some part of the body to create pressure or to reduce inflammation. [< L *compressare,* ult. < *com–* together + *premere* press] —**com·pressed′,** *adj.* —**com·pres′sion,** *n.* —**com·pres′sive,** *adj.*

compressed air, air that has been put under extra pressure to increase its force when released and used in the operation of drills, brakes, sprayers, etc.

com·press·i·ble (kəm pres′ə bəl), *adj.* that can be compressed. —**com·press′i·bil′i·ty,** *n.*

com·pres·sor (kəm pres′ər), *n.* **1** one that compresses. **2** machine for compressing air, gas, etc.

com·prise, com·prize (kəm prīz′), *v.,* **-prised, -pris·ing; -prized, -priz·ing.** consist of; include. [< F *compris,* pp. of *comprendre* < L *comprehendere.* See COMPREHEND.] —**com·pris′a·ble, com·priz′a·ble,** *adj.*

com·pro·mise (kom′prə mīz), *v.,* **-mised, -mis·ing,** *n.* —*v.* **1** settle (a dispute) by agreeing that each will give up a part of what is demanded. **2** put under suspicion; put in danger. —*n.* **1** settlement of a dispute by a partial yielding on both sides. **2** result of such a settlement. **3** anything halfway between two different things. **4** a putting under suspicion. [< F < L *compromissum.* See COM–, PROMISE.] —**com′pro·mis′er,** *n.*

comp·trol·ler (kən trōl′ər), *n.* =controller (def. 1). —**comp·trol′ler·ship,** *n.*

com·pul·sion (kəm pul′shən), *n.* **1** act of compelling; use of force; force. **2** state of being compelled. —**com·pul′sive,** *adj.* —**com·pul′sive·ly,** *adv.*

com·pul·so·ry (kəm pul′sə ri), *adj.* **1** required. **2** using force. —**com·pul′so·ri·ly,** *adv.* —**com·pul′so·ri·ness,** *n.*

com·punc·tion (kəm pungk′shən), *n.* the pricking of conscience; regret; remorse. [< LL *compunctio* < L, < *com–* + *pungere* prick]

com·pute (kəm pūt′), *v.,* **-put·ed, -put·ing.** **1** do by arithmetical work; reckon; calculate. **2** use a computer. [< L, < *com–* up + *putare* reckon. Doublet of COUNT[1].] —**com·put′a·ble,** *adj.* —**com·put′a·bil′i·ty,** *n.* —**com·pu·ta′tion,** *n.*

com·put·er (kəm pūt′ər), *n.* **1** an electronic machine which processes, stores, and retrieves data. **2** person or thing that computes, esp. one skilled in computing. —**com·put′er·ist,** *n.*

com·put·er·ize (kəm pū′tə rīz), *v.,* **–ized, –iz·ing. 1** adapt to a computer: *computerized an entire process.* **2** install or equip with computers: *plan to computerize the factory.* —**com·put′er·i·za′tion,** *n.*

computerized axial tomography, X-ray photography processed by computer that produces cross-sectional views of the body; CAT scan.

computer language, system of words and symbols used for programming computers.

computer literacy, knowledge and ability to use computers. —**com·pu′ter-lit′er·ate,** *adj.*

computer science, science of computers, including design, programming, and operation. —**computer scientist.**

computer virus, subprogram surreptitiously inserted into a computer that causes it to malfunction. Such computer viruses are inserted through Internet access to individual computers or an entire computer system.

com·rade (kom′rad), *n.* **1** companion and friend; partner. **2** a fellow member of a political party, etc. [< F < SP. *camarada* roommate, ult. < L *camera* CHAMBER] —**com′rade·ship,** *n.*

con[1] (kon), *adv.* against a proposition, opinion, etc. —*n.* reason, person, etc., against. [short for L *contra* against]

con[2] (kon), *v.,* **conned, con·ning.** learn enough to remember; study. [var. of *can*[1]]

con[3] (kon), *adj., v.,* **conned, con·ning.** *Slang.* —*adj.* confidence, as in *con game, con man.* —*v.* to swindle. [short for *confidence*]

con[4] (kon), *n.* =convict.

con-, *prefix.* form of **com-** before *n.*

con·cave (*adj., v.* kon kāv′, kon′kāv, kong′–; *n.* kon′kāv, kong′–), *adj., n., v.,* **–caved, –cav·ing.** —*adj.* hollow and curved like the inside of a circle or sphere. —*n.* a concave surface or thing. —*v.* make concave. [< L, < *com-* + *cavus* hollow] —**con·cave′ly,** *adv.* —**con·cave′ness,** *n.*

con·cav·i·ty (kon kav′ə ti), *n., pl.* **–ties. 1** a concave condition or quality. **2** a concave surface or thing.

con·ceal (kən sēl′), *v.* **1** hide. **2** keep secret. [< OF < L, < *com-* + *celare* hide] —**con·ceal′a·ble,** *adj.* —**con·ceal′er,** *n.* —**con·ceal′ment,** *n.*

con·cede (kən sēd′), *v.,* **–ced·ed, –ced·ing. 1** admit as true; admit. **2** give (what is asked or claimed); grant; yield. [< L, < *com-* + *cedere* yield] —**con·ced′ed·ly,** *adv.* —**con·ced′er,** *n.*

con·ceit (kən sēt′), *n.* **1** too high an opinion of oneself or of one's ability, importance, etc. **2** a witty thought or expression. **3** imagination; fancy.

con·ceit·ed (kən sēt′id), *adj.* having too high an opinion of oneself or one's ability, importance, etc.; vain. —**con·ceit′ed·ly,** *adv.* —**con·ceit′ed·ness,** *n.*

con·ceiv·a·ble (kən sēv′ə bəl), *adj.* that can be conceived or thought of; imaginable. —**con·ceiv′a·bil′i·ty, con·ceiv′a·ble·ness,** *n.* —**con·ceiv′a·bly,** *adv.*

con·ceive (kən sēv′), *v.,* **–ceived, –ceiv·ing. 1** form in the mind; think up; imagine. **2** have an idea or feeling; think. **3** put in words; express. **4** become pregnant. [< OF < L *concipere* take in < *com-* + *capere* take] —**con·ceiv′er,** *n.*

con·cen·trate (kon′sən trāt), *v.,* **–trat·ed, –trat·ing,** *n.* —*v.* **1** bring or come together to one place. **2** pay close attention; focus the mind. **3** make stronger, purer, or more intense; condense. —*n.* something that has been concentrated. [< L *com-* + *centrum* CENTER] —**con′cen·tra′tor,** *n.*

con·cen·tra·tion (kon′sən trā′shən), *n.* **1** a concentrating or being concentrated. **2** close attention. **3** something that has been concentrated.

concentration camp, camp where political enemies, prisoners of war, and interned foreigners are held.

con·cen·tric (kən sen′trik), *adj.* having the same center. —**con·cen′tri·cal,** *adj.* —**con·cen′tri·cal·ly,** *adv.* —**con′cen·tric′i·ty,** *n.*

con·cept (kon′sept), *n.* general notion; idea of a class of objects; idea. [< L *conceptus,* pp. of *concipere* CONCEIVE]

con·cep·tion (kən sep′shən), *n.* **1** act or power of conceiving. **2** a being conceived. **3** a becoming pregnant. **4** idea; impression. **5** design; plan. —**con·cep′tive,** *adj.*

con·cep·tu·al (kən sep′chü əl), *adj.* having to do with concepts or general ideas. —**con·cep′tu·al·ly,** *adv.*

con·cern (kən sėrn′), *v.* have to do with; have an interest for; be the business or affair of. —*n.* **1** whatever has to do with a person or thing; important matter; business affair. **2** interest. **3** a troubled state of mind; worry; anxiety; uneasiness. **4** a business company; firm. **5** relation; reference.

concern oneself, a take an interest; be busy. **b** be troubled or worried; be anxious or uneasy. [< Med.L, relate to, < L *com-* together + *cernere* sift]

con·cern·ing (kən sėr′ning), *prep.* having to do with; regarding; relating to; about.

con·cert (*n., adj.* kon′sėrt, –sərt; *v.* kən sėrt′), *n.* **1** a musical performance in which several musicians or singers take part. **2** agreement; harmony; union. —*adj.* used in concerts; for concerts. —*v.* arrange by agreement; plan or make together.

in concert, all together. [< F < Ital. *concerto* CONCERTO]

con·cert·ed (kən sėr′tid), *adj.* arranged by agreement; planned or made together; combined.

con·cer·ti·na (kon′sėr tē′nə), *n.* a small musical instrument somewhat like an accordion.

con·cer·to (kən cher′tō), *n., pl.* **–tos.** a long musical composition for one or

more principal instruments, such as a violin, piano, etc., accompanied by an orchestra. [< Ital. < L *concentus* symphony, harmony, ult. < *com-* together + *canere* sing]

con·ces·sion (kən sesh′ən), *n.* **1** a conceding. **2** anything conceded or yielded; admission; acknowledgment. **3** something conceded or granted by a government or controlling authority; grant. **4** place rented for a small business, as a newsstand, etc.

conch (kongk; konch), *n., pl.* **conchs** (kongks), **con·ches** (kon′chiz). a large, spiral sea shell. [< L < Gk. *konche*]

con·ci·erge (kon′si ėrzh′), *n.* **1** person who manages reservations and registers guests at a hotel or inn. **2** =innkeeper. **3** doorkeeper. **4** janitor. [< F *concierge* warden]

con·cil·i·ate (kən sil′i āt), *v.,* **–at·ed, –at·ing. 1** win over; soothe. **2** gain (good will, regard, favor, etc.) by friendly acts. **3** reconcile; bring into harmony. [< L *conciliatus < concilium* COUNCIL] —**con·cil′i·a′tion,** *n.* —**con·cil′i·a′tor,** *n.*

con·cil·i·a·to·ry (kən sil′i ə tô′ri; –tō′–), **con·cil·i·a·tive** (–i ā′tiv), *adj.* tending to win over, soothe, or reconcile. —**con·cil′i·a·to′ri·ly,** *adv.* —**con·cil′i·a·to′ri·ness,** *n.*

con·cise (kən sīs′), *adj.* expressing much in few words; brief but full of meaning. [< L *concisus < com-* + *caedere* cut] —**con·cise′ly,** *adv.* —**con·cise′ness,** *n.*

con·ci·sion (kən sizh′ən), *n.* **1** quality or state of being concise; brevity. **2** a cutting up or off.

con·clave (kon′klāv; kong′–), *n.* **1** a private meeting. **2** a meeting of the cardinals for the election of a pope. **3** rooms where the cardinals meet in private for this purpose. [< L, < *com-* with + *clavis* key]

con·clude (kən klüd′), *v.,* **–clud·ed, –clud·ing. 1** end; finish. **2** say in ending. **3** arrange; settle. **4** find out by thinking; reach (certain facts or opinions) as a result of reasoning; infer. **5** decide; resolve. [< L *concludere < com-* up + *claudere* close] —**con·clud′er,** *n.*

con·clu·sion (kən klü′zhən), *n.* **1** end. **2** the last main division of a speech, essay, etc. **3** a final result; outcome. **4** arrangement; settlement. **5** decision, judgment, or opinion reached by reasoning.

in conclusion, finally; lastly; to conclude.

con·clu·sive (kən klü′siv), *adj.* decisive; convincing; final. —**con·clu′sive·ness,** *n.*

con·coct (kon kokt′; kən–), *v.* prepare; make up. [< L *concoctus < com-* together + *coquere* cook] —**con·coct′er,** *n.* —**con·coc′tion,** *n.*

con·com·i·tant (kon kom′ə tənt; kən–), *adj.* accompanying; attending. —*n.* an accompanying thing, quality, or circumstance; accompaniment. [< L, < *com-* + *comitari* accompany] —**con·com′i·tance,** *n.* —**con·com′i·tant·ly,** *adv.*

con·cord (kon′kôrd; kong′–), *n.* **1** agreement; harmony; peace. **2** a harmonious combination of tones sounded together. **3** treaty. [< F < L *concordia,* ult. < *com–* together + *cor* heart]

Con·cord (kong′kərd), *n.* **1** town in E Massachusetts; the second battle of the American Revolution, April 19, 1775. **2** capital of New Hampshire, in the S part.

con·cord·ance (kon kôr′dəns; kən–), *n.* **1** agreement; harmony. **2** an alphabetical list of the principal words of a book with references to the passages in which they occur.

con·cord·ant (kon kôr′dənt; kən–), *adj.* agreeing; harmonious. —**con·cord′ant·ly,** *adv.*

con·cor·dat (kon kôr′dat), *n.* agreement; compact. [< F < LL *concordatum,* pp. of *concordare* make harmonious]

con·course (kon′kôrs; kong′–; –kōrs), *n.* **1** a running, flowing, or coming together. **2** crowd. **3** place where crowds come. **4** a large open space in a public building. **5** boulevard. [< OF < L *concursus* < *com–* together + *currere* run]

con·crete (*adj., n., and v.* **1** kon′krēt, kon krēt′; *v.* **2** kon krēt′), *adj., n., v.,* –**cret·ed,** –**cret·ing.** —*adj.* **1** existing as an actual object; real. **2** specific; particular. **3** naming a thing. *Sugar* is a concrete noun; *sweetness* is an abstract noun. **4** made of concrete. **5** formed into a mass; solid; hardened —*n.* mixture of crushed stone or gravel, sand, cement, and water that hardens as it dries. —*v.* **1** cover with concrete. **2** form or mix into a mass; harden into a mass. [< L *concretus* < *com–* together + *crescere* grow] —**con·crete′ness,** *n.*

con·cre·tion (kon krē′shən), *n.* **1** a forming into a mass; a solidifying. **2** a solidified mass; hard formation.

con·cu·bine (kong′kyə bīn; kon′–), *n.* **1** woman who lives with a man without being legally married to him. **2** wife who has an inferior rank, rights, etc. [< L, < *com–* with + *cubare* lie] —**con·cu′bi·nage,** *n.*

con·cu·pis·cent (kon kū′pə sənt), *adj.* **1** eagerly desirous. **2** lustful; sensual. [< L *concupiscens,* ult. < *com–* (intensive) + *cupere* desire] —**con·cu′pis·cence,** *n.*

con·cur (kən kėr′), *v.,* –**curred,** –**cur·ring.** **1** be of the same opinion; agree. **2** work together. **3** come together; happen at the same time. [< L, < *com–* together + *currere* run]

con·cur·rence (kən kėr′əns), *n.* **1** having the same opinion; agreement. **2** a working together. **3** a happening, at the same time. **4** a coming together. Also, **concurrency.**

con·cur·rent (kən kėr′ənt), *adj.* **1** happening at the same time. **2** cooperating. **3** agreeing; consistent; harmonious. **4** coming together; meeting in a point. —**con·cur′rent·ly,** *adv.*

con·cus·sion (kən kush′ən), *n.* **1** a sudden, violent shaking; shock. **2** injury to the brain, spine, etc., caused by a blow, fall, or other shock. [< L *concussio* < *con·cutere* shake violently < *com–* (intensive) + *quatere* shake]

con·demn (kən dem′), *v.* **1** express strong disapproval of. **2** pronounce guilty of a crime or wrong. **3** doom: *condemned to death.* **4** declare not sound or suitable for use. **5** take for public use under special provision of the law. [< OF < L, < *com–* + *damnare* cause loss to, condemn] —**con·dem′na·ble** *adj.* —**con·dem′na·to′ry,** *adj.* —**con·demn′er,** *n.* —**con·demn′ing·ly,** *adv.*

con·dem·na·tion (kon′dem nā′shən; –dəm–), *n.* **1** a condemning or being condemned. **2** cause or reason for condemning.

con·den·sa·tion (kon′den sā′shən), *n.* **1** a condensing or being condensed. **2** something condensed; condensed mass. **3** act of changing a gas or vapor to a liquid.

con·dense (kən dens′), *v.,* –**densed,** –**dens·ing.** **1** make or become denser or more compact. **2** make stronger; concentrate. **3** change from a gas or vapor to a liquid. **4** put into fewer words; express briefly. [<L, < *com–* + *densus* thick] —**con·den′sa·ble, con·den′si·ble,** *adj.* **con·den′sa·bil′i·ty, con·den′si·bil′i·ty,** *n.*

con·dens·er (kən den′sər), *n.* **1** person or thing that condenses something **2** device for receiving and holding a charge of electricity. **3** apparatus for changing gas or vapor into a liquid. **4** strong lens or lenses for concentrating light upon a small area.

con·de·scend (kon′di send′), *v.* come down willingly or graciously to the level of one's inferiors in rank. [< LL *condescendere.* See COM–, DESCEND.] —**con′de·scend′ence,** *n.*

con·de·scend·ing (kon′di sen′ding), *adj.* **1** coming down in a pleasant manner to the level of one's inferiors. **2** haughty or patronizing. —**con′de·scen′sion,** *n.*

con·dign (kən dīn′), *adj.* deserved; adequate; fitting: *condign punishment.* [< F < L *condignus* very worthy < *com–* completely + *dignus* worthy]

con·di·ment (kon′də mənt), *n.* something used to give flavor and relish to food, such as pepper and spices. [< L *condimentum* spice < *condire* put up, preserve]

con·di·tion (kən dish′ən), *n.* **1** state in which a person or thing is. **2** good condition: *keep in condition.* **3** rank; social position. **4** thing on which something else depends. **5** something demanded as an essential part of an agreement. —*v.* **1** put in good condition. **2** subject to a condition. **3** adapt or modify by shifting a response to a different stimulus.

conditions, set of circumstances. **on condition that,** if. [< L *condicio* agreement < *com–* together + *dicere* say] —**con·di′tion·er,** *n.*

con·di·tion·al (kən dish′ən əl), *adj.* **1** depending on something else; not absolute; limited. **2** expressing or containing a condition. —**con·di′tion·al′i·ty,** *n.* —**con·di′tion·al·ly,** *adv.*

con·di·tion·ed (kən dish′ənd), *adj.* **1** subject to certain conditions. **2** in or having a certain kind of condition. **3** based on or caused by psychological conditioning: *conditioned response.*

con·di·tion·ing (kən dish′ə ning), *n.* process of shaping the behavior of a person or animal by exposure to particular stimuli that cause a new response.

con·do (kon′dō), *n., pl.* –**dos.** *Informal.* =condominium.

con·dole (kən dōl′), *v.,* –**doled,** –**dol·ing.** express sympathy; sympathize. [< L, < *com–* with + *dolere* grieve, suffer] —**con·do′lence, con·dole′ment,** *n.* —**con·dol′er,** *n.* —**con·dol′ing·ly,** *adv.*

con·dom (kon′dəm), *n.* thin rubber sheath used by males to prevent the spread of AIDS and as a contraceptive device.

con·do·min·i·um (kon′də min′ē əm), *n.* **1 a** apartment house in which apartments are owned as separate pieces of real estate. **b** apartment in such a building. **2** joint control, esp. by two or more countries over another country or its government. [< NL < L *com–* with + *dominium* lordship < *dominus* master]

con·done (kən dōn′), *v.,* –**doned,** –**don·ing.** forgive; overlook. [< L, < *com–* up + *donare* give] —**con′do·na′tion,** *n.* —**con·don′er,** *n.*

con·dor (kon′dər), *n.* a large American vulture with a bare neck and head. [< Sp. < Peruvian *cuntur*]

con·duce (kən düs′; –dūs′), *v.,* –**duced,** –**duc·ing.** lead; contribute; be favorable. [< L, < *com–* together + *ducere* lead] —**con·duc′er,** *n.* —**con·du′cive,** *adj.* —**con·du′cive·ness,** *n.*

con·duct (*n.* kon′dukt; *v.* kən dukt′), *n.* **1** behavior; way of acting. **2** direction; management. **3** leading; guidance. [< v.] —*v.* **1** act in a certain way; behave: *conduct herself like a lady.* **2** direct; manage. **3** direct (an orchestra, etc.) as leader. **4** lead; guide. **5** transmit (heat, electricity, etc.); be a channel for. [< L *conductus* < *com–* together + *ducere* lead] —**con·duct′i·ble,** *adj.* —**con·duct′i·bil′i·ty,** *n.* —**con·duc′tive,** *adj.*

con·duct·ance (kən duk′təns), *n.* power of conducting electricity as affected by the shape, length, etc., of the conductor.

con·duc·tion (kən duk′shən), *n.* **1** transmission of heat, electricity, etc., by the transferring of energy from one particle to another. **2** a conveying: *conduction of water in a pipe.*

con·duc·tiv·i·ty (kon′duk tiv′ə ti), *n.* power of conducting heat, electricity, etc.

con·duc·tor (kən duk′tər), *n.* **1** person who conducts; director; manager; leader; guide. **2** director of an orchestra, chorus, etc. **3** person in charge of a streetcar, bus, railroad train, etc. **4** thing that transmits heat, electricity, light, sound, etc. **5** a lightning rod.

con·duit (kon′dit; –dü it), *n.* **1** channel or pipe for carrying liquids long distances. **2** tube or underground passage for electric wires. [< OF < Med.L *conductus* a leading, a pipe < L, contraction < *com*- together + *ducere* draw]

cone (kōn), *n., v.,* **coned, con·ing.** —*n.* **1** solid with a flat, round base that tapers evenly to a point at the top. **2** surface traced by a moving straight line, one point of which is fixed, that constantly touches a fixed curve. **3** anything shaped like a cone. **4** a cone-shaped, edible shell filled with ice cream. **5** part that bears the seeds on pine, cedar, fir, and other evergreen trees. **6** in machines, a cone-shaped part. —*v.* shape like a cone. [< L < Gk. *konos* pine cone, cone]

co·ney (kō′ni), *n., pl.* **co·neys.** =cony.

con·fec·tion (kən fek′shən), *n.* piece of candy, candied fruit, sugared nut, jam, etc. [< L *confectio* < *com*- up + *facere* make]

con·fec·tion·er (kən fek′shən ər), *n.* person who makes and sells candies, ice cream, etc.

con·fec·tion·er·y (kən fek′shən er′i), *n., pl.* **-er·ies. 1** candies, sweets, etc.; confections. **2** business of making or selling confections. **3** place where confections are made or sold; candy shop.

con·fed·er·a·cy (kən fed′ər ə si), *n., pl.* **-cies. 1** union of countries or states; group of people joined together for a special purpose. **2** league; alliance. **3** conspiracy.

the Confederacy, group of eleven S states that seceded from the United States in 1860 and 1861.

con·fed·er·ate (*adj., n.* kən fed′ər it; *v.* kən fed′ər āt), *adj., n., v.,* **-at·ed, -at·ing.** —*adj.* joined together for a special purpose; allied. —*n.* **1** country, person, etc., joined with another for a special purpose; ally; companion. **2** accomplice; partner in crime. —*v.* join (countries, people, etc.) together for a special purpose; ally.

Confederate, a person who lived in and supported the Confederacy. **b** of or belonging to the Confederacy. [< L, < *com*- together + *foedus* league]

con·fed·er·a·tion (kən fed′ər ā′shən), *n.* **1** a joining or being together in a league; federation. **2** group of countries, states, etc., joined together for a special purpose; league.

the Confederation, the confederation of the American states from 1781 to 1789.

con·fer (kən fėr′), *v.,* **-ferred, -fer·ring. 1** consult together; exchange ideas; talk things over. **2** give; bestow: *confer a medal.* [< L, *com*- together + *ferre* bring] —**con·fer′ment,** *n.*

con·fer·ee (kon′fər ē′), *n.* person who takes part in a conference.

con·fer·ence (kon′fər əns), *n.* **1** a meeting of interested persons to discuss a particular subject. **2** consultation with a person or a group of persons. **3** association of schools, churches, etc., joined together for some special purpose. **4** act of bestowing; conferment.

con·fer·ral (kən fėr′əl), *n.* a giving or bestowing.

con·fess (kən fes′), *v.* **1** acknowledge; admit; own up. **2** admit one's guilt. **3** tell (one's sins) to a priest in order to obtain forgiveness. **4** acknowledge one's belief in or adherence to. [< LL *confessare,* ult. < *com*- + *fateri* confess] —**con·fess′ed·ly,** *adv.* —**con·fess′er,** *n.*

con·fes·sion (kən fesh′ən), *n.* **1** acknowledgment; admission; owning up. **2** admission of guilt. **3** the telling of one's sins to a priest in order to obtain forgiveness. **4** thing confessed. **5** acknowledgment of belief; profession of faith. **6** belief acknowledged; creed.

con·fes·sion·al (kən fesh′ən əl), *n.* a small booth where a priest hears confessions. —*adj.* of or having to do with confession.

con·fes·sor (kən fes′ər), *n.* **1** person who confesses. **2** priest who has the authority to hear confessions.

con·fet·ti (kən fet′i), *n.* **1** bits of colored paper thrown about at carnivals, weddings, etc. **2** candies. [< Ital., pl., comfits. See CONFECTION.]

con·fi·dant (kon′fə dant′; kon′fə dant), *n.* person trusted with one's secrets, private affairs, etc.; close friend.

con·fi·dante (kon′fə dant′; kon′fə dant), *n.* a female confidant.

con·fide (kən fīd′), *v.,* **-fid·ed, -fid·ing. 1** tell as a secret. **2** entrust secrets, private affairs, etc. **3** hand over (a task, person, etc.) in trust; give to another for safekeeping. **4** put trust; have faith. [< L, < *com*- completely + *fidere* trust]

con·fi·dence (kon′fə dəns), *n.* **1** firm belief; trust. **2** firm belief in oneself and one's abilities. **3** boldness; too much boldness. **4** a feeling of trust; assurance that a person will not tell others what is said. **5** thing told as a secret. —*adj.* having to do with swindling that takes advantage of the victim's confidence.

confidence game, fraud in which the swindler persuades his victim to trust him.

confidence man, swindler who persuades his victim to trust him.

con·fi·dent (kon′fə dənt), *adj.* **1** firmly believing; certain; sure. **2** sure of oneself and one's abilities. **3** too bold; too sure. —*n.* close, trusted friend; confidant. —**con·fi·dent·ly,** *adv.*

con·fi·den·tial (kon′fə dən′shəl), *adj.* **1** told or written as a secret. **2** showing confidence. **3** trusted with secrets, private affairs, etc. —**con′fi·den′ti·al·i-**

ty, *n.* —**con′fi·den′tial·ly,** *adv.* —**con′fi·den′tial·ness,** *n.*

con·fig·u·ra·tion (kən fig′yə rā′shən), *n.* **1** the relative position of parts; manner of arrangement. **2** form; shape; outline. —**con·fig′u·ra′tion·al,** *adj.*

con·fine (*v.* kən fīn′; *n.* kon′fīn), *v.,* **-fined, -fin·ing.** —*v.* **1** keep within limits: restrict. **2** keep indoors; shut in. **3** imprison. —*n.* Usually, **confines.** boundary; border; limit.

be confined, give birth to a child. [< F, < *confins,* pl., bounds < L *confinium,* ult. < *com*- together + *finis* end, border] —**con·fine′ment,** *n.*

con·firm (kən fėrm′), *v.* **1** make certain. **2** approve; consent to. **3** strengthen; make firmer. **4** admit to full membership in a church. [< OF < L, < *com*- + *firmus* firm] —**con·firm′a·ble,** *adj.*

con·fir·ma·tion (kon′fər mā′shən), *n.* **1** a confirming. **2** thing that confirms; proof. **3** ceremony of admitting a person to full membership in a church.

con·firm·a·to·ry (kən fėr′mə tô′ri; –tō′–), **con·firm·a·tive** (–mə tiv), *adj.* confirming.

con·firmed (kən fėrmd′), *adj.* **1** firmly established; proved. **2** habitual; constant; chronic: *a confirmed invalid.* —**con·firm′ed·ly,** *adv.* —**con·firm′ed·ness,** *n.*

con·fis·cate (kon′fis kāt), *v.,* **-cat·ed, -cat·ing. 1** seize for the public treasury. **2** seize by authority; take and keep. [< L, orig., lay away in a chest, < *com*- + *fiscus* chest, public treasury] —**con′fis·ca′tion,** *n.* —**con′fis·ca′tor,** *n.*

con·fis·ca·to·ry (kən fis′kə tô′ri; –tō′–), *adj.* **1** of or like confiscation; tending to confiscate. **2** confiscating.

con·fla·gra·tion (kon′flə grā′shən), *n.* a big fire. [< L *conflagratio* < *com*- up + *flagrare* burn]

con·flate (kən flāt′), *v.,* **-flat·ed, -flat·ing. 1** bring or put together from various elements. **2** form (a text, etc.) by the combination of two readings. —**con·fla′tion,** *n.*

con·flict (*v.* kən flikt′; *n.* kon′flikt), *v.* **1** fight; struggle. **2** be directly opposed; disagree; clash. —*n.* **1** fight; struggle. **2** direct opposition; disagreement; clash. [< L *conflictus* < *com*- together + *fligere* strike] —**con·flic′tion,** *n.* —**con·flic′tive,** *adj.*

con·flu·ence (kon′flü əns), *n.* **1** a flowing together, as of two rivers. **2** a coming together of people or things; throng. [< L, < *com*- together + *fluere* flow] —**con′flu·ent,** *adj.*

con·flux (kon′fluks), *n.* =confluence.

con·form (kən fôrm′), *v.* **1** act according to law or rule; be in agreement with generally accepted standards. **2** correspond in form or character. **3** make similar. **4** adapt. [< OF < L, < *com*- + *formare* shape < *forma* a shape] —**con·form′er,** *n.*

con·form·a·ble (kən fôr′mə bəl), *adj.* **1** similar. **2** adapted; suited. **3** in agreement; agreeable; harmonious. 4 obedient; submissive. —**con·form′a·ble·ness,** *n.* —**con·form′a·bly,** *adv.*

con·form·ance (kən fôr′məns), *n.* =conformity.

con·for·ma·tion (kon′fôr mā′shən), *n.* 1 form of a thing resulting from the arrangement of its parts. 2 a symmetrical arrangement of the parts of a thing. 3 a conforming; adaptation.

con·form·ism (kən fôr′miz əm), *n.* 1 principle or policy of conformity. 2 belief or insistence on conformity in thought and behavior.

con·form·ist (kən fôr′mist), *n.* person who conforms.

con·form·i·ty (kən fôr′mə ti), *n., pl.* **-ties.** 1 similarity; corresponding; agreement. 2 action in agreement with generally accepted standards. 3 submission.

con·found (kon found′, kən– *for 1-3;* kon′found′ *for 4), v.* 1 confuse; mix up. 2 be unable to tell apart. 3 surprise and puzzle. 4 damn. *Confound* is used as a mild oath. [< OF < L, < *com*– together + *fundere* pour] —**con·found′er,** *n.*

con·found·ed (kon′foun′did; kən–), *adj.* 1 damned. *Confounded* is used as a mild oath. 2 hateful; detestable. —**con·found′ed·ly,** *adv.*

con·frere (kon′frār), *n.* fellow member; colleague. [< OF *confrere* < ML *confrater* < L *com*– together + *frāter* brother]

con·front (kən frunt′), *v.* 1 meet face to face; stand facing. 2 face boldly; oppose. 3 bring face to face; place before. [< F < Med.L, < L *com*– together + *frons* forehead] **con′fron ta′tion, con front′ment,** *n.*

Con·fu·cius (kən fū′shəs), *n.* 551?–478 B.C., Chinese philosopher and moral teacher. —**Con·fu′cian,** *adj., n.* —**Con·fu′cian·ism,** *n.* —**Con·fu′cian·ist,** *n.*

con·fuse (kən fūz′), *v.,* **-fused, -fus·ing.** 1 mix up; throw into disorder. 2 be unable to tell apart; mistake (one thing for another). 3 make uneasy and ashamed; embarrass. [< F < L *confusus,* pp. of *confundere.* See CONFOUND.] —**con·fus′ed·ly,** *adv.* —**con·fus′ed·ness,** *n.* —**con·fus′ing·ly,** *adv.*

con·fu·sion (kən fū′zhən), *n.* 1 act or fact of confusing. 2 confused condition; disorder. 3 failure to distinguish clearly. 4 uneasiness and shame. —**con·fu′sion·al,** *adj.*

con·fute (kən fūt′), *v.,* **-fut·ed, -fut·ing.** 1 prove to be false or incorrect. 2 make useless. [< L *confutare*] —**con′fu·ta′tion,** *n.* —**con·fut′er,** *n.*

Cong., 1 Congregation. 2 Congress; Congressional.

con·geal (kən jēl′), *v.* 1 freeze. 2 thicken; stiffen. [< OF < L, < *com*– up + *gelare* freeze] —**con·geal′a·ble,** *adj.* —**con·geal′er,** *n.* —**con·geal′ment,** *n.*

con·gen·ial (kən jēn′yəl), *adj.* 1 having similar tastes and interests; getting on well together. 2 agreeable; suitable: *he seeks more congenial work.* [< L, < *com*–

together + *genialis* < *genius* spirit] —**con·ge′ni·al′i·ty,** *n.* —**con·gen′ial·ly,** *adv.*

con·gen·i·tal (kən jen′ə təl), *adj.* present at birth. [< L *congenitus* born with. See GENITAL.] —**con·gen′i·tal·ly,** *adv.*

con·ger (kong′gər), or **conger eel,** *n.* a large ocean eel that is caught for food along the coasts of Europe. [< OF < L < Gk. *gongros*]

con·ge·ries (kon jir′ēz, kon′jər ēz), *n. sing. or pl.* collection; heap; mass.

con·gest (kən jest′), *v.* 1 fill too full; over-crowd. 2 cause too much blood or mucus to gather in (one part of the body). 3 become too full of blood or mucus. [< L *congestus* < *com*– together + *gerere* carry] —**con·ges′tion,** *n.* —**con·ges′tive,** *adj.*

con·glom·er·ate (*v.* kən glom′ər āt; *adj., n.* kən glom′ər it), *v.,* **-at·ed, -at·ing, ** *adj., n.* —*v.* gather in a rounded mass. —*adj.* 1 gathered into a rounded mass; clustered. 2 made up of miscellaneous materials gathered from various sources. —*n.* 1 mass formed of fragments. 2 rock consisting of pebbles, gravel, etc., held together by a cementing material. 3 corporation or business composed of several different and separate companies. [< L, < *com*– + *glomus* ball] —**con·glom′er·a′tion,** *n.*

Con·go (kong′gō), *n.* 1 **Democratic Republic of the,** republic in C Africa, formerly Zaire or the Belgian Congo. 2 **Republic of the,** republic in W C Africa on the Atlantic, formerly part of French Equatorial Africa.

congo eel or **snake,** an eel like amphibian that has very small, weak legs.

con·grat·u·late (kən grach′ə lāt), *v.,* **-lated, -lat·ing.** express one's pleasure at the happiness or good fortune of. [< L, < *com* + *gratulari* show joy] —**con·grat′u·la′tor,** *n.* —**con·grat′u·la·to′ry,** *adj.*

con·grat·u·la·tion (kən grach′ə lā′shən), *n.* 1 act of congratulating. 2 Usually, **congratulations.** expression of pleasure at another's happiness or good fortune.

con·gre·gate (kong′grə gāt), *v.,* **-gat·ed, -gat·ing,** *adj.* —*v.* come together into a crowd or mass. —*adj.* assembled; collected. [< L *congregatus* < *com*– together + *grex* flock]

con·gre·ga·tion (kong′grə gā′shən), *n.* 1 act of congregating. 2 a gathering of people or things; assembly. 3 group of people gathered together for religious worship. 4 a religious community or order with a common rule but not under solemn vows.

con·gre·ga·tion·al (kong′grə gā′shən əl), *adj.* 1 of a congregation; done by a congregation. 2 **Congregational,** of or belonging to Congregationalism or Congregationalists.

con·gre·ga·tion·al·ism (kong′grə gā′shən əl iz′əm), *n.* 1 system of church government in which each individual church governs itself. 2 **Congregation-**

alism, principles and system of organization of a Protestant denomination in which each individual church governs itself. —**con′gre·ga′tion·al·ist, Con′gre·ga′tion·al·ist,** *n., adj.*

con·gress (kong′gris), *n.* 1 the lawmaking body of a nation, esp. of a republic. 2 **Congress, a** the national lawmaking body of the United States, consisting of the Senate and House of Representatives. **b** its session of two years. 3 formal meeting of representatives to discuss some subject. —*v.* meet in congress. [< L *congressus* < *com*– together + *gradi* go]

con·gres·sion·al (kən gresh′ən əl), *adj.* 1 of a congress. 2 **Congressional,** of Congress.

con·gress·man (kong′gris mən), *n., pl.* **-men.** Often, **Congressman.** 1 member of Congress. 2 member of the House of Representatives.

con·gress·wom·an (kong′gris wùm′ ən), *n., pl.* **-wom·en.** a female congresswoman.

con·gru·ent (kong′grù ənt), *adj.* 1 agreeing; harmonious. 2 exactly coinciding. [< L, < *congruere* agree] —**con′gru·ence, con′gru·en·cy,** *n.* —**con′gru·ent·ly,** *adv.*

con·gru·i·ty (kən grü′ə ti), *n., pl.* **-ties.** 1 agreement; harmony. 2 the exact coincidence of lines, angles, figures, etc. 3 point of agreement.

con·gru·ous (kong′grù əs), *adj.* 1 agreeing; harmonious. 2 fitting; appropriate. 3 exactly coinciding. —**con′gru·ous·ly,** *adv.* —**con′gru·ous·ness,** *n.*

con·ic (kon′ik), **con·i·cal** (–ə kəl), *adj.* 1 cone-shaped; like a cone. 2 of a cone. —**con′i·cal·ly,** *adv.*

co·ni·fer (kō′nə fər; kon′ə–), *n.* any of a large group of trees and shrubs, most of which are evergreen and bear cones. [< L, < *conus* cone (< Gk. *konos*) + *ferre* to bear] —**co·nif′er·ous,** *adj.*

conj., 1 conjugation. 2 conjunction.

con·jec·tur·al (kən jek′chər əl), *adj.* 1 involving conjecture. 2 inclined to conjecture. —**con·jec′tur·al·ly,** *adv.*

con·jec·ture (kən jek′chər), *n., v.,* **-tured, -tur·ing.** —*n.* 1 formation of an opinion without sufficient evidence for proof; guessing. 2 a guess. —*v.* guess. [< L *conjectura* < *com*– together + *jacere* throw] —**con·jec′tur·a·ble,** *adj.* —**con·jec′tur·ably,** *adv.* —**con·jec′tur·er,** *n.*

con·join (kən join′), *v.* unite. —**conjoin′er,** *n.*

con·joint (kən joint′; kon′joint), *adj.* 1 joined together; united. 2 joint. —**conjoint′ly,** *adv.*

con·ju·gal (kon′jə gəl), *adj.* 1 of marriage; having to do with marriage. 2 of husband and wife. [< L *conjugalis* < *com*– with + *jugum* yoke] —**con′jugal·ly,** *adv.*

con·ju·gate (*v.* kon′jə gāt; *adj., n.* kon′jə git, –gāt), *v.,* **-gat·ed, -gat·ing,** *adj., n.* —*v.* 1 give the forms of (a verb) according to a systematic arrangement. 2 join together; couple. —*adj.* joined together; coupled. —*n.* word derived from the same root as another. [< L, < *com-* with + *jugum* yoke] —**con′ju·ga′tive**, *adj.* —**con′ju·ga′tor**, *n.*

con·ju·ga·tion (kon′jə gā′shən), *n.* **1** systematic arrangement of the forms of a verb. **2** group of verbs having similar forms in such an arrangement. **3** act of giving the forms of a verb according to such an arrangement. **4** a joining together; a coupling.

con·junc·tion (kən jungk′shən), *n.* **1** act of joining together; union; combination. **2** word that connects words, phrases, clauses, or sentences. **3** the apparent nearness of two or more celestial bodies. [< L *conjunctio* < *com-* with + *jungere* join]

con·junc·ti·va (kon′jungk tī′və), *n., pl.* **-vas, -vae** (–vē) the mucous membrane that covers the inner surface of the eyelids.

con·junc·tive (kən jungk′tiv), *adj.* **1** joining together. **2** joined together; joint. **3** like a conjunction. *When* is a conjunctive adverb. —*n.* a conjunctive word; conjunction. —**con·junc′tive·ly**, *adv.*

con·junc·ti·vi·tis (kən jungk′tə vī′tis), *n.* inflammation of the conjunctiva.

con·ju·ra·tion (kon′jŭ rā′shən), *n.* **1** act of invoking by a sacred name. **2** magic form of words used in conjuring; magic spell.

con·jure (kun′jər; kon′–), *v.,* **-jured, -jur·ing. 1** compel (a spirit, devil, etc.) to appear or disappear by magic words. **2** summon a devil, spirit, etc. **3** cause to be or happen by magic. **4** practice magic.
conjure up, a cause to appear in a magic way. **b** cause to appear in the mind. [< OF < L *conjurare* make a compact < *com-* together + *jurare* swear] —**con′jur·er, con′jur·or**, *n.*

conk (kongk), *Slang.* **conk out,** break down. [dial. < *conk*(er) a blow on the nose < *conk* nose < *conch* shell]

con man, confidence man; swindler.

Conn., Connecticut.

con·nect (kə nekt′), *v.* **1** join (one thing to another); link (two things together). **2** join in some business or interest. **3** associate in the mind. [< L, < *com-* together + *nectere* tie] —**con·nect′ed·ly**, *adv.* —**con·nect′er, con·nec′tor**, *n.*

con·nect·ed (kə nek′tid), *adj.* **1** joined together; fastened together. **2** linked by telephone, cell phone, or email. **3** joined in a sequence. **4** having social ties and associates.

Con·nect·i·cut (kə net′ə kət), *n.* one of the New England states in NE United States.

con·nec·tion (kə nek′shən), *n.* **1** act of connecting. **2** condition of being joined together; union. **3** thing that connects. **4** any kind of practical relation with another thing. **5** group of people associated in some way. **6** thinking of persons or things together. **7** a relative. —**con·nec′tion·al**, *adj.*

con·nec·tive (kə nek′tiv), *adj.* that connects. —*n.* **1** thing that connects. **2** word used to connect words, phrases, and clauses. Conjunctions and relative pronouns are connectives. —**con·nec′tive·ly**, *adv.* —**con·nec·tiv′i·ty**, *n.*

connective tissue, tissue that connects, supports, or encloses other tissues and organs in the body.

conn·ing tower (kon′ing), a small tower on the deck of a submarine, used as an entrance and as a place for observation.

con·nip·tion (kə nip′shən), *n.* or **conniption fit,** *Informal.* fit of hysterical excitement.
conniptions, hysterics.

con·niv·ance (kə nīv′əns), **con·niv·an·cy** (–ən si), *n.* **1** act of conniving. **2** pretended ignorance or secret encouragement of wrongdoing.

con·nive (kə nīv′), *v.,* **-nived, -niv·ing. 1** give aid to wrongdoing by not telling of it, or by helping it secretly. **2** cooperate secretly. [< L *connivere* shut the eyes, wink < *com-* together + *niv-* press] —**con·niv′er**, *n.*

con·nois·seur (kon′ə sėr′), *n.* expert; critical judge. [< F, ult. < L, < *co-* + *gnoscere* recognize]

con·no·ta·tion (kon′ə tā′shən), *n.* **1** a connoting. **2** what is suggested in addition to the simple meaning. —**con′no·ta′tive**, *adj.* —**con′no·ta′tive·ly**, *adv.*

con·note (kə nōt′), *v.,* **-not·ed, -not·ing.** suggest in addition to the literal meaning; imply. [< Med.L, < L *com-* with + *notare* to NOTE]

con·nu·bi·al (kə nü′bi əl; –nū′–), *adj.* of or having to do with marriage. [< L, < *com-* + *nubere* marry] —**con·nu′bi·al′i·ty**, *n.* —**con·nu′bi·al·ly**, *adv.*

con·quer (kong′kər), *v.* **1** get by fighting; win in war. **2** overcome by force; defeat. **3** be victorious. [< OF < L, < *com-* + *quaerere* seek] —**con′quer·a·ble**, *adj.* —**con′quer·ing**, *adj.* —**con′quer·ing·ly**, *adv.* —**con′quer·or**, *n.*

con·quest (kon′kwest; kong′–), *n.* **1** act of conquering. **2** thing conquered; land, people, etc., conquered. **3** person whose love or favor has been won. [< OF, < *conquerre* CONQUER]

con·quis·ta·dor (kon kwis′tə dôr′), *n., pl.* **-dors, -dores. 1** a Spanish conqueror in North or South America during the 16th century. **2** conqueror. [< Sp., < *conquistar* CONQUER]

cons., 1 consecrated. **2** consonant. **3** constitutional. **4** construction.

Cons., 1 Conservative. **2** Consolidated. **3** Constable. **4** Constitution. **5** Consul. **6** Consulting.

con·san·guin·e·ous (kon′sang gwin′i əs), *adj.* descended from the same parent or ancestor. [< L, < *com-* together + *sanguis* blood] —**con′san·guin′e·ous·ly**, *adv.* —**con′san·guin′·i·ty**, *n.*

con·science (kon′shəns), *n.* **1** ideas and feelings within a person that warn him of what is wrong. **2** conscientiousness.

[< OF < L *conscientia* < *com-* + *scire* know] —**con′science·less**, *adj.*

con·sci·en·tious (kon′shi en′shəs), *adj.* **1** careful to do what one knows is right; controlled by conscience. **2** done with care to make it right. —**con′sci·en′tious·ly**, *adv.* —**con′sci·en′tious·ness**, *n.*

conscientious objector, person whose beliefs forbid him to take an active part in warfare.

con·scion·a·ble (kon′shən ə bəl), *adj.* according to conscience; just. —**con′scion·a·bly**, *adv.*

con·scious (kon′shəs), *adj.* **1** aware; knowing. **2** able to feel. **3** known to oneself; felt: *conscious guilt.* **4** meant; intended: *a conscious lie.* **5** self-conscious; shy; embarrassed. [< L *conscius* < *com-* + *scire* know] —**con′scious·ly**, *adv.*

con·scious·ness (kon′shəs nis), *n.* **1** state of being conscious; awareness. **2** all the thoughts and feelings of a person. **3** awareness of what is going on about one.

con·script (*v.* kən skript′; *adj., n.* kon′skript), *v.* **1** compel by law to enlist in the army or navy; draft. **2** take for government use. —*adj.* conscripted; drafted. —*n.* a conscripted soldier or sailor. [< L *conscriptus* < *com-* down + *scribere* write] —**con·scrip′tion**, *n.*

con·se·crate (kon′sə krāt), *v.,* **-crat·ed, -crat·ing**, *adj.* —*v.* **1** set apart as sacred; make holy: *a church is consecrated to worship.* **2** devote to a purpose. —*adj. Archaic.* consecrated. [< L *consecratus* < *com-* + *sacer* sacred] —**con′se·cra′tion**, *n.* —**con′se·cra′tor**, *n.*

con·sec·u·tive (kən sek′yə tiv), *adj.* **1** following without interruption; successive. **2** made up of parts that follow each other in logical order. [< F, < L *consecutus* following closely < *com-* up + *sequi* follow] —**con·sec′u·tive·ly**, *adv.* —**con·sec′u·tive·ness**, *n.*

con·sen·su·al (kən sen′shü əl), *adj.* happening or done by mutual consent.

con·sen·sus (kən sen′səs), *n.* general agreement. [< L, < *consentire* CONSENT]

con·sent (kən sent′), *v.* agree; give approval or permission. —*n.* **1** agreement; permission. **2** harmony; accord. [< OF < L, < *com-* together + *sentire* feel, think] —**con·sent′er**, *n.*

con·se·quence (kon′sə kwens; –kwəns), *n.* **1** act or fact of following something as its effect. **2** result; effect. **3** a logical result; deduction; inference. **4** importance.
in consequence, as a result; therefore.
in consequence of, as a result of; because of.
take the consequences, accept what happens as a result of one's actions.

con·se·quent (kon′sə kwent; –kwənt), *adj.* **1** following as an effect; resulting. **2** following as a logical conclusion. **3** logically consistent. —*n.* thing that follows something else; result; effect. [< L *consequens,* ppr. of *consequi.* See CONSECUTIVE.]

con·se·quen·tial (kon´sə kwen´shəl), *adj.* 1 following as an effect; resulting. 2 important. 3 self-important; pompous. —**con´se·quen´ti·al´i·ty**, *n.* —**con´se·quen´tial·ly**, *adv.* —**con´se·quen´tial·ness**, *n.*

con·se·quent·ly (kon´sə kwent li;–kwənt-), *adv.* as a result; therefore.

con·ser·van·cy (kən sėr´ven si), *n.* 1 conservation of natural resources. 2 organization dedicated to conservation of open spaces, wildlife, etc. 3 area protected from development by such an organization.

con·ser·va·tion (kon´sər vā´shən), *n.* 1 a protecting from harm, loss, or from being used up. 2 the official protection and care of forests, rivers, etc. 3 forest, etc., under official protection and care. —**con´ser·va´tion·al**, *adj.* —**con´ser·va´tion·ist**, *n.*

conservation of energy, principle that the total amount of energy in the universe does not vary.

con·serv·a·tive (kən sėr´və tiv), *adj.* 1 inclined to keep things as they are; opposed to change. 2 Often, **Conservative.** of or belonging to a political party that opposes changes in national institutions. 3 cautious; moderate. —*n.* 1 a conservative person. 2 Often, **Conservative.** member of a conservative political party. 3 means of preserving. —**con·serv´a·tism, con·serv´a·tive·ness,** *n.* —**con·serv´a·tive·ly**, *adv.*

con·ser·va·tor (kən sėr´və tər), *n.* 1 preserver; guardian, esp. of old documents, works of art, etc. 2 legal guardian or administrator of a business or property.

con·serv·a·to·ry (kən sėr´və tô´ri; –tō-), *n., pl.* **-ries.** 1 greenhouse or glass-enclosed room for growing and displaying plants and flowers. 2 *U.S.* school for instruction in music, art, or oratory. 3 preservative.

con·serve (*v.* kən sėrv´; *n.* kon´sėrv, kən sėrv´), *v.,* **-served, -serv·ing,** *n.* —*v.* 1 protect from harm, loss, or from being used up. 2 preserve (fruit) with sugar. [< L, < *com–* + *servare* preserve] —*n.* Often, **conserves.** fruit preserved in sugar; jam. [< F, < *conserver.* See v.] —**con·serv´a·ble**, *adj.* —**con·serv´er**, *n.*

con·sid·er (kən sid´ər), *v.* 1 think about in order to decide. 2 think to be; think of as. 3 allow for; take into account. 4 be thoughtful of (others and their feelings). [< L *considerare,* orig., examine the stars, < *com–* + *sidus* star]

con·sid·er·a·ble (kən sid´ər ə bəl), *adj.* 1 worth thinking about; important. 2 not a little; much. —**con·sid´er·a·bly**, *adv.*

con·sid·er·ate (kən sid´ər it), *adj.* 1 thoughtful of others' feelings. 2 deliberate. —**con·sid´er·ate·ly**, *adv.* —**con·sid´er·ate·ness**, *n.*

con·sid·er·a·tion (kən sid´ər ā´shən), *n.* 1 act of thinking about in order to decide. 2 something thought of as a reason. 3 money or other payment. 4 thoughtfulness for others and their feelings.

in consideration of (or **for**), **a** because of. **b** in return for.

take into consideration, take into account.

under consideration, being thought about.

con·sid·er·ing (kən sid´ər ing), *prep.* taking into account; making allowance for. —*adv.* taking everything into account: *he does very well, considering.*

con·sign (kən sīn´), *v.* 1 hand over; deliver. 2 transmit; send. 3 set apart; assign. 4 transmit, as by public carrier, esp. for safekeeping or sale. [< F < L *consignare* furnish with a seal < *com–* + *signum* seal] —**con·sign´a·ble**, *adj.* —**con´sign·ee´**, *n.* —**con·sign´or, con·sign´er**, *n.*

con·sign·ment (kən sīn´mənt), *n.* 1 act of consigning. 2 shipment sent to a person or company for safekeeping or sale.

on consignment, delivered to a person or company without payment until the goods are sold.

con·sist (kən sist´), *v.* 1 be made up; be formed. 2 agree; be in harmony.

consist in, be contained in; be made up of. [< L, come to a stand, exist, consist, < *com–* + *sistere* stand]

con·sist·en·cy (kən sis´tən si), **con·sist·ence** (-təns), *n., pl.* **-cies; -ces.** 1 degree of firmness or stiffness. 2 a keeping to the same principles, course of action, etc. 4 harmony; agreement.

con·sist·ent (kən sis´tənt), *adj.* 1 keeping or inclined to keep to the same principles, course of action, etc. 2 in agreement; in accord. 3 cohering. —**con·sist´ent·ly**, *adv.*

con·sis·to·ry (kən sis´tə ri), *n., pl.* **-ries.** 1 a church council or court. 2 place where it meets.

con·so·la·tion (kon´sə lā´shən), *n.* 1 comfort. 2 a comforting person, thing, or event. —**con·sol´a·to´ry**, *adj.*

con·sole¹ (kən sōl´), *v.,* **-soled, -sol·ing.** comfort. [< L, < *com–* + *solari* soothe] —**con·sol´a·ble**, *adj.* —**con·sol´er**, *n.*

con·sole² (kon´sōl), *n.* 1 the desklike part of an organ containing the keyboard, stops, and pedals. 2 a heavy, ornamental bracket. [< F]

con·sol·i·date (kən sol´ə dāt), *v.,* **-dat·ed, -dat·ing.** 1 unite; combine; merge. 2 make or become solid. 3 organize and strengthen (a newly captured position) so that it can be used against the enemy. [< L, < *com–* + *solidus* solid] —**con·sol´i·da´tion**, *n.*

con·sol·ing (kən sōl´ing), *adj.* that consoles. —**con·sol´ing·ly**, *adv.*

con·som·mé (kon´sə mā´), *n.* a clear soup made by boiling meat in water. [< F, pp. of *consommer* CONSUMMATE]

con·so·nant (kon´sə nənt), *n.* 1 a sound during the articulation of which the breath stream is impeded to a greater or lesser degree, as the sound of *b* in *boy* or the sound of *f* in *fast.* 2 a letter representing such a sound. —*adj.* 1 harmonious; in agreement; in accord. 2 agreeing in sound. 3 =consonantal. [< L, < *com–* together + *sonare* sound] —**con´so·nance**, *n.* —**con´so·nant·ly**, *adv.*

con·so·nan·tal (kon´sə nan´təl), *adj.* having to do with a consonant or its sound.

con·sort (*n.* kon´sôrt; *v.* kən sôrt´), *n.* 1 husband or wife. 2 an associate. 3 ship accompanying another. —*v.* 1 associate. 2 agree; accord. [< F < L, sharer, < *com–* with + *sors* lot]

con·sor·ti·um (kən sôr´shi əm), *n., pl.* **-ti·a** (-shi ə). 1 legal partnership; association. 2 an agreement among bankers of several nations to give financial aid to another nation or to finance a project too large for only one entity to support. 3 group, association, etc. joined by a similar agreement. [< L, partnership]

con·spic·u·ous (kən spik´yu əs), *adj.* 1 easily seen. 2 worthy of notice; remarkable. [< L *conspicuus* visible < *com–* + *specere* look at] —**con·spic´u·ous·ly**, *adv.* —**con·spic´u·ous·ness**, *n.*

con·spir·a·cy (kən spir´ə si), *n., pl.* **-cies.** 1 secret planning with others to do something wrong. 2 plot. —**con·spir´a·tor**, *n.*

con·spire (kən spīr´), *v.,* **-spired, -spir·ing.** 1 plan secretly with others to do something wrong; plot. 2 act together. [< L, < *com–* together + *spirare* breathe] —**con·spir´a·to´ri·al**, *adj.* —**con·spir´er**, *n.*

con·sta·ble (kon´stə bəl, kun´-), *n.* a police officer; policeman. [< OF < LL *comes stabuli* count of the stable; later, chief household officer] —**con´sta·ble·ship´**, *n.*

con·stab·u·lar·y (kən stab´yə ler´i), *n., pl.* **-lar·ies.** 1 constables of a district. 2 police force organized like an army; state police.

con·stant (kon´stənt), *adj.* 1 always the same; not changing. 2 never stopping. 3 happening often or again and again. 4 faithful; loyal; steadfast. —*n.* 1 thing that is always the same. 2 quantity assumed to be invariable throughout a given discussion. [< L, < *com–* (intensive) + *stare* stand] —**con´stan·cy**, *n.*

Con·stan·tine the Great (kon´stən tīn; –tēn), A.D. 288?–337, Roman emperor from 324 to 337, who established the city of Constantinople.

Con·stan·ti·no·ple (kon´stan tə nō´pəl), *n.* former name of Istanbul.

con·stant·ly (kon´stənt li), *adv.* 1 without change. 2 without stopping. 3 often.

con·stel·la·tion (kon´stə lā´shən), *n.* 1 a group of stars. 2 division of the heavens occupied by such a group. [< LL, < L *com–* together + *stella* star]

con·ster·na·tion (kon´stər nā´shən), *n.* great dismay; paralyzing terror. [< L, < *consternare* terrify, var. of *consternere* lay low < *com–* + *sternere* strew]

con·sti·pate (kon'stə pāt), v., **-pat·ed, -pat·ing.** cause constipation in. [< L, < *com-* together + *stipare* press] —**con'sti·pat´ed,** adj.

con·sti·pa·tion (kon'stə pā'shən), n. sluggish condition of the bowels.

con·stit·u·en·cy (kən stich'ü ən si), n., pl. **-cies. 1** voters in a district. **2** the district; the people living there.

con·stit·u·ent (kən stich'ü ənt), adj. **1** forming a necessary part; that composes. **2** appointing; electing. **3** having the power to make or change a political constitution. —n. **1** a necessary part of a whole; component. **2** person who votes or appoints; voter.

con·sti·tute (kon'stə tüt; –tūt), v., **-tut·ed, -tut·ing. 1** make up; form. **2** appoint; elect. **3** set up; establish. [< L *constitutus* < *com-* + *statuere* set up]

con·sti·tu·tion (kon'stə tü'shən; –tū´–), n. **1** way in which a person or thing is organized; nature; makeup: *a healthy constitution.* **2** system of fundamental principles according to which a nation, state, or group is governed. **3** document stating these principles. **4** appointing; making. **5 Constitution,** the constitution by which the United States is governed. It was drawn up in 1787 and became effective in 1788.

con·sti·tu·tion·al (kon'stə tü'shən əl; –tū´–), adj. **1** of or in the constitution of a person or thing. **2** of, in, or according to the constitution of a nation, state, or group. **3** for one's health. —n. walk or other exercise taken for one's health. —**con´sti·tu'tion·al·ly,** adv.

con·sti·tu·tion·al·i·ty (kon'stə tü´shən al'ə ti; –tū´–), n. quality of being constitutional.

con·strain (kən strān'), v. **1** force; compel. **2** confine; imprison. **3** repress; restrain. [< OF *constreindre* < L, < *com-* together + *stringere* pull tightly] —**con·strain'a·ble,** adj. —**con·strain'er,** n.

con·strained (kən strānd'), adj. forced. —**con·strain'ed·ly,** adv.

con·straint (kən strānt'), n. **1** confinement. **2** restraint. **3** forced or unnatural manner. **4** force; compulsion. [< OF, < *constreindre* CONSTRAIN]

con·strict (kən strikt'), v. draw together; contract; compress. [< L *constrictus,* of *constringere* CONSTRAIN] —**con·stric'tion,** n. —**con·stric'tive,** adj.

con·stric·tor (kən strik'tər), n. **1** snake that kills its prey by squeezing it with its coils. **2** person or thing that constricts.

con·struct (v. kən strukt'; n. kon'strukt), v. **1** put together; build. **2** draw (a figure, etc.) so as to fulfill given conditions. —n. thing constructed. [< L *constructus* < *com-* up + *struere* pile] —**con·struc'tor, con·struct'er,** n.

con·struc·tion (kən struk'shən), n. **1** act of constructing. **2** way in which a thing is constructed. **3** thing constructed; a building. **4** meaning; explanation; interpretation. **5** arrangement of words in a sentence, clause, phrase, etc. —**con·struc'tion·al,** adj. —**con·struc'tion·ist,** n.

con·struc·tive (kən struk'tiv), adj. **1** tending to construct; building up; helpful. **2** structural. **3** not directly expressed; inferred. —**con·struc'tive·ly,** adv. —**con·struc'tive·ness,** n.

con·strue (kən strü'), v., **-strued, -stru·ing. 1** show the meaning of; explain; interpret. **2** translate. **3** analyze the arrangement and connection of words in (a sentence, clause, phrase, etc.). [< L *construere* CONSTRUCT] —**con·stru'a·ble,** adj. —**con·stru'er,** n.

con·sul (kon'səl), n. **1** government official who lives in a foreign city and looks after business interests of his or her own country. **2** either of the two chief magistrates of the ancient Roman republic. [< L, prob. orig., one who consults the senate] —**con'su·lar,** adj. —**con'sul·ship,** n.

con·su·late (kon'sə lit), n. **1** the duties, authority, and position of a consul. **2** a consul's term of office. **3** an official residence or offices of a consul.

consul general, pl. **consuls general,** consul of the highest rank.

con·sult (kən sult'), v. **1** seek information or advice from; refer to. **2** exchange ideas; talk things over. **3** take into consideration; have regard for. [< L, < *consulere* take counsel, consult] —**con·sult'a·ble,** adj.

con·sult·an·cy (kən sul'tən si), n., pl. **-cies.** work or business of a consultant.

con·sult·ant (kən sul'tənt), n. **1** person who consults another. **2** person who gives professional or technical advice.

con·sul·ta·tion (kon'səl tā'shən), n. **1** act of consulting. **2** a meeting to exchange ideas or talk things over. —**con·sult'a·tive,** adj.

con·sume (kən süm'), v., **-sumed, -sum·ing. 1** use up. **2** eat or drink up. **3** destroy; burn up. **4** waste away; be destroyed. **5** spend; waste (time, money, etc.). [< L, < *com-* + *sumere* take up] —**con·sum'a·ble,** adj.

con·sum·er (kən süm'ər), n. **1** person or thing that consumes. **2** person who uses food, clothing, or anything grown or made by producers.

con·sum·er·ism (kən süm'ər izm), n. **1** movement to protect the consumer from shoddy products, misleading information in marketing products, and to protect the environment from damage caused by manufacturing and production practices. **2** concentration on constantly expanding both the production of consumer goals and the market for them. —**con·sum'er·ist,** n.

Consumer Price Index, measure of increases or decreases in prices paid by consumers for certain goods and services.

con·sum·mate (v. kon'sə māt; adj. kon´-sə mət, kən sum'it), v., **-mat·ed, -mat·ing,** adj. —v. **1** complete; fulfill. **2** complete (a marriage) by sexual intercourse. —adj. complete; perfect; in the highest degree. [< L, < *consummare* bring to a peak < *com-* + *summa* highest degree] —**con·sum'mate·ly,** adv. —**con'sum·ma´tor,** n.

con·sum·ma·tion (kon'sə mā'shən), n. completion; fulfillment.

con·sump·tion (kən sump'shən), n. **1** act of using up; use. **2** amount used up. **3** destruction. **4** a wasting disease of the lungs or of some other part of the body; tuberculosis of the lungs.

con·sump·tive (kən sump'tiv), adj. **1** having or likely to have tuberculosis of the lungs. **2** of tuberculosis of the lungs. **3** tending to consume; destructive; wasteful. —n. person who has tuberculosis of the lungs. —**con·sump'tive·ly,** adv. —**con·sump'tive·ness,** n.

cont., **1** containing; contents. **2** continued.

con·tact (kon'takt), n. **1** condition of touching; touch. **2** connection. —v. *Colloq.* get in touch with; make a connection with. [< L *contactus* a touching < *com-* + *tangere* touch]

contact lens, thin plastic lens to correct vision which covers the front of the eyeball and is held in place by the fluid of the eye.

con·ta·gion (kən tā'jən), n. **1** the spreading of disease by contact. **2** disease spread in this way; contagious disease. **3** means by which disease is spread. **4** the spreading of any influence from one person to another. [< L *contagio* touching. See CONTACT.]

con·ta·gious (kən tā'jəs), adj. **1** spread by contact: *scarlet fever is a contagious disease.* **2** causing contagious diseases. —**con·ta'gious·ly,** adv. —**con·ta'gious·ness,** n.

con·tain (kən tān'), v. **1** have within itself; hold as contents; include. **2** be capable of holding. **3** be equal to: *a pound contains 16 ounces.* **4** control; hold back; restrain: *to contain one's anger.* **5** be divisible by without a remainder: *12 contains 2, 3, 4, and 6.* [< OF < L, < *com-* in + *tenere* hold] —**con·tain'a·ble,** adj.

con·tain·er (kən tān'ər), n. box, can, jar, etc., used to hold something.

con·tain·ment (kən tān'mənt), n. the confinement of a hostile or potentially hostile political or military force within existing geographical boundaries.

con·tam·i·nate (kən tam'ə nāt), v., **-nat·ed, -nat·ing.** make impure by contact. [< L *contaminatus* < *com-* + *tag-* touch. See CONTACT.] —**con·tam'i·nant, con·tam´i·na'tion,** n. —**con·tam'i·na´tive,** adj. —**con·tam'i·na´tor,** n.

contd., continued.

con·temn (kən tem'), v. treat with contempt; despise; scorn. [< L, < *com-* + *temnere* disdain, orig., cut] —**con·temn'-er, con·tem'nor,** n.

con·tem·plate (kon'təm plāt), v., **-plat·ed, -plat·ing. 1** look at for a long time; gaze at. **2** think about for a long time; study carefully. **3** meditate. **4** expect; intend. [< L, < *contemplari* survey < *com-* + *templum* restricted area marked off for the taking of auguries] —**con′tem·pla′·tive,** *adj.* —**con′tem·pla′tor,** *n.*

con·tem·pla·tion (kon′təm plā′shən), *n.* **1** act of looking at or thinking about something for a long time. **2** deep thought; meditation. **3** expectation; intention.

con·tem·po·ra·ne·ous (kən tem′pə rā′ni əs), *adj.* belonging to the same period of time. —**con·tem′po·ra′ne·ous·ly,** *adv.* —**con·tem′po·ra′ne·ous·ness,** *n.*

con·tem·po·rar·y (kən tem′pə rer′i), *adj., n., pl.* **-rar·ies.** —*adj.* **1** belonging to or living in the same period of time. **2** of the same age or date. —*n.* **1** person who belongs to the same period of time as another or others. **2** person, magazine, etc., of the same age or date. [< L *com-* + *temporarius* < *tempus* time]

con·tempt (kən tempt′), *n.* **1** the feeling that a person, act, or thing is mean, low, or worthless; scorn; a despising. **2** condition of being scorned or despised; disgrace. **3** disobedience to or open disrespect for the rules or decisions of a law court, a lawmaking body, etc. [< L *contemptus.* See CONTEMN.]

con·tempt·i·ble (kən temp′tə bəl), *adj.* deserving contempt or scorn. —**con·tempt′i·bil′i·ty, con·tempt′i·ble·ness,** *n.* —**con·tempt′i·bly,** *adv.*

con·temp·tu·ous (kən temp′chü əs), *adj.* showing contempt; scornful. —**con·temp′tu·ous·ly,** *adv.* —**con·temp′tu·ous·ness,** *n.*

con·tend (kən tend′), *v.* **1** fight; struggle. **2** take part in a contest; compete. **3** argue; dispute. **4** declare to be a fact; maintain as true. [< L, < *com-* (intensive) + *tendere* stretch] —**con·tend′er,** *n.*

con·tent¹ (kon′tent), *n.* **1** Usually, **contents.** what is contained. **2** facts and ideas stated, as in a book or speech. **3** power of containing; capacity. **4** amount contained; volume. [< L *contentum,* pp. of *continere* CONTAIN]

con·tent² (kən tent′), *v.* satisfy; please; make easy in mind. —*adj.* **1** satisfied; pleased. **2** easy in mind. **3** willing; ready. —*n.* contentment.

content oneself, be contented. [< F < L *contentus,* pp., restrained. See CONTAIN.]

con·tent·ed (kən ten′tid), *adj.* satisfied; pleased; easy in mind. —**con·tent′ed·ly,** *adv.* —**con·tent′ed·ness,** *n.*

con·ten·tion (kən ten′shən), *n.* **1** argument; dispute; quarrel. **2** statement or point that one has argued for. **3** an arguing; disputing; quarreling. **4** struggle; contest.

con·ten·tious (kən ten′shəs), *adj.* **1** quarrelsome. **2** characterized by contention. —**con·ten′tious·ly,** *adv.* —**con·ten′tious·ness,** *n.*

con·tent·ment (kən tent′mənt), *n.* satisfaction; being pleased; ease of mind.

con·test (*n.* kon′test; *v.* kən test′), *n.* **1** trial to see which can win; competition. **2** fight; struggle. **3** argument; dispute. [< *v.*] —*v.* **1** try to win. **2** fight for; struggle for. **3** argue against; dispute about. **4** take part in a contest. [< F < L *contestari* call to witness < *com-* + *testis* witness] —**con·test′a·ble,** *adj.* —**con·test′er,** *n.*

con·test·ant (kən tes′tənt), *n.* **1** person who takes part in a contest. **2** person who contests, as election returns, etc.

con·text (kon′tekst), *n.* parts directly before and after a word, sentence, etc., that influence its meaning. [< L, < *com-* + *texere* weave] —**con·tex′tu·al,** *adj.* —**con·tex′tu·al·ly,** *adv.*

con·ti·gu·i·ty (kon′tə gū′ə ti), *n., pl.* **-ties.** condition of being contiguous.

con·tig·u·ous (kən tig′yü əs), *adj.* **1** in actual contact; touching. **2** adjoining; near. [< L *contiguus* < *com-* + *tag-* touch. See CONTACT.] —**con·tig′u·ous·ly,** *adv.* —**con·tig′u·ous·ness,** *n.*

con·ti·nence (kon′tə nəns), **con·ti·nen·cy** (-nən si), *n., pl.* **-ces; -cies.** **1** self-control; self-restraint; moderation. **2** chastity.

con·ti·nent¹ (kon′tə nənt), *n.* **1** one of the seven great masses of land on the earth; North America, South America, Europe, Africa, Asia, Australia, or Antarctica. **2** mainland.

the Continent, the mainland of Europe. [< L, < *continere* CONTAIN]

con·ti·nent² (kon′tə nənt), *adj.* **1** showing restraint with regard to the desires or passions. **2** chaste. [see CONTINENT¹] —**con′ti·nent·ly,** *adv.*

con·ti·nen·tal (kon′tə nen′təl), *adj.* **1** of or characteristic of a continent. **2** **Continental. a** belonging to or characteristic of the mainland of Europe. **b** of or having to do with the American colonies at the time of the American Revolution. —*n.* **1 Continental,** soldier of the American army during the American Revolution. **2** piece of American paper money issued during the American Revolution.

Continental Congress, either of two legislative assemblies representing the American colonies from 1774 to 1781. The Second Continental Congress adopted the Declaration of Independence in 1776.

Continental Divide, 1 ridge in W North America that separates streams flowing toward the Pacific from those flowing toward the Atlantic or the Arctic; Great Divide. **2** often, **continental divide.** any line that separates streams flowing to opposite sides of any continent.

continental drift, slow movement of the earth's landmasses.

continental shelf, shallow portion of the earth's seabed bordering most continents, usually not more than 100 fathoms deep.

con·tin·gen·cy (kən tin′jən si), *n., pl.* **-cies. 1** an accidental happening; unexpected event; chance. **2** a happening or

event depending on something that is uncertain; possibility.

con·tin·gent (kən tin′jənt), *adj.* **1** conditional; depending on something not certain. **2** liable to happen or not to happen; possible; uncertain. **3** happening by chance; accidental; unexpected. —*n.* **1** share of soldiers, laborers, etc., furnished as an addition to a large force from other sources. **2** group that is part of a larger group. **3** accidental or unexpected event. [< L *contingens* touching < *com-* + *tangere* to touch] —**con·tin′gent·ly,** *adv.*

con·tin·u·al (kən tin′yü əl), *adj.* **1** never stopping. **2** repeated many times; very frequent. —**con·tin′u·al·ly,** *adv.*

con·tin·u·ance (kən tin′yü əns), *n.* **1** =continuation. **2** *Law.* adjournment or postponement until a future time.

con·tin·u·a·tion (kən tin′yü ā′shən), *n.* **1** act of going on with a thing after stopping. **2** a being continued. **3** anything by which a thing is continued; added part. **4** act or fact of not stopping.

con·tin·ue (kən tin′ū), *v.,* **-tin·ued, -tin·u·ing. 1** keep up; keep on; go on. **2** begin again. **3** last; endure. **4** stay. **5** cause to stay. **6** postpone; adjourn. [< L *continuare* < *continere* hold together. See CONTAIN.] —**con·tin′u·a·ble,** *adj.* —**con·tin′u·er,** *n.*

con·ti·nu·i·ty (kon′tə nü′ə ti; -nū′-), *n., pl.* **-ties. 1** state or quality of being continuous. **2** a continuous or connected whole. **3** the detailed plan of a motion picture.

con·tin·u·ous (kən tin′yü əs), *adj.* without a stop or break; connected; unbroken. —**con·tin′u·ous·ly,** *adv.* —**con·tin′u·ous·ness,** *n.*

con·tin·u·um (kən tin′yü əm), *n., pl.* **-tin·u·a** (-tin′yü ə). continuous quantity, series, etc. [< L]

con·tort (kən tôrt′), *v.* twist or bend out of shape; distort. [< L *contortus* < *com-* + *torquere* twist] —**con·tor′tion,** *n.* —**con·tor′tive,** *adj.*

con·tor·tion·ist (kən tôr′shən ist), *n.* person who can twist or bend the body into odd and unnatural positions.

con·tour (kon′tur), *n.* outline of a figure. —*v.* mark with lines showing the contour of. —*adj.* **1** showing topographical outlines, as hills, valleys, etc.: *a contour map.* **2** following natural ridges and furrows or general contour to avoid erosion: *contour planting.* [< F < Ital. *contorno,* ult. < L *com-* + *tornus* turning lathe < Gk. *tornos*]

contra-, *prefix.* in opposition; against, as in *contradistinction.* [< L *contra*]

con·tra·band (kon′trə band), *adj.* against the law; prohibited: *contraband trade.* —*n.* **1** goods imported or exported contrary to law; smuggled goods. **2** trading contrary to law; smuggling. [< Sp. < Ital., < *contra-* against (< L) + *bando* < LL *bandum* ban < Gmc.]

con·tra·bass (kon′trə bās′), —*n.* **1** the lowest bass voice or instrument. **2** large stringed instrument shaped like a cello and having a very low bass tone; double bass. —*adj.* having to do with such instruments.

con·tra·cep·tion (kon´trə sep´shən), *n.* prevention of conception. [< *contra-* + *(con)ception*] —**con´tra·cep´tive,** *adj., n.*

con·tract (*v.* kən trakt´ *for 1–3,* kon´trakt, kən trakt´ *for 4; n.* kon´trakt), *v.* **1** draw together; shrink. **2** shorten (a word, etc.) by omitting some of the letters or sounds. **3** get; acquire. **4** make a contract; agree by contract. —*n.* **1** agreement. **2** a written agreement that can be enforced by law. [< L *contractus* < *com–* together + *trahere* draw] —**con·tract´ed,** *adj.* —**con·tract´i·ble,** *adj.* —**con·trac´tive,** *adj.*

con·trac·tile (kən trak´təl), *adj.* **1** capable of contracting. **2** producing contraction. —**con´trac·til´i·ty,** *n.*

con·trac·tion (kən trak´shən), *n.* **1** process of contracting. **2** state of being contracted. **3** something contracted; shortened form. *Can't* is a contraction of *cannot.*

con·trac·tor (kon´trak tər; kən trak´tər), *n.* person who agrees to furnish materials or to do a piece of work for a certain price.

con·trac·tu·al (kən trak´chù əl), *adj.* of, or having the nature of, a contract. —**con·trac´tu·al·ly,** *adv.*

con·tra·dict (kon´trə dikt´), *v.* **1** deny (a statement, rumor, etc.). **2** deny the words of (a person). **3** be contrary to; disagree with. [< L *contradictus* < *contra* in opposition + *dicere* say] —**con´tra·dict´a·ble,** *adj.* —**con´tra·dict´er, con´tra·dic´tor,** *n.*

con·tra·dic·tion (kon´trə dik´shən), *n.* **1** act of denying what has been said. **2** statement that contradicts another; denial. **3** disagreement; opposition. **4** inconsistency.

con·tra·dic·to·ry (kon´trə dik´tə ri), *adj.* **1** contradicting; contrary; in disagreement. **2** inclined to contradict.

con·tra·dis·tinc·tion (kon´trə dis tingk´shən), *n.* distinction by opposition or contrast.

con·trail (kon´trāl), *n.* vapor trail left by an aircraft flying at a high altitude.

con·tral·to (kən tral´tō), *n., pl.* **-tos,** *adj.,* —*n.* **1** the lowest woman's voice. **2** part to be sung by the lowest woman's voice. **3** person who sings this part. **4** formerly, the highest male voice. —*adj.* of or for a contralto. [< Ital., < *contra–* counter to (< L) + *alto* high < L *altus*]

con·trap·tion (kən trap´shən), *n.* contrivance; device; gadget.

con·tra·pun·tal (kon´trə pun´təl), *adj.* **1** of or having to do with counterpoint. **2** according to the rules of counterpoint. [< Ital. *contrapunto* COUNTERPOINT]

con·tra·ri·ety (kon´trə rī´ə ti), *n., pl.* **-ties.** **1** a being contrary. **2** something contrary.

con·tra·ri·wise (kon´trer i wīz´; *for 3, also* kən trãr´i wīz´), *adv.* **1** in the opposite way or direction. **2** on the contrary. **3** perversely.

con·tra·ry (kon´trer i; *for adj. 4, also* kən trãr´i), *adj., n., pl.* **-ries,** *adv.* —*adj.* **1** opposed; opposite; completely different. **2** opposite in direction, position, etc. **3** unfavorable: *a contrary wind.* **4** opposing others; stubborn; perverse. —*n.* fact or quality that is the opposite of something else; the opposite. —*adv.* in opposition. [< AF < L *contrarius* < *contra* against] —**con´tra·ri·ly,** *adv.* —**con´tra·ri·ness,** *n.*

con·trast (*n.* kon´trast; *v.* kən trast´), *n.* **1** a striking difference. **2** person, thing, event, etc., that shows differences when put side by side with another. —*v.* **1** compare (two things) so as to show their differences. **2** show differences when compared. [< F < Ital. < LL, < L *contra–* against + *stare* stand] —**con·trast´a·ble,** *adj.*

con·tra·vene (kon´trə vēn´), *v.,* **-vened, -ven·ing.** **1** conflict with; oppose. **2** violate; infringe. [< LL, < L *contra–* against + *venire* come] —**con´tra·ven´er,** *n.* —**con´tra·ven´tion,** *n.*

con·trib·ute (kən trib´yùt), *v.,* **-ut·ed, -ut·ing.** **1** give (money, help, etc.) along with others. **2** write (articles, stories, etc.) for a newspaper or magazine.

contribute to, help bring about. [< L, bring together, collect, < *com–* together + *tribuere* bestow] —**con·trib´ut·a·ble,** *adj.* —**con·trib´u·tive, con·trib´u·to´ry,** *adj.* —**con·trib´u·tive·ly,** *adv.* —**con·trib´u·tor,** *n.*

con·tri·bu·tion (kon´trə bū´shən), *n.* **1** act of giving money, help, etc., along with others. **2** money, help, etc., given; gift. **3** article, story, etc., written for a newspaper or magazine.

con·trite (kən trīt´; kon´trīt), *adj.* **1** broken in spirit by a sense of guilt; penitent. **2** showing deep regret and sorrow. [< L *contritus* crushed < *com–* (intensive) + *terere* rub, grind] —**con·trite´ly,** *adv.* —**con·trite´ness, con·tri´tion,** *n.*

con·triv·ance (kən trīv´əns), *n.* **1** thing invented; mechanical device. **2** act or manner of contriving. **3** power or ability of contriving. **3** power or ability of contriving.

con·trive (kən trīv´), *v.,* **-trived, -triv·ing.** **1** invent; design. **2** plan; scheme; plot. **3** manage. **4** bring about. [< OF, < *con–* (< L *com–*) + *trover* find < VL, start, rouse, < L *turbare* stir up < *turba* commotion] —**con·triv´er,** *n.*

con·trol (kən trōl´), *n., v.,* **-trolled, -trol·ling.** —*n.* **1** power; authority; direction. **2** a holding back; a keeping down; restraint: *he lost control of his temper.* **3** means of restraint; check. **4** device that controls a machine. **5** standard of comparison for testing the results of scientific experiments. —*v.* **1** have power or authority over; direct. **2** hold back; keep down; restrain. **3** regulate. [< F *contrôler,* ult. < OF *contrerolle* register < *contre* against (< L *contra*) + *rôle* ROLL] —**con·trol´la·ble,** *adj.* —**con·trol´la·bil´i·ty,** *n.* —**con·trol´ment,** *n.*

con·trol·ler (kən trōl´ər), *n.* **1** Also, **comptroller.** person employed to supervise expenditures, etc. **2** person who controls. **3** device that controls or regulates. —**con·trol´ler·ship,** *n.*

con·tro·ver·sial (kon´trə vėr´shəl), *adj.* **1** of controversy. **2** open to controversy; debatable. **3** fond of controversy. —**con´tro·ver´sial·ist,** *n.* —**con´tro·ver´sial·ly,** *adv.*

con·tro·ver·sy (kon´trə vėr´si), *n., pl.* **-sies.** **1** debate; dispute. **2** quarrel; wrangle. [< L, < *contro–* against + *versus,* pp. of *vertere* turn]

con·tro·vert (kon´trə vėrt; kon´trə vėrt´), *v.* **1** dispute; deny. **2** discuss; debate.

con·tu·ma·cious (kon´tù mā´shəs; -tyù–), *adj.* stubbornly rebellious; obstinately disobedient. [< L, < *contumax* insolent < *tumere* swell up] —**con´tu·ma´cious·ly,** *adv.* —**con´tu·ma´cious·ness, con´tu·ma·cy,** *n.*

con·tu·me·ly (kon´tù mə li, -tyù–; kən tü´mə li, -tū´–), *n., pl.* **-lies.** **1** insulting words or actions; humiliating treatment. **2** a humiliating insult. [< L *contumelia,* orig., insolent action < *tumere* swell up] —**con´tu·me´li·ous,** *adj.*

con·tuse (kən tüz´; -tūz´), *v.,* **-tused, -tus·ing.** =bruise. [< L *contusus* < *com–* (intensive) + *tundere* to pound]

con·tu·sion (kən tü´zhən; -tū´–), *n.* =bruise.

co·nun·drum (kə nun´drəm), *n.* **1** riddle whose answer involves a pun or play on words. **2** any puzzling problem.

con·va·lesce (kon´və les´), *v.,* **-lesced, -lesc·ing.** make progress toward health. [< L *convalescere* < *com–* + *valere* be strong]

con·va·les·cence (kon´və les´əns), *n.* **1** a gradual recovery of health and strength after illness. **2** time during which one is convalescing. —**con´va·les´cent,** *adj., n.*

con·vec·tion (kən vek´shən), *n.* **1** act of conveying. **2** the transfer of heat from one place to another by the circulation of heated particles of a gas or liquid. [< L *convectio* < *com–* together + *vehere* carry] —**con·vec´tion·al,** *adj.* —**con·vec´tive,** *adj.* —**con·vec´tor,** *n.*

con·vene (kən vēn´), *v.,* **-vened, -ven·ing.** meet for some purpose; assemble. [< L, < *com–* together + *venire* come] —**con·ven´er,** *n.*

con·ven·ience (kən vēn´yəns), *n.* **1** fact or quality of being convenient. **2** a convenient condition or time. **3** comfort; advantage. **4** anything handy or easy to use; thing that saves trouble or work.

convenience food, prepared and packaged food that can be stored and served when convenient.

con·ven·ient (kən vēn´yənt), *adj.* **1** saving trouble; well arranged; easy to reach or use; handy. **2** easily done; not troublesome.

convenient to, near. [< L *conveniens,* ppr. of *convenire* meet, agree, be suitable. See CONVENE.] —**con·ven′ient·ly,** *adv.*

con·vent (kon′vent), *n.* **1** community of nuns; group of women living together who devote their lives to religion. **2** building or buildings in which they live. [< AF < L *conventus* assembly < *convenire* CONVENE] —**con·ven′tu·al,** *adj.*

con·ven·ti·cle (kən ven′tə kəl), *n.* **1** a secret meeting, esp. for religious reasons. **2** place of such a meeting. [< L *conventiculum,* dim. of *conventus* meeting. See CONVENT.]

con·ven·tion (kən ven′shən), *n.* **1** a meeting for some purpose; gathering; assembly. **2** delegates to a meeting or assembly. **3** agreement. **4** general agreement; common consent; custom. **5** custom approved by general agreement; rule based on common consent. [< L *conventio < convenire* CONVENE]

con·ven·tion·al (kən ven′shən əl), *adj.* **1** depending on conventions; customary. **2** established by general consent. **3** formal; not natural; not original. **4** following custom rather than nature. —**con·ven′tion·al·ism,** *n.* —**con·ven′tion·al·ly,** *adv.*

con·ven·tion·al·i·ty (kən ven′shən al′-ə ti), *n.,* *pl.* **-ties. 1** conventional quality or character. **2** conventional behavior; adherence to custom. **3** a conventional custom or rule.

con·ven·tion·al·ize (kən ven′shən əl īz), *v.,* **-ized, -iz·ing. 1** make conventional. **2** draw in a conventional manner. —**con·ven′tion·al·i·za′tion,** *n.*

conventional wisdom, generally accepted attitude or opinion; popular belief.

con·verge (kən vèrj′), *v.,* **-verged, -verg·ing. 1** tend to meet in a point. **2** cause to converge. [< LL, < L *com-* together + *vergere* incline]

con·ver·gence (kən èr′jəns), **con·ver·gen·cy** (-jən si), *n.,* *pl.* **-ces; -cies. 1** act, process, or fact of converging. **2** tendency to meet in a point. **3** point of meeting. —**con·ver′gent,** *adj.*

con·ver·sant (kən vèr′sənt; kon′vər-), *adj.* **1** familiar by use or study. **2** intimately associated. —**con·ver′sant·ly,** *adv.*

con·ver·sa·tion (kon′vər sā′shən), *n.* exchange of thoughts by talking informally.

con·ver·sa·tion·al (kon′vər sā′shən əl), *adj.* **1** of or having to do with conversation. **2** fond of conversation; good at conversation. —**con′ver·sa′tion·al·ly,** *adv.*

con·ver·sa·tion·al·ist (kon′vər sā′-shən ə list), *n.* person who is fond of or good at conversation.

con·verse[1] (*v.* kən vèrs′; *n.* kon′vèrs), *v.,* **-versed, -vers·ing,** *n.* —*v.* talk informally together. —*n.* conversation. [< OF < L, live with < *com-* with + *versari* live, be busy < *verti* to turn] —**con·vers′er,** *n.*

con·verse[2] (*adj.* kən vèrs′, kon′vèrs; *n.* kon′vèrs), *adj.* **1** opposite; contrary. **2** reversed in order; turned about. —*n.* **1** thing that is opposite or contrary. **2** thing that is turned around. [< L *conversus* turned around, pp. of *convertere* CONVERT] —**con·verse′ly,** *adv.*

con·ver·sion (kən vèr′zhən; –shən), *n.* act of converting. —**con·ver′sion·al,** *adj.*

con·vert (*v.* kən vèrt′; *n.* kon′vèrt), *v.* **1** change; turn. **2** change from unbelief to faith; change from one religion, party, etc., to another. **3** take and use unlawfully. **4** turn the other way around; invert; transpose. **5** exchange for an equivalent: *convert bank notes into gold.* —*n.* person who has been converted. [< L, < *com-* around + *vertere* turn]

con·vert·er, con·ver·tor (kən vèr′tər), *n.* **1** person or thing that converts. **2** machine for changing the form of an electric current. **3** furnace in which pig iron is changed into steel.

con·vert·i·ble (kən vèr′tə bəl), *adj.* **1** capable of being converted. **2** of an automobile, having a top that may be folded down. —*n.* automobile with a folding top. —**con·vert′i·bil′i·ty,** *n.* —**con·vert′i·bly,** *adv.*

con·vex (*adj.* kon veks′, kən–, kon′veks; *n.* kon′veks), *adj.* curved out. —*n.* a convex surface, part, or thing. [< L *convexus* vaulted, prob. < *com-* around + *vac-bend*] —**con·vex′i·ty,** *n.* —**convex′ly,** *adv.*

con·vey (kən vā′), *v.* **1** carry; transport. **2** transmit; conduct. **3** express; make known; communicate. **4** transfer the ownership of (property) from one person to another. [< OF *conveier* < VL, set on the road, accompany < L *com-* with + *via* road. Doublet of CONVOY.] —**con·vey′a·ble,** *adj.*

con·vey·ance (kən vā′əns), *n.* **1** act of carrying. **2** thing that carries people and goods; vehicle. **3** transfer of the ownership of property from one person to another.

con·vey·or, con·vey·er (kən vā′ər), *n.* **1** person or thing that conveys. **2** device that carries things from one place to another.

con·vict (*v.* kən vikt′; *n.* kon′vikt), *v.* **1** prove guilty. **2** declare guilty. —*n.* **1** person convicted by a court. **2** person serving a prison sentence. [< L *convictus,* pp. of *convincere* CONVINCE.]

con·vic·tion (kən vik′shən), *n.* **1** act of proving or declaring guilty. **2** state of being proved or declared guilty. **3** act of convincing (a person). **4** a being convinced. **5** firm belief. —**con·vic′tion·al,** *adj.*

con·vince (kən vins′), *v.,* **-vinced, -vinc·ing.** persuade by argument or proof. [< L, < *com-* + *vincere* overcome] —**con·vinc′er,** *n.* —**con·vin′ci·ble,** *adj.*

con·vinc·ing (kən vin′sing), *adj.* that convinces. —**con·vinc′ing·ly,** *adv.* —**con·vinc′ing·ness,** *n.*

con·viv·i·al (kən viv′i əl), *adj.* **1** fond of eating and drinking with friends. **2** of or suitable for a feast or banquet. [< LL, < *convivium* feast < *com-* with + *vivere* live] —**con·viv′ial′i·ty,** *n.* —**con·viv′i·al·ly,** *adv.*

con·vo·ca·tion (kon′və kā′shən), *n.* **1** a calling together. **2** an assembly. —**con′vo·ca′tion·al,** *adj.*

con·voke (kən vōk′), *v.,* **-voked, -vok·ing.** call together; summon to assemble. [< L, < *com-* together + *vocare* call] —**con·vok′er,** *n.*

con·vo·lute (kon′və lüt), *adj., v.,* **-lut·ed, -lut·ing.** —*adj.* coiled. —*v.* to coil. [< L *convolutus < com-* up + *volvere* roll] —**con′vo·lute′ly,** *adv.*

con·vo·lut·ed (kon′və lü′tid), *adj.* **1** having convolutions; twisted. **2** *Fig.* complicated; twisting: *a convoluted explanation.*

con·vo·lu·tion (kon′və lü′shən), *n.* **1** a coiling, winding, or twisting together. **2** coil; winding; twist. **3** an irregular fold or ridge on the surface of the brain.

con·voy (*v.* kən voi′, kon′voi; *n.* kon′voi), *v.* accompany in order to protect. —*n.* **1** act of convoying. **2** an escort; protection. **3** warships, soldiers, etc., that convoy; protecting escort. **4** fleet, supplies, etc., accompanied by a protecting escort. [< F *convoyer.* Doublet of CONVEY.]

con·vulse (kən vuls′), *v.,* **-vulsed, -vuls·ing. 1** shake violently. **2** throw into a fit of laughter; cause to shake with laughter. [< L *convulsus < com-* (intensive) + *vellere* tear]

con·vul·sion (kən vul′shən), *n.* **1** a violent, involuntary contracting and relaxing of the muscles; spasm; seizure. **2** fit of laughter. **3** a violent disturbance. —**con·vul′sive,** *adj.* —**con·vul′sive·ly,** *adv.*

co·ny (kō′ni), *n., pl.* **-nies. 1** rabbit fur. **2** *Archaic.* rabbit. Also, **coney.** [< OF *conil* < L *cuniculus* rabbit < Iberian]

coo (kü), *n., v.,* **cooed, coo·ing.** —*n.* a soft, murmuring sound made by doves or pigeons. —*v.* **1** make this sound. **2** murmur softly; speak in a soft, loving manner. [imit.] —**coo′er,** *n.*

cook (kük), *v.* **1** prepare (food) by using heat. **2** undergo cooking; be cooked. **3** act as cook; work as cook. **4** subject (anything) to the action of heat. **5** tamper with. [< n.] —*n.* person who cooks. [< LL *cocus* < L *coquus*]

cook·book (kük′bük′), *n.* book of recipes containing directions for cooking.

cook·er (kük′ər), *n.* apparatus or container to cook things in.

cook·er·y (kük′ər i), *n., pl.* **-er·ies. 1** art of cooking. **2** room or place for cooking.

cook·ie (kük′i), *n., pl.* **-ies. 1** small, flat cake. **2** *Slang.* **a** person: *one tough cookie.* **b** familiar address for a girl or woman. Also, **cooky.**

that's how (or **the way**) **the cookie crumbles,** *Informal.* that is the way things are. [< Du. *koekje* little cake]

cook·out (kŭk′out′), *n.* cooking and eating of a meal out-of-doors.

cool (kül), *adj.* **1** somewhat cold; more cold than hot. **2** allowing or giving a cool feeling: *cool clothes.* **3** *Fig.* not excited; calm. **4** *Fig.* having little enthusiasm or interest. **5** *Fig.* bold; impudent. **6** without exaggeration or qualification: *a cool million dollars.* **7** *Informal.* great; excellent. —*n.* something cool; cool part, place, or time: *the cool of the evening.* —*v.* **1** become cool. **2** make cool. **cool one's heels**, *Colloq.* be kept waiting for a long ime. [OE *cōl*] —**cool′ish**, *adj.* —**cool′ly**, *adv.* —**cool′ness**, *n.*

cool·ant (kül′ənt), *n.* a cooling medium, used for machinery, etc.

cool·er (kül′ər), *n.* **1** apparatus or container that cools foods or drinks, or keeps them cool. **2** anything that cools. **3** *Slang.* jail.

Cool·idge (kül′ij), *n.* **Calvin,** 1872–1933, the 30th president of the United States, 1923–29.

coo·lie, coo·ly (kü′li), *n., pl.* **–lies.** an unskilled, native laborer in China, India, etc. [prob. < Tamil *kuli* hire, hired servant]

coon (kün), *n. Colloq.* =raccoon.

coop (küp; kŭp), *n.* **1** a small cage or pen for chickens, rabbits, etc. **2** any small confining structure. —*v.* **1** keep or put in a coop. **2** confine in a very small space. [ME *coupe* basket < L *cupa* cask]

co-op (kō′op; kō op′), *n. Colloq.* **1** cooperative store. **2** cooperative apartment.

coop·er (küp′ər; kŭp′-), *n.* man who makes or repairs barrels, casks, etc. —*v.* make or repair (barrels, casks, etc.). [? < MDu., MLG *kuper* < L *cuparius* < *cupa* cask]

Coo·per (kü′pər; kŭp′ər), *n.* **James Fenimore,** 1789–1851, American novelist.

coop·er·age (küp′ər ij; kŭp′–), *n.* **1** work done by a cooper. **2** shop of a cooper.

co·op·er·ate (kō op′ər āt), *v.,* **–at·ed, –at·ing.** work together. [< LL, < *co–* together + *operari* to work] —**co·op′er·a′tor,** *n.*

co·op·er·a·tion (kō op′ər ā′shən), *n.* **1** act of working together; united effort or labor. **2** combination of persons for purposes of production, purchase, or distribution for their joint benefit.

co·op·er·a·tive (kō op′ər ā′tiv; –op′rə tiv), *adj.* **1** wanting or willing to work together with others. **2** of, having to do with, or being a cooperative. —*n.* organization in which the profits and losses are shared by all members. —**co·op′er·a′tive·ly,** *adv.* —**co·op′er·a′tive·ness,** *n.*

co-opt (kō′opt), *v.* **1 a** take over; secure for oneself or other purposes. **b** commandeer. **2** choose or elect a new member by voting. [< L *cooptare* < *com–* together with + *optare* choose, elect]

co·or·di·nate (*adj.,* –nit, –nāt; *v.* kō ôr′də nāt), *adj., n., v.,* **–nat·ed, –nat·ing.** —*adj.* **1** equal in importance; of equal rank. **2** made up of coordinate parts. **3** joining words, phrases, or clauses of equal grammatical importance. *And* and *but* are coordinate conjunctions. —*n.* **1** a coordinate person or thing. **2** *Math,* any of two or more magnitudes that define the position of a point, line, or plane by reference to a fixed figure, system of lines, etc. —*v.* **1** make coordinate; make equal in importance. **2** arrange in proper order or relation; harmonize; adjust [< L *co–* with + *ordinatus,* pp. of *ordinare* regulate] —**co·or′di·nate·ly,** *adv.* —**co·or′di·nate·ness,** *n.* —**co·or′di·na′tive,** *adj.* —**co·or′di·na′tor,** *n.*

co·or·di·na·tion (kō ôr′də nā′shən), *n.* act of coordinating.

coot (küt), *n.* **1** a wading and swimming bird with short wings and lobate toes. **2** *Colloq.* fool; simpleton. [? < Du. *koet*]

coot·ie (küt′i), *n. Slang.* louse.

cop[1] (kop), *n., Informal.* policeman. [OE *coppian*]

cop[2] (kop), *v.,* **copped, cop·ping. 1** capture; catch; nab: *cop a prize.* **2** steal. **cop a plea,** plead guilty to a lesser charge, esp. to receive a smaller penalty. **cop out,** *Slang.* **a** back out; refuse to become involved. **b** avoid or escape. [perhaps < OF *caper* seize]

cop·out (kop′out′), *n.* **1** refusal to become involved; a backing out. **2** person who refuses to be involved or backs out.

co·part·ner (kō pärt′nər), *n.* a fellow partner; associate. —**co·part′ner·ship,** *n.*

cope[1] (kōp), *v.,* **coped, cop·ing.** struggle or contend (*with*), esp. on even terms or successfully. [< F *couper* strike < *coup* COUP]

cope[2] (kōp), *n., v.,* **coped, cop·ing.** —*n.* **1** a long cape worn by priests during certain religious rites. **2** anything like a cope, such as a canopy, the sky, etc. —*v.* cover with a cope. [< Med.L *capa* cloak, var. of LL *cappa* hood]

co·peck (kō′pek), *n.* =kopeck.

Co·pen·ha·gen (kō′pən hā′gən; –hä′–), *n.* capital of Denmark.

Co·per·ni·cus (kə pėr′nə kəs), *n.* **Nikolaus,** 1473–1543, Polish astronomer. —**Co·per′ni·can,** *adj.*

cope·stone (kōp′stōn′), *n.* **1** the top stone of a wall. **2** a finishing touch. [< *cope*[2] + *stone*]

cop·i·able (kop′ē ə bəl), *adj.* that can be copied, esp. on a copier.

cop·i·er (kop′i ər), *n.* **1** machine that makes photograph copies. **2** =imitator. **3** =copyist.

co·pi·lot (kō′pī′lət), *n.* assistant or second pilot in an aircraft.

cop·ing (kōp′ing), *n.* the top layer of a brick or stone wall, usually sloping. [< *cope*[2]]

coping saw, a narrow saw in a U-shaped frame, used to cut curves.

co·pi·ous (kō′pi əs), *adj.* **1** plentiful; abundant. **2** containing much matter. **3** containing many words. [< L, < *copia* plenty] —**co′pi·ous·ly,** *adv.* —**co′pi·ous·ness,** *n.*

cop·per[1] (kop′ər), *n.* **1** a tough, reddish-brown metallic element, Cu, that is easily shaped into thin sheets or fine wire and resists rust. **2** thing made of copper. **3** a reddish brown. —*v.* cover with copper. —*adj.* **1** of copper. **2** reddish-brown. [< L *cuprum,* for earlier *aes Cyprium* metal of Cyprus] —**cop′per·y,** *adj.*

cop·per[2] (kop′ər), *n.* =policeman. [< *cop*[1] + *–er*[1]]

cop·per·as (kop′ər əs), *n.* ferrous sulfate, $FeSO_47H_2O$, used in dyeing, inkmaking, medicine, and photography. [< F < Med. L (*aqua*) *cuprosa* (water) of COPPER]

cop·per·head (kop′ər hed′), *n.* **1** a poisonous North American snake related to the water moccasin and the rattlesnake. **2 Copperhead,** a Northerner sympathetic with the South during the Civil War.

cop·per·plate (kop′ər plāt′), *n.* **1** a thin, flat piece of copper on which a design, writing, etc., is engraved or etched. **2** an engraving, picture, or print made from a copperplate. **3** copperplate printing or engraving.

cop·per·smith (kop′ər smith′), *n.* person who makes things out of copper.

cop·ra (kop′rə), *n.* the dried meat of coconuts. [< Pg. < Malayalam *koppara*]

copse (kops), **cop·pice** (kop′is), *n.* a thicket of small trees, bushes, etc. [< OF *coupeiz* a cutover forest < *couper* cut. See COUP.]

Copt (kopt), *n.* native of Egypt, descended from the ancient Egyptians.

cop·ter (kop′tər), *n.* =helicopter.

Cop·tic (kop′tik), *n.* the former language of the Copts. —*adj.* of or by the Copts.

cop·u·la (kop′yə lə), *n., pl.* **–las, –lae** (–lē). **1** verb that connects the subject and the predicate, usually some form of *be.* **2** something that connects. [< L, bond, < *co–* together + *apere* fasten. Doublet of COUPLE.] —**cop′u·lar,** *adj.*

cop·u·late (kop′yə lāt), *v.,* **–lat·ed, –lat·ing.** have sexual intercourse. [< L *copulatus,* pp. of *copulare.* See COPULA.] —**cop′u·la′tion,** *n.*

cop·u·la·tive (kop′yə lā′tiv; –lə–), *n.* copulative word. —*adj.* **1** connecting. *Be* is a copulative verb; *and* is a copulative conjunction. **2** pertaining to copulation. —**cop′u·la′tive·ly,** *adv.*

cop·y (kop′i), *n., pl.* **cop·ies,** *v.,* **copied, cop·y·ing.** —*n.* **1** thing made like another. **2** thing made to be followed as a pattern or model. **3** one of a number of books, newspapers, magazines, pictures, etc., made at the same printing. **4** material ready to be set in type. —*v.* **1** follow as a pattern or model; imitate. **2** =photocopy. [< F < Med.L *copia* transcript < L, plenty]

copying machine, =copier.

cop·y·ist (kop′i ist), *n.* **1** person who makes written copies. **2** imitator.

cop·y·right (kop′i rīt′), *n.* the exclusive right to make and sell a certain book, picture, etc. —*adj.* protected by copyright. —*v.* protect by getting a copyright. —**cop′y·right′a·ble,** *adj.* —**cop′y·right′er,** *n.*

co·quet (kō ket′), *v.,* **–quet·ted, –quet·ting. 1** flirt. **2** trifle. [< F, < *coquet,* dim. of *coq* cock] —**co′quet·ry,** *n.*

co·quette (kō ket′), *n.* woman who tries to attract men merely to please her vanity; flirt. [< F. See COQUET.] —**coquet′tish,** *adj.* —**co·quet′tish·ly,** *adv.* —**co·quet′tish·ness,** *n.*

cor., 1 corner. **2** coroner. **3** corpus. **4** corrected; correction. **5** correspondence; correspondent; corresponding.

cor·a·cle (kôr′ə kəl; kor′–), *n.* a small, light boat made by covering a wooden frame with waterproof material. [< Welsh < *corwg*]

cor·al (kôr′əl; kor′–), *n.* **1** a stony substance consisting of the skeletons of very small sea animals called polyps. **2** polyp that secretes a skeleton of coral and forms large, branching colonies by budding. **3** a deep pink; red. —*adj.* **1** made of coral. **2** deep-pink; red. [< OF < L < Gk. *koral(l)ion*]

coral reef, reef consisting mainly of coral.

Coral Sea, part of the Pacific at the NE Australian coast.

coral snake, any of several species of small, poisonous American snakes, most of which are banded with alternating rings of red, yellow, and black.

cor·bel (kôr′bəl), *n., v.,* **–beled, –bel·ing.** —*n.* bracket of stone, etc., on a wall. —*v.* furnish with corbels; support by corbels. [< OF, dim. of *corp* raven < L *corvus*]

cord (kôrd), *n.* **1** a thick string; very thin rope. **2** influence that binds or restrains. **3** *Elect.* a pair of covered wires with fittings to connect an iron, lamp, etc., with a socket. **4** Also, **chord.** structure in an animal body that is somewhat like a cord: *the spinal cord.* **5** ridge on cloth. **6** cloth with ridges on it; corduroy. **7** measure of cut wood; 128 cubic feet. —*v.* **1** fasten or tie with a cord. **2** pile (wood) in cords.

cords, corduroy pants or trousers. [< OF < L < Gk. *chorde* gut. Doublet of CHORD².] —**cord′ed,** *adj.* —**cord′er,** *n.*

cord·age (kôr′dij), *n.* **1** cords; ropes. The cordage of a ship is its rigging. **2** quantity of wood measured in cords.

cor·date (kôr′dāt), *adj.* heart-shaped. [< NL, < L *cor* heart] —**cor′date·ly,** *adv.*

cord·ed (kôr′did), *adj.* **1** ribbed. **2** fastened with a cord; bound with cords. **3** cut and piled in cords.

cor·dial (kôr′jəl), *n.* liqueur. —*adj.* sincere; hearty; warm; friendly. [< Med.L, < L *cor* heart] —**cor′dial·ly,** *adv.* —**cor′dial·ness,** *n.*

cor·dial·i·ty (kôr jal′ə ti; –ji al′–), *n., pl.* **–ties.** cordial quality or feeling; heartiness; friendliness.

cor·dil·le·ra (kôr′dəl yär′ə; kôr dil′ər ə), *n.* W a long mountain range. [< Sp.,

ult. < L *chorda* rope, CORD] —**cor′dil·le′ran,** *adj.*

cord·ite (kôr′dīt), *n.* a smokeless gunpowder composed chiefly of nitroglycerin and guncotton. [< cord, n. + –ite²]

cor·don (kôr′dən), *n.* **1** line or circle of people or things placed at intervals as a guard. **2** cord, braid, or ribbon worn as an ornament or badge of honor. [< F, < *corde* CORD]

cor·don bleu (kôr dôn blœ′), *pl.* **cor·dons bleus** (kôr dôn blœ′). **1** high honor; great distinction. **2** person of great distinction in a particular field, esp. a renowned chef. [< F *cordon bleu* blue ribbon]

cor·do·van (kôr′də vən; kôr dō′vən), *n.* kind of soft, fine-grained leather. —*adj.* of or having to do with this leather.

cor·du·roy (kôr′də roi; kôr′də roi′), *n.* **1** a thick cotton cloth with close, velvetlike ridges. **2 corduroys,** corduroy trousers. —*adj.* made of corduroy. [appar. < F *corde du roi* king's cord]

cord·wood (kôrd′wůd′), *n.* **1** wood sold or piled in cords. **2** wood cut in 4-foot lengths.

core (kôr; kōr), *n., v.,* **cored, cor·ing.** —*n.* **1** the central part, containing the seeds, of fruits like apples and pears. **2** the central or most important part: *the core of an argument.* —*v.* take out the core. [ME]

co·re·op·sis (kô′ri op′sis; kō′–), *n.* plant with yellow, red and yellow, or reddish flowers shaped like daisies. [< NL, < Gk. *koris* bedbug + *opsis* appearance; from the shape of the seed]

co·re·spond·ent (kō′ri spon′dənt; kôr′i–; kor′–), *n. Law.* person accused of adultery with a husband or wife being sued for divorce.

co·ri·an·der (kô′ri an′dər; kō′–), *n.* **1** plant whose aromatc, seedlike fruits are used in cooking and in medicine. **2** the fruit. [< F < L < Gk. *koriandron,* var. of *koriannon*]

Cor·inth (kôr′inth; kor′–), *n.* seaport in S Greece. In ancient times, Corinth was a center of commerce, art, and luxury.

Co·rin·thi·an (kə rin′thi ən), *adj.* **1** of or having to do with Corinth or its people. **2** noting or pertaining to the most elaborate of the three types of Greek architecture. **3** luxurious. —*n.* **1** native or inhabitant of Corinth. **2 Corinthians,** either of two books of the New Testament, written by the Apostle Paul to the Christians of Corinth.

cork (kôrk), *n.* **1** a light, thick, outer bark of a kind of oak, used for bottle stoppers, floats for fishing lines, etc. **2** Also, **cork oak.** the tree. **3** shaped piece of cork. **4** any stopper for a bottle, etc. **5** the protective outer bark of woody plants. —*v.* **1** stop up with a cork. **2** restrain. **3** blacken with burnt cork. —*adj.* of cork. [< Sp. *alcorque* < Ar. < L *quercus* oak] —**cork′y,** *adj.*

cork·age (kôr′kij), *n.* charge made by a restaurant for serving a patron's wine,

rather than wine offered by the restaurant.

cork·er (kôr′kər), *n.* **1** *Slang.* **a** someone remarkable. **b** something marvelous or astonishing. **2** person or device that corks.

cork·screw (kôrk′skrü′), *n.* tool for removing corks from bottles. —*v.* move or advance in a spiral or zigzag course. —*adj.* spiral.

corm (kôrm), *n.* a bulblike underground stem. [< NL < Gk. *kormos* stripped tree trunk < *keirein* shear]

cor·mo·rant (kôr′mə rənt), *n.* **1** a large, greedy sea bird with a pouch under its beak. **2** a greedy person. —*adj.* greedy. [< OF *cormareng* < *corp* raven (< L *corvus*) + *marenc* of the sea (< L *mare*)]

corn¹ (kôrn), *n.* **1** kind of grain that grows on large ears; maize; Indian corn. **2** plant that it grows on. **3** in England, grain in general, esp. wheat. **4** in Scotland and Ireland, oats. **5** Also, **corn whiskey,** whiskey made from corn. **6** *Informal.* something trite or sentimental. —*v.* preserve (meat) with strong salt water or by dry salt. [OE] —**corned,** *adj.*

corn² (kôrn), *n.* a hardening of the skin, usually on a toe. [< OF, horn, < L *cornu*]

Corn Belt, area of the midwestern United States where corn is a major crop.

corn bread, bread made of corn meal.

corn·cob (kôrn′kob′), *n.* **1** the central, woody part of an ear of corn. **2** a tobacco pipe with a bowl hollowed out of a piece of dried corncob.

cor·ne·a (kôr′ni ə), *n.* the transparent part of the outer coat of the eyeball. The cornea covers the iris and the pupil. [< Med. L *cornea* (*tela*) horny (web) < L *cornu* horn] —**cor′ne·al,** *adj.*

cor·nel (kôr′nəl), *n.* **1** in Europe, a shrub or small tree with yellow flowers. **2** in the United States, the flowering dogwood. [< G < Med.L *cornolius* < L *cornus*]

cor·nel·ian (kôr nēl′yən), *n.* =carnelian.

cor·ner (kôr′nər), *n.* **1** the point or place where lines or surfaces meet. **2** the place where two streets meet. **3** piece to protect or decorate a corner. **4** small, private place. **5** place that is far away; region. **6** an awkward position. **7** a buying up of the available supply of some stock or article to raise its price. —*adj.* **1** at a corner. **2** for a corner. —*v.* **1** put or drive into a corner. **2** force into a difficult position. **3** buy up all or nearly all that can be had of (something) to raise its price. **4** (of an automobile) round sharp curves at relatively high speeds.

around the corner, in the near future; happening soon.

cut corners, a shorten the way by going across corners. **b** save money, effort, time, etc. by cutting down.

paint oneself into a corner, get into a situation that is impossible to get out of.

the four corners of the earth, the furthest parts of the world; far away and everywhere.

turn the corner, pass the worst or most dangerous point. [< AF var. of OF *cornere* < L *cornu* horn, tip]

cor·nered (kôr′nərd), *adj.* **1** without hope of escape or relief. **2** having a corner or corners.

cor·ner·stone (kôr′nər stōn′), *n.* **1** stone at the corner of two walls that holds them together. **2** main part on which something rests; basis.

cor·ner·wise (kôr′nər wīz′), **cor·ner·ways** (–wāz′), *adv.* **1** with the corner in front; forming a corner. **2** diagonally.

cor·net (kôr net′ *for 1;* kôr′nit, kôr net′ *for 2*), *n.* **1** a wind instrument somewhat like a trumpet, usually made of brass. **2** piece of paper rolled into a cone and twisted at one end, used to hold candy, nuts, etc. [< OF, < L *cornu* horn] —**cor·net′ist, cor·net′ist,** *n.*

corn·flow·er (kôrn′flou′ər), *n.* plant with blue, pink, white, or purple flowers; bachelor's-button.

corn·husk (kôrn′husk′), *n.* husk of an ear of corn. —**corn′husk′ing,** *n.*

cor·nice (kôr′nis), *n., v.,* –**niced,** –**nic·ing.** —*n.* a projecting ornamental molding along the top of a wall, pillar, building, etc. —*v.* furnish or finish with a cornice. [< F < Ital. < Med.Gk. *koronis* copestone < Gk., something bent]

Cor·nish (kôr′nish), *adj.* of or having to do with Cornwall, its people, or their former language. —*n.* the ancient Celtic language of Cornwall. —**Cor′nish·man,** *n.*

corn meal, meal made from Indian corn ground up.

corn oil, vegetable oil made from corn, used in salads and cooking.

corn pone, *S.* a flat, usually rectangular loaf of corn meal shaped by hand.

corn·row (kôrn′rō), *n.* one of a series of flat, narrow braids that covers the head.

corn silk, the glossy threads or styles at the end of an ear of corn.

corn·stalk (kôrn′stôk′), *n.* stalk of Indian corn.

corn·starch (kôrn′stärch′), *n.* a starchy flour made from Indian corn, used to thicken puddings, etc.

corn sugar, sugar made from cornstarch.

corn syrup, syrup made from cornstarch, used esp. in baked goods and confections. Also, **corn sirup.**

cor·nu·co·pi·a (kôr′nə kō′pi ə), *n.* **1** a horn-shaped container or ornament. **2** horn of plenty, overflowing with fruits and flowers. [< LL, for L *cornu copiae* horn of plenty]

Corn·wal·lis (kôrn wôl′is; –wol′is), *n.* **Charles,** 1738–1805, British general who surrendered to George Washington at Yorktown, 1781.

corn·y (kôr′ni), *adj.,* **corn·i·er, corn·i·est.** *Slang.* trite; unsophisticated, overly sentimental.

co·rol·la (kə rol′ə), *n.* the internal envelope or floral leaves of a flower; the petals. [< L, garland, dim. of *corona* crown]

cor·ol·lar·y (kôr′ə ler′i; kor′–), *n., pl.* –**lar·ies.** **1** an additional proposition that can be easily inferred from a proved proposition. **2** inference. **3** a natural consequence or result. [< LL *corollarium* < L, gift, < *corolla* garland. See COROLLA.]

co·ro·na (kə rō′nə), *n., pl.* –**nas,** –**nae** (–nē). **1** ring of light or halo seen around the sun or moon. **2** the top of the head. **3** the appendage on the inner side of the corolla of some plants. [< L, crown. Doublet of CROWN.] —**co·ro′nal,** *adj.*

cor·o·nar·y (kôr′ə ner′i; kor′–), *adj.* **1** pertaining to or resembling a crown. **2** of or designating either or both of the two arteries that supply blood to the muscular tissue of the heart. —*n.* **1** coronary thrombosis. **2** *Informal.* heart attack. [< L *coronarius* encircling < *corona* crown]

coronary thrombosis, thrombosis of the heart, involving a blockage of a coronary artery.

cor·o·na·tion (kôr′ə nā′shən; kor′–), *n.* ceremony of crowning a king, emperor, etc.

cor·o·ner (kôr′ə nər; kor′–), *n.* **1** a local official who investigates before a jury any unnatural death. **2 coroner's jury,** group of persons chosen to witness the investigation. [< AF *corouner* officer of the crown < *coroune* CROWN] —**cor′o·ner·ship′,** *n.*

cor·o·net (kôr′ə nit; –net; kor′–), *n.* **1** a small crown worn as a mark of high rank. **2** circlet of anything worn around the head as an ornament. [< OF *coronet,* dim. of *corone* CROWN] —**cor′o·net·ed,** *adj.*

Corp., corp., **1** Corporal. **2** Corporation.

cor·po·ral[1] (kôr′pə rəl), *adj.* of the body: *corporal punishment.* [< L *corporalis* < *corpus* body] —**cor′po·ral′i·ty,** *n.* —**cor′po·ral·ly,** *adv.*

cor·po·ral[2] (kôr′pə rəl), *n.* the lowest noncommissioned army officer, next below a sergeant and next above a private. [< F < Ital. *caporale < capo* head < L *caput*] —**cor′po·ral·ship′,** *n.*

cor·po·rate (kôr′pə rit), *adj.* **1** of or forming a corporation; incorporated. **2** combined. [< L, < *corporare* form into a body < *corpus* body] —**cor′po·rate·ly,** *adv.*

cor·po·ra·tion (kôr′pə rā′shən), *n.* **1** group of persons who obtain a charter giving them as a group certain legal rights and privileges distinct from those of the individual members of the group. **2** group of persons with authority to act as a single person. **3** prominent abdomen.

cor·po·re·al (kôr pô′ri əl; –ō′–), *adj.* **1** of or for the body; bodily. **2** material; tangible. [< L *corporeus < corpus* body] —**cor·po′re·al′i·ty, cor·po′re·al·ness,** *n.* —**cor·po′re·al·ly,** *adv.*

corps (kôr; kōr), *n., pl.* **corps** (kôrz; kōrz). **1** branch of specialized military service,

such as the Signal Corps. **2** a tactical unit usually consisting of two or more divisions, and smaller than an army. **3** group of people organized for working together. [< F. See CORPSE.]

corps de ballet (kôr′də ba lā′), group of ballet dancers, esp. those who are members of a company other than soloists. [< F]

corpse (kôrps), *n.* a dead human body. [< OF < L *corpus* body]

cor·pu·lence (kôr′pyə ləns), **cor·pu·len·cy** (–lən si), *n.* fatness. [< L, < *corpus* body] —**cor′pu·lent,** *adj.* —**cor′pu·lent·ly,** *adv.*

cor·pus (kôr′pəs), *n., pl.* –**po·ra** (–pə rə). **1** a body. **2** a complete collection of writings, laws, etc. [< L, body]

corpus cal·lo·sum (kə lō′səm), *pl.* **corpora callosa.** band of nerve fibers that connects the cerebral hemispheres of the brain in humans and other mammals.

cor·pus·cle (kôr′pəs əl; –pus–), *n.* any of the cells that float in the blood, lymph, etc., carrying oxygen and carbon dioxide or destroying disease germs. [< L *corpusculum,* dim. of *corpus* body] —**cor·pus′cu·lar,** *adj.*

cor·pus de·lic·ti (kôr′pəs di lik′tī), *Law.* **1** the actual facts that prove a crime or offense has been committed. **2** body of a murdered person. [< L, body of the crime]

corpus lu·te·um (lü′tē əm), *pl.* **corpora lutea. 1** yellow endocrine mass formed in the ovary from the rupture of the sac that contained a mature ovum. **2** extract made from the corpus luteum of a cow or hog, used in certain medical treatment.

cor·ral (kə ral′), *n., v.,* –**ralled,** –**ral·ling.** —*n.* an enclosed space for keeping or for capturing horses, cattle, etc. —*v.* **1** drive into or keep in a corral. **2** surround; capture. [< Sp., < *corro* ring]

cor·rect (kə rekt′), *adj.* **1** free from mistakes or faults; right. **2** in good taste; proper. —*v.* **1** change to what is right; remove mistakes from. **2** alter to agree with some standard: *correct the reading of a barometer.* **3** mark the errors of. **4** find fault with to improve; punish. **5** counteract (something hurtful); cure. [< L *correctus,* pp. of *corrigere* make straight < *com-* + *regere* direct] —**cor·rect′ly,** *adv.* —**cor·rect′ness,** *n.* —**cor·rec′tor,** *n.*

cor·rec·tion (kə rek′shən), *n.* **1** act of correcting. **2** thing put in place of an error or mistake. **3** punishment; rebuke; scolding. —**correc′tion·al,** *adj.*

cor·rec·tive (kə rek′tiv), *adj.* tending to correct; making better. —*n.* something that tends to correct anything that is wrong or hurtful. —**cor·rec′tive·ly,** *adv.*

cor·re·late (kôr′ə lāt; kor′–), *v.,* –**lat·ed,** –**lat·ing,** *adj., n.* —*v.* **1** have a mutual relation. **2** bring into proper relation with one another. *adj.* correlated. —*n.*

either of two related things. [< com- + relate

cor·re·la·tion (kôr′ə lā′shən; kor′-), n. 1 the mutual relation of two or more things. 2 a correlating or being correlated.

cor·rel·a·tive (kə rel′ə tiv), adj. 1 mutually dependent; each implying the other. 2 having a mutual relation and commonly used together. Conjunctions used in pairs, such as either . . . or and both . . . and, are correlative words. —n. either of two closely related things. —**cor·rel′a·tiv′i·ty,** n. —**cor·rel′a·tive·ly,** adv.

cor·re·spond (kôr′ə spond′; kor′-), v. 1 be in harmony; agree. 2 be similar: the arms of a man correspond to the wings of a bird. 3 exchange letters. [< Med.L, < L com- together, with + respondere answer] —**cor′re·spond′ing,** adj. —**cor′re·spond′ing·ly,** adv.

cor·re·spond·ence (kôr′ə spon′dəns; kor′-), n. 1 agreement; harmony. 2 similarity in structure or function. 3 exchange of letters; letter writing. 4 letters.

correspondence course, lessons in a certain subject given by a correspondence school.

cor·re·spond·ent(kôr′ə spon′dənt;kor′-), n. 1 person who exchanges letters with another. 2 person employed by a newspaper or magazine to send news from a distant place. 3 thing that corresponds to something else. —adj. corresponding; in agreement. —**cor′re·spond′ent·ly,** adv.

cor·ri·dor (kôr′ə dər; -dôr; kor′-), n. 1 a long hallway. 2 a narrow strip of land connecting two parts of a country or an inland country with a seaport. [< F < Pr. corredor < correr run < L currere]

cor·ri·gi·ble (kôr′ə jə bəl; kor′-), adj. 1 that can be corrected. 2 open to correction. [< LL, < L corrigere CORRECT] —**cor′ri·gi·bil′i·ty,** n. —**cor′ri·gi·bly,** adv.

cor·rob·o·rate (kə rob′ə rāt), v., -rat·ed, -rat·ing. make more certain; confirm. [< L, < corroborare strengthen < com- + robur oak] —**cor·rob′o·ra′tion,** n. —**cor·rob′o·ra′tor,** n.

cor·rob·o·ra·tive (kə rob′ə rā′tiv; -rə tiv), **cor·rob·o·ra·to·ry** (-rə tô′ri; -tō′-), adj. confirming. —**cor·rob′o·ra′tive·ly,** adv.

cor·rode (kə rōd′), v., -rod·ed, -rod·ing. 1 eat away gradually. 2 become corroded. [< L, < com- + rodere gnaw] —**cor·rod′i·ble,** adj.

cor·ro·sion (kə rō′zhən), n. 1 act or process of corroding. 2 a corroded condition. 3 product of corroding.

cor·ro·sive (kə rō′siv), adj. 1 producing corrosion; corroding; eating away. 2 Fig. wearing to the mind or emotions: the corrosive effects of stress. —n. substance that corrodes. —**cor·ro′sive·ly,** adv. —**cor·ro′sive·ness,** n.

cor·ru·gate (v. kôr′ə gāt, kor′-; adj. kôr′ə git, -gāt, kor′-), v., -gat·ed, -gat·ing,

adj. —v. 1 bend or shape into a row of wavelike folds. 2 wrinkle; furrow. —adj. wrinkled; furrowed. [< L, < com- + ruga wrinkle]

cor·ru·gat·ed (kôr′ə gā tid; kor′-), adj. bent or shaped into a wavelike ridge: a strong, corrugated tin roof.

cor·ru·ga·tion (kôr′ə gā′shən; kor′-), n. 1 a corrugating. 2 a being corrugated. 3 one of a series of wavelike ridges.

cor·rupt (kə rupt′), adj. 1 evil; wicked. 2 influenced by bribes; dishonest. 3 a incorrect because of alterations, as a text. b considered inferior by some because of change in meaning or form, or deviation from standard usage, as a language, dialect, form, etc. 4 rotten; decayed. —v. 1 make evil or wicked. 2 bribe. 3 a make incorrect by changing, as a text. b cause to differ from standard usage, as a form, meaning, dialect, etc. 4 rot; decay. 5 become corrupt. [< L corruptus < com- + rumpere break] —**corrupt′er,** n. —**cor·rupt′ing·ly,** adv. —**cor·rupt′ly,** adv. —**cor·rupt′ness,** n.

cor·rupt·i·ble (kə rup′tə bəl), adj. 1 that can be corrupted; that can be bribed. 2 liable to be corrupted; perishable. —**cor·rupt′i·bil′i·ty, corrupt′i·ble·ness,** n. —**cor·rupt′i·bly,** adv.

cor·rup·tion (kə rup′shən), n. 1 a making or being made evil or wicked. 2 evil conduct; wickedness. 3 bribery; dishonesty. 4 a a making incorrect by changing, as a text. b a causing to differ from standard usage, as a form, meaning, dialect, etc. c an instance of this: a corrupt form of a word. 5 rot; decay. 6 thing that causes corruption.

cor·sage (kôr säzh′), n. bouquet to be worn at a woman's waist or her shoulder, etc. [< F, < OF cors body < L corpus]

cor·sair (kôr′sār), n. 1 pirate. 2 a pirate ship. 3 privateer. [< F < Ital. < VL cursarius runner < L cursus a run]

corse·let (kôrs′lit for 1; kôr′sə let′ for 2), n. Also, **cors·let.** armor for the body. [< F, double dim. of OF cors body < L corpus]

cor·set (kôr′sit), n. Often, **corsets.** a woman's stiff, close-fitting undergarment, worn about the waist and hips to support or shape the body. [< F, dim. of OF cors body < L corpus]

Cor·si·ca (kôr′sə kə), n. French island in the Mediterranean, SE of France. —**Cor′si·can,** adj., n.

cor·tege, cor·tège (kôr tāzh′; -tezh′), n. 1 procession. 2 group of followers, attendants, etc.; retinue. [< F < Ital. corteggio < corte COURT]

cor·tex (kôr′teks), n., pl. -ti·ces (-tə sēz). 1 bark. 2 a the outer layers of an internal organ, as of the kidney. b layer of gray matter that covers most of the surface of the brain. [< L, bark] —**cor′ti·cal,** adj. —**cor′ti·cal·ly,** adv.

cor·ti·sone (kôr′tə zōn), n. hormone derived from the cortex of the adrenal

gland, used experimentally in controlling arthritis.

co·run·dum (kə run′dəm), n. an extremely hard mineral consisting of aluminum oxide, Al_2O_3, used as an abrasive. [< Tamil kurundam. Cf. Skt. kuruvinda ruby.]

cor·us·cate (kôr′əs kāt; kor′-), v., -cat·ed, -cat·ing. give off flashes of light; sparkle. [< L, < coruscus flashing] —**cor′us·ca′tion,** n.

cor·vette, cor·vet (kôr vet′), n. warship with sails and only one tier of guns. [prob. < MDu. korf a kind of ship < corbis basket]

cor·ymb (kôr′imb; -im; kor′-), n. a flat cluster of flowers in which the outer flowers blossom first. [< L < Gk. korymbos top, cluster] —**co·rym′bose,** adj. —**co·rym′bose·ly,** adv.

co·ry·za (kə rī′zə), n. cold in the head. [< L < Gk. koryza catarrh]

cos (kos; kôs), n. kind of lettuce. [from the island of Cos in the Aegean]

cos, cosine.

Co·sa No·stra (kō′zə nōs′tra, nos′-), =Mafia. [< Italian cosa nostra our thing]

co·se·cant (kō sē′kənt; -kant), n. the secant of the complement of a given angle or arc.

co·sign (kō sīn′), v. act as cosignatory of. —**co·sign′er,** n.

co·sig·na·to·ry (kō sig′nə tô′ri; -tō′-), adj., n., pl. -ries. —adj. signing along with another or others. —n. one who so signs.

co·sine (kō′sīn), n. sine of the complement of a given angle or arc.

cos·met·ic (koz met′ik), n. preparation for beautifying the skin, etc. —adj. beautifying. [< Gk. kosmetikos of order, adornment < kosmos order]

cos·mic (koz′mik), adj. 1 of or belonging to the cosmos; having to do with the whole universe. 2 vast. [< Gk. kosmikos < kosmos order, world] —**cos′mi·cal·ly,** adv.

cosmic dust, fine particles of matter in outer space, often forming clouds.

cosmic rays, rays of very short wave lengths and very great penetration, coming to the earth esp. from the sun and interstellar space.

cos·mog·o·ny (koz mog′ə ni), n., pl. -nies. 1 origin of the universe. 2 theory of its origin. [< Gk. kosmogonia < kosmos world + gignesthai be born]

cos·mog·ra·phy (koz-mog′rə fi), n., pl. -phies. science that deals with the general appearance and structure of the universe. [< Gk., < kosmos world + graphein write]

cos·mol·o·gy (koz mol′ə ji), n. science or theory of the universe, its parts, and laws. —**cos′mo·log′i·cal,** adj.

cos·mo·naut (koz′mə nôt), n. astronaut, esp. a Russian astronaut. [< Russ. kosmonaut]

cos·mo·pol·i·tan (koz′mə pol′ə tən), *adj.* 1 belonging to all parts of the world; widely spread. 2 free from national or local prejudices; feeling at home in any part of the world. —*n.* a cosmopolitan person or thing.

cos·mo·pol·i·tan·ism (koz′mə pol′ə tə niz′əm), *n.* 1 cosmopolitan character or quality. 2 belief that people are citizens of the world, rather than of a nation or region.

cos·mop·o·lite (koz mop′ə līt), *n.* 1 a cosmopolitan person. 2 animal or plant found in all or many parts of the world. [< Gk., < *kosmos* world + *polites* citizen < *polis* city]

cos·mos (koz′məs; –mos), *n.* 1 the universe thought of as an orderly, harmonious system. 2 any complete system that is orderly and harmonious. 3 plant with white, pink, or purple flowers, that blooms in the fall. [< NL < Gk. *kosmos* order, world]

Cos·sack (kos′ak; –ək), *n.* one of a people living in S Russia, noted as horsemen.

cos·set (kos′it), *n.* a pet lamb; a pet. [< v.] —*v.* treat as a pet; pamper. [< unrecorded OE *cossettan* to kiss < *coss* a kiss]

cost (kôst; kost), *n., v.,* **cost, cost·ing.** —*n.* 1 price paid. 2 loss; sacrifice. —*v.* be obtained at the price of; require.

at all costs or **at any cost,** by all means; no matter what must be done.

costs, expenses of a lawsuit or case in court. [< OF, < *coster* < L, < *com-* + *stare* stand]

cos·tal (kos′təl), *adj.* 1 of or pertaining to a rib or ribs. 2 bearing ribs. [< Med.L, < L *costa* rib]

Cos·ta Ri·ca (kos′tə rē′kə; kôs′–; kōs′–), country in Central America. —**Costa Rican.**

cost-ef·fec·tive (kôst′ə fek′tiv, kost′–), *adj.* effective in terms of the relation of cost to anticipated or actual benefits. —**cost′-ef·fec′tive·ness ,** *n.*

cos·ter (kos′tər; kôs′–), or **cos·ter·mon·ger** (–mung′gər; –mong′–), *n. Esp. Brit.* person who sells fruit, vegetables, fish, etc., in the street. [< *costard* a kind of English apple]

cos·tive (kos′tiv; kôs′–), *adj.* 1 constipated. 2 producing constipation. 3 *Fig.* stingy. [< OF < L *constipatus,* pp. See CONSTIPATE.] —**cos′tive·ly,** *adv.* —**cos′tive·ness,** *n.*

cost·ly (kôst′li; kost′–), *adj.,* **–li·er, –li·est.** 1 of great value. 2 costing much. 3 *Archaic.* costing too much. —**cost′li·ness,** *n.*

cost-of-liv·ing index (kôst′əv liv′ing, kost′–), Consumer Price Index.

cos·tume (*n.* kos′tüm, –tüm; *v.* kos tüm′, –tüm′), *n., v.,* **–tumed, –tum·ing.** —*n.* 1 style of dress, etc., including the way the hair is worn, kind of jewelry, etc. 2 dress belonging to another time or place, worn on the stage, etc. 3 a complete set of outer garments. —*v.* provide a costume for; dress. [< F < Ital.

< VL *consuetumen* custom. Doublet of CUSTOM.]

costume jewelry, jewelry made from inexpensive metals and imitation gems, often showy, colorful, and beautiful.

cos·tum·er (kos tüm′ər; –tüm′–), **cos·tumi·er** (–tüm′i ər; –tüm′–), *n.* person who makes, sells, or rents costumes or dresses.

co·sy (kō′zi), *adj.,* **co·si·er, co·si·est,** *n., pl.* **co·sies.** =cozy. —**co′si·ly,** *adv.* —**co′si·ness,** *n.*

cot (kot), *n.* 1 a narrow, portable bed, esp. one made of canvas. 2 *Brit.* crib. [< Anglo-Ind. < Hind. *khāt.* Cf. Skt. *khatvā.*]

cot, cotangent.

co·tan·gent (kō tan′jənt), *n.* tangent of the complement of a given angle or arc. —**co′tan·gen′tial,** *adj.*

cote (kōt), *n.* 1 shelter or shed for small animals, etc. 2 *Brit.* cottage. [OE. See COT².]

co·te·rie (kō′tə ri), *n.* set or circle of acquaintances; group of people who often meet socially. [< F, association for holding land, < *cotier* COTTER²]

co·ter·mi·nous (kō tėr′mə nəs), *adj.* 1 having the same boundaries or limits; coextensive. 2 having a common boundary; bordering.

co·til·lion (kə til′yən), *n.* 1 any large, formal dancing party. 2 dance with complicated steps and much changing of partners. It is led by one couple. [< F, orig., petticoat, dim. of *cotte* COAT]

cot·tage (kot′ij), *n.* 1 a small house. 2 house at a summer resort. [see COT², –AGE]

cottage cheese, a soft, white cheese made from the curds of sour milk.

cottage indusry, 1 system of production where workers produce goods for someone else in the home using their own equipment. 2 any small, busy enterprise based in the home. 3 *Fig.* apparently endless output of something from an individual or group.

cot·tag·er (kot′ij ər), *n.* person who lives in a cottage.

cot·ter¹ (kot′ər), *n.* 1 pin that is inserted through a slot to hold small parts of machinery, etc., together. 2 =cotter pin.

cot·ter², **cot·tar** (kot′ər), *n.* a Scottish peasant who works for a farmer and is allowed to use a small cottage and a plot of land. [< Med.L *cotarius* < *cota* < OE *cot* COT²]

cotter pin, a metal pin, usually split at one end, inserted through a hole or slot to hold parts of machinery together.

cot·ton (kot′ən), *n.* 1 soft, white fibers in a fluffy mass around the seeds of a plant of the mallow family. 2 plant or plants that produce these fibers. 3 thread of cotton fibers. 4 cloth made of cotton thread. —*adj.* made of cotton. —*v. Informal.* take a liking.

cotton on (to), *Informal.* understand; catch on. [< OF < Ital. < Ar. *quṭn*] —**cot′ton·y,** *adj.*

cotton batting, soft, fluffy cotton pressed into thin layers.

Cotton Belt, region of the S United States where cotton is extensively grown.

cotton gin, machine for separating the fibers of cotton from the seeds.

cot·ton·mouth (kot′ən mouth′), *n.* =water moccasin.

cot·ton·seed (kot′ən sēd′), *n., pl.* **–seeds** or (*esp. collectively*) **–seed.** seed of cotton, used for making cottonseed oil, fertilizer, cattle food, etc.

cottonseed oil, oil pressed from cottonseed, used for cooking, for making soap, etc.

cot·ton·tail (kot′ən tāl′), *n.* a common American wild rabbit.

cot·ton·wood (kot′ən wüd′), *n.* 1 an American poplar tree having cottonlike tufts on the seeds. 2 its soft wood.

cotton wool, 1 raw cotton, before or after picking. 2 =cotton batting.

cot·y·le·don (kot′ə lē′dən), *n.* an embryo leaf in the seed of a plant; the first leaf, or one of the first pair of leaves, growing from a seed. [< L < Gk. *kotyledon* cup-shaped hollow < *kotyle* small vessel] —**cot′y·le′don·al,** *adj.* —**cot′y·le′don·ous,** *adj.*

couch (kouch), *n.* 1 thing made to sleep or rest on. 2 place to sleep or rest in: *a grassy couch.* —*v.* 1 lay on a couch. 2 put in words; express. 3 lie hidden ready to attack. [< OF, < *coucher* lay in place < L, < *com-* + *locare* place < *locus* a place] —**couch′er,** *n.*

couch·ant (kouch′ənt), *adj.* lying down, but with the head raised. [< F, ppr. See COUCH.]

cou·gar (kü′gər), *n.* a large, tawny American wildcat; puma; mountain lion. [< F < NL < Tupi-Guarani]

cough (kôf; kof), *v.* force air from the lungs with sudden effort and noise. —*n.* 1 act of coughing. 2 repeated acts of coughing. 3 a diseased condition of the lungs, etc., that causes coughing.

cough up, a expel from the throat by coughing. **b** *Fig.* give; bring out; produce. [ME *coghen* < OE *cohhetan*]

could (kùd), *v.* pt. of **can.**

could·n't (kūd′ənt), could not.

cou·lee (kü′li), *n.* 1 a deep ravine or gulch. A coulee is usually dry in summer. 2 stream of lava. [< F, < *couler* flow < L *colare* strain]

cou·lomb (kü lom′), *n.* quantity of electricity furnished by a current of one ampere in one second. [for C. A. de *Coulomb,* French physicist]

coul·ter (kōl′tər), *n.* =colter.

coun·cil (koun′səl), *n.* 1 group of people called together to give advice, talk things over, or settle questions. 2 a small group of people elected by citizens to make laws for and govern a city or town. 3 an ecclesiastical assembly for deciding matters of doctrine or discipline. [< OF < L *concilium* < *com-* together + *calare* call]

coun·cil·man (koun′səl mən), *n.*, *pl.* **-men.** member of the council of a city or town.

council of war, conference to talk over and decide on matters of importance.

coun·cil·wo·man (koun′səl wŭm′ən), *n.* female member of the council of a city or town.

coun·ci·lor (koun′sə lər), *n.* a council member. **—coun′ci·lor·ship′,** *n.*

coun·sel (koun′səl), *n.,* *v.,* **-seled, -sel·ing.** **—***n.* **1** act of exchanging ideas; act of talking things over. **2** advice. **3** lawyer or group of lawyers. **4** design; plan. **—***v.* **1** give advice to; advise. **2** recommend. **3** exchange ideas; consult together; deliberate. [< OF < L *consilium* < *consulere* consult, orig., convoke < *com-* together + *sel-* take]

coun·se·lor (koun′sə lər), *n.* **1** person who gives advice; adviser. **2** lawyer. **—coun′se·lor·ship′,** *n.*

count[1] (kount), *v.* **1** name the numbers up to. **2** add; find how many. **3** take into account. **4** depend; rely. **5** be included in counting. **6** have an influence of value. **7** consider. **—***n.* **1** a finding out how many. **2** the total number; amount. **3** an accounting. **4** ten seconds counted to give a fallen boxer time to rise. **5** each charge in a formal accusation.

count for, amount to; be worth.

count in, *Informal.* include: *count me in to help.*

count off, divide into groups of equal size by counting.

count out, a fail to consider. **b** declare (a fallen boxer) the loser after failing to rise within 10 seconds. [< OF < L < *com-* up + *putare* reckon. Doublet of COMPUTE.] **—count′a·ble,** *adj.*

count[2] (kount), *n.* a European nobleman having a rank about the same as that of an English earl. [< OF < L *comes* companion < *com-* with + *ire* go]

count·down (kount′doun′), *n.* **1** period of time preceding the firing of a rocket, spacecraft, etc. **2** the calling out of the passing minutes (and seconds, in the last stage) of this period.

coun·te·nance (koun′tə nəns), *n.,* *v.,* **-nanced, -nanc·ing. —***n.* **1** expression of the face. **2** face; features. **3** approval; encouragement. **4** calmness; composure. **—***v.* approve; encourage. [< OF < Med.L *continentia* demeanor < L, self-control. See CONTINENT[2].]

count·er[1] (koun′tər), *n.* **1** *Esp. U.S.* **a** a long table in a store, restaurant, etc. **b** =countertop. **2** a piece of wood, metal, etc., used to count, as in card games. **3** an imitation coin. [< OF, < *conter* COUNT[1]]

count·er[2] (koun′tər), *n.* **1** person who counts. **2** a machine for counting.

coun·ter[3] (koun′tər), *adv.* in the opposite direction; opposed; contrary. **—***adj.* opposite; contrary. **—***v.* go or act counter to; oppose. **—***n.* **1** that which is opposite

or contrary to something else. **2** a stiff piece inside the back of a shoe around the heel. **3** part of a ship's stern from the water line to the end of the curved part. [< F < L *contra* against]

counter-, *combining form.* **1** against; in opposition to, as in *counteract.* **2** in return, as in *counterattack.* **3** that corresponds; so as to correspond, as in *counterpart.* [see COUNTER[3]]

coun·ter·act (koun′tər akt′), *v.* act against; neutralize the action or effect of; hinder. **—coun′ter·ac′tion,** *n.* **—coun′ter·ac′tive,** *adj.,* *n.*

coun·ter·at·tack (*n.* koun′tər ə tak′; *v.* koun′tər ə tak′), *n.* attack made to counteract an attack. **—***v.* attack in return.

coun·ter·bal·ance (*n.* koun′tər bal′əns; *v.* koun′tər bal′əns), *n.,* *v.,* **-anced, -anc·ing. —***n.* **1** weight balancing another weight. **2** influence, power, etc., balancing another. **—***v.* act as a counterbalance to; offset.

counter check, check which a depositor can obtain from the bank for withdrawal of funds from his or her account.

coun·ter·claim (*n.* koun′tər klām′; *v.* koun′tər klām′), *n.* an opposing claim; claim made by a person to offset a claim made against him. **—***v.* make a counterclaim. **—coun′ter·claim′ant,** *n.*

coun·ter·clock·wise (koun′tər klok′wīz′), *adv., adj.* in the direction opposite to that in which the hands of a clock go.

coun·ter·cul·ture (koun′tər kul′chər), *n.* culture of esp. young people opposed to the standards and norms of the traditional culture. **—coun′ter·cul′tur·al,** *adj.*

coun·ter·feit (koun′tər fit), *v.* **1** copy (money, handwriting, pictures, etc.) in order to deceive or defraud. **2** resemble closely. **3** pretend; dissemble. **—***n.* copy made to deceive or defraud and passed as genuine. **—***adj.* made to deceive or defraud. [< OF *contrefait* imitated < *contre-* against (< L *contra-*) + *faire* make < L *facere*] **—coun′ter·feit′er,** *n.*

coun·ter·in·sur·gen·cy (koun′tər in sėr′jen si), *n.* **1** guerrilla warfare waged against a force viewed as hostile, such as an occupying force in a country. **2** military action taken against guerrillas or other insurgents. **—coun′ter·in·sur′gent,** *adj., n.*

coun·ter·in·tel·li·gence (koun′tər in tel′ə jəns), *n.* activity or measures taken to cause confusion or cast doubt on information obtained by spies from other countries or entities.

coun·ter·ir·ri·tant (koun′tər ir′ə tənt), *n.* **1** something used to produce irritation in one place in order to relieve irritation elsewhere. **2** *Fig.* any problem, concern, etc. that distracts from a primary source of irritation.

coun·ter·mand (*v.* koun′tər mand′, -mänd′; *n.* koun′tər mand, -mänd), *v.* **1** withdraw or cancel (an order, command, etc.). **2** recall or stop by a contrary order.

—*n.* command, etc., that revokes a previous one. [< OF, < L *contra-* against + *mandare* order]

coun·ter·of·fen·sive (koun′tər ə fen′siv), *n.* aggressive action on a large scale undertaken by a defending force to seize the initiative from the attacking force.

coun·ter·pane (koun′tər pān′), *n.* quilt; coverlet. [alter. of *counterpoint* quilt < OF]

coun·ter·part (koun′tər pärt′), *n.* **1** copy; duplicate. **2** person or thing closely resembling another. **3** person or thing that complements another.

coun·ter·plot (*n., v.* koun′tər plot′; *v. also* koun′tər plot′), *n.,* *v.,* **-plot·ted, -plot·ting. —***n.* plot to defeat another plot. **—***v.* devise a counterplot.

coun·ter·point (koun′tər point′), *n.* *Music.* **1** melody added to another as an accompaniment. **2** art of adding melodies to a given melody according to fixed rules.

coun·ter·poise (koun′tər poiz′), *n.,* *v.,* **-poised, -pois·ing. —***n.* **1** weight balancing another weight. **2** influence, power, etc., balancing or offsetting another. **—***v.* act as a counterpoise to; offset. [< OF *countrepeis* < *contre-* against (< L *contra-*) + *peis* weight < L *pensum*]

coun·ter·rev·o·lu·tion (koun′tər rev′ə lü′shən), *n.* revolution against a government established by a previous revolution. **—coun′terrev′o·lu′tion·ar′y,** *adj., n.* **—coun′ter·rev′o·lu′tion·ist,** *n.*

coun·ter·shaft (koun′tər shaft′; -shäft′), *n.* shaft that transmits motion from the main shaft to the working part of a machine.

coun·ter·sign (*n., v.* koun′tər sīn′; *v. also* koun′tər sīn′), *n.* **1** password given in answer to the challenge of a sentinel. **2** signature added to another signature to confirm it. **—***v.* sign (something already signed by another) to confirm it. **—coun′ter·sig′na·ture,** *n.*

coun·ter·sink (*v., n.* koun′tər singk′; *v. also* koun′tər singk′), *v.,* **-sunk, -sink·ing,** *n.* **—***v.* **1** enlarge the upper part of (a hole) to make room for the head of a screw, bolt, etc. **2** sink the head of (a screw, bolt, etc.) into such a hole so that it is even with or below the surface. **—***n.* **1** a countersunk hole. **2** tool for countersinking holes.

coun·ter·spy (koun′tər spī), *n.* person who works to uncover or counteract the activities of enemy spies.

coun·ter·ten·or (koun′tər ten′ər), *n.* **1** highest range of a male voice, higher than a tenor and sometimes falsetto. **2** singer who has such a voice. **3** music for this voice.

coun·ter·top (koun′tər top′), *n.* shelf on the top of a cabinet, used as a workspace, esp. in a kitchen.

coun·ter·weight (koun′tər wāt′), *n.* weight that balances another weight.

count·ess (koun′tis), *n.* **1** wife or widow of an earl or a count. **2** woman whose rank is equal to that of an earl or a count.

counting house or **room,** building or office used for keeping accounts and doing business.

count·less (kount′lis), *adj.* too many to count; very many; innumerable.

coun·tri·fied, coun·try·fied (kun′tri fīd), *adj.* like the country; rural.

coun·try (kun′tri), *n., pl.* **–tries,** *adj.* —*n.* 1 land; region; district. 2 all the land of a nation. 3 **a** people of a nation. **b** the public, esp. as a body of voters. 4 land where a person was born or is a citizen. 5 land without many houses; rural district. —*adj.* 1 of the country; rural. 2 rustic. [< OF < VL *contrata* what lies opposite < L *contra* against]

coun·try-and-west·ern (kun′trē ən wes′-tərn), *n.* stylized form of country music, usually played on amplified instruments.

country club, club in the country near a city.

coun·try·man (kun′tri mən), *n., pl.* **–men.** 1 man of one's own country. 2 man who lives in the country.

country music, 1 folk music of rural areas of the United States, played with banjo, guitar, harmonica, etc., and, sometimes, improvised instruments. 2 =country-and-western.

coun·try·side (kun′tri sīd′), *n.* 1 rural district; country. 2 certain section of the country. 3 its people.

coun·try·wom·an (kun′tri wŭm′ən), *n., pl.* **–wom·en.** 1 woman of one's own country. 2 woman living in the country.

coun·ty (koun′ti), *n., pl.* **–ties.** 1 in the United States, the political unit next below the state. 2 one of the chief districts into which a state or country, as Great Britain and Ireland, is divided. 3 people of a county. [< AF *counté* < *counte* COUNT²]

county seat, town or city where the county government is located.

coup (kü), *n., pl.* **coups** (küz). 1 a sudden, brilliant action. 2 =coup d'état. [< F < L < Gk. *kolaphos*]

coup de grâce (kü′ də gräs′), *pl.* **coups de grâce.** 1 action that gives a merciful death to a suffering animal or person. 2 *Fig.* the finishing stroke. [< F, lit., stroke of grace]

coup d'é·tat (kü′ dā tä′), a sudden and decisive measure in politics, esp. one affecting a change of government illegally or by force. [< F, lit., stroke of state]

cou·pe (küp), *n.* 1 a closed, two-door automobile seating two to five people. 2 a closed carriage with a seat for the driver outside. [< F, pp. of *couper* cut. See COUP.]

cou·ple (kup′əl), *n., v.,* **–pled, –pling.** —*n.* 1 two things of the same kind that go together; pair. 2 **a** two people who live together or are partners. **b** two people who are partners in a dance.

—*v.* join together; join together in pairs. [< OF *cople* < L *copula* bond. Doublet of COPULA.] —**cou′pler,** *n.*

cou·plet (kup′lit), *n.* 1 two successive lines of poetry, esp. two that rhyme and are equally long. 2 couple; pair.

cou·pling (kup′ling), *n.* 1 act or process of joining together. 2 device for joining together parts of machinery. 3 device used to join together two railroad cars. 4 device or arrangement for transferring electrical energy from one circuit to another.

cou·pon (kü′pon; kü′–), *n.* 1 a printed statement of interest due on a bond, which can be cut from the bond and presented for payment. 2 part of a ticket, advertisement, ration book, etc., that gives the person who holds it certain rights. [< F, < *couper* cut. See COUP.]

cour·age (kèr′ij), *n.* bravery; fearlessness. [< OF *corage* < *cuer* heart < L *cor*]

cou·ra·geous (kə rā′jəs), *adj.* full of courage; brave; fearless. —**cou·ra′geous·ly,** *adv.* —**coura′geous·ness,** *n.*

cour·i·er (kèr′i ər; kúr′–), *n.* messenger sent in haste. [< F *courrier* < Ital. < L *currere* run]

course (kôrs; kōrs), *n., v.,* **coursed, coursing.** —*n.* 1 onward movement. 2 direction taken. 3 way of doing. 4 way; path. 5 group of similar things arranged in some regular order. 6 regular order. 7 series of studies in a school, college, or university. 8 one of the studies. 9 part of a meal served at one time. 10 place for races or games. 11 layer of bricks, stones, shingles, etc.; row. —*v.* 1 race; run. 2 hunt with dogs.

in due course, at the proper time.

in the course of, during.

of course, a surely. **b** as should be expected.

run its (or **one's**) **course, a** be completed. **b** come to an end. [< F *cours* < L *cursus,* a running and < F *course* < Ital. *corsa* a running < L *currere* run]

cours·er (kôr′sər; kōr′–), *n. Poetic.* a swift horse.

court (kôrt; kōrt), *n.* 1 space enclosed by walls or buildings. 2 a short street. 3 area marked off for a game, as for tennis. 4 a stately dwelling. 5 residence where a sovereign lives; royal palace. 6 household of a sovereign. 7 sovereign and advisers as a ruling power. 8 **a** place where justice is administered. **b** judge or judges. 9 attention paid to get favor. 10 act of making amorous advances. —*v.* 1 try to please. 2 make amorous advances to. 3 try to get; seek: *court danger.*

out of court, without the aid or sponsorship of a law court: *settle a dispute out of court.* [< OF < L *cohors* enclosure, retinue. Doublet of COHORT.]

cour·te·ous (kèr′ti əs), *adj.* polite; thoughtful of others. [< OF *corteis* < *cort* COURT] —**cour′teous·ly,** *adv.* —**cour′te·ous·ness,** *n.*

cour·te·san (kôr′tə zən; kōr′–; kèr′–), *n.* a prostitute. [< F < Ital. *cortigiana* woman of the court < *corte* COURT]

cour·te·sy (kèr′tə si), *n., pl.* **–sies.** 1 polite behavior; thoughtfulness for others. 2 polite act; thoughtful act. [< OF *cortesie* < *corteis* COURTEOUS]

courtesy call, short visit or telephone call paid by one person to another as an act of respect or as required by etiquette.

court·house (kôrt′hous′; kōrt′–), *n.* 1 a building where law courts are held. 2 a building used for the government of a county.

cour·ti·er (kôr′ti ər; kōr′–), *n.* 1 person often present at the court of a king, prince, etc. 2 person who tries to win the favor of another.

court·ly (kôrt′li; kōrt′–), *adj.,* **–li·er, –li·est.** 1 suitable for a king's court; elegant. 2 trying hard to please one's superior; flattering. —**court′li·ness,** *n.*

court-mar·tial (kôrt′mär′shəl; kōrt′–), *n., pl.* **courts-mar·tial,** *v.,* **–tialed, –tial·ing.** —*n.* 1 court of army or navy officers for trying offenders against military or naval laws. 2 trial by such a court. —*v.* try by such a court.

court·room (kôrt′rüm′; –rùm′; kōrt′–), *n.* room where a law court is held.

court·ship (kôrt′ship; kōrt′–), *n.* making love; wooing.

court·yard (kôrt′yärd′; kōrt′–), *n.* space enclosed by walls, in or near a large building.

cous·cous (kùs′kùs′), *n.* coarse ground wheat, cooked and served with meat or broth, esp. in N African dishes.

cous·in (kuz′ən), *n.* 1 son or daughter of one's uncle or aunt. 2 a distant relative. 3 term used by one sovereign in speaking to another sovereign or to a great nobleman. [< F < L *consobrinus* mother's sister's child < *com–* together + *soror* sister] —**cous′in·ly,** *adj., adv.* —**cous′in·ship,** *n.*

cous·in-ger·man (kuz′ən jèr′mən), *n., pl.* **cous·ins-ger·man.** son or daughter of one's uncle or aunt; first cousin.

cou·ture (kü tùr′, kü tyr′), *n.* 1 business of designing and making clothing, esp. dresses. 2 designers and dressmakers.

cou·tu·ri·er (kü tür′iər; *Fr.* kü ty ryā′), *n.* a dressmaker and dress designer, esp. of expensive and unusual fashions. [< F]

co·va·lence (kō vā′ləns), *n.* total of the pairs of electrons one atom can share with surrounding atoms.

cove (kōv), *n.,* a small, sheltered bay; inlet on the shore. [OE *coja* chamber]

cov·e·nant (kuv′ə nənt), *n.* 1 a solemn agreement between two or more persons or groups to do or not to do a certain thing; compact. 2 in the Bible, the solemn promises of God to man. 3 a legal contract; formal agreement that is legal. —*v.* solemnly agree. [< OF, < *covenir* < L *convenire.* See CONVENE.] —**cov′e·nant·er,** *n.*

cov·er (kuv′ər), *v.* **1** put something over. **2** clothe; wrap up. **3** be thick over. **4** protect; shelter. **5** go over; travel. **6** include; make up. **7** be enough for. **8** have within range. **9** act as a reporter or photographer of: *to cover a fire for a newspaper.* —*n.* **1** thing that covers. **2** protection; shelter.

break cover, come out in the open.

cover up, a cover completely. **b** *Fig.* hide; conceal.

from cover to cover, from the first to the last page of a book; beginning to end.

under cover, a hidden; secret; disguised. **b** secretly. [< OF < L, < *co–* up + *operire* cover] —**cov′er·er,** *n.* —**cov′er·less,** *adj.*

cov·er·age (kuv′ər ij), *n.* **1** amount covered by something. **2** risks covered by an insurance policy.

cover charge, in some restaurants and nightclubs, a charge made for service, music, etc.

covered wagon, a wagon having a removable canvas cover.

cov·er·ing (kuv′ər ing), *n.* thing that covers.

cov·er·let (kuv′ər lit), **cov·er·lid** (–lid), *n.* **1** an outer covering for a bed; bedspread. **2** any covering.

cover letter, letter accompanying a package, proposal, resume, etc., that explains or confirms what is being sent. Also, **covering letter** or **note.**

cover story, lead or most important article or story in a magazine, associated with the illustration on its cover.

cov·ert (kuv′ərt; kō′vərt), *adj.* **1** sheltered. **2** secret; disguised: *covert glances.* —*n.* shelter; hiding place. [< OF, pp. of *covrir* cover] —**cov′ert·ly,** *adv.* —**cov′ert·ness,** *n.*

cov·er·up (kuv′ər up′), *n.* **1** something that conceals or disguises a defect, crime, or malfeasance. **2** garment that completely covers another garment.

cov·et (kuv′it), *v.* desire eagerly (esp. something that belongs to another). [< OF *coveitier,* ult. < L *cupere* desire] —**cov′et·a·ble,** *adj.* —**cov′et·er,** *n.*

cov·et·ous (kuv′ə təs), *adj.* overly desirous (esp. of things that belong to others).—**cov′etous·ly,**adv.—**cov′et·ous·ness,** *n.*

cov·ey (kuv′i), *n., pl.* **-eys. 1** brood of partridges, quail, etc. **2** small flock; group. [< OF, < *cover* incubate < L *cubare* lie]

cow¹ (kou), *n., pl.* **cows,** (*Archaic* or *Dial.*) **kine** (kīn). **1** female of a bovine family, esp. of the domestic species that furnishes milk. **2** female of various other large animals: *an elephant cow.* **3** *Slang.* term of contempt for a woman. [OE *cū*]

cow² (kou), *v.* make afraid; frighten. [< Scand. *kūga*]

cow·ard (kou′ərd), *n.* person who lacks courage or is afraid. —*adj.* **1** lacking courage; cowardly. **2** showing fear. [< OF *coart* < *coe* tail < L *cauda*]

cow·ard·ice (kou′ər dis), *n.* lack of courage; being easily made afraid.

cow·ard·ly (kou′ərd li), *adj.* **1** lacking courage. **2** of a coward. —*adv.* fit for a coward. —**cow′ard·li·ness,** *n.*

cow·boy (kou′boi′), *n.* man who works on a ranch, at rodeos, etc.

cow·er (kou′ər), *v.* **1** crouch in fear or shame. **2** draw back tremblingly from another's threats, blows, etc. [< Scand. *kūra* sit moping]

cow·girl (kou′gėrl′), *n.* woman who works on a ranch, at rodeos, etc.

cow hand, person who works on a cattle ranch.

cow·herd (kou′hėrd′), *n.* person whose work is looking after cattle.

cow·hide (kou′hīd′), *n.,* **1** hide of a cow. **2** leather made from it. **3** strong leather whip.

cowl (koul), *n.* **1** a monk's cloak with a hood. **2** the hood itself. **3** anything shaped like a cowl. **4** metal covering over an airplane engine. **5** a covering for the top of a chimney to increase the draft. —*v.* **1** put a monk's cowl on. **2** cover with a cowl or something resembling a cowl. [< LL *cuculla,* var. of L *cucullus* hood] —**cowled,** *adj.*

cow·lick (kou′lik′), *n.* a small tuft of hair that will not lie flat.

cowl·ing (koul′ing), *n.* metal covering over the engine of an airplane.

cow·man (kou′mən), *n., pl.* **-men, 1** an owner of cattle; ranchman. **2** cowboy; cowherd.

co·work·er (kō wėr′kər), *n.* person who works with another.

cow·pea (kou′pē′), *n.* **1** plant that has very long pods, used as food for cattle, fertilizer, etc. **2** seed of this plant.

cow·pox (kou′poks′), *n.* contagious viral disease of cows causing small pustules on cows' udders. Vaccine for smallpox is obtained from cows that have cowpox.

cow·rie, cow·ry (kou′ri), *n., pl.* **-ries.** a yellow shell formerly used as money in some parts of Africa and Asia. [< Hind. *kaurī*]

cow·slip (kou′slip), *n.* **1** a wild plant with yellow flowers; marsh marigold. **2** an English primrose. [OE, < *cū* cow + *slyppe* slime]

cox (koks), *n.* =coxswain.

cox·comb (koks′kōm′), *n.* **1** a vain, empty-headed man; conceited dandy. **2** =cockscomb. **3** a cap resembling a cock's comb, worn by clowns or jesters. [var. of *cock's comb*]

cox·swain (kok′sən; –swān′), *n.* person who steers a boat, racing shell, etc. Also, **cockswain.**

coy (koi), *adj.* **1** shy; modest; bashful. **2** pretending to be shy. [< F *coi* < L *quietus* at rest. Doublet of QUIET¹ and QUIT, adj.] —**coy′ly,** *adv.* —**coy′ness,** *n.*

coy·o·te (kī ō′tē; kī′ōt), *n., pl.* **-tes** or (*esp. collectively*) **-te. 1** a prairie wolf of North America. **2** person hired to guide illegal immigrants from Latin America to the United States. [< Mex.Sp. < Nahuatl *koyotl*]

coy·pu (koi′pü), *n., pl.* **-pus** or (*esp. collectively*) **-pu.** a large ratlike water animal of South America. Its fur is called nutria. [< Sp. < Araucanian (S Am. Ind. linguistic stock) *koypu*]

coz·en (kuz′ən), *v.* =cheat. —**coz′en·er,** *n.*

co·zy (kō′zi), *adj.,* **co·zi·er, co·zi·est,** *n., pl.* **co·zies.** —*adj.* warm and comfortable; snug. —*n.* padded cloth cover to keep a teapot warm. Also, **cosy.** [< Scand. (Norw.) *koselig*] —**co′zi·ly,** *adv.* —**co′zi·ness,** *n.*

cp., 1 compare. **2** coupon.

C.P.A., Certified Public Accountant.

cpd., compound.

CPI, Consumer Price Index.

Cpl., cpl., Corporal.

CPU, central processing unit.

CPR, cardiopulmonary resuscitation.

Cr, chromium.

cr., credit; creditor.

crab¹ (krab), *n., v.,* **crabbed, crab·bing.** —*n.* **1** a shellfish that has a short, broad body with the abdomen or tail folded under, four pairs of legs, and one pair of pincers. **2** a cross, ill-natured person. **3 Crab,** Cancer, a constellation of the zodiac. —*v.* catch crabs for eating. [OE *crabba*] —**crab′ber,** *n.*

crab² (krab), *n.* =crab apple.

crab³ (krab), *v.,* **crabbed, crab·bing.** *Colloq.* find fault (with); criticize. [cf. MDu. *krabben* scratch, quarrel]

crab apple, 1 any of various small, very sour apples, used for making jelly. **2** tree that bears crab apples.

crab·bed (krab′id), *adj.* **1** Also, **crab′by.** peevish; ill-natured; cross. **2** hard to understand. **3** hard to read or decipher. [< *crab¹*]

crab grass, a coarse grass that spreads rapidly and spoils lawns, etc.

crack (krak), *n.* **1** place, line, surface, or opening made by breaking without separating into parts. **2** a sudden, sharp noise. **3** blow that makes a sudden, sharp noise. **4** a narrow opening. **5** instant; moment. **6** *Slang.* try; effort. **7** *Slang.* joke. **8** potent, free-based form of cocaine. —*v.* **1** break without separating into parts. **2** break with a sudden, sharp noise. **3** make or cause to make a sudden, sharp noise. **4** hit with a sudden, sharp noise. **5** make or become harsh and shrill: *his voice cracked.* **6** give way; break down. **7** tell (a joke, etc.). **8** break into: *crack a safe.*

crack down, take stern measures.

crack up, a suffer a mental collapse. **b** crash; go to pieces. **c** *Informal.* laugh or cause to laugh uncontrollably. [OE *cracian*]

crack-brained (krak′brānd′), *adj.* crazy; insane. —**crack brain.**

crack·co·caine (krak′kō kān′, –kō′kān), *n.* crack (*n.,* def. 8).

crack·down (krak′doun′), *n.* taking sudden and stern measures to end a practice, activity, etc.

cracked (krakt), *adj.* 1 broken without separating into parts. 2 harsh and shrill. 3 crazy; insane.

crack·er (krak′ər), *n.* 1 a thin, crisp biscuit. 2 =firecracker. 3 a small, paper roll used as a party favor, which explodes when pulled at both ends. 4 *U.S. Dialect.* poor white person living in the hills and backwoods regions of Georgia, Florida, etc. 5 person or instrument that cracks.

crack·head (krak′hed′), *n. Slang.* person addicted to crack.

crack·ing (krak′ing), *n.* process of changing certain hydrocarbons in petroleum and other oils into lighter hydrocarbons by heat and pressure to produce gasoline. —*adj. Informal.* 1 vigorous; brisk. 2 thorough; complete. —*adv. Informal.* thoroughly.

get cracking, *Informal.* make a vigorous start; get going.

crack·le (krak′əl), *v.,* **–led, –ling,** *n.* —*v.* make slight, sharp sounds. —*n.* 1 a slight, sharp sound, such as paper makes when crushed. 2 surface containing very small cracks of some kinds of china, glass, etc. [< *crack*]

crack·ling (krak′ling), *n.* 1 the crisp, browned skin of roasted pork. 2 Usually, **cracklings.** *Dial.* crisp part left after lard has been fried out of hog's fat.

crack·pot (krak′pot), *n.* eccentric or crazy person. —*adj.* eccentric; impractical.

crack-up (krak′up′), *n.* 1 crash; smash. 2 a mental or physical breakdown.

cra·dle (krā′dəl), *n., v.,* **–dled, –dling.** —*n.* 1 a baby's little bed, usually on rockers. 2 place where a thing begins its growth. 3 frame to support a ship, aircraft, or other large object while it is being built, repaired, lifted, etc. 4 box on rockers to wash gold from earth. 5 frame attached to a scythe for laying grain evenly as it is cut. —*v.* 1 put or rock in a cradle; hold as in a cradle. 2 shelter or train in early life. 3 support in a cradle. 4 wash in a cradle. 5 cut with a cradle scythe.

rob the cradle, *Informal.* choose as a partner or marry someone much younger than oneself. [OE *cradol*]

craft (kraft; kräft), *n.* 1 special skill. 2 trade or work requiring special skill. 3 members of a trade requiring special skill. Carpenters are a craft. 4 skill in deceiving others; slyness; trickiness. 5 (*pl. in use*) boats, ships, or aircraft. 6 a boat, ship, or aircraft. [OE *cræft*]

crafts·man (krafts′mən; kräfts′–), *n., pl.* **–men.** 1 a skilled workman. 2 artist. —**crafts′man·ship,** *n.*

craft·y (kraf′ti; kräf′–), *adj.,* **craft·i·er, crafti·est.** skillful in deceiving others; sly; tricky. —**craft′i·ly,** *adv.* —**craft′i·ness,** *n.*

crag (krag), *n.* a steep, rugged rock rising above others. [< Celtic] —**crag′gy, crag′ged,** *adj.* —**crag′gi·ness,** *n.*

cram (kram), *v.,* **crammed, cram·ming.** 1 force; stuff. 2 fill too full. 3 eat too fast or too much. 4 stuff with knowledge or information, esp. for an examination. 5 learn hurriedly. [OE *crammian* < *crimman* insert] —**cram′mer,** *n.*

cramp¹ (kramp), *n.* 1 a metal bar bent at both ends, used for holding together blocks of stone, timbers, etc. 2 clamp. 3 something that confines or hinders; limitation; restriction. —*v.* 1 fasten together with a cramp. 2 confine in a small space; limit; restrict. —*adj.* 1 confined; limited; restricted. 2 hard to read; difficult to understand. [< MDu. *cramp(e)*, MLG *krampe*]

cramp² (kramp), *n.* 1 a sudden, painful contracting of muscles from chill, strain, etc. 2 a paralytic affection of particular muscles. —*v.* cause to have a cramp. **cramps,** very sharp pains in the abdomen. [< MDu. See CRAMP¹.]

cram·pon (kram′pon), *n.* 1 spiked plate on the sole of a shoe or boot to prevent slipping, used in logging, mountain climbing, etc. 2 strong iron bar used for lifting; grappling iron.

cran·ber·ry (kran′ber′i; –bər i), *n., pl.* **–ries.** 1 a firm, sour, dark-red berry, used for jelly, sauce, etc. 2 a small shrub that the berries grow on. [< LG *kraanbere*]

crane (krān), *n., v.,* **craned, cran·ing.** —*n.* 1 machine with a long, swinging arm, for lifting and moving heavy weights. 2 a swinging metal arm in a fireplace, used to hold a kettle over the fire. 3 a large wading bird with very long legs and a long neck. 4 any of various herons, esp. the great blue heron. —*v.* 1 move by, or as if by, a crane. 2 stretch out (one's neck). [OE *cran*]

crane fly, any of several insects which have long legs; the daddy-longlegs of Great Britain.

cra·ni·ol·o·gy (krā′ni ol′ə ji), *n.* science that deals with the size, shape, and other characteristics of skulls. —**cra′ni·o·log′i·cal,** *adj.* —**cra′ni·o·log′i·cal·ly,** *adv.* —**cra′ni·ol′o·gist,** *n.*

cra·ni·om·e·try (krā′ni om′ə tri), *n.* science of measuring skulls; measurement of skulls. —**cra′ni·o·met′ric,** *adj.* —**cra′ni·o·met′ri·cal·ly,** *adv.* —**cra′ni·om′etrist,** *n.*

cra·ni·um (krā′ni əm), *n., pl.* **–ni·ums, –ni·a** (–ni ə). the skull. [< LL < Gk. *kranion*] —**cra′ni·al,** *adj.*

crank (krangk), *n.* 1 part or handle of a machine connected at right angles to another part to transmit motion. 2 *Informal. Fig.* person with odd notions or habits. 3 *Informal. Fig.* a cross or ill-tempered person. —*v.* 1 work or start by means of a crank. 2 bend into the shape of a crank.

crank out, produce rapidly and steadily.

crank up, get ready; get started. [OE *cranc*]

crank·case (krangk′kās′), *n.* a heavy, metal case enclosing the crankshaft, connecting rods, etc., of an internal-combustion engine.

crank·shaft (krangk′shaft′; –shäft′), *n.* shaft turned by cranks operated by the movement of the pistons in a gasoline engine.

crank·y (krang′ki), *adj.,* **crank·i·er, crank·i·est.** 1 cross; irritable; ill-natured. 2 odd; queer. —**crank′i·ly,** *adv.* —**crank′i·ness,** *n.*

cran·ny (kran′i), *n., pl.* **–nies.** a small, narrow opening; crack; crevice. [< F *cran* fissure < Med.L *crena* notch] —**cran′nied,** *adj.*

crape (krāp), *n.* =crepe

crap·pie (krap′i), *n.* a small freshwater fish, used for food.

crap (krap), *n. Slang.* nonsense; rubbish. —*v.* talk nonsense.

crap around, *Slang.* waste time foolishly.

craps (kraps), *n.* a gambling game played with two dice.

crap·shoot (krap′shüt), *n.* unplanned event or undertaking whose outcome is extremely uncertain; gamble.

crap·shoot·er (krap′shüt′ər), *n.* person who plays craps.

crash¹ (krash), *n.* 1 a sudden, loud noise. 2 a falling, hitting, or breaking with force and a loud noise. 3 sudden ruin; severe failure in business. 4 of an airplane, a fall to the earth or a bad landing. —*v.* 1 make a sudden, loud noise. 2 fall, hit, or break with force and a loud noise. 3 move or go with force and a loud noise. 4 be suddenly ruined; fail in business. 5 land in such a way as to damage or wreck an aircraft; make a very bad landing. 6 cause (an aircaft) to land in such a way. 7 fail, as of a computer. 8 *Slang.* go to (a party, etc.) although not invited. —*adj.* of something used to rescue persons involved in a crash: *a crash boat.* [blend of *craze* shatter and *mash*] —**crash′er,** *n.*

crash² (krash), *n.* a coarse linen cloth, used for towels, curtains, upholstering, etc. [prob. < Russ.; cf. Russ. *krashenina* colored linen]

crash program, plan of action involving maximum effort and speed.

crass (kras), *adj.* 1 gross; stupid. 2 thick; coarse. [< L *crassus* thick] —**crass′ly,** *adv.* —**crass′ness,** *n.*

crate (krāt), *n., v.,* **crat·ed, crat·ing.** —*n.* a large frame, box, basket, etc., used to pack glass, fruit, etc., for shipping or storage. —*v.* pack in a crate. [< L *cratis* wickerwork] —**crat′er,** *n.*

cra·ter (krā′tər), *n.* 1 depression around the opening of a volcano. 2 a bowl-shaped hole. [< L < Gk. *krater* bowl < *kra–* mix]

cra·vat (krə vat′), *n.* 1 =necktie. 2 =neckcloth; scarf. [< F *cravate,* special use of *Cravate* Croat]

crave (krāv), *v.,* **craved, crav·ing.** 1 long for; yearn or; desire strongly. 2 ask earnestly; beg. [OE *crafian* demand]

cra·ven (krā′vən), *adj.* cowardly. —*n.* coward. —**cra′ven·ly,** *adv.* —**cra′ven·ness,** *n.*

crav·ing (krāv′ing), *n.* strong desire; longing.

craw (krô), *n.* **1** crop of a bird or insect. **2** stomach of any animal.

stick in one's craw, *Informal.* be unpalatable or unacceptable. [ME *crawe*]

craw·fish (krô′fish′), *n., pl.* **-fish·es** or (*esp. collectively*) **-fish,** *v. Am.* —*n.* any of numerous crustaceans much like small lobsters. —*v.* back out of something; retreat. [var. of *crayfish*]

crawl (krôl), *v.* **1** move slowly, pulling the body along the ground: *worms crawl.* **2** move slowly on hands and knees. **3** move slowly. **4** swarm with crawling things. **5** feel creepy. —*n.* **1** a crawling; slow movement. **2** a fast way of swimming by overarm strokes. [appar. < Scand. (Dan.) *kravle*] —**crawl′er,** *n.* —**crawl′ing·ly,** *adv.*

crawl space, small open space above the ceiling or under the floor of a house where pipes, heat ducts, etc. are located.

crawl·y (krôl′i), *adj.* creepy.

cray·fish (krā′fish′), *n., pl.* **-fish·es** or (*esp. collectively*) **-fish.** =crawfish. [< OF *crevice* < Gmc.; akin to CRAB[1]]

cray·on (krā′on; -ən), *n., v.,* **-oned, -on·ing.** —*n.* **1** stick of white or colored chalk or wax or charcoal used for drawing or writing. **2** drawing made with crayons. —*v.* draw with a crayon or crayons. [< F, < *craie* chalk < L *creta*]

craze (krāz), *n., v.,* **crazed, craz·ing.** —*n.* **1** something everybody is very much interested in for a short time; fad. **2** a tiny crack in the glaze of pottery, etc. —*v.* **1** make or become crazy. **2** make tiny cracks all over the surface of (a dish, etc.). **3** become minutely cracked. [appar. < Scand. (Sw.) *krasa* break in pieces] —**crazed,** *adj.*

cra·zy (krā′zi), *adj.,* **-zi·er, -zi·est. 1** having a diseased mind; insane. **2** showing insanity. **3** unreasonably eager or enthusiastic. **4** not strong or sound; frail.

like crazy, without let-up; like mad: *he ran like crazy.* —**cra′zi·ly,** *adv.* —**cra′zi·ness,** *n.*

crazy quilt, patchwork quilt.

creak (krēk), *v.* squeak loudly. —*n.* a creaking noise. [ME *creken* < OE *cræcettan* croak]

creak·y (krēk′i), *adj.,* **creak·i·er, creak·i·est.** likely to creak; creaking. —**creak′i·ly,** *adv.* —**creak′i·ness,** *n.*

cream (krēm), *n.* **1** the oily, yellowish part of milk. **2** food made of cream; food like cream. **3** an oily preparation put on the skin to make it smooth and soft. **4** a yellowish white. **5** the best part. —*v.* **1** put cream in. **2** take cream from. **3** form like cream on the top; foam; froth. **4** cook with cream. **5** make into a smooth mixture like cream. —*adj.* **1** containing cream: *cream soup.* **2** yellowish-white. [< OF *cresme* < LL *crama* cream < Gaulish,

and < Eccl.L *chrisma* ointment < Gk., < *chriein* anoint]

cream cheese, a soft, bland, white cheese.

cream·er (krēm′ər), *n.* **1** a small pitcher. **2** apparatus for separating cream from milk.

cream·er·y (krēm′ər i), *n., pl.* **-er·ies. 1** place where butter and cheese are made. **2** place where cream, milk, and butter are sold or bought.

cream of tartar, a very sour, white powder, $KHC_4H_4O_6$, used in cooking and in medicine.

crease[1] (krēs), *n., v.,* **creased, creas·ing.** —*n.* line or mark made by folding; fold; wrinkle. —*v.* **1** make a crease or creases in. **2** become creased. —**creas′er,** *n.*

crease[2] (krēs), *n.* =creese.

cre·ate (krē āt′), *v.,* **-at·ed, -at·ing. 1** cause to be; bring into being; make. **2** make by giving a new character, function, or status to. **3** be the first to represent (a role in a play, or the like). **4** give rise to; cause. [< L, < *creare*]

cre·a·tion (krē ā′shən), *n.* **1** a creating or being created. **2** all things created; the universe. **3** thing created. **4** an artistic product.

the Creation, the creating of the universe by God. —**cre·a′tion·al,** *adj.*

cre·a·tion·ism (krē ā′shə niz′əm), *n.* doctrine that the earth and its inhabitants were created by God as they are now and did not evolve over time. —**cre·a′tion·ist,** *n.*

cre·a·tive (krē ā′tiv), *adj.* **1** having the power to create; inventive; productive. **2** constructive; purposeful. —*n. Informal.* creative person; person who does creative work. —**cre·a′tive·ly,** *adv.* —**cre·a′tive·ness, cre·a·tiv′i·ty,** *n.*

cre·a·tor (krē ā′tər), *n.* **1** person who creates. **2 the Creator,** God. —**cre·a′tor·ship,** *n.*

cre·a·ture (krē′chər), *n.* **1** a living person or animal. **2** a farm animal. **3** person who is completely under the influence of another. **4 a** anything created: *creature of her imagination.* **b** *Fig.* result or product developed from something else. [< L *creatura.* See CREATE.]

crèche (kresh; krāsh), *n.* model of the Christ child in the manger with attendant figures, often displayed at Christmas.

cre·dence (krē′dəns), *n.* belief. [< Med.L, < L *credere* believe]

cre·den·tial (kri den′shəl), *n.* **1** that which gives a title to credit or confidence. **2** Usually, **credentials.** letters of introduction; references.

cred·i·ble (kred′ə bəl), *adj.* believable; reliable; trustworthy. [< L, < *credere* believe] —**cred′i·bil′i·ty, cred′i·ble·ness,** *n.* —**cred′i·bly,** *adv.*

cred·it (kred′it), *n.* **1** belief; faith; trust. **2** trust in a person's ability and intention to pay. **3** money in a person's bank account, etc. **4** time allowed for delayed payment. **5** unit of academic work

counting toward graduation. **6** reputation in money matters. **7** honor; praise. **8** Usually, **credits. a** acknowledgment of contributions by various people to a book, film, etc. **b** a listing of such contributors. —*v.* **1** believe; have faith in; trust. **2** give credit in a bank account, etc. **3** acknowledge; thank. **4** put an academic credit on the record of.

credit to, ascribe to; attribute to.

credit with, give recognition to.

give credit to, have faith in; trust.

on credit, on a promise to pay later.

to one's credit, bring honor to; worthy of approval. [< F < Ital. < L *creditum* a loan < *credere* trust, entrust]

cred·it·a·ble (kred′it ə bəl), *adj.* bringing honor or praise. —**cred′it·a·ble·ness, cred′it·a·bil′i·ty,** *n.* —**cred′it·a·bly,** *adv.*

credit card, card that allows its holder to make purchases, obtain cash, etc. on credit; plastic.

cred·i·tor (kred′i tər), *n.* **1** person who gives credit. **2** person to whom a debt is owed.

credit union, cooperative association that makes loans to its members at low rates of interest.

cre·do (krē′dō; krā′dō), *n., pl.* **-dos.** =creed. [< L, I believe]

cre·du·li·ty (krə dül′ə ti; -dū-), *n.* a too great readiness to believe.

cred·u·lous (krej′ə ləs), *adj.* **1** too ready to believe; easily deceived. **2** characterized by credulity. **3** caused by credulity. —**cred′u·lous·ly,** *adv.* —**cred′u·lous·ness,** *n.*

creed (krēd), *n.* **1** a brief statement of the essential points of religious belief as approved by some church. **2** any statement of faith, principles, opinions, etc. [< L *credo* I believe]

creek (krēk; krik), *n.* a small stream. [appar. < MDu. *crēke,* and/or Scand. *kriki* nook]

Creek (krēk), *n., pl.* **Creek** or **Creeks. 1** member of a group of American Indians of the S United States, now living mostly in Oklahoma. **2** the Muskhogean language of these people.

creel (krēl), *n.* basket for holding fish. [? < F *creil,* ult. < L *cratis* wickerwork]

creep (krēp), *v.,* **crept, creep·ing,** *n.* —*v.* **1** move with the body close to the ground or floor. **2** move slowly. **3** grow along the ground or over a wall by means of clinging stems, as ivy. **4** feel as if things were creeping over the skin. **5** move in a timid, stealthy, or servile manner. **6** slip slightly out of place. —*n.* a creeping.

the creeps, *Informal.* feeling of horror, as if something were creeping along one's skin. [OE *crēopan*]

creep·er (krēp′ər), *n.* **1** person or thing that creeps. **2** any plant that grows along a surface, sending out rootlets from the stem.

creep·y (krēp′i), *adj.,* **creep·i·er, creep·i·est. 1** having a feeling as if things were creeping over one's skin; frightened. **2** causing such a feeling.

creese (krēs), *n.* dagger with a wavy blade, used by the Malays. Also, **crease, kris.** [< Malay *kris*]

cre·mate (krē′māt; kri māt′), *v.,* **–mat·ed, –mat·ing.** burn (a dead body) to ashes. [< L, < *cremare* burn] **—cre·ma′tion,** *n.* **—cre′ma·tor,** *n.*

cre·ma·to·ry (krē′mə tô′ri; –tō′–; krem′ ə–), *n., pl.* **–ries,** *adj.* **—n. 1** furnace for cremating. **2** building that has a furnace for cremating. **—adj.** of or having to do with cremating.

cre·nate (krē′nāt), *adj.* with a scalloped edge. [< NL, < Med.L *crena* notch] **—cre′nate·ly,** *adv.* **—cre·na′tion,** *n.*

cren·el·ate (kren′əlāt), *v.,* **–at·ed, –at·ing.** furnish with battlements. [< F *créneler* < *crenel* notch, ult. < Med.L *crena*] **—cren′el·a′tion,** *n.*

Cre·ole (krē′ōl), *n.* **1** a white person descended from the French who settled in Louisiana. **2** a French or Spanish person born in Spanish America or the West Indies. **—adj.** of or having to do with the Creoles. [< F < Sp. < Pg. *crioulo* < *criar* bring up < L *creare* create]

cre·o·sote (krē′ə sōt), *n., v.,* **–sot·ed, –sot·ing. —n. 1** an oily liquid with a penetrating odor, obtained by distilling wood tar, used as a preservative, etc. **2** a similar substance obtained from coal tar. **—v.** treat with creosote. [orig., meat preservative; < Gk. *kreo–* (for *kreas* flesh) + *soter* savior < *sozein* save]

crepe, crêpe (krāp), *n.* **1** a thin silk, cotton, rayon, or woolen cloth with a crinkled surface. **2** Also, **crepe paper.** tissue paper that looks like crepe. **3** light, thin pancake. **4** =crepe rubber. **5** black crepe used as a sign of mourning: *decked out in blackest crepe.* Also, **crape.** [< F < L *crispa* curled]

crepe rubber, crude rubber with a crinkled surface, used for the soles of shoes.

crep·i·tate (krep′ə tāt), *v.,* **–tat·ed, –tat·ing.** crackle; rattle. [< L, < *crepitare* crackle < *crepare* crack] **crep′i·ta′tion,** *n.*

crept (krept), *v.* pt. and pp. of **creep.**

cre·pus·cu·lar (kri pus′kyə lər), *adj.* **1** of twilight; resembling twilight; dim; indistinct. **2** appearing or flying by twilight. [< L *crepusculum* twilight]

cre·scen·do (krə shen′dō), *n., pl.* **–dos,** *adj., adv.* **—n.** a gradual increase in force or loudness. **—adj., adv.** gradually increasing in force or loudness. [< Ital., ppr. of *crescere* increase < L]

cres·cent (kres′ənt), *n.* **1** shape of the moon in its first or last quarter. **2** anything having this or a similar shape. **—adj. 1** shaped like the moon in its first or last quarter. **2** growing; increasing. [< L, ppr. of *crescere* grow]

cress (kres), *n.* =watercress. [OE *cresse*]

cres·set (kres′it), *n.* a metal container for burning oil, wood, etc., to give light. [< OF]

crest (krest), *n.* **1** comb, tuft, etc., on the head of a bird or animal. **2** decoration, plumes, etc., on the top of a helmet. **3** decoration at the top of a coat of arms. **4** an ornamental part which surmounts a wall, the ridge of a roof, etc. **5** the top part; top of a hill, wave, etc.; ridge; peak; summit. **6** the highest or best of its kind. **—v. 1** furnish with a crest. **2** form into a crest. [< OF < L *crista* tuft] **—crest′ed,** *adj.* **—crest′less,** *adj.*

crest·fall·en (krest′fôl′ən), *adj.* with bowed head; dejected; discouraged. **—crest′fall′en·ly,** *adv.* **—crest′fall′en·ness,** *n.*

cre·ta·ceous (kri tā′shəs), *adj.* like chalk; containing chalk. [< L, < *creta* chalk]

Cre·ta·ceous (kri tā′shəs), *n.* **1** last geologic period of the Mesozoic era, characterized by the formation of chalk deposits. **2** rocks formed during this period.

Crete (krēt), *n.* a Greek island in the Mediterranean, SE of Greece. **—Cre′tan,** *adj., n.*

cre·tin (krē′tən), *n.* very stupid person; idiot. [< F < Swiss dial. < L *Christianus* Christian; came to mean "man," then "fellow," then "poor fellow"]

cre·tin·ism (krē′tən iz əm), *n.* a congenital condition due to a deficiency in the thyroid gland, resulting in mental and physical retardation.

cre·vasse (krə vas′), *n., v.,* **–vassed, –vassing. —n. 1** a deep crack or crevice in the ice of a glacier. **2** break in a levee. **—v.** fissure with crevasses. [< F, CREVICE]

crev·ice (krev′is), *n.* a narrow split or crack. [< OF *crevace* < VL *crepacia* < L *crepare* crack] **—crev′iced,** *adj.*

crew¹ (krü), *n.* **1** people needed to do work on a ship, or to row a boat. **2** group of people working or acting together. **3** crowd; gang. **4** crew cut. [< OF *creüe* increase, recruit < *creistre* grow, L *crescere*]

crew² (krü) *v.* pt. of **crow¹.**

crew neck, round, close-fitting neck on a sweater or T-shirt. **—crew′-necked,** *adj.*

crib (krib), *n., v.,* **cribbed, crib·bing. —n. 1** a small bed with high sides to keep a baby from falling out. **2** rack or manger for horses and cows to eat from. **3** building or box for storing grain, salt, etc. **4** framework of logs or timbers used in building. **5** *Informal.* use of another's words or ideas as one's own. **6** *Informal.* notes or helps that are unfair to use in doing schoolwork. **7** a small room or house. **—v. 1** provide with a crib. **2** *Informal.* use (another's words or ideas) as one's own. **3** *Informal.* use notes unfairly in doing schoolwork. **4** shut up in a small space. [OE *cribb*] **—crib′ber,** *n.*

crib·bage (krib′ij), *n.* a card game for two, three, or four people.

crib death, =sudden infant death syndrome.

crick (krik), *n.* a sudden, painful muscular cramp. **—v.** cause a crick in.

crick·et¹ (krik′it), *n.* a black insect of the grasshopper family. [< OF *criquet;* imit.]

crick·et² (krik′it), *n.* **1** an outdoor game played by two teams of eleven players each, with ball, bats, and wickets. **2** fair play; good sportsmanship. **—v.** play this game. [< OF *criquet* goal post, stick, prob. < MDu. *cricke* stick to lean on] **—crick′et·er,** *n.*

crick·et³ (krik′it), *n.* a small stool.

cri·er (krī′ər), *n.* **1** official who shouts out public announcements. **2** person who shouts out announcements of goods for sale. **3** person who cries.

crime (krīm), *n.* **1** a wrong act that is against the law. **2** violation of law. **3** a wrong act; sin. [< OF < L *crimen* < *cernere* judge, decide]

Cri·me·a (krī mē′ə; kri-), *n.* peninsula in SW Ukraine, on the N coast of the Black Sea. **—Cri·me′an,** *adj.*

crim·i·nal (krim′ə nəl), *n.* person guilty of a crime. **—adj. 1** guilty of crime. **2** having to do with crime. **3** like crime; wrong; sinful. **—crim′i·nal′i·ty,** *n.* **—crim′i·nal·ly,** *adv.*

crim·i·nol·o·gy (krim′ə nol′ə ji), *n.* study of crimes and criminals. **—crim′i·no·log′ic, crim′i·no·log′i·cal,** *adj.* **—crim′i·nol′o·gist,** *n.*

crimp (krimp), *v.* press into small, narrow folds; make wavy. **—n. 1** a crimping. **2** something crimped; fold; wave. **3** a waved or curled lock of hair.

put a crimp in, hinder. [OE *gecrympan*] **—crimp′er,** *n.* **—crimp′y,** *adj.*

crim·son (krim′zən), *n.* a deep red. **—adj.** deep-red. **—v.** turn deep red. [< Ital. or Sp. < Ar. *qirmizī* < Skt. *kṛmi*-insect]

cringe (krinj), *v.,* **cringed, cring·ing,** *n.* **—v. 1** shrink or crouch in fear. **2** try to get favor or attention by servile behavior. **—n.** a cringing. [ME *crengen* < OE *cringan* give way] **—cring′er,** *n.*

crin·kle (kring′kəl), *v.,* **–kled, –kling,** *n.* **—v. 1** wrinkle; ripple. **2** rustle: *paper crinkles when it is crushed.* **—n. 1** wrinkle; ripple. **2** rustle. [ME *crenkle(n)* < OE *crincan* bend] **—crin′kly,** *adv.*

cri·noid (krī′noid; krin′oid), *n.* a flower-shaped sea animal, usually anchored by a stalk. **—adj.** of or like a crinoid. [< Gk., < *krinon* lily]

crin·o·line (krin′ə lin; –lēn), *n.* **1** a stiff cloth used as a lining. **2** petticoat of crinoline to hold a skirt out. **3** a hoop skirt. [< F < Ital., < *crino* horsehair (< L *crinia* hair) + *lino* thread (< L *linum*)]

crip·ple (krip′əl), *n., v.,* **–pled, –pling. —n.** lame person or animal; one that cannot use a leg or arm properly. **—v. 1** make a cripple of. **2** *Fig.* damage; disable; weaken. [OE *crypel;* akin to CREEP] **—crip′pler,** *n.*

cri·sis (krī′sis), *n., pl.* **–ses** (–sēz). **1** turning point in a disease, toward life or death. **2** *Fig.* deciding event in the course of anything. **3** time of danger or anxious waiting. [< L < Gk., < *krinein* decide]

crisis center, headquarters from which disaster relief is managed, medical and psychological help is made available, evacuation plans, etc. formed.

crisp (krisp), *adj.* **1** hard and thin; breaking easily with a snap. **2** fresh; sharp and clear; bracing: *crisp winter air.* **3** clear-cut; decisive. —*v.* make or become crisp. [< L *crispus* curled] —**crisp′ly,** *adv.* —**crisp′ness,** *n.*

crisp·er (kris′pər), *n.* thing that crisps, as a drawer in a refrigerator for vegetables or a heated box for crackers, etc.

crisp·y (kris′pi), *adj.,* **crisp·i·er, crisp·i·est.** crisp.

criss·cross (kris′krôs′; –kros′), *adj.* made or marked with crossed lines; crossed. —*adv.* crosswise. —*v.* mark or cover with crossed lines. —*n.* mark or pattern made of crossed lines. [alter. of *Christ's cross*]

cri·te·ri·on (krī tir′i ən), *n., pl.* **-te·ri·a** (-tir′i ə), **-te·ri·ons.** rule or standard for making a judgment; test. [< Gk., < *krinein* judge]

crit·ic (krit′ik), *n.* **1** person who makes judgments of the merits and faults of books, music, plays, etc. **2** person whose profession is writing such judgments for a newspaper, etc. **3** person who finds fault. [< L < Gk. *kritikos* critical < *krinein* judge]

crit·i·cal (krit′ə kəl), *adj.* **1** inclined to find fault or disapprove. **2** skilled as a critic. **3** coming from one who is skilled as a critic: *a critical judgment.* **4** belonging to the work of a critic. **5** of a crisis: *the critical moment.* **6** full of danger or difficulty. **7** of supplies, labor, or resources, essential for the work or project but existing in inadequate supply. —**crit′i·cal·ly,** *adv.* —**crit′ical·ness,** *n.*

critical mass, 1 minimum amount of fissionable material needed to support a self-sustaining chain reaction. **2** *Fig.* point at which conditions or opinions combine to produce change (of policy, direction, etc.).

crit·i·cism (krit′ə siz əm), *n.* **1** disapproval; faultfinding. **2** the making of judgments; analysis of merits and faults. **3** a critical comment, essay, review, etc.

crit·i·cize (krit′ə sīz), *v.,* **-cized, -ciz·ing.** **1** disapprove; find fault with. **2** judge or speak as a critic. —**crit′i·ciz′a·ble,** *adj.* —**crit′i·ciz′er,** *n.*

cri·tique (kri tēk′), *n.* **1** art of criticism. **2** a critical essay or review. [< F < Gk. *kritike (techne)* the critical art. See CRITIC.]

crit·ter (krit′ər), *n. Informal.* creature; animal.

croak (krōk), *n.* a deep, hoarse cry, as of a frog, crow, or raven. —*v.* **1** make such a sound. **2** utter in a deep, hoarse voice. **3** be always prophesying misfortune; grumble. **4** *Slang.* die. [< OE *crǣcettan*]

croak·er (krōk′ər), *n.* **1** one that croaks. **2** any of various fishes that make a croaking or grunting noise.

Cro·a·tia (krō ā′shə), *n.* country in SE Europe. —**Cro′at,** *n.* —**Cro·a′tian,** *adj., n.*

cro·chet (krō shā′), *v.,* **-cheted** (–shād′), **-chet·ing** (–shā′ing), *n.* —*v.* knit (sweaters, lace, etc.) with a single needle having a hook at one end. —*n.* knitting done in this way. [< F, dim. of *croc* hook < Gmc.]

crock (krok), *n.* pot or jar made of baked clay. [OE *crocc(a)*]

crock·er·y (krok′ər i), *n.* dishes, jars, etc., made of baked clay; earthenware.

croc·o·dile (krok′ə dīl), *n.* a large, lizardlike reptile with a thick skin, long narrow head, and webbed feet. [< OF < L < Gk. *krokodeilos,* earlier, lizard]

crocodile tears, false or insincere grief.

croc·o·dil·i·an (krok′ə dil′i ən), *adj.* of or like a crocodile. —*n.* any of a group of reptiles that includes crocodiles, alligators, etc.

cro·cus (krō′kəs), *n., pl.* **cro·cus·es, cro·ci** (-sī). **1** a small flowering plant that grows from a bulblike stem, usually blooming very early in the spring. **2** the flower. [< L < Gk. *krokos* < Semitic]

Croe·sus (krē′səs), *n.* **1** a very rich king of Lydia from 560 to 546 B.C. **2** a very rich person.

croft (krôft; kroft), *n.* **1** *Brit.* a small enclosed field. **2** a very small rented farm. [OE] —**croft′er,** *n.*

crois·sant (kwä sän′, krä sänt′), *n.* rich, buttery roll of bread shaped like a crescent. [< F *croissant* crescent]

croix de guerre (krwä′ də gār′), a French medal given to soldiers for bravery under fire.

Cro-Mag·non (krō mag′non), *adj.* belonging to a group of prehistoric people who lived in SW Europe. —*n.* person of this group.

crom·lech (krom′lek), *n.* **1** circle of upright stones built in prehistoric times. **2** a dolmen. [< Welsh, < *crom* bent + *llech* flat stone]

Crom·well (krom′wel; –wəl), *n.* **Oliver,** 1599–1658, English general, Puritan leader, and lord protector of the Commonwealth, 1653–58.

crone (krōn), *n.* a shrunken old woman. [< MDu. < F *carogne* carcass, hag. See CARRION.]

cro·ny (krō′ni), *n., pl.* **-nies.** a very close friend; chum.

crook (krůk), *v.* hook; bend; curve. —*n.* **1** hook; bend; curve. **2** a hooked, curved, or bent part. **3** a shepherd's staff. **4** a dishonest person; thief; swindler. [appar. < Scand *krōkr*]

crook·ed (krůk′id *for 1 and 2;* krůkt *for 3*), *adj.* **1** not straight; bent; curved; twisted. **2** *Fig.* dishonest. **3** having a crook. —**crook′ed·ly,** *adv.* —**crook′ed·ness,** *n.*

croon (krün), *v.* **1** hum, sing, or murmur in a low tone. **2** sing in a low voice with exaggerated emotion. —*n.* low humming, singing, or murmuring. [< Scand. *krauna* murmur] —**croon′er,** *n.*

crop (krop), *n., v.,* **cropped, crop·ping.** —*n.* **1** product grown or gathered for

use, esp. for use as food. **2** the yield of any product in a season: *a large corn crop.* **3** a baglike swelling of a bird's food passage where food is prepared for digestion. **4** a short whip with a loop instead of a lash. —*v.* **1** plant and cultivate a crop. **2** cut; cut short.

crop out or **up, a** appear; come to the surface. **b** turn up unexpectedly. [OE *cropp* sprout, craw]

crop·per (krop′ər), *n.* **1** person or thing that crops. **2** person who raises a crop, esp. on shares.

cro·quet (krō kā′), *n.* an outdoor game played by knocking wooden balls through small wire arches with mallets. [< F, dial. var. of *crochet.* See CROCHET.]

cro·quette (krō ket′), *n.* a small mass of chopped meat, fish, etc., coated with crumbs and fried. [< F, < *croquer* crunch]

cro·sier (krō′zhər), *n.* an ornamental staff carried by or before bishops or certain abbots. Also, **crozier.** [< F, crook bearer, < VL *croccia* crook < Gmc.]

cross (krôs; kros), *n.* **1** stick or post with another across it. **2** the symbol (✝) of the Christian religion. **3** two intersecting lines (× +). **4** burden of duty; suffering; trouble. **5** a mixing of kins, breeds, or races. **6** result of such mixing. —*v.* **1** mark with a cross. **2** draw a line across. **3** move across. **4** meet and pass: *my letter to her and hers to me crossed.* **5** oppose; hinder. **6** cause (different kinds, breeds, races, etc.) to interbreed. —*adj.* **1** crossing; lying or going across. **2** opposing; counter. **3** in a bad temper. **4** mixed in kind, breed, or race.

cross over, a go from one homologous chromosome to another during meiosis. **b** die.

the Cross, a the cross on which Christ died. **b** Christ's sufferings and death; the Atonement. **c** the Christian religion. [< OIrish *cros* < L *crux.* Doublet of CRUX.] —**cross′ly,** *adv.* —**cross′ness,** *n.*

cross-, *combining form.* **1** cross-shaped, as in *cross-stitch.* **2** moving across, as in *cross country.* **3** opposite, as in *cross-purposes.* **4** from one to another, as in *cross-fertilization.*

cross·bar (krôs′bär′; kros′–), *n.* bar, line, or stripe going crosswise.

cross·beam (krôs′bēm′; kros′–), *n.* a large beam that crosses another or extends from wall to wall.

cross·bones (krôs′bōnz′; kros′–), *n. pl.* two large bones placed crosswise, symbolizing death.

cross·bow (krôs′bō′; kros′–), *n.* a medieval weapon with a bow and a grooved stock in the middle to direct the arrows, stones, etc. —**cross′bow′man,** *n.*

cross·bred (krôs′bred′; kros′–), *adj.* produced by crossbreeding. —*n.* a crossbreed.

cross·breed (krôs′brēd′; kros′–), *v.,* **-bred, -breed·ing,** *n.* —*v.* breed by mixing kinds, breeds, or races. —*n.* individual or breed produced by crossbreeding.

cross bun, =hot cross bun.

cross-coun·try (krôs′kun′tri; kros′–), *adj.* across open country instead of by road.

cross-cur·rent or **cross-cur·rent** (krôs′-kėr ənt; kros′–), *n.* **1** current of air blowing across another. **2** *Fig.* opposing tendency or trend.

cross-cut (krôs′kut′; kros′–), *adj., n., v.,* **–cut, –cut·ting.** —*adj.* **1** used or made for cutting across. **2** cut across. —*n.* **1** a cut across. **2** short cut. —*v.* cut across.

cross-dress (krôs′dres′; kros′–), *v.* dress in the clothing of the opposite sex. —**cross′-dress′er,** *n.,* —**cross′-dress′-ing,** *n.*

cross-ex·am·ine (krôs′ig zam′ən; kros′–), *v.,* **–ined, –in·ing. 1** question (a witness for the opposing side) closely to test the truth of his evidence. **2** examine closely or severely. —**cross′-ex·am′i·na′tion,** *n.* —**cross′-ex·am′in·er,** *n.*

cross-eyed (krôs′īd′; kros′–), *n.* having strabismus, esp. the form in which both eyes turn toward the nose.

cross-fer·ti·li·za·tion (krôs′fėr′tə lə-z ā′shən; kros′–), *n.* fertilization of one flower by pollen from another.

cross-fer·ti·lize (krôs′fėr′tə līz; kros′–), *v.,* **–lized, –liz·ing.** cause the cross-fertilization of.

cross-fire (krôs′fīr′; kros′–), *n.* **1** gunfire coming from opposite directions so as to cross. **2** *Fig.* verbal attack from several people at once.

cross-grained (krôs′grānd′; kros′–), *adj.* having the grain running across the regular grain.

cross hairs, fine hairs stretched across the focal point of an optical instrument to define the line of sight.

(caught) in the cross hairs, in view as a target of verbal attack or as being responsible for something.

cross-hatch (krôs′hach′; kros′–), *v.* mark or shade with two sets of parallel lines crossing each other.

cross·ing (krôs′ing; kros′–), *n.* **1** place where things cross each other. **2** place at which a street, river, etc., may be crossed. **3** act of crossing. **4** voyage across water.

cross-patch (krôs′pach′; kros′–), *n.* a cross, bad-tempered person.

cross-piece (krôs′pēs′; kros′–), *n.* piece that is placed across something.

cross-pol·li·nate (krôs′pol′ə nāt; kros′–), *v.,* **–nat·ed, –nat·ing.** cause cross-fertilization in. —**cross′-pol′li·na′tion,** *n.*

cross-pur·pose (krôs′pėr′pəs; kros′–), *n.* opposing or contrary purpose.

at cross-purposes, a misunderstanding each other's purpose. **b** acting under such a misunderstanding.

cross-ques·tion (krôs′kwes′chən; kros′–), *v.* =cross-examine.

cross-re·fer (krôs′ri fėr′; kros′–), *v.,* **–ferred, –fer·ring. 1** refer from one part to another. **2** make a cross reference.

cross reference, reference from one part of a book, index, etc., to another.

cross·road (krôs′rōd′; kros′–), *n.* **1** road that crosses another. **2** road connecting main roads. **3** Often, **crossroads** (*sing. in use*). **a** place where roads cross. **b** meeting place, esp. for people living far apart.

cross section, 1 act of cutting anything across. **2** piece cut in this way. **3** *Fig.* representative sample.

cross-stitch (krôs′stich′; kros′–), *n.* **1** one stitch crossed over another, forming an X. **2** embroidery made with this stitch. —*v.* embroider or sew with this stitch.

cross trees, two horizontal bars of wood near the top of a ship's mast.

cross·wise (krôs′wīz′; kros′–), **cross·ways** (–wāz′), *adv.* **1** so as to cross; across. **2** in the form of a cross. **3** opposite to what is required; wrongly.

cross·word puzzle (krôs′wėrd′; kros′–), puzzle with sets of squares to be filled in with words, one letter to each square. Synonyms or definitions of the words are given with numbers corresponding to numbers in the squares.

crotch (kroch), *n.* **1** a forked piece or part. **2** place where the human body divides into the two legs. [var. of *crutch*] **crotched,** *adj.*

crotch·et (kroch′it), *n.* **1** an odd notion; unreasonable whim. **2** a small hook or hooklike part. [< OF *crochet.* See CROCHET.]

crotch·et·y (kroch′ə ti), *adj.* **1** full of odd notions or unreasonable whims. **2** of the nature of a crotchet. —**crotch′et·i·ness,** *n.*

cro·ton (krō′tən), *n.* a tropical shrub or tree of Asia with a strong odor. The seeds of a croton tree yield an oil (**cro·ton oil**) used in medicine. [< NL < Gk. *kroton* tick[2]]

Croton bug, a small cockroach; water bug. [< *Croton (water) bugs,* numerous in New York City after the Croton aqueduct began to bring water to the city]

crouch (krouch), *v.* **1** stoop low with bent legs like an animal ready to spring, or in hiding. **2** bow down in a timid manner. —*n.* **1** act or state of crouching. **2** a crouching position. [< OF *crochir* < *croc* hook < Gmc.]

croup[1] (krüp), *n.* inflammation or diseased condition of the throat and windpipe characterized by a hoarse cough and difficult breathing. [? < *croup,* v., blend of *croak* and *whoop*] —**croup′y,** *adj.*

croup[2] (krüp), *n.* rump of a horse, etc. [< F *croupe* < Gmc.]

crou·pi·er (krü′pi ər), *n.* attendant at a gambling table who rakes in the money and pays the winners. [< F, < *croupe* CROUP[2]; orig., one who rides behind]

crou·ton (krō′ton), *n.* a small piece of toasted or fried bread, often served in soup. [< F, < *croûte* CRUST]

crow[1] (krō), *n., v.,* **crowed** (or **crew** for 2), **crowed, crow·ing.** —*n.* **1** a loud cry made by a rooster. **2** a happy sound made by a baby. —*v.* **1** make the happy sound of a baby. **2** make the cry of a cock. **3** show happiness and pride; boast. [OE *crāwan;* imit.]

crow[2] (krō), *n.* **1** a large, glossy-black bird that has a harsh cry or caw. **2** any similar bird, such as ravens, magpies, jays, etc.

as the crow flies, in a straight line; in or by the shortest way.

eat crow, *Informal.* be forced to do something very disagreeable and humiliating. [OE *crāwe*]

Crow (krō), *n.* member of a tribe of American Indians formerly living in Wyoming and Montana, now living in Montana.

crow·bar (krō′bär′), *n.* a strong iron or steel bar, used as a lever.

crowd (kroud), *n.* **1** a large number of people together. **2** people in general; the masses. **3** group; set. [< v.] —*v.* **1** collect in large numbers. **2** fill; fill too full. **3** push; shove. [OE *crūdan* press] —**crowd′ed,** *adj.*

crow·foot (krō′fut′), *n., pl.* **–foots.** buttercup or other plant with leaves shaped somewhat like a crow's foot.

crown (kroun), *n.* **1** head covering for a king, queen, etc. **2** royal power. **3** a king, queen, etc. **4** wreath for the head. **5** honor; reward. **6** the highest part; top. **7** part of a tooth above the gum. —*v.* **1** make king, queen, etc. **2** honor; reward. **3** cover the highest part of: *a fort crowns the hill.* **4** add the finishing touch to. **5** put a crown on. **6** make a king of (a checker moved across the checkerboard).

the Crown, a royal power. **b** government of Great Britain in its legal capacity. [< AF < L *corona* garland, wreath. Doublet of CORONA.] —**crown′er,** *n.*

crown glass, very clear glass used in optical instruments.

crown prince, the oldest living son of a king, queen, etc.; heir apparent to a kingdom.

crown princess, 1 wife of a crown prince. **2** girl or woman who is heir apparent to a kingdom.

crow's-foot (krōz′fut′), *n., pl.* **–feet.** Usually, **crow's-feet.** wrinkle at the outer corner of the eye.

crow's-nest (krōz′nest′), *n.* **1** a small, enclosed platform near the top of a mast, used by the lookout. **2** any similar platform ashore.

cro·zier (krō′zhər), *n.* =crosier.

CRT, cathode-ray tube.

cru (krü, French krʏ), *n., pl.* **crus** (krüz, French krʏ). vintage of wine produced in a French vineyard. [< F *crû,* pp. of *croître* to grow]

cru·cial (krü′shəl), *adj.* **1** very important; critical; decisive. **2** very trying; severe. [<NL(medical)<L*crux*cross] —**cru′cial·ly,** *adv.*

cru·ci·ble (krü′sə bəl), *n.* **1** container in which metals, ores, etc., can be melted. **2**

a severe test or trial. [< Med.L *crucibulum*, origi., night lamp]

cru·ci·fix (krü′sə fiks), *n.* **1** a cross with the figure of Christ crucified on it. **2** a cross. [< LL *crucifixus* fixed to a cross < *crux* cross + *fixus*, pp. of *figere* fasten]

cru·ci·fix·ion (krü′sə fik′shən), *n.* act of crucifying.

Crucifixion, a the putting to death of Christ on the cross. **b** picture, statue, etc., of this.

cru·ci·form (krü′sə fôrm), *adj.* shaped like a cross. —**cru′ci·form′ly,** *adv.*

cru·ci·fy (krü′sə fī), *v.,* **–fied, –fy·ing. 1** put to death by nailing or binding the hands and feet to a cross. **2** *Fig.* treat severely; torture. [< OF < LL *crucifigere.* See CRUCIFIX.] —**cru′ci·fi′er,** *n.*

crud (krud), *n. Slang.* **1** anything disgusting or worthless; filth. **2** disgusting or dirty person. —**crud′dy,** *adj.*

crude (krüd), *adj.,* **crud·er, crud·est. 1** in a natural or raw state; unrefined. **2** not mature; unripe. **3** rough; coarse: *a crude log cabin.* **4** lacking finish, grace, taste, or refinement: *crude manners.* —*n.* =crude oil. [< L *crudus* raw] —**crude′ly,** *adv.* —**crude′ness, cru′di·ty,** *n.*

cru·el (krü′əl), *adj.* **1** fond of causing pain to others and delighting in their suffering. **2** showing a cruel nature: *cruel acts.* **3** causing pain and suffering: *a cruel war.* [< F < L *crudelis* rough. See CRUDE.] —**cru′el·ly,** *adv.* —**cru′elness,** *n.*

cru·el·ty (krü′əl ti), *n., pl.* **–ties. 1** readiness to give pain to others or to delight in their suffering. **2** a cruel act.

cru·et (krü′it), *n.* a glass bottle to hold vinegar, oil, etc., for the table. [< OF, dim. of *cruie* pot < Gmc.]

cruise (krüz), *v.,* **cruised, cruis·ing, *n.*** —*v.* **1** sail about from place to place on pleasure or business; sail over or about. **2** journey or travel over or about: *taxis cruise the streets to find a fare.* **3** fly in an airplane at the speed of maximum efficiency. —*n.* a cruising voyage. [< Du. *kruisen* < *kruis* < L *crux* cross]

cruis·er (krüz′ər), *n.* **1** warship with less armor and more speed than a battleship. **2** airplane, taxi, etc., that cruises. **3** a police car connected with headquarters by radio.

crul·ler (krul′ər), *n.* a twisted doughnut. [appar. < Du., < *krullen* curl]

crumb (krum), *n.* **1** a very small piece of bread, cake, etc., broken from a larger piece. **2** the soft inside part of bread. **3** a little bit: *a crumb of comfort.* —*v.* **1** break into crumbs. **2** cover with crumbs for frying or baking. [OE *cruma*] —**crumb′y,** *adj.*

crum·ble (krum′bəl), *v.,* **–led, –bling. 1** break into very small pieces or crumbs. **2** fall into pieces; decay. [earlier *crimble* < OE *gecrymman* < *cruma* crumb]

crum·bly (krum′bli), *adj.,* **–bli·er, –bli·est.** easily crumbled. —**crum′bli·ness,** *n.*

crum·my (krum′i), *adj. Informal.* **1** repulsive; dirty. **2** worthless; unsatisfactory.

crum·pet (krum′pit), *n. Esp. Brit.* cake baked on a griddle, that is thicker than a pancake and is usually toasted after being baked. [OE *crompeht* a cake]

crum·ple (krum′pəl), *v.,* **–pled, –pling, *n.*** —*v.* **1** crush together; wrinkle. **2** *Colloq.* collapse. —*n.* wrinkle made by crushing something together. [< OE *crump* bent]

crunch (krunch), *v.* **1** crush noisily with the teeth. **2** crush or grind noisily. —*n.* act or sound of crunching. —**crunch′y,** *adj.*

crup·per (krup′ər), *n.* strap attached to the back of a harness and passing under a horse's tail. [< OF *cropiere* < *crope* CROUP²]

cru·sade (krü sād′), *n., v.,* **–sad·ed, –sad·ing.** —*n.* **1** Often, **Crusade.** any one of the Christian military expeditions between the years 1096 and 1272 to recover the Holy Land from Muslim rule. **2** war having a religious purpose and approved by the church. **3** a vigorous campaign against a public evil or in favor of some new idea. —*v.* take part in a crusade. [blend of earlier *crusado* (< Sp. *cruzada*) and *croisade* (< F < Pr., from a verb meaning "take the cross"). See CROSS.] —**cru·sad′er,** *n.*

cruse (krüz; krüs), *n.* jug, pot, or bottle made of earthenware. [< MDu. *croes*]

crush (krush), *v.* **1** squeeze together violently so as to break or bruise. **2** wrinkle or crease by wear or rough handling. **3** break into fine pieces by grinding or pounding. **4** subdue; conquer. —*n.* **1** violent pressure like grinding or pounding. **2** mass of people crowded close together. **3** *Informal.* **a** sudden or ardent infatuation. **b** object of a sudden or ardent infatuation. [appar. < OF *croissir* < Gmc.] —**crush′er,** *n.*

Cru·soe (krü′sō), *n.* **Robinson,** shipwrecked hero of a book of the same name by Daniel Defoe.

crust (krust), *n.* **1** the hard, outside part of bread. **2** piece of this; any hard, dry piece of bread. **3** the baked outside covering of a pie. **4** *Informal. Fig.* impudence; gall; nerve. **5** any hard outside covering. **6** the solid outside part of the earth. —*v.* **1** cover or become covered with a crust. **2** form or collect into a crust. [< L *crusta* rind]

crus·ta·cean (krus tā′shən), *n.* any of a group of water animals with hard shells, jointed bodies and appendages, and gills for breathing, including crabs, lobsters, shrimps, etc. —*adj.* of or belonging to this group. [< NL, < L *crusta* shell, rind]

crust·y (krus′ti), *adj.,* **crust·i·er, crust·i·est. 1** having a crust; hard; crustlike. **2** *Fig.* harsh in manner, speech, etc. —**crust′i·ly,** *adv.* —**crust′i·ness,** *n.*

crutch (kruch), *n.* **1** support to help a lame person walk that is a stick with a crosspiece at the top to fit under the arm or on the forearm and hand. **2** *Fig.* anything like a crutch in shape or use; support; prop. **3** a forked support or part.

—*v.* support with or as with a crutch; prop or sustain. [OE *crycc*]

crux (kruks), *n.* **1** the essential part; the most important point. **2** a puzzling or perplexing question. [< L, cross. Doublet of CROSS.]

cry (krī), *v.,* **cried, cry·ing, *n., pl.* cries.** —*v.* **1** make sounds showing pain, fear, sorrow, etc. **2** shed tears; weep. **3** (of animals) give forth characteristic calls. **4** call loudly; shout. **5** announce in public. —*n.* **1** sound made by a person or animal that shows pain, fear, anger, or sorrow. **2** fit of weeping. **3** noise or call of an animal: *the cry of the crow.* **4** the yelping of hounds in the chase. **5** a shout: *a cry for help.* **6** general opinion; public report.

a far cry, a a long way. **b** a great difference.

cry for, a beg for. **b** need very much.

cry out a call loudly. **b** scream; yell. [< OF < L *quiritare*]

cry·ing (krī′ing), *adj.* **1** that cries. **2** demanding attention; very bad.

cry·o·gen·ics (krī ə jen′iks), *n.* branch of physics concerned with the behavior of matter at very low temperatures. —**cry′o·gen′ic,** *adj.* —**cry′o·gen′i·cist,** *n.*

crypt (kript), *n.* an underground room or vault. [< L < Gk. *kryptos* hidden. Doublet of GROTTO.]

cryp·tic (krip′tik), **cryp·ti·cal** (–tə kəl), *adj.* having a hidden meaning; mysterious. [< LL < Gk. *kryptos* hidden] —**cryp′ti·cal·ly,** *adv.*

cryp·to·gam (krip′tə gam), *n.* old term for plant having no seeds, as ferns and mosses. [< NL < Gk. *kryptos* hidden + *gamos* marriage] —**cryp′to·gam′ic, cryp·tog′a·mous,** *adj.*

cryp·to·gram (krip′tə gram), *n.* something written in secret code or cipher.

cryp·to·graph (krip′tə graf; –gräf), *n.* **1** cryptogram. **2** a system of secret writing. —**cryp′to·graph′ic, cryp′to·graph′i·cal,** *adj.*

cryp·tog·ra·phy (krip tog′rə fi), *n.* process or art of writing in secret characters. —**cryp·tog′ra·pher,** *n.*

crys·tal (kris′təl), *n.* **1** a clear, transparent mineral, a kind of quartz, that looks like ice. **2** piece of crystal cut to form an ornament. **3** very transparent glass. **4** glass over the face of a watch. **5** a regularly shaped piece with angles and flat surfaces into which a substance solidifies. —*adj.* **1** made of crystal. **2** clear and transparent like crystal. [< OF < L < Gk. *krystallos* clear ice]

crys·tal·line (kris′təl in; –ēn; –īn), *adj.* **1** consisting of crystals; solidified in the form of crystals. **2** made of crystal. **3** clear and transparent like crystal.

crys·tal·lize (kris′təl īz), *v.,* **–lized, –liz·ing. 1** form into crystals; solidify into crystals. **2** form into definite shape. **3** coat with sugar. —**crys′tal·liz′a·ble,** *adj.* —**crys′tal·li·za′tion,** *n.*

crys·tal·log·ra·phy (kris′tə log′rə fi), *n.* science that deals with the form, structure, and properties of crystals. —**crys′tal·log′ra·pher,** *n.*

Cs, cesium.

C.S.T., CST, or **c.s.t.,** Central Standard Time.

CT, 1 (*zip code*) Connecticut. **2** Also, **C.T.** Central Time.

Cu, copper.

cu., cubic.

cub (kub), *n.* **1** a young bear, fox, lion, etc. **2** an inexperienced or awkward boy.

Cu·ba (kū′bə), *n.* country on the largest island in the West Indies, S of Florida. —**Cu′ban,** *adj., n.*

cub·by (kub′i), or **cub·by·hole** (-hōl′) *n.* a small, enclosed space.

cube (kūb), *n., v.,* **cubed, cub·ing.** —*n.* **1** solid with six equal, square sides. **2** product obtained when a number is cubed: *the cube of 4 is 64.* —*v.* **1** make or form into the shape of a cube. **2** use (a number) three times as a factor: *5 cubed is 125.* [< L < Gk. *kybos* cube, die]

cube root, number used as the factor of a cube: *the cube root of 125 is 5.*

cu·bic (kū′bik), **cu·bi·cal** (-bə kəl), *adj.* **1** shaped like a cube. **2** having length, breadth, and thickness. **3** having to do with or involving the cubes of numbers. —**cu′bi·cal·ly,** *adv.*

cu·bi·cle (kū′bə kəl), *n.* a very small room or compartment. [< L *cubiculum* bedroom < *cubare* lie]

cubic measure, system of measurement of volume in cubic units. 1728 cubic inches = 1 cubic foot.

cub·ism (kūb′iz əm), *n.* method of painting, drawing, and sculpture in which objects are represented by cubes and other geometrical figures rather than by realistic details. —**cub′ist,** *n.* —**cu·bis′tic,** *adj.*

cu·bit (kū′bit), *n.* an ancient measure of length, about 18 to 22 inches. [< L *cubitum* elbow, cubit]

cu·boid (kū′boid), *adj.* shaped like a cube. —*n.* something shaped like a cube. —**cu·boi′dal,** *adj.*

cuck·old (kuk′əld), *n.* husband of an unfaithful wife. —*n.* make a cuckold of. [< OF *cucuault* < *coucou* cuckoo]

cuck·oo (kúk′ü; *esp. for adj.* kü′kü), *n., pl.* **-oos,** *adj.* —*n.* **1** bird whose call sounds much like its name. The common European cuckoo lays its eggs in the nests of other birds instead of hatching them itself. **2** the American cuckoo, which builds its own nest. **3** call of the cuckoo. —*adj. U.S. Informal.* crazy; silly. [imit.]

cuckoo clock, clock with a toy bird that makes a sound like the European cuckoo to mark the hours and half-hours.

cu·cum·ber (kū′kum bər), *n.* **1** vegetable that has a green skin with firm flesh inside, used in salads and for pickles. **2** vine that it grows on. [< OF < L *cucumis*]

cud (kud), *n.* mouthful of food that cattle and similar animals bring back into the mouth from the first stomach for a slow, second chewing. [OE *cudu,* var. of *cwidu*]

cud·dle (kud′əl), *v.,* **-dled, -dling,** *n.* —*v.* **1** hold closely and lovingly in one's arms or lap. **2** lie close and snug; curl up. **3** hug. —*n.* hug. —**cud′dly,** *adj.*

cudg·el (kuj′əl), *n., v.,* **-eled, -el·ing.** —*n.* a short, thick stick used as a weapon; club. —*v.* beat with a cudgel.

take up the cudgels for, defend strongly. [OE *cycgel*]

cue¹ (kū), *n.* **1** hint or suggestion as to what to do or when to act. **2** in a play, the last word or words of one actor's speech that is the signal for another to come on the stage, begin speaking, etc. [prob. < F *queue* tail, end; with ref. to the end of a preceding actor's speech. See QUEUE.]

cue² (kū), *n.* **1** =queue. **2** a long, tapering stick used for striking the ball in billiards, pool, etc. [var. of *queue*]

cuff¹ (kuf), *n.* **1** band around the wrist, either attached to a sleeve or separate. **2** turned-up fold around the bottom of the legs of trousers. **3** =handcuff.

off the cuff, without preparation; impromptu. [ME *cuffe* glove]

cuff² (kuf), *v., n.* hit with the hand; slap. [cf. Sw. *kuffa* push]

cui·rass (kwi ras′), *n.* **1** piece of armor for the body made of a breastplate and a plate for the back fastened together. **2** the breastplate alone. [< F *cuirasse* < Ital. < VL < LL *coriacea (vestis)* (garment) of leather < L *corium* leather; form infl. by F *cuir* leather < L *corium*]

cui·sine (kwi zēn′), *n.* **1** style of cooking or preparing food. **2** food. [< F < L *cocina,* var. of *coquina* < *coquus* a cook]

cuisse (kwis), *n.* piece of armor to protect the thigh. [< F, thigh, < L *coxa* hip]

cul-de-sac (kul′də sak′; kŭl′–), *n.* street or passage open at only one end; blind alley. [< F, bottom of the sack]

cu·lex (kū′leks), *n., pl.* **-li·ces** (-lə sēz). the most common mosquito of North America and Europe. [< L, gnat]

cu·li·nar·y (kū′lə ner′i; kŭl′ə–), *adj.* **1** having to do with cooking. **2** used in cooking. [< L, < *culina* kitchen]

cull (kul), *v.* **1** pick out; select. **2** pick over; make selections from. —*n.* something picked out as being inferior or worthless. [< OF < L *colligere* COLLECT]

culm (kulm), *n.* the jointed stem of grasses, usually hollow. [< L *culmus* stalk]

cul·mi·nate (kul′mə nāt), *v.,* **-nat·ed, -nat·ing.** reach its highest point; reach a climax. [< LL *culminatus* < L *culmen,* earlier *columen* top]

cul·mi·na·tion (kul′mə nā′shən), *n.* **1** the highest point; climax. **2** a reaching the highest point.

cu·lottes (kyü lots′), *n. pl.* woman's skirt divided into two legs but sewn in such a way that the cloth falls like a skirt.

cul·pa·ble (kul′pə bəl), *adj.* deserving blame. [< F < L, < *culpa* fault] —**cul′pa-**

bil′i·ty, cul′pa·ble·ness, *n.* —**cul′pa·bly,** *adv.*

cul·prit (kul′prit), *n.* **1** person guilty of a fault or crime: offender. **2** prisoner in court accused of a crime.

cult (kult), *n.* **1** system of religious worship. **2** great admiration for a person, thing, idea, etc.; worship. **3** group showing such admiration; worshipers. [< L *cultus* worship < *colere* cultivate]

cul·ti·va·ble (kul′tə və bəl), **cul·ti·vat·a·ble** (-vāt′ə bəl), *adj.* that can be cultivated. —**cul′ti·va·bil′i·ty,** *n.*

cul·ti·vate (kul′tə vāt), *v.,* **-vat·ed, -vat·ing.** **1** prepare and use (land) to raise crops by plowing it, planting seeds, and taking care of the growing plants. **2** loosen the ground around (growing plants) to kill weeds, etc. **3** *Fig.* improve; develop, as by education. **4** *Fig.* give time, thought, and effort to. **5** *Fig.* seek better acquaintance with. [< Med.L, < *cultivare* < *cultivus* under cultivation < L *cultus* pp. of *colere* till] —**cul′ti·vat′ed,** *adj.*

cul·ti·va·tion (kul′tə vā′shən), *n.* **1** act of cultivating. **2** improvement; development. **3** the giving of time and thought to improving and developing (the body, mind, or manners). **4** culture.

cul·ti·va·tor (kul′tə vā′tər), *n.* **1** person or thing that cultivates. **2** a tool or machine used to loosen the ground and destroy weeds.

cul·tur·al (kul′chər əl), *adj.* of or having to do with culture. —**cul′tur·al·ly,** *adv.*

cul·ture (kul′chər), *n., v.,* **-tured, -tur·ing.** —*n.* **1** fineness of feelings, thoughts, tastes, manners, etc. **2** civilization of a given race or nation at a given time. **3** development of the mind or body by education, training, etc. **4** cultivation. **5** colony or growth of germs of a given kind that has been carefully made. —*v.* **1** cultivate. **2** grow in a medium. [< F < L *cultura* a tending. See CULT.]

cul·tured (kul′chərd), *adj.* **1** having or showing culture; refined. **2** produced or raised by culture.

culture shock, disorientation a person feels when thrust into a foreign culture or a new way of life.

cul·vert (kul′vərt), *n.* a small channel for water crossing under a road, railroad, canal, etc.

cum·ber (kum′bər), *v.* **1** burden; trouble. **2** hinder; hamper. —*n.* hindrance. [prob. < OF *combrer* impede < *combre* barrier < Celtic]

Cum·ber·lands (kum′bər landz), *n.* plateau of the Appalachian Mountains, extending from SW Virginia to N Alabama.

cum·ber·some (kum′bər səm), **cum·brous** (-brəs), *adj.* **1** clumsy; unwieldy. **2** burdensome. —**cum′ber·some·ly, cum′brous·ly,** *adv.* —**cum′ber·some·ness, cum′brous·ness,** *n.*

cum·in (kum′ən), *n.* **1** small plant of the Mediterranean region, belonging to the parsley family, whose seedlike fruits are used in cooking and medicine. **2** its seedlike fruit.

cum lau·de (kùm lou′dē; kum lô′dē), with praise or honor. [< L]

cum·quat (kum′kwot), *n.* =kumquat.

cu·mu·late (*v.* kŭ′myə lāt, *adj.* kŭ′myə lit, –lāt), *v.,* **–lat·ed, –lat·ing,** *adj.* —*v.* heap up; accumulate. —*adj.* heaped up. [< L, < *cumulus* heap] —**cu′mu·la′tion,** *n.*

cu·mu·la·tive (kŭ′myə lā′tiv; –lə tiv), *adj.* increasing or growing in amount, force, etc., by additions. —**cu′mu·la′tive·ly,** *adv.* —**cu′mu·la′tive·ness,** *n.*

cu·mu·lo·nim·bus or **cu·mu·lo·nim·bus** (kŭ′myə lō nim′bəs), *n., pl.* **–bus·es, –bi** (–bi). huge vertical cloud formation, reaching heights between 1600 and 20,000 feet; thunderland.

cu·mu·lo·stra·tus or **cu·mu·lo·stra·tus** (kŭ′myə lō strā′təs), *n., pl.* **–ti** (–ti). cumulus cloud with its base spread out horizontally, like a stratus cloud.

cu·mu·lus (kŭ′myə ləs), *n., pl.* **–li** (–lī). **1** cloud made up of rounded heaps with a flat bottom. **2** heap. [< L, heap] —**cu′mu·lous,** *adj.*

cu·ne·ate (kŭ′ni it; –āt), *adj.* wedge-shaped. [< L, < *cuneus* wedge]

cu·ne·i·form (kū nē′ə fôrm; kū′ni ə fôrm′), **cu·ni·form** (kū′nəfôrm), *adj.* wedge-shaped. —*n.* cuneiform writing of ancient Babylonia, Assyria, Persia, etc. [< L *cuneus* wedge + –FORM]

cun·ning (kun′ing), *adj.* **1** clever in deceiving; sly. **2** skillful; clever. **3** *Informal.* pretty and dear; attractive. —*n.* **1** slyness in getting what one wants. **2** skill; cleverness. [OE *cunning* < *cunnan* know (how). See CAN[1].] —**cun′ning·ly,** *adv.* —**cun′ning·ness,** *n.*

cup (kup), *n., v.,* **cupped, cup·ping.** —*n.* **1** dish to drink from. **2** cupful. **3** in cooking, a half pint. **4** thing shaped like a cup. The petals of some flowers form a cup. **5** ornamental cup, vase, etc., given to the winner of a contest. **6** thing to be endured or experienced; fate. **7** in golf, the hole. —*v.* **1** shape like a cup. **2** take or put in a cup.

cup of tea, a suited to one's taste or interest or pleasure. **b** a kind of thing; matter: *her behavior was a different cup of tea.*

in one's cups, drunk. [< LL *cuppa;* cf. L *cupa* tub]

cup·bear·er (kup′bâr′ər), *n.* person who fills and passes around the cups in which drinks are served.

cup·board (kub′ərd), *n.* **1** closet or cabinet with shelves for dishes, food, etc. **2** *Esp. Brit.* any small closet.

cup·cake (kup′kāk′), *n.* a small cake baked in a cup-shaped tin.

cup·ful (kup′fûl), *n., pl.* **–fuls.** as much as a cup holds.

Cu·pid (kū′pid), *n.* **1** the Roman god of love, son of Venus, identified with the Greek god Eros. **2 cupid,** a winged baby used as a symbol of love.

cu·pid·i·ty (kū pid′ə ti), *n.* eager desire; greed. [< L, < *cupidus* desirous < *cupere* long for, desire]

cu·po·la (kū′pə lə), *n.* **1** a rounded roof; dome. **2** a small dome or tower on a roof. [< Ital. < LL *cupula,* dim. of L *cupa* tub]

cu·pre·ous (kū′pri əs), *adj.* **1** of or containing copper. **2** copper-colored.

cu·pric (kū′prik), *adj.* of or containing divalent copper.

cu·prite (kyü′prīt), *n.* mineral that is an important ore of copper.

cu·prous (kū′prəs), *adj.* of or containing monovalent copper.

cu·prum (kū′prəm), *n.* copper. [< L. See COPPER.]

cur (kėr), *n.* **1** a worthless dog; mongrel. **2** an ill-bred, worthless person. [ME *curre*]

cur., **1** currency. **2** current.

cur·a·ble (kyür′ə bəl), *adj.* that can be cured. —**cur′a·bil′i·ty, cur′a·ble·ness,** *n.* —**cur′a·bly,** *adv.*

Cu·ra·çao (kyür′ə sō′; kü′rä sou′), *n.* **1** group of Dutch islands in the West Indies. **2** the largest island of this group. **3 curaçao,** liqueur or cordial flavored with orange peel.

cu·ra·cy (kyür′ə si), *n., pl.* **–cies.** the position, rank, or work of a curate.

cu·ra·re, cu·ra·ri (kyü rä′rē), *n.* a poisonous, resinlike substance obtained from a tropical vine. [< Carib *kurare*]

cu·rate (kyür′it), *n.* clergyman who is an assistant to a pastor, rector, or vicar. [< Med.L, < *cura* cure (def. 5) < L, care]

cur·a·tive (kyür′ə tiv), *adj.* having the power to cure; curing; tending to cure. —*n.* means of curing.

cu·ra·tor (kyü rā′tər), *n.* person in charge of all or part of a museum, library, etc. [< L, < *curare* care for < *cura* care] —**cu′ra·to′ri·al,** *adj.* —**cu·ra′tor·ship,** *n.*

curb (kėrb), *n.* **1** a raised border of concrete, stone, or wood along the edge of a pavement, etc. **2** check; resraint. **3** chain or strap fastened to a horse's bit and passing under its lower jaw, used to restrain the horse. **4** market that deals in stocks and bonds not listed on the regular stock exchange. —*v.* **1** hold in check; restrain. **2** provide with a curb. [< F < L *curvus* bent]

curb bit, a horse's bit having a curb.

curb·ing (kėr′bing), *n.* **1** material for making a curb. **2** a raised border of concrete, etc.; curb.

curb·stone (kėrb′stōn′), *n.* stone or stones forming a curb.

cur·cu·li·o (kėr kū′li ō), *n., pl.* **–li·os.** a snout beetle, esp. one that destroys fruit. [< L]

curd (kėrd), *n.* Often, **curds.** the thick part of milk that separates from the watery part when milk sours. —*v.* form into curds; curdle. [ME *curd, crud*] —**curd′y,** *adj.*

cur·dle (kėr′dəl), *v.,* **–dled, –dling. 1** form into curds. **2** thicken.

curdle the blood, horrify; terrify. [< *curd*]

cure (kyür), *v.,* **cured, cur·ing,** *n.* —*v.* **1** make well; bring back to health. **2** get rid of. **3** preserve (meat) by drying and salting. —*n.* **1** act or fact of curing. **2** treatment that brings a person back to health. **3** medicine that is a remedy. **4** way of curing meat. **5** spiritual charge; religious care. [< F < L *cura* care, concern] —**cure′less,** *adj.* —**cur′er,** *n.*

cu·ré (kyü rā′), *n.* a parish priest. [< F. See CURATE.]

cure-all (kyür′ôl′), *n.* remedy supposed to cure all diseases or evils.

cur·few (kėr′fū), *n.* **1** a ringing of a bell at a fixed time every evening as a signal, as for children to come off the streets. **2** bell ringing such a signal: *"the curfew tolls the knell of parting day."* **3** time when it is rung. **4** in the Middle Ages, a signal to put out lights and cover fires. [< AF, < *covrir* cover + *feu* fire < L *focus* hearth]

cu·ri·a (kyür′i ə), *n., pl.* **cu·ri·ae** (kyür′i ē). group of high officials who assist the Pope in the government and administration of the Roman Catholic Church.

cu·rie (kyür′ē; kü rē′), *n.* unit of radioactivity. [for Mme. *Curie*]

cu·ri·o (kyür′i ō), *n., pl.* **cu·ri·os.** object valued as a curiosity. [short for *curiosity*]

cu·ri·os·i·ty (kyür′i os′ə ti), *n., pl.* **–ties. 1** an eager desire to know. **2** a strange, rare, or novel object. **3** an interesting quality, as from strangeness.

cu·ri·ous (kyür′i əs), *adj.* **1** eager to know. **2** too eager to know; prying. **3** interesting because strange, unusual, etc. **4** very careful; exact. **5** very odd; eccentric. [< OF < L *curiosus* inquisitive, full of care, ult. < *cura* care] —**cu′ri·ous·ly,** *adv.* —**cu′ri·ous·ness,** *n.*

cu·ri·um (kyür′i əm), *n.* an element, Cm, produced by bombardment of plutonium and uranium by helium ions. [for Mme. *Curie*]

curl (kėrl), *v.* **1** twist into rings; roll into coils. **2** twist out of shape; bend into a curve. —*n.* **1** a curled lock of hair. **2** anything like it. **3** a curling or being curled. [ME *curle(n), crulle(n) < crul* curly]

curl·er (kėr′lər), *n.* **1** person or thing that curls. **2** a device on which hair is twisted to make it curl.

cur·lew (kėr′lü), *n., pl.* **–lews** or (*esp. collectively*) **–lew.** a wading bird with a long, thin bill. [< OF *courlieu;* imit.]

curl·i·cue (kėr′li kū), *n.* a fancy twist, curl, flourish, etc.

curl·ing (kėr′ling), *n.* game played on the ice in which large, smooth stones are slid at a target.

curl·y (kėr′li), *adj.,* **curl·i·er, curl·i·est. 1** curling; wavy. **2** having curls. —**curl′i·ly,** *adv.* —**curl′i·ness,** *n.*

cur·mudg·eon (kər muj′ən), *n.* a rude, stingy, bad-tempered person; miser. —**cur·mudg′eonly,** *adv.*

cur·rant (kėr′ənt), *n.* **1** a small, seedless raisin, used in cakes, etc. **2** a small, sour, edible berry that grows in bunches on certain shrubs. **3** bush that bears currants. [< AF *(raisins de) Corauntz* raisins of Corinth]

cur·ren·cy (kėr′ən si), *n., pl.* **-cies.** **1** money in actual use in a country. **2** a passing from person to person; circulation: *people who spread a rumor give it currency.* **3** general use or acceptance; common occurrence.

cur·rent (kėr′ənt), *n.* **1** a flow. **2** flow of electricity along a wire, etc. **3** course; movement; general direction. —*adj.* **1** going around; passing from person to person. **2** generally used or accepted; commonly occurring. **3** of the present time: *the current issue of a magazine.* [< L *currens*, ppr. of *currere* run] —**cur′rent·ly**, *adv.*

cur·ric·u·lar (kə rik′yə lər), *adj.* having to do with a curriculum.

cur·ric·u·lum (kə rik′yə ləm), *n., pl.* **-lums, -la** (-lə). course of study or set of courses of study in a school, college, etc. [< L, race course, chariot, dim. of *currus* chariot < *currere* run]

curriculum vi·tae (vī′ti), *pl.* **curricula vitae.** *Latin.* **1** short summary of a person's background, education, experience, etc.; resume. **2** course of a person's life.

cur·ry[1] (kėr′i), *v.,* **-ried, -ry·ing.** **1** rub and clean (a horse, etc.) with a brush or currycomb. **2** prepare (tanned leather) for use by soaking, scraping, beating, coloring, etc.

curry favor, seek a person's favor by insincere flattery, constant attentions, etc. [< OF *correiier* put in order < *con-* (< L *com-*) + *reiier* arrange < Gmc.] —**cur′ri·er**, *n.*

cur·ry[2] (kėr′i), *n., pl.* **-ries,** *v.,* **-ried, -ry·ing.** —*n.* **1** a peppery sauce or powder containing a mixture of spices, seeds, vegetables, etc. **2** stew flavored with curry. —*v.* prepare or flavor with curry. [< Tamil *kari*]

cur·ry·comb (kėr′i kōm′), *n.* brush with metal teeth for rubbing and cleaning a horse. —*v.* use a currycomb on.

curse (kėrs), *v.,* **cursed** or **curst, curs·ing,** *n.* —*v.* **1** ask God to bring evil or harm on. **2** bring evil or harm on. **3** swear; swear at; blaspheme. —*n.* **1** the words that a person says when he asks God to curse someone or something. **2** something that is cursed. **3** harm or evil that comes as if in answer to a curse. **4** cause of evil or harm. **5** word or words used in swearing.

be cursed with, have and suffer from. [OE *cūrs, n., cūrsian,* v.] —**curs′er**, *n.*

curs·ed (kėr′sid; kėrst), *adj.* **1** under a curse. **2** deserving a curse; evil; hateful; damnable. —**curs′ed·ly**, *adv.* —**curs′ed·ness**, *n.*

cur·sive (kėr′siv), *adj.* written with the letters joined together: *ordinary handwriting is cursive.* —*n.* letter made to join

other letters. [< Med.L, < *cursus,* pp. of L *currere* run] —**cur′sive·ly**, *adv.*

cur·sor (kėr′sər), *n.* **1** movable mark or pointer on a computer screen that opens a program or file or indicates where an insertion, deletion, or other operation begins. **2** sliding glass of an optical instrument having a fine line on it to facilitate sighting.

cur·so·ry (kėr′sə ri), *adj.* hasty and superficial; without attention to details. [< LL *cursorius* of a race < *currere* run] —**cur′so·ri·ly**, *adv.* —**cur′so·ri·ness**, *n.*

curt (kėrt), *adj.* **1** short; brief; **2** rudely brief; abrupt: *a curt way of talking.* [< L *curtus* cut short] —**curt′ly**, *adv.* —**curt′ness**, *n.*

cur·tail (kėr tāl′), *v.* cut short; cut off part of; reduce; lessen. [< *curtal,* adj., cut short (esp. of tails) < OF < L *curtus*; infl. by *tail*] —**cur·tail′er**, *n.* —**cur·tail′ment**, *n.*

cur·tain (kėr′tən), *n.* **1** piece of material hung to shut off, cover, hide, or decorate something. **2** thing that covers or hides. —*v.* **1** provide with a curtain; shut off with a curtain; decorate with a curtain. **2** cover; hide.

curtain off, separate or divide with a curtain.

curtains, *Slang.* **a** the end. **b** death.

draw the curtain over (or **on**), conceal.

raise the curtain, reveal. [< OF < LL *cortina*]

curtain call, call for an actor, musician, etc., to return to the stage and acknowledge the applause of the audience.

curtain raiser, 1 short play or performance given before the main entertainment, performance, etc. **2** *Fig.* something small or insignificant used to introduce something much bigger or important.

curt·sy, curt·sey (kėrt′si), *n., pl.* **-sies; -seys;** *v.,* **-sied, -sy·ing; -seyed, -sey·ing.** —*n.* bow of respect or greeting by women, consisting of bending the knees and lowering the body slightly. —*v.* make a curtsy. [var. of *courtesy*]

cur·va·ture (kėr′və chər; -chùr), *n.* **1** a curving. **2** a curved piece or part; curve.

cur·va·ceous (kėr vā′shəs), *adj. Informal.* having a well-formed, attractive female figure. —**cur·va′ceous·ly**, *adv.*

curve (kėrv), *n., v.,* **curved, curv·ing,** *adj.* —*n.* **1** line that has no straight part. **2** something having the shape of a curve; bend: *curves in a road.* **3** baseball thrown to curve just before it reaches the batter. **4** a line or lines that can be defined by an equation or equations. —*v.* **1** bend so as to form a curve. **2** move in the course of a curve. —*adj.* curved.

throw a curve, play a trick; deal unfairly with. [< L *curvus* bending]

cur·vet (*n.* kėr′vit; *v.* kėr vet′, kėr′vit), *n., v.,* **-vet·ted, -vet·ting; -vet·ed, -vet·ing.** —*n.* leap in the air made by a horse, in which all the legs are off the ground for a second. —*v.* **1** make such a leap. **2**

make (a horse) leap in this way. [< Ital. *corvetta,* dim. of *corvo* CURVE]

cur·vi·lin·e·ar (kėr′və lin′i ər), **cur·vi·lin·e·al** (-i əl), *adj.* consisting of or enclosed by curved lines.

cur·vy (kėr′vi), *adj.,* **-vi·er, -vi·est. 1** *Informal.* =curvaceous. **2** having a curve or curves.

cush·ion (kùsh′ən), *n.* **1** a soft pillow or pad used to sit, lie, or kneel on. **2** anything used or shaped like a cushion. **3** the elastic lining of the sides of a billiard table. **4** something to counteract a sudden shock, jar, or jolt. —*v.* **1** put or seat on a cushion; support with cushions. **2** protect from sudden shocks or jars with a cushion, esp. a cushion of steam. [< OF *coussin,* prob. < VL *coxinum* < L *coxa* hip]

cusp (kusp), *n.* **1** a pointed end; point. A crescent has two cups. **2** a blunt or pointed protuberance of the crown of a tooth.

on the cusp, at the edge or beginning: *on the cusp of adolescence.* [< L *cuspis*]

cus·pid (kus′pid), *n.* tooth having one cusp; canine tooth. —**cus′pi·dal**, *adj.*

cus·pi·date (kus′pə dāt), **cus·pi·dat·ed** (-dāt′id), *adj.* having a sharp, pointed end.

cuss (kus), *Informal.* —*n.* **1** curse. **2** an insignificant or troublesome person or animal. —*v.* curse. [var. of *curse*]

cus·tard (kus′tərd), *n.* a baked or boiled pudding made of eggs, sugar, milk, etc. [var. of *crustade* < F < Pr. *croustado* pasty < L *crustare* encrust < *crusta* crust]

cus·to·di·an (kus tō′di ən), *n.* person in charge; caretaker: *the custodian of a museum.* —**cus·to′di·an·ship′**, *n.*

cus·to·dy (kus′tə di), *n., pl.* **-dies. 1** keeping; care. **2** a being confined or detained; imprisonment.

in custody, in the care of the police; in prison.

take into custody, arrest. [< L, < *custos* guardian] —**cus·to′di·al**, *adj.*

cus·tom (kus′təm), *n.* **1** a usual action; habit. **2** habit maintained for so long that it has almost the force of law. **3** the regular business given by a customer. **4 customs, a** taxes paid to the government on things brought in from a foreign country. **b** department of the government that collects these taxes. —*adj.* **1** made specially for individuals; made to order. **2** making things to order. [< OF < VL *consuetumen* < L *com-* + *suescere* accustom. Doublet of COSTUME.]

cus·tom·ar·y (kus′təm er′i), *adj.* **1** according to custom; as a habit; usual. **2** holding or held by custom; established by custom, as distinguished from law. —**cus′tom·ar′i·ly**, *adv.* —**cus′tom·ar′i·ness**, *n.*

cus·tom-built (kus′təm bilt′), *adj.* built to order; not ready-made.

cus·tom·er (kus′təm ər), *n.* **1** person who buys. **2** person; fellow.

custom house, a building where taxes on things brought into a country are collected.

cus·tom·ize (kus′tə mīz), v., **–ized, –iz·ing.** make specially for a customer; make to order.

cus·tom-made (kus′təm mād′), adj. made to order; not ready-made.

cut (kut), v., **cut, cut·ting,** adj., n. —v. **1** separate, open, or remove with something sharp: cut meat, timber, etc. **2** wound with a knife, saw, etc. **3** reduce; decrease. **4** pass; go: cut through the woods. **5** divide by crossing: a brook cuts that field. **6** hit or strike sharply. **7** hurt the feelings of. **8** Slang. be absent from (a class, lecture, etc.). **9** dissolve: gasoline cuts grease. —adj. **1** that has been cut. **2** shaped or formed by cutting. **3** reduced: cut prices. —n. **1** wound or opening made by cutting. **2** passage, channel, etc., made by cutting or digging. **3** piece cut off or cut out. **4** way in which a thing is cut; style; fashion. **5** reduction. **6** a sharp blow or stroke. **7** action or speech that hurts the feelings. **8** Slang. absence from a class, lecture, etc. **9** Slang. share of booty, etc.

a cut above, superior to (someone or something).

cut across, go straight across or through.

cut and dried, a ready for use. **b** Fig. dull; uninteresting.

cut and run, make off quickly.

cut back, a reduce or curtail. **b** shorten by cutting off the end. **c** reverse direction suddenly.

cut down, a cause to fall by cutting. **b** Fig. reduce; decrease. **c** kill. **d** injure or disable.

cut in, a go in suddenly. **b** break in; interrupt.

cut it out, Slang. stop it; quit it.

cut loose, a separate from; break a connection or relation. **b** run away. **c** act without restraint.

cut off, a remove by cutting. **b** shut off. **c** stop suddenly. **d** break; interrupt.

cut out, a remove by cutting. **b** leave out. **c** get the better of. **d** make by cutting. **e** Slang. stop doing something.

cut up, cut to pieces. [ME cutte(n)]

cu·ta·ne·ous (kū tā′ni əs), adj. of or having to do with the skin. [< Med.L, < L cutis skin]

cut·a·way (kut′ə wā′), n. coat having the lower part cut back in a curve from the waist.

cut·back (kut′bak′), n. **1** a scheduled slowing down of any industrial operation: a cutback in steel production. **2** reduction: a cutback in the defense budget.

cute (kūt), adj., **cut·er, cut·est. 1** pleasing or attractive because pretty, dear, dainty, etc. **2** clever; shrewd. [var. of acute] **—cute′ly,** adv. **—cute′ness,** n.

cute·sy (kut′si), adj., **–si·er, –si·est.** Informal. consciously cute; affected.

cut glass, glass shaped or decorated by grinding and polishing. **—cut′-glass′,** adj.

cu·ti·cle (kū′tə kəl), n. **1** outer skin. **2** the hardened skin around the edges of the fingernail or toenail. [< L cuticula, dim. of cutis skin]

cut·ie (kū′ti), n., Informal. **1** attractive, lively young woman. **2** someone or something shrewd, surprising, or clever. Also, **cutey.**

cut·lass, cut·las (kut′ləs), n. a short, heavy, slightly curved sword. [< F coutelas < L culter knife]

cut·ler (kut′lər), n. person who makes, sells, or repairs knives, scissors, and other cutting instruments. [< F, < coutel small knife < L cultellus, dim. of culter knife]

cut·ler·y (kut′lər i), n. **1** knives, scissors, and other cutting instruments. **2** knives, forks, spoons, etc., for table use. **3** business of a cutler.

cut·let (kut′lit), n. **1** slice of meat for broiling or frying. **2** a flat, fried cake of chopped meat or fish. [< F côtelette, ult. < costa rib]

cut·off (kut′ôf′; –of′), n. **1** a short way across or through. **2** a stopping of the passage of steam or working fluid to the cylinder of an engine. **3** mechanism or device that does this.

cutoffs, pants, esp. blue jeans, cut off at the knee and not hemmed.

cut·out (kut′out′), n. **1** shape or design to be cut out: some books have cutouts. **2** device for disconnecting an engine from its muffler. **3** device for breaking an electric current.

cut·purse (kut′pėrs′), n. =pickpocket.

cut rate, price lower than the usual price: buy appliances at a cut rate.

cut·ter (kut′ər), n. **1** person who cuts. **2** tool or machine for cutting: a meat cutter. **3** a small, light sleigh, usually pulled by one horse. **4** a small sailboat with one mast. **5** boat belonging to a warship, used to carry people and supplies to and from the ship. **6** a small, armed ship used by the coast guard.

cut·throat (kut′thrōt′), n. murderer. —adj. **1** murderous. **2** relentless; merciless; severe.

cut·ting (kut′ing), n. **1** thing cut off or cut out. **2** a small shoot cut from a plant to grow a new plant. **3** a newspaper or magazine clipping. **4** act of one that cuts. —adj. **1** that cuts; sharp. **2** hurting the feelings; sarcastic. **—cut′ting·ly,** adv.

cut·tle·fish (kut′əl fish′), or **cuttle** (kut′əl), n., pl. **–fish·es** or (esp. collectively) **–fish; –tles.** a saltwater mollusk with ten sucker-bearing arms and a hard, internal shell. One kind of cuttlefish squirts out an inky fluid when frightened. [OE cudele cuttlefish]

cut·up (kut′up′), n. Slang. person who shows off or plays tricks.

cut·wa·ter (kut′wô′tər; –wot′ər), n. the front part of a ship's prow.

cut·worm (kut′wėrm′), n. caterpillar that cuts off the stalks of young plants near the ground.

CV, curriculum vitae.

cwt., hundredweight.

–cy, suffix. **1** office, position, or rank of, as in captaincy. **2** quality, state, condition, or fact of being, as in bankruptcy. [< F -cie, < L -cia, Gk. -kia]

cy·an·ic (sī an′ik), adj. **1** of cyanogen; containing cyanogen. **2** blue.

cyanic acid, a colorless, poisonous liquid, HOCN.

cy·a·nide (sī′ə nīd; –nid), **cy·a·nid** (–nid), n. **1** salt of hydrocyanic acid. **2** potassium cyanide, KCN, a powerful poison.

cy·an·o·gen (sī an′ə jən), n. **1** a colorless, poisonous, inflammable gas, C_2N_2, with the odor of bitter almonds. **2** a univalent radical, CN, consisting of one atom of carbon and one of nitrogen.

cy·a·no·sis (sī′ə nō′sis), n. blueness or lividness of the skin, caused by lack of oxygen in the blood. [< NL < Gk. kyanosis darkblue color] **—cy′a·not′ic,** adj.

cyber–, combining form. **1** of or having to do with computers, as in cyberphobia. **2** created by or existing only in a computer, as in cyberspace.

cy·ber·net·ics (sī′bər net′iks), n. comparative study of complex calculating machines and the human nervous system in order to understand better the functioning of both systems. **—cy′ber·net′ic,** adj.

cy·ber·pho·bi·a (sī′bər fō′bē ə), n. extreme, unreasonable fear of computers. **—cy′ber·phobe,** n. **—cyber·pho′bic,** adj.

cy·ber·space (sī′bər spās′), n. =virtual reality.

cy·cad (sī′kad), n. a large, tropical, palmlike plant with a cluster of long, fernlike leaves at the top. [< NL < Gk. kykas]

cyc·la·men (sik′lə mən; –men), n. plant of the same family as the primrose, with heart-shaped leaves and snowy white, purple, pink, or crimson flowers, whose five petals bend backward. [< NL < L < Gk. kyklaminos]

cy·cle (sī′kəl), n., v., **–cled, –cling.** —n. **1** period of time or complete process of growth or action that repeats itself in the same order. Spring, summer, autumn, and winter make a cycle. **2** a complete set or series. **3** all the stories, poems, legends, etc., about a great hero or event. **4** a very long period of time; age. **5** Physics. a complete or double alteration or reversal of an alternating electric current. —v. **1** pass through a cycle; occur over and over again in the same order. **2** ride a bicycle, tricycle, etc. [< LL < Gk. kyklos] **—cy′cler,** n.

cy·clic (sī′klik; sik′lik), **cy·cli·cal** (sī′klə kəl; sik′lə–), adj. **1** of a cycle. **2** moving or occurring in cycles. **3** arranged in a ring.

cy·clist (sī′klist), n. rider of a bicycle, tricycle, etc.

cy·cloid (sī′kloid), adj. like a circle; somewhat circular.

cy·clom·e·ter (sī klom′ə tər), n. instrument that measures the distance that a wheel travels by recording the revolutions that it makes.

cy·clone (sī′klōn), *n.* **1** a very violent windstorm; tornado. **2** storm moving around and toward a calm center of low pressure, which also moves. [< Gk. *kyklon,* ppr. of *kyklóein* move around in a circle] —**cy·clon′ic, cy·clon′i·cal,** *adj.* —**cy·clon′i·cal·ly,** *adv.*

cy·clo·pe·di·a (sī′klə pē′di ə), *n.* an encyclopedia. [shortened form of *encyclopedia*] —**cy′clo·pe′dic,** *adj.* —**cy′clo·pe′dist,** *n.*

Cy·clops (sī′klops), *n., pl.* **Cy·clo·pes** (sī klō′pēz). *Gk. Legend.* one of a group of one-eyed giants. [< L < Gk., < *kyklos* circle + *ops* eye] —**Cy′clo·pe′an,** *adj.*

cy·clo·ram·a (sī′klə ram′ə; -rä′mə), *n.* a large picture of a landscape, battle, etc., on the wall of a circular room. [< Gk. *kyklos* circle + *horama* spectacle] —**cy′clo·ram′ic,** *adj.*

cy·clo·tron (sī′klə tron), *n.* apparatus that sends out electrons at very high velocities to disintegrate atoms. [< Gk. *kyklos* circle + E *-tron* (as in *neutron*)]

cyg·net (sig′nit), *n.* a young swan.

cyl., cylinder; cylindrical.

cyl·in·der (sil′ən dər), *n.* **1** a solid bounded by two equal, parallel circles and a curved surface formed by moving a straight line of fixed length so that its ends always lie on the two parallel circles. **2** volume of such a solid. **3** any long, round object, solid or hollow, with flat ends. **4** the piston chamber of an engine. [< L < Gk., < *kylindein* to roll]

cy·lin·dri·cal (sə lin′drə kəl), **cy·lin·dric** (-drik), *adj.* shaped like a cylinder; having the form of a cylinder. —**cy·lin′dri·cal′i·ty,** *n.* —**cy·lin′dri·cal·ly,** *adv.*

cym·bal (sim′bəl), *n.* one of a pair of brass plates, used as a musical instrument. [< L < Gk., < *kymbe* hollow of a vessel] —**cym′bal·ist,** *n.*

cyme (sīm), *n.* a flower cluster in which there is a flower at the top of the main stem and of each branch of the cluster. [< L < Gk. *kyma* something swollen, sprout] —**cy′mose,** *adj.*

Cym·ry (kim′ri), *n.* the Welsh people. —**Cym′ric,** *adj. n.*

cyn·ic (sin′ik), *n.* **1** person inclined to believe that the motives for people's actions are insincere and selfish. **2** a sneering, sarcastic person. **3 Cynic,** member of a group of ancient Greek philosophers who taught that self-control is the essential part of virtue, and despised pleasure, money, and personal comfort. —*adj.* **1** cynical. **2 Cynic,** of or having to do with the Cynics or their doctrines. [< L < Gk. *kynikos* doglike < *kyon* dog]

cyn·i·cal (sin′ə kəl), *adj.* **1** doubting the worth of life. **2** sneering; sarcastic. —**cyn′i·cal·ly,** *adv.* —**cyn′i·cal·ness,** *n.*

cyn·i·cism (sin′ə siz əm), *n.* **1** cynical quality or disposition. **2** a cynical remark.

cyn·o·sure (sī′nə shùr; sin′ə-), *n.* **1** center of attraction, interest, or attention. **2** something used for guidance or direction. [< L < Gk. *kynosoura* dog's tail < *kyon* dog + *oura* tail]

cy·pher (sī′fər), *n., v.* =cipher.

cy·press (sī′prəs), *n.* **1** an evergreen tree of the South, with hard wood and dark leaves. **2** its wood. **3** any of various similar plants such as the European **"true" cypress,** and the **"standing cypress"** of the United States. [< OF < L *cypressus* < Gk. *kyparissos*]

cyp·ri·noid (sip′rə noid), *n.* any of a large group of freshwater fishes, including the carps, suckers, goldfishes, breams, most freshwater minnows, etc. —*adj.* of or belonging to this group. [< L *cyprinus* carp (< Gk.) + -OID]

Cyp·ri·ot (sip′ri ət), *adj.* of Cyprus. —*n.* a native or inhabitant of Cyprus. Also, **Cypriote.**

Cy·prus (sī′prəs), *n.* an island and republic in the E Mediterranean, S of Turkey, divided between its Turkish Cypriot and Greek Cypriot populations.

Cy·ril·lic (si ril′ik), *adj.* of or having to do with the alphabet used for Russian and other Slavic languages, based on an ancient Slavic alphabet. [< *Cyril,* apostle to the Slavs, who developed an earlier alphabet from which the Cyrillic alphabet was derived]

cyst (sist), *n.* **1** an abnormal, saclike growth in animals or plants. Cysts usually contain liquid and diseased matter. **2** a saclike structure in animals or plants. [< NL < Gk. *kystis* pouch, bladder] —**cyst′ic,** *adj.*

-cyte, *combining form.* cell, as in *lymphocyte.*

Cyth·er·e·a (sith′ər ē′ə), *n.* Gk. Myth. Aphrodite. —**Cyth′er·e′an,** *adj.*

cyto- *combining form.* cell or cells, as in *cytoplasm.*

cy·to·gen·et·ics (sī′tō jə net′iks), *n.* branch of biology dealing with the relation of cells to heredity and variation.

cy·tol·o·gy (sī tol′ə ji), *n.* branch of biology that deals with the formation, structure, and function of the cells of animals and plants. [< Gk. *kytos* receptacle, cell + -LOGY —**cy′to·log′ic, cy′to·log′i·cal,** *adj.* —**cy′to·log′i·cal·ly,** *adv.* —**cy·tol′o·gist,** *n.*

cy·to·plasm (sī′tə plaz əm), **cy·to·plast** (-plast), *n.* the living substance or photoplasm of a cell, exclusive of the nucleus. —**cy′to·plas′mic,** *adj.*

czar (zär), *n.* **1** emperor. It was the title of the emperors of Russia. **2** autocrat; person with absolute power. Also, **tsar, tzar.** [< Russ. *tsar* < Old Church Slavic < Gothic < L *Caesar* Caesar]

czar·e·vitch (zär′ə vich), *n.* **1** the eldest son of a Russian czar. **2** son of a Russian czar. Also, **tsarevitch, tzarevitch.**

cza·ri·na (zä rē′nə), *n.* wife of a czar; Russian empress. Also, **tsarina, tzarina.**

Czech (chek), *n.* **1** member of the most westerly branch of the Slavs. Bohemians, Moravians, and Silesians are Czechs. **2** their Slavic language. —*adj.* of or having to do with the Czech language or people. —**Czech′ic, Czech′ish,** *adj.*

Czech·o·slo·va·ki·a, (chek′ə slō vä′ki ə; -vak′i ə), *n.* former country in C Europe. —**Czech′o·slo·va′ki·an,** *adj., n.*

Czech Republic, republic in C Europe, formerly part of Czechoslovakia.

D, d (dē), *n., pl.* **D's; d's.**
1 the fourth letter of the alphabet. **2** the second note or tone of the musical scale of C major. **3** the Roman numeral for 500.

D, deuterium.

D., 1 December. **2** Democrat; Democratic. **3** Dutch.

d., 1 day. **2** dead. **3** degree. **4** died. **5** dollar. **6** dose.

D.A., District Attorney.

dab (dab), *v.,* **dabbed, dab·bing,** *n.* —*v.* **1** touch lightly; tap. **2** put on with light strokes. —*n.* **1** a quick, light touch or blow; a tap. **2** a small, soft or moist mass. **3** a little bit. [ME] —**dab′ber,** *n.*

dab·ble (dab′əl), *v.,* **-bled, -bling. 1** dip (hands, feet, etc.) in and out of water; splash. **2** do superficially; work a little: *dabble at painting.* [< Flem. *dabbelen*] —**dab′bler,** *n.*

dace (dās), *n., pl.* **dac·es** or (*esp. collectively*) **dace.** any of several small freshwater fish. [ME *darse* < OF *dars* DART]

dachs·hund (däks′hund΄; –hunt΄; daks′–; dash′–), *n.* dog that is small, with a long body and very short legs. [< G, < *dachs* badger + *hund* dog]

Da·cron (dā′kron), *n. Trademark.* a synthetic wrinkle- and abrasion-resistant fiber used for shirts, suits, etc.

dac·tyl (dak′təl), *n.* a metrical foot of three syllables (– ˘ ˘), one accented followed by two unaccented, or, in classical verse, one long followed by two short. [< L < Gk. *daktylos* finger] —**dac·tyl′ic,** *adj., n.*

dad (dad), *n.* father.

dad·dy (dad′i), *n., pl.* **-dies.** father.

dad·dy-long·legs (dad′ilông′legz΄; –long′–), *n., pl.* **-legs.** U.S. **1** animal similar to a spider, with a small body and very long, thin legs. **2** =crane fly.

da·do (dā′dō), *n., pl.* **-does, -dos. 1** the lower part of the wall of a room when it is decorated differently from the upper part. **2** part of a pedestal between the base and the cap. [< Ital. DIE²]

Daed·a·lus (ded′ə ləs), *n. Gk. Legend.* a skillful worker who made wings for flying and built the labyrinth in Crete.

dae·mon (dē′mən), *n.* **1** *Gk. Myth.* **a** a supernatural being. **b** an inferior deity. **2** demon. [< L < Gk. *daimon*] —**dae·mon′ic,** *adj.*

daf·fo·dil (daf′ə dil), *n.* **1** narcissus with yellow flowers and long, slender leaves. **2** the flower. **3** yellow. [var. of *affodill* < VL < L < Gk. *asphodelos*]

daff·y (daf′i), *adj.,* **daff·i·er, daff·i·est.** *Informal.* foolish; silly; crazy.

daft (daft; däft), *adj.* **1** silly; foolish. **2** crazy. [cf. OE *gedæfte* gentle] —**daft′ness,** *n.*

dag·ger (dag′ər), *n.* **1** a small weapon with a short, pointed blade, used for stabbing. **2** sign (†) used in printing to refer the reader to a footnote, etc. [prob. < obs. *dag* slash]

da·guerre·o·type (də ger′ə tīp; –i ə tīp), *n., v.,* **-typed, -typ·ing.** —*n.* **1** an early method of photography in which the pictures were made on silvered metal plates. **2** picture made in this way. —*v.* photograph by this process. [for L. J. M. *Daguerre,* inventor]

dahl·ia (dal′yə; däl′–), *n.* **1** a tall plant of the aster family that has large, showy flowers in the autumn. **2** the flower. [< NL; named for A. *Dahl,* botanist]

dai·kon (dī′kən), *n.* Japanese radish with a long, white and sweet root, grown in the United States. [< Jap. *daikon* great root]

Dail Eir·eann (dôl ār′ən; doil), or **Dail,** *n.* the lower house of parliament of the Irish Republic.

dai·ly (dā′li), *adj., n., pl.* **-lies,** *adv.* —*adj.* done, happening, or appearing every day, or every day but Sunday. —*n.* newspaper appearing every day, or every day but Sunday. —*adv.* every day; day by day.

dain·ty (dān′ti), *adj.,* **-ti·er, -ti·est,** *n., pl.* **-ties.** —*adj.* **1** having delicate beauty; fresh and pretty. **2** having or showing delicate tastes and feeling; particular. **3** good to eat; delicious. **4** too particular; overnice. [< n.] —*n.* something very good to eat; a delicious bit of food. [< OF < L. *dignitas* worthiness < *dignus* worthy] —**dain′ti·ly,** *adv.* —**dain′ti·ness,** *n.*

dair·y (dār′i), *n., pl.* **dair·ies. 1** room or building where milk and cream are kept and made into butter and cheese. **2** farm where milk and cream are produced and butter and cheese made. **3** store or company that sells milk, butter, etc. **4** business of producing milk, butter, etc. [ME *deierie* < *deie* maid (OE *dæge* breadmaker]

dair·y·ing (dār′i ing), *n.* business of operating a dairy or dairy farm.

da·is (dā′is; dās), *n.* a raised platform in a hall or large room for a throne, seats of honor, etc. [< OF < L *discus* quoit, DISH]

dai·sy (dā′zi), *n., pl.* **-sies, 1** plant of the aster family whose flowers or petals are usually white or pink around a yellow center. **2** a tall plant of the same family whose flower heads have a yellow disk and white rays; the common "white daisy" of the U.S.

push up the daisies, *Slang.* be in the grave. [OE *dæges* edge day's eye] —**dai′sied,** *adj.*

Da·kar (dä kär′), *n.* seaport and capital of Senegal.

Da·lai La·ma (dä lī′ lä′mə), the chief priest of the religion of Lamaism in Tibet and Mongolia. Also, **Grand Lama.**

dale (dāl), *n.* valley. [OE *dæl*]

dal·li·ance (dal′i əns), *n.* **1** flirtation. **2** a playing; trifling.

dal·ly (dal′i), *v.,* **-lied, -ly·ing. 1** act in a playful manner. **2** flirt (with danger, temptation, a person, etc.); trifle. **3** be idle; loiter. **4** waste (time). [< OF *dalier* chat] —**dal′li·er,** *n.*

Dal·ma·tian (dal mā′shən), *n.* a large, short-haired dog, usually white with black spots; coach dog.

dam¹ (dam), *n., v.,* **dammed, dam·ming.** —*n.* **1** wall built to hold back flowing water. **2** water held back by a dam. **3** anything resembling a dam. —*v.* **1** provide with a dam; hold back (water, etc.) by means of a dam. **2** hold back; block up. [ME]

dam² (dam), *n.* **1** the female parent of four-footed animals. **2** mother. [var. of *dame*]

dam·age (dam′ij), *n., v.,* **-aged, -ag·ing.** —*n.* **1** harm or injury that lessens value or usefulness. **2 damages,** money necessary to make up for some harm done to a person or his property. —*v.* harm or injure so as to lessen value or usefulness; harm; hurt. [< OF, < *dam* < L *damnum* loss, hurt] —**dam′age·a·ble,** *adj.* —**dam′ag·ing·ly,** *adv.*

damage control, any means used to contain damage caused by an accident, financial loss, adverse publicity, etc.

dam·a·scene (dam′ə sēn; dam΄ə sēn′), *v.,* **-scened, -scen·ing,** *adj., n.* —*v.* ornament (metal) with inlaid gold or silver or with a wavy design. —*adj.* of or like such an ornament. —*n.* the ornament or design itself. [< L < Gk. *Damaskenos* of Damascus]

Da·mas·cus (də mas′kəs), *n.* capital of Syria, a very ancient trading center.

Damascus steel, ornamented steel, used in making swords, etc.

dam·ask (dam′əsk), *n.* **1** silk woven with an elaborate pattern. **2** linen with woven designs. **3** damascened metal. **4** a rose color; pink. —*v.* make damask. —*adj.* **1** of or named after the city of Damascus. **2** made of damask. **3** pink; rose-colored. [< L < Gk. *Damaskos* Damascus]

dame (dām), *n.* **1** an elderly woman. **2** *Informal.* woman. **3** in Great Britain, **a** title given to a woman who has received an honorable rank corresponding to that of a knight. **b** the legal title of the wife or widow of a knight or baronet (in ordinary use, *Lady*). [< OF < L *domina* mistress]

damn (dam), *v.* **1** declare (something) to be bad or inferior; condemn. **2** cause to fail; ruin. **3** doom to eternal punishment; condemn to hell. **4** swear or swear at by saying "damn"; curse. —*n.* a saying of "damn"; curse. [< OF < L *damnare* condemn < *damnum* loss] —**damn′er,** *n.*

dam·na·ble (dam′nə bəl), *adj.* **1** abominable; outrageous; detestable. **2** deserving damnation. —**dam′na·ble·ness,** *n.* —**dam′na·bly,** *adv.*

dam·na·tion (dam nā′shən), *n.* **1** a damning or being damned; condemnation. **2** condemnation to eternal punishment. **3** curse. —**dam′na·to΄ry,** *adj.*

damned (damd), *adj.* **1** condemned as bad or inferior. **2** doomed to eternal punishment. **3** cursed; abominable. —*n.*

Usually, **the damned,** the souls in hell. —*adv.* very.

damned·est (dam'dist), *adj.* most damned. —*n. Informal.* greatest possible effort; utmost.

Dam·o·cles (dam'ə klēz), *n.* flatterer and courtier of Dionysius, king of Syracuse, who enjoyed a banquet given by Dionysius until he saw a sword hung by a single hair above his head.

Da·mon (dā'mən), *n. Rom. Legend.* a man who pledged his life for his friend Pythias, who was sentenced to death.

damp (damp), *adj.* slightly wet; moist. —*n.* 1 moisture. 2 thing that checks or deadens. 3 dejection; discouragement. 4 any harmful gas that collects in mines, such as firedamp. —*v.* 1 make moist or slightly wet. 2 check; deaden. 3 stifle; suffocate. 4 extinguish.

damp down, stifle or check; suppress. [< MDu. or MLG] —**damp'ly,** *adv.* —**damp'ness,** *n.*

damp·en (dam'pən), *v.* 1 moisten. 2 depress; discourage. —**damp'en·er,** *n.*

damp·er (dam'pər), *n.* 1 person or thing that depresses. 2 a movable plate to control the draft in a stove or furnace. 3 device for checking vibration, as of piano strings.

dam·sel (dam'zəl), *n.* girl; maiden. [< OF *dameisele,* ult. < L *domina* DAME]

damsel fly or **dam·sel·fly** (dam'zəl flī'), insect similar to the dragonfly, but smaller; devil's-darning-needle.

dam·son (dam'zən), *n.* 1 a small, dark-purple plum. 2 tree that it grows on. [< L (*prunum*) *damascenum* (plum) of Damascus]

Dan (dan), *n.* a Hebrew tribe that migrated to N Palestine.

Dan., 1 Daniel. 2 Danish.

Da·na·i·des (də nā'ə dēz), *n. pl. Gk. Legend.* the fifty daughters of **Danaus** (dan'i əs), a Greek king. All but one killed their husbands on their wedding night, and were condemned to draw water with a sieve forever in Hades.

dance (dans; däns), *v.,* **danced, danc·ing,** *n., adj.* —*v.* 1 move in rhythm, usually in time with music. 2 do or take part in (a dance). 3 jump up and down; move in a lively way. 4 bob up and down. —*n.* 1 movement in rhythm, usually in time with music. 2 some special group of steps, etc. 3 one round of dancing. 4 piece of music for dancing. 5 party where people dance. 6 movement up and down; lively movement. —*adj.* of or for dancing. [< OF *danser,* prob. < Gmc.] —**dan'ce·a·ble,** *adj.* —**danc'er,** *n.* —**danc'ing·ly,** *adv.*

dance·hall (dans'hôl, däns'–), *n.* dance music composed of various styles that are electronically mixed and accompanied by rapping.

dance hall, a public hall or room in which dances are held.

dan·de·li·on (dan'də lī'ən), *n.* weed with deeply notched leaves and bright-yellow flowers. [< F *dent de lion* lion's tooth; from toothed leaves]

dan·der (dan'dər), *n. Informal.* temper; anger.

get one's dander up, get angry.

dan·di·fy (dan'də fī), *v.,* **–fied, –fy·ing.** make dandylike or foppish. —**dan'di·fi·ca'tion,** *n.*

dan·dle (dan'dəl), *v.,* **–dled, –dling.** 1 move (a child) up and down on one's knees or in one's arms. 2 pet; pamper. —**dan'dler,** *n.*

dan·druff (dan'drəf), *n.* small, whitish scales of dry skin that form on the scalp.

dan·dy (dan'di), *n., pl.* **–dies,** *adj.,* **–di·er, –di·est.** —*n.* 1 man who is too careful of his dress and appearance. 2 an excellent or first-rate thing. —*adj.* 1 of a dandy; too carefully dressed. 2 excellent; first-rate. —**dan'dy·ism,** *n.*

Dane (dān), *n.* 1 native or inhabitant of Denmark. 2 person of Danish descent.

Dane·law (dān'lô'), *n.* 1 set of laws enforced by the Danes when they held NE England in the 9th and 10th centuries A.D. 2 part of England under these laws.

dan·ger (dān'jər), *n.* 1 chance of harm; nearness to harm; risk; peril. 2 thing that may cause harm. [< OF *dangier* < L *dominium* sovereignty < *dominus* master]

dan·ger·ous (dān'jər əs), *adj.* likely to cause harm; not safe; risky. —**dan'ger·ous·ly,** *adv.* —**dan'ger·ous·ness,** *n.*

dan·gle (dang'gəl), *v.,* **–gled, –gling,** *n.* —*v.* 1 hang and swing loosely. 2 hold or carry (a thing) so that it swings loosely. 3 hang about; follow. 4 cause to dangle. —*n.* 1 act or fact of dangling. 2 something that dangles. [< Scand. (Dan.)] —**dan'gler,** *n.*

dangling participle (dang'gling), participle not clearly connected with the word it modifies, as in "lying in bed, crickets chirp loudly," *lying* is a dangling participle.

Dan·iel (dan'yəl), *n.* 1 Hebrew prophet in the Bible. 2 book of the Bible that tells about him.

Dan·ish (dān'ish), *adj.* of or having to do with the Danes, their language, or Denmark. —*n.* language of the Danes.

dank (dangk), *adj.* unpleasantly damp; moist; wet. —**dank'ly,** *adv.* —**dank'ness,** *n.*

dan·seur (dän sœr'), *n.* male dancer, esp. in a ballet. [< F]

dan·seuse (dän sœz'), *n., pl.* **–seuses** (–sœz'). a woman dancer in a ballet. [< F]

Dan·ube (dan'ūb), *n.* river flowing from SW Germany into the Black Sea. —**Dan·u'bi·an,** *adj.*

dap·per (dap'ər), *adj.* 1 neat; trim; spruce. 2 small and active. [cf. MDu. *dapper* agile, strong] —**dap'per·ly,** *adv.* —**dap'per·ness,** *n.*

dap·ple (dap'əl), *adj., n., v.,* **–pled, –pling.** —*adj.* spotted: *a dapple horse.* —*n.* 1 a spotted appearance or condition. 2 animal with a spotted or mottled skin. —*v.* mark or become marked with spots. [cf. Scand. *depill* spot]

DAR or **D.A.R.,** Daughters of the American Revolution.

Dar·da·nelles (där'də nelz'), *n.* strait between Europe and Asia, connecting the Sea of Marmara with the Aegean Sea. In ancient times it was called the Hellespont.

dare (dãr), *v.,* **dared** or **durst, dared, dar·ing,** *n.* —*v.* 1 have courage; be bold; be bold enough. 2 have courage for; not be afraid of; be bold enough for. 3 meet and resist; face and defy. 4 challenge. —*n.* a challenge. [OE *dearr* (inf., *durran*)] —**dar'er,** *n.*

dare·dev·il (dãr'dev'əl), *n.* a reckless person. —*adj.* reckless.

dar·ing (dãr'ing), *n.* courage to take risks; boldness. —*adj.* courageous; bold. —**dar'ing·ly,** *adv.* —**dar'ing·ness,** *n.*

Da·ri·us I (də rī'əs), 558?–486? B.C., king of Persia from 521 to 486? B.C.

dark (därk), *adj.* 1 without light; with very little light. 2 not light-colored: *a dark complexion.* 3 nearly black. 4 hard to understand. 5 secret; hidden. 6 ignorant. 7 evil. 8 gloomy —*n.* 1 absence of light. 2 night. 3 a dark color. 4 secrecy. 5 ignorance.

after dark, after night has fallen.

in the dark, without knowledge or information.

keep dark, not tell about.

whistle in the dark, try to be brave or hopeful in a frightening or difficult situation. [OE *deorc*] —**dark'ish,** *adj.* —**dark'ish·ness,** *n.* —**dark'ly,** *adv.* —**dark'ness,** *n.*

Dark Ages or **dark ages,** the early part of the Middle Ages, from about A.D. 500 to about 1000.

dark·en (där'kən), *v.* make or become dark or darker. —**dark'en·er,** *n.*

dark horse, an unexpected winner that little is known about.

dark·room (därk'rüm'; –rùm'), *n.* room arranged for developing photographs.

dar·ling (där'ling), *n.* person very dear to another; person much loved. —*adj.* very dear; much loved. [OE *dēorling* < *dēore* DEAR]

darn[1] (därn), *v.* mend by making rows of stitches back and forth across a hole, torn place, etc. —*n.* 1 act of darning. 2 place so mended. [< dial. F *darner* mend < *darne* piece < Breton *darn*] —**darn'er,** *n.*

darn[2] (därn), *v.* damn; curse.

not give a darn, be completely indifferent. [< *damn;* infl. by *tarnal* (informal for *eternal*)] —**darned,** *adj., adv.*

dart (därt), *n.* 1 a slender, pointed weapon to be thrown or shot. 2 a sudden, swift movement. 3 stinger of an insect. 4 seam to make a garment fit better. —*v.* 1 throw or shoot suddenly and swiftly. 2 move suddenly and swiftly. 3 send suddenly. [< OF < Gmc.]

dart·er (där′tər), *n.* **1** animal or person that moves suddenly and swiftly. **2** a small freshwater fish, somewhat like a perch, that darts away very rapidly. **3** a swimming bird that has a long neck and darts at its prey.

Dar·win (där′wən), *n.* **Charles,** 1809–82, English scientist, famous for his theory of evolution. **—Dar·win′i·an,** *adj., n.*

Dar·win·ism (där′wən iz əm), *n.* doctrine maintained by Charles Darwin respecting the origin of species as derived by descent, with variation, from parent forms through the natural selection of those best adapted to survive in the struggle for existence. **—Dar′win·ist,** *n., adj.*

dash (dash), *v.* **1** throw. **2** splash. **3** rush. **4** strike violently against something. **5** ruin: *our hopes were dashed.* **6** discourage; abash. **—***n.* **1** a splash. **2** a rush. **3** a smash. **4** thing that discourages. **5** a small amount. **6** a short race. **7** mark (—) used in writing or printing. **8** a long sound used in sending messages by telegraph. **9** energy; spirit; liveliness. **10** =dashboard.
  dash off, do, make, go, write, etc. quickly. [ME *dasche(n)*] **—dash′er,** *n.*

dash·board (dash′bôrd′; -bōrd′), *n.* **1** the panel with instruments and gauges in an automobile, airplane, etc. **2** protection on the front of a boat, etc., that prevents mud or water from being splashed into it.

dash·er (dash′ər), *n.* **1** person or thing that dashes. **2** paddle for stirring cream in an ice cream freezer or butter churn.

da·shi·ki (də shē′ki), *n.* loose garment like a shirt, often embroidered or of printed fabric, put on by pulling over the head. [< W African word]

dash·ing (dash′ing), *adj.* **1** full of energy and spirit; lively. **2** stylish; showy. **—dash′ing·ly,** *adv.*

das·tard (das′tərd), *n.* a mean coward; sneak. **—***adj.* mean and cowardly; sneaking. [ME, orig., a dullard, appar. < *dased,* pp. of DAZE] **—das′tard·ly,** *adj.* **—das′tard·li·ness,** *n.*

dat., dative.

da·ta (dā′tə; dat′ə; dä′tə), *n.* **1** pl. of **da·tum. 2** things known or granted; facts. **3** information stored in a computer.

da·ta·bank (dā′tə bangk′; dat′ə-; dä′tə-), or **data bank. 1** large collection of records stored on a computer system from which data can be selected and extracted for use on another computer or computer system. **2** such a computer system with its data. **3** place where such a data storage system is located. **4** any data storage system.

da·ta·base (dā′tə bās′; dat′ə-; dä′tə-), *n.* or **data base. 1** collection of records or information, stored on a computer and arranged so that they are accessible to the user. **2** =databank.

data processing, creation, arrangement, and storage of electronic records and information on a computer.

date[1] (dāt), *n., v.,* **dat·ed, dat·ing. —***n.* **1** time when something happens. **2** statement of time. **3** period of time. **4** appointment for a certain time. **5** person of the opposite sex with whom an appointment is made. **—***v.* **1** put a date on. **2** give a date to. **3** have a date on it. **4** have its origin: *that house dates from the 18th century.* **5** make a social appointment with (a person of the opposite sex).
  out of date, old; not presently in use.
  to date, till now; yet.
  up to date, a in fashion; modern. **b** up to the present time; current. [< F < Med.L *data,* pp. fem. of L *dare* give] **—dat′a·ble, date′a·ble,** *adj.*

date[2] (dāt), *n.* **1** the sweet fruit of a kind of palm tree. **2** date palm. [< OF < L < Gk. *daktylos* date, finger]

dat·ed (dāt′id), *adj.* **1** showing a date on it. **2** out-of-date.

date·less (dāt′lis), *adj.* **1** without a date. **2** endless; unlimited. **3** so old that it cannot be given a date. **4** old but still interesting. **5** without a companion for a social engagement.

date line, 1 an imaginary line agreed upon as the place where each calendar day first begins. It runs north and south through the Pacific, mostly along the 180th meridian. **2** line in a letter, newspaper, etc., giving the date when it was written or issued.

date palm, a palm tree on which dates grow.

da·tive (dā′tiv), *adj.* showing the indirect object of a verb. In "Give me the book," *me* is in the dative case. **—***n.* **1** the dative case. **2** word in this case. [< L *dativus* of giving < *datus,* pp. of *dare* give] **—da′tive·ly,** *adv.*

da·tum (dā′təm; dat′əm; dä′təm), *n., pl.* **da·ta.** fact from which conclusions can be drawn. [< L, (thing) given, pp. of *dare*]

daub (dôb), *v.* **1** coat or cover with plaster, clay, mud, etc. **2** make dirty; soil; stain. **3** paint unskillfully. **—***n.* **1** anything daubed on. **2** act of daubing. **3** a badly painted picture. [< F < L, < *de-* + *albus* white] **—daub′er,** *n.*

daugh·ter (dô′tər), *n.* **1** a female child. **2** a female descendant. **3** girl or woman related in the same way that a child is related to its parents. **4** anything thought of as a daughter in relation to its origin. [OE *dohtor* **—daugh′ter·ly,** *adj.*

daughter cell, one of two new cells formed when an old cell divides.

daughter chromosome, one of the two chromosomes which come from equal division of a single chromosome in a mother cell.

daugh·ter-in-law (dô′tər in lô′), *n., pl.* **daugh·ters-in-law.** wife of one's son.

daunt (dônt; dänt), *v.* **1** frighten. **2** discourage. [< OF *danter* < L *domitare* < *domare* tame]

daunt·less (dônt′lis; dänt′-), *adj.* not to be frightened or discouraged; brave. **—daunt′less·ly,** *adv.* **—daunt′less·ness,** *n.*

dau·phin (dô′fən), *n.* title of the oldest son of the king of France, from 1349 to 1830. [< F, orig. a family name]

Da·vid (dā′vid), *n.* the second king of Israel.

da Vin·ci (də vin′chi), **Leonardo,** 1452–1519, Italian painter, architect, and scientist.

dav·it (dav′it; dā′vit), *n.* a curved arm at the side of a ship, used to hold or lower a small boat, anchor, etc. [< AF *daviot*]

Da·vy Jones (dā′vi jōnz′), the sailor's devil.

Davy Jones's locker, grave of those who die at sea; bottom of the ocean.

daw (dô), *n.* =jackdaw. [ME *dawe*]

daw·dle (dô′dəl), *v.,* **–dled, –dling.** waste time; idle; loiter. **—daw′dler,** *n.*

dawn (dôn), *n.* **1** the first light in the east; daybreak. **2** beginning. **—***v.* **1** grow bright or clear. **2** grow clear to the eye or mind. **3** begin; appear: *a new era is dawning.* [< *dawning,* prob. < Scand. (Dan.) *dagning*]

day (dā), *n.* **1** time between sunrise and sunset. **2** the 24 hours of day and night (called a **mean solar day**). **3** hours for work: *an eight-hour day.* **4** time taken by some specified celestial body to make one complete turn on its axis: *the moon's day.* **5** time; period: *in days of old; he has had his day.* **6** conflict; contest.
  any day, *Informal.* **a** every time; always. **b** in every way.
  call it a day, *Informal.* stop work or other activity.
  day after (or **by**) **day,** each day; daily.
  day in, day out, every day; continuously.
  from day to day, each day.
  in this day and age, at the present time.
  that'll be the day, *Informal.* it will never happen. [OE *dæg*]

day·break (dā′brāk′), *n.* time when it first begins to get light in the morning.

day·dream (dā′drēm′), *n.* **1** dreamy thought about pleasant things. **2** a pleasant plan or fancy, unlikely to come true. **—***v.* think dreamily about pleasant things. **—day′dream′er,** *n.*

Day-Glo (dā′glō′), *n.* trademark for color, esp. in marking pens, that is fluorescent and vivid. **—***adj.* having such brilliant, fluorescent color.

day laborer, manual worker paid by the day.

day·light (dā′līt′), *n.* **1** light of day. **2** daytime. **3** dawn; daybreak. **4** publicity; openness.
  daylights, *Slang.* vital parts; insides: *scared the daylights out of me.*

day·light-sav·ing time (dā′līt′ sāv′ing), time that is one hour faster than standard time, usually used during the summer to give more daylight after working hours.

Day of Atonement, Yom Kippur.

day school, a private school for students who live at home.

day·time (dā′tīm′), *n.* time when it is day.

daze (dāz), *v.,* **dazed, daz·ing,** *n.* —*v.* **1** confuse and bewilder; cause to feel stupid; stun. **2** dazzle. —*n.* a dazed condition; bewilderment; stupor. [ME *dase(n).* Cf. Scand. *dasa* make tired.] —**daz′ed·ly,** *adv.*

daz·zle (daz′əl), *v.,* **-zled, -zling,** *n.* —*v.* **1** hurt (the eyes) with too bright light or with quick-moving lights. **2** overcome (the sight or the mind) by brightness, display, etc. —*n.* act or fact of dazzling; bewildering brightness. [< *daze*] —**daz′zler,** *n.* —**daz′zling·ly,** *adv.*

dB or **db,** decibel.

DBA or **dba,** doing business as.

DC, 1 *(zip code)* District of Columbia. **2** direct current.

D.C., 1 also, **d.c.** direct current. **2** District of Columbia.

D-day (dē′dā′), *n.* **1** day on which a previously planned military attack is to be made, or on which any important undertaking is to begin. **2** June 6, 1944, the day Allies landed on the beaches of Normandy in World War II.

DE, *(zip code)* Delaware.

de-, *prefix.* **1** do the opposite of, as in *decentralize, demobilize.* **2** down, as in *depress, descend.* **3** away; off, as in *deport.* **4** entirely; completely, as in *despoil.* [< L *de* from, away]

de·ac·ces·sion (dē′ak sesh′ən), *v.* sell off or auction paintings, sculpture, etc. from a museum collection, usually to raise funds. Also, **deaccess.**

dea·con (dē′kən), *n.* **1** officer of a church who helps the minister in church duties not connected with the preaching. **2** member of the clergy next below a priest in rank. [< L < Gk. *diakonos* servant] —**dea′con·ry, dea′con·ship,** *n.*

dea·con·ess (dē′kən is), *n.* **1** woman who is an official assistant in church work, esp. in caring for the sick and poor. **2** a female deacon.

de·ac·ti·vate (dē ak′tə vāt), *v.,* **-vat·ed, -vat·ing. 1** =demobilize. **2** make inactive. **3** stop the use of. **-de·ac′ti·va′tion,** *n.*

dead (ded), *adj.* **1** no longer living. **2** without life. **3** not active; dull; quiet. **4** without force, power, spirit, or feeling. **5** no longer in use. **6** out of play. **7** worn-out. **8** sure; certain. **9** complete; absolute: *dead silence.* —*adv.* **1** completely; absolutely: *dead wrong.* **2** directly; straight. —*n.* **1** dead person or persons. **2** time of greatest darkness, cold, etc.: *the dead of night.* [OE *dēad*] —**dead′ness,** *n.*

dead beat, *Slang.* **1** person who avoids payment of obligations. **2** loafer. **-dead′-beat′,** *adj.*

dead·en (ded′ən), *v.* **1** make dull or weak: *some drugs deaden pain.* **2** make sound-proof. —**dead′en·er,** *n.*

dead end, 1 street, passage, etc., closed at one end. **2** *Fig.* point at which any progress, advancement, etc. is impossible. —**dead′-end′,** *adj., v.*

dead heat, race that ends in a tie.

dead letter, 1 letter that cannot be delivered. **2** law, rule, etc., that is not enforced.

dead·line (ded′līn′), *n.* the latest possible time to do something.

dead·lock (ded′lok′), *n.* a complete standstill. —*v.* bring or come to a deadlock.

dead·ly (ded′li), *adj.,* **-li·er, -li·est,** *adv.* —*adj.* **1** causing death; fatal. **2** like death. **3** until death: *deadly enemies.* **4** extreme; intense. —*adv.* **1** extremely. **2** like death. **3** as if dead. —**dead′li·ness,** *n.*

dead pan, an expressionless face.

dead reckoning, finding one's position by means of a compass and calculations based on speed, time elapsed, and direction from a known position.

Dead Sea, salt lake between Israel and Jordan.

dead·wood (ded′wüd′), *n.* **1** dead branches or trees. **2** *Fig.* useless people or things. **3** *Fig.* conventional word or phrase that adds nothing to the meaning of a sentence.

deaf (def), *adj.* **1** not able to hear. **2** not able to hear well. **3** *Fig.* not willing to hear; heedless: *deaf to all requests.*

deaf and dumb, unable to hear and speak. [OE *dēaf*] —**deaf′ly,** *adv.* —**deaf′ness,** *n.*

deaf·en (def′ən), *v.* **1** make deaf. **2** stun with noise. **3** drown out by a louder sound. **4** make soundproof. —**deaf′en·ing·ly,** *adv.*

deaf-mute (def′mūt′), *n.* person who cannot hear or speak.

deal¹ (dēl), *v.,* **dealt** (delt), **deal·ing,** *n.* —*v.* **1** have to do: *arithmetic deals with numbers.* **2** act; behave. **3** do business: *a butcher deals in meat.* **4** give: *one fighter dealt the other a blow.* **5** give a share of; distribute. —*n.* **1** a business arrangement. **2** arrangement; plan. **3** in cardplaying, the distribution of cards. **4** quantity; amount.

a good (or **great**) **deal, a** a large part, portion, or amount (of something). **b** to a great extent or degree. [OE *dælan*] —**deal′er, deal′er·ship,** *n.*

deal² (dēl), *n.* board of pine or fir wood. [< MLG or MDu. *dele*]

deal·ing (dēl′ing), *n.* Usually, **dealings. a** business relations. **b** friendly relations.

dean (dēn), *n.* **1** member of the faculty of a college or university who has charge of the studies of the students. **2** head of a division or school in a college or university. **3** a high official of a church, often one in charge of a cathedral. **4** member who has belonged to a group longest. [< OF < LL *decanus* master of ten < *decem* ten] —**dean′ship,** *n.*

dean·er·y (dēn′ər i), *n., pl.* **-er·ies. 1** position or authority of a dean. **2** residence of a dean.

dear (dir), *adj.* **1** much loved; precious. **2** (as a form of address at the beginning of letters) much valued; highly esteemed. **3** high-priced; costly. —*n.* a dear one. —*adv.* **1** with affection; fondly. **2** at a high price. —*interj.* exclamation of surprise. [OE *dēore*] —**dear′ly,** *adv.* —**dear′ness,** *n.*

dearth (dėrth), *n.* **1** scarcity; lack. **2** scarcity of food; famine. [ME *derthe < dere* hard]

dear·y or **dear·ie** (dir′ē), *n. pl.* **dear·ies.** *Informal.* dear one; darling.

death (deth), *n.* **1** the ending of any form of life. **2** any ending that is like dying. **3** being dead. **4** any condition like being dead.

at death's door, almost dead; dying.

be death on, be well-equipped to handle; able to deal with firmly.

catch one's death, *Informal.* catch a bad cold.

in at the death, *Fig.* present at the end of something.

put to death, a kill or execute. **b** killed.

to death, beyond endurance; excessively.

to the death, to the last extremity; to the bitter end. [OE *dēath*] —**death′like′,** *adj.*

death·bed (deth′bed′), *n.* **1** bed on which a person dies. **2** the last hours of life. —*adj.* during the last hours of life: *a deathbed confession.*

death·blow (deth′blō′), *n.* **1** blow that kills. **2** thing that puts an end (to something).

death cup, a poisonous mushroom that has a cuplike enlargement at the base of the stem.

death·less (deth′lis), *adj.* never dying; living forever; immortal; eternal. —**death′less·ly,** *adv.* —**death′less·ness,** *n.*

death·ly (deth′li), *adj.* **1** like that of death. **2** causing death; deadly. **3** *Poetic.* of death. —*adv.* **1** as if dead. **2** extremely.

death rate, proportion of the number of deaths per year to the total population or to some other stated number.

death row, block or row of cells where criminals condemned to death are held.

death's-head (deths′hed′), *n.* a human skull used as a symbol of death.

death·trap (deth′trap′), *n.* **1** unsafe building or structure where the risk of fire or collapse is great. **2** any extremely dangerous situation.

Death Valley, valley in E California; the lowest land in the Western Hemisphere, 276 ft. below sea level.

death·watch (deth′woch′; -wôch′), *n.* watch kept beside a dying or dead person.

de·ba·cle (dā bä′kəl; di-; -bak′əl), *n.* disaster; overthrow; downfall. [< F, < *dé-* + *bâcler* to bar]

de·bar (di bär′), *v.,* **-barred, -bar·ring.** bar out; shut out; prevent. —**de·bar′ment,** *n.*

de·bark (di bärk′), *v.* go or put ashore from a ship or aircraft; disembark.

[< F, < dé- + barque BARK³] **—de′bar·ka′tion,** *n.*

de·base (di bās′), *v.,* **–based, –bas·ing.** make low or lower; lessen the value of. [< *de-* + *(a)base*] **—de·base′ment,** *n.* **—de·bas′er,** *n.*

de·bate (di bāt′), *v.,* **–bat·ed, –bat·ing.** *—v.* **1** discuss reasons for and against (something); consider. **2** argue about (a question, topic, etc.) in a public meeting. *—n.* **1** discussion of reasons for and against. **2** a public argument for and against a question in a meeting. [< OF, < *de-* + *batre* BEAT] **—de·bat′a·ble,** *adj.* **—de·bat′er,** *n.*

de·bauch (di bôch′), *v.* **1** corrupt morally; seduce. **2** corrupt; pervert; deprave. *—n.* excessive indulgence in sensual pleasures. [< F *débaucher* entice from duty] **—de·bauch′ed·ly,** *adv.* **—de·bauch′er,** *n.* **—de·bauch′ment,** *n.*

deb·au·chee (deb′ô chē′; –shē′), *n.* a corrupt, dissipated, or depraved person.

de·bauch·er·y (di bôch′ər i), *n., pl.* **–er·ies. 1** excessive indulgence in sensual pleasures. **2** seduction from duty, virtue, or morality.

de·ben·ture (di ben′chər), *n.* a written acknowledgment of a debt. [< *debentur* there are owing. See DEBIT.]

de·bil·i·tate (di bil′ə tāt), *v.,* **–tat·ed, –tat·ing.** weaken. **—de·bil′i·tat′ed,** *adj.* **—de·bil′i·ta′tion,** *n.* **—de·bil′i·ta′tive,** *adj.*

de·bil·i·ty (di bil′ə ti), *n., pl.* **–ties.** weakness. [< L, < *debilis* weak]

deb·it (deb′it), *n.* **1** entry of something owed in an account. **2** the left-hand side of an account where such entries are made. *—v.* **1** enter on the debit side of an account. **2** charge with a debt. [< L *debitum* (thing) owed, pp. of *debere*]

debit card, bank card that allows a bank customer to charge purchases directly against funds in an account as well as make deposits and withdrawals at an automatic teller machine.

deb·o·nair, deb·o·naire, or **deb·on·naire** (deb′ə nãr′), *adj.* **1** cheerful. **2** pleasant; courteous. [< OF, < *de bon aire* of good disposition] **—deb′o·nair′ness,** *n.*

de·bouch (di büsh′), *v.* come out from a narrow or confined place into open country. [< F, < *dé-* + *bouche* mouth < L *bucca*] **—de·bouch′ment,** *n.*

de·brief (di brēf′), *v.* **1** question (someone) closely to obtain as much information as possible upon their return from a mission or assignment. **2** *Fig.* question (anyone) closely.

de·bris (də brē′; dā′brē), *n.* **1** scattered fragments; ruins; rubbish. **2** mass of stones, fragments of rocks, etc. [< F, < OF, < *de-* + *brisier* break]

debt (det), *n.* **1** something owed to another. **2** liability or obligation to pay or render something. **3** sin. [< OF *dete* < L *debitum* (thing) owed, pp. of *debere*]

debt·or (det′ər), *n.* person who is in debt.

de·bug (di bug′), *v.,* **–bugged, –bug·ging. 1** remove or fix the defects of. **2** find

and remove hidden listening and other surveillance devices.

de·bunk (di bungk′), *v.* remove nonsense or sentimentality from. **—de·bunk′er,** *n.*

De·bus·sy (də bū′si; *Fr.* də by sē′), *n.* Claude A., 1862–1918, French composer.

de·but (dā′bū; dā bū′; di–), *n.* **1** a first public appearance, as on the stage. **2** a first formal appearance in society. [< F *débuter* make the first stroke < *dé-* + *but* goal]

deb·u·tante (deb′yə tänt; –tant; deb′-yə tänt′), *n.* **1** girl during her first season in society. **2** woman making a debut.

Dec., December.

dec., **1** deceased. **2** decimeter.

deca–, *prefix.* ten, as in *decagram.* [< Gk. *deka*]

dec·ade (dek′ād), *n.* **1** ten years. **2** group of ten. [< F < LL < Gk. *dekas* group of ten < *deka* ten]

de·ca·dence (di kā′dəns; dek′ə dəns), **de·ca·den·cy** (–dən si), *n.* a falling off; decline; decay. [< F < Med.L, < L *de-* + *cadere* fall]

de·ca·dent (di kā′dənt; dek′ə dənt), *adj.* falling off; declining; growing worse. *—n.* a decadent person. **—de·ca′dent·ly,** *adv.*

dec·a·gon (dek′ə gon), *n.* a plane figure having 10 angles and 10 sides. **—de·cag′o·nal,** *adj.*

dec·a·gram (dek′ə gram), *n.* weight equal to 10 grams.

dec·a·he·dron (dek′ə hē′drən), *n., pl.* **–drons, –dra** (–drə). a solid figure having 10 surfaces. **—dec′a·he′dral,** *adj.*

de·cal (dē′kal; di kal′), *n.* **1** design or picture treated so that it will stick fast to glass, wood, etc. **2** process of applying these designs or pictures. [< F *décalcomanie,* < *décalquer* transfer a tracing + *manie* MANIA]

dec·a·li·ter (dek′ə lē′tər), *n.* measure of volume equal to 10 liters.

Dec·a·logue, Dec·a·log (dek′ə lôg; –log), *n.* the Ten Commandments. Exod. 20:2–17.

dec·a·me·ter (dek′ə mē′tər), *n.* measure of length equal to 10 meters.

de·camp (di kamp′), *v.* **1** depart quickly or secretly. **2** leave a camp. **—de·camp′ment,** *n.*

de·cant (di kant′), *v.* pour off (liquor or a solution) gently without disturbing the sediment. [< Med.L, < *de-* + *canthus* lip < Gk. *kanthos* corner of the eye] **—de′can·ta′tion,** *n.*

de·cant·er (di kan′tər), *n.* **1** a bottle used to decant. **2** a glass bottle used for serving wine or liquor.

de·cap·i·tate (di kap′ə tāt), *v.,* **–tat·ed, –tat·ing.** behead. [< LL < *de-* + L *caput* head] **—de·cap′i·ta′tion,** *n.*

dec·a·pod (dek′ə pod), *n.* **1** crustacean having ten legs or arms, such as lobsters and crabs. **2** mollusk having ten legs or arms, such as squid. *—adj.* having ten legs or arms.

dec·a·syl·la·ble (dek′ə sil′ə bəl), *n.* line of poetry having ten syllables. **—dec′a·syl·lab′ic,** *adj.*

de·cath·lon (di kath′lon), *n.* an athletic contest having ten parts, such as racing, jumping, etc., won by the person having the highest total score. [< DECA– + Gk. *athlon* contest] **—de·cath′lete,** *n.*

de·cay (di kā′), *v.* **1** rot. **2** grow less in power, strength, beauty, etc. *—n.* **1** process of rotting. **2** loss of power, strength, beauty, etc. **3** loss in quantity of a radioactive substance through disintegration of its component nuclei. [< OF, < *de-* + *cair* < L *cadere* fall]

de·cease (di sēs′), *n., v.,* **–ceased, –ceas·ing.** *—n.* death. *—v.* die. [< F < L *decessus* < *de-* + *cedere* go]

de·ceased (di sēst′), *adj.* dead. *—n.* the **deceased,** a dead person.

de·ce·dent (di sē′dənt), *n.* a dead person.

de·ceit (di sēt′), *n.* **1** act or fact of deceiving, lying, or cheating. **2** a dishonest trick. **3** deceitful quality; deceitfulness.

de·ceit·ful (di sēt′fəl), *adj.* **1** ready or willing to deceive or lie. **2** deceiving; fraudulent. **—de·ceit′ful·ly,** *adv.* **—de·ceit′ful·ness,** *n.*

de·ceive (di sēv′), *v.,* **–ceived, –ceiv·ing. 1** make (a person) believe as true something that is false; mislead. **2** use dishonest tricks. [< OF *deceiver* < L, < *de-* + *capere* take] **—de·ceiv′er,** *n.* **—de·ceiv′ing·ly,** *adv.*

de·cel·er·ate (dē sel′ər āt), *v.,* **–at·ed, –at·ing.** decrease the velocity of; slow down. [< *de-* + *(ac)celerate*] **—de·cel′er·a′tion,** *n.* **—de·cel′er·a′tor,** *n.*

De·cem·ber (di sem′bər), *n.* the 12th and last month of the year. It has 31 days. [< L, < *decem* ten; from the order of the early Roman calendar]

de·cen·cy (dē′sən si), *n., pl.* **–cies. 1** state or quality of being decent. **2** propriety of behavior. **3** a proper regard for modesty or delicacy. **4 decencies,** suitable acts.

de·cen·ni·al (di sen′i əl), *adj.* **1** of or for ten years. **2** happening every ten years. *—n.* tenth anniversary. [< L *decennium* decade < *decem* ten + *annus* year] **—de·cen′ni·al·ly,** *adv.*

de·cent (dē′sənt), *adj.* **1** proper and right. **2** conforming to the standard of good taste. **3** good enough; fairly good. **4** not severe; rather kind. [< L *decens* becoming, fitting, ppr. of *decere*] **—de′cent·ly,** *adv.* **—de′cent·ness,** *n.*

de·cen·tral·ize (dē sen′trəl īz), *v.,* **–ized, –iz·ing.** spread or distribute (authority, power, etc.). **—decen′tral·i·za′tion,** *n.*

de·cep·tion (di sep′shən), *n.* **1** act of deceiving. **2** state of being deceived. **3** thing that deceives; illusion. **4** fraud; sham.

de·cep·tive (di sep′tiv), *adj.* apt or tending to deceive. **—de·cep′tive·ly,** *adv.* **—de·cep′tive·ness,** *n.*

deci–, *prefix.* one tenth of, as in *decigram.* [< L *decem* ten, *decimus* tenth]

dec·i·bel (des′ə bel), *n.* unit for measuring the loudness of sounds.

de·cide (di sīd′), *v.,* **–cid·ed, –cid·ing. 1** settle (a question, dispute, etc.) by giving victory to one side. **2** make up one's mind; resolve. **3** cause (a person) to reach a decision. [< L *decidere* cut off < *de–* + *caedere* cut]

de·cid·ed (di sīd′id), *adj.* **1** clear; definite; unquestionable. **2** firm; determined. **—de·cid′ed·ly,** *adv.* **—de·cid′ed·ness,** *n.*

de·cid·u·ous (di sij′ü əs), *adj.* **1** falling off at a particular season or stage of growth, as horns. **2** shedding leaves annually. [< L, < *de–* + *cadere* fall] **—de·cid′u·ous·ly,** *adv.* **—de·cid′u·ous·ness,** *n.*

dec·i·gram (des′ə gram), *n.* weight equal to ¹⁄₁₀ of a gram.

dec·i·li·ter (des′ə lē′tər), *n.* measure of volume equal to ¹⁄₁₀ of a liter.

dec·i·mal (des′ə məl), *adj.* based upon ten or tenths; increasing by tens, as the metric system. *—n.* a decimal fraction. [< L *decimus* tenth] **—dec′i·mal·ly,** *adv.*

decimal fraction, fraction whose denominator is ten or some power of ten.

decimal point, period placed before a fraction expressed in decimal figures, as in 2.03, .623.

dec·i·mate (des′ə māt), *v.,* **–mat·ed, –mat·ing.** destroy much of; kill a large part of. [< L *decimatus,* pp. of *decimare* take a tenth, ult. < *decem* ten] **—dec′i·ma′tion,** *n.* **—dec′i·ma′tor,** *n.*

dec·i·me·ter (des′ə mē′tər), *n.* measure of length equal to ¹⁄₁₀ of a meter.

de·ci·pher (di sī′fər), *v.* **1** make out the meaning of (bad writing, an unknown language, or anything puzzling). **2** translate (a message in code) into plain language by using a key. **—de·ci′pher·a·ble,** *adj.* **—de·ci′pher·ment,** *n.*

de·ci·sion (di sizh′ən), *n.* **1** the deciding or settling of a question, dispute, etc. **2** judgment reached or given, as by a court. **3** a making up of one's mind. **4** firmness; determination.

de·ci·sive (di sī′siv), *adj.* **1** having or giving a clear result. **2** having or showing decision. **—de·ci′sive·ly,** *adv.* **—de·ci′sive·ness,** *n.*

deck (dek), *n.* **1** floor or platform extending from side to side of a ship. **2** part or floor resembling it: *the deck of an airplane.* **3** open porch built on to a house. **4** pack of playing cards. *—v.* cover; dress: *decked out in fine clothes.*

clear the deck (or **decks**), **a** remove unnecessary objects from the deck of a warship, to prepare for action. **b** *Fig.* make ready for any action.

hit the deck, a get up from bed. **b** drop on the ground or floor.

on deck, *Informal.* present; on hand.

stack the deck, a arrange a deck of cards dishonestly. **b** *Fig.* prepare circumstances in advance. [< MDu. *dec* roof]

deck hand, sailor who works on deck.

de·claim (di klām′), *v.* **1** recite in public; make a formal speech. **2** speak or write for effect. [< L, < *de–* + *clamare* cry]

dec·la·ma·tion (dek′lə mā′shən), *n.* **1** act or art of reciting in public. **2** selection of poetry, prose, etc., for reciting. **3** a speaking or writing for effect. **—de·clam′a·to′ry,** *adj.*

dec·la·ra·tion (dek′lə rā′shən), *n.* **1** act of declaring. **2** thing declared. **3** statement of goods, etc., for taxation. **4** a formal announcement.

Declaration of Independence, a public statement adopted by the Continental Congress on July 4, 1776, in which the American colonies declared themselves free and independent of Great Britain.

de·clare (di klãr′), *v.,* **–clared, –clar·ing. 1** announce publicly or formally; make known; proclaim: *declare a dividend.* **2** say openly or strongly. **3** make a statement of (goods, etc.) for taxation. [< L, < *de–* + *clarus* clear] **—de·clar′a·tive, de·clar′a·to′ry,** *adj.* **—de·clar′er,** *n.*

dé·clas·sé (dā kla sā′), *adj.* reduced in rank or social standing; degraded.

de·clas·si·fy (dē′klas′ə fī), *v.,* **–fied, –fy·ing.** remove (documents, codes, etc.) from the list of restricted, confidential, or secret information. **—de·clas′si·fi′a·ble,** *adj.* **—de·clas′si·fi·ca′tion,** *n.*

de·clen·sion (di klen′shən), *n.* **1** the giving of the different endings to nouns, pronouns, and adjectives according to their case. **2** group of words whose endings for the different cases are alike. **3** a downward movement, bend, or slope. **—de·clen′sion·al,** *adj.*

dec·li·na·tion (dek′lə nā′shən), *n.* **1** a downward bend or slope. **2** decline; deterioration. **3** difference in direction between true north and magnetic north at any given point. **4** the angular distance of a star, planet, etc., from the celestial equator.

de·cline (di klīn′), *v.,* **–clined, –clin·ing,** *n. —v.* **1** refuse. **2** refuse politely. **3** bend or slope down. **4** grow less in strength, power, value, etc.; grow worse; decay. **5** give the different cases or case endings of (a noun, pronoun, or adjective). *—n.* **1** a falling; a sinking: *a decline in prices.* **2** a downward slope. **3** a losing of strength, power, value, etc.; a growing worse. **4** the last part of anything. [< L, < *de–* + *clinare* bend] **—de·clin′a·ble,** *adj.* **—de·clin′er,** *n.*

de·cliv·i·ty (di kliv′ə ti), *n., pl.* **–ties.** a downward slope. [< L, < *de–* + *clivus* slope]

de·coct (di kokt′), *v.* extract desired substances from (herbs, etc.) by boiling. [< L *decoctus* < *de–* + *coquere* cook] **—de·coc′tion,** *n.*

de·code (dē kōd′), *v.,* **–cod·ed, –cod·ing.** translate (secret writing) from code into ordinary language. **—de·cod′er,** *n.*

dé·colle·tage (dā′kol tàzh′), *n.* **1** neck of a dress or blouse cut low to expose the shoulders. **2** dress or blouse cut this way. [< F (literally) bare the neck] **—dé′colle·té′,** *adj.*

de·com·pose (dē′kəm pōz′), *v.,* **–posed, –pos·ing. 1** decay; rot. **2** separate (a substance) into what it is made of. **—de′com·pos′a·ble,** *adj.* **—de′com·po·si′tion,** *n.*

de·com·press (dē′kəm pres′), *v.* **1** remove the pressure from. **2** lessen the pressure of air on. **3** *Fig.* reduce pressure or stress on oneself. **—de′com·pres′sion,** *n.*

decompression chamber, airtight space in which a person exposed to abnormal air pressure is gradually accustomed to normal air pressure.

decompression sickness, painful condition caused by nitrogen bubbles in the blood that form when a person moves too suddenly from abnormal air pressure to normal pressure; the bends.

de·con·tam·i·nate (dē′kən tam′ə nāt), *v.,* **–nat·ed, –nat·ing. 1** free from poison gas or harmful radioactive agents. **2** free from any sort of contamination. **—de′con·tam′i·na′tion,** *n.*

de·con·trol (dē′kən trōl′), *v.,* **–trolled, –trol·ling,** *n. —v.* remove controls from: *decontrol prices. —n.* removing of controls.

dé·cor or **dé·cor** (dā kôr′), *n.* decoration. [< F, < *décorer* DECORATE]

dec·o·rate (dek′ə rāt), *v.,* **–rat·ed, –rat·ing. 1** make beautiful; adorn. **2** paint or paper (a room, etc.). **3** give a medal, ribbon, etc., to (a person) as an honor. [< L *decoratus* < *decus* adornment] **—dec′o·ra′tive,** *adj.* **—dec′o·ra′tive·ly,** *adv.* **—dec′o·ra′tive·ness,** *n.* **—dec′o·ra′tor,** *n.*

dec·o·ra·tion (dek′ə rā′shən), *n.* **1** act of decorating. **2** thing used to decorate; ornament. **3** medal, ribbon, etc., given as an honor.

dec·o·rous (dek′ə rəs; di kô′rəs; –kō′–), *adj.* well-behaved; acting properly. **—dec′o·rous·ly,** *adv.* **—dec′o·rous·ness,** *n.*

de·co·rum (di kô′rəm; –kō′–), *n.* **1** propriety of action, speech, dress, etc. **2** observance or requirement of polite society. [< L, (that which is) seemly]

de·coy (*v.* di koi′; *n.* dē′koi, di koi′), *v.* **1** lure (wild birds, animals, etc.) into a trap or within gunsho. **2** lead or tempt into danger. *—n.* **1** an artificial bird used to lure birds into a trap or within gunshot. **2** place into which wild birds or animals are lured. **3** any person or thing used to lead or tempt into danger. [< Du. *de kooi* the cage < L *cavea* cave] **—de·coy′er,** *n.*

de·crease (*v.* di krēs; *n.* dē′krēs, di krēs′), *v.,* **–creased, –creas·ing,** *n. —v.* become or make less. *—n.* **1** a becoming less. **2** amount by which a thing becomes or is made less. [< OF < L, < *de–* + *crescere* grow] **—de·creas′ing·ly,** *adv.*

de·cree (di krē′), *n., v.,* **–creed, –cree·ing.** *—n.* something ordered or settled by authority. *—v.* order or settle by authority. [< OF < L *decretum* < *de-* + *cernere* decide]

de·crim·i·nal·ize (di krim'ə na līz'), *v.*, **–ized, –iz·ing.** declare no longer a criminal act or offense. **—de·crim'i·nal·i·za'tion,** *n.*

de·crep·it (di krep'it), *adj.* broken down or weakened by old age. [< L *decrepitus* broken down < *de-* + *crepare* creak] **—de·crep'it·ly,** *adv.*

de·crep·i·tude (di krep'ə tüd; –tūd), *n.* feebleness, usually from old age; decrepit condition.

de·cre·scen·do (dē'krə shen'dō; dā'–), *n.*, *pl.* **–dos,** *adj., adv.* —*n.* a gradual decrease in force or loudness; diminuendo. —*adj., adv.* with a gradual decrease in force or loudness. [< Ital.]

de·cre·tal (di krē'təl), *n.* decree or reply by the Pope settling some question of doctrine or ecclesiastical law.

de·cry (di krī'), *v.*, **–cried, –cry·ing. 1** condemn. **2** make little of; try to lower the value of. [< OF *décrier.* See DE-, CRY.] **—de·cri'al,** *n.* **—de·cri'er,** *n.*

de·cum·bent (di kum'bənt), *adj.* **1** reclining. **2** lying or trailing on the ground with the end tending to climb. [< L *decumbens,* ppr. of *decumbere* lie down]

ded·i·cate (ded'ə kāt), *v.*, **–cat·ed, –cat·ing. 1** set apart for a sacred or solemn purpose. **2** give up wholly or earnestly, as to some person or end. **3** address (a book, poem, etc.) to a friend or patron as a mark of affection, gratitude, etc. [< L, < *de-* + *dicare* proclaim] **—ded'i·ca'tive, ded'i·ca·to'ry,** *adj.*

ded·i·ca·tion (ded'ə kā'shən), *n.* **1** a setting apart or being set apart for a sacred or solemn purpose. **2** words dedicating a book.

de·duce (di düs'; –dūs'), *v.*, **–duced, –duc·ing. 1** infer from a general rule or principle. **2** trace the course, descent, or origin of. [< L, < *de-* + *ducere* lead] **—de·duc'i·ble,** *adj.*

de·duct (di dukt'), *v.* take away; subtract. [< L *deductus,* pp. See DEDUCE.] **—de·duct'i·ble,** *adj.*

de·duc·tion (di duk'shən), *n.* **1** act of taking away; subtraction. **2** amount deducted. **3** a logical inference from a general rule or principle. **—de·duc'tive,** *adj.* **—de·duc'tive·ly,** *adv.*

deed (dēd), *n.* **1** thing done; act. **2** a brave, skillful, or unusual act. **3** action; doing; performance. **4** a written or printed agreement legally transferring ownership, esp. of real estate. —*v.* transfer by a deed. [OE *dēd*]

deem (dēm), *v.* think; believe; consider. [OE *dēman* < *dōm* judgment]

deep (dēp), *adj.* **1** going far down or back: *a deep hole.* **2** far down or back. **3** in depth: *50 feet deep.* **4** low in pitch. **5** strong and dark in color. **6** intense; extreme: *deep sleep.* **7** hard to understand. **8** with the mind fully taken up: *deep in thought.* —*adv.* **1** far down or back. **2** of time, far on. —*n.* **1** a deep

place. **2** the most intense part: *the deep of winter.*

the deep, the sea. [OE *dēop*] **—deep'ly,** *adv.* **—deep'ness,** *n.*

deep·en (dēp'ən), *v.* make or become deeper.

deep-freeze (dēp'frēz'), —*n.* container for freezing and storing food.

deep-fry (dēp'frī'), *v.* fry food in deep, hot grease, oil, etc.

deep-root·ed (dēp'rüt'id; –rut'–), *adj.* **1** deeply rooted. **2** firmly fixed.

deep-seat·ed (dēp'sēt'id), *adj.* **1** far below the surface. **2** firmly fixed.

deep-set (dēp'set'), *adj.* **1** set deeply. **2** firmly fixed.

deer (dir), *n., pl.* **deer, deers. 1** a swift, graceful animal of a group that have hoofs and chew the cud. A male deer has horns or antlers, which are shed and grow again every year. **2** any of a group of animals including deer, elk, moose, and caribou. [OE *dēor* animal]

deer·hound (dir'hound'), *n.* hound with a shaggy coat, related to the greyhound.

deer·skin (dir'skin'), *n.* **1** skin of a deer. **2** leather made from it.

def., 1 defective. **2** defendant. **3** deferred. **4** definite. **5** definition.

de·face (di fās'), *v.*, **–faced, –fac·ing.** spoil the appearance of; mar. [< obs. F *defacer.* See DISFACE.] **—de·face'a·ble,** *adj.* **—de·face'ment,** *n.* **—de·fac'er,** *n.*

de fac·to (dē fak'tō), in fact; in reality. [< L, from the fact]

de·fal·cate (di fal'kāt; –fôl'–), *v.*, **–cat·ed, –cat·ing.** steal or misuse money trusted to one's care. [< L *defalcatus* < *de-* + *falx* sickle] **—de'fal·ca'tion,** *n.* **—de·fal'ca·tor,** *n.*

de·fame (di fām'), *v.*, **–famed, –fam·ing.** attack the good name of; harm the reputation of; speak evil of; slander. [< OF < L, < *de-* + *fama* rumor] **—def'a·ma'tion,** *n.* **—de·fam'a·to'ry,** *adj.* **—de·fam'er,** *n.*

de·fault (di fôlt'), *n.* **1** failure to do something or to appear somewhere when due; neglect. **2** in sports, failure to compete in a scheduled match. **3** failure to pay when due. —*v.* **1** fail to do something or appear somewhere when due. **2** fail to pay when due.

in default of, lacking; not having. [< OF *defaute* < *defaillir.* See FAULT.] **—de·fault'er,** *n.*

de·feat (di fēt'), *v.* **1** win a victory over; overcome. **2** frustrate; thwart. **3** make useless. —*n.* a defeating or being defeated. [< OF < LL, < L *dis-* un- + *facere* do] **—de·feat'er,** *n.*

de·feat·ism (di fēt'iz əm), *n.* attitude or behavior of a person who expects, wishes for, or admits the defeat of his country, cause, party, etc. **—de·feat'ist,** *n.*

def·e·cate (def'ə kāt), *v.*, **–cat·ed, –cat·ing.** have a movement of the bowels. [< L, < *de-* from + *faeces,* pl., dregs] **—def'e·ca'tion,** *n.*

place. **2** the most intense part: *the deep of winter.*

de·fect (di fekt'; dē'fekt), *n.* **1** fault; blemish; imperfection. **2** lack of something essential to completeness; a falling short. —*v.* forsake one's own country, group, etc. for another, esp. another that is opposed to it in political or social doctrine. [< L *defectus* want < *deficere* fail. See DEFICIENT.] **—de·fec'tor,** *n.*

de·fec·tion (di fek'shən), *n.* **1** a falling away from loyalty, duty, religion, etc.; desertion. **2** failure.

de·fec·tive (di fek'tiv), *adj.* **1** having a flaw or blemish; not perfect. **2** subnormal in behavior or intelligence. **3** lacking one or more of the usual forms of grammatical inflection. —*n.* person who has some defect of body or mind. **—de·fec'tive·ly,** *adv.* **—de·fec'tive·ness,** *n.*

de·fence (di fens'), *n. Brit.* defense. **—de·fence'less,** *adj.* **—de·fence'less·ly,** *adv.* **—de·fence'less·ness,** *n.*

de·fend (di fend'), *v.* **1** guard from attack or harm. **2** act, speak, or write in favor of. **3** contest (a lawsuit). **4** make a defense. [< OF < L *defendere* ward off] **—de·fend'a·ble,** *adj.* **—de·fend'er,** *n.*

de·fend·ant (di fen'dənt), *n.* person accused or sued in a law court.

de·fense (di fens'), *n.* **1** act of defending or protecting. **2** thing that defends or protects. **3** act of defending oneself, as in boxing or fencing. **4** team or players defending a goal in a game. **5** action, speech, or writing in favor of something. **6** answer of a defendant to an accusation or lawsuit against him or her. **7** a defendant and his or her lawyers. [< OF < L *defensa* < *defendere* DEFEND] *adj.* **—de·fense'less·ly,** *adv.* **—de·fense'less·ness,** *n.* **—de·fen'si·bil'i·ty, de·fen'si·ble·ness,** *n.* **—de·fen'si·bly,** *adv.*

defense mechanism, 1 any self-protective action by an organism. **2** psychological reaction to limit emotional damage that could be caused by dwelling on very unpleasant feelings or experiences.

de·fen·si·ble (di fen'sə bəl), *adj.* **1** that can be defended. **2** *Fig.* justifiable; proper. **—de·fen'si·bil'i·ty,** *n.* **—de·fen'si·bly,** *adv.*

de·fen·sive (di fen'siv), *adj.* **1** ready to defend; defending. **2** for defense. **3** of defense. —*n.* **1** position or attitude of defense. **2** thing that defends. **—de·fen'sive·ly,** *adv.* **—de·fen'sive·ness,** *n.*

de·fer¹ (di fėr'), *v.*, **–ferred, –fer·ring.** put off; delay. [< L *differre.* See DIFFER.] **—de·fer'ment,** *n.* **—de·fer'rer,** *n.*

de·fer² (di fėr'), *v.*, **–ferred, –fer·ring.** yield in judgment or opinion; submit courteously. [< F < L, < *de-* down + *ferre* carry] **—de·fer'rer,** *n.*

def·er·ence (def'ər əns), *n.* **1** a yielding to the judgment or opinion of another; courteous submission. **2** great respect.

in deference to, out of respect for.

pay (or **show**) **deference to,** yield or submit to.

def·er·en·tial (def´ər en'shəl), *adj.* showing deference; respectful. —**def´er·en'tial·ly**, *adv.*

de·fi·ance (di fi'əns), *n.* **1** a standing up against authority and refusing to recognize or obey it; open resistance. **2** challenge to meet in a contest, to do something, or to prove something. [< OF. See DEFY.]

de·fi·ant (di fi'ənt), *adj.* showing defiance; challenging; openly resisting. —**de·fi'ant·ly**, *adv.* —**de·fi'ant·ness**, *n.*

de·fi·bril·late (di fi'brə lāt), *v.,* –**lat·ed**, –**lat·ing**. to cause fibrillating heart muscles to relax, esp. by means of electric shock. —**de·fi´bril·la'tion, de·fi´bril·la'tor**, *n.*

de·fi·cien·cy (di fish'ən si), *n., pl.* –**cies**. **1** lack or absence of something needed or required; incompleteness. **2** amount by which something falls short or is too small.

de·fi·cient (di fish'ənt), *adj.* **1** incomplete; defective. **2** not sufficient in quantity, force, etc. [< L *deficiens* failing < *de–* + *facere* do] —**de·fi'cient·ly**, *adv.*

def·i·cit (def'ə sit), *n.* amount by which a sum of money falls short; shortage. [< L, it is wanting. See DEFICIENT.]

de·fi·er (di fi'ər), *n.* person who defies.

de·file¹ (di fil'), *v.,* –**filed**, –**fil·ing**. **1** make filthy or dirty; make disgusting in any way. **2** destroy the purity or cleanness of; corrupt. [alter. of *defoul* (< OF *defouler* trample down, violate) after obs. *file* befoul < OE *fȳlan* < *fūl* foul] **de·file'ment**, *n.* —**de·fil'er**, *n.*

de·file² (di fil'; dē'fil), *v.,* –**filed**, –**fil·ing**, *n.* —*v.* march in a line. —*n.* a narrow way or passage, esp. a steep and narrow valley. [< F, special use of pp. of *défiler* march by files < *dé–* off + *file* FILE¹]

de·fine (di fin'), *v.,* –**fined**, –**fin·ing**. **1** make clear the meaning of; explain. **2** make clear; make distinct. **3** fix; settle. **4** settle the limits of. [< F < L *definire* to limit < *de–* + *finis* end] —**de·fin'a·ble**, *adj.* —**de·fin'a·bly**, *adv.* —**de·fin'er**, *n.*

def·i·nite (def'ə nit), *adj.* **1** clear; exact; not vague. **2** limited; restricted. **3** limiting; restricting. The English definite article is *the.* —**def'i·nite·ness**, *n.*

def·i·nite·ly (def'ə nit li), *adv.* **1** in a definite manner. **2** certainly.

def·i·ni·tion (def´ə nish'ən), *n.* **1** act of defining. **2** statement that makes clear the meaning of a word; explanation. **3** capacity of a lens to give a clear, distinct image. **4** clearness.

de·fin·i·tive (di fin'ə tiv), *adj.* **1** conclusive; final. **2** limiting; defining. —*n.* word that limits or defines a noun. *The, this, all, none,* etc., are definitives. —**de·fin'i·tive·ly**, *adv.* —**de·fin'i·tive·ness**, *n.*

de·flate (di flāt'), *v.,* –**flat·ed**, –**flat·ing**. **1** let air or gas out of (a balloon, tire, football, etc.). **2** reduce the amount of; reduce. [< L, < *de–* off + *flare* blow] —**de·fla'tor**, *n.*

de·fla·tion (di flā'shən), *n.* **1** act of letting the air or gas out: *the deflation of a tire.* **2** reduction. **3** reduction of the amount of available money in circulation. **4** increase in the value of money so that prices go down. —**de·fla'tion·ar´y**, *adj.*

de·flect (di flekt'), *v.* bend or turn aside; change the direction of. [< L, < *de–* away + *flectere* bend] —**de·flec'tion**, *n.* —**de·flec'tive**, *adj.* —**de·flec'tor**, *n.*

de·flow·er (dē flou'ər), *v.* **1** strip flowers from. **2** spoil; ruin. **3** deprive of virginity; ravish.

de·fo·li·ant (di fō'lē ənt), *n.* chemical spray used to remove the leaves of plants and trees.

de·fo·li·ate (di fō'lē āt), *v.,* –**at·ed**, –**at·ing**. remove the leaves of (a plant or tree), esp. with a chemical spray. [< L *defoliare* + *–ate¹*] —**de·fo´li·a'tion**, *n.*

de·for·est (dē fôr'ist; –for'–), *v.* clear of trees. —**de·for´est·a'tion**, *n.* —**de·for'est·er**, *n.*

de·form (di fôrm'), *v.* **1** spoil the form or shape of. **2** make ugly. **3** change the form of; transform. —**de´for·ma'tion**, *n.* —**de·formed'**, *adj.*

de·form·i·ty (di fôr'mə ti), *n., pl.* –**ties**. **1** part that is not properly formed. **2** condition of being improperly formed. **3** an improperly formed person or thing. **4** ugliness.

de·fraud (di frôd'), *v.* take money, rights, etc., away from by fraud; cheat. [< L *defraudare.* See DE–, FRAUD.]

de·fray (di frā'), *v.* pay (costs or expenses). [< F, < *dé–* + *frai* cost] —**de·fray'a·ble**, *adj.* —**de·fray'al, de·fray'ment**, *n.* —**de·fray'er**, *n.*

de·frost (dē frôst'; -frost'), *v.* **1** remove frost or ice from. **2** thaw. —**de·frost'er**, *n.*

deft (deft), *adj.* skillful; nimble. [var. of *daft*] —**deft'ly**, *adv.* —**deft'ness**, *n.*

de·funct (di fungkt'), *adj.* dead; extinct. [< L *defunctus* finished < *de–* + *fungi* perform] —**de·funct'ness**, *n.*

de·fuse (dī fūz'), –**fused**, –**fus·ing**. **1** remove the fuse from a bomb or other explosive device. **2** *Fig.* lessen the effects of criticism or opposition.

de·fy (di fi'), *v.,* –**fied**, –**fy·ing**. **1** resist boldly or openly. **2** withstand; resist. **3** challenge (a person) to do or prove something. [< OF *desfier* < VL, < L *dis–* + *fidus* faithful]

deg., degree.

de·gen·er·a·cy (di jen'ər ə si), *n.* degenerate condition.

de·gen·er·ate (*v.* di jen'ər āt; *adj., n.* di jen'ər it), *v.,* –**at·ed**, –**at·ing**, *adj., n.* —*v.* **1** decline in physical, mental, or moral qualities; grow worse. **2** *Biol.* sink to a lower or less organized type. —*adj.* showing a decline in physical, mental, or moral qualities. —*n.* person having an evil and unwholesome character. [< L, ult. < *de–* + *genus* race, kind] —**de·gen'er·ate·ly**, *adv.* —**de·gen'er·ate·ness**, *n.* —**de·gen'er·a´tive**, *adj.*

de·gen·er·a·tion (di jen´ə rā'shən), *n.* **1** process of declining or deteriorating. **2** deterioration of the body caused by disease, injury, etc. **3** degenerate condition. **4** slow change in an organism, species, etc., to a less highly developed form.

deg·ra·da·tion (deg rə dā'shən), *n.* **1** a degrading. **2** a being degraded. **3** degraded condition. **3** a wearing down by erosion.

de·grade (di grād'), *v.,* –**grad·ed**, –**grad·ing**. **1** reduce to a lower rank; take away a position, an honor, etc., from. **2** make worse; debase. **3** wear down by erosion. [< Eccl.L < L *de–* + *gradus* step, grade] —**de·grad'er**, *n.*

de·gree (di grē'), *n.* **1** stage or step in a scale or process. **2** amount; extent. **3** unit for measuring temperature. **4** unit for measuring angles or arcs. **5** rank. **6** rank or title given by a college or university to a student whose work fulfills certain requirements, or to a person as an honor. **7** one of the three stages in the comparison of adjectives or adverbs. *Fastest* is the superlative degree of *fast.* **8** the relative measure of guilt: *murder in the first degree.*

by degrees, gradually.

to a degree, a to a large amount; to a great extent. **b** somewhat; rather. [< OF *degre* < VL, < *degradare* divide into steps < LL, DEGRADE]

de·his·cence (di his'əns), *n.* a bursting open, esp. of seed capsules, etc., to scatter the seeds. [< L *dehiscens,* ult. < *de–* + *hiare* gape] —**de·his'cent**, *adj.*

de·horn (di hôrn'), *v.* remove the horns from. —**de·horn'er**, *n.*

de·hy·drate (dē hī'drāt), *v.,* –**drat·ed**, –**drat·ing**. **1** deprive (a chemical compound) of water or the elements of water. **2** take moisture from. **3** lose water or moisture. —**de´hy·dra'tion, de´hy·dra'tor**, *n.*

de·ice (dī īs'), *v.,* –**iced**, –**ic·ing**, prevent or remove ice formation from (a surface).

de·ic·er (dē īs'ər), *n.* device, esp. used on aircraft, to prevent or remove ice formation.

de·i·fy (dē'ə fī), *v.,* –**fied**, –**fy·ing**. **1** make a god of. **2** worship or regard as a god. [< OF < LL *deificare* < *deus* god + *facere* make] —**de´i·fi·ca'tion**, *n.* —**de'i·fi´er**, *n.*

deign (dān), *v.* **1** condescend. **2** condescend to give (an answer, a reply, etc.). [< OF < L, < *dignus* worthy]

de·ism (dē'iz əm), *n.* **1** belief that God exists entirely apart from our world and does not influence the lives of human beings. **2** belief in God without accepting any particular religion. [< L *deus* god] —**de'ist**, *n.* —**de·is'tic, de·is'ti·cal**, *adj.* —**de·is'ti·cal·ly**, *adv.*

de·i·ty (dē'ə ti), *n., pl.* –**ties**. **1** god or goddess. **2** divine nature; being a god. **3 the Deity,** God. [< F < L *deitas* < *deus* god]

dé·jà vu (dā´zhä vü'), **1** feeling that one has already experienced something before. **2** realizing that one has experienced or seen something before, often too many times to be interesting. [< F (literally) already seen]

de·ject·ed (di jek′tid), *adj.* in low spirits; sad; discouraged. —**de·ject′ed·ly,** *adv.* —**de·ject′ed·ness,** *n.*

de·jec·tion (di jek′shən), *n.* lowness of spirits; sadness; discouragement. [< L *dejectio* < *de–* down + *jacere* throw]

de ju·re (dē jùr′ē), *Latin.* by right; legal.

del., 1 delegate. 2 delete. 3 delivery.

Del., Delaware.

Del·a·ware (del′ə wãr), *n.* an E state of the United States. —**Del′a·war′e·an,** *adj., n.*

de·lay (di lā′), *v.* **1** put off till a later time. **2** make late; keep waiting; hinder. **3** be late; wait; go slowly. —*n.* **1** act of delaying. **2** fact of being delayed. [< OF, < *de–* + *laier* leave, let, prob. < Celtic] —**de·lay′er,** *n.*

de·lec·ta·ble (di lek′tə bəl), *adj.* very pleasing; delightful. [< OF < L, < *delectare* DELIGHT] —**de·lec′ta·ble·ness,** *n.* —**de·lec′ta·bly,** *adv.*

de·lec·ta·tion (dē′lek tā′shən), *n.* delight.

del·e·gate (*n.* del′ə gāt, –git; *v.* del′ə gāt), *n., v.,* –**gat·ed,** –**gat·ing.** —*n.* **1** person given power or authority to act for others; representative. **2** representative of a territory in the United States House of Representatives. **3** member of the lower branch of the legislature in Maryland, Virginia, and West Virginia. —*v.* **1** appoint or send (a person) as a delegate. **2** give over (one's power or authority) to another as agent or deputy. [< L, < *de–* + *legare* send with a commission]

del·e·ga·tion (del′ə gā′shən), *n.* **1** act of delegating. **2** fact of being delegated. **3** group of delegates.

de·lete (di lēt′), *v.,* –**let·ed,** –**let·ing.** strike out or take out (anything written or printed). [< L, pp. of *delere* destroy] —**de·le′tion,** *n.*

del·e·te·ri·ous (del′ə tir′i əs), *adj.* harmful; injurious. [< NL < Gk. *deleterios,* ult. < *deleesthai* hurt] —**del′e·te′ri·ous·ly,** *adv.*

delft (delft), **delf** (delf), or **delftware** (delft′wãr′), *n.* kind of glazed earthenware made in Holland, often decorated in blue.

del·i (de′i), *n., pl.* del·is. *Informal.* delicatessen.

Del·hi (del′i), *n.* city in N India, a former capital of the Mogul empire.

de·lib·er·ate (*adj.* di lib′ər āt; *v.* di lib′ər āt), *adj., v.,* –**at·ed,** –**at·ing.** —*adj.* **1** carefully thought out; made or done on purpose. **2** slow and careful in deciding what to do. **3** not hurried; slow. —*v.* **1** think over carefully; consider. **2** discuss reasons for and against something; debate. [< L, < *de–* + *librare* weigh] —**de·lib′er·ate·ly,** *adv.* —**de·lib′er·ate·ness,** *n.* —**de·lib′er·a·tor,** *n.*

de·lib·er·a·tion (di lib′ər ā′shən), *n.* **1** careful thought. **2** discussion of reasons for and against something; debate: *the*

deliberations of Congress. **3** slowness and care.

de·lib·er·a·tive (di lib′ər ā′tiv), *adj.* **1** for deliberation; having to do with deliberation: *Congress is a deliberative body.* **2** characterized by deliberation. —**de·lib′er·a′tive·ly,** *adv.* —**de·lib′er·a′tive·ness,** *n.*

del·i·ca·cy (del′ə kə si), *n., pl.* –**cies.** **1** slightness and grace. **2** subtle quality. **3** fineness of feeling for small differences; sensitiveness. **4** need of care, skill, or tact. **5** thought or regard for the feelings of others. **6** a shrinking from what is offensive. **7** susceptibility to illness; weakness. **8** a choice kind of food.

del·i·cate (del′ə kit), *adj.* **1** pleasing to the taste; mild; soft: *delicate foods.* **2** easily torn; thin. **3** requiring careful handling: *a delicate situation.* **4** very rapidly responding to slight changes of condition: *delicate instruments.* **5** easily hurt or made ill: *a delicate child.* **6** subtle. **7** considerate. [< L *delicatus* pampered] —**del′i·cate·ly,** *adv.* —**del′i·cate·ness,** *n.*

del·i·ca·tes·sen (del′ə kə tes′ən), *n. Am.* **1** (*sing. in use*) store that sells prepared foods, such as cooked meats, salads, relishes, etc. **2** (*pl. in use*) the foods. [< G, pl. of *delikatesse* delicacy < F]

de·li·cious (di lish′əs), *adj.* **1** very pleasing to taste or smell. **2** very pleasing; delightful. [< OF < LL, < *deliciae* a delight < *delicere* entice. See DELIGHT.] —**de·li′cious·ly,** *adv.* —**deli′cious·ness,** *n.*

de·light (di līt′), *n.* **1** great pleasure; joy. **2** thing that gives great pleasure. —*v.* **1** please greatly. **2** have great pleasure. [< OF *delit,* ult. < L *delectare* to charm < *delicere* entice < *de–* + *lacere* entice] —**de·light′ed,** *adj.* —**de·light′ed·ly,** *adv.* —**de·light′ed·ness,** *n.* —**de·light′er,** *n.*

de·light·ful (di līt′fəl), *adj.* very pleasing; giving joy. —**de·light′ful·ly,** *adv.* —**de·light′ful·ness,** *n.*

De·li·lah (di lī′lə), *n.* **1** woman who betrayed Samson, her lover, to the Philistines. Judges 16. **2** a false, treacherous woman; temptress.

de·lim·it (di lim′it), *v.* fix the limits of; mark the boundaries of. —**de·lim′i·ta′tion,** *n.* —**de·lim′i·ta′tive,** *adj.*

de·lin·e·ate (di lin′i āt), *v.,* –**at·ed,** –**at·ing.** **1** trace the outline of. **2** draw; sketch. **3** describe in words. [< L, < *de–* + *linea* line] —**de·lin′e·a′tion,** *n.* —**de·lin′e·a′tor,** *n.*

de·lin·quen·cy (di ling′kwən si), *n., pl.* –**cies.** **1** failure to do what is required by law or duty; guilt. **2** fault; offense.

de·lin·quent (di ling′kwənt), *adj.* **1** failing to do what is required by law or duty. **2** owed and not paid. **3** having to do with delinquents. —*n.* a delinquent person; offender; criminal. [< L, < *de–* + *linquere* leave] —**de·lin′quent·ly,** *adv.*

del·i·quesce (del′ə kwes′), *v.,* –**quesced,** –**quesc·ing.** become liquid by absorbing moisture from the air. [< L, < *de–* +

liquere be liquid] —**del′i·ques′cence,** *n.* —**del′i·ques′cent,** *adj.*

de·lir·i·ous (di lir′i əs), *adj.* **1** temporarily out of one's senses. **2** wildly excited. **3** caused by delirium. —**de·lir′i·ous·ly,** *adv.* —**de·lir′i·ous·ness,** *n.*

de·lir·i·um (di lir′i əm), *n., pl.* –**lir·i·ums,** –**lir·i·a** (–lir′i ə). **1** a temporary disorder of the mind, as during fevers, characterized by wild excitement, irrational talk, and hallucinations. **2** any wild excitement that cannot be controlled. [< L, < *delirare* rave, be crazy < *de lira* (*ire*) (go) out of the furrow (in plowing)]

de·liv·er (di liv′ər), *v.* **1** carry and give out; distribute: *the postman delivers letters.* **2** give up; hand over. **3** give forth in words: *the jury delivered its verdict.* **4** strike; throw: *deliver a blow.* **5** set free; rescue. **6** help (a woman) give birth to a child. **deliver oneself of,** speak; give out. [< F < L *deliberare* set free < *de–* + *liber* free] —**de·liv′er·a·ble,** *adj.* —**de·liv′er·er,** *n.*

de·liv·er·ance (di liv′ər əns), *n.* **1** act of setting free or state of being set free. **2** a formal expression of opinion or judgment.

de·liv·er·y (di liv′ər i; –liv′ri), *n., pl.* –**er·ies.** **1** act or fact of delivering or distributing: *parcel-post delivery.* **2** a giving up; handing over. **3** way of giving a speech, lecture, etc. **4** act or way of striking, throwing, etc. **5** rescue; release. **6** giving birth to a child; childbirth. **7** anything that is delivered.

dell (del), *n.* a small, sheltered glen or valley, usually with trees in it. [OE]

de·louse (dē lous′; –louz′), *v.,* –**loused,** –**lous·ing.** remove lice from.

Del·phi (del′fī), *n.* town in ancient Greece where an oracle of Apollo was located. —**Del′phic, Del′phi·an,** *adj.*

Delphic oracle, oracle of Apollo at Delphi.

del·phin·i·um (del fin′i əm), *n.* larkspur. [< NL < Gk., < *delphin* dolphin; from shape of nectar gland]

del·ta (del′tə), *n.* **1** deposit of earth and sand that collects at the mouths of some rivers and is usually three-sided. **2** the fourth letter of the Greek alphabet (Δ or δ). **3** anything shaped like a triangle. **4** =delta wing.

delta wing, aircraft wing shaped like a triangle that provides more speed and lift. —**del′ta-wing′,** *adj.*

del·toid (del′toid), *adj.* triangular. —*n.* a large, triangular muscle of the shoulder.

de·lude (di lüd′), *v.,* –**lud·ed,** –**lud·ing.** mislead; deceive. [< L, < *de–* (to the detriment of) + *ludere* play] —**de·lud′er,** *n.*

del·uge (del′ūj), *n., v.,* –**uged,** –**ug·ing.** —*n.* **1** a great flood. **2** a heavy fall of rain. **3** any overwhelming rush. —*v.* **1** to flood. **2** overwhelm.

the Deluge, the great flood in the days of Noah. Gen. 7 [< OF < L *diluvium* < *dis–* away + *luere* wash]

de·lu·sion (di lü′zhən), *n.* **1** a deluding or being deluded. **2** a false notion or belief.

3 a fixed belief maintained in the face of indisputable evidence to the contrary.

de·lu·sive (di lü′siv), *adj.* deceptive; false; unreal. —**de·lu′sive·ly,** *adv.* —**de·lu′sive·ness,** *n.*

de·lu·so·ry (di lü′sə ri), *adj.* delusive; deceptive.

de·luxe (də lŭks′; –lüks′), *adj.* of exceptionally good quality; elegant. [< F]

delve (delv), *v.,* **delved, delv·ing. 1** search carefully for information. **2** *Archaic or Dial.* dig. [OE *delfan*] —**delv′er,** *n.*

Dem., Democrat; Democratic.

de·mag·net·ize (dē mag′nə tīz), *v.,* **–ized, –iz·ing.** deprive of magnetism. —**de′mag·net·i·za′tion,** *n.* —**de·mag′net·iz′er,** *n.*

dem·a·gog·ic (dem′ə goj′ik; –gog′ik), **dem·a·gog·i·cal** (–ə kəl), *adj.* of or like a demagogue. —**dem′a·gog′i·cal·ly,** *adv.*

dem·a·gogue, dem·a·gog (dem′ə gôg; –gog), *n.* a popular leader who stirs up the people in order to get something for him or herself. [< Gk., < *demos* people + *agogos* leader < *agein* lead]

dem·a·gogu·er·y (dem′ə gôg′ər i;–gog′–), *n.* methods or principles of a demagogue.

dem·a·go·gy (dem′ə gō′ji;–gôg′i;–gog′i), *n. Esp. Brit.* **1** demagoguery. **2** character of a demagogue.

de·mand (di mand′; –mänd′), *v.* **1** ask for as a right. **2** ask for with authority. **3** require; need. —*n.* **1** act of demanding. **2** thing demanded. **3** claim; requirement. **4** desire and ability to buy.

in demand, wanted.

on demand, upon request. [< L, < *de–* + *mandare* to order] —**de·mand′a·ble,** *adj.* —**de·mand′er,** *n.*

de·mar·cate (dē′mär kāt, di mär′–), *v.,* **–cat·ed, –cat·ing. 1** set and mark the limits of. **2** *Fig.* distinguish.

de·mar·ca·tion (dē′mär kā′shən), *n.* **1** act of setting and marking the limits. **2** *Fig.* separation; distinction. Also, **demarkation.** [< Sp., < *de–* off + *marcar* mark]

de·mean[1] (di mēn′), *v.* lower in dignity or standing; humble. [< *de–* + *mean*[2]; formed after *debase*]

de·mean[2] (di mēn′), *v.* behave or conduct (oneself). [< OF, < *de–* + *mener* lead < L *minare* drive]

de·mean·or (di mēn′ər), *n.* way a person looks and acts; behavior. [ME *demenure* < *demenen* behave]

de·ment·ed (di men′tid), *adj.* insane; crazy. [< L, < *de–* out of + *mens* mind] —**de·ment′ed·ly,** *adv.* —**de·ment′ed·ness,** *n.*

de·men·tia (di men′shə), *n.* a partial or complete loss of mind.

de·mer·it (dē mer′it), *n.* **1** fault; defect. **2** mark against a person's record for poor work or unsatisfactory behavior.

de·mesne (di mān′; –mēn′), *n.* **1** land or land and buildings possessed as one's own. **2** house and land belonging to a lord and used by him. **3** domain; realm. [< AF *demeyne* DOMAIN]

demi–, *prefix.* half, as in *demigod.* [< F *demi* half < VL < L, < *dis–* apart + *medius* middle]

dem·i·god (dem′i god′), *n.* **1** god that is partly human. **2** a minor or lesser god.

dem·i·god·dess (dem′i god′is), *n.* a female demigod.

dem·i·john (dem′i jon), *n.* a large bottle of earthenware enclosed in wicker.

de·mil·i·ta·rize (dē mil′ə tə rīz), *v.,* **–rized, –riz·ing.** free from military control. —**de·mil′ita·ri·za′tion,** *n.*

dem·i·mon·daine (dem′i mon′dān), *n.* woman of the demimonde. [< F]

dem·i·monde (dem′i mond; dem′i mond′), *n.* **1** class of women whose reputation and morals are doubtful. **2** woman of this class; demimondaine. **3** prostitutes as a group. **4** those who live and work on the margins of conventional, reputable society. [< F, half-world]

de·mise (di mīz′), *n.* death. [appar. < AF, pp. of *desmettre* put away < *des–* away (< L *dis–*) + *mettre* put < L *mittere* let go, send]

dem·i·sem·i·qua·ver (dem′i sem′i kwä′-vər), *n. Music.* a thirty-second note.

dem·i·tasse (dem′i tas′; –täs′), *n.* a very small cup of coffee. [< F, half-cup]

dem·o (dem′ō), *n., pl.* **dem·os.** *Informal.* **1** recording sent to record companies, agents, etc. as a demonstration of a new song, album, group, etc. **2** demonstration. **3** =demonstrator.

de·mo·bi·lize (dē mō′bə līz), *v.,* **–lized, –li·zing.** disband (troops, etc.). —**de·mo′bi·li·za′tion,** *n.*

de·moc·ra·cy (di mok′rə si), *n., pl.* **–cies. 1** government that is run directly or indirectly by the people who live under it. **2** country, state, or community having such a government. **3** treatment of others as one's equals. **4 Democracy. a** the principles of the Democratic Party. **b** its members collectively. [< F < Gk., < *demos* people + *kratos* rule]

dem·o·crat (dem′ə krat), *n.* **1** person who believes that a government should be run by the people who live under it. **2** person who holds or acts on the belief that all people are his equals. **3 Democrat.** member of the Democratic Party. —**de·moc′ra·tism,** *n.*

dem·o·crat·ic (dem′ə krat′ik), *adj.* **1** of a democracy; like a democracy. **2** treating all classes of people as one's equals. **3 Democratic.** of the Democratic Party.

Democratic Party, one of the two main political parties in the United States.

de·moc·ra·tize (di mok′rə tīz), *v.,* **–tized, –tiz·ing.** make or become democratic. —**de·moc′ra·ti·za′tion,** *n.*

de·mog·ra·phy (di mog′rə fi), *n.* science dealing with statistics of births, deaths, diseases, etc., of a community. —**de·mog′ra·pher,** *n.* —**de′mo·graph′ic,** *adj.*

de·mol·ish (di mol′ish), *v.* **1** pull or tear down; destroy. **2** *Fig.* defeat utterly, as in

a sports event or competitive situation. [< F < L *demoliri* tear down < *de–* + *moles* mass] —**de·mol′ish·er,** *n.* —**de·mol′ish·ment,** *n.*

dem·o·li·tion (dem′ə lish′ən; dē′mə–), *n.* destruction; ruin.

de·mon (dē′mən), *n.* **1** an evil spirit; devil; fiend. **2** a very wicked or cruel person. **3** an evil influence. **4** person who has great energy or vigor. **5** an attendant or guiding spirit. **6** =daemon. [(defs. 1–5) < L < Gk. *daimonion* divine (thing), in Christian writings, evil spirit; (def. 6) see DAEMON]

de·mon·e·tize (dē mon′ə tīz; –mun′–), *v.,* **–tized, –tiz·ing.** deprive of its standard value as money. —**de·mon′e·ti·za′tion,** *n.*

de·mo·ni·ac (di mō′ni ak), *adj.* Also, **de·mo·ni·a·cal** (dē′mə nī′ə kəl). **1** of demons. **2** devilish; fiendish. **3** raging; frantic. —*n.* person supposed to be possessed by an evil spirit. —**de′mo·ni′a·cal·ly,** *adv.*

de·mon·ic (di mon′ik), *adj.* **1** of or caused by evil spirits. **2** influenced by a guiding spirit.

de·mon·ol·o·gy (dē′mən ol′ə ji), *n.* study of demons or of beliefs about demons. —**de′mon·ol′o·gist,** *n.*

de·mon·stra·ble (di mon′strə bəl; dem′ən–), *adj.* capable of being proved. —**de·mon′stra·bil′i·ty,** *n.* —**de·mon′stra·bly,** *adv.*

dem·on·strate (dem′ən strāt), *v.,* **–strat·ed, –strat·ing. 1** establish the truth of; prove. **2** explain by using examples, experiments, etc. **3** advertise the merits of (a thing for sale). **4** show openly; exhibit. **5** show feeling or political opinion by a parade, meeting, etc. [< L, < *de–* + *monstrare* show]

dem·on·stra·tion (dem′ən strā′shən), *n.* **1** clear proof. **2** explanation with the use of examples, experiments, etc. **3** advertising or making known some new product or process in a public place. **4** an open show or exhibition, as of feeling, ability, etc. **5** show of feeling or political opinion by a parade, meeting, etc.

de·mon·stra·tive (di mon′strə tiv), *adj.* **1** expressing one's affections freely and openly. **2** showing clearly; explanatory. **3** giving proof; conclusive. **4** pointing out. *This* and *that* are demonstrative pronouns and also demonstrative adjectives. —*n.* pronoun or adjective that points out. —**de·mon′stra·tive·ly,** *adv.* —**de·mon′stra·tive·ness,** *n.*

de·mon·stra·tor (dem′ən strā′tər), *n.* **1 a** person or thing that demonstrates. **b** vehicle, appliance, etc., used by a dealer to demonstrate its use. **2** person who demonstrates at a meeting, parade, etc.

de·mor·al·ize (di môr′əl īz; –mor′–), *v.,* **–ized, iz·ing. 1** corrupt the morals of. **2** weaken the spirit, courage, or discipline of; dishearten. **3** throw into confusion or disorder. —**de·mor′al·i·za′tion,** *n.* —**de·mor′al·iz′er,** *n.*

de·mote (di mōt'), v., -mot·ed, -mot·ing. put back to a lower grade; reduce in rank. [< de- + (pro)mote] —de·mo'tion, n.

de·mur (di mėr'), v., -murred, -mur·ring, n. —v. object. —n. an objection. [< OF < L, < de- + morari delay]

de·mure (di myür'), adj., -mur·er, -mur·est. 1 falsely proper; unnaturally modest; coy. 2 serious; sober. [< obs. mure, adj., demure < OF < L maturus mature] —de·mure'ly, adv.

de·mur·rer (di mėr'ər), n. 1 person who objects. 2 objection.

den (den), n., v., denned, den·ning. —n. 1 place where a wild animal lives. 2 place where thieves or the like have their headquarters. 3 a small and cozy private room. —v. inhabit a den. [OE denn]

de·nar·i·us (di när'i əs), n., pl. -nar·i·i (-när'i ī). an ancient Roman coin. [< L, containing here (here, ten times the value of an as²) < deni ten at a time]

de·na·tion·al·ize (dē nash'ən əl īz;–nash'-nəl-), v., -ized, -iz·ing. 1 deprive of national rights, scope, etc. 2 return to private ownership. —de·na'tion·al·i·za'tion, n.

de·nat·u·ral·ize (dē nach'ə rəl īz; –nach'-rəl-), v., -ized, -iz·ing. 1 make unnatural. 2 take citizenship from. —de·nat'u·ral·i·za'tion, n.

de·na·ture (dē nā'chər), v., -tured, -tur·ing. 1 change the nature of. 2 make (alcohol, food, etc.) unfit for drinking or eating without destroying for other purposes. —de·na'tur·a'tion, n.

den·drite (den'drīt), n. the branching part at the receiving end of a nerve cell. [< Gk., < dendron tree]

de·neu·tral·ize (dē nü'trəl īz; –nü'–), v., -ized, -iz·ing. abolish the neutral status of (a country, territory, etc.). —de·neu'tral·i·za'tion, n.

den·gue (deng'gā; –gi), n. an infectious fever wth skin rash and severe pain in the joints and muscles. [< Sp., < Swahili (lang. of C Africa) kidinga popo]

de·ni·al (di nī'əl), n. 1 act of saying that something is not true. 2 act of saying that one does not hold to or accept: a public denial of communism. 3 a refusing.

de·ni·er¹ (di nī'ər), n. person who denies.

den·ier² (den'yər; də nir'), n. unit of weight used to express the fineness of silk, rayon, or nylon yarn. [< OF < L denarius DENARIUS]

den·im (den'əm), n. a heavy, coarse cotton cloth for overalls, etc.

denims, overalls or trousers made of denim. [short for F serge de Nîmes serge of Nîmes]

den·i·zen (den'ə zən), n. 1 inhabitant; occupant. 2 a foreign word, plant, animal, etc., that has been adopted. —v. make (one) a denizen; naturalize. [< OF denzein < denz within < LL < L de from + intus within]

Den·mark (den'märk), n. a small country in N Europe.

de·nom·i·nate (v. di nom'ə nāt; adj. di nom'ə nit, –nāt), v., -nat·ed, -nat·ing, adj. —v. give a name to; name. —adj. called by a specific name. [< L, < de- + nomen name]

de·nom·i·na·tion (di nom'ə nā'shən), n. 1 name for a group or class of things. 2 a religious group or sect. 3 class or kind of units: a coin of low denomination.

de·nom·i·na·tion·al (di nom'ə nā'-shən əl; –nāsh'nəl), adj. having to do with some religious denomination or denominations; controlled by a religious denomination. —de·nom'i·na'tion·al·ly, adv.

de·nom·i·na·tion·al·ism (di nom'ə nā'-shən əl iz'əm; –nāsh'nəl-), n. 1 denominational principles. 2 division into denominations.

de·nom·i·na·tive (di nom'ə nā'tiv; –nə tiv), adj. 1 giving a distinctive name; naming. 2 formed from a noun or an adjective. To center is a denominative verb. —n. a denominative word. —de·nom'i·na'tive·ly, adv.

de·nom·i·na·tor (di nom'ə nā'tər), n. 1 number below the line in a fraction, stating the size of the parts in their relation to the whole. 2 person or thing that names.

de·no·ta·tion (dē'nō tā'shən), n. 1 meaning, esp. the exact, literal meaning. The denotation of home is "place where one lives," but it has many connotations. 2 indication; denoting. —de'no·ta'tive, adj.

de·note (di nōt'), v., -not·ed, -not·ing. 1 be the sign of; indicate. 2 be a name for; mean. [< F < L, < de- + notare note < nota mark]

de·noue·ment (dā'nü mäN'), n. solution of a plot in a play, a story, etc.; outcome; end. [< F, < dénouer untie < L dis- + nodus knot]

de·nounce (di nouns'), v., -nounced, -nounc·ing. 1 condemn publicly; express strong disapproval of. 2 inform against; accuse. 3 give formal notice of the termination of (a treaty, etc.). [< OF < L, < de- + nuntiare announce < nuntius messenger] —de·nounce'ment, de·nounc'er, n.

dense (dens), adj., dens·er, dens·est. 1 closely packed together; thick. 2 Fig. stupid. [< L densus] —dense'ly, adv. —dense'ness, n.

den·si·ty (den'sə ti), n., pl. -ties. 1 dense condition or quality; compactness; thickness. 2 Fig. stupidity. 3 a quantity of matter in a unit of volume. b quantity of electricity in a unit of area. c quantity of anything in a unit of area. 4 specific gravity.

dent (dent), n. 1 hollow made by a blow or pressure. 2 weak spot. —v. 1 make a dent in. 2 become dented. [ME dente, var. of dint]

dent., dental; dentist; dentistry.

den·tal (den'təl), adj. 1 of or for the teeth. 2 of or for a dentist's work. 3 produced by placing the tip of the tongue against or near the upper front teeth. —n. a dental sound. [< L dens tooth]

den·tate (den'tāt), adj. having tooth-like projections; toothed; notched. —den'tate·ly, adv.

den·tine (den'tān; –tin), den·tin (–tin), n. the hard, bony material that forms the main part of a tooth.

den·tist (den'tist) n. doctor who cares for the teeth, including cleaning, repairing, and extracting teeth, and supplying artificial teeth.

den·tist·ry (den'tis tri), n. work, art, or occupation of a dentist.

den·ti·tion (den tish'ən), n. 1 growth of teeth; teething. 2 kind, number, and arrangement of the teeth.

den·ture (den'chər), n. 1 set of artificial teeth. 2 set of teeth.

de·nude (di nüd'; –ūd'), v., -nud·ed, -nud·ing. 1 make bare; strip. 2 lay (a rock, etc.) bare by removing what lies above. —de'nu·da'tion, n.

de·nun·ci·a·tion (di nun'si ā'shən;–shi–), n. 1 strong, public disapproval. 2 act of informing against; accusation. 3 formal notice of the intention to end a treaty, etc.

de·nun·ci·a·to·ry (di nun'si ə tô'ri; –shi–; –tō'–), adj. condemning; accusing.

Den·ver (den'vər), n. capital of Colorado, in the central part.

de·ny (di nī'), v., -nied, -ny·ing. 1 declare (something) is not true. 2 say that one does not hold to or accept. 3 refuse. 4 disown.

deny oneself, do without the things one wants. [< F < L, < de- + negare say no]

de·o·dor·ant (dē ō'dər ənt), n. preparation that destroys odors. —adj. that destroys odors.

de·o·dor·ize (dē ō'dər īz), v., -ized, -iz·ing. destroy the odor of. —de·o'dor·i·za'tion, n. —de·o'dor·iz'er, n.

de·ox·y·ri·bo·nu·cle·ase (dē ok'sə rī'-bō nü'klē ās; –nyü–), n. enzyme involved in the hydrolysis of deoxyribo-nucleic acid.

de·ox·y·ri·bo·nu·cle·ic acid (dē ok'sə rī'-bō nu klē'ik; –nyü–), acid present in the nucleus of all cells, crucial to the transmission of genetic characteristics; DNA. [< deoxyribose + nucleic acid]

dep., 1 depart; departure. 2 department. 3 deposit. 4 deputy.

de·part (di pärt'), v. 1 go away; leave. 2 turn away; change (from). 3 die. [< OF, < LL departire divide < L de- + partire < pars part]

de·part·ed (di pär'tid), n. Usually, the departed. dead person or persons. —adj. 1 dead. 2 gone; past.

de·part·ment (di pärt'mənt), n. 1 separate part; division: the fire department. 2 one of the administrative districts into which France is divided. 3 a chief division of governmental administration. —de'part·men'tal, adj. —de'part·men'tal·ly, adv.

department store, store that sells many kinds of articles arranged in separate departments.

de·par·ture (di pär′chər), *n.* **1** act of going away; act of leaving. **2** a turning away; change.

de·pend (di pend′), *v.* **1** rely; trust. **2** rely for support or help. **3** be controlled or influenced by something else.

depend on, be controlled or influenced by. [< OF < L, < *de-* from + *pendere* hang]

de·pend·a·ble (di pen′də bəl), *adj.* reliable; trustworthy. —**de·pend′a·bil′i·ty, de·pend′a·ble·ness,** *n.* —**de·pend′a·bly,** *adv.*

de·pend·ence (di pen′dəns), *n.* **1** reliance on another for support or help. **2** reliance; trust. **3** fact of being controlled or influenced by something else: *the dependence of crops on the weather.* **4** person or thing relied on.

de·pend·en·cy (di pen′dən si), *n., pl.* **-cies.** **1** country or territory controlled by another country. **2** dependence. **3** thing that depends on another for existence, support, or help.

de·pend·ent (di pen′dənt), *adj.* **1** relying on another for support or help. **2** controlled or influenced by something else. **3** hanging down. **4 a** (of a variable) relying on the value of an independent variable. **b** (of an equation) that can be derived from another equation. —*n.* person who relies on another for support or help.

de·pict (di pikt′), *v.* represent by drawing, painting, or describing; show; picture; portray. [< L *depictus* < *de-* + *pingere* paint] —**de·pict′er,** *n.* —**de·pic′tion,** *n.*

de·pil·a·to·ry (di pil′ə tô′ri; -tō′-), *adj., n., pl.* **-ries.** —*adj.* capable of removing hair. —*n.* paste, liquid, or other preparation for removing hair. [< L, < *de-′* + *pilus* hair]

de·plane (di plān′), *v.* **-planed, -plan·ing.** get off a plane.

de·plete (di plēt′), *v.,* **-plet·ed, -plet·ing.** empty; exhaust. [< L *depletus* empty < *de-* + *-plere* fill] —**de·ple′tion,** *n.* —**de·ple′tive,** *adj.*

de·plor·a·ble (di plôr′ə bəl; -plōr′-), *adj.* **1** to be deplored; lamentable. **2** wretched; miserable. —**de·plor′a·bly,** *adv.*

de·plore (di plôr′; -plōr′), *v.,* **-plored, -plor·ing.** be very sorry about; lament. [< L, < *de-* + *plorare* weep]

de·ploy (di ploi′), *v.* **1** spread out forces from a column into a long battle line. **2** place forces in readiness for use at a later time. **3** *Fig.* draw on; use: *deploy tact and patience.* [< F, < *dé-* (< L *dis-*) + *ployer* < L *plicare* fold] —**de·ploy′ment,** *n.*

de·po·nent (di pō′nənt), *n.* person who testifies in writing under oath. [< L, < *de-* away, down + *ponere* put]

de·pop·u·late (dē pop′yə lāt), *v.,* **-lat·ed, -lat·ing.** deprive of inhabitants. —**de·pop′u·la′tion,** *n.* —**de·pop′u·la′tor,** *n.*

de·port (di pôrt′; -pōrt′), *v.* **1** banish; expel; remove. **2** behave or conduct (oneself) in a particular manner. [< F < L, < *de-* away + *portare* carry]

de·por·ta·tion (dē′pôr tā′shən; -pōr-), *n.* expulsion; banishment.

de·port·ment (di pôrt′mənt; -pōrt′-), *n.* way a person acts; behavior; conduct.

de·pose (di pōz′), *v.,* **-posed, -pos·ing.** **1** put out of office or a position of authority: *depose a government.* **2** declare under oath; testify. [< OF, < *de-* down + *poser* POSE] —**de·pos′a·ble,** *adj.* —**de·pos′al,** *n.*

de·pos·it (di poz′it), *v.* **1** put down; lay down; leave lying. **2** put (money) in a bank. **3** put in a place for safekeeping. **4** pay as a pledge to do something or to pay more later. —*n.* **1** something laid down or left lying. **2** thing put in a place for safekeeping. **3** money put in a bank. **4** money paid as a pledge to do something or to pay more later. **5** mass of some mineral in rock or in the ground.

on deposit, in a bank or vault. [< L *depositus* < *de-* away + *ponere* put]

de·pos·i·tar·y (di poz′ə ter′i), *n., pl.* **-tar·ies.** **1** person or company that receives something for safekeeping; trustee. **2** =depository.

dep·o·si·tion (dep′ə zish′ən; dē′pə-), *n.* **1** act of deposing. **2 a** testimony. **b** a sworn statement in writing. **3** act of depositing. **4** thing deposited; deposit.

de·pos·i·tor (di poz′ə tər), *n.* **1** person who deposits. **2** person who deposits money in a bank.

de·pos·i·to·ry (di poz′ə tô′ri; -tō′-), *n., pl.* **-ries.** **1** place where a thing is put for safekeeping; storehouse. **2** trustee.

de·pot (dē′pō; *Mil.* dep′ō), *n.* **1** a bus or railroad station. **2** storehouse; warehouse. **3** place where military supplies are stored. [< F < L *depositum.* See DEPOSIT.]

de·prave (di prāv′), *v.,* **-praved, -prav·ing.** make bad; corrupt. [< L, < *de-* + *pravus* crooked, wrong] —**de·prav′er,** *n.*

de·praved (di prāvd′), *adj.* corrupt; perverted.

de·prav·i·ty (di prav′ə ti), *n., pl.* **-ties.** **1** wickedness; corruption. **2** a corrupt act; bad practice.

dep·re·cate (dep′rə kāt), *v.,* **-cat·ed, -cat·ing.** express strong disapproval of; protest against. [< L, plead in excuse, avert by prayer < *de-* + *precari* pray] —**dep′re·cat′ing·ly,** *adv.* —**dep′re·ca′tion,** *n.* —**dep′re·ca′tor,** *n.*

dep·re·ca·to·ry (dep′rə kə tô′ri; -tō′-), *adj.* **1** deprecating. **2** apologetic. —**dep′re·ca′to·ri·ly,** *adv.* —**dep′re·ca·to′ri·ness,** *n.*

de·pre·ci·ate (di prē′shi āt), *v.,* **-at·ed, -at·ing.** **1** lessen the value or price of. **2** lessen in value, as money. **3** speak slightingly of; belittle. [< L, < *de-* + *pretium* price] —**de·pre′ca′tor,** *n.*

de·pre·ci·a·tion (di prē′shi ā′shən), *n.* **1** a lessening or lowering in value. **2** a speaking slightingly of; a belittling.

de·pre·ci·a·to·ry (di prē′shi ə tô′ri; -tō′-), *adj.* tending to depreciate, disparage, or undervalue.

dep·re·da·tion (dep′rə dā′shən), *n.* act of plundering; robbery; a ravaging. [< L, < *de-* + *praeda* booty]

de·press (di pres′), *v.* **1** make sad or gloomy; cause to have low spirits. **2** press down; push down; lower. **3** lower in pitch. **4** lower in amount or value: *depress prices.* **5** reduce the activity of; weaken. [< OF, < L *depressus* < *de-* + *premere* press] —**de·press′ing·ly,** *adv.* —**de·pres′sor,** *n.*

de·pres·sant (di pres′ənt), —*adj.* decreasing the rate of vital activities. —*n.* medicine that lessens pain or excitement; sedative.

de·pressed (di prest′), *adj.* **1** sad; gloomy; low-spirited. **2** pressed down; lowered: *depressed profits.* **3** flattened down; broader than high.

de·pres·sion (di presh′ən), *n.* **1** act of pressing down. **2** depressed condition. **3** a low place; hollow. **4 a** sadness; gloominess; low spirits. **b** psychological condition characterized by long-lasting despair and hopelessness. **5** reduction of economic activity; dullness of trade. **6** angular distance of an object below the horizon. —**de·pres′sive,** *adj.* —**de·pres′sive·ly,** *adv.*

dep·ri·va·tion (dep′rə vā′shən), *n.* act of depriving; state of being deprived.

de·prive (di prīv′), *v.,* **-prived, -priv·ing.** **1** take away from by force. **2** keep from having or doing. [< OF, < *de-* (< L *de-*) + *priver* deprive < L, orig., exempt]

dept., 1 department. **2** deputy.

depth (depth), *n.* **1** quality of being deep; deepness. **2** distance from top to bottom. **3** distance from front to back. **4** the deepest part: *in the depths of the earth.* **6** the most central part: *in the depth of the forest.* **7** profound penetration: *depth of mind.*

beyond (or **out of) one's depth, a** in water that is too deep. **b** beyond one's abilities, training, etc.

in depth, deep; detailed. [ME, < OE *dēop* deep]

depth charge, an explosive charge dropped from a ship or airplane and arranged to explode at a certain depth under water.

depth perception, ability to perceive distance between objects and their spatial relationship to the observer.

dep·u·ta·tion (dep′yə tā′shən), *n.* **1** act of deputing. **2** group of persons appointed to act for others.

de·pute (di pūt′), *v.,* **-put·ed, -put·ing.** **1** appoint to do one's work or to act in one's place. **2** give (work, power, etc.) to another. [< F < LL, assign < L, consider as < *de-* + *putare* think, count]

dep·u·tize (dep′yə tīz), *v.*, **-tized, -tiz·ing.** 1 appoint as deputy. 2 act as deputy.

dep·u·ty (dep′yə ti), *n., pl.* **-ties,** *adj.* —*n.* 1 person appointed to do the work or to act in the place of another: *a sheriff's deputy.* 2 representative in certain law-making assemblies. —*adj.* acting as a deputy.

der., derivation; derivative; derived.

de·rail (dē rāl′), *v.* 1 cause (a train, etc.) to run off the rails. 2 run off the rails. —**de·rail′ment,** *n.*

de·range (di rānj′), *v.*, **-ranged, -rang·ing.** 1 disturb the order or arrangement of. 2 make insane. [< F *déranger.* See DE-, RANGE.] —**de·ranged′,** *adj.* —**de·range′ment,** *n.*

Der·by (dèr′bi; *Brit.* där′bi), *n., pl.* **-bies.** 1 a horse race: *the Kentucky Derby.* 2 race, as of automobiles or airplanes. 3 **derby,** a stiff hat with a rounded crown and narrow brim.

der·e·lict (der′ə likt), *adj.* 1 abandoned; deserted; forsaken. 2 failing in one's duty; negligent. —*n.* 1 ship abandoned at sea. 2 any worthless, discarded thing. 3 person with no home, job, family, etc. [< L *derelictus* < *de-* wholly + *re-* behind + *linquere* leave]

der·e·lic·tion (der′ə lik′shən), *n.* 1 failure in one's duty; negligence. 2 abandonment; desertion; forsaking.

de·ride (di rīd′), *v.*, **-rid·ed, -rid·ing.** laugh at in scorn; ridicule. [< L, < *de-* at + *ridere* laugh] —**de·rid′er,** *n.* —**de·rid′ing·ly,** *adv.*

de ri·gueur (də rē gœr′), *French.* required by etiquette; according to custom; proper.

de·ri·sion (di rizh′ən), *n.* 1 scornful laughter; ridicule; contempt. 2 an object of ridicule.

de·ri·sive (di rī′siv), **de·ri·so·ry** (-sə ri), *adj.* mocking; ridiculing. —**de·ri′sive·ly,** *adv.*

deriv., derivation; derivative; derived.

der·i·va·tion (der′ə vā′shən), *n.* 1 act or fact of deriving. 2 state of being derived. 3 source; origin. 4 theory of the development or origin of a word. —**der′i·va′tion·al,** *adj.*

de·riv·a·tive (di riv′ə tiv), *adj.* derived; not original. —*n.* 1 something derived. 2 a word formed by adding a prefix or suffix to another word. 3 *Chem.* substance obtained from another by substituting a different element.

de·rive (di rīv′), *v.*, **-rived, -riv·ing.** 1 obtain from a source or origin: *derive pleasure from travel.* 2 come from a source or origin; originate. 3 trace (a word, custom, etc.) from or to a source or origin. 4 *Chem.* obtain (a compound) from another by substituting a different element. [< F < L *derivare* lead off, draw off < *de-* + *rivus* stream] —**de·riv′a·ble,** *adj.* —**de·riv′er,** *n.*

der·ma (dèr′mə), *n.* 1 the sensitive layer of skin beneath the epidermis. 2 =skin. [< Gk., skin] —**der′mal,** *adj.*

der·ma·tol·o·gy (dèr′mə tol′ə ji), *n.* science that deals with the skin and its diseases. —**der′ma·to·log′i·cal,** *adj.* —**der′ma·tol′o·gist,** *n.*

der·mis (dèr′mis), *n.* =derma. —**der′mic,** *adj.*

der·o·gate (der′ə gāt), *v.*, **-gat·ed, -gat·ing.** 1 take away; detract. 2 become worse; degenerate. [< L, < *de-* away from + *rogare* ask] —**der′o·ga′tion,** *n.*

de·rog·a·to·ry (di rog′ə tô′ri; -tō′-), **de·rog·a·tive** (-ə tiv), *adj.* 1 disparaging; belittling. 2 lessening the value; detracting. —**de·rog′a·to′ri·ly, de·rog′a·tive·ly,** *adv.*

der·rick (der′ik), *n.* 1 machine with a long arm for lifting and moving heavy objects. 2 towerlike framework over an oil well, gas well, etc. [for *Derrick,* a hangman at Tyburn, London]

der·vish (dèr′vish), *n.* member of any of various Muslim orders. [< Turk. < Pers. *darvīsh*]

desc., descendant.

des·cant (*v.* des kant′, dis-; *n.* des′kant), *v.* 1 talk at great length; discourse. 2 sing or play a melody with another melody. —*n.* **a** part music. **b** melody to be played or sung with another melody. [< OF < Med. L, < L *dis-* + *cantus* song < *canere* sing]

de·scend (di send′), *v.* 1 go or come down from a higher place to a lower place. 2 go from earlier to later time. 3 go from greater to less. 4 lower oneself; stoop. 5 slope downward. 6 be handed down from parent to child. 7 make a sudden attack. [< OF < L, < *de-* + *scandere* climb] —**de·scend′a·ble,** *adj.*

de·scend·ant (di sen′dənt), *n.* 1 person born of a certain family or group. 2 offspring; child. —*adj.* Also, **descendent.** descending.

de·scent (di sent′), *n.* 1 a coming down or going down. 2 a downward slope. 3 way or passage down; means of descending. 4 family line; ancestry. 5 a sudden attack.

de·scribe (di skrīb′), *v.*, **-scribed, -scrib·ing.** 1 tell or write about. 2 give a picture or account of in words. 3 draw the outline of; trace. [< L, < *de-* + *scribere* write] —**de·scrib′a·ble,** *adj.* —**de·scrib′er,** *n.*

de·scrip·tion (di skrip′shən), *n.* 1 act of describing. 2 composition or account that describes or gives a picture in words. 3 kind; sort: *people of every description.* 4 act of drawing in outline.

de·scrip·tive (di skrip′tiv), *adj.* describing; using description. —**de·scrip′tive·ly,** *adv.* —**de·scrip′tive·ness,** *n.*

de·scry (di skrī′), *v.*, **-scried, -scry·ing.** catch sight of; be able to see; make out. [< OF *descrier* proclaim. See DIS-, CRY.]

des·e·crate (des′ə krāt), *v.*, **-crat·ed, -crat·ing.** disregard the sacredness of. [< *de-* + (con)*secrate*] —**des′e·crat′er, des′e·cra′tor,** *n.* —**des′e·cra′tion,** *n.*

de·seg·re·gate (dē seg′rə gāt), *v.*, **-gat·ed, -gat·ing.** 1 abolish segregation in. 2 of a place or institution, become desegregated.

de·seg·re·ga·tion (dē seg′rə gā′shən), *n.* abolishment of the practice of segregating blacks from whites, esp. in the U.S. public schools.

de·sen·si·tize (dē sen′sə tīz), *v.*, **-tized, -tiz·ing.** make less sensitive. —**de·sen′si·ti·za′tion,** *n.* —**de·sen′si·tiz′er,** *n.*

des·ert¹ (dez′ərt), *n.* 1 a dry, barren region, usually sandy and without trees. 2 region that is not inhabited or cultivated; wilderness. —*adj.* 1 dry; barren. 2 not inhabited or cultivated; wild. [< OF < Eccl.L *desertum,* (thing) abandoned, pp. See DESERT².]

de·sert² (di zèrt′), *v.* 1 go away and leave; abandon; forsake. 2 run away from duty. 3 leave military service without permission. [< F < LL *desertare* < L *deserere* abandon < *de-* DIS- + *serere* join] —**de·sert′er,** *n.*

de·sert³ (di zèrt′), *n.* Usually, **deserts.** what is deserved; suitable reward or punishment: *the robber got his just deserts in prison.* [< OF *deserte,* pp. of *deservir* DESERVE]

de·ser·tion (di zèr′shən), *n.* 1 a deserting, esp. in violation of duty or obligation. 2 state of being deserted.

de·serve (di zèrv′), *v.*, **-served, -serv·ing.** have a claim or right to; be worthy of. [< F < L *deservire* serve well < *de-* + *servire* serve] —**de·serv′er,** *n.*

de·serv·ed·ly (di zèr′vid li), *adv.* justly.

de·serv·ing (di zèr′ving), *adj.* 1 that deserves; worthy (of something). 2 worth helping.

des·ic·cate (des′ə kāt), *v.*, **-cat·ed, -cat·ing.** 1 dry thoroughly. 2 preserve by drying thoroughly. [< L, < *de-* out + *siccus* dry] —**des′ic·ca′tion,** *n.* —**des′ic·ca′tive,** *adj.*

de·sid·er·a·tum (di sid′ər ā′təm; -ä′təm), *n., pl.* **-ta** (-tə). something desired or needed. [< L, pp. of *desiderare* long for]

de·sign (di zīn′), *n.* 1 a drawing, plan, or sketch made to serve as a pattern: *design for a machine.* 2 arrangement of detail, form, and color in painting, etc.: *a wallpaper design.* 3 a plan in mind to be carried out. 4 intention. —*v.* 1 make a first sketch of; plan out. 2 make drawings, sketches, plans, etc. 3 form in the mind; contrive. [< F < L, < *de-* + *signum* mark]

des·ig·nate (*v.* dez′ig nāt; *adj.* dez′ig nit, -nāt), *v.*, **-nat·ed, -nat·ing,** *adj.* —*v.* 1 point out; indicate definitely. 2 name; entitle. 3 select for duty, office, etc.; appoint. —*adj.* appointed; selected. [< L *designatus,* pp. See DESIGN.] —**des′ig·na′tive,** *adj.* —**des′ig·na′tor,** *n.*

designated hitter, baseball player who bats for the pitcher for a whole game but does not play in the field.

des·ig·na·tion (dez′ig nā′shən), *n.* 1 act of designating. 2 a descriptive title; name. 3 appointment; selection.

de·sign·ed·ly (di zīn′id li), *adv.* purposely.

de·sign·er (di zīn′ər), *n.* 1 person who designs: *a dress designer.* 2 plotter;

schemer. —*adj.* 1 designed by and labeled as the work of a particular fashion designer. 2 made or altered for a particular purpose: *designer foods; designer drugs.*

de·sign·ing (di zīn′ing), *adj.* 1 scheming; plotting. 2 showing plan or forethought. —*n.* art of making designs. —**de·sign′ing·ly,** *adv.*

de·sir·a·ble (di zīr′ə bəl), *adj.* worth wishing for; worth having. —**de·sir′a·bil′i·ty, de·sir′a·ble·ness,** *n.* —**de·sir′a·bly,** *adv.*

de·sire (di zīr′), *v.,* –**sired,** –**sir·ing,** *n.* —*v.* 1 wish for; wish strongly for. 2 express a wish for; ask for. 3 crave sexually. —*n.* 1 wish; strong wish. 2 an expressed wish; request. 3 thing desired. 4 sexual craving; lust. [< OF < L *desiderare* long for]

de·sir·ous (di zīr′əs), *adj.* having or showing desire; full of desire; desiring.

de·sist (di zist′), *v.* stop; cease. [< OF < L, < *de-* + *sistere* stop]

desk (desk), *n.* 1 piece of furniture with a flat or sloping top on which to write or to rest books for reading. 2 lectern; pulpit. 3 **a** music stand. **b** position in an orchestra: *first cello desk.* 4 department or special location in an organization: *an information desk; the China desk at the State Department.* [< Med.L *desca* < Ital. *desco* < L *discus* quoit, DISH < Gk. *diskos*]

Des Moines (də moin′), capital of Iowa, in the central part.

des·o·late (*adj.* des′ə lit; *v.* des′ə lāt), *adj., v.,* –**lat·ed,** –**lat·ing.** —*adj.* 1 laid waste; devastated; barren. 2 not lived in; deserted. 3 unhappy; wretched; forlorn. 5 dreary; dismal. —*v.* 1 make unfit to live in; lay waste. 2 deprive of inhabitants. 3 make lonely, unhappy, or forlorn. [< L, < *de-* + *solus* alone] —**des′o·late·ly,** *adv.* —**des′o·late·ness,** *n.* —**des′o·lat′er, des′o·la′tor,** *n.*

des·o·la·tion (des′ə lā′shən), *n.* 1 act of making desolate. 2 a lonely or deserted condition. 3 great sadness; sorrow.

de·spair (di spār′), *n.* 1 loss of hope; hopelessness. 2 person or thing that causes despair. —*v.* lose hope; be without hope. [< OF < L, < *de-* + *sperare* to hope] —**de·spair′ing,** *adj.* —**de·spair′ing·ly,** *adv.* —**de·spair′ing·ness,** *n.*

des·patch (dis pach′), *v., n.* =dispatch.

des·per·a·do (des′pər ä′dō; –ä′dō), *n., pl.* –**does,** –**dos.** a bold, reckless criminal. [< OSp. See DESPERATE.]

des·per·ate (des′pər it), *adj.* 1 not caring what happens because hope is gone. 2 with little or no hope of improvement; very serious. 3 ready to run any risk. [< L *desperatus,* pp. See DESPAIR.] —**des′per·ate·ly,** *adv.* —**des′per·ate·ness,** *n.*

des·per·a·tion (des′pər ā′shən), *n.* act or fact of despairing; despair.

des·pi·ca·ble (des′pi kə bəl; des pik′ə bəl), *adj.* to be despised; contemptible. —**des′pi·ca·ble·ness,** *n.* —**des′pica·bly,** *adv.*

de·spise (di spīz′), *v.,* –**spised,** –**spis·ing.** look down on; feel contempt for. [< OF

< L, < *de-* down + *specere* look at] —**de·spis′er,** *n.*

de·spite (di spīt′), *n., v.,* –**spit·ed,** –**spit·ing,** *prep.* —*n.* 1 malice; spite. 2 insult; injury. —*v.* treat with contempt. —*prep.* in spite of. [< OF < L *despectus* a looking down upon < *de-* + *specere* look at]

de·spoil (di spoil′), *v.* rob; plunder. [< OF < L, < *de-* + *spoliare* strip < *spolium* armor, booty] —**de·spoil′er,** *n.* —**de·spoil′ment, de·spo′li·a′tion,** *n.*

de·spond (di spond′), *v.* lose heart, courage, or hope. [< L, < *de-* + *spondere* lose heart] —**de·spond′ing,** *adj.* —**de·spond′ing·ly,** *adv.*

de·spond·en·cy (di spon′dən si), **de·spond·ence** (–dəns), *n., pl.* –**cies;** –**ces.** loss of courage or hope. —**de·spond′ent,** *adj.*

des·pot (des′pət; –pot), *n.* 1 tyrant; oppressor. 2 monarch having unlimited power; absolute ruler. [< OF < Med.Gk. *despotes* master < Gk.]

des·pot·ic (des pot′ik), *adj.* of a despot; tyrannical. —**des·pot′i·cal·ly,** *adv.*

des·pot·ism (des′pət iz əm), *n.* 1 tyranny; oppression. 2 government by a monarch having unlimited power.

des·sert (di zėrt′), *n.* a course served at the end of a meal, such as pie, fruit, ice cream, etc. [< F, < *desservir* clear the table < *des-* (< L *dis-*) + *servir* serve < L]

des·ti·na·tion (des′tə nā′shən), *n.* 1 place to which a person or thing is going or is being sent. 2 a setting apart for a particular purpose.

des·tine (des′tən), *v.,* –**tined,** –**tin·ing.** 1 set apart for a particular purpose or use; intend. 2 cause by fate.

destined for, a intended for: *destined for glory.* **b** bound for: *ships destined for England.* [< OF < L *destinare* make fast, < *de-* + *stare* stand]

des·ti·ny (des′tə ni), *n., pl.* –**nies.** 1 what becomes of a person or thing in the end; one's lot or fortune. 2 what will happen in spite of all efforts to change or prevent it. 3 fate.

des·ti·tute (des′tə tüt; –tūt), *adj.* lacking necessary things such as food, clothing, and shelter.

destitute of, having no; without [< L, < *destituere* forsake < *de-* away + *statuere* put, place]

des·ti·tu·tion (des′tə tü′shən; –tū′–), *n.* 1 destitute condition; extreme poverty. 2 lack.

de·stroy (di stroi′), *v.* 1 break to pieces; make useless; ruin, spoil. 2 put an end to; do away with. 3 deprive of life; kill. 4 counteract the effect of; make void. [< OF < VL < L, < *de-* un- + *struere* pile, build] —**de·stroy′a·ble,** *adj.*

de·stroy·er (di stroi′ər), *n.* 1 person or thing that destroys. 2 a relatively small, very fast warship used to attack submarines, for escort duty, etc.

de·struct·i·ble (di struk′tə bəl), *adj.* capable of being destroyed. —**de·struct′i·bil′i·ty,** *n.*

de·struc·tion (di struk′shən), *n.* 1 act of destroying. 2 state of being destroyed. 3 cause or means of destroying.

de·struc·tive (di strukt′iv), *adj.* 1 tending to destroy. 2 causing destruction. 3 tearing down; not helpful. —**de·struc′tive·ly,** *adv.* —**de·struc′tive·ness,** *n.*

des·ue·tude (des′wə tüd; –tūd), *n.* disuse. [< F < L *desuetudo* < *de-* dis- + *suescere* accustom]

des·ul·to·ry (des′əl tô′ri; –tō′–), *adj.* 1 jumping from one thing to another; unconnected. 2 without aim or method. [< L *desultorius* of a leaper, ult. < *de-* down + *salire* leap] —**des′ul·to′ri·ly,** *adv.* —**des′ul·to′ri·ness,** *n.*

de·tach (di tach′), *v.* 1 loosen and remove; unfasten; separate. 2 send away on special duty. [< F, formed with *dé-* (< L *dis-*) after *attacher* ATTACH] —**de·tach′a·ble,** *adj.* —**de·tach′er,** *n.*

de·tached (di tacht′), *adj.* 1 separate from others; isolated. 2 not influenced by others or by one's own interests and prejudices.

de·tach·ment (di tach′mənt), *n.* 1 separation. 2 group of soldiers or ships sent on some special duty. 3 a standing apart; aloofness. 4 freedom from prejudice or bias; impartiality.

de·tail (*n.* di tāl′, dē′tāl; *v.* di tāl′), *n.* 1 a small or unimportant part. 2 a dealing with small things one by one. 3 a minor decoration or subordinate part in a building, picture, machine, etc. 4 a small group selected for or sent on some special duty. —*v.* 1 tell fully; give the particulars of. 2 select for or send on special duty.

in detail, part by part; fully. [< F, < *détailler* cut in pieces < *de-* + *tailler* cut]

de·tailed (di tāld′; dē′tāld), *adj.* 1 having many details. 2 exact.

de·tain (di tān′), *v.* 1 hold back; keep from going; delay. 2 keep in custody; confine. [< OF < L, < *de-* + *tenere* hold] —**de·tain′er,** *n.* —**de·tain′ment,** *n.*

de·tect (di tekt′), *v.* find out; discover. [< L *detectus* < *de-* un- + *tegere* cover] —**de·tect′a·ble, de·tect′i·ble,** *adj.*

de·tec·tion (di tek′shən), *n.* 1 a finding out; discovery. 2 a being found out or discovered.

de·tec·tive (di tek′tiv), *n.* policeman or other person whose work is finding information secretly, discovering who committed a crime, etc. —*adj.* pertaining to detectives and their work.

de·tec·tor (di tek′tər), *n.* person or thing that detects.

de·ten·tion (di ten′shən), *n.* 1 act of detaining. 2 state of being detained; delay. 3 confinement.

de·ter (di tėr′), *v.,* –**terred,** –**ter·ring.** discourage; keep back; hinder. [< L, < *de-* from + *terrere* frighten] —**de·ter′ment,** *n.*

de·ter·gent (di tėr′jənt), *adj.* cleansing. —*n.* a detergent substance. [< L, < *de-* off + *tergere* wipe]

de·te·ri·o·rate (di tir′i ə rāt), v., **-rat·ed, -rat·ing.** make or become worse; depreciate. [< L, < *deterior* worse] **—de·te′ri·o·ra′tion,** n. **—de·te′ri·o·ra′tive,** adj.

de·ter·mi·na·ble (di tėr′mə nə bəl), adj. capable of being settled or decided.

de·ter·mi·nant (di tėr′mə nənt), n. thing that determines. —adj. determining.

de·ter·mi·nate (di tėr′mə nit), adj. **1** with exact limits; fixed; definite. **2** settled; positive. **3** having the primary and each secondary axis ending in a flower or bud. **—de·ter′mi·nate·ly,** adv. **—de·ter′mi·nate·ness,** n.

de·ter·mi·na·tion (di tėr′mə nā′shən), n. **1** act of settling beforehand. **2** finding out the exact amount or kind, by weighing, measuring, or calculating. **3** result of finding out exactly; conclusion. **4** settlement; decision. **5** firmness of purpose.

de·ter·mi·na·tive (di tėr′mə nā′tiv; -nə tiv), adj. determining. —n. thing that determines. **—de·ter′mi·na′tive·ly,** adv. **—de·ter′mi·na′tive·ness,** n.

de·ter·mine (di tėr′mən), v., **-mined, -min·ing. 1** make up one's mind firmly; resolve. **2** settle; decide. **3** find out exactly; fix. **4** fix the geometrical position of. **5** be the deciding factor in reaching a certain result. **6** limit; define. [< OF < L *determinare* set limits to < *de-* + *terminus* end] **—de·ter′min·er,** n.

de·ter·mined (di tėr′mənd), adj. firm; resolute. **—de·ter′mined·ly,** adv. **—de·ter′mined·ness,** n.

de·ter·min·ism (di tėr′mən iz əm), n. doctrine that human actions and all events are the necessary results of antecedent causes. **—de·ter′min·ist,** n., adj.

de·ter·rent (di tėr′ənt; -ter′-), adj. deterring; restraining. —n. something that deters. **—de·ter′rence,** n.

de·test (di test′), v. dislike very much; hate. [< F < L *detestari* curse while calling the gods to witness < *de-* + *testis* witness] **—de·test′a·ble,** adj. **—de·test′a·bil′i·ty, de·test′a·ble·ness,** n. **—de·test′a·bly,** adv. **—de·test′er,** n.

de·tes·ta·tion (dē′tes tā′shən), n. **1** very strong dislike; hatred. **2** a detested person or thing.

de·throne (dē thrōn′), v., **-throned, -thron·ing.** deprive of the power to rule; remove from a throne; depose. **—de·throne′ment,** n. **—de·thron′er,** n.

det·o·nate (det′ə nāt), v., **-nat·ed, -nat·ing.** explode with a loud noise. [< L, < *de-* (intensive) + *tonare* thunder] **—det′o·na′tion,** n. **—det′o·na′tor,** n.

de·tour (dē′tur; di tùr′), n. **1** road that is used when the main or direct road cannot be traveled. **2** a roundabout way. —v. **1** use a detour. **2** cause to use a detour. [< F, < *détour* turn aside < *dé-* (< L *dis-*) + *tourner* turn]

de·tox (n. dē′toks, v. di toks′), n. Informal. =detoxification. —v. =detoxify.

de·tox·i·fi·ca·tion (di tok′sə fə kā′shən), n. **1** process of removing poison from. **2** a being detoxified. Also, **detoxication.**

de·tox·i·fy (di tok′sə fī), v., **-fied, -fy·ing. 1** remove poison or its effects from. **2** be detoxified. Also, **detoxicate.**

de·tract (di trakt′), v. take away. [< L *detractus* < *de-* away + *trahere* draw] **—de·trac′tion,** n. **—de·trac′tive,** adj. **—de·trac′tor,** n.

de·train (di trān′), v. get off a railroad train. **—de·train′ment,** n.

det·ri·ment (det′rə mənt), n. **1** damage; injury; harm. **2** something that causes damage or harm. [< L *detrimentum* < *de-* away + *terere* wear]

det·ri·men·tal (det′rə men′təl), adj. damaging; injurious; harmful. **—det′ri·men′tal·ly,** adv.

de·tri·tus (di trī′təs), n. particles of rock or other material worn away from a mass. [< L, a rubbing away]

deuce[1] (dūs; dūs), n. **1** in a game of cards or dice, two. **2** a playing card marked with a 2. **3** the side with two spots in dice. **4** a tie score at 40 each in a tennis game, or 5 games each in a set. [< OF *deus* two < L *duos,* accus. of *duo* two]

deuce[2] (dūs; dūs), interj. exclamation of annoyance meaning "bad luck," "the mischief," "the devil." [prob. < LG *duus* DEUCE[1], an unlucky throw at dice]

deu·ced (dū′sid, dū′-; düst, düst), adj. devilish; excessive. —adv. devilishly; excessively. **—deu′ced·ly,** adv.

Deut., Deuteronomy.

deu·te·ri·um (dü tir′i əm; dū-), n. an isotope of hydrogen, D, whose molecules weigh twice as much as those of ordinary hydrogen; heavy hydrogen. [< NL < Gk. *deutereion,* neut., having second place < *deuteros* second]

deu·ter·on (dü′tər on; dū′-), n. the nucleus of deuterium, consisting of one proton and one neutron that have parallel spins. [< Gk. *deuteron,* neut. of *deuteros* second (with ref. to deuterium as H[2])]

Deu·ter·on·o·my (dü′tər on′ə mi; dū′-), n. the fifth book of the Old Testament. [< L < Gk., < *deuteros* second + *nomos* law]

de·val·u·ate (dē val′yù āt), v., **-at·ed, -ating.** =devalue. **—de·val′u·a′tion,** n.

de·val·ue (dē val′ū), v., **-val·ued, -val·u·ing.** lessen the value of.

dev·as·tate (dev′əs tāt), v., **-tat·ed, -tat·ing.** make desolate; destroy; ravage. [< L, < *de-* + *vastus* waste] **—dev′as·tat′ing·ly,** adv. **—dev′as·ta′tion,** n. **—dev′as·ta′tor,** n.

de·vel·op (di vel′əp), v. **1** bring or come into being or activity; grow. **2** make or become bigger, better, fuller, more useful, etc. **3** Music. elaborate (a theme) by changes of rhythm, melody, or harmony. **4** make or become known; reveal. **5** treat with chemicals to bring out a photograph. [< F *développer* unwrap] **—de·vel′op·a·ble,** adj.

de·vel·op·er (di vel′əp ər), n. **1** person or thing that develops. **2** chemical used to bring out the picture on a photographic film.

de·vel·op·ment (di vel′əp mənt), n. **1** a developing. **2** a developed stage, state, or result. **3** housing built on open land or to replace older buildings. **—de·vel′op·men′tal,** adj.

de·vi·ant (dē′vi ənt), n. anyone or anything that diverges from what is considered the norm.

de·vi·ate (dē′vi āt), v., **-at·ed, -at·ing.** turn aside (from a way, course, rule, truth, etc.); diverge. [< LL, < *de-* aside + *via* way] **—de′vi·a′tion,** n. **—de′vi·a′tor,** n.

de·vice (di vīs′), n. **1** machine; apparatus. **2** plan; scheme; trick. **3** a pattern or an ornament. **4** picture or design on a coat of arms.

leave to one's own devices, leave to do as one thinks best. [fusion of ME *devis* separation, talk + *devise* design, emblem, plan; both < OF < L *divisus,* pp. of *dividere* DIVIDE]

dev·il (dev′əl), n., v., **-iled, -il·ing,** interj. —n. **1** an evil spirit; fiend; demon. **2** a wicked or cruel person. **3** a very clever, energetic, or reckless person. —v. **1** bother; tease; torment. **2** prepare (food) with hot seasoning. —interj. exclamation of disgust, anger, etc.

devil of a, devilish; confounded.

go to the devil, go to ruin.

like the devil, with great energy.

raise the devil, Informal. cause trouble; create a disturbance.

the Devil, Satan.

the devil to pay, much trouble ahead. [< L < Gk. *diabolos* slanderer < *dia-* across, against + *ballein* throw]

dev·iled (dev′əld), adj. highly seasoned: *deviled ham.*

dev·il·fish (dev′əl fish′), n., pl. **-fish·es** or (esp. collectively) **-fish. 1** a large, odd-shaped fish related to the shark; giant ray. **2** =octopus.

dev·il·ish (dev′əl ish; dev′lish), adj. **1** like a devil. **2** mischievous; daring. **3** very great; extreme. —adv. Colloq. extremely. **—dev′il·ish·ly,** adv. **—dev′il·ish·ness,** n.

dev·il·ment (dev′əl mənt), n. devilish behavior.

dev·il's advocate (dev′əlz), **1** person who argues against a popular position or cause or for an unpopular position or cause. **2** person in the Roman Catholic Church appointed to argue against a proposed canonization or beatification.

dev·il·try (dev′əl tri), n., pl. **-tries.** U.S. **1** wicked behavior. **2** daring behavior; mischief. **3** great cruelty or wickedness.

de·vi·ous (dē′vi əs), adj. **1** winding; twisting. **2** straying from the right course; not straightforward. [< L, < *de-* out of + *via* the way] **—de′vi·ous·ly,** adv. **—de′vi·ous·ness,** n.

de·vise (di vīz′), v., **-vised, -vis·ing,** n. —v. **1** think out; plan; contrive; invent. **2** give or leave (land, buildings, etc.) by a will. —n. **a** a giving or leaving of land, buildings, etc., by a will. **b** a will or part of a will doing this. **c** land, buildings, etc., given or left in this way. [< OF *deviser* dispose in portions, arrange, ult. < L *dividere* DIVIDE] —**de·vis′a·ble**, *adj.* —**de·vis′er, de·vi′sor**, *n.*

de·vis·ee (di vīz′ē′; dev′ə zē′), *n.* person to whom land, etc., is devised.

de·vi·tal·ize (dē vī′təl īz), *v.*, **-ized, -iz·ing.** take the life or vitality of. —**de·vi′·tal·i·za′tion**, *n.*

de·void (di void′), *adj.* lacking (*of*): *devoid of sense.* [< OF, < *des–* (< L *dis–*) + *voidier* VOID]

dev·o·lu·tion (dev′ə lü′shən), *n.* 1 transfer of (authority, responsibility, etc.) to another. 2 granting of self-government to a dependency.

de·volve (di volv′), *v.*, **-volved, -volv·ing.** 1 transfer (duty, work, etc.) to someone else. 2 be handed down to someone else; be transferred. [< L, < *de–* down + *volvere* roll] —**de·volve′ment**, *n.*

De·vo·ni·an (də vō′nē ən), *n.* 1 geological period of the Paleozoic era marked by the appearance of fish, amphibians, and wingless insects. 2 rocks formed during this period. —*adj.* of or having to do with the Devonian era or its rocks.

de·vote (di vōt′), *v.*, **-vot·ed, -vot·ing.** 1 give up (oneself, one's money, time, or efforts) to some person, purpose, or service. 2 dedicate; consecrate. [< L *devotus* < *de–* entirely + *vovere* vow] —**de·vote′ment**, *n.*

de·vot·ed (di vōt′id), *adj.* 1 loyal; faithful. 2 dedicated; consecrated. —**de·vot′ed·ly**, *adv.* —**de·vot′ed·ness**, *n.*

dev·o·tee (dev′ə tē′), *n.* person deeply devoted to something, such as a religion.

de·vo·tion (di vō′shən), *n.* 1 deep, steady affection; loyalty; faithfulness. 2 act of devoting or state of being devoted. **devotions,** religious worship; prayers. —**de·vo′tion·al**. —**de·vo′tion·al·ly**, *adv.*

de·vour (di vour′), *v.* 1 eat (usually said of animals). 2 eat like an animal; eat hungrily. 3 consume; waste; destroy: *a devouring disease.* 4 swallow up; engulf. 5 *Fig.* take in with eyes or ears in a hungry, greedy way: *devour a book.* [< OF < L, < *de–* down + *vorare* gulp] —**de·vour′er**, *n.* —**de·vour′ing·ly**, *adv.*

de·vout (di vout′), *adj.* 1 active in worship and prayer; religious. 2 devoted; earnest; sincere. [< OF < L *devotus*, pp. See DEVOTE.] —**de·vout′ly**, *adv.* —**de·vout′ness**, *n.*

dew (dü; dū), *n.* 1 moisture from the air that condenses and collects in small drops on cool surfaces during the night. 2 anything fresh or refreshing like dew. —*v.* wet with dew; moisten. [OE *dēaw*] —**dew′less**, *adj.*

dew·ber·ry (dü′ber′i; dū′-), *n., pl.* **-ries.** 1 a blackberry vine that grows along the ground. 2 fruit of one of these vines.

dew·claw (dü′klô′, dū–), *n.* useless claw or hoof on some animals.

dew·drop (dü′drop′; dū′-), *n.* a drop of dew.

dew·lap (dü′lap′; dū′-), *n.* a loose fold of skin under the throat of cattle and some other animals. [< dew (orig. and meaning uncert.) + lap < OE *læppa* pendulous piece)

dew point, temperature of the air at which dew begins to form.

dew·y (dü′i; dū′i), *adj.*, **dew·i·er, dew·i·est.** 1 wet with dew. 2 refreshing. —**dew′i·ness**, *n.*

dex·ter (deks′tər), *adj.* of or on the right-hand side. [< L, right]

dex·ter·i·ty (deks ter′ə ti), *n.* 1 skill in using the hands. 2 skill in using the mind; cleverness.

dex·ter·ous (deks′tər əs; –trəs), *adj.* 1 having or showing skill in using the hands. 2 having or showing skill in using the mind; clever. Also, **dextrous.** —**dex′ter·ous·ly**, *adv.* —**dex′ter·ous·ness**, *n.*

dex·tral (deks′trəl), *adj.* right; right-hand. —**dex·tral′i·ty**, *n.* —**dex′tral·ly**, *adv.*

dex·trose (deks′trōs), *n.* a sugar, $C_6H_{12}O_6$, less sweet than cane sugar; a form of glucose.

dex·trous (deks′trəs), *adj.* =dexterous. —**dex′trous·ly**, *adv.* —**dex′trous·ness**, *n.*

dg. or **dg,** decigram.

DH or **dh,** designated hitter.

di (dē), *n.* tone of the musical scale, intermediate between do and re.

di–, *prefix.* twice; double; twofold, as in *dioxide.* [< Gk. *dis*]

di·a·be·tes (dī′ə bē′tis; –tēz), *n.* disease in which the digestive system is unable to absorb normal amounts of sugar and starch. [< NL < Gk., a passer-through < *dia–* through + *bainein* go] —**di′a·bet′ic**, *adj., n.*

di·a·bol·ic (dī′ə bol′ik), **di·a·bol·i·cal** (–ə kəl), *adj.* 1 like the Devil; very cruel or wicked. 2 having to do with the Devil or devils. [< LL < Gk. *diabolikos.* See DEVIL.] —**di′a·bol′i·cal·ly**, *adv.*

di·a·crit·ic (dī′ə krit′ik), *adj.* diacritical. —*n.* a diacritical mark. [< Gk. *diakritikos* < *dia–* apart + *krinein* separate]

di·a·crit·i·cal (dī′ə krit′ə kəl), *adj.* used to distinguish. —**di′a·crit′i·cal·ly**, *adv.*

diacritical mark, mark like ¨ ^ ´ or ` placed over or under a letter to indicate pronunciation, etc.

di·a·dem (dī′ə dem), *n.* crown. [< L < Gk. *diadema* < *dia–* across + *deein* bind]

di·aer·e·sis (dī er′ə sis), *n., pl.* **-ses** (–sēz). =dieresis.

diag. 1 diagonal. 2 diagram.

di·ag·nose (dī′əg nōs′; –nōz′), *v.*, **-nosed, -nos·ing.** make a diagnosis of.

di·ag·no·sis (dī′əg nō′sis), *n., pl.* **-ses** (–sēz). 1 act or process of finding out what disease a person or animal has by examination and careful study of the symptoms. X rays and blood tests are used in diagnosis. 2 careful study of the facts about something to find out its essential features, faults, etc. 3 decision reached after a careful study of symp-

toms or facts. [< NL < Gk., < *dia–* apart + *gignoskein* learn to know] —**di′ag·nos′tic**, *adj.* —**di′ag·nos·ti′cian**, *n.*

di·ag·o·nal (dī ag′ə nəl), *n.* 1 a straight line that cuts across in a slanting direction, often from corner to corner. 2 any slanting line, row, course, etc. —*adj.* 1 taking the direction of a diagonal; slanting; oblique. 2 having slanting lines, ridges, etc. 3 connecting two corners that are not next to each other. [< L, < Gk. *diagonios* from angle to angle < *dia–* across + *gonia* angle] —**di·ag′o·nal·ly**, *adv.*

di·a·gram (dī′ə gram), *n., v.*, **-gramed, -gram·ing.** —*n.* an outline, a plan, a drawing, a figure, a chart, or a combination of any of these made to show clearly what a thing is or how it works. —*v.* make a diagram of. [< L < Gk. *diagramma* < *dia–* apart, out + *graphein* mark] —**di′a·gram·mat′ic, di′a·gram·mat′i·cal**, *adj.* —**di′a·gram·mat′i·cal·ly**, *adv.*

di·al (dī′əl), *n., v.*, **-aled, -al·ing.** —*n.* 1 a marked surface on which time is shown by a moving pointer or shadows. 2 disk with numbers, etc., on which the amount of water, pressure, etc., is shown by a pointer. 3 plate, disk, etc., of a radio with numbers, letters, etc., on it for tuning in to a radio station. 4 part of an automatic telephone used in making telephone calls. —*v.* 1 show on a telephone dial. 2 call by means of a telephone dial. [appar. < Med.L (*rota*) *dialis* daily (wheel) < L *dies* day]

dial., dialect; dialectal.

di·a·lect (dī′ə lekt), *n.* 1 form of speech characteristic of a fairly definite region: *the Scottish dialect.* 2 words and pronunciations used by certain professions, classes of people, etc. 3 one of a group of closely related languages. Some of the dialects descended from the Latin language are French, Italian, Spanish, and Portuguese. [< L < Gk. *dialektos*, ult. < *dia–* between + *legein* speak]

di·a·lec·tal (dī′ə lek′təl), *adj.* of a dialect; like that of a dialect. —**di′a·lec′tal·ly**, *adv.*

di·a·lec·tic (dī′ə lek′tik), *n.* 1 art or practice of logical discussion. 2 Also, **dialectics.** the principles of logic. —*adj.* 1 pertaining to logical discussion. 2 dialectal.

di·a·lec·ti·cian (dī′ə lek tish′ən), *n.* person skilled in dialectic or dialectics; logician.

di·a·logue, di·a·log (dī′ə lôg; –log), *n.* 1 conversation. 2 a literary work in the form of a conversation. 3 conversation in a play, story, etc. [< L < Gk., < *dia-* between + *logos* speech] —**di′a·logu′er**, *n.*

di·al·y·sis (dī al′ə sis), *n., pl.* **-ses** (–sēz). 1 separation of crystalloids from colloids in solution by diffusion through a membrane. 2 separation of waste matter from the blood as a treatment for kidney failure. [< Gk., < *dia-* apart + *lyein* loose] —**di·a·lyt′ic,** *adj.*

diam., diameter.

di·a·mag·net·ic (dī′ə mag net′ik), *adj.* repelled by a magnet. —**di′a·mag·net′i·cal·ly,** *adv.* —**di′a·mag′net·ism,** *n.*

di·am·e·ter (dī am′ə tər), *n.* **1** a straight line passing from one side to the other through the center of a circle, sphere, etc. **2** the length of such a line; width; thickness. [< OF < L < Gk., < *dia-* across + *metron* measure]

di·a·met·ric (dī′ə met′rik), **di·a·met·ri·cal** (–rə kəl), *adj.* **1** of or along a diameter. **2** exactly opposite. —**di′a·met′ri·cal·ly,** *adv.*

dia·mond (dī′mənd; dī′ə–), *n.* **1** a form of pure carbon in crystals, the hardest known substance, used as a precious stone. **2** a plane figure shaped like this ◊. **3** a playing card with one or more red designs like a diamond on it. **4** space inside the lines that connect the bases in baseball. —*adj.* made of diamonds.

diamond in the rough, person having good qualities but lacking refinement. [< OF < Med.L *diamas,* alter. of L *adamas* ADAMANT]

dia·mond·back (dī′mənd bak′; dī′ə–), *n.* **1** any rattlesnake with diamond-shaped markings on its back. **2** Also, **diamondback terrapin.** turtle that has diamond-shaped markings on its shell.

Di·an·a (dī an′ə), *n.* the Roman goddess of the hunt and of the moon and protectress of women.

di·a·pa·son (dī′ə pā′zən; –sən), *n. Music.* **1** melody, strain. **2** the whole range of a voice or instrument. **3** either of two principal stops in an organ. [< L < Gk., < *dia pason (chordon)* across all (the notes of the scale)]

di·a·per (dī′ə pər; dī′pər), *n.* piece of cloth or other absorbent material used as part of a baby's underclothing. —*v.* put a diaper on. [< OF < Med.Gk. *diaspros* < *dia-* (intensive) + *aspros* white]

di·aph·a·nous (dī af′ə nəs), *adj.* transparent. [< Med.L < Gk., < *dia-* through + *phainein* show] —**di·aph′a·nous·ly,** *adv.*

di·a·phragm (dī′ə fram), *n.* **1** a partition of muscles and tendons separating the cavity of the chest from the cavity of the abdomen. **2** a vibrating disk in a telephone. **3** device for controlling the light entering a camera, microscope, etc. **4** contraceptive device. —*v.* **1** furnish with a diaphragm. **2** act upon by a diaphragm. [< LL < Gk. *diaphragma* < *dia-* across + *phrassein* fence] —**di′a·phrag·mat′ic,** *adj.*

di·ar·rhe·a (dī′ə rē′ə), *n.* too many and too loose movements of the bowels. [< L < Gk., < *dia-* through + *rheein* flow]

di·a·ry (dī′ə ri), *n., pl.* **-ries. 1** account written down each day, of what one has done, thought, etc. **2** book for keeping such an account, with a blank space for each day of the year. [< L *diarium* < *dies* day] —**di′a·rist,** *n.*

di·a·stase (dī′ə stās), *n.* enzyme that changes starch into dextrin and maltose during digestion, germination of seeds, etc. [< F < Gk. *diastasis* separation < *dia-* apart + *sta-* stand] —**di′a·stat′ic,** *adj.*

di·as·to·le (dī as′tə lē), *n.* **1** the normal, rhythmical dilation of the heart, esp. that of the ventricles. **2** the lengthening of a syllable which is regularly short. [< LL < Gk., expansion < *dia-* apart + *stellein* send] —**di·as·tol′ic,** *adj.*

di·as·tro·phism (dī as′trə fiz əm), *n.* action of the forces which have caused the deformation of the earth's crust, producing continents, mountains, etc. [< Gk. *diastrophe* distortion < *dia-* apart + *strephein* twist] —**di′a·stroph′ic,** *adj.*

di·a·ther·my (dī′ə thėr′mi), *n.* **1** method of treating diseases by heating the tissues beneath the skin with an electric current. **2** apparatus for doing this. [< F < Gk. *dia-* through + *therme* heat] —**di′a·ther′mic,** *adj.*

di·a·tom (dī′ə tom; –tem), *n.* anyone of the microscopic, one-celled aquatic algae that have hard shells. —**di′a·to·ma′ceous,** *adj.*

di·a·tom·ic (dī′ə tom′ik), *adj.* **1** having two atoms in each molecule. **2** =bivalent.

di·a·ton·ic (dī′ə ton′ik), *adj.* of or using the tones of a standard major or minor scale. [< L < Gk., < *dia-* through + *tonos* tone]

di·a·tribe (dī′ə trīb), *n.* a bitter and violent denunciation of some person or thing. [< L < Gk. *diatribe* pastime, study, discourse < *dia-* away + *tribein* wear]

di·ba·sic (dī ba′sik), *adj.* having two hydrogen atoms that can be replaced by two atoms or radicals of a base in forming salts.

dib·ble (dib′əl), *n., v.,* **-bled, -bling.** —*n.* a pointed tool for making holes in the ground for seeds, young plants, etc. —*v.* make a hole in (the ground) with or as with a dibble. —**dib′bler,** *n.*

dice (dīs), *n. pl., sing.* **die,** *v.,* **diced, dic-ing.** —*n.* **1** small cubes with a different number of spots (one to six) on each side, used in playing games and gambling. **2** game played with dice. **3** small cubes. —*v.* **1** play dice. **2** cut into small cubes.

load the dice, *Informal.* make sure of the outcome ahead of time.

no dice, a no; refusal. **b** in vain. —**dic′er,** *n.*

dic·ey (dī′sē), *adj. Informal.* uncertain; risky.

di·chot·o·my (dī kot′ə mi), *n., pl.* **-mies. 1** division into two parts. **2** branching by repeated divisions into two parts. [< L < Gk. *dichotomos* cut in half < *dicha* in two + *temnein* cut] —**di·chot′o·mous, di·cho·tom′ic,** *adj.*

di·chrom·ic (dī krō′mik), *adj.* having or showing only two colors.

di·chro·mat·ic (dī′krō mat′ik), *adj.* **1** having two colors. **2** showing two color phases. **3** of or having dichromatism.

di·chro·ma·tism (dī′krō′mə tizm), *n.* **1** quality or condition of being dichromatic. **2** color blindness where only two colors are seen.

Dick·ens (dik′ənz), *n.* **Charles,** 1812–70, English novelist.

dick·ens (dik′ənz), *n., interj.* =devil.

dick·er (dik′ər), *v.* trade by barter or by petty bargaining; haggle. —*n.* a petty bargain. [< *dicker,* n., a lot of ten hides]

dick·ey, dick·y, or **dick·ie** (dik′i), *n., pl.* **dick·eys; dick·ies; dick·ies. 1** shirt front that can be detached. **2** any small bird.

di·cot·y·le·don (dī kot′ə lē′dən; dī′kot–), *n.* a flowering plant that has two seed leaves. Also, **dicot.** —**di·cot′y·le′don·ous,** *adj.*

dict., **1** dictator. **2** dictionary.

dic·ta (dik′tə), *n., pl.* of **dictum.**

dic·tate (*v.* dik′tāt, dik tāt′; *n.* dik′tāt), *v.,* **-tat·ed, -tat·ing,** *n.* —*v.* **1** say or read (something) aloud for another person or other persons to write down. **2** command with authority; give orders that must be obeyed. —*n.* direction or order that is to be carried out or obeyed. [< L *dictatus,* pp. of *dictare* say often < *dicere* tell, say]

dic·ta·tion (dik tā′shən), *n.* **1** act of saying or reading (something) aloud for another person or persons to write down. **2** words said or read aloud to be written down. **3** act of commanding with authority. —**dic·ta′tion·al,** *adj.*

dic·ta·tor (dik′tā tər; dik tā′–), *n.* **1** person exercising absolute authority, esp. over a country. **2** one who dictates. —**dic′ta·tor·ship′,** *n.*

dic·ta·to·ri·al (dik′tə tô′ri əl; –tō′–), *adj.* **1** of or like that of a dictator. **2** imperious; domineering; overbearing. —**dic′ta·to′ri·al·ly,** *adv.*

dic·tion (dik′shən), *n.* **1** manner of expressing ideas in words; style of speaking or writing. **2** manner of using the voice in speaking; the utterance or enunciation of words.

dic·tion·ar·y (dik′shən er′i), *n., pl.* **-ar·ies.** book containing a selection of the words of a language or of some special subject, arranged alphabetically, with explanations of their meanings and other information about them.

dic·tum (dik′təm), *n., pl.* **-tums, -ta** (–tə). **1** a formal comment; authoritative opinion. **2** maxim; saying. [< L, (thing) said, pp. of *dicere* say]

did (did), *v.* pt. of **do**[1].

di·dac·tic (dī dak′tik; di–), **di·dac·ti·cal** (–tə kəl), *adj.* **1** intended to instruct. **2** inclined to instruct others; teacherlike. [< Gk. *didaktikos* < *didaskein* teach] —**di·dac′ti·cal·ly,** *adv.* **di·dac′ti·cism,** *n.*

did·dle (did′əl), *v.,* **-dled, -dling.** *Informal.* **1** waste (time). **2** swindle. **3** ruin; undo.

diddle away, waste a small amount at a time. —**did′dler,** *n.*

did·n't (did′ənt), did not.

didst (didst), *v. Archaic.* did. "Thou didst" means "You did."

die[1] (dī), v., **died, dy·ing. 1** cease to live; stop living; become dead. **2** come to an end; lose force or strength; stop. **3** lose spiritual life. **4** suffer as if dying. **5** want very much; be very desirous.

die away or **down,** stop or end little by little; lose force or strength gradually.

die hard, a resist to the very end. **b** persist.

die off, die one after another until all are gone.

die out, a lose force or strength gradually. **b** cease or end completely. [OE *diegan*]

die[2] (dī), n., pl. **dice** for 1, **dies** for 2, v., **died, die·ing. —n. 1** one of a set of dice. **2** any tool or apparatus for shaping, cutting, or stamping things. —v. to shape with a die.

the die is cast, the decision is made and cannot be changed. [< OF < L *datum* (thing) given (i.e., by fortune), pp. of *dare* give]

di·e·cious (dī ē′shəs), adj. =dioecious. —**di·e′cious·ly,** adv.

die·hard (dī′härd′), adj. resisting to the very end; refusing to give in. —n. person who resists vigorously to the end.

di·e·lec·tric (dī′i lek′trik), adj. conveying electricity otherwise than by conduction; nonconducting: *dry air is dielectric.* —n. a dielectric substance, such as glass, rubber, or wood. —**di′e·lec′tri·cal·ly,** adv.

di·er·e·sis (dī er′ə sis), n., pl. **-ses** (-sēz). two dots (¨) placed over the second of two consecutive vowels to indicate that the second vowel is to be pronounced in a separate syllable, as in coöperate. Also, **diaeresis.** [< LL < Gk. *diairesis* separation, division < *dia-* apart + *haireein* take] —**di′e·ret′ic,** adj.

die·sel engine or **motor** (dē′zəl; -səl), an internal-combustion engine that burns oil with heat caused by the compression of air.

di·et[1] (dī′ət), n., v., **-et·ed, -et·ing. —n. 1** the usual food and drink for a person or animal. **2** a special selection of food and drink eaten during sickness, or to gain or lose weight. —v. keep to a diet. [< OF < L < Gk. *diaita* way of life] —**di′et·er,** n.

di·et[2] (dī′ət), n. **1** a formal assembly. **2** the national lawmaking body in certain countries. [< Med.L *dieta* day's work, session of councilors, ult. identical with *diet*[1] but infl. by L *dies* day]

di·e·tar·y (dī′ə ter′i), adj., n., pl. **-tar·ies.** —adj. having to do with diet. —n. system of diet.

di·e·tet·ic (dī′ə tet′ik), **di·e·tet·i·cal** (-ə kəl), adj. having to do with diet. —**di′e·tet′i·cal·ly,** adv.

di·e·tet·ics (dī′ə tet′iks), n. science that deals with the amount and kinds of food needed by the body.

di·e·ti·tian, di·e·ti·cian (dī′ə tish′ən), n. person trained to plan meals that have the proper proportion of various kinds of food.

dif., difference; different.

dif·fer (dif′ər), v. **1** be unlike; be different. **2** have or express a different opinion; disagree.

differ from, a be unlike; disagree. **b** vary. [< F < L *differe* set apart, differ < *dis-* apart + *ferre* carry]

dif·fer·ence (dif′ər əns; dif′rəns), n., v., **-enced, -enc·ing. —n. 1** condition of being different. **2** way of being different; point in which people or things are different. **3** amount by which one quantity is different from another. **4** condition of having a different opinion; disagreement. **5** dispute. —v. make different.

make a difference, a give different treatment. **b** have an effect or influence; matter.

split the difference, a divide what is left in half. **b** compromise.

dif·fer·ent (dif′ər ənt; dif′rənt), adj. **1** not alike; not like. **2** not the same; separate; distinct. **3** not like others or most others; unusual. —**dif′fer·ent·ly,** adv.

dif·fer·en·tial (dif′ər en′shəl), adj. **1** of a difference; showing a difference; depending on a difference. **2** distinguishing; distinctive. **3** pertaining to distinguishing characteristics or specific differences. **4** *Math.* pertaining to or involving differentials: *differential calculus.* **5** *Physics.* concerning the difference of two or more motions, pressures, etc. —n. **1** a differential duty or rate; the difference involved. **2** *Math.* an infinitesimal difference between consecutive values of a variable quantity. **3** arrangement of gears in an automobile that allows one of the rear wheels to turn faster than the other in going round a corner or curve. —**dif′fer·en′tial·ly,** adv.

dif·fer·en·ti·ate (dif′ər en′shi āt), v., **-at·ed, -at·ing. 1** make different. **2** become different. **3** make a distinction between. —**dif′fer·en′ti·a′tion,** n. —**dif′fer·en′ti·a′tor,** n.

dif·fi·cult (dif′ə kult; -kəlt), adj. **1** hard to understand. **2** hard to deal with, get along with, or please. —**dif′fi·cult·ly,** adv.

dif·fi·cul·ty (dif′ə kul′ti; -kəl ti), n., pl. **-ties. 1** fact or condition of being difficult. **2** hard work; much effort. **3** trouble. **4** financial trouble. **5** thing that is difficult; obstacle. **6** disagreement. [< L *difficultas* < *difficilis* hard < *dis-* + *facilis* easy]

dif·fi·dent (dif′ə dənt), adj. lacking in self-confidence; shy. —**dif′fi·dence,** n. —**dif′fi·dent·ly,** adv. [< L, ult. < *dis-* + *fidere* trust]

dif·fract (di frakt′), v. break up by diffraction. [< L *diffractus* < *dis-* up + *frangere* break]

dif·frac·tion (di frak′shən), n. **1** a breaking up of a ray of light into a series of light and dark bands or into colored bands of the spectrum. **2** a similar

breaking up of sound waves, electricity, etc.

dif·frac·tive (di frak′tiv), adj. causing or pertaining to diffraction. —**dif·frac′tive·ly,** adv. —**dif·frac′tive·ness,** n.

dif·fuse (v. di fūz′; adj. di fūs′), v., **-fused, -fus·ing,** adj. —v. **1** spread out so as to cover a larger space or surface; scatter widely. **2** mix together by spreading into one another, as gases and liquids do. —adj. **1** not drawn together at a single point; spread out. **2** using many words where a few would do. [< L *diffusus* < *dis-* in every direction + *fundere* pour] —**dif·fuse′ly,** adv. —**dif·fuse′ness,** n. —**dif·fus′er, dif·fu′sor,** n.

dif·fu·sion (di fū′zhən), n. **1** act or fact of diffusing. **2** a being widely spread or scattered; diffused condition. **3** a mixing together of the molecules of gases, etc. by spreading into one another. **4** use of too many words; wordiness.

dif·fu·sive (di fū′siv), adj. **1** tending to diffuse. **2** showing diffusion. **3** using too many words; wordy. —**dif·fu′sive·ly,** adv. —**dif·fu′sive·ness,** n.

dig (dig), v., **dug, dig·ging,** n. —v. **1** use a shovel, spade, hands, claws, or snout in making a hole or in turning over the ground. **2** make (a hole, cellar, etc.) by removing material. **3** get by digging: *dig clams.* **4** make a careful search or inquiry (for information or into some author). **5** understand; comprehend. —n. **1** act of digging. **2** *Fig.* a thrust or poke; a sarcastic remark. **3** *Informal.* archaeological excavation.

dig in, a dig trenches for protection. **b** work hard. **c** establish oneself in a position; stubbornly resist moving or changing. **d** eat with enthusiasm.

dig into, *Informal.* **a** work hard at. **b** hand over, esp. after having been asked more than once: *dig into his pockets.*

dig up, a unearth. **b** excavate. **c** discover; uncover. [ME *dygge(n),* prob. < F *diguer* < Gmc.]

di·gest (v. də jest′, dī-; n. dī′jest), v. **1** change (food) in the stomach and intestines so that the body can absorb it. **2** undergo this process. **3** understand and absorb mentally. **4** condense; summarize. —n. information condensed; summary: *a digest of law.* [< L *digestus,* pp. of *digerere* separate, dissolve < *dis-* apart + *gerere* carry] —**di·gest′er,** n.

di·gest·i·ble (də jes′tə bəl; dī-), adj. capable of being digested; easily digested. —**di·gest′i·bil′i·ty,** n.

di·ges·tion (də jes′chən; dī-), n. **1** the digesting of food. **2** ability to digest. **3** act of digesting.

di·ges·tive (də jes′tiv; dī-), adj. **1** of or for digestion. **2** helping digestion. —n. something that aids digestion.

dig·ger (dig′ər), n. **1** person that digs. **2** the part of a machine that turns up the ground. **3** any tool for digging.

dig·gings (dig′ingz), n. pl. **1** place where digging is being done, as an archaeological site. **2** material that is dug out. **3** place to live.

dig·it (dij′it), *n.* **1** finger or toe. **2** any of the figures 0, 1, 2, 3, 4, 5, 6, 7, 8, 9 Sometimes 0 is not called a digit. [< L *digitus* finger]

dig·it·al (dij′ə təl), *adj.* **1** of a digit or digits. **2** having digits. **3** of or having to do with a binary code. —*n.* key of an organ, piano, etc., played with the fingers. —**dig′it·al·ly,** *adv.*

digital camera, an electronic camera that takes picture in digital form.

digital computer, kind of computer which uses numbers, esp. as a binary code, to carry out instructions and process information.

dig·i·tal·is (dij′ə tal′is; –tā′lis), *n.* **1** medicine used for stimulating the heart, obtained from the leaves and seeds of the foxglove. **2** foxglove. [< L, < *digitus* finger; from shape of corolla]

dig·i·tate (dij′ə tāt), **dig·i·tat·ed** (–tāt′id), *adj.* **1** having fingers or toes. **2** having radiating divisions like fingers. —**dig′i·tate·ly,** *adv.*

dig·i·ti·za·tion (dij′ə tə zā′shən), *n.* a converting into digital form.

dig·i·tize (dij′ə tīz), *v.,* **–ized, –iz·ing. 1** convert to digital form. **2** use the fingers to count or manipulate something.

dig·ni·fied (dig′nə fīd), *adj.* having dignity; noble; stately. —**dig′ni·fied′ly,** *adv.*

dig·ni·fy (dig′nə fī), *v.,* **–fied, –fy·ing. 1** give dignity to; make noble, worthwhile, or worthy. **2** give a high-sounding name to. [< OF < L, < *dignus* worthy + *facere* make]

dig·ni·tar·y (dig′nə ter′i), *n., pl.* **–tar·ies.** person who has a position of honor.

dig·ni·ty (dig′nə ti), *n., pl.* **–ties. 1** proud and self-respecting character or manner; stateliness. **2** degree of worth, honor, or importance. **3** a high office, rank, or title. **4** worth; nobleness. [< OF < L, < *dignus* worthy]

di·graph (dī′graf; –gräf), *n.* two letters used together to spell a single sound, as *ea* in *each* or *head.* —**di·graph′ic,** *adj.*

di·gress (də gres′; dī–), *v.* turn aside; get off the main subject in talking or writing. [< L *digressus* < *dis–* aside + *gradi* to step]

di·gres·sion (də gresh′ən; dī–), *n.* a turning aside; a getting off the main subject in talking or writing. —**di·gres′sion·al,** *adj.*

di·gres·sive (də gres′iv; dī–), *adj.* tending to digress; digressing. —**di·gres′sive·ly,** *adv.* —**di·gres′sive·ness,** *n.*

di·he·dral (dī hē′drəl), *adj.* **1** having two plane surfaces. **2** formed by two plane surfaces. **3** making a dihedral angle. —*n.* the figure formed by two intersecting plane surfaces. [< Gk. *di–* two + *hedra* seat] —**di·he′dral·ly,** *adv.*

dike (dīk), *n., v.,* **diked, dik·ing.** —*n.* **1** a bank of earth or a dam built as a defense against flooding by a river or the sea. **2** ditch or channel for water. **3** a fissure in a stratum filled with deposited matter. —*v.* **1** provide with dikes. **2** drain with a ditch or channel for water. Also, **dyke.** [< Scand. *dīk;* akin to DITCH] —**dik′er,** *n.*

Di·lan·tin (dī lan′tin), *n. Trademark.* a white, powdery drug, $C_{15}H_{11}N_2O_2Na$, used in controlling epilepsy.

di·lap·i·dat·ed (də lap′ə dāt′id), *adj.* falling to pieces; partly ruined or decayed through neglect. [< L *dilapidatus,* pp. of *dilapidare* lay low (with stones) < *dis–* (intensive) + *lapidare* to stone < *lapis* stone]

di·lap·i·da·tion (də lap′ə dā′shən), *n.* a falling to pieces; decayed condition.

dil·a·ta·tion (dil′ə tā′shən; dī′lə–), *n.* =dilation.

di·late (dī lāt′; də–), *v.,* **–lat·ed, –lat·ing. 1** make or become larger or wider. **2** speak or write in a very complete or detailed manner. **3** set forth at length. [< L, < *dis–* apart + *latus* wide] —**di·lat′a·ble,** *adj.* —**di·la′tor,** *n.*

di·la·tion (dī lā′shən; də–), *n.* **1** act of dilating; enlargement; widening. **2** dilated condition. **3** a dilated part.

dil·a·to·ry (dil′ə tô′ri; –tō–), *adj.* **1** tending to delay; not prompt. **2** causing delay. —**dil′a·to′ri·ly,** *adv.* —**dil′a·to′ri·ness,** *n.*

di·lem·ma (də lem′ə; dī–), *n.* **1** situation requiring a choice between two evils. **2** any perplexing situation; a difficult choice. **3** argument forcing an opponent to choose one of two alternatives equally unfavorable to him. [< LL < Gk., < *di–* two + *lemma* premise]

dil·et·tan·te (dil′ə tan′tē; –tänt′), *n., pl.* **–tes, –ti** (–tē), *adj.* —*n.* **1** lover of the fine arts. **2** person who follows some art or science as an amusement or in a trifling way. **3** trifler. —*adj.* having to do with dilettantes. [< Ital., < *dilettare* DELIGHT] —**dil′et·tant′ish,** *adj.* —**dil′et·tant′ism,** *n.*

dil·i·gence (dil′ə jəns), *n.* a working hard; careful effort; being diligent; industry. [< F < L *diligentia.* See DILIGENT.]

dil·i·gent (dil′ə jənt), *adj.* **1** hard-working; industrious. **2** careful and steady. [< L *diligens,* ppr. of *diligere* value highly, love < *dis–* apart + *legere* choose] —**dil′i·gent·ly,** *adv.*

dill (dil), *n.* **1** spicy seeds or leaves used to flavor pickles. **2** plant that they grow on. [OE *dile*]

dill pickle, a cucumber pickle flavored with dill.

dil·ly (dil′i), *n., pl.* **–lies.** *Slang.* person or thing that is unique or outstanding.

dil·ly-dal·ly (dil′i dal′i), *v.,* **–lied, –ly·ing.** waste time; loiter; trifle.

di·lute (də lüt′; dī–), *v.,* **–lut·ed, –lut·ing,** *adj.* —*v.* **1** make weaker or thinner by adding water or some other liquid. **2** weaken; lessen. **3** become diluted. —*adj.* weakened or thinned by the addition of water or other liquid. [< L, < *dis–* apart + *luere* wash] —**di·lute′ness,** *n.*

di·lu·tion (də lü′shən; dī–), *n.* **1** act of diluting. **2** fact or state of being diluted. **3** something diluted.

di·lu·vi·al (də lü′vi əl; dī–), **di·lu·vi·an** (–ən), *adj.* of, having to do with, or caused by a flood. [< L, < *diluvium* DELUGE]

dim (dim), *adj.,* **dim·mer, dim·mest,** *v.,* **dimmed, dim·ming.** —*adj.* **1** not bright; not clear; not distinct. **2** not clearly seen, heard, or understood. **3** not seeing, hearing, or understanding clearly. —*v.* make or become dim. [OE *dimm*] —**dim′ly,** *adv.* —**dim′ness,** *n.*

dim., dimin., **1** diminuendo. **2** diminutive.

dime (dīm), *n.* a coin of the United States and of Canada, worth 10 cents.

a dime a dozen, very cheap or plentiful. [< OF < L *decima (pars)* tenth (part) < *decem* ten]

di·men·sion (də men′shən), *n.* **1** measurement of length, breadth, or thickness. **2** size; extent. [< F < L *dimensio* < *dis–* out + *metiri* measure] —**di·men′sion·al,** *adj.* —**di·men′sionless,** *adj.*

di·min·ish (də min′ish), *v.* **1** make or become smaller in size, amount, or importance; lessen; reduce. **2** lessen in esteem; degrade. **3** cause to taper. **4** *Music.* lessen (an interval) by a half step. [blend of *diminue* < L, < *dis–* (intensive) + *minuere* lessen) and *minish* (< OF < VL *minutiare,* ult. < L *minutus* small)] —**di·min′ish·a·ble,** *adj.*

di·min·u·en·do (də min′yü en′dō), *n., pl.* **–dos,** *adj., adv.* —*n.* **1** a gradual lessening of loudness. **2** passage to be played or sung with a diminuendo. —*adj., adv.* with a diminuendo. [< Ital., ppr. of *diminuire* diminish]

dim·i·nu·tion (dim′ə nü′shən; –nū′–), *n.* a diminishing; a lessening; decrease.

di·min·u·tive (də min′yə tiv), *adj.* **1** small; tiny. **2** *Gram.* expressing smallness or affection. —*n.* **1** a small person or thing. **2** word or part of a word expressing smallness. The suffixes *–let* and *–kin* are diminutives. —**di·min′u·tive·ly,** *adv.* —**di·min′u·tive·ness,** *n.*

dim·i·ty (dim′ə ti), *n., pl.* **–ties.** a thin cotton cloth woven with heavy threads at intervals in stripes or checks, used for dresses, curtains, etc. [< Ital. < Gk. *dimitos* of double thread < *di–* double + *mitos* warp thread]

dim·mer (dim′ər), *n.* **1** person or thing that dims. **2** device that dims an electric light or automobile headlight.

dim·ple (dim′pəl), *n., v.,* **–pled, –pling.** —*n.* **1** a small hollow, usually in the cheek or chin. **2** any small, hollow place. —*v.* **1** make or show dimples in. **2** form dimples. [ME *dympull*]

dim sum, Chinese steamed dumplings, filled with meat, vegetables, etc. [< Cantonese *dim sum*]

dim·wit (dim′wit′), *n. Informal.* stupid or foolish person. —**dim′wit′ted,** *adj.* —**dim′wit′ted·ly,** *adv.* —**dim′wit′ted·ness,** *n.*

din (din), *n., v.,* **dinned, din·ning.** —*n.* a loud, confused noise that lasts. —*v.* **1** make a din. **2** strike with din. **3** say over and over. [OE *dynn*]

dine (dīn), *v.,* **dined, din·ing. 1** eat dinner. **2** give a dinner to or for.

dine out, eat dinner away from home. [< F *dîner* < VL *disjejunare* to breakfast < *dis–* + *jejunium* fast]

din·er (dīn'ər), *n.* **1** person who is eating dinner. **2** a railroad car in which meals are served. **3** restaurant, esp. one shaped like such a car.

di·nette (dī net'), *n.* a small dining room.

ding (ding), *v.* make a sound like a bell; ring continuously. —*n.* **1** sound made by a bell. **2** small dent or scratch on the body of a car, surfboard, etc. [imit.]

ding·bat (ding'bat), *n. Slang.* **1** gadget. **2** odd or stupid person.

ding-dong (ding'dông'; –dong'), *n.* sound made by a bell or anything like a bell; continuous ringing. [imit.]

din·ghy (ding'gi), *n., pl.* **–ghies. 1** a small rowboat. **2** a small boat used as a tender by a large boat. [< Hind. *diṅgī*]

din·go (ding'gō), *n., pl.* **–goes.** Australian wild dog that hunts alone or in packs. [< a native name]

din·gy (din'ji), *adj.,* **–gi·er, –gi·est.** dirty-looking; not bright and fresh; dull. —**din'gi·ly,** *adv.* —**din'gi·ness,** *n.*

dining car, a railroad car in which meals are served.

dining room, room in which meals are served.

dink·y (dingk'i), *adj.,* **dink·i·er, dink·i·est.** small; insignificant.

din·ner (din'ər), *n.* **1** the main meal of the day. **2** a formal meal in honor of some person or occasion. [< F *dîner* dine; inf. used as n.]

di·no·saur (dī'nə sôr), *n.* any of a group of extinct reptiles. [< NL < Gk. *deinos* terrible + *sauros* lizard]

dint (dint), *n.* **1** force. **2** =dent. —*v.* =dent. [OE *dynt*] —**dint'less,** *adj.*

di·oc·e·san (dī os'ə sən; dī'ə sē'sən), *adj.* of or having to do with a diocese. —*n.* bishop of a diocese.

di·o·cese (dī'ə sis; –sēs), *n.* district over which a bishop has authority. [< OF < LL < L < Gk. *dioikesis* province, diocese]

di·oe·cious (dī ē'shəs), *adj.* having male and female flowers in separate plants. Also, **diecious.** [< NL *dioecia* < Gk. *di–* double + *oikos* house] —**di·oe'cious·ly,** *adv.*

Di·o·ny·sus (dī'ə nī'səs), *n.* Greek god of wine; Bacchus. —**Di'o·ny'sian,** *adj.*

di·o·ram·a (dī'ə ram'ə; –rä'mə), *n.* picture that is arranged and lighted to appear very realistic. [< F < Gk. *dia–* through + *horama* sight]

di·ox·ide (dī ok'sīd; –sid), **di·ox·id** (–sid), *n.* oxide containing two atoms of oxygen and one of a metal or other element.

dip (dip), *v.,* **dipped** or **dipt, dip·ping,** *n.* —*v.* **1** put under water or any liquid and lift quickly out again. **2** go under water and come quickly out again. **3** take up in the hollow of the hand or with a pail, pan, or other container. **4** put (one's hand, a spoon, etc.) into to take out something. **5** lower and raise again quickly: *the flag is dipped as a kind of salute.* **6** sink or drop down: *a bird dips in its flight.* **7** slope downward. —*n.* **1** a dipping of any kind, esp. a plunge into and out of a tub of water, the sea, etc. **2** mixture in which to dip something: *chips with creamy dip.* **3** that which is taken out or up by dipping. **4** a sudden drop. **5** amount of slope down.

dip into, a take something out. **b** read or look at for a short time; glance at. [OE *dyppan*]

diph·the·ri·a (dif thir'i ə; dip–), *n.* infectious disease of the throat, usually accompanied by a high fever and formation of membranes that hinder breathing. [< F < Gk. *diphthera* hide]

diph·thong (dif'thông; –thong; dip'–), *n.* a vowel sound made up of two identifiable vowel sounds in immediate sequence and pronounced in one syllable, as *oi* in *point* and *ai* in *ice.* [< F < LL < Gk., < *di–* double + *phthongos* sound] —**diph·thong'al,** *adj.*

dip·loid (dip'loid), *adj.* having twice the usual number of chromosomes for a species. —*n.* a diploid organism or cell.

di·plo·ma (di plō'mə), *n., pl.* **–mas, –ma·ta** (–mə tə). **1** certificate given by a school, college, or university to its graduating students. **2** any certificate that bestows certain rights, privileges, honors, etc. [< L < Gk., paper folded double, ult. < *diploos* double]

di·plo·ma·cy (di plō'mə si), *n., pl.* **–cies. 1** management of relations between nations. **2** skill in managing such relations. **3** skill in dealing with others; tact. [< F, < *diplomate* diplomat]

dip·lo·mat (dip'lə mat), *n.* **1** representative of a nation who is located in a foreign country to look after the interests of his or her own nation in the foreign country. **2** a tactful person.

dip·lo·mat·ic (dip'lə mat'ik), *adj.* **1** of or having to do with diplomacy. **2** skillful in dealing with others; tactful. —**dip'lo·mat'i·cal·ly,** *adv.*

dip·per (dip'ər), *n.* **1** person or thing that dips. **2** a long-handled cup or larger vessel for dipping water or other liquids. **Dipper,** either of two groups of stars in the northern sky somewhat resembling the shape of a dipper; Big Dipper or Little Dipper.

dip·py (dip'i), *adj.* **–i·er, –i·est.** *Informal.* silly; foolish.

dip·stick (dip'stik'), *n.* rod with a graduated scale on it for measuring the amount of liquid inside a container, as the oil in the engine of a car.

dipt (dipt), *v.* pt. and pp. of **dip.**

dip·ter·ous (dip'tər əs), *adj.* **1** having two winglike parts. **2** belonging to the order including mosquitoes, gnats, and houseflies, characterized by one pair of membranous wings. [< L < Gk., < *di–* two + *pteron* wing]

dip·tych (dip'tik), *n.* **1** ancient writing tablet in two pieces, and hinged so that it could be closed. **2** a pair of paintings or carvings hinged together. **3** something folded into two leaves. [< LL < Gk. *diptychos* folded double]

dire (dīr), *adj.,* **dir·er, dir·est.** causing great fear or suffering; dreadful. [< L *dirus*] —**dire'ly,** *adv.* —**dire'ness,** *n.*

di·rect (də rekt'; dī–), *v.* **1** manage; control; guide. **2** give orders; command. **3** tell or show the way. **4** point (to); aim (at). **5** put the address on (a letter, package, etc.). **6** address (words, etc.) to a person. **7** turn (a thing) straight to. —*adj.* **1** proceeding in a straight line; straight. **2** in an unbroken line of descent. **3** immediate. **4** without anyone or anything in between: *a direct tax.* **5** frank; plain. **6** absolute: *the direct opposite.* —*adv.* directly. [< L *directus,* pp. of *dirigere* set straight < *dis–* apart + *regere* guide] —**di·rect'ness,** *n.*

direct current, a steady electric current that flows in one direction.

di·rec·tion (də rek'shən; dī–), *n.* **1** guidance; management; control: *the direction of a play or movie.* **2** order; command. **3** a knowing or telling what to do; instruction. **4** course taken by a moving body, such as a ball. **5** any way in which one may face or point. **6** tendency.

di·rec·tion·al (də rek'shən əl; dī–), *adj.* **1** of or having to do with direction in space. **2** fitted for determining the direction from which signals come, or for signaling in one direction only.

di·rect·ly (də rekt'li; dī–), *adv.* **1** in a direct line or manner; straight. **2** immediately; at once.

direct mail, mail sent by a business or other organization directly to potential customers or supporters, usually to advertise a product or obtain a contribution.

direct object, a grammatical term denoting the person or thing upon which the verb directly acts.

di·rec·tor (də rek'tər; dī–), *n.* **1** person who directs, esp. one who directs the production of a play or motion picture. **2** one of the persons chosen to direct the affairs of a company or institution. —**di·rec'to·ri·al,** *adj.* —**di·rec'tor·ship,** *n.*

di·rec·tor·ate (də rek'tər it; dī–), *n.* **1** position of a director. **2** group of directors.

di·rec·to·ry (də rek'tə ri; –tri; dī–), *n., pl.* **–ries,** *adj.* —*n.* **1** book of names and addresses. **2** book of rules or instructions. **3** group of directors; directorate. —*adj.* directing; advisory.

direct primary, election in which the voters of a political party choose the candidates of their party for office.

dire·ful (dīr'fəl), *adj.* dire; dreadful; terrible. —**dire'ful·ly,** *adv.* —**dire'ful·ness,** *n.*

dirge (dėrj), *n.* a funeral song or tune. [contraction of L *dirige* DIRECT (imperative of *dirigere*), first word in office for the dead]

dir·i·gi·ble (dir′ə jə bəl; də rij′ə-), *n.* balloon that can be steered. —*adj.* capable of being directed. [< L *dirigere* to DIRECT] —**dir′i·gi·bil′i·ty**, *n.*

dirk (dėrk), *n.* dagger. —*v.* stab with a dirk.

dirn·dl (dėrn′dəl), *n.* 1 an Alpine peasant girl's costume consisting of a blouse, a tight bodice, and a full skirt. 2 dress imitating it. [< South G dial., girl, dim. of *dirne* maid]

dirt (dėrt), *n.* 1 mud, dust, earth, or anything like them. 2 loose earth; soil. 3 unclean action, thought, or speech. [ME *drit,* ? short for OE *drīting* excrement]

dirt-cheap (dėrt′chēp′), *adj.* very cheap.

dirt farmer, person who has practical experience in doing his own farming.

dirt·y (dėr′ti), *adj.* **dirt·i·er, dirt·i·est,** *v.,* **dirt·ied, dirt·y·ing.** —*adj.* 1 soiled by dirt; unclean. 2 not clear or pure in color; clouded. 3 low; mean; vile. 4 unclean in action, thought, or speech. 5 causing a great amount of radioactive fallout: *dirty bombs.* 6 stormy; windy. —*v.* make dirty; soil. —**dirt′i·ly,** *adv.* —**dirt′i·ness,** *n.*

dis-, *prefix.* 1 opposite of, as in *discontent.* 2 reverse of, as in *disentangle.* 3 apart; away, as in *dispel.* [< L; also, *di-, dif-*]

dis·a·bil·i·ty (dis′ə bil′ə ti), *n., pl.* **-ties.** 1 a disabled condition. 2 something that disables. 3 something that disqualifies.

dis·a·ble (dis ā′bəl), *v.,* **-bled, -bling.** 1 deprive of ability of power; make useless; cripple. 2 disqualify legally. —**dis·a′ble·ment,** *n.*

dis·a·buse (dis′ə būz′), *v.,* **-bused, -bus-ing.** free from deception or error.

di·sac·cha·ride (disak′ə rīd, -ər id), *n.* any one of a group of carbohydrates, such as lactose or sucrose, that are changed into two simple sugars by hydrolosis. Also, **disaccharid.**

dis·ad·van·tage (dis′əd van′tij; -văn′-), *n., v.,* **-taged, -tag·ing.** —*n.* 1 lack of advantage; unfavorable condition: *a deaf person is at a disadvantage in school.* 2 loss; injury. —*v.* subject to a disadvantage.

dis·ad·van·ta·geous (dis ad′vən tā′jəs; dis′ad-), *adj.* causing disadvantage; unfavorable. —**dis·ad′van·ta′geous·ly,** *adv.* —**dis·ad′van·ta′geous·ness,** *n.*

dis·af·fect (dis′ə fekt′), *v.* make unfriendly, disloyal, or discontented. —**dis′af·fec′-tion,** *n.*

dis·af·fect·ed (dis′ə fek′tid), *adj.* unfriendly; disloyal; discontented.

dis·a·gree (dis′ə grē′), *v.,* **-greed, -gree-ing.** 1 fail to agree; differ. 2 quarrel; dispute. 3 have a bad effect; be harmful.

dis·a·gree·a·ble (dis′ə grē′ə bəl), *adj.* 1 not to one's liking; unpleasant. 2 bad-tempered; cross. —**dis′a·gree′a·ble-ness,** *n.* —**dis′a·gree′a·bly,** *adv.*

dis·a·gree·ment (dis′ə grē′mənt), *n.* 1 failure to agree; difference of opinion. 2 quarrel; dispute. 3 difference; unlikeness.

dis·al·low (dis′ə lou′), *v.* refuse to allow; deny the truth or value of; reject. —**dis′al·low′ance,** *n.*

dis·ap·pear (dis′ə pir′), *v.* 1 pass from sight. 2 pass from existence; be lost. —**dis′ap·pear′ance,** *n.*

dis·ap·point (dis′ə point′), *v.* 1 fail to satisfy or please; leave (one) wanting or expecting something. 2 fail to keep a promise to. 3 keep from happening; oppose and defeat.

dis·ap·point·ment (dis′ə point′mənt), *n.* 1 state of being or feeling disappointed. 2 person or thing that causes disappointment. 3 act or fact of disappointing.

dis·ap·pro·ba·tion (dis′ap rə bā′shən), *n.* disapproval.

dis·ap·prov·al (dis′ə prüv′əl), *n.* 1 opinion or feeling against; expression of an opinion against; dislike. 2 refusal to consent; rejection.

dis·ap·prove (dis′ə prüv′), *v.,* **-proved, -prov·ing.** 1 have or express an opinion against. 2 show dislike (*of*). 3 refuse consent to; reject. —**dis′ap·prov′ing-ly,** *adv.*

dis·arm (dis ärm′), *v.* 1 take weapons away from. 2 stop having an army and navy; reduce or limit the size of an army, navy, etc. 3 remove suspicion from; make friendly; calm the anger of. 4 make harmless.

dis·ar·ma·ment (dis är′mə mənt), *n.* 1 act of disarming. 2 reduction or limitation of armies, navies, and their equipment.

dis·arm·ing (dis är′ming), *adj.* able to allay fear or suspicion; friendly and calm.

dis·ar·range (dis′ə rānj′), *v.,* **-ranged, -rang·ing.** disturb the arrangement of; put out of order. —**dis′ar·range′ment,** *n.*

dis·ar·ray (dis′ə rā′), *n.* 1 disorder; confusion. 2 disorder of clothing. —*v.* put into disorder or confusion.

dis·as·sem·ble (dis′ə sem′bəl), *v.,* **-bled, -bling.** take apart. —**dis′as·sem′bly,** *n.*

dis·as·so·ci·ate (dis ə sō′shē āt), *v.,* **-at-ed, -at·ing.** =dissociate. —**dis′as·so·ci·a′-tion,** *n.*

dis·as·ter (di zas′tər; -zäs′-), *n.* event that causes much suffering or loss; great misfortune. [< F < Ital. < L *dis-* without + *astrum* star < Gk. *astron*]

dis·as·trous (di zas′trəs; -zäs′-), *adj.* bringing disaster; causing great danger, suffering, loss, etc. —**dis·as′trous-ly,** *adv.*

dis·a·vow (dis′ə vou′), *v.* deny that one knows about, approves of, or is responsible for; disclaim. —**dis′a·vow′al,** *n.* —**dis′a·vow′er,** *n.*

dis·band (dis band′), *v.* 1 disperse; scatter. 2 dismiss from service. —**dis·band′-ment,** *n.*

dis·bar (dis bär′), *v.,* **-barred, -bar·ring.** deprive (a lawyer) of the right to practice law. —**dis·bar′ment,** *n.*

dis·be·lief (dis′bi lēf′), *n.* lack of belief; refusal to believe.

dis·be·lieve (dis′bi lēv′), *v.,* **-lieved, -liev-ing.** 1 have no belief in. 2 reject as not believable. —**dis′be·liev′er,** *n.*

dis·bur·den (dis bėr′dən), *v.* 1 relieve of a burden. 2 get rid of (a burden). —**dis-bur′den·ment,** *n.*

dis·burse (dis bėrs′), *v.,* **-bursed, -burs-ing.** pay out; expend. [< OF, < *des-* (< L *dis-*) + *bourse* purse < LL *bursa* < Gk. *byrsa* leather, wineskin] —**dis·burs′a-ble,** *adj.* —**dis·burse′ment,** *n.* —**dis-burs′er,** *n.*

disc (disk), *n.* 1 disk. 2 compact disk.

disc., 1 discount. 2 discovered.

dis·card (*v.* dis kärd′; *n.* dis′kärd), *v.* 1 give up as useless or worn out; throw aside. 2 get rid of (useless or unwanted playing cards) by throwing them aside or playing them. 3 throw out an unwanted card. —*n.* 1 act of throwing aside as useless. 2 thing thrown aside as useless or not wanted. 3 unwanted cards thrown aside; card played as useless. [see DIS-, CARD]

dis·cern (di zėrn′; -sėrn′), *v.* 1 perceive; see clearly. 2 recognize as distinct or different; distinguish. [< F < L, < *dis-* off + *cernere* separate] —**dis·cern′er,** *n.* —**dis-cern′i·ble,** *adj.* —**dis·cern′i·bly,** *adv.*

dis·cern·ing (di zėr′ning; -ser′-), *adj.* shrewd; acute; discriminating. —**dis-cern′ing·ly,** *adv.*

dis·cern·ment (di zėrn′mənt; -sėrn′), *n.* 1 keenness in perceiving and understanding; good judgment; shrewdness. 2 act of discerning.

dis·charge (*v.* dis chärj′; *n. also* dis′chärj), *v.,* **-charged, -charg·ing,** *n.* —*v.* 1 unload (a ship); unload (cargo) from a ship; unload. 2 fire; shoot; *discharge a gun.* 3 release; let go; dismiss; get rid of: *discharge an employee.* 4 come or pour forth. 5 rid of an electric charge. 6 pay (a debt, etc.). 7 perform (a duty). 8 cancel or set aside (a court order). —*n.* 1 an unloading. 2 a firing off of a gun, a blast, etc. 3 a release; a letting go; a dismissing. 4 a giving off; a letting out. 5 thing given off or let out. 6 rate of flow. 7 transference of electricity between two charged bodies when placed in contact or near each other. [see DIS-, CHARGE] —**dis-charge′a·ble.** *adj.* —**dis·charg′er,** *n.*

dis·ci·ple (di sī′pəl), *n., v.,* **-pled, -pling.** —*n.* 1 believer in the thought and teaching of a leader; follower. 2 one of the followers of Jesus. —*v.* cause to become a follower. [< L *discipulus* pupil < unrecorded *discipere* grasp, apprehend] —**dis·ci′ple·ship,** *n.*

Disciples of Christ, Protestant religious sect that bases its teachings on the New Testament only.

dis·ci·pli·nar·i·an (dis′ə plə nār′i ən), *n.* person who enforces discipline or who believes in strict discipline. —*adj.* disciplinary.

dis·ci·pli·nar·y (dis′ə plə ner′i), *adj.* **1** having to do with discipline. **2** for discipline.

dis·ci·pline (dis′ə plin), *n., v.,* **-plined, -plining.** —*n.* **1** training esp. training of the mind or character. **2** trained condition of order and obedience. **3** order among school pupils, soldiers, or members of any group. **4** a particular system of rules for conduct. **5** punishment. **6** branch of instruction or education. —*v.* **1** train; bring to a condition of order and obedience; bring under control. **2** punish. [< L *disciplina.* See DISCIPLE.] —**dis·ci·plin·er,** *n.*

dis·claim (dis klām′), *v.* **1** refuse to recognize as one's own; deny connection with. **2** give up all claim to.

dis·claim·er (dis klām′ər), *n.* **1** a disclaiming. **2** person who disclaims.

dis·close (dis klōz′), *v.,* **-closed, -closing. 1** open to view; uncover. **2** make known; reveal. —**dis·clos′er,** *n.*

dis·clo·sure (dis klō′zhər), *n.* **1** act of disclosing. **2** thing disclosed.

dis·co (dis′kō), *n., pl.* **-cos. 1** =discotheque. **2** music played in a discotheque. —*adj.* of or having to do with a disco: *the disco scene.* —*v.,* **-coed, -co·ing.** dance to disco.

dis·cog·ra·phy (dis kog′rə fi), *n.* **1** list of recordings or writings about them. **2** history of recordings and performers. —**dis·cog′ra·pher,** *n.* —**dis′co·graph′ic, dis′co·graph′i·cal,** *adj.*

dis·coid (dis′koid), *adj.* flat and circular; disklike

dis·col·or (dis kul′ər), *v.* **1** change or spoil the color of; stain. **2** become changed in color. —**dis′col·or·a′tion, dis·col′or·ment,** *n.*

dis·com·fit (dis kum′fit), *v.* **1** defeat; rout. **2** defeat the plans or hopes of; frustrate. **3** embarrass greatly; confuse. [< OF, ult. < *dis-* + *conficere* accomplish]

dis·com·fi·ture (dis kum′fi chər), *n.* **1** defeat; rout. **2** defeat of plans or hopes; frustration. **3** confusion.

dis·com·fort (dis kum′fərt), *v.* **1** disturb the comfort of. **2** distress; sadden. **3** make uncomfortable or uneasy. —*n.* **1** thing that causes discomfort. **2** lack of comfort; uneasiness.

dis·com·mode (dis′kə mōd′), *v.,* **-mod·ed, -mod·ing.** disturb; trouble; inconvenience.

dis·com·pose (dis′kəm pōz′), *v.,* **-posed, -pos·ing.** disturb the self-possession of; make uneasy; bring into disorder. —**dis′com·pos′ed·ly,** *adv.* —**dis′com·pos′ing·ly,** *adv.*

dis·com·po·sure (dis′kəm pō′zhər), *n.* state of being disturbed; uneasiness; embarrassment.

dis·con·cert (dis′kən sèrt′), *v.* **1** disturb the self-possession of; confuse. **2** upset; disorder. —**dis′con·cert′ing·ly,** *adv.* —**dis′con·cer′tion,** *n.*

dis·con·cert·ed (dis′kən sèrt′id), *adj.* disturbed; confused. —**dis′con·cert′ed·ly,** *adv.*

dis·con·nect (dis′kə nekt′), *v.* undo or break the connection of; unfasten. —**dis′con·nec′tion,** *n.*

dis·con·nect·ed (dis′kə nek′tid), *adj.* **1** not connected; separate. **2** incoherent; broken. —**dis′con·nect′ed·ly,** *adv.* —**dis′con·nect′ed·ness,** *n.*

dis·con·so·late (dis kon′sə lit), *adj.* **1** without hope; forlorn. **2** unhappy; cheerless. [< Med.L, < L *dis-* + *consolatus,* pp. of *consolari* CONSOLE¹] —**dis′con′so·late·ly,** *adv.* —**dis′con·so·la′tion, dis·con′so·late·ness,** *n.*

dis·con·tent (dis′kən tent′), *adj.* not content; dissatisfied. —*n.* Also, **discontent·ment.** dislike of what one has uneasiness; restlessness. —*v.* dissatisfy; displease.

dis·con·tent·ed (dis′kən ten′tid), *adj.* not contented; not satisfied. —**dis′con·tent′ed·ly,** *adv.* —**dis′con·tent′ed·ness,** *n.*

dis·con·tin·ue (dis′kən tin′yù), *v.,* **-tin·ued, -tin·u·ing. 1** put an end to. **2** cease. —**dis′con·tin′u·ance, dis′con·tin′u·a′tion,** *n.* —**dis′con·tin′u·er,** *n.*

dis·con·tin·u·ous (dis′kən tin′yù əs), *adj.* broken; interrupted. —**dis′conti·nu′i·ty, dis′con·tin′u·ous·ness,** *n.* —**dis′con·tin′u·ous·ly,** *adv.*

dis·cord (*n.* dis′kôrd; *v.* dis kôrd′), *n.* **1** difference of opinion; disagreement. **2** a lack of harmony in notes sounded at the same time. **3** harsh, clashing sounds. —*v.* be out of harmony; disagree. [< OF < *discors* discordant < *dis-* apart + *cor* heart]

dis·cord·ant (dis kôr′dənt), *adj.* **1** not in harmony: *a discordant note in music.* **2** not in agreement; not fitting together. **3** harsh; clashing. —**dis·cord′ance, discord′an·cy,** *n.*

dis·co·theque or **dis·co·thèque** (diskətek), *n.* club where recorded music is played for dancing. [< F, lit., disk collection]

dis·count (*v.* dis′kount, dis kount′; *n.* dis′kount), *v.* **1** deduct (a certain percentage) of the amount or cost. **2** allow for exaggeration; believe only part of. **3** lend money, deducting the interest in advance. —*n.* **1** deduction from the amount or cost. **2** interest deducted in advance.

at a discount, a at less than the usual price. **b** *Fig.* in low esteem. [< OF, < *des-* (< L *dis-*) + *conter* COUNT¹] —**dis′count·a·ble,** *adj.* —**dis′count·er,** *n.*

dis·coun·te·nance (dis koun′tə nəns), *v.,* **-nanced, -nanc·ing. 1** refuse to approve; discourage. **2** abash.

dis·cour·age (dis kèr′ij), *v.,* **-aged, -ag·ing. 1** lessen the hope or confidence of. **2** try to prevent by disapproving; frown upon. **3** prevent; hinder. [< OF, < *des-* (< L *dis-*) + *corage* COURAGE] —**dis·cour′age·a·ble,** *adj.* —**dis·cour′age·ment,** *n.* —**dis·cour′ag·er,** *n.* —**dis·cour′ag·ing·ly,** *adv.*

discouraged worker, unemployed person who has stopped looking for a job.

dis·course (*n.* dis′kôrs, -kōrs, dis kôrs′, -kōrs′; *v.* dis kôrs′, -kōrs′), *n., v.,* **-coursed, -cours·ing.** —*n.* **1** a formal speech or writing: *a lecture is a discourse.* **2** conversation; talk. —*v.* **1** speak or write formally. **2** converse; talk. [< F < Med.L, < L, < *dis-* in different directions + *currere* run] —**dis·cours′er,** *n.*

dis·cour·te·ous (dis kèr′ti əs), *adj.* not courteous; rude; impolite. —**dis·cour′te·ous·ly,** *adv.* —**dis·cour′te·ous·ness,** *n.*

dis·cour·te·sy (dis kèr′tə si), *n., pl.* **-sies. 1** lack of courtesy; rudeness; impoliteness. **2** a rude or impolite act.

dis·cov·er (dis kuv′ər), *v.* see or learn of for the first time; find out. [< OF, < *des-* (< L *dis-*) + *covrir* COVER] —**dis·cov′er·a·ble,** *adj.* —**dis·cov′er·er,** *n.*

dis·cov·er·y (dis kuv′ər i; -kuv′ri), *n., pl.* **-eries. 1** act of discovering. **2** thing discovered.

dis·cred·it (dis kred′it), *v.* **1** cast doubt on; destroy belief, faith, or trust in. **2** refuse to believe; decline to trust or have faith in. —*n.* **1** loss of belief, faith, or trust; doubt. **2** loss of good name or standing; disgrace. **3** thing that causes loss of good name or standing; disgrace.

dis·cred·it·a·ble (dis kred′it ə bəl), *adj.* bringing discredit. —**dis·cred′it·a·bly,** *adv.*

dis·creet (dis krēt′), *adj.* careful and sensible in speech and action; wisely cautious. [< OF < Med.L < L *discretus,* pp., separated. See DISCERN.] —**dis·creet′ly,** *adv.* —**dis·creet′ness,** *n.*

dis·crep·an·cy (dis krep′ən si), *n., pl.* **-cies. 1** lack of consistency; difference; disagreement. **2** an example of inconsistency.

dis·crep·ant (dis krep′ənt), *adj.* disagreeing; different; inconsistent. [< L, < *dis-* differently + *crepare* sound] —**dis·crep′ant·ly,** *adv.*

dis·crete (dis krēt′), *adj.* **1** separate; distinct. **2** consisting of distinct parts. [< L *discretus,* separated, pp. See DISCERN.] —**dis·crete′ly,** *adv.* —**dis·crete′ness,** *n.*

dis·cre·tion (dis kresh′ən), *n.* **1** freedom to judge or choose. **2** good judgment; carefulness in speech or action; wise caution.

dis·cre·tion·ar·y (dis kresh′ən er′i), *adj.* left to one's own judgment.

dis·crim·i·nate (*v.* dis krim′ə nāt; *adj.* diskrim′ə nit), *v.,* **-nat·ed, -nat·ing,** *adj.* —*v.* **1** make or see a difference. **2** make a distinction. **3** distinguish. —*adj.* having discrimination; making nice distinctions. [< L *discriminatus* distinguished < *discrimen* separation < *discernere* DISCERN] —**dis·crim′i·nate·ly,** *adv.* —**dis·crim′inat′ing,** *adj.* —**dis·crim′i·nat′ing·ly,** *adv.* —**discrim′i·na′tor,** *n.*

dis·crim·i·na·tion (dis krim′ə nā′shən), *n.* **1** act of making or recognizing differences and distinctions. **2** ability to make fine distinctions. **3** the making of a difference in favor of or against.

dis·crim·i·na·tive (dis krim′ə nā′tiv), **dis·crim·i·na·to·ry** (−ə nə tô′ri; −tō′−), *adj.* **1** discriminating. **2** showing discrimination. —**dis·crim′i·na′tive·ly,** *adv.*

dis·cur·sive (dis kėr′siv), *adj.* wandering or shifting from one subject to another; rambling. —**dis·cur′sive·ly,** *adv.* —**dis·cur′sive·ness,** *n.*

dis·cus (dis′kəs), *n.* a heavy, circular plate of stone or metal, used in athletic games as a test of skill and strength in throwing. [< L < Gk. *diskos*]

dis·cuss (dis kus′), *v.* consider from various points of view; talk over. [< L *discussus* < *dis−* apart + *quatere* shake] —**dis·cus′sant,** *n.*

dis·cus·si·ble (dis kus′ə bəl), *adj.* able to be discussed. Also, **discussable.**

dis·cus·sion (dis kush′ən), *n.* a going over the reasons for and against; discussing things.

dis·dain (dis dān′), *v.* look down on; consider beneath oneself; scorn. —*n.* act of disdaining; feeling of scorn. [< OF, < *des−* (< L *dis−*) + *deignier* DEIGN]

dis·dain·ful (dis dān′fəl), *adj.* feeling or showing disdain. —**dis·dain′ful·ly,** *adv.* —**disdain′ful·ness,** *n.*

dis·ease (di zēz′), *n., v.,* −**eased,** −**eas·ing.** —*n.* **1** sickness; illness. **2** any particular illness. —*v.* affect with disease. [< OF, < *des−* (< L *dis−*) + *aise* EASE] —**dis·eased′,** *adj.*

dis·em·bark (dis′em bärk′), *v.* land from a ship, airplane, etc. —**dis′em·bar·ka′tion, dis′em·bark′ment,** *n.*

dis·em·bar·rass (dis′em bar′əs), *v.* **1** disengage. **2** free from uneasiness.

dis·em·bod·y (dis′em bod′i), *v.,* −**bod·ied,** −**bod·y·ing.** separate (a soul, spirit, etc.) from the body. —**dis′em·bod′i·ment,** *n.*

dis·em·bow·el (dis′em bou′əl), *v.,* −**eled,** −**el·ing.** take or rip out the bowels of. —**dis′em·bow′el·ment,** *n.*

dis·en·chant (dis′en chant′; −chänt′), *v.* free from a magic spell or illusion. —**dis′en·chant′er,** *n.* —**dis′en·chant′ment,** *n.*

dis·en·cum·ber (dis′en kum′bər), *v.* free from a burden, annoyance, or trouble.

dis·en·fran·chise (dis′en fran′chīz), *v.,* −**chised,** −**chis·ing.** =disfranchise. —**dis′en·fran′chise·ment,** *n.*

dis·en·gage (dis′en gāj′), *v.,* −**gaged,** −**gag·ing.** **1** free from an engagement, pledge, obligation, etc. **2** detach; loosen. —**dis′en·gage′ment,** *n.*

dis·en·tan·gle (dis′en tang′gəl), *v.,* −**tan·gled,** −**tan·gling.** free from tangles or complications; untangle. —**dis′en·tan′gle·ment,** *n.*

dis·es·tab·lish (dis′es tab′lish), *v.* withdraw state recognition or support from (a church). —**dis′es·tab′lish·ment,** *n.*

dis·es·teem (dis′es tēm′), *v., n.* scorn; dislike.

dis·fa·vor (dis fā′vər), *n.* **1** dislike; disapproval. **2** state of being regarded with dislike or disapproval. —*v.* regard with dislike; disapprove.

dis·fig·ure (dis fig′yər), *v.,* −**ured,** −**ur·ing.** spoil the appearance of; hurt the beauty of. —**dis·fig′ure·ment,** *n.* —**dis·fig′ur·er,** *n.*

dis·fran·chise (dis fran′chīz), *v.,* −**chised,** −**chis·ing.** **1** take the rights of citizenship away from. **2** take a right or privilege from. —**disfran′chise·ment,** *n.* —**dis·fran′chis·er,** *n.*

dis·gorge (dis gôrj′), *v.,* −**gorged,** −**gorg·ing.** **1** throw up what has been swallowed. **2** pour forth; discharge. **3** give up unwillingly.

dis·grace (dis grās′), *n., v.,* −**graced,** −**grac·ing.** —*n.* **1** loss of honor or respect; shame. **2** cause of disgrace. **3** loss of favor or trust. —*v.* **1** cause disgrace to. **2** dismiss in disgrace. [< F < Ital. *disgrazia.* See DIS−, GRACE.] —**dis·grac′er,** *n.*

dis·grace·ful (dis grās′fəl), *adj.* causing loss of honor or respect; shameful. —**dis·grace′ful·ly,** *adv.* —**dis·grace′ful·ness,** *n.*

dis·grun·tle (dis grun′təl), *v.,* −**tled,** −**tling.** fill with bad humor or discontent. [< *dis−* + obs. *gruntle* to grunt, grumble] —**dis·grun′tle·ment,** *n.*

dis·guise (dis gīz′), *v.,* −**guised,** −**guis·ing,** *n.* —*v.* **1** make a change in clothes and appearance to hide who one really is or to look like someone else. **2** hide what (a thing) really is; make (a thing) seem like something else. —*n.* **1** use of a changed or unusual dress and appearance in order not to be known. **2** clothes, actions, etc., used to hide who one really is or to make a person look like someone else. **3** a false or misleading appearance; deception; concealment. [< OF, < *des−* (< L *dis−*) + *guise* GUISE] —**dis·guis′ed·ly,** *adv.* —**dis·guis′er,** *n.*

dis·gust (dis gust′), *n.* strong dislike; sickening dislike. —*v.* arouse disgust in. [< early modern F, < *des−* (< L *dis−*) + *goust* taste < L *gustus*] —**dis·gust′ing·ly,** *adv.*

dis·gust·ed (dis gus′tid), *adj.* filled with disgust. —**dis·gust′ed·ly,** *adv.* —**dis·gust′ed·ness,** *n.*

dis·gust·ing (dis gus′ting), *adj.* that disgusts; distasteful. —**dis·gust′ing·ly,** *adv.*

dish (dish), *n.* **1** anything to serve food in, such as a plate, platter, bowl, cup, or saucer. **2** amount of food served in a dish. **3** the food served. **4** thing shaped like a dish. **5** *Slang.* something in accord with one's taste or preference. **6** *Slang.* pretty young woman or girl. —*v.* **1** serve (food) by putting it in a dish. **2** make concave.

dish it out, *Informal.* **a** criticize someone severely. **b** physically abuse someone.

dish out (or **up**), **a** serve food. **b** *Fig.* reveal; dispense information: *dish out gossip.* **c** *Informal.* administer; inflict: *dish out punishment.* [< L *discus* dish, DISCUS]

dis·ha·bille (dis′ə bēl′), *n.* informal, careless dress. [< F *déshabillé,* pp. < *dés−* (< L *dis−*) + *habiller* dress]

dis·har·mo·ny (dis här′mə ni), *n., pl.* −**nies.** lack of harmony; discord.

dish·cloth (dish′klôth′; −kloth′), *n.* cloth to wash dishes with.

dis·heart·en (dis här′tən), *v.* discourage; depress. —**dis·heart′en·ing·ly,** *adv.* —**dis·heart′en·ment,** *n.*

di·shev·eled (di shev′əld), *adj.* **1** rumpled; mussed; disordered; untidy. **2** hanging loosely or in disorder: *disheveled hair.*

dis·hon·est (dis on′ist), *adj.* not honest. —**dishon′est·ly,** *adv.*

dis·hon·es·ty (dis on′əs ti), *n., pl.* −**ties.** **1** lack of honesty. **2** a dishonest act.

dis·hon·or (dis on′ər), *n.* **1** loss of honor or reputation; shame; disgrace. **2** cause of dishonor. —*v.* cause or bring dishonor to.

dis·hon·or·a·ble (dis on′ər ə bəl), *adj.* **1** causing loss of honor; shameful; disgraceful. **2** without honor. —**dis·hon′or·a·ble·ness,** *n.* —**dis·hon′or·a·bly,** *adv.*

dish·pan (dish′pan′), *n.* pan in which to wash dishes.

dish·rag (dish′rag′), *n.* =dishcloth.

dish·tow·el (dish′tou′əl), *n.* cloth for drying dishes.

dish·wash·er (dish′wosh′ər; −wôsh′), appliance for washing dishes, glasses, etc.

dish·wa·ter (dish′wô′tər; −wo tər), *n.* **1** gray, soapy water in which dishes have been washed. **2** water in which to wash dishes. **3** *Fig.* anything like dishwater, esp. something old or bland.

dish·y (dish′i), *adj. Slang.* attractive.

dis·il·lu·sion (dis′i lü′zhən), *v.* free from illusion. —*n.* a freeing or being freed from illusion. —**dis′il·lu′sion·ment,** *n.* —**dis′il·lu′sive,** *adj.*

dis·in·cli·na·tion (dis′in klə nā′shən), *n.* unwillingness.

dis·in·cline (dis′in klīn′), *v.,* −**clined,** −**clin·ing.** make or be unwilling.

dis·in·fect (dis′in fekt′), *v.* destroy the disease germs in. —**dis′in·fec′tion,** *n.* —**dis′infec′tor,** *n.*

dis·in·fect·ant (dis′in fek′tənt), *n.* means for destroying disease germs. Alcohol, iodine, and carbolic acid are disinfectants. —*adj.* destroying disease germs.

dis·in·form (dis′in fôrm′), *v.* give out false information to mislead.

dis·in·for·ma·tion (dis′in fər mā′shən), *n.* false information intended to mislead. [< Russ.]

dis·in·gen·u·ous (dis′in jen′yu̇ əs), *adj.* not frank; insincere. —**dis′in·gen′u·ous·ly,** *adv.* —**dis′in·gen′u·ous·ness,** *n.*

dis·in·her·it (dis′in her′it), *v.* prevent from inheriting; deprive of an inheritance. —**dis′inher′it·ance,** *n.*

dis·in·te·grate (dis in′tə grāt), *v.,* −**grat·ed,** −**grat·ing.** **1** separate into small parts or bits. **2** change in nuclear structure through bombardment by charged particles. —**dis·in′te·gra·ble,** *adj.* —**dis·in′te·gra′tion,** *n.* —**dis·in′te·gra′tor,** *n.*

dis·in·ter (dis´in tèr´), v., **-terred, -ter·ring. 1** take out of a grave or tomb; dig up. **2** discover and reveal. —**dis´in·ter´ment**, n.

dis·in·ter·est (dis in´tər ist; –trist), n. lack of interest; indifference.

dis·in·ter·est·ed (dis in´tər is tid; –tris tid; –tər es´tid), adj. **1** free from selfish motives; impartial; fair. **2** U.S. not interested. —**dis·in´ter·est·ed·ly**, adv. —**dis·in´ter·est·ed·ness**, n.

dis·join (dis join´), v. separate.

dis·joint (dis joint´), v. **1** take apart at the joints. **2** put out of order. **3** put out of joint; dislocate. —**dis·joint´ed**, adj. —**dis·joint´ed·ly**, adv. —**dis·joint´ed·ness**, n.

dis·junc·tion (dis jungk´shən), n. a disjoining or being disjoined; separation.

dis·junc·tive (dis jungk´tiv), adj. **1** causing separation. **2** showing a contrast between two ideas, words, etc. **3** involving alternatives: a disjunctive proposition. —n. statement involving alternatives. —**dis·junc´tive·ly**, adv.

disk (disk), n. **1** a round, flat, thin object. **2** a round, flat surface, or an apparently round, flat surface: the sun's disk. **3** a roundish, flat part in a plant or animal. **4** a compact disk or phonograph record. Also, **disc.** [< L discus DISCUS] —**disk´like´**, adj.

disk brake, automobile brake that consists of a revolving disk attached to the wheel and flat plates that press against the disk. Also, **disc brake.**

disk drive, device in a computer that transfers data or instructions between the computer and a storage disk.

disk harrow, harrow with a row of sharp, revolving disks used in preparing ground for planting or sowing.

disk jockey, announcer for a radio program or entertainment, as for a party, consisting chiefly of recorded music.

dis·like (dis līk´), n., v., **-liked, -lik·ing.** —n. a feeling of not liking; a feeling against. —v. not like; object to; have a feeling against. —**dis·lik´a·ble**, adj.

dis·lo·cate (dis´lō kāt), v., **-cat·ed, -cat·ing. 1** put out of joint. **2** put out of order; disturb; upset. —**dis´lo·ca´tion**, n.

dis·lodge (dis loj´), v., **-lodged, -lodg·ing.** drive or force out of a place, position, etc. —**dis·lodg´ment**, n.

dis·loy·al (dis loi´əl), adj. not loyal; unfaithful. —**dis·loy´al·ly**, adv.

dis·loy·al·ty (dis loi´əl ti), n., pl. **-ties. 1** lack of loyalty. **2** a disloyal act.

dis·mal (diz´məl), adj. **1** dark; gloomy. **2** dreary; miserable. —**dis´mal·ly**, adv. —**dis´mal·ness**, n.

dis·man·tle (dis man´təl), v., **-tled, -tling. 1** strip of covering, equipment, furniture, etc. **2** pull down; take apart. [< OF desmanteler. See DIS-, MANTLE.] —**dis·man´tlement**, n.

dis·may (dis mā´), n. loss of courage because of fear of what is about to happen. —v. trouble greatly; make afraid.

[ME desmayen < AF < VL, deprive of strength < L ex- + unrecorded Frankish magan have strength]

dis·mem·ber (dis mem´bər), v. **1** separate or divide into parts. **2** cut or tear the limbs from. —**dis·mem´ber·ment**, n.

dis·miss (dis mis´), v. **1** send away; allow to go. **2** remove from office or service. **3** put out of mind; stop thinking about. **4** refuse to consider (a complaint, plea, etc.) in a law court. [< L dismissus, var. of dimissus < dis- away + mittere send] —**dis·miss´al**, n.

dis·mis·sive (dis mis´iv), adj. **1** tending to dismiss. **2** showing lack of interest or concern: a dismissive remark.

dis·mount (dis mount´), v. **1** get off a horse, bicycle, etc. **2** throw or bring down from a horse; unhorse. —**dis·mount´a·ble**, adj.

dis·o·be·di·ent (dis´ə bē´di ənt), adj. refusing or failing to obey. —**dis´o·be´di·ence**, n. —**dis´o·be´di·ent·ly**, adv.

dis·o·bey (dis´ə bā´), v. refuse or fail to obey. —**dis´o·bey´er**, n.

dis·o·blige (dis´ə blīj´), v., **-bliged, -blig·ing. 1** refuse or fail to oblige. **2** give offense to. —**dis´o·blig´ing**, adj. —**dis´o·blig´ing·ly**, adv.

dis·or·der (dis ôr´dər), n. **1** lack of order; confusion. **2** public disturbance; riot. **3** sickness; disease. —v. **1** destroy the order of; throw into confusion. **2** cause sickness in.

dis·or·dered (dis ôr´dərd), adj. **1** lacking order; jumbled. **2** sick.

dis·or·der·ly (dis ôr´dər li), adj. **1** not orderly; in confusion. **2** causing disorder; unruly. —adv. in a disorderly manner. —**dis·or´der·li·ness**, n.

dis·or·gan·ize (dis ôr´gən īz), v., **-ized, -iz·ing.** throw into confusion and disorder. —**disor´gan·i·za´tion**, n. —**disor´gan·iz´er**, n.

dis·o·ri·ent (dis ôr´ə ent), v. **1** cause to lose one's sense of direction. **2** Fig. cause one to feel confused or embarrassed. Also, **disorientate.** —**dis·o´ri·en·ta´tion**, n.

dis·own (dis ōn´), v. refuse to recognize as one's own.

dis·par·age (dis par´ij), v., **-aged, -ag·ing. 1** speak slightingly of; belittle. **2** lower the reputation of; discredit. [< OF desparagier match unequally < des- (< L dis-) + parage rank, lineage < L par equal. See PEER[1].] —**dis·par´age·ment**, n. —**dis·par´ag·er**, n. —**dis·par´ag·ing·ly**, adv.

dis·pa·rate (dis´pə rit), adj. essentially different; unlike. [< L, < dis- apart + parare get] —**dis´pa·rate·ly**, adv. —**dis´pa·rate·ness**, n.

dis·par·i·ty (dis par´ə ti), n., pl. **-ties.** inequality; difference.

dis·pas·sion (dis pash´ən), n. freedom from emotion or prejudice; impartiality.

dis·pas·sion·ate (dis pash´ən it), adj. free from emotion or prejudice; calm; impartial. —**dis·pas´sion·ate·ly**, adv. —**dis·pas´sion·ate·ness**, n.

dis·patch (dis pach´), v. **1** send off to some place or for some purpose. **2** get (something) done promptly or speedily. **3** give the death blow to; kill. —n. **1** a sending off (of a letter, a messenger, etc.). **2** a written message, such as special news or government business. **3** promptness; speed. **4** a putting to death; a killing. Also, **despatch.** [< Ital. dispacciare hasten or Sp. despachar] —**dis·patch´er**, n.

dis·pel (dis pel´), v., **-pelled, -pel·ling.** drive away and scatter; disperse. [< L, < dis- away + pellere drive] —**dis·pel´ler**, n.

dis·pen·sa·ble (dis pen´sə bəl), adj. **1** that may be done without; unimportant. **2** that may be forgiven, condoned, or declared not binding. **3** capable of being dispensed or administered. —**dis·pen´sa·bil´i·ty, dis·pen´sa·ble·ness**, n.

dis·pen·sa·ry (dis pen´sə ri), n., pl. **-ries.** place where medicines and medical advice are given free or for a very small charge.

dis·pen·sa·tion (dis´pən sā´shən; –pen–), n. **1** act of distributing: the dispensation of charity to the poor. **2** thing given out or distributed. **3** rule; management: England under the dispensation of Elizabeth. **4** official permission to disregard a rule. —**dis´pen·sa´tion·al**, adj. —**dis´pen·sa´tor**, n.

dis·pen·sa·to·ry (dis pen´sə tô´ri; –tō´–), n., pl. **-ries. 1** book that tells how to prepare and use medicines. **2** dispensary.

dis·pense (dis pens´), v., **-pensed, -pens·ing. 1** give out; distribute. **2** carry out; put in force; apply. **3** prepare and give out: a druggist dispenses medicines.

dispense with, a do away with. **b** get along without. [< OF < L dispensare weigh out < dis- out + pendere weigh] —**dis·pens´er**, n.

dis·perse (dis pèrs´), v., **-persed, -pers·ing.** spread in different directions; scatter. [< F < L dispersus < dis- in every direction + spargere scatter] —**dis·per´sal**, n. —**dis·pers´ed·ly**, adv. —**dis·pers´er**, n. —**dis·pers´i·ble**, adj. —**dis·per´sive**, adj.

dis·per·sion (dis pèr´zhən; –shən), n. **1** Also, **dispersal. a** a dispersing. **b** a being dispersed. **2** the separation of light into its different colors, as by a prism.

dis·pir·it (dis pir´it), v. depress; discourage. —**dis·pir´it·ed**, adj. —**dis·pir´it·ed·ly**, adv.

dis·place (dis plās´), v., **-placed, -plac·ing. 1** put something else in the place of. **2** remove from a position of authority. **3** move from its usual place or position.

displaced person, a person forced out of his or her native country by war, famine, or threat of captivity, esp. a European during World War II.

dis·place·ment (dis plās´mənt), n. **1** act of displacing. **2** a being displaced. **3** weight of the volume of water displaced by a ship or other floating object. **3** psychological defense mechanism that shifts an emotional response from one object to another, unrelated object.

dis·play (dis plā′), *v.* **1** expose to view; show. **2** show in a special way, so as to attract attention. —*n.* **1** a displaying; exhibition. **2** a showing off; ostentation. [< OF < L *displicare* scatter. See DEPLOY.] —**dis·play′er,** *n.*

dis·please (dis plēz′), *v.,* **–pleased, –pleas·ing.** not please; offend; annoy.

dis·pleas·ure (dis plezh′ər), *n.* the feeling of being displeased; slight anger; annoyance.

dis·port (dis pôrt′; –pōrt′), *v.* amuse (oneself); sport; play. [< OF, < *des-* (< L *dis-*) away from + *porter* carry < L *portare*]

dis·pos·a·ble (dis pōz′ə bəl), *adj.* capable of being disposed of.

dis·pos·al (dis pōz′əl), *n.* **1** act of getting rid (of something). **2** sale. **3** a settling of affairs. **4** act of putting in a certain order or position; arrangement.

at or **in one's disposal,** ready for one's use or service at any time.

dis·pose (dis pōz′), *v.,* **–posed, –pos·ing.** **1** put in a certain order or position; arrange. **2** make ready or willing. **3** make liable or subject.

dispose of, a get rid of. **b** give away. **c** sell. [< OF, < *dis-* (< L) variously + *poser* place (see POSE)] —**dis·pos′er,** *n.*

dis·po·si·tion (dis′pə zish′ən), *n.* **1** one's natural way of acting toward others or of thinking about things; nature: *a cheerful disposition.* **2** tendency; inclination: *a disposition to argue.* **3** act of putting in order or position; arrangement: *the disposition of soldiers in battle.* **4** management; settlement: *a court's disposition of a complaint.* **5** disposal: *a large income at one's disposition.*

dis·pos·sess (dis′pə zes′), *v.* force to give up the possession of a house, land, etc.; oust. **dis′pos·ses′sion,** *n.* —**dis′pos·ses′sor,** *n.*

dis·proof (dis prüf′), *n.* **1** a disproving; refutation. **2** fact, reason, etc., that disproves something.

dis·pro·por·tion (dis′prə pôr′shən; –pōr′–), *n.* lack of proper proportion; lack of symmetry. —*v.* make disproportionate.

dis·pro·por·tion·al (dis′prə pôr′shən əl; –pōr′–), *adj.* disproportionate. —**dis′pro·por′tion·al·ly,** *adv.*

dis·pro·por·tion·ate (dis′prə pôr′shən it; –pōr′–), *adj.* out of proportion; lacking in proper proportion. —**dis′pro·por′tion·ate·ly,** *adv.* —**dis′pro·por′tion·ate·ness,** *n.*

dis·prove (dis prüv′), *v.,* **–proved, –prov·ing.** prove false or incorrect; refute. —**dis·prov′a·ble,** *adj.*

dis·put·a·ble (dis pūt′ə bəl; dis′pyü tə bəl), *adj.* liable to be disputed; uncertain. —**dis·put′a·bil′i·ty,** *n.* —**dis·put′a·bly,** *adv.*

dis·pu·tant (dis′pyü tənt; dis pū′–), *adj.* engaged in argument or controversy.

—*n.* person who takes part in a dispute or debate.

dis·pu·ta·tion (dis′pyü tā′shən), *n.* **1** debate; controversy. **2** dispute.

dis·pu·ta·tious (dis′pyü tā′shəs), **dis·puta·tive** (dis pūt′ə tiv), *adj.* fond of disputing; inclined to argue. —**dis′pu·ta′tious·ly,** *adv.* —**dis′pu·ta′tious·ness,** *n.*

dis·pute (dis pūt′), *v.,* **–put·ed, –put·ing,** *n.* —*v.* **1** discuss; argue; debate. **2** quarrel. **3** declare not true; call in question. **4** fight against; resist. **5** try to win. —*n.* **1** argument; debate. **2** a quarrel.

beyond dispute, a not to be debated or questioned. **b** final; agreed to. [< L, examine, discuss, argue < *dis-* item by item + *putare* calculate] —**dis·put′er,** *n.*

dis·qual·i·fi·ca·tion (dis′kwol ə fə kā′shən), *n.* **1** a disqualifying. **2** a being disqualified. **3** something that disqualifies.

dis·qual·i·fy (dis kwol′ə fī), *v.,* **–fied, –fy·ing.** **1** make unable to do something. **2** declare unfit or unable to do something.

dis·qui·et (dis kwī′ət), *v.* make uneasy or anxious; disturb. —*n.* uneasiness; anxiety.

dis·qui·e·tude (dis kwī′ə tüd; –tūd), *n.* anxiety.

dis·qui·si·tion (dis′kwə zish′ən), *n.* a long or formal speech or writing about a subject. [< L *disquisitio,* ult. < *dis-* (intensive) + *quaerere* seek]

dis·re·gard (dis′ri gärd′), *v.* **1** pay no attention to; take no notice of. **2** treat without proper regard or respect; slight. —*n.* **1** lack of attention; neglect. **2** lack of proper regard or respect. —**dis′re·gard′ful,** *adj.*

dis·re·pair (dis′ri pār′), *n.* bad condition.

dis·rep·u·ta·ble (dis rep′yə tə bəl), *adj.* **1** having a bad reputation. **2** not respectable. —**dis·rep′u·ta·bil′i·ty,** *n.* —**dis·rep′u·ta·bly,** *adv.*

dis·re·pute (dis′ri pūt′), *n.* disgrace; discredit; disfavor.

dis·re·spect (dis′ri spekt′), *n.* lack of respect. —*v.* treat or consider with a lack of respect. —**dis′re·spect′ful,** *adj.* —**dis′re·spect′ful·ly,** *adv.* —**dis′re·spect′ful·ness,** *n.*

dis·robe (dis rōb′), *v.,* **–robed, –rob·ing.** undress. —**dis·robe′ment,** *n.* —**dis·rob′er,** *n.*

dis·rupt (dis rupt′), *v.* break up; split. [< L *disruptus* < *dis-* apart + *rumpere* break] —**disrupt′er,** *n.* —**dis·rup′tion,** *n.* —**dis·rup′tive,** *adj.*

dis·sat·is·fac·tion (dis′sat is fak′shən), *n.* discontent; displeasure.

dis·sat·is·fac·to·ry (dis′sat is fak′tə ri), *adj.* causing discontent; unsatisfactory.

dis·sat·is·fy (dis sat′is fī), *v.,* **–fied, –fy·ing.** fail to satisfy; displease.

dis·sect (di sekt′; dī–), *v.* **1** separate or divide the parts of (an animal, plant, etc.) in order to examine or study the structure. **2** examine carefully part by part; analyze. [< L < *dis-* apart + *secare* cut] —**dis·sec′tion,** *n.* —**dis·sec′tor,** *n.*

dis·sect·ed (di sek′tid; dī–), *adj.* **1** cut or divided into many parts. **2** deeply cut into numerous segments. **3** cut up by irregular valleys.

dis·sem·ble (di sem′bəl), *v.,* **–bled, –bling.** **1** disguise or hide (one's real feelings, thoughts, plans, etc.). **2** pretend; feign. [alter., after *resemble,* of obs. *dissimule* dissimulate] —**dis·sem′bler,** *n.*

dis·sem·i·nate (di sem′ə nāt), *v.,* **–nat·ed, –nat·ing.** scatter widely; spread abroad. [< L, < *dis-* in every direction + *semen* seed] —**dis·sem′i·na′tion,** *n.* —**dis·sem′i·na′tive,** *adj.* —**dis·sem′i·na′tor,** *n.*

dis·sen·sion (di sen′shən), *n.* **1** a disputing; a quarreling. **2** hard feeling caused by a difference in opinion.

dis·sent (di sent′), *v.* **1** differ in opinion; disagree. **2** refuse to conform to the rules and beliefs of an established church. —*n.* **1** difference of opinion; disagreement. **2** refusal to conform to the rules and beliefs of an established church. [< L, < *dis-* differently + *sentire* think, feel] —**dis·sent′er,** *n.*

dis·sen·tient (di sen′shənt), *adj.* dissenting. —*n.* person who dissents. —**dis·sen′tience,** *n.*

dis·ser·ta·tion (dis′ər tā′shən), *n.* a formal discussion of a subject; treatise. [< L *dissertatio* < *dis-* + *serere* join words]

dis·serv·ice (dis sėr′vis), *n.* harm; injury.

dis·sev·er (di sev′ər), *v.* sever; separate. —**dis·sev′er·ance,** *n.*

dis·si·dent (dis′ə dənt), *adj.* disagreeing; dissenting. —*n.* person who disagrees or dissents. —**dis′si·dence,** *n.*

dis·sim·i·lar (di sim′ə lər), *adj.* not similar; unlike; different. —**dis·sim′i·lar′i·ty,** *n.* —**dis·sim′i·lar·ly,** *adv.*

dis·si·mil·i·tude (dis′si mil′ə tüd; –tūd), *n.* unlikeness; difference.

dis·sim·u·late (di sim′yə lāt), *v.,* **–lated, –lat·ing.** disguise; dissemble. —**dis·sim′u·la′tion,** *n.* —**dis·sim′u·la′tor,** *n.*

dis·si·pate (dis′ə pāt), *v.,* **–pat·ed, –pat·ing.** **1** spread in different directions; scatter. **2** disappear; dispel. **3** spend foolishly. **4** indulge too much in sensual or foolish pleasures. [< L, < *dis-* in different directions + *sipare* throw] —**dis′si·pat′er, dis′si·pa′tor,** *n.* —**dis′si·pa′tive,** *adj.*

dis·si·pat·ed (dis′ə pāt′id), *adj.* indulging too much in sensuous or foolish pleasures; dissolute. —**dis′si·pat′ed·ly,** *adv.* —**dis′si·pat′ed·ness,** *n.*

dis·si·pa·tion (dis′ə pā′shən), *n.* **1** a dissipating or being dissipated. **2** too much indulgence in evil or foolish pleasures.

dis·so·ci·ate (di sō′shi āt), *v.,* **–at·ed, –at·ing.** **1** break the connection or association with; separate. **2** *Chem.* separate or decompose by dissociation. [< L, < *dis-* apart + *socius* ally]

dis·so·ci·a·tion (di sō′si ā′shən; –shi ā′–), *n.* **1** act of dissociating or state of being dissociated. **2** separation or decomposition of a chemical substance into simpler constituents. —**dis·so′ci·a′tive,** *adj.*

dis·sol·u·ble (di sol′yə bəl), *adj.* capable of being dissolved. —**dis·sol′u·bil′i·ty, dis·sol′u·ble·ness,** *n.*

dis·so·lute (dis′ə lüt), *adj.* living an immoral life; very wicked; dissipated. [< L *dissolutus*, pp. of *dissolvere* DISSOLVE] —**dis′so·lute·ly,** *adv.* —**dis′so·lute·ness,** *n.*

dis·so·lu·tion (dis′ə lü′shən), *n.* 1 a breaking up into parts. 2 the breaking up of an assembly by ending its session. 3 ruin; destruction.

dis·solve (di zolv′), *v.,* **-solved, -solv·ing.** 1 make or become liquid, esp. by putting or being put into a liquid. 2 break up; end: *dissolve a partnership.* 3 fade away. [< L, < *dis-* (intensive) + *solvere* loose] —**dis·solv′a·ble,** *adj.* —**dis·solv′er,** *n.*

dis·so·nance (dis′ə nəns), **dis·so·nan·cy** (-nən si), *n., pl.* **-nan·ces; -cies.** combination of sounds that is not harmonious; discord. [< L, < *dis-* differently + *sonare* to sound]

dis·so·nant (dis′ə nənt), *adj.* 1 harsh in sound. 2 out of harmony. —**dis′so·nant·ly,** *adv.*

dis·suade (di swād′), *v.,* **-suad·ed, -suad·ing.** persuade not to do something. [< L, < *dis-* against + *suadere* to urge] —**dis·suad′er,** *n.* **dis·sua′sion,** *n.* —**dis·sua′sive,** *adj.*

dist., 1 distance. 2 district.

dis·taff (dis′taf; -täf), *n.* 1 the female sex; woman or women. 2 woman's work or affairs. 3 a split stick that holds the wool, flax, etc., for spinning. [OE, < *dis-* (see DIZEN) + *stœf* staff]

distaff side, the mother's side of a family.

dis·tal (dis′təl), *adj.* away from the center; forming the end part: *distal feathers.*

dis·tance (dis′təns), *n., v.,* **-tanced, -tanc·ing.** —*n.* 1 space in between. 2 a being far away. 3 place far away. 4 lack of friendliness or familiarity; reserve. —*v.* leave far behind; do much better than.

dis·tant (dis′tənt), *adj.* 1 far away in space. 2 away. 3 far apart in time, relationship, likeness, etc.; not close. 4 not friendly. [< F < L *distans* < *dis-* off + *stare* stand] —**dis′tant·ly,** *adv.*

dis·taste (dis tāst′), *n.* dislike.

dis·taste·ful (dis tāst′fəl), *adj.* unpleasant; disagreeable; offensive. —**dis·taste′ful·ly,** *adv.* —**dis·taste′ful·ness,** *n.*

dis·tem·per[1] (dis tem′pər), *n.* an infectious disease of dogs and other animals, accompanied by a short, dry cough and a loss of strength. [< LL *distemperare* mix improperly. See DIS-, TEMPER.]

dis·tem·per[2] (dis tem′pər), *n.* paint made by mixing the colors with eggs or glue instead of oil. [< OF *destemprer* < Med.L, soak, < LL, mix thoroughly. See DIS-, TEMPER.]

dis·tend (dis tend′), *v.* stretch out; expand. [< L, < *dis-* apart + *tendere* stretch] —**dis·ten′si·ble,** *adj.* —**dis·ten′si·bil′i·ty,** *n.* —**dis·ten′tion,** *n.*

dis·tich (dis′tik), *n., pl.* **-tichs.** two lines of verse together that make complete sense; couplet. [< L < Gk., < *di-* two + *stichos* line]

dis·till (dis til′), *v.,* **-tilled, -till·ing.** 1 heat (a liquid, or other substance) and condense the vapor given off. 2 obtain by distilling. 3 extract; refine. 4 fall in drops; drip. [< L, < *de-* down + *stillare* to drop < *stilla* drop] —**dis·till′a·ble,** *adj.*

dis·til·late (dis′tə lit; -lāt), *n.* a distilled liquid; something obtained by distilling.

dis·til·la·tion (dis′tə lā′shən), *n.* 1 a distilling. 2 something distilled; extract; essence.

dis·till·er (dis til′ər), *n.* 1 person or thing that distills. 2 person or business that makes whiskey, rum, brandy, etc.

dis·till·er·y (dis til′ər i), *n., pl.* **-er·ies.** place where distilling is done.

dis·tinct (dis tingkt′), *adj.* 1 not the same; separate. 2 not alike; different. 3 clear; plain. 4 unmistakable; decided. [< L *distinctus,* pp. of *distinguere* DISTINGUISH] —**dis·tinct′ness,** *n.*

dis·tinc·tion (dis tingk′shən), *n.* 1 act of distinguishing; making a difference: *he gave every child 10 dollars without distinction.* 2 difference. 3 point of difference; special quality or feature. 4 honor: *the soldier served with distinction.* 5 mark or sign of honor. 6 excellence; superiority. **a distinction without a difference,** false or artificial difference.

dis·tinc·tive (dis tingk′tiv), *adj.* distinguishing from others; special; characteristic. —**dis·tinc′tive·ly,** *adv.* —**dis·tinc′tive·ness,** *n.*

dis·tinct·ly (dis tingkt′li), *adv.* 1 clearly; plainly. 2 unmistakably; decidedly.

dis·tin·guish (dis ting′gwish), *v.* 1 tell apart; see or show the difference in. 2 see or hear clearly. 3 be a special quality or feature of. 4 make famous or well-known. [< L, < *dis-* between + *stinguere* to prick] —**dis·tin′guish·a·ble,** *adj.* —**dis·tin′guish·a·bly,** *adv.*

dis·tin·guished (dis ting′gwisht), *adj.* famous; well-known.

dis·tort (dis tôrt′), *v.* 1 pull or twist out of shape. 2 change from the truth. [< L *distortus* < *dis-* (intensive) + *torquere* twist] —**dis·tort′ed,** *adj.* —**dis·tort′ed·ly,** *adv.* —**dis·tort′ed·ness,** *n.* —**dis·tort′er,** *n.*

dis·tor·tion (dis tôr′shən), *n.* 1 a twisting out of shape. 2 *Fig.* exaggeration or twisting of a fact. 3 distorted form or image. 4 change of a sound or light wave creating inaccurate reproduction during transmission. —**dis·tor′tion·al,** *adj.*

dis·tract (dis trakt′), *v.* 1 draw away (the mind, attention, etc.). 2 confuse; disturb; bewilder. 3 put out of one's mind; make insane. [< L *distractus* < *dis-* away + *trahere* draw] —**dis·tract′ed,** *adj.* —**dis·tract′ed·ly,** *adv.* —**dis·tract′er,** *n.* —**dis·tract′ing,** *adj.* —**dis·tract′ing·ly,** *adv.* —**dis·trac′tive,** *adj.*

dis·trac·tion (dis trak′shən), *n.* 1 act of distracting. 2 thing that distracts. 3 confusion of mind; disturbance of thought. 4 relief from continued thought, grief, or effort. **to distraction,** to a point of complete confusion; craziness.

dis·traught (dis trôt′), *adj.* 1 distracted. 2 crazed. [var. of obs. *distract,* adj. See DISTRACT.]

dis·tress (dis tres′), *n.* 1 great pain or sorrow; anxiety; trouble. 2 something that causes distress; misfortune. 3 dangerous condition; difficult situation: *ship in distress.* —*v.* cause pain, grief, or suffering to. [< OF *distrece,* ult. < L *districtus* < *dis-* apart + *stringere* draw] —**dis·tress′ful,** *adj.* —**dis·tress′ful·ly,** *adv.* —**dis·tress′ing,** *adj.* —**dis·tress′ing·ly,** *adv.*

dis·trib·ute (dis trib′yüt), *v.,* **-ut·ed, -ut·ing.** 1 divide and give out in shares. 2 spread; scatter. 3 divide into parts. 4 arrange; classify. [< L, < *dis-* individually + *tribuere* assign] —**dis·trib′ut·a·ble,** *adj.*

dis·tri·bu·tion (dis′trə bū′shən), *n.* 1 act of distributing. 2 way of being distributed. 3 thing distributed. 4 the distributing to consumers of goods grown or made by producers. —**dis′tri·bu′tion·al,** *adj.*

dis·trib·u·tive (dis trib′yə tiv), *adj.* 1 of or having to do with distribution; distributing. 2 referring to each individual of a group considered separately. —**dis·trib′u·tive·ly,** *adv.* —**dis·trib′u·tive·ness,** *n.*

dis·trib·u·tor, dis·trib·ut·er (dis trib′yə tər), *n.* 1 person or thing that distributes. 2 person or company that distributes to consumers the goods grown or made by producers. 3 part of a gasoline engine that distributes electric current to the spark plugs.

dis·trict (dis′trikt), *n.* 1 portion of a country; region. 2 portion of a country, state, or city serving as a unit for policing, fire prevention, political representation, etc. —*v.* divide into districts. [< LL *districtus* district < L *distringere.* See DISTRESS.]

district attorney, lawyer who handles cases for the government for a certain district.

District of Columbia, district in the E United States belonging to the federal government.

dis·trust (dis trust′), *v.* have no confidence in; be suspicious of. —*n.* lack of trust or confidence; suspicion. —**dis·trust′ful,** *adj.* —**dis·trust′ful·ly,** *adv.*

dis·turb (dis tèrb′), *v.* 1 destroy the peace, quiet, or rest of. 2 break in upon with noise or change. 3 put out of order. 4 make uneasy; trouble. [< L < *dis-* (intensive) + *turbare* agitate < *turba* commotion] —**dis·turb′er,** *n.* —**dis·turb′ing·ly,** *adv.*

dis·turb·ance (dis tèr′bəns), *n.* 1 a disturbing or being disturbed. 2 thing that disturbs. 3 confusion; disorder.

dis·un·ion (dis ūn′yən), *n.* 1 separation; division. 2 lack of unity; disagreement.

dis·u·nite (dis′yu̇ nīt′), *v.*, **-nit·ed, -nit·ing. 1** separate; divide. **2** destroy the unity of. —**dis·u′ni·ty,** *n.*

dis·use (*n.* dis ūs′; *v.* dis ūz′), *n., v.,* **-used, -us·ing.** —*n.* lack of use. —*v.* stop using.

ditch (dich), *n.* a long, narrow place dug in the earth, usually used to carry off water. —*v.* **1** dig a ditch in. **2** *Informal.* get rid of. [OE *dīc*] —**ditch′er,** *n.*

dith·er (dith′ər), *n.* **1** a tremble; shiver; quiver. **2** a confused, excited condition.

dits·y or **dits·ey** (dit′si), *adj.* flighty; unpredictable; dizzy.

dit·to (dit′ō), *n., pl.* **-tos,** *adv.* —*n.* **1** the same as was said before; the same. **2** mark (″) that stands for ditto. —*adv.* as said before; likewise. [< Ital., said, < L *dictus,* pp. of *dicere* say]

dit·ty (dit′i), *n., pl.* **-ties.** a short, simple song or poem. [< OF *ditié* < L *dictatum* (thing) dictated, pp. of *dictare* DICTATE]

ditty bag, a small bag used to hold needles, thread, buttons, etc.

ditz (dits), *n.* flighty, unpredictable person.

ditz·y (dit′si), *adj.* =ditsy.

di·u·ret·ic (dī′yu̇ ret′ik), *adj.* causing an increase in the flow of urine. —*n.* drug that does this. [< LL < Gk., < *dia-* through + *oureein* urinate]

di·ur·nal (dī ėr′nəl), *adj.* **1** occurring every day; daily. **2** of or belonging to the daytime. **3** lasting a day. [< LL *diurnalis* < L *dies* day. Doublet of JOURNAL.] —**di·ur′nal·ly,** *adv.*

div., 1 divide; divided. **2** dividend. **3** division.

di·va (dē′və), *n., pl.* **-vas.** prima donna. [< Ital. < L, goddess]

di·va·lent (dī vā′lənt), *adj.* having a valence of two.

dive (dīv), *v.,* **dived** or **dove, dived, div·ing,** *n.* —*v.* **1** plunge head first into water. **2** go down or out of sight suddenly. **3** (of an airplane) plunge downward at a steep angle. —*n.* **1** act of diving. **2** the downward plunge of an airplane. **3** a low, cheap place for drinking and gambling. [OE *dȳfan*] —**div′er,** *n.*

dive-bomb (dīv′bom′), *v.* plunge at a target.

dive bomber, airplane used to bomb a target by making an almost vertical dive straight at it. —**dive bombing.**

di·verge (də vėrj′; dī-), *v.,* **-verged, -verg·ing. 1** move or lie in different directions from the same point. **2** differ; vary; deviate. [< LL, < *dis-* in different directions + *vergere* slope] —**di·ver′gence, di·ver′gen·cy,** *n.* —**di·ver′gent,** *adj.* —**di·ver′gent·ly,** *adv.*

di·vers (dī′vərz), *adj.* several different; various. [< OF < L *diversus,* pp. of *divertere* DIVERT]

di·verse (də vėrs′; dī-), *adj.* **1** different; unlike. **2** varied: *a person of diverse interests.* [var. of *divers;* now regarded as immediately from L] —**di·verse′ly,** *adv.* —**di·verse′ness,** *n.*

di·ver·si·fy (də vėr′sə fī; dī-), *v.,* **-fied, -fy·ing.** give variety to; vary. —**di·ver′si·fi·ca′tion,** *n.* —**di·ver′si·fi′er,** *n.*

di·ver·sion (də vėr′zhən; -shən; dī-), *n.* **1** a turning aside. **2** amusement; entertainment; pastime.

di·ver·sion·ar·y (də vėr′zhən er′i; -shən-, dī-), *adj.* of or like a diversion or feint, esp. in military tactics.

di·ver·si·ty (də vėr′sə ti; dī-), *n., pl.* **-ties. 1** complete difference. **2** variety.

di·vert (də vėrt′; dī-), *v.* **1** turn aside. **2** amuse; entertain. [< F < L, < *dis-* aside + *vertere* turn] —**di·vert′er,** *n.* —**di·ver′tive,** *adj.*

di·ver·tic·u·li·tis (dī′vər tik′yə lī′tis), *n.* inflammation of a sac, esp. in the intestine.

di·ver·tic·u·lum (dī vər tik′yə ləm), *n., pl.* **-lums, -la** (-lə). tubular sac branching off from a canal or cavity. [< L]

di·ver·ti·men·to (di ver ti men′tō), *n., pl.,* **-tos, -ti** (-ti). **1** light instrumental composition, usually in several movements. **2** a diversion, esp. a pleasant one. [< Ital.]

di·ver·tisse·ment (dē ver tēs mäN′), *n.* amusement; entertainment. [< F]

di·vest (də vest′; dī-), *v.* **1** strip; rid; free. **2** force to give up; deprive. [< Med.L *divestire* < OF, < *des-* away (< L *dis-*) + *vestir* < L *vestīre* clothe]

di·vide (də vīd′), *v.,* **-vid·ed, -vid·ing,** *n.* —*v.* **1** separate into parts: *a brook divides the field.* **2** separate into equal parts: *divide 8 by 2, and you get 4.* **3** give some of to each; share: *the children divided the candy among them.* **4** disagree or cause to disagree; differ or cause to differ in feeling, opinion, etc.: *jealousy divided us.* —*n.* ridge of land between two regions drained by different river systems. [< L *dividere*] —**di·vid′a·ble,** *adj.* —**di·vid′er,** *n.*

di·vid·ed (də vīd′id), *adj.* **1** separated. **2** (of a leaf) cut to the base so as to form distinct portions.

div·i·dend (div′ə dend), *n.* **1** number or quantity to be divided by another: *in 8 + 2, 8 is the dividend.* **2** money to be shared by those to whom it belongs. If a company makes a profit, it declares a dividend. [< L, (thing) to be divided]

di·vid·er (də vīd′ər), *n.* **1** person or thing that divides. **2** Usually, **dividers.** instrument for dividing lines, etc.; compasses.

div·i·na·tion (div′ə nā′shən), *n.* **1** act of foreseeing the future or foretelling the unknown. **2** a skillful guess or prediction. —**di·vin′a·to′ry,** *adj.*

di·vine (də vīn′), *adj., n., v.,* **-vined, -vin·ing.** —*adj.* **1** of God or a god. **2** by or from God. **3** to or for God; sacred; holy. **4** like God or a god; heavenly. **5** *Informal.* very excellent. —*n.* clergyman; minister; priest. —*v.* find out or foretell. [< OF < L *divinus* of a deity < *divus* deity] —**di·vine′ly,** *adv.* —**di·vine′ness,** *n.* —**di·vin′er,** *n.*

divining rod, a forked stick supposed to be useful in locating water, oil, metal, and other things underground.

di·vin·i·ty (də vin′ə ti), *n., pl.* **-ties. 1** a divine being; a god. **2** divine nature or quality. **3** study of God, religion, and divine things; theology.

the Divinity, God; the Deity.

di·vis·i·ble (də viz′ə bəl), *adj.* **1** capable of being divided. **2** capable of being divided without leaving a remainder. —**di·vis′i·bil′i·ty,** *n.* —**di·vis′i·bly,** *adv.*

di·vi·sion (də vizh′ən), *n.* **1** a dividing or being divided. **2** act of giving some to each; a sharing. **3** process of dividing one number by another. **4** thing that divides. **5** part; group; section. **6** part of an army consisting of two or three brigades of infantry and a certain amount of cavalry, artillery, etc., usually commanded by a major general. **7** difference of opinion, thought, or feeling; disagreement. —**di·vi′sion·al,** *adj.*

division of labor, a dividing up of work so that each person has a certain part to do.

di·vi·sive (də vī′siv), *adj.* tending to cause disagreement or division.

di·vi·sor (də vī′zər), *n.* number or quantity by which another is divided: *in 8 + 2, 2 is the divisor.*

di·vorce (də vôrs′; -vōrs′), *n., v.,* **-vorced, -vorc·ing.** —*n.* **1** the legal ending of a marriage. **2** a complete separation —*v.* **1** end legally a marriage between. **2** separate from by divorce: *Mrs. Smith divorced her husband.* **3** separate. [< OF < L *divortium* separation < *divertere* DIVERT]

di·vor·cé (də vôr′sā′; -vōr′-), *n.* divorced man. [< F]

di·vor·cee (də vôr′sē′; -vōr′-), *n.* divorced person.

di·vor·cée (də vôr′sā′; -vōr′-), *n.* divorced woman. [< F]

div·ot (div′ət), *n.* a small piece of turf or earth dug up by a golf club in making a stroke.

di·vulge (də vulj′), *v.,* **-vulged, -vulg·ing.** make known; make public; tell; reveal: *the traitor divulged secret plans to the enemy.* [< L *divulgare* make common < *dis-* + *vulgus* common people] —**di·vulge′ment,** *n.* —**di·vulg′er,** *n.*

div·vy (div′i), *v.,* **-vied, -vy·ing.** *Informal.* Also, **divvy up.** share; divide.

Dix·ie (dik′si), *n.* the S states of the United States.

Dix·ie·land (dik′si land), *n.* style of jazz originally from New Orleans.

diz·zy (diz′i), *adj.,* **-zi·er, -zi·est,** *v.,* **-zied, -zy·ing.** —*adj.* **1** disposed to fall; not steady; stagger. **2** confused; bewildered. **3** causing dizziness: *a dizzy height.* **4** *Informal.* silly; foolish. —*v.* make dizzy. [OE *dysig* foolish] —**diz′zi·ly,** *adv.* —**diz′zi·ness,** *n.*

DJ or **D.J.,** disk jockey.

Dja·kar·ta (jə kär′tə), *n.* seaport and capital of Indonesia, in NW Java. Also, **Jakarta.**

dkg., decagram.

dkl., decaliter.

dkm., decameter.

dl., decaliter.

dm., decimeter.

DMZ, demilitarized zone.

DNA, deoxyribonucleic acid, the substance responsible for the transmission of inherited characteristics. Also, **DNA-ase.**

DNA fingerprint, genetic fingerprint, unique to each individual, used as a means of identification. —**DNA fingerprinting.**

DNA profile, =DNA fingerprint.

do[1] (dü), *v., pres.* **do, does, do;** *pt.* **did;** *pp.* **done;** *ppr.* **do·ing;** *n.* —*v.* **1** perform: *do your work.* **2** act: *do or die.* **3** finish: *that's done!* **4** make: *Walt Disney did a movie about the seven dwarfs.* **5** behave: *do wisely.* **6** put in order: *do the dishes.* **7** fare: *how do you do?* **8** be satisfactory: *this hat will do.* **9** cook: *the roast will be done in an hour.* **10** traverse: *we did 80 miles in an hour.* **11** *Do* has special uses where it has no definite meaning: **a** in asking questions: *do you like milk?* **b** in emphasizing a verb: *I do want to go.* **c** in standing for a verb already used: *my dog goes where I do.* **d** in expressions that contain *not: people talk; animals do not.* **e** in inverted constructions after the adverbs *rarely, hardly, little,* etc.: *rarely did she laugh.* —*n. Colloq.* a festive party.

do away with, a abolish. **b** kill.

do by, act or behave toward; treat.

do for, ruin or damage: *The car is done for.*

do in, a ruin. **b** *Informal.* kill. **c** exhaust: *done in by the move.*

do or die, try as hard as possible.

do out of, swindle.

do over, a do once again. **b** redecorate.

do up, wrap up.

do without, manage without something. [OE *dōn*]

do[2] (dō), *n.* the first and last tone of a musical scale. [substituted for *ut.* See GAMUT.]

do., ditto.

DOA, dead on arrival.

do·a·ble (dü′ə bəl), *adj.* that can be done.

dob·bin (dob′ən), *n.* a slow, gentle horse.

Do·ber·man pin·scher (dō′bər mən pin′-shər), a medium-sized dog with short, dark hair.

doc (dok), *n. Informal.* doctor.

doc., document.

do·cent (dō′sənt), *n.* **1** lecturer at a university, esp. one who is a graduate student. **2** guide who conducts museum tours.

doc·ile (dos′əl), *adj.* **1** easily managed; obedient. **2** easily taught; willing to learn. [< F < L *docilis* < *docere* teach] —**doc′ile·ly,** *adv.* —**do·cil′i·ty,** *n.*

dock[1] (dok), *n.* **1** platform built on the shore or out from the shore; wharf; pier. **2** water between two piers. **3** place where a ship may be repaired, often built watertight so that the water may be pumped out. —*v.* **1** bring (a ship) to a dock. **2** come into a dock. [< MDu. or MLG *docke*]

dock[2] (dok), *n.* the solid, fleshy part of an animal's tail. —*v.* **1** cut short; cut the end off. **2** cut down; reduce: *dock wages for lateness.* [OE *–docca,* as in *finger-docca* finger muscle]

dock[3] (dok), *n.* place where an accused person stands in a law court. [cf. Flem. *dok* pen]

dock[4] (dok), *n.* a large weed with sour and bitter leaves. [OE *docce*]

dock·age (dok′ij), *n.* **1** place to dock ship. **2** charge for using a dock. **3** the docking of ships.

dock·et (dok′it), *n., v.,* **-et·ed, -et·ing.** —*n.* **1** list of lawsuits to be tried by a court. **2** *U.S.* any list of matters to be considered by some group of people. **3** label or ticket giving the contents of a package, document, etc. —*v.* **1** enter on a docket. **2** make a summary or list of. **3** mark with a docket.

dock·yard (dok′yärd′), *n.* place where ships are built, equipped, and repaired.

doc·tor (dok′tər), *n.* **1** person licensed to treat diseases or physical disorders; physician or surgeon. **2** any person who treats diseases: *a witch doctor.* **3** person who has received one of the highest degrees given by a university: *a Doctor of Philosophy.* **4** the academic degree held by such a person. **5** *Archaic.* a learned man; teacher. —*v.* **1** practice medicine. **2** treat diseases in (a person, animal, etc.). **3** tamper with. [< OF < L, teacher, < *docere* teach] —**doc′tor·al,** *adj.*

doc·tor·ate (dok′tər it), *n.* degree of doctor given by a university.

doc·tri·nar·i·an (dok trə när′i ən), *n.* an impractical theorist.

doc·trine (dok′trən), *n.* **1** what is taught as the belief of a church, nation, etc. **2** what is taught; teachings. [< F < L *doctrina* < *doctor* DOCTOR] —**doc′tri·nal,** *adj.* —**doc′tri·nal·ly,** *adv.*

doc·u·dra·ma (dok′yə drä′mə), *n.* television drama based on facts. [< *documentary + drama*]

doc·u·ment (*n.* dok′yə mənt; *v.* dok′yə ment), *n.* something written, printed, etc., that gives information or proof of some fact. —*v.* **1** provide with documents. **2** prove or support by means of documents. [< L *documentum* example, proof < *docere* show] —**doc′u·men·ta′tion,** *n.*

doc·u·men·ta·ry (dok′yə men′tə ri), *adj., n., pl.* **-ries.** —*adj.* **1** of, pertaining to, or like a document or documents. **2** verified in writing. **3** presenting or recording factual information in an artistic fashion: *a documentary film.* —*n.* a documentary motion picture.

dod·der (dod′ər), *v.* shake; tremble; totter.

Do·dec·a·nese Islands (dō′dek ə nēs′; –nēz′; dō dek′ə–), group of Greek Islands in the Aegean Sea, off SW Turkey.

dodge (doj), *v.,* **dodged, dodg·ing,** *n.* —*v.* **1** move quickly to one side. **2** move quickly in order to get away from (a person, a blow, or something thrown). **3** get away from by some trick. —*n.* **1** sudden movement to one side. **2** a clever trick or ruse.

dodge ball, game whose object is to avoid being hit by a rubber ball thrown by a surrounding ring of players.

dodg·em (doj′əm), *n.,* or **dodgem car.** any one of various kinds of small cars ridden for entertainment at fairs and amusement parks.

dodg·er (doj′ər), *n.* **1** person who dodges. **2** a shifty or dishonest person.

do·do (dō′dō), *n., pl.* **–dos, –does.** a large, clumsy bird unable to fly. Dodoes are now extinct. [< Pg. *doudo* fool]

doe (dō), *n.* a female deer, antelope, rabbit, or hare. [OE *dā*]

Doe (dō), *n.* **John,** name used in legal documents, etc., to mean anyone.

do·er (dü′ər), *n.* person who does something.

does (duz), *v.* third pers. sing., pres. indic. of **do**[1].

doe·skin (dō′skin′), *n.* **1** skin of a female deer. **2** leather made from it. **3** a smooth, soft woolen cloth.

does·n't (duz′ənt), does not.

do·est (dü′ist), *v. Archaic.* do.

do·eth (dü′ith), *v. Archaic.* does.

doff (dof; dôf), *v.* take off; remove, as a hat. [contraction of *do off*]

dog (dôg; dog), *n., v.,* **dogged, dog·ging.** —*n.* **1** a domesticated carnivorous animal (of the genus *Canis*), kept as a pet, for hunting, etc. **2** any animal of the family that includes wolves, foxes, and jackals. **3** a male dog, fox, wolf, etc. **4** any of various animals somewhat like a dog, such as the prairie dog. **5** a low, worthless man. **6** andiron. —*v.* hunt or follow like a dog. [OE *docga*]

go to the dogs, be ruined.

dog·catch·er (dôg′kach′ər; dog′–), *n.* person employed to catch stray dogs.

dog days, period of very hot and uncomfortable weather during July and August.

doge (dōj), *n.* the chief magistrate of Venice or Genoa when they were republics. [< Venetian Ital. < L *dux* leader. Doublet of DUCE, DUKE.]

dog-ear (dôg′ir′; dog′–), *n.* a folded-down corner of a page in a book. —*v.* fold down the corner of (the page or pages of a book). Also, **dog's-ear** —**dog′-eared′,** *adj.*

dog·fight (dôg′fīt′; dog′–), *n.* an engagement of fighter planes at close quarters with the enemy. —**dog′fight′,** *v.*

dog·fish (dôg′fish′; dog′–), *n., pl.* **-fish·es** or (*esp. collectively*) **-fish.** any of several kinds of small shark, as the **spiny dogfish** of the North Atlantic coast.

dog·ged (dôg′id; dog′–), *adj.* stubborn: *dogged determination.* **—dog′ged·ly,** *adv.* **—dog′ged·ness,** *n.*

dog·ger·el (dôg′ər əl; dog′–), **dog·grel** (dôg′rəl; dog′–), *n.* very poor poetry that is not artistic in form or meaning. **—adj.** of or like doggerel; not artistic; poor.

dog·gie (dôg′i, dog′i), *n.* **1** little dog. **2** pet name for a dog. Also, **doggy.**

dog·gy (dôg′i; dog′i), *adj.,* **-gi·er, -gi·est.** like a dog.

doggy bag, bag given to a customer in a restaurant with leftover food from the meal in it.

dog·house (dôg′hous′; dog′–), *n.* a small house or shelter for a dog.
in the doghouse, out of favor.

do·gie (dō′gi), *n. W.* a motherless calf on the range or in a range herd.

dog·ma (dôg′mə; dog′–), *n., pl.* **-mas, -ma·ta** (-mə tə). **1** belief taught or held as true, esp. by a church. **2** doctrine. **3** opinion asserted in a positive manner as if it were authoritative. [< L < Gk., opinion, < *dokeein* think]

dog·mat·ic (dôg mat′ik; dog–), **dog·mat·i·cal** (-ə kəl), *adj.* **1** having to do with dogma. **2** asserting opinions as if one were the highest authority; positive; overbearing. **3** asserted without proof. **—dog·mat′i·cal·ly,** *adv.* **—dog·mat′i·cal·ness,** *n.*

dog·ma·tism (dôg′mə tiz əm; dog′), *n.* positive or authoritative assertion of opinion. **—dog′ma·tist,** *n.*

dog·ma·tize (dôg′mə tīz; dog′–), *v.,* **-tized, -tiz·ing.** speak or write in a dogmatic way. **—dog′ma·ti·za′tion,** *n.* **—dog′ma·tiz′er,** *n.*

do-good·er (dü′gůd′ər), *n.* a person who is overly eager to correct or set things right.

Dog Star, 1 Sirius. **2** Procyon.

dog tag, 1 *Informal.* identification tag worn by a member of the military. **2** identification tag attached to a dog's collar.

dogtooth violet, dog's-tooth violet, a small plant of the lily family that has yellow, white, or purple flowers; adder's-tongue.

dog·trot (dôg′trot′; dog′–), *n.* a gentle trot.

dog·watch (dôg′woch′; -wôch′; dog′–), *n.* one of the two two-hour periods of work on a ship, from 4 to 6 P.M. and from 6 to 8 P.M.

dog·wood (dôg′wůd′; dog′–), *n.* **1** tree with pink or white flowers that bloom in the spring. **2** its hard wood.

doi·ly (doi′li), *n., pl.* **-lies.** a small piece of linen, lace, paper, etc., used under plates, vases, etc. [after a London dry-goods dealer]

do·ing (dü′ing), *n.* action.

doings, a things done; actions. **b** behavior; conduct.

dol·drum (dol′drəm; dōl′–), *n.* a calm, windless region of the ocean near the equator.

doldrums, dullness; low spirits.

dole (dōl), *n., v.,* **doled, dol·ing. —n. 1** portion of money, food, etc., given in charity. **2** a small portion. **—v. 1** deal out in portions to the poor. **2** give in small portions. [OE *dāl* part; akin to DEAL[1]]

dole·ful (dōl′fəl), *adj.* sad; mournful; dreary; dismal. **—dole′ful·ly,** *adv.* **—dole′ful·ness,** *n.*

doll (dol), *n.* **1** a child's plaything made to look like a baby, child, or grown person. **2** a pretty girl or woman without much intelligence. **3** *Slang.* nice person: *he's a doll.* **—v.** *Informal.* dress (*up*) in a stylish or showy way. [pet name for *Dorothy*]

dol·lar (dol′ər), *n.* **1** a unit of money in the United States, equivalent to 100 cents. **2** a similar unit of money in Canada, Australia, etc.

bet one's bottom dollar, a bet the last money one has. **b** be certain or sure.

dollars to doughnuts, sure thing; certainty. [earlier *daler* < LG; corresponds to HG *Joachimsthaler* coin of St. Joachim's valley (in Bohemia)]

doll·y (dol′i), *n., pl.* **doll·ies. 1** a child's name for a doll. **2** a small, low frame with wheels, used to move heavy things.

dol·man sleeve (dol′mən), *n.,* sleeve of a woman's dress or coat that is fitted at the wrist and cut full above the forearm. [ult. < Turk. *dōlāmān*]

dol·men (dol′mən), *n.* a prehistoric tomb made by laying a large, flat stone across several upright stones. [< F]

dol·o·mite (dol′ə mīt), *n.* a rock consisting of calcium and magnesium carbonate. [for M. *Dolomieu,* geologist]

do·lor (dō′lər), *n. Poetic.* sorrow; grief. [< OF < L *dolor*]

dol·or·ous (dol′ər əs; dō′lər–), *adj.* **1** mournful; sorrowful. **2** grievous; painful. **—dol′or·ous·ly,** *adv.* **—dol′or·ous·ness,** *n.*

dol·phin (dol′fən), *n.* a small whale that has a beaklike snout. [< OF *daulphin* < L < Gk. *delphis*]

dolt (dōlt), *n.* a dull, stupid person.

dolt·ish (dōl′tish), *adj.* dull and stupid. **—dolt′ish·ly,** *adv.* **—dolt′ish·ness,** *n.*

-dom, *suffix.* **1** position, rank, or realm of a ___, as in *kingdom.* **2** condition of being ___, as in *martyrdom.* **3** all those who are ___, as in *heathendom.* [OE *-dōm*]

do·main (dō mān′), *n.* **1** territory under the control of one ruler or government. **2** land owned by one person; estate. **3** field of thought, action, etc. **4** space on the Internet used and controlled by a particular website. [< F *domaine* < L, < *dominus* lord, master]

dome (dōm), *n., v.,* **domed, dom·ing. —n. 1** a large, rounded roof on a circular

or many-sided base. **2** something high and rounded: *the dome of the sky.* **—v. 1** cover with a dome. **2** shape like a dome. **3** rise or swell as a dome does. [< F < LL, roof, house, < Gk. *doma*]

do·mes·tic (də mes′tik), *adj.* **1** of the home, household, or family affairs. **2** fond of home and family life. **3** not wild; tame. **4** of one's own country; not foreign. **5** made in one's own country; native. **—n.** servant in a household. [< L, ult. < *domus* house] **—do·mes′ti·cal·ly,** *adv.*

do·mes·ti·cate (də mes′tə kāt), *v.,* **-cat·ed, -cat·ing. 1** change (animals, savages, or plants) from a wild to a tame state; tame. **2** make fond of home and family life. **3** cause to be or feel at home; naturalize. **—do·mes′ti·ca′tion,** *n.*

do·mes·tic·i·ty (dō′mes tis′ə ti), *n., pl.* **-ties. 1** home and family life. **2** fondness for home and family life.

dom·i·cile (dom′ə səl; -sīl), *n., v.,* **-ciled, -cil·ing. —n. 1** house; home; residence. **2** place of permanent residence. **—v. 1** settle in a domicile. **2** dwell; reside. [< F < L *domicilium* < *domus* house + *colere* dwell] **—dom′i·cil′i·ar·y,** *adj.*

dom·i·nance (dom′ə nəns), **dom·i·nan·cy** (-nən si), *n., pl.* **-ces; -cies.** a being dominant; rule; control.

dom·i·nant (dom′ə nənt), *adj.* **1** most influential; ruling. **2** occupying a commanding position. **3** based on or pertaining to the dominant note in a scale. **4** of a characteristic that reappears in a larger number of offspring than a contrasting characteristic. **—n.** the fifth note in a scale. **—dom′i·nant·ly,** *adv.*

dominant character, one character that prevails over another when a pair of characters is present in the germ plasm, as in eye color, where brown prevails over blue.

dom·i·nate (dom′ə nāt), *v.,* **-nat·ed, -nat·ing. 1** control or rule by strength or power. **2** rise high above; hold a commanding position over. [< L, < *dominus* lord, master] **—dom′i·na′tive,** *adj.* **—dom′i·na′tor,** *n.*

dom·i·na·tion (dom′ə nā′shən), *n.* act or fact of dominating; control; rule.

dom·i·neer (dom′ə nir′), *v.* rule (over) at one's own will; tyrannize. [< Du. < F < L *dominari.* See DOMINATE.]

dom·i·neer·ing (dom′ə nir′ing), *adj.* inclined to domineer; arrogant. **—dom′i·neer′ing·ly,** *adv.* **—dom′i·neer′ing·ness,** *n.*

Do·min·i·can (də min′ə kən), *adj.* **1** of Saint Dominic or the religious order founded by him. **2** of the Dominican Republic. **—n. 1** friar or nun belonging to the Dominican order. **2** native or inhabitant of the Dominican Republic.

Dominican Republic, republic in the E part of the island of Hispaniola, in the West Indies.

do·min·ion (də min′yən), *n.* **1** supreme authority; rule; control. **2** territory under

the control of one ruler or government.
3 a self-governing territory. [< obs. F
< Med.L *dominio,* alter. of L *dominium*
ownership]

Dominion Day, July 1, a national holiday
in Canada in honor of the establishment
of the Dominion of Canada in 1867.

dom·i·no[1] (dom′ə nō), *n., pl.* **–noes, –nos.**
a loose cloak with a small mask covering
the upper part of the face, worn esp. at
masquerades. [< F < L *dominus* lord,
master]

dom·i·no[2] (dom′ə nō), *n., pl.* **–noes. 1
dominoes** (*sing. in use*), game played
with flat, oblong pieces having dots
marked on one side. **2** one of these
pieces.

don[1] (don), *n.* **1 Don,** Mr.; Sir (Spanish
title). **2** Spanish lord or gentleman. **3**
distinguished person. **4** head, fellow,
or tutor of a college at Oxford or Cam-
bridge University. [< Sp. < L *dominus*
lord, master]

don[2] (don), *v.,* **donned, don·ning.** put on
(clothing, etc.). [contraction of *do on*]

Do·ña (dō′nyä), *n.* **1** Lady; Madam (Spanish title). **2 doña,** Spanish lady. [< Sp. < L
domina mistress]

do·nate (dō′nāt), *v.,* **–nat·ed, –nat·ing.**
give; contribute. [< L, < *donum* gift]

do·na·tion (dō nā′shən), *n.* **1** act of giving
or contributing. **2** gift; contribution.

done (dun), *adj.* **1** completed; finished;
ended. **2** cooked enough. —*v.* pp. of
do[1].

don·jon (dun′jən; don′–), *n.* a large,
strongly fortified tower of a castle. [var.
of *dungeon*]

Don Juan (don′ wän′; jü′ən), **1** a legendary Spanish nobleman who led a dissolute life. **2** person leading an immoral
life.

don·key (dong′ki; dung′–), *n., pl.* **–keys.
1** a small animal somewhat like a horse
but with longer ears, a shorter mane, and
a tuft of hair on the end of its tail. **2** a
stubborn or stupid person.

donkey engine, a small steam engine.

don·na (don′ə), *n.* **1** a lady. **2 Donna,** title
of respect; Madam. [< Ital. < L *domina*
mistress]

do·nor (dō′nər), *n.* person who contrib-
utes; giver. [< AF < L *donator* < *donare*
DONATE] **—do′nor·ship,** *n.*

donor card, card that permits use of the
cardholder's organs for transplantation
in the case of his or her sudden death, as
in an automobile accident.

do-noth·ing (dü′nuth′ing), *n.* **1** person
who is reluctant to take action that
would change or upset existing conditions. **2** lazy, idle person.

Don Qui·xo·te (don′ ki hō′tē), hero of a
satire of chivalry.

don't (dōnt), do not.

doo·dad (dü′dad), *n.* Colloq. a fancy, trifling ornament.

doo·dle (dü′dəl), *v.,* **–dled, –dling,** *n.*
—*v.* make drawings, etc., while talking

or thinking. —*n.* a meaningless drawing
or mark.

doo·dle·bug (dü′dəl bug′), *n.* larva of
the ant lion.

doo·hick·ey (dü′hik′i), *n. Informal.* thing;
gadget.

doom (düm), *n.* **1** fate. **2** an unhappy or
terrible fate; ruin; death. **3** judgment;
sentence. —*v.* **1** destine to an unhappy
or terrible fate. **2** fix as a sentence or fate:
the emperor will doom her in death. [OE
dōm law, judgment]

dooms·day (dümz′dā′), *n.* end of the
world; day of God's final judgment of
humankind.

door (dôr; dōr), *n.* **1** a movable part to
close an opening in a wall. A door turns
on hinges or slides open and shut. **2**
any movable part that suggests a door.
3 doorway. **4** room, house, or building
to which a door belongs: *his house is
three doors down the street.* **5** way to get
something.

darken one's door, appear at one's
door.

next door to, close-by or close to.

show the door, ask to leave: *showed
them the door.*

slam (or **close**) **the door** (on), reject
or end any contact or association (with
someone or something). [OE *duru*]

door·bell (dôr′bel′; dōr′–), *n.* bell to be
rung on the outside of a door as a signal
that someone wishes to have the door
opened.

door·jamb (dôr′jam′; dōr′–), **door·post**
(–pōst′), *n.* the upright piece forming
the side of a doorway.

door·keep·er (dôr′kēp′ər; dōr′–), *n.* **1**
person who guards a door or entrance.
2 doorman.

door·knob (dôr′nob′; dōr′–), *n.* handle
on a door.

door·man (dôr′mən; –man′; dōr′–), *n.,
pl.* **–men. 1** person whose work is opening the door of a hotel, store, apartment
house, etc., for people going in or out. **2**
person who guards a door.

door·mat (dôr′mat′; dōr′–), *n.* **1** mat
used for wiping dirt from the bottom of
one's shoes before entering a building. **2**
Fig. person easily led or used by others.

door·nail (dôr′nāl′; dōr′–), *n.* nail with
a large head.

dead as a doornail, entirely dead.

door·sill (dôr′sil′; dōr′–), *n.* threshold.

door·step (dôr′step′; dōr′–), *n.* step leading from an outside door to the ground.

door·way (dôr′wā′; dōr′–), *n.* an opening
in a wall where a door is.

door·yard (dôr′yärd′; dōr′–), *n.* yard near
the door of a house; yard around a
house.

dope (dōp), *n., v.,* **doped, dop·ing.** —*n.* **1
a** harmful, narcotic drug, such as opium,
morphine, etc. **b** a drug addict. **2** *Racing
Slang.* drug given to a horse to stimulate
it. **3** *Slang.* information; forecast; prediction. **4** a very stupid person. —*v. Slang.*
give dope to.

dope out, a figure out. **b** predict.
[< Du. *doop* dipping sauce < *doopen* dip]
—dop′er, *n. Slang.*

Dor·ic (dôr′ik; dor′–), *adj.* of or having
to do with the oldest and simplest of the
Greek kinds of architecture.

dorm (dôrm), *n.* dormitory.

dor·man·cy (dôr′mən si), *n.* dormant
state.

dor·mant (dôr′mənt), *adj.* **1** sleeping. **2**
quiet as if asleep. **3** inactive. Plant bulbs
stay dormant during the cold of winter.
[< OF, ppr. of *dormir* sleep < L *dormire*]

dor·mer (dôr′mər), *n.* **1** Also, **dormer
window.** an upright window that projects from a sloping roof. **2** the projecting part of a roof that contains such a
window. [< OF < L *dormitorium* DOR-
MITORY]

dor·mi·to·ry (dôr′mə tô′ri; –tō′–), *n., pl.*
–ries. 1 *U.S.* a building with many sleeping rooms. **2** a sleeping room containing
several beds. [< L, < *dormire* sleep]

dor·mouse (dôr′mous′), *n., pl.* **–mice.** a
small animal that looks somewhat like a
squirrel and sleeps all winter.

dor·sal (dôr′səl), *adj.* of, on, or near the
back. [< LL < L *dorsum* back] **—dor′sal-
ly,** *adv.*

do·ry (dô′ri; dō′–), *n., pl.* **–ries.** rowboat with a flat bottom and high sides.
[< Central Am. Ind.]

DOS, disk operating system.

dos·age (dōs′ij), *n.* **1** amount of a medicine to be taken at one time. **2** the giving
of medicine in doses.

dose (dōs), *n., v.,* **dosed, dos·ing.** —*n.* **1**
amount of a medicine to be given or
taken at one time. **2** amount of anything
given at one time as a remedy, treatment,
etc. —*v.* give medicine to in doses; treat
with medicine. [< F < LL < Gk. *dosis* a
giving < *didonai* give] **—dos′er,** *n.*

dos·si·er (dos′i ā; –i ər), *n.* collection of
documents about some subject. [< F]

dost (dust), *v. Archaic.* do.

dot (dot), *n., v.,* **dot·ted, dot·ting.** —*n.* **1** a
tiny round mark; very small spot; point.
2 *Music.* a point after a note or rest that
makes it half again as long. **3** a short
sound used in sending messages by telegraph or radio. —*v.* **1** mark with a dot or
dots. **2** be here and there in.

on the dot, at exactly the right time. [OE
dott head of a boil] **—dot′ter,** *n.*

dot·age (dōt′ij), *n.* weak-minded and
childish condition caused by old age.
[< *dote*]

do·tard (dō′tərd), *n.* person who is weak-
minded and childish because of old age.
[< *dote*]

dote (dōt), *v.,* **dot·ed, dot·ing.** be weak-
minded and childish because of old age.

dote on or **upon,** be foolishly fond of.
[ME *doten*] **—dot′er,** *n.* **—dot′ing,** *adj.*
—dot′ing·ly, *adv.*

doth (duth), *v. Archaic.* does.

dot·ty (dot′i), *adj.,* **–ti·er, –ti·est. 1**
unsteady; shaky; feeble. **2** full of dots.

Douay Bible or **Version,** an English translation of the Latin Vulgate Bible, made by a group of Roman Catholics.

dou·ble (dub′əl), *adj., adv., n., v.,* **–bled, –bling.** —*adj.* **1** twice as much, as many, as large, as strong, etc. **2** for two. **3** made of two like parts: *double doors.* **4** having two beats (or some multiple of two) to the measure. **5** made of two unlike parts; combining two in one. *Bear* has a double meaning: *carry* and *animal.* **6** insincere; deceitful; false. **7** having more than one set of petals. —*adv.* **1** twice. **2** two together. —*n.* **1** number or amount that is twice as much. **2** person or thing just like another. **3** in motion pictures, a person who acts in the place of a leading actor or actress. **4** hit by which a batter gets to second base in baseball. —*v.* **1** make twice as much or twice as many. **2** be used for another; be the double of. **3** serve two purposes; play two parts: *the maid doubled as cook.* **4** fold; bend: *he doubled his fists in anger.*

double back, a fold over. **b** go back the same way one came.

doubles, game with two players on each side.

double up, a fold or curl up. **b** bend over. **c** share a room, bed, etc. with another.

on the double, a quickly. **b** in double time. [< OF < L *duplus*] —**dou′ble·ness,** *n.* —**dou′bler,** *n.*

double agent, spy who works for two opposing or rival groups.

double bar, double vertical line on a music staff that indicates the end of a movement or composition.

double bass, a musical instrument shaped like a cello but much larger, with a very low bass tone; bass viol.

double bassoon, a large bassoon, an octave lower in pitch than the ordinary bassoon.

double boiler, pair of cooking pans, one of which fits down into the other.

dou·ble-breast·ed (dub′əl bres′tid), *adj.* overlapping enough to make two thicknesses across the breast and having two rows of buttons.

double chin, soft fold of skin under the chin.

dou·ble-cross (dub′əl krôs′; –kros′), *v.* promise to do one thing and then do another; be treacherous to. —**dou′ble-cross′er,** *n.*

double cross, act of treachery.

double dagger, mark (‡) used to refer the reader to another section or to a note in a book.

dou·ble-deal·ing (dub′əl dēl′ing), *n., adj.* pretending to do one thing and then doing another; deceiving. —**dou′ble-deal′er,** *n.*

dou·ble-du·ty (dub′əl dü′ti; –dū′–), *adj.* serving two functions.

dou·ble-en·ten·dre (dü blän tän′drə), *n.* word or expression with two meanings.

One meaning is often improper. [< obs. F, lit., to be taken two ways]

double entry, system of bookkeeping in which each transaction is written down twice, once on the credit side of the account and once on the debit side.

dou·ble-faced (dub′əl fāst′), *adj.* **1** pretending to be what one is not; hypocritical; deceitful. **2** having two faces or aspects.

double fault, the making of two successive improper serves in tennis.

dou·ble-head·er (dub′əl hed′ər), *n.* in baseball, two games on the same day in immediate succession.

double helix, spiral structure of a DNA molecule, made up of two helical strands of nucleotides. **2** molecule of DNA.

dou·ble-joint·ed (dub′əl join′tid), *adj.* having joints of the fingers, arms, etc., that can bend in unusual ways.

dou·ble-park (dub′əl pärk′), *v.* park (a car, etc.) beside another car which is occupying the area specified for parking. —**dou′ble-park′ing,** *n.*

double play, play in baseball in which two players are put out.

double pneumonia, pneumonia involving both lungs.

dou·ble-quick (dub′əl kwik′), *n.* the next quickest step to a run in marching. —*adj.* very quick. —*adv.* in double-quick time. —*v.* march in double-quick step.

dou·blet (dub′lit), *n.* **1** a man's close fitting jacket. **2** one of two words in a language, derived from the same original but coming by different routes, as *guard* and *ward.*

doublets, two dice showing the same number when thrown.

double talk, speech that is purposely incoherent, but that is made to seem serious by mixing in normal words, intonations, etc.

double time, 1 in the U.S. Army, a rate of marching in which 180 paces, each of 3 feet, are taken in a minute. **2** =double-quick.

dou·ble·tree (dub′əl trē′), *n.* crossbar on a carriage, wagon, plow, etc.

dou·bloon (dub lün′), *n.* a former Spanish gold coin. [< F *doublon* or < Sp. *doblón* < *doble* DOUBLE]

dou·bly (dub′li), *adv.* **1** twice; twice as. **2** two at a time.

doubt (dout), *v.* **1** not believe; not be sure of; feel uncertain about. **2** be uncertain. —*n.* **1** lack of belief or sureness; uncertainty.

beyond or **without doubt,** surely; certainly.

no doubt, a surely; certainly. **b** probably. [< OF *douter* < L *dubitare*] —**doubt′a·ble,** *adj.* —**doubt′er,** *n.* —**doubt′ing·ly,** *adv.*

doubt·ful (dout′fəl), *adj.* **1** in doubt; not sure; uncertain. **2** causing doubt; open to question or suspicion. —**doubt′ful·ly,** *adv.* —**doubt′ful·ness,** *n.*

doubt·less (dout′lis), *adv.* **1** surely; certainly. **2** probably. —*adj.* sure; cer-

tain. —**doubt′less·ly,** *adv.* —**doubt′less-ness,** *n.*

douche (düsh), *n., v.,* **douched, douching.** —*n.* **1** jet of water applied on or into any part of the body. **2** application of a douche. **3** spray, syringe, or other device for applying a douche. —*v.* **1** apply a douche to. **2** take a douche. [< F < Ital. *doccia,* ult. < L *ducere* lead]

dough (dō), *n.* **1** a soft, thick mixture of flour, liquid, and other materials for baking. **2** any soft, thick mass like this. **3** *Slang.* money. [OE *dāg*]

dough·nut or **do·nut** (dō′nut′), *n.* a small, brown cake, usually ring-shaped, cooked in deep fat.

dough·y (dō′i), *adj.,* **dough·i·er, dough·i·est.** of or like dough.

Douglas fir, a very tall evergreen tree common in the W United States.

Doug·lass (dug′ləs), *n.* **Frederick,** 1817–95, black American leader who opposed slavery.

dour (dùr; dour), *adj.* **1** gloomy; sullen. **2** *Scot.* stern; severe. [< L *durus* hard, stern]

douse (dous), *v.,* **doused, dous·ing. 1** plunge into water or any other liquid. **2** throw water over; extinguish. **3** *Informal.* put out (a light); extinguish. —**dous′er,** *n.*

dove[1] (duv), *n.* **1** bird with a thick body, short legs, and a beak enlarged at the tip; pigeon. **2** *Fig.* person opposed to war and use of force; peace-loving person. [OE *dufe–;* akin to DIVE]

dove[2] (dōv), *v. U.S.* pt. of **dive.**

dove·cote (duv′kōt′), **dove·cot** (–kot′), *n.* a small house or shelter for doves or pigeons.

Do·ver (dō′vər), *n.* **1 Strait of,** a narrow channel or strait between N France and SE England. **2** capital of Delaware.

dove·tail (duv′tāl′), *n.* **1** projection at the end of a piece of wood, metal, etc., that can be fitted into a corresponding opening at the end of another piece to form a joint. **2** the joint formed in this way. —*v.* **1** fasten, join, or fit together with projections that fit into openings. **2** fit together exactly. **3** *Fig.* fit together well or harmoniously.

dov·ish (duv′ish), *adj.* **1** like a dove. **2** *Fig.* opposing war or war of force; anxious for peaceful resolution.

dow·a·ger (dou′ə jər), *n.* **1** widow who holds some title or property from her dead husband. **2** a dignified, elderly lady. [< OF *douagere* (def. 1) < *douage* DOWER]

dow·dy (dou′di), *adj.,* **–di·er, –di·est,** *n., pl.* **–dies.** —*adj.* poorly dressed; not neat; not stylish; shabby. —*n.* woman whose clothes are dowdy. —**dow′di·ly,** *adv.* —**dow′di·ness,** *n.*

dow·el (dou′əl), *n., v.,* **–eled, –el·ing.** —*n.* peg on a piece of wood, metal, etc., to fit into a corresponding hole on another piece to form a joint. —*v.* fasten with dowels.

dow·er (dou′ər), *n.* **1** a widow's share for life of her dead husband's property. **2** dowry. **3** a natural gift, talent, or quality; endowment. —*v.* provide with a dower; endow. [< OF < Med.L *dotarium*, < LL *dotare* endow < L *dos* dowry]

down[1] (doun), *adv.* **1** in or to a lower place or condition. **2** to a position or condition that is difficult, dangerous, etc.: *the dogs ran down the fox.* **3** to a later time or person: *hand down a house.* **4** to a smaller amount, degree, etc. **5** actually: *get down to work.* **6** in writing: *take down what I say.* —*prep.* down along, through, or into: *walk down a street.* —*adj.* **1** in a lower place or condition. **2** going or pointed down. **3** sick; ill: *she is down with a cold.* **4** sad; discouraged: *he felt down about his failure.* **5** behind an opponent by a certain number. —*v.* **1** put down; get down: *he downed the medicine at one swallow.* **2** lie down: *down, Fido!* —*n.* **1** a downward movement. **2** piece of bad luck. **3** chance to move a football forward.

be down on, be angry at; have a grudge against.

down and out, without money, friends, or other resources.

down with, a put down. **b** cast out. [var. of *adown*]

down[2] (doun), *n.* soft feathers or hair; fluff. [< Scand. *dūnn*]

down[3] (doun), *n.* **1** mound or ridge of sand heaped up by the wind; dune. **2** Usually, **downs.** rolling, grassy land. [OE *dūn* hill]

down·beat (doun′bēt′), *n.* **1** first beat in a bar of music. **2** conductor's gesture indicating this. —*adj.* gloomy; dejected.

down·cast (doun′kast′; -käst′), *adj.* **1** directed downward. **2** dejected; sad; discouraged.

down·er (dou′nər), *n. Informal.* **1** sedative drug. **2** dull, disappointing experience.

down·fall (doun′fôl′), *n.* **1** overthrow; ruin. **2** a heavy rain or snow. —**down′fall′en,** *adj.*

down·grade (doun′grād′), *n., adj., adv., v.,* **-grad·ed, -grad·ing.** —*n.* a downward slope. —*adj., adv.* downward. —*v.* move to a lower position with a smaller salary. —**down′grad′ing,** *adj., n.*

down·heart·ed (doun′här′tid), *adj.* dejected. —**down′heart′ed·ly,** *adv.* —**down′heart′ed·ness,** *n.*

down·hill (doun′hil′), *adv.* down the slope of a hill; downward. —*adj.* **1** sloping downward; tending downward. **2** worse.

down·link (doun′lingk′), *n.* transmission of signals from a spacecraft to a receiver on the ground. **2** receiver for such signals.

down·load (doun′lōd′), *v.* transfer data from one computer to another or to a printer, CD, etc.

down·pour (doun′pôr′; -pōr′), *n.* a heavy rain.

down·right (doun′rīt′), *adj.* **1** thorough; complete. **2** plain; positive. —*adv.* thoroughly; completely. —**down′right′ly,** *adv.* —**down′right′ness,** *n.*

down·stairs (doun′stārz′), *adv.* **1** down the stairs. **2** on a lower floor. —*adj.* on a lower floor. —*n.* lower floor or floors.

down·stream (doun′strēm′), *adv., adj.* with the current of a stream; down a stream.

down·swing (doun′swing′), *n.* **1** downward movement or course. **2** a swinging down, as of an arm.

down·time (doun′tīm′), *n.* time in which a worker, machine, department, etc., is inactive.

down-to-earth (doun′tə èrth′), *adj.* practical; realistic.

down·town (doun′toun), *n.* the commercial section or main district of a town. —*adv., adj.* **1** to, toward, or in the lower part of a town. **2** to or in the main part of a town.

down·trod·den (doun′trod′ən), **down-trod** (-trod′), *adj.* **1** oppressed. **2** trodden down.

down·turn (doun′tèrn′), *n.* downward trend, esp. in business activity.

down·ward (doun′wərd), *adv.* Also, **down′wards.** toward a lower place or condition. —*adj.* moving or tending toward a lower place or condition.—**down′ward·ly,** *adv.*—**down′ward·ness,** *n.*

down·y (doun′i), *adj.,* **down·i·er, down·i·est. 1** of soft feathers or hair. **2** covered with soft feathers or hair. **3** like down; soft; fluffy. —**down′i·ness,** *n.*

dow·ry (dou′ri), *n., pl.* **-ries. 1** money, property, etc., that a woman brings to her husband when she marries him. **2** a natural gift, talent, or quality. Also, **dower.** [< AF *dowarie*]

dowse (douz), *v.,* **dowsed, dows·ing.** use a divining rod to locate water, etc. —**dows′er,** *n.*

dox·ol·o·gy (doks ol′ə ji), *n., pl.* **-gies.** hymn or statement praising God. [< Med.L. < Gk., < *doxa* glory, praise + *-logos* speaking] —**dox′o·log′i·cal,** *adj.* —**dox′o·log′ical·ly,** *adv.*

doy·en (doi′ən), *n.* senior member of a group; dean. [< F]

doy·enne (doi′en), *n.* female senior member of a group; dean. [< F]

doz., dozen; dozens.

doze (dōz), *v.,* **dozed, doz·ing,** *n.* —*v.* sleep lightly; be half asleep. —*n.* a light sleep; a nap.

doze off, fall into a doze. [cf. Dan. *döse* make dull] —**doz′er,** *n.*

doz·en (duz′ən), *n., pl.* **-ens** or (*after a number*) **-en.** group of 12 [< OF *dozeine* < *douse* twelve < L *duodecim*] —**doz′enth,** *adj.*

DP or **D.P.** displaced person.

Dr, Doctor.

Dr. 1 debtor. **2** doctor. **3** drive.

dr., 1 debtor. **2** dram; drams.

drab[1] (drab), *n., adj.* **drab·ber, drab·best.** —*n.* a dull, brownish gray. —*adj.* **1** dull; monotonous; unattractive. **2** dull brownish-gray. [appar. var. of *drap* cloth < F. See DRAPE.] —**drab′ly,** *adv.* —**drab′ness,** *n.*

drachm (dram), *n.* drachma.

drach·ma (drak′mə), *n., pl.* **-mas, -mae** (-mē). **1** a unit of Greek money. **2** an ancient Greek silver coin, varying in value. [< L < Gk. *drachme* handful < *drassesthai* grasp]

dra·co·ni·an or **Dra·co·ni·an** (drə kō′nē ən), *adj.* severe; cruel; harsh. [in reference to the severe laws of the Athenian legislator *Draco*]

draft (draft; dräft), *n.* **1** current of air. **2** device for regulating a current of air: *the draft of a furnace.* **3** a plan; a sketch. **4** a rough copy: *a draft of a speech.* **5** selection of persons for some special purpose: *men supplied to the army by draft.* **6** act of pulling loads; pulled. **7** Usually, **draught. a** the pulling in of a net to catch fish. **b** quantity of fish caught in a net. **8** a written order from one person or bank to another, requiring the payment of a stated amount of money. **9** Usually, **draught.** depth of water that a ship needs for floating. **10** Usually, **draught.** act of drinking: he *emptied the glass at one draft.* —*v.* **1** make a plan or sketch of. **2** write out a rough copy of. **3** select for some special purpose. —*adj.* **1** for pulling loads: *a big, strong horse or ox is a draft animal.* **2** Usually, **draught.** drawn from a barrel when ordered. [var. of *draught*] —**draft′er,** *n.*

draft·ee (draf t′; dräf-), *n.* person who is drafted for military service.

drafts (drafts; dräfts), *n. pl.* U.S. spelling of **draughts.**

drafts·man (drafts′mən; dräfts′-), *n., pl.* **-men.** person who makes plans or sketches, as of buildings and machines. —**drafts′man·ship,** *n.*

draft·y (draf′ti; dräf′-), *adj.,* **draft·i·er, draf·ti·est. 1** in a current of air. **2** having many currents of air. **3** causing a current of air. —**draft′i·ly,** *adv.* —**draft′i·ness,** *n.*

drag (drag), *v.,* **dragged, drag·ging,** *n.* —*v.* **1** pull or move along heavily or slowly. **2** go too slowly. **3** pull a net, hook, harrow, etc., over or along for some purpose. **4** be drawn or hauled along; trail on the ground. —*n.* **1** net, hook, etc., used in dragging. **2** act of dragging. **3** thing dragged. **4** anything that holds back; hindrance.

drag in, bring an unrelated topic into a conversation or discussion.

drag on, continue or go on too long. [ME *dragge(n)*]

drag·gle (dag′əl), *v.,* **-gled, -gling.** make or become wet or dirty by dragging through mud, water, dust, etc.

drag·net (drag′net′), *n.* **1** net pulled over the bottom of a river, pond, etc., or along the ground. **2** *Fig.* means of finding or catching.

drag·on (drag′ən), *n.* a huge, fierce animal supposed to look like a snake with wings and claws, often breathing out fire and smoke. [< OF < L < Gk. *drakon*]

drag·on·fly (drag′ən flī′), *n., pl.* **–flies.** a large, harmless insect, with a long, slender body and two pairs of gauzy wings, that catches flies, mosquitoes, etc.

dra·goon (drə gün′), *n.* soldier who fights on horseback. —*v.* **1** oppress or persecute by dragoons. **2** compel by oppression or persecution. [< F *dragon* DRAGON, pistol, (later) soldier]

drag race, 1 a race to test acceleration, in which cars compete over a measured distance (**drag strip**). **2** such a race on a highway or busy thoroughfare. —**drag′-rac′er,** *n.*

drain (drān), *v.* **1** draw off or flow off slowly. **2** empty or dry by draining. **3** use up little by little; deprive. —*n.* **1** channel or pipe for carrying off water or other liquid. **2** anything that drains. **3** a slow taking away.
go down the drain, a become worthless. **b** be ignored or forgotten. [OE *drēahnian;* akin to DRY] —**drain′a·ble,** *adj.* —**drain′er,** *n.*

drain·age (drān′ij), *n.* **1** act or process of draining. **2** system of channels or pipes for carrying off water or waste of any kind. **3** what is drained off. **4** area that is drained.

drainage basin, area that is drained by a river and its tributaries.

drain·pipe (drān′pīp′), *n.* pipe for carrying off water or other liquid.

drake (drāk), *n.* a male duck. [ME]

dram (dram), *n.* **1** a small weight. In apothecaries' weight, 8 drams make one ounce; in avoirdupois weight, 16 drams make one ounce. **2** a fluid dram. **3** a small drink of intoxicating liquor. [< OF < L *drachma* DRACHMA]

dra·ma (drä′mə; dram′ə), *n.* **1** story written to be acted out by actors on a stage. **2** series of happenings that seem like those of a play. [< LL < Gk., play, deed < *draein* do]

Dram·a·mine (dram′ə mēn), *n. Trademark.* drug used as a remedy for motion sickness.

dra·mat·ic (drə mat′ik), *adj.* **1** of drama; having to do with plays. **2** seeming like a drama or play; exciting. —**dra·mat′i·cal·ly,** *adv.*

dra·mat·ics (drə mat′iks), *n.* **1** (*sing. or pl. in use*) art of acting or producing plays. **2** (*pl. in use*) plays given by amateurs. **3** *Informal.* dramatic behavior.

dram·a·tis per·so·nae (dram′ə tis pər·sō′nē), characters or actors in a play. [< L]

dram·a·tist (dram′ə tist), *n.* writer of plays; playwright.

dram·a·tize (dram′ə tīz), *v.*, **–tized, –tiz·ing. 1** make a drama of; arrange in the form of a play. **2** show or express in a dramatic way. —**dram′a·ti·za′tion,** *n.* —**dram′a·tiz′er,** *n.*

dram·a·tur·gy (dram′ə tėr′ji), *n.* art of writing or producing dramas. [< Gk. *dramatourgia* < *drama* DRAMA + *–ourgos* making < *ergon* work] —**dram′a·tur′gic, dram′a·tur′gi·cal,** *adj.* —**dram′a·tur′gist,** *n.*

drank (drangk), *v.* pt. of **drink.**

drape (drāp), *v.*, **draped, drap·ing,** *n.* —*v.* **1** cover or hang with cloth falling loosely in folds. **2** arrange (clothes, hangings, etc.) in graceful folds. **3** fall in folds. —*n.* cloth hung in graceful folds; hanging. [< F < *drap* cloth < LL *drappus*]

drap·er (drāp′ər), *n.* **1** *Esp. Brit.* dealer in cloth or dry goods. **2** person that drapes.

dra·per·y (drā′pər i), *n., pl.* **–per·ies. 1** clothing or hangings arranged in graceful folds. **2** graceful arrangement of hangings or clothing. **3** cloth or fabric.

dras·tic (dras′tik), *adj.* acting with force or violence; extreme. [< Gk. *drastikos* effective < *draein* do] —**dras′ti·cal·ly,** *adv.*

draught (draft; dräft), *n., v., adj.* =draft. [ME *draht* < OE *dragan* draw] —**draught′er,** *n.*

draughts (drafts; dräfts), *n. pl. Brit. (sing. in use)* =checkers.

draughts·man (drafts′mən; dräfts′–), *n., pl.* **–men.** =draftsman. —**draughts′man·ship,** *n.*

Dra·vid·i·an (drə vid′i ən), *adj.* of or having to do with the non-Aryan races in S India and Sri Lanka. —*n.* **1** member of any of these races. **2** languages spoken by them.

draw (drô), *v.*, **drew, drawn, draw·ing,** *n.* —*v.* **1** pull; drag: *a horse draws a wagon.* **2** pull out: *he drew his hand from his pocket; draw a pail of water from the well.* **3** move: *we drew near the fire to get warm.* **4** attract: *a parade draws a crowd.* **5** make a picture or likeness of with pencil, pen, chalk, crayon, etc. **6** write (an order to pay money). **7** be a drain. **8** make a current of air to carry off smoke: *a chimney draws.* **9** breathe in. **10** finish with neither side winning. **11** stretch. **12** shrink. **13** (of a ship) need for floating; sink to a depth of. —*n.* **1** act of drawing. **2** thing that attracts. **3** a tie in a game. **4** a land basin into or through which water drains; valley.
beat to the draw, a draw a gun sooner than an opponent. **b** do anything sooner than an opponent or competitor.
draw away, get ahead of others in a race.
draw back, recoil; retreat.
draw down, use up or be used up.
draw in, a entice. **b** contract; tighten.
draw on, a approach. **b** *Fig.* make use of: *draw on experience.*
draw oneself up, stand up straight.
draw out, a persuade to talk. **b** extend: *draw out the introductions.*

draw up, a arrange in order: *drew up in a line.* **b** write out or compose. **c** stop or pull up. [OE *dragan*]

draw·back (drô′bak′), *n.* something unfavorable or unpleasant; disadvantage; hindrance.

draw·bridge (drô′brij′), *n.* bridge that can be wholly or partly lifted, lowered, or moved to one side.

draw·ee (drô ē′), *n.* person for whom an order to pay money is written.

drawer (drôr for 1; drô′ər for 2 and 3), *n.* **1** box that slides in and out of a chest, desk, table, etc. **2** person or thing that draws. **3** person who writes an order to pay money.

drawers (drôrz), undergarment fitting over the legs and around the waist.

draw·ing (drô′ing), *n.* **1** picture or likeness made with pencil, pen, chalk, crayon, etc. **2** the making of such pictures or likenesses. **3** act of a person or thing that draws anything.

drawing board, board on which paper is fastened for drawing.
on the drawing board, being developed or designed; incomplete.

drawing card, person or thing that attracts people to a show or event.

drawing room, room for receiving or entertaining guests; parlor. [for *withdrawing room*]

draw·knife (drô′nīf′), or **drawing knife,** *n., pl.* **–knives.** blade with a handle at each end, used to shave off surfaces. Also, **drawshave.**

drawl (drôl), *v.* talk in a slow, lazy way. —*n.* a slow, lazy way of talking. [appar. akin to DRAW] —**drawl′er,** *n.* —**drawl′ing·ly,** *adv.*

drawn (drôn), *v.* pp. of **draw.**

draw·shave (drô′shāv′), *n.* =drawknife.

dray (drā), *n.* a low, strong cart for hauling heavy loads. —*v.* transport or carry on a cart. [OE *drœg*– drag < *dragan* draw]

dray·age (drā′ij), *n.* charge for hauling a load on a dray.

dread (dred), *v.* look forward to with fear. —*n.* **1** fear, esp. fear of something that may happen. **2** person or thing inspiring fear. **3** awe. —*adj.* **1** dreaded; dreadful. **2** awe-inspiring. [OE *drēdan*]

dread·ful (dred′fəl), *adj.* **1** causing dread; awe-inspiring. **2** very bad; very unpleasant. —**dread′ful·ly,** *adv.* —**dread′ful·ness,** *n.*

dream (drēm), *n., v.,* **dreamed** or **dreamt** (dremt), **dream·ing.** —*n.* **1** something thought, felt, seen, or heard during sleep. **2** something as unreal as a dream. **3** state in which a person has dreams. **4** something having great beauty or charm. —*v.* **1** have dreams. **2** think of (something) as possible; imagine. **3** spend in dreaming.
dream up, create (an invention, etc.) mentally. [OE *drēam* joy, music] —**dream′er,** *n.* —**dream′ing·ly,** *adv.* —**dream′less,** *adj.*

dream·y (drēm′i), *adj.*, **dream·i·er, dream·iest. 1** full of dreams. **2** like a dream; vague; dim: *a dreamy recollection.* **3** impractical: *a dreamy person.* **4** causing dreams; soothing. —**dream′i·ly,** *adv.* —**dream′i·ness,** *n.*

drear·y (drir′i), *adj.*, **drear·i·er, drear·i·est. 1** dull; gloomy; cheerless; depressing. **2** *Archaic.* sad; sorrowful. [OE *drēorig*] —**drear′i·ly,** *adv.* —**drear′i·ness,** *n.*

dreck (drek), *n. Slang.* worthless junk.

dredge[1] (drej), *n., v.,* **dredged, dredg·ing.** —*n.* **1** machine with a scoop or series of buckets for removing mud, sand, or other materials from the bottom of a river, harbor, etc. **2** apparatus with a net, used for gathering oysters, etc. —*v.* **1** clean out or deepen (a channel, harbor, etc.) with a dredge. **2** bring up or gather with a dredge. [ME *dreg;* akin to DRAG] —**dredg′er,** *n.*

dredge[2] (drej), *v.,* **dredged, dredg·ing.** sprinkle: *dredge meat with flour.* [appar. < *dredge,* n., grain mixture] —**dredg′er,** *n.*

dregs (dregz), *n.* **1** solid bits of matter that settle to the bottom of a liquid. **2** the most worthless part. [< Scand. *dreggjar*] —**dreg′gy,** *adj.*

drench (drench), *v.* wet thoroughly; soak. —*n.* **1** a thorough wetting; a soaking. **2** something that drenches. **3** solution for soaking. [OE *drencan* < *drincan* drink] —**drench′er,** *n.*

dress (dres), *n., adj., v.,* **dressed** or **drest, dress·ing.** —*n.* **1** the outer garment worn by women and girls. **2** an outer covering. **3** clothes. **4** formal clothes. [< v.] —*adj.* **1** of or for a dress. **2** of formal dress; characterized by formal dress. [< v.] —*v.* **1** put clothes on. **2** decorate; trim. **3** make ready for use. **4** arrange (hair). **5** put a medicine, bandage, etc., on (a wound or sore). **6** form in a straight line: *the captain ordered the soldiers to dress their ranks.*

dress down, a scold; rebuke. **b** beat; thrash.

dress up, put best clothes on. [< OF *dresser* arrange, ult. < L *directus* straight. See DIRECT.]

dres·sage (dres′ij; dre säzh′), *n.* technique of guiding a horse through various paces without obvious signals. [< F]

dress·er[1] (dres′ər), *n.* person who dresses (himself, another person, a shop window, or a wound).

dress·er[2] (dres′ər), *n.* **1** piece of furniture with drawers for clothes, and sometimes a mirror; bureau. **2** piece of furniture with shelves for dishes. [< early F *dresseur.* See DRESS.]

dress·ing (dres′ing), *n.* **1** what is put on or in something to get it ready for use. **2** sauce for salads, fish, meat, etc. **3** a stuffing of bread crumbs, seasoning, etc., for chicken, turkey, etc. **4** medicine, bandage, etc., put on a wound or sore. **5** a scolding or beating.

dress·ing-down (dres′ing doun′), *n.* a scolding; rebuke.

dressing gown, loose robe worn while dressing or resting.

dressing table, small table with a mirror at which a woman can sit to fix her hair, apply makeup, etc.

dress·mak·er (dres′māk′ər), *n.* person whose work is making dresses, etc. —*adj.* of women's apparel, characterized by delicate flowing lines, hand finishing, and decoration. —**dress′mak′ing,** *n.*

dress rehearsal, rehearsal of a play with costumes and scenery just as for a regular performance.

dress·y (dres′i), *adj.,* **dress·i·er, dress·i·est.** *Colloq.* **1** fond of wearing showy clothes. **2** stylish; fashionable. —**dress′i·ness,** *n.*

drest (drest), *v.* pt. and pp. of **dress.**

drew (drü), *v.* pt. of **draw.**

drib·ble (drib′əl), *v.,* **-bled, -bling,** *n.* —*v.* **1** flow or let flow in drops, small amounts, etc.; trickle. **2** let saliva run from the mouth. **3** move (a ball) along by bouncing it or giving it short kicks. —*n.* **1** a dropping; dripping; trickle. **2** act of dribbling a ball. [< *drib,* var. of *drip*] —**drib′bler,** *n.*

drib·let (drib′lit), *n.* a small amount.

dried (drīd), *v.* pt. and pp. of **dry.**

dri·er (drī′ər), *adj.* comparative of **dry.** —*n.* **1** person or thing that dries. **2** =dryer. **3** substance put in paint, varnish, etc., to make it dry more quickly.

drift (drift), *v.* **1** carry or be carried along, as by currents of water or air. **2** go along without knowing or caring where one is going. **3** heap or be heaped up, as by the wind. [< n.] —*n.* **1** a drifting. **2** direction of drifting. **3** tendency; trend; meaning. **4** snow, sand, etc., heaped up by the wind. **5** current of water or air caused by the wind. **6** a driving movement or force. **7** distance that a ship or aircraft is off its course because of currents. [ME, a driving, < OE *drīfan* DRIVE] —**drift′er,** *n.*

drift·age (drif′tij), *n.* **1** a drifting. **2** the distance drifted. **3** what has drifted.

drift·net (drift′net′), *n.* long fishing net held up along the top edge by floats or buoys, esp. for catching herring.

drift·wood (drift′wùd′), *n.* wood drifting in the water or washed ashore by water.

drill[1] (dril), *n.* **1** tool or machine for boring holes. **2** method of teaching or training by having the learners do a thing over and over again. **3** group instruction and training in physical exercises or in marching, handling a gun, etc. **4** snail that bores into and destroys oysters. —*v.* **1** bore a hole in; pierce with a drill. **2** teach by having learners do a thing over and over again. **3** do or cause to do military or physical exercises. [< Du. *dril* < *drillen* to bore] —**drill′er,** *n.*

drill[2] (dril), *n.* **1** machine for planting seeds in rows. **2** a small furrow to plant seeds in. **3** row of planted seeds. —*v.* plant in small furrows. —**drill′er,** *n.*

drill[3] (dril), *n.* a strong, twilled cotton or linen cloth, used for overalls, linings, etc. [short for *drilling* < G *drillich* < L *trilix* of three threads < *tri-* three + *licium* thread]

drill[4] (dril), *n.* baboon of W Africa, smaller than the mandrill. [prob. < African name]

drill instructor, officer who drills soldiers in marching, handling guns, etc.

drill·mas·ter (dril′mas′tər; -mäs′-), *n.* **1** =drill instructor. **2** *Fig.* person who drills others in anything: *a class that needs the skills of a drillmaster.*

dri·ly (drī′li), *adv.* dryly.

drink (dringk), *v.,* **drank, drunk.** *n.* —*v.* **1** swallow (liquid). **2** take and hold; absorb: *the dry ground drank up the rain.* **3** drink alcoholic liquor. **4** drink in honor of. —*n.* **1** liquid swallowed or to be swallowed. **2** alcoholic liquor. **3** too much drinking of alcoholic liquor.

drink to, drink in honor of. [OE *drincan*] —**drink′a·ble,** *adj., n.* —**drink′er,** *n.*

drip (drip), *v.,* **dripped** or **dript** (dript), **dripping,** *n.* —*v.* **1** fall or let fall in drops. **2** be so wet that drops fall. —*n.* **1** a falling in drops. **2** liquid that falls in drops. [OE *dryppan* < *dropa* a drop]

drip·ping (drip′ing), *n.* function of a thing which drips.

drippings, a liquids that have dripped down. **b** melted fat and juices that drip down from meat while roasting.

drive (drīv), *v.,* **drove, driv·en, driv·ing,** *n.* —*v.* **1** make go: *grief drove her insane.* **2** force: *hunger drove him to steal.* **3** direct the movement of (an automobile, horse, etc.). **4** work hard. **5** dash or rush with force. **6** bring about: *drive a bargain.* **7** hit very hard and fast: *drive a golf ball.* —*n.* **1** trip in an automobile, carriage, etc. **2** road to drive on. **3** vigor; energy: *an ambitious man with drive.* **4** pressure: *hunger is a strong drive in humankind.* **5** a special effort of a group for some purpose: *a drive to get money for charity.* **6** a very hard, fast hit. **7** a driving.

drive at, mean; intend. [OE *drīfan*]

drive-in (drīv′in′), *n.* place where customers may make purchases, eat, attend movies, etc., while seated in their cars.

driv·el (driv′əl), *v.,* **-eled, -el·ing.** *n.* —*v.* **1** let saliva run from the mouth. **2** flow like saliva running from the mouth. **3** talk or say in a stupid, foolish manner; talk silly nonsense. **4** waste (time, energy, etc.) in a stupid, foolish way. —*n.* **1** saliva running from the mouth. **2** stupid, foolish talk; silly nonsense. [OE *dreflian*] —**driv′el·er,** *n.*

driv·en (driv′ən), *v.* pp. of **drive.** —*adj.* carried along and gathered into heaps by the wind.

driv·er (drīv′ər), *n.* **1** person or thing that drives. **2** person who directs the movement of an automobile, horses, etc. **3** person who makes people work very hard. **4** a golf club with a wooden head, used in hitting the ball from the tee. **5** any of several tools used in forcing things in, on, out, or through. **6** in machinery, a part that transmits force or motion.

drive shaft, shaft that transmits power from the engine to various working parts of a machine, esp. in an automobile where the drive shaft connects to the rear axle.

drive·way (drīv′wā′), *n.* a private road that leads from a house to the street.

driz·zle (driz′əl), *v.,* **–zled, –zling.** *n.* rain in very small drops like mist. [? < ME *drese* to fall < OE *drēosan*] **—driz′zly,** *adj.*

droll (drōl), *adj.* amusingly odd; humorously quaint. [< F *drôle* (orig. *n.*) good fellow < Du. *drol* little fat fellow]

droll·er·y (drōl′ər i), *n., pl.* **–er·ies. 1** laughable trick. **2** quaint humor. **3** jesting.

drom·e·dar·y (drom′ə der′i; drum′–), *n., pl.* **–dar·ies.** a swift camel for riding, usually the one-humped camel of Arabia. [< LL *dromedarius* < Gk. *dromas kamelos* running camel < *dromos* a running]

drone[1] (drōn), *n.* **1** a male honeybee. **2** person not willing to work; idler; loafer. [OE *drān*]

drone[2] (drōn), *v.,* **droned, dron·ing,** *n.* **—v. 1** make a deep, continuous, humming sound. **2** talk or say in a monotonous voice. **—n.** a deep, continuous, humming sound: *the drone of motor.* [akin to DRONE[1]]

drool (drül), *v.* let saliva run from the mouth as a baby does. **—n.** saliva running from the mouth. [contraction of DRIVEL]

droop (drüp), *v.* **1** hang down; bend down. **2** become weak; lose strength and energy. **3** be sad and gloomy. **—n.** a bending position; hanging down. [< Scand. *drūpa*] **—droop′ing·ly,** *adv.* **—droop′y,** *adj.*

drop (drop), *n., v.,* **dropped, drop·ping. —n. 1** a small amount of liquid in a roundish shape. **2** a very small amount of liquid. **3** anything roundish like a drop. **4** a sudden fall. **5** distance down; length of a fall: *a drop of 200 feet.* **—v. 1** fall or let fall in drops. **2** fall suddenly; cause to fall. **3** fall dead, wounded, or tired out. **4** go or make lower; sink. **5** leave out; omit. **6** stop; end: *let a matter drop.* **7** come casually or unexpectedly. **8** give or express casually: *drop a hint.* **9** of animals: **a** give birth to. **b** be born.

at the drop of a hat, immediately and without urging.

drop back, go toward the rear.

drop behind, fall behind.

drop by, visit casually, without an invitation.

drop in the bucket, very little in comparison to a whole.

drop off, a go away; disappear. **b** go to sleep. **c** leave someone or something at a destination.

drop out, a withdraw from school or college before completing a course or term. **b** withdraw from society, esp. because of disillusionment with it.

drops, liquid medicine given in drops. [OE *dropa*]

drop-forge (drop′fôrj′; –fōrj′), *v.,* **–forged, –forg·ing.** beat (hot metal) into shape with a very heavy hammer or weight. **—drop′-forg′er,** *n.* **drop forging.**

drop hammer, a very heavy weight lifted by machinery and then dropped on the metal to be beaten into shape.

drop kick, kick given to a football as it touches the ground after being dropped.

drop-kick (drop′kik′), *v.* give (a football) a drop kick. **—drop′-kick′er,** *n.*

drop leaf, hinged leaf of a table that folds down when not in use. **—drop′leaf′,** *adj.*

drop·let (drop′lit), *n.* a tiny drop.

drop·per (drop′ər), *n.* **1** person or thing that drops. **2** glass or plastic tube with a hollow rubber cap at one end and a small opening at the other end from which a liquid can be made to fall in drops.

dro·soph·i·la (drō sof′ə lə), *n., pl.* **–lae** (–lē). a small fly whose larvae feed on fruit and decaying plants; fruit fly. [< NL < Gk. *drosos* dew + *philos* loving]

dross (drôs; dros), *n.* **1** waste or scum that comes to the surface of melting metals. **2** waste material; rubbish. [OE *drōs*]

drought (drout), *n.* **1** a long period of dry weather; continued lack of rain. **2** lack of moisture; dryness. [OE *drūgath;* akin to DRY] **—drought′y,** *adj.*

drove[1] (drōv), *v.* pt. of **drive.**

drove[2] (drōv), *n., v.,* **droved, drov·ing. —n. 1** group of cattle, sheep, hogs, etc., moving or driven along together; herd; flock. **2** many people moving along together; crowd. **—v. 1** drive (cattle) to market. **2** deal in (cattle). [OE *drāf*]

dro·ver (drō′vər), *n.* **1** man who drove cattle, sheep, hogs, etc., to market. **2** dealer in cattle.

drown (droun), *v.* **1** die under water or other liquid because of lack of air to breathe. **2** kill by keeping under water or other liquid. **3** cover with water; flood. **4** be stronger or louder than. **5** get rid of; suppress. [OE *druncnian;* akin to DRINK] **—drown′er,** *n.*

drowse (drouz), *v.,* **drowsed, drows·ing,** *n.* **—v. 1** be sleepy; be half asleep. **2** make sleepy. **3** pass (time) in drowsing. **—n.** being half asleep; sleepiness. [OE *drūs(i)an* sink, become slow]

drow·sy (drou′zi), *adj.,* **–si·er, –si·est. 1** half asleep; sleepy. **2** causing sleepiness; lulling. **3** caused by sleepiness. **—drow′si·ly,** *adv.* **—drow′si·ness,** *n.*

drub (drub), *v.,* **drubbed, drub·bing,** *n.* **—v. 1** beat with a stick; whip soundly. **2** defeat by a large margin in a fight, game, contest, etc. **—n.** a blow; thump; knock. [? < Ar. *ḍaraba* beat] **—drub′ber,** *n.*

drub·bing (drub′ing), *n.* **1** a beating. **2** a thorough defeat.

drudge (druj), *n., v.,* **drudged, drudg·ing. —n.** person who does hard, tiresome, or disagreeable work. **—v.** do such work. [ME *drugge(n);* cf. OE *drēogan* work, suffer] **—drudg′er,** *n.*

drudg·er·y (druj′ər i), *n., pl.* **–er·ies.** hard, uninteresting, or disagreeable work.

drug (drug), *n., v.,* **drugged, drug·ging. —n. 1** substance (other than food) that, when taken into the body, produces a change in it. If the change helps the body, the drug is a medicine; if the change harms the body, the drug is a poison. **2** substance that causes drowsiness; narcotic. **—v. 1** give harmful drugs to. **2** put a harmful or poisonous drug in (food or drink). **3** affect or overcome (the body or senses) in a way not natural: *the wine had drugged him.* [< OF *drogue,* ? < Du. *drog,* akin to E DRY] **—drug′less,** *adj.*

drug·gist (drug′ist), *n. U.S.* person licensed to fill prescriptions; pharmacist.

drug·store (drug′stôr′; –stōr′), *n.* pharmacy.

Dru·id (drü′id), *n.* Often, **druid.** member of a religious order of priests, prophets, poets, etc., among the ancient Celts of Britain, Ireland, and France. **—dru·id′ic, dru·id′i·cal,** *adj.* **—dru′id·ism,** *n.*

drum (drum), *n., v.,* **drummed, drum·ming. —n. 1** a musical instrument that makes a sound when it is beaten. A drum is hollow with a covering stretched tightly over the ends. **2** sound made when a drum is beaten; sound like this. **3** anything shaped somewhat like a drum. **4** part around which something is wound in a machine. **5** drumshaped container to hold oil, food, etc. **6** membrane covering the hollow part of the ear. **7** the hollow part of the middle ear. **—v. 1** beat or play a drum. **2** beat, tap, or strike again and again. **3** force into one's mind by repeating over and over.

beat the drum or **drums,** give vigorous support to or advocate enthusiastically for something.

drum out, dismiss or send away in disgrace.

drum up, a call together: *drum up a quorum.* **b** solicit; obtain: *drum up business.* [< *drumslade* drummer < Du. or LG *trommelslag* drumbeat]

drum·beat (drum′bēt′), *n.* sound made when a drum is beaten.

drum·head (drum′hed′), *n.* **1** parchment or membrane stretched tightly over the end of a drum. **2** =eardrum.

drum·lin (drum′lən), *n.* ridge or oval hill formed by deposit from a glacier. [for *drumling,* dim. of *drum* ridge < Scotch Gaelic and Irish *druim* ridge]

drum major, leader or director of a marching band.

drum·mer (drum′ər), *n.* person who plays a drum.

drum·stick (drum′stik′), *n.* **1** stick for beating a drum. **2** the lower half of the leg of a cooked chicken, turkey, etc.

drunk (drungk), *adj.* **1** overcome with alcoholic liquor; intoxicated. **2** very much excited or affected. —*n.* **1** person who is drunk. **2** spell of drinking alcohol liquor. —*v.* pp. of **drink.**

drunk·ard (drungk′ərd), *n.* person who is often drunk.

drunk·en (drungk′ən), *adj.* **1** drunk. **2** caused by or resulting from being drunk. **3** often drinking too much alcohol liquor. —**drunk′en·ly,** *adv.* —**drunk′en·ness,** *n.*

dru·pa·ceous (drü pā′shəs), *adj.* **1** like a drupe. **2** producing drupes.

drupe (drüp), *n.* fruit whose seed is contained in a hard pit or stone surrounded by soft, pulpy flesh, as cherries, peaches, etc. [< NL < L *druppa* very ripe olive < Gk. *drypepa,* accus. of *drypeps* ripening on the tree]

drupe·let (drüp′lit), *n.* a small drupe. A raspberry or blackberry is a mass of drupelets.

dry (drī), *adj.,* **dri·er, dri·est,** *v.,* **dried, dry·ing,** *n.,* *pl.* **drys.** —*adj.* **1** not wet; not moist. **2** having little or no rain. **3** not giving milk. **4** having no water in or on it. **5** wanting a drink; thirsty. **6** not liquid; solid: *dry measure.* **7** showing no feeling: *dry humor.* **8** not interesting; dull. **9** without butter: *dry toast.* **10** without mucus: *a dry cough.* **11** free from sweetness or fruity flavor: *dry wine.* **12** having or favoring laws against selling alcohol. —*v.* make or become dry.

dry up, a make or become completely dry. **b** stop talking. [OE *drȳge*]

dry cell, a small, portable device that produces electric current. It is an electric cell made with absorbent material so that its contents cannot spill.

dry-clean (drī′klēn′), *v.* clean (clothes, etc.) with naphtha, benzine, etc., instead of water. —**dry cleaner.** —**dry cleaning.**

dry dock, dock from which the water can be pumped out. Dry docks are used for building or repairing ships.

dry-dock (drī′dok′), *v.* **1** place in a dry dock. **2** go into dry dock.

dry·er (drī′ər), *n.* machine or appliance that removes water by heat or air, as a clothes or hair dryer. Also, **drier.**

dry farming, way of farming land in regions where there is no irrigation and little rain.

dry goods, cloth, ribbon, lace, etc.

dry ice or **Dry Ice,** *Trademark.* a very cold, white solid formed when carbon dioxide is greatly compressed and then cooled, used as a refrigerant.

dry·ly (drī′li), *adv.* in a dry manner. Also, **drily.**

dry measure, 1 system for measuring such things as grain, vegetables, or fruit. In the United States: 2 pints = 1 quart; 8 quarts = 1 peck; 4 pecks = 1 bushel. **2** measurement of dry things.

dry·ness (drī′nis), *n.* a being dry; dry quality.

dry rot, decay of seasoned wood, causing it to crumble to a dry powder, due to various fungi.

dry run, a practice test or session.

Ds, dysprosium. Also, **Dy.**

D.S., D.Sc., Doctor of Science.

D.S.C., Distinguished Service Cross.

D.S.T. or **DST,** Daylight Saving Time.

du·al (dü′əl; dū′–), *adj.* **1** of two; showing two. **2** consisting of two parts; double; twofold. [< L *dualis* < *duo* two] —**du′al·ly,** *adv.*

du·al·ism (dü′əl iz əm; dū′–), *n.* **1** dual condition. **2** doctrine of philosophy that all the phenomena of the universe can be explained by two separate and distinct substances or principles, such as mind and matter. —**du′al·ist,** *n.* —**du′al·is′tic,** *adj.*

du·al·i·ty (dü al′ə ti; dū–), *n.,* *pl.* **-ties.** dual condition or quality.

dub[1] (dub), *v.,* **dubbed, dub·bing. 1** make (a man) a knight by striking his shoulder lightly with a sword. **2** give a title to; call; name. [OE *dubbian*]

dub[2] (dub), *v.,* **dubbed, dub·bing,** *n.* —*v.* add sounds on a motion-picture film. —*n.* **1** the sounds thus added. **2** the act or process of dubbing. [short for *double*]

du·bi·ous (dü′bi əs; dū′–), *adj.* **1** doubtful; uncertain. **2** of questionable character; probably bad. [< L *dubiosus* < *dubius* doubtful < *du–* two] —**du′bi·ous·ly,** *adv.* —**du′bi·ous·ness,** *n.*

Dub·lin (dub′lən), *n.* capital of the Republic of Ireland.

du·cal (dü′kəl; dū′–), *adj.* of a duke or dukedom. —**du′cal·ly,** *adv.*

duc·at (duk′ət), *n.* gold or silver coin formerly used in some European countries. [< F < Ital. *ducato* < Med.L < L *dux* leader]

duch·ess (duch′is), *n.* **1** wife or widow of a duke. **2** lady with a rank equal to a duke's.

duch·y (duch′i), *n.,* *pl.* **duch·ies.** territory under the rule of a duke or duchess; dukedom.

duck[1] (duk), *n.* **1** a wild or tame swimming bird with a short neck, short legs, and webbed feet. Most ducks have broad, flat bills. **2** the female duck. **3** flesh of a duck used for food. **4** *Slang.* a fellow; chap. [OE *dūce*; akin to DUCK[2]]

duck[2] (duk), *v.* **1** dip or plunge suddenly under water and out again. **2** lower the head or bend the body suddenly to keep from being hit, seen, etc. **3** avoid. —*n.* **1** a sudden dip or plunge under water and out again. **2** a sudden lowering of the head or bending of the body. [ME *duke(n)*]

duck[3] (duk), *n.* a strong, cotton or linen cloth with a lighter and finer weave than canvas, used for sails, tents, etc. [< Du. *doek* cloth]

duck·bill (duk′bil′), or **duckbilled platy·pus,** *n.* a small water mammal that lays eggs and has webbed feet and a beak like a duck. Also, **platypus.**

duck·ling (duk′ling), *n.* a young duck.

duck·pins (duk′pinz′), *n.* game similar to bowling played with smaller balls and pins.

duck·weed (duk′wēd′), *n.* a very small flowering plant that grows in water.

duck·y (duk′i), *adj.,* **duck·i·er, duck·i·est.** *Informal.* **1** charming. **2** marvelous; wonderful. —*n.,* *pl.* **duckies.** dear; darling; sweetie.

duct (dukt), *n.* **1** tube, pipe, or channel for carrying liquid, air, wires, etc. **2** tube in the body for carrying a bodily fluid: *tear ducts.* [< L, < *ducere* lead] —**duct′less,** *adj.*

duc·tile (duk′təl), *adj.* **1** capable of being hammered out thin or drawn out into a wire, as gold or copper. **2** easily molded or shaped, as wax. **3** easily managed or influenced; docile. —**duc·til′i·ty,** *n.*

ductless gland, gland without a duct whose secretion passes directly into the blood or lymph circulating through it; endocrine gland. The thyroid and the spleen are ductless glands.

dud (dud), *n.* **1** shell or bomb that did not explode. **2** failure. **3** useless person or thing.

duds, a clothes. **b** possessions.

dude (düd; dūd), *n.* **1** city-bred person, esp. one who vacations on a ranch. **2** *Slang.* handsome male. —**dud′ish,** *adj.*

dude ranch, ranch that is run as a tourist resort.

dudg·eon (duj′ən), *n.* anger; resentment. **in high dudgeon,** very angry; resentful.

due (dü; dū), *adj.* **1** owed as a debt; to be paid as a right. **2** proper; suitable; rightful: *due reward.* **3** as much as needed; enough. **4** promised to come, be ready, be paid, etc.; expected. —*n.* thing owed as a debt or to be paid as a right. —*adv.* straight; directly; exactly: *due east.*

become or **fall due,** become payable.

dues, amount of money owed or to be paid.

due to, caused by.

give a person his or **her due,** be fair; do justice. [< OF *deü,* pp. of *devoir* owe < L *debere*]

du·el (dü′əl; dū′-), *n.,* *v.,* **-eled, -el·ing.** —*n.* **1** a formal fight between two people armed with swords or firearms, arranged to settle a quarrel, etc. **2** any fight or contest between two opponents: *duel of wits.* —*v.* fight a duel. [< F < Med.L *duellum* < L (archaistic for *bellum*) war] —**du′el·er,** *n.* —**du′el·ist,** *n.*

du·en·na (dü en′ə; dū–), *n.* **1** (in Spain and Portugal) an elderly woman who is the governess and chaperon of a young girl. **2** governess; chaperon. [< Sp. < L *domina* mistress. See DOMINATE.]

due process or **due process of law,** legal protections to which a person is entitled.

du·et (dü et'; dū–), *n.* **1** piece of music to be sung or played by two people. **2** two singers or players performing together. [< Ital. *duetto,* dim. of *duo* DUO]

duf·fel or **duf·fle bag** (duf'əl), a bag of stout material.

duffel coat, duffle coat, coat of coarse wool that goes to the knees, with a hood and toggle closings. Also, **duffer.**

duff·er (duf'ər), *n.* **1** useless, clumsy, or incompetent person. **2** =duffel coat.

dug (dug), *v.* pt. and pp. of **dig.**

du·gong (dü'gong), *n.* a large, fish-shaped mammal of tropical seas with flipperlike forelimbs and a crescent-shaped tail. [< Malay *dūyong*]

dug·out (dug'out'), *n.* **1** small shelter at the side of a baseball field, used by players who are not at bat or not in the game. **2** boat made by hollowing out a large log.

duke (dük; dūk), *n.* **1** nobleman ranking next below a prince. **2** prince who rules a small state or country called a duchy. **3 dukes,** *Slang.* fists. [< OF < L *dux* leader. Doublet of DOGE, DUCE.] **—duke'dom,** *n.*

dul·cet (dul'sit), *adj.* soothing, esp. to the ear; sweet; pleasing. [< F *doucet,* dim. of *doux* sweet < L *dulcis*]

dul·ci·mer (dul'sə mər), *n.* instrument with strings, played by striking the strings with two hammers. [< OF < L *dulcis* sweet + *melos* song (< Gk.)]

dull (dul), *adj.* **1** not sharp or pointed. **2** not bright or clear. **3** stupid. **4** insensitive. **5** not interesting; boring. **6** having little spirit; not active. **7** not felt sharply: *a dull pain.* —*v.* **1** make dull. **2** become dull. **3** *Fig.* reduce sensitivity to people, events, etc. [ME *dul*] **—dull'ness, dul'ness,** *n.* **—dul'ly,** *adv.*

dull·ard (dul'ərd), *n.* a stupid person who learns very slowly.

dull·ish (dul'ish), *adj.* somewhat dull.

dulse (duls), *n.* any of several coarse, edible seaweeds that have red fronds. [< Irish and Scotch Gaelic *duileasg*]

du·ly (dü'li; dū'–), *adv.* **1** according to what is due; as due; properly; suitably; rightfully. **2** as much as is needed; enough. **3** when due; at the proper time.

Du·ma (dü'mə), *n.* **1** elected legislature of Russia. **2** national legislature of Russia from 1906–17. **3** Usually, **duma.** an elective council. [< Russ.]

dumb (dum), *adj.* **1** not able to speak: *dumb animals.* **2** silenced for the moment by fear, surprise, shyness, etc. **3** that does not speak; silent. **4** stupid; dull. [(defs. 1–3) OE; (def. 4) < G *dumm* stupid] **—dumb'ly,** *adv.* **—dumb'ness,** *n.*

dumb·bell (dum'bel'), *n.* **1** short bar of wood or iron with large, heavy, round ends, used to exercise the muscles of the arms, back, etc. **2** *Slang.* a very stupid person.

dumb·wait·er (dum'wāt'ər), *n.* a small box with shelves, pulled up and down a shaft to send dishes, food, rubbish, etc., from one floor to another.

dum·found, dumb·found (dum'-found'), *v.* amaze and make unable to speak; bewilder; confuse. [< *dumb* + (con)*found*] **—dum'found'er, dumb'found'er,** *n.*

dum·my (dum'i), *n., pl.* **-mies,** *adj.* —*n.* **1** figure of a person, used to display clothing in store windows, to shoot at in rifle practice, to tackle in football, etc. **2** *Informal.* a stupid person; blockhead. **3** an imitation; counterfeit. **4** person supposedly acting for himself, but really acting for another. **5** in card games, **a** player whose cards are laid face up on the table and played by his partner. **b** hand of cards played in this way. —*adj.* **1** imitation; counterfeit; sham. **2** acting for another while supposedly acting for oneself.

dump (dump), *v.* **1** empty out. **2** put (goods) on the market in large quantities and at a low price. —*n.* **1** place for unloading rubbish. **2** place for storing ammunition or other supplies.

dump on, *Slang.* **a** attack with words. **b** criticize severely. [? < Scand. (Dan.) *dumpe* fall with a thud] **—dump'er,** *n.*

dump·ling (dump'ling), *n.* **1** a rounded piece of dough, boiled or steamed and served with meat. **2** a small pudding made by enclosing fruit in a piece of dough and baking or steaming it.

dumps (dumps), *n. pl. Informal.* low spirits.

dump·ster (dump'stər), *n.* large bin for refuse that can be mechanically lifted onto a trailer and hauled away or emptied into a garbage truck.

dump truck, truck that can be unloaded by tipping up the bed.

dump·y (dump'i), *adj.,* **dump·i·er, dump·i·est.** short and fat. **—dump'i·ly,** *adv.* **—dump'i·ness,** *n.*

dun¹ (dun), *v.,* **dunned, dun·ning,** *n.* —*v.* demand payment of a debt from, again and again. —*n.* demand for payment of a debt. [appar. < obs. *dun* make a DIN < Scand. *duna* to thunder]

dun² (dun), *n.* a dull, grayish brown. —*adj.* dull grayish-brown. [OE *dunn,* ? < Celtic]

dunce (duns), *n.* a stupid person. [< *Duns*(*man*), name applied by attackers to any follower of *Duns Scotus,* theologian]

dunce cap, a tall, cone-shaped cap formerly worn as a punishment by a child who was slow in learning lessons in school.

dun·der·head (dun'dər hed'), *n.* a stupid, foolish person; dunce; blockhead.

dune (dün; dūn), *n.* mound or ridge of loose sand heaped up by the wind. [< F < MDu. *dūne;* akin to DOWN³]

dung (dung), *n.* waste matter from animals; manure. —*v.* put dung on as a fertilizer. [OE] **—dung'y,** *adj.*

dun·ga·ree (dung'gə rē'), *n.* **1** a coarse cotton cloth, used for work clothes, sails, etc. **2 dungarees,** trousers or clothing made of this cloth. [< Hind. *dungrī*]

dun·geon (dun'jən), *n.* **1** a dark underground room to keep prisoners in. **2** =donjon. —*v.* confine in a dungeon; imprison. [< OF *donjon* < Gmc.]

dung·hill (dung'hil), *n.* **1** heap of dung. **2** a vile place or person.

dunk (dungk), *v.* **1** dip (something, esp. food) into a liquid: *dunk doughnuts into coffee.* **2** drop a basketball into the basket. —*n.* **1** a dunking. **2** =dunk shot. [< LG *dunken* dip] **—dunk'er,** *n.*

dunk shot, shot in basketball in which the player jumps high enough to drop the ball into the basket.

dun·lin (dun'lən), *n., pl.* **-lins** or (*esp. collectively*) **-lin.** a small wading bird that has a broad black stripe across the abdoment during the breeding season. [dim. of *dun²*]

dun·nage (dun'ij), *n.* **1** baggage or clothes. **2** branches, mats, etc., placed around a cargo to protect it from damage by water or chafing.

du·o (dü'ō; dū'ō), *n.* **1** =duet. **2** *Fig.* a pair. [< Ital. < L, two]

du·o·dec·i·mal (dü'ō des'ə məl; dū'–), *adj.* pertaining to twelfths or to twelve; proceeding by twelves. —*n.* **1** one twelfth. **2** one of a system of numerals, the base of which is twelve instead of ten.

duodecimals, system of counting by twelves.

du·o·de·num (dü'ō dē'nəm; dū'–), *n., pl.* **-na** (-nə). the first part of the small intestine, just below the stomach. [< Med.L < L *duodeni* twelve each; with ref. to its length, about twelve finger breadths] **—du'o·de'nal,** *adj.*

dup., duplicate.

dupe (düp, dūp), *n., v.,* **duped, dup·ing.** —*n.* **1** person easily deceived or tricked. **2** *Informal.* =duplicate. —*v.* **1** deceive; trick. **2** =duplicate. [< F < L *upupa* hoopoe (a bird)] **—dup'er,** *n.*

du·ple (dü'pəl; dū'–), *adj.* **1** double. **2** having two or a multiple of two beats to the measure. [< L *duplus* double]

duple time, two-part time; two beats to the measure.

du·plex (dü'pleks; dū'–), *adj.* double; twofold. —*n.* =duplex apartment. [< L < *du-* two + *plicare* fold] **—du·plex'i·ty,** *n.*

duplex apartment, an apartment having rooms on two floors.

du·pli·cate (*adj., n.* dü'plə kit, dū'–; *v.* dü'plə kāt, dū'–), *adj., n., v.,* **-cat·ed, -cat·ing.** —*adj.* **1** exactly like something else. **2** double. —*n.* **1** one of two things exactly alike. **2 in duplicate,** in two forms exactly alike. —*v.* make an exact copy of; repeat exactly. [< L, < *duplicare* double. See DUPLEX.] **—du'pli·ca'tion,** *n.*

du·plic·i·ty (dü plis′ə ti; dū–), *n., pl.* **-ties.** deceitfulness in speech or action; treachery.

du·ra·ble (dúr′ə bəl; dyúr′–), *adj.* lasting a long time; not soon injured or worn out. [< F < L, < *durare* to last, harden < *durus* hard] —**du′ra·bil′i·ty, du′ra·ble·ness,** *n.* —**du′ra·bly,** *adv.*

du·ra ma·ter (dúr′ə mā′tər), tough outer membrane covering the brain and spinal cord.

du·ra·tion (dú rā′shən; dyú–), *n.* length of time; time during which anything continues.

du·ress (dú res′, dyú–; dúr′es, dyúr′–), *n.* compulsion. [< OF < L *duritia* hardness < *durus* hard]

dur·ing (dúr′ing; dyúr′–), *prep.* **1** through the whole time of. **2** at some time in; in the course of. [ppr. of obs. *dure* ENDURE]

du·rum (dúr′əm; dyúr′–), or **durum wheat,** *n.* a hard wheat from which the flour used in macaroni, spaghetti, etc., is made.

dusk (dusk), *n.* **1** time just before dark. **2** shade; gloom. —*adj.* dark-colored; dusky. [var. of OE *dux* dark]

dusk·y (dus′ki), *adj.,* **dusk·i·er, dusk·i·est. 1** somewhat dark; dark-colored. **2** dim; obscure. **3** gloomy. —**dusk′i·ly,** *adv.* —**dusk′i·ness,** *n.*

dust (dust), *n.* **1** fine, dry earth; any fine powder. **2** earth; ground. **3** what is left of a dead body after decay. **4** cloud of dust in the air. **5** disturbance. **6** humble condition. **7** a worthless thing. —*v.* **1** get dust off. **2** soil with dust. **3** sprinkle (with dust, powder, etc.).

bite the dust, *Slang.* **a** fall dead or wounded. **b** be defeated, humiliated, or eliminated.

dust off, reintroduce later.

gather dust, be neglected; ignored.

let the dust settle, allow circumstances, conditions, etc., to return to normal. [OE *dūst*] —**dust′less,** *adj.*

dust bowl, area, esp. in the W part of the United States, where dust storms were frequent.

dust devil, small whirlwind that picks up and carries dust.

dust·er (dus′tər), *n.* **1** person or thing that dusts. **2** cloth, brush, etc., used to get dust off things. **3** a dust storm.

dust jacket, the jacket of a book.

dust·pan (dust′pan′), *n.* a flat, broad pan to sweep dust into from the floor.

dust storm, a strong wind carrying clouds of dust across or from a dry region.

dust·up (dust′up′), *n. Informal.* controversy; noisy quarrel.

dust·y (dus′ti), *adj.,* **dust·i·er, dust·i·est. 1** covered with dust; filled with dust. **2** like dust; dry and powdery. **3** having the color of dust; grayish. —**dust′i·ly,** *adv.* —**dust′i·ness,** *n.*

Dutch (duch), *adj.* of or having to do with the Netherlands, its people, or their language. —*n.* **1 the Dutch, a** the people of the Netherlands. **b** the people of Germany. The ancestors of the Pennsylvania Dutch came from Germany, not from the Netherlands. **2** language of the Netherlands.

go Dutch, have each person pay for him or herself.

in Dutch, in trouble.

Dutch door, door divided across the middle allowing the top half to be opened and the bottom remain latched.

Dutch·man (duch′mən), *n., pl.* **-men.** native or inhabitant of the Netherlands.

Dutch·man's-breech·es (duch′mənz-brich′iz), *n. sing. and pl.* **1** a spring wild flower shaped somewhat like breeches. **2** the plant that bears it.

Dutch oven, a heavy iron kettle with a close-fitting cover.

du·te·ous (dü′ti əs; dū′–), *adj.* dutiful; obedient. —**du′te·ous·ly,** *adv.* —**du′te·ous·ness,** *n.*

du·ti·a·ble (dü′ti ə bəl; dū′–), *adj.* on which a duty or tax must be paid.

du·ti·ful (dü′tə fəl; dū′–), *adj.* **1** performing the duties one owes; obedient. **2** required by duty; proceeding from or expressing a sense of duty. —**du′ti·ful·ly,** *adv.* —**du′ti·ful·ness,** *n.*

du·ty (dü′ti; dū′–), *n., pl.* **-ties. 1** thing that a person ought to do; thing that is right to do: *sense of duty.* **2** thing that a person has to do in his or her work; action required by one's occupation or position: *off duty on weekends; on duty today.* **3** tax on articles brought into or taken out of a country, made, sold, etc. [< AF *dueté* < *du* DUE]

DVD (dē′vē′dē′), digital video disk, digital recording of pictures and sound.

dwarf (dwôrf), *n.* **1** person, animal, or plant much smaller than the usual size for its kind. **2** in fairy tales, an ugly little man with magic power. —*adj.* much smaller than the usual size of its kind; checked in growth. —*v.* **1** keep from growing large; check in growth. **2** cause to seem small by contrast or by distance: *that tall building dwarfs the other.* [OE *dweorg*] —**dwarf′ness,** *n.*

dwarf·ish (dwôr′fish), *adj.* like a dwarf; smaller than usual. —**dwarf′ish·ly,** *adv.* —**dwarf′ish·ness,** *n.*

dwell (dwel), *v.,* **dwelled, dwell·ing.** make one's home; live.

dwell on, a think, write, or speak about for a long time. **b** put stress on. [OE *dwellan* delay] —**dwell′er,** *n.*

dwell·ing (dwel′ing), *n.* house to live in; place in which one lives.

dwin·dle (dwin′dəl), *v.,* **-dled, -dling.** become smaller and smaller; shrink; diminish. [dim. of obs. *dwine* < OE *dwīnan* waste away]

Dy, dysprosium. Also, **Ds.**

dye (dī), *n., v.,* **dyed, dye·ing.** —*n.* **1** a coloring matter used to color cloth, hair, etc.; liquid containing this. **2** color produced by such coloring matter; tint; hue. —*v.* **1** color (cloth, hair, etc.) by putting in a liquid containing coloring matter. **2** color; stain. [OE *dēag*]

dyed-in-the-wool (dīd′in t͞hə wùl′), *adj.* **1** dyed before being woven into cloth. **2** thoroughgoing, complete.

dye·ing (dī′ing), *n.* the coloring of fabrics with dye.

dy·er (dī′ər), *n.* person whose business is dyeing fabrics.

dye·stuff (dī′stuf′), *n.* substance yielding a dye or used as a dye, as indigo.

dy·ing (dī′ing), *adj.* **1** about to die. **2** coming to an end. **3** of death; at death. —*n.* death.

dyke (dīk), *n., v.,* **dyked, dyk·ing.** =dike.

dy·nam·ic (dī nam′ik), **dy·nam·i·cal** (–ə kəl), *adj.* **1** having to do with energy or force in motion. **2** having to do with dynamics. **3** active; energetic; forceful. [< Gk. *dynamikos* < *dynamis* power < *dynasthai* be powerful] —**dy·nam′i·cal·ly,** *adv.*

dy·nam·ics (dī nam′iks), *n.* **1** (*sing. in use*) branch of physics dealing with the action of force on bodies either at motion or at rest. Dynamics includes kinematics, kinetics, and statics. **2** (*pl. in use*) forces, physical or moral, at work in any field.

dy·na·mism (dī′nə miz əm), *n.* quality of being dynamic; energetic; forceful.

dy·na·mite (dī′nə mīt), *n., v.,* **-mit·ed, -mit·ing.** —*n.* a powerful explosive used in blasting rock, tree stumps, etc. —*v.* blow up or destroy with dynamite. —**dy′na·mit′er,** *n.*

dy·na·mo (dī′nə mō), *n., pl.* **-mos. 1** machine that changes mechanical energy into electric energy and produces electric current. **2** motor which turns electrical energy into mechanical energy. **3** *Fig.* dynamic person; innovator.

dy·na·mom·e·ter (dī′nə mom′ə tər), *n.* apparatus to measure force.

dy·nast (dī′nast; –nəst), *n.* **1** member of a dynasty; hereditary ruler. **2** any ruler. [< L < Gk., < *dynasthai* be powerful]

dy·nas·ty (dī′nəs ti; *esp. Brit.* din′əs–), *n., pl.* **-ties. 1** series of rulers who belong to the same family. **2** period of time during which a dynasty rules. —**dy·nas′tic, dy·nas′ti·cal,** *adj.* —**dy·nas′ti·cal·ly,** *adv.*

dyne (dīn), *n.* amount of force that, acting on a mass of one gram for one second, gives it a velocity of one centimeter per second. [< F < Gk. *dynamis* power < *dynasthai* be powerful]

dys-, *prefix.* bad, abnormal, defective, as in *dyslexia.*

dys·en·ter·y (dis′ən ter′i), *n.* a painful disease of the intestines, producing diarrhea with blood and mucus. [< OF < L < Gk., < *dys-* bad + *entera* intestines] —**dys′en·ter′ic,** *adj.*

dys·func·tion (dis fungk′shən), *n.* 1 abnormal function, as of an organ or joint; malfunction. 2 not acting or behaving as expected: *economic dysfunction; political dysfunction.* —**dys·func′tion·al,** *adj.*

dys·lex·ia (dis lek′sē ə), *n.* inability to read properly. —**dys·lex′ic,** *n., adj.*

dys·pep·si·a (dis pep′si ə; –shə), *n.* poor digestion; indigestion. [< L < Gk., < *dys*– bad + *pep*– cook, digest]

dys·pep·tic (dis pep′tik), *adj.* 1 pertaining to dyspepsia. 2 suffering from dyspepsia. 3 gloomy; pessimistic. —*n.* person who has dyspepsia. —**dys·pep′ti·cal·ly,** *adv.*

dys·pro·si·um (dis prō′si əm; –shi–), *n.* a rare element, Dy or Ds, the most magnetic substance known. [< NL < Gk. *dysprositos* hard to get at]

dys·tro·phy (dis′trə fi), *n.* 1 defective nutrition. 2 defective development. 3 degeneration: *muscular dystrophy.*

dz., dozen; dozens.

E, e (ē), *n., pl.* **E's; e's. 1** the fifth letter of the alphabet. **2** the third tone of the scale of C major.

E, E., 1 East; east; Eastern; eastern. **2** English.

e, electronic.

ea., each.

each (ēch), *adj.* every one of two or more considered separately or one by one: *each dog has a name.* —*pron.* each one: *each went his way.* —*adv.* for each; to each; apiece: *these pencils are a dime each.* [OE *ǣlc* < *ā* ever + *gelīc* alike]

each other, 1 each the other: *they struck each other,* that is, they struck, *each* striking *the other.* **2** one another: *they struck at each other.*

ea·ger (ē′gər), *adj.* **1** wanting very much. **2** characterized by intensity of desire or feeling: *eager looks.* [< OF < L *acer* keen] —**ea′ger·ly,** *adv.* —**ea′ger·ness,** *n.*

eager beaver, *Informal.* very hardworking, ambitious person.

ea·gle (ē′gəl), *n.* **1** a large bird of prey that has keen eyes and powerful wings. **2** picture of an eagle, or object shaped like an eagle, used as an emblem on a flag, stamp, etc. [< OF < L *aquila*]

eagle eye, careful, sharp watch or lookout.

ea·gle-eyed (ē′gəl īd′), *adj.* able to see far and clearly.

ea·glet (ē′glit), *n.* a young eagle.

ear[1] (ir), *n.* **1** part of the body by which human beings and animals hear; organ of hearing. **2** the external ear; visible part of the ear. **3** sense of hearing. **4** ability to distinguish small differences in sounds. **5** listening.

be all ears, listen eagerly; pay careful attention.

believe one's ears, have trust in the truth of what one hears.

bend one's ear, hold in conversation too long.

fall on deaf ears, not be listened to; receive no attention.

have or **keep an ear to the ground,** pay attention to what people are thinking or saying so that one can act accordingly.

lend an ear, listen.

(play) by ear, perform without preparation or using written music, etc.

turn a deaf ear, refuse to listen or pay attention.

up to the ears, thoroughly involved; almost overcome.

wet behind the ears, too young; inexperienced. [OE *ēare*]

ear[2] (ir), *n.* part of certain plants, such as corn, wheat, etc., that contains the grains. —*v.* grow ears; form ears. [OE *ēar*]

ear·ache (ir′āk′), *n.* pain in the ear.

ear·drum (ir′drum′), *n.* a thin membrane across the middle ear that vibrates when sound waves strike it; tympanic membrane.

earl (ėrl), *n.* a British nobleman ranking below a marquis and above a viscount. [OE *eorl*] —**earl′dom, earl′ship,** *n.*

ear·ly (ėr′li), *adv., adj.,* **–li·er, –li·est.** —*adv.* **1** in the first part. **2** before the usual time: *call me early.* **3** long ago. **4** soon. —*adj.* **1** of or occurring in the first part: *in early life.* **2** occurring before the usual time: *have an early dinner.* **3** occurring far back in time: *in early times.* **4** occurring in the near future: *an early reply.*

early on, at or from the beginning. [OE, < *ǣr* ere + *-līce* -LY[1]] —**ear′li·ness,** *n.*

early bird, person who gets up or arrives early; one who gains by acting promptly.

ear·mark (ir′märk′), *n.* **1** mark made on the ear of an animal to show who owns it. **2** a special mark, quality, or feature that gives information about a person or thing; sign. —*v.* **1** make an earmark on; identify or give information about. **2** set aside for some special purpose.

ear·muffs (ir′mufs′), *n. pl.* pair of coverings to put over the ears to keep them warm.

earn (ėrn), *v.* **1** receive for work or service; be paid. **2** do enough work for; deserve; be worth. **3** bring or get as deserved. [OE *earnian*] —**earn′er,** *n.*

ear·nest[1] (ėr′nist), *adj.* **1** firm in purpose; serious. **2** important: *"Life is real, life is earnest."* —*n.* **in earnest,** sincere. [OE *eornost*] —**ear′nest·ly,** *adv.* —**ear′nest·ness,** *n.*

ear·nest[2] (ėr′nist), *n.* part given or done in advance as a pledge for the rest, or to bind a bargain. [ME *ernes,* appar. alter. (by assoc. with *-NESS*) of *erres* < OF, pl. < L *arra* < Gk. *arrhabon* < Heb. *'ērābōn*]

earn·ing (ėrn′ing), *n.* act of gaining. **earnings,** money earned; wages; profits.

ear·phone (ir′fōn′), *n.* receiver that is fastened over the ear; headphone.

ear·ring (ir′ring′), *n.* ornament for the ear.

ear·shot (ir′shot′), *n.* distance a sound can be heard; range of hearing: *he was out of earshot and could not hear our shouts.*

ear tag, metal or plastic identification tag attached to the ear of an animal.

earth (ėrth), *n.* **1** planet on which we live; the third planet from the sun, and the fifth in size. **2** inhabitants of this planet. **3** this world (often in contrast to heaven and hell). **4** ground; soil; dirt. **5** connection of an electrical conductor with the earth.

come back to earth, stop dreaming and get back to practical matters. [OE *eorthe*]

earth·en (ėr′thən), *adj.* **1** made of earth. **2** made of baked clay.

earth·en·ware (ėr′thən wār′), *n.* **1** baked clay dishes, containers, etc. **2** baked clay.

earth·light (ėrth′līt), *n.* =earthshine.

earth·ly (ėrth′li), *adj.,* **–li·er, –li·est. 1** having to do with the earth, not with heaven. **2** possible; conceivable: *for no earthly reason.* —**earth′li·ness,** *n.*

earth·quake (ėrth′kwāk′), *n.* a shaking of the earth, caused by the sudden move-

ment of rock masses or by changes beneath the surface.

earth science, any science dealing with the earth, as geology, meteorology, or oceanography.

earth·shak·ing (ėrth′shā′king), *adj.* unusually great or important. Also, **earth-shattering.**

earth·shine (ėrth′shīn′), *n.* faint light on that part of the moon not directly illuminated by the sun. It is light reflected from earth and most easily seen just before and after the new moon. Also, **earthlight.**

earth·ward (ėrth′wərd), *adv.* Also, **earthwards.** toward the earth. —*adj.* at or toward the earth.

earth·work (ėrth′wėrk′), *n.* **1** bank of earth piled up for a fortification. **2** a moving of earth in engineering operations.

earth·worm (ėrth′wėrm′), *n.* a reddishbrown worm that lives in the soil; angleworm.

earth·y (ėr′thi), *adj.,* **earth·i·er, earth·i·est. 1** of or like earth or soil. **2** not spiritual; worldly. **3** not refined; coarse. —**earth′i·ness,** *n.*

ear trumpet, a trumpet-shaped instrument held to the ear as an aid in hearing.

ear·wax (ir′waks′), *n.* the sticky, yellowish substance in the canal of the outer ear.

ear·wig (ir′wig′), *n.* a beetlelike insect. Supposedly it creeps into the ear. [OE, < *ēare* ear + *wicga* beetle, worm]

ease (ēz), *n., v.,* **eased, eas·ing.** —*n.* **1** freedom from pain or trouble; comfort. **2** freedom from trying hard; lack of effort; readiness: *he writes with ease.* **3** freedom from constraint; natural or easy manner. —*v.* **1** give relief or comfort to. **2** lessen; lighten: *some medicines ease pain.* **3** move slowly and carefully: *he eased the big box through the narrow door.*

at ease, a free from pain or trouble; comfortable. **b** with the body relaxed and the feet apart.

ease in, break in slowly.

ease off or **up, a** lessen. **b** lighten. **c** slow down.

ease out, encourage to leave a position.

ill at ease, uncomfortable.

take one's ease, rest; make oneself comfortable. [< OF *aise* comfort, opportunity < VL *adjacens* neighborhood < L, *ADJACENT*] —**eas′er,** *n.*

ea·sel (ē′zəl), *n.* a support or upright frame for a picture, blackboard, etc. [< Du. *ezel* easel, lit., ass < L *asinus*]

ease·ment (ēz′mənt), *n.* a right held by one person in land owned by another.

eas·i·ly (ēz′ə li), *adv.* in an easy manner; with little effort.

eas·i·ness (ēz′i nis), *n.* **1** quality, condition, or state of being easy. **2** carelessness; indifference.

east (ēst), *n.* **1** direction of the sunrise; direction just opposite west. **2**

Also, **East.** part of any country toward the east. **3. East.** region from Maine through Maryland in the United States. —*adj.* **1** lying toward or situated in the east. **2** originating in or coming from the east: *an east wind.* —*adv.* **1** toward the east. **2** in the east.

down East, a New England. **b** the E part of New England.

the East, the Orient. [OE *ēast*]

East·er (ēs′tər), *n.* day for celebrating Christ's rising from the dead. [OE *ēastre,* orig., name of dawn goddess < *ēast* EAST]

Easter Island, island in the S Pacific, 2000 miles W of Chile, and belonging to it.

east·er·ly (ēs′tər li), *adj., adv.* **1** toward the east. **2** from the east. —**east′er·li·ness,** *n.*

east·ern (ēs′tərn), *adj.* **1** toward the east. **2** from the east. **3** of or in the east.

Eastern, a of or in the E part of the United States. **b** of or in the countries in Asia; Oriental. —**east′ern·most,** *adj.*

Eastern Church, 1 group of Christian churches in E Europe, W Asia, and Egypt that do not recognize the Pope as spiritual leader. **2** the Orthodox Church.

east·ern·er (ēs′tər nər), *n.* native or inhabitant of the east.

Easterner, native or inhabitant of the E part of the United States.

Eastern Hemisphere, the half of the world that includes Europe, Asia, Africa, and Australia.

East·er·tide (ēs′tər tīd′), *n.* Easter time.

East Indies, 1 the collective name given to India, Indochina, and the Malay Archipelago. **2** the islands of the Malay Archipelago. —**East Indian.**

east·ward (ēst′wərd), *adv.* Also, **eastwards.** toward the east. —*adj.* **1** toward the east. **2** east.

eas·y (ēz′i), *adj.,* **eas·i·er, eas·i·est,** *adv.* —*adj.* **1** requiring little effort; not hard: *easy work.* **2** free from pain, discomfort, trouble, or worry: *easy circumstances.* **3** giving comfort or rest: *an easy chair.* **4** not harsh; not severe; not strict: *easy terms.* **5** not fast; slow: *an easy pace.* —*adv.* **1** with little effort. **2** easily.

easy come, easy go, something easily gotten can just as easily be lost.

easy does it, be careful.

go easy on, a be gentle or kindly with. **b** use with restraint.

take it easy, *Informal.* not over-exert or push oneself. [< OF *aisié,* pp. of *aaisier* set at ease < *a–* (< L *ad–*) + *aise* at EASE]

eas·y·go·ing (ēz′i gō′ing), *adj.* taking matters easily; not worrying.

easy mark, *Informal.* person who is easily imposed on.

eat (ēt), *v.,* **ate, eat·en** (ēt′ən), **eat·ing. 1** chew and swallow (food). **2** have a meal. **3** destroy: *acid eats metal.* **4** wear away; waste away. **5** make by eating.

eat one's words, take back what one has said; retract.

eat out, eat away from home.

eat up, a eat all of. **b** use up; waste away: *extravagance ate up his inheritance.* [OE *etan*] —**eat′er,** *n.*

eat·a·ble (ēt′ə bəl), *adj.* fit to eat. —*n.* Usu. **eatables.** things fit to eat; edibles.

eau de cologne or **Eau de Co·logne** (ō′ də kə lōn′), =cologne. [< F, water of Cologne, where it was first made]

eaves (ēvz), *n. pl.* the lower edge of a roof that projects beyond a wall. [OE *efes*]

eaves·drop (ēvz′drop′), *v.,* **–dropped, –drop·ping.** listen to what one is not supposed to hear; listen secretly to private conversation. —**eaves′drop′per,** *n.* —**eaves′drop′ping,** *n.*

ebb (eb), *n.* **1** a flowing of the tide away from the shore; fall of the tide. **2** a growing less or weaker; decline. **3** point of decline. —*v.* **1** flow out; fall. **2** grow less or weaker; decline. [OE *ebba*]

ebb and flow, 1 movement of the tides. **2** *Fig.* changes in circumstances, similar to the tides.

ebb tide, tide that flows away from shore.

E·bo·la (i bō′lə) **virus,** virus that causes hemorrhagic fever.

eb·on·y (eb′ən i), *n., pl.* **–on·ies,** *adj.* —*n.* **1** a hard, heavy, durable wood, used for the black keys of a piano, the backs and handles of brushes, ornamental woodwork, etc. **2** a tropical tree that yields this wood. —*adj.* **1** made of ebony. **2** like ebony; black; dark. [< L < Gk., < *ebenos* ebony < Egypt. *hebni*]

e·bul·lient (i bul′yənt), *adj.* overflowing with enthusiasm, liveliness, etc. [< L, < *ex–* out + *bullire* boil] —**e·bul′lience, e·bul′lien·cy,** *n.* —**e·bul′lient·ly,** *adv.*

ec·cen·tric (ik sen′trik), *adj.* **1** out of the ordinary; odd; peculiar. **2** not having the same center. **3** off center; having its axis set off center. **4** not circular in form. —*n.* an eccentric person. [< Med.L < L *eccentrus* < Gk., < *ex–* out + *kentron* center] —**ec·cen′tri·cal·ly,** *adv.*

ec·cen·tric·i·ty (ek′sən tris′ə ti; –sen–), *n., pl.* **–ties. 1** something queer or out of the ordinary; oddity; peculiarity. **2** eccentric quality or condition.

eccl., ecclesiastical.

Ec·cle·si·as·tes (i klē′zi as′tēz), *n.* book of the Old Testament. [< LL < Gk. *ekklesiastes* preacher, ult. < *ex–* out + *kaleein* call]

ec·cle·si·as·tic (i klē′zi as′tik), *n.* clergyman. —*adj.* ecclesiastical.

ec·cle·si·as·ti·cal (i klē′zi as′tə kəl), *adj.* of or having to do with the church or the clergy. —**ec·cle′si·as′ti·cal·ly,** *adv.*

ECG, electrocardiogram.

ech·e·lon (esh′ə lon), *n.* **1** a steplike arrangement of troops, ships, etc. **2** level of command. —*v.* form into a steplike arrangement. [< F, round of a ladder < *échelle* ladder < L *scala*]

e·chid·na (i kid′nə), *n., pl.* **–nas, –nae** (–nē). a small, egg-laying, ant-eating animal of Australia with a covering of

spines and a long, slender snout. [< L < Gk., viper]

e·chi·no·derm (i kī′nə dėrm; ek′i nə–), *n.* starfish, sea urchin, or other similar small sea animal with a stony shell and a body whose parts are arranged radially. [< NL, < Gk. *echinos,* sea urchin, orig., hedgehog + *derma* skin]

e·chi·nus (i kī′nəs), *n.* **1** sea urchin. **2** simple, rounded molding at the top of a Doric column.

ech·o (ek′ō), *n., pl.* **ech·oes,** *v.,* **ech·oed, echo·ing.** —*n.* **1** a sounding again; a repeating of a sound. **2** person who repeats the words or imitates the feelings, acts, etc., of another. **3** imitation of the feelings, acts, etc., of another. —*v.* **1** sound again; repeat or be repeated in sound; reflect sounds. **2** repeat (the words) or imitate (the feelings, acts, etc.) of another. [< L < Gk.] —**ech′o·er,** *n.*

e·cho·ic (i kō′ik), *adj.* **1** like an echo. **2** imitative of sound, as the words "caw" and "buzz"; onomatopoeic.

ech·o·lo·ca·tion (ek′ō lō ka′shən), *n.* **1** method of finding the distance to an object and its direction by measuring the length of time it takes sound or radio waves echoed from the object to reach the source of the waves, used in radar and sonar. **2** use of echoes as directional signals by some mammals, such as bats and whales.

echo sounding, method of finding the depth of a body of water by measuring how long it takes sound waves echoed from the bottom to reach a receiver at the surface.

é·clair (ā klār′), *n.* an oblong puff or piece of pastry filled with whipped cream or custard and covered with icing. [< F, lightning, ult. < L *exclarare* lighten < *ex–* out + *clarus* clear]

é·clat (ā klä′), *n.* **1** a brilliant success. **2** fame; glory. **3** burst of applause or approval. [< F]

ec·lec·tic (ek lek′tik), *adj.* **1** selecting and using what seems best from various sources. **2** from various sources. [< Gk. *eklektikos* < *ex–* out + *legein* pick] —**ec·lec′ti·cism,** *n.*

e·clipse (i klips′), *n., v.,* **e·clipsed, e·clips·ing.** —*n.* **1** a darkening of the sun, moon, etc., when some other celestial body is in a position that cuts off its light. A **solar eclipse** occurs when the moon is between the sun and the earth. **2** loss of importance or reputation; failure for a time. —*v.* **1** cut off or obscure the light from; darken. **2** cut off or obscure the importance of; surpass. [< OF < L < Gk. *ekleipsis* < *ex–* out + *leipein* leave]

e·clip·tic (i klip′tik), *n.* path that the sun appears to travel in one year. It is the great circle of the celestial sphere, cut by the plane containing the orbit of the earth. —*adj.* Also, **e·clip′ti·cal. 1** of this circle. **2** having to do with eclipses.

ec·logue (ek′lôg; –log), *n.* a short poem about country life, esp. a dialogue between shepherds. [< L < Gk. *ekloge* a selection. See ECLECTIC.]

eco-, *prefix.* of the environment or ecology; ecological, as in *ecocatastrophe.*

e·co·ca·tas·tro·phe (ē′kə ca tas′trə fē; ek′ə–), *n.* enormous or worldwide ecological disaster.

e·co·cide (ē′kə sīd; ek′ə–), *n.* destruction of the earth's environment by failure to control pollution, overuse of resources, etc.

e·col·o·gy (ē kol′ə ji), *n.* branch of biology that deals with the relation of living things to their environment and to each other. [< Gk. *oikos* house + –LOGY] —**ec′o·log·ic, ec′o·log′i·cal,** *adj.* —**ec′o·log′i·cal·ly,** *adv.* —**e·col′o·gist,** *n.*

econ., economic; economics; economy.

e·co·nom·ic (ē′kə nom′ik; ek′ə–), *adj.* **1** of or pertaining to economics. Economic problems have to do with the production, distribution, and consumption of wealth. **2** having to do with the management of the income, supplies, and expenses of a household, community, government, etc.

e·co·nom·i·cal (ē′kə nom′ə kəl; ek′ə–), *adj.* **1** avoiding waste; saving: *an efficient engine is economical of fuel.* **2** having to do with economics. —**e′co·nom′i·cal·ly,** *adv.*

e·co·nom·ics (ē′kə nom′iks; ek′ə–), *n.* science of the production, distribution, and consumption of wealth. Economics deals with the material welfare of humankind and the problems of capital, labor, wages, prices, tariffs, taxes, etc.

e·con·o·mist (ē kon′ə mist; i–), *n.* **1** an expert in economics. **2** person who is economical.

e·con·o·mize (ē kon′ə mīz; i–), *v.,* –**mized,** –**miz·ing. 1** manage so as to avoid waste; use to the best advantage. **2** cut down expenses. —**e·con′omiz′er,** *n.*

e·con·o·my (ē kon′ə mi; i–), *n., pl.* –**mies. 1** a making the most of what one has; freedom from waste in the use of anything; thrift. **2** managing affairs and resources so as to avoid waste; management. **3** system of managing the production, distribution, and consumption of goods: *feudal economy.* [< L < Gk. *oikonomia* < *oikos* house + *nemein* manage]

economy class, travel class on an airplane, train, etc., that is less luxurious and less expensive than first class.

e·con·o·my-size (i kon′ə mi sīz′), *adj.* in a large package and priced at less per unit than a regular size package.

e·co·sphere (i′kə sfir; ek′ə–), *n.* region suitable to sustain life; biosphere.

e·co·sys·tem (ē′kə sis′təm; ek′ə–), *n.* system of lining organisms and their physical environment, including food, water, weather, predators, etc.

e·co·tour·ism (ē′kō tŭr′izm; ek′ō–), *n.* travel to an area that preserves the natural environment. —**e′co·tour′, e′co·tour′ist,** *n.*

ec·ru, (ek′rü), *n., adj.* pale brown; light tan. [< F, raw, unbleached, var. of *cru* raw < L *crudus*]

ec·sta·sy (ek′stə si), *n., pl.* –**sies. 1** state of great joy; thrilling or overwhelming delight; rapture. **2** amphetamine-based drug. [< L < Gk. *ekstasis* trance, distraction < *ex–* out + *histanai* to place]

ec·stat·ic (ik stat′ik), *adj.* Also, **ec·stat′i·cal. 1** full of or tending to show ecstasy. **2** caused by ecstasy. —**ec·stat′i·cal·ly,** *adv.*

ECT, electroconvulsive therapy.

ecto-, *combining form.* to or on the outside, as in *ectoplasm =outer portion of cytoplasm.* [< Gk. *ekto–*]

ec·to·derm (ek′tə dėrm), *n.* the outer layer of cells formed during the development of the embryos of animals. —**ec′to·der′mal,** *adj.*

-ectomy, *combining form.* surgical removal of a particular part of the body, as in *appendectomy =surgical removal of the appendix.*

ec·to·plasm (ek′tə plaz əm), *n.* the outer portion of the cytoplasm of a cell. —**ec′to·plas′mic,** *adj.*

ec·to·ther·mic (ek′tə thėr′mik), *adj.* receiving heat from the outside; cold-blooded. —**ec′to·ther′mous,** *adj.* —**ec′to·ther′my,** *n.*

Ec·ua·dor (ek′wə dôr), *n.* country in NW South America. —**Ec′ua·do′re·an, Ec′ua·do′ri·an,** *adj., n.*

ec·u·men·i·cal (ek′yù men′ə kəl), **ec·u·men·ic** (–men′ik), *adj.* **1** general; universal. **2** of or representing the whole Christian Church. [< L *oecumenicus* < Gk., < *oikoumene* (*ge*) inhabited (world), ult. < *oikos* dwelling] —**ec′u·men′i·cal·ly,** *adv.*

ec·u·men·ism (ek′yù mə niz əm), *n.* principle of worldwide Christian harmony and unity, esp. in the Protestant Church.

ec·ze·ma (ek′sə mə; ig zē′–), *n.* a skin inflammation characterized by itching and the formation of patches of red scales. [< NL < Gk. *ekzema* < *ex–* out + *zeein* boil]

-ed, *suffix.* **1** forming the past tense. **2** forming the past participle. **3** with various meanings: **a** having; supplied with, as in *bearded, long-legged, pale-faced, tender-hearted.* **b** having the characteristics of, as in *honeyed.* [OE]

ed., **1** edited; edition; editor. **2** educated.

E·dam cheese (ē′dam; ē′dəm), or **Edam,** *n.* a round, yellow cheese made in Holland, usually covered with red wax on the outside. [after village in Holland]

ed·dy (ed′i), *n., pl.* –**dies,** *v.,* –**died,** –**dy·ing.** —*n.* water, air, etc., moving against the main current and having a whirling motion; small whirlpool or whirlwind. —*v.* move against the main current in a whirling motion; whirl. [? < OE *ed–* turning + *ēa* stream]

e·del·weiss (ā′dəl vīs), *n.* a small Alpine plant having very small white flowers and surrounding leaves covered with white fuzz. [< G, < *edel* noble + *weiss* white]

e·de·ma (i dē′mə), *n., pl.* –**ma·ta** (–mə tə). a watery swelling in the tissues of the body. [< NL < Gk., < *oidos* tumor]

E·den (ē′dən), *n.* **1** garden where Adam and Eve lived at first. **2** *Fig.* delightful spot; paradise.

e·den·tate (ē den′tāt), *adj.* toothless. —*n.* one of a group of animals that are toothless or lack front teeth, as anteaters, armadillos, and sloths. [< L, < *ex–* without + *dens* tooth]

edge (ej), *n., v.,* **edged, edg·ing.** —*n.* **1** line or place where something ends; part farthest from the middle; side. **2** brink; verge. **3** a thin, sharp side that cuts. **4** sharpness; keenness. **5** advantage. —*v.* **1** put an edge on; form an edge on. **2** move in a sidewise manner or little by little. **3** border.

edge in, manage to get in.

edge out, win by a narrow margin.

on edge, a disturbed; uncomfortable. **b** impatient.

on the edge of, about to (do something).

take the edge off, deprive of force, strength, or enjoyment. [OE *ecg*] —**edged,** *adj.* —**edg·er,** *n.*

edge·ways (ej′wāz′), *adv.* with the edge forward; in the direction of the edge. Also, **edgewise.**

get a word in edgeways, manage to say a few words.

edg·ing (ej′ing), *n.* border or trimming on or for an edge.

edg·y (ej′i), *adj.,* **edg·i·er, edg·i·est. 1** having a sharp edge. **2** impatient; irritable. **3** *Fig.* unconventional.

ed·i·ble (ed′ə bəl), *adj.* fit to eat. —*n.* Usually, **edibles.** things fit or intended for eating. [< LL, < L *edere* eat] —**ed′i·bil′i·ty, ed′i·ble·ness,** *n.*

e·dict (ē′dikt), *n.* a public order or command by some authority; decree. [< L, < *ex–* out + *dicere* say] —**e·dic′tal,** *adj.*

ed·i·fi·ca·tion (ed′ə fə kā′shən), *n.* moral improvement; spiritual benefit; instruction.

ed·i·fice (ed′ə fis), *n.* a building, esp. a large or imposing building. [< F < L *aedificium* < *aedis* temple (pl., house) + *facere* make]

ed·i·fy (ed′ə fī), *v.,* –**fied,** –**fy·ing. 1** improve morally; benefit spiritually; instruct. **2** build; construct. [< F < L *aedificare* build (up). See EDIFICE.] —**ed′i·fi′er,** *n.*

Ed·in·burgh (ed′ən bėr′ō), *n.* capital of Scotland.

ed·it (ed′it), *v.* **1** prepare (another person's writings) for publication. **2** have charge of (a newspaper, magazine, etc.) and decide what shall be printed.

edit down, make shorter by editing.

edit out, delete in editing. [< L *editus* < *ex–* out + *dare* give; partly < *editor*]

edit., edited; edition; editor.

e·di·tion (i dish′ən), *n.* **1** all the copies of a book, newspaper, etc., issued about the same time. **2** form in which a book is printed or published: *a three-volume edition.*

ed·i·tor (ed′ə tər), *n.* **1** person who edits. **2** person who writes editorials. [< L. See EDIT.] —**ed′i·tor·ship′**, *n.*

ed·i·to·ri·al (ed′ə tô′ri əl; –tō′–), *adj.* of or having to do with an editor; by an editor. —*n.* article in a newspaper or magazine written by the editor or under his or her direction, giving an opinion or attitude of the paper. —**ed′i·to′ri·al·ly**, *adv.*

ed·i·to·ri·al·ize (ed′ə tô′ri əl īz; –tō′–), *v.,* –**ized,** –**iz·ing. 1** write an editorial. **2** express one's opinions publicly, esp. in a newspaper. **3** write news articles as if they were editorials.

Ed·mon·ton (ed′mən tən), *n.* city in SW Canada; the capital of Alberta.

E.D.T., e.d.t., Eastern daylight time.

.edu, domain address for educational organizations on the Internet.

ed·u·ca·ble (ej′ŭ kə bəl), *adj.* capable of being educated.

ed·u·cate (ej′ŭ kāt), *v.,* –**cat·ed,** –**cat·ing. 1** develop in knowledge, skill, ability, or character by training, study, etc. **2** send to school. [< L *educatus,* pp. of *educare* bring up, raise, akin to *educere* EDUCE]

ed·u·ca·tion (ej′ŭ kā′shən), *n.* **1** development in knowledge, or skill, by teaching, or study. **2** knowledge or skill, developed by teaching, or study. **3** science or art that deals with teaching and learning. —**ed′u·ca′tor,** *n.*

ed·u·ca·tion·al (ej′ŭ kā′shən əl), *adj.* **1** of or having to do with education. **2** giving education; tending to educate. —**ed′u·ca′tion·al·ist, ed′u·ca′tion·ist,** *n.* —**ed′u·ca′tion·al·ly,** *adv.*

ed·u·ca·tive (ej′ŭ kā′tiv), *adj.* that educates.

e·duce (i düs′; i dūs′), *v.,* **e·duced, e·duc·ing.** bring out; develop. [< L, < *ex–* out + *ducere* lead] —**e·duc′i·ble,** *adj.* —**e·duc′tion,** *n.*

-ee, *suffix.* **1** person who is ___, as in *absentee.* **2** person who is ___ed, as in *appointee.* **3** person to whom something is ___ed, as in *mortgagee.* [< F *–é,* masc. pp. ending]

E.E., Electrical Engineer.

EEG, electroencephalogram; electroencephalograph.

eel (ēl), *n.* a long, slippery fish shaped like a snake and lacking ventral fins. [OE *ǣl*] —**eel′like′,** *adj.*

eel·grass (ēl′gras′; –gräs′), *n.* a North Atlantic sea plant with long, narrow leaves.

eel·pout (ēl′pout′), *n.* **1** a small, eellike saltwater fish. **2** the burbot.

e'en (ēn), *adv.* Poetic. even.

e'er (ār), *adv.* Poetic. ever.

-eer, *suffix.* **1** one who is concerned or deals with, as in *auctioneer, charioteer.* **2** person who produces, as in *pamphleteer,*

sonneteer. **3** be concerned or deal with, as in *electioneer.* [< F *–ier*]

ee·rie, ee·ry (ir′i), *adj.,* –**ri·er,** –**ri·est. 1** causing fear; strange; weird. **2** timid because of superstition. [ME *eri,* var. of *erg,* OE *earg* cowardly] —**ee′ri·ly,** *adv.* —**ee′ri·ness,** *n.*

ef·face (i fās′), *v.,* –**faced,** –**fac·ing. 1** rub out; destroy; wipe out. **2** keep (oneself) from being noticed. [< F, < *es–* (< L *ex–*) away + face FACE] —**ef·face′a·ble,** *adj.* —**ef·face′ment,** *n.* —**ef·fac′er.** *n.*

ef·fect (i fekt′), *n.* **1** whatever is produced by a cause; something made to happen by a person or thing; result. **2** power to produce results; force; influence. **3** impression produced. **4** combination of color or form in a picture, etc. **5** purport; intent; meaning. —*v.* produce as a result; bring about.

effects, personal property; belongings; goods.

for effect, for show; to impress or influence others.

in effect, a in result; really. **b** in operation.

into effect, in action; in force.

of no effect, useless.

take effect, become active.

to the effect, with the meaning or purpose. [< L *effectus < ex– + facere* make] —**ef·fect′er,** *n.* —**ef·fect′i·ble,** *adj.*

ef·fec·tive (i fek′tiv), *adj.* **1** producing the desired effect. **2** active. **3** striking; impressive.—**ef·fec′tive·ly,***adv.*—**ef·fec′tive·ness,** *n.*

ef·fec·tu·al (i fek′chù əl), *adj.* **1** producing the effect desired: *quinine is an effectual preventive for malaria.* **2** valid. —**ef·fec′tu·al·i·ty,** *n.* —**ef·fec′tu·al·ly,** *adv.*

ef·fec·tu·ate (i fek′chù āt), *v.,* –**at·ed,** –**at·ing.** cause; accomplish. —**ef·fec′tu·a′tion,** *n.*

ef·fem·i·nate (i fem′ə nit), *adj.* lacking in manly qualities; showing unmanly weakness or delicacy; womanish. [< L, < *ex– + femina* woman] —**ef·fem′i·na·cy,** *n.* —**ef·fem′i·nate·ly,** *adv.* —**ef·fem′i·nate·ness,** *n.*

ef·fer·ent (ef′ər ənt), *adj.* conveying outward from a central organ or point. Efferent nerves carry impulses from the brain to the muscles. —*n.* an efferent nerve or blood vessel. [< L, < *ex–* out + *ferre* carry]

ef·fer·vesce (ef′ər ves′), *v.,* –**vesced,** –**vesc·ing. 1** give off bubbles of gas; bubble. **2** be lively; be excited. [< L *effervescere* boil up < *ex–* out + *fervere* be hot] —**ef′fer·ves′cence, ef′fer·ves′cen·cy,** *n.* —**ef′fer·ves′cent,** *adj.*

ef·fete (i fēt′), *adj.* unable to produce; worn out; exhausted. [< L *effetus* worn out by bearing < *ex–* out + *fe–* breed, bear] —**ef·fete′ness,** *n.*

ef·fi·ca·cious (ef′ə kā′shəs), *adj.* producing the desired results; effective. —**ef′fi·ca′cious·ly,** *adv.* —**ef′fi·ca′cious·ness,** *n.*

ef·fi·ca·cy (ef′ə kə si), *n.,* pl. –**cies.** power to produce a desired effect or result;

effectiveness. [< L, < *efficere* accomplish. See EFFICIENT.]

ef·fi·cien·cy (i fish′ən si), *n.,* pl. –**cies. 1** ability to produce the effect wanted without waste of time, energy, etc. **2** efficient operation.

ef·fi·cient (i fish′ənt), *adj.* **1** able to produce the effect wanted without waste of time, energy, etc. **2** producing an effect. [< L *efficiens < ex– + facere* do, make] —**ef·fi′cient·ly,** *adv.*

ef·fi·gy (ef′ə ji), *n.,* pl. –**gies.** statue, etc., of a person; image.

burn or **hang in effigy,** burn or hang a stuffed image of a person to show hatred or contempt. [< F < L *effigies < ex–* out + *fingere* form] —**ef·fi′gi·al,** *adj.*

ef·flo·resce (ef′lô res′; –lō–), *v.,* –**resced, -resc·ing. 1** burst into bloom. **2** change from crystals to powder by loss of water. **3** become covered with a crusty deposit when water evaporates. [< L *efflorescere < ex–* out + *flos* flower]

ef·flo·res·cence (ef′lô res′əns; –lō–), **ef·flo·res·cen·cy** (–ən si), *n.,* pl. –**cen·ces; -cies. 1** a blooming; a flowering. **2** mass of flowers or anything resembling it. **3** a change in which crystals lose water and become powder. **4** powder formed in this way. **5** eruption on the skin; rash. **6** a crusty deposit formed when water evaporates from a solution. —**ef′flo·res′cent,** *adj.*

ef·flu·ent (ef′lù ənt), *adj.* flowing out or forth. —*n.* Often, **ef′flu·ence. 1** that which flows out or forth; outflow. **2** stream flowing out of another stream, lake, etc. [< L, < *ex–* out + *fluere* flow]

ef·flu·vi·um (i flü′vi əm), *n.,* pl. –**vi·a** (–vi ə), –**vi·ums.** vapor or odor. [< L. See EFFLUENT.] —**ef·flu′vi·al,** *adj.*

ef·fort (ef′ərt), *n.* **1** exertion of power, physical or mental; use of energy and strength to do something; trying hard. **2** hard try; strong attempt. **3** result of effort; thing done with effort; achievement. [< F < OF, < *esforcier* force, exert < L *ex–* out + *fortis* strong] —**ef′fort·less,** *adj.* —**ef′fort·less·ly,** *adv.* —**ef′fort·less·ness,** *n.*

ef·fron·ter·y (i frun′tər i), *n.,* pl. –**ter·ies.** shameless boldness; impudence. [< F < OF *esfront* shameless < L *ex–* out + *frons* brow]

ef·ful·gent (i ful′jənt), *adj.* shining brightly; radiant. [< L, < *ex* forth + *fulgere* shine] —**ef·ful′gence,** *n.* —**ef·ful′gent·ly,** *adv.*

ef·fuse (*v.* i fūz′; *adj.* i fūs′), *v.,* –**fused, -fus·ing,** *adj.* —*v.* pour out; spill; shed. —*adj.* **1** spread out. **2** profuse. [< L *effusus < ex–* out + *fundere* pour]

ef·fu·sion (i fū′zhən), *n.* **1** a pouring out. **2** unrestrained expression of feeling, etc., in talking or writing.

ef·fu·sive (i fū′siv), *adj.* showing too much feeling; too emotional. —**ef·fu′sive·ly,** *adv.* —**ef·fu′sive·ness,** *n.*

EFT, electronic funds transfer.

eft (eft), *n. U.S.* a small newt. [OE *efete*. See NEWT.]

e.g., for example. [< L *exempli gratia*]

e·gal·i·tar·i·an (i gal´ə ter´ē ən), *n.* person who believes that all people are equal. —*adj.* believing that all people are equal.

e·gal·i·tar·i·an·ism (i gal´ə ter´e ə niz´əm), *n.* belief in equality, esp. social equality.

egg[1] (eg), *n.* **1** a roundish body covered with a shell or membrane that is laid by the female of birds, reptiles, and fishes. Their offspring come from these eggs. **2** anything shaped like a hen's egg. **3** a female germ cell. —*v.* prepare (food) with eggs.

egg on one's face, humiliation; extreme embarrassment.

have or **put all one's eggs in one basket,** risk all on one effort, chance, etc.

walk on eggs or **eggshells,** be extremely careful or cautious. [< Scand.]

egg[2] (eg), *v.* urge; encourage: *the boys egged him on to fight.* [< Scand. *eggja* < *egg* edge]

egg·beat·er (eg´bē´tər), *n.* **1** utensil with revolving blades for beating eggs, cream, etc. **2** *Informal.* =helicopter.

egg cell, the reproductive cell produced by a female plant or animal.

egg cream, drink made of chocolate syrup, milk, and soda water.

egg foo yung (eg´fū´yung´), fried omelet filled with Chinese vegetables, pork, etc., and served with a sauce.

egg·nog (eg´nog´), *n.* drink made of eggs, milk, and sugar, often containing whiskey, brandy, or wine. [< *egg*[1] + *nog* strong ale]

egg·plant (eg´plant´; -plänt´), *n.* **1** plant with a large, oval, purple-skinned fruit. **2** the fruit, used as a vegetable.

egg roll, thin dough wrapped around a filling of Chinese vegetables, pork, etc., to form a roll which is fried.

egg·shell (eg´shel´), *n.* **1** shell covering an egg. **2** a creamy white. —*adj.* **1** like an eggshell; very thin and delicate. **2** creamy-white.

eg·lan·tine (eg´lən tīn; -tēn), *n.* a wild rose with pink flowers; sweetbrier. [< F, dim. of OF *aiglent* < VL *aculentus* < L *acus* needle]

e·go (ē´gō; eg´ō), *n., pl.* **e·gos. 1** the individual as a whole in his capacity to think, feel, and act; self. **2** conceit. [< L, I]

e·go·ism (ē´gō iz əm; eg´ō-), *n.* **1** seeking the welfare of oneself only; selfishness. **2** talking too much about oneself; conceit. —**e´go·ist,** *n.*

e·go·is·tic (ē´gō is´tik; eg´ō-), **e·go·is·ti·cal** (-tə kəl), *adj.* **1** seeking the welfare of oneself only; selfish. **2** talking too much about oneself; conceited. —**e´go·is·ti·cal·ly,** *adv.*

e·go·tism (ē´gə tiz əm; eg´ə-), *n.* **1** excessive use of *I, my,* and *me;* habit of thinking, talking or writing too much of oneself. **2** selfishness. —**e´go·tist,** *n.*

ego trip, something done to boost one's reputation or self-satisfaction.

e·go·tis·tic (ē´gə tis´tik; eg´ə-), **e·go·tis·ti·cal** (-tə kəl), *adj.* **1** characterized by egotism; conceited. **2** selfish. —**e´go·tis´ti·cal·ly,** *adv.*

e·gre·gious (i grē´jəs), *adj.* **1** outrageous; flagrant. **2** remarkable; extraordinary. [< L *egregius* < *ex-* out + *grex* herd, flock] —**e·gre´gious·ly,** *adv.* —**e·gre´gious·ness,** *n.*

e·gress (ē´gres), *n.* **1** a going out. **2** way out; exit. **3** right to go out. [< L *egressus* < *ex-* out + *gradi* step, go]

e·gret (ē´gret; eg´ret), *n.* **1** heron with tufts of beautiful, long plumes. **2** one of its plumes; aigrette. **3 snowy egret,** the North American egret. [< F *aigrette*]

E·gypt (ē´jipt), *n.* country in NE Africa.

Egypt., Egyptian.

E·gyp·tian (i jip´shən), *adj.* of or having to do with Egypt or its people. —*n.* **1** native or inhabitant of Egypt. **2** language of the ancient Egyptians.

Egyptian cotton, cotton with fine, long, silky fibers, grown esp. in the United States.

E·gyp·tol·o·gy (ē´jip tol´ə ji), *n.* science or study of the history, language, etc., of ancient Egypt. —**E·gyp´to·log´i·cal,** *adj.* —**E´gyp·tol´o·gist,** *n.*

eh (ā, e), *interj.* exclamation meaning what, as a question, or yes, as an answer.

EHF or **ehf,** extremely high frequency.

ei·der (ī´dər), *n.* **1** eider duck. **2** its down. [< Scand. *æthr*]

ei·der·down (ī´dər down´) or **eider down, 1** the soft feathers of the eider duck, used as stuffing. **2** quilt stuffed with these feathers. [< Scand. *œthar-dūn*]

eider duck, a large, northern sea duck with very soft feathers on its breast.

Eif·fel Tower (ī´fəl), a lofty tower in Paris.

eight (āt), *n.* **1** a cardinal number, one more than seven. **2** symbol of this number; 8. —*adj.* one more than seven; 8. [OE *eahta*]

eight ball, a black-colored ball in the game of pool carrying the number 8. **behind the eight ball,** in a difficult situation.

eight·een (ā´tēn´), *n.* **1** a cardinal number, eight more than ten. **2** symbol of this number; 18. —*adj.* eight more than ten; 18. —**eight´eenth´,** *adj., n.*

eight·fold (āt´fōld´), *adj.* **1** eight times as much or as many. **2** having eight parts. —*adv.* eight times as much or as many.

eighth (ātth), *adj.* **1** next after the seventh; last in a series of 8. **2** being one of 8 equal parts. —*n.* **1** next after the seventh; last in a series of 8. **2** one of 8 equal parts. **3** one octave.

eighth note, a short musical note; one eighth of a whole note; quaver.

eight·y (ā´ti), *n., pl.* **eight·ies,** *adj.* —*n.* **1** a cardinal number, eight times ten. **2** sym-

bol of this number; 80. —*adj.* eight times ten; 80. —**eight´i·eth,** *adj., n.*

ein·stein·i·um (īn stīn´i əm), *n.* rare, radioactive, artificial element, E, produced as a by-product of nuclear fission. [named for Albert *Einstein*]

Eir·e (ār´ə), *n.* the Republic of Ireland.

Ei·sen·how·er (ī´zən how´ər), **Dwight David,** 1890–1969, American general, 34th president of the United States, 1953–61.

ei·ther (ē´ŧħər; ī´-), *adj.* **1** one or the other of two: *either hat.* **2** each of two: *either side.* —*pron.* one or the other of two: *either of the hats.* —*adv.* any more than another: *if you do not go, I shall not go either.* —*conj.* one or the other of two: *either come or go.* [OE *ǣgther* < *ǣghwœther* each of two < *ā* always + *gehwœther* each of two. See WHETHER.]

e·jac·u·late (i jak´yə lāt), *v.,* **-lat·ed, -lat·ing. 1** say suddenly and briefly; exclaim. **2** eject; discharge. [< L, < *ex-* out + *jaculum* javelin < *jacere* throw] —**e·jac´u·la´tive,** *adj.* —**e·jac´u·la´tor,** *n.*

e·jac·u·la·tion (i jak´yə lā´shən), *n.* **1** exclamation. **2** discharge.

e·jac·u·la·to·ry (i jak´yə lə tô´ri; -tō´-), *adj.* **1** said suddenly. **2** discharging.

e·ject (i jekt´), *v.* throw out; expel. [< L *ejectare,* ult. < *ex-* out + *jacere* throw] —**e·jec´tion, e·ject´ment,** *n.* —**e·jec´tive,** *adj.* —**e·jec´tor,** *n.*

eke (ēk), *v.,* **eked, ek·ing. eke out, a** supply what is lacking to; supplement. **b** barely make (a living). [dial. var. of obs. *eche* to augment < OE *ēcan* < OE *ēaca* addition]

EKG, electrocardiogram.

el (el), *n.* **1** =ell. **2** an elevated railroad.

e·lab·o·rate (*adj.* i lab´ə rit; *v.* i lab´ə rāt), *adj., v.,* **-rat·ed, -rat·ing.** —*adj.* worked out with great care; having many details; complicated. —*v.* **1** work out with great care; add details to. **2** talk, write, etc., in great detail; give added details. [< L, < *ex-* out + *labor* work] —**e·lab´o·rate·ly,** *adv.* —**e·lab´o·rate·ness,** *n.* —**e·lab´o·ra´tive,** *adj.* —**e·lab´o·ra´tor,** *n.*

e·lab·o·ra·tion (i lab´ə rā´shən), *n.* **1** an elaborating. **2** a being elaborated. **3** something elaborated.

é·lan (ā län´), *n.* enthusiasm; liveliness. [< F, < *élancer* to dart]

e·land (ē´lənd), *n.* a large African antelope with twisted horns. [< Du., elk]

e·lapse (i laps´), *v.,* **e·lapsed, e·laps·ing.** slip away; glide by; pass. [< L *elapsus* < *ex-* away + *labi* glide]

e·las·mo·branch (i las´mə brangk; i laz´-), *n.* fish whose skeleton is formed of cartilage and whose gills are thin and platelike. [< NL < Gk. *elasmos* metal plate + *branchia* gills]

e·las·tic (i las´tik), *adj.* **1** having the quality of springing back to its original size, shape, or position after being stretched, squeezed, etc. **2** springing back; springy: *an elastic step.* **3** recovering quickly from low spirits, etc.; buoyant. **4** easily altered to suit changed conditions; flexible; adaptable. —*n.* **1** tape, cloth, etc., woven partly of rubber. **2** a rubber band. [< NL < Gk. *elastikos* driving, propulsive < *elaunein* drive] —**e·las′ti·cal·ly,** *adv.* —**e·las′tic′i·ty,** *n.*

e·las·ti·cized (i las′tə sīzd), *adj.* woven with elastic or made with elastic.

e·late (i lāt′), *v.,* **e·lat·ed, e·lat·ing.** put in high spirits; make joyful or proud. [< L, < *ex*- out, away + *latus,* pp. to *ferre* carry] —**e·lat′er,** *n.*

e·lat·ed (i lāt′id), *adj.* in high spirits; joyful; proud. —**e·lat′ed·ly,** *adv.*

e·la·tion (i lā′shən), *n.* high spirits; joyous pride; exultant gladness.

E layer, layer of the ionosphere, 50 to 90 miles above the surface of the earth. Also, **E region.**

el·bow (el′bō), *n.* **1** joint between the upper and lower arm. **2** anything resembling a bent elbow. —*v.* push with the elbow or elbows.

rub elbows with, mix with, as at a party or in a crowd: *a chance to rub elbows with celebrities.*

up to the elbows, a very busy. **b** deeply involved. [OE *elnboga.* See ELL[1], BOW[2].]

elbow grease, *Informal.* energy; hard work: *a lot of elbow grease went into the job.*

el·bow·room (el′bō rüm′; –rüm′), *n.* plenty of room; enough space to move or work in.

eld (eld), *n. Archaic.* **1** old age. **2** old times; former times. [OE *ældu* < *ald* old]

eld·er[1] (el′dər), *adj.* born, produced, or formed before something else; older; senior: *my elder brother.* —*n.* **1** an older person. **2** one of the influential men of a tribe or community. **3** any of various important officers in certain churches. [OE *eldra,* comp. of *ald* old]

el·der[2] (el′dər), *n.* =elderberry. [OE *ellærn*]

el·der·ber·ry (el′dər ber′i), *n., pl.* **-ries. 1** shrub or tree with black or red berries, sometimes used in making wine. **2** berry of this plant.

eld·er·ly (el′dər li), *adj.* somewhat old; beyond middle age; near old age. —*n.* **the elderly,** the old; old people. —**eld′er·li·ness,** *n.*

eld·er·ship (el′dər ship), *n.* **1** office or position of an elder in a church. **2** group or court of elders; presbytery.

elder statesman, wise or experienced older person turned to for advice, esp. as former government official or politician.

eld·est (el′dist), *adj.* oldest (of brothers and sisters or of a group). [OE, superl. of *ald* old]

El·do·ra·do (el′də rä′dō; –rä′–), **El Dorado,** *n., pl.* **-dos. 1** a legendary city of great wealth. **2** any fabulously wealthy place.

elec., electric; electrical; electricity.

e·lect (i lekt′), *v.* **1** choose or select for an office by voting. **2** choose. —*adj.* **1** elected but not yet in office. **2** chosen;

selected. —*n.* **the elect, a** people chosen by God for salvation and eternal life. **b** people who belong to a group with special rights and privileges. [< L *electus* < *ex*- out + *legere* choose]

elect., electric; electrical; electricity.

e·lec·tion (i lek′shən), *n.* **1** choice. **2** a choosing by vote.

e·lec·tion·eer (i lek′shən ir′), *v.* work for the success of a candidate or party in an election. —**e·lec′tion·eer′er,** *n.* —**e·lec′tion·eer′ing,** *n.*

e·lec·tive (i lek′tiv), *adj.* **1** chosen by an election: *elective officials.* **2** filled by an election: *an elective office.* **3** having the right to vote in an election. **4** open to choice; not required. —*n.* course of study that may be taken, but is not required. —**e·lec′tive·ly,** *adv.* —**e·lec′tive·ness,** *n.*

e·lec·tor (i lek′tər), *n.* **1** one having the right to vote in an election. **2** member of the electoral college. **3** one of the princes who had the right to elect the emperor of the Holy Roman Empire. —**e·lec′tor·al,** *adj.*

electoral college, group of people chosen by the voters to elect the president and vice-president of the United States.

e·lec·tor·ate (i lek′tər it), *n.* **1** the persons having the right to vote in an election. **2** territory under the rule of an elector of the Holy Roman Empire.

e·lec·tric (i lek′trik), *adj.* Also, **e·lec′tri·cal. 1** of electricity; having to do with electricity. **2** charged with electricity. **3** producing electricity. **4** run by electricity. **5** exciting; thrilling. [< NL *electricus* < L < Gk. *elektron* amber (which, under friction, has the property of attracting)] —**e·lec′tri·cal·ly,** *adv.*

electrical storm, =thunderstorm.

electric chair, chair used in electrocuting criminals.

electric eel, a large, eellike fish of South America that can give strong electric shocks.

electric eye, a photoelectric cell. An electric eye can operate a mechanism to open a door when its invisible beam is interrupted.

e·lec·tri·cian (i lek′trish′ən; ē′lek–) *n.* person whose work is installing or repairing electric wires, lights, motors, etc.

e·lec·tric·i·ty (i lek′tris′ə ti; ē′lek–), *n.* **1** form of energy that can produce light, heat, magnetism, and chemical changes, and which can be generated by friction, induction, or chemical changes. **2** an electric current; flow of electrons.

e·lec·tri·fy (i lek′trə fī), *v.,* **-fied, -fy·ing. 1** charge with electricity. **2** equip to use electricity. **3** give an electric shock to. **4** excite; thrill. —**e·lec′tri·fi·ca′tion,** *n.* —**e·lec′tri·fi′er,** *n.*

electro–, *combining form.* **1** electric, as in *electromagnet.* **2** electrically, as in *electropositive.* **3** electricity. [< Gk. *elektron* amber]

e·lec·tro·car·di·o·gram (i lek′trō kär′dē ə gram), *n.* tracing or record of a cardiograph.

e·lec·tro·car·di·o·graph (i lek′trō kär′dē ə graf; –gräf), *n.* instrument that measures the electrical impulses of each heartbeat. —**e·lec′tro·car′di·o·graph′ic,** *adj.* —**e·lec′tro·car′di·og′ra·phy,** *n.*

e·lec·tro·chem·is·try (i lek′trō kem′is tri), *n.* branch of chemistry that deals with chemical changes produced by electricity and the production of electricity by chemical changes. —**e·lec′tro·chem′i·cal,** *adj.*

e·lec·tro·con·vul·sive (i lek′trō kən vul′siv) **therapy** or **treatment,** =electroshock therapy.

e·lec·tro·cute (i lek′trə kūt), *v.,* **-cut·ed, -cut·ing.** kill by electricity. [< *electro-* + (*exe*) *cute*] —**e·lec′tro·cu′tion,** *n.*

e·lec·trode (i lek′trōd), *n.* either of the two terminals of a battery or any other source of electricity. [< *electro-* + Gk. *hodos* way]

e·lec·tro·dy·nam·ics (i lek′trō dī nam′iks), *n.* branch of physics that deals with the action of electricity or with electric currents. —**e·lec′tro·dy·nam′ic, e·lec′tro·dy·nam′i·cal,** *adj.*

e·lec·tro·en·ceph·a·lo·gram (i lek′trō en sef′ə lə gram), *n.* tracing or record made by an electroencephalograph.

e·lec·tro·en·ceph·a·lo·graph (i lek′trō en sef′ə lə graf; –gräf), instrument that measures the electrical impulses of the brain. —**e·lec′tro·en·ceph′a·lo·graph′ic,** *adj.* —**e·lec′tro·en·ceph′a·log′ra·phy,** *n.*

e·lec·trol·y·sis (i lek′trol′ə sis; ē′lek–), *n.* **1** decomposition of a chemical compound into ions by the passage of an electric current through a solution of it. **2** removal of excess hair, moles, etc., by destruction with an electrified needle.

e·lec·tro·lyte (i lek′trə līt), *n.* **1** solution that will conduct a current. **2** compound whose solution is a conductor. [< *electro-* + Gk. *lytos* dissoluble < *lyein* loose] —**e·lec′tro·lyt′ic,** —**e·lec′tro·lyt′i·cal,** *adj.* —**e·lec′tro·lyt′i·cal·ly,** *adv.*

e·lec·tro·lyze (i lek′trə līz), *v.,* **-lyzed, -lyz·ing.** decompose by electrolysis. —**e·lec′tro·ly·za′tion,** *n.* —**e·lec′tro·lyz′er,** *n.*

e·lec·tro·mag·net (i lek′trō mag′nit), *n.* piece of iron that becomes a strong magnet when electricity passes through wire coiled around it. —**e·lec′tro·mag·net′ic,** *adj.*

e·lec·tro·mag·net·ism (i lek′trō mag′nə tiz əm), *n.* **1** magnetism as produced by electric currents. **2** branch of physics that deals with this.

e·lec·tro·mo·tive (i lek′trə mō′tiv), *adj.* of or producing a flow of electricity.

electromotive force, force that causes an electric current to flow, produced by differences in electrical charge or potential.

e·lec·tron (i lek′tron), *n.* unit charge of negative electricity. All atoms are composed of electrons and protons. [< *electric* + *-on* (as in *ion,* etc.)] —**e·lec′tron′ic,** *adj.*

e·lec·tro·neg·a·tive (i lek′trō neg′ə tiv), *adj.* charged with negative electricity.

electron gun, device that guides the flow of electrons and greatly increases the speed of atomic particles.

electronic art, art made, displayed, and sometimes controlled by a computer.

electronic funds transfer, system for transferring funds by computer from one bank to another or one account to another.

electronic mail, messages created on one computer and sent to another; email or Email.

electronic music, music created electronically.

e·lec·tron·ics (i lek′tron′iks; ē′lek–), *n.* **1** branch of physics that deals with electrons and their movement through transistors, semiconductors, etc., and has made development of radar, television, computers, etc., possible. **2** industry or business of producing electronic products: *continued growth in electronics.*

electron microscope, microscope that uses beams of electrons instead of beams of light, and has much higher power than any ordinary microscope.

e·lec·tro·plate (i lek′trə plāt′), *v.,* **–plat·ed, –plat·ing,** *n.* —*v.* cover with a coating of metal by means of electrolysis. —*n.* silverware, etc., covered in this way. —**e·lec′tro·plat′er,** *n.*

e·lec·tro·pos·i·tive (i lek′trō poz′ə tiv), *adj.* charged with positive electricity.

e·lec·tro·shock (i lek′trō shok′) **therapy** or **treatment,** treatment of mental disorder by passing electric current through the brain.

e·lec·tro·stat·ics (i lek′trə stat′iks), *n.* branch of physics dealing with objects charged with electricity. —**e·lec′tro·stat′ic,** *adj.*

e·lec·trum (i lek′trəm), *n.* a pale-yellow alloy of gold and silver, used by the ancients. [< L < Gk. *elektron*]

el·ee·mos·y·nar·y (el′ə mos′ə ner′i; el′i ə–), *adj.* **1** charitable. **2** free. **3** supported by charity. [< LL, < L *eleemosyna* ALMS]

el·e·gance (el′ə gəns), **el·e·gan·cy** (–gən si), *n., pl.* **–gan·ces; –cies.** refined grace and richness; luxury free from showiness.

el·e·gant (el′ə gənt), *adj.* having or showing good taste; gracefully and richly refined. [< L *elegans*] —**el′e·gant·ly,** *adv.*

el·e·gi·ac (el′ə jī′ak; –ək; i lē′ji ak), *adj.* Also, **el′e·gi′a·cal. 1** of or suitable for an elegy. **2** sad; mournful; melancholy.

el·e·gize (el′ə jīz), *v.,* **–gized, –giz·ing. 1** compose an elegy. **2** lament in an elegy.

el·e·gy (el′ə ji), *n. pl.* **–gies.** a mournful or melancholy poem; poem that is a lament for the dead. [< F < L < Gk. *elegeia,* ult. < *elegos* mournful poem]

elem., element; elementary; elements.

el·e·ment (el′ə mənt), *n.* **1** one of the simple substances, such as gold, hydro-

gen, etc., that cannot be separated into simpler parts by ordinary means; substance composed of atoms that are chemically alike. **2** one of the parts of which anything is made up. **3** one of the four substances—earth, water, air, and fire—that were once thought to make up all other things. **4** natural or suitable surroundings.

be in one's element, be where one feels at home, at ease.

the elements, a the simple, necessary parts to be learned first; the basics. **b** atmospheric forces: *not a night to be out in the elements.* [< L *elementum* rudiment, first principle]

el·e·men·tal (el′ə men′təl), *adj.* **1** of the forces of nature. **2** simple but powerful: *hunger is an elemental feeling.* **3** being a necessary or essential part. **4** elementary. —**el′e·men′tal·ly,** *adv.*

el·e·men·ta·ry (el′ə men′tə ri; –tri), *adj.* **1** of or dealing with the simple, necessary parts to be learned first; introductory. **2** made up of only one chemical element; not a compound. —**el′e·men′ta·ri·ly,** *adv.* —**el′e·men′ta·ri·ness,** *n.*

elementary particle, one of the fundamental units of which all matter is composed, including the electron, proton, and neutron, neutrino, photon, and others.

elementary school, 1 school of five or six grades followed by middle school. **2** school of eight grades, followed by a four-year high school.

el·e·phant (el′ə fənt), *n., pl.* **–phants** or (*esp. collectively*) **–phant.** a heavy mammal, with a long trunk and ivory tusks, that is the largest four-footed animal now living. [< OF < L Gk. *elephas* elephant, ivory, prob. < Egypt.]

el·e·phan·ti·a·sis (el′ə fən tī′ə sis; –fan–), *n.* disease in which parts of the body, usually the legs, become greatly enlarged, caused by parasitic worms that block the flow of lymph.

el·e·phan·tine (el′ə fan′tin; –tīn; –tēn), *adj.* **1** like an elephant; huge; heavy; clumsy; slow. **2** of elephants.

elev., elevation.

el·e·vate (el′ə vāt), *v.,* **–vat·ed, –vat·ing. 1** lift up; raise. **2** raise in rank or station. [< L, < *ex–* out + *levare* lighten, raise]

el·e·vat·ed (el′ə vāt′id), *adj.* **1** lifted up; raised; high. **2** dignified; lofty; noble. —*n.* a street railway raised above the ground.

el·e·va·tion (el′ə vā′shən), *n.* **1** a raised place; high place. **2** height above the earth's surface or above sea level. **3** a raising or being raised. **4** loftiness; nobility.

el·e·va·tor (el′ə vā′tər), *n.* **1** thing that raises or lifts up. **2** a moving platform or cage to carry people and things up and down in a building, mine, etc. **3** a building for storing grain. **4** an adjustable surface that causes an airplane to go up or down.

elevator shaft, a vertical passageway for an elevator.

e·lev·en (i lev′ən), *n.* **1** a cardinal number, one more than ten. **2** symbol of this number; 11. **3** team of eleven players. —*adj.* one more than ten; 11. [OE *endleofan* one left (over ten)] —**e·lev′-enth,** *adj., n.*

eleventh hour, the latest possible moment.

elf (elf), *n., pl.* **elves. 1** a tiny, mischievous fairy. **2** a small, mischievous person. [OE *ælf*] —**elf′like′,** *adj.*

elf·in (el′fən), *adj.* of or suitable for elves; like an elf's. —*n.* elf.

elf·ish (el′fish), *adj.* elflike; elfin; mischievous. —**elf′ish·ly,** *adv.* —**elf′ish·ness,** *n.*

el·hi (el′hī′), *adj.* of or having to do with both the lower, elementary grades and the upper, high school grades.

e·lic·it (i lis′it), *v.* draw forth: *elicit a reply, elicit applause.* [< L *elicitus* < *ex–* out + *lacere* entice] —**e·lic′i·ta′tion,** *n.* —**e·lic′i·tor,** *n.*

e·lide (i līd′), *v.,* **e·lid·ed, e·lid·ing.** omit or slur over in pronunciation. The *e* in *the* is elided in "th' inevitable hour." [< L, < *ex–* out + *laedere* dash] —**e·lid′i·ble,** *adj.*

el·i·gi·bil·i·ty (el′ə jə bil′ə ti), *n., pl.* **–ties.** fitness; qualification; desirability.

el·i·gi·ble (el′ə bəl), *adj.* fit to be chosen; properly qualified; desirable. —*n.* an eligible person. [< F < LL < L *eligere* pick out, choose. See ELECT.] —**el′i·gi·bly,** *adv.*

e·lim·i·nate (i lim′ə nāt), *v.,* **–nat·ed, –nat·ing. 1** get rid of; remove. **2** pay no attention to; leave out of consideration; omit. **3** get rid of (an unknown quantity) by combining algebraic equations. **4** execute. [< L, *ex–* off + *limen* threshold] —**e·lim′i·na′tion,** *n.* —**e·lim′i·na′tive,** *adj.* —**e·lim′i·na′tor,** *n.*

e·li·sion (i lizh′ən), *n.* suppression of a vowel or a syllable. In poetry it generally consists in omitting a final vowel when the next word has an initial vowel.

e·lite (i lēt′; ā–), *n.* the choice or distinguished part; the best people. —*adj.* distinguished: *an elite group.* [< F, fem. pp. of *élire* pick out < L *eligere.* See ELECT.] —**e·lit′ist,** *n.*

e·lit·ism (i lēt′iz əm), *n.* **1** rule or government by an elite. **2** belief in or support for such rule or government.

e·lix·ir (i lik′sər), *n.* **1** substance allegedly having the power of changing lead, iron, etc., into gold or of lengthening life indefinitely. **2** a universal remedy; cure-all. [< Med.L < Ar. *al-iksīr* (def. 1), prob. < Gk. *xerion* drying powder used on wounds < *xeros* dry]

E·liz·a·beth (i liz′ə bəth), *n.* 1533–1603, queen of England from 1558 to 1603, daughter of Henry VIII.

E·liz·a·be·than (i liz′ə bē′thən; –beth′ən), *adj.* of the time of Queen Elizabeth. —*n.* person, esp. a writer, of the time of Queen Elizabeth.

Elizabethan sonnet, type of sonnet written by Shakespeare and many other Elizabethans.

elk (elk), *n.*, *pl.* **elks** or (*esp. collectively*) **elk.** 1 a large deer of N Europe and Asia. It has antlers like a moose. 2 a large, reddish deer of North America; wapiti. [appar. < AF form of OE *eolh*]

ell¹ (el), *n.* an old measure of length, equal to 45 inches. [OE *eln* length of lower arm]

ell² (el), *n.* 1 something shaped like an L. 2 an extension of a building at right angles to it. Also, **el.**

el·lipse (i lips′), *n.* a plane curve, the path of a point that moves so that the sum of its distances from two fixed points remains the same. [< L *ellipsis* ELLIPSIS]

el·lip·sis (i lip′sis), *n.*, *pl.* **-ses** (-sēz). 1 omission of a word or words needed to complete the grammatical construction of a sentence. *Example:* She is as tall as her brother (is tall). 2 marks (… or ***) used to show an omission in writing or printing. [< L < Gk., < *elleipein* come short, leave out]

el·lip·ti·cal (i lip′tə kəl), **el·lip·tic** (-tik), *adj.* 1 like an ellipse; of an ellipse. 2 showing ellipsis; having a word or words omitted. —**el·lip′ti·cal·ly,** *adv.*

elm (elm), *n.* 1 a tall, graceful shade tree. 2 its hard, heavy wood. [OE]

el·o·cu·tion (el′ə kū′shən), *n.* 1 art of speaking or reading clearly and effectively in public; art of public speaking. 2 manner of speaking or reading in public. [< L *elocutio* < *ex-* out + *loqui* speak] —**el′o·cu′tion·ar′y,** *adj.* —**el′o·cu′tion·ist,** *n.*

e·lon·gate (i lông′gāt; i long′-), *v.*, **-gat·ed, -gat·ing.** *adj.* —*v.* lengthen; extend; stretch. —*adj.* 1 lengthened. 2 long and thin: *the elongate leaf of the willow.* [< L, < *ex-* out + *longus* long] —**e·lon′ga′tion,** *n.*

e·lope (i lōp′), *v.* **e·loped, e·lop·ing.** 1 run away with a lover. 2 run away; escape. [< AF *aloper* < ME *lope(n)* run. See LOPE.] —**e·lope′ment,** *n.* —**e·lop′er,** *n.*

el·o·quence (el′ə kwens), *n.* 1 flow of speech that has grace and force. 2 power to win by speaking; art of speaking so as to stir the feelings. [< L *eloquentia* < *ex-* out + *loqui* speak]

el·o·quent (el′ə kwənt), *adj.* 1 having eloquence. 2 very expressive. —**el′o·quent·ly,** *adv.*

El Sal·va·dor (el sal′və dôr), country in W Central America.

else (els), *adj.* 1 other; different. 2 in addition. —*adv.* 1 instead. 2 differently. 3 otherwise; if not.

or else, a or face the consequences. **b** otherwise. [OE *elles*]

else·where (els′hwãr), **else·with·er** (-hwith′ər), *adv.* somewhere else; in or to some other place.

e·lu·ci·date (i lü′sə dāt), *v.*, **-dat·ed, -dat·ing.** make clear; explain. [LL, < L *ex-* out + *lucidus* bright] —**e·lu′ci·da′tion,**

n. —**e·lu′ci·da′tive,** *adj.* —**e·lu′ci·da′tor,** *n.*

e·lude (i lüd′), *v.*, **e·lud·ed, e·lud·ing.** 1 slip away from; escape by cleverness, quickness, etc. 2 escape discovery by; baffle. [< L, < *ex-* out + *ludere* play] —**e·lud′er,** *n.* —**e·lu′sion,** *n.*

e·lu·sive (i lü′siv), **e·lu·so·ry** (-sə ri), *adj.* 1 hard to describe or understand; baffling. 2 tending to elude. —**e·lu′sive·ly,** *adv.* —**e·lu′sive·ness,** *n.*

e·lu·vi·um (i lü′vē əm), *n.* deposit of soil created by the disintegration of rocks at the site or by being deposited as dust by winds. —**e·lu′vi·al,** *adj.* —**e·lu′vi·a′tion,** *n.*

elves (elvz), *n.* pl. of **elf.**

elv·ish (el′vish), *adj.* elfish; elflike. —**elv′ish·ly,** *adv.*

E·ly·si·um (i lizh′i əm; i liz′-; i lizh′əm), *n.* 1 *Gk. Myth.* place where heroes and virtuous people lived after death. 2 any place or condition of perfect happiness; paradise. —**E·ly′sian,** *adj.*

em (em), *n.*, *pl.* **ems.** 1 the letter M, m. 2 unit for measuring the amount of print in a line, page, etc.

'em (əm), *pron.*, *pl. Informal.* them.

e·ma·ci·ate (i mā′shi āt), *v.*, **-at·ed, -at·ing.** make unnaturally thin; cause to lose flesh or waste away. [< L, ult. < *ex-* + *macies* leanness] —**e·ma′ci·a′tion,** *n.*

email or **Email** (i′māl′), *n.* messages sent by computer; electronic mail. Also, **e-mail** or **E-mail.**

em·a·nate (em′ə nāt), *v.*, **-nat·ed, -nat·ing.** come forth. [< L, < *ex-* out + *manare* flow] —**em′a·na′tion,** *n.* —**em′a·na′tive,** *adj.*

e·man·ci·pate (i man′sə pāt), *v.*, **-pat·ed, -pat·ing.** release from slavery or restraint; set free. [< L *emancipatus* < *ex-* away + *manceps* purchaser < *manus* hand + *capere* take] —**e·man′ci·pa′tion,** *n.* —**e·man′ci·pa′tive,** *adj.* —**e·man′ci·pa′tor,** *n.*

e·mas·cu·late (*v.* i mas′kyə lāt; *adj.* i mas′kyə lāt; -lāt), *v.*, **-lat·ed, -lat·ing,** *adj.* —*v.* 1 remove the male glands of; castrate. 2 destroy the force of; weaken. —*adj.* deprived of vigor; weakened; effeminate. [< L *emasculatus* < *ex-* away + *masculus* male] —**e·mas′cu·la′tion,** *n.* —**e·mas′cu·la′tor,** *n.*

em·balm (em bäm′), *v.* 1 treat (a dead body) with drugs, chemicals, etc., to keep it from decaying. 2 keep in memory; preserve. 3 fill with sweet scent; perfume. —**em·balm′er,** *n.* —**em·balm′ment,** *n.*

em·bank (em bangk′), *v.* protect, enclose, or confine with a raised bank of earth, stones, etc.

em·bank·ment (em bangk′mənt), *n.* 1 a raised bank of earth, stones, etc., used to hold back water, support a roadway, etc. 2 an embanking.

em·bar·go (em bär′gō), *n.*, *pl.* **-goes,** *v.*, **-goed, -go·ing.** —*n.* 1 order of a government forbidding ships to enter or

leave its ports. 2 any restriction put on commerce by law. 3 restriction; restraint; hindrance. —*v.* lay an embargo on; forbid to enter or leave port. [< Sp., < *embargar* restrain < VL *in-* in + *barra* BAR]

em·bark (em bärk′), *v.* 1 go on board ship. 2 put on board ship. 3 set out; start. 4 involve (a person) in an enterprise; invest (money) in an enterprise. [< F *embarquer.* See EN-, BARK³.] —**em′bar·ka′tion, em′bar·ca′tion,** *n.* —**em·bark′ment,** *n.*

em·bar·rass (em bar′əs), *v.* 1 disturb (a person); make self-conscious. 2 involve in difficulties; hinder. 3 burden with debt; involve in financial difficulties. [< F, lit., to block < Ital., < *imbarrare* to bar < VL *barra* BAR —**em·bar′rass·ing,** *adj.* —**em·bar′rass·ing·ly,** *adv.* —**em·bar′rass·ment,** *n.*

em·bas·sa·dor (em bas′ə dər; -dôr), *n.* =ambassador.

em·bas·sy (em′bə si), *n.*, *pl.* **-sies.** 1 ambassador and his staff of assistants. 2 the official residence, offices, etc., of an ambassador in a foreign country. 3 position or duties of an ambassador. 4 a special errand; important mission; official message. [< OF < Ital. < Pr. < Gothic *andbahti* service, ult. < Gaulish *ambactus*]

em·bat·tle¹ (em bat′əl), *v.*, **-tled, -tling.** prepare for battle; form into battle order. [see EN-, BATTLE]

em·bat·tle² (em bat′əl), *v.*, **-tled, -tling.** provide with battlements; fortify. [< *en-* + obs. *battle,* v., furnish with battlements]

em·bed (em bed′), *v.*, **-bed·ded, -bed·ding.** 1 put in a bed; plant. 2 fix or enclose in a surrounding mass: *made of metal embedded in concrete.* 3 insert a journalist into a military unit to accompany the soldiers on missions and file news reports based on direct experience. Also, **imbed.**

em·bel·lish (em bel′ish), *v.* 1 decorate; adorn; ornament. 2 make more interesting by adding real or imaginary details; elaborate. [< OF *embellir* < *en-* in (< L *in-*) + *bel* handsome < L *bellus*] —**em·bel′lish·er,** *n.* —**em·bel′lish·ment,** *n.*

em·ber (em′bər), *n.* piece of wood or coal still glowing in the ashes of a fire. [OE *æmerge*]

em·bez·zle (em bez′əl), *v.*, **-zled, -zling.** steal (money, securities, etc., entrusted to one's care). [< AF *enbesiler* < *en-* + *beseler* destroy] —**em·bez′zle·ment,** *n.* —**em·bez′zler,** *n.*

em·bit·ter (em bit′ər) *v.* make bitter; make more bitter: *embittered by loss.*

em·bla·zon (em blā′zən), *v.* 1 display conspicuously. 2 decorate; adorn. 3 praise highly; honor publicly. —**em·bla′zon·er,** *n.* —**em·bla′zon·ment, em·bla′zon·ry,** *n.*

em·blem (em′bləm), *n.* 1 representation of an invisible quality, idea, etc., by some connection of thought; symbol. The dove is an emblem of peace. **2** a heraldic device. [< L, inlaid work < Gk. *emblema* insertion < *en-* in + *ballein* throw]

em·blem·at·ic (em´blə mat'ik), **em·blem·at·i·cal** (–ə kəl), *adj.* used as an emblem; symbolical. The dove is emblematic of peace. **—em´blem·at´i·cal·ly**, *adv.*

em·bod·y (em bod'ē), *v.*, **–bod·ied, –body·ing. 1** put into visible form; express in definite form. **2** bring together and include in a book, system, etc.; organize. **3** make part of an organized book, law, system, etc.; incorporate. **—em·bod'i·ment,** *n.*

em·bold·en (em bōl'dən), *v.* make bold; encourage.

em·bo·lism (em'bə liz əm), *n.* obstruction of a blood vessel by a clot, a bit of fat, or other obstacle. [< L < Gk. *embolismos.* See EMBLEM.] **—em´bo·lis'mic,** *adj.*

em·bo·lus (em'bə ləs), *n., pl.* **–li** (–lī). a solid material in the vascular system.

em·bos·om (em büz'əm; –bü'zəm), *v.* **1** surround; enclose; envelop. **2** embrace; cherish.

em·boss (em bôs; –bos'), *v.* decorate with a design, pattern, etc., that stands out from the surface. [See EN-, BOSS²] **—em·boss'er,** *n.* **—em·boss'ment,** *n.*

em·bow·er (em bou'ər), *v.* enclose in a shelter of leafy branches.

em·brace (em brās'), *v.*, **–braced, –bracing,** *n.* **—v. 1** clasp or hold in the arms to show love or friendship; hug. **2** *Fig.* take up; take for oneself; accept: *embrace the Christian religion.* **3** include; contain. **4** surround; enclose. **—n. 1** an embracing; a hug. **2** an accepting. [< OF < VL, < L *in-* in + *brachium* arm] **—em·brace'a·ble,** *adj.* **—em·brace'ment,** *n.* **—em·brac'er,** *n.*

em·bra·sure (em brā'zhər), *n.* an opening in a wall for a gun, with sides that spread outward. [< F, < *embraser* widen an opening]

em·broi·der (em broi'dər), *v.* **1** ornament (cloth, leather, etc.) with a design, pattern, etc., of stitches. **2** make or put (a design, pattern, etc.) on cloth, leather, etc., with stitches. **3** *Fig.* add imaginary details to; exaggerate. [see EN-, BROIDER] **—em·broi'der·er,** *n.*

em·broi·der·y (em broi'dər i), *n., pl.* **–der·ies. 1** art of working raised and ornamental designs in cloth, leather, etc., with a needle; embroidering. **2** embroidered work or material. **3** *Fig.* imaginary details; exaggeration.

em·broil (em broil'), *v.* **1** involve (a person, country, etc.) in a quarrel. **2** throw (affairs, etc.) into a state of confusion. **—em·broil'er,** *n.* **—em·broil'ment,** *n.*

em·bry·o (em'brī ō), *n., pl.* **bry·os,** *adj.* **—n. 1** animal during the period of its growth from the fertilized egg until its organs have developed so that it can live independently. **2** an undeveloped plant within a seed. **—adj.** embryonic; undeveloped; not mature. [< Med.L < Gk. *embryon,* < *en-* in + *bryein* swell]

embryol., embryology.

em·bry·ol·o·gy (em´brī ol'ə ji), *n.* study of the formation and development of embryos. **—em´bry·o·log'i·cal, em´bry·o·log'ic,** *adj.* **—em´bry·ol'o·gist,** *n.*

em·bry·on·ic (em´brī on'ik), *adj.* **1** of the embryo. **2** undeveloped; not mature.

em·cee (em'sē'), *n., v.,* **–ceed, –cee·ing.** *U.S.* **—n.** master of ceremonies. **—v.** act as master of ceremonies of. Also, **M.C.** [< pronunciation of *M.C.*]

e·meer (ə mir'), *n.* =emir.

e·mend (i mend'), **e·men·date** (ē'men-dāt), *v.,* **e·mend·ed, e·mend·ing; e·men·dat·ed, e·men·dat·ing.** suggest changes to free (a faulty text, document, etc.) from errors; correct; improve. [< L, < *ex-* away + *menda* fault] **—e·mend'a·ble,** *adj.* **—e´men·da'tion,** *n.* **—e·men'da·to´ry,** *adj.*

em·er·ald (em'ər əld; em'rəld), *n.* a bright-green precious stone; transparent green beryl. **—adj.** bright-green. [< OF *esmeralde* < L < Gk. *smaragdos*]

e·merge (i mėrj'), *v.,* **–e·merged, e·merging.** come out; come into view. [< L, < *ex-* out + *mergere* dip] **—e·mer'gence,** *n.* **—e·mer'gent,** *adj.*

e·mer·gen·cy (i mėr'jən si), *n., pl.* **–cies. —n.** a sudden need for immediate action. **—adj.** for use in time of sudden need.

e·mer·i·tus (i mer'ə təs), *adj.* honorably discharged; retired from active service, but still holding one's rank and title. **—n.** person honorably discharged or retired. [< L, < *ex-* to the end + *merere* serve]

e·mer·sion (i mėr'zhən; –shən), *n.* an emerging.

em·er·y (em'ər i), *n.* a hard, dark mineral, an impure corundum, used for grinding, smoothing, and polishing. [< F < Ital. < VL *smericulum* < Med.Gk. *smeris* < Gk. *smyris* abrasive powder]

emery board, thin, flat, small piece of cardboard, coated with emery powder and used as a nail file.

e·met·ic (i met'ik), *adj.* causing vomiting. **—n.** medicine or treatment that causes vomiting. [< L < Gk. *emetikos* < *emeein* vomit]

em·i·grant (em'ə grənt), *n.* person who leaves his own country or region to settle in another. **—adj.** leaving one's own country or region to settle in another.

em·i·grate (em'ə grāt), *v.,* **–grat·ed, –grat·ing.** leave one's own country or region to settle in another. [< L, < *ex-* out + *migrare* to move. See MIGRATE.] **—em'i·gra'tion,** *n.*

e·mi·gré or **é·mi·gré** (em'ə grā), *n., pl.* **–grés** (–grāz). **1** emigrant. **2** member of a refugee group. [< F]

em·i·nence (em'ə nəns), *n.* **1** rank or position above all or most others; high standing; fame. **2** a high place; lofty hill. **3 Eminence,** title of honor given to a cardinal in the Roman Catholic Church. [< L *eminentia* < *ex-* out + *minere* jut]

em·i·nent (em'ə nənt), *adj.* **1** distinguished; exalted. **2** conspicuous; noteworthy. **3** high; lofty. **4** projecting. **—em'i·nent·ly,** *adv.*

eminent domain, right of government to take private property for public use. The owner must be paid for the property taken.

e·mir (ə mir'), *n.* **1** Arabic title for a chief, prince, or military leader. **2** title of the descendants of Muhammad. Also, **emeer.** [< Ar. *amīr* commander]

e·mir·ate (ə'mir it), *n.* **1** rank or authority of an emir. **2** state or territory led by an emir.

em·is·sar·y (em'ə ser´i), *n., pl.* **–sar·ies,** *adj.* **—n. 1** person sent on a mission or errand. **2** a secret agent; spy. **—adj.** of, or acting as, an emissary. [< L *emissarius.* See EMIT.]

e·mis·sion (i mish'ən), *n.* **1** act or fact of emitting. **2** thing emitted. **—e·mis'sive,** *adj.*

e·mit (i mit'), *v.,* **e·mit·ted, e·mit·ting. 1** give off; send out. **2** put into circulation; issue. **3** utter; voice. [< L, < *ex-* out + *mittere* send] **—e·mit'ter,** *n.*

Em·man·u·el (i man'yü əl), *n.* =Immanuel.

Em·my (em'i), *n., pl.* **–mies.** a small statuette awarded annually by the Academy of Television Arts and Sciences for excellence in television.

e·mol·lient (i mol'yənt), *adj.* softening; soothing. **—n.** something that softens and soothes. [< L < *emollire* soften < *ex-* + *mollis* soft]

e·mol·u·ment (i mol'yə mənt), *n.* profit from an office or position; fee. [< L, profit, ult. < *ex-* out + *molere* grind]

e·mote (i mōt'), *v.,* **e·mot·ed, e·mot·ing. 1** act, esp. in an exaggerated manner. **2** show emotion. **—e·mo'tive,** *adj.* **—e´mo·tiv'i·ty,** *n.*

e·mo·tion (i mō'shən), *n.* a strong feeling, as of fear, anger, love, joy, etc. [< F, (after *motion*) < *émouvoir* stir up < L, < *ex-* out + *movere* move] **—e·mo'tion·al,** *adj.* **—e·mo´tion·al'i·ty,** *n.* **—e·mo'tion·al·ly,** *adv.* **—e·mo'tion·less,** *adj.*

e·mo·tion·al·ism (i mō'shən əl iz´əm), *n.* **1** emotional quality or character. **2** an appealing to the emotions. **3** tendency to display emotion too easily.

Emp., emperor; empire; empress.

em·pan·el (em pan'əl), *v.,* **–eled, –el·ing,** =impanel.

em·pa·thize (em'pə thīz), *v.,* **–thized, –thiz·ing.** feel empathy.

em·pa·thy (em'pə thi), *n.* the complete understanding of another's feelings, motives, etc. [< Gk., < *en-* in + *pathos* feeling] **—em·path'ic,** *adj.*

em·per·or (em'pər ər), *n.* man who is the ruler of an empire. [< OF < L *imperator* commander < *in-* in + *parare* to order] **—em'per·or·ship´,** *n.*

em·pha·sis (em'fə sis), *n., pl.* **–ses** (–sēz). **1** special force; stress; importance. **2** special force given to particular syllables, words, or phrases. [< L < Gk., < *emphainein* indicate < *en-* in + *phainein* show]

em·pha·size (em′fə sīz), v. **-sized, -sizing.** give special force to; stress.

em·phat·ic (em fat′ik), adj. **1** spoken or done with force or stress; strongly expressed. **2** attracting attention; striking. —**em·phat′i·cal·ly,** adv.

em·pire (em′pīr), n. **1** group of countries or states under the same ruler or government: *the Roman Empire.* **2** country ruled by an emperor or empress: *the Japanese Empire.* **3** absolute power; supreme authority. **4** *Fig.* large business or group of businesses controlled by one group or family or an individual: *a media empire.* [< OF < L *imperium.* See EMPEROR.]

em·pir·ic (em pir′ik), n. **1** person who lacks theoretical or scientific knowledge and relies entirely on practical experience. **2** person without regular or proper training; quack. —adj. =empirical. [< L < Gk. *empeirikos* < *en-* in + *peira* experience, experiment]

em·pir·i·cal (em pir′ə kəl) adj. **1** based on experiment and observation. **2** based entirely on practical experience. —**em·pir′i·cal·ly,** adv.

em·pir·i·cism (em pir′ə siz əm), n. **1** use of methods based on experiment and observation. **2** undue reliance upon experience; unscientific practice; quackery. —**em·pir′i·cist,** n.

em·place·ment (em plās′mənt), n. **1** space or platform for a heavy gun or guns. **2** an assigning to a place; locating.

em·ploy (em ploi′), v. **1** use the services of; give work and pay to. **2** use. **3** engage the attention of; keep busy; occupy. —n. a being employed; service for pay; employment. [< F < L, *in-* in + *plicare* fold] —**em·ploy′a·ble,** adj.

em·ploy·ee (em ploi′ē; em′ploi ē′), n. person who works for some person or firm for pay.

em·ploy·er (em ploi′ər), n. **1** person or firm that employs one or more persons. **2** user.

em·ploy·ment (em ploi′mənt), n. **1** an employing or being employed. **2** what a person is doing; business. **3** use.

em·po·ri·um (em pô′ri əm; -pō′-), n., pl. **-po·ri·ums, -po·ri·a** (-pô′ri ə; -pō′-), **1** center of trade; marketplace. **2** a large store selling many different things. [< L < Gk. *emporion* < *emporos* merchant, traveler < *en-* on + *poros* voyage]

em·pow·er (em pou′ər), v. **1** give power to. **2** enable; permit. —**em·pow′er·ment,** n.

em·press (em′pris), n. **1** wife of an emperor. **2** woman who is the ruler of an empire.

emp·ty (emp′ti), adj. **-ti·er, -ti·est,** v., **-tied, -ty·ing,** n., pl. **-ties.** —adj. **1** with nothing or no one in it. **2** not real; meaningless: *an empty threat has no force.* —v. **1** pour out or take out the contents of; make empty. **2** become empty. **3**

flow out; discharge. —n. something with nothing or no one in it.

empty of, having no: *a city empty of people.* [OE *æmtig* < *æmetta* leisure] —**emp′ti·ly,** adv. —**emp·ti·ness,** n.

emp·ty-hand·ed (emp′ti han′did), adj. having nothing in the hands; bringing or taking nothing, esp. of value.

empty set, mathematical set that has no members; null set.

em·py·re·al (em pir′i əl; em′pə rē′əl, -pī–), adj. celestial; heavenly.

em·py·re·an (em′pə rē′ən; -pī–), n. **1** region of pure light. **2** sky; firmament. —adj. =empyreal. [< LL < Gk. *empyrios, empyros* < *en-* in + *pyr* fire]

e·mu (ē′mū), n. a large, flightless Australian bird resembling an ostrich but smaller. [< Moluccan *emeu*]

em·u·late (em′yə lāt), v., **-lat·ed, -lat·ing.** try to equal or excel. [< L, < *aemulus* striving to equal] —**em′u·la′tion,** n. —**em′u·la′tive,** adj.

em·u·lous (em′yə ləs), adj. wishing to equal or excel. —**em′u·lous·ly,** adv. —**em′u·lous·ness,** n.

e·mul·si·fy (i mul′sə fī), v., **-fied, -fy·ing.** make into an emulsion. —**e·mul′si·fi·ca′tion,** n. —**e·mul′si·fi′er,** n.

e·mul·sion (i mul′shən), n. **1** liquid that is a mixture of liquids that do not dissolve in each other. **2** a coating on a photographic film, plate, etc., that is sensitive to light. [< NL *emulsio* < L *ex-* out + *mulgere* milk]

en (en), n. **1** the letter N, n. **2** half of the width of an em in printing.

en-, *prefix.* **1** cause to be; make, as in *enable, enfeeble.* **2** put in; put on, as in *encircle, enthrone.* **3** other meanings, as in *enact, encourage, entwine. En-* often changes the meaning of a verb little or not at all. [< OF < L *in-*; before *b, p,* or *m* the form becomes *em-*]

-en, *suffix.* **1** cause to be; make, as in *blacken, sharpen.* **2** cause to have, as in *heighten, strengthen.* **3** become, as in *sicken, soften.* **4** come to have; gain, as in *lengthen.* **5** made of, as in *silken, wooden.* **6** *-en* is used to form past participles of strong verbs, as in *fallen, shaken.* **7** *-en* is used to form the plural of a few nouns, as in *children, oxen.* [OE]

en·a·ble (en ā′bəl), v., **-bled, -bling.** give ability, power, or means to; make able. —**en·a′bler′,** n.

en·act (en akt′), v. **1** pass (a bill) giving it validity as law; make into a law. **2** play the part of; act out; play. —**en·ac′tor,** n.

en·act·ment (en akt′mənt), n. **1** an enacting. **2** a being enacted. **3** law.

e·nam·el (i nam′əl), n., v., **-eled, -el·ing** —n. a glasslike substance melted and then cooled to make a smooth, hard surface. **2** paint or varnish used to make a smooth, hard, glossy surface. **3** the smooth, hard, glossy outer layer of the teeth. **4** thing covered or decorated with enamel. [< v.] —v. cover or decorate with enamel. [< AF *enamayller* < *en-* on

(< L *in-*) + *amayl* (OF *esmail*) enamel < Gmc.] —**e·nam′el·er,** n. —**e·nam′el·work′,** n.

e·nam·el·ware (i nam′əl wār), n. pots, pans, and household appliances, etc., made of metal coated with enamel.

en·am·or (en am′ər), v. arouse to love; charm: *her beauty enamored the prince.* [< OF *enamourer* < *en-* in (< L *in-*) + *amour* love < L *amor*] —**en·am′ored,** adj.,

cnc., enclosure.

en·camp (en kamp′), v. **1** make a camp. **2** stay in a camp. —**en·camp′ment,** n.

en·cap·su·late (en kap′sə lāt), v. **-lat·ed, -lat·ing. 1** enclose in a capsule. **2** encase in a covering. **3** *Fig.* capture an idea, atmosphere, mood, etc., in words.

en·case (en kās′), v., **-cased, -cas·ing. 1** put in a case. **2** cover completely; enclose.

-ence, *suffix.* **1** act, fact, quality, or state of ___ing, as in *abhorrence, indulgence.* **2** quality or state of being ___ent, as in *absence, confidence, competence, prudence.* [< L *-entia*]

en·ceph·a·li·tis (en sef′ə lī′tis), n. inflammation of the brain caused by injury, infection, poison, etc. —**en·ceph′a·lit′ic,** adj.

en·ceph·a·lon (en sef′ə lon), n. the brain. [< NL < Gk., < *en-* in + *kephale* head] —**en′ce·phal′ic,** adj.

en·chain (en chān′), v. **1** put in chains; fetter. **2** attract and fix firmly; hold fast. —**en·chain′ment,** n.

en·chant (en chant′; -chänt′), v. **1** use magic on; put under a spell. **2** delight greatly; charm. [< F < L *in-* against + *cantare* chant]

en·chant·er (en chan′tər; -chän′-), n. one that enchants.

en·chant·ing (en chan′ting; -chän′-), adj. **1** very delightful; charming. **2** bewitching. —**en·chant′ing·ly,** adv.

en·chant·ment (en chant′mənt; -chänt′-), n. **1** an enchanting or being enchanted. **2** something that enchants.

en·chan·tress (en chant′ris; -chänt′-), n. woman who enchants.

en·chi·la·da (en chi lä′də), n. rolled tortilla filled with cheese, peppers, meat, etc. served with a spicy sauce.

the whole enchilada, the entire affair, business, etc.

en·ci·pher (en sī′fər), v. put a message into cipher.

en·cir·cle (en sèr′kəl), v., **-cled, -cling. 1** form a circle around; surround. **2** go in a circle around. —**en·cir′cle·ment,** n.

encl., enclosed; enclosure.

en·clave (en′klāv), n. **1** country or district surrounded by a foreign territory. **2** *Fig.* any small group isolated or separate from a larger one surrounding it. **3** *Fig.* any small area isolated from a surrounding area. [< F, < *enclaver* enclose]

en·close (en klōz′), v., **-closed, -clos·ing. 1** shut in on all sides; surround. **2** put a wall or fence around. **3** put in an envelope along with a letter, etc. **4** contain.

en·clo·sure (en klō′zhər), *n.* **1** an enclosing or being enclosed. **2** an enclosed place. **3** thing that encloses. **4** thing enclosed.

en·code (en kōd′), *v.,* **-cod·ed, -cod·ing.** put a message into code.

en·co·mi·um (en kō′mi əm), *n., pl.* **-miums, -mi·a** (-mi ə), an elaborate expression of praise; high praise; eulogy. [< LL < Gk. *enkomion,* neut. < *en-* in + *komos* revelry] —**en·co′miast,** *n.* —**en·co′mi·as′tic,** *adj.* —**enco′mi·as′ti·cal·ly,** *adv.*

en·com·pass (en kum′pəs), *v.* **1** surround completely; shut in on all sides; encircle. **2** enclose; contain. —**en·com′passment,** *n.*

en·core (äng′kôr; -kōr; än′-), *interj., n., v.,* **-cored, -cor·ing.** —*interj.* once more; again. —*n.* **1** demand by the audience for the repetition of a song, etc., or for another appearance of the performer or performers. **2** repetition of a song, etc., in response to such a demand. **3** an additional song, etc., given in response to such a demand. —*v.* make such a demand for (a performer, etc.) by applauding. [< F]

en·coun·ter (en koun′tər), *v.* **1** meet unexpectedly. **2** meet with (difficulties, opposition, etc.). **3** meet as an enemy; meet in a fight or battle. —*n.* **1** a meeting, esp. an unexpected one. **2** a meeting of enemies; fight; battle. [< OF < VL, < L *in-* + *contra* against]

en·cour·age (en kėr′ij), *v.* **-aged, -ag·ing.** **1** give courage to; increase the hope or confidence of; urge on **2** be favorable to; help; support. [< OF, < *en-* in + *corage* COURAGE] —**en·cour′ag·er,** *n.* —**encour′ag·ing·ly,** *adv.*

en·cour·age·ment (en kėr′ij mənt), *n.* **1** an encouraging. **2** a being encouraged. **3** thing that encourages.

en·croach (en krōch′), *v.* **1** go beyond proper or usual limits. **2** trespass upon the property or rights of another; intrude. [< OF, < *en-* in (< L *in-*) + *croc* hook < Gmc.] —**en·croach′er,** *n.* —**encroach′ment,** *n.*

en·crust (en krust′), *v.* **1** cover with a crust or hard coating: *every surface was encrusted with ice.* **2** form a crust. **3** decorate with a layer of jewels, gold, etc. Also, **incrust.** —**en′crus·ta′tion,** *n.*

en·crypt (en kript′), *v.* put into cipher or code. —**en·cryp′tion,** *n.*

en·cum·ber (en kum′bər), *v.* **1** hold back (from running, doing, etc.); hinder; hamper. **2** make difficult to use; fill; obstruct. **3** weigh down; burden. [< OF, < *en* in + *combre* barrier, prob. < Celtic]

en·cum·brance (en kum′brəns), *n.* **1** anything that encumbers; hindrance; obstruction; burden. **2** claim, mortgage, etc., on property.

-ency, *suffix.* **1** act, fact, quality, or state of ___ing, as in *dependency.* **2** quality or state of being ___ent, as in *frequency.* **3** other meanings, as in *agency, currency.* [< L *-entia*]

ency. or **encyc.** encyclopedia.

en·cyc·li·cal (en sik′lə kəl; -sī′klə-), **encyc·lic** (-lik), *n.* letter about the general welfare of the church from the pope to his clergy. —*adj.* intended for wide circulation. [< LL *encyclicus* < Gk., < *en-* in + *kyklos* circle]

en·cy·clo·pe·di·a (en sī′klə pē′di ə), *n.* book or series of books giving information, arranged alphabetically, on all branches of knowledge. [< LL < Gk. *enkyklopaideia,* for *enkyklios paideia* well-rounded education] —**en·cy′clo·pe′dic,** *adj.* —**en·cy′clo·pe′dist,** *n.*

en·cyst (en sist′), *v.* enclose or become enclosed in a cyst or sac. —**en·cyst′ment,** *n.*

end (end), *n.* **1** the last part; conclusion. **2** place where a thing stops. **3** purpose; object. **4** result; outcome. **5** death; destruction. **6** part left over; remnant; fragment. **7** player at either end of the line in football. —*v.* **1** bring or come to an end; stop; finish. **2** destroy; kill. **3** form the end of; be the end of.

at loose ends, not settle; disordered.

end to end, one end against another: *tables placed end to end.*

end up, wind up; come out: *end up in trouble.*

in the end, finally.

keep or **hold one's end up,** do one's part.

make both ends meet, spend or use only as much as one has.

no end, *Informal.* very much: *no end of fun.*

on end, a upright. **b** one after another: *little sleep for nights on end.*

put an end to, a stop: *put an end to such nonsense.* **b** destroy; kill. [OE *ende*] —**end′er,** *n.*

en·dan·ger (en dān′jər), *v.* cause danger to; expose to loss or injury. —**en·dan′ger·ment,** *n.*

en·dan·gered (en dān′jerd), *adj.* facing possible extinction: *endangered species.*

en·dear (en dir′), *v.* make dear. —**en·dear′ing·ly,** *adv.*

en·dear·ment (en dir′mənt), *n.* **1** an endearing. **2** thing that endears. **3** act or word showing love or affection; caress.

en·deav·or (en dev′ər), *v.* try hard; attempt earnestly; make an effort; strive. —*n.* an earnest attempt; effort. [< *en-* + F *devoir* duty] —**en·deav′or·er,** *n.*

en·dem·ic (en dem′ik), *adj.* regularly found in a particular people or locality. —*n.* an endemic disease. [< Gk. *endemos* native < *en-* in + *demos* people] —**endem′i·cal·ly,** *adv.*

end·ing (en′ding), *n.* **1** the last part; end. **2** death. **3** letter or syllable added to a word or stem to change its meaning or to show its relationship to other words; inflection. The common plural ending in English is *s* or *es.*

en·dive (en′dīv; än′dēv), *n.* **1** kind of chicory with finely divided, curly leaves, used for salads. **2** kind of chicory that looks like very smooth white celery, also used for salads. [< OF < Med.L < Med.Gk. < L *intibum*]

end·less (end′lis), *adj.* **1** having no end; never stopping; lasting or going on forever. **2** with the ends joined for continuous action: *an endless chain.* —**end′lessly,** *adv.* —**end′less·ness,** *n.*

end·most (end′mōst), *adj.* nearest to the end; last; farthest.

endo-, *combining form.* within; inside; inner, as in *endocarp, endoplasm.* [< Gk.]

en·do·car·di·um (en′dō kär′di əm) *n.* smooth membrane that lines the cavities of the heart.

en·do·carp (en′dō kärp), *n.* the inner layer of a ripened ovary of a plant.

en·do·crine (en′dō krin; -krin), *adj.* of or having to do with the endocrine glands. —*n.* **1** an endocrine gland. **2** its secretion. [< *endo-* + Gk. *krinein* separate]

endocrine gland, any of various glands that produce secretions that pass directly into the blood stream instead of into a duct, as the thyroid gland.

en·do·cri·nol·o·gy (en′dō kri nol′ə ji; -krī-), *n.* science that deals with the endocrine glands, esp. their role in the body and disease. —**en′do·cri′no·log′ical,** *adj.* —**en′do·cri·nol′o·gist,** *n.*

en·do·derm (en′dō dėrm), *n.* inner layer of cells formed in an embryo. [< *endo-* + Gk. skin] —**en′do·der′mal,** *adj.*

en·dog·e·nous (en doj′ə nəs), *adj.* growing from the inside; originating within. —**en·dog′e·nous·ly,** *adv.*

en·do·me·tri·um (en′dō mē′trē əm) *n.* inner lining of the uterus. [< NL *endometrium* < Gk. *éndon* within + *mētra* womb] —**en′do·me′tri·al,** *adj.*

en·do·plasm (en′dō plaz əm), *n.* the inner portion of the cytoplasm of a cell. —**en′do·plas′mic,** *adj.*

en·dor·phin (en dôr′fin), *n.* any one of a group of substances in the brain that reduce the sense of pain and are involved in other responses.

en·dorse (en dôrs′), *v.* **-dorsed, -dorsing. 1** write one's name, comment, etc., on the back of (a check or other document). **2** approve; support. [alter. of ME *endosse(n)* <OF, < *en-* on + *dos* back < L *dorsum*] —**en·dors′a·ble,** *adj.* —**en·dor′see′,** *n.* —**en·dorse′ment,** *n.* —**en·dors′er,** *n.*

en·do·skel·e·ton (en′dō skel′ə tən), *n.* internal skeleton of vertebrates and related forms.

en·do·sperm (en′dō spėrm), *n.* nourishment for the embryo enclosed with it in the seed of a plant.

en·dow (en dou′), *v.* **1** give money or property to provide an income for. **2** provide with some ability, quality, or talent: *nature endowed her with both beauty and brains.* [< OF, < *en-* (< L in-) + *douer* endow < L *dotare*] —**en·dow′er**, *n.*

en·dow·ment (en dou′mənt), *n.* **1** an endowing. **2** money or property given to provide an income. **3** Usually, **endowments.** talent, esp. a natural, inborn talent; ability.

end product, portion remaining after something is processed; the result of a processing.

end table, small table suitable to put beside a chair or couch.

en·due (en dü′; -dū′), *v.,* **-dued, -du·ing.** provide with a quality or power.

en·dur·ance (en dúr′əns; -dyūr-), *n.* **1** power to last or keep on. **2** power to put up with, bear, or stand.

en·dure (en dúr′; -dyūr′), *v.* **-dured, -dur·ing. 1** keep on; last. **2** undergo; bear; tolerate. [< OF < LL < L, make hard < *in-* + *durus* hard] —**en·dur′a·ble,** *adj.* —**en·dur′a·bly,** *adv.*

en·dur·ing (en dúr′ing; -dyūr′-), *adj.* lasting; permanent. —**en·dur′ing·ly,** *adv.* —**en·dur′ing·ness,** *n.*

end use, the particular function which a resource or product serves or is limited to.

end·ways (end′wāz′), **end·wise** (-wīz′), *adv.* **1** on end; upright. **2** with the end forward; in the direction of the end. **3** lengthwise. **4** end to end.

en·e·ma (en′ə mə), *n., pl.* **en·e·mas, e·nem·a·ta** (i nem′ə tə). injection of liquid into the rectum to flush the bowels. [< Gk., < *en-* in + *hienai* send]

en·e·my (en′ə mi), *n., pl.* **-mies,** *adj.* —*n.* **1** person or group that hates and tries to harm another. **2** a hostile force, nation, army, fleet, or air force; person, ship, etc., of a hostile nation. **3** anything harmful; *frost is an enemy of plants.* —*adj.* of an enemy. [< OF < L, < *in-* not + *amicus* friendly]

en·er·get·ic (en′ər jet′ik), *adj.* full of energy; eager to work; full of force; active. —**en′er·get′i·cal·ly,** *adv.*

en·er·gize (en′ər jīz), *v.,* **-gized, -giz·ing.** give energy to. —**en′er·giz′er,** *n.*

en·er·gy (en′ər ji), *n., pl.* **-gies. 1** active strength or force; healthy power; vigor. **2** strength; force; power. **3** *Physics.* capacity for doing work. [< LL < Gk., < *energos* active < *en-* in + *ergon* work]

energy crisis, severe shortage of electricity, gas, etc., or of the fuels used to produce energy.

en·er·vate (en′ər vāt), *v.* **-vat·ed, -vat·ing.** lessen the vigor or strength of; weaken. [< L, < *ex-* away + *nervus* sinew, nerve] —**en′er·va′tion,** *n.* —**en′er·va′tor,** *n.*

en·fee·ble (en fē′bəl), *v.,* **-bled, -bling.** make feeble; weaken. —**en·fee′ble·ment,** *n.* —**en·fee′bler,** *n.*

en·fi·lade (en′fə lād′),*n., v.,* **-lad·ed, -lad·ing.** —*n.* **1** gunfire directed from the side at a line of troops or a position held by them. **2** situation exposed to such raking gunfire. —*v.* fire guns at (a line of troops or the position held by them) from the

side. [< F, < *enfiler* thread, pierce < *en-* on (< L *in-*) + *fil* thread < L *filum*]

en·fold (en fōld′), *v.* **1** fold in; wrap up. **2** embrace; clasp. —**en·fold′er,** *n.* —**en·fold′ment,** *n.*

en·force (en fôrs′; -fōrs′), *v.,* **-forced, -forc·ing. 1** force obedience to; put into force: *judges enforce the laws.* **2** force; compel: *the bandits enforced obedience by threats of violence.* [< OF, ult. < L *in-* + *fortis* strong] —**en·force′a·ble,** *adj.* —**en·for′ced·ly,** *adv.* —**en·force′ment,** *n.* —**en·forc′er,** *n.*

en·fran·chise (en fran′chīz), *v.,* **-chised, -chis·ing. 1** give the right to vote. **2** set free; release from slavery or restraint. —**en·fran′chise·ment,** *n.* —**en·fran′chis·er,** *n.*

Eng., England; English.

eng., 1 engineer; engineering. **2** engraved; engraving.

en·gage (en gāj′), *v.,* **-gaged, -gag·ing. 1** bind by a pledge; bind oneself; promise; pledge. **2** promise or pledge to marry. **3** keep busy; occupy: *study engages much of my time.* **4** keep oneself busy; be active: *engaged in a game of chess.* **5** hire; employ; reserve (seats, rooms, etc.). **6** catch and hold; attract: *engage attention.* **7** fit into; lock together: *gears that engage.* **8** start a battle with; attack. [< F, < *engage* under pledge] —**en·gag′er,** *n.*

en·gaged (en gājd′), *adj.* **1** promised or pledged to marry. **2** busy; occupied. **3** involved in a fight or battle.

en·gage·ment (en gāj′mənt), *n.* **1** act of engaging. **2** fact or condition of being engaged. **3** promise; pledge. **4** promise to marry. **5** a meeting with someone at a certain time; appointment. **6** period of being hired; time of use or work. **7** fight; battle.

en·gag·ing (en gāj′ing), *adj.* attractive; pleasing; charming. —**en·gag′ing·ly,** *adv.* —**en·gag′ing·ness,** *n.*

en·gen·der (en jen′dər), *v.* bring into existence; produce; cause. [< OF < L, < *in-* in + *generare* create] —**en·gen′der·er,** *n.* —**en·gen′der·ment,** *n.*

en·gine (en′jən), *n.* **1** machine that applies power to some work, esp. a machine that can start others moving. **2** machine that pulls a railroad train. **3** machine; device; instrument: *big guns are engines of war.* **4** =fire engine. [< OF < L *ingenium* inborn qualities, talent < *in-* + *gen-* create]

en·gi·neer (en′jə nir′), *n.* **1** person who runs an engine. **2** person who plans, builds, or manages engines, machines, roads, bridges, canals, railroads, forts, etc.; expert in engineering. **3** member of a group that does engineering work in the army or navy. —*v.* **1** plan, build, direct, or work as an engineer. **2** *Fig.* manage cleverly; guide skillfully: *engineer a successful fund-raiser.*

en·gi·neer·ing (en′jə nir′ing), *n.* science, work, or profession of an engineer; planning, building, or managing engines,

machines, roads, bridges, canals, railroads, forts, etc.

Eng·land (ing′glənd), *n.* the largest division of Great Britain, in the S part. —**Eng′land·er,** *n.*

Eng·lish (ing′glish), *adj.* of or having to do with England, its people, or their language. —*n.* **1** the people of England collectively. **2** the English language, including Old English or Anglo-Saxon (before 1100), Middle English (about 1100–1500), and Modern English (from about 1500). **3** the English used in a certain locality or by a certain group. [OE *Englisc* < *Engle* the English people]

English Channel, strait between England and France.

English English, English as spoken in England.

English horn, a wooden musical instrument resembling an oboe, but larger and having a lower tone.

Eng·lish·ism (ing′gli shiz əm), *n.* **1** deep affection and loyalty to England or its customs. **2** word or expression from British English. **3** very English custom or characteristic.

English ivy, =ivy (def. 1).

Eng·lish·man (ing′glish mən), *n., pl.* **-men. 1** native or inhabitant of England. **2** one whose ancestry is English.

English muffin, flat muffin made with yeast dough, baked on a griddle, and served toasted.

English sparrow, a small, brownish-gray bird, now very common in America.

Eng·lish·wom·an (ing′glish wùm′ən), *n., pl.* **-wom·en. 1** woman who is a native or inhabitant of England. **2** woman whose ancestry is English.

en·gorge (en gôrj′), *v.,* **-gorged, -gorg·ing. 1** eat greedily. **2** fill with food until stuffed. **3** collect too much blood in one part of the body. —**en·gorge′ment,** *n.*

engr., 1 engineer. **2** engraved; engraver.

en·graft (en graft′; -gräft′), *v.* insert or graft (a shoot from one tree or plant) into or on another.

en·grave (en grāv′), *v.* **-graved, -grav·ing. 1** carve artistically; decorate by engraving. **2** cut in lines on a metal plate, block of wood, etc., for printing. **3** print from such a plate, block, etc. **4** impress deeply. [< *en-* + *grave*³ —**en·grav′er,** *n.*

en·grav·ing (en grāv′ing), *n.* **1** art of an engraver; cutting lines in metal plates, blocks of wood, etc., for printing. **2** picture printed from an engraved plate, block, etc. **3** an engraved plate, block, etc.; engraved design or pattern.

en·gross (en grōs′), *v.* **1** occupy wholly; take up all the attention of. **2** copy or write in large letters; write a beautiful copy of. [(def. 1) < *in gross* < F *en gros* in a lump; (def. 2) < AF, < *en-* in + *grosse* large writing, document. See GROSS.] —**en·gross′er,** *n.* —**en·gross′ing,** *adj.* —**en·gross′ment,** *n.*

en·gulf (en gulf′), *v.* swallow up; overwhelm; submerge.

en·hance (en hans´; –häns´), v., **-hanced, -hanc·ing.** make greater; add to; heighten. [< AF var. of OF *enhaucier* < *en-* on, up + *haucier* raise. See HAWSER.] —**en·hance´ment,** n. —**en·hanc´er,** n.

e·nig·ma (i nig´mə), n. a baffling or puzzling problem, situation, person, etc. [< L < Gk. *ainigma* < *ainissesthai* speak darkly < *ainos* fable] —**en´ig·mat´ic,** adj. —**en´ig·mat´i·cal·ly,** adv.

en·join (en join´), v. **1** order; direct; urge. **2** forbid; prohibit: *the judge enjoined him from infringing on the rights of his neighbors.* [< OF *enjoindre* < L, attack, charge < *in-* on + *jungere* join] —**en·join´er,** n.

en·joy (en joi´), v. **1** have or use with joy; be happy with; take pleasure in. **2** have as an advantage or benefit. **enjoy oneself,** have a good time. [< OF, < *en-* + *joir* enjoy < L *gaudere*] —**en·joy´a·ble,** adj. —**en·joy´a·ble·ness,** n. —**en·joy´a·bly,** adv. —**en·joy´er,** n.

en·joy·ment (en joi´mənt), n. **1** an enjoying. **2** thing enjoyed. **3** joy; happiness; pleasure.

enl., **1** enlarged. **2** enlisted.

en·large (en lärj´), v., **-larged, -larg·ing.** make or become larger; increase in size. —**en·larg´er,** n.

en·large·ment (en lärj´mənt), n. **1** an enlarging or being enlarged. **2** anything that is an enlarged form of something else. An enlargement is often made from a small photograph. **3** thing that enlarges something else; addition.

en·light·en (en līt´ən), v. give the light of truth and knowledge to; free from prejudice, ignorance, etc. —**en·light´en·er,** n. —**en·light´en·ment,** n.

en·light·en·ment (en lī´tən mənt), n. **1** a being enlightened; information; instruction. **2** **the Enlightenment,** philosophical movement in Europe in the 18th century that stressed rationalism and intellectual freedom.

en·list (en list´), v. **1** enroll in some branch of the military service. **2** induce to join in some cause or undertaking; secure the help or support of. —**en·list´er,** n.

enlisted man or **woman,** *Esp. U.S.* member of the armed forces who is not a commissioned officer or cadet.

en·list·ee (en lis´tē; –lis´tē´), n. person who enlists in the military.

en·list·ment (en list´mənt), n. **1** an enlisting. **2** a being enlisted. **3** time for which a person enlists.

en·liv·en (en līv´ən), v. make lively, active, gay, or cheerful. —**en·liv´en·er,** n. —**en·liv´en·ment,** n.

en masse (en mas´; än mäs´), in a group; all together. [<F]

en·mesh (en mesh´), v. catch in a net; enclose in meshes; entangle.

en·mi·ty (en´mə ti), n., pl. **-ties.** the feeling that enemies have for each other; hate. [OF *ennemistie* < VL < L *inimicus* ENEMY]

en·no·ble (en nō´bəl), v., **-bled, -bling. 1** give a title or rank of nobility to. **2** raise in the respect of others; dignity; exalt. —**en·no´ble·ment,** n. —**en·no´bler,** n.

en·nui (än´wē), n. a feeling of weariness and discontent from lack of occupation or interest; boredom. [< F. See ANNOY.]

e·nor·mi·ty (i nôr´mə ti), n., pl. **-ties. 1** extreme wickedness; outrageousness. **2** an extremely wicked crime; outrageous offense. **3** huge size.

e·nor·mous (i nôr´məs), adj. **1** extremely large; huge. **2** extremely wicked; outrageous. [< L, < *ex-* out of + *norma* pattern] —**e·nor´mous·ly,** adv. —**e·nor´mous·ness,** n.

e·nough (i nuf´), adj. adequate for the need or want. —n. an adequate quantity or number. —adv. **1** sufficiently; adequately. **2** quite; fully: *he is willing enough to take a tip* —interj. stop! no more! [OE *genōg*]

en·pas·sant (än pä sän´), French. **1** in passing: *mention en passant.* **2** move with a pawn in chess that leads to the pawn's immediate capture.

en·plane (en plān´), v., **-planed, -plan·ing.** go aboard an aircraft.

en pointe or **en pointes** (än pwaNt´), French. on the toes, in ballet.

en·quire (en kwīr´), v., **-quired, -quir·ing.** =inquire. —**en·quir´y,** n.

en·rage (en rāj´), v., **-raged, -rag·ing.** put into a rage; make very angry. —**en·rage´ment,** n.

en·rap·ture (en rap´chər), v., **-tured, -tur·ing.** fill with great delight; entrance.

en·rich (en rich´), v. **1** make rich or richer: *an education enriches the mind.* **2** raise the nutritive value of (a food) by adding vitamins and minerals in processing. —**en·riched´,** adj.

en·rich·ment (en rich´mənt), n. **1** a being enriched: *enrichment of understanding from experience.* **2** thing that enriches: *vitamin enrichment in bread; music brings enrichment.*

en·roll, en·rol (en rōl´), v., **-rolled, -roll·ing. 1** write in a list. **2** have one's name written in a list. **3** make a member. **4** become a member. **5** enlist. —**en·roll´er,** n.

en·roll·ment, en·rol·ment (en rōl´mənt), n. **1** an enrolling. **2** number enrolled.

en route (än rüt´), on the way. [< F]

Ens., Ensign.

en·sconce (en skons´), v., **-sconced, -sconc·ing. 1** shelter safely; hide. **2** settle comfortably and firmly. [< *en-* + *sconce* fortification, prob. < Du. *schans*]

en·sem·ble (än säm´bəl), n. **1** all the parts of a thing considered together; general effect. **2** a united performance of the full number of singers, musicians, etc. **3** group of musicians or the musical instruments used in taking part in such a performance. **4** a complete, harmonious costume. [< F, < VL < L *in-* + *simul* at the same time]

en·shrine (en shrīn´), v. **-shrined, -shrin·ing. 1** enclose in a shrine. **2** keep sacred; cherish. —**en·shrine´ment,** n.

en·shroud (en shroud´), v. cover with, or as with, a shroud; hide; veil: *fog enshrouded the ship.*

en·sign (en´sən; en´sīn, *esp. for* 1), n. **1** flag; banner: *the ensign of the United States is the Stars and Stripes.* **2** the lowest commissioned officer in the navy. **3** sign of one's rank, position, or power; symbol of authority. [< OF < L *insignia* INSIGNIA] —**en´sign·ship, en´sign·cy,** n.

en·slave (en slāv´), v., **-slaved, -slav·ing.** make a slave or slaves of; take away freedom from. —**en·slave´ment,** n. —**en·slav´er,** n.

en·snare (en snār´), v., **-snared, -snar·ing.** catch in a snare; trap. —**en·snare´ment.** n. —**en·snar´er,** n.

en·sue (en sü´), v., **-sued, -su·ing.** come after; happen as a result; follow. The ensuing year means the next year. [< OF *ensivre* < L, < *in-* upon + *sequi* follow]

en·sure (en shùr´), v., **-sured, -sur·ing. 1** make sure or certain. **2** make sure of getting; secure. **3** make safe; protect. [< AF, < *en-* (< L *in-*) + *seür* SURE]

-ent, suffix. **1** ___ing, as in *absorbent, indulgent, coincident.* **2** one that ___s, as in *correspondent, president, superintendent.* **3** other meanings, as in *competent, confident.* [< L *-ens (-ent-)*]

en·tab·la·ture (en tab´lə chər), n. part of a building resting on the top of columns. [< Ital. *intavolatura* < *in-* on (< L *in-*) + *tavola* board, tablet < L *tabula*]

en·tail (en tāl´), v. **1** impose; require. **2** limit the inheritance of (property, etc.) to a specified line of heirs so that it cannot be left to anyone else. —n. **1** an entailing. **2** an entailed inheritance. **3** order of descent specified for an entailed estate. —**en·tail´ment,** n.

en·tan·gle (en tang´gəl), v., **-gled, -gling. 1** get twisted up and caught; tangle. **2** get into difficulty; involve. **3** perplex; confuse. —**en·tan´gle·ment,** n.

en·tente (än tänt´), n. **1** an understanding; agreement between two or more governments. **2** parties to an understanding; governments that have made an agreement. [< F]

en·ter (en´tər), v. **1** go into; come into: *enter a room.* **2** go in; come in: *Do not enter.* **3** become a part or member of; join: *enter the Boy Scouts.* **4** cause to join or enter; obtain admission for: *enter a dog in a show.* **5** begin; start. **6** write or put in a book, list, etc. **7** put in regular form; record: *the injured man entered a complaint in court.* [< OF < L *intrare* < *intro* inwards, *intra* within] —**en´ter·a·ble,** adj.

en·ter·ic (en ter´ik), adj. =intestinal. [< Gk., < *entera* intestines]

en·ter·i·tis (en´tə rī´tis), n. inflammation of the intestines.

en·ter·prise (en´tər prīz), n. **1** an important, difficult, or dangerous undertaking. **2** an undertaking; project: *a business enterprise.* **3** readiness to start projects; courage and energy in starting projects.

[< OF, < *entre–* between (< L *inter–*) + *prendre* take < L *prehendere*]

en·ter·pris·ing (en'tər prīz'ing), *adj.* courageous and energetic in starting projects. **—en'ter·pris'ing·ly,** *adv.*

en·ter·tain (en'tər tān'), *v.* **1** interest; please; amuse. **2** have as a guest. **3** have guests; provide entertainment for guests. **4** take into the mind; consider. [< F, < *entre–* among (< L *inter–*) + *tenir* hold < L *tenere*] **—en'ter·tain'er,** *n.*

en·ter·tain·ing (en'tər tān'ing), *adj.* interesting; pleasing; amusing. **—en'ter·tain'ing·ly,** *adv.* **—en'ter·tain'ing·ness,** *n.*

en·ter·tain·ment (en'tər tān'mənt), *n.* **1** an entertaining. **2** a being entertained. **3** thing that interests, pleases, or amuses.

en·thrall, en·thral (en thrôl'), *v.,* **-thralled, -thrall·ing. 1** captivate; fascinate; charm. **2** make a slave of; enslave. **—en·thrall'er,** *n.* **—en·thrall'ing,** *adj.* **—en·thrall'ing·ly,** *adv.* **—en·thrall'ment, en·thral'ment,** *n.*

en·throne (en thrōn'), *v.,* **-throned, -thron·ing. 1** set on a throne. **2** invest with authority, esp. as a sovereign or as a bishop. **—en·throne'ment,** *n.*

en·thuse (en thüz'), *v.* **-thused, -thus·ing. 1** become enthusiastic; show enthusiasm. **2** fill with enthusiasm. [< *enthusiasm*]

en·thu·si·asm (en thü'zi az əm), *n.* eager interest; zeal. [< LL < Gk., < *entheos* god-possessed < *en–* In + *theos* god]

en·thu·si·ast (en thü'zi ast), *n.* person who is filled with enthusiasm.

en·thu·si·as·tic (en thü'zi as'tik), *adj.* full of enthusiasm; eagerly interested. **—en·thu'si·as'ti·cal·ly,** *adv.*

en·tice (en tīs'), *v.,* **-ticed, -tic·ing.** tempt by arousing hopes or desires; attract by offering some pleasure or reward. [< OF *enticier* stir up, incite < *en–* in (< L *in–*) + L *titio* firebrand] **—en·tice'ment,** *n.* **—en·tic'er,** *n.* **—en·tic'ing·ly,** *adv.*

en·tire (en tīr'), *adj.* **1** having all the parts or elements; whole; complete. **2** not broken; having an unbroken outline. [< OF < L *integer* < *in–* not + *tag–* touch] **—en·tire'ly,** *adv.* **—en·tire'ness,** *n.*

en·tire·ty (en tīr'ti), *n., pl.* **-ties. 1** wholeness; completeness. **2** a complete thing; the whole.

in its entirety, wholly; completely.

en·ti·tle (en tī'təl), *v.,* **-tled, -tling. 1** give the title of; call by the name of. **2** give a claim or right to.

en·ti·ty (en'tə ti), *n., pl.* **-ties. 1** something that has a real and separate existence either actually or in the mind. **2** being; existence. [< LL *entitas* < L *ens,* ppr. of *esse* be]

en·tomb (en tüm'), *v.* place in a tomb; bury. **—en·tomb'ment,** *n.*

en·to·mo·log·i·cal (en'tə mə loj'ə kəl), *adj.* of or pertaining to entomology. **—en'to·mo·log'i·cal·ly,** *adv.*

en·to·mol·o·gy (en'tə mol'ə ji), *n.* branch of zoology that deals with insects.

[< Gk. *entomon* insect + –LOGY] **—en'to·mol'o·gist,** *n.*

en·tou·rage (än'tů räzh'), *n.* family, servants, attendants, and others accompanying a person. [< F, < *entourer* surround]

en·trails (en'tralz; -trəlz), *n.pl.* **1** the inner parts of a human or animal. **2** intestines; bowels. [< OF < LL *intralia* < L *interanea* < *inter* within]

en·train (en trān'), *v.* **1** get on a train. **2** put on a train. **—en·train'ment,** *n.*

en·trance[1] (en'trəns), *n.* **1** act of entering. **2** place by which to enter; door, passageway, etc. **3** freedom or right to enter; permission to enter. [< OF, < *entrer* ENTER]

en·trance[2] (en trans'; -träns'), *v.,* **-tranced, -tranc·ing. 1** put into a trance. **2** fill with joy; delight; charm. **—en·trance'ment,** *n.* **—en·tranc'ing,** *adj.* **—en·tranc'ing·ly,** *adv.*

en·trant (en'trənt), *n.* person who enters.

en·trap (en trap'), *v.,* **-trapped, -trap·ping. 1** catch in a trap. **2** bring into difficulty or danger; deceive; trick. **—en·trap'ment,** *n.*

en·treat (en trēt'), *v.* ask earnestly; beg and pray; implore. [< OF, < *en–* (< L *in–*) + *traitier* TREAT] **—en·treat'ing·ly,** *adv.* **—en·treat'ment,** *n.*

en·treat·y (en trēt'i), *n., pl.* **-treat·ies.** an earnest request; prayer.

en·tree (än'trā), *n.* **1** freedom or right to enter; access. **2** U.S. the main dish of food at dinner or lunch. [< F, fem. pp. of *entrer* ENTER]

en·trench (en trench'), *v.* **1** surround with a trench; fortify with trenches. **2** establish firmly. **3** trespass; encroach; infringe. **—en·trench'ment,** *n.*

en·tre·pre·neur (än'trə prə nèr'), *n.* person who organizes and manages a business or industrial enterprise, taking the risk of loss and getting the profit when there is one. [< F, < *entreprendre* undertake. See ENTERPRISE.] **—en'tre·pre·neur'i·al,** *adj.*

en·tro·py (en'trə pi), *n.* **1** measure of the amount of energy that cannot be used in a system. **2** measure of randomness or unpredictability, as in an isolated physical system or an electronic system. [< G *Entropie* < Gk. *en–* in + *tropé* a turning]

en·trust (en trust'), *v.* **1** charge with a trust; trust. **2** give the care of; hand over for safe-keeping.

en·try (en'tri), *n., pl.* **-tries. 1** act of entering. **2** place by which to enter; way to enter: *a vestibule is an entry.* **3** thing written or printed in a book, list, etc. Each word explained in a dictionary is an entry. **4** person or thing that takes part in a contest. [< OF, < *entrer* ENTER]

en·twine (en twīn'), *v.,* **-twined, -twin·ing. 1** twine together. **2** twine around. **—en·twine'ment,** *n.*

e·nu·mer·ate (i nümər āt'; -nū'-), *v.,* **-at·ed, -at·ing. 1** name one by one; give a list of. **2** count. **—e·nu'mer·a'tion,**

n. **—e·nu'mer·a'tive,** *adj.* **—e·nu'mer·a'tor,** *n.*

e·nun·ci·ate (i nun'si āt; -shi-), *v.* **-at·ed, -at·ing. 1** pronounce (words): *a well-trained actor enunciates very distinctly.* **2** state definitely; announce: *after many experiments the scientist enunciated a new theory.* [< L, < *ex–* out + *nuntius* messenger] **—e·nun'ci·a'tion,** *n.* **—e·nun'ci·a'tive,** *adj.* **—e·nun'ci·a'tor,** *n.*

en·vel·op (en vel'əp), *v.,* **-oped, -op·ing,** *n.* **—v. 1** wrap; cover. **2** surround: *our soldiers enveloped the enemy.* **3** hide; conceal: *fog enveloped the village.* **—n.** =envelope. [< OF, < *en–* in (<L *in–*) + *voloper* wrap] **—en·vel'op·er,** *n.*

en·ve·lope (en'və lōp; än'–), *n.* **1** a folded and gummed paper cover in which a letter or anything flat can be mailed. **2** a covering; wrapper. **3** bag that holds the gas in a balloon.

push or **stretch the envelope,** go beyond what is usual or expected. [< F *enveloppe* < *envelopper* ENVELOP]

en·vel·op·ment (en vel'əp mənt), *n.* **1** an enveloping. **2** a being enveloped. **3** thing that envelops; wrapping; covering.

en·ven·om (en ven'əm), *v.* **1** make poisonous. **2** fill with bitterness, hate, etc.

en·vi·a·ble (en'vi ə bəl), *adj.* to be envied; desirable; worth having. **—cn'vi·a·ble·ness,** *n.* **—en'vi·a·bly,** *adv.*

en·vi·ous (en'vi əs), *adj.* full of envy; feeling or showing envy. **—en'vi·ous·ly,** *adv.* **—en'vi·ous·ness,** *n.*

en·vi·ron (en vī'rən), *v.* surround; enclose. [< OF *environner* < *environ* around < *en–* in (< L *in–*) + *viron* circle]

en·vi·ron·ment (en vī'rən mənt), *n.* **1** surroundings. **2** all of the surrounding conditions and influences that affect the development of a living thing. **3** act or fact of surrounding. **—en·vi'ron·men'tal,** *adj.*

en·vi·ron·men·tal·ism (en vī'rən mən'tə liz əm), *n.* **1** belief that the environment is a more important factor in shaping behavior than heredity. **2** study of the environment in order to determine how to lessen damage to it, esp. through human activities.

en·vi·ron·men·tal·ist (en vī'rən mən'tə list), *n.* **1** person dedicated to solving problems in the environment caused by human activity, esp. pollution. **2** person dedicated to protecting the environment.

en·vi·rons (en vī'rənz), *n.pl.* surrounding districts; suburbs.

en·vis·age (en viz'ij), *v.,* **-aged, -ag·ing. 1** look in the face of. **2** contemplate. **3** form a mental picture of. [< F *envisager.* See EN–, VISAGE.]

en·vi·sion (en vizh'ən), *v.* see or imagine, as if in a vision.

en·voy (en'voi), *n.* **1** messenger. **2** diplomat ranking next below an ambassador and next above a minister. [< OF, < *envoier* send < VL, < L *in via* on the way]

en·vy (en′vi), *n., pl.* **–vies,** *v.,* **–vied, –vy·ing.** —*n.* **1** discontent or ill will at another's good fortune because one wishes it had been his. **2** the object of such feeling. —*v.* feel envy for or because of. [< OF *envie* < L *invidia,* ult. < *invidere* look with enmity at < *in–* against + *videre* see] —**en′vi·er,** *n.* —**en′vy·ing·ly,** *adv.*

en·wrap (en rap′), *v.,* **–wrapped, –wrapping.** wrap.

en·zyme (en′zīm; –zim), *n.* a chemical substance, produced in living cells, that can cause changes in other substances without being changed itself. Pepsin is an enzyme. [< Med.Gk. *enzymos* leavened < *en–* in + *zyme* leaven] —**en′zymat′ic,** *adj.*

E·o·cene (ē′ə sēn), *n.* **1** second epoch of the Tertiary period of the Cenozoic era, when the bottommost rocks were formed and some ancestors of mammals appeared. **2** rocks formed during this epoch. —*adj.* of or having to do with this epoch or its rocks. [< Gk. *ēōs* dawn + *kainos* recent]

e·o·hip·pus (ē ō hip′əs), *n.* any one of an extinct genus of horses that was the ancestor of modern horses. [< NL *Eohippus* < Gk. *ēōs* dawn + *hippos* horse]

e·o·lith (ē′ə lith), *n.* primitive stone tool from an early stage of human culture. [< Gk. *ēōs* dawn + *lithos* stone]

e·o·lith·ic (ē′ə lith′ik), *adj.* pertaining to an early stage of human culture, characterized by the use of very primitive stone instruments. [< Gk. *eos* dawn + *lithos* stone]

e·on (ē′ən; ē′on), *n.* **1** indefinitely long period of time: *waited eons for a plane.* **2** one billion years, in geology and astronomy. [< L <Gk. *aion*].

E·o·zo·ic (ē′ə zō′ik), *n.* **1** geological period before the Paleozoic, when life first appeared. **2** rock formed during this period. —*adj.* of or having to do with this period or its rocks. [< Gk. *ēōs* dawn + *zōion* animal + E –*ic*]

EPA, Environmental Protection Agency (of the U.S. government).

ep·au·let, ep·au·lette (ep′ə lət), *n.* ornament on the shoulder of a uniform. [< F, dim. of *épaule* shoulder]

é·pée or **e·pee** (ā pā′), *n.* sword used in fencing.

e·phed·rine, e·phed·rin (i fed′rin), *n.* drug, $C_{10}H_{15}ON$, used to relieve hay fever, asthma, head colds, etc. [< NL *ephedra* < L, horsetail (a plant) < Gk.]

e·phem·er·a (i fem′ər ə), *n., pl.* **–er·ae** (–ə rē), **–er·as. 1** someone or something of momentary interest or importance. **2** =May fly.

e·phem·er·al (i fem′ər əl), *adj.* lasting for only a day; lasting for only a very short time; very short-lived. [< Gk. *ephemeros* liable to be cut short < *epi–* subject to + *hemera* the day (of destiny)] —**e·phem′er·al·ly** *adv.*

e·phem·er·id (i fem′ər id), *n.* =May fly.

E·phe·sian (i fē′zhən), *adj.* of Ephesus or its people. —*n.* **1** native or inhabitant of Ephesus. **2 Ephesians,** book of the New Testament written in the name of the Apostle Paul to the Christians at Ephesus.

epi–, *prefix.* on; upon; above; in addition; among: *epiglottis = on the windpipe; epilogue = spoken in addition.*

ep·ic (ep′ik), *n.* a long poem that tells of the adventures of one or more great heroes. An epic is written in a dignified, majestic style, and often gives expression to the ideals of a nation or race. The *Iliad,* the *Aeneid,* and *Paradise Lost* are epics. —*adj.* Also, **ep′i·cal. 1** of or having to do with an epic. **2** like an epic; grand in style; heroic [< L < Gk. *epikos* < *epos* word, story] —**ep′i·cal·ly,** *adv.*

ep·i·ca·lyx (ep′ə kā′liks; –kal′iks), *n.* ring of bracts at the base of a flower that looks like an outer calyx.

ep·i·car·di·um (ep′ə kär′dē əm), *n., pl.* **–di·a** (–di ə). innermost layer of the pericardium, which encloses the heart. [< *epi–* upon + *pericardium*]

ep·i·carp (ep′ə kärp), *n.* the outer layer of a fruit or ripened ovary of a plant. The skin of a pear is the epicarp.

ep·i·cene (ep′ə sēn), *adj.* **1** belonging to or having the characteristics of male and female. **2** of no definite kind or sex. [< L < Gk. *epikoinos* common gender]

ep·i·cen·ter (ep′ə sen′tər), *n.* point of focus for the vibrations of an earthquake.

ep·i·cot·yl (ep′ə kot′əl), *n.* stem or axis above the cotyledons in the plant embryo. [< *epi–* above + Gk. *kotýlē* small vessel or hollow]

ep·i·cure (ep′ə kyúr), *n.* person who has a refined taste in eating and drinking and cares much about foods and drinks. [Anglicized var. of *Epicurus*]

ep·i·cu·re·an (ep′ə kyù rē′ən), *adj.* **1** like an epicure; fond of pleasure and luxury. **2** fit for an epicure. **3 Epicurean,** of Epicurus or his philosophy. —*n.* **1** person fond of pleasure and luxury; epicure. **2** believer in the philosophy of Epicurus.

Ep·i·cu·re·an·ism (ep′ə kyù rē′ən iz em), *n.* **1** philosophy or principles of Epicurus or his followers. **2** Also, **epicureanism.** belief or practice of this philosophy.

Ep·i·cu·rus (ep′ə kyúr′əs), *n.* 342?–270 B.C., Greek philosopher who taught that happiness is the highest good and that virtue alone produces happiness.

ep·i·cy·cle (ep′ə sī′kəl), *n.* **1** circle that rolls around the inside or outside of the circumference of another circle. **2** small circle whose center moves round in the circumference of a larger circle, formerly used to explain the motion of planets. [< LL *epicyclus* < Gk. *epi–* on + *kyklos* circle] —**ep′i·cy′clic,** *adj.*

ep·i·dem·ic (ep′ə dem′ik), *n.* **1** the rapid spreading of a disease so that many people have it at the same time. **2** the rapid spread of an idea, fashion, etc. —*adj.* affecting many people at the same time; widespread. [< F *épidémie* < Med.L < Gk., < *epi–* among + *demos* people] —**ep′i·dem′i·cal·ly,** *adv.*

ep·i·de·mi·ol·o·gy (ep′ə dē′mē ol′ə ji), *n.* branch of medicine concerned with the causes, spread, and control of disease, esp. within a community. [< E *epidemic* + –*ology* study of] —**ep′i·de′mi·ol·o·log′i·cal,** *adj.* —**ep′i·de′mi·ol′o·gist,** *n.*

ep·i·der·mis (ep′ə dèr′mis), *n.* **1** the outer layer of the skin. **2** the outer covering on the shells of many mollusks. **3** any of various other outer layers of invertebrates. **4** a skinlike layer of cells in seed plants and ferns. [< LL < Gk., < *epi–* on + *derma* skin] —**ep′i·der′mal, ep′i·der′mic,** *adj.*

ep·i·der·moid (ep′ə dèr′moid), **ep·i·der·moi·dal** (–dèr moi′dəl), *adj.* resembling epidermis.

ep·i·glot·tis (ep′ə glot′is), *n.* a thin, triangular plate of cartilage that covers the entrance to the windpipe during swallowing, so that food, etc., does not get into the lungs. [< LL < Gk., < *epi–* on + *glotta* tongue] —**ep′i·glot′tal,** *adj.*

ep·i·gram (ep′ə gram), *n.* **1** a short, pointed or witty saying. **2** a short poem ending in a witty or clever turn of thought. [< L < Gk., < *epi–* on + *graphein* write] —**ep′i·gram·mat′ic, ep′i·gram·mat′i·cal,** *adj.* —**ep′i·gram·mat′i·cal·ly,** *adv.*

ep·i·gram·ma·tize (ep′ə gram′ə tīz), *v.,* **–tized, –tiz·ing. 1** express by epigrams. **2** make epigrams.

ep·i·graph (ep′ə graf), *n.* **1** inscription on a building, tomb, etc. **2** quotation at the beginning of a book, chapter, etc., that indicates a main idea or theme.

e·pig·ra·phy (i pig′rə fi), *n.* **1** inscriptions. **2** branch of knowledge that deals with the deciphering and interpretation of inscriptions. —**e·pig′ra·phist, e·pig′ra·pher,** *n.*

ep·i·lep·sy (ep′ə lep′si), *n.* a chronic nervous disease whose attacks cause convulsions and unconsciousness. [< LL < Gk., *epilepsia* seizure, ult. < *epi–* on + *lambanein* take]

ep·i·lep·tic (ep′ə lep′tik), *adj.* **1** of or having to do with epilepsy. **2** having epilepsy. —*n.* person who has epilepsy.

ep·i·logue, ep·i·log (ep′ə lôg; –log), *n.* **1** the concluding part of a novel, poem, etc. **2** speech or poem after the end of a play. It is addressed to the audience and is spoken by one of the actors. [< F < L < Gk., ult. < *epi–* in addition + *legein* speak]

e·piph·a·ny (i pif′ə ni), *n.* **1** appearance or revelation, esp. of a deity. **2** *Fig.* sudden insight or revelation about something: *an epiphany caused her to see the relationship very clearly.* **3 the Epiphany,** January 6, the anniversary of the coming of the Wise Men to Christ at Bethlehem. [< OF *epiphany* < LL, < Gk. *epipháneia* < *epi–* upon + *phainein* to show]

ep·i·phyte (ep'ə fīt), *n.* plant that grows on another plant for support, but not for nourishment. Many mosses, lichens, and orchids are epiphytes. [< Gk. *epi-* on + *phyton* plant] —**ep´i·phyt´ic, ep´i·phyt´i·cal,** *adj.* —**ep´i·phyt´i·cal·ly,** *adv.*

e·pis·co·pa·cy (i pis'kə pə si), *n., pl.* **-cies.** 1 government of a church by bishops. 2 bishops as a group. 3 position, rank, or term of office of a bishop; episcopate.

e·pis·co·pal (i pis'kə pəl), *adj.* 1 of or having to do with bishops. 2 governed by bishops. 3 **Episcopal,** of or having to do with the Church of England, or certain Protestant churches of the United States, such as the Protestant Episcopal Church. [< LL, < L *episcopus* BISHOP —**e·pis´co·pal·ly,** *adv.*

E·pis·co·pa·lian (i pis´kə pāl'yən; -pā´li ən), *n.* member of the Protestant Episcopal Church. —*adj.* Episcopal.

e·pis·co·pate (i pis'kə pit; -pāt), *n.* 1 position, rank, or term of office of a bishop. 2 district under the charge of a bishop; bishopric. 3 bishops as a group.

ep·i·sode (ep'ə sōd), *n.* a single happening or group of happenings in real life or a story. [< Gk. *episodion,* neut., coming in besides, ult. < *epi-* on + *eis* into + *hodos* way] —**ep´i·sod´ic, ep´i·sod´i·cal,** *adj.* —**ep´i·sod´i·cal·ly,** *adv.*

e·pis·te·mol·o·gy (i pis´tə mol'ə ji), *n.* part of philosophy that deals with the origin, nature, and limits of knowledge. [< Gk. *episteme,* knowledge + -LOGY] —**e·pis´te·mo·log´i·cal,** *adj.* —**e·pis´te·mo·log´i·cal·ly,** *adv.* —**e·pis´te·mol´o·gist,** *n.*

e·pis·tle (i pis'əl), *n.* 1 letter, usually a long, instructive letter written in formal or elegant language. 2 **Epistle, a** letter written by one of Christ's Apostles. The Epistles make up 21 books of the New Testament. **b** selection from one of these, read as part of Mass or of the Anglican service of Holy Communion. [< L < Gk. *epistole,* ult. < *epi-* to + *stellein* send]

e·pis·to·lar·y (i pis'tə ler´i), *adj.* 1 carried on by letters; contained in letters. 2 of letters; suitable for writing letters.

ep·i·taph (ep'ə taf; -täf), *n.* a short statement in memory of a dead person, usually put on his or her tombstone. [< L < Gk. *epitaphion* funeral oration < *epi-* at + *taphos* tomb] —**ep´i·taph´ic,** *adj.* —**ep´i·taph´ist,** *n.*

epi·tha·la·mi·um (ep´ə thə lā´mē əm), *n., pl.* **-mi·ums, -mi·a** (-mi ə), poem or song in honor of someone or a couple newly married. [< *epithalamium* < Gk. *epithalámion*]

ep·i·the·li·um (ep´ə thē'li əm), *n., pl.* **-li·ums, -li·a** (-li ə). a thin layer of cells forming a tissue that covers surfaces and lines hollow organs. [< NL, < Gk. *epi-* on + *thele* nipple] —**ep´i·the´li·al,** *adj.*

ep·i·thet (ep'ə thet), *n.* a descriptive expression; adjective or noun expressing some quality or attribute, as in "Richard the Lion-Hearted." [< L < Gk. *epitheton* added < *epi-* on + *tithenai* place] —**ep´i·thet´ic, ep´i·thet´i·cal,** *adj.*

e·pit·o·me (i pit'ə mē), *n.* 1 a condensed account; summary. 2 a condensed representation of something; something or part that is typical or representative of the whole. [< L < Gk., < *epi-* into + *temnein* cut] —**e·pit'o·mist** *n.*

e·pit·o·mize (i pit'ə mīz), *v.,* **-mized, -miz·ing.** make an epitome of; summarize. —**e·pit'o·miz´er,** *n.*

ep·i·zo·ot·ic (ep´ə zō ot'ik), *adj.* temporarily prevalent among animals. —*n.* an epizootic disease. [< Gk. *epi-* among + *zoion* animal]

e plu·ri·bus u·num (ē plür'ə bəs ū'nəm), *Latin.* out of many, one; the motto on the official seal of the United States. It was once the official motto of the United States, but since 1956 the official motto has been "In God We Trust."

ep·och (ep'ək), *n.* 1 period of time; era. 2 period of time in which striking things happened. 3 the starting point of such a period. 4 the dividing line between geological periods. [< Med.L < Gk. *epoche* a stopping, fixed point in time < *epi-* up + *echein* hold] —**ep'och·al,** *adj.*

ep·o·nym (ep'ə nim), *n.* 1 person or imaginary character from whom a place gets or is thought to get its name. 2 name that is a synonym for something: *cardigan is an eponym for the Earl of Cardigan.*

ep·on·y·mous (ep on'ə məs), *adj.* giving one's name to a nation, tribe, place, etc. Romulus is the eponymous hero of Rome. [< Gk., < *epi-* to + *onyma* (dial.) name]

ep·ox·y (e pok'si), *adj.* of or referring to a large group of compounds, used esp. in the manufacture of plastics, adhesives, etc., that contain oxygen, which acts as a bridge between two radicals or molecules: *epoxy glue.* —*n., pl.* **-ox·ies.** =epoxy resin. [< *ep-* + *oxygen*]

epoxy resin, a synthetic resin made from an epoxy compound that hardens after being shaped under heat.

ep·si·lon (ep'sə lon; -lən), *n.* the fifth letter of the Greek alphabet (E, ε).

eq., 1 equal. 2 equation. 3 equivalent.

eq·ua·ble (ek'wə bəl; ē'kwə-), *adj.* changing little; uniform; even; tranquil. [< L, < *aequare* make uniform < *aequus* even, just] —**eq´ua·bil´i·ty, eq'ua·ble·ness,** *n.* —**eq'ua·bly,** *adv.*

e·qual (ē'kwəl), *adj., n., v.,* **e·qualed, e·qual·ing.** —*adj.* 1 the same in amount, size, number, value, degree, rank, etc.; as much; neither more nor less. 2 the same throughout; even; uniform. —*n.* person or thing that is equal. —*v.* 1 be equal to. 2 make or do something equal to.

equal to, able to; strong enough for; brave enough for; etc. [< L *aequus* even, just]

e·qual·i·ty (i kwol'ə ti), *n., pl.* **-ties.** a being equal; sameness in amount, size, number, value, degree, rank, etc.

e·qual·ize (ē'kwəl īz), *v.,* **-ized, -iz·ing.** 1 make equal. 2 make even or uniform. —**e´qual·i·za'tion,** *n.* —**e'qual·iz´er,** *n.*

e·qual·ly (ē'kwəl i), *adv.* in an equal manner; in or to an equal degree; so as to be equal.

e·qua·nim·i·ty (ē´kwə nim'ə ti; ek'wə-), *n.* evenness of mind or temper; calmness. [< L, < *aequus* even + *animus* mind, temper]

e·quate (i kwāt'), *v.,* **e·quat·ed, e·quat·ing.** 1 state to be equal; put in the form of an equation. 2 consider, treat, or represent as equal. 3 make equal. [< L *aequatus* made equal < *aequus* equal]

e·qua·tion (i kwā'zhən; -shən), *n.* 1 statement of equality between two quantities. *Examples:* $(4 \times 8) + 12 = 44$. $C = 2\pi r$. 2 expression using chemical formulas and symbols showing the substances used and produced in a chemical change. *Example:* $HCl + NaOH = NaCl + H_2O$. 3 an equating or being equated.

e·qua·tor (i kwā'tər), *n.* 1 an imaginary circle around the middle of the earth, halfway between the North Pole and the South Pole. 2 a similarly situated circle on any celestial or spherical body. 3 an imaginary circle in the sky corresponding to that of the earth. [< LL *aequator* (*diei et noctis*) equalizer (of day and night). See EQUAL.] —**e´qua·to'ri·al,** *adj.* **e´qua·to'ri·al·ly** *adv.*

eq·uer·ry (ek'wər i), *n., pl.* **-ries.** 1 officer of a household who has charge of the horses or who accompanies his master's carriage. 2 attendant on a royal or noble person. [< F *écurie* stable < Gmc.; infl. by L *equus* horse]

e·ques·tri·an (i kwes'tri ən), *adj.* 1 of horsemen or horsemanship; having to do with horseback riding. 2 on horseback; mounted on horseback. —*n.* rider or performer on horseback. [< L *equestris* of a horseman < *equus* horse]

e·ques·tri·enne (i kwes´tri en'), *n.* a woman rider or performer on horseback. [< F]

equi-, *combining form.* 1 equal, as in *equivalence.* 2 equally, as in *equidistant.* [< L *aequus* equal]

e·qui·an·gu·lar (ē´kwi ang'gyə lər), *adj.* having all angles equal, as a square.

e·qui·dis·tant (ē´kwə dis'tənt), *adj.* equally distant. —**e´qui·dis'tance,** *n.* —**e´qui·dis'tant·ly,** *adv.*

e·qui·lat·er·al (ē´kwə lat'ər əl), *adj.* having all sides equal. —*n.* figure having all sides equal. —**e´qui·lat'er·al·ly,** *adv.*

e·qui·lib·ri·um (ē´kwə lib'ri əm), *n.* 1 state of balance; condition in which opposing forces exactly balance or equal each other. 2 mental poise. [< L, ult. < *aequus* equal + *libra* balance]

e·quine (ē'kwīn), *adj.* of horses; like a horse; like that of a horse. —*n.* a horse. [< L, < *equus* horse]

e·qui·noc·tial (ē´kwə nok'shəl), *adj.* 1 having to do with either equinox. 2 occurring at or near the equinox:

equinoctial gales. **3** at or near the earth's equator.

e·qui·nox (ē′kwə noks), *n.* either of the two times in the year when the center of the sun crosses the celestial equator, and day and night are of equal length all over the earth, occurring about March 21 (**vernal equinox**) and September 22 (**autumnal equinox**). [Med.L < L, < *aequus* equal + *nox* night]

e·quip (i kwip′), *v.,* **e·quipped, e·quip·ping. 1** furnish with all that is needed; fit out; provide. **2** fit up; array. [< F *équiper* < OF *esquiper* < Scand. *skipa* to man (a ship)]

eq·ui·page (ek′wə pij), *n.* **1** carriage. **2** carriage with its horses, driver, and servants. **3** equipment; outfit.

e·quip·ment (i kwip′mənt), *n.* **1** act of equipping. **2** anything used in or provided for equipping; outfit.

e·qui·poise (ē′kwə poiz; ek′wə–), *n.* **1** state of balance. **2** a balancing force; counterbalance.

e·qui·po·ten·tial (ē′kwə pə ten′shəl), *adj.* in physics, having equal potential: *equipotential surfaces.*

eq·ui·se·tum (ek′wə sē′təm), *n., pl.* **-tums, -ta** (-tə) **1** genus of plants with hard, rough, unbranched stems. **2** =horsetail. [< NL < L, < *equus* horse + *saeta* (coarse) hair]

eq·ui·ta·ble (ek′wə tə bəl), *adj.* **1** fair; just. **2** *Law.* pertaining to or dependent upon equity. —**eq′ui·ta·ble·ness,** *n.* —**eq′ui·ta·bly,** *adv.*

eq·ui·ty (ek′wə ti), *n., pl.* **-ties. 1** fairness; justice. **2** what is fair and just. **3** system of rules and principles based on fairness and justice. **4** amount that a property is worth beyond what is owed on it. [< L, < *aequus* even, just]

e·quiv·a·lence (i kwiv′ə ləns), **e·quiv·a·len·cy** (-lən si), *n., pl.* **-len·ces; -cies.** a being equivalent; equality in value, force, significance, etc.

e·quiv·a·lent (i kwiv′ə lənt), *adj.* **1** equal in value, area, force, effect, meaning, etc. **2** having the same extent. A triangle and a square of equal area are equivalent. —*n.* **1** something equivalent. **2** *Chem.* the number of parts by weight in which an element will combine with or displace 8 parts of oxygen or 1 part of hydrogen. [< LL, < L *aequus* equal + *valere* be worth] —**e·quiv′a·lent·ly,** *adv.*

e·quiv·o·cal (i kwiv′ə kəl), *adj.* **1** having two or more meanings; intentionally vague or ambiguous. **2** undecided; uncertain. **3** questionable; suspicious. [< LL *aequivocus* ambiguous < L *aequus* equal + *vocare* call] —**e·quiv′o·cal·ly,** *adv.* —**e·quiv′o·cal·ness,** *n.*

e·quiv·o·cate (i kwiv′ə kāt), *v.,* **-cat·ed, -cat·ing. 1** use expressions of double meaning in order to mislead. **2** avoid the truth; lie. —**e·quiv′o·ca′tion,** *n.* —**e·quiv′o·ca′tor,** *n.*

-er[1], *suffix.* **1** person or thing that ___s, as in *admirer, burner.* **2** person living in ___, as in *New Yorker, villager.* **3** person that makes or works with ___, as in *hatter, tiler, tinner.* **4** person or thing that is or has ___, as in *six-footer, three-master, fiver.* [OE *-ere*]

-er[2], *suffix forming the comparative degree.* **1** of adjectives, as in *softer, smoother.* **2** of adverbs, as in *slower.* [OE *-ra, -re*]

Er, erbium.

e·ra (ir′ə; ē′rə), *n.* **1** a historical period distinguished by certain important or significant happenings. **2** period of time starting from some important or significant happening, date, etc. **3** one of five very extensive periods of time in geological history. [< LL, var. of *aera* number, epoch, prob. same word as L *aera* counters (for reckoning), pl. of *aes* brass]

e·rad·i·ca·ble (i rad′ə kə bəl), *adj.* that can be eradicated.

e·rad·i·cate (i rad′ə kāt), *v.,* **-cat·ed, -cat·ing. 1** get rid of entirely; destroy completely. **2** pull out by the roots. [< L, < *ex-* out + *radix* root] —**e·rad′i·ca′tion,** *n.* —**e·rad′i·ca′tive,** *adj.* —**e·rad′i·ca′tor,** *n.*

e·rase (i rās′), *v.* **e·rased, e·ras·ing. 1** rub out; scrape out. **2** remove all trace of; blot out. [< L *erasus* < *ex-* out + *radere* scrape] —**e·ras′a·ble,** *adj.*

e·ras·er (i rās′ər), *n.* thing for erasing marks made with pencil, ink, chalk, etc.

E·ras·mus (i raz′məs), *n.* 1466?–1536, Dutch scholar and humanist, a leader of the Renaissance movement.

e·ra·sure (i rā′shər; -zhər), *n.* **1** an erasing. **2** an erased word, letter, etc. **3** place where a word, letter, etc., has been erased.

er·bi·um (ėr′bi əm), *n.* a rare metallic element, Er, of the yttrium group. [< NL, < (*Ytt*)*erb*(*y*), Swedish place name]

ere (ār), *prep.* before. —*conj.* **1** sooner than; rather than. **2** before. [OE *ǣr*]

e·rect (i rekt′), *adj.* **1** straight up; upright. **2** raised; bristling. —*v.* **1** put straight up; set upright. **2** build; form. **3** in geometry, draw; construct. **4** put together; set up. [< L *erectus* < *ex-* up + *regere* direct] —**e·rect′er, e·rec′tor,** *n.* —**e·rec′tion,** *n.* —**e·rect′ly,** *adv.* —**e·rect′ness,** *n.*

e·rec·tile (i rek′təl), *adj.* **1** capable of being erected. **2** that can become distended and rigid: *erectile tissues in animals.* —**e·rec′til′i·ty,** *n.*

E region, =E layer.

ere·long (ār′lông′; -long′), *adv.* before long; soon.

e·rep·sin (i rep′sin), *n.* enzyme complex in intestinal and pancreatic juices that breaks down proteins into amino acids.

erg (ėrg), *n.* unit for measuring work or energy. It is the amount of work done by one dyne acting through a distance of one centimeter. [< Gk. *ergon* work]

er·go (ėr′gō), *adv., conj.* therefore. [<L]

er·go·nom·ics (ėr gə nom′iks), *n.* study of the relationship of people to their work and work environment, esp. to fit jobs to the abilities of individuals and to improve the design of office furniture and equipment. [< *ergo-* work + economics] —**er′go·nom′ic,** *adj.* —**er′go·nom′i·cal·ly,** *adv.*

er·got (ėr′gət; -got), *n.* **1** disease of rye caused by a fungus. **2** a hard, dark body produced by this disease. **3** medicine made from this body, used to stop bleeding and to contract unstriped muscles. [< F < OF *argot* cock's spur]

er·i·ca·ceous (er′ə kā′shəs), *adj.* belonging to the heath family. Heather, azalea, and rhododendron are ericaceous plants.

Er·ic·sson (er′ik sən), *n.* **Leif,** Viking chieftain and son of Eric the Red. He probably discovered North America about A.D. 1000.

Er·ic the Red (er′ik), born A.D. 950?, Viking chief who discovered Greenland about A.D. 982.

E·rie (ir′i), *n.* **1 Lake,** one of the five Great Lakes, between the United States and Canada. **2** member of an Iroquoian tribe of American Indians formerly living along the S and E shores of Lake Erie.

Erie Canal, canal in New York State between Buffalo and Albany.

Er·in (er′ən; ir′–), *n. Poetic.* Ireland.

Er·i·tre·a (er′ə trē′ə), *n.* a country on the Red Sea in NE Africa.

Er·i·tre·an (er′ə trē′ən), *n.* native or inhabitant of Eritrea. —*adj.* of or having to do with Eritrea.

er·mine (ėr′mən), *n., pl.* **-mines** or (*esp. collectively*) **-mine. 1** weasel of northern climates. It is brown in summer, but white with a black-tipped tail in winter. **2** its soft, white fur, used for women's coats, trimming, etc. **3** position, rank, or duties of a judge. [< OF < Gmc.]

erne, ern (ėrn), *n.* eagle that lives near the sea. [OE *earn*]

e·rode (i rōd′), *v.,* **e·rod·ed, e·rod·ing. 1** eat into; eat or wear away gradually. **2** form by a gradual eating or wearing away. [< L, < *ex-* away + *rodere* gnaw]

E·ros (ir′os; er′–), *n.* the Greek god of love, the son of Aphrodite, identified by the Romans with Cupid.

e·ro·sion (i rō′zhən), *n.* **1** a gradual eating or wearing away. **2** a being eaten or worn away. —**e·ro′sive,** *adj.*

e·ro·sion·al (i rō′zhə nəl), *adj.* **1** causing erosion: *erosional winds.* **2** produced by erosion: *an erosional canyon.* —**e·ro′sion·al·ly,** *adv.*

e·rot·ic (i rot′ik), **e·rot·i·cal** (-ə kəl), *adj.* of or having to do with sexual love. [< Gk. *erotikos* of Eros] —**e·rot′i·cal·ly,** *adv.* —**e·rot′i·cism,** *n.*

err (ėr; er), *v.* **1** go wrong; make mistakes. **2** be wrong; be mistaken or incorrect. **3** do wrong; sin. [< OF < L *errare* wander] —**err′ing,** *adj.* —**err′ing·ly,** *adv.*

er·rand (er′ənd), *n.* **1** a trip to do something. **2** what one is sent to do. [OE *ǣrende*]

er·rant (er′ənt), *adj.* **1** traveling in search of adventure; wandering; roving. **2** wrong; mistaken; incorrect. [< F, ppr. of OF *errer* travel (< VL *iterare* < L *iter* journey), blended with F *errant,* ppr. of *errer* ERR] **—er′rant·ly,** *adv.*

er·rant·ry (er′ənt ri), *n., pl.* **-ries.** conduct or action of a knight-errant.

er·rat·ic (i rat′ik), *adj.* **1** not steady; uncertain; irregular. **2** queer; odd: *erratic behavior.* [< L, < *errare* err] **—er·rat′i·cal·ly,** *adv.*

er·ro·ne·ous (ə rō′ni əs; e-), *adj.* incorrect. **—er·ro′ne·ous·ly,** *adv.* **—er·ro′ne·ous·ness,** *n.*

er·ror (er′ər), *n.* **1** something wrong; what is incorrect; mistake. **2** condition of being wrong, mistaken, or incorrect. **3** wrongdoing; sin. **4** faulty play in a game that gives an advantage to the opponent. [< OF < L. See ERR.]

er·satz (er′zäts), *adj., n.* substitute: *ersatz rubber.* [< G]

Erse (ėrs), *n.* **1** Scotch Gaelic. **2** the Celtic language of Ireland. **—adj.** of either of these languages. [Scot. var. of *Irish*]

erst (ėrst), *adv. Archaic.* formerly; long ago. [OE *ǣrst,* superl. of *ǣr* ere]

erst·while (ėrst′hwīl′), *adv.* some time ago; in time past; formerly. **—adj.** former; past.

e·ruct (i rukt′), *v.* belch. [< L, < *ex-* out + *ructare* belch]

e·ruc·tate (i ruk′tāt), *v.,* **-tat·ed, -tat·ing.** belch. **—e·ruc′ta′tion,** *n.* **—e·ruc′ta·tive,** *adj.*

er·u·dite (er′ů dīt; er′yů), *adj.* scholarly; learned. [< L *eruditus* instructed < *ex-* away + *rudis* rude] **—er′u·dite′ly,** *adv.* **—er′u·dite′ness,** *n.*

er·u·di·tion (er′ů dish′ən; er′yů–), *n.* acquired knowledge; scholarship; learning. **—er′u·di′tion·al,** *adj.*

e·rupt (i rupt′), *v.* **1** burst forth. **2** throw forth. **3** break out in a rash. The skin erupts during measles. [< L *eruptus* < *ex-* out + *rumpere* burst]

e·rup·tion (i rup′shən), *n.* **1** a bursting forth. **2** a throwing forth of lava, etc., from a volcano or of hot water from a geyser. **3** a breaking out in a rash. **4** red spots on the skin; rash. **—e·rup′tive,** *adj.*

-ery, *suffix.* **1** place for _____ing, as in *cannery, hatchery.* **2** place for _____s, as in *nunnery.* **3** occupation or business of a _____, as in *cookery.* **4** state or condition of a _____, as in *slavery.* **5** qualities, actions, etc., of a _____, as in *knavery.* **6** _____s as a group, as in *machinery.* [< OF *erie*]

e·ryth·ro·blast (i rith′rō blast), cell with a nucleus, found in bone marrow, from which red corpuscles develop. [< *erythro-* red blood cell + Gk. *blastós* germ, sprout]

e·ryth·ro·cyte (i rith′rō sīt), *n.* =red blood cell. [< *erythro-* red + *-cyte* cell]

Es, einsteinium.

es·ca·late (es′kə lāt), *v.,* **-lat·ed, -lat·ing. 1** increase or decrease in relation to some index, esp. automatically, in relation to the consumer price index and government benefits. **2** expand or increase by degrees: *each goal escalated the fans' excitement.* **3** move on an escalator or as if on one. [< *escalator*] **—es′ca·la′tion,** *n.*

es·ca·la·tor (es′kə lā′tər), *n.* **1** moving stairway, based on the endless chain. **2** someone or something that escalates. [Originally a Trademark, < *escala*de ladder + elev*ator*]

es·cal·lop, es·cal·op (es kol′əp; –kal′–), *v.* bake in a cream sauce or with bread crumbs. **—n.** scallop. [(orig. n.) < OF *escalope* shell < Gmc.] **—es·cal′loped,** *adj.*

es·ca·pade (es′kə pād; es′kə pād′), *n.* a breaking loose from rules or restraint; wild adventure or prank. [< F < Ital., < *scappare* ESCAPE]

es·cape (es kāp′), *v.,* **-caped, -cap·ing,** *n.* **—v. 1** get free; get out and away. **2** keep free or safe from; avoid. **3** come out of without being intended: *a cry escaped her lips.* **4** fail to be noticed or remembered by: *his name escapes me.* **—n. 1** an escaping. **2** way of escaping. **3** an avoiding of reality. [< OF *escaper,* ult. < L *ex-* out of + *cappa* cloak] **—es·cap′er,** *n.*

es·ca·pee (es′kə pē′; es kāp′ē), *n.* person who has escaped.

es·cape·ment (es kāp′mənt), *n.* device in a timepiece by which the motion of the wheels and of the pendulum or balance wheel are accommodated to each other.

es·cape-proof (es kāp′prüf′), *adj.* secure against escape: *an escapeproof cage.*

escape velocity, minimum speed necessary to overcome the pull of earth's gravitational field or another attracting body.

es·cap·ism (es kāp′iz əm), *n.* a habitual avoidance of unpleasant realities by recourse to imagination and fiction. **—es·cap′ist,** *n.*

es·car·got (es kár gō′), *n., pl.* **-gots** (–gō′, –gōz). *French.* a snail, esp. served as food.

es·ca·role (es′kə rōl), *n.* a broad-leaved kind of endive, used for salads.

es·carp·ment (es kárp′mənt), *n.* **1** a steep slope; cliff. **2** ground made into a steep slope in a fortification. [< F < Ital. *scarpa* < Gmc.]

-escent, *suffix.* coming to be or do something; in the process of _____ing, as in *pubescent.*

es·chew (es chü′), *v.* avoid as bad or harmful; shun. [< OF *eschiver* < Gmc.]

es·cort (*n.* es′kôrt; *v.* es kôrt′), *n.* **1** one or a group going with another to give protection, show honor, etc. **2** act of going with another as an escort. **3** woman who accompanies and entertains a man. **—v.** go with as an escort. [< F < Ital. *scorta* < *scorgere* guide < L *ex-* + *corrigere* CORRECT]

es·crow (es′krō; es krō′), *n.* deed, bond, or other written agreement put in charge of a third person until certain conditions are fulfilled.

in escrow, in the care of someone, by agreement, who is a third party. [< AF var. of OF *escroue* scrap, scroll < Gmc.]

es·cutch·eon (es kuch′ən), *n.* shield or shield-shaped surface on which a coat of arms is put. [< OF *escuchon,* <L *scutum* shield]

-ese, *suffix.* **1** of or pertaining to, as in *Japanese* art. **2** native or inhabitant of, as in *Portuguese.* **3** language of, as in *Chinese.* [< OF *-eis* < L *-ensis*]

Es·ki·mo (es′kəm ō), *n., pl.* **-mos, -mo,** *adj.* **—n. 1** the indigenous people living near the Arctic from the tip of Russia, across N America to Greenland. **2** the language or culture of these people. [< Dan. < F < Algonquian *eskimantsis* raw-flesh-eaters]

Eskimo dog, a strong dog formerly much used to pull sledges.

e·so·phag·e·al (ē′sə faj′ē əl), *adj.* of or connected with the esophagus.

e·soph·a·gus (ē sof′ə gəs), *n., pl.* **-gi** (–jī). passage for food from the mouth to the stomach; gullet. [< NL < Gk., < *oiso-* carry + *phagein* eat]

es·o·ter·ic (es′ə ter′ik), *adj.* **1** understood only by the select few; intended for an inner circle of disciples, scholars, etc. **2** secret; confidential. [< Gk. *esoterikos,* ult. < *eso* within] **—es′o·ter′i·cal·ly,** *adv.*

ESP, extrasensory perception.

esp., especially.

es·pa·drille (es′pə dril), *n.* casual shoe with a rope sole and, usually, a canvas upper. [< F]

es·pal·ier (es pal′yər), *n.* **1** framework upon which trees and shrubs grow. **2** tree or shrub trained to grow this way. [< F]

es·pe·cial (es pesh′əl), *adj.* **1** special; particular. **2** exceptional in amount or degree. [< OF < L *specialis* SPECIAL]

es·pe·cial·ly (es pesh′əl i), *adv.* particularly; chiefly.

Es·pe·ran·to (es′pə rän′tō; –ran′–), *n.* simple artificial language for international use.

es·pi·o·nage (es′pi ə nij; es′pi ə näzh), *n.* use of spies; spying. [< F, < *espion* spy < Ital. *spione* < *spia* spy]

es·pla·nade (es′plə näd′; –näd′), *n.* **1** an open, level space used for public walks or drives. **2** an open space between a fortress and a town. [< F < Sp., ult. < L *ex-* out + *planus* level]

es·pous·al (es pouz′əl), *n.* an espousing; adoption (of a cause, etc.).

es·pouse (es pouz′), *v.,* **-poused, -pous·ing. 1** marry. **2** take up or make one's own; *espouse a cause.* [< OF < L *sponsare* < *sponsus* betrothed, pp. of *spondere* betroth] **—es·pous′er,** *n.*

es·pres·so (es pres′ō), *n.* strong, dark-roasted coffee brewed in a special machine by an infusion of steam and usually served black. [< Ital.]

espresso bar, shop that specializes in serving espresso coffee.

es·prit (es prē′), *n.* lively wit; spirit. [< F < L *spiritus* SPIRIT]

es·prit de corps (es prē′ də kôr′), *French.* a sense of loyalty, shared interests, and responsibility to some group.

es·py (es pī′), *v.,* **–pied, –py·ing.** see; spy. [< OF *espier* <Gmc.]

-esque, *suffix.* 1 in the ____ style; resembling the ____ style, as in *Romanesque.* 2 like a ____, as in *statuesque.* [< F < Ital. *-esco*]

es·quire (es kwīr′; es′kwīr), **1** in the Middle Ages, a young man of noble family who attended a knight until he himself was made a knight. **2** Englishman ranking next below a knight. **3 Esquire,** title of respect placed after a man's last name. [< OF < L *scutarius* shieldbearer < *scutum* shield]

-ess, *suffix.* female, as in *heiress, hostess, lioness.* [< F *-esse* < L *-issa* < Gk.]

es·say (*n.* 1 es′ā; *n.* 2 es ′ā, e sā′; *v.* e sā′), *n.* 1 a literary composition on a certain subject. An essay is usually shorter and less methodical than a treatise. 2 try; attempt. —*v.* try; attempt. [< OF < L *exagium* a weighing] —**es·say′er,** *n.*

es·say·ist (es′ā ist), *n.* writer of essays.

es·sence (es′əns), *n.* 1 that which makes a thing what it is; necessary part or parts; important feature or features. 2 any concentrated substance that has the characteristic flavor, fragrance, or effect of the plant, fruit, etc., from which it is obtained. 3 perfume. [< L. < *esse* be]

es·sen·tial (ə sen′shəl), *adj.* 1 needed to make a thing what it is; necessary; very important. 2 of, like, or constituting the essence of a substance. 3 of the highest sort; in the highest sense: *essential happiness.* —*n.* an absolutely necessary element or quality; fundamental feature. [< Med.L *essentialis.* See ESSENCE.] —**es·sen′tial·ly,** *adv.* —**es·sen′tial·ness,** *n.*

-est, *suffix forming the superlative degree.* 1 of adjectives, as in *warmest.* 2 of adverbs, as in *slowest.*

E.S.T., EST, or **e.s.t.,** Eastern Standard Time.

es·tab·lish (es tab′lish), *v.* 1 set up permanently: *establish a business.* 2 settle in a position; set up in business. 3 bring about permanently; cause to be accepted: *establish a custom.* 4 show beyond dispute; prove: *establish a fact.* [< OF *establir* < L *stabilire* make STA-BLE[2]] —**es·tab′lish·er,** *n.*

established church, 1 church that is a national institution recognized and supported by the government. **2 Established Church,** =Church of England.

es·tab·lish·ment (es tab′lish mənt), *n.* 1 an establishing. 2 a being established. 3 something established; an institution. A household, business, church, or army is an establishment.

the Establishment, a ruling groups or institutions of a country; power structure. **b** powerful or influential people, as a group in an institution or in society.

es·tate (es tāt′), *n.* 1 a large piece of land belonging to a person; landed property. 2 that which a person owns; property; possessions. 3 condition or stage in life. [< OF < L *status* state]

es·teem (es tēm′), *v.* 1 have a favorable opinion of; regard highly. 2 think; consider. —*n.* a very favorable opinion; high regard. [< OF < L *aestimare* value]

es·ter (es tər), *n.* 1 compound in which the acid hydrogen of an acid is replaced by the organic radical of an alcohol. Animal and vegetable fats and oils are esters. 2 any salt containing a hydrocarbon radical.

Es·ther (es′tər), *n.* 1 the Jewish wife of a Persian king, who saved her people from massacre. 2 book of the Old Testament that tells her story.

es·ti·ma·ble (es′tə mə bəl), *adj.* 1 worthy of esteem; deserving high regard. 2 capable of being estimated or calculated. —**es′ti·ma·ble·ness,** *n.* —**es′ti·ma·bly,** *adv.*

es·ti·mate (*n.* es′tə mit; –māt; *v.* es′tə māt), *n., v.,* **–mat·ed, –mat·ing.** —*n.* 1 judgment or opinion about how much, how many, how good, etc. 2 statement of what certain work will cost, made by one willing to do the work. —*v.* 1 have an opinion of. 2 fix the worth, size, amount, etc., esp. in a rough way; calculate approximately. [< L *aestimatus,* pp. of *aestimare* value] —**es′ti·ma′tive,** *adj.* —**es′ti·ma′tor,** *n.*

es·ti·ma·tion (es′tə mā′shən), *n.* 1 judgment; opinion. 2 esteem; respect. 3 act or process of estimating.

Es·to·ni·a (es tō′ni ə), *n.* a small country in N Europe, on the Baltic Sea. —**Es·to′ni·an,** *adj., n.*

es·top (es top′), *v.,* **–topped, –top·ping.** 1 in law, prevent from asserting or doing something contrary to a previous assertion or act. 2 stop; bar; obstruct. [< OF, < *estoupe* tow < L *stuppa*]

es·top·pel (es top′əl), *n.* 1 legal prevention from asserting or doing something contrary to a previous assertion or act. 2 act or process of estopping.

es·trange (es trānj′), *v.,* **–tranged, –trang·ing.** 1 turn (a person) from affection to indifference, dislike, or hatred; make unfriendly; separate: *a quarrel had estranged him from his family.* 2 keep apart; keep away. [< OF < L, < *extraneus* STRANGE] —**es·trange′ment,** *n.* —**es·trang′er,** *n.*

es·tro·gen (es′trə jən), *n.* any of various hormones which induce a series of physiological changes in females, esp. in the reproductive or sexual organs. —**es′tro·gen′ic,** *adj.*

es·trous (es′trəs), *adj.* of or having to do with the estrus.

es·trus (es′trəs), *n.* periodic and regularly recurring period when females of the lower mammals are physiologically able to conceive and willing to mate. [< NL *estrus* ult. < Gk. *oîstros* gadfly]

es·tu·ar·y (es′chü er′i), *n., pl.* **-ar·ies.** 1 a broad mouth of a river into which the tide flows. 2 inlet of the sea. [< L, < *aestus* tide] —**es′tu·ar′i·al,** *adj.*

-et, *suffix.* little, as in *owlet, islet.* This meaning has disappeared in most words formed by adding *-et.* [< OF]

ETA, estimated time of arrival.

e·ta (ā′tə; ē′tə), *n.* the seventh letter of the Greek alphabet (H, η).

et al., 1 and elsewhere. 2 and others. [(def.1) < L *et alibi;* (def. 2) < L *et alii*]

etc., et cetera.

et cet·er·a (et set′ə rə; set′rə), and others; and the rest; and so forth; and so on; and the like [< L]

etch (ech), *v.* 1 engrave (a drawing or design) on metal, glass, etc., by means of acid. When filled with ink, the lines of the design will reproduce a copy on paper. 2 engrave a drawing or design on by means of acid. 3 make drawings or designs by this method. [< Du. < G *ätzen;* akin to EAT] —**etch′er,** *n.*

etch·ing (ech′ing), *n.* 1 picture or design printed from an etched plate. 2 an etched plate; etched drawing or design. 3 art of an etcher; process of engraving a drawing or design on metal, glass, etc., by means of acid.

ETD, estimated time of departure.

e·ter·nal (i tėr′nəl), *adj.* 1 without beginning or ending; lasting throughout all time. 2 always and forever the same. 3 seeming to go on forever; occurring very frequently. —*n.* the Eternal, God. [< L *aeternalis,* ult. < *aevum* age] —**e·ter′nal·ly,** *adv.* —**e·ter′nal·ness,** *n.*

Eternal City, the, Rome.

e·ter·ni·ty (i tėr′nə ti), *n., pl.* **-ties.** 1 time without beginning or ending; all time. 2 the endless period after death; future life. 3 a seemingly endless period of time.

eth·ane (eth′ān), *n.* a colorless, odorless, inflammable gas, C_2H_6. It is a hydrocarbon present in natural gas and illuminating gas.

eth·a·nol (eth′ə nōl, –nol), *n.* 1 =ethyl alcohol. 2 alcohol-based fuel made from grains, including corn, wheat, and barley, and often mixed with gasoline for use in automobiles. [< *ethane* + *–ol* derived from alcohol]

e·ther (ē′thər), *n.* 1 a colorless, strong-smelling liquid, $(C_2H_5)_2O$, that burns and evaporates readily. Its fumes cause unconsciousness when deeply inhaled. Ether is used as a solvent for fats and resins. 2 a the upper regions of space beyond the earth's atmosphere; clear sky. **b** the invisible, elastic substance formerly supposed to be in space. [< Gk. *aither* upper air]

e·the·re·al (i thir′i əl), *adj.* 1 light; airy; delicate: *ethereal beauty.* 2 not of the earth; heavenly. —**e·the′re·al′i·ty,** *n.* —**e·the′re·al·ly,** *adv.* —**e·the′re·al·ness,** *n.*

eth·ic (eth′ik), *adj.* =ethical. —*n.* ethics; system of ethics. [< L < Gk., < *ethos* moral character]

eth·i·cal (eth′ə kəl), *adj.* **1** having to do with standards of right and wrong; of ethics or morality. **2** in accordance with formal or professional rules of right and wrong. —**eth′i·cal′i·ty,** *n.* —**eth′i·cal·ly,** *adv.* —**eth′i·cal·ness,** *n.*

eth·ics (eth′iks), *n.* **1** (*sing. in use*) study of standards of right and wrong; that part of science and philosophy dealing with moral conduct, duty, and judgment. **2** (*pl. in use*) formal or professional rules of right and wrong; system of conduct or behavior.

E·thi·o·pi·a (ē′thi ō′pi ə), *n.* **1** country in E Africa. **2** an ancient region in NE Africa, S of Egypt.

E·thi·o·pi·an (ē′thi ō′pi ən), *adj.* of or having to do with Ethiopia or its people. —*n.* native or inhabitant of Ethiopia.

E·thi·op·ic (ē′thi op′ik; –ō′pik), *adj.* of or having to do with the ancient language of Ethiopia or the church using this language. —*n.* the ancient language of Ethiopia.

eth·nic (eth′nik) *adj.* **1** having to do with the various cultures, languages, and characteristics of different people, special to them. **2** of or having to do with people from another country or culture. **3** of or for ethnics. —*n.* member of an ethnic group. [< L <Gk., < *ethnos* nation] —**eth′ni·cal·ly,** *adv.*

ethnic cleansing, use of force and violence to clear a geographic area of an ethnic group.

eth·nic·i·ty (eth nis′ə ti), *n.* ethnic heritage; cultural or national background.

ethno–, *combining form.* people; nation; culture; as in *ethnocentric.*

eth·no·cen·tric (eth′nō sen′trik), *adj.* believing one's own culture or national origin superior to another. —**eth′no·cen′trism,** *n.*

eth·nog·ra·phy (eth nog′rə fi), *n.* the scientific description and classification of the various races of people. —**eth·nog′ra·pher,** *n.* —**eth′no·graph′ic, eth′no·graph′i·cal,** *adj.* —**eth′no·graph′i·cal·ly,** *adv.*

eth·nol·o·gy (eth nol′ə ji), *n.* science that deals with the various races of people, their origin, distribution, characteristics, customs, institutions, and culture. —**eth′no·log′ic, eth′no·log′i·cal,** *adj.* —**eth′no·log′ical·ly,** *adv.* —**eth·nol′o·gist,** *n.*

e·thos (ē′thos), *n.* **1** spirit or nature of a particular group, institution, etc. **2** qualities or characteristics that distinguish a particular culture or group. [< NL < Gk. *ethos* character, nature]

eth·yl (eth′əl), *n.* a univalent radical, $-C_2H_5$, in many organic compounds. Ordinary alcohol contains ethyl.

ethyl alcohol, ordinary alcohol, C_2H_5OH, made by the fermentation of grain, sugar, etc.

eth·yl·ene (eth′ə lēn), *n.* a colorless, inflammable gas, C_2H_4, with an unpleasant odor, used as a fuel and anesthetic, and for coloring and ripening citrus fruits.

e·ti·ol·o·gy (ē′ti ol′ə ji), *n.* **1** an assigning of a cause. **2** science that deals with origins or causes. **3** theory of the causes of disease. [< L < Gk., < *aitia* cause + –*logos* treating of] —**e′ti·o·log′i·cal,** *adj.* —**e′ti·o·log′i·cal·ly,** *adv.* —**e′ti·ol′o·gist,** *n.*

et·i·quette (et′ə ket), *n.* **1** conventional rules for conduct or behavior in polite society. **2** formal rules or conventions governing conduct in a profession, official ceremony, etc.: *medical etiquette.* [< F < Gmc.]

Et·na (et′nə), *n.* **Mount,** volcano in NE Sicily.

E·tru·ri·a (i trŭr′i ə) *n.* an ancient country in W Italy.

E·trus·can (i trŭs′kən), **E·tru·ri·an** (i trŭr′i ən), *adj.* of or having to do with Etruria, its people, their language, art, or customs. —*n.* **1** native or inhabitant of Etruria. **2** language of Etruria.

et seq., and the following; and that which follows. [< L *et sequens*]

–ette, *suffix.* **1** little, as in *kitchenette, statuette.* **2** female, as in *farmerette, suffragette.* **3** substitute for, as in *leatherette.* [< F, fem. of –*et* –ET]

é·tude (ā tüd′; ā tūd′), *n.* **1** piece of music intended to develop skill in technique. **2** such a composition intended for performance. [< F, study]

et·y·mol·o·gy (et ə mol′ə ji), *n., pl.* –**gies.** **1** account or explanation of the origin and history of a word. **2** a historical study dealing with linguistic changes, esp. a study dealing with individual word origins. [< L < Gk., < *etymon* the original sense or form of a word (neut. of *etymos* true, real) + –*logos* treating of] —**et′y·mo·log′i·cal,** *adj.* —**et′y·mo·log′i·cal·ly,** *adv.* —**et′y·mol′o·gist,** *n.*

eu–, *prefix.* good; well; true as in *eulogy, euphony.* [< Gk.]

EU, European Union.

Eu, europium.

eu·ca·lyp·tus (ū′kə lip′təs), *n., pl.* –**tus·es,** –**ti** (–tī). a very tall tree that originated in Australia. It is valued for its timber and for an oil made from its leaves. [< NL, < Gk. *eu–* well + *kalyptos* covered; with ref. to bud covering]

eu·car·y·ote (ū kar′i ōt), *n.* cell having a visible nucleus or an organism with visible nuclei. Also, **eukaryote.** [< *eu–* good, true + Gk. *káryon* nut, kernel]

Eu·cha·rist (ū′kə rist), *n.* **1** sacrament of the Lord's Supper; Holy Communion. **2** the consecrated bread and wine used in this sacrament. [< LL < Gk. *eucharistia* thankfulness, the Eucharist] —**Eu′cha·ris′tic,** *adj.*

eu·chre (ūkər), *n., v.,* –**chred,** –**chring,** —*n.* a simple card game for two, three, or four players, using the 32 (or 28, or 24) highest cards. —*v.* defeat (the side that declared the trump) at euchre.

Eu·clid (ū′klid), *n.* Greek mathematician who wrote a book on geometry about 300 B.C.

Eu·clid·e·an, Eu·clid·i·an (ū′klid′li ən), *adj.* of Euclid or his principles of geometry.

eu·gen·ic (u jen′ik), *adj.* **1** having to do with improvement of the race; improving the offspring produced; improving the race. **2** possessing good inherited characteristics. [< Gk. *eugenes* well-born < *eu–* well + *genos* birth] —**eu·gen′i·cal·ly,** *adv.*

eu·gen·ics (ū jen′iks), *n.* science of improving the human race. Eugenics would apply the same principles to human beings that have long been applied to animals and plants. —**eu·gen′i·cist,** *n.*

eu·lo·gist (ū′lə jist), *n.* person who eulogizes.

eu·lo·gis·tic (ū′lə jis′tik), *adj.* praising highly. —**eu′lo·gis′ti·cal·ly,** *adv.*

eu·lo·gize (ū′lə jīz), *v.,* –**gized,** –**giz·ing.** praise very highly. —**eu′lo·giz′er,** *n.*

eu·lo·gy (ū′lə ji), *n., pl.* –**gies.** speech or writing in praise of a person, action, etc.; high praise. [< Gk. *eulogia* < *eu–* well + *legein* speak]

eu·nuch (ū′nək), *n.* **1** a castrated man. **2** a castrated man in charge of a harem or the household of an Oriental ruler. [< L < Gk., < *eune* bed + *echein* keep]

eu·phe·mism (ū′fə miz əm), *n.* **1** use of a mild or indirect expression instead of one that is harsh or unpleasantly direct. **2** a mild or indirect expression used in this way. "Pass away" is a common euphemism for "die." [< Gk., < *eu–* good + *pheme* speaking] —**eu′phe·mist,** *n.* —**eu′phe·mis′tic,** *adj.* —**eu′phe·mis′ti·cal·ly,** *adv.*

eu·phe·mize (ū′fə mīz), *v.,* –**mized,** –**miz·ing. 1** employ euphemism. **2** express by euphemism. —**eu′phe·miz′er,** *n.*

eu·phon·ic (ū fon′ik), *adj.* **1** having to do with euphony. **2** euphonious. —**eu·phon′i·cal·ly,** *adv.* —**eu·phon′i·cal·ness,** *n.*

eu·pho·ni·ous (ū fō′ni əs), *adj.* sounding well; pleasing to the ear; harmonious. —**eu·pho′ni·ous·ly,** *adv.* —**eu·pho′ni·ous·ness,** *n.*

eu·pho·ni·um (ū fō′ni əm), *n.* a brass musical instrument like a tuba, having a loud, deep tone.

eu·pho·ny (ū′fə ni), *n., pl.* –**nies. 1** agreeableness of sound; pleasing effect to the ear; agreeableness of speech sounds as uttered or combined in utterance. **2** tendency to change sounds so as to favor ease of utterance. [< LL < Gk., < *eu–* good + *phone* sound]

eu·phor·bi·a (ū fôr′bi ə), *n.* any of a genus of plants with acrid, milky juice and small, inconspicuous flowers; spurge. Some euphorbias resemble cacti. [< L, < *Euphorbus*, a Greek physician]

eu·pho·ri·a (ū fô′ri ə; –fō′–), *n.* sense of well-being and expansiveness. [< NL < Gk., < *eu* well + *pherein* to bear] —**euphor′ic,** *adj.*

Eu·phra·tes (ū frā′tēz), *n.* river in SW Asia, flowing from E Turkey into the Persian Gulf. It joins the Tigris River in Iraq.

Eur., Europe; European.

Eur·a·sia (yùr ā′zhə; –shə), *n.* Europe and Asia. —**Eur·a′sian,** *adj., n.*

eu·re·ka (yù rē′kə), *interj.* I have found it! (the motto of California). [< Gk.]

Eu·rip·i·des (yù rip′ə dēz), *n.* 480?–406? B.C., Greek tragic poet.

eu·ro (yùr′ō), currency of the European Union.

Euro- or **euro-,** *combining form.* European, esp. of the European Union, as in *Eurodollar.*

Eu·ro·bank (yùr′ō bangk′), *n.* bank of the European Union. esp. the central bank.

Eu·ro·dol·lar (yùr′ō dol′ər), *n.* a U.S. dollar held by banks and financial institutions of the European Union.

Eu·rope (yùr′əp), *n.* continent W of Asia.

Eu·ro·pe·an (yùr′ə pē′ən), *adj.* of or having to do with Europe or its people. —*n.* native or inhabitant of Europe.

European Community, former name of the European Union.

Eu·ro·pe·an·ize (yùr′ə pē′ən īz), *v.,* –**ized,** –**iz·ing.** make European in appearance, habit, way of life, etc.

European plan, system of charges to guests in a hotel by which the price covers the room, but not the meals (distinguished from *American plan*).

European Union, economic, political, and social union of European countries, founded in 1993, formerly called the European Community.

eu·ro·pi·um (yù rō′pi əm), *n.* a rare metallic element, Eu, of the same group as cerium. [< NL, < L *Europa* Europe < Gk.]

Eu·ryd·i·ce (yù rid′ə sē), *n.* Gk. Myth. the wife of Orpheus, who freed her from Hades by the charm of his music, but lost her again when he turned back to see if she was following.

Eu·sta·chi·an tube (ū stā′ki ən; –stā′shən), a slender canal between the pharynx and the middle ear.

Eu·ter·pe (ū tèr′pē), *n.* the Greek Muse of music and lyric song.

eu·tha·na·sia (ū′thə nā′zhə), *n.* a painless killing, esp. to end a painful and incurable disease. [< Gk., < *eu*– easy + *thanatos* death]

eu·tro·phi·ca·tion (ū′trə fə kā′shən), *n.* too great an amount of nutrients in ponds, lakes, etc., causing excess growth of algae and plants and a reduction of oxygen in the water. [< Gk. *eutrophos* thriving, nourishing]

Eux·ine Sea (ūk′sin), an ancient name for the Black Sea.

ev, eV or **EV,** electron volt.

e·vac·u·ate (i vak′yù āt), *v.,* –**at·ed,** –**at·ing.** 1 leave empty; withdraw from: *the soldiers evacuated the fort.* 2 withdraw; remove: *evacuate flood victims.* 3 make empty: *evacuate the bowels.* [< L, < *ex*– out + *vacuus* empty] —**e·vac′u·a′tion,** *n.* —**e·vac′u·a′tor,** *n.*

e·vac·u·ee (i vak′yù ē; i vak′yù ē′), *n.* one who is removed to a place of greater safety.

e·vade (i vād′), *v.,* **e·vad·ed, e·vad·ing.** 1 get away from by trickery; avoid by cleverness. 2 elude [< L, < *ex*– away + *vadere* go] —**e·vad′a·ble, e·vad′i·ble,** *adj.* —**e·vad′er,** *n.* —**e·vad′ing·ly,** *adv.*

e·val·u·ate (i val′yù āt), *v.,* –**at·ed,** –**at·ing.** find the value or the amount of; fix the value of. —**e·val′u·a′tion, e·val′u·a′tor,** *n.*

ev·a·nesce (ev′ə nes′), *v.,* –**nesced,** –**nesc·ing.** disappear; fade away; vanish. [< L *evanescere* < *ex*– out + *vanus* insubstantial]

ev·a·nes·cence (ev′ə nes′əns), *n.* 1 gradual disappearance; vanishing. 2 tendency not to last long: *evanescence of the northern lights.*

ev·a·nes·cent (ev′ə nes′ənt), *adj.* tending to disappear or fade away; able to last only a short time. —**ev′a·nes′cent·ly,** *adv.*

e·van·gel·i·cal (ē′van jel′ə kəl; ev′ən–), *adj.* Also, **e′van·gel′ic.** 1 of, concerning, or according to the four Gospels or the New Testament. 2 of or having to do with the Protestant churches that emphasize Christ's atonement and salvation by faith as the most important parts of Christianity, as the Methodists and Baptists. 3 evangelistic. —*n.* 1 an adherent of evangelical doctrines. 2 member of an evangelical church.[E *evangel* + –*ical, evangel* < LL, < Gk. *evangelion* good tidings, ult. < *eu*– good + *angellein* announce] —**e′van·gel′i·cal·ism,** *n.* —**e′van·gel′i·cal·ly,** *adv.*

e·van·ge·lism (i van′jə liz əm), *n.* 1 a preaching of the Gospel; earnest effort for the spread of the Gospel. 2 work of an evangelist. 3 belief in the doctrines of an evangelical church or party.

e·van·ge·list (i van′jə list), *n.* 1 preacher of the Gospel. 2 a traveling preacher who stirs up religious feeling in revival services or camp meetings. 3 **Evangelist,** any of the writers of the four Gospels; Matthew, Mark, Luke, or John. —**e·van′ge·lis′tic, e·van′ge·lis′ti·cal,** *adj.* —**e·van′ge·lis′ti·cal·ly,** *adv.*

e·van·ge·lize (i van′jə līz), *v.,* –**lized,** –**liz·ing.** 1 preach the Gospel to. 2 convert to Christianity by preaching. —**e·van′ge·li·za′tion,** *n.* —**e·van′ge·liz′er,** *n.*

e·vap·o·rate (i vap′ə rāt), *v.,* –**rat·ed,** –**rat·ing.** 1 change from a liquid or solid into a vapor. 2 remove water or other liquid from: *heat is used to evaporate milk.* 3 give off moisture. 4 vanish; disappear. [< L, < *ex*– out + *vapor* VAPOR] —**e·vap′o·ra′tion,** *n.* —**e·vap′o·ra′tive,** *adj.* —**e·vap′o·ra′tor,** *n.*

e·va·sion (i vā′zhən), *n.* 1 a getting away from something by trickery; an avoiding by cleverness. 2 an attempt to escape an argument, a charge, a question, etc. 3 means of evading; trick or excuse used to avoid something.

e·va·sive (i vā′siv; –ziv), *adj.* tending or trying to evade. "Perhaps" is an evasive answer. —**e·va′sive·ly,** *adv.* —**e·va′sive·ness,** *n.*

eve (ēv), *n.* 1 evening or day before a holiday or some other special day: *Christmas Eve.* 2 time just before. 3 *Poetic.* evening. [var. of *even²*]

Eve (ēv), *n.* in the Bible, the first woman, Adam's wife.

e·ven¹ (ē′vən), *adj.* 1 level; flat; smooth. 2 at the same level. 3 regular; uniform. 4 equal. 5 leaving no remainder when divided by 2. 6 exact. —*v.* make even. —*adv.* 1 evenly. 2 just; exactly. 3 indeed. 4 fully; quite: *faithful even unto death.* 5 though one would not expect it: *even the least noise disturbs her.* 6 still; yet

break even, have equal gains and losses.

even if, in spite of the fact that.

even out, become level; balance.

even though, although.

get even, get revenge.

e·ven² (ē′vən), *n. Poetic.* evening. [OE *æfen*]

e·ven·hand·ed (ē′vən han′did), *adj.* impartial; fair; just.

eve·ning (ēv′ning), *n.* 1 the last part of day and early part of night; time between sunset and bedtime. 2 *S U.S.* afternoon. 3 the last part: *the evening of life.* —*adj.* in the evening; of the evening; for the evening. [OE *æfnung* < *æfnian* become evening < *æfen* evening]

evening dress, 1 formal clothes for evening. 2 woman's formal clothing, esp. a long dress.

evening primrose, a tall plant with spikes of fragrant yellow or white flowers that open in the evening.

evening star, a bright planet seen in the western sky after sunset.

e·ven·song (ē′vən sông′; –song′), *n.* a church service said or sung in the late afternoon or early evening; vespers.

e·vent (i vent′), *n.* 1 a happening. 2 result; outcome. 3 item or contest in a program of sports.

at or **in all events,** in any case; whatever happens.

in any event, in any case; anyhow.

in the event of, in case of.

in the event that, if it should happen that. [< L, < *ex*– out + *venire* come]

e·ven-tem·pered (ē′vən tem′pərd), *adj.* not easily disturbed or angered; calm.

e·vent·ful (i vent′fəl), *adj.* 1 full of events; having many unusual events. 2 having important results; important. —**e·vent′ful·ly,** *adv.* —**e·vent′ful·ness,** *n.*

example 223

e·vent·ing (i ven′ting), *n.* equestrian competition, which includes dressage, jumping, etc.

e·ven·tu·al (i ven′chù əl), *adj.* **1** coming in the end; final. **2** depending on uncertain events; possible. —**e·ven′tu·al·ly,** *adv.*

e·ven·tu·al·i·ty (i ven′chù al′ə ti), *n., pl.* **-ties.** a possible occurrence or condition; possibility.

e·ven·tu·ate (i ven′chù āt), *v.,* **-at·ed, -at·ing.** come out in the end; happen finally; result.

ev·er (ev′ər), *adv.* **1** at any time: *was there ever a man with such bad luck.* **2** at all times: *ever at your service.* **3** continuously: *ever since.* **4** at all; by any chance; in any case.

ever so, very: *ever so cold today.* [OE *ǣfre*]

Ev·er·est (ev′ər ist), *n.* **Mount,** peak in the Himalayas in S Tibet, the highest in the world.

ev·er·glade (ev′ər glād′), *n.* **1** a large tract of low, wet ground partly covered with tall grass; large swamp or marsh. **2 Everglades,** a swampy region in S Florida.

ev·er·green (ev′ər grēn′), *adj.* having green leaves all the year. —*n.* **1** an evergreen plant, as pine, spruce, cedar, ivy, etc. **2 evergreens,** evergreen twigs or branches used for decoration, esp. at Christmas; greens.

ev·er·last·ing (ev′ər las′ting; -läs′-), *adj.* **1** lasting forever. **2** lasting a long time. **3** lasting too long; tiresome. —*n.* **1** eternity. **2** flower that keeps its shape and color when dried.

the Everlasting, God. —**ev′er·last′ing·ly,** *adv.* —**ev′er·last′ing·ness,** *n.*

ev·er·more (ev′ər môr′; -môr′), *adv., n.* always; forever.

e·ver·sion (i vėr′zhən; -shən), *n.* a turning of an organ, structure, etc., inside out. —**e·ver′si·ble,** *adj.*

e·vert (i vėrt′), *v.* turn inside out. [< L, < *ex-* out + *vertere* turn]

eve·ry (ev′ri), *adj.* **1** all, regarded singly or separately; each and all. **2** all possible: *we showed him every consideration.*

every last, all; every one.

every now and then, from time to time.

every other, each first, third, fifth, etc., or second, fourth, sixth, etc. [< OE *ǣfre* ever + *ǣlc* each]

eve·ry·bod·y (ev′ri bod′i), *pron.* every person; everyone: *everybody likes the new teacher.*

eve·ry·day (ev′ri dā′), *adj.* **1** of every day; daily. **2** for every ordinary day; not for Sundays or holidays. **3** not exciting; usual. —**eve′ry·day′ness,** *n.*

eve·ry·one (ev′ri wun; -wən), *pron.* every person; everybody: *everyone took his purchases home.*

eve·ry·place (ev′ri plās), *adv.* =everywhere.

eve·ry·thing (ev′ri thing), *pron.* every thing; all things. —*n.* something extremely important; very important thing.

eve·ry·where (ev′ri hwãr), *adv.* in every place; in all places.

e·vict (i vikt′), *v.* expel by a legal process from land, a building, etc.; eject (a tenant). [< L *evictus* < *ex-* out + *vincere* conquer] —**e·vic′tion,** *n.* —**e·vic′tor,** *n.*

ev·i·dence (ev′ə dəns), *n., v.,* **-denced, -denc·ing.** —*n.* **1** whatever makes clear the truth or falsehood of something. **2** facts established and accepted in a court of law. **3** person who gives testimony in a court of law; witness: *state's evidence.* **4** indication; sign. —*v.* make easy to see or understand; show clearly; prove.

in evidence, easily seen or noticed.

turn state's evidence, (of someone involved in a crime) offer to be a witness against another or others also involved in the crime. [< L, < *ex-* out + *videns,* ppr. of *videre* to see]

ev·i·dent (ev′ə dənt), *adj.* easy to see or understand; clear; plain. —**ev′i·den′tial,** *adj.* —**ev′i·dent·ly,** *adv.*

e·vil (ē′vəl), *adj.* **1** bad; wrong; sinful; wicked. **2** causing harm or injury. —*n.* **1** something bad; sin; wickedness. **2** thing that causes harm or injury. —*adv.* badly. [OE *yfel*] —**e′vil·ly,** *adv.* —**e′vil·ness,** *n.*

e·vil·do·er (ē′vəl dü′ər), *n.* person who does evil. —**e′vil·do′ing,** *n.*

evil eye, the supposed power of causing harm or bringing bad luck to others by looking at them.

e·vil-mind·ed (ē′vəl mīn′did), *adj.* having an evil mind; wicked; malicious.

e·vince (i vins′), *v.,* **e·vinced, e·vinc·ing.** **1** show clearly; reveal. **2** show that one has (a quality, trait, etc.). [< L, < *ex-* out + *vincere* conquer] —**e·vin′ci·ble, e·vin′cive,** *adj.*

e·vis·cer·ate (i vis′ər āt), *v.,* **-at·ed, -at·ing.** **1** remove the bowels from; disembowel. **2** deprive of something essential. [< L, < *ex-* out + *viscera* VISCERA] —**e·vis′cer·a′tion,** *n.*

e·voke (i vōk′), *v.,* **e·voked, e·vok·ing.** call forth; bring out. [< L, < *ex-* out + *vocare* call] —**ev′o·ca′tion** *n.* —**e·vok′er,** *n.*

ev·o·lu·tion (ev′ə lü′shən), *n.* **1** any process of formation or growth; gradual development: *the evolution of modern chemistry from alchemy.* **2** theory that all living things developed from a few simple forms of life. **3** movement that is a part of a definite plan, design, or series. —**ev′o·lu′tion·ar′y, ev′o·lu′tion·al,** *adj.* —**ev′o·lu′tion·al·ly,** *adv.*

ev·o·lu·tion·ist (ev′ə lü′shən ist), *n.* student of, or believer in, the theory of evolution.

e·volve (i volv′), *v.,* **e·volved, e·volv·ing.** **1** develop gradually; work out. **2** develop by a process of growth and change to a more highly organized condition. [< L, < *ex-* out + *volvere* roll] —**e·volv′er,** *n.*

ewe (ū), *n.* a female sheep. [OE *ēowu*]

ew·er (ū′ər), *n.* a widemouthed water pitcher. [< AF < VL *aquaria* < L *aquarius* for drawing water < *aqua* water]

ex (eks), *n.* former wife, husband, or partner.

ex-, *prefix.* **1** out of; from; out, as in *exclude, exit, export.* **2** utterly; thoroughly, as in *excruciating, exasperate.* **3** former; formerly, as in *ex-member, ex-president, ex-soldier.* [< L *ex-* out of, without; also, *e-* (before *b, d, g, h, l, m, n, r, v*), and *ef-* (before *f*)]

Ex., Exodus.

ex., **1** example. **2** except.

ex·ac·er·bate (ig zas′ər bāt; ek sas′-), *v.,* **-bat·ed, -bat·ing.** **1** make a condition worse, as pain, discomfort, disease, etc. **2** irritate (feelings). —**ex·ac′er·ba′tion,** *n.*

ex·act (ig zakt′), *adj.* **1** without any error or mistake; strictly correct. **2** strict; severe; rigorous. —*v.* **1** demand and get; force to be paid. [< L *exactus,* pp. of *exigere* weigh accurately < *ex-* out + *agere* weigh] —**ex·act′a·ble,** *adj.* —**ex·act′er, ex·ac′tor,** *n.* —**ex·act′ness,** *n.*

ex·act·ing (ig zak′ting), *adj.* **1** requiring much; making severe demands; hard to please. **2** requiring effort, care, or attention. —**ex·act′ing·ly,** *adv.* —**ex·act′ing·ness,** *n.*

ex·ac·tion (ig zak′shən), *n.* **1** an exacting. **2** thing exacted, as taxes, fees, etc.

ex·ac·ti·tude (ig zak′tə tüd; -tud), *n.* exactness.

ex·act·ly (ig zakt′li), *adv.* **1** in an exact manner; accurately; precisely. **2** just so; quite right.

ex·ag·ger·ate (ig zaj′ər āt), *v.,* **-at·ed, -at·ing.** **1** make (something) greater than it is; overstate: *exaggerate a misfortune.* **2** increase or enlarge abnormally. **3** say or think something is greater than it is. [< L, < *ex-* out, up + *agger* heap] —**ex·ag′ger·at′ed,** *adj.* —**ex·ag′ger·a′tion,** *n.* —**ex·ag′ger·a′tor,** *n.*

ex·alt (ig zôlt′), *v.* **1** raise in rank, honor, power, character, quality, etc. **2** fill with pride, joy, or noble feeling. **3** praise; honor; glorify. [< L, < *ex-* out, up + *altus* high] —**ex·alt′ed·ly,** *adv.* —**ex·alt′er,** *n.*

ex·al·ta·tion (eg′zôl tā′shən), *n.* **1** an exalting. **2** a being exalted. **3** lofty emotion; rapture.

ex·am (ig zam′), *n.* examination.

ex·am·i·na·tion (ig zam′ə nā′shən), *n.* **1** an examining or being examined. **2** test of knowledge or qualifications; list of questions. **3** answers given in such a test. **4** *Law.* a formal interrogation.

ex·am·ine (ig zam′ən), *v.,* **-ined, -in·ing.** **1** look at closely and carefully. **2** test the knowledge or qualifications of; ask questions of. [< F < L *examinare* < *examen* a weighing. See EXACT.] —**ex·am′in·a·ble,** *adj.* —**ex·am′in·er,** *n.*

ex·am·i·nee (ig zam′ə nē′), *n.* person who is being examined.

ex·am·ple (ig zam′pəl; -zäm′-), *n., v.,* **-pled, -pling.** —*n.* **1** one taken to show what others are like; case that shows something; sample. **2** person or thing to be imitated; model; pattern. **3** warning to others: *make an example of rioters by* *arresting the leaders.* —*v.* **1** be an example of; exemplify. **2** set an example to. [< OF < L *exemplum.* See EXEMPT.]

ex·as·per·ate (ig zas′pər āt; –zäs′–), *v.*, **–at·ed, –at·ing.** irritate very much; annoy extremely; make angry. [< L, < *ex–* thoroughly + *asper* rough] —**ex·as′per·at′er**, *n.* —**ex·as′per·at′ing·ly**, *adv.*

ex·as·per·a·tion (ig zas′pər ā′shən; –zäs′–), *n.* extreme annoyance; irritation; anger.

exc., 1 excellent. **2** except.

Exc., Excellency.

Ex·cal·i·bur (eks kal′ə bər), *n.* the magic sword of King Arthur.

ex ca·the·dra (eks kə thē′drə; kath′ə–), *Latin.* with authority; from the seat of authority.

ex·ca·vate (eks′kə vāt), *v.*, **–vat·ed, –vat·ing. 1** make hollow; hollow out. **2** make by digging; dig. **3** dig out; scoop out. **4** get or uncover by digging. [<L, < *ex–* out + *cavus* hollow] —**ex′ca·va′tion**, *n.* —**ex′ca·va′tor**, *n.*

ex·ceed (ik sēd′), *v.* **1** go beyond; overstep. **2** be more or greater than others; surpass. [< F < L, < *ex–* out + *cedere* go] —**ex·ceed′er**, *n.*

ex·ceed·ing (ik sēd′ing), *adj.* surpassing; very great; unusual; extreme. —**ex·ceed′-ing·ly**, *adv.*

ex·cel (ik sel′), *v.*, **–celled, –cel·ling. 1** be better than; do better than. **2** be better than others; do better than others. [< F < L *excellere*)

ex·cel·lence (ek′sə ləns), *n.* **1** a being better than others; superiority. **2** an excellent quality or feature.

ex·cel·len·cy (ek′sə lən si), *n.*, *pl.* **–cies**, excellence.

Excellency, title of honor used in speaking to or of a president, governor, ambassador, bishop, etc.

ex·cel·lent (ek′sə lənt), *adj.* unusually good; better than others. —**ex′cel·lent-ly**, *adv.*

ex·cel·si·or (*adj.* ik sel′si ôr; *n.* ik sel′-si ər), *adj.* ever upward; higher. —*n.* short, thin, curled shavings of soft wood. [< L, comparative of *excelsus* high, pp. of *excellere* excel]

ex·cept (ik sept′), *prep.* Also, **ex·cept′-ing.** leaving out; other than. —*v.* **1** take out; leave out; exclude: *present company excepted.* **2** make objection.

except for a with the exception of: *everyone laughed except for me.* **b** were it not for: *except for the rain, a perfect day.* [< L *exceptus* < *ex–* out + *capere* take]

ex·cep·tion (ik sep′shən), *n.* **1** a leaving out. **2** person or thing left out. **3** an unusual instance; case that does not follow the rule. **4** objection.

take exception, a object. **b** be offended.

ex·cep·tion·a·ble (ik sep′shən ə bəl), *adj.* objectionable. —**ex·cep′tion·a·bly**, *adv.*

ex·cep·tion·al (ik sep′shən əl), *adj.* out of the ordinary; unusual. —**ex·cep′tion-al·ly**, *adv.*

ex·cerpt (*n.* ek′sėrpt; *v.* ik sėrpt′), *n.* a selected passage; quotation. —*v.* take out; select (a passage) from; quote. [< L *excerptum* < *ex–* out + *carpere* pluck]

ex·cess (*n.* ik ses′; *adj.* ek′ses, ik ses′), *n.* **1** more than enough; part that is too much. **2** amount or degree by which one thing is more than another. **3** action that goes beyond what is necessary or just. —*adj.* extra: *excess baggage.*

in excess of, more than.

to excess, too much: *party to excess.* [< L *excessus* < *ex–* out + *cedere* go; akin to EXCEED]

ex·ces·sive (ik ses′iv), *adj.* too much; too great; going beyond what is necessary or right. —**ex·ces′sive·ly**, *adv.* —**ex·ces′-sive·ness**, *n.*

exch., 1 exchange. **2** exchequer.

ex·change (iks chānj′), *v.*, **–changed, –chang·ing,** *n.* —*v.* **1** give (for something else). **2** give and take (one thing in return for another); change for another. **3** be taken in a trade. —*n.* **1** an exchanging. **2** what is exchanged. **3** place where things are exchanged. Stocks are bought, sold, and traded in a stock exchange. **4** varying rate or sum in one currency given for a fixed sum in another currency. [< OF < VL, < *ex–* out + *cambiare* change<Celtic] —**ex·change′a·ble**, *adj.* —**ex·change′a·bil′i·ty**, *n.* —**ex·chang′er**, *n.*

exchange rate, amount that one country's currency is worth in terms of another's: *exchange rate of $1.20 for one euro.*

exchange student, student participating in a program of trading students between countries or institutions.

ex·cheq·uer (iks chek′ər; eks′chek ər), *n.* **1** treasury of a state or nation. **2** treasury. **3 Exchequer,** department of the British government in charge of its finances and the public revenues. [< OF *eschequier* chessboard; because accounts were kept on a table marked in squares]

ex·cise¹ (ek′sīz; –sīs; ik sīz′), *n.* tax on the manufacture, sale, or use of certain articles made, sold, or used within a country. [appar. < MDu. < OF *acceis* tax, ult. < L *ad–* to + *census* tax]

ex·cise² (ik sīz′), *v.*, **–cised, –cis·ing.** cut out; remove. [< L *excisus* < *ex–* out + *caedere* cut] —**ex·cis′a·ble**, *adj.* —**ex·ci′sion**, *n.*

ex·cit·a·ble (ik sīt′ə bəl), *adj.* capable of being excited; easily excited. —**ex·cit′a-bil′i·ty, ex·cit′a·ble·ness**, *n.* —**ex·cit′a-bly**, *adv.*

ex·ci·ta·tion (ek′sī tə′shən), *n.* **1** an exciting. **2** a being excited.

ex·cite (ik sīt′), *v.*, **–cit·ed, –cit·ing. 1** stir up the feelings of. **2** arouse. **3** stir to action; stimulate. [< L *excitare*, ult. < *ex–* out + *ciere* set in motion] —**ex·cit′ed**, *adj.* —**ex·cit′ed·ly**, *adv.* —**ex·cit′er**, *n.*

ex·cite·ment (ik sīt′mənt), *n.* **1** an exciting; arousing. **2** state of being excited. **3** thing that excites.

ex·cit·ing (ik sīt′ing), *adj.* arousing; stirring. —**ex·cit′ing·ly**, *adv.*

ex·claim (iks klām′), *v.* say or speak suddenly in surprise or strong feeling; cry out. [< F < L, < *ex–* + *clamare* cry out] —**ex·claim′er**, *n.*

ex·cla·ma·tion (eks′klə mā′shən), *n.* **1** an exclaiming. **2** thing exclaimed. *Ah!* and *oh!* are exclamations. —**ex·clam′a·to′ry**, *adj.*

exclamation mark or **point,** punctuation mark (!) that shows a word, phrase, etc., was exclaimed.

ex·clude (iks klüd′), *v.*, **–clud·ed, –clud·ing. 1** shut out; keep out. **2** drive out and keep out; expel. [< L *excludere* < *ex–* out + *claudere* shut] —**ex·clud′a·ble**, *adj.* —**ex·clud′er**, *n.* —**ex·clu′sion**, *n.*

ex·clu·sive (iks klü′siv; –ziv), *adj.* **1** shutting out all others. **2** each shutting out the other: *exclusive terms.* **3** not divided or shared with others; single; sole: *an exclusive right.* **4** very particular about choosing friends, members, patrons, etc.: *an exclusive club.* —**ex·clu′sive·ly**, *adv.* —**ex·clu′sive·ness**, *n.*

ex·com·mu·ni·cate (eks′kə mū′nə kāt), *v.*, **–cat·ed, –cat·ing.** cut off from membership in a church; —**ex′com·mu′ni-ca′tion**, *n.* —**ex′com·mu′ni·ca′tor**, *n.*

ex·co·ri·ate (iks kô′ri āt; –kō′–), *v.*, **–at-ed, –at·ing.** denounce violently. [< LL, < *ex–* off + *corium* hide, skin] —**ex-co′ri·a′tion**, *n.*

ex·cre·ment (eks′krə mənt), *n.* waste matter discharged from the bowels. [< L *excrementum*, ult. < *ex–* out + *cernere* sift] —**ex′cre·men′tal**, *adj.*

ex·cres·cence (iks kres′əns), **ex·cres·cen-cy** (–ən si), *n.*, *pl.* **–cen·ces; –cies**, an unnatural growth; disfiguring addition, as a wart. [< L, < *ex–* out + *crescere* grow] —**ex·cres′cent**, *adj.*

ex·crete (iks krēt′), *v.*, **–cret·ed, –cret·ing.** discharge (waste matter) from the body; separate (waste matter) from the blood or tissues. [< L *excretus*, pp. See EXCRE-MENT.] —**ex·cre′tion**, *n.* —**ex·cre′tive, ex′cre·to′ry**, *adj.*

ex·cru·ci·ate (iks krü′shi āt), *v.*, **–at·ed, –at·ing.** crucify; torture. [< L *excruciatus* < *ex–* utterly + *cruciare* to torture < *crux* cross] —**ex·cru′ci·at′ing**, *adj.* —**ex·cru′ci·at′ing·ly**, *adv.*

ex·cul·pate (eks′kul pāt; iks kul′–), *v.*, **–pat·ed, –pat·ing.** free from blame; prove innocent. [< L *ex–* out + *culpa* guilt] —**ex′cul·pa′tion**, *n.* —**ex·cul′pa-to′ry**, *adj.*

ex·cur·sion (iks kėr′zhən; –shən), *n.* **1** a short journey made with the intention of returning; pleasure trip. **2** a wandering from the subject; deviation; digression. [< L *excursio* < *ex–* out + *currere* run] —**ex·cur′sion·ist**, *n.*

ex·cur·sive (iks kėr′siv), *adj.* off the subject; wandering; rambling. —**ex·cur′sive-ly**, *adv.* —**ex·cur′sive·ness**, *n.*

ex·cuse (*v.* iks kūz′; *n.* iks kūs′), *v.*, **–cused, –cus·ing**, *n.* —*v.* **1** overlook (a fault, etc.);

pardon; forgive. **2** give a reason or apology for; try to clear of blame. **3** be a reason or explanation for; clear of blame. **4** free from duty or obligation; let off. —*n.* **1** a real or pretended reason or explanation. **2** act of excusing.

excuse oneself, a ask to be pardoned. **b** ask to be allowed to leave. [< OF < L *excusare* < *ex-* away + *causa* cause] —**ex·cus'a·ble,** *adj.* —**ex·cus'a·bly,** *adv.* —**ex·cus'er,** *n.*

ex·ec (ig zek'), *n. Informal.* executive.

exec., executive; executor.

ex·e·cra·ble (ek'sə krə bəl), *adj.* abominable; detestable. —**ex'e·cra·bly,** *adv.*

ex·e·crate (ek'sə krāt), *v.,* **-crat·ed, -crat·ing. 1** abhor; loathe; detest. **2** curse. [< L *execratus,* ult. < *ex-* completely + *sacer* accursed] —**ex'e·cra'tion,** *n.* —**ex'e·cra'tive,** *adj.* —**ex'e·cra'tor,** *n.*

ex·e·cute (ek'sə kūt), *v.,* **-cut·ed, -cut·ing. 1** carry out; do. **2** put into effect; enforce. **3** put to death according to law. **4** make according to a plan or design. **5** make (a deed, contract, etc.) legal by signing, sealing, or doing whatever is necessary. [< Med.L *executare,* ult. < L *ex-* out + *sequi* follow] —**ex'e·cut'a·ble,** *adj.* —**ex'e·cut'er,** *n.*

ex·e·cu·tion (ek'sə kū'shən), *n.* **1** an executing. **2** a being executed. **3** mode or style of performance. **4** infliction of capital punishment. **5** effective action.

ex·e·cu·tion·er (ek'sə kū'shən ər), *n.* person who puts criminals to death according to law.

ex·ec·u·tive (ig zek'yə tiv), *adj.* **1** having to do with carrying out or managing affairs. **2** having the duty and power of putting the laws into effect. —*n.* **1** person who carries out or manages affairs. **2** person, group, or branch of government that has the duty and power of putting the laws into effect. **3** Usually, **Executive.** the President of the United States.

the Executive, executive branch of the U.S. government. —**ex·ec'u·tive·ly,** *adv.*

Executive Mansion, the White House in Washington, D.C.

executive privilege, *U.S.* right not to testify in court or before Congress, asserted by members of the executive branch of the Federal government to protect them from having to reveal national secrets, private meetings, etc.

executive session, meeting of a legislative body that is closed to the public, usually to consider sensitive matters.

ex·ec·u·tor (ig zek'yə tər *for 1;* ek'sə kū'tər *for 2*), *n.* **1** person named in a will to carry out the provisions of the will. **2** person who executes plans, laws, etc. —**ex·ec'u·to'ri·al,** *adj.*

ex·ec·u·trix (ig zek'yə triks), *n., pl.* **ex·ec·u·tri·ces** (ig zek'yə trī'sēz), **ex·ec·u·trix·es.** a woman executor.

ex·e·ge·sis (ek'sə jē'sis), *n., pl.* **-ses** (-sēz). **1** a scholarly explanation or interpretation of the Bible. **2** an explanatory note. [< Gk., < *ex-* out + *hegeesthai* lead,

guide] —**ex'e·get'ic,** *adj.* —**ex'e·get'i·cal·ly,** *adv.*

ex·em·plar (ig zem'plər; -plär), *n.* **1** model; pattern. **2** a typical case; example.

ex·em·pla·ry (ig zem'plə ri; eg'zəm pler'i), *adj.* **1** being a good model or pattern: *exemplary conduct.* **2** serving as a warning to others: *exemplary punishment.* **3** serving as an example; typical. [< L *exemplaris.* See EXAMPLE.] —**ex·em'pla·ri·ly,** *adv.* —**ex·em'pla·ri·ness,** *n.*

ex·em·pli·fy (ig zem'plə fī), *v.,* **-fied, -fy·ing.** show by example; be an example of. —**ex·em'pli·fi·ca'tion,** *n.*

ex·em·pli gra·ti·a (ig zem'plī grā'shi ə), *Latin.* for example; for instance.

ex·empt (ig zempt'), *v.* free from a duty, obligation, rule, etc., to which others are subject; release. —*adj.* freed from a duty, obligation, rule, etc.; released. —*n.* an exempt person. [< L *exemptus* < *ex-* out + *emere* take] —**ex·empt'i·ble,** *adj.* —**ex·emp'tion,** *n.*

ex·er·cise (ek'sər sīz), *n., v.,* **-cised, -cis·ing.** —*n.* **1** active use to give practice and training or to cause improvement. **2** thing that gives practice and training or causes improvement. —*v.* **1** give exercise to; train. **2** take exercise. **3** carry out in action; perform. **4** make uneasy; annoy. **exercises, a** physical regimen; activities; *do exercises daily.* **b** ceremony: *graduation exercises.* [< OF < L *exercitium* < *exercere* not allow to rest < *ex-* + *arcere* keep away] —**ex'er·cis'a·ble,** *adj.* —**ex'er·cis'er,** *n.*

ex·ert (ig zėrt'), *v.* use actively; put into action. [< L, thrust out, < *ex-* out + *serere* attach] —**ex·er'tive,** *n.*

ex·er·tion (ig zėr'shən), *n.* **1** effort. **2** a putting into use; active use; use.

ex·hale (eks hāl'), *v.,* **-haled, -hal·ing. 1** breathe out. **2** give off (air, vapor, smoke, odor, etc.). [< F < L, < *ex-* out + *halare* breathe] —**ex'ha·la'tion,** *n.*

ex·haust (ig zôst'), *v.* **1** empty completely. **2** use up. **3** tire very much. **4** draw off: *exhaust the air in a jar.* **5** leave nothing important to be found out or said about; study or treat thoroughly. —*n.* **1** the escape of used steam, gasoline, etc., from a machine. **2** means or way for used steam, gasoline, etc., to escape from an engine. **3** the used steam, gasoline, etc., that escapes. [< L *exhaustus* < *ex-* out, off + *haurire* draw] —**ex·haust'er,** *n.* —**ex·haust'i·ble,** *adj.* —**ex·haust'i·bil'i·ty,** *n.*

ex·haust·ed (ig zôs'tid), *adj.* **1** used up: *exhausted grain stores.* **2** worn out.

ex·haus·tion (ig zôs'chən), *n.* **1** an exhausting. **2** a being exhausted. **3** extreme fatigue.

ex·haus·tive (ig zôs'tiv), *adj.* leaving out nothing important; thorough; comprehensive. —**ex·haus'tive·ly,** *adv.* —**ex·haus'tive·ness,** *n.*

ex·hib·it (ig zib'it), *v.* **1** show; display. **2** show publicly. **3** show in court as evidence; submit for consideration or

inspection. —*n.* **1** show; display. **2** thing or things shown publicly. **3** a public show. **4** thing shown in court as evidence. [< L *exhibitus* < *ex-* out + *habere* hold] —**ex·hib'i·tor, ex·hib'it·er,** *n.*

ex·hi·bi·tion (ek'sə bish'ən), *n.* **1** a showing; display: *an exhibition of bad manners.* **2** a public show. **3** thing or things shown publicly; exhibit.

ex·hi·bi·tion·ism (ek'sə bish'ən iz əm), *n.* **1** an excessive tendency to show off one's abilities. **2** tendency to show what should not be shown. —**ex'hi·bi'tion·ist,** *n.*

ex·hil·a·rate (ig zil'ə rāt), *v.,* **-rat·ed, -rat·ing.** make merry or lively; put into high spirits; stimulate. [< L, < *ex-* thoroughly + *hilaris* merry] —**ex·hil'a·rat'ing,** *adj.* —**ex·hil'a·rat'ing·ly,** *adv.* —**ex·hil'a·ra'tion,** *n.*

ex·hort (ig zôrt'), *v.* urge strongly; advise or warn earnestly. [< L, < *ex-* + *hortari* urge strongly] —**ex'hor·ta'tion,** *n.* —**ex·hor'ta·tive, ex·hor'ta·to'ry,** *adj.* —**ex·hort'er,** *n.*

ex·hume (eks hūm'; ig zūm'), *v.,* **-humed, -hum·ing. 1** take out of a grave or the ground; dig up. **2** reveal. [< Med.L, < L *ex-* out of + *humus* ground] —**ex'hu·ma'tion** *n.*

ex·i·gen·cy (ek'sə jən si), **ex·i·gence** (-jəns), *n., pl.* **-cies; -gen·ces. exigencies.** an urgent need; demand for immediate action or attention; situation demanding immediate action or attention; emergency.

ex·i·gent (ek'sə jənt), *adj.* **1** demanding immediate action or attention; urgent. **2** demanding a great deal; exacting. [< L *exigens,* ppr. of *exigere* EXACT]

ex·ile (eg'zīl; ek'sīl), *v.,* **-iled, -il·ing,** *n.* —*v.* force (a person) to leave his or her country or home; banish. —*n.* **1** a being exiled; banishment. **2** an exiled person. **3** any prolonged absence from one's own country. [< OF < L *exilium*] —**ex·il'ic,** *adj.*

ex·ist (ig zist'), *v.* **1** have actual existence; be; be real. **2** continue to be; live; have life. **3** be present; occur. [< F < L, < *ex-* forth + *sistere* stand] —**ex·ist'ent,** *adj.*

ex·ist·ence (ig zis'təns), *n.* **1** real or actual being; being. **2** continued being; living; life. **3** occurrence; presence. **4** thing that exists.

ex·is·ten·tial·ism (eg'zis ten'shəl iz əm; ek'sis-), *n.* philosophy stressing the need for personal initiative in a world lacking purpose. —**ex'is·ten'tial,** *adj.* —**ex'is·ten'tial·ist,** *n.*

ex·it (eg'zit; ek'sit), *n.* **1** way out. **2** a going out; departure. **3** act of leaving the stage. —*v.* **1** leave; depart; go out. **2** go out; depart; leave (stage direction for an actor to leave the stage). **dis·so·ci·a·tion** [< L, goes out; also < L *exitus* a going out < *ex-* out + *ire* go]

ex li·bris (eks lī'bris; lē'-), *Latin.* from the library (of).

exo– *prefix.* outside; outside of; outer: *exosphere* = *outer layer of the atmosphere.* [< Gk. *exō* without]

ex·o·at·mos·phere (ek´sō at´mə sfir), *n.* =exosphere. —**ex´o·at´mos·pher´ic,** *adj.*

ex·o·bi·ol·o·gy (ek´sō bī ol´ə ji), *n.* study of life on other planets or celestial bodies. —**ex´o·bi´o·log´i·cal,** *adj.* —**ex´o·bi·ol´o·gist,** *n.*

ex·o·crine (ek´sə krīn; –krin), *adj.* **1** secreting to the outside, through a duct or cavity; *exocrine glands, such as the mammary glands.* **2** of or having to do with exocrine secretions. [< *exo–* + Gk. *krínein* to separate]

Exod., Exodus.

ex·o·dus (ek´sə dəs), *n.* a going out; departure.

Exodus, a departure of the Israelites from Egypt. **b** Exodus, second book of the Old Testament. [< L < Gk., < *ex–* out + *hodos* way]

ex of·fi·ci·o (eks ə fish´i ō), because of one's office. [< L] —**ex´-of·fi´ci·o,** *adj.*

ex·og·a·my (ek sog´ə mē), *n.* practice of marrying only outside of one's tribe or group. [< *exo–* + *–gamy*] —**ex·og´a·mous,** *adj.*

ex·og·e·nous (eks oj´ə nəs), *adj.* **1** having stems that grow by the addition of layers of wood on the outside under the bark. **2** originating from the outside. [< NL *exogenus* growing on the outside. < Gk. *exo–* outside + *gen–* bear, produce] —**ex·og´e·nous·ly,** *adv.*

ex·on·er·ate (ig zon´ər āt), *v.,* **at·ed, at·ing.** free from blame. [< L, < *ex–* off + *onus* burden] —**ex·on´er·a´tion,** *n.* —**ex·on´er·a´tive,** *adj.*

ex·or·bi·tant (ig zôr´bə tənt), *adj.* exceeding what is customary, proper, or reasonable; very excessive. [< L, < *ex–* out of + *orbita* track. See ORBIT.] —**ex·or´bi·tance, ex·or´bi·tan·cy,** *n.* —**ex·or´bi·tant·ly,** *adv.*

ex·or·cise, ex·or·cize (ek´sôr sīz), *v.,* **–cised, –cis·ing; –cized, –ciz·ing. 1** drive out (an evil spirit) by prayers, ceremonies, etc. **2** free (a person or place) from an evil spirit. [< LL < Gk. *exorkizein* bind by oath < *ex–* + *horkos* oath] —**ex´or·cis´er, ex´or·ciz´er,** *n.*

ex·or·cism (ek´sôr siz əm), *n.* **1** an exorcising. **2** prayers, ceremonies, etc., used in exorcising. —**ex´or·cist,** *n.*

ex·o·sphere (ek´sə sfir), *n.* the outermost atmospheric layer in which the ionosphere begins to merge with interplanetary space, about 300 miles above the earth's surface.

ex·ot·ic (ig zot´ik), *adj.* foreign; strange; rare. —*n.* anything exotic. [< L < Gk. *exotikos* < *exo* outside < *ex–* out of] —**ex·ot´i·cal·ly,** *adv.*

exp., **1** expenses. **2** export. **3** express.

ex·pand (iks pand´), *v.* **1** increase in size; enlarge; swell. **2** spread out; open out; unfold; extend. **3** express in fuller form or greater detail. [< L, < *ex–* out + *pan-*

dere spread. Doublet of SPAWN.] —**expand´er,** *n.*

ex·panse (iks pans´), *n.* a large, unbroken space or stretch; wide, spreading surface.

ex·pan·sion (iks pan´shən), *n.* **1** an expanding. **2** a being expanded; increase in size, volume, etc. **3** amount or degree of expansion. **4** an expanded part or form.

ex·pan·sive (iks pan´siv), *adj.* **1** capable of expanding; tending to expand. **2** wide; spreading. **3** taking in much or many things; broad; extensive. **4** showing one's feelings freely and openly; effusive. —**expan´sive·ly,** *adv.* —**ex·pan´sive·ness,** *n.*

ex·pa·ti·ate (iks pā´shi āt), *v.,* **–at·ed, –at·ing.** write or talk much. [< L, < *exspatiari* walk about < *ex–* out + *spatium* space] —**ex·pa´ti·a´tion,** *n.* **·ex·pa´ti·a´tor,** *n.*

ex·pa·tri·ate (*v.* eks pā´tri āt; *adj., n.* eks pā´tri it, –āt), *v.,* **–at·ed, –at·ing,** *adj., n.* —*v.* banish; exile. —*adj.* expatriated. —*n.* an expatriated person; exile. [< LL, < *ex–* out of + *patria* fatherland] —**ex·pa´tri·a´tion,** *n.*

ex·pect (iks pekt´), *v.* **1** look forward to; think likely to come or happen. **2** look forward to with reason or confidence; desire and feel sure of getting. **3** think; suppose; guess.

be expecting, be pregnant. [< L, < *ex–* out + *specere* look]

ex·pect·an·cy (iks pek´tən si), **ex·pect·ance** (–təns), *n., pl.* **–cies; –an·ces.** expectation.

ex·pect·ant (iks pek´tənt), *adj.* **1** having expectations; expecting. **2** showing expectation. **3** pregnant. —*n.* person who expects something. —**ex·pect´ant·ly,** *adv.*

ex·pec·ta·tion (eks´pek tā´shən), *n.* **1** an expecting or being expected; anticipation. **2** thing expected. **3** ground for expecting something; prospect.

ex·pec·to·rant (iks pek´tə rənt), *Med.* —*adj.* causing or helping the discharge of phlegm, etc. —*n.* an expectorant medicine.

ex·pec·to·rate (iks pek´tə rāt), *v.,* **–rat·ed, –rat·ing.** cough up and spit out (phlegm, etc.); spit. [< L, < *ex–* out of + *pectus* breast] —**ex·pec´to·ra´tion,** *n.*

ex·pe·di·en·cy (iks pē´di ən si), **ex·pe·di·ence** (–əns), *n., pl.* **–cies; –enc·es. 1** suitability for bringing about a desired result; desirability or fitness under the circumstances. **2** personal advantage; self-interest.

ex·pe·di·ent (iks pē´di ənt), *adj.* **1** fit for bringing about a desired result; desirable or suitable under the circumstances. **2** giving or seeking personal advantage; based on self-interest. —*n.* a useful means of bringing about a desired result. [< L *expediens,* ppr. of *expedire* to free from a net, set right < *ex–* out + *pes* foot] —**ex·pe´di·ent·ly,** *adv.*

ex·pe·dite (eks´pə dīt), *v.,* **–dit·ed, –dit·ing.** make easy and quick; speed up. [< L *expeditus.* See EXPEDIENT.]

ex·pe·dit·er (eks´pə dīt´ər), *n.* **1** person who is responsible for supplying raw materials or delivering finished products on schedule.

ex·pe·di·tion (eks´pə dish´ən), *n.* **1** journey for some special purpose. **2** group of people, ships, etc., that make such a journey. **3** efficient and prompt action.

ex·pe·di·tion·ar·y (eks´pə dish´ən er´i), *adj.* of or making up an expedition: *an expeditionary force.*

ex·pe·di·tious (eks´pə dish´əs), *adj.* efficient and prompt. —**ex´pe·di´tious·ly,** *adv.*

ex·pel (iks pel´), *v.,* **–pelled, –pel·ling. 1** force out; force to leave. **2** put out; dismiss permanently. [< L, < *ex–* out + *pellere* drive] —**ex·pel´la·ble,** *adj.* —**ex·pel´ler,** *n.*

ex·pend (iks pend´), *v.* spend; use up. [< L, < *ex–* out + *pendere* weigh, pay. Doublet of SPEND.] —**ex·pend´er,** *n.*

ex·pend·a·ble (iks pen´də bəl), *adj.* **1** that can be expended. **2** worth giving up or sacrificing to the enemy or to destruction for strategic reasons. —*n.* Usually, **expendables.** expendable persons or things.

ex·pend·i·ture (iks pen´di chər; –chůr), *n.* **1** act of expending. **2** cost; expense.

ex·pense (iks pens´), *n.* **1** an expending; paying out money; outlay. **2** cost; charge. **3** cause of spending. **4** loss; sacrifice.

at the expense of, a paid for by someone else. **b** with the loss or sacrifice of: *work long hours at the expense of time with family.*

expenses, a costs involved in doing something: *expenses for the sheep are included.* **b** money paid to reimburse someone for doing a job; *paid travel plus expenses.* [< AF < LL *expensa.* See EXPEND.]

ex·pen·sive (iks pen´siv), *adj.* costly; high-priced. —**ex·pen´sive·ly,** *adv.* —**ex·pen´sive·ness,** *n.*

ex·pe·ri·ence (iks pir´i əns), *n., v.,* **–enced, –enc·ing.** —*n.* **1** what has happened to one; anything or everything observed, done, or lived through. **2** an observing, doing, or living through things: *people learn by experience.* **3** skill, practical knowledge, or wisdom gained by observing, doing, or living through things. —*v.* have happen to one. [< of < L, < *experiri* test < *ex–* out + *peri–* try] —**ex·per´i·en´tial,** *adj.*

ex·pe·ri·enced (iks pir´i ənst), *adj.* **1** having had experience. **2** taught by experience. **3** skillful or wise because of experience.

ex·per·i·ment (*v.* iks per´ə ment; *n.* iks per´ə mənt), *v.* try in order to find out; make trials or tests: *experimenting with dyes to get the color wanted.* —*n.* **1** test or trial to find out something: *a cooking experiment.* **2** a conducting of such tests or trials: *scientists test out theories by experiments.* [< L *experi-*

mentum. See EXPERIENCE.] —**ex·per'i·ment'er**, *n.*

ex·per·i·men·tal (iks per'ə men'təl), *adj.* **1** based on experiments: *chemistry is an experimental science.* **2** used for experiments. **3** based on experience, not on theory or authority. —**ex·per´i·men'tal·ly**, *adv.*

ex·per·i·men·ta·tion (iks per'ə men tā'shən), *n.* an experimenting.

ex·pert (*n.* eks'pėrt; *adj.* iks pėrt', eks'pėrt), *n.* person who knows a great deal about some special thing. —*adj.* **1** very skillful; knowing a great deal about some special thing. **2** from an expert; requiring or showing knowledge about some special thing. [< L *expertus,* pp. of *experiri* test. See EXPERIENCE.] —**ex·pert'ly**, *adv.* —**ex·pert'ness**, *n.*

ex·pi·ate (eks'pi āt), *v.,* **-at·ed, -at·ing.** make amends for (a wrong, sin, etc.); atone for. [< L, < *ex-* completely + *piare* appease < *pius* devout] —**ex'pi·a·ble**, *adj.* —**ex'pi·a'tion**, *n.* —**ex'pi·a'tor**, *n.*

ex·pi·a·tory (eks'pi ə tô'ri; -tō´-), *adj.* intended to expiate; expiating; atoning.

ex·pi·ra·tion (ek'spə rā'shən), *n.* **1** a coming to an end. **2** a breathing out. —**ex·pir'a·to'ry**, *adj.*

ex·pire (ik spīr'), *v.,* **-pired, -pir·ing. 1** come to an end. **2** die. **3** breathe out: *used air is expired from the lungs.* [< L, < *ex-* out + *spirare* breathe] —**ex·pir'er**, *n.*

ex·pi·ry (ek spīr'i), *n.* **1** end; expiration: *a warrantee's expiry.* **2** dying; death.

ex·plain (iks plān'), *v.* **1** make plain or clear; tell how to do. **2** tell the meaning of; interpret. **3** give reasons for; account for.

explain away, give excuses for: *could not explain away his behavior.*

explain oneself, a make one's meaning clear. **b** give reasons for one's behavior. [< L, < *ex-* out + *planus* flat] —**ex·plain'a·ble**, *adj.* —**ex·plain'er**, *n.* —**ex·plan'a·to'ry**, *adj.* —**ex·plan'a·to'ri·ly**, *adv.*

ex·pla·na·tion (eks'plə nā'shən), *n.* **1** an explaining. **2** thing that explains. **3** interpretation.

ex·ple·tive (eks'plə tiv), *adj.* filling out a sentence or line; completing. —*n.* **1** something that fills out a sentence or line. **2** oath or meaningless exclamation. [< LL *expletivus* < *ex-* out + *plere* fill] —**ex'ple·tive·ly**, *adv.*

ex·pli·ca·ble (eks'plə kə bəl; iks plik'ə-), *adj.* capable of being explained.

ex·pli·cate (eks'plə kāt), *v.,* **-cat·ed, -cat·ing. 1** develop (a principle, doctrine, etc.). **2** explain. —**ex´pli·ca'tion**, *n.*

ex·plic·it (iks plis'it), *adj.* **1** clearly expressed; distinctly stated; definite. **2** not reserved; frank; outspoken. [< L, < *ex-* un- + *plicare* fold] —**ex·plic'it·ly**, *adv.* —**ex·plic'it·ness**, *n.*

ex·plode (iks plōd'), *v.,* **-plod·ed, -plod·ing. 1** blow up; burst with a loud noise. **2** cause to explode. **3** burst forth noisily; *explode with laughter.* **4** cause to be

rejected; destroy belief in. [< L *explodere* drive out by clapping < *ex-* out + *plaudere* clap] —**ex·plod'er**, *n.*

ex·plod·ed view (ik splō' did), diagram or drawing that shows the parts of a mechanism, construction, etc., separated but placed in relation to one another.

ex·ploit (*n.* eks'ploit, iks ploit'; *v.* iks ploit'), *n.* a bold, unusual act; daring deed. —*v.* **1** make use of; turn to practical account. **2** make unfair use of; use selfishly for one's own advantage. [< OF < VL *explicitum* achievement < L, pp. neut. of *explicare* unfold, settle. See EXPLICIT.] —**ex·ploit'a·ble**, *adj.* —**ex´ploi·ta'tion**, *n.* —**ex·ploit'a·tive**, *adj.* —**ex·ploit'er**, *n.*

ex·plore (iks plôr'; -plōr'), *v.,* **-plored, -plor·ing. 1** travel in (little known lands or seas) for the purpose of discovery. **2** go over carefully; look into closely; examine. [< L *explorare* spy out, orig., cry out (at sight of game or enemy) < *ex-* out + *plorare* weep) —**ex´plo·ra'tion**, *n.* —**ex·plor'a·to´ry, ex·plor'a·tive**, *adj.* —**ex·plor'er**, *n.*

ex·plo·sion (iks plō'zhən), *n.* **1** a blowing up; a bursting with a loud noise. **2** loud noise caused by this. **3** a noisy bursting forth; outbreak; *explosions of anger.*

ex·plo·sive (iks plō'siv; -ziv), *adj.* **1** of or for explosion; tending to explode. **2** tending to burst forth noisily. —*n.* an explosive substance. —**ex·plo'sive·ly**, *adv.* —**ex·plo'sive·ness**, *n.*

ex·po (eks'pō), *n.,* *pl.* **-pos.** *Informal.* exposition (def. 1).

ex·po·nent (iks pō'nənt), *n.* **1** person or thing that explains, interprets, etc. **2** person or thing that stands as an example, type or symbol of something: *Lincoln is a famous exponent of self-education.* **3** index or small number written above and to the right of an algebraic symbol or a quantity to be used as a factor, as in a^3. [< L *exponens.* See EXPOUND.]

ex·po·nen·tial (iks'pō nen'shəl), *adj.* **1** of or involving an algebraic exponent. **2** *Fig.* greater or more than ordinary: *exponential growth.* —**ex´po·nen'tial·ly**, *adv.*

ex·port (*v.* iks pôrt', -pōrt', eks'pôrt, -pōrt; *n.* eks'pôrt, -pōrt), *v.* send (goods) out of one country for sale and use in another. —*n.* **1** article exported. **2** an exporting. [< L, < *ex-* away + *portare* carry] —**ex·port'a·ble**, *adj.* —**ex´por·ta'tion**, *n.* —**ex·port'er**, *n.*

ex·pose (iks pōz'), *v.,* **-posed, -pos·ing. 1** lay open; leave unprotected; uncover. **2** show openly; display: *goods are exposed for sale in a store.* **3** make known; show up; reveal: *he exposed the plot.* **4** allow light to reach and act on (a photographic film or plate). [< OF, < *ex-* forth + *poser* put, POSE] —**ex·pos'er**, *n.*

ex·po·sé (eks'pō zā'), *n.* a showing up of crime, dishonesty, etc. [< F. See EXPOSE.]

ex·po·si·tion (eks'pə zish'ən), *n.* **1** a public show or exhibition. **2** a detailed explanation. **3** speech or writing explaining a process or idea.

ex·pos·i·tor (iks poz'ə tər), *n.* person or thing that explains; expounder, interpreter.

ex·pos·i·to·ry (iks poz'ə tô'ri; -tō´-), **ex·pos·i·tive** (-ə tiv), *adj.* explaining; serving or helping to explain

ex post fac·to (eks' pōst' fak'tō), made or done after something, but applying to it. [< Med.L *ex postfacto* from what is done afterward]

ex·pos·tu·late (iks pos'chə lāt), *v.,* **-lat·ed, -lat·ing.** reason earnestly with a person, protesting against something he or she means to do or has done; remonstrate. [<L, *ex-* (intensive) + *postulare* demand] —**ex·pos´tu·la'tion**, *n.* —**expos'tu·la´tor**, *n.* —**ex·pos'tu·la·to´ry**, *adj.*

ex·po·sure (iks pō'zhər), *n.* **1** an exposing. **2** a being exposed. **3** position in relation to the sun and wind: *a southern exposure.* **4** time during which light reaches and acts on a photographic film or plate. **5** a putting off without shelter; abandoning.

ex·pound (iks pound'), *v.* **1** make clear; explain; interpret. **2** set forth or state in detail. [< OF < L, < *ex-* forth + *ponere* put] —**ex·pound'er**, *n.*

ex·press (iks pres'), *v.* **1** put into words: *your thoughts are well expressed.* **2** show by look, voice, or action; reveal: *express feeling in one's tone.* **3** show by a sign, figure, etc.; indicate. **4** send by express. **5** press out; squeeze out: *express the juice of grapes.* —*adj.* **1** clear; definite. **2** for a particular purpose; special. **3** exact. **4** having to do with express. **5** traveling fast and making few stops: *an express train.* **6** for fast traveling: *an express highway.* —*n.* **1** message sent for a particular purpose. **2** a quick or direct means of sending things. **3** train, bus, elevator, etc., traveling fast and making few stops. —*adv.* by express; directly.

express oneself, say what one is thinking. [< L *expressus* < *ex-* out + *premere* press] —**ex·press'er**, *n.* —**ex·press'i·ble**, *adj.*

ex·pres·sion (iks presh'ən), *n.* **1** a putting into words. **2** word or group of words used as a unit. **3** a showing by look, voice, or action. **4** look that shows feeling. **5** a bringing out the meaning or beauty of something read, sung, etc. **6** a showing of a characteristic: *genetic expression.* **7** symbol or group of symbols expressing some mathematical fact. —**ex·pres'sion·less**, *adj.* —**ex·pres'sion·less·ness**, *n.*

ex·pres·sive (iks pres'iv), *adj.* **1** serving as a sign or indication; expressing. **2** full of expression; having much feeling, meaning, etc. —**ex·pres'sive·ly**, *adv.* —**ex·pres'sive·ness**, *n.*

ex·press·ly (iks pres'li), *adv.* **1** clearly; plainly; definitely. **2** on purpose.

ex·pres·so (iks pres'ō), *n.* =espresso.

ex·press·way (iks pres'wā´), *n.* an express highway.

ex·pro·pri·ate (eks prō'pri āt), *v.,* **-at·ed, -at·ing. 1** take (land, etc.) out of the owner's possession, esp. for public use. **2** put (a person) out of possession; dispossess. [< Med.L, < *ex-* away from + *proprius* one's own] —**ex·pro´pri·a´tion,** *n.* —**ex·pro'pri·a´tor,** *n.*

ex·pul·sion (iks pul'shən), *n.* **1** an expelling; forcing out. **2** a being expelled or forced out: *expulsion from school.* —**ex·pul'sive,** *adj.*

ex·punge (iks punj'), *v.,* **-punged, -pung·ing.** remove completely; blot out; erase. [< L, < *ex-* out + *pungere* prick] —**ex·pung'er,** *n.*

ex·pur·gate (eks'pər gāt), *v.,* **-gat·ed, -gat·ing.** remove objectionable passages or words from (a book, letter, etc.); purify. [< L, < *ex-* out + *purgare* purge] —**ex´pur·ga'tion,** *n.* —**ex'pur·ga·tor,** *n.*

ex·qui·site (eks'kwi zit; iks kwiz'it), *adj.* **1** very lovely; delicate. **2** sharp; intense. **3** of highest excellence; most admirable: *exquisite taste and manners.* [< L *exquisitus* < *ex-* out + *quaerere* seek] —**ex'qui·site·ly,** *adv.* —**ex'qui·site·ness,** *n.*

ext., 1 extension. **2** external. **3** extinct. **4** extra. **5** extract.

ex·tant (eks'tənt; iks tant'), *adj.* still in existence. [< L *extans* < *ex-* out, forth + *stare* stand]

ex·tem·po·ra·ne·ous (iks tem´pə rā'ni əs), **ex·tem·po·ra·ry** (-tem'pə rer´i), *adj.* **1** spoken or done without preparation; offhand: *an extemporaneous speech.* **2** made for the occasion: *my newspaper became an extemporaneous umbrella.* [< LL, < L *ex tempore* according to the moment] —**ex·tem´po·ra'ne·ous·ly, ex·tem'po·rar´i·ly** *adv.* —**ex·tem´po·ra'ne·ous·ness, ex·tem'po·rar´i·ness,** *n.*

ex·tem·po·re (iks tem'pə rē), *adv.* without preparation; offhand. —*adj.* extemporaneous. [< L]

ex·tem·po·rize (iks tem'pə rīz), *v.,* **-rized, -riz·ing. 1** speak, play, sing, or dance, composing as one proceeds. **2** compose offhand; make for the occasion. —**ex·tem´po·ri·za'tion,** *n.* —**ex·tem'po·riz´er,** *n.*

ex·tend (iks tend'), *v.* **1** stretch out. **2** straighten out. **3** lengthen. **4** widen; enlarge. **5** give grant. [< L, < *ex-* out + *tendere* stretch] —**ex·tend'ed,** *adj.* —**ex·tend'ed·ly,** *adv.* —**ex·tend'i·ble,** *adj.*

extended family, family and near relatives, such as aunts, uncles, cousins, grandparents, living together in one household.

ex·tend·er (iks ten'dər), *n.* **1** thing that extends. **2** a cheap substance added to one that is scarce and expensive, to make it last longer.

ex·ten·si·ble (iks ten'sə bəl), *adj.* capable of being extended. —**ex·ten´si·bil'i·ty, ex·ten'si·ble·ness,** *n.*

ex·ten·sion (iks ten'shən), *n.* **1** an extending. **2** a being extended. **3** an extended part; addition. **4** range; extent. —**ex·ten'sion·al,** *adj.*

ex·ten·sive (iks ten'siv), *adj.* **1** of great extent. **2** affecting many things; comprehensive. **3** depending on the use of large areas: *extensive agriculture.* —**ex·ten'sive·ly,** *adv.* —**ex·ten'sive·ness,** *n.*

ex·ten·sor (iks ten'sər; -sôr), *n.* muscle that extends or straightens out a limb or other part of the body.

ex·tent (iks tent'), *n.* **1** size, space, length, amount, or degree to which a thing extends. **2** something extended; extended space.

ex·ten·u·ate (iks ten'yu āt), *v.,* **-at·ed, -at·ing. 1** make (guilt, a fault, offense, etc.) seem less; excuse in part. **2** make thin or weak; diminish. [< L, < *ex-* out + *tenuis* thin] —**ex·ten´u·a'tion,** *n.* —**ex·ten'u·a´tive,** *adj.* —**ex·ten'u·a´tor,** *n.*

extenuating circumstances, circumstances that make guilt for an offense, etc., seem less.

ex·te·ri·or (iks tir'i ər), *n.* an outer surface or part; outward appearance; outside: *a harsh exterior but a kind heart.* —*adj.* **1** on the outside; outer. **2** coming from without; happening outside. [< L, < *exterus* outside < *ex* out of] —**ex·te'ri·or·ly,** *adv.*

exterior angle 1 any one of four angles formed outside two parallel lines intersected by a straight line. **2** angle formed by one side of a closed polygon and the extension of an adjacent side.

ex·ter·mi·nate (iks tėr'mə nāt), *v.,* **-nat·ed, -nat·ing.** destroy completely. [< LL, < L, drive out < *ex-* out of + *terminus* boundary] —**ex·ter´mi·na'tion,** *n.* —**ex·ter'mi·na´tor,** *n.*

ex·ter·nal (iks tėr'nəl), *adj.* **1** on the outside; outer. **2** to be used on the outside of the body. **3** having to do with outward appearance or show; superficial. **6** having to do with international affairs; foreign. —*n.* **1** an outer surface or part; outside. **2 externals,** clothing, manners, outward acts, or appearances. [< L *externus* outside < *exterus* outside < *ex* out of] —**ex·ter'nal·ly,** *adv.*

external ear, the outermost part of the ear, at the side of the head.

external fertilization, fertilization of an egg or human ovum outside the body; in vitro fertilization.

ex·tinct (iks tingkt'), *adj.* **1** no longer in existence. **2** no longer active; extinguished: *an extinct volcano.* [< L *exstinctus,* pp. of *exstinguere.* See EXTINGUISH.]

ex·tinc·tion (iks tingk'shən), *n.* **1** an extinguishing. **2** a being extinguished; extinct condition. **3** a doing away with completely; wiping out; destruction.

ex·tin·guish (iks ting'gwish), *v.* **1** put out; quench. **2** put an end to; do away with; wipe out; destroy. [< L, < *ex-* out + *stinguere* quench] —**ex·tin'guish·a·ble,**

adj. —**ex·tin'guish·a·bly,** *adv.* —**ex·tin'guish·er,** *n.* —**ex·tin'guish·ment,** *n.*

ex·tir·pate (eks'tər pāt; iks tėr'pāt), *v.,* **-pat·ed, -pat·ing. 1** remove completely; destroy totally. **2** tear up by the roots. [< L, < *ex-* out + *stirps* root] —**ex´tir·pa'tion,** *n.* —**ex'tir·pa´tive,** *adj.* —**ex'tir·pa´tor,** *n.*

ex·tol, ex·toll (iks tōl'; -tol'), *v.,* **-tolled, -tol·ling.** praise highly. [< L, < *ex-* up + *tollere* raise] —**ex·tol'ler,** *n.* —**ex·tol'ment, ex·toll'ment,** *n.*

ex·tort (iks tôrt'), *v.* obtain (money, a promise, etc.) by threats, force, fraud, or illegal use of authority. [< L *extortus* < *ex-* out + *torquere* twist] —**ex·tort'er,** *n.* —**ex·tor'tive,** *adj.*

ex·tor·tion (iks tôr'shən), *n.* **1** act of extorting. **2** anything obtained by extorting.

ex·tor·tion·ar·y (iks tôr'shən er´i), *adj.* characterized by or given to extortion.

ex·tor·tion·ate (iks tôr'shən it), *adj.* characterized by extortion. —**ex·tor'tion·ate·ly,** *adv.*

ex·tor·tion·er (iks tôr'shən ər), **ex·tor·tion·ist** (-ist), *n.* person who is guilty of extortion.

ex·tra (eks'trə), *adj.* more, greater, or better than what is usual, expected, or needed. —*n.* **1** something in addition to what is usual, expected, or needed. **2** an additional charge. **3** person who is employed by the day to play minor parts in motion pictures. —*adv.* more than usually. [prob. short for *extraordinary*]

extra-, *prefix.* outside; beyond; besides, as in *extraordinary.* [< L]

ex·tract (*v.* iks trakt'; *n.* eks'trakt), *v.* **1** pull out or draw out, usually with some effort: *extract a tooth, extract a confession.* **2** obtain by pressure, suction, etc.: *oil is extracted from olives.* **3** deduce: *extract a principle from a collection of facts.* **4** take out; select (a passage) from a book, speech, etc. —*n.* **1** something drawn out or taken out; passage taken from a book, speech, etc. **2** a concentrated preparation of a substance: *vanilla extract.* [< L *extractus* < *ex-* out + *trahere* draw] —**ex·tract'a·ble, ex·tract'i·ble,** *adj.* —**ex·trac'tive,** *adj.,* *n.* —**ex·trac'tor,** *n.*

ex·trac·tion (iks trak'shən), *n.* **1** an extracting. **2** a being extracted. **3** descent; origin.

ex·tra·cur·ric·u·lar (eks´trə kə rik'yə lər), *adj.* outside the regular course of study: *football is an extracurricular activity.*

ex·tra·dite (eks'trə dīt), *v.,* **-dit·ed, -dit·ing. 1** give up or deliver (a fugitive or prisoner) to another nation or legal authority for trial or punishment. **2** obtain the extradition of (such a person). [< *extradition*] —**ex'tra·dit´a·ble,** *adj.*

ex·tra·di·tion (eks´trə dish'ən), *n.* surrender of a fugitive or prisoner by one state, nation, or legal authority to another for trial or punishment. [< L, < *ex-* out + *tradere* trade]

ex·tra·mar·i·tal (eks′trə mar′ə təl), *adj.* outside the bonds of marriage: *extramarital affair.* —**ex′tra·mar′i·tal·ly,** *adv.*

ex·tra·ne·ous (iks trā′ni əs), *adj.* from outside; not belonging; foreign. [< L, < *extra* outside < *ex-* out of. Doublet of STRANGE.] —**ex·tra′ne·ous·ly,** *adv.* —**ex·tra′ne·ous·ness,** *n.*

ex·traor·di·nar·y (iks trôr′də ner′i; *esp.* for 2 eks′trə ôr′–), *adj.* **1** beyond what is ordinary; most unusual; very remarkable. **2** outside of, additional to, or ranking below the regular class of officials; special. [< L, < *extra ordinem* out of the (usual) order] —**ex·traor′di·nar′i·ly,** *adv.* —**ex·traor′di·nar′i·ness,** *n.*

ex·trap·o·late (iks trap′ə lāt), *v.,* –**lat·ed,** –**lat·ing.** predict from facts: *extrapolate a storm's course from pressure gradients.*

ex·tra·sen·so·ry (eks′trə sen′sə ri), *adj.* not within ordinary sense perception.

extrasensory perception, the perceiving of thoughts, actions, etc., in other than a normal fashion; mental telepathy.

ex·tra·ter·ri·to·ri·al (eks′trə ter′ə tô′-ri əl; –tō′–), *adj.* beyond territorial limits or jurisdiction, as persons resident in a country but not subject to its laws. —**ex′tra·ter′ri·to′ri·al′i·ty,** *n.* —**ex′tra·ter′ri·to′ri·al·ly,** *adv.*

ex·trav·a·gance (iks trav′ə gəns), *n.* **1** careless and lavish spending; wastefulness. **2** a going beyond the bounds of reason; excess.

ex·trav·a·gant (iks trav′ə gənt), *adj.* **1** spending carelessly and lavishly; wasteful. **2** beyond the bounds of reason; excessive; exorbitant. [< Med.L, < *extra–* outside + *vagari* wander] —**ex·trav′a·gant·ly,** *adv.*

ex·trav·a·gan·za (iks trav′ə gan′zə), *n.* a fantastic play, piece of music, etc. [blend of Ital. *stravaganza* peculiar behavior, and E *extra*]

ex·tra·ve·hic·u·lar (iks′trə vi hik′yə lər), *adj.* **1** outside a spacecraft in space. **2** of or for activity, esp. repairs, outside an orbiting spacecraft.

ex·treme (iks trēm′), *adj.,* –**trem·er,** –**trem·est,** *n.* —*adj.* **1** much more than usual; very great; very strong. **2** at the very end; farthest possible; last. —*n.* **1** something extreme; one of two things as far or as different as possible from each other. **2** an extreme degree. **3** *Math.* the first or last term in a proportion or series.
go to extremes, do or say too much. [< L *extremus,* superl. of *exterus* outer] —**ex·treme′ly,** *adv.* —**ex·treme′ness,** *n.*

extreme sports, active sports that include danger as part of their appeal, including skydiving, bungee-jumping, snowboarding, etc.

extreme unction, =annointing of the sick.

ex·trem·ism (iks trē′miz əm), *n.* tendency to go to extremes, or pleasure in going to extremes.

ex·trem·ist (iks trēm′ist), *n.* **1** person who goes to extremes. **2** person who has extreme ideas or favors extreme measures.

ex·trem·i·ty (iks trem′ə ti), *n., pl.* –**ties. 1** the very end; farthest possible place; last part or point. **2** extreme need, danger, suffering, etc. **3** an extreme degree. **4** an extreme action.

extremities, hands and feet.

ex·tri·cate (eks′trə kāt), *v.,* –**cat·ed,** –**cat·ing.** set free (from entanglements, difficulties, embarrassing situations, etc.); release. [< L, < *ex-* out of + *tricae* perplexities] —**ex′tri·ca·ble,** *adj.* —**ex′tri·ca·bil′i·ty,** *n.* —**ex′tri·ca·bly,** *adv.* —**ex′-tri·ca′tion,** *n.*

ex·trin·sic (eks trin′sik), *adj.* **1** not essential or inherent. **2** being outside of a thing; coming from without; external. [< later L *extrinsecus* outer < earlier L, from outside, < unrecorded OL *extrim* from outside + *secus* following] —**ex-trin′si·cal·ly,** *adv.*

ex·tro·vert (eks′trə vėrt), *n.* person more interested in what is going on around him or her than in his or her own thoughts and feelings. [< *extro–* (var. of *extra–* outside) + L *vertere* turn]

ex·trude (iks trüd′), *v.,* –**trud·ed,** –**trud·ing. 1** thrust out; push out. **2** stick out; protrude. [< L, < *ex-* out + *trudere* thrust] —**ex·tru′sion,** *n.* —**ex·tru′sive,** *adj*

ex·u·ber·ance (ig zü′bər əns), *n.* fact, quality, state, or condition of being exuberant. [< L, < *exuberare* grow luxuriantly < *ex-* thoroughly + *uber* fertile]

ex·u·ber·ant (ig zü′bər ənt), *adj.* **1** very abundant; overflowing; lavish. **2** profuse in growth; luxuriant. —**ex·u′ber-ant·ly,** *adv.*

ex·ude (ig züd′; ik süd′), *v.,* –**ud·ed,** –**ud-ing. 1** ooze. **2** give forth. [< L, < *ex-* out + *sudare* to sweat] —**ex′u·da′tion,** *n.*

ex·ult (ig zult′), *v.* be very glad; rejoice greatly. [< L *exsultare* < *ex-* forth + *salire* leap] —**ex′ul·ta′tion,** *n.* —**ex·ult′ing-ly,** *adv.*

ex·ult·ant (ig zul′tənt), *adj.* rejoicing greatly; exulting. —**ex·ult′ant·ly,** *adv.*

ex·ur·ban·ite (eks′ėr′bən īt), *n.* person who lives in the exurbs. [< *ex-* (def. 1, ? also def. 3) + (sub)*urbanite*]

ex·ur·bi·a (eks′ėr′bi ə), *n.* the exurbs.

ex·urbs (eks′ėrbz), *n. pl.* region outside a large city, between the suburbs and the country. [< *ex-* + (sub)*urbs*]

-ey, *suffix.* full of; containing; like, as in *clayey, skyey.* [var. of –*y*¹]

eye (ī), *n., v.,* **eyed, eye·ing** or **eye·ing.** —*n.* **1** organ of the body by which people and animals see; organ of sight. **2** the colored part of the eye; iris. **3** region surrounding the eye: *the blow gave him a black eye.* **4** ability to see small differences in things: *an eye for color.* **5** look; watchful look; view; opinion: *in the eye of the law.* **6** thing shaped like or suggesting an eye: *the eye of a storm.* —*v.*

look at; watch: *the dog eyed the stranger.*
an eye for an eye, punishment equal in severity to the injury.
be all eyes, watch or look eagerly.
catch one's eye, attract one's notice.
cry one's eyes out, cry copiously; be very upset.
easy on the eyes, *Informal.* good-looking; attractive.
have an eye to or **for,** pay attention to: *an eye for opportunity.*
in the public eye, often seen in public; recognized by the public.
keep an eye on, watch.
keep one's eyes peeled, *Informal.* be watchful, alert.
knock one's eyes out, *Informal.* overcome with wonder or delight.
lay or **set eyes on,** see; notice: *first laid eyes on her yesterday.*
make eyes at, flirt with.
open one's eyes, cause one to see what is true or actually happening.
see eye to eye, agree.
shut one's eyes to, refuse to see or consider.
turn a blind eye, ignore; disregard.
with an eye to, keeping in mind; considering: *a choice made with an eye to public opinion.*
with one's eyes open, fully aware of the circumstances or possible risks.
without batting an eye, without any reaction; with no emotion. [OE *eage*]

eye·ball (ī′bôl′), *n.* the ball-shaped part of the eye, without the lids and bony socket. —*v. Slang.* watch carefully.

eyeball to eyeball, face to face with an adversary.

eye·brow (ī′brou′), *n.* **1** arch of hair above the eye. **2** the bony ridge that it grows on.
raise an eyebrow or **eyebrows,** cause disapproval, doubt, discomfort, amazement: *a lifestyle that raised eyebrows in the town.*

eye-catch·ing (ī′kach′ing), *adj.* **1** attractive. **2** easily noticed.

eye cup, small cup shaped to fit around the eye, used for washing or medicating the eye.

eye·ful (ī′fúl), *n.* **1** as much as the eye can take in. **2** a good look. **3** *Informal. Fig.* good-looking person.

eye·glass (ī′glas′; ī′gläs′), *n.* lens to aid poor vision.

eyeglasses, pair of glass lenses to help vision.

eye·lash (ī′lash′), *n.* one of the hairs on the edge of the eyelid.

eye·let (ī′lit), *n.* **1** a small, round hole for a lace or cord to go through. **2** a metal ring around such a hole to strengthen it.

eye·lid (ī′lid′), *n.* the movable fold of skin over the eye.

eye·lin·er (ī′lī′nər), *n.* **1** cosmetic applied to the edge of the eyelid to accentuate the shape of the eye. **2** applicator for eyeliner.

eye opener or **eye-open·er** (ī′ō′pə nər), *n.* *Informal.* surprising event or information.

eye·piece (ī′pēs′), *n.* lens nearest to the eye of the user in a telescope, microscope, etc.

eye shadow, cosmetic applied to the eyelids.

eye·shot (ī′shot′), *n.* range of vision.

eye·sight (ī′sīt′), *n.* **1** power of seeing; sight. **2** range of vision; view.

eye·sore (ī′sôr′; ī′sōr′), *n.* thing unpleasant to look at.

eye·strain (ī′strān′), *n.* a tired or weak condition of the eyes caused by using them too much, reading in a dim light, etc.

eye·tooth (ī′tüth′), *n., pl.* **–teeth.** an upper canine tooth.

eye·wit·ness (ī′wit′nis), *n.* person who actually sees or has seen some act or happening.

E·ze·ki·el (i zē′ki əl; i zēk′yəl), *n.* book of the Old Testament.

F, f (ef), *n.*, *pl.* **F's; f's. 1** the sixth letter of the alphabet. **2** the fourth note of the scale of C major.

F, 1 fluorine. Also, **Fl. 2** French.

F., 1 Fahrenheit. **2** February. **3** Friday.

f., 1 feminine. **2** folio. **3** following.

fa (fä), *n.* the fourth note of the musical scale. [see GAMUT]

fa·ble (fā'bəl), *n.*, *v.*, **-bled, -bling. —n. 1** story made up to teach a lesson. **2** an unntrue story; falsehood. —*v.* **1** tell or write fables. **2** lie. [< OF < L *fabula* < *fari* speak] —**fa'bled,** *adj.* —**fa'bler,** *n.*

fab·ric (fab'rik), *n.* **1** woven or knitted material; cloth. **2** thing constructed of combined parts; framework: *cultural fabric of the country.* [< F < L *fabrica* workshop. Doublet of FORGE[1].]

fab·ri·cate (fab'rə kāt), *v.*, **-cat·ed, -cat·ing. 1** build; construct; manufacture. **2** make up; invent (stories, lies, excuses, etc.). **3** forge (a document). —**fab'ri·ca'tion,** *n.* —**fab'ri·ca'tor,** *n.*

fab·u·lous (fab'yə ləs), *adj.* **1** not believable; amazing. **2** of or belonging to a fable; imaginary. [< L < *fabula* FABLE] —**fab'u·lous·ly,** *adv.* —**fab'u·lous·ness,** *n.*

fa·cade or **fa·çade** (fə säd'), *n.* the front part or principal side of a building. [< F, < *face* FACE]

face (fās), *n.*, *v.*, **faced, fac·ing. —n. 1** the front part of the head. **2** look; expression. **3** a look made by distorting the face. **4** outward appearance. **5** the front part; right side; surface: *the face of a clock or building.* **6** boldness; impudence. **7** dignity; self-respect: *face is very important to Asian peoples.* —*v.* **1** be opposite (to). **2** stand before. **3** meet bravely or boldly; oppose and resist. **4** present itself to: *a crisis faced us.* **5** cover or line with a different material.

face down, confront fearlessly.

face to face, a with faces toward each other. **b** in the actual presence: *come face to face with failure.*

face up to, confront something with full awareness of its importance, difficulty, etc.

fall (flat) on one's face. *Informal.* fail.

fly in the face of, defy

in the face of, a in the presence of. **b** in spite of.

in your face, confrontational; aggressive.

show one's face, be present; be seen.

to one's face, in one's presence. [< F, ult. < L *facies* form] —**face'a·ble,** *adj.* —**face'less,** *adj.*

face card, king, queen, or jack in a deck of cards.

face·down (fās'down'), *n.* direct confrontation. —*adj.* with the face downward: *facedown on the sidewalk.*

face·lift (fās'lift'), *n.* **1** surgery to remove wrinkles and fat deposits on the face. **2**

Fig. any superficial change to improve the image or appearance of something.

face·off (fās'ôf'; -of'), *n.* **1** act of putting the puck in play in ice hockey. **2** *Fig.* confrontation between opponents.

fac·et (fas'it), *n.*, *v.*, **-et·ed, -et·ing. —n. 1** any one of the small, polished surfaces of a cut gem. **2** thing like the facet of a gem. —*v.* cut facets on. [< F *facette*, dim. of *face* FACE]

fa·ce·tious (fə sē'shəs), *adj.* **1** having the habit of joking. **2** said in fun; not to be taken seriously. [< L *facetia* jest < *facetus* witty] —**fa·ce'tious·ly,** *adv.* —**fa·ce'tious·ness,** *n.*

face value, 1 value stated on a bond, check, note, etc. **2** apparent worth, meaning, etc.

fa·cial (fā'shəl), *adj.* **1** of the face. **2** for the face. —*n.* massage or treatment of the face. —**fa'cial·ly,** *adv.*

fac·ile (fas'əl), *adj.* **1** easily done, used, etc.: *a facile task.* **2** moving, acting, working, etc., with ease: *a facile pen.* **3** of easy manners or temper; agreeable; yielding: *a facile nature.* [< L *facilis* easy < *facere* do] —**fac'ile·ly,** *adv.* —**fac'ile·ness,** *n.*

fa·cil·i·tate (fə sil'ə tāt), *v.*, **-tat·ed, -tat·ing.** make easy; lessen the labor of; assist. —**fa·cil'i·ta'tion,** *n.*

fa·cil·i·ty (fə sil'ə ti), *n.*, *pl.* **-ties. 1** absence of difficulty; ease. **2** power to do anything easily, quickly, and smoothly. **3** something that makes an action easy; aid; convenience.

facilities, place built or reserved for special use or to provide special service: *playground facilities; sports facilities.*

fac·ing (fās'ing), *n.* **1** a covering of different material for ornament, protection, etc. **2** material put around the edge of cloth to protect or trim it.

fac·sim·i·le (fak sim'ə lē), *n.*, *v.*, **-led, -le·ing,** *adj.* —*n.* **1** an exact copy or likeness; perfect reproduction. **2** process for transmitting printed matter and reproducing it on a receiving set; fax. —*v.* make a facsimile of. —*adj.* of a facsimile. [< L *fac* make! + *simile* like]

fact (fakt), *n.* **1** thing known to be true or to have really happened. **2** what is true or has really happened; truth; reality. **3** thing supposed to be true: *we doubted his facts.*

as a matter of fact, in point of actual fact; indeed.

in fact, truly; really. [< L *factum* (thing) done, pp. of *facere* do. Doublet of FEAT.]

fac·tion (fak'shən), *n.* **1** group of people in a political party, church, club, etc., acting together or having a common end in view. **2** strife; discord. [< L *factio* party, orig., a doing < *facere* do. Doublet of FASHION.] —**fac'tion·al,** *adj.* —**fac'tion·al·ism,** *n.*

fac·tious (fak'shəs), *adj.* **1** fond of causing faction. **2** of or caused by faction. —**fac'tious·ly,** *adv.* —**fac'tious·ness,** *n.*

fac·ti·tious (fak tish'əs), *adj.* developed by effort; not natural; forced; artificial.

[< L *facticius* artificial] —**fac·ti'tious·ly,** *adv.* —**fac·ti'tious·ness,** *n.*

fac·tor (fak'tər), *n.* **1** element, condition, quality, etc., that helps to bring about a result. **2** any of the numbers, algebraic expressions, etc., that form a product when multiplied together. **3** person who does business for another; agent. —*v.* separate into mathematical factors. —**fac'tor·ship,** *n.*

fac·to·ry (fak'tə ri; -tri), *n.*, *pl.* **-ries.** a building or group of buildings where things are manufactured. —**fac'to·ry·like',** *adj.*

fac·to·tum (fak tō'təm), *n.* person employed to do all kinds of work. [< Med.L, < L *fac* do! + *totum* the whole]

fac·tu·al (fak'chù əl), *adj.* concerned with fact; consisting of facts. —**fac'tu·al·ly,** *adv.*

fac·ul·ty (fak'əl ti), *n.*, *pl.* **-ties. 1** power to do some special thing, esp. a power of the mind. **2 a** teachers of a school, college, or university. **b** department of learning: *faculty of theology.* [< L *facultas* < *facilis* FACILE]

fad (fad), *n.* something everybody is very much interested in for a short time; craze; rage. —**fad'dish,** *adj.* —**fad'dist,** *n.*

fade (fād), *v.*, **fad·ed, fad·ing. 1** lose color or brightness. **2** lose freshness or strength; wither. **3** die away; disappear.

fade in, of film or television, appear slowly.

fade out, of film or television, disappear slowly. [< OF, < *fade* VAPID]

fade-in (fād'in'), *n.* scene in a motion picture or on television that slowly appears and brightens.

fade-out (fād'out'), *n.* **1** scene in a motion picture or on television that slowly disappears. **2** a gradual disappearance.

fag[1] (fag), *v.*, **fagged, fag·ging, 1** work hard or until wearied. **2** tire by work.

fag out, tire completely.

fag[2] (fag), *n. Slang.* male homosexual; faggot.

fag end, remnant.

fag·got (fag'ət), *n. Slang.* male homosexual.

fag·ot (fag'ət), *n.* bundle of sticks or twigs tied together. [< OF]

Fahr., Fahrenheit.

Fahr·en·heit (far'ən hīt), *adj.* of, based on, or according to a scale for measuring temperature on which 32 degrees marks the freezing point of water and 212 degrees the boiling point. [after G. D. *Fahrenheit,* physicist]

fai·ence (fī äns'; fä-) *n.* brightly decorated, fine earthenware.

fail (fāl), *v.* **1** not succeed; be unable to do or become. **2** not do; neglect. **3** be of no use or help to; be not enough; become weak; die away; be unable to pay what one owes. **4** give or receive a mark of failure.

without fail, without failing to do; certainly. [< OF *faillir,* ult. < L *fallere* deceive]

fail·ing (fāl′ing), *n.* 1 failure. 2 fault; defect. —*prep.* in the absence of; lacking. —*adj.* that fails. —**fail′ing·ly**, *adv.*

faille (fīl; fāl), *n.* a soft, ribbed silk or rayon cloth. [< F]

fail-safe (fāl′sāf′), *adj.* 1 having protection from a failure built in. 2 guaranteed foolproof, safe.

fail·ure (fāl′yər), *n.* 1 a being unable to do or become. 2 a not doing; neglecting. 3 a being not enough; falling short. 4 becoming weak; dying away. 5 a being unable to pay what one owes. 6 person or thing that has failed.

fain (fān), *Archaic.* —*adv.* willingly. —*adj.* willing. [OE *fægen*]

faint (fānt), *adj.* 1 not clear or plain; dim. 2 weak; feeble. 3 ready to faint; about to faint. —*v.* lose consciousness temporarily. —*n.* condition in which a person lies unconscious. [< OF, pp. of *faindre* FEIGN] —**faint′er**, —**faint′ish**, *adj.* —**faint′ly**, *adv.* —**faint′ness**, *n.*

faint-heart·ed (fānt′här′tid), *adj.* lacking courage; cowardly; timid. —**faint′-heart·ed·ly**, *adv.*—**faint′-heart′ed-ness**, *n.*

fair¹ (fãr), *adj.* 1 not favoring one more than the other or others; just; honest. 2 according to the rules. 3 pretty good; average. 4 not dark; light. 5 clear; sunny. 6 beautiful. 7 clean; easily read. —*adv.* in a fair manner.
fair and square, a just; honest: *fair and square deal.* **b** justly; honestly: *win fair and square.* [OE *fæger*] —**fair′ish**, *adj.* —**fair′ness**, *n.*

fair² (fãr), *n.* 1 display of goods, products, etc. 2 a gathering of people to buy and sell, often held in a certain place at regular times during the year: *a county fair.* 3 a combined entertainment and sale of articles. [< OF < LL *feria* holiday]

fair ball, ball hit to or over the legal playing area.

fair game, 1 animals or birds that can be lawfully hunted. 2 *Fig.* someone or something it is permissible to attack.

fair·ground (fãr′ground′), field or other outdoor area where a fair is held.

fair-haired (fãr′hãrd′), *adj.* 1 having light-colored hair; blond. 2 *Fig.* favored: *the fair-haired one advanced rapidly.*

fair·ly (fãr′li), *adv.* 1 justly; honestly. 2 rather; somewhat.

fair-mind·ed (fãr′mīn′did), *adj.* not prejudiced; just; impartial. —**fair′-mind′ed-ness**, *n.*

fair sex, females.

fair·way (fãr′wā′), *n.* 1 an unobstructed passage or way. 2 the mowed and tended area between the tee and putting green.

fair-weath·er (fãr′weŧ′ər), *adj.* 1 of or fitted for fair weather. 2 *Fig.* weakening or failing in time of need: *fair-weather friend.*

fair·y (fãr′i), *n.*, *pl.* **fair·ies**, *adj.* —*n.* a tiny supernatural being, very lovely and delicate, supposed to help or harm human beings. —*adj.* 1 of fairies. 2 like a fairy;

lovely; delicate. [< OF *faerie* < *fae* FAY] —**fair′y·like′**, *adj.*

fair·y·land (fãr′i land′), *n.* 1 the imaginary place where the fairies live. 2 an enchanting and pleasant place.

fairy tale, 1 story about fairies, elves, or other magical beings. 2 a lie.

fait ac·com·pli (fe tä kôn plē′), *French.* thing done and no longer worth opposing.

faith (fāth), *n.* 1 a believing without proof; trust. 2 belief in God, religion, or spiritual things. 3 what is believed. 4 religion. 5 a being faithful; loyalty.
break faith, break a promise.
in bad faith, dishonestly.
keep faith, keep a promise.
keep the faith, remain true to one's convictions or beliefs. [< OF *feit* < L *fides*]

faith·ful (fāth′fəl), *adj.* 1 worthy of trust; doing one's duty; loyal. 2 true; accurate. —*n.* **the faithful, a** true believers. **b** loyal supporters. —**faith′ful·ly**, *adv.* —**faith′ful·ness**, *n.*

faith healing, method of curing disease or affliction by prayer and religious faith. —**faith healer.**

faith·less (fāth′lis), *adj.* 1 unworthy of trust; not loyal. 2 without faith; unbelieving. —**faith′less·ly**, *adv.* —**faith′less·ness**, *n.*

fake (fāk), *v.*, **faked, fak·ing**, *n.*, *adj.* —*v.* make to seem satisfactory; falsify; counterfeit. —*n.* 1 fraud; deception. 2 one who fakes. —*adj.* intended to deceive; false. —**fak′er**, *n.*

fak·er·y (fā′kər i), *n.* fraud; deceit.

fa·kir (fə kir′; fā′kər), *n.* 1 a Muslim holy man who lives by begging. 2 a Hindu ascetic. [< Ar. *faqīr* poor]

fal·con (fôl′kən; fô′kən), *n.* 1 hawk trained to hunt and kill birds and small game. 2 a swift-flying hawk having a short, curved, notched bill. [< OF < LL *falco*]

fal·con·ry (fôl′kən ri; fô′kən–), *n.* 1 sport of hunting with falcons. 2 the training of falcons to hunt. —**fal′con·er**, *n.*

fal·de·ral (fal′də ral), **fal·de·rol** (–rol), *n.* =folderol.

fall (fôl), *v.*, **fell, fall·en, fall·ing** *n.* —*v.* 1 drop or come down from a higher place: *the snow falls fast.* 2 come down suddenly from an erect position. 3 become bad or worse: *he was tempted and fell.* 4 be captured, destroyed, or killed. 5 pass into a certain condition: *he fell asleep; night falls.* 6 come; happen: *Christmas falls on Sunday.* 7 become lower or less: *prices fell sharply.* 8 be divided: *fall into five parts.* 9 slope downward: *the land falls gradually.* —*n.* 1 a dropping from a higher place. 2 amount that falls: *a heavy fall of snow.* 3 distance that anything falls. 4 a coming down suddenly from an erect position. 5 a becoming bad or worse. 6 capture; destruction. 7 a lowering; becoming less. 8 a downward slope. 9 season of the year between summer and winter; autumn.
fall apart, a crumble; disintegrate. **b** *Fig.* become very emotional.

fall away, a withdraw support or allegiance. **b** fade; languish.
fall back, retreat.
fall flat, utterly fail.
fall for, a be duped or taken in by. **b** fall in love with; be attracted to.
fall in, a take a place in formation and come to attention. **b** meet: *fell in with some bad characters.* **c** agree.
fall off, become less: *productivity fell off.*
fall on, a attack. **b** come upon: *fall on a solution.*
fall out, a leave a place in formation. **b** quarrel.
fall through, fail.
fall under, belong under; be classified as.
falls, waterfall; cascade; cataract.
the Fall, the sin of Adam and Eve in yielding to temptation. [OE *feallan*]

fal·la·cious (fə lā′shəs), *adj.* 1 deceptive; misleading. 2 logically unsound; erroneous. —**fal·la′cious·ly**, *adv.* —**fal·la′cious-ness**, *n.*

fal·la·cy (fal′ə si), *n.*, *pl.* **–cies.** 1 a false idea; mistaken belief; error. 2 mistake in reasoning; misleading or unsound argument. [< L, ult. < *fallere* deceive]

fall·en (fôl′ən), *v.* pp. of **fall.** —*adj.* 1 dropped. 2 on the ground; down flat. 3 degraded. 4 overthrown; destroyed. 5 dead.

fall guy, *Slang.* person left in a difficult situation.

fal·li·ble (fal′ə bəl), *adj.* 1 liable to be deceived or mistaken; liable to err. 2 liable to be erroneous, inaccurate, or false. [< Med.L, < L *fallere* deceive] —**fal′li·bil′i·ty, fal′li·ble·ness**, *n.* —**fal′li·bly**, *adv.*

falling star, =meteor.

Fal·lo·pi·an tubes (fə lō′pi ən), pair of slender tubes through which ova from the ovaries pass to the uterus.

fall·out (fôl′out′), *n.* 1 the radioactive particles or dust that fall to the earth after an atomic explosion. 2 *Fig.* aftermath of a quarrel, unpopular decision, scandal, etc.

fal·low¹ fal′ō), *adj.* plowed and left unseeded for a season or more; uncultivated; inactive. —*n.* 1 land plowed and left unseeded for a season or more. 2 the plowing of land without seeding it for a season in order to destroy weeds, improve the soil, etc. —*v.* plow and harrow (land) without seeding. [OE *fealg*]

fal·low² (fal′ō), *adj.* pale yellowish-brown. [OE *fealu*]

fallow deer, a small European deer with a yellowish coat that is spotted with white in the summer.

false (fôls), *adj.*, **fals·er, fals·est**, *adv.* —*adj.* 1 not true; not correct; wrong. 2 not truthful; lying. 3 not loyal; not faithful. 4 used to deceive; deceiving: *false weights.* 5 not real; artificial: *false teeth.* 6 improperly called or named. The false acacia is really a locust tree. —*adv.*

in a false manner. [< L *falsus* < *fallere* deceive] —**false′ly,** *adv.* —**false′ness,** *n.*

false·hood (fôls′hůd), *n.* 1 quality of being false. 2 something false. 3 lying. 4 a lie.

fal·set·to (fôl set′ō), *n., pl.* –**tos,** *adj., adv.* —*n.* an unnaturally high-pitched voice, esp. in a man. —*adj.* that sings in a falsetto. —*adv.* in a falsetto. [< Ital., dim of *falso* FALSE]

fal·si·fy (fôl′sə fī), *v.,* –**fied,** –**fy·ing.** 1 make false; misrepresent. 2 lie. 3 disprove. —**fal′si·fi·ca′tion,** *n.* —**fal′si·fi′er,** *n.*

fal·si·ty (fôl′sə ti), *n., pl.* –**ties.** 1 a being false; incorrectness. 2 deceitfulness. 3 that which is false.

fal·ter (fôl′tər), *v.* 1 lose courage; draw back; hesitate; waver. 2 move unsteadily; stumble; totter. 3 speak in hesitating, broken words; stammer. —*n.* faltering sound. [cf. Scand. *faltrask* be cumbered] —**fal′ter·er,** *n.* —**fal′ter·ing·ly,** *adv.*

fame (fām), *n., v.,* **famed, fam·ing.** —*n.* 1 a being very well known; having much said or written about one. 2 what is said about one; reputation. —*v.* make famous. [< obs. F < L *fama* < *fari* speak]

famed (fāmd), *adj.* made famous; celebrated; well-known.

fa·mil·ial (fə mil′yəl), *adj.* 1 of or like a family. 2 genetic; inherited through the genes.

fa·mil·iar (fə mil′yər), *adj.* 1 well-known. 2 widely used. 3 well-acquainted. 4 close; personal; intimate. 5 not formal; friendly. 6 too friendly; presuming. —*n.* a familiar friend. [< OF < L *familiaris.* See FAMILY.] —**fa·mil′iar·ly,** *adv.*

fa·mil·iar·i·ty (fə mil′yar′ə ti), *n., pl.* –**ties.** 1 close acquaintance. 2 freedom of behavior suitable only to friends. 3 instance of such behavior.

fa·mil·iar·ize (fə mil′yər īz), *v.,* –**ized,** –**iz·ing.** 1 make well acquainted. 2 make well known. —**fa·mil′iar·i·za′tion,** *n.*

fam·i·ly (fam′ə li; fam′li), *n., pl.* –**lies.** 1 father, mother, and their children. 2 children of a father and mother. 3 group of people living in the same house. 4 all of a person's relatives. 5 group of related people; tribe. 6 group of related or similar things. 7 *Biol.* group of related animals or plants ranking below an order and above a genus. [< L *familia* household < *famulus* servant]

family name, the last name of all the members of a certain family; surname.

family planning, limitation of the size of a family by birth control.

family tree, 1 diagram that shows the relationships of ancestors and members of a family. 2 genealogy of a family.

fam·ine (fam′ən), *n.* 1 starvation. 2 lack of food in a place; time of starving. 3 a very great lack of anything. [< F, ult. < L *fames* hunger]

fam·ish (fam′ish), *v.* be or make extremely hungry; starve. —**fam′ish·ment,** *n.*

fa·mous (fā′məs), *adj.* very well known; noted. [< AF < L, < *fama* FAME] —**fa′mous·ly,** *adv.* —**fa′mous·ness,** *n.*

fan¹ (fan), *v.,* **fanned, fan·ning.** —*n.* 1 instrument or device to make a current of air. It causes a cooling breeze, blows dust away, etc. 2 thing spread out like an open fan. 3 a striking out in baseball. —*v.* 1 make a current of (air) with a fan, etc. 2 direct a current of air with a fan, etc.: *fan a fire.* 3 stir up; arouse: *bad treatment fanned their dislike into hate.* 4 spread out: *fanned her cards.* 5 strike out in baseball.

fan out, spread out: *searchers fanned out.* [< L *vannus* fan for winnowing grain] —**fan′ner,** *n.*

fan² (fan), *n.* 1 an enthusiastic follower of a sport, hobby, etc. 2 admirer of an actor, writer, etc. [short for *fanatic*]

fa·nat·ic (fə nat′ik), *n.* person who is carried away beyond reason by his beliefs. —*adj.* enthusiastic or zealous beyond reason. [< L, < *fanum* temple] —**fa·nat′i·cism,** *n.*

fa·nat·i·cal (fə nat′ə kəl), *adj.* unreasonably enthusiastic; extremely zealous. —**fa·nat′i·cal·ly,** *adv.*

fan belt, strong rubber belt rotated by the crankshaft of an engine that turns the cooling systems, generator, etc. of an automobile.

fan·cied (fan′sid), *adj.* imagined; imaginary.

fan·ci·er (fan′si ər), *n.* person who is especially interested in something, as dogs, etc.

fan·ci·ful (fan′si fəl), *adj.* 1 showing fancy; quaint; odd. 2 influence by fancy; imaginative. 3 imaginary; unreal. —**fan′ci·ful·ly,** *adv.* —**fan′ci·ful·ness,** *n.*

fan·cy (fan′si), *n., pl.* –**cies,** *v.,* –**cied,** –**cy·ing,** *adj.,* –**ci·er,** –**ci·est.** —*n.* 1 imagination. 2 thing imagined. 3 a liking; fondness. —*v.* 1 imagine. 2 be fond of; like. —*adj.* 1 made or arranged specially to please. 2 decorated; ornamental. 3 requiring much skill: *fancy skating.* 4 costing extra to please the taste, etc.: *fancy fruit.* [contraction of *fantasy*]

fan·cy-free (fan′si frē′), *adj.* free from influence.

fan·cy·work (fan′si wėrk′), *n.* ornamental needlework; embroidery, crocheting, etc.

fan·dan·go (fan dang′gō), *n., pl.* –**gos.** a lively Spanish dance in three-quarter time. [< Sp.]

fan·fare (fan′fār), *n.* 1 a short tune or call sounded by trumpets, bugles, etc. 2 a loud show of activity, talk, etc.; showy flourish. [< F, < *fanfarer,* v., < Sp. < Ar.]

fang (fang), *n.* 1 a long, pointed tooth of a dog, wolf, snake, etc. 2 a long, slender, tapering part of anything. [OE] —**fanged,** *adj.* —**fang′less,** *adj.* —**fang′like′,** *adj.*

fan·light (fan′līt′), *n.* 1 a semicircular window with bars spread out like an

open fan. 2 any semicircular or other window over a door.

fan·tail (fan′tāl′), *n.* 1 tail, end, or part spread out like an open fan. 2 pigeon whose tail spreads out like an open fan.

fan·ta·si·a (fan tā′zhi ə; –zhə; –zi ə), *n.* musical composition following no fixed form or style. [< Ital. See FANTASY.]

fan·ta·size (fan′tə sīz), *v.,* –**sized,** –**siz·ing.** imagine; speculate fantastically.

fan·tas·tic (fan tas′tik), **fan·tas·ti·cal** (–tə kəl), *adj.* 1 very odd or queer: *weird, fantastic shadows.* 2 very fanciful; capricious: *a fantastic idea.* 3 unreal: *superstition causes fantastic fears.* —**fan·tas′ti·cal·ly,** *adv.* —**fan·tas′ti·cal·ness,** **fan·tas′ti·cal·i·ty,** *n.*

fan·ta·sy (fan′tə si; –zi), *n., pl.* –**sies.** 1 play of the mind; imagination. 2 a wild, strange fancy; caprice; whim. 4 fantasia. [< OF < L < Gk. *phantasia* appearance, image, ult. < *phainein* show]

far (fär), *adj.,* **far·ther, far·thest,** *adv.* —*adj.* 1 distant; not near: *a far country.* 2 more distant: *the far side of the hill.* —*adv.* 1 a long way off in time or space. 2 very much.

as far as, to the distance, point, or degree that.

by far, very much.

far and away, very much.

far and near, everywhere.

far and wide, everywhere.

far be it from me, I do not dare or want.

far from it, not at all; by no means.

far out, *Informal.* unconventional.

go far, a last long. **b** tend very much. **c** get ahead.

how far, to what distance, point, or degree.

in so far as, to the extent that.

so far, a to this or that point. **b** until now or then.

so far as, to the extent that.

so far so good, until now everything has been safe or satisfactory. [OE *feorr*]

far·ad (far′əd), *n.* a unit of electrical capacity. It is the capacity of a condenser that, when charged with one coulomb, gives a pressure of one volt. [for Michael Faraday]

far·a·way (fär′ə wā′), *adj.* 1 distant. 2 dreamy.

farce (färs), *n., v.,* **farced, farc·ing.** —*n.* 1 play full of ridiculous happenings, absurd actions, etc. 2 broad humor. 3 ridiculous mockery; absurd pretense. [< F, lit., stuffing, ult. < L *farcire* stuff] —**far′cial,** *adj.*

far·ci·cal (fär′sə kəl), *adj.* of or like a farce; absurd; improbable. —**far′ci·cal·i·ty, far′ci·cal·ness,** *n.* —**far′ci·cal·ly,** *adv.*

far cry, a long way; great distance.

fare (fãr), *n., v.,* **fared, far·ing.** —*n.* 1 sum of money paid to ride on a plane, bus, etc. 2 passenger on a plane, bus, etc. 3 food. [blend of OE *faer* and *faru*] —*v.*

1 get along; do. **2** turn out; happen. [OE *faran*] —**far′er**, *n.*

Far East, China, Japan, and other parts of E Asia. —**Far Eastern.**

fare·well (fãr′wel′), *interj.* good-by; good luck. —*n.* **1** expression of good wishes at parting; good-by. **2** departure; leave-taking. —*adj.* of farewell; parting; last.

far-fetched (fãr′fecht′), *adj.* not coming naturally; forced; strained.

far-flung (fãr′flung′), *adj.* widely spread; covering a large area.

fa·ri·na (fə rē′nə), *n.* flour or meal made from grain, potatoes, beans, nuts, etc. [< L, < *far* grits]

far·i·na·ceous (far′ə nā′shəs), *adj.* consisting of flour or meal; starchy; mealy.

farm (färm), *n.* **1** piece of land used to raise crops or animals. **2** thing like a farm. A sheet of water for cultivating oysters is an oyster farm. **3** a minor-league baseball team belonging to or associated with a major-league club. —*v.* **1** raise crops or animals on a farm. **2** cultivate (land). **3** take proceeds or profits of (a tax, undertaking, etc.) on paying a fixed sum. **4** let out (taxes, revenues, an enterprise, etc.) to another for a fixed sum or percentage. **5** be a farmer.

farm out, a subcontract to another person, company, etc. **b** assign to a minor-league baseball team. [< F, ult. < L *firmus* firm]

farm·er (fär′mər), *n.* **1** person who raises crops or animals on a farm; person who runs a farm. **2** person who takes a contract for the collection of taxes by agreeing to pay a certain sum to the government.

farm hand, person who works on a farm.

farm·house (färm′hous′), *n.* house on a farm.

farm·ing (fär′ming), *n.* **1** business of raising crops or animals on a farm; agriculture. **2** practice of letting out the collection of public revenue. **3** condition of being let out at a fixed sum. —*adj.* of or pertaining to farms.

farm·stead (färm′sted), *n.* farm with its buildings.

farm·yard (färm′yärd′), *n.* yard connected with the farm buildings or enclosed by them.

far·o (fãr′ō), *n.* a gambling game played by betting on the order in which certain cards will appear. [appar. alter. of *Pharaoh*]

far-off (fãr′ôf′; -of′), *adj.* distant.

far-reach·ing (fãr′rēch′ing), *adj.* having a wide influence or effect; extending far.

far·ri·er (far′i ər), *n.* person who shoes horses. [< OF < L, < *ferrum* iron]

far·ri·er·y (far′i ər i), *n., pl.* **-er·ies.** work of a farrier.

far·row (far′ō), *n.* litter of pigs. —*v.* give birth to a litter of pigs. [OE *fearh*]

far-see·ing (fär′sē′ing), *adj.* **1** able to see far. **2** looking ahead; planning wisely for the future.

far-sight·ed (fär′sīt′id), *adj.* **1** able to see far. **2** seeing distant things more clearly than near ones. **3** *Fig.* looking ahead; planning wisely for the future. —**far′-sight′ed·ly,** *adv.* —**far′-sight′ed·ness,** *n.*

far·ther (fär′ŧħər), *comparative of* **far.** —*adj.* **1** more distant. **2** more; additional: *do you need farther help?* —*adv.* **1** at or to a greater distance. **2** at or to a more advanced point. **3** in addition; also. [ME *ferther*]

far·ther·most (fär′ŧħər mōst), *adj.* most distant; farthest.

far·thest (fär′ŧħist), *superlative of* **far.** —*adj.* **1** most distant. **2** longest. —*adv.* **1** to or at the greatest distance. **2** most. [ME *ferthest*]

far·thin·gale (fär′ŧħing gāl), *n.* a hoop skirt worn in England from about 1550 to about 1650. [< F < Sp., < *verdugo* rod]

fas·ces (fas′ēz), *n.pl., sing.* **fas·cis** (fas′is). bundle of rods or sticks containing an ax with the blade projecting, carried before a Roman magistrate as a symbol of authority. [< L, pl. of *fascis* bundle]

fas·ci·cle (fas′ə kəl), *n.* **1** a small bundle. **2** a close cluster of flowers, leaves, etc. **3** a single part of a printed work issued in sections. [< L *fasciculus,* dim. of *fascis* bundle] —**fas′ci·cled,** *adj.*

fas·ci·nate (fas′ə nāt), *v.,* **-nat·ed, -nat·ing.** **1** attract very strongly; enchant by charming qualities. **2** hold motionless by strange power, terror, etc. Snakes are said to fascinate small birds. [< L, < *fascinum* spell] —**fas′ci·nat′ed·ly,** *adv.* —**fas′ci·nat′ing,** *adj.* —**fas′ci·nat′ing·ly,** *adv.* —**fas′ci·na′tor,** *n.*

fas·ci·na·tion (fas′ə nā′shən), *n.* **1** a fascinating or being fascinated. **2** very strong attraction; charm; enchantment.

fas·cism (fash′iz əm), *n.* **1** a strongly nationalistic movement in favor of government control of business. **2** any system of government in which property is privately owned, but all industry and business is regulated by a strong national government. [< Ital., < *fascio* bundle (as political emblem) < L *fascis*]

fas·cist (fash′ist), *n.* **1** person who favors and supports fascism. **2** **Fascist,** person who favored and supported Fascism in Italy. —*adj.* of or having to do with fascism or fascists. —**fas·cis′tic, Fas·cis′tic,** *adj.*

fash·ion (fash′ən), *n.* **1** manner; way. **2** the prevailing style; current use in clothes, manners, speech, etc. **3** fashionable people. —*v.* make; shape; form.

after or **in a fashion,** in some way or other; not very well. [< OF < L *factio* a doing or making. Doublet of FACTION.] —**fash′ion·er,** *n.*

fash·ion·a·ble (fash′ən ə bəl; fash′nə bəl), *adj.* **1** following the fashion; in fashion; stylish. **2** of, like, or used by people of fashion. —**fash′ion·a·ble·ness,** *n.* —**fash′ion·a·bly,** *adv.*

fast¹ (fast; fäst), *adj.* **1** quick; rapid; swift. **2** indicating a time ahead of the correct time. **3** not restrained in pleasures; too wild. **4** firm; secure; tight: *a fast hold on a rope.* **5** loyal; faithful. **6** that will not fade easily. —*adv.* **1** quickly; rapidly; swiftly. **2** firmly; securely; tightly. **3** thoroughly; completely; soundly: *he was fast asleep.*

play fast and loose, say one thing and do another; be tricky, insincere, or unreliable.

pull a fast one, play a trick; deceive. [OE *fæst*]

fast² (fast; fäst), *v.* go without food; go without certain kinds of food. —*n.* **1** a fasting. **2** day or time of fasting. [OE *fæstan*]

fast day, day observed by fasting, esp. a day regularly set apart by a church.

fas·ten (fas′ən; fäs′-), *v.* **1** fix firmly in place; tie; lock; shut. **2** attach; connect: *he tried to fasten the blame upon his companions.* **3** direct; fix: *the dog fastened his eyes on the stranger.* [OE *fæstnian* < *fæst* fast¹] —**fas′ten·er,** *n.*

fas·ten·ing (fas′ən ing; fas′ning; fäs′-), *n.* thing used to fasten something, as a lock, bolt, clasp, hook, button, etc.

fast food, food that is cooked and served quickly, as hamburgers, chicken, etc. —**fast-food,** *adj.*

fas·tid·i·ous (fas tid′i əs), *adj.* hard to please; extremely refined or critical; easily disgusted. [< L, < *fastidium* loathing] —**fas·tid′i·ous·ly,** *adv.* —**fas·tid′i·ous·ness,** *n.*

fast·ness (fast′nis; fäst′-), *n.* **1** a strong, safe place; stronghold. **2** a being fast.

fast-track (fast′trak′), *v.,* **-tracked, -track·ing.** arrange or move for consideration, action, etc., as soon as possible: *fast-track emergency relief.*

on the fast track, moving forward quickly. —**fast′-track′,** *adj.*

fat (fat), *n., adj.,* **fat·ter, fat·test,** *v.,* **fat·ted, fat·ting.** —*n.* **1** a white or yellow, oily substance formed in the bodies of animals. **2** animal tissue containing this substance. **3** any of a class of organic compounds of which the natural fats are usually mixtures. **4** the richest or best part. —*adj.* **1** consisting of or containing fat; oily: *fat meat.* **2** fertile: *fat land.* **3** profitable: *a fat office.* **4** plentiful. **5** too fat; obese. —*v.* make fat; become fat. [OE *fætt,* orig. pp., fatted] —**fat′ly,** *adv.* —**fat′ness,** *n.*

fa·tal (fā′təl), *adj.* **1** causing death. **2** causing destruction or ruin. **3** important; decisive; fateful. [< L, < *fatum* FATE] —**fa′tal·ly,** *adv.* —**fa′tal·ness,** *n.*

fa·tal·ism (fā′təl iz əm), *n.* **1** belief that fate controls everything that happens. **2** submission to everything that happens as inevitable. —**fa′tal·ist,** *n.* —**fa′tal·is′tic,** *adj.* —**fa′tal·is′ti·cal·ly,** *adv.*

fa·tal·i·ty (fā tal′ə ti; fə-), *n., pl.* **-ties.** **1** a fatal accident or happening; death. **2** a fatal influence or effect.

fat cat, 1 big contributor to political parties. **2** person who is very highly paid and expects special privileges, deference, etc.

fate (fāt), *n., v.,* **fat·ed, fat·ing.** —*n.* **1** power supposed to fix beforehand and control everything that happens. **2** what is caused by fate. **3** what becomes of a person or thing. **4** death; ruin. —*v.* destine. [< L *fatum* (thing) spoken (i.e., by the gods), pp. of *fari* speak]

fat·ed (fāt′id), *adj.* determined by fate.

fate·ful (fāt′fəl), *adj.* **1** controlled by fate. **2** determining what is to happen; important; decisive. **3** showing what fate decrees; prophetic. **4** causing death, destruction, or ruin; disastrous. —**fate′ful·ly,** *adv.* —**fate′ful·ness,** *n.*

Fates (fāts), *n.pl. Gk. and Roman Myth.* the three goddesses supposed to control human life.

fa·ther (fä′t͟hər), *n.* **1** a male parent. **2** person who is like a father. **3** a male ancestor; forefather. **4** person who helped to make something; founder; inventor; author. **5** title of respect used in addressing priests. —*v.* **1** be the father of. **2** take care of as a father does; act as a father to. **3** make; originate. **the Father,** God. [OE *fæder*] —**fa′ther·hood,** *n.* —**fa′ther·less,** *adj.* —**fa′ther·less·ness,** *n.*

fa·ther-in-law (fä′t͟hər in lô′), *n., pl.* **fathers-in-law.** father of one's husband or wife.

fa·ther·land (fä′t͟hər land′), *n.* one's native country; land of one's ancestors.

fa·ther·ly (fä′t͟hər li), *adj.* **1** of a father. **2** like a father; kindly. —*adv.* in the manner of a father. —**fa′ther·li·ness,** *n.*

fath·om (fat͟h′əm), *n., pl.* **fath·oms** or (*esp. collectively*) **fath·om,** *v.* —*n.* a unit of measure equal to 6 feet, used mostly in measuring the depth of water and the length of ships' ropes, cables, etc. —*v.* **1** measure the depth of. **2** get to the bottom of; understand fully. [OE *fæthm* width of the outstretched arms] —**fath′om·a·ble,** *adj.* —**fath′om·er,** *n.* —**fath′om·less,** *adj.* —**fath′om·less·ly,** *adv.*

fa·tigue (fə tēg′), *n., v.,* **-tigued, -ti·guing,** *adj.* —*n.* **1** weariness. **2** hard work; effort. **3** a weakening (of metal) caused by long-continued use or strain. —*v.* **1** cause fatigue in; weary. **2** weaken by much use or strain. —*adj.* pertaining to fatigue.

fatigues, work clothes, of the military. [< F, ult. < L *fatigare* tire] —**fa·tigue′less,** *adj.*

Fa·ti·ma (fə tē′mə; fat′i mə), *n.* A.D. 606?–632, only daughter of Muhammad.

fat·ling (fat′ling), *n.* calf, lamb, kid, or pig fattened to be killed for food.

fat·ten (fat′ən), *v.* make fat; become fat. —**fat′ten·er,** *n.*

fat·tish (fat′ish), *adj.* somewhat fat. —**fat′tish·ness,** *n.*

fat·ty (fat′i), *adj.,* **-ti·er, -ti·est. 1** of fat; containing fat. **2** like fat; oily; greasy. —**fat′ti·ly,** *adv.* —**fat′ti·ness,** *n.*

fatty acid, any one of a group of organic acids, found in animal and vegetable fats and oils.

fa·tu·i·ty (fə tü′ə ti; -tū′-), *n., pl.* **-ties.** self-satisfied stupidity; silliness.

fat·u·ous (fach′ù əs), *adj.* stupid but self-satisfied; foolish; silly. [< L *fatuus* foolish] —**fat′u·ous·ly,** *adv.* —**fat′u·ous·ness,** *n.*

fat·wa (fat′wä), *n.* directive from a Muslim leader. [Ar., edict]

fau·cet (fô′sit), *n.* device containing a valve for controlling the flow of water or other liquid from a pipe, tank, barrel, etc. [< F *fausset* < *fausser* bore through]

fault (fôlt), *n.* **1** something that is not as it should be. **2** mistake. **3** cause for blame. **4** a break in a rock or vein with part pushed up or down. **5** failure to serve the ball into the right place in tennis and similar games. —*v. Geol.* suffer or cause a fault. **at fault,** observing blame; wrong. **find fault,** pick out faults; complain. **find fault with,** object to; criticize. **in fault,** deserving blame; wrong. **to a fault,** too much; very. [< OF *faute,* ult. < L *fallere* deceive]

fault·find·ing (fôlt′fīn′ding), *n., adj.* finding fault; complaining, pointing out faults. —**fault′find′er,** *n.*

fault·less (fôlt′lis), *adj.* without a single fault; free from blemish or error; perfect. —**fault′less·ly,** *adv.* —**fault′less·ness,** *n.*

fault·y (fôl′ti), *adj.,* **fault·i·er, fault·i·est. 1** having faults; containing blemishes or errors; wrong; imperfect. **2** blamable. —**fault′i·ly,** *adv.* —**fault′i·ness,** *n.*

faun (fôn), *n. Roman Myth.* deity that helped farmers and shepherds, represented as looking like a man, but with the ears, horns, tail, and sometimes the legs, of a goat. [< L *Faunus* a pastoral deity]

fau·na (fô′nə), *n.* animals of a given region or time. [< NL, orig. (in LL) name of a rural goddess]

faux pas (fō′ pä′), *pl.* **faux pas** (fō′ päz′), slip in speech, conduct, manners, etc.; breach of etiquette; blunder. [< F]

fa·vor (fā′vər), *n.* **1** kindness. **2** liking; approval. **3** more than fair treatment; too great kindness. **4** gift; token. —*v.* **1** show kindness to. **2** like; approve. **3** give more than fair treatment to. **4** help. **5** treat gently: *the dog favors his sore foot.* **6** look like: *the girl favors her mother.* **curry favor,** try to win favor from someone by insincere or constant flattery, attention, etc. **in favor of, a** on the side of; supporting. **b** to the advantage of; helping. [< OF < L, < *favere* show kindness to] —**fa′vored,** *adj.* —**fa′vor·er,** *n.* —**fa′vor·ing·ly,** *adv.*

fa·vor·a·ble (fā′vər ə bəl; fāv′rə-), *adj.* **1** favoring; approving. **2** being to one's advantage; helping: *a favorable wind.* —**fa′vor·a·ble·ness,** *n.* —**fa′vor·a·bly,** *adv.*

fa·vor·ite (fā′vər it; fāv′rit), *adj.* liked better than others; liked very much. —*n.* **1** one liked better than others. **2** one expected to win a contest.

favorite son, politician supported by his or her state's delegation for nomination as a presidential candidate at a national convention.

fa·vor·it·ism (fā′vər ə tiz′əm; fāv′rə-), *n.* a favoring of one or some more than others; having favorites.

fawn¹ (fôn), *n.* **1** deer less than a year old. **2** a light, yellowish brown. —*adj.* light yellowish-brown. [< OF *faon,* ult. < L *fetus* fetus]

fawn² (fôn), *v.* **1** cringe and bow; act slavishly. **2** (of dogs, etc.) show fondness by crouching, wagging the tail, licking the hand, etc. [OE *fagnian* < *fægen* fain] —**fawn′er,** *n.* —**fawn′ing·ly,** *adv.*

fax (faks), *n., pl.* **faxes. 1** =fax machine. **2** copy of document, etc., sent or received on a fax machine. [< *facsimilie*]

fax machine, electronic device for sending, receiving, and printing out documents, etc., over telephone lines.

fay (fā), *n.* =fairy. [< OF, ult. < L *fatum* FATE]

faze (fāz), *v.,* **fazed, faz·ing.** disturb; worry; bother. [var. of *feeze,* OE *fēsian* drive]

FBI or **F.B.I.,** *U.S.* Federal Bureau of Investigation.

F.C.C., FCC, Federal Communications Commission.

F clef, the bass clef in music.

FDA or **F.D.A.,** Food and Drug Administration.

Fe, iron. [< L *ferrum*]

fe·al·ty (fē′əl ti), *n., pl.* **-ties. 1** loyalty and duty owed by a vassal to his feudal lord. **2** loyalty; faithfulness; allegiance. [< OF < L *fidelitas.* Doublet of FIDELITY.]

fear (fir), *n.* **1** a being afraid; feeling that danger or evil is near; dread. **2** cause for fear; danger: *there is no fear of our losing.* **3** an uneasy feeling; anxious thought. —*v.* **1** feel fear. **2** feel fear of. **3** feel concern. **for fear of (a thing),** in order to prevent (that thing) from occurring. **without fear or favor,** impartially; justly. [OE *fær* peril] —**fear′er,** *n.* —**fear′less,** *adj.* —**fear′less·ly,** *adv.* —**fear′less·ness,** *n.*

fear·ful (fir′fəl), *adj.* **1** causing fear; terrible; dreadful. **2** full of fear; afraid. **3** showing fear; caused by fear. **4** very bad, unpleasant, ugly, etc. —**fear′ful·ly** *adv.* —**fear′ful·ness,** *n.*

fear·some (fir′səm), *adj.* **1** causing fear; frightful. **2** timid; afraid. —**fear′some·ly,** *adv.* —**fear′some·ness,** *n.*

fea·si·ble (fē′zə bəl), *adj.* **1** capable of being done or carried out easily. **2** likely; probable. **3** suitable; convenient. [< OF *faisable,* ult. < L *facere* do] —**fea′si·bil′i·ty, fea′si·ble·ness,** *n.* —**fea′si·bly,** *adv.*

feast (fēst), *n.* **1** an elaborate meal prepared for some special occasion and for a number of guests. **2** a religious festival or celebration. —*v.* **1** have a feast. **2** provide with a feast. **3** give pleasure or joy to. [< OF < L *festa* festal ceremonies] —**feast′er,** *n.*

feat (fēt), *n.* a great or unusual deed; act showing great skill, strength, etc. [< OF < L *factum* (thing) done. Doublet of FACT.]

feath·er (feth′ər), *n.* **1** one of the light, thin growths that cover a bird's skin. **2** something like a feather in shape or lightness. —*v.* **1** supply or cover with feathers. **2** grow like feathers. **3** turn the edge of a blade in the direction of movement.

feather in one's cap, thing to be proud of.

feather one's nest, take advantage of chances to get rich.

in fine feather, in good health, high spirits, etc.

make feathers fly, cause trouble.

ruffle (someone's) feathers, irritate.

smooth (someone's) feathers, soothe; smooth over. [OE *fether*] —**feath′ered,** *adj.* —**feath′er·less,** *adj.* —**feath′er·like′,** *adj.*

feath·er·brain (feth′ər brān′), *n.* a silly, foolish, weak-minded person. —**feath′er·brained′,** *adj.*

feath·er·weight (feth′ər wāt′), *n.* **1** a very light thing or person. **2** boxer who weighs less than 126 pounds and more than 118 pounds. —*adj.* very light.

feath·er·y (feth′ər i), *adj.* **1** having feathers; covered with feathers. **2** like feathers. **3** light; flimsy. —**feath′er·i·ness.** *n.*

fea·ture (fē′chər), *n., v.,* **-tured, -tur·ing.** —*n.* **1** part of the face. The nose, mouth, chin, and forehead are features. **2** a distinct part or quality; thing that stands out and attracts attention. **3 a** main film being shown. **b** a special article, comic strip, etc., in a newspaper. —*v.* be a feature of. [< OF < L *factura* < *facere* do] —**fea′ture·less,** *adj.*

Feb., February.

fe·brile (fē′brəl; feb′rəl), *adj.* **1** of fever; feverish. **2** caused by fever. [< Med.L *febrilis.* See FEVER.]

Feb·ru·ar·y (feb′rú er′i; feb′yú–), *n., pl.* **-ar·ies.** the second month of the year. It has 28 days except in leap years, when it has 29. [< L, *februa,* pl., the feast of purification celebrated on Feb. 15]

fe·ces (fē′sēz), *n.pl.* waste matter discharged from the intestines. [< L *faeces,* pl., dregs] —**fe′cal,** *adj.*

feck·less (fek′lis), *adj.* **1** futile; ineffective. **2** weak; helpless. [< *feck* vigor, var. of *fect* < *effect*] —**feck′less·ly,** *adv.* —**feck′less·ness,** *n.*

fe·cund (fē′kənd; fek′ənd), *adj.* fruitful; productive; fertile. [< F < L *fecundus*] —**fe·cun′di·ty,** *n.*

fed¹ (fed), *v.* pt. and pp. of **feed.**

fed up, disgusted or bored: *fed up with meetings.*

fed² (fed), *n. Informal.* Federal agent.

Fed (fed), *n. Informal.* **1** Federal Reserve System. **2** Federal Reserve Bank. **3** Federal Reserve Board of Governors.

fed·er·al (fed′ər əl; fed′rəl), *adj.* **1** formed by an agreement between groups establishing a central organization. **2** of or having to do with such a central organization.

Federal, a of or having to do with the central government of the United States. **b** supporting the Constitution. **c** supporting the central government of the United States during the Civil War.

Federal, supporter or soldier of the central government of the United States during the Civil War. [< L *foedus* compact] —**fed′er·al·ly,** *adv.*

Federal Bureau of Investigation, bureau of the Department of Justice established to investigate violations of Federal laws.

fed·er·al·ism (fed′ər əl iz′əm; fed′rəl–), *n.* federal principles of government.

Federalism, principles of the Federalist Party.

fed·er·al·ist (fed′ər əl ist; fed′rəl–), *n.* **1** advocate of a federal union among the colonies during and after the War of Independence. **2** person who favors the federal principle of government. —*adj.* of federalism or the Federalists.

ederalist, member of the Federalist Party in the United States. —**fed′er·al·is′tic,** *adj.*

Federalist Party, a political party in the United States that favored the adoption of the Constitution and a strong central government. It existed from about 1791 to about 1816.

fed·er·al·ize (fed′ər əl īz; fed′rəl–), *v.,* **-ized, -iz·ing. 1** unite into a federal union. **2** bring under control of the federal government. —**fed′er·al·i·za′tion,** *n.*

fed·er·ate (*v.* fed′ər āt; *adj.* fed′ər it, fed′rit), *v.,* **-at·ed, -at·ing,** *adj.* —*v.* form into a federation. —*adj.* federated. [< L *foederatus* leagued together. See FEDERAL.]

fed·er·a·tion (fed′ər ā′shən), *n.* **1** formation of a political unity out of a number of separate states, etc. **2** union by agreement, often a union of states or nations. —**fed′er·a′tive,** *adj.* —**fed′er·a′tive·ly,** *adv.*

fe·do·ra (fi dô′rə; –dō′–), *n.* a soft felt hat with a curved brim.

fee (fē), *n.* **1** sum of money asked or paid for a service or privilege; charge. Doctors and lawyers get fees for their services. **2** right to keep and use land; fief. **3** an inherited estate in land. **4** ownership. [< AF *fieu* < Gmc.]

fee·ble (fē′bəl), *adj.,* **-bler, -blest.** weak; ineffective: *a feeble attempt.* [< OF < L < *flebilis* lamentable < *fiere* weep] —**fee′ble·ness,** *n.* —**fee′blish,** *adj.* —**fee′bly,** *adv.*

fee·ble-mind·ed (fē′bəl mīn′did), *adj.* lacking normal intelligence. —**fee′ble-mind′ed·ly,** *adv.* —**fee′ble-mind′ed·ness,** *n.*

feed (fēd), *v.,* **fed, feed·ing,** *n.* —*v.* **1** give food to. **2** eat. **3** supply with material: *feed a machine; praise fed his vanity.* —*n.* **1** food for animals. **2** a supplying with material. **3** the material supplied. [OE *fēdan* < *fōda* food] —**feed′er,** *n.*

feed·back (fēd′bak′), *n.* **1** the return of the results of a process, or a part of them, to the same or an earlier stage of the process, as a self-criticizing or regulating mechanism. **2** the return of the energy in an electronic circuit from the output to the input, either in positive phase to amplify or in negative phase to control the output.

feed·bag (fēd′bag′), *n.* bag for grain that hangs from a horse's head, enabling the animal to feed; nosebag.

feel (fēl), *v.,* **felt, feel·ing,** *n.* —*v.* **1** touch: *feel this cloth.* **2** try to touch; try to find by touching: *feel in all your pockets.* **3** find out by touching; be aware of: *feel the cool breeze.* **4** have the feeling of being; be: *she feels sure.* **5** seem: *the air feels cold.* **6** experience. —*n.* **1** touch: *the feel of silk.* **2** a feeling: *a feel of frost in the air.* **3** the sense of touch. [OE *fēlan*]

feel·er (fēl′ər), *n.* **1** person or thing that feels. **2** a special part of an animal's body for touching, as an insect's antenna. **3** remark, question, etc., made to find out what others are thinking or planning.

feel·ing (fēl′ing), *n.* **1** act or condition of one that feels. **2** sense of touch. **3** a being conscious; awareness. **4** emotion; sympathy. **5** opinion. —*adj.* sensitive. **feelings,** sympathies; susceptibilities: *hurt one's feelings.* —**feel′ing·ly,** *adv.*

feet (fēt), *n.* pl. of **foot.**

feign (fān), *v.* **1** put on a false appearance of; pretend. **2** make up to deceive: *feign an excuse.* [< OF *feindre* (*feign–*) < L *fingere* form] —**feigned,** *adj.* —**feign′ed·ly,** *adv.* —**feign′er,** *n.* —**feign′ing·ly,** *adv.*

feint (fānt), *n.* **1** false appearance; pretense. **2** movement intended to deceive. —*v.* make a pretended blow. [< F, < *feindre* FEIGN]

feis·ty (fīs′ti), *adj.,* **feist·i·er, feist·i·est.** full of high spirits; lively.

feld·spar (feld′spär′; fel′–), *n.* any of several crystalline minerals composed mostly of aluminum silicates. Also, **felspar.** [< *feld–* (< G *feldspat,* lit. field spar) + *spar*³]

fe·lic·i·tate (fə lis′ə tāt), *v.,* **-tat·ed, -tat·ing.** formally express good wishes to; congratulate. [< LL, < *felix* happy] —**fe·lic′i·ta′tion,** *n.*

fe·lic·i·tous (fə lis′ə təs), *adj.* **1** well chosen for the occasion; unusually appropriate. **2** having a gift for apt speech. —**fe·lic′i·tous·ly,** *adv.* —**fe·lic′i·tous·ness,** *n.*

fe·lic·i·ty (fə lis′ə ti), *n., pl.* **-ties. 1** happiness; bliss. **2** good fortune; blessing. **3** a pleasing aptness in expression. **4** a happy turn of thought; well-chosen phrase.

fe·line (fē′līn), *adj.* **1** of or belonging to the cat family. **2** catlike; stealthy. —*n.* any animal belonging to the cat family, such as lions, tigers, and panthers. [< L *felis* cat] —**fe′line·ly**, *adv.* —**fe′line·ness, fe·lin′i·ty.** *n.*

fell¹ (fel), *v.* pt. of **fall.**

fell² (fel), *v.* **1** cause to fall; knock down. **2** cut down (a tree). **3** turn down and stitch one edge of (a seam) over the other. —*n.* seam made by felling. [OE *fellan* < *feallan* fall] —**fell′a·ble,** *adj.* —**fell′er,** *n.*

fell³ (fel), *adj.* **1** cruel; fierce; terrible: *a fell blow.* **2** deadly; destructive: *a fell disease.* [< OF < VL *fello.* See FELON¹.] —**fell′ness,** *n.*

fell⁴ (fel), *n.* skin or hide of an animal. [OE; akin to FILM]

fel·loe (fel′ō), *n.* the circular rim of a wheel into which the outer ends of the spokes are inserted. [var. of *felly,* OE *felg*]

fel·low (fel′ō), *n.* **1** man; boy. **2** companion; comrade; associate. **3** a graduate student who has a fellowship in a university or college. —*adj.* belonging to the same class; united by the same work, aims, etc.: *fellow citizens, fellow workers.* [< Scand. *fēlagi* partner (lit., fee-layer)]

fel·low·ship (fel′ō ship), *n.* **1** companionship. **2** a taking part with others; sharing. **3** group of people having similar tastes, interests, etc.; brotherhood. **4** position or sum of money given to a graduate student in a university or college to enable him or her to go on with his or her studies.

fel·on¹ (fel′ən), *n.* person who has committed a serious crime. [< OF, ult. < L *fellare* suck (obscene)]

fel·on² (fel′ən), *n.* a very painful infection on a finger or toe, usually near the nail.

fe·lo·ni·ous (fə lō′ni əs), *adj.* that is a felony; criminal. —**fe·lo′ni·ous·ly,** *adv.* —**fe·lo′ni·ous·ness,** *n.*

fel·o·ny (fel′ə ni), *n., pl.* **–nies.** crime more serious than a misdemeanor. Murder and burglary are felonies.

fel·spar (fel′spär′), *n.* feldspar.

felt¹ (felt), *v.* pt. and pp. of **feel.**

felt² (felt), *n.* cloth made by rolling and pressing together wool, hair, or fur, used to make hats, slippers, etc. —*adj.* made of felt. —*v.* **1** make into felt. **2** cover with felt. [OE]

felt-tip (felt′tip′), *n.* or **felt tip pen,** pen with a hard felt tip, esp. for labeling.

fem., feminine.

fe·male (fē′māl), *n.* **1** woman or girl. **2** animal belonging to the sex that brings forth young. **3** plant having a pistil and no stamens. —*adj.* **1** of or pertaining to women or girls. **2** belonging to the sex that brings forth young. **3** having pistils. **4** designating some part of a machine, connection, etc., into which a corresponding part fits. [< OF < L *femella,*

dim. of *femina* woman; form infl. by *male*] —**fe·mal′i·ty,** *n.*

fem·i·nine (fem′ə nin), *adj.* **1** of women or girls. **2** like a woman; womanly. **3** like that of a woman; not suited to a man. **4** of or belonging to the female sex. **5** of the gender to which names of females belong. *Actress, queen,* and *cow* are feminine nouns. —*n.* **a** the feminine gender. **b** word or form in the feminine gender. [< OF < L, < *femina* woman] —**fem′i·nine·ly,** *adv.* —**fem′i·nin′i·ty, fem′i·nine·ness,** *n.*

fem·i·nism (fem′ə niz əm), *n.* **1** doctrine that favors more rights and activities for women. **2** feminine nature or character. —**fem′i·nist,** *n.* —**fem′i·nis′tic,** *adj.*

femme fa·tale (fam fä tál′), *French.* a dangerously fascinating or alluring woman; siren.

fe·mur (fē′mər), *n., pl.* **fe·murs, fem·o·ra,** (fem′ə rə). the thighbone. [< L, thigh] —**fem′o·ral,** *adj.*

fen (fen), *n.* marsh; swamp; bog. [OE *fenn*]

fence (fens), *n., v.,* **fenced, fenc·ing.** —*n.* **1** railing, wall, or other means of enclosing a yard, garden, field, farm, etc., to show where it ends or to keep people or animals out or in. **2** person who buys and sells stolen goods. —*v.* **1** put a fence around; enclose. **2** fight with swords or foils. **3** parry; evade.

mend (one's) fences, improve one's relations or standing.

on the fence, not having made up one's mind which side to take; doubtful; hesitating.

sit on the fence, remain uncommitted or undecided about something. [var. of *defence*] —**fence′less,** *adj.* —**fence′less·ness,** *n.* —**fence′like′,** *adj.* —**fenc′er,** *n.*

fenc·ing (fen′sing), *n.* **1** art of fighting with swords or foils. **2** material for fences.

fend (fend), *v.* defend; resist.

fend for oneself, provide for oneself; get along by one's own efforts. [var. of *defend*]

fend·er (fen′dər), *n.* **1** anything that keeps or wards something off. **2** guard or protection over the wheel of an automobile, motorcycle, etc.; mudguard. **3** a metal guard, frame, or screen in front of a fireplace to keep hot coals and sparks from the room. [var. of *defender*]

fend·er-bend·er (fen′dər ben′dər), *n.* minor automobile collision.

Fe·ni·an (fē′ni ən; fēn′yən), *n.* member of an Irish secret organization founded in the United States about 1858 for the purpose of overthrowing English rule in Ireland. —*adj.* of or having to do with the Fenians. —**Fe′ni·an·ism,** *n.*

fen·nel (fen′əl), *n.* a tall plant with yellow flowers, used in medicine and cooking. [< VL *fenuclum,* ult. < L *fenum* hay]

fe·ral (fir′əl), *adj.* **1** wild; untamed. **2** brutal; savage. [< L *fera* beast]

fer-de-lance (fer də läns′), *n.* a large poisonous snake of tropical America. [< F, iron (tip) of a lance]

fer·ment (*v.* fər ment′; *n.* fèr′ment), *v.* **1** undergo a gradual chemical change, becoming sour or alcoholic and giving off bubbles of gas. **2** cause this chemical change in. **3** cause unrest in; excite; agitate. **4** be excited; seethe with agitation or unrest. —*n.* **1** substance causing fermentation: *yeast is a ferment.* **2** excitement; agitation; unrest: *national ferment.* [< L *fermentum* < *fervere* boil] —**fer·ment′a·ble,** *adj.*

fer·men·ta·tion (fèr′men tā′shən), *n.* **1** act or process of fermenting. **2** excitement; agitation; unrest. **3** a change, as becoming sour or alcoholic and giving off bubbles of gas, caused by a ferment.

fer·mi·um (fer′mi əm), *n.* a rare, radioactive, artificial element, Fm, produced as a by-product of nuclear fission. [named for Enrico *Fermi*]

fern (fèrn), *n.* plant that has roots, stems, and leaves, but no flowers, and reproduces by spores instead of seeds. [OE *fearn*] —**fern′like′,** *adj.* —**fern′y,** *adj.*

fe·ro·cious (fə rō′shəs), *adj.* savagely cruel; fierce. [< L, < *ferox* fierce] —**fe·ro′cious·ly,** *adv.* —**fe·roc′i·ty, fe·ro′cious·ness,** *n.*

fer·ret (fer′it), *n.* a white or yellowish-white weasel used for killing rats, hunting rabbits, etc. —*v.* **1** hunt with ferrets. **2** hunt; search. [< OF *fuiret,* ult. < L *fur* thief] —**fer′ret·er,** *n.*

fer·ric (fer′ik), *adj.* **a** of or containing iron. **b** containing trivalent iron. [< L *ferrum* iron]

Fer·ris wheel (fer′is), a large, revolving wheel with seats hanging from its rim, used in carnivals, amusement parks, etc. [for G. W. G. *Ferris,* its inventor]

fer·rous (fer′əs), *adj.* **a** of or containing iron. **b** containing divalent iron.

fer·ru·gi·nous (fə rü′jə nəs), *adj.* **1** of or containing iron; like that of iron. **2** reddish-brown like rust. [< L, < *ferrugo* iron rust < *ferrum* iron]

fer·rule (fer′əl; –ül), *n., v.,* **–ruled, –rul·ing.** —*n.* **1** a metal ring or cap put around the end of a cane, umbrella, etc. **2** a metal ring or short tube. —*v.* supply with a ferrule. Also, **ferule.** [< OF, ult. < L *viriola,* dim of *viriae* bracelets]

fer·ry (fer′i), *n., pl.* **–ries,** *v.,* **–ried, –ry·ing.** —*n.* **1** place where boats carry people and goods across a river or narrow stretch of water. **2** the boat used; ferryboat. [< v.] —*v.* **1** carry (people and goods) back and forth across a river or narrow stretch of water. **2** go across in a ferryboat. [OE *ferian* < *fær* fare]

fer·ry·boat (fer′i bōt′), *n.* boat used for ferrying.

fer·ry·man (fer′i mən), *n., pl.* **–men.** person who owns or has charge of a ferry.

fer·tile (fèr′təl), *adj.* **1** able to produce much; rich in things that aid growth, development, etc. **2** capable of reproduction; able to produce seeds, fruit, young, etc. **3** *Biol.* capable of developing into a new individual; fertilized. [< L *fertilis* < *ferre* bear] —**fer′tile·ly,** *adv.* —**fer′tile·ness,** *n.*

fer·til·i·ty (fėr til′ə ti), *n.* a being fertile.

fer·ti·lize (fėr′tə līz), *v.,* **-lized, -liz·ing. 1** make fertile; make able to produce much. **2** put fertilizer on. **3** unite with (an egg cell) in fertilization; impregnate. —**fer′ti·liz′a·ble,** *adj.* —**fer′ti·li·za′tion,** *n.*

fer·ti·liz·er (fėr′tə līz′ər), *n.* substance put on land to make it able to produce more, as manure.

fer·ule[1] (fer′əl; –ül), *n., v.,* **-uled, -ul·ing.** —*n.* stick or ruler used for punishing children by striking them on the hand. —*v.* punish with a stick or ruler. [< L *ferula* rod]

fer·ule[2] (fer′əl; –ül), *n., v.,* **-uled, -ul·ing.** =ferrule.

fer·vent (fėr′vənt), *adj.* showing warmth of feeling; very earnest. [< F < L *fervens* boiling] —**fer′ven·cy, fer′vent·ness,** *n.* —**fer′vent·ly,** *adv.*

fer·vid (fėr′vid), *adj.* showing great warmth of feeling; intensely emotional. [< L, < *fervere* boil] —**fer′vid·ly,** *adv.* —**fer′vid·ness,** *n.*

fer·vor (fėr′vər), *n.* great warmth of feeling; intense emotion. [< OF < L. See FERVENT.]

fes·cue (fes′kū), *n.* a tough grass used for pasture. [< OF, ult. < L *festuca*]

fes·tal (fes′təl), *adj.* of a feast, festival, or holiday; joyous; festive. [< OF < LL < L *festum* feast] —**fes′tal·ly,** *adv.*

fes·ter (fes′tər), *v.* **1** form pus. **2** cause pus to form. **3** cause irritation or pain; rankle. [< n.] —*n.* sore that forms pus; small ulcer. [< OF < L *fistula* pipe, ulcer]

fes·ti·val (fes′tə vəl), *n.* **1** day or special time of rejoicing or feasting, often in memory of some great happening. **2** celebration; entertainment: *a music festival.* **3** merrymaking; revelry. —*adj.* having to do with a festival. [< Med.L, ult. < L *festum* feast]

Festival of Lights, =Hanukkah.

fes·tive (fes′tiv), *adj.* of or for a feast, festival, or holiday; joyous; merry. —**fes′tive·ly,** *adv.* —**fes′tive·ness,** *n.*

fes·tiv·i·ty (fes tiv′ə ti), *n., pl.* **-ties. 1** festive activity; thing done to celebrate. **2** gaiety; merriment. **3 festivities,** festive proceedings.

fes·toon (fes tün′), *n.* a hanging curve of flowers, leaves, ribbons, etc. —*v.* **1** decorate with festoons. **2** form into festoons; hang in curves. [< F < Ital. *festone* < *festa* festival, feast]

fet·a (fet′ə), *n.* Greek cheese made from goat's or sheep's milk and cured in brine.

fe·tal (fē′təl), *adj.* **1** of a fetus. **2** like that of a fetus.

fetch (fech), *v.* **1** go and get; bring. **2** cause to come; succeed in bringing. **3** be sold for. —*n.* act of fetching. [OE *feccan*] —**fetch′er,** *n.*

fetch·ing (fech′ing), *adj. Informal.* attractive; charming. —**fetch′ing·ly,** *adv.*

fete (fāt), *n., v.,* **fet·ed, fet·ing,** —*n.* festival; entertainment; party. —*v.* honor with a fete; entertain: *the engaged couple were feted by their friends.* [< F, feast]

fet·id (fet′id; fē′tid), *adj.* smelling very bad; stinking. [< L *foetidus* < *foetere* to smell] —**fet′id·ly,** *adv.* —**fet′id·ness, fe·tid′i·ty,** *n.*

fe·tish (fē′tish; fet′ish), *n.* **1** any material thing supposed to have magic power. **2** anything regarded with unreasoning reverence or devotion. [< F < Pg. *feitiço* charm < L *facticius* artificial] —**fe′tish·like′,** *adj.*

fet·ish·ism (fē′tish iz əm; fet′ish–), *n.* belief in fetishes; worship of fetishes. —**fe′tish·ist,** *n.* —**fe′tish·is′tic,** *adj.*

fet·lock (fet′lok), *n.* **1** tuft of hair above a horse's hoof on the back part of the leg. **2** part of a horse's leg where this tuft grows. [ME *fetlok*]

fet·ter (fet′ər), *n.* **1** chain or shackle for the feet to prevent escape. **2** Usually, **fetters.** anything that shackles or binds; restraint. —*v.* **1** bind with fetters; chain the feet of. **2** bind; restrain. [OE *feter;* akin to FOOT]

fet·tle (fet′əl), *n.* condition; trim: *the horse is in fine fettle.* [? < ME *fettel(en)* gird up, < OE *fetel* belt]

fet·tuc·cine or **fet·tu·ci·ne** (fet′ə chē′ni), *n.* **1** flat, thin Italian noodles. **2** dish made with these noodles, usually with a sauce and cheese. Also, **fettuccini** or **fettucini.**

fe·tus (fē′təs), *n.* an animal embryo during the later stages of its development. [< L]

feud[1] (fūd), *n.* **1** a long and deadly quarrel between families, often passed down from generation to generation. **2** bitter hatred between two persons, groups, etc. **3** quarrel. —*v.* carry on a feud; quarrel endlessly. [var. of ME *fede* < OF < OHG *fehida* enmity] —**feu′dal,** *adj.*

feud[2] (fūd), *n.* a feudal estate; fief. [< Med.L *feudum* < Gmc.]

feu·dal (fū′dəl), *adj.* **1** of or having to do with feudalism. **2** of or having to do with feuds or fiefs. [< Med.L *feudalis.* See FEUD[2].] —**feu′dal·ly,** *adv.*

feu·dal·ism (fū′dəl iz əm), *n.* the feudal system or its principles and practices. **feu′dal·ist,** *n.* —**feu′dal·is′tic,** *adj.*

feudal system, the social, economic, and political system of Europe in the Middle Ages, under which vassals held land in return for military and other services to the lord owning the land.

feu·da·to·ry (fū′də tô′ri; –tō′–), *adj., n., pl.* **-ries.** —*adj.* owing feudal services to a lord. —*n.* a feudal estate; fief.

fe·ver (fē′vər), *n.* **1** an unhealthy condition of the body in which the temperature is higher than normal. **2** any of various diseases that cause fever, such as typhoid fever. **3** *Fig.* an excited, restless condition. **4** *Fig.* fad; enthusiasm. —*v.* **1** affect with fever; heat. **2** become feverish. [< L *febris*] —**fe′vered,** *adj.* —**fe′ver·less,** *adj.*

fe·ver·few (fē′vər fū), *n.* a perennial plant of the aster family with small, white, daisylike flowers. [< LL *febrifug(i)a* FEBRIFUGE]

fe·ver·ish (fē′vər ish), *adj.* **1** having fever. **2** causing fever. **3** infested with fever. **4** excited; restless. —**fe′ver·ish·ly,** *adv.* —**fe′ver·ish·ness,** *n.*

fe·ver·ous (fē′vər əs), *adj.* =feverish. —**fe′ver·ous·ly,** *adv.*

fe·ver·root (fē′vər rüt′; –rùt′), *n.* a coarse plant sometimes used for medicine.

fever sore, =cold sore.

few (fū), *adj.* not many. —*n.* a small number.

quite a few, a good many.

the few, the minority: *the few determined to be heard.* [OE *fēawe*] —**few′ness,** *n.*

fey (fā), *adj.* **1** like a fairy or elf. **2** saucy; lively. [< OE *fæge*]

fez (fez), *n., pl.* **fez·zes.** a felt cap, usually red, ornamented with a long, black tassel, formerly worn by Turkish men. [< Turk.; named after *Fez,* Morocco]

ff, fortissimo.

ff., and the following; and what follows.

f-hole (ef′hōl′), *n.* one of the two f-shaped openings in the body of a violin, cello, etc.

fi·an·cé (fē′än sā′; fē′än sā), *n.* man engaged to be married. [< F, betrothed]

fi·an·cée (fē′än sā′; fē′än sā), *n.* woman engaged to be married. [< F]

fi·as·co (fi as′kō), *n., pl.* **-cos, -coes.** failure; breakdown. [< F < Ital., flask]

fi·at (fī′ət; –at), *n.* **1** an authoritative order or command; decree. **2** sanction. [< L, let it be done]

fib (fib), *n., v.,* **fibbed, fib·bing.** lie about some small matter. [? < *fibble-fable* < *fable*] —**fib′ber,** *n.*

fi·ber (fī′bər), *n.* **1** a threadlike part; thread: *a muscle is made up of many fibers.* **2** substance made up of threads or threadlike parts. Hemp fiber can be spun into rope. **3** texture: *cloth of coarse fiber.* **4** character; nature. **5** a threadlike root of a plant. [< F < L *fibra*]

fi·ber·fill (fī′bər fil′), *n.* synthetic, soft fiber, used as padding for cushions, mattresses, coats, etc., and as stuffing for toys.

Fi·ber·glas (fī′bər glas′; –gläs′), *n. Trademark.* =fiberglass.

fi·ber·glass (fī′bər glas′; –gläs′), *n.,* a very fine, flexible glass fiber that can be made into insulating material, fabrics, canoes, etc., when combined with plastic.

fi·bril (fī′brəl), *n.* a small fiber.

fi·bril·la·tion (fī′brə lā′shən), *n.* slight tremor in a muscle, esp. of the heart.

fi·brin (fī′brən), *n.* **1** a tough, elastic, yellowish protein formed when blood clots. **2** gluten in plants. —**fi′brin·ous,** *adj.*

fi·brin·o·gen (fī brin′ə jən), *n.* protein, esp. found in the blood and lymph, involved in the coagulation of the blood.

fi·bro·blast (fī′brə blast), *n.* cell from which fibrous tissue is formed, immediately after an injury.

fi·broid (fī′broid), *adj.* composed of fibers. —*n.* tumor composed of fibers or fibrous tissue.

fi·brous (fī′brəs), *adj.* composed of fibers; having fibers; like fiber.

fi·bro·vas·cu·lar (fī′brō vas′kyə lər), made of woody fibers and ducts in plants.

fibrovascular bundle, bundle of minute ducts surrounded by long fibers, such as the vein on a leaf.

fib·u·la (fib′yə lə), *n., pl.* **–lae** (–lē) **–las. 1** the outer and thinner of the two bones in the human lower leg. It extends from knee to ankle. **2** a similar bone in the hind leg of animals. [< L, clasp, brooch] —**fib′u·lar,** *adj.*

fick·le (fik′əl), *adj.* likely to change without reason; changing; not constant. [OE *ficol*]

fic·tion (fik′shən), *n.* **1** novels, short stories, and other prose writings that tell about imaginary people and happenings. **2** an imaginary account or statement; made-up story. [< L *fictio* < *fingere* to form, fashion] —**fic′tion·al,** *adj.* —**fic′tion·al·ly,** *adv.*

fic·ti·tious (fik tish′əs), *adj.* **1** not real; imaginary; made-up: *characters in novels are usually fictitious.* **2** assumed in order to deceive; false: *the criminal used a fictitious name.* —**ficti′tious·ly,** *adv.* —**fic·ti′tious·ness,** *n.*

fid·dle (fid′əl), *n., v.,* **–dled, –dling.** —*n.* =violin. —*v.* **1** play on a violin. **2** make aimless movements; trifle: *he fiddled away the whole day doing absolutely nothing.*

play second fiddle, take a secondary part. [OE *fithele* (recorded in *fithelere* fiddler); prob. akin to *viol*] —**fid′dler,** *n.*

fiddler crab, small, burrowing crab found on the east coast of the United States. Also, **fiddler.**

fid·dle·sticks (fid′əl stiks′), *interj.* nonsense! rubbish!

fid·dly (fid′lē), *Informal.* requiring much attention or care to do; fussy.

fi·del·i·ty (fī del′ə ti; fə–), *n., pl.* **–ties. 1** faithfulness to a trust or vow; steadfast faithfulness. **2** accuracy; exactness. [< L *fidelitas,* ult. < *fides* faith. Doublet of FEALTY.]

fidg·et (fij′it), *v.* **1** move about restlessly; be uneasy. **2** make uneasy. —*n.* **1** condition of being restless or uneasy. **2** person who moves about restlessly. [< obs. *fidge* move restlessly] —**fidg′et·y,** *adj.* —**fidg′et·i·ness,** *n.*

fi·du·ci·ar·y (fī dü′shi er′i; –dū′–), *adj., n., pl.* **–ar·ies.** —*adj.* **1** held in trust: *fiduciary estates.* **2** holding in trust. A fiduciary possessor is legally responsible for what belongs to another. **3** depending upon public trust and confidence for its value. Paper money that cannot be redeemed in gold or silver is fiduciary currency. —*n.* trustee. [< L, < *fiducia* trust]

fie (fī), *interj.* for shame! shame! [< OF]

fief (fēf), *n.* **1** piece of land held on condition of giving military and other services to the lord owning the land. **2** the land or territory so held. [< F < Gmc.]

field (fēld), *n.* **1** land with few or no trees. **2** piece of land used for crops or pasture. **3** piece of land used for sports or contests. **4** land yielding some product: *an oil field.* **5** a battlefield. **6** a broad surface: *a field of ice.* **7** sphere of activity or operation. **8** *Physics.* space throughout which a force operates: *a magnetic field.* —*v.* **1** stop or catch and return (a ball) in baseball, cricket, etc. **2** act as a fielder in baseball, cricket, etc. —*adj.* **1** of or pertaining to fields. **2** growing or living in fields. **3** performed on a field, not on a track.

play the field, a engage in a wide variety of activities or endeavors. **b** go out with many different members of the opposite sex.

take the field, begin a battle, campaign, game, etc. [OE *feld*]

field day, 1 day for outdoor sports contests. **2** day when members of the military perform mock maneuvers. **3** *Fig.* day of unusual pleasure or success.

field·er (tēl′dər), *n.* baseball player who is stationed around or outside the diamond to stop the ball and throw it in.

field goal 1 a goal in football counting 3 points made by a drop kick. **2** a toss in basketball into the basket made during regular play, not as a result of a foul.

field hand, person hired as a farm laborer.

field house, 1 building near an athletic field, esp. for storage of equipment. **2** building used for indoor athletics.

field trip, trip away from a school to allow students to see things or places first-hand.

field work, scientific or technical work done in the field by surveyors, geologists, etc. —**field′work′er,** *n.*

fiend (fēnd), *n.* **1** an evil spirit; devil. **2** a very wicked or cruel person. **3** person who gives himself up to some habit, practice, game, etc.; devotee.

the Fiend, the Devil. [OE *fēond*] —**fiend′like′,** *adj.*

fiend·ish (fēn′dish), *adj.* very cruel or wicked; devilish. —**fiend′ish·ly,** *adv.* —**fiend′ish·ness,** *n.*

fierce (firs), *adj.* **fierc·er, fierc·est. 1** savage; wild: *a fierce lion.* **2** raging; violent: *a fierce wind.* **3** very eager or active; ardent: *fierce efforts.* [< OF < L *ferus* wild] —**fierce′ly,** *adv.* —**fierce′ness,** *n.*

fier·y (fīr′i; fī′ər i), *adj.,* **fier·i·er, fier·i·est, 1** containing fire; burning; flaming. **2** like fire; very hot; flashing; glowing. **3** full of feeling or spirit; ardent: *a fiery speech.* **4** easily aroused or excited: *a fiery temper.* —**fier′i·ly,** *adv.* —**fier′i·ness,** *n.*

fi·es·ta (fī es′tə), *n.* **1** a religious festival; saint's day. **2** holiday; festivity. [< Sp., FEAST]

fife (fīf), *n., v.,* **fifed, fif·ing.** —*n.* a small, shrill musical instrument like a flute. —*v.* play on a fife. [< G *pfeife* pipe] —**fif′er,** *n.*

fif·teen (fif′tēn′), *n.* **1** a cardinal number, five more than ten. **2** symbol of this number; 15. —*adj.* five more than ten; 15. —**fif′teenth′,** *adj., n.*

fifth (fifth), *adj.* **1** next after the fourth; last in a series of 5. **2** being one of 5 equal parts. —*n.* **1** next after the fourth; last in a series of 5. **2** one of 5 equal parts. **3 a** one fifth of a gallon (U.S.), a measure used for alcoholic beverages. **b** bottle or container holding a fifth. —**fifth′ly,** *adv.*

Fifth Amendment, part of the Bill of Rights that protects a person from being a witness against himself or herself.

take the Fifth, refuse to answer a question, under oath, by citing the protection of the Fifth Amendment.

fif·ty (fif′ti), *n., pl.* **–ties,** *adj.* —*n.* **1** a cardinal number, five times ten. **2** symbol of this number; 50. —*adj.* five times ten; 50. —**fif′ti·eth,** *adj., n.*

fif·ty-fif·ty (fif′ti fif′ti), *adv., adj.* in or with equal shares.

fig (fig), *n.* **1** a small, soft, sweet fruit that grows in warm regions, eaten fresh or dried like dates and raisins. **2** tree that figs grow on. **3** very small amount: *I don't care a fig for your opinion.* [< OF < Pr., ult. < L *ficus* fig tree]

fig., 1 figurative; figuratively. **2** figure; figures.

fig-eat-er (fig′ēt ər), *n.* a large, green-and-red beetle that feeds on ripe fruit; southern June bug.

fight (fīt), *n., v.,* **fought, fight·ing.** —*n.* **1** struggle; battle; conflict. **2** an angry dispute. **3** power or will to fight. [< v.] —*v.* **1** take part in a fight. **2** war against. **3** get or make by fighting.

fight back, resist; strive against.

fight it out, fight to a clear decision or victory.

fight shy of, keep away from; avoid.

show fight, be ready to resist or fight. [OE *feohtan*] —**fight′a·ble,** *adj.*

fight·er (fīt′ər), *n.* **1** one who or that which fights. **2** a professional boxer. **3** armed airplane used mainly for attacking the enemy.

fig·ment (fig′mənt), *n.* something imagined; made-up story. [< L *figmentum* < *fingere* to form, fashion]

fig·ur·a·tion (fig′yə rā′shən), *n.* **1** form; shape. **2** act of forming; shaping. **3** act of decorating with figures or designs. **4** in music, ornamenting with grace notes, trills, etc.

fig·ur·a·tive (fig′yər ə tiv), *adj.* **1** using words out of their literal meaning to add beauty or force. **2** representing by a likeness or symbol. **—fig′ur·a·tive·ly,** *adv.* **—fig′ur·a·tive·ness,** *n.*

fig·ure (fig′yər), *n., v.,* **–ured, –ur·ing.** **—n. 1** symbol for a number, as 1, 2, 3, 4, etc. **2** form; shape: *she saw dim figures moving.* **3** form enclosing a surface or space. Circles, triangles, and spheres are geometrical figures. **4** person; character: *a great figure in history.* **5** way in which a person looks or appears: *the poor old woman was a figure of distress.* **6** picture; drawing; diagram; illustration. **7** set of movements in dancing or skating. **—v. 1** use figures to find the answer to a problem; reckon; compute. **2** conclude; judge. **3** be conspicuous; appear: *the names of great leaders figure in the story of human progress.*

figure in, take into account; include.

figure on, a depend on; rely on. **b** consider as a part of a plan or undertaking.

figure out, a understand. **b** calculate; estimate. [< F < L *figura fingere* form] **—fig′ur·er,** *n.*

fig·ured (fig′yərd), *adj.* decorated with a design or pattern; not plain.

figure eight, 1 exercise in figure skating in which the skater traces in the ice the shape of an 8. **2** similar maneuver done by a pilot of a plane in flight.

fig·ure·head (fig′yər hed′), *n.* person who is the head in name only, and has no real authority or responsibility.

figure of speech, expression in which words are used out of their literal meaning or out of their ordinary use to add beauty or force. Similes and metaphors are figures of speech.

fig·ur·ine (fig′yər ēn′), *n.* a small ornamental figure made of stone, pottery, metal, etc.; statuette. [< F < Ital. *figurina*]

fig·wort (fig′wèrt′), *n.* **1** a tall, coarse plant with small, greenish-purple or yellow flowers that have a disagreeable odor. **2** any similar plant.

Fi·ji (fē′jē), *n.* **1** Fiji Islands. **2** native of these islands. **—Fi′ji·an,** *adj., n.*

Fiji Islands, group of islands in the S Pacific, N of New Zealand.

fil·a·ment (fil′ə mənt), *n.* **1** a very fine thread; very slender, threadlike part. **2** wire that gives off light in an electric lightbulb. **3** the stalklike part of a stamen that supports the anther. [< LL, < L *filum* thread]

fil·bert (fil′bərt), *n.* a cultivated hazelnut. [for St. *Philibert,* because the nuts ripen about the time of his day]

filch (filch), *v.* steal in small quantities; pilfer. **—filch′er,** *n.*

file[1] (fīl), *n., v.,* **–filed, fil·ing. —n. 1** place for keeping papers in order. **2** set of papers kept in order. **3** line of people or things one behind another. **—v. 1** put away in order. **2** march or move in a file. **3** make application.

on file, in a file; put away and kept in

order. [< F *fil* thread (< L *filum*) and F *file* row (ult. < LL *filare* spin a thread)] **—fil′er,** *n.*

file[2] (fīl), *n., v.,* **filed, fil·ing. —n.** a steel tool with many small ridges or teeth on it. Its rough surface is used to smooth or wear away hard substances. **—v.** smooth or wear away with a file. [OE *fīl*] **—fil′er,** *n.*

file·fish (fīl′fish′), *n., pl.* **-fish·es** or (*esp. collectively*) **-fish.** fish whose skin is covered with many very small spines instead of scales.

fi·let (fi lā; fil′ā), *n.* **1** net or lace having a square mesh. **2** fillet (def. 2). **—v.** =fillet. [< F. See FILLET.]

fi·let mi·gnon (fi lā′mēn′yon, min yon′), *n., pl.* **fi·lets mi·gnons** (fi lā′ mēn′yon, min yon′). thick, round slice of beef, cut from the tenderloin and either broiled or sautéed.

fil·i·al (fil′i əl), *adj.* **1** of a son or daughter; due from a son or daughter. **2** *Genetics.* of any generation following that of the parents. [< LL, < L *filius* son, *filia* daughter] **—fil′i·al·ly,** *adv.*

fil·i·bus·ter (fil′ə bus′tər), *n.* the deliberate hindering of the passage of a bill in a legislature by long speeches or other means of delay. **—v.** deliberately hinder the passage of a bill by long speeches or other means of delay. [< Sp. < Du. *vrijbuiter* freebooter] **—fil′i·bus·ter·er,** *n.*

fil·i·gree (fil′ə grē), *n., v.,* **-greed, -gree-ing,** *adj.* **—n.** very delicate, lacelike ornamental work of gold or silver wire. **—v.** ornament with filigree. **—adj.** Also, **fil′i·greed′.** ornamented with filigree; made into filigree. [for *filigrane* < F < Ital. < L *filum* thread + *granum* grain]

fil·ings (fil′ingz), *n.pl.* small pieces removed by a file.

Fi·li·pi·na (fil′ə pē na), *n.* female native of the Philippines.

Fil·i·pi·no (fil′ə pē′nō), *n., pl.* **-nos.** native of the Philippines. **—adj.** =Philippine.

fill (fil), *v.* **1** put into until there is room for no more; make full: *fill a cup.* **2** become full: *the hall filled rapidly.* **3** take up all the space in: *the crowd filled the hall.* **4** supply what is needed for: *a store fills orders.* **5** stop up or close by putting something in: *a dentist fills decayed teeth.* **6** hold and do the duties of (a position, office, etc.). **—n. 1** enough to fill something. **2** something that fills.

fill in, a fill with something. **b** complete by filling: *fill in the questionnaire.*

fill out, a make larger; swell. **b** complete by filling: *fill out a form.*

fill up, fill. [OE *fyllan* < *full* full]

fill·er (fil′ər), *n.* **1** person or thing that fills. **2** thing put in to fill something.

fil·let (fil′it; *n. 3 and v., usually* fi lā′, fil′ā), *n.* **1** a narrow band, ribbon, etc., **2** Also, **filet.** slice of fish, meat, etc., without bones or fat. **—v.** Also, **filet.** cut (fish, meat, etc.) into fillets. [< F, dim. of *fil* < L *filum* thread]

fill·ing (fil′ing), *n.* thing put in to fill something.

Fill·more (fil′môr; -mōr), *n.* **Millard,** 1800–74, the 13th president of the United States, 1850–53.

fil·ly (fil′i), *n., pl.* **-lies.** a female colt; young mare. [? < Scand. *fylja;* akin to FOAL]

film (film), *n.* **1** a very thin layer, sheet, surface, or coating. **2** roll or sheet of thin, flexible material, such as cellulose, used in making photographs and coated with an emulsion sensitive to light. **3** a motion picture. **—v. 1** cover or become covered with a film: *her eyes filmed with tears.* **2** make a motion picture of.

films, motion pictures. [OE *filmen;* akin to FELL[4]]

film·y (fil′mi), *adj.,* **film·i·er, film·i·est. 1** of or like a film; very thin. **2** covered with a film. **—film′i·ly,** *adv.* **—film′i·ness,** *n.*

fil·ter (fil′tər), *n.* **1** device for straining out substances from a liquid or gas by passing it slowly through felt, paper, sand, charcoal, etc. **2** felt, paper, sand, charcoal, or other porous material used in such a device. **3** device for controlling certain light rays, electric currents, etc. **—v. 1** pass through a filter; strain. **2** act as a filter for. **3** pass or flow very slowly. **4** remove or control by a filter. [< Med.L. *filtrum* felt < Gmc.] **—fil′ter·er,** *n.*

fil·ter·a·ble (fil′tər ə bəl), *adj.* **1** that can be filtered. **2** that passes through a filter. **—fil′ter·a·bil′i·ty, fil′ter·a·ble·ness,** *n.*

filth (filth), *n.* **1** foul, disgusting dirt. **2** obscene words or thoughts; vileness; moral corruption. [OE *fylth* < *fūl* foul]

filth·y (fil′thi), *adj.,* **filth·i·er, filth·i·est. 1** disgustingly dirty; foul. **2** vile. **—filth′i·ly,** *adv.* **—filth′i·ness,** *n.*

fil·trate (fil′trāt), *n., v.,* **-trat·ed, -trat-ing. —n.** liquid that has been passed through a filter. **—v.** pass through a filter. **—fil·tra′tion.** *n.*

fin (fin), *n.* **1** a movable winglike part of a fish's body. **2** thing shaped or used like a fin. [OE *finn*] **—fin′less,** *adj.* **—fin′like′,** *adj.*

fi·na·gle (fə nā′gəl), *v.,* **-gled, -gling. 1** manage craftily or cleverly. **2** cheat. **—fi·na′gler,** *n.*

fi·nal (fī′nəl), *adj.* **1** at the end; last; with no more after it. **2** settling the question; not to be changed: *a decision of the Supreme Court is final.* **—n.** something final.

finals, the last or deciding set in a series of contests, examinations, etc. [< L, < *finis* end]

fi·na·le (fi nä′lē), *n.* **1** the last part of a piece of music or a play. **2** the last part; end. [< Ital., FINAL]

fi·nal·ist (fī′nəl ist), *n.* person who takes part in the deciding set in a series of contests, etc.

fi·nal·i·ty (fī nal′ə ti), *n., pl.* **-ties. 1** a being final, finished, or settled. **2** something final; final act, speech, etc.

fi·nal·ize (fī′nəl īz), v., **-ized, -iz·ing.** make final or definite. —**fi′nal·i·za′tion,** n.

fi·nal·ly (fī′nəl i), adv. **1** at the end; at last. **2** so as to decide or settle the question.

fi·nance (fə nans′; fī–; fī′nans), n., v., **-nanced, -nanc·ing.** —n. money matters. —v. **1** provide money for. **2** manage the finances of.

finances, money matters; money; funds; revenue. [< OF, ending, settlement of a debt, ult. < *fin* end < L *finis;* akin to FINE[2]]

fi·nan·cial (fə nan′shəl; fī–), adj. having to do with money matters or the management of large sums of money. —**fi·nan′cial·ly,** adv.

fin·an·cier (fin′ən sir′; fī′nən-), n. person skilled in finance.

fin·back (fin′bak′), n. or **finback whale.** kind of baleen whale having a large fin on its back.

finch (finch), n. a small songbird having a cone-shaped bill, as sparrows, buntings, and canaries. [OE *finc*]

find (fīnd), v., **found, find·ing,** n. —v. **1** come upon; happen on; meet with: *find a bug in the sugar.* **2** look for and get; obtain: *find favor with the public.* **3** discover: *an astronomer finds a new star; can you find time to do this?* **4** see; know; feel; perceive: *he found himself growing sleepy.* **5** arrive at; reach: *water finds its level.* **6** declare: *the jury founds the accused innocent.* —n. **1** a finding. **2** thing found.

find oneself, learn one's abilities and how to make good use of them.

find out, learn about; come to know; discover. [OE *findan*] —**find′a·ble,** adj.

find·er (fīn′dər), n. person or thing that finds.

fin de siè·cle (faN də syā′klə), *French,* end of the century.

find·ing (fīn′ding), n. **1** discovery. **2** thing found. **3** decision reached after an inquiry; verdict of a jury.

findings, results of an inquiry or research.

fine[1] (fīn), adj., **fin·er, fin·est,** adv. —adj. **1** very good; excellent: *a fine sermon, a fine view, a fine scholar.* **2** very small or thin: *fine wire.* **3** sharp: *a tool with a fine edge.* **4** not coarse or heavy; delicate: *fine linen.* **5** subtle: *the law makes fine distinctions.* **6** clear; bright: *fine weather.* —adv. very well; excellently.

cut it fine, allow very little leeway or margin, esp. of time. [< OF *fin,* ult. < L *finire* finish] —**fine′ly,** adv. —**fine′ness,** n.

fine[2] (fīn), n., v. **fined, fin·ing.** —n. sum of money paid as a punishment. —v. cause to pay a fine.

in fine, a finally. **b** in a few words; briefly. [< OF < L *finis* end; in Med.L, settlement, payment]

fine arts, arts depending upon taste and appealing to the sense of beauty; painting, drawing, sculpture, and architecture. Literature, music, dancing, and acting are also often included in the fine arts.

fine-grained (fīn′grānd′), adj. having a fine, close grain.

fin·er·y (fīn′ər i), n., pl. **-er·ies.** showy clothes, ornaments, etc.

fi·nesse (fə nes′), n. v., **-nessed, -ness·ing.** —n. **1** delicacy of execution; skill. **2** the skillful handling of a delicate situation to one's advantage; craft; stratagem. —v. **1** use finesse. **2** bring or change by finesse. [< F, < *fin* FINE[1]]

fin·ger (fing′gər), n. **1** one of the five end parts of the hand, esp. the four besides the thumb. **2** part of a glove that covers a finger. **3** anything shaped or used like a finger. —v. touch or handle with the fingers; use the fingers on.

burn one's fingers, be hurt by doing something unwise.

keep one's fingers crossed, hope for the best.

lay or **put a finger on,** touch; meddle with.

lift a finger, make some sort of effort.

point the or **a finger at,** blame; accuse.

put one's finger on, point out exactly.

slip through one's fingers, fail to take advantage of something; miss an opportunity. [OE.] —**fin′ger·er,** n. —**fin′ger·less,** adj.

fin·ger·ing (fing′gər ing), n. **1** a touching or handling with the fingers; using the fingers. **2** signs marked on a piece of music to show how the fingers are to be used in playing it.

fin·ger·nail (fing′gər nāl′), n. a hard layer of horn at the end of a finger.

finger paint, thickened watercolors, applied to paper with the fingers. —**finger painting.**

fin·ger·print (fing′gər print′), n. impression of the markings on the inner surface of the last joint of a finger or thumb. —v. take the fingerprints of.

fin·i·al (fin′i əl; fī′ni–), n. ornament on top of a roof or lamp, end of a pew in church, etc. [< Med.L *finium* final settlement (prob. orig., end) < L *finis*]

fin·ick·y (fin′ə ki), adj. too dainty or particular; too precise; fussy. [appar. < *fine*[1]]

fi·nis (fī′nis; fin′is), n. end. [< L]

fin·ish (fin′ish), v. **1** bring (action, speech, etc.) to an end; end. **2** bring (work, affairs, etc.) to completion; complete: *he started the race but did not finish it.* **3** use up completely: *finish a spool of thread.* **4** perfect; polish. **5** prepare the surface of in some way: *finish cloth with nap.* —n. **1** end. **2** perfection. **3** way in which the surface is prepared. **4** thing used to finish something.

finish off, a complete: *finish off that job.* **b** overcome completely; defeat: *finish off an adversary.* **c** kill.

finish up, a complete. **b** use up.

finish with, a complete: *finish with that job.* **b** have nothing to do with (some-

one). [< OF *fenir* < L *finire*] —**fin′ished,** adj. —**fin′ish·er,** n.

fi·nite (fī′nīt), adj. having limits or bounds; not infinite: *death ends man's finite existence.* —n. what is finite; something finite. [< L *finitus* finished] —**fi′nite·ly,** adv. —**fi′nite·ness,** n.

fink (fingk), n. **1** informer. **2** strikebreaker.

Fin·land (fin′lənd), n. **1** country in N Europe. **2** Gulf of, part of the Baltic Sea, south of Finland. —**Fin′land·er, Finn,** n.

fin·nan had·die (fin′ən had′i) or **haddock** (had′ək), smoked haddock. [for *Findhorn haddock;* from name of town in Scotland]

finned (find), adj. having a fin or fins.

Finn·ish (fin′ish), adj. of or having to do with Finland, its people, or their language. —n. language of Finland.

fin whale, =finback.

fiord (fyôrd; fyōrd), n. a long, narrow bay of the sea between high banks or cliffs. Also, **fjord.** [< Norw., earlier *fjorthr;* akin to FIRTH]

fir (fėr), n. **1** tree somewhat like a pine. **2** its wood. [OE *fyrh*]

fire (fīr), n., v., **fired, fir·ing.** —n. **1** flame, heat, and light caused by burning. **2** something burning. **3** fuel arranged to burn: *light a fire.* **4** something that suggests a fire because it is hot, glowing, brilliant, or light: *the fire in a diamond.* **5** passion, fervor, excitement, etc. **6** severe trial or trouble. **7** the shooting or discharge of guns, etc. —v. **1** cause to burn. **2** tend the fire of: *fire a furnace.* **3** dry with heat; bake. Bricks are fired to make them hard. **4** arouse; excite; inflame. **5** discharge (gun, bomb, gas mine, etc.) **6** dismiss from a job, etc.

catch fire, a begin to burn. **b** gain enthusiastic support or acceptance: *the campaign finally caught fire.*

fire away, a fire guns; shoot. **b** *Fig.* bombard with questions or talk.

fire off, a discharge guns. **b** launch a rocket. **c** send in haste and anger: *fire off a letter of complaint.*

hang fire, be slow in doing or completing something, esp. because of uncertainty.

on fire, a burning. **b** full of a feeling or spirit or ardor.

open fire, begin shooting or throwing.

play with fire, meddle with something dangerous.

set fire to, cause to burn.

under fire, a exposed to shooting from enemy guns. **b** attacked; blamed. [OE *fȳr*] —**fir′er,** n.

fire alarm, device or signal that warns of fire.

fire·arm (fīr′ärm′), n. gun, pistol, or other weapon to shoot with.

fire·ball (fīr′bôl′), n. great billowing mass of fire produced by an explosion.

fire boat, boat equipped to put out fires on ships or docks.

fire·box (fīr′boks′), *n.* place for the fire in a furnace, boiler, etc.

fire·brand (fīr′brand′), *n.* **1** piece of burning wood. **2** person who arouses strife or angry feeling in others.

fire break, strip of ground cleared of grass, trees, etc., to stop the progress of a fire.

fire·brick (fīr′brik′), *n.* brick that can stand great heat, used to line furnaces and fireplaces.

fire company, organized group of firefighters.

fire·crack·er (fīr′krak′ ər), *n.* a paper roll containing gunpowder and a fuse.

fire·damp (fīr′damp′), *n.* methane, a gas formed in coal mines, dangerously explosive when mixed with certain proportions of air.

fire department, 1 department of a city, town, etc., organized and equipped to fight fires. **2** people hired or who volunteer to serve in such a department.

fire·dog (fīr′dôg′; –dog′), *n.* =andiron.

fire engine, machine for throwing water, chemicals, etc., to put out fires.

fire escape, stairway, ladder, etc., in or on a building, to use in case of fire.

fire extinguisher, container filled with chemicals which, when sprayed upon fire, extinguish it.

fire·fight·er (fīr′fī′ tər) *n.* or **fire fighter,** person whose work is putting out fires.

fire·fly (fīr′flī′), *n., pl.* –**flies.** a small beetle that gives off flashes of light when it flies at night; lightning bug.

fire·house (fīr′hous′), *n.* building where fine department equipment is kept and where firefighters sometimes live while on duty.

fire·man (fīr′mən), *n., pl.* –**men. 1** =firefighter. **2** person whose work is taking care of the fire in a furnace, boiler, etc.

fire·place (fīr′plās′), *n.* place built in the wall of a room or outdoors to hold a fire.

fire·pow·er (fīr′pou′ ər), *n.* the total number of bullets, directed missiles, etc., that can be fired at an enemy or target in a given instant.

fire·proof (fīr′prüf′), *adj.* that will not burn; almost impossible to burn. —*v.* make fireproof.

fire·side (fīr′sīd′), *n.* **1** space around a fireplace or hearth. **2** home. **3** home life. —*adj.* beside the fire: *fireside comfort.*

fire station, =firehouse.

fire·trap (fīr′trap′), *n.* **1** a building hard to get out of when it is on fire. **2** a building that will burn very easily.

fire·wa·ter (fīr′wô′ tər; –wot′–), *n.* strong alcoholic drink. The American Indians called whiskey, gin, rum, etc., firewater.

fire·weed (fīr′wēd′), *n.* any of various weeds which grow on land that has been burned over.

fire·wood (fīr′wůd′), *n.* wood to make a fire.

fire·works (fīr′wėrks′), *n. pl.* **1** firecrackers, bombs, rockets, etc., that make a loud noise or a beautiful, fiery display at night. **2** display of these.

firing line, 1 line of soldiers placed to shoot. **2** soldiers forming this line.

on the firing line, in a position to be attacked by opponents in a controversy, campaign, etc.

fir·kin (fėr′kən), *n.* **1** quarter of a barrel, used as a measure of capacity. **2** a small wooden cask for butter, etc. [ME *ferdekyn* < MDu. *verdelkijn,* dim. of *verdel* lit., fourth part]

firm[1] (fėrm), *adj.* **1** not yielding easily to pressure or force; solid; hard: *firm ground.* **2** tightly fastened or fixed: *a candle firm in its socket.* **3** not easily changed; steady: *a firm purpose; a firm price.* —*v.* make or become firm. [< L *firmus*] —**firm′ly,** *adv.* —**firm′ness,** *n.*

firm[2] (fėrm), *n.* a business company or partnership. [< Ital. < Sp., Pg. *firma* signature, ult. < L *firmus* firm[1]]

fir·ma·ment (fėr′mə mənt), *n.* arch of the heavens; sky. [< L. ult. < *firmus* firm[1]]

first (fėrst), *adj.* **1** before all others. anything else. **2** most important. **3 a** highest in pitch. **b** playing or signing the part highest in pitch. —*adv.* **1** before anything else: *the good die first.* **2** for the first time. **3** rather; sooner: *I'll go to jail first.* —*n.* person, thing, place, etc., that is first. [OE *fyrst*]

first aid, emergency treatment given to an injured person before a doctor comes. —**first′-aid′,** *adj.*

first base, 1 the first of the bases from the home plate in baseball. **2** player stationed there.

first-born (fėrst′bôrn′), *adj.* born first; oldest. —*n.* the first-born child.

first-class (fėrst′klas′; –kläs′), *adj.* of the highest class or best quality; excellent. —*adv.* on or by first-class accommodations. —**first class.**

first-hand (fėrst′hand′), *adj., adv.* from the original source; direct.

first lady, the wife of the president of the United States.

first lieutenant, officer ranking below a captain and above a second lieutenant.

first·ling (fėrst′ling), *n.* the first of its kind.

first·ly (fėrst′li), *adv.* in the first place; first.

first person, form of a pronoun or verb used to refer to the speaker. *I, me, my,* and *we, us, our* are pronouns of the first person.

first-rate (fėrst′rāt′), *adj.* **1** of the highest class. **2** excellent; very good.

first sergeant, a master sergeant in direct charge of a company or similar unit under the commissioned officer in command.

first-string (fėrst′string′), *adj.* **1** of or having to do with the best and starting players on a team. **2** best; first-rate; excellent.

firth (fėrth), *n. Esp. Scot.* a narrow arm of the sea; estuary of a river. [< Scand. *firthir,* pl. of *fjörthr;* akin to FIORD]

fis·cal (fis′kəl), *adj.* **1** financial. **2** having to do with public finance. [< L, < *fiscus* purse] —**fis′cal·ly,** *adv.*

fish (fish), *n., pl.* **fish·es** or (*esp. collectively*) **fish,** *v., adj.* —*n.* **1** a vertebrate animal that lives in water and has gills instead of lungs for breathing. Fish are usually covered with scales and have fins for swimming. In popular use, whales and dolphins are called fish, and certain invertebrates are called shellfish. **2** flesh of fish used for food. —*v.* **1** catch fish; try to catch fish. **2** try to catch fish in. **3** search. **4** find and pull: *he fished the map from the back of the drawer.* —*adj.* of or pertaining to fishes, fishing, or the sale of fish.

fish out of water, person who is out of his or her usual environment, and uncomfortable; stranger.

Fishes, =Pisces.

neither fish nor fowl, person or thing not easily classified. [OE *fisc*] —**fish′a·ble,** *adj.* —**fish′less,** *adj.* —**fish′like′,** *adj.*

fish·er (fish′ər), *n.* **1** =fisherman. **2** a slender animal like a weasel but larger.

fish·er·man (fish′ər mən), *n., pl.* –**men. 1** person who fishes for a living or for pleasure. **2** ship used in fishing.

fish·er·y (fish′ər i), *n., pl.* –**er·ies. 1** business or industry of catching fish. **2** place for catching fish.

fish farm, place where fish are raised for food, usually in ponds or submerged pens.

fish hawk, large bird that feeds on fish; osprey.

fish·hook (fish′hůk′), *n.* hook used for catching fish.

fish·ing (fish′ing), *n.* the catching of fish for a living or for pleasure.

fishing rod, a long pole with a line attached to it, used in catching fish.

fish story, fabrication; tall tale.

fish·wife (fish′wīf′), *n., pl.* –**wives.** woman who sells fish.

fish·y (fish′i), *adj.,* **fish·i·er, fish·i·est. 1** like a fish in smell, taste, or shape. **2** of fish. **3** full of fish. **4** doubtful; unlikely; suspicious. —**fish′i·ly,** *adv.* —**fish′i·ness,** *n.*

fis·sion (fish′ən), *n.* **1** a splitting apart; division into parts. **2** method of reproduction in which the body of the parent divides to form two or more independent individuals. **3** the splitting that occurs when the nucleus of an atom under bombardment absorbs a neutron. [< L *fissio.* See FISSILE.]

fis·sion·a·ble (fish′ən ə bəl), *adj.* capable of nuclear fission: *fissionable material.*

fis·sure (fish′ər), *n., v.,* –**sured,** –**sur·ing.** —*n.* **1** split or crack; long, narrow opening. **2** a splitting apart; division into parts. —*v.* split apart; divide into parts.

fist (fist), *n.* **1** hand closed tightly. **2** symbol used in printing. [OE *fӯst*]

fist·i·cuff (fis'tə kuf'), *n.* blow with the fist.

fisticuffs, a fight with the fists. **b** blows with the fists.

fis·tu·la (fis'chù lə), *n., pl.* **-las, -lae** (-lē). 1 tube or pipe. 2 a tubelike sore. [< L., pipe, ulcer] **—fis'tu·lous, fis'tu·lar,** *adj.*

fit[1] (fit), *adj.* **fit·ter, fit·test,** *v.,* **fit·ted, fit·ting,** *n.* **—adj.** 1 having the necessary qualities; suitable. 2 right; proper. 3 ready; prepared: *fit for service.* 4 in good health. **—v.** 1 be fit; be fit for. 2 have the right size or shape for. 3 make fit. 4 prepare. 5 equip. **—n.** 1 manner in which one thing fits another: *a tight fit.* 2 process of fitting. 3 thing that fits: *this coat is a good fit.*

fit out or **up,** outfit with necessary things.

fit to be tied, *Informal.* very upset or annoyed. [ME *fyt*] **—fit'ly,** *adv.* **—fit'ness,** *n.* **—fit'ter,** *n.*

fit[2] (fit), *n.* 1 a sudden, sharp attack: *a fit of colic; fit of epilepsy; a fit of anger.* 2 a short period of doing one thing.

by fits and starts, starting and stopping in an irregular fashion.

throw or **have a fit,** *Informal.* become very angry or overly excited. [OE *fitt* conflict]

fitch (fich), *n.* 1 polecat of Europe. 2 its fur, yellowish with dark markings. [? < MDu. *vitsche*]

fit·ful (fit'fəl), *adj.* going on and then stopping awhile; irregular. **—fit'ful·ly,** *adv.* **—fit'ful·ness,** *n.*

fit·ting (fit'ing), *adj.* right; proper; suitable. **—n.** 1 making fit. 2 a trying on unfinished clothes to see if they will fit.

fittings, furnishings; fixtures. **—fit'ting·ly,** *adv.* **—fit'ting·ness,** *n.*

five (fīv), *n.* 1 a cardinal number, one more than four. 2 symbol for this number; 5. 3 team of five players. **—adj.** one more than four; 5. [OE *fíf*]

five·fold (fīv'fōld'), *adj.* 1 five times as much or as many. 2 having five parts. **—adv.** five times as much or as many.

fix (fiks), *v.,* **fixed, fix·ing,** *n.* **—v.** 1 make or become firm; fasten tightly: *fix a post in the ground.* 2 settle; set: *fix a price.* 3 direct or hold (eyes, attention, etc.) steadily. 4 become rigid: *fixed in terror.* 5 put definitely: *fix the blame.* 6 treat to keep fading. 7 mend; repair. 8 put in order; arrange: *fix one's hair.* 9 put in a condition or position favorable to oneself: *fix a race.* **—n.** 1 position hard to get out of. 2 point on a map or chart at which two lines of position cross one another.

fix up, a mend; repair. **b** put in order; arrange. [< F. ult. < L *fixus* fixed] **—fix'a·ble,** *adj.* **—fix'er,** *n.*

fix·a·tion (fiks ā'shən), *n.* 1 fixing or being fixed. 2 treatment to keep something from fading. 3 a morbid attachment.

fix·a·tive (fik'sə tiv), *adj.* that prevents fading. **—n.** substance used to prevent fading.

fixed (fikst), *adj.* 1 not movable; firm. 2 settled; set; definite. 3 steady. 4 made rigid. 5 permanent. 6 put order. 7 prearranged dishonestly. **—fix'ed·ly,** *adv.* **—fix'ed·ness,** *n.*

fixed star, star whose position in relation to other stars appears not to change.

fix·ing (fik'sing), *n.* act of one who or that which fixes.

fixings, trimmings.

fix·i·ty (fik'sə ti), *n., pl.* **-ties.** 1 permanence; steadiness; firmness. 2 something fixed.

fix·ture (fiks'chər), *n.* 1 thing put in place to stay: *electric light fixtures.* 2 person or thing that stays in one place, job, etc.

fizz (fiz), *v.,* **fizzed, fizz·ing.** make a hissing sound. **—n.** a hissing sound. **—fizz'er,** *n.*

fiz·zle (fiz'əl), *v.,* **-zled, -zling,** *n.* **—v.** hiss or sputter weakly. **—n.** 1 a hissing; sputtering. 2 failure.

fizz·y (fiz'i), *adj.,* **fizz·i·er, fizz·i·est.** that fizzes.

fjord (fyôrd; fyord), *n.* =fiord.

FL, fluorine. Also, **F.**

fl., 1 flourished. 2 fluid.

FL, *(zip code)* Florida.

Fla., Florida.

flab (flab), *n. Informal.* 1 anything soft or flabby; esp. excess flesh. 2 *Fig.* excess of anything: *a story full of flab.*

flab·ber·gast (flab'ər gast), *v. Informal.* make speechless with surprise; astonish greatly; amaze. [? blend of *flap* or *flabby* + *aghast*]

flab·by (flab'i), *adj.,* **-bi·er, -bi·est,** lacking firmness or force; soft. [var. of earlier *flappy* < *flap*] **—flab'bi·ly,** *adv.* **—flab'bi·ness,** *n.*

flac·cid (flak'sid), *adj.* limp; weak: *flaccid muscles.* [< L, < *flaccus* flabby] **—flac·cid'i·ty, flac'cid·ness,** *n.* **—flac'cid·ly,** *adv.*

fla·con (flä kôn'), *n.* a small bottle with a stopper, used for perfume, smelling salts, etc. [< F. See FLAGON.]

flag[1] (flag), *n., v.,* **flagged, flag·ging.** **—n.** piece of cloth with a color or pattern that stands for some country, city, party, club, etc., or which gives some information or signal. **—v.** 1 stop or signal by a flag: *flag a train.* 2 communicate by a flag: *flag a message.*

flag down, stop by waving or other signal.

flags, a feathers on the second joint of a bird's wing. **b** long feathers on the lower parts of certain birds' legs.

wave the flag, excite patriotic or other emotion. [? < *flag*[3]]

flag[2] (flag), *n.,* 1 iris with blue, purple, yellow, or white flowers and sword-shaped leaves. 2 =sweet flag. [cf. Dan. *flœg*]

flag[3] (flag), *v.,* **flagged, flag·ging.** get tired; grow weak; droop. [cf. earlier Du. *vlaggheren* flutter]

flag[4] (flag), *n., v.,* **flagged, flag·ging.** **—n.** =flagstone. **—v.** pave with flagstones. [var. of *flake*]

Flag Day, June 14, the anniversary of the day in 1777 when the flag of the United States was adopted.

flag·el·late (flaj'ə tāt), *v.,* **-lat·ed, -lat·ing,** *adj.* **—v.** whip; flog. **—adj.** Also, **flag'el·lat'ed.** 1 shaped like a whiplash. 2 having flagella. [< L, *flagellum* whip] **—flag'el·la'tion,** *n.* **—flag'el·la'tor,** *n.*

fla·gel·lum (flə jel'əm), *n., pl.* **-la** (-lə), **-lums.** 1 a long, whiplike tail or part, which is an organ of locomotion in certain cells, bacteria, protozoa, etc. 2 runner of a plant. [< L, whip]

flag·eo·let (flaj'ə let'), *n.* a wind instrument somewhat like a flute. [< F, dim. of OF *flajol* flute, ult. < L *flare* blow]

flag·ging[1] (flag'ging), *adj.* drooping; tired; weak. **—flag'ging·ly,** *adv.*

flag·ging[2] (flag'ing), *n.* 1 flagstones. 2 pavement made of flagstones.

flag·man (flag'man'), *n.* person who signals with a flag or sign, esp. at road construction sites.

flag·on (flag'ən), *n.* 1 container for liquids, usually having a handle and a spout, and often a cover. 2 a large bottle, holding about two quarts. 3 contents of a flagon. [< OF *flascon.* Cf. FLASK.]

flag·pole (flag'pōl'), **flag·staff** (-staf'; -stäf'), *n.* pole from which a flag is flown.

fla·gran·cy (flā'grən si), **fla·grance** (-grəns), *n.* flagrant nature or quality.

fla·grant (flā'grənt), *adj.* notorious; outrageous; scandalous. [< L *flagrans* burning] **—fla'grant·ly,** *adv.*

flag·ship (flag'ship'), *n.* ship that carries the officer in command of a fleet or squadron and displays his flag.

flag·stone (flag'stōn'), *n.* a large, flat stone, used for paving walks, etc.

flail (flāl), *n.* instrument for threshing grain by hand. **—v.** 1 strike with a flail. 2 beat; thrash. [< LL *flagellum* < L, whip]

flair (flâr), *n.* 1 keen perception: *a flair for bargains.* 2 talent: *a flair for making clever rhymes.* [< F, scent < *flairer* smell < L *fragrare*]

flak (flak), *n.* fire from anti-aircraft guns. [for *Fl.A.K.,* G abbrev. of *flieger-abwehr-kanone* anti-aircraft cannon]

flake (flāk), *n., v.,* **flaked, flak·ing.** **—n.** 1 a small, light mass; soft, loose bit: *a flake of snow.* 2 a thin, flat piece or layer: *flakes of rust.* 3 *Informal.* odd or unreliable person. **—v.** 1 come off in flakes; take off, chip, or peel in flakes. 2 form into flakes. [? < Scand. (Dan.) (sne) *flage* (snow) flake]

flak·y (flāk'i), *adj.,* **flak·i·er, flak·i·est.** 1 consisting of flakes. 2 easily broken or separated into flakes. 3 *Informal.* odd or crazy. **—flak'i·ly,** *adv.* **—flak'i·ness,** *n.*

flam·boy·ant (flam boi'ənt, *adj.* 1 gorgeously brilliant; flaming. 2 very ornate. 3 having wavy lines. [< F, flaming. See FLAMBEAU.] **—flam·boy'ance,** *n.* **—flam·boy'ant·ly,** *adv.*

flame (flām), *n. v.,* **flamed, flam·ing.** **—n.** 1 one of the glowing, red or yellow tongues of light that shoot out from a blazing fire. **2** a burning gas or vapor. **3** a burning with flames; blaze. **4** thing that suggests flame. —*v.* **1** burn with flame; blaze. **2** shine brightly; give out a bright light. **3** burst out quickly and hotly.

flame out, suddenly fail to function.

flame up, suddenly burst into flames.

the flames, fire, as an instrument of death or destruction. [< OF < L *flamma*] —**flame′less,** *adj.* —**flam′er,** *n.*

fla·men·co (flə meng′kō), *n.* gypsy dancing, music, etc., of a style characteristic of Andalusia. [< Sp.]

flame·out (flām′out′), *n.* the sudden failure of a jet engine to function, esp. while the aircraft containing it is in flight.

flame·proof (flām′prüf′), *adj.* not liable to burn, esp. a material treated with flame retardant.

flame thrower, weapon that throws a spray of oil that ignites in the air.

flam·ing (flām′ing), *adj.* **1** burning with flames. **2** like a flame; very bright; brilliant. **3** *Fig.* violent; vehement. —**flam′ing·ly.** *adv.*

fla·min·go (flə ming′gō), *n., pl.* –**gos,** –**goes.** tropical wading bird with very long legs and feathers that vary from pink to scarlet. [< Pg. < Sp. < Pr. *flamenc* < *flama* FLAME]

flam·ma·ble (flam′ə bəl), *adj.* =inflammable.

Flan·ders (flan′dərz; flän′–), *n.* district in W Belgium, N France, and SW Netherlands.

flange (flanj), *n., v.,* **flanged, flang·ing.** —*n.* a projecting edge, rim, collar, etc., on an object for keeping it in place, attaching it to another object, strengthening it, etc. —*v.* provide with a flange. [var. of *flanch,* n., < *flanch,* v., < OF *flanchir* bend; akin to *flank*]

flank (flangk), *n.* **1** side of an animal or person between the ribs and the hip. **2** piece of beef cut from this part. **3** side. **4** the far right or left side of an army, fleet, etc. —*v.* **1** be at the side of: *high buildings flanked the alley.* **2** get around the far right or left side of. **3** attack from or on the side. [< OF *flanc* <Gmc.] —**flank′er,** *n.*

flan·nel (flan′əl), *n.* a soft, warm woolen cloth. **2** a soft, warm cotton cloth with a fuzzy nap.

flannels, clothes made of flannel.

flan·nel·et (flan′əl et′), *n.* =flannel.

flap (flap), *v.,* **flapped, flap·ping.** *n.* —*v.* **1** swing or sway about loosely and with more or less noise: *curtains flapped in the open windows* **2** move (wings, arms, etc.) up and down. **3** strike noisily with something broad and flat. —*n.* **1** a flapping motion. **2** noise caused by flapping. **3** blow from something broad and flat. **4** a broad, flat piece, usually hanging or fastened at one edge only. **5** hinged section on an airplane, a wing which can be

moved to assist a take-off or a landing. **6** *Informal.* noisy anger or excitement; commotion: *in a flap over harsh criticism.* [prob. imit.]

flap·jack (flap′jak′), *n.* =griddlecake.

flap·per (flap′ər), *n.* a flap (def. 4).

flare (flãr), *v.,* **flared, flar·ing,** *n.* —*v.* **1** flame up briefly or unsteadily, sometimes with smoke. **2** spread out in the shape of a bell: *the sides of a ship flare from the keel to the deck.* —*n.* **1** a bright, unsteady light or blaze. **2** a dazzling light used for signaling. **3** a sudden outburst. **4** a spreading out into a bell shape. **5** part that spreads out.

flare up or **out, a** flame up. **b** *Fig.* burst into anger, violence, etc. [cf. Norw. *flara* blaze]

flare-up (flãr′up′), *n.* **1** outburst of flame. **2** *Fig.* a sudden outburst of anger, violence, etc.

flar·ing (flãr′ing), *adj.* **1** flaming. **2** gaudy. **3** spreading gradually outward in form.

flash (flash), *n.* **1** a sudden, brief light or flame: *a flash of lightning.* **2** a sudden, brief feeling or display: *a flash of wit.* **3** a very brief time; instant. —*v.* **1** give out a sudden, brief light or flame. **2** come suddenly; pass quickly. [appar. imit.] —**flash′er,** *n.* —**flash′ing·ly,** *adv.*

flash·back (flash′bak′), *n.,* **1** break in the narrative of a novel, film, etc., to show something which happened in the past. **2** vivid recollection of something which happened in one's past.

flash bulb, a portable electric device used to make bright flashes for taking photographs indoors or at night.

flash·card (flash′kärd′), *n.* card with a letter, word, number, etc., on it, used to drill basic skills such as arithmetic and word recognition.

flash flood, a very sudden, violent flooding of a river, stream, etc.

flash·light (flash′lit′), *n.* a portable electric light, operated by batteries.

flash point, 1 temperature at which a flammable substance will catch fire. **2** *Fig.* point at which disagreement turns into hostility.

flash·y (flash′i), *adj.,* **flash·i·er, flash·i·est. 1** very bright for a short time; flashing. **2** showy; gaudy. —**flash′i·ly,** *adv.* —**flash′i·ness,** *n.*

flask (flask; fläsk), *n.* **1** any bottle-shaped container. **2** a small bottle with flat sides, made to be carried in the pocket. [OE *flasce.* Cf. LL *flasca* < Gmc.]

flat¹ (flat), *adj.,* **flat·ter, flat·test,** *n., adv., v.,* **flat·ted, flat·ing.** —*adj.* **1** smooth and level; even: *flat land.* **2** spread out; at full length. **3** not very deep or thick: *a plate is flat.* **4** with little air in it: *a flat tire.* **5** positive: *a flat refusal.* **6** without much life, interest, flavor, etc.: *flat food.* **7** not shiny or glossy: *a flat yellow.* **8** below the true pitch. —*n.* **1** something flat. **2** a flat part. **3** flat land. **4** sign (♭) that lowers a tone or note one half step below natural pitch. **5** tire with little air in it.

—*adv.* **1** *Music.* below the true pitch. **2** in a flat manner. **3** in a flat position. —*v.* make or become flat.

fall flat, fail completely; have no effect or interest. [< Scand. *flatr*] —**flat′ly,** *adv.* —**flat′ness,** *n.* —**flat′tish,** *adj.*

flat² (flat), *n.* apartment or set of rooms on one floor. [alter. of *flet,* OE *flett*]

flat·bed (flat′bed′), *n.* flat trailer for carrying containers, large equipment, etc.

flat·boat (flat′bōt′), *n.* a large boat with a flat bottom, often used on a river or canal.

flat·car (flat′kär′), *n.* a railroad freight car without a roof or sides.

flat·fish (flat′fish′), *n., pl.* –**fish·es** or (*esp. collectively*) –**fish.** fish with a flat body, and with both eyes on the side kept uppermost when lying flat.

flat·foot (flat′fùt′), *n., pl.* –**feet. 1** foot with a flattened arch. **2** =policeman.

flat·foot·ed (flat′fùt′id), *adj.* **1** having feet with flattened arches. **2** not to be changed or influenced; firm; uncompromising.

catch one flat-footed, catch one not ready; be unprepared. —**flat′foot′ed·ly,** *adv.* —**flat′-foot′ed·ness,** *n.*

flat·i·ron (flat′ī′ərn), *n.* =iron

flat silver, silver knives, forks, etc.

flat·ten (flat′ən), *v.* make or become flat. —**flat′ten·er,** *n.*

flat·ter (flat′ər), *v.* **1** praise too much. **2** show to be better looking than what is true: *this picture flatters her.* **3** try to win over by flattering.

flatter oneself, be pleased to know or think. [? extended use to ME *flateren* float, FLUTTER] —**flat′ter·er,** *n.* —**flat′ter·ing,** *adv.*

flat·ter·y (flat′ər i), *n., pl.* –**ter·ies, 1** act of flattering. **2** words of praise, usually untrue or overstated.

flat·top (flat′top′), *n.* an aircraft carrier.

flat·u·lent (flach′ə lənt), *adj.* **1** having gas in the stomach or intestines. **2** pompous in speech or behavior; vain; empty. [< F < L *flatus* a blowing] —**flat′u·lence,** *n.* —**flat′u·lent·ly,** *adv.*

flat·ware (flat′wãr′), *n.* **1** knives, forks, and spoons, esp of silver. **2** plates and other flat dishes.

flat·worm (flat′wèrm′), *n.* worm with a flat body, that lives in water or as a parasite on some animal.

flaunt (flônt; flänt), *v.* **1** show off: *flaunt riches in public.* **2** wave proudly: *banners flaunting in the breeze.* —*n.* a flaunting. [? <Scand. (Norw.) *flanta* gad about] —**flaunt′er,** *n.* —**flaunt′ing·ly,** *adv.* —**flaunt′y,** *adj.*

flau·tist (flô′tist), *n.* =flutist.

fla·vor (flā′vər), *n.* **1** taste, esp. a characteristic taste: *chocolate and vanilla have different flavors.* **2** thing used to give a certain taste to food or drink; flavoring. **3** a characteristic quality: *stories that have a flavor of the sea.* **4** aroma; odor. —*v.* **1** give an added taste to; season. **2** give a characteristic quality to.

[< OF *flaur*, ult. < L *fragrare* emit odor] —**fla′vor·er**, *n.* —**fla′vor·less**, *adj.*

fla·vor·ing (flā′vər ing; flāv′ring), *n.* thing used to give a certain taste to food or drink.

flaw (flô, *n.* 1 a defective place; crack. 2 fault; defect. —*v.* make or become defective; crack. [< Scand. (Sw.) *flaga*]

flaw·less (flô′lis), *adj.* without a flaw. —**flaw′less·ly**, *adv.* —**flaw′less·ness**, *n.*

flax (flaks), *n.* 1 plant with small, narrow leaves, blue flowers, and slender stems about two feet tall. Linseed oil is made from its seeds. 2 the threadlike fibers of this plant, spun into linen thread. [OE *fleax*]

flax·en (flak′sən), *adj.* 1 made of flax. 2 like the color of flax; pale-yellow: *flaxen hair.*

flax·seed (flaks′sēd´), *n.* seeds of flax.

flay (flā), *v.* 1 strip off the skin or outer covering of. 2 *Fig.* scold severely; criticize without pity or mercy. [OE *flēan*] —**flay′er**, *n.*

flea (flē), *n.* a small, wingless, jumping insect that lives as a parasite on animals, sucking their blood. [OE *flēah*]

flea·bane (flē′bān´), *n.* plant supposed to drive away fleas.

flea collar, narrow strip of plastic treated with a substance to repel and kill fleas, worn as a collar by cats and dogs.

flea market, market, often outdoors, where a wide variety of items are for sale, esp. used furniture, clothes, books, jewelry, etc.

fleck (flek), *n.* 1 spot or patch of color, light, etc. 2 a small particle; flake. —*v.* sprinkle with spots or patches of color, light, etc.; speckle. [? < Scand. *flekkr*] —**flecked**, *adj.*

flec·tion (flek′shən), *n.* 1 a bending. 2 a bent part; bend. [< L *flexio* < *flectere* bend] —**flec′tion·al**, *adj.*

fledge (flej), *v.*, **fledged**, **fledg·ing**. 1 grow the feathers needed for flying. 2 bring up (a young bird) until it is able to fly. 3 provide or cover with feathers. [cf. OE *unfligge* unfledged, unfit to fly]

fledg·ling (flej′ling), *n.* 1 a young bird just able to fly. 2 a young inexperienced person.

flee (flē), *v.*, **fled** (fled), **flee·ing**. 1 run away; try to get away by running. 2 run away from. 3 go quickly; move swiftly. [OE *flēon*] —**fle′er**, *n.*

fleece (flēs), *n.*, *v.*, **fleeced**, **fleec·ing**. —*n.* 1 wool that covers a sheep or similar animal. 2 quantity of wool cut from a sheep at one time. —*v.* 1 cut the fleece from. 2 rob; cheat; swindle. [OE *flēos*] —**fleeced**, *adj.* —**fleece′less**, *adj.* —**fleec′er**, *n.*

fleec·y (flēs′i), *adj.*, **fleec·i·er**, **fleec·i·est**. 1 like a fleece. 2 covered with fleece. —**fleec′i·ly**, *adv.* —**fleec′i·ness**, *n.*

fleet[1] (flēt), *n.* 1 group of warships under one command; navy. 2 any group of boats sailing together. 3 group of airplanes, automobiles, etc., moving or working together. [OE *flēot* < *flēotan* float]

fleet[2] (flēt), *adj.* swift; rapid. [< v.] —*v.* pass swiftly; move rapidly. [OE *flēotan* float] —**fleet′ly**, *adv.* —**fleet′ness**, *n.*

fleet·ing (flēt′ing), *adj.* passing swiftly; moving rapidly; soon gone. —**fleet′ing·ly**, *adv.* —**fleet′ing·ness**, *n.*

Flem., Flemish.

Flem·ing (flem′ing), *n.* 1 native of Flanders. 2 a Belgian whose native language is Flemish.

Flem·ish (flem′ish), *adj.* of or having to do with Flanders, its people, or their language. —*n.* 1 the people of Flanders. 2 their language.

flesh (flesh), *n.* 1 a soft substance of the body that covers the bones and is covered by skin. 2 meat. 3 body, not the soul or spirit. 4 the bad side of human nature. 5 family or relatives by birth. 6 the soft part of fruits or vegetables.
in the flesh, **a** alive. **b** in person. [OE *flæsc*] —**flesh′less**, *adj.*

flesh-col·ored (flesh′kul´ərd), *adj.* pinkish-white with a tinge of yellow.

flesh·y (flesh′i), *adj.*, **flesh·i·er**, **flesh·i·est**. 1 having much flesh; fat. 2 of or like flesh. 3 pulpy. —**flesh′i·ness**, *n.*

fleur-de-lis (flèr´də lē´; -lēs´), *n.*, *pl.* **fleurs-de-lis** (flèr´də lēz´). 1 design or device used in heraldry. 2 the royal coat of arms of France. 3 the iris flower or plant. [< F, lily flower]

flew (flü), *v.* pt. of **fly**[2].

flex (fleks), *v.* bend. [< L *flexus* bent]

flex·i·ble (flek′sə bəl), *adj.* 1 easily bent; not stiff; bending without breaking. 2 easily adapted or managed. [< F < L *flexibilis*. See FLEX.] —**flex′i·bil′i·ty**, **flex′i·ble·ness**, *n.* —**flex′i·bly**, *adv.*

flex·or (flek′sər), *n.* any muscle that bends some part of the body.

flex·time (fleks′tīm´), *n.* working hours set to the convenience of the employee that may begin earlier or end later than usual. [< *flexible* + *time*]

flex·ure (flek′shər), *n.* 1 a bending; curving. 2 bend; curve. —**flex′ur·al**, *adj.*

flib·ber·ti·gib·bet (flib′ər ti jib´it), *n.* a frivolous, flighty person.

flick (flik), *n.* 1 a quick, light blow; sudden, snapping stroke. 2 the light, snapping sound of such a blow or stroke. 3 streak; splash; fleck. 4 *Slang*. a motion picture. —*v.* 1 strike lightly with a quick, snapping blow. 2 make a sudden, snapping stroke with: *the boys flicked wet towels at each other.* 3 flutter; move quickly and lightly. [prob. imit.] —**flick′er**, *n.*

flick·er[1] (flik′ər), *v.* 1 shine with a wavering light; burn with an unsteady flame. 2 move quickly and lightly in and out or back and forth: *the tongue of a snake flickers.* —*n.* 1 a wavering, unsteady light or flame. 2 a quick, light movement. [OE *flicorian*] —**flick′er·ing·ly**, *adv.*

flick·er[2] (flik′ər), *n.* woodpecker of North America with golden-yellow feathers

on the underside of the wings. [? imit. of its note]

fli·er (flī′ər), *n.* 1 person or thing that flies. 2 an aviator. 3 =handbill. Also, **flyer.**

flight[1] (flīt), *n.* 1 act or manner of flying. 2 distance a bird, bullet, airplane, etc., can fly. 3 group of things flying through the air together. 4 trip in an aircraft. 5 a soaring above or beyond what is ordinary. 6 set of stairs or steps between landings of a building. [OE *flyht*; akin to FLY[2]]

flight[2] (flīt), *n.* act of fleeing; running away. [ME *fliht* < OE *flēon* flee]

flight attendant, steward or stewardess on an aircraft.

flight·less (flīt′lis), *adj.* unable to fly.

flight recorder, recording device that makes a record of speed, course, and other data, esp. of use in analyzing the cause of a crash; black box.

flight·y (flīt′i), *adj.*, **flight·i·er**, **flight·i·est**. likely to have sudden fancies; full of whims; frivolous. —**flight′i·ly**, *adv.* —**flight′i·ness**, *n.*

flim·sy (flim′zi), *adj.*, **-si·er**, **-si·est**. 1 light and thin; frail. 2 lacking seriousness or sense; trivial: *a flimsy excuse.* [? < alter. of *film*] —**film′si·ly**, *adv.* —**film′si·ness**, *n.*

flinch (flinch), *v.* draw back from difficulty, danger, or pain; shrink. —*n.* a drawing back. [prob. < OF *flenchir* < unrecorded Frankish *hlankjan* bend. Cf. G *lenken*.] —**flinch′er**, *n.* —**flinch′ing·ly**, *adv.*

fling (fling), *v.*, **flung**, **fling·ing**. —*v.* 1 throw with force; throw: *fling a stone.* 2 plunge; kick. 3 put suddenly or violently: *fling him into jail.* —*n.* 1 a sudden throw. 2 plunge; kick. 3 time of doing as one pleases. 4 a lively Scottish dance.
have a fling at, try; attempt. [? akin to Scand. *flengja* flog] —**fling′er**, *n.*

flint (flint), *n.* 1 a very hard, gray or brown stone that makes a spark when struck against steel. 2 piece of this used with steel to light fires, explode gunpowder, etc. 3 *Fig.* anything very hard or unyielding. [OE]

flint·lock (flint′lok´), *n.* 1 gunlock in which a flint striking against steel makes sparks that explode the gunpowder. 2 an old-fashioned gun with such a gunlock.

flint·y (flin′ti), *adj.*, **flint·i·er**, **flint·i·est**. 1 consisting of flint; containing flint. 2 *Fig.* like flint; very hard; unyielding. —**flint′i·ly**, *adv.* —**flint′i·ness**, *n.*

flip[1] (flip), *v.* **flipped**, **flip·ping**, *n.*, *adj.*, **flip·per**, **flip·pest**. —*v.* 1 toss or move with a snap of a finger and thumb. 2 jerk: *the branch flipped back.* 3 flick. —*n.* 1 a smart tap; snap. 2 a sudden jerk. —*adj.* flippant. [prob. imit.]

flip[2] (flip), *n.* a hot drink containing beer, ale, cider, or the like, with sugar and spice. [n. use of *flip*[1], v.]

flip-flop (flip′flop´), *n.* 1 reversal: *a flip-flop on policy.* 2 acrobatic stunt. 3 Often, **flip-flops.** rubber sandals held on the foot by a thong. —*v.* turn about; reverse.

flip·pan·cy (flip'ən si), *n., pl.* –**cies.** a being flippant.

flip·pant (flip'ənt), *adj.* smart or pert in speech; not respectful. [cf Scand. *fleipa* babble] —**flip'pant·ly,** *adv.* —**flip'pant-ness,** *n.*

flip·per (flip'ər), *n.* **1** a broad, flat limb esp. adapted for swimming. Seals have flippers. **2** swimming aid made of rubber and shaped like a frog's foot, worn on the swimmer's foot.

flip side, opposite or reverse of something.

flirt (flèrt), *v.* **1** make love without meaning it. **2** trifle; toy: *he flirted with the idea of going to Europe.* **3** move quickly; flutter. —*n.* **1** person who makes love without meaning it. **2** a quick movement or flutter. [imit.] —**flirt'er,** *n.* —**flirt'ing·ly,** *adv.*

flir·ta·tion (flèr tā'shən), *n.* **1** a making love without meaning it. **2** a love affair that is not serious. —**flir·ta'tious,** *adj.* —**flir·ta'tious·ly,** *adv.* —**flir·ta'tious-ness,** *n.*

flit (flit), *v.,* **flit·ted, flit·ting,** *n.* —*v.* **1** fly lightly and quickly; flutter. **2** pass quickly. —*n.* a light, quick movement. [? < Scand. *flytjask*] —**flit'ter,** *n.*

flit·ter (flit'ər), *v., n.* =flutter.

float (flōt), *v.* **1** stay on top of or be held up by air, water, or other liquid. **2** move with a moving liquid; drift: *the boat floated out to sea.* **3** rest or move in a liquid, the air, etc. **4** set going as a company. —*n.* **1** anything that stays up or holds up something else in water. **2** a raft. **3** a low, flat car that carries something to be shown in a parade. [OE *flotian*] —**float'a·ble,** *adj.* —**float'er,** *n.*

float·ing (flōt'ing), *adj.* **1** that floats. **2** not fixed; not staying in one place; moving around.

floating ribs, ribs not attached to the breastbone; last two pairs of ribs.

flock[1] (flok), *n.* **1** group of animals of one kind keeping, feeding, or herded together, esp. of sheep, goats, or birds. **2** a large group; crowd. **3** people of the same church group. —*v.* go or gather in a flock; come crowding. [OE *flocc*]

floe (flō), *n.* field or sheet of floating ice. [< Scand. (Norw.) *flo*]

flog (flog; flôg), *v.,* **flogged, flog·ging.** whip very hard; beat with a whip, stick, etc. —**flog'ger,** *n.*

flood (flud), *n.* **1** flow of water over what is usually dry land. **2** a great outpouring of anything: *flood of light, flood of words.* **3** a flowing of the tide toward the shore. —*v.* **1** flow over. **2** fill much fuller than usual. **3** fill, cover, or overcome like a flood. **4** flow like a flood.

the Flood, the water that covered the earth in the time of Noah. Gen. 7 [OE *flōd*] —**flood'a·ble,** *adj.* —**flood'er,** *n.* —**flood'less,** *adj.*

flood control, control of rivers that tend to overflow by the use of dams, levees, dikes, extra outlets, reforestation, etc.

flood·gate (flud'gāt'), *n.* **1** gate in a canal, river, stream, etc., to control the flow of water. **2** *Fig.* thing that controls any flow or passage.

flood·light (flud'līt'), *n.* **1** lamp that gives a broad beam of light. **2** a broad beam of light from such a lamp. —*v.* illuminate by such a lamp.

floor (flôr; flōr), *n.* **1** the inside bottom covering of a room. **2** story of a building. **3** a flat surface at the bottom. **4** part of a room or hall of a lawmaking body, etc. **5** privilege to speak in a lawmaking body, etc. The chairman decides who has the floor. **6** part of an exchange where buying and selling of stocks, bonds, etc., is done. **7** of prices, amounts, etc., the lowest level. —*v.* **1** put a floor in or over. **2** knock down. **3** defeat. **4** confuse; puzzle. [OE *flōr*] —**floor'less,** *adj.*

floor·board (flôr'bôrd'; flōr'-), *n.* **1** one of the boards making up a wooden floor. **2** Usually, **floorboards.** the floor of an automobile, esp. where the driver sits.

floor·ing (flôr'ing; flōr'-), *n.* **1** floor. **2** floors. **3** material for making floors.

floor leader, member of a lawmaking body chosen to direct the members who belong to his or her political party.

floor plan, diagram of the layout of the floor of a building, showing the location and size of various rooms, windows, etc., and drawn to scale.

floor show, entertainment presented at a night club.

flop (flop), *v.,* **flopped, flop·ping,** *n.* —*v.* **1** move loosely or heavily; flap around clumsily. **2** fall, throw, or move heavily. **3** change or turn suddenly. **4** fail. —*n.* **1** a flopping. **2** sound made by flopping. **3** failure. [imit. var. of *flap*] —**flop'per,** *n.*

flop·py (flop'i), *adj.,* –**pi·er,** –**pi·est.** flopping; tending to flop. —**flop'pi·ly,** *adv.* —**flop'pi·ness,** *n.*

floppy disk, small disk for storing computer data.

flo·ra (flô'rə; flō'-), *n.* plants of a particular region or time. [< L]

flo·ral (flô'rəl; flō'-) *adj.* **1** of flowers; having to do with flowers. **2** resembling flowers. —**flo'ral·ly,** *adv.*

Flor·ence (flôr'əns; flor'-), *n.* city in C Italy. —**Flor'en·tine,** *adj., n.*

flo·res·cence (flō res'əns; flō-), *n.* **1** act of blossoming. **2** condition of blossoming. **3** period of blossoming. [< NL *florescentia,* ult. < L *florere* flourish] —**flo·res'cent,** *adj.*

flo·ret (flô'rit; flō'-), **1** a small flower. **2** one of the small flowers in a flower head of a composite plant.

flor·id (flôr'id; flor'-), *adj.* **1** highly colored; ruddy: *a florid complexion.* **2** elaborately ornamented; flowery; showy; ornate. [< L *floridus* < *flos* flower] —**flo·rid'i·ty, flor'id·ness,** *n.* —**flor'id·ly,** *adv.*

Flor·i·da (flôr'ə də; flor'-), *n.* a state in the extreme SE part of the United States. —**Flo·rid'i·an, Flor'i·dan,** *adj., n.*

flor·in (flôr'ən; flor'-), *n.* **1** a gold coin issued at Florence in 1252. **2** any of various gold or silver coins used in different countries of Europe since then. [< F Ital. *fiorino* Florentine coin marked with a lily, ult. < L *flos* flower]

flo·rist (flô'rist; flō'-; flor'ist), *n.* person who raises or sells flowers.

floss (flôs; flos), or **floss silk,** *n.* **1** short loose silk fibers. **2** a shiny, untwisted silk thread made from such fibers. **3** soft, silky fluff or fibers.

floss·y (flôs'i; flos'i), *adj.,* **floss·i·er, floss·i·est.** **1** of floss. **2** like floss.

flo·ta·tion (flō tā'shən), *n.* a floating or launching.

flo·til·la (flō til'ə), *n.* **1** a small fleet. **2** fleet of small ships. [< Sp., dim. of *flota* fleet]

flot·sam (flot'səm), *n.* wreckage of a ship or its cargo found floating on the sea. [< AF *floteson* < *floter* float < OE]

flounce[1] (flouns), *v.,* **flounced, flounc-ing,** *n.* —*v.* go with an angry or impatient fling of the body: *she flounced out of the room in a rage.* —*n.* an angry or impatient fling of the body. [< Scand. (Sw.) *flunsa* plunge]

flounce[2] (flouns), *n., v.,* **flounced, flounc-ing.** —*n.* a wide ruffle used to trim a dress, skirt, etc. —*v.* trim with a flounce or flounces. [var. of *frounce* < OF *fronce* wrinkle]

floun·der[1] (floun'dər), *v.* **1** struggle awkwardly without making much progress; plunge about. **2** be clumsy or confused and make mistakes. —*n.* a floundering. —**floun'der·ing·ly,** *adv.*

floun·der[2] (floun'dər), *n., pl.* –**ders** or (*esp. collectively*) –**der.** flatfish that has a large mouth. [< AF *flo(u)ndre* < Scand. (Norw.) *flundra*]

flour (flour), *n.* **1** a fine, powdery substance made by grinding and sifting wheat or other grain. **2** any fine, soft powder. —*v.* cover with flour. [special use of *flower* (i.e., the flower of the meal)] —**flour'less,** *adj.* —**flour'y,** *adj.*

flour·ish (flèr'ish), *v.* **1** grow or develop with vigor; thrive; do well. **2** be in the best time of life or activity. **3** wave (a sword, arm, etc.) in the air. **4** make a showy display. —*n.* **1** a waving in the air. **2** a showy decoration in writing. **3** a showy trill or passage in music. **4** a showy display. [< OF *florir,* ult. < L *flos* flower] —**flour'ish·er,** *n.* —**flour'ish-ing,** *adj.* —**flour'ish·ing·ly,** *adv.*

flout (flout), *v.* treat with contempt or scorn; mock; scoff at. —*n.* contemptuous speech or act; insult; mockery; scoffing. [var. of *flute,* v.] —**flout'er,** *n.* **flout'ing·ly,** *adv.*

flow (flō), *v.* **1** run like water; circulate. **2** pour out; pour along: *the audience flowed out of the theater.* **3** move easily or smoothly; glide. **4** hang loose and waving: *flowing curtains before an open* window. —n. 1 act of flowing: *flow of blood.* 2 any continuous movement. 3 rate of flowing. 4 current; stream. 5 rise of the tide. [OE *flōwan*]

flow·er (flou′ər), n. 1 part of a plant that produces the seed; blossom; bloom. 2 plant grown for its blossoms. 3 any of several kinds of reproductive structures in lower plants, such as the mosses. 4 the finest part. 5 time of being at one's best. —v. 1 have flowers; produce flowers. 2 cover or decorate with flowers. 3 be at one's best.

in flower, flowering.

in full flower, at peak competence and achievement; flourishing. [< OF < L *flos*]

flow·ered (flou′ərd), adj. 1 having flowers. 2 covered or decorated with flowers.

flow·er·et (flou′ər it), n. a small flower; floret.

flow·er·ing (flou′ər ing), adj. having flowers.

flow·er·pot (flou′ər pot′), n. pot to hold dirt for a plant to grow in.

flow·er·y (flou′ər i), adj., **-er·i·er, -er·i·est.** 1 having many flowers. 2 containing many fine words and fanciful expressions. —**flow′er·i·ly,** adv. —**flow′er·i·ness,** n.

flown (flōn), v. pp. of **fly**[2].

fl. oz., fluid ounce.

flu (flü), n. =influenza.

flub (flub), v., **flubbed, flub·bing.** Informal. do (something) very clumsily; make a mess of.

fluc·tu·ate (fluk′chù āt), v., **-at·ed, -at·ing.** rise and fall; change continually; vary irregularly. [< L, < *fluctus* wave] —**fluc′tu·a′tion,** n.

flue (flü), n. tube, pipe, or other enclosed passage for conveying smoke, hot air, etc.

flu·ent (lü′ənt), adj. 1 flowing smoothly or easily: *speak fluent French.* 2 speaking or writing easily and rapidly. [< L *fluens* flowing] —**flu′en·cy, flu′ent·ness,** n. —**flu′ent·ly,** adv.

fluff (fluf), n. 1 soft, light, downy particles. 2 a downy mass: *a fluff of fur.* —v. shake or puff out (hair, feathers, etc.) into a soft, light mass. —**fluff′er,** n.

fluff·y (fluf′i), adj., **fluff·i·er, fluff·i·est.** 1 soft and light like fluff: *whipped cream is fluffy.* 2 covered with fluff; downy: *fluffy baby chicks.* —**fluff′i·ly,** adv. —**fluff′i·ness,** n.

flu·id (flü′id), n. any liquid or gas; any substance that flows. Water, mercury, air, and oxygen are fluids. —adj. 1 in the state of a fluid; like a fluid; flowing. 2 changing easily; not fixed. [< L, < *fluere* flow] —**flu·id′ic,** adj. —**flu·id′i·ty, flu′id·ness,** n. —**flu′id·ly,** adv.

fluid dram, one eighth of a fluid ounce.

fluid ounce, measure for liquids. In the United States, 16 fluid ounces = 1 pint.

fluke[1] (flük), n. 1 either of the two points of an anchor. 2 the barbed head or barb of an arrow, harpoon, etc. [? special use of *fluke*[3]]

fluke[2] (flük), n. a lucky chance; fortunate accident.

fluke[3] (flük), n. =flatfish. [OE *flōc*]

fluk·y (flük′i), adj., **fluk·i·er, fluk·i·est.** obtained by chance rather than by skill.

flume (flüm), n. 1 a deep, narrow valley with a stream running through it. 2 a large, inclined through or chute for carrying water. [< OF < L *flumen* river < *fluere* flow]

flum·mox (flum′əks), v. Informal. cause confusion; bewilder.

flung (flung), v. pt. and pp. of **fling.**

flunk (flungk), —v. 1 fail in school work. 2 cause to fail. 3 mark or grade as having failed. —n. failure.

flunk·y (flungk′i), n., pl. **flunk·ies.** a flattering, fawning person.

flu·o·resce (flü′ə res′), v., **-resced, -resc·ing.** give off light by fluorescence.

flu·o·res·cence (flü′ə res′əns), n. 1 a giving off of light by a substance when it is exposed to certain rays (X rays and ultraviolet rays). 2 property of a substance that causes this. 3 light given off in this way. —**flu′o·res′cent,** adj.

fluorescent lamp, an electric lamp containing gas or vapor which produces light (**fluorescent light**) when electric current is introduced. —**fluorescent lighting.**

fluor·i·date (flur′ə dāt; flü′ə rə-), v., **-dat·ed, -dat·ing.** add small amounts of fluorine to drinking water, esp. to decrease tooth decay. [< *fluoridation*]

fluor·i·da·tion (flur′ə dā′shən; flü′ə rə-), n. act or process of fluoridating. [< *fluoride*]

flu·o·ride (flü′ə rīd; -rid), **flu·o·rid** (-rid) n. compound of fluorine and another element or radical.

flu·o·rine (flü′ə rēn; -rin), **flu·o·rin** (-rin), n. a poisonous, greenish-yellow gas, F or Fl, that is a very active element similar to chlorine. —**flu·or′ic,** adj.

flu·o·rite (flü′ə rīt), **flu·or·spar** (flü′-ôr spär′; -ər-) n. calcium fluoride, CaF_2, a transparent, crystalline mineral that occurs in many colors.

fluor·o·scope (flur′ə skōp; flü′ə rə-), n. device containing a fluorescent screen for examining objects exposed to X rays, etc.

flur·ry (flėr′i), n., pl. **-ries,** v., **-ried, -ry·ing.** —n. 1 a sudden gust. 2 a sudden, gusty shower or snowfall. 3 sudden excitement, confusion, or commotion. —v. 1 excite; confuse; disturb. 2 fall in a sudden shower of snow.

flush[1] (flush), v. 1 blush; glow. 2 flow rapidly: *embarrassment caused the blood to flush to her cheeks.* 3 wash or cleanse with a rapid flow of water. —n. 1 blush; glow. 2 rapid flow. 3 glowing vigor; freshness: *the first flush of youth.* 4 fit of feeling very hot. [? connected with *flash, blush*]

flush[2] (flush), adj. 1 even; level. 2 well supplied: *flush with money.* 3 abundant; plentiful. —adv. 1 so as to be level; evenly. 2 directly; squarely. —v. make even; level. [? extended use of *flush*[1]]

flush[3] (flush), v. 1 fly or start up suddenly, as a bird. 2 cause to fly or start up suddenly.

flush[4] (flush), n. a hand all of one suit in cards. [cf. F *flus, flux* < L *fluxus* flow]

flus·ter (flus′tər), v. make or become nervous and excited; confuse. —n. nervous excitement; confusion. [cf. Scand. *flaustr* bustle and *flaustra* be flustered]

flute (flüt), n., v., **flut·ed, flut·ing.** —n. 1 a long, slender, pipelike instrument with a series of finger holes or keys along the side. It is played by blowing across a hole near one end. 2 a long, round groove, as in cloth, a column, etc. —v. 1 play on a flute. 2 make long, round grooves in. [< OF < Pr. *flauta,* ult. < L *flatus* blown] —**flute′like′,** adj.

flut·ed (flü′tid), adj. 1 having long, round grooves. 2 *Fig.* like a flute in sound: *fluted bird song.*

flut·ing (flüt′ing), n. decoration made of flutes.

flut·ist (flüt′ist), n. person who plays a flute.

flut·ter (flut′ər), v. 1 wave back and forth quickly and lightly. 2 flap the wings; flap. 3 move restlessly. 4 tremble: *her heart fluttered.* 5 confuse; excite. —n. 1 a fluttering. 2 confused or excited condition. [OE *flotorian* < *flēotan* float] —**flut′ter·er,** n. —**flut′ter·ing·ly,** adv.

flux (fluks), n. 1 a flow; flowing. 2 a flowing in of the tide. 3 continuous change. 4 an unnatural discharge of blood or liquid matter from the body. 5 substance used to help metals or minerals melt together. —v. 1 cause a discharge in; purge. 2 melt together. [< L *fluxus* < *fluere* flow]

fly[1] (flī), n., pl. **flies.** 1 a housefly. 2 any of a large group of insects, including houseflies, mosquitoes, gnats, May flies, etc. 3 fishhook with feathers, silk, tinsel, etc., on it to make it look like an insect. [OE *flēoge*]

fly[2] (flī), v., **flew, flown, fly·ing;** n., pl. **flies.** —v. 1 move through the air with wings. 2 float in the air. 3 cause to fly. 4 travel through the air in an aircraft. 5 go rapidly. 6 run away; flee. —n. 1 flap to cover buttons on clothing. 2 flap forming the door of a tent. 3 ball hit high in the air with a bat. [OE *flēogan*]

fly·blown (flī′blōn′), adj. 1 tainted by the eggs or larvae of flies. 2 spoiled.

fly-by-night (flī′bī nīt′), adj. not reliable; not to be trusted.

fly-cast·ing (flī′kas′ting; -käs′-), n., or **fly casting.** sport of fishing with rod and reel, with an artificial fly as bait.

fly·catch·er (flī′kach′ər), n. any of a family of songless, perching birds having small, weak feet, short necks, and large heads with broad, flattened bills hooked at the tip.

fly·er (flī′ər), n. =flier.

fly-fish (flī′fish′), v. fish with flies as bait. —**fly′-fish′er,** n. —**fly′-fish′ing,** n.

fly·ing (flī′ing), adj. 1 that flies; moving through the air. 2 floating in the air. 3 swift; hasty.

flying buttress, an arched support or brace built against the wall of a building to resist outward pressure.

flying colors, success; victory.

flying fish, a tropical fish that has winglike fins and can leap through the air.

flying jib, a small, triangular sail set in front of the regular jib.

flying machine, =aircraft.

flying saucer, any of various mysterious disklike objects reportedly seen flying over the United States and Mexico, since 1947; UFO.

fly·leaf (flī′lēf′), n., pl. **-leaves.** a blank sheet of paper at the beginning or end of a book, pamphlet, etc.

fly·o·ver (flī′ō′vər), n. a mass flight of aircraft over a city, reviewing stand, etc.

fly paper, strip of paper with a sticky coating, used to trap flies.

fly·speck (flī′spek′), n. a tiny spot left by a fly. —v. make flyspecks on.

fly·weight (flī′wāt′), n. boxer who weighs not more than 112 pounds.

fly·wheel (flī′hwēl′), n. a heavy wheel attached to machinery to keep the speed even.

fm, 1 fathom. 2 from.

Fm, fermium.

FM, F.M., frequency modulation.

f number, focal length of a camera lens.

foal (fōl), n. a young horse, donkey, etc.; colt or filly. —v. give birth to (a foal). [OE fola]

foam (fōm), n. mass of very small bubbles. —v. 1 form or gather foam. 2 break into foam. [OE fām] —**foam′less,** adj.

foam rubber, rubber processed so that it is soft and porous, used for cushions, etc.

foam·y (fōm′i), adj., **foam·i·er, foam·i·est.** 1 covered with foam; foaming. 2 made of foam. 3 like foam. —**foam′i·ly,** adv. —**foam′i·ness,** n.

fob¹ (fob), n. 1 a small pocket in trousers or breeches to hold a watch, etc. 2 a short watch chain, ribbon, etc., that hangs out of a watch pocket. [cf. dial. HG fuppe pocket]

fob² (fob), v., **fobbed, fob·bing.** cheat; trick.

fob off, put off or get rid of by a trick.

f.o.b., F.O.B., free on board.

fo·cal (fō′kəl), adj. of a focus; having to do with a focus. —**fo′cal·ly,** adv.

focal length, distance of the focus from the optical center of a lens.

fo·cus (fō′kəs), n., pl. **-cus·es, -ci** (-sī), v., **-cused, -cus·ing.** —n. 1 point where rays of light, heat, etc., meet after being bent by a lens, curved mirror, etc. 2 distance of this point from the lens,

curved mirror, etc. 3 correct adjustment of a lens, the eye, etc., to make a clear image. 4 the central point. —v. 1 bring (rays of light, heat, etc.) to a point. 2 adjust (a lens, the eye, etc.) to make a clear image. 3 concentrate: he focused his mind on his lessons.

in focus, clear; distinct.

out of focus blurred; indistinct. [< L, hearth] —**fo′cus·er,** n.

focus group, group of people brought together to give their opinions about something, such as a political issue, a proposed policy, etc.

fod·der (fod′ər), n. coarse food for horses, cattle, etc. [OE fōdor < fōda food]

foe (fō), n. enemy. [OE fāh hostile]

fog (fog; fôg), n., v., **fogged, fog·ging.** —n. 1 cloud of fine drops of water just above the earth's surface; thick mist. 2 a confused or puzzled condition. —v. 1 cover with fog. 2 confuse; puzzle. [< foggy]

fog bank, a dense mass of fog.

fog·gy (fog′i; fôg′i), adj., **-gi·er, -gi·est.** 1 having much fog; misty. 2 confused; puzzled. [< fog long grass; orig., marshy] —**fog′gi·ly,** adv. —**fog′gi·ness,** n.

fog·horn (fog′hôrn′; fôg′–), n. horn that warns ships in foggy weather.

fo·gy (fō′gi), n., pl. **-gies.** person who is behind the times. —**fo′gy·ish,** adj.

foi·ble (foi′bəl), n. a weak point; weakness. [< F, older form of modern faible FEEBLE]

foil¹ (foil), v. prevent from carrying out (plans, attempts, etc.); turn aside or hinder. [< OF fuler trample, full (cloth). See FULLER.]

foil² (foil), n. 1 metal beaten, hammered, or rolled into a very thin sheet. 2 anything that makes something else look or seem better by contrast. —v. 1 cover or back with metal foil. 2 set off by contrast. [< F < L folia leaves]

foil³ (foil), n. a long, narrow sword with a knob or button on the point to prevent injury, used in fencing.

foist (foist), v. 1 palm off as genuine; impose slyly. 2 insert secretly or slyly. [prob. < dial. Du. vuisten take in hand < vuist fist]

fol., 1 folio. 2 following.

fold¹ (fōld), v. 1 bend or double over on itself. 2 bring close to the body. 3 wrap; enclose. 4 fail in business; close up. —n. 1 layer of something folded. 2 a hollow place made by folding. 3 bend in rock after its stratification.

fold in, mix an ingredient into a batter by gently turning it over and over, esp. a cake batter.

fold up, a make or become smaller and flatter by folding. **b** collapse. **c** Informal. fail completely. [OE fealdan]

fold² (fōld), n. 1 pen to keep sheep in. 2 church family; church. —v. put or keep (sheep) in a pen. [OE falod]

-fold, suffix. 1 times as many; times as great, as in tenfold. 2 formed or divided

into ____ parts, as in manifold. [OE –feald]

fold·er (fōld′ər), n. 1 person or thing that folds. 2 holder for papers, made by folding a piece of stiff paper. 3 a small book made of one or more folded sheets.

fo·li·a·ceous fō′li ā′shəs), adj. 1 leaflike; leafy. 2 made of leaflike plates or thin layers. [< L, < folia leaves.]

fo·li·age (fō′li ij), n. 1 leaves. 2 decoration made of carved or painted leaves, flowers, etc. [alter. of F feuillage, ult. < L folia leaves]

fo·li·ate (adj. fō′li it, –āt; v. fō′li āt), adj., v., **-at·ed, -at·ing.** —adj. having leaves; covered with leaves. —v. put forth leaves.

fo·li·a·tion (fō′li ā′shən), n. 1 a growing of leaves; putting forth of leaves. 2 a being in leaf. 3 decoration with leaflike ornaments. 4 the consecutive numbering of leaves of a book.

fo·lic acid (fō′lik), part of the vitamin B complex, found in green leaves and animal tissue.

fo·li·o (fō′li ō), n., pl. **-li·os,** adj., v., **-li·oed, -li·o·ing.** —n. 1 a large sheet of paper folded once to make two leaves, or four pages, of a book, etc. 2 book having pages made by folding large sheets of paper once. 3 a page number of a book, etc. —adj. of the largest size; made of large sheets of paper folded once. —v. number the leaves of a book, pamphlet, etc. [< L, abl. of folium leaf]

folk (fōk), n., pl. **folk, folks,** adj. —n. 1 people. 2 tribe; nation. —adj. of or having to do with the common people, their beliefs, legends, customs, etc.

folks a people. **b** members of one's own family. [OE folc]

folk art, art originating among ordinary people that is a direct expression of their lives.

folk dance, 1 dance originating and handed down among the common people. 2 music for it.

folk·lore (fōk′lôr′; –lōr′), n. beliefs, legends, customs, etc., of a people, tribe, etc. **folk′lor′ist,** n. —**folk′lor·is′tic,** adj.

folk music, music originating and handed down among the common people.

folk song, 1 song originating and handed down among the common people. 2 song imitating this.

folk·sy (fōk′si), adj., **-si·er, -si·est.** 1 appealing to ordinary people; informal. 2 sociable.

folk tale or **story,** story or legend originating and handed down among the common people.

folk·way (fōk′wā′), n. custom or habit that has grown up within a social group and is common among the members of this group.

fol·li·cle (fol′ə kəl), n. 1 a small cavity, sac, or gland. Hair grows from follicles. 2 a dry, one-celled seed vessel. Milkweed pods are follicles. [< L folliculus, dim of follis bellows] —**fol·lic′u·lar,** adj.

fol·low (fol′ō), v. 1 go or come after. 2 result from; result. 3 go along with; accompany. 4 pursue. 5 take as a guide; use; obey. 6 keep the eyes or mind on: *follow a story.* 7 be concerned with: *follow the career of an artist.* —n. act of following.

as follows, the following.

follow out, carry out to the end: *follow out a plan.*

follow through, continue a stroke or motion through to its end.

follow up, a follow closely. **b** carry out to the end. **c** increase the effect of. [OE *folgian*] —**fol′low·a·ble,** adj.

fol·low·er (fol′ō ər), n. 1 person or thing that follows. 2 person who follows the ideas or beliefs of another. 3 attendant; servant. 4 a male admirer; beau.

fol·low·ing (fol′ō ing), n. followers; attendants. —adj. that follows; next after.

the following, persons, things, items, etc., now to be named, related, described, etc.

fol·low-through (fol′ō thrü′), n. 1 continuation of a movement or stroke in sports. 2 continuation of something undertaken, as a plan, idea, etc.

fol·low-up (fol′ō up′), n. 1 act of carrying out to an end or completion. 2 further action on something in order to reach a goal, get a positive response, etc. 3 newspaper story that follows an initial story about something.

fol·ly (fol′i), n., pl. **–lies. 1** being foolish; lack of sense; unwise conduct. 2 a foolish act, practice, or idea; something silly. 3 a costly but foolish undertaking. [< OF, < *fol* foolish. See FOOL.]

fo·ment (fō ment′), v. promote; foster (trouble, rebellion, etc.) [< LL *fomentare*, ult. < L *fovere* to warm]

fond (fond), adj. 1 liking: *fond of children.* 2 loving: *a fond look.* 3 cherished: *fond remembrances.* [ME *fonned*, pp. of *fonne(n)* be foolish] —**fond′ly,** adv. —**fond′ness,** n.

fon·dle (fon′dəl), v., **–dled, –dling.** pet; caress. [< *fond*, v., special use of *fond*, adj.] —**fon′dler,** n.

fon·due (fon′dü; fon dü′), n. 1 traditionally, a combination of melted cheese and wine, eaten on small pieces of bread dipped into it. 2 any similar dish of a sauce into which small pieces of food are dipped. [< F, fem. pp. of *fondre* melt]

font¹ (font), n. 1 basin holding water for baptism. 2 basin for holy water. 3 fountain; source. [< L *fons* SPRING]

font² (font). n. in printing, a complete set of type of one size and style. [< F *fonte* < *fondre* melt]

food (füd), n. 1 what an animal or plant takes in to enable it to live and grow. 2 what is eaten: *give food to the hungry.* 3 a particular kind or article of food. 4 what sustains or serves for consumption in any way: *food for thought.* [OE *fōda*] —**food′less,** adj.

food chain, 1 natural system of animals feeding on each other, esp. higher animals feeding on lower animals. 2 *Fig.* any system in which members of one group are dependent on another group: *economic food chain.*

food·ie (fü′dē), n. person with an unusual interest in food.

food processor, 1 business that prepares agricultural products for sale as food, esp. by canning, freezing, etc. 2 small appliance that chops, slices, and minces food.

food·stuff (füd′stuf′), n. material for food.

fool (fül), n. 1 person without sense; unwise or silly person. 2 clown formerly kept by a king or lord to amuse people; jester. 3 person who has been deceived or tricked; dupe. —v. 1 act like a fool for fun; play; joke. 2 make a fool of; deceive; trick.

fool around, waste time foolishly.

fool with, meddle foolishly with. [< OF *fol* madman, prob. < LL *follis* empty-headed < L, bag, bellows]

fool·er·y (fül′ər i), n., pl. **–er·ies.** foolish action or behavior.

fool·har·dy (fül′här′di), adj., **–di·er, –di·est.** foolishly bold; rash. —**fool′har′di·ly,** adv. —**fool′har′di·ness,** n.

fool·ish (fül′ish), adj. 1 like a fool; without sense; unwise; silly. 2 ridiculous. 3 trifling. —**fool′ish·ly,** adv. —**fool′ish·ness,** n.

fool·proof (fül′prüf′), adj. so safe or simple that even a fool can use or do it.

fool's gold, mineral that looks like gold, iron pyrites or copper pyrites.

foot (fut), n., pl. **feet,** v. —n. 1 the end part of a leg; part that a person, animal, or thing stands on. 2 end toward which the feet are put. 3 bottom; base. 4 part that covers the foot. 5 measure of length, twelve inches. 6 one of the parts into which a line of poetry is divided. —v. 1 walk. 2 add. 3 pay (a bill, etc.).

get a foot in the door, enter into or begin a desirable arrangement.

on foot, walking.

put one's foot down, act firmly, decisively.

under foot, in the way. [OE *fōt*]

foot·age (fut′ij), n. length in feet.

foot-and-mouth disease, a dangerous, contagious disease of cattle and some other animals, characterized by blisters in the mouth and around the hoofs.

foot·ball (fut′bôl′), n. 1 game played with a large, inflated leather ball by two teams of eleven players each on a field with a goal at each end. 2 ball used in this game. 3 any game or ball like this.

foot·board (fut′bôrd′; –bōrd′), n. 1 board or small platform to be used as a support for the feet. 2 an upright piece across the foot of a bed.

foot·bridge (fut′brij′), n. bridge for people on foot only.

foot-can·dle (fut′kan′dəl), n. unit for measuring illumination. It is the amount of light produced by a standard candle at a distance of one foot.

foot·ed (fut′id), adj. having a certain kind or number of feet: *a four-footed animal.*

foot·fall (fut′fôl′), n. sound of steps coming or going; footstep.

foot·hill (fut′hil′), n. a low hill at the base of a mountain or mountain range.

foot·hold (fut′hōld′), n. 1 place to put the feet; support for the feet; surface to stand on. 2 a firm footing or position.

foot·ing (fut′ing), n. 1 a firm placing of the feet. 2 place to put the feet; surface to stand on. 3 condition; position; relationship: *the United States and Canada are on a friendly footing.*

foot·lights (fut′līts′), n. pl. 1 row of lights at the front of a stage. 2 profession of acting.

foot·loose (fut′lüs′), adj. free to go anywhere or do anything.

foot·man (fut′mən), n., pl. **–men.** a male servant who opens doors, waits on the table, etc.

foot·note (fut′nōt′), n. note at the bottom of a page about something on the page.

foot·path (fut′path′; –päth′), n. path for people on foot only.

foot·pound (fut′pound′), n. quantity of energy needed to raise a weight of one pound to a height of one foot.

foot·print (fut′print′), n. mark made by a foot.

foot soldier, infantryman.

foot·sore (fut′sôr′; –sōr′), adj. having sore feet from much walking.

foot·step (fut′step′), n. 1 sound of steps coming or going. 2 footprint. 3 distance covered in one step. 4 step on which to go up or down.

foot·stool (fut′stül′), n. a low stool to put the feet on when sitting.

foot·wear (fut′wâr′), n. shoes, slippers, stockings, etc.

foot·work (fut′wèrk′), n. way of using the feet.

fop (fop), n. a vain man who is very fond of fine clothes and has affected manners. —**fop′per·y,** n. —**fop′pish,** adj. —**fop′pish·ly,** adv. —**fop′pish·ness,** n.

for (fôr; *unstressed* fər), prep. 1 in place of: *use boxes for chairs.* 2 in favor of: *who did he vote for?* 3 representing: *a lawyer acts for a client.* 4 in order to become, have, keep, go, etc.: *he ran for his life; hunting for her cat; left for New York.* 5 suited to: *books for children.* 6 because of: *punished for stealing.* 7 in honor of: *a party given for her.* 8 with a feeling toward: *longing for home.* 9 throughout; during: *work for an hour.* 10 as being: *know for a fact.* 11 to the amount of: *a check for $20.* —conj. because: *we can't go, for it is raining.* [OE]

for·age (fôr′ij; for′–), n., v., **–aged, –ag·ing.** —n. 1 food for horses, cattle, etc. 2 a hunting or searching for food. —v. 1 hunt or search for food. 2 get by hunting or searching about. **3** hunt; search about. **4** plunder. [< F, < OF *fuerre* fodder < Gmc.] —**for′ag·er,** *n.*

fo·ram·i·nif·er·a (fô ram′ə nif′ər ə; fō–), *n. pl.* group of tiny, one-celled sea animals, most of which have shells with tiny holes in them. [< NL, < L *foramen* a small opening + *ferre* to bear] —**fo·ram′i·nif′er·al, fo·ram′i·nif′er·ous,** *adj.*

for·as·much as (fôr′əz much′ az), in view of the fact that; since; because.

for·ay (fôr′ā; for′ā), *n.* a raid for plunder. —*v.* plunder; lay waste; pillage. [akin to FORAGE. Cf. OF *forrer* forage.] —**for′ay·er,** *n.*

for·bear[1] (fôr bãr′), *v.,* **–bore, –borne, –bearing. 1** hold back; keep from doing, saying, using, etc. **2** be patient; control oneself. [OE *forberan*] —**for·bear′er,** *n.* —**for·bear′ing·ly,** *adv.*

for·bear[2] (fôr′bãr), *n.* forebear; ancestor.

for·bear·ance (fôr bãr′əns), *n.* **1** act of forbearing. **2** patience; self-control.

for·bid (fər bid′), *v.,* **–bade** (–bad′) or **–bad** (–bad′), **–bid·den** or **–bid, –bid·ding.** order (one) not to do something; make a rule against; prohibit. [OE *forbēodan*] —**for·bid′der,** *n.*

for·bid·ding (fər bid′ing), *adj.* causing fear or dislike; looking dangerous or unpleasant. —**for·bid′ding·ly,** *adv.* —**for·bid′ding·ness,** *n.*

force (fôrs; fōrs), *n., v.,* **forced, forc·ing.** —*n.* **1** strength; power. **2** strength used against a person or thing; violence. **3** power to control, influence, etc.; effectiveness. **4** group of people working or acting together: *our office force.* **5** group of soldiers, sailors, policemen, etc. **6** cause that produces, changes, or stops the motion of a body. —*v.* **1** use force on. **2** compel. **3** compel a baseball player to leave one base and try in vain to reach the next. **4** make or drive by force. **5** get or take by force. **6** break open or through by force. **7** urge to violent effort. **8** hurry the growth of. **9** make by unnatural effort: *force a laugh.*

by force of, by dint of; by virtue of: *by force of personality alone.*

forces, armed forces.

in force, a in effect; binding; valid. **b** with full strength. [< F, ult. < L *fortis* strong] —**force′a·ble,** *adj.* —**force′less,** *adj.* —**forc′er,** *n.*

forced (fôrst; fōrst), *adj.* **1** made, compelled, or driven by force: *forced labor.* **2** made by an unnatural effort: *a forced smile.*

forced march, an unusually long, fast march.

force·ful (fôrs′fəl; fōrs′–), *adj.* full of force; strong; powerful; vigorous; effective. —**force′ful·ly,** *adv.* —**force′ful·ness,** *n.*

for·ceps (fôr′seps; –səps), *n.* small pincers or tongs used by surgeons, dentists, etc., or seizing, holding, and pulling. [< L, < *formus* hot + *capere* take]

for·ci·ble (fôr′sə bəl; fôr′–), *adj.* **1** made or done by force; using force: *a forcible entrance into a house.* **2** having or showing force; powerful; convincing: *a forcible speaker.* —**for′ci·ble·ness,** *n.* —**for′ci·bly,** *adv.*

ford (fôrd; fōrd), *n.* place where a river or other body of water is not too deep to cross by walking through the water. —*v.* cross by a ford. [OE] —**ford′a·ble,** *adj.* —**ford′less,** *adj.*

Ford (fôrd; fōrd), **Gerald Rudolph,** 1913–2006, 38th president of the United States, 1974–77.

fore (fôr; for), *adj., adv.* at the front; toward the beginning or front; forward. [adj. use of *fore*–] —*n.* the forward part; front. [< adj.] —*interj.* shout of warning to persons ahead who are liable to be struck by the ball.

fore–, *prefix.* **1** front; in front; at or near the front, as in *foremast.* **2** before; beforehand, as in *foresee.* [OE *for(e)*]

fore-and-aft (fôr′ənd aft′; for′–; –äft′), *adj.* lengthwise on a ship; from bow to stern.

fore and aft, 1 at or toward both bow and stern of a ship. **2** lengthwise on a ship.

fore·arm[1] (fôr′ärm′; for′–), *n.* that part of the arm between the elbow and wrist.

fore·arm[2] (fôr ärm′; for′–), *v.* prepare for trouble ahead of time; arm beforehand.

fore·bear (fôr′bãr; for′–), *n.* ancestor; forefather. Also, **forbear.**

fore·bode (fôr bōd′; for′–), *v.,* **–bod·ed, –bod·ing. 1** give warning of; predict. **2** have a feeling that something bad is going to happen. —**fore·bod′ing,** *n., adj.* —**fore·bod′ing·ly,** *adv.*

fore·brain (fôr′brān′; for′–), *n.* the front section of the brain.

fore·cast (fôr′kast′; for′–; –käst′), *v.,* **–cast** or **–cast·ed, –cast·ing,** *n.* —*v.* prophesy; predict; plan ahead: *forecast earnings.* —*n.* prophecy; prediction: *a gloomy forecast.* —**fore′cast′er,** *n.*

fore·cas·tle (fōk′səl; fôr′kas′əl; for′–; –käs′–), *n.* **1** the upper deck in front of the foremast. **2** sailor's quarters in a merchant ship.

fore·close (fôr klōz′; for′–), *v.,* **–closed, –clos·ing. 1** shut out; prevent; exclude. **2** take away the right to redeem (a mortgage). [< OF *forclos* excluded < *for–* out (< Frankish *for–* and L *foris*) + *clore* shut < L *claudere*] —**fore·clos′a·ble,** *adj.*

fore·clo·sure (fôr klō′zhər; for′–), *n.* the foreclosing of a mortgage.

fore·doom (fôr düm′; for′–), *v.* doom beforehand.

fore·fa·ther (fôr′fä′ᵺər; for′–), *n.* ancestor.

fore·fin·ger (fôr′fing′gər; for′–), *n.* finger next to the thumb, first finger; index finger.

fore·foot (fôr′fůt′; for′–), *n., pl.* **–feet.** one of the front feet of an animal having four or more feet.

fore·front (fôr′frunt′; for′–), *n.* place of greatest importance, activity, etc.

fore·gath·er (fôr gaᵺ′ər; for–), *v.* =forgather.

fore·go[1] (fôr gō′; for–), *v.,* **–went, –gone, –go·ing.** =forgo. —**fore·go′er,** *n.*

fore·go[2] (fôr gō′; for–), *v.,* **–went, –gone, –go·ing.** precede; go before. —**fore·go′er,** *n.*

fore·go·ing (fôr′gō′ing, for′–; fôr′gō′ing, for′–), *adj.* preceding; previous.

fore·gone (fôr gôn′, for–, –gon′; fôr′gôn, for′–, –gon), *adj.* that has gone before; previous.

foregone conclusion, 1 fact that was almost surely known beforehand. **2** a predictable result.

fore·ground (fôr′ground′; for′–), *n.* part of a picture or scene nearest the observer; part toward the front.

fore·hand (fôr′hand′; for′–), *adj.* **1** foremost. **2** made with the palm of the hand turned forward. —*n.* **1** a forehand stroke. **2** position in front or above; advantage.

fore·hand·ed (fôr′han′did; for′–), *adj.* **1** providing for the future; prudent; thrifty. **2** done beforehand; early. —**fore′hand′ed·ness,** *n.*

fore·head (fôr′id; for′id; fôr′hed′), *n.* **1** part of the face above the eyes. **2** a front part.

for·eign (fôr′ən; for′–), *adj.* **1** outside one's own country. **2** coming from outside one's own country: *foreign money.* **3** having to do with other countries: *foreign trade.* **4** not belonging; not related: *foreign to her nature; a foreign substance in the blood.* [< OF *forain,* ult. < L *foras* outside] —**for′eign·ness,** *n.*

foreign affairs, a country's relations with other countries.

for·eign-born (fôr′ən bôrn′; for′–), *adj.* born in another country.

for·eign·er (fôr′ən ər; for′–), *n.* person from another country; alien.

foreign exchange, 1 the settling of accounts between people in different countries. **2** currency and bills used to settle such accounts.

foreign office, *Brit.* the government department in charge of foreign affairs.

Foreign Service, part of the Department of State of the United States, providing people to serve in embassies abroad and in Washington, D.C.

fore·know (fôr nō′; for′–), *v.,* **–knew, –known, –know·ing.** know beforehand. —**fore·know′a·ble,** *adj.* —**fore′knowl·edge,** *n.*

fore·leg (fôr′leg′; for′–), *n.* one of the front legs of an animal having four or more legs. Also, **forelimb.**

fore·lock (fôr′lok′; for′–), *n.* lock of hair that grows just above the forehead.

fore·man (fôr′mən; for′–), *n., pl.* **–men. 1** person in charge of a group of workers or of some part of a factory. **2** chairperson of a jury.

fore·mast (fôr′mast′; for′–; –mäst′), *n.* mast nearest the bow of a ship.

fore·most (fôr′mōst; fôr′–), *adj.* first in rank, order, place, etc. —*adv.* first: *fall head foremost.*

fore·noon (fôr′nün′; fôr′–), *n.* time between early morning and noon.

fo·ren·sic (fə ren′sik), *adj.* of or suitable for a law court or public debate. [< L *forensis* < *forum* forum] —**fo·ren′sics,** *n.*

fore·or·dain (fôr′ôr dān′; fōr′–), *v.* ordain beforehand; predestine.

fore·paw (fôr′pô′; fōr′–), *n.* a front paw.

fore·run (fôr run′; fōr–), *v.,* **–ran, –run, –run·ning. 1** precede. **2** be a sign or warning of (something to come).

fore·run·ner (fôr′run′ər, fôr ′–; fôr run′ər, fôr–), *n.* **1** person that is sent before; herald. **2** sign or warning of something to come. **3** ancestor.

fore·sail (fôr′sāl′; fōr′–; *Naut.* –səl), *n.* **1** the principal sail on the foremast of a schooner. **2** the lowest sail on the foremast of a square-rigged ship.

fore·see (fôr sē′; fōr–), *v.,* **–saw, –seen, –see·ing.** see or know beforehand. —**fore·see′a·ble,** *adj.* —**fore·se′er,** *n.*

fore·shad·ow (fôr shad′ō; fōr–), *v.* indicate beforehand; be a warning of.

fore·sheet (fôr′shēt′; fōr′–), *n.* one of the ropes used to hold a foresail in place.

fore·shore (fôr′shôr′; fōr′shôr′), *n.* part of the shore between the high-water mark and low-water mark.

fore·short·en (fôr shôr′tən; fōr–), *v.* represent (lines, etc.) as of less than true length in order to give the proper impression to the eye.

fore·sight (fôr′sīt′; fōr′–), *n.* **1** power to see or realize beforehand what is likely to happen. **2** careful thought for the future; prudence. **3** a looking ahead; view into the future. —**fore′sight′ed,** *adj.* —**fore′sight′ed′ness,** *n.*

fore·skin (fôr′skin′; fōr′–), *n.* fold or skin that covers the end of the penis; prepuce.

for·est (fôr′ist; for′–), *n.* **1** a large area of land covered with trees; thick woods; woodland. **2** the trees themselves. —*v.* plant with trees; change into a forest. [< OF, ult. < L *foris* out of doors] —**for′est·ed,** *adj.* —**for′est·less,** *adj.* —**for′est·like′,** *adj.*

fore·stall (fôr stôl′; fōr–), *v.* **1** prevent by acting first. **2** deal with (a thing) in advance; anticipate; be ahead of. [ME *forstalle(n)* < OE *foresteall* prevention] —**fore·stall′er,** *n.*

for·est·a·tion (fôr′is tā′shən; for′–), *n.* the planting or taking care of forests.

fore·stay (fôr′stā′; fōr′–), *n.* rope or cable reaching from the foremast to the bowsprit.

for·est·ed (fôr′ə stid; for′–), *adj.* covered with trees; wooded.

for·est·er (fôr′is tər; for′–), *n.* person in charge of a forest who looks after the trees and guards against fires.

forest preserve, forest protected by the government or other organizations from sale for development, commercial exploitation, etc. Also, **forest reserve.**

for·est·ry (fôr′is tri; for′–), *n.* science of planting and taking care of forests.

fore·taste (*n.* fôr′tāst′, fōr′–; *v.* fôr tāst′, fōr–), *n., v.,* **–tast·ed, –tast·ing.** —*n.* a preliminary taste; anticipation. —*v.* taste beforehand; anticipate.

fore·tell (fôr tel′; fōr–), *v.,* **–told, –tell·ing.** tell or show beforehand; predict; prophesy. —**fore·tell′er,** *n.*

fore·thought (fôr′thôt′; fōr′–), *n.* **1** previous thought or consideration; planning. **2** careful thought for the future; prudence.

fore·top (fôr′top′; fōr′), *n.* platform at the top of the foremast.

fore·top·mast (fôr′top′mast′; fōr′–; –mäst′), *n.* mast next above the foremast.

fore·top·sail (fôr′top′sāl′; fōr′–; *Naut.* –səl), *n.* sail next above the foresail.

for·ev·er (fər ev′ər), *adv.* **1** for always; without ever coming to an end. **2** all the time; always.

for·ev·er·more (fər ev′ər môr′; –mōr′), *adv.* forever.

fore·warn (fôr wôrn′; fōr–), *v.* warn beforehand.

fore·went (fôr went′; fōr–), *v.* pt. of **forego.**

fore·wo·man (fôr′wùm′ən, fōr′–), *n., pl.* **–wom·en. 1** women in charge of a group of workers or some part of production in a factory. **2** chairwoman of a jury.

fore·word (fôr′wèrd′; fōr′–), *n.* introduction; preface.

for·feit (fôr′fit), *v.* lose or have to give up as a penalty for some act, neglect, fault, etc. —*n.* **1** thing lost or given up as a penalty; fine. **2** loss or giving up as a penalty. —*adj.* lost or given up as a penalty. [< OF *forfait* < *forfaire* transgress < *for-* wrongly (< Frankish *for-* and L *foris* outside) + *faire* do < L *facere*] —**for′feit·a·ble,** *adj.* —**for′feit·er,** *n.*

for·fei·ture (fôr′fi chər), *n.* **1** a forfeiting. **2** penalty; fine.

for·gath·er (fôr gaŧħ′ər), *v.* **1** gather together; assemble; meet. **2** meet by accident. **3** be friendly; associate.

for·gave (fər gāv′), *v.* pt. of **forgive.**

forge[1] (fôrj; fōrj), *n., v.,* **forged, forg·ing.** —*n.* **1** place with fire where metal is heated very hot and then hammered into shape. **2** a blacksmith's shop; smithy. **3** where iron or other metal is melted and refined. —*v.* **1** heat (metal) very hot and then hammer into shape. **2** make; shape; form. **3** make or write (something false). **4** sign (another's name) falsely to deceive. [< OF, ult. < L *fabrica* workshop. Doublet of FABRIC.] —**forge′a·ble,** *adj.* —**forg′er,** *n.*

forge[2] (fôrj; fōrj), *v.,* **forged, forg·ing.** move forward slowly but steadily.

for·ger·y (fôr′jər i; fōr′–), *n., pl.* **–ger·ies. 1** act of forging a signature, etc. **2** something made or written falsely to deceive.

for·get (fər get′), *v.,* **–got, –got·ten** or **–got, –get·ting. 1** let go out of the mind; fail to remember; be unable to remember. **2** omit or neglect without meaning to.

forget it, take no notice; don't mention it, esp. a favor. [OE *forgietan*]

for·get·ful (fər get′fəl), *adj.* **1** apt to forget; having a poor memory. **2** heedless. **3** causing to forget. —**for·get′ful·ly,** *adv.* —**for·get′ful·ness,** *n.*

for·get-me-not (fər get′mē not′), *n.* any of several small plants with hairy leaves and clusters of small blue or white flowers.

for·give (fər giv′), *v.,* **–gave, –giv·en, –giv·ing. 1** give up the wish to punish or get even with; pardon; excuse. **2** give up all claim to; not demand payment for: *forgive a debt.* [OE *forgiefan*] —**for·giv′a·ble,** *adj.* —**for·giv′er,** *n.*

for·give·ness (fər giv′nis), *n.* **1** act of forgiving; pardon. **2** willingness to forgive.

for·giv·ing (fər giv′ing), *adj.* that forgives; willing to forgive. —**for·giv′ing·ly,** *adv.* —**for·giv′ing·ness,** *n.*

for·go (fôr gō′), *v.,* **–went, –gone, –go·ing. 1** do without; give up. **2** refrain; forbear. [OE *forgān*] —**for·go′er,** *n.*

for·got (fər got′), *v.* pt. and pp. of **forget.**

for·got·ten (fər got′ən), *v.* pp. of **forget.**

fork (fôrk), *n.* **1** instrument with a handle and two or more long, pointed parts at one end. **2** anything shaped like a fork, as the place where a tree, road, or stream divides into branches. **3** one of the branches into which anything is divided. —*v.* **1** lift, throw, or dig with a fork. **2** have a fork or forks; divide into branches.

fork over, *Informal.* hand over; pay out. [< L *furca*] —**fork′less,** *adj.* —**fork′like′,** *adj.*

forked (fôrkt), *adj.* **1** having a fork or forks. **2** zigzag: *forked lightning.* —**fork′ed·ly,** *adv.* —**fork′ed·ness,** *n.*

fork lift, 1 device with prongs for lifting and lowering a load. **2** small tractor or truck equipped with this device.

for·lorn (fôr lôrn′), *adj.* **1** left alone; neglected; deserted. **2** wretched in feeling or looks; unhappy. [OE *forloren* lost, pp. of *forlēosan*] —**for·lorn′ly,** *adv.* —**for·lorn′ness,** *n.*

form (fôrm), *n.* **1** appearance apart from color or materials; shape. **2** shape of the body of a person or animal. **3** thing that gives shape to something; mold. **4** an orderly arrangement of parts. The effect of a work of music comes from its form as well as its content. **5** way of doing something; manner; method: *his form in running is bad.* **6** a set way of doing something; formality; ceremony. **7** document with printing or writing on it and blank spaces to be filled in. **8** kind; sort: *heat and light are forms of energy.* **9** shapes of a word to express different relationships. *Boys* is the plural form of *boy.* —*v.* **1** give shape to; make. **2** take shape: *clouds form in the sky.* **3**

become: *water forms ice when it freezes.* **4** organize; establish: *we formed a club.* **5** arrange in some order: *the soldiers formed into lines.* [< OF < L *forma* form, mold]

-form, *suffix.* **1** shaped, as in *cruciform.* **2** (number of) forms, as in *multiform.* [< L *-formis*]

for·mal (fôr′məl), *adj.* **1** with strict attention to outward forms and ceremonies; not familiar and homelike. **2** according to set customs or rules. **3** clear and definite: *a contract is a formal agreement.* **4** very regular; orderly. [< L *formalis.* See FORM.] —**for′mal·ly,** *adv.* —**for′mal·ness,** *n.*

form·al·de·hyde (fôr mal′də hīd), *n.* a colorless gas, CH$_2$O, with a sharp, irritating odor. It is used as a preservative.

for·mal·ism (fôr′məl iz əm), *n.* strict attention to outward forms and ceremonies. —**for′mal·ist,** *n.* —**for′mal·is′tic,** *adj.*

for·mal·i·ty (fôr mal′ə ti), *n., pl.* **-ties. 1** outward form; ceremony. **2** attention to forms and customs. **3** stiffness of behavior or arrangement. **4** something done merely for form's sake.

for·mal·ize (fôr′məl īz), *v.,* **-ized, -iz·ing. 1** make formal. **2** give a definite form to. —**for′mal·i·za′tion,** *n.* —**for′mal·iz′er,** *n.*

for·mat (fôr′mat), *n.* **1** shape, size, and general arrangement of a book, magazine, etc. **2** plan or arrangement of anything: *format at a debate.* —*v.,* **-mat·ted, -mat·ting. 1** design or plan the arrangement of something: *format a brochure.* **2** put into a format. [< F < L (*liber*) *formatus* (book) formed (in a special way)]

for·ma·tion (fôr mā′shən), *n.* **1** a forming or being formed. **2** arrangement; order: *troops in battle formation.* **3** thing formed. **4** series of layers or deposits of the same kind of rock or mineral.

form·a·tive (fôr′mə tiv), *adj.* **1** forming; molding. **2** used to form words. The suffixes *-ly* and *-ness* are formative endings. —**form′a·tive·ly,** *adv.* —**form′a·tive·ness,** *n.*

for·mer[1] (fôr′mər), *adj.* **1** first of two. **2** earlier; past; long past. [ME *formere,* a comparative patterned after *formest* foremost]

form·er[2] (fôr′mər), *n.* person or thing that forms.

for·mer·ly (fôr′mər li), *adv.* in the past; some time ago.

form-fit·ting (fôrm′fit′ing), *adj.* close-fitting: *a form-fitting jacket.*

for·mic acid (fôr′mik), a colorless liquid, CH$_2$O$_2$, that is irritating to the skin. It occurs in ants, spiders, nettles, etc. [< L *formica* ant]

for·mi·da·ble (fôr′mə də bəl), *adj.* hard to overcome; hard to deal with; to be dreaded. [< L, < *formidare* dread] —**for′mi·da·ble·ness, for′mi·da·bil′i·ty,** *n.* —**for′mi·da·bly,** *adv.*

form·less (fôrm′lis), *adj.* without definite or regular form; shapeless. —**form′less·ly,** *adv.* —**form′less·ness,** *n.*

form letter, letter so phrased that it may be sent to many different people.

For·mo·sa (fôr mō′sə), *n.* =Taiwan.

for·mu·la (fôr′myə lə), *n., pl.* **-las, -lae** (-lē). **1** recipe; prescription: *formula for making soap.* **2** expression showing by chemical symbols the composition of a compound. The formula for water is H$_2$O. **3** expression showing by algebraic symbols a rule, principle, etc. **4** a set form of words, esp. one which by much use has partly lost its meaning. "How do you do?" is a polite formula. [< L, dim. of *forma* form]

for·mu·la·ic (fôr′myə lā′ik), *adj.* based on or consisting of formulas: *a formulaic plot.*

for·mu·lar·y (fôr′myə ler′i), *n., pl.* **-lar·ies,** *adj.* —*n.* **1** collection of formulas. **2** a set form of words; formula. —*adj.* having to do with formulas.

for·mu·late (fôr′myə lāt), *v.,* **-lat·ed, -lat·ing. 1** state definitely; express in systematic form. **2** express in a formula; reduce to a formula. —**for′mu·la′tion,** *n.* —**for′mu·la′tor,** *n.*

for·ni·cate (fôr′nə kāt), *v.,* **-cat·ed, -cat·ing.** commit fornication. [< Eccl.L, < *fornix* brothel] —**for′ni·ca′tor,** *n.*

for·ni·ca·tion (fôr′nə kā′shən), *n.* a sexual act between unmarried persons.

for·sake (fôr sāk′), *v.,* **-sook** (-sùk′), **-sak·en, -sak·ing.** give up; leave alone; leave. [OE, < *for-* + *sacan* dispute, deny]

for·sak·en (fôr sāk′ən), *v.* pp. of **forsake.** —*adj.* deserted; abandoned; forlorn. —**for·sak′en·ly,** *adv.*

for·sooth (fôr süth′), *adv. Archaic.* in truth; indeed. [OE *forsōth*]

for·swear (fôr swâr′), *v.,* **-swore, -sworn, -swear·ing. 1** renounce on oath; swear or promise solemnly to give up. **2** be untrue to one's sworn word or promise; perjure (oneself). —**for·swear′er,** *n.*

for·syth·i·a (fôr sith′i ə; -sī′thi ə), *n.* shrub having many bell-shaped, yellow flowers in early spring before its leaves come out. [< NL; named for W. *Forsyth,* horticulturist]

fort (fôrt; fōrt), *n.* a strong building or place that can be defended against an enemy. [< F < L *fortis* strong]

forte[1] (fôrt; fōrt), *n.* something a person does very well; strong point. [< F *fort* < L *fortis* strong]

for·te[2] (fôr′tē), *adj., adv.* in music, loud. [< Ital., strong, < L *fortis*]

forth (fôrth; fōrth), *adv.* **1** forward; onward. **2** into view or consideration; out. **3** away. [OE]

forth·com·ing (fôrth′kum′ing; fōrth′-), *adj.* **1** about to appear; approaching. **2** ready when wanted: *she needed help, but none was forthcoming.*

forth·right (fôrth′rīt′, fôrth′-; fôrth′rīt′, fōrth′-), *adj.* frank and outspoken; straight-forward; direct: *forthright criticism.* —**forth′right′ness,** *n.*

forth·with (fôrth′with′; fōrth′-; -with′), *adv.* at once; immediately.

for·ti·fi·ca·tion (fôr′tə fə kā′shən), *n.* **1** a fortifying. **2** fort, wall, ditch, etc., used in fortifying. **3** a fortified place. **4** the enriching of foods, as with vitamins.

for·ti·fy (fôr′tə fī), *v.,* **-fied, -fy·ing. 1** build forts, walls, etc.; strengthen against attack; provide with forts, walls, etc. **2** give support to; strengthen. **3** enrich the nutritive value of (a food) by adding vitamins and minerals in processing. [< F < LL, ult. < L *fortis* strong + *facere* make] —**for′ti·fi′a·ble,** *adj.* —**for′ti·fi′er,** *n.*

for·tis·si·mo (fôr tis′ə mō), *adj., adv.* in music, very loud. [< Ital., superlative of *forte* strong]

for·ti·tude (fôr′tə tüd; -tūd), *n.* courage in facing pain, danger, or trouble; firmness of spirit. [< L, < *fortis* strong]

Fort La·my (lä mē′), capital of Chad, in the S part.

fort·night (fôrt′nīt; -nit), *n.* two weeks.

fort·night·ly (fôrt′nīt li), *adv., adj., n., pl.* **-lies.** —*adv.* once in every two weeks. —*adj.* appearing or happening once in every two weeks. —*n.* periodical published every two weeks.

FORTRAN or **For·tran** (fôr′tran), *n.* computer language based on algebraic notation. [< *Fo*rmula *tran*slation]

for·tress (fôr′tris), *n.* a fortified place; fort.

for·tu·i·tous (fôr tü′ə təs; -tū′-), *adj.* happening by chance; accidental: *a fortuitous meeting.* [< L *fortuitus,* ult. < *fors* chance] —**for·tu′i·tous·ly,** *adv.* —**for·tu′i·tous·ness,** *n.*

for·tu·i·ty (fôr tü′ə ti; -tū′-), *n., pl.* **-ties.** chance; accident.

for·tu·nate (fôr′chə nit), *adj.* **1** having good luck; lucky. **2** bringing good luck; having favorable results. [< L, < *fortuna* fortune] —**for′tu·nate·ly,** *adv.* —**for′tu·nate·ness,** *n.*

for·tune (fôr′chən), *n., v.,* **-tuned, -tun·ing.** —*n.* **1** good luck; prosperity. **2** what is going to happen to a person; fate. **3** what happens; luck; chance. **4** a great deal of money or property; riches; wealth. **5** position in life. —*v.* happen; chance. [< OF < L *fortuna*] —**for′tune·less,** *adj.*

for·tune-tell·er (fôr′chən tel′ər), *n.* person who claims to be able to tell what will happen to people. —**for′tune·tell′ing,** *adj., n.*

for·ty (fôr′ti), *n., pl.* **-ties,** *adj.* —*n.* **1** a cardinal number, four times ten. **2** symbol of this number; 40. —*adj.* four times ten; 40. [OE *fēowertig*] —**for′ti·eth,** *adj., n.*

for·ty-nin·er (fôr′ti nīn′ər), *n.* person who went to California to seek gold in 1849.

forty winks, *Informal.* short nap.

fo·rum (fô′rəm; fō′–), *n., pl.* **fo·rums, fo·ra** (fô′rə; fō′–). **1** the public square or marketplace of an ancient Roman town. **2** assembly for discussing questions of public interest. **3** a law court; tribunal. [< L]

for·ward (fôr′wərd), *adv.* Also, **for′wards.** **1** ahead; onward: *run forward.* **2** toward the front: *come forward.* **3** under or into consideration: *bring forward a plan.* —*adj.* **1** toward the front: *the forward part of a ship.* **2** far ahead; advanced: *a child forward for his age.* **3** ready; eager: *forward with his answers.* **4** pert; bold: *forward behavior.* —*v.* **1** send on further: *forward mail.* **2** help along: *forward hopes.* —*n.* player whose position is in the front line in certain games. [OE *forweard*] —**for′ward·er,** *n.* —**for′ward·ly,** *adv.* —**for′ward·ness,** *n.*

for·went (fôr went′), *v.* pt. of **forgo.**

fos·sa (fos′ə), *n., pl.* **fos·sae** (fos′ē). a shallow depression or pit in a bone, etc. [< L, ditch]

fosse, foss (fôs; fos), *n.* ditch; trench; canal; moat. [< F < L *fossa* ditch]

fos·sil (fos′əl), *n.* **1** the hardened remains or traces of animals or plants. **2** a very old-fashioned person, set in his or her ways. —*adj.* **1** forming a fossil; of the nature of a fossil. **2** belonging to the outworn past: *fossil ideas.* [< F < L *fossilis* dug up < *fodere* dig] —**fos′sil·like′,** *adj.*

fossil fuel, coal, oil, and gas.

fos·sil·ize (fos′ə līz), *v.,* –**ized,** –**iz·ing.** **1** change into a fossil; turn into stone. **2** make or become antiquated, set, stiff, or rigid. —**fos′sil·i·za′tion,** *n.*

fos·ter (fôs′tər; fos′–), *v.* **1** help the growth or development of. **2** bring up; rear. —*adj.* in the same family, but not related by birth: *a foster brother.* [OE *fōstrian* nourish, *fōster* nourishment; akin to FOOD] —**fos′ter·er,** *n.*

fought (fôt), *v.* pt. and pp. of **fight.**

foul (foul), *adj.* **1** very dirty; nasty; smelly. **2** very wicked; vile. **3** against the rules; unfair: *a foul stroke.* **4** hitting against: *one boat foul of the wharf.* **5** tangled up; caught: *cut the foul rope.* **6** clogged up: *the chimney is foul.* **7** unfavorable; stormy: *foul weather.* **8** pertaining to a ball not hit within the playing area. —*v.* **1** make or become dirty; soil; defile. **2** hit a ball so that it falls outside the base lines. **3** hit against: *one boat fouled the other.* **4** get tangled up with; catch. **6** clog up. —*n.* **1** unfair play. **2** ball hit so that it falls outside the base lines.

foul up, bungle.

go, fall, or **run foul of, a** hit against and get tangled up with. **b** get into trouble or difficulties with. [OE *fūl*] —**foul′ly,** *adv.* —**foul′ness,** *n.*

fou·lard (fü lärd′; fə–), *n.* a soft, thin fabric made of silk, rayon, or cotton, used for neckties, dresses, etc. [< F < Swiss F *foulat* cloth that has been cleansed and thickened]

foul line, 1 in baseball, either the line from home to first base, or from home to third base, with their unmarked continuations. **2** in basketball, line in front of each basket from which free throws are made. **3** line beyond which a broad jumper, javelin thrower, etc. cannot step.

found[1] (found), *v.* pt. and pp. of **find.**

found[2] (found), *v.* **1** establish; set up: *the Pilgrims founded a colony at Plymouth.* **2** rest for support; base: *he founded his claim on facts.* [< OF < L, < *fundus* bottom]

found[3] (found), *v.* melt and mold (metal); make of molten metal; cast. [< F < L *fundere* pour]

foun·da·tion (foun dā′shən), *n.* **1** part on which the other parts rest for support; base. **2** basis; ground: *foundation of an argument.* **3** a founding or establishing. **4** a being founded or established. **5** institution founded and endowed. **6** fund that supports a charity, research, etc. —**foun·da′tion·al,** *adj.*

foun·der[1] (foun′dər), *v.* **1** fill with water and sink. **2** break down; go lame; stumble. [< OF *foundrer,* ult. < L *fundus* bottom]

found·er[2] (foun′dər), *n.* person who founds or establishes something.

found·er[3] (foun′dər), *n.* person who casts metals.

found·ling (found′ling), *n.* baby or child found deserted. [ME *fundeling;* akin to FIND]

found·ry (foun′dri), *n., pl.* –**ries.** place where metal is melted and molded.

fount (fount), *n.* **1** fountain. **2** source. [< L *fons* spring]

foun·tain (foun′tən), *n.* **1** stream of water rising into the air. **2** spring of water. **3** place to get a drink. **4** source; origin. [< OF < LL *fontana* of a spring < L *fons* spring] —**foun′tain·less,** *adj.* — **foun′tain·like′,** *adj.*

foun·tain·head (foun′tən hed′), *n.* **1** source of a stream. **2** original source.

four (fôr; fō), *n.* **1** a cardinal number, one more than three. **2** symbol for this number; 4. —*adj.* one more than three; 4. [OE *fēower*]

four-flush·er (fôr′flush′ər; fōr′–), *n.* person who pretends to be more or other than he or she really is; bluffer.

four·fold (fôr′fōld′; fōr′–), *adj.* **1** four times as much or as many. **2** having four parts. —*adv.* four times as much or as many.

four-foot·ed (fôr′fut′id; fōr′–), *adj.* having four feet.

4-H club or **Four-H club** (fôr′āch′; fōr′–), a club in a nationwide system dedicated to teaching agricultural skills to young people.

four-in-hand (fôr′in hand′; fōr′–), *n.* **1** necktie tied in a slip knot with the ends left hanging. **2** carriage pulled by four horses. —*adj.* **1** tied in a slip knot. **2** pulled by four horses.

four-post·er (fôr′pōs′tər; fōr′–), *n.* bed with four tall corner posts, originally for supporting curtains.

four·score (fôr′skôr′; fōr′skōr′), *adj., n.* four times twenty; 80.

four·square (*adj.* fôr′skwär′, fōr′–; *n.* fôr′skwär′, fōr′–), *adj.* **1** =square. **2** frank; outspoken. **3** not yielding; firm. —*n.* =a square. —**four′square′ly,** *adv.* —**four′square′ness,** *n.*

four·teen (fôr′tēn′; fōr′–), *n.* **1** a cardinal number, four more than ten. **2** symbol of this number; 14. —*adj.* four more than ten; 14. —**four′teenth′,** *adj., n.*

fourth (fôrth; fōrth), *adj.* **1** next after the third; last in a series of 4. **2** being one of 4 equal parts. —*n.* **1** next after the third; last in a series of 4. **2** one of 4 equal parts. **3** *Music.* **a** tone on the 4th degree from a given tone that is counted as the 1st. **b** interval between such tones. **c** combination of such tones. —**fourth′ly,** *adv.*

fourth dimension, dimension in addition to length, width, and thickness. Time can be thought of as a fourth dimension. —**fourth′-di·men′sion·al,** *adj.*

fourth estate, newspapers or newspaper workers; journalism or journalists.

Fourth of July, holiday in honor of the adoption of the Declaration of Independence on July 4, 1776; Independence Day.

fowl (foul), *n., pl.* **fowls** or (*esp. collectively*) **fowl. 1** any bird. **2** any of several kinds of large birds used for food, such as the hen, rooster, and turkey. **3** flesh of a fowl used for food. [OE *fugol*] —**fowl′er,** *n.*

fowling piece, a light gun for shooting wild birds.

fox (foks), *n.* **1** a wild animal somewhat like a dog. **2** its fur. **3** *Fig.* sly, crafty person. —*v.* **1** trick by being sly and crafty. **2** became discolored; cause to become discolored. [OE] —**fox′like′,** *adj.*

fox·fire (foks′fīr′), *n.* phosphorescent light given off by decaying wood.

fox·glove (foks′gluv′), *n.* plant with tall stalks having many bell-shaped flowers.

fox·hole (foks′hōl′), *n.* hole in the ground for protection against enemy fire.

fox·hound (foks′hound′), *n.* hound with a keen sense of smell, bred and trained to hunt foxes.

fox·tail (foks′tāl′), *n.* **1** tail of a fox. **2** grass with brushlike spikes of flowers.

fox terrier, a small, active dog of a breed once trained to drive foxes from their holes.

fox trot, 1 dance with short, quick steps. **2** music for it.

fox-trot (foks′trot′), *v.,* –**trot·ted,** –**trot·ting.** dance the fox trot.

fox·y (fok′si), *adj.,* **fox·i·er, fox·i·est. 1** like a fox; sly; crafty. **2** discolored; stained. —**fox′i·ly,** *adv.* —**fox′i·ness,** *n.*

foy·er (foi′ər; foi′ā), *n.* **1** an entrance hall in a theater or hotel furnished with sofas and chairs where people can relax;

lobby. **2** an entrance hall. [< F, ult. < L *focus* hearth]

fp or **FP, 1** foot-pound. **2** freezing point.

fpm or **f.p.m.,** feet per minute.

fps or **f.p.s.,** feet per second.

Fr, francium.

Fr., 1 Father. **2** French. **3** Friday.

fr., 1 fragment. **2** *pl.* **fr., frs.** franc. **3** from.

fra·cas (frā′kəs), *n.* a noisy quarrel or fight; disturbance; brawl. [< F < Ital. *fracasso* < *fracassare* smash]

frac·tion (frak′shən), *n.* **1** one or more of the equal parts of a whole. **2** a very small part, amount, etc.: fragment. [< LL *fractio* < L *frangere* break] —**frac′tion·al,** *adj.* —**frac′tion·al·ly,** *adv.*

frac·tious (frak′shəs), *adj.* cross; peevish; unruly.—**frac′tious·ly,** *adv.* —**frac′tious·ness,** *n.*

frac·ture (frak′chər), *v.* **-tured, -tur·ing,** *n.* —*v.* break; crack. —*n.* **1** a breaking of a bone or cartilage. **2** a breaking or being broken. **3** break; crack.[< F < L *fractura* < *frangere* break] —**frac′tur·al,** *adj.*

frag·ile (fraj′əl), *adj.* easily broken, damaged, or destroyed; delicate; frail. [< L *fragilis*; akin to *frangere* break. Doublet of FRAIL.] —**frag′ile·ly,** *adv.* —**fra·gil′i·ty, frag′ile·ness,** *n.*

frag·ment (frag′mənt), *n.* **1** a broken piece; part broken off. **2** an incomplete or disconnected part. **3** part of an incomplete or unfinished work. [< L *fragmentum* < *frangere* break] —**frag·men′tal,** *adj.*

frag·men·tar·y (frag′mən ter′i), *adj.* made up of fragments; incomplete; disconnected. —**frag′men·tar′i·ly,** *adv.* —**frag′men·tar′i·ness,** *n.*

frag·men·ta·tion (frag′mən tā′shən), *adj.* denoting a bomb, grenade, etc., that scatters pieces of its contents on explosion.

fra·grance (frā′grəns), *n., pl.* **-granc·es.** a sweet smell; pleasing odor.

fra·grant (frā′grənt), *adj.* having a pleasing odor; sweet-smelling. [< L *fragrans* smelling, emitting odor] —**fra′grant·ly,** *adv.*

frail (frāl), *adj.* **1** not very strong; weak. **2** easily broken, damaged, or destroyed. **3** liable to yield to temptation. [< OF < L *fragilis*. Doublet of FRAGILE.] —**frail′ly,** *adv.* —**frail′ness,** *n.*

frail·ty (frāl′ti), *n., pl.* **-ties. 1** a being frail. **2** liability to yield to temptation.

frame (frām), *n., v.,* **framed, fram·ing.** —*n.* **1** support over which something is stretched or built: *frame of a house.* **2** body. **3** way in which a thing is put together. **4** border in which a thing is set: *a picture frame.* [< v.] —*v.* **1** put together; plan; make. **2** put a border around. **3** prearrange falsely; make seem guilty. [OE *framian* to profit < *fram* forth] —**frame′less,** *adj.* —**fram′er,** *n.*

frame of mind, way of thinking or feeling; disposition; mood.

frame-up (frām′up′), *n. Informal.* **1** a secret and dishonest arrangement made

beforehand. **2** arrangement made to have a person falsely accused.

frame·work (frām′werk′), *n.* **1** support over which a thing is stretched or built. **2** way in which a thing is put together; structure.

franc (frangk), *n.* **1** unit of money in France, Belgium, and Switzerland. **2** coin worth one franc. [< OF < *Francorum Rex* king of the Franks, on early coins]

France (frans; fräns), *n.* country in W Europe.

fran·chise (fran′chīz), *n.* **1** privilege or right granted by a government: *a franchise to operate buses on the city streets.* **2** right to vote. [< OF, < *franc* free; akin to FRANK] —**fran′chised,** *adj.* —**fran′chise·ment,** *n.*

Fran·cis·can (fran sis′kən), *n.* member of a religious order founded by Saint Francis in 1209. —*adj.* of this religious order.

fran·ci·um (fran′si əm), *n.* a rare radioactive element, Fr.

fran·gi·ble (fran′jə bəl), *adj.* breakable. [< OF < L *frangere* break] —**fran′gi·bil′i·ty, fran′gi·ble·ness,** *n.*

fran·glais or **Fran·glais** (frän glā′), *n.,* spoken French that contains many English words and expressions. [< F *franglais,* < *français* French + an*glais* English]

frank (frangk), *adj.* free in expressing one's real thoughts, opinions, and feelings; not afraid to say what one thinks. —*v.* send (a letter, package, etc.) without charge. —*n.* **1** mark to show that a letter, package, etc., is to be sent without charge. **2** right to send letters, packages, etc., without charge. [< OF, free, sincere (orig., a Frank) < Gmc.] —**frank′a·ble,** *adj.* —**frank′er,** *n.* —**frank′ly,** *adv.* —**frank′ness,** *n.*

Frank (frangk), *n.* member of a group of German tribes that conquered northern Gaul in the sixth century A.D.

Frank·en·stein (frangk′ən stīn), *n.* **1 a** man in a story, who creates a monster that he cannot control. **b** the monster itself. **2** *Fig.* thing that causes the ruin of its creator. [from novel by Mary Shelley]

Frank·fort (frangk′fərt), *n.* capital of Kentucky, in the N part.

frank·furt·er (frangk′fər tər), *n.* a reddish sausage made of beef and pork. [< G, of Frankfort]

frank·in·cense (frangk′in sens), *n.* a fragrant resin from certain Asiatic or African trees. [< OF *franc encens* pure incense]

Frank·ish (frangk′ish), *adj.* of or having to do with the Franks. —*n.* the language of the Franks.

Frank·lin (frangk′lən), *n.* **Benjamin,** 1706–90, American statesman, author, and scientist.

fran·tic (fran′tik), *adj.* very much excited. [< OF < L < Gk. *phrenitikos* < *phre-*

nitis FRENZY. Doublet of PHRENETIC.] —**fran′tic·ly,** *adv.* —**fran′tic·ness,** *n.*

frappe (frap), *n.* **1** =milkshake. **2** =frappé. [< F]

frap·pé (fra pā′), —*adj.* iced; cooled. —*n.* **1** fruit juice sweetened and frozen. **2** any frozen and blended or iced food or drink. [< F, chilled, beaten]

fra·ter·nal (frə tėr′nəl), *adj.* brotherly. [< L *fraternus* brotherly < *frater* brother] —**fra·ter′nal·ism,** *n.* —**fra·ter′nal·ly,** *adv.*

fraternal twins, twins coming from two separately fertilized egg cells.

fra·ter·ni·ty (frə tėr′nə ti), *n., pl.* **-ties. 1** group of men or boys joined together for fellowship or for some other purpose. **2** group having the same interests, kind of work, etc.

frat·er·nize (frat′ər nīz), *v.,* **-nized, -niz·ing.** associate in a brotherly way; be friendly. —**frat′er·ni·za′tion,** *n.* —**frat′er·niz′er,** *n.*

frat·ri·cide[1] (frat′rə sīd; frā′trə–), *n.* act of killing one's brother or sister. [< L, < *frater* brother + *cidium* a killing] —**frat′ri·cid′al,** *adj.*

frat·ri·cide[2] (frat′rə sīd; frā′trə–), *n.* person who kills his own brother or sister. [< L, < *frater* brother + –*cida* killer]

Frau (frou), *n., pl.* **Fraus** (frouz), *Ger.* **Frau·en** (frou′ən). *German.* **1** Mrs. **2** wife.

fraud (frôd), *n.* **1** deceit; cheating; dishonesty. **2** a dishonest act, statement, etc.; something done to deceive; trick. **3** *Esp. U.S.* person who is not what he pretends to be. [< OF < L *fraus* cheating]

fraud·u·lent (frôj′ə lənt; frôd′yū–), *adj.* **1** deceitful; cheating; dishonest. **2** intended to deceive. **3** done by fraud. —**fraud′u·lence,** *n.* —**fraud′u·lent·ly,** *adv.*

fraught (frôt), *adj.* loaded; filled. [< MDu. or MLG *vracht* freight]

Fräu·lein (froi′līn), *n., pl.* **Fräu·leins,** *Ger.* **Fräu·lein.** *German* **1** Miss. **2** an unmarried woman; young lady. **3** fraülein. unmarried, young German woman.

fray[1] (frā), *n.* a noisy quarrel; fight. [var. of *affray*]

fray[2] (frā), *v.* **1** separate into threads; make or become ragged or worn along the edge. **2** wear away; rub. [< F *frayer* < L *fricare* rub]

fraz·zle (fraz′əl), *v.,* **-zled, -zling,** *n. Esp. U.S.* —*v.* **1** tear to shreds; fray; wear out. **2** tire out; weary. —*n.* frazzled condition.

freak (frēk), *n.* **1** something very queer or unusual. **2** unconventional person. **3** *Fig.* devotee of anything: *a movie freak.* **4** drug addict. —*adj.* very queer or unusual.

freak out, become overly excited. [cf. OE *frīcian* dance] —**freak′ish,** *adj.* —**freak′ish·ly,** *adv.* —**freak′ish·ness,** *n.*

freck·le (frek′əl), *n., v.,* **-led, -ling.** —*n.* a small, light-brown spot on the skin. —*v.* **1** cover with freckles. **2** become marked or spotted with freckles. [prob. alter. of *frecken* < Scand. *freknur, pl.*] —**freck′led, freck′ly**, *adj.*

Fred·er·ic·ton (fred′rik tən; fred′ər ik–), *n.* capital of New Brunswick, Canada.

free (frē), *adj.*, **fre·er, fre·est**, *adv.*, *v.*, **freed, free·ing**. —*adj.* **1** not under another's control; having liberty; able to do, act, or think as one pleases. **2** not held back, fastened, or shut up; released; loose. **3** not hindered: *having a free hand.* **4** open to all: *a free port.* **5** without cost, tax, or duty. **6** not following rules, forms, or words exactly; not strict. **7** not combined with something else: *oxygen exists free in air.* —*adv.* **1** without cost, payment, or return. **2** freely. —*v.* **1** relieve from any kind of burden, bondage, or slavery; make free. **2** let loose; release. **3** clear: *freed of suspicion.*
for free, without charge or cost.
free and easy, relaxed; natural.
free from or **of,** having no; without.
free with, giving or using freely; generous. [OE *frēo, frīo*] —**free′ly**, *adv.* —**free′ness,** *n.*

free·base (frē′bās′), *v.*, **-based, -bas·ing**. remove impurities from (cocaine). —*n.* pure cocaine.

free·bie or **free·bee** (frē′bē), *n. Informal.* something obtained without charge.

free·board (frē′bôrd′; –bōrd′), *n.* part of a ship's side between the water line and the deck or gunwale.

free·boot·er (frē′büt′ər), *n.* pirate; buccaneer. [< Du. *vrijbuiter* < *vrij* free + *buit* booty]

free·born (frē′bôrn′), *adj.* born free, not in slavery.

free city, city forming an independent state.

freed·man (frēd′mən), *n., pl.* **-men.** man freed from slavery.

free·dom (frē′dəm), *n.* **1** state or condition of being free. **2** not being under another's control; power to do, say, or think as one pleases; liberty. **3** free use: *guests have freedom of our home.* **4** undue familiarity. **5** ease of movement or action.

freedom fighter, person who actively opposes or fights against a repressive government.

freed·wom·an (frēd′wum′ən), *n., pl.* **-wom·en.** woman freed from slavery.

free enterprise, right of private business to organize and operate under open competition with a minimum of government regulation; private enterprise.

free fall, 1 movement of a body in flight influenced only by the force of gravity. **2** period before the parachute opens during a jump. **3** *Fig.* any unrestrained decline: *in a financial free fall.*

free·hand (frē′hand′), *adj.* done by hand without using instruments, measurements, etc.

free·hand·ed (frē′han′did), *adj.* **1** generous; liberal. **2** having the hands free.

free·hold (frē′hōld′), *n.* **1** piece of land held for life or with the right to transfer it to one's heirs. **2** the holding of land in this way. —**free′hold′er,** *n.*

free·lance (frē′lans′; –läns′), *v.,* **-lanced, -lanc·ing.** work as a freelancer. Also, **free·lance.**

free·lanc·er (frē′lan′sər), *n.* **1** skilled worker, esp. an artist, editor, etc., who is hired by different employers to do a particular job. **2** writer, artist, etc., who sells work to anyone who will buy it. Also, **free-lancer.** —**free′lance′, free′-lance′,** *adj.*

free·man (frē′mən), *n., pl.* **-men. 1** person who is not not a slave or a serf. **2** person who has civil or political freedom; citizen.

free market, market regulated by the economic forces of supply and demand without much government interference into its operation.

Free·ma·son (frē′mā′sən), *n.* member of a worldwide secret society; Mason. —**free′ma·son′ic,** *adj.*

Free·ma·son·ry (frē′mā′sən ri), *n.* **1** principles or doctrines of the society of Freemasons. **2** **freemasonry,** natural fellowship.

free press, a press not censored or controlled by the government.

free-spo·ken (frē′spō′kən), *adj.* speaking freely; saying what one thinks; frank. —**free′-spo′ken·ly,** *adv.* —**free′-spo′ken·ness,** *n.*

free-stand·ing or **free-stand·ing** (frē′-stan′ding), *adj.* able to stand or standing by itself; independent.

free·stone (frē′stōn′), *n.* **1** stone, such as limestone or sandstone, that can easily be cut without splitting. **2** fruit having a stone that is easily separated from the pulp. —*adj.* having a fruit stone that is easily separated from the pulp.

free·style or **free-style** (frē′stīl′), *adj.* executed in any form or manner: *freestyle competition.* —*n.* freestyle contest or competition, as of figure skating or swimming.

free·think·er (frē′thingk′ər), *n.* person who forms his religious opinions independently of authority or tradition. —**free′think′ing,** *n., adj.* —**free thought.**

free trade, trade unrestricted by taxes, imposts, or differences of treatment; esp. international trade free from protective duties, subject only to tariff for revenue. —**free′trad′er,** *n.*

free verse, poetry not restricted by the usual rules about meter, rhyme, etc.

free·way (frē′wā′), *n.* a high-speed highway for which no tolls are charged.

free·wheel·ing (frē′hwē′ling), *adj.* **1** acting freely, without restraint. **2** coasting.

free·will (frē′wil′), *adj.* of one's own accord; voluntary: *a freewill offering.*

free will, will free from outside restraints; voluntary choice; freedom of decision.

freeze (frēz), *v.,* **froze, fro·zen, freez·ing,** *n.* —*v.* **1** turn into ice; harden by cold. **2** make or become very cold. **3** kill or injure by frost. **4** cover or become covered with ice; clog with ice. **5** make or become stiff and unfriendly. **6** chill or be chilled with fear, etc. **7** become motionless. **8 a** fix a price at a definite amount. **b** make (funds, bank balances, etc.) unusable and inaccessible by government decree. —*n.* **1** a freezing or being frozen. **2** period during which there is freezing weather.

freeze out, force out; get rid of; exude. [OE *frēosan*]

freeze-dry (frēz′drī′), *v.,* **-dried, -dry·ing.** remove the moisture in foods or other organic substances by freezing and then evaporating the ice that has formed. Something freeze-dried does not need refrigeration.

freez·er (frēz′ər), *n.* **1** machine to freeze ice cream. **2** a refrigerator cabinet (for frozen foods, ice cream, etc.) within which a temperature below the freezing point is maintained.

freezing point, temperature at which a liquid freezes. The freezing point of water is 32 degrees F. or 0 degrees C.

freight (frāt), *n.* **1** load of goods carried on a truck, plane, train, etc. **2** the carrying of goods on a truck, plane, train, etc. **3** charge for this. **4** large truck or train for carrying goods. **5** *Fig.* load; burden —*v.* **1** load with freight. **2** carry as freight. **3** send as freight. **4** load; burden. [< MDu. or MLG *vrecht*] —**freight′less,** *adj.*

freight·er (frāt′ər), *n.* large truck or ship for carrying freight.

French (french), *adj.* of or having to do with France, its people, or their language. —*n.* **1** people of France. **2** their language. —**French′man,** *n.*

French Canadian, 1 Canadian whose ancestors came from France. **2** French, as spoken in Canada.

French doors, pair of glass doors that are hinged and open in the middle. Also, **French windows.**

french fries (frīz), potatoes cut into thin strips and fried in deep fat.

french-fry (french′frī′), *v.,* **-fried, -fry·ing.** fry in deep fat; deep-fry.

French horn, a brass wind instrument that has a mellow tone.

French·i·fy (fren′chə fī), *v.,* **-fied, -fy·ing.** make French or like the French.

French Revolution, revolution in France from 1789 to 1799, which changed France from a monarchy to a republic.

french toast, slices of bread dipped in a mixture of egg and milk and then fried.

fre·net·ic (frə net′ik), *adj.* frantic; frenzied. [var. of *phrenetic*] —**fre·net′i·cal·ly,** *adv.*

fren·zy (fren′zi), *n., pl.* **-zies,** *v.,* **-zied, -zy·ing.** —*n.* brief fury; near madness; very great excitement. —*v.* make frantic. [< OF < L *phrenesis,* ult. < Gk. *phren* mind] —**fren′zied,** *adj.*

fre·quen·cy (frē′kwən si), *n., pl.* –**cies. 1** a frequent occurrence. **2** rate of occurrence. **3** number of complete cycles per second of an alternating current.

frequency modulation, 1 a deliberate modulation of the frequency of the transmitting wave in broadcasting to align with the changes in sounds or images being broadcast. **2** a broadcasting system, relatively free of static, using this method of modulation.

fre·quent (*adj.* frē′kwənt; *v.* fri kwent′), *adj.* occurring often, near together, or every little while. —*v.* go often to; be often in. [< L *frequens* crowded] —**frequent′er,** *n.* —**fre′quent·ly,** *adv.*

fre·quen·ta·tive (fri kwen′tə tiv), *adj. Gram.* expressing frequent repetition of an action.

fres·co (fres′kō), *n., pl.* –**coes, –cos. 1** act or art of painting with water colors on damp, fresh plaster. **2** picture or design so painted. [< Ital., cool, fresh] —**fres′co·er,** *n.*

fresh (fresh), *adj.* **1** newly made, arrived, or obtained: *fresh footprints.* **2** new; recent: *a fresh start.* **3** not salty. **4** not spoiled; not stale. **5** not artificially preserved. **6** not wearied; vigorous; lively. **7** looking healthy or young. **8** pure; cool; refreshing: *a fresh breeze.* **9** too bold; impudent. —*n.* spring, pool, or stream of fresh water. [OE *fersc;* but infl. in form by OF *freis,* fem. *fresche* < Gmc.] —**fresh′ness,** *n.*

fresh·en (fresh′ən), *v.* make fresh; become fresh. —**fresh′en·er,** *n.*

fresh·et (fresh′it), *n.* **1** flood caused by heavy rains or melted snow. **2** rush of fresh water flowing into the sea.

fresh·ly (fresh′li), *adv.* in a a fresh manner.

fresh·man (fresh′mən), *n., pl.* –**men,** *adj.* —*n.* **1** student in the first year of high school or college. **2** beginner. —*adj.* of these students.

fresh·wa·ter (fresh′wô′tər; –wot′ər), *adj.* of or living in water that is not salty.

fret[1] (fret), *v.,* **fret·ted, fret·ting,** *n.* —*v.* **1** be or make peevish, unhappy, discontented, or worried. **2** eat away; wear; rub. —*n.* peevish complaining; worry; discontented condition. [OE *fretan* eat] —**fret′ter,** *n.*

fret[2] (fret), *n., v.,* **fret·ted, fret·ting.** —*n.* an ornamental pattern made of straight lines bent or combined at angles. —*v.* decorate with fretwork. [< OF *frete*]

fret[3] (fret), *n.* any of a series of ridges of wood, ivory, or metal on a guitar, banjo, etc., to produce different tones on the strings. —**fret′ted,** *adj.*

fret·ful (fret′fəl), *adj.* apt to fret; peevish. —**fret′ful·ly,** *adv.* —**fret′ful·ness,** *n.*

fret·work (fret′wėrk′), *n.* **1** ornamental openwork or carving. **2** anything patterned like fretwork.

Fri., Friday.

fri·a·ble (frī′ə bəl), *adj.* easily crumbled. [< L, < *friare* crumble] —**fri′a·bil′i·ty, fri′a·ble·ness,** *n.*

fri·ar (frī′ər), *n.* member of certain religious orders of the Roman Catholic Church. [< OF < L *frater* brother]

fri·ar·y (frī′ər i), *n., pl.* –**ar·ies. 1** a building or buildings where friars live; monastery. **2** brotherhood of friars.

fric·as·see (frik′ə sē′), *n., v.,* –**seed, –see·ing.** —*n.* meat cut up, stewed, and served in a sauce made with its own gravy. —*v.* prepare (meat) in this way. [< F, < *fricasser* mince and cook in sauce]

fric·a·tive (frik′ə tiv), —*adj.* pronounced by forcing the breath through a narrow opening formed by placing the tongue or lips near or against the palate, teeth, etc.; spirant. *F, v, s,* and *z* are fricative consonants. —*n.* a fricative consonant.

fric·tion (frik′shən), *n.* **1** a rubbing of one object against another; rubbing. **2** resistance to motion of surfaces that touch. **3** conflict of differing ideas, opinions, etc.; disagreement. [< L, < *fricare* rub] —**fric′tion·al,** *adj.* —**fric′tion·al·ly,** *adv.* —**fric′tion·less,** *adj.*

Fri·day (frī′di; –dā), *n.* **1** the sixth day of the week, following Thursday. **2** servant of Robinson Crusoe. **3** any faithful servant or devoted follower. [OE *Frīgedaeg* Frigg's day]

fridge (frij), *n.* refrigerator.

fried (frīd), *adj.* cooked in hot fat. —*v.* pt. and pp. of **fry**[1].

friend (frend), *n.* **1** person who knows and likes another. **2** person who favors and supports. **3** person who belongs to the same side or group. **4 Friend,** member of the Society of Friends, a religious group opposed to war and to taking oaths; Quaker.

be friends with, be a friend of; like.

make friends with, become a friend of; come to like. [OE *frēond*] —**friend′ed,** *adj.* —**friend′less,** *adj.* —**friend′less·ness,** *n.*

friend at court, person who can help one with others; influential friend.

friend·ly (frend′li), *adj.,* –**li·er, –li·est,** *adv.* —*adj.* **1** of a friend; having the attitude of a friend. **2** like a friend; like a friend's. **3** on good terms; not hostile. **4** wanting to be a friend: *a friendly dog.* **5** favoring and supporting; favorable. —*adv.* in a friendly manner; as a friend. —**friend′li·ly,** *adv.* —**friend′li·ness,** *n.*

friend·ship (frend′ship), *n.* **1** state of being friends. **2** the liking between friends. **3** friendly feeling or behavior.

fri·er (frī′ər), *n.* **1** appliance for frying: *an electric frier.* **2** small chicken, or other fowl, suitable for frying. Also, **fryer.**

fries (frīz), *n.* =french fries.

frieze (frēz), *n.* **1** a horizontal band of decoration around a room, building, mantel, etc. **2** a horizontal band, often ornamented with sculpture, between the cornice and architrave of a building. [< F *frise*]

frig·ate (frig′it), *n.* a three-masted, sailing warship of medium size. [< F < Ital. *fregata*]

frigate bird, a strong-flying, tropical sea bird that steals other birds' food.

fright (frīt), *n.* **1** sudden fear; sudden terror. **2** *Informal.* person or thing that is ugly, shocking, or ridiculous. [OE *fryhto*]

fright·en (frīt′ən), *v.* **1** fill with fright; make afraid; scare. **2** drive (away, off, etc.) by scaring. —**fright′en·er,** *n.* —**fright′en·ing·ly,** *adv.*

fright·ful (frīt′fəl), *adj.* **1** that should cause fright; dreadful; terrible. **2** ugly; shocking. **3** *Informal.* disagreeable; unpleasant. **4** *Informal.* very great. —**fright′ful·ly,** *adv.* —**fright′ful·ness,** *n.*

frig·id (frij′id), *adj.* **1** very cold: *a frigid climate.* **2** cold in feeling or manner; stiff; chilling: *a frigid greeting.* [< L, ult. < *frigus* cold] —**fri·gid′i·ty, frig′id·ness,** *n.* —**frig′id·ly,** *adv.*

Frigid Zone, region within the Arctic or the Antarctic Circle.

fri·jol (frē′hōl), **fri·jole** (frē′hōl; frē hō′lē), *n., pl.* **fri·joles** (frē′hōlz; frē hō′lēz; *Sp.* frē hō′lās). kind of bean much used for food in Mexico and SW United States. [< Sp.]

frill (fril), *n.* **1** a ruffle. **2** thing added merely for show; useless ornament; affectation of dress, manner, speech, etc. **3** fringe of feathers, hair, etc., around the neck of a bird or animal. —*v.* decorate with a ruffle; adorn with ruffles. —**frill′er,** *n.* —**frill′y,** *adj.*

fringe (frinj), *n., v.,* **fringed, fring·ing.** —*n.* **1** border or trimming made of threads, cords, etc., either loose or tied together in small bunches. **2** anything like this; border: *a fringe of hair hung over her forehead.* —*v.* **1** make a fringe for. **2** be a fringe for: *bushes fringed the road.* [< OF < L *fimbria*] —**fringe′less,** *adj.* —**fringe′like′,** *adj.* —**fring′y,** *adj.*

fringe benefit, compensation other than wages, as insurance, pensions, etc., or privileges, received by an employee of a company.

frip·per·y (frip′ər i), *n., pl.,* –**per·ies.** cheap, showy clothes; gaudy ornaments. [< F *friperie,* ult. < *frepe* rag]

Fris., Frisian.

Fris·bee (friz′bē), *n.* trademark for a saucer-shaped disk, usually made of plastic, that skims through the air when thrown. **2 frisbee,** any similar disk. [< *Frisby,* the name of a bakery whose pie plates inspired the disc]

Fris·co (fris′kō), *n. Informal.* San Francisco.

Fri·sian (frizh′ən), *adj.* of or having to do with Friesland (in the northern Netherlands), its people, or their language. —*n.* **1** native or inhabitant of Friesland or certain nearby islands. **2** language spoken in Friesland and certain nearby islands, a W Germanic dialect.

frisk (frisk), *v.* **1** run and jump about playfully; skip and dance joyously; frolic. **2** search (a person) for concealed weapons, stolen goods, etc., by running a hand quickly over his or her clothes. [orig. *adj.*, < F *frisque*] —**frisk′er,** *n.*

frisk·y (fris′ki), *adj.*, **frisk·i·er, frisk·i·est.** playful; lively. —**frisk′i·ly,** *adv.* —**frisk′i·ness,** *n.*

frit·ter[1] (frit′ər), *v.* waste little by little. [< *fritters* small pieces, ? alter. of *fitters*] —**frit′ter·er,** *n.*

frit·ter[2] (frit′ər), *n.* a small cake of batter, sometimes containing fruit or other food, fried in fat. [< F *friture,* ult. < L *frigere* fry]

fritz (frits), *n. Informal.* **on the fritz,** not working properly; broken down.

fri·vol·i·ty (fri vol′ə ti), *n., pl.* **–ties. 1** a being frivolous. **2** a frivolous act or thing.

friv·o·lous (friv′ə ləs), *adj.* **1** lacking in seriousness or sense; silly. **2** of little worth or importance; trivial. [< L *frivolus*] —**friv′o·lous·ly,** *adv.* —**friv′o·lous·ness,** *n.*

friz, frizz (friz), *v.,* **frizzed, friz·zing,** *n., pl.* **friz·zes,** —*v.* **1** form into small, crisp curls; curl. **2** form into little tufts: *cloth with a frizzed nap.* —*n.* hair arranged in close, untidy curls. [appar. < F *friser*]

friz·zle (friz′əl), *v.,* **–zled, –zling.** form into small, crisp curls; curl. [? akin to OE *frīs* curly] —**friz′zler,** *n.*

friz·zly (friz′li), *adj.* full of small, crisp curls; curly.

friz·zy (friz′i), *adj.* =frizzly. —**friz′zi·ly,** *adv.* —**friz′zi·ness,** *n.*

fro (frō), *adv.* from; back.
to and fro, first one way and then back again; back and forth. [< Scand. *frā;* akin to FROM]

frock (frok), *n.* gown; dress. —*v.* clothe in a frock. [< OF *froc*] —**frock′less,** *adj.*

frog[1] (frog; frôg), *n., v.,* **frogged, frog·ging.** —*n.* **1** a small, leaping animal with webbed feet, that lives in or near water. **2** animal like this. **3** horny substance in the middle of the bottom of a foot of a horse, donkey, etc. —*v.* hunt frogs. [OE *frogga*] —**frog′like′,** *adj.*

frog[2] (frog; frôg), *n.* an ornamental fastening for a coat or dress. [? < Pg. *froco* < L *floccus* flock[2]]

frog·man (frog′man), *n., pl.* **–men.** person trained and equipped for underwater operations of various kinds.

frol·ic (frol′ik), *n., v.,* **–icked, –ick·ing,** *adj.* —*n.* **1** a gay prank; fun. **2** a merry game or party. [< v. or adj.] —*v.* play; have fun; make merry. [< adj.] —*adj.* full of fun; merry. [< Du. *vrolijk* < MDu. *vro* glad] —**frol′ick·er,** *n.*

frol·ic·some (frol′ik səm), *adj.* full of fun; merry; playful. —**frol′ic·some·ly,** *adv.* —**frol′ic·some·ness,** *n.*

from (from; frum; *unstressed* frəm), *prep.* **1** out of: *a train from New York.* **2** out of the possession of: *take the book from her.* **3** beginning with: *from that time*

forward. **4** caused by: *act from a sense of duty.* **5** as being unlike: *tell one tree from another.* [OE *from*]

frond (frond), *n.* **1** a divided leaf of a fern, palm, etc. **2** a leaflike part of a seaweed, lichen, etc. [< L *frons* leaf] —**frond′ed,** *adj.*

front (frunt), *n.* **1** the first part. **2** part that faces forward. **3** part that faces a street or road: *the front of a house.* **4** thing fastened or worn on the front. **5** place where fighting is going on; line of battle. **6** land facing a street, river, etc. **7** an outward appearance of wealth, importance, etc. **8** person or thing that serves as a cover for illicit or illegal activities. **9** the dividing surface between two dissimilar air masses. —*adj.* of, on, in, or at the front. —*v.* **1** have the front toward; face. **2** meet face to face; oppose.
in front of, in a place or position before.
up front, a in advance. **b** *Fig.* straightforward; open. [< L *frons,* lit., forehead]

front·age (frun′tij), *n.* **1** front of a building or of a lot. **2** length of this front. **3** land facing a street, river, etc.

fron·tal (frun′təl), *adj.* **1** of, on, in, or at the front. **2** of the forehead. —*n.* bone of the forehead. —**fron′tal·ly,** *adv.*

fron·tier (frun tir′; frun′tir; frŏn′tir), *n.* **1** *U.S.* the farthest part of a settled country, where the wilds begin. **2** an uncertain or undeveloped region: *the frontiers of science.* —*adj.* of or on the frontier. [< OF *front* FRONT]

fron·tiers·man (frun tirz′mən), *n., pl.* **–men.** person who lives on the frontier.

fron·tis·piece (frun′tis pēs; fron′–), *n.* **1** a front part. **2** picture facing the title page of a book. [< F < LL *frontispicium,* lit., looking at the forehead < L *frons* forehead + *specere* look]

front-page (frunt′pāj′), *adj.* suitable for the front page of a newspaper; important.

frost (frost; frôst) *n.* **1** freezing condition with temperature below the point at which water freezes. **2** ice crystals formed when water vapor in the air condenses at a temperature below freezing. **3** coldness of manner or feeling. —*v.* **1** cover with frost. **2** cover with anything that suggests frost. **3** kill or injure by frost. [OE] —**frost′less,** *adj.* —**frost′like′,** *adj.*

frost·bite (frost′bīt′; frost′–), *n., v.,* **–bit, –bit·ten, –bit·ing.** —*v.* injury to the body caused by severe cold. —*v.* injure by severe cold. —**frost′bit·ten,** *adj.*

frost·ing (frôs′ting; fros′–), *n.* mixture of sugar, eggs, water, etc., for covering a cake.

frost·y (frôs′ti; fros′–), *adj.,* **frost·i·er, frost·i·est. 1** cold enough for frost. **2** covered with frost. **3** cold in manner or feeling; unfriendly. —**frost′i·ly,** *adv.* —**frost′i·ness,** *n.* —**frost′less,** *adj.*

froth (frôth; froth), *n.* **1** foam. **2** trivial talk, etc. —*v.* **1** give out froth; foam. **2** cover with foam. **3** cause to foam. [ME

frothe; ? < Scand. *frotha;* but cf. OE *āfrēothan,* v.] —**froth′er,** *n.*

froth·y (frôth′i; froth′i), *adj.* **froth·i·er, froth·i·est. 1** foamy. **2** trifling; unimportant. —**froth′i·ly,** *adv.* —**froth′i·ness,** *n.*

fro·ward (frō′wərd; frō′ərd), *adj.* not easily managed; willful; contrary. [< *fro* + *-ward*] —**fro′ward·ly,** *adv.* —**for′ward·ness,** *n.*

frown (froun), *n.* **1** a drawing together of the brows, usually in deep thought or in strong feeling. **2** any expression or show of disapproval. —*v.* **1** wrinkle the forehead in annoyance or disapproval. **2** look displeased or angry. [< OF *froignier* < Celtic] —**frown′er,** *n.* —**frown′ing·ly,** *adv.*

frowz·y (frouz′i), *adj.,* **frowz·i·er, frowz·i·est.** slovenly; untidy. —**frowz′i·ly,** *adv.* —**frowz′i·ness,** *n.*

froze (frōz), *v.* pt. of **freeze.**

fro·zen (frō′zən), *adj.* **1** turned into ice; hardened by cold. **2** very cold **3** killed or injured by frost. **4** covered or clogged with ice. **5** cold and unfeeling. **6** too frightened to move. **7** made impossible to sell or exchange: *frozen assets.* —*v.* pp. of **freeze.** —**fro′zen·ly,** *adv.* —**fro′zen·ness,** *n.*

fruc·ti·fy (fruk′tə fī), *v.,* **–fied, –fy·ing. 1** bear fruit. **2** make fruitful; fertilize. [< F < L, < *fructus* fruit + *facere* make] —**fruc′ti·fi·ca′tion,** *n.*

fruc·tose (fruk′tōs), *n.* fruit sugar, $C_6H_{12}O_6$, a carbohydrate found in all sweet fruits and in honey.

fru·gal (frü′gəl), *adj.* **1** avoiding waste; saving: *a frugal housekeeper.* **2** costing little; barely sufficient: *a frugal meal.* [< L, < *frugi* economical] —**fru·gal′i·ty, fru′gal·ness,** *n.* —**fru′gal·ly,** *adv.*

fruit (früt), *n.* **1** product of a tree, bush, shrub, or vine that is good to eat. **2** part of a plant that contains the seeds. A fruit is the ripened ovary of a flower and the tissues connected with it. **3** the useful product of plants: *the fruits of the earth.* **4** product; result. —*v.* have or produce fruit. [< OF < L *fructus*] —**fruit′like′,** *adj.*

fruit·cake (früt′kāk′), *n.,* or **fruit cake.** heavy, rich cake made with candied fruits, nuts, spices, and often, brandy.

fruit·er·er (früt′ər ər), *n.* dealer in fruit.

fruit fly, a small fly whose larvae feed on decaying fruits and vegetables.

fruit·ful (früt′fəl), *adj.* **1** producing much fruit. **2** producing much of anything. **3** having good results; bringing benefit or profit. —**fruit′ful·ly,** *adv.* —**fruit′ful·ness,** *n.*

fru·i·tion (frü ish′ən), *n.* **1** condition of having results; fulfillment; attainment. **2** pleasure that comes from possession or use. **3** condition of producing fruit. [< LL, < *frui* enjoy]

fruit·less (früt′lis), *adj.* **1** having no results; useless; unsuccessful. **2** producing no fruit; barren. —**fruit′less·ly,** *adv.* —**fruit′less·ness,** *n.*

fruit sugar, =fructose.

fruit·y (früt′ī), *adj.,* **fruit·i·er, fruit·i·est.** tasting or smelling like fruit. —**fruit′i·ness,** *n.*

frump (frump), *n.* woman who is frumpish.

frump·ish (frump′ish), *adj.* shabby and out of style in dress.

frump·y (frump′ī), *adj.,* **frump·i·er, frump·i·est.** =frumpish. —**frump′i·ly,** *adv.* —**frump′i·ness,** *n.*

frus·trate (frus′trāt), *v.,* **-trat·ed, -trat·ing. 1** bring to nothing; make useless or worthless; foil; defeat. **2** thwart; baffle. [< L, < *frustra* in vain] —**frus′trat·er,** *n.* —**frus·tra′tion,** *n.* —**frus′tra·tive,** *adj.*

fry¹ (frī), *v.,* **fried, fry·ing,** *n., pl.* **fries.** —*v.* cook in hot fat. —*n.* fried food; dish of fried meat, fish, etc. [< F < L *frigere*]

fry² (frī), *n., pl.* **fry.** a young fish. [cf. Scand. *frjö* seed]

fry·er (frī′ər), *n.* **1** =frier (def. 1). **2** fowl (chicken, duck, etc.) intended for frying.

fry·ing (frī′ing)**,pan,**flat pan with a handle and made of iron, stainless steel, or other metals, used for frying food.

out of the frying pan (and) into the fire, from one bad situation to another, possibly worse.

ft., 1 foot; feet. 2 fort.

fuch·sia (fū′shə), *n.* shrub with handsome pink, red, or purple flowers that droop from the stems. [< NL; named for L. *Fuchs,* botanist]

fudge (fuj), *n., interj., v.,* **fudged, fudging.** —*n.* **1** a soft candy made of sugar, milk,butter,etc.**2** nonsense.—*interj.* nonsense! bosh! —*v.* **1** do or make in a perfunctory way. **2** talk nonsense. **3** fake.

fu·el (fū′əl), *n., v.,* **-eled, -el·ing.** —*n.* **1** thing that can be burned to make a fire. Coal and oil are fuels. **2** thing that keeps up or increases a feeling. —*v.* **1** supply with fuel. **2** get fuel. [< OF *feuaile,* ult. < L *focus* hearth] —**fu′el·er,** *n.*

fuel cell, device which produces electricity from a chemical reaction between oxygen and a gaseous fuel such as hydrogen.

fuel injection, the spraying of gasoline or other fuel directly into the combustion chamber of an internal-combustion engine.

fuel rod, long rod of nuclear fuel, used in a nuclear reactor.

fu·gi·tive (fū′jə tiv), *n.* person who is fleeing or who has fled. —*adj.* **1** fleeing; having fled; runaway. **2** lasting only a very short time; passing swiftly. [< F < L, < *fugere* flee] —**fu′gi·tive·ly,** *adv.* —**fu′gi·tive·ness,** *n.*

fugue (fūg), *n.* composition based on one or more short themes in which different voices or instruments repeat the same melody with slight variations. [< F < Ital. < L *fuga* flight] —**fugue′like′,** *adj.*

-ful, *suffix.* **1** full of, as in *cheerful.* **2** having; characterized by, as in *careful,*

thoughtful. **3** having a tendency to, as in *harmful, mournful.* **4** enough to fill, as in *cupful, handful.* **5** other meanings, as in *manful, useful.* [see FULL, adj.]

ful·crum (ful′krəm), *n., pl.* **-crums, -cra** (-krə). support on which a lever turns or is supported. [< L, bedpost, < *fulcire* to support]

ful·fill, ful·fil (ful fil′), *v.,* **-filled, -filling. 1** carry out (a promise, etc.); cause to happen or take place. **2** do or perform (a duty); obey. **3** satisfy (a requirement, etc.); serve (a purpose). **4** finish; complete [OE *fullfyllan*] —**ful·fill′er,** *n.* —**ful·fill′ment, ful·fil′ment,** *n.*

full (ful), *n.* the greatest size, amount, extent, volume, etc. —*v.* make or become full. —*adj.* **1** able to hold no more; filled: *a full cup.* **2** complete; entire: *a full supply.* **3** more than enough to satisfy; well supplied. **4** plump; round. **5** strong and distinct: *a full voice.* **6** made with wide folds or much cloth. —*adv.* **1** completely; entirely. **2** straight; directly: *the blow hit him full in the face.*

full of,a filled with.**b** completely absorbed with: *full of his new job.*

in full, a to or for the complete amount. **b** written or said with all the words. [OE] —**full′ness,** *n.* —**ful′ly,** *adv.*

full·back (ful′bak′), *n.* player whose position is farthest behind the front line.

full blast, *Informal.* in full operation; at highest speed and full capacity.

full-blood·ed (ful′blud′id), *adj.* **1** of pure race, breed, etc. **2** vigorous; hearty.

full-blown (ful′blōn′), *adj.* **1** in full bloom. **2** *Fig.* fully developed: *full-blown flu.*

full dress, formal clothes worn in the evening or on important occasions.

full-dress (ful′dress′), *adj.* **1** pertaining to full dress: *a full-dress dinner.* **2** complete; formal: *a full-dress conference.*

full-grown (ful′grōn′), *adj.* mature.

full moon, the moon seen as a whole circle.

full·ness (ful′nis), *n.* quality or condition of being full.

full-time (ful′tōm′), *adj., adv.* for the amount of time usually spent at work: *full-time work; start full-time next week.* —**full′-tim′er,** *n.*

ful·mi·nate (ful′mə nāt), *v.,* **-nat·ed, -nating. 1** thunder forth in speech or writing; denounce violently. **2** explode violently. [< L, < *fulmen* lightning] —**ful′mi·na′tion,** *n.* —**ful′mi·na′tor,** *n.*

ful·ness (ful′nis), *n.* =fullness.

ful·some (ful′səm; ful′-), *adj.* so much as to be disgusting; offensive. [< *full* + *-some*¹; infl. in meaning by *foul*] —**ful′some·ly,** *adv.* —**ful′some·ness,** *n.*

fum·ble (fum′bəl), *v.,* **-bled, -bling,** *n.* —*v.* **1** grope or handle awkwardly. **2** fail to hold (a ball). —*n.* **1** an awkward groping or handling. **2** failure to hold a ball. [cf. LG *fummeln*] —**fum′bler,** *n.* —**fum′bling,** *adj., n.* —**fum′bling·ly,** *adv.*

fume (fūm), *v.,* **fumed, fum·ing,** *n.* —*v.* **1** give off fumes. **2** make angry complaints; show anger or irritation. —*n.* Often, **fumes.** vapor, gas, or smoke, esp. if harmful, strong, or odorous. [< OF < L *fumus* smoke] —**fume′less,** *adj.* —**fum′er,** *n.* —**fum′ing·ly,** *adv.*

fu·mi·gate (fū′mə gāt), *v.,* **-gat·ed, -gating.** disinfect with fumes; expose to fumes. [< L *fumigatus* < *fumus* fume] —**fu′mi·ga′tion,** *n.* —**fu′mi·ga′tor,** *n.*

fun (fun), *n., adj.* —*n.* playfulness; merry play; amusement; joking. —*adj. Informal.* amusing: *a fun time.*

for or **in fun,** playfully; as a joke.

make fun of or **poke fun at,** laugh at; ridicule. [? orig. v., var. of obs. *fon* befool]

func·tion (fungk′shən), *n.* **1** proper work; normal action or use; purpose. **2** a formal public or social gathering for some purpose. **3** quantity whose value depends on, or varies with, the value given to one or more related quantities. —*v.* work; be used; act. [< L *functio* < *fungi* perform] —**func′tion·less,** *adj.*

func·tion·al (fungk′shən əl), *adj.* **1** having to do with a function or functions. **2** having a function; working; acting. —**func′tion·al·ly,** *adv.*

functional illiteracy, unable to read or write above a basic level. —**functional illiterate.**

func·tion·ar·y (fungk′shən er′ī), *n., pl.* **-aries.** person charged with a function or office.

function word, word whose function in a sentence is mainly to express relationships between other elements or to express grammatical meanings.

fund (fund), *n.* **1** sum of money set aside for a special purpose. **2** stock or store ready for use; supply: *a fund of information.* —*v.* **1** set aside a sum of money. **2** change (a debt) from short to long term.

funds, a money ready to use. **b** money. [< L *fundus* bottom, piece of land]

fun·da·men·tal (fun′də men′təl), *adj.* of or forming a foundation or basis; essential. —*n.* **1** principle, rule, law, etc., that forms a foundation or basis. [< NL, < L *fundamentum* foundation, ult. < *fundus* bottom] —**fun′da·men·tal′i·ty,** *n.* —**fun′da·men′tal·ly,** *adv.*

fun·da·men·tal·ism (fun′də men′təl iz əm), *n.* **1** the belief that the words of the Bible were inspired by God and should be believed and followed literally. **2** movement in certain Protestant churches upholding this belief. —**fun′da·men′tal·ist,** *n., adj.*

fu·ner·al (fū′nər əl; fūn′rəl), *n.* **1** ceremonies performed when a dead person's body is buried or burned. **2** procession taking a dead person's body to the place where it is buried or burned. —*adj.* of or suitable for a funeral. [< LL *funeralis* < L *funus* funeral, death]

fu·ne·re·al (fū nir′i əl), *adj.* **1** of or suitable for a funeral. **2** gloomy; dismal. —**fu·ne′re·al·ly,** *adv.*

fun·gi·cide (fun′jə sīd), *n.* any substance that destroys fungi. [< L *fungus* + *-cida* killer] —**fun′gi·cid′al,** *adj.*

fun·gous (fung′gəs), *adj.* **1** of a fungus or fungi; like a fungus; spongy. **2** caused by a fungus.

fun·gus (fung′gəs), *n., pl.* **fun·gi** (fun′jī), **fun·gus·es,** *adj.* —*n.* **1** plant without flowers, leaves, or green coloring water. Mushrooms are fungi. **2** something that grows or springs up rapidly like a mushroom. **3** a diseased, spongy growth on the skin. —*adj.* =fungous. [< L; prob. akin to Gk. *sphongos* sponge] —**fun′gus·like′,** *adj.*

funk¹ (fungk), —*n.* **1** fear; panic. **2** feeling of depression; bad mood. —*v.* shrink from; shirk.

funk² (fungk), *n.* type of blues, influenced by gospel and African rhythms.

funk·y (fung′ki), *adj.* **1** of or like the blues; sad; earthy. **2** fearful; panicky. **3** hip; cool.

fun·nel (fun′əl), *n., v.,* **-neled, -nel·ing.** —*n.* **1** a small, tapering tube with a wide, cone-shaped mouth. **2** anything shaped like a funnel. **3** a round, metal chimney; smokestack. —*v.* **1** pass or feed through a funnel. **2** converge. [< OF < LL < L, < *in-* in + *fundere* pour] —**fun′nel·like′,** *adj.*

fun·ny (fun′i), *adj.,* **-ni·er, -ni·est,** *n., pl.* **-nies.** —*adj.* **1** causing laughter; amusing. **2** strange; queer; odd. —*n.* **funnies, a** comic strips. **b** section of a newspaper devoted to them. —**fun′ni·ly,** *adv.* —**fun′ni·ness,** *n.*

funny bone, part of the elbow over which a nerve passes.

fur (fėr), *n, v.,* **furred, fur·ring.** —*n.* **1** the soft hair covering the skin of certain animals. **2** skin with such hair on it. **3** Usually, **furs.** garment made of fur. **4** a coating of foul or waste matter like fur. [< v.] —*v.* **1** make, cover, trim, or line with fur. **2** coat with foul or waste matter like fur.

furs, a coat, wrap, etc., made of fur. **b** animal skins with fur on them.

make the fur fly, cause trouble or a quarrel or fight. [< OF *forrer* line, encase < *forre* sheath < Gmc.] —**fur′less,** *adj.*

fur., **1** furlong. **2** furnished.

fur·be·low (fėr′bə lō), *n.* bit of elaborate trimming. —*v.* trim in an elaborate way. [alter. of *falbala* < Rom.]

fur·bish (fėr′bish), *v.* **1** brighten by rubbing or scouring; polish. **2** restore to good condition; make usable again. [< OF *forbir* polish < Gmc.] —**fur′bish·er,** *n.*

Fu·ries (fyur′iz), *n. pl. Gk. and Roman Myth.* the three spirits of revenge.

fu·ri·ous (fyur′i əs), *adj.* **1** intensely violent; raging. **2** full of wild, fierce anger. **3** of unrestrained energy, speed, etc.: *furi-*

ous activity. [< L, < *furia* fury] —**fu′ri·ous·ly,** *adv.* —**fu′ri·ous·ness,** *n.*

furl (fėrl), *v.* roll up; fold up: *furl a flag.* —*n.* roll or coil of something furled. [< F *ferler* < AF *ferlier* < *fer* firm (< L *firmus*) + *lier* bind < L *ligare*] —**furl′er,** *n.*

fur·long (fėr′lông; –long), *n.* measure of distance equal to one eighth of a mile. [OE *furlang* < *furh* furrow + *lang* long]

fur·lough (fėr′lō), *n.* leave of absence, esp. for a soldier. —*v.* give leave of absence to. [< Du. *verlof*]

fur·nace (fėr′nis), *n.* **1** an enclosed structure to make a very hot fire in, used to heat buildings. **2** a very hot place. [< OF < L *fornax* < *fornus* oven] —**fur′nace·like′,** *adj.*

fur·nish (fėr nish), *v.* **1** supply; provide. The sun furnishes heat. **2** supply (a room, house, etc.) with furniture, equipment, etc. [< OF *furnir* accomplish < Gmc.] —**fur′nish·er,** *n.*

fur·nish·ings (fėr′nish ingz), *n. pl.* **1** furniture or equipment for a room, house, etc. **2** accessories of dress; articles of clothing.

fur·ni·ture fėr′nə chər), *n.* **1** movable articles needed in a room, house, etc. **2** articles needed; equipment. [< F *fourniture.* See FURNISH.]

fu·ror (fyur′ôr), *n.* **1** outburst of wild enthusiasm or excitement. **2** craze; mania. **3** madness; frenzy. [< F *fureur* < L, < *furere* rage]

furred (fėrd), *adj.* **1** having fur. **2** made, covered, trimmed, or lined with fur.

fur·ri·er (fėr′i ər), *n.* person whose work is preparing furs or making and repairing fur coats, etc.

fur·ring (fėr′ing), *n.* **1** act of covering, trimming, or lining with fur. **2** the fur used. **3** thin strips of wood nailed to beams, walls, etc.

fur·row (fėr′ō), *n.* **1** a long, narrow groove or track cut in the ground by a plow. **2** any long, narrow groove or track. **3** wrinkle. —*v.* **1** plow. **2** make furrows in. **3** wrinkle. [OE *furh*] —**fur′row·er,** *n.* —**fur′row·less,** *adj.* —**fur′row·like′,** *adj.,* —**fur′row·y,** *adj.*

fur·ry (fėr′i), *adj.,* **-ri·er, -ri·est. 1** of fur. **2** covered with fur. **3** looking or feeling like fur. —**fur′ri·ness,** *n.*

fur·ther (fėr′ŧʜər), *compar. adj. and adv.,* *superl.* **fur·thest** (fėr′ŧʜist), *v.* —*adj.* **1** farther; more distant: *on the further side.* **2** more: *have you any further need of me?* —*adv.* **1** at or to a greater distance: *seek no further for happiness.* **2** to a greater extent: *inquire further into the matter.* **3** also; besides: *say further.* —*v.* help forward; promote. [OE *furthra,* adj., *furthor,* adv., < *forth* forth] —**fur′ther·er,** *n.*

fur·ther·ance (fėr′ŧʜər əns), *n.* act of furthering; helping forward; promotion.

fur·ther·more (fėr′ŧʜər môr; –mōr), *adv.* moreover; also; besides.

fur·ther·most (fėr′ŧʜər mōst), *adj.* furthest.

fur·tive (fėr′tiv), *adj.* **1** done stealthily; secret: *a furtive glance.* **2** sly; stealthy; shifty: *a furtive manner.* [< L, < *fur* thief] —**fur′tive·ly,** *adv.* —**fur′tive·ness,** *n.*

fu·ry (fyur′i), *n., pl.* **-ries. 1** wild, fierce anger; rage. **2** violence; fierceness.

like fury, violently; very rapidly. [< L *furia*]

furze (fėrz), *n.* a low, prickly, evergreen shrub with yellow flowers, common on waste lands in Europe; gorse. [OE *fyrs*] —**furz′y,** *adj.*

fuse¹ (fūz), *n.* **1** part of a circuit that melts and breaks the connection when the current becomes dangerously strong. **2** =a fuze (def. 1). [< Ital. < L *fusus* spindle] —**fuse′less,** *adj.* —**fuse′like′,** *adj.*

fuse² (fūz), *v.,* **fused, fus·ing. 1** melt; melt together. Copper and zinc are fused to make brass. **2** blend; unite. [< L *fusus* poured, melted]

fu·se·lage (fū′zə läzh; –lij; –sə–), *n.* framework of the body of an airplane that holds passengers, cargo, etc. [< F, < *fuselé* spindle-shaped. See FUSE¹.]

fu·si·ble (fū′zə bəl), *adj.* that can be fused or melted. —**fu′si·bil′i·ty, fu′si·ble·ness,** *n.* —**fu′si·bly,** *adv.*

fu·sil·ier, fu·sil·eer (fū′zə lir′), *n.* formerly, a soldier armed with a light flintlock musket. [< F, < *fusil* musket]

fu·sil·lade (fū′zə lād′), *n., v.,* **-lad·ed, -lad·ing.** —*n.* **1** discharge of many firearms. **2** something that resembles a fusillade: *a fusillade of questions.* —*v.* attack or shoot down by a fusillade. [< F, < *fusiller* shoot < *fusil* musket]

fu·sion (fū′zhən), *n.* **1** a melting; melting together; fusing. **2** a blending; union. **3** a fused mass. **4** the combining of two nuclei to create a nucleus of greater mass. **5** blend of jazz and other popular musical styles.

fu·sion·ist (fū′zhən ist), *n.* person taking part in a union of political parties or factions. —**fu′sion·ism,** *n.*

fuss (fus), *n.* much bother about small matters; useless talk and worry. —*v.* **1** make a fuss. **2** make nervous or worried; bother. —**fuss′er,** *n.*

fuss·y (fus′i), *adj.,* **fuss·i·er, fuss·i·est. 1** inclined to fuss; hard to please; very particular. **2** much trimmed; elaborately made. **3** full of details; requiring much care. —**fuss′i·ly,** *adv.* —**fuss′i·ness,** *n.*

fust·y (fus′ti), *adj.,* **fust·i·er, fust·i·est. 1** having a stale smell; musty; moldy; stuffy. **2** old-fashioned; out-of-date. [< *fust,* n., < OF wine cask, < L *fustis* cudgel] —**fust′i·ly,** *adv.* —**fust′i·ness,** *n.*

fu·tile (fū′təl), *adj.* **1** not successful; useless. **2** not important; trifling. [< L *futilis* pouring easily, worthless < *fundere* pour] —**fu′tile·ly,** *adv.* —**fu·til′i·ty, fu′tile·ness,** *n.*

fu·ton (fū′ton), *n.* **1** padded Japanese floor mattress. **2** such a mattress, folded on a frame and used as a couch or a bed, when unfolded. [< Jap.]

fu·ture (fū′chər), *n.* **1** time to come; what is to come; what will be. **2** chance of success or prosperity. **3** a future tense or verb form. —*adj.* **1** that is to come; that will be; coming. **2** expressing or indicating time to come. *Shall go* or *will go* is the future tense of *go.*

futures, things, esp. stocks and commodities, bought or sold to be received or delivered at a future date and at a certain price. [< L *futurus,*

future participle of *esse* be] —**fu′ture·less,** *adj.*

fu·tu·ri·ty (fū tür′ə ti; –tyür′–), *n., pl.* **–ties. 1** future. **2** a future state or event. **3** quality of being future.

fuze (fūz), *n.* **1** a slow-burning wick or other device to detonate a shell, bomb, etc. **2** =fuse[1].

fuzz (fuz), *n.* loose, light fibers or hairs; down. —*v.* make or become fuzzy. [cf. Du. *voos* spongy]

fuzz·y (fuz′i), *adj.,* **fuzz·i·er, fuzz·i·est. 1** of or like fuzz. **2** covered with fuzz. **3** blurred; indistinct. —**fuzz′i·ly,** *adv.* —**fuzz′i·ness,** *n.*

fwd., forward.

–fy, *suffix.* **1** make; cause to be; change into, as in *simplify, intensify.* **2** become, as in *solidify.* **3** other meanings, as in *modify, qualify.* [< F *–fier* < L *–ficare* < *facere* do, make]

FYI, for your information.

G, g (jē), *n., pl.* **G's; g's.**
1 the seventh letter of the alphabet. **2** the fifth note in the scale of C major.

G, 1 general (audience), a film rating. **2** German. Also, **Ger.**

g., 1 conductance. **2** gram.

GA, (*zip code*) Georgia.

Ga, gallium.

Ga., Georgia.

gab (gab), *n., v.,* **gabbed, gab·bing.** *Informal.* chatter; gabble.

gab·ar·dine, gab·er·dine (gab′ər dēn; gab′ər dēn′), *n.* a closely woven woolen or cotton cloth having small, diagonal ribs on its surface, used for raincoats, suits, etc. [< Sp. *gabardina*]

gab·ble (gab′əl), *v.,* **-bled, -bling,** *n.* —*v.* **1** talk rapidly with little of no meaning; jabber. **2** make rapid, meaningless sounds: *the geese gabbled.* —*n.* rapid talk with little or no meaning. [< *gab,* var. of *gob* < Scotch Gaelic, mouth] —**gab′bler,** *n.*

gab·by (gab′i), *adj.,* **-bi·er, -bi·est,** talkative.

ga·ble (gā′bəl), *n., v.,* **-bled, -bling.** —*n.* **1** end of a ridged roof, with the three-cornered piece of wall that it covers. **2** an end wall with a gable. **3** a triangular ornament or canopy over a door, window, etc. —*v.* build or form as a gable. [< OF *gable* < Scand. *gafl*] —**ga′bled,** *adj.* —**ga′ble·like′,** *adj.*

gable roof, roof that forms a gable at one or both ends.

Ga·bon (gä bôn′), *n.* republic in W C Africa on the Atlantic.

Ga·bri·el (gā′bri əl), *n.* archangel who acts as God's messenger.

gad[1] (gad), *v.,* **gad·ded, gad·ding,** *n.* —*v.* move about restlessly; go about looking for pleasure or excitement. —*n.* a gadding. [< *gad*ling companion, wanderer] —**gad′der,** *n.*

gad[2], **Gad** (gad), *n., interj.* word used as a mild oath, exclamation of surprise, etc.

gad·fly (gad′flī′), *n., pl.* **-flies. 1** fly that stings cattle, horses, etc. **2** an irritating or annoying person.

gadg·et (gaj′it), *n.* a small mechanical device or contrivance; any ingenious device.

gadg·et·ry (gaj′ə tri), *n.* **1** gadgets. **2** making or using gadgets.

gad·o·lin·i·um (gad′ə lin′i əm), *n.* a rare metallic element, Gd.

Gael (gāl), *n.* **1** a Scottish Highlander. **2** Celt born or living in Scotland or the Isle of Man, or, occasionally, in Ireland.

Gael·ic (gāl′ik), *adj.* of or having to do with the Gaels or their language. —*n.* language of the Gaels.

gaff (gaf), *n.* **1** a strong hook or barbed spear for pulling large fish out of the water. **2** spar or pole extending along the upper edge of a fore-and-aft sail. —*v.* hook or pull (a fish) out of the water with a gaff.

stand the gaff, hold up well under strain or punishment. [< OF *gaffe* < Celtic]

gaffe (gaf), *n.* blunder; faux pas. [< F]

gag (gag), *n., v.,* **gagged, gag·ging.** —*n.* **1** something thrust into a person's mouth to keep him or her from talking, crying out, etc. **2** anything used to silence a person; restraint or hindrance to free speech. **3** an amusing remark or trick; joke. —*v.* **1** put a gag into; keep from talking, crying out, etc., with a gag. **2** force to keep silent; restrain or hinder from free speech. **3** choke or strain in an effort to vomit. [prob. imit.] —**gag′ger,** *n.*

gage (gāj), *n., v.,* **gaged, gag·ing.** =gauge. —**gag′er,** *n.*

gag·gle (gag′əl), *n.* **1** honking sound of a goose. **2** flock of geese. **3** *Informal. Fig.* group of people or things. —*v.,* **-gled, -gling.** make the honking sound of a goose. [prob. imit.]

gai·e·ty (gā′ə ti), *n., pl.* **-ties. 1** cheerful liveliness; merriment. **2** gay entertainment. **3** bright appearance. Also, **gayety.**

gai·ly (gā′li), *adv.* **1** as if gay; happily; merrily. **2** brightly; showily. Also, **gayly.**

gain (gān), *v.* **1** get; obtain; secure. **2** get as an increase, addition, advantage, or profit; make a profit; benefit. **3** make progress; advance; improve. **4** be the victor in; win. **5** get to; arrive at. —*n.* **1** act of gaining or getting anything. **2** what is gained; increase; addition; advantage; profit. **3** getting wealth.

gain on, come closer to; get near to.

gains, profits; earnings; winnings. [< OF *gaaigner* < Gmc.] —**gain′a·ble,** *adj.*

gain·er (gān′ər), *n.* **1** person or thing that gains. **2** a fancy dive in which the diver turns a back somersault in the air.

gain·ful (gān′fəl), *adj.* bringing in money or advantage; profitable. —**gain·ful·ly,** *adv.* —**gain′ful·ness,** *n.*

gain·say (*v.* gān sā′; *n.* gān′sā′), *v.,* **-said, -say·ing,** *n.* —*v.* deny; contradict; dispute. —*n.* contradiction. [< *gain–* against + *say*] —**gain·say′er,** *n.*

gainst, 'gainst (genst), *prep., conj.* =against.

gait (gāt), *n.* kind of steps used in going along; way of walking or running. [< Scand. *gata* way] —**gait′ed,** *adj.*

gai·ter (gā′tər), *n.* **1** a covering for the lower leg or ankle, made of cloth, leather, etc. **2** shoe with an elastic strip in each side. [< F *guêtre*]

gal (gal), *n. Informal.* girl.

gal., gallon; gallons.

ga·la (gā′lə; gal′ə), *n.* festive occasion; festival. —*adj.* of festivity; for a festive occasions; with festivities. [< F < Ital. < OF *gale* merriment]

ga·lac·tic (gə lak′tik), *adj.* **1** of or having to do with the Milky Way or other galaxies. **2** of milk; obtained from milk. [< Gk. *galaktikos* < *gala* milk]

Gal·a·had (gal′ə had), *n.* **Sir,** noblest and purest knight of the Round Table, who found the Holy Grail.

gal·an·tine (gal′ən tēn), *n.* veal, chicken, or other white meat boned, tied up, boiled, and then served cold with its own jelly. [< F]

Ga·lá·pa·gos Islands (gə lä′pə gəs; –gōs), group of islands in the Pacific, 600 miles west of and belonging to Ecuador.

Ga·la·tia (gə lā′shə), *n.* an ancient country in C Asia Minor that later became a Roman province. —**Ga·la′tian,** *adj., n.*

Ga·la·tians (gə lā′shənz), *n.pl.* book of the New Testament, written by the Apostle Paul.

gal·ax·y (gal′ək si), *n., pl.* **-ax·ies. 1** a brilliant or splendid group. **2** a portion of space in which stars are clustered relatively thickly. Our Milky Way is only one of over a million such galaxies. **3** **Galaxy,** =Milky Way. [< LL *galaxias* < Gk., < *gala* milk]

gale[1] (gāl), *n.* **1** a very strong wind. **2** wind with a velocity of 25 to 75 miles per hour. **3** a noisy outburst: *gales of laughter.*

gale[2] (gāl), *n.* shrub with fragrant leaves that grows in marshy places. [OE *gagel*]

ga·le·na (gə lē′nə), *n.* a metallic, gray ore containing much lead sulfide, PbS. It is the most important source of lead. [< L]

Ga·li·cia (gə lish′ə), *n.* region in C Europe, now divided between Poland and Russia.

Gal·i·le·an[1] (gal′ə lē′ən), *adj.* of or having to do with Galilee or its people. —*n.* native or inhabitant of Galilee.

Gal·i·le·an[2] (gal′ə lē′ən), *adj.* of or having to do with Galileo.

Gal·i·lee (gal′ə lē), *n.* **1** region in N Israel that was a Roman province in the time of Christ.

Gal·i·le·o (gal′ə lē′ō; –lā′ō), *n.* 1564–1642, Italian astronomer, first to use the telescope and prove that the earth goes around the sun.

gal·i·ot (gal′i ət), *n.* **1** a small, fast galley moved with oars and sails. **2** a single-masted Dutch cargo or fishing boat. [< OF *galiote,* dim. of *galie,* ult. < Med.Gk. *galea*]

gall[1] (gôl), *n.* **1** a bitter, yellow, brown, or greenish liquid secreted by the liver and stored in the gall bladder; bile of animals. **2** gall bladder. **3** anything very bitter or harsh. **4** bitterness; hate. **5** *U.S.* too great boldness; impudence. [OE *galla*]

gall[2] (gôl), *v.* **1** make or become sore by rubbing: *the rough strap galled the horse's skin.* **2** annoy; irritate. —*n.* **1** a sore spot on the skin caused by rubbing. **2** cause of annoyance or irritation. [extended use of *gall*[1]]

gall[3] (gôl), *n.* lump or ball that forms on the leaves, stems, or roots of plants where they have been injured by insects or fungi. [< F < L *galla*]

gal·lant (*adj.* *1–3* gal′ənt; *adj.* *4* gə lant′, gal′ənt; *n.* gal′ənt, gə lant′), *adj.* **1** noble; brave; daring. **2** grand; fine; stately. **3** showy. **4** very polite and attentive to women. —*n.* **1** a spirited or courageous man. **2** man who wears showy clothes. **3** man who is very polite and attentive to women. [< OF *galant,* ppr. of *galer* make a show. See GALA.] —**gal′lant·ly,** *adv.* —**gal′lant·ness,** *n.*

gal·lant·ry (gal′ən tri), *n., pl.* **–ries. 1** the conduct of a gallant. **2** noble spirit or conduct; dashing courage. **3** great politeness and attention to women. **4** a gallant act or speech. **5** showy display.

gall bladder, sac attached to the liver, in which excess gall or bile is stored until needed.

gal·le·on (gal′i ən; gal′yən), *n.* a large, high ship, usually with three or four decks. [< Sp. *galeón* < *galea* GALLEY]

gal·ler·y (gal′ər i; gal′ri), *n., pl.* **–ler·ies. 1** a projecting upper floor in a church, theater, or hall for part of the audience; a balcony. **2** people who sit there. **3** a long, narrow room or passage; hall. **4** room or building where works of art are shown. **5** collection of works of art. **6** room or building where shooting is practiced, etc. [< Ital. *galleria*]

gal·ley (gal′i), *n., pl.* **–leys. 1** a long, narrow ship of former times having oars and sails. **2** kitchen of a ship. **3** =galley proof. [< OF *galee,* ult. < Med.Gk. *galea*]

galley proof, proof printed from type.

galley slave, 1 person compelled or condemned to row a galley. **2** drudge.

gall·fly (gôl′flī′), *n., pl.* **–flies.** insect that causes galls on plants.

Gal·lic (gal′ik), *adj.* **1** of or having to do with Gaul or its people. **2** French.

Gal·li·cism, gal·li·cism (gal′ə siz əm), *n.* a French idiom or expression.

gal·li·na·ceous (gal′ə nā′shəs), *adj.* belonging to a large group of birds that nest on the ground and fly only short distances. [< L, < *gallina* hen]

gall·ing (gôl′ing), *adj.* that galls; chafing.

gal·li·nule (gal′ə nül; –nūl), *n.* any of certain long-toed wading birds of the rail family, as the moor hen of Europe.

gal·li·um (gal′i əm), *n.* a shining, white metal, Ga, with a low melting point. It is an element similar to mercury. [< NL, ? < L *gallus* cock, trans of *Lecoq* (de Boisbaudran), the discoverer]

gal·li·vant (gal′ə vant), *v.* go about seeking pleasure; gad about. [? < *gallant*]

gall·nut (gôl′nut′), *n.* a nutlike gall on plants.

gal·lon (gal′ən), *n.* a measure for liquids, equal to 4 quarts. The U.S. gallon equals 231 cubic inches and 3.785 liters. [< OF *galon*]

gal·lop (gal′əp), *n.* **1** the fastest gait of a horse or other four-footed animal. In a gallop, all four feet are off the ground together once in each stride. **2** a ride at a gallop. **3** rapid motion; rapid progress. —*v.* **1** ride at a gallop. **2** go at a gallop. **3** go very fast; hurry. [< F *galoper* < Gmc.] —**gal′lop·er,** *n.*

gal·lows (gal′ōz), *n., pl.* **–lows·es** or **–lows. 1** a wooden frame made of a crossbar on two upright posts, used for hanging criminals. **2** hanging as a punishment. [OE *galga*]

gall·stone (gôl′stōn′), *n.* a pebblelike mass that sometimes forms in the gall bladder or its duct.

ga·lore (gə lôr′; –lōr′), *adv.* in abundance. [< Irish *go leór*]

ga·losh (gə losh′), *n.* Usually, **galoshes.** a plastic or rubber overshoe covering the ankle, worn in wet or snowy weather. Also, **golosh.** [< F *galoche*]

gals., gallons.

gal·van·ic (gal van′ik), *adj.* **1** producing an electric current by chemical action. **2** of or caused by an electric current.

gal·va·nism (gal′və niz əm), *n.* electricity produced by chemical action. [for Luigi *Galvani*]

gal·va·nize (gal′və nīz), *v.,* **–nized, –niz·ing. 1** apply an electric current to. **2** arouse suddenly; startle. **3** cover (iron or steel) with a thin coating of zinc to prevent rust. —**gal′va·ni·za′tion,** *n.* —**gal′va·niz′er,** *n.*

Gam·bi·a (gam′bi ə), *n.* republic in W Africa.

gam·bit (gam′bit), *n.* **1** way of opening a game of chess by purposely sacrificing a pawn or a piece to gain some advantage. **2** *Fig.* any action or move, esp. at the beginning of something, intended to gain an advantage. [< F < Pr. *cambi* an exchange]

gam·ble (gam′bəl), *v.,* **–bled, –bling,** *n.* —*v.* **1** play games of chance for money. **2** take a risk; take great risks in business, speculation, etc. **3** bet; wager. —*n.* a risky venture or undertaking. [prob. akin to *game,* v.] —**gam′bler,** *n.* —**gam′bling,** *n.*

gam·bol (gam′bəl), *n., v.,* **–boled, –bol·ing.** —*n.* a running and jumping about in play; caper; frolic. —*v.* frisk about; run and jump about in play. [< F *gambade* < Ital., ult. < *gamba* leg]

gam·brel (gam′brəl), *n.* gambrel roof. [< OF *gamberel* < *gambe* leg < LL *gamba*]

gambrel roof, roof having two slopes on each side. The lower slope is usually steeper than the upper one.

game¹ (gam), *n., adj.,* **gam·er, gam·est,** *v.,* **gamed, gam·ing.** —*n.* **1** way of playing; pastime; amusement. **2** things needed to play a game. **3** contest with certain rules. **4** number of points required to win. **5** plan; scheme; *we discovered his game.* **6** wild animals, birds, or fish hunted or caught for sport or for food. —*adj.* **1** having to do with game, hunting, or fishing: *game laws protect wild life.* **2** brave; plucky: *the losing team put up a game fight.* —*v.* **1** gamble. **2** manipulate (rules or a system or process) to one's advantage.

ahead of the game, doing well rather than suffering a loss, esp. financial loss.

games, athletic contests.

play games, avoid facing something; act evasively.

play the game, follow the rules; be a good sport.

the game is up, the plan or scheme has failed. [OE *gamen* joy] —**game′ly,** *adv.* —**game′ness,** *n.*

game² (gām), *adj.* lame; crippled.

game of chance, game that depends on luck, not skill.

gam·ete (gam′ēt; gə mēt′), *n.* reproductive cell capable of uniting with another to form a fertilized cell that can develop into a new plant or animal. [< NL < Gk. *gamete* wife, *gametes* husband, ult. < *gamos* marriage] —**ga·met′ic** *adj.*

ga·me·to·cyte (gə mē′tə sīt), *n.* cell that produces gametes by division.

ga·me·to·gen·e·sis (gam′ə tə jen′ə sis), *n.* formation or development of gametes.

ga·me·to·phyte (gə mē′tə fīt), *n.* part or structure producing gametes.

game warden, official whose duty it is to enforce the game laws in a certain district.

gam·in (gam′ən), *n.* a neglected boy left to roam about the streets. [< F]

gam·ing (gām′ing), *n.* the playing of games of chance for money; gambling.

gam·ma (gam′ə), *n.* **1** the third letter of the Greek alphabet (Γ, γ). **2** the third in any series or group.

gamma glob·u·lin (glob′yə lin), a constituent of the human blood. Gamma globulin contains antibodies.

gamma rays, penetrating electromagnetic radiations of very high frequency given off by radium and other radioactive substances.

gam·o·pet·al·ous (gam′ə pet′əl əs), *adj.* having the petals joined to form a tube-shaped corolla. [< Gk. *gamos* marriage + E *petal*]

gam·o·sep·al·ous (gam′ə sep′əl əs), *adj.* having the sepals joined together.

gam·ut (gam′ət), *n.* **1** the whole series of recognized musical notes. **2** the entire range of anything: *the gamut of feeling from hope to despair.* [contraction of Med.L *gamma ut* < *gamma* G, the lowest tone, + *ut,* later do.

gam·y (gām′i), *adj.,* **gam·i·er, gam·i·est. 1** having a strong taste or smell like the flesh of wild animals or birds; slightly tainted. **2** abounding in game. **3** brave; plucky. —**gam′i·ly,** *adv.* —**gam′i·ness,** *n.*

gan·der (gan′dər), *n.* a male goose. [OE *gandra*]

gang (gang), *n.* **1** group of people acting or going around together. **2** group of people working together under one foreman. **3** set of similar tools or machines arranged to work together. —*v.* form a gang.

gang up on, *Informal.* oppose or attack as a group. [OE, a going]

gang·land (gang′land′; –lənd), *n.* **1** the world of gangs or gangsters. **2** territory controlled by a gang or a gangster organization. —*adj.* of or having to do with gangland.

gan·gling (gang′gling), *adj.* awkwardly tall and slender; lank and loosely built. [appar. ult. < *gang*, v.]

gan·gli·on (gang′gli ən), *n., pl.* **-gli·a** (-gli ə), **-gli·ons** group of nerve cells forming a nerve center, esp. outside of the brain or spinal cord [< LL < Gk.]

gang·plank (gang′plangk′), *n.* a movable bridge used in getting on and off a ship, etc.

gan·grene (gang′grēn; gang grēn′), —*n.* decay of a part of a living person or animal when the blood supply is interfered with by injury, infection, freezing, etc. [< L < Gk. *gangraina*] —**gan′gre·nous,** *adj.*

gang·ster (gang′stər), *n.* member of a gang of criminals.

gang·ster·ism (gang′stə riz əm), *n.* **1** crimes committed by organized gangs. **2** crimes and activities of gangsters. **3** crime.

gang·way (gang′wā′), *n.* **1** =passageway. **2** passageway on a ship. **3** =gangplank. —*interj.* get out of the way! stand aside and make room!

gan·net (gan′it), *n.* a large, fish-eating sea bird somewhat like a pelican, but with long, pointed wings and a shorter tail. [OE *ganot*]

gan·oid (gan′oid), *adj.* of fishes, having hard scales of bone overlaid with enamel. —*n.* a ganoid fish. [< Gk. *ganos* brightness]

gant·let[1] (gônt′lit; gant′-; gänt′-), *n.* punishment in which the offender had to run between two rows of men who struck him with clubs or other weapons as he passed. [< Sw. *gatlopp* < *gata* lane + *lopp* course]

gant·let[2] (gônt′lit; gant′-; gänt′-) *n.* =gauntlet[1].

gap (gap), *n., v.,* **gapped, gap·ping.** —*n.* **1** a broken place; opening. **2** an empty part; unfilled space; blank. **3** a wide difference of opinion, character, etc. **4** a pass through mountains. —*v.* make a gap. [< Scand.; akin to GAPE]

gape (gāp; gap), *v.,* **gaped, gap·ing,** *n.* —*v.* **1** open wide. **2** open the mouth wide; yawn. **3** stare with the mouth open. —*n.* **1** a wide opening. **2** act of opening the mouth wide; yawning. **3** an openmouthed stare. [< Scand. *gapa*]

gar (gär), *n., pl.* **gars** or (*esp. collectively*) **gar.** =garfish. [for *garfish*]

G.A.R., Grand Army of the Republic.

ga·rage (gə räzh′; -räj′), *n., v.,* **-raged, -rag·ing.** —*n.* place where automobiles are kept; shop for repairing automobiles. —*v.* put or keep in a garage. [< F, < *garer* put in shelter]

garage sale, private sale of household items, including furniture, dishes, appliances, etc., often held in a garage or on a lawn; yard sale.

garb (gärb), *n.* **1** way one is dressed; clothing. **2** outward covering, form, or

appearance. —*v.* clothe. [< F < Ital. *garbo* grace]

gar·bage (gär′bij), *n.* **1** waste animal or vegetable matter from a kitchen, store, etc.; scraps of food to be thrown away. **2** *Informal. Fig.* anything worthless or contemptible.

gar·ban·zo (gär bän′zō), *n., pl.* **-zos.** =chickpea. [< Sp. *garbanzo*]

gar·ble (gär′bəl), *v.,* **-bled, -bling.** make unfair or misleading selections from (facts, statements, writings, etc.); omit parts of in order to misrepresent. [< Ital. < Ar. *gharbala* sift, prob. < LL *cribellare,* ult < *cribrum* sieve] —**gar′bler,** *n.*

gar·den (gär′dən), *n.* **1** piece of ground used for growing vegetables, herbs, flowers, or fruits. **2** park or place where people go for amusements or to see things that are displayed. —*v.* take care of a garden; make a garden; work in a garden. —*adj.* **1** growing or grown in a garden; for a garden. **2** common; ordinary. [< OF *gardin* < Gmc.] —**gar′den·er,** *n.* —**gar′den·like′,** *adj.*

gar·de·nia (gär dē′nyə; -ni ə), *n.* **1** a fragrant, roselike, white flower with waxy petals. **2** shrub having these flowers. [< NL; named for A. *Garden,* botanist]

Gar·field (gär′fēld), *n.* **James,** 1831–81, the 20th president of the United States, in 1881.

gar·fish (gär′fish′), *n., pl.* **-fish·es** or (*esp. collectively*) **-fish.** fish with a long, slender body and long, narrow jaws. [< *gar* (OE *gar* spear) + *fish*]

Gar·gan·tu·a (gär gan′chù ə), *n.* a goodnatured giant in a satire by Rabelais.

Gar·gan·tu·an or **gar·gan·tu·an** (gär gan′chù ən), *adj.* huge; gigantic; over-sized.

gar·gle (gär′gəl), *v.,* **-gled, -gling,** *n.* —*v.* wash or rinse (the throat) with a liquid kept in motion by the breath. —*n.* liquid used for gargling. [prob. imit.]

gar·goyle (gär′goil), *n.* spout for carrying off rain water, ending in a grotesque head that projects from the gutter of a building. [< OF *gargouille.* Cf. L *gargulio* gullet.] —**gar′goyled,** *adj.*

gar·ish (gãr′ish), *adj.* unpleasantly bright; glaring; showy; gaudy. [ult. < obs. *gaure* stare] —**gar′ish·ly,** *adv.* —**gar′ish·ness,** *n.*

gar·land (gär′lənd), *n.* **1** wreath of flowers, leaves, etc. **2** book of short literary selections, esp. poems. —*v.* decorate with garlands. [< OF *garlande*]

gar·lic (gär′lik), *n.* **1** plant like an onion whose strong-smelling bulb is composed of small sections called cloves. **2** bulb or clove of this plant, used to season meats, salads, etc. [OE *gārlēac* < *gār* spear + *lēac* leek] —**gar′lick·y,** *adj.*

gar·ment (gär′mənt), *n.* **1** article of clothing. **2** an outer covering. [< OF *garnement* < *garnir* fit out. See GARNISH.] —**gar′ment·less,** *adj.*

garment bag, bag of plastic or other flexible fabric with a zipper opening, for protecting clothes while traveling or in storage.

gar·ner (gär′nər), *v.* gather and store away. [< n.] —*n.* storehouse for grain. [< OF < L *granarium* < *granum* grain]

gar·net (gär′nit), *n.* **1** a hard, vitreous silicate mineral occurring in a number of varieties. A deep-red, variety is used as a gem. **2** a deep red. —*adj.* deep-red. [< OF *grenat* < Med.L *granatum* < L, pomegranate] —**gar′net·like′,** *adj.*

gar·nish (gär′nish), *n.* **1** something laid on or around food as a decoration. **2** decoration; trimming. —*v.* **1** decorate (food). **2** decorate; trim. [< OF *garnir* provide, defend < Gmc.] —**gar′nish·er,** *n.*

gar·nish·ee (gär′nish ē′), *v.,* **-nish·eed, -nish·ee·ing,** *n.* —*v.* attach (money or property) by legal authority in payment of a debt. —*n.* person served with a notice of garnishment.

gar·nish·ment (gär′nish mənt), *n.* **1** decoration; trimming. **2** a legal notice warning a person to hold in his possession property that belongs to the defendant in a lawsuit until the plaintiff's claims have been settled.

gar·ni·ture (gär′nə chər), *n.* decoration; trimming; garnish.

gar·ret (gar′it), *n.* space in a house just below a sloping roof; attic. [< OF *garite* < *garir* defend < Gmc.]

gar·ri·son (gar′ə sən), *n.* **1** soldiers stationed in a fort, town, etc., to defend it. **2** place that has a garrison. —*v.* **1** station soldiers in (a fort, town, etc.) to defend it. **2** occupy (a fort, town, etc.) as a garrison. [< OF *garison* < *garir.* See GARRET.]

gar·rote, gar·rotte, ga·rotte (gə rōt′; -rot′), *n., v.,* **-rot·ed, -rot·ing; -rot·ted, -rot·ting.** —*n.* **1** a Spanish method of executing a person by strangulation with an iron collar. **2** the iron collar used for this. **3** a strangling and robbery. —*v.* **1** execute by garroting. **2** strangle and rob. [< Sp., stick for twisting cord] —**gar·rot′er, gar·rot′ter, ga·rot′ter,** *n.*

gar·ru·lous (gar′ə ləs; -yə-), *adj.* **1** talking too much about trifles. **2** wordy. [< L, < *garrire* chatter] —**gar·ru′li·ty, gar′ru·lous·ness,** *n.* —**gar′ru·lous·ly,** *adv.*

gar·ter (gär′tər), *n.* **1** band or strap to hold up a stocking or sock. **2 Garter, Order of the. a** oldest and most prestigious knighthood in Great Britain, established about 1349. **b** its badge. —*v.* fasten with a garter. [< OF *gartier* < *garet* bend of the knee]

garter snake, a small, harmless, brownish or greenish snake with long yellow stripes.

gas (gas), *n., pl.* **gas·es,** *v.,* **gassed, gassing.** —*n.* **1** any fluid substance that can expand without limit; not a solid or liquid. **2** any mixture of gases that can be burned, esp. that obtained from coal and other substances. **3** air. **4** substance used in warfare that poisons, suffocates, etc. **5** gasoline. —*v.* **1** attack with gas in warfare. **2** supply with gasoline. **3** *Informal.* talk idly.

gas up, fill a tank with gasoline.

step on the gas, accelerate; go faster. [alter. of Gk. *chaos* chaos; coined by J. B. van Helmont, physicist] —**gas′less,** *adj.*

Gas·con (gas′kən), *n.* native of Gascony. —*adj.* of Gascony or its people.

Gas·co·ny (gas′kə ni), *n.* region in SW France.

gas·e·ous (gas′i əs), *adj.* in the form of gas; of or like a gas. —**gas′e·ous·ness,** *n.*

gas guzzler, automobile or other vehicle that burns more than an average amount of gasoline. —**gas-′guz′zling,** *adj.*

gash (gash), *n.* a long, deep cut or wound. [< *v.*] —*v.* make a long, deep cut or wound in. [earlier *garsh* < OF *garser* scarify]

gas·i·fy (gas′ə fī), *v.,* **-fied, -fy·ing.** change into a gas. —**gas′i·fi′a·ble,** *adj.* —**gas′i·fi·ca′tion,** *n.* —**gas′i·fi′er,** *n.*

gas·ket (gas′kit), *n.* ring or strip of rubber, metal, plaited hemp, etc., packed around a piston, pipe joint, etc., to keep steam, gas, etc., from escaping.

gas mask, mask with a filter containing chemicals to neutralize poisonous gases, etc.

gas·o·line (gas′ə lēn; gas′ə lēn′), *n.* a colorless liquid that evaporates and burns very easily, made by distilling petroleum, used chiefly as a fuel.

gasp (gasp; gäsp), *n.* a catching of the breath with open mouth, as if out of breath or surprised. —*v.* **1** catch the breath with difficulty; breathe with gasps. **2** utter with gasps. [< Scand. *geispa* yawn]

gas·ser (gas′ər), *n.* **1** natural gas well or boring. **2** *Slang.* something remarkable.

gas·sy (gas′i), *adj.,* **-si·er, -si·est. 1** full of gas; containing gas. **2** like gas.

gas·tric (gas′trik), *adj.* of or near the stomach. [< Gk. *gaster* stomach]

gastric juice, the digestive fluid secreted by glands in the lining of the stomach. It contains pepsin and other enzymes and hydrochloric acid.

gas·trin (gas′trin), *n.* hormone that promotes secretion of gastric juice.

gas·tri·tis (gas trī′tis), *n.* inflammation of the stomach, esp. of its mucous membrane. —**gas·trit′ic,** *adj.*

gas·tro·en·ter·i·tis (gas′trō en′tə rī′tis), *n.* inflammation of the lining of the stomach and intestines.

gas·tro·en·ter·ol·o·gy (gas′tro en′tə rol′ə jē), *n.* a branch of medicine that deals with disorders and function of the stomach and intestines. —**gas′tro·en′ter·ol′o·gist,** *n.*

gas·tron·o·my (gas tron′ə mi), *n.* art or science of good eating. [< F < Gk., < *gaster* stomach + *nomos* law] —**gas′tro·nom′ic, gas′tro·nom′i·cal,** *adj.* —**gas′tro·nom′i·cal·ly,** *adv.* —**gas·tron′o·mist,** *n.*

gas·tro·pod (gas′trə pod), *n.* mollusk with a disklike organ of locomotion on the ventral surface of its body. —*adj.* of such mollusks. [< NL, < Gk. *gaster* stomach + *-podos* footed < *pous* foot]

gas·tru·la (gas′trŭ lə), *n., pl.* **-lae** (-lē). state in the development of all many-celled animals, when the embryo is usually saclike and composed of two layers of cells. [< NL, dim. of Gk. *gaster* stomach] —**gas′tru·lar,** *adj.*

gas turbine, turbine powered by the gas obtained from combustion of a fuel.

gas turbine engine, engine that obtains power from a gas turbine, as a jet engine.

gat (gat), *n. Slang.* a revolver or pistol. [for *Gatling gun*]

gate (gāt), *n.* **1** a movable part or frame to close an opening in a wall or fence. **2** =gateway. **3** way to get something. **4** door, valve, etc., to stop or control the flow of water in a pipe, dam, lock, etc. **5** number of people who pay to see a contest, exhibition, etc. **6** amount of money received from them. [OE *gatu,* pl. of *geat*] —**gate′less,** *adj.* —**gate′like′,** *adj.* —**gate′man,** *n.*

gate-crash (gāt′crash′), *v., Informal.* attend an event without an invitation or a ticket.

gate crasher, person who attends a function, party, etc. without an invitation ticket; uninvited guest.

gated community, private housing development with access controlled by a security system.

gate·way (gāt′wā′), *n.* **1** an opening in a wall or fence where a gate is. **2** way to go in or out; way to get to something.

gath·er (gath′ər), *v.* **1** bring into one place or group. **2** come together; assemble. **3** pick and collect; take: *farmers gather their crops.* **4** get or gain little by little: *gather speed.* **5** put together in the mind; conclude; infer. **6** pull together in folds: *gather a skirt to fit at the waist.* —*n.* one of the little folds between stitches when cloth is gathered.

gather up, pick up. [OE *gaderian* < *geador* together] —**gath′er·a·ble,** *adj.* —**gath′er·er,** *n.*

gath·er·ing (gath′ər ing), *n.* **1** act of one that gathers. **2** meeting; assembly; party; crowd.

gauche (gōsh), *adj.* awkward; clumsy; tactless. [< F, left] —**gauche′ly,** *adv.* —**gauche′ness,** *n.*

gau·che·rie (gō′shə rē′), *n.* **1** awkwardness; tactlessness. **2** an awkward or tactless movement, act, etc.

gau·cho (gou′chō), *n., pl.* **-chos.** cowboy of mixed Spanish and Indian descent in the southern plains of South America. [< Sp.]

gaud (gôd), *n.* a cheap, showy ornament. [appar. < AF, < *gaudir* rejoice < L *gaudere*]

gaud·y (gôd′i), *adj.,* **gaud·i·er, gaud·i·est.** too bright and gay to be in good taste; showy but cheap. —**gaud′i·ly,** *adv.* —**gaud′i·ness,** *n.*

gauge (gāj), *n., v.,* **gauged, gaug·ing.** —*n.* **1** standard measure; scale of standard measurements; measure. **2** instrument for measuring. **3** means of estimating or judging. **4** size; capacity; extent. —*v.* **1** measure accurately; find the size of with a gauge. **2** estimate; judge. Also, **gage.** [< OF *gauger*] —**gauge′a·ble,** *adj.*

Gaul (gôl), *n.* **1** an ancient country in W Europe. It included France, Belgium, the Netherlands, and parts of Switzerland, Germany, and N Italy. **2** one of the Celtic inhabitants of ancient Gaul. **3** a Frenchman.

Gaul·ish (gô′lish), *adj.* of or having to do with ancient Gaul or its people. —*n.* Celtic language of the ancient Gauls.

gaunt (gônt; gänt), *adj.* **1** very thin and bony; with hollow eyes and a starved look. **2** looking bare and gloomy; desolate; grim. —**gaunt′ly,** *adv.* —**gaunt′ness,** *n.*

gaunt·let¹ (gônt′lit; gänt′-), *n.* **1** a stout, heavy glove, usually of leather covered with plates of iron or steel, that was part of a knight's armor. **2** a stout, heavy glove with a wide, flaring cuff. **3** the wide, flaring cuff. Also, **gantlet.**

run the gauntlet, a run between two rows of men who strike the victim as he passes. **b** *Fig.* endure harsh criticism or unfriendly attacks from all sides.

throw down the gauntlet, challenge. [< OF *gantelet,* dim. of *gant* glove < Gmc.] —**gaunt′let·ed,** *adj.*

gaunt·let² (gônt′lit; gänt′-), *n.* =gantlet¹.

Gau·ta·ma (gô′tə mə; gou′-), *n.* Buddha.

gauze (gôz), *n.* **1** a very thin, light cloth, easily seen through. **2** a thin haze. [< F *gaze;* named for *Gaza,* Palestine] —**gauze′like′,** *adj.*

gauz·y (gôz′i), *adj.,* **gauz·i·er, gauz·i·est,** like gauze; thin and light as gauze. —**gauz′i·ly,** *adv.* —**gauz′i·ness,** *n.*

gave (gāv), *v.* pt. of **give.**

gav·el (gav′əl), *n.* a small mallet used by a presiding officer to signal for attention or order. [OE *gafeluc* spear < Welsh]

ga·vi·al (gā′vi əl), *n.* a large crocodile of India that has a long, slender snout. [< F < Hind. *ghariyāl*]

ga·votte, ga·vot (gə vot′), *n.* **1** dance like a minuet but much more lively. **2** music for it. [< F < Pr. *gavoto* < *Gavots* Alpine people]

gawk (gôk), *n.* an awkward person; clumsy fool. —*v. Informal.* stare rudely or stupidly. [? < dial. *gaulick*(*-handed*) left(*-handed*)]

gawk·y (gôk′i), *adj.,* **gawk·i·er, gawk·i·est.** awkward; clumsy. —**gawk′i·ly,** *adv.* —**gawk′i·ness,** *n.*

gay (gā), *adj.,* **gay·er, gay·est. 1** happy and full of fun; merry. **2** bright-colored; showy. **3** homosexual. —*n.* a homosexual. [< F *gai*] —**gay′ness,** *n.*

gay·e·ty (gā′ə ti), *n., pl.* **-ties.** =gaiety.

gay·ly (gā′li), *adv.* =gaily.

gaze (gāz), *v.,* **gazed, gaz·ing,** *n.* —*v.* look long and steadily. —*n.* a long, steady look. [cf. Scand. (dial. Norw.) *gasa*] —**gaz′er,** *n.*

ga·ze·bo (gə zē′bō), *n., pl.* **-bos** or **-boes. 1** summerhouse, balcony, etc., that affords a fine view. **2** screened structure, usually with a canvas roof, for eating and relaxing outdoors. [? < *Egaze* + < *-bo* I shall]

ga·zelle (gə zel′), *n.* a small, graceful antelope of Africa and Asia that has soft, lustrous eyes. [< F < Ar. *ghazāl*] —**ga·zelle′like′**, *adj.*

ga·zette (gə zet′), *n., v.,* **-zet·ted, -zet·ting.** —*n.* **1** a newspaper. **2** an official government journal containing lists of appointments, promotions, etc. —*v.* publish, list, or announce in a gazette. [< F < Ital. *gazzetta*, orig., coin; from price of paper]

gaz·et·teer (gaz′ə tir′), *n.* dictionary of geographical names.

gaz·pa·cho (gäs pä′chō), *n.* spicy soup of pureed tomatoes, peppers, onions, etc., served cold. [< Sp. *gazpacho*]

G clef, the treble clef.

Gd, gadolinium.

GDP gross domestic product.

Ge, germanium.

gear (gir), *n.* **1** wheel having teeth that fit into the teeth of another wheel of the same kind. **2** arrangement of fixed and moving parts for transmitting or changing motion; mechanism; machinery. **3** working order; adjustment: *chimes on the clock are out of gear; plans in gear for a celebration.* **4** equipment needed for some purpose. —*v.* **1** connect by gears. **2** fit or work together; mesh. **3** provide with gear; equip.

in gear, a connected to the motor. **b** *Fig.* in working order.

out of gear, a not connected to the motor. **b** *Fig.* not in working order.

shift gears, a change from one gear to another. **b** *Fig.* change one's attitude or approach to something. [appar. < Scand. *gervi, görvi*] —**gear′less,** *adj.*

gear·ing (gir′ing), *n.* set of gears, chains, etc., for transmitting motion or power; gears.

gear·shift (gir′shift′), *n.* device for connecting a motor, etc., to any of several sets of gears.

gear·wheel (gir′hwēl′), *n.* wheel having teeth that fit into the teeth of another wheel of the same kind; cogwheel.

geck·o (gek′ō), *n., pl.* **geck·os, geck·oes.** a small, harmless, insect-eating lizard with suction pads on its feet so that it can walk on ceilings, walls, etc. [< Malay *gēkoq;* imit.]

GED, General Educational Development (test).

gee (jē), *interj.* exclamation or mild oath.

geese (gēs), *n.* pl. of **goose.**

Gei·ger counter (gī′gər), device which detects and counts ionizing particles. It is used to measure radioactivity, test cosmic-ray particles, etc. [after H. *Geiger,* physicist]

gei·sha (gā′shə; gē′-), *n., pl.* **-sha, -shas.** Japanese young woman trained as an entertainer and companion for men. [< Jap.]

gel (jel), *n., v.,* **gelled, gel·ling.** —*n.* **1** a jellylike or solid material formed from a colloidal solution. **2** jellylike preparation for holding the hair in place. —*v.* form a gel. Egg white gels when it is cooked. [for *gelatin*]

gel·a·tin (jel′ə tən), **gel·a·tine** (-tən; -tēn), *n.* **1** an odorless, tasteless substance obtained by boiling animal tissues, bones, hoofs, etc. used in making jellied desserts, glue, etc. **2** any of various vegetable substances having similar properties. [< F < Ital., < *gelata* jelly < L *gelare* freeze] —**gel′a·tin·like′,** *adj.*

ge·lat·i·nous (jə lat′ə nəs), *adj.* **1** jellylike. **2** of or containing gelatin. —**ge·lat′i·nous·ly,** *adv.* —**ge·lat′i·nous·ness,** *n.*

ge·la·to (jə lä′tō), *n., pl.* **-ti** (-tē). rich and creamy Italian ice cream. [< Ital. *gelato* < *gelare* to freeze < L *gelāre*]

geld (geld), *v.,* **geld·ed** or **gelt, geld·ing.** remove the male glands of (a horse or other animal); castrate. [< Scand. *gelda* castrate]

geld·ing (gel′ding), *n.* a gelded horse or other animal.

gem (jem), *n., v.,* **gemmed, gem·ming.** —*n.* **1** a precious stone; jewel. **2** *Fig.* person or thing that is very precious, beautiful, etc. —*v.* set or adorn with gems, or as if with gems. [< F < I. *gemma* gem, bud] —**gem′like′,** *adj.*

gem·i·nate (jem′ə nāt), *v.,* **-nat·ed, -nat·ing,** *adj.* —*v.* make or become double; combine in pairs. —*adj.* combined in a pair or pairs; coupled. [< L, < *geminus* twin] —**gem′i·nate·ly,** *adv.* —**gem′i·na′tion,** *n.*

Gem·i·ni (jem′ə nī), *n.pl., gen.* **Gem·i·no·rum** (jem′ə nô′rəm; -nō′-). **1** a northern constellation in the zodiac containing two bright stars. **2** the third sign of the zodiac; the Twins. **3** Castor and Pollux, the twin sons of Zeus.

gem·mate (jem′āt), *v.,* **-mat·ed, -mat·ing.** put forth buds; reproduce by budding.

gem·ol·o·gy (je mol′ə ji), *n.* science of gems, including their uses and characteristics. —**gem·ol′o·gist,** *n.*

gems·bok (gemz′bok′), *n.* a large antelope of South Africa, having long, straight horns and a long, tufted tail. [< Afrikaans < G, < *gemse* chamois + *bock* buck]

Gen., **1** General. **2** Genesis.

gen., **1** gender. **2** general. **3** genitive.

gen·darme (zhän′därm), *n., pl.* **-darmes** (-därmz). policeman with military training. [< F, < *gens d'armes* men of arms]

gen·der (jen′dər), *n.* **1 a** in many languages, the grouping of nouns into a series of classes, such as masculine, feminine, neuter, etc. **b** one of such classes. **2** sex: *male gender.* [< OF < L *genus* kind, sort]

gene (jēn), *n.* element of a chromosome transmitted from parent to offspring and composed mainly of DNA. Genes are carriers of hereditary traits that determine the characteristics of offspring. [< Gk. *genea* breed, kind]

ge·ne·al·o·gy (jē′ni al′ə ji; jen′i-; -ol′-), *n., pl.* **-gies.** **1** account of the descent of a person or family from an ancestor or ancestors. **2** descent of a person or family from an ancestor; pedigree; lineage, **3** the making or investigation of such accounts; study of pedigrees. [< L < Gk., ult. < *genea,* generation + *-logos* treating of] —**ge′ne·a·log′i·cal, ge′ne·a·log′ic,** *adj.* —**ge′ne·a·log′i·cal·ly,** *adv.* —**ge′ne·al′o·gist,** *n.*

gene mapping, the process of determining the positions of genes on a molecule of DNA.

gene pool, all of the genes of a specific species, considered as a whole or in relation to a particular area.

gen·er·a (jen′ər ə), *n.* pl. of **genus.**

gen·er·al (jen′ər əl; jen′rəl), *adj.* **1** of all; for all; from all: *the general welfare.* **2** widespread: *general interest in sports.* **3** not special: *a general reader.* **4** not detailed; sufficient for practical purposes: *general instructions.* **5** forming a group: *"cat" is a general term for cats, lions, and tigers.* **6** in chief; of highest rank: *the postmaster general.* —*n.* **1** officer ranking above a colonel. **2** head of a religious order.

in general, usually; for the most part. [< L *generalis* of a (whole) class < *genus* class, race] —**gen′er·al·ness,** *n.*

General Assembly, 1 legislature of certain states of the United States. **2** the legislative body of the United Nations.

gen·er·al·is·si·mo (jen′ər əl is′ə mō; jen′rəl-), *n., pl.* **-mos.** commander in chief of all or several armies in the field. [< Ital., superlative of *generale* general]

gen·er·al·i·ty (jen′ər al′ə ti), *n., pl.* **-ties. 1** a general statement; word or phrase not definite enough to have much meaning or value. **2** general quality or condition. **3** a general principle or rule. **4** the greater part; main body; mass.

gen·er·al·ize (jen′ər əl īz; jen′rəl-), *v.,* **-ized, -iz·ing. 1** make into one general statement. **2** infer (a general rule) from particular facts. **3** talk indefinitely or vaguely; use generalities. **4** make general; bring into general use or knowledge. —**gen′er·al·i·za′tion,** *n.* —**gen′er·al·iz′er,** *n.*

gen·er·al·ly (jen′ər əl i; jen′rəl i), *adv.* **1** in most cases; usually. **2** for the most part; widely. **3** in a general way; without giving details.

general officer, in the military, an officer holding a rank above colonel.

general practitioner, a physician who has not trained in a medical specialty.

gen·er·al·ship (jen′ər əl ship′; jen′rəl-), *n.* **1** ability as a general; skill in commanding an army. **2** skillful management; leadership. **3** rank, commission, authority, or term of office of a general.

general staff, group of high army officers who make plans for war or national defense.

general store, store that sells a variety of goods, as clothing, hardware, groceries, etc.

gen·er·ate (jen′ər āt), v., **–at·ed, –at·ing. 1** produce; cause to be: *friction generates heat.* **2** produce (offspring). [< L, < *genus* race]

gen·er·a·tion (jen′ər ā′shən), n. **1** all the people born about the same time. **2** time from the birth of one generation to the birth of the next generation; about 20–30 years. **3** one step or degree in the descent of a family. **4** production: *generation of electricity.* **5** descent; genealogy. —**gen′er·a′tive,** *adj.*

generation gap, differences in attitudes and values between one generation and another, as between parents and their children.

gen·er·a·tor (jen′ər ā′tər), n. **1** machine that changes mechanical energy into electrical energy; dynamo. **2** person or thing that generates.

ge·ner·ic (jə ner′ik), adj. **1** applied to, or referring to, a group or class; general. **2** having to do with a class or group of similar things; inclusive. **3** not registered as a trademark: *generic drugs.* —**ge·ner′i·cal·ly,** *adv.*

gen·er·os·i·ty (jen′ər os′ə ti), n., pl. **–ties. 1** a being generous; willingness to share with others; unselfishness. **2** nobleness of mind; absence of meanness. **3** a generous act.

gen·er·ous (jen′ər əs), adj. **1** willing to share with others; unselfish. **2** having or showing a noble mind; willing to forgive; not mean. **3** large; plentiful. **4** fertile: *generous fields.* [< L *generosus* of noble birth < *genus* race, stock] —**gen′er·ous·ly,** *adv.* —**gen′er·ous·ness,** *n.*

Gen·e·sis (jen′ə sis), n. **1** the first book of the Old Testament, that gives an account of the creation of the world. **2 genesis,** origin; creation. [< L < Gk.]

gen·et (jen′it), n. =jennet.

gene therapy, treatment of inherited disorders by replacement of the defective genes which cause them.

ge·net·ic (jə net′ik), adj. **1** having to do with origin and natural growth. **2** of or having to do with genetics. [< Gk. *genetikos* < *genesis* origin, creation] —**ge·net′i·cal·ly,** *adv.*

genetic code, combinations of nucleotides occurring in the DNA or RNA of a chromosome, which determines hereditary characteristics.

genetic engineering, alteration of genetic material to change particular characteristics.

genetic fingerprint, =DNA fingerprint.

ge·net·ics (jə net′iks), n. science dealing with the principles of heredity and variation in animals and plants. —**ge·net′i·cist** n.

Geneva Convention, agreement between nations providing for the neutrality of the members and buildings of the medical departments on battlefields. It was first formulated at Geneva, Switzerland, in 1864.

Gen·ghis Khan (jeng′gis kän′), 1162–1227, Mongol conqueror of C Asia.

gen·ial (jēn′yəl), adj. **1** smiling and pleasant; cheerful and friendly: *a genial welcome.* **2** helping growth; pleasantly warming; comforting: *genial sunshine.* [< L *genialis,* lit., belonging to the GENIUS] —**ge′ni·al′i·ty, gen′ial·ness,** n. —**gen′ial·ly,** *adv.*

ge·nie (jē′ni), n. spirit; jinni. [< F *génie*]

gen·i·tal (jen′ə təl), adj. having to do with reproduction or the sex organs. [< L *genitalis,* ult. < *gignere* beget]

gen·i·tals (jen′ə təlz), n.pl. the external sex organs.

gen·i·tive (jen′ə tiv), —n. **1** case in certain languages showing possession, source, origin, etc. **2** word or construction in this case. —adj. of this case; in this case; having to do with its forms or constructions. [< L *genitivus* of origin] —**gen′i·ti′val,** adj. —**gen′i·ti′val·ly,** *adv.*

gen·ius (jēn′yəs; jē′ni əs), n., pl. **gen·ius·es** for 1–4, **ge·ni·i** (jē′ni ī) for 5. **1** very great natural power of mind. **2** person having such power. **3** great natural ability of some special kind: *genius for acting.* **4** the special character or spirit of a person, nation, age, language, etc. **5** either of two spirits, one good and one evil, supposed to influence a person′s fate. [< L, tutelary spirit, male generative power]

gen·o·cide (jen′ə sīd), n. systematic extermination of a cultural or racial group. [< Gk. *genos* race + E *–cide* killing < L *caedere* to kill; coined by R. Lemkinn in 1944] —**gen′o·cid′al,** adj.

gen·ome (jē′nōm), n. all of the genetic material contained in the chromosomes of a particular organism: *the human genome.* —**ge·nom′ic,** adj.

gen·o·type (jē′nō tīp), n. genetic makeup of an organism, as distinguished from its outward appearance. —**gen′o·typ′ic, gen′o·typ′i·cal,** adj.

gen·re (zhän′rə), n. **1** kind; sort; style. **2** style or kind of painting, etc., that shows scenes from ordinary life. [< F < L *genus* kind]

gent (jent), n. man; gentleman.

gen·teel (jen tēl′), adj. **1** belonging or suited to polite society. **2** polite; well-bred; fashionable. [< F *gentil* < L *gentilis.* Doublet of GENTILE, GENTLE.] —**gen·teel′ly,** adv. —**gen·teel′ness,** n.

gen·tian (jen′shən), n. plant with funnel-shaped, usually blue flowers, stemless leaves, and bitter juice. [< L *gentiana;* said to be named for *Gentius,* king of Illyria (ancient country on the Adriatic)]

gen·tile, Gen·tile (jen′tīl), n. **1** person who is not a Jew. **2** heathen; pagan.

—adj. **1** not Jewish. **2** heathen; pagan. [< LL *gentilis* foreign < L, of a people, national. Doublet of GENTEEL, GENTLE.]

gen·til·i·ty (jen til′ə ti), n., pl. **–ties. 1** gentle birth; membership in the aristocracy or upper class. **2** good manners. **3** refinement.

gen·tle (jen′təl), adj., **–tler, –tlest,** v., **–tled, –tling.** —adj. **1** not severe, rough, or violent; mild: *a gentle tap.* **2** soft; low: *a gentle sound.* **3** moderate: *a gentle wind.* **4** kindly; friendly: *a gentle disposition.* **5** easily handled or managed: *a gentle dog.* **6** of good family; wellborn. **7** refined; polite. —v. tame (a horse). [< OF < L *gentilis* of the (same) family, national < *gens* family, nation. Doublet of GENTEEL, GENTILE.] —**gen′tle·ness,** n. —**gen′tly,** adv.

gen·tle·folk (jen′təl fōk′), **gen·tle·folks** (–fōks′), n.pl. people of good family and social position.

gen·tle·man (jen′təl mən), n., pl. **–men. 1** man of good family and social position. **2** man who is honorable and well-bred. **3** (as a polite term) any man. —**gen′tle·man·like′,** adj.

gen·tle·man·ly (jen′təl mən li), adj. like a gentleman; suitable for a gentleman; polite; well-bred. —**gen′tle·man·li·ness,** n.

gentleman′s agreement, agreement binding as a matter of honor, not legally.

gen·tle·wom·an (jen′təl wům′ən), n., pl. **–wom·en. 1** woman of good family and social position. **2** a well-bred woman; lady. —**gen′tle·wom′an·ly,** adj. —**gen′tle·wom′an·li·ness,** n.

gen·try (jen′tri), n. **1** people of good family and social position. **2** people of any particular class. [alter. of *gentrice* < OF *genterise,* ult. < *gentil* GENTLE]

gen·u·flect (jen′yů flekt), v. bend the knee as an act of reverence or worship. [< Med.L, < L *genu* knee + *flectere* bend] —**gen′u·flec′tor,** n.

gen·u·flec·tion (jen′yů flek′shən), n. a bending of the knee as an act of reverence or worship.

gen·u·ine (jen′yů ən), adj. **1** actually being what it seems or is claimed to be; real; true. **2** without pretense; sincere; frank. [< L *genuinus,* native, ult. < *gignere* beget] —**gen′u·ine·ly,** adv. —**gen′u·ine·ness,** n.

ge·nus (jē′nəs), n., pl. **gen·er·a** (jen′ər a), **ge·nus·es. 1** kind; sort; class. **2** group of related animals or plants ranking below a family and above a species. The scientific name of an animal or plant consists of the genus written with a capital letter and the species written with a small letter.

geo– combining form. **1** earth; of the earth, as in *geocentric.* **2** geology, as in *geophysics.* **3** geographical, as in *geopolitics.*

ge·o·cen·tric (jē′ō sen′trik), adj. **1** as viewed or measured from the earth′s center. **2** having or representing the earth as a center. [< *geo*– earth (< Gk. *ge*) + Gk. *kentron* center] —**ge′o·cen′tri·cal·ly,** *adv.*

ge·od·e·sy (ji od′ə si), **ge·o·det·ics** (jē′ə det′iks), *n.* branch of applied mathematics dealing with the shape and dimensions of the earth, the determination of the shape and area of large tracts on its surface, variations in terrestrial gravity, and the exact position of geographical points. [< NL < Gk. *geodaisia* < *ge* earth + *daiein* divide] —**ge′o·des′ic, ge′o·des′i·cal,** *adj.* —**ge·od′e·sist,** *n.*

ge·o·det·ic (jē′ə det′ik), *adj.* having to do with geodesy. —**ge′o·det′i·cal·ly,** *adv.*

ge·og·ra·phy (jē og′rə fi), *n., pl.* –**phies.** 1 study of the earth's surface, climate, continents, countries, peoples, industries, and products. 2 the surface features of a place or region. [< L < Gk., < *ge* earth + *graphein* describe] —**ge·og′ra·pher,** *n.* —**ge′o·graph′i·cal, ge′o·graph′ic,** *adj.* —**ge′o·graph′i·cal·ly,** *adv.*

geol., geology; geologic.

ge·ol·o·gy (ji ol′ə ji), *n., pl.* –**gies.** 1 science that deals with the earth's crust, the layers of which it is composed, and their history. 2 features of the earth's crust in a place or region; rocks, rock formation, etc., of a particular area. [< NL, < Gk. *ge* earth + *–logos* treating of] —**ge′o·log′ic, ge′o·log′i·cal,** *adj.* —**ge′o·log′i·cal·ly,** *adv.* —**ge·ol′o·gist,** *n.*

geom., geometry; geometric.

ge·om·e·tri·cian (ji om′ə trish′ən; jē′əm ə), *n.* person trained in geometry.

geometric progression, also **geometrical progression.** =progression (def. 2).

ge·om·e·trid (ji om′ə trid), *n.* any of a group of gray or greenish moths with slender bodies, whose larvae ar called measuring worms or inchworms.

ge·om·e·try (ji om′ə tri), *n.* branch of mathematics that deals with lines, angles, surfaces, and solids. Geometry includes the definition, comparison, and measurement of squares, triangles, circles, cubes, cones, spheres, etc. [< L < Gk., < *ge* earth + *–metres* measurer] —**ge′o·met′ric, ge′o·met′ri·cal,** *adj.* —**ge′o·met′ri·cal·ly,** *adv.*

ge·o·phys·ics (jē′ō fiz′iks), *n.* science dealing with the relations between the features of the earth and the forces that produce them. —**ge′o·phys′i·cist,** *n.*

ge·o·po·lit·i·cal (jē′ō pə lit′ə kəl), *adj.* pertaining to or involved in geopolitics. —**ge′o·po·lit′i·cal·ly,** *adv.* —**ge′o·pol·i·ti′cian,** *n.*

ge·o·pol·i·tics (jē′ō pol′ə tiks), *n.* study of government and its policies as affected by physical geography.

George (jôrj), *n.* 1 **Saint,** died A.D. 303?, Christian martyr, the patron saint of England. 2 **III,** 1738–1820, king of England, 1760–1820.

Geor·gia (jôr′jə), *n.* a S state of the United States. —**Geor′gian,** *adj., n.*

ge·o·sci·ence (jē′ō sī′əns), *n.* any science of the solid earth, as geology, geophysics, etc. —**ge′o·sci′en·tist,** *n.*

ge·o·ther·mal (jē′ə thėr′məl), *adj.* of or having to do with the internal heat of the earth.

ge·ot·ro·pism (ji ot′rə piz əm), *n. Biol.* response to gravity. **Positive geotropism** is a tendency to move down into the earth. **Negative geotropism** is a tendency to move upward. [< *geo*– earth (< Gk. *ge*) + Gk. *tropikos* < *trope* turning] —**ge′o·trop′ic,** *adj.* —**ge′o·trop′i·cal·ly,** *adv.*

Ger., 1 Also, **G.** German. 2 Germany. 3 Also, **Gmc.** Germanic.

ger., gerund.

ge·ra·ni·um (jə rā′ni əm), *n.* 1 a cultivated plant having large clusters of showy flowers or fragrant leaves. 2 a wild plant having pink or purple flowers, deeply notched leaves, and long, pointed pods. [< L < Gk., < *geranos* crane; from resemblance of seed pod to crane's bill]

ger·bil (jėr′bil), *n.* small rodent with short front legs and long back legs, native to desert regions, used in research and kept as pets. Also, **gerbille.**

ger·fal·con (jėr′fôl′kən; –fô′–), *n.* a large falcon of the arctic. Also, **gyrfalcon.** [< OF *gerfaucon* < Gmc.]

ger·i·at·rics (jer′i at′riks), *n.* science dealing with the study of old age and its diseases. [< Gk. *geras* old age + *iatreia* healing] —**ger′i·at′ric,** *adj.* —**ger′i·a·tri′cian,** *n.*

germ (jėrm), *n.* 1 a microscopic animal or plant that causes disease. 2 the earliest form of a living thing; seed; bud. 3 origin. [< F < L *germen* sprout] —**germ′less,** *adj.*

Ger·man (jėr′mən), *n.* 1 native or inhabitant of Germany. 2 language of Germany, esp. that used in literature, on the radio, etc. —*adj.* of Germany, its people, or their language.

ger·man (jėr′mən), *adj.* 1 having the same parents. Children of the same father and mother are **brothers-german,** or **sisters-german.** 2 related as a child of one's uncle or aunt. A **cousin-german** is a first cousin. [< OF < L *germanus*]

ger·mane (jėr mān′), *adj.* closely connected; to the point; pertinent. [var. of *german*]

Ger·man·ic (jėr man′ik), *adj.* 1 German. 2 Teutonic. —*n.* a branch of the Indo-European language family, customarily divided into **East Germanic** (Gothic), **North Germanic** (the Scandinavian languages), and **West Germanic** (English, Frisian, Dutch, German).

ger·ma·ni·um (jėr mā′ni əm), *n.* a rare metallic element, Ge, with a grayish-white color. Its compounds resemble those of tin.

German measles, a contagious disease resembling measles, but much less serious.

German shepherd, =police dog.

German silver, a white alloy of copper, zinc, and nickel, used for ornaments, utensils, etc.

Ger·ma·ny (jėr′mə ni), *n.* country in C Europe.

germ cell, 1 cell that can produce a new individual; egg or sperm cell. 2 cell from which an egg or sperm cell develops. 3 fertilized ovum.

ger·mi·cide (jėr′mə sīd), *n.* any substance that kills germs, esp. disease germs. [< *germ* + *–cide* < L *–cida* killer < *caedere* to kill] —**ger′mi·cid′al,** *adj.*

ger·mi·nal (jėr′mə nəl), *adj.* 1 of germs or germ cells. 2 like that of germs or germ cells. 3 in the earliest stage of development.

ger·mi·nant (jėr mə nənt), *adj.* germinating.

ger·mi·nate (jėr′mə nāt), *v.,* –**nat·ed, –nat·ing.** start growing or developing; sprout. —**ger′mi·na′tion,** *n.* —**ger′mi·na′tor,** *n.*

germ plasm or **plasma,** 1 =germ cells. 2 chromosomes in germ cells.

germ warfare, the spreading of germs to produce disease among the enemy in time of war.

ger·on·tol·o·gy (jer′ən tol′ə ji), *n.* branch of science dealing with the phenomena and problems of old age. —**ger′on·to·log′i·cal,** *adj.* —**ger′on·tol′o·gist,** *n.*

ger·ry·man·der (ger′i man′dər; jer′–), *n.* arrangement of the political divisions of a state, county, etc., made to give one political party an unfair advantage in elections. —*v.* 1 arrange the political divisions of (a state, county, etc.) to give one political party an unfair advantage in elections. 2 manipulate unfairly. [< *Gerry* + (*sala*)*mander*; Gov. Gerry's party redistricted Mass. in 1812, and Essex Co. became roughly salamander-shaped]

ger·und (jer′ənd), *n.* a verb form used as a noun; verbal noun. [< LL *gerundium,* ult. < L *gerere* bear] —**ge·run′di·al,** *adj.*

ge·run·dive (jə run′div), *n.* 1 a Latin verb form used as an adjective, frequently expressing the idea of necessity or duty. 2 an analogous verbal adjective in other languages. —**ger′un·di′val,** *adj.* —**ge·run′dive·ly,** *adv.*

Ge·sta·po (gə stä′pō; –shtä′–), *n.* an official organization of secret police in Germany under Hitler. [< G *ge*(*heime*) *sta*(*ats*) *po*(*lizei*) secret state police]

ges·tate (jes′tāt), *v.,* –**tat·ed, –tat·ing.** 1 carry (young) in the uterus from conception to birth. 2 form and develop (a project, idea, etc.). [< L *gestare* carried < *gestare* carry] —**ges·ta′tion,** *n.*

ges·tic·u·late (jes tik′yə lāt), *v.,* –**lat·ed, –lat·ing.** 1 make or use gestures. 2 make or use many vehement gestures. [< L *gesticulatus,* ult. < *gestus* gesture] —**ges·tic′u·la′tor,** *n.* —**ges·tic′u·la·to′ry, ges·tic′u·la′tive,** *adj.*

ges·tic·u·la·tion (jes tik′yə lā′shən), *n.* 1 act of gesticulating. 2 gesture.

ges·ture (jes′chər), *n., v.,* **–tured, –tur-ing.** —*n.* **1** movement of the hands, arms, or any parts of the body, used instead of words or with words to help express an idea or feeling. **2** the use of such movements. **3** any action for effect or to impress others: *her refusal was merely a gesture; she really wanted to go.* —*v.* make or use gestures. [< Med.L *gestura* < L *gerere* to bear, conduct] —**ges′tur·er,** *n.*

get (get), *v.,* **got** or (*Archaic*) **gat, got** or (*esp. U.S.*) **got·ten, get·ting,** *n.* —*v.* **1** obtain by effort; gain; win: *get first prize; get a reputation.* **2** come to be; become: *get sick; get to be friends.* **3** commit to memory; learn: *get one's lessons.* **4** receive: *get a gift; get ten days in jail; get skill through practice.* **5** catch or contract (a disease or illness). **6** succeed in finding (a thing or a person). **7** bring into a particular position, situation, or condition: *get a fire under control.* **8** cause to be or do; persuade: *we got him to speak; he got me nervous.* **9** be obliged to: *we have got to die sometime.* **10** come to or arrive in a place specified or implied: *his plane got in yesterday.* **11** *Slang.* understand (a person or idea). —*n.* offspring of an animal.

get across, a make clear or convincing. **b** succeed.

get along, a go away. **b** advance. **c** manage; succeed; prosper. **d** agree.

get around, a go from place to place. **b** become widely known; spread. **c** deceive; trick.

get away, a go away. **b** escape. **c** start.

get away with, a get the advantage of. **b** succeed in taking or doing something.

get back at, get revenge.

get behind, support; endorse.

get by, a pass. **b** not be noticed or caught.

get down on, develop a dislike for.

get even, retaliate.

get into, a find out about. **b** get control of.

get off, a come down from or out of. **b** escape. **c** start. **d** say or express (a joke, witticism).

get off on, a start: *got off on our way.* **b** drift into: *easy to get off on other subjects.*

get on, a go up on or into. **b** put on. **c** advance. **d** manage; succeed; agree.

get out, a go out. **b** take out. **c** go away; escape. **d** become known; publish.

get over, a recover from; overcome. **b** make clear or convincing.

get there, succeed.

get through, secure favorable action on.

get together, meet; assemble; come to an agreement.

get up, a get out of bed, etc. **b** stand up. **c** prepare; arrange. [< Scand. *geta*] —**get′ta·ble, get′a·ble,** *adj.* —**get′ter,** *n.*

get·a·way (get′ə wā′), *n.* **1** act of getting away; escape. **2** start of a race.

Geth·sem·a·ne (geth sem′ə nē), *n.* garden near Jerusalem, the scene of Jesus's agony, betrayal, and arrest. Matt. 26:36.

get-out (get′out′), *n. Informal.* way of escape.

as all get-out, as much as possible; extremely: *pretty as all get-out.*

get-to·geth·er (get′tù geth′ər), *n.* an informal social gathering or party.

Get·tys·burg (get′iz bėrg), *n.* town in S Pennsylvania; Civil War battle, July 1–3, 1863.

get-up (get′up′), *n. Informal.* **1** dress; costume. **2** initiative; energy; ambition.

get-up-and-go (get′up′ən gō′), *n. Informal.* energy; drive; spunk.

gew-gaw (gū′gô), *n.* a showy trifle; bauble.

gey·ser (gī′zər), *n.* spring that sends a column of hot water and steam into the air at intervals. [< Icelandic *Geysir,* name of a spring in Iceland, < *geysa* gush]

Gha·na (gä′nə), *n.* country in W Africa, formerly the Gold Coast.

ghast·ly (gast′li; gäst′–), *adj.,* **–li·er, –li·est,** *adv.* —*adj.* **1** horrible: *a ghastly wound.* **2** like a dead person or ghost; deathly pale. **3** shocking: *a ghastly failure.* —*adv.* in a ghastly manner; deathly. [OE *gāstlic* < *gāst* ghost] —**ghast′li·ness,** *n.*

ghat (got), *n.* in India: **1** landing place. **2** mountain pass. [< Hind.]

gher·kin (gėr′kən), *n.* **1** small, prickly cucumber often used for pickles. **2** a young, green cucumber used for pickles. [< earlier Du. *agurkje,* dim. of *agurk* < G < Slavic < Med.Gk., ult. < Pers. *angorah* watermelon]

ghet·to (get′ō), *n., pl.* **–tos. 1** part of a city where a racial group was required to live. **2** part of a city where one racial or ethnic group lives, usually for social or economic reasons. **3** *Fig.* any place where only people similar to each other live. [< Ital.]

ghet·to·ize (get′ō īz), *v.,* **–ized, –iz·ing.** segregate; enclose in an area.

ghost (gōst), *n.* **1** spirit of a dead person. It is supposed to live in another world and appear to living people as a pale, dim, shadowy form. **2** a faint image; slightest suggestion: *not a ghost of a chance.* **3** a ghost writer. —*v. Informal.* be a ghost writer for.

give up the ghost, die. [OE *gāst*] —**ghost′like′,** *adj., adv.*

ghost·ly (gōst′li), *adj.,* **–li·er, –li·est. 1** like a ghost; pale, dim, and shadowy. **2** spiritual; religious. —**ghost′li·ness,** *n.*

ghost town, town empty of all residents and business.

ghost-write (gōst′rīt′), *v.,* **–wrote, –writ-ten, –writ·ing.** write (something) for an employer who is the ostensible author.

ghost writer, person who writes something for another who takes the credit.

ghoul (gül), *n.* **1** a horrible demon in Oriental stories, believed to feed on corpses. **2** person who robs graves or corpses. **3** person who enjoys what is revolting, brutal, and horrible. [< Ar. *ghūl*] —**ghoul′ish,** *adj.* —**ghoul′ish·ly,** *adv.* —**ghoul′ish·ness,** *n.*

GI (jē′ī′), *adj., n., pl.* —*adj.* **1** from government issue: *GI equipment.* **2** or for enlisted army personnel: *a GI obstacle course.* —*n.* an enlisted soldier; serviceman [< the initial letters of the phrase "Government Issue"]

gi·ant (jī′ənt), *n.* **1** an imaginary being having human form, but larger and more powerful than a man. **2** person or thing of unusual size, strength, importance, etc. —*adj.* like a giant; unusually big and strong; huge. [< OF < L < Gk. *gigas*]

gi·ant·ess (jī′ən tis), *n.* a woman giant.

giant star, bright star of great size and low density.

gib·ber (jib′ər; gib′–), *v.* chatter senselessly; talk rapidly and indistinctly. —*n.* senseless chattering.

gib·ber·ish (jib′ər ish; gib′–), *n.* senseless chatter; rapid, indistinct talk; jargon.

gib·bet (jib′it), *n., v.,* **–bet·ed, –bet·ing.** —*n.* **1** an upright post with a projecting arm at the top, from which the bodies of criminals were hung after execution. **2** =gallows. —*v.* hang on a gibbet. [< OF *gibet,* dim. of *gibe* club]

gib·bon (gib′ən), *n.* a small, long-armed ape of SE Asia and the East Indies, that lives in trees. [< F]

gib·bous (gib′əs), *adj.* curved out; humped. A gibbous moon is more than half full but less than full. [< L *gibbus* a hump]

gibe (jīb), *v.* **gibed, gib·ing,** *n.* —*v.* jeer; scoff; sneer. —*n.* a sneering or sarcastic remark. Also, **jibe.** [? < OF *giber* handle roughly < *gibe* staff] —**gib′er,** *n.*

gib·let (jib′lit), *n.* Usually, **giblets.** the heart, liver, or gizzard of a fowl. [< OF *gibelet* stew of game]

Gi·bral·tar (jə brôl′tər), *n.* **1** seaport and fortress on a high rock at the S tip of Spain. It is a British colony. **2 Rock of,** the large rock on which this fortress stands. **3 Strait of,** strait between Africa and Europe, connecting the Mediterranean Sea with the Atlantic.

gid·dy (gid′i), *adj.,* **–di·er, –di·est,** *v.,* **–died, –dy·ing.** —*adj.* **1** having a confused, whirling feeling in one's head; dizzy. **2** likely to make dizzy; causing dizziness. **3** rarely or never serious; flighty. [OE *gydig* mad, possessed (by an evil spirit) < *god* a god] —**gid′di·ly,** *adv.* —**gid′di·ness,** *adv.*

gift (gift), *n.* **1** thing given; present. **2** act of giving: *get a thing by gift.* **3** natural ability; special talent. —*v.* present with a gift or gifts; endow. [< Scand.; akin to *give*]

gift·ed (gif′tid), *adj.* having natural ability or special talent: *a gifted musician.*

gig (gig), *n.* **1** a light, two-wheeled carriage drawn by one horse. **2** a long, light ship's boat moved by oars or sails.

giga-, *combining form.* one billion, as in *gigahertz.*

gig·a·bit (gig′ə bit′), *n.* unit of information equal to one billion bits.

gig·a·hertz (gig′ə hėrts), *n.* one billion hertz.

gi·gan·tic (jī gan′tik), *adj.* like a giant; unusually big; huge; enormous. —**gi·gan′ti·cal·ly**, *adv.* —**gi·gan′tic·ness**, *n.*

gi·gan·tism (jī gan′tiz əm), *n.* **1** condition of overdeveloped growth of the body. **2** unusual growth of a plant. **3** tendency to extremely large size: *the gigantism of these new buildings.* Also, **giantism.**

gig·gle (gig′əl), *v.*, **-gled, -gling,** *n.* —*v.* laugh in a silly or undignified way. —*n.* a silly or undignified laugh. [< *giglet* laughing girl] —**gig′gler,** *n.* —**gig′gling·ly,** *adv.* —**gig′gly,** *adj.*

gig·o·lo (jig′ə lō), *n., pl.* **-los.** man who is paid for being a dancing partner or escort for a woman. [< F]

Gi·la monster (hē′lə), a large, poisonous lizard of Arizona and New Mexico, covered with beadlike, orange-and-black scales. [after *Gila* River, Arizona]

gild¹ (gild), *v.,* **gild·ed** or **gilt, gild·ing. 1** cover with a thin layer of gold or similar material; make golden. **2** make (a thing) look bright and pleasing. **3** make (a thing) seem better than it is. [OE *gyldan* < *gold*] —**gild′a·ble,** *adj.* —**gild′ed,** *adj.* —**gild′er,** *n.* —**gild′ing,** *n.*

gild² (gild), *n.* =guild. —**gilds′man,** *n.*

gill¹ (gil), *n.* part of the body of a fish, tadpole, crab, etc. by which it breathes in water. [< Scand. (Sw.) *gäl*] —**gilled,** *adj.* —**gill′·like′,** *adj.*

gill² (jil), *n.* measure for liquids; one fourth of a pint. [< OF *gille* wine measure]

gil·lie (gil′i), *n.* Scot. **1** attendant of a hunter or fisherman. **2** follower; servant. [< Scotch Gaelic *gille* lad]

gill net, fishing net designed to catch fish by their gills.

gil·ly·flow·er (jil′i flou′ər), *n.* any of various flowers that have a spicy fragrance. [< OF < L < Gk. *karyophyllon* clove tree < *karyon* clove + *phyllon* leaf]

gilt (gilt), *v.* pt and pp. of **gild¹.** —*n.* a thin layer of gold or similar material with which a thing is gilded. —*adj.* gilded.

gilt-edged (gilt′ejd′), *adj.* **1** having gilded edges. **2** of the very best quality.

gim·bals (jim′bəlz; gim′-), *n.pl.* device for keeping an object horizontal. A ship's compass is supported on gimbals. [ult. < OF *gemel* twin < L *gemellus*]

gim·crack (jim′krak′), *n.* a showy, useless trifle. —*adj.* showy but useless.

gim·crack·er·y (jim′krak′ər i), *n., pl.* **-er·ies.** showy, useless trifles, collectively.

gim·let (gim′lit), *n.* a small tool with a screw point, for boring holes. [< OF *guimbelet*]

gim·let-eyed (gim′lit īd′), *adj.* having eyes that are sharp and piercing.

gim·mick (gim′ik), *n. U.S. Informal.* any tricky device.

gimp¹ (gimp), *n.* a braidlike trimming made of silk, worsted, or cotton. [< F *guimpe* < Gmc. Doublet of GUIMPE.]

gimp² (gimp), *v.* walk with a limp. —*n. Informal.* **1** lame person. **2** a limp.

gin¹ (jin), *n.* a strong alcoholic drink, usually flavored with juniper berries. [short for *geneva* liquor]

gin² (jin), *n., v.,* **ginned, gin·ning.** —*n.* **1** machine for separating cotton from its seeds. **2** trap; snare. —*v.* **1** separate (cotton) from its seeds. **2** catch in a gin.

gin up, *Informal.* stir up; excite. [< OF *engin* ENGINE]

gin³ (jin), *n.* =gin rummy.

gin·ger (jin′jər), *n.* **1** spice made from the root of a tropical plant, used for flavoring and in medicine. **2** the root, often preserved in syrup or candied. **3** the plant. [< LL < L < Gk. < Prakrit (an ancient lang. of India) *singabēra*] —**gin′ger·y,** *adj.*

ginger ale, a nonalcoholic, bubbling drink flavored with ginger.

ginger beer, an English drink similar to ginger ale, but made with fermenting ginger.

gin·ger·bread (jin′jər bred′), *n.* **1** cake flavored with ginger and sweetened with molasses. **2** something showy and elaborate, but not in good taste. —*adj.* gaudy.

gin·ger·ly (jin′jər li), *adv.* with extreme care or caution. —*adj.* extremely cautious. —**gin′ger·li·ness,** *n.*

gin·ger·snap (jin′jər snap′), *n.* a thin, crisp cooky flavored with ginger.

ging·ham (ging′əm), *n.* a cotton cloth made from colored threads, usually in stripes, plaids, or checks. [< F < Malay *ginggang,* orig., striped]

gin·gi·vi·tis (jin′jə vī′təs), *n.* inflammation of the gums. [< L *gingīva* gum²]

gink·go (ging′kō; jing′kō), **ging·ko** (ging′kō), *n., pl.* **-goes; -koes.** a large, ornamental tree of China and Japan with fan-shaped leaves and edible nuts. [< Jap.]

gin rummy (jin), a kind of rummy in which players form sequences and matching combinations and lay down their hands when having ten or less points.

gin·seng (jin′seng), *n.* **1** a low plant with a thick, branched root. **2** this root, much used in medicine by the Chinese. [< Chinese *jên shên; jên* = man]

gi·raffe (jə raf′; -räf′), *n.* a large African mammal with a very long neck and legs and a spotted skin, the tallest of living animals. [< F < Ar. *zarāfah*]

gird (gėrd), *v.,* **girt** or **gird·ed, gird·ing. 1** put a belt or girdle around. **2** fasten with a belt or girdle. **3** surround; enclose. **4** get ready for action. **5** clothe; furnish. [OE *gyrdan*]

gird·er (gėr′dər), *n.* a main supporting beam. A tall building or big bridge often has steel girders for its frame. [< *gird*]

gir·dle (gėr′dəl), *n., v.,* **-dled, -dling.** —*n.* **1** belt, sash, cord, etc., worn around the waist. **2** anything that surrounds or encloses. **3** support like a corset worn about the hips or waist. —*v.* **1** form a

girdle around; encircle. **2** kill (a tree) by cutting a ring around its trunk. **3** put a girdle on or around. [OE *gyrdel.* See GIRD.] —**gir′dle·like′,** *adj.* —**gir′dler,** *n.*

girl (gėrl), *n.* **1** a female child. **2** a young, unmarried woman. **3** a female servant. **4** sweetheart. **5** *Informal.* woman of any age. [OE *gyrl-* in *gyrlgyden* virgin goddess] —**girl′ish,** *adj.* —**girl′ish·ly,** *adv.* —**girl′ish·ness,** *n.*

girl·friend (gėrl′frend′), *n.* **1** young man's sweetheart or steady companion. **2** female companion. Also, **girl friend.**

girl·hood (gėrl′hůd), *n.* **1** time or condition of being a girl. **2** girls as a group.

girl·ie (gėr′li), *n. Informal.* a little girl.

girl scout, member of the Girl Scouts.

Girl Scouts, organization for girls that seeks to develop health, character, and useful skills.

girt (gėrt), *v.* **1** pt. and pp. of **gird. 2** put a girth around. **3** fasten with a girth.

girth (gėrth), *n.* **1** the measure around anything: *man of large girth.* **2** strap or band that keeps a saddle, pack, etc., in place on a horse's back. —*v.* **1** measure in girth. **2** fasten with a strap or band. [< Scand. *gjörth* girdle; akin to GIRD]

gist (jist), *n.* the essential part; main idea; substance of a longer statement [< OF, (it) consists (in), depends (on) < L *jacet* it lies]

give (giv), *v.,* **gave, giv·en, giv·ing,** *n.* —*v.* **1** hand over: *my brother gave me his watch, please give me a drink, give one's word.* **2** let have; furnish; provide: *give aid to the needy; give advice; give a long account.* **3** deal; administer; allot: *give one a blow; give a contract; give credit to another.* **4** produce: *give a lecture, a play, etc.* **5** put forth; utter: *give a cry.* **6** cause; occasion: *give trouble.* **7** yield to force or pressure. —*n.* a yielding to force or pressure; elasticity.

give away, a give as a present. **b** hand over (a bride) to a bridegroom. **c** betray a secret, esp. unintentionally; expose (a person).

give back, return.

give in, a admit defeat; yield. **b** hand in.

give it to (someone), punish; scold.

give off, send out; put forth: *give off a glow.*

give or take, about; more or less: *coming soon, give or take a week.*

give out, a send out; put forth. **b** distribute; make known. **c** become used up or worn out.

give up, a hand over; deliver; surrender. **b** stop having, doing, or trying. **c** have no more hope for. **d** devote entirely. [< Scand. (Dan.) *give*] —**giv′er,** *n.*

give-and-take (giv′ən tāk′), *n.* **1** an even or fair exchange; mutual concession. **2** good-natured banter; exchange of talk.

give·a·way (giv′ə wā′), *n.* an unintentional revelation; exposure; betrayal.

give·back (giv′bak′), *n.* a return or concession of benefits in a labor contract, usually in exchange for something from management, such as job security, etc.

giv·en (giv'ən), *adj.* **1** stated; fixed; specified. **2** inclined; disposed. **3** assigned as a basis of calculating, reasoning, etc. **4** known. —*v.* pp. of **give**.

given name, name given to a person in addition to a family name. *John is the given name of John Smith.*

Gi·za (gē'zə), *n.* city in NE Egypt, the location of the great Pyramids and the Sphinx.

giz·mo (giz'mō), *n. Informal.* gadget; contraption.

giz·zard (giz'ərd), *n.* a bird's second stomach, where the food from the first stomach is ground up fine. [< OF, ult. < L *gigeria* cooked entrails of a fowl]

Gk., Greek, Also, **Gr.**

Gl, glucinum (beryllium).

gla·brous (glā'brəs), *adj.* without hair or down; smooth. [< L *glaber* smooth]

gla·cé (gla sā', *adj.* **1** covered with sugar, frosting, or icing. **2** frozen. **3** finished with a glossy surface. [< F, pp. of *glacer* impart a gloss to]

gla·cial (glā'shəl), *adj.* **1** of ice or glaciers; having much ice or many glaciers. **2** relating to a glacial epoch or period. **3** made by the action of ice or glaciers. **4** very cold; icy. [< L, < *glacies* ice] —**gla·cial·ly**, *adv.*

glacial epoch, 1 =Ice Age; Pleistoscene. **2** any time when the earth was largely covered by glaciers.

gla·ci·ate (glā'shi āt), *v.*, **-at·ed, -at·ing. 1** cover with ice or glaciers. **2** act on by ice or glaciers. —**gla·ci·a·tion**, *n.*

gla·cier (glā'shər), *n.* a large mass of ice formed from snow on high ground wherever winter snowfall exceeds summer melting. Glaciers move very slowly down a mountain or along a valley. [< F, ult. < L *glacies*] —**gla·ciered**, *adj.*

glad (glad), *adj.*, **glad·der, glad·dest. 1** happy; pleased. **2** bringing joy; pleasant. **3** bright; gay. [OE *glæd* bright, shining] —**glad'ly**, *adv.* —**glad'ness**, *n.*

glad·den (glad'ən), *v.* make or become glad. —**glad'den·er**, *n.*

glade (glād), *n.* **1** an open space in a wood or forest. **2** a marshy tract of low ground covered with grass. [prob. akin to *glad*]

glad hand, the hand extended in cordial greeting. —*v.*, **glad-hand.** make a show of being everyone's friend.

glad-hand·er (glad'hand'ər), *n.* person who makes a show of being friendly to all.

glad·i·a·tor (glad'i ā'tər), *n.* **1** in ancient Rome, a slave, captive, or paid fighter who fought at the public shows. **2** a skilled contender in any field or cause. [< L, < *gladius* sword] —**glad'i·a·to'ri·al**, *adj.*

glad·i·o·lus (glad'i ō'ləs; glə dī'ə–), **glad·i·o·la** (–lə), *n., pl.* **-li** (–lī), **-lus·es; -las.** kind of iris with spikes of large, handsome flowers in various colors. [< L, dim. of *gladius* sword]

glad·some (glad'səm), *adj.* **1** glad; joyful; cheerful. **2** causing gladness.

—**glad'some·ly**, *adv.* —**glad'some-ness**, *n.*

glam (glam), *n.* **1** glamour. **2** form of heavy-metal rock music.

glam·or·ize (glam'ər īz), *v.,* **-ized, -iz·ing.** make (someone or something) glamorous.

glam·or·ous (glam'ər əs), *adj.* full of glamour; fascinating. —**glam'or·ous-ly**, *adv.*

glam·our, glam·or (glam'ər), *n.* **1** mysterious fascination; alluring charm. **2** a magic spell or influence; enchantment. [alter. of *grammar* or its var. *gramarye* occult learning; orig., a spell]

glance (glans; gläns), *n., v.,* **glanced, glanc·ing.** —*n.* **1** a quick look. **2** flash of light; gleam. **3** a glancing off; deflected motion; swift, oblique movement. —*v.* **1** direct in a quick look. **2** flash with light; gleam. **3** direct obliquely. **4** hit and go off at a slant. [var. of ME *glace(n)* strike a glancing blow < OF *glacier* to slip]

gland (gland), *n.* organ in the body by which certain substances are separated from the blood and changed into some secretion for use in the body, such as bile, or into a product to be discharged from the body, such as sweat. [< F *glande*, ult. < L *glandula*, dim. of *glans* acorn] —**gland'less**, *adj.* —**gland'like'**, *adj.*

glan·ders (glan'dərz), *n.* a serious contagious disease of horses, mules, etc., accompanied by swellings beneath the lower jaw and a profuse discharge from the nostrils. [< OF *glandre* GLAND] —**glan'der·ous**, *adj.*

glan·du·lar (glan'jə lər), *adj.* of or like a gland; having glands.

glare¹ (glār), *n., v.,* **glared, glar·ing.** —*n.* **1** a strong, bright light; light that shines so brightly it hurts the eyes. **2** a fierce, angry stare. **3** too great brightness and showiness. —*v.* **1** give off a strong, bright light; shine so brightly as to hurt the eyes. **2** stare fiercely and angrily. [ME *glaren.* Cf. OE *glæren* glassy.]

glare² (glār), —*n.* a bright, smooth surface. —*adj.* bright and smooth. [extended use of *glare¹*]

glar·ing (glār'ing), *adj.* **1** very bright; dazzling. **2** staring fiercely and angrily. **3** too bright and showy. **4** conspicuous. —**glar'ing·ly**, *adv.* —**glar'ing·ness**, *n.*

glar·y (glār'i), *adj.* glaring.

glass (glas; gläs), *n.* **1** a hard, brittle substance that is usually transparent, made by melting sand with soda, potash, lime, or other substances. **2** thing to drink from made of glass. **3** as much as a glass holds. **4** thing or things made of glass. A windowpane, a mirror, or a telescope is a glass. —*v.* put glass in; cover or protect with glass. —*adj.* made of glass.

glasses, a pair of lenses to correct defective eyesight; eyeglasses; spectacles. **b** field glasses; binoculars.

(see, look at, etc.) **through rose-colored glasses**, view something in the most favorable way possible. [OE *glæs*]

glass blowing, art or process of shaping glass by blowing while it is still hot and soft. —**glass blower.**

glass·ful (glas'fúl; gläs'–), *n., pl.* **-fuls.** as much as a glass holds.

glass snake, a legless, snakelike lizard of the S United States, whose tail breaks off very easily.

glass·ware (glas'wār'; gläs'–), *n.* articles made of glass.

glass·y (glas'i; gläs'i), *adj.*, **glass·i·er, glass·i·est. 1** like glass; smooth; easily seen through. **2** having a fixed, stupid stare. —**glass'i·ly**, *adv.* —**glass'i·ness**, *n.*

glau·co·ma (glô kō'mə), *n.* disease of the eye, characterized by hardening of the eyeball and gradual loss of sight. [< Gk. *glaukoma.* See GLAUCOUS.] —**glau-co'ma·tous**, *adj.*

glau·cous (glô'kəs), *adj.* **1** light bluish-green. **2** covered with whitish powder as plums and grapes are. [< L < Gk. *glaukos* gray]

glaze (glāz), *v.,* **glazed, glaz·ing**, *n.* —*v.* **1** put glass in; cover with glass. **2** make a smooth, glassy surface or glossy coating on (china, food, etc.). **3** become smooth, glassy, or glossy: *eyes glazed over.* —*n.* **1** a smooth, glassy surface or glossy coating: *the glaze on a china cup.* **2** a coating of smooth ice. [ME *glase(n)* < *glas* GLASS] —**glaz'er**, *n.* —**glaz'ing**, *n.* —**glaz'y**, *adj.* —**glaz'i·ness**, *n.*

gla·zier (glā'zhər), *n.* person whose work is putting glass in windows, picture frames, etc.

gleam (glēm), *n.* **1** flash or beam of light. **2** a short or faint light. **3** a faint show: *a gleam of hope.* —*v.* **1** flash or beam with light. **2** shine with a short or faint light. [OE *glǣm*]

glean (glēn), *v.* **1** gather (grain) left on a field by reapers. **2** gather little by little or slowly: *glean the facts.* [< OF < LL *glennare* < Celtic] —**glean'er**, *n.*

glee (glē), *n.* **1** joy; delight; mirth. **2** song for three or more voices singing different parts, usually without instrumental accompaniment. [OE *glēo*]

glee club, group organized for singing songs.

glee·ful (glē'fəl), *adj.* filled with glee; merry; joyous. —**glee'ful·ly**, *adv.* —**glee'ful·ness**, *n.*

glen (glen), *n.* a small, narrow valley. [< Scotch Gaelic *gle(a)nn*] —**glen'like'**, *adj.*

glen·gar·ry (glen gar'i), *n., pl.* **-ries.** a Scottish cap with straight sides and a creased top, often having short ribbons at the back. [after *Glengarry,* valley in Scotland]

glen plaid, cloth or design of narrow checks or crisscross stripes in subtle colors. [< *Glenurquhart plaid,* after the name of a valley in Scotland]

glib (glib), *adj.,* **glib·ber, glib·best. 1** speaking or spoken smoothly and easily. **2** speaking or spoken too smoothly and easily to be sincere: *a glib excuse.* [short for *glibbery* slippery. Cf. Du. *glibberig.*] —**glib′ly,** *adv.* —**glib′ness,** *n.*

glide (glīd), *v.,* **glid·ed, glid·ing,** *n.* —*v.* **1** move along smoothly, evenly, and easily. **2** pass gradually, quietly, or imperceptibly. **3** of an aircraft, come down slowly at a slant without using a motor. —*n.* **1** a smooth, even, easy movement. **2** of an aircraft, act of gliding. **3** a slur. **4** sound made in passing from one speech sound to another. [OE *glīdan*] —**glid′ing·ly,** *adv.*

glide path, path of an aircraft or spacecraft as it comes in for a landing.

glid·er (glīd′ər), *n.* **1** aircraft resembling an airplane without a motor. Rising air currents keep it in the air. **2** person or thing that glides. **3** seat, suspended in a frame, that swings.

glim·mer (glim′ər), *n.* **1** a faint, unsteady light. **2** a vague idea; dim notion; faint glimpse. —*v.* **1** shine with a faint, unsteady light. **2** appear faintly or dimly. [cf. OE *gleomu* splendor] —**glim′mer·ing,** *n.* —**glim′mer·ing·ly,** *adv.*

glimpse (glimps), *n., v.,* **glimpsed, glimps·ing.** —*n.* **1** a short, quick view. **2** a short, faint appearance. —*v.* **1** catch a short, quick view of. **2** look quickly; glance. [akin to *glimmer*] —**glimps′er,** *n.*

glint (glint), *v., n.* gleam; flash. [cf. dial. Sw. *glinta*]

glis·sade (gli säd′; –säd′), *n.* **1** slide over ice or snow descending a slope. **2** slide down any surface. **3** gliding or sliding ballet step. —*v.,* **-sad·ed, -sad·ing.** make a glissade; slide. [< F *glissade* < *glisser* to slide]

glis·san·do (gli sän′dō), *adj.* played with a gliding effect, by sliding one finger across the piano keys. —*n.* passage played glissando. [Italianization of F *glissant,* ppr. of *glisser* to slide]

glis·ten (glis′ən), *v., n.* sparkle; glitter; shine. [OE *glisnian*] —**glis′ten·ing·ly,** *adv.*

glitch (glich), *n. Informal.* minor difficulty or obstacle. [perhaps < Yiddish *glitsh* a slipping]

glit·ter (glit′ər), *v.* **1** shine with a bright, sparkling light. **2** be bright and showy. —*n.* **1** a bright, sparkling light. **2** brightness; showiness. [cf. Scand. *glitra*] —**glit′ter·ing, glit′ter·y,** *adj.* —**glit·ter·ing·ly,** *adv.*

gloam·ing (glōm′ing), *n. Poetic.* evening twilight; dusk. [OE *glōmung* < *glōm* twilight]

gloat (glōt), *v.* gaze intently; ponder with pleasure; stare: *the miser gloated over his gold.* [cf. Scand. *glotta* smile scornfully] —**gloat′er,** *n.* —**gloat′ing·ly,** *adv.*

glob (glob), *n.* lump; blob.

glob·al (glōb′əl), *adj.* **1** shaped like a globe. **2** worldwide. —**glob′al·ly,** *adv.*

glob·al·ism (glōb′ə liz əm), *n.* **1** principle that the world and its peoples are interdependent. **2** concern for the whole world, with national self-interest playing a subsidiary role.

global village, the world seen as resembling a village because of instant electronic communication, which makes distance less important and less of an obstacle.

global warming, gradual warming of the earth's atmosphere, caused by concentration of gases, esp. carbon dioxide in the atmosphere.

globe (glōb), *n., v.,* **globed, glob·ing.** —*n.* **1** anything round like a ball; sphere. **2** earth; world. **3** sphere with a map of the earth or sky on it. **4** anything rounded like a globe. —*v.* gather or form into a globe. [< F < L *globus*]

globe·fish (glōb′fish′), *n., pl.* **-fish·es** or (*esp. collectively*) **-fish.** fish that can make itself nearly ball-shaped by drawing in air.

globe·trot·ter (glōb′trot′ər), *n.* person who travels widely over the world. —**globe′trot′ting,** *n., adj.*

glo·bose (glō′bōs), *adj.* =globular. —**glo′bose·ly,** *adv.* —**glo·bos′i·ty,** *n.*

glob·u·lar (glob′yə lər), *adj.* **1** shaped like a globe or globule; spherical. **2** consisting of globules. —**glob′u·lar′i·ty,** *n.* —**glob′u·lar·ly,** *adv.*

glob·ule (glob′ūl), *n.* a very small ball; tiny drop.

glob·u·lin (glob′yə lin), *n.* any one of a group of proteins, found in plant and animal tissues, and a constituent of human blood plasma.

glock·en·spiel (glok′ən spēl′), *n.* instrument consisting of a series of small, tuned bells, metal bars, or tubes mounted in a frame and struck by two little hammers. [< G, < *glocke* bell + *spiel* play]

glom (glom), *v.,* **-glommed, glom·ming.** *Slang.* **1** grab; steal. **2** look at; glimpse: *glom a pretty girl.*

glom on to, *Slang.* grab; hold on to. [< *Dial.* *glaum*]

glom·er·ate (glom′ər it), *adj.* clustered together; collected into a rounded mass. [< L, < *glomus* ball] —**glom′er·a′tion,** *n.*

gloom (glüm), *n.* **1** deep shadow; darkness; dimness. **2** low spirits; sadness. —*v.* **1** be or become dark, dim, or dismal. **2** be in low spirits; feel miserable. [OE *glōm* twilight]

gloom·y (glüm′i), *adj.,* **gloom·i·er, gloom·i·est. 1** dark; dim. **2** in low spirits; sad; melancholy. **3** causing low spirits; discouraging; dismal. —**gloom′i·ly,** *adv.* —**gloom′i·ness,** *n.*

glop (glop), *n. Slang.* anything unpleasant or sticky; goo. —**glop′py,** *adj.* [prob. imit.]

Glo·ri·a (glô′ri ə; glō′–), *n.* song of praise to God, or its musical setting. [<L]

glo·ri·fy (glô′rə fī; glō′–), *v.,* **-fied, -fy·ing. 1** give glory to; make glorious. **2** praise; honor; worship. **3** make more beautiful or splendid. [< OF < L, < *gloria* glory + *facere* make] —**glo′ri·fi′a·ble,** *adj.* —**glo′ri·fi·ca′tion,** *n.* —**glo′ri·fi′er,** *n.*

glo·ri·ous (glô′ri əs; glō′–), *adj.* **1** having or deserving glory; illustrious. **2** giving glory. **3** magnificent; splendid. —**glo′ri·ous·ly,** *adv.* —**glo′ri·ous·ness,** *n.*

glo·ry (glô′ri; glō′–), *n., pl.* **-ries,** *v.,* **-ried, -ry·ing.** —*n.* **1** great praise and honor; fame; renown. **2** that which brings praise and honor; source of pride and joy. **3** radiant beauty; brightness; magnificence; splendor or greatest prosperity. **4** heaven. —*v.* be proud; rejoice.

in one's glory, feeling great satisfaction or pleasure. [< OF < L *gloria*]

gloss[1] (glôs; glos), *n.* **1** a smooth, shiny surface; luster. **2** an outward appearance or surface that covers wrong underneath. —*v.* **1** put a smooth, shiny surface on. **2** smooth over; make seem right: *gloss over a mistake.* [cf. Scand. *glossi* flame] —**gloss′er,** *n.*

gloss[2] (glôs; glos), *n.* **1** explanation; interpretation; comment. **2** glossary. **3** translation inserted between the lines of a text printed in a foreign language. —*v.* **1** comment on; explain; annotate. **2** make glosses. [< L < Gk. *glossa,* lit., tongue] —**gloss′er,** *n.*

glos·sa·ry (glos′ə ri; glôs′–), *n., pl.* **-ries.** list of special, technical, or difficult words with explanations or comments: *glossary of Shakespeare's plays.* [< L, < *glossa* GLOSS[2]] —**glos′sa·rist,** *n.*

glos·su·la·li·a (glos′ə lā′lē ə; glôs′–), *n.* **1** utterance of words or sounds without recognizable meaning. **2** speaking in tongues; ecstatic speech, esp. in a religious context. [< Gk. *glôssa* tongue + *laliá* speech]

gloss·y (glôs′i; glos′i), *adj.,* **gloss·i·er, gloss·i·est.** smooth and shiny. —**gloss′i·ly,** *adv.* —**gloss′i·ness,** *n.*

glot·tal (glot′əl), *adj.* **1** of the glottis. **2** produced in the glottis. H in *hope* is a glottal sound.

glot·tis (glot′is), *n.* an opening at the upper part of the windpipe, between the vocal cords. [< NL < Gk., ult. < *glotta* tongue]

glove (gluv), *n., v.,* **gloved, glov·ing.** —*n.* **1** a covering for the hand, usually with separate places for each of the four fingers and the thumb. **2** a boxing glove. —*v.* **1** cover with a glove; provide with gloves. **2** serve as a glove for.

fit like a glove, fit or suit perfectly.

handle with kid gloves, treat gently; handle carefully.

take off the gloves or **take the gloves off,** become aggressive; get tough. [OE *glōf*] —**glove′less,** *adj.* —**glove′like′,** *adj.*

glov·er (gluv′ər), *n.* person who makes or sells gloves.

glow (glō), *n.* **1** shine from something that is red-hot or white-hot; similar shine. **2** brightness: *the glow of sunset.* **3** *Fig.* a warm feeling or color of the body: *the glow of health.* **4** *Fig.* an eager look on the face: *glow of excitement.* —*v.* **1** shine as if red-hot or white-hot. **2** show a warm color; be red or bright. **3** *Fig.* be eager or passionate. [OE *glōwan*] —**glow′ing,** *adj.* —**glow′ing·ly,** *adv.*

glow·er (glou′ər), *v.* stare angrily; scowl. —*n.* an angry or sullen look. [? < obs. *glow,* v., stare] —**glow′er·ing·ly,** *adv.*

glow·worm (glō′wėrm′), *n.* any insect larva or wormlike insect that glows in the dark.

glu·ca·gon (glü′kə gon), *n.* hormone secreted by the pancreas that raises the blood sugar level. It is used to treat diabetes and tumors. [< *glucose*]

glu·cose (glü′kōs), *n.* **1** kind of sugar, $C_6H_{12}O_6$, occurring in fruits. **2** syrup made from starch.

glue (glü), *n., v.,* **glued, glu·ing.** —*n.* **1** substance used to stick things together, often made by boiling the hoofs, skins, and bones of animals in water. **2** any similar sticky substance. —*v.* **1** stick together with glue. **2** fasten tightly; attach firmly. [< OF *gluz* < LL *glutis*] —**glue′like′,** *adj.* —**glu′er,** *n.*

glue·y (glü′i), *adj.* **glu·i·er, glu·i·est. 1** like glue; sticky. **2** smeared with glue.

glum (glum), *adj.* **glum·mer, glum·mest.** gloomy; dismal; sullen. —**glum′ly,** *adv.* —**glum′ness,** *n.*

glu·on (glü′on), *n.* particle believed to hold together the constituents of quarks. [< *glue* + *-on* nuclear particle]

glut (glut), *v.,* **glut·ted, glut·ting,** *n.* —*v.* **1** fill full; feed or satisfy fully. **2** fill too full; supply too much for. —*n.* **1** a full supply; great quantity. **2** too great a supply. [< obs. *glut,* n., GLUTTON < OF]

glu·ten (glü′tən), *n.* a tough, sticky substance that remains in flour when the starch is taken out. [< L, glue] —**glu′te·nous,** *adj.*

glu·ti·nous (glü′tə nəs), *adj.* sticky. —**glu′ti·nous·ly,** *adv.* —**glu′ti·nous·ness, glu′ti·nos′i·ty,** *n.*

glut·ton (glut′ən), *n.* **1** a greedy eater; person who eats too much. **2** *Fig.* person who never seems to have enough of something. [< OF < L *gluto*]

glut·ton·ous (glut′ən əs), *adj.* greedy about food; having the habit of eating too much. —**glut′ton·ous·ly,** *adv.* —**glut′ton·ous·ness,** *n.*

glut·ton·y (glut′ən i), *n., pl.* **-ton·ies.** excess in eating.

glyc·er·in (glis′ər in), **glyc·er·ine** (-in; -ēn), *n.* a colorless, syrupy, sweet liquid, $C_3H_8O_3$, obtained from fats and oils, used in ointments, lotions, antifreeze solutions, and explosives.

glyc·er·ol (glis′ər ōl; -ol), *n.* =glycerin.

gly·co·gen (glī′kə jən), *n.* a starchlike substance in the liver and other animal tissues that is changed into sugar as needed.

glyph (glif), *n.* **1** hieroglyph or other similar symbol. **2** pictorial symbol used to substitute for a word: *international airport glyphs.*

gm., gram; grams.

G-man (jē′man′), *n., pl.* **-men.** a special agent of the U.S. Department of Justice; agent of the FBI.

Gmc., Germanic. Also, **Ger.**

gnarl (närl), *n.* knot in wood; hard, rough lump. —**gnarled, gnarl′y,** *adj.*

gnash (nash), *v.* strike or grind (the teeth) together; grind together. [var. of *gnast,* appar. < Scand. *gnastan* gnashing]

gnat (nat), *n.* any of various small, two-winged insects or flies. Most gnats are bloodsucking and make bites that itch. [OE *gnætt*] —**gnat′like′,** *adj.*

gnaw (nô), *v.,* **gnawed, gnawed** or **gnawn** (nôn), **gnaw·ing. 1** bite at and wear away. **2** make by biting. **3** wear away; consume; corrode. **4** torment. [OE *gnagan*] —**gnaw′er,** *n.* —**gnaw′ing,** *adj.* —**gnaw′ing·ly,** *adv.*

gneiss (nīs), *n.* rock like granite, but with flatter crystals in more nearly parallel layers. [< G] —**gneiss′ic,** *adj.*

gnoc·chi (nôk′ki), *n.pl.* small Italian dumplings.

gnome (nōm), *n.* dwarf supposed to live in the earth and guard precious treasures. [< F < NL *gnomus*] —**gnom′ish,** *adj.*

gno·mon (nō′mon), *n.* pointer on a sundial, etc., that shows the time of day. [< Gk., indicator, < *gignoskein* know]

Gnos·tic (nos′tik), *n.* believer in Gnosticism. *adj.* Also, **Gnos′ti·cal.** of Gnosticism or Gnostics. [< Gk. *gnostikos* of knowledge < *gignoskein* know]

Gnos·ti·cism (nos′tə siz əm), *n.* the mystical religious and philosophical doctrine of pre-Christian and early Christian times.

GNP, gross national product

gnu (nü; nū), *n., pl.* **gnus** or (*esp. collectively*) **gnu.** an African antelope with an oxlike head and a long tail; wildebeest. [< Kaffir *nqu*]

go (gō), *v.,* **went, gone, go·ing.** *n., pl.* **goes.** —*v.* **1** move along or away; leave; proceed: *go straight home, go to the city.* **2** act; work; run: *the clock goes.* **3** become: *go mad, go hungry.* **4** put oneself: *don't go to any trouble for me, go under an alias.* **5** extend; reach: *his memory goes far back.* **6** be given or sold: *first prize goes to you.* **7** turn out; have a certain result: *how did the game go?* **8** belong: *this book goes up there, certain colors go together.* **9** have certain words: *How does the song go?* **10** carry authority; be done without any question: *what he says goes.* **11** break down; give way: *Her hearing is going.* —*n.* **1** act of going. **2** try; attempt; chance. **3** something successful.

go about, a be busy at; work on. **b** move from place to place. **c** turn around; change direction.

go along (with), cooperate (with); agree (with).

go around, a move from place to place: *went around, looking for a job.* **b** be enough to give some to all.

go at, a attack. **b** *Fig.* work at energetically: *go at a problem.*

go back on, break one's word.

go behind, investigate the real or hidden reasons for.

go by, a pass. **b** be guided by; follow. **c** be known by.

go down, a descend; decline; sink. **b** be defeated; lose. **c** work out; play out: *the plan went down badly.*

go for, a try to get. **b** favor; support. **c** attack. **d** be attracted by or to: *he goes for beauty over brains.*

go for broke, try wholeheartedly.

go into, a enter into: *go into a fury; go into medicine.* **b** be contained in: *much experience goes into a performance.* **c** investigate.

go in with, join.

go it alone, do something without help; act independently.

go off, a leave; depart. **b** explode. **c** take place; happen. **d** stop; discontinue: *go off a food.*

go on, a go ahead. **b** behave: *go on like a fool.* **c** happen: *what went on last night?*

go out, a stop; end. **b** go to a party, dinner, etc. **c** go on strike.

go over, a look at carefully. **b** do or read again. **c** succeed.

go through, a go to the end of; do all of. **b** undergo; experience. **c** search. **d** be accepted: *the loan went through.*

go through with, carry out to completion.

go together, a harmonize; complement: *dress, hat, and scarf all went together perfectly.* **b** keep steady company as lovers.

go under, be ruined; fail; sink.

go up, a ascend. **b** increase. **c** be built.

go with, a accompany. **b** be in harmony with.

go without, not have.

let go, a allow to escape. **b** give up one's hold. **c** fail to keep in good condition.

let oneself go, a give way to one's feelings or desires. **b** fail to keep oneself in good health or condition.

on the go, always moving or acting. [OE *gān*] —**go′er,** *n.*

goad (gōd), *n.* **1** a sharp-pointed stick for driving cattle, etc. **2** anything that drives or urges one on. —*v.* drive on; urge on; act as a goad to. [OE *gād*] —**goad′like′,** *adj.*

go·a·head (gō′ə hed′), —*n.* action of going forward; ambition; spirit; authority to proceed. —*adj.* disposed to push ahead.

goal (gōl), *n.* **1** place where a race ends. **2** place to which players try to advance a ball, etc., in certain games. **3** score or points won by advancing a ball, etc.,

to this place. **4** thing wanted. [ME *gol*]
—**goal′less,** *adj.*

goal·keep·er (gōl′kēp′ər), **goal·ie** (gōl′i),
n. player who tries to prevent the ball,
etc., from reaching the goal in certain
games.

goat (gōt), *n., pl.* **goats** or (*esp. collectively*) **goat. 1** a cud-chewing mammal
with hollow horns and long, usually
straight hair, closely related to the sheep,
but stronger, less timid, and more active.
2 the Rocky Mountain goat. **3 Goat,**
Capricorn. **4** *Slang.* person made to
suffer for the mistakes of others; scapegoat.

get one's goat, make a person angry
or annoyed; tease someone. [OE *gāt*]
—**goat′like′,** *adj.*

goat·ee (gō tē′), *n.* a pointed beard on a
man's chin.

goat·herd (gōt′hėrd′), *n.* person who
tends goats.

goat·skin (gōt′skin′), *n.* **1** skin of a goat. **2**
leather made from it.

goat·suck·er (gōt′suk′ər), *n.* bird with a
flat head, wide mouth, and long wings
that flies at night and feeds on flying
insects.

gob[1] (gob), *n.* sailor in the navy.

gob[2] (gob), *n.* lump; mass. [appar. < OF
gobe]

gob·bet (gob′it), *n.* lump; mass. [< OF
gobet, dim. of *gobe* gob[2]]

gob·ble[1] (gob′əl), *v.,* **–bled, –bling.** eat fast
and greedily; swallow quickly in big
pieces.

gobble up, seize upon eagerly. [< *gob*[2]]
—**gob′bler,** *n.*

gob·ble[2] (gob′əl), *v.,* **–bled, –bling,** *n.* —*v.*
make the throaty sound that a turkey
does. —*n.* this sound. [imit.]

gob·ble·dy·gook, gob·ble·de·gook (gob′-
əl di gük′), *n.* speech or writing whose
meaning is obscured by excessive use
of technical terminology, involved sentences, and big words.

gob·bler (gob′lər), *n.* a male turkey.

go·be·tween (gō′bi twēn′), *n.* person who
goes back and forth between others with
messages, proposals, etc.; intermediary.

gob·let (gob′lit), *n.* a drinking glass with
a base and stem. [< OF *gobelet,* dim. of
gobel cup]

gob·lin (gob′lən), *n.* a mischievous sprite
or elf in the form of an ugly-look-
ing dwarf. [< F *gobelin* < MHG *kobold*
demon]

go·cart or **go·cart** (gō′kärt′), *n.* **1** child's
cart, a seat on wheels that can be ridden.
2 an infant's walker. **3** a light carriage.

God (god), *n.* **1** the maker and ruler of
the world; Supreme Being. **2 god, a** a
being thought of as superior to nature
and to human beings and considered
worthy of worship. **b** idol. **c** god. **3** *Fig.*
person intensely admired and respected.
[OE]

god·child (god′chīld′), *n., pl.* **–chil·dren.**
child for whom a grown-up person
takes vows at its baptism.

god·daugh·ter (god′dô′tər), *n.* a female
godchild.

god·dess (god′is), *n.* **1** a female god. **2**
a very beautiful or charming woman.
—**god′dess·hood, god′dess·ship,** *n.*

god·fa·ther (god′fä′ᵗħər), *n.* man who
takes vows for a child when it is baptized.

God-giv·en (god′giv′ən), *adj.* **1** given by
God. **2** very welcome and suitable.

God·head (god′hed), *n.* **1** God. **2** divine
nature; divinity.

god·hood (god′hùd), *n.* divine character;
divinity.

god·less (god′lis), *adj.* **1** not believing
in God; not religious. **2** wicked; evil.
—**god′less·ly,** *adv.* —**god′less·ness,** *n.*

god·like (god′līk′), *adj.* **1** like God or a
god; divine. **2** suitable for God or a god.
—**god′like′ness,** *n.*

god·ly (god′li), *adj.,* **–li·er, –li·est.** obeying God's laws; religious; pious; devout.
—**god′li·ly,** *adv.* —**god′li·ness,** *n.*

god·moth·er (god′muᵗħ′ər), *n.* woman
who takes vows for a child when it is
baptized.

god·par·ent (god′pār′ənt), *n.* godfather
or godmother.

god·send (god′send′), *n.* something
unexpected and very welcome, as if sent
from God.

god·son (god′sun′), *n.* a male godchild.

God·speed (god′spēd′), *n.* wish of success to a person starting on a journey.

go·fer (gō′fər), *n.* person, esp. an office
assistant, who runs errands for someone. [< *go for,* as a pun on gopher]

go-get·ter (gü′get′ər), *n.* an energetic person who gets what he seeks.

gog·gle (gog′əl), *n., v.,* **–gled, –gling,** *adj.*
—*n.* Usually, **goggles.** large, close-fitting
spectacles to protect the eyes from light,
dust, etc. —*v.* stare with bulging eyes.
—*adj.* bulging: *a frog has goggle eyes.*
[ME *gogel(en)*] —**gog′gle-eyed′,** *adj.*

go·ing (gō′ing), *n.* **1** a going away. **2**
condition of the ground or road for
walking, riding, etc. —*adj.* **1** moving;
acting; working; running. **2** that goes; that
can or will go.

be going to, about to.

get going, begin.

going concern, company, store, etc., that
is doing business.

go·ings-on (gō′ingz on′), *n. pl.* or **goings
on,** actions or events, esp. involving
questionable behavior.

goi·ter, goi·tre (goi′tər), *n.* **1** disease of
the thyroid gland, that often causes a
large swelling in the neck. **2** the swelling.
[< F *goitre,* ult. < L *guttur* throat]

gold (gōld), *n.* **1** a shiny, bright-yellow,
precious metal, used for making coins
and jewelry. Gold is a chemical element.
Symbol: Au. **2** coins made of gold. **3**
money in large sums; wealth; riches. **4**
a bright, beautiful, or precious thing or
material: *a heart of gold.* —*adj.* **1** made
of gold. **2** of or like gold. **3** bright-yellow. [OE]

gold-brick (gōld′brik′), —*v.* pretend illness to avoid duties. —*n.* Also, **gold′-
brick′er.** person, esp. in the army or
navy, who avoids duty or shirks work.

Gold Coast, region in W Africa, largely
included in Ghana.

gold digger, *Slang.* woman who tries by
various schemes to get money from
men.

gold dust, gold in a fine powder.

gold·en (gōl′dən), *adj.* **1** made of gold. **2**
containing gold. **3** shining like gold. **4**
extremely favorable, valuable, or important. **5** very happy and prosperous;
flourishing. —**gold′en·ly,** *adv.* —**gold′en-
ness,** *n.*

golden parachute, award of generous
benefits and payment to an employee.

gold·en·rod (gōl′dən rod′), *n.* plant that
blooms in the autumn and has many
small yellow flowers on tall, branching
stalks.

golden rule, rule of conduct set forth by
Jesus.

gold-filled (gōld′fild′), *adj.* made of cheap
metal covered with a layer of gold.

gold·finch (gōld′finch′), *n.* **1** a small
American songbird. The male is yellow
marked with black. **2** a European songbird with yellow on its wings.

gold·fish (gōld′fish′), *n., pl.* **–fish·es** or
(*esp. collectively*) **–fish.** a small, reddish-
golden fish.

gold leaf, gold beaten into very thin
sheets.

gold rush, 1 a sudden rush of people to a
place where gold has just been found. **2**
sudden rush to buy something valuable.

gold·smith (gōld′smith′), *n.* person
whose work is making articles of gold.

gold standard, 1 use of gold as the
standard of value for the money of a
country. **2** *Fig.* the very best of something.

golf (golf; gôlf), *n.* an outdoor game
played with a small, hard ball and a set
of long-handled clubs having wooden
or iron heads. The player tries to hit the
ball into a series of holes with as few
strokes as possible. —*v.* play this game.
—**golf′er,** *n.*

Go·li·ath (gə lī′əth), *n.* in the Bible, a
giant whom David killed with a stone
from a sling.

gol·ly (gol′i), *interj.* exclamation of wonder, pleasure, surprise, as a substitute
for "God."

go·losh (gə losh′), *n.* =galosh.

Go·mor·rah, Go·mor·rha (gə môr′ə;
–mor′–), *n.* in the Bible, a wicked city
destroyed, together with Sodom, by fire
from heaven. Gen. 18 and 19.

gon·ad (gon′ad; gō′nad), *n.* organ in
which reproductive cells develop. Ovaries and testes are gonads. [< NL < Gk.
gone seed] —**gon′ad·al, go·na′di·al, go-
nad′ic,** *adj.*

gon·a·do·tro·pin (gon′ə də trop′in, gə-
nad′ə–), *n.* hormone which stimulates
the gonads.

gon·do·la (gon′də lə), *n.* **1** a long, narrow boat with a high peak at each end, used on the canals of Venice. **2** car that hangs under a dirigible and holds the motors, passengers, etc. [< dial. Ital., < *gondolar* rock]

gondola car, a freight car that has low sides and no top.

gon·do·lier (gon′də lir′), *n.* man who poles a gondola.

gone (gôn; gon), *adj.* **1** moved away; left. **2** lost: *a gone cause.* **3** dead. **4** used up. **5** failed; ruined. —*v.* pp. of **go.**

far gone, much advanced; deeply involved.

gon·er (gôn′ər; gon′–), *n. Informal.* person or thing that is dead, ruined, past help, etc.

gong (gông; gong), *n.* a metal disk with a turned-up rim, that makes a loud noise when struck. [< Malay] —**gong′like′,** *adj.*

gon·or·rhe·a (gon′ə rē′ə), *n.* a contagious sexually transmitted disease that causes inflammation of the genital and urinary organs. [< LL < Gk., < *gonos* seed + *rhoia* flow] —**gon′or·rhe′al,** *adj.*

goo (gü), *n. Informal.* something thick or sticky.

goo·ber (gü′bər), *n. S., Informal.* peanut. [< Bantu]

good (gůd), *adj.* **bet·ter, best,** *n., interj.* —*adj.* **1** having the right qualities; desirable: *a good book.* **2** right; proper: *do what seems good to you.* **3** well-behaved: *a good boy.* **4** kind; friendly: *say a good word for me.* **5** reliable; dependable: *good judgment.* **6** agreeable; pleasant: *a good time.* **7** satisfying; full: *a good day.* **8** skillful; clever: *a good manager.* —*n.* **1** benefit: *work for the common good.* **2** that which is good: *find the good in people.* —*interj.* that is good!

as good as, almost the same as; practically.

feel good, feel well or elated.

for good, forever; finally; permanently.

good for, a able to do, live, or last. **b** able to pay. **c** worth.

make good, a make up for. **b** carry out; fulfill. **c** succeed. [OE *gōd*]

Good Book, Bible.

good-by, good-bye (gůd′bī′), *interj., n., pl.* **–bys; –byes.** farewell. [contraction of *God be with ye*]

good-for-noth·ing (gůd′fər nuth′ing), *adj.* worthless; useless. —*n.* person who is worthless or useless.

Good Friday, Friday before Easter, observed in commemoration of Christ's crucifixion.

good-heart·ed (gůd′här′tid), *adj.* kind and generous. —**good′-heart′ed·ly,** *adv.* —**good′-heart′ed·ness,** *n.*

Good Hope, Cape of, cape near the SW tip of Africa.

good-hu·mored (gůd′hū′mərd; –ū′–), *adj.* cheerful; pleasant. —**good′-hu′mored·ly,** *adv.* —**good′-hu′mored·ness,** *n.*

good-look·ing (gůd′lůk′ing), *adj.* having a pleasing appearance; handsome.

good·ly (gůd′li), *adj.,* **–li·er, –li·est. 1** pleasant; excellent: *a goodly land.* **2** good-looking: *a goodly youth.* **3** considerable: *a goodly quantity.* —**good′li·ness,** *n.*

good morning, form of greeting said in the morning.

good-na·tured (gůd′nā′chərd), *adj.* pleasant; kindly; cheerful; agreeable. —**good′-na′tured·ly,** *adv.* —**good′-na′tured·ness,** *n.*

good·ness (gůd′nis), *n.* **1** quality or state of being good; kindness; friendliness. —*interj.* exclamation of surprise.

good night, form of farewell said at night.

goods (gůdz), *n.pl.* **1** personal property; belongings. **2** thing or things for sale; wares. **3** material for clothing; cloth.

Good Samaritan, person who is unselfish in helping others.

good-tem·pered (gůd′tem′pərd), *adj.* easy to get along with. —**good′tem′pered·ly,** *adv.*

good will, 1 kindly or friendly feeling. **2** cheerful consent; willingness. **3** reputation and steady trade that a business has with its customers.

good·y (gůd′i), *n., pl.* **good·ies,** *interj.* —*n.* something very good to eat. —*interj.* exclamation of pleasure. [< *good*]

good·y-good·y (gůd′i gůd′i), *n.* person who makes a display of how good he or she is. —*adj.* good, in an artificial way.

goose (güs), *n. pl.,* **geese 1** a wild or tame web-footed swimming bird, like a duck but larger and having a longer neck. **2** a female goose. **3** a silly person.

cook one's goose, ruin one's reputation, chance to advance, succeed, etc. [OE *gōs*] —**goose′like′,** *adj.*

goose·ber·ry (güs′ber′i; güz′–), *n., pl.* **–ries. 1** a small, sour berry somewhat like a currant but larger, used to make pies, tarts, jam, etc. **2** the thorny bush that it grows on.

goose egg, 1 egg of a goose. **2** *Slang.* zero, esp. in sports.

goose pimples, a rough condition of the skin caused by cold or fear. Also, **goose bumps, goose flesh.**

goose·neck (güs′nek′), *n.* anything long and curved like a goose's neck, such as a movable support for a lamp.

goose step, a marching step in which the leg is swung high with a straight, stiff knee.

goose-step (güs′step′), *v.,* **–stepped, –step·ping.** march with a goose step.

G.O.P., the "Grand Old Party" (the Republican Party in the United States).

go·pher (gō′fər), *n.* **1** *S., W.* a burrowing, ratlike rodent with large cheek pouches. **2** ground squirrel. [? < early United States F, *gaufre,* lit., honeycomb; with ref. to burrowing]

Gor·di·an knot (gôr′di ən). **cut the Gordian knot,** use a quick, easy way out of a difficulty. [with ref. to the knot tied by *Gordius,* king of Phrygia, and cut by Alexander the Great]

gore¹ (gôr; gōr), *n.* blood that is shed; thick blood; clotted blood. [OE *gor* dirt, dung]

gore² (gôr; gōr), *v.,* **gored, gor·ing.** wound with a horn or tusk: *the savage bull gored the farmer.* [ME *gorre(n)*]

gore³ (gôr; gōr), *n., v.,* **gored, gor·ing.** —*n.* a long, triangular piece of cloth put or made in a skirt, sail, etc., to give greater width or change the shape. —*v.* put or make a gore in. [OE *gāra* point < *gār* spear] —**gored,** *adj.* —**gor′ing,** *n.*

gorge (gôrj), *n., v.,* **gorged, gorg·ing.** —*n.* **1** a deep, narrow valley, usually steep and rocky. **2** *Archaic.* throat; gullet. —*v.* eat greedily until full; stuff with food. [< OF, ult. < LL *gurges* throat, jaws < L, abyss, whirlpool] —**gorg′er,** *n.*

gor·geous (gôr′jəs), *adj.* richly colored; splendid: *a gorgeous sunset.* [< OF *gorgias* fashionable] —**gor′geous·ly,** *adv.* —**gor′geous·ness,** *n.*

Gor·gon (gôr′gən), *n. Gk. Legend.* any of three horrible sisters who had snakes for hair and whose look turned the beholder to stone. [< L < Gk., < *gorgos* terrible]

Gor·gon·zo·la (gôr′gən zō′lə), *n.* a strong, white Italian cheese that looks and tastes much like Roquefort cheese.

go·ril·la (gə ril′ə), *n.* **1** a very large human-like ape of Africa. **2** *Informal.* a strong and unrefined man. [< NL < Gk. < an African lang.] —**go·ril′la·like′,** *adj.*

gor·mand (gôr′mənd), *n.* =gourmand.

gor·mand·ize (gôr′mən dīz), *v.,* **–ized, –iz·ing.** stuff oneself with food; eat very greedily; gorge. [orig. n., < F *gourmandise* gluttony] —**gor′mand·iz′er,** *n.*

gor·y (gôr′i; gōr′i), *adj.,* **gor·i·er, gor·i·est.** bloody. —**gor′i·ly,** *adv.* —**gor′i·ness,** *n.*

gosh (gosh), *interj.* exclamation or mild oath.

gos·hawk (gos′hôk′), *n.* a powerful, short-winged hawk, formerly much used in falconry. [OE *gōshafoc* < *gōs* goose + *hafoc* hawk]

gos·ling (goz′ling), *n.* a young goose.

gos·pel (gos′pəl), *n.* **1** the teachings of Jesus and the Apostles. **2** Usually, **Gos·pel.** any one or part of the first four books of the New Testament, by Matthew, Mark, Luke, and John. **3** the absolute truth. —*adj.* **1** evangelical. **2** of or pertaining to the gospel. [OE *gōdspel* good tidings (i.e., of the Nativity) < *gōd* good + *spel* spell²]

gos·sa·mer (gos′ə mər), *n.* **1** film or thread of cobweb. **2** a very thin, light cloth. **3** anything very light and thin. —*adj.* Also, **gos′sa·mer·y.** very light and thin; filmy. [ME *gossomer* goose summer, name for "Indian summer," the season for goose and cobwebs]

gos·sip (gos′ip), *n., v.,* **–siped, –sip·ing.** —*n.* **1** idle talk, not always true, about other people and their affairs. **2** person who gossips a good deal. —*v.* repeat what one knows, or the idle talk that one hears, about other people and their affairs. [OE *godsibb,* orig., godparent < *god* God + *sibb* relative] —**gos′sip·er,** *n.* —**gos′sip·ing,** *n.* —**gos′sip·ing·ly,** *adv.* —**gos′sip·y,** *adj.*

got (got), *v.* pt. and pp. of **get.**

Goth (goth), *n.* **1** member of a Teutonic tribe that overran the Roman Empire in the third, fourth, and fifth centuries A.D. **2** an uncivilized person; barbarian.

Goth·ic (goth′ik), *n.* **1** style of architecture using pointed arches and high, steep roofs, developed in W Europe during the Middle Ages from about 1150 to 1550. **2** language of the Goths. —*adj.* **1** of Gothic architecture. **2** of the Goths or their language. **3** also, **gothic.** (of a story, novel, etc.) dark and mysterious, complicated. —**Goth′i·cal·ly,** *adv.*

got·ten (got′ən), *v.* pp. of **get.**

gou·ache (gu̇′wäsh), *n.* **1** opaque water color, made from a mixture of pigment and gum. **2** method of painting with gouache. **3** painting made this way. [< F *gouache* < Ital. *guazzo* water colors]

gouge (gouj), *n., v.,* **gouged, goug·ing.** —*n.* **1** chisel with a curved blade. **2** groove or hole made by gouging. —*v.* **1** cut with a gouge. **2** dig out; force out. **3** *Informal.* trick; cheat. [< F < LL *gulbia*] —**goug′er,** *n.*

gou·lash (gu̇′läsh), *n.* stew made of beef or veal and vegetables, usually highly seasoned. [< Hung. *gulyás* (*hús* herdsman's (meat)]

gourd (gôrd; gōrd; gu̇rd), *n.* **1** the hard-shelled fruit of certain vines. **2** cup, bowl, bottle, rattle, etc., made from a dried shell of this fruit. **3** vine that gourds grow on. **4** any plant of the family to which cucumbers, pumpkins, and muskmelons belong. [< F < OF *cohorde* < L *cucurbita*] —**gourd′like′,** *adj.* —**gourd′-shaped,** *adj.*

gour·mand (gu̇r′mənd), *n.* person who is fond of good eating. [< F, gluttonous < *gourmet* gourmet]

gour·met (gu̇r′mā), *n.* person who is expert in judging and choosing fine foods, wines, etc.; epicure. [< F < OF *groumet* wine tester]

gout (gout), *n.* a painful disease of the joints, often characterized by a swelling of the big toe. [< OF < L *gutta* a drop, in Med.L, gout]

gout·y (gout′i), *adj.,* **gout·i·er, gout·i·est. 1** diseased or swollen with gout. **2** of gout; caused by or causing gout. —**gout′i·ly,** *adv.* —**gout′i·ness,** *n.*

Gov., Governor.

gov., **1** government. **2** governor.

gov·ern (guv′ərn), *v.* **1** rule; control; manage. **2** exercise a directing or restraining influence over; determine: *motives governing a person's decision.* **3** hold back; restrain; check: *govern one's temper.* [< OF < L < Gk. *kybernaein* steer] —**gov′ern·a·ble,** *adj.*

gov·ern·ance (guv′ər nəns), *n.* rule; control.

gov·ern·ess (guv′ər nis), woman who teaches children in a private house.

gov·ern·ment (guv′ərn mənt; -ər-), *n.* **1** act of governing; rule or authority over a country, state, district, etc. **2** person or persons ruling a country, state, district, etc.; administration. **3** system of ruling: *republican government.* **4** country, state, district, etc., ruled. —**gov′ern·men′tal,** *adj.* —**gov′ern·men′tal·ly,** *adv.*

gov·er·nor (guv′ər nər; guv′nər), *n.* **1** official elected as the executive head of a state of the United States. **2** official appointed to govern a province, city, fort, etc. **3** an automatic device that keeps a machine going at a certain speed.

governor general, *pl.* **governors general.** governor who has subordinate or deputy governors under him. —**gov′er·nor-gen′er·al·ship′,** *n.*

gov·er·nor·ship (guv′ər nər ship′; guv′nər-), *n.* position or term of office of governor.

govt., Govt., government.

gown (goun), *n.* **1** a woman's dress. **2** a loose outer garment worn to show position, profession, etc., as that of a judge. **3** nightgown or dressing gown. —*v.* put a gown on; dress in a gown. [< OF < LL *gunna*]

GP, (gē′pē′), general practitioner.

Gr., 1 Grecian. **2** Greece. **3** Also, **Gk.** Greek.

gr., 1 grain. **2** gram. **3** gravity. **4** gross.

grab (grab), *v.,* **grabbed, grab·bing,** *n.* —*v.* seize suddenly; snatch. —*n.* **1** a snatching; a sudden seizing. **2** that which is grabbed. [cf. MDu. *grabben*] —**grab′ber,** *n.*

grab bag, 1 bag in which an assortment of objects is hidden and from which a person takes one, without knowing what it will be. **2** *Fig.* a variety or odd assortment: *grab bag of ideas.*

grab·by (grab′i), *adj.,* **-bi·er, -bi·est.** greedy; grasping.

grace (grās), *n., v.,* **graced, grac·ing.** —*n.* **1** beauty of form, movement, or manner; pleasing or agreeable quality. **2** good will; favor. **3** mercy; pardon. **4** favor and love of God. **5** a short prayer of thanks before or after a meal. **6** favor shown by granting a delay. **7** allowance of time. —*v.* **1** give or add grace to; set off with grace. **2** do a favor or honor to.

fall from grace, a fall out of favor. **b** return to bad habits, sinful ways, etc.

in one's good or **bad graces,** liked or disliked by one; approved of or disapproved of.

Grace, *Class. Myth.* one of the three sister goddesses controlling beauty and charm in people and in nature.

with good grace, willingly; pleasantly. [< F < L *gratia* < *gratus* **pleasing**]

grace·ful (grās′fəl), *adj.* having or showing grace; beautiful in form, movement, or manner. —**grace′ful·ly,** *adv.* —**grace′ful·ness,** *n.*

grace·less (grās′lis), *adj.* **1** without grace. **2** not caring for what is right or proper. —**grace′less·ly,** *adv.* —**grace′less·ness,** *n.*

grace note, note not essential to the harmony or melody, added for embellishment.

gra·cious (grā′shəs), *adj.* pleasant; kindly; courteous. —*interj.* exclamation of surprise. [< OF < L *gratiosus*] —**gra′cious·ly,** *adv.* —**gra′cious·ness, gra′ci·os′i·ty,** *n.*

grack·le (grak′əl), *n.* kind of blackbird. [< L *graculus* jackdaw]

grad., graduate; graduated.

gra·da·tion (grā dā′shən), *n.* **1** a change by steps or stages; gradual change. **2** Usually, **gradations.** step, stage, or degree in a series. **3** act or process of grading. [< L *gradatio.* See GRADE.] —**gra·da′tion·al,** *adj.* —**gra·da′tion·al·ly,** *adv.*

grade (grād), *n., v.,* **grad·ed, grad·ing.** —*n.* **1** any one division of a school arranged according to the pupils' progress. **2** degree in a scale of rank, quality, value, etc. **3** group of people or things having the same rank, quality, value, etc. **4** number or letter that shows how well one has done. **5** slope of a road, railroad track, etc. **6** amount of slope. —*v.* **1** place in classes; arrange in grades; sort. **2** give a grade to. **3** make more nearly level. **4** change gradually.

make the grade, overcome difficulties. [< F < L *gradus* step, degree]

grade crossing, place where a railroad crosses a street or another railroad on the same level.

grad·er (grād′ər), *n.* **1** person or thing that grades. **2** person who is in a certain grade at school.

grade school, =elementary school.

gra·di·ent (grā′di ənt), *n.* **1** rate at which a road, railroad track, etc., rises. **2** the sloping part of a road, etc. **3** rate at which temperature or pressure changes. **4** rate of change of any variable. [< L *gradiens* walking. See GRADE.]

grad·u·al (graj′u̇ əl), *adj.* by degrees too small to be separately noticed; little by little. —**grad′u·al·ly,** *adv.* —**grad′u·al·ness,** *n.*

grad·u·al·ism (graj′u̇ ə liz′əm), *n.* principle of gradual change. —**grad′u·al·ist,** *n.*

grad·u·ate (*v.* graj′u̇ āt; *n., adj.* graj′u̇ it), *v.,* **-at·ed, -at·ing,** *n., adj.* —*v.* **1** finish a course of study at a school, college, or university and receive a diploma or other document saying so. **2** give a diploma to for finishing a course of study. **3** mark with degrees for measuring. A thermometer is graduated. —*n.* **1** person who has graduated. **2** container marked with degrees for measuring. —*adj.* **1** that is a graduate: *a graduate student.* **2** of or for graduates. [< Med.L *graduatus.* See GRADE.] —**grad′u·a′tor,** *n.*

graduate school, part of a university or college that offers studies leading to master's and doctor's degrees.

grad·u·a·tion (graj´ù ā´shən), *n.* **1** a graduating from a school, college, or university. **2** graduating exercises. **3** a marking with degrees for measuring. **4** mark or set of marks to show degrees for measuring.

graf·fi·ti (grə fē´ti), *n.* spray-painted pictures or words on buildings, bridges, subway cars, etc. [< Ital. *graffito, pl. graffiti,* scribbling < Gk. *gráphein,* draw, write]

graft[1] (graft; gräft), *v.* **1** insert (a shoot, bud, etc.) from one tree or plant into a slit in another so that it will grow there permanently. **2** produce or improve (fruit, flower, etc.) by grafting. **3** transfer (a piece of skin, bone, etc.) from one part of the body to another so that it will grow there permanently. **4** *Fig.* insert or impose on: *graft new work onto earlier writings.* —*n.* **1** shoot, bud, etc., used in grafting. **2** act of grafting. **3** piece of skin, bone, etc., transferred in grafting. [earlier, *graff* < OF < L < Gk. *grapheion* stylus < *graphein* write; from similarity of shape] —**graft´er,** *n.* —**graft´ing,** *n.*

graft[2] (graft; gräft), —*n.* **1** the taking of money dishonestly in connection with public business. **2** money dishonestly taken or obtained. —*v.* make money dishonestly through one's job, esp. in political positions. —**graft´er,** *n.*

gra·ham (grā´əm), *adj.* made from unsifted whole wheat or whole-wheat flour. [for S. Graham, reformer of dietetics]

Grail (grāl), *n.* the Holy Grail. [< OF < Med.L *gradale* plate, or < VL *cratale* < *crater* bowl < Gk.]

grain (grān), *n.* **1** a seed of wheat, oats, and similar cereal grasses. **2** plants that these seeds or seedlike fruits grow on. **3** a tiny, hard particle of sand, salt, sugar, etc. **4** the smallest unit of weight. One pound avoirdupois equals 7000 grains. **5** the smallest possible amount; tiniest bit: *grain of truth.* **6** arrangement or direction of fibers in wood, layers in stone, etc. **7** the rough surface of leather. **8** natural character; disposition. —*v.* form into grains.

go against the grain, be contrary to what someone believes or wants.

with a grain of salt, with skepticism; with reservations. [< OF < L *granum* grain, seed] —**grained,** *adj.* —**grain´er,** *n.* —**grain´less,** *adj.* —**grain´y,** *adj.*

grain alcohol, ethyl alcohol, often made from grain.

grained (grānd), *adj.* **1** having the lines and markings of wood. **2** painted to look like wood or marble.

grain elevator, a building for storing grain.

gram (gram), *n.* unit of weight in the metric system. Twenty-eight grams weigh about one ounce avoirdupois. [< F < LL < Gk. *gramma* small weight < *graphein* write]

-gram, *combining form.* **1** something written; message, as in *cablegram, telegram, monogram.* [< Gk. *-gramma* something written, ult. < *graphein* write] **2** grams; of a gram, as in *kilogram, milligram.* [< Gk., < *gramma* small weight, ult. < *graphein* write]

gram., grammar; grammatical.

gram·mar (gram´ər), *n.* **1** study and classification of the classes, forms, sounds, and uses of words of a particular language. **2** statements about the use of words. **3** the elements of any subject: *grammar of painting.* [< OF < L < Gk. *grammatike (techne)* (art) of letters, ult. < *graphein* write]

gram·mar·i·an (grə mār´i ən), *n.* expert in grammar.

grammar school, 1 a public school in the United States having the grades between preschool and high school. **2** *Brit.* a secondary school.

gram·mat·i·cal (grə mat´ə kəl), *adj.* **1** according to correct use of words. **2** of grammar. —**gram·mat´i·cal·ly,** *adv.* —**gram·mat´i·cal·ness,** *n.*

gram·mo·lec·u·lar (gram´mə lek´yə lər), *adj.* of or having to do with a gram molecule.

gram molecule, amount of an element or compound that equals its molecular weight expressed in grams.

gram·pus (gram´pəs), *n.* **1** a large, fierce dolphin; killer whale. **2** a small, toothed whale. [earlier *grapays* < OF < Med.L *crassus piscis* fat fish]

gran·a·ry (gran´ə ri; grān´–), *n., pl.* **–ries. 1** place where grain is stored. **2** region having much grain. [< L, < *granum* grain]

grand (grand), *adj.* **1** large and of fine appearance: *grand mountains.* **2** fine; noble; stately: *grand music.* **3** very high in rank; chief: *grand jury.* **4** important; main: *the grand staircase.* **5** complete: *grand total.* **6** very satisfactory. —*n. Informal.* a thousand dollars. [< OF < L *grandis* big] —**grand´ly,** *adv.* —**grand´ness,** *n.*

gran·dam (gran´dam), **gran·dame** (–dām), *n.* **1** =grandmother. **2** old woman. [< AF *graund dame.* See GRAND, DAME.]

grand·aunt (grand´ant´; –änt´), *n.* =great-aunt.

Grand Canyon, a deep gorge of the Colorado River, in N Arizona.

grand·child (grand´chīld´), *n., pl.* **–children.** child of one's son or daughter.

grand·daugh·ter (grand´dô´tər), *n.* daughter of one's son or daughter.

gran·dee (gran dē´), *n.* **1** a Spanish or Portuguese nobleman of the highest rank. **2** person of high rank or great importance. [< Sp., Pg. *grande.* See GRAND.]

gran·deur (gran´jər; –jùr), *n.* greatness; majesty; nobility; dignity; splendor.

grand·fa·ther (grand´fä´thər), *n.* **1** father of one's father or mother. **2** =forefather. —**grand´fa´ther·ly,** *adj.*

grandfather clause, provision that allows an existing right or privilege to continue, despite its being withdrawn by a new law. [< *grandfather clause* a provision in some S U.S. states that made voting difficult for blacks]

gran·dil·o·quent (gran dil´ə kwənt), *adj.* using lofty or pompous words. [< L, < *grandis* grand + *loquens* speaking] —**gran·dil´o·quence,** *n.* —**gran·dil´o·quent·ly,** *adv.*

gran·di·ose (gran´di ōs), *adj.* **1** grand in an imposing or impressive way. **2** grand in an affected or pompous way; trying to seem magnificent. [< F < Ital. *grandioso*] —**gran´di·ose·ly,** *adv.* —**gran´di·os´i·ty,** *n.*

grand jury, jury chosen to investigate accusations and bring an indictment against the accused if there is enough evidence for trial before an ordinary jury.

grand·ma (grand´mä´; gram´mä´; gram´ə), *n. Informal.* grandmother.

grand·moth·er (grand´muth´ər), *n.* **1** mother of one's father or mother. **2** ancestress. —**grand´moth´er·ly,** *adj.*

grand·neph·ew (grand´nef´ū; –nev´ū), *n.* son of one's nephew or niece.

grand·niece (grand´nēs´), *n.* daughter of one's nephew or niece.

Grand Old Party, the Republican Party.

grand opera, a musical drama in which all the speeches are sung to the accompaniment of an orchestra.

grand·pa (grand´pä; gram´pä´; gram´pə), *n. Informal.* grandfather.

grand·par·ent (grand´pār´ənt), *n.* grandfather or grandmother.

grand·sire (grand´sīr´), *n. Archaic.* **1** =grandfather. **2** =forefather. **3** an old man.

grand·son (grand´sun´), *n.* son of one's son or daughter.

grand·stand (grand´stand´), *n.* the principal seating place for people at an athletic field, race track, etc. —*v.* **–standed, –standing.** do something showy or meant to impress.

grandstand play, something done to win applause, attract attention, etc.

grand·un·cle (grand´ung´kəl), *n.* =great-uncle.

grange (grānj), *n.* **1** farm. **2** Grange, organization of farmers for the improvement of their welfare. [< OF < VL *granica* < L *granum* grain]

grang·er (grān´jər), *n.* =farmer.

gran·ite (gran´it), *n.* a hard igneous rock made of grains of other rocks, chiefly quartz and feldspar. [< Ital. *granito* grained, ult. < L *granum* grain] —**gran´ite·like´,** *adj.* —**gra·nit´ic,** *adj.*

gran·ny (gran´i), *n., pl.* **–nies.** *Informal.* **1** =grandmother. **2** an old woman. **3** a fussy person.

granny knot, knot differing from a square knot in having the ends crossed the wrong way.

gra·no·la (grə nō'lə), *n.* mixture of cereals, nuts, raisins, etc., sold as breakfast food or as a natural-food snack.

grant (grant; gränt), *v.* **1** give what is asked; allow. **2** admit to be true; accept without proof; concede. **3** bestow or confer (a right, etc.) by formal act; transfer or convey (the ownership of property), esp. by deed or writing. —*n.* **1** thing granted, such as a privilege, right, sum of money, or tract of land. **2** act of granting.

take for granted, assume to be true; use as proved or agreed to. [< OF *granter,* var. of *creanter,* promise, authorize, ult. < L *credens* trusting] —**grant'a·ble,** *adj.* —**gran·tee',** *n.* —**grant'er, grant'or,** *n.*

Grant (grant), **Ulysses S.,** 1822–85, American general, 18th president of the United States, 1869–77.

gran·u·lar (gran'yə lər), *adj.* **1** consisting of or containing grains or granules. **2** resembling grains or granules. —**gran'u·lar'i·ty,** *n.* —**gran'u·lar·ly,** *adv.*

gran·u·late (gran'yə lāt), *v.,* **–lat·ed, –lat·ing. 1** form into grains or granules. **2** roughen on the surface. **3** become granular; develop granulations. —**gran'u·lat'ed,** *adj.* —**gran'u·lat'er, gran'u·la'tor,** *n.* —**gran'u·la'tion,** *n.* —**gran'u·la'tive,** *adj.*

gran·ule (gran'ūl), *n.* **1** a small grain. **2** a small bit or spot like a grain. [< LL *granulum,* dim. of *granum* grain]

grape (grāp), *n.* **1** a small, round fruit that grows in bunches on a vine. **2** =grapevine. **3** a dark, purplish red. [< OF, bunch of grapes, < *graper* pick grapes < *grape* hook < Gmc.] —**grape'less,** *adj.* —**grape'like',** *adj.*

grape·fruit (grāp'früt), *n.* a pale-yellow citrus fruit like an orange, but larger and sourer.

grape·shot (grāp'shot'), *n.* cluster of small iron balls used as a charge for cannon.

grape sugar, sugar formed in all green plants, but esp. in grapes; dextrose.

grape·vine (grāp'vīn'), *n.* **1** vine that bears grapes. **2 a** way by which reports are mysteriously spread. **b** a baseless report.

graph (graf; gräf), *n.* **1** line or diagram showing how one quantity depends on or changes with another. **2** any line or lines representing a series of relations. —*v.* draw (such a line or diagram); draw a line representing some change, equation, or function. [for *graphic formula.* See GRAPHIC.]

-graph, *combining form.* **1** make a picture, draw, or write, as in *photograph.* **2** machine that makes a picture, draws, or writes, as in *seismograph.* **3** drawn or written, as in *autograph.* **4** something drawn or written, as in *lithograph.* [< Gk. *gráphein* write]

graph·ic (graf'ik), *adj.* **1** lifelike; vivid. **2** of or about diagrams and their use. **3** shown by a graph. **4** of or about draw-

ing, painting, engraving, or etching: *the graphic symbols.* **5** of or used in handwriting: *graphic symbols.* **6** written; inscribed. [< L < Gk., < *gráphein* write] —**graph'i·cal·ly, graph'ic·ly,** *adv.* —**graph'i·cal·ness,** *n.*

graphic arts, drawing, painting, engraving, etc., esp. as applied to making prints and designing books.

graph·ics (graf'iks), *n.* **1** art or science of drawing, esp. mechanical drawing. **2** illustrative material included in a book or other printed materials. **3** layout, type, and design generated by a computer.

graph·ite (graf'īt), *n.* a soft, black form of carbon with a metallic luster, used for lead in pencils and for lubricating machinery. [< G *graphit* < Gk. *graphein* write] —**gra·phit'ic,** *adj.*

graph paper, paper ruled into squares, used for making graphs and diagrams.

grap·nel (grap'nəl), *n.* **1** instrument with one or more hooks for seizing and holding. **2** a small anchor with three or more hooks. [< OF *grapin* hook, dim. of *grape* hook]

grap·ple (grap'əl), *v.,* **–pled, –pling,** *n.* —*v.* **1** seize and hold fast; grip or hold firmly. **2** struggle; fight. **3** use a grapnel; search for with a grapnel. [< n.] —*n.* **1** a seizing and holding fast; firm grip or hold. **2** =grapnel. [< OF *grapil* hook] —**grap'pler,** *n.*

grappling iron, =grapnel.

grasp (grasp; gräsp), *v.* **1** seize and hold fast by closing the fingers around. **2** understand. —*n.* **1** a seizing and holding tightly; clasp of the hand. **2** power of seizing and holding. **3** control; possession. **4** understanding.

grasp at, a try to take hold of. **b** accept eagerly. [ME *graspe(n)*; akin to GROPE] —**grasp'a·ble,** *adj.* —**grasp'er,** *n.*

grasp·ing (gras'ping; gräs'–), *adj.* **1** eager to get all that one can; greedy. **2** that grasps. —**grasp'ing·ly,** *adv.* —**grasp'ing·ness,** *n.*

grass (gras; gräs), *n.* **1** any of various plants that cover fields, lawns, and pastures. **2** land covered with grass; pasture. **3** plant that has jointed stems and long, narrow leaves. Wheat, corn, and bamboo are grasses. **4** *Slang.* marijuana. —*v.* cover with grass. [OE *græs*; akin to GREEN, GROW] —**grass'less,** *adj.* —**grass'like',** *adj.*

grass·hop·per (gras'hop'ər; gräs'–), *n.* insect with strong legs and wings for jumping.

grass·land (gras'land'; gräs'–), *n.* land with grass on it, used for pasture.

grass roots, the ordinary citizens of a region or state taken all together.

grass snake, any of various harmless snakes that are gray-green in color and live in meadows.

grass widow, a woman divorced or separated from her husband.

grass widower, a man divorced or separated from his wife.

grass·y (gras'i; gräs'i), *adj.,* **grass·i·er, grass·i·est. 1** covered with grass. **2** of or like grass. —**grass'i·ness,** *n.*

grate[1] (grāt), *n., v.,* **grat·ed, grat·ing.** —*n.* **1** framework of iron bars to hold a fire. **2** framework of bars over a window or opening; grating. —*v.* furnish with a grate or grating. [< Med.L < Ital. < LL *cratis,* L, hurdle] —**grate'less,** *adj.* —**grate'like',** *adj.*

grate[2] (grāt), *v.,* **—grat·ed, grat·ing. 1** make (a grinding sound); sound harshly. **2** rub with a harsh sound: *the door grated on its hinges.* **3** have an annoying or unpleasant effect: *rude manners grate.* **4** wear down or grind off in small pieces: *grate cheese.* [< OF *grater* < Gmc.]

grat·er (grāt'ər), *n.* kitchen tool for shredding cheese, vegetables, etc.

grate·ful (grāt'fəl), *adj.* **1** feeling gratitude; thankful. **2** pleasing; welcome. [< obs. *grate* agreeable (< L *gratus*) + *full*] —**grate'ful·ly,** *adv.* —**grate'ful·ness,** *n.*

grat·i·fy (grat'ə fī), *v.,* **–fied, –fy·ing. 1** give pleasure or satisfaction to; please. **2** satisfy; indulge. [< F < L, < *gratus* pleasing + *facere* make, do] —**grat'i·fi·ca'tion,** *n.* —**grat'i·fi'er,** *n.* —**grat'i·fy'ing·ly,** *adv.*

grat·ing[1] (grāt'ing), *n.* framework of bars over a window or opening.

grat·ing[2] (grāt'ing), *adj.* harsh or unpleasant. —**grat'ing·ly,** *adv.*

grat·is (grat'is; grā'tis), *adv., adj.* free of charge. [< L, ult. < *gratia* favor]

grat·i·tude (grat'ə tüd; –tūd), *n.* kindly feeling because of a favor received; thankfulness. [< LL, < *gratus* thankful]

gra·tu·i·tous (grə tü'ə təs; –tū'–), *adj.* **1** freely given or obtained; free. **2** without reason or cause. —**gra·tu'i·tous·ly,** *adv.* —**gra·tu'i·tous·ness,** *n.*

gra·tu·i·ty (grə tü'ə ti; –tū'–), *n., pl.* **–ties. 1** present of money in return for service; tip. **2** present; gift. [< Med.L, gift, appar. < L *gratuitus* free]

grave[1] (grāv), *n.* **1** hole dug in the ground where a dead body is to be buried. **2** mound or monument over it. **3** any place that becomes the receptacle of what is dead: *a watery grave.*

dig one's own grave, cause one's own downfall or ruin. [OE *græf.* See GRAVE[3].]

grave[2] (grāv), *adj.,* **grav·er, grav·est,** *n.* —*adj.* **1** important; weighty; momentous. **2** serious; threatening: *a grave situation.* **3** dignified; sober; solemn. **4** having a particular accent (`) that may indicate pitch, quality of sound (as in French *père*), or syllabic value (as in *belovèd*). —*n.* the grave accent. [< F < L *gravis* serious] —**grave'ly,** *adv.* —**grave'ness,** *n.*

grave[3] (grāv), *v.,* **graved, graved** or **grav·en, grav·ing.** engrave; carve. [OE *grafan*] —**grav'er,** *n.*

grav·el (grav'əl), *n., v.,* **–eled, –el·ing.** —*n.* pebbles and rock fragments coarser than sand. —*v.* lay or cover with gravel. [< OF *gravele,* dim. of *grave* sand, seashore < Celtic] —**grav′el·ly,** *adj.*

grav·en (grāv′ən), *adj.* engraved; carved; sculptured: *graven image.* —*v.* pp. of **grave**[3].

grave·stone (grāv′stōn′), *n.* stone that marks a grave.

grave·yard (grāv′yärd′), *n.* place for burying the dead; cemetery; burial ground.

grav·i·tate (grav′ə tāt), *v.,* –**tat·ed,** –**tat·ing.** 1 move or tend to move by gravitation. 2 settle down; sink. 3 tend to go; be strongly attracted: *unemployed workers gravitated to the city.* [< NL, ult. < L *gravis* heavy]

grav·i·ta·tion (grav′ə tā′shən), *n.* 1 a force that attracts bodies toward one another. b a moving or tendency to move caused by this force. 2 a natural tendency toward some point or object of influence. —**grav′i·ta′tion·al,** *adj.* —**grav′i·ta′tion·al·ly,** *adv.*

grav·i·ty (grav′ə ti), *n., pl.* –**ties.** 1 the natural force that causes objects to move or tend to move toward the center of the earth. Gravity causes objects to have weight. 2 the natural force that makes objects move or tend to move toward each other; gravitation. 3 heaviness; weight. 4 seriousness; solemnity; earnestness. 5 critical character; importance. [< L, < *gravis* heavy]

gra·vy (grā′vi), *n., pl.* –**vies.** 1 juice that comes out of meat in cooking. 2 sauce for meat, potatoes, etc., made from this juice. 3 *Fig.* profit or gain secured without effort. [ME *grave,* a mistaken writing of OF *grané* properly grained, seasoned, ult. < L *granum* grain]

gravy boat, small dish, shaped somewhat like a boat, for serving gravy or sauce.

gravy train, *Informal.* something that yields money or profit without much effort.

gray (grā), *n.* 1 color made by mixing black and white. 2 gray cloth or clothing. —*adj.* 1 having a color between black and white. 2 having gray hair. 3 dark; gloomy; dismal. —*v.* make or become gray. [OE *grǣg*] —**gray·ly,** *adv.* —**gray′ness,** *n.*

gray·beard (grā′bird′), *n.* old man.

gray·ish (grā′ish), *adj.* somewhat gray.

gray·lag (grā′lag′), *n.* a wild, gray goose that is common in Europe. [< *gray* + *lag;* because these birds migrate south at a very late date]

gray·ling (grā′ling), *n.* a freshwater fish somewhat like a trout.

gray matter, 1 grayish tissue in the brain and spinal cord that contains nerve cells and some nerve fibers. 2 *Informal.* intelligence; brains.

graze[1] (grāz), *v.,* **grazed, graz·ing.** 1 feed on growing grass. 2 put (cattle, sheep, etc.) to feed on growing grass or a pasture. [OE *grasian* < *grǣs* grass] —**graz′er,** *n.*

graze[2] (grāz), *v.,* **grazed, graz·ing,** *n.* —*v.* 1 touch lightly in passing; rub lightly

(against). 2 scrape the skin from. —*n.* 1 a grazing. 2 a slight wound made by grazing. —**graz′ing·ly,** *adv.*

graz·ing (grāz′ing), *n.* growing grass that cattle, sheep, etc., feed on; pasture.

grease (*n.* grēs; *v.* grēs, grēz), *n., v.,* **greased, greas·ing.** —*n.* 1 soft animal fat. 2 any thick, oily substance. —*v.* 1 smear with grease; put grease on. 2 cause to run smoothly by greasing. 3 *Slang.* give money as a bribe or tip. [< OF, ult. < L *crassus* fat] —**grease′less,** *adj.* —**greas′er,** *n.*

grease·ball (grēs′bôl′), *n. Informal.* person who seems untrustworthy, slippery.

grease gun, device shaped like a tube that has a piston which forces grease out through a nozzle or small opening to lubricate bearings, tracks, etc.

greas·y (grēs′i; grēz′i), *adj.,* **greas·i·er, greas·i·est.** 1 smeared with grease; having grease on it. 2 containing much grease. 3 like grease; smooth; slippery. —**greas′i·ly,** *adv.* —**greas′i·ness,** *n.*

greasy spoon, *Informal.* restaurant serving cheap, sometimes greasy, food.

great (grāt), *adj.* 1 big; large: *a great crowd.* 2 more than usual; much: *great ignorance, a great talker.* 3 important; famous: *a great composer.* 4 much in use; favorite: *that is a great habit of his.* 5 *Informal.* very good; fine: *a great party.* [OE *grēat*] —**great′ly,** *adv.* —**great′ness,** *n.*

great-aunt (grāt′ant′; -änt′), *n.* aunt of one's father or mother, grandaunt.

Great Britain, England, Scotland, and Wales. It is the largest island of Europe.

great circle, any circle on the surface of a sphere having its plane passing through the center of the sphere.

great·coat (grāt′kōt′), *n.* a heavy overcoat.

Great Dane, one of a breed of large, powerful, short-haired dogs.

Great Divide, the Rocky Mountains of N America.

great-heart·ed (grāt′här′tid), *adj.* 1 noble; generous. 2 brave; fearless. —**great′-heart′ed·ness,** *n.*

Great Lakes, series of lakes between the United States and Canada; Lakes Ontario, Erie, Huron, Michigan, and Superior.

Great Plains, a semiarid region just east of the Rocky Mountains in the United States and SW Canada.

great-un·cle (grāt′ung′kəl), *n.* uncle of one's father or mother; granduncle.

grebe (grēb), *n.* a diving bird like a loon, having feet not completely webbed and a pointed bill. [< F]

Gre·cian (grē′shən), *adj., n.* Greek.

Gre·co-Ro·man (grē′kō rō′mən), *adj.* Greek and Roman.

Greece (grēs), *n.* country in S Europe, on the Mediterranean Sea.

greed (grēd), *n.* extreme or excessive desire, esp. for money. [OE *grǣd*] —**greed′less,** *adj.*

greed·y (grēd′i), *adj.,* **greed·i·er, greed·i·est.** 1 wanting to get more than one's share; having a very great desire to possess something. 2 wanting to eat or drink a great deal in a hurry; piggish. [OE *grǣdig*] —**greed′i·ly,** *adv.* —**greed′i·ness,** *n.*

Greek (grēk), *adj.* of Greece, its people, or their language. —*n.* 1 native or inhabitant of Greece. 2 language of Greece.

Greek fire, = wildfire.

Greek Orthodox Church, 1 Christian church of the countries in communion or doctrinal agreement with the patriarch of Constantinople. 2 Also, **Greek Church.** part of this church that constitutes the established church in Greece.

green (grēn), *n.* 1 color of most growing plants, grass, and leaves. 2 green coloring matter, dye, paint, etc. 3 grassy land or a plot of grassy ground as a town common. 4 a putting green. 5 Usually, **Green.** person, esp. a politician, or group dedicated to preservation of the environment. —*adj.* 1 having the color green. 2 covered with growing plants, grass, leaves, etc.: *green fields.* 3 not dried, cured, seasoned, or otherwise prepared for use. 4 not ripe; not fully grown. 5 not trained or experienced; not mature; easily fooled. 6 having a pale, sickly color. —*v.* make or become green.

greens, a green leaves and branches used for decoration. b leaves and stems of plants used for food: *salad greens.* [OE *grēne;* akin to GRASS, GROW] —**green′ish,** *adj.* —**green′ness,** *n.*

green algae, bright, grass-green algae living mainly in fresh water.

green·back (grēn′bak′), *n.* paper money having the back printed in green.

green bean, green string bean.

green·bri·er (grēn′brī′ər), *n.* a climbing smilax with prickly stems and green leaves.

green card, identification card issued to a registered alien resident of the United States that permits him or her to work.

green·er·y (grēn′ər i), *n., pl.* –**er·ies.** green plants, grass, or leaves; verdure.

green-eyed (grēn′īd′), *adj.* jealous.

green·gage (grēn′gāj′), *n.* a large plum with a light-green skin and pulp. [after Sir Wm. *Gage,* who introduced it into England]

green·gro·cer (grēn′grō′sər), *n.* person who sells fresh vegetables and fruit. —**green′gro′cer·y,** *n.*

green·horn (grēn′hôrn′), *n.* person without experience. [with ref. to the green horns of young oxen]

green·house (grēn′hous′), *n.* a building with a glass roof and glass sides kept warm for growing plants; hothouse. —*adj.* of or having to do with the greenhouse effect.

greenhouse effect, absorption and retention of the sun's radiation in the earth's atmosphere, causing an increase in temperature.

greenhouse gas, gas in the atmosphere, such as ozone and carbon dioxide, that traps the sun's radiation.

Green·land (grēn′lənd), *n.* the largest island in the world, belonging to Denmark. It lies NE of North America.

green light, official permission to proceed on a particular task or undertaking.

Green Mountains, part of the Appalachian Mountains extending through Vermont.

green·room (grēn′rüm′; -rûm′), *n.* room in old theaters for the use of actors and actresses when they are not on the stage.

green·sward (grēn′swôrd′), *n.* green grass.

green tea, tea whose leaves have been withered by steam.

green thumb, a remarkable ability to grow flowers, vegetables, etc., esp. as a hobby.

Green·wich (grin′ij; gren′-; -ich), *n.* borough in SE London, England. Longitude is measured east and west of Greenwich.

Green·wich Village (gren′ich), section of New York City, famous as a district for artists and writers.

green·wood (grēn′wùd′), *n.* forest in spring and summer when the trees are green.

greet (grēt), *v.* **1** speak or write to in a friendly, polite way. **2** address; salute. **3** receive: *his speech was greeted with cheers.* **4** present itself to; meet. [OE *grētan*] **—greet′er,** *n.*

greet·ing (grēt′ing), *n.* act or words of a person who greets another; welcome.

greetings, friendly wishes, as on a special occasion.

gre·gar·i·ous (grə gār′i əs), *adj.* **1** fond of being with others. **2** living in flocks, herds, or other groups. [< L *gregarius* < *grex* flock] **—gre·gar′i·ous·ly,** *adv.* **—gre·gar′i·ous·ness,** *n.*

Gre·go·ri·an calendar (grə gô′ri ən; -gō′-), calendar now in use in the United States and most other countries, introduced by Pope Gregory XIII in 1582. It is a correction of the calendar of Julius Caesar.

Gregorian chant, vocal music having free rhythm and a limited scale, used in the Roman Catholic Church.

grem·lin (grem′lən), *n.* an imaginary elf that troubles the pilots of airplanes.

gre·nade (grə nād′), *n.* a small bomb, usually hurled by hand. [< F < Sp. *granada* pomegranate (lit., having grains) < L *granatus.* See GARNET.]

gren·a·dier (gren′ə dir′), *n.* member of a special regiment of guards in the British army; originally, a soldier who threw grenades; later, a very tall foot soldier. [< F, < *grenade* GRENADE] **—gren′a·dier′i·al,** *adj.* **—gren′a·dier′ly,** *adv.*

gren·a·dine (gren′ə dēn′; gren′ə dēn), *n.* syrup made from pomegranate or

currant juice. [< F *grenadin.* See GRENADE.]

grew (grü), *v.* pt. of **grow.**

grey (grā), *n., adj., v.* =gray. **—grey′ly,** *adv.* **—grey′ness,** *n.*

grey·hound (grā′hound′), *n.* one of a breed of tall, slender, swift dogs. [prob. < Scand. *greyhundr* < *grey* bitch + *hundr* dog]

grid (grid), *n.* **1** framework of parallel iron bars; grating; gridiron. **2** the lead plate in a storage battery. **3** network or system of electric lines that delivers electricity to a region or country: *midwestern power grid.* [short for *gridiron*]

grid·dle (grid′əl), *n., v.,* **-dled, -dling.** **—n.** a heavy, flat plate of metal to cook griddlecakes, etc. **—v.** cook on a griddle. [< unrecorded OF *gredil;* cf. OF *grediller singe.* See GRILL.]

grid·dle·cake (grid′əl kāk′), *n.* thin, flat cake of batter cooked on a griddle; pancake; flapjack.

grid·i·ron (grid′ī ′ərn) *n.* **1** a cooking utensil consisting of a framework of parallel iron bars or wires, usually with a handle. **2** any framework or network that looks like a gridiron. **3** a football field. [ME *gredire* GRIDDLE; final element assimilated to *iron*]

grid·lock (grid′lok′), *n.* **1** stoppage of vehicular traffic on city streets caused by heavy volume. **2** any stoppage, as of telephone service or complex negotiations.

grief (grēf), *n.* **1** deep sadness caused by trouble or loss; heavy sorrow. **come to grief, a** have trouble; fail. **b** cause of sadness or sorrow. [< OF, < *grever* GRIEVE] **—grief′less,** *adj.*

griev·ance (grēv′əns), *n.* a real or imagined wrong; reason for being angry or annoyed; cause for complaint.

grieve (grēv), *v.,* **grieved, griev·ing. 1** feel grief; be very sad. **2** cause to feel grief; make very sad; afflict. [< OF *grever,* ult. < L *gravis* heavy] **—griev′er,** *n.* **—griev′ing·ly,** *adv.*

griev·ous (grēv′əs), *adj.* **1** hard to bear; causing great pain or suffering. **2** flagrant; atrocious: *a grievous wrong.* **3** causing grief. **4** full of grief; showing grief: *a grievous cry.* **—griev′ous·ly,** *adv.* **—griev′ous·ness,** *n.*

grif·fin, grif·fon (grif′ən), *n. Gk. Myth.* creature with the head and wings of an eagle, and the body of a lion. [< OF *grifon* < L *gryphus,* var. of *gryps* < Gk.]

grill (gril), *n.* **1** a cooking utensil consisting of a framework of parallel iron bars for broiling meat, fish, etc.; gridiron. **2** dish of broiled meat, fish, etc. **3** restaurant or dining room that specializes in serving broiled meat and fish. **—v.** **1** broil. **2** torture with heat. **3** question severely and persistently: *the detectives grilled the prisoner until he finally confessed.* [< F *gril,* ult. < LL *cratis* grate < L, hurdle] **—grill′er,** *n.*

grille (gril), *n.* an openwork metal structure or screen, used as a gate, door,

or window. [< F < L *craticula* < *cratis* hurdle] **—grilled,** *adj.*

grim (grim), *adj.,* **grim·mer, grim·mest. 1** without mercy; stern; harsh; fierce. **2** not yielding; not relenting: *grim determination.* **3** looking stern, fierce, or harsh. **4** horrible; ghastly: *grim scenes of destruction.* [OE *grimm* fierce] **—grim′ly,** *adv.* **—grim′ness,** *n.*

gri·mace (grə mās′; grim′is), *n., v.,* **-maced, -mac·ing. —n.** twisting of the face; ugly or funny smile. **—v.** make grimaces. [< F < Sp. *grimazo* panic] **—gri·mac′er,** *n.*

grime (grīm), *n., v.,* **grimed, grim·ing.** **—n.** dirt rubbed deeply and firmly into a surface. **—v.** cover with grime; make very dirty. [? OE *grīma* mask]

grim·y (grīm′i), *adj.,* **grim·i·er, grim·i·est.** covered with grime; very dirty. **—grim′i·ly,** *adv.* **—grim′i·ness,** *n.*

grin (grin), *v.,* **grinned, grin·ning,** *n.* **—v. 1** smile broadly. **2** show, make, or express by smiling broadly: *he grinned approval.* **—n.** a broad smile. [OE *grennian*] **—grin′ner,** *n.* **—grin′ning·ly,** *adv.*

Grinch or **grinch** (grinch), *n. Informal.* person who spoils the pleasure of others; spoilsport. [< *How the Grinch Stole Christmas,* a children's story by Dr. Seuss (Theodor Seuss Geisel)]

grind (grīnd), *v.,* **ground** or (*Rare*) **grinded, grind·ing,** *n.* **—v. 1** crush into bits or into powder. **2** crush by harshness or cruelty. **3** sharpen, smooth, or wear by rubbing on something rough. **4** rub harshly (on, into, against, or together): *grind one's heel into the ground.* **5** work by turning a crank: *to grind an ice cream freezer.* **6** work or study long and hard. **—n. 1** act of grinding. **2** long, hard work or study. **3** person who works long and hard at his studies. [OE *grindan*] **—grind′ing·ly,** *adv.*

grind·er (grīn′dər), *n.* **1** person or thing that grinds. **2** person or machine that sharpens tools. **3** a molar.

grind·stone (grīnd′stōn′), *n.* a flat, round stone set in a frame and turned to sharpen tools and knives, or to smooth and polish things.

have, keep, or **put one's nose to the grindstone,** work long and hard.

grin·ga (gring′gə), *n., pl.* **-gas.** among Latinos, a woman gringo. [< Mex. Sp. fem. of *gringo*]

grin·go (gring′gō), *n., pl.,* **-gos.** among Latinos, term for a foreigner, esp. for an American or Englishman. [< Mex. Sp. < Sp., gibberish]

grip (grip), *n., v.,* **gripped** (gript) or **gript** (gript), **grip·ping. —n. 1** a firm hold; seizing and holding tight; tight grasp. **2** power of gripping. **3** handle. **4** special way of shaking hands. **5** firm control. **6** mental grasp. **7** sudden, sharp pain. **8** influenza. **9** a stagehand. **—v. 1** take a firm hold on; seize and hold tight. **2** get and keep the interest and attention of: *an exciting story grips you.* [OE gripe < grīpan to grasp] —**grip′per,** n. —**grip′ping·ly,** adv.

gripe (grīp), v., **griped, grip·ing,** n. —v. **1** clutch tightly; pinch. **2** cause pain in the bowels. **3** U.S. complain. —n. **1** fast hold; gripping; clutch. **2** grasp; control. **3** U.S. complaint. [OE grīpan]

grippe (grip), n. =influenza. [< F < Russ. khrip hoarseness]

grip·ping (grip′ing), adj. catching and holding the attention or interest. —**grip′ping·ly,** adv.

gris·ly (griz′li), adj., **-li·er, -li·est.** frightful; horrible; ghastly. [OE grislic] —**gris′li·ness,** n.

grist (grist), n. **1** grain to be ground. **2** grain that has been ground; meal or flour.

grist for (or **to**) **one's mill,** something useful, profitable, or advantageous for one. [OE grīst < grindan grind]

gris·tle (gris′əl), n. =cartilage. [OE]

gris·tly (gris′li), adj., **-tli·er, -tli·est.** of, containing, or like gristle.

grist mill, mill for grinding grain.

grit (grit), n., v., **grit·ted, grit·ting.** —n. **1** very fine gravel or sand. **2** a coarse sandstone. **3** courage; pluck. —v. grate; grind: grit one's teeth. [OE grēot] —**grit′less,** adj.

grits (grits), n.pl. **1** coarsely ground corn, oats, etc., with the husks removed. **2** coarse hominy. [OE gryttan, pl.]

grit·ty (grit′i), adj., **-ti·er, -ti·est, 1** of or containing grit; like grit; sandy. **2** courageous; plucky. —**grit′ti·ly,** adv. —**grit′ti·ness,** n.

griz·zled (griz′əld), adj. **1** grayish; gray. **2** gray-haired. [< grizzle gray hair, (adj.) gray < OF grisel, dim. of gris gray < Gmc.]

griz·zly (griz′li), adj., **-zli·er, -zli·est,** n., pl. **-zlies.** —adj. **1** grayish; gray. **2** gray-haired. —n. =grizzly bear.

grizzly bear, a large, fierce, gray or brownish-gray bear of W North America.

groan (grōn), n. a deep-throated sound expressing grief, pain, or disapproval; short moan. —v. **1** give a groan or groans. **2** be loaded or overburdened. **3** express by groaning. [OE grānian] —**groan′er,** n. —**groan′ing,** n., adj. —**groan′ing·ly,** adv.

gro·cer (grō′sər), n. person who sells food and household supplies. [< OF grossier, ult. < L grossus thick]

gro·cer·y (grō′sər i; grōs′ri), n., pl. **-cer·ies.** store that sells food and household supplies.

groceries, food and household supplies sold by a grocer.

grog (grog), n. Esp. Brit. **1** drink made of rum or other alcohol, diluted with water. **2** any strong alcohol. [short for grogram, nickname of Brit. Admiral Vernon, from his grogram cloak]

grog·gy (grog′i), adj., **-gi·er, -gi·est.** shaky; unsteady. —**grog′gi·ly,** adv. —**grog′gi·ness,** n.

groin (groin), n. **1** part of the body where the thigh joins the abdomen. **2** a curved line where two vaults of a roof cross. —v. build with groins. [ME grynde, infl. by loin]

grom·met (grom′it), n. **1** a metal eyelet. **2** ring of rope, used as an oarlock, to hold a sail on its stays, etc. [< obs. F gromette curb of bridle < gourmer curb]

groom (grüm), n. **1** man or boy who has charge of horses. **2** =bridegroom. **3** Archaic. manservant. —v. **1** feed and take care of (horses); rub down and brush. **2** take care of the appearance of; make neat and tidy. **3** prepare (a person) to run for a position or political office. [ME grom(e) boy] —**groom′er,** n.

grooms·man (grümz′mən), n., pl. **-men.** man who attends the bridegroom at a wedding.

groove (grüv), n., v., **grooved, groov·ing.** —n. **1** a long, narrow channel or furrow, esp. one cut by a tool. **2** a fixed way of doing things. —v. **1** make a groove in. **2** be in good form. **3** have a fine time; have fun.

in the groove, Informal. **a** in best form. **b** current; fashionable. [OE grōf ditch] —**groove′less,** adj. —**groove′like′,** adj. —**groov′er,** n.

groov·y (grü′vi), adj., **groov·i·er, groov·i·est.** Informal. great; excellent; cool.

grope (grōp), v., **groped, grop·ing. 1** feel about with the hands. **2** search blindly and uncertainly. **3** find by feeling about with the hands. [OE grāpian, akin to grīpan to grasp] —**grop′er,** n. —**grop′ing·ly,** adv.

gros·beak (grōs′bēk′), n. finch with a cone-shaped bill. [< F, gros large + bec beak]

gros·grain (grō′grān′), n. a closely woven silk or rayon cloth with heavy cross threads and a dull finish. —adv. having heavy cross threads and a dull finish [var. of grogram]

gross (grōs), adj., n., pl. **gross·es** for 1, **gross** for 2. —adj. **1** with nothing taken out; whole; entire: gross receipts. **2** very bad; outrageous; glaring: gross errors. **3** Fig. coarse; vulgar. **4** too big and fat; overfed. **5** thick; heavy; dense: the gross growth of a jungle. —n. **1** whole sum; total amount. **2** unit consisting of twelve dozen; 144.

gross out, Informal. disgust. [< OF < L grossus thick] —**gross′ly,** adv. —**gross′-ness,** n.

gross domestic product, total value of goods and services produced in a nation during a particular period of time, excluding foreign investments and payments.

gross national product, total value of all goods and services produced in a nation during a particular period of time.

gro·tesque (grō tesk′), adj. **1** odd or unnatural in shape, appearance, manner, etc.; fantastic; queer. **2** ridiculous; absurd. [< F < Ital. grottesco < grotta grotto] —**gro·tesque′ly,** adv. —**gro·tesque′ness,** n.

grot·to (grot′ō), n., pl. **-toes, -tos. 1** cave. **2** an artificial cave made for coolness or pleasure. [< Ital. grotta < L < Gk. krypte vault. Doublet of CRYPT.]

grouch (grouch), v. be sulky or ill-tempered; complain. —n. **1** a sulky person. **2** a sulky, discontented feeling. [var. of obs. grutch < OF groucher murmur]

grouch·y (grouch′i), adj., **grouch·i·er, grouch·i·est.** sulky; sullen; discontented. —**grouch′i·ly,** adv. —**grouch′i·ness,** n.

ground[1] (ground), n. **1** the solid part of the earth's surface. **2** soil; dirt. **3** particular piece of land; land for some special purpose. **4** Often, **grounds.** foundation for what is said, thought, claimed, or done; basis; reason. **5** underlying surface; background: a blue pattern on a white ground. **6** connection of an electrical conductor with the earth. —adj. of, on, at, or near the ground. —v. **1** put on the ground. **2** run aground. **3** establish firmly. **4** have a basis. **5** instruct in first principles: well grounded in grammar. **6** connect (an electric wire) with the earth.

break ground, a plow up soil. **b** begin building. **c** Fig. begin something, as a venture.

cover ground, a go over a certain distance. **b** travel. **c** do a certain amount of work, etc.

gain ground, a advance; progress. **b** Fig. become more common or widespread.

get off the ground, go forward; start.

give ground, retreat; yield.

grounds, a land or area for some purpose: fair grounds. **b** land, lawns, and gardens around a house. **c** small bits that sink to the bottom of a drink such as coffee or tea; dregs; sediment.

hold one's ground, not retreat or yield.

lose ground, a retreat; yield. **b** Fig. become less widespread or common.

run into the ground, wear out; overdo: run a joke into the ground.

shift one's ground, use a different defense or argument.

stand one's ground, refuse to retreat or yield. [OE grund bottom]

ground[2] (ground), v. pt. and pp. of **grind.**

ground cover, low plants and vines planted to prevent soil from eroding and to enrich it.

ground crew, people responsible for servicing an aircraft while at an airport.

ground·er (groun′dər), n. baseball hit to bound or roll along the ground.

ground floor, the most advantageous position in relation to a business deal, etc.

ground hog, =woodchuck.

ground·less (ground′lis), adj. without foundation, basis, or reason. —**ground′less·ly,** adv. —**ground′less-ness,** n.

ground·nut (ground′nut′), n. **1** any of various plants having edible underground parts, such as the peanut. **2** the edible tuber, pod, or the like, of such a plant.

ground pine, a low, creeping evergreen, a kind of club moss, used for Christmas decorations and the like.

ground plan, 1 plan of a floor of a building. **2** first or fundamental plan.

ground rule, one of a basic set of rules, in a sport or any activity.

ground squirrel, any one of various burrowing rodents belonging to the squirrel family, esp. the chipmunk.

ground swell, broad, deep waves caused by a distant storm, earthquake, etc.

ground water, water from a spring or well.

ground·work (ground'werk´), *n.* foundation; basis.

group (grüp), *n.* **1** number of persons or things together. **2** number of persons or things belonging or classed together. **3** number of persons or things that act as a unit. —*v.* **1** form into a group. **2** put in a group. **3** arrange in groups. [< F < *gruppo*]

group·er (grüp'ər), *n., pl.* **-ers** or (*esp. collectively*) **-er.** a large food fish of warm seas. [< Pg. *garupa*]

group·ie (grü'pē), *n. Informal.* **1** adolescent girl who is a fan of a rock group or a celebrity, attending performances, following them, etc. **2** any devotee.

group·ing (grü'ping), *n.* **1** placement or way of being placed in a group. **2** people or things in a group.

grouse[1] (grous), *n., pl.* **grouse.** a game bird with feathered legs. The prairie chicken, sage hen, and ruffed grouse of the United States are different kinds. —**grouse'like´,** *adj.*

grouse[2] (grous), *v.,* **groused, grous·ing,** *n.* —*v.* grumble; complain. —*n.* complaint. —**grous'er,** *n.*

grout (grout), *n.* thin plaster or mortar used to fill cracks, esp. around tiles, and finish walls, etc. —*v.* use or finish with grout.

grove (grōv), *n.* group of trees standing together; orchard. [OE *gráf*]

grov·el (gruv'əl; grov'-), *v.,* **-eled, -el·ing.** lie face downward; crawl at someone's feet; humble oneself. [< *groveling,* orig. adv., < phrase *on grufe* prone < Scand. *á grúfu*] —**grov'el·er,** *n.* —**grov'el·ing·ly,** *adv.*

grow (grō), *v.,* **grew, grown, grow·ing. 1** become bigger by taking in food, as plants and animals do: *a tree growing.* **2** become greater; increase: *his fame grew.* **3** become attached: *grow fast to the wall.* **4** become: *grow cold, grow rich.* **5** cause to grow; produce; raise: *grow corn, grow a beard.*

grow on or **upon, a** have an increasing effect or influence on: *the habit simply grew on me.* **b** become liked or admired by: *the story grows on you.*

grow out of, a outgrow. **b** be a result of; develop from.

grow up, a advance to or arrive at full growth. **b** be produced; develop. [OE *grōwan;* akin to GRASS, GREEN] —**grow'er,** *n.*

growl (groul), *v.* **1** make a deep, low, angry sound. **2** express by growling. —*n.* a deep, low, angry sound; deep, warning snarl. [prob. imit.] —**growl'er,** *n.* —**growl'ing·ly,** *adv.*

grown (grōn), *adj.* **1** arrived at full growth. **2** covered with a growth. —*v.* pp. of **grow.**

grown-up (*adj.* grōn'up´; *n.* grōn'up´), *adj.* **1** adult. **2** characteristic of or for adults. —*n.* adult.

growth (grōth), *n.* **1** process of growing; development. **2** amount of growing or developing; increase. **3** what has grown or is growing: *a thick growth of bushes covered the ground.* **4** an unhealthy mass of tissue formed in or on the body, as a tumor.

grub (grub), *n., v.,* **grubbed, grub·bing.** —*n.* **1** a wormlike form or larva of an insect, esp. the smooth, thick larva of a beetle. **2** *Slang.* food. [< v.] —*v.* **1** dig. **2** root out of the ground; dig up. [ME *grubbe(n)*] —**grub'ber,** *n.*

grub·by (grub'i), *adj.,* **-bi·er, -bi·est. 1** dirty; grimy. **2** infested with grubs. —**grub'bi·ly,** *adv.* —**grub'bi·ness,** *n.*

grub·stake (grub'stāk´), *n., v.,* **-staked, -stak·ing.** *W. Informal.* —*n.* food, outfit, money, etc., supplied to a prospector on the condition of sharing in whatever is found. —*v.* supply with a grubstake. —**grub'stak´er,** *n.*

grudge (gruj), *n., v.,* **grudged, grudg·ing.** —*n.* sullen feeling against. —*v.* **1** envy the possession of. **2** give unwillingly. [var. of obs. *grutch* < OF *groucher*] —**grudg'er,** *n.* —**grudg'ing·ly,** *adv.*

gru·el (grü'əl), *n., v.,* **-eled, -el·ing.** —*n.* a thin, almost liquid food made by boiling oatmeal, etc., in water or milk. —*v.* subject to an exhausting or tiring experience. [< OF, ult. < Gmc.] —**gru·el'ing,** *adj.*

grue·some (grü'səm), *adj.* revolting in a ghastly way; horrible. [< *grue* to shudder. Cf. MDu., MLG *gruwen.*] —**grue'some·ly,** *adv.* —**grue'some·ness,** *n.*

gruff (gruf), *adj.* **1** deep and harsh; hoarse. **2** rough; rude; unfriendly; bad-tempered. [< Du. *grof*] —**gruff'ly,** *adv.* —**gruff'ness,** *n.*

grum·ble (grum'bəl), *v.,* **-bled, -bling,** *n.* —*v.* **1** mutter in discontent; complain in a bad-tempered way. **2** express by grumbling. —*n.* mutter of discontent; bad-tempered complaint. [akin to OE *grymettan* roar, and GRIM] —**grum'bler,** *n.* —**grum'bling·ly,** *adv.*

grump (grump), *n.* an ill-humored person.

grump·y (grump'i), *adj.,* **grump·i·er, grump·i·est.** surly; ill-humored; gruff. —**grump'i·ly,** *adv.* —**grump'i·ness,** *n.*

grunt (grunt), *n.* **1** the deep, hoarse sound that a hog makes. **2** sound like this. —*v.* **1**

make this sound. **2** say with this sound. **3** *Informal.* soldier who fights at the front. [OE *grunnettan* < *grunian* grunt] —**grunt'er,** *n.* —**grunt'ing·ly,** *adv.*

grunt·work (grunt'werk´), *n.* menial work, either as a laborer or at the bottom of an organization.

Gru·yère (gri yãr'; grü–), *n.* variety of firm, light-yellow cheese made from whole milk. [after *Gruyère,* district in Switzerland]

gua·ca·mo·le (gwä´kə mō'lã; –li), *n.* mashed avocado, usually seasoned with cilantro, onions, tomatoes, and lime juice, esp. used as an accompaniment for Latin American food. [< Mex. Sp. < Nahuatl]

Guam (gwäm), *n.* a U.S. island in the W Pacific, east of the Philippines.

gua·nine (gwä'nēn; –nin), *n.* one of the bases of DNA and RNA and found in the nucleic acids in all cells.

gua·no (gwä'nō), *n., pl.* **-nos. 1** manure of sea birds found esp. on islands near Peru, used for fertilizing. **2** fertilizer made from fish. [< Sp. < Quechua (Ind. lang. of Peru) *huanu*]

guar·an·tee (gar´ən tē'), *n., v.,* **-teed, -tee·ing.** —*n.* **1** a promise to pay or do something if another fails; pledge to replace goods if they are not as represented. **2** person who so promises. —*v.* **1** stand back of; give a guarantee for; assure genuineness or permanence of. **2** undertake to secure for another. **3** make secure (against or from). **4** engage to do (something). [prob. var. of *guaranty*]

guar·an·tor (gar´ən tôr'; –tər), *n.* person who makes or gives a guarantee.

guar·an·ty (gar'ən ti), *n., pl.* **-ties,** *v.,* **-tied, -ty·ing.** —*n.* **1** act or fact of giving security. **2** pledge or promise given as security; security. **3** person who acts as guarantee. —*v.* guarantee. [< OF *guarantie* < *guarant* warrant < Gmc. Doublet of WARRANTY.]

guard (gärd), *v.* **1** keep safe; watch over carefully; defend; protect. **2** keep in check; prevent from getting out; hold back. —*n.* **1** somebody or something that guards. **2** anything that gives protection. **3** careful watch. **4** in football, player at either side of the center. **5** in basketball, either of two players defending the goal.

off (one's) guard, not prepared for a sudden attack or threat; not watchful; not alert.

on (one's) guard, ready for a sudden attack or threat; alert. [< F *garder,* v., *garde,* n. < Gmc. Doublet of WARD.] —**guard'er,** *n.*

guard·ed (gär'did), *adj.* **1** kept safe; carefully watched over; protected. **2** careful; cautious. —**guard'ed·ly,** *adv.* —**guard'ed·ness,** *n.*

guard·house (gärd'hous´), *n.* **1** a building occupied by soldiers on guard. **2** a building used as a jail for soldiers.

guard·i·an (gär′di ən), *n.* **1** person appointed by law to take care of the affairs of someone who cannot take care of them himself or herself. **2** any person who takes care of somebody or something. —*adj.* protecting: *a guardian angel.* —**guard′i·an·ship′,** *n.*

guards·man (gärdz′mən), *n., pl.* **-men. 1** guard. **2** *U.S.* soldier who belongs to the National Guard.

Gua·te·ma·la (gwä′tə mä′lə), *n.* **1** country in NW Central America. **2** Also, **Guatemala City.** its capital. —**Gua′te·ma′lan,** *adj.*

gua·va (gwä′və), *n.* **1** a tropical American tree or shrub with a yellowish, pear-shaped fruit. **2** the fruit, used for jelly, jam, etc. [< Sp. *guayaba*]

gua·yu·le (gwä ü′lä), *n.* a small shrub growing in Mexico and Texas. Rubber is obtained from its juice. [< a Mexican lang.]

gu·ber·na·to·ri·al (gü′bər nə tô′ri əl; -tô′-; gü′-), *adj.* of or having to do with a governor. [< L *gubernator,* orig., pilot. See GOVERN.]

gudg·eon (guj′ən), *n.* **1** a small European freshwater fish. It is easily caught and often used for bait. **2** =minnow. [< OF *goujon,* ult. < L *gobius,* a kind of fish < Gk. *kobios*]

Guern·sey (gėrn′zi), *n., pl.* **-seys. 1** any of a breed of dairy cattle resembling the Jersey, but somewhat larger. **2** a British island in the English Channel.

guer·ril·la, gue·ril·la (gə ril′ə), *n.* fighter in a war carried on by independent bands which harass the enemy by sudden raids, plundering supplies, etc. —*adj.* of or by guerrillas. [< Sp., dim. of *guerra* war]

guess (ges), *v.* **1** form an opinion without really knowing: *guess the height of a building.* **2** get right by guessing: *guess a riddle.* **3** *Esp. U.S.* think; believe; suppose: *I guess I can get there.* —*n.* opinion formed without really knowing. [prob. < Scand. (Sw.) *gissa*] —**guess′er,** *n.* —**guess′ing·ly,** *adv.*

guess·ti·mate (*n.* ges′tə mit; *v.* ges′tə māt), *n., v.* **-mat·ed, -mat·ing.** —*n.* estimate based on a guess. —*v.* make an estimate based on guessing. [< *guess* + *es*timate]

guess·work (ges′wėrk′), *n.* work, action, or results based on guessing; guessing.

guest (gest), *n.* **1** person who is received and entertained at one's home, club, etc.; person who is not a regular member; visitor. **2** person staying at a hotel, boarding house, etc. [< Scand. *gestr.* Cf. OE *giest.*] —**guest′less,** *adj.*

guest worker, person who enters a country to work, esp. to fill a temporary labor shortage. [< G *gastarbeiter* guest worker]

guff (guf), *n. Informal.* **1** nonsense. **2** backtalk. [imit.]

guf·faw (gu fô′), *n.* a loud, coarse burst of laughter. —*v.* laugh loudly and coarsely.

Gui·a·na (gē ä′nə; -an′ə), *n.* region in N South America including French Guiana, Guyana, and Surinam.

guid·ance (gīd′əns), *n.* **1** a guiding; leadership; direction. **2** thing that guides.

guide (gīd), *v.,* **guid·ed, guid·ing,** *n.* —*v.* **1** show the way; lead; conduct; direct. **2** manage; control. —*n.* **1** person, who shows the way, leads, conducts, or directs. **2** mark, sign, etc., to direct the eye or mind. **3** =guidebook. [< OF *guider* < Gmc.] —**guid′a·ble,** *adj.* —**guide′less,** *adj.* —**guid′er,** *n.*

guide·book (gīd′bùk′), *n.* book of directions and information, eps. one for travelers.

guided missile, projectile that can be guided accurately often for great distances by transmitted electronic impulses.

guide·line (gīd′līn′), *n.* **1** Usually, **guide·lines. 1** principle, policy, or set of rules. **2** a rope or rail that serves as a guide.

guide·post (gīd′pōst′), *n.* post with signs and directions on it for travelers.

guide word, word at the top of a page that indicates what is on that page, as in a dictionary.

gui·don (gī′dən), *n.* **1** a small flag or streamer carried as a guide by soldiers. **2** flag, streamer, or pennant of a company, regiment, etc. [< F <Ital. *guidone*]

guild (gild), *n.* **1** society for mutual aid or for some common purpose: *the Ladies' Auxiliary Guild of the church.* **2** in the Middle Ages, a union of the men in one trade formed to keep standards high and to look out for the interests of their trade. [< Scand. *gildi*]

guil·der (gil′dər), *n.* **1** a silver coin or unit of money in the Netherlands. **2** coin formerly used in the Netherlands, Germany, or Austria. [alter. of *gulden*]

guild·hall (gild′hôl′), *n.* hall in which a guild meets.

guilds·man (gildz′mən), *n., pl.* **-men.** member of a guild.

guile (gīl), *n.* crafty deceit; craftiness; sly tricks. [< OF < Gmc. Doublet of WILE.]

guile·ful (gīl′fəl), *adj.* crafty and deceitful; sly and tricky. —**guile′ful·ly,** *adv.* —**guile′ful·ness,** *n.*

guile·less (gīl′lis), *adj.* without guile. —**guile′less·ly,** *adv.* —**guile′less·ness,** *n.*

guil·le·mot (gil′ə mot), *n.* any of several arctic diving birds of the auk family with narrow bills. [< F, prob. < *Guillaume* William]

guil·lo·tine (*n.* gil′ə tēn; *v.* gil′ə tēn′), *n., v.,* **-tined, -tin·ing.** —*n.* machine for beheading persons by means of a heavy blade that slides down between two grooved posts. —*v.* behead with this machine. [< F; named for J. I. *Guillotin,* physician and advocate of its use]

guilt (gilt), *n.* **1** fact or state of having done wrong; being guilty; being to blame. **2** guilty action or conduct. [OE *gylt* offense]

guilt·less (gilt′lis), *adj.* not guilty; free from guilt; innocent. —**guilt′less·ly,** *adv.* —**guilt′less·ness,** *n.*

guilt·y (gil′ti), *adj.,* **guilt·i·er, guilt·i·est. 1** having done wrong; deserving to be blamed and punished: *the jury pronounced the prisoner guilty of murder.* **2** knowing or showing that one has done wrong: *a guilty conscience.* —**guilt′i·ly,** *adv.* —**guilt′i·ness,** *n.*

guimpe (gimp; gamp), *n.* blouse worn under a dress and showing at the neck or at the neck and arms. [< F < Gmc. Doublet of GIMP.]

guin·ea (gin′i), *n.* **1** a former English gold coin worth 21 shillings. **2** guinea fowl.

Guin·ea (gin′i) republic in W Africa on the Atlantic, formerly including French, Portuguese, and Spanish colonies.

Guin·ea-Bis·sau (gin′i bi sou′), *n.* country in W Africa, formerly Portuguese Guinea.

guinea fowl, a domestic fowl somewhat like a pheasant, having dark-gray feathers with small, white spots.

guinea hen, 1 =guinea fowl. **2** a female guinea fowl.

guinea pig, 1 a short-eared, tailless animal like a big, fat, harmless rat, often used for laboratory experiments. **2** any person or thing serving as a subject for experiment or observation.

guise (gīz), *n.* **1** style of dress; garb: *the soldier went in the guise of a monk.* **2** external appearance; aspect; semblance. **3** assumed appearance; pretense: *under the guise of friendship.* [< OF < Gmc.]

gui·tar (gə tär′), *n.* a musical instrument having six strings, played with the fingers. [< Sp. *guitarra* < Gk. *kithara* cithara. Doublet of CITHARA and ZITHER.] —**gui·tar′ist,** *n.* —**gui·tar′like′,** *adj.*

gu·lag or **Gu·lag** (gü′lag, gü lag′), *n.* **1** prison camp for intellectuals, dissidents, and criminals, esp. in the former Soviet Union. **2** *Fig.* an isolated place or situation, like a prison. [< Russ. acronym for Chief Administration of Camps]

gulch (gulch), *n.* a deep, narrow ravine with steep sides, esp. one marking the course of a stream or torrent.

gulf (gulf), *n.* **1** a large bay; arm of an ocean or sea extending into the land. **2** a very deep break or cut in the earth. **3** any wide separation: *a gulf between old friends.* **4 the Gulf,** the Gulf of Mexico. [< F < Ital., ult. < Gk. *kolpos,* orig., bosom] —**gulf′like′,** *adj.*

Gulf Stream, current of warm water flowing north from the Gulf of Mexico along the Atlantic coast to Newfoundland, where it turns northeast toward the British Isles.

gull¹ (gul), *n.* a graceful, gray-and-white bird with long wings, webbed feet, and a thick, strong beak, living on or near large bodies of water. [? < Welsh *gwylan*]

gull² (gul), *v.* deceive; cheat. —*n.* person who is easily deceived or cheated.

Gul·lah (gul′ə), *n.* **1** one of a group of blacks living along the coast of South Carolina and Georgia and on the islands off the coast. **2** dialect of English spoken by the Gullahs.

gul·let (gul′it), *n.* **1** passage for food from the mouth to the stomach; esophagus. **2** throat, [< OF, ult. < L *gula* throat]

gul·li·ble (gul′ə bəl), *adj.* easily deceived. —**gul′li·bil′i·ty,** *n.* —**gul′li·bly,** *adv.*

gul·ly (gul′i), *n., pl.* **-lies.** a narrow gorge; ditch made by running water. [? var. of *gullet*]

gulp (gulp), *v.* **1** swallow eagerly or greedily. **2** keep in; choke back. **3** gasp; choke. —*n.* **1** act of swallowing. **2** amount swallowed at one time; mouthful. [imit.] —**gulp′er,** *n.* —**gulp′ing·ly,** *adv.*

gum[1] (gum), *n., v.,* **gummed, gum·ming.** —*n.* **1** a sticky juice, obtained from or given off by certain trees and plants, used to make candy, medicine, and mucilage. **2** =chewing gum. **3** substance on the back of a stamp, the flap of an envelope, etc.; glue. —*v.* **1** smear, stick together, or stiffen with gum. **2** give off gum; form gum. **3** make or become sticky; clog with something sticky.

gum up, *Informal.* put out of order. [< OF < L < Gk. *kommi*] —**gum′like′,** *adj.* —**gum′mer,** *n.*

gum[2] (gum), *n.* Often **gums.** flesh around the teeth. —*v.,* **gummed, gumming.** chew with the gums. [OE *gōma* palate]

gum·bo (gum′bō), *n., pl.* **-bos. 1** the okra plant. **2** its sticky pods. **3** soup thickened with okra pods. [of African origin]

gum·drop (gum′drop′), *n.* a stiff, jelly-like piece of candy made of gelatin, etc., sweetened and flavored.

gum·my (gum′i), *adj.,* **-mi·er, -mi·est. 1** sticky like gum. **2** covered with gum. **3** giving off gum. —**gum′mi·ness,** *n.*

gump·tion (gump′shən), *n.* **1** initiative; energy. **2** good judgment.

gum·shoe (gum′shü′), *n.* detective.

gum tree, a sweet gum, tupelo, eucalyptus, or other tree that yields gum.

gun (gun), *n., v.,* **gunned, gun·ning.** —*n.* **1** rifle, cannon, or other weapon with a long metal tube for shooting bullets, shot, etc. **2** pistol or revolver. **3** anything resembling a gun in use or shape. —*v.* **1** shoot with a gun; hunt with a gun. **2** accelerate rapidly.

gun down, a shoot down. **b** *Fig.* destroy; kill: *gun down a proposal.*

gun for, a have as a target; aim for. **b** shoot.

jump the gun, a start a race before the starting gun. **b** begin before anyone else; get a head start.

stick to one's guns, refuse to retreat or change position. [< OF *engan* engine, trap, snare, ult. < L *canna* reed] —**gun′less,** *adj.*

gun·boat (gun′bōt′), *n.* a small warship that can be used in shallow water.

gun·cot·ton (gun′kot′ən), *n.* explosive made by treating cotton with nitric and sulfuric acids.

gun·fire (gun′fīr′), *n.* the shooting of a gun or guns.

gun·lock (gun′lok′), *n.* part of a gun by which the charge is fired.

gun·man (gun′mən), *n., pl.* **-men.** man who uses a gun to rob, kill, etc.

gun metal, 1 dark-gray metal used for chains, handles, etc. **2** dark gray. **3** a bronze formerly used to make guns. —**gun′-met′al,** *adj.*

gun·nel[1] (gun′əl), *n.* =gunwale.

gun·nel[2] (gun′əl), *n.* a small N Atlantic fish resembling a perch.

gun·ner (gun′ər), *n.* **1** person trained to fire artillery; soldier who handles and fires cannon. **2** a navy officer in charge of a ship's guns. **3** person who hunts with a gun.

gun·ner·y (gun′ər i), *n.* **1** art and science of constructing and managing big guns. **2** use of guns; shooting of guns. **3** guns collectively.

gun·ning (gun′ing), *n.* hunting with a gun.

gun·ny (gun′i), *n., pl.* **-nies. 1** a strong, coarse fabric used for sacks, bags, etc. **2** Also, **gunny sack.** sack, etc., made of this. [< Hind. *goni*]

gun·pow·der (gun′pou′dər), *n.* powder that explodes with force when brought into contact with fire, used esp. in gunnery.

gun·run·ning (gun′run′ing), *n.* the bringing of guns and ammunition into a country illegally. —**gun′run′ner,** *n.*

gun·ship (gun′ship′), *n.* helicopter armed with guns and rockets, used in battle.

gun·shot (gun′shot′), *n.* **1** shot fired from a gun. **2** the shooting of a gun. **3** distance that a gun will shoot.

gun·smith (gun′smith′), *n.* person whose work is making or repairing small guns.

gun·stock (gun′stok′), *n.* the wooden support to which the barrel of a gun is fastened.

gun·wale (gun′əl), *n.* the upper edge of a ship's or boat's side. Also, **gunnel.**

gup·py (gup′i), *n., pl.* **-pies.** a very small, brightly colored, viviparous fish of tropical fresh water. [for R. J. L. *Guppy*]

gur·gle (gėr′gəl), *v.,* **-gled, -gling,** *n.* —*v.* **1** flow or run with a bubbling sound. **2** make a bubbling sound. —*n.* a bubbling sound. [? imit.]

gur·ney (gėr′ni) *n.* **1** wheeled stretcher for transporting patients. **2** wheeled canvas cart. [*orig. uncert.*]

gu·ru (gü′rü), *n.* **1** religious leader; spiritual guide, esp. in Hinduism. **2** any leader or expert.

gush (gush), *v.* **1** rush out suddenly; pour out. **2** talk in a silly way about one's affections or enthusiasms. **3** give forth suddenly or very freely. —*n.* **1** rush of water or other liquid from an enclosed place. **2** silly, emotional talk. [prob. imit.] —**gush′ing,** *adj.* —**gush′ing·ly,** *adv.*

gush·er (gush′ər), *n.* **1** *Esp. U.S.* an oil well that gives oil in large quantities without pumping. **2** a gushy person.

gush·y (gush′i), *adj.,* **gush·i·er, gush·i·est.** showing silly feeling; effusive; sentimental.

gus·set (gus′it), *n.* a triangular piece of material inserted to give greater strength or more room. [< OF *gousset* < *gousse* husk]

gust (gust), *n.* **1** a sudden, violent rush of wind. **2** a sudden burst of rain, smoke, sound, etc. **3** outburst of anger, enthusiasm, etc. [< Scand. *gustr*]

gus·to (gus′tō), *n., pl.* **-tos.** keen relish; hearty enjoyment. [< Ital., orig., taste < L *gustus*]

gust·y (gus′ti), *adj.,* **gust·i·er, gust·i·est. 1** coming in gusts; windy; stormy. **2** marked by outbursts: *gusty laughter.* —**gust′i·ly,** *adv.* —**gust′i·ness,** *n.*

gut (gut), *n., v.,* **gut·ted, gut·ting.** —*n.* **1** intestine. **2** a tough string made from the intestines of a sheep, cat, etc., used for violin strings, tennis rackets, etc. —*v.* **1** remove the entrails of; disembowel. **2** plunder or destroy the inside of.

guts, a pluck; courage; endurance. **b** entrails; bowels. [OE *guttas,* pl.] —**gut′ter,** *n.*

Gu·ten·berg (gü′tən bėrg), *n.* **Johann,** 1398?–1468, German printer, supposedly the first European to print from movable type.

gut·ter (gut′ər), *n.* **1** channel along the side of a street or road to carry off water; low part of a street beside the sidewalk. **2** channel or trough along the lower edge of a roof to carry off rain water. **3** channel; groove. **4** *Fig.* a low, miserable place or situation. —*v.* **1** form gutters in. **2** flow or melt in streams. [< OF *goutiere,* ult. < L *gutta* drop] —**gut′ter·like′,** *adj.* —**gut′ter·y,** *adj.*

gut·ter·snipe (gut′ər snīp′), *n. Informal.* **1** gamin who lives in the streets. **2** person without breeding or decency.

gut·tur·al (gut′ər əl), *adj.* **1** of the throat. **2** formed in the throat; harsh. [< NL, < L *guttur* throat] —**gut′tur·al′i·ty,** *n.* —**gut′tur·al·ly,** *adv.* —**gut′tur·al·ness,** *n.*

guy[1] (gī), *n., v.,* **guyed, guy·ing.** —*n.* rope, chain, wire, etc., attached to something to steady or secure it. —*v.* steady or secure with a guy or guys. [< OF *guie* guide, ult. < Gmc.]

guy[2] (gī), *n.* **1** fellow; chap. **2** *Informal.* attractive man. [for *Guy* Fawkes]

Guy·a·na (gē ä′nə; -an′ə), *n.* republic in NE South America; formerly the British colony of British Guiana.

guz·zle (guz′əl), *v.,* **-zled, -zling.** drink greedily; drink too much. —**guz′zler,** *n.*

gym (jim), *n.* =gymnasium.

gym·na·si·um (jim nā′zi əm), *n., pl.* **-si·ums, -si·a** (-zi ə). room, building, etc., fitted up for physical exercise or training and for indoor athletic sports. [< L < Gk. *gymnasion,* ult. < *gymnos* naked]

gym·nast (jim′nast), *n.* expert in gymnastics. [< Gk., < *gymnazein* exercise. See GYMNASIUM.]

gym·nas·tic (jim nas′tik), *adj.* having to do with bodily exercise or activities. —**gym·nas′ti·cal·ly,** *adv.*

gym·nas·tics (jim nas′tiks), *n.* physical exercises for developing the muscles.

gym·no·sperm (jim′nə spėrm), *n.* any of a large group of plants having the seeds exposed, not enclosed in ovaries. The pine, fir, and spruce, which bear seeds on the surface of cone scales instead of in pods, are gymnosperms. [< NL < Gk., < *gymnos* naked + *sperma* seed] —**gym′no·sper′mous,** *adj.*

gy·ne·col·o·gy (gī′nə kol′ə ji), *n.* branch of medical science that deals with the functions and diseases peculiar to women. [< Gk. *gyne* woman + –LOGY] —**gy′ne·co·log′ic** *adj.* **gy′ne·co·log′i·cal,** *adj.* —**gy′ne·col′o·gist,** *n.*

gyp (jip), *v.,* **gypped, gyp·ping,** *n.* U.S. *Slang.* —*v.* cheat; swindle. —*n.* **1** a cheat or swindle. **2** a swindler. [shortened from *gypsy*] —**gyp′per,** *n.*

gyp·sum (jip′səm), *n.* a hydrated calcium sulfate, CaSO₄·2H₂O, a mineral used for making plaster of Paris, fertilizer, etc. [< L < Gk. *gypsos*]

Gyp·sy (jip′si), *n., pl.* –**sies,** *adj.* —*n.* **1** person belonging to a group of people who probably came from India originally; Romany. **2** Romany, the language of the Gypsies. **3** **gypsy,** *U.S.* person who resembles a Gypsy or lives a wandering life. **4** =gypsy cab. —*adj.* **gypsy, a** of the Gypsies. **b** resembling a Gypsy or gypsy. [ult. < *Egyptian*] —**gyp′sy·like′,** *adj.*

gypsy cab, taxicab that is not licensed to cruise the streets looking for passengers.

gypsy moth, a brownish or white moth whose larvae eat the leaves of trees.

gy·rate (jī′rāt; jī rāt′), *v.,* –**rat·ed,** –**rat·ing.** move in a circle or spiral. [< L, < *gyrus* circle < Gk. *gyros*] —**gy·ra′tion,** *n.* —**gy·ra′tor,** *n.* —**gy′ra·to′ry,** *adj.*

gyr·fal·con (jėr′fôl′kən; –fô′–), *n.* =gerfalcon.

gy·ro·com·pass (jī′rō kum′pəs), *n.* compass using a gyroscope intead of a magnetic needle to point to the geographic North Pole instead of to the magnetic pole.

gyr·o (jī′rō), *n., pl.* **gyr·os.** sandwich esp. of roast pork or lamb, served rolled up on thin bread. [< Gk. *gyros* circle, spiral]

gy·ro·scope (jī′rə skōp), *n.* a heavy wheel or disk mounted so that its axis can turn freely in one or more directions. A spinning gyroscope tends to resist change in the direction of its axis. —**gy′ro·scop′·ic,** *adj.* —**gy′ro·scop′i·cal·ly,** *adv.*

gy·ro·sta·bi·liz·er (jī′rō stā′bə līz′ər), *n.* device for stabilizing a seagoing vessel by counteracting its rolling motion.

gyve (jīv), *n., v.,* **gyved, gyv·ing.** —*n.* Usually, **gyves.** shackle, esp. for the leg; fetter. —*v.* fetter; shackle.

H, h (āch), *n., pl.* **H's; h's.** the eighth letter of the alphabet.

H, 1 henry (unit of inductance). **2** hydrogen.

h., H., 1 high. **2** hits. **3** hour.

Ha, hahnium (radioactive element).

ha (hä), *interj.* **1** exclamation of surprise, joy, triumph, etc. **2** sound of a laugh.

ha·be·as cor·pus (hā′bi əs kôr′pəs), writ requiring that a prisoner be brought before a judge or into court to decide whether he or she is being held lawfully. [L, you may have the person]

hab·er·dash·er (hab′ər dash′er), *n.* dealer in men's wear.

hab·er·dash·er·y (hab′ər dash′ər i; –dash′ri), *n., pl.* **-er·ies.** shop of a haberdasher.

hab·it (hab′it), *n.* **1** tendency to act in a certain way or to do a certain thing; usual way of acting: *habit of waking early.* **2** the distinctive dress or costume worn by members of a religious order. **3** a woman's riding suit. **4** the characteristic form, mode of growth, etc., of an animal or plant.

break a habit, stop doing something habitual.

kick the habit, stop doing something that had become a habit, esp. smoking. [< OF < L *habitus* < *habere* hold, live in, stay]

hab·it·a·ble (hab′ə tə bəl), *adj.* fit to live in. —**hab′it·a·bil′i·ty, hab′it·a·ble·ness,** *n.* —**hab′it·a·bly,** *adv.*

hab·it·ant (hab′ə tənt), *n.* inhabitant. [< F < L, ppr. of *habitare* live in]

hab·i·tat (hab′ə tat), *n.* **1** place where an animal or plant naturally lives or grows. **2** a dwelling place. [< L *habitat* it inhabits]

hab·i·ta·tion (hab′ə tā′shən), *n.* **1** place to live in. **2** an inhabiting.

ha·bit·u·al (hə bich′ü əl), *adj.* **1** done by habit; caused by habit: *a habitual smile.* **2** being or doing something by habit: *a habitual reader.* **3** often done, seen, or used: *ice and snow are a habitual sight in arctic regions.* —**ha·bit′u·al·ly,** *adv.* —**ha·bit′u·al·ness,** *n.*

ha·bit·u·ate (hə bich′ü āt), *v.,* **-at·ed, -at·ing.** make used (to); accustom. —**ha·bit′u·a′tion,** *n.*

ha·bit·u·é (hə bich′ü ā′), *n.* a person who has the habit of going to any place frequently. [< F]

ha·ci·en·da (hä′si en′də), *n.* a large ranch; landed estate; country house [< Sp < L *facienda* (things) to be done < *facere* do]

hack¹ (hak), *v.* **1** cut roughly or unevenly; deal cutting blows. **2** give short, dry coughs. —*n.* **1** a rough cut. **2** a short, dry cough. [OE –*haccian*] —**hack′er,** *n.*

hack² (hak), *n.* **1** *U.S.* carriage for hire. **2** taxi. **3** an old or worn-out horse. **4** person hired to do routine literary work; drudge. —*v.* drive a taxi. —*adj.* working or done merely for money. [short for *hackney*]

hack·ber·ry (hak′ber′i), *n., pl.* **-ries. 1** tree related to the elm that has small, cherrylike fruit. **2** the fruit.

hack·er (hak′ər), *n.* **1** person who spends time fooling around. **2** person skilled at using and programming computers, esp. someone who illegally enters and manipulates a computer system, causing it to malfunction.

hack·le¹ (hak′əl), *n.* **1** one of the long, slender feathers on the neck of certain birds. **2** the neck plumage of certain birds. [ME *hakell;* akin to HECKLE] —**hack′ler,** *n.*

hack·le² (hak′əl), *v.,* **-led, -ling.** cut roughly; hack; mangle [< *hack¹*]

hack·ney (hak′ni), *n., pl.* **-neys,** *adj., v.,* **-neyed, -ney·ing.** —*n.* **1** horse for ordinary riding. **2** carriage for hire. —*adj.* hired. —*v.* use too often; make commonplace. [< OF *haquenee*]

hack·neyed (hak′nid), *adj.* used too often; commonplace.

hack·saw (hak′sô′), *n.* saw for cutting metal, consisting of a narrow, fine-toothed blade fixed in a frame.

hack·work (hak′wėrk′), *n.* unoriginal or tiresome work, esp. writing done by a hack.

had (had), *v.* pt. and pp. of **have.**

had·dock (had′ək), *n., pl.* **-docks** or (*esp. collectively*) **-dock.** a food fish of the N Atlantic, somewhat like a cod, but smaller. [ME *haddok*]

Ha·des (hā′dēz), *n.* **1** *Gk. Myth.* home of the dead, below the earth. **2** hades, hell. [< Gk. *Haides*]

hadj (haj), *n.* —hajj.

hadj·i (haj′i), *n., pl.* **-is.** =hajji.

had·n't (had′ənt), had not.

haf·ni·um (haf′ni əm; häf′–), *n.* a rare metallic element, Hf, somewhat like zirconium. [< *Hafnia,* L name for Copenhagen]

haft (haft; häft), *n.* handle (of a knife, sword, dagger, etc.). —*v.* furnish with a handle or hilt; set in a haft. [OE *hæft*]

hag (hag) *n.* **1** a very ugly old woman, esp. one who is vicious or malicious. **2** witch. [ME *hagge,* akin to OE *hægtesse* witch, fury] —**hag′gish,** *adj.* —**hag′like′,** *adj.*

hag fish (hag′fish′), *n., pl.* **-fish·es** or (*esp. collectively*) **-fish.** a small saltwater fish shaped like an eel, that attaches itself to other fish by its round mouth and bores into them with its horny teeth.

Hag·ga·dah (hə gä′də), *n., pl.* **-doth** (–dōth). legend in the Talmud that explains the law.

hag·gard (hag′ərd), *adj.* wild-looking from pain, fatigue, worry, hunger, etc. —**hag′gard·ly,** *adv.* —**hag′gard·ness,** *n.*

hag·gis (hag′is), *n. Scot.* heart, lungs, and liver of a sheep mixed with suet and oatmeal and boiled in the stomach of the animal.

hag·gle (hag′əl), *v.,* **-gled, -gling. 1** dispute about a price or the terms of a bargain; wrangle. **2** mangle in cutting;

hack. [< *hag* chop < Scand. *höggva*] —**hag′gler,** *n.*

hag·i·og·ra·phy (hā′jē og′rə fi; hag′ē–), *n.* **1** literature that deals with the lives of saints. **2** *Fig.* biography that idolizes its subject. —**hag′i·og′ra·pher,** *n.*

hag·i·ol·o·gy (hā′ji ol′ə ji; hag′i–), *n., pl.* **-gies. 1** literature that deals with the lives and legends of saints. **2** list of saints. [< Gk. *hagios* holy + –LOGY] —**hag′i·o·log′i·cal,** *adj.* —**hag′i·ol′o·gist,** *n.*

hag·rid·den (hag′rid′ən), *adj.* worried or tormented, as if by witches.

hahn·i·um (hä′nē əm), *n.* element 105. [< NL hahnium < Otto *Hahn* (1879–1968), German radiochemist]

hail¹ (hāl), *v.* **1** shout in welcome to; greet; cheer. **2** greet as: *they hailed him leader.* **3** call loudly to; shout to. —*n.* **1** greeting; cheer. **2** a loud call; shout. —*interj. Poetic.* greetings! welcome!

hail from, come from. [< Scand. *heill* health] —**hail′er,** *n.*

hail² (hāl), *n.* **1** small, roundish pieces of ice coming down from the clouds in a shower; frozen rain. **2** shower like hail: *a hail of bullets.* —*v.* **1** come down in hail. **2** pour down or upon in a shower like hail. [OE *hægel*]

hail·stone (hāl′stōn′), *n.* a small, roundish piece of ice coming down from the clouds.

hail·storm (hāl′stôrm′), *n.* storm with hail.

hair (hãr), *n.* **1** a fine, threadlike growth from the skin of people and animals. **2** mass of such growths. **3** a fine, threadlike growth from the outer layer of plants. **4** a very narrow space; something very small; least degree.

by a hair's breadth, by the least amount imaginable.

get in one's hair, bother one; be a nuisance to one.

let one's hair down, a be relaxed. **b** be candid.

make one's hair stand on end, frighten or alarm one.

split hairs, make too fine distinctions.

tear one's hair, be extremely upset, with worry.

turn a hair, show a reaction, as of embarrassment or discomfort. [OE *hēr*] —**hair′less,** *adj.* —**hair′less·ness,** *n.* —**hair′like′,** *adj.*

hair·cloth (hãr′klôth′; –kloth′), *n.* cloth made of horsehair or camel's hair, used to cover furniture, stiffen garments, etc.

hair·cut (hãr′kut′), *n.* act or manner of cutting the hair. —**hair′cut′ter,** *n.*

hair·do (hãr′dü′), *n., pl.* **-dos.** way of arranging the hair.

hair·dress·er (hãr′dres′ər), *n.* person whose work is taking care of people's hair or cutting it. —**hair′dress′ing,** *n., adj.*

hair·line (hãr′līn′), *n.* **1** a very thin line. **2** line where hair growth ends on the head and forehead.

hair·piece (hãr′pēs′), *n.* **1** toupee. **2** small wig worn by women as part of a hairdo.

hair·pin (hãr′pin′), *n.* pin, usually a U-shaped piece of wire, shell, or plastic, used by women to keep the hair in place.

hair·rais·ing (hãr′rāz′ing), *adj.* making the hair stand on end; terrifying.

hair's-breadth, hairs·breadth (hãrz′-bredth′), *n.* a very small space or distance. —*adj.* extremely narrow or close.

hair shirt, 1 a rough shirt or girdle made of horsehair, worn as a penance. **2** *Fig.* adoption of austerity or self-sacrifice.

hair·split·ting (hãr′split′ing), *n., adj.* making too fine distinctions. —**hair′-split·ter,** *n.*

hair·spring (hãr′spring′), *n.* a fine, hair-like spring that regulates the motion of the balance wheel in a watch or clock.

hair trigger, trigger that operates by very slight pressure.

hair·y (hãr′i), *adj.,* **hair·i·er, hair·i·est. 1** covered with hair; having much hair. **2** of or like hair. —**hair′i·ness,** *n.*

Hai·ti (hã′ti), *n.* republic in the western part of the island of Hispaniola. —**Hai′ti·an,** *adj., n.*

hajj or **haj** (haj), *n.* pilgrimage to Mecca, a requirement that each Muslim undertake at least once. Also, **hadj.** [< Ar. *ḥajj*]

haj·ji (haj′i), *n., pl.* **-jis.** Muslim who has made a pilgrimage to Mecca. Also, **hadji.** [< Ar.*ḥājjī,* var. of *ḥajj*]

hake (hāk), *n., pl.* **hakes** or (*esp. collectively*) **hake.** a sea fish related to the cod. [? < Scand. (Norw.) *hakefisk,* lit., hook fish; from the hooklike growth under the lower jaw]

hal·berd (hal′bərd), **hal·bert** (–bərt), *n.* weapon that is both a spear and a battle-ax, used in warfare in the 15th and 16th centuries. [< F *hallebarde* < Ital. *alabarda*]

hal·cy·on (hal′si ən), *adj.* calm; peaceful; happy. [< L < Gk., var. of *alkyon* kingfisher]

hale¹ (hāl), *adj.,* **hal·er, hal·est.** strong and well; healthy. [OE *hāl*] —**hale′ness,** *n.*

hale² (hāl), *v.,* **haled, hal·ing. 1** compel to go. **2** drag by force.[< OF *haler* < Gmc. Doublet of HAUL.]

Hale (hāl), *n.* Nathan, 1755–76, American patriot hanged as a spy by the British.

half (haf; häf), *n., pl.* **halves,** *adj., adv.* —*n.* **1** one of two equal (or approximately equal) parts. **2** one of two equal periods in certain games. **3** a half hour: *half past ten.* —*adj.* **1** forming a half; being or making half of. **2** not complete; being only part of: *a half truth.* —*adv.* **1** to half of the full amount or degree: *a glass half full of milk.* **2** partly: *half aloud.* **3** almost: *half dead from hunger.*
not half bad, fairly good. [OE]

half-and-half (haf′ənd haf′; häf′ənd häf′), *adj.* **1** half one thing and half another. **2** not clearly one thing or the other. —*adv.* in two equal parts. —*n. U.S.* mixture of milk and cream.

half-back (haf′bak′; häf′–), *n.* football player whose position is behind the forward line.

half-baked (haf′bākt′; häf′–), *adj.* **1** not cooked enough. **2** not fully worked out; incomplete. **3** not experienced; showing poor judgment.

half-blood (haf′blud′; häf′–), *n.* **1** =half-breed. **2** person related to another person through one parent only. —**half′-blood′-ed,** *adj.*

half blood, relationship between persons who are related through one parent only.

half-breed (haf′brēd′; häf′–), *n.* person whose parents are of different races.

half brother, brother related through one parent only.

half-caste (haf′kast′; häf′käst′), *n.* =half-breed.

half cock, position of the hammer of a gun when it is pulled back halfway and locked.

half-cocked (haf′kokt′,häf-),*adj.* **1** having the hammer of a gun pulled back halfway. **2** *Informal. Fig.* done or said without thought beforehand; absurd.
go off half-cocked, speak or act without thinking first.

half dollar, a silver coin of the United States and Canada, worth 50 cents.

half-heart·ed (haf′här′tid; häf′–), *adj.* lacking courage, interest, or enthusiasm. —**half′-heart′ed·ly,** *adv.* —**half′-heart′-ed·ness,** *n.*

half hitch, an easily unfastened knot, formed by passing the end of a rope under and over its standing part and then inside the loop.

half hour, *n.* **1** thirty minutes. **2** the halfway point in an hour.

half-hour (haf′our′; häf′–), *adj.* of or lasting a half hour. —**half′-hour′ly,** *adv.*

half-life (haf′lif′; häf′–), *n.* time in which half of the original radiant energy of an element is given off, used to measure radioactivity.

half-mast (haf′mast′; häf′mäst′), *n.* position halfway down from the top of a mast, staff, etc.

half moon, 1 moon when only half of its surface appears bright. **2** something shaped like a half moon or crescent. —**half′-moon′,** *adj.*

half nelson, hold in wrestling accomplished by hooking one arm under an opponent's armpit and putting the hand on the back of his neck.

half note, note in music held half as long as a whole note; minim.

half·pen·ny (hā′pə ni; hāp′ni), *n., pl.* **half·pen·nies** (hā′pə niz; hāp′niz), **half·pence** (hā′pəns), *adj.* —*n.* coin worth half a British penny. —*adj.* **1** worth only a halfpenny. **2** having little value.

half sister, sister related through one parent only.

half-staff (haf′staf′, häf–), *adj.* =half-mast.

half step, difference in pitch between two adjacent keys on a piano; semitone.

half tone, =half step.

half-track (haf′trak′; häf′–), *n.* vehicle that has wheels in front and short tracks in the rear for driving, used to carry personnel and weapons.

half-way (haf′wā′; häf′–), *adv.* half the way: *halfway home.* —*adj.* **1** midway: *a halfway house.* **2** not going far enough; incomplete.
go or **meet halfway,** do one's share to be friendly or agreeable with.

halfway house, 1 place where people recovering from a mental condition or illness live and receive care before going home. **2** place where former prisoners live under supervision to become accustomed to life outside prison.

half-wit (haf′wit′; häf′–), *n.* **1** a feeble-minded person. **2** a stupid, foolish person.

half-wit·ted (haf′wit′id; häf′–), *adj.* **1** feeble-minded. **2** very stupid; foolish. —**half′-wit′ted·ly,** *adv.* —**half′-wit′ted-ness,** *n.*

hal·i·but (hal′ə bət; hol′–), *n., pl.* **-buts** or (*esp. collectively*) **-but.** a large flatfish much used for food, often weighing several hundred pounds. [ME *halybutte* < *haly* holy + *butte* flatfish; eaten on holy days]

Hal·i·fax (hal′ə faks), *n.* seaport in SE Canada, the capital of Nova Scotia.

hal·ite (hal′īt; hā′līt), *n.* a native rock salt. [< NL, < Gk. *hals* salt]

hal·i·to·sis (hal′ə tō′sis), *n.* bad or offensive breath. [< NL, < L *halitus* breath]

hall (hol), *n.* **1** *U.S.* way to go through a building; passageway. **2** passageway or room at the entrance of a building. **3** a large room for holding meetings, parties, banquets, etc. **4** a building for public business: *the town hall.* [OE *heall*]

hal·le·lu·jah, hal·le·lu·iah (hal′ə lü′yə), *interj.* praise ye the Lord! —*n.* a rendering of this. Also, **alleluia.** [< Heb. *hallēlū-yāh* praise ye Yah (Jehovah)]

hal·liard (hal′yərd), *n.* =halyard.

hall·mark (hol′märk′), *n.* **1** an official mark indicating standard of purity, put on gold and silver articles. **2** mark or sign of genuineness or good quality. —*v.* put a hallmark on. [from Goldsmiths' *Hall* in London, the seat of the Gold-smiths' Company, by whom the stamping was legally regulated]

hal·loo (hə lü′), *interj., n., pl.* **-loos,** *v.,* **-looed, -loo·ing.** —*interj.* **1** shout to make hounds run faster. **2** call or shout to attract attention. —*n., v.* shout; call.

hal·low¹ (hal′ō), *v.* **1** make holy; make sacred. **2** honor as holy or sacred. [OE *hālgian* < *hālig* holy]

hal·low² (hə lō′), *interj., n., v.* =halloo.

hal·lowed (hal′ōd; *in worship, often* hal′-ō id), *adj.* **1** made holy; sacred; consecrated. **2** honored or observed as holy. —**hal′lowed·ness,** *n.*

Hal·low·een (hal′ō ēn′; hol′–), *n.* evening of October 31, preceding All Saints' Day. [for *Allhallow-even*]

hal·lu·ci·nate (hə lü′sə nāt), *v.*, **–nat·ed**, **–nat·ing.** to affect with or have hallucinations. [< L *alucinātus, pp.* of *alucinārī* wander (in the mind); dream + E–*ate*[1]]

hal·lu·ci·na·tion (hə lü′sə nā′shən), *n.* **1** apparent perception of an object or sound that is not really present. **2** the object or sound apparently perceived illusion. —**hal·lu′ci·na·to′ry**, *adj.*

hal·lu·cin·o·gen (hə lü′sə nə jən), *n.* substance, esp. a drug, that produces hallucinations.

hall·way (hôl′wā′), *n.* **1** way to go through a building. **2** passageway or room at the entrance of a building.

ha·lo (hā′lō), *n.*, *pl.* **–los, –loes**, *v.*, **–loed**, **–lo·ing.** —*n.* **1** ring of light around the sun, moon, or other shining body. **2** a golden circle of light represented about the head of a saint, etc. **3** glory or glamour that surrounds an idealized person or thing: *a halo of romance surrounds King Arthur and his knights.* —*v.* surround with a halo. [< L (def. 1) < Gk. *halos* disk, threshing floor (with ref. to circular path of the oxen)] —**ha′lo·like′**, *adj.*

hal·o·gen (hal′ə jən), *n.* any one of the elements iodine, bromine, chlorine, and fluorine, that combine directly with metals to form salts. [< Gk. *hals* salt + *gennaein* to produce]

halt[1] (hôlt), *v.* stop for a time, as in marching. [< n.] —*n.* a temporary stop.

call a halt, order a stop. [< F *halte* < G *halt* < *halten* to stop]

halt[2] (hôlt), *v.* **1** be in doubt; hesitate; waver: *words halt in embarrassment.* **2** be faulty or imperfect: *a halting line of verse.* **3** *Archaic.* be lame. —*adj.* **1** flawed; not smoothly flowing, as of writing, an argument, etc. **2** *Archaic.* lame. —*n. Archaic.* lameness. [OE *healt*, adj.] —**halt′ing·ly**, *adv.* —**halt′ing·ness**, *n.*

hal·ter (hôl′tər), *n.* **1** rope, strap, etc., for leading or tying an animal. **2** an abbreviated shirt for women which fastens behind the neck and across the back. —*v.* put a halter on; tie with a halter. [OE *hælftre*]

halve (hav; häv), *v.*, **halved, halv·ing. 1** share equally: *halve expenses on a trip.* **2** reduce to half: *halve the time of doing the work.* [< *half*]

halves (havz; hävz), *n. pl.* of **half.**

by halves, a partly. **b** in a half-hearted way.

go halves, share equally.

hal·yard (hal′yərd), *n.* rope or tackle used on a ship to raise or lower a sail, yard, flag, etc. Also, **halliard.** [ME *hallyer* < HALE[2]]

ham (ham), *n.*, *v.*, **hammed, ham·ming.** —*n.* **1** salted and smoked meat from the upper part of a hog's hind leg. **2** the upper part of an animal's hind leg, used for food. **3** a poor actor or performer. **4** an amateur radio operator. —*v.* overact.

ham it up, overact; ham: *an interview is not the time to ham it up.*

hams, back of the thigh and buttock:

cramped from crouching on their hams. [OE *hamm*]

Ham (ham), *n.* in the Bible, the second son of Noah.

ham·a·dry·ad (ham′ə drī′əd; –ad), *n. Gk. Myth.* a wood nymph supposed to live and die with the tree she dwelt in; dryad. [< L < Gk. *Hamadryas* < *hama* together (with) + *drys* tree]

ham·burg (ham′bėrg), *n.* =hamburger.

ham·burg·er (ham′bėr gər), *n.* **1** ground beef, usually shaped into round, flat cakes and fried or broiled. **2** sandwich made with this meat. [< G, pertaining to *Hamburg*]

Ham·il·ton (ham′əl tən), *n.* **1 Alexander,** 1757–1804, American statesman, the first secretary of the treasury. **2** capital of Bermuda.

Ham·it·ic (ham it′ik; hə mit′–), *adj.* of or having to do with a group of languages in N and E Africa, including ancient Egyptian, Berber, Ethiopian, etc.

ham·let (ham′lit), *n.* a small village. [< OF *hamelet*, dim. of *hamel* village < Gmc.; akin to HOME]

Ham·let (ham′lit), *n.* **1** one of Shakespeare's greatest tragedies, first printed in 1603. **2** the principal character in this play.

ham·mer (ham′ər), *n.* **1** tool with a metal head and a handle, used to drive nails and beat metal into shape. **2** anything shaped or used like a hammer: **a** mallet or gavel used by an auctioneer. **b** cock of a gun or pistol. —*v.* **1** drive, hit, or work with a hammer. **2** beat into shape with a hammer. **3** fasten by using a hammer. **4** hit again and again. **5** force by many efforts. **6** work out with much effort.

come or **go under the hammer,** be sold at auction.

hammer (away) at, a keep working at. **b** keep insisting on.

hammer out, a shape by beating with a hammer. **b** *Fig.* work out; devise. [OE *hamor*] —**ham′mer·er**, *n.* —**ham′mer·less**, *adj.* —**ham′mer·like′**, *adj.*

ham·mer·head (ham′ər hed′), *n.* shark whose wide head looks somewhat like a double-headed hammer.

hammer lock, a wrestling hold in which an opponent's arm is twisted and held behind his back.

ham·mock (ham′ək), *n.* a hanging bed or couch made of canvas, netted cord, etc. [< Sp. *hamaca* < Carib] —**ham′mock·like′**, *adj.*

ham·per[1] (ham′pər), *v.* hold back; hinder. [ME *hampre(n)*]

ham·per[2] (ham′pər), *n.* a large basket, usually with a cover. [var. of *hanaper* < OF, < *hanap* cup < Gmc.]

ham·ster (ham′stər), *n.* small rodent with a short tail and large cheek pouches, often kept as a pet and used in laboratory research.

ham·string (ham′string′), *n.*, *v.*, **–strung** or (*Rare*) **–stringed, –string·ing.** —*n.* **1** one of the tendons at the back of the knee in humans. **2** the great tendon at

the back of the hock of a fourfooted animal. —*v.* **1** cripple by cutting the hamstring. **2** destroy activity, efficiency, etc., of.

Han·cock (han′kok), *n.* **John,** 1737–93, American statesman, the first signer of the Declaration of Independence.

hand (hand), *n.* **1** the end part of an arm; part that a person grasps and holds things with. **2** anything resembling a hand. **3** a hired worker: *a farm hand.* **4** Often, **hands.** possession; control: *this is no longer in my hands.* **5** part or share in doing something: *he had no hand in the matter.* **6** side: *at her left hand stood two men.* **7** source: *she heard the story at second hand.* **8** style of handwriting: *in a clear hand.* **9** round of applause: *the winner got a big hand.* **10** promise of marriage. **11** measure using breadth of a hand; 4 inches. **12** cards held by a player in a card game. **13** one round of a card game. —*v.* **1** give with the hand; pass; pass along: *please hand me the butter.* **2** help with the hand: *the polite boy handed the lady into her car.* —*adj.* of, for, by, or in the hand.

at first hand, from direct knowledge or experience.

at hand, a within reach; near; close. **b** ready.

by hand, a by using the hands, not machinery **b** by special messenger.

change hands, pass from one person to another.

force one's hand, make a person act before he or she had planned to or to do something disliked.

(from) hand to mouth, without provision for the future.

give or **lend** or **bear a hand,** help; assist.

hand and foot, thoroughly; completely.

hand and glove, in close relationship.

hand in hand, a holding hands. **b** *Fig.* together.

hands down, without question; easily.

in hand, a under control. **b** in possession.

lay hands on, a seize; take; got. **b** arrest. **c** attack; harm.

on hand, a near; close. **b** ready.

on the other hand, considering the other side.

out of hand, beyond control: *behavior completely out of hand.*

show one's hand, reveal one's intentions.

throw up one's hands, give up; admit failure.

wash one's hands of, have nothing more to do with; give up on. [OE] —**hand′less**, *adj.*

hand·bag (hand′bag′), *n.* woman's small bag for money, keys, cosmetics, etc.

hand·ball (hand′bôl′), *n.* **1** game played by hitting a small ball against a wall with the hand. **2** ball used in this game.

hand·bill (hand′bil′), *n.* a printed announcement to be handed out to people.

hand·book (hand′bük′), *n.* **1** a small book of reference; manual. **2** guidebook for tourists.

hand·breadth (hand′bredth′), *n.* breadth of a hand, used as a measure. It varies from 2½ to 4 inches. Also, **hand's-breadth.**

hand·cart (hand′kärt′), *n.* a small cart pulled or pushed by hand.

hand·clasp (hand′klasp′; –kläsp′), *n.* grasp of a person's hand, as in agreement or greeting.

hand·craft (hand′kraft′), *v.* make or fashion by hand. —*n.* =handicraft.

hand·cuff (hand′kuf′), *n.* Usually, **handcuffs.** one of a pair of metal clasps joined by a short chain and fastened around the wrists. —*v.* put handcuffs on.

–handed, *suffix.* **1** having or using a hand or hands: *a two-handed stroke.* **2** having a certain kind or number of hands, as in *left-handed.*

hand·ed·ness (han′did nis), *n.* preference of using one hand over the other.

Han·del (han′dəl), *n.* **George Frederick,** 1685–1759, German musical composer.

hand·ful (hand′fül), *n., pl.* **–fuls. 1** as much or as many as the hand can hold. **2** a small number or quantity. **3** person or thing that is hard to manage.

hand·i·cap (han′di kap), *n., v.,* **–capped, –cap·ping.** —*n.* **1** race, contest, game, etc., in which the better contestants are given certain disadvantages, or the poorer ones certain advantages, so that all have an equal chance to win. **2** disadvantage or advantage given. **3** something that puts a person at a disadvantage; hindrance. —*v.* **1** give a handicap to. **2** put at a disadvantage; hinder. [for *hand in cap;* appar. with ref. to an old game] —**hand′i·cap′per,** *n.*

hand·i·craft (han′di kraft; –kräft), *n.* **1** skill with the hands. **2** trade or art requiring skill with the hands. [alter. of *handcraft,* patterned after *handiwork*] —**hand′i·crafts′man,** *n.* —**hand′i·crafts′man·ship,** *n.*

hand·i·work (han′di werk′), *n.* **1** work done with the hands. **2** work that a person has done herself or himself. **3** result of a person's action. [OE *handgeweorc* handwork]

hand·ker·chief (hang′kər chif), *n.* **1** a soft, square piece of cloth used for wiping the nose, face, eyes, etc. **2** piece of cloth worn over the head or around the neck; kerchief.

han·dle (han′dəl), *n., v.,* **–dled, –dling.** —*n.* part of a thing made to be held or grasped by the hand. —*v.* **1** touch, feel, hold, or move with the hand; use the hands on. **2** manage; direct; control. **3** behave or act when handled: *this car handles easily.* **4** deal with; treat. **5** deal in; trade in: *that store handles meat and groceries.*

fly off the handle, lose one's temper; get angry.

get or **have a handle on,** grasp; understand. [OE < *hand*] —**han′dled,** *adj.* —**han′dle·less,** *adj.*

handle bar. Often, **handle bars.** the bar, usually curved, in front of the rider, by which a bicycle, etc., is guided.

han·dler (han′dlər), *n.* **1** person or thing that handles. **2** person who helps to train a boxer or who acts as his second.

hand·made (hand′mād′), *adj.* made by hand, not by machinery; not machine-made.

hand·maid (hand′mād′), **hand·maid·en** (–mād′ən), *n.* **1** a female servant. **2** a female attendant.

hand-me-down (hand′mē doun′), *n.* something passed from one person to another; something used or second-hand.

hand organ, a large music box that is made to play tunes by turning a crank.

hand·out (hand′out′), *n.* **1** portion of food, money, etc. handed out: *to give a handout to a beggar.* **2** written material given to reporters as news, but often contrived to serve some purpose of publicity, propaganda, etc.

hand·picked (hand′pikt′), *adj.* **1** picked by hand. **2** carefully selected. **3** unfairly selected.

hand·rail (hand′rāl′), *n.* railing used as a guard or support on a stairway, platform, etc.

hand's-breadth (handz′bredth′), *n.* =hand-breadth.

hand·shake (hand′shāk′), *n.* a clasping and shaking each other's hands in friendship.

hand·some (han′səm), *adj.,* **–som·er, –som·est. 1** good-looking; pleasing in appearance. **2** fairly large; considerable: *a handsome sum of money, a handsome gift.* [ME, eacy to handle, ready at hand < *hand* + *–some*[1]] —**hand′some·ly,** *adv.* —**hand′some·ness,** *n.*

hands-on (handz′on′, –ôn′), *adj.* personally involved.

hand·spring (hand′spring′), *n.* spring or leap in which a person turns heels over head while balancing on one or both hands.

hand·stand (hand′stand′), *n.* a balancing on one's hands with the feet in the air.

hand-to-hand (hand′tə hand′), *adj.* close together; at close quarters.

hand-to-mouth (hand′tə mouth′), *adj.* not providing for the future; not thrifty.

hand·work (hand′werk′), *n.* work done by hand, not by machinery.

hand·writ·ing (hand′rīt′ing), *n.* **1** writing by hand; writing with pen, pencil, etc. **2** manner or style of writing. —**hand′writ′ten,** *adj.*

hand·y (han′di), *adj.,* **hand·i·er, hand·i·est. 1** easy to reach or use; saving work; convenient. **2** skillful with the hands. **3** easy to handle or manage. —**hand′i·ly,** *adv.* —**hand′i·ness,** *n.*

handy man, person who does odd jobs.

hang (hang), *v.,* **hung** or (*esp. for execution or suicide*) **hanged, hang·ing,** *n.* —*v.* **1** fasten or be fastened to something above. **2** fasten or be fastened so as to swing or turn freely: *hang a door on its hinges.* **3** put to death by hanging with a rope around the neck. **4** cover

or decorate with things that hang: *hang a window with curtains.* **5** bend down; droop: *he hung his head in shame.* **6** be doubtful or undecided; hesitate. **7** loiter; linger: *hang at the mall.* —*n.* **1** way that a thing hangs. **2** way of using or doing; idea. **3** a trifle: *not care a hang.*

hang around with, *Informal.* spend time with.

hang back, be reluctant to move ahead.

hang on, a hold tightly to. **b** be unwilling to let go, stop, or leave. **c** depend on. **d** consider or listen to very carefully.

hang out, a put up outdoors, as a flag or laundry. **b** lean out. **c** spend time with. **d** *Slang.* live or stay.

hang together, a support each other. **2** *Fig.* make sense; be coherent.

hang tough, be resolute or firm.

hang up, a put on a hook, peg, etc. **b** end a telephone call. [OE *hangian*] —**hang′a·ble,** *adj.*

hang·ar (hang′ər), *n.* shed for aircraft. [< F, ? < Gmc.]

hang·dog (hang′dôg′; –dog′), *adj.* ashamed; sneaking; degraded.

hang·er (hang′ər), *n.* **1** person who hangs things: *a paper hanger.* **2** tool or machine that hangs things. **3** thing on which something else is hung: *a coat hanger.*

hang·er-on (hang′ər on′; –ôn′), *n., pl.* **hang·ers-on. 1** follower; dependent. **2** an undesirable follower. **3** person who often goes to a place.

hang glider, device like a large kite under which a person hangs from a harness and steers with a bar, used for the sport of hang gliding.

hang gliding, sport of soaring on air currents in a hang glider.

hang·ing (hang′ing), *n.* **1** death by hanging with a rope around the neck. **2** Often, **hangings.** thing that hangs from a wall, bed, etc. —*adj.* fastened to something above.

hang·man (hang′mən), *n., pl.* **–men.** person who puts criminals to death by hanging them.

hang·nail (hang′nāl′), *n.* bit of skin that hangs partly near a fingernail.

hang·out (hang′out′), *n.* a rendezvous, esp. for criminals or gangs.

hang·o·ver (hang′ō′vər), *n.* **1** something that remains from an earlier time or condition. **2** condition the morning after drinking too much alcoholic liquor.

hang-up (hang′up′), *n. Informal.* problem or anxiety that keeps a person from moving forward.

hank (hangk), *n.* **1** coil; loop. **2** skein. [appar. < Scand. *hönk*]

han·ker (hang′kər), *v.* wish; crave. —**hank′er·er,** *n.* —**han′ker·ing,** *n.*

han·kie (hang′ki), *n.* handkerchief.

han·ky-pan·ky (hang′ki pang′ki), *n.* **1** underhanded or illegal conduct. **2** trickery; shenanigans. [prob. alter. of *hocus-pocus*]

Han·ni·bal (han′ə bəl), *n.* 247–183? B.C., a Carthaginian general who invaded Italy.

han·som (han′səm), *n.* a two-wheeled cab for two passengers, drawn by one horse, with the driver on a seat high up behind the cab. [from name of early designer of such cabs]

han·ta·vi·rus (han′tə vī′rəs), *n.* virus carried by rodents that causes respiratory and kidney infections that are sometimes fatal. [< *Hanta* genus name < river in Korea]

Ha·nuk·kah or **Ha·nuk·ka** (hä′nu̇ kä; hä′–), annual Jewish Feast of Lights or Feast of Dedication, usually in December, when a candle is lit on each day of the Feast. Also, **Chanukah.**

hap (hap), *n. Archaic.* chance; luck. [< Scand. *happ*]

hap·haz·ard (*n.* hap′haz′ərd; *adj., adv.* hap′haz′ərd), *n.* chance. —*adj.* random; not planned: *haphazard answers.* —*adv.* by chance; at random. —**hap′haz′ard·ly,** *adv.* —**hap′haz′ard·ness,** *n.*

hap·less (hap′lis), *adj.* unlucky; unfortunate. —**hap′less·ly,** *adv.* —**hap′less·ness,** *n.*

hap·loid (hap′loid), *adj.* having the number of sets of chromosomes usual for a species; monoploid. —*n.* haploid organism or cell; monoploid. [< Gk. *haploûs* single + E *-oid*]

hap·pen (hap′ən), *v.* **1** take place; occur: *nothing happens here.* **2** be or take place by chance: *accidents will happen.* **3** have the fortune; chance: *I happened to sit by Mary.* **4** be done (to): *something has happened to this lock.*

happen on, a meet. **b** find. [ME *happene(n)* < HAP]

hap·pen·ing (hap′ən ing), *n.* thing that happens; event; occurrence.

hap·pen·stance (hap′ən stans), *n.* accidental or chance occurrence. [< *happen* + circum*stance*]

hap·py (hap′i), *adj.,* **–pi·er, –pi·est. 1** feeling or showing pleasure and joy; glad. **2** lucky; fortunate: *by a happy chance, I found the money.* **3** clever and fitting; apt; successful and suitable. [ME, < HAP] —**hap′pi·ly,** *adv.* —**hap′pi·ness,** *n.*

hap·py-go-luck·y (hap′i gō luk′i), *adj.* taking things easily; trusting to luck. —*adv.* by mere chance.

har·a·ki·ri (har′ə kir′i; hä′rə–), **har·a·kar·i** (–kar′i; –käri), *n.* suicide by ripping open the abdomen with a knife, the national form of honorable suicide in Japan. Also, **hari-kari.** [< Jap., belly cut]

ha·rangue (hə rang′), *n., v.,* **–rangued, –rangu·ing.** —*n.* **1** a noisy speech. **2** a long, pompous speech. —*v.* **1** address in a harangue. **2** deliver a harangue. [< OF *arenge* < Gmc.] —**ha·rangu′er,** *n.*

har·ass (har′əs; hə ras′), *v.* **1** trouble by repeated attacks; harry. **2** disturb; worry; torment. [< F *harasser* < OF *harer* set a dog on] —**har′ass·er,** *n.* —**har′ass·ing·ly,** *adv.* —**har′ass·ment,** *n.*

har·bin·ger (här′bin jər), *n.* one that goes ahead to announce another's coming; forerunner. —*v.* announce beforehand; announce. [< OF *herbergere* provider of shelter (hence, one who goes ahead), ult. < *herberge* lodging < Gmc.]

har·bor (här′bər), *n.* **1** place of shelter for ships and boats. **2** any place of shelter. —*v.* **1** give shelter to; give a place to hide: *a dog that harbors fleas.* **2** keep or nourish in the mind: *harbor unkind thoughts.* [OE *hereborg* lodgings < *here* army + *beorg* shelter] —**har′bor·er,** *n.* —**har′bor·less,** *adj.*

har·bor·age, (här′bər ij), *n.* **1** shelter for ships and boats. **2** any shelter.

harbor master, officer who has charge of a port and enforces the rules respecting it.

hard (härd), *adj.* **1** solid and firm to the touch; not soft. **2** firmly formed; tight: *a hard knot.* **3** needing much ability, effort, or time; difficult: *a hard problem.* **4** causing much pain, trouble, care, etc.; severe: *a hard illness.* **5** stern; unfeeling: *be hard on a person.* **6** not pleasant; harsh: *a hard face.* **7** acting or done with energy, persistence, etc.: *a hard worker.* **8** containing mineral salts that interfere with the action of soap: *hard water.* **9** *U.S.* containing much alcohol: *hard liquor.* **10** pronounced as the *c* and *g* in *corn* and *get.* —*adv.* **1** so as to be hard, solid, or firm: *frozen hard.* **2** firmly; tightly: *hold hard.* **3** with difficulty: *breathe hard.* **4** with effort or energy: *try hard.* **5** close; near: *the house stands hard by the bridge.*

hard and fast, that cannot be changed; strict.

hard of hearing, somewhat deaf.

hard up, needing money or anything very badly. [OE *heard*] —**hard′ness,**

hard·ball (härd′bôl′), *n.* =baseball. —*adj.* tough; rough.

play hardball, be rough and uncompromising.

hard-bit·ten (härd′bit′ən), *adj.* stubborn; unyielding; dogged.

hard-boiled (härd′boild′), *adj.* **1** boiled until hard. **2** *Informal.* not easily influenced by the feelings.

hard coal, =anthracite.

hard copy, copy typed or written or printed out from a computer on paper.

hard-core (härd′kôr′; –kōr), *adj.* **1** unyielding; persistent: *hard-core nationalism, hard-core poverty.* **2** addictive: *hard-core drugs.*

hard core, the permanent or most persistent part of any thing or group; central or vital part.

hard·en (har′dən), *v.* **1** make or become hard or capable of endurance. **2** make or become unfeeling or pitiless. —**hard′en·er,** *n.*

hard goods, machinery, vehicles, and other heavy goods. —**hard′-goods,** *adj.*

hard·hat (härd′hat′), *n.* or **hard hat, 1** rigid, protective hat worn by construction workers. **2** a construction worker.

hard-head·ed (härd′hed′id), *adj.* **1** not easily excited or deceived. **2** stubborn; obstinate. —**hard′-head′ed·ly,** *adv.* —**hard′-head′ed·ness,** *n.*

hard-heart·ed (härd′här′tid), *adj.* without pity; cruel; unfeeling. —**hard′-heart′ed·ly,** *adv.* —**hard′-heart′ed·ness,** *n.*

hard-hit·ting (härd′hit′ing), *adj.* vigorous; aggressive; powerful.

har·di·hood (här′di hu̇d), *n.* boldness; daring.

Har·ding (här′ding), *n.* **Warren Gamaliel,** 1865–1923, the 29th president of the United States, 1921–23.

hard landing, crash landing, esp. of a spacecraft.

hard line, unyielding adherence to a policy, attitude, etc. —**hard′-line′,** *adj.* —**hard′-lin′er,** *n.*

hard·ly (härd′li), *adv.* **1** only just; barely: *he had hardly reached there, when it began to snow.* **2** not quite: *hardly strong enough.* **3** probably not: *he will hardly come now.* **4** with trouble or effort: *a hardly won contest.* **5** harshly; severely: *deal hardly with a person.*

hard-nosed (härd′nōzd′), *adj.* stubborn.

hard palate, the front, bony part of the roof of the mouth.

hard·pan (härd′pan′), *n.* hard, firm, underlying earth.

hard-pressed (härd′prest′), *adj.* under severe pressure; in difficulty.

hard·ship (härd′ship), *n.* something hard to bear; hard condition of living.

hard·tack (härd′tak′), *n.* a very hard, dry biscuit, eaten by sailors.

hard·ware (härd′wār′), *n.* **1** articles made from metal, as locks, screws, etc. **2** military equipment, as tanks, guns, etc., as distinguished from manpower.

hard·wood (härd′wu̇d′), *n.* **1** any hard, compact wood. **2** in forestry, any tree that has broad leaves or does not have needles. **3** wood of such a tree, as the oak or maple.

har·dy (här′di), *adj.,* **–di·er, –di·est. 1** able to bear hard treatment, fatigue, etc.; strong; robust. **2** able to withstand the cold of winter in the open air: *hardy plants.* **3** bold; daring. [< OF *hardi,* pp. of *hardir* harden < Gmc.] —**har′di·ly,** *adv.* —**har′di·ness,** *n.*

hare (hār), *n., pl.* **hares** or (*esp. collectively*) **hare. 1** a gnawing animal very much like a rabbit but larger, having long ears, long hind legs, a short tail, and a divided upper lip. **2** a rabbit. [OE *hara*] —**hare′like′,** *adj.*

hare·bell (hār′bel′), *n.* a slender plant with blue, bell-shaped flowers; bluebell.

hare-brained (hār′brānd′), *adj.* giddy; heedless; reckless.

hare·lip (hār′lip′), *n.* a congenital deformity caused when parts of the lip fail to grow together before birth. —**hare′lipped′,** *adj.*

har·em (hār′əm), *n.* **1** part of a Muslim house where the women live. **2** its occupants; the wives, female relatives, female servants, etc., of a Muslim household. [< Ar. *ḥarīm* forbidden]

har·i-kar·i (har′i kar′i; hä′ri kä′ri), *n.* =harakiri.

hark (härk), *v.* listen.

hark back, go back; turn back. [ME *herkien*]

hark·en (här′kən), v. hearken. [OE *heorcnian*] —**hark′en·er,** n.

har·le·quin (här′lə kwin; –kin), n. **1.** Often, **Harlequin.** character in comedy and pantomime who is usually masked, has a costume of varied colors, and carries a wooden sword. **2** a mischievous person; buffoon. —*adj.* varied in color; many-colored. [< F; OF var. of *Herlequin* < ME *Herle King* King Herla (mythical figure); modern meaning in French is from Ital. *arlecchino* < F *Harlequin*]

har·lot (här′lət), n. =prostitute. [< OF, vagabond]

har·lot·ry (här′lət ri), n. =prostitution.

harm (härm), n. **1.** hurt; damage. **2** evil; wrong. —*v.* damage; injure; hurt. [OE *hearm*] —**harm′er,** n.

harm·ful (härm′fəl), adj. causing harm; injurious; hurtful. —**harm′ful·ly,** adv. —**harm′ful·ness,** n. pernicious.

harm·less (härm′lis), adj. causing no harm; that would not harm anyone or anything. —**harm′less·ly,** adv. —**harm′less·ness,** n.

har·mon·ic (här mon′ik), adj. **1** having to do with harmony. **2** musical. **3** indicating a series of oscillations accompanying a fundamental frequency. —*n.* overtone. [< L < Gk. *harmonikos* harmonic, musical. See HARMONY.] —**har·mon′i·cal·ly,** adv.

har·mon·i·ca (här mon′ə kə), n. an oblong musical instrument with metal reeds, played by the mouth; mouth organ.

har·mon·ics (här mon′iks), n. science of musical sounds.

har·mo·ni·ous (här mō′ni əs), adj. **1** agreeing in feelings, ideas, or action: *play together in a harmonious group.* **2** arranged so that the parts are orderly or pleasing; going well together: *harmonious colors.* **3** sweet-sounding; musical. —**har·mo′ni·ous·ly,** adv. —**har·mo′ni·ous·ness,** n.

har·mo·ni·um (här mō′ni əm), n. a small organ with metal reeds.

har·mo·nize (här′mə nīz), v., –nized, –niz·ing. **1** bring into harmony or agreement. **2** be in harmony or agreement: *the colors in the room harmonized.* **3** add tones to (a melody) to make successive chords. —**har′mo·ni·za′tion,** n. —**har′mo·niz′er,** n.

har·mo·ny (här′mə ni), n., pl. –nies. **1** agreement of feeling, ideas, or actions; getting along well together: *work in perfect harmony.* **2** an orderly or pleasing arrangement of parts; going well together: *harmony of colors in a picture.* **3 a** sounding together of notes in a chord. **b** study of chords and of relating them to successive chords. [< F < L < Gk. *harmonia* concord, a joining < *harmos* joint]

har·ness (här′nis), n. combination of leather straps, bands, and other pieces used to connect a horse or other animal to a carriage, wagon, plow, etc. —*v.* **1** put harness on. **2** cause to produce power.

in harness, in or at one's regular work. [< OF *harneis* < Scand.] —**har′ness·er,** n. —**har′ness·less,** adj. —**har′ness·like′,** adj.

Har·old II (har′əld), 1022?–1066, the last Saxon king of England, defeated by William the Conqueror in 1066.

harp (härp), n. instrument with strings set in a triangular frame, played by plucking the strings with the fingers. —*v.* play on a harp.

harp on, keep on tiresomely talking or writing about; refer continually to. [OE *hearpe*] —**harp′er,** n. —**harp′ist,** n. —**harp′like′,** adj.

har·poon (här pün′), n. a barbed spear with a rope tied to it, used for catching whales and other sea animals. —*v.* strike, catch, or kill with a harpoon. [(? < Du.) < F *harpon* < L *harpe* sickle, hook < Gk.] —**har·poon′er,** n. —**harpoon′like,** adj.

harp·si·chord (härp′sə kôrd), n. a stringed instrument like a piano, used from about 1550 to 1750. [< obs. F *harpechorde* < *harpe* (< Gmc.) + *chorde* CHORD²]

Har·py (här′pi), n., pl –pies. **1** Gk. Legend. any of several filthy, greedy monsters having women's heads and birds' bodies, wings, and claws. **2 harpy,** a very greedy person; person who preys upon others. [< L < Gk. *harpyia*, prob. akin to *harpazein* snatch]

har·que·bus (här′kwə bəs), n. an old form of portable gun, used before muskets. Also **arquebus.** [< F < Ital. < Du. *haakbus*, lit., hook gun]

har·ri·dan (har′ə dən), n. a bad-tempered, disreputable old woman.

har·ri·er¹ (har′i ər), n. a small hound of the kind used to hunt hares. [appar. < *hare*]

har·ri·er² (har′i ər), n. **1** person who harries. **2** hawk that preys on small animals.

Har·ris·burg (har′is bėrg), n. capital of Pennsylvania, in the S part.

Har·ri·son (har′ə sən), n. **1 Benjamin,** 1833–1901, the 23rd president of the United States, 1889–93. **2** his grandfather, **William Henry,** 1773–1841, American general and ninth president of the United States, in 1841.

har·row (har′ō), n. a heavy frame with iron teeth or upright disks, used on plowed fields for breaking up clods, covering seeds, etc. —*v.* **1** draw a harrow over (land, etc.). **2** hurt; wound. **3** arouse uncomfortable feelings in; distress; torment. [ME *harwe*] —**har′row·er,** n. —**har′row·ing,** adj. —**har′row·ing·ly,** adv.

har·ry (har′i), v., -ried, -ry·ing. **1** raid and rob with violence. **2** keep troubling; worry; torment. [OE *hergian* < *here* army]

harsh (härsh), adj. **1** rough to the touch, taste, eye, or ear; sharp and unpleasant.

2 without pity; cruel; severe. **3** rugged; bleak: *a harsh climate.* [var. of ME *harsk* < Scand. (Dan.) *harsk* rancid] —**harsh′ly,** adv. —**harsh′ness,** n.

hart (härt), n., pl. **harts** or (*esp. collectively*) **hart. 1** a male red deer after its fifth year. **2** a male deer; stag. [OE *heorot*]

har·te·beest (här′tə bēst; härt′bēst′), n., pl. -beests or (*esp. collectively*) -beest. a large, swift African antelope with ringed, curved horns bent backward at the tips. [< Afrikaans, hart beast]

Hart·ford (härt′fərd), n. capital of Connecticut, in the C part.

harts·horn (härts′hôn′), n. smelling salts.

har·um-scar·um (hār′əm skār′əm), adj. reckless; rash. —*adv.* recklessly; wildly. —*n.* **1** a reckless person. **2** reckless behavior. [appar. < *hare* frighten + *scare*]

har·vest (här′vist), n. **1** a reaping and gathering in of grain and other food crops, usually in the late summer or early autumn. **2** time or season when grain, fruit, etc., are gathered in. **3** one season's yield of any natural product; crop. **4** *Fig.* result; consequences. —*v.* gather in and bring home for use. [OE *hœrfest*]

har·vest·er (här′vis tər), n. **1** person who works in a harvest field; reaper. **2** machine for harvesting crops, esp. grain.

har·vest·man (här′vist mən), n., pl. -men. **1** person who harvests. **2** =daddy-longlegs.

harvest moon, full moon at harvest time or about September 23.

has (haz), v. 3rd pers. sing. pres. indic. of **have.**

has-been (haz′bin′), n. person or thing whose best days are past.

hash (hash), n. **1** mixture of cooked meat, potatoes, etc., chopped into small pieces and fried or baked. **2** *Fig.* mixture; jumble. **3** *Fig.* mess; muddle. **4** *Informal.* hashish. [< v.] —*v.* **1** chop into small pieces. **2** mess; muddle. [< F *hacher* < *hache* hatchet]

Hash·em·ite (hash′ə mit), adj. of or having to do with the royal dynasty of Jordan and the former royal dynasty of Iraq. —*n.* member of this dynasty, claiming descent from Muhammad. Also, **Hashimite.**

hash·ish, hash·eesh (hash′ēsh), n. the dried flowers, top leaves, and tender parts of Indian hemp, used for its narcotic effect. [< Ar. *hashīsh* dried hemp leaves]

Ha·sid·ic (hə sid′ik), adj. of or having to do with the Hasidim or their beliefs.

Has·i·dim (has′i dim; hä′si-; hä′sē-), n. members of a pious and mystical Jewish sect founded in the 1700s. **2** members of a Jewish sect founded about 200 B.C. [< Heb. *hasidim* pious ones]

has·n't (haz′ənt), has not.

hasp (hasp; häsp), *n.* clasp or fastening for a door, window, trunk, box, etc., esp. one that fits over a staple or into a hole and is fastened by a peg, padlock, etc. [var. of OE *hœpse*]

has·sle (has′əl), *n.* struggle; contest. —*v.,* **-sled, -sling.** *Informal.* **1** struggle. **2** harass; annoy. [appar. < Southern U.S. dial. *hassle* pant, breathe noisily (cf. E dial. *hussle,* same meaning), frequentative of E dial. *hoose* cough, wheeze; related to *wheeze*]

has·sock (has′ək), *n.* **1** a thick cushion to rest the feet on, sit on, or kneel on. **2** tuft or bunch of coarse grass. [OE *hassuc* coarse grass]

hast (hast), *v. Archaic.* 2nd pers. sing. pres. indic. of **have.**

haste (hāst), *n.* **1** a trying to be quick; hurrying: *the emergency king's business required haste.* **2** quickness without thought or care: *haste makes waste.*
in haste, a in a hurry; quickly. **b** without careful thought; rashly.
make haste, hurry; be quick. [< OF < Gmc.]

has·ten (hās′ən), *v.* **1** cause to be quick; speed; hurry: *hasten everyone off to bed.* **2** be quick; go fast: *hasten to explain.* —**has′ten·er,** *n.*

hast·y (hās′ti), *adj.,* **hast·i·er, hast·i·est. 1** hurried; quick: *a hasty visit.* **2** not well thought out; rash: *a hasty decision.* **3** easily angered; quick-tempered. —**hast′i·ly,** *adv.* —**hast′i·ness,** *n.*

hasty pudding, mush made of corn meal.

hat (hat), *n., v.,* **hat·ted, hat·ting.** —*n.* a covering for the head, usually with a brim. —*v.* cover or furnish with a hat.
hold on to your hat, prepare for a shock or surprise.
pass the hat, ask for contributions; take up a collection.
talk through one's hat, talk about something without much knowledge of the subject.
wear two (or **many** or **several**) **hats,** have more than one job; have many responsibilities. [OE *hœtt*] —**hat′less,** *adj.* —**hat′like′,** *adj.*

hat·band (hat′band′), *n.* band around the crown of a hat, just above the brim.

hatch[1] (hach), *v.* **1** bring forth (young) from an egg or eggs. **2** keep (an egg or eggs) warm until the young come out. **3** come out from the egg: *three chickens hatched today.* **4** arrange; plan, esp. secretly; plot. —*n.* **1** act of hatching. **2** the brood hatched. [ME *hacche(n)*] —**hatch′er,** *n.*

hatch[2] (hach), *n.* **1** an opening in a ship's deck through which the cargo is put in. **2** an opening in the floor or roof of a building, etc. **3** a trap door covering such an opening. [OE *hœcc*]

hatch·er·y (hach′ər i; hach′ri), *n., pl.* **-er·ies.** place for hatching eggs of fish, hens, etc.

hatch·et (hach′it), *n.* a small ax with a short handle, for use with one hand.

bury the hatchet, make peace. [< OF *hachette,* dim. of *hache* ax. See HASH.] —**hatch′et·like′,** *adj.*

hatch·et-faced (hach′it fāsd′), *adj.* having a narrow face with sharp features.

hatchet job, *Informal.* ruthless criticism.

hatch·ing (hach′ing), *n.* fine, parallel lines drawn, cut, or engraved close together.

hatch·way (hach′wā′), *n.* **1** an opening in the deck of a ship to the lower part. **2** a similar opening in a floor, roof, etc.

hate (hāt), *v.,* **hat·ed, hat·ing,** *n.* —*v.* **1** dislike very strongly: *do good to them that hate you.* **2** dislike: *I hate to study.* —*n.* **1** a strong dislike. **2** object of hatred. [OE *hatian*] —**hate′a·ble,** *adj.* —**hat′er,** *n.*

hate·ful (hāt′fəl), *adj.* **1** causing hate; to be hated. **2** feeling hate; showing hate. —**hate′ful·ly,** *adv.* —**hate′ful·ness,** *n.*

hath (hath), *v. Archaic.* 3rd pers. sing. pres. indic. of **have.**

ha·tred (hā′trid), *n.* very strong dislike; hate.

hat·ter (hat′ər), *n.* person who makes or sells hats.

haugh·ty (hô′ti), *adj.,* **-ti·er, -ti·est. 1** too proud of oneself and too scornful of others: *a haughty man.* **2** showing pride and scorn: *a haughty smile.* [< *haut* or *haught* < F *haut* < L *altus* high; form infl. by OG *hauh* high] —**haugh′ti·ly,** *adv.* —**haugh′ti·ness,** *n.*

haul (hôl), *v.* pull or drag with force: *haul logs to a mill with horses.* —*n.* **1** act of hauling; hard pull. **2** load hauled. **3** distance that a load is hauled. **4** amount won, taken, etc., at one time; catch: *a good haul of fish.*
haul off, move one's arm back before delivering a blow.
haul up, a change the course of (a ship). **b** bring up for a reprimand. [< F *haler* < Gmc. Doublet of HALE[2].] —**haul′er,** *n.*

haul·age (hôl′ij), *n.* **1** act of hauling. **2** charge made for hauling.

haunch (hônch; hänch), *n.* **1** part of the body around the hip; the hip. **2** a hind quarter of an animal. **3** leg and loin of a deer, sheep, etc., used for food. [< OF *hanche* < Gmc.]

haunt (hônt; hänt), *v.* **1** go often to; visit frequently: *ghosts were supposed to haunt the old house.* **2** be often with; come often to: *memories of his youth haunted the old man.* —*n.* Often, **haunts.** place frequently gone to or often visited: *a swimming pool is a favorite haunt of boys in summer.* [< OF *hanter* < OE *hāmettan* shelter (cf. HOME)] —**haunt′er,** *n.* —**haunt′ing·ly,** *adv.*

haunt·ed (hôn′tid; hän′-), *adj.* visited or frequented by ghosts.

Ha·van·a (hə van′ə), *n.* capital of Cuba, on the NW coast.

have (hav; *unstressed* həv, əv), *v., pres. indic. sing.* **have, have, has,** *pl.* **have;** *pt. and pp.* **had;** *ppr.* **hav·ing. 1** hold; possess; own: *I have a house in the country.* **2** cause to: *have him shut the door.* **3** be obliged: *men have to eat.* **4** take; get:

have a seat. **5** engage in; experience: *have fun, have a talk with him.* **6** allow; permit: *he won't have any noise while he is reading.* **7** keep; retain; know: *he has the directions in mind, have an idea.* **8** hold an advantage over: *you have him there.* **9** become the father or mother of. **10** *Have* is used with past participles to express completed action (the perfect tense): *they have come.*
have at, a hit; attack. **b** attack with words.
have done (with), stop; finish.
have had it, *Informal.* **a** become disgusted. **b** be finished or unable to advance.
have it in for, have a grudge against.
have it out, fight or argue until a question is settled.
have on, wear.
have to do with, a be connected to. **b** pertain to. [OE *habban*]

ha·ven (hā′vən), *n.* **1** harbor; port. **2** place of shelter and safety. —*v.* shelter in a haven. [OE *hœfen*] —**ha′ven·less,** *adj.*

have-not (hav′not′), *n.* person or country that has little or no property or wealth.

have·n't (hav′ənt), have not.

hav·er·sack (hav′ər sak), *n.* bag used by soldiers and hikers to carry food. [< F < LG *habersack* oat sack]

hav·oc (hav′ək), *n., v.,* **-ocked, -ock·ing.** —*n.* very great destruction or injury. —*v.* devastate.
play havoc with, injure severely; ruin; destroy. [< AF var. of OF *havot* plundering, devastation] —**hav′ock·er,** *n.*

haw[1] (hô), *n.* **1** the red berry of the hawthorn. **2** the hawthorn. [OE *haga*]

haw[2] (hô), *interj., n.* a stammering sound between words. —*v.* make this sound; stammer.

haw[3] (hô), *interj.* word of command to horses, oxen, etc., directing them to turn to the left. —*v.* turn to the left.

Ha·wai·i (hə wī′ē; -wä′yə), *n.* **1** a group of islands in the N Pacific, the 50th state of the United States. **2** the largest of the Hawaiian Islands. —**Ha·wai′ian,** *adj., n.*

hawk[1] (hôk), *n.* **1** bird of prey with a strong hooked beak, large curved claws, short rounded wings, and a long tail. **2** bird of prey like a hawk; buzzard or kite. **3** person who is eager for war. —*v.* hunt with trained hawks. [OE *hafoc*] —**hawk′er,** *n.* —**hawk′ing,** *n.* —**hawk′ish, hawk′like′,** *adj.*

hawk[2] (hôk), *v.* **1** carry (goods) about for sale as a street peddler does. **2** spread (a report) around. [< *hawker* peddler, prob. < MLG HUCKSTER.] —**hawk′er,** *n.*

hawk[3] (hôk), *v.* clear the throat noisily. —*n.* a noisy effort to clear the throat. [prob. imit.]

hawk-eyed (hôk′īd′), *adj.* having sharp eyes like a hawk.

hawk moth, a large moth with a long body and narrow wings.

hawks·bill turtle (hôks′bil′), **hawk's-bill,** or **hawksbill,** *n.* a sea turtle whose mouth is shaped like a hawk's beak and whose horny plates furnish tortoise shell.

hawse (hôz; hôs), *n.* **1** part of a ship's bow having holes for hawsers or cables to pass through. **2** one of these holes. **3** space between the bow of a ship at anchor and her anchors. [< Scand. *hāls*]

hawse·hole (hôz´hōl´; hôs´–), *n.* hole in a ship's bow for a hawser to pass through.

haw·ser (hô´zər; –sər), *n.* a large rope or small cable, esp. one used for mooring or towing ships. [appar. < AF *hauceour* < OF *haucier* hoist, ult. < L *altus* high]

haw·thorn (hô´thôrn), *n.* a thorny shrub or tree with clusters of white, red, or pink blossoms and small, red berries called haws.

hay (hā), *n.* grass, alfalfa, clover, etc., cut and dried for use as food for cattle, horses, etc. —*v.* cut and dry grass, alfalfa, clover, etc., for hay.
hit the hay, *Informal.* go to bed.
make hay, a cut and dry grass for animal feed. **b** take advantage of an opportunity without delay.
make hay while the sun shines, take advantage of an opportunity before it vanishes. [OE *hēg*; akin to HEW]

hay·cock (hā´kok´), *n.* a small pile of hay, shaped like a cone, in a field.

Hay·dn (hī´dən; hā´–), *n.* **Franz Joseph,** 1732–1809, Austrian composer.

Hayes (hāz), *n.* **Rutherford B.,** 1822–93, the 19th president of the United States, 1877–81.

hay fever, allergy to the pollen of ragweed and other plants that has symptoms like a cold.

hay·field (hā´fēld´), *n.* field where grass, alfalfa, clover, etc., is grown or cut for hay.

hay·loft (hā´lôft´; –loft´), *n.* place in a stable or barn where hay is stored.

hay·mow (hā´mou´), *n.* **1** =hayloft. **2** heap of hay stored in a barn.

hay·seed (hā´sēd´), *n.* **1** seed shaken out of hay. **2** *U.S. Informal.* person from the country; farmer.

hay·stack (hā´stak´), **hay·rick** (–rik´), *n.* a large pile of hay outdoors.

hay·wire (hā´wīr´), *adj. Informal.* **1** in a mess; in utter confusion. **2** crazy; insane.

haz·ard (haz´ərd), *n.* **1** risk; danger; peril: *at all hazards.* **2** chance. —*v.* **1** take a chance with; risk; venture. **2** expose to risk. [< OF *hasard* < Ar. *az-zahr* the die] —**haz´ard·a·ble,** *adj.* —**haz´ard·er,** *n.* —**haz´ard·less,** *adj.*

hazard light, flashing light to warn of a traffic hazard such as a disabled vehicle, esp. this device on an automobile.

haz·ard·ous (haz´ər dəs), *adj.* dangerous; risky; perilous. —**haz´ard·ous·ly,** *adv.* —**haz´ard·ous·ness,** *n.*

haze¹ (hāz), *n.* **1** a small amount of mist, smoke, dust, etc., in the air. **2** vagueness of the mind; slight confusion. [cf. E dial. *haze* to drizzle, be foggy]

haze² (hāz), *v.,* **hazed, haz·ing.** in schools, universities, etc., force (a fellow student, esp. a freshman) to do unnecessary or ridiculous tasks; bully. [< OF *haser* irritate, annoy] —**haz´er,** *n.* —**haz´ing,** *n.*

ha·zel (hā´zəl), *n.* **1** shrub or small tree whose light-brown nuts are good to eat. **2** a light brown. —*adj.* **1** light-brown. **2** of or pertaining to the hazel. [OE *hæsel*]

ha·zel·nut (hā´zəl nut´), *n.* nut of the hazel.

ha·zy (hā´zi), *adj.,* **-zi·er, -zi·est. 1** full of haze; misty; smoky: *hazy air.* **2** rather confused; vague; obscure: *hazy ideas.* —**ha´zi·ly,** *adv.* —**ha´zi·ness,** *n.*

H-bomb (āch´bom´), *n.* the hydrogen bomb.

HDL, high-density lipoprotein, a component of cholesterol in the blood that contains more protein than fats, and so is sometimes called good cholesterol.

he (hē; *unstressed* ē, i), *pron., nom.,* **he;** *poss.,* **his,** of him, of his; *obj.,* **him;** *pl. nom.,* **they;** *poss.,* **theirs,** their, of them, of theirs; *obj.,* **them;** *n., pl.* **he's.** —*pron.* **1** boy, man, or male animal spoken about or mentioned before. **2** anyone: *he who hesitates is lost.* —*n.* boy; man; male animal. [OE *hē*]

He, helium.

head (hed), *n., adj., v.* —*n.* **1** the top part of the human body where the eyes, ears, and mouth are. **2** the corresponding part of an animal's body. **3** the top or foremost part of anything: *the head of a pin, the head of column of troops.* **4** chief person; leader: *the crowned heads of England.* **5** anything rounded like a head: *head of lettuce, head of a boil.* **6** the striking part of a tool or implement. **7** piece of skin stretched tightly over the end of a drum, tambourine, etc. **8** the higher or more important part of anything: *head of a lake, head of a coin.* **9** mind; understanding; intelligence; intellect: *have a good head for mathematics.* **10** topic; point: *four main heads.* **11** a decisive point; crisis: *bring matters to a head.* **12** force or pressure gained little by little: *a head of steam, the movement has gathered head.* **13** source of a river or stream. **14** foam; froth. —*adj.* **1** at the head, top, or front: *the head division of a parade.* **2** coming from in front: *a head wind.* **3** chief; leading; directing. —*v.* **1** be or go at the head, top, or front of: *head a parade.* **2** move or face (toward): *head a boat toward shore.* **3** be the head or chief of: *head a business.* **4** put a head on: *head a report.*
come to a head, a (of an infection) fill with pus. **b** *Fig.* come to a point of crisis or need for a decision.
give one his or **her head,** allow someone to do what he or she wants to do.
go to one's head, a affect one's mind. **b** make one dizzy. **c** make one conceited.
head off, a get in front of and turn back or aside. **b** prevent.

keep one's head, remain calm.
lose one's head, get excited; lose one's self-control.
out of one's head, *Informal.* crazy; insane.
over one's head, a beyond one's understanding. **b** higher authority.
turn one's head, make one conceited. [OE *hēafod*]

head·ache (hed´āk´), *n.* **1** pain in the head. **2** thing, situation, etc., that is the cause of great bother, vexation, etc.

head·dress (hed´dres´), *n.* a covering or decoration for the head.

–headed, *suffix.* **1** having a certain kind of head, as in *long-headed.* **2** having a specified number of heads, as in *two-headed.*

head·er (hed´ər), *n.* **1** person, tool, or machine that puts on or takes off heads of grain, pins, nails, etc. **2** a plunge or dive headfirst.

head·first (hed´fèrst´), *adv.* **1** with the head first. **2** hastily; rashly.

head·fore·most (hed´fôr´mōst; –fōr´–), *adv.* headfirst.

head·gear (hed´gir´), *n.* a covering for the head; hat, cap, etc.

head·hunt·ing (hed´hun´ting), *n.* practice among some tribes of taking the heads of enemies as signs of victory, manhood, etc.

head·hunt·er (hed´hun´tər), *n.* **1** person who practices head-hunting. **2** *Informal.* person who finds executives for businesses.

head·ing (hed´ing), *n.* **1** part forming the head, top, or front. **2** something written or printed at the top of a page. **3** title of a page, chapter, etc; topic. **4** direction in which a ship or aircraft is moving.

head·land (hed´lənd), *n.* point of land jutting out into water; cape.

head·less (hed´lis), *adj.* **1** having no head. **2** without a leader.

head·light (hed´līt´), *n.* **1** a bright light at the front of an automobile, locomotive, etc. **2** light at a masthead.

head·line (hed´līn´), *n., v.,* **-lined, -lin·ing.** —*n.* words printed at the top of an article in a newspaper, indicating what it is about. —*v.* **1** furnish with a headline. **2** give prominence to; call attention to. **3** be the main attraction.

head·long (hed´lông; –long), *adv., adj.* **1** =headfirst. **2** with great haste and force. **3** in too great a rush; rash; rashly.

head·man (hed´man´; –mən), *n., pl.* **-men.** chief; leader.

head·mas·ter (hed´mas´tər; –mäs´–), *n.* person in charge of a school, esp. of a private school; principal. —**head´mas´ter·ship,** *n.*

head·mis·tress (hed´mis´tris), *n.* a woman headmaster.

head·most (hed´mōst), *adj.* first; foremost.

head·on (hed´on´; -ôn´), *adj.* with the head or front first.

head·phone (hed´fōn´), *n.* receiver held on the head, against the ears.

head·piece (hed′pēs′), *n.* 1 piece of armor for the head; helmet. 2 hat, cap, or other covering for the head.

head·quar·ters (hed′kwôr′tərz), *n. pl. or sing.* 1 place from which the chief or commanding officer of an army, police force, etc., sends out orders. 2 center from which any organization is controlled and directed; main office.

head·rest (hed′rest′), *n.* support for the head, as on a dentist chair or on the back of an automobile seat.

head·room (hed′rüm′; –rum′), *n.* empty space above, as in an aircraft cabin or a doorway.

head·ship (hed′ship), *n.* position of head; chief authority.

head·stall (hed′stôl′), *n.* part of a bridle or halter that fits around a horse's head.

head·stone (hed′stōn′), *n.* stone set at the head of a grave.

head·stream (hed′strēm′), *n.* stream that is the source of a larger stream.

head·strong (hed′strông′; –strong′), *adj.* 1 rashly or foolishly determined to have one's own way; hard to control or manage; obstinate. 2 showing rash or foolish determination to have one's own way. —**head′strong′ness,** *n.*

heads-up (hedz′up′), *n.* advance warning about something. —*interj.* exclamation to warn something, esp. a fly ball, is headed toward a person.

head·wait·er (hed′wāt′ər), *n.* person in charge of the waiters in a restaurant, hotel, etc.

head·wa·ters (hed′wô′tərz; –wot′ərz), *n.pl.* sources or upper parts of a river.

head·way (hed′wā′), *n.* 1 motion forward: *the ship made headway against the tide.* 2 progress with work, etc. 3 a clear space overhead in a doorway or under an arch, bridge, etc.; clearance.

head wind, wind blowing straight against the front of a ship, etc.

head·y (hed′i), *adj.,* **head·i·er, head·i·est.** 1 hasty; rash. 2 apt to affect the head and make one dizzy; intoxicating. —**head′i·ly,** *adv.* —**head′i·ness,** *n.*

heal (hēl), *v.* 1 make whole, sound, or well; bring back to health; cure (a disease or wound). 2 become whole or sound; get well. [OE *hǣlan < hāl* whole] —**heal′er,** *n.* —**heal′ing,** *n.* —**heal′ing·ly,** *adv.*

health (helth), *n.* 1 a being well; freedom from sickness. 2 condition of body or mind: *in poor health.* 3 a drink in honor of a person, with a wish for health and happiness: *drink a health to the bride.* [OE *hǣlth < hāl* whole]

health·ful (helth′fəl), *adj.* giving health; good for the health. —**health′ful·ly,** *adv.* —**health′ful·ness,** *n.*

health·y (hel′thi), *adj.,* **health·i·er, health·i·est.** 1 having good health. 2 showing good health: *a healthy appearance.* 3 =healthful. —**health′i·ly,** *adv.* —**health′i·ness,** *n.*

heap (hēp), *n.* 1 pile of many things thrown or lying together: *a heap of sand.*

2 a large amount. —*v.* 1 form into a heap; gather in heaps. 2 give generously or in large amounts. 3 fill full or more than full: *heap a plate with food.* [OE *hēap*] —**heap′er,** *n.*

hear (hir), *v.,* **heard** (hèrd), **hear·ing,** *interj.* —*v.* 1 perceive by the ear: *hear sounds.* 2 be able to perceive by the ear: *he cannot hear well.* 3 listen to: *hear a person's explanation.* 4 be told; receive news or information: *hear from a friend.* —*interj.* **hear! hear!** shouts of approval; cheering.

hear from, receive news or information from.

hear one out, listen to someone to the end.

not hear of it, not agree to or allow something to happen. [OE *hēran*] —**hear′er,** *n.*

hear·ing (hir′ing), *n.* 1 sense by which sound is perceived: *the old man's hearing is poor.* 2 act or process of perceiving sound: *be within hearing.* 3 chance to be heard: *the judge gave both sides a hearing in court.*

heark·en (här′kən), *v.* 1 listen; listen attentively. 2 *Poetic.* listen to; give heed to; hear. Also, **harken.** [OE *hercnian, heorcnian*] —**heark′en·er,** *n.*

hear·say (hir′sā′), *n.* common talk; gossip.

hearse (hèrs), *n.* automobile, carriage, etc., for carrying a dead person to the grave. [< OF < L *hirpex* harrow; orig., a frame like a harrow]

heart (härt), *n.* 1 a hollow, muscular organ that pumps the blood throughout the body by contracting and dilating. 2 feelings; emotions: *a kind heart, give one's heart, have no heart.* 3 spirit; courage; enthusiasm: *take heart.* 4 the innermost or most important part: *heart of the forest, the very heart of the matter.* 5 figure shaped somewhat like this ♥. 6 a playing card with one or more red, heart-shaped figures.

after one's own heart, just as one likes it.

at heart, basically; actually.

by heart, a by memory. **b** from memory.

get to the heart of, find out the truth of.

hearts (*sing. in use*), game in which the players try to get rid of cards in this suit.

lose one's heart to, fall in love with.

take heart, be encouraged.

with all one's heart, sincerely. [OE *heorte*]

heart·ache (härt′āk′), *n.* sorrow; grief.

heart attack, sudden malfunction of the heart.

heart·beat (härt′bēt′), *n.* pulsation of the heart, including one complete contraction and dilation.

heart·break (härt′brāk′), *n.* a crushing sorrow or grief. —**heart′break′er,** *n.* —**heart′break′ing,** *adj.* —**heart′break′ing·ly,** *adv.*

heart·bro·ken (härt′brō′kən), *adj.* crushed with sorrow or grief. —**heart′bro′ken·ly,** *adv.* —**heart′bro′ken·ness,** *n.*

heart·burn (härt′bèrn′), *n.* a burning feeling in the stomach, often rising to the chest and throat.

heart·ed (här′tid), *adj.* having a heart (of the kind mentioned): *good-hearted.*

heart·en (här′tən), *v.* encourage; cheer up.

heart failure, inability of the heart to function properly, resulting in inadequate blood flow from the heart.

heart·felt (härt′felt′), *adj.* sincere; genuine.

hearth (härth), *n.* 1 floor of a fireplace. 2 home; fireside. [OE *heorth*]

hearth·stone (härth′stōn′), *n.* 1 stone forming a hearth. 2 home; fireside.

heart·i·ly (här′tə li), *adv.* sincerely; with enthusiasm; thoroughly.

heart·i·ness (här′ti nis), *n.* 1 vigor. 2 sincerity.

heart·land (härt′land′), *n.* 1 area or region that is the center of or important to a country, industry, etc. 2 an area thought to represent the personality or character of a country.

heart·less (härt′lis), *adj.* 1 without kindness or sympathy. 2 without courage, spirit, or enthusiasm. —**heart′less·ly,** *adv.* —**heart′less·ness,** *n.*

heart-rend·ing (härt′ren′ding), *adj.* causing mental anguish; very distressing. —**heart′rend′ing·ly,** *adv.*

heart·sick (härt′sik′), *adj.* sick at heart; very much depressed; very unhappy. —**heart′sick′ness,** *n.*

heart-strik·en (härt′strik′ən), *adj.* struck to the heart with grief; shocked with fear; dismayed.

heart·strings (härt′stringz′), *n.pl.* deepest feelings; strongest affections.

heart·throb (härt′throb′), *n.* person who is the object of passionate affection.

heart-to-heart (härt′tə härt′), *adj.* without reserve; frank; sincere.

heart·warm·ing (härt′wôr′ming), *adj.* arousing warm, friendly feeling; endearing.

heart·wood (härt′wüd′), *n.* the hard, central wood of a tree.

heart·y (här′ti), *adj.* **heart·i·er, heart·i·est,** *n., pl.* **heart·ies.** —*adj.* 1 warm and friendly; genuine; sincere: *a hearty welcome.* 2 strong and well; vigorous: *a hearty old man, a hearty laugh.* 3 with plenty to eat; abundant: *a hearty meal, a hearty eater.* —*n.* 1 a fellow sailor; sailor. [< *heart*] —**heart′i·ness,** *n.*

heat (hēt), *n.* 1 degree of hotness; temperature. 2 sensation of warmth. 3 form of energy that consists of the motion of the molecules of a substance. The rate of motion determines the temperature. 4 warmth or intensity of feeling. 5 *Informal.* pressure; coercion. 6 one trial in a race. 7 sexual excitement in female animals. —*v.* 1 make hot or warm; become hot or warm. 2 *Fig.* fill with strong feeling; excite; become excited.

heat up, a make or become hot. **b** *Fig.* increase the level of intensity, excitement, etc.

turn the heat on, *Informal.* put pressure on, esp. increase effort to achieve a result. [OE *hātu;* akin to HOT] —**heat′ed,** *adj.* —**heat′less,** *adj.*

heat·ed·ly (hēt′id li), *adv.* in a vigorous, angry, or excited manner.

heat·er (hēt′ər), *n.* stove, furnace, or other apparatus that gives heat or warmth.

heat exchanger, device to transfer heat from one medium to another to be utilized as a source of power, as in a gas turbine, etc.

heath (hēth), *n.* **1** open, waste land with heather or low bushes growing on it, but few or no trees. **2** a low bush growing on such land. Heather is one kind of heath. **one's native heath,** place where one was born or brought up. [OE *hǣth*] —**heath′like′,** *adj.* —**heath′y,** *adj.*

hea·then (hē′then), *n.,* pl. **-thens, -then,** *adj.* —*n.* **1** person who is not a Christian, Jew, or Muslim. **2** an irreligious person. —*adj.* **1** of or having to do with the heathen. **2** irreligious. [OE *hǣthen* < *hǣth* heath] —**hea′then·ish,** *adj.* —**hea′then·ish·ly,** *adv.* —**hea′then·ish·ness,** *n.* —**hea′then·ism,** *n.* —**hea′then·ness,** *n.*

heath·er (heth′ər), *n.* a low, evergreen shrub with stalks of small, rosy-pink, bell-shaped flowers, covering many heaths of Scotland and N England. [? < *heath*] —**heath′er·y,** *adj.*

heat lightning, flashes of lightning without any thunder, seen esp. on hot summer evenings.

heat shield, coating of a material that is extremely resistant to heat to protect the nose of a missile or spacecraft from the intense heat of reentry in the atmosphere.

heat·stroke (hēt′strōk′), *n.* collapse or sudden illness caused by too much heat.

heat wave, a long period of very hot weather.

heave (hēv), *v.,* **heaved** or (*esp. Naut.*) **hove, heav·ing,** *n.* —*v.* **1** lift with force or effort: *heave a heavy box into a wagon, heave the anchor overboard.* **2** pull with force or effort; haul: *they heaved on the rope.* **3** give a deep, heavy breath. **4** rise and fall alternately: *waves heave in a storm.* **5** try to vomit; vomit. —*n.* act or fact of heaving.

heaves (*sing. in use*), disease of horses characterized by difficult breathing, coughing, and heaving of the flanks.

heave to, stop a ship; stop. [OE *hebban*] —**heav′er,** *n.*

heav·en (hev′ən), *n.* **1** in Christian use, the place of God and the angels. **2** **Heaven,** God: *the will of Heaven.* **3** place or condition of greatest happiness. **4** Usually, **heavens.** the upper air; sky. [OE *heofon*]

heav·en·ly (hev′ən li), *adj.* **1** divine; holy: *our heavenly Father.* **2** like heaven: *a heavenly spot.* **3** of or in the heavens:

the moon and other heavenly bodies. —**heav′en·li·ness,** *n.*

heav·en·ward (hev′ən wərd), *adv.* Also, **heav′en·wards.** toward heaven. —*adj.* directed toward heaven.

Heav·i·side layer (hev′i sīd), the ionosphere's second layer, which reflects radio waves of frequencies produced in short-wave broadcasting.

heav·y (hev′i), *adj.,* **heav·i·er, heav·i·est,** *n.,* pl. **heav·ies,** *adv.* —*adj.* **1** hard to lift or carry; of great weight. **2** of great amount, force, or intensity; greater than usual: *heavy rain.* **3** hard to bear or endure: *heavy taxes, heavy food, heavy reading.* **4** weighted down; laden: *eyes heavy with sleep.* **5** cloudy: *a heavy sky.* **6** thick; coarse: *heavy features.* **7** clumsy; slow: *a heavy walk.* **8** loud and deep: *the heavy roar of cannon.* **9** of large size: *heavy artillery.* **10** not risen enough: *heavy bread.* **11** among isotopes, indicating one possessing a greater atomic weight. —*n.* **1** a heavy person or thing. **2** villain in a play. —*adv.* **1** in a heavy manner; heavily.

hang heavy, pass slowly, boringly. [OE *hefig* < *hebban* heave] —**heav′i·ly,** *adv.* —**heav′i·ness,** *n.*

heavy cream, cream that has a high butterfat content and can be whipped.

heav·y-du·ty (hev′i dü′ti; -dyü′-), *adj.* built to withstand hard use, exposure to the weather, etc.

heav·y-hand·ed (hev′i han′did), *adj.* clumsy or awkward, of the hand or touch.

heav·y-heart·ed (hev′i här′tid), *adj.* sad; gloomy. —**heav′y-heart′ed·ness,** *n.*

heavy hydrogen, deuterium, D.

heavy metal, rock music that has a heavy beat and harsh, amplified instrumental effects. —**heav′y-met′al,** *adj.*

heav·y-set or **heav·y·set** (hev′i set′), *adj.* having a broad, stocky build.

heavy water, water formed of oxygen and heavy hydrogen, D_2O, similar to ordinary water, but 1.1 times as heavy.

heav·y·weight (hev′i wāt′), *n.* **1** person or thing of much more than average weight. **2** boxer or wrestler who weighs 175 pounds or more. **3** person who has much intelligence or importance.

Heb., 1 Hebrew. **2** Hebrews.

He·bra·ic (hi brā′ik), *adj.* of or having to do with the Hebrews or their language or culture; Hebrew. —**He·bra′i·cal·ly,** *adv.*

He·brew (hē′brü), *n.* **1** Jew; Israelite. **2** the ancient language of the Jews, in which the Old Testament was recorded. **3** the present-day language of Israel. —*adj.* Jewish.

He·brews (hē′brüz), *n.* book of the New Testament.

Heb·ri·des (heb′rə dēz), *n. pl.* group of Scotch islands off NW Scotland. —**Heb′ri·de′an,** *adj.*

Hec·a·te (hek′ə tē), *n. Gk. Myth.* the goddess of the moon, earth, and infernal regions, later associated with magic and witchcraft. Also, **Hekate.**

heck·le (hek′əl), *v.,* **-led, -ling.** harass and annoy by asking many bothersome questions, etc. [< *heckle,* n., ME *hekele;* akin to HACKLE[1]] —**heck′ler,** *n.* —**heck′ling,** *n.*

hec·tare (hek′tār), *n.* measure of area in the metric system, equal to 100 ares, 10,000 square meters, or 2.471 acres. [< F < Gk. *hekaton* hundred + F *are* ARE[2]]

hec·tic (hek′tik), *adj.* **1** very excited or exciting. **2** feverish. [< L < Gk. *hektikos* habitual, consumptive] —**hec′ti·cal·ly,** *adv.*

hecto-, *prefix.* hundred, as in *hectogram, hectoliter.* [< Gk. *hekaton*]

hec·to·gram (hek′tə gram′), *n.* unit of weight in the metric system, equal to 100 grams (3.527 ounces).

hec·to·li·ter (hek′tə lē′tər), *n.* unit of capacity in the metric system, equal to 100 liters (2.8378 bushels or 26.4 gallons).

Hec·tor (hek′tər), *n. Gk. Legend.* in the *Iliad,* a son of Priam, the bravest of the Trojans, who was killed by Achilles.

hec·tor (hek′tər), *v.* **1** bluster; bully. **2** tease.

Hec·u·ba (hek′yu bə), *n. Gk. Legend.* in the *Iliad,* the wife of Priam and mother of Hector.

he'd (hēd; *unstressed* ēd, id, hid), **1** he had. **2** he would.

hedge (hej), *n., v.,* **hedged, hedg·ing,** —*n.* **1** Also, **hedge·row** (hej′rō′). a thick row of bushes or small trees, planted as a fence or boundary. **2** any barrier or boundary. **3** act of hedging. —*v.* **1** put a hedge around. **2** enclose or separate with a hedge. **3** avoid giving a direct answer or taking a definite stand. **4** protect (a bet, etc.) by taking some offsetting risk. [OE *hecg*] —**hedg′er,** *n.*

hedge·hog (hej′hog′; -hôg′), *n.* **1** the porcupine. **2** any of a group of small European mammals that have spines on the back.

he·don·ism (hē′dən iz əm), *n.* doctrine that pleasure or happiness is the highest good. [< Gk. *hedone* pleasure] —**he′don·ist,** *n., adj.* —**he′do·nis′tic,** *adj.* —**he′do·nis′ti·cal·ly,** *adv.*

heed (hēd), *v.* give careful attention to; take notice of. —*n.* careful attention. [OE *hēdan*] —**heed′er,** *n.* —**heed′ing·ly,** *adv.*

heed·ful (hēd′fəl), *adj.* careful; attentive. —**heed′ful·ly,** *adv.* —**heed′ful·ness,** *n.*

heed·less (hēd′lis), *adj.* careless; thoughtless. —**heed′less·ly,** *adv.* —**heed′less·ness,** *n.*

heel[1] (hēl), *n.* **1** the back part of a person's foot, below the ankle. **2** part of a stocking or shoe that covers the heel. **3** part of a shoe or boot that is under the heel. **4** part of the hind leg of an animal that corresponds to a person's heel. **5** anything shaped, used, or placed at an end like a heel, such as an end crust of bread, etc. —*v.* **1** follow closely. **2** put a heel or heels on.

down at the heel or **heels,** shabby.

drag one's heels, act slowly or reluctantly; delay.

take to one's heels, run away.

under the heel or **heels of,** controlled by; dominated by. [OE *hēla*] **—heel′less,** *adj.*

heel[2] (hēl), *v.* lean over to one side; tilt: *the ship heeled as it turned.* —*n.* act of heeling. [alter. of earlier *heeld* < OE *h(i)eldan* < *heald* inclined]

heel[3] (hēl), *n. Informal.* a hateful or odious person [special use of *heel*[1]]

heeled (hēld), *adj.* provided with money.

heel·er (hēl′ər), *n.* follower or hanger-on of a political boss.

heft (heft), *n.* **1** weight; heaviness. **2** the greater part; bulk. —*v.* **1** judge the weight or heaviness of by lifting. **2** lift; heave. [< *heave*]

heft·y (hef′ti), *adj.,* **heft·i·er, heft·i·est. 1** weighty; heavy. **2** big and strong.

he·gem·o·ny (hi jem′ə ni; hej′ə mō′ni), *n., pl.* **-nies.** political domination, esp. the leadership or domination of one state in a group; leadership. [< Gk. < *hegemon* leader] **—heg′e·mon′ic,** *adj.*

He·gi·ra (hi jī′rə; hej′ə-), *n.* **1** flight of Muhammad from Mecca to Medina in A.D. 622. **2** **hegira,** departure; flight. Also, **Hejira.**

heif·er (hef′ər), *n.* a young cow that has not had a calf. [OE *hēahfore*]

heigh (hā; hī), *interj.* =hey.

height (hīt), *n.* **1** measurement from top to bottom; how high a thing is; elevation above ground, sea level, etc. **2** a fairly great distance up. **3** a high point or place; hill. **4** the highest part; top. **5** the highest point; greatest degree: *the height of folly.* [OE *hīehthu* < *hēah* high]

height·en (hīt′ən), *v.* **1** make or become higher. **2** make or become stronger or greater; increase. **—height′en·er,** *n.*

Heim·lich maneuver (hīm′lik), technique to stop someone from choking on food caught in the windpipe. [< Henry J. *Heimlich,* American physician who devised it]

hei·nous (hā′nəs), *adj.* very wicked; extremely offensive; hateful. [< OF *haïnos,* ult. < OF *haïr* hate < Gmc.] **—hei′nous·ly,** *adv.* **—hei′nous·ness,** *n.*

heir (ãr), *n.* **1** person who receives, or has the right to receive, someone's property or title after the death of its owner. **2** person who inherits anything. —*v.* inherit. [< OF < L *heres* heir] **—heir′less,** *adj.*

heir apparent, *pl.* **heirs apparent.** person who will be heir if he or she lives longer than the one holding the property or title.

heir·ess (ãr′is), *n.* **1** a female heir. **2** woman or girl inheriting great wealth.

heir·loom (ãr′lüm′), *n.* possession handed down from generation to generation. [< *heir* + *loom,* orig., implement]

heir presumptive, *pl.* **heirs presumptive.** person who will be heir unless a nearer relative is born.

held (held), *v.* pt. and pp. of **hold**[1].

Hel·e·na (hel′ə nə), *n.* capital of Montana, in the W part.

Helen of Troy (hel′ən), *Gk. Legend.* the beautiful wife of King Menelaus of Sparta. Her abduction by Paris led to the Trojan War.

hel·i·cal (hel′ə kəl), *adj.* having to do with, or having the form of, a helix; spiral. **—hel′i·cal·ly,** *adv.*

hel·i·ces (hel′ə sēz), *n.* pl. of **helix.**

hel·i·cop·ter (hel′ə kop′tər; hē′lə-), *n.* an aircraft lifted from the ground and kept in the air by horizontal propellers; choppers. [< F, < Gk. *helix* spiral + *pteron* wing]

he·li·o·cen·tric (hē′li ō sen′trik), *adj.* **1** viewed or measured from the sun's center. **2** having or representing the sun as a center. [< Gk. *helios* sun + *kentron* center]

he·li·o·trope (hē′li ə trōp; hēl′yə-), *n.* **1** plant with clusters of small, fragrant purple or white flowers. **2** a pinkish purple. **3** =bloodstone. —*adj.* pinkish-purple. [< L < Gk., < *helios* sun + *-tropos* turning]

he·li·ot·ro·pism (hē′li ot′rə piz əm), *n.* tendency that makes a plant turn itself toward the light.

hel·i·pad (hel′ə pad′; hē′lə-), *n.* small, paved area for helicopters to take off or land on, as at a hospital.

hel·i·port (hel′ə pôrt; hē′lə-; -pōrt), *n.* airport designed esp. for helicopters.

he·li·um (hē′li əm), *n.* a rare, very light, inert gaseous element, He, that will not burn, much used in balloons and dirigibles. [< NL, < Gk. *helios* sun]

he·lix (hē′liks), *n., pl.* **hel·i·ces** (hel′ə sēz), **he·lix·es. 1** spiral, as a screw thread or a watch spring. **2** a spiral ornament. [< L < Gk., a spiral]

hell (hel), *n.* **1** in Christian use, a place where wicked persons are punished after death. **2** the powers of evil. **3** abode of the dead; Hades. **4** any place or state of wickedness, torment, or misery. [OE]

he'll (hēl), **1** he will. **2** he shall.

Hel·las (hel′əs), *n.* Greece.

hell·bend·er (hel′ben′dər), *n.* a large salamander that is common in the Ohio River and its tributaries.

hell·bent (hel′bent′), *adj. Slang.* recklessly determined.

hell·cat (hel′kat′), *n.* **1** a mean, spiteful woman. **2** witch.

hel·le·bore (hel′ə bôr; -bōr), *n.* **1** any of several plants of the buttercup family with showy flowers that bloom before spring. **2** any of several tall plants of the lily family. [< L < Gk. *helleboros*]

Hel·lene (hel′ēn), *n.* Greek.

Hel·len·ic (he len′ik; -lē′nik), *adj.* **1** Greek. **2** of Greek history, language, or culture from 776 B.C. to the death of Alexander the Great in 323 B.C.

Hel·len·ism (hel′ən iz əm), *n.* **1** ancient Greek culture or ideals. **2** adoption or imitation of Greek speech, ideals, or customs. **3** idiom or expression peculiar to the Greek language. **—Hel′len·ist,** *n.* **—Hel′len·is′tic, Hel′len·is′ti·cal,** *adj.*

Hel·len·ize (hel′ən īz), *v.,* **-ized, -iz·ing. 1** make Greek in character. **2** use or imitate the Greek language, ideals, or customs. **—Hel′len·i·za′tion,** *n.* **—Hel′len·iz′er,** *n.*

Hel·les·pont (hel′əs pont), *n.* an ancient name of the Dardanelles.

hell·fire (hel′fīr′), *n.* fire of hell; punishment in hell.

hel·lion (hel′yən), *n. Informal.* a mischievous, troublesome person.

hell·ish (hel′ish), *adj.* **1** fit to have come from hell; devilish; fiendish. **2** of hell. **—hell′ish·ly,** *adv.* **—hell′ish·ness,** *n.*

hel·lo (he lō′; hə-), *interj., n., pl.* **-los,** *v.,* **-loed, -lo·ing.** —*interj.* **1** exclamation to attract attention or express greeting. **2** exclamation of surprise. —*n.* **1** call of greeting or surprise. **2** call to attract attention. —*v.* shout or call to attract attention or in greeting or surprise.

helm (helm), *n.* **1** handle or wheel by which a ship is steered. **2** the entire steering apparatus. **3** position of control or guidance. —*v.* steer. [OE *helma*] **—helm′less,** *adj.*

hel·met (hel′mit), *n.* a covering, usually metal, which protects the head. [< OF, < Gmc.] **—hel′met·ed,** *adj.*

hel·minth (hel′minth), *n.* an intestinal worm, such as the tapeworm, etc. [< Gk. *helmins*]

helms·man (helmz′mən), *n., pl.* **-men.** person who steers a ship.

Hel·ot, hel·ot (hel′ət; hē′lət), *n.* **1** slave or serf in ancient Sparta. **2** slave; serf. [< L < Gk. *Heilos,* prob. akin to Gk. *haliskesthai* be captured] **—hel′ot·ism,** *n.* **—hel′ot·ry,** *n.*

help (help), *v.,* **helped, help·ing,** *n.* —*v.* **1** provide with what is needed or useful; aid; assist: *help out a friend, help someone with his work.* **2** make better; relieve: *this will help your cough.* **3** avoid; keep from: *he can't help yawning.* **4** give food to: *help her to some cake.* —*n.* **1** thing done or given in helping; aid; assistance. **2** person or thing that helps. **3** a hired helper or group of hired helpers. **4** means of making better; remedy. [OE *helpan*] **—help′a·ble,** *adj.* **—help′er,** *n.*

help·ful (help′fəl), *adj.* giving help; useful. **—help′ful·ly,** *adv.* **—help′ful·ness,** *n.*

help·ing (help′ing), *n.* portion of food served to a person at one time.

help·less (help′lis), *adj.* **1** not able to help oneself; weak. **2** without help, protection, etc. **—help′less·ly,** *adv.* **—help′less·ness,** *n.*

help·mate (help′māt′), *n.* companion and helper; wife or husband.

Hel·sin·ki (hel′sing ki), *n.* seaport and capital of Finland.

hel·ter-skel·ter (hel′tər skel′tər), *adv.* with headlong, disorderly haste. —*adj.* carelessly hurried; confused.

Hel·ve·tia (hel vē′shə), *n. Poetic.* Switzerland.

hem[1] (hem), *n., v.,* **hemmed, hem·ming.** —*n.* border or edge on a garment; edge made by folding over the cloth and sewing it down. —*v.* fold over and sew down the edge of (cloth).

hem in, around, or **about, a** surround on all sides. **b** keep from getting away or moving freely. [OE *hemm*] —**hem′mer,** *n.*

hem² (hem), *interj., n., v.,* **hemmed, hem·ming.** —*interj., n.* sound like clearing the throat, used to attract attention or show doubt or hesitation. —*v.* **1** make this sound. **2** hesitate in speaking. [imit.]

hem·a·tite (hem′ə tīt; hē′mə–), *n.* an important iron ore, Fe_2O_3, that is reddish-brown when powdered. [< L < Gk. *haimatites* bloodlike < *haima* blood] —**hem′a·tit′ic,** *adj.*

hem·a·tol·o·gy (hem′ə tol′ə ji; hē′mə–), *n.* branch of physiology that deals with the structure, constituents, and diseases of the blood, and the organs that produce the blood. —**hem′a·tol′o·gist,** *n.*

hemi–, *prefix.* half, as in *hemisphere.* [< Gk.]

he·mip·ter·ous (hi mip′tər əs), *adj.* belonging to a large group of insects including bedbugs, chinch bugs, lice, and aphids. [< Gk. *hemi–* half + *pteron* wing]

hem·i·sphere (hem′ə sfir), *n.* **1** half of a sphere or globe. **2** half of the earth's surface. [< F < L < Gk., < *hemi–* half + *sphaira* sphere] —**hem′i·spher′i·cal,** *adj.* —**hem′i·spher′i·cal·ly,** *adv.*

hem·i·stich (hem′ə stik), *n.* **1** half a line of verse. **2** an incomplete line of verse. [< L < Gk., < *hemi–* half + *stichos* row]

hem·line (hem′līn′), *n.* edge or hem of a garment, esp. of a skirt.

hem·lock (hem′lok), *n.* **1** a poisonous plant of the carrot family, with spotted stems, finely divided leaves, and small white flowers. **2** poison made from it. **3** an evergreen tree of the pine family with small cones and drooping branches, whose bark is used in tanning. **4** its wood. [OE *hymlice*]

he·mo·glo·bin (hē′mə glō′bən; hem′ə–), *n.* the protein matter in the red corpuscles of the blood that carries oxygen from the lungs to the tissues, and carbon dioxide from the tissues to the lungs. [for *hematoglobulin,* ult. < Gk. *haima* blood + L *globulus,* dim. of *globus* globe]

he·mo·phil·i·a (hē′mə fil′i ə; hem′ə–), *n.* an inherited condition in which the blood does not clot normally, resulting in excessive bleeding from the slightest cut. [< NL, < Gk. *haima* blood + *philia* affection, tendency] —**he′mo·phil′i·ac,** *n.*

hem·or·rhage (hem′ə rij; hem′rij), *n.* discharge of blood, as a nosebleed. [< L < Gk. *haimorrhagia,* ult. < *haima* blood + *rhegnynai* break, burst] —**hem′or·rhag′ic,** *adj.*

hemorrhagic fever, viral disease transmitted to human by rodents, insects, ticks, etc., characterized by fever, internal bleeding, and shock.

hem·or·rhoids (hem′ə roidz), *n.pl.* painful swellings formed by the dilation of blood vessels near the anus; piles. [< L < Gk., ult. < *haima* blood + –*rhoos* flowing] —**hem′or·rhoi′dal,** *adj.*

hemp (hemp), *n.* **1** a tall Asiatic plant whose tough fibers are made into heavy string, rope, coarse cloth, etc. **2** the tough fibers of this plant. **3** hashish or other drug obtained from some kinds of hemp. [OE *henep*] —**hemp′en,** *adj.*

hem·stitch (hem′stich′), *v.* hem along a line from which threads have been drawn out, gathering the cross threads into a series of little groups. —*n.* **1** the stitch used. **2** ornamental needlework made by hemstitching. —**hem′stitch′er,** *n.*

hen (hen), *n.* **1** a female domestic fowl. **2** female of other birds. [OE *henn*]

hen·bane (hen′bān′), *n.* a coarse, bad-smelling plant with sticky, hairy leaves and clusters of yellowish-brown flowers, poisonous to fowls.

hence (hens), *adv.* **1** as a result of this; therefore: *it is very late, hence go to bed.* **2** from now; from this time onward: *years hence.* **3** from this source or origin. **4** from here: *a mile hence.* —*interj.* go away! [ME *hennes* < OE *heonan* + –*s,* adv. ending]

hence·forth (hens′fôrth′; –fôrth′), **hence·for·ward** (–fôr′wərd), *adv.* from this time on.

hench·man (hench′mən), *n., pl.* –**men.** a trusted attendant or follower. [ME *henxstman* < OE *hengest* horse + MAN; orig., a groom]

hen·e·quen (hen′ə kin), *n.* **1** a yellow fiber from leaves of an agave of Yucatán, used for making binder twine, ropes, coarse fabrics, etc. **2** plant that yields this fiber. [< Sp. < native Yucatán word]

hen·house (hen′hous′), *n.* house for poultry.

hen·na (hen′ə), *n., adj., v.,* –**naed,** –**na·ing.** —*n.* **1** a dark, reddish-brown dye used on the hair. **2** tree of Asia and Africa from whose leaves this dye is made. —*adj.* reddish-brown. —*v.* dye or color with henna. [< Ar. *ḥinnā′*]

hen·ner·y (hen′ər i), *n., pl.* –**ner·ies.** place where fowls are kept.

hen·peck (hen′pek′), *v.* domineer over; browbeat. —**hen′pecked′,** *adj.*

Hen·ry (hen′ri), *n.* **1 Patrick,** 1736–99, American patriot, orator, and statesman. **2 VIII,** 1491–1547, king of England, 1509–47.

hen·ry (hen′ri), *n., pl.* –**ries,** –**rys.** unit of electrical inductance. When a current varying at the rate of one ampere per second induces an electromotive force of one volt, the circuit has an inductance of one henry. [after J. *Henry,* physicist]

he·pat·ic (hi pat′ik), *adj.* **1** of or having to do with the liver. **2** acting on the liver as a medicine. [< L < Gk., < *hepar* liver]

he·pat·i·ca (hi pat′ə kə), *n.* a low plant with delicate purple, pink, or white flowers that bloom early in the spring. [< NL, ult. < Gk. *hepar* liver; leaf thought to resemble the liver in shape]

hep·a·ti·tis (hep′ə tī′tis), *n.* **1** inflammation of the liver. **2** contagious disease of the liver caused by a virus and characterized by inflammation of the liver, fever, and jaundice. There are two types, A and B. [< Gk. *hépar, hépatos* liver]

hep·ta·gon (hep′tə gon), *n.* a plane figure having seven angles and seven sides. [< L < Gk., < *hepta* seven + *gonia* angle] —**hep·tag′o·nal,** *adj.*

her (hèr; *unstressed* hər, ər), *pron.* the objective case of **she:** *I like her.* —*adj.* the possessive form of **she;** of her; belonging to her; done by her: *her look, her book, her work.* [OE *hire*]

her., heraldic; heraldry.

He·ra (hir′ə), *n.* Gk. Myth. goddess, wife of Zeus and queen of gods and men.

her·ald (her′əld), *n.* **1** formerly, an officer who carried messages, made announcements, arranged public ceremonies, and regulated armorial bearings. **2** forerunner; harbinger: *dawn is the herald of day.* —*v.* **1** bring news of; announce. **2** go before and announce the coming of. [< Med.L *heraldus* < Rom. < Gmc.]

he·ral·dic (he ral′dik), *adj.* of or having to do with heraldry or heralds. —**he·ral′di·cal·ly,** *adv.*

her·ald·ry (her′əld ri), *n., pl.* –**ries. 1** science or art dealing with coats of arms and tracing family descent. **2** coat of arms.

herb (èrb; hèrb), *n.* **1** plant whose leaves or stems are used for medicine, seasoning, food, or perfume. Sage, mint, and lavender are herbs. **2** a flowering plant whose stems live only one season. Peonies, buttercups, corn, wheat, cabbage, lettuce, etc., are herbs. **3** =herbage. [< OF < L *herba*] —**herb′less,** *adj.* —**herb′like′,** *adj.*

her·ba·ceous (hèr bā′shəs), *adj.* **1** of an herb; like an herb; having stems that are soft and not woody. **2** like a leaf; green.

herb·age (èr′bij; hèr′–), *n.* **1** herbs. **2** grass. **3** the green leaves and soft stems of plants.

herb·al (hèr′bəl; èr′–), *adj.* of herbs. —*n.* book about herbs.

herb·al·ist (hèr′bəl ist; hèr′–), *n.* **1** person who gathers or deals in herbs. **2** formerly, a botanist.

her·bar·i·um (hèr bār′i əm), *n., pl.* –**bar·i·ums,** –**bar·i·a** (–bār′i ə), **1** collection of dried plants systematically arranged. **2** room or building where such a collection is kept.

her·bi·cide (hèr′bə sīd; hèr′–), *n.* substance used to kill weeds; weedkiller. [< *herb* + –*cide* killer] —**her′bi·ci′dal,** *adj.*

her·biv·o·rous (hèr biv′ə rəs), *adj.* feeding on grass or other plants. [< NL, < L *herba* herb + *vorare* devour]

her·cu·le·an, Her·cu·le·an (hèr kū′li ən; hèr′kyə lē′ən), *adj.* **1** of great strength, courage, or size; very powerful. **2** requiring great strength, courage, or size; hard to do.

Her·cu·les (hėr′kyə lēz), *n.* **1** *Class. Legend.* hero famous for his great strength. **2** a northern constellation.

herd (hėrd), *n.* **1** number of animals together, esp. large animals: *a herd of cows, a herd of elephants.* **2** a large number of people. **3** the common people; rabble. —*v.* **1** join together; flock together. **2** form into a flock, herd, or group. **3** tend or take care of (cattle, sheep, etc.).

ride herd on, keep within limits; control. [OE *heord*] —**herd′er,** *n.*

herds·man (hėrdz′mən), *n., pl.* **-men.** person who takes care of a herd.

here (hir), *adv.* **1** in this place; at this place: *place it here.* **2** to this place: *come here.* **3** at this time; now. **4** in this life. —*n.* **1** this place. **2** this life. —*interj.* answer showing that one is present when the roll is called.

here and there, in this place and that at intervals.

here's to (you)!, a wish of health, happiness, or success to.

neither here nor there, off the subject; unimportant. [OE *hēr*]

here·a·bout (hir′ə bout′), **here·a·bouts** (-bouts′), *adv.* about this place; around here; near here.

here·af·ter (hir af′tər; –äf′–), *adv.* **1** after this; in the future. **2** in life after death. —*n.* **1** the future. **2** life after death.

here·by (hir bī′), *adv.* by this means; in this way.

he·red·i·ta·ble (hə red′ə tə bəl), *adj.* that can be inherited. —**he·red′i·ta·bil′i·ty,** *n.* —**he·red′i·ta·bly,** *adv.*

he·red·i·tar·y (hə red′ə ter′i), *adj.* **1** coming by inheritance: *a hereditary title.* **2** holding a position by inheritance: *a hereditary ruler.* **3** transmitted or caused by heredity: *hereditary color blindness.* —**he·red′i·tar′i·ly,** *adv.* —**he·red′i·tar′i·ness,** *n.*

he·red·i·ty (hə red′ə tē), *n., pl.* **-ties. 1** the transmission of genetic physical or mental characteristics from parent to offspring. **2** qualities that have come to offspring from parents. [< L *hereditas* < *heres* heir]

Her·e·ford (hėr′fərd; her′ə fərd), *n.* one of a breed of beef cattle having a red body, white face, and white markings under the body.

here·in (hir in′), *adv.* **1** in this place. **2** in this matter; in view of this.

here·in·af·ter (hir′in af′tər; –äf′–), *adv.* afterward in this document, statement, etc.

here·of (hir ov′; –uv′), *adv.* of this; about this.

here·on (hir on′; –ôn′), *adv.* **1** on this. **2** immediately after this.

here's (hirz), here is.

her·e·sy (her′ə sē), *n., pl.* **-sies. 1** belief different from the accepted belief of a church, school, profession, etc. **2** the holding of such a belief. [< OF < L < Gk.

hairesis a taking, choosing < *haireein* take]

her·e·tic (her′ə tik), *n.* person who holds a belief that is different from the accepted belief of his or her church, school, profession, etc. —*adj.* holding such a belief.

he·ret·i·cal (hə ret′ə kəl), *adj.* **1** of or having to do with heresy or heretics. **2** containing heresy; characterized by heresy. —**he·ret′i·cal·ly,** *adv.*

here·to (hir tü′), *adv.* to this place, thing, etc.

here·to·fore (hir′tə fôr′; –fōr′), *adv.* before this time; until now.

here·un·to (hir′un tü′), *adv.* **1** unto this. **2** until this time.

here·up·on (hir′ə pon′; –pôn′), *adv.* **1** upon this. **2** immediately after this.

here·with (hir with′; –with′), *adv.* **1** with this. **2** by this means; in this way.

her·it·a·ble (her′ə tə bəl), *adj.* **1** capable of being inherited. **2** capable of inheriting. —**her′it·a·bil′i·ty,** *n.* —**her′it·a·bly,** *adv.*

her·it·age (her′ə tij), *n.* what is or may be handed on to a person from his or her ancestors; inheritance. [< OF, < *heriter* inherit < LL, ult. < L *heres* heir]

her·maph·ro·dite (hėr maf′rə dīt), *n.* **1** animal or plant having the reproductive organs of both sexes. **2** person or thing that combines two opposite qualities. —*adj.* of or like a hermaphrodite. [< L < Gk. *Hermaphroditos* Hermaphroditus, son of Hermes and Aphrodite, who became united in body with a nymph] —**her·maph′ro·dit′ic,** *adj.*

Her·mes (her′mēz), *n.* Gk. Myth. god who was the messenger of Zeus and the other gods.

her·met·ic (hėr met′ik), **her·met·i·cal** (–ə kəl), *adj.* airtight. [< Med.L *hermeticus* < *Hermes* Hermes] —**her·met′i·cal·ly,** *adv.*

her·mit (hėr′mit), *n.* person who goes away from other people and lives by himself, esp. one who does so for religious reasons; anchorite. [< OF < LL < Gk. *eremites* < *eremia* desert < *eremos* solitary] —**her·mit′ic, her·mit′i·cal,** *adj.* —**her·mit′i·cal·ly,** *adv.* —**her′mit·like′,** *adj.*

her·mit·age (hėr′mə tij), *n.* **1** home of a hermit. **2** place to live away from other people.

hermit crab, a soft-bodied crab that lives in the empty shells of snails, whelks, etc.

her·ni·a (hėr′nē ə), *n., pl.* **-ni·as, -ni·ae** (-nē ē), protrusion of a part of the intestine or some other organ through a break in its surrounding walls; rupture. [< L] —**her′ni·al,** *adj.*

he·ro (hir′ō), *n., pl.* **-roes. 1** person admired for bravery, great deeds, or noble qualities. **2** the most important person in a story, play, poem, etc. [ult. < L < Gk. *heros*]

He·rod·o·tus (hə rod′ə təs), *n.* 484?–425 B.C., Greek historian, called "the father of history."

he·ro·ic (hi rō′ik), *adj.* Also, **he·ro′i·cal. 1** like a hero in deeds, or qualities. **2** of or about heroes and their deeds: *heroic poetry.* **3** unusually daring or bold. —*n.* a heroic poem.

heroics, a high-sounding language. **b** words, feelings, or actions that seem grand or noble but are only for effect. —**he·ro′i·cal·ly,** *adv.* —**he·ro′i·cal·ness, he·ro′ic·ness,** *n.*

heroic couplet, two successive lines of poetry in iambic pentameter that rhyme.

heroic verse, iambic pentameter couplets.

her·o·in (her′ō in), *n.* a poisonous, habit-forming drug made from morphine.

her·o·ine (her′ō in), *n.* **1** woman or girl admired for her great deeds or noble qualities. **2** the most important female person in a story, play, poem, etc. [< L < Gk., fem. of *heros* hero]

her·o·ism (her′ō iz əm), *n.* **1** actions and qualities of a hero or heroine; great bravery; daring courage. **2** a very brave act or quality.

her·on (her′ən), *n.* a wading bird with a long neck, long bill, and long legs. [< OF *hairon* < Gmc.]

her·pes (hėr′pēz), *n.* viral disease of the skin or mucous membrane characterized by clusters of blisters, such as cold sores and shingles. [< L < Gk., shingles, < *herpein* creep] —**her·pet′ic,** *adj.*

her·pes·vi·rus (hėr′pēz vī′rəs), *n.* any one of a group of viruses, including the viruses that cause chicken pox and herpes.

her·pe·tol·o·gy (hėr′pə tol′ə jē), *n.* branch of zoology dealing with reptiles. [< Gk. *herpeton* reptile (< *herpein* creep) + -LOGY] —**her′pe·to·log′i·cal,** *adj.* —**her′pe·tol′o·gist,** *n.*

her·ring (her′ing), *n., pl.* **-rings** or (*esp. collectively*) **-ring.** a small food fish of the N Atlantic. [OE *hǣring*]

her·ring·bone (her′ing bōn′), *adj.* having a zigzag pattern or arrangement. —*n.* a zigzag pattern or arrangement.

hers (hėrz), *pron.* **1** of her; belonging to her. **2** the one or ones belonging to her.

her·self (hėr self′), *pron.* **1** the emphatic form of **she** or **her:** *she herself did it.* **2** the reflexive form of **her:** *she hurt herself.* **3** her real self: *in those fits she is not herself.*

hertz (hėrts), *n.* unit of frequency equivalent to one cycle per second.

hertz·i·an wave (hert′sē ən), an electromagnetic radiation, such as the wave used in communicating by radio, produced by irregular fluctuation of electricity in a conductor. [first investigated by H. R. *Hertz,* physicist]

he's (hēz; *unstressed* ēz, iz, hiz), **1** he is. **2** he has.

hes·i·tan·cy (hez′ə tən sē), **hes·i·tance** (hez′ə təns), *n., pl.* **-cies; -tanc·es.** hesitation; doubt; indecision.

hes·i·tant (hez′ə tənt), *adj.* hesitating; doubtful; undecided. **—hes′i·tant·ly,** *adv.*

hes·i·tate (hez′ə tāt), *v.,* **-tat·ed, -tat·ing.** 1 hold back because one feels doubtful; be undecided. 2 feel that perhaps one should not: *I hesitated to ask you.* 3 pause. 4 speak with stops or pauses. [< L *haesitare* < *haerere* stick fast] **—hes′i·tat′er, hes′i·ta′tor,** *n.* **—hes′i·tat′ing·ly,** *adj.* **—hes′i·tat′ing·ly,** *adv.*

hes·i·ta·tion (hez′ə tā′shən), *n.* 1 a hesitating; doubt; indecision; unwillingness; delay. 2 a speaking with short stops or pauses.

Hes·per·us (hes′pər əs), *n.* the evening star.

Hes·sian (hesh′ən), *adj.* of Hesse or its people. *—n.* 1 native or inhabitant of Hesse. 2 *U.S.* a German soldier hired by England to fight against the Americans during the American Revolution.

heter-, hetero-, *combining form.* other; different, as in *heterogeneous.* [< Gk., < *heteros*]

het·er·o·dox (het′ər ə doks), *adj.* rejecting the regularly accepted beliefs or doctrines; differing from an acknowledged standard; not orthodox. [< LL < Gk., < *heteros* other + *doxa* opinion]

het·er·o·dox·y (het′ər ə dok′si), *n., pl.* **-dox·ies.** 1 rejection of regularly accepted beliefs or doctrines; opposite of orthodoxy. 2 belief, doctrine, or opinion not in agreement with what is regularly accepted.

het·er·o·ga·mete (het′ər ō gə mēt′), *n.* either of two gametes, differing in character or behavior, which can unite with the other to form a zygote, as an egg and a sperm.

het·er·o·ge·ne·ous (het′ər ə jē′ni əs; -jēn′yəs), *adj.* 1 different in kind; unlike; not at all similar; varied. 2 made up of unlike elements or parts; miscellaneous. [< Med.L *heterogeneus,* ult. < Gk. *heteros* other + *genos* kind] **—het′er·o·ge·ne′i·ty, het′er·o·ge′ne·ous·ness,** *n.* **—het′er·o·ge′ne·ous·ly,** *adv.*

het·er·o·sex·u·al (het′ər ə sek′shu əl), *adj.* 1 of or having to do with the different sexes. 2 having to do with or showing an interest in a person of the opposite sex. *—n.* a heterosexual person.

hew (hū), *v.,* **hewed, hewed** or **hewn** (hūn), **hew·ing.** 1 cut with an ax, sword, etc. 2 cut into shape; form by cutting: *hew stone for building.* 3 cut down; fell with cutting blows. [OE *hēawan*] **—hew′er,** *n.*

hex (heks), *—v.* practice witchcraft on; bewitch. [< n.] *—n.* a magic spell. [< G *hexe* witch]

hex·a·gon (hek′sə gon), *n.* a plane figure having six angles ad six sides. [< LL < Gk., ult. < *hex* six + *gonia* angle] **—hex·ag′o·nal,** *adj.* **—hex·ag′o·nal·ly,** *adv.*

hex·a·gram (hek′sə gram), *n.* a six-pointed star formed by two equilateral triangles.

hex·a·he·dron (hek′sə hē′drən), *n., pl.* **-drons, -dra** (-drə). a solid figure having six faces. [< Gk., < *hex* six + *hedra* surface] **—hex′a·he′dral,** *adj.*

hex·am·e·ter (heks am′ə tər), *adj.* of poetry, consisting of six feet or measures. *—n.* poetry having six feet or measures in each line. [< L < Gk., < *hex* six + *metron* measure]

hex·a·pod (hek′sə pod), *n.* a true insect; arthropod having six feet. *—adj.* having six feet. [< Gk., < *hex* six + *pous* foot]

hey (hā), *interj.* sound made to attract attention, to express surprise or other feeling, or to ask a question.

hey·day (hā′dā′), *n.* period of greatest strength, vigor, spirits, prosperity, etc.

Hf, hafnium.

hf., half.

HG, High German.

Hg, mercury.

hi (hī), *interj.* hello! how are you?

HI, (*zip code*) Hawaii.

H.I., Hawaiian Islands.

hi·a·tus (hī ā′təs), *n., pl.* **-tus·es, -tus.** 1 an empty space; gap. 2 interruption of continuity: *several hiatuses in the testimony.* [< L, gap, < *hiare* gape]

hi·ba·chi (hi bä′chi), *n.* small, portable grill that burns charcoal, used for cooking or heating. [< Jap. *hibachi* < *hi* fire + *bachi* bowl, pot]

hi·ber·nal (hī bėr′nəl), *adj.* of winter; wintry.

hi·ber·nate (hī′bər nāt), *v.,* **-nat·ed, -nat·ing.** spend the winter in sleep or in an inactive condition, as bears and woodchucks do. [< L, < *hibernus* wintry] **—hi′ber·na′tion,** *n.*

Hi·ber·ni·a (hī bėr′ni ə), *n. Poetic.* Ireland. **—Hi·ber′ni·an,** *n., adj.*

hi·bis·cus (hə bis′kəs; hī-), *n.* plant, shrub, or tree with large, showy, bell-shaped flowers. [< L]

hic·cup, hic·cough (hik′up; -əp), *n.* an involuntary catching of the breath. *—v.* catch the breath in this way.

hick (hik), *—n.* an unsophisticated person. *—adj.* of or like hicks.

hick·o·ry (hik′ə ri; hik′ri), *n., pl.* **-ries.** 1 North American tree whose nuts are good to eat. 2 its tough, hard wood. [< Am.Ind.]

hid·den (hid′ən), *adj.* concealed; secret; mysterious; obscure. *—v.* pp. of **hide**[1].

hide[1] (hīd), *v.,* **hid** (hid), **hid·den** or **hid, hid·ing.** 1 put or keep out of sight; conceal. 2 cover up; shut off from sight. 3 keep secret. [OE *hȳdan*] **—hid′er,** *n.*

hide[2] (hīd), *n., v.,* **hid·ed, hid·ing.** *—n.* skin of an animal, either raw or tanned. *—v.* beat; thrash.

neither hide nor hair, nothing whatsoever. [OE *hȳd*]

hide-and-seek (hīd′ənd sēk′), *n.* children's game in which some hide and others try to find them.

hide·a·way (hīd′ə wā′), *n.* =hideout.

hide·bound (hīd′bound′), *adj.* narrow-minded and stubborn.

hid·e·ous (hid′i əs), *adj.* 1 very ugly; frightful: *a hideous monster.* 2 revolting to the moral sense: *a hideous crime.* [< OF *hide* fear, horror] **—hid′e·ous·ly,** *adv.* **—hid′e·ous·ness,** *n.*

hide·out or **hide-out** (hīd′out′), *n.* place for hiding or being alone.

hid·ing[1] (hīd′ing), *n.* 1 concealment. 2 place to hide.

hid·ing[2] (hīd′ing), *n.* a beating.

hi·er·ar·chy (hī′ər är′ki), *n., pl.* **-chies.** 1 system of persons, etc., which has higher and lower ranks. 2 body of church officials of different ranks, as archbishops, bishops, priests, etc. 3 government by priests. [< Med.L < Gk., < *hieros* sacred + *archos* ruler] **—hi′er·ar′chic, hi′er·ar′chi·cal,** *adj.* **—hi′er·ar′chi·cal·ly,** *adv.*

hi·er·at·ic (hī′ər at′ik), **hi·er·at·i·cal** (-ə kəl), *adj.* having to do with a form of Egyptian writing used by the early priests in their records. Hieratic writing is a simplified form of hieroglyphics. [< L < Gk., ult. < *hieros* sacred] **—hi′er·at′i·cal·ly,** *adv.*

hier·o·glyph·ic (hīr′ə glif′ik), *n.* 1 picture or symbol of an object standing for a word, idea, or sound, used by ancient Egyptians, etc. 2 a secret symbol. *—adj.* 1 of or written in hieroglyphics. 2 symbolical.

hieroglyphics, letter or word that is hard to read. [< LL < Gk., < *hieros* sacred + *glyphe* carving] **—hier′o·glyph′i·cal·ly,** *adv.*

hig·gle·dy-pig·gle·dy (hig′əl di pig′əl di), *adv.* in jumbled confusion. *—adj.* jumbled; confused.

high (hī), *adj.* 1 of more than usual height; tall: *a high building.* 2 far above the ground or some base: *an airplane high in the air.* 3 extending to or down from a height: *a high leap.* 4 above others in rank, quality, character, etc.: *high office.* 5 greater, stronger, or better than average: *high temperature, high costs, high crimes.* 6 chief; main: *the high altar.* 7 not low in pitch; shrill; sharp: *a high voice.* 8 slightly tainted. 9 stimulated or dazed by narcotics or alcoholic drink. *—adv.* at or to a high point, place, rank, amount, degree, price, pitch, etc.: *the eagle flies high. —n.* 1 something that is high. 2 region or area of high barometric pressure.

on high, a high above; up in the air. **b** in heaven. [OE *hēah*]

on a high, stimulated; excited.

high·ball (hī′bôl′), *n.* whiskey, brandy, etc., mixed with soda water or ginger ale and served with ice in a tall glass.

high·born (hī′bôrn′), *adj.* of noble birth.

high·boy (hī′boi′), *n.* a tall chest of drawers on legs.

high·brow (hī′brou′), *n.* person who cares a great deal about knowledge and culture. *—adj.* of or suitable for a highbrow.

high·er-up (hī′ər up′), *n. Informal.* one occupying a superior position.

high·fa·lu·tin (hī′fə lü′tən), *adj. Informal.* pompous; bombastic.

high·fi·del·i·ty (hī′fə del′ə ti; –fī–), *adj.* indicating reproduction of the full audio range with a minimum of distortion.

high·fli·er (hī′flī′ər), *n.* person who is extravagant or has pretentious ideas.

high·flown (hī′flōn′), *adj.* aspiring; extravagant.

high·fre·quen·cy (hī′frē′kwən si), *adj.* of a frequency having from 1.5 to 30 megacycles per second.

High German, the literary and official language of Germany, a development of the dialects of the highlands in C and S Germany.

high·grade (hī′grād′), *adj.* superior.

high·hand·ed (hī′han′did), *adj.* bold; arbitrary; domineering; overbearing. —**high′-hand′ed·ly,** *adv.* —**high′-hand′ed·ness,** *n.*

high·hat (hī′hat′), *adj.* 1 stylish; grand. 2 snobbish.

high jump, event in which the contestants try to jump as high as possible.

high·land (hī′lənd), *n.* country or region that is higher and hillier than the neighboring country.

High·land·er (hī′lən dər), *n.* native or inhabitant of the Highlands of Scotland.

Highland fling, a lively dance of the Highlands of Scotland.

High·lands (hī′ləndz), *n.pl.* a mountainous region in N and W Scotland.

high·level (hī′lev′əl), *adj.* 1 of high rank; important. 2 having or reaching great height. 3 highly radioactive.

high-level language, computer programming language that uses words.

high·light (hī′līt′), *n., v.,* –**light·ed,** –**light·ing.** —*n.* Also, **high light.** 1 effect or representation of bright light. 2 part of a painting, photograph, etc., in which light is represented as falling with full force. 3 the most conspicuous or interesting part, event, scene, etc. —*v.* 1 cast a bright light on. 2 make prominent.

high·ly (hī′li), *adv.* 1 in a high degree; very. 2 favorably. 3 at a high price.

high·mind·ed (hī′mīn′did), *adj.* having or showing high principles and feelings. —**high′-mind′ed·ly,** *adv.* —**high′-mind′ed·ness,** *n.*

high·ness (hī′nis), *n.* 1 a being high; height. 2 **Highness,** title of honor given to members of royal families.

high·pitched (hī′picht′), *adj.* 1 of high tone or sound; shrill. 2 having a steep slope.

high·pow·ered (hī′pou′ərd), *adj.* 1 having much power. 2 *Fig.* energetic; vigorous; aggressive.

high·pres·sure (hī′presh′ər), *adj., v.,* –**sured,** –**sur·ing.** —*adj.* 1 having or using more than the usual pressure. 2 using strong, vigorous methods. —*v.* use strong, vigorous methods in selling, etc.

high·pro·file (hī′prō′fīl), *adj.* attracting attention; well-known; conspicuous.

high·rise (hī′rīz′), *adj.* of or having to do with a tall apartment building.

high·road (hī′rōd′), *n.* 1 a main road; highway. 2 a direct and easy way.

high school, school attended after the elementary school. —**high′-school′,** *adj.*

high seas, the open ocean, outside the authority of any country.

high·sound·ing (hī′soun′ding), *adj.* having an imposing or pretentious sound.

high·spir·it·ed (hī′spir′it id), *adj.* 1 proud. 2 courageous. 3 spirited; fiery.

high spot an outstanding part or feature. **hit the high spots, a** go through with great speed. **b** mention a few points briefly.

high·strung (hī′strung′), *adj.* very sensitive; easily excited; nervous.

high·test (hī′test′), *adj.* passing high requirements or tests.

high tide, 1 the highest level of the tide. 2 time when the tide is highest.

high time, time just before it is too late.

high·toned (hī′tōnd′), *adj.* 1 high in tone or pitch. 2 dignified; fashionable.

high treason, treason against one's government.

high water, 1 highest level of water. 2 =high tide.

high-wa·ter mark (hī′wô′tər; -wot′ər), 1 the highest level reached by a body of water. 2 any highest point.

high·way (hī′wā′), *n.* 1 a public road. 2 a main road or route.

high·way·man (hī′wā′mən), *n., pl.* –**men.** man who robs travelers on the public road.

hi·jack (hī′jak′), *v.* rob or take by force, esp. goods being transported or possession of a vehicle, aircraft, etc. —**hi′jack′er,** *n.*

hike (hīk), *v.,* **hiked, hik·ing,** *n.* —*v.* 1 take a long walk; tramp; march. 2 move, draw, or raise with a jerk. —*n.* 1 a march or tramp. 2 increase. —**hik′er,** *n.*

hi·lar·i·ous (hə lār′i əs; hī–), *adj.* very merry. —**hi·lar′i·ous·ly,** *adv.* —**hi·lar′i·ous·ness,** *n.*

hi·lar·i·ty (hə lar′ə ti; hī–), *n.* great mirth. [< L, < *hilaris, hilarus* gay < Gk. *hilaros*]

hill (hil), *n.* 1 a raised part on the earth's surface, not so big as a mountain. 2 a little heap or pile: *an ant hill.*

over the hill, too old; on the way down.

the Hill, Capitol Hill in Washington, D.C.; Congress. [OE *hyll*]

hill·bil·ly (hil′bil′i), *n., pl.* –**lies.** person who lives in the backwoods or a mountain region, esp. in the South.

hill·ock (hil′ək), *n.* a little hill. —**hill′ock·y,** *adj.*

hill·side (hil′sīd′), *n.* side of a hill.

hill·top (hil′top′), *n.* top of a hill.

hill·y (hil′i), *adj.,* **hill·i·er, hill·i·est.** 1 having many hills. 2 like a hill; steep. —**hill′i·ness,** *n.*

hilt (hilt), *n.* handle of a sword, dagger, etc.

up to the hilt, completely. [OE] —**hilt′ed,** *adj.*

hi·lum (hī′ləm), *n., pl.* –**la** (–lə). mark or scar on a seed at the point of attachment to the seed vessel. [< L, trifle]

him (him; *unstressed* im), *pron.* the objective case of **he:** *take him home.*

Him·a·la·yas (him′ə lā′əz; hə mäl′yəz), *n.pl.* a mountain range extending for 1600 miles along the N border of India. —**Him′a·la′yan,** *adj.*

him·self (him self′; *unstressed* im self′), *pron.* 1 the emphatic form of **he** or **him:** *he himself did it.* 2 the reflexive form of **him:** *he hurt himself.* 3 his real self: *he feels like himself again.*

hind[1] (hīnd), *adj.,* **hind·er, hind·most** or **hind·er·most.** back; rear. [see HINDER[2], BEHIND]

hind[2] (hīnd), *n., pl.* **hinds** or (*esp. collectively*) **hind.** a female deer, usually a female red deer after its third year. [OE]

Hind., Hindustani.

hin·der[1] (hin′dər), *v.* keep back; hold back; get in the way of; make difficult; stop; prevent. [OE *hindrian*] —**hin′der·er,** *n.* —**hin′der·ing·ly,** *adv.*

hind·er[2] (hīn′dər), *adj.* hind; back; rear. [cf. OE *hinder* and *hindan* in back, behind]

Hin·di (hin′di), *n.* 1 an Indo-European vernacular language of N India. 2 form of Hindustani.

hind·most (hīnd′mōst), *adj.* furthest behind; last.

hind·quar·ter (hīnd′kwôr′tər), *n.* the hind leg and loin of a carcass of beef, lamb, etc.

hin·drance (hin′drəns), *n.* 1 person or thing that hinders; obstacle. 2 act of hindering.

hind·sight (hīnd′sīt′), *n.* ability to see, too late, what should have been done.

Hin·du (hin′dü), *n., pl.* –**dus;** *adj.* —*n.* 1 member of a native people of India, esp. one who speaks an Indo-European language. 2 person who believes in Hinduism. —*adj.* having to do with the Hindus, their languages, or their religion.

Hin·du·ism (hin′dü iz əm), *n.* the religious and social system of the Hindus.

Hin·du·stan (hin′dü stän′; –stan′), *n.* 1 India. 2 part of India north of the Deccan.

Hin·du·sta·ni (hin′dü stä′ni; –stan′i), *adj.* having to do with India, its people, or their languages. —*n.* the commonest language of India.

hinge (hinj), *n., v.,* **hinged, hing·ing.** —*n.* 1 joint on which a door, gate, cover, lid, etc., moves back and forth. 2 a critical point. —*v.* 1 furnish with hinges; attach by hinges. 2 hang or turn on a hinge. 3 depend. [OE *henge-*; akin to HANG] —**hinged,** *adj.*

hin·ny (hin′i), *n., pl.* –**nies.** a mulelike animal that is the offspring of a male horse and a female donkey. [< L *hinnus* < Gk. *innos*]

hint (hint), *n.* a slight sign; indirect suggestion. —*v.* give a slight sign of; suggest indirectly.

hint at, give a hint of; suggest. [appar. < *hent,* v., seize, OE *hentan*] —**hint′er,** n. —**hint′ing·ly,** adv.

hin·ter·land (hin′tər land′), n. **1** land or district behind a coast; back country. **2** remote parts; background. [< G]

hip[1] (hip), n. the projecting part on a person where the leg joins the body; joint formed by the upper thighbone and pelvis. [OE *hype*] —**hip′like′,** adj.

hip[2] (hip), n. pod containing the ripe seed of a rose bush. [OE *hēope*]

hip·bone (hip′bōn′), n. either of the two wide bones that, with the backbone, form the pelvis in mammals.

hip hop, rap music for dancing that has a strong beat.

hip joint, joint formed by the hipbone and thighbone.

hip·po (hip′ō), n., pl. **-pos.** *Informal.* hippopotamus.

Hip·poc·ra·tes (hi pok′rə tēz), n. 460?–357? B.C., Greek physician, called "the father of medicine." —**Hip′po·crat′ic,** adj.

Hippocratic oath, a famous oath describing the duties and obligations of a physician.

hip·po·drome (hip′ə drōm), n. **1** arena or building for a circus, rodeo, etc. **2** in ancient Greece and Rome, an oval track for horse races and chariot races, surrounded by tiers of seats for spectators. [< L < Gk., < *hippos* horse + *dromos* course]

hip·po·pot·a·mus (hip′ə pot′ə məs), n., pl. **-mus·es, -mi** (-mī). a huge, thick-skinned, hairless mammal found in and near the rivers of Africa. [< L < Gk., < *hippos* horse + *potamos* river]

hir·cine (hėr′sīn; –sin), adj. of goats; resembling a goat. [< L, < *hircus* goat]

hire (hīr), v., **hired, hir·ing,** n. —v. **1** pay for the use of (a thing) or the work or services of (a person). **2** give the use of (a thing) or the work or services of (a person) in return for payment. [OE *hȳrian,* < n.] —n. **1** payment for such use or work. **2** a hiring. [OE *hȳr*] —**hir′a·ble, hire′a·ble,** adj. —**hir′er,** n.

hire·ling (hīr′ling), n. person who works only for money, without interest or pride in the task. —adj. to be had for hire; mercenary.

Hir·o·shi·ma (hir′ə shē′mə), n. seaport in W Japan, largely destroyed by an atomic bomb.

hir·sute (hėr′süt), adj. hairy. [< L *hirsutus*] —**hir′sute·ness,** n.

his (hiz; *unstressed* iz), pron. **1** of him; belonging to him: *this is his.* **2** the one or ones belonging to him: *the others are not his.* —adj. of him; belonging to him: *this is his book.* [OE, gen. of *hē* he]

His·pan·ic (his pan′ik), n. person living in the United States who is of Spanish or Latin-American descent. —adj. **1** =Spanish. **2** =Latin-American; Latino.

His·pan·io·la (his′pən yō′lə), n. the second largest island in the West Indies, divided into the Dominican Republic and the republic of Haiti.

hiss (his), v. **1** make a sound like *ss.* Geese and snakes hiss. **2** show disapproval of or scorn for by hissing: *hiss poor acting.* **3** force or drive by hissing: *hiss him off the stage.* —n. a sound like *ss.* [imit.] —**hiss′er,** n.

hist (hist), interj. be still! listen!

hist., historian; historical; history.

his·ta·mine (his′tə mēn; –min), n. an amine, $C_5H_9N_3$, released by the body in allergic reactions. It lowers the blood pressure, etc.

his·tol·o·gy (his tol′ə ji), n. science of the tissues of animals and plants; study of the structure, esp. the microscopic structure, of organic tissues. [< Gk. *histos* web + -LOGY] —**his′to·log′i·cal,** adj. —**his·tol′o·gist,** n.

his·to·ri·an (his tô′ri ən; –tō′–), n. **1** person who writes about history. **2** scholar who is an authority on history.

his·tor·ic (his tôr′ik; –tor′–), adj. **1** famous or important in history. **2** =historical.

his·tor·i·cal (his tôr′ə kəl; –tor′–), adj. **1** of or having to do with history. **2** according to history; based on history. **3** known to be real or true; in history, not in legend. **4** =historic. —**his·tor′i·cal·ly,** adv. —**his·tor′i·cal·ness,** n.

his·to·ri·og·ra·pher (his tô′ri og′rə fər; –tō′–), n. historian. —**his·to′ri·og′ra·phy,** n.

his·to·ry (his′tə ri; his′tri), n., pl. **-ries. 1** statement of what has happened. **2** story of a person or a nation; systematic written account. **3** a known past: *this ship has a history.*

make history, a influence the course of history. **b** do something remarkable, historic. [< L < Gk. *historia* inquiry, record, history. Doublet of STORY[1].]

his·tri·on·ic (his′tri on′ik), adj. **1** having to do with actors or acting. **2** theatrical; insincere. [< L, < *histrio* actor < Etruscan *(h)ister*] —**his′tri·on′i·cal·ly,** adv.

his·tri·on·ics (his′tri on′iks), n. pl. **1** dramatic representation; theatricals; dramatics. **2** a theatrical or insincere manner, expression, etc.

hit (hit), v., **hit, hit·ting,** n. —v. **1** come against with force; give a blow to; strike; knock. **2** propel by a stroke: *hit the ball over the fence.* **3** have a painful effect on; affect severely. **4** of an engine, ignite the mixture in a cylinder: *the car hits on all cylinders.* —n. **1** a blow; stroke. **2** a getting to what is aimed at. **3** a successful attempt, performance, or production: *the song was a hit.* **4** ball so struck that the batter can get to the first base safely, and perhaps further.

hit it off, get along well together; agree.

hit on or upon, a come on; meet with; get to. **b** find, esp. by accident; guess correctly.

hit or miss, by chance; at random. [< Scand. *hitta*] —**hit′ter,** n.

hit-and-run (hit′ən run′), adj. of or having to do with hitting a person or vehicle and driving away, rather than stopping to see what happened.

hitch (hich), v. **1** move or pull with a jerk; move jerkily. **2** harness to a cart or conveyance. **3** fasten with a hook, ring, rope, strap, etc. **4** become fastened or caught; catch. —n. **1** a short, sudden pull or jerk; jerky movement. **2** a fastening; catch. **3** obstacle; hindrance: *the performance went off without a hitch.* **4** kind of knot used for temporary fastening. [ME *hyche(n)*] —**hitch′er,** n.

hitch·hike (hich′hīk), v., **-hiked, -hik·ing.** travel by getting free rides from passing automobiles. —**hitch′hik′er,** n.

hith·er (hiŧħ′ər), adv. to this place; toward this place; here: *come hither.* —adj. on this side; nearer. [OE *hider;* akin to HERE]

hith·er·to (hiŧħ′ər tü′), adv. up to this time; until now.

hith·er·ward (hiŧħ′ər wərd), **hith·er·wards** (–wərdz), adv. toward this place; hither.

Hit·tite (hit′īt), n. **1** member of an ancient people in Asia Minor and Syria, existing from about 2000 B.C. until about 1200 B.C. **2** language of the Hittites. —adj. of or having to do with the Hittites or their language.

HIV, human immunodeficiency virus, which causes AIDS.

hive (hīv), n., v., **hived, hiv·ing.** —n. **1** house or box for bees to live in. **2** a large number of bees living together. **3** a busy, swarming place full of people or animals. **4** a swarming crowd. —v. put (bees) in a hive. [OE *hȳf*]

hives (hīvz), n. any of various diseases in which the skin itches and shows patches of red.

H.M., His Majesty; Her Majesty.

H.M.S., His (Her) Majesty's Service; His (Her) Majesty's Ship.

ho (hō), interj. **1** exclamation of scornful laughter, joy, or surprise. **2** exclamation to attract attention.

Ho, holmium.

hoa·gy or **hoa·gie** (hōg′i), n., pl. **-gies.** hero sandwich.

hoar (hôr; hōr), adj. hoary. —n. hoarfrost. [OE *hār*]

hoard (hôrd; hōrd), n. what is saved and stored away; things stored. —v. save and store away. [OE *hord*] —**hoard′er,** n.

hoar·frost (hôr′frôst′; hōr′–; –frost′), n. white frost.

hoar·hound (hôr′hound′; hōr′–), n. =horehound.

hoarse (hôrs; hōrs), adj., **hoars·er, hoars·est. 1** sounding rough and deep. **2** having a rough voice. [OE *hās;* infl. by Scand. *hāss*] —**hoarse′ly,** adv. —**hoarse′ness,** n.

hoar·y (hôr′i; hōr′i), adj., **hoar·i·er, hoar·i·est. 1** white or gray. **2** white or gray with age. **3** old; ancient. —**hoar′i·ness,** n.

hoax (hōks), n. a mischievous trick, esp. a made-up story. —v. play a mischievous trick on; deceive in fun or to injure. (prob. alter. of *hocus*] —**hoax′er,** n.

hob[1] (hob), n. shelf at the back or side of a fireplace.

hob² (hob), *n.* =hobgoblin; elf. [ME, for *Rob* (*Robert* or *Robin*)]

Ho·bart (hō′bärt; –bərt), *n.* capital of Tasmania.

hob·ble (hob′əl), *v.*, **-bled, -bling,** *n.* —*v.* **1** walk awkwardly; limp. **2** tie the legs of (a horse, etc.) together. **3** =hinder. —*n.* **1** an awkward walk; limp. **2** rope or strap used to hobble a horse, etc. [ME *hobelen.* Cf. Du. *hobbelen* to rock.] —**hob′bler,** *n.* —**hob′bling,** *adj.*

hob·by (hob′i), *n., pl.* **-bies.** something a person especially likes to work at or study apart from his or her main business; any favorite pastime, topic of conversation, etc. [ME *hobyn* small horse]

hob·by·horse (hob′i hôrs′), *n.* **1** stick with a horse's head, used as a toy horse by children. **2** a rocking horse.

hob·gob·lin (hob′gob′lən), *n.* **1** goblin; elf. **2** bogy. [< *hob²* + *goblin*]

hob·nail (hob′nāl′), *n.* a short nail with a large head formerly used to protect the soles of heavy shoes. [< *hob* peg + *nail*] —**hob′nailed**′, *adj.*

hob·nob (hob′nob′), *v.*, **-nobbed, -nobbing.** associate intimately; talk together on familiar terms. [from drinking phrase *hob or nob* give or take, ult. OE *hæbbe* have + *næbbe* not have]

ho·bo (hō′bō), *n., pl.* **-bos, -boes.** a tramp or vagrant.

Hob·son's choice (hob′sənz), choice of taking the thing offered or nothing. [from T. *Hobson,* who rented the horse nearest his stable door or none]

hock¹ (hok), *n.* joint in the hind leg of a horse, cow, etc., above the fetlock joint. [OE *hōh*]

hock² (hok), *n.* kind of white Rhine wine. [for *Hockamore,* alter. of *Hochheimer*]

hock³ (hok), *v.* **1** pawn. **in hock,** in debt. [orig. *n.* Cf. Du. *hok* pen, jail.]

hock·ey (hok′i), *n.* game played by two teams on ice or on a field, where players hit a rubber disk or ball with curved sticks to drive it across a goal.

ho·cus-po·cus (hō′kəs pō′kəs), *n., v.,* **-cused, -cusing.** —*n.* **1** form of words used in conjuring. **2** trickery; deception. —*v.* play tricks on; deceive. [sham Latin used by jugglers, etc.]

hod (hod), *n.* trough or tray with a long handle, used for carrying bricks, mortar, etc., on the shoulder. [cf. MDu. *hodde*]

hodge·podge (hoj′poj′), *n.* a disorderly mixture; mess; jumble. [var. of *hotchpot* < OF *hochepot* ragout]

Hodg·kin's disease (hoj′kinz), cancer of the lymphatic system. [< Thomas *Hodgkin* (1798–1866), English physician who described it]

hoe (hō), *n., v.,* **hoed, hoe·ing.** —*n.* tool with a small blade set across the end of a long handle, used to loosen soil and cut weeds. —*v.* **1** loosen, dig, or cut with a hoe. **2** use a hoe. [< OF *houe* < Gmc.] —**hoe′like**′, *adj.*

hoe·cake (hō′kāk′), *n.* S. kind of bread made of corn meal.

hoe·down (hō′doun′), *n.* **1** noisy, unrestrained dance, esp. a square dance. **2** music for this dance.

hog (hog; hôg), *n., v.,* **-hogged, hogging.** —*n.* **1** pig. **2** a full-grown pig, raised for food. **3** a selfish, greedy, or dirty person. —*v. Slang.* take more than one's share of. [OE *hogg*]

ho·gan (hō′gôn), *n.* Navaho Indian dwelling made with logs and covered by earth with a hole at the top for smoke to escape. [< Athapaskan (Navaho) *hóghan* house]

hog·gish (hog′ish; hôg′–), *adj.* **1** like a hog; very selfish; greedy. **2** dirty; filthy. —**hog′gish·ly,** *adv.* —**hog′gish·ness,** *n.*

hog·nose snake (hog′nōz′; hôg′–), a harmless North American snake with an upturned snout.

hogs·head (hogz′hed; hôgz′–), *n.* **1** a large barrel that contains from 63 to 140 gallons. **2** a liquid measure, equal to 63 gallons.

hog-tie (hog′tī′; hôg′–), *v.,* **-tied, -tying.** tie all four feet together.

hog·wash (hog′wosh′; –wôsh′; hôg′–), *n.* **1** swill. **2** worthless stuff; nonsense.

ho-hum (hō′hum′), *interj.* sound made to express boredom or indifference. —*adj.* boring; indifferent: *a ho-hum performance.*

hoi pol·loi (hoi′pə loi′), the masses. [< Gk.]

hoist (hoist), *v.* raise on high; lift up, often with ropes and pulleys. —*n.* **1** a hoisting; lift. **2** elevator or other apparatus for hoisting heavy loads. [earlier *hoise* < Du. *hijschen*] —**hoist′er,** *n.*

hoi·ty-toi·ty (hoi′ti toi′ti), *interj.* exclamation showing surprise and some contempt. —*adj.* **1** giddy; flighty. **2** inclined to put on airs; haughty. —*n.* **1** flightiness. **2** haughtiness.

Hok·kai·do (hō′kī′dō), *n.* the second largest island in Japan.

ho·kum (hō′kəm), *n. Slang.* **1** sentimental matter introduced merely for effect. **2** humbug; nonsense; bunk. [? < *hocus*]

hold¹ (hōld), *v.,* **held, held** or (*Archaic*) **hold·en, hold·ing,** *n.* —*v.,* **1** take in the hands or arms and keep: *hold a child.* **2** keep in some position or condition: *please hold still, hold your breath.* **3** defend: *hold the fort.* **4** contain: *this theater holds 500 people.* **5** occupy: *hold an office.* **6** keep or support; adhere; be true: *hold a belief, hold to a purpose, the rule holds in all cases.* **7** consider: *hold human life cheap.* **8** continue: *the good weather held.* **9** decide legally: *the court holds him guilty.* —*n.* **1** act of holding: *release one's hold.* **2** thing to hold by, as a handle. **3** a controlling force or influence: *have a secret hold on a person.* **4** way of holding one's opponent; grasp or grip.

get hold of, get; obtain.

hold back, keep back; keep from acting.

hold down, a keep down; keep under control. **b** have and keep: *hold down a job.*

hold forth, a talk; preach. **b** offer.

hold in, a keep in; restrain. **b** keep silence: *held in her criticism.*

hold off, keep at a distance; keep from acting or attacking.

hold on, a keep one's hold. **b** keep on; continue. **c** stop!

hold out, a continue; last. **b** extend. **c** offer.

hold over, a keep for future consideration. **b** stay in office beyond the regular term.

hold up, a keep from falling; support. **b** show; display. **c** continue; last; endure. **d** stop. **e** stop by force and rob.

no hold or **holds barred,** no restraint; complete freedom of action or expression.

on hold, a awaiting someone to take or resume a telephone call. **b** *Fig.* put off; delayed. [OE *healdan*]

hold² (hōld), *n.* interior of a ship below the deck. [var. of *hole*]

hold·er (hōl′dər), *n.* **1** person who holds something. **2** thing to hold something else with.

hold·ing (hōl′ding), *n.* **1** land; piece of land. **2** Often, **holdings.** property in stocks or bonds.

holding action, 1 a military operation that seeks merely to prevent an enemy advance. **2** any undertaking that resembles this: *a holding action against inflation.*

holding company, company that owns stocks or bonds of other companies and often controls them.

hold·out (hōld′out′), *n.* refusal to compromise or come to an agreement on something, esp. in order to exact a higher place, better terms, etc.

holding pattern, 1 flight pattern of an aircraft waiting to land at an airport. **2** *Fig.* any maneuver that delays a decision or action, esp. one that continues for a long period.

hold·up (hōld′up′), *n.* **1** act of stopping by force and robbing. **2** a stopping.

hole (hōl), *n., v.,* **holed, hol·ing.** —*n.* **1** an open place: *a hole in a sweater.* **2** a hollow place. **3** place dug by an animal to live in. **4** a small, dark, dirty place. **5** flaw; defect. **6** embarrassing position. —*v.* make holes in.

pick holes or **shoot full of holes,** find fault with; criticize.

hole up, a go into a hole for the winter. **b** hide; withdraw. [OE *hol*] —**hole′less,** *adj.* —**hole′y,** *adj.*

hol·i·day (hol′ə dā), *n.* **1** day when one does not work; day for pleasure and enjoyment. **2** Now usually, **holy day.** a religious festival. —*adj.* suited to a holiday. [OE *hāligdæg* holy day]

ho·li·ness (hō′li nis), *n.* **1** a being holy. **2** **Holiness,** title used of the Pope.

Hol·land (hol′ənd), *n.* =the Netherlands. —**Hol′land·er,** *n.*

hol·low (hol′ō), *adj.* **1** having nothing, or only air, inside; empty. A pipe is hollow. **2** cup-shaped: *a hollow wooden bowl.* **3** as if coming from something hollow; dull: *a hollow voice.* **4** *Fig.* not real or sincere; false; worthless: *hollow promises, hollow praise.* **5** deep and sunken: *hollow eyes and cheeks.* —*n.* **1** a hollow place; hole; *a hollow in the road.* **2** valley: *Sleepy Hollow.* —*v.* make hollow; bend or dig out to a hollow shape. [OE *holh,* n.] —**hol′low·ly,** *adv.* —**hol′low·ness,** *n.*

hol·ly (hol′i), *n., pl.* **–lies. 1** tree or shrub with shiny, sharp-pointed, green leaves and bright-red berries. **2** the leaves and berries used as Christmas decorations. [OE *holegn*]

hol·ly·hock (hol′i hok), *n.* a tall plant with clusters of large, showy flowers of various colors. [ME *holihoc* < *holi* holy + *hoc* mallow (OE *hocc*)]

hol·mi·um (hōl′mi əm), *n.* a rare metallic element, Ho, belonging to the yttrium group. [< NL; named for *Stockholm*]

holm oak (hōm), an evergreen oak of S Europe with leaves like those of the holly. [OE *holegn* holly + *āc* oak]

hol·o·caust (hol′ə kôst), *n.* **1** an offering all of which is burned. **2** complete destruction by fire, esp. of animals or human beings. **3** great or wholesale destruction.

the Holocaust, mass extermination of Jews by the Nazis during World War II. [< L < Gk., < *holos* whole + *kaustos* burned] —**hol′o·caus′tal, hol′o·caus′-tic,** *adj.*

hol·o·gram (hol′ə gram), *n.* record or reproduction of an image produced by holography.

hol·o·graph[1] (hol′ə graf; –gräf), *adj.* wholly written in the handwriting of the person in whose name it appears: *a holograph will.* —*n.* a holograph manuscript, letter, document, etc. [< LL < Gk., < *holos* whole + *graphe* writing] —**hol′o·graph′ic,** *adj.*

hol·o·graph[2] (hol′ə graf), *v.* produce a hologram of. —**ho·log′ra·pher,** *n.* —**hol′o·graph′ic,** *adj.*

ho·log·ra·phy (ho lôg′rə fē, –log′–), *n.* method of photography which uses laser light to record a three-dimensional image on a plate or film. [< *holo-* whole; entire + *–graphy*]

Hol·stein (hōl′stīn; –stēn), **Holstein-Friesian** (–frē′zhən), *n.* any of a breed of large, black-and-white dairy cattle.

hol·ster (hōl′stər), *n.* a leather case for a pistol, attached to a belt or a horseman's saddle. [cf. Du. *holster*] —**hol′stered,** *adj.*

ho·ly (hō′li), *adj.,* **–li·er, –li·est,** *n., pl.* **–lies.** —*adj.* **1** set apart to the service of God; declared sacred: *a holy day.* **2** like a saint; spiritually perfect; very good. **3** worthy of reverence. [OE *hālig*]

Holy City, 1 city considered sacred by the adherents of any religion. Jerusalem, Rome, and Mecca are Holy Cities. **2** heaven.

Holy Communion, 1 a sharing in the Lord's Supper as a part of church worship. **2** celebration of the Lord's Supper.

holy day, a religious festival, esp. one not occurring on Sunday, as Good Friday, etc.

Holy Ghost, spirit of God; third person of the Trinity.

Holy Grail, cup or dish supposed to have been used by Christ at the Last Supper.

Holy Land, Palestine.

holy orders, the rite or sacrament of ordination.

Holy Roman Empire, empire in W and C Europe regarded as the continuation of the Roman Empire.

Holy Scriptures, the Bible; scripture (def. 2).

Holy See, position or authority of the Pope.

Holy Spirit, = Holy Ghost.

ho·ly·stone (hō′li stōn′), *n., v.,* **–stoned, –ston·ing.** —*n.* piece of soft sandstone used for scrubbing the wooden decks of ships. —*v.* scrub with a holystone.

Holy Week, week before Easter.

Holy Writ, the Bible; the Scriptures.

hom·age (hom′ij; om′–), *n.* **1** respect; reverence: *pay homage to a great leader.* **2** a formal acknowledgment by a vassal that he owed loyalty and service to his lord. [< OF, < *hom* man, vassal < L *homo*].

hom·bre (ôm′brä), *n. Spanish.* man.

hom·burg (hom′bėrg), *n.* a man's soft felt hat with the crown dented in at the top.

home (hōm), *n., adj., adv., v.,* **homed, hom·ing.** —*n.* **1** a place where a person or family lives. **2** place where a person was born or brought up. **3** place where an animal or plant lives; habitat. **4** place where a person can rest and be safe. **5** place where people who are old, sick, blind, etc., may live: *a nursing home.* **6** in sports and games, goal. **7** *Baseball.* home plate. —*adj.* having to do with one's own home or country. —*adv.* at, to, or toward one's own home or country: *go home.* **2** to the place where it belongs; to the thing aimed at: *strike home.* **3** to the heart or center; deep in: *drive a nail home.* —*v.* **1** go home. **2** have a home.

at home, a in one's own home or country. **b** at ease; comfortable. **c** ready to receive visitors.

bring home, make clear, emphatic, or realistic.

home (in) on, a (of a guided missile), reach a target. **b** *Fig.* focus on; concentrate on. [OE *hām*] —**home′like′,** *adj.*

home·boy (hōm′boi′), *n.* **1** boy or man from one's own neighborhood or community, esp. one who embodies the attitudes, dress. etc., of a particular area. **2** inner-city young person, esp. one associated with a neighborhood or gang.

home·bred (hōm′bred′), *adj.* native; domestic.

home·brew (hōm′brü′), *n.* beer or other alcoholic liquor made at home.

home economics, science and art that deals with the management of a household.

home-grown (hōm′grōn′), *adj.* **1** grown or made at home; produced locally. **2** *Fig.* produced domestically; not imported.

home·land (hōm′land′), *n.* one's native land.

home·less (hōm′lis), *adj.* having no home. —*n.* **the homeless,** people, considered as a group, who do not have a place to live. —**home′less·ly,** *adv.* —**home′less·ness,** *n.*

home·ly (hōm′li), *adj.,* **–li·er, –li·est. 1** not good-looking; ugly; plain. **2** suited to home life; simple; everyday: *homely pleasures.* **3** of plain manners; unpretending. —**home′li·ness,** *n.*

home·made (hōm′mād′), *adj.* made at home.

ho·me·op·a·thy (hō′mi op′ə thi; hom′i–), *n.* method of treating disease by drugs, given in very small doses, which would in large doses produce in a healthy person symptoms similar to those of the disease. [< Gk. *homoios* similar + –PATHY] —**ho′me·o·path, ho′me·op′a·thist,** *n.* —**ho′me·o·path′ic,** *adj.* —**ho′me·o·path′i·cally,** *adv.*

home plate, block or slab beside which a player stands to bat the ball, and to which he must return, after hitting the ball and rounding the bases, in order to score.

hom·er (hōm′ər), *n.* **1** = home run. **2** a homing pigeon.

Ho·mer (hōm′ər), *n.* about the 10th cent. B.C., the great epic poet of ancient Greece; author of the *Iliad* and the *Odyssey.*

Ho·mer·ic (hō mer′ik), *adj.* **1** by Homer. **2** of or pertaining to Homer or his poems. **3** in the style of Homer.

Homeric laughter, loud, hearty laughter.

home rule, local self-government.

home run, run made by a player on a hit that enables him, without aid from fielding errors of the opponents, to make the entire circuit of the bases without a stop.

home-school·ing (hōm′skü′ling), *n.* instruction of children by parents at home, rather than at a public or private school. —**home′-school′,** *v.* —**home′-school′er,** *n.*

home·sick (hōm′sik′), *adj.* longing for home. —**home′sick′ness,** *n.*

home·spun (hōm′spun′), *adj.* **1** spun or made at home. **2** *Fig.* not polished; plain; simple. —*n.* **1** cloth made of yard spun at home. **2** a strong, loosely woven cloth similar to it.

home·stead (hōm′sted), *n.* **1** house with its land and other buildings; farm with its buildings. **2** parcel of 160 acres of public land granted to a settler under certain conditions by the U.S. government. —**home′stead·er,** *n.*

home stretch, 1 part of a track over which the last part of a race is run. **2** the last part.

home·ward (hōm′wərd), *adv.* Also, **home′wards.** toward home. —*adj.* being in the direction of home.

home·work (hōm′wėrk′), *n.* **1** work done at home. **2** lesson to be studied or prepared outside the classroom.

home·y (hōm′i), *adj.,* **hom·i·er, hom·i·est.** like home; cozy and comfortable.

hom·i·cide[1] (hom′ə sīd; hō′mə–), *n.* the killing of one human being by another. Intentional homicide is murder. [< OF < L, < *homo* man + *–cidium* act of killing] **—hom′i·cid′al,** *adj.* **—hom′i·cid′al·ly,** *adv.*

hom·i·cide[2] (hom′ə sīd; hō′mə–), *n.* person who kills a human being. [< OF < L, < *homo* man + *–cida* killer]

hom·i·let·ics (hom′ə let′iks), *n.,* art of composing and preaching sermons. [< LL < Gk., affable, ult. < *homileein* associate with. See HOMILY.] **—hom′i·let′ic,** *adj.* **—hom′i·let′i·cal·ly,** *adv.*

hom·i·ly (hom′ə li), *n., pl.* **–lies.** **1** sermon, usually on some part of the Bible. **2** a serious moral talk or writing. [< OF < LL < Gk. *homilia* < *homilios* throng < *homou* together]

homing pigeon, pigeon trained to fly home from great distances carrying written messages.

hom·i·nid (hom′ə nid), *adj.,* having to do with or resembling any one of a family of primates that includes humans. **—n.** a hominid animal.

hom·i·noid (hom′ə noid), *adj.,* of or like a human. **—n.** a hominoid animal. [< NL *Hominidas* the family name < L *homō* man + E *–oid*]

hom·i·ny (hom′ə ni), *n.,* corn hulled and coarsely ground or crushed, usually eaten boiled. [< Algonkian]

ho·mo (hō′mō), *n., pl.* **hom·i·nes** (hom′-ə nēz). man. [< L]

Ho·mo e·rec·tus (hō′mō i rek′təs), an extinct species of human being whose fossil remains show walked upright. [< NL *homō ērēctus* erect man]

ho·mo·ge·ne·ous (hō′mə jē′ni əs; –jēn′-yəs; hom′ə–), *adj.* **1** of the same kind; similar. **2** composed of similar elements or parts. [< Med.L < Gk., < *homos* the same + *genos* kind] **—ho′mo·ge·ne′i·ty, ho′mo·ge′ne·ous·ness,** *n.* **—ho′mo·ge′ne·ous·ly,** *adv.*

ho·mog·e·nize (hə moj′ə nīz), *v.,* **–nized, –niz·ing.** make homogeneous. In homogenized milk the fat is distributed evenly throughout and does not rise in the form of cream.

hom·o·graph (hom′ə graf; –gräf; hō′mə–), *n.* word having the same spelling as another, but a different origin and meaning. *Mail,* meaning "letters," and *mail,* meaning "armor," are homographs. [< Gk., < *homos* the same + *graphe* writing] **—hom′o·graph′ic,** *adj.*

Ho·mo hab·i·lis (hō′mō hab′ə ləs), an extinct species of human being thought to be the earliest toolmaker. [< L *homō habilis* skillful man]

ho·mol·o·gous (hō mol′ə gəs), *adj.* **1** corresponding in position, value, etc. **2** corresponding in type of structure and in origin. The wing of a bird and the foreleg of a horse are homologous. [< Gk., agreeing, < *homos* same + *logos* reasoning, relation]

ho·mol·o·gy (hō mol′ə ji), *n., pl.* **–gies.** correspondence in position, proportion, value, structure, origin, etc.

hom·o·nym (hom′ə nim), *n.* word having the same pronunciation as another, but a different meaning. *Meat* and *meet* are homonyms. [< L < Gk., < *homos* same + *onyma* (dial.) name] **—hom′o·nym′ic,** *adj.*

hom·o·phone (hom′ə fōn; hō′mə–), *n.,* **1** letter or symbol having the same sound as another. The letters *c* and *k* are homophones in the word *cork.* **2** =homonym. [< Gk., < *homos* same + *phone* sound]

ho·moph·o·ny (hō mof′ə ni; hom′ə fō′ni), *n.* **1** sameness of sound. **2** music having one part or melody predominating. **—hom′o·phon′ic, ho·moph′o·nous,** *adj.*

ho·mop·ter·ous (hō mop′tər əs), *adj.,* belonging to a group of insects (including the aphids and cicadas) with mouth parts adapted to sucking and wings of the same texture throughout. [< Gk. *homos* same + *pteron* wing]

Ho·mo sa·pi·ens (hō′mō sā′pi enz), man; human being; the species including all humankind. [L, lit., man having sense]

ho·mo·sex·u·al (hō′mə sek′shù əl), *adj.,* pertaining to or manifesting sexual feelings for one of the same sex. **—n.** a homosexual person. [< Gk. *homos* same + L *sexus* sex] **—ho′mo·sex′u·al′i·ty,** *n.*

ho·mo·zy·gote (hō′mə zī′gōt; –zig′ōt; hom′ə–), *n.,* an animal or plant whose chromosomes contain an identical pair of genes and reproduces without variation of genus, form, etc. **—ho′mo·zy′gous,** *adj.* **—ho′mo·zy′gous·ly,** *adv.*

ho·mun·cu·lus (hō mung′kyə ləs), *n., pl.* **–li** (–lī). a little man. [< L, dim. of *homo* man]

Hon., Honorable; Honorary.

Hon·du·ras (hon dùr′əs; –dyùr′əs), *n.* country in N Central America. **—Hon·du′ran,** *adj., n.*

hone (hōn), *n., v.,* **honed, hon·ing.** **—n.** a fine-grained whetstone on which to sharpen cutting tools. **—v.** sharpen on a hone. [OE *hān* a stone]

hon·est (on′ist), *adj.* **1** not lying, cheating, or stealing; truthful: *an honest man.* **2** obtained by fair and upright means: *honest profits.* **3** frank; open: *honest opposition.* **4** not mixed; genuine; pure: *honest goods.* [< OF < L *honestus* < *honos* honor] **—hon′est·ly,** *adv.*

hon·es·ty (on′is ti), *n.* fairness and uprightness.

hon·ey (hun′i), *n., pl.* **hon·eys** *adj., v.,* **hon·eyed** or **hon·ied, hon·ey·ing. —n.** **1** a thick sweet, yellow liquid, that bees make out of the drops they collect from flowers. **2** drop of sweet liquid, found in many flowers. **3** *Fig.* sweetness. **4** darling; dear. **—v.** **1** sweeten with or as with honey. **2** talk sweetly; flatter. [OE *hunig*] **—hon′ey·like′,** *adj.*

hon·ey·bee (hun′i bē′), *n.* bee that makes honey.

hon·ey·comb (hun′i kōm′), *n.* **1** structure of wax containing rows of six-sided cells formed by bees, in which to store honey, pollen, and their eggs. **2** anything like this. **—adj.** like a honeycomb: *a honeycomb pattern.* **—v.** **1** make like a honeycomb. **2** pierce with many holes. **3** permeate: *the city is honeycombed with crime.*

hon·ey·dew (hun′i dü′; –dū′), *n.* **1** a sweet substance on the leaves of certain plants in hot weather. **2** a sweet substance on leaves and stems, secreted by tiny insects called aphids. **3** =honeydew melon.

honeydew melon, a variety of melon with sweet, green flesh and a smooth, whitish skin.

hon·eyed (hun′id), *adj.* **1** sweetened with honey. **2** laden with honey. **3** *Fig.* sweet as honey.

honey locust, a thorny North American tree with long, divided leaves and large, flat pods containing sweet pulp.

hon·ey·moon (hun′i mün′) *n.* **1** vacation spent together by a newly married couple. **2** the first month of marriage. **3** period of good relations, as in diplomacy or business, esp. at the beginning of an association. **—v.** spend or have a honeymoon. **—hon′ey·moon′er,** *n.*

hon·ey·suck·le (hun′i suk′əl), *n.* **1** shrub or vine with small, fragrant flowers. **2** any of various similar plants. **—hon′ey·suck′led,** *adj.*

honk (hongk; hôngk), *n.* **1** cry of the wild goose. **2** any similar sound: *honk of a taxi.* **—v.** make such a sound. [imit.] **—honk′er,** *n.*

honk·y-tonk (hong′ki tongk′; hông′-ki tôngk′), *n.* a cheap saloon, cabaret, etc. **—adj.** of or having to do with the music or entertainment in such a place.

Hon·o·lu·lu (hon′ə lü′lü), *n.* seaport and capital of Hawaii.

hon·or (on′ər), *n.* **1** glory; fame; renown; good name. **2** sense of what is right or proper. **3 Honor,** title used in speaking to or of a judge, mayor, etc. **—v.** **1** respect greatly; regard highly. **2** accept and pay (a bill, etc.) when due.

do the honors, act as host or hostess.

honors, a course of study in a particular field more intensive or rigorous than required for an ordinary degree. **b** recognition given a student for excellence in academic work. [< OF < L *honos, honor*] **—hon′or·er,** *n.*

hon·or·a·ble (on′ər ə bəl), *adj.* **1** honest; upright. **2** causing or bringing honor. **3 Honorable,** title of respect before the names of certain officials. **—hon′or·a·ble·ness,** *n.* **—hon′or·a·bly,** *adv.*

hon·o·rar·i·um (on′ə rār′i əm), *n., pl.* **–rar·i·ums, –rar·i·a** (–rār′i ə). fee for professional services on which no fixed price is set.

hon·or·ar·y (on′ər er′i), *adj.* **1** given or done as an honor. **2** as an honor only: *an honorary secretary.*

hon·or·if·ic (on´ər if´ik), *adj.* **1** doing or giving honor. **2** showing respect or deference. —*n.* an honorific word or phrase. —**hon´or·if´i·cal·ly,** *adv.*

honor system, system of trusting people in schools and other institutions to obey the rules and do their work independently.

hood (hud), *n.* **1** a soft covering for the head and neck, either separate or as part of a cloak. **2** anything like a hood in shape or use. **3** a metal covering over the engine of an automobile. **4** *Informal.* hoodlum. **5** *Informal.* =neighborhood. —*v.* cover with a hood. [OE *hōd*] —**hood´ed,** *adj.* —**hood´less,** *adj.* —**hood´like´,** *adj.*

-hood, *suffix.* **1** state or condition of being, as in, *likelihood.* **2** character or nature of, as in *sainthood.* **3** group, body of, as in *sisterhood.* [OE *-hād*]

hood·ie (hud´i), *n.* jacket with a hood, esp. a sweatshirt.

hood·lum (hud´ləm), *n.* a young rowdy; street ruffian. —**hood´lum·ism,** *n.*

hoo·doo (hü´dü), *n., pl.* **-doos,** *v.,* **-dooed, -doo·ing.** —*n.* **1** person or thing that brings bad luck. **2** bad luck. —*v.* bring or cause bad luck to. [? var. of *voodoo*]

hood·wink (hud´wingk), *v.* mislead by a trick; deceive. —**hood´wink·er,** *n.*

hoo·ey (hü´i), *n.* nonsense. —*interj.* exclamation of disgust or disapproval.

hoof (huf; hüf), *n., pl.* **hoofs** or (*Rare*) **hooves,** *v.* —*n.* **1** a hard, horny covering on the feet of horses, cattle, sheep, pigs, and some other animals. **2** the whole foot of such animals. —*v. Informal.* **1** walk. **2** dance.
on the hoof, alive; not killed and butchered. [OE *hōf*] —**hoofed,** *adj.* —**hoof´er,** *n.* —**hoof´like´,** *adj.*

hoof·beat (huf´bēt´; hüf´-), *n.* sound made by an animal's hoof.

hook (huk), *n.* **1** piece of metal, wood, etc., curved for catching hold of something or for hanging things on. **2** a curved piece of wire for catching fish. **3** anything curved like a hook as a sharp bend or point of land or a curve thrown in baseball. **4** a short, swinging blow. —*v.* **1** attach or fasten with a hook or hooks: *please hook my dress for me.* **2** catch (fish) with a hook. **3** be curved like a hook. **4** throw (a ball) so that it curves. **5** hit with a hook in boxing.
by hook or by crook, in any way at all; by fair means or foul.
hook up, a attach or fasten with a hook or hooks. **b** arrange and connect parts of (a computer, telephone, etc.). **c** *Informal.* meet (a person). [OE *hōc*] —**hook´less,** *adj.* —**hook´like´,** *adj.*

hook·ah (huk´ə), *n.* a tobacco pipe with a long tube by which the smoke is drawn through water. [< Ar. *ḥuqqa* vase, pipe]

hooked (hukt), *adj.* **1** curved or bent like a hook. **2** having hooks.

hooked rug, rug made by pulling yarn or strips of cloth through a piece of canvas, burlap, etc.

hook·er (huk´ər), *n. Informal.* **1** a prostitute. **2** a difficulty or possible problem. **3** something that catches the attention.

hook·up (huk´up´), *n.* **1** arrangement and connection of the parts of a computer, telephone, etc. **2** an effecting of relationships: *a hookup between nations.*

hook·worm (huk´wėrm´), *n.* **1** worm that gets into the intestines and causes a disease characterized by weakness and apparent laziness. **2** the disease.

hook·y (huk´i), *n.* **play hooky,** run away; be absent without reason.

hoo·li·gan (hü´lə gən), *n.* a street ruffian; hoodlum. —**hoo´li·gan·ism,** *n.*

hoop (hüp; hup), *n.* **1** ring or flat band in the form of a circle: *hoop for holding the staves of a barrel.* **2** anything shaped like a hoop. —*v.* fasten together with hoops. [OE *hōp*] —**hooped,** *adj.* —**hoop´er,** *n.* —**hoop´like´,** *adj.*

hoop·la (hüp´lä´), *n. Informal.* any meaningless, showy, or overexuberant activity to gain publicity, promote a product, etc.; ballyhoo.

hoo·poe (hü´pü), *n.* a bright-colored bird with a long, sharp bill and a fanlike crest on its head. [earlier *hoop* < F < L *upupa* (imit.)]

hoop skirt, a woman's skirt worn over a flexible hoop.

hoo·ray (hu rā´), *interj., n., v.* hurrah.

Hoo·sier (hü´zhər), *n.* native or inhabitant of Indiana.

hoot (hüt), *n.* **1** sound that an owl makes. **2** any similar sound. **3** shout to show disapproval or scorn. **4** thing of little value. —*v.* **1** make the sound that an owl makes. **2** make a shout to show disapproval. **3** show disapproval by hooting. **4** force or drive by hooting. [ME *hute(n)*; ? imit.] —**hoot´er,** *n.*

Hoo·ver (hü´vər), **Herbert C.** 1874–1964, the 31st president of the United States, 1929–33.

hooves (hüvz; huvz), *n. Rare.* pl. of **hoof.**

hop¹ (hop), *v.,* **hopped, hop·ping,** *n.* —*v.* **1** spring, or move by springing, on one foot or with all feet at once: *many birds hop.* **2** jump over: *hop a ditch.* **3** jump on (a train, car, etc.). —*n.* a hopping; spring. [OE *hoppian*]

hop² (hop), *n.,* **1** vine having flower clusters that look like small, yellow pine cones. **2** hops, dried flower clusters of the hop vine, used to flavor beer and other malt drinks. [< MDu. *hoppe*]

hope (hōp), *n., v.,* **hoped, hop·ing.** —*n.* **1** a feeling that what one desires will happen. **2** thing that expectation centers in: *he is the hope of the family.* **3** thing hoped for. **4** ground for expectation: *no hope of recovery.* —*v.* wish and expect. [OE *hopa*]

hope chest, chest for storing articles that will be useful after a woman marries.

hope·ful (hōp´fəl) *adj.* **1** feeling or showing hope. **2** causing hope; giving hope; likely to succeed. —*n.* boy or girl thought likely to succeed. —**hope´ful·ly,** *adv.* —**hope´ful·ness,** *n.*

hope·less (hōp´lis), *adj.* **1** feeling no hope. **2** giving no hope: *a hopeless illness.* —**hope´less·ly,** *adv.* —**hope´less·ness,** *n.*

Ho·pi (hō´pi), *n., pl.* **-pis. 1** member of a tribe of Pueblo Indians living largely in stonebuilt towns in N Arizona. **2** their Shoshonean language [< a contraction of Shoshonean *hōpitu* peaceful ones, or *hōpitu shinumu* "peaceful all people," the Hopi tribal name].

hop·lite (hop´līt), *n.* a heavily armed foot soldier of ancient Greece. [< Gk., < *hopla* arms]

hop·per (hop´ər), *n.* **1** person or thing that hops. **2** container to hold something and feed it into another part, usually larger at the top than at the bottom.

hop·scotch (hop´skoch´), *n.* a children's game in which the players hop over the lines of a figure drawn on the ground.

hor., 1 horizon. **2** horizontal.

horde (hôrd; hōrd), *n.* **1** crowd; swarm. **2** a wandering tribe or troop. [< F < G < Polish < Turk. *urdū* camp]

hore·hound (hôr´hound´; hōr´-), *n.* **1** plant with woolly, whitish leaves and clusters of small, whitish flowers. **2** a bitter extract made from the leaves of this plant. **3** candy or cough medicine flavored with it. [OE *hārhūne* < *hār* hoar + *hūne* name of a plant]

ho·ri·zon (hə rī´zən), *adj., n.* **1** line where the earth and sky seem to meet. **2** limit of one's thinking, experience, interest, or outlook. [< OF < L < Gk. *horizon* (*kyklos*) bounding (circle), ult. < *horos* limit]

hor·i·zon·tal (hôr´ə zon´təl; hōr´-), *adj.* **1** parallel to the horizon; at right angles to a vertical line. **2** flat; level. —*n.* a horizontal line, plane, direction, position, etc. —**hor´i·zon·tal´i·ty, hor´i·zon´tal·ness,** *n.* —**hor´i·zon´tal·ly,** *adv.*

hor·mone (hôr´mōn), *n.* **1** substance formed in certain parts of the body that enters the blood stream and influences the activity of some organ, as adrenalin and insulin. **2** any similar substance produced in plants. [< Gk. *hormon* setting in motion] —**hor·mo´nal,** *adj.*

horn (hôrn), *n.* **1** a hard growth, usually curved and pointed, on the heads of cattle, sheep, goats, and some other animals. **2** anything that sticks up on the head of an animal: *a snail's horns.* **3** container made of horn: *a powder horn.* **4** instrument sounded by blowing into the smaller end. **5** device sounded as a warning signal: *a foghorn.* **6** thing shaped like a horn: *a saddle horn.* —*adj.* made of horn. —*v.* furnish with horns.
horn in, meddle or intrude.
horns of a dilemma, two unpleasant choices, one of which must be taken.
lock horns, dispute; quarrel. [OE] —**horned,** *adj.* —**horn´less.** *adj.* —**horn´like´,** *adj.*

Horn (hôrn), *n.* **Cape,** cape on an island at the S tip of South America.

horn·bill (hôrn´bil´), *n.* a large bird having a very large bill with a horn or horny lump on it.

horn·blende (hôrn′blend′), *n.* a common black, dark-green, or brown mineral found in granite and other rocks. [< G] —**horn·blen′dic,** *adj.*

horn·book (hôrn′bŭk′), *n.* page with the alphabet, etc., on it, covered with a sheet of transparent horn and fastened in a frame with a handle, formerly used in teaching children to read.

horned toad, a small lizard with a broad, flat body, short tail, and many spines.

hor·net (hôr′nit), *n.* a large wasp that can give a very painful sting. [OE *hyrnet(u)*]

horn of plenty, =cornucopia.

horn·pipe (hôrn′pīp′), *n.* 1 a lively dance done by one person, formerly popular among sailors. 2 music for it.

horn·swog·gle (hôrn′swog′əl), *v.*, **-gled, -gling.** *Informal.* hoax; cheat.

horn·y (hôr′ni), *adj.*, **horn·i·er, horn·i·est.** 1 made of horn or a substance like it. 2 hard like a horn: *hands horny from work.* 3 having a horn or horns. —**horn′i·ness,** *n.*

ho·rol·o·gist (hō rol′ə jist), *n.* expert in horology.

ho·rol·o·gy (hō rol′ə ji), *n.* 1 science of measuring time. 2 art of making timepieces. —**hor′o·log′i·cal,** *adj.*

hor·o·scope (hôr′ə skōp; hor′-), *n.* 1 position of the planets at the hour of a person's birth, regarded as influencing his life. 2 diagram of the heavens at given times, used in telling fortunes. [< F < L < Gk. < *hora* hour + *skopos* watcher]

hor·ren·dous (hō ren′dəs; ho–), *adj.* horrible; terrible; frightful. —**hor·ren′dous·ly,** *adv.*

hor·ri·ble (hôr′ə bəl; hor′-) *adj.* 1 causing horror; terrible; dreadful; frightful; shocking. 2 extremely unpleasant or amazing. [< OF < L, < *horrere* bristle] —**hor′ri·ble·ness,** *n.* —**hor′ri·bly,** *adv.*

hor·rid (hôr′id; hor′-), *adj.* 1 terrible; frightful. 2 very unpleasant. –**hor′rid·ly,** *adv.* —**hor′rid·ness,** *n.*

hor·ri·fy (hôr′ə fī; hor′-), *v.*, **-fied, -fy·ing.** 1 cause to feel horror. 2 shock very much. —**hor·rif′ic,** *adj.* —**hor′ri·fi·ca′tion,** *n.*

hor·ror (hôr′ər; hor′-), *n.* 1 terror and disgust caused by something frightful. 2 very great disgust. 3 cause of horror. [< L, < *horrere* bristle]

hor·ror-strick·en (hôr′ər strik′ən; hor′-), **hor·ror-struck** (–struk′), *adj.* horrified.

hors d'oeu·vre (ôr′dėrv′; *Fr.* dœ′vrə), *pl.* **d'oeu·vres** (dėrvz′; *Fr.* dœ′vrə). relish or light food served before the regular courses of a meal, as olives, celery, anchovies, etc. [F, apart from (the main) work]

horse (hôrs), *n.*, *pl.* **hors·es** or (*esp. collectively*) **horse,** *v.*, **horsed, hors·ing,** *adj.* —*n.* 1 a four-legged animal with solid hoofs and flowing mane and tail, used from very early times to draw loads, carry riders, etc. 2 cavalry. 3 piece of gymnasium apparatus to jump or vault over. 4 frame with legs to support something; sawhorse. —*v.* 1 provide with a

horse or horses. 2 tease in a rough way; act boisterously. —*adj.* 1 having to do with horses. 2 on horses.

back the wrong horse, support a losing cause, candidate, etc.

beat a dead horse, persist in a fruitless effort.

from the horse's mouth, from an original or well-informed source.

hold one's horses, *Informal.* slow down or stop momentarily.

horse of another or **different color,** another matter altogether; utterly different. [OE *hors*]

horse·back (hôrs′bak′), *n.* the back of a horse. —*adv.* on the back of a horse.

horse chestnut, 1 a shade tree with spreading branches, large leaves, clusters of showy white flowers, and glossy brown nuts. 2 the nut. 3 any tree or shrub of the same family as the horse chestnut.

horse·flesh (hôrs′flesh′), *n.* 1 horses. 2 meat from horses.

horse·fly (hôrs′flī′), *n.*, *pl.* **-flies.** fly that bites horses.

horse·hair (hôrs′hār′), *n.* 1 hair from the mane or tail of a horse. 2 a stiff fabric made of this hair.

horse·hide (hôrs′hīd′), *n.* 1 hide of a horse. 2 leather made from this hide.

horse latitudes, two regions where there is often very calm weather, extending around the world at about 30° north and 30° south of the equator.

horse laugh, a loud, boisterous laugh.

horse·less (hôrs′lis), *adj.* 1 without a horse. 2 not requiring a horse; self-propelled: *automobiles were called horseless carriages.*

horse·man (hôrs′mən) *n.*, *pl.* **-men.** 1 man who rides on horseback. 2 man skilled in riding or managing horses. —**horse′man·ship,** *n.*

horse·play (hôrs′plā′), *n.* rough, boisterous fun.

horse·pow·er (hôrs′pou′ər), *n.* unit for measuring the power of engines, motors, etc.; 1 horsepower = 550 foot-pounds per second.

horse·rad·ish (hôrs′rad′ish), *n.* 1 a tall plant with a white, hot-tasting root that is ground up and used as a relish with meat, oysters, etc. 2 relish made of this root.

horse sense, common sense; plain, practical good sense.

horse·shoe (hôrsh′shü′; hôrs′-), *n.*, *v.*, **-shoed, -shoe·ing.** —*n.* 1 a U-shaped metal plate nailed to a horse's hoof to protect it. 2 thing shaped like a horseshoe. 3 **horseshoes** (*sing. in use*), game in which the players try to throw horseshoes over or near a stake. —*v.* put a horseshoe or horseshoes on. —**horse′sho′er,** *n.*

horseshoe crab, a crablike sea animal with a body shaped like a horseshoe and a long, spiny tail; king crab.

horse·tail (hôrs′tāl′), *n.* a flowerless plant with hollow, jointed stems and scalelike leaves at each joint.

horse-trade (hôrs′trād′), *v.*, **-trad·ed, -trad·ing.** buy or sell shrewdly. —**horse trade, horse trader.**

horse·whip (hôrs′hwip′), *n.*, *v.*, **-whipped, -whip·ping.** —*n.* whip for driving or controlling horses. —*v.* beat with a horsewhip.

horse·wom·an (hôrs′wum′ən), *n.*, *pl.* **-wom·en.** 1 woman who rides on horseback. 2 woman skilled in riding or managing horses.

hors·y (hôr′si), *adj.*, **hors·i·er, hors·i·est.** 1 having to do with horses. 2 fond of horses or horse racing. 3 dressing or talking like people who spend much time with horses. 4 large and awkward in appearance. Also, **horsey.** —**hors′i·ness,** *n.*

hort., horticultural; horticulture.

hor·ta·to·ry (hôr′tə tô′ri; –tō′–), *adj.* serving to urge or encourage; giving advice; exhorting. [< LL, < L *hortari* exhort]

hor·ti·cul·ture hôr′tə kul′chər), *n.* 1 science of growing flowers, fruits, vegetables, etc. 2 cultivation of a garden. [< L *hortus* garden + *cultura* cultivation] —**hor′ti·cul′tur·al,** *adj.* —**hor′ti·cul′tur·ist,** *n.*

ho·san·na (hō zan′ə), *interj.* shout of praise to the Lord. —*n.* a shout of "hosanna." [< LL < Gk. < Heb. *hōshī′āh nna* save now, we pray]

hose (hōz), *n.*, *pl.* **hose,** *v.*, **hosed, hos·ing.** —*n.* 1 stockings. 2 a close-fitting outer garment extending from the waist to the toes, formerly worn by men. 3 tube made of rubber, canvas, or other flexible material, used to carry water or other liquids for short distances. —*v.* put water on with a hose. [OE *hosa*]

Ho·se·a (hō zē′ə; –zā′ə), *n.* 1 book of the Old Testament. 2 its author, a Hebrew prophet who lived in the eighth century B.C.

ho·sier (hō′zhər), *n.* person who makes or sells hosiery.

ho·sier·y (hō′zher i), *n.* 1 hose; stockings; 2 business of a hosier.

hos·pice (hos′pis), *n.* 1 house where travelers can lodge. 2 **a** a place where people who are dying are cared for. **b** special care in the home for people near death. [< F < L *hospitium* < *hospes* guest, host[1]]

hos·pi·ta·ble (hos′pi tə bəl; hos pit′ə–), *adj.* 1 giving a welcome, food and shelter, and friendly treatment to guests or strangers: *a hospitable family.* 2 willing and ready to entertain; receptive: *hospitable to new ideas.* —**hos′pi·ta·ble·ness,** *n.* —**hos′pi·ta·bly,** *adv.*

hos·pi·tal (hos′pi təl) *n.* 1 place where sick or injured people are cared for. 2 similar place for animals. [< OF < Med. L *hospitale* inn. See HOST[1].]

hos·pi·tal·i·ty (hos′pə tal′ə ti), *n.*, *pl.* **-ties.** friendly, generous reception and treatment of guests or strangers. [< L *hospitalitas.* See HOST[1].]

hos·pi·tal·ize (hos′pi təl īz), *v.*, **-ized, -iz·ing.** put in a hospital. —**hos′pi·tal·i·za′tion,** *n.*

host¹ (hōst), *n.* **1** person who receives another at his or her house as a guest. **2** keeper of an inn or hotel. **3** plant or animal in or on which a parasite lives. [< OF < L *hospes* guest, host]

host² (hōst), *n.* **1** a large number; multitude. **2** army. [< OF < LL *hostis* army < L, enemy (orig., stranger)]

Host (hōst), *n.* bread or water used in the Eucharist. [< OF *oiste* < L *hostia* animal sacrificed]

hos·tage (hos'tij), *n.* person given up to another or held by an enemy as a pledge that certain promises, agreements, etc., will be carried out. [< OF, ult. < L *hospes* guest]

hos·tel (hos'təl), *n.* a lodging place, esp. a supervised lodging place for young people on bicycle trips, hikes, etc.; inn; hotel. [< OF < *oste* HOST¹. Doublet of HOTEL.] —**hos'tel·er,** *n.*

hos·tel·ry (hos'təl ri), *n., pl.* –**ries.** inn; hotel.

host·ess (hōs'tis), *n.* **1** woman who receives another person as her guest. **2** woman whose job is to welcome and help guests at a hotel, restaurant, etc. **3** female flight attendant. **4** female innkeeper. **5** woman paid to entertain or dance with guests, travelers, etc.

hos·tile (hos'təl; *sometimes* hos'tīl), *adj.* **1** of an enemy or enemies. **2** opposed; unfriendly; unfavorable. [< L, < *hostis* enemy] —**hos'tile·ly,** *adv.*

hos·til·i·ty (hos til'ə ti), *n., pl.* –**ties. 1** being an enemy; unfriendliness. **2** state of being at war. **3** opposition; resistance. **hostilities,** acts of war; warfare; fighting.

hos·tler (os'lər; hos'–), *n.* person who takes care of horses at an inn or stable. Also, **ostler.**

hot (hot), *adj.,* **hot·ter, hot·test,** *adv.* —*adj.* **1** having much heat: *fire is hot, food too hot to eat.* **2** having a sharp, burning taste: *peppers are hot.* **3** actively conducting current: *a hot wire.* **4** radioactive: *hot debris.* **5** full of strong feeling: *hot with anger.* **6** full of enthusiasm; eager. **7** new; fresh: *a hot scent.* **8** following closely: *in hot pursuit.* **9** obtained illegally. —*adv.* in a hot manner.

hot up, *Informal.* **a** heat something up; warm. **b** *Fig.* make livelier or more exciting.

make it hot for, *Informal.* make trouble or difficulties for. [OE *hāt*] —**hot'ly,** *adv.* —**hot'ness,** *n.*

hot air, empty talk or writing.

hot·bed (hot'bed'), *n.* **1** bed of earth covered with glass and kept warm for growing plants. **2** *Fig.* place favorable to rapid growth, esp. of something unwanted or dangerous.

hot·blood·ed (hot'blud'id), *adj.* **1** easily excited or angered. **2** passionate.

hot cake, =griddle cake.

sell or **go like hot cakes,** sell quickly or well.

hot cross bun, bun marked with a cross, usually eaten during Lent or on Good Friday.

hot dog, 1 a hot frankfurter enclosed in a roll. **2** =frankfurter. **3** skillful athlete. **4** a show-off.

ho·tel (hō tel'), *n.* house or large building that provides lodging, food, etc., to travelers and others. [< F *hôtel* < OF *hostel.* Doublet of HOSTEL.]

hot·foot (hot'fût'), *adv.* in great haste. —*v.* go in great haste; hurry.

hot·head (hot'hed'), *n.* a hot-headed person.

hot·head·ed (hot'hed'id), *adj.* **1** having a fiery temper. **2** impetuous; rash. —**hot'-head'ed·ly,** *adv.* —**hot'-head'ed·ness,** *n.*

hot·house (hot'hous'), *n.* =greenhouse. —*adj.* of or from a greenhouse: *hothouse grapes.*

hot rod, a stripped-down, usually older, automobile with a supercharged motor and other modifications for speed.

hot seat, an uncomfortable situation.

hot·shot or **hot·shot,** (hot'shot'), *n.* highly skilled person, esp. one who seems self-important.

hot spot, 1 dangerous or violent place. **2** popular bar, club, etc.

hot-tem·pered (hot'tem'pərd), *adj.* easily angered.

Hot·ten·tot (hot'ən tot), *n.* **1** member of a South African race having a dark, yellowish-brown complexion. **2** their language.

hot tub, large vat filled with hot water circulated through jets, in which a person or group of people soak, for relaxation or therapy.

hot water, *Informal.* trouble; difficulty.

hou·dah (hou'də), *n.* =howdah.

hough (hok), *n.* =hock¹.

hound (hound), *n.* **1** dog of any of various breeds, most of which hunt by scent and have large, drooping ears and short hair. **2** any dog. **3** person who is very fond of something. —*v.* **1** hunt; chase. **2** urge (on). [OE *hund*]

hour (our), *n.* **1** 60 minutes; $\frac{1}{24}$ of a day. **2** one of the 12 points that measure time from noon to midnight and from midnight to noon. **3** time of day. Some clocks strike the hours. **4** a particular time: *the breakfast hour, the man of the hour.*

hours, a time for something, as for study or doing business: *our hours are 9–5.* **b** usual time for getting up and going to bed: *keeps long hours.* [< OF < L < Gk. *hora* season, time, hour]

hour·glass (our'glas'; –gläs'), *n.* device for measuring time, requiring just an hour for its contents (sand or mercury) to go from the container on top to one on the bottom.

hou·ri (hûr'i; hou'ri), *n., pl.* –**ris.** a young, eternally beautiful girl of the Muslim paradise. [< F < Pers. *ḥūri* < Ar. *ḥūr* black-eyed]

hour·ly (our'li), *adj.* **1** done, happening, or counted every hour. **2** coming very often; frequent. —*adv.* **1** every hour; hour by hour. **2** very often; frequently.

house (*n.* hous; *v.* houz), *n., pl.* **hous·es** (houz'iz), *v.,* **housed, hous·ing.** —*n.* **1** a building in which people live. **2** a building to hold anything: *greenhouse, warehouse.* **3** lawmaking body: *the House of Representatives.* **4** a business firm. **5** theater. **6** audience. **7** family, esp. a noble or royal family. —*v.* **1** put or provide with a house. **2** give shelter to; harbor.

bring down the house, be loudly applauded.

clean house, a thoroughly clean a home. **b** *Fig.* get rid of unsatisfactory employees, practices, etc., in a business or organization.

keep house, manage a home and its affairs; do housework.

on the house, paid for by the owner of the business; free. [OE *hūs*] —**house'less,** *adj.*

house arrest, legally confined to one's house, rather than being in jail.

house·boat (hous'bōt'), *n.* boat used as a place to live in.

house·break·er (hous'brāk'ər), *n.* person who breaks into a house to steal or commit some other crime. —**house'break'ing,** *n.*

house·bro·ken (hous'brō'ken), *adj.* of a dog, cat, etc., trained to live indoors.

house·coat (hous'kōt'), *n.* a light dress-like garment with a long skirt, for casual wear in one's home.

house·fly (hous'flī'), *n., pl.* –**flies.** a two-winged fly that lives around and in houses, feeding on food, garbage, and filth.

house·hold (hous'hōld'), *n.* **1** all the people living in a house; family. **2** home and its affairs. —*adj.* of a household; having to do with a household; domestic: *household expenses.*

house·hold·er (hous'hōl'dər), *n.* **1** person who owns or lives in a house. **2** head of a family.

house·keep·er (hous'kēp'ər), *n.* **1** person who manages a home and its affairs and does the housework. **2** woman who directs the servants that do the housework. —**house'keep',** *v.* —**house'keep'ing,** *n.*

house·lights (hous'līts'), *n.* lights used to illuminate a theater before and after a performance.

house·maid (hous'mād'), *n.* woman servant who does housework.

House of Burgesses, the lower house of the colonial legislature in Virginia or Maryland.

House of Commons, the lower, elective branch of the lawmaking body of Great Britain and Northern Ireland, or of Canada.

house of correction, place of confinement and reform for persons convicted of minor offenses and not regarded as confirmed criminals.

House of Delegates, the lower branch of the legislature in Maryland, Virginia, and West Virginia.

House of Lords, the upper, nonelective branch of the lawmaking body of Great Britain and Northern Ireland, composed of nobles and clergymen of high rank.

House of Representatives, 1 the lower branch of the lawmaking body of the United States. **2** the lower branch of the lawmaking body of certain states of the United States. **3** the lower branch of the Parliament of Australia, or of the general assembly of New Zealand.

house party, entertainment of guests in a home for a few days.

house-sit (hous′sit′), *v.* live in a home and take care of it while the owners or occupants are away. **—house′-sit′ter,** *n.*

house-top (hous′top′), *n.* top of a house; roof.

from the housetops, publicly or loudly.

house·warm·ing (hous′wôr′ming), *n.* party given when a family moves into a new home.

house·wife (hous′wīf′), *n., pl.* **-wives.** woman who is the head of a household. **—house′wife′ly,** *adj.* **—house′wife′li·ness,** *n.*

house·work (hous′wėrk′), *n.* work to be done in housekeeping, such as washing, ironing, cleaning, sweeping, or cooking.

house wrecker, 1 person whose occupation is demolishing houses and other buildings. **2** *Fig.* a disruptive person.

hous·ing (houz′ing), *n.* **1** act of sheltering; provision of homes. **2** houses. **3** shelter; covering. **4** frame or plate to hold part of a machine in place.

hove (hōv), *v.* pt. and pp. of **heave.**

hov·el (huv′əl; hov′–), *n.* **1** house that is small, mean, and unpleasant to live in. **2** an open shed for sheltering cattle, tools, etc. [ME]

hov·er (huv′ər; hov′–), *v.* **1** stay in or near one place in the air: *the two birds hovered over their nest.* **2** wait near at hand. **3** be in an uncertain condition; waver: *the sick man hovered between life and death.* —*n.* **1** act of hovering. **2** state of hovering. [ME *hover(en)* < *hoven* hover] **—hov′er·er,** *n.* **—hov′er·ing·ly,** *adv.*

hov·er·craft (huv′ər kraft; hov′–; –kräft), *n.* vehicle which travels just above the ground or water on a cushion of air created by a system of fans.

how (hou), *adv.* **1** in what way: *tell her how to do it.* **2** to what degree: *how long?* **3** in what state or condition: *tell me how Mrs. Jones is.* **4** why: *how is it you are late?* —*n.* way or manner of doing: *she considered all the hows and wherefores.*

and how, *Informal.* certainly; very much.

how about, *Informal.* would you like to or would you consider: *how about a movie tonight?*

how far, to what point: *how far did they get?* [OE *hū*]

how·dah (hou′də), *n.* seat for persons riding on the back of an elephant. [< Hind. < Ar. *haudaj*]

how·e′er (hou âr′), *conj., adv.* however.

how·ev·er (hou ev′ər), *adv.* **1** to whatever degree or amount; no matter how. **2** in whatever way; by whatever means. —*conj.* nevertheless; yet.

how·itz·er (hou′it sər), *n.* a short cannon for firing shells in a high curve. [earlier *howitz* < Du. < G < Czech *houfnice* catapult]

howl (houl), *v.* **1** give a long, loud, mournful cry. Dogs and wolves howl. **2** give a long, loud cry of pain, rage, scorn, etc. **3** yell; shout: *howl with laughter.* **4** force or drive by howling. —*n.* **1** a long, loud, mournful cry. **2** a loud cry of pain, rage, etc. **3** yell; shout.

howl down, drown out someone's speech with loud sounds like howling. [ME *houle(n)*]

howl·er (houl′ər), *n.* **1** person or thing that howls. **2** a ridiculous mistake; stupid blunder.

how·so·ev·er (hou′sō ev′ər), *adv.* **1** to whatever degree or amount. **2** in whatever way.

how-to (hou′tü), *adj.* showing how something is done.

hoy·den (hoi′den), *n.* a boisterous, romping girl; tomboy. —*adj.* boisterous; rude. Also, **hoiden.** **—hoy′den·ish,** *adj.* **—hoy′den·ish·ly,** *adv.* **—hoy′den·ish·ness,** *n.*

Hoyle (hoil), *n.* **1** book of rules and instructions for playing card games. **2** **according to Hoyle,** according to the rules or customs; fair.

HP, H.P., hp., or **h.p.,** horsepower.

H.Q., h.q., headquarters.

hr., *pl.* **hrs.** hour.

H.R., House of Representatives.

H.R.H., His (Her) Royal Highness.

ht., height.

html, Hyper Text Markup Language, used to format World Wide Web documents.

http, Hyper Text Transfer Protocol, used to determine how messages are formatted and transmitted on the World Wide Web.

hua·ra·ches (hə rä′chiz), *n.* leather sandals that have no heel. [< Mex. Sp. *huaraches*]

hub (hub), *n.* **1** the central part of a wheel. **2** any center of interest, importance, activity, etc.

hub·bub (hub′ub), *n.* a noisy tumult; uproar.

hu·bris (hū′bris), *n.* arrogant self-confidence. [< Gk. *hýbris*]

huck·le·ber·ry (huk′əl ber′i), *n., pl.* **-ries.** **1** a small berry like a blueberry, but darker. **2** shrub that it grows on.

huck·ster (huk′stər), *n.* **1** peddler. **2** person who sells small articles. **3** mean and unfair trader. —*v.* sell; peddle; haggle. [cf. MDu. *hokester.* See HAWK².]

hud·dle (hud′əl), *v.,* **-dled, -dling,** *n.* —*v.* **1** crowd, close: *the sheep huddled together in a corner.* **2** nestle in a heap: *the cat huddled itself on the cushion.* **3** group together behind the line of scrimmage to receive signals. —*n.* **1** a confused heap, mass, or crowd. **2** a grouping of players behind the line of scrimmage to receive signals.

go into a huddle, confer secretly.

Hud·son (hud′sən), *n.* river in E New York State, flowing into New York Bay.

Hudson Bay, a large bay in C Canada.

hue¹ (hū), *n.* **1** color. **2** that quality whereby one color (as red) differs from other colors (as blue, green, etc.). **3** a particular color: *a greenish hue.* [OE *hīw*] **—hued,** *adj.*

hue² (hū), *n.* a shouting.

hue and cry, shouts of alarm or protest. [< F *hu* < *huer*]

huff (huf), *n.* fit of anger or peevishness. —*v.* **1** make angry; offend. **2** puff; blow.

huff·y (huf′i), *adj.,* **huff·i·er, huff·i·est.** **1** offended. **2** easily offended; touchy. **—huff′i·ly,** *adv.* **—huff′i·ness,** *n.*

hug (hug), *v.,* **hugged, hug·ging,** *n.* —*v.* **1** put the arms around and hold close, esp. in affection. **2** cling firmly or fondly to: *hug an opinion.* **3** keep close to: *the boat hugged the shore.* —*n.* a tight clasp with the arms. [cf. Scand. *hugga* comfort]

huge (hūj), *adj.,* **hug·er, hug·est.** extremely large. [< OF *ahuge*] **—huge′ly,** *adv.* **—huge′ness,** *n.*

Hu·gue·not (hū′gə not), *n.* a French Protestant of the 16th and 17th centuries.

hu·la (hü′lə), *n., pl.* **-las,** *v.* **-laed, -la·ing.** —*n.* a native Hawaiian dance. —*v.* dance the hula. [< Hawaiian]

hula hoop, large plastic hoop swung around the body by rotating the hips.

hulk (hulk), *n.* **1** body of an old or worn-out ship. **2** ship used as a prison. **3** a big, clumsy ship. **4** a big, clumsy person or thing. [OE *hulc,* ? < Med.L < Gk. *holkas* merchant ship]

hulk·ing (hul′king), *adj.* big and clumsy.

hull¹ (hul), *n.* **1** the outer covering of a seed. **2** calyx of some fruits, such as the green frill of a strawberry. **3** any outer covering. —*v.* remove the hull or hulls from. [OE *hulu*] **—hull′er,** *n.*

hull² (hul), *n.* body or frame of a ship, exclusive of masts, sails, or rigging. [? same word as *hull¹*]

hul·la·ba·loo (hul′ə bə lü′), *n.* =uproar.

hul·lo (hə lō′), *interj., n., pl.* **-los,** *v.,* **-loed, -lo·ing.** =hello.

hum (hum), *v.,* **hummed, hum·ming,** *n., interj.* —*v.* **1** make a continuous murmuring sound: *the sewing machine hums busily.* **2** sing with closed lips, not sounding words. **3** be busy and active: *make things hum.* —*n.* **1** a continuous murmuring sound: *the hum of the city street.* **2** a singing with closed lips, not sounding words. —*interj.* a low sound like that of the letter *m.* [imit.] **—hum′mer,** *n.*

hu·man (hū′mən), *adj.* **1** of a person or people; that a person or people have: *selfishness is a human weakness, human affairs, beyond human power.* **2** being a person or persons; having the form or qualities of people: *children are human beings, he is more human than his brother.* —*n.* a human being; person. [< OF < L *humanus*] —**hu′man·ness,** *n.*

hu·mane (hū mān′), *adj.* kind; merciful; not cruel or brutal. [var. of *human*] —**hu·mane′ly,** *adv.* —**hu·mane′ness,** *n.*

hu·man·ism (hū′mən iz əm), *n.* **1** study of the humanities. **2** Sometimes, **Humanism,** the principles or culture of the scholars of the Renaissance. —**hu′man·ist,** *n.* —**hu′man·is′tic,** *adj.*

hu·man·i·tar·i·an (hū man′ə tãr′i ən), *adj.* helpful to humanity; philanthropic. —*n.* person who is devoted to the welfare of all human beings. [< *humanity*; patterned after *unitarian,* etc.] —**hu·man′i·tar′i·an·ism,** *n.*

hu·man·i·ty (hū man′ə ti), *n., pl.* **-ties. 1** human beings taken as a group; people: *advances in science help all humanity.* **2** fact of being human; human character or quality. **3** fact of being humane; humane treatment; kindness: *treat animals with humanity.*

the humanities, a the Latin and Greek languages and literatures. **b** languages, literatures, art, etc. **c** branches of learning concerned with humans.

hu·man·ize (hū′mən īz), *v.,* **-ized, -izing. 1** make human; give a human character or quality to. **2** make humane; cause to be kind or merciful. —**hu′man·i·za′tion,** *n.* —**hu′man·iz′er,** *n.*

hu·man·kind (hū′mən kīnd′), *n.* human beings; people; human race; mankind.

hu·man·ly (hū′mən li), *adv.* **1** in a human manner; by human means. **2** according to the feelings, knowledge, or experience of people.

human nature, qualities and characteristics shared by human beings.

hu·man·oid (hū′mə noid), *adj.* of human form; having human characteristics; like a human. —*n.* a humanoid being. Also, **hominoid.**

hum·ble (hum′bəl), *adj.,* **-bler, -blest,** *v.,* **-bled, -bling.** —*adj.* **1** low in position or condition: *a humble place to live.* **2** modest in spirit. **3** courteously respectful: *in my humble opinion.* —*v.* make humble. [< OF < L *humilis* low < *humus* earth] —**hum′ble·ness,** *n.* —**hum′bler,** *n.* —**hum′bly,** *adv.*

hum·ble·bee (hum′bəl bē′), *n.* =bumblebee. [ME *humbalbee,* ult. < *hum*]

humble pie. eat humble pie, be forced to do something very disagreeable and humiliating.

hum·bug (hum′bug′), *n., v.,* **-bugged, -bug·ging.** —*n.* **1** a cheat; sham. **2** quality of falseness, deception, etc. —*v.* deceive with a sham; cheat. —**hum′bug′ger,** *n.*

hum·ding·er (hum ding′ər), *n. Informal.* someone or something remarkable, exceptional.

hum·drum (hum′drum′), *adj.* without variety; dull. —*n.* humdrum routine.

hu·mer·us (hū′mər əs), *n., pl.* **-mer·i** (-mər ī), **1** the long bone in the upper part of the forelimb or arm, from the shoulder to the elbow. **2** the upper part of the forelimb or arm. [< L *umerus*] —**hu′mer·al,** *adj.*

hu·mid (hū′mid), *adj.* moist; characterized by much moisture in the air: *a humid region.* [< L *umidus < umere* be moist] —**hu′mid·ly,** *adv.* —**hu′mid·ness,** *n.*

hu·mid·i·fy (hū mid′ə fī), *v.,* **-fied, -fy·ing.** make humid, moist, or damp. —**hu·mid′i·fi·ca′tion,** *n.* —**hu·mid′i·fi′er,** *n.*

hu·mid·i·ty (hū mid′ə ti), *n.* moistness; amount of moisture in the air.

hu·mi·dor (hū′mə dôr′), *n.* box, jar, etc., for keeping things, esp. tobacco, moist.

hu·mil·i·ate (hū mil′i āt), *v.,* **-at·ed, -at·ing.** lower the pride, dignity, or self-respect of: *humiliated by failure.* [< L, < *humilis* HUMBLE] —**hu·mil′i·at′ing·ly,** *adv.* —**hu·mil′i·a′tion,** *n.*

hu·mil·i·ty (hū mil′ə ti), *n., pl.* **-ties.** humbleness of mind; meekness.

hum·ming·bird (hum′ing bėrd′), *n.* a very small, brightly colored American bird with a long, narrow bill and narrow wings that make a humming sound.

hum·mock (hum′ək), *n.* a very small, rounded hill; knoll; hillock. —**hum′mock·y,** *adj.*

hu·mor (hū′mər; ū′–), *n.* **1** funny or amusing quality: *I see no humor in your tricks.* **2** ability to see or show the funny or amusing side of things. **3** state of mind; mood; disposition: *success puts you in good humor.* **4** fancy; whim. —*v.* give in to the fancies or whims of (a person); indulge: *a sick person has to be humored.* [< L *umor* fluid] —**hu′mor·less,** *adj.*

hu·mor·esque (hū′mər esk′), *n.* a light, playful, or humorous piece of music.

hu·mor·ist (hū′mər ist; ū′–), *n.* a humorous talker; writer of jokes and funny stories. —**hu′mor·is′tic,** *adj.*

hu·mor·ous (hū′mər əs; ū′–), *adj.* full of humor; funny; amusing. —**hu′mor·ous·ly** *adv.* —**hu′mor·ous·ness,** *n.*

hump (hump), *n.* **1** a rounded lump that sticks out. **2** mound. —*v.* **1** raise or bend up into a lump: *the cat humped her back when she saw the dog.* **2** *U.S.* exert (oneself). [cf. Du. *homp* lump] —**humped,** *adj.* —**hump′less,** *adj.*

hump·back (hump′bak′), *n.* **1** =hunchback. **2** a large whale that has a humplike dorsal fin. —**hump′backed′,** *adj.*

humph (humf), *interj., n.* exclamation expressing doubt, disgust, contempt, etc.

Hump·ty-Dump·ty (hump′ti dump′ti), *n.* anything broken or smashed beyond repair, as a plan, idea, etc. [the name of the egg-shaped figure in the nursery rhyme]

hump·y (hump′i), *adj.,* **hump·i·er, hump·i·est. 1** full of humps. **2** humplike.

hu·mus (hū′məs), *n.* soil made from decayed leaves and other vegetable matter, containing valuable plant foods. [< L, earth]

Hun (hun), *n.* **1** member of a warlike Asiatic people who overran E and C Europe between about A.D. 375 and 453. **2** *Fig.* a barbarous, destructive person; vandal.

hunch (hunch), *v.* **1** hump. **2** draw, bend, or form into a lump: *he sat hunched up with his chin between his knees.* **3** move, push, or shove by jerks. —*n.* **1** a hump. **2** a vague feeling or suspicion: *a hunch it would rain.*

hunch·back (hunch′bak′), *n.* person with a hump on his or her back; humpback. —**hunch′backed′,** *adj.*

hun·dred (hun′drəd), *n., pl.* **-dreds** or (*as after a numeral*) **-dred,** *adj.* —*n.* **1** a cardinal number, ten times ten. **2** symbol of this number; 100. —*adj.* ten times ten; 100. [OE] —**hun′dredth,** *adj.*

hun·dred·fold (hun′drəd fōld′), *adj., adv.* a hundred times as much or as many.

hun·dred·weight (hun′drəd wāt′), *n., pl.* **-weights** or (*as after a numeral*) **-weight.** measure of weight, equal to 100 pounds in the United States or 112 pounds in England.

hung (hung), *v.* pt. and pp. of **hang.**

hung up, *Informal.* **a** delayed or stopped. **b** in difficulty; anxious.

hung up on, *Informal.* **a** obsessed with. **b** too attached to.

Hung., 1 Hungarian. **2** Hungary.

Hun·gar·i·an (hung gãr′i ən), *adj.* of Hungary, its people, or their language. —*n.* **1** native or inhabitant of Hungary; Magyar. **2** language of Hungary; Magyar.

Hun·ga·ry (hung′gə ri), *n.* country in C Europe, formerly a part of Austria-Hungary.

hun·ger (hung′gər), *n.* **1** painful feeling or weak condition caused by lack of food. **2** desire or need for food. **3** a strong desire: *a hunger for kindness.* —*v.* **1** feel hunger; be hungry. **2** have a strong desire. [OE *hungor*] —**hun′ger·ing·ly,** *adv.*

hunger strike, refusal to eat until certain demands are granted.

hung·o·ver (hung′ō′vər), *adj.* suffering from a hangover; miserable.

hun·gry (hung′gri), *adj.,* **-gri·er, -griest. 1** feeling a desire or need for food. **2** showing hunger: *a hungry look.* **3** having a strong desire or craving; eager: *hungry for books.* —**hun′gri·ly,** *adv.* —**hun′gri·ness,** *n.*

hunk (hungk), *n.* **1** a big lump or piece. **2** *Informal.* muscular, attractive man.

hunk·er (hung′kər), *v.* crouch on one's haunches.

hunker down, wait patiently or guardedly.

hunt (hunt), *v.* **1** chase or go after (wild animals, game birds, etc.) for food or sport. **2** drive (out, away); pursue. **3** try to find; search carefully: *hunt through drawers.* —*n.* **1** act of hunting. **2** group of persons hunting together. **3** attempt to find something; thorough look; careful search.

hunt down, a hunt for until found or killed. **b** look or search for until found.

hunt up, look for or find by searching: *hunt up old friends.* [OE *huntian*]

hunt·er (hun′tər), *n.* **1** person who hunts. **2** horse or dog for hunting.

hunting horn, horn used in a hunt.

hunt·ress (hun′tris), *n.* woman who hunts.

hunts·man (hunts′mən), *n., pl.* **-men.** hunter.

hur·dle (hèr′dəl), *n., v.,* **-dled, -dling.** —*n.* **1** barrier for people or horses to jump over in a race. **2** obstacle; difficulty. —*v.* **1** jump over. **2** overcome (an obstacle, difficulty, etc.).

hurdles, race in which the runners jump over hurdles. [OE *hyrdel*] —**hur′dler,** *n.*

hur·dy-gur·dy (hèr′di gèr′di), *n., pl.* **-dies.** a barrel organ or street piano played by turning a handle. [? imit.]

hurl (hèrl), *v.* **1** throw with much force. **2** fling forth (words, cries, etc.) violently; utter with vehemence. —*n.* a forcible or violent throw. [cf. LG *hurreln*] —**hurl′er,** *n.*

hurl·y-burl·y (hèr′li bèr′li), *n., pl.* **-burl·ies,** disorder and noise; tumult.

Hu·ron (hyùr′ən), *n.* **1** Lake, the second largest of the five Great Lakes, between the United States and Canada. **2** member of a tribe of Iroquois Indians. —*adj.* of this tribe.

hur·rah (hə rä′; -rô′), **hur·ray** (hə rä′), *interj., n.* shout of joy, approval, etc. —*v.* shout hurrahs; cheer.

hur·ri·cane (hèr′i kān), *n.* **1** a tropical cyclone; storm with violent wind and, usually, very heavy rain. **2** a sudden, violent outburst. [< Sp. *huracán* < Carib]

hur·ried (hèr′id), *adj.* **1** forced to hurry. **2** done or made in a hurry; hasty. —**hur′ried·ly,** *adv.* —**hur′ried·ness,** *n.*

hur·ry (hèr′i), *v.,* **-ried, -ry·ing,** *n., pl.* **-ries.** —*v.* **1** drive, carry, send, or move with more than natural speed. **2** urge to act soon or with great speed. **3** cause to hasten. —*n.* **1** a hurried action. **2** eagerness to have or do quickly.

hurry up! move faster; get a move on. —**hur′ry·ing·ly,** *adv.*

hur·ry-scur·ry (hèr′i skèr′i), *n., pl.* **-ries,** *adj., adv.* —*n.* a hurrying and confusion. —*adj.* hurried and confused. —*adv.* with hurrying and confusion.

hurt (hèrt), *v.,* **hurt, hurt·ing,** *n.* —*v.* **1** cause pain, harm, or damage. **2** suffer pain. **3** have a bad effect on. —*n.* **1** pain; injury; wound. **2** a bad effect; damage; harm. [appar. < OF *hurter* strike < Gmc.] —**hurt′er,** *n.* —**hurt′less,** *adj.*

hurt·ful (hèrt′fəl), *adj.* causing hurt, harm, or damage; injurious. —**hurt′ful·ly,** *adv.* —**hurt′ful·ness,** *n.*

hur·tle (hèr′təl), *v.,* **-tled, -tling. 1** dash or drive violently; rush suddenly; come with a crash: *spears hurtled against shields.* **2** move with a clatter; rush noisily or violently: *the train hurtled past.* [? < *hurt*]

hus·band (huz′bənd), *n.* man who has a wife; married man. —*v.* manage carefully; be saving of: *husband one's resources.* [OE *húsbónda* < *hús* house + *bónda* head of family < Scand. *bóndi*] —**hus′band·less,** *adj.*

hus·band·man (huz′bənd mən), *n., pl.* **-men.** =farmer.

hus·band·ry (huz′bənd ri), *n.* **1** farming. **2** management of one's affairs or resources. **3** careful management.

hush (hush), *v.* **1** stop making a noise; make or become silent or quiet. **2** soothe; calm. —*n.* a stopping of noise; silence; quiet. —*interj.* stop the noise! be silent! keep quiet!

hush up a keep from being told; stop discussion of. **b** be quiet! [< ME *hussht* silent]

hush money, money paid to keep a person from telling something.

hush-pup·py (hush′pup i), *n.* small ball of corn meal, deep-fried.

husk (husk), *n.* **1** the dry outer covering of certain seeds or fruits. An ear of corn has a husk. **2** the dry or worthless outer covering of anything. —*v.* remove the husk from. [ME *huske*] —**husk′er,** *n.*

husk·y[1] (hus′ki), *adj.,* **husk·i·er, husk·i·est,** *n., pl.* **husk·ies.** —*adj.* **1** dry in the throat; hoarse; rough of voice. **2** of, like, or having husks. **3** big and strong. —*n.* a big, strong person. —**husk′i·ly,** *adv.* —**husk′i·ness,** *n.*

Husk·y, husk·y[2] (hus′ki), *n., pl.* **Husk·ies, husk·ies.** an Eskimo dog.

Huss (hus), *n.* **John,** 1369?–1415, Bohemian religious reformer. —**Huss′ite,** *n.*

hus·sar (hù zär′), *n.* a European light-armed cavalry soldier. [< Hung. < OSerbian < Ital. *corsaro* runner. See CORSAIR.]

hus·sy (huz′i; hus′-), *n., pl.* **-sies. 1** a bad-mannered or pert girl. **2** a worthless woman.

hus·tings (hus′tingz), *n. pl. or sing.* platform from which speeches are made in a political campaign. [< Scand. *hústhing* council < *hús* house + *thing* assembly]

hus·tle (hus′əl), *v.,* **-tled, -tling,** *n.* —*v.* **1** hurry. **2** force hurriedly or roughly; jostle rudely. **3** work with tireless energy. —*n.* **1** a hurry. **2** a rough pushing; rude jostling. **3** tireless energy. [< Du. *hutselen* shake] —**hus′tler,** *n.*

hut (hut), *n.* a small, roughly built house; small cabin. [< F < G *hütte*] —**hut′like′,** *adj.*

hutch (huch), *n.* **1** pen for rabbits, etc. **2** box; chest; bin. **3** cabinet with open shelves on top for dishes. —*v.* put in a hutch; hoard. [< OF < Med.L *hutica* chest]

Hu·tu (hü′tü), *n.* member of a Bantu-speaking people of Rwanda and Burundi.

huz·za (hə zä′), *interj., n., pl.* **-zas,** *v.,* **-zaed, -za·ing.** —*interj., n.* a loud shout of joy, encouragement, or applause; hurrah. —*v.* shout huzzas; cheer.

hy·a·cinth (hī′ə sinth), *n.* **1** plant of the lily family that grows from a bulb and has a spike of small, fragrant, bell-shaped flowers. **2** a reddish-orange gem; a variety of zircon. [< L < Gk. *hyakinthos* kind of flower]

hy·a·lu·ron·i·dase (hī′ə lü ron′ə dās), *n.* enzyme that aids the circulation of body fluids.

hy·brid (hī′brid), *n.* **1** offspring of two animals or plants of different species, varieties, etc. A loganberry is a hybrid between a raspberry and blackberry. **2** anything of mixed origin. A word formed of parts from different languages is a hybrid. —*adj.* **1** bred from two different species, varieties, etc. A mule is a hybrid animal. **2** of mixed origin. [< L *hybrida,* var. of *ibrida* mongrel, hybrid] —**hy′brid·ism,** *n.*

hy·brid·ize (hī′brid īz), *v.,* **-ized, -iz·ing. 1** cause to produce hybrids. Botanists hybridize different kinds of plants to get new varieties. **2** produce hybrids. —**hy′brid·i·za′tion,** *n.*

hy·dra (hī′drə), *n., pl.* **-dras, -drae** (-drē). **1** any persistent evil. **2** kind of freshwater polyp, so called because when the body is cut into pieces, each piece forms a new individual. **3 Hydra,** *Gk. Legend.* a monstrous serpent having nine heads. [< L < Gk., water serpent]

hy·dran·gea (hī drān′jə), *n.* shrub with opposite leaves and large, showy clusters of small white, pink, or blue flowers. [< NL, < Gk. *hydor* water + *angeion* vessel, capsule]

hy·drant (hī′drənt), *n.* an upright street fixture from which water may be drawn to fight fires, wash the streets, etc. [< Gk. *hydor* water]

hy·drate (hī′drāt), *n., v.,* **-drat·ed, -drat·ing.** —*n.* compound produced when certain substances unite with water, represented in formulas as containing molecules of water. Washing soda ($NA_2CO_8 \cdot 10H_2O$) is a hydrate. —*v.* become or cause to become a hydrate; combine with water to form a hydrate. [< Gk. *hydor* water] —**hy·dra′tion,** *n.* —**hy′dra·tor,** *n.*

hy·drau·lic (hī drô′lik), *adj.* **1** having to do with water in motion. **2** operated by water or other liquid: *hydraulic brakes.* **3** hardening under water: *hydraulic cement.* [< L < Gk., ult. < *hydor* water + *aulos* pipe] —**hy·drau′li·cal·ly,** *adv.*

hy·drau·lics (hī drô′liks), *n.* science treating of water and other liquids in motion, their uses in engineering, the laws of their actions, etc.

hy·dride (hī′drīd; -drid), **hy·drid** (-drid), *n.* compound of hydrogen with another element or radical.

hydro-, hydr-, *combining form.* **1** of or having to do with water or other liquids, as in *hydrometer, hydrostatics.* **2** combined with hydrogen, as in *hydrochloric, hydrosulfuric.* [< Gk., < *hydor* water]

hy·dro·car·bon (hī′drō kär′bən), *n.* any of a class of compounds containing only hydrogen and carbon, as methane, benzene, and acetylene. Gasoline is a mixture of hydrocarbons.

hy·dro·ceph·a·lus (hī′drō sef′ə ləs), *n.* accumulation of fluid in the skull, esp. in infancy, often causing enlargement of the head. [< NL *hydrocephalus* < Gk. *hýdōr* water + *kephalé* head] —**hy′dro·ce·phal′ic,** *adj.*

hy·dro·chlo·ric acid (hī′drə klô′rik; –klō′–), **a** a colorless gas, HCl, with a strong, sharp odor. **b** an aqueous solution of this.

hy·dro·cor·ti·sone (hī′drō kôr′tə zōn), *n.* an adrenal hormone similar to cortisone, used in treating arthritis.

hy·dro·cy·an·ic acid (hī′drō sī an′ik), =prussic acid.

hy·dro·dy·nam·ics (hī′drō dī nam′iks; –di–), *n.* branch of physics dealing with the forces that water and other liquids exert, often called hydraulics. —**hy′dro·dy·nam′ic,** *adj.*

hy·dro·e·lec·tric (hī′drō i lek′trik), *adj.* of or pertaining to the production of electricity by water power. —**hy′dro·e·lec′tric·i·ty,** *n.*

hy·dro·foil (hī′drō foil), *n.* **1** a fin below the waterline of a boat that raises the hull out of the water at high speeds, enabling the boat to go even faster. **2** a boat with hydrofoils.

hy·dro·gen (hī′drə jən), *n.* a very light, colorless gas, H, that burns easily and weighs less than any other known element. [< F, ult. < Gk. *hydor* water + *geinasthai* produce; form infl. by –*genes* born] —**hy·drog′e·nous,** *adj.*

hy·dro·gen·ase (hī′drə jə nās), *n.* enzyme found in bacteria that can insert or remove hydrogen from organic compounds.

hydrogen bomb, bomb that uses the fusion of atoms to cause an explosion of tremendous force; fusion bomb. Also, **H-bomb.**

hydrogen peroxide, a colorless, unstable liquid, H_2O_2, often used in dilute solution as an antiseptic, bleaching agent, etc.

hy·drog·ra·phy (hī drog′rə fi), *n.* science of the measurement and description of seas, lakes, rivers, etc., with special reference to their use for navigation and commerce. —**hy·drog′ra·pher,** *n.* **hy′dro·graph′ic,** *adj.*

hy·droid (hī′droid), *n.* a very simple form of hydrozoan that grows into branching colonies by budding; polyp. —*adj.* like a polyp.

hy·drol·y·sis (hī drol′ə sis), *n., pl.* –**ses** (–sēz). decomposition that changes a compound into other compounds by taking up the elements of water. —**hy′dro·lyt′ic,** *adj.*

hy·dro·lyze (hī′drə līz), *v.,* –**lyzed,** –**lyz·ing.** decompose by hydrolysis.

hy·drom·e·ter (hī drom′ə tər), *n.* a graduated instrument for finding the specific gravity of liquids.

hy·dro·pho·bi·a (hī′drə fō′bi ə), *n.* **1** rabies. **2** a morbid dread of water. —**hy′dro·pho′bic,** *adj.*

hy·dro·phyte (hī′drə fīt), *n.* any plant that can grow only in water or very wet soil.

hy·dro·plane (hī′drə plān), *n., v.,* –**planed,** –**plan·ing.** —*n.* **1** fast motorboat that glides on the surface of water. **2** airplane provided with floats or with a boatlike underpart, enabling it to take off and land on water; seaplane. **3** structure on an airplane that enables it to float. **4** horizontal rudder on a submarine that enables it to surface and submerge. —*v.* ride in a hydroplane.

hy·dro·pon·ics (hī′drə pon′iks), *n.* the growing of plants in water containing mineral nutrients. [< HYDRO– + L *ponere* to place] —**hy′dro·pon′ic,** *adj.*

hy·dro·pow·er (hī′drō pou′ər), *n.* =hydroelectric power.

hy·dro·sphere (hī′drə sfir), *n.* **1** water on the surface of the globe. **2** water vapor in the atmosphere.

hy·dro·stat·ics (hī′drə stat′iks), *n.* branch of physics that deals with the equilibrium and pressure of liquids. —**hy′dro·stat′ic, hy′dro·stat′i·cal,** *adj.* —**hy′dro·stat′i·cal·ly,** *adv.*

hy·dro·trop·ic (hī′drə trop′ik), *adj.* bending or turning in response to moisture, as the roots of a plant grow toward water. [< *hydro–* + Gk. *trópos* a turning] —**hy·dro·tro′pism,** *n.*

hy·drous (hī′drəs), *adj.* **1** containing water. **2** containing water or its elements in some kind of union, as in hydrates or in hydroxides.

hy·drox·ide (hī drok′sīd; –sid), *n.* any compound consisting of an element or radical combined with one or more hydroxyl radicals.

hy·drox·yl (hī drok′səl), a univalent radical, OH, in all hydroxides.

hy·dro·zo·an (hī′drə zō′ən), *n.* any of a group of invertebrate water animals including hydras, polyps, many jellyfishes, etc. [< NL *Hydrozoa,* genus name < Gk. *hydor* water + *zoion* animal]

hy·e·na (hī ē′nə), *n.* a wolflike, flesh-eating mammal of Africa and Asia. [< L < Gk. *hyaina* < *hys* pig]

hy·giene (hī′jēn; –ji ēn), *n.* rules of health; science of keeping well. [< NL (*ars*) *hygieina* the healthful art < GK., ult. < *hygies* healthy] —**hy′gien·ist,** *n.*

hy·gi·en·ic (hī′ji en′ik; –jē′nik), *adj.* **1** healthful; sanitary. **2** having to do with health or hygiene. —**hy′gi·en′i·cal·ly,** *adv.*

hy·grom·e·ter (hī grom′ə tər), *n.* instrument for determining the amount of moisture in the air. [< Gk. *hygron* moisture (neut. of *hygros* wet) + –METER]

hy·grom·e·try (hī grom′ə tri), *n.* science of determining the amount of moisture in the air.

hy·ing (hī′ing), *v.* ppr. of **hie.**

hy·la (hī′lə), *n.* a tree toad. [< NL < Gk. *hyle* woods]

hy·men (hī′mən), *n.* a fold of mucous membrane extending partly across the opening into the vagina. [< LL < Gk.]

hy·me·ne·al (hī′mə nē′əl), *adj.* having to do with marriage. —*n.* a wedding song.

hy·me·nop·ter·ous (hī′mə nop′tər əs), *adj.* belonging to a group of insects including ants, bees, and wasps. [< Gk., < *hymen* membrane + *pteron* wing] —**hy′me·nop′ter·an,** *n.*

hymn (him), *n.* **1** song in praise of God. **2** any similar song of praise. [< L < Gk., *hymnos*] —**hymn′like′,** *adj.*

hym·nal (him′nəl), *n.* Also, **hymn′book′.** book of hymns. —*adj.* of hymns.

hym·nol·o·gy (him nol′ə ji), *n.* **1** study of hymns, their history, classification, etc. **2** hymns. —**hym′no·log′i·cal,** *adj.* —**hym·nol′o·gist,** *n.*

hy·oid (hī′oid), *n.* the U-shaped bone at the root of the tongue. [< NL < Gk. *hyoeides* U-shaped < Υ (upsilon) + *eidos* form]

hype (hīp), *v.,* **hyped, hyp·ing.** Often, **hype up.** promote; publicize; generate interest in. —*n.* **1** publicity; promotion. **2** exaggeration; trickery: *media hype.*

hy·per (hī′pər), *adj.* too excited or enthusiastic; nervous; jumpy.

hyper–, *prefix.* over; above; beyond; exceedingly; to excess, as in *hyperactive, hypersensitive, hypertension.* [< Gk. *hyper*]

hy·per·ac·tive (hī′pər ak′tiv), *adj.* overly active: *hyperactive imagination.*

hy·per·bo·la (hī pėr′bə lə), *n., pl.* –**las.** a curve formed when a cone is cut by a plane making a larger angle with the base than the side of the cone makes. [< NL < Gk. *hyperbole,* ult. < *hyper–* beyond + *ballein* throw]

hy·per·bo·le (hī pėr′bə lē), *n.* exaggeration for effect. [< L < Gk. See HYPERBOLA.]

hy·per·bol·ic (hī′pər bol′ik), *adj.* **1** of, like, or using hyperbole; exaggerated; exaggerating. **2** of hyperbolas. —**hy′per·bol′i·cal·ly,** *adv.*

hy·per·crit·i·cal (hī′pər krit′ə kəl), *adj.* too critical. —**hy′per·crit′i·cal·ly,** *adv.*

hy·per·gly·ce·mi·a (hī′pər gli sē′mē ə), *n.* abnormally high sugar content in the blood, as in diabetes. —**hy′per·gly·ce′mic,** *adj.*

hy·per·on (hī′pər on), *n.* a very short-lived, unstable particle with a mass between that of the neutron and the deuteron.

hy·per·par·a·site (hī′pər par′ə sīt), *n.* a parasitic organism that lives off another parasite. —**hy′per·par′a·sit·ic,** *adj.* —**hy′per·par′a·sit·ism,** *n.*

hy·per·sen·si·tive (hī′pər sen′sə tiv), *adj.* excessively sensitive. —**hy′per·sen′si·tive·ness, hy′per·sen′si·tiv′i·ty,** *n.*

hy·per·ten·sion (hī′pər ten′shən), *n.* an abnormally high blood pressure.

hy·per·ten·sive (hī′pər ten′siv), —*adj.* having or marked by rising, or unusually high, blood pressure. —*n.* a hypertensive person.

hy·per·text (hī′pər tekst′), *n.* system for storage of computer data that is linked by subject or content, as for a browser.

hy·per·tro·phy (hī pėr′trə fi), *n., pl.* **–phies,** *v.,* **–phied, –phy·ing.** —*n.* enlargement of a part or organ. —*v.* grow too big. [< NL, < Gk. *hyper–* over + *trophe* nourishment] **—hy′per·troph′ic,** *adj.*

hy·per·ven·ti·late (hī′pər ven′tə lāt), **–lat·ed, –lat·ing.** breathe too quickly or too deeply. **—hy′per·ven′ti·la′tion,** *n.*

hy·phen (hī′fən), *n.* mark (-) used to connect the parts of a compound word, or the parts of a word divided at the end of a line, etc. —*v.* hyphenate. [< LL < Gk., in one, hyphen, < *upo–* under + *hen* one].

hy·phen·ate (hī′fən āt), *v.,* **–at·ed, –at·ing.** connect by a hyphen; write or print with a hyphen. **—hy′phen·a′tion,** *n.*

hyp·no·sis (hip nō′sis), *n., pl.* **–ses** (–sēz). state resembling deep sleep, but more active, in which a person has little will of his or her own and little feeling, and acts according to the suggestions of the person who brought about the hypnosis.

hyp·no·ther·a·py (hip′nə ther′ə pi), *n.* **1** treatment of some mental disorders by hypnosis. **2** hypnosis used in place of anesthetics.

hyp·not·ic (hip not′ik), *adj.* **1** of hypnosis. **2** easily hypnotized. **3** causing sleep. —*n.* **1** person who is hypnotized or easily hypnotized. **2** drug or other means of causing sleep. [< LL < Gk. *hypnotikos* putting to sleep < *hypnoein* put to sleep < *hypnos* sleep] **—hyp·not′i·cal·ly,** *adv.*

hyp·no·tism (hip′nə tiz əm), *n.* **1** the inducing of hypnosis. **2** science dealing with hypnosis. **—hyp′no·tist,** *n.*

hyp·no·tize (hip′nə tīz), *v.,* **–tized, –tiz·ing. 1** put into a hypnotic state; cause hypnosis. **2** *Fig.* dominate by suggestion; control, as if by a spell. **—hyp′no·tiz′a·ble,** *adj.* **—hyp′no·ti·za′tion,** *n.* **—hyp′no·tiz′er,** *n.*

hypo–, *prefix.* under; beneath; below; less than; slightly; somewhat, as in *hypodermic.* [< Gk., < *hypo*]

hy·po·chon·dri·a (hī′pə kon′dri ə), *n.* unnatural anxiety about one's health; imaginary illness. [< LL, abdomen, < Gk., *hypo–* under + *chondros* cartilage (of the breastbone); from the supposed seat of melancholy]

hy·po·chon·dri·ac (hī′pə kon′dri ak), *n.* person suffering from hypochondria. —*adj.* suffering from hypochondria.

hy·po·cot·yl (hī′pə kot′əl), *n.* part of the stem below the cotyledons in the embryo of a plant. **—hy′po·cot′y·lous,** *adj.*

hy·poc·ri·sy (hi pok′rə si), *n., pl.* **–sies. 1** act or fact of putting on a false appearance of goodness. **2** pretending to be what one is not. [< OF < LL < Gk. *hypokrisis* acting, dissimulation, ult. < *hypo–* under + *krinein* judge]

hyp·o·crite (hip′ə krit), *n.* **1** person who puts on a false appearance of goodness. **2** person who pretends to be what one is not. [< OF < L < Gk. *hypokrites* actor. See HYPOCRISY.] **—hyp′o·crit′i·cal,** *adj.* **—hyp′o·crit′i·cal·ly,** *adv.*

hy·po·der·mic (hī′pə dėr′mik), *adj.* **1** under the skin. **2** injected under the skin: *a hypodermic needle.* —*n.* **1** dose of medicine injected under the skin. **2** syringe used to inject a dose of medicine under the skin. [< NL, < Gk. *hypo–* under + *derma* skin] **—hy′po·der′mi·cal·ly,** *adv.*

hy·po·der·mis (hī′pə dėr′mis, hip′ə–), *n.* **1** layer of tissue that secretes integuement and lies under the shell or outer covering of some insects, crustaceans, and worms.

hy·po·gly·ce·mi·a (hī′pō glī sē′mē ə), *n.* abnormally low sugar content in the blood. **—hy′po·gly·ce′mic,** *adj.*

hy·po·ten·sion (hī′pō ten′shən), *n.* an abnormally low blood pressure.

hy·pot·e·nuse (hī pot′ə nüs; –nūs), *n.* side of a right-angled triangle opposite the right angle. [< LL < Gk. *hypoteinousa* subtending < *hypo–* under + *teinein* stretch]

hy·po·thal·a·mus (hī′pə thal′ə məs; hip′ə–), *n.* part of the brain under the thalamus, which controls temperature, hunger, thirst, and the pituitary gland. **—hy′po·tha·lam′ic,** *adj.*

hy·poth·e·sis (hī poth′ə sis), *n., pl.* **–ses** (–sēz). **1** something assumed because it seems likely to be a true explanation; theory. **2** proposition assumed as a basis for reasoning. **3** a mere guess. [< NL < Gk., < *hypo–* under + *thesis* a placing]

hy·poth·e·size (hī poth′ə sīz), *v.,* **–sized, –siz·ing. 1** make a hypothesis. **2** assume; suppose.

hy·po·thet·i·cal (hī′pə thet′ə kəl), **hy·po·thet·ic** (–ik), *adj.* **1** of or based on a hypothesis; assumed; supposed. **2** in logic, conditional: *a hypothetical proposition.* **—hy′po·thet′i·cal·ly,** *adv.*

hys·sop (his′əp), *n.* a fragrant, bushy plant of the same family as mint, used for medicine, flavoring, etc. [< L < Gk. *hyssopos* < Semitic]

hys·ter·ec·to·my (his′tər ek′tə mi), *n., pl.* **–mies.** removal of the uterus or a portion of it. [< Gk. *hystera* uterus + *ex–* out + *tomos* cutting]

hys·te·ri·a (his tir′i ə; –ter′–), *n.* **1** a nervous disorder that causes violent fits of laughing and crying, imaginary illnesses, or general lack of self-control. **2** senseless excitement. [< NL, < Gk. *hystera* uterus; because women are thought to be more often affected than men]

hys·ter·ic (his ter′ik), *adj.* hysterical. —*n.* Usually, **hysterics,** fit of hysterical laughing and crying

hys·ter·i·cal (his ter′ə kəl), *adj.* **1** unnaturally excited; showing an unnatural lack of control; unable to stop laughing, crying, etc. **2** suffering from hysteria. **3** of, characteristic of, or pertaining to hysteria. **—hys·ter′i·cal·ly,** *adv.*

Hz, hertz.

I, i (ī), *n., pl.* **I's; i's.** 1 the ninth letter of the alphabet. 2 the Roman numeral for 1.

I (ī), *pron., nom.* **I,** *poss.* **my** or **mine,** *obj.* **me;** *pl. nom.* **we,** *poss.* **ours** or **our,** *obj.* **us;** *n., pl.* **I's.** —*pron.* the nominative case singular of the pronoun of the first person, used by a speaker or writer to denote himself. —*n.* the pronoun *I* used as a noun. [OE *ic*]

I, iodine.

I., 1 Island; Islands. 2 Isle; Isles. 3 Israel; Israeli.

i., interest.

IA, (*zip code*) Iowa.

Ia., Iowa.

IAEA, International Atomic Energy Agency (implementing international cooperation on nuclear issues).

–ial, *suffix.* form of **–al,** as in *adverbial, facial,* etc.

i·am·bic (ī am′bik), *n.* measure in poetry consisting of two syllables, an unaccented followed by an accented. —*adj.* of or containing such measures. Much English poetry is iambic. [< L < Gk. *iambos* + E *–ic*]

–ian, *suffix.* form of **–an,** as in *Bostonian, Episcopalian,* etc.

I-beam (ī′bēm′), *n.* metal beam shaped in cross section like the capital letter I.

I·be·ri·a (ī bir′i ə), *n.* peninsula in SW Europe, occupied by Spain and Portugal. —**I·be′ri·an,** *adj., n.*

i·bex (ī′beks), *n., pl.* **i·bex·es, ib·i·ces** (ib′ə sēz; ī′bə–), or (*esp. collectively*) **i-bex.** a wild goat of Europe, Asia, or Africa, the male of which has very large horns. [< L]

ibid., ib., ibidem.

i·bi·dem (i bī′dem), *adv. Latin.* in the same place; in the same book, chapter, page, etc.

i·bis (ī′bis), *n., pl.* **i·bis·es** or (*esp. collectively*) **i·bis.** a long-legged wading bird like a heron, regarded by ancient Egyptians as sacred. [< L < Gk. < Egyptian]

–ible, *suffix.* that can be ___ed, as in *impressible, perfectible, reducible.* [< OF < L *–ibilis*]

ibn–, *combining form. Arabic.* son; son of: *Abdul ibn-Saud.*

I·bo (ē′bō), *n., pl.* **–bo** or **–bos.** 1 member of a people of W Africa, forming a large part of the population of Nigeria. 2 their language. Also, **Igbo.**

–ic, *suffix.* 1 of or pertaining to, as in *atmospheric, Icelandic.* 2 having the nature of, as in *artistic, heroic.* 3 constituting or being, as in *bombastic, monolithic.* 4 characterized by; containing; made up of, as in *alcoholic, iambic.* 5 made by; caused by, as in *phonographic.* 6 like; like that of; characteristic of, as in *meteoric, sophomoric.* 7 *–ic* implies a smaller proportion of the element than *–ous* implies, as in *sulfuric.* [< F *–ique* or L *–icus* or Gk. *–ikos*]

–ical, *suffix.* 1 *–ic,* as in *geometrical, parasitical, hysterical.* 2 *–ic* specialized or differentiated in meaning, as in *economical.* 3 *–ical* sometimes equals *–al* added to nouns ending in *–ic,* as in *critical, musical.*

Ic·a·rus (ik′ə rəs; ī′kə–), *n. Gk. Legend.* the son of Daedalus, Icarus and his father escaped from Crete by using wings that Daedalus had made. Icarus flew so high that the sun melted the wax by which his wings were attached. —**I·car′i·an,** *adj.*

ICBM, Intercontinental Ballistic Missile.

I.C.C., ICC, Interstate Commerce Commission.

ice (īs), *n., v.,* **iced, ic·ing,** *adj.* —*n.* 1 water made solid by cold; frozen water. 2 layer or surface of ice. 3 something that looks or feels like ice. 4 a frozen dessert usually made of sweetened fruit juice. 5 icing. —*v.* 1 cool with ice; put ice in or around. 2 cover with ice. 3 turn to ice; freeze. 4 cover (cake) with icing. —*adj.* of ice; having to do with ice.

break the ice, a make a beginning. **b** overcome first difficulties in talking or getting acquainted.

ice up, fill up or cover with ice. **on ice,** not being considered; inactive; out of sight.

on thin ice, in a dangerous or difficult position. [OE *īs*] —**ice′less,** *adj.* —**ice′like′,** *adj.*

ice age, 1 the glacial epoch. 2 Usually, **Ice Age.** =Pleistocene.

ice bag, waterproof bag for holding ice, used as a compress to relieve swelling, etc.

ice·berg (īs′bėrg′), *n.* a large mass of ice floating in the sea.

tip of the iceberg, small or insignificant part of something much larger, more serious, etc. [< Dan. *isbjerg,* or Swed. *isberg,* or Du. *ijsberg,* lit., ice mountain]

iceberg lettuce, round-headed lettuce with crisp leaves.

ice·boat (īs′bōt′), *n.* 1 a triangular frame on runners, fitted with sails for sailing on ice. 2 =icebreaker (def. 1).

ice·bound (īs′bound′), *adj.* 1 held fast by ice. 2 shut in or obstructed by ice.

ice·box (īs′boks′), *n.* 1 =refrigerator. 2 an insulated box in which to keep food, liquids, etc., cool with ice, etc.

ice·break·er (īs′brāk′ər), *n.* 1 a strong boat used to break a channel through ice. 2 *Fig.* anything that serves to encourage or enliven conversation.

ice·cap (īs′kap′), *n.* a permanent covering of ice over an area, sloping down on all sides from an elevated center.

ice-cold (īs′kōld′), *adj.* 1 cold as ice. 2 *Fig.* unfeeling.

ice cream, a frozen dessert made of cream or custard sweetened and flavored.

ice cube, small cube-shaped piece of ice, put in a drink to make or keep it cool.

iced (īst), *adj.* 1 cooled with ice; with ice in or around it. 2 covered with ice: *iced highways.* 3 covered with icing.

ice field, a large sheet of ice floating in the sea or covering an area of land.

ice floe, large sheet of ice floating in the sea.

Ice·land (īs′lənd), *n.* a large island republic in the N Atlantic. —**Ice′land′er,** *n.*

Ice·lan·dic (īs lan′dik), *adj.* of or having to do with Iceland, its people, or their language. —*n.* the language of Iceland.

ice·man (īs′man′), *n., pl.* **–men** (–men′). man who sells or handles ice.

ice pack, 1 large area of masses of ice floating in the sea. 2 bag containing ice for application to the body.

ice sheet, a broad, thick sheet of ice covering a very large area for a long time.

ice-skate (īs′skāt′), *v.,* **–skat·ed, –skat·ing.** skate on ice. —**ice′-skat′er,** *n.*

ice skates, a pair of metal runners, usually attached to high shoes, for skating.

ich·neu·mon (ik nü′mən; –nū′–), *n.* 1 a small brown, weasellike animal of Egypt. 2 =ichneumon fly. [< L < Gk., lit., searcher (supposedly for crocodile's eggs), ult. < *ichnos* track]

ichneumon fly, insect that looks like a wasp but does not sting. Its larvae live as parasites in or on other insects, usually killing them.

ich·thy·ol·o·gy (ik′thi ol′ə ji), *n.* branch of zoology dealing with fishes. [< Gk. *ichthys* fish + –LOGY] —**ich′thy·o·log′ic, ich′thy·o·log′i·cal,** *adj.* —**ich′thy·ol′o·gist,** *n.*

ich·thy·or·nis (ik′thē ôr′nis), *n., pl.* **–or·ni·thes** (–ôr′nə thēz). any member of an extinct genus of birds having vertebrae resembling those of fish. [< NL *ichthyornis* genus name < Gk. *ichthys* fish + *órnīs* bird]

ich·thy·o·saur (ik′thi ə sôr′), **ich·thy·o·sau·rus** (ik′thi ə sôr′əs), *n., pl.* **–saurs, –sau·ri** (–sô′rī). an extinct fishlike marine reptile with four paddlelike flippers. [< NL, < Gk. *ichthys* fish + *sauros* lizard]

i·ci·cle (ī′si kəl), *n.* 1 a pointed, hanging stick of ice formed by the freezing of dripping water. 2 anything like an icicle, as glittery tinsel, etc. [ME *isykle* < OE *īs* ice + *gicel* icicle] —**i′ci·cled,** *adj.*

ic·ing (īs′ing), *n.* mixture of sugar with butter, egg white, etc., used to cover cakes.

i·con (ī′kon), *n., pl.* **i·cons, i·co·nes** (ī′kə nēz). 1 in the Eastern Church, a sacred picture or image of Christ, an angel, a saint, etc. 2 picture; image. [< L < Gk. *eikon*]

i·con·ic (ī kon′ik), *adj.* 1 of or having to do with an icon. 2 representative of; quintessential. 3 following or based on a conventional style of art.

i·con·o·clasm (ī kon′ə klaz əm), *n.* 1 ridicule or attack on revered institutions or beliefs viewed as based on superstition or error. 2 practice of destroying icons.

i·con·o·clast (ī kon′ə klast), *n.* 1 person opposed to worshiping images. 2 person who attacks cherished beliefs or institutions as wrong or foolish. [< Med.L

< Med.Gk. *eikonoklastes* < Gk. *eikon* image + *klaein* to break] —**i·con′o·clas′-tic**, *adj.* —**i·con′o·clas′ti·cal·ly**, *adv.*

-ics, *suffix*. **1** facts, principles, science, as in *physics*. **2** methods, system, activities, as in *athletics, politics, tactics*.

i·cy (ī′si), *adj.*, **i·ci·er**, **i·ci·est**. **1** like ice; very cold; slippery. **2** having much ice; covered with ice. **3** of ice. **4** *Fig.* without warm feeling; cold and unfriendly. —**i′ci·ly**, *adv.* —**i′ci·ness**, *n.*

id (id), *n.* the preformed, primitive psychic force in the unconscious, which is the source of instinctive energy essential for propagation and self-preservation. [< G use of L *id* it]

I'd (īd), **1** I should. **2** I would. **3** I had.

ID, (*zip code*) Idaho.

I.D. (ī′dē′), *n.* **1** identity. **2** Also, **ID.** identification. —*v.* identify (someone).

ID card, =identity card.

id., idem.

Ida., Id., Idaho.

I·da·ho (ī′də hō), *n.* a W state of the United States. —**I′da·ho′an**, *adj., n.*

-ide, -id, *suffix*. compound of, as in *chloride, sulfide*. [< *oxide*]

i·de·a (ī dē′ə), *n.* **1** plan, picture, or belief of the mind. **2** thought; fancy; opinion.

i·de·al (ī dē′əl; ī dēl′), *n.* perfect type; model to be imitated; what one would wish to be: *religion holds up high ideals for us to follow.* —*adj.* **1** just as one would wish; perfect: *an ideal day for a picnic.* **2** existing only in thought. A point without length, breadth, or thickness is an ideal object. **3** not practical; visionary.

i·de·al·ism (ī dē′əl iz əm), *n.* **1** an acting according to one's ideals of what ought to be, regardless of circumstances or of the approval or disapproval of others. **2** the cherishing of fine ideals. **3** representing imagined types rather than an exact copy of any person, instance, or situation. **4** belief that all knowledge is of ideas and that it is impossible to know whether there really is a world of objects.

i·de·al·ist (ī dē′əl ist), *n.* **1** person who acts according to his or her ideals; person who has fine ideals. **2** person who neglects practical matters in following ideals.

i·de·al·is·tic (ī dē′əl is′tik), *adj.* **1** having high ideals and acting according to them. **2** forgetting or neglecting practical matters in trying to follow out one's ideals; not practical. **3** of idealism or idealists. —**i·de′al·is′ti·cal·ly**, *adv.*

i·de·al·ize (ī dē′əl īz), *v.*, **-ized**, **-iz·ing.** make ideal; think of or represent as perfect rather than as is actually the case: *Many voters idealize their candidate.* —**i·de′al·i·za′tion**, *n.* —**i·de′al·iz′er**, *n.*

i·de·al·ly (ī dē′əl i), *adv.* **1** according to an ideal; perfectly. **2** in idea or theory.

i·dée fixe (ē dā′fēks′), *pl.* **i·dées fixes** (ē dā′fēks). *French.* fixed idea.

i·dem (ī′dem; id′em), *pron., adj. Latin.* the same as previously given or mentioned.

i·den·ti·cal (ī den′tə kəl), *adj.* **1** the same: *both events happened on the identical day.* **2** exactly alike: *identical houses.* [< Med.L *identicus* < L *idem* same] —**i·den′ti·cal·ly**, *adv.* —**i·den′ti·cal·ness**, *n.*

identical twin, one of twins, of the same sex, developing from a single fertilized ovum.

i·den·ti·fi·ca·tion (ī den′tə fə kā′shən), *n.* **1** an identifying or being identified. **2** something used to identify a person or thing.

i·den·ti·fy (ī den′tə fī), *v.*, **-fied**, **-fy·ing.** **1** recognize as being, or show to be, a certain person or thing; prove to be the same: *identify handwriting.* **2** make the same; treat as the same. **3** connect closely; link; associate (*with*): *identify with the aims of the UN.* —**i·den′ti·fi′a·ble**, *adj.* —**i·den′ti·fi′er**, *n.*

i·den·ti·ty (ī den′tə ti), *n., pl.* **-ties.** **1** individuality; who a person is; what a thing is: *the writer concealed his identity under an assumed name.* **2** exact likeness; sameness: *the identity of the two crimes.*

identity card, card issued to a person to prove his or her identity; ID card.

id·e·o·graph (id′i ə graf′; -gräf′; ī′di-), **id·e·o·gram** (-gram′), *n.* a graphic symbol that represents a thing or an idea without indicating a word for the thing or the idea, as Egyptian hieroglyphics and Chinese characters. [< Gk. *idea* idea + -GRAPH] —**id′e·o·graph′ic, id′e·o·graph′i·cal**, *adj.* —**id′e·o·graph′i·cal·ly**, *adv.*

i·de·o·logue (ī dē′ə lôg; -log), *n.* person occupied by ideas; visionary; idealologist.

i·de·ol·o·gy (ī′di ol′ə ji; id i′-), *n., pl.* **-gies.** **1** set of doctrines; body of opinions. **2** fundamental doctrines and point of view. **3** the combined doctrines, assertions, and intentions of a social or political movement. —**i′de·o·log′ic, i′de·o·log′i·cal**, *adj.* —**i′de·o·log′i·cal·ly**, *adv.* —**i′de·ol′o·gist**, *n.*

ides (īdz), *n.pl.* in the ancient Roman calendar, the 15th day of March, May, July, and October, and the 13th day of the other months. [< F < L *idus* < Etruscan]

id·i·o·cy (id′i ə si), *n., pl.* **-cies.** **1** being an idiot. **2** very great stupidity or folly.

id·i·o·lect (id′i ə lekt), *n.* the way a person speaks his or her native language; individual speech.

id·i·om (id′i əm), *n.* **1** phrase or expression whose meaning cannot be understood from the ordinary meanings of the words in it. "How do you do?" and "I have caught cold" are English idioms. **2** dialect. **3** a people's way of expressing themselves. [< LL < Gk. *idioma*, ult. < *idios* one's own]

id·i·o·mat·ic (id′i ə mat′ik), **id·i·o·mat·i·cal** (-ə kəl), *adj.* **1** using an idiom or idioms. **2** of or concerning idioms. **3** characteristic of a particular language. —**id′i·o·mat′i·cal·ly**, *adv.*

id·i·o·syn·cra·sy (id′i ō sing′krə si; -sin′-), *n., pl.* **-sies.** personal peculiarity. [< Gk.,

< *idios* one's own + *synkrasis* temperament < *syn* together + *kerannymi* mix] —**id′i·o·syn·crat′ic**, *adj.*

id·i·ot (id′i ət), *n.* **1** person born with such slight mental capacities that he or she can never learn to read or count. **2** a very stupid or foolish person. [< L < Gk. *idiotes*, orig., private person < *idios* one's own]

id·i·ot·ic (id′i ot′ik), *adj.* of or like an idiot; very stupid or foolish. —**id′i·ot′i·cal·ly**, *adv.*

id·i·ot sa·vant (id′i ət sə vänt′), *pl.* **idiot savants** or **idiots savants.** person who is mentally retarded but displays a remarkable skill, esp. feats of memory. [< F *idiot savant,* lit. scholarly idiot]

i·dle (ī′dəl), *adj.*, **i·dler**, **i·dlest**, *v.*, **i·dled**, **i·dling.** —*adj.* **1** doing nothing; not busy; not working: *idle hands, money lying idle.* **2** not willing to do things; lazy. **3** useless; worthless: *idle pleasures.* **4** without any good reason, cause, or foundation: *idle fears.* —*v.* **1** be idle; do nothing. **2** waste (time); spend. **3** run slowly without transmitting power. [OE *īdel*] —**i′dle·ness**, *n.* —**i′dler**, *n.* —**i′dly**, *adv.*

i·dol (ī′dəl), *n.* **1** image or other object worshiped as a god. **2** object of extreme devotion. [< OF < L < Gk. *eidolon* image < *eidos* form]

i·dol·a·ter (ī dol′ə tər), *n.* **1** person who worships idols. **2** admirer; adorer; devotee.

i·dol·a·trous (ī dol′ə trəs), *adj.* **1** worshiping idols. **2** having to do with idolatry. **3** blindly adoring. —**i·dol′a·trous·ly**, *adv.* —**i·dol′a·trous·ness**, *n.*

i·dol·a·try (ī dol′ə tri), *n., pl.* **-tries.** **1** worship of idols. **2** worship of a person or thing; extreme devotion. [< OF < L < Gk. < *eidolon* image + *latreia* service]

i·dol·ize (ī′dəl īz), *v.*, **-ized**, **-iz·ing.** **1** worship as an idol. **2** love or admire very much; be extremely devoted to. —**i′dol·i·za′tion**, *n.*

i·dyl, i·dyll (ī′dəl), *n.* **1** a short description in poetry or prose of a simple and charming scene or event, esp. one connected with country life. **2** scene or event suitable for such a description. [< L < Gk. *eidyllion,* dim. of *eidos* form]

i·dyl·lic (ī dil′ik), *adj.* suitable for an idyl; simple and charming. —**idyl′li·cal·ly**, *adv.*

i.e., that is; that is to say. [Latin *id est*]

if (if), *conj.* **1** supposing that; on condition that; in case that: *if you are going, leave now.* **2** whether: *I wonder if he will go.* **3** although; even though: *if he is little, he is strong.* —*n.* condition; supposition. **as if,** as it would be if. [OE *gif*]

if·fy (if′i), *adj.*, **-fi·er**, **-fi·est.** **1** full of ifs. **2** doubtful.

ig·loo (ig′lü), *n., pl.* **-loos.** **1** a dome-shaped hut used by Eskimos, often built of blocks of hard snow. **2** a structure shaped like an igloo. [< Eskimo, house]

ig·ne·ous (ig′ni əs), *adj.* **1** of fire; pertaining to fire. **2** produced by fire, intense heat, or volcanic action. [< L, < *ignis* fire]

ig·nite (ig nīt′), *v.*, **–nit·ed, –nit·ing. 1** set on fire. **2** make intensely hot; cause to glow with heat. **3** take fire; begin to burn. [< L, < *ignis* fire] —**ig·nit′a·ble, ig·nit′i·ble,** *adj.* —**ig·nit′a·bil′i·ty, ig·nit′i·bil′i·ty,** *n.* —**ig·nit′er, ig·ni′tor,** *n.*

ig·ni·tion (ig nish′ən), *n.* **1** a setting on fire. **2** a catching on fire. **3** apparatus for igniting the explosive vapor in the cylinders of an internal-combustion engine. **4** any chemical or mechanical device used to ignite rocket or jet fuel.

ig·no·ble (ig nō′bəl), *adj.* **1** mean; base; without honor. **2** of low birth. [< L, < *in–* not + Old L *gnobilis* noble] —**ig′no·bil′i·ty, ig·no′ble·ness,** *n.* —**ig·no′bly,** *adv.*

ig·no·min·i·ous (ig′nə min′i əs), *adj.* **1** shameful; disgraceful; humiliating. **2** contemptible. —**ig′no·min′i·ous·ly,** *adv.* —**ig′no·min′i·ous·ness,** *n.*

ig·no·min·y (ig′nə min′i), *n., pl.* **–min·ies. 1** loss of one's good name; public shame and disgrace; dishonor. **2** shameful action or conduct. [< L *ignominia* < *in–* not + *nomen* name]

ig·no·ra·mus (ig′nə rā′məs; –ram′əs), *n., pl.* **–mus·es.** an ignorant person. [< L, we do not know]

ig·no·rance (ig′nə rəns), *n.* lack of knowledge; quality or condition of being ignorant.

ig·no·rant (ig′nə rənt), *adj.* **1** knowing little or nothing; without knowledge. **2** uninformed; unaware: *ignorant of the facts.* **3** showing lack of knowledge: *an ignorant remark.* [< L *ignorans* not knowing] —**ig′no·rant·ly,** *adv.*

ig·nore (ig nôr′; –nōr′), *v.,* **–nored, –noring.** pay no attention to; disregard. [< L *ignorare* not know] —**ig·nor′er,** *n.*

i·gua·na (i gwä′nə), *n.* a large climbing lizard found in tropical America. [< Sp. < Carib] —**i·gua′ni·an** *adj., n.*

IHS, first three letters of the name of Jesus in Greek.

i·kon (ī′kon), *n.* icon.

Il, illinium.

IL, (*zip code*) Illinois.

il·e·i·tis (il′i ī′tis), *n.* inflammation of the ileum, due to infection, a tumor, or other cause and involving partial or complete blocking of the passage of food through the small intestine.

il·e·um (il′i əm), *n.* the lowest part of the small intestine. [< LL, var. of *ilium,* sing. to L *ilia* loins, entrails] —**il′e·ac,** *adj.*

i·lex (ī′leks), *n.* **1** =holm oak. **2** =holly. [< L]

il·i·ac (il′i ak), *adj.* of or having to do with the ilium; near the ilium.

Il·i·ad (il′i əd), *n.* a long Greek epic poem about the siege of Ilium, or Troy, supposedly written by Homer. —**Il′i·ad′ic,** *adj.*

il·i·um (il′i əm), *n., pl.* **il·i·a** (il′i ə), the broad upper portion of the hipbone. [< NL < LL, sing. to L *ilia* flank, groin]

Il·i·um (il′i əm), *n.* ancient Troy.

ilk (ilk), *n.* **1** kind; sort.
of that ilk, of that kind or sort. [OE *ilca* same]

ill (il), *adj.,* **worse, worst,** *n., adv.* —*adj.* **1** having some disease; not well; sick. **2** bad; evil; harmful; *an ill deed, an ill wind.* —*n.* **1** sickness; disease. **2** an evil; a harm; a trouble. —*adv.* **1** badly; harmfully. **2** in an unkind manner; harshly; cruelly. **3** with trouble or difficulty; scarcely.
ill at ease, uncomfortable. [< Scand. *illr*]

I'll (īl), **1** I shall, **2** I will.

Ill., Illinois.

ill., illustrated; illustration.

ill-advised (il′əd vīzd′), *adj.* acting or done without enough consideration; unwise. —**ill′-ad·vis′ed·ly,** *adv.*

ill-bred (il′bred′), *adj.* badly brought up; rude.

ill breeding, bad manners; rudeness.

ill-con·sid·ered (il′kən sid′ərd), *adj.* unwise.

ill-dis·posed (il′dis pōzd′), *adj.* unfriendly.

il·le·gal (i lē′əl), *adj.* not lawful; against the law; forbidden by law. —**il·le′gal·ly,** *adv.* —**il·le′gal·ness,** *n.*

il·le·gal·i·ty (il′ē gal′ə ti), *n., pl.* **–ties. 1** unlawfulness. **2** an illegal act.

il·leg·i·ble (i lej′ə bəl), *adj.* very hard or impossible to read. —**il·leg′i·bil′i·ty, il·leg′i·ble·ness,** *n.* —**il·leg′i·bly,** *adv.*

il·le·git·i·mate (il′ə jit′ə mit), *adj.* **1** born of parents who are not married to each other. **2** not according to the law or the rules. —**il′le·git′i·ma·cy, il′le·git′i·mate·ness,** *n.* —**il′le·git′i·mate·ly,** *adv.*

ill-fat·ed (il′fāt′id), *adj.* **1** sure to have a bad fate or end. **2** unlucky.

ill-fa·vored (il′-fā′vərd), *adj.* **1** ugly. **2** offensive. —**ill′-fa′vored·ely,** *adv.* —**ill′-fa′vored·ness,** *n.*

ill feeling, mistrust, animosity.

ill-found·ed (il′foun′did), *adj.* without a good reason or sound basis.

ill-got·ten (il′got′ən), *adj.* acquired by evil or unfair means; dishonestly obtained.

ill health, poor health.

ill humor, cross, unpleasant temper or mood.

ill-hu·mored (il′hū′mərd; –ū′-), *adj.* cross; unpleasant. —**ill′hu′mored·ly,** *adv.* —**ill′-hu′mored·ness,** *n.*

il·lib·er·al (i lib′ər əl), *adj.* **1** not liberal; narrow-minded; prejudiced. **2** stingy; miserly. —**il·lib′er·al′i·ty, il·lib′er·al·ness,** *n.* —**il·lib′er·al·ly,** *adv.*

il·lic·it (i lis′it), *adj.* not permitted by law; forbidden. —**il·lic′it·ly,** *adv.* —**il·lic′it·ness,** *n.*

il·lim·it·a·ble (i lim′it ə bəl), *adj.* limitless; boundless; infinite. —**il·lim′it·a·bil′i·ty, il·lim′it·a·ble·ness,** *n.* —**il·lim′it·a·bly,** *adv.*

Il·li·nois (il′ə noi′; –noiz′), *n.* **1** a Middle Western state of the United States. **2** member of an American Indian tribe

formerly living between the Mississippi and Wabash Rivers. —*adj.* of this tribe. —**Il′li·nois′an,** *adj., n.*

il·liq·uid (i lik′wid), *adj.* **1** not easily converted into cash. **2** not having liquid assets.

il·lit·er·a·cy (i lit′ər ə si), *n., pl.* **–cies. 1** inability to read or write. **2** lack of education.

il·lit·er·ate (i lit′ər it), *adj.* **1** unable to read or write. **2** lacking in education. **3** showing lack of culture. —*n.* an illiterate person. —**il·lit′er·ate·ly,** *adv.* —**il·lit′er·ate·ness,** *n.*

ill-judged (il′jujd′), *adj.* unwise; rash.

ill-man·nered (il′man′ərd), *adj.* having or showing bad manners; impolite; rude. —**ill′-man′nered·ly,** *adv.* —**ill′-man′nered·ness,** *n.*

ill nature, crossness; disagreeableness; spite. —**ill′-na′tured,** *adj.* —**ill′-na′tured·ly,** *adv.* —**ill′-na′tured·ness,** *n.*

ill·ness (il′nis), *n.* sickness; disease.

il·log·i·cal (i loj′ə kəl), *adj.* not logical; not reasonable. —**il·log′i·cal′i·ty, il·log′i·cal·ness,** *n.* —**il·log′i·cal·ly,** *adv.*

ill-spent (il′spent′), *adj.* spent badly; wasted.

ill-starred (il′stärd′), *adj.* unlucky; disastrous.

ill-suit·ed (il′süt′id; –sūt′-), *adj.* unsuitable.

ill temper, bad temper or disposition; crossness. —**ill′-tem′pered,** *adj.* —**ill′-tem′pered·ly,** *adv.* —**ill′-tem′pered·ness,** *n.*

ill-timed (il′tīmd′), *adj.* inappropriate.

ill-treat (il′trēt′), *v.* treat badly or cruelly; do harm to; abuse. —**ill′-treat′ment,** *n.*

il·lu·mi·nate (i lü′mə nāt′), *v.,* **–nat·ed, –nat·ing. 1** light up; make bright. **2** make clear; explain; inform; instruct. **3** decorate with lights. **4** decorate with gold, colors, pictures, and designs: *some old books and manuscripts were illuminated.* [< L *illuminatus,* ult. < *in–* in + *lumen* light] —**il·lu′mi·nat′ing, il·lu′mi·na′tive,** *adj.* —**il·lu′mi·nat′ing·ly,** *adv.* —**il·lu′mi·na′tor,** *n.*

il·lu·mi·na·tion (i lü′mə nā′shən), *n.* **1** a lighting up; a making bright. **2** amount of light; light. **3** a making clear; explanation. **4** decoration with lights. **5** decoration of books and letters with gold, colors, pictures, and designs.

il·lu·mine (i lü′mən), *v.,* **–mined, –mining.** make or become bright; illuminate; light up. —**il·lu′mi·na·ble,** *adj.*

illus., illust., illustrated; illustration.

ill-use (*v.* il′üz′; *n.* il′üs′), *v.,* **–used, –us·ing,** *n.* —*v.* treat badly, cruelly, or unfairly. —*n.* Also, **ill′-us′age.** bad, cruel, or unfair treatment.

il·lu·sion (i lü′zhən), *n.* **1** appearance which is not real; misleading appearance. **2** a false impression, perception, notion, or belief. **3** thing that deceives by giving a false impression or idea: *an optical illusion.* [< L *illusio* < *illudere* mock] —**il·lu′sion·al,** *adj.*

il·lu·sion·ar·y (i lü′zhə ner′i), *adj.* like an illusion; illusory.

il·lu·sive (i lü′siv), *adj.* due to an illusion; unreal; misleading; deceptive. —**il·lu′sive·ly**, *adv.* —**il·lu′sive·ness**, *n.*

il·lu·so·ry (i lü′sə ri), *adj.* illusive. —**il·lu′so·ri·ly**, *adv.* —**il·lu′so·ri·ness**, *n.*

illust., illustrated; illustration.

il·lus·trate (il′əs trāt; i lus′–), *v.*, **–trat·ed**, **–trat·ing.** **1** make clear or explain by stories, examples, comparisons, etc. **2** provide with pictures, diagrams, maps, etc., that explain or decorate. [< L *illustratus* lighted up, ult. < *in–* in + *lustrum* purification] —**il′lus·tra′tor**, *n.*

il·lus·tra·tion (il′əs trā′shən), *n.* **1** picture, diagram, map, etc., used to explain or decorate something. **2** story, example, comparison, etc., used to make clear or explain something. **3** act or process of illustrating.

il·lus·tra·tive (i lus′trə tiv; il′əs trā′–), *adj.* illustrating; used to illustrate; helping to explain. —**il·lus′tra·tive·ly**, *adv.*

il·lus·tri·ous (i lus′tri əs), *adj.* very famous; outstanding. [< L *illustris* lighted up, bright] —**il·lus′tri·ous·ly**, *adv.* —**il·lus′tri·ous·ness**, *n.*

ill will, unkind or unfriendly feeling; dislike; hate. —**ill′-willed′**, *adj.*

ill wind, misfortune; calamity.

il·ly (il′i), *adv.* ill; badly.

I'm (īm), I am.

im·age (im′ij), *n.*, *v.*, **–aged**, **–ag·ing.** —*n.* **1** likeness; picture; copy. **2** likeness made of stone, wood, etc.; statue. **3** picture in the mind; idea. Your memory or imagination forms images of people and things that you do not actually see. **4** description or figure of speech that helps the mind to form forceful or beautiful pictures. Poetry often contains images. **5** symbol: *image of good taste.* **6** public face or perception of a person or organization. —*v.* **1** form an image of. **2** reflect as a mirror does. **3** picture in one's mind; imagine. [< OF < L *imago*]

im·age·ry (im′ij ri), *n.*, *pl.* **–ries. 1** pictures in the mind; things imagined. **2** descriptions and figures of speech that help the mind to form forceful or beautiful pictures. **3** images; statues.

i·mag·i·na·ble (i maj′ə nə bəl), *adj.* that can be imagined. —**i·mag′i·na·ble·ness**, *n.* —**i·mag′i·na·bly**, *adv.*

i·mag·i·nar·y (i maj′ə ner′i), *adj.* existing only in the imagination; not real: *the equator is an imaginary line.* —**i·mag′i·nar′i·ly**, *adv.*

i·mag·i·na·tion (i maj′ə nā′shən), *n.* **1** an imagining; power of forming pictures in the mind of things not present to the senses. **2** ability to create new things or ideas or to combine old ones in new forms. **3** creation of the mind; fancy. —**i·mag′i·na′tion·al**, *adj.*

i·mag·i·na·tive (i maj′ə nā′tiv; –nə tiv), *adj.* **1** showing imagination. **2** able to imagine well; fond of imagining. **3** of

imagination. —**i·mag′i·na′tive·ly**, *adv.* —**i·mag′i·na′tive·ness**, *n.*

i·mag·ine (i maj′ən), *v.*, **–ined**, **–in·ing. 1** picture in one's mind; have an idea: *we can hardly imagine life without electricity.* **2** suppose: *imagine this to be the case.* **3** guess: *I cannot imagine what you mean.* [< F < L, < *imago* image]

im·ag·ing (im′ə jing), *n.* process of creating or transmitting electronic images. —*adj.* of or having to do with electronic images.

i·ma·go (i mā′gō), *n.*, *pl.* **i·ma·gos, i·mag·i·nes** (i maj′ə nēz). insect in the final adult, esp. winged, stage. [< L, image]

im·be·cile (im′bə səl), *n.* **1** person of very weak mind: *an imbecile is almost an idiot.* **2** a very stupid or foolish person. —*adj.* **1** very weak in mind. **2** very stupid or foolish. [< F < L *imbecillus* weak < *in–* without + *bacillus* staff] —**im′be·cile·ly**, *adv.* —**im′be·cil′i·ty**, *n.*

im·bed (im bed′), *v.*, **–bed·ded**, **–bed·ding.** =embed.

im·bibe (im bīb′), *v.*, **–bibed**, **–bib·ing. 1** drink; drink in. **2** absorb. **3** take into one's mind. [< L, < *in–* in + *bibere* drink] —**im·bib′er**, *n.*

im·bro·glio (im brōl′yō), *n.*, *pl.* **–glios. 1** a difficult situation. **2** a complicated disagreement. [< Ital.]

im·bue (im bū′), *v.*, **–bued**, **–bu·ing. 1** fill; inspire: *he imbued his son's mind with the ambition to succeed.* **2** fill with moisture or color. [< L *imbuere*] —**im·bue′ment**, *n.*

imit., imitation, imitative (def. 2).

im·i·ta·ble (im′ə tə bəl), *adj.* that can be imitated. —**im′i·ta·bil′i·ty**, *n.*

im·i·tate (im′ə tāt), *v.*, **–tat·ed**, **–tat·ing. 1** try to be like; follow the example of: *the little boy imitated his father.* **2** make or do something like; copy: *a parrot imitates the sounds it hears.* **3** act like: *John imitated a bear.* **4** be like; look like; resemble: *wood painted to imitate stone.* [< L *imitatus*]

im·i·ta·tion (im′ə tā′shən), *n.* **1** an imitating: *we learn many things by imitation.* **2** a copy: *give us an imitation of a rooster crowing.* —*adj.* not real: *imitation pearls.* **in imitation of**, in order to be like or look like. —**im′i·ta′tion·al**, *adj.*

im·i·ta·tive (im′ə tā′tiv), *adj.* **1** likely or inclined to imitate others: *monkeys are imitative.* **2** imitating; showing imitation. *Bang* and *whiz* are imitative words. **3** not real. —**im′i·ta′tive·ly**, *adv.* —**im′i·ta′tive·ness**, *n.*

im·i·ta·tor (im′ə tā′tər), *n.* person or animal that imitates; mimic.

im·mac·u·late (i mak′yə lit), *adj.* **1** without a spot or stain; absolutely clean. **2** without sin; pure. [< L, < *in–* not + *macula* spot] —**im·mac′u·la·cy, im·mac′u·late·ness**, *n.* —**im·mac′u·late·ly**, *adv.*

Immaculate Conception, doctrine that the Virgin Mary was conceived free of original sin.

im·ma·nence (im′ə nəns), **im·ma·nen·cy** (–nən si), *n.* state of being immanent.

im·ma·nent (im′ə nənt), *adj.* originating within; inherent. [< L, < *in–* in + *manere* stay] —**im′ma·nent·ly**, *adv.*

Im·man·u·el (i man′yù əl), *n.* Christ. Also, **Emmanuel.**

im·ma·te·ri·al (im′ə tir′i əl), *adj.* **1** not important; insignificant. **2** not material; spiritual. —**im′ma·te′ri·al·ly**, *adv.* —**im′ma·te′ri·al·ness**, *n.*

im·ma·ture (im′ə chùr′; –tùr′; –tyùr′), *adj.* not mature; not ripe; not full-grown; not fully developed. —**im′ma·ture′ly**, *adv.* —**im′ma·tur′i·ty, im′ma·ture′ness**, *n.*

im·meas·ur·a·ble (i mezh′ər ə bəl), *adj.* too vast to be measured; boundless; without limits. —**im·meas′ur·a·bil′i·ty, im·meas′ur·a·ble·ness**, *n.* —**im·meas′ur·a·bly**, *adv.*

im·me·di·a·cy (i mē′di ə si), *n.* a being immediate.

im·me·di·ate (i mē′di it), *adj.* **1** coming at once; without delay: *an immediate reply.* **2** with nothing between: *in immediate contact, the immediate result.* **3** closest; nearest: *my immediate neighbor.* **4** pertaining to the present: *our immediate plans.* [< LL *immediatus*, ult. < L *in–* not + *medius* in the middle] —**im·me′di·ate·ness**, *n.*

im·me·di·ate·ly (i mē′di it li), *adv.* **1** at once; without delay. **2** with nothing between. **3** next.

im·me·mo·ri·al (im′ə mô′ri əl; –mō′–), *adj.* extending back beyond the bounds of memory; extremely old. —**im′me·mo′ri·al·ly**, *adv.*

im·mense (i mens′), *adj.* **1** very big; huge; vast. **2** very good. [< L, < *in–* not + *mensus* measured] —**im·mense′ly**, *adv.* —**im·mense′ness**, *n.*

im·men·si·ty (i men′sə ti), *n.*, *pl.* **–ties.** very great or boundless extent; vastness.

im·merse (i mèrs′), *v.*, **–mersed**, **–mers·ing. 1** plunge (something) into a liquid. **2** baptize by dipping (a person) under water. **3** involve deeply; absorb: *immersed in business affairs.* [< L *immersus* < *in–* in + *mergere* plunge] —**im·mer′sion**, *n.*

im·mi·grant (im′ə grənt), *n.* person who comes into a foreign country or region to live: *Canada has many immigrants from Europe.* —*adj.* immigrating.

im·mi·grate (im′ə grāt), *v.*, **–grat·ed**, **–grat·ing.** come into a foreign country or region to live. [< L, < *in–* into + *migrare* move] —**im′mi·gra′tor**, *n.*

im·mi·gra·tion (im′ə grā′shən), *n.* **1** a coming into a foreign country or region to live. **2** immigrants: *the immigration of 1918.*

im·mi·nence (im′ə nəns), **im·mi·nen·cy** (–nən si), *n.* **1** state or fact of being imminent. **2** thing that is imminent; evil or danger about to occur.

im·mi·nent (im′ə nənt), *adj.* likely to happen soon; about to occur. [< L *imminens* overhanging] —**im′mi·nent·ly**, *adv.*

im·mis·ci·ble (i mis′ə bəl), *adj.* incapable of being mixed. —**im·mis′ci·bil′i·ty,** *n.* —**im·mis′ci·bly,** *adv.*

im·mo·bile (i mō′bəl; –bēl), *adj.* **1** not movable; firmly fixed. **2** not moving; not changing; motionless. —**im′mo·bil′i·ty,** *n.*

im·mo·bi·lize (i mō′bə līz), *v.,* –**lized,** –**liz·ing.** make immobile. —**im·mo′bi·li·za′tion,** *n.*

im·mod·er·a·cy (i mod′ər ə si), *n.* =immoderation.

im·mod·er·ate (i mod′ər it), *adj.* not moderate; too much; going too far; extreme; more than is right or proper. —**im·mod′er·ate·ly,** *adv.* —**im·mod′er·ate·ness,** *n.*

im·mod·er·a·tion (i mod′ə rā′shən), *n.* lack of moderation; excess.

im·mod·est (i mod′ist), *adj.* **1** bold and rude. **2** indecent; improper. —**im·mod′est·ly,** *adv.*

im·mod·es·ty (i mod′is ti), *n.* **1** lack of modesty; boldness and rudeness. **2** lack of decency; improper behavior.

im·mo·late (im′ə lāt), *v.,* –**lat·ed,** –**lat·ing.** **1** kill as a sacrifice. **2** sacrifice. [< L *immolatus* sacrificed, orig., sprinkled with sacrificial meal < *in–* on + *mola* sacrificial meal] —**im′mo·la′tion,** *n.* —**im′mo·la′tor,** *n.*

im·mor·al (i môr′əl; i mor′–), *adj.* **1** morally wrong; wicked. Lying and stealing are immoral. **2** lewd; unchaste. —**im·mor′al·ly,** *adv.*

im·mo·ral·i·ty (im′ə ral′ə ti), *n., pl.* –**ties.** **1** wickedness; wrongdoing; vice. **2** lewdness; unchastity. **3** an immoral act.

im·mor·tal (i môr′təl), *adj.* **1** living forever; never dying; everlasting. **2** remembered or famous forever. —*n.* **1** an immortal being. **2** Usually, **immortals** one of the gods of ancient Greek and Roman mythology. **3** person remembered or famous forever: *Shakespeare is one of the immortals.* —**im·mor′tal·ly,** *adv.*

im·mor·tal·i·ty (im′ôr tal′ə ti), *n.* **1** endless life; living forever. **2** fame that lasts forever.

im·mor·tal·ize (i môr′təl īz), *v.,* –**ized,** –**iz·ing.** **1** make immortal. **2** give everlasting fame to. —**im·mor′tal·i·za′tion,** *n.* —**im·mor′tal·iz′er,** *n.*

im·mov·a·ble (i müv′ə bəl), *adj.* **1** that cannot be moved; firmly fixed. **2** not moving; not changing position; motionless. **3** *Fig.* firm; steadfast; unyielding. **4** *Fig.* unfeeling; impassive. —**im·mov′a·bil′i·ty, im·mov′a·ble·ness,** *n.* —**im·mov′a·bly,** *adv.*

im·mune (i mūn′), *adj.* **1** having immunity: **a** exempt, as from taxes, laws, etc. **b** protected against disease, as by inoculation. **2** of or having to do with the immune system. [< L *immunis,* orig., free from obligation]

immune system, the body's system of defense against disease, which destroys viruses, bacteria, or other foreign matter by means of antibodies, T-cells, etc.

im·mu·ni·ty (i mū′nə ti), *n., pl.* –**ties. 1** resistance to disease, poison, etc. **2** freedom or protection from obligation, service, or duty.

im·mu·nize (im′yủ nīz), *v.,* –**nized,** –**niz·ing.** give immunity to; make immune. —**im′mu·ni·za′tion,** *n.*

im·mu·no·bi·ol·o·gy (i mü′nō bī ol′ə ji), *n.* study of biological immunity or immunization.

im·mu·nol·o·gy (im′yủ nol′ə ji), *n.* science of the nature and causation of immunity from diseases. —**im·mu′no·log′ic, im·mu′no·log′i·cal,** *adj.* —**im′mu·nol′o·gist,** *n.*

im·mu·no·ther·a·py (i mü′nō ther′ə pi), *n.* treatment of disease by stimulation or suppression of the body's immune system, as in the case of allergic reactions.

im·mure (i myủr′), *v.,* –**mured,** –**mur·ing. 1** imprison. **2** confine closely. [< Med.L, < L *in–* in + *murus* wall] —**im·mure′ment,** *n.*

im·mu·ta·ble (i mū′tə bəl), *adj.* never changing; unchangeable. —**im·mu′ta·bil′i·ty, im·mu′ta·ble·ness,** *n.* —**im·mu′ta·bly,** *adv.*

IMO, in my opinion.

imp (imp), *n.* **1** a young or small devil or demon. **2** a mischievous child. [OE *impe* a shoot, graft, ult. < VL *imputus* < Gk. *emphytos* engrafted]

imp., 1 imperative. **2** imperfect. **3** imperial. **4** import.

im·pact (im′pakt), *n.* the striking (of one thing against another): *the impact of the two swords broke both of them.* [< L *impactus* struck against. See IMPINGE.] —**im·pac′tion,** *n.*

im·pact·ed (im pak′tid), *adj.* **1** firmly wedged or pressed in place. **2** of a tooth, pressed between the jawbone and another tooth.

im·pair (im pār′), *v.* make worse; damage; weaken. [< OF *empeier,* ult. < L *in–* + *pejor* worse] —**im·pair′er,** *n.* —**im·pair′ment,** *n.*

im·pale (im pāl′), *v.,* –**paled,** –**pal·ing. 1** pierce through with anything pointed; fasten upon anything pointed. **2** torture or punish by thrusting upon a pointed stake. [< F, ult. < L *in–* on + *palus* stake] —**im·pale′ment,** *n.* —**im·pal′er,** *n.*

im·pal·pa·ble (im pal′pə bəl), *adj.* **1** that cannot be perceived by the sense of touch: *sunbeams are impalpable.* **2** very hard for the mind to grasp: *impalpable distinctions.* —**im·pal′pa·bil′i·ty,** *n.* —**im·pal′pa·bly,** *adv.*

im·pan·el (im pan′əl), *v.,* –**eled,** –**el·ing. 1** put on a list for duty on a jury. **2** select (a jury) from the list. Also, **empanel.** —**im·pan′el·ment,** *n.*

im·part (im pärt′), *v.* **1** give a share in; give: *rich furnishings that impart elegance.* **2** communicate; tell: *impart a secret.* [< L, < *in–* in + *pars* part] —**im·part′i·ble,** *adj.*

im·par·tial (im pär′shəl), *adj.* showing no more favor to one side than to the other;

fair; just. —**im·par′tial·ly,** *adv.* —**im·par′tial·ness,** *n.*

im·par·ti·al·i·ty (im′pär shi al′ə ti), *n.* fairness, justice.

im·pass·a·ble (im pas′ə bəl), *adj.* not passable; so that one cannot go through or across. —**im·pass′a·bil′i·ty, im·pass′a·ble·ness,** *n.* —**im·pass′a·bly,** *adv.*

im·passe (im pas′), *n.* **1** position from which there is no escape; deadlock. **2** road or way closed at one end. [< F]

im·pas·si·ble (im pas′ə bəl), *adj.* **1** unable to suffer or feel pain. **2** that cannot be harmed. **3** without feeling; impassive. [< L *impassibilis,* ult. < *in–* not + *pati* suffer] —**im·pas′si·bil′i·ty, im·pas′si·ble·ness,** *n.* —**im·pas′si·bly,** *adv.*

im·pas·sioned (im pash′ənd), *adj.* full of strong feeling; ardent; emotional. —**im·pas′sioned·ly,** *adv.* —**im·pas′sioned·ness,** *n.*

im·pas·sive (im pas′iv), *adj.* **1** without feeling or emotion; unmoved; indifferent. **2** calm; serene. —**im·pas′sive·ly,** *adv.* —**im·pas′sive·ness,** *n.*

im·pas·siv·i·ty (im′pa siv′ə ti), *n.* state of being impassive.

im·pas·to (im päs′tō), *n.* **1** technique of laying paint, esp. oil paint, thickly on a canvas. **2** paint laid on in this manner. [< It. *impasto* < *impastare* beplaster]

im·pa·tience (im pā′shəns), *n.* **1** lack of patience; being impatient. **2** uneasiness and eagerness.

im·pa·ti·ens (im pā′shənz; –shē enz), *n.* plant of the genus that includes balsam, much used in gardens for its colorful flowers in all hues of red. [< NL *impatiens* genus name < L *impatiēns* impatient]

im·pa·tient (im pā′shənt), *adj.* **1** not patient; not willing to bear delay, opposition, pain, bother, etc., calmly. **2** restless: *the horses were impatient to start in the race.* **3** showing lack of patience: *an impatient answer.* —**im·pa′tient·ly,** *adv.* —**im·pa′tient·ness,** *n.*

im·peach (im pēch′), *v.* **1** call in question: *to impeach a person's honor.* **2** charge with wrongdoing; accuse. **3** accuse (a public officer) of wrong conduct during office before a competent tribunal: *a judge may be impeached for taking a bribe.* [< OF *empechier* hinder, ult. < L *in–* on + *pedica* shackle] —**im·peach′a·ble,** *adj.* —**im·peach′a·bil′i·ty,** *n.* —**im·peach′er,** *n.* —**im·peach′ment,** *n.*

im·pec·ca·ble (im pek′ə bəl), *adj.* **1** faultless. **2** sinless. [< LL, < *in–* not + *peccare* sin] —**im·pec′ca·bil′i·ty,** *n.* —**im·pec′ca·bly,** *adv.*

im·pe·cu·ni·ous (im′pi kū′ni əs), *adj.* having little or no money; penniless; poor. [< L, < *in–* not + *pecunia* money] —**im′pe·cu·ni·ous·ly,** *adv.* —**im′pe·cu·ni·ous·ness,** *n.*

im·ped·ance (im pēd′əns), *n.* the apparent resistance in an alternating-current circuit.

im·pede (im pēd'), v., **-ped·ed, -ped·ing.** hinder; obstruct. [< L *impedire* < *in-* on + *pes* foot] —**im·ped'er,** *n.* —**im·ped'ing·ly,** *adv.*

im·ped·i·ment (im ped'ə mənt), *n.* **1** hindrance. **2** defect in speech. —**im·ped·i·men'tal,** *adj.*

im·ped·i·men·ta (im ped´ə men'tə), *n.pl.* **1** baggage. **2** military supplies carried with an army. **3** hindrances. [< L]

im·pel (im pel'), v., **-pelled, -pel·ling. 1** cause to move; drive forward; push along: *the wind impelled the boat to shore.* **2** drive; force; cause: *hunger impelled the lazy man to work.* [< L, < *in-* on + *pellere* push] —**im·pel'ler,** *n.*

im·pend (im pend'), v. **1** be likely to happen soon; be near: *when war impends, wise men try to prevent it.* **2** hang; hang threateningly. [< L, < *in-* over + *pendere* hang]

im·pend·ing (im pen'ding), *adj.* **1** likely to happen soon; imminent. **2** overhanging.

im·pen·e·tra·ble (im pen'ə trə bəl), *adj.* **1** that cannot be entered, pierced, or passed. **2** impossible for the mind to understand; inscrutable. —**im·pen´e·tra·bil'i·ty, im·pen'e·tra·ble·ness,** *n.* —**im·pen'e·tra·bly,** *adv.*

im·pen·i·tent (im pen'ə tənt), *adj.* not penitent; feeling no sorrow or regret for having done wrong. —**im·pen'i·tence, im·pen'i·tent·ness,** *n.* —**im·pen'i·tent·ly,** *adv.*

imper., imperative.

im·per·a·tive (im per'ə tiv), *adj.* **1** not to be avoided; urgent; necessary. **2** expressing a command; peremptory: *an imperative tone.* **3** in grammar, expressing command: *the imperative mood.* —*n.* **1** a command. **2** in grammar, the imperative mood. [< L, < *imperare* order] —**im·per'a·tive·ly,** *adv.* —**im·per'a·tive·ness,** *n.*

im·per·cep·ti·ble (im´pər sep'tə bəl), *adj.* **1** that cannot be perceived or felt. **2** very slight; gradual. —**im´per·cep´ti·bil'i·ty, im´per·cep'ti·ble·ness,** *n.* —**im´per·cep'ti·bly,** *adv.*

imperf., imperfect.

im·per·fect (im per'fikt), *adj.* **1** not perfect; having some defect or fault. **2** not complete; lacking some part. **3** expressing continued or customary action in the past. —*n.* the imperfect tense or verb form. English has no imperfect, but such forms as *was studying* and *used to study* are like the imperfect in other languages. —**im·per'fect·ly,** *adv.* —**im·per'fect·ness,** *n.*

im·per·fec·tion (im´pər fek'shən), *n.* **1** lack of perfection. **2** fault; defect.

im·pe·ri·al (im pir'i əl), *adj.* **1** of or pertaining to an empire or its ruler. **2** of or having to do with the rule or authority of one country over other countries and colonies. **3** supreme; majestic; domineering. —*n.* a small beard left growing beneath the lower lip. [< L, < *imperium* empire] —**im·pe'ri·al·ly,** *adv.* —**im·pe'ri·al·ness,** *n.*

im·pe·ri·al·ism (im pir'i əl iz´əm), *n.* **1** policy of extending the rule or authority of one country over other countries and colonies. **2** an imperial system of government. —**im·pe'ri·al·ist,** *n.* —**im·pe´ri·al·is'tic,** *adj.* —**im·pe´ri·al·is'ti·cal·ly,** *adv.*

im·per·il (im per'əl), v., **-iled, -il·ing.** put in danger. —**im·per'il·ment,** *n.*

im·pe·ri·ous (im pir'i əs), *adj.* **1** haughty; domineering. **2** imperative; urgent. [< L *imperiosus* commanding. See IMPERATIVE.] —**im·pe'ri·ous·ly,** *adv.* —**im·pe'ri·ous·ness,** *n.*

im·per·ish·a·ble (im per'ish ə bəl), *adj.* everlasting; not perishable; indestructible. —**im·per´ish·a·bil'i·ty, im·per'ish·a·ble·ness,** *n.* —**im·per'ish·a·bly,** *adv.*

im·per·ma·nent (im pėr'mə nənt), *adj.* temporary. —**im·per'ma·nence,** *n.* —**im·per'ma·nent·ly,** *adv.*

im·per·me·a·ble (im pėr'mi ə bəl), *adj.* **1** impassable. **2** impervious. —**im·per´me·a·bil'i·ty, im·per'me·a·ble·ness,** *n.* —**im·per'me·a·bly,** *adv.*

impers., impersonal.

im·per·son·al (im pėr'sən əl; –pėrs'nəl), *adj.* **1** referring to all or any persons, not to any special one: *"first come, first served"* is an impersonal remark. **2** having no existence as a person: *electricity is an impersonal force.* **3** of a verb, having nothing but an indefinite *it* for a subject. Example: *rained* in "It rained yesterday." —**im·per'son·al·ize** (im pėr'sə nə līz), v., **-ized, -iz·ing.** make impersonal. —**im·per´son·al·i·za'tion,** *n.*

im·per·son·al·i·ty (im pėr´sən al'ə ti), *n., pl.* **-ties. 1** impersonal character. **2** impersonal thing, force, etc.

im·per·son·al·ly (im pėr'sən əl i; –pėrs'nəl i), *adv.* in an impersonal manner; without personal reference or connection.

im·per·son·ate (im pėr'sən āt), v., **-at·ed, -at·ing. 1** act the part of; *impersonate Hamlet on the stage.* **2** pretend to be; mimic the voice, appearance, and manners of: *impersonate a well-known news commentator.* **3** personify; typify. —**im·per'son·a'tion,** *n.* —**im·per'son·a'tor,** *n.*

im·per·ti·nence (im pėr'tə nəns), **im·per·ti·nen·cy** (–nən si), *n., pl.* **-nenc·es; -cies. 1** impertinent quality. **2** impertinent act or speech. **3** lack of pertinence; irrelevance.

im·per·ti·nent (im pėr'tə nənt), *adj.* **1** saucy; impudent; insolent. **2** not pertinent; not to the point; out of place. —**im·per'ti·nent·ly,** *adv.*

im·per·turb·a·ble (im´pər tėr'bə bəl), *adj.* unexcitable; not easily excited; calm. —**im´per·turb´a·bil'i·ty, im´per·turb'a·ble·ness,** *n.* —**im´per·turb'a·bly,** *adv.*

im·per·vi·ous (im pėr'vi əs), *adj.* **1** not letting things pass through; not allowing passage. **2** not open to argument, suggestions, etc. —**im·per'vi·ous·ly,** *adv.* —**im·per'vi·ous·ness,** *n.*

im·pe·ti·go (im´pə tī'gō), *n.* an infectious skin disease causing pimples filled with pus. [< L, < *impetere* attack < *in-* + *petere* aim for]

im·pet·u·os·i·ty (im pech´u os'ə ti), *n., pl.* **-ties.** sudden or rash energy; ardor.

im·pet·u·ous (im pech'u əs), *adj.* **1** acting hastily, rashly, or with sudden feeling. **2** moving with great force or speed. —**im·pet'u·ous·ly,** *adv.* —**im·pet'u·ous·ness,** *n.*

im·pe·tus (im'pə təs), *n.* **1** force with which a moving body tends to maintain its velocity and overcome resistance. **2** a driving force; incentive. [< L, attack]

im·pi·e·ty (im pī'ə ti), *n., pl.* **-ties. 1** lack of piety or reverence for God. **2** lack of respect. **3** an impious act.

im·pinge (im pinj'), v., **-pinged, -ping·ing. 1** encroach; infringe. **2** hit; strike: *rays of light impinge on the eye.* [< L *impingere* < *in-* on + *pangere* strike] —**im·pinge'ment,** *n.* —**im·ping'er,** *n.*

im·pi·ous (im'pī əs), *adj.* not pious; not having or not showing reverence for God; wicked; profane. —**im·pi'ous·ly,** *adv.* —**im·pi'ous·ness,** *n.*

imp·ish (imp'ish), *adj.* **1** of or like an imp. **2** mischievous. —**imp'ish·ly,** *adv.* —**imp'ish·ness,** *n.*

im·pla·ca·ble (im plā'kə bəl; –plak'ə–), *adj.* that cannot be placated, pacified, or appeased. —**im·pla´ca·bil'i·ty, im·pla'ca·ble·ness,** *n.* —**im·pla'ca·bly,** *adv.*

im·plant (im plant'; –plänt'), v. **1** instill or fix deeply (a desire, opinion, etc.): *a good teacher implants high ideals in children.* **2** plant in the ground, planter, etc. **3** insert in the body: *implant a tooth; implant a pacemaker.* —*n.* any tissue, organ, or artificial substance inserted in the body. —**im´plan·ta'tion,** *n.* —**im·plant'er,** *n.*

im·plau·si·ble (im plô'zə bəl), *adj.* not appearing reasonable, possible, or true; not plausible. —**im·plau´si·bil'i·ty,** *n.* —**im·plau'si·bly,** *adv.*

im·ple·ment (*n.* im'plə mənt; *v.* im'plə ment), *n.* a useful article of equipment; tool; instrument; utensil, such as a plow, ax, shovel, broom, etc. —*v.* **1** provide with implements or other means. **2** provide the power and authority necessary to accomplish or put (something) into effect: *implement a policy.* **3** carry out; get done. [< LL *implementum,* lit., that which fills a need, ult. < *in-* in + *-plere* fill] —**im'ple·men'tal,** *adj.*

im·pli·cate (im'plə kāt), v., **-cat·ed, -cat·ing. 1** show to have a part or to be connected; involve: *the thief's confession implicated two other men.* **2** imply. [< L, < *in-* in + *plicare* fold]

im·pli·ca·tion (im´plə kā'shən), *n.* **1** an implying or being implied: *admit a thing by implication.* **2** indirect suggestion; hint: *no implication of dishonesty.* —**im´pli·ca'tion·al,** *adj.*

im·plic·it (im plis′it), *adj.* **1** meant, but not clearly expressed or distinctly stated; implied: *implicit consent.* **2** without doubting, hesitating, or asking questions; absolute: *implicit obedience.* [< L *implicitus,* pp. of *implicare* IMPLICATE] —**im·plic′it·ly,** *adv.* —**im·plic′it·ness,** *n.*

im·plied (im plīd′), *adj.* involved, indicated, suggested, or understood without express statement.

im·plode (im plōd′), *v.,* **–plod·ed, –plod·ing.** burst inward; collapse. —**im·plo′-sion,** *n.* [< im– (in-²) into + *explode*]

im·plore (im plôr′; –plōr′), *v.,* **–plored, –plor·ing.** **1** beg earnestly for. **2** beg (a person to do some act). [< L, < *in–* toward + *plorare* cry] —**im′plo·ra′-tion,** *n.* —**im·plor′er,** *n.* —**im·plor′ing·ly,** *adv.* —**im·plor′ing·ness,** *n.*

im·ply (im plī′), *v.,* **–plied, –ply·ing. 1** indicate without saying outright; express indirectly; suggest: *her smile implied that she had forgiven us.* **2** involve as a necessary part or condition: *speech implies a speaker.* [< OF *emplier* involve, put (in). See IMPLICATE.]

im·po·lite (im′pə līt′), *adj.* not polite; having or showing bad manners; rude; discourteous. —**im′po·lite′ly,** *adv.* —**im′po·lite′ness,** *n.*

im·pol·i·tic (im pol′ə tik), *adj.* not politic; not expedient; unwise. —**im·pol′i·tic·ly,** *adv.* —**im·pol′i·tic·ness,** *n.*

im·pon·der·a·ble (im pon′dər ə bəl), *adj.* without weight that can be felt or measured. —*n.* something imponderable. —**im·pon′der·a·bil′i·ty, im·pon′der·a·ble·ness,** *n.* —**im·pon′der·a·bly,** *adv.*

im·port (*v.* im pôrt′, –pōrt′, im′pôrt, –pōrt; *n.* im′pôrt, –pōrt), *v.* **1** bring in from a foreign country for sale or use: *we import coffee from Brazil.* **2** mean; signify: *tell me what your remark imports.* **3** be of importance or consequence. —*n.* **1** thing imported: *rubber is a useful import.* **2** an importing; importation. **3** meaning: *what is the import of your remark?* **4** importance. [< L, < *in–* in + *portare* carry] —**im·port′a·ble,** *adj.* —**im·port′a·bil′i·ty,** *n.* —**im·port′er,** *n.*

im·por·tance (im pôr′təns), *n.* quality or fact of being important; consequence; significance.

im·por·tant (im pôr′tənt), *adj.* **1** meaning much; worth noticing or considering; having value or significance. **2** having social position or influence. **3** acting or seeming important. [< F < Med.L *importans* being significant < L, bringing on or in. See IMPORT.] —**im·por′tant·ly,** *adv.*

im·por·ta·tion (im′pôr tā′shən; –pōr–), *n.* **1** act of importing. **2** something imported.

im·por·tu·nate (im pôr′chə nit), *adj.* asking repeatedly; annoyingly persistent. —**im·por′tu·nate·ly,** *adv.* —**im·por′tu·nate·ness,** *n.*

im·por·tune (im′pôr tün′; –tūn′; im pôr′-chən), *v.,* **–tuned, –tun·ing.** ask urgently or repeatedly; trouble with demands.

[< MF < L *importunus* inconvenient] —**im′por·tune′ly,** *adv.* —**im′por-tun′er,** *n.*

im·por·tu·ni·ty (im′pôr tü′nə ti; –tū′–), *n., pl.* **–ties.** persistence in asking; act of demanding again and again.

im·pose (im pōz′), *v.,* **–posed, –pos·ing. 1** put (a burden, tax, punishment, etc.) on. **2** force or thrust one's or its authority or influence on another or others. **3** force or thrust (oneself or one's company) on another or others. **4** pass off (a thing upon a person) to deceive. [< F, < *in–* on + *poser* put, place, POSE] —**im·pos′a·ble,** *adj.* —**im·pos′er,** *n.*

im·pos·ing (im pōz′ing), *adj.* impressive because of size, appearance, dignity, etc.: *the Capitol is an imposing building.* —**im·pos′ing·ly,** *adv.* —**im·pos′ing·ness,** *n.*

im·po·si·tion (im′pə zish′ən), *n.* **1** act or fact of imposing. **2** tax, duty, task, burden, etc. **3** an unfair tax, etc. **4** an imposing upon a person by taking advantage of his good nature. **5** deception; fraud; trick.

im·pos·si·bil·i·ty (im pos′ə bil′ə ti; im′-pos–), *n., pl.* **–ties. 1** quality of being impossible. **2** something impossible.

im·pos·si·ble (im pos′ə bəl), *adj.* **1** that cannot be or happen: *the accident seemed impossible.* **2** not possible to use; not to be done: *few things are impossible.* **3** that cannot be true: *an impossible rumor.* **4** not endurable; very objectionable: *an impossible person.* —**im·pos′si·ble·ness,** *n.* —**im·pos′si·bly,** *adv.*

im·post (im′pōst), *n.* **1** tax on goods brought into a country. **2** tax; tribute. —*v.* fix duties on. [< OF, ult. < L *in–* on + *ponere* place, put]

im·pos·tor (im pos′tər), *n.* **1** person who assumes a false name or character. **2** deceiver; cheat. [< LL, < *imponere* impose. See IMPOST.]

im·pos·ture (im pos′chər), *n.* deception; fraud.

im·po·tence (im′pə təns), **im·po·ten·cy** (–tən si), *n.* lack of power; condition or quality of being impotent.

im·po·tent (im′pə tənt), *adj.* **1** not having power; helpless. **2** lacking in sexual power. —**im′po·tent·ly,** *adv.* —**im′po-tent·ness,** *n.*

im·pound (im pound′), *v.* **1** shut up in a pen or pound. **2** shut up; enclose; confine. **3** put in the custody of a law court: *the court impounded the documents to use as evidence.* —**im·pound′age,** *n.* —**im·pound′er,** *n.*

im·pov·er·ish (im pov′ər ish; –pov′rish), *v.* **1** make very poor. **2** exhaust the strength, richness, or resources of. [< OF *empoveriss–,* ult. < L *in–* + *pau-per* poor] —**im·pov′er·ish·er,** *n.* —**im·pov′er·ish·ment,** *n.*

im·pow·er (im pou′ər), *v.* =empower. —**im·pow′er·ment,** *n.*

im·prac·ti·ca·ble (im prak′tə kə bəl), *adj.* **1** not working well in practice: *impracti-cable suggestions.* **2** that cannot be used:

an impracticable road. —**im·prac′ti·ca-bil′i·ty, im·prac·ti·ca·ble·ness,** *n.* —**im-prac′ti·ca·bly,** *adv.*

im·prac·ti·cal (im prak′tə kəl), *adj.* not practical. —**im·prac′ti·cal′i·ty,** *n.*

im·pre·cate (im′prə kāt), *v.,* **–cat·ed, –cat-ing.** call down (curses, evil, etc.). [< L *imprecatus,* ult. < *in–* on + *prex* prayer] —**im′pre·ca′tion,** *n.* —**im′pre·ca′tor,** *n.*

im·pre·cise (im′pri sīs′), *adj.* not precise, inexact; inaccurate. —**im·pre·ci′sion,** *n.*

im·preg·na·ble (im preg′nə bəl), *adj.* that cannot be overthrown by force; able to resist attack: *an impregnable fortress, an impregnable argument.* [< F, < *in–* not + *pregnable* pregnable] —**im·preg′na-bil′i·ty, im·preg′na·ble·ness,** *n.* —**im-preg′na·bly,** *adv.*

im·preg·nate (im preg′nāt), *v.,* **–nat·ed, –nat·ing. 1** make pregnant; fertilize. **2** fill (with); saturate. [< LL *impraegnatus* made pregnant] —**im′preg·na′tion,** *n.* —**im·preg′na·tor,** *n.*

im·pre·sa·ri·o (im′pre sä′ri ō), *n., pl.* **–sa-ri·os.** organizer or manager of an opera or concert company. [< Ital., < *impresa* undertaking, ult. < L *in–* on + *prehendere* take] —**im′pre·sa′ri·o·ship′,** *n.*

im·press¹ (*v.* im pres′; *n.* im′pres), *v.,* **–pressed, –press·ing,** *n.* —*v.* **1** have a strong effect on the mind or feelings of: *a hero impresses us with his courage.* **2** fix in the mind: *she repeated the words to impress them in her memory.* **3** mark by pressing or stamping; imprint. —*n.* **1** impression; mark; stamp. **2** act of impressing. [< L *impressus < in–* in + *premere* press] —**im·press′er,** *n.* —**im-press′i·ble,** *adj.* —**im·press′i·bil′i·ty,** *n.*

im·press² (im pres′), *v.,* **–pressed, –press-ing. 1** seize by force for public use. **2** force (men) to serve in the navy or army. [< *in-²* + *press²*] —**im·press′ment,** *n.*

im·pres·sion (im presh′ən), *n.* **1** effect produced on a person: *make a bad impression.* **2** idea; notion: *a vague impression.* **3** something produced by pressure; mark, stamp, print, etc.: *impres-sion of a rabbit's feet in the snow.*

im·pres·sion·a·ble (im presh′ən ə bəl), *adj.* sensitive to impressions; easily impressed or influenced. —**im·pres′sion·a·bil′i·ty, im·pres′sion·a·ble·ness,** *n.*

im·pres·sion·ism (im presh′ən iz əm), *n.* **1** style of painting, developed in France in the 1800's that conveys esp. the impression created by light on a person, scene, etc. **2** style of literature concerned with emotional mood and general impressions. **3** style of musical composition that conveys the composer's impressions of an emotion, scene, etc. —**im·pres′-sion·ist,** *n.* —**im·pres′sion·is·tic,** *adj.*

im·pres·sive (im pres′iv), *adj.* able to impress the mind, feelings, conscience, etc.: *an impressive sermon.* —**im·pres′-sive·ly,** *adv.* —**im·pres′sive·ness,** *n.*

im·pri·ma·tur (im′pri mā′tər; –prī–), *n.* **1** an official license to print or publish a book, etc., now usually works sanctioned by the Roman Catholic Church. **2** sanction; approval. [< NL, let it be printed. See IMPRESS[1].]

im·print (*n.* im′print; *v.* im print′), *n.* **1** mark made by pressure; print: *the imprint of a foot in the sand.* **2** impression; mark: *suffering left its imprint on her face.* **3** a publisher's name, with the place and date of publication, on the title page or at the end of a book. —*v.* **1** mark by pressing or stamping; print: *imprint a postmark on an envelope.* **2** press or impress: *a scene imprinted on my memory.* —**im·print′er**, *n.*

im·print·ing (im prin′ting), *n.* process in very young animals that causes them to recognize a parent.

im·pris·on (im priz′ən), *v.* **1** put in prison; keep in prison. **2** confine closely; restrain. —**im·pris′on·ment**, *n.*

im·prob·a·ble (im prob′ə bəl), *adj.* not probable; not likely to happen; not likely to be true. —**im·prob′a·bil′i·ty, im·prob′a·ble·ness**, *n.* —**im·prob′a·bly**, *adv.*

im·promp·tu (im promp′tü; –tū), *adv., adj.* without previous thought or preparation; offhand. —*n.* improvisation. [< *in promptu* in readiness]

im·prop·er (im prop′ər), *adj.* **1** not correct. **2** not suitable. **3** not decent. —**improp′er·ly**, *adv.* —**im·prop′er·ness**, *n.*

improper fraction, fraction greater than 1. *Examples:* ⅔, ⅘.

im·pro·pri·e·ty (im′prə prī′ə ti), *n., pl.* –ties. **1** lack of propriety; quality of being improper. **2** improper conduct, act, expression, etc.

im·prove (im prüv′), *v.,* –**proved,** –**proving.** **1** make or become better: *his health is improving.* **2** increase the value of (land or property). **3** use well; make good use of: *improve your time by studying.*

improve on, make better; do better than. [< AF *emprouer* < OF *en-* in + *prou* profit] —**im·prov′a·ble,** *adj.* —**im·prov′a·bil′i·ty, im·prov′a·ble·ness,** *n.* —**im·prov′a·bly,** *adv.* —**im·prov′er,** *n.* —**im·prov′ing·ly,** *adv.*

im·prove·ment (im prüv′mənt), *n.* **1** a making or becoming better. **2** increase in value. **3** change or addition that increases value: *a house with all modern improvements.* **4** better condition; thing that is better than another; advance.

im·prov·i·dent (im prov′ə dənt), *adj.* lacking foresight; not looking ahead; not careful in providing for the future; not thrifty. —**im·prov′i·dence,** *n.* —**im·prov′i·dent·ly,** *adv.*

im·pro·vise (im′prə vīz), *v.,* –**vised,** –**vising.** **1** compose or utter (verse, music, etc.) without preparation. **2** prepare or provide offhand; extemporize. [< F < Ital. *improvvisare,* ult. < L *in-* not + *pro-* beforehand + *videre* see] —**im′pro·vi·sa′tion,** *n.* —**im′pro·vi·sa′tion·al,** *adj.* —**im′pro·vis′er,** *n.*

im·pru·dence (im prü′dəns), *n.* lack of prudence; imprudent behavior.

im·pru·dent (im prü′dənt), *adj.* not prudent; rash; not discreet. —**im·pru′dent·ly,** *adv.* —**im·pru′dent·ness,** *n.*

im·pu·dence (im′pyə dəns), *n.* lack of shame or modesty; rude boldness.

im·pu·dent (im′pyə dənt), *adj.* without shame or modesty; offensively impertinent; rudely bold. [< L, < *in-* not + *pudere* be modest] —**im′pu·dent·ly,** *adv.* —**im′pu·dent·ness,** *n.*

im·pugn (im pūn′), *v.* call in question; attack by words or arguments; challenge as false. [< OF < L *impugnare* assault < *in-* against + *pugnare* fight] —**im·pugn′a·ble,** *adj.* —**im·pugn′ment,** *n.* —**im·pugn′er,** *n.*

im·pulse (im′puls), *n.* **1** a sudden, driving force or influence; push: *the impulse of hunger.* **2** effect of a sudden, driving force, influence, or tendency to act: *an angry mob influenced more by impulse than by reason.* **3** stimulus transmitted, esp. by nerve cells, and influences action in the muscle, gland, or other nerve cells that it reaches. [< L *impulsus* < *impellere* IMPEL]

im·pul·sion (im pul′shən), *n.* **1** an impelling; driving force. **2** impulse. **3** impetus.

im·pul·sive (im pul′siv), *adj.* **1** acting upon impulse; easily moved. **2** driving onward; impelling; pushing. —**im·pul′sive·ly,** *adv.* —**im·pul′sive·ness,** *n.*

im·pu·ni·ty (im pū′nə ti), *n.* freedom from punishment, injury, or other bad consequences. [< L *impunitas,* ult. < *in-* without + *poena* punishment]

im·pure (im pyùr′), *adj.* **1** not pure; dirty. **2** immoral; corrupt. **3** mixed with something of lower value; adulterated. **4** not of one color, style, etc.; mixed. —**im·pure′ly,** *adv.* —**im·pure′ness,** *n.*

im·pu·ri·ty (im pyùr′ə ti), *n., pl.* –ties. **1** lack of purity; being impure. **2** Often, **impurities.** impure thing or element; thing that makes something else impure.

im·pute (im pūt′), *v.,* –**put·ed,** –**put·ing.** consider as belonging; attribute; charge (a fault, etc.) to a person; blame. [< L, < *in-* in + *putare* reckon] —**im·put′a·ble,** *adj.* —**im′pu·ta′tion,** *n.* —**im·put′a·tive,** *adj.* —**im·put′a·tive·ly,** *adv.* —**im·put′a·tive·ness,** *n.* —**im·put′er,** *n.*

in (in), *prep. In* expresses inclusion, situation, presence, existence, position, and action. **1** inside: *in the box, go in the house.* **2** of: *a dress in silk, one in a hundred, a book in American history.* **3** because of; for: *act in self-defense.* **4** during; while: *in the present time, in crossing the street.* —*adv.* **1** in or into some place, position, condition, etc.: *come in.* **2** present, esp. in one's home or office: *he is not in today.* —*adj.* that is in; being in. —*n.* **1** familiarity or influence over someone or something. **2** access to someone or something.

in for, unable to avoid; sure to get or have.

in for it, *Informal.* in trouble.

in on, aware of; involved.

ins, people in office; or in control.

ins and outs, a twists and turns. **b** details.

in that, because.

in with, a friendly with. **b** partners with. [OE]

In, indium.

IN, (*zip code*) Indiana.

in–[1], *prefix.* not; the opposite of; the absence of, as in *inexpensive, inattention.* [< L; *in-* becomes *il-* before *l, im-* before *b, m,* and *p,* and *ir-* before *r*]

in–[2], *prefix.* in; within; into; toward, as in *inborn, indoors, inland.* [OE]

in., inch; inches.

in·a·bil·i·ty (in′ə bil′ə ti), *n.* lack of ability, power, or means; fact or state of being unable.

in ab·sen·tia (in ab sen′shə), *Latin.* while absent.

in·ac·ces·si·ble (in′ak ses′ə bəl), *adj.* **1** not accessible; that cannot be reached or entered. **2** hard to get at; hard to reach or enter. —**in′ac·ces′si·bil′i·ty, in′ac·ces′si·ble·ness,** *n.* —**in′ac·ces′si·bly,** *adv.*

in·ac·cu·ra·cy (in ak′yə rə si), *n., pl.* –cies. **1** lack of accuracy. **2** error; mistake.

in·ac·cu·rate (in ak′yə rit), *adj.* not exact; containing mistakes. —**in·ac′cu·rate·ly,** *adv.* —**in·ac′cu·rate·ness,** *n.*

in·ac·tion (in ak′shən), *n.* absence of action; idleness.

in·ac·ti·vate (in ak′tə vāt), *v.,* –**vat·ed,** –**vat·ing.** make inactive. —**in·ac′ti·va′tion,** *n.*

in·ac·tive (in ak′tiv), *adj.* not active; idle; sluggish. —**in·ac′tive·ly,** *adv.* —**in·ac′tiv′i·ty, in·ac′tive·ness,** *n.*

in·ad·e·quate (in ad′ə kwit), *adj.* not adequate; not enough; not as much as is required. —**in·ad′e·qua·cy, in·ad′e·quate·ness,** *n.* —**in·ad′e·quate·ly,** *adv.*

in·ad·mis·si·ble (in′əd mis′ə bəl), *adj.* **1** not allowable. **2** not to be admitted. —**in′ad·mis′si·bil′i·ty,** *n.* —**in′ad·mis′si·bly,** *adv.*

in·ad·ver·tence (in′əd vėr′təns), *n., pl.* –enc·es. **1** lack of attention; carelessness. **2** oversight; mistake.

in·ad·ver·tent (in əd vėr′tənt), *adj.* **1** not attentive; heedless; negligent. **2** not done on purpose; caused by oversight. —**in′ad·vert′ent·ly,** *adv.*

in·ad·vis·a·ble (in′əd vīz′bə əl), *adj.* not advisable; unwise; not prudent. —**in′ad·vis′a·bil′i·ty, in′ad·vis′a·ble·ness,** *n.* —**in′ad·vis′a·bly,** *adv.*

in·al·ien·a·ble (in āl′yən ə bəl; –ā′li ən–), *adj.* that cannot be given away or taken away. —**in·al′ien·a·bil′i·ty,** *n.* —**in·al′ien·a·bly,** *adv.*

in·ane (in ān′), *adj.* **1** silly; senseless. **2** empty. [< L *inanis*] —**in·ane′ly,** *adv.* —**in·ane′ness,** *n.*

in·an·i·mate (in an′ə mit), *adj.* **1** lifeless. **2** dull. —**in·an′i·mate·ly,** *adv.* —**in·an′i·mate·ness,** *n.*

in·a·ni·tion (in′ə nish′ən), *n.* **1** emptiness. **2** weakness from lack of food. [< LL, < L *inanire* to empty]

in·an·i·ty (in an′ə ti), *n., pl.* **-ties.** **1** silliness; lack of sense. **2** a silly or senseless act, practice, remark, etc. **3** emptiness.

in·ap·pli·ca·ble (in ap′lə kə bəl; in ′ə plik′-ə bəl), *adj.* not applicable; not appropriate; not suitable. —**in·ap′pli·ca·bil′i·ty, in·ap′pli·ca·ble·ness,** *n.* —**in·ap′pli·ca·bly,** *adv.*

in·ap·pre·ci·a·ble(in ′ə prē′shi ə bəl;–shə -bəl), *adj.* too small to be noticed or felt; very slight. —**in ′ap·pre′ci·a·bly,** *adv.*

in·ap·pro·pri·ate (in ′ə prō′pri it), *adj.* not suitable; not fitting. —**in ′ap·pro′pri·ate·ly,** *adv.* —**in ′ap·pro′pri·ate·ness,** *n.*

in·apt (in apt′), *adj.* **1** not apt; not suitable; unfit. **2** unskillful; awkward. —**in·apt′ly,** *adv.* —**in·apt′ness,** *n.*

in·ap·ti·tude (in ap′tə tüd; –tūd), *n.* **1** unfitness. **2** lack of skill.

in·ar·tic·u·late (in ′är tik′yə lit), *adj.* **1** not distinct; not like regular speech: *an inarticulate mutter.* **2** unable to speak in words; dumb. **3** not jointed. —**in ′ar·tic′u·late·ly,** *adv.* —**in ′ar·tic′u·late·ness,** *n.*

in·ar·tis·tic (in ′är tis′tik), *adj.* not artistic; lacking good taste. —**in ′ar·tis′ti·cal·ly,** *adv.*

in·as·much as (in ′əz much′), **1** because. **2** in so far as.

in·at·ten·tion (in ′ə ten′shən), *n.* lack of attention; negligence.

in·at·ten·tive (in ′ə ten′tiv), *adj.* not attentive; careless; negligent. —**in ′at·ten′tive·ly,** *adv.* —**in ′at·ten′tive·ness,** *n.*

in·au·di·ble (in ô′də bəl), *adj.* that cannot be heard. —**in·au′di·bil′i·ty, in·au′di·ble·ness,** *n.* —**in·au′di·bly,** *adv.*

in·au·gu·ral (in ô′gyə rəl), *adj.* of or for an inauguration. —*n.* **1** inaugural address. **2** inaugural ceremonies.

inaugural address, speech made by a president of the United States, or a governor of a state, when he or she is inaugurated.

in·au·gu·rate (in ô′gyə rāt), *v.,* **-rat·ed, -rat·ing.** **1** install in office with a ceremony. **2** make a formal beginning of; begin. [< L, ult. < *in-* for + *augur* taker of omens] —**in·au′gu·ra′tor,** *n.*

in·au·gu·ra·tion (in ô′gyə rā′shən), *n.* **1** act or ceremony of installing a person in office. **2** formal beginning; beginning. **3** opening for public use with a ceremony or celebration.

in·aus·pi·cious (in ′ôs pish′əs), *adj.* unfavorable; unlucky. —**in ′aus·pi′cious·ly,** *adv.* —**in ′aus·pi′cious·ness,** *n.*

in·board (in′bôrd′; –bōrd′), *adv., adj.* inside the hull of a ship.

in·born (in′bôrn′), *adj.* born in a person; instinctive; natural.

in·bound (in′bound′), *adj.* inward bound.

in·bred (in′bred′), *adj.* **1** inborn; natural: *an inbred courtesy.* **2** bred for generations from ancestors closely related.

in·breed (in′brēd′), *v.,* **-bred, -breed·ing.** **1** breed from closely related animals or plants. **2** produce or develop within.

in·breed·ing (in′brēd ′ing), *n.* breeding from closely related persons, animals, or plants.

inc., 1 inclosure. **2** including. **3** inclusive. **4** Also, **Inc.** incorporated. **5** increase.

In·ca (ing′kə), *n.* **1** member of a South American Indian people who ruled an empire in Peru before the Spanish conquest. **2** ruler or member of the royal family of these people. —**In′can,** *n., adj.*

in·cal·cu·la·ble (in kal′kyə lə bəl), *adj.* **1** too great in number to be counted; numerous. **2** not to be reckoned beforehand. **3** not to be relied on; uncertain. —**in·cal′cu·la·bil′i·ty, in·cal′cu·la·ble·ness,** *n.* —**in·cal′cu·la·bly,** *adv.*

in·can·desce (in ′kən des′), *v.,* **-desced, -des·cing.** glow or cause to glow.

in·can·des·cence (in ′kən des′əns), *n.* red-hot or white-hot condition.

in·can·des·cent (in ′kən des′ənt), *adj.* **1** glowing with heat; red-hot or white-hot. **2** *Fig.* intensely bright; brilliant. **3** pertaining to or containing a material that gives light by incandescence: *an incandescent lamp.* [< L *incandescens* beginning to glow < *in-* + *candere* be gleaming white] —**in ′can·des′cent·ly,** *adv.*

in·can·ta·tion (in ′kan tā′shən), *n.* **1** set of words spoken as a magic charm or to cast a magic spell. **2** use of such words. [< L, ult. < *in-* against + *cantare* chant]

in·ca·pa·ble (in kā′pə bəl), *adj.* **1** without ordinary ability; not efficient; not competent: *incapable workers.*

incapable of, a without the ability, power, or fitness for: *incapable of work.* **b** not susceptible to; not capable of receiving or admitting: *incapable of exact measurement.* —**in·ca ′pa·bil′i·ty,in·ca′pa·ble·ness,** *n.* —**in·ca′pa·bly,** *adv.*

in·ca·pac·i·tant (in ′ka pas′ə tant), *n.* something that incapacitates, as a chemical or drug.

in·ca·pac·i·tate (in ′kə pas′ə tāt), *v.,* **-tat·ed, -tat·ing.** deprive of ability, power, or fitness; disable. —**in ′ca·pac′i·ta′tion,** *n.*

in·ca·pac·i·ty (in ′kə pas′ə ti), *n., pl.* **-ties.** lack of ability, power, or fitness; disability.

in·car·cer·ate (in kär′sər āt), *v.,* **-at·ed, -at·ing.** imprison. [< LL, < L *in-* in + *carcer* jail] —**in·car′cer·a′tion,** *n.* —**in·car′cer·a′tor,** *n.*

in·car·nate (*adj.* in kär′nit, –nāt; *v.* in kär′nāt), *adj., v.,* **-nat·ed, -nat·ing.** —*adj.* embodied in flesh, esp. in human form. —*v.* **1** make incarnate; embody. **2** put into an actual form; realize. [< L, < *in-* + *caro* flesh]

in·car·na·tion (in ′kär nā′shən), *n.* **1** a taking on of human form by a divine being. **2** person or thing that represents some quality or idea. **3 the Incarnation,** the union of divine nature and human nature in the person of Jesus Christ.

in·case (in kās′), *v.,* **-cased, -cas·ing.** =encase. —**in·case′ment,** *n.*

in·cau·tious (in kô′shəs), *adj.* not cautious; heedless; reckless; rash. —**in·cau′tious·ly,** *adv.* —**in·cau′tious·ness,** *n.*

in·cen·di·ar·y (in sen′di er′i), *adj., n., pl.* **-ar·ies.** —*adj.* **1** having to do with the setting of property on fire maliciously. **2** causing fires; used to start a fire: *incendiary bombs.* **3** deliberately stirring up strife or rebellion: *incendiary speeches.* —*n.* **1** person who maliciously sets fire to property. **2** person who deliberately stirs up strife or rebellion. [< L, < *incendium* fire] —**in·cen′di·a·rism,** *n.*

in·cense¹ (in′sens), *n.* **1** substance giving off a sweet smell when burned. **2** perfume or smoke from it. **3** something sweet like incense, such as the perfume of flowers, flattery, or praise. [< LL *incensus* < L *incendere* burn] —**in′cense·less,** *adj.*

in·cense² (in sens′), *v.,* **-censed, -cens·ing.** make very angry; fill with rage. [< L *incensus* kindled] —**in·cense′ment,** *n.*

in·cen·tive (in sen′tiv), *n.* motive; stimulus. —*adj.* inciting; encouraging. [< L *incentivus* striking up the tune < *in-* + *canere* sing]

in·cep·tion (in sep′shən), *n.* a beginning; commencement. [< L *inceptio* < *incipere* begin < *in-* on + *capere* take] —**in·cep′-tive,** *adj.*

in·ces·sant (in ses′ənt), *adj.* never stopping; continued or repeated without interruption. [< LL, < L *in-* not + *cessare* cease] —**in·ces′san·cy, in·ces′sant·ness,** *n.* —**in·ces′sant·ly,** *adv.*

in·cest (in′sest), *n.* crime of sexual intercourse between persons so closely related that their marriage is prohibited by law. [< L *incestum* < *in-* not + *castus* chaste]

in·ces·tu·ous (in ses′chù əs), *adj.* **1** involving incest. **2** guilty of incest. —**in·ces′tu·ous·ly,** *adv.* —**in·ces′tu·ous·ness,** *n.*

inch (inch), *n.* **1** measure of length, $\frac{1}{12}$ of a foot. **2** the amount of rainfall, etc., that would cover a surface to the depth of one inch. **3** the smallest part, amount, or degree; very little bit. —*v.* move slowly or little by little: *a worm inches along.*

by inches or **inch by inch,** slowly; little by little.

every inch, completely.

within an inch of, very near; very close to. [< L *uncia,* orig., a twelfth. Doublet of OUNCE¹]

in·cho·ate (in kō′it), *adj.* just begun; in an early stage; incomplete; undeveloped. [< L *inchoatus* begun] —**in·cho′ate·ly,** *adv.* —**in·cho′ate·ness,** *n.*

inch·worm (inch′wèrm′), *n.* a measuring worm.

in·ci·dence (in′sə dəns), *n.* **1** range of occurrence or influence; way of affecting: *in an epidemic the incidence of disease is widespread.* **2** a falling on; a striking, esp. the direction in which one thing falls on or strikes another, as the angle (**angle of incidence**) that a line or ray of light falling upon a surface makes with a line perpendicular to that surface.

in·ci·dent (in′sə dənt), *n.* **1** a happening; event. **2** event that helps or adds to something else, as a distinct piece of action in a story, play, or poem. —*adj.* liable to happen; belonging: *hardships incident to the life of an explorer.* [< L *incidens* happening < *in-* on + *cadere* to fall]

in·ci·den·tal (in′sə den′təl), *adj.* **1** happening or likely to happen along with something else more important: *discomforts incidental to camping out.* **2** occurring by chance. —*n.* something incidental.

in·ci·den·tal·ly (in′sə den′təl i; –dent′li), *adv.* as an incident along with something else; accidentally.

incidental music, music that accompanies a film, play, etc., to set a mood or engage an audience.

in·cin·er·ate (in sin′ər āt), *v.,* –at·ed, –at·ing. burn to ashes. [< Med.L, < L *in-* into + *cinis* ashes] —**in·cin′er·a′tion,** *n.*

in·cin·er·a·tor (in sin′ər ā′tər), *n.* furnace or other arrangement for burning things.

in·cip·i·ent (in sip′i ənt), *adj.* just beginning; in an early stage. [< L *incipiens* beginning < *in-* on + *capere* take] —**in·cip′i·ence,** *n* —**in·cip′i·ent·ly,** *adv*

in·cise (in sīz′), *v.,* –cised, –cis·ing. **1** cut into. **2** carve; engrave. [< F *inciser,* ult. < *in-* into + *caedere* cut] —**in·cised′,** *adj.*

in·ci·sion (in sizh′ən), *n.* **1** cut made in something; gash. **2** act of incising.

in·ci·sive (in sī′siv), *adj.* sharp; penetrating; piercing; keen: *an incisive criticism.* [< Med.L *incisivus* < L *incidere* INCISE] —**in·ci′sive·ly,** *adv.* —**in·ci′sive·ness,** *n.*

in·ci·sor (in sī′zər), *n.* tooth adapted for cutting; one of the front teeth.

in·cite (in sīt′), *v.,* –cit·ed, –cit·ing. move to action; urge on; stir up; rouse. [< L *incitare,* ult. < *in-* on + *ciere* cause to move] —**in·cite′ment,** *n.* —**in·cit′er,** *n.* —**in·cit′ing·ly,** *adv.*

in·ci·vil·i·ty (in′sə vil′ə ti), *n., pl.* –ties. **1** rudeness; lack of courtesy; impoliteness. **2** a rude or impolite act.

incl., 1 including. **2** inclusive.

in·clem·en·cy (in klem′ən si), *n., pl.* –cies. severity; harshness: *the inclemency of the weather kept us at home.*

in·clem·ent (in klem′ənt), *adj.* **1** rough; stormy. **2** severe; harsh. —**in·clem′ent·ly,** *adv.*

in·cli·na·tion (in′klə nā′shən), *n.* **1** tendency: *an inclination to become fat.* **2** preference; liking: *a strong inclination for sports.* **3** a leaning; a bending; a bowing: *a nod is an inclination of the head.* **4** slope; slant: *the inclination of a roof.* —**in′cli·na′tion·al,** *adj.*

in·cline (*v.* in klīn′; *n.* in′klīn, in klīn′), *v.,* –clined, –clin·ing, *n.* —*v.* **1** be favorable; be disposed; tend: *dogs incline toward*

meat as a food. **2** make favorable or willing; influence: *incline your conscience to obey the law.* **3** slope; slant. **4** lean; bend; bow. —*n.* **1** slope; slant. **2** a sloping surface. [< L, < *in-* + *-clinare* bend] —**in·clined′,** *adj.* —**in·clin′er,** *n.*

inclined plane, plank or other plane surface put at an oblique angle with a horizontal surface.

in·close (in klōz′), *v.,* –closed, –clos·ing. =enclose. —**in·clos′er,** *n.*

in·clo·sure (in klō′zhər), *n.* =enclosure.

in·clude (in klüd′), *v.,* –clud·ed, –clud·ing. **1** contain; comprise: *the farm includes 160 acres.* **2** put in a total, a class, or the like; reckon in a count: *all on board the ship were lost, including the captain.* [< L *includere* < *in-* + *claudere* shut] —**in·clud′i·ble, in·clud′a·ble,** *adj.*

in·clu·sion (in klü′zhən), *n.* **1** an including or being included. **2** thing included.

in·clu·sive (in klü′siv), *adj.* **1** including in consideration; including; comprising: *read pages 10 to 20 inclusive.* **2** including much; including everything concerned: *an inclusive list of expenses.*

inclusive of, including; counting: *$30, inclusive of shipping and handling.* —**in·clu′sive·ly,** *adv.* —**in·clu′sive·ness,** *n.*

in·cog·ni·to (in′kog nē′tō), *adj., adv., n., pl.* –tos. —*adj., adv.* with one's name, character and rank, etc., concealed. —*n.* a disguised state or condition. [< Ital. < L *incognitus* unknown, ult. < *in-* not + *cognoscere* come to know]

in·co·her·ence (in′kō hir′əns), *n., pl.* –enc·es. **1** disconnected thought or speech. **2** lack of logical connection. **3** failure to stick together; looseness.

in·co·her·ent (in′kō hir′ənt), *adj.* **1** disconnected; confused. **2** not sticking together. —**in′co·her′ent·ly,** *adv.*

in·com·bus·ti·ble (in′kəm bus′tə bəl), *adj.* that cannot be burned; fireproof. —**in′com·bus′ti·bil′i·ty, in′com·bus′ti·ble·ness,** *n.* —**in′com·bus′ti·bly,** *adv.*

in·come (in′kum), *n.* what comes in from property, business, labor, etc.; receipts.

income tax, government tax on a person's income.

in·com·ing (in′kum ing), *adj.* coming in.

in·com·men·su·ra·ble (in′kə men′shə rə bəl; –sə rə–), *adj.* **1** that cannot be compared because not measurable in the same units or scale. **2** having no common integral divisor. —**in′com·men′su·ra·bil′i·ty, in′com·men′su·ra·ble·ness,** *n.* —**in′com·men′su·ra·bly,** *adv.*

in·com·men·su·rate (in′kə men′shə rit; –sə rit), *adj.* **1** not in proportion; not adequate. **2** =incommensurable. —**in′com·men′su·rate·ly,** *adv.* —**in′com·men′su·rate·ness,** *n.*

in·com·mo·di·ous (in′kə mō′di əs), *adj.* **1** not roomy enough. **2** inconvenient; uncomfortable. —**in′com·mo′di·ous·ly,** *adv.*

in·com·mu·ni·ca·ble (in′kə mü′nə kə bəl), *adj.* not capable of being communicated

or told. —**in′com·mu′ni·ca·ble·ness,** *n.* —**in′com·mu′ni·ca·bly,** *adv.*

in·com·mu·ni·ca·do (in′kə mü′nə kä′dō), *adj.* deprived of communication with others. [< Sp.]

in·com·pa·ra·ble (in kom′pə rə bəl; –prə bəl), *adj.* **1** without equal; matchless: *incomparable beauty.* **2** not to be compared; unsuitable for comparison. —**in·com′pa·ra·bil′i·ty, in·com′pa·ra·ble·ness,** *n.* —**in·com′pa·ra·bly,** *adv.*

in·com·pat·i·bil·i·ty (in′kəm pat′ə bil′ə ti), *n., pl.* –ties. **1** lack of harmony. **2** incompatible thing, quality, etc.

in·com·pat·i·ble (in′kəm pat′ə bəl), *adj.* **1** not able to live or act together peaceably; opposed in character. **2** inconsistent: *poor eating habits are incompatible with health.* —**in′com·pat′i·ble·ness,** *n.* —**in′com·pat′i·bly,** *adv.*

in·com·pe·tence (in kom′pə təns), *n.* lack of ability, power, or fitness.

in·com·pe·tent (in kom′pə tənt), *adj.* not competent; lacking ability, power, or fitness. —*n.* an incompetent person. —**in·com′pe·tent·ly,** *adv.*

in·com·plete (in′kəm plēt′), *adj.* not complete; lacking some part; unfinished. —**in′com·plete′ly,** *adv.* —**in′com·plete′ness, in′com·ple′tion,** *n.*

in·com·pre·hen·si·ble (in′kom pri hen′sə bəl), *adj.* impossible to understand. —**in′com·pre·hen′si·bil′i·ty, in′com·pre·hen′si·ble·ness,** *n.* —**in′com·pre·hen′si·bly,** *adv.*

in·com·press·i·ble (in′kəm pres′ə bəl), *adj.* not capable of being squeezed into a smaller size. —**in′com·press′i·bil′i·ty,** *n.*

in·con·ceiv·a·ble (in′kən sēv′ə bəl), *adj.* impossible to imagine; unthinkable; incredible. —**in′con·ceiv′a·bil′i·ty, in′con·ceiv′a·ble·ness,** *n.* —**in′con·ceiv′a·bly,** *adv.*

in·con·clu·sive (in′kən klü′siv), *adj.* not decisive; not effective. —**in′con·clu′sive·ly,** *adv.* —**in′con·clu′sive·ness,** *n.*

in·con·gru·i·ty (in′kong grü′ə ti; –kon–; –kən–), *n., pl.* –ties. **1** unfitness; inappropriateness; being out of place. **2** lack of agreement or harmony; inconsistency. **3** something that is incongruous.

in·con·gru·ous (in kong′grü əs), *adj.* **1** out of keeping; not appropriate; out of place. **2** lacking in agreement or harmony; not consistent. —**in·con′gru·ous·ly,** *adv.* —**in·con′gru·ous·ness,** *n.*

in·con·se·quent (in kon′sə kwent; –kwənt), *adj.* not logical; not logically connected. **2** not to the point; off the subject. —**in·con′se·quence,** *n.* —**in·con′se·quent·ly,** *adv.*

in·con·se·quen·tial (in′kon sə kwen′shəl), *adj.* **1** unimportant; trifling. **2** inconsequent. —**in·con′se·quen′tial·ly,** *adv.*

in·con·sid·er·a·ble (in′kən sid′ər ə bəl), *adj.* not worthy of consideration; not important. —**in′con·sid′er·a·ble·ness,** *n.* —**in′con·sid′er·a·bly,** *adv.*

in·con·sid·er·ate (in′kən sid′ər it), *adj.* not thoughtful of the rights and feelings of others. —**in′con·sid′er·ate·ly,** *adv.* —**in′con·sid′er·ate·ness, in′con·sid′er·a′tion,** *n.*

in·con·sist·en·cy (in′kən sis′tən si), *n., pl.* **-cies. 1** lack of agreement or harmony; variance. **2** failure to keep to the same principles, course of action, etc.; changeableness. **3** thing, act, etc., that is inconsistent.

in·con·sist·ent (in′kən sis′tənt), *adj.* **1** lacking in agreement or harmony; at variance. **2** failing to keep to the same principles, course of action, etc.; changeable. —**in′con·sist′ent·ly,** *adv.*

in·con·sol·a·ble (in′kən sōl′ə bəl), *adj.* not to be comforted. —**in′con·sol′a·bil′i·ty, in′con·sol′a·ble·ness,** *n.* —**in′con·sol′a·bly,** *adv.*

in·con·spic·u·ous (in′kən spik′yü əs), *adj.* attracting little or no attention. —**in′con·spic′u·ous·ly,** *adv.* —**in′con·spic′u·ous·ness,** *n.*

in·con·stan·cy (in kon′stən si), *n.* fickleness.

in·con·stant (in kon′stənt), *adj.* not constant; changeable; fickle. —**in·con′stant·ly,** *adv.*

in·con·test·a·ble (in′kən tes′tə bəl), *adj.* not to be disputed; unquestionable. —**in′con·test′a·bil′i·ty, in′con·test′a·ble·ness,** *n.* —**in′con·test′a·bly,** *adv.*

in·con·ti·nence (in kon′tə nəns), *n.* lack of self-restraint.

in·con·ti·nent (in kon′tə nənt), *adj.* without self-restraint. —**in·con′ti·nent·ly,** *adv.*

in·con·tro·vert·i·ble (in′kon trə vèr′tə bəl), *adj.* that cannot be disputed; unquestionable. —**in′con·tro·vert′i·bil′i·ty, in′con·tro·vert′i·ble·ness,** *n.* —**in′con·tro·vert′i·bly,** *adv.*

in·con·ven·ience (in′kən vēn′yəns), *n., v.,* **-ienced, -ienc·ing.** —*n.* **1** lack of convenience or ease; trouble; bother. **2** cause of trouble, difficulty, or bother. —*v.* cause trouble, difficulty, etc., to.

in·con·ven·ient (in′kən vēn′yənt), *adj.* not convenient; troublesome; causing bother or discomfort. —**in′con·ven′ient·ly,** *adv.*

in·cor·po·rate (*v.* in kôr′pə rāt; *adj.* in kôr′pə rit), *v.,* **-rat·ed, -rat·ing,** *adj.* —*v.* **1** make (something) a part of something else; join or combine (something) with something else: *we will incorporate your suggestion in this new plan.* **2** form into a corporation: *incorporate a business.* **3** embody; give material form to: *incorporate one's thoughts in an article.* —*adj.* united; combined; incorporated. [< L, *in-* into + *corpus* body] —**in·cor′po·ra′tive,** *adj.* —**in·cor′po·ra′tor,** *n.*

in·cor·po·ra·tion (in kôr′pə rā′shən), *n.* **1** an incorporating: *the incorporation of air bubbles in the glass spoiled it.* **2** a being incorporated: *incorporation gives a company the power to act as one person.*

in·cor·po·re·al (in′kôr pô′ri əl; -pō′-), *adj.* not made of any material substance; spiritual. —**in′cor·po′re·al·ly,** *adv.*

in·cor·rect (in′kə rekt′), *adj.* **1** not correct; wrong; faulty. **2** not proper. —**in′cor·rect′ly,** *adv.* —**in′cor·rect′ness,** *n.*

in·cor·ri·gi·ble (in kôr′ə jə bəl; in kor′-), *adj.* so firmly fixed (in bad ways, a bad habit, etc.) that nothing else can be expected: *an incorrigible liar.* —*n.* an incorrigible person. —**in·cor′ri·gi·bil′i·ty, in·cor′ri·gi·ble′ness,** *n.* —**in·cor′ri·gi·bly,** *adv.*

in·cor·rupt·i·ble (in′kə rup′tə bəl), *adj.* **1** not to be corrupted; honest. **2** not capable of decay. —**in′cor·rupt′i·bil′i·ty, in′cor·rupt′i·ble·ness,** *n.* —**in′cor·rupt′i·bly,** *adv.*

in·crease (*v.* in krēs′; *n.* in′krēs), *v.,* **-creased, -creas·ing,** *n.* —*v.* **1** make greater or more numerous; make richer or more powerful. **2** become greater; grow in numbers; advance in quality, success, power, etc. —*n.* **1** gain in size, numbers, etc.; growth. **2** result of increasing; increased product.

on the increase, increasing. [< AF var. of OE *encreistre* < L, < *in-* in + *crescere* grow] —**in·creas′a·ble,** *adj.* —**increas′er,** *n.*

in·creas·ing·ly (in krēs′ing li), *adv.* more and more.

in·cred·i·ble (in kred′ə bəl), *adj.* seeming too extraordinary to be possible; unbelievable: *incredible bravery.* —**in·cred′i·bil′i·ty, in·cred′i·ble·ness** *n.* —**in·cred′i·bly,** *adv.*

in·cre·du·li·ty (in′krə dü′lə ti; -dū′-), *n.* lack of belief; doubt.

in·cred·u·lous (in krej′ə ləs), *adj.* **1** not ready to believe; not credulous; doubting. **2** showing a lack of belief. —**in·cred′u·lous·ly,** *adv.* —**in·cred′u·lous·ness,** *n.*

in·cre·ment (in′krə mənt; ing′-), *n.* **1** increase; growth. **2** amount by which something increases. [< L *incrementum* < *increscere* INCREASE] —**in′cre·men′tal,** *adj.*

in·crim·i·nate (in krim′ə nāt), *v.,* **-nat·ed, -nat·ing.** accuse of a crime; show to be guilty: *the thief incriminated two others who helped him steal.* [< LL, < L *in-* against + *crimen* charge] —**in·crim′i·na′tion,** *n.* —**in·crim′i·na′tor,** *n.*

in·crust (in krust′), *v.* =encrust. —**in′crus·ta′tion,** *n.*

in·cu·bate (in′kyə bāt; ing′-), *v.,* **-bat·ed, -bat·ing. 1** sit on (eggs) in order to hatch them. **2** keep (eggs, etc.) warm so that they will hatch or grow. [< L, < *in-* on + *cubare* lie] —**in′cu·ba′tive,** *adj.*

in·cu·ba·tion (in′kyə bā′shən; ing′-), *n.* **1** an incubating or being incubated. **2** stage of a disease from the time of infection until the appearance of the first symptoms. —**in′cu·ba′tion·al,** *adj.*

in·cu·ba·tor (in′kyə bā′tər; ing′-), *n.* **1** apparatus having a box or chamber for keeping eggs at a specific temperature so that they will hatch. **2** a similar apparatus for rearing children born prematurely. **3** apparatus in which bacterial cultures are developed.

in·cu·bus (in′kyə bəs; ing′-), *n., pl.* **-bi** (-bī), **-bus·es. 1** an evil spirit supposed to descend upon sleeping persons. **2** nightmare. **3** an oppressive or burdensome thing. [< Med.L (def. 1), LL (def. 2), < L (def. 2), < L, < *in-* on + *cubare* lie]

in·cul·cate (in kul′kāt; in′kul kāt), *v.,* **-cat·ed, -cat·ing.** impress by repetition; teach persistently. [< L *inculcatus,* orig., trampled in, ult. < *in-* in + *calx* heel] —**in′cul·ca′tion,** *n.* —**in·cul′ca·tor,** *n.*

in·cum·ben·cy (in kum′bən si), *n., pl.* **-cies.** a holding of an office, position, etc., and performance of its duties; term of office.

in·cum·bent (in kum′bənt), *adj.* **1** lying, leaning, or pressing (on). **2** resting (on a person) as a duty: *it is incumbent on a judge to be just.* —*n.* person holding an office, position, church living, etc. [< L *incumbens* lying down on] —**in·cum′bent·ly,** *adv.*

in·cum·ber (in kum′bər), *v.* =encumber.

in·cum·brance (in kum′brəns), *n.* =encumbrance.

in·cu·nab·u·la (in′kyŭ nab′yə lə), *n.pl., sing.* **-lum** (-ləm). books printed before the year 1500. [< L, cradle] —**in′cu·nab′u·lar,** *adj.*

in·cur (in kėr′), *v.,* **-curred, -cur·ring.** run or fall into (something unpleasant); bring (blame, punishment, danger, etc.) on oneself: *the hunter incurred great danger in killing the tiger.* [< L, < *in-* upon + *currere* run]

in·cur·a·ble (in kyŭr′ə bəl), *adj.* not capable of being cured or remedied. —*n.* person having an incurable disease. —**in·cur′a·bil′i·ty, in·cur′a·ble·ness,** *n.* —**in·cur′a·bly,** *adv.*

in·cu·ri·ous (in kyŭr′ əs), *adj.* not curious; without curiosity. —**in′cu·ri·os′i·ty, in·cu′ri·ous·ness,** *n.* —**in·cu′ri·ous·ly,** *adv.*

in·cur·sion (in kėr′zhən; -shən), *n.* invasion; raid; sudden attack. [< L *incursio* < *incurrere.* See INCUR.]

in·cur·sive (in kėr′siv), *adj.* making incursions.

in·cus (ing′kəs), *n., pl.* **in·cu·des.** the middle one of a chain of three small bones in the middle ear of man and other animals. [< L, anvil]

Ind., 1 India. **2** Indian. **3** Indiana.

ind., 1 independent. **2** index. **3** indicative.

in·debt·ed (in det′id), *adj.* in debt; obliged; owing money or gratitude. —**in·debt′ed·ness,** *n.*

in·de·cen·cy (in dē′sən si), *n., pl.* **-cies. 1** lack of decency. **2** an indecent act or word.

in·de·cent (in dē′sənt), *adj.* **1** not decent; in very bad taste; improper: *an indecent lack of gratitude to the man who saved his life.* **2** not modest; morally bad; obscene. —**in·de′cent·ly,** *adv.*

in·de·ci·pher·a·ble (in´di sī´fər ə bəl), *adj.* incapable of being deciphered; illegible. —**in´de·ci´pher·a·bil´i·ty,** *n.*

in·de·ci·sion (in´di sizh´ən), *n.* lack of decision; tendency to delay or to hesitate.

in·de·ci·sive (in´di sī´siv), *adj.* 1 having the habit of hesitating and putting off decisions. 2 not deciding or settling the matter. —**in´de·ci´sive·ly,** *adv.* —**in´de·ci´sive·ness,** *n.*

in·dec·o·rous (in dek´ə rəs; in´di kô´rəs, –kō´–), *adj.* not suitable; improper. —**in·dec´o·rous·ly,** *adv.* —**in·dec´o·rous·ness,** *n.*

in·deed (in dēd´), *adv.* in fact; really; truly; surely. —*interj.* expression of surprise, incredulity, irony, or contempt.

indef., indefinite.

in·de·fat·i·ga·ble (in´di fat´ə gə bəl), *adj.* tireless; untiring. —**in´de·fat´i·ga·bil´i·ty, in´de·fat´i·ga·ble·ness,** *n.* —**in´de·fat´i·ga·bly,** *adv.*

in·de·fen·si·ble (in´di fen´sə bəl), *adj.* 1 that cannot be defended. 2 not justifiable. —**in´de·fen´si·bil´i·ty, in´de·fen´si·ble·ness,** *n.* —**in´de·fen´si·bly,** *adv.*

in·de·fin·a·ble (in´di fīn´ə bəl), *adj.* that cannot be defined. —**in´de·fin´a·ble·ness,** *n.* —**in´de·fin´a·bly,** *adv.*

in·def·i·nite (in def´ə nit), *adj.* 1 not clearly defined; not precise; vague. 2 not limited. —**in·def´i·nite·ly,** *adv.* —**in·def´i·nite·ness,** *n.*

indefinite article, *a* or *an.*

in·del·i·ble (in del´ə bəl), *adj.* 1 that cannot be erased or removed; permanent: *an indelible disgrace.* 2 making an indelible mark: *an indelible pen.* [< L, < *in-* not + *delere* destroy] —**in·del´i·bil´i·ty, in·del´i·ble·ness,** *n.* —**in·del´i·bly,** *adv.*

in·del·i·ca·cy (in del´ə kə si), *n., pl.* **-cies.** lack of delicacy; being indelicate.

in·del·i·cate (in del´ə kit), *adj.* 1 not delicate; coarse; crude. 2 improper; immodest. —**in·del´i·cate·ly,** *adv.* —**in·del´i·cate·ness,** *n.*

in·dem·ni·fi·ca·tion (in dem´nə fə kā´shən), *n.* 1 an indemnifying or being indemnified. 2 compensation; recompense.

in·dem·ni·fy (in dem´nə fī), *v.,* **-fied, -fy·ing.** 1 repay; make good; compensate for damage, loss, or expenses incurred. 2 secure against damage or loss; insure. —**in·dem´ni·fi´er,** *n.*

in·dem·ni·ty (in dem´nə ti), *n., pl.* **-ties.** 1 payment for damage, loss, or expense incurred. 2 security against damage or loss; insurance. [< LL, < L *indemnis* unhurt < *in-* not + *damnum* damage]

in·dent¹ (*v.* in dent´; *n.* in´dent, in dent´), *v.* 1 cut (an edge) so that it looks like a row of teeth; notch. 2 begin (a line) farther from the edge than the other lines. —*n.* 1 a notch. 2 an indenting. [< OF *endenter,* ult. < L *in-* in + *dens* tooth] —**in·dent´er,** *n.*

in·dent² (in dent´), *v.* 1 make a dent in. 2 press in; stamp. [< *in-²* + *dent*]

in·den·ta·tion (in´den tā´shən), *n.* 1 an indenting or being indented. 2 dent; notch; cut. 3 =indention.

in·den·tion (in den´shən), *n.* 1 a beginning of a line farther from the edge than the other lines. 2 blank space left by doing this. 3 =indentation.

in·den·ture (in den´chər), *n., v.,* **-tured, -tur·ing.** —*n.* 1 written agreement. 2 Also, **indentures.** contract by which a person is bound to serve someone else. 3 =indentation. —*v.* bind by a contract for service. [< OF *endenteure* indentation]

in·de·pend·ence (in´di pen´dəns), *n.* freedom from the control, influence, support, or help of another.

Independence Day, the Fourth of July.

in·de·pend·ent (in´di pen´dənt), *adj.* 1 needing, wishing, or getting no help from others: *independent thinking.* 2 acting, working, or esp. voting by one's own ideas. 3 not under another's rule. 4 not depending on others. 5 having an adequate private income. 6 not controlled or influenced by something else; separate; distinct. —*n.* 1 person who is independent in thought or behavior. 2 person who votes without regard to party. —**in·de·pend´ent·ly,** *adv.*

independent clause, =main clause.

in-depth (in´depth´), *adj.* covering all aspects; thorough; complete.

in·de·scrib·a·ble (in´di skrīb´ə bəl), *adj.* that cannot be described; beyond description. —**in´de·scrib´a·bil´i·ty, in´de·scrib´a·ble·ness,** *n.* —**in´de·scrib´a·bly,** *adv.*

in·de·struct·i·ble (in´di struk´tə bəl), *adj.* that cannot be destroyed. —**in´de·struct´i·bil´i·ty, in´de·struct´i·ble·ness,** *n.* —**in´de·struct´i·bly,** *adv.*

in·de·ter·mi·na·ble (in´di tėr´mə nə bəl), *adj.* 1 not capable of being settled or decided. 2 not capable of being ascertained. —**in´de·ter´mi·na·bly,** *adv.*

in·de·ter·mi·nate (in´di tėr´mə nit), *adj.* not determined; indefinite; vague. —**in´de·ter´mi·nate·ly,** *adv.* —**in´de·ter´mi·nate·ness,** *n.*

in·de·ter·mi·na·tion (in´di tėr´mə nā´shən), *n.* 1 lack of determination. 2 an unsettled state.

in·dex (in´deks), *n., pl.* **-dex·es, -di·ces** (–də sēz), *v.* —*n.* 1 list of what is in a book, telling on what pages to find topics, names, etc., usually put at the end of the book and arranged in alphabetical order. 2 thing that points out or shows; sign. 3 Also, **index finger.** finger next to the thumb; forefinger. 4 pointer: *a dial has an index.* 5 number representing an increase or decrease of prices, business activity, etc., *consumer price index.* —*v.* 1 provide with an index; make an index of. 2 enter in an index. [< L, orig., that which points out]

In·di·a (in´di ə). *n.* 1 a peninsular subcontinent in Asia, S of the Himalayas, between the Bay of Bengal and the Arabian Sea, projecting into the Indian Ocean. Now chiefly divided between the republic of India and Pakistan. 2 a republic in S Asia.

India ink, 1 a black pigment consisting of lampblack mixed with a binding material. **2** liquid ink prepared from this pigment.

In·di·a·man (in´di ə mən), *n., pl.* **-men.** a ship in the trade with India.

In·di·an (in´di ən), *n.* 1 an American Indian. 2 any one of the languages of the American Indians. 3 native of India or the East Indies. —*adj.* 1 of or having to do with American Indians. 2 of, living in, or belonging to India or the East Indies.

In·di·an·a (in´di an´ə), *n.* a Middle Western state of the United States. —**In´di·an´i·an,** *adj.,* *n.*

In·di·an·ap·o·lis (in´di ən ap´ə lis), *n.* capital of Indiana, near the center of the state.

Indian club, a bottle-shaped wooden club swung for exercise.

Indian corn, 1 grain that grows on large ears; maize. **2** plant that it grows on.

Indian file, single file.

Indian giver, person who takes back a gift after having bestowed it.

Indian Ocean, ocean S of Asia, E of Africa, and W of Australia.

Indian paintbrush, 1 plant of the figwort family, esp. found in W North America, that has red, pink, or yellow bracts. **2** common weed of North America that has reddish-orange flowers.

Indian pipe, a leafless plant with a solitary flower that looks like a tobacco pipe.

Indian summer, time of mild, dry, hazy weather in late autumn.

India paper, a thin, tough paper, used for Bibles, prayer books, etc.

In·dic (in´dik), *adj.* 1 of or having to do with India. 2 of or indicating the Indian branch of the Indo-Iranian languages, Hindi, Urdu, Sanskrit, etc.

indic., indicative.

in·di·cate (in´də kāt), *v.,* **-cat·ed, -cat·ing.** 1 point out; show; make known: *a thermometer indicates temperature.* 2 be a sign or hint of: *fever indicates sickness.* 3 give a sign or hint of; express: *indicate one's intention.* [< L, < *in-* in + *dicare* proclaim]

in·di·ca·tion (in´də kā´shən), *n.* 1 an indicating. 2 thing that indicates; sign.

in·dic·a·tive (in dik´ə tiv), *adj.* 1 pointing out; showing; being a sign (of); suggestive. 2 expressing or denoting a state, act, or happening as actual or asking a question. In "I go" and "Did I go?" the verbs are in the indicative mood. —*n.* **a** the indicative mood. **b** a verb form in this mood. —**in·dic´a·tive·ly,** *adv.*

in·di·ca·tor (in´də kā´tər), *n.* 1 person or thing that indicates. 2 pointer on the dial that measures something. 3 a measuring or recording instrument. 4 substance used to indicate chemical conditions or changes, as litmus paper.

in·di·ces (in′də sēz), *n.* pl. of **index.**

in·dict (in dīt′), *v.* **1** charge with an offense or crime; accuse. **2** find enough evidence against (an accused person) so that a trial is necessary. [< AF *enditer* INDITE] —**in·dict′a·ble,** *adj.* —**in·dict′er, in·dict′or,** *n.*

in·dict·ment (in dīt′mənt), *n.* **1** a formal accusation, esp. the legal accusation presented by a grand jury. **2** accusation.

in·die (in′dē), *n.* **1** independent producer, esp. of films. **2** film or recording independently produced. —*adj.* of or having to do with an independent production or producer. [< *inde*pendent]

In·dies (in′dēz), *n.pl.* **1** East Indies, India, and the Malay Archipelago. **2** the East Indies. **3** the West Indies.

in·dif·fer·ence (in dif′ər əns; –dif′rəns), *n.* **1** lack of interest or attention. **2** lack of importance: *where we ate was a matter of indifference.*

in·dif·fer·ent (in dif′ər ənt; –dif′rənt), *adj.* **1** having no feeling for or against: *indifferent to an admirer.* **2** impartial; neutral; without preference: *an indifferent decision.* **3** unimportant; not mattering much: *the time for starting is indifferent to me.* **4** neither good nor bad; just fair.

in·dif·fer·ent·ly (in dif′ər ənt li; –dif′rənt–), *adv.* **1** with indifference. **2** without distinction; equally. **3** moderately; tolerably; passably. **4** poorly; badly.

in·di·gence (in′də jəns), *n.* poverty.

in·dig·e·nous (in dij′ə nəs), *adj.* originating in the region or country where found; native. [< L *indigena* native] —**in·dig′e·nous·ly,** *adv.* —**in·dig′e·nous·ness,** *n.*

in·di·gent (in′də jənt), *adj.* poor; needy. [< L *indigens* needing] —**in′di·gent·ly,** *adv.*

in·di·gest·i·ble (in′də jes′tə bəl; –dī–), *adj.* that cannot be digested; hard to digest. —**in′di·gest′i·bil′i·ty, in′di·gest′i·ble·ness,** *n.* —**in′di·gest′i·bly,** *adv.*

in·di·ges·tion (in′də jes′chən; –dī–), *n.* inability to digest food; difficulty in digesting food.

in·dig·nant (in dig′nənt), *adj.* angry at something unworthy, unjust, or mean. —**in·dig′nant·ly,** *adv.*

in·dig·na·tion (in′dig nā′shən), *n.* anger at something unworthy, unjust, or mean; righteous anger. [< L, ult. < *in-* not + *dignus* worthy]

in·dig·ni·ty (in dig′nə ti), *n.,* pl. **-ties.** injury to dignity; an insult; a slight.

in·di·go (in′də gō), *n.,* pl. **-gos, –goes,** *adj.* —*n.* **1** blue dyestuff obtained from certain plants or made artificially. **2** plant from which indigo is obtained. **3** a deep violet blue. —*adj.* deep violet-blue. [< Sp. < L < Gk. *indikon,* orig. adj., Indian]

indigo bunting, a small American finch, the male of which is a deep violet-blue.

in·di·rect (in′də rekt′; –dī–), *adj.* **1** not direct; not straight: *an indirect route.* **2** not directly connected; secondary: *an indirect consequence.* **3** not straightfor-

ward and to the point: *an indirect reply, indirect methods.* —**in′di·rect′ly,** *adv.* —**in′di·rect′ness,** *n.*

in·di·rec·tion (in′də rek′shən; –dī–), *n.* **1** roundabout act, means, etc. **2** dishonesty; deceit.

indirect lighting, diffused light that illuminates without glare.

indirect object, person or thing that is indirectly affected by the action of the verb. The indirect object usually comes before the direct object and shows to whom or for whom something is done. In "I gave John a book," *John* is the indirect object and *book* is the direct object.

indirect tax, tax paid by the consumer in the form of higher prices for the taxed goods or services.

in·dis·cern·i·ble (in′di zėr′nə bəl; –sèr′–), *adj.* imperceptible. —**in′dis·cern′i·ble·ness, in′dis·cern′i·bly,** *adv.*

in·dis·creet (in′dis krēt′), *adj.* not discreet; not wise and judicious; imprudent.—**in′dis·creet′ly,** *adv.* —**in′dis·creet′ness,** *n.*

in·dis·cre·tion (in′dis kresh′ən), *n.* **1** lack of good judgment. **2** an indiscreet act.

in·dis·crim·i·nate (in′dis krim′ə nit), *adj.* **1** with no feeling for differences: *an indiscriminate reader.* **2** confused: *an indiscriminate mass.* —**in′dis·crim′i·nate·ly,** *adv.* —**in′dis·crim′i·nate·ness,** *n.*

in·dis·pen·sa·ble (in′dis pen′sə bəl), *adj.* absolutely necessary: *air is indispensable to life.* —*n.* an indispensable person or thing. —**in′dis·pen′sa·ble·ness,** *n.* —**in′dis·pen′sa·bly,** *adv.*

in·dis·pose (in′dis pōz′), *v.,* **-posed, -pos·ing. 1** make unwilling; make averse. **2** make slightly ill. **3** make unfit or unable.

in·dis·posed (in′dis pōzd′), *adj.* **1** slightly ill. **2** unwilling; without inclination; averse.

in·dis·po·si·tion (in′dis pə zish′ən), *n.* **1** disturbance of health; slight illness. **2** unwillingness; disinclination; aversion.

in·dis·put·a·ble (in′dis pūt′ə bəl; in dis′pyə tə–), *adj.* not to be disputed; undoubtedly true; unquestionable. —**in′dis·put′a·ble·ness,** *n.* —**in′dis·put′a·bly,** *adv.*

in·dis·sol·u·ble (in′di sol′yə bəl), *adj.* not capable of being dissolved, undone, or destroyed; lasting; firm. —**in′dis·sol′u·ble·ness,** *n.* —**in′dis·sol′u·bly,** *adv.*

in·dis·tinct (in′dis tingkt′), *adj.* not distinct; not clear to the eye, ear, or mind. —**in′dis·tinct′ly,** *adv.* —**in′dis·tinct′ness,** *n.*

in·dis·tin·guish·a·ble (in′dis ting′gwish-ə bəl), *adj.* that cannot be distinguished. —**in′dis·tin′guish·a·ble·ness,** *n.* —**in′dis·tin′guish·a·bly,** *adv.*

in·dite (in dīt′), *v.,* **-dit·ed, -dit·ing.** put in words or writing; compose. [< OF *enditer* < L *in-* in + *dictare* DICTATE, express in writing] —**in·dite′ment,** *n.* —**in·dit′er,** *n.*

in·di·um (in′di əm), *n.* a metallic element, In, that is soft, white, malleable, and easily fusible. [< NL, < L *indicum* INDIGO]

in·di·vid·u·al (in′də vij′ù əl), *n.* **1** person. **2** one person, animal, or thing. —*adj.* **1** single; particular; separate: *an individual question.* **2** for one person only: *individual seats.* **3** pertaining or peculiar to one person or thing: *individual tastes, an individual style.* [< Med.L, ult. < L *in-* not + *dividuus* divisible]

in·di·vid·u·al·ism (in′də vij′ù əl iz′əm), *n.* **1** theory that individual freedom is as important as the welfare of the group as a whole. **2** each for himself; selfishness.

in·di·vid·u·al·ist (in′də vij′ù əl ist), *n.* **1** one who lives life for himself or herself and does not try to cooperate with others. **2** supporter of individualism. —**in′di·vid′u·al·is′tic,** *adj.*

in·di·vid·u·al·i·ty (in′də vij′ù al′ə ti), *n.,* pl. **-ties. 1** individual character; sum of the qualities that make a person himself or herself, not someone else. **2** state of being individual; existence as an individual.

in·di·vid·u·al·ize (in′də vij′ù əl īz), *v.,* **-ized, -iz·ing. 1** make individual; give a distinctive character to. **2** consider as individuals; list one by one; specify. —**in′di·vid′u·al·i·za′tion,** *n.* —**in′di·vid′u·al·iz′er,** *n.*

in·di·vid·u·al·ly (in′də vij′ù əl i), *adv.* **1** personally; one at a time; as individuals: *the teacher helps us individually.* **2** each from the others: *people differ individually.*

in·di·vis·i·ble (in′də viz′ə bəl), *adj.* **1** not capable of being divided. **2** not capable of being divided without a remainder. —**in′di·vis′i·bil′i·ty, in′di·vis′i·ble·ness,** *n.* —**in′di·vis′i·bly,** *adv.*

In·do·chi·na (in′dō chī′nə), *n.* the SE peninsula of Asia, comprising Myanmar, the Malay Peninsula, Thailand, Cambodia, Laos, and Vietnam.

In·do·chi·nese (in′dō chī nēz′; –nēs′), *adj.* **1** of or having to do with Indochina, the Mongoloid peoples living there, or their languages. **2** of or having to do with the family of languages comprising these languages and the Tibetan and Chinese groups of languages.—*n.* native or inhabitant of Indochina.

in·doc·tri·nate (in dok′trə nāt), *v.,* **-nat·ed, -nat·ing. 1** teach a doctrine, belief, or principle to. **2** inculcate. [prob. < Med.L, < *in-* in + *doctrinare* teach < L *doctrina* DOCTRINE] —**in·doc′tri·na′tion,** *n.* —**in·doc′tri·na′tor,** *n.*

Indo-, *combining form.* of India; Indian, as in *Indo-European.*

In·do-Eu·ro·pe·an (in′dō yùr′ə pē′ən), *adj.* **1** of India and Europe. **2** of or having to do with a group of related languages spoken in India, W Asia, and Europe. English, German, Latin, Greek, Persian, and Sanskrit are some of the Indo-European languages. —*n.* this group of languages.

In·do-Ger·man·ic (in′dō jèr man′ik), *adj.* =Indo-European.

In·do-Iranian (in′dō i rā′nē ən; –ī–; –i rä–), *adj.* of or having to do with the Indic and Iranian (Persian) branch of Indo-European.

in·do·lence (in′də ləns), *n.* laziness; dislike of work; idleness.

in·do·lent (in′də lənt), *adj.* lazy; disliking work. [< LL, < L *in-* not + *dolere* be in pain] —**in′do·lent·ly,** *adv.*

in·dom·i·ta·ble (in dom′ə tə bəl), *adj.* unconquerable;unyielding.[<LL*indomitabilis,* ult. < L *in-* not + *domare* tame] —**in′dom′i·ta·bil′i·ty, in·dom′i·ta·ble·ness,** *n.* —**in·dom′i·ta·bly,** *adv.*

In·do·ne·sia (in′dō nē′shə; –zhə), *n.* **1 Republic of,** an autonomous republic in the Malay Archipelago, including Java, Sumatra, S and E Borneo, W Timor, Bali, and other islands. **2** =Malay Archipelago. —**In′do·ne′sian,** *adj., n.*

in·door (in′dôr′; –dōr′), *adj.* done, used, etc., in a house or building: *indoor tennis.*

in·doors (in′dôrz′; -dōrz′), *adv.* in or into a house or building.

in·dorse (in dôrs′), *v.,* –dorsed, –dorsing. =endorse.

in·du·bi·ta·ble (in dü′bə tə bəl; –dū′–), *adj.* not to be doubted; certain. —**in·du′bi·ta·ble·ness,** *n.* —**in·du′bi·ta·bly,** *adv.*

in·duce (in düs′; –dūs′), *v.,* –duced, –duc·ing. **1** lead on; influence; persuade: *advertising induces people to buy.* **2** cause; bring about: *some drugs induce sleep.* **3** produce (an electric or magnetic change) without contact. **4** infer by reasoning from particular facts to a general rule or principle. [< L, < *in-* in + *ducere* lead] —**in·duc′er,** *n.* —**in·duc′i·ble,** *adj.*

in·duce·ment (in düs′mənt; –dūs′–), *n.* something that influences or persuades; incentive.

in·duct (in dukt′), *v.* **1** bring in; introduce (into position, office, etc.). **2** put formally in possession of (an office, etc.): *inducted into the office of governor.* **3** U.S. enroll in military service. [< L *inductus,* pp. of *inducere.* See INDUCE.]

in·duct·ance (in duk′təns), *adj.* property of an electrical conductor or circuit that makes induction possible.

in·duc·tee (in duk′tē), *n.* person who is soon to be inducted into military service.

in·duc·tile (in duk′təl), *adj.* not ductile. —**in′duc·til′i·ty,** *n.*

in·duc·tion (in duk′shən), *n.* **1** process by which an object having electrical or magnetic properties produces similar properties in a nearby object, usually without direct contact. **2** reasoning from particular facts to a general rule or principle. **3** conclusion reached in this way. **4** act or ceremony of installing a person in office. **5** enrollment in military service.

in·duc·tive (in duk′tiv), *adj.* **1** of or using induction; reasoning by induction. **2** having to do with electrical or magnetic induction. —**in·duc′tive·ly,** *adv.* —**in·duc′tive·ness,** *n.*

in·dulge (in dulj′), *v.,* –dulged, –dulging. **1** yield to the wishes of; humor: *indulge a sick person.* **2** give way to: *indulge our desires.* **3** give way to one's pleasures; give oneself up to: *indulge in tobacco.* [< L *indulgere*] —**in·dulg′er,** *n.* —**in·dulg′ing·ly,** *adv.*

in·dul·gence (in dul′jəns), *n.* **1** an indulging: *indulgence in rich food.* **2** thing indulged in. **3** favor; privilege. **4** in the Roman Catholic Church, remission of the punishment still due to sin after the guilt has been forgiven.

in·dul·gent (in dul′jənt), *adj.* indulging; kind; almost too kind: *the indulgent mother bought her boy everything he wanted.* —**in·dul′gent·ly,** *adv.*

in·dus·tri·al (in dus′tri əl), *adj.* **1** having to do with or connected with the industries, trades, or manufactures: *industrial workers.* **2** manufacturing rather than agricultural or commercial: *an industrial community.* **3** of or having to do with the workers in industries: *industrial insurance.* —**in·dus′tri·al·ly,** *adv.*

in·dus·tri·al·ism (in dus′tri əl iz′əm), *n.* system of social and economic organization in which large industries are very important and industrial activities or interests prevail.

in·dus·tri·al·ist (in dus′tri əl ist), *n.* person who conducts or owns an industrial enterprise.

in·dus·tri·al·i·za·tion (in dus′tri əl ə zā′shən), *n.* development of large industries as an important feature in a country or a social or economic system.

in·dus·tri·al·ize (in dus′tri əl īz′), *v.,* –ized, –iz·ing. **1** make industrial. **2** organize as an industry.

industrial park, area, usually outside a city or large town, esp. designed and built for manufacturing.

in·dus·tri·ous (in dus′tri əs), *adj.* hardworking. —**in·dus′tri·ous·ly,** *adv.* —**in·dus′tri·ous·ness,** *n.*

in·dus·try (in′dəs tri), *n., pl.* –tries. **1** any branch of business, trade, or manufacture: *the automobile industry.* **2** systematic work or labor. **3** steady effort. [< L *industria*]

–ine[1], *suffix.* of; like; like that of; characteristic of; having the nature of; being, as in *crystalline, elephantine.* [< L *-inus*]

–ine[2], *suffix.* used esp. in the names of chemicals, as in *chlorine, aniline.* [< F < L *-ina*]

in·e·bri·ate (*v.* in ē′bri āt; *n., adj.* in ē′bri it), *v.,* –at·ed, –at·ing, *n., adj.* —*n.* **1** make drunk; intoxicate. **2** intoxicate mentally; excite. —*n.* habitual drunkard; intoxicated person. —*adj.* intoxicated; drunk. [< L, < *in-* + *ebrius* drunk] —**in·e′bri·a′tion,** *n.*

in·e·bri·e·ty (in′i brī′ə ti), *n.* drunkenness.

in·ed·i·ble (in ed′ə bəl), *adj.* not fit to eat. —**in·ed′i·bil′i·ty,** *n.*

in·ef·fa·ble (in ef′ə bəl), *adj.* **1** not to be expressed in words;too great to be described in words. **2** that must not be spoken. [< L *ineffabilis,* ult. < *in-* not + *ex-* out + *fari* speak] —**in·ef′fa·bil′i·ty, in·ef′fa·ble·ness,** *n.* —**in·ef′fa·bly,** *adv.*

in·ef·fec·tive (in′ə fek′tiv), *adj.* **1** not effective; of little use. **2** unfit for work; incapable. —**in′ef·fec′tive·ly,** *adv.* —**in′ef·fec′tive·ness,** *n.*

in·ef·fec·tu·al (in′ə fek′chù əl), *adj.* **1** without effect; useless. **2** not able to produce the effect wanted. —**in′ef·fec′tu·al′i·ty, in′ef·fec′tu·al·ness,** *n.* —**in′ef·fec′tu·al·ly,** *adv.*

in·ef·fi·ca·cious (in′ef ə kā′shəs), *adj.* not able to produce the effect wanted. —**in′ef·fi·ca′cious·ly,** *adv.* —**in′ef·fi·ca′cious·ness, in′ef·fi·cac′i·ty,** *n.*

in·ef·fi·ca·cy (in ef′ə kə si), *n.* inability to produce the effect wanted.

in·ef·fi·cien·cy (in′ə fish′ən si), *n.* inability to get things done.

in·ef·fi·cient (in′ə fish′ənt), *adj.* **1** not able to produce, accomplish, or effect anything without waste of time, energy, etc. **2** not able to get things done. —**in′ef·fi′cient·ly,** *adv.*

in·e·las·tic (in′i las′tik), *adj.* stiff; inflexible; unyielding.

in·e·las·tic·i·ty (in′i las tis′ə ti), *n.* lack of elasticity.

in·el·e·gance (in el′ə gəns), *n., pl.* –gances. **1** lack of good taste. **2** something that is not elegant or graceful.

in·el·e·gant (in el′ə gənt), *adj.* not in good taste; crude; vulgar. —**in·el′e·gant·ly,** *adv.*

in·el·i·gi·ble (in el′ə jə bəl), *adj.* not suitable; not qualified. —*n.* person who is not suitable or not qualified. —**in·el′i·gi·bil′i·ty,** *n.* —**in·el′i·gi·bly,** *adv.*

in·e·luc·ta·ble (in′i luk′tə bəl), *adj.* that cannot be escaped. [< L *ineluctabilis* < *in-* not + *ex-* out of + *luctari* to struggle] —**in′e·luc′ta·bil′i·ty,** *n.* —**in′e·luc′ta·bly,** *adv.*

in·ept (in ept′), *adj.* **1** not suitable; out of place. **2** absurd; foolish. [< L *ineptus* < *in-* not + *aptus* apt] —**in·ept′ly,** *adv.* —**in·ept′ness,** *n.*

in·ept·i·tude (in ept′ə tüd; –tūd), *n.* **1** unfitness; foolishness. **2** a silly or inappropriate act or remark.

in·e·qual·i·ty (in′i kwol′ə ti), *n., pl.* –ties. **1** a being unequal in amount, size, value, rank, etc. **2** lack of evenness or uniformity. **3** *Math.* expression showing that two quantities are unequal, like $a > b$ or $c < d$.

in·eq·ui·ta·ble (in ek′wə tə bəl), *adj.* unfair; unjust. —**in·eq′ui·ta·bly,** *adv.*

in·eq·ui·ty (in ek′wə ti), *n., pl.* –ties. unfairness; injustice.

in·e·rad·i·ca·ble (in′i rad′ə kə bəl), *adj.* that cannot be rooted out or got rid of. —**in′e·rad′i·ca·ble·ness,** *n.* —**in′e·rad′i·ca·bly,** *adv.*

in·ert (in ėrt′), *adj.* **1** having no power to move or act; lifeless. **2** inactive; slow; sluggish. **3** with few or no active properties. Helium and neon are inert gases. [< L *iners* idle, unskilled < *in-* without + *ars* art, skill] —**in·ert′ly**, *adv.* —**in·ert′ness**, *n.*

in·er·tia (in ėr′shə), *n.* **1** tendency to remain in the state one is in and not start changes. **2** tendency of all matter to stay still or to go on moving in the same direction unless acted on by some outside force. [< L, < *iners* INERT] —**in·er′tial**, *adj.*

inertial guidance, a complex gyroscopic navigational system which keeps an aircraft, missile, submarine, etc. on a predetermined course.

in·es·cap·a·ble (in′əs kāp′ə bəl), *adj.* that cannot be escaped or avoided.

in·es·ti·ma·ble (in es′tə mə bəl), *adj.* too good, great, valuable, etc., to be measured or estimated. —**in·es′ti·ma·bly**, *adv.*

in·ev·i·ta·ble (in ev′ə tə bəl), *adj.* not avoidable; sure to happen; certain to come. —*n.* that which is inevitable. —**in·ev′i·ta·bil′i·ty, in·ev′i·ta·ble·ness,** *n.* —**in·ev′i·ta·bly**, *adv.*

in·ex·act (in′ig zakt′), *adj.* not exact; not accurate. —**in′ex·act′ly**, *adv.* —**in′ex·act′ness**, *n.*

in·ex·cus·a·ble (in′iks kūz′ə bəl), *adj.* that ought not to be excused; that cannot be justified. —**in′ex·cus′a·bil′i·ty, in′ex·cus′a·ble·ness,** *n.* —**in′ex·cus′a·bly**, *adv.*

in·ex·haust·i·ble (in′ig zôs′tə bəl), *adj.* **1** that cannot be exhausted; very abundant. **2** tireless. —**in′ex·haust′i·bil′i·ty, in′ex·haust′i·ble·ness,** *n.* —**in′ex·haust′i·bly**, *adv.*

in·ex·o·ra·ble (in ek′sə rə bəl), *adj.* relentless; unyielding; not influenced by prayers or entreaties. [< L, < *in-* not + *ex-* successfully + *orare* entreat] —**in·ex′o·ra·bil′i·ty, in·ex′o·ra·ble·ness,** *n.* —**in·ex′o·ra·bly**, *adv.*

in·ex·pe·di·en·cy (in′iks pē′di ən si), *n.* lack of expediency; being inexpedient.

in·ex·pe·di·ent (in′iks pē′di·ənt), *adj.* not expedient; not practicable, suitable, or wise. —**in′ex·pe′di·ent·ly**, *adv.*

in·ex·pen·sive (in′iks pen′siv), *adj.* not expensive; cheap; low-priced. —**in′ex·pen′sive·ly**, *adv.* —**in′ex·pen′sive·ness,** *n.*

in·ex·pe·ri·ence (in′iks pir′i əns), *n.* lack of experience; lack of skill or wisdom gained from experience. —**in′ex·pe′ri·enced,** *adj.*

in·ex·pert (in eks′pėrt; in′iks pėrt′), *adj.* unskilled. —**in′ex·pert′ly**, *adv.* —**in′ex·pert′ness,** *n.*

in·ex·pi·a·ble (in eks′pi ə bəl), *adj.* that cannot be atoned for: *an inexpiable crime.* —**in·ex′pi·a·ble·ness,** *n.* —**in·ex′pi·a·bly**, *adv.*

in·ex·pli·ca·ble (in eks′pli kə bəl; in′iks plik′ə bəl), *adj.* impossible to explain or understand; mysterious. —**in·ex′pli·ca·bil′i·ty, in·ex′pli·ca·ble·ness,** *n.* —**in·ex′pli·ca·bly**, *adv.*

in·ex·press·i·ble (in′iks pres′ə bəl), *adj.* that cannot be expressed; beyond expression. —**in′ex·press′i·bil′i·ty, in′ex·press′i·ble·ness,** *n.* —**in′ex·press′i·bly**, *adv.*

in·ex·pres·sive (in′iks pres′iv), *adj.* not expressive; lacking in expression. —**in′ex·pres′sive·ly**, *adv.* —**in′ex·pres′sive·ness,** *n.*

in·ex·tin·guish·a·ble (in′iks ting′gwish ə·bəl), *adj.* that cannot be put out or stopped. —**in′ex·tin′guish·a·bly**, *adv.*

in ex·tre·mis (in iks trē′mis), at the point of death. [< L, lit., amid the final things]

in·ex·tri·ca·ble (in eks′tri kə bəl), *adj.* **1** that one cannot get out of. **2** that cannot be disentangled or solved. —**in·ex′tri·ca·bil′i·ty, in·ex′tri·ca·ble·ness.** —**in·ex′tri·ca·bly**, *adv.*

inf., 1 Also, **Inf.** infantry. **2** infinitive. **3** information. **4** infra (below).

in·fal·li·bil·i·ty (in fal′ə bil′ə ti), *n.* absolute freedom from error.

in·fal·li·ble (in fal′ə bəl), *adj.* **1** free from error; that cannot be mistaken. **2** absolutely reliable; sure. —**in·fal′li·ble·ness,** *n.* —**in·fal′li·bly**, *adv.*

in·fa·mous (in′fə məs), *adj.* **1** shamefully bad; extremely wicked. **2** having a very bad reputation; in public disgrace. —**in′fa·mous·ly**, *adv.* —**in′fa·mous·ness,** *n.*

in·fa·my (in′fə mi), *n., pl.* –**mies. 1** very bad reputation; public disgrace. **2** shameful badness; extreme wickedness. [< L, < *in-* without + *fama* (good) reputation]

in·fan·cy (in′fən si), *n., pl.* –**cies. 1** condition or time of being an infant; babyhood. **2** early stage; beginning of development. **3** condition of being under legal age of responsibility.

in·fant (in′fənt), *n.* **1** baby; very young child. **2** person under the legal age of responsibility; a minor. —*adj.* **1** of or for an infant. **2** in an early stage; just beginning to develop. [< L *infans,* orig., not speaking < *in-* not + *fari* speak] —**in′fant·hood,** *n.*

in·fan·ti·cide (in fan′tə sīd), *n.* the killing of a baby. [< L, < *infans* INFANT + *-cidium* act of killing < *caedere* kill] —**in·fan′ti·cid′al,** *adj.*

in·fan·tile (in′fən tīl; –til), *adj.* **1** of an infant or infants; having to do with infants. **2** like an infant; babyish; childish. **3** in an early stage; just beginning to develop.

infantile paralysis, =poliomyelitis.

in·fan·ti·lism (in fan′tə liz əm), *n.* abnormal persistence or appearance of childish traits in adults.

in·fan·try (in′fən tri), *n., pl.* –**tries.** soldiers who fight on foot. [<F < Ital., < *infante, fante* foot soldier, orig., a youth. See INFANT.]

in·fan·try·man (in′fən tri mən), *n., pl.* –**men,** soldier who fights on foot.

in·fat·u·ate (*v.* in fach′ù āt; *adj., n.* in fach′ù it, –āt), *v.,* –**at·ed,** –**at·ing,** *adj., n.* —*v.* inspire with a foolish or extreme pas-sion. —*adj.* infatuated. —*n.* an infatuated person. [< L, < *in-* + *fatuus* foolish]

in·fat·u·at·ed (in fach′ù āt′id), *adj.* extremely adoring; foolishly in love. —**in·fat′u·at′ed·ly**, *adv.*

in·fat·u·a·tion (in fach′ù ā′shən), *n.* foolish love; unreasoning fondness.

in·fect (in fekt′), *v.* **1** cause disease in by introducing germs: *dirt infects an open cut.* **2** influence in a bad way; contaminate: *one bad companion can infect a whole group.* **3** influence by spreading from one to another: *the captain's courage infected his soldiers.* [< L *infectus* dyed, orig., put in < *in-* in + *facere* make] —**in·fec′tor**, *n.*

in·fec·tion (in fek′shən), *n.* **1** causing of disease in people, animals, and plants by the introduction of germs. **2** disease caused in this way. **3** influence, feeling, or idea spreading from one to another. **4** fact or state of being infected.

in·fec·tious (in fek′shəs), *adj.* **1** spread by infection: *measles is an infectious disease.* **2** causing infection. **3** apt to spread. —**in·fec′tious·ly**, *adv.* —**in·fec′tious·ness,** *n.*

in·fec·tive (in fek′tiv), *adj.* =infectious. —**in·fec′tive·ness, in′fec·tiv′i·ty,** *n.*

in·fe·lic·i·tous (in′fə lis′ə təs), *adj.* **1** unsuitable; not appropriate. **2** unfortunate; unhappy. —**in′fe·lic′i·tous·ly**, *adv.*

in·fe·lic·i·ty (in′fə lis′ə ti), *n., pl.* –**ties. 1** unsuitability; inappropriateness. **2** misfortune; unhappiness. **3** something unsuitable; inappropriate word, remark, etc.

in·fer (in fėr′), *v.,* –**ferred,** –**fer·ring. 1** find out by reasoning; conclude: *from the facts known we infer his innocence.* **2** indicate; imply: *ragged clothing infers poverty.* [< L, < *in-* in + *ferre* bring] —**in·fer′a·ble,** *adj.* —**in·fer′a·bly**, *adv.* —**in·fer′rer,** *n.*

in·fer·ence (in′fər əns), *n.* **1** process of inferring. **2** that which is inferred; conclusion.

in·fe·ri·or (in fir′i ər), *adj.* **1** lower in position or rank: *a lieutenant is inferior to a captain.* **2** not so good; lower in quality; worse. **3** below average: *an inferior mind.* —*n.* **1** person who is lower in rank or station. **2** an inferior thing. [< L, compar. of *inferus,* adj., situated below] —**in·fe′ri·or·ly**, *adv.*

in·fe·ri·or·i·ty (in fir′i ôr′ə ti; –or′–), *n.* inferior condition or quality.

inferiority complex, an abnormal or morbid feeling of being inferior to other people.

in·fer·nal (in fėr′nəl), *adj.* **1** of hell; having to do with the lower world. **2** hellish; diabolical. **3** *Informal.* abominable; outrageous. [< LL *infernalis,* ult. < L *inferus* below] —**in′fer·nal′i·ty,** *n.* —**in·fer′nal·ly**, *adv.*

in·fer·no (in fėr′nō), *n., pl.* –**nos. 1** hell. **2** a hell-like place or thing. [< Ital.]

in·fer·tile (in fėr′təl), *adj.* not fertile; sterile. —**in′fer·til′i·ty,** *n.*

in·fest (in fest′), v. trouble or disturb frequently or in large numbers: *mosquitoes infest swamps.* [< L, attack, < *infestus* hostile] —**in′fes·ta′tion,** n. —**in·fest′er,** n.

in·fi·del (in′fə dəl), n. 1 person who does not believe in religion. 2 person who does not accept a particular faith: *Muslims call Christians infidels.* 3 person who does not accept Christianity. —*adj.* 1 not believing in religion. 2 not accepting a particular faith. [< L, < *in-* not + *fides* faith]

in·fi·del·i·ty (in′fə del′ə ti), n., pl. **-ties.** 1 lack of religious faith. 2 unfaithfulness, esp. of husband or wife; disloyalty. 3 an unfaithful or disloyal act.

in·field (in′fēld′), n. 1 a baseball diamond. 2 first, second, and third basemen and shortstop of a baseball team.

in·field·er (in′fēl′dər), n. an infield player.

in·fight·ing (in fī′ting), n. 1 throwing punches in boxing at close quarters. 2 *Fig.* conflict or controversy among close associates: *office infighting.* —**in′fight′,** v. —**in′fight′er,** n.

in·fil·trate (in fil′trāt), v., **-trat·ed, -trat·ing,** n. —*v.* 1 pass into or through by, or as by, filtering: *enemy troops infiltrated the front lines.* 2 filter into or through; permeate. —*n.* that which infiltrates. —**in′fil·tra′tion,** n. —**in·fil′tra·tive,** adj.

infin., infinitive.

in·fi·nite (in′fə nit), adj. 1 without limits or bounds; endless: *the infinite power of God.* 2 extremely great. —*n.* 1 that which is infinite.

the Infinite, God. [< L, < *in-* not + *finis* boundary] —**in′fi·nite·ly,** adv. —**in′fi·nite·ness,** n.

in·fin·i·tes·i·mal (in′fin ə tes′ə məl), adj. so small as to be almost nothing. —*n.* an infinitesimal amount. [< NL *infinitesimus* the "nth" < L *infinitus* INFINITE] —**in′fin·i·tes′i·mal·ly,** adv.

in·fin·i·tive (in fin′ə tiv), n. a form of a verb not limited by person and number. *Examples:* Let him *go.* We want *to go* now. [< LL, < L *infinitus* unrestricted, INFINITE] —**in·fin′i·tive·ly,** adv.

in·fin·i·tude (in fin′ə tüd; -tūd), n. 1 a being infinite. 2 an infinite extent, amount, or number.

in·fin·i·ty (in fin′ə ti), n., pl. **-ties.** 1 state of being infinite. 2 an infinite distance, space, time, or quantity. 3 an infinite extent, amount, or number.

in·firm (in fèrm′), adj. 1 weak; feeble. 2 weak in will or character; not steadfast. —**in·firm′ly,** adv. —**in·firm′ness,** n.

in·fir·ma·ry (in fèr′mə ri), n., pl. **-ries.** place for the care of the infirm, sick, or injured; hospital in a school or institution.

in·fir·mi·ty (in fèr′mə ti), n., pl. **-ties.** 1 weakness; feebleness. 2 sickness; illness.

in·fix (v. in fiks′; n. in′fiks′), v. 1 fix in; drive in. 2 *Fig.* fix in the mind or memory; impress. 3 *Gram.* insert an infix. —*n. Gram.* a formative element inserted within the body of a word.

infl., influenced.

in·flame (in flām′), v., **-flamed, -flaming.** 1 excite; make more violent. 2 become excited with intense feeling. 3 make or become red or hot from disease, etc. [< OF *enflamer* < L, ult. < *in-* + *flamma* flame] —**in·flam′er,** n. —**in·flam′ing·ly,** adv.

in·flam·ma·ble (in flam′ə bəl), adj. 1 easily set on fire. 2 easily excited or aroused. —*n.* something inflammable. —**in·flam′ma·bil′i·ty, in·flam′ma·ble·ness,** n. —**in·flam′ma·bly,** adv.

in·flam·ma·tion (in′flə mā′shən), n. 1 a diseased condition of some part of the body, marked by heat, redness, swelling, and pain. 2 an inflaming or being inflamed.

in·flam·ma·to·ry (in flam′ə tô′ri; -tō′-), adj. 1 tending to excite or arouse. 2 of, causing, or accompanied by inflammation.

in·flate (in flāt′), v., **-flat·ed, -flat·ing.** 1 blow out or swell with air or gas: *inflate a balloon.* 2 swell or puff out: *inflate with pride.* 3 increase (prices or currency) beyond the normal amount. [< L, < *in-* into + *flare* blow] —**in·flat′a·ble,** adj. —**in·flat′er, in·fla′tor,** n.

in·fla·tion (in flā′shən), n. 1 a swelling (with air, gas, pride, etc.). 2 swollen state; too great expansion. 3 a sharp and sudden rise of prices. 4 increase of the currency of a country by issuing much paper money.

in·fla·tion·ar·y (in flā′shən er′i), adj. of or having to do with inflation; tending to inflate.

in·flect (in flekt′), v. 1 change the tone or pitch of (the voice). 2 vary the form of (a word) to show gender, person, tense, etc. 3 bend; curve. [< L, < *in-* in + *flectere* bend] —**in·flec′tive,** adj. —**in·flec′tor,** n.

in·flec·tion (in flek′shən), n. 1 change in the tone or pitch of the voice as in a question with a rising inflection. 2 variation in the form of a word to show gender, person, tense, etc. 3 bend; curve. —**in·flec′tion·al·ly,** adv.

in·flec·tion·al (in flek′shən əl), adj. of, pertaining to, or exhibiting grammatical inflection.

in·flex·i·ble (in flek′sə bəl), adj. 1 firm; unyielding; steadfast. 2 that cannot be changed; unalterable. 3 not easily bent; stiff; rigid. —**in·flex′i·bil′i·ty, in·flex′i·ble·ness,** n. —**in·flex′i·bly,** adv.

in·flict (in flikt′), v. 1 give or cause, as a blow, wound, pain, etc. 2 impose, as a burden, suffering, anything unwelcome, etc. [< L *inflictus* < *in-* on + *fligere* dash] —**in·flict′er, in·flic′tor,** n. —**in·flic′tive,** adj.

in·flic·tion (in flik′shən), n. 1 act of inflicting. 2 something inflicted; pain; suffering; burden; punishment.

in·flo·res·cence (in′flô res′əns; -flō-), n. 1 flowering stage. 2 a arrangement of flowers on the stem or axis. b a flower cluster. [< NL *inflorescentia* < L *in-* in + *flos* flower] —**in′flo·res′cent,** adj.

in·flow (in′flō′), n. 1 a flowing in or into. 2 that which flows in.

in·flu·ence (in′flü əns), n., v., **-enced, -enc·ing.** —*n.* 1 power of persons or things to act on others: *a person may have influence by one's ability or wealth.* 2 person or thing that has such power. —*v.* have power over; change the nature or behavior of: *the moon influences the tides.* [< Med.L *influentia,* orig., a flowing in, ult. < L *in-* in + *fluere* to flow] —**in′flu·enc·er,** n.

in·flu·en·tial (in′flü en′shəl), adj. 1 having influence. 2 using influence; producing results. —**in′flu·en′tial·ly,** adv.

in·flu·en·za (in′flü en′zə), n. an acute contagious disease, like a very bad cold in its symptoms, but much more dangerous and exhausting; flu. [< Ital., INFLUENCE] —**in′flu·en′zal,** adj.

in·flux (in′fluks), n. a flowing in; steady flow. [< LL *influxus,* ult. < L *in-* in + *fluere* flow]

in·form (in fôrm′), v. 1 supply with knowledge, facts, or news; tell. 2 make an accusation or complaint: *one thief informed against the others.* [< L, < *in-* + *forma* form] —**in·form′ing·ly,** adv.

in·for·mal (in fôr′məl), adj. 1 not in the regular or prescribed manner; done without ceremony. 2 used in everyday common talk, but not used in formal talking or writing. —**in·for′mal·ly,** adv.

in·for·mal·i·ty (in′fôr mal′ə ti), n., pl. **-ties.** 1 lack of ceremony. 2 an informal act.

in·form·ant (in fôr′mənt), n. person who gives information to another.

in·for·ma·tion (in′fər mā′shən), n. 1 knowledge; facts; news: *a dictionary gives information about words.* 2 an informing: *a guidebook is for the information of travelers.* 3 accusation or complaint against a person. —**in′for·ma′tion·al,** adj.

information retrieval, process of recovering data from a file, esp. as stored on a computer.

information technology, application of computers to managing data.

in·form·a·tive (in fôr′mə tiv), adj. giving information; instructive.

in·formed (in fôrmd′), adj. having knowledge or information; educated.

in·form·er (in fôr′mər), n. 1 person who makes an accusation or complaint against others: *an informer told the police.* 2 =informant.

in·frac·tion (in frak′shən), n. a breaking of a law or obligation; violation. [< L *infractio* < *in-* in + *frangere* to break]

in·fra·red (in′frə red′), n. the invisible part of the spectrum whose rays have wave lengths longer than those of the red part of the visible spectrum. —*adj.* pertaining to the infrared.

in·fra·struc·ture (in′frə struk′chər), n. underlying elements necessary for any system or structure to function: *the county's crumbling infrastructure, the economic infrastructure.*

in·fre·quen·cy (in frē'kwən si), **in·fre·quence** (–kwəns), *n.* a being infrequent; scarcity; rarity.

in·fre·quent (in frē'kwənt), *adj.* not frequent; occurring seldom or far apart. —**in·fre'quent·ly,** *adv.*

in·fringe (in frinj'), *v.,* **-fringed, -fringing.** 1 violate: *infringe the food and drug law.* 2 trespass; encroach: *infringe upon rights.* [< L, < *in–* in + *frangere* break] —**in·fringe'ment,** *n.* —**in·fring'er,** *n.*

in·fu·ri·ate (in fyür'i āt), *v.,* **-at·ed, -at·ing.** put into a fury; make furious; enrage. [< Med.L, < L *in–* into + *furia* fury] —**in·fu'ri·ate·ly,** *adv.* —**in·fu'ri·at'ing·ly,** *adv.* —**in·fu'ri·a'tion,** *n.*

in·fuse (in fūz'), *v.,* **-fused, -fus·ing.** 1 introduce as by pouring: *the captain infused his own courage into his men.* 2 inspire: *infuse with courage.* 3 steep or soak in a liquid to get something out. [< L *infusus* < *in–* in + *fundere* pour] —**in·fus'er,** *n.*

in·fu·si·ble (in fū'zə bəl), *adj.* that cannot be fused or melted. —**in·fu'si·bil'i·ty, in·fu'si·ble·ness,** *n.*

in·fu·sion (in fū'zhən), *n.* 1 act or process of infusing. 2 intravenous injection of a medication. 3 a liquid extract obtained by steeping or soaking.

in·fu·so·ri·an (in'fyù sô'ri ən; –sō'–), *n.* one of a group of one-celled animals that move by vibrating filaments.

–ing[1], *suffix.* 1 action, result, product, material, etc., of some verb, as in *hard thinking, the art of painting.* 2 action, result, product, material, etc., of some other part of speech, as in *lobstering, offing, shirting.* 3 of one that ___s; of those that ___, as in *smoking habit, printing trade, drinking song.* [ME *-ing,* OE *-ing, -ung*]

–ing[2], *suffix.* 1 element forming the present participle. 2 that ___s, as in *seeing eye, lasting happiness, growing child.* [ME *-ing, -inge*]

in·gen·ious (in jēn'yəs), *adj.* 1 skillful in making; good at inventing. 2 cleverly planned and made. [< L, < *ingenium* natural talent] —**in·gen'ious·ly,** *adv.* —**in·gen'ious·ness,** *n.*

in·ge·nue or **in·gé·nue** (aN'zhə nü), *n., pl.* **-nues.** 1 a simple, innocent girl or young woman, esp. as represented on the stage. 2 actress who plays such a part. [< F, orig. adj., ingenuous]

in·ge·nu·i·ty (in'jə nü'ə ti; –nū'–), *n., pl.* **-ties.** skill in planning, inventing, etc.; cleverness. [< L *ingenuitas* frankness < *ingenuus* ingenuous; infl. by association with *ingenious*]

in·gen·u·ous (in jen'yü əs), *adj.* 1 frank; open; sincere. 2 simple; natural; innocent. [< L *ingenuus,* orig., native, free born] —**in·gen'u·ous·ly,** *adv.* —**in·gen'u·ous·ness,** *n.*

in·gest (in jest'), *v.* take (food, etc.) into the body for digestion. [< L *ingestus* < *in–* in + *gerere* carry] —**in·ges'tion,** *n.* —**in·ges'tive,** *adj.*

in·glo·ri·ous (in glô'ri əs; –glō'–), *adj.* 1 bringing no glory; shameful; disgraceful. 2 having no glory; not famous. —**in·glo'ri·ous·ly,** *adv.* —**in·glo'ri·ous·ness,** *n.*

in·got (ing'gət), *n.* mass of metal, such as gold, silver, or steel, cast into a convenient shape in a mold. [< OE *in–* in + *goten* poured]

in·grained (in grānd'; in'grānd'), *adj.* deeply and firmly fixed; thoroughly imbued: *ingrained honesty.*

in·grate (in'grāt), *n.* an ungrateful person. [< L, < *in–* not + *gratus* thankful]

in·gra·ti·ate (in grā'shi āt), *v.,* **-at·ed, -at·ing.** bring (oneself) into favor: *ingratiate oneself by giving presents.* [< *in–*[2] + L *gratia* favor] —**in·gra'ti·at'ing·ly,** *adv.* —**in·gra'ti·a'tion,** *n.*

in·grat·i·tude (in grat'ə tüd; –tūd), *n.* lack of gratitude; being ungrateful.

in·gre·di·ent (in grē'di ənt), *n.* one of the parts of a mixture: *the ingredients of a cake.* [< L *ingrediens* entering < *in–* in + *gradi* go]

in·gress (in'gres), *n.* 1 a going in: *ingress to a field.* 2 way in; entrance. 3 right to go in. [< L *ingressus* < *ingredi.* See INGREDIENT.] —**in·gres'sion,** *n.* —**in·gres'sive,** *adj.* —**in·gres'sive·ness,** *n.*

in·grown (in'grōn'), *adj.* 1 grown within; grown inward. 2 grown into the flesh.

in·hab·it (in hab'it), *v.* live in (a place, region, house, cave, tree, etc.). [< L, < *in–* in + *habitare* dwell < *habere* have, dwell] —**in·hab'it·a·ble,** *adj.* —**in·hab'it·a·bil'i·ty,** *n.* —**in·hab·i·ta'tion,** *n.* —**in·hab'it·er,** *n.*

in·hab·it·ant (in hab'ə tənt), *n.* person or animal that lives in a place.

in·hal·ant (in hāl'ənt) *n.* 1 medicine to be inhaled. 2 apparatus for inhaling it.

in·hale (in hāl'), *v.,* **-haled, -hal·ing.** draw into the lungs; breathe in (air, gas, fragrance, etc.). [< L, < *in–* in + *halare* breathe] —**in·ha·la'tion,** *n.*

in·hal·er (in hāl'ər), *n.* 1 apparatus used in inhaling medicine. 2 person who inhales.

in·har·mo·ni·ous (in'här mō'ni əs), *adj.* discordant; disagreeing. —**in·har·mo'ni·ous·ly,** *adv.* —**in·har·mo'ni·ous·ness,** *n.*

in·here (in hir'), *v.,* **-hered, -her·ing.** exist; belong to as a quality or attribute: *power inheres in a ruler.* [< L, < *in–* in + *haerere* to stick]

in·her·ent (in hir'ənt; –her'–), *adj.* belonging to (a person or thing) as a quality or attribute: *inherent modesty, inherent probability.* —**in·her'ence,** *n.* —**in·her'ent·ly,** *adv.*

in·her·it (in her'it), *v.* 1 receive as an heir: *the widow inherited the farm.* 2 get or possess from one's ancestors: *she inherits*

her father's blue eyes. [< OF *enheriter,* ult. < L *in–* + *heres* heir] —**in·her'i·tor,** *n.*

in·her·it·a·ble (in her'ə tə bəl), *adj.* 1 capable of being inherited. 2 capable of inheriting; qualified to inherit. —**in·her'it·a·bil'i·ty, in·her'it·a·ble·ness,** *n.*

in·her·it·ance (in her'ə təns), *n.* 1 act or process of inheriting: *he obtained his house by inheritance from an aunt.* 2 right of inheriting. 3 anything inherited: *good health is a fine inheritance.*

in·hib·it (in hib'it), *v.* 1 hinder by obstruction or restriction; restrain: *duty inhibits fear in a crisis.* 2 prohibit; forbid. [< L *inhibitus* < *in–* in + *habere* hold] —**in·hib'it·a·ble,** *adj.* —**in·hib'it·er, in·hib'i·tor,** *n.* —**in·hib'i·tive,** *adj.*

in·hi·bi·tion (in'i bish'ən; in'hi–), *n.* 1 an inhibiting or being inhibited. 2 emotion or other inner force that restrains natural impulses. —**in·hib'i·tive, in·hib'i·to'ry,** *adj.*

in·hos·pi·ta·ble (in hos'pi tə bəl; in'hos·pit'ə bəl), *adj.* 1 not hospitable. 2 providing no shelter; barren: *an inhospitable shore.* —**in·hos'pi·ta·ble·ness,** *n.* —**in·hos'pi·ta·bly,** *adv.*

in·hos·pi·tal·i·ty (in hos'pə tal'ə ti), *n.* lack of hospitality; inhospitable behavior.

in·hu·man (in hū'mən), *adj.* not human; not having the qualities natural to a human being. —**in·hu'man·ly,** *adv.* —**in·hu'man·ness,** *n.*

in·hu·mane (in'hū mān'), *adj.* lacking in compassion, humanity, or kindness. —**in'hu·mane'ly,** *adv.*

in·hu·man·i·ty (in'hū man'ə ti), *n., pl.* **-ties.** 1 inhuman quality; lack of feeling; cruelty; brutality. 2 an inhuman, cruel, or brutal act.

in·im·i·cal (in im'ə kəl), *adj.* 1 unfriendly; hostile. 2 adverse; unfavorable; harmful. [< LL, < L *inimicus* < *in–* not + *amicus* friendly] —**in·im·i'cal'i·ty,** *n.* —**in·im'i·cal'ly,** *adv.*

in·im·i·ta·ble (in im'ə tə bəl), *adj.* that cannot be imitated or copied; matchless. —**in·im'i·ta·bil'i·ty, in·im'i·ta·ble·ness,** *n.* —**in·im'i·ta·bly,** *adv.*

in·iq·ui·tous (in ik'wə təs), *adj.* 1 very unjust. 2 wicked. —**in·iq'ui·tous·ly,** *adv.* —**in·iq'ui·tous·ness,** *n.*

in·iq·ui·ty (in ik'wə ti), *n., pl.* **-ties.** 1 very great injustice. 2 wickedness. 3 a wicked or unjust act. [< L *iniquitas,* ult. < *in–* not + *aequus* just]

i·ni·tial (i nish'əl), *adj., n., v.,* **-tialed, -tial·ing.** —*adj.* occurring at the beginning; first; earliest. —*n.* the first letter of a word. —*v.* mark or sign with initials. [< L *initialis,* ult. < *inire* begin < *in–* in + *ire* go]

i·ni·tial·ly (i nish'əl i), *adv.* at the beginning.

i·ni·ti·ate (*v.* i nish'i āt; *n., adj.* i nish'i it, –āt), *v.,* **-at·ed, -at·ing.** *n., adj., —v.* 1 be the first one to start; begin. 2 admit (a person) by special forms or ceremonies (into mysteries, secret knowledge, or a society). 3 introduce into the knowledge of some art or subject. —*n.* person who is initiated. —*adj.* initiated. [<L *initiatus,* ult. < *inire* begin. See INITIAL.] —**i·ni′ti·a′tor,** *n.*

i·ni·ti·a·tion (i nish′i ā′shən), *n.* **1** an initiating or being initiated. **2** formal admission into a group or society. **3** ceremonies by which one is admitted to a group or society.

initiation fee, fee one pays upon being initiated into a society, club, etc.

i·ni·ti·a·tive (i nish′i ə tiv; –i ā′tiv), *n.* **1** active part in taking the first steps in any undertaking; the lead: *take the initiative in making acquaintances.* **2** readiness and ability to be the one to start a course of action: *a leader must have initiative.* **3** right of citizens outside the legislature to introduce or enact a new law by vote. **4** right to be the first to act, legislate, etc. —**i·ni′ti·a·tive·ly,** *adv.*

i·ni·ti·a·to·ry (i nish′i ə tō′ri; –tō′–), *adj.* **1** first; beginning; introductory. **2** of initiation. —**i·ni′ti·a·to′ri·ly,** *adv.*

in·ject (in jekt′), *v.* **1** force (liquid) into (a passage, cavity, or tissue). **2** throw in: *inject a remark into the conversation.* [< L *injectus* < *in–* + *jacere* to throw] —**in·jec′tion,** *n.* —**in·jec′tor,** *n.*

in·ju·di·cious (in′jü dish′əs), *adj.* showing lack of judgment; unwise; not prudent. —**in′ju·di′cious·ly,** *adv.* —**in′ju·di′cious·ness,** *n.*

in·junc·tion (in jungk′shən), *n.* **1** command; order. **2** a formal order issued by a law court ordering a person or group to do, or refrain from doing, something. [< LL *injunctio* < L *injungere* ENJOIN]

in·jure (in′jər), *v.,* **–jured, –jur·ing. 1** do damage to; harm; hurt. **2** do wrong to; be unfair to. [< *injury*] —**in′jur·er,** *n.*

in·ju·ri·ous (in jůr′i əs), *adj.* **1** causing injury; harmful. **2** wrongful; unfair; unjust. —**in·ju′ri·ous·ly,** *adv.* —**in·ju′ri·ous·ness,** *n.*

in·ju·ry (in′jər i), *n., pl.* **–ju·ries. 1** damage; harm; hurt. **2** wrong; unfairness. [< L *injuria* < *in–* not + *jus* right]

in·jus·tice (in jus′tis), *n.* **1** lack of justice; being unjust. **2** an unjust act.

ink (ingk), *n.* **1** liquid used for writing or printing. **2** dark liquid discharged by cuttlefish for protection. —*v.* put ink in; mark or stain with ink. [< OF *enque* < LL < Gk. *enkauston* < *en* in + *kaiein* burn] —**ink′er,** *n.* —**ink′less,** *adj.* —**ink′like′,** *adj.*

ink·horn (ingk′hôrn′), *n.* a small container formerly used to hold ink, often made of horn. —*adj.* bookish; pedantic.

ink·jet (ingk′jet′), *adj.* of or having to do with high-speed printing that uses jets of ink controlled by a computer to form images on paper.

ink·ling (ingk′ling), *n.* slight suggestion; vague notion; hint. [< OE *inca* doubt]

ink·stand (ingk′stand′), *n.* **1** stand to hold ink and pens. **2** container used to hold ink.

ink·well (ingk′wel′), *n.* container used to hold ink on a desk or table.

ink·y (ingk′i), *adj.,* **ink·i·er, ink·i·est. 1** like ink; dark; black. **2** covered with ink; marked or stained with ink. **3** of ink. —**ink′i·ness,** *n.*

in·laid (in′lād′), *adj.* **1** set in the surface as a decoration or design. **2** decorated with a design or material set in the surface.

in·land (*adj.* in′lənd; *n., adv.,* also in′-land′), *adj.* **1** away from the coast or the border; situated in the interior: *an inland sea.* **2** domestic; not foreign: *inland trade.* —*n.* interior of a country; land away from the border or the coast. —*adv.* in or toward the interior.

in·land·er (in′lən dər), *n.* person who lives in an interior area.

in-law (in′lô′), *n.* relative by marriage.

in·lay (in′lā′), *v.,* **–laid, –lay·ing,** *n.* —*v.* **1** set in the surface as a decoration or design: *inlay strips of gold.* **2** decorate with something set in the surface: *inlay a wooden box with silver.* —*n.* **1** an inlaid decoration, design, or material. **2** a shaped piece of gold, porcelain, etc., cemented in a tooth as a filling. —**in′lay′er,** *n.*

in·let (in′let), *n.* **1** a narrow strip of water extending from a larger body of water into the land or between islands. **2** entrance.

in-line skate (in′līn′), roller skate with the wheels arranged in a line under the boot; rollerblade; blade.

in lo·co pa·ren·tis (in lō′kō pə ren′tis), *Latin.* in the place of a parent; as a parent.

in·mate (in′māt), *n.* person confined in a prison, asylum, hospital, etc.

in me·mo·ri·am (in mə mô′ri əm; –mō′–), in memory (of); to the memory (of). [< L]

in·most (in′mōst), *adj.* **1** farthest in; deepest within: *inmost depths.* **2** most private; most secret: *inmost desire.*

inn (in), *n.* **1** a public house for lodging and caring for travelers. **2** =tavern. [OE, lodging] —**inn′less,** *adj.*

in·nate (i nāt′; in′āt), *adj.* natural; inborn: *an innate talent for drawing.* [< L *innatus* < *in–* + *nasci* be born] —**in·nate′ly,** *adv.* —**in·nate′ness,** *n.*

in·ner (in′ər), *adj.* **1** farther in; inside. **2** more private; more secret: *inner thoughts.* **3** of the mind or soul: *a person's inner life.* —**in′ner·ly,** *adv.* —**in′ner·ness,** *n.*

inner city, central part of a large city, esp. that part which is poor, crowded, and subject to violence.

inner ear, space in the bone behind the middle ear, containing the organs of balance and hearing.

in·ner·most (in′ər mōst), *adj.* farthest in; inmost: *the innermost parts.*

inner tube, separate rubber tube that fits inside a tire and is filled with air.

in·ning (in′ing), *n.* **1** turn of one side in a game; chance to play. **2** *Fig.* Usually,

innings. time a person or party is in power. [OE *innung* a taking in]

inn·keep·er (in′kēp′ ər), *n.* person who owns, manages, or keeps an inn.

in·no·cence (in′ə səns), *n.* **1** freedom from sin, wrong, or guilt. **2** simplicity.

in·no·cent (in′ə sənt), *adj.* **1** doing no wrong; free from sin or wrong; not guilty. **2** without knowledge of evil: *a baby is innocent.* **3** without evil effects; harmless: *innocent amusements.* **4** simple; artless. —*n.* an innocent person. [< L, < *in–* not + *nocere* to harm] —**in′no·cent·ly,** *adv.*

in·noc·u·ous (i nok′yů əs), *adj.* harmless. [< L, < *in–* not + *nocuus* hurtful < *nocere* to harm] —**in·noc′u·ous·ly,** *adv.* —**in·noc′u·ous·ness,** *n.*

in·no·vate (in′ə vāt), *v.,* **–vat·ed, –vat·ing.** make changes; bring in something new or new ways of doing things. [< L, < *in–* + *novus* new] —**in′no·va′tive,** *adj.* —**in′no·va′tor,** *n.*

in·no·va·tion (in′ə vā′shən), *n.* **1** change made in the established way of doing things. **2** making changes; bringing in new things or new ways of doing things. —**in′no·va′tion·al,** *adj.* —**in′no·va′tion·ist,** *n.*

in·nox·ious (i nok′shəs), *adj.* harmless.

in·nu·en·do (in′yů en′dō), *n., pl.* **–does. 1** indirect hint or reference. **2** indirect suggestion against somebody: *spread scandal by innuendo.* [< L, lit., by giving a nod to, *in–* in + *–nuere* nod]

in·nu·mer·a·ble (i nü′mər ə bəl; –nū′–), *adj.* too many to count; very many. —**in·nu′mer·a·ble·ness,** *n.* —**in·nu′mer·a·bly,** *adv.*

in·oc·u·late (in ok′yə lāt), *v.,* **–lat·ed, –lat·ing. 1** infect (a person or animal) with germs that will cause a very mild form of a disease so the individual will not catch that disease. **2** use disease germs to prevent or cure diseases. **3** put bacteria, serums, etc., into: *inoculate soil with bacteria.* [< L *inoculatus* engrafted < *in–* in + *oculus* bud, eye] —**in·oc′u·la′tion,** *n.* —**in·oc′u·la′tive,** *adj.* —**in·oc′u·la′tor,** *n.*

in·of·fen·sive (in′ə fen′siv), *adj.* harmless; not arousing objections. —**in′of·fen′sive·ly,** *adv.* —**in′of·fen′sive·ness,** *n.*

in·op·er·a·ble (in op′ər ə bəl), *adj.* **1** not able to be cured or repaired by surgery. **2** unworkable.

in·op·er·a·tive (in op′ər ā′tiv; –op′rə tiv), *adj.* without effect; not working. —**in·op′er·a·tive·ness,** *n.*

in·op·por·tune (in′op ər tün′; –tūn′), *adj.* coming at a bad time; unsuitable. —**in′op′por·tune′ly,** *adv.* —**in′op·por·tune′ness,** *n.*

in·or·di·nate (in ôr′də nit), *adj.* much too great; excessive; unrestrained. [< L, < *in–* not + *ordo* order] —**in·or′di·na·cy, in·or′di·nate·ness,** *n.* —**in·or′di·nate·ly,** *adv.*

in·or·gan·ic (in′ôr gan′ik), *adj.* **1** not having the organized physical structure of animals and plants: *minerals are inorganic.* 2 not produced by animal or plant activities. 3 not containing organic matter, as certain chemical compounds. —in′or·gan′i·cal·ly, *adv.*

inorganic chemistry, branch of chemistry dealing with all compounds except the organic compounds.

in·put (in′pùt′), *n.* 1 what is put in or taken in. 2 data put into a computer. 3 power supplied to a machine.

in·quest (in′kwest), *n.* a legal inquiry, esp. before a jury, to determine the cause of a death that may possibly have been the result of a crime. [< OF *enqueste,* ult. < L *inquirere* INQUIRE]

in·qui·e·tude (in kwī′ə tüd; –tūd), *n.* restlessness; uneasiness.

in·quire (in kwīr′), *v.,* –**quired, –quir·ing.** 1 try to find out by questions; ask. 2 make a search for information, knowledge, or truth; make an examination of facts or principles. Also, **enquire.** [< L *inquirere* < *in–* into + *quaerere* ask] —**in·quir′er,** *n.* —**in·quir′ing·ly,** *adv.*

in·quir·y (in kwīr′i; in′kwə ri), *n., pl.* –**quir·ies.** 1 an inquiring; an asking. 2 question. 3 search for information, knowledge, or truth; examination of facts or principles.

in·qui·si·tion (in′kwə zish′ən), *n.* 1 a thorough investigation; searching inquiry. 2 official investigation; judicial inquiry. **the Inquisition, a** court appointed by the Roman Catholic Church to discover and suppress heresy and to punish heretics. **b** activities of this court. —**in′qui·si′tion·al,** *adj.*

in·quis·i·tive (in kwiz′ə tiv), *adj.* 1 asking many questions. 2 too curious; prying into other people's affairs. —**in·quis′i·tive·ly,** *adv.* —**in·quis′i·tive·ness,** *n.*

in·quis·i·tor (in kwiz′ə tər), *n.* person who makes an inquisition; official investigator; judicial inquirer. **Inquisitor,** member of the Inquisition.

in·road (in′rōd′), *n.* 1 attack; raid. 2 forcible encroachment: *inroads upon savings.*

in·rush (in′rush′), *n.* rushing in; inflow. —**in′rush′ing,** *n., adj.*

ins., 1 inches. 2 inspector. 3 insurance.

in·sane (in sān′), *adj.* 1 not sane; mentally deranged. 2 for insane people: *an insane asylum.* 3 extremely foolish. —**in·sane′ly,** *adv.* —**in·sane·ness,** *n.*

in·san·i·tar·y (in san′ə ter′i), *adj.* unhealthful. —**in·san′i·tar′i·ness,** *n.*

in·san·i·ty (in san′ə ti), *n., pl.* –**ties.** 1 state of being insane. 2 extreme folly.

in·sa·tia·ble (in sā′shə bəl), *adj.* that cannot be satisfied. —**in·sa′tia·bil′i·ty, in·sa′tia·ble·ness,** *n.* —**in·sa′tia·bly,** *adv.*

in·sa·ti·ate (in sā′shi it), *adj.* never satisfied. —**in·sa′ti·ate·ly,** *adv.* —**in·sa′ti·ate·ness,** *n.*

in·scribe (in skrīb′), *v.,* –**scribed, –scrib·ing.** 1 write, engrave, or mark (words, letters, etc.) on paper, metal, stone, etc. 2 mark or engrave (with words,

letters, etc.). 3 address or dedicate (a book, etc.) informally to a person. 4 *Fig.* impress deeply: *my father's words are inscribed in my memory.* [< L, < *in–* on + *scribere* write] —**in·scrib′a·ble,** *adj.* —**in·scrib′er,** *n.*

in·scrip·tion (in skrip′shən), *n.* 1 something inscribed, as by writing or engraving. A monument or a coin has an inscription on it. 2 informal dedication in a book, on a picture, etc.

in·scru·ta·ble (in skrü′tə bəl), *adj.* that cannot be understood; so mysterious or obscure that one cannot make out its meaning. [< LL, < L *in–* not + *scrutari* examine, ransack < *scruta* trash] —**in·scru′ta·bil′i·ty, in·scru·ta·ble·ness,** *n.* —**in·scru′ta·bly,** *adv.*

in·seam (in′sēm′), *n.* inner or inside seam of a trouser leg, sleeve, or shoe.

in·sect (in′sekt), *n.* 1 a small invertebrate animal with its body divided into three parts (head, thorax, and abdomen), with three pairs of legs, and usually two pairs of wings, as flies, mosquitoes, and beetles. 2 any similar small animal with its body divided into several parts, with several pairs of legs, as spiders, centipedes, etc. [< L *insectum,* lit., divided *in–* into + *secare* to cut] —**in′sect·like′,** *adj.*

in·sec·ti·cide (in sek′tə sīd), *n.* substance for killing insects. —**in·sec′ti·cid′al,** *adj.*

in·sec·tiv·o·rous (in′sek tiv′ə rəs), *adj.* 1 insect-eating; feeding mainly on insects. 2 of or belonging to a group of small mammals including moles, hedgehogs, etc. —**in·sec′ti·vore,** *n.*

in·se·cure (in′si kyùr′), *adj.* 1 not secure; unsafe. 2 *Fig.* uncertain; unsure: *our insecure future.* 3 liable to give way; not firm: *an insecure lock.* —**in′se·cure′ly,** *adv.*

in·se·cu·ri·ty (in′si kyùr′ə ti), *n., pl.* –**ties.** 1 lack of security. 2 *Fig.* feelings of uncertainty. 3 something insecure.

in·sem·i·nate (in sem′ə nāt), *v.,* –**nat·ed, –nat·ing.** 1 sow; implant. 2 impregnate. —**in·sem′i·na′tion,** *n.*

in·sen·sate (in sen′sāt; –sit), *adj.* 1 without sensation. 2 unfeeling: *insensate cruelty.* 3 senseless; stupid: *insensate folly.* —**in·sen′sate·ly,** *adv.* —**in·sen′sate·ness,** *n.*

in·sen·si·bil·i·ty (in sen′sə bil′ə ti), *n., pl.* –**ties.** 1 lack of feeling. 2 lack of consciousness.

in·sen·si·ble (in sen′sə bəl), *adj.* 1 not sensitive; not able to feel or observe: *a blind man is insensible to colors.* 2 not aware: *insensible of the danger.* 3 not able to feel anything; unconscious: *the man hit by the truck was insensible for hours.* 4 not easily felt: *the room grew cold by insensible degrees.* —**in·sen′si·bly,** *adv.*

in·sen·si·tive (in sen′sə tiv), *adj.* 1 not sensitive. 2 slow to feel or notice. —**in·sen′si·tive·ness, in·sen′si·tiv′i·ty,** *n.*

in·sen·ti·ent (in sen′shi ənt; –shənt), *adj.* unable to feel; lifeless. —**in·sen′ti·ence,** *n.*

in·sep·a·ra·ble (in sep′ə rə bəl; –sep′rə bəl), *adj.* that cannot be separated.

—**in·sep′a·ra·bil′i·ty, in·sep′a·ra·ble·ness,** *n.* —**in·sep′a·ra·bly,** *adv.*

in·sert (*v.* in sèrt′; *n.* in′sèrt), *v.* put in; set in: *insert a key into a lock.* —*n.* something set in or to be set in: *an insert of several pages.* [< L, < *in–* in + *serere* entwine] —**in·sert′er,** *n.*

in·ser·tion (in sèr′shən), *n.* 1 an inserting: *the insertion of pictures in a book.* 2 thing inserted. 3 band of lace or embroidery to be sewed at each edge between parts of other material.

in·serv·ice (in′ser′vis), *adj.* while working: *in-service computer courses.*

in·set (*v.* in set′, in′set′; *n.* in′set′), *v.,* –**set, –set·ting,** *n.* —*v.* set in; insert. —*n.* something inserted.

in·shore (in′shōr′; –shōr′), *adj.* near the shore. —*adv.* in toward the shore.

in·side (*n., adj.* in′sīd′; *adv., prep.* in′sīd′), *n.* 1 side or surface that is within; inner part: *the inside of a house.* 2 inward nature. —*adj.* 1 being on the inside: *an inside seat.* 2 done or known by those inside; private; secret: *inside information, the theft was an inside job.* —*adv.* 1 on or to the inside; within. 2 indoors: *go inside.* —*prep.* in; within: *a gift inside a box.*

inside of, in; within the limits of: *be home inside of a week.*

inside out, a so that what is inside is outside; with the outside showing. **b** backwards; confused: *inside out reasoning.* **c** thoroughly: *knew her parts inside out.*

insides, part inside the body; stomach and bowels.

in·sid·er (in′sīd′ər), *n.* 1 person who is inside some place, society, organization, etc. 2 person who is so situated as to understand the actual conditions or facts of a case. 3 person with access to secret information or facts not generally known: *a government insider.*

insider trading, illegal practice of buying or selling shares of stock on the basis of secret information about a company that would affect the value of its stock.

inside track, 1 lane nearest the inside curve of a race course. 2 *Fig.* advantageous position.

in·sid·i·ous (in sid′i əs), *adj.* 1 crafty; tricky; treacherous. 2 working secretly or subtly: *an insidious disease.* [< L, < *insidiae* ambush, ult. < *in–* + *sedere* sit] —**in·sid′i·ous·ly,** *adv.* —**in·sid′i·ous·ness,** *n.*

in·sight (in′sīt′), *n.* 1 a viewing of the inside or inner parts of (something) with understanding. 2 wisdom and understanding in dealing with people or with facts.

in·sig·ni·a (in sig′ni ə), *n.pl., sing.* **in·sig·ne** (in sig′nē). emblems, badges, or other distinguishing marks of a high position, military order, etc. [< L, pl. of *insigne* badge < *in–* on + *signum* mark]

in·sig·nif·i·cance (in′sig nif′ə kəns), *n.* 1 unimportance. 2 meaninglessness.

in·sig·nif·i·cant (in′sig nif′ə kənt), *adj.* **1** having little use or importance. **2** meaningless. —**in′sig·nif′i·cant·ly,** *adv.*

in·sin·cere (in′sin sir′), *adj.* not sincere; not honest or candid; deceitful. —**in′sin·cere′ly,** *adv.*

in·sin·cer·i·ty (in′sin ser′ə ti), *n., pl.* **-ties.** lack of sincerity; hypocrisy.

in·sin·u·ate (in sin′yü āt), *v.,* **-at·ed, -at·ing. 1** push in or get in by an indirect, twisting way: *the spy insinuated himself into the confidence of important army officers.* **2** suggest indirectly; hint. [< L, < *in-* in + *sinus* a curve] —**in·sin′u·at′·ing·ly,** *adv.* —**in·sin′u·a′tive,** *adj.* —**in·sin′u·a′tor,** *n.*

in·sin·u·a·tion (in sin′yü ā′shən), *n.* **1** an insinuating. **2** indirect suggestion against someone. **3** hint; suggestion. **4** act or speech to gain favor.

in·sip·id (in sip′id), *adj.* **1** without much taste. **2** uninteresting; colorless; weak. [< LL *insipidus* < L *in-* not + *sapidus* tasty] —**in·sip′id·ly,** *adv.* —**in·sip′id·ness,** *n.*

in·si·pid·i·ty (in′si pid′ə ti), *n., pl.* **-ties. 1** lack of flavor; lack of interest. **2** something insipid.

in·sist (in sist′), *v.* keep firmly to some demand, some statement, or some position. [< L, < *in-* on + *sistere* take a stand] —**in·sist′er,** *n.*

in·sist·ent (in sis′tənt), *adj.* **1** insisting; continuing to make a strong, firm demand or statement. **2** compelling attention or notice; pressing; urgent. —**in·sist′ence, in·sist′en·cy,** *n.* —**in·sist′ent·ly,** *adv.*

in·snare (in snār′), *v.,* **-snared, -snar·ing.** =ensnare.

in·so·bri·e·ty (in′sə brī′ə ti), *n.* intemperance.

in·so·far (in′sō fär′), or **in so far,** *adv.* to such an extent or degree: *insofar as we know.*

in·sole (in′sōl′), *n.* the inner sole of a shoe or boot.

in·so·lence (in′sə ləns), *n.* bold rudeness; insulting behavior or speech.

in·so·lent (in′sə lənt), *adj.* boldly rude; insulting. [< L *insolens,* orig., unusual < *in-* not + *solere* be wont] —**in′so·lent·ly,** *adv.*

in·sol·u·ble (in sol′yə bəl), *adj.* **1** that cannot be dissolved. **2** that cannot be solved. —**in·sol′u·bil′i·ty, in·sol′u·ble·ness,** *n.* —**in·sol′u·bly,** *adv.*

in·solv·a·ble (in sol′və bəl), *adj.* that cannot be solved.

in·sol·vent (in sol′vənt), *adj.* **1** not able to pay one's debts; bankrupt. **2** pertaining to bankrupts. —*n.* an insolvent person. —**in·sol′ven·cy,** *n.*

in·som·ni·a (in som′ni ə), *n.* inability to sleep; sleeplessness. [< L, < *in-* not + *somnus* sleep] —**in·som′ni·ous,** *adj.*

in·som·ni·ac (in som′nē ak), *n.* person who suffers from insomnia.

in·so·much (in′sō much′), *adv.* **1** to such an extent or degree; so. **2** inasmuch.

in·sou·ci·ance (in sü′si əns), *n.* freedom from care or anxiety; carefree feeling.

in·sou·ci·ant (in sü′si ənt), *adj.* free from care or anxiety. [< F] —**in·sou′ci·ant·ly,** *adv.*

in·spect (in spekt′), *v.* **1** look over carefully; examine. **2** examine officially. [< L *inspectus* < *in-* upon + *specere* look]

in·spec·tion (in spek′shən), *n.* **1** an inspecting. **2** formal or official examination. —**in·spec′tion·al,** *adj.*

in·spec·tor (in spek′tər), *n.* **1** person who inspects. **2** police officer ranking next below a superintendent. —**in·spec′to·ral, in·spec′to·ri·al,** *adj.* —**in·spec′tor·ship,** *n.*

in·spi·ra·tion (in′spə rā′shən), *n.* **1** influence of thought and strong feelings on actions, esp. on good actions: *get inspiration from a speech.* **2** any influence that arouses effort to do well: *the captain was an inspiration to his men.* **3** idea that is inspired. **4** a breathing in; a drawing air into the lungs. —**in′spi·ra′tion·al,** *adj.* —**in′spi·ra′tion·al·ly,** *adv.*

in·spire (in spīr′), *v.,* **-spired, -spir·ing. 1** put thought, feeling, life, force, etc., into: *the speaker inspired the crowd.* **2** cause (thought or feeling): *the leader's courage inspired confidence in others.* **3** affect; influence: *his sly ways inspire me with distrust.* **4** suggest; cause to be told or written: *his enemies inspired false stories about him.* **5** breathe in; breathe in air. [< L, < *in-* in + *spirare* breathe] —**in·spir′a·ble,** *adj.* —**in·spir′er,** *n.* —**in·spir′ing·ly,** *adv.*

in·spir·it (in spir′it), *v.* put spirit into; encourage; hearten. —**in·spir′it·ing·ly,** *adv.*

inst., 1 installment. **2** instant. **3** Also, **Inst.** institute; institution.

in·sta·bil·i·ty (in′stə bil′ə ti), *n.* lack of firmness; liability to give way or change.

in·stall (in stôl′), *v.* **1** place (a person) in office with ceremonies. **2** establish in a place: *install oneself in an easy chair.* **3** put in position for use: *install a telephone.* [< Med.L, < *in-* in (< L) + *stallum* STALL[1] (< Gmc.)] —**in′stal·la′tion,** *n.* —**in·stall′er,** *n.*

in·stall·ment[1] (in stôl′mənt), *n.* **1** part of a sum of money or of a debt to be paid at certain regular times. **2** any of several parts furnished or issued at successive times: *a serial story in a magazine in six installments.* [prob. < *install* pay periodically]

in·stall·ment[2] (in stôl′ mənt), *n.* installation.

installment plan, system of paying for goods in installments.

in·stance (in′stəns), *n., v.,* **-stanced, -stanc·ing.** —*n.* **1** example; case: *an instance of neglect.* **2** stage or step in an action; occasion: *in the first instance.* **3** request; suggestion; urging: *he came at our instance.* —*v.* refer to as an example.

for instance, for example. [< OF < L

instantia insistence < *instans* insistent. See INSTANT.]

in·stant (in′stənt), *n.* **1** particular moment: *stop talking this instant.* **2** moment of time: *he paused for an instant.* —*adj.* **1** immediate; without delay: *instant relief.* **2** pressing; urgent: *an instant need for action.* **3** dehydrated, crystallized, or powdered: *instant coffee.* **4** of the present month; present. [< L *instans* insisting, standing near < *in-* in + *stare* stand]

in·stan·ta·ne·ous (in′stən tā′ni əs), *adj.* occurring, done, or made in an instant. —**in′stan·ta·ne·ous·ly,** *adv.* —**in′stan·ta·ne·ous·ness,** *n.*

in·stant·ly (in′stənt li), *adv.* **1** in an instant; at once; immediately. **2** urgently.

in·stead (in sted′), *adv.* **1** in place (of): *instead of studying, she read a book.* **2** in one's or its place: *let him go instead.*

in·step (in′step), *n.* **1** the upper surface of the human foot between the toes and the ankle. **2** part of a shoe, stocking, etc., over the instep.

in·sti·gate (in′stə gāt), *v.,* **-gat·ed, -gat·ing.** urge on; stir up: *foreign agents instigated a rebellion.* [< L *instigatus*] —**in′sti·ga′tion,** *n.* —**in′sti·ga′tive,** *adj.* —**in′sti·ga′tor,** *n.*

in·still, in·stil (in stil′), *v.,* **-stilled, -still·ing. 1** put in little by little; impart gradually: *reading good books instills a love of literature.* **2** put in drop by drop. [< L, < *in-* in + *stilla* a drop] —**in′stil·la′tion,** *n.* —**in·still′er,** *n.* —**in·still′ment, in·stil′ment,** *n.*

in·stinct[1] (in′stingkt), *n.* **1** natural feeling, knowledge, or power, such as guides animals; unlearned tendency: *an instinct leads birds to fly.* **2** a natural bent, tendency, or gift; talent: *an instinct to govern.* [< L *instinctus,* n. < *instinguere* impel]

in·stinct[2] (in stingkt′), *adj.* charged or filled with something: *the picture is instinct with life and beauty.* [< L *instinctus,* pp. See INSTINCT[1].]

in·stinc·tive (in stingk′tiv), *adj.* of, caused, or done by instinct; born in an animal or person, not learned. —**in·stinc′tive·ly,** *adv.*

in·stinc·tu·al (in stingkt′chù əl), *adj.,* of or having to do with instinct: *an instinctual reaction.*

in·sti·tute (in′stə tüt; -tūt), *v.,* **-tut·ed, -tut·ing,** *n.* —*v.* set up; establish; begin; initiate: *the police instituted an inquiry.* —*n.* **1** organization, building, or society for some special purpose, as an art institute. **2** an established principle, law, custom, organization, or society. [< L *institutus* < *in-* in + *statuere* establish] —**in′sti·tut′er, in′sti·tu′tor,** *n.*

in·sti·tu·tion (in′stə tü′shən; -tū′-), *n.* **1** organization or society for some public or social purpose, as a church, school, hospital, etc. **2** building that houses such an organization or society. **3** established law, custom, organization, or society: *giving presents on Christmas is an* *institution.* **4** setting up; establishing; beginning: *the institution of a savings bank.* **5** *Fig.* familiar person or thing: *the fair has become an institution.*

in·sti·tu·tion·al (in´stə tü´shən əl; –tū´–), *adj.* of, like, or established by an institution. **—in´sti·tu´tion·al·ly,**

in·sti·tu·tion·al·ize (in´stə tü´shən ə līz; –tū´–), *v.,* **–ized, –iz·ing. 1** make into an institution: *institutionalized the annual clambake.* **2** put a person into an institution: *fewer people with mental illness are institutionalized.* **—in´sti·tu´tion·al·i·za´tion,** *n.*

instr., 1 instructor. **2** instrument.

in·struct (in strukt´), *v.* **1** teach. **2** give directions or orders to. **3** inform. [< L *instructus* < *in–* on + *struere* to pile]

in·struc·tion (in struk´shən), *n.* a teaching; knowledge; education.

instructions, directions; orders. **—in·struc´tion·al,** *adj.*

in·struc·tive (in struk´tiv), *adj.* useful for instruction; instructing: *an instructive experience.* **—in·struc´tive·ly,** *adv.* **—in·struc´tive·ness,** *n.*

in·struc·tor (in struk´tər), *n.* **1** teacher. **2** teacher ranking below an assistant professor in American colleges and universities. **—in·struc´tor·ship,** *n.*

in·stru·ment (in´strə mənt), *n.* **1** tool or mechanical device: *a dentist's instruments.* **2** device for producing musical sounds: *stringed instruments.* **3** thing with or by which something is done; a person so made use of; means. **4** a formal legal document, such as a contract. [< L *instrumentum* < *instruere* arrange, INSTRUCT]

in·stru·men·tal (in´strə men´təl), *adj.* **1** acting or serving as a means; useful; helpful. **2** played on or written for instruments. **—in´stru·men´tal·ly,** *adv.*

in·stru·men·tal·ist (in´strə men´təl ist), *n.* person who plays on an instrument.

in·stru·men·tal·i·ty (in´strə men tal´ə ti), *n.,* *pl.* **–ties.** helpfulness as an instrument; agency; means.

in·stru·men·ta·tion (in´strə men tā´shən), *n.* **1** arrangement or composition for instruments. **2** use of instruments.

instrument board, =instrument panel.

in·stru·ment·ed (in´strə ment´id), *adj.* equipped with electronic or other devices necessary for guidance: *a fully instrumented missile.*

instrument flying, directing an airplane by instruments only.

instrument panel, panel with dials, lights, etc., that show how various components or systems connected to it are functioning, as for an automobile, aircraft, or spacecraft.

in·sub·or·di·nate (in´sə bôr´də nit), *adj.* resisting authority; disobedient; unruly. **—n.** one who is insubordinate. **—in´sub·or´di·nate·ly,** *adv.*

in·sub·or·di·na·tion (in´sə bôr´də nā´shən), *n.* resistance to authority; disobedience.

in·sub·stan·tial (in´səb stan´shəl), *adj.* **1** frail; flimsy; weak: *a cobweb is very insubstantial.* **2** unreal; not actual; imaginary: *ghosts are insubstantial.* **—in´sub·stan´ti·al´i·ty,** *n.*

in·suf·fer·a·ble (in suf´ər ə bəl; –suf´rə bəl), *adj.* intolerable; unbearable: *insufferable insolence.* **—in·suf´fer·a·ble·ness,** *n.* **—in·suf´fer·a·bly,** *adv.*

in·suf·fi·cien·cy (in´sə fish´ən si), *n.* too small an amount; lack; deficiency.

in·suf·fi·cient (in´sə fish´ənt), *adj.* not enough. **—in´suf·fi´cient·ly,** *adv.*

in·su·lar (in´sə lər), *adj.* **1** of or having to do with islands or islanders. **2** living or situated on an island. **3** forming an island. **4** narrow-minded; prejudiced. [< LL, < L *insula* island] **—in´su·lar·ism, in´su·lar´i·ty,** *n.* **—in´su·lar·ly,** *adv.*

in·su·late (in´sə lāt), *v.,* **–lat·ed, –lat·ing. 1** keep from losing or transferring electricity, heat, sound, etc. **2** cover or surround (electric wire, etc.) with nonconducting material. **3** set apart; separate from others; isolate. [< L *insulatus* formed into an island < *insula* island]

in·su·la·tion (in´sə lā´shən), *n.* **1** an insulating or being insulated. **2** material used in insulating.

in·su·la·tor (in´sə lā´tər), *n.* that which insulates; nonconductor.

in·su·lin (in´sə lin), *n.* **1** hormone secreted by the pancreas that enables the body to use sugar and other carbohydrates. **2** insulin for treatment of diabetes produced by genetic engineering. [< L *insula* island (i.e., of the pancreas)]

in·sult (*v.* in sult´; *n.* in´sult), *v.* treat with scorn, abuse, or great rudeness: *the rebels insulted the flag by throwing mud on it.* **—n.** an insulting speech or action. [< L *insultare* < *in–* on, at + *salire* to leap] **—in·sult´er,** *n.* **—in·sult´ing,** *adj.* **—in·sult·ing·ly,** *adv.*

in·su·per·a·ble (in sü´pər ə bəl), *adj.* that cannot be passed over or overcome: *an insuperable barrier.* **—in·su´per·a·bil´i·ty, in·su´per·a·ble·ness,** *n.* **—in·su´per·a·bly,** *adv.*

in·sup·port·a·ble (in´sə pôr´tə bəl; –pōr´–), *adj.* unbearable; unendurable; intolerable. **—in´sup·port´a·ble·ness,** *n.* **—in´sup·port´a·bly,** *adv.*

in·sur·a·ble (in shûr´ə bəl), *adj.* capable of being insured; fit to be insured. **—in·sur´a·bil´i·ty,** *n.*

in·sur·ance (in shûr´əns), *n.* **1** an insuring of property, person, or life: *fire insurance.* **2** the business of insuring property, life, etc. **3** amount of money for which a person or thing is insured: *he has $100,000 insurance.* **4** amount of money paid for insurance; premium: *her insurance is $300 a year.*

in·sure (in shûr´), *v.,* **–sured, –sur·ing. 1** arrange for money payment in case of loss of (property, profit, etc.) or accident or death to (a person): *insure antiques.* **2** make safe from financial loss by accident, death, etc., by paying money to an insurance company: *was he insured at the time of the accident?* [var. of *ensure* < AF, < *en–* in + OF *seur* SURE]

in·sured (in shûrd´), *n.* person whose property, life, etc., are insured.

in·sur·er (in shûr´ər), *n.* person or company that insures.

in·sur·gence (in sėr´jəns), *n.* a rising in revolt; rebellion.

in·sur·gen·cy (in sėr´jən si), *n.* **1** =insurgence. **2** revolt against a government, not recognized as a state of war; insurrection: *the insurgency may become all-out civil war.*

in·sur·gent (in sėr´jənt), *n.* person who rises in revolt; rebel. **—adj.** rising in revolt; rebellious. [< L, < *in–* against + *surgere* rise]

in·sur·mount·a·ble (in´sər moun´tə bəl), *adj.* that cannot be overcome. **—in´sur·mount´a·bly,** *adv.*

in·sur·rec·tion (in´sə rek´shən), *n.* an uprising against established authority; revolt. [< LL *insurrectio* < L *insurgere.* See INSURGENT.] **—in´sur·rec´tion·al,** *adj.* **—in´sur·rec´tion·al·ly,** *adv.*

in·sus·cep·ti·ble (in´sə sep´tə bəl), *adj.* not susceptible; not easily influenced. **—in´sus·cep´ti·bil´i·ty,** *n.* **—in´sus·cep´ti·bly,** *adv.*

int., 1 interest. **2** international. **3** intransitive.

in·tact (in takt´), *adj.* with no part missing; untouched; uninjured; whole: *dishes left intact after a fall.* [< L *intactus,* ult. < *in–* not + *tangere* touch] **—in·tact´·ness,** *n.*

in·tagl·io (in tal´yō; –tǟl´–), *n.,* *pl.* **in·tagl·ios. 1** process of engraving by making cuts in a surface. **2** design engraved in this way. [< Ital., ult. < *in–* into + *tagliare* to cut]

in·take (in´tāk´), *n.* **1** place where water, gas, etc., enters a channel, pipe, or other narrow opening. **2** a taking in. **3** amount or thing taken in.

in·tan·gi·ble (in tan´jə bəl), *adj.* **1** not capable of being touched. **2** not easily grasped by the mind. **—n.** something intangible. **—in·tan´gi·bil´i·ty, in·tan´gi·ble·ness,** *n.* **—in·tan´gi·bly,** *adv.*

in·te·ger (in´tə jər), *n.* a whole number as distinguished from a fraction or mixed number. 1, 2, 3, 15, 106, etc., are integers. [< L, whole]

in·te·gral (in´tə grəl), *adj.* **1** necessary to the completeness of the whole; essential. **2** entire; complete. **3** having to do with whole numbers; not fractional. [< LL, < L *integer* whole] **—in´te·gral´i·ty,** *n.* **—in´te·gral·ly,** *adv.*

in·te·grate (in´tə grāt), *v.,* **—grat·ed, –grat·ing. 1** make into a whole; complete. **2** bring together (parts) into a whole. **3** *U.S.* make schools, parks, etc. available to all citizens on an equal basis. [< L, < *integer* whole] **—in´te·gra´tion,** *n.* **—in´te·gra´tive,** *adj.* **—in´te·gra´tor,** *n.*

in·te·grat·ed circuit (in′tə grā′tid), electronic circuit on a chip, esp. of silicon, whose components cannot be moved; microcircuit.

in·teg·ri·ty (in teg′rə ti), *n.* **1** honesty; sincerity; uprightness: *a man of integrity.* **2** wholeness; completeness: *defend the integrity of one's country.* **3** perfect condition; soundness. [< L *integritas.* See INTEGER.]

in·teg·u·ment (in teg′yù mənt), *n.* an outer covering, as a skin or a shell. [< L *integumentum* < *in-* on + *tegere* to cover]

in·tel·lect (in′tə lekt), *n.* **1** power of knowing; understanding. **2** great intelligence; high mental ability: *a man of intellect.* **3** person having high mental ability. [< L *intellectus* < *intelligere.* See INTELLIGENT.]

in·tel·lec·tu·al (in′tə lek′chù əl), *adj.* **1** of the intellect: *intellectual power.* **2** needing or using intelligence: *an intellectual process.* **3** possessing or showing intelligence: *an intellectual type of mind, intellectual tastes.* —*n.* person who is well informed or concerned with the intellect. —**in′tel·lec′tu·al′i·ty, in′tel·lec′tu·al·ness,** *n.* —**in′tel·lec′tu·al·ly,** *adv.*

in·tel·lec·tu·al·ize (in′tə lək′chù ə līz), *v.* **-ized, -iz·ing.** make intellectual; apply understanding or reason to.

in·tel·li·gence (in tel′ə jəns), *n.* **1** ability to learn and know; understanding; mind. **2** knowledge; news; information. **3** the obtaining or distributing of information, esp. secret information. **4** group of persons engaged in obtaining secret information.

intelligence quotient, number used to measure a child's intelligence, obtained by dividing the mental age by the chronological age.

intelligence test, test used to measure mental development.

in·tel·li·gent (in tel′ə jənt), *adj.* having or showing intelligence; able to learn and know; quick at learning. [< L *intelligens* understanding < *inter-* between + *legere* choose] —**in·tel′li·gent·ly,** *adv.*

in·tel·li·gent·si·a (in tel′ə jent′si ə; –gent′–), *n.pl.* persons representing, or claiming to represent, the enlightened opinion of a society. [< Russ. < L *intelligentia.* See INTELLIGENT.]

in·tel·li·gi·ble (in tel′ə jə bəl), *adj.* capable of being understood; comprehensible. [< L, < *intelligere.* See INTELLIGENT.] —**in·tel′li·gi·bil′i·ty, in·tel′li·gi·ble·ness,** *n.* —**in·tel′li·gi·bly,** *adv.*

in·tem·per·ance (in tem′pər əns; –prəns), *n.* **1** lack of moderation or self-control; excess. **2** the excessive use of intoxicating liquor.

in·tem·per·ate (in tem′pər it; –prit), *adj.* **1** not moderate; lacking in self-control; excessive. **2** drinking too much intoxicating liquor. **3** not temperate; severe: *an intemperate winter.* —**in·tem′per·ate·ly,** *adv.* —**in·tem′per·ate·ness,** *n.*

in·tend (in tend′), *v.* **1** have in mind as a purpose; mean; plan: *we intend to go home soon.* **2** design; destine: *a book intended for beginners.* [< L, < *in-* toward + *tendere* stretch] —**in·tend′er,** *n.*

in·tend·ed (in ten′did), *adj.* **1** meant; planned. **2** prospective: *a woman's intended husband.* —*n.* a prospective husband or wife.

in·tense (in tens′), *adj.* **1** very much; very great; very strong: *intense pain.* **2** full of vigorous activity, strong feelings, etc.: *an intense life.* **3** having or showing strong feelings: *an intense person.* [< L *intensus,* pp. of *intendere* strain. See INTEND.] —**in·tense′ly,** *adv.* —**in·tense′ness,** *n.*

in·ten·si·fy (in ten′səfī), *v.,* **-fied, -fy·ing.** make or become intense or more intense; strengthen: *blowing on a fire intensifies the heat.* —**in·ten′si·fi·ca′tion,** *n.* —**in·ten′si·fi′er,** *n.*

in·ten·si·ty (in ten′sə ti), *n., pl.* **-ties.** **1** a being intense; great strength; extreme degree. **2** great strength or violence of feeling. **3** amount or degree of strength of electricity, heat, light, sound, etc., per unit of area, volume, etc.

in·ten·sive (in ten′siv), *adj.* **1** deep and thorough: *an intensive study.* **2** giving force or emphasis; expressing intensity. In "He himself said it," *himself* is an intensive pronoun. —*n.* intensive word, prefix, etc. —**in·ten′sive·ly,** *adv.* —**in·ten′sive·ness,** *n.*

intensive care, hospital care of a patient who is seriously ill that involves constant monitoring and immediate access to lifesaving equipment.

intensive care unit, special unit of a hospital having the equipment and staff to provide intensive care.

in·tent¹ (in tent′), *n.* **1** purpose; intention. **2** meaning; significance.

to all intents and purposes, in almost every way; practically. [< OF *entent, entente* < L *intendere* INTEND]

in·tent² (in tent′), *adj.* **1** very attentive; having the eyes or thoughts earnestly fixed on something; earnest. **2** earnestly engaged; much interested. [< L *intentus,* pp. of *intendere* to strain. See INTEND.] —**in·tent′ly,** *adv.* —**in·tent′ness,** *n.*

in·ten·tion (in ten′shən), *n.* **1** purpose; design; plan: *our intention is to travel next summer.* **2** meaning.

intentions, purposes with respect to marrying.

in·ten·tion·al (in ten′shən əl), *adj.* done on purpose; meant; intended. —**in·ten′tion·al·ly,**

in·ter (in tér′), *v.,* **-terred, -ter·ring.** put (a dead body) into a grave or tomb; bury. [< OF *enterrer,* ult. < L *in-* in + *terra* earth]

inter-, *prefix.* **1** together; one with the other, as in *intercommunicate.* **2** between, as in *interlude.* **3** among a group, as in *interscholastic.* [< L, < *inter,* prep., adv., among, between, during]

in·ter·act (in′tər akt′), *v.* act on each other. —**in′ter·ac′tion,** *n.* —**in′ter·ac′tive,** *adj.*

in·ter·breed (in′tər brēd′), *v.,* **-bred, -breed·ing.** breed by the mating of different kinds; breed by using different varieties or species of animals or plants.

in·ter·ca·lar·y (in tér′kə ler′i), *adj.* inserted in a calendar: *February 29 is an intercalary day.*

in·ter·cede (in′tər sēd′), *v.,* **-ced·ed, -ced·ing.** **1** plead or beg in another's behalf: *Will interceded with the teacher for Dan.* **2** interfere in order to bring about an agreement. [< L, < *inter-* between + *cedere* go] —**in′ter·ced′er,** *n.*

in·ter·cel·lu·lar (in′tər sel′yə lər), *adj.* situated between or among cells.

in·ter·cept (in′tər sept′), *v.* **1** take or seize on the way from one place to another: *intercept a letter.* **2** cut off (light, water, etc.). **3** check; stop: *intercept the flight of a criminal.* **4** mark off between two points or lines. [< L *interceptus* < *inter-* between + *capere* catch] —**in′ter·cep′tion,** *n.* —**in′ter·cep′tive,** *adj.* —**in′ter·cep′tor,** *n.*

in·ter·ces·sion (in′tər sesh′ ən), *n.* act or fact of interceding. —**in′ter·ces′sion·al,** *adj.* —**in′ter·ces′sor,** *n.* —**in′ter·ces′so·ry,** *adj.*

in·ter·change (*v.* in′tər chānj′; *n.* in′tər chānj′), *v.,* **-changed, -chang·ing,** *n.* —*v.* **1** put each of (two or more persons or things) in the place of the other. **2** give and take; exchange: *interchange gifts.* **3** cause to happen by turns; alternate: *interchange severity with indulgence.* —*n.* **1** a putting each of two or more persons or things in the other's place. **2** a giving and taking; exchanging. **3** point at which an express highway connects with another road.

in·ter·change·a·ble (in′tər chān′jə bəl), *adj.* **1** capable of being used in place of each other. **2** able to change places. —**in′ter·change′a·bil′i·ty, in′ter·change′a·ble·ness,** *n.* —**in′ter·change′a·bly,** *adv.*

in·ter·col·le·giate (in′tər kə lē′jit; –ji it), *adj.* between colleges or universities.

in·ter·com (in′tər kom′), *n.* telephone apparatus with which members of the crew of an airplane, office, etc., can talk to each other.

in·ter·com·mu·ni·cate (in′tər kə mū′nə kāt′), *v.,* **-cat·ed, -cat·ing.** communicate with each other. —**in′ter·com·mu′ni·ca′tion,** *n.*

in·ter·con·nect (in′tər kə nekt′), *v.* connect with each other. —**in′ter·con·nec′tion,** *n.*

in·ter·con·ti·nen·tal (in′tər kon′tə nen′təl), *adj.* **1** for use between continents. **2** of more than one continent.

in·ter·course (in′tər kôrs; –kōrs), *n.* **1** communication; dealings between people; exchange of thoughts, services, feelings, etc. **2** sexual intercourse.

in·ter·de·nom·i·na·tion·al (in′tər di nom′ə nā′shən əl; –nāsh′nəl), *adj.* between or involving different religious denominations.

in·ter·de·part·men·tal (in´tər di pärt´men´t əl, –dē´pärt–), *adj.* between departments, as of an agency, school, etc.

in·ter·de·pend·ence (in´tər di pen´dəns), **in·ter·de·pend·en·cy** (–dən si), *n.* dependence on each other; mutual dependence.

in·ter·de·pend·ent (in´tər di pen´dənt), *adj.* dependent each upon the other. —**in´ter·de·pend´ent·ly,** *adv.*

in·ter·dict (*v.* in´tər dikt´; *n.* in´tər dikt), *v.* 1 prohibit; forbid. 2 restrain. 3 cut off from certain church privileges. —*n.* 1 prohibition based on authority; formal order forbidding something. 2 a cutting off from certain church privileges. [< L, < *inter–* between + *dicere* speak] —**in´ter·dic´tion,** *n.* —**in´ter·dic´tive,** *adj.* —**in´ter·dic´tor,** *n.* —**in´ter·dic´to·ry,** *adj.*

in·ter·dis·ci·pli·nar·y (in´tər dis´ə plə ner´i), *adj.* between different fields of study.

in·ter·est (in´tər ist; –trist), *n.* 1 a feeling of wanting to see, do, own, share in: *an interest in sports.* 2 power of arousing such a feeling: *a dull book lacks interest.* 3 share; part; portion: *buy a half interest in a business.* 4 group of people having the same business, activity, etc. 5 advantage; benefit. 6 money paid for the use of money: *the interest on the loan was 5 percent.* —*v.* 1 arouse the attention, curiosity, concern, etc., of: *an exciting story interests you.* 2 cause (a person) to take a share or interest in: *the dealer tried to interest us in buying a car.*
in the interest of, for; to help. [< L, it is of importance, it makes a difference < *inter–* between + *esse* be]

in·ter·est·ed (in´tris tid; –tər es´tid), *adj.* 1 feeling or showing interest. 2 having an interest or share. 3 influenced by personal considerations; prejudiced. —**in´ter·est·ed·ly,** *adv.* —**in´ter·est·ed·ness,** *n.*

in·ter·est·ing (in´tris ting; –tər es´ting), *adj.* arousing interest; holding one's attention. —**in´ter·est·ing·ly,** *adv.* —**in´ter·est·ing·ness,** *n.*

in·ter·face (in´tər fās´), *n., v.,* **-faced, fac·ing.** —*n.* 1 surface lying between two objects or spaces, that forms their shared boundary. 2 connection or relationship between people or things; interaction: *customer interface, computer interface.* —*v.* work together smoothly.

in·ter·faith (in´tər fāth´), *adj.* for or of more than one faith or religion.

in·ter·fere (in´tər fir´), *v.,* **-fered, -fer·ing.** 1 come into opposition; clash: *come on Saturday if nothing interferes.* 2 disturb the affairs of others; meddle. 3 take part for a purpose: *the police interfered to stop the riot.*
interfere with, hinder. [< OF, < L *inter–* between + *ferire* to strike] —**in´ter·fer´er,** *n.* —**in´ter·fer´ing·ly,** *adv.*

in·ter·fer·ence (in´tər fir´əns), *n.* 1 an interfering. 2 the reciprocal action of

waves by which they reinforce or neutralize one another. 3 interruption of a desired radio or television signal by other signals. 4 act of interfering with a football player who is trying to tackle.

in·ter·fer·on (in´tər fir´on), *n.* 1 protein produced by animal cells infected by a virus and released into the bloodstream or cellular fluid, which triggers healthy cells to manufacture an enzyme to fight the infection. 2 this protein produced by genetic engineering and used to treat conditions such as hepatitis and leukemia. [< *interfere* + NL *-on* substance]

in·ter·fuse (in´tər fūz´), *v.,* **-fused, -fus·ing.** 1 be diffused through; permeate. 2 fuse together; blend. [< L *interfusus* < *inter–*between+*fundere*pour] —**in´ter·fu´sion,** *n.*

in·ter·ga·lac·tic (in´tər gə lak´tik), *adj.* located or occurring between galaxies.

in·ter·gen·er·a·tion·al (in´tər jen´ə rā´shə nəl), *adj.* occurring or existing between generations.

in·ter·gla·cial (in´tər glā´shəl), *adj.* happening or formed between two glacial periods.

in·ter·im (in´tər im), *n.* meantime; time between. —*adj.* for the meantime; temporary. [< L, in the meantime < *inter* between]

in·te·ri·or (in tir´i ər), *n.* 1 inside; inner surface or part. 2 part of a region or country away from the coast or border. 3 affairs within a country: *Department of the Interior.* —*adj.* 1 on the inside; inner. 2 away from the coast or border. 3 domestic. [< L, inner] —**in·te´ri·or´i·ty,** *n.* —**in·te´ri·or·ly,** *adv.*

interj., interjection.

in·ter·ject (in´tər jekt´), *v.* throw in between other things; insert abruptly; *interject a witty remark.* [< L *interjectus* < *inter–* between + *jacere* throw] —**in´ter·jec´tor,** *n.*

in·ter·jec·tion (in´tər jek´shən), *n.* 1 an exclamation regarded as a part of speech, as oh! hurrah! 2 an interjecting. 3 something interjected; remark; exclamation. —**in´ter·jec´tion·al,** *adj.* —**in´ter·jec´tion·al·ly,** *adv.*

in·ter·lace (in´tər lās´), *v.,* **-laced, -lac·ing.** 1 cross over and under each other; weave together; intertwine. 2 cross in an intricate manner. —**in´ter·lace´ment,** *n.*

in·ter·lard (in´tər lärd´), *v.* give variety to; mix; intersperse. [< F, < L *inter–* between + *lardum* fat] —**in´ter·lard´ment,** *n.*

in·ter·lay (in´tər lā´), *v.,* **-laid, -lay·ing.** 1 lay between. 2 diversify with something laid between.

in·ter·lay·er (in´tər lā´ər), *n.* layer between two or more layers: *an insulating interlayer for warmth.*

in·ter·leave (in´tər lēv´), *v.,* **-leaved, -leav·ing.** insert a leaf or leaves of paper between the pages.

in·ter·line¹ (in´tər līn´), *v.,* **-lined, -lin·ing.** insert an extra lining between the

outer cloth and the ordinary lining of (a garment).

in·ter·line² (in´tər līn´), *v.,* **-lined, -lin·ing.** write, print, or mark between the lines.

in·ter·lin·e·ar (in´tər lin´i ər), *adj.* 1 inserted between the lines. 2 containing two different languages or versions in alternate lines.

in·ter·lin·ing (in´tər līn´ing), *n.* an extra lining inserted between the outer cloth and the ordinary lining of a garment.

in·ter·link (in´tər lingk´), *v.* link together.

in·ter·lock (in´tər lok´), *v.* lock or join with one another. —**in´ter·lock´er,** *n.*

in·ter·lop·er (in´tər lōp´ər), *n.* intruder.

in·ter·lude (in´tər lüd), *n.* 1 anything thought of as filling the time between two things; interval. 2 piece of music played between the parts of a song, church service, play, etc. 3 entertainment between the acts of a play. [< Med.L, < L *inter–* between + *ludus* play]

in·ter·lu·nar (in´tər lü´nər), *adj.* 1 having to do with the time when the moon is not seen at night. 2 having to do with the period between the old moon and the new moon.

in·ter·mar·ry (in´tər mar´i), *v.,* **-ried, -ry·ing.** 1 become connected by marriage. 2 marry within the family. —**in´ter·mar´riage,** *n.*

in·ter·med·dle (in´tər med´əl), *v.,* **-dled, -dling.** meddle; interfere. —**in´ter·med´-dler,** *n.*

in·ter·me·di·ar·y (in´tər mē´di er´i), *n.,* *pl.* **-ar·ies,** *adj.* —*n.* person who acts for one person with another; go-between. —*adj.* 1 acting between. 2 being between; intermediate.

in·ter·me·di·ate (in´tər mē´di it), *adj.* being or occurring between: *gray is intermediate between black and white.* —*n.* 1 something in between. 2 mediator. [< Med.L, ult. < L *inter–* between + *medius* in the middle] —**in´ter·me´di·ate·ly,** *adv.* —**in´ter·me´di·ate·ness,** *n.*

in·ter·ment (in tèr´mənt), *n.* burial.

in·ter·mez·zo (in´tər met´sō; –med´zō), *n., pl.* **-zos, -zi** (–sē; –zē). 1 a short dramatic or musical entertainment between the acts of a play. 2 a short musical composition between the main divisions of an extended musical work. 3 an independent musical composition of similar character. [< Ital.]

in·ter·mi·na·ble (in tèr´mə nə bəl), *adj.* endless; so long as to seem endless. —**in·ter´mi·na·bly,** *adv.*

in·ter·min·gle (in´tər ming´gəl), *v.,* **-gled, -gling.** mix together; mingle. —**in´ter·min´gle·ment,** *n.*

in·ter·mis·sion (in´tər mish´ən), *n.* 1 time between periods of activity; pause. 2 stopping for a time; interruption: *rain without intermission.*

in·ter·mit·tent (in´tər mit´ənt), *adj.* 1 stopping and beginning again. 2 pausing at intervals. —**in´ter·mit´tence,** *n.* —**in´ter·mit´tent·ly,** *adv.*

in·ter·mix (in´tər miks´), v. mix together; blend. —**in´ter·mix´ture**, n.

in·tern¹ (in tèrn´), v. 1 confine within a country; *intern soldiers in a neutral country.* 2 force to stay in a certain place. [< F *interner* < L *internus* within] —**in·tern´ment**, n.

in·tern² (in´tèrn), person learning a skill, job, etc., while working as an assistant under supervision. —v. act as an intern. [< F *interne*. See INTERN¹.] —**in´tern·ship**, n.

in·ter·nal (in tèr´nəl), adj. 1 inner; inside: *internal injuries, internal evidence.* 2 having to do with affairs within a country; domestic: *internal disturbances.* [< Med.L *internalis*. See INTERN¹.] —**in·ter´nal·ly**, adv.

internal-combustion engine, engine in which the pressure is produced by gas or vapor exploding inside the cylinder and against the piston.

in·ter·nal·ize (in tèr nə līz), v., -**ized,** -**iz·ing.** 1 adopt a habit, custom, mannerism, etc. of another person or group, and make it part of one's personality. 2 keep an emotion, problem, etc., to oneself; repress. —**in·ter´nal·i·za´tion**, n.

internal medicine, branch of medicine that deals with the internal organs of the body and the diagnosis and treatment of their diseases.

in·ter·na·tion·al (in´tər nash´ən əl; -nash´nəl), adj. 1 between or among nations: *an international agreement* 2 having to do with the relations between nations: *international law.* —**in´ter·na´tion·al´i·ty**, n. —**in´ter·na´tion·al·ly**, adv.

International Date Line, date line (def. 1).

in·ter·na·tion·al·ism (in´tər nash´ən əl iz´əm; -nash´nəl-), n. principle of international cooperation for the good of all nations. —**in´ter·na´tion·al·ist**, n.

in·ter·na·tion·al·ize (in´tər nash´ən əl īz; -nash´nəl-), v., -**ized,** -**iz·ing.** make international; bring (territory) under the control of several nations. —**in´ter·na´tion·al·i·za´tion**, n.

international law, law governing the conduct of relations between nations.

in·ter·ne·cine (in´tər nē´sin; -sīn), adj. 1 destructive to both sides. 2 deadly; destructive. [< L *internecinus*, ult. < *inter-* + *nex* slaughter]

in·tern·ee (in´tèr nē´), n. person interned, as a prisoner of war, enemy alien, etc.

In·ter·net (in´tər net´), n. worldwide electronic network that links smaller networks of governments, universities, and individuals into a global communication system.

in·tern·ist (in tèr´nist), n. doctor who treats internal diseases, or those of internal organs that do not respond to surgery.

in·ter·pel·late (in´tər pel´āt; in tèr´pə lāt), v., -**lat·ed,** -**lat·ing.** ask formally in a legislature for an explanation of offi-

cial action or government policy. [< L *interpellatus* interrupted] —**in´ter·pel·la´tion**, n.

in·ter·plan·e·tar·y (in´tər plan´ə ter´i), adj. within the solar system, but not within the atmosphere of the sun or any planet.

in·ter·play (in´tər plā´), n. action or influence on each other: *interplay of light and shadow.*

in·ter·po·late (in tèr´pə lāt), v., -**lat·ed,** -**lat·ing.** 1 alter (a book, passage, etc.) by putting in new words or groups of words. 2 put in new (words, passages, etc.). 3 insert terms or something different) between other terms or things, as in a series. [< L *interpolatus* refurbished] —**in·ter´po·lat´er, in·ter´po·la´tor**, n.

in·ter·po·la·tion (in tèr´pə lā´shən), n. 1 an alteration in a text. 2 words inserted in a text. 3 something added to a series or group of things.

in·ter·po·la·tive (in tèr´pə lā´tiv), adj. altering; changing.

in·ter·pose (in´tər pōz´), v., -**posed,** -**pos·ing.** 1 put between; insert. 2 come between; be between. 3 interrupt. 4 interfere in order to help; intervene: *mother interposed in the dispute.* 5 put in as an interference or interruption. [< F, < *inter-* between + *poser* place, POSE] —**in´ter·pos´er**, n. —**in´ter·pos´ing·ly**, adv.

in·ter·po·si·tion (in´tər pə zish´ən), n. 1 something inserted. 2 an interruption. 3 interference: *the interposition of calming words.*

in·ter·pret (in tèr´prit), v. 1 explain the meaning of: *interpret a dream.* 2 bring out the meaning of: *interpret a part in a play.* 3 understand in a certain way: *interpret silence as consent.* 4 serve as an interpreter; translate. [< L *interpretari* < *interpres* mediary] —**in·ter´pret·a·ble**, adj. —**in·ter´pret·a·bil´i·ty**, n. —**in·ter´pre·tive**, adj. —**in·ter´pre·tive·ly**, adv.

in·ter·pre·ta·tion (in tèr´prə tā´shən), n. 1 an interpreting; explanation: *different interpretations of the same facts.* 2 bringing out the meaning of a dramatic part, music, etc. —**in·ter´pre·ta´tion·al, in·ter´pre·ta´tive**, adj. —**in·ter´pre·ta´tive·ly**, adv.

in·ter·pret·er (in tèr´prə tər), n. 1 person who interprets. 2 person whose business is translating from a foreign language.

in·ter·ra·cial (in´tər rā´shəl), adj. between or involving different racial groups.

in·ter·reg·num (in´tər reg´nəm), n. 1 time between the end of one ruler's reign and the beginning of the next one. 2 any time during which a nation is without its usual ruler. 3 period of inactivity; pause. [< L, < *inter-* between + *regnum* reign]

in·ter·re·late (in´tər ri lāt´), v., -**lat·ed,** -**lat·ing.** connect closely with each other; bring into mutual relation. —**in´ter·re·lat´ed**, adj. —**in´ter·re·la´tion**, n. —**in´ter·re·la´tion·ship**, n.

in·ter·ro·gate (in ter´ə gāt), v., -**gat·ed,** -**gat·ing.** question thoroughly; examine by asking questions: *interrogate a witness.* [< L, *inter-* between + *rogare* ask] —**in·ter´ro·gat´ing·ly**, adv. —**in·ter´ro·ga´tor**, n.

in·ter·ro·ga·tion (in ter´ə gā´shən), n. 1 a questioning. The formal examination of a witness by asking questions is interrogation. 2 a question.

in·ter·rog·a·tive (in´tə rog´ə tiv), adj. asking a question; having the form of a question. —n. a word used in asking a question. —**in´ter·rog´a·tive·ly**, adv.

in·ter·rog·a·to·ry (in´tə rog´ə tô´ri; -tō-), questioning.

in·ter·rupt (in´tə rupt´), v. 1 break in upon (talk, work, rest, a person speaking, etc.); hinder; stop: *do not interrupt the speaker.* 2 make a break in: *interrupt the view.* [< L *interruptus* < *inter-* between + *rumpere* break] —**in´ter·rupt´er**, n.

in·ter·rup·tion (in´tə rup´shən), n. 1 an interrupting: *her frequent interruption was rude.* 2 a being interrupted: *flooding caused interruption in travel.* 3 thing that interrupts. 4 intermission.

in·ter·scho·las·tic (in´tər skə las´tik), adj. between schools: *interscholastic competition.*

in·ter·sect (in´tər sekt´), v. 1 cut or divide by passing through or crossing. 2 cross each other. [< L, < *inter-* between + *secare* cut]

in·ter·sec·tion (in´tər sek´shən), n. 1 an intersecting. 2 point or line where one thing crosses another. —**in´ter·sec´tion·al**, adj.

in·ter·sperse (in´tər spèrs´), v., -**spersed,** -**spers·ing.** scatter here and there among other things: *bushes were interspersed among trees.* [< L *interspersus* < *inter-* between + *spargere* scatter] —**in´ter·sper´sion**, n.

in·ter·state (in´tər stāt´; in´tər stāt´), adj. between states: *interstate commerce.* —n. interstate highway.

in·ter·stel·lar (in´tər stel´ər; in´tər stel´ər), adj. among or between the stars.

in·ter·stice (in tèr´stis), n. a small or narrow space between things or parts; chink. [< LL *interstitium* < L *inter-* between + *stare* to stand] —**in´ter·sti´tial**, adj. —**in´ter·sti´tial·ly**, adv.

in·ter·twine (in´tər twīn´), v., -**twined,** -**twin·ing.** twine, one with another. —**in´ter·twin´ing·ly**, adv.

in·ter·ur·ban (in´tər èr´bən; in´tər èr´bən), adj. between cities or towns: *an interurban railroad.*

in·ter·val (in´tər vəl), n. 1 time or space between: *an interval of a week.* 2 the difference in pitch between two tones. **at intervals, a** now and then. **b** here and there. [< L *intervallum*, orig., space between palisades < *inter-* between + *vallum* wall]

in·ter·vene (in´tər vēn´), v., -**vened,** -**ven·ing.** 1 come between; be between: *a week intervenes between the two holidays.* 2

come in to help settle a dispute: *the President intervened in the strike.* [< L, < *inter–* between + *venire* come] **—in′ter·ven′er, in′ter·ve′nor,** *n.*

in·ter·ven·tion (in′tər ven′shən), *n.* **1** an intervening. **2** interference by one nation in the affairs of another. **—in′ter·ven′tion·al,** *adj.* **—in′ter·ven′tion·ist,** *n.*

in·ter·view (in′tər vū), *n.* **1** a meeting to talk over something special: *an interview with a manager for a job.* **2 a** a meeting between a reporter and a person from whom information is sought for publication. **b** newspaper or magazine article resulting from such a meeting. *—v.* have an interview with; meet and talk with [< F *entrevue,* ult. < L *inter–* between + *videre* see] **—in′ter·view′er,** *n.*

in·ter·weave (in′tər wēv′), *v.,* **-wove** or **-weaved, -wo·ven** or **-wove** or **-weaved, -weav·ing. 1** weave together. **2** intermingle; connect closely. **—in′ter·weave′ment,** *n.* **—in′ter·weav′er,** *n.* **—in′ter·wo′ven,** *adj.*

in·tes·tate (in tes′tāt; -tit), *adj.* **1** having made no will. **2** not disposed of by a will. *—n.* person who has died without making a will. [< L, < *in–* not + *testari* make a will < *testis* witness] **—in·tes′ta·cy,** *n.*

in·tes·ti·nal (in tes′tə nəl), *adj.* of or in the intestines. **—in·tes′ti·nal·ly,** *adv.*

intestinal fortitude, courage; tenacity.

in·tes·tine (in tes′tən), *n.* **1** part of the alimentary canal that extends from the stomach to the anus. **2** a portion of this. The first, narrower and longer portion is the **small intestine** and the other the **large intestine.** [< L *intestina,* neut. pl., internal, ult. < *in* in]

in·ti·ma·cy (in′tə mə si), *n., pl.* **-cies. 1** a being intimate; close acquaintance. **2** a familiar or intimate act.

in·ti·mate¹ (in′tə mit), *adj.* **1** very familiar; known very well; closely acquainted. **2** close; thorough: *intimate knowledge of a matter.* **3** very personal; most private: *intimate affairs of the family.* **4** far within; inmost: *intimate desires of the heart.* *—n.* a close friend. [< L *intimatus* (see INTIMATE²), confused with *intimus* inmost] **—in′ti·mate·ly,** *adv.* **—in′ti·mate·ness,** *n.*

in·ti·mate² (in′tə māt), *v.,* **-mat·ed, -mat·ing. 1** suggest indirectly; hint. **2** announce; notify. [< L *intimatus,* orig., made to sink in, ult. < L *intimus* inmost] **—in′ti·mat′er,** *n.*

in·ti·ma·tion (in′tə mā′shən), *n.* **1** indirect suggestion; hint. **2** announcement; notice.

in·tim·i·date (in tim′ə dāt), *v.,* **-dat·ed, -dat·ing. 1** frighten; make afraid. **2** influence or force by fear. [< Med.L, < L *in–* + *timidus* fearful] **—in·tim′i·da′tion,** *n.* **—in·tim′i·da′tor,** *n.*

in·to (in′tü; *unstressed* in′tu̇, -tə), *prep.* **1** to the inside of; toward the inside; within: *go into the house.* **2** to the condi-

tion of; to the form of: *divided into ten rooms.*

in·tol·er·a·ble (in tol′ər ə bəl), *adj.* unbearable; too much, too painful, etc., to be endured. **—in·tol′er·a·bil′i·ty, in·tol′er·a·ble·ness,** *n.*

in·tol·er·a·bly (in tol′ər ə bli), *adv.* unbearably; beyond endurance.

in·tol·er·ance (in tol′ər əns), *n.* **1** lack of tolerance; unwillingness to let others do and think as they choose, esp. in matters of religion. **2** inability to endure; unwillingness to endure.

in·tol·er·ant (in tol′ər ənt), *adj.* not tolerant; unwilling to let others do and think as they choose, esp. in matters of religion.

intolerant of, not able to endure; unwilling to endure. **—in·tol′er·ant·ly,** *adv.*

in·to·na·tion (in′tō nā′shən; -tə-), *n.* **1** act of intoning. **2** pattern of modulation and inflection in connected speech.

in·tone (in tōn′), *v.,* **-toned, -ton·ing. 1** read or recite in a singing voice; chant. **2** utter with a particular tone. [< Med.L, ult. < L *in–* + *tonus* tone] **—in·ton′er,** *n.*

in to·to (in tō′tō), *Latin,* completely.

in·tox·i·cant (in tok′sə kənt), *n.* any intoxicating agent, as an alcoholic liquor or drug.

in·tox·i·cate (in tok′sə kāt), *v.,* **-cat·ed, -cat·ing. 1** make drunk. **2** excite beyond self-control. [< Med.L, ult. < L *in–* in + *toxicum* poison. See TOXIC.] **—in·tox′i·cat′ed,** *adj.* **—in·tox′i·cat′ing·ly,** *adv.*

in·tox·i·ca·tion (in tok′sə kā′shən), *n.* **1** drunkenness. **2** great emotional excitement.

intra–, *prefix.* within; inside; on the inside. [< L *intra,* prep., adv.]

in·tra·coast·al (in′trə kōs′təl), *adj.* **1** located within a coastal area. **2** of or having to do with intracoastal waterways: *intracoastal travel.*

in·trac·ta·ble (in trak′tə bəl), *adj.* hard to manage; stubborn. **—in·trac′ta·bil′i·ty, in·trac′ta·ble·ness,** *n.* **—in·trac′ta·bly,** *adv.*

in·tra·mu·ral (in′trə myu̇r′əl), *adj.* **1** within a school or college, etc. **2** within the walls; inside, esp. of the body or an organ.

in·tra·mus·cu·lar (in′trə mus′kyə lər), *adj.* in or within a muscle.

intrans., intr., intransitive.

in·tran·si·gence (in tran′sə jəns), **in·tran·si·gen·cy** (-jən si), *n.* uncompromising hostility.

in·tran·si·gent (in tran′sə jənt), *adj.* unwilling to agree or compromise; irreconcilable. *—n.* person who is unwilling to agree or compromise. [< F < Sp., ult. < L *in–* not + *transigere* come to an agreement < *trans–* through + *agere* to drive] **—in·tran′si·gent·ly,** *adv.*

in·tran·si·tive (in tran′sə tiv), *—adj.* of verbs, not taking a direct object. *—n.* an intransitive verb. **—in·tran′si·tive·ly,** *adv.* **—in·tran′si·tive·ness,** *n.*

in·tra·state (in′trə stāt′), *adj.* within a state.

in·tra·u·ter·ine (in′trə ū′tər in; -tə rīn), *adj.* within the uterus.

in·tra·vas·cu·lar (in′trə vas′kyə lər), *adj.* within a blood vessel or vessels.

in·tra·ve·nous (in′trə vē′nəs), *adj.* **1** within a vein or the veins. **2** into a vein. [< INTRA– + L *vena* vein] **—in′tra·ve′nous·ly,** *adv.*

in·trep·id (in trep′id), *adj.* fearless; dauntless; very brave. [< L, < *in–* not + *trepidus* alarmed] **—in′tre·pid′i·ty,** *n.* **—in·trep′id·ly,** *adv.*

in·tri·ca·cy (in′trə kə si), *n., pl.* **-cies. 1** a being intricate; complexity. **2** complication; something involved; intricate proceeding.

in·tri·cate (in′trə kit), *adj.* **1** with many twists and turns; entangled; complicated: *an intricate knot.* **2** very hard to understand; perplexing: *an intricate piece of machinery.* [< L *intricatus* entangled, ult. < *in–* in + *tricae* hindrances] **—in′tri·cate·ly,** *adv.* **—in′tri·cate·ness,** *n.*

in·trigue (*n.* in trēg′, in′trēg; *v.* in trēg′), *n., v.,* **-trigued, -tri·guing.** *—n.* **1** underhand planning; plotting; secret scheming. **2** a crafty plot; secret scheme. *—v.* **1** carry on an underhand plan; scheme secretly; plot. **2** excite the curiosity and interest of. [< F < Ital. < L *intricare* entangle. See INTRICATE.] **—in·tri′guer,** *n.* **—in·tri′guing·ly,** *adv.*

in·trin·sic (in trin′sik), **in·trin·si·cal** (-sə kəl), *adj.* belonging to a thing by its very nature; essential; inherent: *the intrinsic value of a dollar bill is only that of a piece of paper.* [< Med.L *intrinsecus* internal < L, inwardly] **—in·trin′si·cal·ly,** *adv.*

in·tro (in′trō), *n., pl.* **-tros.** *Informal.* **1** social or business introduction. **2** introductory passage of music.

intro., introd., introduction; introductory.

in·tro·duce (in′trə düs′; -dūs′), *v.,* **-duced, -duc·ing. 1** bring in: *introduce a story into the conversation.* **2** put in; insert: *introduce a tube into the throat.* **3** bring into use, notice, knowledge, etc.: *introduce a new word, introduce to biochemistry.* **4** make known: *introduce a speaker.* **5** begin: *introduce a trial with a plea of not guilty.* [< L, < *intro–* in + *ducere* lead] **—in′tro·duc′er,** *n.* **—in′tro·duc′i·ble,** *adj.*

in·tro·duc·tion (in′trə duk′shən), *n.* **1** an introducing: *the introduction of steel made tall buildings easy to build.* **2** a being introduced: *introduction to strangers.* **3** thing that introduces; first part of a book, speech, piece of music, etc., leading up to the main part. **4** thing introduced.

in·tro·duc·to·ry (in′trə duk′tə ri), *adj.* used to introduce; serving as an introduction; preliminary. **—in′tro·duc′tive·ly,** *adv.*

in·tro·spec·tion (in´trə spek´shən), *n.* examination of one's own thoughts and feelings. [< L, < *intro-* into + *specere* to look] —**in´tro·spec´tive,** *adj.* —**in´tro·spec´tive·ly,** *adv.*

in·tro·ver·sion (in´trə vèr´zhən; –shən), *n.* tendency to be more interested in one's own thoughts and feelings than in what is going on around one.

in·tro·vert (*v.* in´trə vèrt´; *n.* in´trə vèrt´), *v.* turn (one's thoughts, etc.) upon oneself. —*n.* person more interested in one's own thoughts and feelings than in what is going on around one; person tending to think rather than act. [< L *intro-* within + *vertere* to turn]

in·trude (in trüd´), *v.,* –**trud·ed,** –**trud·ing. 1** thrust oneself in; come unasked and unwanted. **2** in geology, thrust in; force in. [< L, < *in-* in + *trudere* to thrust] —**in·trud´er,** *n.* —**in·trud´ing·ly,** *adv.*

in·tru·sion (in trü´zhən), *n.* **1** act of intruding. **2** unlawful entry. **3** in geology, **a** the forcing of molten rock into fissures or strata. **b** molten rock forced into fissures or strata.

in·tru·sive (in trü´siv), *adj.* intruding. —**in·tru´sive·ly,** *adv.* —**in·tru´sive·ness,** *n.*

in·tu·it (in tü´it; –tyü´–), *v.,* –**it·ed,** –**it·ing.** know or understand instinctively, without reasoning; perceive. [< L *intuitus,* pp. of *intuëri.* See INTUITION.]

in·tu·i·tion (in´tü ish´ən; –tyü–), *n.* **1** perception of truths, facts, etc., without reasoning. **2** something so perceived. [< LL *intuitio* a gazing at, ult. < *in-* at + *tueri* to look] —**in·tu´i·tion·al,** *adj.* —**in´tu·i´tion·al·ly,** *adv.*

in·tu·i·tive (in tü´ə tiv; –tū´–), *adj.* **1** perceiving by intuition. **2** acquired by intuition: *intuitive knowledge.* —**in·tu´i·tive·ly,** *adv.* —**in·tu´i·tive·ness,** *n.*

In·u·it (in´yü it), *n., pl.* –**it** or –**its. 1** a native person living in the arctic regions of North America; Eskimo. **2** the language of this people; Eskimo. —*adj.* of or having to do with these people or their language.

in·un·date (in´un dāt; in un´dāt), *v.,* –**dat·ed,** –**dat·ing.** overflow; flood. [< L, < *in-* onto + *undare* flow] —**in´un·da´tion,** *n.*

in·ure (in yūr´), *v.,* –**ured,** –**ur·ing. 1** toughen or harden; accustom; habituate. **2** have effect; be useful. [< *in* + obs. *ure* use, *n.* < AF < L *opera* work] —**in·ure´ment,** *n.*

inv., invoice.

in·vade (in vād´), *v.,* –**vad·ed,** –**vad·ing. 1** enter with force or as an enemy; attack: *soldiers invaded the country.* **2** enter as if to take possession: *tourists invaded the city.* **3** interfere with; encroach upon; violate: *invade the rights of others.* [< L, < *in-* in + *vadere* go, walk] —**in·vad´er,** *n.*

in·va·lid¹ (in´və lid), *n.* a sick, weak person not able to get about and do things. —*adj.* **1** not well; weak and sick. **2** of or for an invalid or invalids. —*v.* **1** make weak or sick; disable. **2** remove from

active service because of sickness or injury. [< L, < *in-* not + *validus* strong]

in·val·id² (in val´id), *adj.* not valid; without force or effect. —**in·va·lid´i·ty,** *n.* —**in·val´id·ly,** *adv.*

in·val·i·date (in val´ə dāt), *v.,* –**dat·ed,** –**dat·ing.** make valueless; deprive of force or effect. —**in·val´i·da´tion,** *n.* —**in·val´i·da´tor,** *n.*

in·va·lid·ism (in´və lid iz´əm), *n.* condition of being an invalid; prolonged ill health.

in·val·u·a·ble (in val´yü ə bəl; –yə bəl), *adj.* very precious; valuable beyond measure. —**in·val´u·a·ble·ness,** *n.* —**in·val´u·a·bly,** *adv.*

in·var·i·a·ble (in vãr´i ə bəl), *adj.* always the same; unchangeable; unchanging. —**in·var´i·a·bil´i·ty, in·var´i·a·ble·ness,** *n.* —**in·var´i·a·bly,** *adv.*

in·va·sion (in vā´zhən), *n.* **1** an invading; an attack. **2** interference; encroachment; violation. —**in·va´sive,** *adj.*

in·vec·tive (in vek´tiv), *n.* violent attack in words; abusive language. [< LL *invectivus.* See INVEIGH.] —**in·vec´tive·ly,** *adv.* —**in·vec´tive·ness,** *n.*

in·veigh (in vā´), *v.* make a violent attack in words. [< L, < *in-* against + *vehere* carry] —**in·veigh´er,** *n.*

in·vei·gle (in vē´gəl; –vā´–), *v.,* –**gled,** –**gling.** lead by trickery; entice; allure. [ult. < F *aveugler* make blind < *aveugle* blind, ult. < L *ab-* away + *oculus* eye] —**in·vei´gler,** *n.*

in·vent (in vent´), *v.* **1** make or think out (something new): *Bell invented the telephone.* **2** make up; think up: *invent an excuse.* [< L, < *in-* in + *venire* come] —**in·vent´i·ble,** *adj.* —**in·ven´tor, in·vent´er,** *n.*

in·ven·tion (in ven´shən), *n.* **1** a making something new: *the invention of gunpowder.* **2** thing invented. **3** power of inventing. **4** a made-up story; false statement. —**in·ven´tion·al,** *adj.*

in·ven·tive (in ven´tiv), *adj.* **1** good at inventing. **2** of invention. **3** showing power of inventing: *an inventive mind.* —**in·ven´tive·ly,** *adv.* —**in·ven´tive·ness,** *n.*

in·ven·to·ry (in´vən tô´ri; –tō´–), *n., pl.* –**to·ries,** –*v.,* –**to·ried,** –**to·ry·ing.** —*n.* **1** a detailed list of articles with their estimated value. **2** collection of articles that are or may be so listed; stock. —*v.* make a detailed list of; enter in a list. [< Med.L *inventorium.* See INVENT.] —**in´ven·to´ri·al,** *adj.*

in·verse (in vèrs´, in´vèrs´), *adj.* reversed in position, direction, or tendency; inverted: *DCBA is the inverse order of ABCD.* —*n.* direct opposite: *evil is the inverse of good.* [< L *inversus,* pp. of *invertere* INVERT] —**in·verse´ly,** *adv.*

in·ver·sion (in vèr´zhən; –shən), *n.* **1** an inverting or being inverted. **2** something inverted.

in·vert (in vèrt´), *v.* **1** turn upside down. **2** turn around or reverse in position,

direction, order, etc. [< L, < *in-* + *vertere* to turn] —**in·vert´i·ble,** *adj.*

in·ver·te·brate (in vèr´tə brit; –brāt), *adj.* **1** without a backbone. **2** of or having to do with invertebrates. —*n.* animal without a backbone. All animals except fishes, amphibians, reptiles, birds, and mammals are invertebrates.

in·ver·ter (in vèr´tər), *n.* electrical device that changes direct current into alternating current.

in·vest (in vest´), *v.* **1** use (money) to buy something that is expected to produce a profit, or income, or both: *people invest in stocks, lands, etc.* **2** lay out; spend: *invest large sums in books.* **3** clothe; cover; surround: *darkness invests the earth at night.* **4** give power, authority, or right to: *invest a lawyer with power to act.* **5** install in office: *the mayor was invested in office.* **6** besiege: *the enemy invested in the city.* [< L, < *in-* in + *vestis* clothing] —**in·ves´tor,** *n.*

in·ves·ti·gate (in ves´tə gāt), *v.,* –**gat·ed,** –**gat·ing.** search into; examine closely: *scientists investigate nature.* [< L, < *in-* in + *vestigare* to track, trace] —**in·ves´ti·ga´tive, in·ves´ti·ga·to´ry,** *adj.* —**in·ves´ti·ga´tor,** *n.*

in·ves·ti·ga·tion (in ves´tə gā´shən), *n.* careful search; detailed or careful examination.

in·ves·ti·ture (in ves´tə chər), *n.* a formal investing of a person with an office, dignity, power, right, etc.

in·vest·ment (in vest´mənt), *n.* **1** a laying out of money. **2** amount of money invested. **3** something expected to yield income or profit or both. **4** siege.

in·vest·or (in ves´tər), *n.* person who invests money.

in·vet·er·a·cy (in vet´ər ə si), *n.* settled, fixed condition; habitualness.

in·vet·er·ate (in vet´ər it), *adj.* **1** confirmed in a habit, practice, feeling, etc.; habitual: *an inveterate reader of the newspaper.* **2** long and firmly established. [< L, < *in-* in + *veterascere* grow old < *vetus* old] —**in·vet´er·ate·ly,** *adv.* —**in·vet´er·ate·ness,** *n.*

in·vid·i·ous (in vid´i əs), *adj.* likely to arouse ill will or resentment; giving offense because unfair or unjust. [< L, < *invidia* envy] —**in·vid´i·ous·ly,** *adv.* —**in·vid´i·ous·ness,** *n.*

in·vig·or·ate (in vig´ər āt), *v.,* –**at·ed,** –**at·ing.** give vigor to; fill with life and energy. [< *vigor*] —**in·vig´or·at´ing·ly,** *adv.* —**in·vig´or·a´tion,** *n.* —**in·vig´or·a´tive,** *adj.*

in·vin·ci·ble (in vin´sə bəl), *adj.* not to be overcome; unconquerable. [< L, < *in-* not + *vincere* conquer] —**in·vin´ci·bil´i·ty, in·vin´ci·ble·ness,** *n.* —**in·vin´ci·bly,** *adv.*

in·vi·o·la·ble (in vī´ə lə bəl), *adj.* **1** that must not be violated or injured; sacred. **2** that cannot be violated or injured. —**in·vi´o·la·bil´i·ty, in·vi´o·la·ble·ness,** *n.* —**in·vi´o·la·bly,** *adv.*

in·vi·o·late (in vī′ə lit; –lāt), *adj.* not violated; uninjured; unbroken; not profaned. —**in·vi′o·late·ly**, *adv.*

in·vis·i·ble (in viz′ə bəl), *adj.* **1** not visible; not capable of being seen: *germs are invisible to the naked eye.* **2** out of sight. **3** hidden: *invisible assets.* —**in·vis′i·bil′i·ty, in·vis′i·ble·ness**, *n.* —**in·vis′i·bly**, *adv.*

in·vi·ta·tion (in′və tā′shən), *n.* **1** request to come to some place or to do something. **2** act of inviting. **3** attraction; inducement. —**in′vi·ta′tion·al**, *adj.*

in·vite (in vīt′), *v.*, **–vit·ed, –vit·ing. 1** ask (someone) politely to come to some place or to do something. **2** make a polite request for: *he invited our opinion of his work.* **3** give occasion for: *the letter invites some question.* **4** attract; tempt. [< L *invitare*] —**in·vit′er**, *n.*

in·vit·ing (in vīt′ing), *adj.* attractive; tempting. —**in·vit′ing·ly**, *adv.* —**in·vit′ing·ness**, *n.*

in vit·ro (in vē′trō, vit′rō), in an artificial environment, as a Petri dish or test tube. [< NL *in vitro* < L *in* in; *vitrum* glass]

in vitro fertilization, fertilization of a human ovum outside the body.

in·vo·ca·tion (in′və kā′shən), *n.* act of calling upon in prayer; appeal for help or protection.

in·voice (in′vois), *n., v.,* **–voiced, –voic·ing.** —*n.* list of goods sent to a purchaser showing prices, amounts, shipping charges, etc. —*v.* make an invoice of; enter on an invoice. [earlier *invoyes*, pl. of *invoy*, var. of ENVOY]

in·voke (in vōk′), *v.,* **–voked, –vok·ing. 1** call on in prayer; appeal to for help or protection. **2** ask earnestly for; beg for. **3** call forth by magic. [< L, < *in-* on + *vocare* call] —**in·vok′er,**

in·vo·lu·cre (in′və lü′kər), *n.* circle of bracts around a flower cluster. [< F < L *involucrum* a cover, < *involvere*. See INVOLVE.]

in·vol·un·tar·y (in vol′ən ter′i), *adj.* **1** not voluntary; not done of one's own free will; unwilling: *an involuntary witness.* **2** not done on purpose; not intended: *an involuntary injury.* **3** not controlled by the will: *breathing is mainly involuntary.* —**in·vol′un·tar′i·ly**, *adv.* —**in·vol′un·tar′i·ness**, *n.*

involuntary muscle, =smooth muscle.

in·vo·lute (in′və lüt), *adj.* **1** rolled inward from the edge. **2** having the whorls closely wound, as a spiral shell. [< L *involutus*, pp. of *involvere* INVOLVE.] —**in′vo·lut′ed·ly**, *adv.*

in·volve (in volv′), *v.,* **–volved, –volv·ing. 1** have as a necessary part; take in; include. **2** cause to be implicated; bring (into difficulty, danger, etc.). **3** entangle; complicate: *involved sentences are hard to understand.* **4** take up the attention of; occupy: *involved in working out a puzzle.* [< L, < *in-* in + *volvere* to roll] —**in·volve′ment**, *n.* —**in·volv′er**, *n.*

in·volved (in volvd′), *adj.* entangled; complicated.

in·vul·ner·a·ble (in vul′nər ə bəl), *adj.* that cannot be wounded or injured; proof against attack. —**in·vul′ner·a·bil′i·ty, in·vul′ner·a·ble·ness**, *n.* —**in·vul′ner·a·bly**, *adv.*

in·ward (in′wərd), *adv.* **1** toward the inside: *a passage leading inward.* **2** into the mind or soul: *turn your thoughts inward.* —*adj.* **1** placed within; internal: *the inward parts of the body.* **2** directed toward the inside: *an inward slant of the eyes.* **3** in the mind or soul: *inward peace.*

in·ward·ly (in′wərd li), *adv.* **1** on the inside; within. **2** toward the inside. **3** in the mind or soul. **4** not aloud or openly.

in·ward·ness (in′wərd nis), *n.* **1** inner nature or meaning. **2** spirituality. **3** earnestness.

in·wrought (in rôt′), *adj.* **1** having a decoration worked in. **2** worked in. **3** mixed together; closely blended.

Io, ionium.

I/O, input-output.

i·o·dide (ī′ə dīd; –did), **i·o·did** (–did), *n.* compound of iodine with another element or radical.

i·o·dine (ī′ə dīn; –din) **1** a nonmetallic element, I, consisting of blackish crystals that give off a dense, violet-colored vapor with an irritating odor, used in medicine, in making dyes, in photography, etc. **2** a brown liquid, **tincture of iodine**, used in antiseptics. [< F *iode* iodine < Gk. *iodes* rust-colored < *ios* rust]

i·on (ī′ən; ī′on), *n.* **1** an atom or group of atoms having a negative or positive electric charge as a result of having gained one or more electrons. **2** an electrically charged particle formed in a gas. [< Gk., neut. ppr. of *ienai* go] —**i·on′ic**, *adj.*

–ion, *suffix.* **1** act of ___ing, as in *attraction.* **2** condition or state of being ___ed, as in *adoption.* **3** result of ___ing, as in *abbreviation.* [< F < L *-io, -ionis*]

I·o·ni·a (ī ō′ni ə), *n.* an ancient region on the W coast of Asia Minor, with nearby islands, colonized by the Greeks in very early times. —**I·o′ni·an**, *adj., n.*

I·on·ic (ī on′ik), *adj.* **1** noting or pertaining to the order of Greek architecture having scrolls in the capitals of the columns. **2** of Ionia or its people.

i·o·ni·um (ī ō′ni əm), *n.* a radioactive element, Io, formed from disintegrating uranium.

i·on·ize (ī′ən īz), *v.,* **–ized, –iz·ing.** separate into ions; produce ions in. Acids, bases, and salts ionize in solution. —**i′on·i·za′tion**, *n.* —**i′on·iz′er**, *n.*

i·on·o·sphere (ī on′ə sfir), *n.* a region of ionized layers of air beginning 18 to 28 miles above the earth's surface. —**i·on′o·spher′ic**, *adj.*

i·o·ta (ī ō′tə), *n.* **1** the ninth letter of the Greek alphabet (I, ι). **2** a very small quantity.

I.O.U., IOU (ī′ō′ū′), **1** I owe you. **2** informal note showing a debt.

I·o·wa (ī′ə wə), *n.* a Middle Western state of the United States. —**I′o·wan**, *n.*

ip·so fac·to (ip′sō fak′tō), *Latin.* by that very fact; by the fact itself.

IQ, I.Q., intelligence quotient.

Ir, iridium.

Ir., Ireland; Irish.

I·ran (i ran′; ī–; ē rän′), *n.* country in SW Asia. Formerly called **Persia.**

I·ra·ni·an (i rā′nē ən; ī–; i rä′–), *adj.* of or having to do with Iran, its inhabitants, or their language. —*n.* **1** native or inhabitant of Iran. **2** language of Iran; Persian.

I·raq (i rak′; ē räk′), *n.* country in SW Asia, N of Arabia. Formerly called **Mesopotamia.**

I·ra·qi (ē rä′kē; i rak′i), *n., pl.* **–qis**, *adj.* —*n.* **1** native or inhabitant of Iraq. **2** Arabic as spoken in Iraq. —*adj.* of or having to do with Iraq, its inhabitants, or their language.

i·ras·ci·ble (i ras′ə bəl), *adj.* **1** easily made angry; irritable. **2** showing anger. [< LL, < L *irasci* grow angry < *ira* anger] —**i·ras′ci·bil′i·ty, —i·ras′ci·ble·ness**, *n.* —**i·ras′ci·bly**, *adv.*

i·rate (ī′rāt; ī rāt′), *adj.* angry. [< L, < *ira* anger] —**i′rate·ly**, *adv.*

IRBM, Intermediate Range Ballistic Missile.

ire (īr), *n.* anger; wrath. [< OF < L *ira*] —**ire′ful**, *adj.* —**ire′ful·ly**, *adv.* —**ire′ful·ness**, *n.* —**ire′less**, *adj.*

Ire., Ireland.

Ire·land (īr′lənd), *n.* **1** one of the British Isles divided into the Republic of Ireland and Northern Ireland. **2 Republic of,** the Irish Republic.

ir·i·des·cence (ir′ə des′əns), *n.* changing or play of colors, as in mother-of-pearl, opals, a peacock's feathers, etc. [< L *iris* rainbow < Gk.] —**ir′i·des′cent**, *adj.* —**ir′i·des′cent·ly**, *adv.*

i·rid·i·um (i rid′i əm), *n.* a rare metallic element, Ir, that resembles platinum and is twice as heavy as lead.

i·ris (ī′ris), *n., pl.* **i·ris·es, ir·i·des** (ir′ə dēz; ī′rə–). **1 a** plant with sword-shaped leaves and large flowers with three upright petals and three drooping petallike sepals. **b** the flower. **2** the colored part around the pupil of the eye. [< L < Gk., rainbow]

I·rish (ī′rish), *adj.* of or having to do with Ireland, its people, or their language. —*n.* **1** (*pl. in use*) people of Ireland. **2** the Celtic language spoken in part of Ireland; Gaelic. **3** English as spoken by the Irish.

Irish Gaelic, Celtic language of Ireland; Gaelic.

I·rish·man (ī′rish mən), *n., pl.* **–men.** person of Irish birth or Irish descent.

Irish Republic, an independent republic in C and S Ireland.

Irish setter, a hunting dog with long, silky, reddish-brown hair.

Irish terrier, a small dog with brown wiry hair, somewhat like a small Airedale.

I·rish·wom·an (ī′ rish wŭm′ən), *n.*, *pl.* **-wom·en.** woman of Irish birth or Irish descent.

irk (ėrk), *v.* weary; disgust; annoy; trouble. [ME *irke(n)*]

irk·some (ėrk′səm), *adj.* tiresome; tedious. —**irk′some·ly,** *adv.* —**irk′some·ness,** *n.*

i·ron (ī′ərn), *n.* **1** the commonest and most useful metal, from which tools, machinery, etc., are made. It is a chemical element, Fe. **2** great hardness and strength; firmness: *men of iron.* **3** tool with a flat surface for smoothing cloth or pressing clothes. —*adj.* **1** made of iron; pertaining to iron. **2** like iron; hard or strong; unyielding: *an iron will.* —*v.* smooth or press (cloth, etc.) with a heated iron.

have too many irons in the fire, do too many things at once.

iron out, smooth away or solve (a problem, disagreement, etc.).

irons, chains or bands of iron; handcuffs; shackles.

pump iron, *Informal.* lift weights.

strike while the iron is hot, act while circumstances are favorable. [OE *īren,* ? < Celtic] —**i′ron·like′,** *adj.*

i·ron·clad (ī′ərn klad′), *adj. Fig.* very hard to change or get out of: *an ironclad agreement.* —*n.* warship protected with iron plates.

Iron Curtain, an imaginary wall that separated the former Soviet Union and the nations under its control or influence from the rest of the world.

i·ron·i·cal (ī ron′ə kəl), **i·ron·ic** (–ik), *adj.* **1** expressing one thing and meaning the opposite: *"Speedy" would be an ironical name for a snail.* **2** contrary to what would naturally be expected. —**i·ron′i·cal·ly,** *adv.* —**i·ron′i·cal·ness,** *n.*

i·ron·ing (ī′ərn ing), *n.* **1** the smoothing or pressing of cloth with a heated iron. **2** batch of clothing, etc., that needs to be ironed or has already been ironed.

ironing board, board covered with a smooth cloth, used for ironing clothes.

iron pyrites, mineral, FeS_2, that looks somewhat like gold; fool's gold.

i·ron·sides (ī′ərnsīdz′), *n.pl.* (*sing. in use*) an armor-clad warship.

i·ron·stone (ī′ərn stōn), *n.* **1** any clay, rock, etc., that contains iron; iron ore. **2** hard, white pottery, used for dishes, bathroom fixtures, etc.

i·ron·ware (ī′ərn wār′), *n.* articles made of iron, such as pots, kettles, tools, etc.; hardware.

i·ron·wood (ī′ərn wŭd′), *n.* **1** any of various trees with hard heavy wood. **2** the wood itself.

i·ron·work (ī′ərn wėrk′), *n.* **1** things made of iron. **2** work in iron. —**i′ron·work′er,** *n.*

i·ron·works (ī′ərn wėrks′), *n.*, *pl. or sing.* place where iron is made or worked into iron articles.

i·ro·ny (ī′rə ni), *n.*, *pl.* **-nies. 1** method of expression in which the ordinary meaning of the words is the opposite of the thought in the speaker's mind: *the boys called the very thin boy "Fatty" in irony.* **2** event contrary to what would naturally be expected. [< L < Gk. *eironeia* dissimulation < *eiron* dissembler]

Ir·o·quois (ir′ə kwoi), *n. sing. and pl.* member of a powerful group of American Indian tribes called the Five Nations, formerly living mostly in New York State and Quebec. —**Ir′o·quoi′an,** *adj.*

ir·ra·di·ate (i rā′di āt), *v.*, **-at·ed, -at·ing. 1** shine upon; make bright; illuminate. **2** *Fig.* illuminate or brighten intellectually or spiritually. **3** shine. **4** radiate; give out. **5** treat with ultraviolet rays: *irradiate fruit.* [< L, < *in-* + *radius* ray] —**ir·ra′di·a′tion,** *n.*

ir·ra·tion·al (i rash′ən əl; i rash′nəl), *adj.* **1** not rational; unreasonable: *it is irrational to be afraid of the number 13.* **2** unable to think and reason clearly. **3** that cannot be expressed by a whole number or a common fraction. √3 is an irrational number. —**ir·ra′tion·al′i·ty, ir·ra′tion·al·ness,** *n.* —**ir·ra′tion·al·ly,** *adv.*

irrational number, any number that is not a whole number.

ir·re·claim·a·ble (ir′i klām′ə bəl), *adj.* that cannot be reclaimed. —**ir′re·claim′a·bil′i·ty, ir′re·claim′a·ble·ness,** *n.* —**ir′re·claim′a·bly,** *adv.*

ir·rec·on·cil·a·ble (i rek′ən sīl′ə b əl; i rek′ən sīl′–), *adj.* that cannot be reconciled; that cannot be made to agree; opposed. —**ir·rec′on·cil′a·bil′i·ty, ir·rec′on·cil′a·ble·ness,** *n.* —**ir·rec′on·cil′a·bly,** *adv.*

ir·re·cov·er·a·ble (ir′i kuv′ər ə bəl), *adj.* **1** that cannot be regained or gotten back: *wasted time is irrecoverable.* **2** that cannot be remedied: *irrecoverable sorrow.* —**ir′re·cov′er·a·ble·ness,** *n.* —**ir′re·cov′er·a·bly,** *adv.*

ir·re·deem·a·ble (ir′i dēm′ə bəl), *adj.* **1** that cannot be bought back. **2** that cannot be exchanged for coin: *irredeemable paper money.* **3** beyond remedy; hopeless. —**ir′re·deem′a·bly,** *adv.*

ir·re·den·tist (ir i den′tist), *n.* person or political party that advocates taking over a region of another country because of cultural or ethnic ties. —*adj.* of or having to do with irridentists. [< It. *irredentista* ult. < L *in-* not + *redimere* redeem] —**ir′re·den′tism,** *n.*

ir·re·duc·i·ble (ir′i düs′ə bəl; –dūs′–), *adj.* that cannot be reduced. —**ir′re·duc′i·bil′i·ty, ir′re·duc′i·ble·ness,** *n.* —**ir′re·duc′i·bly,** *adv.*

ir·ref·u·ta·ble (i ref′yə tə bəl; ir′i fūt′ə bəl), *adj.* that cannot be refuted or disproved. —**ir′ref′u·ta·bil′i·ty,** *n.* —**ir·ref′u·ta·bly,** *adv.*

irreg., **1** irregular. **2** irregularly.

ir·reg·u·lar (i reg′yə lər), *adj.* **1** not regular; not according to the usual order or natural way: *irregular breathing.* **2** not smooth; not straight; without symmetry: *an irregular pattern.* **3** not according to law or morals: *irregular behavior.* **4** not a member of an established group: *an irregular soldier.* **5** not inflected in the usual way. *Come* is an irregular verb. —*n.* one that is irregular. —**ir·reg′u·lar·ly,** *adv.*

ir·reg·u·lar·i·ty (i reg′yə lar′ə ti), *n.*, *pl.* **-ties. 1** lack of regularity. **2** something irregular.

ir·rel·e·vant (i rel′ə vənt), *adj.* not to the point; off the subject. —**ir·rel′e·vance, ir·rel′e·van·cy,** *n.* —**ir·rel′e·vant·ly,** *adv.*

ir·re·li·gion (ir′i lij′ən), *n.* **1** lack of religion. **2** hostility to religion; disregard of religion.

ir·re·li·gious (ir′i lij′əs), *adj.* **1** not religious; indifferent to religion. **2** contrary to religious principles; impious. —**ir′re·li′gious·ly,** *adv.* —**ir′re·li′gious·ness,** *n.*

ir·re·me·di·a·ble (ir′i mē′di ə bəl), *adj.* that cannot be remedied; incurable. —**ir′re·me′di·a·ble·ness,** *n.* —**ir′re·me′di·a·bly,** *adv.*

ir·re·mov·a·ble (ir′i müv′ə bəl), *adj.* that cannot be removed. —**ir′re·mov′a·bil′i·ty,** *n.* —**ir′re·mov′a·bly,** *adv.*

ir·rep·a·ra·ble (i rep′ə rə bəl), *adj.* that cannot be repaired or made good. —**ir·rep′a·ra·ble·ness,** *n.* —**ir·rep′a·ra·bly,** *adv.*

ir·re·place·a·ble (ir′i plās′ə bəl), *adj.* not replaceable; impossible to replace with another.

ir·re·press·i·ble (ir′i pres′ə bəl), *adj.* that cannot be repressed or restrained. —**ir′re·press′i·bil′i·ty, ir′re·press′i·ble·ness,** *n.* —**ir′re·press′i·bly,** *adv.*

ir·re·proach·a·ble (ir′i prōch′ə bəl), *adj.* free from blame; faultless. —**ir′re·proach′a·ble·ness,** *n.* —**ir′re·proach′a·bly,** *adv.*

ir·re·sist·i·ble (ir′i zis′tə bəl), *adj.* that cannot be resisted; too great to be withstood. —**ir′re·sist′i·ble·ness,** *n.* —**ir′re·sist′i·bly,** *adv.*

ir·re·so·lute (i rez′ə lüt), *adj.* not resolute; unable to make up one's mind. —**ir·res′o·lute·ly,** *adv.* —**ir·res′o·lute·ness, ir·res′o·lu′tion,** *n.*

ir·re·spec·tive (ir′i spek′tiv), *adj.* regardless: *any person, irrespective of age, may join the club.* —**ir′re·spec′tive·ly,** *adv.*

ir·re·spon·si·ble (ir′i spon′sə bəl), *adj.* **1** without a sense of responsibility. **2** not responsible; that cannot be called to account: *a dictator is an irresponsible ruler.* —*n.* an irresponsible person. —**ir′re·spon′si·bil′i·ty, ir′re·spon′si·ble·ness,** *n.* —**ir′re·spon′si·bly,** *adv.*

ir·re·triev·a·ble (ir′i trēv′ə bəl), *adj.* that cannot be retrieved or recovered; that cannot be recalled or restored to its former condition. —**ir′re·triev′a·bil′i·ty, ir′re·triev′a·ble·ness,** *n.* —**ir′re·triev′a·bly,** *adv.*

ir·rev·er·ence (i rev′ər əns), *n.* **1** lack of reverence; disrespect. **2** act of showing irreverence.

ir·rev·er·ent (i rev′ər ənt), *adj.* not reverent; disrespectful. —**ir·rev′er·ent·ly,** *adv.*

ir·re·vers·i·ble (ir′i vėr′sə bəl), *adj.* not capable of being reversed. —**ir′re·vers′i·bil′i·ty, ir′re·vers′i·ble·ness,** *n.* —**ir′re·vers′i·bly,** *adv.*

ir·rev·o·ca·ble (i rev′ə kə bəl), *adj.* not to be recalled, withdrawn, or annulled: *an irrevocable decision.* —**ir·rev′o·ca·bil′i·ty, ir·rev′o·ca·ble·ness,** *n.* —**ir·rev′o·ca·bly,** *adv.*

ir·ri·gate (ir′ə gāt), *v.,* **-gat·ed, -gat·ing.** 1 supply (land) with water by ditches sprinkling, etc. 2 supply (a wound, cavity in the body, etc.) with a flow of some liquid. [< L, < *in-* + *rigare* wet] —**ir′ri·ga′tion,** *n.* —**ir′ri·ga′tion·al,** *adj.* —**ir′ri·ga′tor,** *n.*

ir·ri·ta·bil·i·ty (ir′ə tə bil′ə ti), *n., pl.* **-ties.** 1 a being irritable; impatience. 2 unnatural sensitiveness (of an organ or part of the body). 3 property that living plant or animal tissue has of responding to a stimulus.

ir·ri·ta·ble (ir′ə tə bəl), *adj.* 1 easily made angry; impatient. 2 unnaturally sensitive or sore. 3 able to respond to stimuli. —**ir′ri·ta·ble·ness,** *n.* —**ir′ri·ta·bly,** *adv.*

ir·ri·tant (ir′ə tənt), *n.* thing that causes irritation. —*adj.* causing irritation. —**ir′ri·tan·cy,** *n.*

ir·ri·tate (ir′ə tāt), *v.,* **-tat·ed, -tat·ing.** 1 arouse to impatience or anger; provoke: *his foolish questions irritated me.* 2 make unnaturally sensitive or sore: *sunburn irritates the skin.* 3 stimulate (an organ, muscle, tissue, etc.) to perform some characteristic action or function. [< L *irritatus* enraged, provoked] —**ir′ri·tat′ing, ir′ri·ta′tive,** *adj.* —**ir′ri·tat′ing·ly,** *adv.* —**ir′ri·ta′tor,** *n.*

ir·rup·tion (i rup′shən), *n.* a breaking or bursting in; violent invasion. [< L *irruptio,* ult. < *in-* in + *rumpere* break] —**ir·rup′tive,** *adj.*

IRS or **I.R.S.,** Internal Revenue Service.

is (iz), *v.* 3rd pers. sing. pres. indic. of **be.** He is, she is, it is.

as is, as it is now; in its present condition. [OE]

is., Is., 1 island. 2 isle.

Isa., Is., Isaiah.

I·saac (ī′zək), *n.* son of Abraham and Sarah, and father of Jacob and Esau. Gen. 21:3.

I·sai·ah (ī zā′ə; ī zī′ə), *n.* 1 Hebrew prophet. 2 book of the Old Testament.

ISBN, International Standard Book Number.

Is·car·i·ot (is kar′i ət), *n.* 1 surname of Judas. 2 a traitor.

-ise, *suffix.* variant of **-ize.**

-ish, *suffix.* 1 somewhat, as in *oldish, sweetish,* 2 resembling; like, as in *a childish man.* 3 like that of; having the characteristics of, as in *a childish idea.* 4 of or pertaining to; belonging to, as in *British, Turkish.* 5 tending to; inclined to, as in *bookish, thievish.* 6 near, but usually somewhat past, as in *fortyish.* [OE *-isc*]

Ish·ma·el (ish′mi əl), *n.* 1 son of Abraham and Hagar, driven into the wilderness by Sarah. Gen. 16. 2 outcast.

Ish·ma·el·ite (ish′mi əl īt), *n.* 1 descendant of Ishmael. 2 outcast.

i·sin·glass (ī′zing glas′; –gläs′), *n.* 1 kind of gelatin obtained from fishes, used for making glue, clearing liquors, etc. 2 thin layers of mica. [alter. of MDu. *huysenblas* sturgeon bladder; infl. by *glass*]

I·sis (ī′sis), *n.* the chief ancient Egyptian goddess, the wife and sister of Osiris, who represented fertility.

isl., 1 *pl.* **isls.** island. 2 isle.

Is·lam (is′ləm; is läm′), *n.* 1 the Muslim religion. 2 Muslims as a group. 3 the countries under Muslim rule. —**Is·lam′ic,** *adj.* —**Is′lam·ism,** *n.* —**Is′lam·ite,** *n., adj.*

Is·lam·ist (is läm′ist), *n.* orthodox Muslim, esp. a militant Muslim.

is·land (ī′lənd), *n.* 1 body of land surrounded by water. 2 something resembling this. 3 a safety area painted in the middle of a busy street. 4 a group of cells distinct from its neighbors in structure or function. —*v.* make into an island. [OE *īgland* < *īg* island + *land* land; spelling infl. by *isle*] —**is′land·less,** *adj.* —**is′land·like′,** *adj.*

is·land·er (ī′lən dər), *n.* native or inhabitant of an island.

isle (īl), **is·let** (ī′lit), *n.* a small island. [< OF < L *insula*]

islets of Lang·er·hans (läng′ər häns), endocrine glands in the pancreas that secrete insulin. Also, **islands of Langerhans.** [< Paul *Langerhans* (1847–88), German physician]

ism (iz′əm), *n.* distinctive doctrine, theory, system, or practice. [See **-ISM.**]

-ism, *suffix.* 1 action; practice, as in *baptism, criticism.* 2 doctrine; system; principle, as in *socialism.* 3 quality; characteristic; state; condition, as in *paganism, Americanism.* 4 illustration; case; instance, as in *witticism.* 5 unhealthy condition caused by, as in *alcoholism.* [< Gk. *-ismos, -isma*]

is·n't (iz′ənt), is not.

iso-, is-, *combining form.* equal; alike, as in *isometric, isotope.* [< Gk., < *isos* equal]

i·so·bar (ī′sə bär), *n.* line on a weather map connecting places having the same average atmospheric pressure. [< Gk., < *isos* equal + *baros* weight] —**i′so·bar′ic,** *adj.*

i·so·cline (ī′sə klīn), *n.* a fold of tightly compressed rock strata. [< *iso-* + Gk. *klīnein* to dip, incline] —**i′so·cli′nal,** *adj.*

i·so·late (ī′sə lāt; is′ə-), *v.,* **-lat·ed, -lat·ing.** 1 place apart; separate from others. 2 separate (an infected person) from other noninfected persons. [< *isolated* < F < Ital. *isolato* < L *insulatus,* ult < *insula* island] —**i′so·la′tion,** *n.*

i·so·la·tion·ist (ī′sə lā′shən ist), *n.* one who objects to his or her country's

participation in international affairs. —**i′so·la′tion·ism,** *n.*

i·so·mer (ī′sə mər), *n.* an isomeric compound.

i·so·mer·ase (ī som′ə rās), *n.* enzyme that initiates the formation of an isomer or isomers.

i·so·mer·ic (ī′sə mer′ik), *adj.* composed of the same elements in the same proportions by weight, but differing in one or more properties because of the difference in arrangement of atoms. [< Gk., < *isos* equal + *meros* part]

i·so·met·ric (ī′sə met′rik), **i·so·met·ri·cal** (-rə kəl), *adj.* pertaining to equality of measure; having equality of measure. —**i′so·met′ri·cal·ly,** *adv.*

isometric exercises, exercises which are intended to strengthen muscles by pushing against an immovable object, as a wall.

i·so·pod (ī′sə pod), *n.* crustacean with a flat, oval body and usually seven pairs of similar legs. —*adj.* of or like an isopod. [< NL *Isopoda* order name < Gk. *isos* equal + *poús, podós* foot]

i·sop·ter·an (ī sop′tər ən), *n.* any one of the order of insects comprising the termites; termite. —*adj.* of or belonging to this order. [< NL *Isopteran* < *iso-* + Gk. *pterón* wing] —**i·sop′ter·ous,** *adj.*

i·sos·ce·les (ī sos′ə lēz), *adj.* having two sides equal. [< LL < Gk., < *isos* equal + *skelos* leg]

i·so·therm (ī′sə thėrm), *n.* line connecting places having the same average temperature. [< ISO- + Gk. *therme* heat] —**i′so·ther′mal,** *adj.* —**i′so·ther′mal·ly,** *adv.*

i·so·tope (ī′sə tōp), *n.* any of two or more elements that have the same chemical properties and the same atomic number, but different atomic weights or radioactive behavior. Hydrogen and heavy hydrogen are isotopes. [< ISO- + Gk. *topos* place] —**i′so·top′ic,** *adj.*

Is·ra·el (iz′ri əl), *n.* 1 republic comprising a portion of Palestine, declared a Jewish state, 1948. 2 name given to the Hebrews. 3 ancient kingdom in N Palestine.

Is·rae·li (iz rā′li), *n., pl.* **-lis,** *adj.* —*n.* citizen or inhabitant of Israel. —*adj.* of or pertaining to Israel.

Is·ra·el·ite (iz′ri əl īt), *n.* Jew; Hebrew. —*adj.* of or pertaining to Israel or the Jews.

Is·sei (ēs′sā′), *n., pl.* **-sei.** a first-generation Japanese living in the United States. [< Jap., first generation]

is·su·ance (ish′ü əns), *n.* an issuing; issue.

is·sue (ish′ü), *v.,* **-sued, -su·ing,** *n.* —*v.* 1 send out; put forth: *issue a bulletin, the government issues stamps.* 2 come out; go out; proceed: *smoke issues from the chimney.* 3 result: *the game issued in a tie.* —*n.* 1 something sent out; quantity (of stamps, copies of a magazine, etc.) sent out at one time. 2 a sending out; a putting forth: *issue of an order.* 3 a flowing out; a discharge: *an issue of blood.* 4 result; outcome: *the issue of the battle.* 5

point to be debated; problem: *the issues of a political campaign.* **6** child or children; offspring.

at issue, in question; to be considered or decided.

make an issue (of), provoke an argument about or make a point of disagreement.

take issue, disagree. [< OF, ult. < L *ex-* out + *ire* go] —**is′su·a·ble,** *adj.* —**is′su·er,** *n.*

-ist, *suffix.* **1** a person who does or makes, as in *theorist, tourist.* **2** one who knows about or has skill with, as in *biologist, flutist.* **3** one engaged in or busy with, as in *horticulturist, machinist.* **4** one who believes in; adherent of, as in *abolitionist, idealist.* [< Gk. *-istes*]

Is·tan·bul (is′tän bül′; –tan–), *n.* a city in European Turkey. Formerly called **Constantinople.**

isth·mi·an (is′mi ən), *adj.* of or having to do with an isthmus.

isth·mus (is′məs), *n., pl.* **-mus·es, -mi** (–mī). a narrow strip of land, having water on either side, connecting two larger bodies of land. [< L < Gk. *isthmos*]

IT, information technology.

it (it), *pron., nom.* **it,** *poss.* **its,** *obj.* **it;** *pl. nom.* **they,** *poss.* **their** *or* **theirs,** *obj.* **them;** *n.* —*pron.* thing, part, animal, or person spoken about: *it rains, it is hard to believe that he is gone, he lorded it over us.* —*n.* person or player who must perform a given task. [OE *hit*]

Ital., It., Italian; Italy.

ital., italic.

I·tal·ian (i tal′yən), *adj.* of Italy, its people, or their language. —*n.* **1** native or inhabitant of Italy. **2** language of Italy.

i·tal·ic (i tal′ik), *adj.* of or in type whose letters slant to the right: *these words are in italic type.* —*n.* **1** an italic type, letter, or number. **2** Often, **italics.** type whose letters slant to the right. [< L, < *Italia* Italy < Gk.]

i·tal·i·cize (i tal′ə sīz), *v.,* **-cized, -ciz·ing.** **1** print in type in which the letters slant to the right. **2** underline with a single line to indicate italics. **3** use italics.

It·a·ly (it′ə li), *n.* country in S Europe on the Mediterranean, including Sicily and Sardinia.

itch (ich), *n.* **1** a tickly, prickling feeling in the skin that makes one want to scratch. **2** a restless, uneasy feeling, longing, or desire for anything. —*v.* **1** have or cause an itching feeling. **2** have an uneasy desire. [OE *gyccan*] —**itch′y,** *adj.* —**itch′i·ness,** *n.*

-ite¹, *suffix.* person associated with, as in *Israelite, Canaanite, laborite.* [< Gk. *-ites*]

-ite², *suffix.* salt of, as in *phosphite, sulfite, nitrite.* [< Gk. *-ites*]

i·tem (ī′təm), *n.* **1** a separate thing or article: *the list contains twelve items.* **2** piece of news; bit of information: *the interesting items in today's paper.* [< L, *adv.,* likewise]

i·tem·ize (ī′təm īz), *v.,* **-ized, -iz·ing.** give each item of; list by items: *itemize the cost of a house.* —**i′tem·i·za′tion,** *n.* —**i′tem·iz′er,** *n.*

it·er·ate (it′ər āt), *v.,* **-at·ed, -at·ing.** repeat. [< L, < *iterum* again] —**it′er·a′tion,** *n.*

it·er·a·tive (it′ər ā′tiv), *adj.* repeating; full of repetitions.

i·tin·er·ant (ī tin′ər ənt; i tin′–), *adj.* traveling from place to place. —*n.* person who travels from place to place. [< LL *itinerans* traveling < L *iter* journey] —**i·tin′er·an·cy, i·tin′er·a·cy,** *n.* —**i·tin′er·ant·ly,** *adv.*

i·tin·er·ar·y (ī tin′ər er′i; i tin′–), *n., pl.* **-ar·ies,** *adj.* —*n.* **1** route of travel; plan of travel. **2** record of travel. —*adj.* **1** of traveling or routes of travel. **2** itinerant.

-itis, *suffix.* inflammation of; inflammatory disease of, as in *bronchitis, tonsillitis.* [< Gk. *-itis,* fem. of *-ites*]

it'll (it′əl), **1** it will. **2** it shall.

its (its), *pron., adj.* of it; belonging to it: *the dog wagged its tail.*

it's (its), **1** it is: *it's going to rain.* **2** it has: *it's rained over a week.*

it·self (it self′), *pron.* **1** emphatic form of it: *the land itself is worth more.* **2** reflexive form of it: *the horse tripped and hurt itself.*

-ity, *suffix.* condition or quality of being; ____ness, as in *brutality, activity, sincerity.* [< F *-ité*]

IV or **i.v.,** intravenous.

I've (īv), I have.

-ive, *suffix.* **1** of or pertaining to, as in *inductive.* **2** tending to; likely to, as in *active, appreciative.* [< L *ivus*]

i·vied (ī′vid), *adj.* overgrown with ivy.

i·vo·ry (ī′və ri; īv′ri), *n., pl.* **-ries,** *adj.* —*n.* **1** a hard white substance composing the tusks of elephants, walruses, etc. **2** substance like ivory. **3** creamy white. —*adj.* **1** made of ivory. **2** of or like ivory. **3** creamy-white. [< AF < L *eboreus* of ivory < *ebur* ivory < Egyptian] —**i′vo·ry·like′,** *adj.*

Ivory Coast, republic in W Africa on the Atlantic.

ivory tower, place or condition of withdrawal from the world of action into a world of ideas and dreams.

i·vy (ī′vi), *n., pl.* **i·vies. 1** Also, **English ivy.** a climbing plant with smooth, shiny, evergreen leaves. **2** any of various other climbing plants that resemble this plant, as *American ivy, poison ivy,* etc. [OE *īfig*] —**i′vy·like′,** *adj.*

-ization, *suffix.* act of or condition of being. *neutralization — the act neutralizing or condition of being neutral.*

-ize, *suffix.* **1** make, as in *legalize, centralize.* **2** become, as in *crystallize, materialize.* **3** engage in; be busy with; use, as in *apologize, theorize.* **4** treat with, as in *circularize, macadamize.* **5** other meanings, as in *alphabetize, criticize, memorize.* Also, **-ise.** [< Gk. *-izein*]

J, j (jā), *n., pl.* **J's; j's.** the tenth letter of the alphabet.

J., 1 journal. **2** judge; justice.

j., joule.

Ja., January. Also, **Jan.**

jab (jab), *v.,* **jabbed, jab·bing,** *n.* —*v.* thrust with something pointed; poke. —*n.* a sharp thrust or poke. [ME *jobbe(n)*; prob. imit.]

jab·ber (jab′ər), *v.* talk very fast in a confused, senseless way; chatter. —*n.* rapid, unintelligible talk; chatter. [prob. imit.] —**jab′ber·er,** *n.* —**jab′ber·ing·ly,** *adv.*

ja·bot (zha bō′; zhab′ō; jab′ō), *n.* ruffle or frill of lace, worn at the throat or down the front of a woman's dress or shirt. [< F, orig., maw of a bird]

jack (jak), *n.* **1** tool or machine for lifting or pushing up heavy weights a short distance. **2** *U.S.* playing card with a picture of a court page on it; knave. **3** metal piece or pebble used in the game of jacks. **4** device to receive a plug. **5** a male donkey. **6** fellow; sailor. —*v.* lift or push up with a jack.

jacks, children's game in which metal pieces or pebbles are tossed and caught or picked up during the bounce of a small rubber ball; jackstones.

jack up, a raise (prices, wages, etc.). **b** push or lift up: *jack up a porch.* [orig. proper name < *Jackie,* var. of *Jankin,* dim. of *John*]

jack·al (jak′ôl; –əl), *n.* a wild dog of Asia and Africa. [< Turk. < Pers. *shaghāl*]

jack·a·napes (jak′ə nāps), *n.* a pert, presuming fellow.

jack·ass (jak′as′; –äs′), *n.* **1** a male donkey. **2** a very stupid person; fool.

jack·boot (jak′büt′), *n.* a large strong boot reaching above the knee.

jack·daw (jak′dô′), *n.* **1** a European crow. **2** one of several kinds of American grackle.

jack·et (jak′it), *n.* **1** a short coat. **2** an outer covering, as the paper cover for a book or the skin of a potato. —*v.* put a jacket on; cover with a jacket. [< OF *jaquet,* dim. of *jaque* tunic < Sp. *jaco* < Ar.] —**jack′et·ed,** *adj.* —**jack′et·less,** *adj.* —**jack′et·like′,** *adj.*

jack·ham·mer (jak′ham′ ər), *n.* pneumatic drill used esp. to break up rock and concrete.

jack-in-the-box (jak′in the boks′), *n.* a toy figure that springs up from a box when the lid is unfastened.

jack-in-the-pulpit (jak′in the pul′pit), *n. Am.* a plant with a greenish, petallike sheath arched over the flower stalk.

jack·knife (jak′nīf′), *n., pl.* **-knives. 1** a large strong pocketknife. **2** kind of dive in which the diver touches his or her feet with the hands before entering the water.

jack of all trades, person who can do many different kinds of work fairly well.

jack-o'-lan·tern (jak′ə lan′tərn), *n.* **1** pumpkin hollowed out and cut to look like a face, used as a lantern at Halloween. **2** =will-o'-the-wisp (def. 1).

jack pot, 1 stakes that accumulate in a poker game until some player wins with a pair of jacks or something better. **2** any large pool of winnings, as in a lottery. **3** *Fig.* any large gain; good fortune.

hit the or **a jackpot, a** win a large prize. **b** have some very good luck.

jack rabbit, a large hare of W North America, having very long legs and ears.

Jack·son (jak′sən), *n.* **1 Andrew,** 1767–1845, the seventh president of the United States, 1829–37. **2** capital of Mississippi, in the C part.

Jack·so·ni·an (jak sō′ni ən), *Am.* —*adj.* of or like Andrew Jackson or his principles. —*n.* follower of Andrew Jackson.

jack·stone (jak′stōn′), *n.* **1** =jack (def. 3). **2 jackstones** (*sing. in use*), =jacks.

jack·straw (jak′strô′), *n.* **1** thin sticks of wood, pointed at each end, or bone, straw, etc., used in a game. **2 jackstraws** (*sing. in use*), game played with a set of these thrown down in a confused pile and picked up one at a time without moving any of the rest of the pile; pickup sticks.

Jac·o·be·an (jak′ə bē′ən), *adj.* of King James I of England or the period of his reign, 1603–25.

Jac·o·bin (jak′ə bin), *n.* **1** member of a radical political club organized in 1789 during the French Revolution. **2** an extreme radical in politics. —**Jac′o·bin·ism,** *n.*

Jac·o·bite (jak′ə bīt), *n.* supporter of James II and his descendants in their claims to the English throne after the English Revolution in 1688.

Jacob's ladder, a rope ladder used on ships.

jac·quard (jə kärd′), *n.* fabric with patterns woven into it. [< F *jacquard* or *jacquart* weaving loom < Joseph *Jacquard* (1752–1834), French weaver who invented it]

jade¹ (jād), *n.* **1** a hard stone, usually green, used for jewels and ornaments. **2** Also, **jade green** sea green. [< F < Sp. (*piedra de*) *ijada* (stone of) colic (jade being supposed to cure this), ult. < L *ilia* flanks] —**jade′like′,** *adj.*

jade² (jād), *n., v.,* **jad·ed, jad·ing.** —*n.* an inferior or worn-out horse. —*v.* **1** wear out; tire; weary. **2** dull by continual use; surfeit; satiate. —**jad′ish,** *adj.*

jad·ed (jād′id), *adj.* **1** weary. **2** satiated. —**jad′ed·ly,** *adv.* —**jad′ed·ness,** *n.*

jae·ger (yā′gər; jā′–), *n.* a sea bird like a gull, that pursues weaker birds and makes them disgorge their prey.

jag (jag), *n., v.,* **jagged, jag·ging.** —*n.* a sharp point sticking out; pointed projection. —*v.* **1** make notches in. **2** cut or tear unevenly.

jag·ged (jag′id), *adj.* with sharp points sticking out. —**jag′ged·ly,** *adv.* —**jag′ged·ness,** *n.*

jag·uar (jag′wär; –yü är′), *n.* a fierce animal of tropical America, much like a leopard, but larger. [< Tupi-Guarani]

jai a·lai (hī′lī′, hī′ə lī′, hī′ə lī′), *n.* game like handball, played on a walled court with a hard ball, which is caught and thrown from a curved wicker basket fastened to the arm; pelota. [< Sp. *jai alai* < Basque *jai* festival + *alai* merry]

jail (jāl), *n.* prison for people awaiting trial or being punished for minor offenses. —*v.* put in jail; keep in jail. [< OF *jaiole,* ult < L *cavea* coop] —**jail′like′,** *adj.*

jail·bird (jāl′bėrd′), *n.* **1** prisoner in jail. **2** person who has been in jail many times.

jail·break (jāl′brāk′), *n.* escape from prison.

jail·er, jail·or (jāl′ər), *n.* keeper of a jail.

ja·la·pe·ño (hä′lä pā′nyō), *n.* hot Mexican pepper, used to flavor dishes, soups, etc.

ja·lop·y (jə lop′i), *n., pl.* **-lop·ies.** an old automobile in bad repair.

jam¹ (jam), *v.,* **jammed, jam·ming,** *n.* —*v.* **1** press tightly; squeeze; crush; push. **2** block up; stick or catch so as not to be worked. **3** make (radio signals, etc.) unintelligible by sending out others of approximately the same frequency. **4** perform a jazz composition with improvised embellishments. —*n.* **1** mass of people or things crowded together: *a traffic jam.* **2** a jamming or being jammed. **3** a difficulty or tight spot. [? imit.]

jam² (jam), *n.* fruit boiled with sugar until thick. [? special use of *jam¹*] —**jam′like′,** *adj.*

Ja·mai·ca (jə mā′kə), *n.* an island country in the West Indies, S of Cuba. —**Ja·mai′can,** *adj., n.*

jamb (jam), *n.* the upright piece forming the side of a doorway, window, fireplace, etc. [< F *jambe,* orig., leg < LL *gamba*]

jam·ba·lay·a (jam′bə lī′ə), *n.* Creole dish made of rice, tomatoes, and spices cooked with shrimp or ham. [probably < Haitian Creole *jambalaya* < Provençal *jambalaia* stew of rice and chicken]

jam·bo·ree (jam′bə rē′), *n.* a noisy party; lively entertainment.

James (jāmz), *n.* **1** the name of two of Christ's disciples. **2** book of the New Testament.

James·town (jāmz′toun′), *n.* a ruined village in SE Virginia; site of the first successful English settlement in North America, in 1607.

jam-packed, jam-packed (jam′pakt′), *adj.* filled to absolute capacity.

jam session, gathering at which musicians improvise on jazz compositions.

Jan., January. Also, **Ja.**

jan·gle (jang′gəl), *v.,* **-gled, -gling,** *n.* —*v.* sound harshly. —*n.* harsh sound. [< OF *jangler*] —**jan′gler,** *n.*

jan·i·tor (jan′ə tər), *n.* person hired to take care of a building, offices, etc. [< L, doorkeeper] —**jan′i·to′ri·al,** *adj.*

Jan·u·ar·y (jan′yü er′i), *n., pl.* **-ar·ies.** the first month of the year. It has 31 days. [< L, < *Janus* Janus]

Ja·nus (jā′nəs), *n.* Roman god of gates and doors, and beginnings and endings, represented with two faces, one looking forward, and the other looking backward.

Jap., Japan; Japanese.

Ja·pan (jə pan′), *n.* an island nation in the Pacific, E of Asia.

ja·pan (jə pan′), *n., v.,* **-panned, -panning.** —*n.* 1 a hard, glossy varnish, used on wood or metal. 2 articles varnished and decorated in the Japanese manner. —*v.* put japan on.

Jap·a·nese (jap′ə nēz′; -nēs′), *adj., n., pl.* **-nese.** —*adj.* of Japan, its people, or their language. —*n.* 1 native of Japan. 2 language of Japan.

Japanese beetle, a small green-and-brown beetle that eats fruits, leaves, and grasses.

jape (jāp), *n., v.,* **japed, jap·ing.** 1 joke; jest. 2 trick. —**jap′er,** *n.*

ja·pon·i·ca (jə pon′ə kə), *n.* 1 camellia. 2 shrub with showy red, pink, or white flowers. [< NL, orig. fem. adj., Japanese]

jar[1] (jär), *n.* 1 a deep container made of glass, earthenware, etc., with a wide mouth. 2 amount that it holds. [< F *jarre,* ult. < Ar. *jarrah*]

jar[2] (jär), *n., v.,* **jarred, jar·ring.** —*n.* 1 a shake; rattle. 2 a harsh, grating noise. 3 a harsh, unpleasant effect; shock. 4 a clash; quarrel. —*v.* 1 make shake; rattle. 2 make a harsh, grating noise. 3 have a harsh, unpleasant effect on; shock. 4 cause to clash; quarrel. [OE *ceorran* creak]

jar·gon (jär′gən; -gon), *n.* 1 confused, meaningless talk or writing. 2 language that is not understood. 3 language of a special group, profession, etc. Doctors, actors, and sailors have jargons. 4 mixture of languages. [< OF, prob. ult. imit.]

jas·mine (jas′mən; jaz′-), *n.* shrub or vine with clusters of fragrant yellow, white, and red flowers. [< F *jasmin* < Ar. < Pers. *yāsmīn*]

jas·per (jas′pər), *n.* 1 a colored quartz, usually red or brown. 2 a green precious stone of ancient times. [< OF *jaspre,* ult. < L < Gk. *iaspis* < Phoenician]

jaun·dice (jôn′dis; jän′-), *n., v.,* **-diced, -dic·ing.** —*n.* 1 disease that causes yellowness of the skin, eyes, and body fluids, and disturbed vision. 2 a disturbed or unnaturally sour mental outlook. —*v.* 1 cause jaundice in. 2 prejudice the mind and judgment of; sour the temper of. [< OF *jaunisse,* ult. < L *galbinus* greenish-yellow]

jaunt (jônt; jänt), *n.* a short pleasure trip or excursion. —*v.* take such a trip.

jaun·ty (jôn′ti; jän′-), *adj.,* **-ti·er, -ti·est.** 1 easy and lively; sprightly; carefree: *jaunty steps.* 2 smart; stylish: *a jaunty little hat.* [< F *gentil* GENTLE] —**jaun′ti·ly,** *adv.* —**jaun′ti·ness,** *n.*

Ja·va (jä′və; jav′ə), *n.* 1 a large island of Indonesia, SE of Asia. 2 **java,** coffee.

Jav·a·nese (jav′ə nēz′; -nēs′), *adj., n., pl.* **-nese.** —*adj.* of Java, its people, or their language. —*n.* 1 native of Java. 2 language of Java.

jave·lin (jav′lin; -ə lin), *n.* a light spear thrown by hand. [< F *javeline*]

jaw (jô), *n.* 1 either of the two bones, or sets of bones, that form the framework of the mouth. 2 either of the parts in a tool or machine that grip and hold. —*v. Informal.* talk; gossip.

jaws, a mouth with its jawbone and teeth. **b** narrow entrance to a valley, mountain pass, channel, etc. [? akin to *chew;* infl. by F *joue* cheek]

jaw·bone (jô′bōn′), *n., v.,* **-boned, bon·ing.** —*n.* 1 bone of either jaw. 2 bone of the lower jaw. —*v.* try to persuade by lecturing, scolding, etc.

jaws of life, device for prying open a door on a crushed vehicle in order to reach an occupant trapped inside.

jay (jā), *n.* 1 a noisy American bird with blue feathers; bluejay. 2 a noisy European bird with a crest. 3 any of various birds of the same family as these two. [< OF]

jay·walk (jā′wôk′), *v.* walk across a street without paying attention to traffic rules. —**jay′walk′er,** *n.* —**jay′walk′ing,** *n.*

jazz (jaz), *n.* music with the accents falling at unusual places; syncopated music. —*adj.* of or like jazz: *a jazz band.* —*v.* play (music) as jazz. [of black American orig.]

jeal·ous (jel′əs), *adj.* 1 fearful that a person one loves may prefer someone else. 2 full of envy; envious: *he is jealous of John's grades.* 3 watchful in guarding something; careful; suspicious: *the dog was a jealous guardian of the child.* [< OF *gelos,* ult. < L *zelus* ZEAL] —**jeal′ous·ly,** *adv.* —**jeal′ous·ness,** *n.*

jeal·ous·y (jel′əs i), *n., pl.* **-ous·ies.** jealous condition or feeling.

jeans (jēnz), *n.* 1 denim pants, often close-fitting. 2 a strong twilled cotton cloth, used for overalls, etc. [prob. < F *Gênes* Genoa]

jeep (jēp), *n.* a small, but powerful, general-purpose automobile with a four-wheel drive. [back formation from *"Jeepers creepers!";* coined by the designer of the vehicle)]

jeer (jir), *v.* make fun rudely or unkindly; mock; scoff. —*n.* a jeering remark; rude, sarcastic comment. —**jeer′er,** *n.* —**jeer′ing·ly,** *adv.*

Jef·fer·son (jef′ər sən), *n.* **Thomas,** 1743–1826, American statesman, third president of the United States, 1801–09. He drafted the Declaration of Independence. —**Jef′fer·so′ni·an,** *adj., n.*

Jefferson City, capital of Missouri.

Je·ho·vah (ji hō′və), *n.* one of the names of God in the Old Testament.

je·june (ji jün′), *adj.* 1 lacking nourishing qualities. 2 flat and uninteresting; unsatisfying. [< L *jejunus,* orig., hungry] —**je·june′ly,** *adv.*

je·ju·num (ji jü′nəm), *n.* the middle portion of the small intestine, between the duodenum and the ileum. [< NL < L, neut. empty]

jell (jel), *v.* become jelly. [< *jelly*]

jel·lied (jel′id), *adj.* 1 turned into jelly; having the consistency of jelly. 2 spread with jelly.

jel·ly (jel′i), *n., pl.* **-lies,** *v.,* **-lied, -ly·ing.** —*n.* 1 a food, soft when hot, but somewhat firm and partly transparent when cold, made by boiling fruit juice and sugar together, cooking bones and meat juice, using gelatin, etc. 2 a jellylike substance. —*v.* become jelly; turn into jelly. [< OF *gelee,* orig., frost, ult. < L *gelare* congeal]

jel·ly·fish (jel′i fish′), *n., pl.* **-fish·es** or (*esp. collectively*) **-fish.** any of a group of invertebrate sea animals with a body formed of a mass of jellylike tissue that is often transparent. Most jellyfish have long trailing tentacles that may bear stinging hairs or feelers.

jel·ly·roll (jel′i rol′), *n.* spongecake spread with jelly and rolled up, with the outside of the roll usually sprinkled with confectioner's sugar.

jen·net (jen′it), *n.* 1 a small Spanish horse. 2 female donkey.

jen·ny (jen′i), *n., pl.* **-nies.** female of certain animals. [orig. proper name, dim. of *Jane,* fem. of *John*]

jeop·ard·ize (jep′ər dīz), *v.,* **-ized, -iz·ing.** risk; endanger; imperil: *soldiers jeopardize their lives in war.*

jeop·ard·y (jep′ər di), *n.* 1 risk; danger; peril: *his life was in jeopardy when the tree fell.* 2 condition of a person on trial for a criminal offense. [< OF *jeu parti* an even or divided game, ult. < L *jocus* play + *pars* part]

Jer., 1 Jeremiah. 2 Jersey.

jer·bo·a (jər bō′ə), *n.* a small, jumping, mouselike mammal of Asia and N Africa. [< NL < Ar. *yarbū*]

Jer·e·mi·ah (jer′ə mī′ə), *n.* 1 a Hebrew prophet who lamented the evils of his time. 2 book of the Old Testament.

Jer·i·cho (jer′ə kō), *n.* an ancient city in Palestine.

jerk[1] (jėrk), *n.* 1 a sudden, sharp pull, twist, or start: *get up with a jerk.* 2 pull or twist of the muscles that one cannot control; twitch. 3 *Informal.* an unsophisticated or stupid person. —*v.* 1 pull or twist suddenly: *jerk one's hand out of hot water.* 2 move with a jerk: *the old wagon jerked along.* [prob. imit.]

jerk[2] (jėrk), *v.* preserve (meat) by cutting it into long thin slices and drying it in the sun. [< Am. Sp. *charquear,* v., < *charquí* < Quechua (Ind. lang. of Peru)]

jer·kin (jėr′kən), *n.* a short coat or jacket, with or without sleeves.

jerk·y[1] (jėr′ki), *adj.,* **jerk·i·er, jerk·i·est.** with sudden starts and stops; with jerks. —**jerk′i·ly,** *adv.* —**jerk′i·ness,** *n.*

jerk·y[2] (jėr′ki), *n.* dried strips of meat, usually beef. [< *jerk*[2] + -*y*[1]]

Je·rome (jə rōm′), *n.* **Saint,** A.D. 340?–420, monk and scholar, author of the Latin translation of the Bible, the Vulgate.

jer·ry-build (jer′i bild′), *v.,* **-built, -build·ing.** build quickly and cheaply of poor materials. **—jer′ry-built′,** *adj.*

Jer·sey (jėr′zi), *n., pl.* **-seys. 1** one of a group of British islands, near the coast of France. **2** one of a breed of small, fawn-colored cattle that came from this island. **3** =New Jersey.

jer·sey (jėr′zi), *n., pl.* **-seys. 1** a close-fitting sweater that is pulled on over the head. **2** a machine-knitted cloth.

Je·ru·sa·lem (jə rü′sə ləm), *n.* city on the Israel-Jordan border, capital of Israel. It is a holy city to Jews, Christians, and Muslims. **—Je·ru′sa·lem·ite′,** *adj., n.*

Jerusalem artichoke, 1 kind of sunflower whose root is edible. **2** its root.

jess (jes), *n.* a short strap fastened around a falcon's leg. [< OF *ges,* ult. < L *jacere* to throw]

Jes·se (jes′i), *n.* father of David, in the Bible.

jest (jest), *n.* **1** joke. **2** act of poking fun; mockery. **3** thing to be mocked or laughed at. **—v. 1** joke. **2** poke fun (at); make fun.

in jest, in fun; not seriously. [< OF *geste,* orig., story, exploit, ult. < L *gerere* accomplish] **—jest′ing·ly,** *adv.*

jest·er (jes′tər), *n.* **1** person who jests. **2** in the Middle Ages, a professional clown.

Je·su (jē′zū; –zü; –sü), *n. Poetic.* Jesus.

Jes·u·it (jezh′ů it; jez′yů–), *n.* member of a Roman Catholic religious order called the Society of Jesus. **—Jes′u·it′ic, Jes′u·it′i·cal,** *adj.* **—Jes′u·it′i·cal·ly,** *adv.*

Je·sus (jē′zəs), or **Jesus Christ,** *n.* founder of the Christian religion.

jet¹ (jet), *n., v.,* **jet·ted, jet·ting. —n. 1** a stream of water, steam, gas, etc., sent with force, esp. from a small opening. **2** a spout or nozzle for sending out a jet. **3** a jet engine. **4** a jet plane. **—v. 1** gush out; shoot forth in a jet or forceful stream. **2** fly by jet. [< F, < *jeter* to throw]

jet² (jet), *n.* **1** a hard black mineral, glossy when polished, used for making beads, buttons, etc. **2** a deep glossy black. **—adj. 1** made of jet. **2** deep glossy black. [< OF < L < Gk. *gagates* < *Gagai,* in Lycia]

jet-black (jet′blak′), *adj.* very black.

jet engine, engine driven by a jet of air or gas; jet-propelled engine.

jet lag, fatigue, apathy, etc., caused by traveling by jet across several time zones in less than a day.

jet·lin·er (jet′līn′ər), *n.* a transport airplane driven by jet propulsion.

jet plane, airplane driven by jet propulsion.

jet propulsion, propulsion in one direction by a jet of air, gas, etc., forced in the opposite direction. **—jet′pro·pelled′,** *adj.*

jet·sam (jet′səm), *n.* **1** goods thrown overboard to lighten a ship in distress and often afterward washed ashore. **2** thing tossed aside as useless.

jet stream, a high-speed air current (up to 250 miles per hour or more) traveling from W to E at high altitudes (six to ten miles).

jet·ti·son (jet′ə sən; –zən), *v.* **1** throw (goods) overboard to lighten a ship in distress or an aircraft waiting to land or preparing to make an emergency landing. **2** throw away; discard. **—n. 1** act of doing this. **2** goods thrown overboard; jetsam. [< AF *getteson,* ult. < L *jacere* throw]

jet·ty (jet′i), *n., pl.* **-ties. 1** structure built out into the water to protect a harbor or influence the current; breakwater. **2** a landing place; pier. [< OF, < *jeter* throw, ult. < L *jacere*]

Jew (jü), *n.* **1** member of a people that formerly lived in Palestine, but now live in many countries. **2** person whose religion is Judaism; Hebrew. **—adj.** Jewish.

jew·el (jü′əl), *n., v.,* **-eled, -el·ing. —n. 1** a precious stone; gem. **2** a valuable ornament to be worn, set with precious stones. **3** person or thing that is very precious. **4** gem or some substitute used as a bearing in a watch. **—v.** set or adorn with jewels or with things like jewels. [< OF *juel,* ult. < L *jocus* joke, game] **—jew′el·like′,** *adj.*

jew·el·er (jü′əl ər), *n.* person who makes, sells, or repairs jewels, jeweled ornaments, watches, etc.

jew·el·ry (jü′əl ri), *n.* jewels.

jew·el·weed (jü′əl wēd′), *n.* =impatiens.

jew·fish (jü′fish′), *n. pl.* **-fish·es** or (*esp. collectively*) **-fish. 1** giant sea bass. **2** any of various other large fishes of warm seas.

Jew·ish (jü′ish), *adj.* of, belonging to, or characteristic of the Jews. **—n.** Yiddish.

Jew·ry (jü′ri), *n., pl.* **-ries. 1** Jews as a group; Jewish people. **2** ghetto. **3** Judea.

jews′-harp, jew′s-harp (jüz′härp′), *n.* a simple musical instrument, held between the teeth and played by striking the free end of a piece of metal with a finger.

Jez·e·bel (jez′ə bəl; –bel), *n.* **1** the wicked wife of Ahab, king of Israel. II Kings 9:7–10, 30–37. **2** a shameless, immoral woman.

jg., j.g., junior grade.

jib¹ (jib), *n.* a triangular sail in front of the foremast. [? < *jib²*]

jib² (jib), *v.,* **jibbed, jib·bing.** =jibe¹.

jibe¹ (jīb), *v.,* **jibed, jib·ing. 1** shift (a sail) from one side of a ship to the other when sailing before the wind. **2** of a sail or boom, shift thus. **3** change the course of a ship so that the sails shift in this way. Also, **jib.** [Du. *gijben*]

jibe² (jīb), *v.,* **jibed, jib·ing,** *n.* =gibe. **—jib′er,** *n.*

jibe³ (jīb), *v.,* **jibed, jib·ing.** be in harmony; agree.

jif·fy (jif′i), **jiff** (jif), *n., pl.* **jif·fies; jiffs.** *Informal.* a very short time; moment.

jig¹ (jig), *n., v.* **jigged, jig·ging. —n. 1** a lively dance, often in triple time. **2** music for it. **—v.** dance a jig.

the jig's up, *Slang.* there's no more chance. [< OF *giguer* dance < *gigue* fiddle] **—jig′like′,** *adj.*

jig² (jig), *n.* **1** fishhook, or set of fishhooks, loaded with a bright metal or having a spoon-shaped piece of bone attached, for drawing through the water. **2** any of various mechanical contrivances or devices, esp. a guide in using a drill, file, etc. [var. of *gauge*]

jig·ger¹ (jig′ər), *n.* **1** a small sail. **2** article, or part; gadget; contraption. **3** a small glass used to measure liquor usually 1½ oz. [< *jig²*]

jig·ger² (jig′ər), *n.* **1** a small flea; chigoe. **2** chigger. [alter. of *chigoe*]

jig·gle (jig′əl), *v.,* **-gled, -gling,** *n. —v.* shake or jerk slightly. **—n.** a slight shake; light jerk; rocky motion. [< *jig¹*]

jig·saw (jig′sô′), *n.* a narrow saw mounted in a frame and worked with an up-and-down motion, used to cut curves or irregular lines.

jigsaw puzzle, picture sawed into irregular pieces that can be fitted together again.

ji·had (ji häd′), *n.* **1** war of religious Muslims against unbelievers. **2** *Fig.* any crusade against a belief or principle. [< Arabic *jihād,* lit. struggle, contest, effort]

jill, Jill (jil), *n.* **1** woman; girl. **2** sweetheart.

jilt (jilt), *v.* cast off (a lover or sweetheart) after giving encouragement. **—jilt′er,** *n.*

Jim Crow (jim′ krō′), **Jim Crow·ism** (krō′iz əm), *Slang.* discrimination against blacks. [Am Eng.]

jim·my (jim′i), *n., pl.* **-mies,** *v.,* **-mied, -my·ing. —n.** a short crowbar used esp. by burglars to force windows, doors, etc., open. **—v.** force open with a jimmy.

jim·son weed (jim′sən), a coarse, bad-smelling weed with white flowers and poisonous, narcotic leaves. [alter. of *Jamestown* (Va.)]

jin·gle (jing′gəl), *n., v.,* **-gled, -gling. —n. 1** sound like that of little bells, or of coins or keys striking together. **2** verse or music that has a jingling sound, esp. short rhyming advertisements. **—v.** make or cause to make a jingling sound: *the sleigh bells jingle, jingle one's money.* [imit.] **—jin′gling·ly,** *adv.* **—jin′gly,** *adj.*

jin·go (jing′gō), *n., pl.* **-goes,** *adj. —n.* person who favors an aggressive foreign policy that might lead to war with other nations. **—adj.** of jingoes; like that of jingoes. **—jin′go·ism,** *n.* **—jin′go·ist,** *n.* **—jin′go·is′tic,** *adj.*

jinn (jin), *n.pl., sing.* **jin·ni** (ji nē′). **1** spirits that can appear in human or animal form. **2** (*sing. in use with pl.* **jinns**) one of these spirits; jinni. Also, **djin, djinn, jin.** [< Ar.]

jin·rik·i·sha, jin·rick·sha (jin rik′shə; –shô), *n.* a small, two-wheeled, hooded carriage pulled by one or more men, formerly used in Japan, China, etc. Also, **rickshaw, ricksha.** [< Jap., < *jin* man + *riki* strength + *sha* vehicle]

jinx (jingks), —*n.* person or thing that brings bad luck. —*v.* bring bad luck to. [< L *iynx* bird used in charms < Gk.]

jit·ney (jit′ni), *n., pl.* **-neys,** small bus that carries passengers, as a private service.

jit·ter (jit′ər), *n.* **jitters,** extreme nervousness. —*v.* be or act very nervous.

jit·ter·y (jit′ər i), *adj.* U.S. nervous.

jiu·jit·su (jü jit′sü), *n.* =jujitsu.

jive (jīv), *n., v.,* **jived, jiv·ing.** Slang. —*n.* swing music. —*v.* perform swing music.

Joan of Arc (jōn′ əv ärk′), 1412–31, French heroine who led armies against the invading English.

job (job), *n., adj., v.,* **jobbed, job·bing.** —*n.* 1 piece of work. 2 work done regularly for pay; employment. 3 anything one has to do. —*adj.* done by the job; hired for a particular piece of work. —*v.* 1 buy (goods) from manufacturers and sell to dealers. 2 let out (work) to different contractors, workmen, etc.

on the job, a while working: *learn on the job.* **b** tending to one's work or duty: *on the job 24/7.* —**job′less,** *adj.* —**job′less·ness,** *n.*

Job (jōb), *n.* 1 a very patient man in the Bible who kept his faith in God in spite of many troubles. 2 book of the Old Testament.

job·ber (job′ər), *n.* person who buys goods from manufacturers and sells to retailers.

job·hold·er (job′hōl′dər), *n.* person regularly employed.

job lot, quantity of goods bought or sold together, often of inferior quality.

jock·ey (jok′i), *n., pl.* **-eys,** *v.,* **-eyed, -ey·ing.** —*n.* person whose occupation is riding horses in races. —*v.* 1 ride (a horse) in a race. 2 trick; cheat. 3 maneuver to get advantage: *the crews were jockeying their boats to get into the best position for the race.* [orig. proper name, < *Jack*] —**jock′ey·ship,** *n.*

jo·cose (jō kōs′), *adj.* jesting; humorous; playful. [< L, < *jocus* jest] —**jo·cose′ly,** *adv.* —**jo·cose′ness, jo·cos′i·ty,** *n.*

joc·u·lar (jok′yə lər), *adj.* funny; joking. [< L, ult. < *jocus* jest] —**joc′u·lar′i·ty,** *n.* —**joc′u·lar·ly,** *adv.*

joc·und (jok′ənd; jō′kənd), *adj.* cheerful; merry; gay. [< var. of L *jucundus* pleasant < *juvare* please] —**jo·cun′di·ty,** *n.*

jodh·purs (jod′pərz), *n.pl.* breeches for horseback riding, loose above the knees and fitting closely below. [< *Jodhpur,* India]

jog¹ (jog), *v.,* **jogged, jog·ging,** *n.* —*v.* 1 shake with a push or jerk: *jog a person's elbow to get his attention.* 2 stir up (one's own or another person's memory). 3 move up and down with a jerking or shaking motion: *the old horse jogged along.* 4 go forward at a regular, slow walk or trot, esp. as exercise. —*n.* 1 a shake, push, or nudge. 2 a hint or reminder: *give one's memory a jog.* 3 a slow walk or trot. [blend of *jot* jolt and *shog* shake] —**jog′ger,** *n.*

jog² (jog), *n.* part that sticks out or in; unevenness in a line or a surface: *a jog in a wall.* [var. of JAG¹]

jog·gle (jog′əl), *v.,* **-gled, -gling,** *n.* —*v.* 1 shake slightly. 2 move with a jerk. —*n.* a slight shake. [< *jog¹*]

John (jon), *n.* 1 one of Christ's Apostles. 2 the fourth book of the New Testament.

John Bull, 1 the typical Englishman. **2** the English nation.

John Doe, a fictitious name used in legal forms or proceedings for the name of an unknown person.

John Hancock, a person's signature. [< the first signer's name on the American Declaration of Independence]

john·ny·cake (jon′i kāk′), *n.* kind of corn bread.

John·ny-jump-up (jon′i jump′up′), *n.* **1** a wild pansy. **2** violet.

John·son (jon′sən), *n.* **1 Andrew,** 1808–75, the 17th president of the United States, 1865–69. **2 Lyndon B.,** 1908–73, the 36th president of the United States, 1963–69.

John the Baptist, man who foretold the coming of Christ and baptized him. Matt. 3.

joie de vi·vre (zhwä də vē′vrə), *French.* joy of living; enjoyment of life.

join (join), *v.* 1 bring or come together; connect; meet: *join hands; two roads join here; the brook joins the river.* 2 combine; unite: *join in marriage; join in a song.* 3 become a member of: *join a club.* 4 adjoin: *his farm joins mine.* —*n.* place or line of joining; seam.

join battle, begin to fight.

join up, enlist in the armed forces. [< OF *joindre* < L *jungere*]

join·er (join′ər), *n.* 1 person or thing that joins. 2 a skilled workman who makes woodwork and furniture.

join·er·y (join′ər i), *n.* skill or trade of a joiner.

joint (joint), *n.* 1 place at which two things or parts are joined. 2 the way parts are joined: *a perfect joint.* 3 in an animal, the parts where two bones move on one another. 4 one of the parts of which a jointed thing is made up: *the middle joint of the finger.* 5 piece of meat cut for cooking. 6 Slang. **a** a cheap, low place, often for the illegal sale of liquor. **b.**any place or establishment. —*v.* 1 connect by a joint or joints. 2 divide at the joints. —*adj.* owned together; done by two or more persons; sharing: *joint owners; joint efforts.*

out of joint, a out of place at the joint. **b** out of order; in bad condition. [< OF, < *joindre* JOIN] —**joint′less,** *adj.*

joint·ly (joint′li), *adv.* together; in common: *the two men owned the newsstand jointly.*

joint-stock company, company or firm whose capital is owned in shares by stockholders.

joist (joist), *n.* one of the parallel pieces of timber to which the boards of a floor or ceiling are fastened. [< OF *giste,* ult. < L *jacere* lie] —**joist′less,** *adj.*

jo·jo·ba (hō hō′bə; hə–), *n.* shrub or small tree of the box family, found in Mexico and SW United States, whose seeds yield an oil used in inks and waxes.

joke (jōk), *n., v.,* **joked, jok·ing.** —*n.* 1 something said or done to make somebody laugh; something amusing: *this was a good joke on me.* 2 person or thing laughed at. —*v.* make a joke; say or do something as a joke. 2 laugh at; make fun of; tease. [< L *jocus*] —**jok′ing·ly,** *adv.*

jok·er (jōk′ər), *n.* 1 person who jokes. 2 an extra playing card used in some games.

jol·li·fi·ca·tion (jol′ə fə kā′shən), *n.* merrymaking.

jol·li·ty (jol′ə ti), *n., pl.* **-ties.** fun; merriment; festivity.

jol·ly (jol′i), *adj.,* **-li·er, -li·est,** *v.,* **-lied, -ly·ing.** —*adj.* full of fun; merry: *a jolly disposition.* —*v.* 1 flatter (a person) to make him feel good or agreeable. 2 make fun of; kid. [< OF *joli,* ? < Gmc.] —**jol′li·ly,** *adv.* —**jol′li·ness,** *n.*

Jolly Rog·er (roj′ər), a pirates' black flag with a skull and crossbones on it.

jolt (jōlt), *v.* move with a shock or jerk; jar; shake up: *the wagon jolted us when the wheel went over a rock.* —*n.* jar; shock; jerk: *stop with a jolt.* —**jolt′er,** *n.* —**jolt′y,** *adj.*

Jo·nah (jō′nə), *n.* 1 in the Bible, a Hebrew prophet thrown overboard during a storm, swallowed by a whale. 2 book of the Old Testament.

jon·gleur (jong′glər; *Fr.* zhôN glœr′), *n.* a wandering minstrel or entertainer in the Middle Ages. [< F < OF *jogleor* juggler. See JUGGLE.]

jon·quil (jong′kwəl; jon′–), *n.* 1 plant of the narcissus family with yellow or white flowers and long slender leaves. 2 the flower. [< F < Sp. *junquillo,* ult. < L *juncus* reed]

Jor·dan (jôr′dən), *n.* country in SW Asia.

Jordan almond, candy made by coating almonds with a hard sugar frosting.

Jo·seph (jō′zəf), *n.* 1 favorite son of Jacob whose jealous brothers sold him into slavery in Egypt. Gen. 37, 39–41. 2 the husband of Mary, the mother of Jesus.

josh (josh), *v.* Informal. make good-natured fun of; tease playfully; banter. —**josh′er,** *n.*

Josh·u·a (josh′ü ə), *n.* 1 successor of Moses. 2 book of the Old Testament.

jos·tle (jos′əl), *v.,* **-tled, -tling,** *n.* —*v.* crowd, strike, or push against; elbow roughly: *we were jostled by the big crowd at the entrance.* —*n.* a jostling; push; knock. [< *joust*] —**jos′tler,** *n.*

jot (jot), *n.*, *v.*, **jot·ted, jot·ting.** —*n.* little bit; very small amount: *not care a jot.* —*v.* write briefly or in haste: *jot down the order.* [< L < Gk. *iota* iota] —**jot′ter,** *n.*

joule (joul; jül), *n.* a unit of work or energy, equal to ten million ergs. [for J. P. *Joule,* scientist]

jounce (jouns), *v.*, **jounced, jounc·ing,** *n.* —*v.* bounce; bump; jolt. —*n.* a jolting movement.

jour·nal (jėr′nəl), *n.* 1 a daily record. 2 account of what happens or of what one thinks or notices, as a diary. 3 newspaper; magazine. 4 book in which every item of business is written down to be entered under the proper account. 5 part of a shaft or axle that turns on a bearing. [< OF < LL *diurnalis.* Doublet of DIURNAL.]

jour·nal·ism (jėr′nəl iz əm), *n.* 1 work of writing for, editing, managing, or producing a newspaper or magazine. 2 newspapers and magazines as a group.

jour·nal·ist (jėr′nəl ist), *n.* person engaged in journalism, as an editor or reporter. —**jour′nal·is′tic,** *adj.* —**jour′nal·is′ti·cal·ly,** *adv.*

jour·ney (jėr′ni), *n.*, *pl.* **-neys,** *v.*, **-neyed, -ney·ing.** —*n.* 1 travel; trip: *a journey around the world.* 2 distance traveled or that one can travel in a certain time. —*v.* take a trip; travel. [< OF *journee,* orig., a day, ult. < L *diurnus* of one day]

jour·ney·man (jėr′ni mən), *n.*, *pl.* **-men.** a qualified workman who has completed an apprenticeship, but has not become an employer or master workman.

joust (just; joust; jüst), *n.* 1 combat between two knights on horseback, armed with lances. 2 *Fig.* an intellectual contest of ideas, opinions, etc. —*v.* 1 fight with lances on horseback. 2 *Fig.* dispute using words; exchange. **jousts,** a tournament. [< OF *jouster,* ult. < L *juxta* beside] —**joust′er,** *n.*

Jove (jōv), *n.* **by Jove,** exclamation of surprise, pleasure, etc. [< L, Jupiter]

jo·vi·al (jō′vi əl), *adj.* good-hearted and full of fun; good-humored and merry. [< L *Jovialis* pertaining to Jupiter (those born under the planet's sign being supposedly cheerful)] —**jo′vi·al·ly,** *adv.* —**jo′vi·al·ness, jo′vi·al′i·ty,** *n.*

jowl[1] (joul; jōl), *n.* 1 part under the jaw; jaw. 2 cheek. [OE *ceafl*]

jowl[2] (joul; jōl), *n.* fold of flesh hanging from the jaw. [akin to OE *ceole* throat]

joy (joi), *n.* 1 a strong feeling of pleasure; gladness; happiness. 2 something that causes gladness or happiness: *"a thing of beauty is a joy forever."* [< OF *joie* < L *gaudia* joys]

joy·ful (joi′fəl), *adj.* 1 glad; happy: *a joyful heart, a joyful look.* 2 causing joy: *joyful news.* —**joy′ful·ly,** *adv.* —**joy′ful·ness,** *n.*

joy·less (joi′lis), *adj.* without joy; sad; dismal: *a joyless prospect.* —**joy′less·ly,** *adv.* —**joy′less·ness,** *n.*

joy·ous (joi′əs), *adj.* joyful; glad; gay. —**joy′ous·ly,** *adv.* —**joy′ous·ness,** *n.*

joy ride, ride in an automobile for pleasure, esp. when the car is driven recklessly. —**joy rider.** —**joy riding.**

joy-ride (joi′rīd′), *v.*, **-rode, -rid·den, -rid·ing.** take a joy ride.

J.P., Justice of the Peace.

Jr., jr., Junior.

ju·bi·lance (jü′bə ləns), *n.* a rejoicing.

ju·bi·lant (jü′bə lənt), *adj.* expressing or showing joy; rejoicing. [< L *jubilans* shouting joy < *jubilum* wild shout] —**ju′bi·lant·ly,** *adv.*

ju·bi·la·tion (jü′bə lā′shən), *n.* a rejoicing; joyful celebration.

ju·bi·lee (jü′bə lē), *n.* 1 time of rejoicing or great joy: *hold a jubilee over a victory.* 2 rejoicing; great joy: *a day of jubilee.* [< OF < LL < Gk. *iobelaios* < Heb. *yōbēl,* orig., trumpet, ram('s horn)]

Ju·da·ic (jüdā′ik), **Ju·da·i·cal** (-ə kəl), *adj.* of the Jews or Judaism; Jewish.

Ju·da·ism (jü′di iz əm; -dā-), *n.* 1 the religion of the Jews. 2 the following of Jewish rules and customs.

Ju·das (jü′dəs), *n.* 1 the disciple who betrayed Christ for money. 2 an utter traitor; person treacherous enough to betray a friend. —**Ju′das·like′,** *adj.*

Jude (jüd), *n.* 1 one of the twelve disciples chosen by Jesus as his Apostles. 2 book of the New Testament.

Ju·de·a, Ju·dae·a (jü dē′ə), *n.* the S part of Palestine when it was a province of the Roman Empire.

Ju·de·an, Ju·dae·an (jü dē′ən), *adj.* 1 of Judea. 2 of the Jews. —*n.* a Jew.

judge (juj), *n.*, *v.*, **judged, judg·ing.** —*n.* 1 a government official appointed or elected to hear and decide cases in a law court. 2 person chosen to settle a dispute or decide who wins. 3 person qualified to form an opinion: *a good judge of cattle.* 4 person who decides: *let me be the judge of that.* —*v.* 1 hear and decide in a law court. 2 settle (a dispute); decide who wins (a race, contest, etc.). 3 form an opinion or estimate (of): *judge the merits of a book.* 4 think; suppose; consider: *I judged the slight to be intentional.* 5 criticize; condemn: *who can judge another?* [< OF < L *judex* < *ius* law + root of *dicere* say] —**judge′less,** *adj.* —**judge′like′,** *adj.* —**judg′er,** *n.*

judge advocate, officer who acts as a prosecutor at a court-martial.

judge·ship (juj′ship), *n.* position, duties, or term of office of a judge.

judg·ment (juj′mənt), *n.* 1 act of judging: *hall of judgment.* 2 decision given by a judge or court. 3 opinion: *it was a bad plan in his judgment.* 4 ability to form opinions; good sense.

judgment day, day of God's final judgment of humankind at the end of the world.

ju·di·ca·to·ry (jü′də kə tô′ri; -tō′-), *adj.*, *n.*, *pl.* **-ries.** —*adj.* of the administration of justice: *a judicatory tribunal.* —*n.*

administration of justice. [< LL *judicatorius,* ult. < L *judex* judge]

ju·di·ca·ture (jü′də kə chər), *n.* 1 administration of justice. 2 position, duties, or authority of a judge. 3 group of judges.

ju·di·cial (jü dish′əl), *adj.* 1 of or having to do with courts, judges, or the administration of justice: *judicial proceedings.* 2 ordered, permitted, or enforced by a judge or a court: *a judicial separation.* 3 of or suitable for a judge: *a judicial mind.* [< L *judicialis,* ult. < *judex* judge] —**ju·di′cial·ly,** *adv.*

ju·di·ci·ar·y (jü dish′i er′i), *n.*, *pl.* **-ar·ies,** *adj.* —*n.* 1 branch of government that administers justice. 2 judges of a country, state, or city. —*adj.* of or having to do with judges or justice.

ju·di·cious (jü dish′əs), *adj.* having, using, or showing good judgment; wise; sensible: *a judicious historian considers facts carefully.* [< F *judicieux,* ult. < L *judex* judge] —**ju·di′cious·ly,** *adv.* —**ju·di′cious·ness,** *n.*

ju·do (jü′dō), *n.* =jujitsu.

jug (jug), *n.* container for liquids with a narrow neck and a handle. [prob. orig. proper name, alter. of *Joan,* fem. of *John*]

jug·gle (jug′əl), *v.*, **-gled, -gling.** 1 do tricks that require skill of hand or eye. 2 do such tricks with: *juggle three balls in the air.* 3 change by trickery: *juggle accounts to hide thefts.* [< OF *jogler* < L *joculari* to joke, ult. < *jocus* jest] —**jug′gler,** *n.*

jug·gler·y (jug′lər i), *n.*, *pl.* **-gler·ies.** 1 sleight of hand. 2 trickery; fraud.

jug·u·lar (jug′yə lər; jü′gyə-), *adj.* 1 of the neck or throat. 2 of the jugular vein. 3 *Fig.* cutthroat; murderous. —*n.* jugular vein. [< NL, < L *jugulum* collarbone, dim. of *jugum* yoke]

jugular vein, one of the two large veins in the neck that return blood from the head to the heart.

juice (jüs), *n.* 1 liquid in fruits, vegetables, and meats. 2 liquid in the body. The gastric juices of the stomach help to digest food. 3 *Informal.* electricity. **juice up,** *Slang.* enliven. **stew in one's own juice,** *Informal.* suffer the consequences of one's own actions. [< OF < L *jus* broth] —**juice′less,** *adj.*

juice box, paper container that holds a single portion of processed juice.

juiced (jüst), *adj.* 1 having electric power. 2 *Fig.* stimulated; pumped up. 3 *Slang.* drunk.

juic·er (jü′sər), *n.* small appliance used to extract juice from fruits and vegetables.

juic·y (jüs′i), *adj.*, **juic·i·er, juic·i·est.** 1 full of juice; having much juice. 2 full of interest; lively. —**juic′i·ly,** *adv.* —**juic′i·ness,** *n.*

ju·jit·su, ju·jut·su (jü jit′sü), *n.* Japanese method of wrestling or fighting without weapons that uses the strength and weight of an opponent to his or her disadvantage. [< Jap., < *jū* soft + *jutsu* art]

juke box (jük), a machine that plays recorded music when coins or bills are deposited in a slot.

Jul., July. Also, **Jy.**

ju·lep (jü′ləp), *n.* drink made of whiskey or brandy, sugar, crushed ice, and fresh mint. [< F < Ar. < Pers. *gulāb,* orig., rose water]

Jul·ian (jül′yən), *adj.* of Julius Caesar.

Julian calendar, calendar in which the average length of a year was 365¼ days. It was introduced by Julius Caesar in 46 B.C.

ju·li·enne (jü′li en′), *adj.* cut in thin strips or small pieces, as potatoes.

Ju·li·et (jü′li et; –ət), *n.* the young heroine of Shakespeare's play *Romeo and Juliet.*

Jul·ius Cae·sar (jül′yəs sē′zər). See **Caesar.**

Ju·ly (jù lī), *n., pl.* **–lies.** the seventh month of the year. It has 31 days. [after *Julius* Caesar]

jum·ble (jum′bəl), *v.,* **–bled, –bling,** *n.* —*v.* mix; confuse: *things strangely jumbled together.* —*n.* a confused mixture. [? imit.]

jum·bo (jum′bō), *n., pl.* **–bos,** *adj.* —*n.* a big, clumsy person, animal, or thing. —*adj.* very big.

jumbo jet, large aircraft that can carry several hundred passengers.

jump (jump), *v.* **1** spring from the ground; leap; bound: *jump up and down..* **2** cause to jump: *jump a horse over a fence.* **3** give a sudden start or jerk: *you made me jump.* **4** rise suddenly: *prices jumped.* **5** in checkers, pass over and capture (an opponent's piece). **6** evade by running away: *jump bail.* —*n.* **1** spring from the ground; leap; bound. **2** thing to be jumped over. **3** distance jumped. **4** a sudden nervous start or jerk. **5** a sudden rise. **6** in checkers, move made to capture an opponent's piece.

get or **have the jump on,** get or have an advantage over.

jump a claim, seize a piece of land claimed by another.

jump at, accept eagerly and quickly.

jump on, blame; scold; criticize. [prob. imit.]

jump cables or **jumper cables,** electric cables used to start the engine of a vehicle with a dead battery by connecting to a live battery.

jump·er[1] (jump′ər), *n.* one that jumps.

jump·er[2] (jump′ər), *n.* **1** a loose jacket. **2** a one-piece dress without sleeves, worn over a blouse. [< *jump* short coat, ? alter. of F *juppe,* ult. < Ar. *jubbah* long open coat]

jumping bean, seed of a Mexican plant containing a larva whose movements cause the seed to jump.

jumping jack, toy man or animal that can be made to jump by pulling a string.

jump shot, in basketball, a shot to the basket made while jumping.

jump-start (jump′stärt′), *v.* **1 a** start an engine in a vehicle by connecting cables

to the battery from an outside source of electricity. **b** start an engine in a vehicle by making the engine turn over while the vehicle is being pushed. **2** *Fig.* start an enterprise or undertaking by extra effort or help.

jump suit or **jump·suit** (jump′süt′), *n.* **1** outfit worn by parachutists. **2** informal or casual one-piece garment resembling a parachutist's outfit.

jump·y (jump′i), *adj.* **jump·i·er, jump·i·est. 1** moving by jumps; making sudden, sharp jerks. **2** easily excited or frightened; nervous. —**jump′i·ness,** *n.*

Jun., **1** June. **2** Also, **Jr.** Junior.

Junc. or **junc.,** junction.

jun·co (jung′kō), *n., pl.* **–cos.** any of several small North American finches often seen in flocks during the winter. [< Sp. < L *juncus* reed]

junc·tion (jungk′shən), *n.* **1** a joining or being joined: *the junction of opposing forces.* **2** place where things join: *highway junction; electrical junction.*

junc·ture (jungk′chər), *n.* **1** point of time. **2** state of affairs, often a crisis. **3** a joining or being joined; junction. [< L *junctura.* Doublet of JOINTURE.]

June (jün), *n.* the sixth month of the year. It has 30 days. [< L *Junius,* a Roman gens]

Ju·neau (jü′nō), *n.* capital of Alaska, in the SE part.

June bug or **beetle,** a large brown beetle of the N United States that appears in June.

jun·gle (jung′gəl), *n.* **1** a wild land thickly overgrown with bushes, vines, trees, etc. **2** a tangled mass. [< Hind. *jangal* < Skt. *jangala* desert]

jungle gym, a framework of ladders and bars for children to climb and swing from.

jun·ior (jün′yər), *adj.* **1** the younger: *John Parker, Junior, son of John Parker.* **2** of lower position, rank, or standing; of more recent appointment: *a junior partner.* **3** of or having to do with juniors in high school or college. —*n.* **1** a younger person. **2** person of lower rank or standing; person of more recent appointment. **3** student in the third year of high school or college. [< L, compar. of *juvenis* young]

junior college, school giving only the first two years of a regular four-year college course.

junior high school, school attended after elementary school, usually consisting of grades 7, 8, and 9.

ju·ni·per (jü′nə pər), *n.* an evergreen shrub or tree with small berrylike cones. [< L *juniperus*]

junk[1] (jungk), *n.* **1** old metal, paper, rags, etc. **2** rubbish; trash. —*v.* throw away or discard as junk.

junk[2] (jungk), *n.* a Chinese sailing ship. [< Pg. *junco,* prob. ult. < Javanese *jong*]

junk art, 1 art, esp. sculpture, made from scrap metal or other cast-off materials. **2** the art of making such works. —**junk artist.**

junk DNA, stretch of DNA on the genome between genes; intron.

jun·ket (jung′kit), *n.* **1** curdled milk, sweetened and flavored. **2** pleasure trip. **3** trip taken by an official at the expense of the government. —*v.* go on a junket. [prob. < dial. OF *jonquette* basket < *jonc* reed < L *juncus*] —**jun′ket·er,** *n.*

junk food, food with little nutritional value.

junk·ie (jung′ki), *n. Informal.* **1** drug addict. **2** *Fig.* any kind of addict: *fashion junkie.*

junk mail, third-class mail; bulk-rate advertising mail.

junk·man (jungk′man′), *n., pl.* **–men.** man who buys and sells old metal, paper, rags, etc.

jun·ta (jun′tə), *n.* **1** revolutionary military governing council. **2** a Spanish or Latin-American council for deliberation or administration. **3** =junto. [< Sp., ult. < L *jungere* join]

jun·to (jun′tō), *n., pl.* **–tos.** a political faction or group, sometimes of a revolutionary character: *Benjamin Franklin's Philadelphia junto.* **2** =junta. [alter. of *junta*]

Ju·pi·ter (jü′pə tər), *n.* the largest planet.

Ju·ras·sic (jù ras′ik), *n.* **1** geological period when birds first appeared. **2** rocks of this period. —*adj.* of this period.

ju·rid·i·cal (jù rid′ə kəl), **ju·rid·ic** (–ik), *adj.* **1** having to do with the administration of justice. **2** of law; legal. [< L, ult. < *jus* law + *dicere* say] —**ju·rid′i·cal·ly,** *adv.*

ju·ris·dic·tion (jür′is dik′shən), *n.* **1** right or power of administering law or justice. **2** authority; power; control. **3** extent of authority: *the judge ruled that the case was not within his jurisdiction.* [< L, ult. < *jus* law + *dicere* say] —**ju′ris·dic′tion·al,** *adj.* —**ju′ris·dic′tion·al·ly,** *adv.*

ju·ris·pru·dence (jür′is prü′dəns), *n.* **1** science or philosophy of law. **2** system of laws. **3** branch of law: *medical jurisprudence.* [< L, < *jus* law + *prudentia* prudence] —**ju′ris·pru·den′tial,** *adj.*

ju·rist (jür′ist), *n.* **1** expert in law. **2** a learned writer on law. [< Med.L *jurista* < L *jus* law]

ju·ris·tic (jù ris′tik), *adj.* of or having to do with jurists or jurisprudence; relating to law. —**ju·ris′ti·cal·ly,** *adv.*

ju·ror (jür′ər), *n.* member of a jury.

ju·ry[1] (jür′i), *n., pl.* **ju·ries. 1** group of persons selected to hear evidence in a law court and sworn to give a decision in accordance with the evidence presented to them. **2** group of persons chosen to give a judgment or to decide a contest and award prizes. [< AF *jurie,* ult. < L *jurare* swear] —**ju′ry·less,** *adj.*

ju·ry[2] (jür′i), *adj.* for temporary use on a ship; makeshift. [prob. ult. < OF *ajurie* help, ult. < L *ad–* + *juvare* aid]

ju·ry·man (jür′i mən), *n., pl.* **–men.** =juror.

just (just), *adj.* **1** right; fair: *a just price.* **2** deserved; merited; well-founded: *just* *anger, a just reward.* **3** lawful: *a just claim.* **4** true; correct: *a just description, just weights.* —*adv.* **1** exactly: *just a pound.* **2** a very little while ago: *he has just gone.* **3** barely: *it just missed the mark.* **4** only; merely: *just an ordinary man.*

just now, a only a short time ago. **b** at present; at this time. [< L *justus* upright < *jus* right] —**just′ly,** *adv.* —**just′ness,** *n.*

jus·tice (jus′tis), *n.* **1** fair dealing: *have a sense of justice.* **2** fairness; rightfulness; well-founded reason: *uphold the justice of our cause, complain with justice.* **3** administration of law; trial and judgment by process of law: *a court of justice.* **4** judge: *the justices of the U.S. Supreme Court.*

bring a person to justice, do what is necessary so that a person will be punished for a crime.

do justice to, a treat fairly. **b** show proper appreciation for.

do oneself justice, do as well as one really can do. [< OF < L *justitia*] —**jus′tice·ship,** *n.*

justice of the peace, a local magistrate who tries minor cases, administers oaths, performs civil marriages, etc.

jus·ti·fi·a·ble (jus′tə fī′ə bəl), *adj.* capable of being justified; that can be shown to be just and right; defensible. —**jus′ti·fi′a·bil′i·ty, jus′ti·fi′a·ble·ness,** *n.* —**jus′ti·fi′a·bly,** *adv.*

jus·ti·fi·ca·tion (jus′tə fə kā′shən), *n.* **1** a justifying or being justified. **2** fact or circumstance that justifies; good reason.

jus·ti·fy (jus′tə fī), *v.,* **–fied, –fy·ing. 1** show to be just or right; give a good reason for: *the fine quality of the cloth justifies its high price.* **2** clear of blame or guilt. —**jus′ti·fi′er,** *n.*

jut (jut), *v.,* **jut·ted, jut·ting,** *n.* —*v.* stick out; project: *the pier juts out into the water.* —*n.* part that sticks out; projection. [var. of *jet*[1]]

jute (jüt), *n.* strong fiber used for making coarse sacks, burlap, rope, etc., obtained from two tropical plants. [< Bengali *jhōto* < Skt. *jūta* mat of hair] —**jute′like′,** *adj.*

Jute (jüt), *n.* member of a Germanic tribe. Some of the Jutes invaded and settled in SE Britain in the fifth century A.D. —**Jut′ish,** *adj.*

Jut·land (jut′lənd), *n.* peninsula of Denmark.

juv., juvenile.

ju·ve·nile (jü′və nəl; –nīl), *adj.* **1** young; youthful; childish. **2** of or for young people: *juvenile books.* —*n.* **1** a young person. **2** actor who plays youthful parts. [< L, < *juvenis* young] —**ju′ve·nile·ly,** *adv.* —**ju′ve·nile·ness, ju′ve·nil′i·ty,** *n.*

juvenile court, law court where cases involving boys and girls are heard.

juvenile delinquent, young person, usually less than 18 years old, who has committed a legal offense.

jux·ta·pose (juks′tə pōz′), *v.,* **–posed, –pos·ing.** put close together; place side by side. [< F, < L *juxta* beside + F *poser* place, POSE] —**jux′ta·po·si′tion,** *n.*

Jy., July. Also, **Jul.**

K, k (kā), *n., pl.* **K's; k's.** the 11th letter of the alphabet.

K[1], potassium.

K[2] (kā), *n.* **1** thousand; 1000. **2** unit of computer memory equal to a binary thousand (1024 bits). [< *kilo–,* prefix for 1000]

K or **K., 1** king; kings. **2** Knight.

k., 1 karat. **2** kilogram. **3** knot.

Kaa·ba (kä′bə), *n.* the sacred shrine of Muslims, a small structure, containing a black stone, in the great mosque at Mecca.

ka·bob (kə bob′), *n.* in India, roast meat. **kabobs,** small pieces of meat and sometimes vegetables, seasoned and roasted on a skewer. [< Hind. *kabāb* < Ar.]

Ka·bu·ki or **ka·bu·ki** (kä bü′ki), *n.* stylized Japanese drama from the 1600's that includes song and dance, extravagant acting, and rich costuming. [< Jap. *kabuki* < *ka* song + *bu* dance + *ki* art]

Ka·bul (kä′bûl), *n.* capital of Afghanistan.

ka·di (kä′di; kä′–), *n., pl.* **–dis.** cadi.

kad·dish (kä′dish), *n.* Also, **Kaddish.** Hebrew prayer of mourning for a deceased family member. [< Ar. *qaddīsh* holy]

Ka·di·ak bear (kä′dē ak; kad′ē–), =Kodiak bear.

Kaf·fir, Kaf·ir (kaf′ər), *n.* **1** member of a Bantu-speaking people in southern Africa. **2** their language. **3 kaffir, kafir,** =kaffir corn.

kaffir corn, kafir corn, a sorghum grown for grain and forage in dry regions.

kaf·tan (kaf′tən; käf tän′), *n.* =caftan.

Kai·ser, kai·ser (kī′zər), *n.* **1** title of the rulers of Germany from 1871 to 1918. **2** title of the rulers of Austria from 1804 to 1918. **3** title of the rulers of the Holy Roman Empire from A.D. 962 to 1806. [< G, < Julius *Caesar*] —**Kai′ser·ship, kai′ser·ship,** *n.*

kale, kail (kāl), *n.* any of various kinds of cabbage that have loose leaves instead of a compact head. Kale looks somewhat like spinach. [var. of *cole*]

ka·lei·do·scope (kə lī′də skōp), *n.* **1** tube containing bits of colored glass and two mirrors. As it is turned, it reflects continually changing patterns. **2** anything that changes continually; a continually changing pattern. [< Gk. *kalos* pretty + *eidos* shape + E –*scope* instrument of viewing < Gk. *skopein* look at] —**ka·lei′do·scop′ic, ka·lei′do·scop′i·cal,** *adj.* —**ka·lei′do·scop′i·cal·ly,** *adv.*

kal·ends (kal′əndz), *n.pl.* =calends.

Kam·chat·ka (kam chat′kə), *n.* peninsula of NE Asia between the Sea of Okhotsk and Bering Sea.

kame (kām), *n.* hill or ridge composed of detritus deposited by a glacier. [< *comb* (special use)]

Ka·nak·a (kə nak′ə; kan′ə kə), *n.* **1** native of Hawaii. **2** native of any island in the S Pacific; South Sea islander. [< Hawaiian, man]

kan·ga·roo[1] (kang′gə rü′), *n., pl.* **–roos** or (*esp. collectively*) **–roo.** mammal of Australia and New Guinea having small forelegs and very strong hind legs, which give it great leaping power. The female kangaroo has a pouch in front in which she carries her young. [prob. < Australian lang.] —**kan′ga·roo′like′,** *adj.*

kan·ga·roo[2] (kang′gə rü′), *adj.* unauthorized; irregular: *a kangaroo court.*

kangaroo rat, a small, mouselike animal of the desert regions of the U.S. and Mexico.

Kans., Kan., Kansas.

Kan·sas (kan′zəs), *n.* a Middle Western state of the United States. —**Kan′san,** *adj., n.*

ka·o·lin, ka·o·line (kā′ə lin), *n.* a fine white clay, used in making porcelain. [< F < Chinese *Kao-ling,* mountain in China]

ka·on (kā′on), *n.* =K-meson.

ka·pok (kā′pok; kap′ək), *n.* the silky fibers around the seeds of a tropical tree, used for stuffing pillows and mattresses. [< Malay *kapoq*]

kap·pa (kap′ə), *n.* the tenth letter (K, κ) of the Greek alphabet.

Ka·ra·chi (kə rä′chi), *n.* former capital of Pakistan, in the W part.

kar·a·kul (kar′ə kəl), *n.* **1** variety of Russian or Asiatic sheep. **2** =caracul. [< *Kara Kul,* lake in Turkestan.

kar·a·o·ke (kar′ē ō′kē), *n.* entertainment at a bar or club, in which patrons sing to the accompaniment of recorded music. [< Jap. *karaoke* empty orchestra]

kar·at (kar′ət), *n.* =carat.

ka·ra·te (kä rä′tā; –ti), *n.* Japanese method of fighting without weapons by striking certain vulnerable parts of the opponent's body. [< Jap.]

ka·ra·te-chop (kä rä′ti chop′), *n. v.,* **–chopped, chop·ping.** —*n.* sharp blow delivered at an angle by the hand, in karate. —*v.* strike with such a blow.

Ka·re·li·a (kə rē′li ə; –rēl′yə), *n.* region of NW Russia, next to Finland.

kar·ma (kär′mə), *n.* **1** in Buddhism and Hinduism, all of the deeds and thoughts of a person's life, believed to determine the quality of an individual's next existence. **2** fate; destiny; kismet. **3** good or bad feelings that are apparently given off by someone or something. [< Skt. *karma*] —**kar′mic,** *adj.*

Kash·mir (kash mir′; kash′mir), *n.* district in N India. Also, **Cashmere.**

Kat·man·du (kät′män dü′), *n.* capital of Nepal.

kar·y·o·type (kar′ē ō tīp′), *n., v.,* **–typed, –typ·ing.** —*n.* **1** characteristics of a set of chromosomes. **2** group of chromosome sets that share one or more characteristics. —*v.* classify chromosome sets by their characteristics. [< *karyo–* cell nucleus + *type*]

Kas·bah (käz bä), *n.* Arab quarter, esp. its shops and markets, in a N African city.

ka·ty·did (kā′ti did), *n.* a large green insect somewhat like a grasshopper. The male makes a shrill noise sounding like "Katy did, Katy didn't."

Kau·ai (kou ī′), *n.* the fourth largest island of Hawaii.

Kau·nas (kou′näs), *n.* capital of Lithuania.

kau·ri, kau·ry (kou′ri), *n., pl.* **–ris; –ries. 1** a tall pine tree that grows in New Zealand. **2** its wood. **3** a resin obtained from it that is used in varnish. [< Maori]

kay·ak (kī′ak), *n.* **1** a covered canoe made of fabric stretched over a light frame with an opening in the middle for one person. **2** a similar canoe used by the Inuit, made of bones and skins. Also, **kaiak.** [< Eskimo (Greenland) *kajakka,* lit. small boat of skins]

Ka·zakh·stan (kə zäk′stän), *n.* country in C Asia on the Caspian Sea.

ka·zoo (kə zü′), *n.* toy instrument which is a tube closed at one end that makes a buzzing sound when it is hummed into. [*imit.*]

kc., kilocycle; kilocycles.

K.C., 1 King's Counsel. **2** Knights of Columbus.

ke·a (kā′ə; kē′ə), *n.* a large, greenish parrot of New Zealand, that kills sheep to feed upon their fat. [< Maori]

ke·bab (kə bob′), *n.* =kabob.

kedge (kej), *v.,* **kedged, kedg·ing,** *n.* —*v.* move (a ship, etc.) by pulling on a rope attached to an anchor that has been dropped some distance away. —*n.* Also, **kedge anchor.** a small anchor used in kedging a boat, etc.

keel (kēl), *n.* the main timber or steel piece that extends the whole length of the bottom of a ship or boat.

on an even keel, horizontal.

keel over, a turn over or upside down; upset. **b** fall over suddenly. **c** faint. [< Scand. *kjölr*]

keel·son (kel′sən; kēl′–), *n.* beam or line of timbers or iron plates fastened along the top of a ship's keel to strengthen it. Also, **kelson.**

keen[1] (kēn) *adj.* **1** sharp; piercing; cutting: *keen wind, keen wit.* **2** able to do its work quickly and accurately: *a keen mind.* **3** full of enthusiasm; eager: *keen about sailing.* [< OE *cēne*] —**keen′ly,** *adv.* —**keen′ness,** *n.*

keen[2] (ken), *n.* a wailing lament for the dead. —*v.* wail; lament. [< Irish *caoine*] —**keen′er,** *n.*

keep (kēp), *v.,* **kept, keep·ing,** *n.* —*v.* **1** have for a long time or forever: *keep a job.* **2** have and not let go: *keep a secret.* **3** take care of: *keep chickens.* **4** have; hold: *keep a thing in mind.* **5** hold back; prevent: *keep from laughing; what is keeping her from coming?* **6** continue; remain; stay: *keep warm under a blanket.* **7** celebrate: *keep Christmas.* —*n.* **1** food and a place to sleep: *he works for his keep.* **2** the strongest part of a castle or fort.

for keeps, a forever: *mine for keeps.* **b** to be kept: *play for keeps.*

keep at, work at; persist.

keep back, a restrain. **b** *Fig.* withhold: *keep back an opinion.*

keep books, make a record of all money received or spent.

keep company, be together.

keep on, continue.

keep to, a follow closely; adhere to: *kept to the plan.* **b** abide by: *keep to a bargain.*

keep up, a continue: *keep up a business.* **b** maintain in good condition: *keep up the garden.* **c** not fall behind: *keep up a diary.*

keep up with, a not fall behind. **b** stay up-to-date: *keep up with the news.* [OE *cēpan* observe]

keep·er (kēp′ər), *n.* **1** person or thing that keeps: *a keeper of promises.* **2** someone or something worth keeping. **3** guard; watchman. **4** guardian; protector. —**keep′er·less,** *adj.*

keep·ing (kēp′ing), *n.* **1** charge; maintenance: *keeping a pet requires care and feeding.* **2** celebration; observance: *the keeping of Thanksgiving Day.* **3** agreement; harmony: *actions are in keeping with promises.* **4** being kept for future use; preservation.

keep·sake (kēp′sāk′), *n.* thing kept in memory of the giver.

keg (keg), *n.* a small barrel, usually holding less than 10 gallons. [< Scand. *kaggi*]

kelp (kelp), *n.* **1** a large, tough, brown seaweed that contains iodine. **2** ashes of seaweed.

kel·pie, kel·py (kel′pi), *n., pl.* –**pies.** a water spirit, usually in the form of a horse, supposed to drown people or warn them of drowning.

kel·son (kel′sən), *n.* =keelson.

Kelt (kelt), *n.* =Celt. —**Kelt′ic,** *adj., n.*

ken (ken), *n.* **1** range of sight. **2** range of knowledge: *what happens on Mars is still beyond our ken.* [OE *cennan* make declaration < *cann* know, can[1]]

Ken., Kentucky.

Ken·ne·dy (ken′ə di), *n.* **John F.,** 1917–63, the 35th president of the United States, 1961–63.

ken·nel (ken′el), *n., v.,* –**neled, –nel·ing.** —*n.* **1** house for a dog or dogs. **2** Often, **kennels.** place where dogs are bred. **3** pack of dogs. —*v.* **1** put or keep in a kennel. **2** take shelter or lodge in a kennel. [< OF *kenel,* ult. < L *canis* dog]

Kent (kent), *n.* **1** county in SE England. **2** an early English kingdom.

Kent·ish (ken′tish), *adj.* of Kent or its people. —*n.* an Anglo-Saxon dialect spoke in the kingdom of Kent.

Ken·tuck·y (kən tuk′i), *n.* a S state of the United States. —**Ken·tuck′i·an,** *adj., n.*

Ken·ya (ken′yə; kēn′yə), *n.* country in E Africa. —**Ken′yan,** *adj., n.*

kept (kept), *v.* pt. and pp. of **keep.**

ker·a·tin (ker′ə tin), *n.* a complex protein, the chief constituent of horn, nails, hair, feathers, etc. [< Gk. *keras* horn]

ker·chief (kėr′chif), *n.* **1** piece of cloth worn over the head or around the neck. **2** =handkerchief. [< OF, < *couvrir* COVER + *chief* head (< L *caput*)]

kerf (kėrf), *n.* **1** cut made by saw, axe, etc. **2** something cut off. [OE *cyrf* < *ceorfan* carve]

ker·fuf·fle (kər fuf′əl), *n. Informal.* minor disagreement or controversy. [? < Scot. *curfuffle* < Scot. Gaelic *car* twist, bend + Scot. *fuffle* disorder]

ker·nel (kėr′nəl), *n.* **1** the softer part inside the hard shell of a nut or inside the stone of a fruit. **2** grain or seed like wheat or corn. **3** the central or most important part. [< OE *cyrnel* < *corn* seed, grain] —**ker′nel·less,** *adj.*

ker·o·sene (ker′ə sēn; ker′ə sēn′), *n.* a thin oil produced by distilling petroleum; coal oil. It is used in lamps and stoves. [< Gk. *kērós* wax]

kes·trel (kes′trəl), *n.* a small European falcon. [prob. < OF *cresserelle,* ult. < L *crista* crest]

ketch (kech), *n.* **1** a fore-and-aft-rigged sailing ship with a large mainmast toward the bow and a smaller mast toward the stern. **2** formerly, a sturdy sailing vessel with two masts. [? < *catch*]

ketch·up (kech′əp), *n.* sauce used with meat, fish, etc. Tomato ketchup is made of tomatoes, onions, salt, sugar, and spices. Also, **catchup, catsup.**

ket·tle (ket′əl), *n.* **1** a metal container for boiling liquids, cooking fruit, etc. **2** =teakettle.

kettle of fish, awkward state of affairs; mess; muddle. [< L *catillus,* dim. of *catinus* vessel]

ket·tle·drum (ket′əl drum′), *n.* drum consisting of a hollow brass or copper hemisphere and a parchment top.

key[1] (kē), *n., pl.* **keys,** *adj., v.* **keyed, key·ing.** —*n.* **1** instrument that locks and unlocks; thing that turns or opens: *key to a door.* **2** thing that explains or answers: *key to a puzzle.* **3** place that commands or gives control of a sea, a district, etc., because of its position: *Gibraltar is the key to the Mediterranean.* **4** an important or essential person, thing, etc. **5** one of a set of parts pressed in playing a piano and in using a computer. **6** scale of notes in music related to one another: *key of B flat.* —*adj.* controlling; very important: *the key industries of a nation.* —*v.* **1** regulate the pitch of: *key a piano up to concert pitch.* **2** adjust; attune: *key a speech to an audience.*

key up, raise the courage or nerve of (to the point of doing something): *players keyed up for the big game.* [OE *cæg*]

key[2] (kē), *n., pl.* **keys.** a low island; reef. [< Sp. < F *quai* < Celtic]

key·board (kē′bôrd′; –bōrd′), *n.* set of keys in a piano, organ, computer, etc.

keyed (kēd), *adj.* **1** having keys: *a keyed flute.* **2** set or pitched in a particular key. **3** fastened or strengthened with a key.

keyed-up (kēd′up′), *adj.* excited; agitated.

key·hole (kē′hōl′), *n.* opening in a lock through which a key is inserted to turn the lock.

key·note (kē′nōt′), *n., v.,* –**not·ed, –not·ing.** —*n.* **1** note on which a scale of tones in music is based. **2** main idea; guiding principle. —*v.* give the keynote speech of.

keynote speech, speech, usually at a political gathering, that presents the principal issues in which those present are interested.

key·pad (kē′pad′), *n.* buttons, arranged as on a calculator, cell phone, telephone, etc.

key signature, sharps or flats placed after the clef at the beginning of a staff of music to indicate the key.

key·stone (kē′stōn′), *n.* **1** middle stone at the top of an arch, holding the other stones or pieces in place. **2** part on which other associated parts depend; essential principle.

key word, word that serves as a guide to find other words, topics, etc., in a list.

kg., kilogram; kilograms.

khak·i (kak′i; kä′ki), *adj., n., pl.* **khak·is.** —*adj.* dull yellowish-brown. —*n.* **1** a dull, yellowish brown. **2** a stout twilled cloth of this color. **3** uniform or uniforms made of this cloth. [< Pers., orig., dusty < *khāk* dust]

kha·lif (kā′lif; kal′if), *n.* =caliph.

khan[1] (kän; kan), *n.* title of a ruler among Tartar or Mongol tribes, or of the emperor of China during the Middle Ages. [< Turk.]

khan[2] (kän; kan), *n.* in Turkey and nearby countries, an inn or place to shelter. [< Pers.]

Khu·fu (kü′fü), *n.* =Cheops.

Khy·ber Pass (kī′bər), a mountain pass between Pakistan and Afghanistan.

kHz, kilohertz.

kib·butz (ki büts′), *n., pl.* **kib·butz·im.** *Hebrew.* a collective farm in Israel.

kib·itz (kib′its), *v.* look on as an outsider and offer unwanted advice. [< Yiddish < colloq. G *kiebitzen* look on at cards < *kiebitz* an annoying onlooker < *kiebetz* plover]

kib·itz·er (kib′it sər), *n.* **1** person offering unwanted advice. **2** meddler. [< *kibitz*]

kick (kik), *v.* **1** strike out with the foot: *the horse kicked the boy.* **2** drive, force, or move by kicking: *kick a ball, kick a goal.* **3** spring back when fired: *this shotgun kicks.* **4** complain; object; grumble. —*n.* **1** act of kicking. **2** recoil of a gun. **3** complaint. **4** thrill, excitement.

kick around, *Informal.* **a** abuse. **b** discuss: *kick around some ideas.*

kick back, *Informal.* **a** relax; do nothing. **b** recoil suddenly and unexpectedly. **c** return a portion of money received as a fee.

kick in, pay what is due or expected.

kick off, put a football in play with a kick.

kick oneself, reproach oneself.

kick up, start; cause.

kick upstairs, *Informal.* promote to a better job. —**kick′er,** *n.*

kick·back (kik′bak′), *n.* amount or portion returned, esp. as a fee.

kick·ball (kik′bôl′), *n.* children's game similar to baseball, but played with a large ball which is kicked, rather than a small ball hit with a bat.

kick·off (kik′ôf′; –of′), *n.* kick that puts a football in a play.

kick·stand (kik′stand′), *n.* metal rod attached to the frame of a bicycle, motor scooter, etc., that keeps the vehicle upright when it is not in use.

kick·y (kik′i), *adj. Informal.* interesting; exciting.

kid[1] (kid), *n.* **1** a young goat. **2** leather made from the skin of young goats, used for gloves and shoes. **3** child. [< Scand. (Dan.)]

kid[2] (kid), *v.,* **kid·ded, kid·ding.** tease playfully; talk jokingly. [? < *kid*[1] in sense of "treat as a child"] —**kid′der,** *n.*

kid·nap (kid′nap), *v.,* **–napped, –nap·ping.** steal (a child); carry off by force; seize and hold against the will by force of fraud. [< *kid*[1] child + *nap* snatch away] —**kid′nap·per,** *n.*

kid·ney (kid′ni), *n., pl.* **–neys. 1** one of the pair of organs in the body that separate waste matter and water from the blood and pass them off through the bladder as urine. **2** kidney or kidneys of an animal, cooked for food. **3** nature; kind; sort. [? < *kiden–,* of uncert. meaning + *ey* egg] —**kid′ney·like′,** *adj.*

kidney bean, 1 a kidney-shaped bean. **2** plant that it grows on. **3** the scarlet runner, a bean that has red flowers.

Kil·i·man·ja·ro (kil′i män jä′rō), *n.* **Mount,** the highest mountain in Africa.

kill[1] (kil), *v.* **1** put to death; cause the death of: *the blow killed him.* **2** put an end to; destroy: *kill odors, kill faith.* **3** cancel (a word, paragraph, item, etc.). **4** defeat or veto (a legislative bill). **5** spoil the effect of: *one color may kill another near it.* **6** use up (time). **7** overcome completely. —*n.* **1** act of killing. **2** animal killed. [ME *kyllen, cullen;* prob. akin to QUELL]

kill[2] (kil), *n. Dial.* stream. [< Du. *kil*]

kill·deer (kil′dir′), **kill·dee** (–dē′), *n., pl.* **–deers** or (*esp. collectively*) **–deer; –dees** or (*esp. collectively*) **–dee.** a small wading bird that has a loud, shrill cry, the commonest plover of North America. [imit. of its call]

killed (kild), *adj.* made inactive; unable to produce disease: *killed virus.*

kill·er (kil′ər), *n.* person, animal, or thing that kills.

killer whale, dolphin that kills and eats large fish, seals, and even whales.

kill·ing (kil′ing), *adj.* **1** deadly; destructive; fatal: *a killing frost.* **2** overpowering; exhausting. —*n. Informal.* a sudden great financial success.

kill·joy (kil′joi′), *n.* person who spoils other people's fun.

kiln (kil; kiln), *n.* furnace or oven for burning, baking, or drying something. —*v.* burn, bake, or dry in a kiln. [< L *culina* kitchen]

ki·lo (kē′lō; kil′ō), *n., pl.* **ki·los. 1** kilogram. **2** kilometer.

kilo–, *prefix.* one thousand, as in *kilogram, kilometer, kilowatt.* [< F]

kil·o·bar (kil′ə bär), *n.* unit of pressure equal to 14,500 pounds per square inch.

kil·o·bit (kil′ə bit′), *n.* unit of electronic information equal to 1000 bits.

kil·o·byte (kil′ə bīt′), *n.* unit of electronic information equal to 1024 bytes.

kil·o·cal·o·rie (kil′ə kal′ə ri), *n.* a large calorie.

kil·o·cy·cle (kil′ə sī′kəl), *n.* **1** 1000 cycles; kilohertz. **2** 1000 cycles per second.

kilog., kilogram; kilograms.

kil·o·gram (kil′ə gram), *n.* unit of mass and weight equal to 1000 grams, or 2.2046 pounds avoirdupois.

kil·o·hertz (kil′ə hèrts′), *n.* 1000 hertz, esp. in radio frequency.

kil·o·li·ter (kil′ə lē′tər), *n.* unit of capacity equal to 1000 liters, or one cubic meter; 264.17 U.S. gallons, or 1.308 cubic yards.

kil·o·me·ter (kil′ə mē′tər; kə lom′ə tər), *n.* distance equal to 1000 meters, or 3280.8 feet. —**kil′o·met′ric,** *adj.*

kil·o·ton (kil′ə tun′), *n.* a measure of atomic power equivalent to the energy released by 1000 tons of high explosive, specifically TNT. [< *kilo–* + *ton* (of explosive energy)]

kil·o·watt (kil′ə wot′), *n.* unit of power equal to 1000 watts.

kil·o·watt-hour (kil′ə wot′our′), *n.* unit of energy equal to the work done by one kilowatt acting for one hour.

kilt (kilt), *n.* a pleated skirt reaching to the knees, worn by men in the Scottish Highlands. [prob. < Scand. (Dan.) *kilte* tuck up] —**kilt′like′,** *adj.*

kil·ter (kil′tər), *n.* good condition; order: *our radio is out of kilter.*

ki·mo·no (kə mō′nə), *n., pl.* **–nos. 1** a loose outer garment held in place by a sash, worn by Japanese men and women. **2** a woman's loose dressing gown. [< Jap.]

kin (kin), *n.* **1** family or relatives; kindred. **2** family relationship; connection by birth or marriage: *what kin is she to you?* —*adj.* related. [OE *cynn*] —**kin′less,** *adj.*

–kin, *suffix.* little, as in *lambkin.* [ME]

kind[1] (kīnd), *adj.* **1** friendly; doing good: *kind words.* **2** gentle: *be kind to animals, a kind master.* [OE (*ge*)*cynde* natural < (*ge*)*cynd* kind[2]]

kind[2] (kīnd), *n.* class; sort; variety: *many kinds of candy.*

in kind, a in goods or produce, not in money. **b** in something of the same sort. **c** in characteristic quality: *difference in kind not merely in degree.*

kind of, nearly; almost; somewhat; rather.

of a kind, a of the same kind; alike. **b** of a poor or mediocre quality: *two boxes and a plank make a table of a kind.* [OE (*ge*)*cynd*]

kin·der·gar·ten (kin′dər gär′tən), *n.* school that educates children from 3 to 6 years old. [< G, < *kinder* children + *garten* garden]

kin·der·gart·ner, kin·der·gar·ten·er (kin′dər gärt′nər), *n.* **1** child who goes to kindergarten. **2** teacher in a kindergarten.

kind-heart·ed (kīnd′här′tid), *adj.* having or showing a kind heart; kindly; sympathetic. —**kind′-heart′ed·ly,** *adv.*

kin·dle (kin′dəl), *v.,* **–dled, –dling. 1** set on fire; light. **2** catch fire; begin to burn. **3** arouse; stir up: *kindle suspicion.* **4** light up; brighten: *the boy's face kindled as he told about the circus.* [prob. ult. < Scand. *kynda* kindle] —**kin′dler,** *n.*

kin·dling (kin′dling), *n.* small pieces of wood for starting a fire.

kind·ly (kīnd′li), *adj.* **–li·er, –li·est,** *adv.* —*adj.* **1** kind; friendly: *kindly faces.* **2** pleasant; agreeable: *a kindly shower.* —*adv.* **1** in a kind or friendly way. **2** pleasantly; agreeably; *he does not take kindly to criticism.* **3** cordially; heartily: *thank you kindly.* —**kind′li·ness,** *n.*

kind·ness (kīnd′nis), *n.* **1** quality of being kind; kind nature. **2** kind treatment. **3** a kind act.

kin·dred (kin′drid), *n.* **1** family or relatives. **2** family relationship; connection by birth or marriage. **3** likeness; resemblance. —*adj.* **1** related: *kindred tribes.* **2** like; similar: *we are studying about dew, frost, and kindred facts of nature.* [< *kin*]

kine (kīn), *n.pl. Archaic.* cows; cattle.

kin·e·mat·ics (kin′ə mat′iks), *n.* branch of physics that deals with the characteristics of different kinds of motion without reference to mass or to causes [< Gk. *kinema* motion < *kineein* move] —**kin′e·mat′ic, kin′e·mat′i·cal,** *adj.*

kin·es·thet·ic (kin′əs thet′ik), *adj.* of or having to do with muscular movement.

ki·net·ic (ki net′ik), *adj.* **1** of motion. **2** caused by motion. [< Gk., < *kineein* move]

ki·net·ics (ki net′iks), *n.* branch of physics that deals with the effects of forces in causing or changing the motion of objects.

kin·folk (kin′fōk′), **kin·folks** (–fōks′), *n.pl. Dial.* kinsfolk.

king (king), *n.* **1** the male ruler of a nation; male sovereign, either with absolute or limited power. **2** man supreme in a certain sphere: *a baseball king.* **3** something considered best or most powerful in its class. **4** the chief piece in chess. **5** piece that has moved entirely across the board in checkers. **6** a playing card bearing a picture of a king. [OE *cyning*] —**king′less,** *adj.*

King Arthur, hero in a group of legends about the knights of the Round Table.

king·bird (king′bėrd′), *n.* a quarrelsome bird that catches and eats insects as it flies.

king cobra, very large and poisonous cobra of SE Asia.

king crab, 1 horseshoe crab. **2** large, edible crab of the N Pacific.

king·dom (king′dəm), *n.* **1** country that is governed by a king or a queen. **2** realm; domain; province: *the mind is the kingdom of thought.* **3** one of the divisions of the natural world: *the animal kingdom, the vegetable kingdom.*

king·fish (king′fish′), *n., pl.* **–fish·es** or (*esp. collectively*) **–fish.** any of several large food fishes of the Atlantic or Pacific coast.

king·fish·er (king′fish´ər), *n.* a bright-colored bird with a large head and a strong beak. The American kingfishers eat fish; some of the European kinds eat insects.

King James Version, English translation of the Bible published in 1611.

king·ly (king′li), *adj.,* **–li·er, –li·est,** *adv.* —*adj.* **1** of a king or kings; of royal rank. **2** fit for a king: *a kingly crown.* **3** like a king; royal; noble. —*adv.* as a king does. —**king′li·ness,** *n.*

king·mak·er (king′mā´kər), *n.* **1** person responsible for someone attaining a throne. **2** powerful politician able to influence or determine the choice of a candidate for office.

king·pin (king′pin´), *n.* **1** pin in front or in the center in bowling games. **2** the most important person or thing.

king post, a vertical post between the apex of a triangular roof truss and a tie beam.

Kings (kingz), *n.pl.* **1** in the Protestant Old Testament, either of two books (I Kings or II Kings). **2** in the Roman Catholic Old Testament, one of four books that include I and II Samuel and I and II Kings.

king's English, correct English.

king's evil, scrofula, a disease that was supposed to be cured by the touch of a king.

king·ship (king′ship), *n.* **1** position, rank, or dignity of a king. **2** rule of a king; government by a king.

king·size (king′sīz´), *adj.* large or long for its kind: *a king-size bed.*

king snake, a large, harmless snake that lives in the S United States. It eats mice and rats and is supposed to kill other snakes.

king's ransom, very large amount of money.

Kings·ton (king′stən), *n.* capital and chief seaport of Jamaica.

kink (kingk), *n.* **1** a twist or curl in thread, rope, hair, etc. **2** pain or stiffness in the muscles of the neck, back, etc.; crick. **3** mental twist; queer idea; odd notion; eccentricity; whim. —*v.* form a kink; make kinks in. [prob. < Du., twist]

kin·ka·jou (king′kə jü), *n.* a yellowish-brown mammal of Central and South America. It resembles a raccoon, but has a long prehensile tail. [< F *quincajou* < Tupi]

kink·y (kingk′i), *adj.,* **kink·i·er, kink·i·est. 1** full of kinks; twisted; curly. **2** *Informal.* strange; eccentric. —**kink′i·ly,** *adv.* —**kink′i·ness,** *n.*

kins·folk (kinz′fōk´), *n.pl.* family; relatives; kin. Also, **kinfolk.**

Kin·sha·sa (kēn shä′sä), *n.* capital of the Democratic Republic of the Congo.

kin·ship (kin′ship), *n.* **1** family relationship. **2** relationship. **3** resemblance.

kins·man (kinz′mən), *n., pl.* **–men.** a male relative.

kins·wom·an (kinz′wùm´ən), *n., pl.* **–wom·en.** a female relative.

ki·osk (ki osk′), *n.* a small building with one or more sides open, used as a news-stand, a bandstand, or an opening to a subway. [< F < Turk. *kiüshk* pavilion]

kip (kip), *n.* hide of a young or under-sized animal.

kip·per (kip′ər), *v.* salt and dry or smoke (herring, salmon, etc.). —*n.* **1** herring, salmon, etc., that has been kippered. **2** male salmon or sea trout during or after the spawning season. [OE *cypera* (def. 2)]

Kir·ghiz (kir gēz′), *n., pl.* **–ghiz, –ghiz·es. 1** a member of a Mongolian people widely scattered over the western part of C Asia. **2** their language.

kirk (kėrk), *n. Scot.* church.

kis·met (kiz′met; kis′–), *n.* fate; destiny. [< Turk. < Ar. *qismat*]

kiss (kis), *v.* **1** touch with the lips as a sign of love, greeting, or respect. **2** touch gently: *a soft wind kissed the treetops.* **3** put, bring, take, etc., by kissing: *kiss away tears.* —*n.* **1** a touch with the lips. **2** a gentle touch. **3** a piece of candy of certain sorts.

kiss and tell, betray a confidence or trust.

kiss off, *Informal.* disregard; dismiss. [OE *cyssan*] —**kiss′a·ble,** *adj.* —**kiss′er,** *n.*

kit (kit), *n.* **1** equipment that a soldier carries. **2** any person's equipment packed for traveling. **3** bag, case, knapsack, etc., for carrying equipment. [prob. < MDu. *kitte*]

kitch·en (kich′ən), *n.* **1** room where food is cooked. **2** cooking department. [ult. < L *coquina* < *coquus* a cook]

kitch·en·ette (kich´ə net′), *n.* a very small, compactly arranged kitchen.

kitchen garden, garden where vegetables and fruit for a family are grown. —**kitchen gardener.**

kitch·en·ware (kich′ən wār´), *n.* kitchen utensils.

kite (kīt), *n., v.,* **kit·ed, kit·ing.** —*n.* **1** a light frame covered with paper or cloth, flown in the air on the end of a long string. **2** hawk with long pointed wings. **3** a fictitious certificate, check, contract, etc., not representing any actual transac-tion, used for raising money or sustaining credit. —*v.* obtain money or credit through kites. [OE *cȳta*]

kith and kin (kith), **1** friends and relatives. **2** kin. [OE *cȳthth* acquaintance, ult. < *cunnan* know]

kitsch or **Kitsch** (kich), *n.* artistic work that lacks merit; junk. [< G *Kitsch* trash] —**kitsch′y, Kitsch′y,** *adj.*

kit·ten (kit′ən), *n.* a young cat. [< var. of OF *cheton,* ult. < LL *cattus* cat]

kit·ten·ish (kit′ən ish), *adj.* **1** like a kitten; playful. **2** coquettish. —**kit′ten·ish·ly,** *adv.* —**kit′ten·ish·ness,** *n.*

kit·ti·wake (kit′i wāk), *n.* kind of sea gull. [imit. of its call]

kit·ty[1] (kit′i), *n., pl.* **–ties. 1** kitten. **2** pet name for a cat. [ult. < *kitten*]

kit·ty[2] (kit′i), *n., pl.* **–ties. 1** stakes in a poker game. **2** money pooled by the players in other games for some special purpose.

ki·va (kē′və), *n.* large room, often underground, used by Pueblo Indians for religious ceremonies and other communal purposes. [< Shoshonean (Hopi) *kiva* sacred chamber]

Ki·wa·nis (ki wä′nis), *n.* an international group of clubs of business and professional men.

ki·wi (kē′wi), *n., pl.* **–wis. 1** =apteryx. **2** fruit of New Zealand, somewhat like a large gooseberry. [< Maori]

K.K.K., KKK, Ku Klux Klan.

kl., kiloliter.

Klan (klan), *n.* =Ku Klux Klan.

Klans·man (klanz′mən), *n., pl.* **–men.** member of the Ku Klux Klan.

klee·nex (klē′neks), *n.* paper handker-chief. [< *Kleenex* trademark for a brand of paper handkerchief]

klep·to·ma·ni·a (klep´tə mā′ni ə), *n.* an insane impulse to steal. [< NL, < Gk. *kleptes* thief + *mania* madness] —**klep′to·ma′ni·ac,** *n.*

klieg light (klēg), a bright, hot arc light used in taking motion pictures. [after *Kliegl* brothers, the inventors]

Klon·dike (klon′dīk), *n.* region in NW Canada, along the Yukon River, famous for its gold fields.

klutz (kluts), *n.* clumsy, awkward person. [< Yiddish *klots,* lit. block, lump] —**klutz′y,** *adj.*

km., 1 kilometer; kilometers. **2** kingdom.

K-mes·on (kā′mes´on; –mē´son; –mez´-on; –mē′zon), *n.* heavy meson having a weight about 967 times that of an electron.

knack (nak), *n.* **1** special skill; power to do something easily. **2** trick; habit.

knack·er (nak′ər), *n.* person who buys useless livestock and sells their hides, hoofs, etc.

knap·sack (nap′sak´), *n.* a canvas bag for carrying clothes, equipment, etc., on the back. [< LG, < *knappen* eat + *sack* sack[1]]

knave (nāv), *n.* **1** a tricky, dishonest person; rogue; rascal. **2** the jack, a playing card with a picture of a servant or soldier on it. [OE *cnafa* boy]

knav·er·y (nāv′ər i; nāv′ri), *n., pl.* **–er·ies.** **1** behavior characteristic of a knave. **2** a tricky, dishonest act.

knav·ish (nāv′ish), *adj.* tricky; dishonest. —**knav′ish·ly,** *adv.* —**knav′ish·ness,** *n.*

knead (nēd), *v.* **1** mix (dough, clay, etc.) by pressing and squeezing, usually with one's hands: *a baker kneads dough.* **2** press and squeeze with the hands; massage. **3** make or shape by kneading. [OE *cnedan*] —**knead′er,** *n.*

knee (nē), *n., v.,* **kneed, knee·ing.** —*n.* **1** the joint between the thigh and the lower leg. **2** any joint corresponding to the human knee or elbow. **3** part of a garment covering the knee. —*v.* strike or touch with the knee.

bring to one's knees, force to yield.

on bended knee, pleading; begging. [OE *cnēo*]

knee·cap (nē′kap′), *n., v.,* **–capped, –capping.** —*n.* a flat, movable bone at the front of the knee; patella. —*v.* shoot a bullet into a person's kneecap, as a form of torture or punishment.

knee-deep (nē′dēp′), *adj.* so deep as to reach the knees.

knee-jerk (nē′jėrk), *adj. Informal. Fig.* without thought: *knee-jerk politician.*

kneel (nēl), *v.,* **knelt** (nelt) or **kneeled, kneel·ing. 1** go down on one's knees or knees. **2** remain in this position. [OE *cnēowlian < cnēo* knee] —**kneel′er,** *n.*

knee·pad (nē′pad′), *n.* pad worn around the knee for protection.

knell (nel), *n.* **1** sound of a bell rung slowly after a death or at a funeral. **2** warning sign of death, failure, etc. **3** a mournful sound. —*v.* **1** ring slowly. **2** give a warning sign of death, failure, etc. **3** make a mournful sound. [OE *cnyllan*]

knew (nü; nū), *v.* pt. of **know.**

Knick·er·bock·er (nik′ər bok′ər), *n.* descendant of the early Dutch settlers of New York.

knick·ers (nik′ərz), *n.pl.* short loose-fitting trousers gathered in at or just below the knee. [< *knicker*bockers]

knick·knack (nik′nak′), *n.* a pleasing trifle; ornament; trinket. Also, **nicknack.**

knife (nīf), *n., pl.* **knives,** *v.,* **knifed, knif·ing.** —*n.* **1** a cutting tool with a sharp-edged blade and handle. **2** a cutting blade in a tool or machine: *the knives of a lawn mower.* —*v.* **1** cut or stab with a knife. **2** try to defeat in an underhand way.

under the knife, undergoing a surgical operation. [OE *cnīf*] —**knife′less,** *adj.* —**knife′like′,** *adj.*

knife edge 1 thin, sharp edge of a knife. **2** anything very sharp and thin. **3** *Fig.* uncertain or precarious situation: *the knife edge of uncertainty.*

knight (nīt), *n.* **1** in the Middle Ages, a man raised to an honorable military rank and pledged to do good deeds. **2** in modern times, a man raised to an honorable rank. **3** piece in the game of

chess. —*v.* raise to the rank of knight. [OE *cniht* boy] —**knight′less,** *adj.*

knight-er·rant (nīt′er′ənt), *n., pl.* **knights-er·rant.** knight traveling in search of adventure.

knight·hood (nīt′hu̇d), *n.* **1** rank or dignity of a knight. **2** character or qualities of a knight. **3** knights as a group or class.

knight·ly (nīt′li), *adj.* of a knight; brave; generous; courteous; chivalrous. —*adv.* as a knight should do; bravely; generously; courteously. —**knight′li·ness,** *n.*

Knights of Columbus, a fraternal society of Roman Catholic men, founded in 1882.

Knight Templar, *pl.* **Knights Templars** *for 1;* **Knights Templar** *for 2.* **1** =Templar (def. 1). **2** member of an order of Masons in the United States.

knish (kə nish′), *n.* small pastry stuffed with potato, cheese, etc., and baked or fried. [< Yiddish *knish*]

knit (nit), *v.,* **knit·ted** or **knit, knit·ting. 1** make (cloth or article of clothing) by looping yarn or thread together with long needles: *mother is knitting a sweater.* **2** form into cloth by looping stitches, not by weaving: *jersey is cloth knitted by machine.* **3** join closely and firmly together; grow together: *a broken bone knits.* **4** draw (the brows) together in wrinkles. [OE *cnyttan < cnotta* knot] —**knit′ter,** *n.*

knit·ting (nit′ing), *n.* knitted work.

knitting needle, one of a pair of long needles used in knitting.

knit·wear (nit′wår′), *n.* clothing made from knitted fabric or knitting.

knives (nīvz), *n.* pl. of **knife.**

knob (nob), *n.* **1** a rounded lump. **2** handle of a door, drawer, etc. **3** a rounded hill or mountain. [cf. MLG *knobbe*] —**knobbed,** *adj.* —**knob′like′,** *adj.*

knob·by (nob′i), *adj.* **–bi·er, –bi·est. 1** covered with knobs. **2** rounded like a knob. —**knob′bi·ness,** *n.*

knock (nok), *v.* **1** hit: *he knocked him on the head.* **2** hit each other: *his knees knocked with fright.* **3** hit and cause to fall: *the car knocked him down.* **4** hit with a noise: *knock on a door.* **5** make a noise, esp. a rattling or pounding noise: *the engine is knocking.* **6** criticize; find fault. —*n.* **1** hit. **2** hit with a noise. **3** act of knocking. **4** sound of knocking: *she did not hear the knock at the door.* **5** sound caused by loose parts: *a knock in the engine.*

knock about, a Also, **knock around.** wander from place to place. **b** suffer harsh treatment: *knocked about by life.*

knock back, *Informal.* eat or drink, esp. without pause.

knock down, take apart.

knock off, a take off; deduct. **b** stop work. **c** make quickly; do quickly. **d** *Informal.* kill.

knock oneself out, exhaust oneself.

knock out, hit so hard as to make helpless or unconscious.

knock together, make or put together hastily. [OE *cnocian*]

knock·a·bout (nok′ə bout′), *adj.* **1** suitable for rough use. **2** noisy; boisterous.

knock·er (nok′ər), *n.* **1** person or thing that knocks. **2** knob, ring, etc., fastened on a door for use in knocking.

knock-kneed (nok′nēd′), *adj.* having legs bent inward at the knees.

knock·off (nok′ôf′; -of′), *n. Informal.* cheap imitation, esp. of an expensive product.

knock·out (nok′out′), *n.* **1** act of knocking out. **2** condition of being knocked out. **3** blow that knocks out. **4** *Informal.* a very attractive person; overwhelming or striking thing. —*adj. Informal.* that knocks out: *a knockout blow.*

knoll (nōl), *n.* a small rounded hill; mound. [OE *cnoll*]

Knos·sos (nos′əs), *n.* the ancient capital of Crete.

knot (not), *n., v.,* **knot·ted, knot·ting.** —*n.* **1** a fastening made by tying or twining together pieces of rope, cord, string, etc. **2** group; cluster: *a knot of people.* **3** a hard mass of wood formed where a branch grows out from a tree, which shows as a roundish, cross-grained piece in a board. **4** tangle, as of hair. **5** a hard lump: *a knot sometimes forms in a tired muscle.* **6 a** unit of speed used on ships; one nautical mile per hour: *the ship averaged 12 knots.* **b** nautical mile, 6080.27 feet. **7** difficulty; problem. —*v.* **1** tie or twine together in a knot. **2** tangle in knots. **3** form (a fringe) by making knots. **4** form into a hard lump. [OE *cnotta*] —**knot′less,** *adj.* —**knot′ted,** *adj.*

knot·hole (not′hōl′), *n.* hole in a board where a knot has fallen out.

knot·ty (not′i), *adj.,* **–ti·er, –ti·est. 1** full of knots: *knotty wood.* **2** difficult; puzzling: *a knotty problem.* —**knot′ti·ness,** *n.*

know (nō), *v.,* **knew, known, know·ing,** *n.* —*v.* **1** be sure of; have information about: *he knows the facts of the case.* **2** be aware of; be acquainted with; be familiar with: *I know her.* **3** have an understanding of; be skilled in: *he knows that subject.* **4** recognize; identify; distinguish: *you will know his house by the red roof.*

in the know, having inside information.

let (someone) know, tell (someone); inform. [OE *cnāwan*] —**know·er,** *n.*

know·a·ble (nō′ə bəl), *adj.* capable of being known. —**know′a·ble·ness,** *n.*

know-how (nō′hou′), *n.* ability to do something.

know·ing (nō′ing), *adj.* **1** having knowledge; well-informed. **2** clever; shrewd. **3** suggesting shrewd or secret understanding of matters: *a knowing look.* —**know′ing·ly,** *adv.* —**know′ing·ness,** *n.*

know-it-all (nō′it ôl′), *n. Informal.* someone who acts as if he or she knows everything.

knowl·edge (nol′ij), *n.* **1** what one knows: *his knowledge of the subject is limited.* **2**

all that is known or can be learned. **3** fact of knowing: *the knowledge of our victory caused great joy.* **4** act of knowing.

knowl·edge·a·ble (nol'ij ə bəl), *adj.* intelligent.

known (nōn), *v.* pp. of **know.**

know-noth·ing (nō'nuth'ing), *n.* an ignorant person.

known quantity, *Fig.* something familiar.

Knt., knight.

knuck·le (nuk'əl), *n., v.,* **-led, -ling.** —*n.* **1** finger joint; joint between a finger and the rest of the hand. **2** knee or hock joint of an animal used as food: *boiled pigs' knuckles.*

knuckle down, apply oneself earnestly; work hard.

knuckle under, submit; yield. [cf. Du. *kneukel* < *knok* bone]

knuckle ball, slow pitch in baseball, thrown from the knuckles and heel of the palm, that curves or drops, making it difficult to hit. —**knuck'le·ball'er,** *n.*

knurl (nėrl), *n.* **1** knot; knob. **2** a small ridge, as on the edge of a coin or round nut. [? < *knur* knot. Cf. MDu. *knorre.*] —**knurled,** *adj.*

knurl·y (nėr'li), *adj.,* **knurl·i·er, knurl·i·est.** =gnarled.

k.o., K.O., knockout.

ko·a·la (kō ä'lə), *n.* a gray, furry mammal of Australia that looks like a small bear and carries its young in a pouch. [< Australian lang.]

Ko·di·ak bear (kō'di ak), large brown bear found in S Alaska and nearby islands. Also, **Kadiak bear.** [< *Kodiak,* name of an island where it lives]

kohl (kōl), *n.* powder used as a cosmetic in Egypt and SW Asia to darken the eyes and the lashes. [< Ar. *kuhl* metallic powder]

kohl·ra·bi (kōl'rä'bi), *n., pl.* **-bies.** vegetable that looks somewhat like a turnip, but is a kind of cabbage. [< G < Ital. *cavoli rape,* ult. < L *caulis* cabbage + *rapa* turnip]

ko·la (kō'lə), *n.* **1** =kola nut. **2** stimulant or tonic made from kola nuts. Also, **cola.** [< African lang.]

kola nut, a bitter brownish nut of a tropical tree. It contains about 3 percent of caffeine.

Ko·mo·do dragon (kə mō'dō), very large lizard of Indonesia; dragon of Komodo; dragon lizard. [< *Komodo,* island where the lizard is found]

ko·peck, ko·pek (kō'pek), *n.* a Russian copper or bronze coin. 100 kopeks = 1 ruble. Also, **copek.** [< Russ. *kopeika*]

Ko·ran (kó rän'; –ran'; kō–), *n.* the sacred book of Muslims. It consists of revela-

tions from Allah to the prophet Muhammad and is a guide to living a Muslim life. Also, **Qur'an, Quran.** [< Ar. *qur'ān* a reading < *qara'a* to read]

Ko·re·a (kô rē'ə; kō–), *n.* a peninsula in E Asia, divided into two republics, North Korea and South Korea. —**Ko·re'an,** *adj., n.*

ko·sher (kō'sHər), *adj.* **1** right or clean according to Jewish ritualistic law. **2** all right; fine; legitimate. —*v.* prepare (food) according to the Jewish law. —*n.* food thus prepared. [< Heb. *kāshēr* proper]

ko·to (kō'tō), large Japanese instrument, somewhat like a zither, with 13 strings plucked by the fingers of both hands. [< Jap.]

kow·tow (kou'tou'), *v.* **1** kneel and touch the ground with the forehead to show deep respect, submission, or worship. **2** show slavish respect or obedience. —*n.* act of kowtowing. [< Chinese *k'o-t'ou,* lit., knock (the) head] —**kow'tow'er,** *n.*

K.P., kitchen police.

Kr. krypton.

kraal (kräl), *n.* **1** village of South African natives, protected by a fence. **2** pen for cattle or sheep in South Africa. [< Afrikaans < Pg. *curral* corral]

kra·ter (krā'tər), *n.* ancient Greek vase or bowl, with painted decoration. [< Gk. *krātēr* < *kerannýnai* mix]

K-ra·tion (kā'rash'ən; –rā'shən), *n.* ration used by troops in the field.

Krebs cycle (krebz), series of chemical reactions by which cells metabolize food into energy. [< Hans A. *Krebs* (1900–81), biochemist who discovered it]

Krem·lin (krem'lin), *n.* citadel of Moscow. The chief offices of the Russian government are in the Kremlin. [< F < Russ. *kreml* < Tatar]

Krish·na (krish'nə), *n.* one of the most important Hindu gods, one of the incarnations of Vishnu.

Kriss Krin·gle (kris' kring'gəl), Santa Claus. [< G *Christkindl, –del* Christ child, Christmas gift]

kro·na (krō'nə), *n., pl.* **-nor** (-nôr). a Swedish or Icelandic silver coin. [< Swed., Icel., crown]

kro·ne¹ (krō'ne), *n., pl.* **-ner** (-ner). a Danish or Norwegian silver coin. [< Dan., Norw., crown]

kro·ne² (krō'nə), *n., pl.* **-nen** (-nən). **1** former German gold coin. **2** former Australian silver coin. [< G, crown]

kryp·ton (krip'ton), *n.* a rare inert gas, Kr, one of the chemical elements. [< NL < Gk., neut. adj., hidden]

KS, *(zip code)* Kansas.

Kt., **1** Also, **kt.** karat. **2** kiloton. **3** Knight.

Kua·la Lum·pur (kwä'lə lùm'pùr'), capital of Malaysia.

ku·dos (kü'dos; kü'–), *n.* glory; fame. [< Gk. *kydos*]

ku·du (kü'dü), *n.* a large, grayish-brown African antelope with white stripes.

kud·zu (kùd'zü), *n.* invasive vine of the pea family, cultivated in China and Japan for its roots and as animal feed. [Jap. *kuzu*]

Ku Klux Klan (kü' kluks' klan'; kü'), **1** a secret society of white people in the S United States formed after the Civil War to regain and maintain their control. **2** a secret society founded in 1915, opposed to blacks, Jews, Catholics, and foreigners.

ku·lak (kü läk'), *n.* a Russian farmer who had poorer peasants working for him. [< Russ., lit., fist]

ku·miss (kü'mis), *n.* fermented mare's or camel's milk used as a drink by Asiatic nomads. [< Russ. < Tatar *kumiz*]

küm·mel (kim'əl), *n.* liqueur flavored with caraway seeds, anise, etc. [< G]

kum·quat (kum'kwot), *n.* **1** a yellow fruit somewhat like a small orange. **2** tree that it grows on. [< Chinese (Cantonese dial.)]

Kurd (kėrd; kùrd), *n.* member of a nomadic and warlike Muslim people living chiefly in Kurdistan. —**Kurd'ish,** *adj.*

Kur·di·stan (kėr'də stan; kùr'di stän'), *n.* an extensive plateau and mountainous region in SW Asia, now divided between Turkey, Iran, and Iraq.

Ku·rile Islands (kùr'il; kü rēl'), chain of 31 small islands N of Japan.

Ku·wait (kù wit'), *n.* **1** a country in NE Arabia. **2** its capital. —**Ku·wai'ti,** *n.*

kv or **k.v.,** kilovolt.

kvetch (kvech), *n., v.* —*n. Informal.* person who constantly complains or criticizes. —*v.* complain; criticize.

kw., kilowatt.

K.W.H., kwh, or **kwhr,** kilowatt-hour.

Kwa·ki·u·tl (kwä'ki ü'təl), *n.* **1** member of any of various groups of American Indians of the N Pacific coast. **2** their Wakashan language.

Kwan·za or **Kwan·zaa** (kwän'zə), *n.* African-American festival celebrated annually from December 25 to January 1 [< Swahili *kwanza,* inf. of *anza* to begin]

KY, *(zip code)* Kentucky.

Ky., Kentucky.

Kyu·shu (kyü'shü) *n.* a large island at the SW end of Japan.

L¹, l (el), *n., pl.* **L's; l's. 1** the 12th letter of the alphabet. **2** Roman numeral for 50.

L² (el), *n., pl.* **L's.** thing shaped like an L; extension to a building at right angles with the main part.

L, 1 Latin. **2** *Physics.* length. **3** Libra.

L., 1 Lake. **2** Late. **3** Latin. **4** Liberal.

l., 1 book. [< L *liber*] **2** latitude. **3** left. **4** length. **5** *pl.* **ll.** line. **6** liter; liters. [< L *libra; libras*]

la (lä), *n.* the sixth tone of the musical scale. [see GAMUT]

La, lanthanum.

LA, (*zip code*) Louisiana.

La., Louisiana.

lab (lab), *n.* laboratory.

Lab., Labrador.

la·bel (lā′bəl), *n., v.,* **–beled, –bel·ing, —n. 1** slip of paper or other material attached to anything and marked to show what or whose it is, or where it is to go. **2** a short phrase used to describe some person, thing, or idea. —*v.* **1** put or write a label on: *the bottle is labeled poison.* **2** put in a class; call; name: *label a man a liar.* [< OF, ? < Gmc.] —**la′bel·er,** *n.*

la·bi·al (lā′bi əl), *adj.* of the lips. [< Med.L, < L *labium* lip] —**la′bi·al·ly,** *adv.*

la·bi·ate (lā′bi āt; –it), *adj.* having one or more liplike parts.

la·bi·um (lā′bi əm), *n., pl.* **–bi·a** (–bi ə). lip or liplike part. [< L]

la·bor (lā′bər), *n.* **1** work; toil. **2** piece of work; task. **3** workers as a group. **4** childbirth. —*v.* **1** work; toil. **2** work hard. **3** elaborate with effort or in detail: *the speaker labored the point.* **4** move slowly and heavily: *the ship labored in the high waves.* **5** be burdened, troubled, or distressed: *labor under a mistake.* **6** be in childbirth. [< OF < L] —**la′bor·ing·ly,** *adv.*

lab·o·ra·to·ry (lab′rə tô′ri; –tō′–; lab′-ə rə–), *n., pl.* **–ries. 1** place where scientific work is done; room or building fitted with apparatus for conducting scientific investigations, experiments, tests, etc.: *a chemical laboratory.* **2** place fitted up for manufacturing chemicals, medicines, explosives, etc.

Labor Day, the first Monday in September, in honor of labor and laborers.

la·bored (lā′bərd), *adj.* done with effort; forced; not easy or natural: *labored politeness.*

la·bor·er (lā′bər ər), *n.* **1** worker. **2** person who does work requiring strength rather than skill or training.

la·bo·ri·ous (lə bô′ri əs; –bō′–), *adj.* **1** requiring much work; requiring hard work: *climbing a mountain is laborious.* **2** hard-working; industrious: *bees are laborious insects.* **3** labored. —**la·bo′ri·ous·ly,** *adv.* —**la·bo′ri·ous·ness,** *n.*

La·bor·ite (lā′bə rīt′), *n.* member of the Labor Party.

Labor Party, a political party organized to protect and promote the interests of workers.

la·bor-sav·ing (lā′bər sāv′ing), *adj.* that takes the place of or lessens labor: *a labor-saving device.*

labor union, association of workers to protect and promote their interests, and for dealing collectively with employers.

Labour Party, British political party. —**La′bour·ite,** *n.*

Lab·ra·dor (lab′rə dôr), *n.* peninsula in NE North America, between Hudson Bay and the Atlantic.

la·bur·num (lə bėr′nəm), *n.* a small tree or shrub with hanging clusters of yellow flowers. [< L]

lab·y·rinth (lab′ə rinth), *n.* **1** place through which it is hard to find one's way; maze. **2** a confusing, complicated arrangement or state of affairs. **3** **Labyrinth,** *Gk. Myth.* maze built by Daedalus for King Minos of Crete. **4** the internal ear. [< L < Gk. *labyrinthos*]

lab·y·rin·thine (lab′ə rin′thin; –thēn), *adj.* **1** of a labyrinth; forming a labyrinth. **2** intricate; confusing.

lac¹ (lak), *n.* a resinous substance deposited on trees in S Asia by certain insects, used in making sealing wax, varnish, etc. [< Hind. < Skt. *lākshā*]

lac² (lak), *n.* in India: **a** 100,000. **b** any large number; great amount. Also, **lakh.** [< Hind. < Skt. *laksha* 100,000]

lace (lās), *n., v.,* **laced, lac·ing.** —*n.* **1** an open weaving or net of fine thread in an ornamental pattern. **2** cord, string, leather strip, etc., for pulling or holding together. **3** gold or silver braid used for trimming: *some uniforms have lace on them.* —*v.* **1** trim with lace. **2** put laces through; pull or hold together with a lace or laces. **3** adorn or trim with narrow braid: *his uniform was laced with gold.* **4** interlace; intertwine. **5** mark with streaks; streak; *a white petunia laced with purple.* **6** lash; beat; thrash.

lace into, a attack; strike repeatedly. **b** criticize severely. [< OF *laz* < L *laqueus* noose. Doublet of LASSO.] —**lace′like′,** *adj.*

lac·er·ate (las′ər āt), *v.,* **–at·ed, –at·ing,** *adj.* —*v.* **1** tear roughly; mangle. **2** wound; hurt (the feelings, etc.). —*adj.* **1** torn; jagged. **2** deeply and irregularly indented: *lacerate leaves.* [< L, < *lacer* mangled]

lac·er·a·tion (las′ər ā′shən), *n.* **1** a lacerating. **2** rough tear; mangled place; wound.

lace·wing (lās′wing′), *n.* insect that has four lacelike wings.

lace·work (lās′wėrk′), *n.* **1** lace. **2** open-work like lace.

lach·ry·mal (lak′rə məl), *adj.* **1** of tears; producing tears. **2** noting, pertaining to, or situated near the lachrymals. —*n.*

lachrymals, glands that produce tears. [< Med.L, < L *lacrima* tear]

lac·ing (lās′ing), *n.* **1** cord, string, etc., for pulling or holding something together. **2** gold or silver braid used for trimming. **3** lashing; beating; thrashing.

lack (lak), *v.* **1** have not enough; need: *a desert lacks water.* **2** be without; have no: *a homeless person lacks a home.* **3** be absent or missing, as something needed or desirable. —*n.* **1** shortage; not having enough: *lack of rest made her tired.* **2** fact or condition of being without: *lack of a fire made him cold.* **3** thing needed: *if you are cold, your lack is heat.* [cf. MDu. *lac,* MLG *lak*]

lack·a·dai·si·cal (lak′ə dā′zə kəl), *adj.* languid; listless; dreamy. —**lack′a·dai′si·cal·ly,** *adv.* —**lack′a·dai′si·cal·ness,** *n.*

lack·ey (lak′i), *n., pl.* **–eys.** —*n.* **1** a slavish follower. **2** a male servant; footman. [< F < Sp. *lacayo* footsoldier]

lack·ing (lak′ing), *adj.* **1** not having enough; deficient. **2** absent; not here. —*prep.* without; not having: *lacking anything better we must use what we have.*

lack·lus·ter (lak′lus′tər), *adj.* not shining or bright; dull. —*n.* a lack of luster.

la·con·ic (lə kon′ik), *adj.* using few words; brief in speech or expression; concise. [< L < Gk. *lakonikos* Spartan; Spartans were noted for pithy speech] —**la·con′i·cal·ly,** *adv.*

lac·quer (lak′ər), *n.* **1** varnish consisting of shellac dissolved in alcohol, used for coating brass. **2** varnish made from the resin of a sumac tree of SE Asia. **3** articles coated with such varnish. —*v.* coat with lacquer. [< F < Pg. *laca* lac¹] **lac′quer·er,** *n.*

la·crosse (lə krôs′; –kros′), *n.* game played with a ball and long-handled rackets by two teams of 10 players each. The players try to send the ball through a goal. [< F]

lac·tase (lak′tās), *n.* enzyme found in some yeasts and the intestines that breaks down lactose. [< *lact*ose + *–ase* suffix denoting enzymes]

lac·tate (lak′tāt), *n., v.,* **–tat·ed, –tat·ing.** —*n.* any salt of lactic acid. —*v.* produce milk.

lac·ta·tion (lak tā′shən), *n.* **1** act of suckling a baby. **2** time during which a mother gives milk. **3** secretion or formation of milk.

lac·te·al (lak′ti əl), *adj.* **1** of or like milk; milky. **2** carrying chyle, a milky liquid formed from digested food. —*n.* any of the tiny vessels that carry this liquid to be mixed with the blood. [< L, < *lac* milk] —**lac′te·al·ly,** *adv.*

lac·tic (lak′tik), *adj.* of or from milk. [< L *lac* milk]

lactic acid, a colorless, odorless acid, $C_3H_6O_3$, formed in sour milk.

lac·to·ba·cil·lus (lak′tō bə sil′əs), *n., pl.* **–cil·li** (–sil′ī). any of a genus of aerobic bacteria that produces lactic acid.

lac·to·fla·vin (lak′tō flā′vin), *n.* =riboflavin.

lac·tose (lak′tōs), *n.* a crystalline sugar, $C_{12}H_{22}O_{11}$, present in milk; milk sugar.

la·cu·na (lə kū′nə), *n., pl.* **–nae** (–nē), **–nas. 1** an empty space; gap; blank: *lacunae in an old manuscript.* **2** a tiny cavity in bones or tissues. [< L, hole]

lac·y (lās′i), *adj.,* **lac·i·er, lac·i·est. 1** of lace. **2** like lace; having an open pattern. **—lac′i·ly,** *adv.* **—lac′i·ness,** *n.*

lad (lad), *n.* youth. [ME *ladde*]

lad·der (lad′ər), *n.* **1** set of rungs or steps fastened to two long sidepieces, for use in climbing. **2** means of climbing higher. [OE *hlǣder*]

lad·die (lad′i), *n. Esp. Scot.* young boy.

lade (lād), *v.,* **lad·ed, lad·en** or **lad·ed, lad·ing. 1** put a burden on; load. **2** dip; scoop; ladle. **3** take on cargo. [OE *hladan*]

lad·en (lād′ən), *adj.* loaded; burdened. **—v.** pp. of **lade.**

lad·ing (lād′ing), *n.* **1** act of loading. **2** load.

la·dle (lā′dəl), *n., v.,* **–dled, –dling.** *n.* **1** a large cup-shaped spoon with a long handle, for dipping out liquids. **—v. 1** dip out. **2** carry in a ladle. [OE *hlœdel* < *hladan* lade] **—la′dle·ful′,** *n.* **—la′dler,** *n.*

la·dy (lā′di), *n., pl.* **–dies. 1** any woman. **2** a well-bred woman; woman of high social position. **3** woman who has the rights or authority of a lord; mistress of a household. **4** noblewoman; woman who has the title of Lady. **5 Lady,** title given to women of certain ranks in the British Empire. [OE *hlǣfdīge,* lit., loaf-kneader]

la·dy·bug (lā′di bug′), **la·dy·bird** (–bėrd′), *n.* a small round beetle with black spots, that eats other insects.

la·dy·fin·ger (lā′di fing′gər), *n.* a small sponge cake shaped somewhat like a finger.

lady in waiting or **lady-in-waiting,** *n., pl.* **ladies in waiting** or **ladies-in-waiting.** lady who is an attendant of a queen or princess.

la·dy·like (lā′di līk′), *adj.* **1** like a lady. **2** suitable for a lady. **—la′dy·like′ness,** *n.*

la·dy·love (lā′di luv′), *n.* woman who is loved by a man; sweetheart.

la·dy·ship (lā′di ship), *n.* rank or position of a lady.

la·dy's-slip·per (lā′diz slip′ər), **la·dy-slip·per** (lā′di–), *n.* wild orchid whose flower looks somewhat like a slipper.

lag (lag), *v.,* **lagged, lag·ging,** *n.* **—v.** move too slowly; fall behind. **—n. 1** a lagging. **2** amount by which a person or thing lags.

la·ger (lä′gər), or **lager beer,** *n.* beer stored from six weeks to six months before being used. [short for G *lagerbier*]

lag·gard (lag′ərd), *n.* person who moves too slowly or falls behind; backward person. **—adj.** slow; falling behind; backward.

la·goon (lə gün′), *n.* **1** pond or small lake connected with a larger body of water. **2** shallow water separated from the sea by low sandbanks. **3** water within a ring-shaped coral island. [< Ital. *laguna* < L *lacuna* pond]

La·gos (lä′gōs; lā′gos), *n.* capital of Nigeria.

la·ic (lā′ik), *adj.* lay; secular. **—n.** layman. [< L *laicus* < Gk., < *laos* people. Doublet of LAY³.] **—la′i·cal·ly,** *adv.*

laid (lād), *v.* pt. and pp. of **lay¹.**

laid up, a stored up; put away for future use. **b** forced to stay indoors or in bed by illness.

laid-back (lād′bak′) or **laid back,** *adj. Informal.* very relaxed; not excitable.

lain (lān), *v.* pp. of **lie².**

lair (lãr), *n.* den or resting place of a wild animal. [OE *leger* < *licgan* lie²]

laird (lãrd), *n. Scot.* owner of land. [Scot. var. of *lord*] **—laird′ly,** *adj.* **—laird′ship,** *n.*

lais·sez faire (les′ā fãr′), **1** principle of letting people do as they please. **2** absence of regulation and interference by government. [< F, allow to do] **—lais′sez-faire′,** *adj.*

la·i·ty (lā′ə ti), *n., pl.* **–ties.** laymen; the people as distinguished from the clergy or from a professional class. [< *lay³*]

lake¹ (lāk), *n.* **1** a large body of water entirely or nearly surrounded by land. **2** a wide place in a river. [< L *lacus*]

lake² (lāk), *n.* a deep-red or purplish-red coloring matter. [< F < Pers. *lāk*]

lake dwelling, house built on piles over a lake in prehistoric times. **—lake dweller.**

lake trout, a gray trout of the lakes of North America.

lakh (lak), *n.* =lac².

Lam., Lamentations.

lam (lam), *n.* a running away.

on the lam, a escaping. **b** in hiding.

la·ma (lä′mə), *n.* a Buddhist priest or monk in Tibet and Mongolia. [< Tibetan *blama*]

La·ma·ism (lä′mə iz əm), *n.* the religious system of the lamas, a form of Buddhism. **—La′ma·ist,** *n.* **—La′ma·is′tic,** *adj.*

la·ma·ser·y (lä′mə ser′i), *n., pl.* **–ser·ies.** monastery of lamas.

La·maze (lə mäz′), *adj.* of or having to do with a popular form of natural childbirth. [< Fernand *Lamaze,* French obstetrician who developed it in the 1950's]

lamb (lam), *n.* **1** a young sheep. **2** meat from a lamb. **3** a young, dear, or innocent person. **—v.** give birth to a lamb or lambs.

like a lamb, a meekly; timidly. **b** easily fooled.

the Lamb, Christ. John 1:29 and 36. [OE] **—lamb′like′,** *adj.*

lam·bast (lam bast′), *v.* =lambaste.

lam·baste (lam bāst′), *v.* **–bast·ed, –basting. 1** beat; thrash. **2** scold roughly.

lamb·da (lam′də), *n.* the 11th letter of the Greek alphabet. (Λ, λ).

lam·bent (lam′bənt), *adj.* **1** moving lightly over a surface: *a lambent flame.* **2** playing lightly and brilliantly over a subject: *a lambent wit.* **3** softly bright: *moon-light is lambent.* [< L *lambens* licking] **—lam′ben·cy,** *n.* **—lam′bent·ly,** *adv.*

lamb·kin (lam′kin), *n.* **1** a little lamb. **2** a young or dear person.

lamb·skin (lam′skin′), *n.* **1** skin of a lamb, esp. with the wool on it. **2** leather made from the skin of a lamb. **3** parchment.

lame (lām), *adj.,* **lam·er, lam·est,** *v.,* **lamed, lam·ing.** **—adj. 1** not able to walk properly; having an injured leg or foot; crippled. **2** stiff and sore. **3** *Fig.* poor; weak; unsatisfactory: *a lame excuse.* **4** *Informal.* naive; unsophisticated. **—v. 1** make lame; cripple. **2** become lame; go lame. [OE *lama*] **—lame′ly,** *adv.* **—lame′ness,** *n.*

la·mé (la mā′; lä–), *n.* a rich fabric made, wholly or partly, of metal threads. [< F, lit., laminated, < *lame* metal leaf]

lame-brained (lām′brānd′), *adj. Informal.* stupid; foolish. **—lame brain.**

lame duck, 1 person who has been defeated for reelection, esp. to Congress, and is serving the last part of his or her term. **2** a disabled or helpless person or thing.

la·mel·la (lə mel′ə), *n., pl.* **–mel·lae** (–mel′ē), **–mel·las.** a thin plate, scale, or layer, esp. of flesh or bone. [< L, dim. of *lamina* thin plate] **—la·mel′lar, lam′el·late,** *adj.*

la·mel·li·branch (lə mel′ə brangk), *n.* any of a class of bivalve mollusks including oysters, mussels, etc. [< *lamella* + *branchia*]

la·ment (lə ment′), *v.* **1** express grief for; mourn: *lament the dead.* **2** regret: *we lamented his absence.* **—n. 1** expression of grief; wail. **2** poem, song, or tune that expresses grief. [< L, < *lamentum* a wailing] **—la·ment′er,** *n.* **—la·ment′ing,** *adj.* **—la·ment′ing·ly,** *adv.*

lam·en·ta·ble (lam ən′tə bəl), *adj.* **1** to be regretted or pitied: *a lamentable accident, a lamentable failure.* **2** sorrowful; mournful. **—lam·en′ta·ble·ness,** *n.* **—lam·en′ta·bly,** *adv.*

lam·en·ta·tion (lam′ən ta′shən), *n.* loud grief; mourning; wailing; cries of sorrow.

Lamentations, book of the Old Testament ascribed by tradition to Jeremiah.

lam·i·na (lam′ə nə), *n., pl.* **–nae** (–nē), **–nas. 1** a thin plate, scale, or layer. **2** the flat wide part of a leaf. [< L]

lam·i·nar (lam′ə nər), *adj.* **1** arranged in thin layers. **2** smooth; not turbulent or rough.

laminar flow, flow of water, air, etc., that is steady and smooth, rather than turbulent or rough.

lam·i·nate (*v.* lam′ə nāt; *adj., n.* lam′ə nāt, –nit), *v.,* **–nat·ed, –nat·ing,** *adj., n.* **—v. 1** split into thin layers. **2** make by putting layer on layer. **3** beat or roll (metal into a thin plate). **4** cover with thin plates. **—adj.** Also, **lam′i·nat′ed.** having, or composed of, thin layers, plates, etc. **—n.** a laminated plastic. **—lam′i·na′tion,** *n.*

lamp (lamp), *n.* **1** thing that gives light, as oil lamps, gas lamps, and electric lamps. **2** something that suggests the light of a lamp. [< OF < L < Gk. *lampas* < *lampein* shine]

lamp·black (lamp′blak′), *n.* a fine black soot consisting of almost pure carbon that is deposited when oil, gas, etc., burn incompletely, used as a coloring matter in paint and ink.

lamp oil, 1 oil used for burning in a lamp. **2** =kerosene.

lam·poon (lam pün′), *n.* piece of malicious or virulent writing that attacks and ridicules a person. —*v.* attack in a lampoon. [< F *lampon* drinking-song < *lampons* let us drink] —**lam·poon′er, lam·poon′ist,** *n.* —**lam·poon′er·y,** *n.*

lam·prey (lam′pri), *n., pl.* **–preys.** a water animal having a body like an eel, gill slits like a fish, no jaws, and a large, round mouth. Some species live on the blood of fish they attach themselves to. [< OF < Med.L *lampreda.* Doublet of LIMPET.]

lamp·shade (lamp′shād′), *n.* shade over a lamp to reduce glare or direct the light.

lance (lans; läns), *n., v.,* **lanced, lanc·ing.** —*n.* **1** a long wooden spear with a sharp iron or steel head: *knights carried lances.* **2** soldier armed with a lance. **3** any instrument like a soldier's lance. **4** =lancet. —*v.* **1** pierce with a lance. **2** cut open with a lancet: *the dentist lanced the gum.* [< F < L *lancea* light Spanish spear]

lan·ce·o·late (lan′si ə lāt; –lit), *adj.* shaped like the head of a lance. [< L, < *lanceola* small LANCE]

lanc·er (lan′sər; län′–), *n.* a mounted soldier armed with a lance.

lan·cet (lan′sit; län′–), *n.* **1** a small, sharp-pointed surgical knife, usually having two sharp edges. **2** lancet arch or window. [< OF *lancette* small LANCE]

lancet arch, narrow, pointed arch.

lancet window, tall, narrow window with a lancet arch at its top.

land (land), *n.* the solid part of the earth's surface: *dry land.* **2** ground; soil: *arable land, common land.* **3** country; region: *mountainous land.* **4** people of a country; nation. —*v.* **1** come to land; bring to land: *the pilot landed the airplane, the ship landed its passengers.* **2** arrive; cause to arrive: *the thief landed in jail.* **3** catch; get: *land a job.*

how the land lies, what the situation is; how things are; state of affairs.

lands, territorial possessions.

make land, see land as a ship approaches a shore. [OE]

lan·dau (lan′dô; -dou), *n.* a four-wheeled carriage with two seats and a top made in two parts that can be folded back. [from name of German town]

land breeze, breeze that blows from land toward the sea.

land bridge, strip of land that connects two land masses: *a land bridge between North America and Mongolia.*

land·ed (lan′did), *adj.* **1** owning land: *landed nobles.* **2** consisting of land: *landed property.*

land·er (lan′dər), *n.* spacecraft designed to land rather than orbit: *pictures from the Mars lander.*

land·fall (land′fôl′), *n.* **1** approach to land from the sea or air; landing. **2** sighting land. **3** land sighted or reached.

land·fill (land′fil′), *n.* **1** place where refuse and debris is deposited and covered with dirt. **2** low-lying land reclaimed by filling it with refuse, etc., or earth and rocks.

land grant, grant of land; gift of land by the government for colleges, railroads, etc.

land·hold·er (land′hōl′dər), *n.* person who owns or occupies land. —**land′hold′ing,** *adj., n.*

land·ing (land′ing), *n.* **1** a coming to land: *the landing of the Pilgrims.* **2** place where persons or goods are landed from a ship: *the steamboat landing.* **3** platform between flights of stairs.

landing craft, any of various kinds of boats or ships used for landing troops or equipment on a shore, esp. during an assault.

landing field, flat field suitable for aircraft to take off and land.

landing gear, wheels, pontoons, etc., under an aircraft.

landing strip, a long, narrow runway for aircraft to take off from and land on.

land·la·dy (land′lā′di), *n., pl.* **–dies. 1** woman who owns buildings or land that she rents to others. **2** mistress of an inn, boarding house, etc.

land·less (land′lis), *adj.* without land; owning no land.

land·locked (land′lokt′), *adj.* **1** shut in, or nearly shut in, by land. **2** living in waters shut off from the sea: *landlocked salmon.*

land·lord (land′lôrd′), *n.* **1** person who owns buildings or land that he or she rents to others. **2** keeper of an inn, lodging house, or boarding house.

land·lub·ber (land′lub′ər), *n.* person not used to being on ships; person clumsy on ships.

land·mark (land′märk′), *n.* **1** something familiar or easily seen, used as a guide. **2** *Fig.* an important fact or event; happening that stands out above others: *invention of the printing press was a landmark in the progress of communication.* **3** historic building, site, etc. **4** stone or other object that marks the boundary of a piece of land. —**land′marked,** *adj.*

land mine, container filled with explosives or chemicals, placed on the ground or lightly covered.

land mass or **land·mass** (land′mas′), *n.* large unbroken area of land, esp. a continent.

land-office business (land′ôf′is; -of′–), *Informal.* rapid or very active business.

Land of Promise, country promised by God to Abraham and his descendants; Canaan. Gen. 15:18; 17:8.

land·own·er (land′ōn′ər), *n.* person who owns land. —**land′own′er·ship,** *n.*

land-poor (land′pur′), *adj.* owning valuable land but lacking cash.

land reform 1 government program of redistribution of land, esp. to those who work on the land. **2** any measure to benefit farmers.

land·scape (land′skāp), *n., v.,* **–scaped, –scap·ing.** —*n.* **1** view of scenery on land. **2** picture showing a land scene. **3** *Fig.* scene of an activity: *the political landscape.* —*v.* make (land) more pleasant to look at by the arrangement of plantings of trees, shrubs, flowers, etc.: *the park is landscaped.* [< Du., < *land* land + –*schap* –ship]

land·slide (land′slīd′), *n.* **1 a** a sliding down of a mass of soil or rock on a steep slope. **b** mass that slides down. **2** overwhelming majority of votes for one political party or candidate.

lands·man (landz′mən), *n., pl.* **–men. 1** man who lives or works on land. **2** inexperienced seaman.

land·ward (land′wərd), *adv.* Also, **land′-wards.** toward the land. *adj.* directed toward the land.

lane (lān), *n.* **1** a narrow way between hedges, walls, houses, or fences; narrow country road. **2** portion of a highway used by traffic going in one direction only. **3** any narrow way: *a lane on a running track.* **4** course or route used by ships or airplanes going in the same direction. [OE]

lang., language.

lang·syne (lang′sīn′; –zīn′), *adv., n. Scot.* —*adv.* long since; long ago. —*n.* time long ago. [see LONG, SINCE]

lan·guage (lang′gwij), *n.* **1** human speech, spoken or written. **2** speech of one nation or race: *the French language.* **3** form, style, or kind of language: *bad language, Shakespeare's language, the language of chemistry.* **4** wording; words: *the language of the Lord's Prayer.* **5** any means of expressing thoughts or feelings: *dogs' language.* [< OF *langage* < *langue* tongue < L *lingua*]

language arts, training in using language, as in speaking, reading, writing.

language laboratory or **language lab,** room equipped with computers, recording devices, etc., esp. for the study and practice in using a language.

lan·guid (lang′gwid), *adj.* **1** drooping; weak; weary; without energy: *people feel languid in hot weather.* **2** without interest or enthusiasm; indifferent: *he is too languid to go anywhere.* **3** sluggish; dull; not brisk or lively: *a languid market.* [< L, < *languere* be faint] —**lan′guid·ly,** *adv.* —**lan′guid·ness,** *n.*

lan·guish (lang′gwish), *v.* **1** become weak or weary; lose energy; droop: *flowers* *languish from lack of water, his vigilance never languished.* **2** long; pine: *she languished for home.* [< F *languir* < L *languere*] —**lan′guish·er,** *n.* —**lan′guish·ment,** *n.*

lan·guish·ing (lang′gwish ing), *adj.* **1** drooping; pining; longing. **2** tender; sentimental; loving. **3** lasting; lingering. —**lan′guish·ing·ly,** *adv.*

lan·guor (lang′gər), *n.* **1** lack of energy; weakness; weariness: *long illness causes languor.* **2** lack of interest or enthusiasm; indifference. **3** softness or tenderness of mood. **4** quietness; stillness: *the languor of a summer afternoon.* [< L] —**lan′guor·ous,** *adj.* —**lan′guor·ous·ly,** *adv.*

lank (langk), *adj.* **1** long and thin; slender; lean. **2** straight and flat; not curly or wavy. [OE *hlanc*] —**lank′ly,** *adv.* —**lank′ness,** *n.*

lank·y (langk′i), *adj.,* **lank·i·er, lank·i·est.** awkwardly long and thin; tall and ungraceful. —**lank′i·ly,** *adv.* —**lank′i·ness,** *n.*

lan·o·lin (lan′ə lin), *n.* fat or grease obtained from wool, used in ointments. [< L *lana* wool]

Lan·sing (lan′sing), *n.* capital of Michigan, in the S part.

lan·tern (lan′tərn) *n.* **1** case to protect a light from wind, rain, etc., having sides of glass or some other material through which the light can shine. **2** room at the top of a lighthouse where the light is. **3** an upright structure on a roof or dome, for letting in light and air or for decoration. [< F < L < Gk. *lampter* torch < *lampein* to shine]

lan·tern-jawed (lan′tərn jôd′), *adj.* having long thin jaws and hollow cheeks.

lan·tha·nide (lan′thə nīd, –nid), *n.* any of the rare-earth elements. [< *lanthanum* + *-ide*]

lan·tha·num (lan′thə nəm), *n.* first of the rare-earth elements, La, one of the most common and belonging to the same group of chemical elements as cerium. [< NL *lanthanum* < Gk. *lanthánein* lie hidden]

lan·yard (lan′yərd), *n.* **1** a short rope or cord used on ships to fasten rigging. **2** cord with a small hook at one end, used in firing certain kinds of cannon. [blend of *lanyer* (< F *lanière* thong) and *yard²*]

La·os (lä′ōs), *n.* country in SE Asia.

La·o·tian (lä ō′shən), *adj.* of or having to do with Laos, its people, or their language. —*n.* native or inhabitant of Laos.

lap¹ (lap), *n.* **1** the front part from the waist to the knees of a person sitting down. **2** clothing that covers it. **3** place where anything rests or is cared for. [OE *læppa*]

lap² (lap), *v.,* **lapped, lap·ping,** *n.* —*v.* **1** lay or lie together, one partly over or beside another: *shingles on a roof lap.* **2** wind or wrap (around); fold (over or about): *he lapped himself in a warm blanket.* **3** surround; envelop: *joy lapped over him.* **4** in a race, get a lap or more ahead

of (other racers). —*n.* **1** lapping over. **2** part that laps over. **3** one time around a race track. [< *lap¹*] —**lap′per,** *n.*

lap³ (lap), *v.,* **lapped, lap·ping,** *n.* —*v.* **1** drink by lifting up with the tongue; *cats and dogs lap up water.* **2** move or beat gently with a lapping sound; splash gently: *little waves lapped against the boat.* —*n.* **1** act of lapping. **2** sound of lapping. **lap up, a** drink or eat greedily and with enjoyment. **b** pay very close attention to. **c** believe without reservation, esp. something questionable. [OE *lapian*] —**lap′per,** *n.*

La Paz (lä päs′), one of the two capitals of Bolivia (Sucre is the other), in the W part.

la·pel (lə pel′), *n.* part of the front of a coat folded back just below the collar. [< *lap¹*]

lap·ful (lap′fùl), *n., pl.* **-fuls.** as much as a lap can hold.

lap·i·dar·y (lap′ə der′i), *n., pl.* **-dar·ies.** person who cuts, polishes, or engraves precious stones. [< L *lapidarius* < *lapis* stone]

lap·in (lap′ən), *n.* **1** rabbit. **2** rabbit fur. [< F]

lap·is laz·u·li (lap′is laz′yù lī), a deep-blue, opaque semiprecious stone used as an ornament. [< Med. L, < L *lapis* stone + Med.L *lazuli,* gen. of *lazulum* lapis lazuli < Ar.]

Lap·land (lap′land), *n.* region in N Norway, Sweden, Finland, and NW Soviet Union. —**Lap′land·er,** *n.*

Lapp (lap), *n.* **1** member of a Mongoloid race living in Lapland. **2** language of the Lapps.

lap·pet (lap′it), *n.* **1** a small flap or fold. **2** a loose fold of flesh or membrane. **3** lobe of the ear. [< *lap¹*]

lap robe, blanket, fur rug, etc., used to keep the lap and legs warm.

lapse (laps), *n., v.,* **lapsed, laps·ing.** —*n.* **1** a slight mistake or error: *a lapse of memory.* **2** a slipping by; a passing away: *a minute is a short lapse of time.* **3** a slipping or falling away from what is right: *a moral lapse, a lapse into savage ways.* **4** a forsaking of a religious faith. —*v.* **1** make a slight mistake or error. **2** slip by; pass away: *the boy's interest soon lapsed.* **3** slip or fall away from what is right. **4** slip back; sink down: *the house lapsed into ruin.* [< L *lapsus* fall < *labi* to slip] —**laps′er,** *n.*

lap·wing (lap′wing′), *n.* a crested plover of Europe, Asia, and N Africa that has a slow, irregular flight and a peculiar wailing cry.

lar·board (lär′bərd; –bôrd; –bōrd), *n.* side of a ship to the left of a person looking from the stern toward the bow; port. —*adj.* on this side of a ship. [ME *laddeborde*]

lar·ce·ny (lär′sə ni), *n., pl.* **-nies. 1** theft. **2** unlawful taking, carrying away, and using of the personal property belonging to another person without his or her

consent. [< AF < L *latrocinium* < *latro* bandit] —**lar′ce·nous,** *adj.*

larch (lärch), *n.* **1** tree of the pine family with small woody cones and needles that fall off in the autumn. **2** its strong, tough wood. [< G, ult. < L *larix*]

lard (lärd), *n.* fat of pigs and hogs, melted down and made clear, used in cooking. —*v.* **1** insert strips of bacon or salt pork in (meat) before cooking. **2** give variety to; enrich: *lard a long speech with stories.* **3** cover or smear with lard or grease. [< OF < L *lardum*] —**lard′like′,** *adj.*

lard·er (lär′dər), *n.* **1** pantry; place where food is kept. **2** stock of food. [< OF *lardier,* ult. <L *lardum* lard]

lard·y (lär′di), *adj.* **1** full of or like lard. **2** plump; fat.

large (lärj), *adj.,* **larg·er, larg·est,** *n.* —*adj.* **1** of great size, amount, or number; big; huge: *a large crowd.* **2** big compared with others of the same sort: *a large apple.* **3** of great scope or range; extensive; broad: *a man of large experience.*

at large, a at liberty; free **b** as a whole; altogether. **c** representing the whole of a state or district, not merely one division of it: *a congressman at large.* [< OF < L *largus* copious] —**large′ness,** *n.*

large-heart·ed (lärj′här′tid), *adj.* generous; big-hearted. —**large′heart′ed·ness,** *n.*

large intestine, wide, lower part of the intestines, where water is absorbed and wastes eliminated, located between the small intestine and the anus.

large·ly (lärj′li), *adv.* to a great extent; mainly: *largely a matter of conjecture.*

large-scale (lärj′skāl′), *adj.* **1** wide; extensive; involving many persons or things: *a large-scale disaster.* **2** made or drawn to a large scale.

lar·gess, lar·gesse (lär′jis), *n.* **1** generous giving. **2** a generous gift or gifts. [< OF, < *large* LARGE]

lar·ghet·to (lär get′ō), *adj., n., pl.* **-ghet-tos.** —*adj.* rather slow. —*n.* passage or piece of music in rather slow time. [< Ital., dim. of *largo* LARGO]

larg·ish (lär′jish), *adj.* rather large.

lar·go (lär′gō), *adj., n., pl.* **-gos.** —*adj.* slow and dignified; stately. —*n.* a slow, stately passage or piece of music. [< Ital. < L *largus* large]

lar·i·at (lar′i ət), *n.* =lasso. [< Sp. *la reata* the rope]

lark¹ (lärk), *n.* **1** a small songbird of Europe, Asia, and N Africa with brown feathers and long hind claws, esp. the skylark. **2** any of several similar songbirds, as the meadow lark. [OE *lāwerce*]

lark² (lärk), *n.* a merry adventure; frolic; prank. —*v.* have fun; play pranks. —**lark′er,** *n.* —**lark′some,** *adj.*

lark·spur (lärk′spėr), *n.* plant whose flowers have a petallike sepal shaped like a spur. Most larkspurs have clusters of blue flowers on tall stalks.

lar·va (lär′və), *n., pl.* **-vae** (–vē). **1** early form of an insect from the time it leaves the egg until it becomes a pupa, as caterpillars, grubs, and maggots. **2** immature form of certain animals that is different in structure from the adult form, as a tadpole. [< L, ghost] —**lar′val,** *adj.*

la·ryn·ge·al (lə rin′ji əl), *adj.* **1** produced or influenced by the larynx. **2** in the larynx. **3** used on the larynx.

lar·yn·gi·tis (lar′ən ji′tis), *n.* inflammation of the larynx.

lar·ynx (lar′ingks), *n., pl.* **la·ryn·ges** (lə rin′jēz), **lar·ynx·es. 1** cavity at the upper end of the windpipe, containing the vocal cords and acting as an organ of voice. **2** similar organ in other mammals, or corresponding structure in other animals. [< Gk.]

la·sa·gna (lə zän′yə), *n., pl.* **-gne** (–yə). **1** dish of wide, flat noodles, tomato sauce, chopped meat, and cheese arranged in layers and cooked. **2** wide, flat noodle. [< Ital. *lasagna* < L *lasanum* cooking pot < Gk. *lásnon* utensil]

las·car (las′kər), *n.* a native sailor of the East Indies. [< Pg., prob. < Urdu (lang. derived from Hindustani) *lashkarī* soldier]

las·civ·i·ous (lə siv′i əs), *adj.* **1** feeling lust. **2** showing lust. **3** causing lust. [< LL, < L *lascivia* playfulness] —**las·civ′i·ous·ly,** *adv.* —**las·civ′i·ous·ness,** *n.*

lase (lāz), *v.,* **lased, las·ing. 1** emit a laser beam. **2** subject to a laser beam or beams.

la·ser (lā′zər), *n.* a device which generates and amplifies light waves of a pure color in a narrow and extremely intense beam of light. —*adj. Fig.* laserlike; focused; sharp: *laser intellect.* [< *l*(ight) *a*(mplification by) *s*(timulated) *e*(mission of) *r*(adiation)]

lash¹ (lash), *n.* **1** the part of a whip that is not the handle. **2** stroke or blow with a whip, etc. **3** a sudden, swift movement. **4** anything that hurts as a blow from a whip does: *the lash of the wind on one's face.* **5** =eyelash. —*v.* **1** beat or drive with a whip, etc.: *he lashed his horse.* **2** wave or beat back and forth: *the wind lashes the sails.* **3** rush violently; pour: *the rain lashed against the windows.* **4** attack severely in words; hurt severely.

lash out, a hit; attack; strike. **b** attack severely in words; scold vigorously. **c** break forth into violent action, excess, or extravagance.

under the or **one's lash,** under the control or supervision of someone. [ME *lassh*]

lash² (lash), *v.* bind with a rope, cord, etc. [? ult. < OF *lache* LACE]

lash·ing¹ (lash′ing), *n.* **1** act of one that lashes. **2** severe attack in words; sharp scolding.

lash·ing² (lash′ing), *n.* rope, cord, etc., used in tying or fastening.

lass (las), *n.* **1** girl; young woman. **2** sweetheart. [ME *lasse*]

las·sie (las′i), *n.* **1** girl. **2** sweetheart.

las·si·tude (las′ə tüd; –tūd), *n.* lack of energy; weakness; weariness. [< L, < *lassus* tired]

las·so (las′ō; las′ü; la sü′), *n., pl.* **-sos, -soes,** *v.,* **-soed, -so·ing.** —*n.* a long rope with a running noose at one end; lariat. —*v.* catch with a lasso. [< Sp. *lazo* < L *laqueus* noose. Doublet of LACE.] —**las′so·er,** *n.*

last¹ (last; läst), *adj.* **1** coming after all others; being at the end; final: *the last page of the book.* **2** most unlikely; least suitable: *that is the last thing one would expect.* **3** extreme. —*adv.* **1** after all others; at the end; finally: *he arrived last.* **2** on the latest or most recent occasion: *when did you last see him?* —*n.* **1** person or thing that is last: *the last in the row.* **2** end: *faithful to the last.*

at last, at the end; after a long time; finally.

breathe one's last, die.

see the last of, not see again. [OE *latost, lætest,* superl. of *læt* late]

last² (last; läst), *v.* **1** go on; hold out; continue to be; endure: *the storm lasted three days.* **2** continue in good condition, force, etc.: *cloth too flimsy to last.*

last out, survive; endure and come through (something). [OE *lǣstan* < *lāst* track; akin to LAST³] —**last′er,** *n.*

last³ (last; läst), *n.* block shaped like a person's foot, on which shoes and boots are formed or repaired.

stick to one's last, pay attention to one's own work; mind one's own business. [OE *lǣste* < *lāst* track] —**last′er,** *n.*

last·ing (las′ting; läs′–), *adj.* that lasts a long time; permanent. —**last′ing·ly,** *adv.*

last·ly (last′li; läst′–), *adv.* finally; in the last place; in conclusion.

last-min·ute (last′min′it), *adj.* at the latest time possible; almost too late.

last rites, =anointing of the sick.

last straw, last of a series of troublesome things that finally causes a collapse, outburst, etc.

Last Supper, supper of Jesus and his disciples on the evening before he was crucified.

Lat., Latin.

lat., latitude.

latch (lach), *n.* catch for fastening a door, gate, or window, consisting of a movable piece of metal or wood that fits into a notch, opening, etc. [< v.] —*v.* fasten with a latch. [OE *lǣccan* grasp]

latch·key (lach′kē′), *n.* key used to draw back or unfasten the latch of a door.

latch·string (lach′string′), *n.* string used to unfasten the latch of a door.

late (lāt), *adj.,* **lat·er** or **lat·ter, lat·est** or **last,** *adv.,* **lat·er, lat·est** or **last.** —*adj.* **1** happening, coming, etc., after the usual or proper time: *too late for the train.* **2** happening, coming, etc., at an advanced time: *success late in life.* **3** recent: *the late war.* **4** recently dead or gone out of office: *the late professor.* —*adv.* **1** after the usual or proper time: *he worked late.* **2** at an advanced time: *late in the afternoon.* **3** recently but no longer.

of late, lately; a short time ago; recently. [OE *lǣt*] —**late′ness,** *n.*

lateen sail, a triangular sail held up by a long yard on a short mast.

Late Latin, the Latin language from about A.D. 300–700.

late·ly (lāt′li), *adv.* a short time ago; recently.

la·ten·cy (lā′tən si), *n.* latent condition or quality.

la·tent (lā′tənt), *adj.* present but not active; hidden; concealed: *latent germs.* [< L *latens* lying hidden]

lat·er·al (lat′ər əl), *adj.* of the side; at the side; from the side; toward the side: *a lateral branch of a family is a branch not in the direct line of descent.* —*n.* **1** a lateral part or outgrowth. **2** a lateral pass in football. [< L < *latus* side] —**lat′er·al·ly,** *adv.*

lat·er·ite (lat′ə rīt), *n.* reddish soil rich in iron or aluminum, commonly found in SW Asia, Africa, and other tropical areas. —**lat′er·it′ic,** *adj.*

la·tex (lā′teks), *n., pl.* **lat·i·ces** (lat′ə sēz), **la·tex·es** (lā′tek siz). **1** a milky liquid found in the rubber tree, dandelion, milkweed, etc. **2** any of various emulsions of plastic or synthetic rubber, used in water-based paints, adhesives, etc. [< L, liquid]

lath (lath; läth), *n., pl.* **laths** (lath̄z; laths; läth̄z; läths), *v.* —*n.* **1** one of the thin narrow strips of wood formerly used to form a support for plaster or to make a lattice. **2** a wire cloth or sheet metal with holes in it, used in place of laths. **3** lining made of laths; lathwork; lathing. —*v.* cover or line with laths. [ME *laththe*]

lathe (lāth̄), *n.* machine for holding articles of wood, metal, etc., and turning them against a cutting tool used to shape them. [< Scand. (Dan.) *(dreje) lad* (turning) lathe]

lath·er (lath̄′ər), *n.* **1** foam made from soap and water. **2** foam formed in sweating. —*v.* **1** put lather on. **2** form a lather. **3** become covered with foam. [OE *lēathor*] —**lath′er·er,** *n.* —**lath′er·y,** *adj.*

Lat·in (lat′ən), *n.* **1** language of the ancient Romans. **2** member of any of the peoples whose languages came from Latin, as the Italians, French, Spanish, etc. **3** native or inhabitant of Latium or of ancient Rome. —*adj.* **1** of Latin; in Latin. **2** of the Latin peoples. **3** of Latium or its people.

La·ti·na (lä ti′nä), *n.* a female Latin American.

Latin America, South America, Central America, Mexico, and most of the West Indies. —**Lat′in-A·mer′i·can,** *adj.* —**Latin American.**

Lat·in·ate (lat′ə nāt), *adj.* from or having to do with Latin.

La·ti·no (lä ti′nō), *n.* a Latin American. —*adj.* Latin-American.

lat·ish (lāt′ish), *adj., adv.* rather late.

lat·i·tude (lat′ə tüd; –tūd), *n.* **1** distance north or south of the equator, measured in degrees. 2 place or region having a certain latitude: *the cold latitudes.* 3 room to act; scope; freedom from narrow rules: *you are allowed much latitude in this work; use your own judgment.* [< L, < *latus* wide] —**lat′i·tu′di·nal,** *adj.*

lat·i·tu·di·nar·i·an (lat′ə tü′də när′i ən; –tū′–), *adj.* allowing others their own beliefs; not insisting on strict adherence to established principles, esp. in religious views. —*n.* person who is latitudinarian in outlook or action. —**lat′i·tu′di·nar′i·an·ism,** *n.*

La·ti·um (lā′shi əm), *n.* ancient country in Italy, SE of Rome.

la·trine (lə trēn′), *n.* toilet in a camp, barracks, factory, etc.; privy. [< F < L *latrina*]

lat·ter (lat′ər), *adj.* 1 second of two: *Canada and the United States are in North America; the former lies N of the latter.* 2 later; more recent; nearer the end: *Friday comes in the latter part of the week.* [OE *lœtra* later]

Latter-day Saint, =Mormon.

lat·ter·ly (lat′ər li), *adv.* lately; recently.

lat·tice (lat′is), *n., v.,* –**ticed,** –**tic·ing.** —*n.* 1 structure of crossed wooden or metal strips with open spaces between them. 2 window, gate, etc., having a lattice. —*v.* 1 form into a lattice; make like a lattice. 2 furnish with a lattice. [< OF *lattis* < *latte* lath < Gmc.]

lat·tice·work (lat′is wėrk′), *n.* 1 lattice. 2 lattices.

Lat·vi·a (lat′vi ə), *n.* a small country in N Europe, on the Baltic Sea. —**Lat′vi·an,** *adj., n.*

laud (lôd), *v.* praise. —*n.* 1 praise. 2 song or hymn of praise. 3 **lauds, Lauds.** morning church service with psalms of praise to God. [ult. < L *laus* praise] —**laud′er,** *n.*

laud·a·ble (lôd′ə bəl), *adj.* worthy of praise; commendable. —**laud′a·bil′i·ty, laud′a·ble·ness,** *n.* —**laud′a·bly,** *adv.*

lau·da·num (lô′də nəm), *n.* solution of opium in alcohol, used to lessen pain. [< NL; coined by Paracelsus]

lau·da·tion (lô dā′shən), *n.* praise.

laud·a·to·ry (lôd′ə tô′ri; –tō′–), **laud·a·tive** (–tiv), *adj.* expressing praise.

laugh (laf; läf), *v.* 1 make the sounds and movements of the face and body that show mirth, amusement, scorn, etc. 2 express with laughter: *laugh a reply.* —*n.* act or sound of laughing.

for laughs, for fun; as amusement.

have the last laugh, to get the better of someone after having appeared to have lost.

laugh at, make fun of.

laugh off, pass off or dismiss with a laugh; get out of by laughing.

no laughing matter, a serious matter. [OE *hliehhan*] —**laugh′er,** *n.*

laugh·a·ble (laf′ə bəl; läf′–), *adj.* such as to cause laughter; amusing; funny. —**laugh′a·ble·ness,** *n.* —**laugh′a·bly,** *adv.*

laugh·ing (laf′ing; läf′–), *adj.* 1 that laughs or seems to laugh: *the laughing brook.* 2 accompanied by laughter. —*n.* laughter.

no laughing matter, matter that is serious. —**laugh′ing·ly,** *adv.*

laugh·ing·stock (laf′ing stok′; läf′–), *n.* object of ridicule; person or thing that is made fun of.

laugh·ter (laf′tər; läf′–), *n.* 1 action of laughing. 2 sound of laughing.

laugh track, recorded laughter of an audience, inserted into the sound track of esp. a television show.

launch¹ (lônch; länch), *n.* 1 the largest boat carried by a warship. 2 more or less open motorboat used for pleasure trips, etc. [< Sp., Pg. *lancha* < *lanchar* LAUNCH²]

launch² (lônch; länch), *v.* 1 cause to slide into the water; set afloat: *launch a ship.* 2 push out or put forth on the water or into the air. 3 start; set going; set out: *launch a new business.* 4 throw; hurl; send out: *launch threats against enemies.* 5 burst; plunge: *launch into a violent attack on the government.* —*n.* movement of a boat or ship from the land into the water. [ult. < OF *lancer* < *lance* LANCE] —**launch′er,** *n.*

launch pad or **launching pad, 1** the surface on which a rocket or missile is prepared for launching and from which it is shot into the air. 2 *Fig.* circumstances or place where a campaign, an idea, a new business, etc. gets underway.

laun·der (lôn′dər; län′–), *v.,* 1 wash and iron (clothes, etc.). 2 be able to be washed; stand washing: *some shirts launder well.* 3 *Fig.* remove all trace of illegality from, esp. money; make legitimate. [< OF, ult. < L *lavanda* (things) to be washed < *lavare* wash] —**laun′der·er,** *n.*

laun·der·ette (lôn′də ret′; län′–), *n.* =laundromat. [< *Launderette,* Trademark for a self-service laundry]

laun·dress (lôn′dris; län′–), *n.* woman whose work is washing and ironing clothes, etc.

laun·dro·mat (lôn′drə mat, län′–), *n.* 1 self-service laundry with coin-operated washers and dryers. 2 laundry with attendants who wash, dry, and fold laundry. [< *Laundromat,* Trademark]

laun·dry (lôn′dri; län′–), *n., pl.* –**dries.** 1 room or building where clothes, etc., are washed and ironed. 2 clothes, etc., washed or to be washed.

laundry list, *Fig.* long, itemized list: *a laundry list of complaints.*

laun·dry·wom·an (lôn′dri wům′ ən; län′–), *n., pl.* –**wom·en.** laundress.

lau·re·ate (lô′ri it), *adj.* 1 crowned with a laurel wreath as a mark of honor. 2 honored; distinguished. —*n.* 1 =poet laureate. 2 a person who is honored or given a prize for significant accomplishment in a particular field: *Nobel laureate.* [<L, ult.< *laurus* laurel] —**lau′re·ate·ship′,** *n.*

lau·rel (lô′rəl; lor′əl), *n.* 1 a small evergreen tree with smooth, shiny leaves; bay tree. 2 the leaves. The ancient Greeks and Romans crowned victors with wreaths of laurel. 3 any tree or shrub of the same family as the bay tree. 4 American evergreen shrub, the mountain laurel.

laurels. a honor; fame. **b** victory.

rest on one's laurels, be satisfied with what one has already achieved or been honored for. [< OF, ult. < L *laurus*] —**lau′reled,** *adj.*

la·va (lä′və; lav′ə), *n.* 1 molten rock flowing from a volcano or fissure in the earth. 2 rock formed by the cooling of this molten rock. Some lavas are hard and glassy; others are light and porous. [< dial. Ital., stream, ult. < L *lavare* wash]

lav·a·to·ry (lav′ə tô′ri; –tō′–), *n., pl.* –**ries.** 1 room where a person can wash hands and face. 2 bowl or basin to wash in. 3 bathroom; toilet. [< LL, < L *lavare* wash]

lave (lāv), *v.,* **laved, lav·ing.** *Poetic.* 1 wash; bathe. 2 wash or flow against. [< L *lavare*]

lav·en·der (lav′ən dər), *n.* 1 a pale purple. 2 a small shrub with spikes of fragrant pale-purple flowers, yielding an oil much used in perfumes. 3 its dried flowers, leaves, and stalks, used to perfume or preserve linens, clothes, etc. —*adj.* pale-purple. [< AF < Med.L *lavendula*]

lav·ish (lav′ish), *adj.* 1 very free or too free in giving, using, or spending; prodigal: *lavish with money.* 2 very abundant; more than enough; given or spent too freely: *lavish gifts.* —*v.* give or spend very freely or too freely: *she lavished kindness on her guest.* [ult. < OF *lavasse* flood < *laver* wash < L *lavare*] —**lav′ish·er,** *n.* —**lav′ish·ly,** *adv.* —**lav′ish·ness,** *n.*

law (lô), *n.* 1 body of rules recognized by a state or a community as binding on its members: *English law is different from French law.* 2 one of these rules: *there is a law against driving too fast.* 3 controlling influence of these rules: *maintain law and order, courts of law.* 4 study concerned with these rules; jurisprudence: *study law.* 5 body of rules concerned with a particular subject: *commercial law, criminal law.* 6 legal profession: *enter the law.* 7 statement of phenomena under the same conditions: *the law of gravitation.*

go to law, appeal to law courts; take legal action.

lay down the law, a give orders that must be obeyed. **b** give a scolding.

take the law into one's own hands, act independently of the law in protecting one's rights or to punish someone who has wronged one. [OE *lagu* < Scand.]

law·a·bid·ing (lô′ə bīd′ing), *adj.* obedient to the law; peaceful and orderly.

law·break·er (lô′brāk′ər), *n.* person who breaks the law. —**law′break′ing,** *n., adj.*

law court, place where justice is administered; court of law.

law enforcement officer, police officer, sheriff, or sheriff's deputy, etc.

law·ful (lô′fəl), *adj.* **1** according to law; done as the law directs: *lawful arrest.* **2** allowed by law; rightful: *lawful demands.* —**law′ful·ly,** *adv.* —**law′ful·ness,** *n.*

law·giv·er (lô′giv′ ər), *n.* lawmaker; legislator. —**law′giv′ ing,** *n., adj.*

law·less (lô′lis), *adj.* **1** paying no attention to the law; breaking the law: *lawless criminal.* **2** hard to control; unruly: *lawless passions.* **3** having no laws: *lawless wilderness.* —**law′less·ly,** *adv.* —**law′less·ness,** *n.*

law·mak·er (lô′māk′ ər), *n.* person who helps to make laws; member of a legislature, congress, or parliament; legislator.

law·mak·ing (lô′māk′ ing), *adj.* that makes laws; legislative. —*n.* making the laws; legislation.

law·man (lô′mən), *n., pl.* **-men.** =law enforcement officer.

lawn¹ (lôn), *n.* land covered with grass kept closely cut, esp. near or around a house. [< OF *launde* wooded ground < Celtic] —**lawn′y,** *adj.*

lawn² (lôn), *n.* a thin, sheer linen or cotton cloth. [? ult. < *Laon,* French city]

lawn mower, machine with revolving blades for cutting the grass on a lawn.

lawn sale, outdoor sale of used household goods, clothing, furniture, etc., held outdoors and often to raise funds for charity.

lawn tennis, game in which a ball is hit back and forth over a low net; tennis.

law·suit (lô′süt′), *n.* case in a law court; application to a court for justice.

law·yer (lô′yər), *n.* person whose profession is giving advice about the laws or acting for others in a law court.

lax (laks), *adj.* **1** not firm or tight; loose; slack: *lax cord.* **2** not strict; careless: *lax mental powers, lax scruples.* **3** not exact; vague. [< L *laxus*] —**lax′ly,** *adv.* —**lax′ness,** *n.*

lax·a·tive (lak′sə tiv), *n.* medicine that makes the bowels move. —*adj.* making the bowels move. [< L *laxativus* loosening, ult. < *laxus* loose]

lax·i·ty (lak′sə ti), *n.* lax condition or quality.

lay¹ (lā), *v.,* **laid, lay·ing,** *n.* —*v.* **1** put down; keep down: *lay your hat on the table.* **2** place in a lying-down position or a position of rest: *lay the baby down gently.* **3** place, set, or cause to be in a particular situation or condition: *lay great emphasis on good manners, the scene of the story is laid in New York.* **4** place in a proper position or in orderly fashion: *lay bricks.* **5** bring down; beat down: *a storm laid the crops low.* **6** put cloth, dishes, etc., on (a table). **7** devise; arrange: *lay plans.* **8** present; bring forward: *lay claim to an estate.* **9** impute; attribute: *the theft was laid to him.* **10** of a hen, to produce (an egg or eggs). **11** put down as a bet; wager: *lay five dollars on a horse.* —*n.* way or position in which a thing is laid or lies: *the lay of the land.*

lay aside, away, or **by,** put away for future use; save.

lay down, a declare; state. **b** give; sacrifice. **c** store away for future use.

lay for, lie in wait for.

lay hold of or **on,** grasp, seize.

lay in, provide; save; put aside for the future.

lay into, a beat; thrash. **b** scold.

lay off, a put aside. **b** stop for a time. **c** put out of work.

lay on, a apply. **b** strike; inflict.

lay oneself or **one open,** expose oneself or another (to): *laid himself open to teasing.*

lay out, a spread out. **b** prepare (a dead body) for burial. **c** arrange; plan. **d** spend.

lay over, stop for a time in a place.

lay up, a put away for future use; save. **b** cause to stay in bed or indoors because of illness or injury. **c** put (a ship) in dock. [OE *lecgan* < *licgan* lie²]

lay² (lā), *v.* pt. of **lie²**.

lay³ (lā), *adj.* of ordinary people; not of the clergy, lawyers, doctors, or those learned in the profession in question. [< OF < L *laicus.* Doublet of LAIC.]

lay⁴ (lā), *n.* **1** a short poem to be sung; poem. **2** song; tune. [< OF *lai,* ? < Celtic]

lay·er (lā′ər), *n.* **1** thing that lays. **2** one thickness or fold: *a cake made of layers.* —*v.* form or arrange in layers: *layer two shirts under a sweater for warmth.* **lay′er·ed,** *adj.*

layer cake, cake made of two or more layers put together with frosting, jelly, etc., between.

lay·ette (lā et′), *n.* set of clothes, bedding, etc., for a newborn baby. [< F, < *laie* chest]

lay·man (lā′mən), *n., pl.* **-men.** person outside of any particular profession, esp. one not belonging to the clergy.

lay·off (lā′ôf′; -of′), *n.* **1** a dismissing of workers temporarily. **2** time during which workers are out of work.

lay·out (lā′out′), *n.* **1** act of laying out. **2** arrangement; plan: *the layout of a house or a book.* **3** thing laid or spread out; display.

lay·o·ver (lā′ō ′vər), *n.* a stopping for a time in a place.

Laz·a·rus (laz′ə rəs), *n.* brother of Mary and Martha, whom Jesus raised from the dead. John 11:1–44.

laze (lāz), *v.,* **lazed, laz·ing.** be lazy or idle.

la·zy (lā′zi), *adj.,* **la·zi·er, la·zi·est. 1** not willing to work or be active: *a lazy student.* **2** moving slowly; not very active: *a lazy walk.* —**la′zi·ly,** *adv.* —**la′zi·ness,** *n.*

la·zy·bones (lā′zi bōnz′), *n.* a lazy person.

lb., *pl.* **lbs., lb.** pound; pounds.

l.c., lower case; in small letters, not capital letters.

LDL, low-density lipoprotein, a component of cholesterol in the blood that contains more fats than protein, and so is sometimes called bad cholesterol.

lea (lē), *n.* a grassy field; meadow. [OE *lēah*]

leach (lēch), *v.* **1** dissolve out soluble parts from (ashes, etc.) by running water through slowly. **2** lose soluble parts when water passes through. —*n.* solution obtained by leaching. [OE *leccan* to wet] —**leach′er,** *n.*

lead¹ (lēd), *v.,* **led, lead·ing,** *n.* —*v.* **1** show the way by going along with or in front of: *lead a horse.* **2** bring to a place, condition, etc: *hard work leads to success; one word led to another.* **3** go or be at the head of: *lead a parade; he leads his class.* **4** pass or spend (life, time, etc.): *lead an idle life.* **5** begin; begin with (card or suit named). —*n.* **1** direction; example. **2** first or foremost place; position in advance: *take the lead.* **3** extent of advance. **4** something that leads. **5** the principal part in a play. **6** string, strap, etc., for leading a dog or other animal.

lead off, a begin; start. **b** be the first batter in a baseball inning or the first in the batting lineup.

lead on, persuade or entice to go along with something, esp. on unwise activity or action; gull.

lead up to, a prepare the way for: *dissatisfaction leads up to demonstrations.* **b** approach (a matter, concern, etc.), gradually or in an indirect way. [OE *lēdan*]

lead² (led), *n.* **1** a heavy, easily melted, bluish-gray metal. Lead is a chemical element. *Symbol:* Pb. **2** something made of this metal or an alloy of it. **3** weight on a line used to find out the depth of water; plummet. **4** bullets; shot. **5** a long, thin piece of graphite as used in pencils. —*adj.* made of lead. [OE *lēad*]

lead·en (led′ən), *adj.* **1** made of lead. **2** like lead in any way: **a** heavy. **b** heavy and slow. **c** dull; gloomy. —**lead′en·ly,** *adv.* —**lead′en·ness,** *n.*

lead·er (lēd′ər), *n.* **1** person or thing that leads. **2** a short length of transparent material attaching the lure to a fish line. **leaders,** row of dots or dashes to guide the eye across a printed page. —**lead′er·less,** *adj.* —**lead′er·ship,** *n.*

lead·ing (lēd′ing), *adj.* **1** guiding; directing. **2** most important; chief: *the leading actor in a play.* —**lead′ing·ly,** *adv.*

lead·ing edge (lē′ding), **1** forward edge of an airfoil or propeller blade. **2** forward part; front edge: *leading edge of a weather front.*

lead·ing question (lēd′ing), question so worded that it suggests the answer desired.

lead·off (lēd′ ôf′; -of′), *n.* **1** beginning; first. **2** first batter of an inning or the batting order in a baseball game. —*adj.* that begins or is first: *leadoff speaker.*

leaf (lēf), *n., pl.* **leaves,** *v.* —*n.* **1** one of the thin, flat, green parts that grow on the stem of a tree or other plant. **2** a sheet of paper. **3** a flat movable piece in the top of a table. —*v.* **1** put forth leaves: *the trees leaf out in the spring.* **2** turn the pages of.

in leaf, having leaves: *trees in full leaf.*

take a leaf from one's book, copy or follow one's example.

turn over a new leaf, try to do or be better in the future. [OE *lēaf*] —**leaf'like',** *adj.*

leaf·age (lēf'ij), *n.* leaves; foliage.

leaf bud, a bud producing a stem with leaves only.

leaf·less (lēf'lis), *adj.* having no leaves.

leaf·let (lēf'lit), *n.* **1** a small or young leaf. **2** one of the separate blades or divisions of a compound leaf. **3** a small, flat or folded sheet of printed matter: *advertising leaflets.*

leaf·stalk (lēf'stôk'), *n.* a petiole.

leaf·y (lēf'i), *adj.,* **leaf·i·er, leaf·i·est.** having many leaves; covered with leaves. —**leaf'i·ness,** *n.*

league¹ (lēg), *n.* **1** association of persons, parties, or countries formed to help one another. **2** persons, parties, or countries associated in a league. **3** an association of sports clubs.

in league, associated by agreement; associated. [< OF < Ital., ult. < L *ligare* bind] —**lea'guer,** *n.*

league² (lēg), *n.* measure of distance, usually about 3 miles. [< LL *leuga* < Celtic]

leak (lēk), *n.* **1** hole or crack not meant to be there that lets something in or out: *a leak in the roof.* **2** release of information supposed to be kept secret. **3** leakage. **4** a point where electrical current escapes from a conductor. **5** means of escape. —*v.* **1** go in or out through a hole or crack. **2** let in something which should be kept out; let out something which should be kept in: *his boat leaks.* **3** make or become known gradually: *the secret leaked out.* [< Scand. *leka*]

leak·age (lēk'ij), *n.* **1** a leaking; a going in or out through a leak. **2** that which leaks in or out. **3** amount of leaking.

leak·proof (lēk'prüf'), *adj.* that will not or does not leak: *leakproof boots.*

leak·y (lēk'i), *adj.* **leak·i·er, leak·i·est,** leaking; having a leak or leaks. —**leak'i·ness,** *n.*

lean¹ (lēn), *v.,* **leaned, lean·ing,** *n.* —*v.* **1** stand slanting, not upright; bend: *a small tree leans over in the wind.* **2** rest sloping or slanting: *lean against me.* **3** set or put in a leaning position: *lean the picture against the wall.* **4** depend; rely: *lean on a friend's advice.* **5** bend or turn a little: *lean toward mercy.* —*n.* act of leaning; inclination.

lean, or **bend over backward,** do everything possible to be accommodating. [OE *hleonian*]

lean² (lēn), *adj.* **1** with little or no fat. **2** producing little; scant: *a lean harvest, a*

lean diet. —*n.* meat having little fat. [OE *hlǣne*] —**lean'ly,** *adv.* —**lean'ness,** *n.*

lean·ing (lēn'ing), *n.* tendency; inclination.

lean-to (lēn'tü'), *n., pl.* **-tos.** **1** building attached to another, toward which its supports or roof slants. **2** a crude shelter built against a tree or post. It is usually open on one side.

leap (lēp), *n., v.,* **leaped** or **leapt** (lept; lēpt), **leap·ing.** —*n.* **1** a jump or spring. **2** thing to be jumped. **3** distance covered by a jump. —*v.* **1** jump: *a frog leaps.* **2** jump over: *leap a wall.* **3** move quickly and lightly: *the flames leaped up.*

by leaps and bounds, very fast and very much; swiftly. [OE *hlēapan*]

leap·frog (lēp'frog'; –frôg'), *n.* game in which one player jumps over another who is bending over.

leap year, year having 366 days. The extra day is February 29.

learn (lėrn), *v.,* **learned** or **learnt** (lėrnt), **learn·ing.** **1** gain knowledge of (a subject) or skill in by study, instruction, or experience: *learn French.* **2** acquire knowledge, skill, etc.: *he learns easily.* **3** memorize: *learn a poem by heart.* **4** find out; come to know; hear. [OE *leornian*] —**learn'er,** *n.*

learn·ed (lėr'nid), *adj.* having, showing, or requiring much knowledge; scholarly. —**learn'ed·ly,** *adv.* —**learn'ed·ness,** *n.*

learn·er (lėr'nər), *n.* **1** person who is learning: *a quick learner.* **2** beginner.

learn·ing (lėr'ning), *n.* **1** the gaining of knowledge or skill. **2** possession of knowledge gained by study; scholarship. **3** knowledge.

lear·y (lir'i), *adj.,* **lear·i·er, lear·i·est.** =leery.

lease (lēs), *n., v.,* **leased, leas·ing.** —*n.* **1** contract; the right to use property for a certain length of time, usually by paying rent. **2** length of time for which such an agreement is made. —*v.* **1** give a lease on. **2** take a lease on. **3** be leased.

a new lease on life, chance to live better, happier, or longer. [< AF < L *laxare* loosen < *laxus* loose] —**leas'er,** *n.*

leash (lēsh), *n.* strap, chain, etc., for holding a dog or other animal in check. —*v.* fasten or hold in with a leash; control.

on a short or **tight** or **long leash,** with very little or a great deal of latitude: *work kept her on a short leash.*

strain at the leash, be impatient. [< OF < L *laxa,* fem., loose]

least (lēst), *adj.* less than any other; smallest; slightest: *the least distance.* —*n.* least amount or degree: *that is the least you can do.* —*adv.* to the least extent, amount, or degree: *he liked that book least of all.*

at least or **at the least, a** at the lowest estimate. **b** at any rate; in any case. not in the least, not at all. [OE *lǣst*]

least common denominator, least common multiple of the denominators of

a group of fractions; lowest common denominator.

least common multiple, smallest quantity divisible by two or more given quantities without a remainder; lowest common multiple.

least·wise (lēst'wīz'), **least·ways** (–wāz), *adv.* at least; at any rate.

leath·er (leth'ər), *n.* material made from the skin of animals by removing the hair and then tanning it. —*adj.* made of leather: *leather gloves.* [OE *lether*]

leath·er·back (leth'ər bak'), *n.* tropical sea turtle having a leathery, flexible shell studded with bony plates. It is the largest living turtle.

leath·ern (leth'ərn), *adj.* **1** made of leather. **2** like leather.

leath·er·neck (leth'ər nek'), *n.* a U.S. marine.

leath·er·y (leth'ər i), *adj.* like leather; tough. —**leath'er·i·ness,** *n.*

leave¹ (lēv), *v.,* **left, leav·ing.** **1** go away or go away from: *he left the house.* **2** stop living in, belonging to, or working at or for: *leave a club.* **3** let remain: *leave a window open; the wound left a scar.* **4** forsake; abandon: *he left home.* **5** let remain when one dies; bequeath: *he left a large fortune.* **6** let remain uneaten, unused, unremoved, etc.: *there is some snow left.*

leave off, a stop. **b** drop off; leave someplace: *leave off a package.*

leave out, fail to do, say, or put in; omit. [OE *lǣfan*] —**leav'er,** *n.*

leave² (lēv), *n.* **1** permission; consent: *they gave him leave to go.* **2** permission to be absent from duty. **3** length of time that this lasts.

on leave, absent from duty with permission.

take leave of, say good-by to. [OE *lēaf*]

leave³ (lēv), *v.,* **leaved, leav·ing.** put forth leaves: *trees leave in the spring.* [var. of *leaf*]

leaved (lēvd), *adj.* having leaves or foliage.

leav·en (lev'ən), *n.* **1** any substance, such as yeast, that will cause fermentation and raise dough. **2** a small amount of fermenting dough kept for this purpose. **3** *Fig.* influence that, spreading silently and strongly, changes conditions or opinions. —*v.* **1** raise with a leaven; make (dough) light or lighter. **2** *Fig.* spread through and transform. [< OF < L *levamen* a lifting < *levare* raise]

leav·en·ing (lev'ə ning), *n.* something that leavens; leaven.

leaves (lēvz), *n.* pl. of **leaf.**

leave-tak·ing (lēv'tāk'ing), *n.* act of taking leave; saying good-by.

leav·ing (lēv'ing), *n.* **1** thing left over. **2 leavings,** leftovers; remnants.

Leb·a·non (leb'ə nən), *n.* republic at the E end of the Mediterranean, N of Israel. —**Leb'a·nese',** *adj., n.*

lech·er (lech'ər), *n.* man who indulges in lechery. [< OF *lecheor* licker < *lechier* lick < Gmc.]

lech·er·ous (lech'ər əs), *adj.* lewd; lustful. —**lech'er·ous·ly,** *adv.* —**lech'er·ous·ness,** *n.*

lech·er·y (lech'ər i), *n.* lewdness.

lec·i·thin (les'ə thin), *n.* fatty substance found in plant and animal tissues and used in manufacturing candies, drugs, cosmetics, and paints.

lec·tern (lek'tərn), *n.* a reading desk in a church, esp. the desk from which the lessons are read. [< OF < Med.L *lectrum* < L *legere* read]

lec·ture (lek'chər), *n., v.,* –**tured,** –**tur·ing.** —*n.* 1 speech; planned talk on a chosen subject; such a talk written down or printed. 2 a scolding. —*v.* 1 give a lecture. 2 instruct or entertain by a lecture. 3 scold; reprove. [< LL *lectura* < L *legere* read] —**lec'tur·er,** *n.* —**lec'ture·ship,** *n.*

led (led), *v.* pt. and pp. of **lead**[1].

LED, light-emitting diode, a crystalline semiconductor that emits a red light, used esp. for electronic display, as on a watch.

ledge (lej), *n.* 1 a narrow shelf: *a window ledge.* 2 shelf or ridge of rock. [< ME *legge*(*n*) lay[1]] —**ledged,** *adj.*

ledg·er (lej'ər), *n.* book of accounts in which a business keeps a record of all money transactions. [< ME *legge*(*n*) lay[1]]

ledger line, line added above or below the staff in written music for notes that are too high or too low to be put on the staff. Also, **leger line.**

lee[1] (lē), *n.* 1 shelter. 2 side or part sheltered from the wind. 3 side away from the wind. 4 direction toward which the wind is blowing. —*adj.* 1 sheltered from the wind. 2 on the side away from the wind. 3 in the direction toward which the wind is blowing. [OE *hlēo*]

lee[2] (lē), *n.* Usually, **lees.** dregs; sediment, as from wine. [< F *lie* < Celtic]

leech (lēch), *n.* 1 worm living in ponds and streams that sucks the blood of animals, formerly used to suck blood from sick people. 2 person who tries persistently to get what he or she can out of others. [OE *lǣce*] —**leech'like',** *adj.*

leek (lēk), *n.* vegetable somewhat like an onion, but with larger leaves, a smaller bulb shaped like a cylinder, and a milder flavor. [OE *lēac*]

leer (lir), *n.* a sly sidelong look; evil glance. —*v.* give a sly sidelong look; glance evilly. [? OE *hlēor* cheek] —**leer'ing·ly,** *adv.*

leer·y (lir'i), *adj.* 1 sly. 2 wary.

lee·ward (lē'wərd; lü'ərd), *adj.* 1 on the side away from the wind. 2 in the direction toward which the wind is blowing. —*adv.* toward the lee side. —*n.* side away from the wind.

lee·way (lē'wā'), *n.* 1 extra space at the side; time, money, etc., more than is needed. 2 convenient room or scope

for action. 3 side movement of a ship to leeward, out of its course.

left[1] (left), *adj.* 1 belonging to the side of the less used hand (in most people); having this relation to the front of any object: *the driver sits on the left side of a car.* 2 situated nearer the observer's or speaker's left hand than his or her right. 3 having liberal or radical political views. —*adv.* on or to the left side: *turn left.* —*n.* 1 the left side or hand. 2 Often, **Left.** more radical part of a lawmaking/political group or opinion. 3 *Fig.* people or political parties holding liberal or radical views. [dial. OE *left* (for *lyft*) weak]

left[2] (left), *v.* pt. and pp. of **leave**[1].

Left Bank, section of Paris on the left bank of the Seine, favored by artists, students, etc.

left field, the outfield behind third base, in baseball.

  out in left field, impractical; wrongheaded.

left-hand (left'hand'), *adj.* 1 on or to the left. 2 of, for, or with the left hand.

left-hand·ed (left'han'did), *adj.* 1 using the left hand more easily and readily than the right. 2 done with the left hand. 3 made to be used with the left hand. 4 turning from right to left. 5 clumsy; awkward: *a left-handed excuse.* 6 doubtful; insincere: *a left-handed compliment.* —**left'-hand'ed·ly,** *adv.* —**left'-hand'ed·ness,** *n.* —**left'-hand'er,** *n.*

left·ist (lef'tist), *n.* 1 person who has radical ideas. 2 member of a radical or extreme organization. —*adj.* having radical ideas.

left·o·ver (left'ō'vər), *n.* thing that is left: *scraps of food from a meal are leftovers.* —*adj.* that is left; remaining.

left wing, the radical members, as of a political party. —**left'-wing',** *adj.* —**left'-wing'er,** *n.*

left·y (lef'ti), *n.pl.* –**ties.** *Informal.* 1 left-handed person. 2 =leftist.

leg (leg), *n.* 1 one of the limbs on which humans and animals support themselves and walk. 2 part of a garment that covers a leg. 3 anything shaped or used like a leg. 4 one of the distinct portions or stages of any course: *last leg of a trip.* 5 side of a triangle that is not the base or hypotenuse.

  pull one's leg, fool, trick, or make fun of him.

  stretch one's legs, take a walk. [< Scand. *leggr*] —**leg'less,** *adj.*

leg., 1 legal. 2 legislative; legislature.

leg·a·cy (leg'ə si), *n., pl.* –**cies.** 1 money or other property left to a person by a will. 2 something that has been handed down from an ancestor or predecessor. [< OF < Med.L *legatia* < L *legatum* bequest]

le·gal (lē'gəl), *adj.* 1 of law: *legal knowledge.* 2 of lawyers. 3 according to law; lawful. [< L *legalis* < *lex* law. Doublet of LOYAL.] —**le'gal·ly,** *adv.*

legal age, age at which a person gains full legal rights and responsibilities; majority.

le·gal·ese (lē'gə lēz; –lēs), *n.* jargon of the legal profession.

le·gal·ism (lē'gəl iz əm), *n.* strict adherence to law or prescription. —**le'gal·ist,** *n.* —**le'gal·is'tic,** *adj.*

le·gal·i·ty (li gal'ə ti), *n., pl.* –**ties.** accordance with law; lawfulness.

le·gal·ize (lē'gəl īz), *v.,* –**ized,** –**iz·ing.** make legal; authorize by law; sanction. —**le'gal·i·za'tion,** *n.*

le·gal-sized (lē'gəl sīzd'), *adj.* of a size longer than ordinary, used esp. for documents or legal papers.

legal tender, money that must, by law, be accepted in payment of debts.

leg·ate (leg'it), *n.* 1 ambassador; representative; messenger. 2 a representative of the Pope. [< L *legatus,* orig., provided with a contract < *lex* contract] —**leg'ate·ship,** *n.*

leg·a·tee (leg'ə tē'), *n.* person to whom a legacy is left.

le·ga·tion (li gā'shən), *n.* 1 the diplomatic representative of a country and the staff of assistants. A legation ranks next below an embassy. 2 the official residence, offices, etc., of a diplomatic representative in a foreign country. [< F < L *legatio*] —**le·ga'tion·ar'y,** *adj.*

le·ga·to (li gä'tō), *adj.* smooth and connected; without breaks between successive musical tones. [< Ital., bound]

leg·end (lej'ənd), *n.* 1 story coming down from the past, which many people have believed. The stories about King Arthur and his knights are legends, not history. 2 such stories as a group. 3 inscription on a coin or medal. 4 words, etc., accompanying a picture or diagram; caption. [< OF < Med.L., < L *legenda* (things) to be read < *legere* read]

leg·end·ar·y (lej'ən der'i), *adj.* of a legend or legends; like a legend; not historical.

leg·er·de·main (lej'ər də mān'), *n.* 1 sleight of hand; conjuring tricks; jugglery. 2 trickery. [< F, quick of hand] —**leg'er·de·main'ist,** *n.*

leg·er line (lej'ər), =ledger line.

leg·gings (leg'ingz), *n.pl.* extra outer coverings of cloth or leather for the legs, for use out of doors.

leg·gy (leg'i), *adj.* 1 a having long legs. b having long and shapely legs. 2 too tall, esp. of plants.

Leg·horn (leg'hôrn), *n.* a small kind of domestic fowl.

leg·i·ble (lej'ə bəl), *adj.* 1 that can be read. 2 easy to read; plain and clear. [< LL, < L *legere* read] —**leg'i·bil'i·ty, leg'i·ble·ness,** *n.* —**leg'i·bly,** *adv.*

le·gion (lē'jən), *n.* 1 body of soldiers; army. 2 body of soldiers in the ancient Roman army consisting of 3000 to 6000 foot soldiers and 300 to 700 cavalrymen. 3 great many; very large number. [< OF < L *legio*]

le·gion·ar·y (lē´jən er´i), *adj., n., pl.* **-ar·ies.** —*adj.* of or belonging to a legion. —*n.* soldier of a legion.

le·gion·naire (lē´jən ār´), *n.* member of a legion.

legionnaires' or **legionnaire's disease,** a serious form of pneumonia, sometimes fatal, caused by bacteria. [< an American Legion convention in 1976 where there was an outbreak and the pneumonia was identified]

leg·is·late (lej´is lāt), *v.,* **-lat·ed, -lat·ing.** 1 make laws: *Congress legislates for the United States.* 2 force by legislation: *the council legislated him out of office.*

leg·is·la·tion (lej´is lā´shən), *n.* 1 the making of laws. 2 the laws made.

leg·is·la·tive (lej´is lā´tiv), *adj.* 1 having to do with making laws. 2 having the duty and power of making laws: *Congress is a legislative body.* 3 ordered by law. —**leg´is·la´tive·ly,** *adv.*

leg·is·la·tor (lej´is lā´tər), *n.* lawmaker; member of a legislative body. [< L *legis lator* proposer of a law]

leg·is·la·ture (lej´is lā´chər), *n.* a group of persons that has the duty and power of making laws for a state or country.

le·git (lə jit´), *adj. Informal.* legitimate.

le·git·i·ma·cy (lə jit´ə mə si), *n.* being legitimate or lawful; being recognized as lawful or proper.

le·git·i·mate (*adj.* lə jit´ə mit; *v.* lə jit´ə māt), *adj., v.,* **-mat·ed, -mat·ing.** —*adj.* 1 rightful; lawful; allowed: *a legitimate excuse.* 2 conforming to accepted standards. 3 born of parents who are married. 4 resting on, or ruling by, the principle of hereditary right: *the legitimate title to a throne.* 5 logical: *a legitimate conclusion.* —*v.* make or declare lawful. [< Med.L, < L *legitimus* lawful] —**le·git´i·mate·ly,** *adv.* —**le·git´i·mate·ness,** *n.*

legitimate stage, drama acted on the stage as opposed to motion pictures.

le·git·i·mist (lə jit´ə mist), *n.* supporter of legitimate authority, esp. of claims to rule based on direct descent. —**le·git´i·mism,** *n.*

le·git·i·mize (lə jit´ə mīz), *v.,* **-mized, -miz·ing.** make or declare to be legitimate. —**le·git´i·mi·za´tion,** *n.*

leg·man (leg´man´), *n., pl.* **-men.** 1 newspaper reporter who gathers facts and information by going to the scene of an event. 2 person who does legwork, going out to gather information, deliver messages, etc.

leg·ume (leg´ūm; li gūm´), *n.* 1 plant having a number of seeds in a pod, such as beans, peas, etc. Many legumes can absorb nitrogen from the air. 2 seed pot of such a plant. [< F < L *legumen*]

le·gu·mi·nous (li gū´mə nəs), *adj.* 1 of or bearing legumes. 2 of the same group of plants as beans and peas.

leg warm·ers (wôr´merz), *n.* knitted coverings for the legs that reach from the thighs to the ankles, used esp. by dancers.

leg·work (leg´wèrk´), *n.* work that involves going from place to place, usually to gather information.

lei (lā), *n., pl.* **leis.** wreath of flowers, leaves, etc. [< Hawaiian]

lei·sure (lē´zhər; lezh´ər), *n.* time free from required work in which a person may rest, and do the things he or she likes to do. —*adj.* 1 free; not busy: *leisure hours.* 2 having leisure: *the leisure class.* **at leisure, a** free; not busy. **b** without hurry; taking plenty of time. **at one's leisure,** at one's convenience. [< OF *leisir* < L *licere* be allowed]

lei·sured (lē´zhərd), *adj.* 1 having enough leisure. 2 =leisurely.

lei·sure·ly (lē´zhər li; lezh´ər–), *adj., adv.* without hurry; taking plenty of time. —**lei´sure·li·ness,** *n.*

leit·mo·tif, leit·mo·tiv (līt´mō tēf´), *n.* a short passage in a musical composition, associated throughout the work with a certain person, situation, or idea. [< G *leitmotiv* leading motive]

lem·ming (lem´ing), *n.* a small, mouselike arctic animal, having a short tail and furry feet. [< Norw.]

lem·on (lem´ən), *n.* 1 a sour, light-yellow citrus fruit growing in warm climates. 2 a thorny tree that bears this fruit. 3 a pale yellow. 4 *Fig.* something disagreeable, unpleasant, or worthless. —*adj.* pale-yellow. [< OF < Ar. < Pers. *līmūn*]

lem·on·ade (lem´ən ād´), *n.* drink made of lemon juice, sugar, and water.

le·mur (lē´mər), *n.* animal somewhat like a monkey, but having a foxlike face and woolly fur, found mainly in Madagascar. [< L, specter]

lend (lend), *v.,* **lent, lend·ing.** 1 let another have or use for a time: *lend an umbrella.* 2 give the use of (money) for a fixed or specified amount of payment: *banks lend money and charge interest.* 3 make a loan or loans. 4 give for a time; give: *a becoming dress lends charm to a girl.*

lend itself or **oneself to,** help or be suitable for. [OE *lǣnan* < *lǣn* loan] —**lend´er,** *n.*

length (lengkth; length), *n.* 1 how long a thing is; thing's measurement from end to end; longest way a thing can be measured: *the length of a rope.* 2 distance a thing extends. 3 extent in time: *length of an hour.* 4 long stretch or extent. 5 piece or portion of given length: *a length of rope.*

at length, a at last; finally. **b** in full; with all the details.

go to any length, do everything possible.

keep at arm's length, keep from being too familiar. [OE, < *lang* long¹]

length·en (lengk´thən; length´–), *v.* make, become, or grow longer.

length·wise (lengkth´wīz´; length´–), *adv.* Also, **length·ways** (lengkth´wāz´; length´–). in the direction of the length. —*adj.* directed toward the length.

length·y (lengk´thi; leng´–), *adj.,* **length·i·er, length·i·est.** long; too long. —**length´i·ly,** *adv.* —**length´i·ness,** *n.*

len·ien·cy (lēn´yən si; lē´ni ən–), **len·ience** (–yəns; –ni əns), *n.* mildness; gentleness; mercy.

len·ient (lēn´yənt; lē´ni ənt), *adj.* mild; gentle; merciful. [< L *leniens* softening < *lenis* mild] —**len´ient·ly,** *adv.*

lens (lenz), *n., pl.* **lens·es,** piece of glass or plastic that brings closer together or sends wider apart the rays of light passing through it. The lens of the eye and the lens of a camera form images. The lenses of a telescope make things look larger and nearer. [< L, lentil (which has a biconvex shape)]

lent (lent) *v.* pt. and pp. of **lend.**

Lent (lent), *n.* the forty weekdays before Easter, observed by Christians as a time for fasting and repenting of sins. [OE *lengten* spring < *lang* long¹ (from lengthening days)]

Lent·en, lent·en (len´tən), *adj.* of or during Lent; suitable for Lent.

len·til (len´təl), *n.* 1 plant whose pods contain two seeds shaped like double-convex lenses. Lentils grow mostly in S Europe and Asia. 2 seed of this plant. Lentils are eaten like peas. [< F < L *lenticula,* dim. of *lens* lentil]

len·to (len´tō), *adj., adv.* (of music) slow; slowly. [< Ital., slow]

Le·o (lē´ō), *n., gen.* **Le·o·nis** ((li ō´nis). 1 a northern constellation that was thought of as arranged in the shape of a lion. 2 the fifth sign of the zodiac; the Lion.

Le·o·nid (lē´ə nid), *n., pl.,* **Le·o·nids, Le·on·i·des.** one of the meteor showers that occurs in mid-November, seeming to originate from the constellation Leo.

le·o·nine (lā´ə nīn), *adj.* of or like a lion. [< L, < *leo* LION]

leop·ard (lep´ərd), *n.* 1 a fierce animal of Africa and Asia that has a dull-yellowish skin spotted with black. 2 jaguar or American leopard. [< OF < L < Gk., < *leon* lion + *pardos* leopard]

leop·ard·ess (lep´ər dis), *n.* a female leopard.

le·o·tard (lē´ə tärd), *n.* 1 close-fitting, one-piece garment, worn by dancers and acrobats. 2 Also, **leotards.** =tights. [< F *létard* < Jules *Léotard,* French aerialist of the 1800s]

lep·er (lep´ər), *n.* person who has leprosy. [< OF < L < Gk. *lepra* leprosy. See LEPROUS.]

lep·i·dop·ter·ous (lep´ə dop´tər əs), *adj.* belonging to the group of insects including butterflies and moths. The larvae are wormlike; the adults have four broad wings. [< NL, < Gk. *lepis* scale + *pteron* wing] —**lep´i·dop´ter·an,** *adj., n.*

lep·re·chaun (lep´rə kôn), *n.* in Irish folklore, a sprite or goblin resembling a little old man. [< Irish *lupracan*]

lep·ro·sy (lep´rə si), *n.* an infectious disease, characterized by ulcers and white, scaly scabs. [< *leprous*]

lep·rous (lep′rəs), *adj.* **1** having leprosy. **2** of or like leprosy. [< LL. < *lepra* leprosy < Gk., < *lepein* to peel] —**lep′rous·ly,** *adv.*

les·bian (lez′bi ən), *adj.* pertaining to lesbianism. *n.* a homosexual woman.

les·bi·an·ism (lez′bi ən iz′əm), *n.* homosexual relations between women.

lese-maj·es·ty (lēz′maj′is ti) or **lese maj·esty,** *n.* crime or offense against the sovereign power in a state; treason. Also, **lèse-majesté.** [< F *lèse-majesté* < L *laesa majestas* insulted sovereignty]

le·sion (lē′zhən), *n.* **1** injury; hurt. **2** a diseased condition. [< L *laesio* injury < *laedere* to strike]

Le·so·tho (lə sō′tō), country in S Africa, entirely surrounded by the Republic of South Africa.

less (les), *adj.* **1** smaller; not so much: *less time.* **2** lower in age, rank, or importance: *no less a person than the President.* —*n.* a smaller amount or quantity. —*adv.* to a smaller extent or degree: *less known.* —*prep.* lacking; without; minus: *a year less two days.*

less and less, ever smaller in amount, degree, etc.: *less and less comfortable.*

none the less, nevertheless. [OE *lǣs(sa)*]

-less, *suffix.* **1** without; that has no, as in *childless, homeless.* **2** that does not, as in *ceaseless, tireless.* **3** that cannot be ____ed, as in *countless.* [OE *-lēas*].

les·see (les ē′), *n.* person to whom a lease is granted. —**les·see′ship,** *n.*

less·en (les′ən), *v.* **1** grow or make less; decrease. **2** represent as less; minimize.

less·er (les′ər), *adj.* **1** less; smaller: *the lesser evil.* **2** the smaller or less important of two.

lesser panda, reddish-brown mammal from the Himalayas, resembling and related to the racoon; panda.

les·son (les′ən), *n.* **1** something learned or studied. **2** unit of learning or teaching; what is to be studied or practiced at one time: *a music lesson.* **3** an instructive experience, serving to encourage or warn. **4** selection from the Bible, read as part of a church service. **5** *Fig.* rebuke; lecture. [< OF < L *lectio* reading < *legere* read]

les·sor (les′ôr; les ôr′), *n.* person who grants a lease.

lest (lest), *conj.* **1** for fear that; that ____ not; in order that ____ not: *be careful lest you fall from that tree.* **2** that: *I was afraid lest he should come too late to save us.* [OE *thȳ lǣs the* whereby less]

let (let), *v.,* **let, let·ting. 1** allow; permit: *she is letting her hair grow, let a person on board a ship.* **2** allow to run out: *doctors used to let blood from people to lessen a fever.* **3** rent; hire out: *let a boat by the hour, that house lets for $1000 a month.* **4** assign by contract: *let work to a contractor.* **5** suppose; assume: *let the two lines be parallel.*

let alone, leave alone; not touch or interfere with.

let be, leave alone.

let down, a lower. **b** slow up. **c** disappoint.

let go, release the hold on.

let in, admit; permit to enter.

let in on, share a secret with.

let know, tell.

let loose, set free; release: *an imagination let loose.*

let off, allow to go free.

let on, allow to be known; reveal one's knowledge of.

let out, a permit to go out. **b** make larger. **c** rent. **d** dismiss or be dismissed, as a school or a meeting. **e** make known; disclose.

let up, stop; pause. [OE *lǣtan*]

-let, *suffix.* **1** little, as in *booklet, streamlet.* **2** thing worn as a band on, as in *anklet, armlet.* **3** other meanings, as in *couplet, gauntlet, ringlet.* [< OF *-elet*]

let·down (let′doun′), *n.* **1** a slowing up. **2** disappointment.

le·thal (lē′thəl), *adj.* causing death; deadly: *a lethal dose.* [< L *let(h)alis* < *letum* death]

le·thar·gic (lə thär′jik), *adj.* **1** unnaturally drowsy; sluggish; dull: *a hot, humid day produces a lethargic condition.* **2** producing lethargy. —**le·thar′gi·cal·ly,** *adv.*

leth·ar·gy (leth′ər ji), *n.,* *pl.* **-gies. 1** drowsy dullness; lack of energy; sluggish inactivity. **2** unnatural sleep. [< L < Gk. *lethargia,* ult. < *lethe* forgetfulness)

let's (lets), let us.

Lett (let), *n.* **1** member of a group of people living in Latvia. **2** their language; Lettish.

let·ter (let′ər), *n.* **1** mark or sign (on paper, etc.) that stands for any one of the sounds that make up words. **2** written or printed message. **3** official document granting some right or privilege. **4** exact wording; actual terms: *he kept the letter of a law but not the spirit.* —*v.* **1** mark with letters. **2** inscribe (something) in letters.

letters, a literature. **b** knowledge of literature; literary culture. **c** profession of an author.

to the letter, very exactly; just as one has been told. [< OF < L *littera*] —**let′ter·er,** *n.*

letter box, 1 =mailbox. **2** place to receive and store email on a computer.

letter carrier, person who carries and delivers mail for the United States Postal Service; mailman; postman.

let·tered (let′ərd), *adj.* **1** marked with letters. **2** able to read and write; educated. **3** knowing literature; having literary culture.

let·ter·head (let′ər hed′), *n.* **1** words printed at the top of a sheet of paper, usually a name and address. **2** sheet of paper so printed.

let·ter·ing (let′ər ing), *n.* **1** letters drawn, painted, stamped, etc. **2** a marking with letters; making letters.

letter of credit, document issued by a bank, allowing the person named in it to draw money up to a certain amount from other specified banks.

let·ter·per·fect (let′ər pėr′fikt), *adj.* correct in every detail.

Let·tish (let′ish), *adj.* of the Letts or their language. —*n.* language of the Letts.

let·tuce (let′is), *n.* **1** the large, green leaves of a plant much used in salad. **2** the plant. [< OF < L *lactuca* < *lac* milk]

let·up (let′up′), *n.* stop; pause.

leu·co·cyte (lü′kə sīt), *n.* a white blood corpuscle; one of the tiny white cells in the blood that destroy disease germs. [< Gk. *leukos* white + *kytos* hollow body]

leu·ke·mi·a (lü kē′mi ə; –kēm′yə), *n.* a usually fatal, kind of cancer characterized by a large excess of white corpuscles in the blood.

Lev., Leviticus.

Le·vant (lə vant′), *n.* countries on the Mediterranean Sea, E of Italy. —**Le·van′tine,** *adj., n.*

lev·ee¹ (lev′i), *n.* **1** bank built to keep a river from overflowing. **2** a landing place for boats. [< F, < *lever* raise < L *levare*]

lev·ee², lev·ée (lev′i; le vē′), *n.* reception. [< F *levé, lever.* See LEVEE¹.]

lev·el (lev′əl), *adj., n., v.,* **-eled, -el·ing.** —*adj.* **1** having the same height everywhere; flat; even: *a level floor.* **2** of equal height, importance, etc.: *the table is level with the edge of the window.* **3** even; uniform; steady: *a calm and level tone.* **4** well-balanced; sensible. —*n.* **1** something that is level. **2** instrument for showing whether a surface is level. **3** level position or condition. **4** height: *the flood rose to a level of 60 feet.* **5** position or standard from a social, moral, or intellectual point of view. —*v.* **1** make level; put on the same level. **2** lay low; bring (something) to the level of the ground. **3** raise and hold level for shooting; aim. **4** remove or reduce (differences, etc.); make uniform.

find one's or **its level,** arrive at the natural or proper level.

level off or **out,** come to an equilibrium, neither rising nor falling, or increasing or decreasing.

level with, be honest with; tell the truth to.

one's level best, one's very best; as well as one can do.

on the level, in a fair, straightforward manner. [< OF, ult. < L *libella,* dim. of *libra* balance] —**lev′el·er,** *n.* —**lev′el·ly,** *adv.* —**lev′el·ness,** *n.*

lev·el·head·ed (lev′əl hed′id), *adj.* having good common sense and judgment.

level playing field, competitive situation that is fair, with no person or organization having an unfair advantage.

lev·er (lev′ər; lē′vər), *n.* **1** bar for raising or moving a weight at one end by pushing down at the other end. It must be supported at a point in between. **2** any

bar working on an axis or support. —v.
1 move with a lever. **2** use a lever. [< OF
leveor < *lever* raise < L *levare*] —**lev′er-
like′**, *adj.*

lev·er·age (lev′ər ij; lē′vər–), *n.* **1** action
of a lever. **2** advantage or power gained
by using a lever. **3** *Fig.* increased power
of action.

le·vi·a·than (lə vī′ə thən), *n.* **1** in the
Bible, a huge sea animal. **2** any great and
powerful person or thing. [< LL < Heb.
liwyā·thān dragon, crocodile, prob.
< *lāvāh* twist, wind]

Le·vi's (lē′vīz), *n., pl.* **1** *Trademark.* heavy
blue denim trousers reinforced at strain
points with copper rivets, as made by
Levi Strauss and Company. **2 levis.**
=blue jeans.

lev·i·tate (lev′ə tāt), *v.* **-tat·ed, -tat·ing.**
1 rise or float in the air. **2** cause to rise
or float in the air. [< L *levitas* lightness
(see LEVITY), modeled after *gravitate*]
—**lev′i·ta′tion**, *n.* —**lev′i·ta′tor**, *n.*

Le·vit·i·cus (lə vit′ə kəs), *n.* the third
book of the Old Testament, containing
the ritual for Jewish rites and ceremonies.

lev·i·ty (lev′ə ti), *n., pl.* **-ties.** lightness
of mind, character, or behavior; lack
of proper seriousness or earnestness:
giggling in church shows levity. [< L,
< *levis* light]

lev·u·lose (lev′yə lōs), *n.* fructose. [< L
laevus left; under polarized light its
plane of polarization is turned to the
left]

lev·y (lev′i), *v.,* **lev·ied, lev·y·ing,** *n., pl.*
lev·ies. —*v.* **1** order to be paid: *the government levies taxes to pay its expenses.*
2 collect (men) for an army: *troops are
levied in time of war.* **3** seize by law
for unpaid debts: *a court can levy on a
person's property for unpaid debts.* —*n.* **1**
money collected. **2** men collected for an
army. **3** a levying. [< F *levée* < *lever* raise.
See LEVEE[1].] —**lev′i·er**, *n.*

lewd (lüd), *adj.* **1** lustful; lascivious. **2**
indecent; obscene. [OE *lǣwede* laic]
—**lewd′ly**, *adv.* —**lewd′ness**, *n.*

lex (leks), *n., pl.* **le·ges** (lē′jēz). *Latin.* law.

lex·i·cog·ra·pher (lek′sə kog′rə fər),
n. dictionary maker. [< Gk., < *lexikon*
wordbook + *graphein* write]

lex·i·cog·ra·phy (lek′sə kog′rə fi), *n.* dictionary making —**lex′i·co·graph′ic,
lex′i·co·graph′i·cal**, *adj.* —**lex′i·co-
graph′i·cal·ly**, *adv.*

lex·i·con (lek′sə kən; -kon), *n.* **1** dictionary, esp. of Greek, Latin, or Hebrew. **2**
vocabulary of a language or of a certain
group, activity, etc.: *the lexicon of crime.*
[< Gk. *lexikon* (*biblion*) wordbook]

Leyden jar, device for accumulating fric-
tional electricity, consisting of a glass
jar lined inside and outside with tin foil.
[from *Leyden, Leiden,* Holland]

LG, Low German.

lge., large.

LGK., Late Greek.

lgth., length.

l.h., left hand.

Lha·sa (lä′sə; las′ə), *n.* capital of Tibet.

Li, lithium.

L.I., Long Island.

li·a·bil·i·ty (lī′ə bil′ə ti), *n., pl.* **-ties. 1**
state of being susceptible: *liability to a
disease.* **2** state of being under obligation: *liability for a debt.* **3** debt. **4** thing
to one's disadvantage: *poor handwriting
is a liability.*

li·a·ble (lī′ə bəl; lī′bəl), *adj.* **1** likely;
unpleasantly likely: *glass is liable to
break.* **2** in danger of having, doing, etc.:
we are all liable to diseases. **3** responsible;
bound by law to pay: *liable for damage.*
4 under obligation; subject: *citizens are
liable to jury duty.* [< OF, ult. < L *ligare*
bind] —**li′a·ble·ness**, *n.*

li·aise (lē āz′), *v.,* **-aised, -ais·ing.** meet
with or connect with, esp. to coordi-
nate the work or activity of a group or
groups. [< *liaison*]

li·ai·son (lē′ā zon′; li ā′zon; lē′ə zon;
–zən), *n.* **1** connection between parts of
an army to secure proper cooperation. **2**
connection between groups or persons
for the purpose of working together as
smoothly as possible. **3** unlawful intimacy between a man and a woman. [< F
< L *ligatio* < *ligare* bind]

li·a·na (li ä′nə; -an′ə), **li·ane** (–än′), *n.* a
climbing vine with a woody stem. [< F
liane, earlier *liorne*]

li·ar (lī′ər), *n.* person who tells lies.

lib (lib), *n. Informal.* **1** liberation. **2** lib-
erationist. —*adj.* of or having to do with
liberation or liberationists.

lib., 1 book. [< L *liber*] **2** librarian;
library.

li·ba·tion (lī bā′shən), *n.* **1** a pouring out
of wine, water, etc., as an offering to a
god. **2** wine, water, etc., offered in this
way. [< L, < *libare* pur out]

lib·ber (lib′ər), *n. Informal.* =liberationist.

li·bel (lī′bəl), *n., v.,* **-beled, -bel·ing.** —*n.*
1 a written or printed statement tending
to damage a person's reputation. **2** crime
of writing or printing a libel. **3** any false
or damaging statement about a person.
—*v.* **1** write or print a libel about. **2** make
false or damaging statements about. **3**
institute suit against by means of a libel.
[< L *libellus,* dim. of *liber* book] —**li′bel-
er**, *n.*

li·bel·ous (lī′bəl əs), *adj.* **1** containing a
libel. **2** spreading libels: *a libelous tongue.*
—**li′bel·ous·ly**, *adv.*

lib·er·al (lib′ər əl; lib′rəl), *adj.* **1** generous:
a liberal donation. **2** plentiful; abundant:
a liberal amount. **3** broad-minded; not
narrow in one's ideas: *a liberal thinker.* **4**
favoring progress and reforms: *a liberal
party.* **5** giving the general thought, not
a word-for-word rendering: *a liberal
translation.* —*n.* person favorable to
progress and reforms.

Liberal, member of a Liberal Party. [< L
liberalis befitting free men < *liber* free]
—**lib′er·al·ly**, *adv.* —**lib′er·al·ness**, *n.*

liberal arts, subjects studied for culture
rather than for immediate practical use,
as literature, languages, history, and philosophy.

lib·er·al·ism (lib′ər əl iz′əm; lib′rəl–), *n.*
liberal principles and ideas; belief in
progress and reforms.

lib·er·al·i·ty (lib′ər al′ə ti), *n., pl.* **-ties.**
1 generosity. **2** a gift. **3** broad-mindedness.

lib·er·al·ize (lib′ər əl īz; lib′rəl–), *v.,*
-ized, -iz·ing. make or become liberal. —**lib′er·al·i·za′tion**, *n.* —**lib′er·
al·iz′er**, *n.*

lib·er·al-mind·ed (lib′ər əl mīn′did; lib′-
rəl–), *adj.* broad-minded.

Liberal Party, political party that favors
progress and reforms.

lib·er·ate (lib′ər āt), *v.,* **-at·ed, -at·ing.**
1 set free. **2** free from social biases or
restrictions. [< L, < *liber* free] —**lib′er-
a′tion**, *n.* —**lib′er·a·tor**, *n.*

lib·er·a·tion·ist (lib′ə rā′shə nist), *n.* person who advocates freedom from social
biases or restrictions: *a women's libera-
tionist.*

Li·be·ri·a (lī bir′i ə), *n.* country in W
Africa, founded by freed American black
slaves in 1847. —**Li·be′ri·an**, *adj., n.*

lib·er·tar·i·an (lib′ər tär′ē ən), *n.* **1** person who advocates individual freedom,
esp. in thought and conduct. **2** person
who believes in the least government
possible. —*adj.* of or having to do with
libertarians or libertarianism. —**lib′er-
tar′i·an·ism′**, *n.*

lib·er·tine (lib′ər tēn), *n.* person who
lacks moral restraint, esp. a man.
—*adj.* without moral restraints; dissolute; licentious. [< L *libertinus* freedman,
ult. < *liber* free]

lib·er·tin·ism (lib′ər tēn iz′əm; –tin–), *n.*
behavior of a libertine.

lib·er·ty (lib′ər ti), *n., pl.* **-ties. 1** freedom:
*grant liberty to slaves, land of liberty,
the colonies won their liberty.* **2** right or
power to do as one pleases; power or
opportunity to do something: *liberty
of speech or action.* **3** leave granted to a
sailor to go ashore. **4** right of being in,
using, etc.: *we give our dog the liberty
of the yard.* **5** too great freedom; setting
aside rules and manners.

at liberty, a free. **b** allowed; permitted. **c**
not busy.

take liberties, be too familiar. [< OF
< L, < *liber* free]

Liberty Bell, bell rung in Philadelphia
July 4, 1776, and regarded as a symbol
of liberty.

li·bid·i·nous (lə bid′ə nəs), *adj.* lustful;
lewd. —**li·bid′i·nous·ly**, *adv.* —**li·bid′i-
nous·ness**, *n.*

li·bi·do (lə bē′dō), *n.* **1** sexual desire
or instinct. **2** instinct generally; vital
impulse; the force motivating mental
life. [< L, desire] —**li·bid′i·nal**, *adj.*

Li·bra (lī′brə), *n., gen.* **-brae** (–brē). **1** a
southern constellation that was thought
of as arranged in the shape of a pair of

scales. **2** the seventh sign of the zodiac; the Scales. [< L, a balance]

li·brar·i·an (lī brãr′i ən), *n.* **1** person in charge of a library or part of a library. **2** person trained for work in a library.

li·brar·y (lī′brer′i; lī′brər i), *n., pl.* **-brar·ies.** **1** collection of books. **2** room or building where a collection of books is kept. [< L *librarium* bookcase < *liber* book]

li·bret·tist (lə bret′ist), *n.* writer of a libretto.

li·bret·to (lə bret′ō), *n., pl.* **-tos, -ti** (-tē). **1** words of an opera or other long musical composition. **2** book containing the words. [< Ital., dim. of *libro* book]

Lib·y·a (lib′i ə), *n.* a country in N Africa W of Egypt. —**Lib′y·an,** *adj., n.*

lice (līs), *n.* pl. of louse.

li·cense (lī′səns), *n., v.,* **-censed, -cens·ing.** —*n.* **1** permission given by law to do something: *a license to drive a car.* **2** paper, card, plate, etc., showing such permission: *show your driver's license.* **3** freedom of action, speech, thought, etc., that is permitted or conceded: *poetic license.* **4** too much liberty; abuse of liberty. —*v.* give a license to; permit by law: *a doctor is licensed to practice medicine.* [< OF < L *licentia* < *licere* be allowed] —**li′cens·a·ble,** *adj.* —**li′cens·er,** *n.*

li·cen·see (lī′sən sē′), *n.* person to whom a license is given.

li·cen·ti·ate (lī sen′shi it; ̄at), *n.* **1** person who has a license or permit to practice an art or profession. **2** holder of any of certain European university degrees lower than that of doctor. —**li·cen′ti·ate·ship′,** *n.*

li·cen·tious (lī sen′shəs), *adj.* **1** disregarding commonly accepted rules or principles. **2** lawless; immoral. **3** lewd. [< L, < *licentia* LICENSE] —**li·cen′tious·ly,** *adv.* —**li·cen′tious·ness,** *n.*

li·chen (lī′kən), *n.* plant that looks somewhat like moss and grows in patches on trees, rocks, etc., consisting of a fungus and an alga growing together. —*v.* cover with lichens. [< L < Gk. *leichen*] —**li′chen·like′,** *adj.* —**li′chen·ous,** *adj.*

lich gate (lich), roofed gateway leading into a churchyard, originally where a casket was set down to await escort into the church by a clergyman. Also, **lych gate.** [< *lich* corpse + *gate*]

lic·it (lis′it), *adj.* lawful; permitted. [< L *licitus*] —**lic′it·ly,** *adv.*

lick (lik), *v.* **1** pass the tongue over: *lick a stamp.* **2** lap up with the tongue. **3** make or bring by using the tongue: *the cat licked the plate clean.* **4** pass about or play over like a tongue: *the flames were licking the roof.* **5** beat; thrash; defeat. —*n.* **1** stroke of the tongue over something. **2** place where natural salt is found and where animals go to lick it up. **3** a blow. **4** a small quantity. [OE *liccian*] —**lick′er,** *n.*

lick·ing (lik′ing), *n.* beating; defeat; thrashing.

take a licking, a suffer a beating or defeat. **b** suffer a setback or reverse, esp. in business.

lic·o·rice (lik′ə ris; lik′ris; –rish), *n.* **1** a sweet, black gummy extract obtained from the roots of a European plant used as a flavoring. **2** plant that yields this. **3** its root. **4** candy flavored with this extract. Also, **liquorice.** [< AF < LL < Gk. *glykyrrhiza* < *glykys* sweet + *rhiza* root]

lid (lid), *n.* **1** a movable cover; top: *the lid of a box.* **2** cover of skin that is moved in opening and shutting the eye; eyelid. [OE *hlid*] —**lid′ded,** *adj.* —**lid′less,** *adj.*

lie[1] (lī), *n., v.,* **lied, ly·ing.** —*n.* **1** a false statement, esp. one known to be false by the person who makes it. **2** something intended to give a false impression. [OE *lyge*] —*v.* **1** tell a lie; tell lies. **2** get, bring, put, etc., by lying: *lie oneself out of a difficulty.* **3** convey a false impression.

give the lie to, a show to be false. **b** call a liar; accuse of lying. [OE *lēogan*]

lie[2] (lī), *v.,* **lay, lain, ly·ing,** *n—v.* **1** have one's body in a flat position along the ground or other surface: *lie on the grass, lie down on the couch.* **2** be or stay in a given position state, etc.: *lie idle, the book is lying on the table, the ship lies to the south of us.* **3** exist; have its place; belong: *the cure lies in education.* **4** be buried. —*n.* manner, position, or direction in which something lies.

lie back, lean backward.

lie in, be confined in childbirth.

lie low, conceal oneself.

lie off, stay or be not far from.

lie over, suspend or put off, as travel or business plans.

(not) take (something) lying down, (not) yield or give in to (something). [OE *licgan*] —**li′er,** *n.*

Liech·ten·stein (liH′tən shtīn), *n.* country between SW Germany and NE Switzerland.

lie·der·kranz (lē′dər kränts), *n.* a smooth cheese with a strong odor. [< G, garland, of songs]

liege (lēj), *n.* **1** lord having a right to the homage and loyal service of his vassals. **2** vassal obliged to give homage and loyal service to his lord. —*adj.* having the right to, or obliged to give, homage and loyal service to a lord. [< OF < LL *leticus* < *letus* freedman, ult. < Gmc.] —**liege′man,** *n.*

lien (lēn), *n* legal claim on the property of another for payment of a debt: *the garage owner has a lien upon my automobile until I pay his bill.* [< F < L *ligamen* bond < *ligare* bind]

lieu (lü), *n.* place; stead.

in lieu of, in place of; instead of. [< F < L *locus*]

Lieut., Lieutenant.

lieu·ten·an·cy (lü ten′ən si), *n., pl.* **-cies.** rank, commission, or authority of a lieutenant.

lieu·ten·ant (lü ten′ənt), *n.* **1** person who acts in the place of someone above him in authority. **2** a commissioned army officer ranking next below a captain. **3** a commissioned naval officer ranking next below a lieutenant commander. [< F, < *lieu* a place + *tenant,* ppr. of *tenir* hold < L *tenere*]

lieutenant colonel, a commissioned army officer ranking next below a colonel and next above a major.

lieutenant commander, a commissioned naval officer ranking next below a commander and next above a lieutenant.

lieutenant general, a commissioned army officer ranking next below a general and next above a major general.

lieutenant governor, 1 an officer next in rank to the governor of a state and taking his place during his absence or in the event of his death. **2** official who acts in place of the governor general in a district of province.

life (līf), *n., pl.* **lives 1** living; being alive; quality that people, animals, and plants have and that rocks, dirt, and metals lack. **2** time of being alive: *a short life.* **3** time of existence or action of inanimate things, as a machine. **4** living being; person: *five lives were lost.* **5** living beings considered together: *the desert island had almost no animal or vegetable life.* **6** way of living: *a dull life.* **7** account of a person's life: *a life of Lincoln.* **8** spirit; vigor: *put more life into your work.*

(as) big or **large as life, a** as just as in life. **b** in person.

bring to life, make seem alive: *the story brings that time to life.*

for life, during the rest of one's life.

from life, using a living model: *a painting from life.*

take life, kill.

take one's own life, kill oneself.

true to life, as in or resembling real life. [OE *līf*]

life belt, life preserver made like a belt.

life·blood (līf′blud′), *n.* **1** blood necessary to life. **2** source of strength and energy.

life·boat (līf′bōt′), *n.* strong boat specially built for saving lives at sea or along the coast.

life buoy, life preserver; something to keep a person afloat until rescued.

life expectancy, 1 the average length of time a person can expect to line. **2** average length of time a person of a particular age can expect to live.

life·guard (līf′gärd′), *n.* person employed on a bathing beach to help in case of accident or danger to bathers.

life insurance, 1 system by which a person pays a small sum regularly to have a large sum paid to his or her family or heirs at death. **2** sum paid by the insurance company at death.

life jacket, sleeveless jacket made of waterproof fabric and filled with air or a light material, worn as a life preserver.

life·less (līf'lis), *adj.* **1** without life: *a lifeless planet.* **2** dead: *lifeless bodies on the battlefield.* **3** dull: *a lifeless performance.* —**life'less·ly,** *adv.* —**life'less·ness,** *n.*

life·like (līf'līk'), *adj.* like life; looking as if alive; like the real thing: *a lifelike description.* —**life'like'ness,** *n.*

life line, rope for saving life, such as one thrown to a ship from the shore.

life·long (līf'lông'; –long'), *adj.* lasting all one's life: *a lifelong companion.*

life preserver, a wide belt, jacket, or circular tube, usually made of waterproof fabric filled with air, cork, etc., to keep a person afloat in the water; something to keep a person afloat until rescued.

life·sav·er (līf'sāv'ər), *n.* **1** person who saves people from drowning. **2** person or thing that saves someone from trouble, discomfort, embarrassment, etc. —**life'sav'ing,** *adj., n.*

life science, any science that deals with living matter, as biology, biochemistry, zoology, etc.

life-size (līf'sīz'), *adj.* as big as the living person, animal, etc.: *a life-size statute.*

life span, 1 length of time a plant or animal lives or is likely to live. **2** length of time or possible length of time anything will last or be of use: *the bridge's estimated life span.*

life·style (līf'stīl') or **life style,** *n.* characteristic manner of living of a person or group.

life·time (līf'tīm'), *n.* time of being alive; time during which a life lasts. —*adj.* for life.

life·work (līf'wèrk'), *n.* work that takes or lasts a whole lifetime; main work in life.

lift (lift), *v.* **1** raise; take up; raise into a higher position: *lift a chair.* **2** rise and go; go away: *the darkness lifts.* **3** go up; yield to an effort to raise something: *this window will not lift.* **4** sent up loudly: *lift a voice or cry.* **5** steal; plagiarize: *to lift things from a store, lift a paragraph.* —*n.* **1** an elevating influence. **2** act or fact of lifting. **3** load lifted. **4** distance through which a thing is lifted. **5** a helping hand. **6** ride in a vehicle given to a traveler on foot; free ride. **7** elevator. [<Scand. *lypta* < *lopt* air] —**lift'a·ble,** *adj.* —**lift'er,** *n.*

lift·off (lift'ôf'; –of'), *n.* take-off or launching, esp. of a rocket.

lig·a·ment (lig'ə mənt), *n., pl.* **lig·a·ments, lig·a·men·ta** (lig'ə men'tə). band of strong tissue that connects bones or holds parts of the body in place. [< L *ligamentum* < *ligare* bind]

lig·a·ture (lig'ə chər; –chûr), *n.* **1** anything used to bind or tie up; bandage, cord, etc. **2** thread, string, etc., used to tie up a bleeding artery or vein. **3** a slur or a group of notes in music connected by a slur. **4** two or three letters joined in printing. Æ and ﬀ are ligatures. [< LL *ligatura,* ult. < L *ligare* bind]

light¹ (līt), *n., adj., v.,* **light·ed** or **lit, light·ing.** —*n.* **1** that by which we see; form of radiant energy that acts on the retina of the eye. **2** thing that gives light, as the sun, a lamp, etc. **3** brightness; clearness: *a strong light, light and shade.* **4** daytime. **5** window or other means of letting in light. **6** knowledge; information. **7** public knowledge; open view: *bring to light.* —*adj.* **1** having light. **2** bright; clear: *it is as light as day.* **3** pale in color; whitish. —*v.* **1** give light to; provide with light. **2** make or become bright: *her face lights up when he comes in.* **4** become light: *the sky lights up at dawn.* **5** set fire to: *she lighted the candles.*

according to one's lights, following one's own ideas, intelligence, and conscience in the best way one knows.

come to light, be revealed, exposed.

in (the) light of, a considering. **b** from the point of view of.

see the light (of day), a be born. **b** be made public. **c** get the right idea; understand. [OE *lēoht*]

light² (līt), *adj.* **1** easy to carry; not heavy: *a light load.* **2** of less than standard or usual weight, amount, force, etc.: *a light sleep, light clothing.* **3** of foods, easy to digest. **4** easy to do or bear; not hard or severe. **5** not looking heavy; graceful; delicate: *a light bridge, light on one's feet.* **6** not serious: *light reading, light losses.* **7** not dense: *a light fog, a light soil.* **8** lightly armed or equipped: *light cavalry.* —*adv.* lightly.

make light of, treat as of little importance. [OE *lēoht, līht*]

light³ (līt), *v.,* **light·ed** or **lit, light·ing. 1** come down to the ground: *a bird lighted on the branch.* **2** come by chance: *his eye lighted upon a sentence, the blow lit on his head.*

light into, a attack. **b** scold.

light out, leave suddenly; go away quickly. [OE *līhtan* < *līht* light²]

light bulb, transparent globe or tube that fits into an electric socket to provide light.

light·en¹ (līt'ən), *v.* **1** make light; grow light: *the sky lightens before the dawn.* **2** brighten: *her face lightened.* **3** flash with lightning: *it thundered and lightened outside.* [ME, < *light¹*] —**light'en·er,** *n.*

light·en² (līt'ən), *v.* **1** reduce the load of; have the load reduced. **2** make or become less of a burden: *to lighten taxes.* **3** make or become more cheerful. [ME, < *light²*]

light·er¹ (līt'ər), *n.* thing or person that starts something burning. [ME, < *light¹*]

light·er² (līt'ər), *n.* a flat-bottomed barge used for loading and unloading ships. [< *light²* or ? < Du. *lichter*]

light-fin·gered (līt'fing'gərd), *adj.* thievish; skillful at picking pockets.

light-foot·ed (līt'fût'id), *adj.* stepping lightly. —**light'foot'ed·ly,** *adv.* —**light'-foot'ed·ness,** *n.*

light-head·ed (līt'hed'id), *adj.* **1** dizzy. **2** delirious. **3** frivolous; flighty. —**light'-head'ed·ly,** *adv.* **light'-head'ed·ness,** *n.*

light-heart·ed (līt'här'tid), *adj.* carefree; cheerful. —**light'-heart'ed·ly,** *adv.* —**light'-heart'ed·ness,** *n.*

light heavyweight, boxer who weighs between 161 and 175 pounds.

light·house (līt'hous'), *n.* tower or framework with a bright light that shines far over the water to warn and guide ships.

light industry, industry that produces goods for consumers, as clothing, food, etc.

light·ing (līt'ing), *n.* **1** giving of light; providing with light. **2** way in which lights are arranged. **3** starting to burn.

lightning arrester, device that protects electrical equipment from damage by lightning.

light·ly (līt'li), *adv.* **1** with little weight, force, etc.: *rest lightly on a thing.* **2** to a small degree or extent: *lightly clad.* **3** quickly; easily: *to jump lightly aside.* **4** cheerfully: *take bad news lightly.*

light·ness¹ (līt'nis), *n.* **1** brightness; clearness. **2** paleness; whitishness. **3** amount of light.

light·ness² (līt'nis), *n.* **1** a being light; not being heavy. **2** not being hard or severe. **3** gracefulness; delicacy. **4** being cheerful. **5** lack of proper seriousness.

light·ning (līt'ning), *n.* discharge or flash of electricity in the sky. [< *lighten¹*]

lightning bug, =firefly.

lightning rod, 1 metal rod fixed on a building or ship to conduct lightning into the earth or water. **2** *Fig.* someone or something that attracts criticism or controversy.

light·proof (līt'prüf'), *adj.* that will not let light through; resistant to light: *a lightproof box.*

light rail, system of transportation that uses monorails, streetcars, etc., usually in a city.

light railway, 1 narrow-gauge railway. **2** =light rail

light·ship (līt'ship'), *n.* ship with a bright light that shines far over the water, anchored at a dangerous place to warn and guide ships.

light show, display of colored lights in constantly changing patterns, often accompanied by music.

light·some (līt'səm), *adj.* **1** nimble; lively. **2** happy; gay; cheerful. **3** frivolous. —**light'some·ly,** *adv.* —**light'some·ness,** *n.*

light·weight (līt'wāt'), *n.* **1** person or thing of less than average weight **2** boxer who weighs less than 135 pounds. **3** person who has little intelligence or importance.

light-year (līt'yir'), *n.* **1** distance that light travels in one year; about 6,000,000,000,000 miles. **2** *Fig.* light-years. a very great distance. **3** *Fig.,* **light-years.** a very long time.

lig·ne·ous (lig'ni əs), *adj.* of or like wood; woody. [< L, < *lignum* wood]

lig·nin (lig'nin), *n.* organic substance which, along with cellulose, forms the essential part of woody tissue and accounts for the greater part of the weight of dry wood. [< L *lignum* wood + *-in*, var. of *-ine²*]

lig·nite (lig′nīt), *n.* a dark-brown kind of coal in which the texture of the wood can be seen. [< F, < L *lignum* wood]

lig·num vi·tae (lig′nəm vī′tē), **1** an extremely heavy and hard wood, used for making pulleys, rulers, etc. **2** a tropical tree from which it comes. [< L, wood of life; from its supposed medicinal value]

lik·a·ble, like·a·ble (līk′ə bəl), *adj.* having qualities that win good will or friendship; popular. —**lik′a·ble·ness, like′a·ble·ness,** *n.*

like¹ (līk), *adj., prep., adv., n, conj.,* —*adj.* **1** similar; similar to; resembling something or each other: *our house is like theirs.* **2** characteristic of: *isn't that just like a boy?* **3** prophetic or indicative of: *it looks like rain.* **4** in the right state or frame of mind for: *I feel like working.* —*prep.* in like manner with; similarly to: *she works like a beaver.* —*adv.* **1** probably: *like enough it will rain.* **2** in like manner. —*n.* **1** person or thing like another; match; counterpart or equal. **2** something of similar nature: *wheat, oats, and the like are cereals.* —*conj.* **1** like as; as. **2** as if. **3** *Slang.* as if to say; so to speak: *I thought like wow, this is great.*

and the like, and so forth; and other things.

nothing like, not nearly.

or the like, or other things.

something like, nearly; almost.

tell it (or **say it**) **like it is,** *Informal.* speak frankly; give the facts plainly. [OE *gelī*]

like² (līk), *v.,* **liked, lik·ing,** *n.* —*v.* **1** be pleased with; be satisfied with. **2** wish for; wish. —*n.* **likes,** likings; preferences. [OE *līcian* to please]

–like, *suffix.* **1** like, as in *wolflike.* **2** like that of; characteristic of, as in *childlike.* **3** suited to; fit or proper for, as in *businesslike.* [< *like¹* adj.]

like·li·hood (līk′li hůd), *n.* probability: *is there any great likelihood of rain this afternoon?*

like·ly (līk′li), *adj.,* **-li·er, -li·est,** *adv.* —*adj.* **1** probable: *one likely result of this heavy rain is the rising of the river.* **2** to be expected: *it is likely to be hot in August.* **3** suitable: *is there a likely place to fish?* **4** showing ability: *a likely boy.* —*adv.* probably: *I shall very likely be at home all day.* [< Scand. *līkligr*]

like-mind·ed (līk′mīn′did), *adj.* **1** in agreement: *we are like-minded about the problem.* **2** sharing opinions, attitudes, etc.: *a like-minded friend.*

lik·en (līk′ən), *v.* compare; represent as like.

like·ness (līk′nis), *n.* **1** a resembling; a being alike: *a boy's likeness to his father.* **2** something that is like; copy; picture:

have one's likeness painted. **3** appearance; shape: *assume the likeness of a swan.*

like·wise (līk′wīz′), *adv.* **1** the same: *go and do likewise.* **2** also; moreover; too.

lik·ing (līk′ing), *n.* **1** preference; fondness; kindly feeling: *a liking for apples.* **2** taste; pleasure: *food to your liking.*

li·lac (lī′lək; –lak), *n.* **1** shrub with clusters of tiny fragrant flowers. **2** the cluster of flowers. **3** a pale pinkish purple. —*adj.* pale pinkish-purple. [< F < Sp. < Ar. < Pers. *līlak* < *nīl* indigo]

Lil·li·pu·tian (lil′ə pū′shən), *adj.* very small; tiny; petty. —*n.* a very small person; dwarf.

lilt (lilt), *v.* sing or play (a tune) in a light tripping manner. —*n.* **1** lively song or tune with a swing. **2** a lively, springing movement. [ME *lulte*]

lil·y (lil′i), *n., pl.* **lil·ies,** *adj.* —*n.* **1** any plant of a family of herbs, shrubs, and trees that grow from a bulb, usually have flowers with six parts, and have stemless leaves. **2** the flower. **3** the bulb. **4** any of various related or similar plants, such as the calla lily or water lily. —*adj.* like a lily; white; pale; pure; lovely; delicate. [< L, akin to Gk. *leirion*] —**lily′y·like′,** *adj.*

lil·y-liv·ered (lil′i liv′ərd), *adj.* cowardly.

lily of the valley, *pl.* **lilies of the valley.** plant having tiny, fragrant, bell-shaped, white flowers arranged up and down a single stem.

Li·ma (lē′mə), *n.* capital of Peru.

Li·ma bean (lī′mə), **1** a broad, flat bean used for food. **2** plant that it grows on. [< *Lima* (Peru)]

limb (lim), *n.* **1** leg, arm, or wing. **2** a large branch of a tree. **3** part that projects; branch; arm. **4** person or thing thought of as a branch or offshoot.

limb from limb, into pieces; completely apart.

out on a limb, in a risky or vulnerable position. [OE *lim*] —**limb′less,** *adj.*

lim·ber (lim′bər), *adj.* bending easily; flexible: *limber fingers.* —*v.* make or become limber: *limber up by exercise.* [? < *limp²* or *limb*] —**lim′ber·ly,** *adv.* —**lim′ber·ness,** *n.*

lim·bic lobe (lim′bik), either of the two lobes of the brain, one in each hemisphere.

limbic system, interconnected neural structures in the cortex of the brain, believed to control emotions and certain behavior.

lim·bo (lim′bō), *n.* **1** Often, **Limbo.** a place for those who are not baptized Christians but do not deserve the punishment of sinners. **2** place for people and things forgotten, cast aside, or out of date. [< L (*in*) *limbo* on the edge]

lime¹ (līm), *n., v.,* **limed, lim·ing.** —*n.* a white substance obtained by burning limestone, shells, bones, etc.; calcium oxide; quicklime. Lime is used in making mortar and on fields to improve the soil. —*v.* put lime on. [OE *līm*]

lime² (līm), *n.* **1** a greenish-yellow fruit much like a lemon, but smaller and sourer. **2** tree that it grows on. [< F < ? < Ar. *līma*]

lime³ (līm), *n.* linden tree, often used for shade. [var. of earlier *line* < OE *lind*]

lime·ade (līm′ād′), *n.* drink made of lime juice, sugar, and water.

lime·kiln (līm′kil′; –kiln′), *n.* furnace for making lime by burning limestone, shells, etc.

lime·light (līm′līt′), *n.* **1** a strong light thrown upon the stage of a theater to light up certain persons or objects. **2** center of public attention and interest.

lim·er·ick (lim′ər ik; lim′rik), *n.* kind of nonsense verse of five lines. [appar. from a song about *Limerick,* Ireland]

lime·stone (līm′stōn′), *n.* rock consisting mostly of calcium carbonate, used for building and for making lime. Marble is a kind of limestone.

lim·it (lim′it), *n.* farthest edge or boundary; where something ends or must end: *the limits of the school grounds.* —*v.* set a limit to; restrict: *her food was limited to bread and water.*

limits, a boundaries; bounds. **b** areas or regions.

the limit, as much as, or more than, one can stand. [< OF < L *limes* boundary] —**lim′it·a·ble,** *adj.* —**lim′it·er,** *n.*

lim·i·ta·tion (lim′ə tā′shən), *n.* **1** a limiting. **2** limited condition. **3** a limiting rule or circumstance; restriction.

lim·i·ta·tive (lim′ə tā′tiv), *adj.* limiting.

lim·it·ed (lim′it id), *adj.* kept within limits; restricted. —**lim′it·ed·ly,** *adv.* —**lim′it·ed·ness,** *n.*

limited monarchy, monarchy in which the ruler's powers are limited by law.

lim·it·less (lim′it lis), *adj.* without limits; boundless.

Li·moges (li mōzh′), *n.* porcelain made at Limoges, France.

lim·ou·sine (lim′ə zēn′; lim′ə zēn) *n.* a closed automobile, in which passengers are seated in the back, usually separated from the driver. [< F, < *Limousin,* former French province]

limp¹ (limp), *n.* a lame step or walk. —*v.* walk with a limp. [cf. OE *lemphealt* lame] —**limp′er,** *n.*

limp² (limp), *adj.* lacking stiffness or firmness: *clothes get limp in hot weather.* [akin to Scand. *limpa* indisposition] —**limp′ly,** *adv.* —**limp′ness,** *n.*

lim·pet (lim′pit), *n.* a small shellfish that sticks to rocks. [< LL *lampreda* lamprey. Doublet of **lamprey.**]

lim·pid (lim′pid), *adj.* clear; transparent: *limpid water, limpid eyes.* [< L *limpidus*] —**limpid′i·ty, lim′pid·ness,** *n.* —**lim′pid·ly,** *adv.*

lim·y (līm′i), *adj.,* **lim·i·er, lim·i·est,** **1** of, containing, or resembling lime. **2** smeared with birdlime.

lin·age (līn′ij), *n.* **1** alignment. **2** quantity of printed or written matter estimated in lines. **3** rate of payment by the line.

linch·pin (linch′pin′), *n.* pin inserted through a hole in the end of an axle to keep the wheel on.

Lin·coln (ling′kən), *n.* **1 Abraham,** 1809–65, the 16th president of the United States, 1861–65. **2** capital of Nebraska, in the SE part.

lin·den (lin′dən), *n.* shade tree with heartshaped leaves and clusters of small, fragrant, yellowish flowers. [OE, orig. adj., < *lind* linden, lime³]

line¹ (līn), *n., v.,* **lined, lin·ing. —*n.* 1** piece of rope, cord, or wire: *a fishing line.* **2** a long narrow mark: *draw two lines along the margin.* **3** edge; limit; boundary: *the line between Texas and Mexico.* **4** row of persons or things: *a line of trees, a column of 40 lines.* **5** short letter; note: *drop me a line.* **6** family or lineage: *of noble line.* **7** course; track: *a line of march, a line of policy.* **8** any rope, wire, pipe, hose, etc., running from one point to another: *a telephone line.* **9** a system of transportation: *the main line of a railroad.* **10** field interest; kind of activity: *a good line of hardware.* **11** one of the horizontal lines that make a staff in music. **12** in football, the players lined up even with the ball before the action of a down begins. —*v.* **1** mark with lines on paper, etc. **2** cover with lines: *a face lined by age.* **3** arrange in a line. **4** arrange a line along; form a line along.

all along the line, at every point; everywhere.

along the line, while something else was happening or being done: *changes made along the line.*

bring into line, cause to or change in order to agree or conform.

down the line, in the future: *what happens down the line?*

down (to the end of) the line, to the end; along the whole way.

draw a or **the line,** fix or set a limit.

hold the line, prevent or resist a change or shift.

in line, a in a row. **b** *Fig.* in agreement. **c** in order or succession.

in line with, in agreement with.

lay or **put on the line, a** put at risk. **b** speak frankly.

lines, a outline; contour: *a ship of fine lines; the lines of a suit.* **b** plan; approach; method: *an investigation along the same lines.* **c** words that an actor speaks in a play or film. **d** poetry; verses. **e** trenches or other defenses used in war.

line up, a form up into a line. **b** make readily available: *line up experienced help.*

out of line, a not in agreement. **b** not behaving properly.

toe the line, conform to a standard. [coalescence of OE *līne* line, rope (< *līn* flax) and L *linea* line, linen thread (< *linum* flax)]

line² (līn), *v.,* **lined, lin·ing. 1** put a layer inside of. **2** fill: *line one's pockets with money.* **3** serve as a lining for. [< OE *līn* flax]

lin·e·age (lin′i ij), *n.* **1** descent in a direct line from an ancestor. **2** family; race. [< OF *lignage* < *ligne* line < L *linea*]

lin·e·al (lin′i əl), *adj.* **1** in the direct line of descent: *a lineal descendant.* **2** hereditary. **3** linear. —**lin′e·al·ly,** *adv.*

lin·e·ar (lin′i ər), *adj.* **1** of or in a line or lines. **2** made of lines; making use of lines. **3** long and narrow. [< L, < *linea* line¹] —**lin′e·ar·ly,** *adv.*

linear accelerator, device for accelerating charged particles in a straight line through a vacuum tube or series of tubes.

linear measure, 1 measure of length. **2** system for measuring length in which 12 inches = 1 foot.

line dance, 1 dance in which dancers are arranged in usually a single line. **2** dance in which one or more lines of dancers perform intricate steps in unison. —**line danc·er.** —**line danc·ing.**

line·man (līn′mən), *n., pl.* **-men. 1** person who sets up or repairs telegraph, telephone, or electric wires. **2** center, guard, tackle, or end in football.

lin·en (lin′ən), *n.* **1** cloth or thread made from flax. **2** articles made of linen or some substitute. [OE *līnen,* adj. < *līn* flax]

line of force, *Physics.* line in a field of electrical or magnetic force that indicates the direction in which the force is acting.

lin·er¹ (līn′ər), *n.* **1** ship or airplane belonging to a transportation system. **2** person or thing that makes lines. **3** a baseball hit so that it travels not far above the ground.

lin·er² (līn′ər), *n.* **1** one that lines. **2** a lining. **3** booklet in a CD box or short passage printed on the cover for a recording that gives information about the material that has been recorded.

lines·man (līnz′mən), *n., pl.* **-men. 1** in certain games, person who watches the lines which mark out the field, court, etc., and assists the umpire. **2** lineman.

line-up, line·up (līn′up′), *n.* **1** formation of persons or things into a line: *a police line-up.* **2** *Am.* arrangement of the players in football, baseball, etc., before a play begins.

ling (ling), *n., pl.* **ling, lings.** fish of N Europe and Greenland, used for food. [ME *lenge* < OE *lang* long¹]

–ling, *suffix.* **1** little; unimportant, as in *lordling.* **2** one that is, as in *underling.* **3** one belonging to or concerned with, as in *earthling, hireling.* [OE]

lin·ger (ling′gər), *v.* **1** stay on in a place: *linger in the country.* **2** continue; persist: *traces linger.* **3** go slowly, as if unwilling to leave; loiter. [frequentative of earlier *leng* delay, OE *lengan* < *lang* long¹] —**lin′ger·er,** *n.*

lin·ge·rie (lan′zhə rē′; län′zhə rā′), *n.* women's underwear. [< F, ult. < *linge* linen]

lin·go (ling′gō), *n., pl.* **-goes. 1** language. **2** any speech regarded as outlandish or queer: *writers about baseball use a strange lingo.* [blend of Pr. *lengo* and Ital. *lingua,* both < L *lingua* tongue]

lin·gua fran·ca (ling′gwə frang′kə). **1** a hybrid language, consisting largely of Italian, used by the Latin races in dealing with Arabs, Turks, Greeks, etc. **2** any hybrid language similarly used. [< Ital., Frankish language]

lin·gual (ling′gwəl), *adj.* of the tongue: *a lingual defect.* [< Med.L, <L *lingua* tongue] —**lin′gual·ly,** *adv.*

lin·gui·ne (ling gwē′ni), *n.* pasta, like spaghetti, but flat. [< Ital. *linguine,* pl. of *linguina* (dim.) < *lingua* tongue]

lin·guist (ling′gwist), *n.* **1** person skilled in a number of languages besides his or her own. **2** scientist who studies the structure of language. [< L *lingua* tongue]

lin·guis·tic (ling gwis′tik), *adj.* having to do with language or the study of languages. —**lin·guis′ti·cal·ly,** *adv.*

lin·guis·tics (ling gwis′tiks), *n.* science of language.

lin·i·ment (lin′ə mənt), *n.* liquid for rubbing on the skin to relieve soreness, sprains, bruises, etc. [< LL, < *linere* anoint]

lin·ing (līn′ing), *n.* layer of material covering the inner surface of something: *the lining of a coat, the lining of a water heater.*

link (lingk), *n.* **1** one ring or loop of a chain. **2** anything that joins as a link joins. **3** bond or tie. **4** *Fig.* fact or thought that connects others: *a link in a chain of evidence.* **5** link of a surveying chain used as a measure; 7.92 inches. —*v.* join as a link does; unite or connect.

link up with, meet, esp. by prearrangement. [< Scand. (Sw.) *länk*] —**linked,** *adj.*

link·age (lingk′ij), *n.* **1** a linking or being linked. **2** arrangement or system of links.

linking verb, a verb with little or no meaning of its own that connects a subject with a predicate adjective or noun.

links (lingks), *n. pl.* =golf course. [OE *hlinc* rising ground]

lin·net (lin′it), *n.* a small songbird of Europe, Asia, and Africa. [OE *līnēte* flax-eater; flaxseeds form much of its diet]

li·no·le·um (li nō′li əm), *n.* floor covering made by putting a hard surface of ground cork mixed with oxidized linseed oil on a canvas back. [< L *linum* flax + *oleum* oil]

lin·seed (lin′sēd′), *n.* seed of flax. [OE *līnsǣd* flaxseed]

linseed oil, a yellowish oil pressed from linseed, used in making paints and wood finishes, printing inks, and linoleum.

lin·sey-wool·sey (lin′zi wŭl′zi), or **lin sey,** *n., pl.* **-wool·seys; lin·seys.** a strong coarse fabric made of linen and wool or of cotton and wool. [< OE *līn* linen + *wull* wool]

lint (lint), *n.* **1** a soft down or fleecy material obtained by scraping linen. Lint was formerly much used as a dressing for wounds. **2** tiny bits of thread. [ME *lynet* < OE *līn* flax] —**lint′y,** *adj.*

lin·tel (lin′təl), *n.* a horizontal beam or stone over a door, window, etc., to support the structure above it. [< OF, ult. < L *limes* boundary]

li·on (lī′ən), *n.* **1** a large, strong, tawny animal of the cat family, found in Africa and S Asia. The male has a full, flowing mane of coarse hair. **2** *Fig.* a very brave or strong person. **3** *Fig.* a famous person. **4 Lion,** Leo, a constellation and sign of the zodiac.

throw or **feed to the lions,** abandon or withdraw support, even if it will lead to ruin or destruction. [< OF < L < Gk. *leon*]

li·on·ess (lī′ən is), *n.* a female lion.

li·on·heart·ed (lī′ən här′tid), *adj.* brave.

li·on·ize (lī′ən īz), *v.,* **-ized, -iz·ing.** treat someone as very important. —**li′on·i·za′tion,** *n.*

lion's share, the biggest or best part.

lip (lip), *n., v.,* **lipped, lip·ping,** *adj.* —*n.* **1** either of the two fleshy movable edges of the mouth. **2** folding or bent-out edge of any opening: *the lip of a pitcher.* **3** mouthpiece of a musical instrument. **4** impudent talk. —*v.* **1** touch with the lips. **2** use the lips in playing a wind instrument. **3** murmur. —*adj.* not heartfelt or deep, but just on the surface: *lip worship.*

curl one's lip, raise the upper lip as an expression of contempt.

keep a stiff upper lip, show no emotion; appear brave.

lips, mouth.

read my lips, *Informal.* pay close attention to what I say.

smack one's lips, a open the lips with a sharp sound to express pleasure. **b** *Fig.* express pleasure at the thought of something. [OE *lippa*]

lip·id (lip′id), *n.* any one of a group of organic compounds including the fats, oils, waxes, and sterols, that have an oily feeling and do not dissolve in water. [< Gk. *lípos* fat + *-id*]

lip·o·pro·tein (lip′ə prō′tēn; -tēin), *n.* any one of a class of proteins having a lipid as a component.

lipped (lipt), *adj.* having a lip or lips.

lip reading, understanding of speech by watching the movements of the speaker's lips. —**lip′-read′,** *v.* —**lip reader.**

lip service, help or support consisting only of words; empty or insincere expressions of good will or loyalty: *support limited to lip service.*

lip·stick (lip′stik′), *n.* a small stick of rouge, etc., used for coloring the lips.

lip-sync or **lip-synch** (lip′singk′), *v.* move the lips in synchronization with

sound recorded separately. —**lip sync, lip synch,** *n.*

liq., 1 liquid. **2** liquor.

liq·ue·fac·tion (lik′wə fak′shən), *n.* **1** process of changing into a liquid. **2** liquefied condition.

liq·ue·fy (lik′wə fī), *v.,* **-fied, -fy·ing.** change into a liquid. [< L, < *liquere* be fluid + *facere* make] —**liq′ue·fi′a·ble,** *adj.* —**liq′ue·fi′er,** *n.*

li·queur (li kėr′; -kyür′), *n.* a strong, sweet, highly flavored alcoholic liquor. [< F. Doublet of LIQUOR.]

liq·uid (lik′wid), *n.* substance that is neither a solid nor a gas; substance that flows freely like water. —*adj.* **1** in the form of a liquid; melted: *liquid soap.* **2** clear and bright like water. **3** clear and smooth-flowing in sound: *the liquid notes of a bird.* **4** easily turned into cash: *a liquid investment.* [< L *liquidus* < *liquere* be fluid] —**liq′uid·ly,** *adv.* —**li·quid′i·ty,** *n.* —**liq′uid·ness,** *n.*

liquid air, intensely cold, transparent liquid formed when air is very greatly compressed and then cooled, used esp. as a refrigerant.

liq·ui·date (lik′wə dāt), *v.,* **-dat·ed, -dat·ing. 1** pay (a debt). **2** settle the accounts of (a business, etc.); clear up the affairs of (a bankrupt). **3** get rid of (an undesirable person or thing): *the Russian revolution liquidated the nobility.* **4** kill ruthlessly; exterminate. **5** determine the amount of (indebtedness or damages). —**liq′ui·da′tion,** *n.* —**liq′ui·da′tor,** *n.* —**li·quid′i·ty.** *n.*

liquid crystal, substance that flows like a liquid but has some properties of a crystal, used in digital watches, calculator displays, etc.

liquid measure, 1 measurement of liquids. **2** system for measuring liquids: 2 pints = 1 quart; 4 quarts = 1 gallon.

liquid oxygen, extremely cold, clear liquid formed by cooling pressurized oxygen, used as rocket fuel; lox.

liq·uor (lik′ər), *n.* **1** an alcoholic drink, esp. brandy, gin, rum, and whiskey. **2** any liquid: *pickles are put up in a salty liquor.* [< L. Doublet of LIQUEUR.]

liq·uo·rice (lik′ə ris; lik′ris; -rish), *n.* =licorice.

li·ra (lir′ə), *n., pl.* **li·re** (lir′ā), **li·ras. 1** unit of money in Italy. **2** coin worth a lira. [< Ital. < L *libra* pound]

Lis·bon (liz′bən), *n.* capital of Portugal.

lisle (līl), *n.* a fine, strong, linen or cotton thread, used for making socks, knit shirts, etc. [< F *Lisle,* former name of Lille]

lisp (lisp), *v.* **1** use the sounds of *th,* as in *thin* and *then,* instead of the sound of *s* and the sound of *z* in speaking. **2** speak imperfectly. —*n.* act, habit, or sound of lisping. [ult. < OE *wlisp,* adj., lisping] —**lisp′er,** *n.* —**lisp′ing·ly,** *adv.*

LISP (lisp), *n.* computer programming language that deals with lists, used esp. in artificial-intelligence programs.

lis·some, lis·som (lis′əm), *adj.* **1** lithe; limber; supple. **2** nimble; active. [var. of *lithesome < lithe*] —**lis′some·ly, lis′som·ly,** *adv.* —**lis′some·ness, lis′som·ness,** *n.*

list¹ (list), *n.* series of names, numbers, words, etc.: *a shopping list.* —*v.* make a list of; enter in a list. [< F *liste* < Gmc.]

list² (list), *n.* the edge of cloth, where the material is a little different. [OE *līste*]

list³ (list), *n.* a tipping to one side; tilt: *the list of a ship.* —*v.* tip to one side; tilt.

list⁴ (list), *v. Archaic* listen. [OE *hlystan* < *hlyst* hearing; akin to LISTEN]

lis·ten (lis′ən), *v.* **1** try to hear; attend closely for the purpose of hearing: *listen to the radio.* **2** give heed to advice, temptation, etc.); pay attention.

listen in, listen to others talking on a telephone. [OE *hlysnan;* akin to LIST⁵] —**lis′ten·er,** *n.*

list·er (lis′tər), *n.* plow that throws the dirt to both sides of the furrow. [< *list²*]

list·less (list′lis), *adj.* seeming too tired to care about anything; not interested in things; not caring to be active. —**list′less·ly,** *adv.* —**list′less·ness,** *n.*

list price, price given in a catalog or list; full price.

lists (lists), *n. pl.* **1** place where knights fought in tournaments. **2** *Fig.* any place or scene of combat. [< *list²*]

lit (lit), *v.* pt. and pp. of **light¹** and **light³.**

lit., 1 liter. **2** literal; literally. **3** literature.

lit·a·ny (lit′ə ni), *n., pl.* **-nies. 1** series of prayers by the minister with responses by the congregation. **2** a repeated series. [< LL < Gk. *litaneia* litany, an entreating]

li·tchi (lē′chē), *n., pl.* **-tchis. 1** Also, **litchi nut.** a nut-shaped fruit with a hard, rough skin. **2** the Chinese tree that it grows on. [< Chinese]

lit crit (lit′krit′), *n.* literary criticism.

lite (līt), *adj.* **1 a** reduced in calories: *lite beer.* **b** reduced in weight or content. **2** *Fig.* not serious: *history lite.*

li·ter (lē′tər), *n.* the common measure of capacity in France, Germany, and other countries which use the metric system. One liter equals 1.0567 qt. liquid measure, or .908 qt. dry measure. [< Gk. < F *litre,* ult. *litra* pound]

lit·er·a·cy (lit′ər ə si), *n.* ability to read and write.

lit·er·al (lit′ər əl), *adj.* **1** following the exact words of the original: *a literal translation.* **2** of persons, taking words in their usual meaning, without exaggeration or imagination; matter-of-fact. **3** of meaning, precise; strict: *the literal meaning of a word.* **4** true to fact: *a literal account.* [< LL, < L *lit(t)era* letter] —**lit′er·al′i·ty,** *n.* —**lit′er·al·ly,** *adv.* —**lit′er·al·ness,** *n.*

lit·er·al·ism (lit′ər əl iz′əm), *n.* **1** exact translation or interpretation. **2** exact portrayal in art or literature. —**lit′er·al·ist,** *n.* —**lit′er·al·is′tic,** *adj.*

lit·er·ar·y (lit′ər er′i). *adj.* **1** having to do with literature. **2** knowing much about literature. **3** engaged in literature as a profession. —**lit′er·ar′i·ly,** adv. —**lit′er-ar′i·ness,** n.

lit·er·ate (lit′ər it), adj. **1** able to read and write. **2** acquainted with literature; educated. —n. **1** person who can read and write. **2** educated person.

lit·e·ra·ti (lit′ə rä′ti; –rä′tī), n. pl. scholarly or literary people. [< L, pl., lit., lettered]

lit·e·ra·tim (lit′ə rä′tim), adv. letter for letter; exactly as written. [< Med.L < L lit(t)era letter]

lit·er·a·ture (lit′ər ə chər; –chŭr; lit′rə–), n. **1** writings of a period or of a country, esp. those kept alive by their beauty or style or thought. Shakespeare is a great name in English literature. **2** all the books and articles on a subject: the literature of stamp collecting. **3** profession of a writer. **4** printed matter of any kind. [< F < L lit(t) eratura writing < lit(t)era letter]

lith·arge (lith′ärj; li thärj′), n. a yellow oxide of lead, PbO, used in making glass, glazes for pottery, and driers for paints and varnishes. [< OF < L < Gk., < lithos stone + argyros silver]

lithe (lith̄), **lithe·some** (lit̄h′səm), adj. bending easily; supple. [OE līthe mild] —**lithe′ly,** adv. —**lithe′ness,** n.

lith·i·um (lith′i əm), n. a soft, silverwhite metallic element, Li, similar to sodium. Lithium is the lightest of all metals. [< NL, < Gk. lithos stone]

lith·o·graph (lith′ə graf; –gräf), n. picture, print, etc., made from a flat, specially prepared stone or a metal plate. —v. print from a stone or plate. [< Gk. lithos stone + -GRAPH] —**li·thog′ra·pher,** n.

li·thog·ra·phy (li thog′rə fi), n. art or process of making lithographs. —**lith′o·graph′ical,** adj. —**lith′o·graph′i·cal·ly,** adv.

lith·o·sphere (lith′ə sfir), n. solid portion of the earth.

Lith·u·a·ni·a (lith′ŭ ā′ni ə), n. a small country in N Europe. —**Lith′u·a′ni·an,** adj., n.

lit·i·ga·ble (lit′ə gə bəl), adj. capable of being made the subject of a suit in a law court.

lit·i·gant (lit′ə gənt), n. person engaged in a lawsuit. —adj. **1** engaging in a lawsuit. **2** inclined to go to law.

lit·i·gate (lit′ə gāt), v., –gat·ed, –gat·ing. **1** engage in a lawsuit. **2** contest in a lawsuit. [< L litigatus < lis lawsuit] —**lit′i·ga′tor,** n.

lit·i·ga·tion (lit′ə gā′shən), n. **1** the carrying of of a lawsuit. **2** a going to law.

li·ti·gious (lə tij′əs), adj. **1** having the habit of going to law. **2** that can be disputed in a court of law. **3** of lawsuits. —**li·ti′gious·ly,** adv. —**li·ti′gious·ness,** n.

lit·mus (lit′məs), n. a blue coloring matter, obtained from certain plants.

[< Scand. litmosi dyer's herbs < litr color + mosi moss]

litmus paper, paper treated with litmus. It turns red when put into an acid and back to blue when put into an alkali.

litmus test, decisive test; acid test: the campaign was a litmus test of the candidate's political skills.

li·tre (lē′tər), n. Esp. Brit. liter.

lit·ter (lit′ər), n. **1** things scattered about or left in disorder. **2** disorder; untidiness. **3** young animals produced at one time: a litter of puppies. **4** straw, hay, etc., used as bedding for animals. **5** stretcher for carrying a sick or wounded person. —v. leave odds and ends lying around; scatter things about: litter a yard with bottles and cans. [< AF, ult. < L lectus bed]

lit·te·ra·teur, lit·té·ra·teur (lit′ə rə tėr′), n. literary person; writer or critic of literature.

lit·tle (lit′əl), adj. **less** or **less·er, least;** or **lit·tler, lit·tlest** adv. **less, least;** n. —adj. **1** not great or big; small: a little house, little discomforts, little hope. **2** on a small scale: the little fellows in business. **3** mean; narrow-minded: little thoughts. —adv. **1** in a small amount or degree; slightly: he eats very little. **2** not at all: little did I think it would happen. —n. a small amount, quantity, or degree: add a little, move a little to the left.

little by little, slowly; gradually; by a small amount at a time.

make little of, treat or represent as of little importance.

not a little, much; very.

think little of, a not value much; consider as unimportant or worthless. **b** not hesitate about. [OE lȳtel] —**lit′tle·ness,** n.

Little Bear, Ursa Minor.

Little Dipper, group of stars in the constellation of Ursa Minor (the Little Bear).

little finger, smallest finger, farthest from the thumb.

Little Ice Age, period of the formation of new glaciers, beginning about 5000 years ago and reaching its height about 1700.

lit·tle·neck (lit′əl nek′), n., or **littleneck clam,** young quahog or similar small clam, usually eaten raw.

Little Rock, capital of Arkansas, in the C part.

little theater, small theater or theater group that presents new, experimental plays.

lit·to·ral (lit′ə rəl), adj. **1** of a shore. **2** on the shore. —n. region along the shore. [ult. <L litoralis < litus shore]

li·tur·gi·cal (lə tėr′jə kəl), **li·tur·gic** (–jik), adj. of or used in liturgies; having to do with liturgies. —**li·tur′gi·cal·ly,** adv.

lit·ur·gy (lit′ər ji), n., pl. –gies. form of public worship. Different churches use different liturgies. [< LL < Gk. leitourgia < leitos public + ergon work]

liv·a·ble, live·a·ble (liv′ə bəl), adj. **1** fit to live in: a livable house. **2** easy to live with.

3 worth living; endurable. —**liv′a·ble-ness, live′a·ble·ness,** n.

liv·a·bil·i·ty or **live·a·bil·i·ty** (liv′ə bil′-ə ti), n. condition of being fit to live in.

live[1] (liv), v., **lived, liv·ing. 1** have life; be alive; exist: all creatures have an equal right to live, if I live till May, live on one's income. **2** feed or subsist: live on 1200 calories per day. **3** dwell: live with one's parents.

live down, live so worthily that (some fault or sin) is overlooked or forgotten.

live it up, Informal. enjoy oneself to the fullest extent possible; have a great time.

live up to, act according to; do (what is expected or promised).

live with, accept; be resigned to; put up with. [OE lifian, libban]

live[2] (līv), adj. **1** having life; alive: a live animal. **2** burning or glowing: live coals. **3** of present interest: a live question. **4** still in use or to be used: live steam. **5** carrying an electric current: a live wire. **6** loaded: a live cartridge. **7** not recorded electronically on film: a live show. [var. of alive]

live·cast (līv′kast′), n. television program broadcast as an event is unfolding.

live-in (liv′in′), adj. living in the place where one works: my live-in babysitter. —n. Informal. partner or lover who lives with another in his or her home.

live·li·hood (līv′li hůd), n. means of keeping alive; support: Dickens wrote for a livelihood.

live·long (liv′lông′; –long′), adj. whole length of; whole; entire.

live·ly (līv′li), adj., –li·er, –li·est, adv. —adj. **1** full of life; active; vigorous; spirited: a lively child. **2** exciting: a lively time. **3** bright; vivid: lively green. **4** bounding back quickly: a lively baseball. —adv. in a lively manner. —**live′li·ly,** adv. —**live′li·ness,** n.

liv·en (līv′ən), v. make or become more lively; brighten; cheer up. —**liv′en·er,** n.

live oak (līv), **1** an evergreen oak of the S United States. **2** its hard wood.

liv·er[1] (liv′ər), n. a large, reddish-brown organ in vertebrate animals that secretes bile and helps in the absorption of food. [OE lifer]

liv·er[2] (liv′ər), n. **1** person who lives. **2** person who dwells in a place.

liv·er·ied (liv′ər id; liv′rid), adj. clothed in a livery.

liv·er·wort (liv′ər wėrt′), n. **1** any of various plants somewhat like mosses. **2** =hepatica.

liv·er·wurst (liv′ər wėrst′; –wŭrst′), n. sausage consisting largely of liver. [< G leberwurst liver sausage]

liv·er·y (liv′ər i; liv′ri), n., pl. –er·ies. **1** any special uniform provided for the servants of a household, or adopted by any group or profession. **2** a distinctive dress, badge, or cognizance provided for retainers. **3** Fig. any characteristic dress, garb, or outward appearance. **4** the feeding, stabling, and care of horses for pay; the hiring out of horses and carriages. [< OF *livrée* < *livrer* dispense; orig., provisions dispensed to servants]

liv·er·y·man (liv′ər i mən; liv′ri–), *n., pl.* **-men.** person who works in or keeps a livery stable.

livery stable, stable engaged in the livery business.

lives (līvz), *n.* pl. of **life.**

live·stock (līv′stok′), *n.* farm animals. Cows, horses, sheep, and pigs are livestock.

live wire, 1 wire in which an electric current is flowing. **2** specially alert and enterprising person.

liv·id (liv′id), *adj.* **1** having a dull-bluish or leaden color. **2** discolored by a bruise. [< L *lividus* < *livere* be bluish] —**liv′id·ly,** *adv.* —**liv′id·ness, li·vid′i·ty,** *n.*

liv·ing (liv′ing), *adj.* **1** having life; being alive: *a living plant.* **2** full of life; strong: *a living faith.* **3** in actual existence; still in use: *living language.* **4** of persons who are alive: *within living memory.* **5** true to life; vivid; lifelike: *a living picture.* **6** of life; for living in: *living conditions.* —*n.* **1** act or condition of one that lives. **2** manner of life: *the importance of right living.* **3** means of obtaining what is needed to support life; livelihood. —**liv′ing·ly,** *adv.* —**liv′ing·ness,** *n.*

living quarters, place to live.

living room, room for general family use.

living wage, sufficient pay to buy the necessities of life.

liz·ard (liz′ərd), *n.* any of a large group of reptiles, most of which are small and have long bodies with four legs and a long tail. Chameleons, horned toads, and glass snakes are lizards. [< OF < L *lacertus*]

LL, Late Latin.

ll., lines.

lla·ma (lä′mə), *n., pl.* **-mas** or (*esp. collectively*) **-ma.** a South American animal somewhat like a camel, but smaller and without a hump. [< Sp. < Quechua (Ind. lang. of Peru)]

LL.D., Doctor of Laws.

lo (lō), *interj.* look! see! behold! [OE *lā*]

loach (lōch), *n.* a small European freshwater fish. [< OF *loche*]

load (lōd), *n.* **1** what one is carrying; burden. **2** something that oppresses mind or spirit. **3** in mechanics, weight supported by a structure or part. **4** external resistance overcome by an engine, measured by the power required. **5** one charge of powder and shot for a gun. —*v.* **1** place on or in something for conveyance: *load grain, load a wagon.* **2** burden; oppress. **3** add weight to: *load dice.* **4** put a charge in (a gun).

loads, great quantity or number. [OE *lād* course, carrying. See LODE.] —**load′er,** *n.*

load·ed (lō′did), *adj.* **1** bearing a load. **2** charged with ammunition. **3** *Informal.*

Fig. full of suggestive meaning: *a loaded remark.* **4** *Informal.* very rich.

load·star (lōd′stär), *n.* =lodestar.

load·stone (lōd′stōn′), *n.* **1** stone that attracts iron as a magnet does. **2** something that attracts.

loaf¹ (lōf), *n., pl.* **loaves. 1** bread shaped and baked as one piece. **2** a rather large cake, often baked in the shape of a loaf of bread. **3** food shaped like a loaf of bread. **4** cone-shaped mass of sugar. [OE *hlāf*]

loaf² (lōf), *v.* spend time idly; do nothing.

loaf·er (lōf′ər), *n.* **1** one who loafs. **2** shoe resembling a moccasin, but with sole and heel stitched to the upper.

loam (lōm), *n.* rich, fertile earth; earth in which much humus is mixed with clay and sand. [OE *lām*] —**loam′y,** *adj.*

loan (lōn), *n.* **1** a lending. **2** money lent. **3** anything lent. —*v.* make a loan; lend. [< Scand. *lān*] —**loan′er,** *n.*

loan shark, *Informal.* person who lends money at an extremely high or unlawful rate of interest.

loan word, foreign word that has been anglicized, as *khaki* or *intelligentsia.*

loath (lōth), *adj.* unwilling; reluctant: *the little girl was loath to leave.* Also, **loth.** [OE *lāth* odious]

loathe (lōth), *v.,* **loathed, loath·ing.** feel strong dislike and disgust for; abhor; hate. [OE *lāthian* be hateful < *lāth* odious] —**loath′er,** *n.*

loath·ing (lōth′ing), *n.* strong dislike and disgust; intense aversion. —**loath′ing·ly,** *adv.*

loath·some (lōth′səm), *adj.* disgusting; sickening: *a loathsome stench.* —**loath′some·ly,** *adv.* —**loath′some·ness,** *n.*

loaves (lōvz), *n.* pl. of **loaf¹.**

lob (lob), *n., v.,* **lobbed, lob·bing.** —*n.* a tennis ball hit high to the back of the opponent's court. —*v.* **1** hit (a ball) thus. **2** throw (a ball) hastily or carelessly. —**lob′ber,** *n.*

lo·bar (lō′bər), *adj.* of or having to do with a lobe or lobes.

lo·bate (lō′bāt), **lo·bat·ed** (–id), *adj.* having a lobe or lobes; having the form of a lobe: *the liver is lobate.* —**lo′bate·ly,** *adv.*

lo·ba·tion (lō bā′shən), *n.* **1** a lobate formation. **2** lobe.

lob·by (lob′i), *n., pl.* **-bies,** *v.,* **-bied, -by·ing.** —*n.* **1** entrance hall; passageway: *the lobby of a theater.* **2** person or group that tries to influence legislators. —*v.* **a** try to influence legislators. **b** get or try to get (a bill) passed by lobbying. [< Med. L *lobia* < Gmc. Doublet of LODGE, LOGE, LOGGIA.] —**lob′by·ist,** *n.*

lobe (lōb), *n.* a rounded projecting part: *the lobes of an oak leaf.* The lobe of the ear is the lower rounded end. [< F < LL < Gk. *lobos*] —**lobed,** *adj.*

lo·bel·ia (lō bēl′yə), *n.* plant with blue, red, yellow, or white flowers. [for M. de Lobel, botanist]

lob·lol·ly (lob′lol′i), *n., pl.* **-lies.** *Am.* **1** Also, **loblolly pine.** a pine tree of the S United States that has thick bark and long needles. **2** its coarse, inferior wood.

lob·ster (lob′stər), *n.* an edible sea animal with two big claws in front and eight legs. [OE *loppestre,* prob. < *loppe* spider; from the shape]

lobster pot, a trap to catch lobsters, shaped like a box with slatted sides.

lob·ule (lob′ūl), *n.* **1** a small lobe. **2** part of a lobe. —**lob′u·lar,** *adj.*

lo·cal (lō′kəl), *adj.* **1** of place: *a local address.* **2** having to do with a certain place or places: *the local doctor, local self-government, local news.* **3** of just one part of the body: *a local pain.* **4** making all, or almost all, stops: *a local train.* —*n.* **1** train, bus, etc., that makes all, or almost all, stops. **2** branch or chapter of a labor union. [< L, < *locus* place] —**lo′cal·ly,** *adv.*

local color, customs, peculiarities, etc., of a certain place or period, used in stories and plays to make them seem more real.

lo·cale (lō kal′), *n.* place, esp. with reference to events or circumstances connected with it. [< F *local* LOCAL]

lo·cal·ism (lō′kəl iz əm), *n.* **1** a local expression, custom, etc. **2** =provincialism.

lo·cal·i·ty (lō kal′ə ti), *n., pl.* **-ties. 1** the place; region; area: *a locality known for its peaches.*

lo·cal·ize (lō′kəl īz), *v.,* **-ized, -iz·ing.** make local; fix in, assign, or limit to a particular place or locality: *an infection localized in the foot.* —**lo′cal·iz′a·ble,** *adj.* —**lo′cal·i·za′tion,** *n.*

lo·cate (lō′kāt; lō kāt′), *v.,* **-cat·ed, -cat·ing. 1** establish in a place: *he located his new store on Main Street.* **2** establish oneself in a place: *he went to New York and located there.* **3** find out the exact position of: *the general tried to locate the enemy's camp.* **4** state or show the position of: *locate Boston.*

be located, be situated: *Rome is located in Italy.* [< L, < *locus* place] —**lo′ca·tor,** *n.*

lo·ca·tion (lō kā′shən), *n.* **1** a locating or being located. **2** position; place. **3** plot of ground marked out by boundaries; lot. **4** a place outside of the studio used in making all or part of a motion picture.

loc·a·tive (lok′ə tiv), *adj.* indicating place. —*n.* **1** case used to indicate place in which. **2** word in this case.

loc. cit., in the place cited. [< L *loco citato*]

loch (lok; loH), *n. Scot.* **1** lake: *Loch Lomond.* **2** arm of the sea partly shut in by land. [< Scotch Gaelic]

lo·ci (lō′sī), *n.* pl. of **locus.**

lock¹ (lok), *n.* **1** means of fastening doors, boxes, etc., usually needing a key of special shape to open it. **2** a locking or being locked. **3** part of a canal, dock, etc., in which the level of the water can be changed by letting water in or out to raise or lower ships. **4** part of a gun by which the charge is fired. **5** a kind of hold in wrestling. —*v.* **1** fasten with a lock: *lock the door.* **2** shut (something in or out or up): *lock a prisoner in a cell.* **3** hold fast: *a ship locked in ice, a secret locked in one's heart.* **4** join, fit, jam, or link together: *the girls locked arms.*

lock on, a fix on a target, using an electronic guidance system, radar, etc. **b** fix on and follow a moving object.

lock out, refuse to give work to workers until they accept the employer's terms.

lock, stock, and barrel, *Informal.* completely; totally.

under lock and key, locked up. [OE *loc*]

lock² (lok), *n.* tress of hair.

locks, the hair of the head. [OE *locc*]

lock·down (lok′doun′), *n.* of a building, completely closed so that no one can leave or enter: *the shootings caused a lockdown for several hours.*

lock·er (lok′ər), *n.* **1** one that locks. **2** chest, drawer, closet, or cupboard that can be locked.

lock·et (lok′it), *n.* a small ornamental case of gold, silver, etc., for holding a picture of someone or a lock of hair. It is usually worn around the neck. [< F *loquet* latch, dim. of OF *loc* < Gmc.]

lock·jaw (lok′jô′), *n.* blood poisoning in which the jaws become firmly closed.

lock·nut (lok′nut′), *n.* **1** nut that holds another securely in place. **2** nut that locks in place when securely screwed.

lock·out (lok′out′), *n.* refusal to give work to workers until they accept the employer's terms.

lock·smith (lok′smith′), *n.* person who makes or repairs locks and keys.

lock step, 1 way of marching in step very close together. **2** *Fig.* rigid arrangement or way of doing something.

lock·up (lok′up′), *n.* =jail.

lock washer, metal washer placed under a nut to keep it from loosening.

lo·co (lō′kō), *n., pl.* **–cos,** *adj.* —*n.* **1** locoweed. **2** disease caused by eating this weed. —*adj. Informal.* crazy. [< Sp., insane]

lo·co·mo·tion (lō′kə mō′shən), *n.* act or power of moving from place to place. Walking, swimming, and flying are common forms of locomotion. [< L *loco* from a place + *motio* motion]

lo·co·mo·tive (lō′kə mō′tiv), *n.* a railroad engine. —*adj.* **1** moving from place to place. **2** having to do with the power to move from place to place.

lo·co·mo·tor (lō′kə mō′tər), *adj.* of or pertaining to locomotion.

locomotor ataxia, a degenerative disease of the spinal cord, marked by loss of control over walking and certain other movements.

lo·co·weed (lō′kō wēd′), *n.* plant of W United States that affects the brains of horses, sheep, etc., that eat it.

lo·cus (lō′kəs), *n., pl.* **lo·ci** (lō′sī), **1** place. **2** curve, surface, or other figure that contains all the points, and only those points, that satisfy a given condition. [< L]

lo·cust (lō′kəst), *n.* **1** any of the grasshoppers with short antennae, certain species of which migrate in great swarms, destroying crops. **2** cicada. **3 a** tree with small rounded leaflets and clusters of sweet-smelling white flowers. **b** its wood, hard and resisting decay. **4** any of various other trees, such as the honey locust. [< L *locusta*]

lo·cu·tion (lō kū′shən), *n.* **1** style of speech: *childish locution.* **2** form of expression: *foreign locutions.* [< L *locutio* < *loqui* speak]

lode (lōd), *n.* vein of metal ore. [OE *lād* course, carrying. See LOAD.]

lo·den (lō′dən), *n.* **1** heavy, waterproof woolen cloth. **2** coat made from this fabric. [< G *Loden* < OHG *lodo*]

lode·star (lōd′stär′), *n.* polestar; North Star.

lode·stone (lōd′stōn′), *n.* =loadstone.

lodge (loj), *v.,* **lodged, lodg·ing,** *n.* —*v.* **1** live in a place for a time. **2** provide with a place to live in or sleep in for a time. **3** get caught or put in a place: *the kite lodged in a tree top.* **4** put before some authority: *lodge a complaint with the police.* —*n.* **1** place to live in; small or temporary house; house. **2** branch of a secret society. **3** den of a beaver or otter. [OF *loge* arbor, covered walk < Gmc. Doublet of LOBBY, LOGE, LOGGIA.]

lodg·er (loj′ər), *n.* person who lives in a rented room in another's house.

lodg·ing (loj′ing), *n.* place to live in for a time.

lodgings, a rented room or rooms in a house, not in a hotel.

lo·ess (lō′is; lœs), *n.* a yellowish-brown loam, usually deposited by the wind. [< G *löss*]

loft (lôft; loft), *n.* **1** attic. **2** room under the roof of a barn. **3** gallery in a church or hall. **4** *U.S.* upper floor of a business building or warehouse. —*v.,* **1** throw or hit a ball, stone, etc., high into the air. **2** launch into space. [< Scand. *lopt* air, sky]

loft·y (lôf′ti; lof′–), *adj.,* **loft·i·er, loft·i·est.** **1** very high: *lofty mountains.* **2** exalted; dignified; grand: *lofty aims.* **3** proud; haughty: *a lofty contempt for others.* —**loft′i·ly,** *adv.* —**loft′i·ness,** *n.*

log (lôg; log), *n., v.,* **logged, log·ging,** *adj.* —*n.* **1** length of wood just as it comes from the tree. **2** daily record of a ship's voyage. **3** record of an airplane trip, performance of an engine, etc. **4** any daily record: *telephone log.* **5** float for measuring the speed of a ship. —*v.* **1** cut down trees, cut them into logs, and get them out of the forest. **2** enter in a daily record. **3** enter in a ship's log. —*adj.* made of logs: *a log house.* [ME *logge*]

log., logarithm.

lo·gan·ber·ry (lō′gən ber′i), *n., pl.* **–ries.** a large, purplish-red fruit of a bramble developed from a cross between a blackberry and a red raspberry. [after J. H. *Logan,* its first grower]

log·a·rithm (lôg′ə riᵺ əm; log′–), *n.* **1** exponent of the power to which a fixed number (usually 10) must be raised in order to produce a given number. If the fixed number is 10, the logarithm of 1000 is 3. **2** one of a system of such exponents used to shorten calculations in mathematics. [< NL, < Gk. *logos* proportion + *arithmos* number] —**log′a·rith′mic,** *adj.* —**log′a·rith′mi·cal·ly,** *adv.*

log·book (lôg′bùk′; log′–), *n.* book in which a daily record of a ship's voyage, airplane's trip, etc., is kept.

loge (lōzh), *n.* box in a theater or opera house. [< F < Gmc. Doublet of LOBBY, LODGE, LOGGIA.]

log·ger (lôg′ər; log′–), *n.* person whose work is logging.

log·ger·head (lôg′ər hed′; log′–) *n.* **1** a stupid person. **2** Also, **loggerhead turtle,** a large-headed turtle of the Atlantic.

at loggerheads, disputing; at enmity. [< *log* + *head*]

log·gia (loj′ə), *n., pl.* **log·gias.** gallery or arcade open to the air on at least one side. [<Ital. < Gmc. Doublet of LOBBY, LODGE, LOGE.]

log·ging (lôg′ing; log′–), *n.* work of cutting down trees, cutting them into logs, and getting them from the forest.

log·ic (loj′ik), *n.* **1** reasoning; use of argument. **2** reason; sound sense. **3** science of proof or of reasoning. **4** the nonarithmetical operations in a computer or the circuitry performing such logical operations. [< LL < Gk. *logike* (*techne*) reasoning (art) < *logos* word]

log·i·cal (loj′ə kəl), *adj.* **1** reasoning correctly. **2** reasonable; reasonably expected. **3** having to do with logic; according to the principles of logic. —**log′i·cal′i·ty, log′i·cal·ness,** *n.* —**log′i·cal·ly,** *adv.*

lo·gi·cian (lō jish′ən), *n.* expert in logic.

lo·gis·tic (lō jis′tik), **lo·gis·ti·cal** (–tə kəl), *adj.* of or having to do with logistics.

lo·gis·tics (lō jis′tiks), *n.* the science of transportation and supply. [< F *logistique* logistics < MF *logistique* (infl. by meaning of pertaining to calculation) < *logis* lodging]

log·jam (lôg′jam′, log′–), *n.* **1** a blockage of the movement of logs floating downstream. **2** *Fig.* lack of movement; deadlock.

log·roll (lôg′rōl′; log′–), *v. Informal.* **1** get (a bill) passed by logrolling. **2** take part in logrolling. —**log′roll′er,** *n.*

log·roll·ing (lôg′rōl′ing; log′–), *n.* **1** giving of political aid in return for a like favor. **2** rolling logs by treading on them, esp. as a sport.

log·wood (lôg′wùd′; log′–), *n.* **1** the heavy brownish-red wood of a tropical American tree, used in dyeing. **2** the tree.

lo·gy (lō′gi), *adj.,* **–gi·er, –gi·est.** *U.S.* heavy; sluggish; dull. [cf. Du. *log*]

–logy, *combining form.* **1** account, doctrine, or science of, as in *biology.* **2** speaking; discussion, as in *eulogy.* [< Gk., in a few cases < *logos* word, discourse, but usually < –*logos* treating of]

loin (loin), *n.* **1** Usually, **loins.** part of the body between the ribs and the hipbones. The loins are on both sides of the backbone. **2** piece of meat from this part of an animal.

gird (up) one's loins, get ready for action. [< OF *loigne,* ult. < L *lumbus*]

loin·cloth (loin′klôth′; –kloth′), *n.* piece of cloth worn around the hips and between the thighs by native peoples of warm countries.

loi·ter (loi′tər), *v.* **1** linger idly; stop along the way. **2** spend (time) idly: *loiter the hours away.* [< MDu. *leuteren* be loose] —**loi′ter·er,** —**loi′ter·ing·ly,** *adv.*

loll (lol), *v.* **1** recline or lean in a lazy manner: *loll on a sofa.* **2** hang loosely or droop: *a dog's tongue lolls out in hot weather.* —*n.* a lolling. [ME *lolle(n)*] —**loll′er,** *n.*

lol·li·pop, lol·ly·pop (lol′i pop), *n.* piece of hard candy on the end of a small stick.

Lom·bard (lom′bärd; –bərd; lum′–), *n.* **1** member of a Germanic tribe which in the sixth century A.D. conquered the part of N Italy since known as Lombardy. **2** native or inhabitant of Lombardy. —**Lom·bar′dic,** *adj.*

Lon·don (lun′dən), *n.* capital of Great Britain in SE England. —**Lon′don·er,** *n.*

lone (lōn), *adj.* **1** alone; solitary: *a lone survivor.* **2** lonesome; lonely: *a lone life.* **3** standing apart; isolated: *a lone house.* [var. of *alone*]

lone·ly (lō′li), *adj.,* **–li·er, –li·est.** **1** feeling oneself alone and longing for company or friends: *she was lonely when among strangers.* **2** without many people: *a lonely road.* **3** alone: *a lonely tree.* —**lone′li·ly,** *adv.* —**lone′li·ness,** *n.*

lon·er (lōn′ər), *n.* **1** person who is or prefers to be alone. **2** independent person: *a political loner.*

lone·some (lōn′səm), *adj.,* **–som·er, –som·est.** **1** feeling lonely **2** making one feel lonely. —**lone′some·ly,** *adv.* —**lone′some·ness,** *n.*

long¹ (lông; long), *adj.,* **long·er, long·est,** *adv., n.* —*adj.* **1** measuring much, or more than usual, from end to end in space or time: *a long distance.* **2** having a specified length in space or time: *five feet long.* **3** far-reaching; extending to a great distance in space or time: *a long memory, a long sight.* **4** of vowels or syllables, taking a comparatively long time to speak. —*adv.* **1** throughout the whole length of: *all night long.* **2** for a long time: *a reform long advocated.* **3** at a point of time far distant from the time indicated: *long before, long since.* —*n.*

1 a long time: *for long, before long.* **2** a long sound.

as long as, provided that.

before long, soon.

so long as, provided that. [OE *lang*] —**long′ish,** *adj.*

long² (lông; long), *v.* wish very much; desire greatly. [OE *langian* < *lang* long¹]

long., longitude.

long·boat (lông′bōt′; long′–), *n.* the largest and strongest boat carried by a sailing ship.

long·bow (lông′bō′; long′–), *n.* bow drawn by hand and discharging a long, feathered arrow (distinguished from *crossbow*).

long-dis·tance (lông′dis′təns; long′–), *adj.* **1** of or having to do with telephone service to another town, city, etc. **2** involving great distances.

long division, method of dividing large numbers, in which each step is written out.

long-drawn (lông′drôn′; long′–), *adj.* lasting a long time; prolonged to great length. Also, **long-drawn-out.**

lon·gev·i·ty (lon jev′ə ti), *n.* long life. [< L *longaevitas,* ult. < *longus* long + *aevum* age]

long·hand (lông′hand′; long′–), *n.* ordinary writing, not shorthand or typewriting.

long·horn (lông′hôrn′; long′–), *n.* one of a breed of beef cattle having very long horns.

long house, large communal dwelling of N American Indians, esp. the Iroquois, and various other tribal societies elsewhere.

long·ing (lông′ing; long′–), *n.* earnest desire: *a longing for home.* —*adj.* having or showing earnest desire: *a child's longing look at a window full of toys.* —**long′ing·ly,** *adv.*

lon·gi·tude (lon′jə tüd; –tūd), *n.* **1** distance E or W on the earth's surface, measured in degrees from a certain meridian. **2** length. [< L *longitudo* length < *longus* long]

lon·gi·tu·di·nal (lon′jə tü′də nəl; –tū′–), *adj.* **1** of length; in length. **2** running lengthwise: *our flag has longitudinal stripes.* **3** of longitude. —**lon′gi·tu′di·nal·ly,** *adv.*

long johns (jonz), *Informal.* long, warm underwear.

long jump, 1 jump to cover the greatest length of ground; broad jump. **2** contest to execute the longest jump.

long-lived (lông′livd′; long′–; –livd′), *adj.* living or lasting a long time.

long-range (lông′rānj′; long′–), *adj.* looking ahead; future: *long-range plans.*

long-run (lông′run′; long′–), *adj.* happening or continuing over a long period of time. —*n.* a long period of time: *plans for the long-run.*

long·shore·man (lông′shôr′mən; long′–; –shōr′–), *n., pl.* **–men.** person whose work is loading and unloading ships.

long shot, an attempt to do something that probably will not succeed but that offers the possibility of great reward.

not by a long shot, not at all.

long-sight·ed (lông′sīt′id; long′–), *adj.* **1** farsighted; focusing at more than the right distance. **2** having foresight; wise.

long-stand·ing (lông′stan′ding; long′–), *adj.* having lasted for a long time.

long-suf·fer·ing (lông′suf′ər ing; long′–; –suf′ring), *adj.* enduring trouble, pain, or injury long and patiently. —*n.* long and patient endurance of trouble, pain, or injury.

long suit, 1 *Fig.* strong attribute; a strength. **2** suit of cards of which one holds the most.

long-term (lông′tėrm′; long′–), *adj.* of or involving a long period of time.

long-time, long-time (lông′tīm′; long′–), *adj.* for a long time; of long standing.

long-wind·ed (lông′win′did; long′–), *adj.* talking or writing at great lengths; tiresome. —**long′-wind′ed·ly,** *adv.* —**long′-wind′ed·ness,** *n.*

long·wise (lông′wīz′; long′–), **long·ways** (–wāz′), *adv.* =lengthwise.

look (lůk), *v.* **1** see; try to see; direct the eyes: *he looked this way.* **2** direct the mind: *look into the matter.* **3** search: *find without looking.* **4** face; have a view: *our house looks on a garden.* **5** seem; appear: *she looks pale.* **6** express or suggest by looks: *look daggers at a person.* —*n.* act of looking: *a careful look.*

look after, attend to; take care of.

look back, remember; recollect.

look down on, despise; scorn.

look forward to, anticipate with pleasure.

look in (on), make a short visit (to someone).

look into, examine; investigate: *look into their complaint.*

look on, a watch without taking part. **b** regard; consider: *look on as a friend.*

look out, be careful; watch out.

look over, examine; inspect: *look over papers.*

looks, appearance; aspect: *admire her good looks; the looks of things are not good.*

look to, a attend to; take care of. **b** turn to for help.

look up, a find; refer to. **b** call on; visit.

look upon, regard; consider.

look up to, respect; admire. [OE *lōcian*] —**look′er,** *n.*

look·er-on (lůk′ər on′; –ôn′), *n., pl.* **look·ers-on.** person who watches without taking part; spectator.

looking glass, =mirror.

look-out (lůk′out′), *n.* **1** a careful watch for someone to come or for something to happen. **2** person or group that keeps such a watch. **3** place from which to watch. **4** crow's-nest.

loom¹ (lüm), *n.* machine for weaving cloth. [OE (*ge*)*lōma* implement]

loom² (lüm), *v.* **1** appear indistinctly: *an iceberg loomed through the thick fog.* **2** appear in a vague, unusually large, or threatening shape: *disaster loomed ahead.*

loon¹ (lün), *n.* a large diving bird that has a loud wild cry. [earlier *loom* < Scand. *lōmr*]

loon² (lün), *n.* a worthless or stupid person.

loon·y (lün´i), *adj.,* **loon·i·er, loon·i·est.** *adj.* crazy. Also, **looney. —loon´i·ness,** *n.*

loop (lüp), *n.* **1** the shape of a curved string, ribbon, bent wire, etc., that crosses itself. In writing, *b* and *g* have loops. **2** thing, bend, course, or motion shaped like this. **3** a fastening or ornament formed of cord, etc., bent and crossed. **4** a complete vertical turn or revolution. —*v.* **1** make a loop of. **2** make loops in. **3** fasten with a loop. **4** form a loop or loops.

in the loop, part of the process.

out of the loop, outside the process, esp. the political process. [ME *loupe,* ? < Celtic] **—loop´er,** *n.*

loop·hole (lüp´hōl´), *n.* **1** a small opening in a wall to shoot through, look through, or let in light and air. **2** means of escape: *find a loophole in the law.* [? < MDu. *lupen* peer]

loose (lüs), *adj.,* **loos·er, loos·est,** *v.,* **loosed, loos·ing,** *adv., n.* —*adj.* **1** not fastened: *a loose thread.* **2** not tight: *loose clothing, a loose tooth.* **3** not bound together: *loose papers.* **4** not put up in a box, can, etc.: *loose coffee.* **5** free; not shut in or up: *we let the dog loose at night.* **6** not pressed close together: *loose earth, cloth with a loose weave.* **7** not strict close, or exact: *a loose translation, loose thinking.* **8** moving too freely: *a loose tongue, loose bowels.* —*v.* **1** set free; let go. **2** discharge (an arrow, gun, etc.); shot. **3** make loose; untie; unfasten. —*adv.* in a loose manner.

cut loose, a separate from anything; break a connection or relation. **b** run away; free oneself. **c** *Colloq.* go on a spree.

on the loose, free; without restraint. [< Scand. *lauss*] **—loose´ly,** *adv.* **—loose´ness,** *n.*

loose cannon, *Informal.* person or thing that is out of control.

loose-joint·ed (lüs´join´tid), *adj.* **1** having loose joints; loosely built. **2** able to move freely.

loose-leaf (lüs´lēf´), *adj.* having pages or sheets that can be taken out and replaced.

loos·en (lüs´ən), *v.* **1** make loose or looser; untie; unfasten. **2** become loose or looser. **—loos´en·er,** *n.*

loot (lüt), *n.* **1** spoils; plunder; booty. **2** *Fig. Informal.* presents: *birthday loot.* —*v.* plunder; rob. [< Hind. *lūt*] **—loot´er,** *n.*

lop (lop), *v.,* **lopped, lop·ping. 1** cut; cut off. **2** cut branches, twigs, etc., from. **—lop´per,** *n.*

lope (lōp), *v.,* **loped, lop·ing,** *n.* —*v.* run with a long, easy stride. —*n.* a long, easy stride. [ult. < Scand. *hlaupa* leap] **—lop´er,** *n.*

lop-eared (lop´ird´), *adj.* having ears that hang loosely or droop.

lop·sid·ed (lop´sīd´id), *adj.* larger or heavier on one side than the other; unevenly balanced. **—lop´sid´ed·ly,** *adv.* **—lop´sid´ed·ness,** *n.*

lo·qua·cious (lō kwā´shəs), *adj.* talking much; fond of talking. **—lo·qua´cious·ly,** *adv.*

lo·quac·i·ty (lō kwas´ə ti), *n.* inclination to talk a great deal; talkativeness. [< L, < *loquax* talkative]

lord (lôrd), *n.* **1** owner, ruler, or master; one who has the power. **2** a feudal superior. —*v.* rule; domineer; behave like a lord.

Lord, in Great Britain, a titled nobleman or peer of the realm.

lord it over, domineer over.

the Lord, a God. **b** Christ.

the Lords, the House of Lords; the upper house of the British Parliament. [OE *hlāford* < *hlāf* loaf + *weard* keeper, ward]

lord·ly (lôrd´li), *adj.,* **–li·er, –li·est,** *adv.* —*adj.* **1** like a lord; suitable for a lord; grand; magnificent. **2** haughty; insolent; scornful. —*adv.* in a lordly manner. **—lord´li·ness,** *n.*

Lord's Day, Sunday.

lord·ship (lûrd´ship), *n.* rank or position of a lord.

Lord's Prayer, prayer given by Jesus to his disciples. Matt. 6:9–13.

Lord's Supper, 1 Jesus's last supper with his disciples. **2** Holy Communion.

lore (lôr; lōr), *n.* **1** facts and stories about a certain subject. **2** learning; knowledge. [OE *lār* akin to LEARN]

lorn (lôrn), *adj., Archaic.* **1** forsaken; forlorn. **2** lost; ruined. [OE *–loren,* pp. of *–lēosan* lose. See FORLORN.]

lor·ry (lôr´i; lor´i), *n., pl.* **–ries.** *Brit.* truck.

lo·ry (lôr´i; lōr´–), *n.* any one of various small, brightly colored parrots of Australia. [< Malay *luri*]

lose (lüz), *v.,* **lost, los·ing. 1** not have any longer; have taken away from one by accident, carelessness, parting, death, etc.: *lose one's life, lose a book.* **2** fail to keep, preserve, or maintain; cease to have: *lose patience.* **3** fail to follow with eye, hearing, mind, etc.: *lose words here and there in a speech.* **4** leave behind in a race or contest. **5** wander from; become separated from: *lose one's way.* **6** fail to win: *lose the prize, our team lost.* **7** bring to destruction; ruin: *the ship and its crew were lost.* **8** cause the loss of: *delay lost the battle.*

lose oneself, a let oneself go astray; become bewildered. **b** become absorbed. [OE *–lēosan,* var. of *–lēosan* lose] **—los´a·ble,** *adj.* **—los´er,** *n.*

los·er (lü´zər), *n. Informal.* person who consistently fails; failure.

los·ings (lüz´ingz), *n. pl.* losses.

loss (lôs; los), *n.* **1** a losing or being lost: *loss of life.* **2** person or thing lost. **3** amount lost. **4** harm or disadvantage caused by losing something.

at a loss, puzzled; uncertain; in difficulty.

losses, a number of soldiers killed, wounded, or captured. **b** the greater amount of money spent or invested over money earned. [OE *los*]

lost (lôst; lost), *v.* pt. and pp. of **lose.** —*adj.* **1** no longer possessed or retained: *lost friends, lost articles.* **2** attended with defeat: *a lost battle.* **3** not used to good purpose; wasted: *lost time.* **4** having gone astray. **5** destroyed or ruined. **6** bewildered.

lost in, completely absorbed or interested in.

lost to, a no longer possible or open to. **b** no longer belonging to. **c** insensible to.

lost cause, 1 undertaking that cannot or will not succeed. **2** *Fig.* person who cannot or will not change (behavior, job, etc.).

lost sheep, person who has strayed from the right sort of conduct or religious belief.

lot (lot), *n., adv.* —*n.* **1** object used to decide something by chance: *we drew lots to decide who should be captain.* **2** such a method of deciding: *divide property by lot.* **3** choice made in this way: *the lot fell to me.* **4** what one gets by lot; share or portion. **5** fate; fortune: *a happy lot.* **6** plot of ground. **7** place where motion pictures are made. **8** number of persons or things considered as a group; a collection: *a fine lot of boys.* —*adv.* to a great extent: *a lot better.*

a lot or **lots** or **lots of,** a great many; a great deal: *lots of money.*

cast or **draw lots,** use lots to decide something.

cast or **throw in one's lot with,** share the fate of; become a partner with. [OE *hlot*]

Lot (lot), *n.* in the Bible, a righteous man who was allowed to escape from Sodom before God destroyed it. His wife looked back and was changed into a pillar of salt. Gen. 19:1–26.

Lo·thar·i·o (lō thãr´iō), *n., pl.* **–thar·i·os.** man who makes love to many women; libertine.

lo·tion (lō´shən), *n.* liquid containing medicine, used on the skin to soothe, heal, or cleanse. [< L *lotio* a washing, ult. < *lavere* to wash]

lot·ter·y (lot´ər ri), *n., pl.* **–ter·ies 1** scheme for distributing prizes by lot or chance. In a lottery a large number of tickets are sold, some of which draw prizes. **2** *Fig.* anything in which the outcome is a matter of chance. [< Ital. *lotteria* < *lotto* lot. See LOTTO.]

lot·to (lot′ō), *n.* game played by drawing numbered disks from a bag or box and covering the corresponding numbers on cards. [< Ital., lott, ult. < Gmc.]

lo·tus, lo·tos (lō′təs), *n.* **1** water lily that grows in Egypt and Asia. **2** plant with red, pink, or white flowers, of the same family as the pea. **3** *Gk. Legend.* plant whose fruit was supposed to cause a dreamy and contented forgetfulness in those who ate it. [< L < Gk. *lotos*]

lo·tus-eat·er, lo·tos-eat·er (lō′təs ēt′ər), *n.* person who leads a life of dreamy, indolent ease.

loud (loud), *adj.* **1** making a noise; not quiet or soft. **2** resounding; noisy. **3** clamorous; insistent: *be loud in demands.* **4** showy or flashy: *loud clothes.* —*adv.* in a loud manner. [OE *hlūd*] —**loud′ly,** *adv.* —**loud′ness,** *n.*

loud·ish (loud′ish), *adj.* somewhat loud.

loud·mouth (loud′mouth′), *n. Informal.* person who talks too much, too noisily, or offensively. —**loud′mouthed′,** *adj.*

loud·speak·er (loud′spēk′ər), *n.* device for amplifying the sound of a speaker's voice, music, etc.

Lou·i·si·an·a (lü ē′zi an′ə; lü′i–), *n.* a S state of the United States. —**Lou·i′si·an′an, Lou·i′si·an′i·an,** *adj., n.*

lounge (lounj), *v.,* **lounged, loung·ing,** *n.* —*v.* stand, stroll, sit, or lie at ease and lazily. —*n.* **1** act or state of lounging. **2** a comfortable and informal room in which one can lounge. **3** couch; sofa. —**loung′er,** *n.*

louse (lous), *n., pl.* **lice. 1** a small, wingless insect that infests the hair or skin of people and animals. **2** anything like it. **louse up,** *Informal.* spoil wreck; make a mess of. [OE *lūs*]

lous·y (louz′i), *adj.,* **lous·i·er, lous·i·est. 1** infested with lice. **2** of poor or low quality. **3** dirty; disgusting. —**lous′i·ly,** *adv.* —**lous′i·ness,** *n.*

lout (lout), *n.* an awkward, stupid fellow; boor. [? *n.* use of *v.,* OE *lūtan* bow or *lūtian* skulk] —**lout′ish,** *adj.* —**lout′ish·ly,** *adv.* —**lout′ish·ness,** *n.*

lou·ver (lü′vər), *n.* **1** window or other opening covered with louver boards. **2** a ventilating slit. **3** a louver board. [< OF *lover*] —**lou′vered,** *adj.*

louver boards, horizontal strips of wood, fiberglass, etc. set slanting in a window or other opening, so as to keep out rain, but provide ventilation and light.

lov·a·ble, love·a·ble (luv′ə bəl), *adj.* deserving love; endearing. —**lov′a·bil′i·ty, love′a·bil′i·ty; lov′a·ble·ness, love′a·ble·ness,** *n.* —**lov′a·bly, love′a·bly,** *adv.*

love (luv), *n., v.,* **loved, lov·ing.** —*n.* **1** strong or passionate affection for a person. **2** a loved one; sweetheart. **3** a strong liking: *a love of books.* **4** no score in tennis and certain other games. —*v.* **1** be in love with: *he loves his wife.* **2** caress: *she held the baby and loved him.* **3** like very much; take great pleasure in: *the children love ice cream.*

fall in love, begin to love; come to feel love.

for the love of, for the sake of; because of: *for the love of art.*

in love, feeling love.

in love with, a feeling love for: *in love with a young man.* **b** very fond of: *in love with opera.*

make love, have sexual relations: *"Make love, not war."* [OE *lufu,* n., *lufian,* v.]

love·bird (luv′bėrd′), *n.* a small parrot that shows great affection for its mate.

love knot, an ornamental knot or bow of ribbons as a token of love.

love·less (luv′lis), *adj.* **1** not loving. **2** not loved. —**love′less·ly,** *adv.* —**love′less·ness,** *n.*

love-lies-bleed·ing (luv′līz blēd′ing), *n.* a kind of amaranth having spikes of crimson flowers.

love·lorn (luv′lôrn′), *adj.,* suffering because of love; forsaken by the person whom one loves. —**love′lorn′ness,** *n.*

love·ly (luv′li), *adj.,* **–li·er, –li·est. 1** beautiful in mind or character; beautiful: *a lovely woman.* **2** very pleasing; delightful: *a lovely evening.* —**love′li·ly,** *adv.* —**love′li·ness,** *n.*

love potion, magic drink supposed to cause love for a certain person.

lov·er (luv′ər), *n.* **1** person who loves. **2** person who is in love with another. **3** person who loves someone already married to another; paramour. **4** person having a strong liking: *a lover of books.* **lovers,** two people who are in love with each other. —**lov′er·like′,** *adj.*

love seat, seat or small sofa for two persons.

love·sick (luv′sik′), *adj.* languishing because of love. —**love′sick′ness,** *n.*

lov·ing (luv′ing), *adj.* feeling or showing love; affectionate; fond. —**lov′ing·ly,** *adv.* —**lov′ing·ness,** *n.*

loving cup, a large cup with handles, passed around for all to drink from.

lov·ing-kind·ness (luv′ing kīnd′nis), *n.* kindness coming from love.

low¹ (lō), *adj.* **1** not high or tall: *low walls.* **2** of less than ordinary height, depth, or quantity: *low ground, the well is getting low.* **3** near the ground, floor, or base: *a low shelf.* **4** small in amount, degree, force, value, etc.: *a low price.* **5** not loud; soft: *a low whisper.* **6** humble: *low birth.* **7** unfavorable; poor: *I have a low opinion of his abilities.* **8** *Fig.* depressed or dejected: *low spirits.* **9** mean or base; coarse; vulgar; degraded: *low company.* **10** pertaining to regions near sea level: *low country.* **11** prostrate or dead: *lay one low.* **12** deep: *a low bow.* **13** of sounds, at or toward the bottom of a scale. —*n.* **1** that which is low. **2** arrangement of the gears used for the lowest speed in an automobile and similar machines. **3** an area of low barometric pressure. —*adv.* **1** near the ground, floor, or base: *fly low.* **2** in, at, or to a low portion, point, degree, condition, price, etc.: *the sun*

sank low, supplies are running low. **3** at low pitch; softly: *speak low.* **4** humbly; meanly: *act low.*

lay low, a knock down. **b** kill.

lie low, stay hidden; keep still. [< Scand. *lägr*] —**low′ness,** *n.*

low² (lō), *v.* make the sound of a cow; moo. —*n.* sound a cow makes; mooing. [OE *hlōwan*]

low·boy (lō′boi′), *n.* a low chest of drawers.

low·brow (lō′brou′), *n. Informal.* person who is not or does not claim to be intellectual, cultured, or elegant. —*adj.* **1** being a lowbrow. **2** fit for lowbrows.

Low Countries, Netherlands, Belgium, and Luxemburg. —**low′-coun′try,** *adj.*

low-down (*n.* lō′doun′; *adj.* lō′doun′), *n.* actual facts or truth. —*adj.* low; mean; contemptible.

low-end (lō′end′), *adj.* **1** of or for the low-income consumer. **2** least complicated or expensive version of a line of products.

low·er¹ (lō′ər), *v.* **1** let down; make lower: *lower the flag, lower the volume of a radio.* **2** sink; become lower: *the sun lowered slowly.* —*adj., adv.* comparative of **low.**

low·er² (lou′ər), *v.* **1** look dark and threatening. **2** frown; scowl. —*n.* **1** a dark and threatening look. **2** frown; scowl. [ME *loure(n)*]

lower case, small letters, not capital.

Lower For·ty-eight or **Lower 48** or **lower for·ty-eight** (fôr′te āt′), the states of the United States, with the exception of Alaska and Hawaii.

Lower House, lower house, the more representative branch of a legislature that has two branches.

low·er·ing (lou′ər ing), *adj.* **1** dark and threatening. **2** frowning; scowling. —**low′er·ing·ly,** *adv.*

low·er·most (lō′ər mōst), *adj.* =lowest.

lower world, hell; Hades. Also, **lower regions.**

lowest common denominator, =least common denominator.

lowest common multiple, =least common multiple.

Low German, the Germanic speech of the Low Countries (Dutch, Flemish, etc.) and esp. of N Germany.

low-grade (lō′grād′), *adj.* **1** of inferior quality. **2** not intense enough to be serious, esp. of a fever or infection.

low-key (lō′kē′), *adj.* subdued; understated.

low·land (lō′lənd), *n.* land that is lower and flatter than the neighboring country. —*adj.* of or in the lowlands. —**low′land·er,** *n.*

Low Latin, Latin as spoken in the Middle Ages.

low·ly (lō′li), *adj.,* **–li·er, –li·est,** *adv.* —*adj.* **1** low in rank, station, position, or development: *a lowly corporal, a lowly occupation.* **2** modest in feeling, behavior, or condition; humble: *he held a* *lowly opinion of himself.* —*adv.* humbly; meekly. —**low′li·ness,** *n.*

low-mind·ed (lō′mīn′did), *adj.* mean; vulgar. —**low′-mind′ed·ly,** *adv.* —**low′-mind′ed·ness,** *n.*

low-profile (lō′prō′fīl), *adj.* played down; low-key.

low-spir·it·ed (lō′spir′it id), *adj.* sad; depressed. —**low′-spir′it·ed·ly,** *adv.* —**low′-spir′it·ed·ness,** *n.*

low tide, 1 lowest level of the tide. **2** time when the tide is lowest. **3** lowest point.

low water, 1 lowest level of water. **2** =low tide.

lox[1] (loks), *n.* a kind of smoked salmon. [< Yiddish *laks* < MHG *lacs* salmon]

lox[2] (loks), =liquid oxygen.

loy·al (loi′əl), *adj.* **1** faithful to love, promise, or duty: *a loyal husband.* **2** faithful to one's king, one's government, or one's country: *a loyal citizen.* [< F < L *legalis* < *lex* law. Doublet of LEGAL.] —**loy′al·ly,** *adv.*

loy·al·ist (loi′əl ist), *n.* **1** person who is loyal to his or her government, esp. in time of revolt. **2** Sometimes, **Loyalist,** *Am.* American who favored England at the time of the American Revolution.

loy·al·ty (loi′əl ti), *n., pl.* **-ties.** loyal feeling or behavior; faithfulness.

loz·enge (loz′inj), *n.* **1** design or figure shaped like this ◊. **2** a small tablet of medicine or piece of candy. [< OF *losenge,* ult. < LL *lausa* slab]

Lr, lawrencium.

LSD, lysergic acid diethylamide, a psychedelic drug.

Lt., Lieutenant.

Ltd., ltd., *Esp. Brit.* limited.

Lu, lutetium.

lu·au (lü′ou), *n.* a feast, originally in Hawaii, generally held outdoors, with roast pig as the main dish. [< Haw.]

lub·ber (lub′ər), *n.* **1** a big, clumsy, stupid fellow. **2** a clumsy sailor.

lub·ber·ly (lub′ər li), *adj.* **1** loutish; clumsy; stupid. **2** awkward in the work of a sailor. —*adv.* in a lubberly manner. —**lub′ber·li·ness,** *n.*

lube (lüb), *n.* **1** =lubricant. **2** =lubrication.

lu·bri·cant (lü′brə kənt), *n.* oil, grease, etc., for putting on parts of machines that slide or move against one another, to make them work smoothly and easily. —*adj.* lubricating.

lu·bri·cate (lü′brə kāt), *v.,* **-cat·ed, -cat·ing. 1** make (machinery) smooth and easy to work by putting on oil, grease, etc. **2** make slippery or smooth. [< L, < *lubricus* slippery] —**lu′bri·ca′tion,** *n.* —**lu′bri·ca′tive,** *adj.* —**lu′bri·ca′tor,** *n.*

lu·cent (lü′sənt), *adj.* **1** shining; luminous. **2** letting the light through; clear. [< L *lucens* shining] —**lu′cence, lu′cen·cy,** *n.* —**lu′cent·ly,** *adv.*

lu·cid (lü′sid), *adj.* **1** easy to understand. **2** sane: *an insane person sometimes has lucid intervals.* **3** clear; transparent: *a lucid stream.* **4** shining; bright: *the lucid stars.* [< L *lucidus* < *lux* light] —**lu·cid′i·ty, lu′cid·ness,** *n.* —**lu′cid·ly,** *adv.*

Lu·ci·fer (lü′sə fər), *n.* chief rebel angel who was cast out of heaven; Satan; the Devil.

Lu·cite (lü′sīt), *n. Trademark.* a clear plastic compound used for airplane windows, lenses, etc.

luck (luk), *n.* **1** that which seems to happen or come to one by chance; chance. **2** good luck.

as luck would have it, by chance.

down on one's luck, having bad luck; unlucky.

in luck, having good luck; lucky.

luck out, have something work out well; be lucky.

out of luck, having bad luck; unlucky.

push one's luck, risk one's good fortune; lose one's advantage.

try one's luck, see what one can do.

worse luck, unfortunately. [< MDu, (*ghe*)*luc,* MLG (*ge*)*lucke*]

luck·less (luk′lis), *adj.* having or bringing bad luck; unlucky. —**luck′less·ly,** *adv.*

luck·y (luk′i), *adj.,* **luck·i·er, luck·i·est.** having or bringing good luck. —**luck′i·ly,** *adv.* —**luck′i·ness,** *n.*

lu·cra·tive (lü′krə tiv), *adj.* bringing in money; profitable. —**lu′cra·tive·ly,** *adv.* —**lu′cra·tive·ness,** *n.*

lu·cre (lü′kər), *n.* money considered as a bad influence. [< L *lucrum*]

Lud·dite (lud′īt), *n.* **1** person opposed to automation or mechanization, esp. computerization. **2** person with opinions thought to be outdated. [< *Luddites,* workers in England (1811–16), who destroyed machinery, believing it caused unemployment].

lu·di·crous (lü′də krəs), *adj.* amusingly absurd; ridiculous. [< L *ludicrus* < *ludus* sport] —**lu′di·crous·ly,** *adv.* —**lu′di·crous·ness,** *n.*

luff (luf), —*v.* turn the bow of a ship toward the wind. —*n.* **1** turning the bow of a ship toward the wind. **2** the forward edge of a fore-and-aft sail. [< Du. *loef*]

lug[1] (lug), *v.,* **lugged, lug·ging,** *n.* —*v.* pull along or carry with effort; drag. —*n.* a pull; haul; drag. [< Scand. (Sw.) *lugga* pull by the hair]

lug[2] (lug), *n.* a projecting part used to hold or grip something.

lug[3] (lug), *n.* =lugsail.

lug·gage (lug′ij), *n.* =baggage. [< *lug*[1]]

lug·ger (lug′ər), *n.* boat with lugsails.

lug·sail (lug′sāl′; -səl), *n.* a four-cornered sail held by a yard that slants across the mast.

lu·gu·bri·ous (lù gü′bri əs; -gü′-), *adj.* sad; mournful. [< L *lugubris* < *lugere* mourn] —**lu·gu′bri·ous·ly,** *adv.* —**lu·gu′bri·ous·ness,** *n.*

Luke (lük), *n.* the third book of the New Testament.

luke·warm (lük′wôrm′), *adj.* **1** neither hot nor cold. **2** showing little enthusiasm; half-hearted. [< ME *leuk* tepid + *warm*] —**luke′warm′ly,** *adv.* —**luke′warm′ness,** *n.*

lull (lul), *v.* **1** hush to sleep: *the mother lulled the crying baby.* **2** quiet: *lull one's suspicions.* **3** become calm or more nearly calm: *the wind lulled.* —*n.* **1** period of less noise or violence; brief calm. **2** a soothing sound. [ME *lulle(n)*]

lul·la·by (lul′ə bī), *n., pl.* **-bies,** *v.,* **-bied, -by·ing.** —*n.* song to put a baby to sleep. —*v.* lull with or as with a lullaby.

lum·ba·go (lum bā′gō), *n.* pain in the muscles of the back and in the loins. [< LL, < L *lumbus* loin]

lum·bar (lum′bər), *adj.* of the loin or loins: *the lumbar region.* —*n.* a lumbar vertebra, artery, nerve, etc. [< NL, < L *lumbus* loin]

lum·ber[1] (lum′bər), *n.* **1** timber, logs, beams, boards, etc., roughly cut and prepared for use. **2** household articles no longer in use, old furniture, etc., that takes up room. —*v.* cut and prepare lumber. [orig. useless goods, prob. noun use of LUMBER[2]] —**lum′ber·er,** *n.* —**lum′ber·ing,** *n.*

lum·ber[2] (lum′bər), *v.* move along heavily and noisily. [< ME *lomeren* move slowly, haltingly < Scand.] —**lum′ber·ing,** *adj.*

lum·ber·jack (lum′bər jak′), *n.* person whose work is cutting down trees and getting out the logs.

lum·ber·man (lum′bər mən), *n., pl.* **-men. 1** =lumberjack. **2** person whose work is cutting and preparing timber for use. **3** person whose business is buying and selling timber or lumber.

lum·ber·yard (lum′bər yärd′), *n.* place where lumber and building supplies are stored and sold.

lu·men (lü′mən), *n., pl.* **-mi·na** (-mə-nə). unit of light; the light given out by a point source of one candle power. [< L, light]

lu·mi·nance (lü′mə nəns), *n.* intensity of light in relation to the size of its source.

lu·mi·nar·y (lü′mə ner′i), *n., pl.* **-nar·ies. 1** the sun, moon, or other light-giving body. **2** *Fig.* a famous person. [< Med.L, < L *lumen* light]

lu·mi·nes·cence (lü′mə nes′əns), *n.* emission of light occurring at a temperature below that of incandescent bodies. Luminescence includes phosphorescence and fluorescence. [< L *lumen* light + E -*escence* a beginning to be < L -*escere*] —**lu′mi·nes′cent,** *adj.*

lu·mi·nous (lü′mə nəs), *adj.* **1** shining by its own or reflected light: *the sun and stars are luminous bodies.* **2** full of light; bright. **3** easily understood; clear; enlightening. —**lu′mi·nos′i·ty, lu′mi·nous·ness,** *n.* —**lu′mi·nous·ly,** *adv.*

lum·mox (lum′əks), *n.* an awkward, stupid person.

lump[1] (lump), *n.* **1** solid mass of no particular shape: *a lump of coal.* **2** swelling; bump: *a lump on the head.* —*v.* **1** make lumps of, on, or in. **2** put together; deal with in a mass or as a whole: *we will* *lump all our expenses. —adj.* **1** in lumps; in a lump. **2** including a number of items. [ME]

lump² (lump), *v.* put up with; endure: *if you don't like it, you can lump it.*

lump·ish (lump′ish), *adj.* **1** like a lump; heavy and clumsy. **2** stolid; stupid. **—lump′ish·ly,** *adv.* **—lump′ish·ness,** *n.*

lump·y (lump′i), *adj.,* **lump·i·er, lump·i·est, 1** full of lumps: *lumpy gravy.* **2** covered with lumps: *lumpy ground.* **3** heavy and clumsy: *a lumpy animal.* **—lump′i·ly,** *adv.* **—lump′i·ness,** *n.*

lu·na·cy (lü′nə si), *n., pl.* **–cies. 1** insanity. **2** extreme folly. [< *lunatic*]

lu·na moth or **Lu·na moth** (lü′nə), large moth of North America with light-green wings having a crescent spot and a long tail-shaped end to each hind wing.

lu·nar (lü′nər), *adj.* **1** of the moon. **2** like the moon. **3** crescent-shaped. [< L, < *luna* moon]

lunar month, interval between one new moon and the next, about 29½ days.

lu·na·tic (lü′nə tik), *n.* **1** an insane person. **2** an extremely foolish person. *—adj.* **1** insane. **2** for insane people. [< LL, ult. < L *luna* moon] **—lu·nat′i·cal·ly,** *adv.*

lunatic fringe, those whose zeal in some cause, movement, or ism goes beyond reasonable limits.

lunch (lunch), *n.* **1** a light meal between breakfast and dinner, or breakfast and supper. **2** a light meal. *—v.* eat lunch. [short for *luncheon*] **—lunch′er,** *n.*

lunch·eon (lun′chən), *n.* **1** =lunch. **2** a formal lunch. *—v.* lunch. [< *luncheon* thick piece, hunk, prob. infl. by *lunch* hunk of bread or cheese]

lunch·eon·ette (lun′chən et′), *n.* restaurant that serves lunches and light meals.

lunch·room (lunch′rüm′; –rum′), *n.* **1** room in an office, school, etc., where lunch or snacks can be eaten. **2** =luncheonette.

lung (lung), *n.* one of the pair of breathing organs in vertebrates by means of which the blood receives oxygen and is relieved of carbon dioxide. [OE *lungen*]

lunge (lunj), *n., v.,* **lunged, lung·ing.** *—n.* any sudden forward movement; thrust. *—v.* move suddenly forward; thrust. [ult. < F *allonger,* ult. < L *ad–* toward + *longus* long] **—lung′er,** *n.*

lung·fish (lung′fish′), *n., pl.* **–fish·es.** freshwater fish having a lunglike sac as well as gills and able to obtain oxygen from both the air and water, found in South America, Australia, and Africa.

lung·wort (lung′wèrt′), *n.* plant with blue flowers and spotted leaves.

lu·pine¹ or **lu·pin** (lü′pən), *n.* **1** any of several plants of the same family as peas and beans, that have long spikes of flowers, radiating clusters of grayish, hairy leaflets, and flat pods with beanshaped seeds. **2** one of the seeds. [< L *lupinus, lupinum.* LUPINE².]

lu·pine² (lü′pīn), *adj.* **1** wolflike; fierce. **2** related to the wolf. [< L *lupinus* < *lupus* wolf]

lurch¹ (lèrch), *n.* sudden leaning or roll to one side: *the car gave a lurch and crashed.* *—v.* lean or roll suddenly to one side.

lurch² (lèrch), *n.* **leave in the lurch,** leave in a helpless condition or difficult situation. [< F *lourche,* name of a game]

lure (lùr), *n., v.,* **lured, lur·ing.** *—n.* **1** attraction: *the lure of the sea.* **2** decoy; bait. *—v.* **1** lead away or into something by arousing desire; attract; tempt. **2** attract with a bait. [< OF *leurre* < Gmc.] **—lur′er,** *n.*

lu·rid (lùr′id), *adj.* **1** lighted up with a red or fiery glare: *lurid flashes of lightning.* **2** terrible; sensational; startling: *lurid crimes.* [< L *luridus*] **—lu′rid·ly,** *adv.* **—lu′rid·ness,** *n.*

lurk (lèrk), *v.* **1** stay about without arousing attention; wait out of sight: *a tiger was lurking in the jungle.* **2** be hidden. [appar. < *lour* lower²] **—lurk′er,** *n.* **—lurk′ing·ly,** *adv.*

lus·cious (lush′əs), *adj.* **1** delicious; richly sweet: *a luscious peach.* **2** very pleasing to taste, smell, hear, see, or feel. **—lus′cious·ly,** *adv.* **—lus′cious·ness,** *n.*

lush (lush), *adj.* **1** tender and juicy; growing thick and green. **2** characterized by abundant growth. [? < OF *lasche* LAX] **—lush′ly,** *adv.* **—lush′ness,** *n.*

lust (lust), *n.* **1** strong desire. **2** improper desire or appetite. **3** desire for indulgence of sex. *—v.* have a strong desire: *a miser lusts after gold.* [OE, pleasure]

lus·ter (lus′tər), *n.* **1** bright shine on the surface: *the luster of pearls.* **2** brightness: *her eyes lost their luster.* **3** fame; glory; brilliance. **4** in ceramics, a metallic, sometimes iridescent, glaze. *—v.* put a luster or gloss on. [< F < Ital. *lustro,* ult. < L *lustrare* illuminate]

lust·ful (lust′fəl), *adj.* full of lust; desiring indulgence of sex; sensual; lewd. **—lust′ful·ly,** *adv.* **—lust′ful·ness,** *n.*

lus·trous (lus′trəs), *adj.* having luster; shining; glossy. **—lus′trous·ly,** *adv.* **—lus′trous·ness,** *n.*

lust·y (lus′ti), *adj.,* **lust·i·er, lust·i·est.** strong and healthy; full of vigor. **—lust′i·ly,** *adv.* **—lust′i·ness,** *n.*

lute (lüt), *n.* a stringed musical instrument, formerly much used, having a long neck and a hollow resonant body, played with the fingers of one hand or with a plectrum. [< OF < Pr. < Ar. *al-'ud* the lute]

lu·te·ti·um (lü tē′shi əm), *n.* a rare metallic element, Lu. [< NL, < L *Lutetia* Paris]

Lu·ther·an (lü′thər ən; lüth′rən), *adj.* having to do with Martin Luther or the church that was named for him. *—n.* member of the Lutheran Church. **—Lu′ther·an·ism,** *n.*

Lux·em·burg, Lux·em·bourg (luk′səm bèrg), *n.* **1** a small country between Germany, France, and Belgium. **2** its capital.

lux·u·ri·ance (lung zhùr′i əns; luk shùr′–), *n.* luxuriant growth or productiveness; rich abundance.

lux·u·ri·ant (lung zhùr′i ənt; luk shùr′–), *adj.* **1** growing thick and green. **2** producing abundantly. **3** rich in ornament. [< L *luxurians* luxuriating. See LUXURIATE.] **—lux·u′ri·ant·ly,** *adv.*

lux·u·ri·ate (lung zhùr′i āt; luk shùr′–), *v.,* **–at·ed, –at·ing. 1** indulge in luxury. **2** take great delight. **3** grow very abundantly. [< L *luxuriatus,* ult. < *luxus* excess] **—lux·u′ri·a′tion,** *n.*

lux·u·ri·ous (lung zhùr′i əs; luk shùr′–), *adj.* **1** fond of luxury; tending toward luxury; self-indulgent: *a luxurious age.* **2** giving luxury; very comfortable and beautiful: *a luxurious hotel.* **—lux·u′ri·ous·ly,** *adv.* **—lux·u′ri·ous·ness,** *n.*

lux·u·ry (luk′shə ri; lug′zhə–), *n., pl.* **–ries. 1** comforts and beauties of life beyond what is really necessary. **2** use of the best and most costly food, clothes, houses, furniture and amusements. **3** thing that one enjoys, usually something choice and costly. **4** thing pleasant but not necessary. [< L *luxuria* < *luxus* excess]

-ly¹, *suffix forming adverbs.* **1** in a _____ manner, as *cheerfully, warmly.* **2** in _____ ways or respects, as *financially, medically, physically.* **3** to a _____ degree or extent, as *greatly, slightly, moderately.* **4** in, to, or from a _____ direction, as *northwardly, laterally.* **5** in a _____ place, as *inwardly, thirdly.* **6** at a _____ time, as *recently.* [OE *–līce < līc*]

-ly², *suffix forming adjectives.* **1** like a _____, as *a ghostly form.* **2** like that of a _____; characteristic of a _____, as *a brotherly kiss.* **3** suited to a _____; fit or proper for a _____, as *a manly fight, womanly kindness.* **4** of each or every _____; occurring once per _____, as *hourly, daily, monthly.* **5** being a _____; that is a _____, as *our heavenly home.* [OE *–līc*]

ly·cée (lē sā′), *n.* a French secondary school maintained by the government. [< F. See LYCEUM.]

ly·ce·um (lī sē′əm; lī′si əm), *n.* **1** lecture hall; place where lectures are given. **2** **Lyceum,** an ancient outdoor grove and gymnasium near Athens, where Aristotle taught. [< L < Gk. *Lykeion* (def. 2), from the nearby temple of Apollo, *Lykeios*]

lye (lī), *n.* any strong alkaline solution, used in making soap and in cleaning. Sodium hydroxide and potassium hydroxide are kinds of lye. [OE *lēag*]

ly·ing¹ (lī′ing), *n.* telling a lie; habit of telling lies. *—adj.* false; untruthful: *a lying rumor.* *—v.* ppr. of lie¹.

ly·ing² (lī′ing), *v.* ppr. of lie²: *a book lying on the table.*

ly·ing-in (lī′ing in′), *n.* **1** confinement in childbirth. **2** =childbirth.

lymph (limf), *n.* a nearly colorless liquid in the tissues of the body, somewhat like blood without the red corpuscles. [< L *lympha* clear water]

lym·phat·ic (lim fat′ik), *adj.* **1** of lymph; carrying lymph. **2** sluggish; lacking energy. —*n.* vessel that contains or carries lymph.

lymphatic system, network of small vessels by which lymph circulates throughout the body, transporting food to cells, fats from the small intestine, and wastes to the blood. Also, **lymph system.**

lymph gland, any of the glandlike bodies occurring in the course of the lymphatic vessels, a source of leucocytes, and involved in filtering out microorganisms and bacteria from lymph. Also, **lymphatic gland, lymph node.**

lym·pho·cyte (lim′fə sīt), *n.* one of the colorless cells of lymph. Also, **lymph cell.**

lynch (linch), *v.* **1** put (an accused person) to death without a lawful trial. **2** *Fig.* denounce or criticize vehemently; excoriate. [orig. *Lynch's law,* from Wm. *Lynch* of Va.] —**lynch′er,** *n.* —**lynch′ing,** *n.*

lynx (lingks), *n., pl.* **lynx·es** or (*esp.* collectively) **lynx.** wildcat of the Northern Hemisphere that has a short tail and rather long legs. [< L < Gk.] —**lynx′like′,** *adj.*

lynx-eyed (lingks′īd′), *adj.* having sharp eyes.

ly·on·naise (lī′ə nāz′), *adj.* fried with pieces of onion: *lyonnaise potatoes.* [< F, < *Lyon* Lyons]

lyre (līr), *n.* an ancient stringed musical instrument somewhat like a small harp. [< OF < L < Gk. *lyra*]

lyre·bird (līr′bėrd′), *n.* an Australian bird, the male of which has a long tail that is lyre-shaped when spread.

lyr·ic (lir′ik), *n.* **1** a short poem expressing personal emotion, as a love poem, a lament, etc. **2** words for a song. —*adj.* **1** having to do with lyric poems: *a lyric poet.* **2** of or suitable for singing.

lyr·i·cal (lir′ə kəl), *adj.* **1** emotional; poetic. **2** lyric. —**lyr′i·cal·ly,** *adv.* —**lyr′i·cal·ness,** *n.*

lyr·i·cism (lir′ə siz əm), *n.* **1** lyrical form or expression. **2** outpouring of lyrical enthusiasm. **3** lyric form or character.

lyr·i·cist (lir′ə sist), *n.* **1** person who writes song lyrics, esp. for the musical theater. **2** lyric poet.

ly·sin (lī′sin), *n.* antibodies which are developed in blood serum, capable of causing the dissolution or destruction of bacteria, red blood cells, and other cellular elements. [< Gk. *lysis* a loosening]

ly·so·some (lī′sə sōm), *n.* particle present in the cytoplasm of cells that breaks down foods in the cells. [< Gk. *lýsis* a loosening + *sôma body*]

ly·so·zyme (lī′sə zīm; –zim), *n.* substance similar to an enzyme, found in tears, egg white, and most body fluids, that is able to destroy many kinds of bacteria. [< Gk. *lýsis* a loosening + en*zyme*]

M, m (em), *n., pl.* **M's; m's.** 1 the 13th letter of the alphabet. 2 Roman numeral for 1000.

M, Middle (def. 4).

M., 1 Majesty. 2 Monday. 3 *pl.* **MM.** Monsieur. 4 noon. [< L *meridies*]

m., 1 male. 2 married. 3 masculine. 4 *Mech.* mass. 5 Also, **m** meter. 6 mile. 7 minim. 8 minute. 9 month. 10 noon. [< L *meridies*]

ma (mä), *n. Informal.* mamma; mother.

Ma, masurium.

MA, (*zip code*) Massachusetts.

M.A., Master of Arts.

ma'am (mam; mäm), *n.* madam.

ma·ca·bre (mə kä′brə; –bər), **ma·ca·ber** (-bər), *adj.* gruesome; horrible; ghastly. [< F]

mac·ad·am (mə kad′əm), *n.* 1 small, broken stones, mixed with tar and rolled until solid and smooth to make roads. 2 road made of layers of this. [after J. L. McAdam, engineer]

mac·a·da·mi·a (mak′ə dä′mē ə), *n.* 1 any one of a genus of tall shrubs or trees native to Australia and cultivated in Hawaii. 2 its large, smooth nut.

mac·ad·am·ize (mə kad′əm īz), *v.,* **–ized, –iz·ing.** make or cover (a road) with macadam.

ma·caque (mə käk′), *n.* any of several kinds of monkeys of Asia, the East Indies, and Africa. [< F < Pg. < African lang.]

mac·a·ro·ni (mak′ə rō′ni), *n., pl.* **–nis, –nies.** flour paste dried, usually in the form of hollow tubes, to be cooked for food. [< earlier Ital. *maccaroni*, pl., ult. < LGk. *makaria* barley broth]

mac·a·roon (mak′ə rün′), *n.* a very sweet cookie made of whites of eggs, sugar, and ground almonds or coconut. [< F < Ital. *maccarone*, sing.; for pl., see MACARONI]

ma·caw (mə kô′), *n.* a large parrot with a long tail, brilliant feathers, and a harsh cry, living in South America and Central America. [< Pg. *macao* < Brazilian]

Mac·beth (mək beth′; mak–), *n.* 1 play by Shakespeare. 2 its principal character.

Mac·ca·bees (mak′ə bēz), *n.pl.* two books of the Old Testament Apocrypha, telling about the successful revolts against the Syrians in the second century B.C., led by the Maccabees. —**Mac′ca·be′an,** *adj.*

mace[1] (mās), *n.* 1 a war club used in the Middle Ages. 2 staff used as a symbol of authority: *a chancellor's mace.* 3 bearer of a mace. [< OF]

mace[2] (mās), *n.* spice made from the dried outer covering of nutmegs. [< OF *macis*]

mace[3] (mās), *n., v.* **maced, mac·ing.** —*n.* tear gas in liquid form, used to subdue rioters, etc. —*v.* attack or subdue with mace. [< trademark *Mace*]

mac·er·ate (mas′ər āt), *v.,* **–at·ed, –at·ing.** 1 soften by soaking for some time: *macerate flowers to extract their perfume,* macerate berries. 2 cause to grow thin. 3 become thin; waste away. [< L *maceratus,* pp. of *macerare* soften] —**mac′er·at′er, mac′er·a′tor,** *n.* —**mac′er·a′tion,** *n.*

mach., machinery; machines; machinist.

Mach (mäk; mak), *n.* =Mach number.

ma·chet·e (mə shet′ē; mə shet′; *Sp.* mä chā′tā), *n.* a large heavy knife, used as a tool and weapon. [< Sp.]

ma·chic·o·lat·ed (mə chik′ə lāt′id), *adj.* having machicolations.

ma·chic·o·la·tion (mə chik′ə lā′shən), *n.* an opening in the floor of a projecting gallery or parapet, or in the roof of an entrance, through which missiles, hot liquids, etc., might be cast upon attackers, much used in medieval fortified structures. [< Med.L, < OF < Pr. *machacol* projection, balcony]

mach·i·nate (mak′ə nāt), *v.,* **–nat·ed, –nat·ing.** contrive or devise artfully or with evil purpose; plot; intrigue. [< L, < *machina* MACHINE] —**mach′i·na′tor,** *n.*

mach·i·na·tion (mak′ə nā′shən), *n.* 1 evil or artful plotting; scheming against authority. 2 Usually, **machinations.** evil plot; secret or cunning scheme.

ma·chine (mə shēn′), *n., v.,* **–chined, –chin·ing.** —*n.* 1 arrangement of fixed and moving parts for doing work, each with some special thing to do: *a washing machine.* 2 device for applying power or changing its direction. Levers and pulleys are simple machines. 3 person or group that acts without thinking. 4 group of people controlling a political organization. —*v.* make or finish with a machine. [< F < L < Gk. *mechane* device; means]

machine gun, gun for keeping up a rapid fire of bullets.

ma·chine-gun (mə shēn′gun′), *v.,* **–gunned, –gun·ing.** fire at with a machine gun.

machine language, information or instructions in a code that a computer can process directly, without translation or processing.

ma·chin·er·y (mə shēn′ər i; –shēn′ri), *n., pl.* **–er·ies.** 1 machines: *a factory contains much machinery.* 2 the parts or works of a machine: *machinery is oiled to keep it running smoothly.* 3 any combination of persons or things by which something is kept going or something is done: *judges and courts are a part of the legal machinery.*

machine shop, workshop where people make or repair machines or parts of machines.

machine tool, tool worked by power.

ma·chin·ist (mə shēn′ist), *n.* 1 a skilled worker with machine tools. 2 person who runs a machine. 3 person who makes and repairs machinery.

ma·chis·mo (mä chēs′mō, –chēz′–), *n.* assertive manliness; manly bravado [< Am. Sp. *machismo* < *macho*]

Mach number, number that expresses the speed of an object in relation to the speed of sound in the same medium. Mach 2 denotes a speed twice the speed of sound, or supersonic speed. [< Ernst Mach (1838–1916), Austrian physicist]

ma·cho (mä′chō), *n., pl.* **–chos.** 1 strong, manly male. 2 =machismo. —*adj.* 1 virile; manly. 2 *Fig.* assertive; suggesting strength: *macho design.* [< Sp. *macho,* lit., male]

Ma·chu Pic·chu (mä′chü pē′chü), ancient and fabulous Inca city built on a mountain in SE Peru.

mack·er·el (mak′ər əl; mak′rəl), *n., pl.* **-el,** (*occasionally, esp. with reference to different species*) **-els.** a saltwater fish of the N Atlantic, much used for food. [< OF *maquerel*]

mackerel sky, sky spotted with small, white, fleecy clouds.

mack·i·naw (mak′ə nô), *n.* kind of short coat made of heavy woolen cloth. [after *Mackinac,* trading post in Michigan]

mack·in·tosh, mac·in·tosh (mak′ən tosh), waterproof coat; raincoat. [after C. Macintosh, the inventor]

mac·ra·mé (mak′rə mā), *n.* coarse lace or fringe made by knotting cord or thread. [appar. < Turk. *makrama* napkin]

macro–, *combining form.* 1 large or long, as in *macrobiotic.* 2 abnormally large, as in *macrophage.*

mac·ro·bi·ot·ic (mak′rō bī ot′ik), *adj.* 1 long-lived. 2 tending to lengthen life. 3 of or having to do with a diet of fish, rice, fruits, and vegetables. [< Gk. *makrobíotos* long-lived, prolonging life < *makrós* long + *bíotos* life + E –*ic*] —**mac′ro·bi·ot′ics,** *n.*

mac·ro·ce·phal·ic (mak′rō sə fal′ik), *adj.* having an abnormally large skull or head. Also, **macrocephalous.** —**mac′ro·ceph′a·ly,** *n.*

mac·ro·cosm (mak′rə koz əm), *n.* the universe. [< F < Med.L, < Gk. *makros* great + *kosmos* world] —**mac′ro·cos′mic,** *adj.*

ma·cron (mā′kron; mak′ron), *n.* a straight, horizontal line (-) placed over a vowel to show its sound. *Examples:* cāme, bē. [< Gk. *makron,* neut. adj., long]

mac·ro·phage (mak′rə fāj), *n.* only one of several especially large phagocytes.

mad (mad), *adj.,* **mad·der, mad·dest.** 1 out of one's head; crazy; insane. 2 much excited; wild. 3 foolish; unwise: *mad spending.* 4 blindly and unreasonably fond: *mad about going to dances.* 5 furious; angry. 6 having rabies: *a mad dog.* **like mad,** furiously; very hard, fast, etc. [OE *gemǣdd*]

Mad·a·gas·car (mad′ə gas′kər), *n.* island republic off the SE coast of Africa in the Indian Ocean.

mad·am (mad′əm), *n., pl.* **mad·ams, mes·dames** (mā däm′). 1 a polite title used in speaking to or of a lady. 2 woman who runs a brothel. [< OF *ma dame* my lady. See DAME.]

mad·ame (mad′əm; *Fr.* mä däm′), *n., pl.* **mes·dames.** 1 French title for a married woman. **2** title used by women singers, artists, etc.

mad·cap (mad′kap′), *n.* a very impulsive person. —*adj.* impulsive; hasty; wild.

mad·den (mad′ən), *v.* **1** make or become very angry or excited; irritate greatly. **2** make or become crazy; drive insane. —**mad′den·ing**, *adj.* —**mad′den·ing·ly**, *adv.*

mad·der (mad′ər), *n.* **1** vine with small yellowish flowers. **2** its red root. **3** a red dye made from these roots. **4** red; crimson. [OE *mædere*]

mad·ding (mad′ing), *adj.* **1** crazy; acting as if mad. **2** driving insane; maddening.

made (mād), *v.* pt. and pp. of **make.** —*adj.* **1** built; formed. **2** specially prepared. **3** artificially produced: *made land.* **4** invented: *a made word.* **5** certain of success; successful.

have or **got it made,** *Informal.* assured of success.

Ma·dei·ra (mə dir′ə), *n.* Often, **madeira.** wine made in a group of Portuguese islands NW of Africa.

mad·e·moi·selle (mad′ə mə zel′; *Fr.* mäd mwä zel′), *n., pl.* **mes·dem·oi·selles** (mäd mwä zel′). French title for an unmarried woman; Miss. [< F, orig. *ma demoiselle* my young lady]

made-up (mād′up′), *adj.* **1** put together. **2** invented; untrue. **3** painted, powdered, etc.

mad·house (mad′hous′), *n.* **1** asylum for insane people. **2** place of uproar and confusion.

Mad·i·son (mad′ə sən), *n.* **1 James,** 1751–1836, the fourth president of the United States, 1809–17. **2** capital of Wisconsin, in the S part.

mad·ly (mad′li), *adv.* **1** insanely. **2** furiously. **3** foolishly.

mad·man (mad′man′; –mən), *n., pl.* **-men.** an insane man; crazy person.

mad·ness (mad′nis), *n.* **1** being crazy; loss of one's mind. **2** great rage; fury. **3** folly.

Ma·don·na (mə don′ə), *n.* Mary, the mother of Jesus. [< Ital., my lady]

mad·ras (mad′rəs; mə dras′), *n.* a closely woven cotton cloth, used for shirts, dresses, etc. [after *Madras,* India]

mad·re·pore (mad′rə pôr; –pōr), *n.* kind of coral that forms coral islands and reefs. [< F < Ital. *madrepora*]

Ma·drid (mə drid′), *n.* capital of Spain, in the C part.

mad·ri·gal (mad′rə gəl), *n.* **1** a short poem that can be set to music. **2** song with parts for several voices, sung without instrumental accompaniment. [< Ital. < LL *matricale* original, chief < *matrix* womb]

mael·strom (māl′strəm), *n.* **1** a great or violent whirlpool of water. **2** a violent confusion of feelings, ideas, or conditions. [< earlier Du., < *malen* grind + *stroom* stream]

mae·nad (mē′nad), *n.* woman in a frenzy. [< L < Gk. *mainás, mainádos* mad woman, bacchante] —**mae·nad′ic,** *adj.*

ma·es·to·so (mä′es tō′sō), *adj., adv.* of music, with dignity or majesty; in a stately, majestic manner.

maes·tro (mīs′trō; *Ital.* mä es′trō), *n., pl.* **-tros,** *Ital.* **ma·es·tri** (mä es′trē). **1** a great composer, teacher, or conductor of music. **2** master of any art. [< Ital. < L *magister* master]

Mae West (mā′west′), *n.* inflatable vest worn as a life preserver.

Ma·fi·a or **Maf·fia** (mä′fē ä), *n.* **1** secret criminal organization active in various parts of the world. **2** secret Sicilian organization, engaged in criminal and terrorist activities. **3** Also, **mafia.** any exclusive group, society, etc.: *the medical mafia.* [Ital. *Mafia* secret society of criminals in Sicily < Sicilian *mafia* boldness, bravado prob. < Ar.]

Ma·fi·o·so or **ma·fi·o·so** (mä′fē ō′sō), *n., pl.* **-si** (-sē). member of the Mafia or a mafia.

mag., **1** magazine. **2** magnitude.

mag·a·zine (mag′ə zēn′; mag′ə zēn), *n.* **1** publication appearing regularly and containing stories, articles, etc., by various writers. **2** room in a fort or warship for storing gunpowder and other explosives. **3** a building for storing gunpowder, guns, food, or other military supplies. **4** place for cartridges in a repeating gun. **5** place for film in a camera; receptacle. [< F < Ital., ult. < Ar. *makhzan* storehouse]

Mag·da·lene (mag′də lən), *n.* = Mary Magdalene.

Mag·el·lan·ic cloud (maj′ə lan′ik), either of two luminous patches in the skies south of the equator, which are galaxies nearest to our own. [< Ferdinand *Magellan* (1480?–1521), Portuguese explorer]

ma·gen·ta (mə jen′tə), *n.* **1** a purplish-red dye. **2** a purplish red. —*adj.* purplish-red. [after Battle of *Magenta,* 1859, because discovered in that year]

mag·got (mag′ət), *n.* insect in the wormlike stage just after leaving the egg; legless larva of any of various kinds of flies. [ME *magot*] —**mag′got·y,** *adj.*

Ma·gi (mā′jī; maj′ī), *n.pl., sing.* **Ma·gus** (mā′gəs). the three "Wise Men" from the East, who brought gifts to the infant Jesus. Matt. 2:1 and 2, 7–13.

mag·ic (maj′ik), *n.* **1** the pretended art of making things happen by secret charms and sayings. **2** something that produces results as if by magic; mysterious influence; unexplained power: *the magic of music.* —*adj.* Also, **mag′i·cal. 1** of magic; used by magic; done by magic. **2** like magic; mysterious; unexplained. [< L, ult. < Gk., *magos* astrologer < OPers.] —**mag′i·cal·ly,** *adv.*

ma·gi·cian (mə jish′ən), *n.* **1** person skilled in the use of magic. **2** person skilled in sleight of hand. [< OF *magicien*]

magic marker, 1 marking pen with a broad, felt tip. **2 Magic Marker.** trademark for this kind of pen.

mag·is·te·ri·al (maj′is tir′i əl), *adj.* **1** of a magistrate; suited to a magistrate: *a judge has magisterial rank.* **2** showing authority: *the captain's magisterial voice.* **3** imperious; domineering; overbearing. [< LL, < L *magister* master] —**mag′is·te′ri·al·ly,** *adv.* —**mag′is·te′ri·al·ness,** *n.*

mag·is·tra·cy (maj′is trə si), *n., pl.* **-cies. 1** position, rank, or duties of a magistrate. **2** magistrates as a group. **3** district under a magistrate.

mag·is·trate (maj′is trāt; –trit), *n.* **1** officer of the government who has power to apply the law and put it in force. The President is the chief magistrate of the United States. **2** judge. [< L *magistratus,* ult < *magister* master]

Mag·na Car·ta or **Char·ta** (mag′nə kär′tə), **1** the great charter guaranteeing the personal and political liberties of the people of England. **2** any fundamental constitution guaranteeing civil and political rights. [< Med.L, great charter]

mag·na cum lau·de (mag′nə kùm lou′də; kum lô′dē), with high honors. [< L]

mag·na·nim·i·ty (mag′nə nim′ə ti), *n., pl.* **-ties. 1** magnanimous nature or quality. **2** a magnanimous act.

mag·nan·i·mous (mag nan′ə məs), *adj.* noble in soul or mind; generous in forgiving; free from mean or petty feelings and acts. [< L, < *magnus* great + *animus* spirit] —**mag·nan′i·mous·ly,** *adv.* —**mag·nan′i·mous·ness,** *n.*

mag·nate (mag′nāt), *n.* a great man; important person. [< LL, < L *magnus* great]

mag·ne·sia (mag nē′shə; –zhə), *n.* **1** magnesium oxide, MgO, a white tasteless powder, used as a laxative. **2** = magnesium. [< Med.L < Gk. *he Magnesia lithos* the Magnesian stone (from *Magnesia,* in Thessaly)]

mag·ne·si·um (mag nē′shi əm; –zhi–), *n.* a light, silver-white metallic element, Mg, that burns with a dazzling white light.

mag·net (mag′nit), *n.* **1** piece of iron, steel, etc., that attracts iron or steel. **2** anything that attracts. [< OF < L < Gk. *Magnes* (*lithos*) Magnesian stone. See MAGNESIA.]

mag·net·ic (mag net′ik), *adj.* **1** having the properties of a magnet. **2** of magnetism; producing magnetism. **3** of the earth's magnetism: *the magnetic meridian.* **4** capable of being magnetized. **5** attractive: *a magnetic personality.* —**mag·net′i·cal·ly,** *adv.*

magnetic field, space around a magnet in which it exerts appreciable magnetic force.

magnetic pole, 1 one of the two poles of a magnet. **2 Magnetic Pole,** point on the earth's surface toward which a magnetic needle points. The earth has a **North** and a **South Magnetic Pole.**

magnetic storm, disturbance of the earth's magnetic field, related to solar flares.

magnetic tape, thin paper, plastic, or metal strip coated with iron oxide on which images, sound, or data can be recorded.

mag·net·ism (mag′nə tiz əm), *n.* **1** properties of a magnet; manifestation of magnetic properties. **2** branch of physics dealing with magnets and magnetic properties. **3** power to attract or charm: *a person of great magnetism.*

mag·net·ite (mag′nə tīt), *n.* an important iron ore, Fe_3O_4, that is strongly attracted by a magnet; black iron oxide.

mag·net·ize (mag′nə tīz), *v.,* **–ized, –iz·ing. 1** give the properties of a magnet to. **2** become magnetic. **3** attract or influence (a person). **—mag′net·iz′a·ble,** *adj.* **—mag′net·i·za′tion,** *n.* **—mag′net·iz′er,** *n.*

mag·ne·to (mag nē′tō), *n., pl.* **-tos.** a small machine for producing electricity. In some gasoline engines, a magneto supplies an electric spark to ignite the vapor.

mag·ne·to·e·lec·tric (mag nē′tō i lek′trik), *adj.* of electricity produced by magnets.

mag·ne·to·sphere (mag nē′tə sfir; –net′ə–), *n.* **1** zone of strong magnetic forces that surrounds the earth, extending about 40,000 miles. **2** any similar zone around a celestial body.

magnet school, school with a strong, broad curriculum, designed to attract students from all over a city or from smaller districts.

mag·ni·fi·ca·tion (mag′nə fə kā′shən), *n.* **1** act of magnifying. **2** a magnified condition. **3** a magnified copy, model, or picture.

mag·nif·i·cence (mag nif′ə səns), *n.* richness of material, color, and ornament; grand beauty; splendor. [< OF < L *magnificentia* < *magnificus* noble < *magnus* great + *facere* make]

mag·nif·i·cent (mag nif′ə sənt), *adj.* richly colored or decorated; splendid; grand; stately. [< OF, < *magnificence* MAGNIFICENCE] **—mag·nif′i·cent·ly,** *adv.*

mag·nif·i·co (mag nif′ə kō), *n., pl.* **-coes.** an important person. [< Ital.]

mag·ni·fy (mag′nə fī), *v.,* **-fied, -fy·ing. 1** cause to be or look larger; increase the real or apparent size of an object. **2** make too much of; go beyond the truth in telling: *magnify the facts.* [< L *magnificare* esteem greatly, ult. < *magnus* great + *facere* make] **—mag′ni·fi′er,** *n.*

mag·nil·o·quence (mag nil′ə kwəns), *n.* **1** high-flown, lofty style of speaking or writing. **2** boastfulness. [< L, < *magnus* great + *loquens,* ppr. of *loqui* speak]

mag·nil·o·quent (mag nil′ə kwənt), *adj.* **1** using big and unusual words; in high-flown language. **2** boastful. [< *magniloquence*] **—mag·nil′o·quent·ly,** *adv.*

mag·ni·tude (mag′nə tüd; –tūd), *n.* **1** size. **2** importance. **3** degree of brightness of a star: *stars of the first magnitude are the brightest.* [< L, < *magnus* large]

mag·no·cel·lu·lar system (mag′nō sel′yə lər), visual pathway of specialized cells in the brain of human and other primates that is involved in perception of motion, low contrast light, and depth. Also, **magno system.**

mag·no·lia (mag nōl′yə), *n.,* **1** tree with large white, pink, or purplish flowers. **2** the flower. [< NL, after P. *Magnol,* French botanist.]

mag·num (mag′nəm), *n.* **1** bottle that holds two quarts of alcoholic liquor. **2** amount that it holds. [< L, neut. adj., great]

mag·num o·pus (mag′nəm ō′pəs), **1** a great work of literature or art. **2** person's greatest work. [< L]

mag·pie (mag′pī), *n.* **1** a noisy bird, black and white with a long tail and short wings, related to the jays. **2** person who chatters. [< *Mag,* for *Margaret,* + *pie*[2]]

mag·uey (mag′wā), *n.* plant with fleshy leaves, growing in tropical America and SW United States. A century plant or agave is a maguey. [< Sp. < West Ind. lang.]

Mag·yar (mag′yär; *Hung.* mod′yor), *n.* **1** member of the chief race living in Hungary. **2** their language; Hungarian. —*adj.* of the Magyars or their language; Hungarian. [< Hung.]

ma·ha·ra·ja, ma·ha·ra·jah (mä′hə rä′jə), *n.* title of certain great ruling princes in India. [< Skt., < *mahā–* great + *rājā* rajah]

ma·ha·ra·nee, ma·ha·ra·ni (mä′hə rä′nē), *n.* wife of a maharaja. [< Hind., < Skt. *mahā–* great + *rājñī* queen]

Ma·ha·ri·shi (mä′hə rē′shē), *n.* **1** Hindu spiritual guide or guru. **2** Also, **maharishi.** any guru. [< Skt. *mahā* great + *rishi* sage, seer]

ma·hat·ma (mə hät′mə; –hat′–), *n.* in India, a wise and holy person who has extraordinary powers. [< Skt. < *mahā–* great + *ātman* soul]

Mah·di (mä′di), *n., pl.* **-dis. 1** leader expected by Muslims to appear and establish a reign of righteousness. **2** person who claims to be this leader. [< Ar. *mahdīy* one who is guided correctly, right < *hadā* he led correctly]

Ma·hi·can (mə hē′kən), *n.* **1** =Mohegan. **2** =Mohican.

mah-jong (mä′jong′; –zhong′), *n.* Chinese game played with 144 dominolike pieces. [< Chinese *ma chiang* name of the game, lit. sparrows]

ma·hog·a·ny (mə hog′ə ni), *n., pl.* **-nies,** *adj.* —*n.* **1** a hard reddish-brown wood of a large evergreen tree that grows in tropical America, much used for furniture. **2** the tree itself. **3** a dark reddish brown. —*adj.* **1** made of mahogany. **2** dark reddish-brown. [< West Ind. lang.]

ma·hout (mə hout′), *n.* in the East Indies, driver of an elephant. [< Hind. *mahāut*]

maid (mād), *n.* **1** a young unmarried woman; girl. **2** an unmarried woman. **3** virgin. **4** a woman servant. [shortened from *maiden*]

maid·en (mād′ən), *n.* a young unmarried woman; girl. —*adj.* **1** of a maiden. **2** unmarried; virgin: *a maiden aunt.* **3** new; fresh; untried; unused: *maiden ground.* **4** first: *a ship's maiden voyage.* [OE *mægden*]

maid·en·hair (mād′ən hār′), *n.* a delicate fern with very slender stalks.

maid·en·head (mād′ən hed), *n.* **1** maidenhood; virginity. **2** the hymen.

maid·en·hood (mād′ən hud), *n.* **1** condition of being a maiden. **2** time when one is a maiden.

maid·en·ly (mād′ən li), *adj.* **1** of a maiden. **2** like a maiden; gentle; modest. **3** suited to a maiden. **—maid′en·li·ness,** *n.*

maiden name, a woman's surname before her marriage.

maid of honor, 1 an unmarried woman who is the chief attendant of the bride at a wedding. **2** an unmarried noble lady who attends a queen or princess.

maid·serv·ant (mād′sėr′vənt), *n.* a female servant.

mail[1] (māl), *n.* **1** letters, papers, parcels, etc., sent by the postal system. **2** system by which they are sent, managed by the United States Postal Service. —*v.* send by mail; put in a mailbox. —*adj.* of mail. [< OF *male* wallet < Gmc.] **—mail′a·ble,** *adj.* **—mail′er,** *n.*

mail[2] (māl), *n.* **1** armor made of metal rings or small loops of chain. **2** armor; protective covering. —*v.* cover or protect with mail. [< OF < L *macula* a mesh in network] **—mailed,** *adj.*

mail·box (māl′boks′), *n.* **1** a public box from which mail is collected. **2** a private box to which mail is delivered. **3** location on a computer where email is received and stored.

mail carrier, =letter carrier.

mail drop, address used only to receive mail.

mail·er (mā′lər), *n.* **1** advertisement sent through the mail to individuals. **2** reinforced envelope or box for mailing a letter or small package. **3** machine that stamps and addresses mail. **4** person who mails: *the mailer is unknown.*

mail·man (māl′man′), *n., pl.* **-men.** person who carries or delivers mail; postman; letter carrier.

mail order, order for goods sent by mail.

mail-or·der house (māl′ôr′dər), business that receives orders and sends goods by mail.

maim (mām), *v.* cut off or make useless some part of; cripple; disable: *automobile accidents maim thousands of people each year.* [var. of *mayhem*] **—maim′er,** *n.*

main (mān), *adj.* most important; largest: *the main street of a town.* —*n.* **1** a large pipe for water, gas, etc. **2** *Poetic.* the open sea; ocean.

in the main, for the most part; chiefly; mostly.

with might and main, with all one's strength. [OE *mægen* power]

main clause, clause in a complex sentence that can stand by itself as a sentence; independent clause.

Maine (mān), *n.* a New England state of the United States.

main·frame (mān′frām′), *n.*, or **main frame,** central processor of a computer, esp. of a very large computer network.

main·land (mān′land′; –lənd), *n.* the largest part of a continent; land that is not a small island or peninsula.

main·ly (mān′li), *adv.* for the most part; chiefly; mostly.

main·mast (mān′mast′; –mäst′; –məst), *n.* the principal mast of a ship.

main·sail (mān′sāl′; –səl), *n.* the largest sail of a ship.

main·sheet (mān′shēt′), *n.* rope that controls the angle at which the mainsail is set.

main·spring (mān′spring′), *n.* **1** the principal spring in a clock, watch, etc. **2** the main cause, motive, or influence.

main·stay (mān′stā′), *n.* **1** rope supporting the mainmast. **2** main support.

main·tain (mān tān′), *v.* **1** keep; keep up; carry on: *maintain an action, a business, etc.* **2** defend; uphold: *maintain an opinion.* **3** declare to be true: *he maintained his innocence.* **4** provide for: *he maintained his family.* [< F *maintenir* < L *manu tenere* hold by the hand] —**main·tain′a·ble,** *adj.* **main·tain′er,** *n.*

main·te·nance (mān′tə nəns), *n.* **1** a maintaining: *maintenance of quiet is necessary in a hospital.* **2** a being maintained; support: *a government collects taxes to pay for its maintenance.* **3** enough to support life; means of living: *his small farm provides only a maintenance.*

main·top (mān′top′), *n.* platform on the mainmast.

main·top·mast (mān′top′mast′; –mäst′; –məst), *n.* the second section of the mainmast above the deck.

main·top·sail (mān′top′sāl′; –səl), *n.* sail above the mainsail.

maî·tre d' (mā′trə dē′), *n.* *Informal.* manager of the dining room and staff in a restaurant.

maî·tre d'hô·tel (mā′trə dô tel′), **1** a hotel manager. **2** headwaiter. [< F]

maize (māz), *n.* **1** a kind of grain that grows on large ears; corn; Indian corn. **2** plant that it grows on. **3** the color of ripe corn; yellow. [< Sp. *maíz,* of West Ind. orig.]

Maj., Major.

ma·jes·tic (mə jes′tik), *adj.* grand; noble; dignified; stately. —**ma·jes′ti·cal·ly,** *adv.*

maj·es·ty (maj′is ti), *n., pl.* **–ties. 1** grandeur; nobility; dignity; stateliness. **2** supreme power or authority: *the majesty of the law.*

Majesty, title used in speaking to or of a king, queen, emperor, etc.: *your Majesty.* [< F < L *majestas*]

ma·jol·i·ca (mə jol′ə kə; –yol′–), *n.* kind of enameled Italian pottery richly decorated in colors. [< Ital. *maiolica* Majorca]

ma·jor (mā′jər), *adj.* **1** larger; greater; more important: *take the major share.* **2** elder; senior: *Cato major.* **3** of legal age. —*n.* **1** an army officer ranking next below a lieutenant colonel and next above a captain. **2** person of the legal age of responsibility. **3** subject or course of study to which a student gives most of his or her time and attention. **4** one of two sets of intervals, chords, scales, or keys: *the scale of C major.* —*v.* specialize in a subject or course of study: *major in mathematics.* [< L, compar. of *magnus* great. Doublet of MAYOR.]

ma·jor-do·mo (mā′jər dō′mō), *n., pl.* **–mos. 1** man in charge of a royal or noble household. **2** butler; steward. [< Sp. or Ital. < Med.L *major domus* chief of the household]

major general, an army officer ranking next below a lieutenant general and next above a brigadier general. —**ma′jor·gen′er·al·ship′,** *n.*

ma·jor·i·ty (mə jôr′ə ti; –jor′–), *n., pl.* **–ties. 1** the larger number; greater part; more than half: *the majority of humankind.* **2** a larger number of votes than all the rest. If Smith received 12,000 votes, Adams 7000, and White 3000, Smith had a majority of 2000 and a plurality of 5000. **3** the legal age of responsibility: *attain one's majority.* **4** rank or position of an army major.

major key, musical key based on the major scale.

major league, either of the two chief leagues in American professional baseball.

major scale, a musical scale having eight notes, with half steps instead of whole steps after the third and seventh notes.

make (māk), *v.,* **made, mak·ing,** *n.* —*v.* **1** bring into being; put together; build; form; shape: *make a dress, one big deal made the young businessman.* **2** have the qualities needed for: *wood makes a good fire, a lawyer makes a good legislator.* **3** cause or cause to be: *make trouble, he made me go, make public.* **4** get ready for use; arrange: *make a bed.* **5** get; obtain; acquire; earn: *make a fortune, make a reputation, he made the team.* **6** do; perform: *make a mistake.* **7** amount to; add up to; count as: *two and two make four.* **8** think of as; figure to be: *I make the distance across the room 15 feet.* **9** reach; arrive at: *the ship made port.* **10** go; travel: *make 500 miles an hour in an airplane.* —*n.* **1** way in which a thing is made; style; fashion. **2** kind; brand.

make believe, pretend.

make do, get along; manage.

make fast, fasten firmly.

make it, *Informal.* succeed.

make off, run away; leave suddenly:

heard shouting and made off in that direction.

make off with, steal.

make out, a write out; fill out. **b** show to be; prove or declare. **c** understand. **d** see with difficulty. **e** get along; manage. **f** *Informal.* kiss; make love.

make over, a alter; make different. **b** hand over; transfer ownership of.

make time, go with speed.

make up, a put together; compose; invent. **b** set right; make satisfactory. **c** pay for. **d** become friends again after a quarrel. **e** put powder, eye shadow, etc. on the face. **f** decide: *made up one's mind.*

make up to, try to get the friendship of; flatter.

on the make, *Informal.* working for success, profit, etc. [OE *macian*]

make-be·lieve (māk′bi lēv′), *n.* pretense. —*adj.* pretended.

mak·er (māk′ər), *n.* person or thing that makes.

Maker, God.

make·o·ver (māk′ō′vər), *n.* **1** renovation of a house, room etc. **2** change of a person's appearance, esp. with new hairstyle, makeup, etc.

make·shift (māk′shift′), *n.* something used for a time instead of the right thing; temporary substitute: *when the electric lights went out, we used candles as a makeshift.* —*adj.* used for a time instead of the right thing.

make·up or **make-up** (māk′up′), *n.* **1** way of being put together. **2** nature; disposition: *a nervous makeup.* **3** way in which an actor is dressed and painted to look his or her part. **4** lipstick, mascara, etc., put on the face; cosmetics.

make-work (māk′wėrk′), *n.* unnecessary work to keep a person occupied; busy work.

mak·ing (māk′ing), *n.* **1** cause of a person's success; means of advancement. **2** material or qualities needed.

in the making, in the process of being made; not yet fully developed.

mal–, *combining form.* bad or badly; poor or poorly, as in *malnutrition, maltreat.* [< OF *mal–* < L *male* badly < *malus* bad]

Mal·a·chi (mal′ə kī), *n.* last book of the Old Testament.

mal·a·chite (mal′ə kīt), *n.* a green mineral, $Cu_2(OH)_2CO_3$, used for ornamental articles. [< F < Gk. *malache* mallow (from the similar color)]

mal·ad·just·ed (mal′ə jus′tid), *adj.* badly adjusted.

mal·ad·just·ment (mal′ə just′mənt), *n.* bad adjustment.

mal·a·droit (mal′ə droit′), *adj.* unskillful; awkward; clumsy. —**mal′a·droit′ness,** *n.*

mal·a·dy (mal′ə di), *n., pl.* **–dies.** sickness; illness; disease. [< OF < *malade* ill < L *male habitus* doing poorly]

Mal·a·ga (mal′ə gə), *n.* **1** kind of large, oval, firm, white grape. **2** kind of white wine.

ma·laise (ma lāz′), *n.* **1** vague bodily discomfort. **2** feeling of unease; disturbed condition. [< F, < *mal–* imperfect + *aise* ease]

mal·ap·por·tion·ment (mal′ə pô′shən mənt; –pōr′–), *n.* wrong or unfair assignment of representation in a legislature.

mal·a·prop·ism (mal′ə prop iz′əm), *n.* **1** a ridiculous misuse of words. **2** a misused word. [after Mrs. *Malaprop,* a character in Sheridan's *Rivals,* who constantly misuses words]

ma·lar·i·a (mə lār′i ə), *n.* disease characterized by periodic chills followed by fever and sweating. Malaria is transmitted by the bite of certain kinds of mosquito. [< Ital. < *mala aria* bad air] —**ma·lar′i·al, ma·lar′i·ous,** *adj.*

ma·lar·key or **ma·lar·ky** (mə lär′ki), *n. Informal.* nonsense; baloney.

Ma·la·wi (ma lä′wē), *n.* country in SE Africa.

Ma·lay (mā′lā; mə lā′), **Ma·lay·an** (mə lā′ən), *n.* **1** member of the people living in the Malay Peninsula and nearby islands. **2** their language. —*adj.* of the Malays, their country, or their language.

Ma·lay·a (mə lā′ə), *n.* the Malay Peninsula.

Mal·a·ya·lam (mal′ə yä′ləm), *n.* the Dravidian language spoken on the SW coast of India.

Malay Archipelago, =Malaysia (def. 1).

Malay Peninsula, peninsula in SE Asia, part of Malaysia.

Ma·lay·sia (mə lā′zhə; –shə), *n.* **1** group of islands between SE Asia and Australia; East Indies. Also called **Malay Archipelago. 2** Also, **Federation of Malaysia.** association of Malaya, Sabah, and Sarawak. —**Ma·lay′sian,** *adj., n.*

mal·con·tent (mal′kən tent′), *adj.* discontented; rebellious. —*n.* a discontented person.

mal de mer (mäl də mār′), *French.* seasickness.

male (māl), *n.* **1 a** man or boy. **b** animal of the same sex as a man or boy. **2 a** flower having a stamen but no pistil. **b** plant bearing flowers with stamens and no pistils. —*adj.* **1** belonging to the sex that produces sperm when mature and can father offspring. **2** of or having to do with men, boys, or animals of the same sex as a man or boy: *male aggression; a male club.* **3** of plants, **a** having flowers with stamens, but no pistils. **b** able to fertilize the female. **4** fitting into a corresponding part of a machine. [< OF < L *masculus,* dim. of *mas* male]

mal·e·dic·tion (mal′ə dik′shən), *n.* a curse. [< L. ult. < *male* ill + *dicere* speak]

mal·e·fac·tion (mal′ə fak′shən), *n.* crime; evil deed.

mal·e·fac·tor (mal′ə fak′tər), *n.* criminal; evildoer. [< L, ult. < *male* badly + *facere* do]

ma·lef·i·cence (mə lef′ə səns), *n.* harm; evil. [< L, < *maleficus* wicked < *male* badly + *facere* do]

ma·lef·i·cent (mə lef′ə sənt), *adj.* harmful; evil.

ma·lev·o·lent (mə lev′ə lənt), *adj.* wishing evil to happen to others; showing ill will; spiteful. [< L *malevolens,* ult. < *male* ill + *velle* wish] —**ma·lev′o·lence,** *n.* —**ma·lev′o·lent·ly,** *adv.*

mal·fea·sance (mal fē′zəns), *n.* official misconduct; violation of a public trust or duty. A judge is guilty of malfeasance if he accepts a bribe. [< F *malfaisance,* ult. < *mal–* badly + *faire* do] —**mal·fea′sant,** *adj., n.*

mal·for·ma·tion (mal′fôr mā′shən), *n.* bad shape; faulty structure.

mal·formed (mal fôrmd′), *adj.* badly shaped; having a faulty structure.

mal·func·tion (mal′fungk′shən), *n.* failure to work or perform properly; dysfunction.

Ma·li (mä′li), *n.* a republic in W Africa S of Algeria.

mal·ic acid (mal′ik; mā′lik), an acid, $C_4H_6O_5$, found in certain fruits.

mal·ice (mal′is), *n.* active ill will; wish to hurt others; spite [< OF < L, < *malus* evil]

ma·li·cious (mə lish′əs), *adj.* showing active ill will; wishing to hurt others; spiteful. —**ma·li′cious·ly,** *adv.* —**ma·li′cious·ness,** *n.*

ma·lign (mə līn′), *v.* speak evil of; slander. —*adj.* **1** evil; injurious. **2** hateful; malicious. **3** very harmful; causing death. [< OF < L *malignus* < *malus* evil + gen-birth, nature] —**ma·lign′er,** *n.* —**ma·lign′ly,** *adv.*

ma·lig·nant (mə lig′nənt), *adj.* **1** very evil; very hateful; very malicious. **2** very harmful. **3** very infectious; very dangerous; causing death: *a malignant growth.* [< LL *malignans* acting from malice < *malignus* MALIGN] —**ma·lig′nance, ma·lig′nan·cy,** *n.* —**ma·lig′nant·ly,** *adv.*

ma·lig·ni·ty (mə lig′nə ti), *n., pl.* **–ties. 1** great malice; extreme hate. **2** great harmfulness; dangerous quality; deadliness. **3** malignant act.

ma·lin·ger (mə ling′gər), *v.* pretend to be sick in order to escape work or duty; shirk. [< F *malingre* sickly] —**ma·lin′ger·er,** *n.*

mall (môl; mal), *n.* **1** shopping center, often with shops enclosed in a large building. **2** walkway through a central shopping district. **3** a shaded walk; public walk or promenade. [< OF < L *malleus* hammer]

mal·lard (mal′ərd), *n., pl.* **–lards** or (*esp. collectively*) **–lard.** kind of wild duck. The male has a green head and a white band around his neck. [< OF *mallart,* prob. < Gmc.]

mal·le·a·ble (mal′i ə bəl), *adj.* **1** capable of being hammered or pressed into various shapes without being broken. **2** adaptable; yielding. [< OF, < L *malleare*

hammer, v. < *malleus,* n.] —**mal′le·a·bil′i·ty, mal′le·a·ble·ness,** *n.*

mal·let (mal′it), *n.* a wooden hammer. Specially shaped mallets are used to play croquet and polo. [< OF *maillet,* dim. of *mail* < L *malleus* hammer]

mal·le·us (mal′i əs), *n., pl.* **mal·le·i** (mal′i ī) the outermost of three small bones in the middle ear, shaped like a hammer. [< L, hammer]

mal·low (mal′ō), *n.* **1** an ornamental plant with purple, pink or white flowers, and downy leaves and stems. **2** any plant like this. [< L *malva.* Cf. Gk. *malache.*]

mall rat, *Informal.* young person who spends time socializing at malls.

malm·sey (mäm′zi), *n.* kind of strong sweet wine. [< Med.L *malmasia,* alter. of *Monembasia,* Greek town]

mal·nour·ished (mal nėr′isht), *adj.* lacking nourishment; poorly nourished.

mal·nu·tri·tion (mal′nü trish′ən; –nū–), *n.* poor nourishment; lack of nourishment.

mal·oc·clu·sion (mal′ə klü′zhən), *n.* failure of the teeth in the upper and lower jaws to close or meet properly.

mal·o·dor·ous (mal ō′dər əs), *adj.* smelling bad. —**mal·o′dor·ous·ly,** *adv.* —**mal·o′dor·ous·ness,** *n.*

mal·prac·tice (mal prak′tis), *n.* **1** criminal neglect or unprofessional treatment of a patient by a doctor. **2** wrong practice or conduct in any official or professional position. —**mal′prac·ti′tion·er,** *n.*

malt (môlt), *n.* **1** barley or other grain soaked in water until it sprouts and tastes sweet, used in brewing and distilling alcoholic liquors. **2** beer or ale. —*v.* **1** change into malt. **2** prepare with malt. —*adj.* of malt; containing malt. [OE *mealt*] —**malt′y,** *adj.*

Mal·ta (môl′tə), *n.* **1** country made up of islands in the Mediterranean, S of Sicily. **2** the principal island of this group. —**Mal·tese′,** *adj., n.*

malt·ase (môl′tās), *n.* enzyme, present in saliva and other body fluids and in yeast, that changes maltose to dextrose.

Maltese cat, kind of bluish-gray cat.

Maltese cross, a kind of cross having arms of equal length shaped like arrowheads pointing toward the center.

malt extract, a sugary substance obtained by soaking malt in water.

malt·ose (môl′tōs), *n.* sugar made by the action of diastase on starch, $C_{12}H_{22}O_{11} \cdot H_2O$.

malt sugar, =maltose.

mal·treat (mal trēt′), *v.* treat roughly or cruelly; abuse. —**mal·treat′ment,** *n.*

mam·ba (mam′bə), *n.* any one of a genus of long and slender poisonous snakes of Central and South America, from the same family as the cobra.

mam·bo (mam′bō; mäm′–), *n.* **1** a ballroom dance of Caribbean origin. **2** the music for it. [< Am. Sp.; ? related to *mambi* a festival and dance of the Antilles]

mam·ma[1], **ma·ma** (mä′mə;), *n.* mother. [reduplication of an infantile sound]

mam·ma[2] (mam′ə), *n., pl.* **mam·mae** (mam′ē). =mammary gland. [< L, breast]

mam·mal (mam′əl), *n.* a vertebrate animal that gives milk to its young. Human beings, horses, dogs, lions, rats, and whales are all mammals. [< NL, ult. < L *mamma* breast] —**mam·ma′li·an,** *adj., n.*

mam·ma·ry (mam′ə ri), *adj.* of the mammae or breasts.

mammary gland, milk-producing gland in female mammals.

mam·mo·gram (mam′ə gram), *n.* X-ray photograph of the breast. [< L *mamma* breast + E *–gram*]

mam·mog·ra·phy (ma mog′rə fi), *n.* X-ray examination of the breast.

Mam·mon, mam·mon (mam′ən), *n.* riches thought of as an evil; greed for wealth [< L < Gk. < Aram. *māmōn(ā)* riches]

mam·moth (mam′əth), *n.* a very large, extinct kind of elephant with a hairy skin and long, curved tusks. —*adj.* huge; gigantic. [< earlier Russ. *mammot*]

man (man), *n., pl.* **men,** *v.,* **manned, man·ning.** —*n.* **1** an adult male person. **2** person; human being: *no man knows.* **3** the human race: *man has existed for thousands of years.* **4** a male follower, servant, or employee. **5** husband. **6** one of the pieces used in games such as chess and checkers. —*v.* **1** supply with men: *man a ship with sailors.* **2** serve or operate; get ready to operate: *man the guns.* **3** make strong; brace: *the captive manned himself to endure torture.*

man alive! *Informal.* exclamation expressing disbelief or surprise.

to a man, without exception; all. [OE *mann*]

Man., 1 Manila. **2** Manitoba.

man·a·cle (man′ə kəl), *n., v.,* **–cled, –cling.** —*n.* **1** Usually, **manacles.** handcuff; shackles for the hands. **2** *Fig.* any restraint. [< OF < L *manicula,* dim. of *manicae* sleeves, manacles < *manus* hand]

man·age (man′ij), *v.,* **–aged, –ag·ing,** *n.* —*v.* **1** control; conduct; handle; direct: *manage a business, manage a horse.* **2** succeed in accomplishing; contrive; arrange: *can you manage to keep warm?* **3** get along: *manage on one's income.* [< Ital. *maneggiare* < *mano* hand < L *manus*]

man·age·a·ble (man′ij ə bəl), *adj.* that can be managed. —**man′age·a·bil′i·ty, man′age·a·ble·ness,** *n.* —**man′age·a·bly,** *adv.*

man·age·ment (man′ij mənt), *n.* **1** control; handling; direction. **2** persons that manage a business or an institution.

man·ag·er (man′ij ər), *n.* person who manages. —**man′ag·er·ship′,** *n.*

man·a·ge·ri·al (man′ə jir′i əl), *adj.* of a manager; having to do with management. —**man′a·ge′ri·al·ly,** *adv.*

Ma·na·gua (mə nä′gwə), *n.* capital of Nicaragua.

ma·ña·na (mä nyä′nä), *n., adv.* tomorrow; some time. [< Sp.]

man-at-arms (man′ət ärmz′), *n., pl.* **men-at-arms. 1** soldier. **2** a heavily armed soldier on horseback.

man·a·tee (man′ə tē′), *n.* a sea cow, a large sea mammal with flippers and a flat, oval tail. [< Sp. *manatí* < Carib lang.]

Man·chu (man′chü), *n.* **1** member of a Mongolian people living in Manchuria. The Manchus conquered China in 1644 and ruled it until 1912. **2** their language. —*adj.* of the Manchus, their country, or their language.

Man·chu·ri·a (man chür′i ə), *n.* region in E Asia, including several provinces of China. —**Man·chu′ri·an,** *adj., n.*

man·da·mus (man dā′məs), *n.* a written order from a higher court to a lower court, an official, a city, a corporation, etc., directing that a certain thing be done. [< L, we order]

Man·dan (man′dan), *n.* **1** member of a W Plains tribe of North American Indians. **2** their Siouan language.

man·da·rin (man′də rin), *n.* **1** a Chinese official of high rank. **2 Mandarin,** the main dialect of the Chinese language, spoken esp. by educated people. **3** kind of small, sweet orange with a very loose peel; tangerine. [< Chinese pidgin Eng. < Pg. *mandar* to order (< L *mandere*), blended with Malay *mantrī* < Hind. < Skt. *mantrin* advisor]

mandarin collar, narrow collar that stands up, fashioned with a split at the front.

man·date (*n.* man′dāt; –dit), *n.* **1** command; order. **2** order from a higher court or official to a lower one. **3** the expressed will of voters to their representative. [< L *mandatum,* n. use of neut. pp. of *mandare* order]

man·da·to·ry (man′də tô′ri; –tō′–), *adj.* **1** of or like a mandate; giving a command or order. **2** required by a command or order.

man·di·ble (man′də bəl), *n.* **1** jawbone; jaw, esp. the lower jaw. **2** either part of a bird's beak. **3** organ in insects for seizing and biting. [< L *mandibula* < *mandere* chew]

man·do·lin (man′də lin; man′də lin′), *n.* a musical instrument with a pear-shaped body, having four or more strings, played with a plectrum. [< F < Ital. *mandolino,* dim. of *mandola,* ult. < Gk. *pandoura* three-stringed instrument]

man·drag·o·ra (man drag′ə rə), *n.* a genus of plants belonging to the nightshade family. [< L < Gk. *mandragoras*]

man·drake (man′drāk), *n.* **1** plant with a very short stem and a thick root, used in medicine. **2** the May apple. [by popular etymology < *mandragora*]

man·drel, man·dril (man′drəl), *n.* spindle or bar of a lathe that supports the material being turned. [< F *mandrin*]

man·drill (man′dril), *n.* a large, fierce baboon of W Africa. [< *man + drill* baboon (<African lang.)]

mane (mān), *n.* the long, heavy hair on the back of the neck of a horse, lion, etc. [OE *manu*] —**maned,** *adj.*

man-eat·er (man′ē′tər), *n.* **1** *Fig.* **a** woman who is very aggressive and possessive of men. **b** any extremely aggressive person. **2** =cannibal. **3** animal that attacks or is believed to attack humans for food.

ma·neu·ver (mə nü′vər), *n., v.,* **–vered, –ver·ing.** —*n.* **1** a planned movement of troops or warships. **2** a skillful plan; clever trick. —*v.* **1** perform or cause to perform maneuvers. **2** plan skillfully; use clever tricks. **3** force by skillful plans; get by clever tricks. **4** move or cause to move with skill: *maneuver a car over icy roads.* [< F *manoeuvre,* ult. < L *manu operare* work by hand] —**ma·neu′ver·a·ble,** *adj.* —**ma·neu′ver·a·bil′i·ty,** *n.* —**ma·neu′ver·er,** *n.*

man·ful (man′fəl), *adj.* manly; brave; resolute. —**man′ful·ly,** *adv.* —**man′ful·ness,** *n.*

man·ga·nese (mang′gə nēs; –nēz), *n.* a hard, brittle, grayish-white metallic element, Mn, used in making glass, paints, and medicines. [< F < Ital., alter. of Med.L. *magnesia* MAGNESIA]

mange (mānj), *n.* a skin disease of animals that forms scabs and causes loss of hair. [< OF *manjüe* itch < *mangier* eat < L *manducare* chew]

man·ger (mān′jər), *n.* box or trough in which hay can be placed for horses or cows to eat. [< OF *mangeoire,* ult. < L *manducare* chew]

man·gle (mang′gəl), *v.,* **–gled, –gling. 1** cut or tear (the flesh) roughly. **2** spoil; ruin. [< AF *mangler,* ? < OF *mahaignier.* See MAYHEM.] —**man′gler,** *n.*

man·go (mang′gō), *n., pl.* **–goes, –gos. 1** a slightly sour, juicy fruit with a thick, yellowish-red rind. **2** the tropical tree that it grows on. [< Pg. < Malay < Tamil *mānkāy*]

man·grove (mang′grōv), *n.* a tropical tree that sends down many branches that take root and form new trunks. [< Sp. *mangle* < Malay *manggi-manggi;* infl. by *grove*]

man·gy (mān′ji), *adj.,* **–gi·er, –gi·est. 1** having the mange; with the hair falling out. **2** shabby and dirty. **3** mean; contemptible. —**man′gi·ly,** *adv.* —**man′gi·ness,** *n.*

man·han·dle (man′han′dəl), *v.,* **–dled, –dling. 1** treat roughly; pull or push about. **2** move by human strength without mechanical appliances.

man·hole (man′hōl′), *n.* hole through which a person can enter a sewer, steam boiler, etc., to inspect or repair it.

man·hood (man′hud), *n.* **1** condition or time of being a man. **2** courage; manliness. **3** men as a group.

man-hour (man′our′), *n.* hour of work by one person, used as a time unit in industry.

ma·ni·a (mā′ni ə), *n.* **1** kind of insanity characterized by great excitement and sometimes violence. **2** unusual fondness; craze: *a mania for chocolate.* [< L < Gk., madness]

ma·ni·ac (mā′ni ak), *n.* **1** an insane person; raving lunatic. **2** person who has an intense liking or enthusiasm for something: *a maniac for details.* —*adj.* Also, **ma·ni·a·cal.** insane, raving. —**ma·ni′a·cal·ly,** *adv.*

ma·nic (mā′nik; man′ik), *adj.* **1** of or like mania. **2** suffering from mania.

man·ic-de·pres·sive (man′ik di pres′iv), *adj.* having alternating attacks of mania and depression: *manic-depressive condition.* —*n.* manic-depressive person.

man·i·cot·ti (man′ə kot′i), *n.* noodles formed into tubes, stuffed with cheese, spinach, etc., and baked in a tomato sauce. [< Ital.]

man·i·cure (man′ə kyur), *v.,* —**cured,** —**cur·ing,** *n.* —*v.* care for (the fingernails and hands); trim, clean, and polish (the fingernails). —*n.* care of the hands; trimming, cleaning, and polishing of fingernails. [< F, < L *manus* hand + *cura* care] —**man′i·cur′ist,** *n.*

man·i·fest (man′ə fest), *adj.* apparent to the eye or to the mind; plain; clear. —*v.* **1** show plainly; reveal; display. **2** prove; put beyond doubt. —*n.* list of a ship's cargo. [< L *manifestus* palpable < *manus* hand + ? *fore* seize] **man′i·fest′ly,** *adv.* —**man′i·fest′ness,** *n.*

man·i·fes·ta·tion (man′ə fes tā′shən), *n.* **1** a manifesting or being manifested. **2** thing that manifests: *diving in to rescue the child was a manifestation of courage.* **3** public demonstration.

manifest destiny, popular idea in the United States in the 1840s that westward expansion was inevitable and preordained.

man·i·fes·to (man′ə fes′tō), *n., pl.* —**toes.** **1** a public declaration of intentions, purposes, or motives by an important person or group; proclamation. [< Ital.]

man·i·fold (man′ə fōld), *adj.* **1** of many kinds; many and various: *manifold duties.* **2** having many parts or forms: *the manifold effects of the hurricane.* —*n.* pipe with several openings. [OE *manigfeald*] —**man′i·fold′ly,** *adv.* —**man′i·fold′ness,** *n.*

man·i·kin (man′ə kin), *n.* **1** a little man; dwarf. **2** =mannequin [< Du. *manneken,* dim. of *man* man]

ma·nil·a, ma·nil·la (mə nil′ə), *n.* **1** =Manila hemp. **2** =Manila paper.

Manila hemp, a strong fiber made from the leaves of a Philippine banana plant, used for making ropes and fabrics; abacá.

Manila paper, a strong, brown or brownish-yellow wrapping paper.

man·i·oc (man′i ok; mā′ni-), *n.* =cassava. [< Sp., Pg., < Tupi *manioca*]

ma·nip·u·late (mə nip′yə lāt), *v.,* —**lat·ed,** —**lat·ing.** **1** handle or treat skillfully;

handle: *manipulate the gear shift of an automobile.* **2** *Fig.* manage by clever use of influence, esp. unfair influence: *he so manipulated the ball team that he was elected captain.* **3** *Fig.* change for one's own purpose or advantage: *the bookkeeper manipulated the company's accounts to conceal his theft.* [< F, < L *manipulus* handful] —**ma·nip′u·lat′a·ble,** *adj.* —**ma·nip′u·la′tion,** *n.* —**ma·nip′u·la′tive, ma·nip′u·la·to′ry,** *adj.* —**ma·nip′u·la′tor,** *n.*

man·i·to (man′ə tō), **man·i·tou** (–tü), *n.* spirit worshiped by Algonquian Indians as a force of nature. [< Algonquian]

Man·i·to·ba (man′ə tō′bə), *n.* province in S Canada.

man·kind (man′kīnd′ *for 1;* man′kīnd′ *for 2*), *n.* **1** the human race; all human beings. **2** men; the male sex (as distinguished from women).

man·like (man′līk′), *adj.* **1** like a man. **2** suitable for a man; masculine.

man·ly (man′li), *adj.,* —**li·er,** —**li·est.** **1** like a man; as a man should be. **2** suitable for a man; masculine. —**man′li·ness,** *n.*

man·na (man′ə), *n.* **1** food miraculously supplied to the Israelites in the wilderness. Exod. 16:14–36. **2** *Fig.* food for the soul. **3** *Fig.* a much needed thing that is unexpectedly supplied. [< LL < Gk. < Heb. *mān*]

man·ne·quin (man′ə kin), *n.* **1** woman whose work is wearing new clothes to show how they look; model. **2** figure of a person used by tailors, artists, stores, etc. [< F < Du. See MANIKIN.]

man·ner (man′ər), *n.* **1** way of doing, being done, or happening: *the trouble arose in this manner.* **2** way of acting or behaving: *an austere manner.* **3** characteristic style in art or literature: *verses in the manner of Spenser.* **4** kind or kinds: *all manner of things.*

by all manner of means, most certainly.

by no manner of means, not at all; under no circumstances.

in a manner of speaking, as one might say.

manners, a way of behaving: *good manners.* **b** polite ways of behaving.

to the manner born, accustomed since birth to some way or condition. [< AF *manere,* ult. < L *manus* hand]

man·nered (man′ərd), *adj.* **1** having manners of a certain kind, as in *well-mannered.* **2** affected; artificial; having many mannerisms: *mannered speech.*

man·ner·ism (man′ər iz əm), *n.* **1** too much use of some manner in speaking, writing, or behaving. **2** an odd little trick; queer habit; peculiar way of acting.

man·ner·less (man′ər lis), *adj.* without good manners.

man·ner·ly (man′ər li), *adj.* having or showing good manners; polite. —*adj.* politely. —**man′ner·li·ness,** *n.*

man·ni·kin (man′ə kin), *n.* =mannequin.

man·nish (man′ish), *adj.* **1** characteristic of a man: *a mannish way of holding a baby.* **2** imitating a man: *a mannish style of dress.* —**man′nish·ly,** *adv.* —**man′nish·ness,** *n.*

ma·noeu·vre (mə nü′vər), *n., v.,* —**vred,** —**vring.** =maneuver.

ma·nom·e·ter (mə nom′ə tər), *n.* instrument for measuring the pressure of gases or vapors. [< F, < Gk. *manos* thin + *metron* measure]

man·or (man′ər), *n.* **1** a landed estate, part of which was set aside for the lord and the rest divided among his peasants, who paid the owner rent in goods, services, or money but were legally little more than property of the manor. **2** in colonial America, a large tract of land within which the owner had similar arrangements with the tenants. **3 a** a large estate. **b** the main house on an estate. [< OF *manoir,* orig. v., dwell < L *manere* stay] —**ma·no′ri·al,** *adj.*

man·qué (män kā′), *adj. French.* defective or undeveloped; unfulfilled; frustrated: *a painter manqué.*

man·pow·er (man′pou′ər), *n.* **1** power supplied by the physical work of men. **2** strength thought of in terms of the number of people needed or available.

man·sard (man′särd), or **mansard roof,** *n.* roof with two slopes on each of four sides. [after F. *Mansard,* architect]

manse (mans), *n.* a minister's house; parsonage. [< Med.L *mansa* dwelling, n. use of fem. pp. of L. *manere* stay]

man·serv·ant (man′sėr′vənt), *n., pl.* **men·serv·ants.** a male servant.

man·sion (man′shən), *n.* a large house; stately residence. [< OF < L *mansio* < *manere* stay]

man·slaugh·ter (man′slô′tər), *n.* **1** killing a human being. **2** killing a person unlawfully but without malice.

man·tai·lored (man′tā′lərd), *adj.* tailored for women in the same manner as clothing for men.

man·teau (man′tō), *n., pl.* —**teaus,** —**teaux** (–tōz). mantle; cloak [< F]

man·tel (man′təl), *n.* **1** shelf above a fireplace with its supports. **2** Also, **man′tel·piece′.** the shelf. [var. of *mantle*]

man·til·la (man til′ə), *n.* a lace or silk veil or scarf covering the hair and falling down over the shoulders, often worn by Spanish and Mexican women. [< Sp., dim. of *manta,* ult. < L *mantellum* mantle]

man·tis (man′tis), *n.* insect that holds its forelegs doubled up as if praying. It eats other insects; praying mantis. [NL use of Gk. *mantis* prophet (from its praying posture)]

man·tle (man′təl), *n., v.,* —**tled,** —**tling.** —*n.* **1** a loose cloak without sleeves; cape. **2** *Fig.* anything that covers like a mantle. **3** a tube made of fine netting around a flame that gets so hot it glows and gives light. **4** layer of the earth that lies between the crust and the outer core. —v. **1** cover with a mantle. **2** cover; conceal. [< L *mantellum*]

man·tra (man'trə), *n.* **1** prayer or invocation of Hinduism and Buddhism, sometimes believed to have magical power. **2** any formulaic phrase repeated over and over. [< Skt. *mantra*, lit., instrument of thought]

man·u·al (man'yü əl), *adj.* of the hands; done with the hands: *manual labor.* —n. **1** a small book that helps its readers to understand or use something; handbook. A cookbook is a manual. **2** an organ keyboard played with the hands. [< L, < *manus* hand] —**man'u·al·ly,** *adv.*

man·u·fac·to·ry (man´yə fak'tə ri), *n., pl.* **-ries.** =factory.

man·u·fac·ture (man´yə fak'chər), *v.,* **-tured, -tur·ing,** *n.* —v. **1** make by hand or by machine. A big factory manufactures goods in large quantities by using machines and dividing the work up among many people. **2** make into something useful. **3** *Fig.* invent; make up: *manufacture an excuse.* **4** *Fig.* produce (music, literary work, etc.) in quantity and in a mechanical way: *manufactured three mysteries this year.* —n. **1** act or process of manufacturing. **2** thing manufactured. [< F, ult. < L *manu facere* make by hand]

man·u·fac·tur·er (man´yə fak'chər ər), *n.* person whose business is manufacturing; owner of a factory.

man·u·mis·sion (man´yə mish'ən), *n.* a freeing or a being freed from slavery.

ma·nure (mə nür'; -nyür'), *n., v.,* **-nured, -nur·ing.** —n. substance put on the soil as fertilizer; refuse from stables, etc. —v. put manure in or on. [< AF *maynoverer* work with the hands. See MANEUVER.]

man·u·script (man'yə skript), *n.* book or paper written by hand or with a typewriter. —adj. written by hand or with a typewriter. [< L *manu scriptus* written by hand]

Manx (mangks), *adj.* of the Isle of Man, its people, or their language. —n. **1** (*pl. in use*) people of the Isle of Man. **2** (*sing. in use*) their language.

Manx cat, kind of cat that has no tail.

Manx·man (mangks'mən), *n., pl.* **-men.** native of the Isle of Man.

man·y (men'i), *adj.,* **more, most,** *n.* —adj. consisting of a great number; numerous: *many people, many years ago.* —n. **1** a great number: *did many come? Yes, a great many.* **2** many people or things: *there were many at the dance.* [OE *manig*]

man·za·ni·ta (man´zə nē'tə), *n.* **1** a heath-like evergreen shrub that grows in the W United States. **2** fruit of these shrubs. [< Sp., dim. of *manzana* apple]

Ma·o·ri (mä'ō ri; mou'ri; mä'ri), *n., pl.* **-ris,** *adj.* —n. **1** member of the native people of New Zealand. **2** their language. —adj. of the Maoris or their language.

map (map), *n., v.,* **mapped, map·ping.** —n. **1** drawing representing the earth's surface or part of it, usually showing countries, cities, rivers, seas, lakes, and mountains. **2** drawing representing part of the sky, showing the position of the stars. —v. **1** make a map of; show on a map. **2** plan; arrange in detail: *map out the week's work.*

put on the map, give prominence to; make well-known. [< Med.L *mappa mundi* map of the world (L *mappa* napkin)]

ma·ple (mā'pəl), *n.* **1** tree grown for its shade, its wood, or its sap. There are many kinds of maples, but all have dry fruits with two wings and opposite leaves without stipules. **2** its hard, light-colored wood. **3** flavor of maple sugar or maple syrup. [OE *mapeltrēow* maple tree]

maple sugar, sugar made from the sap of one variety of maple.

maple syrup, syrup made from the sap of one variety of maple.

mar (mär), *v.,* **marred, mar·ring.** spoil the beauty of; damage; injure. [OE *merran* waste]

Mar., March.

mar·a·bou (mar'ə bü), *n.* **1** kind of large stork common in Africa and the East Indies. **2** a furlike trimming made from its soft, downy feathers. [< F]

ma·ra·ca (mə rä'kə; -rak'ə), *n.* percussion instrument made from a dried gourd, or something shaped like a gourd, with dried seeds, pebbles, etc. inside it that rattle when shaken. [< Pg. *maracá* < Brazilian name for gourd]

mar·a·schi·no (mar´ə skē'nō), *n.* a strong, sweet alcoholic drink made from a kind of small black cherry. [< Ital., ult. < L *amarus* sour]

maraschino cherries, cherries preserved in a syrup flavored with maraschino.

mar·a·thon (mar'ə thon), *n.* **1** a foot race of 26 miles, 385 yards. **2** any long race or contest.

ma·raud (mə rôd'), *v.* go about in search of plunder; make raids on for booty. —n. a raid for booty. [< F, < *maraud* rascal] —**ma·raud'er,** *n.* —**ma·raud'ing,** *adj.*

mar·ble (mär'bəl), *n., adj., v.,* **-bled, -bling.** —n. **1** a hard limestone, white or colored, capable of taking a beautiful polish. **2** marbles, collection of sculptures. **3** a small ball of clay, glass, stone, etc., used in games. **4** marbles (*sing. in use*), game played with marbles. —adj. **1** made of marble. **2** *Fig.* like marble; white, hard, cold, or unfeeling. **3** having a pattern like marble. —v. color in imitation of the patterns in marble: *binders marble the edges of some books.*

lose one's marbles, *Informal.* lose one's ability to reason, one's common sense: *seems to have lost his marbles.* [< OF < L < Gk. *marmaros* gleaming stone]

mar·bling (mär'bling), *n.* coloring, graining, or marking that is like the patterns in marble: *handsome marbling on the doors, a marbling of fat throughout the meat.*

Mar·burg disease (mär'bėrg), contagious viral disease that is often fatal, characterized by high fever and hemorrhaging. [< *Marburg,* Germany, where it was identified]

mar·ca·site (mär'kə sīt), *n.* yellow mineral used for ornaments; iron pyrites. [< Med. L < Ar. *marqashīṭā* < Aram.]

march¹ (märch), *v.* **1** walk in time and with steps of the same length. **2** walk or proceed steadily. **3** cause to march or go: *the policeman marched the thief off to jail.* —n. **1** act or fact of marching: *a quick march.* **2** music for marching. **3** distance marched. **4** a long, hard walk. **5** advance; progress: *the march of events.*

on the march, going forward; moving ahead.

steal a march, gain an advantage without being noticed; get ahead of one's competition. [< F *marcher,* earlier, to trample] —**march'er,** *n.*

march² (märch), *n.* land along the border of a country; frontier.

the Marches, lands along the border between England and Wales or Scotland. [< OF *marche* < Gmc.]

March (märch), *n.* the third month of the year, having 31 days. [< OF *marche* < L *Martius* (month) of Mars]

march·ing orders (mär'ching), **1** military orders to move. **2** *Fig.* any instruction to do something. **3** *Informal. Fig.* notification to an employee that he or she has been fired.

mar·chion·ess (mär'shən is), *n.* **1** wife or widow of a marquis. **2** lady equal in rank to a marquis. [< Med.L. *marchionissa* < *marchio* MARQUIS]

march·pane (märch'pān´), *n.* =marzipan.

Mar·di gras (mär'di grä'), the last day before Lent; Shrove Tuesday. [< F, fat Tuesday]

mare¹ (mār), *n.* a female horse, donkey, etc. [OE *mere*]

ma·re² (mär'ē, mä'rē), *n., pl.* **ma·ri·a. 1** dark area on the moon that appears to be flat. **2** similar area on any planet. [< L sea]

mare's-nest (mārz'nest´), *n.* something supposed to be a great discovery that turns out to be a mistake or joke.

mar·ga·rine (mär'jə rin), *n.* a substitute for butter consisting mainly of vegetable fat derived from cottonseed and soybean oils and to a lesser extent from corn and peanut oils; oleomargarine. [< F]

mar·gay (mär'gā), *n.* small long-tailed and spotted wildcat like the ocelot, found from Texas to Brazil. [< F *margay,* alter. of *margaia* < Tupi (Brazil) *mbaracaïa*]

mar·gin (mär'jən), *n.* **1 a** edge; border: *the margin of a lake.* **b** *Fig.* the edge of anything: *at the margins of society.* **2** blank space around the writing or printing on a page. **3** extra amount; amount beyond what is necessary; difference. **4** difference between the cost and selling price of stocks, etc. **5 a** money or security deposited with a broker to protect him from loss on contracts undertaken for the actual buyer or seller. **b** amount of such a deposit: *60 percent margin.* [< L *margo* edge]

mar·gin·al (mär′jə nəl), *adj.* **1** written or printed in a margin. **2** of a margin. **3** on or near the margin of production or profit: *marginal land, marginal business.* **4** *Fig.* existing or occurring on the fringes of anything: *marginal problem; marginal society.* —**mar′gin·al·ly,** *adv.*

mar·grave (mär′grāv), *n.* title of certain German princes. [< MDu. *markgrave* count of the marches]

mar·gue·rite (mär′gə rēt′), *n.* kind of daisy with white petals and a yellow center. [< F < L < Gk. *margarites* pearl]

ma·ri·a·chi (mär′i äch′i), *n.* **1** member of a Mexican band of strolling musicians, traditionally including singers accompanied by accordions and guitars. **2** the band of musicians. **3** music played by such a band. [< Mex. Sp. *mariachi,* prob. < F *mariage* marriage (because orig. they played at weddings)]

mar·i·cul·ture (mar′ə kul chər), *n.* cultivation of marine animals and plants, for food and raw materials; aquaculture.

mar·i·gold (mar′ə gōld), *n.* **1** plant of the aster family with yellow, orange, or red flowers. **2** the flower. [< (the Virgin) *Mary* + *gold*]

mar·i·jua·na (mar′ə wä′nə), *n.* **1** kind of hemp. **2** drug made from its leaves and flowers and smoked in a cigarette for its narcotic effect; hashish. [< Am.Sp.; ? < Am. Ind. word, infl. by name *María Juana* Mary Jane]

ma·rim·ba (mə rim′bə), *n.* a musical instrument somewhat like a xylophone. [< Bantu]

ma·ri·na (mə rē′nə), *n.* a boat basin, esp. one having facilities for rest and recreation of the owners and crews as well as for berthing, repairing, and supplying all types of craft.

mar·i·nate (mar′ə nāt), *v.* **–nat·ed, –nat·ing. 1** steep in a pickle, usually one of vinegar or wine seasoned with herbs, spices, etc. **2** soak in oil and vinegar. [< F *mariner*] —**mar′i·na′tion,** *n.*

ma·rine (mə rēn′), *adj.* **1** of the sea; found in the sea; produced by the sea: *marine animals.* **2** of shipping; of the navy; for use at sea. —*n.* **1** shipping; fleet **2** soldier formerly serving only at sea, now also participating in land and air action. [< F < L, < *mare* sea]

Marine Corps, a separate branch of the U.S. armed forces trained for land, sea, and air action.

mar·i·ner (mar′ə nər), *n.* sailor; seaman. [< AF, < OF *marin* MARINE]

mar·i·o·nette (mar′i ə net′), *n.* a small doll moved by strings or the hands. A marionette show is often given on a miniature stage. [< F, ult. < *Marie* Mary]

Mar·i·po·sa lily (mar′ə pō′sə; –zə), **1** plant with tuliplike flowers that grows in the W United States and Mexico. **2** the flower. [< Sp *mariposa* butterfly]

mar·i·tal (mar′ə təl), *adj.* **1** of marriage; pertaining to marriage: *marital vows.* [< L, < *maritus* married man] —**mar′i·tal·ly,** *adv.*

mar·i·time (mar′ə tīm), *adj.* **1** on or near the sea: *a maritime city.* **2** living near the sea: *maritime peoples.* **3** of the sea; having to do with shipping and sailing: *maritime law.* [< L *maritimus* < *mare* sea]

mar·jo·ram (mär′jə rəm), *n.* a fragrant plant of the same family as mint. **Sweet marjoram** is used in cooking. [< OF *majorane,* ? < L *amaracus* < Gk.]

mark[1] (märk), *n.* **1** trace or impression made by some object on the surface of another: *Your glass left a mark on the table.* **2** line, dot, or other object to show position: *a high-water mark.* **3** line where a race starts. **4** something that is a sign; indication: *a mark of respect.* **5** written or printed stroke or sign: *punctuation marks.* **6** grade or rating: *a failing mark.* **7** cross made by a person who cannot write his or her name. **8** what is usual, proper, or expected; standard: *a tired person does not feel up to the mark.* **9** influence; impression: *a great man leaves his mark on whatever he does.* —*v.* **1** give grades to; rate. **2** make a mark or marks; put a mark or marks on. **3** show clearly; manifest: *a frown marked her displeasure.* **4** distinguish; set off: *many important inventions mark the last 150 years.* **5** pay attention to; notice; observe: *mark my words.*

hit the mark, a succeed in doing what one aimed to accomplish. **b** be exactly right.

make one's mark, succeed; become well-known.

mark down, a write down; note down. **b** mark for sale at a lower price.

mark time, a move the feet as if marching, but without advancing. **b** suspend progress temporarily.

mark up, mark for sale at a higher price.

miss the mark, a fail to do what one tried to do. **b** be not exactly right.

wide of the mark, *Fig.* irrelevant. [< OE *mearc*] —**mark′er,** *n.*

mark[2] (märk), *n.* **1** a unit of money of Germany. **2** coin or paper note equal to the mark. [OE *m(e)arc*]

Mark (märk), *n.* the second book of the New Testament, telling the story of the life of Christ.

marked (märkt), *adj.* **1** having a mark or marks on it. **2** very noticeable; easily recognized: *there is a marked difference between grapes and oranges.* —**mark′ed·ness,** *n.*

mark·ed·ly (mär′kid li), *adv.* in a marked manner or degree; noticeably.

mar·ket (mär′kit), *n.* **1** store for the sale of provisions: *a vegetable market.* **2** space or building in which provisions, cattle, etc., are shown for sale. **3** a meeting of persons for buying and selling. **4** the people so gathered. **5** trade, esp. as regards a particular article: *the cotton market.* **6** opportunity to sell or buy; demand: *lose one's market.* —*v.* **1** buy or sell in a market: *market goods.* **2** carry or send to market.

play the market, speculate on the stock exchange. [< OF < L *mercatus* trade, ult. < *merx* merchandise] —**mar′ket·er,** *n.*

mar·ket·a·ble (mär′kit ə bəl), *adj.* that can be sold; salable. —**mar′ket·a·bil′i·ty,** *n.*

mar·ket·place (mär′kit plās′), *n.* or **market place, 1** place where a market is held. **2** world of business and commerce.

market research, study of what people want to buy, their opinions of products and prices, etc.

market value, price at which an item would be bought or sold in the market at a particular time.

mark·ing (mär′king), *n.* **1** mark or marks. **2** arrangement of marks.

marks·man (märks′mən), *n., pl.* **–men.** person who shoots well. —**marks′man·ship,** *n.*

marl (märl), *n.* soil containing clay and calcium carbonate, used in making cement and as a fertilizer. [< OF < Med. L *margila* < L *marga,* prob. < Celtic] —**marl′y,** *adj.*

mar·lin (mär′lən), *n.* a large sea fish like a sailfish. [short for *marlinespike*]

mar·line (mär′lən), *n.* a small cord wound around the ends of a rope to keep it from fraying. [< Du. *marlijn* < *marren* tie + *lijn* line]

mar·line·spike, mar·lin·spike (mär′lən spīk′), *n.* a pointed iron implement used by sailors to separate strands of rope in splicing, etc.

mar·ma·lade (mär′mə lād), *n.* preserve like jam, made of oranges or of other fruit. [< F < Pg., < *marmelo,* quince, ult. < Gk., < *meli* honey + *melon* apple]

Mar·ma·ra, Marmo·ra (mär′mə rə), *n.* **Sea of,** a small sea between Europe and Asia Minor, connected with the Aegean Sea by the Dardanelles and with the Black Sea by the Bosporus.

mar·mo·re·al (mär môr′ēəl; –mōr′–), *adj.* **1** of marble. **2** cold and smooth or white, like marble. [< L *marmoreus* < *marmor* marble + E –*al*[1]]

mar·mo·set (mär′mə zet), *n.* a very small monkey with a soft thick fur, living in South America and Central America. [< OF *marmouset* grotesque figurine]

mar·mot (mär′mət), *n.* a gnawing animal with a thick body and a bushy tail. Woodchucks and prairie dogs are marmots. [< F *marmotte*]

ma·roon[1] (mə rün′), *n., adj.* very dark brownish-red. [< F < Ital. *marrone* chestnut]

ma·roon[2] (mə rün′), *v.* **1** put (a person) ashore in a lonely place and leave him or her there. **2** leave in a lonely, helpless position. [< F *marron,* ? < Sp. *cimarron* wild < *cimarra* bushes]

marque (märk), *n.* official permission from a government to capture enemy merchant ships. [< F < Pr. *marca* reprisal < *marcar* seize as a pledge, ult. < Gmc.]

mar·quee (mär kē′), *n.* **1** a large tent, often one put up for some outdoor entertainment. **2** a rooflike shelter over an entrance, esp. of a theater or hotel. [< F *marquise* (misunderstood as plural)]

mar·que·try, mar·que·te·rie (mär′kə tri), *n., pl.* **-tries; -te·ries.** inlaid decoration made of small pieces of contrasting wood, ivory, etc., in furniture. [< F, < *marqueter* inlay < *marque* mark[1] < Gmc.]

mar·quis (mär′kwis), *n.* nobleman ranking below a duke and above an earl or count. [< OF, < *march* < Gmc. See MARCH[2].] —**mar′quis·ate,** *n.*

mar·quise (mär kēz′), *n.* **1** wife or widow of a marquis. **2** woman equal in rank to a marquis. [< F]

mar·qui·sette (mär′ki zet′; –kwi–), *n.* a very thin fabric with square meshes, made of cotton, silk, or rayon and often used for window draperies. [< F, dim. of *marquise* marquise]

mar·riage (mar′ij), *n.* **1 a** two people living together as husband and wife; married life. **b** two people living together as partners. **2** ceremony of being married; a marrying. **3** *Fig.* a close union: *a marriage of form and function.* **4** *Fig.* a merger of two enterprises or businesses. [< OF, < *marier* MARRY[1]]

mar·riage·a·ble (mar′ij ə bəl), *adj.* fit for marriage; old enough to marry. —**mar′riagea·bil′i·ty, mar′riage·a·ble·ness,** *n.*

mar·ried (mar′id), *adj.* **1** having a husband or wife or partner. **2** of marriage; of husbands and wives or partners.

mar·row (mar′ō), *n.* **1** the soft tissue that fills the cavities of most bones. **2** *Fig.* the inmost or essential part: *frightened to the marrow.* [OE *mearg*]

mar·ry (mar′i), *v.,* **-ried, -ry·ing. 1** join as husband and wife: *the minister married them.* **2** become married; take a husband or wife: *she married late in life.* **3** give in marriage: *she has married all her daughters.* **4** unite closely.

marry into, become part of (a family) through marriage.

marry off, give in marriage: *children are all married off.* [< OF < L, < *maritus* husband < *mas* male] —**mar′ri·er,** *n.*

Mars (märz), *n.* planet next beyond the earth. It is the fourth in order from the sun.

Mar·seil·laise (mär′sə lāz′), *n.* French national song, written in 1792 during the French Revolution.

mar·seilles (mär sālz′), *n.* a thick cotton cloth woven in figures or stripes, used for bedspreads, etc. [< *Marseilles,* city in France]

marsh (märsh), *n.* low land covered at times by water; soft wet land; swamp. —*adj.* swampy; marshy. [OE *mersc* < *mere* lake]

mar·shal (mär′shəl), *n., v.,* **-shaled, -shal-ing.** —*n.* **1** officer of various kinds, esp. a police officer. **2** an officer of a U.S. Federal court whose duties are like those of a sheriff. **3** a high officer in an army: *Marshal of France.* **4** person arranging the order of march in a parade or of events or ceremonies. —*v.* **1** arrange in order: *he marshaled his facts well.* **2** conduct with ceremony: *marshaled into the presence of the king.* [< OF < LL *mariscalcus* groom < Gmc., lit., horse servant]

marsh gas, =methane.

marsh·mal·low (märsh′mal′ō; *often* –mel′ō), *n.* a soft, white, spongy candy, covered with powdered sugar. [OE *merscmealwe;* orig. made from the root of the marsh mallow]

marsh mallow, plant with pink flowers that grows in marshy places.

marsh marigold, =cowslip.

marsh·y (mär′shi), *adj.,* **marsh·i·er, marsh·iest. 1** soft and wet like a marsh. **2** having many marshes. **3** of marshes. —**marsh′i·ness,** *n.*

mar·su·pi·al (mär sü′pi əl), *n.* animal that carries its young in a pouch. Kangaroos and opossums are marsupials. —*adj.* **1** of a marsupials. **2** having a pouch for carrying the young.

mar·su·pi·um (mär sü′pi əm), *n., pl.* **-pi-a** (-pi ə). pouch or fold of skin on the abdomen of a female marsupial for carrying the young. [< L < var. of Gk. *marsippion,* dim. of *marsippos* pouch]

mart (märt), *n.* market; center of trade. [< Du. *markt* MARKET]

mar·ten (mär′tən), *n., pl.* **-tens** or (*esp. collectively*) **-ten. 1** a slender animal like a weasel, but larger. **2** its valuable fur. [< OF *martrine,* ult. < Gmc.]

mar·tial (mär′shəl), *adj.* **1** of war; suitable for war: *martial music.* **2** fond of fighting; warlike; brave: *martial spirit.* [< L *Martialis* < *Mars* Mars] —**mar′tial·ly,** *adv.*

martial law, rule by the army or militia with special military courts instead of by the usual civil authorities, as during war.

Mar·tian (mär′shən), *adj.* of the planet Mars. —*n.* a supposed inhabitant of the planet Mars.

mar·tin (mär′tən), *n.* swallow with a short beak and a forked or square tail. [from the name *Martin*]

mar·ti·net (mär′tə net′; mär′tə net), *n.* person who enforces very strict discipline. [after J. *Martinet,* French general]

mar·tin·gale (mär′tən gāl), *n.* **1** strap of a horse's harness that prevents the horse from rising on its hind legs or throwing back its head. **2** rope or spar that steadies the jib boom on a ship. [< F]

mar·ti·ni (mär tē′ni), *n., pl.* **-nis.** a cocktail containing gin and dry vermouth.

mar·tyr (mär′tər), *n.* **1** person who chooses to die or suffer rather than renounce his or her faith; person who is put to death or made to suffer greatly for his or her religion or other beliefs. **2** person who suffers great pain or anguish. —*v.* **1** put (a person) to death or torture because of his or her religion or other beliefs. **2** cause to suffer greatly; torture. [< L < Gk., witness] —**mar′tyr·dom,** *n.*

mar·vel (mär′vəl), *n., v.,* **-veled, -vel·ing.** —*n.* something wonderful; astonishing thing: *the marvels of science.* —*v.* be filled with wonder. [< OF < VL < L *mirabilia* wonders, ult. < *mirus* strange]

mar·vel·ous (mär′vəl əs), *adj.* **1** wonderful; extraordinary. **2** improbable. —**mar′vel·ous·ly,** *adv.* —**mar′vel·ous·ness,** *n.*

Marx·ism (märk′siz əm), *n.* political and economic theories of Karl Marx (1818–83) and Friedrich Engels (1820–95).

Marx·ist (märk′sist), *n.* follower of Karl Marx's theories. —*adj.* of Marx or his theories. —**Marx′i·an,** *adj.*

Mar·y (mãr′i), *n.* mother of Jesus. Matt. 1:18–25.

Mar·y·land (mer′ə lənd), *n.* an E state of the United States. —**Mar′y·land·er,** *n.*

mar·zi·pan (mär′zə pan), *n.* paste made of ground almonds and sugar, molded into various forms or used as a filling for pastries and cakes. [< G < Ital. *marzapane* < unrecorded Ar. *martabān* porcelain container]

masc., masculine.

mas·car·a (mas kar′ə), *n.* preparation used for coloring the eyelashes and eyebrows. [< Sp., mask]

mas·cot (mas′kot), *n.* animal, person, or thing supposed to bring good luck. [< F *mascotte,* ult. < Pr. *masco* witch]

mas·cu·line (mas′kyə lin), *adj.* **1** of men; male. **2** like a man; manly; strong; vigorous. **3** of the gender of male names. *King, ram,* and *bull* are masculine nouns. —*n.* **1** masculine gender. **2** word or form in the masculine gender. [< L *masculinus,* ult. < *mas* male] —**mas′cu·line·ly,** *adv.* —**mas′culin′i·ty, mas′cu·line·ness,** *n.*

ma·ser (mā′zər), *n.* device that amplifies or generates microwaves, used in radar and radio astronomy. [< *m*icrowave *a*mplification by *s*timulated *e*mission of *r*adiation]

mash (mash), *n.* **1** a soft mixture; soft mass. **2** a warm mixture of bran or meal and water for horses and other animals. **3** crushed malt or meal soaked in hot water for making beer. —*v.* **1** beat into a soft mass; crush to a uniform mass.

2 mix crushed malt or meal with hot water in brewing. [OE *māsc-*]

mash·er (mash'ər), *n.* **1** one that mashes. **2** *Informal.* man who makes inappropriate advances to women.

mask (mask; mäsk), *n.* **1** a covering to hide or protect the face: *the burglar wore a mask.* **2** *Fig.* thing that hides or disguises: *he hid his evil plans under a mask of friendship.* **3** clay, wax, or plaster likeness of a person's face. —*v.* **1** cover (the face) with a mask. **2** *Fig.* hide; disguise: *a smile masked his disappointment.* [< F < Ital. *maschera* < Ar. *maskhara* laughingstock < *sakhira* to ridicule] —**mask'er,** *n.*

mas·och·ism (mas'ək iz əm; maz'–), *n.* **1** perversion in which sexual pleasure is derived from the experience of physical pain or abuse. **2** any pleasure derived from experiencing misery, pain, or abuse. [after L. von Sacher *Masoch,* who described it in his novels] —**mas'och·ist,** *n.* —**mas'och·is'tic,** *adj.*

ma·son (mā'sən), *n.* **1** man whose work is building with stone or brick. **2** Often, **Mason.** member of the worldwide secret society of Freemasons. [< OF, ult. < VL *maccare* beat < Gmc.]

Ma·son-Dix·on line (mā'sən dik'sən), boundary between Pennsylvania and Maryland, as laid out in 1763–67, formerly thought of as separating the North and the South of the United States or the free and slave states.

ma·son·ic, Ma·son·ic (mə son'ik), *adj.* having to do with the Freemasons or Freemasonry.

Ma·son·ite (mā'sə nīt), *n. Trademark.* type of hard fiberboard with a smooth finish on one side, used on the backs of cabinets, panels, etc.

Mason jar, jar for canning with a metal top that forms a seal. [< John *Mason,* American inventor who patented the jar in 1858]

ma·son·ry (mā'sən ri), *n., pl.* **-ries. 1** work built by a mason; stonework; brickwork. **2** trade or skill of a mason. **3** Often, **Masonry. a** principles or doctrines of the society of Freemasons. **b** members of this society

masque (mask; mäsk), *n.* **1** a former amateur dramatic entertainment in which fine costumes, scenery, music, and dancing were more important than the story. **2** a masked ball; masquerade. [< F. See MASK.] —**mas'quer,** *n.*

mas·quer·ade (mas'kər ād'), *n., v.,* **-aded, -ad·ing.** —*n.* **1** party or dance at which masks and fancy costumes are worn. **2** false pretense; disguise. —*v.* **1** take part in a masquerade. **2** disguise oneself; go about under false pretenses: *the king masqueraded as a beggar.* [< F < Ital., < *maschera* MASK] —**mas'quer·ad'er,** *n.*

mass¹ (mas), *n.* **1** large quantity: *mass of treasure, mass of dough.* **2** majority; greater part: *the mass of the people.* **3** bulk; size: *the mass of a landslide.* **4** quantity of matter a body contains: *the mass of a piece of lead is not changed by melting it.* —*v.* form or collect into a mass; assemble: *mass the peonies behind the roses.*

the masses, the common people; the working classes; the lower classes. [< L *massa* kneaded dough < Gk. *maza* barley bread < *massein* knead]

Mass, mass² (mas), *n.* **1** central service of worship in the Roman Catholic Church and some other churches; Holy Eucharist as a sacrament. **2** music written for certain parts of it. [< LL *missa* < L *mittere* send away]

Mass., Massachusetts.

Mas·sa·chu·setts (mas'ə chü'sits; –zits), *n.* a New England state of the United States.

mas·sa·cre (mas'ə kər), *n., v.,* **-cred, -cring.** —*n.* **1** wholesale, pitiless slaughter of people or animals. **2** *Fig.* any great loss or instance of destruction: *the game turned into a massacre.* —*v.* kill (many people or animals) needlessly or cruelly; slaughter in large numbers. [< F, in OF *macecle* shambles] —**mas'sa·crer,** *n.*

mas·sage (mə säzh'), *n., v.,* **-saged, -sag·ing.** —*n.* a rubbing and kneading of the muscles and joints to make them work better and to increase the circulation of blood. —*v.* give a massage to. [< F, ult. < *masse* mass] —**mas·sag'er, mas·sag'ist,** *n.*

massage parlor, 1 place where massages are given. **2** brothel.

Mas·sa·soit (mas'ə soit), *n.* American Indian chief (1580?–1661) who was friendly to the Pilgrims.

mas·seur (ma sœr'), *n.* person whose work is massaging people. [< F]

mas·seuse (ma sœz'), *n.* female masseur. [< F]

mas·sive (mas'iv), *adj.* **1** big and heavy; large and solid; bulky. **2** *Fig.* imposing; impressive. **3** much larger or more than usual: *a massive crowd; massive bleeding.* —**mas'sive·ly,** *adv.* —**mas'sive·ness,** *n.*

mass media, *n., pl.* of **mass medium.** forms of communication (newspapers, television, films, etc.) that reach a large number of people.

mass meeting, a large public gathering of people to hear or discuss some matter of common interest.

mass noun, a noun that does not form a plural, that usually refers to something uncountable, and that cannot be preceded by *a* or *an.*

mass number, number that indicates, as closely as possible, the atomic weight of an isotope, which equals the sum of protons and neutrons in the nucleus.

mass production, making of goods in large quantities by machinery. —**mass'-pro·duce',** *v.*

mass·y (mas'i), *adj.,* **mass·i·er, mass·i·est.** =massive. —**mass'i·ness,** *n.*

mast¹ (mast; mäst), *n.* **1** a long pole of wood or steel set upright on a ship to support the sails and rigging. **2** any upright pole.

before the mast, as a common sailor. [OE *mæst*]

mast² (mast; mäst), *n.* acorns, chestnuts, beechnuts, etc., esp. as food for pigs. [OE *mæst*]

mas·tec·to·my (mas tek'tə mē), *n., pl.* **-mies.** surgical removal of the breast, usually because it is caucerous. [< Gk. *mastós* breast + *ektomē* a cutting out]

mas·ter (mas'tər; mäs'–), *n.* **1** person who has power or authority; one in control; employer; owner. **2** man at the head of a household. **3** captain of a merchant ship. **4** person whose teachings one follows or accepts. **5** person with much knowledge; expert. **6** a skilled worker; craftsman in business for himself: *master carpenter.* **7** a great artist. **8** picture or painting by a great artist. **9** title of respect for a boy: *young Master George.* —*adj.* **1** being master; of a master: *a master key.* **2** main; controlling. —*v.* **1** become master of; conquer; control. **2** become expert in; become skillful at: *master French.* [< L *magister;* cf. *magis* more] —**mas'ter·less,** *adj.*

mas·ter·ful (mas'tər fəl; mäs'–), *adj.* **1** fond of power or authority; domineering. **2** expert; skillful. —**mas'ter·ful·ly,** *adv.* —**mas'ter·ful·ness,** *n.*

mas·ter·ly (mas'tər li; mäs'–), *adj.* expert; skillful. —*adv.* expertly; skillfully. —**mas'ter·li·ness,** *n.*

mas·ter·mind (mas'tər mīnd'; mäs'–), *n.* person who plans and supervises a scheme of action, usually from behind the scenes. —**mas'ter·mind,** *v.*

master of ceremonies, person in charge of a ceremony or entertainment who makes sure that all its parts occur in the proper order.

mas·ter·piece (mas'tər pēs'; mäs'–), *n.* **1** anything done or made with wonderful skill. **2** person's greatest work.

master sergeant, U.S. Army. the highest ranking noncommissioned officer, formerly next above technical sergeant, next above sergeant first class.

master stroke, very skillful act or achievement.

mas·ter·work (mas'tər wėrk'), *n.* =masterpiece.

mas·ter·y (mas'tər i; –tri; mäs'–), *n., pl.* **-ter·ies. 1** power such as a master has; control: *the mastery of the seas.* **2** the upper hand; victory. **3** great skill; expert knowledge: *mastery of a foreign language.*

mast·head (mast'hed'; mäst'–), *n.* **1** top of a ship's mast. **2** that part of a newspaper or magazine that gives the title, owner, address, rates, etc.

mas·tic (mas'tik), *n.* a yellowish resin used in making varnish, chewing gum, and incense, and as an astringent. [< OF < L < Gk. *mastiche*]

mas·ti·cate (mas′tə kāt), *v.*, **–cat·ed, –cat·ing. 1** chew. **2** reduce to a pulp. [< LL, < *masticare* < Gk. *mastichaein* gnash the teeth] **—mas′ti·ca′tion,** *n.* **—mas′ti·ca′tor,** *n.*

mas·tiff (mas′tif; mäs′–), *n.* a large, strong dog with drooping ears and hanging lips. [< OF *mastin,* ult. < L *mansuetus* tame]

mas·to·don (mas′tə don), *n.* a very large extinct animal much like an elephant. [< NL, < Gk. *mastos* breast + *odon* tooth]

mas·toid (mas′toid), *n.* projection of bone behind the ear. **—adj.** of this bone. [< Gk., < *mastos* breast + *eidos* form]

mas·tur·ba·tion (mas′tər bā′shən), *n.* sexual self-stimulation. [< L *masturbatio,* ult. < *manus* hand + *stuprum* defilement]

mat¹ (mat), *n., v.,* **mat·ted, mat·ting. —n. 1** piece of coarse fabric like a rug, made of woven grass, straw, rope, etc. **2** piece of material to put under a dish, vase, lamp, etc. **3** a large thick pad used to protect wrestlers or gymnasts. **4** anything packed or tangled thickly together: *mat of weeds.* **—v. 1** cover with mats. **2** pack or tangle thickly together. [< LL *matta*]

mat² (mat), *n.* border or background for a picture, between it and the frame. [< F, orig. adj., dull, dead. See MAT³.]

mat³ (mat), *adj., n., v.,* **mat·ted, mat·ting. —adj.** dull; not shiny. **—n.** a dull surface or finish. **—v.** give a dull finish to. [< F, < *mater* subdue, CHECKMATE]

mat·a·dor (mat′ə dôr), *n.* chief performer and person appointed to kill the bull in bullfights. [< Sp., ult. < *mate* dead < Ar. *māt*]

match¹ (mach), *n.* **1** a short, slender piece of wood, pasteboard, etc., tipped with a mixture that takes fire when rubbed on a rough or specially prepared surface. **2** cord prepared to burn at a uniform rate, for firing guns, cannon, etc. [< OF *meiche,* prob. ult. < Gk. *myxa* lamp wick]

match² (mach), *n.* **1** person or thing equal to or like another: *a boy is not a match for a man.* **2** two persons or things that are alike or go well together: *her hat is a match for her coat.* **3** game; contest. **4** marriage. **5** person considered as a possible husband or wife. **—v. 1** be equal to; be a match for: *no one could match him in singing.* **2** be alike; go well together: *the rugs and the wallpaper match.* **3** find one like; get a match for: *match a color.* **4** put in opposition; oppose: *Tom matched his strength against Bob's.* [OE *gemæcca* companion] **—match′a·ble,** *adj.* **—match′er,** *n.*

match·book (mach′bùk′), *n.* folder of paper matches with a strip on the bottom for striking.

match·box (mach′boks′), *n.* box that holds matches, esp. wooden matches, and has a surface for striking on one side.

match·less (mach′lis), *adj.* so great or wonderful that it cannot be equaled.

—match′less·ly, *adv.* **—match′less-ness,** *n.*

match·lock (mach′lok′), *n.* **1** an old form of gun fired by lighting the powder with a wick or cord. **2** the mechanism for firing it.

match·mak·er (mach′māk′ər), *n.* **1** person who arranges, or tries to arrange, marriages for others. **2** person who arranges contests, prize fights, races, etc. **—match′mak′ing,** *n., adj.*

mate¹ (māt), *n., v.,* **mat·ed, mat·ing. —n. 1** one of a pair: *where is the mate to this glove?* **2** husband or wife. **3** assistant: *gunner's mate.* **5** companion; fellow worker. **—v. 1** join in a pair: *birds mate in the spring.* **2** marry. [appar. < MLG *mate* messmate; akin to MEAT]

mate² (māt), *n., v.,* **mat·ed, mat·ing.** defeat in the game of chess. [< OF *mater* CHECKMATE]

ma·té, ma·te³ (mä′tā; mat′ā), *n.* **1** kind of tea made from the dried leaves of a South American plant. **2** the plant. **3** its leaves. [< Sp., < Quechua (Ind. lang. of Peru) *mati* calabash dish]

ma·te·ri·al (mə tir′i əl), *n.* **1** what a thing is made from; matter or articles needed for making or doing something: *dress material, building materials.* **2** fabric: *what is the material of that coat?* **—adj. 1** of, relating to, or involved with matter: *material laws.* **2** of the body: *material comforts.* **3** caring too much for the things of this world and neglecting spiritual needs. **4** that matters; important: *no material objections to the plan.* [< L, < *materia* timber, matter < *mater* trunk (of a tree). Doublet of MATÉRIEL.]

ma·te·ri·al·ism (mə tir′i əl iz′əm), *n.* **1** belief that all action, thought, and feeling can be explained by the movements and changes of matter. **2** tendency to care too much for the things of this world and neglect spiritual needs. **—ma·te′ri·al·ist,** *n.* **—ma·te′ri·al·is′tic,** *adj.* **—ma·te′ri·al·is′ti·cal·ly,** *adv.*

ma·te·ri·al·ize (mə tir′i əl īz), *v.,* **–ized, –iz·ing. 1** become an actual fact; be realized: *our plans did not materialize.* **2** give material form to: *an inventor materializes his ideas by building a model.* **3** appear in bodily form: *a spirit materialized from the smoke of the magician's fire.* **—ma·te′ri·al·i·za′tion,** *n.* **—ma·te′ri·al·iz′er,** *n.*

ma·te·ri·al·ly (mə tir′i əl i), *adv.* **1** physically. **2** considerably; greatly. **3** in matter or substance; not in form.

ma·te·ri·el or **ma·té·ri·el** (mə tir′i el′), *n.* everything used by an army, organization, undertaking, etc.; equipment. [< F, material. Doublet of MATERIAL.]

ma·ter·nal (mə tèr′nəl), *adj.* **1** of or like a mother; motherly. **2** related on the mother's side of the family: *everyone has two maternal grandparents.* **3** received or inherited from a mother. [< F *maternel,* ult. < L *mater* mother] **—ma·ter′nal·ly,** *adv.*

ma·ter·ni·ty (mə tèr′nə ti), *n.* **1** motherhood; being a mother. **2** motherliness; qualities of a mother. **—adj. 1** for a woman soon to have a baby: *a maternity dress.* **2** for a woman in or after childbirth: *maternity hospital.*

math (math), *n. Informal.* mathematics.

do the math, calculate, esp. in terms of cost: *do the math to see if it's worthwhile.*

math., mathematics.

math·e·mat·i·cal (math′ə mat′ə kəl; math-mat′–), **math·e·mat·ic** (–ik), *adj.* **1** of or having to do with mathematics: *mathematical problems.* **2** exact; accurate. **—math′e·mat′i·cal·ly,** *adv.*

math·e·ma·ti·cian (math′ə mə tish′ən; math′mə–), *n.* person skilled in mathematics.

math·e·mat·ics (math′ə mat′iks; math-mat′–), *n.* science dealing with numbers and the measurement, properties, and relationships of quantities. Mathematics includes arithmetic, algebra, geometry, calculus, etc. [pl. of *mathematic* < L < Gk. *mathematikos,* ult. < *manthanein* learn]

mat·i·nee or **mat·i·née** (mat′ə nā′), *n.* a dramatic or musical performance held in the afternoon. [< F, < *matin* morning]

ma·tins (mat′ənz), *n. pl.* **1** first of the seven canonical hours in the breviary. **2** morning prayers in the Church of England. [< OF, < LL *matutinus* of or in the morning]

ma·tri·arch (mā′tri ärk), *n.* **1** mother who is the ruler of a family or tribe. **2** a venerable old woman. [< *matri–* (< L *mater* mother) + *(patri)arch*] **—ma′tri·ar′chal, ma′tri·ar′chic,** *adj.*

ma·tri·ar·chy (mā′tri är′ki), *n., pl.* **–chies.** form of social organization in which the mother is the ruler of a family or tribe, descent being traced through the mother.

ma·tri·cide¹ (mā′trə sīd; mat′rə–), *n.* act of killing one's mother. [< L, < *mater* mother + *–cidium* act of killing] **—ma′tri·cid′al,** *adj.*

ma·tri·cide² (mā′trə sīd; mat′rə–), *n.* person who kills his mother. [< L, < *mater* mother + *–cida* killer]

ma·tric·u·late (mə trik′yə lāt), *v.,* **–lat·ed, –lat·ing.** enroll as a student in a college or university. [< LL *matricula,* dim. of L *matrix* register] **—ma·tric′u·la′tion,** *n.*

mat·ri·mo·ny (mat′rə mō′ni), *n., pl.* **–nies. 1** married life. **2** act of marrying; rite or ceremony of marriage. **3** relation between married persons. [< L *matrimonium* < *mater* mother] **—mat′ri·mo′ni·al,** *adj.* **—mat′ri·mo′ni·al·ly,** *adv.*

ma·trix (mā′triks; mat′riks), *n., pl.* **ma·trices** (mā′trə sēz; mat′rə–), **ma·trix·es.** that which gives origin or form to something enclosed within it. A mold for a casting is a matrix. [< L, womb]

ma·tron (mā′trən), *n.* **1** married woman or widow, esp. a woman with a child or children. **2** woman who manages the household affairs or supervises the inmates of a school, hospital, or other institution: *a police matron.* [< OF < L *matrona* < *mater* mother] —**ma′tron·al**, *adj.* —**ma′tron·like′**, *adj.* —**ma′tron·ly**, *adj.* —**ma′tron·li·ness**, *n.*

matron of honor, a married woman who is the chief attendant of the bride at a wedding.

Matt., Matthew.

mat·ted (mat′id), *adj.* formed into a mat; entangled in a thick mass.

mat·ter (mat′ər), *n.* **1** what things are made of; material. Matter occupies space. **2** some particular kind of substance: *coloring matter.* **3** words written or printed: *reading matter.* **4** grounds; occasion; cause: *matter for complaint, matter of record.* **5** amount; quantity: *a matter of 20 miles.* **6** importance; significance: *a trivial complaint of no matter.* —*v.* be of importance.

for that matter, so far as that is concerned; in fact.

no matter, it is not important; never mind.

no matter what, regardless of something.

what is the matter? what is wrong? [< OF < L *materia,* orig., timber]

matter of course, something to be expected.

matter of fact, something that is based on fact, as contrasted with an opinion or supposition.

as a matter of fact, in truth, in reality.

mat·ter-of-fact (mat′ər əv fakt′), *adj.* dealing with facts; not fanciful; unimaginative: *a matter-of-fact account of the accident.*

Mat·thew (math′ū), *n.* the first book of the New Testament, telling the story of the life of Christ.

mat·ting (mat′ing), *n.* fabric of grass, straw, hemp, or other fiber, for covering floors, etc.

mat·tock (mat′ək), *n.* tool like a pickax, but having a flat blade, used for loosening soil and cutting roots. [OE *mattuc*]

mat·tress (mat′ris), *n.* a covering of strong cloth stuffed with cotton, foam rubber straw, etc., used on a bed frame or as a bed. [< OF < Ital. < Ar. *al-maṭraḥ* the cushion]

mat·u·rate (mach′ù rāt), *v.,* –**rat·ed,** –**rating.** ripen. [< L, < *maturus* ripe]

mat·u·ra·tion (mach′ù rā′shən), *n.* **1** process of developing; maturing *the maturation of an idea.* **2** last stages of development of a germ cell in preparation for fertilization.

ma·ture (mə chŭr′; –tŭr; –tyŭr′), *adj., v.,* –**tured,** –**tur·ing.** —*adj.* **1** ripe; full-grown: *fifty is a mature age.* **2** fully worked out; carefully thought out; fully developed: *mature plans.* **3** due; payable: *a mature loan.* —*v.* **1** come to full

growth; ripen. **2** work out carefully. **3** fall due. [< L *maturus* ripe] —**ma·ture′ly**, *adv.* —**ma·ture′ness**, *n.*

ma·tu·ri·ty (mə chŭr′ə ti; –tŭr–′; –tyŭr′–), *n.* **1** full development; ripeness. **2** a being completed or ready. **3** a falling due; time a debt is payable.

mat·zo (mät′sō), *n., pl.* **matz·oth** (mät′sōth), **matz·os** (mät′sōs; *pop.* –səz), or (*collectively*) **mat·zo.** thin piece of unleavened bread, eaten by Jews esp. during the Passover. [< Heb. *matstsōth,* pl. of *matstsāh,* unleavened bread]

matzo ball, small dumpling made from matzo meal, usually served in soup.

maud·lin (môd′lən), *adj.* **1** sentimental in a weak, silly way: *just a maudlin tale of loss that lacks real understanding.* **2** sentimental and tearful because of drunkenness or excitement. [alter. of Mary *Magdalene,* often painted as weeping]

maul (môl), *n.* a very heavy hammer or mallet. —*v.* beat and pull about; handle roughly: *the lion mauled its keeper badly.* [var. of *mall*]

Mau·ri·ta·ni·a (mô′rə tā′ni ə; –tän′yə), *n.* a republic in W Africa on the Atlantic. —**Mau′rita′nian**, *n., adj.*

Mau·ri·tius (mô rish′əs), *n.* island country, east of Madagascar in the Indian Ocean. —**Mau·ri′tian**, *n., adj.*

mau·so·le·um (mô′sə lē′əm), *n., pl.* –**le·ums, –le·a** (–lē′ə). a large, magnificent tomb. [< L < Gk. *Mausoleion,* tomb of a king, *Mausolus*]

mauve (mōv), *n., adj.* delicate, pale purple. [< F < L *malva* mallow]

ma·ven or **ma·vin** (mā′vən), *n.* an expert or connoisseur: *a food maven.* [< Yiddish *meyvn* < Heb. *mēbhīn,* lit. one who understands]

mav·er·ick (mav′ər ik), *n.* **1** W. calf or other animal not marked with an owner's brand. **2** *Fig.* **a** anyone or anything that is unconventional. **b** one who does not conform to the policies of his group or refuses to fall in with a regular political party. [prob. after S. *Maverick,* Texan who did not brand his cattle]

ma·vis (mā′vis), *n.* a European song thrush. [< OF *mauvis* < Celtic]

maw (mô), *n.* **1** mouth. **2** throat. **3** stomach. [OE *maga*]

mawk·ish (môk′ish), *adj.* **1** sickening. **2** sickly sentimental; weakly emotional. [orig., maggoty < *mawk* maggot < Scand. *mathkr*] —**mawk′ish·ly,** *adv.* —**mawk′ish·ness**, *n.*

max., maximum.

max·il·la (mak sil′ə), *n., pl.* –**il·lae** (–sil′ē). **1** jaw; jawbone; upper jawbone. **2** either of a pair of appendages just behind the mandibles of insects, crabs, etc. [< L, jaw] —**max′il·lar′y**, *adj.*

max·im (mak′səm), *n.* a short rule of conduct; proverb; statement of a general truth. [< F < LL *maxima (propositio)* axiom]

max·i·mal (mak′sə məl), *adj.* greatest possible; maximum.

max·i·mize (mak′sə mīz), *v.* –**mized,** –**miz·ing.** increase to the highest possible amount or degree. —**max′i·mi·za′tion**, *n.*

max·i·mum (mak′sə məm), *n., pl.* –**mums, –ma** (–mə), *adj.* —*n.* the largest or highest amount; greatest possible amount. —*adj.* largest; highest; greatest possible: *the maximum score on the test is 100.* [< L, neut. adj., greatest, superl. of *magnus* great]

may (mā), *auxiliary v., pt.* **might. 1** possibility, opportunity, or permission: *you may enter.* **2** wish or prayer: *may you be very happy.* [OE *mæg* (inf., *magan*)]

May (mā), *n.* the fifth month of the year, having 31 days. [< L *Maius*]

Ma·ya (mä′yə), *n.* **1** member of an ancient American Indian people living in Mexico and Central America. **2** their language. —*adj.* of the Mayas, their culture, or their language. —**Ma′yan**, *adj., n.*

may·be (mā′bi), *adv.* possibly; perhaps.

May Day, May 1, sometimes celebrated by labor parades and meetings.

May·day or **may·day** (mā′dā), *n.* international distress call, used esp. by ships, aircraft, and small craft. [< pronunciation of F *m'aidez* help me]

May·flow·er (mā′flou′ər), *n.* **1** ship on which the Pilgrims came to America in 1620. **2** plant whose flowers blossom in May.

May fly, a slender insect, having the forewings much larger than the hind wings, that dies soon after reaching the adult stage; ephemerid.

may·hem (mā′hem; –əm), *n.* **1** state of chaos and confusion. **2** crime of intentionally maiming a person or causing injury so that he or she is less able to make or defense. [< OF *mahaigne*]

may·on·naise (mā′ə nāz′), *n.* a dressing made of egg yolks, olive oil, vinegar or lemon juice, and seasoning, beaten together until thick. [< F, ult. < *Mahon,* Minorca]

may·or (mā′ər; mār), *n.* the chief official of a city or town. [< OF *maire, maor* < L *major.* Doublet of MAJOR.] —**may′or·ship**, *n.*

may·or·al·ty (mā′ər əl ti; mār′əl ti), *n., pl.* –**ties. 1** position of mayor. **2** mayor's term of office.

May·pole, may·pole (mā′pōl′), *n.* a high pole decorated with flowers or ribbons, around which merrymakers dance.

maze (māz), *n.* **1** network of paths through which it is hard to find one's way. **2** state of confusion; muddled condition. [var. of *amaze*]

ma·zur·ka (mə zėr′kə; –zûr′–), *n.* **1** a lively Polish dance. **2** music for it. [< Polish, woman of Mazovia in Poland]

M.C., 1 Master of Ceremonies. **2** Member of Congress.

mc or **mc.,** megacycle.

Mc·Coy (mə koi′), *n.* **the real,** a genuine person or thing.

Mc·Kin·ley (mə kin′li), *n.* **William,** 1843–1901, the 25th president of the United States, 1897–1901.

Md, mendelevium.

MD, 1 (*zip code*) Maryland. **2** Also, **M.D.** Doctor of Medicine.

Md., Maryland.

mdse., merchandise.

me¹ (mē; *unstressed* mi), *pron.* the objective, or accusative, case of **I:** *the dog bit me, give me a bandage.* —*adj.* concerned only with self: *me-generation.* [OE *mē*]

me² (mē), *n.* third tone of a musical scale. [see GAMUT]

ME, 1 (*zip code*) Maine. **2** Middle English.

Me., Maine.

mead (mēd), *n.* an alcoholic drink made from fermented honey and water. [OE *medu*]

mead·ow (med′ō), *n.* piece of grassy land; field where hay is grown. [OE *mǣdwe*, oblique case of *mǣd* mead¹] —**mead′ow·y,** *adj.*

meadow lark, songbird with a black crescent on a yellow breast.

mea·ger (mē′gər), *adj.* **1** poor; scanty: *meager fare.* **2** thin; lean: *a meager man.* [< F < L *macer* thin] —**mea′ger·ly,** *adv.* —**mea′ger·ness,** *n.*

meal¹ (mēl), *n.* **1** breakfast, lunch, dinner, supper, or tea. **2** food served or eaten at one time. [OE *mǣl*]

meal² (mēl), *n.* **1** ground grain, esp. corn meal. **2** anything ground to a powder. [OE *melu*]

meal·worm (mēl′wėrm′), *n.* or **meal worm,** a beetle larva that feeds on flour and meal.

meal ticket, 1 ticket or pass that allows a person to get a meal. **2** *Informal. Fig.* person or thing that is a source of money.

meal·time (mēl′tīm′), *n.* the usual time for eating a meal.

meal·y (mēl′i), *adj.,* **meal·i·er, meal·i·est. 1** like meal; dry and powdery. **2** of meal. **3** containing meal. **4** pale. —**meal′i·ness,** *n.*

meal·y·bug (mēl′i bug′), *n.* or **mealy bug,** small scale insect that has a soft body covered by a white secretion and causes great damage to citrus trees.

meal·y-mouthed (mēl′i mouᵗh′d′; -moutht′), *adj.* unwilling to tell the straight truth in plain words; using soft words insincerely.

mean¹ (mēn), *v.,* **meant, mean·ing. 1** signify; denote: *what does this word mean?* **2** have as a purpose; have in mind; intend: *I do not mean to go.* [OE *mǣnan*]

mean² (mēn), *adj.* **1** small-minded; stingy: *mean about money, mean thoughts.* **2** low in quality or grade; poor. **3** low in social position or rank; humble. **4** of poor appearance; shabby: *a mean appearance.* **5** hard to manage; bad-tempered: *a mean horse.* [OE *(ge)mǣne* common] —**mean′ly,** *adv.* —**mean′ness,** *n.*

mean³ (mēn), *adj.* halfway between two extremes. —*n.* **1** condition, quality, or course of action halfway between two extremes: *a happy mean between extravagance and stinginess.* **2** quantity having a value intermediate between the values of other quantities.

by all means, certainly; without fail.

by any means, at all; in any possible way; at any cost.

by means of, by the use of; through; with.

by no means, certainly not.

means, a (*sing.* or *pl.* in use) what a thing is done by; agency; method: *by fair means.* **b** (*pl.* in use) wealth: *a man of means.*

means to an end, way of getting or doing something: *a friendship that sadly was only a means to an end.* [< OF < L *medianus* middle < *medius*]

me·an·der (mi an′dər), *v.* **1** follow a winding course. **2** wander aimlessly. [< L < Gk. *Maiandros,* name of a winding river]

mean·ie (mē′nē), *n.* person who is unkind, nasty.

mean·ing (mēn′ing), *n.* what is meant or intended; significance. —*adj.* that means something; expressive. —**mean′ing·ful,** *adj.* —**mean′ing·ful·ly,** *adv.* —**mean′ing·ly,** *adv.*

mean·ing·less (mēn′ing lis), *adj.* without meaning; not significant. —**mean′ing·less·ly,** *adv.* —**mean′ing·less·ness,** *n.*

meant (ment), *v.* pt. and pp. of **mean¹.**

mean·time (mēn′tīm′), **mean·while** (-hwīl′), *n.* time between. —*adv.* in the time between.

mea·sles (mē′zəlz), *n.* **1** an infectious disease characterized by a bad cold, fever, and a breaking out of small red spots on the skin. **2** a similar but much less severe disease; German measles. [ME *maseles;* prob. infl. by ME *mezel* leprous < OF, ult. < L *miser* wretched]

mea·sly (mē′zli), *adj.,* **-sli·er, -sli·est. 1** too little; scanty; very unsatisfactory. **2** of or like measles. **3** infected with measles.

meas·ur·a·ble (mezh′ər ə bəl; māzh′-), *adj.* capable of being measured. —**meas′ur·a·bil′i·ty, meas′ur·a·ble·ness,** *n.* —**meas′ur·a·bly,** *adv.*

meas·ure (mezh′ər; māzh′-), *v.,* **-ured, -ur·ing,** *n.* —*v.* **1** find out the extent, size, quantity, capacity, etc., of something; estimate by some standard: *measure the room.* **2** be of specified measure: *this brick measures 2 x 4 x 8 inches.* **3** get or take by measuring: *measure out a bushel of potatoes.* **4** serve as a measure of: *a ruler measures distance.* **5** compare: *measure one's behavior by the company one is in.* —*n.* **1** size, dimensions, quantity, etc., thus determined: *his waist measure is 30 inches.* **2** instrument for measuring: *a pint measure.* **3** system or unit of measuring: *dry measure.* Inch, quart, pound, and hour are common

measures. **4** quantity or degree; reasonable limit: *angry beyond measure.* **5** bar of music. **6** course of action; procedure: *take measures to relieve suffering.*

for good measure, as an extra.

in a measure, to some degree; partly.

measure out, divide; distribute; deal out.

measure up, have the necessary abilities or qualifications.

take measures, act; take steps.

take one's measure, judge one's character. [< OF < L *mensura,* n., < *mensus,* pp. of *metiri,* v., measure] —**meas′ur·er,** *n.*

meas·ured (mezh′ərd; māzh′-), *adj.* **1** regular; uniform: *a measured pace.* **2** deliberate and restrained: *measured speech.* —**meas′ured·ly,** *adv.*

meas·ure·less (mezh′ər lis; māzh′-), *adj.* too great to be measured; unlimited; vast.

meas·ure·ment (mezh′ər mənt; māzh′-), *n.* **1** way of measuring: *clocks give us a measurement of time.* **2** act or fact of measuring: *the measurement of length by a yardstick is easy.* **3** size or amount found by measuring. **4** system of measuring.

measuring worm, larva of any geometrid; inchworm.

meat (mēt), *n.* **1** animal flesh used as food. Fish and poultry are not usually called meat. **2** food of any kind: *meat and drink.* **3** part that can be eaten: *meat of a nut.* **4** substance; food for thought. [OE *mete*] —**meat′less,** *adj.*

meat·ball (mēt′bôl′), *n.* **1** ball of seasoned chopped meat, usually beef, cooked and served in a sauce, esp. tomato sauce and with spaghetti. **2** *Informal.* dull, uninspired person.

meat·y (mēt′i), *adj.,* **meat·i·er, meat·i·est. 1** of meat; having the flavor of meat. **2** like meat. **3** full of meat. **4** full of substance; giving food for thought: *a meaty speech.*

Mec·ca (mek′ə), *n.* **1** city in W Saudi Arabia. Muslims turn toward Mecca when praying and go there on pilgrimages. **2 mecca,** any place that a person longs to visit or reach. —**Mec′can,** *adj., n.*

me·chan·ic (mə kan′ik), *n.* worker skilled with tools, esp. one who repairs machinery. [< L < Gk., < *mechane* machine]

me·chan·i·cal (mə kan′ə kəl), *adj.* **1** having to do with machinery. **2** made or worked by machinery. **3** like a machine; like that of a machine; automatic; without expression: *her reading is very mechanical.* **4** or in accordance with the science of mechanics. —**me·chan′i·cal·ly,** *adv.*

mechanical engineering, branch of engineering that deals with mechanical power and machinery.

me·chan·ics (mə kan′iks), *n.* **1** branch of physics dealing with the action of forces on bodies and with motion. Mechanics includes kinetics, statics, and kinematics. **2** knowledge dealing with machinery. 3 (*pl. in use*) mechanical part; technique.

mech·a·nism (mek′ə niz əm), *n.* 1 means or way by which something is done; machinery. 2 system of parts working together as the parts of a machine do: *the mechanism of the body.* 3 mechanical part; technique. —**mech′a·nist,** *n.* —**mech′a·nis′tic,** *adj.*

mech·a·nize (mek′ə nīz), *v.,* -**nized,** -**niz·ing.** 1 make mechanical. 2 do by machinery, rather than by hand: *much housework can be mechanized.* 3 replace men or animals by machinery in (a business, etc.). —**mech′a·ni·za′tion,** *n.*

mech·an·o·re·cep·tion (mek′ə nō ri sep′-shən), *n.* response to mechanical stimuli by a sense organ.

mech·an·o·re·cep·tor (mek′ə nō ri sep′-tər), *n.* sense organ that responds to mechanical stimuli, as the sense of hearing.

Med., Medieval.

med., medical; medicine.

med·al (med′əl), *n.* a flat piece of metal with a design or words stamped on it. [< F < Ital. *medaglia,* ult. < L *metallum* metal]

med·al·ist (med′əl ist), *n.* 1 person who has won a medal. 2 person who designs or makes medals.

me·dal·lion (mə dal′yən), *n.* 1 a large medal. 2 design, ornament, etc., shaped like a medal.

med·dle (med′əl), *v.,* -**dled,** -**dling.** busy oneself with other people's things or affairs without being asked or needed. [< OF *medler,* ult. < L *miscere* mix] —**med′dler,** *n.*

med·dle·some (med′əl səm), *adj.* fond of meddling in other people's affairs; meddling. —**med′dle·some·ness,** *n.*

Med. Gk., Medieval Greek.

me·di·a (mē′di ə), *n.* 1 pl. of **medium.** 2 =mass media.

me·di·ae·val (mē′di ē′vəl; med′i–), *adj.* medieval. —**me′di·ae′val·ly,** *adv.*

me·di·al (mē′di əl), *adj.* 1 in the middle. 2 average; ordinary. [< LL, < L *medius* middle]

me·di·an (mē′di ən), *adj.* middle. —*n.* 1 in the middle. 2 the middle number of a series. The median of 1, 3, 4, 8, 9 is 4. 3 =median strip. [< L, < *medius* middle] —**me′di·an·ly,** *adv.*

median strip, strip of land, often landscaped with grass and shrubs, that divides highway lanes for traffic going in opposite directions.

me·di·ate (*v.* mē′di āt; *adj.* mē′di it), *v.,* -**at·ed,** -**at·ing,** *adj.* —*v.* 1 effect by intervening; settle by intervening. 2 be a go-between; act in order to bring about an agreement between persons or sides. 3 be a connecting link. —*adj.* connected, but not directly; connected through some other person or thing. [< LL *mediatus* situated in the middle < L *medius* middle] —**me′di·ate·ly,** *adv.* —**me′di·a′tive,** *adj.*

me·di·a·tion (mē′di ā′shən), *n.* intervention to bring about agreement or reconciliation between persons or sides in a dispute. —**me′di·a′tor,** *n.*

med·ic (med′ik), *n.* 1 a member of a medical battalion in the army. 2 *Informal.* physician. [< L *medicus* physician]

Med·i·caid or **med·i·caid** (med′ə kād), *n.* government program, involving federal, state, and local governments, that provides medical care for needy and disabled children and adults.

med·i·cal (med′ə kəl), *adj.* of or having to do with the science or practice of medicine. [< F < LL, < L *medicus* doctor] —**med′i·cal·ly,** *adv.*

medical examiner. 1 official of a local government, esp. a physician or coroner, who performs autopsies and determines the causes of suspicious deaths. 2 doctor who examines people claiming insurance compensation.

Med·i·care or **med·i·care** (med′ə kār′), *n.* program of the U.S. government to provide medical and hospital care for people 65 years old and older.

med·i·cate (med′ə kāt), *v.,* -**cat·ed,** -**cat·ing.** 1 treat with medicine. 2 put medicine on or in. [< L, < *medicus* healing] —**med′i·ca′tion,** *n.*

me·dic·i·nal (mə dis′ə nəl), *adj.* having value as medicine; healing; helping; relieving. —**medic′i·nal·ly,** *adv.*

med·i·cine (med′ə sən), *n.* 1 substance, drug, or means used to cure disease or improve health. 2 science of curing disease or improving health; skill in healing; doctor's art; treatment of diseases. **take one's medicine,** do what one must; do something one dislikes to do. [< L, < *medicus* doctor]

medicine ball, a large, heavy leather ball tossed from one person to another for exercise.

medicine man, man believed by North American Indians and primitive peoples to have magic power over diseases, evil spirits, and other things.

me·di·e·val (mē′di ē′vəl; med′i–), *adj.* 1 belonging to or having to do with the Middle Ages (the years from about A.D. 500 to about 1450). 2 like that of the Middle Ages. [< L *medium* middle + *aevum* age] —**me′di·e′val·ly,** *adv.*

Medieval Greek, the Greek language from about A.D. 700 to about 1500.

me·di·e·val·ism (mē′di ē′vəl iz əm; med′i–), *n.* 1 spirit, ideals, and customs of the Middle Ages; medieval thought, religion, and art. 2 a medieval belief or custom.

me·di·e·val·ist (mē′di ē′vəl ist; med′i–), *n.* person who knows much about the Middle Ages.

Medieval Latin, the Latin language from about A.D. 700 to about 1500.

med·i·gap (med′ə gap′), *n.* supplementary health insurance that pays for medical costs which Medicare does not cover.

me·di·o·cre (mē′di ō′kər; mē′di ō′kər), *adj.* neither good nor bad; average; ordinary. [< F < L *mediocris,* orig., halfway up < *medius* middle + *ocris* jagged mountain]

me·di·oc·ri·ty (mē′di ok′rə ti), *n., pl.* -**ties.** 1 mediocre quality. 2 mediocre ability or accomplishment. [L *mediocritas*]

Medit., Mediterranean.

med·i·tate (med′ə tāt), *v.,* -**tat·ed,** -**tat·ing.** 1 engage in thought or contemplation; reflect: *monks meditate on holy things for hours at a time.* 2 consider in the mind as something to be done or effected: *the king struck a blow that he had meditated for some time.* [< L *meditatus*] —**med′i·ta′tor,** *n.*

med·i·ta·tion (med′ə tā′shən), *n.* continued thought; reflection, esp. on sacred or solemn subjects.

med·i·ta·tive (med′ə tā′tiv), *adj.* fond of meditating. —**med′ita′tive·ly,** *adv.*

Med·i·ter·ra·ne·an (med′ə tə rā′ni ən; –rān′yən), *n.* a large sea between Europe and Africa. —*adj.* of this sea or the lands around it.

me·di·um (mē′di əm), *adj., n., pl.* -**di·ums,** -**di·a** (–di ə). —*adj.* having a middle position; moderate: *hamburger cooked medium, set at medium speed, a medium temperature.* —*n.* 1 that which is in the middle; neither one extreme nor the other; middle condition. 2 substance or agent through which anything acts; a means: *radio is a medium of communication.* 3 substance in which something can live; environment: *water is the medium in which fish live.* 4 liquid with which paints are mixed. 5 person through whom supposed messages from the world of spirits are sent. [< L, neut. adj., middle]

Med.L, Medieval Latin.

med·lar (med′lər), *n.* 1 fruit that looks like a small brown apple. 2 the small, bushy tree that it grows on. [< OF *meslier* (tree) < *mesle* (fruit), ult. < L < Gk. *mespilon*]

med·ley (med′li), *n., pl.* -**leys,** *adj.* —*n.* 1 mixture of things that ordinarily do not belong together. 2 piece of music made up of parts from other pieces. —*adj.* made up of parts that are not alike; mixed. [< OF *meslée* < *mesler* mix, ult. < L *miscere.* Doublet of MELEE.]

medley relay, 1 swimming event in which teams of swimmers compete, with each team member in turn swimming a different stroke over the course. 2 relay race.

me·dul·la (mi dul′ə), *n., pl.* -**lae** (–ē). 1 =medulla oblongata. 2 the inner substance of an organ or structure. 3 the pith of plants. [< L, marrow]

me·dul·la ob·lon·ga·ta (mi dul′ə ob′-long gä′tə; –gä′tə), the lowest part of the brain, at the top end of the spinal cord. [< NL, prolonged medulla]

med·ul·lar·y (med′ə ler′i; mi dul′ər i), *adj.* of or like medulla or the medulla oblongata.

meek (mēk), *adj.* 1 not easily angered; mild. 2 submitting when ordered about by others. [< Scand. *miūkr* soft] —**meek′ly,** *adv.* —**meek′ness,** *n.*

meet[1] (mēt), *v.,* met, meet·ing, *n.* —*v.* 1 come face to face with; come together or in contact with; join: *where the two streets meet.* 2 be introduced to; become acquainted with. 3 be present at the arrival of: *meet a train.* 4 satisfy; pay: *meet bills.* 5 come together in conflict; fight. 6 come to; experience: *strange sounds met our ears.* 7 assemble: *Congress will meet next month.* —*n.* a meeting; a gathering: *an athletic meet.*

meet up with, meet; spend some time with.

meet with, have; get: *the plan met with approval.* [OE *mētan*]

meet[2] (mēt), *adj.* suitable; proper; fitting. [OE *gemǣte*] —**meet′ly,** *adv.*

meet·ing (mēt′ing), *n.* 1 a coming together. 2 assembly. 3 junction.

meeting house, building used for worship; church.

me·ga (meg′ə), *adj.* *Informal.* huge; extremely important.

mega–, *combining form.* 1 very large, as in *megabucks.* 2 one million, as in *megaton.*

meg·a·bit (meg′ə bit′), *n.* unit of electronic information equal to one million bits. [< *mega*– + *bit*]

meg·a·buck (meg′əbuk′), *Informal.* a million dollars.

megabucks, very large amount of money. [< *mega*– + *buck* dollar]

meg·a·byte (meg′ə bīt′), *n.* unit of electronic information that is about equal to one million bytes. [< *mega*– + *byte*]

meg·a·cy·cle (meg′ə sī′kəl), *n.* a million cycles in radio. [< *mega*– one million times (< Gk. *megas* great) + *cycle* < Gk. *kyklos* circle]

meg·a·lo·ma·ni·a (meg′ə lō mā′ni ə), *n.* delusions of greatness, wealth, etc. [< Gk. *megas* (*megalo*–) great + *mania* madness] —**meg′a·lo·ma′ni·ac,** *n.*

meg·a·lith (meg′ə lith), *n.* very large stone, esp. one used in construction by prehistoric people.

meg·a·lith·ic (meg′ə lith′ik), *adj.* 1 of or having to do with megaliths. 2 of or having to do with a late neolithic culture in W Europe identified with the use of megaliths in building monuments and tombs.

meg·a·lop·o·lis (meg′ə lop′ə lis), *n.* city of enormous size, esp. when thought of as the center of power, wealth, etc., in a country or the world. [< Gk. *mégas, megálou* great + *pólis* city]

meg·a·phone (meg′ə fōn), *n.* a large, funnel-shaped horn used to increase the loudness of the voice or the distance at which it can be heard. [< Gk. *megas* great + *phone* sound]

meg·a·spore (meg′ə spôr; –spōr), *n.* 1 large spore in certain ferns from which the female gametophyte develops. 2 embryo sac in seed plants.

meg·a·ton (meg′ə tun), *n.* a measure of atomic power equivalent to the energy released by one million tons of TNT. [< *mega*– one million times + *ton*]

mei·o·sis (mīō′sis), *n., pl.* –**ses** (–sēz). process that reduces the number of chromosomes in reproductive cells by one half, resulting in the production of gametes or spores; reduction division. [< NL < Gk. *meíōsis* a lessening ult. < *meíōn* less]

mel·an·cho·li·a (mel′ən kō′li ə), *n.* great depression of spirits and gloomy fears. [< LL < Gk., < *melas* black + *chole* bile]

mel·an·chol·y (mel′ən kol′i), *n.* sadness; low spirits; tendency to be sad. —*adj.* 1 sad; gloomy. 2 causing sadness; depressing. —**mel′an·chol′ic,** *adj.* —**mel′an·chol′i·cal·ly,** *adv.*

Mel·a·ne·sia (mel′ə nē′zhə; –shə), *n.* group of islands in the Pacific, NE of Australia.

Mel·a·ne·sian (mel′ə nē′zhən; –shən), *n.* 1 a member of any of the peoples living in Melanesia. 2 the languages of Melanesia. —*adj.* of or relating to Melanesia, its inhabitants, or their languages.

mel·a·nin (mel′ə nin), *n.* dark pigment, esp. the black of skin, hair, and eyes of humans, which helps protect the skin from sunburn and improves vision in bright sunlight. [< Gk. *mélas, –anos* black + E –*in*]

mé·lange (mā länzh′), *n.* mixture; medley. [< F, < *mêler* mix]

Mel·ba toast (mel′bə), very thin, crisp toast.

meld[1] (meld), *n.* in canasta, pinochle, etc., the announcement of any counting combination in a hand. —*v.* make a meld.

meld[2] (meld), *v.* merge; blend. [< prob. verb use of *melled* mingled, blended < ME *mellen* mix, mingle]

me·lee (mā′lā; mā lā′; mel′ā), *n.* a confused fight; hand-to-hand fight among a number of fighters. [< F *mêlée.* Doublet of MEDLEY.]

mel·lif·lu·ent (mə lif′lü ənt), *adj.* mellifluous. —**mel·lif′lu·ence,** *n.* —**mel·lif′lu·ent·ly,** *adv.*

mel·lif·lu·ous (mə lif′lü əs), *adj.* sweetly or smoothly flowing: *the mellifluous speech of the orator.* [< LL, < L *mel* honey + *fluere* to flow] —**mel·lif′lu·ous·ly,** *adv.*

mel·low (mel′ō), *adj.* 1 soft and full-flavored from ripeness; sweet and juicy: *a mellow apple.* 2 fully matured: *mellow wine.* 3 soft and rich: *mellow tones.* 4 softened and made wise by age and experience. —*v.* make or become mellow. [var. of OE *mearu* soft tender] —**mel′low·ly,** *adv.* —**mel′low·ness,** *n.*

me·lo·de·on (mə lō′di ən), *n.* a small reed organ. [see MELODY]

me·lod·ic (mə lod′ik), *adj.* 1 having to do with melody. 2 melodious. —**me·lod′i·cal·ly,** *adv.*

me·lo·di·ous (mə lō′di əs), *adj.* 1 sweet-sounding; pleasing to the ear; musical. 2 producing melody. —**me·lo′di·ous·ly,** *adv.* —**melo′di·ous·ness,** *n.*

mel·o·dra·ma (mel′ə drä′mə; –dram′ə), *n.* 1 a sensational drama with exaggerated appeal to the emotions and, usually, a happy ending. 2 any sensational writing, speech, or action with exaggerated appeal to the emotions. [< F, < Gk. *melos* music + *drama* drama]

mel·o·dra·mat·ic (mel′ə drə mat′ik), *adj.* of, like, or suitable for melodrama; sensational and exaggerated. —**mel′o·dra·mat′i·cal·ly,** *adv.* —**mel′o·dram′a·tist,** *n.*

mel·o·dy (mel′ə di), *n., pl.* –**dies.** 1 sweet music; any sweet sound. 2 succession of single tones in music; tune. 3 the main tune in harmonized music; air. [< LL < Gk. *meloidia,* ult. < *melos* song + *oide* song]

mel·on (mel′ən), *n.* a large juicy fruit that grows on a vine. Watermelons, cantaloupes or muskmelons, and honeydew melons are different kinds. [< F < LL *melo,* short for L *melopepo* < Gk., < *melon* apple + *pepon* gourd]

melt (melt), *v.,* **melt·ed, melt·ed** or **mol·ten, melt·ing,** *n.* —*v.* 1 change from solid to liquid: *great heat melts iron.* 2 dissolve: *sugar melts in water.* 3 change or disappear gradually: *the clouds melted away; pity melted her heart.* —*n.* act of melting. [OE *meltan*] —**melt′a·ble,** *adj.* —**melt′er,** *n.*

melt·down (melt′doun′), *n.* 1 melting of nuclear fuel through its containment vessel and its release into the environment because of a failure of the cooling system. 2 *Informal. Fig.* great emotional upset.

melting point, degree of temperature at which a solid substance melts.

mem·ber (mem′bər), *n.* 1 one belonging to a group: *a member of Congress.* 2 constituent part of a whole: *a member of an equation.* 3 part of a plant, animal, or human body, esp. a leg or arm. [< OF, < L *membrum* limb, part]

mem·ber·ship (mem′bər ship), *n.* 1 fact or state of being a member: *membership in the Boy Scouts.* 2 members. 3 number of members.

mem·brane (mem′brān), *n.* 1 a thin, soft sheet or layer of animal tissue lining or covering some part of the body. 2 a similar layer of vegetable tissue. [< L *membrana* < *membrum* member] —**mem′bra·nous,** *adj.*

me·men·to (mə men′tō), *n., pl.* –**tos,** –**toes.** thing serving as a reminder, warning, or remembrance. [< L, remember!]

mem·o (mem′ō), *n., pl.* **mem·os.** =memorandum.

mem·oir (mem′wär; –wôr), *n.* biography.

memoirs, a record of facts and events written from personal knowledge or special information. **b** autobiography. [< F *mémoire* < L *memoria*. Doublet of MEMORY.]

mem·o·ra·bil·i·a (mem′ə rə bil′i ə), *n. pl.* things or events worth remembering. [< L (pl.). See MEMORABLE.]

mem·o·ra·ble (mem′ə rə bəl), *adj.* worth remembering; not to be forgotten; notable. [< L, ult. < *memor* mindful] —**mem′o·ra·bil′i·ty,** *n.* —**mem′o·ra·bly,** *adv.*

mem·o·ran·dum (mem′ə ran′dəm), *n.,* *pl.* **-dums, -da** (-də). **1** a short written statement for future use; note to aid one's memory. **2** an informal note or report. [< L, (thing) to be remembered]

me·mo·ri·al (mə mô′ri əl; -mō′-), *n.* something that is a reminder of some event or person, such as a statue, an arch or column, a book, or a holiday. —*adj.* helping people to remember: *memorial services.* [< L, < *memoria* MEMORY]

Memorial Day, day for honoring American servicemen and women who died while serving their country. It is celebrated on the last Monday in May, and is generally a legal holiday.

me·mo·ri·al·ize (mə mô′ri əl īz; -mō′-), *v.,* **-ized, -iz·ing.** preserve the memory of; commemorate. —**me·mo′ri·al·i·za′tion,** *n.* —**me·mo′ri·al·iz′er,** *n.*

mem·o·rize (mem′ə rīz), *v.,* **-rized, -riz·ing.** commit to memory; learn by heart. —**mem′o·ri·za′tion,** *n.* —**mem′o·riz′er,** *n.*

mem·o·ry (mem′ə ri; mem′ri), *n.,* *pl.* **-ries. 1** ability to remember. **2** act or fact of remembering: *the memory of things past.* **3** all that a person remembers. **4** person, thing, or event that is remembered. **5** length of time during which the past is remembered: *this has been the hottest summer within my memory.* **6** a system of storing information in computer.

in memory of, to help in remembering; as a reminder of. [< L *memoria* < *memor* mindful. Doublet of MEMOIR.]

men (men), *n. pl.* **1** pl. of **man. 2** human beings; people in general.

men·ace (men′is), *n., v.,* **-aced, -ac·ing.** —*n.* threat: *forest fires are a menace.* —*v.* threaten: *floods menaced the valley with destruction.* [< F < L *minaciae* (pl.), ult. < *minae* projecting points, threats] —**men′ac·ing·ly,** *adv.*

me·nag·er·ie (mə naj′ər i; -nazh′-), *n.* **1** collection of wild animals kept in cages for exhibition. **2** place where such animals are kept. **3** *Fig.* unusual assortment of people. [< F, lit., management of a household]

me·nar·che (mə när′kē; me-), *n.* first menstrual period. [< Gk. *mēn* month + *-archē* a beginning]

mend (mend), *v.* **1** put in good condition again; make whole; repair: *mend a road.* **2** set right; improve: *he should mend*

his manners. **3** get back one's health. —*n.* **1** place that has been mended. **2** a mending; improvement. [var. of *amend*] —**mend′a·ble,** *adj.* —**mend′er,** *n.*

men·da·cious (men dā′shəs), *adj.* **1** lying; untruthful. **2** false; untrue. [< L, < *mendax* lying] —**men·da′cious·ly,** *adv.* —**men·da′cious·ness, men·dac′i·ty,** *n.*

men·de·le·vi·um (men′də lā′vi əm), *n.* a rare, radioactive, artificial element. Mv, produced as a by-product of nuclear fission. [named for D. I. *Mendeleev,* Russian chemist]

Men·de·li·an (men dē′lē ən), *adj.* **1** of or having to do with Gregor Mendel or Mendel's laws. **2** inherited in accord with Mendel's laws.

Mendel's laws, laws describing the inheritance of many characteristics in animals and plants. [< Gregor *Mendel* (1822–84), Austrian monk and botanist who formulated them]

men·di·cant (men′də kənt), *adj.* begging: *mendicant friars ask alms for charity.* —*n.* **1** beggar. **2** a mendicant friar. [< L *mendicans* < *mendicus* beggar] —**men′di·can·cy,** *n.*

men·folk (men′fōk′), *n. pl.* men.

men·ha·den (men hā′dən), *n., pl.* **-den.** a sea fish common along the E coast of the United States. [< Algonquian]

me·ni·al (mē′ni əl; mēn′yəl), *adj.* belonging to or suited to a servant; low; mean. —*n.* servant who does the humblest and most unpleasant tasks. [< AF, < *meiniée* household, ult. < L *mansio* habitation] —**me′ni·al·ly,** *adv.*

me·nin·ges (mə nin′jēz), *n. pl., sing.* **me·ninx** (mē′ningks). the three membranes that surround the brain and spinal cord. [< NL (pl.) < Gk.] —**me·nin′ge·al,** *adj.*

men·in·gi·tis (men′in jī′tis), *n.* a very serious disease in which the membranes surrounding the brain or spinal cord are inflamed. —**men′in·git′ic,** *adj.*

me·nis·cus (mə nis′kəs), *n., pl.* **-nis·cus·es, -nis·ci** (-nis′ī). **1** the curved upper surface of a column of liquid. **2** lens that is convex on one side and concave on the other. [< NL < Gk. *meniskos,* dim. of *mene* moon]

Men·non·ite (men′ən īt), *n.* member of a Christian church opposed to infant baptism, taking oaths, holding public office, and military service.

Me·nom·i·nee (mə nom′ə nē), *n., pl.* **-nees** or **-ne. 1** member of a tribe of Indians of Algonkian descent living in Wisconsin, northern Michigan, and northern Illinois. **2** Algonkian language of this tribe.

men·o·pause (men′ə pôz), *n.* the final cessation of the menses, occurring normally between the ages of 45 and 50. [< NL, < Gk. *men* month + *pausis* pause]

me·nor·ah (mə nôr′ə, -nōr′-), *n.* **1** Also, **Menorah.** candlestick with eight branches, used during the Jewish celebration of Hanukkah. **2 Menorah,**

the seven-branched candlestick in the ancient Temple at Jerusalem. [< Heb.]

mensch (mench), *n. Informal.* decent, respected person. [< Yiddish *mentsch* person < G *Mensch*]

men·ses (men′sēz), *n. pl.* discharge of blood from the uterus that normally occurs every four weeks between puberty and the menopause. [< L, pl. of *mensis* month]

men·stru·al (men′strü əl), *adj.* **1** pertaining to the menses. **2** monthly.

men·stru·ate (men′strü āt), *v.,* **-at·ed, -at·ing.** have a discharge of blood from the uterus, normally at intervals of four weeks. [< LL *menstruatus,* ult. < L *mens* month] —**men′stru·a′tion,** *n.*

men·sur·a·ble (men′shər ə bəl), *adj.* measurable. —**men′sur·a·bil′i·ty,** *n.*

men·su·ra·tion (men′shə rā′shən), *n.* **1** act, art, or process of measuring. **2** branch of mathematics that deals with finding lengths, areas, and volumes. [< LL, ult. < L *mensura* MEASURE]

-ment, suffix forming nouns from verbs or the stems of verbs. **1** act or state or fact of ___ing, as in *enjoyment, management.* **2** state or condition or fact of being ___ed, as in *amazement, astonishment.* **3** product or result of ___ing, as in *pavement.* **4** means or instrument for ___ing, as in *inducement.* [< F < L *-mentum*]

men·tal (men′təl), *adj.* **1** of the mind. *a mental test.* **2** for the mind; done by the mind: *mental arithmetic.* **3** having a mental disease or weakness. **4** for insane people. [< LL, < L *mens* mind]

mental age, measure of the development or natural intelligence of a person, determined by testing.

men·tal·i·ty (men tal′ə ti), *n., pl.* **-ties.** mental capacity; mind.

men·tal·ly (men′təl i), *adv.* **1** in the mind; with the mind. **2** with regard to the mind.

mental reservation, an unexpressed qualification of a statement.

mental telepathy, =extrasensory perception.

men·thol (men′thol; -thôl; -thōl), *n.* a white, crystalline substance, $C_{10}H_{20}O$, obtained from oil of peppermint, used in medicine. [< G, < L *menta* mint + *oleum* oil]

men·tho·lat·ed (men′thə lāt′id), *adj.* containing menthol.

men·tion (men′shən), *v.* speak about; refer to. [< *n.*] —*n.* a short statement (about); reference (to).

make mention of, mention.

not to mention, not even considering; besides. [< OF < L *mentio*] —**men′tion·a·ble,** *adj.* —**men′tion·er,** *n.*

men·tor (men′tər), *n.* a wise and trusted adviser. [< Gk.]

men·u (men′ü; mā′nū), *n.* **1** list of the food served at a meal; bill of fare. **2** the food served. **3** list of options available to the user of a computer program. [< F, small, detailed, < L *minutus* made small. Doublet of MINUTE[2].]

me·ow (mi ou′), *n.* sound made by a cat. —*v.* make this sound. [imit.]

Meph·i·stoph·e·les (mef′ə stof′ə lēz), *n.* a powerful evil spirit; crafty devil. —**Meph′is·to·phe′li·an,** *adj.*

mer·can·tile (mėr′kən til; –tīl), *adj.* **1** of merchants or trade; commercial: *a mercantile firm, mercantile law.* **2** of or pertaining to mercantilism. [< F < Ital., < *mercante* MERCHANT]

mer·can·til·ism (mėr′kən til iz′əm; –tīl–), *n.* **1** system which favored a balance of exports of commodities, over imports, and regulated a nation's agriculture, industry, and trade with that end in view. **2** mercantile principles, practices, or spirit. —**mer′can·til·ist,** *n.*

Mer·ca·tor's projection (mər kā′tərz), method of drawing maps with straight instead of curved lines for latitude and longitude. [after G. *Mercator,* cartographer]

mer·ce·nar·y (mėr′sə ner′i), *adj., n., pl.* **-nar·ies.** —*adj.* **1** working for money only; acting with money as the motive. **2** done for money or gain. —*n.* soldier serving for pay in a foreign army. [< L, < *merces* wages]

mer·cer·ize (mėr′sər īz), *v.,* **-ized, -iz·ing.** treat (cotton thread or cloth) with a chemical solution that strengthens it, gives it a silky luster, and makes it hold dyes better. [after J. *Mercer,* patentee of the process]

mer·chan·dise (mėr′chən dīz; –dīs), *n., v.,* **-dised, -dis·ing.** —*n.* goods for sale; wares; articles bought and sold. —*v.* buy and sell; trade. [< F, < *marchand* MERCHANT] —**mer′chan·dis′er,** *n.*

mer·chant (mėr′chənt), *n.* **1** person who buys and sells. **2** storekeeper. —*adj.* trading; pertaining to trade: *merchant ships.* [< OF *marchëant,* ult. < L *merx* wares]

mer·chant·a·ble (mėr′chən tə bəl), *adj.* marketable.

mer·chant·man (mėr′chənt mən), *n., pl.* **-men.** ship used in commerce.

merchant marine, 1 ships used in commerce. **2** *U.S.* **Merchant Marine.** officers and sailors trained to serve on these ships, patrol U.S. waterways, perform rescues at sea, etc.

mer·ci·ful (mėr′si fəl), *adj.* having mercy; showing or feeling mercy; full of mercy. —**mer′ci·ful·ly,** *adv.* —**mer′ci·ful·ness,** *n.*

mer·ci·less (mėr′si lis), *adj.* without mercy; having no mercy; showing no mercy. —**mer′ci·less·ly,** *adv.* —**mer′ci·less·ness,** *n.*

mer·cu·ri·al (mər kyur′i əl), *adj.* **1** sprightly; quick; changeable; fickle. **2** caused by the use of mercury: *mercurial poisoning.* **3** containing mercury: *a mercurial ointment.* —**mer·cu′ri·al·ly,** *adv.* —**mer·cu′ri·al·ness,** *n.*

mer·cu·ric (mər kyur′ik), *adj.* of compounds, containing mercury in a bivalent state.

mer·cu·rous (mər kyur′əs; mėr′kyə rəs), *adj.* of compounds, containing mercury as a univalent radical.

mer·cu·ry (mėr′kyə ri), *n., pl.* **-ries. 1** a heavy, silver-white metallic element, Hg, that is liquid at ordinary temperatures. **2** column of mercury in a thermometer or barometer. **3 Mercury,** planet nearest the sun. [< L *Mercurius* (def. 3)]

mer·cy (mėr′si), *n., pl.* **-cies. 1** more kindness than justice requires; kindness beyond what can be claimed or expected. **2** kindly treatment; pity. **3** something to be thankful for; blessing. **at the mercy of,** in the power of. [< OF < Med.L *merces* < L, reward]

mere[1] (mir), *adj., superl.* **mer·est.** nothing else than; only; simple: *the cut was the merest scratch.* [< L *merus* pure]

mere[2] (mir), *n. Poetic.* lake; pond. [OE]

mere·ly (mir′li), *adv.* simply; only; and nothing more; and that is all: *merely a matter of form.*

mer·e·tri·cious (mer′ə trish′əs), *adj.* attractive in a showy way; alluring by false charms. [< L, < *meretrix* prostitute < *mereri* earn] —**mer′e·tri′cious·ly,** *adv.* —**mer′e·tri′cious·ness,** *n.*

mer·gan·ser (mər gan′sər), *n., pl.* **-sers** or (*esp. collectively*) **-ser.** any of several kinds of large ducks that have long, slender bills. The male has a crested head. [< NL, < *mergus* diver + *anser* goose]

merge (mėrj), *v.,* **merged, merg·ing.** swallow up or become swallowed up; absorb; combine and absorb; combine: *the twilight merges into darkness.* [< L *mergere* to dip]

merg·er (mėr′jər), *n.* a merging; absorption; combination: *one big company was formed by the merger of four small ones.*

me·rid·i·an (mə rid′i ən), *n.* **1** circle passing through any place on the earth's surface and through the North and South Poles. **2** the half of such a circle from pole to pole. **3** *Fig.* the highest point: *the meridian of life is the prime of life.* [< OF < L *meridianus,* ult. < *medius* middle + *dies* day]

me·ringue (mə rang′), *n.* **1** mixture made of egg whites beaten stiff and sweetened. **2** a small cake, etc., made of this mixture. [< F]

me·ri·no (mə rē′nō), *n., pl.* **-nos. 1** kind of sheep with long, fine wool. **2** wool of this sheep. **3** a soft woolen yarn made from it. [< Sp.]

mer·it (mer′it), *n.* **1** goodness; worth; value: *the merits of Shakespeare's plays are obvious.* **2** thing that deserves praise or reward: *realistic thinking is one of his merits.* **3** often, **merits.** real fact or quality, whether good or bad: *the judge will consider the case on its merits.* —*v.* deserve. [< F < L *meritum* earned]

mer·i·toc·ra·cy (mer′ə tok′rə si), *n.* **1** class of people distinguished by their intellect, talent, or accomplishments. **2** system that advances individuals on the basis of intellect, talent, or accomplishments. [< *merit* + *-ocracy,* as in *aristocracy*]

mer·i·to·ri·ous (mer′ə tô′ri əs; –tō′–), *adj.* deserving reward or praise; having merit; worthy. —**mer′i·to′ri·ous·ly,** *adv.* —**mer′i·to′ri·ous·ness,** *n.*

merit pay, wages paid on the basis of an employee's performance on the job.

merit system, appointment and advancement in the civil service on the basis of performance and merit, as opposed to political affiliation.

mer·maid (mėr′mād′), *n.* maiden in fairy tales having the form of a fish from the waist down. [< *mere*[2] + *maid*]

mer·ri·ment (mer′i mənt), *n.* laughter and gaiety; fun; mirth; merry enjoyment.

mer·ry (mer′i), *adj.,* **-ri·er, -ri·est. 1** laughing; full of fun: *a merry reveler.* **2** joyful: *a merry holiday, merry bells.* **3** *Archaic.* delightful. **make merry,** laugh and be happy; have fun. [OE *myrge*] —**mer′ri·ly,** *adv.* —**mer′ri·ness,** *n.*

mer·ry-an·drew (mer′i an′drü), *n.* clown.

mer·ry-go-round (mer′i gō round′), *n.* **1** set of animals and seats on a platform that goes round and round by machinery. **2** any whirl or rapid round: *a merry-go-round of parties.*

mer·ry·mak·ing (mer′i māk′ing), *n.* **1** laughter and happiness; fun. **2** happy festival; merry entertainment. —*adj.* happy and full of fun; engaged in merrymaking. —**mer′ry·mak′er,** *n.*

me·sa (mā′sə), *n.* a small, high plateau with steep sides. [< Sp. < L *mensa* table]

mé·sal·li·ance (mā zal′i əns; *Fr.* mā zä lyäns′), *n. French.* unsuitable marriage; misalliance.

mes·cal (mes kal′), *n.* **1** an alcoholic drink made from the fermented juice of an agave plant. **2** the plant itself. **3** a small cactus whose buttonlike tops are dried and chewed as a stimulant and hallucinogen by some Indian tribes during religious ceremonies; peyote. [< Sp. < Aztec *mexcalli* liquor]

mes·dames (mā däm′), *n. pl.* **1** pl. of **madam. 2** pl. of **madame. 3** ladies.

mes·de·moi·selles (mād mwä zel′), *n. pl.* of **mademoiselle.**

mesh (mesh), *n.* **1** open space of a net or sieve: *this net has half-inch meshes.* —*v.* **1** catch or be caught in a net. **2** engage or become engaged: *the teeth of the small gear mesh with the teeth of a larger one.* **in mesh,** in gear; fitted together. [cf. OE *mæscre* net]

mes·mer·ism (mes′mər iz əm; mez′–), *n.* hypnotism. [for F. A. *Mesmer,* who popularized the doctrine] —**mes·mer′ic,** *adj.* —**mes·mer′i·cal·ly,** *adv.* —**mes′mer·ist,** *n.*

mes·mer·ize (mes′mər īz; mez′–), *v.,* **-ized, -iz·ing.** =hypnotize. —**mes′mer·i·za′tion,** *n.* —**mes′mer·iz′er,** *n.*

Mes·o·a·mer·i·ca (mes′ō ə mer′əkə; mē′so–), *n.* part of the American continent extending from northern Mexico to the Isthmus of Panama. —**Mes′o·a·mer′i·can,** *adj., n.*

mes·o·carp (mes′ə kärp), *n.* the middle layer of the pericarp, such as the fleshy part of a peach. [< Gk. *mesos* middle + *karpos* fruit]

mes·o·derm (mes′ə dėrm), *n.* the middle layer of cells in an embryo. [< Gk. *mesos* middle + *derma* skin] —**mes′o·der′mal,** *adj.*

mes·o·lith·ic or **Mes·o·lith·ic** (mes′-ə lith′ik), *adj.* of or having to do with the middle period of the Stone Age. —*n.* this period: *people of the mesolithic.* [< Gk. *meso–* middle + *líthos* stone + E *–ic*]

mes·o·sphere (mes′ə sfir), *n.* region of the earth's atmosphere between the stratosphere and ionosphere, about 30–50 miles above the earth's surface, where most ozone is created.

mes·on (mes′on), *n.* a highly unstable heavy electron found in cosmic rays; particle having the same electric charge as an electron, but much greater mass.

mes·quite (mes kēt′; mes′kēt), *n.* tree or shrub growing in the SW United States and in Mexico. [< Am.Sp. *mezquite* < Aztec]

mess (mes), *n.* **1** a dirty or untidy mass or group of things; dirty or untidy condition. **2** confusion; difficulty: *her papers are in a mess.* **3** an unpleasant or unsuccessful affair or state of affairs: *the beggar had made a mess of his life.* **4** group of people who take meals together regularly, esp. such a group in the army or navy. **5** meal of such a group: *the officers are at mess now.* **6** a portion of food that does not look or taste good: *have a mess of beans.* —*v.* **1** make dirty or untidy. **2** make a failure of; confuse; spoil. **3** take one's meals (with).

mess about, mess around, putter around.

mess around with or **about with,** *Informal.* **a** meddle with. **b** fool around with; be involved with. [< OF < L *missus* (thing) put (i.e., on the table)]

mes·sage (mes′ij), *n.* **1** words sent from one person to another. **2** official speech or writing: *the President's message to Congress.* **3** inspired words: *the message of a prophet.*

get the message, *Informal.* fully understand the importance of something. [< OF, ult. < L *missus* sent]

mes·sa·line (mes′ə lēn′; mes′ə lēn), *n.* a thin, soft silk cloth with a surface like satin. [< F]

mes·sen·ger (mes′ən jər), *n.* **1** person who carries a message or goes on an errand. **2** sign that something is coming; forerunner.

messenger RNA, a ribonucleic acid that carries genetic instructions from the DNA to the ribosomes which control the kind of protein or enzyme a cell will produce.

Mes·si·ah (mə sī′ə), *n.* **1** expected deliverer of the Jewish people. **2** in Christian use, Jesus. **3** any savior. [var. of LL *Messias,* < Gk. < Heb. *māshīaḥ* anointed] —**Mes′si·an′ic,** *adj.*

mes·sieurs (mes′ərz; *Fr.* mā syœ′), *n.pl.* **1** pl. of **monsieur. 2** gentlemen.

mess·mate (mes′māt′), *n.* one of a group of people who eat together regularly.

Messrs., *n.* messieurs.

mess·y (mes′i), *adj.,* **mess·i·er, mess·i·est.** in a mess; like a mess; untidy; in disorder; dirty. —**mess′i·ness,** *n.*

mes·ti·za (mes tē′zə), *n.* **1** a woman of mixed ancestry. **2** woman of Spanish and American Indian ancestry. **3** woman of the Philippine Islands having Chinese ancestry.

mes·ti·zo (mes tē′zō), *n., pl.* **–zos, –zoes. 1** person of mixed blood. **2** person of Spanish and American Indian blood. **3** native of the Philippine Islands having Chinese blood. [< Sp., ult. < L *mixtus* mixed]

met (met), *v.* pt. and pp. of **meet**[1].

met., metropolitan.

me·tab·o·lism (mə tab′ə liz əm), *n.* processes of building up food into living matter and using living matter until it is broken down into simpler substances or waste matter, giving off energy. [< Gk. *metabole* change < *meta–* into a different position + *bole* a throwing] —**met′a·bol′ic,** *adj.* —**me·tab′o·lize,** *v.*

met·a·car·pus (met′ə kär′pəs), *n., pl.* **–pi** (–pī). **1** part of a hand between the wrist and the fingers. **2** part of a forefoot between the carpus and the phalanges. [< NL, ult. < Gk. *meta–* after + *karpos* wrist] —**met′a·car′pal,** *adj., n.*

met·al (met′əl), *n., adj., v.,* **–aled, –aling.** —*n.* **1** substance such as iron, silver, copper, and brass. **2** any element whose atoms tend to lend electrons, or any mixture of such elements. **3** broken stone, cinders, etc., used for roads and roadbeds. **4** material; substance: *cowards are not made of the same metal as heroes.* —*adj.* made of metal. —*v.* furnish or cover with metal. [< OF < L < Gk. *metallon,* orig., mine]

metal fatigue, cracking, weakening, or failure of a metal, caused by stress from vibration, tapping, etc.

metall., metallurgic; metallurgy.

me·tal·lic (mə tal′ik), *adj.* **1** of, containing, or consisting of metal. **2** like metal; characteristic of metal; that suggests metal: *a metallic luster, a metallic voice.* —**me·tal′li·cal·ly,** *adv.*

met·al·lif·er·ous (met′əl if′ər əs), *adj.* containing or yielding metal. [< L, < *metallum* metal + *ferre* to bear]

met·al·lur·gy (met′əl ėr′ji), *n.* science or art of separating metals from their ores and refining them for use. [< NL *metallurgia,* ult. < Gk. *metallon* metal + *ergon* work] —**met′al·lur′gic, met′al·lur′gi·cal,** *adj.* —**met′al·lur′gi·cal·ly,** *adv.* —**met′al·lur′gist,** *n.*

met·al·work·ing (met′əl wėr′king), *n.* act or process of making things out of metal. —**met′al·work′,** *n.* —**met′al·work′er,** *n.*

met·a·mor·phism (met′ə môr′fiz əm), *n.* **1** change of form. **2** change in the structure of a rock caused by pressure, heat, etc.

met·a·mor·phose (met′ə môr′fōz; –fōs), *v.,* **–phosed, –phos·ing.** change in form; transform: *the witch metamorphosed people into animals.*

met·a·mor·pho·sis (met′ə môr′fə sis), *n., pl.* **–ses** (–sēz). **1** change of form. **2** the changed form. **3** a noticeable or complete change of character, appearance, or condition. [< L < Gk., ult. < *meta–* over + *morphe* form] —**met′a·mor′phic,** *adj.*

met·a·phase (met′ə fāz), *n.* second stage of mitosis, marked by the arrangement of the pairs of chromosomes along one spindle, or line of minute fibers, in the center of the nucleus of the cell.

met·a·phor (met′ə fər; –fôr), *n.* figure of speech in which a word or phrase that ordinarily means one thing is used of another thing in order to suggest a likeness between the two. [< F < L < Gk. *metaphora* transfer, ult. < *meta–* over + *pherein* carry] —**met′a·phor′ic, met′a·phor′i·cal,** *adj.* **met′a·phori·cal·ly,** *adv.*

met·a·phys·i·cal (met′ə fiz′ə kəl), *adj.* **1** of metaphysics. **2** highly abstract; hard to understand. —**met′a·phys′i·cal·ly,** *adv.*

met·a·phys·ics (met′ə fiz′iks), *n.* branch of philosophy that tries to explain reality and knowledge, the philosophical study of the real nature of the universe. [< Med.L < Med.Gk. (ta) *metaphysika* for Gk. *ta meta ta physika* the (works) after the Physics; with ref. to philosophical works of Aristotle] —**met′a·phy·si′cian,** *n.*

me·tas·ta·sis (mə tas′tə sis), *n., pl.* **–ses.** **1** transfer from one organ or part to another of a function, pain, disease, etc., esp. of cancerous cells. **2** cancerous cells, growth, etc., transferred in this way. [< LL < Gk. *metástasis* removal, ult. < *meta–* changed over + *histánai* place] —**me·tas′ta·size,** *v.*

met·a·tar·sus (met′ə tär′səs), *n., pl.* **–si** (–sī). **1** part of a foot between the ankle and the toes. **2** part (or bony part) of a hind foot between the tarsus and the phalanges. [< NL, < Gk. *meta–* after + *tarsos* flat of the foot] —**met′a·tar′sal,** *adj.*

me·tath·e·sis (mə tath′ə sis), *n., pl.* **–ses** (–sēz). **1** transposition of sounds, syllables, or letters in a word. **2** interchange of atoms between two molecules. **3** transposition; reversal. [< LL < Gk., transposition, ult. < *meta–* over + *tithenai* set] —**met′a·thet′ic, met′a·thet′i·cal,** *adj.*

Met·a·zo·a (met′ə zō′ə), *n. pl.* a large zoological division of the two kingdom system of classification comprising all animals which are composed of more than one cell. [< NL, ult. < Gk. *meta–* after + *zoion* animal] —**met′a·zo′an,** *adj., n.*

mete (mēt), *v.,* **met·ed, met·ing.** give to each a share of; distribute; allot. [OE *metan*]

me·te·or (mē′ti ər), *n.* mass of stone or metal that comes toward the earth from outer space with enormous speed; shooting star. [< L < Gk. *meteoron* (thing) in the air < *meta–* up + *–aoros* lifted < *aeirein* lift]

me·te·or·ic (mē′ti ôr′ik; –or′–), *adj.* 1 consisting of meteors. 2 *Fig.* flashing like a meteor; brilliant and soon ended; swift: *a meteoric career.* —**me′te·or′i·cal·ly,** *adv.*

me·te·or·ite (mē′ti ər īt), *n.* 1 mass of stone or metal that has fallen to the earth from outer space. 2 meteor or meteoroid. —**me′te·or·it′ic,** *adj.*

me·te·or·oid (mē′ti ə roid), *n.* any of the small bodies that travel through space and become meteorites or shooting stars when they enter the earth's atmosphere.

meteorol., 1 meteorology. 2 meteorologic.

me·te·or·ol·o·gy (mē′ti ər ol′ə ji), *n.* science of the atmosphere and weather. —**me′te·or·o·log′ic, me′te·or·o·log′i·cal,** *adj.* —**me′te·or·o·log′i·cal·ly,** *adv.* —**me′te·or·ol′o·gist,** *n.*

me·ter¹ (mē′tər), *n.* 1 unit of length in the metric system; 39.37 inches. 2 the arrangement of beats or accents in a line of poetry. 3 the arrangement of beats in music. [< F < L < Gk. *metron*]

me·ter² (mē′tər), *n.* 1 device for measuring. 2 device for measuring and recording the amount of gas, water, electricity, etc., used. —*v.* measure with a meter. [< *mete¹*]

-meter, *combining form.* 1 device for measuring, as in *speedometer.* 2 meter; 39.37 inches, as in *kilometer.* 3 ___ feet, as in *hexameter.* [< NL *-metrum* Gk. *metron* measure]

me·tered mail (mē′tərd), mail with postage stamped on it by a machine.

meter maid, woman assigned to enforce parking meter regulations.

meth (meth), *n. Informal.* =methamphetamine.

Meth., Methodist.

meth·a·done (meth′ə dōn), *n.* synthetic narcotic used to reduce pain and to treat heroin addiction.

meth·am·phet·a·mine (meth′am fet′ə min), *n.* powerful drug that acts as a stimulant to the central nervous system. [< *methyl* + *amphetamine*]

meth·ane (meth′ān), *n.* a colorless, odorless, inflammable gas, CH_4, the simplest of the hydrocarbons. Methane comes from marshes, petroleum wells, volcanoes, and coal mines.

meth·a·nol (meth′ə nōl; –nol), *n.* =methyl alcohol.

me·thinks (mi thingks′), *v., pt.* **me·thought.** *Archaic.* it seems to me. [OE *mē thyncth* it seems to me]

meth·od (meth′əd), *n.* 1 way of doing something: *method of instruction.* 2 system in doing things; order in thinking: *work with method.*

method in one's madness, sensible purpose in what appears to be foolish. [< L < Gk. *methodos,* orig., pursuit < *meta–* after + *hodos* a traveling]

meth·od·i·cal (mə thod′ə kəl), **me·thod·ic** (–ik), *adj.* according to a method; systematic; orderly. —**me·thod′i·cal·ly,** *adv.* —**me·thod′ical·ness,** *n.*

Meth·od·ism (meth′əd iz əm), *n.* doctrine, organization, and manner of worship of the Methodist Church.

Meth·od·ist (meth′əd ist), *n.* member of a church that had its origin in the teachings and work of John Wesley. —*adj.* of Methodists or Methodism. —**Meth′od·is′tic,** *adj.*

meth·od·ize (meth′əd īz), *v.,* **–ized, –iz·ing.** reduce to a method; arrange with method. —**meth′od·iz′er,** *n.*

meth·od·ol·o·gy (meth′ə dol′ə ji), *n.* 1 system of methods or procedures used in any field, as a type of surgery or teaching. 2 branch of logic concerned with the application of this system to any field of knowledge.

me·thought (mi thôt′), *v. pt.* of **methinks.**

Me·thu·se·lah (mə thü′zə lə), *n.* 1 a man said to have lived 969 years. Gen. 5:27. 2 a very old man.

meth·yl (meth′əl), *n.* a univalent hydrocarbon radical, CH_3. [< F, ult.< Gk. *methy* wine + *hyle* wood]

methyl alcohol, wood alcohol, CH_3OH; methanol.

me·tic·u·lous (mə tik′yə ləs), *adj.* extremely or excessively careful about small details. [< L *meticulosus* < *metus* fear] —**me·tic′u·lous·ly,** *adv.*

mé·tier (mā tyā′), *n.* trade; profession. [< F < L *ministerium.* Doublet of MINISTRY.]

me·ton·y·my (mə ton′ə mi), *n.* use of the name of one thing for that of another which it naturally suggests. *Example:* The pen (power of literature) is mightier than the sword (force). [< LL < Gk. *metonymia,* lit., change of name < *meta–* over + dial. *onyma name*] —**met′o·nym′ic, met′o·nym′i·cal,** *adj.*

me·tre (mē′tər), *n. Esp. Brit.* meter.

met·ric (met′rik), *adj.* 1 of the meter or the system of measurement based on it. 2 metrical.

met·ri·cal (met′rə kəl), *adj.* 1 of meter; having a regular arrangement of accents; written in verse, not in prose. 2 of, pertaining to, or used in measurement. —**met′ri·cal·ly,** *adv.*

met·ri·ca·tion (met′rə kā′shən), *n.* act or process of changing to a metric system.

metric system, a decimal system of measurement that uses the meter (39.37 in.) as its unit of length, the gram (.0022046 pound) as the unit of mass or weight, and the liter (61.024 cu. in. or 1 cubic decimeter) as the unit of volume.

metric ton, 1000 kilograms or 2204.62 avoirdupois pounds.

met·ro·nome (met′rə nōm), *n.* a clocklike device with a pendulum that can be adjusted to tick at different speeds. [< Gk. *metron* measure + *–nomos* regulating] —**met′ro·nom′ic,** *adj.*

me·trop·o·lis (mə trop′ə lis), *n.* 1 the most important city of a country or region: *New York is the metropolis of the United States.* 2 a large, important center: *Chicago is a busy metropolis.* 3 the chief diocese of a church province. [< LL < Gk., < *meter* mother + *polis* city]

met·ro·pol·i·tan (met′rə pol′ə tən), *adj.* of a large city; belonging to large cities: *metropolitan newspapers.* —*n.* 1 person who lives in a large city and knows its ways. 2 bishop who has authority over the bishops of a church province.

met·tle (met′əl), *n.* disposition; spirit; courage.

on one's mettle, ready to do one's best. [var. of *metal*] —**met′tled,** *adj.*

met·tle·some (met′əl səm), *adj.* full of mettle; spirited; courageous.

Mev or **mev** (mev), *n.* million electron volts.

mew¹ (mū), *n.* sound made by a cat; meow. —*v.* make this sound. [imit.]

mew² (mū), *n.* a sea gull; gull. [OE *mǣw*]

mewl (mūl), *v.* cry like a baby; whimper. [imit.]

mews (mūz), *n.* stables built around a court or alley.

Mex., 1 Mexican. 2 Mexico.

Mex·i·co (mek′sə kō), *n.* 1 country in North America, just S of W United States. 2 **Gulf of,** gulf of the Atlantic, S of the United States and E of Mexico. —**Mex′i·can,** *adj., n.*

Mexico City, capital of Mexico, in the C part.

me·zu·zah or **me·zu·za** (me zü′zä), *n., pl.* **–zahs, –za, –zoth** (–zōth). small box, tube, etc., with a parchment scroll inside, attached to the doorpost of an Orthodox Jewish home. [< Heb. *məzuzâ* doorpost]

mez·za·nine (mez′ə nēn), *n.* a low story between two higher stories of a building, usually one just above and extending only part way over the ground floor. [< F < Ital., < *mezzano* middle < L *medianus*]

mez·zo (met′sō; mez′ō), *adj.* middle as the range of a singer's voice or the loudness or softness of a passage; medium; half. [< Ital. < L *medius* middle]

mez·zo-so·pran·o (met′sō sə pran′ō; –prä′nō; mez′ō–), *n., pl.* **–pran·os.** 1 voice between soprano and contralto. 2 singer having such a voice.

mez·zo·tint (met′sō tint′; mez′ō–), *n.* 1 picture engraved on copper or steel by polishing and scraping away parts of a roughened surface. 2 this method of engraving pictures. —*v.* engrave by this method. [< Ital. *mezzotinto* half-tint]

MF, Middle French.

mf., somewhat loud. [< Ital. *mezzo forte*]

mfg., manufacturing.

mfr., pl. **mfrs.** manufacturer.

Mg, magnesium.

mg. or **mg,** milligram; milligrams.

Mgr., 1 Manager. 2 Monsignor.

MHG, Middle High German.

mho (mō), *n., pl.* **mhos.** unit of electrical conductance, equal to the conductance of a body through which one ampere flows. [< reversed spelling of *ohm,* unit of electrical resistance]

mi (mē), *n.* the third tone of the scale. [see GAMUT]

MI, (*zip code*) Michigan.

mi., 1 mile; miles. 2 mill; mills.

mi·as·ma (mī az′mə; mi–), *n., pl.* **–mas, –ma·ta** (–mə tə). harmful vapors arising from rotting organic matter. [< NL < Gk., pollution] **—mi·as′mal, mi′as·mat′ic, mi·as′mic,** *adj.*

mi·ca (mī′kə), *n.* mineral that divides into thin, partly transparent layers; isinglass. [< L, grain, crumb] **—mi·ca′ceous,** *adj.*

Mi·cah (mī′kə), *n.* book of the Old Testament.

mice (mīs), *n.* pl. of **mouse.**

Mich., 1 Michaelmas. 2 Michigan.

Mich·ael·mas (mik′əl məs), *n.* September 29, church festival in honor of the archangel Michael.

Mich·i·gan (mish′ə gən), *n.* a Middle Western state of the United States. **—Mich′i·gan′der, Mich′i·gan·ite,** *n.*

mick·le (mik′əl), *adj., adv., n. Archaic.* much. [OE *micel*]

Mic·mac (mik′mak), *n., pl.* **–mac** or **–macs.** member of an Algonkian Indian tribe of E Canada.

micro–, *combining form.* 1 small; very small, as in *microchip.* 2 one millionth of a ____, as in *microfarad.* 3 that makes much use of the microscope, as in *microbiology.* [< Gk., < *mikros* small]

mi·crobe (mī′krōb), *n.* 1 a microscopic organism, usually one of vegetable nature; germ. 2 bacterium, esp. one causing disease. [< F, < Gk. *mikros* small + *bios* life] **—mi·cro′bi·al, mi·cro′bic,** *adj.*

mi·cro·chip (mī′krō chip′), *n.* =microcircuit.

mi·cro·cir·cuit (mī′krō sėr′kit), *n.* miniaturized electronic circuit, used esp. in computers; integrated circuit. **—mi′cro·cir′cuit·ry,** *n.*

mi·cro·cosm (mī′krō koz əm), *n.* 1 a little world; universe in miniature. 2 man thought of as a miniature representation of the universe. [< F < LL < LGk. *mikros kosmos* little world] **—mi′cro·cos′mic, mi′cro·cos′mi·cal,** *adj.*

mi·cro·far·ad (mī′krō far′əd; –ad), *n.* unit of electrical capacity; one millionth of a farad.

mi·cro·fiche (mī′krə fēsh′), *n., pl.* **–fiches, –fiche** (–fēsh). plastic card or sheet containing microfilms of as many as 100 pages of a book. [< E *micro–* + F *fiche* card]

mi·cro·film (mī′krō film′), *n.* film preserving the contents of newspapers, records, etc., in very small space. —*v.* record on microfilm.

mi·cro·lith (mī′krə lith), *n.* tiny pointed blade, usually made from flint, used as arrow or tools during the Stone Age. [< E *micro–* + Gk. *líthos* stone] **—mi·cro·lith′ic,** *adj.*

mi·crom·e·ter (mī krom′ət ər), *n.* 1 instrument for measuring minute distances, angles, objects, etc., used with a microscope or telescope. 2 micrometer caliper.

micrometer caliper, caliper having a screw with a fine thread, used for very accurate measurement.

mi·cron (mī′kron), *n., pl.* **mi·crons, mi·cra** (mī′krə). one millionth of a meter. *Symbol:* μ [< NL < Gk., neut. adj., small]

Mi·cro·ne·sia (mī′krō nē′zhə; –shə), *n.* group of small islands in the Pacific, E of the Philippines. **—Mi′cro·ne′sian,** *adj., n.*

mi·cro·or·gan·ism (mī′krō ôr′gən iz əm), *n.* animal or vegetable organism too small to be seen except with a microscope, as bacteria.

mi·cro·phone (mī′krə fōn), *n.* instrument that changes sound waves into variations of an electric current.

mi·cro·pro·ces·sor (mī kro pros′əs ər), *n.* very small processing unit for a computer, made as an integrated circuit.

mi·cro·scope (mī′krə skōp), *n.* 1 instrument with a lens or combination of lenses for making small things look larger. 2 an electron microscope. [< NL *microscopium* < Gk. *mikros* small + *skopion* means of viewing < *skopein* look at]

mi·cro·scop·ic (mī′krə skop′ik), *adj.* 1 that cannot be seen without using a microscope; tiny. 2 like a microscope; suggesting a microscope: *a microscopic eye for mistakes.* 3 of a microscope; with a microscope. **—mi′cro·scop′i·cal·ly,** *adv.*

mi·cros·co·py (mī kros′kə pi; mī′krə skō′pi), *n.* use of a microscope; microscopic investigation.

mi·cro·sec·ond (mī′kro sek′ənd), *n.* unit of time equal to one millionth of a second.

mi·cro·spore (mī′krə spôr′; –spōr′), *n.* 1 very small spore of certain ferns, from which a male gametophyte develops. 2 pollen grain of seed plants.

mi·cro·sur·ger·y (mī′krō sėr′jər i), *n.* surgery performed on small or minute structures of the body, as blood vessels or nerves. **—mi′cro·sur′geon,** *n.* **—mi′cro·sur′gi·cal,** *adj.*

mi·cro·wave (mī′krō wāv′), *n.* 1 an electromagnetic wave, usually having a wave length less than thirty centimeters. 2 =microwave oven. —*v.* heat or cook in a microwave oven. **—mi′cro·wave′a·ble,** *adj.*

microwave oven, oven heated by microwaves.

mid (mid), *adj.* in the middle of; middle. [OE *midd*]

mid·air or **mid-air** (mid′ār′), *adj.* up in the air: *a midair collision was averted.* **in midair,** in doubt: *an answer left hanging in mid-air.*

mid-At·lan·tic or **Mid-At·lan·tic** (mid′at lan′tik), *adj.* of or having to do with the E states of New York, New Jersey, and Pennsylvania.

mid·brain (mid′brān′), *n.* the middle segment of the brain.

mid·chan·nel (mid′chan′əl), *n.* the middle part of a channel.

mid·con·ti·nent (mid′kon′tə nənt), *n.* the middle part of a continent.

mid·day (mid′dā′), *n.* middle of the day; noon. —*adj.* of midday.

mid·den (mid′ən), *n.* refuse heap, esp. one from prehistoric times that contains bones, tools, etc., as a record of life at that time. [< ME *mydyng,* appar. < Scand.]

mid·dle (mid′əl), *adj.* 1 halfway between; in the center; at the same distance from either end or side. 2 in between; medium: *a man of middle size.* 3 intermediate, esp. in time. 4 between old and modern: *Middle English.* —*n.* 1 point or part that is the same distance from each end or side or other limit; the central part. 2 the middle part of a person's body; waist. 3 something intermediate. [OE *middel*]

middle age, time of life between youth and old age; period from about 40 to about 55 years old. **—mid′dle-aged′,** *adj.*

Middle Ages, period of European history between ancient and modern times, from about A.D. 50 to about 1450.

Middle America, 1 American middle class, esp. as considered representative of American culture and values. 2 Middle West region of the U.S. **—Middle American.**

Middle Atlantic States or **Region,** E states of New York, New Jersey, and Pennsylvania.

mid·dle·brow (mid′əl brou′), *n. Informal.* person moderately interested in culture or intellectual pursuits, between a highbrow and a low-brow.

middle C, note on the first added line below the treble staff and the first above the bass staff.

middle class, people between the aristocracy or the very wealthy and the peasantry or working class.

middle ear, the tympanum.

Middle East, region from the E Mediterranean to India. The term has no exact geographical limits, but is usually taken to include the Near East. Also, **Mideast.**

Middle English, 1 period in the history of the English language between Old English and Modern English, lasting from about 1100 to about 1475. **2** language of this period.

Middle French, the French language from 1400–1600.

Middle High German, the High German language from 1100–1450.

Middle Low German, the Low German language from 1100–1450.

mid·dle·man (mid′əl man′), *n., pl.* **-men.** trader or merchant who buys goods from the producer and sells them to a retailer or directly to the consumer.

mid·dle·most (mid′əl mōst), *adj.* in the exact middle; nearest the middle; midmost.

mid·dle-of-the-road (mid′əl əv thə rōd′), *adj.* avoiding extremes, as in politics, editorial policy, etc. —**mid′dle-of-the-road′er,** *n.*

middle school, any school for the grades between elementary school and high school.

mid·dle·weight (mid′əl wāt′), *n.* boxer or wrestler who weighs more than 147 pounds and less than 160 pounds.

Middle West, part of the United States W of the Appalachian Mountains, E of the Rocky Mountains, and N of the Ohio River and the S boundaries of Missouri and Kansas. Also, **Midwest.** —**Middle Western.** —**Middle Westerner.**

mid·dling (mid′ling), *adj.* medium in size, quality, grade, etc. —*adv.* moderately; fairly. [< *middle*]

mid·dy (mid′i), *n., pl.* **-dies. 1** mid-shipman. **2** middy blouse.

middy blouse, a loose blouse like a sailor's with a collar that forms a broad flap at the back.

Mid·east (mid′ēst′), *n.* =Middle East.

midge (mij), *n.* a kind of very small insect; gnat. [OE *mycg*]

midg·et (mij′it), *n.* **1** a very small person; dwarf. **2** something very small of its kind. [< *midge*]

mid·i·ron (mid′ī′ərn), *n.* a golf club with a steel or iron head having a face of medium slope.

mid·land (mid′lənd), *n.* the middle part of a country; the interior. —*adj.* in or of the midland.

Mid·lands (mid′ləndz), *n. pl.* the C part of England; the midland counties.

mid·life (mid′līf′), *n.* =middle age. —*adj.* of or in middle age.

mid·most (mid′mōst), *adj.* in the exact middle; nearest the middle.

mid·night (mid′nīt′), *n.* twelve o'clock at night; the middle of the night. —*adj.* of or like midnight; late at night.

midnight sun, sun seen at midnight in the arctic and antarctic regions during summer.

mid·o·cean (mid′ō′shən), *n.* the middle of the ocean: *mid-ocean ridges of both the Atlantic and Pacific.*

mid·point (mid′point′), *n.* middle part of anything.

mid·rib (mid′rib′), *n.* the central vein of a leaf.

mid·riff (mid′rif), *n.* muscular wall separating the chest cavity from the abdomen; diaphragm. [OE *midhrif* < *midd* mid + *hrif* belly]

mid·sec·tion (mid′sek′shən), *n.* **1** middle part of anything. **2** =midriff.

mid·ship (mid′ship′), *adj.* in or of the middle of a ship.

mid·ship·man (mid′ship′mən), *n., pl.* **-men. 1** student at the U.S. Naval Academy at Annapolis. **2** formerly, a boy or young man who assisted the officers of a ship.

mid·ships (mid′ships′), *adv.* =amidships.

midst¹ (midst), *n.* middle.

in the midst of, in the middle of; among; surrounded by.

midst², 'midst (midst), *prep.* amidst; amid.

mid·stream (mid′strēm′), *n.* middle of a stream.

mid·sum·mer (mid′sum′ər), *n.* **1** middle of summer. **2** time around June 21. —*adj.* in the middle of summer.

mid·term (mid′tèrm′), *n.* **1** middle of a term of office, school, etc. **2** examination given students in the middle of a term. —*adj.* occurring or having to do with the midterm.

mid·way (mid′wā′), *adv., adj.* halfway; in the middle. —*n.* **1** middle way or course. **2** place for side shows and other amusements at a fair.

mid·week (mid′wēk′), *n.* the middle of the week. —*adj.* in the middle of the week.

Mid·west (mid′west′), *n.* =Middle West. —**Mid′west′ern,** *adj.* —**Mid′west′ern·er,** *n.*

mid·wife (mid′wīf′), *n., pl.* **-wives.** woman who helps women in childbirth. [OE *mid* with + *wif* woman]

mid·wife·ry (mid′wīf′ə ri; –wīf′ri), *n.* the helping of women in childbirth.

mid·win·ter (mid′win′tər), *n.* **1** middle of winter. **2** the time around December 21. —*adj.* in the middle of winter.

mid·year (mid′yir′), *adj.* happening in the middle of the year. —*n.* **midyears,** midyear examinations.

mien (mēn), *n.* manner of holding the head and body; way of acting and looking: *George Washington had the mien of a soldier.* [prob. < *demean;* infl. by F *mine* expression < Celtic]

miff (mif), —*n.* a peevish fit; petty quarrel. —*v.* **1** be offended; have a petty quarrel. **2** offend slightly.

might¹ (mīt), *v.* pt. of **may.** [OE *mihte*]

might² (mīt), *n.* great power; strength. [OE *miht*]

might·y (mīt′i), *adj.,* **might·i·er, might·i·est,** *adv.* —*adj.* **1** possessing, characterized by, or showing strength or power; powerful; strong: *a mighty ruler, mighty force.* **2** very great: *a mighty*

famine. —*adv.* very. —**might′i·ly,** *adv.* —**might′i·ness,** *n.*

mi·gnon·ette (min′yən et′), *n.* plant with long, pointed clusters of small, fragrant, greenish-white flowers. [< F]

mi·graine (mī′grān), *n.* a severe headache, usually on one side only; sick headache. [< F < LL < Gk. *hemikrania* < *hemi-* half + *kranion* skull]

mi·grant (mī′grənt), *n.* person, animal, bird, or plant that migrates. —*adj.* migrating.

mi·grate (mī′grāt), *v.,* **-grat·ed, -grat·ing. 1** move from one place to settle in another: *pioneers from New England migrated to all parts of the United States.* **2** go from one region to another with the change in the seasons: *most birds migrate to warmer countries in the winter.* [< L *migratus*]

mi·gra·tion (mī grā′shən), *n.* **1** a migrating. **2** number of people or animals migrating together. —**migra′tion·al,** *adj.*

mi·gra·to·ry (mī′grə tô′ri; –tō′–), *adj.* **1** migrating; that migrates. **2** of migration. **3** wandering.

mi·ka·do, Mi·ka·do (mə kä′dō), *n., pl.* **-dos.** title of the emperor of Japan. [< Jap., lit., exalted gate]

mike (mīk), *n.* =microphone.

mil (mil), *n.* unit of length, .001 of an inch, used in measuring the diameter of wires. [< L *mille* thousand]

mil., 1 military. **2** militia.

mi·la·dy (mi lā′di), *n., pl.* **-dies. 1** my lady. **2** an English lady.

milch (milch), *adj.* giving milk; kept for the milk it gives: *a milch cow.* [OE –*milce* milking < *mioluc* milk]

mild (mīld), *adj.* **1** gentle; kind: *a mild, inoffensive man.* **2** warm; temperate; moderate; not harsh or severe: *a mild climate.* **3** soft or sweet to the senses; not sharp, sour, bitter, or strong in taste: *mild cheese.* [OE *milde*] —**mild′ly,** *adv.* —**mild′ness,** *n.*

mil·dew (mil′dü; –dū), *n.* kind of fungus that appears on plants or on paper, clothes, leather, etc. —*v.* cover or become covered with mildew. [OE *mildēaw* honeydew] —**mil′dew·y,** *adj.*

mile (mīl), *n.* **1** unit of measure equal to 5280 feet (a statute mile). **2 geographical** or **nautical mile,** the length of one minute of a great circle of the earth, officially fixed at 6080.27 feet. **3 international nautical** or **air mile,** an official measure equal to 6076.097 feet. [< L *milia* (*passum*), pl. of *mille* (*passus*) a thousand (paces)]

mile·age (mīl′ij), *n.* **1** miles covered or traveled. **2** length, extent, or distance in miles. **3** allowance for traveling expenses at so much a mile.

mile·post (mīl′pōst′), *n.* post or stake marking miles to a place on the distance covered.

mil·er (mīl′ər), *n.* person or animal, esp. a horse, trained or competing in a mile-long race.

mile·stone (mīl′stōn′), *n.* **1** stone set up to show the distance in miles to a certain place. **2** *Fig.* an important event showing progress.

mi·lieu (mē lyœ′), *n.* surroundings; environment. [< F]

mil·i·tant (mil′ə tənt), *adj.* aggressive; fighting; warlike. —*n.* a militant person. [< L, serving as a soldier, ult. < *miles* soldier] —**mil′i·tan·cy,** *n.* —**mil′i·tant·ly,** *adv.*

mil·i·ta·rism (mil′ə tə riz′əm), *n.* **1** policy of making military organization and power very strong. **2** military spirit and ideals. —**mil′ta·rist,** *n.* —**mil′i·ta·ris′tic,** *adj.* —**mil′i·ta·ris′tical·ly,** *adv.*

mil·i·ta·rize (mil′ə tə rīz′), *v.,* **–rized, –riz·ing.** **1** make the military organization of (a country) very powerful. **2** fill with military spirit and ideals. —**mil′i·ta·ri·za′tion,** *n.*

mil·i·tar·y (mil′ə ter′i), *adj.* **1** of soldiers or war. **2** done by soldiers. **3** fit for soldiers. **4** suitable for war; warlike. **5** belonging to the army. —*n.* the army; soldiers. [< L, < *miles* soldier] —**mil′i·tar′i·ly,** *adv.*

military police, soldiers that act as police for the army.

mil·i·tate (mil′ə tāt), *v.,* **–tat·ed, –tat·ing.** act; work; operate (*against* or *in favor of*): *bad weather militated against the success of the picnic.*

mi·li·tia (mi lish′ə), *n.* army of citizens trained for war or any other emergency. [< L < *miles* soldier] —**mi·li′tia·man,** *n.*

milk (milk), *n.* **1** the white liquid secreted by female mammals for the nourishment of their young. **2** any kind of liquid resembling this: *the milk of a coconut.* —*v.* **1** draw milk from (a cow, goat, etc.). **2** yield or produce milk. **3** drain contents, strength, information, wealth, etc., from: *the dishonest treasurer milked the club treasury.* **4** draw sap or poison from: *milk a rattlesnake.* [OE *mioluc*] —**milk′er,** *n.*

milk chocolate, chocolate candy made from chocolate liquor, milk solids, and sugar.

milk·maid (milk′mād′), *n.* **1** woman who milks cows. **2** woman who works in a dairy.

milk·man (milk′man′), *n., pl.* **–men.** person who sells or delivers milk.

milk of magnesia, a milky, white medicine, Mg(OH)$_2$ in water, used as a laxative and antacid.

milk run, routine trip, esp. a flight on a plane.

milk shake, drink made of milk, flavoring, and usually ice cream, beaten together to a smooth, foamy mixture.

milk snake, a small, harmless, gray snake.

milk·sop (milk′sop′), *n.* an unmanly fellow; coward. —**milk′sop′ism,** *n.*

milk sugar, =lactose.

milk tooth, one of the first set of teeth; temporary tooth of a young child or animal.

milk·weed (milk′wēd′), *n.* weed with white juice that looks like milk.

milk·y (mil′ki), *adj.,* **milk·i·er, milk·i·est.** **1** like milk; white as milk; whitish. **2** of milk; containing milk. —**milk′i·ness,** *n.*

Milky Way, 1 a broad band of faint light that stretches across the sky at night. It is made up of countless stars, too far away to be seen separately without a telescope. **2** the galaxy in which these countless stars are found, and which includes the earth, sun, and the planets around the sun.

mill¹ (mil), *n.* **1** machine for grinding grain into meal. **2** building containing such a machine. **3** any machine for crushing or grinding: *a coffee mill.* **4** machine for stamping, pressing, cutting, polishing, etc. **5** building where manufacturing is done. —*v.* **1** grind (grain) into flour or meal. **2** grind into powder or pulp. **3** manufacture. **4** move around in confusion: *the frightened cattle began to mill.* **5** cut fine notches on the edge of (a coin).

go through the mill, *Informal.* **a** undergo thorough training or experience. **b** learn from experience, esp. hard or painful experience.

put through the mill, *Informal.* **a** test; try out. **b** teach by painful experience. [< LL *molinum* < L *mola* millstone]

mill² (mil), *n.* \$.001, or ¹⁄₁₀ of a cent. Mills are used in figuring, but not as coins. [short for L *millesimum* one thousandth < *mille* thousand]

mill·dam (mil′dam′), *n.* **1** dam built in a stream to supply water power for a mill. **2** =millpond.

mil·len·ni·um (mə len′i əm), *n., pl.* **–ni·ums,** **–ni·a** (–ni ə). **1** period of a thousand years. **2** the period of a thousand years during which Christ is expected to reign on earth. Rev. 20:1–7. **3** period of righteousness and happiness. [< NL, < L *mille* thousand + *annus* year] —**mil·len′ni·al,** *adj.*

mil·le·pede (mil′ə pēd′), *n.* =millipede.

mill·er (mil′ər), *n.* **1** one who owns or runs a mill, esp. a flour mill. **2** moth whose wings look as if they were powdered with flour.

mil·let (mil′it), *n.* **1** a very small grain used for food in Asia and Africa. **2** the plant that it grows on, often used for hay. [< F, ult. < L *milium*]

milli–, *combining form.* one thousandth of a ____, as in *millimeter.* [< L, < *mille*]

mil·li·am·pere (mil′i am′pir), *n.* one thousandth of an ampere.

mil·liard (mil′yərd; –yärd), *n.* thousand millions; 1,000,000,000. [< F, < L *mille* thousand]

mil·li·gram (mil′ə gram), *n.* one thousandth of a gram.

mil·li·li·ter (mil′ə lē′tər), *n.* one thousandth of a liter.

mil·li·me·ter (mil′ə mē′tər), *n.* one thousandth of a meter, or .03937 inch.

mil·li·mi·cron (mil′ə mī′kron), *n., pl.* **–cra** (–krə). the thousandth part of a micron.

mil·li·ner (mil′ə nər), *n.* person who makes, trims, or sells women's hats. [var. of *Milaner,* dealer in goods from Milan, Italy, famous for straw]

mil·li·ner·y (mil′ə ner′i; –nər i), *n.* **1** women's hats. **2** business of making, trimming, or selling women's hats.

mill·ing (mil′ing), *n.* **1** business of grinding grain in a mill. **2** manufacturing. **3** cutting ridges on the edge of a coin. **4** the ridges on the edge of a coin.

mil·lion (mil′yən), *n.* **1** one thousand thousand; 1,000,000. **2** a very large number. —*adj.* **1** one thousand thousand; 1,000,000. **2** very many. [< OF < Ital. *milione,* ult. < L *mille* thousand] —**mil′lionth,** *adj., n.*

mil·lion·aire (mil′yən ār′), *n.* **1** person who has a million or more dollars, pounds, francs, etc. **2** very wealthy person.

mil·li·pede (mil′ə pēd), *n.* small, wormlike arthropod that has two pairs of legs for most of its segments. Also, **milliped, millepede.** [< L *millepeda* < *mille* thousand + *pēs, pedis* foot]

mill·pond (mil′pond′), *n.* pond supplying water to drive a mill wheel, esp. one formed by a milldam.

mill·race (mil′rās′), *n.* **1** current of water that drives a mill wheel. **2** channel in which it flows to the mill.

mill·stone (mil′stōn′), *n.* **1** either of a pair of round flat stones for grinding corn, wheat, etc. **2** a heavy burden.

mill·stream (mil′strēm′), *n.* the stream in a millrace.

mill wheel, wheel that supplies power for a mill.

mill·work (mil′wėrk′), *n.* **1** doors, windows, moldings, and other things made in a planing mill. **2** work done in a mill.

mill·wright (mil′rīt′), *n.* **1** person who designs, builds, or sets up mills or machinery for mills. **2** mechanic who sets up and takes care of the machinery in a factory, workshop, etc.

mi·lord (mi lôrd′), *n.* **1** my lord. **2** an English gentleman.

milque·toast (milk′tōst′), *n.* an extremely timorous person. [after comic-strip character, Mr. *Milquetoast*]

milt (milt), *n.* **1** the sperm cells of male fishes with the milky fluid containing them. **2** the reproductive gland in male fishes. [OE *milte*]

Mil·ton·ic (mil ton′ik), *adj.* of or having to do with John Milton (1808–74), English poet. **2** like Milton's literary style; solemn; majestic. Also, **Miltonian.**

mime (mīm), *n., v.,* **mimed, mim·ing.** —*n.* jester; clown. —*v.* imitate; mimic. [< L < Gk. *mimos*] —**mim′er,** *n.*

mi·met·ic (mi met′ik; mī–), *adj.* **1** imitative. **2** make-believe. **3** exhibiting mimicry.

[< Gk. *mimetikos* < *mimeesthai* imitate] —**mi·met′ical·ly,** *adv.*

mim·ic (mim′ik), *v.,* **-icked, -ick·ing,** *n.,* *adj.* —*v.* **1** make fun of by imitating. **2** copy closely; imitate: *a parrot can mimic a person's voice.* **3** resemble closely: *some insects mimic leaves.* —*n.* person or thing that imitates. —*adj.* not real, but imitated or pretended for some purpose. [< L < Gk. *mimikos.* See MIME.]

mim·ic·ry (mim′ik ri), *n., pl.* **-ries. 1** a mimicking. **2 protective mimicry,** close resemblance of an animal to its surroundings or to some other animal.

mi·mo·sa (mi mō′sə; –zə), *n.* tree, shrub, or plant growing in warm regions, and usually having fernlike leaves, and heads or spikes of small flowers. [< NL, < L *mimus* MIME; from mimicry of animal reactions]

min., 1 minimum. **2** minute; minutes.

min·a·ret (min′ə ret′; min′ə ret), *n.* a slender, high tower of a Muslim mosque with one or more projecting balconies, from which a crier calls the people to prayer. [< F or Sp. < Ar. *manārat* lighthouse]

mince (mins), *v.,* **minced, minc·ing,** *n.* —*v.* **1** chop up into very small pieces. **2** speak or do in an affectedly polite or elegant manner. **3** walk wth little short steps. —*n.* =mincemeat.

not to mince matters, speak plainly and frankly. [< OF *mincier,* ult. < L *minutus* small] —**minc′er,** *n.*

mince·meat (mins′mēt′), *n.* mixture of chopped meat, apples, suet, raisins, spices, etc., used as a filling for pies.

make mincemeat of, totally overcome; reduce, as if cut into pieces.

minc·ing (min′sing), *adj.* **1** too polite; too nice. **2** walking with little short steps. —**minc′ing·ly,** *adv.*

mind (mīnd), *n.* **1** that which thinks, feels, and wills; intellect; reason: *be out of one's mind, change one's mind, have a mind to do something.* **2** what one thinks or feels; opinions; sentiments: *speak your mind.* —*v.* **1** remember: *keep safety in mind.* **2** attend to; give heed to: *mind my words! mind the baby.* **3** obey: *mind your father and mother.* **4** feel concern about; object to: *mind parting from a friend.*

bear or **keep in mind,** remember.

be of one mind, have the same opinion.

blow one's mind, *Informal.* shock or greatly surprise.

cross one's mind, occur to one; think of.

have in mind, a remember. **b** think of; consider. **c** intend; plan.

make up one's mind, decide.

put in mind, remind.

set one's mind on, want very much. [OE *gemynd*] —**mind′er,** *n.*

mind-blow·ing (mīnd′blō′ing), *adj. Informal.* **1** very shocking; extremely surprising. **2** causing hallucinations.

mind-bog·gling (mīnd′bog′ling), *adj.* overwhelming; jarring.

mind·ful (mīnd′fəl), *adj.* **1** having in mind: *mindful of the advice.* **2** taking thought; careful: *mindful of every step.* —**mind′ful·ly,** *adv.* —**mind′ful·ness,** *n.*

mind·less (mīnd′lis), *adj.* **1** without intelligence; stupid. **2** not taking thought; careless. —**mind′less·ly,** *adv.*

mind reader, person able to guess the thoughts of others.

mind·set or **mind-set** (mīnd′set′), *n.* way of thinking or feeling; attitude.

mind's eye, mental view; imagination.

mine[1] (mīn), *pron.* the one or ones belonging to me: *your shoes are black; mine are brown.* [OE *mīn*]

mine[2] (mīn), *n., v.,* **mined, min·ing.** —*n.* **1** a large hole or space dug in the earth to get out something valuable. **2** *Fig.* rich or plentiful source: *a dictionary is a mine of information.* **3** container holding an explosive charge that is put under water or shallowly buried. —*v.* **1** dig a mine; make a hole, space, passage, etc., below the earth. **2** dig into (the earth, a hill, etc.) for coal, ore, etc. **3** get (metal, etc.) from a mine. **4** dig in; make (passages, etc.) by digging. **5** lay explosive mines. [< F < Celtic]

mine field, area throughout which explosive mines have been laid.

min·er (mīn′ər), *n.* **1** worker in a mine. **2** machine used to mine.

min·er·al (min′ər əl; min′rəl), *n.* **1** substance obtained by mining. Coal is a mineral. **2** any substance that is neither plant nor animal. —*adj.* containing minerals: *mineral water.* [< OF, ult. < mine MINE[2]]

mineral., mineralogy.

min·er·al·ize (min′ər əl īz; min′rəl–), *v.,* **-ized, -iz·ing.** convert into mineral substance; transform (metal) into an ore. —**min′er·al·i·za′tion,** *n.* —**min′er·al·iz′er,** *n.*

min·er·al·o·gy (min′ər al′ə ji; –ol′ə–), *n.* science of minerals. —**min′er·a·log′i·cal,** *adj.* —**min′er·a·log′i·cal·ly,** *adv.* —**min′er·al′o·gist,** *n.*

mineral oil, 1 oil obtained from the earth. Kerosene is a mineral oil. **2** a colorless, odorless, tasteless oil obtained from petroleum.

mineral water, water containing mineral salts or gases.

min·e·stro·ne (min′ə strō′ni), *n.* a thick soup containing vegetables, vermicelli, etc. [< Ital.]

mine sweeper, ship used for dragging a harbor, the sea, etc., to remove mines laid by an enemy.

min·gle (ming′gəl), *v.,* **-gled, -gling. 1** mix: *two rivers that join mingle their waters.* **2** associate: *mingle with important people.* [ME *mengele(n)* < OE *mengan* mix] —**min′gler,** *n.*

min·i (min′i), *n., pl.* **min·is.** anything smaller than the usual size: *drive a mini.*

—*adj.* smaller than ordinary; miniature: *a hand-held mini computer.*

min·i·a·ture (min′i ə chər; min′ə chər), *n.* **1** anything represented on a small scale: *a miniature of the ship Mayflower.* **2** a very small painting, usually a portrait. —*adj.* done or made on a very small scale; tiny.

in miniature, on a small scale; reduced in size. [< Ital. *miniatura* < Med.L *miniare* illuminate (a manuscript) < L, paint red, < *minium* red lead; confused with L *minutus* small] —**min′i·a·tur·ist,** *n.*

min·i·bike (min′i bīk′), *n.* small motorcycle.

min·i·cam (min′i kam′), *n.* miniature camera.

min·im (min′əm), *n.* **1** the smallest liquid measure, one sixtieth of a dram, or about a drop. **2** a half note in music. **3** a very small amount. [< L *minimus* smallest]

min·i·mal (min′ə məl), *adj.* least possible; at or of a minimum: *minimal help.*

min·i·mize (min′ə mīz), *v.,* **-mized, -miz·ing. 1** reduce to the least possible amount or degree: *minimize the effects of inflation.* **2** state at the lowest possible estimate; make the least of: *minimize the help others have given.* —**min′i·mi·za′tion,** *n.* —**min′i·miz′er,** *n.*

min·i·mum (min′ə məm), *n., pl.* **-mums, -ma** (–mə), *adj.* —*n.* the least possible amount; lowest amount: *eight hours' sleep is the minimum that children should have.* —*adj.* **1** least possible: *minimum age for voting.* **2** lowest: *minimum rate.* [< L, smallest (thing)] —**min′i·mal,** *adj.*

minimum wage, wage agreed upon or fixed by law as the lowest payable to certain employees.

min·ing (mīn′ing), *n.* **1** working mines for ores, coal, etc. **2** business or work of digging coal or ores from mines.

min·ion (min′yən), *n.* servant or follower willing to do whatever he or she is ordered. [< F *mignon* petite, dainty]

min·i·se·ries (min′i sir′ēz), *n., pl.* **-ries.** serial program, esp. for television, having fewer episodes than programs that run for a season.

min·is·ter (min′is tər), *n.* **1** clergyman serving a church; spiritual guide; pastor. **2** person who is given charge of a department of the government: *the Minister of War.* **3** person sent to a foreign country to represent his or her own government: *the United States Minister to France.* —*v.* **1** act as a servant or nurse; be of service: *she ministers to the sick man's wants.* **2** be helpful; give aid; contribute. [< L, servant < *minus* less, after *magister* MASTER]

min·is·te·ri·al (min′is tir′i əl), *adj.* **1** of a minister. **2** of the ministry. **3** suitable for a clergyman. —**min′is·te′ri·al·ly,** *adv.*

min·is·trant (min′is trənt), *adj.* ministering. —*n.* one who ministers.

min·is·tra·tion (min´is trā´shən), *n.* **1** service as a minister of a church. **2** help; aid.

min·is·try (min´is tri), *n., pl.* **-tries. 1** office, duties, or time of service of a minister. **2** ministers of a church. **3** ministers of a government. **4** a government department under a minister. **5** a ministering or serving. [< L *ministerium* office, service; see MINISTER. Doublet of MÉTIER.]

mink (mingk), *n.* **1** a weasellike animal that lives in water part of the time. **2** its valuable brown fur. [appar. Scand. (Sw.) *mänk*]

Minn., Minnesota.

min·ne·sing·er (min´ə sing´ər), *n.* a German lyrical poet and singer of the 12th, 13th, and 14th centuries. [< G, love singer]

Min·ne·so·ta (min´ə sō´tə), *n.* a Middle Western state of the United States. **—Min´ne·so´tan,** *adj., n.*

min·now (min´ō), *n.* **1** a very small freshwater fish. **2** any very tiny fish. [ME *minwe,* OE *myne*]

Mi·no·an (mi nō´ən), *adj.* of or having to do with the ancient civilization of Crete (about 3500–1400 B.C.). **—n.** native or inhabitant of Minoan Crete.

mi·nor (mī´nər), *adj.* **1** smaller; lesser; less important: *a minor fault, a minor poet.* **2** under legal age. **3 a** less by a half step than the corresponding major interval. **b** denoting a scale, mode, or key whose third tone is minor in relation to the fundamental tone. **—n. 1** person under the legal age of responsibility. **2** subject a student gives less time and attention to than a major subject. [< L, lesser]

mi·nor·i·ty (mə nôr´ə ti; mī–; –nor´–), *n., pl.* **-ties,** *adj.* **—n. 1** smaller number or part; less than half. **2** member of a group that is a minority of the population or is treated as a minority: *Latin Americans, women, and other minorities.* **3** condition or time of being under the legal age of responsibility. **—adj.** of or pertaining to a minority.

minor key, musical key or mode based on the minor scale.

minor league, any professional sports league or association, esp. in baseball, other than the major leagues.

minor scale, musical scale of eight notes with whole steps after the second and fifth notes.

min·ster (min´stər), *n. Esp. Brit.* **1** church of a monastery. **2** a large or important church; cathedral. [< LL *monasterium.* Doublet of MONASTERY.]

min·strel (min´strəl), *n.* **1** singer or musician in the household of a lord in the Middle Ages. **2** singer or musician who went about and sang or recited poems, often of his own making. [< OF < LL *ministerialis* < L *ministerium* MINISTRY]

minstrel show, popular entertainment of esp. the 1800s that included singing, dancing, humorous sketches, etc., done by performers in blackface.

min·strel·sy (min´strəl si), *n., pl.* **-sies.** art or practice of a minstrel.

mint[1] (mint), *n.* **1** a sweet-smelling plant used for flavoring. **2** piece of candy flavored with mint. [< L *menta,* akin to Gk. *minthe*]

mint[2] (mint), *n.* **1** place where money is coined by public authority. **2** a large amount: *a million dollars is a mint of money.* **—v. 1** coin (money). **2** make or fabricate; originate. [< L *moneta* mint, money. Doublet of MONEY.] **—mint´er,** *n.*

min·u·end (min´yü end), *n.* number or quantity from which another is to be subtracted. In 100 − 23 = 77, the minuend is 100. [< L *minuendus* to be made smaller < *minus* less]

min·u·et (min´yü et´), *n.* **1** a slow, stately dance. **2** music for it. [< F *menuet,* dim. of *menu* small]

mi·nus (mī´nəs), *prep.* **1** less; decreased by: *5 minus 2 leaves 3.* **2** lacking: *a book minus its cover.* **—adj. 1** less than: *a mark of B minus is not so high as B.* **2** showing subtraction: *the minus sign is −.* **3** less than zero: *if you have no money, and owe someone 3 cents, you have − 3¢.* **—n. 1** Also, **minus sign.** sign (−) meaning that the quantity following it is to be subtracted. **2** minus quantity. **3** deficiency or loss. [< L, less]

min·ute[1] (min´it), *n.* **1** sixty seconds; one sixtieth of an hour. **2** short time; instant: *that'll be over in a minute, come here this minute.* **3** one sixtieth of a degree. 10°10´ means ten degrees and ten minutes.

minutes, a written summary of a conversation, meeting, etc. **b** official record of proceedings of a society, board, committee, etc.

up to the minute, up-to-date. [< OF < LL *minuta* small part. See MINUTE[2].]

mi·nute[2] (mī nüt´; –nūt´; mə–), *adj.* **1** very small: *microscopes are used to study minute organisms.* **2** going into or concerned with very small details: *minute instructions.* [< L *minutus* made small < *minus* less. Doublet of MENU.] **—mi·nute´ly,** *adv.* **—mi·nute´ness,** *n.*

min·ute hand (min´it), hand on a clock or watch that indicates minutes. It moves around the whole dial once in an hour.

min·ute·man (min´it man´), *n., pl.* **-men.** member of the American militia just before and during the Revolution, who were ready for military service at very short notice.

mi·nu·ti·ae (mi nü´shi ē; –nū´–), *n. pl.* very small matters; trifling details. [< L, smallness. See MINUTE[2].]

minx (mingks), *n.* a pert girl.

mir·a·cle (mir´ə kəl), *n.* **1** a wonderful happening that is contrary to or independent of the known laws of nature: *it would be a miracle if the sun should stand still in the heavens for an hour.* **2** something marvelous; a wonder. **3** remarkable example: *a miracle of patience.* [< OF < L *miraculum,* ult. < *mirus* wonderful]

mi·rac·u·lous (mə rak´yə ləs), *adj.* **1** contrary to or independent of the known laws of nature. **2** wonderful; marvelous. **—mi·rac´u·lous·ly,** *adv.* **—mi·rac´u·lous·ness,** *n.*

mi·rage (mə räzh´), *n.* **1** a misleading appearance, usually in the desert or at sea, resulting from a reflection of some distant scene in such a way as to give the impression that it is near. **2** illusion. [< F, < *mirer* look at. See MIRROR.]

mire (mīr), *n., v.,* **mired, mir·ing. —n. 1** soft deep mud; slush. **2** bog; swamp. **—v. 1** get stuck in mire. **2** soil with mud or mire. **3** involve in difficulties. [< Scand. *mȳrr*]

mir·ror (mir´ər), *n.* **1** a looking glass; surface that reflects light. **2** *Fig.* whatever reflects or gives a true description: *that book is a mirror of the times.* **—v.** reflect as a mirror does: *the still water mirrored the trees along the bank.* [< OF *mirour,* ult. < L *mirari* wonder, admire]

mirror image, a reverse image; reflection.

mirror writing, writing in reverse, as if reflected in a mirror.

mirth (mèrth), *n.* merry fun; being joyous; laughter. [OE *myrgth* < *myrge* merry] **—mirth´less,** *adj.* **—mirth´less·ly,** *adv.* **—mirth´less·ness,** *n.*

mirth·ful (mèrth´fəl), *adj.* merry; laughing. **—mirth´ful·ly,** *adv.* **—mirth´ful·ness,** *n.*

mir·y (mīr´i), *adj.,* **mir·i·er, mir·i·est. 1** muddy; swampy. **2** dirty; filthy. **—mir´i·ness,** *n.*

mis–, *prefix.* **1** bad, as in *misformation, misgovernment.* **2** badly, as in *misform, mismade, mismake.* **3** wrong, as in *mispronunciation, misvaluation.* **4** wrongly, as in *misclassify, mislabel.* [OE *mis(s)–,* or in borrowed words < OF *mes–* < OHG *missi–, missa–*]

mis·ad·ven·ture (mis´əd ven´chər), *n.* an unfortunate accident; bad luck; mishap.

mis·al·li·ance (mis´ə lī´əns), *n.* an unsuitable alliance or association, esp. in marriage.

mis·an·thrope (mis´ən thrōp; miz´–), *n.* hater of humankind; person who dislikes or distrusts human beings. [< Gk., < *mis-sein* hate + *anthropos* man] **—mis´an·throp´ic,** *adj.* **—mis´anthrop´i·cal·ly,** *adv.*

mis·an·thro·py (mis an´thrə pi), *n.* hatred, dislike, or distrust of human beings.

mis·ap·ply (mis´ə plī´), *v.,* **-plied, -ply·ing.** apply wrongly; make a wrong application or use of. **—mis´ap·pli·ca´tion,** *n.*

mis·ap·pre·hend (mis´ap ri hend´), *v.* misunderstand. **—mis´ap·pre·hen´sion,** *n.*

mis·ap·pro·pri·ate (mis´ə prō´pri āt), *v.,* **-at·ed, -at·ing. 1** put to a wrong use. **2** use dishonestly as one's own. **—mis´ap·pro´pri·a´tion,** *n.*

mis·be·got·ten (mis′bi got′ən), *adj.* begotten unlawfully; illegitimate.

mis·be·have (mis′bi hāv′), *v.*, **–haved, –hav·ing.** behave badly. —**mis′be·hav′ior,** *n.*

misc., miscellaneous; miscellany.

mis·cal·cu·late (mis kal′kyə lāt), *v.*, **–lat·ed, –lat·ing.** calculate wrongly. —**mis′cal·cu·la′tion,** *n.*

mis·call (mis kôl′), *v.* call by a wrong name.

mis·car·riage (mis kar′ij), *n.* **1** failure: *a miscarriage of justice.* **2** birth of a baby before it is able to live.

mis·car·ry (mis kar′i), *v.*, **–ried, –ry·ing. 1** go wrong: *John's plans miscarried, and he could not come.* **2** have a miscarriage.

mis·ce·ge·na·tion (mis′ə jə nā′shən), *n.* an interbreeding between different races. [< L *miscere* mix + *genus* race]

mis·cel·la·ne·ous (mis′ə lā′ni əs), *adj.* not all of one kind or nature: *a miscellaneous collection containing stones, stamps, birds' nests, and other things.* [< L, < *miscellus* mixed, ult. < *miscere* mix] —**mis′cel·la′ne·ous·ly,** *adv.* —**mis′cel·la′ne·ous·ness,** *n.*

mis·cel·la·ny (mis′ə lā′ni), *n., pl.* **–nies. 1** a miscellaneous collection; mixture. **2 miscellanies,** collection of miscellaneous articles in one book.

mis·chance (mis chans′; –chäns′), *n.* misfortune; bad luck.

mis·chief (mis′chif), *n.* **1** injury, usually done by some person; harm. **2** conduct that causes harm or trouble, often without meaning it. **3** one who does harm, often just in fun. **4** merry teasing: *eyes full of mischief.* [< OF *meschief,* ult. < *mes–* bad (see MIS–) + *chever* come to an end < *chief* head < L *caput*]

mis·chie·vous (mis′chə vəs), *adj.* **1** harmful: *a mischievous belief.* **2** full of mischief; naughty. **3** full of pranks and teasing fun. —**mis′chie·vous·ly,** *adv.* —**mis′chie·vous·ness,** *n.*

mis·ci·ble (mis′ə bəl), *adj.* capable of being mixed. [< L *miscere* mix] —**mis′ci·bil′i·ty,** *n.*

mis·con·ceive (mis′kən sēv′), *v.*, **–ceived, –ceiv·ing.** have wrong ideas about; misunderstand. —**mis′con·ceiv′er,** *n.* —**mis′con·cep′tion,** *n.*

mis·con·duct (*n.* mis kon′dukt; *v.* mis′kən dukt′), *n.* **1** bad behavior. **2** bad management: *misconduct of the business resulted in a loss.* —*v.* **1** behave badly. **2** manage badly.

mis·con·strue (mis′kən strü′), *v.*, **–strued, –stru·ing.** take in a wrong sense; misunderstand. —**mis′con·struc′tion,** *n.*

mis·count (*v.* mis kount′; *n.* mis′kount), *v.* count wrongly. —*n.* wrong count.

mis·cre·ant (mis′kri ənt), *adj.* having very bad morals; base. —*n.* villain. [< OF, < *mes–* wrongly (see MIS–) + *creant,* ppr. of *creire* believe < L *credere*]

mis·cue (mis kū′), *Fig.* error; mistake. [< shot in billiards or pool where the cue slips]

mis·deal (*v.* mis dēl′; *n.* mis′dēl′), *v.*, **–dealt** (–delt′), **–deal·ing,** *n.* —*v.* deal wrongly, esp. at cards. —*n.* a wrong deal. —**mis·deal′er,** *n.*

mis·deed (mis dēd′; mis′dēd′), *n.* a bad act; wicked deed.

mis·de·mean·or (mis′di mēn′ər), *n.* **1** a breaking of the law, not so serious as a felony. Disturbing the peace and breaking traffic laws are misdemeanors. **2** bad behavior: *all were punished for the misdemeanor of a few.*

mis·di·rect (mis′də rekt′; –dī–), *v.* direct wrongly. —**mis′di·rec′tion,** *n.*

mis·do (mis dü′), *v.*, **–did, –done, –do·ing.** do wrongly. —**mis·do′er,** *n.*

mis·em·ploy (mis′em ploi′), *v.* use wrongly or improperly. —**mis′em·ploy′ment,** *n.*

mi·ser (mī′zər), *n.* person who loves money for its own sake; one who lives poorly in order to save money and keep it. [< L, wretched]

mis·er·a·ble (miz′ər ə bəl; miz′rə bəl), *adj.* **1** wretchedly unhappy: *a sick child is often miserable.* **2** causing trouble or unhappiness: *a miserable cold.* **3** poor; mean; wretched: *they live in miserable surroundings.* —*n.* a miserable person; one who is in misery. —**mis′er·a·ble·ness,** *n.* —**mis′er·a·bly,** *adv.*

mi·ser·ly (mī′zər li), *adj.* of, like, or suited to a miser; stingy. —**mi′ser·li·ness,** *n.*

mis·er·y (miz′ər i; miz′ri), *n., pl.* **–er·ies. 1** a miserable, unhappy state of mind: *the misery of having no home or friends.* **2** poor, mean, miserable circumstances: *the misery of poverty.* [< L *miseria* < *miser* wretched]

mis·fire (mis fīr′), *v.*, **–fired, –fir·ing,** *n.* —*v.* **1** fail to be fired or exploded properly. **2** fail: *the joke misfired.* —*n.* instance of misfiring.

mis·fit (*v.* mis fit′; *n.* mis′fit′), *v.*, **–fit·ted, –fit·ting,** *n.* —*v.* fit badly. —*n.* **1** a bad fit. **2** a maladjusted individual.

mis·for·tune (mis fôr′chən), *n.* **1** bad luck. **2** piece of bad luck; unlucky accident.

mis·give (mis giv′), *v.*, **–gave, –giv·en, –giv·ing.** cause to feel doubt, suspicion, or anxiety.

mis·giv·ing (mis giv′ing), *n.* a feeling of doubt, suspicion, or anxiety: *have misgivings about their safety.*

mis·gov·ern (mis guv′ərn), *v.* govern or manage badly. —**mis·gov′ern·ment,** *n.*

mis·guide (mis gīd′), *v.*, **–guid·ed, –guid·ing.** lead into mistakes or wrongdoing; mislead. —**mis·guid′ance,** *n.* —**mis·guid′ed,** *adj.* —**mis·guid′ed·ly,** *adv.* —**mis·guid′er,** *n.*

mis·han·dle (mis han′dəl), *v.*, **–dled, –dling.** handle badly; maltreat.

mis·hap (mis′hap; mis hap′), *n.* an unlucky accident.

mish·mash (mish′mash′), *n.* confused jumble; hodgepodge. [prob. imit. reduplication of *mash*]

mis·in·form (mis′in fôrm′), *v.* **1** give wrong or misleading information to. **2** make a false statement about. —**mis′in·for·ma′tion,** *n.*

mis·in·ter·pret (mis′in tėr′prit), *v.* interpret wrongly; explain wrongly; misunderstand. —**mis′in·ter′pre·ta′tion,** *n.*

mis·judge (mis juj′), *v.*, **–judged, –judg·ing.** judge wrongly or unjustly. —**mis·judg′ment,** *n.*

mis·lay (mis lā′), *v.*, **–laid, –lay·ing. 1** put in the wrong place. **2** put in a place and then forget where it is: *mislay a sweater.* —**mis·lay′er,** *n.*

mis·lead (mis lēd′), *v.*, **–led, –lead·ing. 1** lead astray; cause to go in the wrong direction: *the sign misled the traveler.* **2** cause to do wrong; lead into wrongdoing: *he was misled by his companions.* **3** lead to think what is not so; deceive: *his lies misled me.* —**mis·lead′ing,** *adj.* —**mis·lead′ing·ly,** *adv.*

mis·man·age (mis man′ij), *v.*, **–aged, –ag·ing.** manage badly. —**mis·man′age·ment,** *n.* —**mis·man′ag·er,** *n.*

mis·match (mis mach′), *v.* match badly or unsuitably. —*n.* a bad or unsuitable match, esp. of people.

mis·name (mis nām′), *v.*, **–named, –nam·ing.** call by a wrong name.

mis·no·mer (mis nō′mər), *n.* **1** name that describes wrongly. **2** error in naming. [< OF, < *mes–* wrongly (see MIS–) + *nommer* to name < L *nominare.* See NOMINATE.]

mi·sog·a·my (mi sog′ə mi), *n.* hatred of marriage. [< NL, ult. < Gk. *misos* hatred + *gamos* marriage] —**mi·sog′a·mist,** *n.*

mi·sog·y·ny (mi soj′ə ni), *n.* hatred of women. [< NL, ult. < Gk. *misos* hatred + *gyne* woman] —**mi·sog′y·nist,** *n.* —**mi·sog′y·nous,** *adj.*

mis·place (mis plās′), *v.*, **–placed, –plac·ing. 1** put in the wrong place. **2** put in a place and then forget where it is. **3** give (one's love or trust) to the wrong person. —**mis·place′ment,** *n.*

mis·play (mis plā′), *n.* a wrong play. —*v.* play wrongly.

mis·print (*n.* mis′print′; *v.* mis print′), *n.* mistake in printing. —*v.* print wrongly.

mis·pri·sion (mis prizh′ən), *n.* **1** a wrongful action or omission, esp. by a public official. **2** neglect to give notice of an act of treason or felony. [< OF, ult. < *mes–* wrongly (see MIS–) + *prendre* take < L *prehendere*]

mis·pro·nounce (mis′prə nouns′), *v.*, **–nounced, –nounc·ing.** pronounce incorrectly. —**mis′pro·nun′ci·a′tion,** *n.*

mis·quote (mis kwōt′), *v.*, **–quot·ed, –quot·ing.** quote incorrectly. —**mis′quo·ta′tion,** *n.*

mis·read (mis rēd′), *v.*, **–read** (–red′), **–read·ing. 1** read wrongly: *misread a sentence.* **2** misunderstand; interpret wrongly: *misread directions and get lost.*

mis·rep·re·sent (mis′rep ri zent′), *v.* represent falsely; give a wrong idea of. —**mis′rep·re·sen·ta′tion,** *n.* —**mis′rep·re·sent′er,** *n.*

mis·rule (mis rül′), *n.*, *v.*, **-ruled, -rul-ing.** —*n.* **1** bad or unwise rule. **2** disorder. —*v.* rule badly. —**mis·rul′er**, *n.*

miss[1] (mis), *v.* **1** fail to hit, find, get, meet, attend, use, catch, hear, read, do, solve, etc. **2** let slip by; not seize: *I missed my chance.* **3** escape or avoid: *barely miss being hit.* **4** notice the absence of; feel keenly the absence of: *I miss my mother when she goes away.* —*n.* failure to hit, attain, etc.

miss fire, a of guns, fail to go off; misfire. **b** go wrong; fail: *a scheme certain to miss fire.*

miss out on, a fail to grasp or take advantage of: *miss out on an opportunity.* **b** fail to comprehend: *miss out on the significance of the event.* [OE *missan*]

miss[2] (mis), *n.*, *pl.* **miss·es. 1** girl; young woman. **2 Miss,** title put before a girl's or unmarried woman's name: *Miss Brown, the Misses Brown, the Miss Browns.* [short for *mistress*]

Miss., Mississippi.

mis·sal (mis′əl), *n.* book containing the prayers, etc., for celebrating Mass throughout the year. [< Med.L, < LL *missa* mass]

mis·shape (mis shāp′), *v.*, **-shaped, -shaped** or **-shap·en, -shap·ing.** shape badly; deform; make in the wrong shape. —**mis·shap′en,** *adj.*

mis·sile (mis′əl), *n.* **1** object that is thrown, hurled, or shot, such as a stone, a bullet, an arrow, or a lance. **2** a self-propelled rocket. [< L, ult. < *mittere* send]

miss·ing (mis′ing), *adj.* lacking; wanting; absent; not found; gone: *one book is missing.*

mis·sion (mish′ən), *n.* **1** sending or being sent on some special work; errand: *he was sent on a mission to a foreign government.* **2** group sent on some special business: *a mission was sent by the church.* **3** business on which a mission is sent. **4** station or headquarters of a religious mission. **5** business or purpose in life; calling: *her mission seems to be to help others.* [< L *missio* < *mittere* send] —**mis′sion·al,** *adj.*

mis·sion·ar·y (mish′ən er′i), *n.*, *pl.* **-ar·ies,** *adj.* —*n.* **1** person sent on a religious mission. **2** person who works to advance some cause or idea. —*adj.* of missions or missionaries.

Mis·sis·sip·pi (mis′ə sip′i), *n.* **1** largest river in the United States, flowing south from Minnesota to the Gulf of Mexico. **2** a S state of the United States. —**Mis′sis·sip′pi·an,** *adj., n.*

mis·sive (mis′iv), *n.* a written message; letter. [< Med.L *missivus,* ult. < L *mittere* send]

Mis·sou·ri (mi zùr′i; –ə), *n.* a Middle Western state of the United States. —**Mis·sou′ri·an,** *adj., n.*

mis·speak (mis spēk′), *v.*, **-spoke, -spo-ken, -speak·ing.** speak, utter, or pronounce wrongly or incorrectly.

mis·spell (mis spel′), *v.*, **-spelled, -spell-ing.** spell incorrectly.

mis·spell·ing (mis spel′ing), *n.* an incorrect spelling.

mis·spend (mis spend′), *v.*, **-spent, -spend·ing.** spend foolishly or wrongly; waste.

mis·spent (mis spent′), *adj.* spent foolishly or wrongly. —*v.* pt. and pp. of **misspend.**

mis·state (mis stāt′), *v.*, **-stat·ed, -stat-ing.** make wrong or misleading statements about. —**mis·state′ment,** *n.*

mis·step (mis step′; mis′step), *n.* **1** a wrong step. **2** error or slip in conduct.

mist (mist), *n.* **1** cloud of very fine drops of water in the air; fog. **2** anything that dims, blurs, or obscures. —*v.* **1** come down in mist; rain in very fine drops. **2** be covered with mist; make dim: *tears misted her eyes.* [OE]

mis·tak·a·ble (mis tāk′ə bəl), *adj.* that may be mistaken or misunderstood.

mis·take (mis tāk′), *n.*, *v.*, **-took, -tak·en, -tak·ing.** —*n.* error; blunder; misunderstanding: *I used your towel by mistake.* —*v.* **1** misunderstand (what is seen or heard). **2** take wrongly; take (to be some other person or thing): *mistake a stick for a snake.* **3** make a mistake.

make no mistake (about it), have no doubt. [< Scand. *mistaka*]

mis·tak·en (mis tāk′ən), *adj.* **1** wrong in opinion; having made a mistake: *a mistaken person should admit his error.* **2** wrong; wrongly judged; misplaced: *giving too much is a mistaken kindness.* —*v.* pp. of **mistake.** —**mis·tak′en·ly,** *adv.*

mis·ter (mis′tər), *n.* **1 Mister,** Mr., a title put before a man's name or the name of his office: *Mr. Smith, Mr. President.* **2** sir: *Good morning, mister.* [var. of *master*]

mis·tle·toe (mis′əl tō), *n.* **1** plant with small, waxy, white berries and yellow flowers, that grows as a parasite on certain trees. **2** sprig of mistletoe, often used as a Christmas decoration. [OE *misteltān* < *mistel* mistletoe + *tān* twig]

mis·took (mis tùk′), *v.* pt. of **mistake.**

mis·tral (mis′trəl; mis träl′), *n.* a cold, dry, northerly wind common in S France and neighboring regions. [< F < Pr., orig., dominant, <L *magistralis* < *magister* master]

mis·treat (mis trēt′), *v.* treat badly. —**mis·treat′ment,** *n.*

mis·tress (mis′tris), *n.* **1** the woman who is at the head of a household. **2** woman or country that is in control or can rule: *mistress of the seas.* **3** woman who has a thorough knowledge or mastery: *a mistress of cookery.* **4** a woman teacher. **5** woman who occupies the place of a wife. **6** *Obs.* **Mistress,** title of courtesy for a married woman, usually abbreviated in writing to Mrs. [< OF *maistresse* < *maistre* MASTER]

mis·tri·al (mis trī′əl), *n.* **1** trial having no effect in law because of some error in the proceedings. **2** an inconclusive trial.

mis·trust (mis trust′), *v.* feel no confidence in; doubt: *mistrust one's ability.* —*n.* lack of trust or confidence. —**mis-trust′er,** *n.* —**mis·trust′ful,** *adj.* —**mis·trust′ful·ly,** *adv.* —**mis·trust′ful·ness,** *n.* —**mis·trust′ing·ly,** *adv.* —**mis·trust′less,** *adj.*

mist·y (mis′ti), *adj.*, **mist·i·er, mist·i·est. 1** of mist. **2** characterized by mist; covered with mist. **3** not clearly seen or outlined; vague; indistinct. —**mist′i·ly,** *adv.* —**mist′i·ness,** *n.*

mist·y-eyed (mis′ti īd′), *adj.* **1 a** close to tears. **b** *Fig.* having moist, dreamy eyes. **2** *Fig.* sentimental.

mis·un·der·stand (mis′un dər stand′), *v.*, **-stood, -stand·ing. 1** understand wrongly. **2** take in a wrong sense; give the wrong meaning to. —**mis′un·der·stand′ing,** *n.*

mis·un·der·stood (mis′un dər stùd′), *adj.* not understood; not properly appreciated. —*v.* pt. and pp. of **misunderstand.**

mis·use (*v.* mis ūz′; *n.* mis ūs′), *v.*, **-used, -us·ing,** *n.* —*v.* **1** use for the wrong purpose: *misuse a knife at the table by lifting food with it.* **2** abuse; ill-treat: *misuse horses by loading them too heavily.* —*n.* a wrong or improper use.

mite[1] (mīt), *n.* any of various tiny animals that belong to the same class as spiders and live in foods, on plants, or on other animals. [OE *mīte*]

mite[2] (mīt), *n.* **1** anything very small; little bit. **2** a very small child. [< Mdu., ? ult. identical with *mite*[1]]

mi·ter (mī′tər), *n.*, *v.*, **-tered, -ter-ing.** —*n.* **1** a tall, pointed, folded cap worn by bishops during sacred ceremonies. **2** the bevel on either of the pieces in a miter joint. —*v.* prepare (ends of wood) for joining in a miter joint. [< L < Gk. *mitra* headband] —**mi′tered,** *adj.* —**mi′ter·er,** *n.*

miter box, device with guides for a saw blade for cutting wood at the proper angle to make a miter joint.

miter joint, a right-angled joint made by cutting the ends of two pieces of wood on equal slants.

mit·i·gate (mit′ə gāt), *v.*, **-gat·ed, -gat-ing.** make or become mild; make or become milder; make less severe or less intense: *mitigate a person's anger or pain, mitigate a punishment.* [< L *mitigatus* < *mitis* gentle] —**mit′i·ga·ble,** *adj.* —**mit′i·ga′tion,** *n.* —**mit′i·ga′tive,** *adj.* —**mit′i·ga′tor,** *n.*

mi·to·chon·dri·a (mī′tə kon′drē ə), *n.*, *pl.* of **mitochondrion.** short, thread-like structures in the cytoplasm of cells that contain many enzymes necessary to metabolism. [< Gk. *mitos* a threat + *chóndros* lump]

mi·to·sis (mi tō′sis; mī–), *n.* method of cell division in which the chromain of the nucleus forms into a thread that separates into segments or chromosomes, each of which in turn separates longitudinally into two parts. [< NL, < Gk. *mitos* thread] —**mi·tot′ic,** *adj.*

mitt (mit), *n.* **1** glove used by baseball players. **2** mitten. [short for *mitten*]

mit·ten (mit′ən), *n.* kind of winter glove covering the four fingers together and the thumb separately. [< F *mitaine* half glove]

mix (miks), *v.,* **mixed** or **mixt, mix·ing,** *n.* —*v.* **1** put together; stir well together: *mix ingredients to make a cake.* **2** join: *mix business and pleasure.* **3** associate together; get along together: *people mix well in a group like ours.* —*n.* mixture.

mix it up, *Informal.* fight, esp. fiercely.

mix up, a confuse. **b** involve; concern. [< *mixt* mixed < F < L *mixtus* mixed] —**mix′er,** *n.*

mixed (mikst), *adj.* **1** put together or formed by mixing; of different kinds combined: *mixed candies, mixed emotions.* **2** of different classes, kinds, etc.; not exclusive: *a mixed company.*

mixed bag, *Informal.* mixture, esp. of different things; miscellaneous collection.

mixed doubles, tennis doubles played with a man and a woman on each team.

mixed economy, an economy that is partly based on free-market capitalism and partly under government control.

mixed up, mentally confused; unstable.

mixed media, =multimedia.

mixed number, number consisting of a whole number and a fraction, such as 1½ or 16⅔.

mix·er (mik′sər), *n.* **1** thing that mixes. **2 a** person who mixes or socializes with others: *a good mixer.* **b** a party or get-together for the purpose of meeting different people. **3** soda, etc., used as a drink mixer.

mix·ture (miks′chər), *n.* **1** a mixing or being mixed. **2** what has been mixed. **3** two or more substances mixed together, but not chemically combined.

mix-up (miks′up′), *n.* confusion; mess.

miz·zen (miz′ən), *n.* **1** a fore-and-aft sail on the mizzenmast. **2** =mizzenmast. [< F < Ital. < L *medianus* in the middle]

miz·zen·mast (miz′ən mast′; –mäst′; –məst), *n.* mast nearest the stern in a two-masted or three-masted ship.

ml. or **ml,** milliliter.

MLG, Middle Low German.

Mlle., *pl.* **Mlles.** Mademoiselle.

MM., Messieurs.

mm. or **mm,** millimeter; millimeters.

Mme., *pl.* **Mmes.** Madame.

Mn, manganese.

MN, (*zip code*) Minnesota.

mne·mon·ic (ni mon′ik), *adj.* **1** aiding the memory. **2** of or pertaining to memory. [< Gk., < *mnamnasthai* remember]

Mo, molybdenum.

MO, (*zip code*) Missouri. **2** (em′ō), modus operandi.

Mo., **1** Missouri. **2** Monday.

M.O., m.o., money order.

mo., **1** *pl.* **mos.** month. **2** months.

mo·a (mō′ə), *n.* a large extinct bird of New Zealand, somewhat like an ostrich. [< Maori]

moan (mōn), *n.* **1** a long, low sound of suffering. **2** any similar sound: *the moan of the wind.* —*v.* **1** make moans; utter with a moan. **2** complain; grieve. [ME *man.* Cf. OE *mǣnan* complain.] —**moan′ing·ly,** *adv.*

moat (mōt), *n.* a deep, wide ditch dug around a castle or town as a protection against enemies. Moats were usually kept filled with water. —*v.* surround with a moat. [< OF *mote* mound]

mob (mob), *n.,* *v.,* **mobbed, mob·bing.** —*n.* **1** a large number of people, usually crowded closely together. **2** the common mass of people. **3** a lawless crowd, easily moved to act without thinking. —*v.* **1** crowd around in curiosity, anger, etc. **2** attack with violence, as a mob does. [short for L *mobile vulgus* fickle common people]

mo·bile (mō′bəl; mō′bēl), *adj.* **1** movable; easy to move. **2** moving easily; changing easily: *a mobile mind adapts itself quickly.* —*n.* pieces of metal, wood, etc., suspended on wires or threads and so balanced as to move in a slight breeze. [< L, movable < *movere* move] —**mo·bil′i·ty,** *n.*

mobile home, large house trailer on a more or less permanent site.

mobile phone, =cell phone.

mo·bi·lize (mō′bə līz), *v.,* **-lized, -liz·ing.** **1** assemble and prepare for war; organize for war: *mobilized troops quickly.* **2** put into motion or active use: *mobilize the wealth of a country.* [<F, < *mobile* MOBILE] —**mo′bi·liz′a·ble,** *adj.* —**mo′bi·li·za′tion,** *n.*

mob·ster (mob′stər), *n.* =gangster.

moc·ca·sin (mok′ə sən), *n.* **1** a soft leather shoe or sandal. **2** Also, **water moccasin.** a poisonous snake found in the S part of the United States. [< Algonquian]

mo·cha (mō′kə), *n.* **1** a choice variety of coffee originally coming from Arabia. **2** mixture of coffee and chocolate, used as a flavoring. —*adj.* flavored with coffee or coffee and chocolate.

mock (mok), *v.* **1** laugh at; make fun of. **2** make fun of by copying or imitating. —*adj.* not real; copying; sham; imitation: *a mock battle.* —*n.* an action or speech that mocks. [< OF *mocquer*] —**mock′er,** *n.* —**mock′ing,** *adj.* —**mock′ing·ly,** *adv.*

mock·er·y (mok′ər i), *n.,* *pl.* **-er·ies.** **1** a making fun; ridicule: *their mockery of John hurt his feelings.* **2** person or thing to be made fun of. **3** a bad copy or imitation: *an unfair trial is a mockery of justice.*

mock·ing·bird (mok′ing bėrd′), *n.* songbird of the S United States that imitates the notes of other birds.

mock orange, =syringa.

mock-up (mok′up′), *n.* a full-sized model of an airplane, machine, etc., used for design, testing, teaching, etc.

mod (mod), *adj. Informal.* up-to-date. —*n.* up-to-date, modern style. [< *modern,* British fashion style of the 1960's]

mo·dal (mō′dəl), *adj.* of or having to do with mode, manner, or form. —**mo·dal′i·ty,** *n.* —**mod′al·ly,** *adv.*

mode (mōd), *n.* **1** manner or way in which a thing is done: *his mode of dressing was unusual.* **2** form of a verb that shows whether an act or state is thought of as a fact, command, etc.; mood. [< L *modus* measure]

mod·el (mod′əl), *n.,* *v.,* **-eled, -el·ing,** *adj.* —*n.* **1** a small copy: *a model of a ship.* **2** way in which a thing is made; style: *dresses of that model are becoming to me.* **3** *Fig.* thing or person to be copied or imitated. **4** person who poses for artists, photographers, etc. **5** person who puts on garments in order to show how they look. —*v.* **1** make; shape; fashion; design; plan: *model a bird's nest in clay.* **2** form (something) after a particular model: *model yourself on your father.* **4** be a model. —*adj.* **1** serving as a model. **2** just right or perfect, esp. in conduct: *a model child.* [< F < Ital. *modello,* dim. of *modo* MODE] —**mod′el·er,** *n.*

mo·dem (mō′dəm), *n.* electronic device that converts signals from analog to digital, or vice versa, allowing computer communications over telephone lines to a network, esp. to the Internet. [< *modulator* + *demodulator*]

mod·er·ate (*adj., n.* mod′ər it; *v.* mod′ər āt), *adj., n., v.,* **-at·ed, -at·ing.** —*adj.* **1** kept or keeping within proper bounds; not extreme: *moderate expenses.* **2** not violent; calm: *moderate winds.* —*n.* person who holds moderate opinions. —*v.* **1** make less violent: *the wind is moderating.* **2** act as moderator; preside (over). [< L *moderatus* regulated]

mod·er·a·tion (mod′ər ā′shən), *n.* **1** a moderating. **2** freedom from excess; proper restraint; temperance. **3** calmness; lack of violence.

in moderation, within limits; not going to extremes.

mod·er·a·tor (mod′ər ā′tər), *n.* **1** a presiding officer; chairman. **2** arbitrator; mediator.

mod·ern (mod′ərn), *adj.* **1** of the present time; of times not long past: *television is a modern invention.* **2** up-to-date; not old-fashioned. —*n.* person of modern times. [< LL *modernus* < LL *modo* just now] —**mod′ern·ly,** *adv.* —**mod′ern·ness,** *n.*

Modern English, the English language from about 1500 through the present.

mod·ern·ism (mod′ər niz əm), *n.* **1** modern attitudes or methods; sympathy with what is modern. **2** a modern word or phrase. —**mod′ern·ist,** *n.* —**mod′ern·is′tic,** *adj.*

mo·der·ni·ty (mə dėr′nə ti; mō–), *n., pl.* **-ties.** **1** a being modern. **2** something modern.

mod·ern·ize (mod′ər nīz), v., **-ized, -iz·ing.** make or become modern; bring up to present ways or standards. **—mod′ern·i·za′tion,** n. **—mod′ern·iz′er,** n.

mod·est (mod′ist), adj. 1 not thinking too highly of oneself; not vain; humble. 2 bashful; not bold; shy. 3 not calling attention to one's body; decent. 4 not too great: a modest request, a modest little house. [< L modestus in due measure < modus measure] **—mod′est·ly,** adv.

mod·es·ty (mod′is ti), n., pl. **-ties.** 1 freedom from vanity; being modest or humble. 2 shyness; bashfulness. 3 being decent.

mod·i·cum (mod′ə kəm), n. a small or moderate quantity: a modicum of common sense. [< L, neut., moderate < modus measure]

mod·i·fi·ca·tion (mod′ə fə kā′shən), n. 1 partial alteration or change: a modification of one's claims. 2 modified form; variety.

mod·i·fi·er (mod′ə fī′ər), n. 1 word or group of words that limits another word or group of words. 2 person or thing that modifies.

mod·i·fy (mod′ə fī), v., **-fied, -fy·ing.** 1 change (somewhat): modify the terms of a lease. 2 make less; tone down; make less severe or strong: modify his demands. 3 Gram. limit the meaning of; qualify. Adverbs modify verbs and adjectives. [< L modificare limit < modus measure + facere make] **—mod′i·fi′a·ble,** adj.

mod·ish (mōd′ish), adj. fashionable; stylish **—mod′ish·ly,** adv. **—mod′ish·ness,** n.

mod·u·late (moj′ə lāt), v., **-lat·ed, -lat·ing.** 1 regulate; adjust; vary; soften; tone down. 2 alter (the voice) for expression. 3 change from one key or note to another. 4 attune to a certain pitch or key. 5 vary the frequency of (electrical waves). 6 change (a radio current) by adding sound waves to it. [<L modulatus, ult. < modus measure] **—mod′u·la′tor,** n. **—mod′u·la·to′ry,** adj.

mod·u·la·tion (moj′ə lā′shən), n. 1 a modulating or being modulated. 2 change from one key to another in the course of a piece. 3 a varying of high-frequency waves.

mod·ule (moj′ül), n. 1 a standard or unit for measuring. 2 the size of some part taken as a unit of measure. 3 any standardized, interchangeable unit. 4 unit of a prefabricated dwelling: a house constructed from modules delivered to the site on a truck. [< L modulus, dim. of modus measure. Doublet of MOLD¹.]

mod·u·lar (moj′ů lər), adj. 1 of or having to do with a module or modules. 2 made or built from interchangeable units.

mo·dus op·e·ran·di (mō′dəs op′ə ran′dī), Latin. method or manner of working.

mo·dus vi·ven·di (mō′dəs vi ven′dī), Latin. way of getting along, esp. while waiting for something.

Mo·gul (mō′gul; mō gul′), n. 1 =Mongolian. 2 one of the Mongol conquerors of India in the 16th century or one of their descendants. Also, **Mughal. 3 mogul,** an important person.

mo·hair (mō′hār), n. 1 cloth made from the long, silky hair of the Angora goat. 2 a similar cloth made of wool and cotton or rayon. [ult. < Ar. mukhayyar; conformed to hair]

Mo·ham·med (mō ham′id), n. =Muhammad.

Mo·ham·med·an (mō ham′ə dən), adj., n. Muslim. Also, **Muhammadan.**

Mo·hawk (mō′hôk), n., pl. **-hawk, -hawks.** 1 member of an Iroquois tribe of American Indians formerly living in C New York State. 2 Iroquoian language of the Mohawk.

Mo·he·gan (mō hē′gən), n. member of a tribe of American Indians formerly living in Connecticut and related to the Mohicans.

Mo·hi·can (mō hē′kən), n. member of a tribe of American Indians formerly living in the upper Hudson valley and Connecticut.

Mohs or **Mohs' scale,** scale for classifying the relative hardness of minerals. [< Friedrich Mohs (1773–1839), German mineralogist who developed it]

moi·e·ty (moi′ə ti), n., pl. **-ties.** 1 half. 2 part. [< OF < LL medietas half < L, the middle < medius middle]

moire (mwar; mwa ra′; mo ra′; mo–), n. fabric having a wavelike pattern; watered fabric. [< F, alter. of E mohair]

moi·ré (mwä rā′; mô rā′; mō–), n. 1 =moire. 2 a wavy pattern that results from two other patterns which overlap. —adj. 1 having a wavelike pattern; watered: moiré silk. 2 printed with a wavy pattern to prevent forgery. [< F]

moist (moist), adj. 1 slightly wet; damp: moist ground. 2 rainy: moist weather. [< OF moiste < L mucidus moldy, musty < mucus mucus] **—moist′ly,** adv. **—moist′ness,** n.

moist·en (mois′ən), v. make or become moist. **—moist′en·er,** n.

mois·ture (mois′chər), n. slight wetness; water or other liquid spread in very small drops in the air or on a surface.

mois·tur·ize (mois′chə rīz), v., **-ized, -iz·ing.** add or supply with moisture by use of some agent, esp. a lotion or cream for the skin. **—mois′tur·iz′er,** n.

mo·lar (mō′lər), n. tooth with a broad surface for grinding. A person's back teeth are molars. —adj. 1 adapted for grinding. 2 of the molar teeth. [< L, < mola mill]

mo·las·ses (mə las′iz), n. a sweet syrup obtained in making sugar from sugar cane. [< Pg. < LL mellaceum must < mel honey]

mold¹ (mōld), n. 1 a hollow shape in which anything is formed or cast: pour melted metal into a mold. 2 the shape or form which is given by a mold. 3

model according to which anything is shaped. 4 nature; character. —v. form; shape: mold candles from wax. [< OF modle < L modulus. Doublet of MODULE.] **—mold′a·ble,** adj.

mold² (mōld), n. 1 a woolly or furry, fungous growth, often greenish in color, that appears on food and other animal or vegetable substances when they are left too long in a warm, moist place. 2 any of the fungi that produce such a growth. —v. cover or become covered with mold. [ME moul, earlier muwle(n), prob. infl. by mold³]

mold³ (mōld), n. loose earth; fine, soft, rich soil. [OE molde]

mold·board (mōld′bôrd′; –bōrd′), n. a curved metal plate in a plow, that turns over the earth from the furrow.

mold·er¹ (mōl′dər), v. turn or cause to turn into dust by natural decay; crumble; waste away. [prob. < mold³]

mold·er² (mōl′dər), n. one that molds.

mold·ing (mōl′ding), n. 1 act of shaping. 2 something molden. 3 strip, usually of wood, used to support pictures, to cover electric wires, etc. 4 decorative strip of wood, stone, plaster, etc.

mold·y (mōl′di), adj., **mold·i·er, mold·i·est.** 1 covered with mold: a moldy crust of bread. 2 musty; stale: a moldy smell. **—mold′i·ness,** n.

mole¹ (mōl), n. a congenital spot on the skin, usually brown. [OE māl]

mole² (mōl), n. 1 a small animal that lives underground most of the time. Moles have velvety fur and very small eyes. 2 spy who infiltrates an organization, group, etc. [ME molle]

mole³ (mōl), n. breakwater. [< L moles mass]

mo·lec·u·lar (mə lek′yə lər), adj. having to do with, caused by, or consisting of molecules. **—mo·lec′u·lar·ly,** adv.

molecular biology, branch of biology that deals with the chemical processes of life at the molecular level, esp. cell replication and the transmission of genetic information. **—molecular biologist.**

molecular weight, weight of a molecule expressed as the sum of the atomic weights of all the atoms in a molecule.

mol·e·cule (mol′ə kül), n. 1 the smallest particle into which a substance can be divided without chemical change. 2 a very small particle. [< NL molecula, dim. of L moles mass]

mole·hill (mōl′hil′), n. 1 a small mound or ridge of earth raised up by moles burrowing under the ground. 2 something insignificant.

mole·skin (mōl′skin′), n. 1 skin of the mole used as fur. 2 a strong cotton fabric with a short, soft nap.

mo·lest (mə lest′), v. meddle with and injure; interfere with and trouble; disturb. [< OF < L, < molestus troublesome < moles burden] **—mo′les·ta′tion,** n. **—mo·lest′er,** n.

moll (mol), *n.* **1** a female companion, esp. of a criminal or vagrant. **2** prostitute. [short for *Molly,* familiar var. of *Mary*]

mol·li·fy (mol′ə fī), *v.,* **–fied, –fy·ing.** soften; appease; mitigate: *mollify a person or his wrath.* [< F < LL, < *mollis* soft + *facere* make] —**mol′li·fi·ca′tion,** *n.* —**mol′li·fi′er,** *n.* —**mol′li·fy′ing·ly,** *adv.*

mol·lusk (mol′əsk), *n.* animal having a soft body not composed of segments, and usually covered with a hard shell. Snails, mussels, oysters, and clams are mollusks. [< F < L *molluscus* soft (of a nutshell)] —**mol·lus′can,** *adj., n.*

mol·ly·cod·dle (mol′i kod′əl), *n., v.,* **–dled, –dling.** —*n.* boy or man accustomed to being fussed over and pampered; milksop. —*v.* coddle; pamper. [< *Molly* (familiar var. of *Mary*) + *coddle*] —**mol′ly·cod′dler,** *n.*

Mo·loch (mō′lok), *n.* **1** a Semitic deity whose worship was marked by the sacrifice of children by their parents. **2** *Fig.* anything conceived as requiring frightful sacrifice.

Mo·lo·tov cocktail (mô′lə tôf; –tôv; mol′ə–; mō′lə–), improvised but effective hand grenade made from a gasoline-filled bottle with a rag as a wick. [< V. *Molotov,* Russian diplomat active during the Spanish Civil War where it was used]

molt (mōlt), *v.* shed the feathers, skin, etc., before a new growth. Birds and snakes molt. —*n.* act or time of doing this. [ME *mout* < OE *mūtian* (as in *bemūtian* exchange for) < L *mutare* change] —**molt′er,** *n.*

molt·en (mōl′tən), *adj.* **1** melted: *molten steel.* **2** made by melting and casting: *a molten image.* —*v.* pp. of **melt.**

mo·lyb·de·num (mə lib′də nəm; mol′-ib dē′nəm), *n.* a silver-white metallic element, Mo, of the chromium group. [< NL < L *molybdaena* < Gk., < *molyb-dos* lead]

mom (mom), *n. Informal.* mother.

mom and pop, of or having to do with a small retail business, esp. family-run: *a mom and pop deli.*

mo·ment (mō′mənt), *n.* **1** a very short space of time; instant: *in a moment, all was changed.* **2** a present or other particular point of time: *we both arrived at the same moment.* **3** importance: *a matter of moment.* [< L *momentum* < *movere* move. Doublet of MOMENTUM.]

mo·men·tar·i·ly (mō′mən ter′ə li), *adv.* **1** for a moment: *hesitate momentarily.* **2** at every moment; from moment to moment: *danger momentarily increasing.* **3** at any moment.

mo·men·tar·y (mō′mən ter′i), *adj.* lasting only a moment. —**mo′men·tar′i·ness,** *n.*

mo·men·tous (mō men′təs), *adj.* very important. —**mo·men′tous·ly,** *adv.* —**mo·men′tous·ness,** *n.*

mo·men·tum (mō men′təm), *n., pl.* **–tums, –ta** (–tə). **1** force with which a body moves, the product of its mass and its velocity: *a falling object gains momentum as it falls.* **2** impetus resulting from movement. [< L, moving power. Doublet of MOMENT.]

mom·my (mom′i), *n., pl.* **–mies.** *Informal.* mother.

Mon., 1 Monday. **2** Monsignor.

Mon·a·co (mon′ə kō; mə nak′ō), *n.* a very small country within SE France, on the Mediterranean Sea.

mon·ad (mon′ad; mō′nad), *n.* **1** unit. **2** a very simple single-celled animal or plant. **3** atom, element, or radical having a valence of one. [< LL < Gk. *monas* unit < *monos* alone]

mon·arch (mon′ərk), *n.* **1** king, queen, emperor, etc.; hereditary sovereign; ruler. **2** *Fig.* person or thing like a monarch. **3** = monarch butterfly. [< LL < Gk., < *monos* alone + *archein* rule]

mo·nar·chal (mə när′kəl), **mo·nar·chi·al** (–ki əl), *adj.* **1** of a monarch. **2** characteristic of a monarch. **3** suitable for a monarch. —**mo·nar′chal·ly,** *adv.*

monarch butterfly, large butterfly with orange and black wings that migrates south as far as Mexico in the fall.

mo·nar·chic (mə när′kik), **mo·nar·chi·cal** (–kə kəl), *adj.* **1** of or like a monarch or monarchy. **2** favoring a monarchy. —**mo·nar′chi·cal·ly,** *adv.*

mon·ar·chism (mon′ər kiz əm), *n.* **1** principles of monarchy. **2** advocacy of monarchic principles. —**mon′ar·chist,** *n., adj.* —**mon′ar·chis′tic,** *adj.*

mon·ar·chy (mon′ər ki), *n., pl.* **–chies.** **1** government by a monarch. **2** nation governed by a monarch.

mon·as·ter·y (mon′əs ter′i), *n., pl.* **–ter·ies.** building where monks or nuns live a contemplative life according to fixed rules and under religious vows. [< LL < Gk. *monasterion,* ult. < *monos* alone. Doublet of MINSTER.] —**mon′as·te′ri·al,** *adj.*

mo·nas·tic (mə nas′tik), **mo·nas·ti·cal** (–tə kəl), *adj.* **1** of monks or nuns: *monastic vows.* **2** of monasteries. **3** like that of monks or nuns. —*n.* monk. [< LL < LGk. *monastikos,* ult. < *monos* alone] —**mo·nas′ti·cal·ly,** *adv.*

mo·nas·ti·cism (mənas′tə siz əm), *n.* system or condition of living according to fixed rules, in groups shut off from the world, and devoted to religion.

Mon·day (mun′di; –dā), *n.* the second day of the week, following Sunday.

mo·ne·ran (mə nir′ən), *n.* any plant or animal, such as blue-green algae and bacteria, that does not have a cellular nucleus. [< Gk. *monērēs* individual, solitary + E *-an*]

mon·e·tar·y (mon′ə ter′i; mun′–), *adj.* **1** of the coinage or currency of a country. The monetary unit in the United States is the dollar. **2** of money: *a monetary reward.* [< LL *monetarius.* See MONEY.] —**mon′e·tar′i·ly,** *adv.*

mon·ey (mun′i), *n., pl.* **–eys.** **1** current coin; gold, silver, or other metal made into coins; bank notes, etc., representing gold or silver; any medium of exchange. **2** a particular form or denomination of money. **3** wealth.

coin money, *Informal.* make a great deal of money from a business.

for my money, *Informal.* in my opinion.

in the money, *Informal.* having more than enough money.

make money, a get money. **b** become rich. [< OF < L *moneta* mint, money < *Juno Moneta,* in whose temple money was coined. Doublet of MINT².]

mon·ey·bag (mun′i bag′), *n.* **1** bag for money. **2 moneybags,** *Informal.* **a** wealth; riches. **b** (*sing. in use*) a wealthy or avaricious person.

mon·eyed (mun′id), *adj.* **1** having money; wealthy. **2** consisting of or representing money.

mon·ey·lend·er (mun′i len′dər), *n.* person whose business is lending money at interest.

mon·ey·mak·er or **mon·ey·mak·er** (mun′i mā′kər), *n.* **1** person skilled in earning money and building a fortune. **2** investment or activity that earns a profit.

money order, order for the payment of money, issued at one post office and payable at another.

mon·ger (mung′gər; mong′–), *n. Brit.* dealer in some sort of article: *a fishmonger.* [ult. < L *mango* trader < Gk.]

Mon·gol (mong′gəl; –gol; –gōl), *n.* **1** member of an Asian people now inhabiting Mongolia and nearby parts of China and Siberia. **2** = Mongolian. —*adj.* **1** of this race. **2** = Mongolian.

Mon·go·li·a (mong gō′li ə), *n.* vast region in Asia, N of China and S of W Siberia.

Mon·go·li·an (mong gō′li ən), **1** member of the people native to Asia, as the Chinese, Japanese, etc. **2** their language or languages. **3** native or inhabitant of Mongolia. —*adj.* of Mongolia, the Mongolians, or their languages.

Mon·gol·oid (mong′gəl oid), *adj.* resembling the Mongols; having characteristics of the Mongolian people. —*n.* Mongolian individual.

mon·goose (mong′güs), *n., pl.* **–goos·es.** a slender, ferretlike animal of India, used for destroying rats, and noted for its ability to kill certain poisonous snakes without being harmed. [< Marathi (lang. of W India) *mangūs*]

mon·grel (mung′grəl; mong′–), *n.* animal or plant of mixed breed, esp. a dog. —*adj.* of mixed breed, origin, nature, etc. [cf. OE *gemang* mixture]

mon·ies (mun′iz), *n.pl.* sums of money.

mon·i·tor (mon′ə tər), *n.* **1** pupil in school with special duties, such as helping to keep order and taking attendance. **2** person who gives advice or warning. **3** a large lizard of Africa, Australia, and S Asia. **4** listening device or receiver for surveillance of electronic, telephone, or other communications. **5** screen that displays output from a computer. —*v.* **1** check (radio, telephone, television, or electronic transmissions) by using a monitor, esp. to check the quality of transmission. **2** listen to (telephone, broadcast, or other transmissions) for the purpose of surveillance. [< L, < *monere* admonish] **—mon′i·to′ri·al,** *adj.* **—mon′i·tor·ship′,** *n.*

mon·i·to·ry (mon′ə tô′ri; –tō′–), *adj.* admonishing; warning.

monk (mungk), *n.* man who gives up everything else for religion and enters a monastery to live. [< LL < LGk. *monachos* < Gk., individual, < *monos* alone]

mon·key (mung′ki), *n., pl.* **-keys,** *v.,* **-keyed, -key·ing.** —*n.* **1** one of the group of animals most closely resembling humans. **2** one of the smaller animals in this group, not a chimpanzee, gorilla, or other large ape. **3** person, esp. a child, who is full of mischief. —*v.* play; fool; trifle.

make a monkey (out) of, make a fool of. [prob. < MLG *Moneke,* son of Martin the Ape in story of Reynard]

monkey bars, =jungle gym.

monkey business, *Informal.* trickery; deceit.

mon·key·shine (mung′ki shīn′), *n. Informal* a mischievous trick; clownish joke.

monkey wrench, wrench with a movable jaw that can be adjusted to fit different sizes of nuts.

put or **throw a monkey wrench into,** spoil; ruin.

monk·ish (mungk′ish), *adj.* **1** of a monk; having to do with monks. **2** like a monk; characteristic of a monk. **3** like monks or their way of life. **—monk′ish·ly,** *adv.* **—monk′ish·ness,** *n.*

monks·hood (mungks′hūd′), *n.* a kind of aconite, so called from its hooded flowers.

mon·o (mon′ō), *n. Informal.* mononucleosis.

mono-, *combining form.* one; single, as in *monogamy, monosyllable,* [< Gk., < *monos* single]

mon·o·chrome (mon′ə krōm), *n.* a painting, drawing, print, etc., in a single color or shades of a single color. [< Gk., < *monos* single + *chroma* color] **—mon′o·chro·mat′ic,** *adj.* **—mon′o·chro′mic,** *adj.* **—mon′o·chrom′ist,** *n.*

mon·o·cle (mon′ə kəl), *n.* eyeglass for one eye. [< F < LL, one-eyed, < Gk. *mono–* single + L *oculus* eye] **—mon′o·cled,** *adj.*

mon·o·clon·al antibody (mon′ə klō′nəl), antibody produced by cloning genetically distinct cells which have been fused, used to treat various medical conditions and diagnose cancer. [< *mono–* + *clone* clone + *–al*]

mon·o·cot·y·le·don (mon′ə kot′ə lē′dən), *n.* plant with only one cotyledon. Also, **monocot, monocotyl. —mon′o·cot·y·le′don·ous,** *adj.*

mon·o·cyte (mon′ə sīt), *n.* type of leucocyte in the blood, the largest in size and having a single, well-defined nucleus. [< *mono–* + *–cyte* cell]

mon·o·dy (mon′ə di), *n., pl.* **–dies. 1** a mournful song. **2** poem in which one person laments another's death. **3 a** style of composition in which one part or melody predominates. **b** composition in this style. [< LL < Gk. *monoidia,* ult. < *monos* single + *aeidein* sing] **—mo·nod′ic,** *adj.* **—mo·nod′i·cal·ly,** *adv.*

mo·nog·a·my (mə nog′ə mi), *n.* **1** practice or condition of being married to only one person at a time. **2** habit of having only one mate. [< L < Gk., < *monos* single + *gamos* marriage] **—mo·nog′a·mist,** *n.* **—mo·nog′a·mous,** *adj.*

mon·o·gram (mon′ə gram), *n.* a person's initials combined in one design. [< LL < Gk., < *monos* single + *gramma* letter] **—mon′o·gram·mat′ic,** *adj.* **—mon′o·grammed,** *adj.*

mon·o·graph (mon′ə graf; –gräf), *n.* book or article written on a particular subject: *Darwin's monograph on earthworms.* **—mo·nog′ra·pher,** *n.* **—mon′o·graph′ic,** *adj.*

mon·o·lin·gual (mon′ə ling′gwəl), *adj.* limited to only one language. [< E *mono–* + L *lingua* tongue + E *–al*]

mon·o·lith (mon′ə lith), *n.* **1** a single large block of stone. **2** monument, column, statue, etc., formed of a single large block of stone. **3** *Fig.* culture, political organization, etc., that is rigid and unyielding. [< L < Gk., < *monos* single + *lithos* stone]

mon·o·lith·ic (mon′ə lith′ik), *adj.* **1** of or pertaining to monoliths. **2** *Fig.* comprising an imposing and rigidly uniform whole: *a police state is a monolithic organization.*

mon·o·logue, mon·o·log (mon′ə lôg; –log), *n.* **1** a long speech by one person in a group. **2** entertainment by a single speaker. **3** play for a single actor. **4** part of a play in which a single actor speaks alone. [< F < LGk., < *monos* single + *logos* speech, discourse] **—mon′o·log′ist,** *n.*

mon·o·ma·ni·a (mon′ə mā′ni ə), *n.* **1** insanity on one subject only. **2** unreasonable interest or tendency. **—mon′o·ma′ni·ac,** *n.* **—mon′o·ma·ni′a·cal,** *adj.*

mon·o·mer (mon′ə mər), *n.* single molecule that can combine with others to form a polymer. [< E *mono–* + Gk. *méros* part] **—mon′o·mer′ic,** *adj.*

mo·no·mi·al (mō nō′mi əl), —*adj.* consisting of a single term. —*n.* expression consisting of a single term. [< MONO– + *–nomial,* as in *binomial*]

mon·o·nu·cle·ar (mon′ə nü′klē ər;–nyü′–), *adj.* having only one nucleus. Also, **mononucleate.**

mon·o·nu·cle·o·sis (mon′ə nü′klē ō′sis; –nyü′–), *n.* **1** condition marked by an abnormal increase in the mononuclear leucocytes in the blood. **2** Also, **infec**

tious mononucleosis. infectious disease characterized by an increase of mononuclear leucocytes in the blood, swollen glands, sore throat, fatigue, etc.

mon·o·plane (mon′ə plān), *n.* airplane with only one pair of wings.

mon·o·ploid (mon′ə ploid), *adj.* having one set of unpaired chromosomes; haploid. —*n.* monoploid organism or cell.

mo·nop·o·list (mə nop′ə list), *n.* **1** person who has a monopoly. **2** person who favors monopoly. **—mo·nop′o·lis′tic,** *adj.*

mo·nop·o·lize (mə nop′ə līz), *v.,* **–lized, –liz·ing. 1** have or get exclusive possession or control of: *this firm monopolizes thread production.* **2** occupy wholly; keep entirely to oneself: *the agent monopolized the conversation.* **—mo·nop′o·li·za′tion,** *n.* **—mo·nop′o·liz′er,** *n.*

mo·nop·o·ly (mə nop′ə li), *n., pl.* **–lies. 1** exclusive control of a commodity or service: *the only milk company in town has a monopoly on milk delivery.* **2** such control granted by a government: *an inventor has a monopoly on his invention for a certain number of years.* **3** control that, though not exclusive, enables the person or company to fix prices. **4** a commercial product or service that is exclusively controlled or nearly so. **5** person or company that has a monopoly of some commodity or service. **6** the exclusive possession or control: *no one country has a monopoly of virtue.* [< L < Gk., < *monos* single + *poleein* sell]

mon·o·rail (mon′ə rāl′), *n.* railway in which cars run on a single rail.

mon·o·sac·cha·ride (mon′ə sak′ə rīd; –ər id), *n.* any one of the simple sugars, such as glucose, fructose, etc., that occur naturally or can be formed by hydrolyzing polysaccharides. [< *mono–* + *saccharide*]

mon·o·syl·la·ble (mon′ə sil′ə bəl), *n.* word of one syllable. *Yes* and *no* are monosyllables. **—mon′o·syl·lab′ic,** *adj.* **—mon′o·syl·lab′i·cal·ly,** *adv.*

mon·o·the·ism (mon′ə thē iz′əm), *n.* doctrine or belief that there is only one God. [< MONO– + Gk. *theos* god] **—mon′o·the′ist,** *n.* **—mon′o·the·is′tic,** *adj.* **—mon′o·the·is′ti·cal·ly,** *adv.*

mon·o·tone (mon′ə tōn), *n.* sameness of tone, of style of writing, of color, etc. —*adj.* continuing on one tone; of one tone, style, or color.

mo·not·o·nous (mə not′ə nəs), *adj.* **1** continuing in the same tone. **2** not varying; without change. **3** wearying because of its sameness. **—mo·not′o·nous·ly,** *adv.* **—mo·not′o·nous·ness,** *n.*

mo·not·o·ny (mə not′ə ni), *n.* **1** sameness of tone or pitch. **2** lack of variety. **3** wearisome sameness. [< Gk. *monotonia,* ult. < Gk. *monos* single + *tonos* tone]

mon·o·treme (mon′ə trēm), *n.* one of the lowest order of mammals. Duckbills and echidnas are monotremes. [< MONO– + *trema* hole]

mon·o·va·lent (mo´ə vā′lənt), *adj.* having a valence of one.

mon·ox·ide (mon ok′sīd), *n.* oxide containing one oxygen atom in each molecule.

Mon·roe (mən rō′), *n.* **James,** 1758–1831, the fifth president of the United States, 1817–25.

Monroe Doctrine, doctrine that European nations should not interfere with American nations or try to acquire more territory in the Americas.

Mon·ro·vi·a (mon rō′vi ə), *n.* capital of Liberia.

Mon·sei·gneur, mon·sei·gneur (môN se-nyœr′), *n., pl.* **Mes·sei·gneurs; mes·sei·gneurs** (mā se nyœr′), **1** a French title of honor given to princes, bishops, and other persons of importance. **2** person bearing this title. [< F, my lord. See SEIGNEUR.]

mon·sieur (mə syœ′), *n., pl.* **mes·sieurs** (mā syœ′). Mr.; sir. [< F, earlier *mon sieur* my lord. See SIRE.]

Mon·si·gnor, mon·si·gnor (mon sē′nyər), *n., pl.* **Mon·si·gnors, Mon·si·gno·ri** (mon´sē nyô′ri; –nyô′–), **mon·si·gnors, mon·si·gno·ri. 1** title given to certain dignitaries in the Roman Catholic Church. **2** person having this title. [< Ital., half-trans. of F *monseigneur* MONSEIGNEUR]

mon·soon (mon sün′), *n.* **1** a seasonal wind of the Indian Ocean and S Asia, blowing from the SW from April to October and from the NE during the rest of the year. **2** a rainy season during which this wind blows from the SW. [< Du. < Pg. < Ar. *mausim* season]

mon·ster (mon′stər), *n.* **1** any animal or plant that is out of the usual course of nature. Centaurs, sphinxes, and griffins are imaginary monsters. **2** *Fig.* a huge creature or thing. **3** *Fig.* person too wicked to be human: *he is a monster of cruelty.* —*adj.* huge. [< OF < L *monstrum* divine warning < *monstrare* show]

mon·stros·i·ty (mon stros′ə ti), *n., pl.* **–ties. 1** monster. **2** a monstrous thing. **3** state or character of being monstrous.

mon·strous (mon′strəs), *adj.* **1** huge; enormous. **2** wrongly formed or shaped; like a monster. **3** *Fig.* so wrong or absurd as to be almost unheard of. **4** *Fig.* shocking; horrible; dreadful. —*adv.* very; extremely. —**mon′strous·ly,** *adv.* —**mon′strous·ness,** *n.*

Mont., Montana.

mon·tage (mon täzh′), *n.* **1** the combination of several distinct pictures to make a composite picture. **2** a composite picture so made. **3** the use of a rapid succession of pictures, esp. to suggest a train of thought. [< F, < *monter* MOUNT¹]

mon·ta·gnard or **Mon·ta·gnard** (mon´tən yärd′), *n., pl.* **–gnards** or **–gnard.** member of the aboriginal tribes living in the mountains of Vietnam. —*adj.* of or belonging to the montagnards. [< F, *lit.* mountaineer]

Mon·tan·a (mon tan′ə), *n.* a W state of the United States. —**Mon·tan′an,** *adj., n.*

Mon·te·vi·de·o (mon´tə vi dā′ō; –vid′i ō) *n.* capital of Uruguay.

Mont·gom·er·y (mont gum′ər i; –gum′ri), *n.* capital of Alabama, in the C part.

month (munth), *n.* **1** one of the 12 parts (Jan., Feb., etc.) into which the year is divided. **2** time from any day of one month to the corresponding day of the next month. [OE *mōnath;* akin to *moon*]

month·ly (munth′li), *adj., adv., n., pl.* **–lies.** —*adj.* **1** of or for a month; lasting a month. **2** done, happening, payable, etc., once a month. —*adv.* once a month; every month. —*n.* magazine or periodical published once a month.

Mont·pel·ier (mont pēl′yər), *n.* capital of Vermont, in the C part.

mon·u·ment (mon′yə mənt), *n.* **1** something set up to keep a person or an event from being forgotten. A monument may be a building, pillar, arch, statue, tomb, or stone. **2** anything that keeps alive the memory of a person or an event. **3** enduring or prominent instance; *the professor's researches were monuments of learning.* **4** something set up to mark a boundary. [< L *monumentum* < *monere* remind]

mon·u·men·tal (mon´yə men′təl), *adj.* **1** of a monument. **2** serving as a monument. **3** like a monument. **4** weighty and lasting; important: *The Constitution of the United States is a monumental document.* **5** very great: *monumental ignorance.* —**mon´u·men′tal·ly,** *adv.*

moo (mü), *n., pl.* **moos,** *v.,* **mooed, moo·ing.** —*n.* sound made by a cow. —*v.* make this sound.

mooch (müch), *v. Informal.* **1** steal. **2** beg; get at another person's expense. —**mooch′er,** *n.*

mood¹ (müd), *n.* state of mind or feeling. [OE *mōd* spirit]

mood² (müd), *n.* form of a verb that shows whether the act or state is thought of as a fact, a command, etc.: *the indicative mood.* Also, **mode.** [alter. *of mode;* infl. by *mood¹*]

mood·y (müd′i), *adj.,* **mood·i·er, mood·i·est. 1** likely to have changes of mood. **2** often having gloomy moods. **3** sunk in sadness; gloomy; sullen. —**mood′i·ly,** *adv.* **mood′i·ness,** *n.*

moon (mün), *n.* **1** a celestial body that revolves around the earth once in approximately 28 days and reflects the sun's light so that it looks bright. **2** moon at a certain phase: **new moon** (visible as slender crescent); **half moon** (visible as half circle); **full moon** (visible as circle); **old moon** (waning). **3** a lunar month. **4** moonlight. **5** satellite of any planet. —*v.* wander about idly or gaze listlessly. [OE *mōna*] —**moon′like´,** *adj.*

moon·beam (mün′bēm´), *n.* ray of moonlight.

moon·light (mün′līt´), *n., adj., v.,* **–light·ed, –light·ing.** —*n.* light of the moon.

—*adj.* **1** Also, **moonlit.** having the light of the moon. **2** while the moon is shining; by night. —*v.* to work at a second job, usually at night, to supplement income.

moon·light·er (mün′līt ər), *n.* person who holds more than one job at the same time.

moon·shine (mün′shīn´), *n.* **1** moonlight. **2** intoxicating liquor unlawfully distilled or unlawfully smuggled into the country.

moon·shin·er (mün′shīn´ər), *n.* person who makes intoxicating liquor contrary to law.

moon·stone (mün′stōn´), *n.* a whitish gem with a pearly luster, a variety of feldspar.

moon·struck (mün′struk´), **moon·strick·en** (–strik´ən), *adj.* dazed; crazed.

moor¹ (mur), *v.* **1** put or keep (a ship, etc.) in place by means of ropes or chains fastened to the shore or to anchors. **2** be made secure by ropes, anchors, etc. [ME *more(n).* Cf. OE *mǣrels* mooring rope.]

moor² (mur), *n.* open waste land, esp. if heather grows on it [OE *mōr*]

Moor (mur), *n.* member of Muslim people living in NW Africa. In the eighth century A.D. the Moors conquered Spain. —**Moor′ish,** *adj.*

moor·age (mur′ij), *n.* **1** a mooring or being moored. **2** place for mooring. **3** charge for using a mooring.

moor hen, 1 a female red grouse. **2** any of various wading birds, as the rail, coot, etc.

moor·ings (mur′ingz), *n.pl.* **1** ropes, cables, anchors, etc., by which a ship is fastened. **2** place where a ship is moored.

moor·land (mur′land´; –lənd), *n.* land covered with heather; moor.

moose (müs), *n., pl.* **moose. 1** animal like a large deer, living in Canada and the N United States. **2** the European elk. [< Algonquian]

moot (müt), *adj.* debatable; doubtful: *a moot point.* —*v.* **1** argue. **2** bring forward (a point, subject, case, etc.) for discussion. [OE *mōt* meeting]

moot court, mock court, esp. one held in a law school to give students practice.

mop (mop), *n., v.,* **mopped, mop·ping.** —*n.* **1** bundle of coarse yarn, rags, cloth, etc., fastened at the end of a stick, for cleaning floors, etc. **2** a thick head of hair like a mop. —*v.* **1** wash or wipe up; clean with a mop. **2** wipe.

mop up, finish. [ME *mappe*]

mope (mōp), *v.,* **moped, mop·ing,** *n.* —*v.* be indifferent and silent; be gloomy and sad. —*n.* person who mopes.

the mopes, low spirits: *infected with the mopes.* —**mop′er,** *n.* —**mop′ish,** *adj.* —**mop′ish·ly,** *adv.* —**mop′ish·ness,** *n.*

mo·ped (mō′ped), *n.* well-built bicycle with a motor and powered by either the motor or pedals. [< *motor* + *ped*al]

mop·pet (mop′it), *n.* child. [< obs. *mop* doll]

mop-up (mop′up′), *n.* **1** a cleaning up. **2** killing or capture of defeated troops at the end of a major engagement in a war. —*adj.* of or having to do with a mop-up.

mop·y (mō′pi), *adj.* listless; gloomy; sad.

mo·raine (mə rān′), *n.* mass of rocks, dirt, etc., deposited at the side or end of a glacier. [<F] —**mo·rain′ic,** *adj.*

mor·al (môr′əl; mor′–), *adj.* **1** good in character or conduct; virtuous according to civilized standards of right and wrong; right; just: *a moral act, a moral man.* **2** capable of understanding right and wrong: *a little baby is not a moral being.* **3** having to do with character or with the difference between right and wrong: *a moral question.* **4** teaching a good lesson; having a good influence. —*n.* **1** lesson, inner meaning, or teaching of a fable, a story, or an event. **morals, a** behavior in matters of right and wrong. **b** character. **c** principles in regard to conduct. [< L *moralis* < *mos* custom (pl., manners)]

mo·rale (mə ral′; –räl′), *n.* moral or mental condition as regards courage, confidence, enthusiasm, etc.: *the morale of troops.* [< F, fem. of *moral* MORAL]

mor·al·ist (môr′əl ist; mor′–) *n.* **1** person who thinks much about moral duties, sees the moral side of things, and leads a moral life. **2** person who teaches, studies, or writes about morals. —**mor′al·is′tic,** *adj.*

mo·ral·i·ty (mə ral′ə ti), *n., pl.* **–ties. 1** right or wrong of an action. **2** doing right; virtue. **3** system of morals; set of rules or principles of conduct.

mor·al·ize (môr′əl īz; mor′–) *v.,* **–ized, –iz·ing. 1** think, talk, or write about questions of right and wrong. **2** point out the lesson or inner meaning of. **3** improve the morals of. —**mor′al·i·za′tion,** *n.* —**mor′al·iz′er,** *n.*

mor·al·ly (môr′əl i; mor′–), *adv.* **1** in a moral manner. **2** in morals; as to morals. **3** ethically: *things morally considered.*

moral victory, defeat that has the effect on the mind that a victory would have.

mo·rass (mə ras′), *n.* piece of low, soft, wet ground; swamp. [< Du. *moeras* < OF *marais* < Gmc.]

mor·a·to·ri·um (môr′ə tô′ri əm; mor′–; –tō′–), *n., pl.* **–ri·ums, –ri·a** (–ri ə). **1** a legal authorization to delay payments of money due. **2** period during which such authorization is in effect. **3** any voluntary or negotiated ending of an activity: *declare a moratorium on swearing.* [< NL, < L *morari* delay < *mora* a delay]

mor·bid (môr′bid), *adj.* **1** unhealthy; not wholesome: *a morbid liking for horror.* **2** caused by disease; characteristic of disease; diseased: *cancer is a morbid growth.* **3** frightful; ghastly: *morbid events.* [< L *morbidus* < *morbus* dis-

ease] —**mor·bid′i·ty, mor′bid·ness,** *n.* —**mor′bid·ly,** *adv.*

mor·dant (môr′dənt), *adj.* biting; cutting; sarcastic. —*n.* **1** substance that fixes colors in dyeing. **2** acid that eats into metal. [< OF, ppr. of *mordre* bite < L *mordere*] —**mor′dan·cy,** *n.* —**mor′dant·ly,** *adv.*

mor·dent (môr′dənt), *n.* grace note or embellishment in music. [< G Mordent < It. *mordente,* ppr. of *mordere* bite]

more (môr; mōr), *adj.* (used as comparative of **much** and **many,** with the superlative **most**), *n., adv.* (often used before adjectives and adverbs, and regularly before those of more than two syllables, to form comparatives). —*adj.* **1** greater in number, quantity, amount, degree, or importance: *more men, more help.* **2** further; additional: *take more time.* —*n.* **1** a greater number, quantity, amount, or degree: *the more they have, the more they want.* **2** an additional amount: *tell me more.* —*adv.* **1** in or to a greater extent or degree: *that hurts more.* **2** in addition; further; longer; again: *sing once more.* **be no more,** be dead.

more and more, a increasingly more. **b** to an increasing degree.

more or less, a somewhat: *more or less accurate.* **b** nearly; approximately: *five miles more or less.* [OE *māra*]

mo·rel (mə rel′), *n.* edible mushroom with a brown, spongy cap, regarded as a delicacy. [< F *morille* < Gmc.]

more·o·ver (môr ō′vər; mōr–), *adv.* also; besides; in addition to that: *his power is absolute and, moreover, hereditary.*

mo·res (mô′rēz; mō′–), *n.pl.* traditional rules; customs. [< L, manners]

mor·ga·nat·ic (môr′gə nat′ik), *adj.* designating or pertaining to a form of marriage in which a man of high rank marries a woman of lower rank with an agreement that neither she nor her children shall have any claim to his rank or property. [< NL *morganaticus* morning gift, ult. < OHG *morgan* morning] —**mor′ga·nat′i·cal·ly,** *adv.*

morgue (môrg), *n.* **1** place in which the bodies of unknown persons found dead are kept until they can be identified. **2** in a newspaper office, the reference library. [< F]

mor·i·bund (môr′ə bund; mor′–), *adj.* dying. [< L *moribundus* < *mori* die] —**mor′i·bun′di·ty,** *n.* —**mor′i·bund·ly,** *adv.*

Mor·mon (môr′mən), *n.* member of the Church of Jesus Christ of Latter-day Saints, founded in 1830 by Joseph Smith. —*adj.* of or pertaining to the Mormons or their religion. —**Mor′mon·ism,** *n.*

morn (môrn), *n. Poetic.* morning. [OE *morgen*]

morn·ing (môr′ning), *n.* **1** the early part of the day, ending at noon. **2** dawn. **3** the first or early part of anything. —*adj.* of or in the morning. [ME *morwening* (see MORN); patterned on *evening*]

morning-after pill, oral contraceptive that prevents pregnancy if taken relatively soon after intercourse.

morn·ing-glo·ry (môr′ning glô′ri;–glō–), *n., pl.* **–ries.** a climbing vine with heart-shaped leaves and funnel-shaped blue, lavender, pink, or white flowers.

morning sickness, nausea and vomiting, esp. in the morning, a fairly common symptom of early pregnancy.

morning star, planet, esp. Venus, seen in the eastern sky before sunrise.

Mo·roc·co (mə rok′ō), *n.* country in NW Africa. —**Mo·roc′can,** *adj.*

mo·roc·co (mə rok′ō), *n., pl.* **–cos. 1** a fine leather made from goatskins, used in binding books. **2** leather imitating this.

mo·ron (mô′ron; mō′–), *n.* **1** person of 20 years or more who has the same intelligence as an ordinary child from 8 to 12 years old. **2** *Informal.* a stupid person; dummy. [< Gk., neut., foolish, dull] —**mo·ron′ic,** *adj.*

mo·rose (mə rōs′), *adj.* gloomy; sullen; ill-humored. [< L *morosus,* orig., set in one's ways < *mos* habit] —**mo·rose′ly,** *adv.* —**mo·rose′ness,** *n.*

morph (môrf), *v.* change; transform. [< *morph* a variant form, in biology]

mor·pheme (môr′fēm), *n.* smallest part of a word that has meaning of its own, including words, prefixes, suffixes, etc. [< F *morphème* < Gk. *morphé* form]

mor·phine (môr′fēn), *n.* drug made from opium, used to dull pain and to cause sleep. [< F < G *morphin* < *Morpheus* Morpheus]

mor·phol·o·gy (môr fol′ə ji), *n.* **1** branch of biology that deals with the forms and structure of animals and plants. **2** branch of the science of language that deals with forms of words as affected by inflection, derivation, etc. [< Gk. *morphe* form + –LOGY] —**mor′pho·log′ic, mor′pho·log′i·cal,** *adj.* —**mor′pho·log′i·cal·ly,** *adv.* —**mor·phol′o·gist,** *n.*

morris dance, an old English dance performed by people in fancy costumes.

mor·row (môr′ō; mor′o), *n.* **1** the following day or time. **2** *Archaic.* morning. **3** tomorrow. [ME *morwe,* var. of *morwen* MORN]

Morse code, a telegraphic alphabet made up of dots, dashes, and spaces. [< Samuel F. B. *Morse* (1791–1872), American inventor of the telegraph]

mor·sel (môr′səl), *n.* **1** a small bite; mouthful. **2** piece; fragment. [< OF, dim. of *mors* a bite, ult. < L *mordere* bite]

mor·tal (môr təl), *adj.* **1** sure to die sometime: *all creatures are mortal.* **2** of man: *past all mortal aid.* **3** causing death: *a mortal wound.* **4** to the death: *a mortal enemy.* **5** very great; deadly: *mortal terror.* —*n.* man; human being. [< L *mortalis* < *mors* death] —**mor′tal·ly,** *adv.*

mor·tal·i·ty (môr tal′ə ti), *n.* **1** mortal nature; being sure to die sometime. **2** loss of life on a large scale: *the mortality from automobile accidents is very serious.*

mor·tar[1] (môr′tər), *n.* mixture of lime, sand, and water, or of cement, sand, and water, for holding bricks or stones together. [< OF *mortier* < L *mortarium*]

mor·tar[2] (môr′tər), *n.* **1** bowl of very hard material, in which substances may be pounded to a powder. **2** a short cannon for shooting shells at high angles. [< L *mortarium* (through F for the meaning "cannon")]

mor·tar·board (môr′tər bôrd′; -bōrd′), *n.* an academic cap with a flat, square top.

mort·gage (môr′gij), *n., v.,* **-gaged, -gag·ing.** —*n.* **1** claim on property, given to a person who has loaned money in case the money is not repaid when due. **2** document that gives such a claim. —*v.* **1** give a lender a claim to (one's property) in case a debt is not paid when due. **2** put under some obligation; pledge. [< OF, < *mort* dead (< L *mortuus*) + *gage* pledge, GAGE[1]]

mort·ga·gee (môr′gi jē′), *n.* person to whom property is mortgaged.

mort·ga·gor (môr′gi jər), *n.* person who mortgages his or her property.

mor·ti·cian (môr tish′ən), *n.* undertaker.

mor·ti·fi·ca·tion (môr′tə fə kā′shən), *n.* **1** shame; humiliation. **2** cause of shame or humiliation. **3** a mortifying or being mortified: *the mortification of the body by fasting.*

mor·ti·fy (môr′tə fī), *v.,* **-fied, -fy·ing. 1** make ashamed; humiliate: *a child's misconduct mortifies its parent.* **2** overcome (bodily desires and feelings) by pain and self-denial: *saints often mortified their bodily cravings.* **3** die; decay: *cut off an injured foot that has mortified.* [< OF < L *mortificare* kill < L *mors* death + *facere* make] —**mor′ti·fi·er,** *n.*

mor·tise (môr′tis), *n., v.,* **-tised, -tis·ing.** —*n.* a rectangular hole in one piece of wood cut to receive a projection on another piece (called the tenon) so as to form a joint. —*v.* **1** cut a mortise in. **2** fasten by a mortise. [< F *mortaise* < Ar. *murtazz* fastened]

mor·tu·ar·y (môr′chů er′i), *n., pl.* **-ar·ies,** *adj.* —*n.* **1** building where dead bodies are kept until burial. **2** =morgue. —*adj.* of death or burial. [< Med.L *mortuarium,* ult. < L *mors* death]

mos., months

mo·sa·ic (mō zā′ik), *n.* **1** small pieces of stone, glass, wood, etc., of different colors inlaid to form a picture or design. **2** such a picture or design. **3** anything like a mosaic. —*adj.* formed by, pertaining to, or resembling such work. [< Med.L *mosaicus, musaicus* of the Muses. See MUSE.]

Mo·sa·ic (mō zā′ik), *adj.* of Moses or of writings ascribed to him.

Mosaic law, 1 the ancient laws of the Hebrews ascribed to Moses. **2** part of the Bible where these laws are stated.

Mos·cow (mos′kou; -kō), *n.* capital of Russia.

Mo·ses (mō′ziz; -zis), *n.* the great leader and lawgiver of the Israelites.

mo·sey (mō′zi), *v.,* **-seyed, -sey·ing.** *Informal.* **1** shuffle along. **2** saunter; amble.

Mos·lem (moz′ləm; mos′-), *n., pl.* **-lems, -lem,** *adj.* Muslim.

mosque (mosk), *n.* a Muslim place of worship. [< F < Ital. < Ar. *masjid* < *sajada* prostrate oneself]

mos·qui·to (məs kē′tō), *n., pl.* **-toes, -tos.** a small, thin insect whose female gives a bite or sting that itches. Some kinds transmit malaria; some transmit yellow fever. [< Sp., dim. of *mosca* < L *musca* fly]

mosquito net, piece of fine netting hung on a frame, esp. over a bed, to keep mosquitos away.

moss (môs; mos), *n.* **1** very small, soft, green or brown plants that grow close together like a carpet on the ground, on rocks, on trees, etc. **2** any of various similar plants. [OE *mos* bog]

moss rose, a cultivated rose with moss-like growth on the calyx and stem.

moss·y (môs′i; mos′i), *adj.,* **moss·i·er, moss·i·est. 1** covered with moss: *a mossy bank.* **2** like moss: *mossy green.* —**moss′i·ness,** *n.*

most (mōst), *adj.* (used as superlative of **much** and **many,** with the comparative **more**), *n., adv.* (often used before adjectives and adverbs, and regularly before those of more than two syllables, to form superlatives). —*adj.* **1** the greatest quantity, amount, measure, degree, or number of: *the winner gets the most money.* **2** almost all: *most children like candy.* —*n.* the greatest quantity, amount, degree, or number: *he did most of the work.* —*adv.* **1** in or to the greatest extent or degree: *which hurt most?* **2** almost; nearly.

at most or **at the most,** not more than.

for the most part, mainly; usually.

make the most of, make the best use of.

the most, *Informal.* the ultimate: *his behavior was the most.*

-most, suffix forming superlatives, as in *foremost, inmost, topmost, uttermost.* [ME]

most·ly (mōst′li), *adv.* almost all; for the most part; mainly; chiefly.

mo·tel (mō tel′), *n.* a hotel, usually located near a highway, which provides sleeping, and often eating, accommodations for motorists. [blend of *motor* and *hotel*]

moth (môth; moth), *n., pl.* **moths** (môthz; mothz; môths; moths). **1** a small, winged insect that lays eggs in cloth, fur, etc. Its larvae eat holes in the material. **2** a broad-winged insect very much like a butterfly, but flying mostly at night. [OE *moththe*] —**moth′y,** *adj.*

moth ball, ball of naphthalene, used to keep moths away from wool, silk, fur, etc.

moth·ball (môth′bôl′; moth′-), *v.* **1** clean and cover (something) with a protective film to prepare it for temporary storage.

2 take (ships, aircraft, etc.) out of service for storage.

moth-eat·en (môth′ēt′ən; moth′-), *adj.* **1** having holes made by moths. **2** *Fig.* worn-out; out-of-date.

moth·er[1] (muŧh′ər), *n.* **1** a female parent. **2** person who is like a mother. **3** *Fig.* cause; source: *Necessity is the mother of invention.* **4** head of a female religious community; woman exercising control and responsibility like that of a mother. —*v.* **1** be mother of; act as mother to. **2** acknowledge oneself mother of or assume as one's own. —*adj.* **1** that is a mother. **2** like a mother. **3** of a mother. [OE *mōdor*] —**moth′er·less,** *adj.*

moth·er[2] (muŧh′ər), *n.* a stringy, sticky substance formed in vinegar or on liquids turning to vinegar. Mother consists of bacteria. [special use of *mother*[1]]

mother country, 1 country where a person was born. **2** country in relation to its colonies or its natives.

mother earth, the earth as the source and protector of its inhabitants and resources.

moth·er·hood (muŧh′ər hůd), *n.* **1** state of being a mother. **2** qualities of a mother. **3** mothers.

moth·er-in-law (muŧh′ər in lô′), *n., pl.* **moth·ers-in-law. 1** mother of one's husband or wife. **2** stepmother.

moth·er·land (muŧh′ər land′), *n.* **1** one's native country. **2** land of one's ancestors.

mother lode, rich, large vein of ore.

moth·er·ly (muŧh′ər li), *adj.* **1** of a mother. **2** like a mother; like a mother's; kindly. —**moth′er·li·ness,** *n.*

moth·er-of-pearl (muŧh′ər əv pėrl′), *n.* the hard, rainbow-colored lining of certain shells, used to make buttons and ornaments; nacre.

Mother's Day, the second Sunday of May, set apart in the United States in honor of mothers.

mother ship, 1 aircraft that carries another aircraft, drone, etc., aloft and launches it in flight. **2** ship, aircraft, etc., that acts as a base of operations for other ships or aircraft.

mother superior, woman who is the head of a convent of nuns.

mother tongue, 1 one's native language. **2** language to which other languages owe their origin.

moth·proof (môth′prüf′; moth′-), *adj.* repelling or resisting to moths. —*v.* make repellant or resistant to moths.

mo·tif (mō tēf′), *n.* **1** subject for development or treatment in art, literature, or music. **2** element of a design, painting, etc., which imparts a theme or unity. [< F]

mo·tile (mō′təl), *adj.* able to move by itself. [< L *motus* moved] —**mo·til′i·ty,** *n.*

mo·tion (mō′shən), *n.* **1** change of position or place; movement; moving: *the* *motion of one's hand in writing.* **2** a formal suggestion made in a meeting or law court: *the motion to adjourn was carried.* —*v.* **1** make a movement, as of the hand or head, to show one's meaning. **2** show (a person) what to do by such a motion: *he motioned me out.*

go through the motions, do something automatically or as a habit.

in motion, moving.

motions, movements; actions; activities. [< L *motio* < *movere* move]

mo·tion·less (mō′shən lis), *adj.* not moving. —**mo′tion·less·ly,** *adv.* —**mo′tion·less·ness,** *n.*

motion picture, series of pictures shown on a screen in which people and things seem to move; movie; film.

motion sickness, feeling of dizziness, nausea, etc., experienced when in motion, as in an automobile, etc.

mo·ti·vate (mō′tə vāt), *v.*, **-vat·ed, -vat·ing.** provide with a motive: act upon as a motive. —**mo′ti·va′tion,** *n.*

mo·tive (mō′tiv), *n.* thought or feeling that makes one act: *his motive in going away was a wish to travel.* —*adj.* that makes something move: *steam is the motive power of this engine.* [< Med.L *motivum* moving (impulse) < L *movere* to move]

mot·ley (mot′li), *n., pl.* **-leys,** *adj.* —*n.* suit of more than one color worn by clowns. —*adj.* **1** of different colors like a clown's suit. **2** made up of units not alike: *a motley collection.* [ME *motteley*]

mo·to·cross (mō′tō krôs′), *n.* cross-country motorcycle race. [< F *moto cross* < *moto–* motorcycle + (E) *cross*-country]

mo·tor (mō′tər), *n.* **1** any thing or person that imparts motion, esp. an engine that makes a machine go. **2** an internal-combustion engine. —*adj.* **1** pertaining to a motor. **2** run by a motor. **3** having to do with motion. **4** having to do with bodily movements. Motor nerves arouse muscles to action. [< L, mover < *movere* to move]

mo·tor·boat (mō′tər bōt′), *n.* boat that is run by a motor.

mo·tor·cade (mō′tər kād), *n.* procession or long line of automobiles.

mo·tor·car (mō′tər kär′), *n.* =automobile.

motor coach, =coach.

mo·tor·cy·cle (mō′tər sī′kəl), *n.* a self-propelled, two-wheeled vehicle. —**mo′tor·cy′clist,** *n.*

motor home, motor vehicle that has living accommodations for recreational travel and camping; recreational vehicle.

mo·tor·ist (mō′tər ist), *n.* person who drives or travels in an automobile.

mo·tor·ize (mō′tər īz), *v.,* **-ized, -iz·ing. 1** furnish with a motor. **2** supply (infantry units, cavalry, etc.) with motor-driven vehicles to facilitate maneuverability. —**mo′tor·i·za′tion,** *n.*

mo·tor·man (mō′tər mən), *n., pl.* **-men. 1** person who runs an electric train. **2** person who runs a motor.

motor scooter, two-wheeled vehicle like a small motorcycle.

mot·tle (mot′əl), *v.,* **-tled, -tling,** *n.* —*v.* mark with spots or streaks of different colors. —*n.* a mottled coloring or pattern. [? < *motley*] —**mot′tler,** *n.*

mot·to (mot′ō), *n., pl.* **-toes, -tos.** a brief sentence adopted as a rule of conduct. [< Ital. < L *muttum* grunt, word. Doublet of MOT.]

mould (mōld), *n., v., Esp. Brit.* mold. —**mould′a·ble,** *adj.*

mound (mound), *n.* **1** bank or heap of earth or stones. **2** a small hill. **3** in baseball, the slightly elevated ground from which the pitcher pitches. —*v.* enclose with a mound; heap up. [OE *mund* protection; meaning infl. by *mount*[2]]

mount[1] (mount), *v.* **1** go or get up; get up on: *mount stairs.* **2** move or proceed upwards: *a flush mounts to the brow.* **3** rise; increase; rise in amount: *the costs are mounting.* **4** get on a horse; put on a horse: *mounted the nervous horse with difficulty* **5** put in proper position or order for use: *mount specimens on slides, mount a picture on cardboard.* **6** go or put on (guard) as a sentry or watch does. —*n.* **1** horse provided for riding. **2** a setting; backing; support. **3** act of mounting. **4** manner of mounting. [< OF *monter* < L *mons* mountain] —**mount′a·ble,** *adj.* —**mount′er,** *n.*

mount[2] (mount), *n.* mountain; high hill. [< L *mons*]

moun·tain (moun′tən), *n.* **1** very high hill. **2** something like a high hill: *a mountain of rubbish.* **3** a huge amount. —*adj.* **1** of or pertaining to mountains. **2** living, growing, or found on mountains. **3** resembling or suggesting a mountain.

make a mountain out of a mole hill, assign great importance to something unimportant. [< OF *montaigne* < *mont* MOUNT[2]]

mountain ash, any of several trees of the rose family with pinnate leaves, white flowers, and bright-red berries.

mountain bike, bicycle with a strong frame equipped with multiple gears, for bicycling on rugged terrain.

moun·tain·eer (moun′tə nir′), *n.* **1** person who lives in the mountains. **2** person skilled in mountain climbing. —*v.* climb mountains.

mountain goat, the white antelope of the Rocky Mountains.

mountain gorilla, gorilla of the mountain forests of Congo and Uganda, larger in size and having longer hair than other gorillas.

mountain laurel, an evergreen shrub with glossy leaves and pale-pink flowers.

mountain lion, =cougar.

moun·tain·ous (moun′tə nəs), *adj.* **1** covered with mountain ranges. **2** huge.

mountain sheep, the wild sheep of the Rocky Mountains, including the bighorn.

moun·te·bank (moun′tə bangk), *n.* **1** any person who tries to deceive people; charlatan. **2** person who sells quack medicines in public, appealing to his audience by tricks, stories, jokes, etc. —*v.* act like a mountebank. [< Ital. *montambanco* for *monta in banco* mount-on-bench]

mount·ed (moun′tid), *adj.* **1** on a vehicle, horse, etc. **2** positioned for use: *mounted gun.* **3** on a support; in a jewelry setting.

mount·ing (moun′ting), *n.* support, setting, or the like: *the mounting of a photograph.*

mourn (môrn; mōrn), *v.* **1** grieve. **2** feel or show sorrow over. [OE *murnan*] —**mourn′er,** *n.*

mourn·ful (môrn′fəl; mōrn′–), *adj.* **1** sad; sorrowful. **2** gloomy; dreary. **3** causing, or attended with, sorrow or mourning. —**mourn′ful·ly,** *adv.* —**mourn′ful·ness,** *n.*

mourn·ing (môr′ning; mōr′–), *n.* **1** sorrowing; lamentation. **2** the wearing of black or some other color, to show sorrow for a person's death. **3** a draping of buildings, hanging flags at half-mast, etc., as signs of such sorrow. **4** clothes, draperies, etc., to show such sorrow. —*adj.* of mourning; used in mourning. —**mourn′ing·ly,** *adv.*

mourning dove, a wild dove of North America that makes a mournful sound.

mouse (*n.* mous; *v.* mouz), *n., pl.* **mice** (mīs), *v.,* **moused, mous·ing.** —*n.* **1** a small, gray, gnawing animal. **2** a shy, timid person. **3** device that moves a cursor on a computer screen. *v.* **1** hunt for mice; catch mice for food. **2** search as a cat does; move about as if searching. [OE *mūs*]

mous·er (mouz′ər), *n.* animal that catches mice.

mous·sa·ka (mü′sä kä′), *n.* Greek baked dish made of alternating layers of ground meat and eggplant or zucchini with a topping of dough and cheese.

mousse (müs), *n.* a fancy food made with whipped cream, either frozen or stiffened with gelatin or beaten egg whites: *chocolate mousse, chicken mousse.* [< F, moss, < Gmc.]

mous·y (mous′i), *adj.,* **mous·i·er, mous·i·est. 1** resembling or suggesting a mouse in color, odor, behavior, etc. **2** quiet as a mouse. **3** infested with mice.

mouth (*n.* mouth; *v.* mouᵺ), *n., pl.* **mouths** (mouᵺz), *v.* —*n.* **1** opening through which an animal takes in food. **2** space containing tongue and teeth. **3** an opening suggesting a mouth: *the mouth of a river.* —*v.* **1** seize or rub with the mouth. **2** utter (words) in an affected or pompous way.

foam at the mouth, a be very angry. **b** be too eager.

make one's mouth water, stimulate one's appetite or desire.

mouth off or **shoot one's mouth off,** talk too frankly or indiscreetly. [OE *mūth*] —**mouth·er**, *n.* —**mouth·less**, *adj.*

mouth·ful (mouth'fúl), *n., pl.* **-fuls. 1** amount the mouth can hold. **2** what is taken into the mouth at one time. **3** a small amount; enough to taste. **4** a great deal: *said a mouthful.*

mouth organ, =harmonica.

mouth·piece (mouth'pēs'), *n.* **1** the part of a pipe, horn, etc., that is placed in or against a person's mouth. **2** piece placed at the mouth of something or forming its mouth. **3** guard for the mouth to protect it from injury in sports. **4** *Fig.* person, newspaper, etc., that speaks for others.

mouth·wash (mouth'wosh'; -wôsh'), *n.* antiseptic liquid for rinsing the mouth.

mouth·y (mouth'ĭ; mouth'ī), *adj.,* **mouth·i·er, mouth·i·est.** loud-mouthed. —**mouth'i·ly,** *adv.* —**mouth'i·ness,** *n.*

mov·a·ble (müv'ə bəl), *adj.* **1** that can be moved. **2** that can be carried from place to place as personal possessions can. **3** changing from one date to another in different years. Easter is a movable holy day. —*n.* piece of furniture that is not a fixture but can be moved to another house. —**mov'a·bil·i·ty; mov'a·ble·ness,** *n.* —**mov'a·bly,** *adv.*

move (müv),*v.,* **moved, mov·ing,***n.* —*v.* **1** change place or position: *the trees move.* **2** change one's abode: *we move next week.* **3** make a move in a game: *I move my bishop.* **4** put or keep in motion: *the wind moves the trees.* **5** act: *God moves in a mysterious way.* **6** impel; rouse; excite: *power to move the masses, move men to tears.* **7** make a proposal: *I move that we adjourn.* **8** make progress; go: *the train moves slowly.*—*n.* **1** right or time to move in a game. **2** act of moving; movement. **3** action toward a goal: *a move to disconcert his opponents.*

get a move on, *Informal.* **a** hurry. **b** begin to move.

move in, move one's family, possessions, etc., into a new place to live.

move up, promote or be promoted: *moved up to district manager.*

on the move, moving about. [< AF < L *movere*] —**mov'er,** *n.*

move·ment (müv'mənt), *n.* **1** act or fact of moving: *movements of the legs.* **2** the moving parts of a machine. The movement of a watch consists of many little wheels. **3 a** the kind of rhythm a piece has, its speed, etc. **b** one division of a long musical selection. **4** suggestion of motion in a pointing or sculpture. **5** efforts and results of a group of people working together to bring about some one thing: *women's movement, the movement for gun control.*

mov·ie (müv'ĭ), *n.* a motion picture.

mov·ing (müv'ing), *adj.* **1** that moves. **2** causing motion; actuating. **3** touching; pathetic: *a moving story.* —**mov'ing·ly,** *adv.*

moving picture, =motion picture.

mow[1] (mō), *v.,* **mowed, mowed** or **mown, mow·ing. 1** cut down with a machine or a scythe. **2** cut down grass or grain. **3** destroy in large numbers, as if by mowing. [OE *māwan*] —**mow'er,** *n.*

mow[2] (mou), *n.* **1** place in a barn where hay, grain, or the like is piled or stored. **2** pile or stack of hay, grain, etc., in a barn. [OE *mūga*]

Mo·zam·bique (mō'zəm bēk'), *n.* a country in SE Africa.

M.P., 1 Member of Parliament. **2** Also, **MP.** Military Police.

mph, m.p.h., miles per hour.

Mr., Mr (mis'tər), *pl.* **Messrs.** mister, title put in front of a man's name or the name of his position.

MRE, meals ready to eat, emergency rations, esp. for the military.

mRNA, messenger RNA.

Mrs. or **Mrs** (mis'iz; miz'iz; miz), *pl.* **Mmes.** title put in front of a married woman's name.

Ms. or **Ms** (miz), *n., pl.* **Mses.** or **Mses** title put in front of a woman's name.

Ms., MS., or **ms.,** *pl.* **Mss.; MSS.; mss.** manuscript.

MS, 1 (*zip code*) Mississippi. **2** multiple sclerosis.

M.S., M.Sc., Master of Science.

Msgr., Monsignor.

M.S.T., MST, or **m.s.t.,** Mountain Standard Time.

MT, (*zip code*) Montana.

Mt., *pl.* **Mts.** Mount: *Mt. Everest.*

mt., mtn., *pl.* **mts.: mtns.** mountain.

mu (mū), *n.* the 12th letter of the Greek alphabet (M, μ).

much (much), *adj.,* **more, most,** *adv.,* **more, most,** *n.* —*adj.* in great quantity, amount, or degree: *much money, much time.*—*adv.* **1** to a great extent or degree: *much pleased.* **2** nearly about: *this is much the same as the others.* —*n.* **1** a great deal: *much of this is not true.* **2** a great, important, or notable thing or matter: *the rain did not amount to much.*

much as, a in the same way as. **b** though.

not much of, small in amount or degree of: *not much of a salary, not much of a housekeeper.*

make much of, treat, represent, or consider as of great importance. [var. of OE *micel*] —**much'ness,** *n.*

mu·ci·lage (mū'sə lij), *n.* **1** a gummy substance used to stick things together. **2** substance like glue or gelatin in plants. [< F < LL *mucilago* musty juice < L *mucus* mucus]

mu·ci·lag·i·nous (mū'sə laj'ə nəs), *adj.* **1** sticky; gummy. **2** containing or secreting mucilage.

muck (muk), *n.* **1** dirt; filth. **2** moist farmyard manure. —*v.* **1** soil or make dirty. **2** put muck on.

muck about or **around,** *Informal.* fool around; waste time.

muck out, clean out, esp. a stable.

muck up, *Informal.* ruin; mess up. [< Scand. *myki*] —**muck'y,** *adj.*

muck·rake (muk'rāk'), *v.,* **-raked, -rak·ing.** hunt for and expose corruption. —**muck'rak·er,** *n.*

mu·cous (mū'kəs), *adj.* **1** of or like mucus. **2** containing or secreting mucus.

mucous membrane, lining of the nose, throat, and other cavities that are open to the air.

mu·cus (mū'kəs), *n.* a slimy substance that moistens the linings of the body. [< L]

mud (mud), *n.* soft, sticky, wet earth. [ME *mudde*]

mud·dle (mud'əl), *v.,* **-dled, -dling,** *n.* —*v.* **1** mix up; bring (things) into a mess. **2** make confused or stupid or slightly drunk. **3** think or act in a confused, blundering way. —*n.* mess; disorder; confusion.

muddle through, manage somehow. [< *mud*] —**mud'dler,** *n.*

mud·dy (mud'ĭ), *adj.,* **-di·er, -di·est,** *v.,* **-died, -dy·ing.** —*adj.* **1** of or like mud. **2** having much mud; covered with mud. **3** clouded with mud; dull; not pure: *muddy water, a muddy color.* **4** confused; not clear. —*v.* make or become muddy. —**mud'di·ly,** *adv.* —**mud'di·ness,** *n.*

mud hen, water bird that looks like a large chicken. It lives in marshes.

mud puppy, salamander that lives in water.

mu·ez·zin (mū ez'in), *n.* crier who, at certain hours, calls Muslims to prayer. [< Ar. *mu'adhdhin*]

muff (muf), *n.* **1** a covering of fur or other material for a woman to keep both hands warm. One hand is put in at each end. **2** a clumsy failure to catch a ball that comes into one's hands. —*v.* **1** fail to catch (a ball) when it comes into one's hands. **2** bungle. [< Du. < F *moufle*]

muf·fin (muf'ən), *n.* a small, round cake made of wheat flour, corn meal, or the like, eaten with butter and usually served hot.

muf·fle (muf'əl), *v.,* **-fled, -fling,** *n.* —*v.* **1** dull or deaden (a sound). **2** wrap or cover with something in order to soften or stop the sound. **3** wrap or cover up in order to keep warm and dry. —*n.* a muffled sound. [< OF *enmoufler* wrap up < *moufle* muff]

muf·fler (muf'lər), *n.* **1** thing used to deaden sound: *the muffler of a motor.* **2** wrap or scarf worn around the neck for warmth.

muf·ti (muf'ti), *n., pl.* **-tis.** ordinary clothes, not a uniform. [< Ar. *muftī* (Muslim jurist, judge), with ref. to clothing worn by such an official when not at work]

mug (mug), *n., v.,* **mugged, mug·ging.** —*n.* **1** a heavy earthenware or metal drinking cup with a handle. **2** amount a mug holds. **3** face. —*v.* attack (a person), esp from behind. [cf. Scand. (Norw.) *mugge;* def. 3 from common shape of mugs in earlier times] —**mug'ger,** *n.*

mug·gy (mug′i), *adj.,* **-gi·er, -gi·est.** warm and humid; damp and close. [< *mug* fog < Scand. *mugga*] **—mug′gi·ness,** *n.*

Mu·ham·mad (mə häm′id), *n.* A.D. 570?–632, founder and prophet of Islam, a religion widely practiced in Asia and Africa. Also, **Mohammed.**

mu·ja·hed·din or **mu·ja·he·din** (mü jä′hə dēn), *n. pl.* Muslim guerrilla fighters, esp. in Afghanistan and Iran. Also, **mujahideen, mujahedeen.** [< Ar. *mujähidïn,* pl. of *mujähid* fighter < *jihäd* struggle, fight, jihad]

mu·lat·to (mə lat′ō; myü–), *n., pl.* **-toes. 1** person having one white and one black parent. **2** person having some white and some black ancestry. [< Sp. and *mulato* < *mulo* mule; from hybrid origin]

mul·ber·ry (mul′ber′i), *n., pl.* **-ries. 1** any of various trees such as the **American mulberry** that yields a berrylike fruit or the **white mulberry** whose leaves are used for feeding silkworms. **2** the berrylike fruit of any of these trees. **3** dark purplish red. [OE *mōrberie* < L *morum* mulberry + OE *berie* berry]

mulch (mulch), *n.* straw, leaves, loose earth, etc., spread on the ground around trees or plants, used to protect the roots from cold or heat, to prevent evaporation of moisture from the soil, etc. *—v.* cover with straw, leaves, etc. [OE *mylsc* mellow]

mule¹ (mül), *n.* **1** offspring of the ass and horse, esp. of a male ass and a mare. **2** a stubborn person. [< F < L *mula, mulus*]

mule² (mül), *n.* kind of slipper that leaves the heel uncovered. [< F < Du. < L *mulleus* shoe of red leather]

mule skinner, *Informal.* muleteer.

mu·le·teer (mü′lə tir′), *n.* driver of mules.

mul·ish (mül′ish), *adj.* stubborn; obstinate. **—mul′ish·ly,** *adv.* **—mul′ish·ness,** *n.*

mull¹ (mul), *v.* think (about) without making much progress; ponder.

mull² (mul), *v.* make (wine, beer, etc.) into a warm drink, with sugar, spices, etc.

mul·lah (mul′ə; mŭl′ə), *n.* in Muslim countries, a title of respect for one who is learned in the sacred law. [< Turk., Pers., Hind. *mullä* < Ar. *mawlä*]

mul·lein, mul·len (mul′ən), *n.* weed with coarse, woolly leaves and spikes of yellow flowers. [< AF *moleine*]

mul·let (mul′it), *n., pl.* **-lets** or (*esp. collectively*) **-let.** kind of edible fish. There are red mullets and gray mullets. [< OF *mulet* < L *mullus* red mullet < Gk. *myllos*]

mul·lion (mul′yən), *n.* a vertical bar between the lights of a window, the panels in the wall of a room, or the like. **—mul′lioned,** *adj.*

multi-, *combining form.* **1** having many or several, as in *multiform.* **2** many or several times, as in *multimillionaire.* [< L, < *multus* much, many]

mul·ti·cel·lu·lar (mul′ti sel′yə lər), *adj.* having more than one cell.

mul·ti·col·ored (mul′ti kul′ərd), *adj.* having many colors.

mul·ti·cul·tur·al (mul′ti kul′chər əl), *adj.* having or combining many distinct cultures. **—mul′ti·cul′tur·al·ism, mul′ti·cul′tur·al·ist,** *n.*

mul·ti·far·i·ous (mul′tə fâr′i əs), *adj.* **1** having many different parts, elements, forms, etc. **2** many and various. [< L *multifarius*] **—mul′ti·far′i·ous·ly,** *adv.*

mul·ti·form (mul′tə fôrm), *adj.* having many different shapes, forms, or kinds. **—mul′ti·for′mi·ty,** *n.*

mul·ti·lat·er·al (mul′ti lat′ər əl), *adj.* **1** having many sides; many-sided. **2** involving two or more nations. **—mul′ti·lat′er·al·ly,** *adv.*

mul·ti·me·di·a (mul′ti mē′di ə), *adj.* **1** using or involving the use of various media as films, recordings, etc., for entertainment or instruction; mixed media. **2** involving different communications media, in the same place. *—n.* use of various media at the same time and place.

mul·ti·mil·lion·aire (mul′ti mil′yən âr′), *n.* a millionaire many times over.

mul·ti·na·tion·al (mul′ti nash′ə nel), *adj.* of or involving many countries. *—n.* a company with branches, plants, etc., in many countries.

mul·ti·ple (mul′tə pəl), *adj.* of, having, or involving many parts, elements, relations, etc.: *a man of multiple interests.* *—n.* number that contains another number a certain number of times without a remainder. 12 is a multiple of 3. [< F < LL *multiplus* manifold]

multiple sclerosis, disorder of the nervous system that attacks the brain and spinal cord.

mul·ti·plex (mul′tə pleks), *adj.* **1** of many kinds, elements, etc. **2** transmitting more than one signal on a band, wave, or wire. *—n.* cinema with a number of smaller theaters within it.

mul·ti·pli·cand (mul′tə pli kand′), *n.* number or quantity to be multiplied by another. [< L *multiplicandus* to be multiplied. See MULTIPLY.]

mul·ti·pli·ca·tion (mul′tə plə kā′shən), *n.* **1** a multiplying. **2** a being multiplied.

mul·ti·plic·i·ty (mul′tə plis′ə ti), *n., pl.* **-ties.** a manifold variety; great many.

mul·ti·pli·er (mul′tə plī′ər), *n.* **1** number by which another number is to be multiplied. **2** person or thing that multiplies.

mul·ti·ply (mul′tə plī), *v.,* **-plied, -ply·ing. 1** increase in number or amount. **2** take (a number or quantity) a given number of times. To multiply 16 by 3 means to take 16 three times, making 48. [< OF < L *multiplicare* < *multiplex* manifold] **—mul′ti·pli′a·ble,** *adj.*

mul·ti·stage (mul′ti stāj), *adj.* of a rocket or missile, having two or more propul-

sive sections, each operating after the preceding stage has burned out and separated.

mul·ti·tude (mul′tə tüd; –tūd), *n.* a great many; crowd.

the multitude, the common people. [< L, < *multus* much]

mul·ti·tu·di·nous (mul′tə tü′də nəs; –tū′–), *adj.* **1** very numerous. **2** including many parts, elements, items, or features. **—mul′ti·tu′di·nous·ly,** *adv.* **—mul′ti·tu′di·nous·ness,** *n.*

mul·ti·va·lent (mul′ti vā′lənt; mul tiv′ə–), *adj.* having a valence of three or more. **—mul′ti·va′lence,** *n.*

mum¹ (mum), *adj.* silent; saying nothing. *—interj.* be silent! say nothing!

mum's the word, don't say anything. [ME; ? imit.]

mum² (mum), *n.* chrysanthemum.

Mumbai (mum bī′), *n.* =Bombay.

mum·ble (mum′bəl) *v.,* **-bled, -bling,** *n.* *—v.* speak indistinctly. *—n.* a mumbling. [ME *momele(n),* ? < *mum*] **—mum′bler,** *n.*

mum·bo·jum·bo (mum′bō jum′bō), *n.* nonsense, esp. talk which confuses or obscures. [< name of guardian genius of native African village in W Sudan]

mu·mes·on (myü′mes′on; –mē′son; –mez′on; –mē′zon), *n.* meson having a mass more than 200 times that of an electron; muon. [< Gk. *mu* letter designating a series + E *meson*]

mum·mer (mum′ər), *n.* **1** person who wears a mask, fancy costume, etc., for fun. **2** actor.

mum·mer·y (mum′ər i), *n., pl.* **-mer·ies. 1** performance of mummers. **2** useless or silly show or ceremony. [< OF *mommerie*]

mum·mi·fy (mum′ə fī), *v.,* **-fied, -fy·ing. 1** make (a dead body) into a mummy; make like a mummy. **2** dry or shrivel up. **—mum′mi·fi·ca′tion,** *n.*

mum·my (mum′i), *n., pl.* **-mies,** *v.,* **-mied, -my·ing.** *—n.* **1** a dead body preserved from decay. Egyptian mummies have lasted more than 3000 years. **2** a brown bituminous pigment. *—v.* mummify. [< Med.L < Ar. < Pers. *mümiyä* < *mum* wax]

mumps (mumps), *n. pl.* (*sing. in use*) a contagious disease marked by swelling of the face and difficulty in swallowing. [pl. of obs. *mump* grimace]

munch (munch), *v.* chew vigorously and steadily; chew noisily. [appar. imit.] **—munch′er,** *n.*

munch·ies (mun′chēz), *n.* **1** snack food. **2** hunger: *attack of the munchies.*

mun·dane (mun′dān), *adj.* **1** of this world, not of heaven; earthly. **2** of the universe; of the world. [< F < L, < *mundus* world] **—mun′dane·ly,** *adv.*

mu·nic·i·pal (mü nis′ə pəl), *adj.* **1** of or having to do with the affairs of a city, town, or other municipality. **2** run by a city, town, etc. **3** having local self-government. [< L *municipalis,* ult. < *munia* official duties + *capere* take on] —**mu·nic′i·pal·ly,** *adv.*

mu·nic·i·pal·i·ty (mū nis′ ə pal′ə ti), *n., pl.* **-ties.** city, town, or other district having local self-government.

mu·nif·i·cence (mū nif′ə səns), *n.* very great generosity. [< L, < *munificus* generous, ult. < *munus* gift + *facere* make]

mu·nif·i·cent (mū nif′ə sənt), *adj.* extremely generous. [< *munificence*] —**mu·nif′i·cent·ly,** *adv.*

mu·ni·tion (mū nish′ən), *n.* **munitions,** military materials used in war, such as guns, ammunition, or bombs. —*adj.* pertaining to materials for the military: *A munition plant is a factory for making munitions.* —*v.* provide with materials for the military. [< L, < *munire* fortify]

mu·ral (myŭr′əl), *adj.* **1** on a wall. **2** of a wall; having to do with walls; like a wall. **3** steep. —*n.* picture painted on a wall. [< F < L, < *murus* wall] —**mu′ral·ist,** *n.*

mur·der (mėr′dər), *n.* **1** the unlawful killing of a human being when it is planned beforehand. **2** *Informal. Fig.* anything very unpleasant or difficult: *the exam was murder.* —*v.* **1** kill thus. **2** spoil; do very badly.
get away with murder, do something objectionable without any consequences.
murder will out, a misdeed will be found out. [var. of obs. *murther,* OE *morthor*] —**mur′der·er,** *n.*

mur·der·ess (mėr′dər is), *n.* woman who murders somebody.

mur·der·ous (mėr′dər əs), *adj.* **1** capable of killing: *a murderous blow.* **2** ready to murder: *a murderous villain.* **3** causing murder: *a murderous plot.* —**mur′der·ous·ly,** *adv.*

mu·ri·at·ic acid (myŭr′i at′ik), hydrochloric acid. [< L, < *muria* brine]

murk (mėrk), *n.* darkness; gloom. —*adj. Poetic.* dark; gloomy. [< Scand, *myrkr*]

murk·y (mėr′ki), *adj.,* **murk·i·er, murk·i·est. 1** dark; gloomy. **2** *Fig.* not clear; obscure: *a murky past.* —**murk′i·ly,** *adv.* —**murk′i·ness,** *n.*

mur·mur (mėr′mər), *n.* **1** a soft, low, indistinct sound that rises and falls a little and goes on without breaks: *murmur of a stream, murmur of voices in another room.* **2** a sound in the heart or lungs, esp. an abnormal sound due to a leaky valve in the heart. **3** a softly spoken word or speech. —*v.* **1** make a soft, low, indistinct sound. **2** utter in a murmur. [< L *murmur*] —**mur′mur·er,** *n.* —**mur′mur·ing,** *adj.* —**mur′mur·ing·ly,** *adv.*

mus., 1 museum. **2** music; musical.

mus·ca·dine (mus′kə din; –dīn), *n.* grape of the S United States.

mus·cat (mus′kat; –kət), *n.* a light-colored grape with the flavor or odor of musk. [< F < Pr. < LL *muscatus* with musk < *muscus* musk]

mus·ca·tel (mus′kə tel′), *n.* **1** a strong, sweet wine made from muscat grapes. **2** the muscat grape. [< OF. See MUSCAT.]

mus·cle (mus′əl), *n., v.,* **-cled, -cling.** —*n.* **1** bundle of special tissue that can be tightened or loosened to move a part of the body. **2** this tissue. **3** strength. —*v.* move or lift using only the muscles.
muscle in, force oneself into a situation where one is not wanted. [< F < L *musculus,* dim. of *mus* mouse; from appearance of certain muscles]

mus·cle-bound (mus′əl bound′), *adj.* having some of the muscles stiff or tight, usually as a result of too much exercise.

Mus·co·vite (mus′kə vit), *n., adj.* **1** Russian. **2** of or from Moscow.

Mus·co·vy (mus′kə vi), *n. Archaic.* Russia.

mus·cu·lar (mus′kyə lər), *adj.* **1** of the muscles; influencing the muscles. **2** having well-developed muscles; strong. **3** consisting of muscle. —**mus′cu·lar′i·ty,** *n.* —**mus′cu·lar·ly,** *adv.*

muscular dys·tro·phy (dis′trə fi), a gradual wasting away and weakening of the muscles.

mus·cu·la·ture (mus′kyə lə chər), *n.* system or arrangement of muscles.

muse (mūz), *v.,* **mused, mus·ing. 1** think in a dreamy way; think; meditate. **2** look thoughtfully. **3** say thoughtfully. [< OF *muser* loiter] —**mus′er,** *n.*

Muse (mūz), *n.* **1** *Class. Myth.* one of the nine Greek Goddesses of the fine arts and sciences. **2** Sometimes, **muse.** spirit that inspires a poet or composer. [< OF < L < Gk. *Mousa*]

mu·se·um (mū zē′əm), *n.* building or rooms where a collection of objects illustrating science, art, ancient life, or other subjects is kept. [< L < Gk. *mouseion* seat of the Muses. See MUSE.]

mush¹ (mush), *n.* **1** corn meal boiled in water. **2** a soft, thick mass. **3** *Informal. Fig.* anything weak, sentimental, or silly, esp. talk. [var. of *mash.* Cf. Du. *moes.*]

mush² (mush), *n., v.* journey on foot, usually with a dog sled across snow. [? for *mush on,* alter. of F *marchons* let us advance] —**mush′er,** *n.*

mush·room (mush′rüm; –rŭm), *n.* **1** a small fungus, shaped like an umbrella, that grows very fast. Some mushrooms are good to eat; some are poisonous. **2** anything shaped or growing like a mushroom. —*adj.* **1** of or like a mushroom. **2** of very rapid growth. —*v.* **1** grow very fast. **2** flatten at one end: *A bullet sometimes mushrooms when it hits a very hard object.* [< F *mousseron,* ? < *mousse* moss < Gmc.]

mush·y (mush′i), *adj.,* **mush·i·er, mush·i·est. 1** like mush; pulpy. **2** weakly sentimental. —**mush′i·ness,** *n.*

mu·sic (mū′zik), *n.* **1** art of putting sounds together in various sequences and arrangements that have melody, harmony, and rhythm. **2** such arrangements of sounds, esp. as produced by instruments or the voice. **3** any pleas-

ant sound. **4** written or printed signs for tones.
face the music, meet trouble boldly or bravely.
set to music, provide (the words of a song) with music. [< L < Gk. *mousike* (*techne*) art of the Muse. See MUSE.]

mu·si·cal (mū′zə kəl), *adj.* **1** of music. **2** beautiful or pleasing to the ear; like music. **3** set to music; accompanied by music. **4** fond of music. **5** skilled in music. —*n.* a play with music that advances the plot. —**mu′si·cal·ly,** *adv.* —**mu′si·cal·ness,** *n.*

musical chairs, children's game in which the players march to music around an ever decreasing row of chairs.
play musical chairs, any activity that consists of switching or changing position without achieving a result.

musical comedy, an amusing play in which plot and characterization are less important than singing, dancing, and costumes.

mu·si·cale (mū′zə kal′), *n.* a social gathering to enjoy music. [< F, short for *soirée musicale* musical evening]

music box, box or case containing apparatus for producing music mechanically.

music hall, hall for musical entertainments.

mu·si·cian (mū zish′ən), *n.* **1** person skilled in music. **2** person who sings or who plays on a musical instrument, especially one who does so for pay. **3** composer of music. —**mu·si′cian·ly,** *adj.* —**mu·si′cian·ship,** *n.*

music video, videotape or disk with images that accompany popular music.

mus·ing (mūz′ing), *adj.* dreamy; meditative. —**mus′ing·ly,** *adv.*

musk (musk), *n.* **1** substance with a strong and lasting odor, used in making perfumes. Musk is found in a special gland in the male musk deer. **2** the odor of musk. [< LL < LGk. < Pers. *mushk*]

musk deer, a small, hornless deer of C Asia, the male of which has a gland containing musk.

mus·keg (mus′keg), *n.* **1** bog covered with moss, esp. in the tundra and forest regions of North America and Europe. **2** any of certain mosses.

mus·kel·lunge (mus′kə lunj), *n., pl.* **-lunge.** a large American pike. [< Ojibwa *mashkinonge* great pike]

mus·ket (mus′kit), *n.* kind of old gun. Soldiers used muskets before rifles were invented. [< F < Ital. *moschetto,* orig., a kind of hawk < *mosca* fly < L *musca*]

mus·ket·eer (mus′kə tir′), *n.* soldier armed with a musket.

mus·ket·ry (mus′kit ri), *n.* **1** muskets. **2** shooting with muskets or rifles. **3** soldiers armed with muskets.

musk·mel·on (musk′mel′ən), *n.* kind of sweet, juicy melon; cantaloupe.

Mus·ko·gee (mus kō′gē), *n., pl.* **-gee** or **-gees. 1** tribe of American Indians from the SE United States, including Choctaw, Chickasaw, Creek, Seminole, and others. 2 their language. —**Mus·ko′ge·an,** *adj.*

musk ox, an arctic animal, somewhat like a sheep, that has a musky smell.

musk·rat (musk′rat′), *n., pl.* –**rats** or (*esp. collectively*) –**rat. 1** a water animal of North America, like a rat, but larger. **2** its valuable dark-brown fur.

musk·y (mus′ki), *adj.,* **musk·i·er, musk·i·est.** of musk; like musk; like that of musk.

Mus·lim (muz′ləm; mus′–), *n., pl.* –**lims,** –**lim.** follower of Muhammad and believer in Islam, the religion he founded. —*adj.* of Muhammad, his followers, or Islam, Islamic. [< Ar. *muslim* one who submits < *aslama* submit; akin to SALAAM]

mus·lin (muz′lən), *n.* **1** a thin, fine cotton cloth, used for dresses, curtains, etc. **2** a heavier cotton cloth, used for sheets, undergarments, etc. —*adj.* made of muslin. [F < Ital. *mussolina* < *Mussolo* Mosul, city in Iraq]

muss (mus), *v.* put into disorder; rumple. —*n.* disorder; mess. [var. of *mess*] —**muss′y,** *adj.*

mus·sel (mus′əl), *n.* **1** an edible saltwater mollusk that looks like a small clam, with black shells. **2** a freshwater mollusk whose shells are used in making buttons. [< L *musculus* mussel, MUSCLE]

must[1] (must; *unstressed* məst), *auxiliary verb, pt.* **must,** *n., adj.* —*aux. v.* **1** be obliged to; be forced to: *humans must eat to live.* **2** ought to; should: *I must go home soon.* **3** be certain to (be, do, have, etc.): *I must seem very rude,. you must have that book.* **4** *Must* is sometimes used with its verb omitted: *we must away.* —*n.* something necessary; obligation: *this rule is a must.* —*adj.* demanding attention or doing; necessary: *a must item, must legislation.* [OE *mōste,* pt.]

must[2] (must), *n.* the unfermented juice of the grape; new wine. [< L (*vinum*) *mustum* fresh (wine)]

must[3] (must), *n.* period of dangerous excitement and irritability, esp. among male elephants and camels during mating season. Also, **musth.**

mus·tache (mus′tash; məs tash′), *n.* **1** hair growing on a person's upper lip. **2** bristly hairs near an animal's mouth. [< F < Ital. < Gk. *mystax* upper lip, mouth]

mus·ta·chio (məs tä′shō), *n., pl.* –**chios,** =mustache. —**mus·ta′chioed,** *adj.*

mus·tang (mus′tang), *n.* the small, wild or half-wild horse of the American plains. [< Sp. *mestengo* untamed]

mus·tard (mus′tərd), *n.* **1** a yellow powder or paste used as seasoning to give a pungent taste. **2** plant from whose seeds it is made. [< OF *moustarde,* ult. < L *mustum* MUST[2]]

mus·ter (mus′tər), *v.* **1** assemble, as troops, the crew of a ship, etc.; gather together; collect: *muster soldiers.* **2** summon: *muster up courage.* —*n.* **1** assembly; collection. **2** bringing together of men or troops for review or service. **3** list of those mustered. **4** the number mustered.

muster in, enroll; enlist, esp. for military service.

muster out, discharge, esp. from military service.

pass muster, be inspected and approved; come up to the required standards. [< OF < L *monstrare* show < *monstrum* portent]

mus·ty (mus′ti), *adj.,* –**ti·er,** –**ti·est. 1** having a smell or taste suggesting mold or damp; moldy. **2** stale; out-of-date: *musty laws.* —**mus′ti·ly,** *adv.* —**mus′ti·ness,** *n.*

mu·ta·ble (mü′tə bəl), *adj.* **1** liable to change: *mutable customs.* **2** fickle: *a mutable person.* [< L, < *mutare* change] —**mu′ta·bil′i·ty, mu′ta·ble·ness,** *n.* —**mu′ta·bly,** *adv.*

mu·ta·gen (myü′tə jən), *n.* agent that causes mutation in an organism.—**mu′ta·gen′e·sis,** *n.* —**mu′ta·gen′ic,** *adj.*

mu·tant (mü′tənt), *n.* new variety of plant or animal resulting from mutation.

mu·tate (mü′tāt), *v.,* –**tat·ed,** –**tat·ing. 1** change. **2** produce mutations.

mu·ta·tion (mü tā′shən), *n.* **1** change; alteration. **2** a new feature that appears suddenly in animals or plants and can be inherited. **3** a new variety of animal or plant formed in this way. [< L, < *mutare* change] —**mu·ta′tion·al,** *adj.*

mute (mūt), *adj., n., v.,* **mut·ed, mut·ing.** —*adj.* **1** not making any sound; silent. **2** unable to speak; dumb. **3** (of letters) not pronounced. —*n.* **1** person who cannot speak. **2** clip or pad put on a musical instrument to soften the sound. —*v.* put a clip or pad on a musical instrument to soften the sound. [< L *mutus*] —**mute′ly,** *adv.* —**mute′ness,** *n.*

mu·ti·late (mü′tə lāt), *v.,* –**lat·ed,** –**lat·ing. 1** cut, tear, or break off a part of; injure seriously by cutting, tearing, or breaking off some part. **2** make (a story, song, etc.) imperfect by removing or damaging parts. [< L, < *mutilus* maimed] —**mu′ti·la′tion,** *n.* —**mu′ti·la′tive,** *adj.* —**mu′ti·la′tor,** *n.*

mu·ti·neer (mü′tə nir′), *n.* person who takes part in a mutiny.

mu·ti·nous (mü′tə nəs), *adj.* rebellious. —**mu′ti·nous·ly,** *adv.* —**mu′ti·nous·ness,** *n.*

mu·ti·ny (mü′tə ni), *n., pl.* –**nies,** *v.,* –**nied,** –**ny·ing.** —*n.* open rebellion against lawful authority, esp. by sailors or soldiers against their officers. —*v.* take part in a mutiny; rebel. [< obs. *mutine* revolt < OF, < *mutin* rebellious, ult. < L *movere* move]

mutt (mut), *n.* dog, esp. a mongrel.

mut·ter (mut′ər), *v.* **1** utter low and indistinctly with lips partly closed. **2** complain; grumble. —*n.* **1** act of muttering. **2** muttered words. [< obs. *moot* mur-

mur, OE *mōtian* make a speech < *mōt* meeting] —**mut′ter·er,** *n.* —**mut′ter·ing·ly,** *adv.*

mut·ton (mut′ən), *n.* meat from a sheep. [< OF *moton* < Celtic]

mu·tu·al (mü′chù əl), *adj.* **1** done, said, felt, etc., by each toward the other; given and received: *mutual promises, mutual dislike.* **2** each to the other: *mutual enemies.* **3** belonging to each of several: *our mutual friend.* [< L *mutuus* reciprocal] —**mu′tu·al′i·ty,** *n.* —**mu′tu·al·ly,** *adv.*

muz·zle (muz′əl), *n., v.,* –**zled,** –**zling.** —*n.* **1** nose, mouth, and jaws of a four-footed animal. **2** cover of straps put over an animal's head and jaws to keep it from biting or eating. **3** open front end of a gun, pistol, etc. —*v.* **1** put a muzzle on. **2** compel (a person) to keep silent about something. [< OF, < *muse* muzzle] —**muz′zler,** *n.*

muz·zle·load·er (muz′əl lōd′ər), *n.* gun that is loaded through the muzzle.

MVP, most valuable player, in sports.

mw, milliwatt.

Mw, megawatt.

my (mī), *pron.* belonging to me. —*interj.* exclamation of surprise. [OE *mīn*]

My·an·mar (mī′ən mär′), *n.* country, formerly Burma, in SE Asia on the Bay of Bengal and between India and China.

my·ce·li·um (mī sē′li əm), *n., pl.* –**li·a** (–li ə) the main part of a fungus, consisting of interwoven fibers. [< NL, < Gk. *mykes* mushroom]

My·ce·nae·an (mī′sə nē′ən), *adj.* of or having to do with Mycenae, an ancient city in S Greece, or its civilization, culture, or art that flourished from about 1500 B.C. to 1100 B.C.

my·col·o·gy (mī kol′ə ji), *n.* branch of botany that deals with fungi. [< Gk. *mykes* fungus + –LOGY] —**my·col′o·gist,** *n.*

my·co·tox·in (mī′kə tok′sən), *n.* poison produced by a fungus. [< Gk. *mýkēs* fungus + E *toxin*]

my·e·lin (mī′ə lin), *n.* soft, fatty substance that forms a sheath around certain nerve fibers.

my·na, my·nah (mī′nə), *n.* an Asiatic bird of the starling family. [< Hind. *mainā*]

my·o·car·di·um (mī′ə kär′di əm), *n.* muscle tissue of the heart. [< NL < Gk. *mýs, myós* muscle + *kardía* heart]

my·o·pi·a (mī ō′pi ə), *n.* =near-sightedness. [< NL, < Gk., ult. < *myein* shut + *ops* eye] —**my·op′ic,** *adj.*

myr·i·ad (mir′i əd), *n.* **1** ten thousand. **2** a very great number: *there are myriads of stars.* —*adj.* **1** ten thousand. **2** countless. [< LL < Gk. *myrias* ten thousand, myriad]

myr·i·a·pod (mir′i ə pod′), *n.* arthropod having a wormlike body with many segments and many legs. Centipedes and millepedes are myriapods. [< Gk. *myrias* myriad + *pous* foot]

myrrh (mér), *n.* a fragrant, gummy substance with a bitter taste, used in medicines, perfumes, and incense. It is obtained from a shrub that grows in Arabia and E Africa. [< L < Gk., ult. < Akkadian (group of extinct Semitic langs.) *murrû*]

myr·tle (mèr′təl), *n.* **1** an evergreen shrub of S Europe with shiny leaves, fragrant white flowers, and black berries. **2** a low, creeping, evergreen vine with blue flowers; periwinkle. [< OF *mirtile*, dim. of L *myrtus* < Gk. *myrtos*]

my·self (mī self′), *pron., pl.* **ourselves. 1** the emphatic form of **me** or **I:** *I myself will go.* **2** reflexive form of **me:** *I hurt myself.* **3** my real self; my normal self: *I am not myself today.*

mys·te·ri·ous (mis tir′i əs), *adj.* **1** full of mystery; hard to explain or understand; secret; hidden. **2** suggesting mystery. —**mys·te′ri·ous·ly,** *adv.* —**mys·te′ri·ous·ness,** *n.*

mys·ter·y (mis′tər i; mis′tri), *n., pl.* –**ter·ies. 1** secret; something that is hidden or unknown. **2** secrecy; obscurity. **3** something that is not explained or understood. **4** a religious doctrine that human reason cannot understand. **5** a secret religious rite. [< L < Gk. *mysterion,* ult. < *myein* close (i.e., the lips or eyes)]

mystery play, medieval religious play.

mys·tic (mis′tik), *n.* person who believes that truth or God can be known through spiritual insight. —*adj.* mystical. [< L < Gk. *mystikos.* See MYSTERY[1].]

mys·ti·cal (mis′tə kəl), *adj.* **1** having some secret meaning; mysterious. **2** spiritually symbolic. The lamb and the dove are mystical symbols of the Christian religion. **3** of or concerned with mystics or mysticism. **4** of or having to do with secret rites. —**mys′ti·cal·ly,** *adv.* —**mys′ti·cal·ness,** *n.*

mys·ti·cism (mis′tə siz əm), *n.* **1** beliefs or mode of thought of mystics. **2** doctrine that truth or God may be known through spiritual insight, independent of the mind.

mys·ti·fy (mis′tə fī), *v.,* –**fied,** –**fy·ing. 1** bewilder purposely; puzzle; perplex. **2** make mysterious; involve in mystery. —**mys′ti·fi·ca′tion,** *n.* —**mys′ti·fy′ing·ly,** *adv.*

mys·tique (mis tēk′), *n.* aura of mystery surrounding someone or something. [< F]

myth (mith), *n.* **1** legend or story, usually attempting to account for something in nature. **2** any invented story. **3** an imaginary person or thing. [< NL < LL < Gk. *mythos* word, story]

myth., mythological; mythology.

myth·i·cal (mith′ə kəl), **myth·ic** (–ik), *adj.* **1** of myths; like a myth; in myths. **2** not real; made-up; imaginary. —**myth′i·cal·ly,** *adv.*

my·thol·o·gy (mi thol′ə ji), *n., pl.* –**gies. 1** myths collectively: *Greek mythology.* **2** study of myths. —**myth′o·log′i·cal, myth′o·log′ic,** *adj.* —**myth′o·log′i·cal·ly,** *adv.* —**my·thol′o·gist,** *n.*

myx·o·vi·rus (mik′sə vī′rəs), *n.* one of a group of viruses that cause red blood cells to clump, including the viruses that cause influenza and mumps. [< Gk. *mýxa* mucus + E *virus*]

N, n (en), *n., pl.* **N's; n's.** the 14th letter of the alphabet.

N, 1 nitrogen. **2** North; Northern.

n, an indefinite number.

N., 1 Navy. **2** New. **3** Noon. **4** North; Northern. **5** November.

n., 1 neuter. **2** nominative. **3** north; northern. **4** noun. **5** number.

Na, sodium.

N.A., North America.

NAACP, National Association for the Advancement of Colored People.

nab (nab), *v.,* **nabbed, nab·bing. 1** catch or seize suddenly; grab. **2** arrest. [earlier *nap,* OE *hnæppan* strike]

na·cho (nä′chō), *n., pl.* **-chos.** toasted tortilla chip with a topping of cheese, ground meat, and sauce made with chili peppers, tomato, etc. [< Mexican Sp.]

na·da (nä′də), *n. Informal.* nothing. [< Sp.]

na·dir (nä′dər; –dir), *n.* **1** the point in the heavens directly beneath the place where one stands; the point opposite the zenith. **2** *Fig.* the lowest point of anything. [ult. < Ar. *naẓīr* opposite (i.e., to the zenith)]

nae (nā), *adj., adv. Scot.* no.

NAFTA or **Naf·ta** (naf′tə), *n.* North American Free Trade Agreement, which established a free-trade zone that includes Mexico, Canada, and the United States.

nag[1] (nag), *v.,* **nagged, nag·ging.** irritate or annoy by peevish complaints; scold. [cf. Icel. *nagga* grumble] **—nag′ger,** *n.* **—nag′ging·ly,** *adv.*

nag[2] (nag), *n.* **1** a horse. **2** an inferior horse. [cf. Du. *negge*]

Na·hua·tl (nä′wä təl), *n.* language of the Aztecs, Toltecs, and other American Indian tribes of C Mexico and parts of Central America. **—adj.** of this language.

Na·hum (nä′əm; –həm), *n.* book of the Old Testament.

nai·ad (nä′ad; nī′–), *n., pl.* **-ads, –a·des** (–ə dēz). immature insect, such as the May fly or dragonfly, in one of a series of aquatic stages of development. [< L < Gk. *Naias;* akin to *naein* to flow]

na·if (nä ēf′), *adj.* =naive.

nail (nāl), *n.* **1** a slender piece of metal that holds separate pieces of wood together or for use as a peg after being hammered into place. **2** a thin, horny plate on the upper side of the end of a finger or toe. **—v. 1** fasten with a nail or nails. **2** hold or keep fixed. **3** *Informal.* catch; seize: *nail the deal.*

hit the nail on the head, guess or understand correctly; say or do something just right.

nail down, fix firmly; secure: *nail down a lid, nail down a claim.* [OE *nægel*] **—nail′er,** *n.*

nail·set (nāl′set′), *n.* tool for driving a nail below a surface.

Nai·ro·bi (nī rō′bi), *n.* capital of Kenya, a country in E Africa.

na·ive (nä ēv′), *adj.* simple in nature; like a child; artless; not sophisticated. [< F, fem., < L *nativus* NATIVE] **—na·ive′ly,** *adv.* **—na·ive′ness,** *n.*

na·ive·te (nä ēv′tā′), *n.* **1** unspoiled freshness. **2** a naive action, remark, etc.

na·ked (nā′kid), *adj.* **1** with no clothes on; bare. **2** not covered; stripped: *a naked sword, naked fields.* **3** *Fig.* not protected; exposed. **4** *Fig.* without addition of anything else; plain: *the naked truth.* [OE *nacod*] **—na′ked·ly,** *adv.* **—na′ked·ness,** *n.*

naked eye, eye not helped by a glass, telescope, or microscope.

nam·by-pam·by (nam′bi pam′bi), *adj., n., pl.* **-bies. —adj.** weakly simple or sentimental; insipid: *valentines are often namby-pamby.* **—n. 1** namby-pamby talk or writing. **2** a namby-pamby person. [alter. of *Ambrose* Philips, 18th cent. Brit. poet ridiculed by H. Carey, A. Pope]

name (nām), *n., v.,* **named, nam·ing. —n. 1** word or words by which a person, animal, place, or thing is spoken of or to. **2** word or words applied descriptively; appellation, title, or epithet: *call a person names.* **3** reputation; fame. **—v. 1** give a name to: *name a newborn baby.* **2** call by name; mention by name: *three persons were named in the report.* **3** give the right name for: *can you name these flowers?* **4** mention; speak of; state: *name several reasons.* **5** choose for some duty or office; nominate: *name Mr. Taft for president.*

in name only, supposed to be, but not really so: *the boss in name only.*

in the name of, a with appeal to the name of: *what, in the name of goodness, were you thinking?* **b** acting for.

name names, identify those involved: *even named names to the press.*

name of the game, central or important thing.

you name it, anyone or anything one can think of. [OE *nama*] **—nam′a·ble, name′a·ble,** *adj.* **—nam′er,** *n.*

name-drop·ping (nām′drop′ing), *n.* use of a well-known person's name in conversation, suggesting acquaintance with him or her, in order to make oneself seem important. **—name′-drop,** *v.* **—name-′drop′per,** *n.*

name·less (nām′lis), *adj.* **1** having no name: *a nameless grave.* **2** that cannot be named or described: *a strange, nameless longing.* **3** not named. **—name′less·ness,** *n.*

name·ly (nām′li), *adv.* that is to say.

name·sake (nām′sāk′), *n.* one having the same name as another, esp. one named after another.

nan·ny (nan′i), *n.* **1** woman employed to care for children in a household. **2** *Informal.* nanny goat.

nan·ny goat (nan′i), a female goat.

nano- *combining form.* **1** one-billionth, as in *nanosecond.* **2** extremely small, as in *nanoplankton.*

na·no·plank·ton (nan′ō plang′tən; nan′ə–), *n.* very small plankton.

na·no·sec·ond (nan′ō sek′ənd, nan′ə–), *n.* billionth of a second.

na·no·sur·ger·y (nan′o sur′jər i; nan′ə–), *n.* surgery performed on minute tissues or cells, with the aid of a microscope.

na·no·tech·nol·o·gy (nan′ō tek nol′ə ji; nan′ə–), *n.* machines, tools, procedures, etc., needed to manipulate materials the size of molecules or cells.

Nantes (nants; *Fr.* nänt), *n.* **Edict of,** edict granting religious toleration to French Huguenots in 1598.

nap[1] (nap), *n., v.,* **napped, nap·ping,** **—n.** a short sleep. **—v.** take a short sleep.

napping, off guard; unprepared. [OE *hnappian* sleep lightly]

nap[2] (nap), *n.* the soft, short, woolly threads or hairs on the surface of cloth. [< Mdu. or MLG *noppe*] **—nap′less,** *adj.*

na·palm (nā′päm′; –pälm′), *n.* **1** a chemical substance used to thicken gasoline for use in certain military weapons. **2** the thickened gasoline.

nape (nāp; nap), *n.* the back of the neck. [< ME *nape*]

na·per·y (nā′pər i; nāp′ri), *n.* tablecloths, napkins, and doilies. [< obs. F *napery* < *nape, nappe* < L *mappa* napkin]

naph·tha (nap′thə; naf′–), *n.* a liquid made from petroleum, coal tar, etc., used as fuel and to take spots from clothing. [< L < Gk., orig., an inflammable liquid issuing from the earth]

naph·tha·lene (naf′thə lēn; nap′–), *n.* a white, crystalline hydrocarbon, $C_{10}H_8$, usually prepared from coal tar, used in making moth balls, dyes, disinfectants, etc.

nap·kin (nap′kin), *n.* **1** piece of cloth used at meals for protecting the clothing or for wiping the lips or fingers. **2** any similar piece, such as a baby's diaper or a small towel. [< F *nappe.* See NAPERY.]

napkin ring, ring to hold a rolled-up napkin, often of silver.

na·po·le·on (nə pō′li ən; –pōl′yən), *n.* kind of pastry with a cream or custard filling. [named for the *Napoleons*]

Na·po·le·on (nə pō′li ən; –pōl′yən), *n.* (*Napoleon Bonaparte*), 1769–1821, French general and emperor of France, 1804–15. **—Na·po′le·on′ic,** *adj.*

nar·cis·sism (när sis′iz əm), *n.* excessive love or admiration for oneself. [< G *Narzissismus* < *Narcissus* in Gk. mythology, beautiful youth who loved his own reflection and turned into the flower,] **—nar·cis′sist,** *n.* **—nar′cis·sis′tic,** *adj.*

nar·cis·sus (när sis′əs), *n., pl.* **-cis·sus·es, –cis·si** (–sis′ī). **1** a spring plant with yellow or white flowers and long, slender leaves. It grows from a bulb. **2** the flower. [< L < Gk.; assoc. (from the sedative effect of the plant) with *narke* numbness]

nar·co·lep·sy (när′kə lep′si), *n.* disorder marked by uncontrollable drowsiness in the daytime. [< Gk. *nárkē* numbness + *lépsis* a seizure] —**nar′co·lep′tic**, *n.*

nar·co·sis (när kō′sis), *n.* stupor; insensibility.

nar·co·ter·ror·ism (när′kō ter′ə riz əm), *n.* violent acts committed by drug traffickers against government agents or others trying to control their activities.

nar·cot·ic (när kot′ik), *n.* 1 drug that produces drowsiness, sleep, dullness, or an insensible condition, lessens pain by dulling the nerves, and can be addictive: *opium is a powerful narcotic.* 2 *Fig.* anything that soothes or dulls. —*adj.* 1 having the properties and effects of a narcotic. 2 of or for persons addicted to narcotic drugs. [< L < Gk., < *narkoein* benumb < *narke* numbness]

nar·rate (na rāt′; nar′āt), *v.,* **-rat·ed, -rat·ing.** 1 tell (a story, etc.) of. 2 tell stories, etc. [< L, pp. of *narrare* relate] —**nar·ra′tor**, *n.*

nar·ra·tion (na rā′shən), *n.* 1 act of telling. 2 the form of composition that relates an event or a story. Novels, short stories, histories, and biographies are forms of narration. 3 story; account.

nar·ra·tive (nar′ə tiv), *n.* 1 story. 2 narration; storytelling. —*adj.* that narrates: *a narrative poem.* —**nar′ra·tive·ly**, *adv.*

nar·row (nar′ō), *adj.* 1 not wide; having little width; of less than the specified, understood, or usual width: *narrow cloth.* 2 limited in extent, space, amount, range, scope, opportunity, etc.: *a narrow circle of friends.* 3 with little margin: *a narrow escape.* 4 lacking breadth of view or sympathy; not liberal; prejudiced: *a narrow point of view.* —*n.* **narrows,** the narrow part of a river, strait, sound, valley, pass, etc. —*v.* make or become narrower; decrease in breadth, extent, etc.; limit. [OE *nearu*] —**nar′row·ly**, *adv.* —**nar′row·ness**, *n.*

nar·row·cast·ing (nar′ōkas′ting), *n.* broadcasting by cable television; cable casting. [< *narrow* limited in range + broad*casting*]

nar·row-gauge (nar′ō gāj′), *adj.* having railroad tracks less than 56½ inches apart.

nar·row-mind·ed (nar′ō mīn′did), *adj.* lacking breadth of view or sympathy; prejudiced. —**nar·row-mind′ed·ly**, *adv.* —**nar′row-mind′ed·ness**, *n.*

nar·whal, nar·wal (när′hwəl; -wəl), or **nar·whale** (-hwāl′), *n.* kind of arctic whale whose body is about 16 feet long. The male has a long tusk extending forward from the upper jaw. [< Dan. or Sw. *narhval* < *når* corpse + *hval* whale]

NASA (na′sa), *n.* National Aeronautics and Space Administration, United States government agency, responsible for civilian research and development in aeronautics and aerospace technology.

na·sal (nā′zəl), *adj.* 1 of, in, or from the nose: *a nasal discharge.* 2 requiring the nose passage to be open; spoken through the nose. *M, n,* and *ng* represent nasal

sounds. —*n.* a nasal sound. [< L *nasus* nose] —**na·sal′i·ty**, *n.* —**na′sal·ly**, *adv.*

na·sal·ize (nā′zəl īz), *v.,* **-ized, -iz·ing.** utter or speak with a nasal sound. —**na′sal·i·za′tion**, *n.*

nas·cent (nas′ənt; nā′sənt), *adj.* in the process of coming into existence; just beginning to exist, grow, or develop. [< L *nascens,* ppr. of *nasci* be born] —**nas′cen·cy**, *n.*

Nash·ville (nash′vil), *n.* capital of Tennessee, in the C part.

na·stur·tium (nə stėr′shəm), *n.* 1 plant with yellow, orange, and red flowers, and sharp-tasting seeds and leaves. 2 the flower. [< L, < *nasus* nose + *torquere* twist; from sharp odor]

nas·ty (nas′ti; näs′-), *adj.,* **-ti·er, -ti·est.** 1 disgustingly dirty; filthy. 2 very unpleasant; nasty weather. [cf. Du. *nestig*] —**nas′ti·ly**, *adv.* —**nas′ti·ness**, *n.*

nat., 1 national. 2 native. 3 natural.

na·tal (nā′təl), *adj.* of one's birth: *one's natal day is his birthday.* [< L *natalis,* ult. < *nasci* be born]

natch (nach), *adv. Informal.* naturally; of course.

na·tion (nā′shən), *n.* 1 people occupying the same country, united under the same government, and mostly speaking the same language: *the English nation.* 2 a people, race, or tribe; those having the same descent, language, and history: *the Scottish nation.* [< L *natio* stock, race, ult. < *nasci* be born]

na·tion·al (nash′ən əl; nash′nəl), *adj.* of a nation; belonging to a whole nation: *national laws, a national disaster.* —*n.* citizen of a nation. —**na′tion·al·ly**, *adv.*

national debt, total amount a government of a country owes.

national forest, forest land set aside by the President of the United States, protected and administered by the Federal government.

National Guard, *U.S.* the reserve militia of the individual states of the United States, called or ordered to serve the Federal government in time of war or national emergency.

national income, total taxable income received by all individuals, organizations, and businesses of a country.

na·tion·al·ism (nash′ən əl iz′əm; nash′-nəl-), *n.* 1 patriotic feelings or efforts. 2 desire and plans for national independence. —**na′tion·al·is′tic**, *adj.*

na·tion·al·i·ty (nash′ən al′ə ti), *n., pl.* **-ties.** 1 nation. 2 condition of belonging to a nation. Citizens of the same country have the same nationality. 3 condition of being a nation: *after the American Revolution the colonies attained nationality.*

na·tion·al·ize (nash′ən əl īz; nash′nəl-), *v.,* **-ized, -iz·ing.** 1 make national. 2 bring (land, industries, railroads, etc.) under the control or ownership of a nation. 3 make into a nation. —**na′tion·al·i·za′tion**, *n.*

national park, large area of land of special geologic, historic, or scenic importance, preserved by a national government for the benefit and enjoyment of all citizens.

na·tion·wide (nā′shən wīd′), *adj.* extending throughout the nation: *a nationwide election.*

na·tive (nā′tiv), *n.* 1 person born in a certain place or country. 2 person who has lived most or all of his or her life in a place. 3 one of the original inhabitants of a place, as contrasted with conquerors, settlers, visitors, etc. —*adj.* 1 born in a certain place or country: *people born in New York are native sons and daughters of New York.* 2 belonging to one because of birth: *one's native land, a native costume.* 3 born in a person; natural: *native ability, native courtesy.* 4 that one learns to speak first: *one's native language, a native speaker of English.* 5 produced in a certain place: *tobacco is native to America.* 6 found in nature: *native salt is refined for use, the native beauty of the hills.*

go native, live as the natives do. [< L *nativus* innate, ult. < *nasci* be born] —**na′tive·ly**, *adv.* —**na′tive·ness**, *n.*

Native American, =American Indian.

na·tive-born (nā′tiv bôrn′), *adj.* born in the place or country indicated.

na·tiv·i·ty (nə tiv′ə ti; nā-), *n., pl.* **-ties.** birth.

the Nativity, a birth of Christ. **b** Christmas; December 25.

natl., national.

NATO, North Atlantic Treaty Organization.

nat·ty (nat′i), *adj.,* **-ti·er, -ti·est.** trim and tidy; neatly smart in dress or appearance. —**nat′ti·ly**, *adv.* —**nat′ti·ness**, *n.*

nat·u·ral (nach′ə rəl; nach′rəl), *adj.* 1 a produced by nature; based on some state of things in nature: *scenery has natural beauty, coal and oil are natural products.* b =organic. 2 instinctive; inborn: *natural ability.* 3 coming in the ordinary course of events; normal: *a natural death, a natural response.* 4 instinctively felt to be right and fair: *natural rights.* 5 free from affectation: *a natural manner.* 6 neither sharp nor flat; without sharps and flats. —*n.* 1 that which is natural. 2 a a natural tone or note. b sign (♮) used to cancel the effect of a preceding sharp or flat. c a white key on the piano. 3 an expert by nature. [< L *naturalis.* See NATURE.] —**nat′u·ral·ness**, *n.*

natural childbirth, giving birth to a child without the use of anesthetics or drugs.

natural food, food that is not processed or has no additives.

natural gas, a combustible gas formed naturally in the earth, consisting of methane with hydrogen and other gases.

natural history, the study of animals, plants, minerals, and other things in nature.

nat·u·ral·ism (nach′ə rəl iz′əm; nach′-rəl-), *n.* 1 in art and literature, close adherence to nature and reality. **2** action based on natural instincts.

nat·u·ral·ist (nach′ə rəl ist; nach′rəl–), *n.* **1** person who makes a study of animals and plants. **2** writer or artist who represents life exactly as it is; extreme realist.

nat·u·ral·is·tic (nach′ə rəl is′tik; nach′-rəl-), *adj.* **1** of natural history or naturalists. **2** of naturalism, esp. in art and literature. **3** of or in accordance with nature.

nat·u·ral·ize (nach′ə rəl īz; nach′rəl–), *v.,* **-ized, -iz·ing. 1** admit (a foreigner) to citizenship. **2** adopt (a foreign word or custom). *"Chauffeur" is a French word that has been naturalized in English.* **3** introduce and make at home in another country: *the English oak has been naturalized in parts of Massachusetts.* **4** become like a native. **—nat′u·ral·i·za′tion,** *n.*

natural language, any language that has developed naturally over a long period of time, as opposed to one that is artificially created, as computer language.

natural law, 1 law based on the natural tendency of people to exercise reason in dealing with others and the basis of common law. **2** law of nature.

nat·u·ral·ly (nach′ə rəl i; nach′rəl i), *adv.* **1** in a natural way: *speak naturally.* **2** by nature: *a naturally obedient child.* **3** as might be expected; of course.

natural resources, materials supplied by nature, as minerals and water power.

natural science, science of nature. Zoology, botany, and geology are natural sciences.

natural selection, the process by which animals and plants best adapted to their environment tend to survive.

na·ture (nā′chər), *n.* **1** the world; all things except those made by humans: *the laws of nature.* **2** the instincts or inherent tendencies: *it is against nature for a mother to kill her child.* **3** what a thing really is; quality: *It is the nature of cats to hunt.* **4** sort; kind: *a person of a gentle nature.* [< OF < L *natura* birth, character, ult. < *nasci* be born]

naught (nôt), *n.* **1** nothing. **2** zero; 0. Also, **nought.** [OE *nāwiht* < *nā* no + *wiht* wight]

naugh·ty (nô′ti), *adj.,* **-ti·er, -ti·est. 1** bad; not obedient. **2** somewhat improper. [< *naught* wicked] **—naugh′ti·ly,** *adv.* **—naugh′ti·ness,** *n.*

nau·sea (nô′shə; –shi ə; –si ə), *n.* **1** the feeling that one has when about to vomit. **2** seasickness. **3** extreme disgust; loathing. [< L < Gk., < *naus* ship]

nau·se·ate (nô′shi āt; –si–), *v.,* **-at·ed, -at·ing. 1** cause nausea in; make sick. **2** feel nausea; become sick. **—nau′se·a′tion,** *n.*

nau·seous (nô′shəs; –shi əs), *adj.* **1** causing nausea; sickening. **2** disgusting; loathsome. **—nau′seous·ly,** *adv.* **—nau′seous·ness,** *n.*

naut., nautical.

nau·ti·cal (nô′tə kəl), *adj.* of or having to do with ships, sailors, or navigation. [< L < Gk. *nautikos,* ult. < *naus* ship] **—nau′ti·cal·ly,** *adv.*

nautical mile, about 6080 feet.

nau·ti·lus (nô′tə ləs), *n., pl.* **-lus·es, -li** (–lī). either of two kinds of cephalopod. The **pearly nautilus** has a spiral shell, pearly inside. The **paper nautilis** has saillike arms and a very thin shell. [< L < Gk. *nautilos,* orig., sailor, ult. < *naus* ship]

nav., 1 naval. **2** navigation.

Nav·a·jo, Nav·a·ho (nav′ə hō), *n., pl.* **-jos, -hos.** member of a tribe of American Indians living in New Mexico, Arizona, and Utah.

na·val (nā′vəl), *adj.* **1** of or for warships or the navy: *a naval officer.* **2** having a navy: *the naval powers.* [< L, < *navis* ship]

nave (nāv), *n.* the main part of a church or cathedral between the side aisles. The nave extends from the main entrance to the transepts. [< Med.L < L *navis* ship]

na·vel (nā′vəl), *n.* **1** the mark or scar in the middle of the surface of the abdomen. **2** center; middle. [OE *nafela*]

navel orange, a seedless orange with a small growth resembling a navel at one end.

navig., navigation.

nav·i·ga·ble (nav′ə gə bəl), *adj.* **1** that ships can travel on: *the Mississippi River is deep enough to be navigable.* **2** seaworthy: *the old ship is no longer navigable.* **3** that can be steered. **—nav′i·ga·bil′i·ty, nav′i·ga·ble·ness,** *n.* **—nav′i·ga·bly,** *adv.*

nav·i·gate (nav′ə gāt), *v.,* **-gat·ed, -gat·ing. 1** sail, manage, or steer (a ship, airplane, etc.). **2** sail on or over (a sea or river). **3** travel by water; sail. **4** manage a ship or aircraft. **5** *Fig.* manage to get up, around, over, or through: *navigate a maze of hallways.* [< L, < *navis* ship + *agere* drive]

nav·i·ga·tion (nav′ə gā′shən), *n.* **1** act or process of navigating. **2** art or science of finding a ship's or airplane's position and course. **—nav′i·ga′tion·al,** *adj.*

nav·i·ga·tor (nav′ə gā′tər), *n.* **1** one who sails the seas. **2** one who has charge of the navigating of a ship or who is skilled in navigating. **3** explorer of the seas. **4** one who finds the position and course of an aircraft.

na·vy (nā′vi), *n., pl.* **-vies. 1** all the ships of war of a country, with their personnel and the department that manages them. **2** officers and men and women of the navy. **3** *Archaic or Poetic.* fleet of ships. **4** Also, **navy blue.** a dark blue. [< OF *navie,* ult. < L *navis* ship]

navy bean, the common white bean, dried for use as food, usually in soups or casseroles.

nay (nā), *adv.* **1** no. **2** not only that, but also: *we are willing, nay eager to go.* **—n. 1** no; a denial or refusal. **2** a negative vote or voter. [< Scand. *nei* < *ne* not + *ei* ever]

nay·say (nā′sā′), *v.* oppose; say no to; vote against. **—nay′say′er,** *n.*

Na·zi (nä′tsi; nat′si), *n., pl.* **Na·zis,** *adj.* **—n. 1** member or supporter of the National Socialist German Workers' Party in Germany. **2** often, **nazi.** fascist. **—adj.** of or having to do with the Nazis. [< G, short for *Na(tionalso)zi(alist)* National Socialist]

Na·zism (nä′tsiz əm; nat′siz–), **Na·zi·ism** (nä′tsi iz əm; nat′si–), *n.* the doctrines of the Nazis.

Nb, niobium.

N.B., 1 New Brunswick. **2** (L *nota bene*) Also, **n.b.** note well; observe carefully.

NC, *(zip code)* North Carolina.

N.C., North Carolina.

N.C.O., noncommissioned officer.

Nd, neodymium.

ND, *(zip code)* North Dakota.

N. Dak., N.D., North Dakota.

Ne, neon.

NE, 1 *(zip code)* Nebraska. **2** northeast; northeastern.

N.E., n.e., northeast; northeastern.

Ne·an·der·thal (ni an′dər thôl; –täl), *adj.* **1** of or belonging to a group of prehistoric people living in Europe, N Africa, and C and W Asia during the early Stone Age. **2** like a Neanderthal: *Neanderthal features.* **3** *Fig.* Often, **neanderthal.** reactionary; backward. **—n. 1** extinct species of man, distinguished by a large, heavy skull and lower jaw, and a low forehead, a predecessor of modern man. Also, **Neanderthal man. 2** *Fig.* Often, **neanderthal.** a reactionary. [< *Neanderthal,* Neander Gorge in Germany where Neanderthal fossils were discovered in 1856]

Ne·a·pol·i·tan (nē′ə pol′ə tən), *adj.* of or pertaining to Naples. **—n.** native of Naples.

neap tide (nēp), the lowest level of high tide. Neap tide comes twice a month. [OE *nēp*]

near (nir), *adv.* to or at a short distance; not far: *stand near.* **—adj. 1** close by; not distant; less distant: *the near side.* **2** intimate; familiar: *a near friend.* **3** closely related: *a near cousin.* **4** short; direct: *go by the nearest route.* **5** by a close margin: *a near escape.* **—prep.** close to in space, time, condition, etc.: *regions near the equator.* **—v.** come or draw near; approach: *the ship neared the land.*

near at hand, a within easy reach. **b** not far in the future. [OE *nēar,* compar. of *nēah* nigh] **—near′ness,** *n.*

near·by (nir′bī′), *adj., adv.* near; close at hand: *a nearby house; they went nearby to visit.*

Near East, the countries of SW Asia and, sometimes, the Balkans, Egypt, and Sudan.

near·ly (nir′li), *adv.* **1** almost: *I nearly made the train.* **2** closely: *a fact that concerns you very nearly.*

near-sight·ed (nir′sīt′id), *adj.* seeing distinctly at a short distance only. **—near′-sight′ed·ly,** *adv.* **—near′-sight′ed·ness,** *n.*

neat (nēt), *adj.* **1** clean and in order: *a neat room.* **2** able and willing to keep things in order: *a neat child.* **3** well-formed; in proportion: *a neat design.* **4** skillful; clever: *a neat trick.* [< F < L *nitidus* gleaming < *nitere* shine] —**neat′ly,** *adv.* —**neat′ness,** *n.*

neat·en (nē′tən), *v.* make tidy; put in order.

neath, ′neath (nēth; nē th), *prep. Poetic.* beneath.

Nebr., Neb., Nebraska.

Ne·bras·ka (nə bras′kə), *n.* a Middle Western state of the United States. —**Ne·bras′kan,** *adj., n.*

neb·u·la (neb′yə lə), *n., pl.* **-lae** (-lē), **-las.** a bright spot like a small, bright cloud, visible in the sky at night. [< L, mist] —**neb′u·lar,** *adj.*

neb·u·los·i·ty (neb′yə los′ə ti), *n., pl.* **-ties. 1** cloudlike quality. **2** nebula.

neb·u·lous (neb′yə ləs), *adj.* **1** hazy; vague; indistinct; confused. **2** cloudlike. **3** of or like a nebula or nebulae. [< L, < *nebula* mist] —**neb′u·lous·ly,** *adv.* —**neb′u·lous·ness,** *n.*

nec·es·sar·i·ly (nes′ə ser′ə li), *adv.* **1** because of necessity: *leaves are not necessarily green.* **2** as a necessary result: *war necessarily causes misery and waste.*

nec·es·sar·y (nes′ə ser′i), *adj., n., pl.* **-sar·ies.** —*adj.* **1** that must be, be had, or be done: *death is a necessary end.* **2** involuntary: *hunger is a necessary response.* —*n.* thing impossible to do without: *food, clothing, and shelter are necessaries of life.* [< L, < *necesse* unavoidable, ult. < *ne-* not + *cedere* withdraw]

ne·ces·si·tate (nə ses′ə tāt), *v.,* **-tat·ed, -tat·ing. 1** make necessary: *his broken leg necessitated an operation.* **2** compel; force. —**ne·ces′si·ta′tion,** *n.*

ne·ces·si·ty (nə ses′ə ti), *n., pl.* **-ties, 1** fact of being necessary; extreme need: *the necessity of eating.* **2** that which cannot be done without: *water is a necessity.* **3** that which forces one to act in a certain way: *necessity often drives people to do disagreeable things.* **4** that which is inevitable: *night follows day as a necessity.* **5** need; poverty: *this poor family is in great necessity.*

of necessity, because it must be.

neck (nek), *n.* **1** part of the body that connects the head with the shoulders. **2** part of a garment that fits the neck. **3** a narrow strip of land. **4** the slender part of a bottle, flask, retort, or other container. **5** the long, slender part of a violin, etc., between the body and the head. —*v. Informal.* embrace amorously; hug; caress.

neck and neck, a abreast. **b** even in a race or contest.

stick one's neck out, put oneself in a vulnerable position.

up to one's neck, *Informal.* deeply involved. [OE *hnecca*]

neck·band (nek′band′), *n.* a cloth band worn around the neck, either separately or as part of a garment.

neck·er·chief (nek′ər chif), *n.* cloth worn round the neck.

neck·lace (nek′lis), *n.* string of jewels, gold, silver, beads, etc., worn around the neck as an ornament.

neck·line (nek′līn′), *n.* line around the neck where a garment ends: *a dress with a low neckline.*

neck·tie (nek′tī′), *n.* a narrow band or a tie worn around the neck and tied in front.

neck·wear (nek′wār′), *n.* ties and other articles that are worn around the neck.

ne·crol·o·gist (ne krol′ə jist), *n.* person who prepares or writes obituaries.

ne·crol·o·gy (ne krol′ə ji), *n., pl.* **-gies. 1** list of persons who have died. **2** notice of a person's death. [< Med.L < Gk. *nekros* dead body + -LOGY] —**nec′ro·log′i·cal,** *adj.* —**nec′ro·log′i·cal·ly,** *adv.*

nec·ro·man·cy (nek′rə man′si), *n.* magic; a foretelling of the future by communicating with the dead. [< Med.L, L < Gk., < *nekros* dead body + *manteia* divination; confusion with L *niger* "black" led to interpretation as "black art"] —**nec′ro·man′cer,** *n.*

ne·cro·sis (ne krō′sis), *n., pl.* **-ses** (-sēz). death or decay (of a part of an animal or plant). [< NL < Gk., ult. < *nekros* dead body] —**ne·crot′ic,** *adj.*

nec·tar (nek′tər), *n.* **1** *Gk. Myth.* the drink of the gods. **2** any delicious drink. **3** a sweet liquid found in many flowers. Bees gather nectar and make it into honey. [< L < Gk. *nektar*]

nec·tar·ine (nek′tər ēn′; nek′tər ēn), *n.* a kind of peach having no down on its skin.

née, nee (nā), *adj.* born. [< F, fem. pp. of *naître* be born < L *nasci*]

need (nēd), *n.* **1** lack of a useful or desired thing: *his writing showed need of grammar.* **2** a useful or desired thing that is lacking: *in the jungle their need was fresh water.* **3** necessity: *there is no need to hurry.* **4** a situation or time of difficulty: *a friend in need.* **5** extreme poverty. —*v.* **1** have need of; want; require: *need money.* **2** be necessary: *the rope cuts his hands more than needs.* **3** must; should; have to; ought to: *need she go?*

have need to, must; should; have to; ought to.

if need be, if it has to be. [OE *ned*] —**need′er,** *n.*

need·ful (nēd′fəl), *adj.* needed; necessary. —**need′ful·ly,** *adv.* —**need′ful·ness,** *n.*

nee·dle (nē′dəl), *n., v.,* **-dled, -dling.** —*n.* **1** a very slender tool, sharp at one end and with a hole or eye to pass a thread through, used in sewing. **2** a slender rod used in knitting. **3** rod with a hook at one end used in crocheting, etc. **4** a thin steel pointer on a compass or on electrical machinery. **5** end of a syringe used for injecting something below the skin. **6** the needle-shaped leaf of a fir tree or pine tree. —*v.* **1** sew or pierce with, or as with, a needle. **2** vex by repeated sharp prods, gibes, etc.; goad or incite, as into hurrying. [OE *nēdl*] —**nee′dle-like′,** *adj.*

needle·point (nē′dəl point′), *n.* embroidery made on a coarse, stiff canvas cloth and used to cover chairs, footstools, etc. Also, **needle point.** —**nee′dle-point′,** *adj.*

need·less (nēd′lis), *adj.* not needed; unnecessary. —**need′less·ly,** *adv.* —**need′less·ness,** *n.*

nee·dle·wom·an (nē′dəl wum′ən), *n., pl.* **-wom·en. 1** skillful user of the needle. **2** woman who earns her living by sewing.

nee·dle·work (nē′dəl wėrk′), *n.* work done with a needle; sewing; embroidery.

need·n't (nēd′ənt), need not.

needs (nēdz), *adv.* because of necessity; necessarily: *he needs must go where duty calls.*

need·y (nēd′i), *adj.,* **need·i·er, need·i·est. 1** very poor; not having enough to live on. **2** craving attention or affection: *Katy's needy cats.* —**need′i·ness,** *n.*

ne′er (nãr), *adv. Esp. Poetic.* never.

ne′er-do-well (nãr′dü wel′), *n.* a worthless fellow; good-for-nothing person. —*adj.* worthless; good-for-nothing.

ne·far·i·ous (ni fãr′i əs), *adj.* very wicked; villainous. [< L *nefarius,* ult. < *ne-* not + *fas* right, orig., (divine) decree < *fari* speak] —**ne·far′i·ous·ly,** *adv.* —**ne·far′i·ous·ness,** *n.*

neg., negative; negatively.

ne·gate (ni gāt′; nē′gāt), *v.,* **-gat·ed, -gat·ing.** deny; nullify. [< L *negatus,* pp. of *negare* say no]

ne·ga·tion (ni gā′shən), *n.* **1** a denying; denial: *shaking the head is a sign of negation.* **2** absence or opposite of some positive thing or quality. Darkness is the negation of light.

neg·a·tive (neg′ə tiv), *adj., n., v.,* **-tived, -tiv·ing.** —*adj.* **1** saying no: *his answer was negative.* **2** not positive; consisting in the lack of the opposite: *negative kindness means not being unkind.* **3** tending to emphasize what is wrong or could be wrong: *a negative attitude.* **4** counting down from zero; minus. **5** of the kind of electricity produced on resin when it is rubbed with silk. **6** showing the lights and shadows reversed: *the negative image on a film.* **7** moving or turning away from light, the earth, etc. **8** resisting suggestions; very uncooperative. —*n.* **1** word or statement that says no or denies. **2** the side that says no or denies in an argument. **3** a negative quality or characteristic. **4** a minus quantity. **5** kind of electricity produced on resin when it is rubbed with silk. **6** the negative element in an electric cell. **7** a photographic image in which the lights and shadows are reversed. Prints are made from it.

in the negative, a in favor of denying (a request, suggestion, etc.). **b** saying no; denying. —**neg′a·tive·ly,** *adv.* —**neg′a·tive·ness, neg′a·tiv′i·ty,** *n.*

neg·a·tiv·ism (neg′ə tiv iz′əm), *n.* tendency to say or do the opposite of what is suggested. —**neg′a·tiv·is′tic,** *adj.*

neg·lect (ni glekt′), *v.* **1** give too little care or attention to: *neglect one's health.* **2** leave undone; not attend to: *neglect an order.* **3** omit; fail: *don't neglect to water the plants.* —*n.* **1** act of neglecting; disregard. **2** want of attention to what should be done. **3** a being neglected. [< L *neglectus* < *neg-* not + *legere* pick up]

neg·lect·ful (ni glekt′fəl), *adj.* careless; negligent. —**neg·lect′ful·ly,** *adv.* —**neg·lect′ful·ness** *n.*

neg·li·gee (neg′lə zhā′; neg′lə zhā), *n.* a woman's loose gown, often of fine fabric and worn over a nightgown. [< F, fem. pp. of *négliger* NEGLECT]

neg·li·gence (neg′lə jəns), *n.* **1** lack of proper care or attention; neglect: *negligence was the cause of the accident.* **2** carelessness; indifference. [< L, < *neglegere* NEGLECT]

neg·li·gent (neg′lə jənt), *adj.* **1** neglectful; given to neglect; showing neglect. **2** careless; indifferent. —**neg′li·gent·ly,** *adv.*

neg·li·gi·ble (neg′lə jə bəl), *adj.* that can be disregarded: *a difference of a penny is negligible.* —**neg′li·gi·bil′i·ty, neg′li·gi·ble·ness,** *n.* —**neg′li·gi·bly,** *adv.*

ne·go·tia·ble (ni gō′shə bəl; –shi ə–), *adj.* **1** capable of being negotiated or sold; whose ownership can be transferred. **2** that can be got past or over. —**ne·go′tia·bil′i·ty,** *n.*

ne·go·ti·ate (ni gō′shi āt), *v.,* **–at·ed, –at·ing. 1** talk over and arrange terms: *negotiate for peace.* **2** sell. **3** get past or over: *the car negotiated the sharp curve by slowing down.* [< L, < *negotium* business < *neg-* not + *otium* ease] —**ne·go′ti·a′tor,** *n.*

ne·go·ti·a·tion (ni gō′shi ā′shən), *n.* a negotiating; arrangement: *negotiations for the new school are nearly finished.*

Ne·gro (nē′grō), *n., pl.* **–groes,** *adj.* —*n.* **1** person belonging to any of the black people. **2** a person having some black ancestors. —*adj.* of or pertaining to blacks. [< Sp. < L *niger* black]

Ne·he·mi·ah (nē′ə mī′ə), *n.* book of the Old Testament.

neigh (nā), *n.* sound that a horse makes. —*v.* make such a sound. [OE *hnǣgan*]

neigh·bor (nā′bər), *n.* **1** one who lives near another. **2** person or thing that is near another. —*v.* **1** live or be near (to). **2** adjoin; border on. —*adj.* living or situated near to another. [OE *nēahgebūr* < *nēah* nigh + *gebūr* dweller, countryman] —**neigh′bor·er,** *n.* —**neigh′bor·ing,** *adj.* —**neigh′bor·ly,** *adj.* —**neigh′bor·li·ness,** *n.*

neigh·bor·hood (nā′bər hud), *n.* **1** region near some place or thing. **2** place; district: *a good neighborhood.* **3** people living near one another; people of a place. **4** =the hood. **5** nearness. —*adj.* of or having to do with a neighborhood.

in the neighborhood of, somewhere near; about: *in the neighborhood of $100.*

nei·ther (nē′thər; nī′–), *conj.* **1** not either: *neither you nor I will go.* **2** nor yet: *"they toil not, neither do they spin."* —*adj.* not either: *neither statement is true.* —*pron.* not either. [ME, < *ne* not + EITHER]

nem·a·tode (nem′ə tōd), *adj.* belonging to a class or group of worms characterized by an elongated, unsegmented, cylindrical body. —*n.* such a worm. Hookworms and trichinae are nematodes. [< NL, ult. < Gk. *nema* thread]

Nem·e·sis (nem′ə sis), *n., pl.* **–ses** (–sēz). **1** the Greek goddess of vengeance. **2** **nemesis, a** just punishment for evil deeds. **b** person who punishes another for evil deeds [< Gk., < *nemein* give what is due]

N. Eng., Northern England.

neo–, *combining form.* **1** new. **2** recent. [< Gk., < *neos*]

ne·o·co·lo·ni·al·ism (nē′ō kə lō′ni ə liz′əm), *n.* the supposed policy or practice of a large nation to dominate politically or economically smaller nations, especially former colonies; imperialism. —**ne·o·co·lo′ni·al·ist,** *n., adj.*

ne·o·con (nē′ō kon), *n., adj.* =neoconservative.

ne·o·con·serv·a·tive (nē′ō kən sėr′və tiv), *n.* person who supports a strong presidency, policies favoring business, and an activist foreign policy. —*adj.* of or having to do with neoconservative principles. —**ne′o·con·serv′a·tism,** *n.*

ne·o·dym·i·um (nē′ō dim′i əm), *n.* a rare metallic element, Nd, found in certain rare minerals.

ne·o·lith·ic or **Ne·o·lith·ic** (nē′ə lith′ik), *adj.* of the later Stone Age, when polished stone weapons and tools were made and used: *neolithic man.*

ne·ol·o·gism (ni ol′ə jiz əm), **ne·ol·o·gy** (–ji), *n., pl.* **–gisms; –gies. 1** use of new words or new meanings for old words. **2** a new word; new meaning for an old word. [< F, < Gk. *neos* new + *logos* word]

ne·on (nē′on), *n.* an element, Ne, that is a colorless, odorless gas, forming a very small part of the air. Tubes containing neon are used in electric signs and television sets. [< NL < Gk., new]

ne·o·phyte (nē′ə fīt), *n.* **1** a new convert. **2** beginner; novice. [< L < Gk., < *neos* new + *phyein* to plant]

ne·o·plasm (nē′ō plaz′əm), *n.* abnormal growth of new tissue, as in a tumor. [< E *neo–* + Gk. *plásma* something formed]

Ne·pal (nə pôl′), *n.* country between India and Tibet. —**Nep′a·lese′,** *n.*

neph·ew (nef′ū), *n.* son of one's brother or sister; son of one's brother-in-law or sister-in-law. [< OF < L *nepos*]

ne·phri·tis (ni frī′tis), *n.* inflammation of the kidneys, esp. Bright's disease. [< LL, Gk., < *nephros* kidney] —**ne·phrit′ic,** *adj.*

nep·o·tism (nep′ə tiz əm), *n.* the showing of too much favor by one in power to relatives, esp. by giving them desirable appointments. [< F < Ital., < *nipote* NEPHEW] —**nep′o·tist,** *n.*

Nep·tune (nep′tūn; –tūn), *n.* **1** *Roman Myth.* the god of the sea, identified with the Greek god Poseidon. **2** a large planet too far from the earth to be seen with the naked eye.

nep·tu·ni·um (nep tü′ni əm; –tū′–), *n.* a radioactive element, Np, obtained by bombardment of uranium with neutrons.

ner·va·tion (nėr vā′shən), *n.* arrangement of nerves.

nerve (nėrv), *n., v.,* **nerved, nerv·ing.** —*n.* **1** fiber or bundle of fibers connecting the brain or spinal cord with the eyes, ears, muscles, glands, etc. **2** mental strength; courage. **3** strength; vigor; energy. **4** rude boldness; impudence. —*v.* arouse strength or courage in: *nerve oneself for a struggle.*

get on one's nerves, annoy or irritate one.

nerves, a nervousness. **b** attack of nervousness. [< L *nervus* sinew, tendon]

nerve cell, 1 cell that conducts impulses; neuron. **2** cell body of a neuron.

nerve center, 1 group of nerve cells that act together. **2** *Fig.* any place that is the center of activity, esp. in directing activity.

nerve gas, any poison gas that attacks the central nervous system

nerve·less (nėrv′lis), *adj.* **1** without strength or vigor; feeble; weak. **2** without courage or firmness. **3** without nerves. —**nerve′less·ly,** *adv.* —**nerve′less·ness,** *n.*

nerv·ous (nėr′vəs), *adj.* **1** of the nerves: *the nervous system of the body.* **2** having delicate or easily excited nerves; restless; uneasy. —**nerv′ous·ly,** *adv.* —**nerv′ous·ness,** *n.*

nervous system, system of nerves and nerve cells in a person or animal.

nerv·y (nėr′vi), *adj.,* **nerv·i·er, nerv·i·est. 1** *Informal.* rude and bold. **2** requiring courage or firmness. **3** highly excitable.

nes·cience (nesh′əns; nesh′i əns), *n.* ignorance. [< LL, ult. < L *ne–* not + *scire* know] —**nes′cient,** *adj.*

–ness, *suffix.* **1** quality, state, or condition of being ___, as *blackness, preparedness.* **2** ___ action; ___ behavior, as in some uses of *carefulness, meanness,* [OE *–nes(s)*]

nest (nest), *n.* **1** a structure or place used by birds for laying eggs and rearing young. **2** place used by insects, fishes, turtles, rabbits, or the like, for depositing eggs or young. **3** a snug abode, retreat, or resting place. **4** place that swarms (usually with something bad): *a nest of thieves.* **5** the birds, animals, etc., living in a nest. **6** set or series (often from large to small) such that each fits within another: *nest of drinking cups.* —*v.* **1** build or have a nest. **2** settle or place in, or as if in, a nest. [OE]

nest egg, 1 a natural or artificial egg left in a nest to induce a hen to continue laying eggs there. **2** something laid up as a reserve.

nes·tle (nes′əl), v., **–tled, –tling. 1** settle comfortably or cozily; be sheltered: *the little house nestled among the trees.* **2** press close in affection or for comfort: *nestle up to one's mother.* [OE *nestlian* < *nest*] **—nes′tler,** *n.*

nest·ling (nest′ling), *n.* **1** bird too young to leave the nest. **2** a young child.

net[1] (net), *n., v.,* **net·ted, net·ting. —**n. **1** an open fabric made of string, cord, thread, or hair, knotted together in such a way as to leave holes regularly arranged, as fish net, a mosquito net, a tennis net, etc. **2** anything like a net. **3** a lacelike cloth. **4** a trap or snare. **—**v. **1** catch in a net: *net a fish.* **2** cover, confine, or protect with a net. [OE *nett*] **—net′like′,** *adj.*

net[2] (net), *adj., n., v.,* **net·ted, net·ting. —**adj. remaining after deductions; free from deductions. A net gain or profit is the actual gain after all working expenses have been paid. **—**n. the net weight, profit, price, etc. **—**v. gain: *the sale netted me a good profit.* [< F. See NEAT[1].]

neth·er (neth′ər), *adj.* lower. [OE *neothera*]

Neth·er·lands (neth′ər ləndz), **the.** *n.* a small country in Europe, W of Germany and N of Belgium; Holland. **—Neth′er·land′er,** *n.*

neth·er·most (neth′ər mōst), *adj.* lowest.

nether world, world of the dead; hell.

net·ting (net′ing), *n.* a netted or meshed material: *mosquito netting.*

net·tle (net′əl), *n., v.,* **–tled, –tling. —**n. kind of plant having sharp leaf hairs that sting the skin when touched. **—**v. sting the mind; irritate; provoke; vex. [OE *netele*]

net·work (net′wėrk′), *n.* **1** a netting; net. **2** any netlike combination of things: *a network of railroads.* **3** group of radio or television stations connected together. **4** a number of computers linked to the same server and able to share data. **5** group of people who share interests or work together informally to promote certain goals. **—**v. meet with groups of people informally to promote shared goals and interests.

neu·ral (nůr′əl; nyůr′–), *adj.* of or pertaining to a nerve, neuron, or nervous system. [< Gk. *neuron* nerve]

neu·ral·gia (nů ral′jə; nyů–), *n.* pain, usually sharp, along the course of a nerve. [< NL, < Gk. *neuron* nerve + *algos* pain] **—neu·ral′gic,** *adj.*

neu·ras·the·ni·a (nůr′əs thē′ni ə; nyůr′–; –thēn′yə), *n.* nervous exhaustion or weakness. [< NL, < Gk. *neuron* nerve + *asthenia* weakness] **—neu′ras·then′ic,** *adj.*

neu·ri·tis (nů rī′tis; nyů–), *n.* inflammation of a nerve or nerves. **—neu·rit′ic,** *adj.*

neu·ro·chem·is·try (nůr′ō kem′ə stri; nyůr′–), *n.* branch of biochemistry concerned with the chemicals that are present and affect the nervous system. **—neu′ro·chem′i·cal,** *adj., n.* **—neu′ro·chem′ist,** *n.*

neu·rol·o·gy (nů rol′ə ji; nyů rol′–), *n.* study of the nervous system and its diseases. **—neu′ro·log′i·cal,** *adj.* **—neu·rol′o·gist,** *n.*

neu·ron (nůr′on; nyůr′–), *n.* one of the conducting cells of which the brain, spinal cord, and nerves are composed. [< Gk., nerve] **—neu·ron′ic,** *adj.*

neu·rop·a·thy (nů rop′ə thi; nyů–), *n.* disease of the nervous system. **—neu′ro·path′ic,** *adj.* **—neu′ro·path′i·cal·ly,** *adv.*

neu·rop·ter·ous (nů rop′tər əs; nyů–), *adj.* belonging to an order of insects having two pairs of wings with netlike veins. [< Gk. *neuron* nerve + *pteron* wing]

neu·ro·sis (nů rō′sis; nyů–), *n., pl.* **–ses** (–sēz). a nervous disorder or disease, esp. one without apparent organic change. [< NL, < Gk., < *neuron* nerve]

neu·ro·sur·ger·y (nů′rō sėr′jər i), *n.* surgery of the nervous system, esp. the brain. **—neu′ro·sur′geon,** *n.*

neu·rot·ic (nů rot′ik; nyů–), *adj.* **1** suffering from a nervous disease. **2** too nervous. **—**n. person suffering from neurosis.

neut., neuter.

neu·ter (nü′tər; nū′–), *adj.* **1** neither masculine nor feminine. *It* is a neuter pronoun. **2** having sex organs that are not fully developed. Worker bees are neuter. **3** being on neither side; neutral. **—**n. **1** a neuter word or form. **2** the neuter gender. **3** an animal, plant, or insect that is neuter. [< L, < *ne-* not + *uter* either]

neu·tral (nü′trəl; nū′–), *adj.* **1** on neither side in a quarrel or war. **2** of or belonging to a neutral country or neutral zone: *a neutral port.* **3** neither one thing nor the other; indefinite. **4** having little or no color; grayish. **5** *Elect.* neither positive nor negative. **—**n. **1** a neutral person or country. **2** position of gears when they do not transmit motion from the engine to the wheels or other working parts. [< L *neutralis.* See NEUTER.] **—neu′tral·ly,** *adv.*

neu·tral·ist (nü′trəl ist; nū–), *adj.* practicing or advocating neutrality. **—neu′tral·ism,** *n.*

neu·tral·i·ty (nü tral′ə ti; nū–), *n.* a being neutral; neutral character or status.

neu·tral·ize (nü′trəl īz; nū′–), *v.,* **–ized, –iz·ing. 1** make neutral. **2** keep war out of. **3** make of no effect by some opposite force; counterbalance. **4** make chemically inert. **5** make electrically inert. **—neu′tral·i·za′tion,** *n.* **—neu′tral·iz′er,** *n.*

neutral vowel, *Phonet.* schwa.

neu·tri·no (nü trē′nō; nū–), *n.* *Physics.* a small, uncharged particle, usually considered to have a mass of zero.

neu·tron (nü′tron; nū′–), *n.* *Physics.* particle that is neutral electrically and has about the same mass as a proton. [< *neutr(al)* neither positively nor negatively charged + *-on* (after *electron, proton*)]

neutron bomb, a hydrogen bomb set off with little heat or shock effect. It releases highly lethal, short-lived neutrons.

Nev., Nevada.

Ne·vad·a (nə vad′ə; –vä′də), *n.* a W state of the United States. **—Ne·vad′an,** *adj., n.*

nev·er (nev′ər), *adv.* **1** not ever; at no time: *he never has seen a more perfect copy.* **2** in no case; not at all; to no extent or degree: *never the wiser.* **3** **never so, a** not even so. **b** no matter how. [OE *nǣfre* < *ne* not + *ǣfre* ever]

nev·er·more (nev′ər môr′; –mōr′), *adv.* never again.

nev·er·the·less (nev′ər ᵺə les′), *adv.* however; none the less; for all that; in spite of it.

new (nü; nū), *adj.* **1** never having existed before; now first made, thought out, known or heard of, felt, or discovered: *a new invention, a new path.* **2** lately grown, come, or made; not old: *a new bud.* **3** different; changed; as if new: *he is a new man now, a new country to me.* **4** not yet accustomed: *new to the work.* **5** later; modern; recent: *new dances, new information.* **—**adv. **1** newly; recently or lately; freshly. **2** again; anew. [OE *nīwe*] **—new′ish,** *adj.* **—new′ness,** *n.*

new·born (nü′bôrn′; nū′–), *adj.* **1** recently or only just born. **2** ready to start a new life.

New·cas·tle (nü′kas′əl; –käs′–; nū′–), *n.* **carry coals to Newcastle,** do something unnecessary.

new·com·er (nü′kum′ər; nū′–), *n.* person who has just come or who came not long ago.

New Deal, the policies and measures advocated by President Franklin D. Roosevelt as a means of improving the economic and social welfare of the United States. **—New Dealer.**

New Delhi, the capital of the republic of India.

new·el (nü′əl; nū′–), *n.* the post at the top or bottom of a stairway that supports the railing. [< OF *noiel,* ult. < L *nux* nut; infl. by *noel* bud, ult. < L *nodus* knot]

New England, the NE part of the United States. **—New Englander.**

new·fan·gled (nü′fang′gəld; nū′–), *adj.* **1** lately come into fashion; of a new kind. **2** fond of novelty. [ME *newefangel* < *newe* new + *fange* (*n*) take]

New·found·land (nü′fənd land′, nū′–; nü′fənd land′, nū′–), *n.* **1** a large island in the Atlantic just off the E coast of Canada. **2** a shaggy, intelligent dog like a spaniel, but much larger.

New Greek, Greek language as used after 1500; modern Greek.

New Guin·ea (gin′i), a large island north of Australia.

New Hamp·shire (hamp′shər; –shir), a New England state of the United States. **—New Hampshirite.**

New Jer·sey (jėr′zi), an E state of the United States. **—New Jerseyite.**

New Latin, the Latin language after 1500.

new·ly (nü′li; nū′li), *adv.* **1** lately; recently: *newly wedded.* **2** again; freshly: *a newly revived scandal.* **3** in a new way.

New Mexico, a SW state of the United States. **—New Mexican.**

new moon, moon when seen as a thin crescent with the hollow side on the left.

New Netherland, a former Dutch colony in America, from 1614 to 1664, divided into the colonies of New York and New Jersey.

news (nüz; nūz), *n.* something told as having just happened; information about something that has just happened or will soon happen. **break the news,** make something known; tell something. [ME *newes,* pl. of *newe* that which is new, adj. used as n.]

news·cast (nüz′kast′; -käst′; nūz′-), *n.* a radio or television broadcast of news. **—news′cast′er,** *n.* **—news′cast′ing,** *n.*

news·deal·er (nüz′dēl′ər; nūz′-), *n.* seller of newspapers and magazines.

news·let·ter (nüz′let′ər; nūz′-), *n.* a written or printed letter presenting an informal or confidential coverage of the news.

news·pa·per (nüz′pā′pər; nūz′-; nüs′-; nūs′-), *n.* sheets of paper printed every day or week, telling the news, carrying advertisements, and often having stories, poems, and useful information.

news·print (nüz′print′; nūz′-), *n.* kind of paper on which newspapers are usually printed.

news·reel (nüz′rēl′; nūz′-), *n.* short film showing current events.

news·stand (nüz′stand′; nūz′-), *n.* place where newspapers and magazines are sold.

news·wor·thy (nüz′wėr′thi), *adj.* of great enough interest or importance to be covered by the news media. **—news′wor′thi·ness,** *n.*

news·y (nüz′i; nūz′i), *adj.,* **news·i·er, news·i·est,** *n., pl.* **news·ies.** **—***adj.* full of news. **—***n.* newsboy.

newt (nüt; nūt), *n.* any of various small salamanders that live in water part of the time. [OE *efete;* ME *an ewt* taken as *a newt*]

New Testament, the part of the Bible which contains the life and teachings of Christ recorded by his followers, together with their own experiences and teachings.

New·to·ni·an (nü tō′ni ən; nū-), *adj.* of or by Isaac Newton (1642–1727), English mathematician, physicist, and philosopher: *Newtonian physics.* **—***n.* follower of Newton.

New World, the Western Hemisphere; North America and South America. **—new′-world′, New′-World′,** *adj.*

new year, 1 year approaching or newly begun. **2 New Year, New Year's, a** New Year's Day. **b** the first day or days of the year.

New Year's Day, New Year's, January 1, usually observed as a legal holiday.

New Year's Eve, the evening of December 31.

New York, an E state of the United States. **—New Yorker.**

New Zea·land (zē′lənd), a country in the S Pacific, consisting of two main islands and various small ones. **—New Zealander.**

next (nekst), *adj.* following at once; nearest: *the next train, the next room.* **—***adv.* **1** the first time after this: *when you next come, bring it.* **2** in the place or time or position that is nearest: *his name comes next.* **—***prep.* nearest to: *the house next the church.*

next door to, a in or at the house next to. **b** almost; nearly.

next to, a nearest to. **b** almost; nearly. [OE *nēhst,* superl. of *nēah* nigh]

next-door (nekst′dôr′; -dōr′), *adj.* in or at the next building, house, etc.

next door, 1 the next building, house, etc. **2** very near.

next of kin, the nearest blood relative.

Nez Per·ce (nez′pėrs′), *n., pl.* **Nez Per·ces. 1** member of an American Indian tribe that formerly lived in Idaho, Oregon, and Washington. **2** their Shahaptian language. [F *nez percé,* lit. pierced nose]

N.G., n.g., no good.

NH, *(zip code)* New Hampshire.

N.H., New Hampshire.

Ni, nickel.

ni·a·cin (nī′ə sin), *n.* =nicotinic acid. [from trademark < *ni*(*cotinic*) *ac*(*id*)]

nib (nib), *n., v.,* **nibbed, nib·bing.** **—***n.* **1** point of a pen; either of its parts. **2** tip; point. **3** a bird's bill. **—***v.* furnish with a nib. [var of *neb*]

nib·ble (nib′əl), *v.,* **-bled, -bling,** *n.* **—***v.* **1** eat away with quick, small bites, as a rabbit or a mouse does. **2** bite gently or lightly. **—***n.* a nibbling; small bite. [cf. LG *nibbelen*] **—nib′bler,** *n.*

Nic·a·ra·gua (nik′ə rä′gwə), *n.* country in Central America. **—Nic′a·ra′guan,** *adj., n.*

nice (nīs), *adj.,* **nic·er, nic·est. 1** pleasing; agreeable; satisfactory: *a nice face.* **2** thoughtful; kind: *he was nice to us.* **3** exact; precise; discriminating: *a nice ear for music.* **4** minute; fine; subtle: *a nice distinction.* **5** exacting; particular; hard to please; fastidious; dainty: *nice in his eating.* [< OF, silly. < L *nescius* ignorant < *ne-* not + *scire* know] **—nice′ly,** *adv.* **—nice′ness,** *n.*

Ni·cene Creed (nī sēn′; nī′sēn), a formal statement of the chief tenets of Christian belief, based on that adopted in A.D. 325.

ni·ce·ty (nī′sə ti), *n., pl.* **-ties. 1** exactness; accuracy; delicacy: *require nicety of adjustment.* **2** a fine point; small distinction; detail: *the niceties of scientific measurement.* **3** something dainty or refined: *the niceties of living.*

niche (nich), *n.* **1** a recess or hollow in a wall for a statue, vase, etc. **2** a suitable place or position. [< F, ult. < L *nidus* nest]

nick (nik), *n.* place where a small bit has been cut or broken out; notch; groove. **—***v.* make a nick or nicks in.

in the nick of time, just in time. [cf. OE *gehnycned* wrinkled]

nick·el (nik′əl), *n., v.,* **-eled, -el·ing.** **—***n.* **1** a metallic element, Ni, that looks like silver and is somewhat like iron, much used as an alloy. **2** a coin containing nickel; a United States five-cent piece. **—***v.* cover or coat with nickel. [< Sw. < G *kupfernickel,* lit., copper devil; the ore resembles copper but yields none]

nick·nack (nik′nak′), *n.* knickknack.

nick·name (nik′nām′), *n., v.,* **-named, -nam·ing.** **—***n.* name added to a person's real name or used instead of it. **—***v.* give a nickname to. [ME *ekename; an ekename* taken as *a nekename.* See EKE[2], NAME.]

Nic·o·si·a (nik′ō sē′ə), *n.* capital of Cyprus.

ni·co·ti·a·na (ni kō′tē a′nə), *n.* plant of the nightshade family, esp. one grown for its showy, night-blooming flowers; flowering tobacco.

nic·o·tine (nik′ə tēn), *n.* poison contained in tobacco leaves. [< F; after J. *Nicot,* who introduced tobacco in France]

nic·o·tin·ic acid (nik′ə tin′ik), a vitamin, C_5H_4NCOOH, which prevents pellagra.

nic·ti·tate (nik′tə tāt), *v.,* **-tat·ed, -tat·ing.** wink. [< Med.L *nictitatus,* ult. < L *nictare* wink] **—nic′ti·ta′tion,** *n.*

nictitating membrane, a thin membrane, or inner or third eyelid, present in many animals, capable of being drawn across the eyeball.

niece (nēs), *n.* daughter of one's brother or sister; daughter of one's brother-in-law or sister-in-law. [< OF, ult. < L *neptis*]

nif·ty (nif′ti), *adj.,* **-ti·er, -ti·est.** *Informal.* **1** attractive; stylish. **2** wonderful; swell.

Ni·ger (nī′jər), *n.* republic in W Africa.

Ni·ge·ri·a (nī jir′i ə), *n.* country in W Africa. **—Ni·ge′ri·an,** *adj., n.*

nig·gard·ly (nig′ərd li), *adj.* **1** stingy. **2** meanly small or scanty: *a niggardly gift.* **—***adv.* stingily. **—nig′gard·li·ness,** *n.*

nig·gling (nig′ling), *adj.* of little importance; petty: *niggling criticism.*

nigh (nī), *adv., adj.,* **nigh·er, nigh·est** or **next,** *prep., v.* =near. [OE *nēah*]

night (nīt), *n.* **1** the darkness between evening and morning; the time between sunset and sunrise. **2** the darkness of night; the dark. **3** the darkness of ignorance, sin, sorrow, old age, death, etc. **4** evening; nightfall. **—***adj.* **1** of the night: *the night sky, night manager.* **2** done or used at night: *night flight, night light.*

make a night of it, celebrate most of the night.

night and day, all the time. [OE *niht*]

night·cap (nīt′kap′), *n.* drink taken just before going to bed.

night clothes, clothing worn at night, for sleeping; sleepwear.

night club, place for dancing, eating, and entertainment, open only at night.

night crawler, large earthworm that comes to the surface of the ground at night.

night·dress (nīt′dres′), *n.* =nightgown.

night·fall (nīt′fôl′), *n.* the coming of night.

night·gown (nīt′goun′), *n.* a long, loose garment worn in bed.

night·hawk (nīt′hôk′), *n.* kind of bird that flies and feeds mostly by night.

night·in·gale (nīt′ən gāl; nīt′ing–), *n.* a small, reddish-brown bird of Europe. The males sings sweetly at night as well as in the daytime. [for *nightgale,* OE *nihtegale* < *niht* night + *galan* sing]

night·jar (nīt′jär′), *n.* any one of various birds that are active mostly at night and whose calls can be heard in the night. [< *night* + *jar²* make a harsh sound]

night·life (nīt′līf), n. activity at night, esp. entertainment in clubs and theaters.

night·long (nīt′lông′; –long′), *adj.* lasting all night. —*adv.* through the whole night.

night·ly (nīt′li), *adj.* 1 done, happening, or appearing every night. 2 done, happening, or appearing at night. —*adv.* 1 every night: *performances are given nightly.* 2 at night; by night.

night·mare (nīt′mâr′), *n.* 1 a very distressing dream. 2 a very distressing experience. [< *night* + OE *mare* monster oppressing men during sleep] —**night′mar′ish,** *adj.*

night owl, person who habitually stays up late.

night school, school held in the evening for persons who work during the day.

night·shade (nīt′shād′), *n.* any of various plants belonging to the same genus as the potato and the tomato. The **black nightshade** has black, poisonous berries. The **deadly nightshade,** or belladonna, has red berries.

night·shirt (nīt′shėrt′), *n.* a long, loose shirt worn for sleeping.

night spot, club where music, food, dancing, etc., are offered at night.

night·stick (nīt′stik′), *n.* police officer's club.

night·time (nīt′tīm′), *n.* time between evening and morning.

ni·hil·ism (nī′ə liz əm), *n.* entire rejection of the usual beliefs in religion, morals, government, laws, etc. [< L *nihil* nothing] —**ni′hil·ist,** *n.* —**ni′hil·is′tic,** *adj.*

nil (nil), *n.* =nothing. [< L, earlier *nihil*]

nim·ble (nim′bəl), *adj.,* **–bler, –blest. 1** active and sure-footed; light and quick; quick-moving: *goats are nimble in climbing among the rocks.* 2 quick to understand and to reply; clever: *a nimble mind.* [ME *nymel* < OE *niman* take] —**nim′ble·ness,** *n.* —**nim′bly,** *adv.*

nim·bo·stra·tus (nim′bō strā′təs), *n., pl.* **–ti** (–tē). cloud formation that appears as a dark layer and produces rain or snow.

nim·bus (nim′bəs), *n.,* **–bus·es, –bi** (–bī). **1** a light disk or other radiance about the head of a divine or sacred person in a picture. 2 a bright cloud surrounding a god, person, or thing. 3 =nimbostratus. [< L, cloud]

nin·com·poop (nin′kəm püp), *n.* fool; simpleton; blockhead.

nine (nīn), *n.* **1** a cardinal number, one more than eight. 2 symbol of this number; 9. **3** set of nine persons or things. —*adj.* one more than eight; 9. [OE *nigon*]

nine·fold (nīn′fōld′), *adj.* **1** nine times as much or as many. **2** having nine parts. —*adv.* nine times as much or as many.

nine·pins (nīn′pinz′), *n. (sing. in use)* game in which nine large wooden pins are set up to be bowled down with a ball.

nine·teen (nīn′tēn′), *n.* **1** a cardinal number, nine more than ten. **2** symbol of this number; 19. —*adj.* nine more than ten; 19. —**nine′teenth′,** *adj., n.*

nine·ty (nīn′ti), *n., pl.* **–ties,** *adj.* —*n.* **1** a cardinal number, nine times ten. **2** symbol of this number; 90. —*adj.* nine times ten; 90. —**nine′ti·eth,** *adj., n.*

nin·ny (nin′i), *n., pl.* **–nies.** fool; silly person.

ninth (nīnth), *adj.* **1** next after the eighth; last in a series of 9. **2** being one of 9 equal parts. —*n.* **1** next after the eighth; last in a series of 9. **2** one of nine equal parts. —**ninth′ly,** *adv.*

ni·o·bi·um (nī ō′bi əm), *n.* a steel-gray, rare metallic element, Nb, that resembles tantalum in chemical properties. —**ni·o′bic, ni·o′bous,** *adj.*

nip¹ (nip), *v.,* **nipped, nip·ping,** *n.* —*v.* **1** squeeze tight and suddenly; bite: *the crab nipped my toe.* **2** take off by biting, pinching, or snipping. **3** hurt at the tips; spoil; injure: *plants nipped by frost.* **4** have a sharp, biting effect on: *cold winds nip your ears and nose.* —*n.* **1** a tight squeeze; pinch; sudden bite. **2** injury caused by frost. **3** sharp cold; chill: *there is a nip in the air on a frosty morning.* **4** a small bit.

nip and tuck, very close or even in a race or contest, so that the outcome is in doubt. [ME *nyppen.* Cf. Du. *nijpen.*]

nip² (nip), *n.* a small drink.

nip·per (nip′ər), *n.* **1** one that nips. **2** Usually, **nippers.** pincers, forceps, pliers, or any tool that nips.

nip·ple (nip′əl), *n.* **1** a small projection through which an infant or baby animal gets its mother's milk. **2** a cap for a baby's bottle, made of rubber, latex, or other rubbery substance and shaped like a nipple. **3** anything shaped or used like a nipple.

nip·py (nip′i), *adj.,* **–pi·er, –pi·est.** biting; sharp.

nir·va·na, Nir·va·na (nir vä′nə; –van′ə; nėr–), *n.* the Buddhist idea of heavenly peace; perfect happiness reached by complete absorption of oneself into the supreme universal spirit. [< Skt., extinction, < *nis*– out + *vā*– blow]

Ni·sei (nē′sā′), *n., pl.* **–sei.** a native-born U.S. or Canadian citizen whose parents were Japanese immigrants. [< Jap.]

nit (nit), *n.* **1** egg of a louse or similar insect. **2** a very young louse or similar insect. [OE *hnitu*]

ni·ter (nī′tər), *n.* **1** potassium nitrate, KNO_3, a salt obtained from potash, used in making gunpowder; saltpeter. **2** sodium nitrate, $NaNO_3$, used as fertilizer. [< L < Gk. *nitron*]

nit-pick (nit′pik′), *v.* search for unimportant faults; criticize meanly, pettily. —**nit′-pick′er,** *n.*

ni·trate (nī′trāt), *n., v.,* **–trat·ed, –trating.** —*n.* **1** salt or ester of nitric acid. **2** potassium nitrate, KNO_3, or sodium nitrate, $NaNO_3$, used as a fertilizer. —*v.* treat with nitric acid or a nitrate. —**ni·tra′tion,** *n.*

ni·tric acid (nī′trik), a clear, colorless liquid, HNO_3, that eats into flesh, clothing, metal, and other substances.

ni·trite (nī′trīt), *n.* salt or ester of nitrous acid.

ni·tro·gen (nī′trə jən), *n.* one of the elements, a colorless, odorless, tasteless gas, N, that forms about four-fifths of the air by volume. —**ni·trog′e·nous,** *adj.*

nitrogen cycle, circulation of nitrogen and its compounds by animals and plants. Nitrogen is absorbed from the soil by green plants, consumed in food by animals, and returned to the soil as animal waste and decaying animals and plants.

ni·tro·glyc·er·in (nī′trə glis′ər in), *n.* an oily, explosive liquid, $C_3H_5(NO_3)_3$, made by treating glycerin with nitric and sulfuric acids, used in dynamite.

ni·trous acid (nī′trəs), an acid, HNO_2, known only in solution or its salts.

nitrous oxide, a colorless gas, N_2O, that causes laughing and inability to feel pain; laughing gas, used as an anesthetic by dentists.

nit·wit (nit′wit′), *n.* stupid person.

nix (niks), *n., interj. Informal.* nothing; no. [< G *nichts*]

nix·ie (nik′si), *n.* a female water fairy.

Nixon (nik′sən), *n.* **Richard M.** 1913–94, the 37th president of the United States, 1969–74, and the only to resign.

NJ, *(zip code)* New Jersey.

N.J., New Jersey.

NL, New Latin.

NM, *(zip code)* New Mexico.

N.M., N. Mex., New Mexico.

NNE, N.N.E., direction halfway between north and northeast.

NNW, N.N.W., direction halfway between north and northwest.

no¹ (nō), *n., pl.* **noes, no's,** *adj., adv.* —*n.* **1** word used to deny, refuse, or disagree. **2** denial; refusal. **3** a negative vote or voter: *the noes have it.* [< adv.] —*adj.* not any; not a: *he has no friends.* [var. of *none*] —*adv.* **1** word used to deny, refuse, or disagree: *Will you come? No.* **2** not in any degree; not at all: *he is no better.* **3** not, chiefly in phrases like *whether or no.* [OE *nā* < *ne* not + *ā* ever]

no², No (nō), *n., pl.* **no, nos, No, Nos.** Japanese classical drama. [< Jap.]

No, nobelium.

No., **1** north; northern. **2** Also, **no.** number.

No·bel (nō bel′), *n.* =Nobel prize.

No·bel·ist (nō bel′ist), *n.* a winner of a Nobel prize.

no·be·li·um (nō bē′li əm), *n.* a rare radioactive, artificial element, No. [< *Nobel* Institute, where produced]

Nobel prizes, money prizes established by Alfred B. Nobel (1833–96) to be given annually to those persons who have made the greatest contributions in the fields of physics, chemistry, economics, medicine or physiology, literature, and the promotion of peace.

no·bil·i·ty (nō bil′ə ti), *n., pl.* **–ties. 1** people of noble rank. Earls, counts, princes, and kings belong to the nobility. **2** noble birth; noble rank. **3** noble character.

no·ble (nō′bəl), *adj.,* **–bler, –blest,** *n.* —*adj.* **1** high and great by birth, rank, or title. **2** high and great in character; showing greatness of mind; good: *a noble deed.* **3** excellent; fine; splendid; magnificent: *a noble sight.* —*n.* person high and great birth, rank, or title. [< F < L *nobilis* renowned] —**no′ble·ness,** *n.* —**no′bly,** *adv.*

noble gas, any of a group of gaseous elements that are somewhat rare and do not combine easily with other elements, including helium, neon, argon, krypton, xenon, and radon; inert gas.

no·ble·man (nō′bəl mən), *n., pl.* **–men.** man of noble rank, title, or birth.

no·blesse o·blige (nō bles′ ō blēzh′), *French.* persons of noble rank should behave nobly.

no·ble·wom·an (nō′bəl wùm′ən), *n., pl.* **–wom·en.** woman of noble birth or rank.

no·bod·y (nō′bod i), *pron., n., pl.* **–bod·ies.** —*pron.* no one; no person. —*n.* person of no importance.

no·brain·er (nō′brā′nər), *n.* something that requires little or no thought.

noc·tur·nal (nok tėr′nəl), *adj.* **1** of or in the night: *stars are a nocturnal sight.* **2** active in the night: *the owl is a nocturnal bird.* **3** closed by day, open by night: *a nocturnal flower.* [< LL *nocturnalis,* ult. < L *nox* night] —**noc·tur′nal·ly,** *adv.*

noc·turne (nok′tėrn), *n.* **1** a dreamy or pensive piece of music. **2** *Fig.* something like a nocturne in character, as a poem. [< F]

nod (nod), *v.,* **nod·ded, nod·ding,** *n.* —*v.* **1** bow (the head) slightly and raise it again quickly. **2** say yes by nodding. **3** express by bowing the head: *nod consent.* **4** let the head fall forward and bob about when sleepy or falling asleep. —*n.* a nodding of the head: *he gave us a nod as he passed.* [ME *nodden*] —**nod′der,** *n.*

node (nōd), *n.* **1** knot; knob; swelling. **2** joint in a stem; part of a stem that normally bears a leaf or leaves. [< L *nodus* knot] —**nod′al,** *adj.*

nod·ule (noj′ül), *n.* **1** a small knot, knob, or swelling. **2** a small, rounded mass or lump: *nodules of pure gold.* [< L *nodulus,* dim. of *nodus* knot] —**nod′u·lar,** *adj.*

no·el (nō el′), *n.* **1** a Christmas song; carol. **2 Noel,** Christmas. [< F < L *natalis* natal (i.e. the natal day of Christ) < *nasci* be born]

no-fault (nō′fôlt′), *adj.* eliminating fault or responsibility, esp. as a cause for withholding compensation (in an accident) or as a reason for issuing a judgment against someone (in a lawsuit).

nog·gin (nog′ən), *n.* **1** a small cup or mug. **2** a small drink; one fourth of a pint. **3** *Informal.* a person's head.

no·how (nō′hou′), *adv. Informal.* in no way; not at all.

noise (noiz), *n., v.,* **noised, nois·ing.** —*n.* **1** a sound that is not musical or pleasant. **2** a sound. **3** din of voices and movements; loud shouting; outcry; clamor. —*v.* **1** make a noise. **2** talk much. **3** spread the news of; tell: *it was noised abroad that the king was dying.* [< OF < L *nausea* NAUSEA]

noise·less (noiz′lis), *adj.* making no noise: *a noiseless typewriter.* —**noise′less·ly,** *adv.* —**noise′less·ness,** *n.*

noi·some (noi′səm), *adj.* **1** offensive; disgusting; smelling bad: *a noisome slum.* **2** harmful; injurious: *a noisome pestilence.* [< *noy* (var. of *annoy*) + *some*¹] —**noi′some·ly,** *adv.* —**noi′some·ness,** *n.*

nois·y (noiz′i), *adj.,* **nois·i·er, nois·i·est. 1** making much noise: *a noisy boy.* **2** full of noise: *a noisy street.* **3** having much noise with it: *a noisy game, a noisy quarrel.* —**nois′i·ly,** *adv.* —**nois′i·ness,** *n.*

nom., nominative.

no·mad (nō′mad; nom′ad), *n.* **1** member of a tribe that moves from place to place to have pasture for its cattle. **2** wanderer. —*adj.* **1** wandering from place to place to find pasture. **2** wandering. [< L < Gk., ult. < *nemein* to pasture]

no·mad·ic (nō mad′ik), *adj.* of nomads or their life; wandering; roving. —**no·mad′i·cal·ly,** *adv.*

nom de plume (nom′ də plüm′), a pen name; name used by a writer instead of his or her real name. [formed in E from F words]

no·men·cla·ture (nō′mən klā′chər; nō men′klə–), *n.* set or system of names or terms: *the nomenclature of music.* [< L *nomenclatura* < *nomen* name + *calare* to call]

nom·i·nal (nom′ə nəl), *adj.* **1** being so in name only; not real: *the president is the nominal head of the club, but the secretary is the one who really runs its affairs.* **2** so small that it is not worth considering; unimportant compared with the real value. [< L, < *nomen* name] —**nom′i·nal·ly,** *adv.*

nom·i·nate (nom′ə nāt), *v.,* **–nat·ed, –nat·ing. 1** name as candidate for an office: *three times Bryan was nominated for President, but he was never elected.* **2** appoint for an office or duty: *the President nominated him as Secretary of State.* [< L, ult. < *nomen* name] —**nom′i·na′tor,** *n.* —**nom′i·na′tion,** *n.*

nom·i·na·tive (nom′ə nə tiv; –nā′tiv), *Gram.* —*adj.* **1** showing the subject of a verb and words agreeing with the subject. **2** being in or pertaining to that case. —*n.* **1** the nominative case. **2** a word in that case. *Who* and *I* are nominatives.

nom·i·nee (nom′ə nē′), *n.* person who is nominated.

non–, *prefix.* not; not a; opposite of; lack of; failure of, as in *nonconformity, nonacceptance, nonpayment.* [< L *non* not] **Non–** is a prefix that combines freely with any noun, adjective, or adverb. Some examples are listed below.

non′ad·he′sive
non′ag·gres′sive
non′as·sign′a·ble
non′be·liev′er
non′bel·lig′er·ent
non′co·her′ent
non·com′bat
non′com·pet′i·tive
non·con·sec′u·tive
non′co·op′er·a′tive
non′dem·o·crat′ic·ly
non′dis·crim′i·na′tion
non·earn′ing
non′en·force′ment
non′ex·ist′ence
non·fac′tu·al
non·fad′ing
non·fire′proof′
non′gov·ern·men′tal
non·hu′man
non′id·i·o·mat′ic
non′im·mu′ni·ty
non′in·fec′tious
non′in·flam′ma·ble
non·ir′ri·tant
non′ju·di′cial
non·liv′ing
non′mag·net′ic
non·mem′ber
non·mil′i·tar′y
non′ne·go′tia·ble
non′ob·serv′er
non·op′er·at′ing
non·orth′o·dox
non′par·tic′i·pa′t ion
non′path·o·gen′ic
non·pay′ing
non′per·form′ance
non′po·lit′i·cal
non′pre·scrip′tive
non′pro·duc′ing
non′pro·lif′er·a′tion
non·pun′ish·a·ble
non′re·cip′ro·cal
non′re·new′a·ble
non′res′i·dence
non′re·turn′a·ble
non·sec′u·lar
non·se′rous
non·smok′ing
non′spe·cif′ic
non·stand′ard
non·start′er
non′sub·scrib′er
non·tax′a·ble
non·tech′ni·cal·ly

non·tox'ic
non·trans·fer'a·ble
non·ven'om·ous
non·ver'bal
non·vol'a·tile
non·vot'ing

non·ac·cept·ance (non´ək sep'təns), *n.* failure or refusal to accept.

non·ad·dic·tive (non´ə dik'tiv), *adj.* not causing addiction.

non·a·ge·nar·i·an (non´ə jə nãr'i ən; nō´nə–), *n.* person who is 90 years old or between 90 and 100 years old. —*adj.* 90 years old or between 90 and 100 years old. [< L *nonagenarius* containing ninety]

non·ag·gres·sion (non´ə gresh'ən), *n.* lack of aggression.

non·a·gon (non'ə gon), *n.* a plane figure having nine angles and nine sides. [< L *nonus* ninth + Gk. *gonia* angle]

non·ap·pear·ance (non´ə pir'əns), *n.* fact of not appearing; failure to appear.

non·at·tend·ance (non´ə ten'dəns), *n.* failure to be present.

nonce (nons), *n.* the one or particular occasion or purpose.

for the nonce, for the present time or occasion. [ME (*for then*) *ones* (for the) *once*, taken as (*for the*) *nones*]

nonce word, word formed and used for a single occasion.

non·cha·lance (non'shə ləns; non´shə läns'), *n.* cool unconcern; indifference.

non·cha·lant (non'shə lənt; non´shə länt'), *adj.* without enthusiasm; coolly unconcerned; indifferent. [< F, < *non–* not (< L) + *chaloir* be warm < L *calere*] —**non'cha·lant·ly,** *adv.*

non·com (non'kom´), *n.* a noncommissioned officer.

non·com·bat·ant (non´kəm bat'ənt; –kom'bə tənt), *n.* person who is not a fighter in the army or navy in time of war; civilian. Surgeons are noncombatants even if in the military. —*adj.* not fighting; civilian in wartime.

non·com·mis·sioned (non´kə mish'ənd), *adj.* without a commission; not commissioned. Corporals are noncommissioned officers.

non·com·mit·tal (non´kə mit'əl), *adj.* not committing oneself; not saying yes or no: *"I will think it over" is a noncommittal answer.* —**non´com·mit'tal·ly,** *adv.*

non·com·pli·ance (non´kəm pli'əns), *n.* fact of not complying; failure to comply.

non·con·duc·tor (non´kən duk'tər), *n.* substance that does not readily conduct heat, electricity, etc.

non·con·form·ist (non´kən fôr'mist), *n.* person who refuses to conform to an established church. —**non´con·form'i·ty,** *n.*

non·co·op·er·a·tion (non´kō op´ər ā'shən), *n.* **1** failure or refusal to cooperate. **2** refusal to cooperate with a government for political reasons.

non·de·script (non'di skript), *adj.* not easily classified; not of any one particu-

lar kind. —*n.* a nondescript person or thing. [< NON– + L *descriptus* (to be) described]

none (nun), *pron.* **1** not any: *we have none of that paper left.* **2** no one; not one: *none of these is a typical case.* **3** (*pl. in use*) no persons or things: *none have arrived.* **4** no part; nothing: *she has none of her mother's beauty.* —*adv.* to no extent; in no way; not at all: *our supply is none too great.* [OE *nān* < *ne* not + *ān* one]

non·en·ti·ty (non en'tə ti), *n., pl.* –ties. **1** person or thing of little or no importance. **2** something that does not exist.

non·es·sen·tial (non´ə sen'shəl), *adj.* not essential; not necessary. —*n.* person or thing not essential.

none·such (nun'such´), *n.* person or thing without equal or parallel.

none·the·less (nun´thə les'), *adv.* none the less; never the less.

non·e·vent (non'i vent´), *n.* **1** an event expected to take place that does not actually occur. **2** a well-publicized and greatly anticipated event that turns out to be of little interest or importance.

non·fic·tion (non fik'shən), *n.* prose literature that is not a novel, short story, or other form of writing based on imaginary people and events. Biographies and histories are nonfiction.

non·ful·fill·ment, **non·ful·fil·ment** (non´ful fil'mənt), *n.* failure to fulfill; failure to be fulfilled.

non·in·ter·ven·tion (non´in tər ven'shən), *n.* **1** failure or refusal to intervene. **2** systematic avoidance of any interference by a nation in the affairs of other nations or of its own states, etc.

non·ju·ror (non jùr'ər), *n.* one who refuses to take a required oath.

non·met·al (non'met´əl), *n.* an element not having the character of a metal. Carbon and nitrogen are nonmetals.

no-no (nō'nō´), *n., pl.* –nos. something forbidden or unacceptable.

non·ob·jec·tive (non´əb jek'tiv), *adj.* **1** of art, not representational; abstract. **2** not realistic; lacking objectivity.

non·pa·reil (non´pə rel'), *adj.* having no equal. —*n.* person or thing having no equal. [< F, < *non–* not (< L) + *pareil* equal, ult. < L *par*]

non·par·ti·san (non pär'tə zən), *adj.* **1** not partisan. **2** not supporting, or controlled by, any of the regular political parties.

non·plus (non plus'; non'plus), *v.,* –plused, –plus·ing, *n.* —*v.* puzzle completely; make unable to say or do anything. —*n.* a state of being nonplused. [< L *non plus* no further]

non·pro·duc·tive (non´prə duk'tiv), *adj.* **1** not productive. **2** not directly connected with production. —**non´pro·duc'tive·ness,** *n.*

non·prof·it (non prof'it), *adj.* not for profit; without profit.

non·res·i·dent (non rez'ə dənt), *adj.* **1** not residing in a particular place. **2** not

residing where official duties require one to reside. —*n.* a nonresident person.

non·re·sist·ant (non´ri zis'tənt), *adj.* not resisting; passively obedient. —*n.* one who does not resist authority or force; one who maintains that violence should never be resisted by force. —**non´re·sist'ance,** *n.*

non·re·stric·tive (non´ri strik'tiv), *adj.* (of a modifier) adding descriptive detail.

non·sched·uled (non'skej'úld), *adj.* not operating or proceeding according to a regular schedule: *a nonscheduled airline.*

non·sec·tar·i·an (non´sek tãr'i ən), *adj.* not connected with any religious denomination.

non·sense (non'sens), *n.* words, ideas, or acts without meaning; foolish talk or doings; a plan or suggestion that is foolish.

non·sen·si·cal (non sen'sə kəl), *adj.* foolish; absurd. —**non·sen'si·cal·ly,** *adv.* —**non·sen'si·cal·ness,** *n.*

non se·qui·tur (non sek'wə tər), inference or conclusion that does not follow from the premises. [< L, it does not follow]

non·skid (non'skid'), *adj.* made to resist skidding: *nonskid tires.*

non·stop (non'stop'), *adj., adv.* without stopping.

non·sup·port (non´sə pôrt'; –pōrt'), *n.* **1** lack of support. **2** failure to provide for someone for whom one is legally responsible.

non·un·ion (non ūn'yən), *adj.* **1** not belonging to a trade union. **2** not following trade union rules. **3** not recognizing or favoring trade unions. —**non·un'ion·ism,** *n.* —**non·un'ion·ist,** *n.*

non·vot·er (non vōt'ər), *n.* person who does not vote.

noo·dle¹ (nü'dəl), *n.* a mixture of flour and water, or flour and eggs, like macaroni, but made in flat strips. [< G *nudel*]

noo·dle² (nü'dəl), *n. Informal.* head.

nook (nùk), *n.* **1** a cozy little corner. **2** a hidden spot; sheltered place. [ME *noke*]

noon (nün), *n.* twelve o'clock in the daytime; middle of the day. —*adj.* of noon [< L *nona (hora)* ninth (hour), 3 p.m.; the meaning shifted with a change in time of church service]

noon·day (nün'dā´), *n., adj.* =noon.

no one (nō'wun´), no person; nobody.

noon·time (nün'tīm´), **noon·tide** (–tīd´), *n.* =noon.

noose (nüs), *n., v.,* **noosed, noos·ing.** —*n.* **1** loop with a slip knot that tightens as the string or rope is pulled. **2** =snare. —*v.* make a noose with; tie a noose in. [prob. < OF < L *nodus* knot]

nope (nōp), *adv. Informal.* no.

nor¹ (nôr; *unstressed* nər), *conj.* and not; or not; neither; and not either. *Nor* is used with a preceding *neither* or negative: *not a boy nor a girl stirred.* [OE (unstressed) *nā(hwæ)ther* < *ne* not + *ā(hwæ)ther* either. See OR.]

nor′, nor² (nôr), *n., adj., adv.* =north

Nor., 1 North. 2 Norway.

Nor·dic (nôr′dik), *adj.* designating, belonging to, or pertaining to a race or type characterized by tall stature, blond hair, blue eyes, and long heads. —*n.* member of such a race. Scandinavians are Nordics. [< F, < *nord* north < Gmc.]

norm (nôrm), *n.* standard for a certain group; type; model; pattern: *in mathematics this class is above the norm.* [< L *norma*]

nor·mal (nôr′məl), *adj.* of the usual standard; regular; usual: *the normal temperature of the human body is 98.6 degrees.* —*n.* the usual state or level: *two pounds above normal* [< L *normalis.* See NORM.] —**nor·mal′i·ty, nor′mal·ness,** *n.*

nor·mal·cy (nôr′məl si), *n.* normal condition.

nor·mal·ize (nôr′məl īz), *v.,* –**ized,** –**iz·ing.** make normal. —**nor′mal·i·za′tion,** *n.*

nor·mal·ly (nôr′məl i), *adv.* in the normal way; regularly; if things are normal.

Nor·man (nôr′mən), *n.* 1 member of the mixed race, descended from the Scandinavians who settled in Normandy and from the French. 2 one of the Scandinavian ancestors of these people; Northman. —*adj.* of the Normans or Normandy.

Nor·man-French (nôr′mən french′), *n.* =Anglo-French

nor·ma·tive (nôr′mə tiv), *adj.* establishing a norm or standard: *a normative study of children's language.*

Norse (nôrs), *adj.* 1 of or having to do with ancient Scandinavia, its people, or their language. 2 of or having to do with Norway or its people. —*n.* 1 (*pl. in use*) **a** people of ancient Scandinavia; Norsemen; Northmen. **b** Norwegians. 2 language of the ancient Scandinavians; Old Norse. 3 language of Norway.

Norse·man (nôrs′mən), *n., pl.* –**men.** member of a tall, blond race that lived in ancient Scandinavia; Northman. The Vikings were Norsemen.

north (nôrth), *n.* 1 direction to which a compass needle points; direction to the right as one faces the setting sun. 2 Also, **North.** part of any country toward the north. 3 **North,** the northern part of the United States; the states north of Maryland, the Ohio River, and Missouri. —*adj.* 1 lying toward or situated in the north. 2 originating in or coming from the north. 3 **North,** in the northern part; northern: *North China.* —*adv.* 1 toward the north. 2 in the north. [OE]

North Africa, a region in the northern part of the continent of Africa, especially those countries bordering on or north of the Sahara. —**North African.**

North America, the northern continent of the Western Hemisphere. The United States, Mexico, and Canada are some of the countries in North America. —**North American.**

North Car·o·li·na (kar′ə lī′nə), a S state of the United States. —**North Carolinian.**

North Da·ko·ta (də kō′tə), a Middle Western state of the United States. —**North Dakotan.**

north·east (nôrth′ēst′; nôr′–), *adj.* 1 halfway between north and east. 2 lying toward or situated in the northeast. 3 originating in or coming from the northeast: *a northeast wind.* 4 directed toward the northeast. —*n.* 1 a northeast direction. 2 place that is in the northeast part or direction. —*adv.* 1 toward the northeast. 2 from the northeast. 3 in the northeast.

the Northeast, New England and adjacent states.

north·east·er (nôrth′ēs′tər; nôr–), *n.* wind or storm from the northeast. Also, **nor′easter.**

north·east·er·ly (nôrth′ēs′tər li; nôr′–), *adj., adv.* toward or from the northeast.

north·east·ern (nôrth′ēs′tərn; nôr′–), *adj.* 1 toward the northeast. 2 from the northeast. 3 **Northeastern,** of, having to do with, or in the Northeast.

north·east·ward (nôrth′ēst′wərd; nôr′–), *adv.* Also, **north′east′wards.** toward the northeast. —*adj.* 1 toward the northeast. 2 northeast. —*n.* northeast. —**north′east′ward·ly,** *adj., adv.*

north·er (nôr′ṯẖər), *n.* wind or storm from the north.

north·er·ly (nôr′ṯẖər li), *adj., adv.* 1 toward the north. 2 from the north: *a northerly wind.* —**north′er·li·ness,** *n.*

north·ern (nôr′ṯẖərn), *adj.* 1 toward the north. 2 from the north. 3 of or in the north. 4 **Northern,** of or in the N part of the United States. —**north′ernmost,** *adj.*

north·ern·er (nôr′ṯẖər nər), *n.* 1 native inhabitant of the north. 2 **Northerner,** native or inhabitant of the N part of the United States.

Northern Hemisphere, the half of the earth that is north of the equator.

Northern Ireland, a self-governing district in NE Ireland that is a part of the United Kingdom of Great Britain and Northern Ireland.

northern lights, the aurora borealis.

North Island, the northernmost of the two main islands of New Zealand.

North Korea, country above the thirty-eighth parallel on the Korean peninsula.

north·land (nôrth′lənd), *n.* land in the north; the northern part of a country. —**north′lander,** *n.*

North·man (nôrth′mən), *n., pl.* –**men.** 1 =Norseman. 2 native or inhabitant of northern Europe.

North Pole, northern end of the earth's axis.

North Star, the bright star almost directly above the North Pole.

north·ward (nôrth′wərd, nôr′ṯẖərd), *adv.* Also, **north′wards.** toward the north.

—*adj.* 1 toward the north. 2 north. —*n.* north.

north·ward·ly (nôrth′wərd li), *adj., adv.* 1 toward the north. 2 of winds, from the north.

north·west (nôrth′west′; nôr′–), *adj.* 1 halfway between north and west. 2 lying toward or situated in the northwest. 3 originating in or coming from the northwest: *a northwest wind.* 4 directed toward the northwest. —*n.* 1 a northwest direction. 2 place that is in the northwest part or direction. —*adv.* 1 toward the northwest. 2 from the northwest. 3 in the northwest.

the Northwest, Washington and Oregon.

north·west·er (nôrth′wes′tər; nôr′–), *n.* wind or storm from the northwest.

north·west·er·ly (nôrth′wes′tər li; nôr′–), *adj., adv.* 1 toward the northwest. 2 from the northwest.

north·west·ern (nôrth′wes′tərn; nôr′–), *adj.* 1 toward or from the northwest. 2 of the northwest. 3 **Northwestern,** of, having to do with, or in Washington or Oregon.

north·west·ward (nôrth′west′wərd; nôr′–), *adv.* Also, **north′west′wards.** toward the northwest. —*adj.* 1 toward the northwest. 2 northwest. —*n.* northwest. —**north′west′ward·ly,** *adj., adv.*

Norw., Norway; Norwegian.

Nor·way (nôr′wā), *n.* a mountainous country in N Europe, west and north of Sweden.

Nor·we·gian (nôr wē′jən), *adj.* of Norway, its people, or their language. —*n.* 1 native or inhabitant of Norway. 2 language of Norway.

nos., Nos., or **no's,** numbers.

nose (nōz), *n., v.,* **nosed, nos·ing.** —*n.* 1 part of the face or head just above the mouth, serving as the opening for breathing and as the organ of smell. 2 the organ of smell. 3 sense of smell: *a dog with a good nose.* 4 faculty for perceiving or detecting: *a reporter must have a nose for news.* 5 part that stands out, as the bow of a ship or airplane. —*v.* 1 discover by smell; smell out; sniff. 2 rub with the nose. 3 push with the nose or forward end: *the boat nosed carefully between the rocks.* 4 search (for); pry (into).

follow one's nose, *Fig.* follow one's instincts.

lead by the nose, have complete control over.

look down (or **turn up**) **one's nose at,** treat with contempt or scorn.

nose out, a Also, **nose around.** find out by looking around quietly or secretly. **b** win by a very small margin.

pay through the nose, pay a great deal too much.

under one's nose, in plain sight; very easy to notice. [OE *nosu*]

nose·band (nōz′band′), *n.* part of a bridle that goes over the animal's nose.

nose·bleed (nōz′blēd′), *n.* a bleeding from the nose.

nose cone, the front section of a ballistic missile, designed to carry a bomb to a target or instruments or a person into space.

nose dive, 1 a swift plunge straight downward by an airplane, etc. **2** *Fig.* a sudden, sharp drop.

nose-dive (nōz′dīv′), *v.,* **-dived, -div·ing.** take a nose dive.

nose·gay (nōz′gā′), *n.* =bouquet.

nose·piece (nōz′pēs′), *n.* part of a helmet that covers and protects the nose.

no-show (nō′shō′), *n.* **1** person who neglects to cancel a reservation. **2** person who fails to show up, esp. for an appointment.

nos·tal·gia (nos tal′jə), *n.* =homesickness. [< NL, < Gk. *nostos* homecoming + *algos* pain] **—nos·tal′gic,** *adj.*

nos·tril (nos′trəl), *n.* either of the two openings in the nose. Smells come into the sensitive parts of the nose through the nostrils. [OE *nosthyrl* < *nosu* nose + *thyrel* hole]

nos·trum (nos′trəm), *n.* **1** medicine made by the person who is selling it; quack remedy; patent medicine. **2** a pet scheme for producing wonderful results; a cure-all. [< L, ours, because it is usually prepared by the person recommending it]

nos·y, nos·ey (nōz′i), *adj.,* **nos·i·er, nos·i·est.** prying; inquisitive.

not (not), *adv.* word that says no; a negative: *that is not true.* [unstressed var. of *nought*]

no·ta be·ne (nō′tə bē′nē), *Latin.* note well; observe what follows; take notice.

no·ta·ble (nō′tə bəl), *adj.* worthy of notice; striking; remarkable: *a notable event.* —*n.* person who is notable: *many notables came to the President's reception.* [< L, < *notare* to note] **—no′ta·ble·ness, no′ta·bil′i·ty,** *n.* **—no′ta·bly,** *adv.*

no·ta·rize (nō′tə rīz), *v.,* **-rized, -riz·ing.** certify (a contract, deed, will, etc.).

no·ta·ry public (nō′tə ri), or **notary,** *n.,* *pl.* **no·tar·ies public; notaries.** a public officer authorized to certify deeds and contracts, to record the fact that a certain person swears that something is true, and to attend to other legal matters. [< L *notarius* clerk, ult. < *nota* note]

no·ta·tion (nō tā′shən), *n.* **1** set of signs or symbols used to represent numbers, quantities, or other values: *the Arabic notation (1, 2, 3, 4, etc.).* **2** the representing of numbers, quantities, or other values by symbols or signs. Music has a special system of notation, and so has chemistry. **3** note to assist memory; record; jotting: *make a notation on the margin.* **4** act of noting. **—no·ta′tion·al,** *adj.*

notch (noch), *n.* **1** a V-shaped nick or cut made in an edge or on a curving surface: *the Indians cut notches on a stick to keep count of numbers.* **2** a deep, narrow pass or gap between mountains. **3** *Fig.* grade;

step; degree. —*v.* **1** make a notch or notches in. **2** record by notches; score; tally. [< F *oche* < OF *oschier* to notch; *an och* taken as *a noch*] **—notched,** *adj.* **—notch′er,** *n.*

note (nōt), *n., v.,* **not·ed, not·ing.** —*n.* **1** words written down to remind one of something: *take notes of a lecture.* **2** notice; heed: *take note of.* **3** a very short letter. **4** a single sound made by a musical instrument or voice. **5** a written sign to show the pitch and length of a sound. **6** a bird's song or call. **7** a significant sound or way of expression: *a note of anxiety in her voice, strike the right note in a letter.* **8** distinction, importance, or consequence: *a man of note.* **9** a written promise to pay a certain sum of money at a certain time. —*v.* **1** write down as a thing to be remembered. **2** observe carefully; give attention to; take notice of. **3** mention specially.

compare notes, exchange ideas or opinions.

take notes, write down things to be remembered, as of a conversation or event. [< OF < L *nota* mark] **—note′less,** *adj.* **—not′er,** *n.*

note·book (nōt′bùk′), *n.* **1** book in which to write notes. **2** portable computer about the size of a notebook.

not·ed (nōt′id), *adj.* especially noticed; conspicuous; well-known; celebrated; famous: *Samson was noted for his strength, Shakespeare is the most noted English author.* **—not′ed·ly,** *adv.* **—not′ed·ness,** *n.*

note paper, paper used for writing letters.

note·wor·thy (nōt′wèr′ᵺi), *adj.* worthy of notice; remarkable: *a noteworthy achievement.* **—note′wor′thi·ly,** *adv.* **—note′wor′thi·ness,** *n.*

noth·ing (nuth′ing), *n.* **1** not anything; no thing: *nothing arrived by mail.* **2** thing that does not exist: *create a world out of nothing.* **3** thing of no importance or significance; person of no importance: *people regard him as a nothing.* **4** zero; naught. —*adv.* not at all: *be nothing wiser than before.*

for nothing, a without payment. **b** with no result; in vain.

make nothing of, a be unable to understand: *make nothing of these numbers.* **b** fail to use or do. **c** treat as worthless or unimportant.

think nothing of, a consider as easy to do. **b** treat as worthless or unimportant. [< *no* + *thing*]

noth·ing·ness (nuth′ing nis), *n.* **1** nonexistence. **2** worthlessness. **3** an unimportant or worthless thing.

no·tice (nō′tis), *n., v.,* **-ticed, -tic·ing.** **1** observation; heed; attention: *escape one's notice.* **2** information; warning: *the whistle blew to give notice of quitting time.* **3** a written or printed sign; paper posted in a public place. **4** a warning that one will end an agreement with another

at a certain time: *the servant gave notice.* **5** paragraph or article about something: *the new book got a favorable notice.* —*v.* **1** take notice of; give attention to; perceive: *I noticed a big difference.* **2** mention; refer to.

serve notice, warn; inform; announce.

take notice, give attention; observe; see. [< F < L, < *notus* known]

no·tice·a·ble (nō′tis ə bəl), *adj.* **1** easily seen or noticed. **2** worth noticing. **—no′tice·a·bly,** *adv.*

no·ti·fi·ca·tion (nō′tə fə kā′shən), *n.* **1** a notifying. **2** notice: *have you received a notification of the meeting?*

no·ti·fy (nō′tə fī), *v.,* **-fied, -fy·ing.** give notice to; let know; inform; announce to: *notify us when there will be a test.* [< F < L, < *notus* known + *facere* make] **—no′ti·fi′er,** *n.*

no·tion (nō′shən), *n.* **1** idea; understanding: *he has no notion of what I mean.* **2** opinion; belief: *one common notion is that red hair means a quick temper.* **3** intention: *he has no notion of risking his money.* **4** a foolish idea or opinion.

notions, small useful articles; pins, needles, thread, tape, etc. [< L *notio,* ult. < *noscere* know]

no·tion·al (nō′shən əl), *adj.* **1** having to do with ideas or opinions. **2** in one's imagination or thought only; not real. **3** full of notions; having strange notions; fanciful. **—no′tion·al·ly,** *adv.*

no·to·chord (nō′tə kôrd′), *n.* **1** rod-shaped structure that runs down the back of many of the simplest vertebrates and supports the spinal nerve. **2** similar structure in the embryo of higher vertebrates, replaced by the spinal chord later in development.

no·to·ri·e·ty (nō′tə rī′ə ti), *n., pl.* **-ties. 1** a being famous for something bad; ill fame: *a crime or scandal brings much notoriety to those involved in it.* **2** being widely known. **3** a well-known person.

no·to·ri·ous (nō tô′ri əs, -tō-), *adj.* well-known because of something bad; having a bad reputation. [< Med.L *notorius* < L *notus* known] **—no·to′ri·ous·ly,** *adv.* **—no·to′ri·ous·ness,** *n.*

not·with·stand·ing (not′with stan′ding; -with-), *prep.* in spite of: *he bought it notwithstanding the high price.* —*conj.* in spite of the fact that: *notwithstanding there was need for haste, he still delayed.* —*adv.* in spite of it; nevertheless: *it is raining; but I shall go, notwithstanding.*

nou·gat (nü′gət; -gä), *n.* a kind of soft candy containing nuts. [< F < Pr., ult. < L *nux* nut]

nought (nôt), *n.* =naught. [see NAUGHT]

noun (noun), *n.* word used as the name of a person, place, thing, quality, event, etc. Words like *John, table, school, kindness, skill,* and *party* are nouns. —*adj.* used as a noun. [< OF *nom* < L *nomen* name] **—noun′al,** *adj.*

nour·ish (nèr′ish), *v.* **1** make grow, or keep alive and well, with food; feed:

milk nourishes a baby. **2** maintain; foster: *nourish a hope.* [< OF *noriss-* < L *nutrire* feed] —**nour′ish·er,** *n.* —**nour′ish·ing,** *adj.* —**nour′ish·ing·ly,** *adv.*

nour·ish·ment (nėr′ish mənt), *n.* **1** food. **2** a nourishing or being nourished.

nou·veau riche (nü vō rēsh′), *pl.* **nou·veaux riches** (nü vō rēsh′). *French.* one who has recently become rich; often, one who makes a vulgar display of his or her wealth.

Nov., November.

no·va (nō′və), *n., pl.* **-vae** (-vē) **-vas.** a star that suddenly glows brightly, then gradually fades to its normal brightness. [< L, fem. of *novus* new]

nov·el (nov′əl), *adj.* of a new kind or nature; strange; new: *flying gives people a novel sensation.* —*n.* story with characters and a plot, usually long enough to fill one or more volumes. [< Ital., < L *novella* new things, speech showing originality] —**nov′el·is′tic,** *adj.* —**nov′el·is′ti·cal·ly,** *adv.*

nov·el·ist (nov′əl ist), *n.* writer of novels.

nov·el·la (nō vel′ə; *Ital.* nō vel′lä), *n., pl.* **-las, -le** (-lä). a short novel or story. Also, **novelette.** [< Ital. See NOVEL.]

nov·el·ty (nov′əl ti), *n., pl.* **-ties. 1** newness: *after the novelty of washing dishes wore off, Mary did not want to do it any more.* **2** a new or unusual thing: *staying up late was a novelty to the children.*

novelties, small, unusual articles; toys, cheap jewelry, etc.

No·vem·ber (nō vem′bər), *n.* the 11th month of the year, having 30 days. [< L, < *novem* nine; from the order of the early Roman calendar]

nov·ice (nov′is), *n.* **1** one who is new to what he or she is doing; beginner. **2** person who is received into a religious group on trial before taking vows. [< OF < L, < *novus* new]

no·vi·ti·ate (nō vish′i it; –āt), *n.* **1** period of trial and preparation in a religious order. **2** novice.

no·vo·caine (nō′və kān), *n.* an alkaloid compound, used as a local anesthetic. [< *Novocain,* trademark, < L *novus* new + E (*co*)*caine*]

now (nou), *adv.* **1** at the present time; by this time: *he is here now, the case is probably settled now.* **2** then; next: *if passed, the bill now goes to the president.* —*n.* the present; this time. —*conj.* since; inasmuch as. [OE *nū*]

now·a·days (nou′ə dāz′), *adv.* at the present day; in these times: *nowadays people travel by air.* —*n.* the present day; these times.

no·way (nō′wā), *adv.* nowise.

now·cast (nou′kast′; –käst′), *v.,* **-cast** or **-cast·ed, -cast·ing.** provide a description of weather conditions as they develop. [< *now* + fore*cast*]

no·where (nō′hwãr), *adv.* in no place; at no place; to no place: *go nowhere.*

nowhere near, not at all near or close: *nowhere near finished.*

no-win (nō′win′), or **no win,** *adj.* not likely to have the desired outcome; likely to fail: *a no-win situation.*

no·wise (nō′wīz), *adv.* in no way; not at all.

nox·ious (nok′shəs), *adj.* very harmful; poisonous: *noxious fumes, noxious teachings.* [< L, < *noxa* hurt] —**nox′ious·ly,** *adv.* —**nox′ious·ness,** *n.*

noz·zle (noz′əl), *n.* tip put on a hose, etc., forming an outlet. [dim. of *nose*]

Np, neptunium.

N.T., New Testament.

nth (enth), *adj.* **1** last in the series 1, 2, 3, 4 … n; being of the indefinitely large or small amount denoted by *n.* **2** *Informal. Fig.* too many to count: *called them for the nth time.*

to the nth degree or **power, a** to any degree or power. **b** to the utmost.

nt. wt., net weight.

nu·ance (nü äns′, nū–; nü′äns, nū′–), *n.* **1** shade of expression, meaning, feeling, etc. **2** shade of color or tone. [< F]

nub (nub), *n.* **1** knob; protuberance. **2** point or gist of anything. [appar. var. of *knob*]

nu·cle·ar (nü′kli ər; nū′–), *adj.* **1** forming a nucleus; having to do with nuclei. **2** like a nucleus or core; contained: *nuclear family.*

nuclear fission, fission (def. 3).

nuclear medicine, use of radioactive isotopes in the diagnosis and treatment of disease.

nuclear physics, branch of physics that is concerned with atoms and their nuclear structure.

nuclear reactor, reactor.

nu·cle·ate (*v.* nü′kli āt, nū′–; *adj.* nü′kli it, –āt, nū′–), *v.,* **-at·ed, -at·ing,** *adj.* —*v.* form into a nucleus or around a nucleus. —*adj.* having a nucleus. —**nu′cle·a′tion,** *n.* —**nu′cle·a′tor,** *n.*

nu·cle·us (nü′kli əs; nū′–), *n., pl.* **-cle·i** (-kli ī), **-cle·us·es. 1** a beginning to which additions are to be made. **2** a central part or thing around which other parts or things are collected. **3** a proton, or group of protons and electrons (sometimes including alpha particles), forming the central part of an atom and carrying a positive charge. **4** an active body lying within the protoplasm of a cell of an animal or a plant, without which the cell cannot grow and divide. **5** the dense central part of a comet's head. [< L, < *nux* nut]

nude (nüd; nūd), *adj.* naked; unclothed; bare. —*n.* a naked figure in painting, sculpture, or photography.

the nude, a the naked figure. **b** a naked condition. [< L *nudus*] —**nude′ly,** *adv.* —**nude′ness,** *n.*

nudge (nuj), *v.,* **nudged, nudg·ing,** *n.* —*v.* push slightly; jog with the elbow to attract attention, etc. —*n.* a slight push or jog.

nud·ism (nüd′iz əm; nūd′–), *n.* practice of going naked for health. —**nud′ist,** *n., adj.*

nu·di·ty (nü′də ti; nū′–), *n., pl.* **-ties. 1** nakedness. **2** something naked.

nug·get (nug′it), *n.* **1** lump. **2** lump of native gold. **3** anything valuable: *nuggets of wisdom.* [? < *nug* lump]

nui·sance (nü′səns; nū′–), *n.* thing or person that annoys, troubles, offends, or is disagreeable: *flies are a nuisance.* [< OF, < *nuire* harm < L *nocere*]

null (nul), *adj.* **1** not binding; of no effect; as if not existing: *a promise obtained by force is legally null.* **2** unimportant; useless; meaningless. **3** not any; zero.

null and void, without force or effect; worthless. [< L, < *ne-* not + *ullus* any]

null set, =empty set.

nul·li·fy (nul′ə fī), *v.,* **-fied, -fy·ing. 1** make not binding; render void: *nullify a law.* **2** make unimportant, useless, or meaningless; destroy; cancel. [< L, < *nullus* not any + *facere* make] —**nul′li·fi·ca′tion,** *n.* —**nul′li·fi′er,** *n.*

nul·li·ty (nul′ə ti), *n., pl.* **-ties. 1** futility; nothingness. **2** a mere nothing. **3** something of no legal force or validity.

Num., Numbers.

numb (num), *adj.* having lost the power of feeling or moving: *numb with cold.* —*v.* make numb; dull the feelings of: *numbed with grief.* [ult. < OE *numen* taken, seized] —**numb′ing·ly,** *adv.* —**numb′ly,** *adv.* —**numb′ness,** *n.*

num·ber (num′bər), *n.* **1** word or symbol used in counting; numeral. Two, fourteen, and 26 are numbers. **2** a particular numeral in a series: *a telephone number.* **3** amount of units; sum; total; quantity: *a number of reasons.* **4** a single issue of a periodical. **5** property of words that indicates one, or more persons or things. *Boy* and *ox* are singular in number; *boys* and *oxen* are plural in number. —*v.* **1** mark with a number; assign a number to; distinguish with a number: *the pages of this book are numbered.* **2** be able to show; have: *this city numbers a million inhabitants.* **3** fix the number of; limit: *his days are numbered.* [< OF < L *numerus*] —**num′ber·er,** *n.*

num·ber·less (num′bər lis), *adj.* **1** very numerous; too many to count: *the fish in the sea are numberless.* **2** without a number.

number one, 1 *Informal.* oneself: *take care of number one.* **2** best or first of a group or series.

num·ber-one (num′bər wun′), *adj.* first; leading; principal: *number-one pain-reliever.*

Num·bers (num′bərz), *n.* the fourth book of the Old Testament.

nu·mer·a·ble (nü′mər ə bəl; nū′–), *adj.* that can be counted.

nu·mer·al (nü′mər əl; nū′–), *n.* figure, letter, or word standing for a number; group of figures, letters, or words standing for a number: *Arabic numerals, Roman numerals.* —*adj.* of numbers; standing for a number. [< LL, < L *numerus* number]

nu·mer·ate (nü′mər āt; nū′–), *v.*, **-at·ed, -at·ing.** number; count; enumerate. —**nu′mer·a′tion**, *n.*

nu·mer·a·tor (nü′mər ā′tər; nū′–), *n.* **1** number above the line in a fraction which shows how many parts are taken. In ⅜, *3* is the numerator. **2** person or thing that makes a count.

nu·mer·i·cal (nü mer′ə kəl; nū–), **nu·mer·ic** (–ik), *adj.* **1** of a number; having to do with numbers; in numbers; by numbers. **2** shown by numbers, not by letters: *10 is a numerical quantity.* —**nu·mer′i·cal·ly**, *adv.*

nu·mer·ous (nü′mər əs; nū′–), *adj.* **1** very many. **2** in great numbers. —**nu′mer·ous·ly**, *adv.* —**nu′mer·ous·ness**, *n.*

nu·mis·mat·ics (nü′miz mat′iks; –mis–; nū–), *n.* study of coins and medals. [< F < L *numisma* coin < Gk., < *nomizein* have in use] —**nu′mis·mat′ic**, *adj.* —**nu·mis′ma·tist**, *n.*

num·skull (num′skul′), *n.* a stupid person; blockhead. [for *numb skull*]

nun (nun), *n.* woman who devotes her life to religion and lives under religious vows with a group of women like her. [ult. < LL *nonna*]

nun·ci·o (nun′shi ō), *n., pl.* **–ci·os.** ambassador from the pope to a government. [< Ital. < L *nuntius* messenger]

nun·ner·y (nun′ər i), *n., pl.* **–ner·ies.** building or buildings where nuns live; convent.

nup·tial (nup′shəl), *adj.* of marriage or weddings. —*n.* **nuptials,** a wedding; the wedding ceremony. [< L *nuptialis,* ult. < *nubere* take a husband]

nurse (nėrs), *n., v.,* **nursed, nurs·ing.** —*n.* **1** person who takes care of the sick, the injured, or the old, or is trained to do this. **2** woman who cares for and brings up the young children or babies of another person. **3** one who feeds and protects. —*v.* **1** be a nurse; act as a nurse; work as a nurse. **2** take care of and bring up (another's baby or young child). **3** nourish; protect; make grow: *nurse a plant, nurse a fire.* **4** use or treat with special care: *he nursed his sore arm by using it very little.* **5** give milk to (a baby). [< OF < L *nutricia* < *nutrire* feed, nourish]

nurse·maid (nėrs′mad′), *n.* woman employed to care for children.

nurse practitioner, registered nurse with qualification to provide primary care to patients.

nurs·er·y (nėr′sər i; nėrs′ri), *n., pl.* **–er·ies. 1** room set apart for the use of children and babies. **2** piece of ground or place where young trees and plants are raised for transplanting or sale. **3** *Fig.* place or condition that helps something to grow and develop: *poverty is a nursery of crime.*

nurs·er·y·man (nėr′sər i mən; nėrs′ri–), *n., pl.* **–men.** person who grows or sells young trees and plants.

nursery school, school for children not old enough to go to kindergarten.

nursing home, establishment for long-term care of older people or convalescents.

nurs·ling, nurse·ling (nėrs′ling), *n.* baby that is being nursed.

nur·ture (nėr′chər), *v.,* **-tured, -tur·ing,** *n.* —*v.* **1** rear; bring up; care for; foster; train: *she nurtured the child as if he had been her own.* **2** nourish. [< n.] —*n.* **1** rearing; bringing up; training; education: *the two sisters had received very different nurture, one at home and the other at a convent.* **2** nourishment. [< OF, ult. < L *nutrire* nourish] —**nur′tur·er**, *n.*

nut (nut), *n., v.,* **nut·ted, nut·ting,** *adj.* —*n.* **1** a dry fruit or seed with a hard, woody or leathery shell and a kernel inside which is good to eat. **2** kernel of a nut. **3** a hard, one-seeded fruit that does not open when ripe, such as an acorn. **4** a small block, usually of metal, that screws on to a bolt to tighten or hold something. **5** *Informal.* a queer or crazy person. —*v.* gather nuts; seek for nuts.

hard nut to crack, something difficult to resolve, accomplish, or handle.

nuts, *U.S.* queer; crazy. [OE *hnutu*] —**nut′like′**, *adj.*

nut·crack·er (nut′krak′ər), *n.* **1** instrument for cracking the shells of nuts. **2** any of several birds of the same family as the crow, that feed on nuts.

nut·gall (nut′gôl′), *n.* lump or ball that swells up on an oak tree where it has been injured by an insect.

nut·hatch (nut′hach′), *n.* a small, sharp-beaked bird that feeds on small nuts, seeds, and insects.

nut·meat (nut′mēt′), *n.* kernel of a nut.

nut·meg (nut′meg), *n.* **1** a hard, spicy seed about as big as a marble, obtained from the fruit of an East Indian tree. The seed is grated and used for flavoring food. **2** the tree. [half-trans. of unrecorded OF

nois mugue, var. of *nois muguete,* MUSK nut (*nois* < L *nux*)]

nu·tri·a (nü′tri ə; nū′–), *n.* fur of the coypu. [< Sp. < L *lutra*]

nu·tri·ent (nü′tri ənt; nū′–), *adj.* nourishing. —*n.* a nourishing substance. [< L, ppr. of *nutrire* nourish]

nu·tri·ment (nü′trə mənt; nū′–), *n.* nourishment; food.

nu·tri·tion (nü trish′ən; nū–), *n.* **1** food. **2** series of processes by which food is changed to living tissues. —**nu·tri′tion·al**, *adj.* —**nu·tri′tion·al·ly**, *adv.* —**nu·tri′tion·ist**, *n.*

nu·tri·tious (nü trish′əs; nū–), *adj.* valuable as food; nourishing. —**nu·tri′tious·ly**, *adv.* —**nu·tri′tious·ness**, *n.*

nu·tri·tive (nü′trə tiv; nū′–), *adj.* **1** having to do with foods and the use of foods. **2** nutritious. —**nu′tri·tive·ness**, *n.*

nuts and bolts, essential features or practical details of something, such as a plan.

nut·shell (nut′shel′), *n.* shell of a nut.

in a nutshell, in very brief form; in a few words.

nut·ting (nut′ing), *n.* gathering nuts.

nut·ty (nut′i), *adj.,* **-ti·er, -ti·est. 1** containing many nuts. **2** like nuts; tasting like nuts. **3** *Informal.* queer; crazy. —**nut′ti·ness**, *n.*

nuz·zle (nuz′əl), *v.,* **-zled, -zling. 1** nestle; snuggle; cuddle. **2** poke or rub with the nose; press the nose against. [< *nose;* infl. by *nestle*]

NV, *(zip code)* Nevada.

NW, N.W., or **n.w.,** northwest; northwestern.

NY, *(zip code)* New York.

N.Y. New York.

N.Y.C., New York City.

ny·lon (nī′lon), *n.* an extremely strong, elastic, and durable substance, used to make clothing, bristles, etc.

nymph (nimf), *n., pl.* **nymphs** *for 1, 2,* **nymphs** or **nym·phae** (nim′fē) *for 3.* **1** *Class. Myth.* one of the lesser goddesses of nature, who lived in seas, rivers, springs, hills, woods, or trees. **2** a beautiful or graceful young woman. **3** insect in the stage of development between larva and adult insect. A nymph has no wings. [< OF < L < Gk. *nymphe*] —**nym′phal**, *adj.*

nym·pho·ma·ni·a (nim′fə mā′ni ə), *n.* an extreme and often uncontrollable sexual desire in a woman. —**nym′pho·ma′ni·ac**, *adj., n.*

N.Z., New Zealand.

O¹, o (ō), *n., pl.* **O's; o's.**
1 the 15th letter of the alphabet. **2** something like the letter O in shape.
O² (ō), *interj.* oh!
O, 1 old. **2** oxygen. **3** zero.
O., 1 Ocean. **2** October. **3** Ohio. **4** Old.

oaf (ōf), *n., pl.* **oafs. 1** a very stupid child or man. **2** a deformed, child. **3** a clumsy person. [OE *ælf* elf] **—oaf′ish,** *adj.* **—oaf′ish·ly,** *adv.* **—oaf′ish·ness,** *n.*

oak (ōk), *n.* **1** a large tree with hard, durable wood, jagged leaves, and nuts called acorns. **2** its wood. **3** tree or shrub resembling or suggesting an oak. *—adj.* made of oak: *an oak table.* [OE *āc*] **—oak′en,** *adj.*

oak apple or **gall,** lump or ball on an oak leaf or stem due to injury by an insect.

oa·kum (ō′kəm), *n.* a loose fiber obtained by untwisting and picking apart old ropes. Oakum was used for calking the seams or cracks on ships. [OE *ācumba* offcombings]

oar (ôr; ōr), *n.* **1** pole with a flat end, used in rowing. **2** person who rows. *—v.* row.
put or **stick one's oar in,** meddle; interfere.
rest on one's oars, stop working or trying and take a rest. [OE *ār*] **—oared,** *adj.* **—oar′less,** *adj.*

oar·lock (ôr′lok´; ōr′-), *n.* a notch or U-shaped support in which the oar rests in rowing; rowlock.

oars·man (ōrz′mən; ōrz′-), *n., pl.* **-men.** **1** person who rows. **2** person who rows well. **—oars′man·like´,** *adj.* **—oars′man·ship,** *n.*

OAS, Organization of American States.

o·a·sis (ō ā′sis), *n., pl.* **o·a·ses** (-sēz). a fertile spot in the desert where there is water. [< L, Gk.; appar. < Egyptian] **—o·a′sal,** *adj.*

oat (ōt), *n.* Usually, **oats.** a tall cereal grass whose grain is used in making oatmeal and as a food for horses.
feel one's oats, *Am., Slang.* **a** be lively or frisky. **b** feel pleased or important and show it.
oats, grain of the oat plant.
sow one's wild oats, do the things that wild young people do before settling down. [OE *āte*] **—oat′en,** *adj.*

oath (ōth), *n., pl.* **oaths** (ōᵺz; ōths). **1** a solemn promise or statement that something is true, which God or some holy person or thing is called on to witness. **2** name of God or some holy person or thing used as an exclamation to add force or to express anger. **3** a curse; swearword.
under oath, a bound by an oath. **b** sworn to tell the truth.
upon one's oath, sworn to tell the truth. [OE *āth*]

oat·meal (ōt′mēl´), *n.* **1** oats made into meal; ground oats; rolled oats. **2** cooked cereal made from oatmeal.

ob-, *prefix.* **1** against; in the way; opposing; hindering, as in *obdurate, object.*

2 toward; to, as in *obey, obtrude.* **3** on; over, as in *oblivion, obtuse.* **4** down, away, as in *obese, obsolete.* [< L *ob-* (also, by assimilation to the following consonant, *o-, oc-, of-, op-, os-*)]

OB, obstetrics.

ob., 1 he, she, or it died. [< L *obit*] **2** incidentally. [< L *obiter*]

O·ba·di·ah (ō′bə dī′ə), *n.* book of the Old Testament containing his prophecies.

ob·bli·ga·to (ob′lə gä′tō), *adj., n., pl.* **-tos.** *—adj.* accompanying a solo, but having a distinct character and independent importance. *—n.* such an accompaniment. [< Ital., lit., obliged]

ob·du·rate (ob′də rit; –dyə-), *adj.* **1** stubborn; unyielding: *an obdurate refusal.* **2** hardened in feelings or heart; not repentant: *an obdurate criminal.* [< L, < *ob-* against + *durare* harden] **—ob′du·ra·cy, ob′du·rate·ness,** *n.* **—ob′du·rate·ly,** *adv.*

o·be·di·ence (ō bē′di əns), *n.* act or fact of doing what one is told; submission to authority or law.

o·be·di·ent (ō bē′di ənt), *adj.* doing what one is told; willing to obey. [< L, ppr. of *oboedire* obey] **—o·be′di·ent·ly,** *adv.* **—o·be′di·ent·ness,** *n.*

o·bei·sance (ō bā′səns; ō bē′-), *n.* **1** movement of the body expressing deep respect; deep bow: *the men made obeisance to the king.* **2** deference; homage. [< OF *obeissance* obedience] **—o·bei′sant,** *adj.* **—o·bei′sant·ly,** *adv.*

ob·e·lisk (ob′ə lisk), *n.* a tapering, four-sided shaft of stone with a top shaped like a pyramid. [< L < Gk. *obeliskos,* dim. of *obelos* a spit] **—ob´e·lis′cal,** *adj.*

o·bese (ō bēs′), *adj.* extremely fat. [< L *obesus* < *ob-* away + *edere* eat] **—o·bese′ly,** *adv.* **—o·bese′ness, o·bes′i·ty,** *n.*

o·bey (ō bā′), *v.* **1** do what one is told: *the dog obeyed and went home.* **2** follow the orders of: *obey your father.* **3** yield to the control of: *a car obeys the driver.* [< F < L, < *ob-* to + *audire* give ear] **—o·bey′er,** *n.* **—o·bey′ing·ly,** *adv.*

ob·fus·cate (ob fus′kāt; ob′fus-), *v.,* **-cat·ed, -cat·ing.** darken; obscure; confuse; stupefy: *a man's mind may be obfuscated by liquor.* [< L, < *ob-* + *fuscus* dark] **—ob´fus·ca′tion,** *n.* **—ob·fus′ca·tor,** *n.*

ob-gyn (ō bē´jē′wī ən, ob′gin), *n.* **1** obstetrician and gynecologist. **2** obstetrics and gynecology.

o·bi (ō′bi), *n.* long, broad sash worn tied at the back with a Japanese kimono. [< Jap.]

o·bit (ō′bit, ob′it), *n. Informal.* an obituary. [< OF *obit* death or < L *obitus* death]

o·bit·u·ar·y (ō bich′ù er´i), *n., pl.* **-ar·ies,** *adj.* *—n.* a notice of death, often with a brief account of the person's life. *—adj.* of a death; recording a death. [< Med.L *obituarius,* ult. < L *obire* (*mortem*) meet (death) < *ob-* up to + *ire* go]

obj., object; objective.

ob·ject (*n.* ob′jikt, –jekt; *v.* əb jekt′), *n.* **1** something that can be seen or touched; thing. **2** person or thing toward which feeling, thought, or action is directed: *an object of charity.* **3** thing aimed at; end; purpose. **4** word or group of words toward which the action of the verb is directed or to which a preposition expresses some relation. *—v.* **1** make objections; be opposed; feel dislike: *many people object to loud noise.* **2** give a reason against; bring forward in opposition; oppose: *mother objected that the weather was too wet to play outdoors.* [< L *objectus* < *ob-* toward, against + *jacere* to throw] **—ob·ject′ing·ly,** *adv.* **—ob·jec′tor,** *n.*

ob·jec·tion (əb jek′shən), *n.* **1** something said in objecting; reason or argument against something: *make objections to a plan.* **2** feeling of disapproval or dislike: *an objection to working.*

ob·jec·tion·a·ble (əb jek′shən ə bəl), *adj.* **1** likely to be objected to: *objectionable features of the plan.* **2** unpleasant; disagreeable: *noise is objectionable in church.* **—ob·jec′tion·a·ble·ness,** *n.* **—ob·jec′tion·a·bly,** *adv.*

ob·jec·tive (əb jek′tiv), *n.* **1** something aimed at: *my objective this summer will be learning to play tennis better.* **2** something real and observable. **3 a** the objective case. **b** word in that case. **4** lens or lenses nearest to the thing seen through a telescope, microscope, etc. *—adj.* **1** being the object of endeavor: *an objective point.* **2** existing outside the mind as an actual object and not merely in the mind as an idea; real. **3** about outward things, not about the thoughts and feelings of the speaker, writer, painter, etc.: *a scientist must be objective in his experiments.* **4** showing the object of a verb or the object of a preposition. **—ob·jec′tive·ly,** *adv.* **—ob·jec′tive·ness,** *n.*

ob·jec·tiv·i·ty (ob´jek tiv′ə ti), *n.* intentness on objects external to the mind; external reality.

object lesson, a practical illustration of a principle.

ob·jet d'art (ôb zhä där′), *pl.* **ob·jets d'art** (ôb zhä där′). *French.* a small picture, vase, etc., of some artistic worth.

ob·la·tion (ob lā′shən), *n.* **1** an offering to God or a god. **2** gift for pious use. **3** the offering of bread and wine in the Communion service. [< LL, < *ob-* up to + *latus,* pp. to *ferre* bring]

ob·li·gate (ob′lə gāt), *v.,* **-gat·ed, -gat·ing.** bind morally or legally; pledge: *a witness in court is obligated to tell the truth.* [< L, < *ob-* to + *ligare* bind]

ob·li·ga·tion (ob´lə gā′shən), *n.* **1** duty under the law; duty due to a promise or contract; duty on account of social relationship or kindness received: *a wife's first obligation is to her husband and children.* **2** a binding power (of a law, promise, sense of duty, etc.): *the one who did the damage is under obligation to pay* for it. **3** a binding legal agreement; bond; contract: *the firm was not able to meet its obligations.* **4** fact of being in debt for a favor, service, or the like. **—ob·li·ga·tion·al,** *adj.* **—ob·li·ga·tor,** *n.*

ob·lig·a·to·ry (əb lig′ə tô′ri; -tō′-; ob′lə gə-), *adj.* binding morally or legally; required: *attendance at primary school is obligatory.* **—ob·lig·a·to·ri·ly,** *adv.* **—ob·lig·a·to·ri·ness,** *n.*

o·blige (ə blīj′), *v.,* **o·bliged, o·blig·ing. 1** bind by a promise, contract, duty, etc.; compel; force: *the law obliges parents to send their children to school.* **2** put under a debt of thanks for some favor; do a favor: *Grace obliged the crowd with a song.* [< OF < L, < *ob-* to + *ligare* bind] **—o·blig·ing,** *adj.* **—o·blig·ing·ly,** *adv.*

ob·lique (əb lēk′; *military* əb lik′), *adj.* **1** not straight up and down; not straight across; slanting. **2** not straightforward; indirect: *she made an oblique reference to her illness, but did not mention it directly.* [< L *obliquus*] **—ob·lique′ly,** *adv.* **—ob·liq′ui·ty, ob·lique′ness,** *n.*

oblique angle, any angle that is not a right angle.

ob·lit·er·ate (əb lit′ər āt), *v.,* **-at·ed, -at·ing.** remove all traces of; blot out; destroy: *rain obliterated the footprints.* [< L, < *ob-* + *litera* letter] **—ob·lit·er·a′tion,** *n.*

ob·liv·i·on (əb liv′i ən), *n.* **1** condition of being entirely forgotten: *many ancient cities have long since passed into oblivion.* **2** forgetfulness. [< L, < *oblivisci* forget, orig. even out, smooth over < *ob-* over + root of *lēvis* smooth]

ob·liv·i·ous (əb liv′i əs), *adj.* forgetful; not mindful: *oblivious of my surroundings.* **—ob·liv′i·ous·ly,** *adv.*

ob·long (ob′lông; -long), *adj.* longer than broad: *an oblong loaf of bread.* **—n.** rectangle that is not a square. [< L, < *ob-* + *longus* long]

ob·lo·quy (ob′lə kwi), *n., pl.* **-quies. 1** public reproach; abuse; blame. **2** disgrace; shame. [< LL, ult. < *ob-* against + *loqui* speak]

ob·nox·ious (əb nok′shəs), *adj.* very disagreeable; offensive; hateful: *disgusting table manners are obnoxious.* [< L, ult. < *ob-* + *noxa* injury] **—ob·nox′ious·ly,** *adv.* **—ob·nox′ious·ness,** *n.*

o·boe (ō′bō), *n.* a wooden wind instrument in which a thin, poignant tone is produced by a double reed. [< Ital. < F *hautbois* HAUTBOY] **—o′bo·ist,** *n.*

obs., obsolete; used formerly but not now.

ob·scene (əb sēn′), *adj.* offending modesty or decency; impure; filthy; vile. [< L *obscenus*] **—ob·scene′ly,** *adv.* **—ob·scen′i·ty, ob·scene′ness,** *n.*

ob·scure (əb skyùr′), *adj.,* **-scur·er, -scur·est,** *v.,* **-scured, -scur·ing.** **—adj. 1** not clearly expressed: *an obscure passage in a book.* **2** not well known; attracting no notice: *an obscure poet.* **3** hidden: *an obscure path.* **4** not clear: *obscure sounds,*

an obscure view. **5** dark; dim: *an obscure corner.* **—v.** hide from view; make obscure; dim; darken: *clouds obscure the sun.* [< OF < L, < *ob-* up + *scur-* cover] **—ob·scu·ra′tion, ob·scure′ment,** *n.* **—ob·scure′ly,** *adv.* **—ob·scure′ness,** *n.* **—ob·scur′er,** *n.* **—ob·scur′ing·ly,** *adv.*

ob·scu·ri·ty (əb skyúr′ə ti), *n., pl.* **-ties. 1** lack of clearness; difficulty in being understood: *the obscurity of the passage makes several interpretations possible.* **2** something obscure: *poor writing is full of obscurities.* **3** a being unknown: *Lincoln rose from obscurity to fame.*

ob·se·qui·ous (əb sē′kwi əs), *adj.* polite or obedient from hope of gain or from fear; servile; fawning: *obsequious courtiers.* [< L, ult. < *ob-* after + *sequi* follow] **—ob·se′qui·ous·ly,** *adv.* **—ob·se′qui·ous·ness,** *n.*

ob·serv·a·ble (əb zėr′və bəl), *adj.* **1** that can be or is noticed; noticeable. **2** that can be or is observed: *Lent is observable by some churches.* **—ob·serv′a·ble·ness,** *n.* **—ob·serv′a·bly,** *adv.*

ob·serv·ance (əb zėr′vəns), *n.* **1** act of observing or keeping laws or customs: *the observance of the Sabbath.* **2** act performed as a sign of worship or respect; religious ceremony: *church services are religious observances.* **3** rule or custom to be observed, esp. the rule of a religious order.

ob·serv·ant (əb zėr′vənt), *adj.* **1** quick to notice; watchful; observing: *an observant person.* **2** careful in observing (a law, rule, custom, etc.): *observant of the traffic rules.* **—n.** person who is a strict observer of customs, religious rites, etc. **—ob·serv′ant·ly,** *adv.*

ob·ser·va·tion (ob′zər vā′shən), *n.* **1** act, habit, or power of seeing and noting: *the trained observation of a doctor.* **2** fact of being seen; being seen; notice: *the tramp avoided observation.* **3** something seen and noted. **4** remark. **—ob′ser·va′tion·al,** *adj.* **—ob′ser·va′tion·al·ly,** *adv.*

ob·serv·a·to·ry (əb zėr′və tô′ri; -tō′-), *n., pl.* **-ries.** place or building with a telescope for observing the stars and other heavenly bodies. **—ob·serv′a·to′ri·al,** *adj.*

ob·serve (əb zėrv′), *v.,* **-served, -serv·ing. 1** see and note; notice: *I observed nothing odd in his behavior.* **2** examine for some special purpose; study: *an astronomer observes the stars.* **3** remark: *"Bad weather," the captain observed.* **4** keep; follow in practice: *observe a rule, observe the Sabbath.* [< L, < *ob-* over + *servare* watch, keep] **—ob·serv′er,** *n.* **—ob·serv′ing,** *adj.* **—ob·serv′ing·ly,** *adv.* **—ob·serv′ing·ness,** *n.*

ob·sess (əb ses′), *v.* fill the mind of; keep the attention of; haunt. [< L *obsessus* < *ob-* by + *sedere* sit] **—ob·ses′sive,** *adj.* **—ob·ses′sor,** *n.*

ob·ses·sion (əb sesh′ən), *n.* **1** influence of a feeling, idea, or impulse that a person cannot escape. **2** the feeling, idea, or impulse itself.

ob·sid·i·an (ob sid′i ən), *n.* a hard, dark, glassy rock that is formed when lava cools. [< L *obsidianus;* named for *Obsius,* its discoverer]

ob·so·les·cent (ob′sə les′ənt), *adj.* passing out of use; tending to become out of date. [< L *obsolescens,* ult. < *ob-* + *solere* to be accustomed] **—ob′so·les′cence,** *n.* **—ob′so·les′cent·ly,** *adv.*

ob·so·lete (ob′sə lēt), *adj.* **1** no longer in use: *"eft" (meaning "again") is an obsolete word.* **2** out-of-date: *we still use this machine though it is obsolete.* [< L *obsoletus.* See OBSOLESCENT.] **—ob′so·lete·ly,** *adv.* **—ob′so·lete·ness,** *n.*

ob·sta·cle (ob′stə kəl), *n.* something that stands in the way or stops progress: *blindness is an obstacle in most occupations.* [< OF < L *obstaculum* < *ob-* in the way of + *stare* stand]

ob·ste·tri·cian (ob′stə trish′ən), *n.* physician whose specialty is obstetrics.

ob·stet·rics (ob stet′riks), *n.* branch of medicine concerned with caring for and treating women before, in, and after childbirth. [< L, < *obstetrix* midwife < *ob-* by + *stare* to stand] **—ob·stet′ric, ob·stet′ri·cal,** *adj.*

ob·sti·na·cy (ob′stə nə si), *n., pl.* **-cies. 1** stubbornness. **2** an obstinate act. **—ob′sti·nance,** *n.*

ob·sti·nate (ob′stə nit), *adj.* **1** not giving in; stubborn: *an obstinate person.* **2** hard to control or treat: *an obstinate cough.* [< L *obstinatus,* ult. < *ob-* by + *-stare* stand] **—ob′sti·nate·ly,** *adv.* **—ob′sti·nate·ness,** *n.*

ob·strep·er·ous (əb strep′ər əs), *adj.* **1** noisy; boisterous. **2** unruly; disorderly: *an obstreperous mob.* [< L, < *ob-* against + *strepere* make a noise] **—ob·strep′er·ous·ly,** *adv.* **—ob·strep′er·ous·ness,** *n.*

ob·struct (əb strukt′), *v.* **1** make hard to pass through; block up: *fallen trees obstruct the road.* **2** be in the way of; hinder: *trees obstruct our view of the ocean.* [< L *obstructus* < *ob-* in the way of + *struere* pile] **—ob·struct′er,** *n.* **—ob·struc′tive,** *adj.* **—ob·struc′tive·ly,** *adv.* **—ob·struc′tive·ness,** *n.*

ob·struc·tion (əb struk′shən), *n.* **1** thing that obstructs; something in the way. **2** a blocking; a hindering, esp. persistent attempts to stop business in a legislative assembly, etc. **—ob·struc′tion·ism,** *n.* **—ob·struc′tion·ist,** *n.*

ob·tain (əb tān′), *v.* **1** get or procure through diligence or effort; acquire: *obtain possession of a house, obtain knowledge.* **2** be in use; be customary: *different rules obtain.* [< F < L, < *ob-* to + *tenere* hold] **—ob·tain′a·ble,** *adj.* **—ob·ten′tion,** *n.*

ob·trude (əb trüd′), *v.,* **-trud·ed, -trud·ing. 1** put forward unasked and unwanted; force: *don't obtrude your opinions on others.* **2** come unasked and unwanted; force oneself; intrude. **3** push out; thrust forward. [< L, < *ob-* toward + *trudere* to thrust] **—ob·trud′er,** *n.* **—ob·tru′sion,** *n.*

ob·tru·sive (əb trü′siv), *adj.* inclined to obtrude; intrusive. —**ob·tru′sive·ly**, *adv.* —**ob·tru′sive·ness**, *n.*

ob·tuse (əb tüs′; –tūs′), *adj.* **1** not sharp or acute; blunt. **2** having more than 90° of angle but less than 180°: *an obtuse angle.* **3** slow in understanding; stupid: *too obtuse to take the hint.* **4** not sensitive; dull: *obtuse hearing.* [< L *obtusus* < *ob–* on + *tundere* to beat] —**ob·tuse′ly**, *adv.* —**ob·tuse′ness**, *n.*

ob·verse (*n.* ob′vėrs; *adj.* ob vėrs′, ob′vėrs), *n.* **1** side of a coin, medal, etc., that has the principal design. **2** the face of anything that is meant to be turned toward the observer; front. **3** counterpart. —*adj.* **1** turned toward the observer. **2** being a counterpart to something else. [< L *obversus* < *ob–* toward + *vertere* to turn] —**ob·verse′ly**, *adv.*

ob·vi·ate (ob′vi āt), *v.*, –**at·ed**, –**at·ing**. meet and dispose of; clear out of the way; remove: *a telephone call often obviates the necessity of writing.* [< L, < *obvius* in the way. See OBVIOUS.] —**ob′vi·a′tion**, *n.*

ob·vi·ous (ob′vi əs), *adj.* easily seen or understood; clear to the eye or mind; not to be doubted: *too obvious to need proof.* [< L, < *obviam* in the way < *ob* across + *via* way] —**ob′vi·ous·ly**, *adv.* —**ob′vi·ous·ness**, *n.*

oc·a·ri·na (ok′ə rē′nə), *n.* a musical instrument shaped like a sweet potato, with finger holes and a whistlelike mouthpiece that sounds like a soft flute; sweet potato. [prob. dim. of Ital. *oca* goose; with ref. to the shape]

occas., occasional; occasionally.

oc·ca·sion (ə kā′zhən), *n.* **1** a particular time: *we have met on several occasions.* **2** a special event: *jewels worn only on great occasions.* **3** a good chance; opportunity. **4** cause; reason: *the occasion of the quarrel.* —*v.* cause; bring about: *his odd behavior occasioned a good deal of talk.*

on occasion, now and then; once in a while. [< L *occasio*, ult. < *ob–* in the way of < *cadere* fall]

oc·ca·sion·al (ə kā′zhən əl), *adj.* **1** happening or coming now and then, or once in a while: *occasional thunderstorms.* **2** caused by or used for some special time or event: *occasional poetry.* —**oc·ca′sion·al·ly**, *adv.*

Oc·ci·dent (ok′sə dənt), *n.* **1** countries in Europe and the Americas; the West. **2** **occident,** the west. [< L *occidens* < *ob–* + *cadere* to fall] —**Oc′ci·den′tal, oc′ci·den′tal,** *adj., n.* —**oc′ci·den′tal·ly**, *adv.*

oc·cip·i·tal (ok sip′ə təl), *adj.* of or having to do with the back part of the head or skull. —**oc·cip′i·tal·ly**, *adv.*

oc·clude (o klüd′), *v.*, –**clud·ed**, –**clud·ing.** **1** stop up (a passage, pores, etc.); close. **2** shut in, out, or off. **3** meet closely. [< L *occludere* < *ob–* up + *claudere* to close] —**oc·clu′sion**, *n.* —**oc·clu′sive**, *adj.*

oc·cult (o kult′; ok′ult), *adj.* **1** beyond the bounds of ordinary knowledge; mysterious. **2** outside the laws of the natural world; magical. Astrology and alchemy are occult sciences. [< L *occultus* hidden] —**oc·cult′ism**, *n.* —**oc·cult′ist**, *n.*

oc·cu·pan·cy (ok′yə pən si), *n.* act or fact of occupying; holding (land, houses, a pew, etc.) by being in possession.

oc·cu·pant (ok′yə pənt), *n.* **1** person who occupies. **2** person in actual possession of a house, estate, office, etc.

oc·cu·pa·tion (ok′yə pā′shən), *n.* **1** business; employment; trade. **2** being occupied; possession; occupying: *the occupation of a town by the enemy.* —**oc′cu·pa′tion·al**, *adj.* —**oc′cu·pa′tion·al·ly**, *adv.*

oc·cu·py (ok′yə pī), *v.*, –**pied**, –**py·ing.** **1** take up; fill: *the building occupies an entire block.* **2** keep busy; engage; employ: *sports often occupy a boy's attention.* **3** take possession of: *the enemy occupied our fort.* **4** keep possession of; hold: *a judge occupies an important position.* **5** live in: *the owner and his family occupy the house.* [< OF < L *occupare* seize < *ob–* onto + *cap–* grasp] —**oc′cu·pi′er**, *n.*

oc·cur (ə kėr′), *v.*, –**curred**, –**cur·ring. 1** take place; happen: *storms often occur in winter.* **2** be found; exist: *e occurs in print more than any other letter.* **3** come to mind; suggest itself: *did it occur to you to close the window?* [< L, < *ob–* in the way of + *currere* run]

oc·cur·rence (ə kėr′əns), *n.* **1** an occurring: *the occurrence of storms.* **2** event: *an unexpected occurrence.* —**oc·cur′rent**, *adj.*

o·cean (ō′shən), *n.* **1** the great body of salt water that covers almost three fourths of the earth's surface. **2** any of its five main divisions; the Atlantic, Pacific, Indian, Arctic, and Antarctic Oceans. **3** a vast expanse or quantity. [< L < Gk. *okeanos*] —**o′ce·an′ic**, *adj.*

O·ce·an·i·a (ō′shi an′i ə), *n.* islands of the C and S Pacific.

o·cean·og·ra·phy (ō′shən og′rə fi), *n.* branch of physical geography dealing with the oceans and marine life. —**o′cean·og′ra·pher**, *n.* —**o′cean·o·graph′ic, o′cean·o·graph′i·cal**, *adj.*

o·ce·lot (ō′sə lot; os′ə–), *n.* a spotted wildcat somewhat like a leopard, found from Texas through South America. [< F < Mex. *ocelotl*]

o·cher, o·chre (ō′kər), *n.* **1** any of various earths ranging in coloring from pale yellow to orange, brown, and red, used as pigments. **2** a brownish yellow. [< F < L < Gk., < *ochros* pale yellow] —**o′cher·ous, o′chre·ous**, *adj.*

o′clock (ə klok′), of or by the clock.

OCR, optical character recognition (process by which a computer recognizes letters and converts them into digital form).

Oct., October.

oc·ta·gon (ok′tə gon; –gən), *n.* a plane figure having eight angles and eight sides. —**oc·tag′o·nal**, *adj.* —**oc·tag′on·al·ly**, *adv.*

oc·tane (ok′tān), *n.* a colorless, liquid hydrocarbon, C_8H_{18}, that occurs in petroleum. Higher quality gasoline contains more of it. [< *octo–* eight + *–ane*, as in meth*ane*]

oc·tave (ok′tiv; –tāv), *n.* **1** interval between a note and another note having twice or half as many vibrations per second. **2** the eighth note above or below a given tone. **3** series of notes or of keys of an instrument, filling the interval between a note and its octave. [< L *octavus* eighth] —**oc·ta′val**, *adj.*

oc·ta·vo (ok tā′vō; –tä′–), *n., pl.* –**vos**, *adj.* —*n.* **1** the page size of a book in which each leaf is one eighth of a whole sheet of paper. **2** book having this size, usually about 6 by 9½ inches. —*adj.* having this size. [< Med.L *in octavo* in an eighth]

oc·tet, oc·tette (ok tet′), *n.* **1** a musical composition for eight voices or instruments. **2** eight singers or players. **3** any group of eight. [< *octo–* eight + *–et*, patterned on *duet*, etc.]

oc·to–, oct–, or **octa–,** *combining form.* eight, as in *octopus* and *octagon.* [< Gk., < *okto*]

Oc·to·ber (ok tō′bər), *n.* the tenth month of the year, having 31 days. [< L, < *octo* eight; from the order of the Roman calendar]

oc·to·ge·nar·i·an (ok′tə jə nãr′i ən), *n.* person who is 80 years old or between 80 and 90 years old. —*adj.* 80 years old or between 80 and 90 years old. [< L *octogenarius* containing eighty]

oc·to·pus (ok′tə pəs), *n.* **1** a sea mollusk having a soft body and eight arms with suckers on them. **2** anything like an octopus; powerful, grasping organization with far-reaching influence. [< NL < Gk., < *okto* eight + *pous* foot]

oc·tu·ple (ok′tù pəl; –tyü–), *adj., v.*, –**pled**, –**pling.** —*adj.* eightfold. —*v.* multiply by eight. [< L, < *octo* eight + *–plus* –fold]

oc·u·lar (ok′yə lər), *adj.* **1** of or having to do with the eye: *an ocular muscle.* **2** like an eye. **3** received by actual sight; seen: *ocular proof.* —*n.* eyepiece of a telephone, microscope, etc. [< L, < *oculus* eye] —**oc′u·lar·ly**, *adv.*

oc·u·list (ok′yə list), *n.* doctor skilled in the treatment of eye diseases.

O.D., Officer of the Day.

odd (od), *adj.* **1** left over: *the odd change.* **2** being one of a pair or set of which the rest is missing: *an odd stocking.* **3** extra; occasional; casual: *odd jobs, odd moments.* **4** with some extra: *six hundred odd children.* **5** leaving a remainder of 1 when divided by 2: *the odd numbers of 7, 9, 11.* **6** strange; peculiar; queer: *it is odd that I cannot remember his name.* [< Scand. *odda–*] —**odd′ish**, *adj.* —**odd′ly**, *adv.* —**odd′ness**, *n.*

odd·i·ty (od′ə ti), *n., pl.* **-ties. 1** strangenes; queerness; peculiarity. **2** a strange, queer, or peculiar person or thing.

odds (odz), *n.pl. or sing.* **1** difference in favor of one and against another; advantage. **2** in games, extra allowance given to the weaker side.

at odds, quarreling; disagreeing.

odds and ends, things left over; extra bits; odd pieces; scraps; remnants.

the odds are, the chances are; the probability is.

ode (ōd), *n.* a lyric poem full of noble feeling expressed with dignity. [< F < LL < Gk. *oide*, ult. < *aeidein* sing]

o·di·ous (ō′di əs), *adj.* very displeasing; hateful; offensive. [< L, *odium* odium] **—o′di·ous·ly,** *adv.* **—o′di·ous·ness,** *n.*

o·di·um (ō′di əm), *n.* **1** hatred; dislike. **2** reproach; blame. [< L, < *odisse* to hate]

o·dom·e·ter (ō dom′ə ter), *n.* device to record the distance traveled by a vehicle. [< F *odomètre* < Gk. *hodómetron* < *hodós* way + *métron* measure]

o·don·tol·o·gy (ō don tol′ə ji), *n.* branch of anatomy that deals with the structure, development, and diseases of the teeth. [< *odonto-* teeth + *-logy*] **—o·don′to·log′i·cal,** *adj.* **—o′don·tol′o·gist,** *n.*

o·dor (ō′dər), *n.* **1** smell: *the odor of roses, the odor of garbage.* **2** reputation. **3** fragrance; perfume. [< OF < L] **—o′dor·less,** *adj.*

o·dor·if·er·ous (ō′dər if′ər əs), *adj.* giving forth an odor; fragrant.

o·dor·ous (ō′dər əs), *adj.* giving forth an odor; having an odor; sweet-smelling; fragrant. **—o′dor·ous·ly,** *adv.*

Od·ys·sey (od′ə si), *n., pl.* **-seys. 1** a long Greek epic poem, describing the wandering of Odysseus after the Trojan War. **2** Also, **odyssey.** any long series of wanderings.

OE, O.E., Old English (Anglo-Saxon).

o'er (ôr; ōr), *prep., adv. Poetic or Dial.* over.

of (ov; uv; *unstressed* əv), *prep.* **1** belonging to: *the children of a family.* **2** made from: *a house of bricks.* **3** that has; containing; with: *a house of six rooms, a look of pity.* **4** that is; named: *the city of Chicago.* **5** away from; from: *north of Boston.* **6** having to do with; in regard to; concerning; about: *think well of someone, the hour of prayer, the writings of Shakespeare, die of grief.* **7** before: *ten minutes of six.* [OE (unstressed) *of.* Cf. OFF.]

OF, O.F., Old French.

off (ôf; of), *prep.* **1** not on: *a button is off his coat.* **2** from; away from: *miles off the main road.* **3** *the ship anchored off Maine.* **—adv. 1** from the usual position, condition, etc.: *he took off his hat, an afternoon off, off on a trip.* **2** away: *go off on a journey, Christmas is only five weeks off.* **3** so as to stop or lessen: *turn the water off.* **4** in full; wholly: *clear off the table.* **—adj. 1** not connected; stopped: *the electricity*

is off, off hours. **2** in a specified condition in regard to money, property, etc.: *how well off are we?* **3** not very good; not up to average: *an off season, an off chance.* **—v. Informal. 1** kill; murder. **2** dismiss; ignore. **—interj. 1** go away! stay away!

be off, go away; leave quickly.

off and on, now and then; intermittently.

off with, a take off. **b** away with! [OE (stressed) *of.* Cf. OF.]

off., office; officer; official.

of·fal (ôf′əl; of′əl), *n.* **1** the waste parts of an animal killed for food. **2** garbage; refuse. [< *off* + *fall*]

off-beat (ôf′bēt′), *adj.* unusual; beyond the ordinary, esp. in literature, art, music, etc.

off-Broad·way (ôf′brôd′wā′; of′-), *adj.* **1** produced or located away from Broadway, the theatrical center of New York City. **2** of plays and productions, more experimental; less commercial than Broadway theater.

off-cen·ter (ôf′sen′tər; of′-), *adj.* **1** not in the center. **2** *Fig.* unconventional; odd.

off-col·or (ôf′kul′ər; of′-), *adj.* **1** defective in color. **2** somewhat improper.

of·fend (ə fend′), *v.* **1** hurt the feelings of; make angry; displease. **2** sin. [< OF < L, < *ob-* against + *-fendere* strike] **—of·fend′er,** *n.* **—of·fend′ing·ly,** *adv.*

of·fense (ə fens′), *n.* **1** a breaking of the law; sin: *an offense against God and man.* **2** cause of wrongdoing or displeasure. **3** condition of being offended; hurt feelings; anger. **4** act of offending; hurting someone's feelings: *no offense was meant.* **5** act of attacking: *a gun is a weapon of offense.* **6** those who are attacking. **—of·fense′less,** *adj.*

of·fen·sive (ə fen′siv), *adj.* **1** giving offense; irritating; annoying: *an offensive remark.* **2** unpleasant; disagreeable; disgusting: *an offensive odor.* **3** used for attack; having to do with attack: *offensive weapons.* **—n. 1** position or attitude of attack: *the army took the offensive.* **2** attack. **—of·fen′sive·ly,** *adv.* **—of·fen′sive·ness,** *n.*

of·fer (ôf′ər; of′-), *v.* **1** hold out to be taken or refused; present: *he offered us his help.* **2** propose: *she offered a few ideas.* **3** present in worship: *offer prayers.* **4** present itself; occur: *I will come if the opportunity offers.* **5** attempt; try: *offer to hit.* **—n.** act or fact of offering: *an offer of money, an offer to sing.* [ult. < L, < *ob-* + *ferre* bring] **—of′fer·er,** *n.*

of·fer·ing (ôf′ər ing; ôf′ring; of′-), *n.* **1** the giving of something as an act of worship. **2** contribution. **3** act of one that offers.

of·fer·to·ry (ôf′ər tô′ri; -tō′-; of′-), *n., pl.* **-ries. 1** collection at a religious service. **2** verses said or the music sung or played while the offering is received. **—of′fer·to′ri·al,** *adj.*

off-hand (ôf′hand′; of′-), *adv.* without previous thought or preparation. **—adj.** Also, **off′hand′ed. 1** done or made off-

hand. **2** casual; informal. **—off′hand′ed·ly,** *adv.* **—off′hand′ed·ness,** *n.*

of·fice (of′is; ôf′-), *n.* **1** place in which the work of a position is done; room or rooms for work. **2** position, esp. in the public service. **3** duty of one's position; task; job; work: *a teacher's office is teaching.* **4** staff of persons carrying on work in an office. **5** act of kindnes or unkindness; attention: *through the good offices of a friend, he was able to get a job.* **6** a religious ceremony or prayer. [< OF < L *officium* service]

of·fice-hold·er (of′is hōl′dər; of′-), *n.* a government official.

of·fi·cer (of′ə sər; ôf′ə-), *n.* **1** person who commands others in the army or navy. **2** person who holds a public, church, or government office. **3** person appointed or elected to an administrative position in a club, society, etc. **—v. 1** provide with officers. **2** direct; conduct; manage. **—of′fi·cer·less,** *adj.*

of·fi·cial (ə fish′əl), *n.* **1** person who holds a public position or who is in charge of some public work or duty: *the President and Secretary of State are government officials.* **2** person holding office; officer: *bank officials.* **—adj. 1** of or pertaining to an office: *an official uniform.* **2** having authority: *an official record.* [< L *officialis.* See OFFICE.] **—of·fi′cial·dom,** *n.* **—of·fi′cial·ly,** *adv.*

of·fi·ci·ate (ə fish′i āt), *v.,* **-at·ed, -at·ing. 1** perform the duties of any office or position. **2** perform the duties of a priest or minister. **—of·fi′ci·a′tion,** *n.* **—of·fi′ci·a′tor,** *n.*

of·fi·cious (ə fish′əs), *adj.* too ready to offer services or advice; minding other people's business; fond of meddling. [< L *officiosus* dutiful. See OFFICE.] **—of·fi′cious·ly,** *adv.* **—of·fi′cious·ness,** *n.*

off·ing (ôf′ing; of′-), *n.* **1** the more distant part of the sea as seen from the shore.

in the offing, a just visible from the shore. **b** within sight. **c** not far off; likely.

off·ish (ôf′ish; of′-), *adj.* inclined to keep aloof; distant and reserved in manner. **—off′ish·ly,** *adv.* **—off′ish·ness,** *n.*

off-key (ôf′kē′; of′-), *adj.* **1** not in tune. **2** inappropriate: *an off-key remark.*

off-load (ôf′lōd′; of′-), *v.* **1** unload cargo. **2** sell; dispose of, esp. an investment.

off-road (ôf′rōd′; of′-), *adj.* **1** off or away from paved roads. **2** of or for travel on rough terrain.

off·set (*v.* ôf′set′, of′-; *n.* ôf′set′, of′-), *v.,* **-set, -set·ting,** *n.* **—v.** make up for; balance: *the better roads offset the greater distance.* **—n. 1** something which makes up for something else; compensation: *budget offsets.* **2** process of printing in which the inked impression is first made on a rubber roller and then on the paper, instead of directly on paper. **3** ledge formed on a wall by lessening its thickness above.

off·shoot (ôf′shüt′; of′-), *n.* **1** shoot or branch growing out from the main stem of a plant, tree, etc. **2** *Fig.* anything coming, or thought of as coming, from a main part, origin, etc.

off·shore (ôf′shôr′; –shōr′; of′–), *adv., adj.* off or away from the shore.

off·spring (ôf′spring′; of′–), *n.* what is born from or grows out of something; child or children; descendant.

off-stage (ôf′stāj′; of′–), *adj.* away from the part of the stage that the audience can see.

off-the-cuff (ôf′tḣə kuf′), *adj.* made without preparation; impromptu: *an off-the-cuff speech.* —*adv.* without preparation: *spoke off-the-cuff.*

oft (ôft; oft), *adv. Archaic.* often. [OE]

of·ten (ôf′ən; of′–; –tən), *adv.* in many cases; many times; frequently: *blame is often misdirected, he comes here often.* [ME, < *oft*]

of·ten·times (ôf′ən tīmz′; of′–), **oft·times** (ôft′tīmz′; oft′–), *adv.* often.

o·gee (ō jē′; ō′jē), *n.* **1** an S-shaped curve or line. **2** =ogee arch. [< F *ogive*]

ogee arch, pointed arch having an S-shaped curve on each side, typical of Gothic architecture.

o·gle (ō′gəl), *v.,* **o·gled, o·gling,** *n.* —*v.* look at with desire; make eyes. —*n.* an ogling look. [< Du. *oogelen* < *oog* eye] —**o′gler,** *n.*

o·gre (ō′gər), *n.* giant or monster that supposedly eats people. [< F] —**o′greish, o′grish,** *adj.*

oh, Oh (ō), *interj., n., pl.* **oh's, ohs; Oh's, Ohs.** —*interj.* **1** word used before names in addressing persons: *Oh, Mary, look!* **2** expression of surprise, joy, grief, pain, and other feelings. —*n.* the exclamation, Oh.

OH, (*zip code*) Ohio.

OHG, O.H.G., Old High German.

O·hi·o (ō hī′ō), *n.* a Middle Western state of the United States. —**O·hi′o·an,** *adj., n.*

ohm (ōm), *n.* unit of electrical resistance. One ohm is the resistance of a conductor through which one volt can send a current of one ampere. [named for G. S. *Ohm,* physicist] —**ohm′ic,** *adj.* —**ohm′me·ter,** *n.*

–oid, *suffix.* **1** like; like that of, as in *Mongoloid, amoeboid.* **2** thing like a, as in *spheroid, alkaloid.* [< Gk, < *eidos* form]

oil (oil), *n.* **1** any of several kinds of thick, fatty or greasy liquids that are lighter than water, burn easily, and dissolve in alcohol, but not in water. Mineral oils are used for fuel; animal and vegetable oils are used in cooking and medicine. Essential oils, such as oil of peppermint, are distilled from plants and evaporate quickly. **2 a** petroleum. **b** fuel oil. **3** an oil painting. —*v.* **1** put oil on or in. **2** bribe. [< OF < L *oleum* < Gk. *elaion*] —**oil′er,** *n.*

oil burner, anything that uses oil as fuel, esp. a furnace to heat a building.

oil·cloth (oil′klôth′; –kloth′), *n.* cloth made waterproof by coating it with oil-based paint or oil.

oil of vitriol, sulfuric acid.

oil painting, 1 picture painted with oil colors. **2** art of painting with oil colors.

oil well, well drilled in the earth to get oil.

oil·y (oil′i), *adj.,* **oil·i·er, oil·i·est. 1** of oil. **2** containing oil. **3** covered or soaked with oil. **4** like oil; smooth; slippery. —**oil′i·ly,** *adv.* —**oil′i·ness,** *n.*

oink (oingk), *n.* **1** sound made by a pig. **2** sound made in imitation of a pig; grunt. —*v.* **1** make the sound a pig makes. **2** grunt like a pig. [*imit.*]

oint·ment (oint′mənt), *n.* substance made from oil or fat, often containing medicine, used on the skin to heal or to make it soft and white. [< OF *oignement,* ult. < L *unguere* anoint; form infl. by *anoint*]

O·jib·wa, O·jib·way (ō jib′wā), *n., pl.* **–wa, –was;** **–way, –ways;** *adj.* —*n.* member of a large tribe of American Indians formerly living near the Great Lakes; Chippewa. —*adj.* of this tribe or their Algonkian language.

OK, (*zip code*) Oklahoma.

OK, O.K. (ō′kā′), *adj., adv., v.,* **OK'd, OK'ing; O.K.'d, O.K.'ing;** *n., pl.* **OK's; O.K.'s.** —*adj., adv.* all right; correct; approved. —*v.* endorse; approve. —*n.* approval. [abbreviation of *oll korrect,* alter. of *all correct*]

o·ka·pi (ō kä′pi), *n., pl.* **–pis, –pi.** an African animal like the giraffe, but smaller and with a much shorter neck. [< an African lang.]

o·kay (ō′kā′), *adj., adv., v., n.* =OK.

O·kie (ō′ki), *n. Informal.* a migratory farm worker, originally one from Oklahoma.

Okla., Oklahoma.

O·kla·ho·ma (ō′klə hō′mə), *n.* a S state of the United States. —**O′kla·ho′man,** *adj., n.*

Oklahoma City, capital of Oklahoma, in the C part.

o·kra (ō′krə), *n.* **1** plant cultivated for its sticky pods, which are used in soups and as a vegetable. **2** the pods. [< West African lang.]

OL, Old Latin.

old (ōld), *adj.,* **old·er** or **eld·er, old·est** or **eld·est,** *n.* —*adj.* **1** having existed long; aged: *an old wall.* **2** of age; in age: *the baby is one year old.* **3** not new; made, used, or known long ago; ancient: *an old tomb, the old language.* **4** much worn by age or use: *old clothes.* **5** seeming old; mature; having much experience: *an old hand at driving.* **6** familiar; dear: *good old fellow.* —*n.* time long ago. [OE *ald*] —**old′ish,** *adj.* —**old′ness,** *n.*

old age, years of life from about 65 on.

old country, country an emigrant comes from.

old·en (ōl′dən), *adj. Poetic.* of old; old; ancient.

Old English, 1 period in the history of the English language before 1100. **2** language of this period; Anglo-Saxon.

old-fash·ioned (ōld′fash′ənd), *adj.* **1** of an old fashion: *an old-fashioned dress.* **2** keeping to old ways, ideas, etc.: *an old-fashioned housekeeper.*

Old French, the French language from about A.D. 800 to about 1400.

Old Glory, flag of the United States.

old-growth forest (ōld′grōth′), forest that has reached its final stage of growth or stability.

old guard, very conservative members of an organization, as a political party or a community.

old hand, very skilled or experienced person.

Old High German, form of the German language that was spoken in S Germany from about A.D. 800 to 1100.

Old Icelandic, =Old Norse (def. 2).

Old Latin, the Latin language before the second century B.C.

old-line (ōld′līn′), *adj.* **1** conservative. **2** established.

old maid, 1 woman who has not married and seems unlikely to. **2** *Fig.* a prim, fussy person. **3** children's card game. —**old′maid′ish,** *adj.*

old master, 1 any great painter who lived before 1700. **2** a painting by such a painter.

Old Norse, 1 Scandinavian speech from the Viking period to about 1300. **2** the Icelandic language in the Middle Ages.

Old Saxon, the form of Low German spoken by the Saxons in NW Germany from about A.D. 800 to about 1100.

old school, group of people who have old-fashioned or conservative ideas.

Old Testament, the earlier part of the Bible, which contains the religious and social laws of the Hebrews, a record of their history.

old-time (ōld′tīm′), *adj.* of former times; like old times.

old-tim·er (ōld′tīm′ər), *n.* person who has long been a resident, member, worker, etc.

old wives' tale, a foolish story or belief.

old-world (ōld′wèrld′), *adj.* **1** of or pertaining to the ancient world. **2** belonging to or characteristic of a former period: *old-world courtesy.* **3** Also, **Old-World.** of or pertaining to the Eastern Hemisphere; not American.

Old World, Europe, Asia, and Africa.

o·le·ag·i·nous (ō′li aj′ə nəs), *adj.* oily. [< L, < *olea* olive tree]

o·le·an·der (ō′li an′dər), *n.* a poisonous evergreen shrub with fragrant red, pink, or white flowers. [< Med.L]

o·le·o·mar·ga·rine (ō′li ō mär′jə rēn; –rin), **o·le·o·mar·ga·rin** (–rin), or **o·le·o** (ō′li ō), *n.* a substitute for butter made from animal fats and vegetable oils; margarine.

ol·fac·tion (ol fak′shən), *n.* **1** act of smelling. **2** sense of smell. [< L *olfactus,* pp. of *olfacere* smell at < *olere* emit a smell + *facere* make]

ol·fac·to·ry (ol fak′tə ri), *adj., n., pl.* **-ries.** —*adj.* having to do with smelling; of smell. The nose is an olfactory organ. —*n.* an olfactory organ.

ol·i·garch (ol′ə gärk), *n.* one of the members of an oligarchy.

ol·i·gar·chy (ol′ə gär′ki), *n., pl.* **-chies.** 1 form of government in which a few people have power. 2 country or state having such a government. 3 the ruling few. [< Gk., ult. < *oligos* few + *archos* leader] —**ol′i·gar′chic, ol′i·gar′chi·cal,** *adj.* —**ol′i·gar′chi·cal·ly,** *adv.*

ol·i·gop·o·ly (ol′ə gop′ə li), *n., pl.* **-lies.** economic condition where there are so few producers of a product or services that competition does not affect its price. [< *oligo*- small, few + -*opoly,* as in mon*opoly*] —**ol′i·gop′o·list,** *n.*

ol·ive (ol′iv), *n.* 1 kind of evergreen tree with gray-green leaves that grows in S Europe and other warm regions. 2 fruit of this tree, with a hard stone and bitter pulp. 3 wood of the olive tree. 4 a yellowish green. 5 a yellowish brown. —*adj.* 1 yellowish-green. 2 yellowish-brown. [< F < L *oliva* < Gk. *elaia*]

olive branch, anything offered as a sign of peace.

olive oil, oil pressed from olives, used as food and in medicine.

ol·o·gy (ol′ə ji), *n., pl.* **-gies.** any science or branch of knowledge. [< connective -*o*- + -LOGY]

O·lym·pi·a (ō lim′pi ə), *n.* capital of Washington, in the W part of the state. —**O·lym′pic,** *adj.*

O·lym·pi·ad, o·lym·pi·ad (ō lim′pi ad), *n.* celebration of the modern Olympic games.

O·lym·pi·an (ō lim′pi ən), *adj.* 1 pertaining to Olympia or to Mount Olympus. 2 like a god; heavenly. 3 rather too gracious; magnificent; superior. —*n.* 1 one of the Greek gods who lived on Mount Olympus. 2 a contender in the modern Olympic games.

O·lym·pic games (ō lim′pik), 1 Also, **Olympian games.** contests in athletics, poetry, and music, held every four years by the ancient Greeks in honor of Zeus. 2 Also, **the Olympics,** modern athletic contests imitating the athletic contests of these games.

O·man (ō män′), *n.* country in SE Arabia, on the Arabian Sea.

o·ma·sum (ō mā′səm), *n., pl.* **-sa** (-sə). the third stomach of a cow or other ruminant. It receives the food when it is swallowed the second time. [< L]

om·buds·man (om′budz man′; -mən; om budz′mən), *n., pl.* **-men.** person hired by a government, company, etc., to receive and deal with complaints from employees and the public.

o·meg·a (ō meg′ə; ō mē′gə; ō mä′gə), *n.* 1 the last letter of the Greek alphabet (Ω, ω). 2 the last of any series; end. [< LGk. *o mega* big *o*]

om·e·let, om·e·lette (om′ə lit; om′lit), *n.* eggs beaten up with milk or water, fried or baked, and then folded over. [< F *omelette*]

o·men (ō′mən), *n.* 1 sign of what is to happen; object or event that is believed to mean good or bad fortune. 2 prophetic meaning: *a bird of ill omen.* [< L]

om·i·nous (om′ə nəs), *adj.* of bad omen; unfavorable; threatening: *those clouds look ominous for our picnic.* [< L, < *omen* omen] —**om′i·nous·ly,** *adv.* —**om′i·nous·ness,** *n.*

o·mis·sion (ō mish′ən), *n.* 1 an omitting or being omitted. 2 thing omitted.

o·mit (ō mit′), *v.,* **o·mit·ted, o·mit·ting.** 1 leave out: *omit a letter in a word.* 2 fail to do; neglect: *Mary omitted making her bed.* [< L *omittere* < *ob*- by + *mittere* let go] —**o·mit′tance,** *n.* —**o·mit′ter,** *n.*

om·ni·bus (om′nə bus), *n., pl.* **-bus·es.** —*n.* 1 volume containing many works by one author, or one containing works by many authors: *omnibus of American poetry.* 2 bus. —*adj.* covering many things at once: *an omnibus law.* [< L, for all]

om·ni·far·i·ous (om′nə fãr′i əs), *adj.* of all forms, varieties, or kinds. [< L *omnifarius*] —**om′ni·far′i·ous·ness,** *n.*

om·nip·o·tence (om nip′ə təns), *n.* complete power; unlimited power.

om·nip·o·tent (om nip′ə tənt), *adj.* having all power; almighty. —*n.* **the Omnipotent,** God. [< L, < *omnis* all + *potens* being able] —**om·nip′o·tent·ly,** *adv.*

om·ni·pres·ence (om′nə prez′əns), *n.* presence everywhere at the same time: *God's omnipresence.*

om·ni·pres·ent (om′nə prez′ənt), *adj.* present everywhere at the same time.

om·nis·cience (om nish′əns), *n.* knowledge of everything; complete or infinite knowledge. [< Med.L, < L *omnis* all + *scientia* knowledge]

om·nis·cient (om nish′ənt), *adj.* having complete or infinite knowledge; knowing everything. —**om·nis′cient·ly,** *adv.*

om·niv·o·rous (om niv′ə rəs), *adj.* 1 eating every kind of food. 2 eating both animal and vegetable food. 3 taking in everything; fond of all kinds: *an omnivorous reader.* [< L, < *omnis* all + *vorare* eat greedily] —**om·niv′o·rous·ly,** *adv.* —**om·niv′o·rous·ness,** *n.*

on (on; ôn), *prep.* 1 above and supported by: *on the table.* 2 touching, be around; upon: *the picture on the wall, put the ring on her finger, a house on the shore.* 3 toward: *the workers marched on the Capitol.* 4 by means of; by the use of: *on good authority.* 5 at the time of; during: *they greeted us on our arrival, on Sunday.* 6 in relation to; in connection with; concerning: *a book on animals, on purpose, on an errand.* 7 among: *who is on the committee?* —*adv.* 1 on something: *the roof is on.* 2 to something: *hold on, or you may fall.* 3 toward something: *some played; the others looked on, march on.* 4

in or into a condition, process, manner, or action: *turn the gas on.* 5 forward: *from that day on, head on.* —*adj.* taking place: *the race is on.*

and so on, and more of the same.

on and off, at some times but not at other times.

on and on, without stopping.

on to, aware of: *on to my secret.* [OE]

ON, O.N., Old Norse.

once (wuns), *adv.* 1 one time: *he comes once a day.* 2 at some one time in the past; formerly: *a once powerful nation.* 3 even a single time; ever: *if the facts once become known.* —*n.* a single occasion: *once is enough.* —*conj.* if ever; whenever: *once you cross the river you are safe.*

all at once, suddenly.

at once, a immediately. **b** at one and the same time.

once and again, repeatedly.

once (and) for all, finally or decisively.

once in a while, now and then.

once or twice, a few times. [OE *ānes* < *ān* ONE]

once·o·ver (wuns′ō′vər), *n.* a single or brief inspection.

on·co·gen (ong′kə jen), *n.* agent or virus that causes growth of tumors. [< Gk. *ónkos* tumor, mass + E -*gen* something growing] —**on′co·gen′e·sis,** *n.* —**on′co·gen′ic,** *adj.*

on·co·gene (ong′kə jēn′), *n.* gene that causes growth of tumors. [< Gk. *ónkos* tumor, mass + E *gene*]

on·col·o·gy (ong kol′ə ji), *n.* branch of medicine dealing with tumors. [< Gk. *ónkos* tumor, mass + E -*ology*] —**on′co·log′i·cal,** *adj.* —**on·col′o·gist,** *n.*

on·com·ing (on′kum′ing; ôn′-), *adj.* approaching. —*n.* approach.

one (wun), *n.* 1 a cardinal number, the first and lowest whole number. 2 symbol of this number; 1. 3 a single person or thing: *I gave him the one he wanted.* —*adj.* 1 a single: *one apple, they held one opinion.* 2 some: *one day he will be sorry.* 3 joined together; united: *they replied in one voice.* 4 a certain: *one John Smith was elected.* —*pron.* 1 some person or thing: *one of the poems was selected for the book.* 2 any person or thing: *one must work hard to achieve success.*

all one, all the same.

at one, in agreement or harmony.

make one, a form or be one of a number, assembly, or party. **b** join together; unite in marriage.

one and all, everyone.

one by one, one after another.

one or two, a few.

one up on, *Informal.* an advantage or superiority over. [OE (stressed) *ān.* Cf. A, AN¹.]

one another, one the other: *they struck at one another, they were in one another's way.*

O·nei·da (ō nī′də), *n.* member of an American Indian tribe formerly living in C New York State.

one-liner (wun′lī′nər), *n.* short, witty remark or wisecrack.

one-ness (wun′nis), *n.* **1** singleness. **2** unity. **3** agreement.

one-off (wun′ôf′; –of′), *n.* something done or happening only once. —*adj.* happening or done only once.

one-on-one (wun′on wun′), *adj.* **1** in a team sport, with each player guarding an opponent. **2** between just two people: *a one-on-one meeting.*

on-er-ous (on′ər əs), *adj.* burdensome; oppressive. [< L *onerosus* < *onus* burden] —**on′er-ous-ly,** *adv.* —**on′er-ous-ness,** *n.*

one-self (wun self′), **one's self,** *pron.* one's own self: *one should not praise oneself.* **be oneself, a** have full control of one's mind or body. **b** act naturally.

one-shot (wun′shot′), *adj.* intended to be used or happening only one time.

one-sid-ed (wun′sīd′id), *adj.* **1** seeing only one side of a question; partial; prejudiced. **2** uneven; unequal. **3** having but one side.

one-time (wun′tīm′), *adj.* **1** of the past; former. **2** happening only once: *a one-time opportunity.*

one-track (wun′trak′), *adj.* **1** having only one track. **2** *Informal.* understanding or doing only one thing at a time; narrow.

one-way (wun′wā′), *adj.* **1** moving or allowing movement in only one direction. **2** developing or working in only one direction: *one-way glass.*

on-go-ing (on′gō′ing; ôn′–), *adj.* continuing; not interrupted.

on-ion (un′yən), *n.* **1** a bulblike root with a sharp, strong smell and taste. **2** the plant it grows on. [< F < L *unio* onion, kind of pearl]

on-line or **on-line** (on′līn′; ôn′–), *adj.* connected to a computer network server, esp. to the Internet.

on-look-er (on′lúk′ər; ôn′–), *n.* person who watches without taking part; spectator. —**on′look′ing,** *adj., n.*

on-ly (ōn′li), *adj.* **1** by itself or themselves; sole, single, or few of the kind or class: *an only son.* **2** best; finest: *he is the only writer for my tastes.* —*adv.* **1** merely: *he sold only two.* **2** and no one else; and that is all: *only he remained.* —*conj.* except that; but: *I would have gone only you objected.* **if only,** I wish: *if only wars would cease!* **only too,** very: *she was only too glad to help.* [OE *ānlīc*]

on-o-mat-o-poe-ia (on′ə mat′ə pē′ə), *n.* formation of a name or word by imitating the sound associated with the thing designated, as in *buzz, hum, cuckoo, slap, splash.* [< L < Gk., < *onoma* word, name + *–poios* making] —**on′o-mat-o-poe′ic,** *adj.*

On-on-da-ga (on′ən dô′gə; –dä′–), *n.* member of a tribe of American Indians formerly living in C New York State.

on-rush (on′rush′; ôn′–), *n.* a violent forward rush.

on-rush-ing (on′rush′ing), *adj.* moving rapidly or forcefully forward.

on-set (on′set′; ôn′–), *n.* **1** beginning: *the onset of this disease is gradual.* **2** attack: *the onset of the enemy took us by surprise.*

on-shore (on′shôr′; –shōr′; ôn′–), *adv., adj.* **1** toward the land. **2** on the land.

on-slaught (on′slôt′; ôn′–), *n.* a vigorous attack.

on-to (on′tü; ôn′-), *prep.* **1** on to; to a position on: *climb onto a limb, jump onto the dock.* **2** *Informal.* be familiar with or aware of: *I'm onto your jokes.*

on-tog-e-ny (on toj′ə ni), *n.* development of an organism, or the history of its development. [< Gk. *ṓn, óntos* being + *–géneia* origin]

on-tol-o-gy (on tol′ə ji), *n.* the philosophy of the nature of reality. [< NL *ontologia* < Gk. *ṓn, óntos* being + *–logiā* –logy] —**on′to-log′i-cal,** *adj.* —**on-tol′o-gist,** *n.*

o-nus (ō′nəs), *n.* burden; responsibility. [< L]

on-ward (on′wərd; ôn′–), *adv.* Also, **on′-wards.** toward the front; further on; on; forward: *move onward.* —*adj.* on; further on; toward the front; forward: *an onward movement.*

on-yx (on′iks), *n.* a semiprecious variety of quartz with layers of different colors and shades. [< L < Gk., nail, claw]

o-o-blast (ō′ə blast), *n.* ovum not yet fully developed. [< E *oo–* egg, ovum + Gk. *blastós* germ, sprout]

oo-dles (ü′delz), *n. pl. Informal.* huge amount; loads; tons: *oodles of friends, oodles of fun.*

o-o-gen-e-sis (ō′ə jen′əsis), *n.* development of the ovum. [< *oo–* egg + *genesis*] —**o′o-ge-net′ic,** *adj.*

oomph (ûmf), *n. Informal.* energy; enthusiasm.

ooze[1] (üz), *v.,* **oozed, ooz-ing,** *n.* —*v.* **1** pass out slowly through small openings; leak out slowly and quietly: *his courage oozed away as he waited.* **2** give out slowly: *the cut oozed blood.* [< n.] —*n.* **1** a slow flow. **2** something that oozes. [OE *wōs* juice] —**oo′zy,** *adj.* —**oo′zi-ness,** *n.*

ooze[2] (üz), *n.* a soft mud or slime, esp. at the bottom of a pond, river, or on the ocean bottom. [OE *wāse* mud] —**oo′zy,** *adj.* —**oo′zi-ness,** *n.*

op., **1** opus; opera. **2** opposite.

o-pac-i-ty (ō pas′ə ti), *n., pl.* **-ties. 1** a being opaque; darkness; a being impervious to light. **2** something opaque.

o-pal (ō′pəl), *n.* a mineral, an amorphous form of silica, found in many varieties and colors (often a milky white), certain of which have a peculiar rainbow play of colors and are valued as gems. [< L *opalus* < Gk. *opallios* < Skt. *upala* precious stone] —**o′pal-ine,** *adj.*

o-pal-esce (ō′pəl es′), *v.,* **-esced, -esc-ing.** exhibit a play of colors like that of the opal. —**o′pal-es′cence,** *n.* —**o′pal-es′cent,** *adj.*

o-paque (ō pāk′), *adj.* **1** not letting light through; not transparent. **2** not shining; dark; dull. **3** obscure; hard to understand. —*n.* something opaque. [< L *opacus* dark, shady] —**o-paque′ly,** *adv.* —**o-paque′ness,** *n.*

op art (op), =optical art.

op. cit., in the work cited. [< L *opere citato*]

o-pen (ō′pən), *adj.* **1** that lets (a person or thing) in or out: *an open window.* **2** that permits passing or flowing through, access into, a view into: *an open gate, an open lid, an open valve, an open field, an open book.* **3** that may be shared, used, taken, or taken part in by anyone: *an open market, an open race, an open position.* **4** without protection, restriction, or cover: *an open fire, open to temptation, open season for hunting.* **5** in plain sight; for all to be aware of: *open disregard of rules.* **6** frank and sincere: *an open face.* **7** that is without a definite answer or answers, or has not been settled: *an open question, an open mind.* **8** of a note, produced without aid of slide, key, etc. —*n.* **1** an open or clear space; opening. **2 the open, a** the open country, air, sea, etc. **b** public view or knowledge. —*v.* **1** give access; let pass through: *open a gate or window, the classroom door opens into the hall.* **2** spread out; unfold: *open a newspaper or letter.* **3** set up; establish: *open a new store.* **4** begin; start: *school opens early, open a conversation.* **5** free from hindrance, as from ice: *open a path in the wilderness.* **6** come apart; burst open: *an earthquake opened a crack in the ground.* **open to, a** ready to take; willing to consider: *open to your ideas.* **b** liable to: *worry left him open to all kinds of wild imaginings.* **c** to be had or used by: *the pool is open to everyone.* **open up, a** make or become open. **b** unfold; spread out. **c** begin; start. [OE; akin to UP] —**o′pen-er,** *n.* —**o′pen-ly,** *adv.* —**o′pen-ness,** *n.*

open air, out of doors. —**o′pen-air′,** *adj.*

o-pen-and-shut (ō′pən ən shut′), *adj. Informal.* obvious; straightforward.

open book, 1 someone who does not hide thoughts or motives; a straightforward person. **2** something widely known or readily understood: *their history is an open book.*

open-book (ō′pən buk′), *adj.* of an examination taken with texts and notes available.

open door, 1 free access to all. **2** policy of admitting all nations to a country upon equal terms, esp. for trade. —**o′pen-door′,** *adj.*

o-pen-end-ed (ō′pən en′did), *adj.* **1** not final; able to be revised or adjusted later. **2** not closed at one end. **3** not decided: *open-ended negotiations.*

o-pen-hand-ed (ō′pən han′did), *adj.* generous; liberal. —**o′pen-hand′ed-ly,** *adv.* —**o′pen-hand′ed-ness,** *n.*

o·pen-heart·ed (ō'pən här'tid), *adj.* **1** frank; unreserved. **2** kindly; generous. —**o'pen-heart'ed·ly,** *adv.* —**o'pen-heart'ed·ness,** *n.*

open house, 1 social event to which all are welcome. **2** occasion when a house, school, institution, etc., is open to the public for inspection.

o·pen·ing (ō'pən ing; ōp'ning), *n.* **1** an open or clear space; gap; hole: *an opening in a wall.* **2** the first part; beginning. **3** a formal beginning: *a spring opening to show the new fashions.* **4** place or position that is open or vacant. **5** a favorable chance or opportunity.

open letter, letter addressed to a person but published in a newspaper, magazine, etc.

o·pen-mind·ed (ō'pən mīn'did), *adj.* having or showing a mind open to new arguments or ideas. —**o'pen-mind'ed·ly,** *adv.* —**o'pen-mind'ed·ness,** *n.*

open primary, primary election in which any registered voter of a state, city, etc., can vote without being a member of a political party.

open secret, something secret that is actually widely known.

open ses·a·me (ses'ə mē), **1** password at which doors or barriers fly open. **2** a magical means of obtaining entrance.

open shop, factory, shop, or other establishment that will employ both union and non-union workers.

o·pen·work (ō'pən werk´), *n.* ornamental work that shows openings.

op·er·a[1] (op'ər ə; op'rə), *n.* **1** play that is mostly sung, with costumes, scenery, acting, and music to go with the singing. *Faust* and *Carmen* are well-known operas. **2** branch of art represented by such plays: *the history of opera.* **3** performance of an opera. **4** theater where operas are performed. [< Ital., for *opera in musica* (a dramatic) work to music; *opera* < L, effort (akin to *opus* a work)]

op·er·a[2] (op'ə rə), *n.* pl. of **opus.**

op·er·a·ble (op'ər ə bəl), *adj.* fit for, or admitting of, a surgical operation. —**op'er·a·ble·ness,** *n.* —**op'er·a·bly,** *adv.*

opera glasses, a small binoculars used at the opera and in theaters.

op·er·ate (op'ər āt), *v.,* –**at·ed, –at·ing. 1** be at work; run: *the machinery operates night and day.* **2** manage; keep at work: *who operates this elevator?* **3** produce an effect; work; act: *several causes operated to bring on the war.* **4** produce a desired effect: *the medicine operated quickly.* **5** do something to the body, usually with instruments, to improve health: *the doctor operated on the injured man.* [< L *operatus* < *opus* a work, or *opera* effort] —**op'er·at´a·ble,** *adj.* —**op'er·at´a·ble·ness,** *n.* —**op'er·at´a·bly,** *adv.*

op·er·at·ic (op´ər at'ik), *adj.* of or like the opera. —**op´er·at'i·cal·ly,** *adv.*

op·er·a·tion (op'ər ā'shən), *n.* **1** act or fact of working. **2** the way a thing works: *the operation of a machine.* **3** action;

activity: *the operation of brushing one's teeth.* **4** something done to the body, usually with instruments, to improve health. **5** movements of soldiers, ships, supplies, etc., for war purposes.

in operation, a running; working; in action. **b** in use or effect. —**op´er·a·tion·al,** *adj.*

op·er·a·tive (op'ər ā'tiv; –ə tiv), *adj.* operating; effective: *the laws operative in a community.* —**op'er·a´tive·ly,** *adv.* —**op'er·a´tive·ness,** *n.*

op·er·a·tor (op'ər ā'tər), *n.* **1** person who operates. **2** a skilled worker who operates a machine, telephone, telegraph, etc. **3** person who runs a factory, mine, railroad, etc.

operator gene, gene that regulates the activity of structural genes.

op·er·on (op'ər on), *n.* area of a chromosome that contains the operator gene and the structural genes that produce messenger RNA for a particular process. [*operator* + *-on* unit of genetic material]

op·er·et·ta (op´ər et'ə), *n., pl.* –**tas.** a short, amusing opera.

oph·thal·mi·a (of thal'mi ə), *n.* an acute infection of the membrane around the eye that may affect the eye, causing blindness. [< LL < Gk., < *ophthalmos* eye]

oph·thal·mic (of thal'mik), *adj.* of or having to do with the eye.

oph·thal·mol·o·gy (of´thal mol'ə ji), *n.* science that deals with the structure, functions, and diseases of the eye. —**oph´thal´mo·log'i·cal,** *adj.* —**oph´thal·mol'o·gist,** *n.*

o·pi·ate (ō'pi it; –āt), *n.* **1** drug that contains opium and so dulls pain or brings sleep. **2** anything that quiets. —*adj.* **1** containing opium. **2** bringing sleep or ease. —**o´pi·at'ic,** *adj.*

o·pine (ō pīn'), *v.,* **o·pined, o·pin·ing.** *Humorous.* hold or express an opinion; think. [< L *opinari*] —**o·pin'er,** *n.*

o·pin·ion (ə pin'yən), *n.* **1** what one thinks; belief not so strong as knowledge; judgment. **2** impression; estimate. **3** a formal judgment by an expert; professional advice. [< L *opinio.* See OPINE.] —**o·pin'ion·al,** *adj.* —**o·pin'ion·al·ly,** *adv.* —**o·pin'ioned,** *adj.*

o·pin·ion·at·ed (ə pin'yən āt´id), *adj.* obstinate or conceited with regard to one's opinions; dogmatic. —**o·pin'ion·at´ed·ly,** *adv.* —**o·pin'ion·at´ed·ness,** *n.*

o·pi·oid (ō'pē oid), *n.* synthetic drug like an opiate in its effect.

o·pi·um (ō'pi əm), *n.* a powerful drug that causes sleep and eases pain. It is also used to stimulate and intoxicate. Opium is made from a kind of poppy. [< L < Gk. *opion,* dim. of *opos* vegetable juice]

o·pos·sum (ə pos'əm), *n.* a small mammal that lives mostly in trees, common in the S United States. When caught, it pretends to be dead. [< Algonquian]

opp., 1 opposed. **2** opposite.

op·po·nent (ə pō'nənt), *n.* person who is on the other side in a fight, game, or discussion; person fighting, struggling, or speaking against one. —*adj.* opposing. [< L, < *ob–* against + *ponere* place]

op·por·tune (op´ər tün'; –tūn'), *adj.* fortunate; well-chosen; favorable; suitable. [< L, favorable (of wind), < *ob portum* (*ferens*) (bringing) to port] —**op´por·tune'ly,** *adv.* —**op´por·tune'ness,** *n.*

op·por·tun·ism (op´ər tün'iz əm; –tün'–), *n.* policy or practice of adapting thought and action to particular circumstances rather than to general principles. —**op´por·tun'ist,** *n.* —**op´por·tun·is'tic,** *adj.* —**op´por·tun·is'ti·cal·ly,** *adv.*

opportunistic infection, infection that develops when the immune system is weakened by another condition, such as AIDS or leukemia.

op·por·tu·ni·ty (op´ər tü'nə ti; –tū'–), *n., pl.* –**ties.** a good chance; favorable time; convenient occasion.

op·pos·a·ble (ə pōz'ə bəl), *adj.* **1** capable of being opposed. **2** capable of being placed opposite something else. The human thumb is opposable to the fingers. —**op·pos´a·bil'i·ty,** *n.*

op·pose (ə pōz'), *v.,* –**posed, –pos·ing. 1** be against; be in the way of; act, fight, or struggle against; try to hinder; resist: *a swamp opposed the advance of the enemy.* **2** set up against; place in the way of: *let us oppose good nature to anger.* **3** put in contrast: *love is opposed to hate.* [< OF, < *op–* (< L *ob–*) against + *poser* put, POSE] —**op·posed',** *adj.* —**op·pos'er,** *n.* —**op·pos'ing,** *adj.* —**op·pos'ing·ly,** *adv.*

op·po·site (op'ə zit), *adj.* **1** placed against; as different in direction as can be: *the house straight across the street is opposite to ours.* **2** as different as can be; just contrary. *Sour* is opposite to *sweet.* —*n.* thing or person that is opposite. *Black* is the opposite of *white.* —*prep.* opposite to: *opposite the church.* [< L *oppositus* < *ob–* against + *ponere* place] —**op'po·site·ly,** *adv.* —**op'po·site·ness,** *n.*

op·po·si·tion (op´ə zish'ən), *n.* **1** action against; resistance. **2** a political party opposed to the party in power. —**op´po·si'tion·al,** *adj.*

op·press (ə pres'), *v.* **1** govern harshly; keep down unjustly or by cruelty. **2** weigh down; lie heavily on; burden. [< Med.L *oppressare,* ult. < L *ob–* against + *premere* press] —**op·pres'sor,** *n.*

op·pres·sion (ə presh'ən), *n.* **1** an oppressing: *the oppression of the people by the nobles.* **2** a being oppressed: *they fought against oppression.* **3** cruel or unjust treatment. **4** a heavy, weary feeling.

op·pres·sive (ə pres'iv), *adj.* **1** harsh; severe; unjust. **2** hard to bear; burdensome. —**op·pres'sive·ly,** *adv.* —**op·pres'sive·ness,** *n.*

op·pro·bri·ous (ə prō'bri əs), *adj.* expressing scorn, reproach, or abuse. *Coward, liar,* and *thief* are opprobrious names.

—op·pro'bri·ous·ly, *adv.* —op·pro'bri·ous·ness, *n.*

op·pro·bri·um (ə prō'bri əm), *n.* disgrace or reproach caused by shameful conduct; infamy. [< L, ult. < *ob-* at + *probrum* infamy, reproach]

opt (opt), *v.* choose; desire: *opt to resign.*
opt for, favor; choose.
opt out, decide to back out: *opted out of the chairmanship.* [< F *opter* < L *optāre* choose, desire]

opt., 1 optative. 2 optics. 3 optional.

op·tic (op'tik), *adj.* of the eye; of the sense of sight. [< Med.L < Gk., < *op-* see]

op·ti·cal (op'tə kəl), *adj.* 1 of the eye; visual: *an optical defect.* 2 made to assist sight: *an optical instrument.* 3 of vision and light in relation to each other. —op'ti·cal·ly, *adv.*

op·ti·cian (op tish'ən), *n.* maker or seller of eyeglasses and other optical instruments.

optic nerve, nerve of sight which connects the eye and brain.

op·tics (op'tiks), *n.* science that deals with light and vision.

op·ti·mal (op'tə məl), *adj.* most favorable. —op'ti·mal·ly, *adv.*

op·ti·mism (op'tə miz əm), *n.* 1 tendency to look on the bright side of things. 2 belief that everything will turn out for the best. 3 doctrine that the existing world is the best of all possible worlds. [< NL, < L *optimus* best] —op'ti·mist, *n.* —op'ti·mis'tic, —op'ti·mis'ti·cal, *adj.* —op'ti·mis'ti·cal·ly, *adv.*

op·ti·mize (op'tə mīz), *v.*, —mized, —miz·ing. make the best or most of. —op'ti·mi·za'tion, *n.*

op·ti·mum (op'tə məm), *n.,* *pl.* —mums, —ma (—mə), *adj.* —n. the best or most favorable point, degree, amount, etc., for the purpose. —adj. optimal. [< L]

op·tion (op'shən), *n.* 1 right or freedom of choice. 2 a choosing; choice. 3 right to buy something at a certain price within a certain time. [< L *optio*]

op·tion·al (op'shən əl), *adj.* left to one's choice; not required. —op'tion·al·ly, *adv.*

op·tom·e·try (op tom'ə tri), *n.* 1 measurement of visual powers. 2 practice or art of testing eyes in order to fit them with glasses. [< *opto-* sight [< Gk. *optos* seen] + *-metry* < Gk., < *metron* measure] —op·tom'e·trist, *n.*

op·u·lent (op'yə lənt), *adj.* 1 wealthy; rich. 2 abundant; plentiful. [< L *opulens* < *ops* power, resources] —op'u·lence, op'u·len·cy, *n.* —op'u·lent·ly, *adv.*

o·pus (ō'pəs), *n.,* *pl.* op·e·ra (op'ə rə). a work; composition: *the violinist played his own opus, No. 16.* [< L]

or (ôr; *unstressed* ər), *conj.* 1 word used to express a choice, difference, etc.: *you can go or stay, is it sweet or sour?* 2 and if not; otherwise: *hurry, or you will be late.* 3 that is; being the same: *this is the end or last part.* [OE (unstressed) *ā(hwæ)ther* < *ā* ever + *hwœther* either, whether]

–or, *suffix.* 1 person or thing that ——s, as in *actor, accelerator, orator.* 2 act, state, condition, quality, characteristic, etc., esp. in words from Latin, as in *error, horror.* [< L]

OR, (*zip code*) Oregon.

or·a·cle (ôr'ə kəl; or'–), *n.* 1 answer, often equivocal, given by a god through a priest or priestess, to some question. 2 place where the god gives answers. 3 priest, priestess, or other means by which the god's answer is given. 4 something regarded as an infallible guide or indicator. 5 a very wise person. [< OF < L *oraculum* < *orare,* orig., recite solemnly]

o·rac·u·lar (ô rak'yə lər), *adj.* 1 of or like an oracle. 2 with a hidden meaning that is difficult to make out. 3 very wise. —o·rac'u·lar'i·ty, *n.* —o·rac'u·lar·ly, *adv.*

o·ral (ô'rəl; ō'–), *adj.* 1 spoken; using speech: *an oral agreement.* 2 of the mouth: *the oral opening.* [< L *os* mouth] —o'ral·ly, *adv.* —o'ral·ness, *n.*

or·ange (ôr'inj; or'–), *n.* 1 a round, reddish-yellow, juicy fruit that grows in warm climates. 2 the tree it grows on. 3 fruit or tree that suggests an orange. 4 a reddish yellow. —adj. 1 of or like an orange. 2 reddish-yellow. [< OF < Sp. < Ar. < Pers. *nārang;* in OF blended with *or* gold]

or·ange·ade (ôr'inj ād'; or'–), *n.* drink made of orange juice, sugar, and water.

orange pekoe, a black tea from Sri Lanka (Ceylon) or India.

o·rang·u·tan (ō rang'ü tan'), o·rang·ou·tang (tang'), or o·rang (ō rang'), *n.* a large ape of the forests of Borneo and Sumatra, that has very long arms and long, reddish-brown hair. It lives mostly in trees and eats fruits and leaves. [< Malay, < *orang* man + *utan* wild]

o·rate (ô rāt'; ō–; ô'rāt; ō'rāt), *v.,* o·rat·ed, o·rat·ing. make an oration; talk in a grand manner. [< *oration*]

o·ra·tion (ô rā'shən; ō–), *n.* a formal public speech delivered on a special occasion. [< L, < *orare* speak formally. Doublet of ORISON.]

or·a·tor (ôr'ə tər; or'–), *n.* 1 person who makes an oration. 2 person who can speak very well in public.

or·a·to·ri·o (ôr'ə tô'ri ō; –tō'–; or'–), *n.,* *pl.* —ri·os. a musical composition, usually based on a religious theme, for solo voices, chorus, and orchestra. [< Ital., orig., place of prayer, LL *oratorium* ORATORY²]

or·a·to·ry¹ (ôr'ə tô'ri; –tō'–; or'–), *n.* 1 skill in public speaking; fine speaking. 2 art of public speaking. [< L (*ars*) *oratoria* oratorical (art)] —or'a·tor'i·cal, *adj.* —or'a·tor'i·cal·ly, *adv.*

or·a·to·ry² (ôr'ə tô'ri; –tō'–; or'–), *n.,* *pl.* —ries. a small chapel; room set apart for prayer. [< LL *oratorium* < *orare* pray]

orb (ôrb), *n.* 1 sphere; globe. 2 sun, moon, planet, or star. 3 world. —v. form

into a circle or sphere. [< L *orbis* circle] —orbed, *adj.*

or·bit (ôr'bit), *n.,* *v.,* –bit·ed, –bit·ing. —n. 1 path of the earth or any one of the planets about the sun. 2 path of any celestial body about another celestial body. 3 *Fig.* regular course of life or experience. 4 *Fig.* sphere of influence. —v. 1 travel around (a body) in an orbit. 2 travel in orbit. 3 place (a satellite) in an orbit. 4 of a satellite, etc., arrive in its orbit. [< L *orbita* wheel track < *orbis* wheel, circle] —or'bit·al, *adj.*

or·bit·er (ôr'bit ər), *n.* something, esp. a spacecraft or satellite, that orbits.

or·chard (ôr'chərd), *n.* 1 piece of ground on which fruit trees are grown. 2 trees in an orchard. [OE *ortgeard* < *ort-* (appar. < L *hortus* garden) + *geard* yard¹]

or·ches·tra (ôr'kis trə), *n.* 1 musicians playing at a concert, an opera, or a play. 2 instruments played together by the musicians in an orchestra. 3 part of a theater just in front of the stage, where the musicians sit. 4 the main floor of a theater, esp. the part near the front. [< L < Gk., the space where the dancers performed, ult. < *orcheesthai* to dance] —or·ches'tral, *adj.* —or·ches'tral·ly, *adv.*

or·ches·trate (ôr'kis trāt), *v.,* –trat·ed, –trat·ing. compose or arrange (music) for performance by an orchestra. 2 *Fig.* arrange anything complex or complicated. —or'ches·tra'tion, or'ches·tra'tor, *n.*

or·chid (ôr'kid), *n.* 1 a plant with beautiful, queerly shaped flowers that are formed of three petallike sepals and three petals, one petal being very different from the other two. b its flower. 2 a light purple. —adj. light-purple. [< NL, ult. < L *orchis* < Gk., testicle; from shape of root.]

ord., 1 order. 2 ordinance. 3 ordinary.

or·dain (ôr dān'), *v.* 1 order; fix; decide; appoint: *the law ordains that the murderers shall be hanged.* 2 officially appoint or consecrate as a minister in a Christian church. [< OF < L *ordinare* < *ordo* order] —or·dain'er, *n.* —or·dain'ment, *n.*

or·deal (ôr dēl'; –dē'əl; ôr'dēl), *n.* 1 a severe test or experience: *the ordeal of a visit to the dentist.* 2 in early times, an effort to decide the guilt or innocence of an accused person by making him do something dangerous like holding fire or taking poison. It was supposed that an innocent person would not be harmed by such danger. [OE *ordǽl* judgment]

or·der (ôr'dər), *n.* 1 way one thing follows another: *in order of size, in alphabetical order.* 2 condition in which every part or piece is in its right place: *put a room in order.* 3 condition; state: *my affairs are in good order.* 4 way the world works; way things happen: *the order of nature.* 5 state or condition of things in which the law is obeyed and there is no trouble: *keep order.* 6 command: *the captain's orders.* 7 direction of a court or judge. **8** paper saying that money is to be paid over: *a money order*. **9** statement telling a store what you wish sent. **10** kind or sort: *ability of a high order*. **11** *Biol.* a group in the classifying of plants and animals that is below a class, but higher than a family. **12** brotherhood of monks, friars, or knights: *the Franciscan order*. **13** any one of the typical styles of columns and architecture: *the Doric, Ionic, and Corinthian orders*. **14** portion or serving of food served in a restaurant, etc. —*v.* **1** put in order; arrange: *order one's affairs*. **2** command; bid: *he ordered that the prisoners be handcuffed*. **3** give orders, directions, etc.: *please order for me*. **4** give (a store, etc.) an order for. **5** decide; will: *the gods ordered it otherwise*.

call to order, a ask to be quiet and start work. **b** open a convention or proceeding.

in order, a in obedience to authority: *keep the rebels in order*. **b** permissible, according to the rules: *a vote is in order*. **c** necessary; logical: *a letter of protest is in order*.

in order that, so that; with the purpose that.

in order to, as a means to; to.

in short order, quickly.

on the order of, somewhat like; similar to: *a uniform on the order of a spacesuit*.

order about or **around,** send here and there; tell to do this and that.

out of order, a not working. **b** not arranged properly; disordered. **c** *Fig.* sick.

take orders, become a member of the clergy. [< OF < L *ordo* row, rank] —**or′der·er,** *n.* —**or′der·less,** *adj.*

or·der·ly (ôr′dər li), *adj., n., pl.* **–lies.** —*adj.* **1** in order; with regular arrangement, method, or system. **2** keeping order; well-behaved or regulated. —*n.* **1** a noncommissioned officer or private soldier who attends a superior officer to carry orders, etc. **2** a hospital attendant who keeps things clean and in order. —**or′der·li·ness,** *n.*

or·di·nal (ôr′də nəl), *adj.* showing order or position in a series. First, second, third, etc., are ordinal numbers; one, two, three, etc., are cardinal numbers. —*n.* an ordinal number. [< LL *ordinalis* < L *ordo* order] —**or′di·nal·ly,** *adv.*

or·di·nance (ôr′də nəns), *n.* rule or law made by authority; decree. [< OF, ult. < L *ordinare* arrange, regulate]

or·di·nar·i·ly (ôr′də ner′ə li; *emphatic* ôr′də när′ə li), *adv.* **1** usually; regularly. **2** to the usual extent.

or·di·nar·y (ôr′də ner′i), *adj., n., pl.* **–nar·ies.** —*adj.* **1** usual; regular; customary: *for all ordinary purposes*. **2** somewhat below the average: *the speaker was ordinary and tiresome*. —*n.* person who has authority in his own right, esp. a bishop or a judge. [< L *ordinarius*. See ORDER.] —**or′di·nar′i·ness,** *n.*

or·di·nate (ôr′də nit; –nāt), *n.* a vertical line drawn on a graph to define a point in a system of coordinates.

or·di·na·tion (ôr′də nā′shən), *n.* **1** act or ceremony of ordaining. **2** fact or condition of being ordained.

ord·nance (ôrd′nəns), *n.* **1** cannon; artillery. **2** military weapons of all kinds. [var. of ordinance]

ore (ôr; ōr), *n.* rock, sand, or dirt containing some metal. [OE *ār* brass]

Oreg., Ore., Oregon.

o·reg·a·no (ə reg′ə nō; –rig–; ôr′ə gä′–), *n.* pungent herb whose leaves are used to flavor food. [< Sp. *orégano* < L *oríganum*]

Or·e·gon (ôr′ə gon; –gən; or′–), *n.* a W state of the United States, on the Pacific coast. —**Or′e·go′ni·an** *adj., n.*

org. **1** organization. **2** organic.

.org, organization, part of domain address on the Internet.

or·gan (ôr′gən), *n.* **1** any part of an animal or plant that is composed of various tissues organized to perform some particular function. An eye, lung, stomach, root, stamen, or pistil is an organ. **2** means of action; instrument. A court is an organ of government. **3** means of giving information or expressing opinions; newspaper or magazine that speaks for and gives the views of a political party or some other organization. **4** Also, **pipe organ.** a musical instrument made of pipes of different lengths, which are sounded by air blown by a bellows and played by keys. **5** any of various other musical instruments: **a** a hand organ. **b** a reed organ. **c** a harmonica. [< L < Gk. *organon* instrument < *ergon* work]

or·gan·dy (ôr′gən di), *n., pl.* **–dies.** a fine, thin, stiff muslin, used for dresses.[< F *organdi* < ? *alter.* of *Organzi,* name of a city in C Asia where this fabric was produced]

or·gan·elle (ôr′gə nel′), *n.* specialized part of a cell of single-celled animals that is similar in function to an organ in higher animals.

or·gan·ic (ôr gan′ik), *adj.* **1** of the bodily organs; vital; affecting the structure of an organ: *an organic disease*. **2** produced by animal or plant activities. Starch is an organic compound. **3** having organs, or an organized physical structure, as plants and animals have; not of the mineral kingdom. **4** made up of related parts, but being a unit; coordinated: *the United States is an organic whole made up of 50 states*. **5** of or containing carbon: *organic compounds*. **6** grown or prepared without use of chemical fertilizers or compounds; natural.

or·gan·i·cal·ly (ôr gan′ik li), *adv.* **1** in an organic manner. **2** in organization. **3** as part of an organization.

organic chemistry, branch of chemistry that deals with compounds of carbon.

or·gan·ism (ôr′gən iz əm), *n.* **1** a living body having organs or an organized

structure; individual animal or plant. **2** a very tiny animal or plant. **3** a whole made up of related parts that work together.

or·gan·ist (ôr′gən ist), *n.* person who plays an organ.

or·gan·i·za·tion (ôr′gən ə zā′shən), *n.* **1** group of persons united for some purpose. Churches, clubs, and political parties are organizations. **2** thing made up of related parts, each having a special duty. **3** act or process of organizing; grouping and arranging parts to form a whole. **4** way in which a thing's parts are arranged to work together. —**or′gan·i·za′tion·al,** *adj.*

or·gan·ize (ôr′gən īz), *v.,* **–ized, –iz·ing. 1** put into working order; get together and arrange. **2** combine in a company, party, labor union, etc. **3** furnish with organs. [< LL, < *organum* ORGAN] —**or′gan·iz′a·ble,** *adj.* —**or′gan·iz·a·bil′i·ty,** *n.* —**or′gan·iz′er,** *n.*

or·gan·za (ôr gan′zə), *n.* sheer fabric, esp. of silk, that resembles organdy. [probably alter. of *Organzi;* see ORGANDY]

or·gasm (ôr′gaz əm), *n.* the series of responses at the climax of copulation. [< NL *orgasmus* < Gk. *orgaein* swell, be excited] —**or·gas′tic,** *adj.*

or·gy (ôr′ji), *n., pl.* **–gies.** a wild, drunken revel.

orgies, secret rites or ceremonies in the worship of certain Greek and Roman gods, esp. the god of wine, celebrated with drinking, wild dancing, and singing. [< L < Gk. *orgia* secret rites] —**or′gi·ac, or′gic,** *adj.* —**or′gi·as′tic,** *adj.* —**or′gi·as′ti·cal·ly,** *adv.*

o·ri·el (ô′ri əl; ō′–), *n.* a bay window projecting from the outer face of a wall. [< OF *oriol* porch]

o·ri·ent (*v.* ô′ri ent, ō′–; *n., adj.* ô′ri ənt, ō′–), *v.* **1 orient oneself,** get in the right relations to what one is confronting, or to new facts, principles, etc. **2** find the direction or compass bearings of. **3** turn toward the east or in any indicated direction: *the building is oriented north and south.* —*n.* **1 the Orient,** the East; countries in Asia. China and Japan are important nations of the Orient. **2** *Poetic.* the east. —*adj.* **1** *Poetic.* eastern. **2** rising. [< L *oriens* rising; with ref. to the rising sun]

O·ri·en·tal (ô′ri en′təl; ō′–), *adj.* **1** Eastern; of the Orient. **2 oriental,** eastern. —*n.* native of the East. Turks, Arabs, Iranians, Indians, and Chinese are Orientals. —**o′ri·en·tal·ly,** *adv.*

O·ri·en·tal·ism, o·ri·en·tal·ism (ô′ri en′təl iz əm; ō′–), *n.* **1** Oriental character or characteristics. **2** knowledge of Oriental languages, literature, etc. —**O′ri·en·tal·ist, o′ri·en·tal·ist,** *n.*

o·ri·en·tate (ô′ri en tāt; ō′–), *v.,* **–tat·ed, –tat·ing.** =orient.

o·ri·en·ta·tion (ô′ri en tā′shən; ō′–), *n.* **1** an orienting or being oriented. **2** a finding out of the actual facts or conditions and putting oneself in the right relation to them.

or·i·fice (ôr′ə fis; or′–), *n.* mouth; opening; hole. [< F < L *orificium* < L *os* mouth + *facere* make]

orig., 1 origin. 2 original; originally.

or·i·ga·mi (or′ə gä′mi), *n.* Japanese art of folding paper to make decorative objects, as birds, flowers, etc. [< Jap.]

or·i·gin (ôr′ə jin; or′–), *n.* 1 thing from which anything comes; source; beginning. 2 parentage; ancestry; birth. [< L *origo* < *oriri* rise]

o·rig·i·nal (ə rij′ə nəl), *adj.* 1 belonging to the beginning; first; earliest: *the original settlers.* 2 new; fresh; novel: *plan an original game for the party.* 3 able to do, make, or think something new; inventive. 4 not copied, imitated, or translated from something else. —*n.* 1 thing from which another is copied, imitated, or translated. 2 language in which a book was first written. 3 an unusual person. 4 origin; source. —**o·rig′i·nal·ly,** *adv.* —**o·rig′i·nal·ness,** *n.*

o·rig·i·nal·i·ty (ə rij′ə nal′ə ti), *n.* 1 ability to do, make, or think up something new. 2 freshness; novelty. 3 a being original.

o·rig·i·nate (ə rij′ə nāt), *v.,* —**nat·ed,** —**nat·ing.** 1 cause to be; invent. 2 come into being; begin; arise. —**o·rig′i·na′tion,** *n.* —**o·rig′i·na′tive,** *adj.* —**o·rig′i·na′tor,** *n.*

o·ri·ole (ô′ri ōl; ō′–), *n.* 1 any of several American birds having yellow- or orange-and-black feathers. 2 any of several European birds having yellow-and-black feathers. [< NL *oriolus,* ult. < L *aurum* gold]

or·mo·lu (ôr′mə lü), *n.* alloy of copper and zinc, used to imitate gold. [< F *or moulu* ground gold]

or·na·ment (*n.* ôr′nə mənt; *v.* ôr′nə ment), *n.* 1 something pretty; something to add beauty: *jewelry and vases are ornaments.* 2 use of ornaments. 3 person or act that adds beauty, grace, or honor. —*v.* add beauty to; make more pleasing or attractive; decorate. [< OF < L, < *ornare* adorn]

or·na·men·tal (ôr′nə men′təl), *adj.* 1 of or having to do with ornament. 2 for ornament; used as an ornament. 3 decorative. —*n.* something ornamental. —**or′na·men′tal·ly,** *adv.*

or·na·men·ta·tion (ôr′nə men tā′shən), *n.* 1 an ornamenting or being ornamented. 2 decorations; ornaments.

or·nate (ôr nāt′), *adj.* much adorned; much ornamented. [< L *ornatus* adorned] —**or·nate′ly,** *adv.* —**or·nate′ness,** *n.*

or·ner·y (ôr′nəri), *adj.* 1 mean in disposition; grumpy: *an ornery child; an ornery mule.* [contraction of *ordinary*] —**or′ner·i·ness,** *n.*

or·ni·thol·o·gy (ôr′nə thol′ə ji), *n.* study of birds. [< NL, < Gk. *ornis* bird + –*logos* treating of] —**or′ni·tho·log′i·cal,** *adj.* —**or′ni·thol′o·gist,** *n.*

or·phan (ôr′fən), *n.* child whose parents are dead; child whose father or mother is dead. —*adj.* 1 of or for such children. 2 without a father or mother or both. —*v.* make an orphan of. [< LL < Gk. *orphanos* bereaved] —**or′phan·hood,** *n.*

or·phan·age (ôr′fən ij), *n.* 1 home for orphans. 2 being an orphan.

or·tho·clase (ôr′thə klās; –klāz), *n.* feldspar having two cleavages at right angles to each other. [< Gk. *orthos* straight + *klasis* cleavage] —**or′tho·clas′tic,** *adj.*

or·tho·don·tia (ôr′thə don′shə; –shi ə), or **or·tho·don·tics** (ôr′thə don′tiks), *n.* branch of dentistry that deals with straightening and adjusting teeth. [< NL, < Gk. *orthos* straight + *odon* tooth] —**or′tho·don′tic,** *adj.* —**or′tho·don′tist,** *n.*

or·tho·dox (ôr′thə doks), *adj.* 1 generally accepted, esp. in religion. 2 having generally accepted views or opinions, esp. in religion. 3 approved by convention; usual; customary. [< LL < Gk., < *orthos* correct + *doxa* opinion] —**or′tho·dox′ly,** *adv.*

Orthodox Church, group of Christian churches in E Europe and W Asia that do not recognize the Pope as the supreme head of the Church. Also, **Greek Orthodox Church, Eastern Church.**

or·tho·dox·y (ôr′thə dok′si), *n., pl.* –**dox·ies.** orthodox practice, esp. in religion; being orthodox.

or·thog·ra·phy (ôr thog′rə fi), *n., pl.* –**phies.** 1 correct spelling; spelling considered as right or wrong. 2 art of spelling; study of spelling. [< L < Gk., *orthos* correct + *graphein* write] —**or·thog′ra·pher,** *n.* —**or′tho·graph′ic, or′tho·graph′i·cal,** *adj.* —**or′tho·graph′i·cal·ly,** *adv.*

or·tho·pe·dics (ôr′thə pē′diks), *n.* branch of surgery that deals with the deformities and diseases of bones and joints, esp. in children. [< Gk. *orthos* correct + *paideia* rearing of children < *pais* child] —**or′tho·pe′dic,** *adj.* —**or′tho·pe′dist,** *n.*

or·thop·ter·ous (ôr thop′tər əs), *adj.* belonging to the order of insects including crickets, grasshoppers, cockroaches, etc. [< Gk. *orthos* straight + *pteron* wing]

–**ory,** *suffix.* 1 ____ing, as in *contradictory.* 2 of or pertaining to ____; of or pertaining to ____ion, as in *advisory, auditory.* 3 characterized by ____ion, as in *adulatory.* 4 serving to ____, as in *expiatory.* 5 tending to ____; inclined to ____, as in *conciliatory.* 6 place for ____; establishment for ____ing, as in *depository.* [< L –*orius,* –*orium*]

o·ryx (ô′riks; ō′–), *n., pl.* **o·ryx·es** or (esp. collectively) **o·ryx.** an African antelope with long, nearly straight horns. [< L < Gk., antelope, pickax; with ref. to pointed horns]

OS, O.S., Old Saxon.

Os, osmium.

O·sage (ō′sāj, ō sāj′), *n.* 1 member of an American Indian tribe that originally lived in the area of the Arkansas and Missouri Rivers. 2 their Siouan language. [< Siouan (Osage) *Wazhazhe* war people (name given to one Osage group)]

Os·car or **os·car** (os′kər), *n.* 1 a small statuette awarded annually by the Academy of Motion Picture Arts and Sciences for the best performances, production, photography, etc., during the year. 2 a prize: *you deserve an oscar doing that.* [supposedly from the remark, "He reminds me of my Uncle Oscar," made by the secretary of the Academy upon seeing one of the statuettes]

os·cil·late (os′ə lāt), *v.,* –**lat·ed,** –**lat·ing.** 1 swing or to cause to swing to and fro like a pendulum; move to and fro between two points. 2 vary between opinions, purposes, etc. 3 cause an electric current to alternate at a high frequency. [< L *oscillatus*] —**os′cil·la′tor,** *n.* —**os′cil·la·to′ry,** *adj.*

os·cil·la·tion (os′ə lā′shən), *n.* 1 fact or process of oscillating. 2 a single swing of a vibrating body. 3 a a single forward and backward surge of a charge of electricity. b a rapid change in electromotive force. c a single complete cycle of an electric wave.

os·cine (os′in; –īn), *n.* any of a large group of perching birds that have well-developed vocal organs and usually sing. [< L *oscines,* pl., < *ob-* to + *canere* sing]

–**ose**[1], *suffix.* 1 full of; having much or many, as in *verbose.* 2 inclined to; fond of, as in *jocose.* 3 like, as in *schistose.* [< L –*osus*]

–**ose**[2], *suffix.* used to form chemical terms, esp. names of sugars and other carbohydrates, as in *fructose, lactose,* and of protein derivatives, as in *proteose.* [< F –*ose* in *glucose*]

o·sier (ō′zhər), *n.* 1 kind of willow tree. 2 a tough, flexible branch or twig of this tree. Osiers are woven into baskets. 3 kind of American dogwood. —*adj.* made of osiers. [< F] —**o′siered,** *adj.*

Os·lo (oz′lō; os′–), *n.* capital of Norway, in the SE part.

os·mi·um (oz′mi əm), *n.* a hard, heavy, grayish metallic element, Os, used for electric-light filaments, etc.

os·mose (oz mōs′; os–), *v.,* –**mosed,** –**mos·ing.** subject to or pass by osmosis.

os·mo·sis (oz mō′sis; os–), *n.* 1 tendency of two fluids that are separated by something porous to go through it and become mixed. 2 diffusion or spreading of fluids through a membrane or partition till they are mixed. 3 *Fig.* absorbing something without effort; effortless learning. [Latinized var. of *osmose* < Gk. *osmos* a thrust] —**os·mot′ic,** *adj.* —**os·mot′i·cal·ly,** *adv.*

os·prey (os′pri), *n., pl.* –**preys.** a large hawk that feeds on fish. [ult. < L *ossifraga* < *os* bone + *frangere* break]

os·si·fy (os′ə fī), v., **–fied, –fy·ing.**
1 change into bone; become bone. **2**
harden like bone; make or become fixed,
hard-hearted, or very conservative.
[< L os bone + facere make] —**os′si·fi·
ca′tion,** n.

os·ten·si·ble (os ten′sə bəl), adj. apparent;
pretended; professed: her ostensible purpose was borrowing sugar, but she really
wanted to see the new furniture. [< F < L
ostendere show < ob– toward + tendere
stretch] —**os·ten′si·bly,** adv.

os·ten·ta·tion (os′ten tā′shən), n. a showing off; display intended to impress others. [< L ostentatio, ult. < ob– toward +
tendere stretch]

os·ten·ta·tious (os′ten tā′shəs), adj. **1**
done for display; intended to attract
notice. **2** showing off; liking to attract
notice. —**os′ten·ta′tious·ly,** adv.
—**os′ten·ta′tious·ness,** n.

os·te·o·ar·thri·tis (os′tē ō är thrī′tis), n.
stiffness and pain in the joints caused
by degeneration of the cartilage, esp. in
older people. —**os′te·o·ar·thrit′ic,** adj.

os·te·o·blast (os′tē ə blast), n. bone cell.

os·te·o·gen·e·sis (os′tē ə jen′ə sis), n. formation or growth of bone. —**os′te·o·ge·
net′ic, os′te·o·gen′ic,** adj.

os·te·ol·o·gy (os′ti ol′ə ji), n. branch of
anatomy that deals with bones. [< Gk.
osteon bone + –LOGY] —**os′te·o·log′i·
cal,** adj. —**os′te·ol′o·gist,** n.

os·te·op·a·thy (os′ti op′ə thi), n. treatment of diseases by manipulating the
bones and muscles. [< Gk. osteon bone
+ –PATHY] —**os′te·o·path, os′te·op′a·
thist,** n. —**os′te·o·path′ic,** adj. —**os′te·
o·path′i·cal·ly,** adv.

os·te·o·po·ro·sis (os′tē ō pə rō′sis), n.
disease in which the bones become
weakened, break easily, and heal
slowly.

os·tra·cism (os′trə siz əm), n. **1** banishment from one's native country. **2** a
being shut out from society, from favor,
from privileges, or from association with
one's fellows.

os·tra·cize (os′trə sīz), v., **–cized, –ciz·
ing. 1** banish. **2** shut out from society,
from favor, from privileges, etc. [< Gk., <
ostrakon tile, potsherd; orig. used in bal-
loting] —**os′tra·ciz′a·ble,** adj. —**os′tra·
ciz′er,** n.

os·trich (ôs′trich; os′–), n. **1** a large
African and Arabian bird that can run
swiftly but cannot fly. **2** Fig. person who
hides from or refuses to face reality. [<
OF < LL avis struthio < L avis bird, LL
struthio < Gk. strouthion < strouthos
ostrich]

O.T., OT, or **OT.,** Old Testament.

oth·er (uth′ər), adj. **1** being the remaining
one of two or more: John is here, but the
other boys are at school. **2** additional or
further: he and one other person. **3** not
the same as one or more already mentioned: come some other day. —pron.
another person or thing: each praises the
other, there are others to be considered.

—adv. otherwise; differently: I can't do
other than to go.

every other, every second; alternate: we
buy milk every other day.

of all others, more than all others: of all
others, I like this book.

the other day (night, etc.), recently. [OE
ōther] —**oth′er·ness,** n.

oth·er·wise (uth′ər wīz′), adv. **1** in a different way; differently: I could not do
otherwise. **2** in other ways: he is noisy,
but otherwise a very nice boy. **3** in a
different condition: he reminded me of
what I should otherwise have forgotten.
—adj. different: it might have been otherwise. —conj. or else; if not: come at once;
otherwise you will be too late.

other world, world to come; life after
death.

oth·er·world·ly (uth′ər wērld′li), adj. of
or devoted to another world, such as
the world of mind or imagination, or
the world to come. —**oth′er·world′li·
ness,** n.

o·tol·o·gy (ō tol′ə ji), n. science of the ear
and its diseases. [< Gk. ous (ot–) ear +
–LOGY] —**o′to·log′i·cal,** adj. —**o·tol′o·
gist,** n.

Ot·ta·wa (ot′ə wə; –wä), n. capital of Canada, in SE Ontario.

ot·ter (ot′ər), n., pl. **–ters** or (esp. collectively) **–ter. 1** any of several mammals
related to the minks and weasels, that
are good swimmers and have webbed
toes with claws. **2** fur of any otter. [OE
oter]

Ot·to·man (ot′ə mən), n., pl. **–mans.**
Turk.

ouch (ouch), interj. exclamation expressing sudden pain.

ought[1] (ôt), auxiliary verb. **1** have a duty;
be obliged: you ought to obey your par-
ents. **2** be right or suitable: it ought to be
allowed. **3** be wise: I ought to go before
it rains. **4** be expected: at your age you
ought to know better. **5** be very likely:
the fastest one ought to win the race. [OE
āhte (inf., āgan owe)]

ought[2] (ôt), n., adv. aught; anything.

ought[3] (ôt), n. nought; zero; 0. [var. of
nought, a nought taken as an ought]

ounce[1] (ouns), n. **1** unit of weight, $\frac{1}{16}$ of
a pound in avoirdupois, and $\frac{1}{12}$ of a
pound in troy weight. **2** measure for
liquids; fluid ounce. 16 ounces = 1 pint.
3 a very small amount. [< OF < L uncia
twelfth part. Doublet of INCH.]

ounce[2] (ouns), n. a grayish wild cat of C
Asia with black spots, somewhat like a
leopard. [< OF once for lonce < L lynx
LYNX]

our (our; är), pron. of us; belonging to
us. [OE ūre]

ours (ourz; ärz), pron. **1** of us; belonging to us: this garden is ours. **2** the one
or ones belonging to us: ours is a large
house.

our·self (our self′; är–), pron. myself.

our·selves (our selvz′; är–), pron. pl. **1** the
emphatic form of **we** or **us**: we did it

ourselves. **2** the reflexive form of **us**: we
hurt ourselves.

–ous, suffix. **1** having; having much; full
of, as in joyous. **2** characterized by, as
in zealous. **3** having the nature of, as
in murderous. **4** of or pertaining to, as
in monogamous. **5** like, as in thunder-
ous. **6** committing or practicing, as in
bigamous. **7** inclined to, as in amorous.
8 implying a larger proportion of the
element indicated by the word than
–ic implies. Stannous means containing
tin in larger proportions than a corresponding stannic compound. [< OF
< L –osus]

oust (oust), v. force out; drive out.
[< AF ouster, (cf. F ôter) < L obstare
block, hinder. See OBSTACLE.]

oust·er (ous′tər), n. **1** an ousting, esp. an
illegal forcing of a person out of his or
her property. **2** one that ousts.

out (out), adv. **1** away; forth: rush out, to
go out at noon. **2** not in or at a place,
position, state, etc.: out of fashion, stand
out. **3** to or at an end: fight it out. **4** from
the usual condition, place, position, etc.:
put the light out. **5** into or in existence:
a rash broke out. **6** aloud; loudly: speak
out. **7** from a store, source, etc.: pick
out a new coat, give out the books. **8**
from a state of satisfaction: feel put out.
9 at a money loss: be out ten dollars.
—adj. **1** not in possession or control:
the Democrats are in, the Republicans
out. **2** not in use, action, etc.: the fire is
out. —n. **1** a being out or putting out.
2 a way out; excuse: an easy out. —v. **1**
go or come out. **2** reveal, esp. something
very personal.

on the outs, quarreling; disagreeing.

out and away, by far.

out and out, thoroughly.

out for, looking for; trying to get.

out of, a without: out of milk. **b** because
of: done out of greed.

out of it, not taking part; withdrawn.

out to, eagerly trying to. [OE ūt]

out–, prefix. **1** outward; forth; away, as
in outburst, outgoing. **2** outside; at a
distance, as in outbuilding, outfield, outlying. **3** more than; longer than, as in
outbid, outlive, outnumber. **4** better than,
as in outdo, outrun, outsail.

out·age (ou′tij), n. interruption of the
provision of electricity, telephone service, etc.

out-and-out (out′ən out′), adj. thorough.

out·bid (out bid′), v., **–bid, –bid** or **–bidden, –bid·ding.** bid higher than (some-
one else).

out·board (out′bôrd′; –bōrd′), adj., adv.
1 outside the hull of a ship or boat. **2**
away from the middle of a ship or boat.

outboard motor, a portable gasoline
motor attached to the back of a boat
or canoe.

out·bound (out′bound′), adj. outward
bound.

out·break (out′brāk′), n. **1** a breaking out.
2 riot; public disturbance.

out·build·ing (out′bil′ding), *n.* shed or building built near a main building.

out·burst (out′bėrst′), *n.* a bursting forth.

out·cast (out′kast′; –käst′), *adj.* **1** cast out from home and friends; homeless; friendless. **2** rejected; discarded. —*n.* an outcast person or animal.

out·class (out klas′; –kläs′), *v.* be of higher class than; be much better than.

out·come (out′kum′), *n.* result; consequence.

out·crop (*n.* out′krop′; *v.* out krop′), *n., v.,* –**cropped, -crop·ping.** —*n.* **1** a coming to the surface of the earth: *the outcrop of a vein of coal.* **2** part that comes to the surface. —*v.* come to the surface; appear.

out·cry (out′krī′), *n., pl.* –**cries. 1** a crying out; sudden cry or scream. **2** a great noise or clamor. **3** auction.

out·date (out dāt′), *v.,* –**dat·ed, -dat·ing.** make old-fashioned. —**out·dat′ed,** *adj.*

out·dis·tance (out dis′tэns), *v.,* –**tanced, -tanc·ing.** leave behind; outstrip.

out·do (out dü′), *v.,* –**did, -done, -do·ing.** do more or better than; surpass. —**out·do′er,** *n.*

out·door (out′dôr′; –dōr′), *adj.* done, used, or living outdoors.

out·doors (out′dôrz′; –dōrz′), —*adv.* out in the open air; not indoors or in the house. —*n.* the open air.

out·er (out′эr), *adj.* farther out; outside. —**out′er·most,** *adj., adv.*

outer ear, external ear on the side of the head, including the passage to the middle ear or tympanum.

outer space, 1 space beyond the pull of the earth′s gravity. **2** space beyond the solar system; interstellar space.

out·field (out′fēld′), *n.* **a** the part of the field beyond the diamond or infield. **b** the three players in the outfield.

out·field·er (out′fēl′dэr), *n.* a player positioned in the outfield.

out·fit (out′fit), *n., v.,* –**fit·ted, -fit·ting.** —*n.* **1** all the articles necessary for any undertaking or purpose: *outfit for a camping trip, bride′s outfit.* **2** group working together. —*v.* furnish with everything necessary for any purpose; equip. —**out′fit′ter,** *n.*

out·flank (out flangk′), *v.* **1** go or extend beyond the flank of (an opposing army, etc.); turn the flank of. **2** circumvent.

out·flow (out′flō′), *n.* **1** a flowing out: *an outflow of sympathy.* **2** that which flows out.

out·fox (out foks′), *v.* outsmart.

out·gen·er·al (out jen′эr эl; –jen′rэl), *v.,* –**aled, -al·ing.** get the better of by superior strategy.

out·go (out′gō′), *n., pl.* –**goes.** what goes out or is paid out; amount that is spent.

out·go·ing (out′gō′ing), *adj.* **1** departing; outward bound: *outgoing flights.* **2** leaving a position or office. **3** friendly; sociable.

out·grow (out grō′), *v.,* –**grew, -grown, -grow·ing. 1** grow too large for. **2** grow

beyond or away from; get rid of by growing older. **3** grow faster or taller than.

out·growth (out′grōth′), *n.* **1** a natural development, product, or result. **2** offshoot; something that has grown out. **3** a growing out or forth.

out·guess (out ges′), *v.* get the better of.

out·house (out′hous′), *n.* **1** a separate building used in connection with a main building. **2** outdoor toilet.

out·ing (out′ing), *n.* **1** a short pleasure trip; walk or airing; holiday spent outdoors away from home. **2** a revealing of something very personal.

out·land·ish (out lan′dish), *adj.* **1** not familiar; queer. **2** looking or sounding as if it belonged to a foreign country. —**out·land′ish·ly,** *adv.* —**out·land′ish·ness,** *n.*

out·last (out last′; –läst′), *v.* last longer than.

out·law (out′lô′), *n.* **1** person outside the protection of the law; exile; outcast. **2** a lawless person; habitual criminal. —*v.* **1** make or declare (a person) an outlaw. **2** make or declare illegal: *outlaw war.* **3** deprive of legal force: *an outlawed debt cannot be collected.* [< Scand. *utlagi*] —**out′law′ry,** *n.*

out·lay (*n.* out′lā′; *v.* out lā′), *n., v.,* –**laid, -lay·ing.** —*n.* **1** a spending. **2** amount spent. —*v.* expend: *outlay money in improvements.*

out·let (out′let), *n.* **1** means or place of letting out or getting out: *outlet of a lake, outlet for one′s energies.* **2** market for a product: *electronics outlet.* **3** box in a wall where an electric plug can be inserted to connect a toaster, lamp, etc., to an electrical system.

out·line (out′līn′), *n., v.,* –**lined, -lin·ing.** —*n.* **1** line that shows the shape of an object; line that bounds a figure. **2** a drawing or style of drawing that gives only outer lines. **3** a general plan; rough draft. —*v.* **1** draw the outer line of. **2** give a plan of; sketch. **in outline, a** with only the outline shown. **b** with only the main features: *a story in outline.* —**out′lin′er,** *n.*

out·live (out liv′), *v.,* –**lived, -liv·ing.** live or last longer than.

out·look (out′lùk′), *n.* **1** what one sees on looking out; view: *a pleasant outlook.* **2** what seems likely to happen; prospect: *the outlook for our picnic is not very good.* **3** way of thinking about things; attitude of mind; point of view: *a gloomy outlook on life.* **4** lookout; tower to watch from.

out·ly·ing (out′lī′ing), *adj.* lying outside the boundary; out-of-the-way; remote.

out·ma·neu·ver (out′mэ nü′vэr), *v.,* –**vered, -ver·ing.** outdo in maneuvering; get the better of by maneuvering.

out·mod·ed (out mōd′id), *adj.* out-of-date.

out·most (out′mōst), *adj.* farthest out.

out·num·ber (out num′bэr), *v.* be more than; exceed in number: *outnumbered three to one.*

out-of-bounds (out′эv boundz′), *adj., adv.* **1** outside the usual or accepted limits: *out-of-bounds behavior.* **2** outside a boundary: *the ball rolled out-of-bounds* (adv.), *an out-of-bounds pass.* (adj.).

out-of-date (out′эv dāt′), *adj.* old-fashioned; not in present use.

out-of-doors (out′эv dôrz′; –dōrz′), *adj.* Also, **out-of-door.** outdoor. —*n., adv.* outdoors.

out-of-the-way (out′эv ŧħэ wā′), *adj.* remote; unfrequented; secluded.

out·pa·tient (out′pā′shэnt), *n.* patient receiving treatment at a hospital but not staying there.

out·play (out plā′), *v.* surpass or defeat in playing.

out·post (out′pōst′), *n.* **1** guard, or small number of soldiers, placed at some distance from an army or camp to prevent surprise. **2** place where they are stationed. **3** anything thought of as an outpost or advance guard.

out·pour (*n.* out′pôr′, –pōr′; *v.* out pôr′, –pōr′), *n.* **1** a pouring out. **2** that which is poured out. —*v.* pour out.

out·pour·ing (out′pôr′ing; –pōr′–), *n.* **1** a pouring out. **2** that which is poured out; outflow. **3** unrestrained expression of emotions, thoughts, etc.

out·put (out′pùt′), *n.* **1** amount produced; product or yield: *the daily output of automobiles.* **2** a putting forth: *a sudden output of effort.*

out·rage (out′rāj′), *n., v.,* –**raged, -rag·ing.** —*n.* act showing no regard for the rights or feelings of others; act of violence; offense; insult. —*v.* **1** offend greatly; do violence to; insult. **2** break (the law, a rule of morality, etc.) openly; treat as nothing at all. [< OF, ult < L *ultra* beyond]

out·ra·geous (out rā′jэs), *adj.* **1** that is or involves an outrage. **2** atrocious. **3** very offensive or insulting. —**out·ra′geous·ly,** *adv.* —**out·ra′geous·ness,** *n.*

out·rank (out rangk′), *v.* rank higher than.

out·reach (*v.* out rēch′; *n.* out′rēch′), *v.* **1** reach beyond. **2** reach out; extend. —*n.* **1** a reaching out. **2** length of reach.

out·ride (out rīd′), *v.,* –**rode, -rid·den, -rid·ing. 1** ride faster or better than, as in a competition. **2** of ships, last through (a storm).

out·rig·ger (out′rig′эr), *n.* **1** framework ending in a float, extending outward from the side of a canoe or boat to prevent upsetting. **2** boat equipped with such a framework or brackets.

out·right (out′rīt′), *adv.* **1** altogether; entirely; not gradually: *sell a thing outright.* **2** openly; without restraint: *I laughed outright.* **3** at once. **4** straight out; straight ahead. —*adj.* **1** complete; thorough: *an outright loss.* **2** downright;

straightforward; direct: *an outright refusal.* —**out′right′ness,** *n.*

out·run (out run′), *v.,* **-ran, -run, -run·ning. 1** run faster than. **2** leave behind; run beyond; pass the limits of.

out·sell (out sel′), *v.,* **-sold, -sell·ing. 1** sell more than. **2** sell for more than.

out·set (out′set′), *n.* a beginning.

out·shine (out shīn′), *v.,* **-shone, -shin·ing. 1** shine more brightly than. **2** be more brilliant or excellent than; surpass.

out·side (*n., adj., adv.* out′sīd′; *prep. also* out′sīd′), *n.* **1** side or surface that is out; outer part. **2** space or position without. —*adj.* **1** on the outside; of or near the outside: *the outside leaves, outside noises.* **2** not belonging to a certain group, set, district, etc. **3** reaching the utmost limit: *an outside estimate.* —*adv.* on or to the outside; outdoors. —*prep.* **1** *U.S.* with the exception (of): *outside of John, none of us liked the play.* **2** out of; beyond the limits of.

at the outside, at the utmost limit; at worst.

outside in, so that what should be outside is inside.

out·sid·er (out′sīd′ər), *n.* person not belonging to a particular group, set, company, party, district, etc.

out·size (out′sīz′), *adj.* larger than the usual size. —*n.* article of clothing, etc., larger than the usual size.

out·skirts (out′skèrts′), *n.pl.* the outer parts or edges of a town, district, etc.; outlying parts.

out·smart (out smärt′), *v. U.S.* outdo in cleverness.

out·spo·ken (out′spō′kən), *adj.* frank; not reserved: *outspoken criticism.* —**out′spo′ken·ly,** *adv.* —**out′spo′ken·ness,** *n.*

out·spread (*adj.* out′spred′; *v.* out spred′), *adj., v.,* **-spread, -spread·ing.** spread out.

out·stand·ing (out stan′ding), *adj.* **1** standing out from others; well-known; important. **2** unpaid. **3** projecting. —**out·stand′ing·ly,** *adv.* —**out·stand′ing·ness,** *n.*

out·stretched (out′strecht′), *adj.* extended.

out·strip (out strip′), *v.,* **-stripped, -strip·ping. 1** go faster than; leave behind in a race. **2** do better than; excel.

out·ward (out′wərd), *adj.* **1** going toward the outside; turned toward the outside: *an outward motion.* **2** outer; plain to see: *to all outward appearances.* —*adv.* Also, **out′wards. 1** toward the outside; away. **2** on the outside. —**out′ward·ness,** *n.*

out·ward·ly (out′wərd li), *adv.* **1** on the outside or outer surface. **2** in appearance or outward manifestation.

out·wear (out wār′), *v.,* **-wore, -worn, -wear·ing. 1** wear longer than. **2** wear out.

out·weigh (out wā′), *v.* **1** weigh more than. **2** exceed in value, importance, influence, etc.: *the advantages outweigh the disadvantages.*

out·wit (out wit′), *v.,* **-wit·ted, -wit·ting.** get the better of by being more intelligent; be too clever for. —**out·wit′ter,** *n.*

out·work (out wėrk′), *v.* surpass in working; work harder or faster than.

ou·zel (ü′zəl), *n.* **1** any of various European thrushes, esp. the blackbird. **2** the water ouzel. [OE *ōsle*]

o·va (ō′və), *n.* pl. of **ovum.**

o·val (ō′vəl), *adj.* **1** egg-shaped. **2** shaped like an ellipse. —*n.* something having an oval shape. [< NL, < L *ovum* egg] —**o′val·ly,** *adv.* —**o′val·ness,** *n.*

o·va·ry (ō′və ri), *n., pl.* **-ries. 1** organ of a female in which eggs are produced. **2** part of a plant enclosing the young seeds. [< NL, < L *ovum* egg] —**o·var′i·an,** *adj.*

o·va·tion (ō vā′shən), *n.* an enthusiastic public welcome; burst of loud clapping or cheering. [< L, < *ovare* rejoice]

ov·en (uv′ən), *n.* **1** space in a stove or near a fireplace, for baking food. **2** a small furnace for heating or drying pottery; kiln. [OE *ofen*]

o·ver (ō′vər), *prep.* **1** above: *the roof over one's head, we have a captain over us.* **2** on; upon: *a blanket lying over a bed.* **3** across: *leap over a wall, lands over the sea.* **4** out and down from: *he fell over the edge of the cliff.* **5** more than; beyond: *it costs over ten dollars.* **6** during: *over many years.* **7** concerning; about: *quarrel over a matter.* —*adv.* **1** above: *curtains hung over the window.* **2** so as to cover the surface: *paint over a wall.* **3** to the other side; across any space: *go over to the store, travel all over.* **4** from one to another: *hand the money over.* **5** down: *she went too near the edge and fell over.* **6** so as to bring the lower side up: *turn over a page.* **7** again; in repetition: *ten times over.* **8** from beginning to end: *read a thing over.* —*adj.* at an end: *the play is over.*

over again, once more.

over against, a opposite to; in front of. **b** so as to bring out a difference.

over and above, besides; in addition to.

over and over, again and again.

over with, finished. [OE *ofer*]

over-, *prefix.* **1** too; too much; too long, etc., as in *overcrowded, overfull, overburden, overpay, oversleep.* **2** extra, as in *oversize, overtime.* **3** over, as in *overflow, overlord, overseas, overthrow.*

Over- is a prefix that combines freely with nouns, verbs, adjectives and adverbs. Some examples are listed below.

o′ver·a·bun′dance
o′ver·anx′ious
o′ver·build′
o′ver·bur′den
o′ver·cau′tious
o′ver·con′fi·dence
o′ver·cook′
o′ver′de·vel′op
o′ver·eat′
o′ver·em′pha·size
o′ver·fa·mil′iar
o′ver·heat′
o′ver·in·dulge′
o′ver·in·vest′
o′ver·man′y
o′ver·nice′
o′ver·pay′
o′ver·rate′
o′ver·rich′
o′ver·sen′si·tive
o′ver·sim·plic′i·ty
o′ver·spend′
o′ver·stim′u·late
o′ver·stress′
o′ver·sure′
o′ver·tech′ni·cal
o′ver·tire′
o′ver·use′
o′ver·val′ue

o·ver·act (ō′vər akt′), *v.* act to excess; overdo in acting; act (a part) in an exaggerated manner.

o·ver·ac·tive (ō′vər ak′tiv), *adj.* too active; active to excess. —**o′ver·ac′tive·ly,** *adv.* —**o′ver·ac·tiv′i·ty,** *n.*

o·ver·a·chieve (ō′vər ə chēv′), *v.* **-chieved, -chiev·ing.** do or accomplish more than is expected.

o·ver·a·chiev·er (ō′vər ə chēv′ər), *n.* person, esp. a student, who does better or accomplishes more than is expected.

o·ver·age[1] (ō′vər āj′), *adj.* past the age of eligibility, greatest usefulness, etc.

o·ver·age[2] (ō′vər ij), *n.* amount or quantity over what is needed; surplus.

o·ver·all (ō′vər ôl′), *adj.* **1** from one end to the other. **2** including everything. —*n.* **overalls,** loose trousers worn over clothes to keep them clean, usually having a part that covers the chest fastened with shoulder straps.

o·ver·arm (ō′vər ärm′), *adj., adv.* =overhand (def. 1).

o·ver·awe (ō′vər ô′), *v.,* **-awed, -aw·ing.** overcome or restrain with awe.

o·ver·bal·ance (ō′vər bal′əns), *v.,* **-anced, -anc·ing. 1** be greater than in weight, importance, value, etc. **2** cause to lose balance.

o·ver·bear (ō′vər bār′), *v.,* **-bore, -borne, -bear·ing. 1** overcome by weight or force; oppress; master. **2** bear down by weight or force; overthrow; upset.

o·ver·bear·ing (ō′vər bār′ing), *adj.* inclined to dictate; forcing others to one's own will; domineering. —**o′ver·bear′ing·ly,** *adv.* —**o′ver·bear′ing·ness,** *n.*

o·ver·bid (*v.* ō′vər bid′; *n.* ō′vər bid′), *v.,* **-bid, -bid** or **-bid·den, -bid·ding,** *n.* —*v.* **1** bid more than the value of (a thing). **2** bid higher than (a person). —*n.* a bid that is higher.

o·ver·blown (ō′vər blōn′), *adj.* **1** blown over; overturned by wind. **2** exaggerated; overdone. **3** too ripe: *overblown apples.*

o·ver·board (ō′vər bôrd′; -bōrd′), *adv.* from a ship into the water.

throw overboard, a throw into the water. **b** get rid of; give up; abandon; discard.

o·ver·cast (ō′vər kast′; –käst′), *adj. v.,* **-cast, -cast·ing.** —*adj.* **1** cloudy; dark; gloomy: *the sky was overcast before the storm.* **2** sewed with overcast stitches. —*v.* **1** cover or be covered with clouds or darkness. **2** sew over and through (the edges of a seam) with long stitches to prevent raveling.

o·ver·charge (*v.* ō′vər chärj′; *n.* ō′vər chärj′), *v.,* **-charged, -charg·ing,** *n.* —*v.* **1** charge too high a price. **2** load too heavily. —*n.* **1** charge that is too great. **2** too heavy or too full a load.

o·ver·coat (ō′vər kōt′), *n.* a heavy coat worn over the regular clothing.

o·ver·come (ō′vər kum′), *v.,* **-came, -come, -com·ing. 1** get the better of; win the victory over; conquer: *overcome an enemy, one's faults.* **2** make weak or helpless: *overcome by weariness.* —**o′ver·com′er,** *n.*

o·ver·do (ō′vər dü′), *v.,* **-did, -done, -do·ing. 1** do too much: *she overdid and became tired.* **2** exaggerate. **3** cook too much. **4** exhaust; tire.

o·ver·dose (*n.* ō′vər dōs′; *v.* ō′vər dōs′), *n., v.,* **-dosed, -dos·ing.** —*n.* too big a dose. —*v.* give too large a dose to.

o·ver·draft (ō′vər draft′; –dräft′), *n.* **1** an overdrawing of an account, as at a bank. **2** amount of the excess.

o·ver·draw (ō′vər drô′), *v.,* **-drew, -drawn, -draw·ing.** draw from (a bank account, allowance, etc.) more than one has available.

o·ver·dress (ō′vər dress′), *v.* **1** put on too much clothing, esp. outer clothing. **2** dress too elaborately or formally.

o·ver·due (ō′vər dü′; –dū′), *adj.* more than due; due some time ago but not yet arrived, paid, etc.: *the train is overdue.*

o·ver·es·ti·mate (*v.* ō′vər es′tə māt′; *n.* ō′vər es′tə mit′), *v.,* **-mat·ed, -mat·ing,** *n.* —*v.* estimate at too high a value, amount, etc. —*n.* estimate that is too high. —**o′ver·es·ti·ma′tion,** *n.*

o·ver·ex·tend (ō′vər ik stend′), *v.* **1** spread something too far. **2** *Fig.* undertake too many projects, responsibilities, etc. **3** take on too many financial burdens.

o·ver·flow (*v.* ō′vər flō′; *n.* ō′vər flō′), *v.,* **-flowed, -flown, -flow·ing,** *n.* —*v.* **1** flow over the bounds; cover; flood: *rivers often overflow in the spring.* **2** flow over the top: *my cup is overflowing.* **3** extend out beyond; be too many for: *the crowd overflowed into the hall.* **4** be very abundant: *overflowing kindness.* —*n.* an overflowing; excess. —**o′ver·flow′ing,** *adj.* —**o′ver·flow′ing·ly,** *adv.*

o·ver·grow (ō′vər grō′), *v.,* **-grew, -grown, -grow·ing. 1** grow over. **2** grow too fast; become too big. —**o′ver·grown′,** *adj.*

o·ver·growth (ō′vər grōth′), *n.* growth overspreading or covering something.

o·ver·hand (ō′vər hand′), *adj., adv.* **1** with the hand raised above the shoulder: *pitch overhand.* **2** in sewing, over and over; with stitches passing successively over an edge. —*v.* sew overhand. —**o′ver·hand′ed,** *adj.*

o·ver·hang (*v.* ō′vər hang′; *n.* ō′vər hang′), *v.,* **-hung, -hang·ing,** *n.* —*v.* **1** hang over; project over. **2** hang over so as to darken, sadden, or threaten. —*n.* **1** something that projects: *the overhang of a roof.* **2** amount of projecting.

o·ver·haul (ō′vər hôl′), *v.* **1** examine thoroughly so as to make any repairs or changes that are needed. **2** gain upon; overtake. —**o′ver·haul′ing,** *n.*

o·ver·head (*adv.* ō′vər hed′; *adj., n.* ō′vər hed′), *adv.* in the sky; on the floor above; on high; above: *the stars overhead.* —*adj.* **1** being, working, or passing overhead: *overhead wires.* **2** applying to one and all; general. —*n.* general expenses or charges, such as rent, lighting, heating, taxes, repairs.

o·ver·hear (ō′vər hir′), *v.,* **-heard, -hear·ing.** hear when one is not meant to hear: *overhear what they said.* —**o′ver·hear′er,** *n.*

o·ver·joy (ō′vər joi′), *v.* make extremely joyful. —**o′ver·joyed′,** *adj.*

o·ver·kill (*n.* ō′vər kil′; *v.* ō′vər kil′), *n.* **1** use of much greater force or destructive power than is necessary. **2** *Fig.* use of any remedy much more severe or greater in its force than is reasonable or warranted. —*v.* kill or destroy with excessive force.

o·ver·lad·en (ō′vər lād′ən), *adj.* overloaded.

o·ver·land (ō′vər land′; –lənd), *adv., adj.* on or through land; by land.

o·ver·lap (*v.* ō′vər lap′; *n.* ō′vər lap′), *v.,* **-lapped, -lap·ping,** *n.* —*v.* lap over; cover and extend beyond: *shingles are laid to overlap each other.* —*n.* **1** a lapping over. **2** amount by which one thing laps over another. **3** part that overlaps.

o·ver·lay (*v.* ō′vər lā′; *n.* ō′vər lā′), *v.,* **-laid, -lay·ing,** *n.* —*v.* **1** lay or place (one thing) over or upon another. **2** cover, overspread, or surmount with something, esp. to finish with a layer or applied decoration of something: *wood overlaid with gold.* —*n.* **1** something laid over something else; layer or decoration; covering. **2** transparent sheet laid over an illustration with additional details on it.

o·ver·lie (ō′vər lī′), *v.,* **-lay, -lain, -ly·ing.** lie over or upon.

o·ver·load (*v.* ō′vər lōd′; *n.* ō′vər lōd′), *v.* load too heavily. —*n.* too great a load.

o·ver·look (ō′vər lùk′), *v.* **1** have a view of from above; be higher than: *this high window overlooks half the city.* **2** fail to see: *here are the letters you overlooked.* **3** pay no attention to; excuse: *overlook bad behavior this time.* **4** manage; look after and direct. —*n.* a high place from which a scenic view, battlefield, or historic site can be seen. —**o′ver·look′er,** *n.*

o·ver·lord (ō′vər lôrd′), *n.* person who is lord over another lord or other lords. —**o′ver·lord′ship,** *n.*

o·ver·ly (ō′vər li), *adv.* overmuch; excessively; too.

o·ver·much (ō′vər much′), *adj., adv., n.* too much.

o·ver·night (*adv.* ō′vər nīt′; *adj., n.* ō′vər nīt′), *adv.* **1** during the night: *stay overnight.* **2** on the night before. —*adj.* **1** done, occurring, etc., during the night: *an overnight stop.* **2** for the night: *an overnight bag.* **3** of or pertaining to the night before. —*n.* the previous evening.

o·ver·pass (*v.* ō′vər pas′, –päs′; *n.* ō′vər pas′, –päs′), *v.,* **-passed** or **-past, -pass·ing,** *n.* —*v.* pass over (a region, bounds, etc.). —*n.* bridge over a road, railroad, canal, etc.

o·ver·play (ō′vər plā′), *v.* **1** play (a part, etc.) in an exaggerated manner. **2** play better than; surpass; defeat.

o·ver·pow·er (ō′vər pou′ər), *v.* **1** overcome; master; overwhelm: *overpower one's enemies.* **2** be so much greater that nothing else is felt: *sudden anger overpowered every other feeling.* —**o′ver·pow′er·ing,** *adj.* —**o′ver·pow′er·ing·ly,** *adv.*

o·ver·pro·duc·tion (ō′vər prə duk′shən), *n.* production of more than is needed or can be sold.

o·ver·reach (ō′vər rēch′), *v.* **1** reach over or beyond. **2** reach too far. **3** cheat. **overreach oneself, a** fail or miss by trying for too much. **b** fail by being too crafty or tricky. —**o′ver·reach′er,** *n.*

o·ver·ride (ō′vər rīd′), *v.,* **-rode, -rid·den, -rid·ing. 1** prevail over: *a new rule overriding all previous ones.* **2** act in spite of: *override objections.* **3** ride over; trample on.

o·ver·rule (ō′vər rül′), *v.,* **-ruled, -rul·ing. 1** rule or decide against (a plea, argument, objection, etc.); set aside. **2** prevail over; be stronger than. —**o′ver·rul′ing,** *adj.* —**o′ver·rul′ing·ly,** *adv.*

o·ver·run (*v.* ō′vər run′; *n.* ō′vər run′), *v.,* **-ran, -run, -run·ning,** *n.* —*v.* **1** spread over: *weeds overran the garden.* **2** run or go beyond; exceed: *the speaker overran the time set for him.* —*n.* **1** an overrunning. **2** amount overrunning or carried over. —**o′ver·run′ner,** *n.*

o·ver·seas (*adv.* ō′vər sēz′; *adj.* ō′vər sēz′), *adv.* across the sea; beyond the sea. —*adj.* **1** done, used, or serving overseas. **2** of countries across the sea; foreign.

o·ver·see (ō′vər sē′), *v.,* **-saw, -seen, -see·ing.** look after and direct (work or workers); superintend; manage.

o·ver·se·er (ō′vər sē′ər), *n.* one who oversees, superintends, or looks after the work of others. —**o′ver·se′er·ship,** *n.*

o·ver·shad·ow (ō′vər shad′ō), *v.* **1** be more important than. **2** cast a shadow over.

o·ver·shoe (ō′vər shü′), *n.* a rubber shoe or a felt shoe with a rubber sole worn over another shoe to keep the foot dry and warm.

o·ver·shoot (ō′vər shüt′), *v.,* **-shot, -shoot·ing. 1** shoot over, higher than, or beyond. **2** go over, higher than, or beyond. **3** go too far.

o·ver·shot (*adj.* ō´vər shot´; *v.* ō´vər shot´), *adj.* **1** having the upper jaw projecting beyond the lower. **2** driven by water flowing over from above. —*v.* pt. and pp. of **overshoot.**

o·ver·sight (ō´vər sīt´), *n.* **1** failure to notice or think of something. **2** watchful care.

o·ver·size (ō´vər sīz´), *adj.* too big. —*n.* size larger than the proper or usual size.

o·ver·sleep (ō´vər slēp´), *v.,* **–slept, –sleeping.** sleep too long, or later than a certain time.

o·ver·state (ō´vər stāt´), *v.,* **–stat·ed, –stat·ing.** state too strongly; exaggerate. —**o´ver·state´ment,** *n.*

o·ver·stay (ō´vər stā´), *v.* **1** stay longer than appropriate or expected. **2** wait too long to do or carry out something, as a sale.

o·ver·step (ō´vər step´), *v.,* **–stepped, –step·ping.** **1** go beyond; exceed: *the government overstepped the bounds of its proper functions.* **2** *Fig.* disregard: *overstep the bounds of courtesy.*

o·ver·stock (*v.* ō´vər stok´; *n.* ō´vər stok´), *v.* supply with more than is needed. —*n.* too great a stock or supply.

o·ver·sup·ply (*v.* ō´vər sə plī´; *n.* ō´vər sə plī´), *v.,* **–plied, –ply·ing,** *n., pl.* **–plies.** —*v.* supply in excess. —*n.* an excessive supply.

o·vert (ō´vėrt; ō vėrt´), *adj.* open; evident; not hidden; public: *hitting someone is an overt act.* [< OF, pp. of *ovrir* open < L *aperire*] —**o´vert·ly,** *adv.* —**o´vert·ness,** *n.*

o·ver·take (ō´vər tāk´), *v.,* **–took, –tak·en, –tak·ing.** **1** come up with: *the blue car overtook ours.* **2** come upon suddenly: *a storm overtook the children.*

o·ver·tax (ō´vər taks´), *v.* **1** tax too heavily. **2** put too heavy a burden on. —**o´ver·tax·a´tion,** *n.*

o·ver-the-count·er (ō´vər t͡hə koun´tər), *adj.* generally available for purchase: *over-the-counter drugs.*

o·ver·throw (*v.* ō´vər thrō´; *n.* ō´vər thrō´), *v.,* **–threw, –thrown, –throw·ing,** *n.* —*v.* **1** take away the power of; defeat: *overthrow a king.* **2** put an end to; destroy: *overthrow slavery.* —*n.* a defeat; upset. —**o´ver·throw´er,** *n.*

o·ver·time (ō´vər tīm´), *n.* extra time; time beyond the regular hours. —*adv., adj.* beyond the regular hours.

o·ver·tone (ō´vər tōn´), *n.* a fainter and higher tone heard along with the main or fundamental tone; harmonic.

o·ver·ture (ō´vər chər), *n.* **1** proposal; offer: *the enemy is making overtures for peace.* **2** composition played by the orchestra as an introduction to an opera, oratorio, etc. [< OF < L *apertura* opening. Doublet of APERTURE.]

o·ver·turn (ō´vər tėrn´), *v.* **1** turn upside down. **2** upset; fall down; fall over. **3** overthrow; destroy the power of. —**o´ver·turn´er,** *n.*

o·ver·ween·ing (ō´vər wēn´ing), *adj.* thinking too much of oneself; conceited;

self-confident; presumptuous. [ppr. of *overween* < OVER– + *ween* expect (OE *wēnan*)] —**o´ver·ween´ing·ly,** *adv.* —**o´ver·ween´ing·ness,** *n.*

o·ver·weight (*adj.* ō´vər wāt´; *n.* ō´vər wāt´), *adj.* having too much weight: *a boy overweight for his age.* —*n.* **1** too much weight. **2** extra weight.

o·ver·whelm (ō´vər hwelm´), *v.* **1** overcome completely; crush: *overwhelm with grief.* **2** cover completely as a flood would [< OVER– + *whelm* roll, submerge (ME)] —**o´ver·whelm´ing,** *adj.* —**o´ver·whelm´ing·ly,** *adv.*

o·ver·work (*n.* ō´vər wėrk´; *v.* ō´vər wėrk´), *n., v.,* **–worked** or **–wrought, –work·ing.** —*n.* too much or too hard work. —*v.* **1** work too hard or too long. **2** spend too much work upon; elaborate to excess.

o·ver·wrought (ō´vər rôt´), *adj.* **1** wearied; excited: *overwrought nerves.* **2** too elaborate. **3** overworked.

o·vi·duct (ō´və dukt´), *n.* tube through which the ovum or egg passes from the ovary. [< NL, < L *ovum* egg + *ductus* DUCT]

o·vi·form (ō´və fôrm´), *adj.* egg-shaped. [< L *ovum* egg + –FORM]

o·vip·a·rous (ō vip´ə rəs), *adj.* producing eggs that are hatched after leaving the body. [< L, < *ovum* egg + *parere* bring forth]

o·vi·pos·i·tor (ō´və poz´ə tər), *n.* in certain insects, an organ at the end of the abdomen, by which eggs are deposited. [< L *ovum* egg + *positor* placer < *ponere* to place]

o·void (ō´void), *adj.* egg-shaped.

o·vu·late (ō´vyə lāt), *v.,* **–lat·ed, –lat·ing.** **1** produce ova or oocytes. **2** release ova or oocytes from the ovary. —**o´vu·la´tion,** *n.*

o·vule (ō´vūl), *n.* **1** a little ovum. **2** part of a plant that develops into a seed. [< NL *ovulum,* dim. of L *ovum* egg] —**o´vu·lar,** *adj.*

o·vum (ō´vəm), *n., pl.* **ova** (ō´və). a female germ cell; egg. [< L, egg]

owe (ō), *v.,* **owed, ow·ing.** **1** have to pay; be in debt for: *owe interest on a mortgage.* **2** be obliged or indebted for: *we owe a great deal to our parents.* [OE *āgan*]

ow·ing (ō´ing), *adj.* **1** that owes: *a man owing money.* **2** due; owed: *pay what is owing.*

owing to, on account of; because of; due to; as a result of: *owing to the rain we did not go outdoors.*

owl (oul), *n.* bird with a big head, big eyes, and a short, hooked beak. Owls hunt mice, small birds, etc. at night. [OE *ūle*] —**owl´ish,** *adj.* —**owl´ish·ly,** *adv.* —**owl´ish·ness,** *n.* —**owl´like´,** *adj.*

owl·et (oul´it), *n.* **1** a young owl. **2** a small owl.

own (ōn), *adj.* of oneself or itself; belonging to oneself or itself: *we have our own troubles, the house is her own.* —*n.* the one or ones belonging to oneself or

itself: *come into one's own.* —*v.* **1** possess: *he owns much land.* **2** acknowledge; admit; confess: *he owned his guilt.*

come into one's own, gain recognition that one deserves.

hold one's own, a resist pressure to change one's position, opinion, etc. **b** resist succumbing to illness.

of one's own, belonging to oneself.

on one's own, on one's own account, responsibility, resources, etc. [OE *āgen,* orig. pp. of *āgan* owe] —**own´er,** *n.* —**own´er·less,** *adj.* —**own´er·ship,** *n.*

ox (oks), *n., pl.* **ox·en. 1** the full-grown male of cattle, that has been castrated and is used as a draft animal or for beef. **2** any of a group of mammals with horns and cloven hoofs, including domestic cattle, buffaloes, bison, etc. [OE *oxa*] —**ox´like´,** *adj.*

ox·blood (oks´blud´), *n.* dark red color. —*adj.* of this color: *oxblood leather.*

ox·bow (oks´bō´), *n.* **1** *U.S.* a U-shaped piece of wood placed under and around the neck of an ox, with the upper ends inserted in the bar of the yoke. **2** a U-shaped bend in a river.

ox·cart (oks´kärt´), *n.* cart drawn by oxen.

ox·en (ok´sən), *n.* pl. of **ox.**

ox·eye (oks´ī´), *n.* **1** the common American daisy. **2** any of several plants like it.

ox·ford (oks´fərd), *n.* **1** kind of low shoe. **2** Also, **Oxford gray.** a very dark gray. [after *Oxford,* the city]

Ox·ford (oks´fərd), *n.* very old English university located in Oxford. —**Ox·on´i·an,** *adj., n.*

ox·i·da·tion (ok´sə dā´shən), *n.* **1** an oxidizing. **2** a being oxidized.

ox·ide (ok´sīd; –sid), **ox·id** (–sid), *n.* compound of oxygen with another element or radical. [< F, < *ox(ygène)* oxygen + *(ac)ide* acid]

ox·i·dize (ok´sə dīz), *v.,* **–dized, –diz·ing.** **1** combine with oxygen. When a substance burns or rusts, it is oxidized. **2** rust. **3** lose or cause to lose hydrogen. —**ox´i·diz´a·ble,** *adj.* —**ox´i·di·za´tion,** *n.* —**ox´i·diz´er,** *n.*

ox·y (ok´sē), *adj.* of or like an ox; large; powerful; muscular.

ox·y·gen (ok´sə jən), *n.* gas without color or odor that forms about one fifth of the air. Animals and plants cannot live, and fire will not burn, without oxygen. Oxygen is a chemical element, O, present in a combined form in many substances. [< F, intended as "acidifying (principle)" < Gk. *oxys* sharp + –*genes* born, ult. < *gignesthai* be born]

ox·y·gen·ate (ok´sə jən āt), **ox·y·gen·ize** (–īz), *v.* **–at·ed, –at·ing; –ized, –iz·ing.** **1** treat or combine with oxygen. **2** =oxidize. —**ox´y·gen·a´tion,** *n.*

oxygen mask, device worn over the nose and mouth through which supplementary oxygen is supplied from an attached container or other source. Oxygen masks are used by pilots and crews, astronauts, people who are ill, etc.

ox·y·mo·ron (ok′si môr′on; –mōr′–), *n.* expression that uses words with contradictory meanings or that suggest opposites, as in *constant change, calm winds, open secret,* or *with all deliberate speed.* [< Gk. *oxýmōron* pointedly foolish < *oxýs* sharp + *mōrós* stupid]

o·yez, o·yes (ō′yes; ō′yez), *interj. n.* hear! attend! a cry uttered, by a public or court crier to command silence and attention before a proclamation, etc., is made. [< AF hear ye! < *oyer* hear, var. of *oïr* < L *audire*]

oys·ter (ois′tər), *n.* kind of mollusk much used as food, having a rough, irregular shell in two halves. Oysters are found in shallow water along seacoasts. Some kinds yield pearls. [< OF < L < Gk. *ostreon*]

oyster bed, place where oysters are cultivated or breed.

oz., *pl.* **ozs.** ounce.

o·zone (ō′zōn), *n.* form of oxygen, O_3, with a peculiar odor, produced by electricity and present in the air, esp. after a thunderstorm. [< F, < Gk. *ozein* smell + F *–one,* chem. suffix] —**o′zo·nous,** *adj.*

ozone layer =ozonosphere.

o·zon·o·sphere (ō zon′ə sfir), *n.* region of concentrated ozone in the earth's upper atmosphere, which shields the earth from radiation.

P, p (pē), *n.*, *pl.* **P's; p's.** the 16th letter of the alphabet.
P, 1 phosphorus. **2** pressure.
p., 1 page. **2** participle. **3** past. **4** per. **5** pint.

pa (pä), *n.* papa; father.

Pa, protactinium.

PA, (*zip code*) Pennsylvania.

Pa., Pennsylvania.

P.A. physician's assistant.

p.a., participial adjective.

pab·lum (pab′ləm), *n.* **1** food; sustenance. **2** *Fig.* anything that energizes or sustains. **3** *Fig.* something, esp. an idea or opinion, whose force is lost through oversimplification or other modifications; pap. [< *Pablum,* trademark for a baby's cereal, infl. by *pabulum* < L]

pab·u·lum (pab′yə ləm), *n.* =pablum. [< L, fodder]

PAC, political action committee, group formed by a politician to gather financial support for an election.

pace (pās), *n.*, *v.*, **paced, pac·ing.** —*n.* **1** rate; speed: *a fast pace in walking.* **2** a step. **3** length of a step in walking; about 2½ feet. **4** way of stepping. The walk, trot, and canter are some of the paces of the horse. —*v.* **1 a** set the pace for. **b** *Fig.* be an example for others. **2** walk over with regular steps: *pace the floor.* **3** measure by paces. **4** of horses, move at a pace.
go through the or **one's paces, a** do something to show how well one can do it. **b** do something well, but automatically.
keep pace with, a stay even with, as in walking, jogging, etc. **b** *Fig.* keep up with: *wages did not keep pace with inflation.*
put one through his or **her paces,** try one out; find out what one can do. [< OF < L *passus* step] —**pac′er,** *n.*

pace·mak·er (pās′māk′ər), *n.* **1** person, animal or thing that sets the pace. **2** electronic device implanted near the heart to regulate the heartbeat. —**pace′-mak′ing,** *n.*

pace·set·ter (pās′set′ər), *n.* **1** person, animal or thing that sets the pace. **2** *Fig.* someone or something that is ahead in design, taste, etc., or sets the pace for all others. —**pace′-set′ting,** *adj.*

pach·y·derm (pak′ə dèrm), *n.* a thick-skinned mammal with hoofs, such as the elephant, hippopotamus, and rhinoceros. [< F < Gk., < *pachys* thick + *derma* skin]

pach·y·san·dra (pak′ə san′drə), *n.* low, spreading usually evergreen plant used as ground cover. [< NL]

Pa·cif·ic (pə sif′ik), *n.* the great ocean W of North and South America, extending to Asia and Australia. —*adj.* of, on, or near the Pacific Ocean.

pa·cif·ic (pə sif′ik), *adj.* **1** tending to make peace; making peace. **2** loving peace; not warlike. **3** peaceful; calm; quiet. [< L *pacificus,* ult. < *pax* peace + *facere* make] —**pa·cif′i·cal·ly,** *adv.*

pac·i·fi·ca·tion (pas′ə fə kā′shən), *n.* **1** act of making peaceful or condition of being peaceful. **2** elimination of a rebellion or insurgency.

pac·i·fi·er (pas′ə fī′ər), *n.* **1** person or thing that pacifies. **2** a rubber nipple or ring given to a baby to suck.

pac·i·fism (pas′ə fiz əm), *n.* principle or policy of establishing and maintaining universal peace by settlement of all differences between nations by peaceful means. —**pac′i·fist,** *n.* —**pac′i·fis′tic,** *adj.* —**pac′i·fis′ti·cal·ly,** *adv.*

pac·i·fy (pas′ə fī), *v.*, **-fied, -fy·ing. 1** make calm; quiet down: *pacify a screaming baby.* **2** establish peace throughout: *soldiers were sent to pacify the country.* [< L *pacificare.* See PACIFIC.] —**pac′i·fi′a·ble,** *adj.* —**pac′i·fy′ing·ly,** *adv.*

pack[1] (pak), *n.* **1** bundle of things wrapped up or tied together for carrying. **2** set; lot; a number together: *a pack of thieves, a pack of lies.* **3** a number of animals hunting together; a number of dogs kept together for hunting. **4** a complete set of playing cards, usually 52. **5** floating pieces of ice pushed together. **6** a paste put on the face as a cosmetic treatment. **7** a wrapping of the body in cloths (hot or cold, wet or dry) as a medical treatment. —*v.* **1** put together in a bundle, box, bale, etc.: *pack your clothes in this bag.* **2** fill with things; put one's things into: *pack your trunk.* **3** press or crowd closely together: *a hundred men were packed into one small room.* **4** put into a container to be sold or stored: *meat and fish are often packed in cans.* **5** make tight with something that water, steam, air, etc., cannot leak through.
pack in, cram: *pack in as much sightseeing as possible into one weekend.*
pack it in, stop doing something; quit.
pack off, a send away. **b** go away suddenly.
send packing, send away in a hurry. [< MLG *packe*] —**pack′er,** *n.*

pack[2] (pak), *v.* arrange unfairly. To pack a jury is to fill it unfairly with those who will favor one side.

pack·age (pak′ij), *n.*, *v.*, **-aged, -ag·ing.** —*n.* **1** bundle of things packed or wrapped together; box with things packed in it; parcel. **2** group of things, as services, goods, terms of negotiation, etc. offered together. —*v.* put in a package.

package store, store that sells alcoholic beverages packaged in bottles or containers.

pack animal, animal used for carrying loads.

pack·et (pak′it), *n.* a small package: *a packet of tacks.*

pack horse, horse used to carry packs of goods.

pack·ing (pak′ing), *n.* **1** material used to pack and protect items in shipping. **2** material used to pack valves, pipe joints, etc., to make them watertight. **3** act, process, or work of one that packs.

packing house, place where meat is prepared and packed to be sold.

pack rat, 1 large, furry-tailed rat of North America that stows food, bits of cloth, etc., in its nest. **2** *Fig.* person who hoards or saves, esp. things not needed.

pact (pakt), *n.* agreement; compact [< L *pactum,* orig., agreed]

pad[1] (pad), *n.*, *v.*, **pad·ded, pad·ding.** —*n.* **1** a cushionlike mass of soft material used for comfort, protection, or stuffing. **2** one of the cushionlike parts on the bottom side of the feet of dogs, foxes, and some other animals. **3** foot of a dog, fox, etc. **4** the large floating leaf of the water lily. **5** number of sheets of paper fastened along an edge or edges; tablet. **6** launching pad. —*v.* **1** fill with something soft; stuff: *a padded suit for football.* **2** make (a written paper or speech) longer by using unnecessary words just to fill space. —**pad′der,** *n.*

pad[2] (pad), *v.*, **pad·ded, pad·ding,** *n.* —*v.* **1** walk; tramp; trudge. **2** walk or trot softly. —*n.* a dull sound, as of footsteps on the ground. [< Du. or LG; akin to PATH]

pad·ding (pad′ing), *n.* **1** material used to pad with, such as hair, cotton, or straw. **2** unnecessary words used just to make a speech or a written paper longer.

pad·dle[1] (pad′əl), *n.*, *v.*, **-dled, -dling.** —*n.* **1** a short oar with a broad blade at one end or both ends, used without resting it against the boat. **2** act of paddling; a turn at the paddle. —*v.* **1** move (a boat or canoe) with a paddle or paddles. **2** row gently. **3** beat or strike with a paddle; spank. —**pad′dler,** *n.*

pad·dle[2] (pad′əl), *v.*, **-dled, -dling. 1** move the hands or feet about in water. **2** walk unevenly or unsteadily, like a toddler. —**pad′dler,** *n.*

pad·dle·fish (pad′əl fish′), *n.*, *pl.* **-fish·es** or (*esp. collectively*) **-fish.** a large fish whose long, flat snout looks somewhat like a canoe paddle.

paddle wheel, wheel with paddles around it for propelling a ship on water.

pad·dock (pad′ək), *n.* **1** a small field near a stable or house, used as a pasture. **2** pen for horses at a race track. [var. of *parrock,* OE *pearroc* enclosed space, fence < Med.L *parricus* enclosure. Doublet of PARK.]

pad·dy (pad′i), *n.*, *pl.* **pad·dies. 1** rice. **2** rice in the husk, uncut or gathered. **3** field of rice. [< Malay *padi*]

pad·lock (pad′lok′), *n.* lock that can be put on and removed. It hangs by a curved bar, hinged at one end and snapped shut at the other. —*v.* fasten with a padlock.

pa·dre (pä′drā), *n.* father (used esp. with reference to a priest). [< Ital., Sp., Pg. < L *pater* father]

pae·an (pē′ən), *n.* song of praise, joy, or triumph. [< L < Gk. *paian* hymn to Apollo (called *Paian*)]

pa·gan (pā′gən), *n.* **1** person who is not a Christian, Jew, or Muslim; heathen. The ancient Greeks and Romans were pagans. **2** person who has no religion. —*adj.* **1** having to do with pagans; not Christian, Jewish, or Muslim. **2** not religious. [< L *paganus*, lit., a rustic, later civilian, heathen < *pagus* village] —**pa′gan·dom**, *n.* —**pa′gan·ish**, *adj.* —**pa′gan·ism**, *n.*

pa·gan·ize (pā′gən īz), *v.,* **-ized, -iz·ing.** make or become pagan. —**pa′gan·i·za′tion**, *n.*

page[1] (pāj), *n., v.,* **paged, pag·ing.** —*n.* **1** one side of a leaf or sheet of paper. **2** print or writing on one side of a leaf. **3** a record: *the pages of history, the settling of the West is a page in our history.* —*v.* number the pages of. [< F < L *pagina* < *pangere* fasten]

page[2] (pāj), *n., v.,* **paged, pag·ing.** —*n.* **1** a boy servant; errand boy. **2** youth who attends a person of rank. **3** youth preparing to be a knight. —*v.* try to find (a person) at a hotel, club, etc., by having his or her name called out, as by a loudspeaker, etc. [< OF < Ital., ult. < Gk. *paidion* lad, dim. of *pais* child]

pag·eant (paj′ənt), *n.* **1** an elaborate spectacle; procession in costume; pomp; display: *the coronation of the new king was a splendid pageant.* **2** a public entertainment that represents scenes from history, legend, or the like, esp. a drama or series of scenes. **3** empty show, not reality.

pag·eant·ry (paj′ənt ri), *n., pl.* **-ries. 1** a splendid show; gorgeous display; pomp. **2** mere show; empty display.

pag·er (paj′ər) *n.* someone or something that pages, esp. an electronic device.

pag·i·na·tion (paj′ə nā′shən), *n.* **1** act of numbering the pages of books, etc. **2** the figures with which pages are numbered.

pa·go·da (pə gō′də), *n.* temple with many stories forming a tower. Pagodas are built in India, China, and Japan. [< Pg. *pagode* < Tamil *pagavadi*]

paid (pād), *adj.* **1** receiving money; hired. **2** no longer owed; settled. **3** cashed. —*v.* pt. and pp. of **pay.**

pail (pāl), *n.* **1** a round container for carrying liquids, etc.; bucket. **2** amount a pail holds. [OE *pægel*; ? < Med.L *pagella* a measure]

pail·ful (pāl′fùl), *n., pl.* **-fuls.** amount that fills a pail.

pain (pān), *n.* a feeling of being hurt; suffering. —*v.* cause to suffer; give pain; hurt.

on or **under pain of,** with the punishment or penalty of, unless a certain thing is done.

pains, trouble to do something; effort; care. [< OF < L *poena* penalty < Gk. *poine*] —**pain′less**, *adj.* —**pain′less·ly**, *adv.* —**pain′less·ness**, *n.*

pained (pānd), *adj.* **1** saddened; hurt; distressed. **2** showing or expressing pain, misery, etc.

pain·ful (pān′fəl), *adj.* **1** causing pain; unpleasant; hurting. **2** difficult. —**pain′ful·ly**, *adv.* —**pain′ful·ness**, *n.*

pains·tak·ing (pānz′tāk′ing), *adj.* very careful. —**pains′tak′ing·ly**, *adv.*

paint (pānt), *n.* **1** substance that can be put on a surface to make a layer or film of white, black, or colored material. **2** coloring matter put on the face or body; rouge. [< v.] —*v.* **1** cover or decorate with paint: *paint a house.* **2** use paint. **3** represent (an object, etc.) in colors. **4** make pictures. **5** picture vividly in words. [< OF < L *pingere*] —**paint′a·ble**, *adj.* —**paint′ed**, *adj.* —**paint′y**, *adj.*

paint·brush (pānt′brush′), *n.* brush for putting on paint.

paint·er[1] (pān′tər), *n.* **1** person who paints pictures; artist. **2** person who paints houses, woodwork, etc. [< OF, ult. < L *pictor* < *pingere* to paint]

paint·er[2] (pān′tər), *n.* a rope, usually fastened to the bow of a boat, for tying it to a ship, pier, etc. [? var. of *panter* net < OF < L < Gk. *panthera* net]

paint·er[3] (pān′tər), *n.* the American panther or cougar. [var. of *panther*]

paint·ing (pān′ting), *n.* **1** something painted; picture. **2** act of one that paints. **3** art of representation, decoration, and creating beauty with paints.

pair (pār), *n., pl.* **pairs** or (*sometimes after a numeral*) **pair,** *v.* —*n.* **1** a set of two; two of a kind: *a pair of gloves, pair of sixes.* **2** a single thing of two parts that cannot be used separately: *a pair of scissors.* **3** two people who are a couple. —*v.* **1** arrange in a pair or pairs. **2** join in love and marriage.

pair off, separate into a pair or pairs. [< F < L *paria* (neut. pl.) equals]

pais·ley (pāz′li), *n., pl.* **-leys,** *adj.* —*n.* a soft woolen cloth with a very elaborate and colorful pattern. —*adj.* made of paisley: *a paisley shawl.* [after *Paisley,* Scotland]

pa·ja·mas (pə jä′məz; –jam′əz), *n.pl.* garment to sleep in, etc., consisting of a loose-fitting jacket or top and pants. [< Hind. < Pers., < *pāe* leg + *jāmah* garment]

Pak·i·stan (pak′ə stan; pä′kə stän), *n.* republic in S Asia. —**Pak·i′stan′i**, *n.*

pal (pal), *n., v.,* **palled, pal·ling.** —*n.* comrade; chum; accomplice. —*v.* associate as pals. [< Gypsy, brother]

pal·ace (pal′is), *n.* **1** a grand house for a king, queen, bishop, or some other exalted personage to live in. **2** a very fine house or building. [< OF < L *palatium* Palatine Hill, location of emperor's palace]

pal·a·din (pal′ə din), *n.* **1** one of the twelve knights in attendance on Charlemagne. **2** a knightly defender. [< F < Ital. *paladino.* See PALATINE.]

pal·an·quin (pal′ən kēn′), *n.* a covered couch enclosed by heavy curtains or shutters, and carried by poles resting on men's shoulders; litter. [< Pg. *palanquim.* Cf. Skt. *palyanka* couch.]

pal·at·a·ble (pal′it ə bəl), *adj.* agreeable to the taste; pleasing. —**pal′at·a·bil′i·ty, pal′at·a·ble·ness**, *n.* —**pal′at·a·bly**, *adv.*

pal·a·tal (pal′ə təl), *adj.* of or having to do with the palate.

pal·ate (pal′it), *n.* **1** roof of the mouth. The bony part in front is the **hard palate,** and the fleshy part in back is the **soft palate. 2** sense of taste: *the new flavor pleased his palate.* [< L *palatum*]

pa·la·tial (pə lā′shəl), *adj.* of or like a palace; fit for a palace; magnificent. —**pa·la′tial·ly**, *adv.*

pal·a·tine (pal′ə tīn; –tin), *adj.* having royal rights in one's own territory: *a count palatine.* [< L *palatinus* of the palatium or Palatine Hill, palace]

pa·lav·er (pə lav′ər; –lä′vər), *n.* **1** talk without substance. **2** smooth, persuading talk; fluent talk; flattery. —*v.* **1** talk. **2** talk flatteringly. [< Pg. < L *parabola* story, parable. Doublet of PARABLE, PAROLE.]

pale[1] (pāl), *adj.,* **pal·er, pal·est,** *v.,* **paled, pal·ing.** —*adj.* **1** without much color; whitish. **2** not bright; dim. —*v.* turn pale. [< OF < L *pallidus* < *pallere* be pale. Doublet of PALLID.] —**pale′ly**, *adv.* —**pale′ness**, *n.* —**pal′ish**, *adj.*

pale[2] (pāl), *n.* **1** a long, narrow board, pointed at the top, used for fences. **2** boundary: *outside the pale of civilized society.* [< OF < L *palus.* Doublet of POLE[1].]

paleo-, *combining form.* **1** early or earliest; prehistoric, as in *paleography, Paleozoic.* **2** reactionary, as in *paleoconservative.* [< Gk. *palaio-* < *palaios* ancient]

pa·le·o·bi·ol·o·gy (pā′li ō bī ol′ə ji), *n.* branch of paleontology dealing with fossil plants and animals. —**pa′le·o·bi·ol′o·gist**, *n.*

pa·le·o·con·serv·a·tive (pā′li ō kən sėr′və tiv), *n.* person who has extremely reactionary views. —*adj.* of or having to do with extremely reactionary views, policies, etc. —**pa′le·o·con·serv′a·tism**, *n.*

pa·le·o·e·col·o·gy (pā′li ō ē kol′ə ji), *n.,* study of the relation of living things to their environment in prehistoric times. —**pa′le·o·ec·o·log′i·cal**, *adj.* —**pa′le·o·e·col′o·gist**, *n.*

pa·le·og·ra·phy (pā′li og′rə fi), *n.* **1** ancient writing or ancient forms of writing. **2** study of ancient writings to determine the dates, origins, meaning, etc. [< *paleo-* + *-graphy* writing] —**pa′le·og′ra·pher**, *n.* —**pa′le·o·graph′ic, pa′le·o·graph′i·cal**, *adj.*

pa·le·o·lith·ic (pā′li ə lith′ik), *adj.* of or having to do with the earlier part of the Stone Age, characterized by crudely chipped stone tools. [< *paleo-* + Gk. *lithos* stone]

pa·le·on·tol·o·gy (pā′li on tol′ə ji), *n.* science of the forms of life existing long ago, as represented by fossil animals and plants. [< *paleo-* + Gk. *ón, óntos,* a being + -LOGY] —**pa′le·on′to·log′ic, pa′le·on′to·log′i·cal**, *adj.* —**pa′le·on′tol′o·gist**, *n.*

Pa·le·o·zo·ic (pā′li ə zō′ik), *n.* an old geological era, or a group of rocks, whose fossils represent early forms of life. —*adj.* of this era or these rocks. [< *paleo-* + Gk. *zōē* life + E *-ic*]

pa·le·o·zo·ol·o·gy (pā′li ō zō ol′ə ji), *n.* branch of paleontology that deals with fossil animals. —**pa′le·o·zo′o·log′i·cal,** *adj.* —**pa′le·o·zo·ol′o·gist,** *n.*

Pa·ler·mo (pə lär′mō), *n.* capital of Sicily, in the NW part.

Pal·es·tine (pal′əs tīn), *n.* a former country in SW Asia, between the Mediterranean Sea and the Jordan River, now divided into Israel and lands governed by the Palestinian Authority. —**Pal′es·tin′i·an,** *adj., n.*

pal·ette (pal′it), *n.* 1 a thin, smooth board or something similar, often oval or oblong, with a thumb hole at one end, used by painters to lay and mix colors on. 2 set of colors on this board. 3 choice of colors used by an artist: *a bright palette.* [< F < VL, dim. of *pala* spade]

pal·frey (pôl′fri), *n., pl.* **-freys.** a gentle riding horse, esp. one used by ladies. [< OF < LL, < Gk. *para-* beside + L *veredus* light horse]

pal·imp·sest (pal′imp sest), *n.* parchment or other writing material from which one writing has been erased to make room for another. [< L < Gk. *palimpsestos* scraped again, ult. < *palin* again + *pseein* rub smooth]

pal·ing (pāl′ing), *n.* 1 fence of pales. 2 a pale, as in a fence.

pal·i·sade (pal′ə sād′), *n., v.,* **-sad·ed, -sad·ing.** —*n.* 1 a long, strong wooden stake pointed at the top end. 2 fence of stakes set firmly in the ground to enclose or defend. 3 Usually, **palisades.** line of high, steep cliffs. —*v.* furnish or surround with a palisade. [< F, < *palisser* enclose with pales. See PALE².]

palisade cell, any one of the elongated cells below the epidermis of a leaf, that contains many chloroplasts and is involved in photosynthesis.

pall¹ (pôl), *n.* 1 a heavy cloth of black, purple, or white velvet spread over a coffin, a hearse, or a tomb. 2 something that spreads over or covers, esp. with darkness or gloom: *a pall of smoke.* —*v.* cover with or as with a pall. [< L *pallium* cloak]

pall² (pôl), *v.* 1 become distasteful or very tiresome because there has been too much of it. 2 cloy. [var. of *appall*]

pal·la·di·um¹ (pə lā′di əm), *n.* a rare silver-white metallic element, Pd, harder than platinum. [< NL; named after the asteroid *Pallas*]

pal·la·di·um² (pə lā′di əm), *n.* anything regarded as an important safeguard. [< L < Gk. *palladion,* dim. of Pallas; the statue of Pallas Athena overlooking Troy was thought to protect the city]

pall·bear·er (pôl′bār′ər), *n.* one of the men who walk with the coffin at a funeral.

pal·let¹ (pal′it), *n.* bed of straw; poor bed. [< OF *paillet* < *paille* straw < L *palea*]

pal·let² (pal′it), *n.* 1 a flat blade used by potters and others. 2 a painter's palette. 3 projection on a pawl, or similar projection in a watch, clock, etc. that engages with the wheels. 4 low platform on which goods are stacked for shipment. [var. of *palette*]

pal·li·ate (pal′i āt), *v.,* **-at·ed, -at·ing.** 1 lessen without curing; mitigate: *palliate a disease.* 2 make appear less serious; excuse: *palliate a fault.* [< L, < *pallium* cloak] —**pal′li·a′tion,** *n.* —**pal′li·a′tive,** *adj.* —**pal′li·a′tive·ly,** *adv.* —**pal′li·a′tor,** *n.*

pal·lid (pal′id), *adj.* lacking color; pale: *a pallid complexion.* [< L *pallidus.* Doublet of PALE¹.] —**pal′lid·ly,** *adv.* —**pal′lid·ness,** *n.*

pal·lor (pal′ər), *n.* lack of color from fear, illness, death, etc.; paleness. [< L]

palm¹ (päm), *n.* 1 inside of the hand between the wrist and the fingers. 2 the corresponding part of a glove. 3 width of a hand; 3 to 4 inches. —*v.* 1 conceal in the hand. 2 pass or get accepted (something not good).

in the palm of one's hand, under one's control.

palm off, pass off or get accepted by tricks, fraud, or false representation. [< OF < L *palma*]

palm² (päm), *n.* 1 any of many kinds of trees growing in warm climates, the majority of which are tall and have a bunch of large leaves at the top. 2 branch or leaf of a palm tree as a symbol of victory or triumph. 3 victory; triumph. [< L *palma* palm tree, palm¹] —**pal·ma′ceous,** *adj.*

Pal·ma (päl′mä), *n.* capital of the Balearic Islands.

pal·mate (pal′māt), **pal·mat·ed** (–id), *adj.* 1 shaped like a hand with the fingers spread out. 2 web-footed; webbed. —**pal′mate·ly,** *adv.*

palm·er¹ (päm′ər), *n.* 1 pilgrim returning from the Holy Land bringing a palm branch as a token. 2 pilgrim.

palm·er² (päm′ər), *n.* person who palms or conceals something.

pal·met·to (pal met′ō), *n., pl.* **-tos, -toes.** any of several kinds of palm trees with fan-shaped leaves, abundant on the SE coast of the United States.

palm·is·try (päm′is tri), *n.* art of telling a person's fortune from the lines and marks in the palm of his hand. —**palm′ist,** *n.*

Palm Sunday, the Sunday before Easter Sunday.

palm·top (päm′top′, pälm′–), *n.* very small portable computer, about the size of the palm of the hand.

palm·y (päm′i), *adj.* **palm·i·er, palm·i·est.** 1 abounding in palms; shaded by palms. 2 flourishing; prosperous; glorious.

pal·o·mi·no (pal′ə mē′nō), *n., pl.* **-nos.** a cream-colored horse of Arabian stock.

Its mane and tail are usually lighter colored. [< Sp.]

pal·pa·ble (pal′pə bəl), *adj.* 1 that can be touched or felt. 2 readily seen or heard and recognized; obvious. [< LL, < L *palpare* feel] —**pal′pa·bil′i·ty,** *n.* —**pal′pa·bly,** *adv.*

pal·pi·tate (pal′pə tāt), *v.,* **-tat·ed, -tat·ing.** 1 beat very rapidly: *your heart palpitates when you are excited.* 2 quiver; tremble: *he palpitated with terror.* [< L, < *palpitare* to throb < *palpare* to pat] —**pal′pi·ta′tion,** *n.*

pal·pus (pal′pəs), **palp** (palp), *n., pl.* **pal·pi** (pal′pī); **palps.** the jointed feeler attached to the mouth of insects, spiders, lobsters, etc. Palpi are organs of touch or taste. [< L]

pal·sy (pôl′zi), *n., pl.* **-sies,** *v.,* **-sied, -sy·ing.** —*n.* tremors; inability to control movement of a hand, leg, etc. —*v.* have tremors or shaking. [< OF < L *paralysis.* Doublet of PARALYSIS.] —**pal′sied,** *adj.*

pal·try (pôl′tri), *adj.,* **-tri·er, -tri·est.** almost worthless; trifling; petty; mean. [? < dial. *palt* trash] —**pal′tri·ly,** *adv.* —**pal′tri·ness,** *n.*

pam·pas (pam′pəz; –pəs), *n.pl.* the vast treeless plains of South America, esp. in Argentina. [< Sp. < Peruvian] —**pam·pe′an,** *adj.*

pam·per (pam′pər), *v.* indulge too much; allow too many privileges to: *pamper a child, pamper one's appetite.* [ME *pampere(n)*] —**pam′per·er,** *n.*

pam·phlet (pam′flit), *n.* booklet in paper covers. [< Anglo-L *panfletus,* for *Pamphilet,* popular name for 12th-century poem, "Pamphilus, seu de Amore"]

pam·phlet·eer (pam′flə tir′), *n.* writer of pamphlets. —*v.* write and issue pamphlets.

pan (pan), *n., v.,* **panned, pan·ning.** —*n.* 1 dish for cooking and other household uses, usually broad, shallow, and with no cover. 2 anything like this. The dishes on a pair of scales are called pans. —*v.* 1 criticize severely; reprimand. 2 wash (gravel, sand, etc.) in a pan to get gold.

pan out, turn out. [OE *panne*]

pan-, *combining form.* all, as in *Pan-American, Pan-Christian, pandemonium.* [< Gk. *pas,* masc., *pan,* neut.]

Pan., Panama.

pan·a·ce·a (pan′ə sē′ə), *n.* remedy for all diseases or ills; cure-all. [< L < Gk. *panakeia,* ult. < *pan-* all + *akos* cure] —**pan′a·ce′an,** *adj.*

Pan·a·ma (pan′ə mä; –mô; pan′ə mä′; –mô′), *n.* 1 **Isthmus of,** a narrow neck of land connecting North America with South America. 2 country on the Isthmus of Panama. —**Pan′a·ma′ni·an,** *adj., n.*

Panama Canal, canal cut across the Isthmus of Panama to connect the Atlantic and Pacific Oceans.

Panama hat, or **panama,** *n.* a fine, straw hat woven from the young leaves of a palmlike plant of Central and South America.

Pan·A·mer·i·can (pan´ə mer´ə kən), *adj.* **1** of all Americans. **2** including all the countries of North, Central, and South America. —**Pan´-A·mer´i·can·ism,** *n.*

pan·cake (pan´kāk´), *n., v.,* –**caked,** –**cak·ing.** —*n.* **1** a thin, flat cake of batter, fried in a pan or on a griddle. **2** a quick, almost flat landing made by an airplane. —*v.* make such a landing.

pan·chro·mat·ic (pan´krō mat´ik), *adj.* sensitive to the light of all colors.

pan·cre·as (pan´kri əs), *n.* gland near the stomach that discharges into the intestine a secretion that helps digestion. The pancreas of animals when used for food is called sweetbread. [< NL < Gk., < *pan* all + *kreas* flesh]

pan·cre·at·ic (pan´kri at´ik), *adj.* of the pancreas. The pancreatic juice aids digestion.

pan·da (pan´də), *n.* the giant panda, a bear-like mammal of Tibet, mostly white with black legs.

pan·dem·ic (pan dem´ik), *adj.* **1** extending across a country, region, or the entire world: *a pandemic disease.* **2** universal. —*n.* disease that spreads around the world: *fears of another flu pandemic.*

pan·de·mo·ni·um (pan´də mō´ni əm), *n.* **1** place of wild disorder or lawless confusion. **2** a wild uproar or lawlessness. [< NL, < Gk. *pan*– all + *daimon* demon]

pan·der (pan´dər), *n.* person who helps other people indulge low desires, passions, or vices. —*v.* **1** supply material or opportunity for vices. **2** act as pander for. [from name of character in story told by Boccaccio and Chaucer]

pan·dow·dy (pan dou´di), *n., pl.* –**dies.** a deep apple pie with top crust only.

pane (pān), *n.* a single sheet of glass in a window, a door, or a sash. [< OF < L *pannus* piece of cloth] —**paned,** *adj.*

pan·e·gyr·ic (pan´ə jir´ik), *n.* **1** speech or writing in praise of a person or thing. **2** enthusiastic or extravagant praise. [< L < Gk., < *pan*– all + *agyris* assembly] —**pan´e·gyr´i·cal,** *adj.* —**pan´e·gyr´i·cal·ly,** *adv.* —**pan´e·gyr´ist,** *n.*

pan·el (pan´əl), *n., v.,* –**eled,** –**el·ing.** —*n.* **1** strip or surface that is different in some way from what is around it. A panel is often sunk below or raised above the rest, and used for a decoration. Panels may be on a wall, in a door or other woodwork, on large pieces of furniture, or made as parts of a dress. **2** list of persons called as jurors; the members of a jury. **3** a group formed for discussion. —*v.* **1** arrange in panels; furnish or decorate with panels. **2** list or select for a jury. [< OF, piece, ult. < L *pannus* piece of cloth]

pan·el·ist (pan´əl ist), *n.* person who serves on a discussion panel or jury.

pan·el·ing (pan´əl ing), *n.* panels.

pang (pang), *n.* a sudden, short, sharp pain or feeling: *the pangs of a toothache, a pang of pity.*

pan·go·lin (pang gō´lin), *n.* a scaly, toothless mammal of tropical Asia and Africa; scaly anteater. [< Malay *peng-goling* roller]

pan·han·dle¹ (pan´han´dəl), *n.* **1** handle of a pan. **2** a narrow strip of land projecting like a handle.

pan·han·dle² (pan´han´dəl), *v.,* –**dled,** –**dling.** beg, esp. in the streets. —**pan´han´dler,** *n.*

Pan·hel·len·ic (pan´hə len´ik), *adj.* of or having to do with all of the Greek people or all of Greece.

pan·ic (pan´ik), *n., adj., v.,* –**icked,** –**ick·ing.** —*n.* fear spreading through a multitude of people so that they lose control of themselves; unreasoning fear: *when the theater caught fire, there was a panic.* —*adj.* caused by panic; showing panic. —*v.* go into a state of panic: *the audience panicked when the fire broke out.* [< F < Gk. *Panikos* of Pan (who caused fear)] —**pan´ick·y,** *adv.*

panic attack, feeling of sudden, unreasoning fear.

panic button, switch for use in an emergency, as on an aircraft.

hit the panic button, overreact to a stressful situation.

pan·ic-strick·en (pan´ik strik´ən), *adj.* immobilized by fear; frightened extremely. —**pan´ic-struck´,** *adj.*

pan·i·cle (pan´ə kəl), *n.* a compound raceme; a loose, diversely branching flower cluster: *a panicle of oats.* [< L *panicula,* dim. of *panus* a swelling] —**pan´i·cled,** *adj.*

pan·ni·er (pan´i ər), *n.* basket, esp. one of a pair of considerable size to be slung across the shoulders or across the back of a beast of burden. [< OF < L *panarium* bread basket < *panis* bread]

pan·o·ply (pan´ə pli), *n., pl.* –**plies.** **1** a complete suit of armor. **2** complete equipment or covering: *an Indian in panoply of paint and feathers.* [< Gk. *panoplia* < *pan*– all + *hopla* arms] —**pan´o·plied,** *adj.*

pan·o·ram·a (pan´ə ram´ə; –rä´mə), *n.* **1** a wide, unbroken view of a surrounding region. **2** a complete survey of some subject: *a panorama of history.* **3** a continuously passing or changing scene: *the panorama of city life.* [< PAN– + Gk. *horama* view] —**pan´o·ram´ic,** *adj.* —**pan´o·ram´i·cal·ly,** *adv.* —**pan´o·ram´ist,** *n.*

Pan·pipe or **pan·pipe** (pan´pīp´), *n.* an early musical instrument made of reeds or tubes of different lengths, fastened together in order of their length. Also, **Pan's pipes.**

pan·sy (pan´zi), *n., pl.* –**sies.** **1** variety of violet that has large flowers with flat, velvety petals usually of several colors. **2** the flower. [< F *pensée* thought. Cf. PENSIVE.]

pant¹ (pant), *v.* **1** breathe hard and quickly. **2** speak with short, quick breaths. **3** long eagerly. —*n.* short quick breath. [? < OF *pantoisier* < VL *phantasiare* be oppressed with nightmare. See FANTASY.]

pant² (pant), *n.* =**pants.** —*adj.* of or belonging to pants: *a wide pant leg.*

pan·ta·lets, **pan·ta·lettes** (pan´tə lets´), *n.pl.* long drawers with a frill at the bottom and extending to the ankles, formerly worn by women and girls.

pan·ta·loon (pan´tə lün´), *n.* **1** in modern pantomime, a mean, foolish old man, the butt and accomplice of the clown. **2** pantaloons, trousers. [< F < Ital. *Pantalone,* a comic character in early Italian comedies]

pan·the·ism (pan´thē iz əm), *n.* **1** belief that God and the universe are identical. **2** worship of all the gods. —**pan´the·ist,** *n.* —**pan´the·is´tic,** **pan´the·is´ti·cal,** *adj.* —**pan´the·is´ti·cal·ly,** *adv.*

pan·the·on (pan´thi on; pan thē´ən), *n.* **1 a** temple dedicated to all the gods. **b** all the deities of a people. **2** *Fig.* any group of important or venerated people: *the presidential pantheon of Washington and Lincoln.* [< L < Gk. *pantheion* < *pan*– all + *theos* god]

pan·ther (pan´thər), *n., pl.* –**thers** or (*esp. collectively*) –**ther.** **1** =cougar. **2** =leopard. **3** =jaguar. [< OF < L < Gk.]

pan·to·mime (pan´tə mīm), *n., v.,* –**mimed,** –**mim·ing.** —*n.* **1** a play without words, in which the actors express themselves by gestures. **2** gestures without words. —*v.* express by gestures. [< L < Gk., < *pas* all + *mimos* mimic] —**pan´to·mim´ic,** *adj.* —**pan´to·mim´ist,** *n.*

pan·try (pan´tri), *n., pl.* –**tries.** a small room in which food, dishes, silverware, table linen, etc., are kept. [< AF *panetrie,* ult. < L *panis* bread]

pants (pants), *n.pl.* **1** trousers. **2** drawers, esp. women's. [short for *pantaloons*]

pan·ty or **pan·tie** (pan´ti), *n., pl.* –**ties.** Usually, **panties.** pants with short legs, worn as an undergarment by women and children; underpants.

pan·zer (pan´zər), *adj.* armored. A panzer division consists largely of tanks. [< G, armor]

pap (pap), *n.* **1** a soft food for infants or invalids. **2** *Fig.* statements, opinions, etc., that are so bland and uninteresting they are like baby food. [cf. LG *pappe*]

pa·pa (pä´pə; pə pä´), *n.* father; daddy.

pa·pa·cy (pā´pə si), *n., pl.* –**cies.** **1** position, rank, or authority of the Pope. **2** time during which a pope rules. **3** all the popes. **4** government by the Pope. [< Med.L., < *papa* POPE]

pa·pal (pā´pəl), *adj.* **1** of the Pope: *a papal letter.* **2** of the papacy. **3** of the Roman Catholic Church: *papal ritual.* —**pa´pal·ism,** *n.*

pa·paw (pô´pô), *n.* **1** a small North American tree bearing oblong, edible fruit with many beanlike seeds. **2** this fruit. [< Sp. *papaya.* See PAPAYA.]

pa·pa·ya (pə pä′yə), *n.* **1** a tropical American tree having a straight, palmlike trunk with a tuft of large leaves at the top and edible, melonlike fruit with yellowish pulp. **2** the fruit. [< Sp. (def. 2), < *papayo* (def. 1) < Carib]

pa·per (pā′pər), *n.* **1** a material in thin sheets used for writing, printing, drawing, wrapping packages, covering walls, etc. Paper is made from wood pulp, rags, etc. **2** piece or sheet of paper. **3** document: *an important paper was stolen.* **4** =newspaper. **5** article; essay. **6** paper money. **7** wallpaper. *—adj.* **1** of or pertaining to paper. **2** made of paper: *paper dolls.* **3** existing only on paper: *paper profits. —v.* cover with paper.

on paper, a in writing or print. **b** in theory: *the idea looks good on paper.*

paper over, cover up or smooth out a disagreement, quarrel, etc.

papers, documents telling who or what one is. [< L *papyrus.* Doublet of PAPYRUS.] **—pa′per·er,** *n.* **—pa′per·like′,** *adj.*

pa·per·back (pā′pər bak′), *n.* a small, inexpensive book bound in paper.

paper clip, wire bent into a flat clip to hold papers together.

paper money, money made from paper rather than metal; bills.

paper tiger, person or thing that appears to be strong or threatening, but is really weak.

pa·per·weight (pā′pər wāt′), *n.* a small, heavy object put on papers to keep them from being scattered.

pa·per·work (pā′pər werk′), *n.* clerical work, as the filling in of forms, planning, figuring, etc., incidental to some activity.

pa·per·y (pā′pər i), *adj.* thin like paper.

pa·pier-mâ·ché (pā′pər mə shā′), *n.* a paper pulp mixed with some stiffener such as paste and molded when moist. It becomes hard and strong when dry. *—adj.* made of papier-mâché. [< F, chewed paper]

pa·pil·la (pə pil′ə), *n., pl.* **-pil·lae** (-pil′ē). **1** a small, nipplelike projection. **2** a small vascular process at the root of a hair or feather. **3** one of certain small protuberances concerned with the senses of touch, taste, or smell. [< L, nipple] **—pap′il·lar′y,** *adj.*

pap·il·lo·ma (pap′ə lō′mə), noncancerous tumor of the skin or mucous membrane, as a corn or wart.

pa·pist (pā′pist), *n., adj.* Roman Catholic. [< NL, < L *papa* POPE]

pa·poose, pap·poose (pa püs′), *n.* a North American Indian baby. [< Algonquian *papeisses* < *peisses* child]

pap·ri·ka (pap rē′kə; pap′rə–), *n.* a kind of red pepper not so strong as the ordinary kind. [< Hung.]

Pap test or **smear,** microscopic examination to determine if cancer is present in cells taken from esp. the cervix or uterus. Also, **pap test, pap smear.**

Pap·u·a New Guinea (pap′yü ə; pä′pü ä), a country in the E portion of the island of New Guinea. **—Pap′u·an,** *adj., n.*

pa·py·rus (pə pī′rəs), *n., pl.* **-ri** (–rī). **1** a tall water plant from which the ancient Egyptians, Greeks, and Romans made a kind of paper to write on. **2** a writing material made from the pith of the papyrus plant. **3** an ancient record written on papyrus. [< L < Gk. *papyros.* Doublet of PAPER.]

par (pär), *n.* **1** equality; an equal level: *he is on a par with his brother in intelligence.* **2** average or normal amount, degree, or condition: *feel below par, not up to par.* **3** the value of a bond, note, share of stock, etc., printed on it; face value: *stock selling above par.* **4** the value of the money of one country in terms of another country. *—adj.* **1** average; normal. **2** of or at par.

par for the course, what is to be expected; the usual. [< L, equal]

par., **1** paragraph. **2** parallel.

par·a·ble (par′ə bəl), *n.* a short story used to teach some truth or moral lesson: *Jesus taught in parables.* [< L < Gk. *parabole* comparison < *para–* alongside + *bole* a throwing. Doublet of PALAVER, PAROLE.]

pa·rab·o·la (pə rab′ə lə), *n., pl.* **-las.** a plane curve formed by the intersection of a cone with a plane parallel to a side of the cone. [< NL < Gk., juxtaposition. See PARABLE.]

par·a·bol·ic (par′ə bol′ik), *adj.* pertaining to, of the form of, or resembling a parabola. **—par′a·bol′i·cal·ly,** *adv.*

par·a·chute (par′ə shüt), *n., v.,* **-chut·ed, -chut·ing.** *—n.* an umbrellalike apparatus used in descending safely through the air from a great height. *—v.* **1** descend by, or as if by, a parachute. **2** convey by a parachute. [< F, < *para–* (< Ital., guard against!) + *chute* a fall] **—par′a·chut′ist,** *n.*

pa·rade (pə rād′), *n., v.,* **-rad·ed, -rad·ing.** *—n.* **1** march for display; procession: *the circus had a parade.* **2** group of people walking for display or pleasure. **3** place where people walk for pleasure. **4** a great show or display: *a parade of one's wealth.* **5** a military display or review of troops. *—v.* **1** march through with display: *the performers and animals paraded the streets.* **2** march in procession. **3** make a great show of. **4** come together in military order for review or inspection. [< F < Sp. *parada,* ult. < L *parare* prepare]

par·a·digm (par′ə dim; –dīm), *n.* pattern; example. [< L < Gk. *paradeigma* pattern, ult. < *para–* side by side + *deiknunai* to show] **—par′a·dig·mat′ic,** *adj.*

par·a·dise (par′ə dīs), *n.* **1** heaven. **2** place or condition of great happiness. **3** place of great beauty. [< L < Gk. < OPers. *pairidaēza* park < *pairi–* around + *daēza* wall] **—par′a·dis′al,** *adj.*

par·a·dox (par′ə doks), *n.* **1** statement that may be true but seems to say two opposite things. "More haste, less speed" is a paradox. **2** statement that is false

because it says two opposite things. **3** person or thing that seems to be full of contradictions. [< L < Gk. < *para–* contrary to + *doxa* opinion] **—par′a·dox′i·cal,** *adj.* **—par′a·dox′i·cal·ly,** *adv.* **—par′a·dox′i·cal·ness,** *n.*

par·af·fin, (par′ə fin), *n.* a white, tasteless substance like wax, used for making candles, for sealing jars, etc. [< G, < L *parum* too little + *affinis* related; from its small affinity for other substances] **—par′af·fin′ic,** *adj.*

par·a·gon (par′ə gon), *n.* model of excellence or perfection. [< OF <Ital. *paragone* touchstone]

par·a·graph (par′ə graf; –gräf), *n.* **1** group of sentences that belong together; distinct part of a chapter, letter, or composition. It is customary to begin a paragraph on a new line and to indent this line. **2** a separate note or item of news in a newspaper. **3** sign (¶) used to show where a paragraph begins or should begin. *—v.* divide into paragraphs. [< LL < Gk. *paragraphos* line (in the margin) marking a break in sense < *para–* beside + *graphein* write] **—par′a·graph′er,** *n.* **—par′a·graph′ic,** *adj.* **—par′a·graph′i·cal·ly,** *adv.*

Par·a·guay (par′ə gwā; –gwī), *n.* country in C South America, between Bolivia, Brazil, and Argentina. **—Par′a·guay′an,** *adj., n.*

par·a·keet (par′ə kēt), *n.* any of various small parrots, most of which have slender bodies and long tails. [< OF < Ital. *parrochetto* < *parroco* parish priest]

par·a·le·gal (par′ə lē′gəl), *n.* person trained to assist a lawyer, prepare documents, etc. *—adj.* of or having to do with paralegals or their work. [*para–* near + *legal*]

par·al·lax (par′ə laks), *n.* **1** the change or amount of change in the direction in which an object is seen or photographed, caused by a change in the position of the observer or camera. **2** in astronomy, the parallax of a star observed from two different points is expressed as the angle formed by the difference between the two points and the star. [< Gk. *parallaxis* alternation, ult. < *para–* + *allassein* to change] **—par′al·lac′tic,** *adj.*

par·al·lel (par′ə lel), *adj., n., v.,* **-leled, -lel·ing.** *—adj.* **1** at or being the same distance apart everywhere, like the two rails of a railroad track. **2** having the same direction, course, or tendency. **3** similar; corresponding: *parallel points in the characters of different men.* *—n.* **1** a parallel line or surface. **2** in geography, any of the imaginary circles around the earth parallel to the equator, marking degrees of latitude. **3** thing like or similar to another. **4** comparison to show likeness: *draw a parallel between this winter and last winter. —v.* **1** be at the same distance from: *the street parallels the railroad.* **2** be like; be similar to: *your story closely parallels what he told me.* **3**

find a case which is similar or parallel to. [< L < Gk., < *para allelois* beside one another]

par·al·lel bars, pair of bars parallel to the ground and raised high enough for a gymnast to perform exercises on that strengthen the arm and chest muscles.

par·al·lel·ism (par′ə lel iz′əm), *n.* **1** a being parallel. **2** likeness; similarity; correspondence.

par·al·lel·o·gram (par′ə lel′ə gram), *n.* a four-sided figure whose opposite sides are parallel and equal.

pa·ral·y·sis (pə ral′ə sis), *n., pl.* **-ses** (-sēz). **1** a lessening or loss of the power of motion or sensation in any part of the body. **2** condition of powerlessness or helpless inactivity; crippling: *a paralysis of trade.* [< L < Gk., ult. < *para-* from beside + *lyein* to loose. Doublet of PALSY.] —**par′a·lyt′ic,** *adj., n.*

par·a·lyze (par′ə līz), *v.,* **-lyzed, -lyz·ing.** **1** affect with a lessening or loss of the power of motion or feeling: *his left arm was paralyzed.* **2** make powerless or helplessly inactive; cripple: *fear paralyzed my mind.* —**par′a·ly·za′tion,** *n.*

par·a·me·ci·um (par′ə mē′shi əm; -si əm), *n., pl.* **-ci·a** (-shi ə; -si ə). a one-celled animal shaped like a slender slipper, that is covered with cilia and has a groove along one side leading into an open mouth. Paramecia are free-swimming and usually live in stagnant water. [< NL, < Gk. *paramekes* oblong < *para-* on one side + *mekos* length]

par·a·med·ic¹ (par′ə med′ik), *n.* medical corpsman who parachutes from a plane to give medical assistance in remote, wilderness areas, or as a member of the military, on the battlefield. [< *para*-parachute + *medic*]

par·a·med·ic² (par′ə med′ik), *n.* emergency or auxilliary medical worker. [< *para-* near + *medic*al] —**par′a·med′i·cal,** *adj.*

par·a·mount (par′ə mount), *adj.* chief in importance; above others; supreme. [< AF *paramont* < *par* by (< L *per*) + *amont* up < L *ad montem* to the mountain] —**par′a·mount·ly,** *adv.*

par·a·mour (par′ə mùr), *n.* **1** person who takes the place of a husband or wife illegally. **2** *Archaic.* lover. [< OF, < *par amour* by love < L *per amorem*]

par·a·noi·a (par′ə noi′ə), *n.* a mental derangement, esp. a chronic form of insanity characterized by elaborate delusions. [< NL < Gk., ult < *para-* amiss + *nous* mind] —**par′a·noi′ac,** *adj., n.*

par·a·noid (par′ə noid), *n.* person suffering from paranoia. —**par′a·noid,** *adj.*

par·a·nor·mal (par′ə nor′məl), *adj.* =psychic.

par·a·pet (par′ə pet; -pit), *n.* **1** a low wall or mound of stone, earth, etc., to protect soldiers. **2** a low wall at the edge of a balcony, roof, bridge, etc. [< Ital., < *para* defend! (< L *parare* prepare) + *petto* breast < L *pectus*]

par·a·pher·nal·ia (par′ə fər nāl′yə), *n.pl.* **1** (*pl. in use*) personal belongings. **2** (*sometimes sing. in use*) equipment; outfit. [< Med.L, ult. < Gk., < *para-* besides + *pherne* dowry]

par·a·phrase (par′ə frāz), *v.,* **-phrased, -phras·ing,** *n.* —*v.* state the meaning of (a passage) in other words; translate freely. —*n.* expression of the meaning of a passage in other words. [< F < L < Gk., < *para-* alongside of + *phrazein* say] —**par′a·phras′er,** *n.*

par·a·ple·gi·a (par′ə plē′ji ə), *n.* paralysis of the legs and the lower part of the trunk. [< NL < Gk., paralysis of one side of the body] —**par′a·ple′gic,** *adj., n.*

par·a·pro·fes·sion·al (par′ə prə fesh′-ən əl), *n.* aide specially trained to assist doctors, lawyers, etc. [< *para-* near + *professional*]

par·a·site (par′ə sīt), *n.* **1** animal or plant that lives on, with, or in another, from which it gets its food. **2** person who lives on others without making any useful and fitting return; hanger-on: *beggars and tramps are parasites.* [< L < Gk., <*para-*alongside of+*sitos* food] —**par′a·sit′ic,** *adj.* —**par′a·sit′i·cal·ly,** *adv.*

par·a·sit·ism (par′ə sī′tiz əm), *n.* **1** relationship between a parasite and its host. **2** parasitic infection or infestation. **3** *Fig.* existing as a human parasite, living off others.

par·a·sol (par′ə sôl; -sol), *n.* umbrella used to ward off the rays of the sun. [< F < Ital., < *para* ward off! + *sole* sun]

par·a·thy·roid glands (par′ə thī′roid), small glands near the thyroid glands. Their secretion, which enables the body to use calcium, is necessary for life.

par·a·troop·er (par′ə trüp′ər), *n.* soldier trained to use a parachute for descent from an aircraft into a battle area. [< *para*(*chute*) + *trooper*] —**par′a·troops′,** *n.pl.*

par·boil (pär′boil′), *v.* **1** boil till partly cooked. **2** overheat. [< F < LL, < *per-* thoroughly + *bullire* boil; *par-* confused with *part*]

par·cel (pär′səl), *n., v.,* **-celed, -cel·ing.** —*n.* **1** bundle of things wrapped or packed together; package. **2** container with things packed in it. **3** piece: *a parcel of land.* —*v.* make into a parcel or parcels.

parcel out, divide into, or distribute in, portions. [< OF, ult. < L *particula*, dim. of *pars* apart]

parch (pärch), *v.* **1** dry by heating; roast slightly: *parched corn.* **2** make or become hot, dry, or thirsty. **3** make excessively dry.

par·chee·si, par·che·si, or **par·chi·si** (pär chē′zi), *n.* **1** game somewhat like backgammon, played by moving pieces according to throws of dice. **2** **Parcheesi,** trademark for this game. [< Hind. *pachīsī* < *pachīs* twenty-five (highest throw)]

parch·ment (pärch′mənt), *n.* **1** skin of sheep, goats, etc., prepared for use as a

writing material. **2** manuscript or document written on parchment. **3** paper that looks like parchment. [< OF < LL < Gk. *pergamene* < *Pergamon* Pergamum, whence it came]

par·don (pär′dən), *n.* **1** forgiveness. **2** excuse. **3** a setting free from punishment; ecclesiastical indulgence. [< v.] —*v.* **1** forgive. **2** excuse. **3** set free from punishment: *the governor pardoned the criminal.* [< OF < LL, < L *per-* thoroughly + *donare* give] —**par′don·a·ble,** *adj.* —**par′don·a·ble·ness,** *n.* —**par′don·a·bly,** *adv.* —**par′don·er,** *n.*

pare (pār), *v.,* **pared, par·ing. 1** cut, trim, or shave off the outer part of; peel: *pare an apple.* **2** cut away little by little: *pare down expenses.* [< F < L *parare* make ready. Doublet of PARRY.]

par·e·gor·ic (par′ə gôr′ik; -gor′-), *n.* a soothing medicine containing camphor and a very little opium. —*adj.* soothing. [< LL < Gk. *paregorikos* soothing, ult. < *para-* at the side of + *-agoros* speaking]

paren., pl. parens., parenthesis.

pa·ren·chy·ma (pə reng′kə mə), *n.* **1** the essential tissue of an animal organ as distinguished from connective tissue, etc. **2** the fundamental cellular tissue of plants, which composes the softer parts of leaves, etc., the pulp of fruits, the pith of stems, etc. [< Gk., < *para-* beside + *en-* in + *chyma* what is poured] —**par′en·chym′a·tous,** *adj.*

par·ent (pār′ənt), *n.* **1** father or mother. **2** any animal or plant that produces offspring. **3** *Fig.* source; cause. [< OF < L *parens,* orig. active pp. of *parere* bring forth] —**pa·ren′tal,** *adj.* —**pa·ren′tal·ly,** *adv.* —**par′ent·hood,** *n.*

par·ent·age (pār′ən tij), *n.* **1** descent from parents; family line; ancestry. **2** being a parent.

pa·ren·the·sis (pə ren′thə sis), *n., pl.* **-ses** (-sēz). **1** word, phrase, sentence, etc., inserted within a sentence to explain or qualify something. **2** either or both of two curved lines ( ) used to set off such an expression. [< L < Gk., < *para-* beside + *en-* in + *thesis* placing] —**par′en·thet′ic, par′en·thet′i·cal,** *adj.* —**par′en·thet′i·cal·ly,** *adv.*

pa·ren·the·size (pə ren′thə sīz), *v.,* **-sized, -siz·ing.** insert as or in a parenthesis.

par·ent·ing (pār′ən ting), *n.* process of caring for and rearing children or offspring.

pa·re·sis (pə rē′sis; par′ə-), *n.* an incomplete paralysis that affects the ability to move, but does not affect ability to feel. [< NL < Gk., a letting go, ult. < *para-* by + *hienai* let go] —**pa·ret′ic,** *adj., n.*

par ex·cel·lence (pär ek′sə läns), *French.* above all others of the same sort.

par·fait (pär fā′), *n.* **1** frozen dessert of ice cream layered with fruits, sauce, etc., with whipped cream on top, served in a tall glass. **2** a rich ice cream containing eggs and whipped cream and frozen without stirring. [< F, perfect]

par·he·li·on (pär hē′li ən; –hēl′yən), *n., pl.* **–li·a** (–li ə; –yə). a bright circular spot on a solar halo. [< L < Gk., < *para–* beside + *helios* sun]

pa·ri·ah (pə rī′ə; pä′ri ə), *n.* **1** outcast. **2** Usually, **Pariah.** member of a low caste in S India and Burma. [< Tamil *paraiyar* drummer; because this caste provided the drummers at festivals]

pa·ri·e·tal (pə rī′ə təl), *adj.* of the wall of the body or of one of its cavities. —*n.* Also, **parietal bone.** either of two bones that form part of the side and top of the skull. [< LL, < L *paries* wall]

par·i·mu·tu·el (par′i mū′chü əl), *n.* **1** system of betting on horse races in which those who have bet on the winning horses divide the money lost by the losers. **2** machine for recording such bets. [< F, mutual wager]

par·ing (pãr′ing), *n.* part pared off; skin; rind.

Par·is (par′is), *n.* capital of France, located in N France on the Seine. —**Pa·ri′sian,** *adj., n.*

par·ish (par′ish), *n.* **1** district that has its own church and clergyman. **2** people of a parish. **3** in Louisiana, a county. [< OF < LL < Gk., ult. < *para* near + *oikos* dwelling]

pa·rish·ion·er (pə rish′ən ər; –rish′nər), *n.* member of a parish.

par·i·ty (par′ə ti), *n.* **1** equality with regard to state, quality, degree, etc. **2** similarity or close correspondence. [< L, < *par* equal]

park (pärk), *n.* **1** land set apart for the pleasure of the public. **2** land set apart for wild animals. **3** place to leave an automobile, etc., for a time. —*v.* **1** enclose in a park. **2** leave (an automobile, etc.) for a time in a certain place. [< OF *parc* < L *parricus* enclosure. Doublet of PADDOCK.]

par·ka (pär′kə), *n.* **1** a fur jacket with a hood, worn in Alaska and in NE Asia. **2** a long woolen shirt or jacket with a hood. [< Russ.]

parking lot, open area for parking vehicles, often for a fee.

parking meter, device containing a clock mechanism which is operated by the insertion of coins. It allows an automobile a specified amount of time in a parking area for each coin.

park·way (pärk′wā′), *n.* a broad road with spaces planted with grass, trees, etc.

Parl., Parliament; Parliamentary.

par·lance (pär′ləns), *n.* way of speaking; talk; language. [< OF, < *parler* speak. See PARLEY.]

par·lay (pär′li; –lā), *v.* **1** extend and exploit (something) with conspicuous success: *parlay an idea into a big business.* [alter. of *paroli* < F < Ital., grand cast at dice]

par·ley (pär′li), *n., pl.* **–leys,** *v.,* **–leyed, –ley·ing.** —*n.* **1** conference; informal talk. **2** an informal discussion with an enemy about terms of surrender,

exchange of prisoners, etc. —*v.* discuss terms, esp. with an enemy. [< OF *parlée* < pp. of *parler* speak, ult. < L *parabola* PARABLE]

par·lia·ment (pär′lə mənt), *n.* council or congress that is the highest lawmaking body of a country. [< OF *parlement.* See PARLEY.]

par·lia·men·tar·i·an (pär′lə men tãr′i ən), *n.* one skilled in parliamentary procedure or debate.

par·lia·men·ta·ry (pär′lə men′tə ri; –men′tri), *adj.* **1** of a parliament. **2** done by a parliament. **3** according to the rules and customs of a parliament or other lawmaking body. **4** having a parliament.

par·lor (pär′lər), *n.* **1** room for receiving or entertaining guests; sitting room. **2** room used as a shop; shop: *a beauty parlor.* —*adj.* of or pertaining to a parlor. [< AF *parlur.* See PARLEY.]

Par·me·san (pär′mə zan′; pär′mə zan), *n.* Also, **Parmesan cheese.** a hard, dry Italian cheese made from skim milk. —*adj.* made with this cheese. [< MF *parmesan,* ult. < It. *Parma,* region in Italy]

pa·ro·chi·al (pə rō′ki əl), *adj.* **1** of, for, or in a parish: *a parochial school.* **2** narrow; limited: *a parochial viewpoint.* [< OF < LL, < *parochia* PARISH] —**pa·ro′chi·al·ism,** *n.* —**pa·ro′chi·al·ly,** *adv.*

par·o·dy (par′ə di), *n., pl.* **–dies,** *v.,* **–died, –dy·ing.** —*n.* **1** a humorous imitation of a serious writing. A parody follows the form of the original, but changes its sense to nonsense. **2** a poor imitation. —*v.* **1** make fun of by imitating; make a parody on. **2** imitate poorly. [< L < Gk., < *para–* beside + *oide* song] —**par′o·dist,** *n.*

pa·role (pə rōl′), *n., v.,* **–roled, –rol·ing.** —*n.* **1** conditional release from prison or jail before the full term is served. **2** conditional freedom allowed in place of imprisonment. **3** word of honor: *the prisoner of war gave his parole not to try to escape.* —*v.* put on parole; release on parole. [< F, word, < L *parabola* PARABLE. Doublet of PARABLE, PALAVER.]

pa·ro·lee (pə rōl′ē), *n.* person on parole.

pa·rot·id (pə rot′id), —*adj.* near the ear. The **parotid glands,** one in front of each ear, supply saliva to the mouth through the **parotid ducts.** —*n.* parotid gland. [< L < Gk. *parotis* < *para–* beside + *ous* ear]

par·ox·ysm (par′ək siz əm), *n.* **1** a severe, sudden attack: *a paroxysm of coughing.* **2** fit; convulsion: *a paroxysm of rage.* [< Med.L < Gk., ult. < *para–* + *oxynein* render acute] —**par′ox·ys′mal,** *adj.*

par·quet (pär kā′; –ket′), *n., v.,* **–queted, –quet·ing.** —*n.* an inlaid wooden flooring. —*v.* **1** furnish with an inlaid wooden floor. **2** make (flooring) of inlaid wood. [< F, dim of *parc* PARK]

par·quet·ry (pär′kit ri), *n., pl.* **–ries.** mosaic of wood used for floors, wainscoting, etc.

parr (pär), *n., pl.* **parrs** or (*esp. collectively*) **parr.** a young salmon before it is old enough to go to sea.

par·ra·keet (par′ə kēt), **par·ro·ket,** or **par·ro·quet** (–ket′), *n.* =parakeet.

par·ri·cide[1] (par′ə sīd), *n.* **1** person who kills his or her parent. **2** person who kills anybody whom he or she should revere. [< F < LL, < L *pater* father + *–cida* killer] —**par′ri·cid′al,** *adj.*

par·ri·cide[2] (par′ə sīd), *n.* crime of killing one's parent or parents. [< F < LL, < L *pater* father + *–cidium* act of killing]

par·rot (par′ət), *n.* bird with a stout, hooked bill and often with bright-colored feathers. Some parrots can imitate sounds and repeat words and sentences. —*v.* repeat without understanding. [< F *Perrot,* dim. of *Pierre* Peter]

parrot fever, psittacosis.

par·ry (par′i), *v.,* **–ried, –ry·ing,** *n., pl.* **–ries.** —*v.* ward off; turn aside; evade (a thrust, stroke, weapon, question, etc.). —*n.* **1** act of parrying; avoiding. **2** a special defensive movement in fencing. [< F < Ital. *parare* ward off < L *parare* prepare. Doublet of PARE.]

parse (pärs), *v.,* **parsed, pars·ing. 1** analyze (a sentence) grammatically, telling its parts of speech and their uses in the sentence. **2** describe (a word) grammatically, telling what part of speech it is, its form, and its use in a sentence. **3** make sense: *that statement doesn't parse.* [< L *pars* (*orationis*) part (of speech)] —**pars′er,** *n.*

Par·see, Par·si (pär′sē; pär sē′), *n.* member of a sun-worshiping sect in India descended from the Persians who first settled there in the early part of the eighth century A.D. —**Par′see·ism, Par′si·ism,** *n.*

par·si·mo·ni·ous (pär′sə mō′ni əs), *adj.* too economical; stingy. —**par′si·mo′ni·ous·ly,** *adv.*

par·si·mo·ny (pär′sə mō′ni), *n.* extreme economy; stinginess. [< L *parsimonia* < *parcere* to spare]

pars·ley (pärs′li), *n., pl.* **–leys.** a garden plant with finely divided, fragrant leaves, used to flavor food and to trim platters of meat. [OE *petersilie,* also < OF *peresil;* both < VL *petrosilium* < L < Gk., < *petros* rock + *selinon* parsley]

pars·nip (pärs′nip), *n.* **1** vegetable that is the long, tapering, whitish root of a plant belonging to the same family as the carrot. **2** the plant. [< OF < L *pastinaca* (cf. *pastinare* dig); form infl. by ME *nep* turnip]

par·son (pär′sən), *n.* **1** minister in charge of a parish. **2** any clergyman; minister. [< Med.L *persona* parson. Doublet of PERSON.]

par·son·age (pär′sən ij), *n.* house provided for a minister by a church.

part (pärt), *n.* **1** something less than the whole: *part of an apple, a dime is a tenth part of a dollar, everyone must do his part.* **2** side in a dispute or contest: *he always* *takes his brother's part.* **3** character in a play; the words spoken by a character. **4** a dividing line left in combing one's hair. **5** one of the voices or instruments in music. The four parts in singing are soprano, alto, tenor, and bass. **6** the musical score for a part. **7** ability; talent: *a man of parts.* **8** region; district; place: *in foreign parts.* [< L *pars*] —*v.* **1** divide into two or more pieces. **2** force apart; divide: *the policeman parted the crowd.* **3** go apart; separate: *the friends parted in anger.* **4** comb (the hair) away from a dividing line. —*adj.* less than the whole: *part time.* —*adv.* in some measure or degree; partly.

for one's (own) part, as far as one is concerned.

for the most part, largely, mostly.

in part, to some extent; partly.

part and parcel, a necessary part.

part company (with), end companionship.

part from, go away from; leave.

part with, give up; let go.

take part, take or have a share. [< OF < L *partire* < *pars*, n.] —**part′ed,** *adj.* —**part′er,** *n.*

part., **1** participle. **2** particular.

par·take (pär tāk′), *v.,* **-took, -tak·en, -tak·ing.** **1** eat or drink some; take some. **2** take or have a share.

partake of, a have a share in. **b** have to some extent the nature or character of: *her graciousness partakes of condescension.* [< *partaker,* for *part-taker*] —**par·tak′er,** *n.*

par·the·no·gen·e·sis (pär′thə nō jen′-ə sis), *n.* reproduction without any male element. [< Gk. *parthenos* virgin + E *genesis*] —**par′the·no·ge·net′ic,** *adj.*

Par·thi·a (pär′thi ə), *n.* an ancient country in Asia SE of the Caspian Sea, now a part of NE Iran. —**Par′thi·an,** *adj., n.*

par·tial (pär′shəl), *adj.* **1** not complete; not total: *a partial loss.* **2** inclined to favor one side more than another; favoring unfairly. **3** favorably inclined: *be partial to sports.* [< LL, < L *pars* part] —**par′tial·ly,** *adv.* —**par′tial·ness,** *n.*

par·ti·al·i·ty (pär′shi al′ə ti; -shal′ə-), *n., pl.* **-ties.** **1** a favoring of one more than another or others; favorable prejudice; being partial: *treat all the students without partiality.* **2** a particular liking; fondness: *a partiality for candy.*

par·tic·i·pant (pär tis′ə pənt), *n.* one who shares or participates. —*adj.* participating.

par·tic·i·pate (pär tis′ə pāt), *v.,* **-pat·ed, -pat·ing.** have a share; take part. [< L *participatus,* ult. < *pars* part + *capere* take] —**par·tic′i·pa′tion,** *n.* —**par·tic′i·pa′tor,** *n.* —**par·tic′i·pa·to′ry,** *adj.*

par·ti·cip·i·al (pär′tə sip′i əl), *adj.* of or having to do with a participle, as a **participial adjective** (a *masked* man), a **participial noun** (the fatigue of *marching*). —**par′ti·cip′i·al·ly,** *adv.*

par·ti·ci·ple (pär′tə sip′əl), *n.* a form of a verb used as an adjective. [< OF,

< *participe* a sharing < L *participium.* See PARTICIPATE.]

par·ti·cle (pär′tə kəl), *n.* **1** a very little bit. **2** prefix or suffix. **3** preposition, conjunction, article, or interjection. *In, if, an,* and *ah* are particles. **4** portion of matter so small that it may be treated as a point without length, breadth, or thickness. [< L *particula,* dim. of *pars* part]

particle physics, branch of physics that deals with elementary particles. —**particle physicist.**

par·ti·col·ored (pär′ti kul′ərd), *adj.* colored differently in different parts.

par·tic·u·lar (pər tik′yə lər), *adj.* **1** apart from others; considered separately; single: *that particular chair is already sold.* **2** belonging to some one person, thing, group, occasion, etc.; not general: *a particular characteristic of a skunk is his smell.* **3** different from others; unusual; special: *a particular friend.* **4** hard to please; wanting everything to be just right; very careful. **5** giving details; full of details: *a particular account of the game.* —*n.* an individual part; item; point: *the work is complete in every particular.*

in particular, especially. [< OF < L *particularis.* See PARTICLE.]

par·tic·u·lar·i·ty (pər tik′yə lar′ə ti), *n., pl.* **-ties.** **1** detailed quality; minuteness. **2** special carefulness. **3** attentiveness to details. **4** a particular feature or trait. **5** quality of being hard to please. **6** quality or fact of beig particular.

par·tic·u·lar·ize (pər tik′yə lər īz), *v.,* **-ized, -iz·ing.** **1** mention particularly or individually; treat in detail. **2** mention individuals; give details. —**par·tic′u·lar·i·za′tion,** *n.*

par·tic·u·lar·ly (pər tik′yə lər li), *adv.* **1** in a high degree; especially. **2** in a particular manner; in detail; minutely.

par·tic·u·late (pär tik′yə lit; -lāt), *adj.* of, having to do with, or made up of very small particles. —*n.* small, separate particle, as of dust or fiber. [< L *particula* particle]

part·ing (pär′ting), *n.* **1** departure; going away. **2** a taking leave. **3** division; separation. **4** place of division or separation. —*adj.* **1** given, taken, done, etc., at parting: *a parting request, a parting shot.* **2** departing. **3** dividing; separating.

par·ti·san (pär′tə zən), *n.* **1** a strong supporter of a person, party, or cause; one whose support is based on feeling rather than on reasoning. **2** guerrilla. —*adj.* of or like a partisan. [< F < Ital. *partigiano* < *parte* PART] —**par′ti·san·ship′,** *n.*

par·ti·tion (pär tish′ən), *n.* **1** wall between rooms, etc. **2** division into parts: *the partition of a man's wealth when he dies.* —*v.* divide into parts: *partition a house into rooms.* [< L, < *partire* PART] —**par·ti′tion·ment,** *n.*

part·ly (pärt′li), *adv.* in part; in some measure or degree.

part·ner (pärt′nər), *n.* **1** one who shares. **2** member of a company or firm who shares the risk and profits of the business. **3 a** wife or husband. **b** intimate companion. **4** companion in a dance. **5** player on the same team or side in a game. [var. of *parcener* < AF, < *parçon* PARTITION; infl. by *part*]

part·ner·ship (pärt′nər ship), *n.* **1** a being a partner; joint interest; association: *the partnership of marriage.* **2** company or firm with two or more members who share in the risk and profits of the business. **3** the legal relation between persons who are legally partners in business. **4** the contract creating this relation.

part of speech, any one of the form classes which collectively include the total structure of a language.

par·tridge (pär′trij), *n., pl.* **-tridg·es** or (*esp. collectively*) **-tridge.** **1** any of several kinds of game birds belonging to the same group as the quail, pheasant, and grouse. **2** in the United States, the ruffed grouse or the quail. [< OF < L < Gk. *perdix*]

part song, song with parts in simple harmony for two or more voices, esp. one meant to be sung without an accompaniment.

part-time (pärt′tīm′), *adj., adv.* for less than the usual amount of time: *part-time work.* —**part′-tim′er,** *n.*

par·tu·ri·ent (pär tūr′i ənt; -tyúr′-), *adj.* **1** bringing forth young; about to give birth to young. **2** pertaining to childbirth.

par·tu·ri·tion (pär′tü rish′ən; -tyú-; -chú-), *n.* childbirth. [< L, < *parturire* be in labor, ult. < *parere* to bear]

par·ty (pär′ti), *n., pl.* **-ties,** *adj.* —*n.* **1** group of people doing something together: *a scouting party of three soldiers.* **2** a gathering for pleasure: *on her birthday she had a party and invited her friends.* **3** group of people wanting the same kind of government or action: *the Democratic Party.* **4** one who takes part in, aids, or knows about: *he was a party to our plot.* **5** each of the persons or sides in a contract, lawsuit, etc. —*adj.* of or pertaining to a party. [< OF *partie* < pp. of < *partir* divide, PART]

party line, generally accepted view.

par value, face value.

par·ve·nu (pär′və nü; -nū), *n.* one who has risen to a higher social level than he or she is accustomed to; upstart. [< F, pp. of *parvenir* arrive < L, < *per-* through + *venire* come]

par·vo (pär′vō), *n.* =parvovirus.

par·vo·cel·lu·lar (pär′vō sel′yə lər) **system,** pathway of cells, in the brain of humans and other primates, specialized to process color, form, and contrast.

par·vo·vi·rus (pär′vō vī′rəs), *n.* any one of a group of viruses found in animals, esp. one that causes serious disease in dogs.

pas·chal (pas′kəl), *adj.* **1** of or having to do with the Jewish Passover. **2** of or having to do with Easter; used in Easter celebrations.

pa·sha (pəshä´; pash´ə; pä´shə), *n.* **1** a former Turkish title of rank. **2** a civil or military official of high rank in Turkey. [< Turk., var. of *bāshā < bash* head]

Pash·to (push´tō), *n.* **1** Iranian language of Afghanistan and the Pathan people of Pakistan. **2** =Pathan. [< Pers. *pashtō* Afghan]

Pash·tun or **Pash·ton** (push tün´), *n.* member of a Muslim people of Afghanistan and Pakistan.

pasque·flow·er (pask´flou´ər), *n.* any of several anemones with purple or white flowers that bloom early in the spring. [*pasque* < OF, Easter, < L < Gk. < Heb. *pesaḥ* Passover]

pass (pas; päs), *v.,* **passed, passed** or **past, pass·ing,** *n.* —*v.* **1** go by; move past: *pass another car on the road.* **2** go from one to another; circulate: *his estate passed to his children, the curious coin was passed around.* **3** go across, around, or over: *pass a threshold, he passed a rope around his waist.* **4** go away: *the time for action had already passed.* **5** be successful in (an examination, a course, etc.). **6** ratify or enact: *pass a bill or law.* **7** exceed; surpass: *his performance passed all expectations.* **8** use; spend: *we passed the days pleasantly.* **9** be accepted (for or as): *use silk or a material that will pass for silk.* **10** express; pronounce: *a judge passes sentence on guilty persons.* **11** go without notice: *he was rude, but let that pass.* **12** transfer (the bail, etc.) in football, hockey, and other games. —*n.* **1** act of passing; passage. **2** success in an examination, etc. **3** free ticket. **4** state; condition: *things have come to a strange pass.* **5** a narrow road, path, way, channel, etc. esp. through mountains. **6** the transfer of a ball, etc., as in football.

bring to pass, accomplish; cause to be.

come to pass, take place; happen.

make a pass, flirt with.

pass away, come to an end; die.

pass by, overlook; disregard.

pass off, a fade away. **b** get accepted: *pass off as genuine.* **c** pretend to be: *successfully passed off as a journalist.* **d** dismiss; turn aside: *pass off a criticism.*

pass out, faint; lose consciousness.

pass over, overlook; disregard.

pass up, give up; renounce.

take a pass, a accept the grade of pass in a class rather than take an examination. **b** put off. [< OF *passer,* ult. < L *passus* step] —**pass´er,** *n.*

pass., **1** passenger. **2** passim. **3** passive.

pass·a·ble (pas´ə bəl; päs´-), *adj.* **1** fairly good; moderate: *a passable knowledge of geography.* **2** that can be passed: *a passable river, a passable coin, a passable bill.* —**pass´a·ble·ness,** *n.* —**pass´a·bly,** *adv.*

pas·sage (pas´ij), *n.* **1** hall or way through a building; passageway. **2** means of passing; way through: *passage through a crowd, the guard refused us passage.* **3**

a passing: *the passage of time, a stormy passage.* **4** piece from a speech or writing: *a passage from the Bible.* **5** a making into law by a favoring vote of a legislature: *the passage of a bill.* **6** phrase or other division of a piece of music. [< OF, < *passer* PASS]

pas·sage·way (pas´ij wā´), *n.* way along which one can pass; passage, as a hall or alley.

pass·book (pas´bůk´; päs´-), *n.* a small book in which a bank keeps an account of what a person puts in and takes out of a savings account; bankbook.

pas·sé (pa sā´; pas´ā), *adj.* **1** past. **2** past its usefulness. **3** out of date. [< F, passed]

pas·sel (pas´əl), *n.* a group: *a passel of chattering girls.* [var. of *parcel*]

pas·sen·ger (pas´ən jər), *n.* traveler in a plane, train, bus, boat, etc. [< OF *passagier < passage* PASSAGE]

passenger pigeon, kind of wild pigeon, now extinct, that flew far in a very large flocks.

pass·er-by (pas´ər bī´; päs´-), *n., pl.* **passers-by.** one that passes by.

pas·ser·ine (pas´ər in; –īn), *adj.* belonging or pertaining to the very large group of perching birds, including more than half of all birds. —*n.* a bird that perches. [< L, < *passer* sparrow]

pass-fail (pas´fāl´; päs´-), *adj.* graded only as passing or failing a course.

pas·sim (pas´im), *adv. Latin.* here and there; in various places.

pass·ing (pas´ing; päs´-), *adj.* **1** that passes. **2** transient; fleeting. **3** cursory; incidental. **4** that is now happening. **5** allowing one to pass an examination or test: *75 will be a passing mark.* —*n.* **1** act of one that passes; a going by; a departure. **2** means or place of passing.

in passing, as one proceeds or passes.

pas·sion (pash´ən), *n.* **1** very strong feeling. Hate and fear are passions. **2** violent anger; rage: *he flew into a passion.* **3** an ardent affection or sexual love between two people. **4** very strong liking: *she has a passion for music.* **5** object of a passion: *music is her passion.*

Passion. the sufferings of Jesus on the cross or after the Last Supper. [< OF < L *passio < pati* suffer] —**pas´sion·less,** *adj.* —**pas´sion·less·ly,** *adv.* —**pas´sion·lessness,** *n.*

pas·sion·ate (pash´ən it), *adj.* **1** having or showing strong feelings. **2** easily moved to anger. **3** resulting from strong feeling: *a passionate speech.* —**pas´sion·ate·ly,** *adv.* —**pas´sion·ate·ness,** *n.*

pas·sion·flow·er (pash´ən flou´ər), *n.* **1** plant with showy flowers supposed to suggest the crown of thorns, the wounds, the nails, etc., of Christ's crucifixion. **2** the flower.

Passion Play or **passion play,** play representing the sufferings and death of Christ.

pas·sive (pas´iv), *adj.* **1** not acting in return; just being acted on without itself

acting: *a passive mind or disposition.* **2** not resisting: *the slaves gave passive obedience to their master.* **3** inactive; quiescent; inert. **4** showing the subject as acted on. In "The window was broken by John," *was broken* is in the passive voice. —*n.* **1** a verb form that shows the subject as acted on. **2** the passive voice. [< L *passivus < pati* suffer] —**pas´sive·ly,** *adv.* —**pas´sive·ness, pas·siv´i·ty,** *n.*

passive resistance, peaceful resistance to esp. a government or other authority by refusing to obey a law or rule, etc.

passive restraint, device that automatically protects someone from injury, as a seatbelt or airbag in an automobile.

pass·key (pas´kē´; päs´-), *n., pl.* **–keys.** **1** key for opening several locks. **2** a private key.

Pass·o·ver (pas´ō´vər; päs´-), *n.* an annual feast of the Jews in memory of the sparing of the Hebrews in Egypt. Exod. 12.

pass·port (pas´pôrt; –pōrt; päs´-) *n.* **1** a paper or book giving official permission to travel in a certain country, under the protection of one's own government. **2** *Fig.* anything that gives one admission or acceptance.

pass·word (pas´wėrd´; päs´-), *n.* a secret word that allows a person speaking it to pass a guard.

past (past; päst), *adj.* **1** gone by; ended: *our troubles are past.* **2** having served a term in office: *a past president.* **3** indicating time gone by, or former action or state: *the past tense, a past participle.* —*n.* **1** time gone by; time before; what has happened: *life began far back in the past, our country has a glorious past.* **2** one's past life, esp. if hidden or unknown. **3** the past tense or a verb form in it. —*prep.* **1** beyond; farther on than: *past the mark, it is past noon.* —*adv.* so as to pass by or beyond: *trains go past quite frequently.* —*v.* pp. of **pass.**

pas·ta (päs´tə), *n.* any of certain foods made of flour, eggs, water, and salt, rolled and fashioned into different shapes and then usually dried, such as spaghetti, macaroni, etc. [< Ital.]

paste (pāst), *n., v.,* **past·ed, past·ing.** —*n.* **1** mixture, such as flour and water boiled together, that will stick paper together. **2** dough for pastry. **3** a soft, doughlike mixture. Fish paste is mashed fish. **4** a hard, glassy material used in making imitations of precious stones. —*v.* **1** stick with paste. **2** *Informal.* strike, esp. with a fist; beat. [< OF < LL < Gk., *pasta* porridge]

paste·board (pāst´bôrd´; –bōrd´), *n.* a stiff material made of sheets of paper pasted together or of paper pulp pressed and dried.

pas·tel (pas tel´; pas´tel), *n.* **1** kind of crayon used in drawing. **2** a drawing made with such crayons. **3** a soft, pale shade of some color. [< F < Ital., < LL *pasta* PASTE]

past·er (pās'tər), *n.* someone or something that pastes.

pas·tern (pas'tərn), *n.* the part of a horse's foot between the fetlock and the hoof. [< OF *pasturon,* dim. of *pasture* tether for a horse, ult. < L *pastor* herdsman. See PASTOR.]

pas·teur·ize (pas'chəriz; –tər–), *v.,* **–ized, –iz·ing.** heat (milk, etc.) to a high enough temperature to destroy harmful bacteria, etc. [after L. *Pasteur*] **—pas'teur·i·za'tion,** *n.*

pas·teur·iz·er (pas'chər iz'ər), *n.* equipment for pasteurizing milk, wine, etc.

pas·time (pas'tīm'; päs'–), *n.* a pleasant way of passing time; amusement; recreation.

past master, person who has much experience in any profession, art, etc.

pas·tor (pas'tər; päs'–), *n.* minister in charge of a church; spiritual guide. [< L, shepherd, < *pascere* feed] **—pas'tor·ship,** *n.*

pas·tor·al (pas'tər əl; päs'–), *adj.* **1** of shepherds or country life. **2** simple or naturally beautiful like the country. **3** of a pastor or his duties. —*n.* **1** a pastoral play, poem, or picture. **2** letter from a bishop to his clergy or to the people of his church district. **—pas'tor·al·ism,** *n.* **pas'tor·al·ist,** *n.* **—pas'tor·al·ly,** *adv.*

pas·to·rale (pas'tə räl'; päs'–), *n.* **1** musical composition that evokes the beauty of the countryside. **2** *Fig.* something like a pastorale in character, as a poem. Also, **pastoral.** [< It. *pastorale* pastoral]

pas·tor·ate (pas'tər it; päs'–), **pas·tor·age** (–ij), *n.* **1** position or duties of a pastor. **2** term of service of a pastor. **3** pastors as a group.

past participle, participle that indicates time gone by, or a former action or state. *Played* and *thrown* are past participles in "She has played all day," "The ball should have been thrown to me."

past perfect, *n.* **1** a verb form showing that an event was completed before a given past time; pluperfect. In "He had learned to read before he went to school," *had learned* is the past perfect of *learn.* **2** the past perfect tense or a verb form in it. —*adj.* of or pertaining to this verb form.

pas·tra·mi (pəs trä'mi), *n.* a smoked and well-seasoned cut of beef, usually sliced thin on a sandwich. [< Yiddish]

pas·try (pās'tri), *n., pl.* **–tries. 1** food made of baked flour paste, made rich with lard, butter, or a vegetable shortening. **2** pies, tarts, and other foods wholly or partly made of rich flour paste. [< *paste*]

pas·tur·age (pas'chər ij; päs'–), *n.* **1** the growing grass and other plants for cattle, sheep, or horses to feed on. **2** pasture land.

pas·ture (pas'chər; päs'–), *n., v.,* **–tured, –tur·ing.** —*n.* **1** a grassy field or hillside; grasslands on which cattle, sheep, or horses can feed. **2** the grass and other growing plants. —*v.* **1** put (cattle, sheep, etc.) out to pasture. **2** (of cattle, sheep, etc.) feed on (growing grass, etc.). [< OF < LL *pastura* < L *pascere* feed]

past·y (pās'ti), *adj.,* **past·i·er, past·i·est. 1** like paste. **2** pale. **3** flabby. **—past'i·ness,** *n.*

pat¹ (pat), *v.,* **pat·ted, pat·ting,** *n.* —*v.* **1** strike or tap lightly with something flat: *she patted the dough into a flat cake.* **2** tap with the hand as a sign of sympathy, approval or affection: *pat a dog.* —*n.* **1** a light stroke or tap with the hand or with something flat. **2** sound made by patting. **3** a small mass, esp. of butter, shaped by patting. [OE *potian* push]

pat² (pat), *adj.* apt; suitable: *a pat reply.* —*adv.* aptly; exactly; suitably.

stand pat, hold to things as they are and refuse to change. [prob. special use of *pat¹*] **—pat'ness,** *n.*

patch (pach), *n.* **1** piece put on to mend a hole or a tear. **2** pad over a hurt eye to protect it. **3** piece of ground: *a garden patch.* —*v.* **1** protect or adorn with a patch or patches; put patches on; mend. **2** piece together; make hastily.

patch up, a put an end to; settle. **b** make right hastily or for a time. **c** put together hastily or poorly. [ME *pacche*] **—patch'er,** *n.* **—patch'y,** *adj.* **—patch'i·ly,** *adv.* **—patch'i·ness,** *n.*

patch pocket, flat pocket sewn on the outside of a jacket, coat, etc.

patch test, test for allergy to a substance in which the substance is applied directly to the skin, often with a small pad or patch.

patch·up (pach'up'), *adj.* improvised; makeshift: *a patch-up repair.*

patch·work (pach'wėrk'), *n.* **1** pieces of cloth of various colors or shapes sewed together: *a patchwork quilt.* **2** anything like this.

pate (pāt), *n.* **1** top of the head; head. **2** brains.

pâ·té or **pa·te** (pä tā'), *n.* **1** finely chopped meat, livers, etc., seasoned with herbs and spices, baked and often served cold. **2** pastry filled with meat, vegetables, etc., in a sauce; patty. [< F]

pâ·té de foie gras (pä tā' də fwä grä'), *French.* paste made with livers of specially fattened geese.

pa·tel·la (pə tel'ə), *n., pl.* **–tel·las, –tel·lae** (–tel'ē) =kneecap. [< L, dim. of *patina* pan] **—pa·tel'lar,** *adj.*

pat·ent (*n., adj.* **1** *v.* pat'ənt, *adj.* **2, 3** pā'tənt, pat'ənt), *n.* **1** a government grant to a person by which he or she is the only one allowed to make or sell a new invention for a certain number of years. **2** invention that is patented. **3** an official document from a government giving a right or privilege. —*adj.* **1** given or protected by a patent. **2** evident; plain: *it is patent that cats dislike dogs.* **3** open. —*v.* get a patent for. [< L *patens* lying open] **—pa'ten·cy,** *n.* **—pat'ent·a·ble,** *adj.* **—pat'ent·a-**
bil'i·ty, *n.* **—pat'ent·ee',** *n.* **—pa'tent·ly,** *adv.* **—pat'en·tor,** *n.*

pat·ent leather (pat'ənt), leather with a very glossy, smooth surface, often black.

pa·ter·nal (pə tėr'nəl), *adj.* **1** of or like a father; fatherly. **2** related on the father's side of the family: *a paternal aunt, cousin, etc.* **3** received or inherited from one's father: *Mary's blue eyes were a paternal inheritance.* [< LL, ult. < *pater* father] **—pa·ter'nal·ly,** *adv.*

pa·ter·nal·ism (pə tėr'nəl iz əm), *n.* management of the affairs of a country or group of people in the way that a father manages the affairs of his family and children. **—pa·ter'nal·is'tic,** *adj.* **—pa·ter'nal·is'ti·cal·ly,** *adv.*

pa·ter·ni·ty (pə tėr'nə ti), *n.* **1** being a father; fatherhood. **2** paternal origin: *King Arthur's paternity was unknown.*

pat·er·nos·ter (pat'ər nos'tər; pā'tər–), *n.* **1** the Lord's Prayer, esp. in Latin. **2** one of the beads of a rosary on which the Lord's Prayer is said. [< L, our father]

path (path; päth), *n., pl.* **paths** (paTHz; päTHz). **1** way made by people or animals walking, usually too narrow for automobiles or wagons. **2** walk through a garden or park. **3** line along which a person or thing moves; route; track: *the moon has a regular path through the sky.* **4** way of acting or behaving. [OE *pæth*] **—path'less,** *adj.* **—path'less·ness,** *n.*

Pa·than (pə tän'; pət hän'), *n.* **1** member of a major group of Afghan people living in Afghanistan, Pakistan, and India. **2** an Afghan. —*adj.* of or having to do with the Pathans. [< Hind. *Paṭhān* < Afghan]

pa·thet·ic (pə thet'ik), *adj.* **1** pitiful; arousing pity. **2** of the emotions. [< LL < Gk. *pathetikos,* ult < *pathein* suffer] **—pa·thet'i·cal·ly,** *adv.*

pathetic fallacy, attributing human emotions and characteristics to nature.

path·find·er (path'fīn'dər; päth'–), *n.* one who finds a path or way.

path·o·gen·ic (path'ə jen'ik), *adj.* producing disease. [< *patho–* (< Gk. *pathos* disease) + *–genic* (ult. < Gk. *gen–* produce)] **—path'o·gen,** *n.*

pathol., pathology.

pa·thol·o·gize (pə tho'ə jīz), *v.,* **–gized, –giz·ing.** diagnose and treat, esp. behavior, as evidence of a diseased condition: *pathologize simple naughtiness.*

pa·thol·o·gy (pə thol'ə ji), *n., pl.* **–gies. 1** study of the causes and nature of diseases. **2** unhealthy conditions and processes caused by a disease. [< *patho–* (< Gk. *pathos* disease) + –LOGY] **—path'o·log'ic, path'o·log'i·cal,** *adj.* **—path'o·log'i·cal·ly,** *adv.* **—pa·thol'o·gist,** *n.*

pa·thos (pā'thos), *n.* quality in speech, writing, music, events, or a scene that arouses a feeling of pity or sadness. [< Gk., suffering, feeling]

path·way (path'wā'; päth'–), *n.* path.

–pathy, *suffix.* **1** feeling, as in *antipathy.* **2** disease, as in *neuropathy.* **3** treatment of disease, as in *osteopathy*. [< Gk. -*patheia*]

pa·tience (pā'shəns), *n.* **1** willingness to put up with waiting, pain, trouble, etc.; calm endurance without complaining or losing self-control. **2** long, hard work; steady effort.

pa·tient (pā'shənt), *adj.* **1** willing to put up with waiting, pain, trouble, etc.; enduring calmly without complaining or losing self-control. **2** with steady effort or long, hard work; quietly persevering. —*n.* person who is being treated by a doctor. [< OF < L *patiens* suffering] —**pa'tient·ly**, *adv.*

pat·i·na (pat'ə nə), *n.* **1** film or incrustation, usually green, on the surface of old bronze. **2** film or coloring produced in the course of time on wood or other substance. [< Ital.]

pat·i·o (pat'ī ō; pä'tī ō), *n.*, *pl.* **-i·os. 1** an inner court or yard open to the sky. **2** terrace for outdoor eating, lounging, etc. [< Sp.]

pat·ois (pat'wä), *n.*, *pl.* **pat·ois** (pat'wäz). dialect spoken by the common people of a district: *the patois of the French Canadians.* [< F]

pa·tri·arch (pā'tri ärk), *n.* **1** father and ruler of a family or tribe. **2** person thought of as the father or founder of something. **3** a venerable old man. [< L < Gk., *patria* family + *archos* leader] —**pa'tri·ar'chal, pa'tri·ar'chic,** *adj.* —**pa'tri·ar'chal·ly,** *adv.*

pa·tri·ar·chy (pā'tri är'ki), *n.*, *pl.* **-chies.** form of social organization in which the father is head of the family and in which descent is reckoned in the male line, the children belonging to the father's clan.

pa·tri·cian (pə trish'ən), *n.* **1** noble; aristocrat. **2** member of the nobility of ancient Rome. —*adj.* **1** of high social rank; aristocratic. **2** like or characteristic of an aristocrat. **3** of the patricians. [< L *patricius* of the *patres* (senators, lit., fathers) at Rome] —**pa·tri'cian·ism,** *n.*

pat·ri·cide[1] (pat'rə sīd), *n.* crime of killing one's father. [< LL, < L *pater* father + -*cidium* act of killing] —**pat'ri·cid'al,** *adj.*

pat·ri·cide[2] (pat'rə sīd), *n.* person who kills his or her father. [< Med.L, < L *pater* father + -*cida* killer]

pat·ri·mo·ny (pat'rə mō'ni), *n.*, *pl.* **-nies. 1** property inherited from one's father or ancestors. **2** property belonging to a church, monastery, or convent. **3** any heritage. [< OF < L *patrimonium* < *pater* father] —**pat'ri·mo'ni·al,** *adj.*

pa·tri·ot (pā'tri ət; -ot), *n.* person who loves and loyally supports his or her country. [< LL < Gk. *patriotes*, ult. < *patris* fatherland] —**pa'tri·ot'ic,** *adj.* —**pa'tri·ot'i·cal·ly,** *adv.*

pa·tri·ot·ism (pā'tri ət iz'əm), *n.* love and loyal support of one's country.

pa·trol (pə trōl'), *v.,* **-trolled, -trol·ling,** *n.* —*v.* go around (a town, camp, etc.) to watch or guard. —*n.* **1** people who patrol: *the patrol was changed at mid-*

night. **2** a going of the rounds to watch or guard. **3** group of soldiers, ships, or airplanes, sent out to find out all they can about the enemy. [< F *patrouiller* paddle in mud] —**pa·trol'ler,** *n.*

pa·trol·man (pə trōl'mən), or **pa·trol·wo·man** (pə trōl'wüm'ən), *n.,* *pl.* **-men.** police officer, etc., who patrols a certain district.

pa·tron (pā'trən), *n.* **1** one who buys regularly at a given store. **2** person who gives his or her approval and support to some person, art, cause, or undertaking. **3** a guardian saint or god. [< OF < L *patronus* < *pater* father. Doublet of PATROON.] —**pa'tron·al,** *adj.*

pa·tron·age (pā'trən ij; pat'rən-), *n.* **1** regular business given by customers. **2** favor, encouragement, or support given by a patron. **3** condescending favor: *an air of patronage.* **4** power to give jobs or favors: *the patronage of a Congressman.* **5** political jobs or favors.

pa·tron·ess (pā'trən is; pat'rən-), *n.* **1** a woman patron. **2** lady who helps some entertainment with her name, money, or presence.

pa·tron·ize (pā'trən īz; pat'rən-), *v.,* **-ized, -iz·ing. 1** be a regular customer of; give regular business to. **2** act as a patron toward; support or protect. **3** treat in a condescending way: *we dislike to have anyone patronize us.* —**pa'tron·iz'er,** *n.* —**pa'tron·iz'ing,** *adj.* —**pa'tron·iz'ing·ly,** *adv.*

patron saint, saint regarded as the special guardian of a person, church, city, etc.

pat·ro·nym·ic (pat'rə nim'ik), *n.* name derived from the name of a father or ancestor. Williamson is a patronymic. [< LL < Gk., < *pater* father + *dial. onyma* name]

pa·troon (pə trün'), *n.* owner of a very large estate in land who had certain privileges under the Dutch governments that controlled New York and New Jersey before the British. [< Du. < L *patronus.* Doublet of PATRON.]

pat·ter[1] (pat'ər), *v.,* make rapid taps: *bare feet pattered along the hard floor.* —*n.* series of quick taps or the sound they make. [< PAT[1]]

pat·ter[2] (pat'ər), *n.* **1** rapid and easy talk: *a magician's patter.* **2** talk of a class or group: *the patter of beggars and thieves.* **3** lyrics for a song, often comic, intended to be sung rapidly. —*v.* talk or say rapidly and easily, without much thought. [var. of *pater* in *paternoster*] —**pat'ter·er,** *n.*

pat·tern (pat'ərn), *n.* **1** arrangement of forms and colors; design: *the patterns of wallpaper, rugs, cloth, and jewelry.* **2** model or guide for something to be made. **3** a fine example; model to be followed. —*v.* make according to a pattern: *she patterned herself after her mother.* [< OF *patron* pattern, PATRON]

pat·terned (pat'ərnd), *adj.* having or decorated with patterns.

pat·ty (pat'i), *n.,* *pl.* **-ties. 1** Also, **patty shell,** a hollow form of pastry filled with chicken, oysters, etc. **2** a small, round, flat piece of food or candy. [< F *pâté*]

pau·ci·ty (pô'sə ti), *n.* **1** a small number; fewness. **2** a small amount; scarcity; lack. [< L, < *paucus* few]

paunch (pônch; pänch), *n.* **1** belly; stomach. **2** a large, protruding belly. [< OF *panche* < L *pantex*] —**paunch'y,** *adj.* —**paunch'i·ness,** *n.*

pau·per (pô'pər), *n.* a very poor person; person supported by charity. [< L, poor. Doublet of POOR.]

pau·per·ism (pô'pər iz əm), *n.* poverty.

pau·per·ize (pô'pər īz), *v.,* **-ized, -iz·ing.** make a pauper of. —**pau'per·i·za'tion,** *n.*

pause (pôz), *v.,* **paused, paus·ing,** *n.* —*v.* **1** stop for a time; wait. **2** dwell; linger: *pause upon a word.* —*n.* **1** moment of silence; stop; rest. **2** a brief stop in speaking or reading. **3** *Music.* a sign (⌣ or ⌢) above or below a note, meaning that it is to be held for a longer time.

give pause, a cause to be wait. **b** cause uneasiness. [< F < L < Gk. *pausis* < *pauein* to stop] —**pause'less,** *adj.* —**pause'less·ly,** *adv.* —**paus'er,** *n.* —**paus'ing·ly,** *adv.*

pav·an or **pav·ane** (pav'ən, pə vän'), *n.* slow, stately dance or the music for it. [< F]

pave (pāv), *v.,* **paved, pav·ing. 1** cover (a street, sidewalk, etc.) with a pavement. **2** make smooth or easy; prepare. [< OF *paver,* ult. < L *pavire* beat, tread down] —**pav'er,** *n.*

pave·ment (pāv'mənt), *n.* **1** covering for streets, sidewalks, etc., made of stones, bricks, wood, asphalt, etc. **2** material used for paving.

pa·vil·ion (pə vil'yən), *n.* **1** a light building, usually one somewhat open, used for shelter, pleasure, etc.: *a bathing pavilion.* **2** a large tent raised on posts; tent. —*v.* furnish with a pavilion; enclose or shelter in a pavilion. [< OF < L *papilio* tent, butterfly]

pav·ing (pāv'ing), *n.* **1** material for pavement. **2** pavement.

paw (pô), *n.* **1** foot of an animal having claws. Cats and dogs have paws. **2** *Informal.* hand. —*v.* **1** strike or scrape with the paws or feet: *the cat pawed the mouse.* **2** *Informal.* handle awkwardly, roughly, or in too familiar a manner. [< OF *powe* < Gmc.] —**paw'er,** *n.*

pawl (pôl), *n.* a pivoted bar arranged to catch in the teeth of a ratchet wheel or the like to prevent movement backward or to impart motion.

pawn[1] (pôn), *v.* leave (something) with another person as security that borrowed money will be repaid: *he pawned his watch to buy food.* [< n.] —*n.* something left as security.

in pawn, in another's possession as security; a pledge. [< OF *pan*] —**pawn'er,** *n.*

pawn[2] (pôn), *n.* **1** one of the 16 pieces of lowest value in chess. **2** person or thing used by someone for his own purposes.

[< AF, var. of OF *peon* < LL *pedo* foot soldier < L *pes* foot. Doublet of PEON.]

pawn·bro·ker (pôn′brō′kər), *n.* person who lends money at interest on articles that are left as security for the loan. —**pawn′bro′king,** *n.*

Paw·nee (pô nē′), *n.* member of an American Indian tribe that lived near the forks of the Platte River.

pawn·shop (pôn′shop′), *n.* pawnbroker's shop.

paw·paw (pô′pô), *n.* =papaw.

pay (pā), *v.,* **paid** or (*Obs. except for def. 13*) **payed, pay·ing,** *n.* —*v.* **1** give (a person) what is due for things, work, etc. **2** give money owed: *pay your way, pay a debt.* **3** give; offer: *pay attention.* **4** be profitable; be worth while to: *it wouldn't pay to take that job, it pays to be polite.* **5** reward or punish: *paid for their insults by causing trouble.* **6** suffer; undergo: *the one who does wrong must pay.* **7** let out (a rope, etc.). —*n.* money or equivalent given for things or work; return for favors or hurts.

in the pay of, paid by and working for.

pay as you go, pay or discharge obligations as they are incurred.

pay back, a return money borrowed. **b** *Fig.* give the same treatment as one received. **c** *Fig.* get even with; get revenge on.

pay off, give all the money that is owed; pay in full. [< OF < L *pacare* pacify < *pax* peace] —**pay·ee′,** *n.* —**pay′er,** *n.*

pay·a·ble (pā′ə bəl), *adj.* **1** required to be paid; due: *bills payable.* **2** that may be paid.

pay dirt, 1 earth, ore, etc., containing enough metal to be worth mining. **2** *Fig.* something profitable or beneficial.

pay·load (pā′lōd′), *n.* **1** load carried by a rocket, aircraft, vehicle, etc. **2** missile warhead.

pay·mas·ter (pā′mas′tər; –mäs′–), *n.* person whose job is to pay wages.

pay·ment (pā′mənt), *n.* **1** a paying. **2** amount paid. **3** reward or punishment.

pay·off (pā′ôf′; –of′), *n.* **1** a paying of wages. **2** time of such payment. **3** returns from an enterprise, specific action, etc. **4** climax (of a story, situation, etc.).

pay roll, 1 list of persons to be paid and the amounts that each one is to receive. **2** the total amount to be paid to them.

payt., payment.

Pb, lead. [< L *plumbum*]

PC, (pē′sē′), **1** personal computer. **2** politically correct.

pc., *pl.* **pcs.** piece.

pct., p.c., percent.

Pd, palladium.

pd., paid.

P.D., Police Department.

pea (pē), *n., pl.* **peas. 1** the round seed in the pod of a plant, used as a vegetable. **2** the plant itself. **3** seed or plant like a pea.

(as) like as two peas (in a pod), very much alike; akin. [< *pease,* orig. sing., later taken as a pl.]

peace (pēs), *n.* **1** freedom from war or strife of any kind. **2** public quiet, order, and security. **3** agreement between contending parties to end war: *the Peace of Paris.* **4** freedom from disturbance; quiet; calm: *peace of mind.* *interj.* keep still! stay quiet!

at peace, a not at war or quarreling. **b** quiet; peaceful.

hold or **keep one's peace,** be silent.

make peace, bring about an understanding or settlement of differences between individuals, countries, etc. [< OF < L *pax*]

peace·a·ble (pēs′ə bəl), *adj.* **1** liking peace; keeping peace: *peaceable people refrain from quarreling.* **2** peaceful: *a peaceable reign.* —**peace′a·ble·ness,** *n.* —**peace′a·bly,** *adv.*

Peace Corps, an agency of the U.S. government, set up in 1961 to provide people with technical skills to underdeveloped countries.

peace·ful (pēs′fəl), *adj.* **1** full of peace; quiet; calm. **2** liking peace; keeping peace. **3** of or having to do with peace. —**peace′ful·ly,** *adv.* —**peace′ful·ness,** *n.*

peace·keep·ing (pēs′kē′ping), *adj.* intervening to end hostilities or maintaining an end to hostilities between enemies. —*n.* task or duties of a peacekeeper or peacekeeping force. —**peace′keep′er,** *n.*

peace·mak·er (pēs′māk′ər), *n.* person who makes peace. —**peace′mak′ing,** *n., adj.*

peace officer, police officer, sheriff, or constable.

peace pipe, pipe smoked by American Indians as a token or pledge of peace.

peace·time (pēs′tīm′), *n.* a time of peace. —*adj.* of or having to do with such a time.

peach (pēch), *n.* **1** a juicy, nearly round fruit having a rough stone or pit. **2** tree that it grows on. **3** fruit or tree like a peach. **4** a yellowish pink. **5** *Informal.* someone especially admirable or likable. —*adj.* yellowish-pink. [< OF, ult. < L *Persicum* (*malum*) Persian apple < Gk.]

peach·y (pēch′i), *adj.* **peach·i·er, peach·i·est.** like a peach. —**peach′i·ness,** *n.*

pea·cock (pē′kok′), *n., pl.* **–cocks** or (*esp. collectively*) **–cock.** male peafowl, a showy bird with beautiful green, blue, and gold feathers. The tail feathers have spots like eyes on them and can be spread out and held upright like a fan. [ult. < OE *pēa* (< L *pavo* peafowl) + *cock*¹]

pea·fowl (pē′foul′), *n.* peacock or peahen.

pea green, light green.

pea·hen (pē′hen′), *n.* female of the peacock with less showy feathers and coloration than the male.

pea jacket, a short coat of thick woolen cloth worn by sailors. Also, **peacoat.**

peak (pēk), *n.* **1** the pointed top of a mountain or hill. **2** mountain that stands alone. **3** the highest point. **4** any pointed end or top: *the peak of a beard, the peak of a roof.* **5** the front part or the brim of a cap, which stands out. —*v.* raise straight up; tilt up. [var. of *pick*²]

peaked¹ (pēkt; pēk′id), *adj.* having a peak; pointed.

peak·ed² (pēk′id), *adj.* pale, thin. [< *peak, v.,* look sick]

peal (pēl), *n.* **1** a loud, long sound: *a peal of thunder.* **2** the loud ringing of bells, esp. of a set of bells rung in a certain order. **3** set of bells; chimes. —*v.* sound out in a peal; ring. [ME *pele*]

pea·nut (pē′nut′), *n.* **1** plant of the same family as the pea, whose pods ripen underground and contain large seeds which are used as nuts when roasted. **2** one of these pods containing seeds. **3** one of these seeds.

peanut brittle, hard candy made of melted sugar and peanuts.

peanut butter, food made of peanuts ground until soft and smooth.

pear (pãr), *n.* **1** a sweet, juicy fruit rounded at one end and smaller toward the stem end. **2** tree that it grows on. **3** fruit or plant like a pear. [< LL *pira* < L *pirum*] —**pear′-shaped′,** *adj.*

pearl (pėrl), *n.* **1** a white or nearly white gem that has a soft shine like satin, formed inside the shell of a kind of oyster, or in other similar shellfish. **2** thing that looks like a pearl, such as a dewdrop or a tear. **3** a very fine one of its kind. **4** a very pale, clear, bluish gray. —*adj.* **1** very pale, clear bluish-gray. **2** formed into small, round pieces: *pearl tapioca.* —*v.* hunt or dive for pearls. [< OF *perle;* ? akin to L *perna,* a bivalve] —**pearl′er,** *n.* —**pearl′y,** *adj.* —**pearl′i·ness,** *n.*

pearl gray, a soft, pale, bluish gray.

peas·ant (pez′ənt), *n.* farmer of the working class in Europe. [< AF var. of OF *paysant* < *pays* country, ult. < L *pagus* district]

peas·ant·ry (pez′ənt ri), *n.* peasants.

pease (pēz), *n. Archaic.* pl. of **pea.** [< LL *pisa* < L *pisum* < Gk. *pison*]

peat (pēt), *n.* kind of turf, used as fuel after being dried. Peat is made of partly rotted moss and plants. —**peat′y,** *adj.*

pea·vey, pea·vy (pē′vi), *n., pl.* **–veys; –vies.** a strong stick that is tipped with an iron or steel point and has a hinged hook near the end. Lumbermen use peaveys in managing logs. [after J. Peavey, the inventor]

peb·ble (peb′əl), *n., v.,* **–bled, –bling.** —*n.* a small stone, usually worn and rounded by being rolled about by water. —*v.* prepare (leather) so that it has a grained surface. [OE *pœbbel* (in place names)] —**peb′bled, peb′bly,** *adj.*

pe·can (pi kän′; –kan′; pē′kan), *n.* **1** an olive-shaped nut with a smooth, thin shell, that grows on a kind of hickory tree common in the S United States. **2** tree that it grows on. [< Algonquian *pakan* hard-shelled nut]

pec·ca·dil·lo (pek′ə dil′ō), *n., pl.* **-loes, -los.** a minor sin or fault. [< Sp. *pecadillo,* dim. of *pecado* sin < L *peccatum*]

pec·ca·ry (pek′ə ri), *n., pl.* **-ries** or (*esp. collectively*) **-ry.** kind of wild pig found in South America and as far N as Texas. [< Carib *pakira*]

peck[1] (pek), *n.* **1** unit of dry measure, eight quarts or one fourth of a bushel: *a peck of potatoes.* **2** container holding just a peck, to measure with. **3** a great deal: *a peck of trouble.* [ME *pec*]

peck[2] (pek), *v.* **1** strike and pick with the beak, esp. with pounding movements. **2** make by striking with the beak: *woodpeckers peck holes in trees.* **3** strike at and pick up with the beak: *a hen pecks corn.* **4** *Informal.* eat only a little, bit by bit. **5** find fault. —*n.* **1** stroke made with the beak. **2** hole or mark made by pecking. **3** stiff, unwilling kiss. [akin to *pick*[1]] —**peck′er,** *n.*

peck·ing order (pek′ing), **1** order of dominance, esp. among fowl, in which the dominant bird pecks another weaker bird, and so on down the line. **2** any hierarchical order, as in a group of young people or an office.

pec·tin (pek′tin), *n.* substance that occurs in ripe fruits and makes fruit jelly stiff. [< Gk. *pektos* congealing, curdling < *pegnynai* make stiff]

pec·to·ral (pek′tə rəl), *adj.* of, in, or on the breast or chest. [< L, < *pectus* chest] —**pec′to·ral·ly,** *adv.*

pe·cul·iar (pi kūl′yər), *adj.* **1** strange; odd; unusual. **2** belonging to one person or thing and not to another; special: *this book has a peculiar value.* [< *peculiaris* of one's own < *peculium* property. See PECULATE.] —**pe·cul′iar·ly,** *adv.*

pe·cu·li·ar·i·ty (pi kū′li ar′ə ti), *n., pl.* **-ties. 1** a being peculiar; strangeness; oddness; unusualness. **2** thing or feature that is strange or odd. **3** a distinguishing quality or feature.

pe·cu·ni·ar·y (pi kū′ni er′i), *adj.* of or pertaining to money; in the form of money. [< L, < *pecunia* money. See PECULATE.] —**pe·cu′ni·ar′i·ly,** *adv.*

ped·a·gog·ic (ped′ə goj′ik; -gō′jik), **ped·a·gog·i·cal** (-ə kəl), *adj.* of teachers or teaching; of pedagogy. —**ped′a·gog′i·cal·ly,** *adv.*

ped·a·gogue (ped′ə gog; -gôg), *n.* **1** teacher. **2** a narrow-minded teacher. [< OF < L < Gk. *paidagogos* < *pais* boy + *agogos* leader]

ped·a·go·gy (ped′ə gō′ji; -goj′i), *n.* **1** teaching. **2** science or art of teaching.

ped·al (*n., v.* ped′əl; *adj.* ped′əl, pē′dəl), *n., v.,* **-aled, -al·ing,** *adj.* —*n.* lever worked by the foot; the part on which the foot is placed to move any kind of machinery. Organs and pianos have pedals for changing the tone. —*v.* **1** work or use the pedals of; move by pedals: *he pedaled his bicycle up the hill.* **2** work pedals. —*adj.* of or having to do with the foot or feet.

[< F < Ital. < L *pedale* (thing) of the foot < *pes* foot] —**ped′al·er, ped′al·ist,** *n.*

ped·ant (ped′ənt), *n.* **1** person who displays his or her knowledge in an unnecessary or tiresome way. **2** a dull, narrow-minded teacher or scholar. [< Ital. *pedante,* ult. < Gk. *paideuein* educate] —**pe·dan′tic,** *adj.* —**pe·dan′ti·cal·ly,** *adv.* —**pe·dan′ti·cism,** *n.*

ped·ant·ry (ped′ənt ri), *n., pl.* **-ries. 1** an unnecessary or tiresome display of knowledge. **2** overemphasis on book learning.

ped·dle (ped′əl), *v.,* **-dled, -dling. 1** carry from place to place and sell. **2** sell or deal out in small quantities; *peddle candy.* **3** travel about with things to sell. —**ped′dler, ped′lar,** *n.*

ped·er·as·ty (ped′ər as′ti; pē′dər-), *n.* sexual intercourse of a male with a male, esp. of a man with a boy. [< NL < Gk. *paiderastia* < *pais* boy + *eran* to love] —**ped′er·ast,** *n.*

ped·es·tal (ped′is təl), *n.* **1** base on which a column or statue stands. **2** base of a tall vase, lamp, etc. **3** base; support; foundation. [< F < Ital. *piedestallo* < *pie* foot (< L *pes*) + *di* of + *stallo* STALL[1] (<Gmc.)]

pe·des·tri·an (pə des′tri ən), *n.* person who goes on foot; walker. —*adj.* **1** going on foot; walking. **2** *Fig.* without imagination; dull; slow. [< L *pedester* on foot < *pes* foot] —**pe·des′tri·an·ism,** *n.*

pe·di·a·tri·cian (pē′di ə trish′ən; ped′i-), *n.* doctor who specializes in pediatrics.

pe·di·at·rics (pē′di at′riks; ped′i-), *n.* branch of medicine dealing with children's diseases and the care of babies and children. [pl. of *pediatric* < Gk. *pais* child + *iatreia* medical treatment] —**pe′di·at′ric,** *adj.*

ped·i·cab (ped′ə kab′), *n.* three-wheeled bicycle with a place for one or two passengers, pedaled by a driver. [< L *pēs* foot + E taxi*cab*]

ped·i·cel (ped′ə səl), *n.* a small stalk or stalklike part. [< NL *pedicellus,* ult < L *pes* foot]

ped·i·gree (ped′ə grē), *n.* **1** list of ancestors; family tree. **2** ancestry; line of descent. [appar. < F *pied de grue* foot of a crane; from appearance of 3-branched mark used in genealogies] —**ped′i·greed,** *adj.*

ped·i·ment (ped′ə mənt), *n.* the low triangular part on the front of buildings in the Greek style.

pe·dol·o·gy (pi dol′ə ji), *n.* branch of science concerned with the nature, origin, and use of soils. [< Gk. *pédon* soil + E *-logy*] —**pe′do·log′i·cal,** *adj.* —**pe·dol′o·gist,** *n.*

pe·dom·e·ter (pi dom′ə tər), *n.* instrument for recording the number of steps taken and thus measuring the distance traveled. [< F, < *pedo-* (< L *pes* foot) + *-metre* -METER]

pe·dun·cle (pi dung′kəl), *n.* stalk; stem; stalklike part. [< NL *pedunculus,* dim.

of L *pes* foot] —**pe·dun′cled,** *adj.* —**pe·dun′cu·lar,** *adj.*

peek (pēk), *v.* look quickly and slyly; peep. —*n.* a quick, sly look. [ME *piken*]

peel (pēl), *n.* Also, **peel′ing.** rind or outer covering of fruit, etc. —*v.* **1** strip skin, rind, or bark from. **2** strip: *the Indians peeled the bark from trees to make canoes.* **3** come off: *when I was sunburned, my skin peeled.* [var. of *pill,* appar. < L *pilare* to strip of hair] —**peel′er,** *n.*

peep[1] (pēp), *v.* **1** look through a small or narrow hole or crack. **2** look when no one knows it. **3** look out, as if peeping; come out partly. **4** cause to stick out a little; show slightly. —*n.* **1** a look through a hole or crack; little look. **2** a secret look. **3** the first looking or coming out: *at the peep of day.* [? var. of *peek*] —**peep′er,** *n.*

peep[2] (pēp), *n.* a short, sharp sound made by a young bird. —*v.* make such a sound. [imit.] —**peep′er,** *n.*

peep·hole (pēp′hōl′), *n.* hole through which one may peep, esp. in a door.

peer[1] (pir), *n.* **1** person of the same rank, ability, etc., as another; equal. **2** person who has a title; person who is high and great by birth or rank. A duke or baroness is a peer. [< OF < L *par* equal]

peer[2] (pir), *v.* **1** look closely to see clearly, as a near-sighted person does: *she peered at the tag to read the price.* **2** come out slightly; peep out: *the sun was peering from behind a cloud.* [? var. of *appear*]

peer·age (pir′ij), *n.* **1** rank or dignity of a peer. **2** peers of a country. **3** book giving a list of the peers of a country.

peer·ess (pir′is), *n.* **1** wife or widow of a peer. **2** woman having the rank of peer in her own right.

peer·less (pir′lis), *adj.* without an equal; matchless: *a peerless leader.* —**peer′less·ly,** *adv.* —**peer′less·ness,** *n.*

peeve (pēv), *v.,* **peeved, peev·ing,** *n.* —*v.* make, become, or be peevish. —*n.* an annoyance.

pee·vish (pē′vish), *adj.* cross; fretful; complaining. [ME *pevysh*] —**pee′vish·ly,** *adv.* —**pee′vish·ness,** *n.*

pee·wee (pē′wē), *n.* **1** someone or something very small. **2** =pewee. —*adj.* small.

peg (peg), *n., v.,* **pegged, peg·ging.** —*n.* **1** pin or small bolt of wood, metal, etc., used to hang things on, to make fast a rope or string, to mark the score in a game, etc. **2** a certain amount; degree. **3** wooden leg. —*v.* **1** fasten or hold with or as if with pegs. **2** work hard. **3** aim; throw.

take down a peg, lower the pride of; humble. [appar. < MDu. *pegge*] —**peg′ger,** *n.*

peign·oir (pān wär′; pān′wär), *n.* a woman's dressing gown. [< F, < *peigner* < L *pectinare* to comb < *pecten* a comb]

pe·jor·a·tive (pi jôr′ə tiv; -jor′-; pē′jə rā′tiv; pej′-), *adj.* tending to make worse; disparaging. —*n.* a pejorative form or word. *Poetaster* is a pejorative of *poet*. [< LL, < *pejor* worse]

Pe·king (pē′king′), *n.* =Beijing.

Pe·king·ese (pē′king ēz′; –ēs′) *n., pl.* **-ese,** *adj.* —*n.* **1** a small dog with long hair and a pug nose. **2** native or inhabitant of Peking. —*adj.* of or having to do with Peking or its people.

pe·koe (pē′kō), *n.* kind of black tea. [< Chinese *pek-ho* white down; because the leaves are picked young with the "down" still on them]

pelf (pelf), *n.* money or riches, thought of as bad or degrading. [< OF *pelfre* spoils]

pel·i·can (pel′ə kən), *n.* a large fish-eating water bird with a huge bill and a pouch for storing food. [< LL < Gk. *pelekan,* ? ult. < *pelekys* ax]

pe·lisse (pə lēs′), *n.* **1** coat lined or trimmed with fur. **2** woman's long cloak. [< F, ult. < LL *pelliceus* of fur < *pellis* skin]

pel·lag·ra (pə lag′rə; –lā′grə), *n.* disease marked by eruption on the skin, a nervous condition, and sometimes insanity, caused by improper food. [< Ital.] —**pel·lag′rous,** *adj.*

pel·let (pel′it), *n.* **1** a little ball of mud, paper, food, medicine, etc.; pill. **2** bullet. —*v.* hit with pellets. [< OF *pelote* < L *pila* ball]

pell-mell, pell·mell (pel′mel′), *adv.* **1** in a rushing, tumbling mass or crowd. **2** in headlong haste. —*adj.* headlong; tumultuous. —*n.* violent disorder or confusion. [< F *pêle-mêle,* latter element appar. < *mêler* mix]

pel·lu·cid (pə lü′sid), *adj.* **1** transparent; clear: *a pellucid stream.* **2** clearly expressed; easy to understand: *pellucid language.* [< L *pellucidus,* ult. < *per–* through + *lucere* to shine] —**pel·lu′cid·i·ty, pel·lu′cid·ness,** *n.* —**pel·lu′cid·ly,** *adv.*

pelt¹ (pelt), *v.* **1** throw things at; attack; assail: *pelt a dog with stones.* **2** beat heavily: *the rain came pelting down.* **3** throw: *the clouds pelted rain upon us.* **4** hurry. —*n.* speed: *at full pelt.* —**pelt′er,** *n.*

pelt² (pelt), *n.* **1** skin of a sheep, goat, or small fur-bearing animal, before it is tanned. **2** skin. [prob. < *peltry*]

pel·vis (pel′vis), *n., pl.* **-ves** (–vēz). **1** the basin-shaped cavity formed by the hip-bones and the end of the backbone. **2** a corresponding cavity of any vertebrate. **3** bones forming this cavity. [< L, basin] —**pel′vic,** *adj.*

pem·mi·can (pem′ə kən), *n.* dried meat pounded into a paste with melted fat. [< Cree (N Am. Ind.) *pimikan* < *pimikew* he makes grease]

pen¹ (pen), *n., v.,* **penned, pen·ning.** —*n.* **1** a small instrument with a point used for writing in ink. **2** tool to use in writing with ink. **3** *Fig.* style of writing; writing. —*v.* write. [< OF < L *penna* feather]

pen² (pen), *n., v.,* **penned** or **pent, pen·ning.** —*n.* a small, closed yard for cows, sheep, pigs, chickens, etc. —*v.* **1** shut in a pen. **2** shut in; confine closely. [OE *penn,*]

pen., peninsula.

pe·nal (pē′nəl), *adj.* **1** of, having to do with, or given as punishment: *penal laws, penal labor.* **2** liable to be punished: *robbery is a penal offense.* [< L, < *poena* punishment < Gk. *poine* fine] —**pe′nal·ly,** *adv.*

pe·nal·ize (pē′nəl īz; pen′əl–), *v.,* **-ized, -iz·ing. 1** declare punishable by law or by rule; set a penalty for: *fouls are penalized in most games.* **2** inflict a penalty on; punish: *our team was penalized five yards.* —**pe′nal·i·za′tion,** *n.*

pen·al·ty (pen′əl ti), *n., pl.* **-ties. 1** punishment: *the penalty for speeding is a fine of sixty dollars.* **2** disadvantage imposed on a side or player for breaking rules. **3** disadvantage attached to some act or condition: *the penalties of old age.*

pen·ance (pen′əns), *n.* punishment borne to show sorrow for sin, to make up for a wrong done, and to obtain pardon. [< OF < L *paenitentia* PENITENCE. Doublet of PENITENCE.]

pence (pens), *n. Brit. pl.* of **penny.**

pen·chant (pen′chənt), *n.* a strong taste or liking; inclination: *a penchant for taking long walks.* [< F, ppr. of *pencher* to incline, ult. < L *pendere* hang]

pen·cil (pen′səl), *n., v.,* **-ciled, -cil·ing.** —*n.* **1** a pointed tool to write or draw with. **2** stick of coloring matter, as for makeup. —*v.* **1** use a pencil on. **2** mark or write with a pencil. **3** draw or execute with a pencil.

pencil in, add to a list or schedule tentatively. [< OF, ult. < L *penicillum,* double dim. of *penis* tail] —**pen′cil·er,** *n.* —**pen′cil·ing,** *n.*

pend (pend), *v.* remain undecided. [< L *pendere* hang]

pend·ant (pen′dənt), *n.* a hanging ornament, such as a locket. —*adj.* =pendent.

pend·ent (pen′dənt), *adj.* **1** hanging: *the pendent branches of willow.* **2** overhanging. **3** pending. —*n.* =pendant. —**pend′ent·ly,** *adv.*

pend·ing (pen′ding), *adj.* waiting to be decided or settled: *while the agreement was pending.* —*prep.* **1** while waiting for; until: *pending his return, let us get everything ready.* **2** during: *pending the investigation.*

pen·drag·on (pen drag′ən), *n.* chief leader, title of ancient British chiefs. [< Welsh, < *pen* chief + *dragon* war leader, DRAGON] —**pen·drag′on·ship,** *n.*

pen·du·lous (pen′jə ləs), *adj.* **1** hanging loosely: *the oriole builds a pendulous nest.* **2** swinging. [< L, < *pendere* hang] —**pen′du·lous·ly,** *adv.* —**pen′du·lous·ness,** *n.*

pen·du·lum (pen′jə ləm; –dyə ləm), *n.* weight so hung from a fixed point that it is free to swing to and fro. The movement of the works of a tall clock is timed by a pendulum. [< NL, neut., < L *pendulus* PENDULOUS]

pen·e·tra·ble (pen′ə trə bəl), *adj.* that can be penetrated. —**pen′e·tra·bil′i·ty, pen′e·tra·ble·ness,** *n.* —**pen′e·tra·bly,** *adv.*

pen·e·trate (pen′ə trāt), *v.,* **-trat·ed, -trat·ing. 1** get into or through: *a bullet can penetrate a wall.* **2** pierce through: *our eyes could not penetrate the darkness.* **3** soak through; spread through: *the door penetrated the whole house.* **4** see into; understand: *I could not penetrate the mystery.* [< L *penetratus,* ult. < *penitus* inmost] —**pen′e·tra′tive,** *adj.* —**pen′e·tra′tive·ly,** *adv.*

pen·e·trat·ing (pen′ə trāt′ing), *adj.* **1** sharp; piercing. **2** *Fig.* having an acute mind; understanding thoroughly. —**pen′e·trat′ing·ly,** *adv.*

pen·e·tra·tion (pen′ə trā′shən), *n.* **1** act or power of penetrating. **2** *Fig.* sharpness of intellect; insight.

pen·guin (pen′gwin; peng′–), *n.* a sea bird with flippers for diving and swimming in place of wings for flying.

pen·i·cil·lin (pen′ə sil′in), *n.* an antibiotic made from a penicillium mold. [< *penicillium*]

pen·i·cil·li·um (pen′ə sil′i əm), *n., pl.* **-cil·li·ums, -cil·li·a** (–sil′i ə). any of a certain genus of fungi. The mold on cheese is a penicillium. [< L *penicillus* small brush or tail. See PENCIL.]

pen·in·su·la (pən in′sə lə; –syə–), *n.* piece of land almost surrounded by water, or extending far out into the water. Florida is a peninsula. [< L, < *paene* almost + *insula* island] —**pen·in′su·lar,** *adj.* —**pen·in′su·lar′i·ty,** *n.*

pe·nis (pē′nis), *n., pl.* **-nis·es** (–nis iz), **-nes** (–nēz). the male organ of copulation, and, in mammals, urine is excreted through it. [< L, tail]

pen·i·tence (pen′ə təns), *n.* sorrow for sinning or doing wrong; repentance. [< OF < L *paenitentia* < *paenitere* repent. Doublet of PENANCE.]

pen·i·tent (pen′ə tənt), *adj.* sorry for sinning or doing wrong; repenting. —*n.* **1** person who is sorry for sin or wrongdoing. **2** person who confesses and does penance for his or her sins under the direction of the church. —**pen′i·tent·ly,** *adv.*

pen·i·ten·tial (pen′ə ten′shəl), *adj.* **1** of, showing, or pertaining to penitence: *the penitential psalms express remorse for sin.* **2** of or pertaining to penance. —**pen′i·ten′tial·ly,** *adv.*

pen·i·ten·tia·ry (pen′ə ten′shə ri), *n., pl.* **-ries,** *adj.* —*n.* **1** prison for criminals. **2** a state or Federal prison. —*adj.* **1** making one liable to punishment in a prison: *a penitentiary offense.* **2** used for punishment, discipline, and reformation: *penitentiary measures.* **3** of penance; penitential.

pen·knife (pen′nīf′), *n., pl.* **-knives.** a small pocketknife.

pen·man (pen′mən), *n.*, *pl.* **-men.** **1** writer; author. **2** person whose handwriting is good.

pen·man·ship (pen′mən ship), *n.* writing with pen, pencil, etc.; handwriting.

Penn., Penna., Pennsylvania.

pen name, name used by a writer instead of his or her real name.

pen·nant (pen′ənt), *n.* flag, usually long and narrow, used on ships in signaling, as a school banner, etc. [blend of *pendant* and *pennon*]

pen·nate (pen′āt), *adj.* having feathers; having wings. [< L *penna* feather, wing]

pen·ni·less (pen′i lis), *adj.* without a cent of money; very poor.

pen·non (pen′ən), *n.* **1** a long, triangular flag, originally carried on the lance of a knight. **2** flag or banner. [< OF *penon*, ult. < L *penna* feather] —**pen′noned,** *adj.*

Penn·syl·va·ni·a (pen′səl vā′ni ə; –vān′yə), *n.* an E state of the United States. —**Penn′syl·va′ni·an,** *adj.*, *n.*

Pennsylvania Dutch, 1 the descendants of 17th and 18th century immigrants to SE Pennsylvania from S Germany and Switzerland. **2** dialect of German with English intermixed, spoken by these people.

pen·ny (pen′i), *n.*, *pl.* **pen·nies. 1** cent; copper coin of the U.S. and Canada. 100 pennies = 1 dollar. **2** an English bronze coin.

a pretty penny, a large sum of money. [OE *pending* < *Penda,* king of Mercia]

pen·ny-an·te (pen′ē an′tē), *adj.* of little value; insignificant; cheap. [< *penny ante* poker played for very small sums]

penny pincher or **pen·ny-pinch·er** (pen′ē pin′chər), *n.* mean, miserly person. —**pen′ny-pinch′ing,** *adj.*, *n.*

pen·ny·roy·al (pen′i roi′əl), *n.* **1** plant of the mint family. **2** a fragrant oil made from it.

pen·ny·weight (pen′i wāt′), *n.* 24 grains or ¹⁄₂₀ of an ounce in troy weight.

pen·ny-wise (pen′i wīz′), *adj.* wise in regard to small sums or matters.

pen·ny·worth (pen′i wėrth′), *n.* **1** as much as can be bought for a penny. **2** *Fig.* a small amount.

pe·nol·o·gy (pē nol′ə ji), *n.* science of punishment of crime and management of prisons. [< Gk. *poine* fine + -LOGY] —**pe′no·log′i·cal,** *adj.* —**pe·nol′o·gist,** *n.*

pen pal, person one regularly exchanges letters with, esp. a person one has never met.

pen·sile (pen′səl), *adj.* **1** hanging; pendent. **2** building a hanging nest. [< L *pensilis* < *pendere* hang]

pen·sion[1] (pen′shən), *n.* a regular payment to a person which is not wages. Pensions are often paid because of long service, special merit, injuries received, etc. —*v.* give a pension to.

pension off, retire from service with a pension. [< OF < L *pensio* < *pendere* weigh, pay] —**pen′sion·a·ble,** *adj.* —**pen′sion·ar′y,** *adj.*, *n.*

pen·sion[2] (pän syôn′), *n. French.* boarding house.

pen·sion·er (pen′shən ər), *n.* **1** person who receives a pension. **2** a hireling; dependent.

pen·sive (pen′siv), *adj.* **1** thoughtful in a serious or sad way. **2** melancholy. [< OF, < *penser* think < L *pensare* weight, ponder < *pendere* weigh] —**pen′sive·ly,** *adv.* —**pen′sive·ness,** *n.*

pent (pent), *adj.* closely confined; penned; shut: *pent in the house all winter.* —*v.* pt. and pp. of **pen**[2].

pen·ta·gon (pen′tə gon), *n.* figure having five sides and five angles. [< LL < Gk., < *pente* five + *gonia* angle] —**pen·tag′o·nal,** *adj.* —**pen·tag′o·nal·ly,** *adv.*

pen·ta·he·dron (pen′tə hē′drən), *n.* solid figure having five faces. [< Gk. *pente* five + *-hedron* having bases]

pen·tam·e·ter (pen tam′ə tər), *n.* poetry having five feet or measures in each line. —*adj.* consisting of five feet or measures. [< L < Gk., < *pente* five + *metron* meter]

Pen·ta·teuch (pen′tə tük; –tūk), *n.* the first five books of the Old Testament; Genesis, Exodus, Leviticus, Numbers, and Deuteronomy. [< L < Gk., < *pente* five + *teuchos* vessel, book] —**Pen′ta·teu′chal,** *adj.*

pen·tath·lon (pen tath′lən), *n.* an athletic contest consisting of five different events. The person having the highest total score wins. [< Gk., < *pente* five + *athlon* contest]

pen·ta·va·lent (pen′tə vā′lənt; pen tav′ə–), *adj.* having a valence of five. —*n.* atom or group of atoms have a valence of five.

Pen·te·cost (pen′tə kôst; –kost), *n.* **1** the seventh Sunday after Easter, a Christian festival. **2** a Jewish religious holiday, observed about seven weeks after the Passover. [< L < Gk. *pentekoste (hemera)* fiftieth (day)] —**Pen′te·cos′tal, pen′te·cos′tal,** *adj.*

pent·house (pent′hous′), *n.* apartment or house built on the top of a building. [ME *pentis* < OF *apentis,* ult. < L *appendere* APPEND]

pen·tose (pen′tōs), *n.* any one of the class of simple sugars that have fine carbon atoms in each molecule and are constituents of ribonucleic acid.

pent-up (pent′up′), *adj.* closely confined.

pe·nult (pē′nult; pi nult′), *n.* the next to the last syllable in a word. [< L *paenultima (syllaba)* next-to-last (syllable) < *paene* almost + *ultimus* last] —**pe·nul′ti·mate,** *adj.*, *n.*

pe·num·bra (pi num′brə), *n.*, *pl.* **-brae** (–brē), **-bras. 1** the partial shadow outside of the complete shadow formed by the sun, moon, etc., during an eclipse. **2** the grayish outer part of a sunspot. [< NL, < L *paene* almost + *umbra* shadow] —**pe·num′bral,** *adj.*

pe·nu·ri·ous (pi nùr′i əs; –nyùr′–), *adj.* mean about spending or giving money; stingy. —**pe·nu′ri·ous·ly,** *adv.* —**pe·nu′ri·ous·ness,** *n.*

pen·u·ry (pen′yə ri), *n.* very great poverty. [< L *penuria*]

pe·on (pē′on; –ən), *n.* unskilled or menial worker. [< Mex. Sp. *peón*]

pe·on·age (pē′ən ij), *n.* **1** practice of contracting convicts to do heavy, manual labor. **2** *Fig.* working like a peon.

pe·o·ny (pē′ə ni), *n.*, *pl.* **-nies. 1** a perennial garden plant with large, showy flowers. **2** its flower. [ult. < Gk. *paionia* < *Paion* physician of the gods; from plant's use in medicine]

peo·ple (pē′pəl), *n.*, *pl.* **-ple** or (*for def.* 2) **-ples,** *v.,* **-pled, -pling.** —*n.* **1** men, women, and children; persons. **2** race; nation. **3** body of citizens of a state; the public. **4** persons of a place, class, or group. **5** the common people; lower classes. **6** persons in relation to a superior: *a king rules over his people.* **7** family; relatives. —*v.* fill with people; populate; stock with animals, etc.: *Europe very largely peopled America.* [< AF < L *populus*] —**peo′pler,** *n.*

pep (pep), *n.,* *v.,* **pepped, pep·ping.** —*n.* spirit; energy; vim. —*v.* **pep up,** instill spirit or energy in. [short for *pepper*]

pep·per (pep′ər), *n.* **1** a seasoning with a hot taste, used for soups, meats, vegetables, etc. **2** plant with berries from which pepper is made. **3** any of several hollow, green or red vegetables with many seeds. They are eaten raw or cooked or pickled. **4** =capsicum. —*v.* **1** season or sprinkle with pepper. **2** sprinkle thickly: *peppered with freckles.* **3** hit with small objects sent thick and fast: *we peppered clay pigeons with shot.* [< L < Gk. *piperi*]

pep·per-and-salt (pep′ər ən sôlt′), *adj.* of black and white color, as with graying hair or fabric.

pep·per·corn (pep′ər kôrn′), *n.* a dried berry ground up to make black pepper.

pep·per·grass (pep′ər gras′) common weed with a peppery taste.

pep·per·mint (pep′ər mint), *n.* **1** herb grown for its oil, used in medicine and in candy. **2** this oil. **3** candy flavored with peppermint oil.

pep·per·o·ni (pep′ər ō′nē), *n.* hot, spicy Italian sausage. [< It.]

pep·per·y (pep′ər i), *adj.* **1** full of pepper; like pepper. **2** hot; sharp. **3** having a hot temper; easily made angry. —**pep′per·i·ness,** *n.*

pep·py (pep′i), *adj.,* **-pi·er, -pi·est.** full of pep; energetic; lively; vigorous. —**pep′pi·ly,** *adv.* —**pep′pi·ness,** *n.*

pep·sin (pep′sin), *n.* enzyme that helps to digest meat, eggs, cheese, and other proteins. [< Gk. *pepsis* digestion]

pep·tic (pep′tik), *adj.* **1** promoting digestion; digestive. **2** of or pertaining to pepsin. [< L < Gk., < *peptos* cooked]

pep·tone (pep′tōn), *n.* any of a class of diffusible and soluble substances into which meat, eggs, cheese, and other proteins are changed by pepsin or trypsin. —**pep·ton′ic,** *adj.*

Pe·quot (pē′kwot), *n.* **1** member of a tribe of American Indians in S New England. **2** their language. [*appar.* < Algonkian *Pequatoog* destroyers]

per (pėr; pər), *prep.* **1** for each: *one book per student, $2.50 per pound.* **2** through; by means of. [< L]

per-, *prefix.* **1** through; throughout. **2** thoroughly; utterly; very. **3** the maximum or a large amount of, as in *peroxide.* [< L]

per·ad·ven·ture (pėr′əd ven′chər), *adv.* Archaic. perhaps. —*n.* chance; doubt.

per·am·bu·late (pər am′byə lāt), *v.,* **-lated, -lat·ing.** walk through or about. [< L, < *per-* through + *ambulare* to walk] —**per·am′bu·la′tion,** *n.* —**per·am′bu·la·to′ry,** *adj.*

per an·num (pər an′əm), per year; yearly; for each year: *a salary of $40,000 per annum.*

per·cale (pər kāl′; -kal′), *n.* a closely woven cotton cloth with a smooth finish. [< F < Pers. *pärgālä*]

per cap·i·ta (pər kap′ə tə), for each person: *$200 for five guests or $40 per capita.*

per·ceive (pər sēv′), *v.,* **-ceived, -ceiv·ing. 1** be aware of through the senses; see, hear, taste, smell, or feel. **2** take in with the mind; observe. [< OF < L, < *per-* fully + *capere* grasp] —**per·ceiv′a·ble,** *adj.* —**per·ceiv′a·bly,** *adv.*

per·cent, (pər sent′) **per cent,** *n.* hundredths; parts in each hundred. Five percent (5%) of 40 is the same as ⁵⁄₁₀₀ × 40. [for LL *per centum*]

per cent., per centum, 1 by the hundred. **2** for or in every hundred.

per·cent·age (pər sen′tij), *n.* **1** rate or proportion of each hundred; part of each hundred: *what percentage of children were absent?* **2** part; proportion: *a large percentage of the city's housing was damaged or destroyed.* **3** allowance, commission, discount, rate of interest, etc., figured by per cent. **4** advantage or profit.

per·cen·tile (pər sen′til; -təl; -tīl), *n.* any value in a series of points on a scale arrived at by dividing a group into a hundred equal parts in order of magnitude.

per·cept (per′sept), *n.* **1** that which is perceived. **2** understanding that is the result of perceiving.

per·cep·ti·ble (pər sep′tə bəl), *adj.* that can be perceived. —**per·cep′ti·bil′i·ty,** *n.* —**per·cep′ti·bly,** *adv.*

per·cep·tion (pər sep′shən), *n.* **1** act of perceiving: *his perception of the change came in a flash.* **2** power of perceiving: *a keen perception.* **3** percept. [< L *perceptio* < *percipere* PERCEIVE] —**per·cep′tion·al,** *adj.*

per·cep·tive (pər sep′tiv), *adj.* **1** having to do with perception. **2** having the power of perceiving. —**per·cep′tive·ness,** *n.*

per·cep·tu·al (pər sep′chù əl), *adj.* of or having to do with perception. —**per·cep′tu·al·ly,** *adv.*

perch¹ (pėrch), *n.* **1** bar, branch, or anything else on which a bird can come to rest. **2** a rather high place or position. **3** measure of length; rod; 5½ yards. **4** measure of area; square rod; 30¼ square yards. —*v.* **1** alight and rest; sit. **2** sit rather high. **3** place high up. [< OF < L *pertica* pole] —**perch′er,** *n.*

perch² (pėrch), *n., pl.* **perch·es** or (*esp. collectively*) **perch. 1** kind of small freshwater fish, used for food. **2** a similar saltwater fish. [< OF < L < Gk. *perke*]

per·chance (pər chans′; -chäns′), *adv.* perhaps.

Per·che·ron (pėr′chə ron; -shə-), one of a breed of large and strong horses.

per·cip·i·ent (pər sip′i ənt), *adj.* **1** perceiving. **2** having perception. —*n.* one that perceives. [< L *percipiens.* See PERCEIVE.] —**per·cip′i·ence,** *n.*

per·co·late (pėr′kə lāt), *v.,* **-lat·ed, -lat·ing. 1** drip or drain through small holes or spaces. **2** filter through; permeate. [< L, ult. < *per-* through + *colum* strainer] —**per′co·la′tion,** *n.*

per·co·la·tor (pėr′kə lā′tər), *n.* kind of coffee pot in which boiling water drains through ground coffee.

per·cus·sion (pər kush′ən), *n.* **1** the striking of one body against another with force; stroke; blow. **2** the striking of musical instruments to produce tones. [< L *percussio* < *per-* (intensive) + *quatere* strike, beat] —**per·cus′sion·ist,** *n.* —**per·cus′sive,** *adj.*

percussion instrument, musical instrument (as a drum or cymbal) played by striking it.

per di·em (pər dī′əm), **1** per day; for each day. **2** allowance of so much every day. [< L, per day]

per·di·tion (pər dish′ən), *n.* **1** loss of one's soul and the joys of heaven. **2** hell. **3** utter loss. [< L, < *perdere* destroy < *per-* destruction + *dare* give]

per·e·gri·nate (per′ə grə nāt), *v.,* **-nat·ed, -nat·ing.** travel; journey. —**per′e·grina′tion,** *n.* —**per′e·gri·na′tor,** *n.*

per·e·grine (per′ə grin; -grīn; -grēn), **per·e·grin** (-grin), *n.* a large falcon. [< L *peregrinus* from foreign parts, ult. < *per-* outside + *ager* (*Romanus*) the (Roman) territory. Doublet of PILGRIM.]

per·emp·to·ry (pər emp′tə ri; per′əmp tô ri; -tō-), *adj.* **1** imperious; positive: *a peremptory teacher.* **2** allowing no denial or refusal: *a peremptory command.* **3** leaving no choice; decisive; final; absolute: *a peremptory decree.* [< L *peremptorius* deadly, that puts an end to, ult. < *per-* destruction + *emere,* orig., take] —**per·emp′to·ri·ly,** *adv.* —**per·emp′to·ri·ness,** *n.*

per·en·ni·al (pər en′i əl), *adj.* **1** lasting for a very long time; enduring: *the perennial beauty of the hills.* **2** having underground parts that live more than two years: *perennial garden plants.* —*n.* a perennial plant. [< L *perennis* lasting

< *per-* through + *annus* year] —**per·en′ni·al·ly,** *adv.*

perf., **1** perfect. **2** perforated.

per·fect (*adj., n.* pėr′fikt; *v.* pər fekt′), *adj.* **1** without defect; faultless: *perfect work shows great care.* **2** completely skilled; expert. **3** having all its parts; complete. **4** entire; utter: *a perfect stranger to us.* **5** showing action or state completed at the time of speaking. —*v.* **1** remove all faults from; make perfect: *perfect a plan as it is being tried out.* **2** improve. **3** complete. —*n.* **a** the perfect tense. **b** a verb form in such tense. *Have eaten* is the perfect form of *eat.* [< OF < L *perfectus* completed < *per-* thoroughly + *facere* make, do] —**per·fect′er,** *n.* —**per′fect·ly,** *adv.* —**per′fect·ness,** *n.*

per·fect·i·ble (pər fek′tə bəl), *adj.* capable of becoming, or being made, perfect. —**per·fect′i·bil′i·ty,** *n.*

per·fec·tion (pər fek′shən), *n.* **1** perfect condition; faultlessness; highest excellence. **2** a perfect person or thing. **3** a making complete or perfect: *the perfection of plans.*

to perfection, perfectly. —**per·fec′tion·ist,** *n.*

per·fec·tive (pər fek′tiv), *adj.* tending to make perfect; conducive to perfection. —**per·fec′tive·ly,** *adv.* —**per·fec′tiveness,** *n.*

perfect number, whole number equal to the sum of its factors, such as 6 (equals 1 + 2 + 3) or 28 (equals 1 + 2 + 4 + 7 + 14).

perfect participle, participle expressing action completed before the time of speaking or acting. In "Having written the letter, she mailed it," *having written* is a perfect participle.

perfect pitch, ability to identify a musical tone and name it on the musical scale merely by hearing it.

per·fi·dy (pėr′fə di), *n., pl.* **-dies.** a breaking faith; base treachery; being false to a trust. [< L, ult. < *per-* + *fides* faith] —**per·fid′i·ous** *adj.* —**per·fid′i·ous·ly,** *adv.* —**per·fid′i·ous·ness,** *n.*

per·fo·rate (*v.* pėr′fə rāt; *adj.* pėr′fə rit, -rāt), *v.,* **-rat·ed, -rat·ing,** *adj.* —*v.* make a hole or holes through. —*adj.* pierced. [< L < *per-* through + *forare* bore] —**per′fo·ra′tive,** *adj.* —**per′fo·ra′tor,** *n.*

per·fo·ra·tion (pėr′fə rā′shən), *n.* **1** hole bored or punched through something: *the perforations in a sheet of stamps.* **2** a perforating or being perforated.

per·force (pər fôrs′; -fōrs′), *adv.* by necessity; necessarily.

per·form (pər fôrm′), *v.* **1** do: *perform work.* **2** put into effect; carry out: *perform a task.* **3** act, play, sing, or do tricks in public: *perform a piece of music.* [< AF *perfourmer,* var. of OF *parfournir* < *par-* completely + *-fournir* furnish, finish; infl. by *forme* form] —**per·form′er,** *n.*

per·form·ance (pər fôr′məns), *n.* **1** a performing. **2** thing performed; act; deed. **3** the giving of a play, circus, or other show.

per·fume (*n.* pèr′fūm, pər fūm′; *v.* pər fūm′), *n., v.,* **-fumed, -fum·ing.** —*n.* **1** a sweet smell. **2** liquid having the sweet smell of flowers. —*v.* **1** fill with sweet odor: *flowers perfumed the air.* **2** put a sweet-smelling liquid on. [< F < OItal. < L *per-* through + *fumare* to smoke]

per·fum·er (pər fūm′ər), *n.* **1** maker or seller of perfumes. **2** someone or something that perfumes.

per·fum·er·y (pər fūm′ər i), *n., pl.* **-er·ies.** **1** a perfume. **2** perfumes. **3** business of making or selling perfumes.

per·func·to·ry (pər fungk′tə ri), *adj.* **1** done merely for the sake of getting rid of the duty; mechanical; indifferent: *the little boy gave his face a perfunctory washing.* **2** acting in a perfunctory way. [< LL *perfunctorius,* ult. < L *perfungi* perform < *per-* to the end + *fungi* execute] —**per·func′to·ri·ly,** *adv.* —**per·func′to·ri·ness ,** *n.*

perh., perhaps.

per·haps (pər haps′; pər aps′), *adv.* maybe; possibly. [ME *per happes* by chances. See PER, HAP.]

per·i·anth (per′i anth), *n.* envelope of a flower, including the calyx and the corolla. [< NL, < Gk. *peri-* around + *anthos* flower]

per·i·car·di·tis (per′ə kär dī′tis), *n.* inflammation of the pericardium.

per·i·car·dium (per′ə kär′di əm), *n., pl.* **-di·a** (-di ə). a membranous sac enclosing the heart. [< Gk., < *peri-* around + *kardia* heart] —**per′i·car′di·ac, per′i·car′di·al,** *adj.*

per·i·carp (per′ə kärp), *n.* walls of a ripened ovary or fruit; seed vessel. [< NL < Gk., < *peri-* around + *karpos* fruit] —**per·i·car′pi·al,** *adj.*

per·i·dot (per′ə dot), *n.* semiprecious yellow-green stone used as a gem.

per·i·gee (per′ə jē), *n.* point in the orbit of a celestial body where it comes closest to the earth. [< F < NL < Gk., < *peri-* near + *ge* earth] —**per′i·ge′al,** *adj.*

per·i·he·li·on (per′ə hē′li ən; -hēl′yən), *n., pl.* **-li·a** (-li ə; -yə). point in its orbit where a celestial body comes closest to the sun. [< NL, < Gk. *peri-* near + *helios* sun]

per·il (per′əl), *n., v.,* **-iled, -il·ing.** —*n.* chance of harm; danger. —*v.* put in danger. [< F < L *periculum*]

per·il·ous (per′ə ləs), *adj.* dangerous. —**per′il·ous·ly,** *adv.*

pe·rim·e·ter (pə rim′ə tər), *n.* **1** the outer boundary of a surface or figure. **2** distance around such a boundary. [< L < Gk., < *peri-* around + *metron* measure] —**per′i·met′ric, per′i·met′ri·cal,** *adj.* —**per′i·met′ri·cal·ly,** *adv.*

per·i·na·tal (per′ə nā′təl), *adj.* of the time of an infant's life just before birth and the month following birth. [< Gk. *peri-* around + E *natal*] —**per′i·na′tol·o·gy,** *n.*

per·i·ne·um (per′ə nē′əm), *n., pl.* **-ne·a** (-nē′ə). region of the body between the thighs. [< LL < Gk. *perination*] —**per′i·ne′al,** *adj.*

pe·ri·od (pir′i əd), *n.* **1** portion of time, life, development, history, etc., having certain features or conditions. **2** a class hour devoted to the study of a single subject. **3** the time of one complete cycle of a vibration, current, etc. **4** portion of a game during which there is actual play. **5** time during which a thing lasts, etc. **6** Also, **periods.** menses. **7** dot (.) marking the end of most sentences or showing an abbreviation. —*adj.* characteristic of a certain period of time: *period furniture.* [< L < Gk. *periodos* a going around, cycle < *peri-* around + *hodos* a going]

pe·ri·od·ic (pir′i od′ik), *adj.* **1** occurring, appearing, or done again and again at regular intervals: *periodic attacks of malaria.* **2** happening every now and then: *a periodic fit of clearing up one's desk.*

pe·ri·od·i·cal (pir′i od′ə kəl), *n.* magazine that appears regularly. —*adj.* **1** of periodicals. **2** published at regular intervals. **3** periodic. —**pe′ri·od′i·cal·ly,** *adv.*

pe·ri·o·dic·i·ty (pir′i ə dis′ə ti), *n., pl.* **-ties.** tendency to happen at regular intervals.

periodic table, table in which the elements, arranged in the order of their atomic weights, are shown in related groups.

per·i·os·te·um (per′i os′ti əm), *n., pl.* **-te·a** (-ti ə). the dense fibrous membrane covering the surface of bones except at the joints. [< NL < LL < Gk., < *peri-* around + *osteon* bone] —**per′i·os′te·al,** *adj.*

per·i·pa·tet·ic (per′ə pə tet′ik), *adj.* walking about; traveling from place to place. [< L < Gk., < *peri-* around + *pateein* to walk; with ref. to Aristotle's manner of teaching]

pe·riph·er·al (pə rif′ər əl), *adj.* **1** pertaining to, situated in, or forming an outside boundary. **2** at the outside; external. —**pe·riph′er·al·ly,** *adv.*

pe·riph·er·y (pə rif′ər i), *n., pl.* **-er·ies.** **1** an outside boundary: *the periphery of a circle is called the circumference.* **2** an external surface. [< LL < Gk., < *peri-* around + *pherein* carry]

per·i·phrase (per′ə frāz), *n., v.,* **-phrased, -phras·ing.** —*n.* a roundabout way of speaking or writing; circumlocution. —*v.* express in a roundabout way.

pe·riph·ra·sis (pə rif′rə sis), *n., pl.* **-ses** (-sēz). periphrase. [< L < Gk., ult. < *peri-* around + *phrazein* speak]

per·i·phras·tic (per′ə fras′tik), *adj.* expressed in a roundabout way. —**per′i·phras′ti·cal·ly,** *adv.*

per·i·scope (per′ə skōp), *n.* instrument that allows those in a submarine or trench to obtain a view of the surface. It is a tube with an arrangement of prisms or mirrors that reflect light rays down the tube. [< Gk. *peri-* around + *skopeein* to look] —**per′i·scop′ic,** *adj.*

per·ish (per′ish), *v.* **1** lose life through violence, accident, privation, etc. **2** decay and disappear. **3** be destroyed: *buildings perish in flames.* [< OF *periss-* < L, < *per-* to destruction + *ire* go]

per·ish·a·ble (per′ish ə bəl), *adj.* liable to perish; liable to spoil or decay. —*n.* Usually, **perishables.** something perishable. —**per′ish·a·ble·ness,** *n.*

per·i·stal·sis (per′ə stal′sis), *n., pl* **-ses** (-sēz). movement in the wall of a hollow organ by which it propels its contents onward, esp. the wavelike, circular contractions of the alimentary canal. [< NL < Gk., ult. < *peri-* around + *stellein* wrap] —**per′i·stal′tic,** *adj.*

per·i·style (per′ə stīl), *n.* **1** row of columns surrounding a building, court, or the like. **2** space or court so enclosed. [< F < L < Gk., < *peri-* around + *stylos* pillar]

per·i·to·ne·um (per′ə tō nē′əm), *n., pl.* **-ne·a** (-nē′ə). membrane that lines the walls of the abdomen and covers the organs in it. [< LL < Gk. *peritonaion,* neut. adj., stretched over, ult. < *peri-* around + *teinein* stretch] —**per′i·to·ne′al,** *adj.*

per·i·to·ni·tis (per′ə tə nī′tis), *n.* inflammation of the peritoneum.

per·i·wig (per′ə wig), *n.* wig. [earlier *perewyke.* See PERUKE.]

per·i·win·kle[1] (per′i wing′kəl), *n.* a low, trailing evergreen plant with blue flowers. The American periwinkle is called myrtle. [< L *pervinca;* infl. by *periwinkle*[2]]

per·i·win·kle[2] (per′i wing′kəl), *n.* a sea snail with a thick, cone-shaped, spiral shell, used for food. [OE *pīnewincle; pīne-?* < L *pina* mussel]

per·jure (pèr′jər), *v.,* **-jured, -jur·ing.** make (oneself) guilty of perjury. [< OF < L, < *per-* falsely + *jurare* swear] —**per′jur·er,** *n.*

per·ju·ry (pèr′jər i), *n., pl.* **-ries.** act of swearing that something is true which one knows to be false.

perk[1] (pèrk), *v.* **1** move, lift the head, or act briskly or saucily: *the sparrow perked up his tail.* **2** move or carry oneself briskly, jauntily, or assertively. —*adj.* perky.

perk up, a make trim or smart. **b** brighten up; energize: *flowers perked up the room.* [ME *perke(n)*]

perk[2] (perk), *n. Informal.* perquisite.

perk[3] (perk), *v. Informal.* percolate (coffee): *a pot perked on the stove.*

perk·y (pèr′ki), *adj.,* **perk·i·er, perk·i·est.** smart; brisk; saucy; pert: *a perky squirrel.* —**perk′i·ly,** *adv.* —**perk′i·ness,** *n.*

per·ma·nent (pèr′mə nənt), *adj.* lasting; intended to last: *a permanent filling in a tooth.* —*n. Colloq.* a permanent wave. [< L *permanens* staying to the end < *per-* through + *manere* stay] —**per′ma·nence, per′ma·nen·cy,** *n.* —**per′ma·nent·ly,** *adv.*

per·man·ga·nate (pər mang′gə nāt), *n.* salt of an acid containing manganese, used as an antiseptic solution.

per·me·a·ble (pėr′mi ə bəl), *adj.* that can be permeated. —**per′me·a·bil′i·ty,** *n.*

per·me·ate (pėr′mi āt), *v.,* –**at·ed,** –**at·ing. 1** spread through the whole of; pass through; soak through: *smoke permeated the house.* **2** penetrate. [< L, < *per*– through + *meare* to pass] —**per′me·a′tion,** *n.* —**per′me·a′tive,** *adj.*

per·mis·si·ble (pər mis′ə bəl), *adj.* that may be permitted; allowable. —**per·mis′si·bil′i·ty,** *n.* —**per·mis′si·bly,** *adv.*

per·mis·sion (pər mish′ən), *n.* formal or express allowance or consent.

per·mis·sive (pər mis′iv), *adj.* **1** permitting; allowing. **2** permitted; allowed. —**per·mis′sive·ly,** *adv.* —**per·mis′sive·ness,** *n.*

per·mit (*v.* pər mit′; *n.* pėr′mit, pər mit′), *v.,* –**mit·ted,** –**mit·ting.** —*v.* **1** allow (a person, etc.) to do something: *permit me to explain.* **2** let (something) be done or occur. **3** tolerate. **4** afford opportunity for: *conditions permitting no delay.* —*n.* **1** a formal, written order giving permission to do something: *a permit to fish or hunt.* **2** permission. [< L, < *per*– through + *mittere* let go] —**per·mit′ter,** *n.*

per·mu·ta·tion (pėr′myú tā′shən), *n.* **1** alteration. **2 a** a changing of the order of a set of things; arranging in different orders. **b** such an arrangement or group. The permutations of *a, b,* and *c* are *abc, acb, bac, bca, cab, cba.* [< L, < *per*– across + *mutare* to change]

per·ni·cious (pər nish′əs), *adj.* **1** that will destroy or ruin; causing great harm or damage: *gambling is a pernicious habit.* **2** fatal. [< L *perniciosus,* ult. < *per*– + *nex* death] —**per·ni′cious·ly,** *adv.* —**per·ni′cious·ness,** *n.*

per·o·ra·tion (per′ə rā′shən), *n.* the last part of an oration or discussion. [< L, < *per*– to a finish + *orare* speak formally]

per·ox·ide (pər ok′sīd), *n., v.,* –**id·ed,** –**id·ing.** —*n.* **a** oxide of a given element or radical that contains the greatest, or an unusual, amount of oxygen. **b** hydrogen peroxide. —*v.* bleach (hair) by applying peroxide (def. b).

perp (pėrp), *n. Informal.* person who is indicted for a crime, or who has committed a crime. [< *perp*etrator]

per·pen·dic·u·lar (pėr′pən dik′yə lər), *adj.* **1** upright; standing straight up. **2** at right angles. —*n.* **1** a perpendicular line or plane. **2** a perpendicular position. [< OF < L, < *perpendiculum* plumb line, ult. < *per*– + *pendere* hang] —**per′pen·dic′u·lar′i·ty,** *n.* —**per′pen·dic′u·lar·ly,** *adv.*

per·pe·trate (pėr′pə trāt), *v.,* –**trat·ed,** –**trat·ing.** do or commit (crime, fraud, trick, or anything bad or foolish). [< L, < *per*– (intensive) + *patrare* perform] —**per′pe·tra′tion,** *n.* —**per′pe·tra′tor,** *n.*

per·pet·u·al (pər pech′ú əl), *adj.* **1** lasting forever; eternal: *the perpetual hills.* **2** lasting throughout life: *a perpetual income.* **3** continuous; never ceasing:

a perpetual stream of visitors. [< L, < *perpetuus* continuous] —**per·pet′u·al·ly,** *adv.* —**per·pet′u·al·ness,** *n.*

per·pet·u·ate (pər pech′ú āt), *v.,* –**at·ed,** –**at·ing.** make perpetual; keep from being forgotten. —**per·pet′u·a′tion,** *n.* —**per·pet′u·a′tor,** *n.*

per·pe·tu·i·ty (pėr′pə tü′ə ti; –tū′–), *n., pl.* –**ties** state or fact of being perpetual; existence forever.

per·plex (pər pleks′), *v.* **1** trouble with doubt; puzzle; bewilder. **2** make difficult to understand or settle; confuse. [orig. adj., < L *perplexus* confused < *per*– completely + *plectere* intertwine] —**per·plex′ed·ly,** *adv.* —**per·plex′ing,** *adj.* —**per·plex′ing·ly,** *adv.*

per·plex·i·ty (pər plek′sə ti), *n., pl.* –**ties. 1** perplexed condition; confusion; being puzzled. **2** something that perplexes.

per·qui·site (pėr′kwə zit), *n.* anything received for work besides the regular pay. [< Med.L *perquisitum* (thing) gained, ult. < L *per*– carefully + *quaerere* seek]

Pers., 1 Persia. **2** Persian.

pers., person; personal.

per se (pėr sē′), *Latin.* by itself; in itself; intrinsically.

per·se·cute (pėr′sə kūt), *v.,* –**cut·ed,** –**cut·ing. 1** do harm to again and again; oppress. **2** punish for religious reasons. **3** annoy: *persecuted by silly questions.* [< *persecution*] —**per′se·cu′tive,** *adj.* —**per′se·cu′tor,** *n.*

per·se·cu·tion (pėr′sə kū′shən), *n.* a persecuting or being persecuted. [< L *persecutio,* ult. < *per*– perseveringly + *sequi* follow]

Per·seus (pėr′si əs; pėr′sūs), *n.* group of stars in the northern sky.

per·se·ver·ance (pėr′sə vir′əns), *n.* a sticking to a purpose or an aim; never giving up what one has set out to do.

per·se·vere (pėr′sə vir′), *v.,* –**vered,** –**ver·ing.** continue steadily in doing something hard; persist. [< F < L, < *per*– very + *severus* strict] —**per′se·ver′ing·ly,** *adv.*

Per·sia (pėr′zhə), *n.* = Iran.

Per·sian (pėr′zhən), *adj.* of or pertaining to Persia or modern Iran, its people, or their language. —*n.* **1** native or inhabitant of Persia or modern Iran. **2** language of Persia or modern Iran.

Persian cat, domestic cat that has long hair, originally from Persia and Afghanistan.

Persian lamb, a very curly fur from lambs of Persia and some parts of C Asia.

per·sim·mon (pər sim′ən), *n.* **1** a North American tree with a plumlike fruit containing one to ten seeds. **2** fruit of this tree, very astringent when green but sweet and good to eat when very ripe. [< Algonquian]

per·sist (pər sist′; –zist′), *v.* **1** continue firmly; refuse to stop or be changed. **2** last; stay; endure. **3** say again and again; maintain. [< L, < *per*– to the end + *sistere* stand]

per·sist·ent (pər sis′tənt; –zis′–), *adj.* **1** persisting; having lasting qualities, esp. in the face of dislike, disapproval, or difficulties: *a persistent worker.* **2** lasting; going on; continuing: *a persistent headache.* —**per·sist′ence, per·sist′en·cy,** *n.* —**per·sist′ent·ly,** *adv.*

per·snick·e·ty (pər snik′ə ti), *adj.* **1** too fastidious; fussy. **2** requiring carefulness and precision. Also, **pernickety.** [< Scot.]

per·son (pėr′sən), *n.* **1** man, woman, or child; human being: *four persons saw this.* **2** a human body; bodily appearance: *he has a fine person.* **3** a human being or corporation having legal rights and duties. **4 a** change in a pronoun or verb to show the person speaking (**first person**), the person spoken to (**second person**), or the person or thing spoken of (**third person**). **b** a form of a pronoun or verb giving such indication. *Comes* is third person singular of *come.*

in person, a in one's own individual character. **b** with one's own bodily presence; physically present. [< OF < L *persona* character, mask worn by actor. Doublet of PARSON.]

per·son·a·ble (pėr′sən ə bəl), *adj.* having a pleasing appearance or personality.

per·son·age (pėr′sən ij), *n.* **1** person of importance. **2** person. **3** character in a book, play, etc.

per·son·al (pėr′sən əl; pėrs′nəl), *adj.* **1** individual; private: *a personal letter.* **2** done in person; directly by oneself, not through others or by letter: *a personal visit.* **3** of the body or bodily appearance; *personal beauty.* **4** inclined to make remarks to or ask questions of others: *don't be too personal.* **5** showing person. *I, we, thou, you, he, she, it,* and *they* are the **personal pronouns.** —*n.* a short paragraph in a newspaper about a particular person or persons.

per·son·al·i·ty (pėr′sə nal′ə ti), *n., pl.* –**ties. 1** the personal or individual quality that makes one person be different or act differently from another: *a baby two weeks old does not have much personality.* **2** qualities of a person. **3** person; personage.

per·son·al·ize (pėr′sən əl īz; pėrs′nəl–), *v.,* –**ized,** –**iz·ing. 1** make personal. **2** personify.

per·son·al·ly (pėr′sən əl i; pėrs′nəl i), *adv.* **1** in person; not by the aid of others: *see to the comforts of guests personally.* **2** as far as oneself is concerned. **3** as a person: *we like Mr. Hart personally.*

personal property, possessions that can be moved, in contrast to land, a house, etc.

per·so·na non gra·ta (pėr sō′nə non grä′tə), *Latin.* an unacceptable person.

per·son·i·fi·ca·tion (pėr son′ə fə kā′shən), *n.* **1** a striking example; type. **2** a representing as a person. **3** figure of speech in which a lifeless thing or quality is spoken of as if alive.

per·son·i·fy (pər son′ə fī), *v.,* –**fied,** –**fy·ing. 1** be a type of; embody: *Satan* *personifies evil.* **2** regard or represent as a person. We often personify the sun and moon, referring to the sun as "he" and the moon as "she." —**per·son'i·fi·er,** *n.*

per·son·nel (pėr'sə nel'), *n.* persons employed in any work, business, or service. [< F, personal; adj. used as n.]

per·spec·tive (pər spek'tiv), *n.* **1** art of picturing objects on a flat surface so as to give the appearance of distance. **2** effect of distance on the appearance of objects. **3** *Fig.* effect of the distance of events upon the mind: *get a perspective on what had happened to him.* **4** view of things or facts in which they are in the right relations. —*adj.* drawn so as to show the proper perspective.

in perspective, a drawn or seen according to the rules of perspective. **b** *Fig.* from a particular point of view or attitude. [< Med.L *perspectiva* (*ars*) (science) of optics, ult. < L *per–* through + *specere* look] —**per·spec'tive·ly,** *adv.*

per·spi·ca·cious (pėr'spə kā'shəs), *adj.* keen in observing and understanding; discerning. [< L *perspicax* sharp-sighted, ult. < *per–* through + *specere* to look] —**per·spi·ca'cious·ly** , *adv.* —**per·spi·cac'i·ty,** *n.*

per·spi·cu·i·ty (pėr'spə kū'ə ti), *n.* clearness in expression; ease in being understood.

per·spic·u·ous (pər spik'yu əs), *adj.* clear; easily understood. [< L *perspicuus,* ult. < *per–* through + *specere* to look] —**per·spic'u·ous·ly,** *adv.* —**per·spic'u·ous·ness** , *n.*

per·spi·ra·tion (pėr'spə rā'shən), *n.* **1** sweat. **2** sweating.

per·spire (pər spīr'), *v.,* **–spired, –spir·ing.** sweat. [< L, < *per–* through + *spirare* breathe]

per·suade (pər swād'), *v.,* **–suad·ed, –suad·ing.** win over to do or believe; make willing or sure by urging, arguing, etc. [< L, < *per–* strongly + *suadere* to urge] —**per·suad'a·ble,** *adj.* —**per·suad'er,** *n.*

per·sua·sion (pər swā'zhən), *n.* **1** a persuading: *all our persuasion was of no use; she would not come.* **2** power of persuading. **3** firm belief. **4** religious belief; creed: *all Christians are not of the same persuasion.*

per·sua·sive (pər swā'siv; –ziv), *adj.* able, intended, or fitted to persuade. —**per·sua'sive·ly,** *adv.* —**per·sua'sive·ness,** *n.*

pert (pėrt), *adj.* **1** too forward or free in speech or action; saucy; bold. **2** lively. [for *apert,* ME < OF, open < L *apertus;* infl. by OF *aspert* EXPERT] —**pert'ly,** *adv.* —**pert'ness,** *n.*

per·tain (pər tān'), *v.* **1** belong or be connected as a part, possession, attribute, etc.: *we own the house and the land pertaining to it.* **2** refer; be related. "Pertaining to school" means "having to do with school." **3** be appropriate: *we had turkey and everything else that pertains*

to Thanksgiving Day. [< OF < L, < *per–* across + *tenere* to reach]

per·ti·na·cious (pėr'tə nā'shəs), *adj.* holding firmly to a purpose, action, or opinion; very persistent. [< L *pertinacia* firmness < *per–* very + *tenax* tenacious] —**per'ti·na'cious·ly,** *adv.* —**per'ti·na'cious·ness, per'ti·nac'i·ty,** *n.*

per·ti·nent (pėr'tə nənt), *adj.* having to do with what is being considered; relating to the matter in hand; to the point: *if your question is pertinent, I will answer it.* [< L, ppr. of *pertinere* PERTAIN] —**per'ti·nence, per'ti·nen·cy,** *n.* —**per'ti·nent·ly,** *adv.*

per·turb (pər tėrb'), *v.* disturb greatly; make uneasy or troubled: *my wife was very perturbed by my illness.* [< L, < *per–* thoroughly + *turbare* confuse] —**per·turb'a·ble,** *adj.* —**per'tur·ba'tion,** *n.* —**per·turb'ed·ly,** *adv.*

Pe·ru (pə rü'), *n.* a mountainous country on the W coast of South America. —**Pe·ru'vi·an,** *adj., n.*

pe·ruke (pə rük'), *n.* wig, esp. one worn by men in the 17th and 18th centuries. [< F *perruque*]

pe·rus·al (pə rüz'əl), *n.* a perusing; reading: *the perusal of a letter.*

pe·ruse (pə rüz'), *v.,* **–rused, –rus·ing. 1** read through carefully. **2** read. [orig., use up, [< L *per–* to the end + E *use*] —**pe·rus'a·ble,** *adj.* —**pe·rus'er,** *n.*

per·vade (pər vād'), *v.,* **–vad·ed, –vad·ing.** go or spread its influence, presence, etc., throughout; be throughout; *the odor of pines pervades the air.* [< L, < *per–* through + *vadere* go] —**per·vad'er,** *n.* —**per·va'sion,** *n.* —**per·va'sive·ness,** *n.*

per·va·sive (pə vā'siv), *adj.* **1** widespread: *pervasive corruption nearly destroyed the city.* **2** strong enough to pervade: *the pervasive odor of paint.* —**per·va'sive·ly,** *adv.*

per·verse (pər vėrs'), *adj.* **1** contrary and willful; stubborn: *the perverse child did just what we told him not to do.* **2** wicked. **3** not correct; wrong: *perverse reasoning.* [< L *perversus* turned away. See PER- VERT.] —**per·verse'ly,** *adv.* —**per·verse'- ness, per·ver'si·ty,** *n.*

per·ver·sion (pər vėr'zhən; –shən), *n.* **1** a turning or being turned to what is wrong; change to what is unnatural, abnormal, or wrong. **2** a perverted or distorted form.

per·vert (*v.* pər vėrt'; *n.* pėr'vėrt), *v.* **1** lead or turn from the right way or from the truth: *reading crime comics perverts our taste for good books.* **2** give a wrong meaning to: *his enemies perverted his friendly remark and made it into an insult.* **3** use for wrong purposes or in a wrong way: *a clever criminal perverts his talents.* —*n.* a perverted person. [< L, < *per–* to destruction + *vertere* to turn] —**per·vert'er,** *n.* —**per·vert'i·ble,** *adj.*

per·vi·ous (pėr'vi əs), *adj.* **1** giving passage or entrance: *sand is easily pervious to water.* **2** open to influence, argument,

etc. [< L, < *per–* through + *via* way] —**per'vi·ous·ness,** *n.*

pe·se·ta (pə sā'tə), *n.* unit of money of Spain. [< Sp., dim. of *pesa* weight. See PESO.]

pes·ky (pes'ki), *adj.,* **–ki·er, –ki·est.** *U.S.* troublesome; annoying. [? alter. of *pesty* < *pest*]

pe·so (pā'sō), *n., pl.* **–sos.** unit of money in Spanish-speaking countries. [< Sp., weight < L *pensum,* pp. of *pendere* weigh]

pes·si·mism (pes'ə miz əm), *n.* **1** tendency to look on the dark side of things or to see difficulties and disadvantages. **2** belief that things naturally tend to evil, or that life is not worth while. [< L *pessimus* worst] —**pes'si·mist,** *n.* —**pes'si· mis'tic,** *adj.* —**pes'si·mis'ti·cal·ly,** *adv.*

pest (pest), *n.* thing or person that causes trouble, injuries, or destruction; nuisance. [< L *pestis* plague]

pes·ter (pes'tər), *v.* annoy; trouble; vex. [appar. < OF *empestrer* hobble (an animal); infl. by *pest*]

pes·tif·er·ous (pes tif'ər əs), *adj.* **1** bringing disease or infection. **2** troublesome; annoying. [< L, < *pestis* plague + *ferre* bring] —**pes·tif'er·ous·ly,** *adv.*

pes·ti·lence (pes'tə ləns), *n.* disease that spreads rapidly, causing many deaths. Smallpox, yellow fever, and the plague are pestilences. —**pes·ti·len'tial,** *adj.*

pes·ti·lent (pes'tə lənt), *adj.* **1** often causing death. Smallpox is a pestilent disease. **2** harmful to morals; destroying peace: *the pestilent effects of war.* **3** troublesome; annoying. —**pes'ti·lent·ly,** *adv.*

pes·tle (pes'əl; pes'təl), *n., v.,* **–tled, –tling.** —*n.* tool for pounding or crushing substances into a powder in a mortar. —*v.* pound or crush with a pestle. [< OF, < L *pistillum* < *pinsere* to pound. Doublet of PISTIL.]

pet¹ (pet), *n., adj., v.,* **pet·ted, pet·ting.** —*n.* **1** animal kept as a favorite and treated with affection. **2** a darling; a favorite. —*adj.* **1** treated as a pet. **2** showing affection: *a pet name.* **3** darling; favorite. —*v.* **1** treat as a pet; stroke; pat. **2** fondle and caress one of the opposite sex.

pet² (pet), *n.* fit of peevishness.

pet·al (pet'əl), *n.* one of the parts of a flower that are usually colored. A rose has many petals. [< NL < Gk. *petalon* leaf, orig. neut. adj., outspread] —**pet'aled,** *adj.*

pe·tard (pi tärd'), *n.* an explosive device formerly used in warfare to break doors or gates.

hoist by, with, or **on one's own petard,** caught up by one's own scheme, or compromised by one's own action. [< F, < *péter* break wind, ult. < L *pedere*]

pet·cock (pet'kok'), *n.* a small faucet.

pe·ter (pē'tər), *v.* fail gradually (with *out*): *the gold lode petered out.*

Pe·ter (pē'tər), *n.* either of two books in the New Testament that bear the Apostle Peter's name.

pet·i·ole (pet′i ōl), *n.* the slender stalk by which a leaf is attached to the stem. [< L *petiolus,* dim. of *pes* foot] —**pet′i·o·late,** *adj.*

pet·it (pet′i), *adj.* in law, small; petty; minor: *petit larceny.* [< F, < VL stem *pit-* little. Doublet of PETTY.]

pe·tite (pə tēt′), *adj.* little; of small size; tiny, esp. with reference to a woman or girl. —**pe·tite′ness,** *n.*

pet·it four (pet′i fôr′; fōr′), *pl.* **pet·its fours** (pet′i fôrz′; fōrz′). small cakes with colored icing decoration. [< F, little oven]

pe·ti·tion (pə tish′ən), *n.* **1** a formal request to a superior or to one in authority for some privilege, right, benefit, etc.: *the people signed a petition asking the city council for a new sidewalk.* —*v.* **1** ask earnestly; make a petition to. **2** pray. [< L, < *petere* seek] —**pe·ti′tion·ar′y,** *adj.* —**pe·ti′tion·er,** *n.*

pet·it jury (pet′i), =petty jury.

pe·tit mal (pə tē′ mäl′), mild epilepsy with very short periods of unconsciousness and tremors. [< F, lit., small sickness]

pet·rel (pet′rəl), *n.* any of a number of sea birds, esp. the stormy petrel. [appar. dim. of St. *Peter,* who walked on the sea]

Pe·tri (pē′trē) or **pe·tri dish,** round dish with a cover, used for in vitro fertilization, to culture bacteria, etc. [< Julius *Petri* (1852–1922), German bacteriologist who developed it]

pet·ri·fy (pet′rə fī), *v.,* **-fied, -fy·ing. 1** turn into stone; become stone. **2** harden; stiffen; deaden. **3** paralyze with fear, horror, or surprise. [< F *pétrifier,* ult. < L *petra* stone < Gk.] —**pet′ri·fac′tion, pet′ri·fi·ca′tion,** *n.*

petro-, *combining form.* **1** rock or rocks, as in *petrography.* **2** petroleum, as in *petrolatum.* [< Gk. *petra* rock, *petrus,* stone]

pet·ro·chem·i·cal (pet′rō kem′ə kəl), *n.* a chemical compound or element obtained from petroleum or natural gas or wholly or partly from their hydrocarbons and intended for chemical markets. —**pet′ro·chem′is·try,** *n.*

pet·ro·dol·lars (pet′rō dol′ərz), *n.pl.* dollars earned as profits in oil-producing countries and usually invested in highly industrialized, developed countries.

pe·trog·ra·phy (pi trog′rə fi), *n.* branch of geology that deals with the description and classification of rocks. —**pe·trog′ra·pher,** *n.*

pet·rol (pet′rəl), *n.* Brit. gasoline. [< F < Med.L *petroleum.* Doublet of PETROLEUM.]

pet·ro·la·tum (pet′rə lā′təm), *n.* **1** salve or ointment made from petroleum. **2** mineral oil.

pe·tro·le·um (pə trō′li əm), *n.* an oil liquid found in the earth. Gasoline, kerosene, and paraffin are made from petroleum. [< Med.L, < Gk. *petra* rock, + L *oleum* oil. Doublet of PETROL.]

petroleum jelly, =petrolatum.

pe·trol·o·gy (pi trol′ə ji), *n.* science of rocks, including their origin, structure, changes, etc. —**pet′ro·log′i·cal,** *adj.* —**pe·trol′o·gist,** *n.*

pet·ti·coat (pet′i kōt), *n.* **1** skirt that hangs from the waist or from the shoulders, worn beneath the dress by women, girls, and babies. **2** skirt. —*adj.* female; feminine: *petticoat government.* [orig. *petty coat* little coat]

pet·ti·fog (pet′i fog; -fôg), *v.,* **-fogged, -fog·ging.** carry on a petty or shifty law business. —**pet′ti·fog′ger,** *n.* —**pet′ti·fog′ging,** *n.*

pet·tish (pet′ish), *adj.* peevish; cross. —**pet′tish·ly,** *adv.* —**pet′tish·ness,** *n.*

pet·ty (pet′i), *adj.,* **-ti·er, -ti·est. 1** having little importance or value; small. **2** mean; narrow-minded. **3** lower; subordinate. [< OF *petit.* Doublet of PETIT.] —**pet′ti·ly,** *adv.* —**pet′ti·ness,** *n.*

petty cash, sum of money kept on hand to pay small expenses.

petty jury, group of 12 persons chosen to decide a case in court. Also, **petit jury.**

petty larceny, theft in which the value of the property taken is less than a certain amount.

petty officer, a noncommissioned officer in the navy.

pet·u·lant (pech′ə lənt), *adj.* peevish; subject to little fits of bad temper; irritable over trifles. [< L *petulans,* ult. < *petere* seek, aim at] —**pet′u·lance, pet′u·lan·cy,** *n.* —**pet′u·lant·ly,** *adv.*

pe·tu·ni·a (pə tü′ni ə; -nyə; -tū′-), *n.* **1** plant with funnel-shaped flowers of white, pink, and various shades of purple. **2** the flower. [< NL < F *petun* tobacco; < South Am.Ind.]

pew (pū), *n.* **1** bench with a back, for people to sit on in a church. **2** place in a church set apart for the use of a certain family or group of people. [< OF < L *podia,* pl., elevated place, balcony, PODIUM]

pe·wee (pē′wē), *n.* **1** a small American bird with an olive-colored or gray back. **2** a phoebe or other small flycatcher. [imit.]

pe·wit (pē′wit; pū′it), *n.* **1** the lapwing. **2** the European black-headed gull. **3** pewee. [imit.]

pew·ter (pū′tər), *n.* **1** alloy of tin with lead, copper, or other metals. **2** dishes or other utensils made of this alloy. —*adj.* made of pewter: *a pewter mug.* [< OF *peautre*]

pe·yo·te (pā ō′tē), *n.* **1** stimulant made from the mescal, used by SW and Mexican Indians in religious ceremonies. **2** one of several cacti, esp. the mescal. [< Mex. Sp.]

pf., **1** Also, **pfg.** pfennig. **2** Also, **pfd.** preferred.

Pfc., private first class.

pfen·nig (pfen′ig), *n.,* *pl.* **pfen·nigs, pfen·ni·ge** (pfen′i gə). a German coin. [< G; akin to PENNY]

Pg., **1** Portugal. **2** Portuguese.

PG, Parental Guidance, a film rating (acceptable for a general audience with parents present for younger viewers).

PG-13, Parental Guidance for children under 13, a film rating.

pH, symbol (with a number) that indicates the acidity or alkalinity of soil, water, etc.

pha·e·ton (fā′ə tən), *n.* a light, four-wheeled carriage. [< F, named for *Phaëthon,* son of Helios]

phag·o·cyte (fag′ə sīt), *n.* leucocyte capable of absorbing and destroying waste or harmful material. [< Gk., *phagos* eating + E –*cyte* cell (< Gk. *kytos* hollow container)] —**phag′o·cyt′ic,** *adj.*

pha·lan·ge (fal′ənj), *n.,* *pl.* –**ges** (–jēz). bone of the finger or toe. [< OF < L *phalanx*]

pha·lan·ger (fə lan′jər), *n.* a small, tree-climbing marsupial of the Australian region. [< NL, < Gk. *phalangion* spiderweb < *phalanx* spider; with ref. to webbed toes]

pha·lanx (fā′langks; fal′angks), *n.,* *pl.* **pha·lanx·es, pha·lan·ges** (fə lan′jēz). **1** in ancient Greece, a special battle formation of infantry fighting in close ranks with their shields joined and long spears overlapping each other. **2** a compact or closely massed body of persons, animals, or things. **3** any bone in the fingers or toes. [< L < Gk.]

phal·lus (fal′əs), *n.,* *pl.* **phal·li** (fal′ī), **1** penis. **2** image of the penis, symbolizing the generative power of nature. [< L < Gk. *phallos*] —**phal′lic, phal′li·cal,** *adj.*

phan·tasm (fan′taz əm), *n.* **1** thing seen only in one's imagination; unreal fancy: *the phantasms of a dream or fever.* **2** a supposed appearance of an absent person, living or dead. [< L < Gk. *phantasma* image, ult. < *phainein* show. Doublet of PHANTOM.] —**phan·tas′mal, phan·tas′mic,** *adj.* —**phan·tas′mal·ly,** *adv.*

phan·tas·ma·go·ri·a (fan taz′mə gô′ri ə; –gō′–), *n.* a shifting scene of real things, illusions, imaginary fancies, deceptions, and the like. [< Gk. *phantasma* PHANTASM + ? *agora* assembly] —**phan·tas′ma·go′ri·al, phan·tas′ma·gor′ic,** *adj.*

phan·ta·sy (fan′tə si; –zi), *n.,* *pl.* –**sies.** =fantasy.

phan·tom (fan′təm), *n.* **1** image of the mind: *phantoms of a dream.* **2** a vague, dim, or shadowy appearance; ghost. —*adj.* like a ghost; unreal: *a phantom ship.* [< OF < VL < Gk. *phantasma* image. Doublet of PHANTASM.]

Phar·aoh (fâr′ō), *n.* title given to the kings of ancient Egypt.

Phar·i·see (far′ə sē), *n.* **1** member of an ancient Jewish sect that was very strict in keeping to tradition. **2** person who makes a show of religion.

pharm., **1** pharmaceutic. **2** pharmacopoeia. **3** pharmacy.

phar·ma·ceu·tic (fär′mə sü′tik), **phar·ma·ceu·ti·cal** (–tə kəl), *adj.* pertaining to pharmacy. [< LL < Gk., ult. < *pharmakon* drug, poison] —**phar′ma·ceu′ti·cal·ly,** *adv.*

phar·ma·ceu·tics (fär′mə sü′tiks), *n.* =pharmacy (def. 1).

phar·ma·cist (fär′mə sist), *n.* =druggist.

phar·ma·col·o·gy (fär′mə kol′ə ji), *n.* science of drugs, their preparation, uses, and effects. [< Gk. *pharmakon* drug + –LOGY] —**phar′ma·co·log′i·cal,** *adj.* —**phar′ma·col′o·gist,** *n.*

phar·ma·co·poe·ia (fär′mə kə pē′ə), *n.* book containing an official list and description of drugs and medicines. [< Gk., < *pharmakon* drug + *poieein* make] —**phar′ma·co·poe′ial,** *adj.*

phar·ma·cy (fär′mə si), *n., pl.* –**cies. 1** preparation and dispensing of drugs and medicines; occupation of a druggist; pharmaceutics. **2** place where drugs and medicines are prepared and sold; drugstore. [< LL < Gk., ult. < *pharmakon* drug]

phar·os (fär′os), *n.* lighthouse, beacon. [< L < Gk., *Pharos* of Alexandria (Egypt), famous ancient lighthouse]

pha·ryn·ge·al (fə rin′ji əl; far′in jē′əl), **pha·ryn·gal** (fə ring′gəl), *adj.* pertaining to or connected with the pharynx.

phar·ynx (far′ingks), *n., pl.* **phar·ynx·es, pha·ryn·ges** (fə rin′jēz). tube or cavity that connects the mouth with the esophagus. [< NL < Gk.]

phase (fāz), *n.* **1** one of the changing states or stages of development of a person or thing: *at present John has no use for girls; that is a phase most boys go through.* **2** one side, part, or view (of a subject): *what phase of mathematics are you studying now?* **3** the apparent shape of the moon or of a planet at a given time. **4** a particular stage in a series of periodic changes or movements. **5** a homogeneous part of a heterogeneous system, separated from other parts by definite boundaries.

phase in, introduce gradually.

phase out or **down,** gradually reduce or eliminate. [< NL < Gk. *phasis* appearance < *phainein* show]

Ph.B., Bachelor of Philosophy.

Ph.D., Doctor of Philosophy.

pheas·ant (fez′ənt), *n., pl.* –**ants** or (*esp. collectively*) –**ant. 1** a game bird with a long tail and brilliant feathers. **2** the ruffed grouse. [< AF < Pr. < L < Gk. *phasianos,* lit., Phasian; with ref. to River Phasis in Colchis]

phe·no·bar·bi·tal (fē′nō bär′bə tôl; –tal), *n.* a white powder, used as a hypnotic or sedative.

phe·nol (fē′nōl; –nol), *n.* carbolic acid.

phe·nom·e·nal (fə nom′ə nəl), *adj.* **1** of or pertaining to a phenomenon or phenomena. **2** having the nature of a phenomenon. **3** extraordinary: *a phenomenal memory.* —**phe·nom′e·nal·ly,** *adv.*

phe·nom·e·non (fə nom′ə non), *n., pl.* –**na** (–nə) or (*esp. for def. 2*) –**nons. 1** fact, event, or circumstance that can be observed: *lightning is an electrical phenomenon.* **2** an extraordinary or remarkable thing or person. [< L < Gk. *phainomenon,* neut. ppr. of *phainesthai* appear]

phew (fū), *interj.* exclamation of disgust, impatience, surprise, relief, etc.

phi (fī; fē), *n.* the 21st letter of the Greek alphabet (Φ, φ).

phi·al (fī′əl), *n.* a small bottle; vial. [< F < LL < L *phiala* < Gk. *phiale* a broad flat vessel]

Phi Be·ta Kap·pa (fī′ bā′tə kap′ə; bē′tə), society composed of American college students and graduates who have ranked high in scholarship.

Phil., 1 Philemon. **2** Philippians. **3** Philippine.

Phil·a·del·phi·a (fil′ə del′fi ə; –del′fyə), *n.* city in SE Pennsylvania, site of the Continental Congress and the Constitutional Convention.

phi·lan·der (fə lan′dər), *v.* make love without serious intentions; flirt. [orig. *n.,* < Gk., < *philos* loving + *aner* man; appar. taken as "loving man"] —**phi·lan′der·er,** *n.*

phi·lan·thro·py (fə lan′thrə pi), *n., pl.* –**pies. 1** love of humankind shown by practical kindness and helpfulness to humanity. **2** thing that benefits humanity: *a hospital is a useful philanthropy.* [< LL < Gk., ult. < *philos* loving + *anthropos* man] —**phil′an·throp′ic,** *adj.* —**phil′an·throp′i·cal ·ly,** *adv.* —**phi·lan′thro·pist,** *n.*

phi·lat·e·ly (fə lat′ə li), *n.* the collecting, arranging, and study of postage stamps, stamped envelopes, post cards, etc. [< F, ult. < Gk. *philos* loving + *ateleia* exemption from tax; the stamp indicates the tax is paid] —**phil′a·tel′ic,** *adj.* —**phil′a·tel′i·cal·ly,** *adv.* —**phi·lat′e·list,** *n.*

Phi·le·mon (fə lē′mən), *n.* book of the New Testament written by Paul.

phil·har·mon·ic (fil′här mon′ik; fil′ər–), *adj.* devoted to music; loving music: *a musical club is often called a philharmonic society.* [< F, ult. < Gk. *philos* loving + *harmonia* music]

Phil·ip (fil′əp), *n.* one of the twelve disciples chosen by Jesus as his Apostles.

Phi·lip·pi·ans (fə lip′i ənz), *n.* one of the books of the New Testament, a letter from Paul to the early Christians of Philippi.

Phi·lip·pic (fə lip′ik), *n.* **1** any of several orations by Demosthenes denouncing King Philip of Macedonia. **2** any of several orations by Cicero denouncing Marcus Antonius. **3 philippic,** a bitter attack in words.

Phil·ip·pine (fil′ə pēn), *adj.* of or having to do with the Philippine Islands or their inhabitants.

Philippines, *n., pl.* **1** island country in E Asia, made up of the Philippine Islands.

2 Also, **Philippine Islands.** group of 7083 islands in the W Pacific, SE of Asia and N of Australia.

Phi·lis·tine (fə lis′tin; fil′əs tēn; –tīn), *n.* **1** one of a warlike people in SW Palestine. **2** person who is commonplace in ideas and tastes. —*adj.* **1** of the Philistines. **2** lacking culture; commonplace. —**Phi·lis′tin·ism,** *n.*

phil·o·den·dron (fil′ə den′drən), *n.* a tropical American climbing evergreen plant, often grown as a house plant for its smooth, shiny leaves.

phi·lol·o·gy (fi lol′ə ji), *n.* **1** an older name for linguistics. **2** the study of literary and other records. [< L < Gk., ult. < *philos* loving + *logos* word, speech, story] —**phil′o·log′ic, phil′o·log′i·cal,** *adj.* —**phi·lol′o·gist,** *n.*

phil·o·mel (fil′ə mel), **phil·o·me·la** (fil′ə mē′lə), *n. Poetic.* nightingale.

philos., philosophical; philosophy.

phi·los·o·pher (fə los′ə fər), *n.* **1** person who studies philosophy much. **2** person who has a system of philosophy. **3** person who shows the calmness of philosophy under hard conditions, accepting life and making the best of it.

philosophers' stone, substance believed to have the power to change base metals into gold or silver.

phil·o·soph·i·cal (fil′ə sof′ə kəl), **phil·o·soph·ic** (–ik), *adj.* **1** of philosophy. **2** knowing much about philosophy. **3** devoted to philosophy. **4** wise; calm; reasonable. —**phil′o·soph′i·cal·ly,** *adv.*

phi·los·o·phize (fə los′ə fīz), *v.,* –**phized, –phiz·ing.** think or reason as a philosopher does; try to understand and explain things: *philosophize about life.* —**phi·los′o·phiz′er,** *n.*

phi·los·o·phy (fə los′əfi), *n., pl.* –**phies. 1** study of the truth or principles underlying all knowledge; study of the most general causes and principles of the universe. **2** explanation or theory of the universe. **3** system for guiding life. **4** the broad general principles of a particular subject: *the philosophy of history.* **5** a reasonable attitude; calmness. [< L < Gk., love of wisdom ult. < *philos* loving + *sophos* wise]

phil·ter (fil′tər), *n.* **1** drug or potion used to make a person fall in love. **2** a magic drink. [< F < L < Gk. *philtron* love charm, ult. < *philos* loving]

phle·bi·tis (fli bī′tis), *n.* inflammation of a vein. —**phle·bit′ic,** *adj.*

phle·bot·o·my (fli bot′ə mi), *n.* opening a vein to let blood; bleeding. [< LL < Gk., ult. < *phleps* vein + –*tomos* cutting] —**phle·bot′o·mist,** *n.*

phlegm (flem), *n.* **1** the thick discharge from the nose or throat that accompanies a cold. **2** sluggish disposition or temperament; indifference. **3** coolness; calmness. [< OF < LL < Gk. *phlegma* clammy humor (resulting from heat) < *phlegein* burn]

phleg·mat·ic (fleg mat′ik), *adj.* **1** sluggish; indifferent. **2** cool; calm. —**phleg·mat′i·cal·ly,** *adv.*

phlo·em (flō′em), *n.* tissue in a plant or tree that carries dissolved food downward to the stems and roots. [< G < Gk. *phlóos* bark]

phlox (floks), *n.* **1** plant with clusters of showy flowers in various colors. **2** the flower. [< L < Gk., a plant; lit., flame]

Ph·nom Penh (pə nôm′ pen′), *n.* capital of Cambodia.

pho·bi·a (fō′bi ə), *n.* a morbid or insane fear. [< NL < Gk. -*phobia* < *phobos* fear] —**pho′bic,** *adj.*

phoe·be (fē′bē), *n.* a small American bird with a grayish-olive back, a yellowish breast, and a low crest on the head. [imit., but accommodated to *Phoebe*]

Phoe·ni·cia (fə nish′ə), *n.* an ancient country in W Syria, on the Mediterranean Sea. —**Phoe·ni′cian,** *adj., n.*

phoe·nix (fē′niks), *n.* a mythical bird, the only one of its kind, said to live 500 or 600 years, to burn itself on a funeral pile, and to rise again from the ashes, fresh and beautiful, for another long life. [< L < Gk. *phoinix,* prob. < Egyptian *bonû, bennu* heron]

Phoe·nix (fē′niks), *n.* capital of Arizona, in the C part.

phone[1] (fōn), *n., v.,* **phoned, phon·ing.** telephone.

phone[2] (fōn), *n.* a speech sound. [< Gk.]

phone card, small, electronically coded card used to pay for telephone calls.

pho·neme (fō′nēm), *n.* one of a group of distinctive sounds that make up the words of a language. The words *cat* and *bat* are distinguished by their initial phonemes /k/ and /b/. [< Gk. *phonema* a sound] —**pho·ne′mic,** *adj.*

pho·ne·mics (fə nē′miks), *n.* branch of linguistics dealing with phonemes. —**pho·ne′mi·cist,** *n.*

phonet., phonetics.

pho·net·ic (fə net′ik), *adj.* **1** of or having to do with speech sounds: *phonetic laws.* **2** representing speech sounds: *phonetic symbols.* [< NL < Gk., ult. < *phone* sound] —**pho·net′i·cal·ly,** *adv.*

pho·net·ics (fə net′iks), *n.* science dealing with speech sounds and the art of pronunciation. —**pho·net′i·cian,** *n.*

phon·ic (fon′ik; fō′nik), *adj.* **1** of sound. **2** of speech sounds; phonetic. **3** voiced.

pho·no·graph (fō′nə graf; -gräf), *n.* instrument that records and reproduces sounds. [< *phono-* (< Gk. *phone* sound) + -GRAPH] —**pho′no·graph′ic,** *adj.* —**pho′no·graph′i·cal·ly,** *adv.*

pho·nol·o·gy (fō nol′ə ji), *n.* **1** system of sounds used in a language. **2** study of the sounds of a language, their history and changes. [< *phono-* (< Gk. *phone* sound) + -LOGY] —**pho′no·log′ic, pho′no·log′i·cal,** *adj.* —**pho′no·log′i·cal·ly,** *adv.* —**pho·nol′o·gist,** *n.*

pho·ny, pho·ney (fō′ni), *adj.,* **-ni·er, -ni·est; -ney·er, -ney·est;** *n., pl.* **-nies; -neys.** *Informal.* —*adj.* not genuine; counterfeit; fraudulent. —*n.* fake; pretender. [< *fawney,* a gilt brass ring used by swindlers < Irish]

phos·phate (fos′fāt), *n.* **1** salt or ester of an acid containing phosphorus. **2** fertilizer containing such salts.

phos·phide (fos′fīd; -fid), *n.* compound of phosphorus with a basic element or radical.

phos·pho·resce (fos′fə res′), *v.,* **-resced, -resc·ing.** be luminous without noticeable heat. —**phos′pho·res′cence,** *n.* —**phos′pho·res′cent,** *adj.*

phos·phor·ic (fos fôr′ik; -for′-), *adj.* pertaining to or containing phosphorus, esp. in its higher valence.

phosphoric acid, a colorless, odorless acid, H_3PO_4, containing phosphorus.

phos·pho·rous (fos′fə rəs; fos fô′-; -fō′-), *adj.* pertaining to or containing phosphorus, esp. in its lower valence.

phos·pho·rus (fos′fə rəs), *n., pl.* **-ri** (-rī). a solid nonmetallic element, P, existing in two forms; one yellow, poisonous, inflammable, and luminous in the dark; the other red, nonpoisonous, and less inflammable. [< L < Gk. *phosphoros* the morning star < *phos* light + *pherein* bring]

pho·to (fō′tō), *n., pl.* **-tos.** photograph.

photo-, *combining form.* **1** light, as in *photoelectric.* **2** photograph or photographic, as in *photomontage.* [< Gk. *phos* light]

pho·to·cop·i·er (fō′tō kop′i ər), *n.* machine that produces photographic copies of documents, drawings, etc., and immediately prints them.

pho·to·cop·y (fō′tō kop′i), *n., pl.* **-ies,** *v.,* **-cop·ied, -cop·y·ing.** copy of a document, drawing, etc., made on a photocopier. —*v.,* produce a copy of a document, drawing, etc., on a photocopier.

pho·to·e·lec·tric (fō′tō i lek′trik), *adj.* pertaining to the electricity or electrical effects produced by light.

photoelectric cell, cell, as a solar cell, which produces an electric current in accordance with the intensity of the light falling upon it.

photo finish, 1 a finish to a race so close that a photograph is required to decide the winner. **2** *Fig.* an outcome that is unclear until the last moment.

photog., photography.

pho·to·gen·ic (fō′tə jen′ik), *adj.* **1** photographing very well, esp. in motion pictures: *a photogenic face.* **2** phosphorescent; luminescent. Certain bacteria are photogenic. [< *photo-* + Gk. *-genes* born, produced]

pho·to·graph (fō′tə graf; -gräf), *n.* picture made with a camera that records an image on film, or a digital camera that converts an image into electronic form. A photograph is made by the action of the light rays from the pictured coming through the lens of the camera onto film. —*v.* **1** take a photograph of. **2** take photographs. **3** look (clear, unnatural, etc.) in a photograph: *she does not photograph well.* [< *photo* + -GRAPH]

pho·tog·ra·phy (fə tog′rə fi), *n.* the taking of photographs. —**pho·tog′ra·pher,** *n.* —**pho′to·graph′ic, pho′to·graph′i·cal,** *adj.* —**pho′to·graph′i·cal·ly,** *adv.*

pho·to·jour·nal·ism (fō′tō jèr′nəl iz əm), *n.* journalism that uses photographs rather than text. —**pho′to·jour′nal·ist ,** *n.*

pho·tom·e·try (fō tom′ə tri), *n.* branch of physics dealing with measurements of the intensity of light. —**pho′to·met′ric,** *adj.* —**pho·tom′e·trist,** *n.*

pho·to·mon·tage (fō′tō mon tãzh′; -môn-), *n.* montage that uses photographs.

pho·ton (fō′ton), *n.* quantum unit of light, an element of radiant energy.

pho·to·sen·si·tive (fō′tō sen′sə tiv), *adj.* readily stimulated to action by light. —**pho′to·sen′si·tiv′i·ty,** *n.*

pho·to·syn·the·sis (fō′tō sin′thə sis), *n.* process by which plant cells make sugar from carbon dioxide and water in the presence of chlorophyll and light.

pho·tot·rop·ism (fō tot′rə piz əm), *n.* tendency to turn in response to light. [< *photo-* + Gk. *-tropos* turning] —**pho′to·trop′ic,** *adj.*

pho·to·vol·ta·ic (fō′tō vol tā′ik), *adj.* **1** producing an electric current when exposed to a source of radiant energy, as sunlight. **2** =photoelectric. —**pho′to·vol·ta′ics,** *n.*

phrase (frāz), *n., v.,* **phrased, phras·ing.** —*n.* **1** combination of words: *he spoke in simple phrases.* **2** expression often used: *"call up"* is the common phrase for *"get a telephone connection with."* **3** a short, striking expression. *Examples:* A Fair Deal; a war to end wars; liberty or death. **4** a group of words not containing a subject and predicate and used as a single word. *Examples:* in the house; coming by the church; to eat too fast. **5** a short part of a piece of music, usually containing four measures. —*v.* **1** express in a particular way: *she phrased her excuse politely.* **2** mark off or bring out the phrases of (a piece of music). [< L < Gk. *phrasis* < *phrazein* express] —**phras′al,** *adj.*

phra·se·ol·o·gy (frā′zi ol′ə ji), *n., pl.* **-gies.** selection and arrangement of words; particular way in which a person expresses himself in language: *the phraseology of the Bible.* —**phra′se·o·log′i·cal,** *adj.*

phre·net·ic (fri net′ik), *adj.* =frenetic. [< OF < L < Gk. *phrenetikos.* Doublet of FRANTIC.] —**phre·net′i·cal·ly,** *adv.*

phre·nol·o·gy (fri nol′ə ji), *n.* theory that the shape of the skull shows what sort of mind and character a person has. [< Gk. *phren* mind + -LOGY] —**phre·nol′o·gist,** *n.*

phy·lac·ter·y (fə lak′tər i), *n., pl.* **-ter·ies.** either of two small leather cases containing texts from the Jewish law, worn by orthodox Jews during prayer to remind them to keep the law. [< LL < Gk. *phylakterion* safeguard, ult. < *phylax* watchman]

phy·log·e·ny (fī loj′ə ni), *n., pl.* **-nies.** racial history; the origin and development (of a kind of animal or plant). [< G, < Gk. *phylon* race + *-geneia* origin] **—phy′lo·ge·net′ic, phy′lo·gen′ic,** *adj.* **—phy′lo·ge·net′i·cal·ly,** *adv.*

phy·lum (fī′ləm), *n., pl.* **-la** (-lə). a primary division of the animal or vegetable kingdom, usually equivalent to a subkingdom. [< NL < Gk. *phylon* race, stock]

phys. 1 physical. 2 physician. 3 physics.

phys ed or **phys. ed.** (fiz′ ed′), *n. Informal.* physical education.

phys·ic (fiz′ik), *n.* medicine, esp. one that moves the bowels. [< L < Gk. *physike* (*episteme*) (knowledge) of nature, ult. < *phyein* produce]

phys·i·cal (fiz′ə kəl), *adj.* 1 of the body: *physical exercise.* 2 of matter; material: *the tide is a physical force.* 3 according to the laws of nature: *a physical impossibility.* 4 of the science of physics. **—phys′i·cal·ly,** *adv.*

physical chemistry, branch of chemistry that deals with the physical properties of substances and uses physical methods to solve chemical problems.

physical education, instruction in how to exercise and take care of the body.

physical geography, study of land forms, climate, winds, ocean currents, and all other physical features of the earth.

physically challenged, having a physical disability; disabled.

physical science, 1 physics. 2 physics, chemistry, geology, astronomy, and other sciences of physical facts.

physical therapy, =physiotherapy.

phy·si·cian (fə zish′ən), *n.* doctor of medicine.

physician's assistant, person trained and licensed to dispense basic medical care to patients, write prescriptions, etc., in a practice with a medical doctor.

phys·ics (fiz′iks), *n.* science that deals with matter and energy that do not involve change in composition, or with the action of different forms of energy on matter. Physics studies mechanics, heat, light, sound, and electricity. [pl. of *physic* (= Gk. *ta physika* the natural things)] **—phys′i·cist,** *n.*

phys·i·og·no·my (fiz′i og′nə mi; –i on′ə–), *n., pl.* **-mies.** 1 kind of features or type of face one has; one's face. 2 art of estimating character from the features of the face or the form of the body. [< LL < Gk., < *physis* nature + *gnomon* judge]

physiol., physiological; physiologist; physiology.

phys·i·ol·o·gy (fiz′i ol′ə ji), *n.* 1 science dealing with the normal functions of living things or their organs: *human physiology, plant physiology.* 2 all the functions

and activities of a living thing or of one of its organs. [< L < Gk., < *physis* nature + *-logos* treating of] **—phys′i·o·log′i·cal, phys′i·o·log′ic,** *adj.* **—phys′i·o·log′i·cal·ly,** *adv.* **—phys·i·ol′o·gist,** *n.*

phys·i·o·ther·a·py (fiz′i ō ther′ə pi), *n.* treatment of diseases and defects by physical remedies, such as massage (rather than by drugs). [< *physio–* (< Gk. *physis* nature) + *therapy*]

phy·sique (fi zēk′), *n.* bodily structure, organization, or development: *a man of strong physique.* [< F, physical. See PHYSIC.]

phy·to·chrome (fī′tə krōm), *n.* bluish pigment in plants that is sensitive to light.

pi¹ (pī), *n., pl.* **pis.** 1 ratio of the circumference of any circle to its diameter, usually written as π. (π = 3.141592+.) 2 the 16th letter of the Greek alphabet (Π, π). [def. 1, use of Gk. letter to mean Gk. *periphereia* PERIPHERY]

pi² (pī), *n., v.,* **pied, pi·ing.** —*n.* 1 printing types all mixed up. 2 any confused mixture. —*v.* mix up (type). Also, **pie.**

P.I., Philippine Islands.

pi·a ma·ter (pī′ə mā′tər), innermost layer of the meninges, membranes that surround the brain and spinal cord. [< ML pious mother, ult. < mistranslation of Ar. thin or tender mother]

pi·a·nis·si·mo (pē′ə nis′ə mō), *adj., adv., n., pl.* **-mos, -mi** (-mē). —*adj.* very soft. —*adv.* very softly. —*n.* a passage played this way. [< Ital., superlative of *piano* soft. See PIANO².]

pi·an·ist (pi an′ist; pē′ə nist), *n.* person who plays the piano.

pi·an·o¹ (pi an′ō), *n., pl.* **-an·os.** a large musical instrument whose tones come from many wires. The wires are sounded by hammers that are worked by striking keys on a keyboard. [for *pianoforte*]

pi·a·no² (pi ä′nō), —*adj.* soft. —*adj.* softly. [< Ital. < L *planus* plain. Doublet of PLAIN and PLAN.]

pi·an·o·for·te (pi an′ə fôr′tē, –fôr′–; pi an′ə fôrt, –fōrt), *n.* =piano¹. [< Ital., < *piano* soft + *forte* loud]

pi·as·ter, pi·as·tre (pi as′tər), *n.* 1 coin used in Turkey, Egypt, Lebanon, Syria, etc. 2 a former Spanish silver coin.

pi·az·za (pi az′ə), *n.* 1 a large porch along one or more sides of a house. 2 an open public square in Italian towns. [< Ital. < L < Gk. *plateia* (*hodos*) broad (street). Doublet of PLACE and PLAZA.]

pi·broch (pē′brok), *n.* kind of musical piece performed on the bagpipe, usually warlike or sad. [< Scotch Gaelic *piobaireachd* pipe music, ult. < *piob* pipe]

pi·ca (pī′kə), *n.* 1 size of type, 12 point. 2 this size used as a measure; about ⅙ inch. [< Anglo-L, name of a book of rules concerning holy days, supposed (? erroneously) to be printed in pica]

pic·a·dor (pik′ə dôr), *n.* one of the horsemen who open a bullfight by irritating the bull with pricks of their lances. [< Sp., < *picar* pierce]

pic·a·resque (pik′ə resk′), *adj.* dealing with rogues and their questionable adventures: *a picaresque novel.* [< Sp., < *pícaro* rogue]

pic·a·yune (pik′ə ūn′), *Am.* —*n.* 1 any coin of small value. 2 an insignificant person or thing; trifle. —*adj.* small; petty; mean. [< Louisiana F *picaillon* coin worth 5 cents]

pic·ca·lil·li (pik′ə lil′i), *n.* relish made of chopped pickles, onions, tomatoes, etc., with hot spices.

pic·co·lo (pik′ə lō), *n., pl.* **-los.** a small, shrill flute, sounding an octave higher than the ordinary flute. [< Ital., small]

pick¹ (pik), *v.* 1 choose; select. 2 pull away with the fingers; gather: *we pick fruit and flowers.* 3 use a pick or pickax. 4 pierce, dig into, or break up with something pointed. 5 use something pointed to remove things from: *pick one's teeth, pick a bone.* 6 prepare for use by removing feathers, waste parts, etc. 7 pull apart. 8 use fingers with a plucking motion: *play a banjo by picking its strings.* 9 seek and find occasion for; seek and find: *pick a quarrel.* —*n.* 1 choice; selection. 2 the best or most desirable part. 3 amount of a crop gathered at one time. 4 thing held in the fingers and used to pull on the strings of a musical instrument.

pick a lock, open a lock with a pointed tool, wire, etc.

pick a pocket, steal from a person's pocket.

pick at, a pull at: *pick at a sweater, the bird picked at the suet.* **b** eat only a little of at a time. **c** find fault with; nag.

pick off, a shoot, one at a time. **b** bring down, as an opponent.

pick on, a find fault with. **b** annoy; tease. **c** select, esp. for unwelcome attention.

pick out, a choose; select. **b** distinguish (a thing) from surroundings: *pick out adjectives from a word list.* **c** make out the meaning of something, the notes of a tune, etc., slowly, with effort.

pick over, a look over carefully: *pick over items on sale.* **b** prepare for use: *pick over beans before cooking.*

pick up, a take up: *pick up litter.* **b** get by chance: *pick up a bargain.* **c** learn without being taught: *pick up Spanish.* **d** take up into a vehicle or ship: *pick up passengers.* **e** improve: *pick up quickly after an accident, the economy has picked up.* **f** go faster; increase in speed. **g** tidy up; put in order. [ME *picke(n)*; cf. OE *pīcung* pricking] **—pick′er,** *n.* **—pick′y,** *adj.*

pick² (pik), *n.* 1 a heavy, sharp-pointed tool for breaking earth, rock, etc.; pickax. 2 a sharp-pointed tool: *ice is broken into pieces with a pick.* [ME *picke,* var. of *pik* PIKE¹]

pick·a·back (pik′ə bak′), *adv.* =piggyback.

pick·ax, pick·axe (pik′aks′), *n.* a heavy tool with a sharp point for breaking up dirt, rocks, etc.; pick.

picked (pikt), *adj.* **1** cleaned by picking. **2** specially selected for merit.

pick·er·el (pik′ər əl; pik′rəl), *n., pl.* **-els** or (*esp. collectively*) **-el.** *U.S. and Canada.* kind of large freshwater fish with a long, narrow, pointed head. [dim. of *pike²*]

pick·et (pik′it), *n.* **1** a pointed stake or peg driven into the ground to make a fence, to tie a horse to, etc. **2** a small body of troops, or a single person, posted at some place to watch for the enemy and guard against surprise. **3** person stationed by a labor union near a factory, store, etc., where there is a strike. **4** a person who takes part in a public demonstration or boycott to support a cause; demonstrator. —*v.* **1** enclose with pickets; fence. **2** station pickets at or near: *picket a factory.* **3** act as a picket. [< F, dim. of *pic* a pick. See PICK²] —**pick′et·er,** *n.* —**pick′et·ing,** *n.*

picket fence, fence made of pickets.

pick·ings (pik′ingz), *n.pl.* **1** amount picked. **2** things left over; scraps. **3** *Fig.* profits: *slim pickings for retailers.*

pick·le (pik′əl), *n., v.,* **-led, -ling.** —*n.* **1** salt water, vinegar, or other liquid in which meat and vegetables can be preserved. **2** cucumber preserved in pickle. **3** any other vegetable preserved in pickle. **4** trouble; difficulty. **5** an acid bath for cleaning metal castings, etc. —*v.* **1** preserve in pickle: *she pickled the beets.* **2** clean with acid. [< MDu. *pekel*] —**pick′ler,** *n.*

pick·pock·et (pik′pok it), *n.* person who steals from people's pockets.

pick·up (pik′up′), *n.* **1** a picking up. **2** acceleration; going faster; increase in speed. **3** reception of television images and their conversion into electric waves. **4** a small, light truck for light hauling.

pick-up sticks, =jackstraws.

pick·y (pik′i), *adj.,* **-i·er, -i·est.** **1** choosy. **2** critical; complaining.

pic·nic (pik′nik), *n., v.,* **-nicked, -nicking.** —*n.* **1** a meal in the open air. **2** *Informal.* a very easy job. —*v.* go on a picnic. [< F *piquenique*] —**pic′nick·er,** *n.*

pi·cot (pē′kō), *n.* one of a number of fancy loops in embroidery, tatting, etc., or along the edge of lace, ribbon, etc. —*v.* trim with such loops. [< F, dim. of *pic* a pick. See PICK².]

Pict (pikt), *n.* member of a group of people formerly living in Scotland, esp. N Scotland. —**Pict′ish,** *adj.*

pic·to·graph (pik′tə graf; -gräf), *n.* picture used as a sign or symbol. [< L *pictus* painted + -GRAPH] —**pic′to·graph′ic,** *adj.* —**pic′to·graph′i·cal·ly,** *adv.* —**pic·tog′ra·phy,** *n.*

pic·to·ri·al (pik tô′ri əl; -tō′-), *adj.* **1** pertaining to pictures; expressed in pictures. **2** making a picture for the mind; vivid. **3** illustrated by pictures: *a pictorial magazine.* **4** having to do with painters or painting. —*n.* magazine in which pictures are an important feature. —**pic·to′ri·al·ly,** *adv.*

pic·ture (pik′chər), *n., v.,* **-tured, -turing.** —*n.* **1** a drawing, painting, portrait, or photograph; a print of any of these. **2** scene. **3** something beautiful. **4** a mental image: *memory's pictures.* **5** likeness: *he is the picture of his father.* **6** example; embodiment: *she was the picture of despair.* **7** a motion picture; film. —*v.* **1** draw, paint, etc.; make into a picture. **2** imagine: *it is hard to picture life a hundred years ago.* **3** describe vividly. [< L *pictura* < *pingere* to paint] —**pic′tur·a·ble,** *adj.* —**pic′tur·a·ble·ness,** *n.* —**pic′tured,** *adj.*

pic·tur·esque (pik′chər esk′), *adj.* **1** quaint or interesting enough to be used as the subject of a picture: *a picturesque old mill.* **2** vivid. —**pic′tur·esque′ly,** *adv.* —**pic′tur·esque′ness,** *n.*

picture tube, the cathode-ray tube of a television receiver, the front of which constitutes the screen on which the picture being transmitted is reproduced.

picture window, a large window designed to give a wide view.

picture writing, 1 the recording of events, expression of ideas, etc., by means of pictures. **2** the pictures used to record events, express ideas, etc.

pid·dle (pid′əl), *v.,* **-dled, -dling.** do anything in a trifling or ineffective way. —**pid′dler,** *n.* —**pid′dling,** *adj.*

pidg·in English (pij′ən), one of several forms of English, with reduced grammatical structure and vocabulary, used in W Africa, Australia, Melanesia, and formerly in China, as a trade or communication jargon. [*pidgin,* Chinese alter. of *business*]

pie¹ (pī), *n.* fruit, meat, etc., enclosed in pastry and baked. [ME *pye*]

pie² (pī), *n.* =magpie. [< OF < L *pica*]

pie³ (pī), *n., v.,* **pied, pie·ing.** =pi². [? extended use of *pie¹*]

pie·bald (pī′bôld′), *adj.* spotted in two colors: *a piebald horse.* —*n.* a spotted horse. [appar. < *pie²* + *bald;* with ref. to dark color of magpie]

piece (pēs), *n., v.,* **pieced, piec·ing.** —*n.* **1** one of the parts into which a thing is divided or broken; bit: *piece of land, piece of bread, this set of china has 144 pieces.* **2** coin. **3** a single composition in an art: *a new piece at a theater.* **4** gun; cannon. **5** quantity in which goods are made: *she bought the whole piece of muslin.* **6** figure, disk, block, or the like, used in playing checkers, chess, and other games. —*v.* **1** make or repair by adding or joining pieces. **2** join the pieces of.

(give someone) a piece of one's mind, forcefully say what one thinks; give one's frank opinion.

go to pieces, a collapse physically or mentally; break down. **b** break into pieces.

of a piece, of the same kind; in keeping.

pick up the pieces, restore order; return to a normal condition. [< OF < VL *pettia* fragment < Celtic] —**piec′er,** *n.* —**piec′ing,** *n.*

pièce de ré·sis·tance (pyes də rā zēs täⁿs′), *French.* the main or outstanding article in any collection.

piece·meal (pēs′mēl′), *adv.* **1** piece by piece; a little at a time. **2** piece from piece; to pieces; into fragments. —*adj.* done piece by piece.

piece of cake, *Informal.* something certain to succeed or easily accomplished.

piece of eight, an old Spanish dollar.

piece of work, *Informal.* person with an unusual character, sometimes difficult to deal with.

piece·work (pēs′wėrk′), *n.* work paid for by the amount done, not by the time is takes. —**piece′work′er,** *n.*

pied (pīd), *adj.* having patches of two or more colors; many-colored. [< *pie²;* with ref. to magpie's plumage]

pie in the sky, something very pleasant or desirable and totally impractical or unattainable.

pier (pir), *n.* **1** structure extending into the water, used as a walk or a landing place. **2** breakwater. **3** one of the solid supports on which the arches of a bridge rest; any solid support of masonry. [< Med.L *pera*]

pierce (pirs), *v.,* **pierced, pierc·ing.** **1** go into; go through: *a tunnel pierces the mountain.* **2** make a hole in; bore into or through: *a nail pierced the tire of our car.* **3** force a way; force a way through or into: *the cold pierces to my bones, the wind pierces our shelter.* **4** sound sharply through, as a cry through the air. **5** make a way through with the eye or mind: *pierce a mystery.* [< OF *percier,* ult. < L *pertusus* pierced] —**pierc′er,** *n.* —**pierc′ing,** *adj.* —**pierc′ing·ly,** *adv.* —**pierc′ing·ness,** *n.*

Pierce (pirs), *n.* **Franklin,** 1804–69, the 14th president of the United States, 1853–57.

pier glass, tall mirror, esp. set between windows.

Pierre (pir), *n.* capital of South Dakota.

pi·e·tism (pī′ə tiz əm), *n.* **1** deep piety. **2** pretended piety. —**pi′e·tist,** *n.* —**pi′e·tis′tic, pi′e·tis′ti·cal,** *adj.*

pi·e·ty (pī′ə ti), *n., pl.* **-ties.** **1** a being pious; reverence for God; devotion to religion. **2** dutiful regard for one's parents or other elders. **3** a pious act, remark, belief, etc. [< OF < L *pietas* < *pius* pious. Doublet of PITY.]

pif·fle (pif′əl), *n. Informal.* silly talk; nonsense.

pig (pig), *n.* **1** a swine or hog, a domestic animal raised for its meat. **2** a young hog. **3** pork. **4** *Informal.* person who seems or acts like a pig. **5** an oblong mass of metal that has been run into a mold while hot. **6** *Informal.* greedy, slovenly, or unpleasant person.

pig out, *Informal.* **a** eat a great deal or too much. **b** *Fig.* overindulge. [OE *picg* (in *picg-bred* acorn, lit., pig-bread] —**pig′like′,** *adj.*

pi·geon (pij′ən), *n.* kind of bird with a plump body and short legs; dove. [< OF < VL < LL *pipio* squab]

pigeon English, =pidgin English.

pigeon hawk, a small hawk.

pi·geon·hole (pij′ən hōl′), *n., v.,* –**holed,** –**hol·ing.** —*n.* one of a set of boxlike compartments for holding papers and other articles in a desk, a cabinet, etc. —*v.* **1** put in a pigeonhole; put away. **2** classify and lay aside in memory where one can refer to it. **3** put aside with the idea of dismissing, forgetting, etc.

pi·geon-toed (pij′ən tōd′), *adj.* having the toes or feet turned inward.

pig·ger·y (pig′ər i), *n., pl.* –**ger·ies.** place where pigs are kept.

pig·gish (pig′ish), *adj.* like a pig; greedy; filthy. —**pig′gish·ly,** *adv.* —**pig′gish·ness,** *n.*

pig·gy (pig′i), *n., pl.* –**gies,** *adj.* —*n.* a little pig. —*adj.* greedy.

pig·gy·back (pig′i bak′), *adj.* designating the carrying of anything that usually moves alone by a larger vehicle, etc., as a trailer truck by a railroad flatcar. —*adv.* on the back or shoulders: *liked to ride piggyback.*

piggy bank, 1 a container shaped like a pig that has a slot to slip coins through. **b** any coin bank. **2** *Fig.* savings.

pig-head·ed (pig′hed′id), *adj.* stupidly obstinate or stubborn.

pig iron, crude iron as it first comes from the blast furnace or smelter, usually cast into oblong masses called pigs.

pig·let (pig′lit), *n.* small or baby pig.

pig·ment (pig′mənt), *n.* coloring matter. The color of a person's hair, skin, and eyes is due to pigment in the cells of the body. [< L *pigmentum,* ult. < *pingere* to paint. Doublet of PIMENTO.] —**pig′men·tar′y,** *adj.*

pig·men·ta·tion (pig′mən tā′shən), *n.* deposit of pigment in the tissue of a living animal or plant, causing coloration or discoloration.

pig·my (pig′mi), *n., pl.* –**mies,** *adj.* =pygmy.

pig·skin (pig′skin′), *n.* **1** skin of a pig. **2** leather made from it. **3** football.

pig·sty (pig′stī′), **pig·pen** (–pen′), *n., pl.* –**sties;** –**pens. 1** pen where pigs are kept. **2** *Fig.* a filthy place.

pig·tail (pig′tāl′), *n.* braid of hair hanging from the back of the head.

pike¹ (pīk), *n.* a long wooden shaft with a sharp-pointed metal head; spear. [OE *pīc* pick] —**pike′man,** *n.*

pike² (pīk), *n.* a large freshwater fish with a long, narrow, pointed head. [for *pike-fish.* See PICK².]

pike³ (pīk), *n.* =turnpike. [for *turn-pike*]

pik·er (pīk′ər), *n. Informal.* person who does things in a small or cheap way.

pike·staff (pīk′staf′; –stäf′), *n., pl.* –**staves** (–stāvz′). staff or shaft of a pike or spear.

pi·las·ter (pə las′tər), *n.* a rectangular pillar, esp. when it forms part of a wall from which it projects somewhat. [< F < Ital. *pilastro* < L *pila* pillar] —**pi·las′tered,** *adj.*

pi·laf or **pi·laff** (pi läf′), *n.* dish from the Middle East consisting of rice or cracked wheat boiled with mutton, fowl, or the like, and flavored with spices, raisins, etc. [< Pers. *pilāw*]

pile¹ (pīl), *n., v.,* **piled, pil·ing.** —*n.* **1** many things lying one upon another in a more or less orderly way: *pile of wood.* **2** mass like a hill or mound: *pile of dirt.* **3** a large structure or mass of buildings. **4** *Informal.* a large amount. —*v.* **1** make into a pile; heap evenly; heap up. **2** gather or rise in piles. **3** go in a confused, rushing crowd. [< OF < L *pila* pillar] —**piled,** *adj.*

pile² (pīl), *n.* a heavy beam driven into the earth, often under water, to help support a bridge, wharf, etc. [< L *pilum* javelin]

pile³ (pīl), *n.* **1** a soft, thick nap on velvet, plush, and many carpets. **2** a soft, fine hair or down; wool. [< L *pilus* hair] —**piled,** *adj.*

pile driver, machine that drives piles into the ground by hammering.

piles (pīlz), *n.pl.* swelling of blood vessels at the anus, often painful; hemorrhoids.

pile-up or **pile·up** (pīl′up′), *n.* **1** collision involving many vehicles. **2** accumulation.

pil·fer (pil′fər), *v.* steal in small quantities; steal. [< OF *pelfrer* rob. Cf. PELF.] —**pil′fer·er,** *n.*

pil·grim (pil′grəm), *n.* **1** person who goes on a journey to a sacred or holy place as an act of religious devotion. **2** traveler; wanderer. **3** Pilgrim, one of the Puritan settlers of Plymouth Colony in 1620. [< AF < Med.L *peregrinus* pilgrim < L, foreigner. Doublet of PEREGRINE.]

pil·grim·age (pil′grə mij), *n.* **1** a journey to some sacred or revered place. **2** *Fig.* life thought of as a journey.

pil·ing (pīl′ing), *n.* **1** piles or heavy beams driven into the ground, etc. **2** structure made of piles.

pill (pil), *n.* **1** medicine made up into a tiny ball to be swallowed whole. **2** a very small ball of anything. **3 the pill.** contraceptive in the form of a pill. **4** *Informal.* an unpleasant person. [< MDu. or MLG < L *pilula,* dim. of *pila* ball]

pil·lage (pil′ij), *v.,* –**laged,** –**lag·ing,** *n.* —*v.* rob with violence; plunder: *pirates pillaged the towns along the coast.* —*n.* plunder; robbery. [< OF < *piller* plunder < VL *piliare*] —**pil′lag·er,** *n.*

pil·lar (pil′ər), *n.* **1** a slender, upright structure; column. Pillars are usually made of stone, wood, or metal and used as supports or ornaments for a building. **2** anything slender and upright like a

pillar. **3** an important support, esp. a person of strong character.

from pillar to post, from one thing or place to another without any definite purpose. [< OF *piler,* ult. < L *pila* pile¹] —**pil′lared,** *adj.*

pill-box (pil′boks′), *n.* **1** box, usually shallow and often round, for holding pills. **2** a small, low fortress with very thick walls and roof, for firing weapons, esp. machine guns.

pil·lo·ry (pil′ə ri), *n., pl.* –**ries,** *v.,* –**ried,** –**ry·ing.** —*n.* frame of wood with holes through which a person's head and hands were put, formerly used as a punishment. —*v.* **1** put in the pillory. **2** expose to public ridicule, contempt, or abuse. [< OF *pellori* < Pr. *espilori*]

pil·low (pil′ō), *n.* **1** bag or case filled with feathers, down, or other soft material. **2** cushion; pad. —*v.* rest on a pillow. [ult. < L *pulvinus*] —**pil′low·like′,** *adj.* —**pil′low·y,** *adj.*

pil·low·case (pil′ō kās′), **pil·low·slip** (–slip′), *n.* a cotton or linen cover pulled over a pillow.

pi·lot (pī′lət), *n.* **1** person who steers a ship. **2** person whose business is steering ships in or out of a harbor or through dangerous waters. **3** person who controls an aircraft or spacecraft. **4** device that controls the action of one part of a machine, motor, etc. **5** =pilot light. —*v.* **1** act as the pilot of; steer. **2** guide; lead. [< F < Ital. *pilota*] —**pi′lot·less,** *adj.*

pi·lot·age (pī′lət ij), *n.* **1** piloting. **2** the fee paid for a pilot's service.

pilot biscuit or **bread,** large, flat cracker.

pilot fish, a small, bluish fish found in warm seas, often accompanying sharks.

pilot light, a small flame kept burning all the time and used to ignite a burner, as on a stove or hot water heater.

Pi·ma¹ (pē′ma), *n.,* or **Pima cotton, 1** cotton that is a cross of Egyptian and native cotton, originally raised in Arizona. **2** fine, smooth fabric made from this cotton. [< *Pima,* name of a county in Arizona]

Pi·ma² (pē′ma), or **Pi·man** (pē′mən), *n.* **1** member of a tribe of American Indians living in Arizona and Mexico. **2** their language. —**Pi′man,** *adj.*

pi·men·to (pi men′tō), *n., pl.* –**tos. 1** kind of sweet pepper, used as a vegetable, relish, and stuffing for green olives. **2** =allspice. **3** tree that allspice grows on. [< Sp. < Med.L *pigmentum* spice < LL, vegetable juice, < L, pigment. Doublet of PIGMENT.]

pi·mien·to (pi myen′tō), *n., pl.* –**tos.** a sweet pepper. [< Sp. See PIMENTO.]

pimp (pimp), *n., v.* =pander.

pim·per·nel (pim′pər nel), *n.* **1** a small, scarlet, purple, or white flower that closes in bad weather. **2** plant it grows on. [< OF *pimprenele,* ult. < VL *piperinus* of peppercorns < L *piper* PEPPER]

pim·ple (pim′pəl), *n.* a small, inflamed swelling of the skin. [cf. OE *piplian* grow pimply] **—pim′pled,** *adj.* **—pim′ply,** *adj.*

pin (pin), *n., v.,* **pinned, pin·ning. —n.** **1** a short, slender piece of wire with a point at one end and a head at the other, for fastening things together. **2** badge with a pin or clasp to fasten it to the clothing. **3** ornament that has a pin or clasp; brooch. **4** peg made of wood or metal, used to fasten things together, hold something, hang things, etc. **5** peg in a violin, etc., to which a string is fastened. **6** a bottle-shaped piece of wood used in the game of ninepins, tenpins, etc. **—v. 1** fasten with a pin or pins; put a pin through. **2** *Fig.* fasten or attach firmly to or on; *pin the blame on them, don't pin your hopes on them.* **3** hold fast in one position. **4** bind to an undertaking or pledge.
on pins and needles, very anxious or uneasy.
pin down, fix firmly; establish: *pin down the facts, need to pin down her opinion about this.*
pins, legs: *a toddler unsteady on his pins.* [OE *pinn* peg]

PIN (pin), personal identification number (used with bank cards, credit cards, etc.).

pin·a·fore (pin′ə fôr′; –fōr′), *n.* **1** a child's apron that covers most of the dress. **2** a light dress without sleeves. [< *pin,* v. + *afore*]

pi·ña·ta (pē nyä′tä), *n., pl.* **-tas.** Spanish papier-maché or clay container shaped like a person or animal that holds candy, trinkets, etc., and hung up at Christmas and for other festivities in Latin America, esp. in Mexico. Blindfolded children try to break it with a stick.

pin·ball (pin′bôl′), *n.* game in which a ball rolls down a board studded with pins or pegs into numbered compartments.

pin·cers (pin′sərz), *n.pl. or sing.* **1** tool for gripping and holding tight, made like scissors but with jaws instead of blades. **2** a large claw of crabs, lobsters, etc., which can be used to pinch or nip; pair of claws. [< OF < *pincier* to pinch]

pinch (pinch), *v.* **1** squeeze between two hard edges; squeeze with thumb and forefinger. **2** press so as to hurt; squeeze. **3** cause sharp discomfort or distress to. **4** cause to shrink or become thin: *a face pinched by hunger.* **5** limit closely; stint: *be pinched for space.* **6** be stingy. **7** *Informal.* arrest. **8** *Informal.* steal. **—n. 1** squeeze between two hard edges; squeeze with thumb and forefinger. **2** sharp pressure that hurts; squeeze. **3** as much as can be taken up with the tips of finger and thumb: *a pinch of salt.* **4** sharp discomfort or distress: *the pinch of hunger.* **5** time of special need; emergency. **6** *Informal.* arrest. **7** *Informal.* stealing. [< OF *pincier*] **—pinch·er,** *n.*

pinch·ers (pin′chərz), *n., pl. or sing.* =pincers.

pinch-hit (pinch′hit′), *v.,* **–hit, –hit·ting.** **1** bat for another baseball player when a hit is badly needed. **2** take another's place in an emergency. **—pinch hitter.**

pin·cush·ion (pin′kush′ən), *n.* a small cushion to stick pins in until needed.

pine[1] (pīn), *n.* **1** any of a group of evergreen trees that have cones, and clusters of needle-shaped leaves that grow out from temporary scalelike leaves. Pines are valuable for timber, turpentine, resin, tar, etc. **2** its wood. [< L *pinus*]

pine[2] (pīn), *v.,* **pined, pin·ing. 1** long eagerly; yearn. **2** waste away with pain, hunger, grief, or desire. [OE, < *pīn,* n., torture < L *poena* penalty < Gk. *poine*]

pin·e·al body or **gland** (pin′i əl), a small body in the brain of all vertebrates which secretes various hormones. [< F < L *pinea* pine cone < *pinus* pine]

pine·ap·ple (pīn′ap′əl), *n.* **1** a large, juicy fruit growing in hot climates, that looks somewhat like a large pine cone. **2** plant with slender, stiff leaves that it grows on.

pin·e·y (pīn′i), *adj.,* **pin·i·er, pin·i·est.** =piny.

pin·feath·er (pin′feth′ər), *n.* an undeveloped feather that looks like a small stub.

ping pong (ping′ pong′), *n.* game like tennis, played on a table with small wooden rackets and a light, hollow celluloid ball; table tennis. **—v.** *Fig.* to toss or bounce back and forth, as between doctors or one decision or another. [< *Ping Pong,* trademark]

pin·head (pin′hed′), *n.* **1** the head of a pin. **2** something very small or worthless. **3** *Informal. Fig.* a stupid person; nitwit; dummy. **—pin′head′ed,** *adj.*

pin·ion[1] (pin′yən), *n.* **1** the last joint of a bird's wing. **2** wing. **3** any one of the stiff flying feathers of the wing. **—v. 1** cut off or tie the pinions of (a bird) to prevent flying. **2** bind; bind the arms of; bind (to something). [< OF *pignon,* ult. < L *pinna* feather. Cf. PINION[2].] **—pin′ioned,** *adj.*

pin·ion[2] (pin′yən), *n.* a small gear with teeth that fit into those of a larger gear or rack. [< F *pignon* < OF, battlement, ult. < L *pinna* pinnacle]

pink[1] (pingk), *n.* **1** color obtained by mixing red with white; light or pale red. **2** the highest degree or condition: *in the pink of health.* **3** plant with spicy-smelling flowers of various colors, mostly white, pink, and red. A carnation is a variety of pink. **4** this plant's flower. **—adj.** pale-red. **—pink′ish,** *adj.* **—pink′ish·ness,** *n.*

pink[2] (pingk), *v.* **1** cut the edge of (cloth) in small scallops or notches. **2** ornament with small, round holes. [ME *pynke(n)* < OE *pynca* point] **—pinked,** *adj.* **—pink′er,** *n.*

pink·eye (pingk′ī′), *n.* a contagious disease, a form of conjunctivitis, characterized by inflammation and soreness of the membrane that lines the eyelids and covers the eyeball.

pink·ie (pingk′i), *n.* the smallest finger. Also, **pinky.**

pinking shears, scissors that pink fabric.

pink slip, notification to an employee of dismissal from a job.

pin money, a small amount of money used to buy extra things for one's own use.

pin·na (pin′ə), *n., pl.* **pin·nae** (pin′ē), **pin·nas. 1** feather, wing, or winglike part. **2** outer part of the ear. **3** primary division of a pinnate leaf; leaflet. [< L] **—pin′nal,** *adj.*

pin·nace (pin′is), *n.* **1** a ship's boat. **2** a very small schooner. [< F < Ital. *pinaccia* or Sp. *pinaza,* ult. < L *pinus* pine[1]]

pin·na·cle (pin′ə kəl), *n., v.,* **-cled, -cling. —n. 1** a high peak or point of rock. **2** the highest point. **3** a slender turret or spire. **—v. 1** put on a pinnacle. **2** furnish with pinnacles. [< OF < L *pinnaculum,* dim. of *pinna* wing, point] **—pin′na·cled,** *adj.*

pin·nate (pin′āt; -it), *adj.* **1** like a feather. **2** having leaflets on each side of a stalk. [< L, < *pinna* feather] **—pin′nate·ly,** *adv.*

pi·noch·le (pē′nuk′əl; -nok′-), *n.* game played with 48 cards, in which points are scored according to the value of certain combinations of cards.

pi·ñon (pin′yən; pen′yon), *n.* **1** pine, esp. of the Rocky Mountain region, producing large edible seeds. **2** its seed. [< Sp., < *piña* pine cone]

pin·point (pin′point′), *v.* aim at accurately; determine precisely: *pinpoint the cause of a problem.* **—n. 1** point of a pin. **2** something very small: *pinpoints of light.* **3** an exact location of something, as on a map. **—adj.** extremely accurate or precise: *pictures of pinpoint clarity.*

pin·prick (pin′prik′), *n.* **1** a little hole made by a sharp point. **2** *Fig.* a minor irritation.

pin·stripe (pin′strīp′), *n.* **1** a thin stripe. **2** fabric with thin stripes or a garment made from it. **—pin′striped,** *adj.*

pint (pīnt), *n.* **1** unit of measure equal to half a quart. **2** container holding a pint. [< F < MDu. *pinte* plug]

pin·tle (pin′təl), *n.* pin or bolt, esp. one upon which something turns, as in a hinge. [OE *pintel* penis]

pin·to (pin′tō), *adj., n., pl.* **-tos. —adj.** spotted in two colors; piebald. **—n. 1** a pinto horse. **2** Also, **pinto bean.** a mottled variety of kidney bean. [< Sp., painted]

pin-up (pin′up′), *n.* picture of a very attractive or famous person, pinned up on a wall, usually by admirers personally unacquainted. **—adj. 1** very attractive: *a pin-up girl.* **2** made to hang on a wall: *a pin-up lamp.*

pin·wheel (pin′hwēl′), *n.* **1** kind of firework that revolves when lighted. **2** toy made of a paper wheel fastened to a stick by a pin so that it revolves in the wind.

pin·worm (pin′wèrm′), *n.* a small, threadlike worm infesting the rectum, esp. of children.

pin·y (pīn′ī), *adj.,* **pin·i·er, pin·i·est. 1** abounding with or covered with pine trees: *piny mountains.* **2** pertaining to or suggesting pine trees: *a piny odor.*

pi·o·neer (pī′ə nir′), *n.* **1** person who settles in a part of the country that has not been occupied before except by primitive tribes. **2** person who goes first, or does something first, and so prepares a way for others. —*v.* prepare or open up for others; take the lead in doing. [< F *pionnier* < OF *peon* foot soldier. See PEON.]

pi·ous (pī′əs), *adj.* **1** having or showing reverence for God; religious. **2** done or used from real or pretended religious motives. [< L *pius*] —**pi′ous·ly,** *adv.* —**pi′ous·ness,** *n.*

pip[1] (pip), *n.* seed of an apple, orange, etc. [short for *pippin*]

pip[2] (pip), *n.* a contagious disease of birds, characterized by the secretion of thick mucus in the mouth and throat. [< MDu. < VL *pippita* < L *pituita* phlegm]

pip[3] (pip), *n.* one of the spots on playing cards, dominoes, or dice. [earlier *peep;* orig. uncert.]

pip[4] (pip), *v.,* **pipped, pip·ping.** break through (the shell) to hatch. [? var. of *peep*]

pipe (pīp), *n., v.,* **piped, pip·ing.** —*n.* **1** tube through which a liquid or gas flows. **2** any tubelike thing or part, esp. a tube with a bowl of clay, wood, etc., at one end, for smoking. **3** a musical instrument with a single tube into which the player blows. **4** any one of the tubes in an organ. **5** a shrill sound, voice, or song. **6** a boatswain's whistle. [< VL *pipa* < L *pipare* chirp; (def. 10) < OF] —*v.* **1** carry by means of a pipe or pipes. **2** supply with pipes. **3** play on a pipe. **4** make a shrill noise; sing in a shrill voice. **5** give orders, signals, etc., with a boatswain's whistle. **6** summon by a pipe.

pipe down, be quiet; shut up.

pipes, a set of musical tubes: *the pipes of Pan.* **b** bagpipe.

pipe up, a begin to play (music). **b** *Informal.* speak. [< L *pipare* chirp] —**pip′er,** *n.*

pipe dream, an impractical idea.

pipe·line (pīp′līn′), *n.* **1** line of pipes for carrying oil or natural gas. **2** *Fig.* source of information, usually secret. **3** *Fig.* stages in the development of a new product, design, etc.: *new drugs in the pipeline.*

pipe·line (pīp′līn′), *v.,* **-lined, -lin·ing. 1** carry by a pipeline. **2** provide with a pipeline.

pipe organ, organ (def. 4).

pi·pette, pi·pet (pī pet′; pi–), *n.* a slender pipe or tube for transferring or measuring liquids. [< F, dim. of *pipe* pipe]

pip·ing (pīp′ing), *n.* **1** pipes. **2** material for pipes. **3** a shrill sound. **4** music of pipes. **5** a narrow band of material, sometimes containing a cord, used for trimming along edges and seams. —*adj.* shrill.

piping hot, very hot.

pip·it (pip′it), *n.* a small bird somewhat like a lark, that sings while flying. [imit.]

pip·pin (pip′ən), *n.* any of several kinds of apple. [< OF *pepin*]

pi·quant (pē′kənt), *adj.* **1** stimulating to the mind, interest, etc.: *a piquant bit of news.* **2** pleasantly sharp; stimulating to the taste: *a piquant sauce.* **3** fresh; dashing. [< F, pricking, stinging] —**pi′quan·cy, pi′quant·ness,** *n.* —**pi′quant·ly,** *adv.*

pique (pēk), *n., v.,* **piqued, pi·quing.** —*n.* a feeling of anger at being slighted; wounded pride. —*v.* **1** cause such a feeling in; wound the pride of. **2** arouse; stir up: *the curiosity of the boys was piqued by the locked trunk.* [< F *piquer* prick, sting]

pi·qué (pi kā′), *n.* a cotton fabric with narrow ribs or raised stripes. [< F, quilted, pp. of *piquer* stitch, prick]

pi·ra·cy (pī′rə si), *n., pl.* **-cies. 1** robbery on the sea. **2** act of publishing or using a book, play, piece of music, etc., without permission. **3** taking or using without permission anything assigned by license or contract to another, as a video, recording, drug, etc. [< Med.L < Gk *peirateia*]

pi·rate (pī′rit), *n., v.,* **-rat·ed, -rat·ing.** —*n.* **1** one who attacks and robs ships unlawfully; robber on the sea. **2** ship used by pirates. **3** any pillager. **4** user of another's creation, esp. writing, without permission and for his own gain. —*v.* **1** be a pirate; plunder; rob. **2** publish or use without the author's permission. **3** use illegally. [< L < Gk., < *peiraein* to attack] —**pi·rat′i·cal** (pī rat′ə kəl), *adj.* —**pi·rat′i·cal·ly,** *adv.*

pir·ou·ette (pir′ü et′), *n., v.,* **-et·ted, -et·ting.** —*n.* a turning or whirling about on one foot or on the toes, as in dancing. —*v.* turn or whirl in this way. [< F, spinning top] —**pir′ou·et′ter, pir′ou·et′tist,** *n.*

Pis·ces (pis′ēz), *n. pl., gen.* **Pis·ci·um** (pish′i əm). **1** the Fishes, a northern constellation that was considered to have the shape of fishes. **2** the 12th sign of the zodiac.

pis·mire (pis′mīr′), *n.* ant. [cf. Norw. *myre*]

pis·ta·chi·o (pis tä′shi ō; –tash′i ō), *n., pl.* **-chi·os. 1** a greenish nut having a flavor that suggests almond. **2** a small tree that it grows on. **3** its flavor. **4** a light green. [< Ital. < L < Gk. *pistakion* < *pistake* the tree < OPers.]

pis·til (pis′təl), *n.* part of a flower that produces seeds, consisting, when complete, of an ovary, a style, and a stigma. [< NL *pistillum* < L, PESTLE. Doublet of PESTLE.] —**pis′til·late,** *adj.*

pis·tol (pis′təl), *n.* a small, short gun held and fired with one hand. [< F < G < Czech *pišťal*]

pis·tole (pis tōl′), *n.* a former gold coin of Spain. [< F, coin, PISTOL]

pis·ton (pis′tən), *n.* a short cylinder, or a flat round piece of metal, fitting closely inside a hollow cylinder in which it is moved back and forth by some force, as the pressure of steam. A piston transmits motion by means of a rod (**piston rod**) attached to it. [< F < Ital. *pistone* < *pistare* pound, ult. < L *pistus,* pp. of *pinsere* pound]

pit[1] (pit), *n., v.,* **pit·ted, pit·ting.** —*n.* **1** a hole in the ground. **2** a little hole or scar, such as is left by smallpox. **3** a covered hole used as a trap for wild animals. **4** place where dogs or cocks are made to fight. **5** place where the orchestra sits in a theater, in front of and below the stage. **6** place in a garage or alongside a racetrack for working on cars. —*v.* **1** mark with small pits or scars. **2** set to fight or compete; match: *the little man pitted his brains against the big man's strength.* [ult. < L *puteus* well] —**pit′ted,** *adj.*

pit[2] (pit), *n., v.,* **pit·ted, pit·ting.** —*n.* the hard seed of a cherry, peach, plum, date, etc.; stone. —*v.* remove pits from (fruit). [< Du., kernel]

pitch[1] (pich), *v.* **1** throw; fling; hurl; toss. **2** throw (a baseball, etc.) for the batter to hit. **3** fix firmly in the ground; set up: *pitch a tent.* **4** take up a position; settle. **5** fall or plunge forward. **6** plunge with the bow rising and then falling: *the ship pitched about in the storm.* **7** set at a certain point, degree, or level. **8** determine the key of (a tune, etc.). **9** *Informal.* try to sell; propose: *pitch an idea.* —*n.* **1** throw; fling; hurl; toss. **2** point; position; degree. **3** degree of highness or lowness of a sound. **4** height. **5** act or manner of pitching. **6** that which is pitched. **7** amount of slope.

pitch in, work vigorously. pitch into, attack. [ME *picche(n)*] —**pitch′ing,** *adj., n.*

pitch[2] (pich), *n.* **1** a black, sticky substance made from tar or turpentine, used to seal roofs, to make pavements, etc. **2** resin from certain evergreen trees. —*v.* cover with pitch. [< L *pix*]

pitch-black (pich′blak′), *adj.* very dark.

pitch·blende (pich′blend′), *n.* mineral consisting largely of uranium oxide, occurring in black, pitchlike masses. Pitchblende is a source of radium, uranium, and actinium.

pitch-dark (pich′därk′), *adj.* =pitch-black.

pitched battle, battle with troops properly arranged.

pitch·er[1] (pich′ər), *n.* container for holding and pouring liquids, with a lip on one side and a handle on the other. [< OF *pichier*]

pitch·er[2] (pich′ər), *n.* **1** person who pitches. **2** player on a baseball team who throws the ball for the batter to hit.

pitch·er·ful (pich′ər fúl), *n., pl.* **-fuls.** quantity sufficient to fill a pitcher.

pitcher plant, plant with leaves shaped somewhat like a pitcher.

pitch·fork (pich′fôrk′), *n.* a large fork with a long handle, for lifting and throwing hay, etc. —*v.* lift and throw with a pitchfork.

pitch pine, a pine tree from which pitch or turpentine is obtained.

pitch pipe, small musical whistle used to give a tone for singing or tuning an instrument.

pitch·y (pich′i), *adj.,* **pitch·i·er, pitch·i·est. 1** full of pitch. **2** like pitch; sticky. **3** black. —**pitch′i·ness,** *n.*

pit·e·ous (pit′i əs), *adj.* to be pitied; moving the heart; deserving pity. —**pit′e·ous·ly,** *adv.* —**pit′e·ous·ness,** *n.*

pit·fall (pit′fôl′), *n.* **1** a hidden pit to catch animals in. **2** any trap or hidden danger.

pith (pith), *n.* **1** the central, spongy tissue of plant stems. **2** a similar soft tissue: *pith of an orange.* **3** an important or essential part: *pith of a speech.* **4** strength; energy. [OE *pitha*]

Pith·e·can·thro·pus (pith′ə kan thrō′pəs; –kan′thrə pəs), *n., pl.* **–pi** (–pī). an extinct ape man, whose existence is assumed from remains found in Java, 1891–92. [< NL, < Gk. *pithekos* ape + *anthropos* man]

pith·y (pith′i), *adj.,* **pith·i·er, pith·i·est. 1** full of substance, meaning, force, or vigor: *pithy phrases.* **2** of or like pith. **3** having much pith: *a pithy orange.* —**pith′i·ly,** *adv.* —**pith′i·ness,** *n.*

pit·i·a·ble (pit′i ə bəl), *adj.* **1** to be pitied; moving the heart; deserving pity. **2** deserving contempt; mean; to be scorned. —**pit′i·a·ble·ness,** *n.* —**pit′i·a·bly,** *adv.*

pit·i·ful (pit′i fəl), *adj.* **1** to be pitied; moving the heart; deserving pity. **2** feeling pity; feeling sorrow for the trouble of others. **3** deserving contempt; mean; to be scorned. —**pit′i·ful·ly,** *adv.* —**pit′i·ful·ness,** *n.*

pit·i·less (pit′i lis), *adj.* without pity or mercy. —**pit′i·less·ly,** *adv.* —**pit′i·less·ness,** *n.*

pit stop 1 a pulling off the track while in an auto race to refuel, get a tire replaced, etc. **2 a** a pulling off the highway to get food, fuel, etc., while on a long trip. **b** place to make such a stop.

pit·tance (pit′əns), *n.* **1** a small allowance of money. **2** a small amount or share. [< OF *pitance,* ult. < L *pietas* PIETY]

pi·tu·i·tar·y (pi tü′ə ter′i; –tū′–), *n.* the pituitary gland. [< L, < *pituita* phlegm]

pituitary gland or **body,** a small, oval endocrine gland situated beneath the brain, that secretes hormones that promote growth, stimulate other glands, etc.

pit·y (pit′i), *n., pl.* **pit·ies,** *v.,* **pit·ied, pit·y·ing.** —*n.* **1** sympathy; sorrow for another's suffering or distress; feeling for the sorrows of others. **2** cause for pity or regret; thing to be sorry for. —*v.* feel pity for.

have or **take pity on,** show pity for. [< OF < L *pietas.* Doublet of PIETY.] —**pit′i·er,** *n.* —**pit′y·ing·ly,** *adv.*

piv·ot (piv′ət), *n.* **1** shaft, pin, or point on which something turns. **2** that on which something turns, hinges, or depends; central point. —*v.* **1** mount on, attach by, or provide with a pivot. **2** turn on a pivot. [< F] —**piv′ot·al,** *adj.*

pix (piks), *n.pl. Informal.* pictures.

pix·el (pik′səl), *n.* one of the tiny dots or elements of an image on a computer or television screen. [< *pix* + *el*ement]

pix·y, pix·ie (pik′si), *n., pl.* **pix·ies.** fairy or elf.

piz·za (pēt′sə), *n.* a large, flat pie of bread dough covered with cheese, tomato sauce, spices, etc., and baked. [< Ital.]

pi·zazz (pə zaz′), *n.* exciting or flashy showiness; liveliness; jazziness.

piz·zi·ca·to (pit′sə kä′tō), *adj., n., pl.* **–ti** (–tē). *Music.* —*adj.* played by plucking the strings with the finger instead of using the bow, as on a violin. —*n.* a note or passage so played. [< Ital., picked]

pjs or **p.j.'s.** (pē′jāz′), *n. pl. Informal.* pajamas.

pk., *pl.* **pks. 1** park. **2** peak. **3** peck.

pkg., *pl.* **pkgs.** package.

pl., 1 place. **2** plural.

pla·ca·ble (plā′kə bəl; plak′ə–), *adj.* forgiving; easily quieted; mild. —**pla′ca·bil′i·ty, pla′ca·ble·ness,** *n.* —**pla′ca·bly,** *adv.*

plac·ard (*n.* plak′ärd; *v.* plə kärd′, plak′ärd), *n.* notice to be posted in a public place; poster. —*v.* put placards on or in. [< F, < *plaque* plaque]

pla·cate (plā′kāt; plak′āt), *v.,* **–cat·ed, –cat·ing.** soothe or satisfy the anger of; make peaceful: *placate a person one has offended.* [< L *placatus*] —**pla′cat·er,** *n.* —**pla·ca′tion,** *n.* —**pla′ca·tive, pla′ca·to′ry,** *adj.*

place (plās), *n., v.,* **placed, plac·ing.** —*n.* **1** part of space occupied by a person or thing, as in a town, village, building, office, house, or dwelling. **2** part or spot in something: *the dentist filled the decayed place in the tooth.* **3** position: *books in place on shelves, save a place for me on the bus, it is not my place to find fault.* **4** position at the finish of a race. —*v.* **1** put (in a spot, position, condition, or relation): *place an order, place sentries.* **2** be at the finish of a race: *place last.*

go places, *Informal.* advance rapidly in a career, profession, etc.

in place, in the right position or condition.

in place of, instead of.

out of place, a not in the proper or usual place. **b** inappropriate or ill-timed.

take place, happen; occur. [< L < Gk. *plateia* (*hodos*) broad way < *platys* broad. Doublet of PLAZA and PIAZZA.] —**plac′er,** *n.*

pla·ce·bo (plə sē′bō), *n., pl.* **–bos** or **–boes.** medication or treatment given to

a patient that has no active ingredients, esp. as part of a trial of a new drug.

place kick, kick given a football after it has been put on the ground. —**place′-kick′,** *v.*

place mat, mat of fabric, straw, etc., set on a table with a napkin, glass, and silverware where a person will sit for a meal.

place·ment (plās′mənt), *n.* **1** a placing or being placed; location; arrangement. **2** the finding of work or a job for a person.

pla·cen·ta (plə sen′tə), *n., pl.* **–tae** (–tē), **–tas.** organ by which the fetus is attached to the wall of the womb and nourished. [< NL < L, flat cake, < Gk. *plakounta,* accus., < *plax* flat surface] —**pla·cen′tal,** *adj.*

plac·er (plas′ər), *n.* place where gold or other minerals can be washed out of loose sand or gravel. [< Am.Sp., sandbank; akin to PLAZA]

plac·id (plas′id), *adj.* calm; peaceful; quiet: *a placid lake.* [< L, < *placere* please] —**pla·cid′i·ty, plac′id·ness,** *n.* —**plac′id·ly,** *adv.*

plack·et (plak′it), *n.* an opening or slit at the top of a skirt to make it easy to put on.

pla·gia·rism (plā′jə riz əm), *n.* **1** act of plagiarizing. **2** idea, expression, plot, etc., taken from another and used as one's own. [< L *plagiarius* kidnaper] —**pla′gia·rist,** *n.* —**pla′gia·ris′tic,** *adj.* —**pla′gia·ris′ti·cal·ly,** *adv.*

pla·gia·rize (plā′jə rīz), *v.,* **–rized, –riz·ing.** take and use as one's own (the thoughts, writings, inventions, etc., of another), esp. to take and use (a passage, plot, etc., from the work of another writer). —**pla′gia·riz′er,** *n.*

plague (plāg), *n., v.,* **plagued, pla·guing.** *n.* **1** a disease that spreads rapidly and often causes death. The plague is common in Asia and has several times swept through Europe. **2** thing or person that torments, offends, or is disagreeable. —*v.* **1** cause to suffer from a plague. **2** annoy; bother. [< L *plaga* blow, pestilence < dial. Gk. *plaga* blow] —**pla′guer,** *n.*

plaice (plās), *n., pl.* **plaice** or (*occasionally*) **plaic·es.** a kind of flatfish. [< OF < LL *platessa* flatfish < Gk. *platys* flat]

plaid (plad), *n.* **1** any cloth with a pattern of checks or crisscross stripes. **2** a pattern of this kind. **3** a long piece of woolen cloth, usually having a pattern of checks or stripes in many colors, worn about the shoulders by the Scottish Highlanders. —*adj.* having a pattern of checks or crisscross stripes: *a plaid dress.* [< Scotch Gaelic *plaide*] —**plaid′ed,** *adj.*

plain (plān), *adj.* **1** easy to understand; easily seen or heard; clear. **2** without ornament, decoration, figured pattern, or varied color. **3** not rich or highly seasoned. **4** common; ordinary in manner: *a plain man of the people.* **5** not pretty: *a plain girl.* **6** frank; honest; sincere. **7** flat;

level; smooth. —*adv.* in a plain manner; clearly. —*n.* a flat stretch of land.

plains, prairies. [< OF < L *planus* flat. Doublet of PIANO², PLAN.] —**plain′ish,** *adj.* —**plain′ly,** *adv.* —**plain′ness,** *n.*

plain-clothes man (plān′klōz′; –klōthz′), detective wearing ordinary clothes when on duty.

Plains Indian, a member of any of the North American Indian tribes who lived on the Great Plains and followed the buffalo.

plains·man (plānz′mən), *n., pl.* -**men.** man who lives on the plains.

plain song, vocal music used in the Christian church from the earliest times. Plain song is sung in unison. It is rhythmical, although the beats are not regular.

plain-spo·ken (plān′spō′kən), *adj.* plain or frank in speech.

plaint (plānt), *n.* **1** complaint. **2** *Archaic.* lament.

plain·tiff (plān′tif), *n.* person who begins a lawsuit. [< OF *plaintif* complaining. See PLAINTIVE.]

plain·tive (plān′tiv), *adj.* mournful; sad. [< OF, ult. < L *planctus* complaint] —**plain′tive·ly,** *adv.* —**plain′tive·ness,** *n.*

plait (plāt, plat *for 1*; plāt, plēt *for 2*), *n., v.* **1** braid. **2** pleat. [< OF *pleit,* ult. < L *plicare* to fold] —**plait′ed,** *adj.* —**plait′ing,** **plait′work′,** *n.*

plan (plan), *n., v.,* **planned, plan·ning.** —*n.* **1** way of making or doing something that has been worked out beforehand; scheme of arrangement. **2** a drawing or diagram to show how a garden, a floor of a house, a park, etc., is arranged. **3** a definite intention or undertaking. —*v.* **1** think out beforehand how something is to be made or done; design, scheme, or devise; make plans. **2** make a drawing or diagram of. [< F, lit., a plane, < L *planus;* with ref. to a sketch on a flat surface. Doublet of PLAIN, PIANO².] —**plan′less,** *adj.* —**planned,** *adj.* —**plan′ner,** *n.*

plane¹ (plān), *n., adj., v.,* **planed, plan·ing.** —*n.* **1** any flat or level surface. **2** level; grade: *try to keep your work on a high plane.* **3** =airplane. **4** surface such that if any two points on it are joined by a straight line, the line will be contained wholly in the surface. —*adj.* **1** flat; level. **2** contained in a flat or level surface: *a plane figure, plane geometry.* —*v.* rise slightly out of the water while moving. [< L *planum* level place]

plane² (plān), *n., v.,* **planed, plan·ing.** —*n.* **1** a carpenter's tool with a blade for smoothing or removing wood. **2** machine for smoothing or removing metal. —*v.* **1** smooth with a plane. **2** remove with a plane. [< F, ult. < LL *plana*]

plan·er (plān′ər), *n.* machine for planing wood or for finishing flat surfaces on metal.

plan·et (plan′it), *n.* one of the celestial bodies (except comets and meteors) that move around the sun. Mercury, Venus,

the earth, Mars, Jupiter, Saturn, Uranus, Neptune, and Pluto are planets. [< LL < Gk. *planetes* < *planaesthai* wander]

plan·e·tar·i·um (plan′ə tãr′i əm), *n., pl.* -**i·a** (-i ə). **1** apparatus that shows the movements of the sun, moon, planets, and stars by projecting lights on the inside of a dome. **2** room or building with such an apparatus.

plan·e·tar·y (plan′ə ter′i), *adj.* **1** of a planet; having to do with planets. **2** moving in an orbit.

plan·et·oid (plan′ə toid), *n.* small planet; asteroid. [< *planet* + -*oid*]

plane tree or **plane,** *n.* a tall spreading tree with broad leaves and bare patches on the trunk. The American plane tree is also called the buttonwood or sycamore. [< F < L < Gk. *platanos* < *platys* broad]

plank (plangk), *n.* **1** a long, flat piece of sawed timber thicker than a board. **2** article or feature of the platform of a political party, etc. —*v.* cover or furnish with planks.

walk the plank, a walk off a plank extending from a ship's side over the water. Pirates used to make their prisoners do this. **b** *Fig.* do or experience something unpleasant. [< OF < L *planca*] —**plank′er,** *n.* —**plank′ing,** *n.*

plant (plant; plänt), *n.* **1** a living thing that is not an animal, esp. a living thing that has leaves and roots. Trees, shrubs, herbs, fungi, algae, etc., are plants: *a tomato plant.* **2** the buildings, equipment, etc., for any purpose: *a manufacturing plant.* **3** *Informal.* scheme to trap, trick, mislead, or deceive. —*v.* **1** put or set in the ground to grow. **2** furnish; stock; put seed in: *plant a garden.* **3** set firmly; put; place. **4** establish or set up (a colony, city, etc.). **5** implant (principles, doctrines, etc.). [< L *planta* sprout] —**plant′ing,** *n.*

plan·tain¹ (plan′tən), *n.* **1** kind of large banana. **2** plant that it grows on. [< Sp. *plátano*]

plan·tain² (plan′tan), *n.* a common weed with large, spreading leaves close to the ground and long, slender spikes carrying flowers and seeds. [< OF < L *plantago*]

plan·tar (plan′tər), *adj.* of or having to do with the sole of the foot. [< L *plantāris* < *planta* sole of the foot]

plan·ta·tion (plan tā′shən), *n.* **1** a large farm or estate on which cotton, tobacco, sugar, etc., are grown. The work on a plantation is done by laborers who live there. **2** a large group of trees or other plants that have been planted. **3** colony. [< L *plantatio* a planting. See PLANT.]

plant·er (plan′tər; plän′-), *n.* **1** person who owns or runs a plantation. **2** machine for planting. **3** person who plants.

plan·ti·grade (plan′tə grād), *adj.* walking on the whole sole of the foot. —*n.* a plantigrade animal, as the bear. [< L *planta* sole + *gradi* to walk]

plant louse, =aphid.

plaque (plak), *n.* **1** an ornamental tablet of metal, porcelain, etc. **2** a platelike ornament or badge. **3** film that forms on the teeth, caused by food and bacteria. **4** deposit on the wall of an artery, the result of excess cholesterol in the blood. [< F < Du. *plak* flat board]

plas·ma (plaz′mə), *n.* **1** the liquid part of blood or lymph, as distinguished from the corpuscles. **2** protoplasm. [< LL < Gk., something formed or molded, < *plassein* to mold] —**plas′mic,** *adj.*

plasma cell, cell that produces antibodies.

plas·mid (plaz′mid), *n.* genetic element that replicates independently of the chromosomes, used esp. in DNA research. Also, **plasma gene.** [< *cyto-plasm* + -*id*]

plas·ter (plas′tər; pläs′-), *n.* **1** a soft mixture of lime, sand, and water that hardens in drying. **2** =plaster of Paris. —*v.* **1** cover with plaster. **2** spread with anything thickly. **3** make smooth and flat. **4** apply a plaster to. **5** apply like a plaster. [< Med.L *plastrum* < L *emplastrum* <Gk., < *en-* on + *plassein* to mold] —**plas′ter·er,** *n.* —**plas′ter·ing,** *n.* —**plas′ter·y,** *adj.*

plas·ter·board (plas′tər bôrd′; –bōrd; pläs′-), *n.* large sheets of wallboard made of a layer of plaster pressed between layers of paper.

plaster of Paris, a mixture of powdered gypsum (a white material) and water, which hardens quickly, used for making molds, cheap statuary, etc.

plas·tic (plas′tik), *n.* **1** any of various substances that harden and retain their shape after being molded or shaped when softened by heat, pressure, etc. Glass, acrylic, vulcanite, and nylon are plastics. **2** *Informal.* =credit card. —*adj.* **1** made of plastic: *plastic toys, plastic bottles.* **2** molding or giving shape to material. **3** concerned with molding or modeling. Sculpture is a plastic art. **4** easily molded or shaped. Clay, wax, and plaster are plastic substances. **5** easily influenced; impressionable. [< L < Gk. *plastikos,* ult. < *plassein* to form, shape] —**plas′ti·cal·ly,** *adv.* —**plas·tic′i·ty,** *n.*

plastic surgery, surgery that restores, remedies, or improves the outer appearance of the body. Also, **cosmetic surgery.** —**plastic surgeon.**

plate (plāt), *n., v.,* **plat·ed, plat·ing.** —*n.* **1** dish, usually round, that is almost flat. **2** contents of such a dish: *a plate of cookies.* **3** something having a similar shape: *pass a collection plate in church.* **4** dishes and utensils covered with silver or gold. **5** a thin, flat sheet or piece of metal. **6** a platelike part, organ, or structure. Some reptiles and fishes have a covering of horny or bony plates. **7** something printed from a piece of metal. **8** home base in baseball. **9** piece of firm material with false teeth set into it. **10** one of the massive, constantly moving pieces of the earth's crust. —*v.* cover with a thin layer of silver, gold, or other metal. [< OF, ult. < VL *plattus* flat < Gk. *platys*] —**plate′like′**, *adj.* —**plat′er**, *n.*

pla·teau (pla tō′), *n., pl.* **–teaus, –teaux** (–tōz′). **1** plain in the mountains or at a height above the sea; large, high plain. **2** *Fig.* period with little apparent movement forward, as in learning something or resolving a problem. [< F < OF *platel*, dim. of *plat* flat]

plate·ful (plāt′fůl), *n., pl.* **–fuls.** as much as a plate will hold.

plate glass, thick and very clear glass used for large windows, doors, mirrors, etc.

plate·let (plāt′lit), *n.* sticky, irregularly-shaped cell fragment that is a component of blood and involved in clotting.

plate tectonics, geological science that deals with the movements of the plates of the earth's crust and their connection to geological events, such as earthquakes and the formation of mountains.

plat·form (plat′fôrm), *n.* **1** a raised level surface. There usually is a platform beside the track at a railroad station. A hall usually has a platform for speakers. **2** in a railroad car, the separate floor space at the end. **3** plan of action or statement of principles of a political party. [< F *plateforme* flat form] —**plat′formed,** *adj.*

plat·ing (plāt′ing), *n.* a thin layer of silver, gold, or other metal.

plat·i·num (plat′ə nəm), *n.* **1** a heavy precious metal, Pt, that looks like silver and does not tarnish or melt easily. It is a chemical element. **2** shade of gray suggestive of platinum. [< NL, ult. < Sp. *plata* silver]

plat·i·tude (plat′ə tüd; –tūd), *n.* **1** a dull or commonplace remark, esp. one given out solemnly as if it were fresh and important. **2** flatness; triteness; dullness. [< F, < *plat* flat] —**plat′i·tu′di·nous,** *adj.*

Pla·ton·ic (plə ton′ik), *adj.* **1** of or pertaining to Plato or his philosophy. **2** Also, **platonic.** friendly but not lover-like. **3** idealistic; not practical. —**Pla·ton′i·cal·ly, pla·ton′i·cal·ly,** *adv.*

Pla·to·nism (plā′tə niz əm), *n.* philosophy or doctrines of Plato or his followers. —**Pla′to·nist,** *n.* —**Pla′to·nis′tic,** *adj.*

pla·toon (plə tün′), *n.* **1** group of soldiers acting as a unit. A platoon is smaller than a company. **2** a small group. [< F *peloton* group, little ball, dim. of *pelote* ball. See PELLET.]

plat·ter (plat′ər), *n.* a large, shallow dish for holding or serving food, esp. meat and fish. [< AF *plater* < OF *plat* PLATE]

plat·y·pus (plat′ə pəs), *n., pl.* **–pus·es, –pi** (–pī). –duckbill. [< NL < Gk., < *platys* flat + *pous* foot]

plau·dit (plô′dit), *n.* Usually, **plaudits.** round of applause; enthusiastic expression of approval or praise. [alter. of L *plaudite* applaud!]

plau·si·ble (plô′zə bəl), *adj.* **1** appearing true, reasonable, or fair. **2** apparently worthy of confidence but often not really so: *a plausible liar.* [< L *plausibilis* deserving applause, pleasing < *plaudere* applaud] —**plau′si·bil′i·ty, plau′si·ble·ness,** *n.* —**plau′si·bly,** *adv.*

play (plā), *n.* **1** fun; sport; recreation. **2** a turn, move, or act in a game. **3** act of carrying on a game. **4** a story written for or presented as a dramatic performance; drama. **5** action: *foul play.* **6** light, quick movement or change: *the play of sunlight on leaves.* **7** freedom for action, movement, etc.: *give imagination full play.* **8** operation; working: *easy play in the mechanism.* —*v.* **1** have fun; take part in a game. **2** do; perform: *he played a mean trick.* **3** take part in (a game): *play tag.* **4** act the part of (a character in a play, etc.); act (a drama). **5** act in a specified way: *play sick.* **6** produce (music) on an instrument; perform on (a musical instrument). **7** move (on, over, along): *play a hose on a burning building.* **8** put into action in a game: *play your ten of hearts.* **9** act carelessly; do foolish things: *don't play with matches.* **10** gamble; bet.

bring or **call into play,** begin to use; make active: *years of experience were brought into play.*

in play, a acting; operating: *special forces are now in play.* **b** as a joke.

play back, replay something recorded.

play into the hands of, act so as to give the advantage to.

play on or **upon,** take advantage of; make use of.

play up, exaggerate the importance of.

play up to, try to get the favor of; flatter. [OE *plegan* to exercise] —**play′a·ble,** *adj.*

play·bill (plā′bil′), *n.* program of a play.

play·boy (plā′boi′), *n.* man, usually wealthy, whose chief interest is in having a good time.

play·er (plā′ər), *n.* **1** person who plays. **2** actor in a theater. **3** musician. **4** thing or device that plays.

play·ful (plā′fəl), *adj.* **1** full of fun; fond of playing. **2** joking; not serious. —**play′ful·ly,** *adv.* —**play′ful·ness,** *n.*

play·ground (plā′ground′), *n.* place for outdoor play.

play·house (plā′hous′), *n.* **1** a small house for a child to play in. **2** a toy house for a child; doll house. **3** theater.

playing card, card used in playing games like bridge and poker; one of a set of 52 cards including 4 suits (spades, hearts, diamonds, and clubs) of 13 cards each.

playing field, 1 open area or field where games are played. **2** *Fig.* any area or sphere of competition.

level the playing field, eliminate any advantage one group or individual might have over another.

play·mate (plā′māt′), *n.* one who plays with another.

play-off (plā′ôf′; –of′), *n.* an extra game or round played to settle a tie.

play on words, =pun

play·thing (plā′thing′), *n.* thing to play with; toy.

play·time (plā′tīm′), *n.* time for playing.

play·wright (plā′rīt′), *n.* writer of plays; dramatist.

pla·za (plä′zə; plaz′ə), *n.* a public square in a city or town. [< Sp. < L < Gk. *plateia* broad way. Doublet of PLACE and PIAZZA.]

plea (plē), *n.* **1** request; appeal: *a plea for pity.* **2** excuse; defense: *the man's plea was that he did not see the signal.* **3** answer made by a defendant to a charge against him or her in a law court. [< OF < L *placitum* (that) which pleases]

plead (plēd), *v.,* **plead·ed** or **plead** (pled), **plead·ing. 1** offer reasons for or against; argue as an excuse: *the woman who stole pleaded poverty.* **2** ask earnestly; make an earnest appeal. **3** speak for or against in a law court: *he had a good lawyer to plead his case.* **4** answer to a charge in a law court: *the prisoner pleaded guilty.* [< OF < VL *placitare,* ult. < L *placere* please] —**plead′er,** *n.* —**plead′ing,** *adj.* —**plead′ing·ly,** *adv.*

pleas·ant (plez′ənt), *adj.* **1** pleasing; agreeable; giving pleasure. **2** easy to get along with; friendly. **3** fair; not stormy. [< OF *plaisant,* ppr. of *plaisir* please < L *placere*] —**pleas′ant·ly,** *adv.* —**pleas′ant·ness,** *n.*

pleas·ant·ry (plez′ənt ri), *n., pl.* **–ries. 1** a good-natured joke; witty remark. **2** joking.

please (plēz), *v.,* **pleased, pleas·ing. 1** be agreeable to: *fresh air pleases most people.* **2** wish; think fit: *come if you please.* **3** be the will of. [< OF < L *placere*] —**pleased,** *adj.* —**pleas′ing,** *adj.* —**pleas′ing·ly,** *adv.* —**pleas′ing·ness,** *n.*

pleas·ur·a·ble (plezh′ər ə bəl; plā′zhər–), *adj.* pleasant; agreeable. —**pleas′ur·a·ble·ness ,** *n.* —**pleas′ur·a·bly,** *adv.*

pleas·ure (plezh′ər; plā′zhər), *n.* **1** a feeling of being pleased; enjoyment; delight. **2** something that pleases; cause of joy or delight. **3** one's will, desire, or choice: *what is your pleasure in this matter?*

pleat (plēt), *n.* a flat, usually narrow, fold made in cloth by doubling it on itself. —*v.* fold or arrange in pleats. [var. of *plait*] —**pleat′er,** *n.*

ple·be·ian (pli bē′ən), *n.* **1** one of the common people of ancient Rome. **2** one of the common people. —*adj.* **1** of the plebeians. **2** of the common people. [< L, < *plebs* the common people]

pleb·i·scite (pleb′ə sīt; –sit), *n.* a direct vote by the qualified voters of a state on some important question. [< L, < *plebs* the common people + *scitum* decree]

plec·trum (plek′trəm), *n., pl.* **–trums, –tra** (–trə). a small piece of ivory, horn, metal, etc., used for plucking the strings of a mandolin, lyre, zither, etc. [< L < Gk. *plektron* < *plessein* to strike]

pled (pled), *v.* pt. and pp. of **plead.**

pledge (plej), *n.*, *v.*, **pledged, pledg·ing.**
—*n.* **1** a solemn promise. **2** something that secures or makes safe; security. **3** condition of being held as security. **4** sign; token. —*v.* **1** promise solemnly; bind by a promise. **2** give as security. [< OF < Med.L *plebium* < Gmc.; akin to PLIGHT²] —**pledg′er,** *n.*

Ple·ia·des (plē′ə dēz; plī′-), *n.pl.* group of hundreds of stars. Six can normally be seen with the naked eye.

Pleis·to·cene (plīs′tə sēn), *n.* geological epoch before the present one, during which time both vast glaciers spread across the northern hemispheres and humans were present in Europe; ice age. **2** geological deposits made during this epoch. —*adj.* of or having to do with this epoch or these deposits.

ple·na·ry (plē′nə ri; plen′ə-), *adj.* **1** full; complete; entire; absolute. **2** attended by all of its qualified members. [< LL, < L *plenus* full]

plen·i·po·ten·ti·ar·y (plen′ə pə ten′shi-er′i; -shə ri), *n.*, *pl.* **-ar·ies,** *adj.* —*n.* person, esp. a diplomatic agent, having full power or authority. —*adj.* having or giving full power and authority. [< Med.L, ult. < L *plenus* full + *potens* powerful]

plen·i·tude (plen′ə tüd; -tūd), *n.* fullness; completeness; abundance. [< L, < *plenus* full]

plen·te·ous (plen′ti əs), *adj.* plentiful.

plen·ti·ful (plen′ti fəl), *adj.* more than enough; ample; abundant: *ten gallons of gasoline is a plentiful supply for a seventy-mile trip.*

plen·ty (plen′ti), *n.*, *pl.* **-ties,** *adj.*, *adv.* —*n.* **1** a full supply; all that one needs; large enough number or quantity: *there is plenty of time.* **2** quality or condition of being plentiful; abundance: *years of peace and plenty.* —*adj.* enough; abundant: *six potatoes will be plenty.* —*adv. Informal.* quite; fully: *plenty good enough.* [< OF < L *plenitas* fullness < *plenus* full]

ple·num (plē′nəm), *n. pl.* **-nums, -na** (-nə). full assembly, as of the upper and lower houses of a legislature. [< L, full]

ple·o·nasm (plē′ə naz əm), *n.* **1** use of more words than are necessary to express an idea. *Both of the two twins* is a pleonasm. **2** an unnecessary word, phrase, or expression. [< LL < Gk., ult. < *pleon* more] —**ple′o·nas′tic,** *adj.*

Ple·si·an·thro·pus (plē′sē an′thrə pəs), *n.* early humanlike ape, whose bones were found in South Africa. [< NL < Gk. *plēsíos* near + *anthrōpos* man]

ple·si·o·saur (plē′sē ə sôr), *n.* sea-reptile of the Mesozoic era, which had four flippers, a long neck, and a small head. [< NL < Gk. *plēsíos* near + *saûros* lizard]

pleth·o·ra (pleth′ə rə), *n.* excessive fullness; too much; superabundance. [< NL < Gk.,< *plethein* be full]

pleu·ra (plùr′ə), *n.*, *pl.* **pleu·rae** (plùr′ē). a thin membrane covering the lungs and folded back to make a lining for the thorax or chest cavity. [< NL < Gk., rib] —**pleu′ral,** *adj.*

pleu·ri·sy (plùr′ə si), *n.* inflammation of the thin membrane covering the lungs and lining the thorax. —**pleu·rit′ic,** *adj.*

plex·i·glass (plek′sə glas′; -gläs′), *n.* **1** a light, transparent thermoplastic, often used in place of glass used to make a great many things, including car windows and household items. **2 Plexiglas.** trademark for plexiglass sheets. [< *pl(astic)* + *(fl)exi(ble)* + *glass*]

plex·us (plek′səs), *n.*, *pl.* **-us·es, -us.** network of nerves, blood vessels, etc. [< L, < *plectere* to twine, braid]

pli·a·ble (plī′ə bəl), *adj.* **1** easily bent; flexible; supple: *willow twigs are pliable.* **2** easily influenced; adaptable; yielding: *he is too pliable to be a good leader.* [< F, < *plier* bend] —**pli′a·bil′i·ty, pli′a·ble·ness,** *n.* —**pli′a·bly,** *adv.*

pli·ant (plī′ənt), *adj.* **1** bending easily; flexible; supple. **2** easily influenced; yielding. [< OF, bending. See PLY².] —**pli′an·cy, pli′ant·ness,** *n.* —**pli′ant·ly,** *adv.*

pli·er (plī′ər), *n.* **1** =pliers. **2** one who or that which plies.

pli·ers (plī′ərz), *n.* (*sometimes sing. in use*). small pincers with long jaws, for bending wire, holding small objects, etc.

plight¹ (plīt), *n.* condition or state, usually bad. [< AF *plit*, orig., manner of folding, ult. < L *plicare* to fold; confused with *plight²*]

plight² (plīt), *v.* pledge; promise. —*n.* a solemn promise; pledge.

plight one's troth, a a promise to be faithful. **b** promise to marry. [OE *pliht* danger]

plinth (plinth), *n.* the lower, square part of the base of a column. [< L < Gk. *plinthos*]

Pli·o·cene (plī′ə sēn), *n.* geologic epoch during which humanlike apes appeared, migration of mammals between continents occurred, and the mountains of W America rose.

plod (plod), *v.*, **plod·ded, plod·ding,** *n.* —*v.* **1** walk heavily; trudge: *we plod the path of toil.* **2** work patiently with effort: *plod away at one's lessons.* —*n.* **1** act of plodding; course of plodding. **2** sound as of a heavy tread. —**plod′der,** *n.* —**plod′ding,** *adj.*

plop (plop), *v.*, **plopped, plop·ping. 1** make or cause to make a sound like an object hitting water without a splash. **2** fall with a plop: *plopped into the chair.* —*n.* a sound like an object hitting water without a splash: *the constant plop of a leaking faucet.*

plot (plot), *n.*, *v.*, **plot·ted, plot·ting.** —*n.* **1** a secret plan, esp. an evil one: *two men formed a plot to rob the bank.* **2** plan or main story of a play, novel, poem, etc. **3** a small piece of ground: *a garden plot.* **4** map; diagram. —*v.* **1** plan secretly with others; plan. **2** divide (land) into plots. **3** make a map or diagram of. **4** mark the position of (something) on a map or diagram. [OE, patch of ground; meaning infl. by *complot* a joint plot (< F)] —**plot′less,** *adj.* —**plot′ted,** *adj.* —**plot′ter,** *n.*

plough (plou), *n.*, *v.* =plow.

plov·er (pluv′ər; plō′vər), *n.* bird with a short tail and a bill like that of a pigeon. [< AF, ult. < L *pluvia* rain]

plow (plou), *n.* **1** a big, heavy implement for cutting the soil and turning it over. **2** machine for removing snow; snowplow. —*v.* **1** turn up (soil) with a plow. **2** move as a plow does; advance slowly and with effort. **3** remove with a plow: *plow up old roots.* **4** furrow: *plow a field, wrinkles plowed in one's face by time.* **5** cut the surface of (water).

plow back, reinvest (earnings) in an enterprise.

plow into, collide with; hit: *a car plowed into the fence.*

plow under, completely turn over a field, esp. to allow it to lie fallow.

plow up, a turn over the soil in a field or garden. **b** damage by plowing or turning over: *moles plow up lawns.* [OE *plōg*] —**plow′er,** *n.* —**plow′ing,** *n.*

plow·man (plou′mən), *n.*, *pl.* **-men. 1** person who guides a plow. **2** a farm worker.

plow·share (plou′shār′), *n.* blade of a plow, the part that cuts the soil.

ploy (ploi), *n.* plan or trick used to gain an advantage. [? < em*ploy*]

pluck (pluk), *v.* **1** pull off; pick. **2** pull at; pull; tug; jerk. **3** pull on (the strings of a musical instrument). **4** pull feathers or hair off: *pluck a chicken.* —*n.* **1** act of picking or pulling. **2** courage. [OE *pluccian*] —**plucked,** *adj.* —**pluck′er,** *n.* —**pluck′less,** *adj.* —**pluck′less·ness,** *n.*

pluck·y (pluk′i), *adj.*, **pluck·i·er, pluck·i·est.** having or showing courage. —**pluck′i·ly,** *adv.* —**pluck′i·ness,** *n.*

plug (plug), *n.*, *v.*, **plugged, plug·ging.** —*n.* **1** piece of wood, etc., used to stop up a hole. **2** device to make an electrical connection. **3** hydrant. **4** a spark plug. **5** an advertisement. —*v.* **1** stop up or fill with a plug. **2** work steadily; plod. **3** work steadily for by advertisements or publicity.

plug in, a make an electrical connection by inserting a plug. **b** *Informal. Fig.* be alert or aware (of whatever is current or new). [< MDu. *plugge*] —**plug′ger,** *n.* —**plug′ging,** *n.*, *adj.* —**plug′less,** *adj.* —**plug′like′,** *adj.*

plum (plum), *n.* **1** a roundish, juicy fruit with a smooth skin and a stone or pit. **2** tree that it grows on. **3** raisin in a pudding, cake, etc. **4** sugarplum. **5** something very good or desirable. **6** a dark, bluish purple. [< VL *pruna* < L *prunum* < Gk., *proumnon.* Doublet of PRUNE.] —**plum′like′,** *adj.*

plum·age (plüm′ij), *n.* feathers of a bird: *a parrot has bright plumage.* [< OF, < *plume* PLUME]

plumb (plum), *n.* a small weight used on the end of a line to find the depth of water or to see if a wall is vertical. —*adj.* vertical. —*adv.* vertically. —*v.* **1** make vertical. **2** test or adjust by a plumb line; test; sound: *plumb the depths of the lake.* **3** get to the bottom of: *no one could plumb the mystery.*

out of plumb or **off plumb,** not vertical. [< OF < L *plumbum* lead]

plumb·er (plum'ər), *n.* person whose work is putting in and repairing water pipes and fixtures in buildings. [< OF *plombier,* ult. <L *plumbum* lead]

plumb·ing (plum'ing), *n.* **1** work or trade of a plumber. **2** the water pipes and fixtures in a building: *bathroom plumbing.*

plumb line, line with a plumb at the end.

plume (plüm), *n., v.,* **plumed, plum·ing.** —*n.* **1** a large, long feather; feather. **2** a feather, bunch of feathers, or tuft of hair worn as an ornament on a hat, helmet, etc. —*v.* **1** furnish with plumes. **2** smooth or arrange the feathers of: *the eagle plumed its wing.* [< OF < L *pluma*] —**plumed,** *adj.* —**plume′like′,** *adj.*

plum·met (plum'it), *v.* plunge; drop. [< OF *plommet* < *plomb* lead; see PLUMB]

plum·my (plum'i), *adj.* **-mi·er, -i·est.** **1** full of or like plums: *a rich, plummy purple.* **2** Fig. very good; desirable: *a plummy job.* **3** Fig. mellow: *a plummy voice.*

plump¹ (plump), *adj.* rounded out; attractively fat. —*v.* make plump; become plump. [cf. MDu. *plomp,* MLG plump blunt, thick] —**plump′ly,** *adv.* —**plump′ness,** *n.*

plump² (plump), *v.* fall or drop heavily or suddenly: *all out of breath, she plumped down on a chair.* —*n.* a sudden plunge; heavy fall. —*adv.* **1** heavily or suddenly: *he ran plump into me.* **2** directly; bluntly. —*adj.* direct; downright; blunt. [cf. Du. *plompen,* LG *plumpen,* and *plump¹*] —**plump′er,** *n.*

plum·y (plüm'i), *adj.* **1** having plumes. **2** adorned with plumes. **3** feathery.

plun·der (plun'dər), *v.* **1** rob by force; rob: *pirates plundered the town.* **2** despoil; fleece; embezzle: *the dishonest cashier plundered $10,000 from the bank.* —*n.* **1** things taken in plundering; booty; loot: *they carried off the plunder in their ships.* **2** act of robbing by force. **3** Fig. an excess or great deal of something, as gifts, winnings, profits, etc. [< G *plündern*] —**plun′der·er,** *n.* —**plun′der·ous,** *adj.*

plunge (plunj), *v.,* **plunged, plung·ing,** *n.* —*v.* **1** throw or thrust with force into a liquid, place, or condition. **2** throw oneself (into water, danger, a fight, etc.). **3** rush; dash. **4** pitch suddenly and violently. —*n.* **1** act of plunging. **2** a dive into the water. **3** a rapid dash. [< OF *plungier,* ult. < L *plumbum* lead] —**plung′ing,** *adj.* —**plung′ing·ly,** *adv.*

plung·er (plun'jər), *n.* **1** one that plunges. **2** part of a machine that acts with a plunging motion.

plunk (plungk), *v.* **1** pluck (a banjo, guitar, etc.) **2** throw, push, put, drop, etc., heavily or suddenly. —*n.* act or sound of plunking. —*adv.* with a plunk. [imit.]

plu·per·fect (plü′pèr′fikt), *n., adj.* past perfect. [short for L *plus quam perfectum* more than perfect]

plu·ral (plur'əl), *adj.* **1** containing or pertaining to more than one. **2** designating that class of words or forms which indicate or imply more than one. —*n.* form of a word to show that it means more than one; plural number. *Books* is the plural of *book; men,* of *man; are,* of *is; we,* of *I; these,* of *this.* [< L *pluralis* < *plus* more]

plu·ral·ism (plur'ə liz əm), *n.* **1** character, condition, or an instance of being plural. **2 a** acceptance and support of various minority ethnic and cultural groups within a society. **b** belief in and advocacy of such a social system. —**plu′ral·is′tic,** *adj.*

plu·ral·i·ty (plu ral'ə ti), *n., pl.* **-ties. 1** difference between the largest number of votes and the next largest in an election. **2** the greater number; the majority. **3** a large number; multitude. **4** state or fact of being plural.

plu·ral·ize (plur'əl īz), *v.,* **-ized, -iz·ing.** make plural; express in the plural form.

plu·ral·ly (plur'əl i), *adv.* in the plural number.

plus (plus), *prep.* **1** added to: *3 plus 2 equals 5.* **2** and also: *the work of an engineer requires intelligence plus experience.* —*adj.* **1** and more: *his mark was B plus.* **2** showing addition: *the plus sign.* **3** positive; positively electrified. —*n.* **1** the plus sign. **2** an added quantity. **3** a positive quantity. **4** surplus; gain. [< L, more]

plush (plush), *n.* fabric like velvet but thicker and softer. —*adj.* luxurious; expensive. [< F *pluche,* ult. < L *pilus* hair] —**plushed,** *adj.* —**plush′y,** *adj.* —**plush′i·ness,** *n.*

Plu·to (plü′tō), *n.* planet farthest from the sun, whose planetary status is uncertain. —**Plu·to′ni·an,** *adj.*

plu·toc·ra·cy (plü tok′rə si), *n., pl.* **-cies. 1** government in which the rich rule. **2** a ruling class of wealthy people. [< Gk., < *ploutos* wealth + *kratos* power]

plu·to·crat (plü′tə krat), *n.* **1** person who has power or influence because of his wealth. **2** a wealthy person. —**plu′to·crat′ic,** *adj.* —**plu′to·crat′i·cal·ly,** *adv.*

plu·to·ni·um (plü tō′ni əm), *n.* a radioactive element, Pu, derived from neptunium, important in atomic fission. [< L, neut., < *Pluto*]

plu·vi·al (plü′vi əl), *adj.* **1** of or pertaining to rain; rainy. **2** caused by rain. [< L, < *pluvia* rain]

ply¹ (plī), *v.,* **plied, ply·ing. 1** work with; use: *the dressmaker plies her needle.* **2** keep up work on; work away at or on: *we plied the water with our oars.* **3** urge again and again: *the enemy plied*

our messenger with questions. **4** supply with in a pressing manner: *ply a person with food or drink.* **5** go back and forth regularly between certain places: *a bus plies between the station and the hotel, boats ply the river.* [ult. var. of *apply*] —**ply′er,** *n.*

ply² (plī), *n., pl.* **plies.** thickness; fold; twist. Three-ply rope is made up of three twists. [< F *pli* < OF < L *plicare* to fold]

ply·wood (plī′wùd′), *n.* board or boards made of several thin layers of wood glued together.

Pm, promethium.

P.M., 1 Postmaster. **2** Prime Minister.

p.m., P.M., 1 after noon. [< L *post meridiem*] **2** the time from noon to midnight.

pneu·mat·ic (nü mat'ik; nū–), *adj.* **1** filled with or containing air. **2** worked by air. **3** having to do with air and other gases. **4** pertaining to pneumatics. [< L < Gk., < *pneuma* wind] —**pneu·mat′i·cal·ly,** *adv.*

pneu·mat·ics (nü mat'iks; nū–), *n.* branch of physics that deals with the pressure, elasticity, weight, etc., of air and other gases.

pneu·mo·nia (nü mō′nyə; –ni ə; nū–), *n.* disease in which the lungs are inflamed. [< NL < Gk., < *pneumon* lung] —**pneu·mon′ic,** *adj.*

Po, polonium.

P.O., post office.

poach¹ (pōch), *v.* **1** trespass (on another's land), esp. to hunt or fish. **2** take (game or fish) without any right. [< early F *pocher* poke out < Gmc.; akin to POKE¹] —**poach′er,** *n.*

poach² (pōch), *v.* cook (an egg) by breaking it into boiling water. [< OF *pochier* < *poche* cooking spoon < Celtic] —**poach′a·ble,** *adj.*

pock (pok), *n.* pimple, mark, or pit on the skin, caused by smallpox and certain other diseases. [OE *pocc*] —**pocked,** *adj.*

pock·et (pok'it), *n.* **1** a small bag sewed into clothing. **2** a hollow place; enclosed place: *a pocket of air.* **3** bag at the corner or side of a pool or billiard table. **4** hole in the earth containing gold or other ore; single lump of ore. —*v.* **1** shut in; hem in. **2** place in one's pocket. **3** hold back; suppress; hide: *he pocketed his pride and said nothing.* **4** take secretly or dishonestly: *Tom pocketed all the profits.* —*adj.* **1** meant to be carried in a pocket: *a pocket handkerchief.* **2** small enough to go in a pocket; diminutive.

deep pockets, a great deal of money to invest or spend.

in one's (hip) pocket, under one's control.

live one's pocket, make a profit for oneself, esp. unethically or illegally.

out of pocket, at one's own expense. [< AF *pokete,* dim. of *poke* POKE²] —**pock′et·y,** *adj.*

pock·et·book (pok'it bùk′), *n.* **1** a woman's purse. **2** case for carrying money, papers, etc., in a pocket.

pock·et·ful (pok′it fŭl), *n., pl.* **-fuls.** as much as a pocket will hold.

pock·et·knife (pok′it nīf′), *n., pl.* **-knives.** a small knife with one or more blades that fold into the handle.

pocket veto, method by which the President can veto a bill by failing to sign it within ten days after a session of Congress ends.

pock·mark (pok′märk′), *n.* pock. **—pock′-marked′,** *adj.*

pod (pod), *n., v.,* **pod·ded, pod·ding.** **—***n.* **1** a bivalve shell or case in which plants like beans and peas grow their seeds. **2** a dehiscent fruit or pericarp with more than one seed. **3 a** a rounded, streamlined cover for something carried externally, esp. on the wings of an aircraft. **b** any container shaped like a pod. **—***v.* **1** produce pods. **2** fill out into a pod.

pod·cast·ing (pod′kast′ing), *n.* distribution of digital audio or video files over the Internet to personal computers and esp. portable, hand-held mobile devices. [< *iPod,* trademark for a mobile digital player-receiver + broad*casting*] **—pod′cast′, pod′cast′er,** *n.*

po·di·a·try (pō dī′ə trī), *n.* =chiropody. [< Gk. *pous* foot + E *–iatry* treatment < Gk. *iatreia*] **—po·di′a·trist,** *n.*

po·di·um (pō′di əm), *n., pl.* **-di·a** (–di ə). **1** a raised platform. **2** an animal structure that serves as a foot. [< L < Gk. *podion,* dim. of *pous* foot]

po·em (pō′əm; pōm), *n.* **1** an arrangement of words in lines with a regularly repeated accent; composition in verse. **2** composition showing great beauty or nobility of language or thought. [< L < Gk. *poema,* var. of *poiema* < *poeein,* var. of *poieein* make, compose]

po·e·sy (pō′ə si; –zi), *n., pl.* **-sies.** poetry. [< OF, ult. < L *poesis* < Gk., var. of *poiesis* composition]

po·et (pō′it), *n.* person who writes poetry. [< L < Gk. *poetes*]

po·et·ess (pō′it is), *n.* a female poet.

po·et·ic (pō et′ik), **po·et·i·cal** (–ə kəl), *adj.* **1** having to do with poems or poets. **2** suitable for poems or poets. *Alas, o'er,* and *blithe* are poetic words. **3** consisting of poems. **—po·et′i·cal·ly,** *adv.*

po·et·ics (pō et′iks), *n.* **1** part of literary criticism that deals with the nature and laws of poetry. **2** treatise on poetry.

poet laureate, *pl.* **poets laureate. 1** in Great Britain, poet appointed by the king or queen to write poems in celebration of court and national events. **2** the official poet of any country, state, etc.

po·et·ry (pō′it ri), *n.* **1** poems: *a collection of poetry.* **2** art of writing poems. **3** poetic quality; poetic spirit or feeling. [< LL, < L *poeta* POET]

po·grom (pō grom′; pō′grəm), *n.* an organized massacre, esp. of Jews. [< Russ., devastation]

poi (poi), *n.* a Hawaiian food made of the root of the taro. [< Hawaiian]

poign·ant (poin′ənt; –yənt), *adj.* **1** very painful; piercing: *poignant suffering.* **2** keen; intense: *a subject of poignant interest.* **3** sharp to the taste or smell: *poignant sauces.* [< OF, ppr. of *poindre* prick < L *pungere*] **—poign′an·cy,** *n.* **—poign′ant·ly,** *adv.*

poin·set·ti·a (poin set′i ə), *n.* plant with large, scarlet leaves that look like flower petals. [< NL; named after J. R. *Poinsett,* its discoverer]

point (point), *n.* **1** a sharp end; something having a sharp end. **2** a tiny round mark; dot. **3** place; spot: *stop at this point.* **4** any particular or definite position, condition, or time; degree; stage: *boiling point.* **5** item; detail: *he answered my questions point by point.* **6** a distinguishing mark or quality: *one's good points.* **7** the main idea or purpose; important or essential thing. **8** piece of land with a sharp end sticking out into the water; cape. **9** unit of scoring or measuring: *stock that has gone up a point.* **—***v.* **1** indicate position or direction, or direct attention with, or as if with, the finger. **2** direct a finger, weapon, etc. **3** have a specified direction: *the signboard points north.* **4** of a dog, show the presence of game by standing rigid and looking toward it.

at the point of, in the act of; very near to.

in point of, as regards.

make a point of, insist upon.

on the point of, just about; on the verge of.

point out, show or call attention to.

point up, emphasize; give attention to.

to the point, appropriate to the subject or occasion. [< OF *point* mark, moment and *pointe* sharp point, both ult. < L *pungere* to prick] **—point′a·ble, point′y,** *adj.*

point-blank (point′blangk′), *adj.* **1** aimed straight at the mark. **2** plain and blunt; direct: *a point-blank question.* **—***adv.* **1** straight at the mark. **2** plainly and bluntly; directly: *one boy gave excuses, but the other refused point-blank.*

pointe (point; pwANt), *n.* **1** in ballet, toe, esp. the position on the tip of the toe. **2** the toe of a ballet slipper. [< F]

point·ed (poin′tid), *adj.* **1** having a point or points: *a pointed roof.* **2** sharp; piercing: *a pointed wit.* **3** *Fig.* directed; aimed. **4** *Fig.* emphatic: *he showed her pointed attention.* **—point′ed·ly,** *adv.* **—point′ed·ness,** *n.*

point·er (poin′tər), *n.* **1** one that points. **2** a long, tapering stick used in pointing things out on a map, blackboard, etc. **3** hand of a clock, meter, etc. **4** a short-haired hunting dog trained to show where game is by standing still and directing its nose toward the location. **5** hint; suggestion.

poin·til·lism (pwan′tə liz əm), *n.* technique of painting in which color is applied in dots and is blended by the eye of the observer. **—poin′til·list,** *n.*

point lace, lace made with a needle.

point·less (point′lis), *adj.* **1** without a point. **2** without force or meaning. **—point′less·ly,** *adv.* **—point′less·ness,** *n.*

point man, 1 person at the front of a patrol. **2** someone who is at the front or acts as leader for a team, group, etc.

point of order, question raised during a proceeding of whether or not the rules are being followed.

point of view, 1 position from which objects are considered. **2** attitude of mind.

point·y-head (poin′ti hed′), *Informal.* an intellectual. **—point′y-head′ed,** *adj.*

poise (poiz), *v.,* **poised, pois·ing,** *n.* **—***v.* **1** balance. **2** hold supported or raised: *poise a spear.* **3** hang supported or suspended. **—***n.* **1** balance. **2** general composure; stability. **3** suspense. [< OF *peser* weigh < L *pensare* intensive of *pendere* weigh]

poi·son (poi′zən), *n.* **1** drug or other substance very dangerous to life and health. Strychnine and opium are poisons. **2** anything dangerous or deadly. **—***v.* **1** kill or harm by poison. **2** put poison in or on. **3** have a dangerous or harmful effect on. **—***adj.* poisonous. [< OF < L *potio* potion. Doublet of POTION.] **—poi′son·er,** *n.* **—poi′son·ing,** *n.*

poison ivy, plant with glossy, green, compound leaves of three leaflets each, that causes a painful rash on most people if they touch it.

poi·son·ous (poi′zən əs), *adj.* **1** containing poison; very harmful to life and health. **2** having a dangerous or harmful effect. **—poi′son·ous·ly,** *adv.* **—poi′son·ous·ness,** *n.*

poke (pōk), *v.,* **poked, pok·ing,** *n.* **—***v.* **1** push against with something pointed; thrust into; thrust; push. **2** pry. **3** make by poking. **4** go lazily; loiter. **—***n.* **1** a poking; thrust; push. **2** a slow, lazy person. [ME. Cf. MDu., MLG *poken.*]

poke·ber·ry (pōk′ber′i), *n., pl.* **-ries. 1** berry of the pokeweed. **2** pokeweed.

poke bonnet, bonnet with a projecting brim.

pok·er[1] (pōk′ər), *n.* **1** one that pokes. **2** a metal rod for stirring a fire.

pok·er[2] (pōk′ər), *n.* a card game in which the players bet on the value of the cards that they hold in their hands. [? < F *poque*]

poker face, face that does not show one's thoughts or feelings.

poke·weed (pōk′wēd′), *n.* a tall weed of North America with juicy, purple berries and poisonous roots.

pok·ey[1] (pōk′i), *n. Informal.* jail.

pok·y, pok·ey[2] (pōk′i), *adj.,* **pok·i·er, pok·i·est. 1** puttering; slow; dull. **2** small and dull; petty; mean. **3** shabby. [< *poke*[1]]

pol (pol), *n. Informal.* =politician.

Pol., Polish.

Po·land (pō′lənd), *n.* country in C Europe.

po·lar (pō′lər), *adj.* **1** of or near the North or South Pole: *the polar regions.* **2** having to do with a pole or poles. **3** of the poles of a magnet, electric battery, etc. **4** opposite in character, like the poles of a magnet: *love and hatred are polar feelings or attitudes.* [< Med.L, < L *polus* POLE²]

polar bear, a large, white bear of the arctic regions.

Po·lar·is (pō lăr'is), *n.* the North Star; polestar.

po·lar·i·ty (pō lar'ə ti), *n.* **1** the possession of an axis with reference to which certain physical properties are determined. A magnet or battery has polarity. **2** a positive or negative polar condition, as in electricity. **3** *Fig.* having two opposite personality traits or tendencies.

po·lar·i·za·tion (pō'lər ə zā'shən), *n.* **1** production or acquisition of polarity. **2** process by which gases produced during electrolysis are deposited on electrodes of a cell, giving rise to a reverse electromotive force.

po·lar·ize (pō'lər īz), *v.,* **–ized, –iz·ing.** give polarity to; cause polarization in: *an issue that polarized voters.* —**po'lar·iz'a·ble,** *adj.* —**po'lar·iz'a·bil'i·ty,** *n.* —**po'lar·iz'er,** *n.*

pole¹ (pōl), *n., v.,* **poled, pol·ing.** —*n.* **1** a long, slender piece of wood, etc.: *a telephone pole, a flag pole.* **2** measure of length; rod; 5½ yards. **3** measure of area; square rod; 30¼ square yards. —*v.* make (a boat) go with a pole. [< L *palus* stake. Doublet of PALE².]

pole² (pōl), *n.* **1** either end of the earth's axis. The North Pole and the South Pole are opposite each other. **2** each of the two points in which the earth's axis, when extended, cuts the celestial sphere, about which the stars seem to revolve. **3** either of two parts where opposite forces are strongest. A magnet or battery has both a positive pole and a negative pole. **4** either end of the axis of any sphere.

poles apart, widely differing, esp. in opinion or point of view. [< L < Gk. *polos*]

Pole (pōl), *n.* native or inhabitant of Poland.

pole·cat (pōl'kat'), *n.* **1** a small, dark-brown European animal with a very disagreeable odor. **2** the North American skunk.

po·lem·ic (pə lem'ik), *n.* **1** argument; dispute; controversy. **2** a vigorous controversialist. —*adj.* Also, **po·lem'i·cal.** of controversy or disagreement; of dispute. [< Gk. *polemikos* belligerent < *polemos* war] —**po·lem'i·cal·ly,** *adv.*

po·lem·ics (pə lem'iks), *n.* art or practice of disputation or controversy, esp. in theology.

pole·star (pōl'stär'), *n.* **1** the North Star. **2** a guiding principle; guide.

pole-vault (pōl'vôlt'), *v.* perform a vault over a high, horizontal bar by using a long pole. —**pole vault, pole'-vault'er, pole'-vault'ing,** *n.*

po·lice (pə lēs'), *n., v.,* **–liced, –lic·ing.** —*n.* **1** persons whose duty is keeping order and arresting people who break the law. **2** department of government that keeps order and arrests persons who break the law. **3** regulation and control of a community, esp. with reference to matters of public order, safety, health, morals, etc.; public order. —*v.* keep order in: *police the streets.* [< F < L < Gk. *politeia* polity. Doublet of POLICY¹, POLITY.]

police dog, a kind of large, strong dog that looks like a wolf; German shepherd.

po·lice·man (pə lēs'mən), *n., pl.* **–men.** member of the police.

police state, state strictly policed by governmental authority, thus demonstrating only a minimum of social, economic, and political liberty.

po·lice·wom·an (pə lēs'wum'ən), *n., pl.* **–wom·en.** woman who is a member of the police.

pol·i·cy¹ (pol'ə si), *n., pl.* **–cies. 1** plan of action; way of management: *it is a poor policy to promise more than you can do.* **2** practical wisdom; prudence: *policy, not sentiment.* **3** political skill or shrewdness. [< OF < L < Gk. *politeia* polity. Doublet of POLICE, POLITY.]

pol·i·cy² (pol'ə si), *n., pl.* **–cies.** a written agreement about insurance. [< F < Ital. *pólissa* < L < Gk. *apodeixis* declaration]

pol·i·cy·hold·er (pol'ə si hōl'dər), *n.* one who holds an insurance policy.

po·li·o (pō'li ō), *n.* =poliomyelitis.

po·li·o·my·e·li·tis (pō'li ō mī'ə lī'tis; pol'i ō–), *n.* **1** =infantile paralysis. **2** any inflammation of the gray matter of the spinal cord. [< NL, < Gk. *polios* gray + *myelos* marrow]

pol·ish (pol'ish), *v.* **1** make smooth and shiny, esp. by friction: *polish shoes.* **2** put into a better condition; improve. —*n.* **1** substance used to give smoothness or shine: *silver polish.* **2** polished condition; smoothness. **3** culture; elegance; refinement.

polish off, get done with; finish. [< OF *poliss–* < L *polire*] —**pol'ished,** *adj.* —**pol'ish·er,** *n.*

Pol·ish (pōl'ish), *adj.* of or pertaining to Poland, its people, or their language. —*n.* language of Poland.

po·lite (pə līt'), *adj.* **1** having or showing good manners; behaving properly. **2** refined; elegant. [< L *politus* polished] —**po·lite'ly,** *adv.* —**po·lite'ness,** *n.*

pol·i·tic (pol'ə tik), *adj.* **1** wise in looking out for one's own interests; prudent: *a politic person.* **2** scheming; crafty. **3** political: *the state is a body politic.* [< L < Gk., ult. < *polis* city-state] —**pol'i·tic·ly,** *adv.*

po·lit·i·cal (pə lit'ə kəl), *adj.* **1** of or concerned with politics. **2** having to do with citizens or government: *treason is a political offense.* **3** of politicians or their methods. —**po·lit'i·cal·ize,** *v.* —**po·lit'i·cal·ly,** *adv.*

political science, science of the principles and conduct of government.

pol·i·ti·cian (pol'ə tish'ən), *n.* **1** person who gives much time to political affairs; person who is experienced in politics. **2** person active in politics chiefly for his or her own profit or that of his or her party. **3** person holding a political office.

po·lit·i·cize (pə lit'ə sīz), *v.,* **–cized, –ciz·ing.** make political; give a political character to. —**po·lit'i·ci·za'tion,** *n.*

po·lit·i·co (pə lit'ə kō), *n., pl.* **–cos.** =politician. [< It. or Sp.]

pol·i·tics (pol'ə tiks), *n. sing. or pl.* **1** management of political affairs: *Franklin D. Roosevelt was engaged in politics for many years.* **2** political principles or opinions. **3** political methods or maneuvers.

pol·i·ty (pol'ə ti), *n., pl.* **–ties. 1** government. **2** a particular form or system of government. **3** community with a government; state. [< obs. F < L < Gk. *politeia,* ult. < *polis* city-state. Doublet of POLICE, POLICY¹.]

Polk (pōk), *n.* **James K,** 1795–1849, the 11th president of the United States, 1845–49.

pol·ka (pōl'kə; pō'–), *n., v.,* **–kaed, –ka·ing.** —*n.* **1** a kind of lively dance. **2** music for it. —*v.* dance a polka. [< F < G, prob. < Slavic]

pol·ka dot (pō'kə), **1** dot or round spot repeated to form a pattern on cloth. **2** pattern or fabric with such dots. —**pol'ka-dot'ted,** *adj.*

poll (pōl), *n.* **1** a voting; collection of votes. **2** number of votes cast. **3** the results of these votes. **4** list of persons, esp. a list of voters. **5** a survey of public opinion concerning a particular subject. —*v.* **1** receive (as votes). **2** vote; cast (a vote). **3** take or register the votes of.

polls, place where votes are cast and counted. [cf. MDu. *pol(le)* top, MLG *pol* head]

pol·len (pol'ən), *n.* a fine, yellowish powder formed on the anthers of flowers. Grains of pollen carried to the pistils of flowers fertilize them. [< L, mill dust]

pol·li·nate (pol'ə nāt), *v.,* **–nat·ed, –nat·ing.** carry pollen from stamens to pistils of; shed pollen on. —**pol'li·na'tion, pol'li·na'tor,** *n.*

pol·li·wog, pol·ly·wog (pol'i wog), *n.* =tadpole. [cf. ME *polwigle.* See POLL, WIGGLE.]

poll·ster (pōl'stər), *n.* one who takes a public-opinion poll.

poll tax, a tax on every person, or on every person of a specified class, esp. as a prerequisite to the right to vote in public elections.

pol·lute (pə lüt'), *v.,* **–lut·ed, –lut·ing. 1** make dirty; defile: *to pollute water.* **2** desecrate. [< L *pollutus*] —**pol·lu'tant, pol·lut'er,** *n.* —**pol·lu'tion,** *n.*

Pol·lux (pol'əks), *n.* one of the two brightest stars in the constellation Gemini.

Pol·ly·an·na (pol'i an'ə), *n.* an irrepressible optimist. [from the heroine of stories by Eleanor Porter, American writer]

po·lo (pō′lō), *n.* a game played by men on horseback with long-handled mallets and a wooden ball. [? ult. < Tibetan *pulu*] —**po′lo·ist,** *n.*

polo coat, double-breasted overcoat with a belted back, made of a soft wool such as camel's hair.

pol·o·naise (pol′ə nāz′; pō′lə–), *n.* **1** a slow, stately dance in three-quarter time. **2** music for it. [< F, fem. adj., lit., Polish]

po·lo·ni·um (pə lō′ni əm), *n.* a radioactive element, Po, occurring in pitchblende. [< NL, < Med.L *Polonia* Poland]

polo shirt, knit shirt with a collar, a buttoned opening at the neck, and, usually, short sleeves.

pol·ter·geist (pōl′tər gīst′), *n.* ghost or spirit that slams doors or makes noises that are unexplainable. [< G < *poltern* make a noise + *Geist* spirit, ghost]

pol·troon (pol trün′), *n.* a wretched coward. [< F < Ital., < *poltro* lazy, orig., bed] —**pol·troon′er·y,** *n.* —**pol·troon′-ish,** *adj.*

poly-, *combining form.* more than one; many; extensive, as in *polyangular, polylinguist, polynuclear.* [< Gk.,< *polys* much, many]

pol·y·an·thus (pol′i an′thəs), *n.* **1** =oxlip. **2** kind of narcissus bearing clusters of small, yellow or white flowers. [< NL < Gk., < *polys* many + *anthos* flower]

pol·y·chrome (pol′i krōm), *adj.* having many colors; decorated or done in many colors. —*n.* work of art done with various colors. [< F < Gk. *polýchrōmos* < *polýs* many + *chroma* color]

pol·y·es·ter (pol′i es′tər), *n.* any of the synthetic resins used in making paints, films, synthetic fibers, construction plastics, etc.

pol·y·eth·yl·ene (pol′i eth′ə lēn), *n.* an odorless, flexible, chemically inert plastic made by polymerizing ethylene, used in industry, for garden hose, freezer containers, etc.

po·lyg·a·my (pə lig′ə mi), *n.* practice or condition of having more than one wife at the same time. [< Gk., < *polys* many + *gamos* marriage] —**po·lyg′a·mist,** *n.* —**po·lyg′a·mous,** *adj.*

pol·y·glot (pol′i glot), *adj.* **1** knowing several languages. **2** written in several languages. —*n.* person who knows several languages. [< Gk., < *polys* many + *glotta* tongue] —**pol′y·glot′tal, pol′y·glot′tic,** *adj.*

pol·y·gon (pol′i gon), *n.* a plane figure having more than four angles and four sides. [< L < Gk., < *polys* many + *gonia* angle] —**po·lyg′o·nal,** *adj.* —**po·lyg′o·nal·ly,** *adv.*

pol·y·he·dron (pol′i hē′drən), *n., pl.* **-drons, -dra** (-drə). a solid figure having many faces. [< NL < Gk., < *polys* many + *hedra* seat, side] —**pol′y·he′dral,** *adj.*

pol·y·mer (pol′i mər), *n.* any of two or more polymeric compounds. Nylon and cellulose are polymers.

pol·y·mer·ic (pol′i mer′ik), *adj.* having the same elements combined in the same proportions by weight, but differing in molecular weight and in chemical and physical properties. Acetylene, C_2H_2, and benzene, C_6H_6, are polymeric compounds. [< Gk., < *polys* many + *meros* part]

pol·y·mer·ize (pol′i mər īz; pə lim′ər–), *v.,* **-ized, -iz·ing.** combine so as to form a polymer. —**po·lym′er·ism,** *n.* —**pol′y·mer·i·za′tion,** *n.*

pol·y·mor·phous (pol′i môr′fəs), **pol·y·mor·phic** (-fik), *adj.* having, assuming, or passing through many or various forms, stages, etc. [< Gk., < *polys* many + *morphe* form] —**pol′y·mor′phism,** *n.*

Pol·y·ne·sia (pol′ə nē′zhə; –shə), *n.* group of many small islands in the Pacific, E of Australia and the Philippines.

Pol·y·ne·sian (pol′ə nē′zhən; –shən), *n.* **1** member of the brown race inhabiting Polynesia. **2** the languages of Polynesia, including Maori, Hawaiian, etc. —*adj.* of or pertaining to Polynesia, its inhabitants, or their languages.

pol·y·no·mi·al (pol′i nō′mi əl), *n.* an algebraic expression consisting of two or more terms. *ab, x^2y,* and *$3npq$* are monomials; *$ab+x^2y$* and *$pq-p^2+q$* are polynomials. —*adj.* consisting of two or more terms. *Homo sapiens* is a polynomial expression. [< POLY- + *-nomial,* as in *binomial*]

pol·yp (pol′ip), *n.* **1** a rather simple form of water animal, not much more than a saclike stomach with fingerlike tentacles around the edge to gather in food. Polyps often grow in colonies, with their bases connected. Corals and sea anemones are polyps. **2** tumor arising from a mucous or serous surface. [< F < L < Gk., < *polys* many + *pous* foot]

pol·y·phon·ic (pol′i fon′ik), *adj.* having two or more voices or parts, each with an independent melody, but all harmonizing; contrapuntal.

po·lyph·o·ny (pə lif′ə ni), *n.* polyphonic composition; counterpoint. [< Gk., < *polys* many + *phone* voice]

pol·y·ploid (pol′i ploid), *adj.* having three or more sets of chromosomes. —*n.* an organism or cell that has three or more sets of chromosomes. [< *poly-* + ha*ploid*]

pol·y·sac·cha·ride (pol′i sak′ə rīd), *n.* a carbohydrate, such as starch, dextrin, and insulin, that can be decomposed into two or more simple sugars.

pol·y·sty·rene (pol′i stī′rēn), *n.* colorless and transparent plastic used to make appliances, insulation, toys, synthetic rubber, etc.

pol·y·syl·la·ble (pol′i sil′ə bəl), *n.* word of more than three syllables. —**pol·y·syl·lab′ic,** *adj.* —**pol′y·syl·lab′i·cal·ly,** *adv.*

pol·y·tech·nic (pol′i tek′nik), *adj.* pertaining to or dealing with many arts or sciences: *a polytechnic school.* —*n.* a technical school.

pol·y·the·ism (pol′i thē iz′əm), *n.* belief in more gods than one. The religion of the Greeks was polytheism. [< F, ult. < Gk. *polys* many + *theos* god] —**pol′y·the′ist,** *n.* —**pol′y·the·is′tic, pol′y·the·is′ti·cal,** *adj.*

pol·y·un·sat·u·rate (pol′i un sach′ər it; –ə rāt), *n.* a polyunsaturated oil or fat, as in some vegetable and fish oils, that have a low cholesterol content.

pol·y·un·sat·u·rat·ed (pol′i un sach′-ə rā tid), *adj.* having many double and triple bonds and free valences, esp. some oils and fats derived from plants.

pom·ace (pum′is), *n.* apple pulp or similar fruit pulp before or after the juice has been pressed out. [ult. < Med.L *pomacium* cider < L *pomum* apple]

po·ma·ceous (pə mā′shəs), *adj.* belonging to the same family of plants as the apple.

po·made (pə mād′; –mäd′), *n., v.,* **-mad-ed, -mad·ing.** —*n.* a perfumed ointment for the scalp and hair. —*v.* put pomade on. [< F < Ital. *pommata* < L *pomum* fruit]

pome (pōm), *n.* apple or any fruit like it; fruit consisting of firm, juicy flesh surrounding a core that contains several seeds. Apples, pears, and quinces are pomes. [< OF, ult. < L *pomum* apple]

pome·gran·ate (pom′gran′it; pum′–; pum gran′it), *n.* **1** a reddish-yellow fruit with a thick skin, red pulp, and many seeds. **2** tree it grows on. [< OF, < *pome* fruit (ult. < L *pomum*) + *grenate* having grains, < L *granum* grain]

Pom·er·a·ni·an (pom′ər ā′ni ən), *n.* a small dog with a sharp nose, pointed ears, and long, thick, silky hair.

pom·mel (pum′əl; pom′–), *n., v.,* **-meled, -mel·ing.** —*n.* **1** part of a saddle that sticks up at the front. **2** a rounded knob on the hilt of a sword, dagger, etc. —*v.* beat with the fists; strike; beat. Also, **pummel.** [< OF *pomel,* ult. < L *pomum* apple] —**pom′mel·er,** *n.*

po·mol·o·gy (pə mol′ə ji), *n.* branch of science that deals with fruits and fruit growing. [< NL *pomologia.* See POME, –LOGY.] —**po′mo·log′i·cal,** *adj.* —**po·mol′o·gist,** *n.*

pomp (pomp), *n.* **1** a stately display; splendor; magnificence: *the king was crowned with great pomp.* **2** a showy display. [< OF < L < Gk. *pompe* parade]

pom·pa·dour (pom′pə dôr; –dōr), *n.* **1** arrangement of a woman's hair in which it is puffed high over the forehead. **2** arrangement of a man's hair in which it is brushed straight up and back from the forehead. [from the Marquise de *Pompadour*]

pom·pa·no (pom′pə nō), *n., pl.* **-nos. 1** a food fish of the West Indies and neighboring coasts of North America. **2** a somewhat similar fish of the California coast. [< Sp.]

pom-pom (pom′pom), *n.* **1** =pompon (def. 1). **2** ball of colored strips of paper or fabric, used esp. by cheerleaders.

pom·pon (pom′pon), *n.* **1** an ornamental tuft or ball of feathers, silk, or the like, worn on a hat or dress, on the shoes, etc. **2** kind of chrysanthemum or dahlia with very small, rounded flowers. [< F, < *pompe* POMP]

pom·pous (pom′pəs), *adj.* **1** trying to seem magnificent; fond of display; acting proudly; self-important: *a pompous manner.* **2** (of language, style, etc.) ostentatiously lofty. **3** magnificent; stately. —**pom·pos′i·ty, pom′pous·ness,** *n.* —**pom′pous·ly,** *adv.*

pon·cho (pon′chō), *n., pl.* –**chos.** a large piece of cloth, often waterproof, with a slit in the middle for the head to go through. [< Am. Sp. < Araucanian (S Am.Ind.) *pontho*]

pond (pond), *n.* body of still water, smaller than a lake. Ponds are often artificially formed. [orig. var. of *pound*[3]] —**pond′y,** *adj.* Am.

pon·der (pon′dər), *v.* consider carefully; meditate. [< OF < L *ponderare* weigh < *pondus* weight] —**pon′der·a·ble,** *adj.* —**pon′der·a·bil′i·ty,** *n.* —**pon′der·er,** *n.* —**pon′der·ing·ly,** *adv.*

pon·der·ous (pon′dər əs), *adj.* **1** very heavy. **2** heavy and clumsy. **3** dull; tiresome. [< L, < *pondus* weight] —**pon′der·ous·ly,** *adv.* —**pon′der·ous·ness, pon′der·os′i·ty,** *n.*

pone (pōn), *n.* S. **1** bread made of corn meal. **2** loaf or cake of this bread. [< Algonquian]

pon·gee (pon jē′), *n.* kind of soft silk, usually left in natural brownish-yellow color. [? < dial. Chinese *pun-chī* home-woven]

pons or **pons Va·ro·li·i** (ponz′və rō′lē ī), bundles of nerve fibers just above the medulla oblongata in the brain, one of which connects the two lobes of the cerebellum and the other, connects the medulla with the cerebrum. [< NL Varoli's bridge < Constanzo *Varoli* (?1543–75) Italian anatomist]

pon·tiff (pon′tif), *n.* **1** the Pope. **2** bishop. **3** a high priest; chief priest. [< F < L *pontifex,* a high priest of Rome, prob. < *pons* bridge + *facere* make]

pon·tif·i·cal (pon tif′ə kəl), *adj.* **1** of or pertaining to the Pope; papal. **2** of or pertaining to a bishop. —**pon·tif′i·cal·ly,** *adv.*

pon·tif·i·cate (pon tif′ə kit; –kāt), *n., v.,* –**cat·ed, –cat·ing.** —*n.* office or term of office of a pontiff. —*v.* speak pompously.

pon·toon (pon tün′), *n.* **1** a low, flat-bottomed boat. **2** such a boat, or some other floating structure, used as one of the supports of a temporary bridge. **3** a sealed box containing air, used in raising sunken boats, etc. **4** either of the two boat-shaped parts of an airplane, for landing on or taking off from water. [< F < L *ponto* < *pons* bridge]

po·ny (pō′ni), *n., pl.* –**nies. 1 a** kind of small horse. **b** any small horse. **2**

Informal. **a** translation of a book, which a pupil uses instead of his or her own translation. **b** notes or other aids used to help with schoolwork; crib.

pony up, pay a bill or debt; settle up. [< F *poulenet,* < L *pullus* foal]

pony express, system of carrying mail, etc., by men on fast ponies or horses.

pony tail, hairstyle in which the hair is pulled back and fastened close to the head with the ends hanging free, like a tail.

pooch (püch), *n.* dog.

pood (püd), *n.* a Russian weight equal to about 36 pounds. [< Russ., ult. < L *pondus* weight]

poo·dle (pü′dəl), *n.* one of a breed of pet dogs with thick hair. Some poodles have wiry, curly hair; others have long, silky hair. [< G *pudel* < dial. G *pudeln* splash water]

pooh (pü), *interj., n.* exclamation of contempt.

pooh-pooh (pü′pü′), *v.* express contempt for; make light of. —*interj.* exclamation of contempt.

pool[1] (pül), *n.* **1** a small body of still water; small pond. **2** a still, deep place in a stream. **3** tank of water to swim or bathe in. [OE *pōl*]

pool[2] (pül), *n.* **1** game played on a special table with six pockets. The players try to drive balls into the pockets with long sticks called cues. **2** things or money put together by different persons for common advantage. —*v.* put (things or money) together for common advantage. [< F *poule* booty, orig., hen < LL *pulla* chick]

pool·room (pül′rüm′; -rüm′), *n.* **1** room or place in which the game of pool is played. **2** place where people bet on races.

poop[1] (püp), *n.* **1** Also, **poop deck.** deck at the stern above the ordinary deck, often forming the roof of a cabin. **2** stern of a ship. [< OF <Ital. < L *puppis* stern]

poop[2] (püp), *v. Informal.* make or become very tired; exhaust.

poop out, *Informal.* **a** stop; quit. **b** fail to do something: *pooped out on the party.*

poor (pùr), *adj.* **1** having few things or nothing; needy. **2** not good in quality; lacking something needed. **3** needing pity; unfortunate. **4** not favorable: *a poor chance for recovery.* —*n.* **the poor,** persons who are needy; poor people. [< OF < L *pauper.* Doublet of PAUPER.] —**poor′ly,** *adv., adj.* —**poor′ness,** *n.*

pop[1] (pop), *v.,* **popped, pop·ping,** *n., adv.* —*v.* **1** make a short, quick, explosive sound. **2** move, go, or come suddenly or unexpectedly. **3** burst open with a pop. **4** heat (popcorn) until it bursts with a pop. **5** hit a short, high ball over the infield. **6** *Informal.* swallow pills, esp. as a drug habit. —*n.* **1** a short, quick, explosive sound. **2** a nonalcoholic carbonated drink. —*adv.* with a pop; suddenly; unexpectedly.

a pop, *Informal.* apiece; for each: *soda was $1 a pop.*

pop out, hit a fly ball which is caught by a fielder in baseball. [imit.]

pop[2] (pop), *adj.* **1** popular. **2** having to do with pop art. —*n.* pop art.

pop[3] (pop), *n.* **1** father. **2** any older man. [short for *papa*]

pop., 1 popular. **2** population.

pop art, a form of painting and sculpture that uses themes of a popular nature, such as comic strips and advertisements. —**pop artist.**

pop·corn (pop′kôrn′), *n.* **1** kind of Indian corn, the kernels of which burst open and puff out when heated. **2** the white, puffed-out kernels.

Pope, pope (pōp), *n.* the supreme head of the Roman Catholic Church: *the Pope, the last three popes.* [< LL *papa* pope < L, tutor, bishop, < Gk. *pap(p)* as father]

pop·eyed (pop′īd′), *adj.* having bulging, large eyes: *a pop-eyed look of surprise.*

pop fly, high fly ball in baseball that is easy to catch.

pop·gun (pop′gun′), *n.* a toy gun that shoots with a popping sound.

pop·in·jay (pop′in jā), *n.* a vain, over-talkative person; conceited, silly person. [< OF < Sp. < Ar. *babbaghā′* < Pers.]

pop·ish (pōp′ish), *adj.* pertaining to the Roman Catholic Church. —**pop′ish·ly,** *adv.* —**pop′ish·ness,** *n.*

pop·lar (pop′lər), *n.* **1** any of several trees that grow very rapidly and produce light, soft wood, such as the cottonwood and the aspen. **2** wood of such a tree. [< OF *poplier* < L *populus*]

pop·lin (pop′lən), *n.* a ribbed fabric, made of silk and wool, cotton and wool, cotton, or with some synthetic yarns. [< F < Ital. *papalina,* fem., papal, from the papal capital of Avignon]

pop·o·ver (pop′ō′vər), *n.* a very light and hollow muffin.

pop·per (pop′ər), *n.* **1** one that pops. **2** a wire basket or metal pan used for popping popcorn.

pop·py (pop′i), *n., pl.* –**pies. 1** kind of plant with showy red, yellow, or white flowers. **2** the extract from any of these plants. Opium is made from one kind of poppy. **3** the flower. **4** a bright red. [ult. < L *papaver*]

pop·py·cock (pop′i kok′), *n., interj.* nonsense; bosh.

poppy seed, seed of the poppy; used to flavor bread, cakes, etc.

pop·si·cle (pop′sə kəl), *n.* ice cream or fruit-flavored ice frozen on a stick. [< *Popsicle,* Trademark]

pop·u·lace (pop′yə lis), *n.* the common people. [< F < Ital. *popolaccio,* ult. < L *populus* people]

pop·u·lar (pop′yə lər), *adj.* **1** liked by most people: *a popular song.* **2** of the people; by the people; representing the people: *the United States has a popular government.* **3** widespread among many people; common. **4** suited to or intended for ordinary people: *popular prices.* [< L, < *populus* people] —**pop′u·lar·ly,** *adv.*

pop·u·lar·i·ty (pop′yə lar′ə ti), *n.* a being liked generally.

pop·u·lar·ize (pop′yə lər īz), *v.,* **–ized, –iz·ing.** make popular. —**pop′u·lar·i·za′tion,** *n.* —**pop′u·lar·iz′er,** *n.*

popular vote, the vote of the entire electorate thought of as including all the people.

pop·u·late (pop′yə lāt), *v.,* **–lat·ed, –lat·ing. 1** inhabit: *the city was densely populated.* **2** furnish with inhabitants: *hobbits populated the woods.* [< Med.L *populatus,* ult. < L *populus* people] —**pop′u·la′tor,** *n.*

pop·u·la·tion (pop′yə lā′shən), *n.* **1** people of a city or a country. **2** the number of people. **3** part of the inhabitants distinguished in any way from the rest: *the infant population.* **4** act or process of furnishing with inhabitants.

pop·u·lism (pop′yə liz əm), *n.* **1** belief that politics should be concerned with the needs and hopes of ordinary people, as opposed to the powerful. **2** political advocacy of that belief.

pop·u·list (pop′yə list), *n.* **1** supporter or advocate of populism. [< *Populist*] **2 Populist.** member of a political party formed in the United States in 1891 that advocated government control of the railroads, etc. [< L *populus* people + E *–ist*] —**Pop′u·lism,** *n.* —**Pop′u·lis′tic, pop′u·lis′tic,** *adj.*

pop·u·lous (pop′yə ləs), *adj.* full of people; having many people per square mile. —**pop′u·lous·ly,** *adv.* —**pop′u·lous·ness,** *n.*

pop-up (pop′up′), *n.* **1** a high fly ball, in baseball. **2** illustration mounted in a book or card that pops up, becoming three-dimensional when the book or card is opened. —*adj.* of or having to do with something that pops up.

por·ce·lain (pôr′sə lin, pōr′–; pôrs′lin, pōrs′–), *n.* very fine earthenware; china. [< F < Ital. *porcellana* a kind of shell]

porch (pôrch; pōrch), *n.* **1** a covered entrance to a building. **2** veranda. [< OF < L *porticus.* Doublet of PORTICO.]

por·cine (pôr′sīn; –sin), *adj.* **1** of pigs or hogs. **2** like or characteristic of pigs or hogs. [< L, < *porcus* pig]

por·cu·pine (pôr′kyə pīn), *n.* rodent covered with spines or quills. [< OF *porcespin,* ult. < L *porcus* pig + *spina* thorn]

pore¹ (pôr), *v.,* **pored, por·ing. 1** study long and steadily: *he would rather pore over a book than play.* **2** meditate or ponder intently. —**por′er,** *n.*

pore² (pôr; pōr), *n.* a very small opening. Sweat comes through the pores in the skin. [< F < L <Gk. *poros,* lit., passage]

por·gy (pôr′gi), *n., pl.* **–gies** or (*esp. collectively*) **–gy.** any of various saltwater food fishes, such as the scup and the sea bream.

pork (pôrk; pōrk), *n.* **1** meat of a pig or hog used for food. **2** money supplied

by federal or state appropriations, taxes, etc., spent to confer local benefits for political reasons. [< OF < L *porcus* pig] —**pork′like′,** *adj.*

pork barrel, =pork (def. 2).

pork·er (pôr′kər; pōr′–), *n.* pig, esp. one fattened to eat.

pork·y (pôr′ki; pōr′–), *adj.* of or like pork; fat.

porn (pôrn), *n. Informal.* =pornography. —*adj.* =pornographic.

por·no (pôr′nō), *n. Informal.* =pornography. —*adj.* =pornographic.

por·no·graph·ic (pôr′nə graf′ik), *adj.* of or having to do with pornography; obscene.

por·nog·ra·phy (pôr nog′rə fi), *n.* obscene writings or pictures. [ult. < Gk. *porne* harlot + *–graphos* writing about]

po·rous (pô′rəs; pō′–), *adj.* full of pores or tiny holes; permeable by water, air, etc. Cloth, blotting paper, and ordinary flowerpots are porous. —**po·ros′i·ty, po′rous·ness,** *n.* —**po′rous·ly,** *adv.*

por·phy·ry (pôr′fə ri), *n., pl.* **–ries.** a hard, red or purplish rock of Egypt containing white crystals. [< F, ult. < Gk. *porphyra* purple dye of shellfish] —**por′phy·rit′ic,** *adj.*

por·poise (pôr′pəs), *n., pl.* **–pois·es** or (*esp. collectively*) **–poise. 1** a sea animal from five to eight feet long, somewhat like a small whale. Porpoises eat fish. **2** any of several other small sea animals, as the common dolphin. [< OF *porpeis,* ult. < L *porcus* hog + *piscis* fish]

por·ridge (pôr′ij; por′–), *n.* food made of oatmeal or other cereal boiled in water or milk. [var. of *pottage*]

por·rin·ger (pôr′in jər; por′–), *n.* a small dish from which soup, porridge, bread and milk, etc., can be eaten.

port¹ (pôrt; pōrt), *n.* **1** place where ships and boats can be sheltered from storms; harbor. **2** place where ships and boats can load and unload; city or town with a harbor. **3** port of entry. [< L *portus*]

port² (pôrt; pōrt), *n.* =porthole. [< L *porta* gate]

port³ (pôrt; pōrt), *n.* the left side of a ship, when facing the bow. —*adj.* on the left side of a ship. —*v.* turn or shift to the left side.

port⁴ (pôrt; pōrt), *n.* way of holding one's head and body; bearing. [< F < L *portare* carry]

port⁵ (pôrt; pōrt), *n.* a strong, sweet wine that is dark red or tawny. [from *Oporto,* Portuguese city]

Port., Portugal; Portuguese.

port·a·ble (pôr′tə bəl; pōr′–), *adj.* capable of being carried; easily carried. —**port′a·bil′i·ty,** *n.*

por·tage (pôr′tij; pōr′–), *n.* **1** a carrying of boats, provisions, etc., overland from one river, lake, etc., to another. **2** place over which this is done. **3** cost of carrying. —*v.* carry (boats, goods, etc.) overland from one river or lake to another. [< OF < *porter* to carry]

por·tal (pôr′təl; pōr′–), *n.* door, gate, or entrance, usually an imposing one. [< Med.L, < L *porta* gate]

portal vein, large vein carrying blood to the liver from other organs.

Port-au-Prince (pôrt′ō prins′; pōrt′–), *n.* seaport and capital of Haiti.

port·cul·lis (pôrt kul′is; pōrt–), *n.* a strong gate or grating of iron sliding up and down in grooves, used to close the gateway of an ancient castle or fortress. [< OF *porte coleice* sliding gate, ult. < L *porta* gate + *colare* filter through]

por·tend (pôr tend′; pōr–), *v.* indicate beforehand; be a portent of: *black clouds portend a storm.* [< L, < *por–* before + *tendere* extend]

por·tent (pôr′tent; pōr′–), *n.* **1** a warning of coming evil; sign; omen. **2** ominous or fateful significance.

por·ten·tous (pôr ten′təs; pōr–), *adj.* **1** indicating evil to come; ominous; threatening. **2** amazing; extraordinary. —**por·ten′tous·ly,** *adv.* —**por·ten′tous·ness,** *n.*

por·ter¹ (pôr′tər; pōr′–), *n.* person employed to carry burdens or baggage. [< OF, ult. < L *portare* carry]

por·ter² (pôr′tər; pōr′–), *n.* **1** doorkeeper; gatekeeper. **2** =janitor. [< OF < LL, < L *porta* gate]

por·ter³ (pôr′tər; pōr′–), *n.* a heavy, dark-brown beer. [short for *porter's ale* (i.e., ale for a *porter¹*)]

por·ter·house (pôr′tər hous′; pōr′–), or **porterhouse steak,** *n.* a choice beefsteak containing the tenderloin. [supposedly so called because made popular about 1814 by the keeper of a New York porterhouse (place where porter and other liquors were sold)]

port·fo·li·o (pôrt fō′li ō; pōrt–), *n., pl.* **–li·os. 1** brief case. **2** position and duties of a cabinet member or a minister of state. [< Ital. *portafoglio,* ult. < L *portare* carry + *folium* sheet, leaf]

port·hole (pôrt′hōl′; pōrt′–), *n.* **1** an opening in a ship's side to let in light and air. **2** opening through which to shoot, as in a wall, or side of a ship. Also, **port.**

por·ti·co (pôr′tə kō; pōr′–), *n., pl.* **–coes, –cos.** roof supported by columns, forming a porch or a covered walk. [< Ital. < L *porticus.* Doublet of PORCH.] —**por′ti·coed,** *adj.*

por·tion (pôr′shən; pōr′–), *n.* **1** part; share. **2** quantity of food served for one person. **3** the part of an estate that goes to an heir; property inherited. **4** one's lot; fate. —*v.* **1** divide into parts or shares. **2** give (a thing to a person) as share; give a portion, inheritance, etc., to. [< OF < L *portio*] —**por′tion·er,** *n.* —**por′tion·less,** *adj.*

Portland cement, kind of cement made by burning limestone and clay in a kiln, used in making mortar and concrete.

port·ly (pôrt′li; pōrt′–), *adj.,* **–li·er, –li·est. 1** stout; corpulent. **2** stately; dignified. [< *port⁴*] —**port′li·ness,** *n.*

por·trait (pôr′trit; –trāt; pōr′–), *n.* **1** picture of a person, esp. of the face. **2** picture in words; description. [< F, orig. pp. of *portraire* portray] —**por′trait·ist**, *n.*

por·trai·ture (pôr′tri chər; pōr′–), *n.* **1** act of portraying. **2** portrait.

por·tray (pôr trā′; pōr–), *v.* **1** picture in words; describe. **2** make a picture of. **3** represent on the stage. [< OF < L, < *pro-* forth + *trahere* draw] —**por·tray′a·ble**, *adj.* —**por·tray′al**, *n.* —**por·tray′er**, *n.*

Por·tu·gal (pôr′chə gəl; pōr′–), *n.* country in SW Europe, just W of Spain.

Por·tu·guese (pôr′chə gēz′; –gēs′; pōr′–), *n., pl.* **–guese**, *adj.* —*n.* **1** native or inhabitant of Portugal. **2** language of Portugal. Portuguese is also the chief language of Brazil. —*adj.* of or pertaining to Portugal, its people, or their language.

Portuguese man-of-war, *pl.* **Portuguese men-of-war**. large hydrozoan, distinguished by its brilliant coloring and strong sting.

por·tu·lac·a (pôr′chə lak′ə; pōr′–), *n.* a low-growing plant with thick, fleshy leaves and variously colored flowers. [< L, purslane]

pos., **1** positive. **2** possessive.

pose (pōz), *n., v.,* **posed, pos·ing.** —*n.* **1** position of the body; way of holding the body. **2** attitude assumed for effect; pretense; affectation: *she takes the pose of being an invalid when really she is well and strong.* —*v.* **1** hold a position: *he posed an hour for his portrait.* **2** put in a certain position; put: *the artist posed him before painting his picture.* **3** put on an attitude for effect; make a false pretense: *he posed as a rich man though he owed more than he owned.* **4** put forward for discussion; state: *pose a question.* [< F *poser* < LL *pausare* pause < L *pausa* a pause; in Romance lang. infl. by stem *pos–* of L *ponere* place (from meaning "cause to pause, set down") and influence spread to many compounds, e.g., *compose, dispose, oppose*]

pos·er[1] (pōz′ər), *n.* person who poses.

pos·er[2] (pōz′ər), *n.* a very puzzling problem.

po·seur (pō zèr′), *n.* an affected person; one who poses to impress others. [< F, < *poser* pose]

posh (posh), *adj.* elegant; luxurious. [*uncert.*]

pos·it (poz′it), *v.* lay down or assume as a fact or principle; affirm; postulate. [< L *positus,* pp. of *ponere* set, place]

po·si·tion (pə zish′ən), *n.* **1** place where a thing or person is. **2** way of being placed: *sit in a more comfortable position.* **3** proper place: *the army maneuvered for position before attacking.* **4** job. **5** rank; standing, esp. high standing. **6** way of thinking; set of opinions: *what is your position on this question?* —*v.* **1** place in a particular spot or position. **2** locate; find the position of. **3** place (a product)

to sell to a particular market or type of buyer. [< L *positio* < *ponere* to set] —**po·si′tion·al**, *adj.*

pos·i·tive (poz′ə tiv), *adj.* **1** admitting of no question; without doubt; sure. **2** too sure; too confident: *her positive manner annoys people.* **3** definite; emphatic. **4** that can be thought of as real and present. Light is a positive thing; darkness is only the absence of light. **5** that definitely does something or adds something; practical: *don't just make criticisms; give us some positive help.* **6** counting up from zero; plus: *five above zero is a positive quantity.* **7** of the kind of electricity produced by rubbing glass with silk; lacking electrons. —*n.* **1** a positive degree, quantity, quality, or characteristic. **2** plate in a battery from which the current flows into the wire. **3** the simple form of an adjective or adverb, as distinct from the comparative and superlative. *Fast* is the positive; *faster* is the comparative; *fastest* is the superlative. [< L *positivus,* ult. < *ponere* to set] —**pos′i·tive·ly**, *adv.* —**pos′i·tive·ness**, *n.*

pos·i·tron (poz′ə tron), *n.* particle having the same magnitude of mass and charge as an electron, but exhibiting a positive charge; positive electron.

poss., **1** possession. **2** possessive.

pos·se (pos′ē), *n.* group of men summoned by a sheriff to help him: *the posse pursued the thief.* [< Med.L, power, < L, v., be able]

pos·sess (pə zes′), *v.* **1** own; have. **2** hold as property; hold; occupy. **3** control; influence strongly. **4** control by an evil spirit: *he fought like one possessed.* [< OF, < *possession* < L, < *possidere* possess] —**pos·sessed′**, *adj.* —**pos·ses′sor**, *n.* —**pos·ses′sor·ship**, *n.*

pos·ses·sion (pə zesh′ən), *n.* **1** a possessing; holding. **2** ownership. **3** thing possessed; property. **4** territory under the rule of a country: *Puerto Rico is a possession of the United States.* **5** domination by a particular feeling, idea, etc. **6** self-control.

pos·ses·sive (pə zes′iv), *adj.* **1** of possession. **2** showing possession. *My, your, his,* and *our* are possessive forms of the pronouns. **3** desirous of ownership: *a possessive nature.* **4** asserting or claiming ownership: *a possessive manner.* —*n.* **1** the possessive case. **2** possessive form of a word. In "the boy's books," *boy's* is a possessive. —**pos·ses′sive·ly**, *adv.* —**pos·ses′sive·ness**, *n.*

pos·si·bil·i·ty (pos′ə bil′ə ti), *n., pl.* **–ties.** **1** a being possible: *there is a possibility that the train may be late.* **2** a possible thing or person.

pos·si·ble (pos′ə bəl), *adj.* **1** that can be; that can be done; that can happen: *come if possible.* **2** that can be true or a fact: *it is possible that he went.* **3** that can be done, chosen, etc., properly: *the only possible candidate.* [< L, < *posse* be able]

pos·si·bly (pos′ə bli), *adv.* **1** by any possibility; no matter what happens: *I cannot possibly go.* **2** perhaps: *possibly you are right.*

pos·sum (pos′əm), *n.* =opossum.

play possum, put on a false appearance; pretend.

post[1] (pōst), *n.* **1** piece of timber, metal, or the like, set upright, usually as a support: *posts of a door or bed.* **2** post, line, etc., where a race starts or ends. —*v.* **1** fasten (a notice) up in a place where it can easily be seen. **2** make known by, or as if by, a posted notice; make public: *post a reward.* **3** protect (land) from trespassers by putting up notices. **4** put (a name) in a list that is published or posted up. **5** cover (a wall, etc.) with notices or bills. [< L *postis*]

post[2] (pōst), *n.* **1** place where a soldier, police officer, etc., is stationed. **2** military station; fort. **3** job or position. **4** a trading station, esp. in unsettled country. —*v.* **1** station at a post; place troops at a particular point: *post guards at the door.* **2** deposit: *post bail.* **3** appoint to a military or diplomatic post. [< F < Ital. < L *positus* stationed] —**post′ed**, *adj.*

post[3] (pōst), *n.* **1** an established system for carrying letters, papers, packages, etc.; the mail. **2** one of a series of fixed stations along a route for furnishing men and horses to carry letters, etc., and supply service to travelers. —*v.* **1** send by post; mail. **2** travel with speed; hasten. **3** move the body up and down, in the saddle, in rhythm with a horse's trot. **4** inform. —*adv.* by post; speedily. [< F < Ital. < L *posita,* fem., placed] —**post′ed**, *adj.*

post–, *prefix.* after, as in *postgraduate, postmortem, postscript.* [< L, < *post,* prep., adv., after, behind]

post·age (pōs′tij), *n.* amount paid on anything sent by mail.

postage meter, machine that stamps a letter with postage and a postmark.

postage stamp, an official stamp placed on mail to show that postage has been paid.

post·al (pōs′təl), *adj.* having to do with mail and post offices. —*n.* Also, **postal card.** post card.

Postal Service, independent agency of the United States government, responsible for handling mail and passports, selling postage stamps, etc.

post card, **1** a card with a government postage stamp printed on it. **2** any card, esp. one with a picture on one side, for sending a message by mail.

post·date (pōst′dāt′), *v.,* **–dat·ed, –dat·ing.** give a later date than the true date to (a letter, check, etc.)

post·er (pōs′tər), *n.* a large printed sheet or notice put up in some public place.

pos·te·ri·or (pos tir′i ər), *adj.* **1** situated behind; back; rear; hind. **2** later; coming after. [< L, compar. of *posterus* subsequent < *post* after] —**pos·te′ri·or·ly,** *adv.*

pos·ter·i·ty (pos ter′ə ti), *n.* **1** generations of the future. **2** all of a person's descendants. [< L, < *posterus.* See POSTERIOR.]

pos·tern (pōs′tərn; pos′-), *n.* **1** a back door or gate. **2** any small door or gate. —*adj.* **1** of or like a postern. **2** rear; lesser: *the castle had a postern door.* [< OF *posterne,* ult. < L *posterus* behind. See POSTERIOR.]

post·grad·u·ate (pōst graj′ù it), —*n.* student who continues studying in college or at school after graduation. —*adj.* **1** taking a course of study after graduation. **2** of or for postgraduates.

post·haste (pōst′hāst′), *n.* great haste. —*adv.* very speedily; in great haste.

post·hole (pōst′hōl′), *n.* hole in the ground or wall to hold a post.

post horse, horse hired by travelers.

post·hu·mous (pos′chù məs), *adj.* **1** born after the death of the father. **2** published after the death of the author. **3** happening after death. [< LL *posthumus,* var. of L *postumus* last; *h* by confusion with *humus* earth, in sense of "burial"] —**post′hu·mous·ly,** *adv.*

pos·til·ion, pos·til·lion (pōs til′yən; pos–), *n.* man who rides one of the horses drawing a carriage. [< F *postillon*]

post·lude (pōst′lüd), *n.* a concluding musical piece or movement. [< *post–* + (*pre*)*lude*]

post·man (pōst′mən), *n., pl.* –**men.** =letter carrier.

post·mark (pōst′märk′), *n.* an official mark stamped on mail to cancel the postage stamp and record the place and date of mailing. —*v.* stamp with a postmark.

post·mas·ter (pōst′mas′tər; –mäs′–), *n.* person in charge of a post office. —**post′mas′ter·ship,** *n.*

postmaster general, *pl.* **postmasters general.** person at the head of the postal system of a country.

post·me·rid·i·an (pōst′mə rid′i ən), *adj.* occurring after noon; of or pertaining to the afternoon.

post me·rid·i·em (pōst mə rid′i əm), after noon. *Abbrev.:* p.m., P.M. [< L, after midday]

post·mis·tress (pōst′mis′tris), *n.* woman in charge of a post office.

post·mod·ern (post′mod′ərn), *adj.* **1** rejecting twentieth-century modernism, in art and architecture. **2** rejecting or reevaluating modern culture, society, or politics, etc. —**post′-mod′ern·ism,** *n.* —**post′-mod′ern·ist,** *n., adj.*

post·mor·tem (pōst môr′təm), *adj.* after death. —*n.* =autopsy. [< L, after death]

post·na·tal (pōst nā′təl), *adj.* after birth.

post office, 1 place where mail is handled and postage stamps are sold. **2** Often, **Post Office.** =Postal Service.

post·paid (pōst′pād′), *adj.* with the postage paid for.

post·par·tum (post pär′təm), *adj.* occurring after childbirth. [< L *post* after + *partum* giving birth]

post·pone (pōst pōn′), *v.,* –**poned,** –**pon·ing.** put off till later; put off to a later time; delay. [< L, < *post–* after + *ponere* put] —**post·pon′a·ble,** *adj.* —**post·pone′ment,** *n.* —**post·pon′er,** *n.*

post·pran·di·al (pōst pran′di əl), *adj.* after-dinner: *postprandial speeches.* [< POST– + L *prandium* lunch]

post·rid·er (pōst′rīd′ ər), *n.* man who carried mail on horseback.

post road, 1 road or route over which mail was carried. **2** road with stations which furnished horses.

post·script (pōst′skript), *n.* addition to a letter, written after the writer's name has been signed. [< L *postscriptum,* orig. neut. pp., < *post–* after + *scribere* write] —**post′script·al,** *adj.*

post·trau·mat·ic (post′trô mat´ik), *adj.* occurring after a wound, injury, or shock.

post-traumatic stress disorder, psychiatric disorder caused by experiencing or witnessing life-threatening events, such as warfare, violent assault, or terrorist attack.

pos·tu·late (*n.* pos′chə lit; *v.* pos′chə lāt), *n., v.,* –**lat·ed,** –**lat·ing.** —*n.* a fundamental principle; necessary condition: *one postulate of geometry is that a straight line may be drawn between any two points.* —*v.* **1** assume without proof as a basis of reasoning; take for granted. **2** require; demand; claim. [< L *postulatum,* orig. neut. pp., demanded] —**pos′tu·la′tion,** *n.* —**pos′tu·la′tor,** *n.*

pos·ture (pos′chər), *n., v.,* –**tured,** –**tur·ing.** —*n.* **1** position of the body; way of holding the body: *good posture is important for health.* **2** condition; situation; state. —*v.* **1** take a certain posture. **2** put in a certain posture. [< F < L *positura* < *ponere* to place] —**pos′tur·er, pos′tur·ist,** *n.*

post·war (pōst′wôr′), *adj.* after the war.

po·sy (pō′zi), *n., pl.* –**sies. 1** flower. **2** bunch of flowers; bouquet. [var. of *poesy*]

pot (pot), *n., v.,* **pot·ted, pot·ting.** —*n.* **1** a round, deep container made of metal or earthenware. There are many different kinds of pots. **2** pot and what is in it; amount a pot can hold. **3** basket used to catch fish, lobsters, etc. **4** all the money bet at one time. **5** *Informal.* marijuana. —*v.* put into a pot.

go to pot, deteriorate; go to ruin. [OE *pott*]

po·ta·ble (pō′tə bəl), *adj.* fit for drinking. —*n.* Usually, **potables.** anything drinkable. [< LL, < L *potare* to drink] —**po′ta·bil′i·ty,** *n.*

pot·ash (pot′ash′), *n.* **1** any of several substances made from wood ashes and used in soap, fertilizers, etc., mainly impure potassium carbonate. **2** =potassium. [< Du. *potasch,* lit., pot ash]

po·tas·si·um (pə tas′i əm), *n.* a soft, silver-white metallic element, K, occurring in nature only in compounds. [< NL < E *potash*]

potassium nitrate, a colorless, crystalline substance, KNO_3, used as an oxidizing agent, in gunpowder, explosives, etc.; niter; saltpeter.

po·ta·to (pə tā′tō), *n., pl.* –**toes. 1** a starchy tuber that is a main item in the food of many countries; Irish potato. **2** plant producing these tubers, and having trumpet-shaped flowers that are white or white with blue stripes. **3** =sweet potato. [< Sp. *patata* < Haitian]

potato beetle or **bug,** beetle with black and yellow stripes that damages potato plants.

potato chip, a thin slice of raw potato fried in deep fat.

pot·bel·ly (pot′bel′i), *n., pl.* –**lies.** a distended or protuberant belly. —**pot′bel′-lied,** *adj.*

pot·boil·er (pot′boil′ər), *n.* work of literature or art produced merely to make a living.

pot cheese, variety of cottage cheese.

po·tent (pō′tənt), *adj.* powerful; having great power: *a potent remedy for a disease, his good deeds had potent effects on his comrades.* [< L *potens*] —**po′ten·cy, po′tence, po′tent·ness,** *n.* —**po′tent·ly,** *adv.*

po·ten·tate (pō′tən tāt), *n.* **1** person having great power. **2** king, queen, emperor, or other ruler.

po·ten·tial (pə ten′shəl), *adj.* **1** possible as opposed to actual; capable of coming into being or action. **2** noting energy which is due to position and not to motion. A suspended weight has potential energy. —*n.* **1** something potential; possibility. **2** amount of electromotive force needed to electrify a point; voltage. A high potential is necessary to transmit an electric current over a long distance. [< LL, ult. < L *potens* potent] —**po·ten′ti·al′i·ty,** *n.* —**po·ten′tial·ly,** *adv.*

potential energy, energy because of position or composition, as opposed to actual motion. A raised weight has potential energy.

pot·hole (pot′hōl′), **1** round hole or cavity in paving on a road: *a pothole deep enough to break an axel.* **2** deep, round hole in a river bed. **3** round entrance in the ground to a cave directly below.

po·tion (pō′shən), *n.* a drink, esp. one that is used as a medicine or poison, or in magic. [< L *potio.* Doublet of POISON.]

pot·luck (pot′luk′), *n.* whatever food happens to be ready or on hand for a meal.

pot·pie (pot′pī′), *n.* **1** a baked meat pie. **2** stew with dumplings.

pot·pour·ri (pō′pù rē′; pot pür′i), *n.* **1** a musical or literary medley. **2** a fragrant mixture of dried flower petals and spices. [< F, trans. of Sp. *olla podrida* rotten pot < L *olla* pot, VL *putrita,* fem. pp. of *putrire* to rot < L *puter* soft, rotten]

pot·sherd (pot'shėrd´), *n.* a broken piece of earthenware. [< *pot* + *sherd,* var. of *shard*]

pot shot, 1 shot taken at game merely to provide a meal, with little regard to the rules of sport. **2** quick shot at an animal or person from close range without careful aim. **3** Often **potshots.** *Fig.* unfocused or random criticism.

pot·tage (pot'ij), *n.* a thick soup of vegetables and meat. [< OF *potage* < *pot* pot < Gmc.]

pot·ted (pot'id), *adj.* **1** put into a pot. **2** cooked and preserved in pots or cans.

pot·ter (pot'ər), *n.* person who makes pots, dishes, vases, etc., out of clay. [OE *pottere* < *pott* pot]

potter's field, piece of ground used for burying people who have no friends or money.

potter's wheel, a rotating horizontal disk upon which clay is molded into dishes, etc.

pot·ter·y (pot'ər i), *n., pl.* **-ter·ies. 1** pots, dishes, vases, etc., made from clay and hardened by heat. **2** art or business of making them. **3** place where they are made.

pot·ty (pot'ē), *n. Informal.* toilet, esp. in children's talk.

pouch (pouch), *n.* **1** bag; sack: *a messenger's pouch.* **2** a baglike fold of skin: *a kangaroo carries its young in a pouch.* —*v.* **1** put into a pouch. **2** form a pouch. [< OF *pouche, poche* < Gmc., akin to POKE[2]] —**pouched,** *adj.*

poul·ter·er (pōl'tər ər), *n.* dealer in poultry.

poul·tice (pōl'tis), *n., v.,* **-ticed, -tic·ing.** —*n.* a soft, moist mass of mustard, herbs, etc., applied to the body as a medicine. —*v.* put a poultice on. [ult. < L *pultes,* pl. of *puls* mush]

poul·try (pōl'tri), *n.* chickens, turkeys, geese, ducks, etc. [< OF, < *poulet* PULLET]

pounce (pouns), *v.,* **pounced, pounc·ing.** *n.* —*v.* **1** come down with a rush and seize. **2** dash, come, or jump suddenly. —*n.* a sudden swoop or pouncing.

pound[1] (pound), *n., pl.* **pounds** or (*esp. collectively*) **pound. 1** unit of weight. 1 pound avoirdupois = 16 ounces. 1 pound troy = 12 ounces. **2** unit of money of Great Britain. [< L *pondo,* orig., *libra pondo* a pound by weight]

pound[2] (pound), *v.* **1** hit hard again and again; hit heavily: *he pounded the door with his fist.* **2** beat hard; throb: *after running fast you can feel your heart pound.* **3** make into a powder or pulp by pounding. —*n.* **1** act of pounding. **2** a heavy or forcible blow. [OE *pūnian*] —**pound´er,** *n.*

pound[3] (pound), *n.* **1** an enclosed place in which to keep stray animals. **2** enclosure for keeping, confining, or trapping ani-

mals. **3** place of confinement. —*v.* shut up in a pound; confine. [OE *pund-*]

pound·age (poun'dij), *n.* weight, in pounds.

pound·al (poun'dəl), *n.* amount of force that, acting for one second on a mass of one pound, gives it a velocity of one foot per second. 1 poundal = 13,825 dynes.

pound cake, cake made with a pound of sugar and a pound of butter for each pound of flour, and plenty of eggs.

pound-fool·ish (pound'fül'ish), *adj.* foolish or careless in regard to large amounts of money.

pour (pôr; pōr), *v.* flow in a steady stream. —*n.* **1** a pouring. **2** a heavy rain. [ME *poure(n)*] —**pour´er,** *n.* —**pour´ing·ly,** *adv.*

pout (pout), *v.* thrust or push out the lips, as a displeased or sulky child does. —*n.* a pushing out of the lips when displeased or sulky. (ME *poute(n)*) —**pout´er,** *n.* —**pout´ing·ly,** *adv.*

pout·y (pout'i), *adj.* inclined to pout; peevish.

pov·er·ty (pov'ər ti), *n.* **1** condition of being poor: *their tattered clothing indicated their great poverty.* **2** lack of what is needed: *poverty of the soil. Fig.* **3** a small amount: *poverty of ideas.* [< OF < L *paupertas* < *pauper* poor]

pov·er·ty-strick·en (pov'ər ti strik´ən), *adj.* extremely poor.

POW, prisoner of war.

pow·der (pou'dər), *n.* **1** a solid reduced to dust by pounding, crushing, or grinding. **2** some special kind of powder: *face powder.* **3** gunpowder. —*v.* **1** make into powder. **2** become powder. **3** sprinkle or cover with powder. **4** apply powder (to the face, etc.). **5** sprinkle: *ground powdered with snow.* [< OF *poudre* < L *pulvis* dust] —**pow´der·er,** *n.* —**pow´der·y,** *adj.*

powder blue, a light blue.

powder horn, flask for carrying gunpowder, made of an animal's horn.

powder keg, 1 small barrel for storing or transporting gun powder. **2** *Fig.* someone or something likely to explode without warning.

powder puff, a soft puff or pad for applying powder to the skin.

powder room, women's lavatory, esp. one with a dressing table, mirrors, etc.

pow·er (pou'ər), *n.* **1** strength; might; force: *medicine of great healing power.* **2** ability to do or act: *her power of concentration.* **3** control; authority; influence; right: *the power of the mayor's office.* **4** person, thing, body, or nation having influence. **5** energy or force that can do work: *flowing water produced power for the mills.* **6** product of a number multiplied by itself. 16 is the 4th power of 2. **7** capacity of an instrument to magnify. The higher the power of a microscope the more details you can see.

in power, having control or authority. [ME, n. < AF, v. < OF *poër* < VL *potere* for L *posse* be able] —**pow'ered,** *adj.*

pow·er·boat (pou'ər bōt´), *n.* boat propelled by an engine on board; motorboat.

pow·er·ful (pou'ər fəl), *adj.* **1** having great power or force; mighty; strong. **2** great in number or degree. —**pow'er·ful·ly,** *adv.* —**pow'er·ful·ness,** *n.*

pow·er·house (pou'ər hous´), *n.* **1** building containing boilers, engines, dynamos, etc., for generating power. **2** *Informal. Fig.* **a** energetic, attractive person. **b** very effective or successful group.

pow·er·less (pou'ər lis), *adj.* without power; helpless. —**pow'er·less·ly,** *adv.* —**pow'er·less·ness,** *n.*

power of attorney, a written statement giving one person legal power to act for another.

power plant, 1 =powerhouse (def. 1). **2** motor or engine.

power station, =powerhouse.

pow·wow (pou'wou´), —*n.* **1** an American Indian ceremony, usually accompanied by magic, feasting, and dancing, performed for the cure of disease, success in hunting, etc. **2** council or conference of or with American Indians. **3** any conference or meeting. —*v.* hold a powwow; confer. [< Algonquian]

pox (poks), *n.* any disease that covers the body or parts of the body with sores, such as chicken pox or smallpox. [var. of *pocks,* pl. of POCK]

pp., 1 pages. **2** past participle. **3** pianissimo.

P.P., Parcel Post.

p.p., 1 parcel post. **2** past participle. **3** post-paid.

ppr., p.pr., present participle.

Pr, praseodymium.

Pr., Provençal.

pr., 1 *pl.* **prs.** pair. **2** present. **3** price.

PR, 1 public relations. **2** (*zip code*) Puerto Rico.

P.R., Puerto Rico.

prac·ti·ca·ble (prak'tə kə bəl), *adj.* **1** that can be done; capable of being put into practice: *a practicable idea.* **2** that can be used: *a practicable road.* [< F, < *pratiquer* PRACTICE; infl. by Med.L *practicare* to practice] —**prac'ti·ca·bil'i·ty, prac'ti·ca·ble·ness,** *n.* —**prac'ti·ca·bly,** *adv.*

prac·ti·cal (prak'tə kəl), *adj.* **1** having to do with action or practice rather than thought or theory. **2** fit for actual practice: *a practical scheme.* **3** useful: *a practical suggestion.* **4** having good sense: *a practical mind.* **5** engaged in actual practice or work: *a practical farmer.* **6** being such in effect; virtual: *so damaged as to be a practical loss.* [< earlier *practic* < LL < Gk. *praktikos* < *prassein* do] —**prac'ti·cal'i·ty, prac'ti cal ness,** *n.*

practical joke, trick played on a person to have a laugh at him or her.

prac·ti·cal·ly (prak'tik li), *adv.* **1** really; in effect: *The mayor practically runs the town.* **2** almost; nearly: *Home is practically around the corner.* **3** in a practical way; in a useful way: *plan practically*. **4** by actual practice.

prac·tice (prak'tis), *n., v.,* **-ticed, -tic· ing.** —*n.* **1** action done many times over for skill: *practice develops skill*. **2** skill gained by experience or exercise: *he was out of practice at batting*. **3** action or process of doing or being something: *a plan not workable in actual practice*. **4** the usual way; custom: *the practice of a business to bill monthly*. **5** business of a doctor or lawyer: *Dr. Adams sold his practice*. [< v.] —*v.* **1** do (some act) again and again to learn to do it well: *practice the piano*. **2** do usually; make a custom of: *practice good manners*. **3** follow, observe, or use day after day: *practice moderation in eating*. **4** work at or follow as a profession, act, or occupation. [< OF *practiser,* ult. < LL *practicus* PRACTICAL] —**prac'tic·er,** *n.*

prac·ticed (prak'tist), *adj.* experienced; skilled; expert; proficient.

prac·ti·tion·er (prak tish'ən ər; -tish'nər), *n.* person engaged in the practice of a profession: *a medical practitioner.*

prag·mat·ic (prag mat'ik), **prag·mat·ical** (-ə kəl), *adj.* concerned with practical results or values; of or pertaining to pragmatism: *a pragmatic philosophy.* [< L < Gk. *pragmatikos* efficient, ult. < *prassein* do] —**prag·mat'i·cal·ly,** *adv.* —**prag·mat'i·cal·ness ,** *n.*

prag·ma·tism (prag'mə tiz əm), *n.* philosophy that tests the value and truth of ideas by their practical consequences. —**prag'ma·tist,** *n.*

Prague (präg), *n.* capital of the Czech Republic.

prai·rie (prãr'i), *n.* a large area of level or rolling land with grass but no trees. [< F, ult. < L *pratum* meadow]

prairie chicken, any of several grouse of the prairies of North America.

prairie dog, animal like a woodchuck but smaller. Prairie dogs bark.

prairie schooner, a large covered wagon used by emigrants in crossing the plains of North America before the railroads were built; covered wagon.

prairie wolf, =coyote.

praise (prāz), *n., v.,* **praised, prais·ing.** —*n.* saying that a thing or person is good; words that tell the worth or value of a thing or person. —*v.* **1** express approval or admiration of. **2** worship in words or song: *praise God.*

damn with faint praise, give such unenthusiastic approval that it seems like a condemnation.

sing the praises of, praise openly and enthusiastically. [< OF *preisier,* ult. < L *pretium* price] —**prais'er,** *n.*

praise·wor·thy (prāz'wer′ᵺi), *adj.* worthy of praise; deserving approval. —**praise′wor′thi·ly,** *adv.* —**praise′wor′thi·ness,** *n.*

pra·line (prä'lēn), *n.* a small cake of brown candy made of sugar and nuts, usually pecans or almonds. [< F; invented by the cook of Marshal Duplessis-*Praslin*]

prance (prans; präns), *v.,* **pranced, prancing,** *n.* —*v.* **1** spring about on the hind legs: *horses prance when they feel lively.* **2** move gaily or proudly; swagger. —*n.* a prancing. —**pranc'er,** *n.* —**pranc'ing· ly,** *adv.*

prank (prangk), *n.* piece of mischief; playful trick. —**prank'ish,** *adj.* —**prank'ish·ly,** *adv.* —**prank'ish·ness,** *n.* —**prank'ster,** *n.*

pra·se·o·dym·i·um (prā′zi ō dim'i əm), *n.* a rare metallic element, Pr, of the same group as cerium. [< NL, ult. < Gk. *prasios* leek-green + E (*di*)*dymium,* a rare element, < Gk. *didymos* twin]

prate (prāt), *v.,* **prat·ed, prat·ing,** *n.* —*v.* talk a great deal in a foolish way. —*n.* empty or foolish talk. [cf. MDu., MLG *praten*] —**prat'er,** *n.* —**prat'ing·ly,** *adv.*

prat·tle (prat'əl), *v.,* **-tled, -tling,** *n.* —*v.* **1** talk as a child does; tell freely and carelessly. **2** talk or tell in a foolish way. **3** sound like baby talk; babble. —*n.* **1** simple, artless talk. **2** baby talk; foolish talk. **3** a sound like baby talk; babble. [< *prate*] —**prat'tler,** *n.* —**prat'tling·ly,** *adv.*

prawn (prôn), *n.* any of several edible shellfish much like shrimp but larger. [ME *prane*]

pray (prā), *v.* **1** speak to God in worship; offer worship. **2** ask earnestly: *pray God for help or to help.* **3** bring or get by praying. [< OF < L *precari* < *prex* prayer] —**pray'er,** *n.*

prayer (prãr), *n.* **1** act of praying. **2** thing prayed for. **3** form of words to be used in praying. **4** form of worship. **5** an earnest or humble request. [< OF *preiere,* ult. < L *prex* prayer] —**prayer'ful,** *adj.* —**prayer'ful·ly,** *adv.* —**prayer'fulness,** *n.*

praying mantis, =mantis.

pre-, *prefix.* before in place, time, order, or rank, as in *prepay, prevision, prewar.* [< L *prae-*]

preach (prēch), *v.* **1** speak publicly on a religious subject; deliver (a sermon). **2** make known by preaching; proclaim: *preach the Gospel.* **3** give earnest advice, sometimes annoying or meddlesome advice. [< OF < L *praedicare* declare, preach. Doublet of PREDICATE.] —**preach'ing,** *n.* —**preach'ing·ly,** *adv.*

preach·er (prēch'ər), *n.* person who preaches; clergyman; minister.

pre·am·ble (prē'am ′bəl), *n.* a preliminary statement; introduction to a speech or a writing. [< F < Med.L *praeambulum,* orig. neut. adj., walking before, ult. < L *prae-* before + *ambulare* to walk]

pre·ar·range (prē′ə rānj′), *v.,* **-ranged, -rang·ing.** arrange beforehand. —**pre′ar·range′ment,** *n.*

Pre-Cam·bri·an or **Pre·cam·bri·an** (prē′kam'brē ən), *n.* earliest geological era. —*adj.* of this period or its rocks.

pre·can·cer·ous (prē′kan'sər əs), *adj.* of or showing a condition that could become cancerous: *precancerous changes in some cells.*

pre·car·i·ous (pri kãr'i əs), *adj.* **1** dependent on the will or pleasure of another. **2** not safe or secure; uncertain; dangerous; risky: *a soldier leads a precarious life.* [< L *precarius,* orig., obtainable by entreaty, ult. < *prex* prayer] —**pre·car'ious·ly,** *adv.* —**pre·car'i·ous·ness,** *n.*

pre·cau·tion (pri kô'shən), *n.* **1** a taking care beforehand: *proper precaution is prudent.* **2** care taken beforehand; thing done beforehand to ward off evil or secure good results. —**pre·cau'tionar′y, pre·cau'tion·al,** *adj.*

pre·cede (prē sēd′), *v.,* **-ced·ed, -ceding. 1** go before; come before: *Herbert Hoover preceded Franklin Roosevelt as President.* **2** be higher than in rank or importance: *a major precedes a captain.* [< L, < *prae-* before + *cedere* go]

prec·e·dence (pres'ə dəns; pri sēd'əns), **prec·e·den·cy** (-dən si), *n., pl.* **-denc·es; -den·cies. 1** act or fact of preceding. **2** higher position or rank; greater importance: *take precedence over all others.* **3** right to precede others in ceremonies or social affairs; social superiority.

prec·e·dent (*n.* pres'ə dənt; *adj.* pri sēd′ənt, pres'ə dənt), *n.* case that may serve as an example or reason for a later case. —*adj.* preceding. [< L *praecedens.* See PRECEDE.] —**prec′e·den'tial,** *adj.* —**pre′ced·ent·ly,** *adv.*

pre·ced·ing (prē sēd'ing), *adj.* going before; coming before; previous.

pre·cept (prē'sept), *n.* rule of action or behavior; maxim. [< L *praeceptum,* orig. neut. pp., enjoined, anticipated < *prae-* before + *capere* take]

pre·ces·sion (prē sesh'ən), *n.* act, fact, or condition of going first; precedence. —**pre·ces'sion·al,** *adj.*

pre·cinct (prē'singkt), *n.* **1** district within certain boundaries, for governmental, administrative, or other purposes: *an election precinct, a police precinct.* **2** space within a boundary: *the school precincts.* **3** Often, **precincts.** boundary; limit. [< Med.L *praecinctum,* orig. neut. pp., enclosed < *prae-* before + *cingere* gird]

pre·cious (presh'əs), *adj.* **1** worth much; valuable. Gold, platinum, and silver are often called the precious metals. **2** much loved; dear. **3** too nice; overrefined. —*adv. Informal.* very: *precious little time to talk.* —*n.* darling. [< OF < L *pretiosus* < *pretium* value] —**pre'cious·ly,** *adv.* —**pre'cious·ness,** *n.*

prec·i·pice (pres'ə pis), *n.* a very steep cliff; almost vertical slope. [< F < L, < *praeceps* steep, lit. headlong, < *prae-* first + *caput* head]

pre·cip·i·tant (pri sip'ə tənt), *adj.* **1** very sudden or abrupt. **2** acting in a hasty or rash manner. **3** falling or rushing headlong. —*n.* substance that causes another substance in solution in a liquid to be deposited in solid form. —**pre·cip'itance, pre·cip'i·tan·cy,** *n.* —**pre·cip'itant·ly,** *adv.*

pre·cip·i·tate (*v.* pri sip′ə tāt; *adj., n.* pri sip′ə tāt, –tit), *v.,* **–tat·ed, –tat·ing,** *adj., n.* —*v.* **1** hasten the beginning of; bring about suddenly: *precipitate a war.* **2** throw headlong; hurl. **3** separate (a substance) out from a solution as a solid. **4 a** condense from vapor in the form of rain, dew, etc. **b** be condensed in this way. —*adj.* **1** very hurried; sudden: *a precipitate drop in the temperature.* **2** with great haste and force; plunging or rushing; hasty; rash. **3** headlong. —*n.* **1** substance, usually crystalline, separated out from a solution as a solid. **2** condensed moisture, usually in the form of rain or snow. [< L, < *praeceps* headlong. See PRECIPICE.] —**pre·cip′i·tate·ly,** *adv.* —**pre·cip′i·tate·ness**, *n.* —**pre·cip′i·ta′·tive,** *adj.* —**pre·cip′i·ta′tor,** *n.*

pre·cip·i·ta·tion (pri sip′ə tā′shən), *n.* **1** act or state of precipitating; throwing down or falling headlong. **2** a sudden bringing on: *precipitation of a quarrel without warning.* **3** unwise or rash rapidity; sudden haste. **4** the depositing of moisture in the form of rain, dew, or snow. **5** the separating out of a substance from a solution as a solid.

pre·cip·i·tous (pri sip′ə təs), *adj.* **1** like a precipice; very steep: *precipitous cliffs.* **2** hasty; rash. —**pre·cip′i·tous·ly,** *adv.* —**pre·cip′i·tous·ness**, *n.*

pre·cise (pri sīs′), *adj.* **1** exact; accurate; definite: *the precise sum was 34½ cents.* **2** careful. **3** strict; scrupulous. [< L *praecisus* abridged < *prae–* in front + *caedere* to cut] —**pre·cise′ly,** *adv.* —**pre·cise′ness,** *n.*

pre·ci·sion (pri sizh′ən), *n.* accuracy; exactness: *precision of a machine.* —**pre·ci′sion·ist,** *n.*

pre·clude (pri klüd′), *v.,* **–clud·ed, –clud·ing.** shut out; make impossible; prevent. [< L, < *prae–* before + *claudere* to shut] —**pre·clu′sion,** *n.* —**pre·clu′sive,** *adj.* —**pre·clu′sive·ly,** *adv.*

pre·co·cious (pri kō′shəs), *adj.* developed earlier than usual. [< L *praecox,* ult. < *prae–* before (its name) + *coquere* ripen] —**pre·co′cious·ly,** *adv.* —**pre·co′cious·ness, pre·coc′i·ty,** *n.*

pre-Co·lum·bi·an (prē′kə lum′bi ən), *adj.* of or having to do with the period before the arrival of Columbus in the New World; of the American culture before the 1400s.

pre·con·ceive (prē′kən sēv′), *v.,* **–ceived, –ceiv·ing.** form an idea or opinion of beforehand. —**pre′con·cep′tion,** *n.*

pre·con·di·tion (prē′kən dish′ən), *n.* requirement that must be satisfied beforehand; prerequisite.

pre·cur·sor (pri kėr′sər), *n.* forerunner. [< L *praecursor,* ult. < *prae–* before + *currere* run]

pre·cur·so·ry (pri kėr′sə ri), *adj.* indicative of something to follow; introductory.

pred., predicate.

pre·date (prē dāt′), *v.,* **–dat·ed, –dat·ing.** **1** give a date earlier than the actual date.

2 give an earlier date to: *experts predated the Greek vase by two centuries.* **3** begin earlier: *generally poor sales predate the present manager.*

pre·da·tion (pri dā′shən), *n.* **1** act or habit of preying upon other animals. **2** act of plundering or robbing.

pred·a·to·ry (pred′ə tô′ri; –tō′–), *adj.* **1** preying upon other animals. Hawks and owls are predatory birds. **2** of or inclined to plundering or robbery. [< L, ult. < *praeda* prey] —**pred′a·to′ri·ly,** *adv.* —**pred′a·to′ri·ness,** *n.*

pre·de·cease (prē′di sēs′), *v.,* **–ceased, –ceas·ing.** die before (another).

pred·e·ces·sor (pred′ə ses′ər), *n.* **1** person holding a position or office before another: *John Adams was Jefferson's predecessor.* **2** thing that came before another. **3** ancestor; forefather. [< LL *praedecessor,* ult. < *prae–* before + *decedere* retire]

pre·des·ti·nate (*v.* prē des′tə nāt; *adj.* prē des′tə nit, –nāt), *v.,* **–nat·ed, –nat·ing,** *adj.* —*v.* **1** decree or ordain beforehand. **2** foreordain by divine purpose. —*adj.* foreordained. —**pre·des′ti·na′tor,** *n.*

pre·des·ti·na·tion (prē′des tə nā′shən), *n.* **1** an ordaining beforehand; destiny; fate. **2** doctrine that by God's decree certain souls will be saved and others lost.

pre·des·tine (prē des′tən), *v.,* **–tined, –tin·ing.** determine or settle beforehand; foreordain.

pre·de·ter·mine (prē′di tėr′mən), *v.,* **–mined, –min·ing.** **1** determine or decide beforehand. **2** direct or impel beforehand (to something). —**pre′de·ter′mi·na·ble,** *adj.* —**pre′de·ter′mi·na′·tion,** *n.*

pre·di·a·bet·ic (prē′dī ə bet′ik), *adj.* showing a tendency to develop diabetes, as established by blood tests. —**pre·di′a·be′tes,** *n.*

pre·dic·a·ment (pri dik′ə mənt), *n.* **1** an unpleasant, difficult, or dangerous situation. **2** any condition, state, or situation. [< LL *praedicamentum* quality, category < L *praedicare* PREDICATE]

pred·i·cate (*n., adj.* pred′ə kit; *v.* pred′ə kāt), *n., adj., v.,* **–cat·ed, –cat·ing.** —*n.* word or words expressing what is said about the subject. Examples: Men *work.* The men *dug wells.* The men *are soldiers.* —*adj.* belonging to the predicate. In "Horses are strong," *strong* is a **predicate adjective.** —*v.* **1** found or base (a statement, action, etc.) on something. **2** declare, assert, or affirm to be real or true: *most religions predicate life after death.* [< L, < *prae–* before + *dicare* make known. Doublet of PREACH.] —**pred′i·ca′tion,** *n.* —**pred′i·ca′tive,** *adj.* —**pred′i·ca′tive·ly,** *adv.*

pre·dict (pri dikt′), *v.* tell beforehand; prophesy. [< L, < *prae–* before + *dicere* say] —**pre·dict′a·ble,** *adj.* —**pre·dic′·tive,** *adj.* —**pre·dic′tive·ly,** *adv.* —**pre·dic′tor,** *n.*

pre·dic·tion (pri dik′shən), *n.* **1** act of predicting. **2** thing predicted; prophecy.

pre·di·gest (prē′di jest′, –dī–), *v.* **1** treat food with chemicals or enzymes to make it more easily digested, as for an invalid. **2** *Fig.* process beforehand for public consumption: *commentators predigest the day's news for us.* —**pre′di·ges′tion,** *n.*

pre·di·lec·tion (prē′də lek′shən; pred′ə–), *n.* a liking; preference. [< F, ult. < L *prae–* before + *diligere* choose]

pre·dis·pose (prē′dis pōz′), *v.,* **–posed, –pos·ing.** give an inclination or tendency to; make liable or susceptible: *a cold predisposes a person to other diseases.* —**pre′dis·po·si′tion** *n.*

pre·dom·i·nant (pri dom′ə nənt), *adj.* **1** having more power, authority, or influence than others; superior. **2** prevailing; most noticeable. —**pre·dom′i·nance,** *n.* —**pre·dom′i·nant·ly,** *adv.*

pre·dom·i·nate (pri dom′ə nāt), *v.,* **–nat·ed, –nat·ing.** be greater in power, strength, influence, or numbers. —**pre·dom′i·nat′ing·ly,** *adv.* —**pre·dom′i·na′·tion,** *n.* —**pre·dom′i·na′tor,** *n.*

pree·mie (prē′mē), *n.* premature infant.

pre·em·i·nent (pri em′ə nənt), *adj.* standing out above all others; superior to others. —**pre·em′i·nence,** *n.* —**pre·em′i·nent·ly,** *adv.*

pre·empt (pri empt′), *v.* **1** secure before someone else can; acquire or take possession of beforehand: *the cat had preempted the comfortable chair.* **2** settle on (land) with the right to buy it before others. [< *preemption*] —**pre·emp′tive,** *adj.* —**pre·emp′tive,** *adj.*

pre·emp·tion (pri emp′shən), *n.* a preempting or being preempted. [< L *prae–* before + *emptio* buying < *emere* to buy]

preen (prēn), *v.* **1** smooth or arrange (the feathers) with the beak, as a bird does. **2** dress (oneself) carefully. —**preen′er,** *n.*

pre·ex·ist (prē′ig zist′), *v.* exist beforehand, or before something else. —**pre′ex·ist′ence,** *n.* —**pre′ex·ist′ent,** *adj.*

pref., **1** preface. **2** preferred. **3** prefix.

pre·fab (prē fab′), *n.* prefabricated structure, esp. a dwelling: *prefabs sprouting like mushrooms.* —*adj.* of or having to do with a prefabricated structure: *prefab construction.*

pre·fab·ri·cate (prē fab′rə kāt), *v.,* **–cat·ed, –cat·ing.** make all standardized parts of (a house, etc.). The erection of a prefabricated house requires merely the assembling of the various sections. —**pre·fab′ri·cat′ed,** *adj.* —**pre·fab′ri·ca′tion,** *n.*

pref·ace (pref′is), *n., v.,* **–aced, –ac·ing.** —*n.* introduction to a book, writing, or speech: *this book has a preface written by the author.* —*v.* **1** introduce by written or spoken remarks; give a preface to. **2** be a preface to; begin. [< OF, ult. < L, < *prae–* before + *fari* speak] —**pref′ac·er,** *n.*

pref·a·to·ry (pref′ə tô′ri; –tō′–), **pref·a·to·ri·al** (pref′ə tô′ri əl; –tō′–), *adj.* of or like a preface; given as a preface; introductory; preliminary. **—pref′a·to′ri·ly, pref′a·to′ri·al·ly,** *adv.*

pre·fect (prē′fekt), *n.* **1** title of various military and civil officers in ancient Rome and elsewhere. **2** the chief administrative official of a department of France. [< L *praefectus,* orig. pp., put in charge < *prae-* in front + *facere* make] **—pre·fec′to·ral, pre′fec·to′ri·al,** *adj.*

pre·fec·ture (prē′fek chər), *n.* office, jurisdiction, territory, or official residence of a prefect. **—pre·fec′tur·al,** *adj.*

pre·fer (pri fer′), *v.,* **-ferred, -fer·ring. 1** like better; choose rather. **2** put forward; present: *in a few words he preferred his claim to the property.* **3** promote; advance. [< L, < *prae-* before + *ferre* carry] **—pre·fer′rer,** *n.*

pref·er·a·ble (pref′ər ə bəl; pref′rə bəl), *adj.* to be preferred; more desirable. **—pref′er·a·bil′i·ty, pref′er·a·ble·ness,** *n.* **—pref′er·a·bly,** *adv.*

pref·er·ence (pref′ər əns; pref′rəns), *n.* **1** act or attitude of liking better: *my preference is for beef rather than lamb.* **2** thing preferred; first choice: *Helen's preference in reading is a detective story.* **3** a prior favor, choice, right, or claim. **4** favoritism.

pref·er·en·tial (pref′ər en′shəl), *adj.* of, giving, or receiving preference. **—pref′er·en′tial·ly,** *adv.*

pre·fer·ment (pri fer′mənt), *n.* **1** advancement; promotion. **2** position or office giving social or financial advancement, esp. one in the church.

pre·fig·ure (prē fig′yər), *v.,* **-ured, -ur·ing. 1** represent beforehand by a figure or type. **2** imagine to oneself beforehand. **—pre′fig·u·ra′tion, pre·fig′ure·ment,** *n.* **—pre·fig′ur·a·tive,** *adj.*

pre·fix (*n.* prē′fiks; *v.* prē fiks′), *n.* a syllable, syllables, or word put at the beginning of a word to change its meaning or to form a new word, as in *prepaid, unlike.* **—***v.* put before. We prefix *Mr.* to a man's name. [< L *praefixus* < *prae-* in front + *figere* fix] **—pre′fix·al,** *adj.*

pre·flight (prē′flīt′), *adj.* before takeoff or launch: *preflight checks.*

preg·na·ble (preg′nə bəl), *adj.* open to attack; assailable. **—preg′na·bil′i·ty,** *n.*

preg·nan·cy (preg′nən si), *n., pl.* **-cies.** pregnant quality or condition.

preg·nant (preg′nənt), *adj.* **1** having an embryo or embryos developing in the uterus; being with child or young. **2** filled; loaded. **3** fertile; rich; abounding. **4** very significant. [< L *praegnans* < *prae-* before + *gen-* to bear] **—preg′nant·ly,** *adv.*

pre·hen·sile (pri hen′səl), *adj.* adapted for seizing, grasping, or holding on. Many monkeys have prehensile tails. [< F, ult. < L *prehendere* to grasp] **—pre′hen·sil′i·ty,** *n.*

pre·his·tor·ic (prē′his tôr′ik; -tor′-), **pre·his·tor·i·cal** (-ə kəl), *adj.* of or belong-ing to periods before recorded history. **—pre′his·tor′i·cal·ly,** *adv.*

pre·his·to·ry or **pre-his·to·ry** (prē his′tə ri; -tri), *n.* history before the time of keeping or making a record; prehistoric times or events.

pre·judge (prē juj′), *v.,* **-judged, -judg·ing.** judge beforehand; judge without knowing all the facts. **—pre·judg′er,** *n.* **—pre·judg′ment,** *n.*

prej·u·dice (prej′ə dis), *n., v.,* **-diced, -dic·ing. —***n.* **1** opinion formed without taking time and care to judge fairly: *a prejudice against doctors.* **2** harm; injury. **—***v.* **1** cause a prejudice in; fill with prejudice: *one unfortunate experience prejudiced him against all lawyers.* **2** damage; harm; injure. [< F < L, < *prae-* before + *judicium* judgment]

prej·u·di·cial (prej′ə dish′əl), *adj.* causing prejudice or disadvantage; hurtful. **—prej′u·di′cial·ly,** *adv.*

prel·a·cy (prel′ə si), *n., pl.* **-cies. 1** position or rank of a prelate. **2** prelates.

prel·ate (prel′it), *n.* clergyman of high rank, such as a bishop. [< Med.L, < L *praelatus* one preferred, orig. pp. to L *praeferre* PREFER] **—prel′ate·ship,** *n.*

prelim., preliminary.

pre·lim·i·nar·y (pri lim′ə ner′i), *adj., n., pl.* **-nar·ies. —***adj.* coming before the main business; leading to something more important. **—***n.* a preliminary step; something preparatory. [< NL, ult. < L *prae-* before + *limen* threshold] **—pre·lim′i·nar′i·ly,** *adv.*

prel·ude (prel′ūd; prē′lüd), *n., v.,* **-ud·ed, -ud·ing. —***n.* **1** anything serving as an introduction; preliminary performance: *the organ prelude to a church service.* **2 a** a prefatory or introductory musical piece to a larger composition, such as a fugue or suite. **b** a brief musical composition, usually based on a short figure or motive. **—***v.* be a prelude or introduction to. [< F < Med.L, ult. < L *prae-* before + *ludere* play]

pre·mar·i·tal (prē mar′ə təl), *adj.* before marriage: *premarital sex.*

pre·ma·ture (prē′mə chûr′; -tûr′; -tyùr′), *adj.* **1** before the proper time; too soon. **2** overhasty; precipitate. **—pre′ma·ture′ly,** *adv.* **—pre′ma·ture′ness, pre′ma·tu′ri·ty,** *n.*

pre·med (prē′med), *n. Informal.* student preparing for medical studies. **—***adj.* preparing for medical studies. **Also, pre·medical.**

pre·med·i·tate (prē med′ə tāt), *v.,* **-tat·ed, -tat·ing.** consider or plan beforehand: *a deliberate, premeditated murder.* **—pre·med′i·tat′ed,** *adj.* **—pre·med′i·tat′ed·ly,** *adv.* **—pre′med·i·ta′tion,** *n.* **—pre·med′i·ta′tor,** *n.*

pre·mier (*n.* pri mir′, prē′mi ər; *adj.* prē′mi ər, prem′yər), *n.* prime minister. **—***adj.* first in rank; chief. [< F, first < L *primarius* PRIMARY] **—pre·mier′ship,** *n.*

pre·miere or **pre·mière** (pri mir′; prə myâr′), *n., v.,* **-miered, -mier·ing** or -mièred, -mièr·ing. **—***n.* a first public performance or showing. **—***v.* **1** give the first public performance or showing. **2** appear or perform for the first time. [< F, orig. fem. of *premier.* See PREMIER.]

prem·ise (*n.* prem′is; *v.* pri mīz′), *n., v.,* **-ised, -is·ing. —***n.* **1** a statement assumed to be true and used to draw a conclusion. *Example:* Major premise: Children should go to school. Minor premise: He is a child. Conclusion: He should go to school. **2 premises, a** house or building with its grounds. **b** property forming the subject of a document. **—***v.* set forth as an introduction or explanation; mention beforehand. [< Med.L *praemissa,* orig. fem. pp., < L *prae-* before + *mittere* send]

pre·mi·um (prē′mi əm), *n.* **1** reward; prize: *some magazines give premiums for obtaining new subscriptions.* **2** something more than the ordinary price or wages. **3** amount of money paid for insurance: *he pays premiums on his life insurance four times a year.* **4** *Fig.* unusual or unfairly high value: *put a premium on being neat and on time.*

at a premium, a at more than the usual value or price. **b** very valuable; much wanted. [< L *praemium* reward]

pre·mo·ni·tion (prē′mə nish′ən; prem′ə-), *n.* a forewarning. [< earlier F < L, ult. < *prae-* before + *monere* warn]

pre·na·tal (prē nā′təl), *adj.* previous to birth. **—pre·na′tal·ly,** *adv.*

pre·nup·tial (prē nup′shəl), *adj.* before marriage; premarital: *prenuptial agreements are legally binding.*

pre·oc·cu·py (pri ok′yə pī), *v.,* **-pied, -py·ing. 1** take up all the attention of: *the question of getting to New York preoccupied her mind.* **2** occupy beforehand; take possession of before others: *our favorite seats had been preoccupied.* **—pre·oc′cu·pan·cy,** *n.* **—pre·oc′cu·pa′tion,** *n.* **—pre·oc′cu·pied,** *adj.*

pre·op (prē′op′), *adj. Informal.* =preoperative.

pre·op·er·a·tive (prē op′ər ə tiv; -ə rā tiv), before surgery: *a preoperative blood test.*

pre·or·dain (prē′ôr dān′), *v.* decide or settle beforehand; foreordain. **—pre′or·dain′ment, pre′or·di·na′tion,** *n.*

prep., **1** preparatory. **2** preposition.

pre·pack·age (prē pak′ij), *v.,* **-aged, -ag·ing** wrap, weigh, and price, esp. foods, before putting out for sale: *the market prepackages fruit, vegetables, and meat.*

pre·pack·aged (prē pak′ijd), *adj.* arranged or sold as a unit: *prepackaged tours.*

pre·paid (prē pād′), *v.* pt. and pp. of **prepay.**

prep·a·ra·tion (prep′ə rā′shən), *n.* **1** a preparing. **2** a being prepared: *A good sleep helps in preparation for a busy day.* **3** thing done to prepare for something. **4** medicine, food, or other substance made by a special process.

pre·par·a·to·ry (pri par′ə tô′ri; -tō′-), *adj.* **1** of or for preparation; preparing: *a* *preparatory school.* **2** as an introduction; preliminary: *a preparatory statement.* —**pre·par′a·to´ri·ly,** *adv.*

pre·pare (pri pãr′), *v.,* **-pared, -par·ing. 1** make ready; get ready. **2** make by a special process. [< L, < *prae–* before + *parere* make ready] —**pre·par′ed·ly,** *adv.* —**pre·par′er,** *n.*

pre·par·ed·ness (pri pãr′id nis; -pãrd′-nis), *n.* a being prepared; readiness.

pre·pay (prē pā′), *v.,* **-paid, -pay·ing. 1** pay in advance. **2** pay for in advance. —**pre·pay′a·ble,** *adj.* —**pre·pay′ment,** *n.*

pre·pon·der·ant (pri pon′dər ənt), *adj.* **1** weighing more; being stronger or more numerous; having more power or influence. **2** chief; most important. —**pre·pon′der·ance, pre·pon′der·an·cy,** *n.* —**pre·pon′der·ant·ly,** *adv.*

pre·pon·der·ate (pri pon′dər āt), *v.,* **-at·ed, -at·ing. 1** be greater than; outweigh. **2** be greater than something else in weight, power, force, influence, number, amount, etc.: *oaks and maples preponderate in our woods.* **3** be chief; be most important. [< L *praeponderatus* outweighed, ult. < *prae–* before + *pondus* weight] —**pre·pon′der·at´ing·ly,** *adv.* —**pre·pon´der·a′tion,** *n.*

prep·o·si·tion (prep′ə zish′ən), *n.* word that shows certain relations between other words. *With, for, by,* and *in* are prepositions in the sentence "A man *with* rugs *for* sale walked *by* our house, *in* the morning." [< L *praepositio,* ult. < *prae–* before + *ponere* place] —**prep′o·si′tion·al,** *adj.* —**prep′o·si′tion·al·ly,** *adv.*

pre·pos·sess (prē′pə zes′), *v.* **1** fill with a favorable feeling or opinion. **2** fill with a feeling or opinion. —**pre′pos·sess′ing,** *adj.* —**pre′pos·sess′ing·ly,** *adv.* —**pre′pos·sess′ing·ness,** *n.* —**pre′pos·ses′sion,** *n.*

pre·pos·ter·ous (pri pos′tər əs; -trəs), *adj.* contrary to nature, reason, or common sense; absurd; senseless. [< L *praeposterus* in reverse order, ult. < *prae–* before + *post* after] —**pre·pos′ter·ous·ly,** *adv.* —**pre·pos′ter·ous·ness,** *n.*

prep·pie or **prep·py** (prep′i), *adj.* of or resembling someone attending a private preparatory school. —*n.* student who attends a preparatory school. [< *prep* school + *–ie*]

prep school, *Informal.* private preparatory school.

pre·quel (prē′kwəl), *n.* book, film, television series, etc., which tells a story of what happened before the story on which it is based. [< *pre–* + *sequel*]

pre·re·cord (prē′ri kôrd′), *v.* record in advance, esp. a television program.

pre·req·ui·site (prē rek′wə zit), *n.* something required beforehand: *a high-school course is the usual prerequisite to college work.* —*adj.* required beforehand.

pre·rog·a·tive (pri rog′ə tiv), *n.* right or privilege that nobody else has: *the government has the prerogative of coining money.* [< L *praerogativa,* orig. fem. adj., asked to vote first, ult. < *prae–* before + *rogare* ask]

Pres., President.

pres., **1** present. **2** pressure.

pres·age (*n.* pres′ij; *v.* pri saj′), *n., v.,* **-aged, -ag·ing.** —*n.* **1** sign felt as a warning; omen. **2** prophetic significance: *an occurrence of dire presage.* **3** a feeling that something is about to happen. —*v.* give warning (of); predict: *some people think that a circle around the moon presages a storm.* [< L, ult. < *prae–* before + *sagus* prophetic] —**pre·sag′er,** *n.* —**pre·sag′ing·ly,** *adv.*

pres·by·ter (prez′bə tər; pres′-), *n.* **1** an elder in the early Christian church. **2** in the Presbyterian church, a minister or a lay elder. **3** in the Episcopal church, a minister or a priest. [< L, elder, < Gk. *presbyteros,* compar. of *presbys* old. Doublet of PRIEST.] —**pres·byt′er·al,** *adj.*

Pres·by·te·ri·an (prez′bə tir′i ən; pres′-), *adj.* **1** being or naming a Protestant denomination or church governed by elected presbyters or elders all of equal rank. **2** of the Presbyterian church. —*n.* member of the Presbyterian church. —**Pres′by·te′ri·an·ism,** *n.*

pres·by·ter·y (prez′bə ter′i, pres′-), *n., pl.* **-ter·ies. 1** in the Presbyterian church, a meeting or court of all the ministers and certain of the elders within a district. **2** district under the jurisdiction of such a meeting or court. **3** part of a church set aside for the clergy.

pre·school (prē′skül′), *adj.* before the age of going to regular school.

pre·sci·ence (prē′shi əns; presh′i-), *n.* knowledge of things before they exist or happen; foreknowledge; foresight. [< LL < L *praesciens* < *prae–* before + *scire* know] —**pre′sci·ent,** *adj.* —**pre′sci·ent·ly,** *adv.*

pre·scribe (pri skrīb′), *v.,* **-scribed, -scrib·ing. 1** order; direct: *good citizens do what the laws prescribe.* **2** order as a remedy or treatment: *the doctor prescribed an antibiotic.* [< L, < *prae–* before + *scribere* write] —**pre·scrib′er,** *n.*

pre·script (*n.* prē′skript; *adj.* pri skript′, prē′skript), *n.* **1** that which is prescribed. **2** order; direction. —*adj.* prescribed.

pre·scrip·tion (pri skrip′shən), *n.* **1** order; direction. **2** a written direction for preparing and using a medicine. **3** the medicine. —**pre·scrip′tive,** *adj.* —**pre·scrip′tive·ly,** *adv.* —**pre·scrip′tive·ness,** *n.*

pres·ence (prez′əns), *n.* **1** fact or condition of being present in a place. **2** place where a person is: *the messenger was admitted to my presence.* **3** physical nearness, as of an audience, or a person of very high rank: *the knight retired from the royal presence.* **4** appearance; bearing: *man of noble presence.* **5** something present, esp. a ghost, spirit, or the like.

in the presence of, in the sight or company of. [< OF < L, < *praesens* PRES-ENT[1]]

presence of mind, ability to think calmly and quickly when taken by surprise.

pres·ent[1] (prez′ənt), *adj.* **1** being in the place or thing in question; at hand, not absent. **2** at this time; being or occurring now. **3** denoting action now going on or a state now existing. *Go* is the present tense; *went* is the past tense. —*n.* **1** the present time: *at present people need courage.* **2** the present tense or a verb form in that tense. [< L *praesens* < *prae–* before + *esse* be]

pre·sent[2] (*v.* pri zent′; *n.* prez′ənt), *v.* **1** give: *he presented a gift to his hostess, the carpenter presented his bill.* **2** offer; set forth: *present an argument, the waiter presented a choice of dessert to each guest.* **3** offer to view or notice: *the new City Hall presents a fine appearance.* **4** bring before the public: *our school presented a play.* **5** introduce: *presented at court.* —*n.* thing given; gift.

present arms, bring a rifle, etc., to a vertical position in front of the body. [< OF < L *praesentare* < *praesens* PRES-ENT[1]] —**pre·sent′er,** *n.*

pre·sent·a·ble (pri zen′tə bəl), *adj.* **1** fit to be seen; suitable in appearance. —**pre·sent′a·bil′i·ty, pre·sent′a·ble·ness,** *n.* —**pre·sent′a·bly,** *adv.*

pres·en·ta·tion (prez′ən tā′shən; prē′zen-), *n.* **1** a giving: *presentation of an award.* **2** gift. **3** a bringing forward; offering to be considered: *the presentation of a plan.* **4** an offering to be seen; showing: *the presentation of a play.* **5** a formal introduction. —**pres′en·ta′tion·al,** *adj.*

pres·ent-day (prez′ənt dā′), *adj.* of the present time.

pre·sen·ti·ment (pri zen′tə mənt), *n.* a feeling or impression that something is about to happen; vague sense of approaching misfortune; foreboding. [< MF, ult. < L *prae–* before + *sentire* to sense]

pres·ent·ly (prez′ənt li), *adv.* before long; soon: *the clock will strike presently.*

pre·sent·ment (pri zent′mənt), *n.* **1** presentation. **2** representation on the stage or by a portrait.

present participle, participle that expresses present time. *Examples: rising* prices, *growing* fear of war.

present perfect, tense indicating action now completed, constructed in English by *have* with a past participle. In "I have completed my work," *have completed* is a present perfect.

present tense, tense that expresses time that is now.

pres·er·va·tion·ist (prez′ər va′shə nist), *n.* person who supports and works to preserve things from the past: *preservationists saved Grand Central Station from demolition.*

pre·serv·a·tive (pri zèr′və tiv), *n.* any substance that will prevent decay or injury: *salt is a preservative for meat.* —*adj.* that preserves.

pre·serve (pri zerv′), *v.,* –**served,** –**serving,** *n.* —*v.* **1** keep from harm or change; keep safe; protect. **2** keep up; maintain. **3** keep from spoiling: *ice helps to preserve food.* **4** prepare (food) to keep it from spoiling. Boiling with sugar, salting, smoking, and pickling are different ways of preserving food. —*n.* **1** Usually, **preserves.** fruit cooked with sugar and sealed from the air. **2** place where wild animals or fish are protected. [< OF < LL, < *prae–* before + *servare* keep] —**pre·serv′a·ble,** *adj.* —**pres′er·va′tion,** *n.* —**pre·serv′er,** *n.*

pre·set (prē′set′), *v.,* –**set,** –**set·ting.** set in advance; adjust beforehand: *the clock was preset for this time zone.*

pre·side (pri zīd′), *v.,* –**sid·ed,** –**sid·ing. 1** hold the place of authority; have charge of a meeting. **2** have authority; have control. [< L, < *prae–* before + *sedere* sit] —**pre·sid′er,** *n.*

pres·i·den·cy (prez′ə dən si; prez′dən si), *n., pl.* –**cies. 1** Often, **Presidency.** office of president. **2** time during which a president is in office.

pres·i·dent (prez′ə dənt; prez′dənt), *n.* **1** the chief officer of a company, college, society, club, etc. **2** Often, **President.** the highest executive officer of a republic. [< L *praesidens* presiding. See PRESIDE.] —**pres′i·den′tial,** *adj.* —**pres′i·den′tial·ly,** *adv.*

pres·i·dent-e·lect (prez′ə dənt i lekt′; prez′dənt–), *n.* president elected but not yet inaugurated.

press[1] (pres), *v.* **1** use force or weight steadily against; push with steady force. **2** squeeze; squeeze out. **3** clasp; hug. **4** make smooth; flatten: *press clothes.* **5** push forward; keep pushing. **6** urge (a person); keep asking; insist on. **7** weigh heavily upon (the mind, a person, etc.); demand prompt action. —*n.* **1** a pressing; pressure; push. **2** pressed condition. **3** any of various instruments or machines for exerting pressure: *a clothes press.* **4** printing press. **5** establishment for printing books, etc. **6** newspapers and periodicals and those who write for them. **7** urgency; hurry.

go to press, begin to be printed. [< OF < L *pressare* < *premere* to press] —**press′er,** *n.*

press[2] (pres), *v.* **1** force into service, usually naval or military. **2** seize and use. [earlier *prest* < OF *prester* furnish, ult. < L *praesto* ready]

press agent, agent in charge of publicity for a person, organization, etc.

press box, enclosed place, usually high above the field of play in a sports arena, stadium, etc., where sports reporters can watch and report on a game.

press conference, meeting of reporters with a public figure or politician where information is given out and questions from the reporters are answered; news conference.

press release, news item or publicity piece given to the news media by an individual or group, usually to call attention to or create interest in an activity, book, etc.

press·ing (pres′ing), *adj.* requiring immediate action or attention; urgent. —**press′ing·ly,** *adv.* —**press′ing·ness,** *n.*

pres·sure (presh′ər), *n.* **1** the continued action of a weight or force: *the pressure of the wind filled the sails of the boat.* **2** force per unit of area: *there is a pressure of 20 pounds to the inch on this tire.* **3** *Fig.* state of trouble or strain: *pressure of poverty.* **4** *Fig.* a compelling force or influence: *he changed his mind under pressure from others.* **5** *Fig.* need for prompt or decisive action; urgency: *pressure of business.* [< OF < L *pressura* < *premere* to press] —**pres′sur·al,** *adj.*

pressure cooker, an airtight apparatus for cooking with steam under pressure.

pressure group, any business, professional, or labor group which attempts to further its interests in the state or national legislatures.

pres·sur·ize (presh′ər īz), *v.,* –**ized,** –**iz·ing. 1** keep the atmospheric pressure inside of the cabin of an aircraft or spacecraft at a normal level in spite of the altitude. **2** subject to very high or increasing pressure.

pres·tige (pres tēzh′; pres′tij), *n.* reputation, influence, or distinction based on what is known of one's abilities, achievements, opportunities, associations, etc. [< F, magic spell, ult. < L *praestigiae* tricks] —**pres·ti′gous,** *adj.* —**pres·ti′gous·ly,** *adv.*

pres·to (pres′tō), *adv., adj., n., pl.* –**tos.** —*adv.* quickly. —*adj.* quick. —*n.* a quick part in a piece of music. [< Ital., ult. < L *praesto,* adv., ready]

pre·sume (pri züm′), *v.,* –**sumed,** –**sum·ing. 1** take for granted without proving; suppose: *the law presumes innocence until guilt is proved.* **2** take upon oneself; venture; dare: *may I presume to tell you you are wrong?* **3** take an unfair advantage (used with *on* or *upon*): *don't presume on a person's good nature by borrowing from him every week.* [< L *praesumere* take for granted < *prae–* before + *sumere* take] —**pre·sum′a·ble,** *adj.* —**pre·sum′a·bly,** *adv.* —**pre·sum′ed·ly,** *adv.* —**pre·sum′er,** *n.* —**pre·sum′ing·ly,** *adv.*

pre·sump·tion (pri zump′shən), *n.* **1** act of presuming. **2** thing taken for granted: *since he had the stolen jewels, the presumption was that he was the thief.* **3** cause or reason for presuming; probability. **4** unpleasant boldness: *it is presumption to go to a party when one has not been invited.*

pre·sump·tive (pri zump′tiv), *adj.* **1** based on likelihood; presumed. **2** giving ground for presumption or belief: *presumptive evidence of his guilt.* —**pre·sump′tive·ly,** *adv.*

pre·sump·tu·ous (pri zump′chù əs), *adj.* acting without permission or right; too bold; forward. —**pre·sump′tu·ous·ly,** *adv.* —**pre·sump′tu·ous·nes s,** *n.*

pre·sup·pose (prē′sə pōz′), *v.,* –**posed,** –**pos·ing. 1** take for granted in advance; assume beforehand: *let us presuppose that he wants more money.* **2** require as a necessary condition; imply: *a fight presupposes fighters.* —**pre′sup·po·si′tion,** *n.*

pret., preterit.

pre·teen or **pre-teen** (prē′tēn′), *n.* young person close to the teenage years. —*adj.* nearly a teenager.

pre·tend (pri tend′), *v.* **1** make believe. **2** claim falsely: *she pretends to like you, but talks about you behind your back.* **3** claim falsely to have: *she pretended illness.* **4** claim: *I don't pretend to be a musician.* **5** lay claim: *James Stuart pretended to the English throne.* **6** venture; attempt: *I cannot pretend to judge between them.* [< L, < *prae–* before + *tendere* to stretch] —**pre·tend′ed,** *adj.* —**pre·tend′ed·ly,** *adv.* —**pre·tend′ing·ly,** *adv.*

pre·tend·er (pri ten′dər), *n.* **1** person who pretends. **2** person who makes claims to a throne without just right.

pre·tense (pri tens′; prē′tens), *n.* **1** make-believe; pretending. **2** a false appearance: *under pretense of picking up the handkerchief, she took the money.* **3** a false claim: *the girls made a pretense of knowing the boys' secret.* **4** claim. **5** a showing off; display: *her manner is free from pretense.* **6** anything done to show off. [< AF *pretensse,* ult. < L *praetendere* PRETEND]

pre·ten·sion (pri ten′shən), *n.* **1** claim: *the young prince has pretensions to the throne.* **2** a putting forward of a claim. **3** a pretentious display.

pre·ten·tious (pri ten′shəs), *adj.* **1** making claims to excellence or importance: *a pretentious person, book, or speech.* **2** doing things for show or to make a fine appearance: *a pretentious style of entertaining guests.* [< F *prétentieux,* ult. < L *praetendere* PRETEND] —**pre·ten′tious·ly,** *adv.* —**pre·ten′tious·ness,** *n.*

pret·er·it, pret·er·ite (pret′ər it), —*n.* a verb form that expresses occurrence in the past; past tense. *Obeyed* is the preterit of *obey; spoke,* of *speak;* and *saw,* of *see.* —*adj.* expressing past time. [< L *praeteritus,* ult. < *praeter–* past + *ire* go]

pre·ter·nat·u·ral (prē′tər nach′ə rəl; –nach′rəl), *adj.* **1** out of the ordinary course of nature; abnormal. **2** due to something above or beyond nature; supernatural. [< Med.L, ult. < L *praeter–* beyond + *natura* NATURE] —**pre′ter·nat′u·ral·ly,** *adv.* —**pre′ter·nat′u·ral·ness,** *n.*

pre·text (prē′tekst), *n.* a false reason concealing the real reason; pretense; excuse. [< L, ult. < *prae–* in front + *texere* to weave]

Pre·to·ri·a (pri tô′ri ə; –tō′–), *n.* the administrative capital of the Republic of South Africa, in the NE part.

pret·ti·fy (prit′ə fī), *v.*, **–fied, –fy·ing.** make pretty, esp. overly pretty.

pret·ty (prit′i), *adj.*, **–ti·er, –ti·est,** *adv.* —*adj.* 1 pleasing to look at; fine or lovely, as opposed to grand, striking, or elegant. 2 too dainty or delicate. 3 *Usually ironically.* excellent: *a pretty state of affairs.* 4 fine; nice: *pretty weather.* —*adv.* fairly; rather.

pretty much or **nearly** or **well,** almost; nearly: *pretty much anyone can do this.*

sitting pretty, in an excellent position or situation. [OE *prǣttig* cunning < *prǣtt* trick] —**pret′ti·ly,** *adv.* —**pret′ti·ness,** *n.* —**pret′ty·ish,** *adj.*

pret·zel (pret′səl), *n.* a hard biscuit, usually in the form of a knot, salted on the outside. [< G *brezel* < L, ult. < Gk. *brachion* arm]

pre·vail (pri vāl′), *v.* 1 exist in many places; be in general use. 2 be the most usual or strongest. 3 be the stronger; win the victory; succeed. 4 be effective.

prevail on, upon, or **with,** persuade. [< L, < *prae–* before + *valere* have power]

pre·vail·ing (pri vāl′ing), *adj.* 1 that prevails; having superior force or influence; victorious. 2 in general use; common. —**pre·vail′ing·ly,** *adv.* —**pre·vail′ing·ness,** *n.*

prev·a·lent (prev′ə lənt), *adj.* widespread; in general use; common: *colds are prevalent in the winter.* [< L *praevalens,* ppr. of *praevalere* PREVAIL] —**prev′a·lence,** *n.* —**prev′a·lent·ly,** *adv.*

pre·var·i·cate (pri var′ə kāt), *v.*, **–cat·ed, –cat·ing.** turn aside from the truth in speech or act; lie. [< L *praevaricatus* having made a sham accusation, ult. < *prae–* before + *varicus* straddling < *varus* crooked] —**pre·var′i·ca′tion,** *n.* —**pre·var′i·ca′tor,** *n.*

pre·vent (pri vent′), *v.* 1 keep (from). 2 keep from happening: *rain prevented the game.* 3 hinder. [< L, < *prae–* before + *venire* come] —**pre·vent′a·ble, pre·vent′i·ble,** *adj.* —**pre·vent′er,** *n.*

pre·ven·tion (pri ven′shən), *n.* 1 a preventing. 2 something that prevents.

pre·ven·tive (pri ven′tiv), **pre·vent·a·tive** (–tə tiv), *adj.* that prevents: *preventive measures against disease.* —*n.* something that prevents: *vaccination is a preventive against smallpox.* —**pre·ven′tive·ly,** *adv.* —**pre·ven′tive·ness,** *n.*

preventive medicine, practice of medicine that focuses on the prevention of disease, as opposed to its treatment.

pre·view (prē′vū′), *n.* 1 a previous view, inspection, survey, etc. 2 the advance showing of scenes from a motion picture. —*v.* view beforehand.

pre·vi·ous (prē′vi əs), *adj.* coming or going before; that came before; earlier.

previous to, before. [< L *praevius* leading the way < *prae–* before + *via* road] —**pre′vi·ous·ly,** *adv.* —**pre′vi·ous·ness,** *n.*

pre·vi·sion (prē vizh′ən), *n.* foresight; foreknowledge. —**pre·vi′sion·al,** *adj.*

pre·war (prē′wôr′), *adj.* before the war.

prey (prā), *n.* 1 animal hunted or seized for food, esp. by another animal: *mice and birds are the prey of cats.* 2 habit of hunting and killing other animals for food: *bird of prey.* 3 person or thing injured; victim: *be a prey to fear or disease.* —*v.* **prey on** or **upon, a** hunt or kill for food. **b** be a strain upon; injure; irritate. **c** rob; plunder. [< OF < L *praeda*] —**prey′er,** *n.*

price (prīs), *n.*, *v.*, **priced, pric·ing.** —*n.* 1 amount for which a thing is sold or can be bought. 2 reward offered for the capture of a person alive or dead. 3 *Fig.* what must be given, done, undergone, etc., to obtain a thing: *the price of success.* 4 value; worth. —*v.* 1 put a price on; set the price of. 2 ask the price of; find out the price of.

at any price, regardless of cost.

beyond or **without price,** so valuable it cannot be assigned a price; priceless. [< OF < L *pretium*] —**priced,** *adj.* —**pric′er,** *n.*

price·less (prīs′lis), *adj.* extremely valuable. —**price′less·ness,** *n.*

prick (prik), *n.* 1 a sharp point. 2 a little hole or mark made by a sharp point. 3 a pricking. 4 a sharp pain. —*v.* 1 make a hole in with a sharp point. 2 mark with a sharp point. 3 cause sharp pain to. 4 spur; urge on.

prick up, point upward. [OE *prica* point] —**pricked,** *adj.* —**prick′ing,** *adj.* —**prick′ing·ly,** *adv.*

prick·er (prik′ər), *n.* 1 something with a sharp point, as a thorn. 2 someone or something that pricks.

prick·le (prik′əl), *n.*, *v.*, **–led, –ling.** —*n.* 1 a small, sharp point; thorn; spine. 2 a stinging or smarting sensation. —*v.* feel a prickly or smarting sensation. [OE *pricel* < *prica* point]

prick·ly (prik′li), *adj.*, **–li·er, –li·est.** 1 having many sharp points like thorns. 2 sharp and stinging; itching. —**prick′li·ness,** *n.*

prickly pear, 1 a pear-shaped, edible fruit of a species of cactus. 2 plant that it grows on.

pride (prīd), *n.*, *v.*, **prid·ed, prid·ing.** —*n.* 1 a high opinion of one's own worth or possessions. 2 pleasure or satisfaction in something concerned with oneself: *take pride in keeping our house clean.* 3 something that one is proud of. 4 too high an opinion of oneself. —*v.* **pride oneself on,** be proud of. [OE *prȳde* < *prūd* PROUD] —**pride′ful,** *adj.* —**pride′ful·ly,** *adv.* —**pride′ful·ness,** *n.* —**pride′less,** *adj.*

priest (prēst), *n.* 1 clergyman or minister of a Christian church. 2 a special servant of a god. [ult. < L *presbyter.* Doublet of PRESBYTER.] —**priest′hood,** *n.* —**priest′less,** *adj.* —**priest′like′,** *adj.*

priest·ess (prēs′tis), *n.* woman who serves at an altar or in sacred rites.

priest·ly (prēst′li), *adj.*, **–li·er, –li·est.** 1 of or pertaining to a priest. 2 suitable for a priest. —**priest′li·ness,** *n.*

prig (prig), *n.* 1 person who is too particular about speech and manners, and takes pride in being better than others. 2 stuffy, humorless person. —**prig′gish,** *adj.* —**prig′gish·ly,** *adv.* —**prig′gish·ness,** *n.*

prim (prim), *adj.*, **prim·mer, prim·mest.** stiffly precise, neat, proper, or formal. —**prim′ly,** *adv.* —**prim′ness,** *n.*

pri·ma·cy (prī′mə si), *n.*, *pl.* **–cies.** 1 a being first in order, rank, importance, etc. 2 position or rank of a church primate. [< Med.L, < L *primas* of first rank. See PRIMATE.]

pri·ma don·na (prē′mə don′ə), *pl.* **pri·ma don·nas.** 1 the principal woman singer in an opera; diva. 2 *Fig.* person who is very sensitive and moody. [<Ital., first lady]

pri·ma fa·ci·e (prī′mə fā′shi ē; fā′shi), at first view; before investigation. [< L, abl. of *prima facies* first appearance]

pri·mal (prī′məl), *adj.* 1 of early times; first; primeval. 2 chief; fundamental. [< Med.L, < L *primus* first] —**pri′mal·ly,** *adv.*

prim·a·quine (prim′ə kwin), *n.* a synthetic compound used in treating malaria.

pri·ma·ri·ly (prī′mer′ə li; –mə rə–; prī mār′ə li), *adv.* 1 chiefly; principally. 2 at first; originally.

pri·ma·ry (prī′mer′i, –mə ri), *adj.*, *n.*, *pl.* **–ries.** —*adj.* 1 first in time; first in order. 2 from which others have come; original; fundamental. 3 first in importance; chief. —*n.* 1 anything that is first in order, rank, or importance. 2 a primary color. 3 election in which members of a party choose candidates for office. [< L *primarius* first in rank < *primus* first] —**pri′ma·ri·ness,** *n.*

primary accent, 1 the strongest accent in the pronunciation of a word. 2 mark (′) used to show this.

primary care, basic medical care for most illnesses, which is provided before specialized treatment for more serious medical problems.

primary colors, pigments or colors that yield all other colors when mixed together. Red, yellow, and blue are the primary colors in pigments.

pri·mate (prī′mit; –māt), *n.* 1 any of the highest order of animals, including humans, apes, and monkeys. 2 archbishop or bishop ranking above all other bishops in a country or church province. [< L *primas* of first rank < *primus* first] —**pri′mate·ship,** *n.* —**pri·ma′tial,** *adj.*

prime¹ (prīm), *adj.* 1 first in rank; chief: *Hard work was the prime reason for success.* 2 first in time or order; fundamental; original. 3 first in quality; first-rate; excellent: *in the prime years of life.* 4 the prime rate. 5 that cannot be divided without a remainder by any whole number except itself and 1. 7, 11, and 13 are prime numbers. **6** having no common divisor but 1. 2 is prime to 9. —*n.* **1** the best time; best condition, or part. **2** a prime number. [ult. < L *primus* first] —**prime′ness,** *n.*

prime² (prīm), *v.,* **primed, prim·ing. 1** supply (a gun) with powder. **2** cover (a surface) with a first coat of paint or oil so that paint will not soak in. **3** equip (a person) with information, words, etc. **4** pour water into (a pump) to start action.

prime meridian, meridian from which the longitude east and west is measured. It passes through Greenwich, England, and its longitude is O°.

prime minister, the chief minister of a government; the head of the cabinet.

prime mover, person or thing that initiates or does the most in an undertaking.

prim·er¹ (prim′ər), *n.* **1** a first book in reading. **2** a first book; beginner's book. [< Med.L *primarius* PRIMARY]

prim·er² (prīm′ər), *n.* **1** person or thing that primes. **2** cap or cylinder containing a little gunpowder, used for firing a charge. **3** point or sealer applied to a surface as a first coat.

prime rate, lowest rate of interest charged by a bank for a loan to a large business.

pri·me·val (prī mē′vəl), *adj.* **1** of the first ages, esp. of the world. **2** dating from the first ages or earliest times. **3** characteristic of the first ages or earliest times; primitive. [< L *primaevus* early in life < *primus* first + *aevum* age] —**pri·me′val·ism,** *n.* —**pri·me′val·ly,** *adv.* —**pri·me′val·ness,** *n.*

prim·ing (prīm′ing), *n.* **1** powder or other material used to set fire to an explosive. **2** a first coat of paint, sizing, etc.

prim·i·tive (prim′ə tiv), *adj.* **1** of early times; of long ago: *primitive people often lived in caves.* **2** first of the kind: *primitive Christians.* **3** very simple; such as people had early in human history. **4** original; primary. [< L, ult. < *primus* first] —**prim′i·tive·ly,** *adv.* —**prim′i·tive·ness,** *n.* —**prim′i·tiv·ism,** *n.*

pri·mo·gen·i·tor (prī′mə jen′ə tər), *n.* **1** ancestor; forefather. **2** the earliest ancestor. [< LL, < L *primus* first + *genitor* begetter]

pri·mo·gen·i·ture (prī′mə jen′ə chər), *n.* **1** state, condition, or fact of being the first-born of the children of the same parents. **2** right or principle of inheritance or succession by the first-born. [< Med.L *primogenitura,* ult. < L *primus* first + *gignere* beget] —**pri′mo·gen′i·tal,** *adj.*

pri·mor·di·al (prī môr′di əl), *adj.* **1** existing at the very beginning; primitive. **2** original; elementary. [< L, < *primordium* beginning] —**pri·mor′di·al·ism,** *n.* —**pri·mor′di·al′i·ty,** *n.* —**pri·mor′di·al·ly,** *adv.*

primp (primp), *v.* **1** dress (oneself) for show. **2** dress carefully.

prim·rose (prim′rōz′), *n.* **1** any of a large group of plants with flowers of various colors. The common primrose of Europe is pale yellow. **2** the flower. —*adj.* pale-yellow. [<Med.L *prima rosa* first rose]

prin., principal.

prince (prins), *n.* **1** a male member of a royal family; esp., in Great Britain, a son or grandson of a king or queen. **2** sovereign. **3** ruler of a small state subordinate to a king or emperor. **4** the greatest or best of a group; chief. [< OF < L *princeps* chief] —**prince′dom,** *n.* —**prince′like′,** *adj.* —**prince′ship,** *n.*

prince consort, prince who is the husband of a queen or empress ruling in her own right.

Prince Edward Island, province of Canada on an island in the Gulf of St. Lawrence, just N of Nova Scotia.

prince·ly (prins′li), *adj.,* **–li·er, –li·est. 1** of a prince or his rank; royal. **2** like a prince; noble. **3** fit for a prince; magnificent. —**prince′li·ness,** *n.*

Prince of Wales, title conferred on the eldest son, or heir apparent, of the British sovereign.

prin·cess (prin′ses; –sis), *n.* **1** daughter of a king or queen; daughter of a king's or queen's son. **2** wife or widow of a prince. **3** woman having the rank of a prince. —**prin′cess·ly,** *adv.*

prin·ci·pal (prin′sə pəl), *adj.* most important; main; chief. —*n.* **1** a chief person; one who gives orders. **2** the head, or one of the heads, of a primary or secondary school. **3** sum of money on which interest is paid. **4** money or property from which income is received. **5** person who hires another person to act for him or her. [< L *principalis* < *princeps* chief] —**prin′ci·pal·ship′,** *n.*

prin·ci·pal·i·ty (prin′sə pal′ə ti), *n., pl.* **–ties. 1** a small state or country ruled by a prince. **2** country from which a prince gets his title. **3** supreme power.

prin·ci·pal·ly (prin′sə pəl i; –sip li), *adv.* for the most part; chiefly; mainly.

principal parts, the main parts of a verb, from which the rest of its forms can be derived.

prin·ci·pate (prin′sə pāt), *n.* **1** a chief place or authority. **2** =principality. [< L, < *princeps* chief]

prin·ci·ple (prin′sə pəl), *n.* **1** truth that is a foundation for other truths: *the principles of democratic government.* **2** a fundamental belief: *religious principles.* **3** rule of action or conduct: *make it a principle to save some money each week.* **4** uprightness; honor: *a man of principle.* **5** rule of science explaining how things act: *the principle by which a machine works.* [< OF < L *principium* < *princeps* chief]

print (print), *v.* **1** use type, blocks, plates, etc., and ink or dye to stamp words,

pictures, designs, etc., on paper or the like. **2** produce books, newspapers, etc., by printing press. **3** make (words or letters) the way they look in print instead of in writing: *print your name clearly.* **4** stamp with designs, patterns, pictures, etc.: *machines print wallpaper, cloth, etc.* —*n.* **1** printed words, letters, etc.: *this book has clear print.* **2** picture or design printed from a block or plate. **3** cloth with a pattern printed on it. **4** mark made by pressing or stamping: *the print of a foot.* **5 a** photograph produced from a negative. **b** photograph electronically produced from a digital camera.

in print, a in printed form. **b** of books, etc., still available from the publisher.

out of print, no longer sold by the publisher.

print out, print output from a computer. [< OF *priente,* ult. < L *premere* to press] —**print′a·ble,** *adj.* —**print′er,** *n.* —**print′less,** *adj.*

print., printing.

print·ing (prin′ting), *n.* **1** the producing of books, newspapers, etc., by impression from movable types, plates, etc. **2** printed words, letters, etc. **3** all the copies printed at one time. **4** letters made like those in print.

printing press, machine for printing from types, plates, etc.

print·out (print′out′), *n.* printed output from a computer.

pri·or¹ (prī′ər), *adj.* coming before; earlier: *a prior engagement.*

prior to, coming before in time, order, or importance; earlier than; before. [< L]

pri·or² (prī′ər), *n.* officer usually ranking next below an abbot, in a monastery or religious house. [< Med.L, n. use of L *prior* PRIOR¹] —**pri′or·ate, pri′or·ship,** *n.*

pri·or·ess (prī′ər is), *n.* woman holding a position corresponding to that of a prior.

pri·or·i·ty (prī ôr′ə ti; –or′–), *n., pl.* **–ties. 1** a being earlier in time. **2** a coming before in order or importance: *fire engines have priority over other traffic.*

pri·o·ry (prī′ə ri), *n., pl.* **–ries.** a religious house governed by a prior or prioress.

prism (priz′əm), *n.* **1** solid whose bases or ends have the same size and shape and are parallel to one another, and each of whose sides has two pairs of parallel edges. **2** a transparent prism, usually with three-sided ends, that separates white light passing through it into the colors of the rainbow. [< LL < Gk. *prisma* < *priein* to saw] —**pris′mal,** *adj.*

pris·mat·ic (priz mat′ik), *adj.* **1** of or like a prism. **2** formed by a transparent prism. **3** varied in color; brilliant. —**pris·mat′i·cal·ly,** *adv.*

pris·on (priz′ən), *n.* place where a person is shut up against his or her will, esp. a public building where criminals are confined. [< OF < L *prehensio* arrest < *prehendere* seize]

pris·on·er (priz′ən ər; priz′nər), *n.* **1** person who is confined in prison. **2** person taken by the enemy in war. **3** person arrested and held for trial.

pris·sy (pris′i), *adj.,* **–si·er, –si·est. 1** too careful and fussy. **2** too easily shocked; overnice.

pris·tine (pris′tēn; –tin; –tīn), *adj.* as it was in its earliest time or state; original; primitive. [< L *pristinus*]

prith·ee (priᵗʰ′i), *interj. Archaic.* I pray thee: *prithee, come hither.*

pri·va·cy (prī′və si), *n., pl.* **–cies. 1** condition of being private; being away from others. **2** absence of publicity; secrecy.

pri·vate (prī′vit), *adj.* **1** not for the public; for just a few special people or for one: *a private car.* **2** not public; individual; personal: *my private opinion.* **3** secret; confidential: *a private source.* **4** secluded: *some private corner.* **5** having no public office: *a private citizen.* —*n.* a common soldier, not an officer.

in private, a not publicly. **b** secret. [< L *privatus* apart from the state, orig. pp., set apart, deprived < *privus* one's own. Doublet of PRIVY.] —**pri′vate·ly,** *adv.* —**pri′vate·ness,** *n.*

private detective or **private investigator,** detective who is not on a police force and can be hired by a private individual to do investigative work.

private enterprise, business as conducted without public (governmental) control or ownership; free enterprise.

pri·va·teer (prī′və tir′), *n.* **1** an armed ship owned by private persons and holding a government commission to attack and capture enemy ships. **2** commander or one of the crew of a privateer.

private eye, *Informal.* —private detective.

private school, educational institution that is not part of the public educational system.

pri·va·tion (prī vā′shən), *n.* **1** lack of the comforts or of the necessities of life. **2** loss; absence. [< L *privatio.* See PRIVATE.]

priv·et (priv′it), *n.* any of several evergreen shrubs with small leaves, much used for hedges.

priv·i·lege (priv′ə lij), *n., v.,* **–leged, –leging.** —*n.* a special right, advantage, or favor. —*v.* give a privilege to. [< L *privilegium* law applying to one individual < *privus* individual + *lex* law] —**priv′i·leged,** *adj.*

priv·i·ly (priv′ə li), *adv.* secretly.

priv·y (priv′i), *adj., n., pl.* **priv·ies.** —*adj.* private. —*n.* a small outhouse used as a toilet.

privy to, having secret or private knowledge of. [< OF < L *privatus.* Doublet of PRIVATE.]

privy council, group of personal advisers to a ruler. —**privy councilor.**

prix fixe (prē′fēks′), *French.* **1** meal offered by a restaurant at a fixed price:

tonight's prix fixe is a good buy. **2** price of this meal.

prize¹ (prīz), *n.* **1** reward won after trying against other people. **2** reward worth working for. —*adj.* **1** given as a prize. **2** that has won a prize. **3** worthy of a prize. [var. of ME *prise* PRICE]

prize² (prīz), *n.* thing or person that is taken or captured, esp. an enemy's ship taken at sea. [< F *prise,* n., seizure < L *prehensa,* fem. pp., seized]

prize³ (prīz), *v.,* **prized, priz·ing. 1** value highly. **2** estimate the value of. [< OF *prisier,* var. of *preisier* PRAISE] —**prized,** *adj.*

prize⁴ (prīz), *v.,* **prized, priz·ing.** *Esp. Brit.* raise or move by force; pry.

prize court, a court that makes decisions concerning ships and other property captured at sea during a war.

prize fight, fight with fists which people pay money to see. —**prize fighter.** —**prize fighting.**

pro¹ (prō), *adv., n., pl.* **pros.** —*adv.* in favor of; for. —*n.* reason in favor of. The pros and cons of a question are the arguments for and against it.

pro² (prō), *n., pl.* **pros,** *adj.* professional. [short for *professional*]

pro–, *prefix.* **1** before, as in *proscenium.* **2** forward, as in *proceed, project.* **3** forth; out, as in *prolong, proclaim.* **4** on the side of; in favor of; in behalf of, as in *pro-British.* [def. 1 < Gk. *pro;* defs. 2, 3, 4 < L *pro*]

pro·ac·tive (prō ak′tiv), acting in advance to affect the outcome of something.

prob., probably.

prob·a·bil·i·ty (prob′ə bil′ə ti), *n., pl.* **–ties. 1** quality or fact of being likely or probable; chance. **2** something likely to happen: *a storm is one of the probabilities for tomorrow.*

in all probability, probably.

prob·a·ble (prob′ə bəl), *adj.* **1** likely to happen: *cooler weather is probable.* **2** likely to be true: *the probable cause of the accident.* [< L, < *probare* PROVE] —**prob′a·bly,** *adv.*

pro·bate (prō′bāt), *n., adj., v.,* **–bat·ed, –bat·ing.** —*n.* the official proving of a will as genuine. —*adj.* of or concerned with the probating of wills: *a probate court.* —*v.* prove by legal process the genuineness of (a will). [< L *probatum,* orig., neut. pp., made good < *probus* good]

pro·ba·tion (prō bā′shən), *n.* **1** trial or testing of conduct, character, qualifications, etc.: *on probation in a job.* **2** any act or process of testing: *admitted to college on probation.* **3** system of letting certain kinds of offenders against the law go without receiving the punishment which they are sentenced to, esp. of jail, unless there is a further offense. —**pro·ba′tion·al, pro·ba′tion·ar′y,** *adj.*

pro·ba·tion·er (prō bā′shən ər), *n.* person who is on probation. —**pro·ba′tion·er·ship′,** *n.*

probe (prōb), *v.,* **probed, prob·ing,** *n.* —*v.* **1** search into; examine thoroughly; investigate. **2** search; penetrate: *probe into a secret.* **3** examine or explore with a probe. —*n.* **1** a thorough examination; investigation. **2** investigation, usually by a legislative body, in an effort to discover evidences of law violation. **3** a slender instrument with a rounded end for exploring the depth or direction of a wound, a cavity in the body, etc. [< LL *proba,* n., < L *probare* PROVE. Doublet of PROOF.] —**prob′er,** *n.* —**prob′ing,** *adj.* —**prob′ing·ly,** *adv.*

pro·bi·ty (prō′bə ti; prob′ə–), *n.* uprightness; honesty; high principle. [< L, < *probus* righteous]

prob·lem (prob′ləm), *n.* **1** question; difficult question. **2** matter of doubt or difficulty. **3** something to be worked out: *a problem in arithmetic.* —*adj.* that causes difficulty: *a problem child.* [< L < Gk. *problema* < *proballein* propose < *pro–* forward + *ballein* to throw]

prob·lem·at·ic (prob′ləm at′ik), **prob·lem·at·i·cal** (–ə kəl), *adj.* having the nature of a problem; doubtful; uncertain; questionable. —**prob′lem·at′i·cal·ly,** *adv.*

pro·bos·cis (prō bos′is), *n., pl.* **–bos·cis·es** (–bos′is iz), **–bos·ci·des** (–bos′ə dēz). **1** an elephant's trunk. **2** a long, flexible snout. **3** the mouth parts of some insects, developed to great length for sucking. [< L < Gk. *proboskis*]

pro·car·y·ote (prō kar′i ōt), *n.* cell or organism lacking a well-defined nucleus or nuclei.

pro·ce·dure (prə sē′jər), *n.* **1** way of proceeding; method of doing things. **2** the customary manners or ways of conducting business: *legal procedure.* **3** medical or dental surgery. [< F, < *procéder* PROCEED] —**pro·ce′dur·al,** *adj.*

pro·ceed (*v.* prə sēd′; *n.* prō′sēd), *v.* **1** go on after having stopped; move forward: *please proceed with your story.* **2** carry on any activity: *he proceeded to light the fire.* **3** come forth; issue; go out: *heat proceeds from fire.* —*n.* Usually, **proceeds,** money obtained from a sale, etc. [< L, < *pro–* forward + *cedere* to move] —**pro·ceed′er,** *n.*

pro·ceed·ing (prə sēd′ing), *n.* action; conduct; what is done.

proceedings, a action in a case in a law court. **b** record of what was done at the meetings of a society, club, etc.

proc·ess (pros′es), *n.* **1** set of actions or changes in a special order: *by what process is cloth made from wool?* **2** part that grows out or sticks out. **3** a written command or summons to appear in a law court. —*v.* treat or prepare by some special method. —*adj.* treated or prepared by some special method. [< F < L *processus* progress < *procedere* PROCEED]

pro·ces·sion (prə sesh′ən), *n.* **1** something that moves forward; persons marching or riding: *a funeral procession.* **2** an orderly moving forward: *march in procession.*

pro·ces·sion·al (prə sesh′ən əl), *adj.* **1** of a procession. **2** used or sung in a procession. —*n.* processional music. —**pro·ces′sion·al·ly,** *adv.*

pro·ces·sor (pros′əs ər), *n.* **1 a** person who prepares foods before distribution and sale. **b** small appliance that chops and mixes foods. **2** unit of a computer that processes data; central processing unit.

pro·choice (prō′chois′), *adj.* favoring a woman's right to choose whether or not to continue a pregnancy; supporting the right to have an abortion.

pro·claim (prə klām′), *v.* make known publicly and officially; declare publicly: *war was proclaimed, proclaim him king.* [< L, < *pro-* forth + *clamare* to shout] —**pro·claimed′,** *adj.* —**pro·claim′er,** *n.*

proc·la·ma·tion (prok′lə mā′shən), *n.* an official announcement; public declaration: *the President's annual Thanksgiving proclamation.* —**pro·clam′a·to′ry** *adj.*

pro·cliv·i·ty (prō kliv′ə ti), *n., pl.* **-ties.** tendency; inclination. [< L, ult. < *pro-* forward + *clivus* slope]

pro·cras·ti·nate (prō kras′tə nāt), *v.,* **-nat·ed, -nat·ing.** put things off until later; delay; delay repeatedly. [< L *procrastinatus,* ult. < *pro-* forward + *cras* tomorrow] —**pro·cras′ti·na′tion,** *n.* —**pro·cras′ti·na′tor,** *n.*

pro·cre·ate (prō′kri āt), *v.,* **-at·ed, -at·ing. 1** become father to; beget. **2** produce offspring. **3** bring into being; produce. [< L, < *pro-* forth + *creare* create] —**pro′cre·a′tion,** *n.* —**pro′cre·a′tive,** *adj.* —**pro′cre·a′tor,** *n.*

proc·tor (prok′tər), *n.* **1** official in a university or school who keeps order. **2** person employed to manage another's case in a law court. [short for *procurator*] —**proc·to′ri·al,** *adj.* —**proc′tor·ship,** *n.*

pro·cure (prə kyúr′), *v.,* **-cured, -cur·ing. 1** obtain by care or effort; get: *procure evidence.* **2** bring about; cause: *procure a person's death.* [< L *procurare* manage, ult. < *pro-* before + *cura* care] —**pro·cur′a·ble,** *adj.* —**pro·cure′ment,** *n.* —**pro·cur′er,** *n.*

prod (prod), *v.,* **prod·ded, prod·ding,** *n.* —*v.* **1** poke or jab with something pointed: *prod an animal with a stick.* **2** stir up; urge on: *prod a lazy boy.* —*n.* **1** poke; thrust. **2** a sharp-pointed stick; goad. [OE *prod-,* as in *prodbor* borer] —**prod′der,** *n.*

prod·i·gal (prod′ə gəl), *adj.* spending too much; wasting money or other resources; wasteful. —*n.* person who is wasteful or extravagant; spendthrift. [< earlier F, ult. < L *prodigus* wasteful] —**prod′i·gal·ly,** *adv.*

prod·i·gal·i·ty (prod′ə gal′ə ti), *n., pl.* **-ties. 1** wasteful or reckless extravagance. **2** rich abundance; profuseness.

pro·di·gious (prə dij′əs), *adj.* **1** very great; enormous; huge. **2** wonderful; marvel-

ous. —**pro·di′gious·ly,** *adv.* —**pro·di′gious·ness,** *n.*

prod·i·gy (prod′ə ji), *n., pl.* **-gies. 1** marvel; wonder: *an infant prodigy.* **2** a marvelous example. [< L *prodigium* omen]

pro·duce (*v.* prə düs′, -dūs′; *n.* prod′üs, -ūs, prō′düs, -dūs), *v.,* **-duced, -duc·ing,** *n.* —*v.* **1** make: *this factory produces stoves, hens produce eggs.* **2** bring about; cause: *hard work produces success.* **3** bring forward; show: *produce your proof.* **4** bring (a play, etc.) before the public. —*n.* what is produced; yield: *vegetables are a garden's produce.* [< L, < *pro-* forth + *ducere* bring] —**pro·duc′i·ble,** *adj.*

pro·duc·er (prə düs′ər; -dūs′-), *n.* **1** one that produces. **2** person who grows or makes things that are to be used or consumed by others. **3** person who has general charge of the production of motion pictures, plays, etc.

producer goods, machinery, tools, raw materials, etc., used in the production of other articles.

prod·uct (prod′əkt), *n.* **1** that which is produced; result of work or of growth: *factory products, farm products.* **2** number or quantity resulting from multiplying.

pro·duc·tion (prə duk′shən), *n.* **1** act of producing; creation. **2** something that is produced.

pro·duc·tive (prə duk′tiv), *adj.* **1** producing; bringing forth: *hasty words are productive of quarrels.* **2** producing food or other articles of commerce: *productive labor.* **3** producing abundantly; fertile: *a productive farm.* —**pro·duc′tive·ly,** *adv.* —**pro′duc·tiv′i·ty, pro·duc′tive·ness,** *n.*

Prof., prof., professor.

pro·fane (prə fān′), *adj., v.,* **-faned, -fan·ing.** —*adj.* **1** not sacred; worldy: *profane literature.* **2** with contempt or disregard for holy things: *profane language.* —*v.* **1** treat (holy things) with contempt or disregard. **2** put to wrong or unworthy use. [< F < L *profanus* not sacred < *pro-* in front (outside) of + *fanum* shrine] —**pro·fane′ly,** *adv.* —**pro·fane′ness,** *n.* —**pro·fan′er,** *n.*

pro·fan·i·ty (prə fan′ə ti), *n., pl.* **-ties. 1** use of profane language; swearing. **2** a being profane; lack of reverence.

pro·fess (prə fes′), *v.* **1** lay claim to; claim: *I don't profess to be an expert.* **2** declare openly: *he professed his loyalty to the United States.* **3** declare one's belief in: *Christians profess Christ and the Christian religion.* [< *professed*] —**pro·fess′ing,** *adj.*

pro·fessed (prə fest′), *adj.* **1** alleged; pretended. **2** avowed or acknowledged; openly declared. **3** having taken the vows of, or been received into, a religious order. [< L *professus* < *pro-* forth + *fateri* confess] —**pro·fess′ed·ly,** *adv.*

pro·fes·sion (prə fesh′ən), *n.* **1** occupation requiring an education, esp. law, medicine, teaching, or the ministry. **2** people engaged in such an occupation.

3 act of professing; open declaration: *a profession of friendship.*

pro·fes·sion·al (prə fesh′ən əl; -fesh′nəl), *adj.* **1** of or pertaining to a profession; appropriate to a profession: *the professional gravity of a doctor.* **2** engaged in a profession: *a professional man.* **3** making a business or trade of something that others do for pleasure: *a professional ballplayer.* **4** undertaken or engaged in by professionals rather than amateurs: *professional tennis.* —*n.* person who does this. —**pro·fes′sion·al·ism ,** *n.* —**pro·fes′sion·al·ly,** *adv.*

pro·fes·sion·al·ize (prə fesh′ən əl īz; -fesh′nəl-), *v.,* **-ized, -iz·ing.** make or become professional. —**pro·fes′sion·al·i·za′tion,** *n.*

pro·fes·sor (prə fes′ər), *n.* **1** teacher of the highest rank in a college or university. **2** person who professes. [< L. See PROFESSED.] —**pro·fes′sor·dom,** *n.* —**pro′fes·so′ri·al,** *adj.* —**pro′fes·so′ri·al·ly,** *adv.*

prof·fer (prof′ər), *v.* offer for acceptance: *proffer services.* —*n.* an offer made: *proffers of peace.* [< AF *proffrir* < *pro-* forth (<L *pro-*) + *offrir* OFFER] —**prof′fer·er,** *n.*

pro·fi·cien·cy (prə fish′ən si), *n., pl.* **-cies.** a being proficient; knowledge; skill.

pro·fi·cient (prə fish′ənt), *adj.* advanced in any art, science, or subject; skilled; expert: *proficient in music.* [< L *proficiens* making progress < *pro-* forward + *facere* make] —**pro·fi′cient·ly,** *adv.*

pro·file (prō′fīl), *n., v.,* **-filed, -fil·ing.** —*n.* **1** a side view. **2** outline. **3** a short and vivid biographical sketch. —*v.* **1** draw a profile of. **2** portray vividly in a biographical sketch. [< Ital., < *profilare* draw in outline < L *pro-* forth + *filum* thread] —**pro′fil·ist,** *n.*

prof·it (prof′it), *n.* **1** Often, **profits.** gain from a business; what is left when the cost of carrying on the business is subtracted from the money taken in. **2** gain from any transaction. **3** advantage; benefit. —*v.* **1** make profit; gain in a material sense. **2** get advantage; gain; benefit: *profit by one's mistakes.* **3** be an advantage or benefit. [< OF < L *profectus* advance < *proficere.* See PROFICIENT.] —**prof′it·er,** *n.* —**prof′it·less,** *adj.* —**prof′it·less·ly,** *adv.*

profit margin, the amount that the selling price of a product is greater than the cost of producing it.

profit sharing, the sharing of profits by employers with employees.

prof·it·a·ble (prof′it ə bəl), *adj.* **1** yielding a financial profit. **2** giving a gain or benefit; useful. —**prof′it·a·ble·ness,** *n.* —**prof′it·a·bly,** *adv.*

prof·it·eer (prof′ə tir′), *n.* person who makes an unfair profit by taking advantage of public necessity. —*v.* seek or make such excessive profits. —**prof′it·eer′ing,** *n.*

prof·li·ga·cy (prof′lə gə si), *n.* **1** reckless extravagance. **2** great wickedness; vice.

prof·li·gate (prof'lə git), *adj.* **1** recklessly extravagant. **2** very wicked; shamelessly bad. —*n.* person who is shamelessly extravagant or wicked. [< L *profligatus* ruined] —**prof'li·gate·ly**, *adv.* —**prof'li·gate·ness**, *n.*

pro for·ma (prō fôr'mə), *Latin.* for the sake of form; only as a matter of form.

pro·found (prə found'), *adj.* **1** very deep: *a profound sleep.* **2** deeply felt; very great: *profound respect.* **3** going far deeper than what is easily understood: *a profound thinker.* **4** low: *a profound bow.* [< OF < L *profundus* < *pro–* away + *fundus* bottom] —**pro·found'ly**, *adv.* —**pro·fun'di·ty, pro·found'ness**, *n.*

pro·fuse (prə fūs'), *adj.* **1** very abundant: *profuse thanks.* **2** spending or giving freely; lavish; extravagant: *profuse with one's money.* [< L *profusus* poured forth < *pro–* forth + *fundere* pour] —**pro·fuse'ly**, *adv.* —**pro·fuse'ness**, *n.*

pro·fu·sion (prə fū'zhən), *n.* **1** great abundance. **2** extravagance; lavishness. —**pro·fu'sive**, *adj.*

pro·gen·i·tor (prō jen'ə tər), *n.* ancestor in the direct line; forefather. [< L, < *pro–* forth + *gignere* beget] —**pro·gen'i·to'ri·al**, *adj.* —**pro·gen·i·tor·ship'**, *n.*

pro·gen·i·ture (prō jen'ə chər), *n.* **1** a begetting; birth. **2** =progeny.

prog·e·ny (proj'ə ni), *n., pl.* **-nies.** children; offspring; descendants. [< OF < L *progenies*. See PROGENITOR.]

pro·ges·ter·one (prō jes'tər ōn), **pro·ges·tin** (–jes'tin), *n.* a hormone, $C_{21}H_{30}O_2$, derived from a body which develops in the ovary.

prog·no·sis (prog nō'sis), *n., pl.* **-ses** (–sēz). **1** forecast of the probable course of a disease. **2** estimate of what will probably happen. [< LL < Gk., ult. < *pro–* before + *gignoskein* recognize] —**prog·nos'tic**, *adj.*

prog·nos·ti·cate (prog nos'tə kāt),*v.*,**-cat·ed, -cat·ing.** predict from facts; forecast. —**prog·nos·ti·ca'tion**, *n.* —**prog·nos'ti·ca'tive**, *adj.* —**prog·nos'ti·ca'tor**, *n.*

pro·gram (prō'gram; –grəm), *n., v.,* **-grammed, -gram·ming.** —*n.* **1** list of items or events; list of performers, etc.: *the program filled four pages.* **2** items composing an entertainment: *the entire program was delightful.* **3** plan of what is to be done: *a school program.* **4** a set of instructions fed into a computer. —*v.* **1** arrange plans of operation for (a computing mechanism, automation system, group of workers, etc.). **2** put (an item) on a program, as in a theatrical entertainment, plan of operation, etc. [< LL < Gk. *programma* proclamation, ult. < *pro–* forth + *graphein* write] —**pro'gram·mat'ic**, *adj.*

prog·ress (*n.* prog'res, *v.* prə gres'), *n.* **1** advance; growth; development; improvement: *the progress of the arts and sciences.* **2** a moving forward; going ahead: *make rapid progress on a journey.* —*v.* **1** get better; advance; develop: *we progress in learning step by step.* **2** move forward; go ahead: *the war had progressed some time.* [< L *progressus,* ult. < *pro–* forward + *gradi* walk]

pro·gres·sion (prə gresh'ən), *n.* **1** a moving forward; going ahead: *a slow method of progression.* **2** succession of quantities in which there is always the same relation between each quantity and the one succeeding it. 2, 4, 6, 8, 10 are in **arithmetical progression.** 2, 4, 8, 16 are in **geometrical progression.** —**pro·gres'sion·al**, *adj.*

pro·gres·sive (prə gres'iv), *adj.* **1** making progress; advancing to something better; improving: *a progressive nation.* **2** favoring progress; wanting improvement in government, etc. **3** moving forward; going ahead. **4** going from one to the next. **5** in grammar, showing a continuation of action: *"is reading" is is a progressive form of "read."* —*n.* person who favors progress. —**pro·gres'sive·ly**, *adv.* —**pro·gres'sive·ness**, *n.*

pro·hib·it (prō hib'it), *v.* **1** forbid by law or authority: *picking flowers in the park is prohibited.* **2** prevent. [< L *prohibitus* < *pro–* away + *habere* keep] —**pro·hib'i·ted**, *adj.*

pro·hi·bi·tion (prō'ə bish'ən), *n.* **1** act of prohibiting or forbidding. **2** law or order that prohibits. **3** law or laws against making or selling alcoholic liquors. —**pro'hi·bi'tion·ist**, *n.*

pro·hib·i·tive (prō hib'ə tiv), *adj.* prohibiting; preventing. —**pro·hib'i·tive·ly**, *adv.* —**pro·hib'i·tive·ness**, *n.*

proj·ect (*n.* proj'ekt; *v.* prə jekt'), *n.* **1** a plan; scheme. **2** an undertaking; enterprise. **3** Also, **projects.** group of apartment buildings, esp. public housing, built and run as a unit. —*v.* **1** plan; scheme. **2** stick out: *the rocky point projects far into the water.* **3** throw or cast forward: *a cannon projects shot.* **4** cause to fall on a surface: *motion pictures are projected on the screen, trees project shadows on the grass.* [< L *projectus* < *pro–* forward + *jacere* to throw] —**project'ed**, *adj.* —**pro·ject'ing**, *adj.*

pro·jec·tile (prə jek'təl), *n.* object that can be thrown, hurled, or shot, such as a stone or bullet. —*adj.* **1** capable of being thrown, hurled, or shot. **2** forcing forward; impelling.

pro·jec·tion (prə jek'shən), *n.* **1** part that projects or sticks out. **2** a sticking out. **3** a throwing or casting forward: *the projection of a cannon ball from a cannon.* **4** the casting forward on a screen of an image from a film projector. **5** *Fig.* forecast of what is likely to happen on the basis of what has happened before. **6** in psychology, the attribution to someone else one's own thoughts, feelings, etc.

pro·jec·tor (prə jek'tər), *n.* apparatus for projecting a picture on a screen.

pro·lac·tin (prō lac'tin), *n.* a pituitary hormone that causes the mammary glands to produce milk. [< *pro–* + *lac* milk + E *–in*]

pro·le·tar·i·an (prō'lə tãr'i ən), *adj.* of or belonging to the proletariat. —*n.* person belonging to the proletariat. [< L *proletarius* furnishing the state only with children < *proles* offspring] —**pro'le·tar'i·an·ism**, *n.*

pro·le·tar·i·at (prō'lə tãr'i ət), *n.* class of people that depend on daily work for a living; laboring class.

pro·life (prō'līf'), *adj.* =right-to-life.

pro·lif·er·ate (prō lif'ə rāt), *v.,* **-at·ed, -at·ing.** **1** grow or multiply parts, as in budding or cellular division. **2** spread; multiply: *websites proliferate overnight, it seems.* —**pro·lif'er·a'tion**, *n.*

pro·lif·ic (prə lif'ik), *adj.* **1** producing offspring abundantly. **2** producing much: *a prolific tree.* [< Med.L, < L *proles* offspring + *facere* make] —**pro·lif'i·ca·cy, pro·lif'ic·ness**, *n.* —**pro·lif'ic·ly**, *adv.*

pro·lix (prō liks'; prō'liks), *adj.* using too many words; too long; tedious. [< L *prolixus* stretched out] —**pro·lix'i·ty, pro·lix'ness**, *n.* —**pro·lix'ly**, *adv.*

pro·logue, pro·log (prō'lôg; –log), *n.* **1** speech or poem addressed to the audience by one of the actors at the beginning of a play. **2** introduction to a novel, poem, or other literary work. **3** any introductory act or event. [< L < Gk. < *pro–* before + *logos* speech]

pro·long (prə lông'; –long'), *v.* make longer; extend. [< LL, < *pro–* forth + *longus* long] —**pro·long'a·ble**, *adj.* **pro'long a'tion, pro·long'ment**, *n.* —**pro·longed'**, *adj.* —**pro·long'er**, *n.*

prom (prom), *n.* formal. dance given by a college or high-school class. [short for *promenade*]

prom·e·nade (prom'ə nād'; –näd'), *n., v.,* **-nad·ed, -nad·ing.** —*n.* **1** walk for pleasure or display: *the Easter promenade.* **2** a public place for such a walk. **3** march of all the guests at the opening of a formal dance. —*v.* **1** walk about or up and down for pleasure or for display. **2** walk through. [< F, < *promener* take for a walk] —**prom'e·nad'er**, *n.*

pro·me·thi·um (prə mē'thi əm), *n.* a rare metallic element, Pm. Formerly, **illinium.**

prom·i·nence (prom'ə nəns), *n.* **1** quality or fact of being prominent. **2** something that juts out, esp. upward.

prom·i·nent (prom'ə nənt), *adj.* **1** well-known; important: *a prominent citizen.* **2** easy to see: *a single tree in a field is prominent.* **3** standing out; projecting: *some insects have prominent eyes.* [< L *prominens* < *pro–* forward + *men–* jut] —**prom'i·nent·ly**, *adv.*

pro·mis·cu·ous (prə mis'kyu əs), *adj.* **1** mixed and in disorder: *a promiscuous heap of clothing.* **2** making no distinctions; not discriminating: *promiscuous friendships.* [< L *promiscuus* < phrase *pro miscus* as common < *miscere* mix]

—pro·mis′cu·ous·ly, *adv.* —pro·mis′cu-ous·ness, prom′is·cu′i·ty, *n.*

prom·ise (prom′is), *n., v.,* -ised, -is·ing. —*n.* 1 words, said or written, binding a person to do or not to do something. 2 indication of what may be expected: *the clouds give promise of rain.* 3 indication of future excellence; something that gives hope of success: *a young scholar who shows promise.* —*v.* 1 make a promise of (something) to (a person, etc.). 2 give one's word; make a promise. 3 give indication or hope of; give ground for expectation. [< L *promissum,* orig. neut. pp., promised < *pro-* before + *mittere* put] —prom′is·er, *n.*

Promised Land, 1 country promised by God to Abraham and his descendants; Canaan. Gen. 15:18; 17:1–8. 2 heaven. 3 Also, **promised land.** *Fig.* any place thought of as wonderful.

prom·is·ing (prom′is ing), *adj.* likely to turn out well; hopeful. —prom′is·ing-ly, *adv.*

prom·is·so·ry (prom′ə sô′ri; –sō′–), *adj.* containing a promise.

promissory note, a written promise to pay a stated sum of money to a certain person at a certain time.

prom·on·to·ry (prom′ən tô′ri; –tô′–), *n., pl.* -ries. a high point of land extending from the coast into the water; headland. [< Med.L *promontorium,* var. of L *promunturium*] —prom′on·to′-ri·al, *adj.*

pro·mote (prə mōt′), *v.,* -mot·ed, -mot·ing. 1 raise in rank, condition, or importance: *promoted to tenth grade, be promoted from clerk to manager.* 2 help to grow or develop; help to success: *promote peace.* 3 help to organize; start: *promote a new company.* 4 further the sale of (an article) by advertising. [< L *promotus* < *pro-* forward + *movere* to move] —pro·mot′a·ble, *adj.* —pro·mot′er, *n.* —pro·mo′tion, *n.* —pro·mo′-tive, *adj.*

prompt (prompt), *adj.* 1 ready and willing; on time; quick: *be prompt to obey.* 2 done at once; made without delay: *prompt punishment.* —*v.* 1 cause (someone) to do something: *his curiosity prompted him to ask questions.* 2 give rise to; suggest; inspire: *a kind thought prompted the gift.* 3 remind (a learner, speaker, actor) of the words or actions needed. [< L *promptus,* orig. pp., brought forth < *pro-* forward + *emere* orig., take. Doublet of PRONTO.] —prompt′er, *n.* —prompt′ly, *adv.* —prompt′ness, promp′ti·tude, *n.*

pro·mul·gate (prō mul′gāt; prom′əl gāt), *v.,* -gat·ed, -gat·ing. 1 proclaim formally; announce officially: *promulgate the king's decree.* 2 spread far and wide: *promulgate knowledge.* [< L, < *pro-* forth + unrecorded *mulgare,* intensive of *mulgere,* orig., to press] —pro′mul·ga′-tion, *n.* —pro·mul′ga·tor, *n.*

pron., 1 pronoun. 2 pronunciation.

prone (prōn), *adj.* 1 inclined; liable: *we are prone to think evil of people we dislike.* 2 lying face down. 3 lying flat. [< L *pronus*] —prone′ly, *adv.* —prone′ness, *n.*

prong (prông; prong), *n.* one of the pointed ends of a fork, antler, etc. [ME *prange*] —pronged, *adj.*

prong·horn (prông′hôrn′; prong′–), *n., pl.* -horns or (*esp. collectively*) -horn. animal like an antelope, found on the plains of W North America.

pro·nom·i·nal (prō nom′ə nəl), *adj.* of pronouns; having the nature of a pronoun. —pro·nom′i·nal·ly, *adv.*

pro·noun (prō′noun), *n.* 1 one of the parts of speech, comprising words used to indicate without naming. 2 a word that does this; word used instead of a noun. *Examples:* I, we, you, he, it, they, who, whose, which, this, mine, whatever. [< F < L, < *pro-* in place of + *nomen* noun]

pro·nounce (prə nouns′), *v.,* -nounced, -nounc·ing. 1 make the sounds of; speak: *pronounce your words clearly.* 2 give an opinion or decision: *only an expert should pronounce on this case.* 3 declare (a person or thing) to be: *the doctor pronounced her cured.* 4 declare formally or solemnly: *the judge pronounced sentence on the criminal.* [< OF < L, ult. < *pro-* forth + *nuntius* announcement] —pro·nounce′a·ble, *adj.* —pro·nounc′er, *n.*

pro·nounced (prə nounst′), *adj.* strongly marked; decided. —pro·nounc′ed·ly, *adv.*

pro·nounce·ment (prə nouns′mənt), *n.* 1 a formal statement. 2 opinion; decision.

pro·nun·ci·a·tion (prə nun′si ā′shən), *n.* 1 way of pronouncing: *this book gives the pronunciation of each main word.* 2 a pronouncing.

proof (prüf), *n.* 1 way or means of showing beyond doubt the truth of something: *Have you proof of what you say?* 2 establishment of the truth of anything. 3 act of testing; trial. 4 condition of having been tested and approved. —*adj.* of tested value against something: *proof against being taken by surprise.* [< OF *prueve* < LL *proba* < L *probare* prove. Doublet of PROBE.] —proof′less, *adj.*

-proof, *suffix.* protected against; safe from, as in *fireproof, stainproof.*

proof·read (prüf′rēd′), *v.,* -read (–red′), -read·ing. read and mark errors to be corrected. —proof′read′er, *n.*

prop (prop), *v.,* propped, prop·ping, *n.* —*v.* 1 hold up by placing a support under or against. 2 support; sustain. —*n.* thing or person used to support another. [cf. MDu. *proppe*] —prop′less, *adj.*

prop·a·gan·da (prop′ə gan′də), *n.* 1 systematic efforts to spread opinions or beliefs. 2 opinions or beliefs thus spread. [< NL *congregatio de propaganda fide* congregation concerning propagating the faith] —prop′a·gan′dism, *n.*

—prop′a·gan′dist, *n.* —prop′a·gan-dis′tic, *adj.*

prop·a·gan·dize (prop′ə gan′dīz), *v.,* -dized, -diz·ing. 1 propagate or spread (doctrines, etc.) by propaganda. 2 carry on propaganda.

prop·a·gate (prop′ə gāt), *v.,* -gat·ed, -gat·ing. 1 produce offspring. 2 increase in number: *trees propagate themselves by seeds.* 3 spread (news, knowledge, etc.): *propagate the principles of science.* 4 pass on; send further: *sound is propagated by vibrations.* [< L *propagatus*] —prop′a·ga·ble, *adj.* —prop′a·ga·bil′i-ty, *n.* —prop′a·ga′tion, *n.* —prop′a·ga′-tive, *adj.* —prop′a·ga′tor, *n.*

pro·pane (prō′pān), *n.* colorless, flammable gas, used as a fuel, refrigerant, or solvent.

pro·pel (prə pel′), *v.,* -pelled, -pel·ling. drive forward; force ahead: *propel a boat by oars.* [< L, < *pro-* forward + *pellere* to push] —pro·pel′la·ble, *adj.*

pro·pel·lant (prə pel′ənt), *n.* something that propels, esp. the fuel of a missile or rocket.

pro·pel·lent (prə pel′ənt), *adj.* propelling. —*n.* one that propels.

pro·pel·ler (prə pel′ər), *n.* 1 device consisting of a revolving hub with blades, for propelling boats, airplanes, etc. 2 one that propels.

pro·pen·si·ty (prə pen′sə ti), *n., pl.* -ties. a natural inclination or bent. [< L *propensus* inclined < *pro-* forward + *pendere* hang]

prop·er (prop′ər), *adj.* 1 correct; right; fitting: *night is the proper time to sleep, and bed the proper place.* 2 according to recognized usage: *use a word in its proper sense.* 3 strictly so called; in the strict sense of the word: *no shellfish are fishes proper.* 4 decent; respectable: *proper conduct.* 5 belonging exclusively or distinctively: *qualities proper to a substance.* [< OF < L *proprius*] —prop′er·ly, *adv.* —prop′er·ness, *n.*

proper fraction, a fraction less than 1, as $\frac{2}{8}$, $\frac{1}{8}$, $\frac{3}{4}$, and $\frac{199}{200}$.

proper noun, noun naming a particular person or thing, as *John* or *Chicago.*

prop·er·ty (prop′ər ti), *n., pl.* -ties. 1 thing or things owned; possession or possessions. 2 piece of land or real estate. 3 quality or power belonging specially to something: *soap has the property of removing dirt.* **properties,** furniture, weapons, etc. (everything except scenery and clothes), used in staging a play. [< OF *propriete* < L, < *proprius* one's own] —prop′er·tied, *adj.*

property tax, tax on real estate and personal property.

pro·phase (prō′fāz), *n.* first stage of both mitosis and meiosis. [< *pro-* + *phase*]

proph·e·cy (prof′ə si), *n., pl.* -cies. 1 a foretelling of future events. 2 thing told about the future. [< OF < L < Gk., < *prophetes* PROPHET]

proph·e·sy (prof′ə sī), v., **–sied, –sy·ing.**
1 tell what will happen; foretell; predict.
2 speak when or as if divinely inspired.
—**proph′e·si′er,** n.

proph·et (prof′it), n. **1** person who tells
what will happen. **2** person who preaches
what he thinks has been revealed to
him. **3 the Prophets,** books of the Old
Testament written by prophets. [< L
< Gk. *prophetes,* ult. < *pro–* before + *pha-
nai* speak] —**proph′et·hood, proph′et·
ship,** n.

proph·et·ess (prof′it is), n. a woman
prophet.

pro·phet·ic (prə fet′ik), **pro·phet·i·cal**
(–ə kəl), adj. **1** belonging to a prophet;
such as a prophet has: *prophetic power.* **2**
containing prophecy: *a prophetic saying.*
3 giving warning of what is to happen;
foretelling. —**pro·phet′i·cal·ly,** adv.

pro·phy·lac·tic (prō′fə lak′tik; prof′ə–),
adj. protecting from disease. —n. medicine or treatment that protects against
disease. [< Gk. *prophylaktikos,* ult. < *pro–*
before + *phylassein* to guard] —**pro′phy·
lac′ti·cal·ly,** adv.

pro·phy·lax·is (prō′fə lak′sis; prof′ə–),
n. **1** protection from disease. **2** treatment to prevent disease. [< NL, < Gk.
pro– before + *phylaxis* protection]

pro·pi·ti·ate (prə pish′i āt), v., **–at·ed, –at·
ing.** prevent or reduce the anger of; win
the favor of; appease or conciliate. [< L,
ult. < *propitius* PROPITIOUS] —**pro·pi′ti·
a′tion,** n. —**pro·pi′ti·a′tor,** n. —**pro·
pi′ti·a·to′ry,** adj. **pro·pi′ti·a′tive,** adj.

pro·pi·tious (prə pish′əs), adj. **1** favorable:
propitious weather for our trip. **2** favorably inclined; gracious. [< L *propitius,*
orig., falling forward < *pro–* forward +
petere go toward] —**pro·pi′tious·ly,** adv.
—**pro·pi′tious·ness,** n.

pro·po·nent (prə pō′nənt), n. **1** person
who makes a proposal or proposition. **2**
favorer; supporter.

pro·por·tion (prə pôr′shən; –pōr′–),
n. **1** relation in size, number, amount,
or degree of one thing compared to
another: *each man's pay will be in proportion to his work.* **2** a proper relation
between parts: *his short legs were not
in proportion to his long body.* **3** part;
share: *a large proportion of Nevada is
desert.* **4** an equality of ratios. *4 is to
2 as 10 is to 5 is a proportion.* —v. fit
(one thing to another) so that they go
together: *the designs in that rug are well
proportioned.*

proportions, a size; extent. **b** dimensions. [< L, < phrase *pro portione* in
relation to the part] —**pro·por′tion·a·
ble,** adj. —**pro·por′tioned,** adj. —**pro·
por′tion·less,** adj.

pro·por·tion·al (prə pôr′shən əl; –pôrsh′-
nəl; –pōr′–), adj. in the proper proportion; corresponding: *the increase in price
is proportional to the improvement in the
car.* —n. one of the terms of a proportion in mathematics. —**pro·por′tion-
al′i·ty,** n. —**pro·por′tion·al·ly,** adv.

pro·por·tion·ate (prə pôr′shən it; –pôrsh′-
nit; –pōr′–), adj. in the proper proportion; proportioned; proportional. —**pro-
por′tion·ate·ly,** adv.

pro·pos·al (prə pōz′əl), n. **1** what is proposed; plan; suggestion. **2** offer of marriage.

pro·pose (prə pōz′), v., **–posed, –pos·ing.**
1 put forward for consideration, discussion, acceptance, etc.; suggest. **2** present (the name of someone) for office,
membership, etc. **3** intend; plan. **4** make
an offer of marriage. [< F, < *pro–* forth
(< L) + *poser* POSE] —**pro·pos′a·ble,** adj.
—**pro·posed′,** adj. —**pro·pos′er,** n.

prop·o·si·tion (prop′ə zish′ən), n. **1** what
is offered to be considered; proposal.
2 statement. **3** statement that is to be
proved true. **4** problem to be solved.
—**prop′o·si′tion·al,** adj. —**prop′o·si′-
tion·al·ly,** adv.

pro·pound (prə pound′), v. put forward;
propose: *propound a theory.* [earlier *pro-
pone* < L, < *pro–* before + *ponere* set]
—**pro·pound′er,** n.

pro·pri·e·tar·y (prə prī′ə ter′i), adj., n.,
pl. **-tar·ies.** —adj. **1** belonging to a pro-
prietor: *proprietary rights.* **2** holding
property: *the proprietary class.* **3** owned
by a private person or company: *a proprietary medicine.* —n. owner or group
of owners.

pro·pri·e·tor (prə prī′ə tər), n. owner.
[alter. of *proprietary* < LL, < L *proprietas*
property, ownership < *proprius* one's
own] —**pro·pri′e·to′ri·al,** adj. —**pro·
pri′e·to′ri·al·ly,** adv. —**pro·pri′e·tor·
ship′,** n. —**pro·pri′e·to′ry,** adj.

pro·pri·e·tress (prə prī′ə tris), n. a woman
owner or manager.

pro·pri·e·ty (prə prī′ə ti), n., pl. **-ties. 1**
quality of being proper; fitness. **2** proper
behavior. [< L, < *proprius* proper]

props (props), n.pl. =properties (items
used in staging a play).

pro·pul·sion (prə pul′shən), n. **1** a driving forward or onward. **2** a propelling
force or impulse. —**pro·pul′sive, pro·
pul′so·ry** adj.

pro ra·ta (prō rā′tə; rä′tə), in proportion.
[< L *pro rata (parte)* according to the
portion figured (for each)]

pro·rate (prō rāt′; prō′rāt′), v., **-rat·ed,
-rat·ing.** distribute or assess propor-
tionally. [< *pro rata*] —**pro·rat′a·ble,**
adj.

pro·sa·ic (prō zā′ik), adj. like prose; matter-of-fact; ordinary; not exciting. —**pro-
sa′i·cal·ly,** adv. —**pro·sa′ic·ness,** n.

pro·sce·ni·um (prō sē′ni əm), n., pl. **-ni-
a** (–ni ə). part of the stage in front of the
curtain. [< L < Gk., < *pro–* in front of +
skene stage, orig., tent]

pro·sciut·to (prō shü′tō), n., pl. **-ti**
(–tē), **-tos.** air-cured ham that is spiced,
served in very thin slices, often with
melon. [< It.]

pro·scribe (prō skrīb′), v., **-scribed,
-scrib·ing. 1** prohibit as wrong or dangerous; condemn. **2** put outside of the
protection of the law; outlaw. **3** forbid to
come into a certain place; banish. [< L,
< *pro–* openly, publicly + *scribere* write]
—**pro·scrib′er,** n. —**pro·scrip′tion,** n.
—**pro·scrip′tive,** adj. —**pro·scrip′tive-
ly,** adv. —**pro·scrip′tive·ness,** n.

prose (prōz), n., adj., v., **prosed, pros·
ing.** —n. **1** the ordinary form of spoken
or written language; plain language not
arranged in verses. **2** dull, ordinary talk.
—adj. **1** of or in prose. **2** lacking imagination; matter-of-fact; commonplace.
—v. talk or write in a dull, commonplace way. [< F < L *prosa (oratio)* straight
(speech), ult. < *pro–* forward + *vertere* to
turn] —**pro′sa·ist, pros′er,** n.

pros·e·cute (pros′ə kūt), v., **-cut·ed, -cut·
ing. 1** bring before a court of law: *reckless drivers will be prosecuted.* **2** carry
out; follow up: *he prosecuted an inquiry
into reasons for the company's failure.*
3 carry on (a business or occupation).
[< L *prosecutus* pursued < *pro–* forth
+ *sequi* follow] —**pros′e·cut′a·ble,** adj.
—**pros′e·cu′tor,** n. —**pros′e·cu′tor·
ship,** n.

prosecuting attorney, =district attorney.

pros·e·cu·tion (pros′ə kū′shən), n. **1** the
carrying on of a lawsuit. **2** side that
starts action against another in a law
court. **3** a carrying out; following up.

pros·e·lyte (pros′ə līt), n., v., **-lyt·ed, -lyt·
ing.** —n. person who has been con-
verted from one opinion, religious
belief, etc., to another. —v. convert from
one opinion, religious belief, etc., to
another. [< L < Gk. *proselytos,* orig., one
from another land] —**pros′e·lyt′er,** n.
—**pros′e·lyt′ism,** n.

pros·e·lyt·ize (pros′ə līt īz′; –lə tīz′), v.,
-ized, -iz·ing. make converts. —**pros′e·
lyt′i·za′tion,** n. —**pros′e·lyt·iz′er,** n.

pros·o·dy (pros′ə di), n. science of poetic
meters and versification. [< L < Gk., all
the features (accent, modulation, etc.)
that characterize speech < *pros* in addition to + *oide* song, poem] —**pro·sod′ic,
pro·sod′i·cal,** adj. —**pro·sod′i·cal·ly,**
adv. —**pros′o·dist,** n.

pros·pect (pros′pekt), n. **1** thing expected
or looked forward to. **2** act of looking
forward; expectation: *the prospect of a
vacation is pleasant.* **3** Also, **prospects.**
outlook for the future. **4** person who
may become a customer, candidate, etc.
5 view; scene: *the prospect from the
mountain.* —v. search: *prospect for gold.*
in prospect, expected; looked forward
to. [< L, ult. < *pro–* forward + *specere* to
look] —**pros′pect·less,** n.

pro·spec·tive (prə spek′tiv), adj. probable; expected. —**pro·spec′tive·ly,** adv.
—**pro·spec′tive·ness,** n.

pros·pec·tor (pros′pek tər; prə spek′–), n.
one who explores or examines a region
for gold, silver, oil, etc.

pro·spec·tus (prə spek′təs), n. a statement describing and advertising something, esp. to attract buyers or investors.
[< L, PROSPECT]

pros·per (pros′pər), *v.* **1** be successful; have good fortune; flourish. **2** make successful. [< OF < L, < *prosperus* prosperous] —**pros′per·er**, *n.* —**pros′per·ing·ly**, *adv.*

pros·per·i·ty (pros per′ə ti), *n.*, *pl.* –**ties.** prosperous condition; good fortune; success.

pros·per·ous (pros′pər əs), *adj.* **1** successful; thriving; doing well; fortunate. **2** favorable; helpful. [< L *prosperus*] —**pros′per·ous·ly**, *adv.* —**pros′per·ous·ness**, *n.*

pros·tate (pros′tāt), or **prostate gland**, *n.* a gland surrounding the male urethra in front of the bladder. [< Med.L < Gk. *prostates* one standing in front. ult. < *pro-* before + *stenai* to stand] —**pro·stat′ic**, *adj.*

pros·ti·tute (pros′tə tüt; –tūt), *n.*, *v.*, –**tut·ed**, –**tut·ing.** —*n.* **1 a** woman who has sexual relations for hire with men. **b** person who engages in sexual acts for money. **2** *Fig.* person who does base things for money or gain. —*v.* **1** put to an unworthy or base use. **2** submit to providing sex for gain or hire. [< L *prostitutus* < *pro-* publicly + *statuere* cause to stand] —**pros′ti·tu′tion**, *n.* —**pros′ti·tu′tor**, *n.*

pros·trate (pros′trāt), *v.*, –**trat·ed**, –**trat·ing**, *adj.* —*v.* **1** lay down flat; cast down: *the captives prostrated themselves before the conqueror.* **2** *Fig.* make very weak or helpless; exhaust: *sickness often prostrates people.* —*adj.* **1** lying flat with face downward. **2** lying flat. **3** *Fig.* overcome; helpless: *a prostrate enemy.* [< L *prostratus* < *pro-* forth + *sternere* strew] —**pros·tra′tion**, *n.*

pros·y (prōz′i), *adj.*, **pros·i·er**, **pros·i·est.** like prose; commonplace; dull; tiresome. —**pros′i·ly**, *adv.* —**pros′i·ness**, *n.*

prot·ac·tin·i·um (prōt′ak tin′i əm), *n.* a very rare radioactive metallic element, Pa.

pro·tag·o·nist (prō tag′ə nist), *n.* **1** the main character in a play, story, or novel. **2** any person who has a central role. [< Gk., ult. < *protos* first + *agon* contest]

pro·te·an (prō′ti ən; prō tē′ən), *adj.* readily assuming different forms or characters; exceedingly variable. [< *Proteus*]

pro·te·ase (prō′tē ās), *n.*, any of various enzymes, such as pepsin, that break down proteins into simpler compounds.

pro·tect (prə tekt′), *v.* **1** shield from harm or danger; shelter; defend; guard. **2** guard (home industry) against foreign goods by taxing any which are brought into the country. [< L *protectus* < *pro-* in front + *tegere* to cover] —**pro·tect′ing**, *adj.* —**pro·tect′ing·ly**, *adv.* —**pro·tect′ing·ness**, *n.* —**pro·tec′tor**, *n.* —**pro·tec′tor·ship**, *n.*

pro·tec·tion (prə tek′shən), *n.* **1** act of protecting; condition of being kept from harm; defense: *we have the police for our protection.* **2** thing or person that prevents damage: *an apron is a protec-*

tion when doing dirty work. **3** system of taxing foreign goods to make them less competitive than domestically produced goods; the opposite of free trade. **4** payment to gangsters as protection from harrassment or violence by them or their associates. —**pro·tec′tion·ism**, *n.* —**pro·tec′tion·ist**, *n.*

pro·tec·tive (prə tek′tiv), *adj.* **1** being a defense; protecting: *the hard protective covering of a turtle.* **2** preventing injury to those around: *a protective device on a machine.* **3** discouraging importation of foreign goods by putting a high tax or duty on them. —**pro·tec′tive·ly**, *adv.* —**pro·tec′tive·ness**, *n.*

pro·tec·tor·ate (prə tek′tər it), *n.* a weak country under the protection and partial control of a strong country.

pro·té·gé (prō′tə zhā), *n.* person under the protection or kindly care of another. [< F, pp. of *protéger* < L *protegere* PROTECT]

pro·tein (prō′tēn; –tē in), *n.* a complex compound containing nitrogen that is a necessary part of the cells of animals and plants. —*adj.* of or containing protein. [< G, < Gk. *proteios* of the first quality]

pro tem., pro tempore.

pro tem·po·re (prō tem′pə rē), *Latin.* for the time being; temporarily.

pro·test (*n.* prō′test; *v.* prə test′), *n.* **1** statement that denies or objects strongly: *yield after protest.* **2** a solemn declaration: *a protest of innocence.* **3** public demonstration against something esp. a government action or position. —*v.* **1** make objections; object to: *protest a decision.* **2** declare solemnly; assert: *the accused man protested his innocence.*
under protest, unwillingly; with objection. [< OF < L, ult. < *pro-* forth + *testis* witness] —**pro·test′er**, *n.* —**pro·test′ing·ly**, *adv.*

Prot·es·tant (prot′is tənt), *n.* **1** a member of any of certain Christian churches which ultimately have split off from the Roman Catholic Church since the sixteenth century. Baptists, Presbyterians, Methodists, Quakers, and many others are Protestants. **2 protestant,** person who protests.

Protestant Episcopal Church, a Protestant church in the U.S. that has about the same principles and beliefs as the Church of England.

Prot·es·tant·ism (prot′is tənt iz′əm), *n.* **1** the religion of Protestants. **2** their principles and beliefs. **3** Protestants or Protestant churches as a group.

prot·es·ta·tion (prot′is tā′shən), *n.* **1** a solemn declaration; protesting. **2** a formal dissent or disapproval; protest.

pro·to·col (prō′tə kol; –kôl), *n.* **1** a first draft or record from which a document, esp. a treaty, is prepared. **2** rules of etiquette of the diplomatic corps. [< OF < Med.L < Gk. *protokollon* a first leaf (with date and contents) glued onto a papyrus

roll < *protos* first + *kolla* glue] —**pro′to·col′ic**, *adj.*

pro·ton (prō′ton), *n.* a tiny particle smaller than an atom carrying one unit of positive electricity. All atoms are built up of electrons and protons. [< Gk., neut. adj., first]

pro·to·plasm (prō′tə plaz əm), *n.* living matter; the substance that is the physical basis of life; the living substance of all plant and animal cells. [< G, < Gk. *protos* first + *plasma* something molded < *plassein* mold] —**pro′to·plas′mic**, *adj.*

pro·to·type (prō′tə tīp), *n.* the first or primary type of anything; the original or model: *a modern ship has its prototype in the hollowed log of early people.* —**pro′to·typ′al**, **pro′to·typ′ic**, **pro′to·typ′i·cal**, *adj.*

Pro·to·zo·a (prō′tə zō′ə), *n.pl.* phylum or subkingdom of protozoans. [< NL, pl., < Gk. *protos* first + *zoion* animal]

pro·to·zo·an (prō′tə zō′ən), *n.* animal that consists of a single cell. —*adj.* belonging or pertaining to the single-celled animals. —**pro′to·zo′al**, **pro′to·zo′ic**, *adj.*

pro·tract (prō trakt′), *v.* **1** draw out; lengthen in time: *protract a visit.* **2** slide out; thrust out; extend. **3** draw by means of a scale and protractor. [< L *protractus* < *pro-* forward + *trahere* drag] —**pro·tract′ed**, *adj.* —**pro·tract′ed·ly**, *adv.* —**pro·tract′ed·ness**, *n.* —**pro·trac′tion**, *n.* —**pro·trac′tive**, *adj.*

pro·trac·tile (prō trak′təl), *adj.* capable of being lengthened out, or of being thrust forth.

pro·trac·tor (prō trak′tər), *n.* instrument for drawing or measuring angles.

pro·trude (prō trüd′), *v.*, –**trud·ed**, –**trud·ing.** **1** thrust forth; stick out: *the saucy child protruded her tongue.* **2** be thrust forth; project: *her teeth protrude too far.* [< L, *pro-* forward + *trudere* to thrust] —**pro·tru′sion**, *n.* —**pro·tru′sive**, **pro·trud′ent**, *adj.* —**pro·tru′sive·ly**, *adv.* —**pro·tru′sive·ness**, *n.*

pro·tu·ber·ance (prō tü′bər əns; –tū′–), **pro·tu·ber·an·cy** (–ən si) *n.*, *pl.* –**anc·es;** –**cies. 1** protuberant quality or condition. **2** part that sticks out; bulge; swelling.

pro·tu·ber·ant (prō tü′bər ənt; –tū′–), *adj.* bulging out; sticking out; prominent. [< LL *protuberans* bulging, ult. < *pro-* forward + *tuber* lump] —**pro·tu′ber·an′tial**, *adj.* —**pro·tu′ber·ant·ly**, *adv.*

proud (proud), *adj.* **1** thinking well of oneself. **2** feeling or showing pleasure or satisfaction: *proud to call him a friend.* **3** having a sense of what is due oneself, one's position, or character: *too proud to fight.* **4** thinking too well of oneself; haughty; arrogant. **5** highly honorable, creditable, or gratifying: *a proud moment.* **6** majestic; magnificent: *proud cities.*

proud of, thinking well of; being well satisfied with. [< OF *prod, prud* valiant < LL *prode* of use < L *prōdesse* be useful] —**proud′ly,** *adv.* —**proud′ness,** *n.*

Prov., 1 Provençal. 2 Proverbs.

prov., provincialism.

prove (prüv), *v.,* **proved, proved** or **prov·en, prov·ing.** 1 establish as true; make certain. 2 be found to be: *this book proved interesting.* 3 try out; test; subject to some testing process: *prove a new gun.* [< OF < L *probare* < *probus* worthy] —**prov′a·ble,** *adj.* —**prov′a·ble·ness,** *n.* —**prov′a·bly,** *adv.* —**prov′er,** *n.*

prov·e·nance (prov′ə nəns), *n.* origin, as the history of a painting or source of an object. [< F < MF *provenir* come forth, originate < L *prōvidēre* come forth, originate]

Pro·ven·çal (prō′vən säl′; prov′ən-), *n.* 1 native or inhabitant of Provence. 2 language of Provence.

prov·en·der (prov′ən dər), *n.* dry food for animals, such as hay or corn. [< OF < L *praebenda.* See PREBEND.]

prov·erb (prov′ėrb), *n.* 1 a short wise saying used for a long time by many people. 2 *Fig.* a well-known example: *he is a proverb of wastefulness.* 3 **Proverbs,** book of the Old Testament made up of sayings of the wise men of Israel, including Solomon.

pro·ver·bi·al (prə vėr′bi əl), *adj.* 1 of proverbs; expressed in a proverb; like a proverb: *proverbial wisdom.* 2 that has become a proverb: *the proverbial stitch in time.* 3 well-known: *the proverbial loyalty of dogs.* **pro·ver′bi·al·ly,** *adv.*

pro·vide (prə vīd′), *v.,* **-vid·ed, -vid·ing.** 1 supply; furnish: *sheep provide us with wool.* 2 take care for the future: *provide for old age.* 3 state as a condition beforehand: *the rules provide that dues must be paid monthly.* 4 get ready; prepare beforehand. [< L, < *pro-* ahead + *videre* see. Doublet of PURVEY.] —**pro·vid′a·ble,** *adj.* —**pro·vid′er,** *n.*

pro·vid·ed (prə vīd′id), *conj.* on the condition that; if: *she will go provided her friends can go also.*

prov·i·dence (prov′ə dəns), *n.* 1 God's care and help. 2 care for the future; good management.

Providence, God.

Prov·i·dence (prov′ə dəns), *n.* capital of Rhode Island, in the NE part.

prov·i·dent (prov′ə dənt), *adj.* 1 having or showing foresight: *provident people lay aside money for their families.* 2 economical; frugal. [< L *providens.* See PROVIDE.] —**prov′i·dent·ly,** *adv.*

prov·i·den·tial (prov′ə den′shəl), *adj.* 1 of or proceeding from divine power or influence. 2 fortunate. —**prov′i·den′tial·ly,** *adv.*

pro·vid·ing (prə vīd′ing), *conj.* on the condition that: *I shall go providing it doesn't rain.*

prov·ince (prov′ins), *n.* 1 one of the main divisions of a country. Canada is made up of provinces instead of states. 2 proper work or activity. 3 an ancient Roman territory outside Italy, ruled by a Roman governor.

the provinces, part of a country outside the capital or the largest cities. [< F < L *provincia*]

pro·vin·cial (prə vin′shəl), *adj.* 1 of a province. 2 belonging or peculiar to some particular province or provinces rather than to the whole country; local: *provincial English.* 3 lacking refinement or polish; narrow: *a provincial point of view.* —*n.* 1 person born or living in a province. 2 a provincial person. —**pro·vin′ci·al′i·ty,** *n.* —**pro·vin′cial·ly,** *adv.*

pro·vin·cial·ism (prə vin′shəl iz əm), *n.* 1 provincial manners, habit of thought, etc. 2 narrow-mindedness. 3 word, expression, or way of pronunciation peculiar to a district of a country.

pro·vi·sion (prə vizh′ən), *n.* 1 statement making a condition: *a provision of the lease is that the rent must be paid promptly.* 2 a taking care for the future: *make provision for a child's welfare.* 3 care taken for the future; arrangement made beforehand: *there is a provision for making the building larger if necessary.* 4 that which is made ready; supply; stock. —*v.* supply with provisions.

provisions, supply of food and drinks. —**pro·vi′sion·er,** *n.*

pro·vi·sion·al (prə vizh′ən əl), *adj.* for the time being; temporary: *a provisional agreement, a provisional governor.* —**pro·vi′sion·al·ly,** *adv.*

pro·vi·so (prə vī′zō), *n., pl.* **-sos, -soes.** sentence or part of a sentence in a contract, or other agreement, that states a condition; condition: *Tom was promoted with the proviso that he was to be put back if he failed any subject.* [< L, it being provided. < *providere* PROVIDE]

pro·vi·so·ry (prə vī′zə ri), *adj.* 1 containing a proviso; conditional. 2 provisional. —**pro·vi′so·ri·ly,** *adv.*

prov·o·ca·tion (prov′ə kā′shən), *n.* 1 act of provoking. 2 something that stirs one up; cause of anger: *angry without provocation.*

pro·voc·a·tive (prə vok′ə tiv), *adj.* 1 irritating; vexing. 2 tending or serving to call forth action, thought, laughter, anger, etc.: *a remark provocative of mirth.* —*n.* something that rouses or irritates. —**pro·voc′a·tive·ly,** *adv.* —**pro·voc′a·tive·ness ,** *n.*

pro·vo·ca·teur (prô vô kà tœr′), person who provokes trouble or incites violence, esp. one secretly hired or ordered to do this. [< F *(agent) provocateur*]

pro·voke (prə vōk′), *v.,* **-voked, -vok·ing.** 1 make angry; vex. 2 stir up; excite: *an insult provokes a person to anger.* 3 bring about; start into action; cause. [< L, < *pro-* forth + *vocare* to call] —**pro·**

vok′er, *n.* —**pro·vok′ing,** *adj.* —**pro·vok′ing·ly,** *adv.*

prov·ost (prov′əst), *n.* 1 person appointed to superintend or preside, such as the head of certain colleges or churches. 2 the chief magistrate in a Scottish town. [< Med.L *propositus* for *praepositus,* orig. pp. < *prae-* at the head of + *ponere* to place] —**prov′ost·ship,** *n.*

pro·vost marshal (prō′vō), 1 in the army, an officer acting as head of police in a camp or district. 2 in the navy, an officer charged with the safekeeping of prisoners until their trial by court-martial.

prow (prou), *n.* 1 the pointed front part of a ship or boat; bow. 2 something like it. [< F < Ital. < L < Gk. *proira*]

prow·ess (prou′is), *n.* 1 bravery; daring. 2 brave or daring acts. 3 unusual skill or ability. [< OF *proece* < *prod* valiant. See PROUD.] —**prow′ess·ful,** *adj.*

prowl (proul), *v.* 1 go about slowly and secretly hunting for something to eat or steal: *many wild animals prowl at night.* 2 wander. —*n.* act of prowling.

on the prowl, out looking or hunting; prowling about. [ME *prolle(n)*] —**prowl′er,** *n.* —**prowl′ing·ly,** *adv.*

prox·i·mal (prok′sə məl), *adj.* situated toward the point of origin or attachment. [< L *proximus* nearest] —**prox′i·mal·ly,** *adv.*

prox·i·mate (prok′sə mit), *adj.* 1 next; nearest. 2 approximate. [< LL *proximatus* approached < *proximus* nearest] —**prox′i·mate·ly,** *adv.* —**prox′i·mate·ness,** *n.*

prox·im·i·ty (proks im′ə ti), *n.* nearness: *she and her cat enjoy the proximity of the fire.* [< L, < *proximus* nearest]

prox·y (prok′si), *n., pl.* **prox·ies.** 1 action of a deputy or substitute. 2 agent; deputy; substitute. 3 a writing authorizing a proxy to act or vote for a person. 4 vote so given. [ME *prokecye,* alter. of *procuracy* the office of proctor. See PROCURE.]

prs., pairs.

prude (prüd), *n.* person who is too proper or too modest about sex; person who puts on extremely proper or modest airs. [< F, ult. < OF *prod* worthy. See PROWESS.] —**prud′ish,** *adj.* —**prud′ish·ly,** *adv.* —**prud′ish·ness,** *n.*

pru·dence (prü′dəns), *n.* 1 wise thought before acting; good judgment. 2 good management; economy.

pru·dent (prü′dənt), *adj.* planning carefully ahead of time; sensible; discreet: *a prudent man saves part of his wages.* [< L *prudens,* var. of *providens* PROVIDENT] —**pru′dent·ly,** *adv.*

pru·den·tial (prü den′shəl), *adj.* of, marked by, or showing prudence. —**pru·den′tial·ly,** *adv.*

prud·er·y (prüd′ər i), *n., pl.* **-er·ies.** 1 extreme modesty or propriety, esp. when not genuine. 2 a prudish act or remark.

prune[1] (prün), *n.* 1 kind of dried sweet plum. 2 *Fig.* an unpleasant, sour person.

[< F < L < Gk. *proumnon.* Doublet of PLUM.]

prune² (prün), *v.,* **pruned, prun·ing. 1** *Fig.* cut out useless or undesirable parts from: *prune a story to its essentials.* **2** cut superfluous or undesirable twigs or branches from (a bush, tree, etc.). [< OF *proognier*] —**prun′er,** *n.*

pruning hook, implement with a hooked blade, used for pruning vines, etc.

pru·ri·ent (prŭr′i ənt), *adj.* having lustful thoughts or wishes. [< L *pruriens* itching, being wanton] —**pru′ri·ence, pru′ri·en·cy,** *n.* —**pru′ri·ent·ly,** *adv.*

Prussian blue, a deep-blue pigment, essentially a cyanogen compound of iron.

prus·sic acid (prus′ik), hydrocyanic acid.

pry¹ (prī), *v.,* **pried, pry·ing,** *n., pl.* **pries.** —*v.* look with curiosity; peep: *she is always prying into other people's affairs.* —*n.* an inquisitive person. [ME *prie(n)*] —**pry′ing·ly,** *adv.*

pry² (prī), *v.,* **pried, pry·ing,** *n., pl.* **pries.** —*v.* **1** raise or move by force. **2** get with much effort: *I pried the secret out of him.* [< n.] —*n.* lever for prying. [< *prize* a lever, taken as a pl.]

Ps., Psalm; Psalms.

P.S., 1 postscript. **2** Public School.

psalm (säm), *n.* a sacred song or poem. —*v.* celebrate or praise in psalms.

Psalm, any of the 150 sacred songs or hymns that together form a book of the Old Testament. [< LL < Gk. *psalmos*]

Psalms (sämz), *n.pl.* book of the Old Testament consisting of 150 psalms.

Psal·ter (sôl′tər), *n.* **1** the Book of Psalms. **2** Sometimes, **psalter.** a prayer book containing the Psalms for liturgical or devotional use. [< L < Gk. *psalterion,* orig., stringed instrument < *psallein* pluck]

pseu·do (sü′dō), *adj.* **1** false; sham; pretended. **2** having only the appearance of. [< Gk. *pseudes* false]

pseu·do·sci·ence (sü′dō sī′əns), *n.* false or fake science: *the theory is based on pseudoscience.* —**pseu′do·sci′en·tif·ic,** *adj.* —**pseu′do·sci′en·tist ,** *n.*

pseu·do·nym (sü′də nim), *n.* name used by an author instead of his or her real name. [< Gk. *pseudonymon < pseudes* false + dial. *onyma* name]

pshaw (shô), *interj., n.* exclamation expressing impatience, contempt, etc.

psi (sī; psē), *n.* the 23rd letter of the Greek alphabet (Ψ, ψ).

psi or **p.s.i.,** pounds per square inch.

psit·ta·co·sis (sit′ə kō′sis), *n.* a contagious disease of parrots and other birds, communicable to people; parrot fever. [< NL, < Gk. *psittakos* parrot]

pso·ri·a·sis (sə rī′ə sis), *n.* a chronic skin disease characterized by dry, scaling patches. [< NL < Gk., ult. < *psora* itch]

PST, P.S.T., or **p.s.t.,** Pacific Standard Time.

psych (sīk), *n. Informal.* psychology. —*v.* **1** use psychology on: *psych an opponent,*

psych out their strategy. **2** create excitement; stimulate: *psych up for the game.* [< *psychology*]

psy·che (sī′kē), *n.* **1** the human soul or spirit. **2** the mind.

psy·che·del·ic (sī′kə del′ik), *adj.* **1** producing hallucinations along with a feeling of heightened awareness, expanded consciousness, liberated creativity, etc. **2** brightly colored, wildly patterned, suggesting a hallucinogenic state. —*n.* **1** drug that produces such sensations. **2** person who uses such a drug.

psy·chi·a·try (sī kī′ə tri; si–), *n.* study and treatment of mental diseases. [< PSYCHO– + Gk. *iatreia* cure] —**psy′-chi·at′ric,** *adj.* —**psy′chi·at′ri·cal·ly,** *adv.* —**psy·chi′a·trist,** *n.*

psy·chic (sī′kik), *adj.* Also, **psy′chi·cal. 1** of the soul or mind; mental. **2** supernatural. **3** especially susceptible to psychic influences. —*n.* medium (def. 5). [< Gk., < *psyche* soul, mind] —**psy′chi·cal·ly,** *adv.*

psy·cho (sī′kō), *n., pl.* **-chos.** *Informal.* a psychopathic person. —*adj. Informal.* psychopathic.

psycho-, psych-, *combining form.* mind, as in *psychoanalysis.* [< Gk. *psyche* soul, mind]

psy·cho·a·nal·y·sis (sī′kō ə nal′ə sis), *n.* **1** the minute examination of a mind to discover the underlying mental causes producing certain mental and nervous disorders. **2** analysis of mind or personality. —**psy′cho·an′a·lyst,** *n.* —**psy′cho·an′a·lyt′ic, psy′cho·an′a·lyt′i·cal,** *adj.* —**psy′cho·an′a·lyt′i·cal·ly,** *adv.*

psy·cho·an·a·lyze (sī′kō an′ə līz), *v.,* **-lyzed, -lyz·ing.** examine by psychoanalysis. —**psy′cho·an′a·lyz′er,** *n.*

psychological warfare, systematic efforts to affect morale, loyalty, etc., esp. of large national groups.

psy·chol·o·gy (sī kol′ə ji), *n., pl.* **-gies. 1** the science of mind. Psychology tries to explain why people act, think, and feel as they do. **2** the mental states and processes of a person or persons; mental nature and behavior: *Mrs. Jones knew her husband's psychology.* [< NL, < Gk. *psyche* soul, mind + *-logos* treating of] —**psy′cho·log′i·cal,** *adj.* —**psy′cho·log′i·cal·ly,** *adv.* —**psy·chol′o·gist,** *n.*

psy·cho·path (sī′kə path), *n.* person who suffers from a mental disorder.

psy·cho·path·ic (sī′kə path′ik), *adj.* **1** of or characteristic of mental disorders. **2** having a mental disorder.

psy·chop·a·thy (sī kop′ə thi), *n.* mental disease or disorder.

psy·cho·sis (sī kō′sis), *n., pl.* **-ses** (–sēz). any severe form of mental disturbance or disease, which can also be part of a physical disease. [< NL < Gk., < *psyche* soul, mind] —**psy·chot′ic,** *adj.*

psy·cho·so·mat·ic (sī kō sə mat′ik), *adj.* of or pertaining to both mind and body, esp. how the mind can affect the body.

psy·cho·ther·a·py (sī′kō ther′ə pi), *n.* treatment of disease by mental influences.

Pt, platinum.

pt., *pl. (for 1, 3, 4)* **pts. 1** part. **2** past tense. **3** pint. **4** point.

P.T.A., Parent-Teacher Association.

ptar·mi·gan (tär′mə gən), *n., pl.* **-gans** or (*esp. collectively*) **-gan.** any of several kinds of grouse found in mountainous and cold regions. [< Scotch Gaelic *tärmachan*]

pter·o·dac·tyl (ter′ə dak′təl), *n.* an extinct flying reptile that had wings somewhat like a bat's. [< Gk. *pteron* wing + *daktylos* finger, toe]

P.T.O., please turn over (a page).

Ptol·e·ma·ic (tol′ə mā′ik), *adj.* of or having to do with the astronomer Ptolemy. The **Ptolemaic system** of astronomy taught that the earth was the fixed center of the universe.

pto·maine (tō′mān; tō mān′), *n.* a substance, often poisonous, produced in decaying matter. Improperly canned foods may contain ptomaines and can cause food poisoning. [< Ital., < Gk. *ptoma* corpse]

PTSD, post-traumatic stress disorder.

Pu, plutonium.

pub (pub), *n.* public house (def. 1).

pu·ber·ty (pū′bər ti), *n.* the physical beginning of manhood and womanhood. Puberty comes at about 14 in boys and about 12 in girls. [< L *pubertas < pubes* adult]

pu·bes·cent (pū bes′ənt), *adj.* **1** arriving or arrived at puberty. **2** covered with down or fine short hair. [< L *pubescens* reaching puberty < *pubes* adult] —**pu·bes′cence,** *n.*

pu·bis (pū′bis), *n., pl.* **-bes** (–bēz). part of either hipbone that, with the corresponding part of the other, forms the front of the pelvis. [< NL os pubis bone of the groin] —**pu′bic,** *adj.*

pub·lic (pub′lik), *adj.* **1** of, belonging to, serving, or concerning the people as a whole: *public affairs, a public park, a public official.* **2** done, made, acting, etc., for the people as a whole: *public relief.* **3** known to many or all; not private: *the fact became public.* —*n.* **1** the people in general; all the people. **2** a particular section of the people; clientele: *a popular actor has a large public.*

in public, not in private or secretly; openly. [< L *publicus,* ult. < *populus* the people] —**pub′lic·ly,** *adv.*

pub·li·can (pub′lə kən), *n.* **1** *Brit.* keeper of a pub. **2** a tax collector of ancient Rome.

pub·li·ca·tion (pub′lə kā′shən), *n.* **1** book, newspaper, or magazine; anything that is published. **2** the printing and selling of books, newspapers, magazines, etc. **3** act of making known; fact or state of being made known; public announcement. [< L, ult. < *publicus* PUBLIC]

public defender, attorney paid from public funds to defend a person accused of a crime who does not have enough money to hire an attorney.

public domain, lands belonging to the state or federal government.

in the public domain, of works, material, etc., available for unrestricted use because unprotected by copyright or patent.

public enemy, person who is a menace to the public.

public health, 1 general level of health of a whole community. **2** measures taken by a government agency to maintain or improve the general level of health in a community, state, or country.

public house, 1 *Brit.* place where alcoholic liquor is sold to be drunk; saloon. **2** inn; hotel.

pub·li·cist (pub′lə sist), *n.* **1** person skilled or trained in law or in public affairs. **2** writer on law, politics, or public affairs.

pub·lic·i·ty (pub lis′ə ti), *n.* **1** public notice: *the publicity that actors desire.* **2** measures used for getting, or the process of getting, public notice: *a campaign of publicity for a new automobile.* **3** being public; being seen by or known to everybody: *in the publicity of the street.*

pub·li·cize (pub′lə sīz), *v.,* **-cized, -ciz-ing.** give publicity to.

public opinion, opinion of the people in a country, community, etc.

public relations, activities of an organization that are concerned with giving the public a better understanding of its policies and purposes, by giving out news through various media.

public school, 1 a free school maintained by taxes. **2** in England, an endowed private boarding school.

public servant, person who works for the government.

pub·lic-spir·it·ed (pub′lik spir′it id), *adj.* having or showing an unselfish desire for the public good.

public utility, company formed or chartered to render services to the public, such as a company furnishing electricity or gas, a railroad, a bus line, etc.

public works, things built by the government at public expense and for public use, such as roads, docks, canals, and waterworks.

pub·lish (pub′lish), *v.* **1** prepare and offer (a book, paper, map, piece of music, etc.) for sale or distribution. **2** make publicly or generally known: *don't publish the faults of your friends.* **3** announce formally or officially. [< OF *publier,* ult. < L *publicus* PUBLIC; modeled after *punish,* etc.] **—pub′lish·a·ble,** *adj.*

pub·lish·er (pub′lish ər), *n.* person or company whose business is to publish books, newspapers, magazines, etc.

puck (puk), *n.* **1** a mischievous spirit; goblin. **2** a rubber disk used in the game of ice hockey. [OE *pūca* goblin] **—puck′ish,** *adj.* **—puck′ish·ness,** *n.*

puck·er (puk′ər), *v.* draw into wrinkles or irregular folds: *pucker one's brow.* **—n.** an irregular fold; wrinkle. [appar. < *poke*²]

pud·ding (pùd′ing), *n.* **1 a** a soft cooked food, usually sweet, as rice pudding. **b** rich cake often made with nuts and fruits, usually cooked by steaming. **2** kind of sausage. **3** anything soft like a pudding.

pud·dle (pud′əl), *n., v.,* **-dled, -dling.** **—n.** **1** a small pool of water, esp. dirty water. **2** a small pool of any liquid. **3** wet clay and sand stirred into a paste. **—v. 1** make wet or muddy. **2** mix up wet clay and sand to stop water from running through. **3** stir (melted iron) along with an oxidizing agent to make wrought iron. [cf. OE *pudd* ditch] **—pud′dler,** *n.* **—pud′dly,** *adj.*

pud·dling (pud′ling), *n.* act or process of converting pig iron into wrought iron by stirring the molten metal along with an oxidizing agent.

pudg·y (puj′i), *adj.,* **pudg·i·er, pudg·i·est.** short and fat or thick. **—pudg′i·ly,** *adv.* **—pudg′i·ness,** *n.*

pueb·lo (pweb′lō), *n., pl.* **-los. 1** an Indian village built of adobe and stone. There were many pueblos in the SW United States. **2 Pueblo,** an Indian living in a pueblo. [< Sp., people, < L *populus*]

pu·er·ile (pū′ər il), *adj.* foolish for a grown person to say or do; childish. [< L, < *puer* boy] **—pu′er·ile·ly,** *adv.* **—pu′er·il′i·ty, pu′er·ile·ness,** *n.*

pu·er·per·al (pū ėr′pər əl), *adj.* of or pertaining to childbirth. [< NL, ult. < L *puer* child + *parere* to bear]

Puer·to Ri·co (pwer′tō rē′kō), island in the E part of the West Indies. It is a self-governing commonwealth affiliated with the United States. **—Puerto Rican.**

puff (puf), *v.* **1** blow or come with short, quick blasts: *the engine puffed, smoke puffed out of the chimney.* **2** breathe quick and hard. **3** *Fig.* swell with air or pride: *he puffed out his cheeks.* **4** arrange in soft, round masses. **5** *Fig.* praise in exaggerated language. **—n. 1** a short, quick blast: *a puff of wind.* **2** act or process of swelling. **3** a soft round mass, as of hair. **4** a light pastry filled with whipped cream, jam, etc. **5** *Fig.* extravagant praise. [OE *pyffan*] **—puff′y,** *adj.* **—puff′i·ly,** *adv.* **—puff′i·ness,** *n.*

puff adder, a large and very poisonous African snake that puffs up the upper part of its body when excited.

puff·ball (puf′bôl′), *n.* any of various ballshaped fungi characterized by spore cases that give off a cloud of tiny spores when suddenly broken.

puff·er (puf′ər), *n.* **1** person or thing that puffs. **2** any of various fishes capable of inflating the body.

puff·er·y (puf′ər i), *n., pl.* **-er·ies.** exaggerated praise.

puf·fin (puf′ən), *n.* a sea bird of the N Atlantic that has a high, narrow, furrowed, parti-colored bill. [ME *poffin*]

pug (pug), *n.* **1** a small, tan dog with a curly tail and a short, turned-up nose. **2** pug nose.

pu·gi·lism (pū′jəliz əm), *n.* art of fighting with the fists; boxing. [< L *pugil* boxer] **—pu′gi·list,** *n.* **—pu′gi·lis′tic,** *adj.* **—pu′gi·lis′ti·cal·ly,** *adv.*

pug·na·cious (pug nā′shəs), *adj.* having the habit of fighting; fond of fighting; quarrelsome. [< L *pugnax,* ult. < *pugnus* fist] **pug·na′cious·ly,** *adv.* **—pug·nac′i·ty, pug·na′cious·ness,** *n.*

pug nose, a short, turned-up nose. **—pug′nosed′,** *adj.*

puke (pūk), *n., v.,* **puked, puk·ing.** *Informal.* =vomit.

Pu·litz·er Prize (pū′lit sər; pùl′it–), any one of various annual prizes for the best American drama, novel, biography, history, book of verse, editorial, and cartoon, established by **Joseph Pulitzer,** an American journalist, 1847–1911, and first awarded in 1917.

pull (pùl), *n.* **1** draw or haul toward oneself or itself, or in a particular direction, or into a particular position: *pull a sled up a hill, pull at one's tight collar.* **2** move or draw out, usually with effort or force: *the bus pulled out of the station, pull a tooth, yarn pulls apart easily.* **3** tear; rip: *pull down an old shed.* **4** stretch too far; strain: *the runner pulled a ligament in his leg.* **5** hold back, esp. to keep from winning: *pull one's punches in a fight.* **6** perform; carry through: *don't pull any tricks.* **—n. 1** act or effort of pulling. **2** force expended in pulling. **3** handle, rope, ring, or other thing to pull by. **4** influence; advantage.

pull for, give help to; support: *pull for a favorite to win.*

pull in, *Informal.* **a** arrest: *pull in the suspect.* **b** arrive: *pull in about midnight.*

pull off, *Informal.* succeed in.

pull oneself together, gather one's faculties, energy, etc.

pull over, move a car to the side of a road and stop.

pull through, get through a difficult or dangerous situation.

pull together, work in harmony; get on together. [OE *pullian*] **—pull′er,** *n.*

pul·let (pùl′it), *n.* a young hen, usually less than a year old. [< OF *poulette,* dim. of *poule* hen < L *pulla*]

pul·ley (pùl′i), *n., pl.* **-leys. 1** wheel with a grooved rim in which a rope can run, and so change the direction of the pull. **2** set of such wheels used to increase the power applied. [< OF *poulie,* ult. < Gk. *polos* axle]

pull·out (pùl′out′), *n.* **1** withdrawal of troops. **2** something that pulls out, as a folded picture in a magazine or book.

pull·o·ver (pùl′ō vər), *n.* sweater put on by pulling it over the head.

pul·mo·nar·y (pùl′mə ner′i), *adj.* **1** of or having to do with the lungs. Tuberculosis and pneumonia are pulmonary diseases. **2** having lungs. [< L, < *pulmo* lung]

pulp (pulp), *n.* **1** the soft part of any fruit or vegetable. **2** the soft inner part of a tooth, containing blood vessels and nerves. **3** any soft wet mass. Paper is made from wood pulp. —*v.* reduce to pulp. [< L *pulpa*] —**pulp′er,** *n.* —**pulp′y,** *adj.* —**pulp′i·ness,** *n.*

pul·pit (pul′pit), *n.* platform or raised structure in a church from which the minister preaches.
the pulpit, preachers or preachings. [< LL *pulpitum* < L, scaffold, platform]

pulp·wood (pulp′wud´), *n.* **1** wood reduced to pulp for making paper. **2** wood suitable for making paper.

pul·sar (pul′sär), *n.* source of radio waves emitted in regular bursts from space: *pulsars located in the Milky Way.* [< *pulse* + *-ar,* as in *quasar*]

pul·sate (pul′sāt), *v.,* **-sat·ed, -sat·ing. 1** expand and contract rhythmically; beat; throb. **2** vibrate; quiver. [< L *pulsatus,* pp. of *pulsare,* frequentative of *pellere* to beat. Doublet of PUSH.] —**pul·sa′tion,** *n.* —**pul′sa·tive** *adj.*

pulse[1] (puls), *n., v.,* **pulsed, puls·ing.** —*n.* **1** the beating of the heart; changing flow of blood in the arteries caused by the beating of the heart. **2** any regular, measured beat. **3** feeling; sentiment: *the pulse of the nation.* —*v.* beat; throb; vibrate. [< L *pulsus* < *pellere* to beat]

pulse[2] (puls), *n.* peas, beans, and lentils, used as food. [< OF < L *puls* porridge]

pul·ver·ize (pul′vər īz), *v.,* **-ized, -iz·ing. 1** grind to powder or dust. **2** become dust. **3** break to pieces; demolish. [< LL *pulverizare* < L *pulvis* dust] —**pul′ver·iz′a·ble,** *adj.* —**pul′ver·i·za′tion,** *n.* —**pul′ver·iz′er,** *n.*

pu·ma (pu′mə), *n.* =cougar [< Sp. < Quechua (S Am.Ind.)]

pum·ice (pum′is), *n., v.,* **-iced, -ic·ing.** —*n.* Also, **pumice stone,** a light, spongy stone thrown up from volcanoes, used for cleaning, smoothing, and polishing. —*v.* clean, smooth, or polish with pumice. [< OF < L *pumex*] —**pu·mi′ceous,** *adj.*

pum·mel (pum′əl), *v.,* **-meled, -mel·ing.** =pommel.

pump[1] (pump), *n.* apparatus or machine for forcing liquids, air, or gas into or out of things. —*v.* **1** move (liquids, air, etc.) by a pump. **2** blow air into. **3** move up and down like a pump handle: *he pumped my hand.* **4** get or try to get information out of.
pump up, *Informal.* excite; enthuse. [appar. < F *pompe,* ? < Gmc.] —**pump′er,** *n.*

pump[2] (pump), *n.* a low shoe with no fasteners.

pum·per·nick·el (pum′pər nik´əl), *n.* a heavy, dark bread made of unbolted rye. [< G]

pump·kin (pump′kin; pung′kin), *n.* **1** large, roundish, orange-yellow fruit of a trailing vine, used for making pies, as food for stock, etc. **2** vine that it grows on. [alter. (with substitution of -KIN) of earlier *pumpion* < L < Gk. *pepon*]

pun (pun), *n., v.,* **punned, pun·ning.** —*n.* a humorous use of a word where it can have different meanings; play on words. —*v.* make puns. —**pun′ner,** *n.* —**pun′ning·ly,** *adv.*

punch[1] (punch), *v.* **1** hit with the fish. **2** herd or drive cattle. —*n.* **1** a quick thrust or blow. **2** vigorous force or effectiveness.
beat to the punch, do something before anyone else.
pull (one's) punches, hold back, act or speak with caution.
punch out, *Informal.* beat; hit, esp. someone already knocked down or injured. [? var. of *pounce*] —**punch′er,** *n.*

punch[2] (punch), *v.* **1** pierce, cut, stamp, force, or drive with a punch: *the train conductor punches tickets.* **2** make (a hole) with a punch or any pointed instrument. —*n.* **1** a tool or apparatus for piercing, perforating, or stamping materials, impressing a design, forcing nails, etc. **2** tool for making holes. [short for *puncheon* a stamping tool used by goldsmiths] —**punch′er,** *n.*

punch[3] (punch), *n.* drink made of different liquids mixed together. [prob. < Hind. *panc* five, through number of ingredients in drink]

Punch (punch), *n.* a hook-nosed, hump-backed doll who quarrels violently with his wife Judy in the puppet show **Punch and Judy.**
pleased as Punch, very much pleased. [var. of *punchinello*]

punch-drunk (punch′drungk´), *adj.* **1** uncoordinated and confused as the result of concussion to the brain, esp. of a boxer. **2** *Fig.* dazed; confused.

pun·cheon (pun′chən), *n.* **1** a large cask for liquor. **2** amount that it holds. [< OF *poinchon,* ult. < L *pungere* pierce]

pun·chi·nel·lo (pun´chə nel′ō), *n., pl.* **-los, -loes.** clown. [< dial. Ital. *Pulcinella.* prob. ult. < L *pullus* chick]

punching bag, 1 a leather or canvas bag, filled to make it hard, to be hung up and punched with the fists for exercise. **2** *Fig.* person or thing that endures another's anger, frustration, etc.

punch line, line in a play or book or at the end of a monologue that sums up the story or makes a point, often humorously.

punch·y (pun′chi), *adj.* **1** forceful; sharp: *punchy writing.* **2** dazed; confused.

punc·til·i·ous (pungk til′i əs), *adj.* **1** very careful and exact: *be punctilious in obeying the doctor's orders.* **2** paying strict attention to details of conduct and ceremony. —**punc·til′i·ous·ly,** *adv.* —**punc·til′i·ous·ness,** *n.*

punc·tu·al (pungk′chü əl), *adj.* prompt; on time: *punctual to the minute.* [< Med.L, < L *punctus* POINT] —**punc´tu·al′i·ty, punc´tu·al·ness,** *n.* —**punc′tu·al·ly,** *adv.*

punc·tu·ate (pungk′chü āt), *v.,* **-at·ed, -at·ing. 1** use periods, commas, and other marks to help make the meaning clear. **2** put punctuation marks in. **3** interrupt now and then. **4** give point or emphasis to: *he punctuated his remarks with gestures.* [< Med.L, < L *punctus* POINT] —**punc′tu·a′tor,** *n.*

punc·tu·a·tion (pungk´chü ā′shən), *n.* use of periods, commas, and other marks to help make the meaning clear.
punctuation marks, marks used in writing or printing to help make the meaning clear, such as periods, commas, question marks, colons, etc.

punc·ture (pungk′chər), *n., v.,* **-tured, -tur·ing.** —*n.* **1** hole made by something pointed. **2** act or process of puncturing. —*v.* **1** make a hole in with something pointed. **2** have or get a puncture. **3** reduce, spoil, or destroy as if by a puncture. [< L *punctura* < *pungere* prick] —**punc′tur·a·ble,** *adj.*

pun·dit (pun′dit), *n.* **1** a very learned Hindu. **2** any very learned person; expert; authority. **3** *Fig.* commentator, esp. one who regularly appears on television. [< Hind. < Skt. *pandita* learned]

pun·gent (pun′jənt), *adj.* **1** sharply affecting the organs of taste and smell: *the pungent smell of burning oil.* **2** sharp; biting: *pungent criticism.* **3** stimulating to the mind; keen; lively: *a pungent wit* [< L *pungens* pricking] —**pun′gen·cy,** *n.* —**pun′gent·ly,** *adv.*

Pu·nic (pyü′nik), *adj.* of or having to do with Carthage or its people. —*n.* language of the Carthaginians. [< L *Pūnicus* < *Poenus* a Carthaginian]

pun·ish (pun′ish), *v.* **1** cause pain, loss, or discomfort to for some fault or offense: *punish a disobedient child, punish theft.* **2** deal with severely, roughly, or greedily. [< OF *puniss-* < L, < *poena* penalty] —**pun′ish·a·ble,** *adj.* —**pun´ish·a·bil′i·ty, pun′ish·a·ble·ness,** *n.* —**pun′ish·er,** *n.*

pun·ish·ment (pun′ish mənt), *n.* **1** a punishing or being punished. **2** something inflicted as a penalty in punishing. **3** pain, suffering, or loss. **4** severe or rough treatment.

pu·ni·tive (pū′nə tiv), **pu·ni·to·ry** (-tô´ri; -tō-), *adj.* **1** concerned with punishment. **2** inflicting punishment. —**pu′ni·tive·ly,** *adv.* —**pu′ni·tive·ness,** *n.*

punk (pungk), *n.* **1** a preparation that burns very slowly. **2** decayed wood used as tinder. **3** young hoodlum. **4 a** =punk rock. **b** style and culture of the punk rock. **5** young, inexperienced person. —*adj.* **1** poor or bad in quality: *a punk car.* **2** not good; miserable: *a punk day altogether.* **3** of or having to do with punk rock. [? < Am.Ind.]

punk rock, rock music having a strong beat and aggressive, rough style. —**punk rocker,**

pun·ster (pun′stər), *n.* person fond of making puns.

punt (punt), *n.* **1** a shallow, flat-bottomed boat having square ends, usually moved by pushing with a pole against the bottom of a river, etc. **2** kick given to a football dropped from the hands before it touches the ground. —*v.* **1** propel (a boat) by pushing with a pole against the bottom of a river, pond, etc. **2** kick (a football) before it touches the ground after dropping it from the hands. [< L *ponto*] —**punt′er,** *n.*

pu·ny (pū′ni), *adj.,* **-ni·er, -ni·est. 1** of less than usual size and strength; weak. **2** petty; not important. [< OF *puisne* laterborn < *puis* (ult. < L *postea*) afterwards + *ne* born < L *natus*] —**pu′ni·ly,** *adv.* —**pu′ni·ness,** *n.*

pup (pup), *n., v.,* **pupped, pup·ping.** —*n.* **1** a young dog; puppy. **2** a young fox, wolf, seal, etc. —*v.* bring forth pups. [var. of *puppy*]

pu·pa (pū′pə), *n., pl.* **-pae** (-pē), **-pas. 1** stage between the larva and the adult in the development of many insects. **2** form of an insect in this stage. Most pupae are inactive and some, such as those of many moths, are enclosed in a tough case or cocoon. [special NL use of L, girl, doll] —**pu′pal,** *adj.*

pu·pil¹ (pū′pəl), *n.* person who is learning in school or being taught by someone. [< OF < L *pupillus, pupilla* ward < *pupus* boy, *pupa* girl] —**pu′pil·like′,** *adj.*

pu·pil² (pū′pəl), *n.* the expanding and contracting opening in the iris of the eye, through which light passes to the retina. [< L *pupilla,* orig., little doll, dim. of *pupa* girl, doll]

pup·pet (pup′it), *n.* **1** a small doll. **2** figure made to look like a person and moved by wires, strings, or the hands. **3** *Fig.* anybody who is not independent, waits to be told how to act, and does what somebody else says. [earlier *poppet* < F, < L *pupa* girl, doll]

pup·pet·eer (pup′ə tir′), *n.* person who manipulates puppets.

pup·pet·ry (pup′ə tri), *n.* **1** art of making and working puppets, and putting on puppet shows. **2** action or movements of puppets.

pup·py (pup′i), *n., pl.* **-pies.** a young dog. [prob. < F *poupée* doll, ult. < L *pupa*] —**pup′py·hood,** *n.*

pup tent, small tent.

pur (pėr), *n., v.,* **purred, pur·ring.** =purr.

pur·blind (pėr′blīnd′), *adj.* **1** nearly blind. **2** slow to discern or understand. [earlier *pur blind* pure blind] —**pur′blind′ly,** *adv.* —**pur′blind′ness,** *n.*

pur·chase (pėr′chəs), *v.,* **-chased, -chasing,** *n.* —*v.* **1** get by paying a price; buy. **2** get in return for something: *purchase safety at the cost of happiness.* **3** hoist, haul, or draw by the aid of some mechanical device. —*n.* **1** act of buying. **2** thing bought. **3** a firm hold to help move something or to keep from slipping. [< AF *purchacer* pursue <

pur– forth (< L *pro-*) + *chacer* CHASE¹] —**pur′chas·a·ble,** *adj.* —**pur′chas·er,** *n.*

pure (pyūr), *adj.* **1** not mixed with anything else; unadulterated; genuine: *pure gold.* **2** perfectly clean; spotless: *a pure white apron.* **3** perfect; correct; without defects: *speak pure French.* **4** nothing else than; mere; sheer: *pure accident.* **5** with no evil; without sin; chaste: *the pure in heart.* **6** abstract or theoretical (opposed to *applied*): *pure mathematics.* **7** of unmixed descent: *a pure Irish family.* —*n.* that which is pure. [< OF < L *purus*] —**pure′ly,** *adv.* —**pure′ness,** *n.*

pu·rée, pu·ree (pyū rā′; pyūr′ā), *n., v.,* **-réed, -ré·ing; -reed, -re·ing.** —*n.* **1** food cooked until soft and pushed through a sieve or ground up raw to a smooth consistency. **2** a thick soup. —*v.* make into a purée. [< F, *purer* to strain]

pur·ga·tive (pėr′gə tiv), *n.* medicine that empties the bowels. —*adj.* purging. —**pur′ga·tive·ly,** *adv.* —**pur′ga·tive·ness,** *n.*

pur·ga·to·ry (pėr′gə tô′ri; -tō′-), *n., pl.* **-ries. 1** in the belief of the Roman Catholics, a temporary condition or place in which the souls of those who have died penitent are purified from venial sin or the effects of sin by punishment. **2** any condition or place of temporary suffering or punishment. [< Med.L *purgatorium,* orig. neut. adj., purging < L *purgare* PURGE] —**pur′ga·to′ri·al,** *adj.*

purge (pėrj), *v.,* **purged, purg·ing,** *n.* —*v.* **1** wash away all that is not clean from; make clean. **2** clear or any undesired thing or person, such as air in a water pipe or opponents in a nation. **3** empty (the stomach or intestinal tract). —*n.* **1** act of purging. **2** medicine that purges. **3** elimination of undesired persons from a nation or party. [< OF < L *purgare* cleanse, ult. < *purus* pure + *agere* drive] —**purge′a·ble,** *adj.* —**purg′er,** *n.*

pu·ri·fy (pyūr′ə fī), *v.,* **-fied, -fy·ing.** make pure. [< OF < L, < *purus* pure + *facere* make] —**pu′ri·fi·ca′tion,** *n.* —**pu′ri·fi′er,** *n.*

pur·ist (pyūr′ist), *n.* **1** person who is extremely careful to be correct in speech, manner of expression, etc. **2** person who is overly concerned with correctness. —**pur′ism,** *n.*

Pu·ri·tan (pyūr′ə tən), *n.* **1** member of a group in the Church of England during the 16th and 17th centuries who wanted simpler forms of worship and stricter morals. Many Puritans settled in New England. **2** **puritan,** person who is very strict in morals and religion. —*adj.* **1** of the Puritans. **2** **puritan,** very strict in morals and religion. —**Pu′ri·tan·ism, pu′ri·tan·ism,** *n.*

pu·ri·tan·i·cal (pyūr′ə tan′ə kəl), **pu·ri·tan·ic** (-ik), *adj.* very strict or too strict in morals or religion. —**pu′ri·tan′i·cal·ly,** *adv.* —**pu′ri·tan′i·cal·ness,** *n.*

pu·ri·ty (pyūr′ə ti), *n.* **1** freedom from dirt or mixture; clearness; cleanness. **2**

freedom from evil; innocence. **3** freedom from foreign or inappropriate elements or characteristics; correctness: *purity of style.* [< L, < *purus* pure]

purl¹ (pėrl), *v.* flow with rippling motions and a murmuring sound. —*n.* a purling motion or sound. [? < Scand. (Norw.) *purla*]

purl² (pėrl), *v.* knit with inverted stitches. —*n.* inversion of stitches in knitting, producing a ribbed appearance. [< *pirl* twist, of uncert. orig.]

pur·lieu (pėr′lü), *n.* **1** piece of land on the border of a forest. **2** one's haunt or resort; one's bounds. **3** any bordering, neighboring, or outlying region or district. [alter. of earlier *puraley* (infl. by F *lieu* place) < AF, < *poraler* go through]

pur·loin (pėr loin′), *v.* steal. [< AF *purloigner* remove < *pur–* forth (< L *pro-*) + *loin* afar < L *longe*] —**pur·loin′er,** *n.*

pur·ple (pėr′pəl), *n., adj., v.,* **-pled, -pling.** —*n.* **1** a dark color made by mixing red and blue. **2** purple cloth or clothing, esp. as worn by emperors, kings, etc., to indicate high rank. **3** imperial, royal, or high rank: *a prince is born to the purple.* —*adj.* **1** of the color of purple. **2** imperial; royal. **3** brilliant; gorgeous; gaudy. —*v.* make or become purple. [< L < Gk. *porphyra,* a shellfish, or the purple dye from it] —**pur′plish, pur′ply,** *adj.*

purple martin, a large, blue-black swallow of the United States.

pur·port (*v.* pər pôrt′, -pōrt′, pėr′pôrt, -pōrt; *n.* pėr′pôrt, -pōrt), *v.* **1** claim; profess: *the document purported to be official.* **2** have as its main idea; mean. —*n.* meaning; main idea. [< AF, < *pur–* forth (< L *pro-*) + *porter* carry < L *portare*] —**pur′port·less,** *adj.*

pur·pose (pėr′pəs), *n.* **1** something one has in mind to get or do; plan; aim; intention. **2** object or end for which a thing is made, done, used, etc. **on purpose,** with a purpose; not by accident. **to good purpose,** with good results. **to little** or **no purpose,** with few or no results. [< OF *purposer* PROPOSE] —**pur′pose·ful,** *adj.* —**pur′pose·ful·ly,** *adv.* —**pur′pose·less,** *adj.* —**pur′pose·less·ness,** *n.*

pur·pose·ly (pėr′pəs li), *adv.* on purpose; intentionally.

purr (pėr), *n.* a low murmuring sound such as a cat makes when pleased. —*v.* make this sound. Also, **pur.** [imit.]

purse (pėrs), *n., v.,* **pursed, purs·ing.** —*n.* **1** a little bag or case for carrying money around with one. **2** money; resources; treasury. **3** sum of money: *a purse was made up for the victims of the fire.* —*v.* draw together; press into folds or wrinkles. [< LL < Gk. *byrsa* hide, skin]

purs·er (pėr′sər), *n.* officer who keeps the accounts of a ship, pays wages, and attends to other matters of business.

purs·lane (pėrs′lān; -lin), *n.* a common plant that has small, yellow flowers and small, thick leaves. [< OF *porcelaine,* alter. of L *porcilaca,* var. of *portulaca*]

pur·su·ance (pər sü′əns), *n.* a following; carrying out; pursuit: *in pursuance of his duty, the policeman risked his life.*

pur·su·ant (pər sü′ənt), *adj.* **pursuant to,** following; acting according to; in accordance with. —**pur·su′ant·ly,** *adv.*

pur·sue (pər sü′), *v.,* **-sued, -su·ing. 1** follow to catch or kill; chase. **2** try to get; follow; seek: *pursue a wise course, pursue pleasure.* **3** carry on; keep on with: *pursue the study of French.* **4** continue to annoy or trouble: *pursue a teacher with questions.* [< AF *pursuer* < L *prosequi.* See PROSECUTE.] —**pur·su′a·ble,** *adj.* —**pur·su′er,** *n.*

pur·suit (pər süt′), *n.* **1** act of pursuing: *in pursuit of a fleeing enemy.* **2** the pursuing of something to be gained or attained: *pursuit of wealth.* **3** occupation: *literary pursuits.*

pu·ru·lent (pyůr′ə lənt; pyůr′yə-), *adj.* **1** full of pus; discharging pus; like pus. **2** *Fig.* rotten; corrupt. [< L *purulentus* < *pus* pus] —**pu′ru·lence,** *n.* —**pu′ru·lent·ly,** *adv.*

pur·vey (pər vā′), *v.* supply (food or provisions); provide; furnish: *purvey meat for an army.* [< AF *porveier* < L *providere.* Doublet of PROVIDE.] —**pur·vey′a·ble,** *adj.* —**pur·vey′or,** *n.*

pur·vey·ance (pər vā′əns), *n.* **1** a purveying. **2** provisions; supplies.

pur·view (pèr′vū), *n.* range of operation, activity, concern, etc.; scope; extent. [< AF *purveu,* orig. pp. of *porveier* purvey]

pus (pus), *n.* a yellowish-white liquid formed by inflammation of infected tissue in the body, that consists of white blood cells, bacteria, serum, etc. [< L] —**pus′sy,** *adj.*

push (půsh), *v.* **1** move (something or someone) away by pressing: *push him outdoors.* **2** press hard: *push with all one's might.* **3** go by force: *push on at rapid pace.* **4** make go forward; urge: *he pushed his plans cleverly, push a claim.* **5** extend: *Alexander pushed his conquests still farther east.* **6** urge the use, sale, etc., of. —*n.* **1** act of pushing. **2** hard effort; determined advance. **3** force; energy.

push around, *Informal.* bully; harass.

push off, a move from the shore or a dock. **b** leave.

push on, move ahead; keep on. [< OF < L *pulsare* beat, PULSATE. Doublet of PULSATE.] —**push′er,** *n.* —**push′ing,** *adj.* —**push′ing·ly,** *adv.*

push back, refute. [< military use, force back, repel]

push·cart (půsh′kärt′), *n.* a light cart pushed by hand.

push·o·ver or **push-o·ver** (půsh′ō′vər), *n. Informal.* **1** something very easy to do. **2** person very easy to beat in a contest. **3** person who is easily swayed or influenced.

push·up or **push-up** (půsh′up), *n.* exercise done by raising and lowering the body, from face-down on the floor, using only the arms.

push·y (půsh′i), *adj.,* **push·i·er, push·i·est.** assertive; aggressive.

pu·sil·lan·i·mous (pū′sə lan′ə məs), *adj.* cowardly; mean-spirited; faint-hearted. [< L, < *pusillus* little + *animus* courage] —**pu′sil·la·nim′i·ty,** *n.* —**pu′sil·lan′i·mous·ly,** *adv.*

puss (pus), *n.* =cat.

puss·y (pus′i), *n., pl.* **puss·ies.** =cat.

puss·y·foot (pus′i fůt′), *v., n., pl.* **-foots.** *Informal.* —*v.* **1** move softly and cautiously to avoid being seen. **2** be cautious and timid about revealing one's opinions or committing oneself. —*n.* person who pussyfoots. —**puss′y·foot′er,** *n.* —**puss′y·foot′ing,** *n., adj.*

pussy willow, a small American willow with silky catkins.

pus·tule (pus′chůl), *n.* **1** pimple containing pus. **2** any swelling like a pimple or blister, such as the pustules of chicken pox. [< L, < *pus* pus] —**pus′tu·lar,** *adj.*

put (půt), *v.,* **put, put·ting,** *n.* —*v.* **1** cause to be in some place or position; place; lay: *put your hand in mine.* **2** cause to be in some state, condition, position, relation, etc.: *put a room in order, put one in a doctor's care, put a tax on gasoline.* **3** express: *a teacher should put things clearly.* **4** take one's course; go; turn; proceed: *the ship put out to sea.* **5** assign; attribute: *he put a wrong construction on my action.* —*n.* a throw or cast.

put across, get acceptance of; convince.

put aside or **by, a** save for future use. **b** discard.

put away, a save for future use. **b** *Fig.* consume food, drink, or a meal. **c** *Informal.* put in jail or a mental hospital. **d** *Informal.* kill.

put down, a put an end to; supress. **b** write down. **c** pay as a down payment. **d** *Informal. Fig.* slight; belittle. **e** land (an aircraft). **f** kill: *put down our old dog.*

put forward, suggest; propose.

put in, a spend (time) as specified. **b** enter port. **c** enter a place for safety, supplies, etc. **d** plant.

put off, a lay aside; postpone. **b** ask or cause to wait. **c** prevent or stop from: *put off the book by its foul language.*

put on, a produce (a play or other entertainment). **b** take on oneself: *put on the pounds.* **c** pretend: *put on a happy smile.* **d** *Informal.* tease; joke: *he was just putting you on.*

put one over on, trick; deceive.

put out, a extinguish (fire). **b** confuse; embarrass; offend. **c** distract, disturb, or interrupt. **d** destroy (an eye). **e** cause to be out in a game. **f** publish.

put through, carry out successfully.

put to it, force to a course; put in difficulty: *put to it to finish the job on time.*

put up, a offer; give; show: *put up the furniture for sale.* **b** build: *put up a house.*

c lay aside: *put up all thought of vacation.* **d** preserve (fruits, etc.). **e** give lodging or food to: *put up strangers.* **f** incite: *someone put them up to this.*

put upon, impose upon; take advantage of; victimize: *feel put upon by the criticism and advice of friends.*

put up with, bear with patience; tolerate. [cf. OE *putung* impulse]

pu·ta·tive (pū′tə tiv), *adj.* supposed; reputed. [< L, < *putare* think] —**pu′ta·tive·ly,** *adv.*

put-down (půt′down′), *n.* slight; snub.

pu·tre·fac·tion (pū′trə fak′shən), *n.* decay; rotting. —**pu′tre·fac′tive,** *adj.*

pu·tre·fy (pū′trə fī), *v.,* **-fied, -fy·ing.** rot; decay. [< OF < L, ult. < *puter* rotten + *fieri* become] —**pu′tre·fi′er,** *n.*

pu·tres·cent (pū tres′ənt), *adj.* **1** becoming putrid; rotting. **2** pertaining to putrefaction. [< L *putrescens* growing rotten, ult. < *puter* rotten] —**pu·tres′cence,** *n.*

pu·trid (pū′trid), *adj.* **1** rotten; foul. **2** thoroughly corrupt or depraved; extremely bad. [< L *putridus,* ult. < *puter* rotten] —**pu′trid·ly,** *adv.* —**pu′trid·ness,** *n.*

putt (put), *v.* strike (a golf ball) gently and carefully in an effort to make it roll into the hole. —*n.* the stroke itself. [var. of *put*]

put·ter[1] (put′ər), *v.* keep busy in a rather useless way. [var. of *potter*[2]] —**put′ter·er,** *n.*

putt·er[2] (put′ər), *n.* **1** person who putts. **2** a golf club used in putting.

putt·er[3] (půt′ər), *n.* one that puts.

putt·ing green (put′ing), the smooth turf or sand around a golf hole.

put·ty (put′i), *n., pl.* **-ties,** *v.,* **-tied, -ty·ing.** —*n.* a soft mixture of whiting and linseed oil, used for fastening panes of glass, etc. —*v.* stop up or cover with putty. [< F *potée,* orig., potful < *pot* pot] —**put′ti·er,** *n.*

put-up (půt′up′), *adj.* planned beforehand, or deliberately, in a secret or crafty manner: *a put-up job.*

puz·zle (puz′əl), *n., v.,* **-zled, -zling.** —*n.* **1** a hard problem. **2** problem or task to be done for fun. **3** puzzled condition. —*v.* **1** make unable to answer, solve, or understand something; perplex. **2** exercise one's mind on something hard.

puzzle out, find out by thinking or trying hard.

puzzle over, think hard about; try hard to do or work out. —**puz′zle·ment,** *n.* —**puz′zler,** *n.*

Pvt., Private.

PX, P.X., Post Exchange.

pyg·my (pig′mi), *n., pl.* **-mies,** *adj.* —*n.* **1** a very small person; dwarf. **2 Pygmy,** member of any of various races of Africa, SE Asia, Philippine Islands, etc. —*adj.* very small. [< L < Gk. *pygmaioi,* orig. pl. adj., dwarfish < *pygme* cubit, fist]

py·lon (pī′lon), *n.* a tall steel framework used to carry high-tension wires across country. [< Gk., gateway, < *pyle* gate]

py·lo·rus (pī lô′rəs; –lō′–; pə–), *n., pl.* **–ri** (–rī). the opening that leads from the stomach into the intestine. [< LL < Gk. *pyloros,* orig., gatekeeper < *pyle* gate + *horos* watching] —**py·lor′ic,** *adj.*

Pyong·yang (pyung′yäng′), *n.* capital of North Korea.

py·or·rhe·a (pī′ə rē′ə), *n.* disease of the gums in which pockets of pus form about the teeth, the gums shrink, and the teeth become loose. [< NL, < Gk. *pyon* pus + *rhoia* a flow < *rhein* to flow] —**py′or·rhe′al,** *adj.*

pyr·a·mid (pir′ə mid), *n.* **1** a solid having triangular sides meeting in a point. **2** thing or things having the form of a pyramid. **3 the Pyramids,** the huge, massive stone pyramids, serving as royal tombs, built by the ancient Egyptians. —*v.* **1** be or put in the form of a pyramid. **2** raise or increase (costs, wages, etc.) gradually. [< L < Gk. *pyramis* < Egyptian] —**py·ram′i·dal,** *adj.* —**py·ram′i·dal·ly,** *adv.* —**pyr′a·mid′ic, pyr′amid′i·cal,** *adj.* —**pry′a·mid′i·cal·ly,** *adv.*

pyre (pīr), *n.* **1** pile of wood for burning a dead body. **2** any pile to be burned. [< L *pyra* < Gk., < *pyr* fire]

py·ret·ic (pī ret′ik), *adj.* **1** of or having to do with fever. **2** producing fever. **3** feverish. [< NL, < Gk. *pyretos* fever < *pyr* fire]

pyr·i·dox·ine (pir′ə dok′sēn; –sin), *n.* vitamin B_6, $C_8H_{11}O_3N$, essential to human nutrition, found in wheat germ, fish liver, etc.

py·ri·tes (pī rī′tēz; pə–; pī′rīts), *n.* **1** iron pyrites, a mineral which has a yellow color and glitters so that it suggests gold; fool's gold. **2** any of various compounds of sulfur and a metal. [< L < Gk., flint, < *pyr* fire]

py·ro·clas·tic (pī′rə klas′tik; pir′ə–), *adj.* made up of rock fragments and lava from a volcanic eruption.

py·rog·ra·phy (pī rog′rə fi; pi–), *n.* art of burning designs on wood, leather, etc. [< *pyro–* (< Gk. *pyr* fire) + *–graphy* (< Gk. *graphein* write)] —**py′ro·graph′ic,** *adj.*

py·ro·ma·ni·a (pī′rə mā′ni ə), *n.* an insane desire to set things on fire. [< *pyro–* (< Gk., *pyr* fire) + *mania*] —**py′ro·ma′ni·ac** *n.*

py·ro·tech·nics (pī′rə tek′niks), *n.* **1** Also, **py′ro·tech′ny. a** the making of fireworks. **b** use of fireworks. **c** display of fireworks. **2** a brilliant or sensational display. [< *pyro–* (< Gk. *pyr* fire) + *technics*] —**py′ro·tech′nic, py′ro·tech′ni·cal,** *adj.*

py·rox·y·lin, py·rox·y·line (pī rok′sə lin), *n.* any of various substances made by nitrating certain forms of cellulose, as guncotton.

Pyr·rhic victory (pir′ik), victory won at too great cost, so named after **Pyr·rhus** (pir′əs), a Greek king, 318?–272 B.C., who invaded Italy and won a battle but with an enormous loss of life.

py·thon (pī′thon; –thən), *n.* **1** any of several large snakes of the Old World that are related to the boas and kill their prey by crushing. **2** any large boa. [< L < Gk.]

Q, q (kū), *n., pl.* **Q's; q's.** the 17th letter of the alphabet.

Q., question.

q., 1 quart. 2 question.

qt., 1 quantity. 2 *pl.* **qt., qts.** quart.

q.t. (kyü′tē′), *n.* **on the q.t.,** in secret; quietly.

quaa·lude (kwā′lüd), *n.* sedative drug used as a narcotic and thought to be addictive. [< *trademark* Quaalude]

quack¹ (kwak), *n.* sound a duck makes. —*v.* make such a sound. [imit.] —**quack′y,** *adj.*

quack² (kwak), *n.* 1 dishonest person who pretends to be a doctor. 2 an ignorant pretender to knowledge or skill of any sort. —*adj.* 1 used by quacks. 2 not genuine. [short for *quacksalver* quack doctor < Du.] —**quack′er·y,** *n.* —**quack′ish,** *adj.* —**quack′ish·ly,** *adv.*

quad¹ (kwod), *n.* quadrangle of a college.

quad² (kwod), *n.* quadruplet.

quad³ (kwod), quaalude.

quad·ran·gle (kwod′rang′gəl), *n.* 1 a four-sided space or court wholly or nearly surrounded by buildings. 2 the buildings around a quadrangle. 3 =quadrilateral. [< LL *quadrangulum* < L *quadri–* four + *angulus* angle] —**quad·ran′gu·lar** *adj.* —**quad·ran′gu·lar·ly,** *adv.*

quad·rant (kwod′rənt), *n.* 1 quarter of a circle or of its circumference. 2 instrument used in astronomy, navigation, etc., for measuring altitudes. [< L *quadrans* a fourth]

quad·rat·ic (kwod rat′ik), —*adj.* involving a square or squares, but no higher powers. $x^2 + 3x + 2 = 12$ is a **quadratic equation.** —*n.* a quadratic equation. —**quad·rat′i·cal·ly,** *adv.*

quad·rat·ics (kwod rat′iks), *n.* branch of algebra that deals with quadratic equations.

quad·ra·ture (kwod′rə chər), *n.* 1 act of squaring. 2 the finding of a square equal in area to a given surface bounded by a circle or other curve. [< L *quadratura.* See QUADRATE.]

quad·ren·ni·al (kwod ren′i əl), *adj.* 1 occurring every four years: *a quadrennial presidential election.* 2 of or for four years. [< L *quadriennium* < *quadri–* four + *annus* year] —**quad·ren′ni·al·ly,** *adv.*

quad·ri·lat·er·al (kwod′rə lat′ər əl), *adj.* having four sides and four angles. —*n.* a plane figure having four sides and four angles. [< L, < *quadri–* four + *latus* side]

qua·drille (kwə dril′), *n.* 1 a square dance for four couples. 2 music for it. [< F < Sp. *cuadrilla* troop < *cuadro* battle square < L *quadrus* square]

quad·ril·lion (kwod ril′yən), *n.* 1 in the United States and France, 1 followed by 15 zeros. 2 in Great Britain, 1 followed by 24 zeros. [< F, < *quadri–* four (< L) + MILLION] —**quad·ril′lionth,** *adj., n.*

quad·ru·ped (kwod′rů ped), *n.* animal that has four feet. —*adj.* having four feet.

[< L, < *quadru–* four + *pes* foot] —**quad·ru′pe·dal,** *adj.*

quad·ru·ple (kwod′rù pəl; kwod rū′–), *adj., n., v.,* **-pled, -pling.** —*adj.* 1 fourfold; consisting of four parts; including four parts or parties. 2 four times; four times as great. —*n.* number, amount, etc., four times as great as another. —*v.* make or become four times as great. [< L *quadruplus* < *quadru–* four + *–plus* fold] —**quad′ru·ply,** *adv.*

quad·ru·plet (kwod′rù plit; kwod rū′–), *n.* 1 one of four children born at a birth. 2 group of four.

quad·ru·pli·cate (*adj., n.* kwod rū′plə kit; *v.* kwod rū′plə kāt), *adj., v.,* **-cat·ed, -cat·ing,** *n.* —*adj.* fourfold; quadruple. —*v.* make fourfold; quadruple. —*n.* one of four things, esp. four copies of a document, exactly alike. [< L *quadruplicatus,* ult. < *quadru–* four + *plicare* to fold] —**quad·ru′pli·ca′tion ,** *n.*

quaff (kwäf; kwaf; kwôf), *v.* drink in large draughts; drink freely. —*n.* a quaffing. —**quaff′er,** *n.*

quag·gy (kwag′i; kwog′i), *adj.,* **-gi·er, -gi·est.** miry; swampy. [prob. < *quag* bog] —**quag′gi·ness,** *n.*

quag·mire (kwag′mīr′; kwog′–), *n.* 1 a boggy or miry place. 2 a difficult situation. [< *quag* bog + *mire*] —**quag′mir′y,** *adj.*

qua·hog, qua·haug (kwô′hog, –hôg; kwəhog′, –hôg′), *n.* a roundish, edible American clam; hard clam. [< Algonquian]

quail¹· (kwāl), *n., pl.* **quails** or (*esp. collectively*) **quail.** any of various game birds belonging to the same group as fowls and partridges, esp. the bobwhite. [< OF *quaille* < Gmc.]

quail² (kwāl), *v.* be afraid; lose courage; shrink back in fear: *the slave quailed at his master's look.* —**quail′er,** *n.*

quaint (kwānt), *adj.* strange or odd in an interesting, pleasing, or amusing way. [< OF *cointe* pretty < L *cognitus* known] —**quaint′ly,** *adv.* —**quaint′ness,** *n.*

quake (kwāk), *v.,* **quaked, quak·ing,** *n.* —*v.* shake; tremble: *quake with fear.* —*n.* 1 a shaking; trembling. 2 earthquake. [OE *cwacian*] —**quak′er,** *n.* —**quak′ing,** *adj.* —**quak′ing·ly,** *adv.* —**quak′y,** *adj.*

Quak·er (kwāk′ər), *n.* member of a Christian group called the Society of Friends. Quakers refuse to go to war or to take oaths; their clothes, manners, and religious services are very plain and simple. —**Quak′er·ish,** *adj.* —**Quak′er·ism,** *n.* —**Quak′er·ly,** *adj.*

qual·i·fi·ca·tion (kwol′ə fə kā′shən), *n.* 1 that which makes a person fit for a job, task, office, etc.: *to know the way is one qualification for a guide.* 2 that which limits, changes, or makes less free and full: *his pleasure had one qualification; his friends could not enjoy it, too.* 3 modification; limitation; restriction: *the statement was made without any qualification.*

qual·i·fied (kwol′ə fīd), *adj.* 1 having the desirable or required qualifications;

fitted; adapted. 2 modified; limited; restricted. —**qual′i·fied·ly,** *adv.* —**qual′i·fied·ness,** *n.*

qual·i·fy (kwol′ə fī), *v.,* **-fied, -fy·ing.** 1 make fit or competent: *qualify oneself for a job.* 2 become fit; show oneself fit: *when did he qualify?* 3 make less strong; change somewhat; limit; modify: *qualify your statement that dogs are loyal by adding "usually."* [< Med.L, < L *qualis* of what sort + *facere* make] —**qual′i·fi′a·ble,** *adj.* —**qual′i·fi′er,** *n.* —**qual′i·fy′ing·ly,** *adv.*

qual·i·ta·tive (kwol′ə tā′tiv), *adj.* concerned with quality or qualities. —**qual′i·ta′tive·ly,** *adv.*

qualitative analysis, testing of something to find out what chemical substances are in it.

qual·i·ty (kwol′ə ti), *n., pl.* **-ties.** 1 something special about an object or person that makes it what it is: *one quality of sugar is sweetness, she has many fine qualities.* 2 the kind that anything is: *that is a poor quality of cloth.* 3 fineness; merit; excellence: *look for quality rather than quantity.* 4 the character of sounds aside from pitch and volume or intensity. [< L, < *qualis* of what sort]

quality control 1 inspection of goods during the manufacturing process to maintain their quality. 2 *Fig.* any system for monitoring the quality of something.

qualm (kwäm), *n.* 1 a sudden disturbing feeling in the mind; misgiving: *I tried the test with some qualms.* 2 disturbance or scruple of conscience: *have some qualms about asking for a favor.* 3 a feeling of faintness or sickness, esp. of nausea, that lasts for just a moment. [OE *cwealm* pain] —**qualm′ish,** *adj.* —**qualm′ish·ly,** *adv.* **qualm′ish·ness,** *n.*

quan·da·ry (kwon′də ri; –dri), *n., pl.* **-ries.** state of perplexity or uncertainty; dilemma.

quan·ti·fy (kwon′tə fī), *v.,* **-fied, -fy·ing.** 1 find the quantity of; measure. 2 express as a quantity: *impossible to quantify such pleasure.* [< ML *quantificare* < L *quantus* how much + *facere* make] —**quan·ti·fi′er,** *n.*

quan·ti·ta·tive (kwon′tə tā′tiv), *adj.* 1 concerned with quantity. 2 that can be measured. —**quan′ti·ta′tive·ly,** *adv.* —**quan′ti·ta′tive·ness,** *n.*

quantitative analysis, a testing of something to find out how much there is of each chemical substance in it.

quan·ti·ty (kwon′tə ti), *n., pl.* **-ties.** 1 amount: *use equal quantities of nuts and raisins in the cake.* 2 a large amount; large number: *a baker buys flour in quantity.* 3 length of a note in music. [< L, < *quantus* how much]

quan·tum (kwon′təm), *n., pl.* **-ta** (–tə). **a** the smallest amount of energy capable of existing independently. **b** this amount of energy regarded as a unit. —*adj.* of sudden importance or effect: *a quantum shift of opinion.* [< L, neut. adj., how much]

quantum jump, 1 change in the orbit of an electron within an atom that occurs when a quantum of energy is lost or gained. **2** *Fig.* =quantum leap.

quantum leap, a huge and sudden advance.

quantum mechanics, quantum theory applied to the physical measurement of the structure and interactions of atomic and subatomic particles.

quantum physics, quantum theory as applied to physics on an atomic level.

quantum theory, theory that whenever energy is transferred, the transfer occurs in pulsations or stages rather than continuously, and that the amount transferred during each stage is a definite quantity.

quark (kwôrk), *n.* one of two basic constituents of matter, confined within protons, neutrons, and mesons. [< "three quarks," a phrase in James Joyce's novel, *Finnegans Wake*]

quar·an·tine (kwôr′ən tēn; kwor′–), *v.,* **–tined, –tin·ing,** *n.* —*v.* **1** keep away from others for a time to prevent the spread of an infectious disease: *farms in the area were quarantined.* **2** *Fig.* isolate for a time for any reason. —*n.* **1** state of being quarantined: *the kennel was in quarantine for three weeks.* **2** detention, isolation, and other measures taken to prevent the spread of an infectious disease. **3** time or place where people, animals, plants, ships, etc., are held until it is sure that they have no infectious diseases, insect pests, etc. **4** isolation or exclusion of a person or group judged to be undesirable: *amounting to a virtual quarantine of the country.* [< Ital., < *quaranta* forty < L *quadraginta*; with ref. to 40 days as the orig. period of isolation]

quar·rel[1] (kwôr′əl; kwor′–), *n., v.,* **–reled, –rel·ing.** —*n.* **1** an angry dispute or disagreement; breaking off of friendly relations. **2** cause for a dispute or disagreement; reason for breaking off friendly relations: *a bully likes to pick quarrels.* **3** cause for complaint. —*v.* **1** dispute or disagree angrily; break off friendly relations. **2** find fault: *it is impossible to quarrel with such a careful analysis of the facts.* [< OF < L *querella,* var. of *querela* complaint] —**quar′rel·er,** *n.*

quar·rel[2] (kwôr′əl; kwor′–), *n.* bolt or arrow used with a crossbow. [< OF < Med.L *quadrellus,* dim. of L *quadrus* square]

quar·rel·some (kwôr′əl səm; kwor′–), *adj.* too ready to quarrel; fond of fighting and disputing. —**quar′rel·some·ness,** *n.*

quar·ry[1] (kwôr′i; kwor′i), *n., pl.* **–ries,** *v.,* **–ried, –ry·ing.** —*n.* place where stone is dug, cut, or blasted out for use in building. —*v.* obtain from a quarry. [< Med.L *quareia,* ult. < L *quadrus* square] —**quar′ri·er,** *n.*

quar·ry[2] (kwôr′i; kwor′i), *n., pl.* **–ries.** **1** animal chased in a hunt; game; prey. **2** anything hunted or eagerly pursued. [< OF, < *cuir* hide < L *corium*]

quart (kwôrt), *n.* **1** measure for liquids, equal to one fourth of a gallon. **2** measure for dry things, equal to one eighth of a peck. **3** container holding a quart. [< F < L *quarta,* fem. adj., fourth]

quar·ter (kwôr′tər), *n.* **1** one fourth; half of a half; one of four equal or corresponding parts. **2** one fourth of a dollar; 25 cents. **3** one fourth of an hour. **4** one fourth of a year; 3 months. **5** one of the four periods of the moon, lasting about 7 days each. **6** region; place; section; district; group: *the Mexican quarter.* **7** point of the compass; direction: *in what quarter is the wind?* **8** mercy shown a defeated enemy in sparing his or her life. —*v.* **1** divide into quarters. **2** give a place to live in: *soldiers were quartered in the town.* —*adj.* being one of four equal parts.

at close quarters, very close together; almost touching.

quarters, a place to live or stay. **b** proper position or station. [< OF < L *quartarius* a fourth < *quartus* fourth]

quar·ter·back (kwôr′tər bak′), *n.* one of four players behind the line.

quar·ter·deck (kwôr′tər dek′), *n.* part of the upper deck between the mainmast and the stern, used esp. by the officers of a ship.

quar·tered (kwôr′tərd), *adj.* **1** divided into quarters. **2** furnished with rooms or lodging.

quar·ter·fi·nal (kwôr′tər fi′nəl), *n.* game or match that takes place just before the semifinal round in a tournament. —*adj.* of or having to do with this round in a tournament. —**quar′ter·fi′nal·ist ,** *n.*

quarter horse, horse bred originally to race a quarter-mile course, now used for polo, riding, and, by cowboys, to separate cattle.

quar·ter·ly (kwôr′tər li), *adj., adv., n., pl.* **–lies** —*adj.* happening, done, etc., four times a year. —*adv.* once each quarter of a year. —*n.* magazine published every three months.

quar·ter·mas·ter (kwôr′tər mas′tər; –mäs′–), *n.* **1** in the army, an officer who has charge of providing quarters, clothing, fuel, transportation, etc., for troops. **2** in the navy, an officer on a ship who has charge of the steering, the compasses, signals, etc. —**quar′ter·mas′ter·ship,** *n.*

quarter note, note equal to one fourth of a whole note.

quarter rest, rest in music equal in length to a quarter note.

quarter section, piece of land, usually square, containing 160 acres.

quar·ter·staff (kwôr′tər staf′; –stäf′), *n., pl.* **–staves** (–stāvz′). an old English weapon consisting of a stout pole 6 to 8 feet long, tipped with iron.

quar·tet, quar·tette (kwôr tet′), *n.* **1** group of four musicians (singers or players). **2** piece of music for four voices or instruments. **3** any group of four. [< F < Ital., < *quarto* fourth < L *quartus*]

quar·tile (kwôr′tīl; –təl), *n.* one of four points on a statistical scale that has the same frequency as the other three. If a student is ranked in the upper quartile of everyone who took a particular test, he or she would be among the 25% who did better than the remaining 75%.

quar·to (kwôr′tō), *n., pl.* **–tos,** *adj.* —*n.* **1** the page size, usually about 9 by 12 inches, of a book in which each leaf is one fourth of a whole sheet of paper. **2** book having this size. —*adj.* having this size. [< Med.L *in quarto* in the fourth (of a sheet)]

quartz (kwôrts), *n.* a very hard mineral composed of silica, SiO_2. Common quartz crystals are colorless and transparent, but amethyst, jasper, and many other colored stones are also quartz. [< G *quarz*]

qua·sar (kwā′sär; kwä–; –zär), *n.* celestial object larger than a star, characterized by emissions of powerful blue light and radio waves. [< *quasi–* + stell*ar* (radio source)]

quash[1] (kwosh), *v.* put down completely; crush: *quash a revolt.* [< OF *quasser* < L *quassare* shatter, intensive of *quatere* to shake]

quash[2] (kwosh), *v.* make void; annul. [< OF < LL *cassare* < *cassus* null; infl. in OF by *quasser* QUASH[1]]

qua·si (kwā′sī; –zī; kwä′si; –zi), *adj.* seeming; not real; halfway. —*adv.* seemingly; not really; partly; almost. [< L]

quasi–, *prefix.* form of **quasi** used in combination, as in *quasi-official.*

qua·si·ju·di·cial (kwä′si jü dish′əl; –zi–; kwä′–), *adj.* having some of the aspects and authority of the judiciary but not under the authority a judiciary.

quat·rain (kwot′rān), *n.* stanza or poem of four lines. [< F, < *quatre* four < L *quattuor*]

qua·ver (kwā′vər), *v.* **1** shake tremulously; tremble: *the old man's voice quavered.* **2** trill in singing or in playing on an instrument. **3** sound, speak, or sing in trembling tones. —*n.* **1** a quavering or tremulous shake, esp. in the voice. **2** trill in singing or in playing on an instrument. **3** an eighth note. [frequentative of *quave* shake, ME *cwavien*] —**qua′ver·er,** *n.* —**qua′ver·ing·ly,** *adv.* —**qua′ver·y,** *adj.*

quay (kē), *n.* a solid landing place where ships load and unload, often built of stone. [< OF *kay* < Celtic]

Que., Quebec.

quea·sy (kwē′zi), *adj.,* **–si·er, –si·est. 1** inclined to nausea; easily upset. **2** tending to unsettle the stomach. **3** uneasy; uncomfortable. **4** squeamish; fastidious. —**quea′si·ly,** *adv.* —**quea′si·ness,** *n.*

Que·bec (kwi bek′), *n.* **1** province in E Canada. **2** its capital, on the St. Lawrence River. —**Que·bec′er, Que·bec′ker.** *n.*

Qué·bé·cois (kā bā kwä′), *n., pl.* **–cois.** *French.* person from Quebec.

Quech·ua (kech′wä), *n.* **1** member of the dominant Indian group of the Inca empire. **2** their language, dialects of which are still spoken in parts of W South America.

Quech·uan (kech′wən), *adj.* of or having to do with the Quechuas, their language, or civilization. —*n.* =Quechua.

queen (kwēn), *n.* **1** wife of a king. **2** a woman ruler. **3** woman who is very important stately, or beautiful. **4** a fully developed female in a colony of bees, ants, etc., that lays eggs. There is usually only one queen in a hive of bees. **5** a playing card bearing a picture of a queen. **6** piece in chess that can move in any straight or diagonal row. **7** the chief, best, finest, etc.: *the rose, queen of flowers.* **8** (often an unfriendly use) a male homosexual. —*v.* act like a queen. [OE *cwēn*] —**queen′dom,** *n.* —**queen′hood, queen′ship,** *n.* —**queen′less,** *adj.* —**queen′like′,** *adj.*

Queen Anne's lace, the wild carrot, that bears a dainty white bloom.

queen·ly (kwēn′li), *adj.,* **–li·er, –li·est,** *adv.* —*adj.* **1** of a queen; fit for a queen. **2** like a queen; like a queen's. —*adv.* in a queenly manner; as a queen does. —**queen′li·ness,** *n.*

queen-size (kwēn′sīz′), *adj.* larger than a regular size, esp. wider and longer. Also, **queen-sized.**

queer (kwir), *adj.* **1** strange; odd: *a queer remark for her to make.* **2** quirky; peculiar: *a queer little house.* **3** homosexual. —*n.* a homosexual. —*v. Informal.* spoil; ruin. [< G *quer* oblique] —**queer′er,** *n.* —**queer′ish,** *adj.* —**queer′ly,** *adv.* —**queer′ness,** *n.*

quell (kwel), *v.* **1** put down (disorder, rebellion, etc.); subdue: *quell a mutiny.* **2** put an end to; extinguish: *quell one's hopes.* **3** quiet or allay (feelings, etc.). [OE *cwellan* to kill] —**quell′er,** *n.*

quench (kwench), *v.* **1** put an end to; stop: *quench a thirst.* **2** drown out; put out: *water will quench a fire.* [OE, as in *ācwencan*] —**quench′a·ble,** *adj.* —**quench′er,** *n.* —**quench′less,** *adj.*

quern (kwėrn), *n.* primitive mill turned by hand for grinding grain. [< OE *cweorn*]

quer·u·lous (kwer′ə ləs; kwer′yə–), *adj.* **1** complaining; faultfinding. **2** fretful; peevish. [< L *querulus* < *queri* complain] —**quer′u·lous·ly,** *adv.* —**quer′u·lous·ness,** *n.*

que·ry (kwir′i), *n., pl.* **–ries,** *v.,* **–ried, –ry·ing.** —*n.* question; inquiry. —*v.* **1** ask; ask about; inquire into. **2** express doubt about. [< Med.L *quere* < L *quaere* ask!]

que·sa·di·lla (kā sə di′yə), *n.* tortilla filled with cheese, meat, etc. folded in half and toasted in a pan. [< Sp. *queso* cheese + tort*illa*]

quest (kwest), *n.* **1** search; hunt. **2** expedition of knights. **3** object sought for. —*v.* search or seek for; hunt. [< OF < VL *quaesita* < L *quaerere* seek] —**quest′er,** *n.* —**quest′ful,** *adj.*

ques·tion (kwes′chən), *n.* **1** thing asked; sentence in interrogative form, addressed

to someone to get information: *what was your question?* **2** matter to be talked over, investigated, considered, etc.; problem: *the question of prohibition.* **3** proposal to be voted on. —*v.* **1** ask in order to find out; seek information from. **2** doubt; dispute: *I question the truth of his story.*

beg the question, a accept as proved or correct the thing being argued about. **b** raise another or more fundamental question: *saying they shouldn't have been there begs the question of how they got there.*

beside the question, off the subject.

beyond or **without question,** not to be disputed.

call in or **into question,** dispute; challenge.

in question, under consideration or discussion.

out of the question, impossible. [< AF < L *quaestio,* ult. < *quaerere* ask] —**ques′tion·ar·y,** *adj., n.* —**ques′tion·er,** *n.* —**ques′tion·ing,** *n.* —**ques′tion·ing·ly,** *adv.*

ques·tion·a·ble (kwes′chən ə bəl), *adj.* **1** open to question or dispute; doubtful; uncertain. **2** of doubtful propriety, honesty, morality, respectability, or the like. —**ques′tion·a·ble·ness,** *n.* —**ques′tion·a·bly,** *adv.*

question mark, mark (?) put after a question in writing or printing.

ques·tion·naire (kwes′chən âr′), *n.* list of questions, usually a written or printed list.

quet·zal (ket säl′), **que·zal** (kāsäl′), *n.* a Central American bird having brilliant golden-green and scarlet plumage. The male has long, flowing tail feathers. [< Sp. < Mex. *quetzalli,* the bird's tail feather]

queue (kū), *n., v.,* **queued, queu·ing.** —*n.* **1** braid of hair hanging down from the back of the head. **2** *Esp. Brit.* a long line of people, automobiles, etc. —*v. Esp. Brit.* form or stand in a long line. [< F < L *coda,* var. of *cauda* tail]

quib·ble (kwib′əl), *n., v.,* **–bled, –bling.** —*n.* an unfair and petty evasion of the point or truth by using words with a double meaning: *a legal quibble.* —*v.* evade the point or the truth by twisting the meaning of words. —**quib′bler,** *n.*

quick (kwik), *adj.* **1** fast and sudden; swift: *a quick turn.* **2** coming soon; prompt: *a quick reply.* **3** not patient; hasty: *a quick temper.* **4** acting quickly; ready; lively. **5** understanding or learning quickly. —*n.* **1** the tender, sensitive flesh under a fingernail or toenail. **2** the tender, sensitive part of one's feelings: *their insults cut him to the quick.* **3** living persons: *the quick and the dead.* —*adv.* quickly. [OE *cwic* alive] —**quick′ish,** *adj.* —**quick′ness,** *n.*

quick·en (kwik′ən), *v.* **1** move more quickly; hasten: *quicken your pace.* **2** stir up; make alive: *quicken one's imagination.* **3** become more alive or alive: *his pulse quickened.* —**quick′en·er,** *n.*

quick fix, *Informal.* hasty remedy, esp. for a problem that should be given careful attention and thought: *apply the usual sloppy quick fix.*

quick-freeze (kwik′frēz′), *v.,* **–froze, –fro·zen, –freez·ing.** subject (food) to rapid freezing to prepare it for storing at freezing temperatures. —**quick freezing.**

quick·lime (kwik′līm′), *n.* a white, alkaline substance obtained by burning limestone and used for making mortar; unslaked lime.

quick·ly (kwik′li), *adv.* in a quick manner.

quick·sand (kwik′sand′), *n.* soft, wet sand, very deep, that will not support one's weight.

quick·sil·ver (kwik′sil′vər), *n.* the metal mercury. —*v.* coat with mercury.

quick·step (kwik′step′), *n.* **1** step used in marching in quick time. **2** a lively dance step. **3** music in a brisk march rhythm.

quick-tem·pered (kwik′tem′pərd), *adj.* easily angered.

quick time, a fast speed of marching. In quick time, soldiers march four miles an hour.

quick-wit·ted (kwik′wit′id), *adj.* having a quick mind; mentally alert. —**quick′-wit′ted·ly,** *adv.* —**quick′-wit′ted·ness,** *n.*

quid (kwid), *n., pl.* **quid.** *Brit. Slang.* former British unit of one pound, or 20 shillings.

quid·di·ty (kwid′ə ti), *n., pl.* **–ties. 1** essence. **2** quibble. [< Med.L *quidditas* whatness < L *quid* what]

quid pro quo (kwid′ prō kwō′), *Latin.* compensation; one thing in return for another.

qui·es·cence (kwī es′əns), *n.* absence of activity; quietness.

qui·es·cent (kwī es′ənt), *adj.* quiet; still; motionless; inactive. [< L *quiescens* resting < *quies,* n., rest] —**qui·es′cent·ly,** *adv.*

qui·et[1] (kwī′ət), *adj.* **1** not moving or moving very little; not active: *a quiet current, quiet games.* **2** free from disturbance; tranquil: *a quiet neighborhood.* **3** not giving offense or causing disorder; peaceable: *quiet neighbors.* **4** free from fuss; in good taste: *quiet manners quiet colors.* —*v.* make or become quiet. —*adv.* quietly. [< L *quietus* resting, ult. < *quies* quiet[2]. Doublet of COY and QUIT, *adj.*] —**qui′et·er,** *n.* —**qui′et·ly,** *adv.* —**qui′et·ness,** *n.*

qui·et[2] (kwī′ət), *n.* **1** state of rest; stillness; absence of motion or noise. **2** freedom from disturbance; peace. [< L *quies*]

qui·e·tude (kwī′ə tüd; –tūd), *n.* quietness; stillness; calmness.

Quil·e·ute (kwil′ə yüt), *n., pl.* **–ute, –utes.** member of a tribe of North American Indians living on the NW coast of the United States. **2** their language.

quill (kwil), *n.* **1** a large, stiff feather. **2** the hollow stem of a feather. **3** anything made from the hollow stem of a feather, such as a pen, toothpick, etc. **4** a stiff, sharp hair or spine. A porcupine has quills on its back. [ME *quil*]

quilt (kwilt), *n.* **1** bedcover made of two pieces of cloth with a soft pad between, held in place by lines of stitching. **2** bedcover. **3** anything resembling a quilt. —*v.* **1** make quilts. **2** stitch together with a soft lining: *quilt a bathrobe.* **3** sew in lines or patterns. [< OF L *culcita* cushion] —**quilt′ed.** *adj.* —**quilt′er.** *n.*

quilt·ing (kwil ting), *n.* **1** quilted work on articles of clothing, bed covers, etc. **2** fabric suited to making a quilt.

quilting bee, a gathering of women to put a quilt together and do the quilting on it.

quince (kwins), *n.* **1** a hard, yellowish fruit, used for preserves. **2** tree it grows on. **3** a similar shrub or tree grown for its blossoms. [orig. pl. of ME *quyne* < OF *cooin* < L *cotoneum*]

qui·nine (kwī′nīn), *n.* **1** a bitter, colorless, crystalline drug made from the bark of a cinchona tree, used for malaria and fevers. **2** any of various compounds of quinine that are used as medicine. [< Sp. *quina* < Quechua (S Am.Ind.) *kina* bark]

quinine water, a carbonated drink containing a small amount of quinine and a little lemon, lime, or orange juice.

quin·quen·ni·al (kwin kwen′i əl), *adj.* **1** occurring every five years. **2** of or for five years. [< L *quinquennium* < *quinque* five + *annus* year]

quin·sy (kwin′zi), *n.* tonsillitis with pus; very sore throat with an abscess in the tonsils. [< Med.L *quinancia* < LL < Gk. *kynanche,* orig., dog′s collar < *kyon* dog + *anchein* choke]

quint (kwint), *n.* *Informal.* a quintuplet.

quin·tes·sence (kwin tes′əns), *n.* **1** pure essence; purest form. **2** the most perfect example of something. [< Med.L *quinta essentia* fifth essence, trans. of Gk. *pempte ousia*]

quin·tes·sen·tial (kwin′tə sen′shəl), *adj.* having the nature of a quintessence; of the purest or most perfect kind.

quin·tet, quin·tette (kwin tet′), *n.* **1** group of five musicians (singers or players). **2** piece of music for five voices or instruments. **3** any group of five. [< F < Ital., < *quinto* fifth < L *quintus*]

quin·til·lion (kwin til′yən), *n.* **1** in the United States and France, 1 followed by 18 zeros. **2** in Great Britain, 1 followed by 30 zeros. [< L *quintus* fifth + E MILLION] —**quin·til′lionth,** *adj., n.*

quin·tu·ple (kwin′tù pəl; -tyù-; kwin tü′pəl; -tü′-), *adj., v.,* –**pled,** –**pling,** *n.* —*adj.* **1** fivefold; consisting of five parts. **2** five times as great. —*v.* make or become five times as great. —*n.* number, amount, etc., five times as great as another. [< F, < L *quintus* fifth; patterned on *quadruple*]

quin·tu·plet (kwin′tù plit; -tyù-; kwin tü′plit; -tü′-; -tup′lit), *n.* **1** one of five children born at a birth. **2** any group or combination of five.

quip (kwip), *n., v.,* **quipped, quip·ping.** —*n.* **1** a clever or witty saying. **2** a sharp, cutting remark. **3** something odd or strange. —*v.* make quips. [for earlier *quippy* < L *quippe* indeed!, I dare say] —**quip′ster,** *n.*

quire (kwīr), *n.* 24 or 25 sheets of paper of the same size and quality. [< OF *quaier,* ult. < L *quaterni* four each]

quirk (kwėrk), *n.* **1** a peculiar way of acting. **2** a sudden twist or turn. —**quirk′y,** *adj.*

quirt (kwėrt), *n.* riding whip with a short, stout handle and a lash of braided leather. [? < Sp. *cuerda* cord]

quit (kwit), *v.,* **quit** or **quit·ted, quit·ting,** *adj.* —*v.* **1** stop: *the men quit work when the whistle blew.* **2** leave: *he quit his room in anger.* **3** free; clear; rid. —*adj.* free; clear; rid: *I gave him money to be quit of him.* [(v.) < OF < Med.L *quietare* discharge < L *quietus* QUIET[1]; (adj.) < OF *quite* < L *quietus.* Doublet of QUIET[1] and COY.]

quit·claim (kwit′klām′), *n.* **1** the giving up of a claim. **2** document stating that somebody gives up a claim. —*v.* give up claim to (a possession, etc.).

quite (kwī), *adv.* **1** completely; wholly; entirely: *a hat quite out of fashion.* **2** actually; really; positively: *quite the thing.* **3** to a considerable extent or degree: *quite pretty.* [orig. adj., var. of *quit* in sense of "clear"]

Qui·to (kē′tō), *n.* capital of Ecuador, in the N part.

quits (kwits), *adj.* on even terms by repayment or retaliation.

be quits with, get even with; have revenge on.

call it quits, give up on something; stop.

quit·ter (kwit′ər), *n.* person who gives up easily.

quiv·er[1] (kwiv′ər), *v., n.* shake; shiver; tremble. [cf. OE *cwiferlīce* actively] —**quiv′er·ing,** *adj.* —**quiv′er·ing·ly,** *adv.*

quiv·er[2] (kwiv′ər), *n.* case to hold arrows. [< AF *quiveir,* prob. < Gmc.] —**quiv′ered,** *adj.*

Qui·xo·te (kē hō′tē; kwik′sət), *n.* =Don Quixote.

quix·ot·ic (kwiks ot′ik), **quix·ot·i·cal** (-ə kəl), *adj.* **1** resembling Don Quixote; extravagantly chivalrous or romantic. **2** visionary; not practical. —**quix·ot′i·cal·ly,** *adv.*

quiz (kwiz), *v.,* **quizzed, quiz·zing,** *n., pl.* **quiz·zes.** —*v.* examine informally by questions; test the knowledge of. —*n.* an informal written or oral examination; test. —**quiz′zer,** *n.* —**quiz′zing,** *adj.* —**quiz′zing·ly,** *adv.*

quiz·zi·cal (kwiz′ə kəl), *adj.* odd; queer; comical. —**quiz′zi·cal·ness,** *n.* —**quiz′zi·cal·ly,** *adv.*

quoin (koin; kwoin), *n.* **1** an external angle of a wall or building. **2** stone forming an outside angle of a wall; cornerstone. **3** a wedge-shaped piece of

wood, metal, etc., esp. one in an arch. [var. of *coin*]

quoit (kwoit), *n.* a heavy, flattish iron or rope ring thrown to encircle a peg stuck in the ground or to come as close to it as possible.

quoits (*sing. in use*)**,** game so played. The game of quoits is often played with horseshoes.

Quon·set hut (kwon′sit), a prefabricated metal building with a semicircular roof. [first used at *Quonset* (R.I.) naval air base]

quo·rum (kwô′rəm; kwō′-), *n.* number of members of any society or assembly that must be present if the business done is to be legal or binding. [< L, of whom]

quot., quotation.

quo·ta (kwō′tə), *n.* **1** share of a total due from or to a particular district, state, person, etc. **2 a** percentage of a total of women, minorities, etc., who must be hired or admitted to a school or profession to achieve a fair representation and prevent discrimination. **b** any number that restricts admission, immigration, etc. [< Med.L, < L *quota pars* how large a part]

quo·ta·ble (kwōt′ə bəl), *adj.* **1** that can be quoted. **2** that can be quoted with propriety. **3** suitable for quoting. —**quot′a·bil′i·ty, quot′a·ble·ness,** *n.* —**quot′a·bly,** *adv.*

quo·ta·tion (kwō tā′shən), *n.* **1** somebody's words repeated exactly by another person; passage quoted from a book, speech, etc.: *from what author does this quotation come?* **2** quoting: *quotation is a habit of some preachers.* **3** the stating of the current price of a stock, commodity, etc. **4** the price so stated: *what was today's market quotation on wheat?* —**quo·ta′tion·al,** *adj.* —**quo·ta′tion·al·ly,** *adv.*

quotation mark, one of a pair of marks (" ") used to indicate the beginning and end of a quotation. Also, **quote mark.**

quote (kwō), *v.,* **quot·ed, quot·ing,** *n.* —*v.* **1** repeat the exact words of; give words or passages from. **2** repeat exactly the words of another or a passage from a book. **3** bring forward as an example or authority. **4** give the price of. —*n.* **1** quotation. **2** a quotation mark. [< Med.L *quotare* number chapters < L *quotus* which (in sequence)] —**quot′er,** *n.*

quoth (kwōth), *v. Archaic.* said. [pt. of *queathe* [OE *cwethan*]. See BEQUEATH.]

quo·tient (kwō′shənt), *n.* number obtained by dividing one number by another. [< L *quotiens* how many times]

q.v., which see. [< L *quod vide*]

qwer·ty (kwėr′ti), *n. Informal.* arrangement of the keys on a computer or typewriter keyboard. [< the letters on the first six alphabetical keys of a keyboard]

R, r (är), *n., pl.* **R's; r's.** the 18th letter of the alphabet. **the three R's,** reading, writing, and arithmetic.

R., restricted (audience, in respect to age), a film rating.

R., 1 railroad; 2 Republican. 3 River.

r., 1 radius. 2 road.

ra (rä), *n.* second tone of a musical scale. [See GAMUT]

Ra (rä), *n.* the sun god and supreme deity in Egyptian mythology.

Ra, radium.

Ra·bat (rə bät′), *n.* capital of Morocco on the Atlantic coast.

rab·bet (rab′it), *n., v.,* **-bet·ed, -bet·ing.** —*n.* 1 cut, groove, or slot made on the edge or surface of a board or the like, to receive the end or edge of another piece of wood shaped to fit it. 2 joint so made. —*v.* 1 cut or form a rabbet in. 2 join with a rabbet. [< OF *rabat* a beating down < *rabattre.* See REBATE.]

rab·bi (rab′ī), *n., pl.* **-bis.** teacher of the Jewish religion; pastor of a Jewish congregation. [< L < Heb., my master]

rab·bin·i·cal (rə bin′ə kəl), **rab·bin·ic** (–ik), *adj.* of or pertaining to rabbis, their learning, writings, etc. —**rab·bin′i·cal·ly,** *adv.*

rab·bit (rab′it), *n.* 1 a burrowing mammal about as big as a cat, with soft fur and long ears. 2 its fur. [ME *rabet*]

rab·ble (rab′əl), *n.* a disorderly crowd; mob.

the rabble, *Contemptuous.* the lower classes. [cf. Du. *rabbelen* prattle]

rab·id (rab′id), *adj.* 1 unreasonably extreme; fanatical; violent. 2 furious; raging. 3 having rabies; mad. [< L *rabidus* < *rabere* be mad] —**rab′id·ly,** *adv.* —**rab′id·ness,** *n.*

ra·bies (rā′bēz), *n.* =hydrophobia (def. 1). [< L, madness]

rac·coon (ra kün′), *n.* 1 a small, grayish flesh-eating mammal with a bushy, ringed tail, that lives mostly in trees and is active at night. 2 its fur. [< Algonquian]

race¹ (ras), *n., v.,* **raced, rac·ing.** —*n.* 1 contest of speed, as in running, driving, riding, sailing, etc. 2 Often, **races.** a series of horse races run at a set time over a regular course. 3 any contest that suggests a race: *a political race.* 4 a strong or fast current of water. 5 channel leading water to or from a place where its energy is utilized. —*v.* 1 engage in a contest of speed. 2 try to beat in a contest of speed; run a race with. 3 run, move, or go swiftly. 4 of a motor, wheel, etc., run too fast. [< Scand. *rās*]

race² (rās), *n.* 1 a great division of humans having certain physical characteristics in common: *there are few genetic differences among the various races.* 2 group of persons connected by common descent or origin. 3 a particular variety of animals or plants. 4 a natural kind of living

creatures: *the human race.* [< F < Ital. *razza*], *adj.* —**ra′cial·ly,** *adv.*

ra·ceme (rā sēm′; rə–), *n.* a simple flower cluster having its flowers on nearly equal stalks along a stem, the lower flowers blooming first. The lily of the valley has racemes. [< L *racemus* cluster. Doublet of RAISIN.] —**ra·cemed′,** *adj.* —**rac′e·mose,** *adj.*

rac·er (rā′sər), *n.* 1 person or thing, as a boat, car, horse, etc., that races. 2 harmless snake of North America, able to move very quickly.

race·horse (rās′hôrs′), *n.* horse bred, trained, and kept for racing.

race track or **course,** ground laid out for racing.

ra·cial (rā′shəl), *adj.* 1 of or having to do with a race of people, animals, or plants. 2 because of or involving race: *racial discrimination, racial harmony.*

ra·cial·ism (rā′shəl iz em) unreasoning fear of another racial group; extreme racial prejudice.

rac·ism (rās′iz əm), *n.* 1 exaggeration of inherent racial differences. 2 prejudice in favor of certain races. —**rac′ist,** *n.*

rack¹ (rak), *n.* 1 frame with bars, shelves, or pegs to hold, arrange, or keep things on, such as a hat rack, tool rack, or baggage rack. 2 framework set on a wagon for carrying hay, straw, etc. 3 instrument formerly used for torturing people by stretching them. 4 cause or condition of great suffering in body or mind. 5 bar with pegs or teeth on one edge, into which teeth on the rim of a wheel can fit. —*v.* 1 hurt very much: *racked with grief.* 2 stretch; strain.

on the rack, in great pain; suffering very much. [prob. < MDu. or MLG *recke*]

rack² (rak), *n.* =wreck. [var. of *wrack*]

rack³ (rak), *n.* a horse's gait, similar to a pace; single-foot. —*v.* go thus.

rack·et¹ (rak′it), *n.* 1 a loud noise; loud talk; din. 2 *Informal.* a dishonest scheme for getting money from people by threatening violence or damage. 3 *Informal.* any dishonest scheme. 4 *Slang.* occupation. [? imit.]

rack·et², **rac·quet** (rak′it), *n.* a light, wide bat made of a network of strings stretched on a frame, used for games like tennis. [< F *raquette* < Ar. *rāḥa* palm of the hand]

rack·et·eer (rak′ə tir′), *n.* person who extorts money by threatening violence or damage. —*v.* extort money by threatening violence or damage. —**rack′et·eer′ing,** *n.*

rac·on·teur (rak′on tėr′), *n.* person clever in telling stories, anecdotes, etc. [< F]

ra·coon (ra kün′), *n.* =raccoon.

rac·y (rās′ī), *adj.,* **rac·i·er, rac·i·est.** 1 vigorous; lively. 2 having an agreeably peculiar taste or flavor. 3 =risqué. —**rac′i·ly,** *adv.* —**rac′i·ness,** *n.*

ra·dar (rā′där), *n.* 1 instrument for determining the distance and direction of unseen objects by the reflection of radio

waves. 2 process by which the reflection of the radio waves is measured.

below or **under the radar,** *Fig.* not observed or known about; hidden: *these problems were below the radar for a long time.*

on the or **one's radar (screen),** *Fig.* aware of and dealing with something, esp. a problem. [short for *ra(dio) d(etecting) a(nd) r(anging)*]

ra·di·al (rā′di əl), *adj.* arranged like or in radii or rays. —*n.* Usually, **radials.** =radial tire. —**ra′di·al·ly,** *adv.*

radial tire, automobile tire strengthened by cords that are placed at right angles to the treads.

ra·di·ance (rā′di əns), **ra·di·an·cy** (–ən si), *n.* 1 vivid brightness. 2 =radiation.

ra·di·ant (rā′di ənt), *adj.* 1 shinning; bright; beaming: *a radiant smile.* 2 sending out rays of light or heat: *the sun is a radiant body.* 3 sent off in rays from some source; radiated. [< L *radians* beaming < *radius* ray]

radiant energy, energy in the form of waves of light, heat, or electricity sent through space, esp. electromagnetic waves.

ra·di·ate (rā′di āt), *v.,* **-at·ed, -at·ing,** *adj.* —*v.* 1 give out rays of: *the sun radiates light and heat.* 2 issue in rays. 3 give out; send forth: *her face radiates joy.* 4 spread out from a center: *roads radiate from the city.* —*adj.* radiating from a center. [< L *radiatus.* See RADIANT.] —**ra′di·ate·ly,** *adv.* —**ra′di·a′tive,** *adj.*

ra·di·a·tion (rā′di ā′shən), *n.* 1 act or process of giving out rays of light, heat, sounds, or electricity. 2 energy radiated; ray or rays. 3 act or process of giving off radioactive rays as the result of the decay of a radioactive substance. 4 rays given off by this decay.

radiation sickness, a systematic disease resulting from overexposure to radioactivity.

ra·di·a·tor (rā′di ā′tər), *n.* 1 a heating device consisting of a set of pipes through which steam or hot water passes. 2 device for cooling circulating water, as on an automobile.

rad·i·cal (rad′ə kəl), *adj.* 1 going to the root; fundamental. 2 favoring extreme changes or reforms; extreme. —*n.* 1 person who favors extreme changes or reforms. 2 an atom or group of atoms acting as a unit in chemical reactions. Ammonium (NH_4) is a radical in NH_4OH. 3 the sign ($\sqrt{\ }$) put before an expression to show that some root of it is to be extracted. [< LL, < L *radix* root] —**rad′i·cal·ism, rad′i·cal·ness,** *n.* —**rad′i·cal·ly,** *adv.*

rad·i·cal·ize (rad′ə kə līz), *v.,* **-ized, -iz·ing.** make or become radical. —**rad′i·cal·i·za′tion,** *n.*

ra·di·i (rā′di ī), *n. pl.* of radius.

ra·di·o (rā′di ō), *n., pl.* **-di·os,** *adj., v.,* **-di·oed, -di·o·ing.** —*n.* 1 way of sending and receiving words, music, etc., by electric waves, without connecting wires. 2 apparatus for receiving and making audible the sounds so sent. —*adj.* 1 of, pertaining to, used in, or sent by radio. 2 of or having to do with electric frequencies higher than 15,000 per second. —*v.* transmit or send out by radio. [independent use of *radio-*, abstracted from *radiotelegraphy*, etc.]

radio-, *combining form.* 1 radio, as in *radiotelegraphy.* 2 radial, as in *radiosymmetrical.* 3 radiant energy, as in *radiograph.* 4 radioactive, as in *radioisotope.* [< *radius*]

ra·di·o·ac·tive (rā′di ō ak′tiv), *adj.* 1 giving off radiant energy in the form of alpha, beta, or gamma rays by the breaking up of atoms. 2 *Fig.* explosive; poisonous: *the relationship had become radioactive.* —**ra′di·o·ac·tiv′i·ty**, *n.*

radio astronomy, branch of astronomy that uses radio waves emitted by distant stellar objects to locate and study them. —**radio astronomer,** *n.* —**ra·di·o·as′-tro·nom′i·cal**, *adj.*

ra·di·o·bi·ol·o·gy (rā′di ō bī ol′ə ji), *n.* branch of biology dealing with the effects of radioactivity on living organisms. —**ra′di·o·bi′o·log′i·cal**, *adj.* —**ra′di·o·bi·ol′o·gist**, *n.*

ra·di·o·car·bon (rā′di ō kär′bən), *n.* carbon 14.

ra·di·o·chem·i·cal (rā′di o kem′ə kəl), *adj.* of or having to do with radiochemistry. —*n.* chemical that has had radioisotopes added to it.

ra·di·o·chem·is·try (rā′di ō kem′ə stri), *n.* branch of chemistry dealing with radioactive substances. —**ra′di·o·chem′-ist**, *n.*

ra·di·o·i·so·tope (rā′di ō ī′sə tōp), *n.* a radioactive isotope derived artificially from an element not normally radioactive, often as a by-product of atomic research, the operation of an atomic furnace, etc.

ra·di·o·sonde (rā′di ō sond′), *n.* a radio transmitter dropped by parachute to broadcast temperature, humidity, etc.

ra·di·o·tel·e·graph (rā′di ō tel′ə graf; -gräf), *n.* telegraph worked by radio. —*v.* telegraph by radio. —**ra′di·o·tel′e·graph′ic**, *adj.*

ra·di·o·te·leg·ra·phy (rā′di ō tə leg′rə fi), *n.* telegraphing by radio.

ra·di·o·tel·e·phone (rā′di ō tel′ə fōn), *n., v.,* **-phoned, -phon·ing.** —*n.* Also, **ra′di·o·phone′.** a radio transmitter using voice communication. —*v.* telephone by radio.

ra·di·o·te·leph·o·ny (rā′di ō tə lef′ə ni), *n.* radio communication by means of voice signals.

ra·di·o·tel·e·scope (rā di ō tel′ə skōp), *n.* large network of wires on a frame forming an antenna that can receive radio signals from outer space, used to find new stars, track satellites, etc.

rad·ish (rad′ish), *n.* 1 a small, crisp root with a red or white skin, used as a relish and in salads. 2 the plant. [< L *radix* root]

ra·di·um (rā′di əs), *n.* a radioactive metallic element, Ra, found in very small amounts in uranium ores. [< NL, < L *radius* ray]

ra·di·us (rā′di əs), *n., pl.* **-di·i** (-di ī), **-di·us·es.** 1 any line going straight from the center to the outside of a circle or a sphere. 2 a circular area measured by the length of its radius. 3 that one of the two bones of the forearm which is on the thumb side. [< L, ray, spoke of a wheel. Doublet of RAY¹.]

ra·don (rā′don), *n.* a rare element, Rn, a radioactive gas by given off by the decay of radium. [< *radium*]

R.A.F., Royal Air Force (of Great Britain).

raf·fi·a (raf′i ə), *n.* 1 fiber from the leafstalks of a species of palm growing in Madagascar, used in making baskets, etc. 2 the raffia palm. [< Malagasy (the language of Madagascar)]

raf·fle (raf′əl), *n., v.,* **-fled, -fling.** —*n.* sale in which many people each pay a small sum for a chance of getting an article. —*v.* 1 sell (an article) by a raffle. 2 hold a raffle. [ME *rafle* a dice game < OF, plundering, stripping, ult. <Du. *rafelen* ravel, pluck]

raft¹ (raft; räft), *n.* logs or boards fastened together to make a floating platform. [< Scand. *raptr* log]

raft² (raft; räft), *n.* a large number; abundance. [var. of *raff* heap < *riffraff*]

raft·er (raf′tər; räf′-), *n.* a slanting beam of a roof. [OE *ræfter*]

rag¹ (rag), *n.* 1 a torn or waste piece of cloth. 2 a small piece of cloth. —*adj.* made from rags.

rags, clothing that is much worn or torn. [< Scand. *rögg* shaggy tuft]

rag² (rag), *v.,* **ragged, rag·ging,** *n.* —*v.* 1 scold. 2 tease. —*n.* a ragging.

rag·a·muf·fin (rag′ə muf′ən), *n.* a ragged, child.

rage (rāj), *n., v.,* **raged, rag·ing.** *n.* 1 violent anger: *a voice quivering with rage.* 2 fierce violence; fury: *the rage to kill.* 3 what everybody wants for a short time; the fashion. —*v.* 1 be furious with anger; speak or act with furious anger. 2 act violently; move, proceed, or continue with great violence: *a storm is raging.* [< OF < VL *rabia* < L *rabies*] —**rage′ful,** *adj.* —**rage′ful·ly,** *adv.*

rag·ged (rag′id), *adj.* 1 worn or torn into rags. 2 wearing torn or badly worn-out clothing. 3 not straight and tidy; rough: *a dog's ragged coat.* 4 having loose shreds or bits. 5 having rough or sharp points; uneven; jagged: *ragged rocks* —**rag′ged·ly,** *adv.* —**rag′ged·ness,** *n.*

rag·lan (rag′lən), *n.* a loose topcoat or overcoat with sleeves cut so as to continue up to the collar. [after Lord *Raglan*, British general]

ra·gout (ra gü′), *n.* a highly seasoned stew of meat and vegetables. [< F, < *ragoûter* restore the appetite]

rag·time (rag′tīm′), *n.* 1 musical rhythm with accents falling at unusual places. 2 music with such rhythm, a form of jazz.

rag·weed (rag′wēd′), *n.* any of several coarse weeds of the aster family whose pollen is one of the most common causes of hay fever.

rah (rä), *interj., n.* =hurrah.

raid (rād), *n.* 1 attack; sudden attack. 2 an entering and seizing what is inside: *a police raid.* 3 *Fig.* an attempt to lure employees or athletes away from an employer or team. —*v.* attack suddenly. [northern form of OE *rād* a riding. Cf. ROAD.] —**raid′er,** *n.*

rail¹ (rāl), *n.* 1 bar of wood or of metal. There are stair rails, fence rails, rails protecting monuments, etc. 2 one of the two parallel bars of a railroad track. 3 railroad: *ship by rail.* 4 the upper part of the bulwarks of a ship. —*v.* 1 furnish with rails. 2 enclose with rails: *rail in a yard, rail off the barnyard.* [< OF < L *regula* straight rod. Double of RULE.]

rail² (rāl), *v.* complain bitterly; use violent and reproachful language. [< F *railler*, ult. < LL *ragere* to scream. Doublet of RALLY².] —**rail′er,** *n.*

rail³ (rāl), *n., pl.* **rails** or (*esp. collectively*) **rail.** any of numerous small birds with short wings, narrow bodies, strong legs, long toes, and a harsh cry, that live in marshes and swamps. [< F *râle* < VL *rascla*; prob. imit.]

rail·ing (rāl′ing), *n.* 1 fence made of rails. 2 material for rails. 3 rails.

rail·ler·y (rāl′ər i), *n., pl.* **-ler·ies.** 1 good-humored ridicule; joking; teasing. 2 a bantering remark. [< F *raillerie.* See RAIL².]

rail·road (rāl′rōd′), *n.* 1 road or track with parallel steel rails on which the wheels of the cars go. 2 tracks, stations, trains, and other property of a system of transportation that uses rails, together with the people who manage them. —*v.* 1 send by railroad; carry on a railroad. 2 work on a railroad. 3 *Fig.* send along quickly or too quickly to be fair. —**rail′road′er,** *n.* —**rail′road′ing,** *n.*

rail·way (rāl′wā′), *n.* 1 railroad. 2 track made of rails.

rai·ment (rā′mənt), *n. Archaic.* clothing; garments. [short for *arraiment.* See ARRAY.]

rain (rān), *n.* 1 water falling in drops from the clouds. 2 the fall of such drops. 3 *Fig.* a thick, fast fall of anything: *a rain of rockets, a rain of abuse.* —*v.* 1 fall in drops of water. 2 fall like rain. 3 pour like rain; send like rain. [OE *regn*] —**rain′less,** *adj.*

rain·bow (rān′bō′), *n.* bow or arch of seven colors (violet, indigo, blue, green, yellow, orange, and red) seen sometimes in the sky, or in mist or spray, when the sun shines on it from behind the viewer.

rain check, 1 ticket for future use, given to the spectators at a baseball game or other outdoor performance stopped by rain. **2** *Fig.* a promise to do something in the future that cannot be done now: *a rain check on an invitation.*

rain·coat (rān′kōt′), *n.* a waterproof coat worn for protection from rain.

rain·drop (rān′drop′), *n.* drop of rain.

rain·fall (rān′fôl′), *n.* **1** shower of rain. **2** amount of water in the form of rain, snow, etc., falling within a given time and area.

rain forest large and dense area of forest found in areas of consistently abundant rain, esp. in the tropics.

rain·mak·er (rān′māk′ər), *n.* **1** one who seeks to produce rain, as by supernatural or artificial means. **2** *Fig.* person, esp. an executive, supposed to be able to expand the business of a firm. —**rain′mak′ing,** *n., adj.*

rain·storm (rān′stôrm′), *n.* storm with much rain.

rain·y (rān′i), *adj.,* **rain·i·er, rain·i·est. 1** having rain; having much rain. **2** bringing rain. **3** wet with rain. —**rain′i·ness,** *n.*

rainy day, future time of need: *keep it for a rainy day.*

raise (rāz), *v.,* **raised, rais·ing,** *n.* —*v.* **1** lift up: *raise one's hand.* **2** set upright: *raise the overturned lamp.* **3** cause to rise: *raise a cloud of dust.* **4** put or take into a higher position; make higher or nobler; elevate: *raise a man to manager.* **5** increase in amount, degree, force, volume, etc.: *raise the temperature, raise the rent, raise your voice.* **6** gather together; collect; manage to get: *the leader raised an army.* **7** breed; grow; rear: *raise wheat, dogs, or children.* **8** cause; bring about; utter: *raise a shout, a funny remark raises a laugh.* **9** build; create; set up: *raise a monument.* **10** *Fig.* rouse; stir up: *the dog raised a rabbit from the underbrush, raise a commotion.* **11** bring back to life: *raise the dead.* **12** put an end to: *raise the siege of a fort.* —*n.* **1** increase in amount, price, pay, etc. **2** amount of such an increase. [< Scand. *reisa*] —**rais′a·ble,** *adj.* —**rais′er,** *n.*

rai·sin (rā′zən), *n.* a sweet dried grape. [< OF < L *racemus* grape cluster. Doublet of RACEME.]

raj (räj), *n.* in India, rule; dominion.

ra·jah (rä′jə), *n.* ruler or chief in India, Java, Borneo, etc. [< Hind. *rājā* < Skt.] —**ra′jah·ship,** *n.*

rake¹ (rāk), *n., v.,* **raked, rak·ing.** —*n.* a longhandled tool having a bar at one end with teeth in it, used for smoothing the soil or gathering together loose leaves, hay, straw, etc. —*v.* **1** move with a rake: *rake the leaves off the grass.* **2** gather; gather together. **3** search carefully. **4** fire guns along the length of (a ship, line of soldiers, etc.). [OE *raca*]

rake² (rāk), *n.* a profligate or dissolute person. [short for *rakehell* a roué]

rak·ish (rāk′ish), *adj.* **1** smart; jaunty; dashing. **2** immoral; dissolute. —**rak′ish·ly,** *adv.* —**rak′ish·ness,** *n.*

Ra·leigh (rô′li), *n.* capital of North Carolina, in the C part.

ral·ly (ral′i), *v.,* **-lied, -ly·ing,** *n., pl.* **-lies.** —*v.* **1** bring together; bring together again; get in order again: *rally the fleeing troops.* **2** come together in a body for a common purpose or action. **3** come to the assistance of a person, party, or cause: *he rallied to the side of his friend.* **4** recover health and strength: *the sick man may rally now.* **5** recover more or less from a drop in price: *the market rallied.* —*n.* **1** act or fact of rallying; recovery. **2** a coming together; mass meeting: *a political rally.* **3** act or fact of hitting the ball back and forth several times in tennis and similar games. [< F *rallier* < *re-* again + *allier* ALLY]

ram (ram), *n., v.,* **rammed, ram·ming.** —*n.* **1** a male sheep. **2** machine or part of a machine that strikes heavy blows. —*v.* **1** butt against; strike head on, strike violently. **2** push hard; drive down or in by heavy blows.

Ram, Aries. [OE *ramm*] —**ram′mer,** *n.*

RAM (ram), random-access memory (storage of accessible data in a computer).

ram·ble (ram′bəl), *v.,* **-bled, -bling,** *n.* —*v.* **1** wander about. **2** talk or write about first one thing and then another with no useful connections. **3** spread irregularly in various directions: *vines rambled over the wall.* —*n.* a walk for pleasure, not to go to any special place. —**ram′bler,** *n.*

ram·bunc·tious (ram bungk′shəs), *adj.* wild and uncontrollable; unruly; boisterous.

ram·e·kin (ram′ə kin), *n.* **1** a small, separately cooked portion of some food, esp. one topped with cheese and bread crumbs. **2** a small baking dish holding enough for one portion. [< F *ramequin* < Du.]

ram·i·fi·ca·tion (ram′ə fə kā′shən), *n.* **1** a spreading or branching out. **2** result of spreading out or dividing; off shoot. **3** *Fig.* consequence.

ram·i·fy (ram′ə fī), *v.,* **-fied, -fy·ing.** divide or spread out into branchlike parts. [< F < Med. L, < L *ramus* branch + *facere* make]

ramp¹ (ramp), *n.* a sloping way connecting two different levels of a building, road, etc.; slope.

ramp up, increase the level or intensity of: *ramp up a public relations campaign.* [< F *rampe* < *ramper.* See RAMP².]

ramp² (ramp), *v.* **1** rush wildly about; behave violently. **2** jump or rush with fury. [< F *ramper* creep]

ram·page (*n.* ram′pāj; *v.* ram pāj′, ram′-pāj), *n., v.,* **-paged, -pag·ing.** —*n.* fit or rushing wildly about; wild outbreak. —*v.* rush wildly about; behave violently; rage. [? < *ramp²*]

ramp·ant (ram′pənt), *adj.* **1** growing without any check; unrestrained; unchecked. **2** angry; excited; violent. [< OF, ramp-

ing] —**ramp′an·cy,** *n.* —**ramp′ant·ly,** *adv.*

ram·part (ram′pärt), *n.* **1** a wide bank of earth, often with a wall on top, built around a fort to help defend it. **2** anything that defends; protection. [< F, < *remparer* fortify, ult. < L *re-* back + *ante* before + *parare* prepare]

ram·rod (ram′rod′), *n.* **1** rod for ramming down the charge in a gun that is loaded from the muzzle. **2** rod for cleaning the gun barrel.

ram·shack·le (ram′shak′əl), *adj.* loose and shaky; likely to come apart. [? ult. < *ransack*]

ran (ran), *v.* pt. of **run.**

ranch (ranch), *n.* **1** a very large farm and its buildings for raising cattle, horses, etc. **2** any farm or farming establishment: *a chicken ranch.* **3** persons employed or living on a ranch. —*v.* work on or manage a ranch. [< Sp., group of persons who eat together] —**ranch′er,** *n.*

ran·che·ro (ran chär′ō; rän–), *n., pl.* **-ros.** *SW U.S.* **1** rancher. **2** ranch hand. [< Am. Sp.; see RANCH]

ranch house, 1 a one-story dwelling, like most houses on a ranch, having a low roof. **2** main house on a ranch, where the owner or manager and family live.

ran·cho (ran′chō; rän′–), *n. SW U.S.* **1** ranch. **2** hut for a herdsman. [< Am. Sp.; see RANCH]

ran·cid (ran′sid), *adj.* **1** stale; spoiled: *rancid fat.* **2** tasting or smelling like stale fat or butter. [< L *rancidus* < *rancere* be rank] —**ran′cid·ly,** *adv.* —**ran′cid·ness,** *n.*

ran·cor (rang′kər), *n.* bitter resentment or ill will; extreme hatred or spite. [< OF < LL, rankness, < L *rancere* be rank] —**ran′cor·ous,** *adj.* —**ran′cor·ous·ly,** *adv.* —**ran′cor·ous·ness,** *n.*

r & b, R & B, or **R and B,** rhythm and blues.

R & D, R and D, research and development.

ran·dom (ran′dəm), *adj.* by chance; with no plan. —*n.* **at random,** by chance; with no plan or purpose. [< OF *randon* rapid rush] —**ran′dom·i·za′tion,** *n.* —**ran′dom·ize,** *v.*

random access, access to data or programs in a computer memory according to the needs of the user and without having to close one program to access another. —**ran′dom-ac′cess,** *adj.*

ra·nee (rä′ni), *n.* wife of a rajah. Also, **rani.** [< Hind. *rānī* < Skt. *rājnī*]

rang (rang), *v.* pt. of **ring².**

range (rānj), *n., v.,* **ranged, rang·ing,** *adj.* —*n.* **1** distance between certain limits; extent: *a range of prices from 5 cents to 25 dollars.* **2** distance a gun can shoot. **3** place to practice shooting. **4** land for grazing. **5** row or line of mountains. **6** stove for cooking. [< v.] —*v.* **1** vary within certain limits: *prices ranging from $5 to $10.* **2** wander over: *buffalo once ranged these plains.* **3** run in a line;

extend: *a boundary ranging east and west.* **4** be found; occur: *a plant ranging from Canada to Mexico.* —*adj.* of or on land for grazing. [< OF *ranger* array, ult. < *reng* line, RANK¹]

rang·er (rān′jər), *n.* **1** person employed to guard a tract of forest. **2** one of a body of armed people employed in ranging over a region to police it. —**rang′er·ship**, *n.*

Ran·goon (rang gün′), *n.* capital and chief port of Myanmar, in the S part.

rang·y (rān′ji), *adj.,* **rang·i·er, rang·i·est.** slender and long-limbed: *a rangy horse.* —**rang′i·ness**, *n.*

ra·ni (rä′ni), *n.* = ranee.

rank¹ (rangk), *n.* **1** row or line, usually of soldiers, placed side by side. **2** position; grade; class: *the rank of colonel, in the first rank.* **3** high position: *a duke is a man of rank.* —*v.* **1** arrange in a row or line. **2** have a certain rank: *New York State ranks first in wealth.* **3** put in some special order in a list: *rank the states for area.* **4** outrank: *a major ranks a captain.*
close ranks, a come into close formation of troops. **b** *Fig.* come together for mutual support: *the family closed ranks.*
pull rank, use one's position, esp. to impose one's will.
ranks, a army; soldiers. **b** rank. [ult. < OF *reng* < Gmc.]

rank² (rangk), *adj.* **1** large and coarse: *rank grass.* **2** growing richly. **3** producing a dense but coarse growth: *rank swamp land.* **4** having a strong, bad smell or taste: *rank potatoes.* **5** *Fig.* strongly marked; extreme: *rank ingratitude.* **6** coarse; not decent. [OE *ranc* proud] —**rank′ly**, *adv.* —**rank′ness**, *n.*

rank and file, 1 a common soldiers, not officers. **b** the common people. **2** ordinary members, as opposed to officials, of a group or organization.

ran·kle (rang′kəl), *v.,* **-kled, -kling.** be sore; cause soreness; continue to give pain: *the insult rankled.* [ult. < OF *draoncler* < Med.L *dracunculus* sore, dim. of L *draco* serpent]

ran·sack (ran′sak), *v.* **1** search thoroughly through: *ransack the desk for the lost letter.* **2** rob; plunder. [< Scand. *rannsaka,* lit., search a house < *rann* house + –*saka* search] —**ran′sacker**, *n.*

ran·som (ran′səm), *n.* price paid or demanded before a captive is set free. —*v.* **1** obtain the release of (a captive) by paying a price. **2** redeem. [< OF *rançon* < L *redemption.* Doublet of REDEMPTION.] —**ran′som·er**, *n.*

rant (rant), *v.* speak wildly, extravagantly, violently, or noisily. —*n.* an extravagant, violent, or noisy speech.
rant and rave, scold and shout wildly. [< MDu. *ranten*] —**rant′er**, *n.* —**rant′ing·ly**, *adv.*

rap¹ (rap), *n., v.,* **rapped, rap·ping.** —*n.* **1** a quick, light blow; a light, sharp knock. **2** blame; rebuke: *take the rap.* —*v.* **1** knock sharply; tap. **2** say sharply: *rap out an answer.* [? imit.]

rap² (rap), *v.,* **rapped, rap·ping. 1** talk; chat. **2** talk rhythmically or in rhyme. **3** perform rap music. —*n.* **1** easy talk; chat. **2** rapid, rhyming talk. **3** = rap music.

rap³ (rap), *n.* the least bit: *not give a rap about that.*

ra·pa·cious (rə pā′shəs), *adj.* **1** seizing by force; plundering. **2** grasping; greedy. **3** of animals, living by the capture of prey. [< L *rapax* grasping < *rapere* seize] —**ra·pa′cious·ly**, *adv.* —**ra·pa′cious·ness**, *n.* —**ra·pac′i·ty**, *n.*

rape¹ (rāp), *n., v.,* **raped, rap·ing.** —*n.* **1** a seizing and carrying off by force. **2** the crime of having sexual intercourse with a woman or girl forcibly and against her will. —*v.* **1** seize and carry off by force. **2** force (a woman or girl) to have sexual intercourse against her will. [< L *rapere* seize] —**rap′ist**, *n.*

rape² (rāp), *n.* a small plant whose leaves are used as food for sheep and hogs and whose seeds yield an oil (**rape oil**) that is used as a lubricant, etc. [< L *rapa, rapum*]

rap·id (rap′id), *adj.* **1** moving, acting, or doing with speed: *a rapid worker.* **2** going on or forward at a fast rate: *rapid growth.* —*n.* Usually, **rapids.** part of a river's course where the water rushes quickly. [< L *rapidus* < *rapere* hurry away] —**ra·pid′i·ty, rap′id·ness**, *n.* —**rap′id·ly**, *adv.*

rapid transit, system of rapid transportation in a city, as subways, elevated trains, etc.

ra·pi·er (rā′pi ər), *n.* a light sword used for thrusting. [< MF *rapière* < *râpe* grater, RASP; with ref. to the perforated guard]

rap·ine (rap′ən), *n.* robbing by force and carrying off; plundering. [< L *rapina*]

rap music, a type of popular music with a strong beat, accompanied by rapid, rhyming talk.

rap·pel (ra pel′), *v.,* **-pelled, -pel·ling.** slide down a vertical surface, as a cliff, building, rock face, etc., using ropes securely fastened above the person descending to control his or her descent. [< F *rappeler*; see REPEAL]

rap·per (rap′ər), *n.* **1** person who plays or performs rap music. **2** person who raps.

rap·port (ra pôrt′; –pōrt′; *Fr.* rä pôr′), *n.* agreement; harmony. [< F, < *rapporter* bring back]

rap·proche·ment (rä prôsh mäN′), *n.* establishment or renewal of friendly relations. [< F, < *rapprocher* bring near]

rap·scal·lion (rap skal′yən), *n.* rascal; rogue; scamp. [earlier *rascallion* < *rascal*]

rapt (rapt), *adj.* **1** lost in delight. **2** so busy thinking of or enjoying one thing that one does not know what else is happening. **3** carried away in body or spirit from earth, life, or ordinary affairs. **4** showing or caused by a rapt condition. [< L *raptus* seized] —**rapt′ly**, *adv.* —**rapt′ness**, *n.*

rap·tor (rap′tər; –tôr), *n.* bird of prey, as an eagle or hawk.

rap·to·ri·al (rap tô′ri əl; –tō′–), *adj.* **1** adapted for seizing prey. **2** belonging or pertaining to an order of birds of prey, such as the eagles, hawks, etc. (ult. < L *raptor* robber < *rapere* seize]

rap·ture (rap′chər), *n.* **1** a strong feeling that absorbs the mind; very great joy. **2** Often, **raptures.** expression of great joy. [< *rapt*]

rap·tur·ous (rap′chər əs), *adj.* full of rapture; expressing or feeling rapture. —**rap′tur·ous·ly**, *adv.* —**rap′tur·ous·ness**, *n.*

rare¹ (rār), *adj.,* **rar·er, rar·est. 1** seldom seen or found: *a rare bird.* **2** not happening often; unusual: *a rare event.* **3** thin; not dense. [< L *rarus*] —**rare′ness**, *n.*

rare² (rār), *adj.,* **rar·er, rar·est.** not cooked much: *a rare steak.* [OE *hrēr*]

rare·bit (rār′bit), *n.* = Welsh rabbit.

rare earth, oxide of a rare-earth metal.

rare-earth elements or **metals** (rār′erth′), rare metallic elements having atomic numbers 57 to 71.

rar·e·fy (rār′ə fī), *v.,* **-fied, -fy·ing. 1** make or become less dense. **2** refine; purify. [< L, < *rarus* rare + *facere* make] —**rar′e·fac′tion**, *n.* —**rar′e·fac′tive**, *adj.*

rare·ly (rār′li), *adv.* **1** seldom; not often: *things rarely seen.* **2** unusually; unusually well: *a rarely carved panel.*

rar·ing (rār′ing), *adj.* eager; anxious: *raring to begin.* [< ppr. *rare,* var. of *rear²*]

rar·i·ty (rér′ə ti), *n., pl.* **-ties. 1** something rare. **2** fewness; scarcity. **3** lack of density; thinness.

ras·cal (ras′kəl), *n.* a bad, dishonest person. Sometimes *rascal* is used jokingly, as when one calls a child a little rascal. —*adj.* low; mean; dishonest. [< OF *rascaille* < *rasque* filth, ult. < L *radere* scratch] —**ras·cal′i·ty**, *n.* —**ras′cal·ly**, *adv.*

rase (rāz), *v.,* **rased, ras·ing.** = raze.

rash¹ (rash), *adj.* too hasty; careless; reckless; taking too much risk. [ME *rasch* quick] —**rash′ly**, *adv.* —**rash′ness**, *n.*

rash² (rash), *n.* a breaking out with many small red spots on the skin. Scarlet fever causes a rash. [< OF *rasche,* ult. < L *radere* scratch]

rash·er (rash′ər), *n.* a thin slice of bacon or ham for frying or broiling.

rasp (rasp; räsp), *v.* **1** make a harsh, grating sound: *the file rasped, rasp out a command.* **2** have a harsh or irritating effect (on); grate: *rasp on one's nerves.* **4** scrape with a rough instrument. —*n.* **1** harsh, grating sound. **2** a coarse file with pointlike teeth. [< OF *rasper* < Gmc.] —**rasp′ing**, *adj.*

rasp·ber·ry (raz′ber′i; –bri; räz′–), *n., pl.* **-ries. 1** a small fruit, usually red or black, that grows on bushes. **2** bush that it grows on. **3** *Informal.* sound of disapproval or derision made with the tongue and lips. [< earlier *raspis* raspberry + *berry*]

rasp·y (ras′pi; räs′–), *adj.*, **rasp·i·er, rasp-i·est. 1** harsh; grating. **2** *Fig.* irritating.

rat (rat), *n.*, *v.*, **rat·ted, rat·ting.** —*n.* **1** a long-tailed rodent like a mouse but larger. Rats are gray, black, brown, or white. **2** a low mean, disloyal person. —*interj.* **rats,** exclamation of irritation or impatience. —*v.* **1** hunt for rats; catch rats. **2** behave in a low, mean, disloyal way.
rat on, *Informal.* expose: *how could you rat on a friend?*
smell a rat, suspect a trick or scheme. [OE *rætt*]

rat·a·ble (rāt′ə bəl), *adj.* capable of being rated. —**rat′a·bil′i·ty, rat′a·ble·ness,** *n.* —**rat′a·bly,** *adv.*

ra·tan (ra tan′), *n.* =rattan.

ratch·et (rach′it), *n.*, *v.* —*n.* wheel or bar with teeth that come against a catch so that motion is permitted in one direction but not in the other. Also, **ratch.** —*v.* **1** move with a ratchet. **2** move as if using a ratchet: *ratchet up the pace of the discussions.* [< F < Ital. *rocchetto*, ult. < Gmc.]

rate (rāt), *n.*, *v.*, **rat·ed, rat·ing.** —*n.* **1** quantity, amount, or degree measured in proportion to something else: *the rate of interest is 6 cents on the dollar.* **2** degree of speed or progress: *a rapid rate.* **3** price: *we pay the regular rate.* **4** class; grade; rating. —*v.* **1** put a value on. **2** consider; regard. **3** put in a certain class or grade, as a ship or sailor.
at any rate, a in any case; under any circumstances. **b** at least.
at that or **this rate,** in that or this case; under such circumstances. [< OF < Med.L *rata* (*pars*) fixed (amount), pp. of L *reri* reckon] —**rat′er,** *n.*

rath·er (rath′ər; räth′–), *adv.* **1** more readily; more willingly: *I would rather stay than go.* **2** more truly: *late Monday night or, rather, early Tuesday morning.* **3** to some extent; somewhat; more than a little: *rather good.*
had rather, would more willingly; prefer to. [OE *hrathor*, compar. of *hrathe* quickly].

raths·kel·ler (räts′kel ́ər), *n.* restaurant selling alcoholic drinks, usually below street level. [< G, < *rat*(*haus*) town hall + *keller* cellar]

rat·i·fy (rat′ə fī), *v.*, **-fied, -fy·ing.** confirm; approve: *the Senate must ratify a treaty to make it binding.* [< OF < Med.L, ult. < L *ratus* fixed + *facere* make] —**rat′i·fi·ca′tion, rat′i·fi ́er,** *n.*

rat·ing (rāt′ing), *n.* **1** class; grade. **2** position in a class or grade: *the rating of a seaman.* **3** an amount fixed as a rate: *a rating of 80% in English.* **4** estimate of credit standing.

ra·ti·o (rā′shi ō; –shō), *n.*, *pl.* **-ti·os. 1** relative magnitude. "He has sheep and cows in the ratio of 10 to 3" means that he has ten sheep for every three cows. **2** quotient. The ratio of 6 to 10 is %10. **3** proportional relation; rate. [< L, reckoning, < *reri* reckon. Doublet of RATION, REASON.]

ra·tion (rash′ən; rā′shən), *n.* **1** a fixed allowance of food; daily allowance of food for a person or animal: *a balanced ration.* **2** portion of anything dealt out: *rations of sugar, of coal, etc.* —*v.* **1** supply with rations: *ration an army.* **2** allows only certain amounts to: *ration citizens when supplies are scarce.* **3** distribute in limited amounts: *ration food to the public in wartime.* [< F < Med.L *ratio* < L, reckoning. Doublet of RATIO, REASON.] —**ra′tion·ing,** *n.*

ra·tion·al (rash′ən əl; rash′nəl), *adj.* **1** sensible; reasonable; reasoned out: *act in a rational way.* **2** able to think and reason clearly: *as children grow older, they become more rational.* **3** of reason; based on reasoning. **4** expressible in finite terms; involving no root that cannot be extracted. [< L *rationalis.* See RATIO.] —**ra′tion·al′i·ty,** *n.* —**ra′tion·al·ly,** *adv.*

ra·tion·ale (rash ́ə nal′), *n.* **1** basic reason: *rationale for becoming a veterinarian.* **2** principle: *the rationale of a policy.* [< L *ratiōnāle,* neut. of *ratiōnālis* rational]

ra·tion·al·ism (rash′ən əl iz′əm; rash′-nəl–), *n.* principle or habit of accepting reason as the supreme authority in matters of opinion, belief, or conduct. —**ra′tion·al·ist,** *n.* —**ra′tion·al·is′tic,** *adj.* —**ra′tion·al·is′ti·cal·ly,** *adv.*

ra·tion·al·ize (rash′ən əl īz; rash′nəl–), *v.*, **-ized, -iz·ing. 1** make rational or conformable to reason. **2** treat or explain in a rational manner. **3** find (often unconsciously) an explanation or excuse for. **4** find excuses for one's desires. —**ra′tion-al·i·za′tion,** *n.* —**ra′tion·al·iz ́er,** *n.*

rat·line, rat·lin (rat′lən), *n.* one of the small ropes that cross the shrouds of a ship, used as steps for going aloft.

rat race, *Informal.* routine that is irrationally busy without much accomplished: *the commuter rat race.*

rats·bane (rats′bān′), *n.* any poison for rats.

rat·tan (ra tan′), *n.* **1** kind of palm with a very long stem. **2** stems of such palm trees, used for wickerwork, canes, etc. **3** cane or switch made from a piece of such a stem. [ult. < Malay *rotan*]

rat·ter (rat′ər), *n.* animal, esp. a cat or dog, that catches rats.

rat·tle (rat′əl), *v.*, **-tled, -tling,** *n.* —*v.* **1** make a number of short, sharp sounds. **2** move with short, sharp sounds: *the cart rattled down the street.* **3** talk quickly, on and on. **4** confuse; embarrass. —*n.* **1** a number of short, sharp sounds: *the rattle of empty bottles.* **2** sound in the throat, occurring in some diseases of the lungs and also often just before death. **3** toy, instrument, etc., that makes a noise when it is shaken. **4** series of horny pieces at the end of a rattlesnake's tail. [ME *ratelen;* prob. imit.]

rat·tle·brain (rat′əl brān′), *n.* a giddy, thoughtless person. —**rat′tle·brained′,** *adj.*

rat·tler (rat′lər), *n.* **1** =rattlesnake. **2** something that rattles.

rat·tle·snake (rat′əl snāk′), *n.* a poisonous snake with a thick body and a broad triangular head, that makes a rattling noise with its tail.

rat·tle·trap (rat′əl trap′), *n.* **1** a rattling, rickety wagon or other vehicle. **2** any shaky, rattling object.

rat·ty (rat′i), *adj.*, **-ti·er, -ti·est. 1** of or like rats. **2** full of rats. **3** shabby.

rau·cous (rô′kəs), *adj.* hoarse; harsh-sounding. [< L *raucus*] —**rau′cous·ly,** *adv.* —**rau′cous·ness, rau′ci·ty,** *n.*

rav·age (rav′ij), *v.*, **-aged, -ag·ing,** *n.* —*v.* lay waste; damage greatly; destroy. —*n.* violence; destruction; great damage. [< F, < *ravir* RAVISH] —**rav′ag·er,** *n.*

rave (rāv), *v.*, **raved, rav·ing. 1** talk wildly: *an excited, angry person raves.* **2** talk with too much enthusiasm: *she raved about her food.* **3** howl; roar; rage. —*n.* **1** praise that is too enthusiastic. **2** *Informal.* wild party. [? < OF *raver,* var. of *rêver* to dream]

rav·el (rav′əl), *v.*, **-eled, -el·ing,** *n.* —*v.* **1** separate the threads of; fray. **2** make plain or clear; unravel. **3** become tangled, involved, or confused. —*n.* an unraveled thread or fiber. [prob. < MDu. *ravelen*] —**rav′el·er,** *n.*

rav·el·ing (rav′əl ing; rav′ling), *n.* something raveled out; a thread drawn from a woven or knitted fabric.

ra·ven (rā′vən), *n.* a large black bird like a crow but larger. —*adj.* deep, glossy black. [OE *hræfn*]

rav·en·ing (rav′ən ing), *adj.* greedy and hungry.

rav·en·ous (rav′ən əs), *adj.* **1** very hungry. **2** greedy. **3** rapacious. —**rav′en·ous·ly,** *adv.* —**rav′en·ous·ness,** *n.*

ra·vine (rə vēn′), *n.* a long, deep, narrow gorge worn by running water.

rav·ing (rāv′ing), *adj.* **1** that raves; delirious; frenzied; raging: *a raving lunatic.* **2** extraordinary: *a raving beauty, a raving success.* **3** of or having to do with a rave: *put on my raving shoes.* —*n.* delirious, incoherent talk.

rav·i·o·li (rav ́i ō′li), *n.pl.* small, thin pieces of dough filled with chopped meat, cheese, etc., cooked in boiling water and served with a seasoned tomato sauce. [< Ital., ult. < L *rapum* beet]

rav·ish (rav′ish), *v.* **1** fill with delight. **2** carry off by force. **3** rape. [< OF *raviss-* < L *rapere* seize] —**rav′ish·er,** *n.* —**rav′ish·ment,** *n.*

rav·ish·ing (rav′ish ing), *adj.* very delightful; enchanting. —**rav′ish·ing·ly,** *adv.*

raw (rô), *adj.* **1** not cooked: *raw oysters.* **2** in the natural state; not manufactured, treated, or prepared: *raw materials, raw hides.* **3** not experienced; not trained: *a raw soldier.* **4** damp and cold: *raw weather.* **5** with the skin off; sore: *a raw spot.* **6** brutally or coarsely frank. **7** *Informal.* harsh; unfair: *a raw deal.* —*n.* raw flesh. [OE *hrēaw*] —**raw′ly,** *adv.* —**raw′ness,** *n.*

raw-boned (rô′bōnd′), *adj.* gaunt.

raw·hide (rô′hīd′), *n., v.,* **–hid·ed, –hid-ing. —*n.* 1** the untanned skin of cattle. **2** rope or whip made of this. —*v.* whip with a rawhide.

ray[1] (rā), *n.* **1** line or beam of light. **2** any stream of particles moving in the same line. **3** a thin line like a ray, coming out from a center. **4** part like a ray. The petals of a daisy and the arms of a starfish are rays. **5** *Fig.* a slight trace; faint gleam. —*v.* send forth in rays; radiate. [< OF < L *radius.* Doublet of RADIUS.]

ray[2] (rā), *n.* any of several varieties of fishes, related to the sharks, that have broad, flat bodies with very broad pectoral fins. [< F < L *raia*]

ray·on (rā′on), *n.* fiber or fabric made from cellulose treated with chemicals. Rayon is used instead of silk, wool, and cotton. [< *ray*[1]]

raze (rāz), *v.,* **razed, raz·ing.** tear down; destroy completely. [< F *raser* scrape, ult. < L *radere*]

ra·zor (rā′zər), *n.* tool with a sharp blade to shave with. [< OF *rasor* < *raser.* See RAZE.]

ra·zor·back (rā′zər bak′), *n.* **1** kind of thin, half-wild hog with a ridged back. **2** sharp ridge on a hill or mountain.

razz (raz), *Informal.* —*v.* laugh at; make fun of. —*n.* derision. [< *raspberry*]

raz·zle-daz·zle (raz′əl daz′əl), *Informal.* —*n.* performance that is fast, flashy, or showy and may also trick the eye. —*adj.* spectacular; flashy.

razz·ma·tazz (raz′mə taz′), *n. Informal.* **1** = razzle-dazzle. **2** nonsense: *the usual advertising razzmatazz.*

Rb, rubidium.

R.C., 1 Red Cross. **2** Roman Catholic.

rd., 1 Also, **Rd.** road. **2** rod; rods.

re[1] (rā; rē), *n.* the second tone of a scale. [see GAMUT]

re[2] (rē), *prep.* with reference to; about; concerning. [for L *in re* in the matter of]

Re, rhenium.

re-, *prefix.* **1** again; anew; once more, as in *reappear, rebuild, reheat, reopen.* **2** back, as in *recall, repay, replace.* [< L; also (before vowels), *red–*]

The meaning of each of the following words is found by adding *again* or *anew* to the main part.

re′ad·just′
re′ap·pear′
re′as·sem′ble
re′as·sess′
re·build′
re·con′sti·tute
re·cop′y
re′de·pos′it
re′de·vel′op
re·ed′it
re′en·act′
re·fash′ion
re·heat′
re·in·vent′
re′in·vig′or·ate
re·is′sue
re·lo′cate

re·num′ber
re·o′pen
re·phrase′
re·read′
re′sale′
re·start′
re·test′
re·think′
re·vi′tal·ize
re·word′

reach (rēch), *v.* **1** get to; come to; arrive at: *reach the top of a hill, the end of a book, an agreement, etc.* **2** stretch; stretch out: *reach toward or after something.* **3** extend in space, time, operation, effect, influence, etc. (to): *the power of Rome reached to the ends of the known world, the radio reaches millions.* **4** get in touch with by anything extended, cast, etc.; touch: *the anchor reached bottom, I cannot reach the top of the wall.* **5** move to touch or seize something; try to get: *the man reached for a pencil.* **6** amount to; be equal to: *sums reaching a considerable amount.* —*n.* **1** a stretching out; reaching: *make a reach for the rope.* **2** extent or distance of reaching: *out of one's reach.* **3** *Fig.* range; power; capacity: *the reach of the mind.* **4** a continuous stretch or extent. [OE *rǣcan*] —**reach′a·ble,** *adj.* —**reach′er,** *n.*

re·act (ri akt′), *v.* **1** act back; have an effect on the one that is acting: *unkindness often reacts on the unkind person.* **2** act in response: *dogs react to kindness by showing affection, react against an injustice.* **3** act chemically: *acids react on metals.*

re·ac·tion (ri ak′shən), *n.* **1** action in the opposite direction: *fever is a common reaction from a chill.* **2** a political tendency toward a previous state of affairs. **3** action or feeling in response to some influence or force: *our reaction to a joke is to laugh.* **4** action of two substances on each other. —**re·ac′tive,** *adj.*

re·ac·tion·ar·y (ri ak′shən er′i), *adj., n., pl.* **-ar·ies.** —*adj.* marked by or favoring reaction; extremely conservative. —*n.* person who favors reaction, esp. in politics.

re·ac·ti·vate (ri ak′tə vāt), *v.,* **-vat·ed, -vat·ing.** return or restore to active duty or service: *reactivate several national guard units.*

re·ac·tor (ri ak′tər), *n.* a special assembly for the production of a limited release of nuclear energy, intended for splitting nuclei; pile; nuclear reactor.

read[1] (rēd), *v.,* **read** (red), **read·ing. 1** get the meaning of (writing or printing): *the blind read with their fingers, he reads himself to sleep.* **2** speak (printed or written words): *read this story to me.* **3** show by letters, figures, signs, etc.: *the thermometer reads 70 degrees.* **4** give as the word or words in a particular passage: *for "fail," a misprint, read "fall."* **5** study: *read law.* **6** understand; interpret: *a prophet reads the future, read a hostile intent in a letter.*

read out of, expel from (a political party, etc.). [OE *rǣdan* counsel]

read[2] (red), *adj.* having knowledge gained by reading; informed. [orig. pp. of *read*[1]]

read·a·ble (rēd′ə bəl), *adj.* **1** easy to read; interesting. **2** capable of being read. —**read′a·bil′i·ty, read′a·ble·ness,** *n.* —**read′a·bly,** *adv.*

re·ad·dress (rē′ə dres′), *v.* **1** put a new address on a letter, package, etc. **2** direct one's attention or energy to again: *readdress a problem.*

read·er (rēd′ər), *n.* **1** person who reads. **2** person employed to read manuscripts and estimate their fitness for publication. **3** book for learning and practicing reading.

read·ing (rēd′ing), *n.* **1** act or process of getting the meaning of writing or printing. **2** a speaking out loud of written or printed words; public recital. **3** written or printed matter read or to be read. **4** thing shown by letters, figures, or signs: *the reading of the thermometer was 96 degrees.* **5** the form of a given word or passage in a particular edition of a book: *no two editions have the same reading for that passage.* **6** *Fig.* interpretation: *a different reading of the play.* —*adj.* used in or for reading.

read·out (rēd′out′), *n.* **1** display of data on a computer screen. **2** transmission of data, as from a space probe.

read·y (red′i), *adj.,* **read·i·er, read·i·est,** *v.,* **read·ied, read·y·ing,** *n.* —*adj.* **1** prepared for action or use at once; prepared: *dinner is ready, ships ready for battle.* **2** willing: *ready to face trial.* **3** quick: *a ready welcome, too ready to find fault.* **4** quick in thought or action; dexterous: *ready wit.* **5** immediately available: *ready money.* —*v.* make ready; prepare. —*n.* condition or position of being fit for action. [< OE *rǣde* ready] —**read′i·ly,** *adv.* —**read′i·ness,** *n.*

read·y-made (red′i mād′), *adj.* made for anybody who will buy; not made to order.

Rea·gan (rā′gən), *n.* **Ronald Wilson,** 1911–2004, the 40th president of the United States, 1981–89.

re·a·gent (rē ā′jənt), *n.* substance used to detect the presence of other substances by the chemical reactions it causes.

re·al[1] (rē′əl; rēl), *adj.* **1** existing as a fact; not imagined or made up; actual; true: *a real experience, the real reason.* **2** genuine: *a real diamond.* **3** noting or pertaining to immovable property. Lands and houses are called real property. **4** either rational or irrational, not imaginary.

get real, *Informal.* be realistic. [< LL *realis* < L *res* matter] —**re′al·ness,** *n.*

re·al[2] (rē′əl; *Sp.* rā äl′), *n., pl.* **re·als,** *Sp.* **re·a·les** (rā ä′lās). a former small Spanish silver coin. [< Sp. < L *regalis* regal. Doublet of REGAL, ROYAL.]

real estate, land together with the buildings, trees, water, etc. on it.

re·al·ism (rē′əl iz əm), *n.* **1** practical tendency. **2** in art and literature, the picturing of life as it actually is. **3** doctrine that material objects have a real existence independent of our consciousness of them. —**re′al·ist,** *n.* —**re′al·is′tic,** *adj.* —**re′al·is′ti·cal·ly,** *adv.*

re·al·i·ty (ri al′ə ti), *n., pl.* **–ties. 1** actual existence; true state of affairs: *ghosts have no place in reality.* **2** a real thing; actual fact.

in reality, really; actually; in fact; truly.

re·al·i·za·tion (rē′əl ə zā′shən), *n.* **1** clear understanding; full awareness; perception. **2** a realizing or being realized.

re·al·ize (rē′əl īz), *v.,* **–ized, –iz·ing. 1** understand clearly; be fully aware of: *she realizes how hard you worked.* **2** make real; bring into actual existence. **3** obtain as a return or profit: *he realized $10,000.* —**re′al·iz′a·ble,** *adj.* —**re′al·iz′er,** *n.*

real-life (rē′əl līf′), *adj.* taken from life; not imagined.

re·al·ly (rē′əl i; rēl′i), *adv.* **1** actually: *things as they really are.* **2** genuinely; truly: *really extraordinary.* **3** indeed: *Oh, really?*

realm (relm), *n.* **1** kingdom. **2** region or sphere in which something rules or prevails. **3** a particular field of something: *the realm of biology.* [< OF *reialme* < *reial* REGAL]

real time, 1 time within which something is actually taking place. **2** infinitesimal amount of time that passes between putting data into a computer and receiving it in processed form.

real-time (rē′əl tīm′), *adj.* nearly instantaneous as with text messaging on a cell phone or on-line: *real-time conversation online.*

real·tor (rēl′tər; rē′əl–; –tôr), *n.* person engaged in the real estate business. [< trademark *Realtor*]

re·al·ty (rē′əl ti), *n.* =real estate.

real wages, wages measured in actual purchasing power.

ream¹ (rēm), *n.* 480 or 500 sheets of paper of the same size and quality. [< OF < Sp. < Ar. *rizmah* bundle]

ream² (rēm), *v.* enlarge or shape (a hole). [OE *rȳman* enlarge < *rūm* room]

ream·er (rēm′ər), *n.* tool for reaming.

reap (rēp), *v.* **1** cut (grain). **2** gather (a crop). **3** *Fig.* get as a return or reward: *reap profits.* [OE *repan*] —**reap′a·ble,** *adj.* —**reap′er,** *n.*

re·ap·praise (rē′ə prāz′), *v.,* **–praised, –prais·ing.** give new consideration to the worth, desirability, etc. of. —**re′ap·prais′al,** *n.*

rear¹ (rir), *n.* **1** the back part; back. **2** space or position behind, or at the back of, anything. **3** the last part of an army, fleet, etc. —*adj.* at or in the back.

at or **in the rear of,** behind. [var. of *arrear*] —**rear′most,** *adj.*

rear² (rir), *v.* **1** make grow; help to grow; bring up: *rear children.* **2** set up; build: *rear a temple.* **3** raise; lift up: *rear one's*

head. **4** of an animal, rise on the hind legs; rise. [OE *rǣran* raise < *rīsan* rise] —**rear′er,** *n.*

rear admiral, a naval officer ranking next above a commodore and next below a vice-admiral.

re·arm (rē ärm′), *v.* **1** arm again; arm oneself again. **2** supply with new or better weapons. —**re·ar′ma·ment,** *n.*

re·ar·range (rē′ə rānj′), *v.,* **–ranged, –rang·ing. 1** arrange in a new or different way. **2** arrange again. —**re′ar·range′ment,** *n.*

rear·ward (rir′wərd), *adv., adj.* toward or in the rear.

rea·son (rē′zən), *n.* **1** cause; motive: *I have my own reasons for doing this.* **2** justification; explanation: *there is no reason for sloppy work.* **3** ability to think and draw conclusions: *she will use her reason to solve the problem.* **4** right thinking; good sense: *listen to reason.* —*v.* **1** think; think logically: *humans can reason.* **2** draw conclusions or inferences from facts or premises. **3** consider; discuss; argue.

by reason of, on account of; because of.

in or **within reason,** that is reasonable or sensible.

reason out, think through and draw a conclusion about.

stand to reason, be reasonable, sensible.

with (good) reason, justifiably; properly. [< OF < L *ratio.* Doublet of RATIO, RATION.] —**rea′son·er,** *n.*

rea·son·a·ble (rē′zən ə bəl; rēz′nə–), *adj.* **1** according to reason; sensible; not foolish. **2** not asking too much; fair; just. **3** not high in price; inexpensive. **4** able to reason. —**rea′son·a·ble·ness, rea′son·a·bil′i·ty,** *n.* —**rea′son·a·bly,** *adv.*

rea·son·ing (rē′zən ing; rēz′ning), *n.* **1** process of drawing conclusions from facts. **2** reasons; arguments.

re·as·sure (rē′ə shùr′), *v.,* **–sured, –sur·ing. 1** restore to confidence. **2** assure again or anew. —**re′as·sur′ance,** *n.* —**re′as·sur′ing·ly,** *adv.*

re·bate (rē′bāt; ri bāt′), *n., v.,* **–bat·ed, –bat·ing.** —*n.* return of part of money paid; partial refund; discount. —*v.* give as a rebate. [< OF *rabattre* beat down < *re*- back + *abattre* ABATE] —**re′bat·er,** *n.*

reb·el (*n., adj.* reb′əl; *v.* ri bel′), *n., adj., v.,* **–belled, re·bel·ling.** —*n.* person who resists or fights against authority instead of obeying. [< v.] —*adj.* defying law or authority: *the rebel army.* —*v.* **1** resist or fight against law or authority. **2** feel a great dislike or opposition. [< OF < L *rebellare,* ult. < *re*- again + *bellum* war. Doublet of REVEL.]

re·bel·lion (ri bel′yən), *n.* **1** active, armed resistance to one's government. **2** resistance to any power or restriction.

re·bel·lious (ri bel′yəs), *adj.* **1** defying authority; acting like a rebel. **2** hard to treat or deal with. **3** of or characteristic of rebels or rebellion. —**re·bel′lious·ly,** *adv.* —**re·bel′lious·ness,** *n.*

re·bound (*v.* ri bound′; *n.* rē′bound′, ri bound′), *v.* spring back. —*n.* a springing back.

re·buff (ri buf′), *n.* a blunt or sudden check to a person who makes advances, offers help, makes a request, etc. —*v.* give a rebuff to. [< F < Ital. *ribuffo*]

re·buke (ri būk′), *v.,* **–buked, –buk·ing,** *n.* —*v.* express disapproval of; reprove. —*n.* expression of disapproval; scolding. [< AF *rebuker.* Cf. OF *rebuchier* < *re*- back + *buchier* to strike] —**re·buk′er,** *n.* —**re·buk′ing·ly,** *adv.*

re·bus (rē′bəs), *n.* representation of a word or phrase by pictures suggesting the syllables or words. A picture of a cat on a log is a rebus for *catalog.* [< L, by means of objects]

re·but (ri but′), *v.,* **–but·ted, –but·ting.** oppose by evidence on the other side or by argument; try to disprove. [< AF, OF *reboter* < *re*- back + *boter* BUTT²] —**re·but′ter,** *n.*

re·but·tal (ri but′əl), *n.* a rebutting.

rec., 1 receipt. **2** recipe. **3** record.

re·cal·ci·trant (ri kal′sə trənt), *adj.* resisting authority or control; disobedient. —*n.* person who is recalcitrant. [< L *recalcitrans* kicking back, ult. < *re*- back + *calx* heel] —**re·cal′ci·trance, re·cal′ci·tran·cy,** *n.*

re·call (*v.* ri kôl; *n.* ri kôl′, rē′kôl′), *v.* **1** call back to mind; remember. **2** call back; order back: *the ambassador was recalled.* **3** take back; withdraw: *recall an edition of a book.* **4** remove (a public official) from office by vote of the people. —*n.* **1** a recalling to mind. **2** a calling back; ordering back. **3** a taking back; revocation; annulment. **4** removal of a public official from office by vote of the people. —**re·call′a·ble,** *adj.*

re·cant (ri kant′), *v.* **1** take back formally or publicly; withdraw or renounce (a statement, opinion, purpose, etc.): *after careful study the scholar recanted his first opinion.* **2** renounce an opinion or allegiance: *the prisoner would not recant.* [< L *recantare,* ult. < *re*- back + *canere* sing] —**re′can·ta′tion,** *n.* —**re·cant′er,** *n.*

re·ca·pit·u·late (rē′kə pich′ə lāt), *v.,* **–lat·ed, –lat·ing.** repeat or recite the main points of; tell briefly; sum up. —**re′ca·pit′u·la′tion,** *n.* —**re′ca·pit′u·la′tive, re·ca·pit′u·la·to′ry,** *adj.* —**re′ca·pit′u·la′tor,** *n.*

re·cap·ture (rē kap′chər), *v.,* **–tured, –tur·ing,** *n.* —*v.* capture again; have again. —*n.* a taking or being taken a second time.

re·cast (*v.* rē kast′, –käst′; *n.* rē′kast′, –käst′), *v.,* **–cast, –cast·ing,** *n.* —*v.* **1** cast again or anew. **2** make over; remodel. —*n.* a recasting.

recd., rec′d., received.

re·cede (ri sēd′), *v.,* **–ced·ed, –ced·ing 1** go or move backward: *he receded from view.* **2** slope backward: *a receding chin.* **3** withdraw: *recede from a plan.* [< L, < *re*- back + *cedere* go] —**re′ced′ence,** *n.*

re·ceipt (ri sēt′), *n.* **1** a written statement that money, a package, a letter, etc., has been received. **2** a receiving or being received: *on receipt of the news he went home.* **4** recipe. —*v.* write on (a bill, etc.) that something has been received or paid for.

receipts, money received; amount or quantity received. [< OF < L *recepta,* fem. pp. of *recipere* RECEIVE]

re·ceiv·a·ble (ri sēv′ə bəl), *adj.* **1** fit for acceptance. **2** on which payment is to be received. —*n.* **receivables,** assets, esp. payments, due from others.

re·ceive (ri sēv′), *v.,* **–ceived, –ceiv·ing. 1** take (something offered or sent): *receive gifts.* **2** be given; get: *receive a letter from home.* **3** experience; suffer; endure: *receive a blow.* **4** take; support; bear; hold: *the boat received a heavy load.* **5** take or let into the mind: *a theory widely received.* **6** let into one's house, society, etc.: *receive a person into the church.* **7** change electrical waves into sound signals in television, radio, cell phones, etc. [< OF < L, < *re–* back + *capere* take]

re·ceiv·er (ri sēv′ər), *n.* **1** person who receives. **2** part of a telephone held to the ear. **3** a receiving set for radio, television, etc. **4** person appointed to take charge of the property of others.

re·ceiv·er·ship (ri sēv′ər ship), *n. Law.* **1** position of a receiver in charge of the property of others. **2** condition of being in the control of a receiver.

re·cent (rē′sənt), *adj.* **1** done or made not long ago: *recent events.* **2** not long past; modern. *a recent period in history.* [< L *recens*] —**re′cent·ly,** *adv.* —**re′cent·ness, re′cen·cy,** *n.*

re·cep·ta·cle (ri sep′tə kəl), *n.* any container or place used to put things in to keep them conveniently. Bags, baskets, and vaults are all receptacles. [< L *receptaculum,* ult. < *recipere* RECEIVE]

re·cep·tion (ri sep′shən), *n.* **1** act or fact or receiving: *calm reception of bad news.* **2** manner of receiving: *a warm reception.* **3** a gathering to receive and welcome people. **4 a** quality of the sound or picture in a television, radio, etc. **b** act or process of receiving a wireless transmission on a cell phone, television, etc.

re·cep·tion·ist (ri sep′shən ist), *n.* person employed to receive callers, as in a doctor's office.

re·cep·tive (ri sep′tiv), *adj.* able, quick, or willing to receive ideas, suggestions, impressions, etc. —**re·cep′tive·ly,** *adv.* —**re′cep·tiv′i·ty, re·cep′tive·ness,** *n.*

re·cep·tor (ri sep′tər), *n.* cell or group of cells sensitive to stimuli; sense organ.

re·cess (*n.* rē′ses for 1, ri ses′, rē′ses for 2 and 3; *v.* ri ses′), *n.* **1** time during which work stops: *there will be a short recess before the next meeting.* **2** part in a wall set back from the rest; alcove; niche. **3** an inner place or part; quiet, secluded place. —*v.* **1** take a recess: *the convention recessed until this afternoon.* **2** place in a recess; set

back. **3** make a recess in: *recess a wall.* [< L *recessus* a retreat < *recedere* RECEDE]

re·ces·sion (ri sesh′ən), *n.* **1** a sloping backward. **2** an indented place in a wall, etc. **3** withdrawal. **4** period of temporary business reduction, shorter and less extreme than a depression. [< L *recessio* < *recedere* RECEDE]

re·ces·sion·al (ri sesh′ən əl), *adj.* sung or played while the clergy and the choir retire from the church at the end of a service. —*n.* a recessional hymn or piece of music.

re·ces·sive (ri ses′iv), *adj.* likely to go back; receding. —*n.* recessive character or gene. —**re·ces′sive·ly,** *adv.*

recessive character, the one of any pair of opposite characters that is latent and subordinate in an animal or plant, when both are present in the germ plasm.

re·cid·i·vism (ri sid′ə viz əm), *n.* a relapse or tendency to fall back into former ways, esp. into crime. [< L *recidere* fall back] —**re·cid′i·vist,** *adj., n.*

rec·i·pe (res′ə pē) *n.* **1** set of directions for preparing something to eat. **2** set of directions for preparing any thing or result. [< L, take! imperative of *recipere* take, RECEIVE]

re·cip·i·ent (ri sip′i ənt), *n.* person or thing that receives something. [< L *recipiens.* See RECEIVE.] —**re·cip′i·ence,** *n.*

re·cip·ro·cal (ri sip′rə kəl), *adj.* **1** in return: *although I gave him many presents, I had no reciprocal gifts from him.* **2** mutual: *reciprocal liking.* —*n.* **1** thing which is reciprocal to something else; counterpart. **2** number so related to another that when multiplied together they give 1. 3 is the reciprocal of ⅓, and ⅓ is the reciprocal of 3. [< L *reciprocus* returning] —**re·cip′ro·cal′i·ty,** *n.* —**re·cip′ro·cal·ly,** *adv.*

re·cip·ro·cate (ri sip′rə kāt), *v.,* **–cat·ed, –cat·ing. 1** give, do, feel, or show in return: *reciprocate favors.* **2** move or cause to move with an alternating backward and forward motion. [< L, < *reciprocus* returning] —**re·cip′ro·ca′tion,** *n.* —**re·cip′ro·ca′tive, re·cip′ro·ca·to′ry,** *adj.*

rec·i·proc·i·ty (res′ə pros′ə ti), *n.* **1** reciprocal state; mutual action. **2** a mutual exchange, esp. an exchange of special privileges in regard to trade between two countries.

re·cit·al (ri sīt′əl), *n.* **1** a musical entertainment, given usually by a single performer. **2** act of reciting; telling facts in detail. **3** story; account.

rec·i·ta·tion (res′ə tā′shən), *n.* **1** a reciting. **2** a reciting of a prepared lesson by pupils before a teacher. **3** a repeating of something from memory. **4** piece repeated from memory.

rec·i·ta·tive (res′ə tə tēv′), *n.* **1** a style of music halfway between speaking and singing. Operas often contain long passages of recitative. **2** passage, part, or piece in this style.

re·cite (ri sīt′), *v.,* **–cit·ed, –cit·ing. 1** say over; repeat: *recite a lesson or a poem.* **2** repeat something from memory; say part of a lesson. **3** give an account of in detail: *recite one's adventures.* [< L *recitare* < *re–* again + *citare* appeal to] —**re·cit′er,** *n.*

reck·less (rek′lis), *adj.* rash; heedless; careless. —**reck′less·ly,** *adv.* —**reck′less·ness,** *n.*

reck·on (rek′ən), *v.* **1** find the number or value of; count: *reckon the cost before you decide.* **2** consider; judge; account: *he is reckoned the best speller in the class.* **3** *Colloq.* think; suppose. **4** depend; rely: *you can reckon on our help.*

reckon with, take into consideration. [OE (*ge*)*recenian*] —**reck′on·er,** *n.*

reck·on·ing (rek′ən ing; rek′ning), *n.* **1** method of computing; count; calculation. **2** settlement of an account. **3** calculation of the position of a ship.

re·claim (ri klām′), *v.* **1** bring back to a useful, good condition. **2** demand the return of. —**re·claim′a·ble,** *adj.* —**re·claim′er,** *n.*

rec·la·ma·tion (rek′lə mā′shən), *n.* a reclaiming or being reclaimed; restoration to a useful, good condition.

re·cline (ri klīn′), *v.,* **–clined, –clin·ing.** lean back; lie or lay down. [< L, < *re–* back + *clinare* lean]

re·clin·er (ri klīn′ər), *n.* **1** a chair that can be adjusted to a reclining position. **2** person who reclines.

rec·luse (rek′lüs, ri klüs′), *n.* person who lives shut up or withdrawn from the world, as for religious or personal reasons. [< OF < L *reclusus* shut up < *re–* back + *claudere* shut] —**re·clu′sion,** *n.*

rec·og·ni·tion (rek′əg nish′ən), *n.* **1** a knowing again; recognizing or being recognized: *by a good disguise he escaped recognition.* **2** acknowledgment: *insist on complete recognition of rights.* **3** favorable notice; acceptance. **4** a formal acknowledgment conveying approval or sanction. [< L *recognitio*]

re·cog·ni·zance (ri kog′nə zəns; –kon′ə–), *n. Law.* **1** bond binding a person to do some particular act. **2** sum of money to be forfeited if the act is not performed. [< OF *recognoissance* < *reconoistre* RECOGNIZE. Doublet of RECONNAISSANCE.]

rec·og·nize (rek′əg nīz), *v.,* **–nized, –niz·ing. 1** know again: *I could scarcely recognize my old friend.* **2** identify: *recognize a person from a description.* **3** acknowledge; accept; admit: *recognize an official's authority.* **4** take notice of: *wait till the chairman recognizes you.* **5** show appreciation of. **6** acknowledge and agree to deal with: *recognize a new government that has come to power.* [< OF *reconoistre* < L, < *re–* again + *com–* (intensive) + (*g*)*noscere* learn. Doublet of RECONNOITER.] —**rec′og·niz′a·ble,** *adj.* —**rec′og·niz′a·bly,** *adv.* —**rec′og·niz′er,** *n.*

rec·og·nized (rek′əg nīzd), *adj.* acknowledged; accepted; admitted: *a recognized authority.*

re·coil (*v.* ri koil´; *n.* ri koil´, rē´koil), *v.* **1** draw back; shrink back: *recoil at seeing a snake.* **2** spring back: *the gun recoiled when I fired, revenge often recoils on the avenger.* —*n.* a recoiling. [< OF *reculer*] —**re·coil´er,** *n.*

rec·ol·lect (rek´ə lekt´), *v.* call back to mind; remember. —**rec´ol·lec´tion,** *n.* —**rec´ol·lec´tive,** *adj.*

re·col·lect (rē´kə lekt´), *v.* **1** collect again. **2** recover control of (oneself).

re·com·bi·nant DNA (ri kom´bi nənt), genetic material produced in the laboratory by combining bits of DNA from different cells or by transplantation of such fragments into cells from other life forms.

re·com·bi·na·tion (ri kom bi nā´shən), *n.* **1** a recombining; continuing anew. **2** the forming of new genetic combinations in an offspring not present in either parent.

rec·om·mend (rek´ə mend´), *v.* **1** speak in favor of; suggest favorably. **2** advise. **3** make pleasing or attractive: *the position of the camp recommends it as a summer home.* **4** hand over for safekeeping. —**rec´om·mend´a·ble,** *adj.* —**rec´om·mend´er,** *n.*

rec·om·men·da·tion (rek´ə men dā´shən), *n.* **1** a recommending. **2** anything that recommends a person or thing. **3** words of advice or praise. **4** thing recommended.

re·com·mit (rē´kə mit´), *v.,* **-mit·ted, -mit·ting. 1** commit again. **2** refer again to a committee. —**re´com·mit´ment, re´com·mit´tal,** *n.*

rec·om·pense (rek´əm pens), *v.,* **-pensed, -pens·ing.** —*v.* **1** pay (a person); pay back; reward. **2** make a fair return for (an action, anything lost, damage done, hurt received, etc.). —*n.* payment; reward; return; amends. [< LL *recompensare,* ult. < L *re-* back + *com-* with, against + *pendere* weigh out in payment]

rec·on·cile (rek´ən sīl), *v.,* **-ciled, -cil·ing. 1** make friends again. **2** settle (a quarrel, disagreement, etc.). **3** make agree; bring into harmony: *reconcile the facts with her story.* **4** make satisfied; make no longer opposed: *reconcile oneself to a long recovery.* [< L, ult. < *re-* back + *concilium* bond of union] —**rec´on·cil´a·ble,** *adj.* —**rec´on·cil´a·bil´i·ty, rec´on·cil´a·ble·ness,** *n.* —**rec´on·cil´a·bly,** *adv.* —**rec´on·cil´er,** *n.*

rec·on·cil·i·a·tion (rek´ən sil´i ā´shən), *n.* **1** a reconciling; bringing together again in friendship. **2** a being reconciled; settlement or adjustment of disagreements, differences, etc. —**rec´on·cile´ment,** *n.* —**rec´on·cil´i·a·to´ry,** *adj.*

rec·on·dite (rek´ən dīt; ri kon´dīt), *adj.* **1** hard to understand; profound. **2** little known; obscure: *recondite writings.* **3** concealed. [< L *reconditus* stored away, ult. < *re-* back + *com-* up + *dare* put] —**rec´on·dite·ly,** *adv.* —**rec´on·dite·ness,** *n.*

re·con·di·tion (rē´kən dish´ən), *v.* put in good condition by repairing, making over, etc.

re·con·nais·sance (ri kon´ə səns), *n.* examination or survey, esp. for military purposes. [< F. Doublet of RECOGNIZANCE.]

rec·on·noi·ter, rec·on·noi·tre (rek´-ə noi´tər; rē´kə-), *v.,* **-tered, -ter·ing; -tred, -tring.** approach and examine or observe in order to learn something; make a survey of (the enemy, the enemy's strength or position, a region, etc.). [< F. Doublet of RECOGNIZE.] —**rec´on·noi´ter·er, rec´on·noi´trer,** *n.*

re·con·sid·er (rē´kən sid´ər), *v.* consider again. —**re´con·sid´er·a´tion,** *n.*

re·con·sti·tut·ed (rē kon´stə tü´tid; -tyü´-), *adj.* **1** brought back to an original form or consistency: *reconstituted foods; reconstituted drugs.* **2** made from used or recycled materials: *reconstituted wood.*

re·con·struct (rē´kən strukt´), *v.* **1** rebuild; make over. **2** bring back or rebuild in an original form. —**re´con·struc´tive,** *adj.*

re·con·struc·tion (rē´kən struk´shən), *n.* **1** a reconstructing. **2** thing reconstructed. **3 Reconstruction, a** process by which the Southern states after the Civil War were reorganized and their relations with the national government were reestablished. **b** period when this was done, 1865–77.

re·cord (*v.* ri kôrd; *n., adj.* rek´ərd), *v.* **1** set down in writing so as to keep for future use: *record what the speaker says.* **2** put in some permanent form; keep for remembrance: *we record history in books.* **3 a** put music, words, or sounds on a phonograph disk. **b** put images and sound on a magnetic tape or digital disk. —*n.* **1** thing written or kept. **2** an official written account: *a secretary keeps a record of what is done at a meeting.* **3** an official copy of a document. **4** disk used on a phonograph. **5** the known facts about what a person, animal, ship, etc., has done: *a fine record at school.* **6** the best yet done; best amount, rate, speed, etc., yet attained: *hold the record for the high jump.* **7** a recording or being recorded: *what happened is a matter of record.* —*adj.* making or affording a record: *a record wheat crop.*

break a or **the record,** surpass an established record.

go on record, state publicly.

off the record, not to be quoted or recorded: *an interview off the record.*

on record, recorded; known: *on record in support of strong environmental policies.* [< OF < L *recordari* remember, ult. < *re-* back + *cor* heart, mind]

re·cord·er (ri kôr´dər), *n.* **1** person whose business is to make and keep records. **2** part of a machine that records. **3** flutelike wind instrument. —**re·cord´er·ship,** *n.*

re·cord·ing (ri kôr´ding), *n.* **1** a tape, digital disk, or phonograph record. **2**

the original transcription of any sound or combination of sounds.

re·count[1] (ri kount´), *v.* tell in detail; give an account of: *recount the happenings of the day.* [< OF, < *re-* again + *conter* relate, COUNT[1]]

re·count[2], **re-count** (*n.* rē´kount´, rē kount´; *v.* rē kount´), *n.* a second count. —*v.* count again.

re·coup (ri küp´), *v.* **1** make up for: *he recouped his losses.* **2** repay. [< F, < *re-* back + *couper* cut] —**re·coup´ment,** *n.*

re·course (rē´kôrs; -kōrs; ri kôrs´; -kōrs´), *n.* **1** an appealing; turning for help or protection. **2** person or thing appealed to or turned to for help or protection.

have recourse to, appeal to; turn to for help. [< OF < L *recursus* retreat, ult. < *re-* back + *currere* run]

re·cov·er (ri kuv´ər), *v.* **1** get back (something lost, taken away, or stolen). **2** make up for (something lost or damaged): *recover lost time.* **3** bring back or get back to life, health, one's senses, or normal condition. **4** get back to the proper position or condition: *he started to fall but recovered himself.* **5** obtain by judgment in a law court. **6** regain in usable form; reclaim. Many useful substances are now recovered from materials that used to be thrown away. [< OF < L *recuperare.* Doublet of RECUPERATE.] —**re·cov´er·a·ble,** *adj.* —**re·cov´er·er,** *n.*

re·cov·er (rē kuv´ər), *v.* put a new cover on.

re·cov·er·y (ri kuv´ər i; -kuv´ri), *n., pl.* **-er·ies. 1** a recovering. **2** a coming back to health or normal condition. **3** a getting back something that was lost, taken away, or stolen. **4** a getting back to a proper position or condition.

recovery room, room in a hospital where patients are monitored as they recover from surgery.

rec·re·ant (rek´ri ənt), *adj.* **1** cowardly. **2** disloyal; traitorous. —*n.* **1** coward. **2** traitor. [< OF, confessing oneself beaten, ult. < L *re-* back + *credere* believe] —**rec´re·ance, rec´re·an·cy,** *n.* —**rec´re·ant·ly,** *adv.*

rec·re·ate (rek´ri āt), *v.,* **-at·ed, -at·ing. 1** refresh with games, pastimes, exercises, etc. **2** take recreation. [< L *recreatus* restored < *re-* again + *creare* create] —**rec´re·a´tive,** *adj.*

re·cre·ate (rē´kri āt´), *v.,* **-at·ed, -at·ing.** create anew. —**re´-cre·a´tion,** *n.*

rec·re·a·tion (rek´ri ā´shən), *n.* play; amusement. Walking, gardening, and reading are quiet forms of recreation. —**rec´re·a´tion·al,** *adj.*

recreational vehicle, vehicle used for recreation, esp. a bus or truck fitted with beds, kitchen, etc.

re·crim·i·nate (ri krim´ə nāt), *v.,* **-nat·ed, -nat·ing.** accuse (someone) in return. [< Med.L, ult. < L *re-* back + *crimen* charge] —**re·crim´i·na´tion,** *n.* —**re·crim´i·na·tive, re·crim´i·na·to´ry,** *adj.*

re·cruit (ri krüt′), *n.* **1** a newly enlisted soldier or sailor. **2** a new member of any group or class. —*v.* **1** get (men or women) to join an army or navy. **2** strengthen or supply (an army, navy, etc.) with new men and women. **3** get (new members). **4** replenish. [< F *recruter* < OF *recrue* new growth, ult. < L *re-* back + *crescere* grow] —**re·cruit′er,** *n.* —**re·cruit′ment,** *n.*

rec·tal (rek′təl), *adj.* of the rectum.

rec·tan·gle (rek′tang gəl), *n.* a four-sided figure with four right angles. [< LL, < L *rectus* right + *angulus* angle]

rec·tan·gu·lar (rek tang′gyə lər), *adj.* shaped like a rectangle. —**rec·tan′gu·lar′i·ty,** *n.* —**rec·tan′gu·lar·ly,** *adv.*

rec·ti·fy (rek′tə fī), *v.,* **-fied, -fy·ing. 1** make right; put right; adjust; remedy: *admit a mistake and be willing to rectify it.* **2** change (an alternating current) into a direct current. **3** purify; refine. [< LL, < L *rectus* right + *facere* make] —**rec′ti·fi′a·ble,** *adj.* —**rec′ti·fi·ca′tion,** *n.* —**rec′ti·fi′er,** *n.*

rec·ti·lin·e·ar (rek′tə lin′i ər), *adj.* **1** forming a straight line. **2** bounded or formed by straight lines. [< L *rectus* straight + E *linear*] —**rec′ti·lin′e·ar·ly,** *adv.*

rec·ti·tude (rek′tə tüd; -tūd), *n.* upright conduct or character; honesty; righteousness. [< LL, < L *rectus* straight]

rec·tor (rek′tər), *n.* **1** clergyman in the Protestant Episcopal Church or the Church of England who has charge of a parish. **2** priest in the Roman Catholic Church who has charge of a congregation or religious house. [< L, ruler, < *regere* to rule] —**rec·to′ri·al,** *adj.* —**rec′tor·ship,** *n.*

rec·to·ry (rek′tə ri; rek′tri), *n., pl.* **-ries.** a rector's house.

rec·tum (rek′təm), *n.* the lowest part of the large intestine. [< NL, for L *intestinum rectum* straight intestine]

re·cum·bent (ri kum′bənt), *adj.* lying down; reclining; leaning. [< L *recumbens* reclining] —**re·cum′ben·cy,** *n.* —**re·cum′bent·ly,** *adv.*

re·cu·per·ate (ri kü′pər āt; -kü′-), *v.,* **-at·ed, -at·ing. 1** recover from sickness, exhaustion, loss, etc. **2** regain. [< L *recuperatus* recovered. Doublet of RECOVER.] —**re·cu′per·a′tion,** *n.* —**re·cu′per·a′tive,** *adj.* —**re·cu′per·a′tive·ness,** *n.* —**re·cu′per·a′tor,** *n.*

re·cur (ri kėr′), *v.,* **-curred, -cur·ring. 1** come up again; occur again; be repeated: *leap year recurs every four years.* **2** return in thought or speech. [< L, < *re-* back + *currere* run]

re·cur·rent (ri kėr′ənt), *adj.* **1** recurring; occurring again; repeated. **2** turned back so as to run in the opposite direction. —**re·cur′rence,** *n.* —**re·cur′rent·ly,** *adv.*

re·curve (ri kėrv′), *v.,* **-curved, -curving.** curve back; bend back.

re·cy·cla·ble (ri sī′klə bəl), *n.* something that can be recycled. —*adj.* that can be recycled.

re·cy·cle (rē sī′kəl), *v.,* **-cled, -cling. 1** treat or process used materials so that they can be used again. **2** go through a cycle or process again: *recycle the wash.* **3** reuse, esp. an idea or fashion.

red (red), *n., adj.,* **red·der, red·dest.** —*n.* **1** the color of blood. **2** any shade of that color. **3** a red pigment or dye. **4** red cloth or clothing. **5** a red or reddish person, animal, or thing. **6 Red,** radical; revolutionary. Communists, extreme socialists, and anarchists were called Reds. —*adj.* **1** having the color of blood, being like it, or suggesting it. **2** sore; inflamed. **3** blushing. **4 Red,** of or having to do with the former Soviet Union.

in the red, in debt; losing money.

see red, become very angry. [OE *rēad*] —**red′dish,** *adj.* —**red′ness,** *n.*

re·dact (ri dakt′), *v.* put into literary form; prepare for publication; edit. [< L *redactus* reduced < *re-* back + *agere* bring] —**re·dac′tion,** *n.* —**re·dac′tor,** *n.*

red algae, large group of red or purple marine algae, including many seaweeds. Certain red algae secrete calcium and are involved in building coral reefs.

red·breast (red′brest′), *n.* robin.

red·bud (red′bud′), *n.* tree that has many small, pink, budlike flowers early in the spring.

red corpuscle, small red blood cell, formed in bone marrow, which carries oxygen from the lungs to body tissues. Also, **red blood cell, erythrocyte.**

Red Cross, an international organization to care for the sick and wounded in war and to relieve suffering caused by floods, fire, diseases, and other calamities.

red deer, 1 deer native to the forests of Europe and Asia, and formerly very abundant in England. **2** the common American deer in its summer coat.

red·den (red′ən), *v.* **1** make or become red. **2** blush.

re·deem (ri dēm′), *v.* **1** buy back: *property on which money has been lent is redeemed when the loan is paid back.* **2** pay off: *we redeemed the mortgage.* **3** carry out; make good; fulfill: *we redeem a promise by doing what we said we would.* **4** set free; rescue; save: *redeemed from sin.* **5** make up for; balance: *a redeeming feature.* [< *redimere* < *re-* back + *emere* buy] —**re·deem′a·ble,** *adj.*

re·deem·er (ri dēm′ər), *n.* **1** person who redeems: *a redeemer of lost souls.* **2 Redeemer,** Jesus.

re·demp·tion (ri demp′shən), *n.* **1** a redeeming. **2** a being redeemed. **3** deliverance; rescue. **4** deliverance from sin; salvation. [< L *redemptio* < *redimere* REDEEM. Doublet of RANSOM.] —**re·demp′tive, re·demp′to·ry,** *adj.*

re·de·ploy (rē′di ploi′), *v.* **1** change the position of troops from one theater of war to another. **2 a** move someone or something from one place to another. **b** shift someone or something to another task. —**re′de·ploy′ment.** *n.*

red flag, 1 symbol of rebellion, revolution, etc. **2** sign of danger. **3** *Fig.* thing that stirs up anger.

red-hand·ed (red′han′did), *adj.* **1** having hands red with blood. **2** in the very act of crime. —**red′-hand′ed·ly,** *adv.* —**red′-hand′ed·ness,** *n.*

red·head (red′hed′), *n.* **1** person having red hair. **2** kind of duck resembling the canvasback, that has a red head. —**red′head′ed,** *adj.*

red herring, 1 the common smoked herring. **2** something used to draw attention away from the real issue.

red-hot (red′hot′), *adj.* **1** red with heat; very hot. **2** *Fig.* very enthusiastic; excited; violent. **3** *Fig.* fresh from the source.

re·di·rect (rē′də rekt′; -dī-), *v.* direct again or anew. —*adj.* noting or pertaining to a second examination of a witness by the party calling him or her after cross-examination. —**re′di·rec′tion,** *n.*

re·dis·trict (rē dis′trikt), *v.* divide into districts again, esp. voting districts.

red lead, red oxide of lead, Pb_3O_4, used in paint, in making glass, etc.

red-let·ter (red′let′ər), *adj.* **1** memorable; especially happy. **2** marked by red letters.

re·do (rē′dü′), *n.* **1** something done again: *the teacher allowed a redo of the test.* **2** =rehash.

red·o·lent (red′ə lənt), *adj.* **1** having a pleasant smell; fragrant. **2** smelling strongly; giving off an odor: *a house redolent of fresh paint.* **3** suggesting thoughts or feelings: *"Ivanhoe" is a name redolent of romance.* [< L *redolens* emitting scent < *re-* back + *olere* to smell] —**red′o·lence, red′o·lent·ly,** *adv.*

re·dou·ble (rē dub′əl), *v.,* **-bled, -bling,** *n.* —*v.* **1** double again. **2** increase greatly; double. **3** repeat; echo. **4** double back. **5** in games, double an opponent's double. —*n.* act of redoubling; a double of a double. [< F *redoubler*] —**re·dou′ble·ment,** *n.*

re·doubt (ri dout′), *n.* a small fort standing alone. [< F *redoute* < Ital. < Med.L *reductus* retreat < *reducere*. See REDUCE.]

re·doubt·a·ble (ri dout′ə bəl), *adj.* that should be feared or dreaded. [< OF, < *redouter* dread < *re-* again + *douter* DOUBT] —**re·doubt′a·ble·ness,** *n.* —**re·doubt′a·bly,** *adv.*

re·dound (ri dound′), *v.* come back as a result; contribute. [< OF < L *redundare* overflow, ult. < *re-* back + *unda* wave]

red pepper, 1 plant that has a podlike fruit that turns red when ripe. The sweet pepper and cayenne are kinds of red pepper. **2** =cayenne pepper.

re·dress (*v.* ri dres′; *n.* rē′dres; ri dres′), *v.* set right; repair; remedy: *redress the wrongs of the poor.* —*n.* a setting right; reparation; relief. [< F, < *re-* again + *dresser* (see DRESS)] —**re·dress′a·ble,** *adj.*

red·start (red′stärt′), *n.* a fly-catching warbler of America. [< *red* + *start* tail]

red tape, too much attention to details and forms. **—red'-tape',** *adj.*

red tide, red or brown discoloration of coastal waters caused by an accumulation of huge numbers of red or brown algae.

red·top (red'top'), *n.* kind of grass grown for forage and pasture.

re·duce (ri düs'; –dūs'), *v.,* **–duced, –duc·ing. 1** make or become less; make smaller; decrease: *reduce expenses, reduce weight.* **2** make lower in degree, intensity, etc.: weaken; dilute. **3** bring down; lower: *misfortune reduced that poor woman to begging.* **4** bring to a certain state, form, or condition; change: *reduce a noisy class to order, reduce a statement to writing.* **5** conquer; subdue. **6 a** combine with hydrogen. **b** remove oxygen from. **c** change (a compound) so that the valence of the positive element is lower. [< L, < *re-* back + *ducere* bring] **—re·duc'er,** *n.* **—re·duc'i·ble,** *adj.* **—re·duc'i·bil'i·ty,** *n.* **—re·duc'i·bly,** *adv.*

reducing agent, any chemical substance that reduces or removes the oxygen in a compound.

re·duc·tion (ri duk'shən), *n.* **1** a reducing or being reduced. **2** amount by which a thing is reduced. **3** form of something produced by reducing; copy of something on a smaller scale. **—re·duc'tion·al,** *adj.* **—re·duc'tive,** *adj.*

reduction division, =meiosis.

re·dun·dan·cy (ri dun'dən si), **re·dun·dance** (–dəns), *n., pl.* **–cies; danc·es. 1** more than is needed. **2** a redundant thing, part, or amount. **3** the use of too many words for the same idea.

re·dun·dant (ri dun'dənt), *adj.* **1** extra; not needed. **2** using too many words for the same idea; wordy. [< L, ppr. of *redundare* REDOUND] **—re·dun'dant·ly,** *adv.*

re·du·pli·cate (*v.* ri dü'plə kāt, –dü–; *adj.* ri dü'plə kit, –kāt, –dü'–), *v.,* **–cat·ed, –cat·ing,** *adj.* **—v.** double; repeat. **—adj.** doubled or repeated. **—re·du'pli·ca'tion,** *n.* **—re·du'pli·ca'tive,** *adj.*

red·wing (red'wing'), *n.* North American blackbird, of which the male has a red patch on each wing. Also, **red-winged blackbird.**

red·wood (red'wůd'), *n.* **1** a California evergreen tree that sometimes grows to a height of 300 feet. **2** its brownish-red wood.

re·ech·o (rē ek'ō), *v.,* **–ech·oed, –ech·o·ing,** *n., pl.* **–ech·oes.** **—v.** echo back. **—n.** echo of an echo.

reed (rēd), *n.* **1** a kind of tall grass with a hollow jointed stalk that grows in wet places. **2** such stalks. **3** thing made from the stalk of a reed or anything like it, as a musical instrument played by blowing through it or an arrow. **4 a** a thin piece of wood, plastic, or metal in a musical instrument that produces sound when a current of air moves it. **b** =reed instrument. **—adj.** producing tones by means of reeds: *a reed organ.* [OE *hrēod*]

reed instrument, musical instrument, such as a clarinet, that produces musical tones by means of a vibrating reed, or an oboe, which has two reeds.

reed·y (rēd'i), *adj.,* **reed·i·er, reed·i·est. 1** full of reeds. **2** made of a reed or reeds. **3** like a reed or reeds. **4** sounding like a reed instrument: *a thin, reedy voice.* **—reed'i·ness,** *n.*

reef¹ (rēf), *n.* a narrow ridge of rocks or sand at or near the surface of the water. [ult. < Scand. *rif*]

reef² (rēf), *n.* part of a sail that can be rolled or folded up to reduce its size. **—v.** reduce the size of (a sail) by rolling or folding up a part of it. [< Scand. *rif* rib, reef. Cf. REEF¹.]

reef·er¹ (rēf'ər), *n.* **1** one who reefs. **2** a short coat of thick cloth, originally worn esp. by sailors and fishermen. [< *reef²*]

reef·er² (rēf'ər), *n. Slang.* cigarette containing marijuana. [< *reef²,* in sense of "roll up"]

reef knot, =square knot.

reek (rēk), *n.* a strong, unpleasant smell; vapor. **—v. 1** send out vapor or a strong, unpleasant smell. **2** be wet with sweat or blood. [OE *rēc*] **—reek'er,** *n.* **—reek'y,** *adj.*

reel¹ (rēl), *n.* **1** frame turning on an axis, for winding thread, yarn, a fish line, rope, wire, etc. **2** spool; roller. **3** spool for film. **—v. 1** wind on a reel. **2** draw with a reel or by winding: *reel in a fish.*

reel off, say, write, or make in a quick, easy way. [OE *hrēol*]

reel² (rēl), *v.* **1** sway, swing, or rock under a blow, shock, etc. **2** sway in standing or walking. **3** be in a whirl; be dizzy. **—n.** a reeling or staggering movement. [special use of *reel¹*]

reel³ (rēl), *n.* **1** a lively dance. **2** music for it. [special use of *reel²*]

re·en·act·ment or **re·en·act·ment** (rē'en akt'mənt), *n.* **1** enact again, as a law. **2** re-creation of a historical event. **—re'en·act', re'-en·act',** *v.* **—re'en·ac'tor, re'-en·ac'tor,** *n.*

re·en·force (rē'en fôrs'; –fōrs'), *v.,* **–forced, –forc·ing.** -reinforce. **—re'en·force'ment,** *n.*

re·en·try (rē'en'tri), *n.* an entering again or return, esp. of a spacecraft into the earth's atmosphere.

reeve (rēv), *v.,* **reeved** or **rove, reev·ing.** pass (a rope) through a hole, ring, etc.

ref (ref), *n. Informal.* a referee.

ref., **1** referee. **2** reference. **3** referred.

re·fec·to·ry (ri fek'tə ri), *n., pl.* **–ries.** a room for meals, esp. in a monastery or convent. [< LL *refectorium,* ult. < L *reficere* refresh < *re-* again + *facere* make]

re·fer (ri fėr'), *v.,* **–ferred, –fer·ring. 1** direct attention: *the minister often refers to the Bible.* **2** relate; apply: *the rule refers only to special cases.* **3** send or direct for information, help, or action: *we referred him to the boss.* **4** turn for information or help: *writers often refer to a dictionary.* **5** hand over; submit: *let's refer the dispute*

to the umpire. **6** consider as belonging or due; assign: *many people refer their failures to bad luck.* [< L, < *re-* back + *ferre* take] **—ref'er·a·ble, re·fer'ra·ble,** *adj.* **—re·fer'rer,** *n.*

ref·er·ee (ref'ər ē'), *n., v.,* **–eed, –ee·ing.** **—n. 1** a judge of play in games and sports. **2** person to whom something is referred for decision or settlement. **—v.** act as referee; act as referee in.

ref·er·ence (ref'ər əns), *n.* **1** direction of the attention: *this history contains many references to larger histories.* **2** statement, book, etc., to which the attention is directed: *you will find that reference on page 16.* **3** use for information or help: *a dictionary is a book of reference.* **4** person who can give information about another person's character or ability. **5** statement about someone's character or ability. **6** relation; respect; regard: *a test without reference to age.* **—adj.** used for information or help: *a reference library.*

in or **with reference to,** about; concerning.

make reference to, mention. **—ref'er·en'tial,** *adj.* **—ref'er·en'tial·ly,** *adv.*

ref·er·en·dum (ref'ər en'dəm), *n., pl.* **–dums, –da** (–də). **1** process of submitting a law already passed by the lawmaking body to a direct vote of the citizens for approval or rejection. **2** the submitting of any matter to a direct vote. [< L, that which must be referred. See REFER.]

ref·er·ent (ref'ər ənt), *n.* object or class of objects, act, situation, quality, idea, or fancy to which a word refers.

re·fer·ral (ri fėr'əl), *n.* **1** direction or assignment of someone or something to a place or person for a particular purpose: *a referral to a lawyer.* **2** person who is referred: *our patients are mainly referrals.*

re·fill (*v.* rē fil'; *n.* rē'fil'), *v.* fill again. **—n.** material to refill a thing. **—re·fill'a·ble,** *adj.*

re·fine (ri fīn'), *v.,* **–fined, –fin·ing. 1** free from impurities: *sugar, oil, and metals are refined before being used.* **2** make or become fine, polished, or cultivated: *reading good books helps to refine one's speech.* **3** make very fine, subtle, or exact. **—re·fin'er,** *n.*

re·fined (ri fīnd'), *adj.* **1** freed from impurities: *refined sugar.* **2** freed or free from grossness, coarseness, crudeness, vulgarity, or the like. **3** subtle: *refined distinctions.* **4** minutely precise: *refined measurements.* **—re·fin'ed·ly,** *adv.*

re·fine·ment (ri fīn'mənt), *n.* **1** fineness of feeling, taste, manners, or language. **2** act or result of refining. **3** improvement.

re·fin·er·y (ri fīn'ər i), *n., pl.* **–er·ies.** a building and machinery for purifying metal, sugar, petroleum, or other things.

re·fit (rē fit'), *v.,* **–fit·ted, –fit·ting,** *n.* **—v. 1** fit, prepare, or equip for use again. **2** get fresh supplies. **—n.** a refitting.

re·flect (ri flekt′), v. **1** turn back or throw back (light, heat, sound, etc.): *the sidewalks reflect heat on a hot day.* **2** give back an image; give back a likeness or image of: *a mirror reflects your face and body.* **3** reproduce or show like a mirror: *the newspaper reflected the owner's opinions.* **4** think; think carefully: *take time to reflect before doing important things.* **5** cast blame, reproach, or discredit: *bad behavior reflects on home training.* **6** serve to cast or bring: *a brave act reflects credit on the person who does it.* [< L, < *re-* back + *flectere* to bend] —**re·flect′er**, *n.* —**re·flect′i·ble**, *adj.*

re·flec·tion (ri flek′shən), *n.* **1** a reflecting or being reflected. **2** something reflected. **3** likeness; image. **4** thinking; careful thinking: *on reflection, the plan seemed too dangerous.* **5** idea or remark resulting from careful thinking; idea; remark. **6** remark, action, etc., that casts blame or discredit.

angle of reflection, angle which a ray of light, or the like, reflected from a surface, makes with a perpendicular to that surface at the point of reflection. —**re·flec′tion·al**, *adj.*

re·flec·tive (ri flek′tiv), *adj.* **1** reflecting: *a reflective surface.* **2** thoughtful: *a reflective look.* —**re·flec′tive·ly**, *adv.* —**re·flec′tive·ness, re′flec·tiv′i·ty,** *n.*

re·flec·tor (ri flek′tər), *n.* any thing, surface, or device that reflects light, heat, sound, etc.

re·flex (*adj., n.* rē′fleks; *v.* ri fleks′), *adj.* **1** not voluntary; coming as a direct response to a stimulation of some sensory nerve cells. Sneezing is a reflex act. **2** bent back; turned back. —*n.* **1** action in direct response to a stimulation of some nerve cells. Sneezing, vomiting, and shivering are reflexes. **2** something reflected; image; reflection: *a law should be a reflex of the will of the people.* —*v.* bend back; turn back. [< L *reflexus*, pp. of *reflectere*. See REFLECT.] —**re·flex′i·ble**, *adj.* —**re·flex′i·bil′i·ty,** *n.* —**re′flex·ly,** *adv.*

re·flex·ive (ri flek′siv), —*adj.* **1** of a verb, expressing an action in which the object of the action is the same as the subject. **2** of a pronoun, indicating that it is the same as a preceding person or thing. —*n.* a reflexive verb or pronoun. In "The boy hurt himself," *hurt* and *himself* are reflexives. —**re·flex′ive·ly,** *adv.* —**re·flex′ive·ness, re′flex·iv′i·ty,** *n.*

re·flux (rē′fluks), *n.* a flowing back; the ebb of a tide.

re·for·est (rē fôr′ist; –for′–), *v.* replant (woodland) with trees. —**re′for·est·a′tion,** *n.*

re·form (ri fôrm′), *v.* **1** improve by some alteration of form, arrangement, etc.: *reform the calendar.* **2** change from worse to better: *reform a bad boy by understanding treatment.* **3** cause (a person) to abandon wrong or evil ways of life or conduct, and to adopt right ones.

4 put an end to (abuses, disorders, etc.); correct (errors, etc.). —*n.* **1** improvement by alteration of arrangement, etc. **2** an instance of this: *political reform, social reforms.* **3** changing one's manner of life, conduct, etc., for the better. [< L, ult. < *re-* again + *forma* form] —**re·form′a·ble,** *adj.* —**re·form′a·tive,** *adj.* —**re·formed′,** *adj.* —**re·form′ist,** *n.*

re-form (rē fôrm′), *v.* **1** form again. **2** take a new shape.

ref·or·ma·tion (ref′ər mā′shən), *n.* **1** a reforming or being reformed; change for the better; improvement. **2 Reformation,** the religious, social, and political movement in Europe in the 16th century that led to the establishment of Protestant churches. —**ref′or·ma′tion·al,** *adj.*

re·form·a·to·ry (ri fôr′mə tô′ri; –tō′–), *adj., n., pl.* **-ries.** —*adj.* serving to reform; intended to reform. —*n.* Also, **reform school.** formerly, a residential, custodial institution for reforming young offenders against the laws; a prison for young criminals.

re·form·er (ri fôr′mər), *n.* person who reforms, or tries to reform, some state of affairs, custom, etc.; supporter of reforms.

re·fract (ri frakt′), *v.* bend (a ray) from a straight course: *water refracts light.* [< L *refractus* broken up < *re-* back + *frangere* to break] —**re·frac′tive,** *adj.* —**re·frac′tive·ly,** *adv.* —**re·frac′tive·ness, re′frac·tiv′i·ty,** *n.* —**re·frac′tor,** *n.*

re·frac·tion (ri frak′shən), *n.* the turning or bending of a ray of light when it passes obliquely from one medium into another of different density.

re·frac·to·ry (ri frak′tə ri), *adj.* **1** hard to manage; stubborn; obstinate: *mules are refractory.* **2** not yielding readily to treatment: *a refractory cough.* **3** hard to melt, reduce, or work. —**re·frac′to·ri·ly,** *adv.* —**re·frac′to·ri·ness,** *n.*

re·frain[1] (ri frān′), *v.* hold oneself back: *refrain from wrongdoing.* [< OF < L, < *re-* back + *frenum* bridle]

re·frain[2] (ri frān′), *n.* **1** phrase or verse repeated regularly in a song or poem. **2** music for it. [< OF, ult. < VL *refrangere* break off. See REFRACT.]

re·fran·gi·ble (ri fran′jə bəl), *adj.* capable of being refracted. [< *re-* + L *frangere* to break] —**re·fran′gi·bil′i·ty, re·fran′gi·ble·ness,** *n.*

re·fresh (ri fresh′), *v.* make or become fresh again; renew. [< OF, < *re-* again + *fresche* fresh] —**re·fresh′ing,** *adj.* —**re·fresh′ing·ly,** *adv.* —**re·fresh′ing·ness,** *n.*

re·fresh·er (ri fresh′ər), *adj.* serving to reinstate knowledge or abilities, or to bring a person new needed knowledge. —*n.* person or thing that refreshes.

re·fresh·ment (ri fresh′mənt), *n.* **1** a refreshing or being refreshed. **2** thing that refreshes.

refreshments, food or drink.

re·fried beans (rē′frīd′), dried beans that have been cooked, mashed, and then fried, and served hot by frying again.

re·frig·er·ant (ri frij′ər ənt), *adj.* **1** refrigerating; cooling. **2** reducing bodily heat or fever. —*n.* **1** something that cools. **2** a liquid convertible into a gas at low temperature, used in mechanical refrigeration.

re·frig·er·ate (ri frij′ər āt), *v.,* **-at·ed, -at·ing.** make or keep cold or cool. [< L *refrigeratus,* ult. < *re-* again + *frigus* cold] —**re·frig′er·a′tion,** *n.*

re·frig·er·a·tor (ri frij′ər ā′tər), *n.* appliance or room for keeping foods, etc., cool, usually by mechanical means.

ref·uge (ref′ūj), *n.* shelter or protection from danger, trouble, etc. [< OF < L, < *re-* back + *fugere* flee]

ref·u·gee (ref′yə jē′; ref′yə jē), *n.* person who flees for refuge or safety, esp. to a foreign country, as in time of persecution or war.

re·ful·gent (ri ful′jənt), *adj.* shining brightly; radiant; splendid. [< L, < *re-* back + *fulgere* shine] —**re·ful′gence,** *n.* —**re·ful′gent·ly,** *adv.*

re·fund[1] (*v.* ri fund′; *n.* rē′fund), *v.* pay back. —*n.* return of money paid. [< L, < *re-* back + *fundere* pour] —**re·fund′er,** *n.*

re·fund[2] (rē fund′), *v.* change (a debt, loan, etc.) into a new form. [< *re-* + *fund*]

re·fur·bish (rē fėr′bish), *v.* polish up again; do up anew; brighten; renovate.

re·fus·al (ri fūz′əl), *n.* **1** act of refusing. **2** right to refuse or take a thing before it is offered to others.

re·fuse[1] (ri fūz′), *v.,* **-fused, -fus·ing. 1** decline to accept; reject: *refuse an offer.* **2** deny (a request, demand, invitation); decline to give, do, or grant: *refuse admittance, refuse to discuss the question.* [< OF *refuser* < L *refusus,* pp. of *refundere.* See REFUND[1].] —**re·fus′a·ble,** *adj.* —**re·fus′er,** *n.*

ref·use[2] (ref′ūs), *n.* useless stuff; waste; rubbish. —*adj.* discarded. [< OF *refus,* pp. of *refuser* REFUSE[1]]

ref·u·ta·tion (ref′yə tā′shən), *n.* the disproving of a claim, opinion, or argument.

re·fute (ri fūt′), *v.,* **-fut·ed, -fut·ing.** prove (a claim, opinion, or argument) to be false or incorrect. [< L *refutare*] —**ref′u·ta·ble,** *adj.* —**ref′u·ta·bil′i·ty,** *n.* —**ref′u·ta·bly,** *adv.* —**re·fut′er,** *n.*

reg., **1** regiment. **2** register; registered. **3** regular; regularly. **4** regulation.

re·gain (ri gān′), *v.* **1** get again or anew; recover: *regain health.* **2** get back to; reach again: *regain the shore.* —**re·gain′a·ble,** *adj.* —**re·gain′er,** *n.* —**re·gain′ment,** *n.*

re·gal (rē′gəl), *adj.* **1** belonging to a king; royal. **2** kinglike; fit for a king. [< L *regalis* < *rex* king. Doublet of ROYAL, REAL[2].] —**re′gal·ly,** *adv.*

re·gale (ri gāl′), *v.,* **-galed, -gal·ing. 1** entertain agreeably; delight with something pleasing. **2** entertain with a choice repast; feast. [< F, ult. < MDu. *wale* wealth] —**re·gale′ment,** *n.*

re·ga·li·a (ri gā′li ə; –gāl′yə), *n.pl.* **1** the emblems of royalty. Crowns, scepters, etc., are regalia. **2** the emblems or decorations of any society, order, etc. [< L, royal things, neut. pl. of *regalis* REGAL]

re·gard (ri gärd′), *v.* **1** consider; think of: *he is regarded as the best doctor in town.* **2** think highly of; care for; respect: *she always regards her parents' wishes.* **3** heed: *none regarded her screams.* **4** look at; look closely at; watch: *he regarded me sternly.* —*n.* **1** consideration; thought; care: *have regard for the feelings of others.* **2** a look; steady look. **3** esteem; favor; good opinion. **4** point; particular matter.

as regards, with respect to; concerning.

in or **with regard to,** about; concerning; relating to.

regards, good wishes; an expression of esteem.

without regard to, not considering. [< F, < *re–* back + *garder* GUARD] —**re·gard′a·ble,** *adj.* —**re·gard′er,** *n.*

re·gard·ful (ri gärd′fəl), *adj.* **1** heedful; observant; mindful. **2** considerate; respectful. —**re·gard′ful·ly,** *adv.* —**re·gard′ful·ness,** *n.*

re·gard·ing (ri gär′ding), *prep.* with regard to; concerning; about: *a prophecy regarding the future.*

re·gard·less (ri gärd′lis), *adj.* having or showing no regard; careless. —*adv.* **1** without regard. **2** with complete disregard of expense or consequence. —**re·gard′less·ly,** *adv.* —**re·gard′less·ness,** *n.*

re·gat·ta (ri gat′ə), *n.* **1** a boat race. **2** a series of boat races. [< dial. Ital.]

re·gen·cy (rē′jən si), *n., pl.* –**cies.** **1** position, office, or function of a regent or group of regents. **2** government consisting of regents. **3** time during which there is a regency.

re·gen·er·ate (*v.* ri jen′ər āt; *adj.* ri jen′-ər it), *v.,* –**at·ed,** –**at·ing,** *adj.* —*v.* **1** grow again; form (new tissue, a new part, etc.) to replace what is lost. **2** reform. **3** improve the moral condition of; put new life and spirit in. **4** increase amplification by transferring power from the output circuit to the input circuit. —*adj.* made over in better form; formed anew morally or spiritually. [< L *regeneratus* made over, ult. < *re–* again + *genus* birth] —**re·gen′er·a·cy,** *n.* —**re·gen′er·a′tion,** *n.* —**re·gen′er·a′tive,** *adj.* —**re·gen′er·a′tive·ly,** *adv.* —**re·gen′er·a′tor,** *n.*

re·gent (rē′jənt), *n.* **1** person who rules when the regular ruler is absent or unfit. **2** member of a governing board. —*adj.* acting as a regent. [< L *regens* ruling] —**re′gent·ship,** *n.*

reg·gae (reg′ā; rä′gä), *n.* lively and rhythmical music from the West Indies, influenced by rhythm and blues. [< Jamaican E, of *uncert. orig.*]

reg·i·cide (rej′ə sīd), *n.* **1** person who kills a king. **2** crime of killing a king. [< L *rex* king + E –*cide* < L –*cida* killer (def. 1), –*cidium* killing]

re·gime (ri zhēm′; rā–), *n.* **1** system of government or rule; prevailing system. **2** system of living; regimen. [< F < L *regimen.* Doublet of REGIMEN.]

reg·i·men (rej′ə men; –mən), *n.* set of rules or habits of diet, exercise, or manner of living intended to improve health, reduce weight, etc. [< L, < *regere* to rule. Doublet of REGIME.]

reg·i·ment (*n.* rej′ə mənt; *v.* rej′ə ment), *n.* **1** unit of an army consisting of several companies of soldiers organized into one large group, usually commanded by a colonel. A regiment is larger than a battalion and smaller than a brigade. **2** a large number. —*v.* **1** form into a regiment or organized group. **2** treat in a strict or uniform manner: *a totalitarian state regiments its citizens.* [< LL *regimentum* rule < *regere* to rule]

reg·i·men·tal (rej′ə men′təl), *adj.* of or pertaining to a regiment. —**reg′i·men′tal·ly,** *adv.*

reg·i·men·ta·tion (rej′ə men tā′shən), *n.* **1** formation into organized or uniform groups. **2** a making uniform. **3** subjection to control.

re·gion (rē′jən), *n.* **1** any large part of the earth's surface: *the region of the equator.* **2** place; space; area: *an unhealthful region.* **3** part of the body: *the region of the heart.* **4** sphere; domain: *the region of art.* [< L *regio* direction < *regere* to direct]

re·gion·al (rē′jən əl), *adj.* of or in a particular region: *a regional storm.* —**re′gion·al·ly,** *adv.*

reg·is·ter (rej′is tər), *n.* **1** list; record: *a register of attendance is kept in our school.* **2** book in which a list or record is kept. **3** thing that records. A cash register shows the amount of money taken in. **4** range of a voice or an instrument. —*v.* **1** write in a list or record: *register the names of the new members.* **2** have one's name written in a list or record: *a person must register before he or she can vote.* **3** indicate; record: *the thermometer registers 90 degrees.* **4** show (surprise, joy, anger, etc.) by the expression on one's face or by actions. **5** have (a letter, parcel, etc.) recorded in a post office, paying extra postage for special care in delivery. [< Med.L *registrum* < L *regestum,* neut. pp., recorded < *re–* back + *gerere* carry] —**reg′is·tra·ble,** *adj.*

reg·is·tered (rej′is tərd), *adj.* **1** recorded: *registered trademark.* **2** certified as specially qualified: *a registered nurse.* **3** sent by registered mail to show delivery of a parcel or letter. **4** pedigreed: *a registered breed.*

reg·is·trar (rej′is trär; rej′is trär′), *n.* official who keeps a register; official recorder. [var. of *registrer* < *register*]

reg·is·tra·tion (rej′is trā′shən), *n.* **1** a registering. **2** an entry in a register. **3** number of people registered. —**reg′is·tra′tion·al,** *adj.*

reg·is·try (rej′is tri), *n., pl.* –**tries.** **1** a registering; registration. **2** place where

a register is kept; office of registration. **3** book in which a list or record is kept; register.

reg·nant (reg′nənt), *adj.* **1** ruling. **2** exercising sway or influence; predominant. **3** prevalent; widespread. [< L *regnans* ruling < *regnum* kingdom]

re·gress (*v.* ri gres′; *n.* rē′gres), *v.* go back; move in a backward direction. —*n.* a going back; movement backward. [< L *regressus* a return < *re–* back + *gradi* go] —**re·gres′sion,** *n.*

re·gret (ri gret′), *n., v.,* –**gret·ted,** –**gret·ting.** —*n.* **1** sorrowful longing for what is gone; sense of loss: *it is a matter of regret that I could not see my mother before leaving.* **2** the feeling of being sorry for some fault, act, etc., of one's own: *regret for injustice done.* **4** Usually, **regrets.** a polite reply declining an invitation. —*v.* feel regret about.

regrets, feelings of sorrow for what is lost, gone, done, or past recall. [< OF *regreter* < OE *grētan,* cry, greet] —**re·gret′ful,** *adj.* —**re·gret′ful·ly,** *adv.* —**re·gret′ful·ness,** *n.* —**re·gret′ta·ble,** *adj.* —**re·gret′ta·bly,** *adv.*

reg·u·lar (reg′yə lər), *adj.* **1** fixed by custom or rule; usual; normal: *six o'clock was his regular hour of rising.* **2** following some rule or principle; according to rule: *a period is the regular ending for a sentence.* **3** coming, acting, or done again and again at the same time: *Sunday is a regular holiday.* **4** steady; habitual: *a regular customer.* **5** even in size, spacing, or speed; well-balanced: *regular features, regular teeth.* **6** orderly; methodical: *lead a regular life.* **7** properly fitted or trained: *our regular crossing guard.* **8** *Informal.* thorough; complete: *a regular tease.* **9** permanently organized: *the regular army.* —*n.* **1** member of a regularly paid group of any kind: *the fire department is made up of regulars and volunteers.* **2** a party member who faithfully stands by the party. [< L, < *regula* RULE] —**reg′u·lar′i·ty,** *n.* —**reg′u·lar·ly,** *adv.*

reg·u·lar·ize (reg′yə lər īz′), *v.,* –**ized,** –**iz·ing.** make regular. —**reg′u·lar·i·za′tion,** *n.*

reg·u·late (reg′yə lāt), *v.,* –**lat·ed,** –**lat·ing.** **1** control by rule, principle, or system: *private schools regulate the behavior of students.* **2** keep at some standard: *regulate the temperature of the room.* **3** adjust so as to ensure correct working: *regulate a watch.* **4** put in good condition: *regulate digestion.* [< LL, < L *regula* RULE] —**reg′u·lat′a·ble, reg′u·la·ble,** *adj.* —**reg′u·la′tive,** *adj.*

reg·u·la·tion (reg′yə lā′shən), *n.* **1** control by rule, principle, or system: *without regulation there can be no cooperation between men.* **2** rule; law: *traffic regulations.* —*adj.* **1** according to or required by a regulation; standard: *a regulation uniform.* **2** usual; ordinary.

reg·u·la·tor (reg′yə lā′tər), *n.* **1** person or thing that regulates. **2** device in a clock or watch to make it go faster or slower. —**reg′u·la·to′ry,** *adj.*

re·gur·gi·tate (rē gėr′jə tāt), *v.,* –**tat·ed,** –**tat·ing. 1** rush, surge, or flow back, as liquids, gases, undigested food, etc. **2** throw up, as food from the stomach. [< Med.L *regurgitatus,* ult. < L *re–* back + *gurges* whirlpool] —**re·gur′gi·ta′tion,** *n.*

re·hab (rē′hab), *n.* **1** treatment, physical therapy, etc., to restore a person's ability to walk, care for himself or herself, etc. **2** place where such treatment is provided.

re·ha·bil·i·tate (rē′hə bil′ə tāt), *v.,* –**tat·ed,** –**tat·ing. 1** restore to a good condition; make over in a new form: *rehabilitate an old house.* **2** restore to former standing, rank, rights, privileges, reputation, etc. **3** restore to good health or to an improved ability to walk, care for oneself, etc., with medical treatment, physical therapy, etc. [< Med.L., ult. < L *re–* again + *habilis* fit (see ABLE)] —**re·ha·bil′i·ta′tion,** *n.*

re·hash (*v.* rē hash′; *n.* rē′hash), *v.* deal with again; work up (old material) in a new form. —*n.* **1** a rehashing. **2** something old put in a different form.

re·hearse (ri hėrs′), *v.,* –**hearsed,** –**hears·ing. 1** practice (a play, part, etc.) for a public performance. **2** drill or train (a person, etc.) by repetition. **3** tell in detail; repeat. [< OF, < *re–* again + *hercier* to harrow, ult. < L *hirpex* rake] —**re·hears′al,** *n.* —**re·hears′er,** *n.*

reign (rān), *n.* **1** period of power of a ruler: *Queen Victoria's reign lasted sixty-four years.* **2** royal power. **3** existence everywhere; prevalence. —*v.* **1** be a ruler: *a king reigns over his kingdom.* **2** exist everywhere; prevail: *on a still night silence reigns.* [< OF < L *regnum* < *regere* to rule]

re·im·burse (rē′im bėrs′), *v.,* –**bursed,** –**burs·ing.** pay back: *you reimburse a person for expenses made for you.* [< *re–* + obs. *imburse* < Med.L., < L *in–* into + LL *bursa* purse; patterned on F *rembourser*] —**re·im·burse′ment,** *n.* —**re·im·burs′er,** *n.*

re·im·port (*v.* rē′im pôrt′, –pôrt′; *n.* rē im′-pôrt, –pōrt), *v.* import (something previously exported. —*n.* reimportation.

re·im·por·ta·tion (rē′im pôr tā′shən; –pōr–) *n.* **1** an importing of something previously exported. **2** goods reimported.

rein (rān), *n.* **1** a long, narrow strap or line fastened to a bridle or bit, by which to guide and control an animal. **2** a means of control and direction. —*v.* **1** check or pull with reins. **2** guide and control.

give rein to, let move or act freely, without guidance or control.

keep a tight rein on, provide close control or constant guidance to.

rein in, a slow or stop by using the reins. **b** *Fig.* slow down or cause a pause in (an activity).

seize or **take the reins,** assume control. [< OF *rene,* ult. < L *retinere* hold back, RETAIN]

re·in·car·nate (rē′in kär′nāt), *v.,* –**nat·ed,** –**nat·ing.** give a new body to (a soul). —**re′in·car·na′tion,** *n.*

rein·deer (rān′dir′), *n., pl.* –**deer.** kind of large deer with branching horns, living in northern regions, used to pull sleighs and also for meat. [< Scand. *hreindýri* < *hreinn* reindeer + *dýr* animal]

re·in·force (rē′in fôrs′; –fōrs′), *v.,* –**forced,** –**forc·ing. 1** strengthen with new force or materials: *reinforce an army, a bridge, etc.* **2** strengthen: *reinforce an argument, etc.* —**re′in·forc′er,** *n.*

reinforced concrete, concrete with metal embedded in it to make the structure stronger.

re·in·force·ment (rē′in fôrs′mənt; –fōrs′–), *n.* **1** act of reinforcing. **2** a being reinforced. **3** something that reinforces.

reinforcements, extra soldiers or warships.

re·in·state (rē′in stāt′), *v.,* –**stat·ed,** –**stat·ing.** restore to a former position or condition; establish again. —**re′in·state′ment,** *n.*

re·in·vig·or·ate (rē′in vig′ə rāt), *v.,* –**at·ed,** –**at·ing.** give new vigor to; reenergize. –**re′in·vig′or·a′tion,** *n.*

re·it·er·ate (rē it′ər āt), *v.,* –**at·ed,** –**at·ing.** say or do several times; repeat (an action, demand, etc.) again and again. [< L, ult. < *re–* again + *iterum* again] —**re·it′er·a′tion,** *n.* —**re·it′er·a′tive,** *adj.* —**re·it′er·a′tive·ly,** *adv.*

re·ject (*v.* ri jekt′; *n.* rē′jekt), *v.* **1** refuse to take, use, believe, accept, acknowledge, hear, consider, grant, etc.: *he tried to join the army but was rejected.* **2** throw away as useless or unsatisfactory: *reject all apples with soft spots.* —*n.* a rejected person or thing. [< L *rejectus* < *re–* back + *jacere* to throw] —**re·ject′a·ble,** *adj.* —**re·ject′er,** *n.* —**re·ject′ing·ly,** *adv.* —**re·jec′tion,** *n.*

re·joice (ri jois′), *v.,* –**joiced,** –**joic·ing. 1** be glad; be filled with joy. **2** make glad; fill with joy. [< OF *rejoiss–,* ult. < L *re–* again + *gaudere* be glad] —**re·joic′er,** *n.* —**re·joic′ing,** *n.* —**re·joic′ing·ly,** *adv.*

re·join[1] (rē join′), *v.* **1** join or unite again. **2** join the company of again. [< *re–* + *join*]

re·join[2] (ri join′), *v.* answer; reply. [< F, < *re–* back + *joindre* join]

re·join·der (ri join′dər), *n.* an answer to a reply; response.

re·ju·ve·nate (ri jü′və nāt), *v.,* –**nat·ed,** –**nat·ing.** make young or vigorous again; give youthful qualities to. [< *re–* + L *juvenis* young] —**re·ju′ve·na′tion,** *n.* —**re·ju′ve·na′tor,** *n.*

re·lapse (ri laps′), *v.,* –**lapsed,** –**laps·ing,** *n.* —*v.* fall or slip back into a former state, way of acting, etc.: *relapse into silence.* —*n.* a relapsing. [< L *relapsus* < *re–* back + *labi* to slip] —**re·laps′er,** *n.*

re·late (ri lāt′), *v.,* –**lat·ed,** –**lat·ing. 1** give an account of; tell: *the traveler related his adventures.* **2** connect in thought or meaning: *"better" and "best" are related*

to *"good."* **3** be connected in any way: *we are interested in what relates to ourselves.* [< L *relatus,* pp. to *referre* < *re–* back + *ferre* bring] —**re·lat′er,** *n.* pertain.

re·lat·ed (ri lāt′id), *adj.* **1** connected. **2** belonging to the same family; connected by a common origin. —**re·lat′ed·ness,** *n.*

re·la·tion (ri lā′shən), *n.* **1** connection in thought or meaning: *your answer has no relation to the question.* **2** connection between persons, groups, countries, etc.: *the relation of mother and child.* **3** person who belongs to the same family as another, such as a father, brother, aunt, etc.; relative. **4** reference; regard: *we must plan with relation to the future.* **5** act of telling; account: *we were interested in his relation of his adventures.* —**re·la′tion·al,** *adj.*

re·la·tion·ship (ri lā′shən ship), *n.* **1** connection. **2** connection between two people who live together as a couple. **3** condition of belonging to the same family.

rel·a·tive (rel′ə tiv), *n.* **1** person who belongs to the same family as another, such as father, brother, aunt, etc. **2** a relative pronoun, adjective, or adverb. —*adj.* **1** related or compared to each other: *consider the relative merits of your proposal and mine.* **2** depending for meaning on a relation to something else. *East* is a relative term. **3** introducing a subordinate clause; referring to another person or thing. In "The man who wanted it is gone," *who* is a relative pronoun, and *who wanted it* is a relative clause.

relative to, a about; concerning. **b** in proportion to. —**rel′a·tive·ness,** *n.*

rel·a·tive·ly (rel′ə tiv li), *adv.* **1** in a relative manner; in relation to something else; comparatively: *a relatively small difference.* **2** in relation or with reference (*to*): *the value of one thing relatively to other things.* **3** in proportion (*to*): *a subject little understood relatively to its importance.*

rel·a·tiv·i·ty (rel′ə tiv′ə ti), *n.* **1** a being relative. **2** character of being relative rather than absolute, as ascribed to motion or velocity. **3** theory expressed in certain equations by the twentieth century physicist, Albert Einstein. According to it, the only velocity we can measure is velocity relative to some body; observers will obtain the same value for the velocity of light which, in a vacuum, is constant; and the mass of a moving body increases with its velocity.

re·lax (ri laks′), *v.* **1** loosen up; make or become less stiff or firm: *relax when you dance.* **2** make or become less strict or severe; lessen in force: *discipline is relaxed on the last day of school.* **3** reduce strain and worry; be lazy and carefree: *take a vacation and relax.* **4** weaken. [< L *relaxare,* ult. < *re–* back + *laxus* loose. Doublet of RELEASE.] —**re·lax′ed·ly,** *adv.* —**re·lax′er,** *n.*

re·lax·a·tion (rēlak sā′shən), *n.* **1** a loosening: *relaxation of the muscles.* **2** a lessening of strictness, severity, force, etc. **3** relief from work or effort; recreation; amusement.

re·lay (rē′lā; ri lā′), *n.* **1** a fresh supply, esp. or horses or men. **2** a relay race. **3** one part of a relay race. **4** an electromagnetic device in which a weak current controls a stronger current, used in transmitting telegraph or telephone messages over long distances. —*v.* **1** take and carry farther. **2** transmit by relay. [< OF *relais* reserve pack of hounds, etc., ult. < *re-* back + *laier* leave < Gmc.]

re·lay (rē lā′), *v.,* **–laid, –lay·ing.** lay again.

re·lay race (rē′lā), race in which each member of a team runs only his or her share of the way.

re·lease (ri lēs′), *v.,* **–leased, –leas·ing,** *n.* —*v.* **1** let go; let loose: *the prisoner was released.* **2** set free; relieve: *release from a promise.* **3** give up (legal right, claim, etc.); make over to another (property, etc.). **4** permit to be published, shown, sold, etc. —*n.* **1** a letting go; setting free: *the release of the slaves.* **2** freedom; relief: *release from pain.* **3** part that releases other parts of a machine. **4** permission for publication, exhibition, sale, etc. **5** article, statement, etc., distributed for publication. [< OF *relaissier* < L *relaxare.* Doublet of RELAX.] —**re·leas′a·ble,** *adj.* —**re·lease′ment,** *n.* —**re·leas′er,** *n.*

re·lease (rē lēs′), *v.,* **–leased, –leas·ing.** lease again.

rel·e·gate (rel′ə gāt), *v.,* **–gat·ed, –gat·ing.** **1** send away, usually to a lower position or condition. **2** send into exile; banish. **3** hand over (a matter, task, etc.). [< L, < *re-* back + *legare* to despatch] —**rel′e·ga·ble,** *adj.* —**rel′e·ga′tion,** *n.*

re·lent (ri lent′), *v.* become less harsh or cruel; be more yielding and merciful. [ult. < L *re-* again + *lentus* slow] —**re·lent′ing·ly,** *adv.*

re·lent·less (ri lent′lis), *adj.* without pity; unyielding; harsh. —**re·lent′less·ly,** *adv.* —**re·lent′less·ness,** *n.*

rel·e·vant (rel′ə vənt), *adj.* bearing upon or connected with the matter in hand; to the point: *be sure your questions are relevant.* [< L *relevans* refreshing, ult. < *re-* back + *levis* light] —**rel′e·vance, rel′e·van·cy,** *n.* —**rel′e·vant·ly,** *adv.*

re·li·a·ble (ri lī′ə bəl), *adj.* worthy of trust; that can be depended on: *reliable sources of news.* —**re·li′a·bil′i·ty, re·li′a·ble·ness,** *n.* —**re·li′a·bly,** *adv.*

re·li·ance (ri lī′əns), *n.* **1** trust; dependence. **2** confidence. **3** thing on which one depends.

re·li·ant (ri lī′ənt), *adj.* **1** relying; depending. **2** confident. **3** relying on oneself.

rel·ic (rel′ik), *n.* **1** thing, custom, etc., that remains from the past. **2** something belonging to a holy person, kept as a sacred memorial. **3** keepsake; souvenir. **relics,** remains; ruins. [< OF < L *reliquiae,* pl., remains]

re·lief (ri lēf′), *n.* **1** the lessening of, or freeing from, a pain, burden, difficulty, etc. **2** something that lessens or frees from pain, burden, difficulty, etc.; help given to poor people, victims of disaster, etc.; aid; help. **3** something that makes a pleasing change or lessens strain. **4** release from a post of duty, as by the coming of a substitute. **5** change of persons on duty. **6** persons who relieve others from duty; person who does this. **7** projection of figures and designs from a surface in sculpture. drawing, painting, etc. **8** figure or design standing out from the surface from which it is cut, shaped, or stamped.

in relief, standing out from a surface.

on relief, receiving aid from public funds; on welfare. [< OF, < *relever* RELIEVE]

relief map, map that shows the different heights of a surface by using shading, colors, solid materials, etc.

relief pitcher, pitcher who comes into a baseball game to take the place of another pitcher.

re·lieve (ri lēv′), *v.,* **–lieved, –liev·ing.** **1** make less; make easier; reduce the pain or trouble of: *aspirin will relieve a headache.* **2** set free: *your coming relieves me of the bother of writing a long letter.* **3** bring aid to; help: *soldiers were sent to relieve the fort.* **4** give variety or a pleasing change to: *a black dress relieved by red trimming.* **5** free (a person on duty) by taking his or her place. **6** make stand out more clearly. [< OF < L *relevare* lighten. See RELEVANT.] —**re·liev′a·ble,** *adj.*

re·liev·er (ri lēv′ər), *n.* **1** someone or something that relieves. **2** =relief pitcher.

re·li·gion (ri lij′ən), *n.* **1** recognition of and belief in a superhuman power or powers to whom obedience, reverence, and worship are due. **2** any system of faith and worship of a Supreme Being or a god or gods: *the Christian religion, the religion of the Muslims.* **3** sense of obligation. [< L *religio* respect for what is sacred]

re·li·gi·os·i·ty (ri lij′i os′ə ti), *n.* **1** affectation of religious feeling. **2** piety; religious sentiment.

re·li·gious (ri lij′əs), *adj.* **1** of or connected with religion: *religious meetings.* **2** much interested in religion; devoted to the worship of God or gods: *an intensely religious person.* **3** strict: *religious care.* —*n.* monk, nun, friar, etc.; member of a religious order. —**re·li′gious·ly,** *adv.* —**re·li′gious·ness,** *n.*

re·lin·quish (ri ling′kwish), *v.* **1** give up; desist from: *relinquish all hope.* **2** give over (to); renounce or surrender (a possession, right, etc.). [< OF *relinquiss-,* ult. < L *re-* behind + *linquere* leave] —**re·lin′quish·er,** *n.* —**re·lin′quish·ment,** *n.*

rel·i·quar·y (rel′ə kwer′i), *n.,* pl. **–quar·ies.** a small box or other receptacle for a relic or relics. [< OF *reliquaire* < *relique* RELIC]

rel·ish (rel′ish), *n.* **1** a pleasant taste; good flavor: *hunger gives relish to simple food.* **2** something to add flavor to food. Olives and pickles are relishes. **3** liking; appetite; enjoyment. —*v.* **1** make pleasing to the taste. **2** like the taste or flavor of. **3** take pleasure in; enjoy. [earlier *reles* < OF, remainder, < *relesser* RELEASE] —**rel′ish·a·ble,** *adj.* —**rel′ish·er,** *n.* —**rel′ish·ing·ly,** *adv.*

re·luc·tance (ri luk′təns), **re·luc·tan·cy** (–tən si), *n.* **1** a reluctant feeling or action; unwillingness. **2** slowness in action because of unwillingness.

re·luc·tant (ri luk′tənt), *adj.* **1** unwilling; showing unwillingness. **2** slow to act because unwilling. [< L *reluctans* struggling against, ult. < *re-* back + *lucta* wrestling] —**re·luc′tant·ly,** *adv.*

re·ly (ri lī′), *v.,* **–lied, –ly·ing.** depend; trust: *rely on your own efforts.* [< OF < L *religare* bind fast < *re-* back + *ligare* bind]

rem (rem), *n.,* pl. **rem, rems.** measure of radiation absorbed, equaling one roentgen of X rays or gamma rays. [< roentgen + equivalent + *man*]

REM (rem), *n.* period during sleep when the eyes move frequently and rapidly. [< rapid + eye + movement]

re·main (ri mān′), *v.* **1** continue in a place; stay: *remain in the city.* **2** continue without change as to some form, state, or quality specified: *remain active in business.* **3** be left after a part, quantity, or number has been taken away or destroyed: *the years of life that remain.* **4** be left as not included; be still to be dealt with: *some objections remain.* —*n.* **remains, a** what is left. **b** a dead body. [< OF < L, < *re-* back + *manere* stay]

re·main·der (ri mān′dər), *n.* **1** the part left over; the rest: *if you take 2 from 9, the remainder is 7.* **2** copies of a book left over after the sale has practically ceased.

re·make (*v.* ri māk′; *n.* ri′māk), *v.,* **–made, –mak·ing.** make again; make over. —*n.* something remade, as a film.

re·mand (ri mand′; –mänd′) *v.* **1** send back. **2** send back (a prisoner or an accused person) to prison. —*n.* a remanding. [< LL, < L *re-* back + *mandare* consign] —**re·mand′ment,** *n.*

re·mark (ri märk′), *v.* **1** say, write, or comment casually. **2** notice; observe: *did you remark his expression?* —*n.* **1** something said in few words; short statement. **2** act of noticing; observation. [< F, < *re-* again + *marquer* to mark]

re·mark·a·ble (ri mär′kə bəl), *adj.* worthy of notice; unusual. —**re·mark′a·ble·ness,** *n.* —**re·mark′a·bly,** *adv.*

re·me·di·a·ble (ri mē′di ə bəl), *adj.* that can be remedied or cured. —**re·me′di·a·bly,** *adv.*

re·me·di·al (ri mē′di əl), *adj.* remedying; curing; helping; relieving: *remedial reading.* —**re·me′di·al·ly,** *adv.*

rem·e·dy (rem′ə di), *n.,* pl. **–dies,** *v.,* **–died, –dy·ing.** —*n.* **1** a means of removing or relieving diseases or any bad condition; cure. **2** legal means of enforcing a right or redressing a wrong. —*v.* put or make right; cure. [< L *remedium*] —**rem′e·di·less,** *adj.*

re·mem·ber (ri mem′bər), *v.* **1** have (something) come into the mind again; call to mind; recall. **2** keep in mind; take care not to forget. **3** have memory: *dogs remember.* **4** make a gift to; reward; tip. **5** mention (a person) as sending friendly greetings; recall to the mind of another. [< OF < L, ult. < *re-* again + *memor* mindful of] —**re·mem′ber·a·ble,** *adj.* —**re·mem′ber·er,** *n.*

re·mem·brance (ri mem′brəns), *n.* **1** power to remember; act of remembering; memory. **2** state of being remembered. **3** keepsake; souvenir. **remembrances,** greetings.

re·mind (ri mīnd′), *v.* make (one) think (of something); cause to remember. —**re·mind′er,** *n.*

rem·i·nisce (rem′ə nis′), *v.,* **-nisced, -nisc·ing.** talk or think about past experiences or events.

rem·i·nis·cence (rem′ə nis′əns), *n.* **1** a remembering; recalling past happenings, etc. **2** Often, **reminiscences.** account of something remembered; recollection. [< L, ult. < *reminisci* remember] —**rem′i·nis′cent,** *adj.* —**rem′i·nis′cent·ly,** *adv.*

re·miss (ri mis′), *adj.* careless; slack; neglectful; negligent: *be remiss in one's duty.* [< L *remissus* < *re-* back + *mittere* send] —**re·miss′ness,** *n.*

re·mis·si·ble (ri mis′ə bəl), *adj.* that can be remitted. —**re·mis′si·bil′i·ty,** *n.*

re·mis·sion (ri mish′ən), *n.* **1** a letting off (from debt, punishment, etc.). **2** pardon; forgiveness. **3** a lessening (of pain, force, labor, etc.).

re·mit (ri mit′), *v.,* **-mit·ted, -mit·ting, 1** send money to a person or place: *enclosed is our bill; please remit.* **2** refrain from carrying out; refrain from exacting; cancel: *remit a punishment or fine.* **3** pardon; forgive: *power to remit sins.* **4** make less; decrease: *remit one's efforts.* [< L *remittere* send back. See REMISS.] —**re·mit′ta·ble,** *adj.* —**re·mit′tal,** *n.* —**re·mit′ter,** *n.*

re·mit·tance (ri mit′əns), *n.* **1** a sending money to someone at a distance. **2** the money that is sent.

re·mit·tent (ri mit′ənt), *adj.* lessening for a time; lessening at intervals. —**re·mit′tent·ly,** *adv.*

rem·nant (rem′nənt), *n.* a small part left: *the remnant of an ancient scroll, a fabric remnant.* [< OF *remenant,* ppr. of *remenoir* REMAIN]

re·mod·el (rē mod′əl), *v.,* **-eled, -el·ing. 1** model again. **2** make over: *remodel an old barn into a house.*

re·mon·strance (ri mon′strəns), *n.* protest; complaint.

re·mon·strant (ri mon′strənt), *adj.* remonstrating; protesting. —*n.* person

who remonstrates. —**re·mon′strant·ly,** *adv.*

re·mon·strate (ri mon′strāt), *v.,* **-strat·ed, -strat·ing. 1** say in protest; object. **2** reason or plead in protest. [< Med.L *remonstratus* pointed out, ult. < L *re-* back + *monstrum* sign] —**re·mon′stra′tion,** *n.* —**re·mon′stra·tive,** *adj.* —**re·mon′stra·tor,** *n.*

re·morse (ri môrs′), *n.* deep, painful regret for having done wrong. [< L *remorsus* torment, ult. < *re-* back + *mordere* to bite] —**re·morse′ful,** *adj.* —**re·morse′ful·ly,** *adv.* —**re·morse′ful·ness,** *n.* —**re·morse′less,** *adj.* —**re·morse′less·ness,** *n.*

re·mote (ri mōt′), *adj.,* **-mot·er, -mot·est. 1** far away; far off: *a remote country.* **2** out of the way; secluded: *a remote village.* **3** distant: *a remote relative.* **4** *Fig.* slight; faint: *I haven't the remotest idea what you mean.* [< L *remotus,* pp. of *removere* REMOVE] —**re·mote′ly,** *adv.* —**re·mote′ness,** *n.*

re·mount (*v.* rē mount′; *n.* rē′mount′, rē mount′), *v.* **1** mount again: *remount a drawing, remount a horse.* **2** furnish with fresh horses. —*n.* a fresh horse, or a supply of fresh horses, for use.

re·mov·a·ble (ri müv′ə bəl), *adj.* that can be removed. —**re·mov′a·bil′i·ty, re·mov′a·ble·ness,** *n.* —**re·mov′a·bly,** *adv.*

re·mov·al (ri müv′əl), *n.* **1** a removing; taking away: *after the removal of the soup, fish was served.* **2** change of place: *removal to larger quarters.* **3** dismissal from an office or position.

re·move (ri müv′), **-moved, -mov·ing,** *n.* —*v.* **1** move from a place or position; take off; take away: *remove your hat.* **2** get rid of; put an end to: *remove all doubt.* **3** kill. **4** dismiss from an office or position: *the governor removed the mayor for failing to do his duty.* **5** go or move away. —*n.* a moving away. **2** change of residence. **3** *Fig.* step or degree of distance: *at every remove the mountain seemed smaller, only one remove from failure.* [< OF < L, < *re-* back + *movere* to move] —**re·mov′er,** *n.*

re·moved (ri müvd′), *adj.* **1** distant; remote. **2** separated by one or more steps or degrees of relationship.

re·mu·ner·ate (ri mū′nər āt), *v.,* **-at·ed, -at·ing.** pay for work, services, trouble, etc.; reward. [< L *remuneratus,* ult. < *re-* back + *munus* gift] —**re·mu′ner·a′tion,** *n.* —**re·mu′ner·a′tive,** *adj.* —**re·mu′ner·a′tive·ly,** *adv.* —**re·mu′ner·a′tor,** *n.*

ren·ais·sance (ren′ə säns′; ren′ə säns; ri nā′səns), *n.* revival; new birth.
the Renaissance, a the great revival of art and learning in Europe during the 14th, 15th, and 16th centuries. **b** period of time when this revival occurred. **c** style of art, architecture, etc., of this period. [< F, < *renaître* be born again, ult. < L *renasci.* See RENASCENT.]
Renaissance man, person having knowledge of a wide variety of subjects.

re·nal (rē′nəl), *adj.* of or pertaining to the kidneys. [< L, < *ren* kidney]

re·nas·cence (ri nas′əns; -nā′səns), *n.* **1** revival; new birth; renewal. **2** a being renascent.
the Renascence, =the Renaissance.

re·nas·cent (ri nas′ənt; -nā′sənt), *adj.* being born again; reviving; springing again into being or vigor. [< L, < *re-* again + *nasci* be born]

rend (rend), *v.,* **rent, rend·ing. 1** pull apart violently; tear: *wolves will rend a lamb.* **2** split: *lightning rent the tree.* **3** disturb violently: *a mind rent by doubt.* **4** remove with force or violence. [OE *rendan*] —**rend′er,** *n.*

ren·der (ren′dər), *v.* **1** cause to become; make: *an accident has rendered him helpless.* **2** give: *render thanks, what service has he rendered?* **3** offer for consideration, approval, payment, etc.; hand in; report: *the treasurer rendered an account of all the money spent.* **4** pay as due: *render tribute to a conqueror.* **5** bring out the meaning of; represent: *the actor rendered the part of Hamlet well.* **6** melt (fat, etc.); clarify or extract by melting. **7** forcibly transport a person to a secret location. [< OF *rendre* < L *reddere* give as due, pay < *re-* as due + *dare* give; infl. by L *prendere* take] —**ren′der·a·ble,** *adj.* —**ren′der·er,** *n.*

ren·dez·vous (rän′də vü), *n., pl.* **-vous** (-vüz), *v.,* **-voused** (-vüd), **-vous·ing** (-vü′ing). —*n.* **1** an appointment or engagement to meet at a fixed place or time; meeting by agreement. **2** a meeting place; gathering place. —*v.* meet at a rendezvous. [< F, < *rendez-vous* betake yourself!]

ren·di·tion (ren dish′ən), *n.* **1** a rendering. **2** the rendering of a dramatic part. **3** translation. **4** forcible transportation of a person to a secret location.

ren·e·gade (ren′ə gād), *n.* deserter from a religious faith, a political party, etc.; traitor. —*adj.* deserting; disloyal; like a traitor. [< Sp. < Med.L *renegatus* denied. See RENEGE.]

re·nege (ri nig′), *v.,* **-neged, -neg·ing.** back out; fail to keep a promise. [< Med.L, < L *re-* back + *negare* deny] —**re·neg′er,** *n.*

re·new (ri nü′; -nū′), *v.* **1** make new again; make like new; restore. **2** begin again; get again; say, do, or give again: *renew an attack, renew one's efforts.* **3** replace by new material or a new thing of the same sort; fill again. **4** give or get for a new period: *renew a lease.* —**re·new′a·ble,** *adj.* —**re·new′ed·ly,** *adv.*

re·new·al (ri nü′əl; -nū′-), *n.* a renewing or being renewed.

ren·net (ren′it), *n.* substance containing rennin, used for making cheese and junket. [ME, < *rennen* RUN]

ren·nin (ren′in), *n.* enzyme in the gastric juice that coagulates or curdles milk.

re·nounce (ri nouns′), *v.,* **-nounced, -nounc·ing. 1** declare formally that one gives up; give up entirely; give up:

renounce a right, claim, or title. **2** disown; cast off: *renounce a wicked son.* [< F < L, ult. < *re-* back + *nuntius* message] **—re·nounce'ment**, *n.*

ren·o·vate (ren'ə vāt), *v.,* **-vat·ed, -vat·ing.** make new again; make like new; restore to good condition. [< L, ult. < *re-* again + *novus* new] **—ren'o·va'·tion**, *n.* **—ren'o·va'tor**, *n.*

re·nown (ri noun'), *n.* fame. [< AF *renoun,* ult. < L *re-* repeatedly + *nomen* name] **—re·nowned'**, *adj.*

rent¹ (rent), *n.* regular payment for the use of property. *—v.* **1** pay for the use of (property): *we rent a house from Mr. Smith.* **2** receive pay for the use of (property): *he rents several other houses.* **3** be leased or let for rent: *this farm rents for $25,000 a year.* [< OF *rente,* ult. < L *reddere* RENDER] **—rent'a·ble**, *adj.* **—rent'er**, *n.*

rent² (rent), *n.* a torn place; tear; split. *—adj.* torn; split. *—v.* pt. and pp. of **rend.** [orig. v., var. of *rend*]

rent·al (ren'təl), *n.* amount received or paid as rent. *—adj.* of or in rent.

re·nun·ci·a·tion (ri nun'si ā'shən), *n.* a giving up of a right, title, possession, etc.; renouncing.

re·open (rē ō'pən), *v.* **1** open again: *reopened the safe.* **2** resume: *reopen talks, reopen classes.*

re·or·gan·i·za·tion (rē ôr gən ə zā'shən), *n.* **1** reorganizing. **2** being reorganized.

re·or·gan·ize (rē ôr'gən īz), *v.,* **-ized, -iz·ing. 1** organize anew; form again; arrange in a new way. **2** form a new company to operate (a business in the hands of a receiver). **—re·or·gan·iz'er**, *n.*

rep (rep), *n. Informal.* **1** representative: *a sales rep.* **2** Also, **Rep.** repertory theater. **Rep., 1** Representative. **2** Republican.

re·pair¹ (ri pār'), *v.* **1** put in good condition again; mend: *he repairs shoes.* **2** make up for: *how can I repair the harm done? —n.* **1** act or work of repairing: *make repairs on the school building.* **2** instance or piece of repairing. **3** condition fit to be used: *keep the roads in repair.* **4** condition with respect to repairing: *a house in bad repair.* [< L, < *re-* again + *parare* prepare] **—re·pair'a·ble**, *adj.* **—re·pair'er**, *n.* **—re·pair'man**, *n.*

re·pair² (ri pār'), *v.* go (to a place). [< OF < LL *repatriare* return to one's own country. Doublet of REPATRIATE.]

rep·a·ra·ble (rep'ə rə bəl), *adj.* that can be repaired or remedied. **—rep'a·ra·bly**, *adv.*

rep·a·ra·tion (rep'ə rā'shən), *n.* **1** a giving of satisfaction or compensation for wrong or injury done. **2** compensation for wrong or injury. **3** Usually, **reparations.** compensation for the devastation of territory during war. **4** a repairing or being repaired. **—re·par'a·tive, re·par'a·to'ry**, *adj.*

rep·ar·tee (rep'ər tē'), *n.* **1** a witty reply or replies. **2** talk characterized by clever and witty replies. **3** cleverness and wit in making replies. [< F, < *repartir* reply, ult. < L *re-* back + *pars* part]

re·past (ri past'; -päst'), *n.* **1** meal; attractive meal; food. **2** a taking of food. [< OF, ult. < L *re-* again + *pascere* feed]

re·pa·tri·ate (rē pā'tri āt), *v.,* **-at·ed, -at·ing.** send back or restore to one's own country: *the prisoners of war were repatriated.* [< LL *repatriatus,* ult. < L *re-* back + *patria* native land. Doublet of REPAIR².] **—re·pa'tri·a'tion**, *n.*

re·pay (ri pā'), *v.,* **-paid, -pay·ing. 1** pay back; give back: *repay money borrowed.* **2** make return for: *repay a kindness.* **3** make return to: *the boy's success repaid the teacher for her efforts.* **—re·pay'a·ble**, *adj.* **—re·pay'er**, *n.* **—re·pay'ment**, *n.*

re·peal (ri pēl'), *v.* do away with; revoke; abrogate: *the Stamp Act was finally repealed.* *—n.* act of repealing; abrogation: *vote for the repeal of a law.* [< AF *repeler,* alter. of OF *rapeler* < *re-* back + *apeler* to call. See APPEAL.] **—re·peal'a·ble**, *adj.* **—re·peal'er**, *n.*

re·peat (ri pēt'), *v.* **1** do or make again: *repeat an error.* **2** say again: *repeat a word for emphasis.* **3** say over; recite: *repeat a poem from memory.* **4** say after another says: *repeat the oath after me.* **5** tell to another or others: *do not repeat the secret.* *—n.* **1** a repeating. **2** thing repeated. **3 a** passage of music to be repeated. **b** sign indicating this, usually a row of dots.

repeat oneself, say again what one has already said. [< L *repetere* attack again < *re-* again + *petere* aim at] **—re·peat'a·ble**, *adj.* **—re·peat'ed**, *adj.* **—re·peat'ed·ly**, *adv.*

re·peat·er (ri pēt'ər), *n.* **1** gun that fires several shots without reloading. **2** one that repeats. **3 a** student who does not move into the next grade. **b** student who repeats a course. **4** person who is sent to prison again and again.

re·pel (ri pel'), *v.,* **-pelled, -pel·ling. 1** force back; drive back or away: *repel the enemy.* **2** cause to move apart or away: *oil and water repel each other.* **3** be displeasing to; cause disgust in: *her manner repels me.* **4** refuse to admit or accept; reject: *repel a suggestion.* [< L, < *re-* back + *pellere* to drive] **—re·pel'lence**, *n.* **—re·pel'ler**, *n.*

re·pel·lent (ri pel'ənt), *adj.* **1** unattractive; disagreeable. **2** repelling; driving back.

re·pent (ri pent'), *v.* **1** feel sorry for sin and seek forgiveness. **2** feel sorry for; regret: *repent one's choice.* [< OF *repentir,* ult. < L *re-* repeatedly + *paenitere* cause to regret] **—re·pent'er**, *n.*

re·pent·ance (ri pen'təns), *n.* **1** sorrow for doing wrong. **2** sorrow; regret. **—re·pent'ant**, *adj.* **—re·pent'ant·ly**, *adv.*

re·per·cus·sion (rē'pər kush'ən), *n.* **1** an indirect influence or reaction from an event. **2** sound flung back; echo. **3** a springing back; rebound; recoil. [< L *repercussio,* ult. < *re-* back + *per-* thoroughly + *quatere* to beat] **—re'per·cus'sive**, *adj.*

rep·er·toire (rep'ər twär; -twôr), *n.* the list of plays, operas, parts, pieces, etc., that a company or performer is prepared to perform. [< F < LL *repertorium.* Doublet of REPERTORY.]

rep·er·to·ry (rep'ər tô'ri; -tō'-), *n., pl.* **-ries. 1** =repertoire. **2** store or stock of things ready for use. [< LL *repertorium* inventory, ult. < *reperire* find, get. Doublet of REPERTOIRE.]

rep·e·ti·tion (rep'ə tish'ən), *n.* a repeating: *repetition helps learning.* **2** thing repeated. **—re·pet'i·tive**, *adj.*

rep·e·ti·tious (rep'ə tish'əs), *adj.* full of repetitions; repeating in a tiresome way. **—rep'e·ti'tious·ly**, *adv.* **—rep'e·ti'tious·ness**, *n.*

re·pine (ri pīn'), *v.,* **-pined, -pin·ing.** be discontented; fret; complain. [< *re-* + *pine²*]

re·place (ri plās'), *v.,* **-placed, -plac·ing. 1** fill or take the place of; supersede. **2** get another in place of. **3** put back; put in place again; restore. **—re·place'a·ble**, *adj.* **—re·place'ment**, *n.* **—re·plac'er**, *n.*

re·plen·ish (ri plen'ish), *v.* fill again; provide a new supply for: *replenish a wardrobe.* [< OF *repleniss-,* ult. < L *re-* again + *plenus* full] **—re·plen'ish·er**, *n.* **—re·plen'ish·ment**, *n.*

re·plete (ri plēt'), *adj.* abundantly supplied; filled. [< L, < *re-* again + *plere* fill] **—re·ple'tion, re·plete'ness**, *n.*

rep·li·ca (rep'lə kə), *n.* copy; reproduction: *a replica of the famous statue at the museum.* [< Ital., < *replicare* reproduce. See REPLY.]

rep·li·cate (rep'lə kāt), *v.,* **-cat·ed, -cat·ing.** duplicate; copy.

re·ply (ri plī'), *v.,* **-plied, -ply·ing, *n.,* pl. -plies.** *—v.* **1** answer in words or writing: *reply to a question.* **2** answer by suitable action: *reply to the enemy's fire.* **3** return as an answer: *not know what to reply.* *—n.* **1** act of replying. **2** an answer in words or writing; response. **3** answer by some action: *his reply was a blow.* [< OF < L *replicare* unroll < *re-* back + *plicare* to fold]

re·po (rē'pō), *n. Informal.* **a** something repossessed: *the car is a repo.* **b** repossession.

re·port (ri pôrt'; -pōrt'), *n.* **1** account of something seen, heard, read, done, or considered. **2** an account officially expressed, generally in writing. **3** the sound of a shot or an explosion. **4** common talk; rumor. **5** reputation. *—v.* **1** make a report of; announce. **2** give a formal account of; state officially. **3** take down in writing; write an account of. **4** make a report. **5** present; present oneself: *report for duty at 9 a.m.* **6** announce as a wrongdoer; denounce. [< OF < L, < *re-* back + *portare* carry] **—re·port'a·ble**, *adj.* **—re·port'ed·ly**, *adv.*

re·port·er (ri pôr'tər; -pōr'-), *n.* **1** person who reports. **2** person who gathers news for a newspaper. **—rep'or·to'ri·al**, *adj.*

re·pose¹ (ri pōz'), *n., v.,* **-posed, -pos·ing.** *—n.* **1** rest; sleep: *do not disturb her*

repose. 2 quietness; ease: *repose of manner.* **3** peace; calmness. —*v.* **1** lie at rest: *repose upon a bed.* **2** lay to rest: *repose yourself in the hammock.* [< F < LL, cause to rest, < *re-* again + *pausare* to pause] —**re·pose′ful,** *adj.* —**re·pose′ful·ly,** *adv.* —**re·pose′ful·ness,** *n.*

re·pose² (ri pōz′), *v.,* **-posed, -pos·ing.** put; place: *repose trust.* [< L *repos-* < *reponere* replace. See POSE.]

re·pos·i·to·ry (ri poz′ə tô´ri; -tō´-), *n., pl.* **-ries.** place or container where things are stored or kept.

re·pos·sess (rē´pə zes′), *v.* possess again; get possession of again. —**re´pos·ses′-sion,** *n.*

re·pous·sé (rə pü sā′), *adj.* **1** in relief; raised by hammering, esp. on thin metal, on the reverse side. **2** ornamental in this manner. —*n.* work ornamental this way. [< F]

rep·re·hend (rep´ri hend′), *v.* reprove (a person), as for a fault; rebuke; blame. [< L, orig., pull back < *re-* back + *prehendere* grasp]

rep·re·hen·si·ble (rep´ri hen′sə bəl), *adj.* deserving reproof, rebuke, or blame. —**rep´re·hen′si·bil′i·ty, rep´re·hen′si·ble·ness,** *n.* —**rep´re·hen′si·bly,** *adv.*

rep·re·hen·sion (rep´ri hen′shən), *n.* reproof; rebuke; blame.

rep·re·sent (rep´ri zent′), *v.* **1** stand for; be a sign or symbol of: *the stars in our flag represent the states, represent speech by writing.* **2** act in place of; speak and act for: *we chose a committee to represent us.* **3** act the part of: *each child will represent an animal at the party.* **4** show in a picture, statue, carving, etc.; give a likeness of; portray. **5** describe; set forth: *represent a scheme as safe.* **6** bring before the mind; make one think of. [< L, < *re-* back + *praesentare* to PRESENT²] —**rep′re·sent′a·ble,** *adj.*

rep·re·sen·ta·tion (rep´ri zen tā′shən), *n.* **1** act of representing. **2** condition or fact of being represented: *"Taxation without representation is tyranny."* **3** representatives considered as a group. **4** likeness; picture; model. **5** protest; complaint. **6** account; statement: *false representations.* —**rep′re·sen·ta′tion·al,** *adj.* —**rep′re·sen·ta′tion·al·ly,** *adv.*

rep·re·sent·a·tive (rep´ri zen′tə tiv), *n.* **1** person appointed to act or speak for others. **2** example; type. —*adj.* **1** having its citizens represented by chosen persons. **2** representing. **3** enough like all those of its kind to stand for all the rest. **Representative,** member of the House of Representatives. —**rep′re·sent′a·tive·ly,** *adv.* —**rep′re·sent′a·tive·ness,** *n.*

re·press (ri pres′), *v.* **1** prevent from acting; check: *repress an impulse to cough.* **2** keep down; put down: *the dictator repressed the revolt.* [< L *repressus* < *re-* back + *premere* press] —**re·press′er,** *n.* —**re·press′i·ble,** *adj.* —**re·pres′sive,** *adj.*

re·pres·sion (ri presh′ən), *n.* **1** act of repressing. **2** state of being repressed.

re·prieve (ri prēv′), *v.,* **-prieved, -priev·ing,** *n.* —*v.* **1** delay the execution of (a person condemned to death). **2** give relief from any evil or trouble. —*n.* **1** delay in carrying out a punishment, esp. of the death penalty. **2** temporary relief from any evil or trouble. [prob. var. of *reprove* in sense of "retest"]

rep·ri·mand (rep′rə mand; -mänd), *n.* a severe or formal reproof. —*v.* reprove severely or formally. [< F *réprimande* < *réprimer* REPRESS]

re·print (*v.* rē print′; *n.* rē′print´), *v.* print again; print a new impression of. —*n.* a reprinting; a new impression of printed work.

re·pris·al (ri prīz′əl), *n.* injury done in return for injury, esp. by one nation to another. [< OF *reprisaille,* ult. < L *reprehendere* REPREHEND]

re·proach (ri prōch′), *n.* **1** blame or disgrace. **2** cause or occasion of blame or discredit. —*v.* blame. [< F *reprocher*] —**re·proach′a·ble,** *adj.* —**re·proach′er,** *n.* —**re·proach′ing·ly,** *adv.* —**re·proach′-less,** *adj.*

re·proach·ful (ri prōch′fəl), *adj.* full of or expressing reproach. —**re·proach′ful·ly,** *adv.* —**re·proach′ful·ness,** *n.*

rep·ro·bate (rep′rə bāt), *n., adj., v.,* **-bat·ed, -bat·ing.** —*n.* an unprincipled scoundrel. —*adj.* corrupt; unprincipled. —*v.* disapprove; condemn; censure. [< LL *reprobatus* reproved < L *re-* dis- + *probare* approve. Doublet of REPROVE.] —**rep′ro·ba′tion,** *n.* —**rep′ro·ba′tive,** *adj.*

re·pro·duce (rē´prə düs′; -dūs′), *v.,* **-duced, -duc·ing.** **1** produce again: *a radio reproduces sounds.* **2** make a copy of: *a camera will reproduce a picture.* **3** produce offspring: *most plants reproduce by seeds.* —**re´pro·duc′er,** *n.* —**re´pro·duc′i·ble,** *adj.*

re·pro·duc·tion (rē´prə duk′shən), *n.* **1** a reproducing or being reproduced. **2** a copy. **3** process by which animals and plants produce individuals like themselves.

re·pro·duc·tive (rē´prə duk′tiv), *adj.* **1** that reproduces. **2** for or concerned with reproduction. —**re´pro·duc′tive·ly,** *adv.* —**re´pro·duc′tive·ness,** *n.*

re·proof (ri prüf′), *n.* words of blame or disapproval.

re·prove (ri prüv′), *v.,* **-proved, -prov·ing.** express disapproval of; find fault with; rebuke; blame. [< OF < LL *reprobare.* Doublet of REPROBATE.] —**re·prov′a·ble,** *adj.* —**re·prov′al,** *n.* —**re·prov′er,** *n.* —**re·prov′ing·ly,** *adv.*

rep·tile (rep′təl; -tīl), *n.* a cold-blooded animal that creeps or crawls, such as a snake, lizard, turtle, alligator, or crocodile. —*adj.* of or like a reptile; crawling; creeping. [< LL, orig. neut. adj., < L *repere* crawl]

rep·til·i·an (rep til′i ən), *adj.* of or pertaining to reptiles. —*n.* a reptile.

re·pub·lic (ri pub′lik), *n.* nation or state in which the citizens elect representatives to manage the government. [< L *res publica* public interest, state]

re·pub·li·can (ri pub′lə kən), *adj.* **1** of a republic; like that of a republic. **2** favoring a republic. **3 Republican,** of or having to do with the Republican Party. —*n.* **1** person who favors a republic. **2 Republican.** member of the Republican Party.

re·pub·li·can·ism (ri pub′lə kən iz´əm), *n.* **1** republican government. **2** republican principles; adherence to republican principles.

Republicanism, principles or policies of the Republican Party.

Republican Party, one of the two main political parties in the United States.

re·pu·di·ate (ri pū′di āt), *v.,* **-at·ed, -at·ing.** **1** refuse to accept; reject: *repudiate a doctrine.* **2** refuse to acknowledge or pay: *repudiate a debt.* **3** cast off; disown: *repudiate a son.* [< L, < *repudium* divorce] —**re·pu´di·a′tion,** *n.* —**re·pu´di·a′tive,** *adj.* —**re·pu´di·a′tor,** *n.*

re·pug·nance (ri pug′nəns), **re·pug·nan·cy** (-nən si), *n.* strong dislike, distaste, or aversion.

re·pug·nant (ri pug′nənt), *adj.* **1** distasteful; disagreeable; offensive. **2** objecting; averse; opposed. [< L *repugnans* resisting < *re-* back + *pugnare* to fight] —**re·pug′nant·ly,** *adv.*

re·pulse (ri puls′), *v.,* **-pulsed, -puls·ing,** *n.* —*v.* **1** drive back; repel. **2** refuse to accept; reject: *she coldly repulsed him.* —*n.* **1** a driving back; being driven back: *after the second repulse, the enemy surrendered.* **2** refusal; rejection. [< L *repulsus,* pp. of *repellere* REPEL] —**re·puls′er,** *n.*

re·pul·sion (ri pul′shən), *n.* **1** strong dislike or aversion. **2** repulse; repelling or being repelled. **3** action of bodies that repel each other, or an inherent force by which bodies are forced apart.

re·pul·sive (ri pul′siv), *adj.* **1** causing strong dislike or aversion: *snakes are repulsive to some people.* **2** tending to drive back or repel. —**re·pul′sive·ly,** *adv.* —**re·pul′sive·ness,** *n.*

rep·u·ta·ble (rep′yə tə bəl), *adj.* having a good reputation; well thought of; in good repute. —**rep′u·ta·ble·ness,** *n.* —**rep′u·ta·bly,** *adv.*

rep·u·ta·tion (rep′yə tā′shən), *n.* **1** what people think and say the character of a person or thing is; character in the opinion of others. **2** good name; good reputation. **3** fame.

re·pute (ri pūt′), *n., v.,* **-put·ed, -put·ing.** —*n.* **1** reputation. **2** good reputation. —*v.* suppose to be; consider; suppose: *he is reputed the richest man in the state.* [< L, < *re-* over + *putare* think]

re·put·ed (ri pūt′id), *adj.* accounted or supposed to be such: *the reputed author.* —**re·put′ed·ly,** *adv.*

re·quest (ri kwest′), *v.* **1** ask for; ask as a favor: *request a loan from the bank.* **2** ask: *he requested her to go with him.* —*n.* **1** act of asking: *at our request.* **2** what is asked for: *grant my request*. **3** state of being asked for or sought after: *a good dancer is in great request*.

by request, in response to a request. [< OF *requeste*, ult. < L *re-* again + *quaerere* ask]

req·ui·em, Req·ui·em (rek′wi əm; rē′-kwi–), *n*. **1** Mass for the dead; musical church service for the dead. **2** music for it. [< L, accus. of *requies* rest; the first word of the Mass]

re·quire (ri kwīr′), *v.*, **–quired, –quir·ing**. **1** have need for; need; want: *we shall require more help*. **2** make necessary; demand; order; command: *circumstances require us to submit*. [< L *requirere*. See REQUEST.] **—re·quir′er**, *n*.

re·quire·ment (ri kwīr′mənt), *n*. **1** need; thing needed: *patience is a requirement in teaching*. **2** demand; thing demanded: *fulfill all requirements for graduation*.

req·ui·site (rek′wə zit), *adj*. required by circumstances; needed; necessary: *the qualities requisite for a leader*. *—n*. thing needed: *food and air are requisites for life*. **—req′ui·site·ly,** *adv*. **—req′ui·site·ness,** *n*.

req·ui·si·tion (rek′wə zish′ən), *n*. **1** act of requiring. **2** a demand made, esp. a formal written demand. **3** state of being required for use or called into service. *—v*. **1** demand or take by authority. **2** make demands upon.

re·quit·al (ri kwīt′əl), *n*. repayment; payment; return.

re·quite (ri kwīt′), *v.*, **–quit·ed, –quit·ing**. **1** pay back; make return for: *requite evil with good*. **2** make retaliation for; avenge. **3** make return to. [< *re-* + *quite*, var. of *quit*] **—re·quite′ment,** *n*. **—re·quit′er,** *n*.

rere·dos (rir′dos), *n*. a screen or a decorated part of the wall behind an altar. [< AF, ult. < *rere* REAR[1] + *dos* back (< L *dossus*, var. of *dorsum*)]

re·route (ri rüt′; –rout′), *v.*, **–rout·ed, –rout·ing**. send or direct by a new or different route.

re·scind (ri sind′), *v*. deprive of force; repeal; cancel: *rescind a law or treaty*. [< L, < *re-* back + *scindere* to cut] **—re·scind′a·ble,** *adj*. **—re·scind′er,** *n*. **—re·scind′ment,** *n*.

re·scis·sion (ri sizh′ən), *n*. a rescinding.

res·cue (res′kū), *v.*, **–cued, –cu·ing**, *n*. *—v*. save from danger, capture, harm, etc.; free; deliver. *—n*. a saving or freeing from danger, capture, harm, etc. [< OF *rescoure*, ult. < L *re-* back + *ex* out + *quatere* to shake] **—res′cu·er,** *n*.

re·search (ri sėrch′; rē′sėrch), *n*. a careful hunting for facts or truth; inquiry; investigation. *—v*. make researches. [< MF *recerche*. See RE–, SEARCH.]

re·search·er (ri sėr′chər; rē′sėr–), *n*. person who does research; investigator.

re·seat (rē sēt′), *v*. **1** seat again. **2** put a new seat on.

re·sect (ri sekt′), *v*. remove or cut out part of, as a surgical procedure. **—re·sec′tion,** *n*. **—re·sec′tion·al,** *adj*.

re·sem·blance (ri zem′bləns), *n*. likeness; similar appearance: *twins often show great resemblance*.

re·sem·ble (ri zem′bəl), *v.*, **–bled, –bling**. be like or similar to; have likeness to in form, figure, or qualities. [< OF *resembler*, ult. < L *re-* again + *similis* similar] **—re·sem′bler,** *n*.

re·sent (ri zent′), *v*. feel injured and angry at; feel indignation at: *resent an insult*. [< F *ressentir*, ult. < L *re-* back + *sentire* feel] **—re·sent′er,** *n*. **—re·sent′ful,** *adj*. **—re·sent′ful·ness,** *n*.

re·sent·ment (ri zent′mənt), *n*. the feeling that one has at being injured or insulted; indignation.

res·er·va·tion (rez′ər vā′shən), *n*. **1** a keeping back; hiding in part; something not expressed: *a mental reservation*. **2** a limiting condition: *agree without reservation*. **3** land set aside for a special purpose. **4** arrangement to keep a thing for a person; securing of accommodations, etc. **5** something reserved.

re·serve (ri zėrv′), *v.*, **–served, –serv·ing**, *n.*, *adj*. *—v*. **1** keep back; hold back: *reserve criticism*. **2** set apart: *time reserved for recreation*. **3** save for use later: *reserve enough money for your fare home*. **4** set aside for the use of a particular person or persons: *reserve a table*. *—n*. **1** the actual cash in a bank or assets that can be turned into cash quickly: *banks must keep a reserve of money*. **2** body of soldiers kept ready to help the main army in battle. **3** public land set apart for a special purpose: *a forest reserve*. **4** anything kept back for future use: *a good reserve of energy*. **5** fact, state, or condition of being kept, set apart, or saved for use later: *keep some cash in reserve*. **6** habit of keeping back or restraining one's thoughts, feelings, and affairs to oneself; self-restraint. *—adj*. kept in reserve; forming a reserve.

reserves, members of the armed forces not in active service but ready to serve if needed. [< L, < *re-* back + *servare* keep]

reserve bank, one of the twelve banks that make up the U.S. Federal Reserve.

re·served (ri zėrvd′), *adj*. **1** kept in reserve; kept by special arrangement. **2** set apart. **3** self-restrained in action or speech. **—re·serv′ed·ly,** *adv*. **—re·serv′ed·ness,** *n*.

re·serv·ist (ri zėr′vist), *n*. soldier or sailor not in active service but available if needed.

res·er·voir (rez′ər vwär; –vôr), *n*. **1** place where water is collected and stored for use. **2** anything to hold a liquid. **3** place where anything is collected and stored. **4** a great supply. [< F, < *réserver* RESERVE]

re·set (*v*. rē set′; *n*. rē′set′), *v.*, **–set, –set·ting**, *n*. *—v*. set again: *the broken arm must be reset*. *—n*. **1** act of resetting. **2** thing reset.

re·shape (ri shāp′), *v.*, **–shaped, –shap·ing**. **1** form into a new or different shape. **2** *Fig*. redesign: *reshape a proposal*.

re·shuf·fle (ri shuf′əl), *v.*, **–fled, –fling**. **1** shuffle again: *reshuffle cards*. **2** *Fig*. rearrange; reorganize: *reshuffle a department*.

re·side (ri zīd′), *v.*, **–sid·ed, –sid·ing**. **1** live (in or at) for a long time; dwell. **2** be (in); exist (in): *her charm resides in her happy smile*. **3** of rights, powers, etc., be vested in; rest in. [< L *residere* < *re-* back + *sedere* settle] **—re·sid′er,** *n*.

res·i·dence (rez′ə dəns), *n*. **1** house; home. **2** act or fact of residing. **3** period of residing in a place.

in residence, living in a place while on duty or doing active work.

res·i·den·cy (rez′ə dən si), *n.*, *pl*. **–cies**. residence.

res·i·dent (rez′ə dənt), *n*. **1** person living in a place, not a visitor. **2** an official sent to live in a foreign land to represent his or her country. *—adj*. **1** dwelling in a place; residing. **2** living in a place while on duty or doing active work. **3** of birds, not migratory.

res·i·den·tial (rez′ə den′shəl), *adj*. **1** of, pertaining to, or fitted for residences. **2** pertaining to residence: *residential qualifications*.

re·sid·u·al (ri zij′ü əl), *adj*. of or forming a residue; remaining; left over. *—n*. remainder.

res·i·due (rez′ə dü; –dū), *n*. what remains after a part is taken; remainder. [< F < L *residuum*, neut. adj., left over. Doublet of RESIDUUM.]

re·sign (ri zīn′), *v*. give up a job, position, etc.; give back; renounce.

resign oneself, submit quietly; adapt oneself without complaint. [< OF < L *resignare* unseal, ult. < *re-* back + *signum* seal]

res·ig·na·tion (rez′ig nā′shən), *n*. **1** act of resigning. **2** a written statement giving notice that one resigns. **3** patient acceptance; quiet submission.

re·signed (ri zīnd′), *adj*. accepting what comes without complaint. **—re·sign′ed·ly,** *adv*. **—re·sign′ed·ness,** *n*.

re·sil·i·ence (ri zil′i əns; –zil′yəns), **re·sil·i·en·cy** (–i ən si; –yən si), *n*. **1** elasticity. **2** cheerfulness.

re·sil·i·ent (ri zil′i ənt; –zil′yənt), *adj*. **1** springing back; returning to the original form or position after being bent, compressed, or stretched. **2** readily recovering; buoyant; cheerful. [< *resiliens* < *re-* back + *salire* to jump]

res·in (rez′ən), *n*. a sticky yellow or brown substance that flows from certain plants and trees, esp. the pine and fir. It is also derived chemically and is used in medicine and varnish. The harder portion remaining after heating is called rosin. [< L *resina*] **—res′in·ous,** *adj*. **—res′in·ous·ly,** *adv*. **—res′in·y,** *adj*.

re·sist (ri zist′), *v*. **1** act against; strive against; oppose: *resist the adoption of a plan*. **2** strive successfully against; keep from: *unable to resist laughing*. **3** withstand the action or effect of (an acid, storm, etc.): *resist rust.* [< L, < *re-* back + *sistere* make a stand] —**re·sist′er**, *n.* —**re·sist′i·ble**, *adj.* —**re·sist′i·bil′i·ty**, *n.*

re·sist·ance (ri zis′təns), *n.* 1 act of resisting. 2 power to resist: *resistance to disease.* 3 thing or act that resists; opposing force; opposition. 4 people in a country occupied or controlled by another country who organize and fight for their freedom: *the French resistance in World War II.* 5 property of a conductor that opposes the passage of a current and changes electric energy into heat. —**re·sist′ant**, *adj.*

re·sis·tiv·i·ty (ri′zis tiv′ə ti), *n., pl.* **-ties.** electrical resistance of a given substance.

re·sis·tor (ri zis′tər), *n.* a conducting body or device used in an electric circuit, etc., because of its resistance.

res·o·lute (rez′ə lüt), *adj.* 1 firmly determined; set or fixed in purpose. 2 firm and bold in pursuing purposes. [< L *resolutus,* pp. of *resolvere* RESOLVE] —**res′o·lute·ly**, *adv.* —**res′o·lute·ness**, *n.*

res·o·lu·tion (rez′ə lü′shən), *n.* 1 act of resolving or determining. 2 thing decided on; thing determined. 3 determination. 4 a formal expression of opinion. 5 act or result of solving; solution.

re·solve (ri zolv′), *v.,* **-solved, -solv·ing,** *n.* —*v.* 1 make up one's mind; determine; decide: *resolve to do better work.* 2 break into parts; break up; distinguish parts within: *resolve a spectrum into its various lines.* 3 answer and explain; solve: *his letter resolved all our doubts.* 4 decide by vote: *it was resolved that our school have a lunchroom.* 5 change: *the assembly resolved itself into a committee.* —*n.* 1 thing determined on: *he kept his resolve to do better.* 2 firmness in carrying out a purpose; determination. [< L, < *re-* un- + *solvere* loosen] —**re·solv′a·ble**, *adj.* —**re·solv′a·bil′i·ty**, *n.* —**re·solv′er**, *n.*

re·solved (ri zolvd′), *adj.* determined; resolute. —**re·solv′ed·ly**, *adv.* —**re·solv′ed·ness**, *n.*

res·o·nance (rez′ə nəns), *n.* 1 resounding quality; being resonant: *the resonance of an organ.* 2 a reinforcing and prolonging of sound by reflection or by vibration of other objects. 3 condition of an electrical circuit adjusted to allow the greatest flow of current at a certain frequency, such as in a radio to receive sound waves.

res·o·nant (rez′ə nənt), *adj.* 1 resounding; continuing to sound; echoing. 2 tending to increase or prolong sounds. 3 of or in resonance, as of a radio. [< L *resonans,* ult. < *re-* back + *sonus* sound] —**res′o·nant·ly**, *adv.*

res·o·na·tor (rez′ə nā′tər), *n.* something that produces resonance; appliance for increasing sound by resonance.

re·sort (ri zôrt′), *v.* 1 go; go often: *many people resort to the beaches in hot weather.* 2 turn for help: *resort to violence.* —*n.* 1

an assembling; going to often: *a park is a place of popular resort in good weather.* 2 place people go to: *a summer resort.* 3 act of turning for help. 4 person or thing turned to for help. [< OF, < *re-* back + *sortir* go out] —**re·sort′er**, *n.*

re·sound (ri zound′), *v.* 1 give back sound; echo. 2 sound loudly. 3 be filled with sound. 4 repeat loudly; proclaim loudly; celebrate. [< L, ult. < *re-* back + *sonus* sound] —**re·sound′er**, *n.* —**re·sound′ing·ly**, *adv.*

re·source (ri sôrs′; -sōrs′; rē′sôrs; -sōrs), *n.* 1 any source of supply, support, or aid. 2 any means of getting success or getting out of trouble. 3 skill in meeting difficulties, getting out of trouble, etc. **resources, a** the actual and potential wealth of a country. **b** means of raising money and supplies; funds. **c** available means or capabilities of any kind. [< F *ressource,* ult. < L *re-* again + *surgere* rise]

re·source·ful (ri sôrs′fəl; -sōrs′-), *adj.* good at thinking of ways to do things; quick-witted. —**re·source′ful·ly**, *adv.* —**re·source′ful·ness**, *n.*

re·spect (ri spekt′), *n.* 1 honor; esteem: *show respect to those who are older.* 2 consideration; regard: *show respect for other people's property.* 3 point; matter; detail: *a plan unwise in many respects.* 4 relation; reference: *plan with respect to the future.* —*v.* 1 feel or show honor or esteem for: *respect the President.* 2 show consideration for: *respect the feelings of others.* 3 relate to; refer to.

in or **with respect to,** in or with relation or reference to: *controversy in respect to the scoring of admissions tests.*

respects, expressions of respect; regards. [< L *respectus,* pp. of *respicere* look back, have regard for < *re-* back + *specere* to look] —**re·spect′er**, *n.*

re·spect·a·bil·i·ty (ri spek′tə bil′ə ti), *n., pl.* **-ties.** 1 respectable quality or condition. 2 respectable social standing.

re·spect·a·ble (ri spek′tə bəl), *adj.* 1 worthy of respect; having a good reputation: *respectable citizens obey the laws.* 2 having fair social standing; honest and decent: *his parents were poor but respectable people.* 3 fairly good; moderate in size or quality: *a respectable but not brilliant record.* 4 good enough to use; fit to be seen. —**re·spect′a·ble·ness**, *n.* —**re·spect′a·bly**, *adv.*

re·spect·ful (ri spekt′fəl), *adj.* showing respect; polite. —**re·spect′ful·ly**, *adv.* —**re·spect′ful·ness**, *n.*

re·spect·ing (ri spek′ting), *prep.* with regard to; about; concerning.

re·spec·tive (ri spek′tiv), *adj.* belonging to each; particular; individual: *go to your respective rooms.*

re·spec·tive·ly (ri spek′tiv li), *adv.* as regards each one in his or her turn or in the order mentioned.

res·pi·ra·tion (res′pə rā′shən), *n.* 1 act of inhaling and exhaling; breathing. 2 a

single breath. 3 the processes by which an animal, plant, or living cell secures oxygen from the air or water, distributes it, combines it with substances in the tissues, and gives off carbon dioxide.

res·pi·ra·tor (res′pə rā′tər), *n.* 1 a device, usually of gauze, worn over the nose and mouth to prevent inhaling harmful substances. 2 device used in giving artificial respiration.

res·pi·ra·to·ry (res′pə rə tô′ri; -tō′-; ri spīr′ə-), *adj.* pertaining to or used for breathing.

re·spire (ri spīr′), *v.,* **-spired, -spir·ing.** inhale and exhale; breathe. [< L, < *re-* regularly + *spirare* breathe]

res·pite (res′pit), *n., v.,* **-pit·ed, -pit·ing.** —*n.* 1 time of relief and rest; lull. 2 a putting off; delay, esp. in carrying out a sentence of death; reprieve. —*v.* give a respite to. [< OF < VL *respectus* delay < LL, expectation, < L *respectare* wait for. See RESPECT.]

re·splend·ent (ri splen′dənt), *adj.* very bright; shining; splendid: *the queen was resplendent with jewels.* [< L *resplendens* glittering < *re-* back + *splendere* to shine] —**re·splend′ence, re·splend′en·cy**, *n.* —**re·splend′ent·ly**, *adv.*

re·spond (ri spond′), *v.* 1 answer; reply. 2 act in answer; react: *nerves respond to a stimulus.* [< OF < L, < *re-* in return + *spondere* to promise]

re·spond·ent (ri spon′dənt), *adj.* answering; responding. —*n.* 1 person who responds. 2 defendant, esp. in a divorce case.

re·sponse (ri spons′), *n.* 1 an answer by word or act. 2 words said or sung by the congregation or choir in answer to the minister. 3 reaction of body or mind to a stimulus. [< L *responsum,* orig. neut. pp. of *respondere* RESPOND]

re·spon·si·bil·i·ty (ri spon′sə bil′ə ti), *n., pl.* **-ties.** 1 a being responsible; obligation: *a little child does not feel much responsibility.* 2 thing for which one is responsible. A task, a debt, and little children to care for are responsibilities.

re·spon·si·ble (ri spon′sə bəl), *adj.* 1 obliged or expected to account (for): *each pupil is responsible for the care of the books given him.* 2 deserving credit or blame: *the bad weather is responsible for the small attendance.* 3 trustworthy; reliable: *a responsible person should take care of the money.* 4 involving obligation or duties: *the presidency is a very responsible position.* —**re·spon′si·ble·ness**, *n.* —**re·spon′si·bly**, *adv.*

re·spon·sive (ri spon′siv), *adj.* 1 making answer; responding: *a responsive glance.* 2 easily moved; responding readily: *be responsive to kindness.* —**re·spon′sive·ly**, *adv.* —**re·spon′sive·ness**, *n.*

rest[1] (rest), *n.* 1 sleep: *have a good night's rest.* 2 ease after work or effort; freedom from anything that tires, troubles, disturbs, or pains; quiet: *rest after work.* 3 absence of motion: *bring a machine to* *rest.* **4** support: *rest for each arm.* **5 a** pause in music. **b** mark to show such a pause. **6** death; the grave. —*v.* **1** be asleep or still; be free from work, effort, care, trouble, etc.: *lie down and rest.* **2** stop moving; be inactive: *the ball rested at the bottom of the hill.* **3** be supported; lean: *the ladder rests against the wall.* **4** be fixed: *our eyes rested on the open book.* **5** rely (on); depend; base: *our hope rests on you.* **6** be found; be present: *in a democracy, government rests with the people.* **7** be dead; lie in the grave. **8** end the introduction of evidence in (a case at law): *the lawyer rested her case.*

at rest, a asleep. **b** not moving. **c** free from pain, trouble, etc. **d** dead.

lay to rest, a bury. **b** *Fig.* end, as a disagreement.

rest up, have or get an adequate rest. [OE]

rest² (rest), *n.* what is left; those that are left. —*v.* continue to be: *you may rest assured that I will keep my promise.* [< F *reste,* ult. < L *restare* be left < *re–* back + *stare* stand]

res·tau·rant (res′tə rənt, –ränt; –trənt, –tränt), *n.* place to buy and eat a meal. [< F, orig. ppr. of *restaurer* RESTORE]

res·tau·ra·teur (res′tə rə tér′), *n.* keeper of a restaurant.

rest·ful (rest′fəl), *adj.* **1** full of rest; giving rest. **2** quiet; peaceful. —**rest′ful·ly,** *adv.* —**rest′ful·ness,** *n.*

res·ti·tu·tion (res′tə tü′shən; –tū′–), *n.* **1** a giving back of what has been lost or taken away. **2** act of making good any loss, damage, or injury. [< L *restitutio,* ult. < *re–* again + *statuere* set up]

res·tive (res′tiv), *adj.* **1** restless; uneasy. **2** hard to manage. **3** refusing to go ahead; balky. [< OF *restif* motionless < *rester* REST², v.] —**res′tive·ly,** *adv.* —**res′tive·ness,** *n.*

rest·less (rest′lis), *adj.* **1** unable to rest; uneasy: *the dog seemed restless.* **2** without rest or sleep; not restful: *a restless night.* **3** rarely or never still or quiet; always moving. —**rest′less·ly,** *adv.* —**rest′less·ness,** *n.*

res·to·ra·tion (res′tə rā′shən), *n.* **1** restoring or being restored; bringing back to a former condition. **2** something restored.

the Restoration, a the reestablishment of the monarchy in 1660 under Charles II of England. **b** period from 1660 to 1688 in England during which Charles II and James II reigned.

re·stor·a·tive (ri stôr′ə tiv; –stōr′–), *adj.* capable of restoring; tending to restore health or strength. —*n.* something that does so.

re·store (ri stôr′; –stōr′), *v.,* **–stored, –stor·ing. 1** bring back; establish again: *restore order.* **2** bring back to a former condition or to a normal condition: *the old house has been restored.* **3** give back; put back: *restore stolen goods to the owner.* [< OF < L *restaurare*] —**re·stor′er,** *n.*

re·strain (ri strān′), *v.* **1** hold back; keep down; keep in check; keep within limits: *restrain your curiosity.* **2** keep in prison; confine. [< OF < L *restringere* RESTRICT] —**re·strain′a·ble,** *adj.* —**re·strain′ed·ly,** *adv.* —**re·strain′er,** *n.*

re·straint (ri strānt′), *n.* **1** a restraining or being restrained. **2** means of restraining. **3** tendency to restrain natural feeling; reserve.

re·strict (ri strikt′), *v.* keep within limits; confine: *restrict the membership to twelve.* [< L *restrictus* < *re–* back + *stringere* draw tight] —**re·strict′ed,** *adj.* —**re·strict′ed·ly,** *adv.*

re·stric·tion (ri strik′shən), *n.* **1** a restricting or being restricted. **2** something that restricts; limiting condition or rule: *restrictions on the use of the playground.*

restriction enzyme, enzyme that cuts strands of DNA at certain points into fragments that can be used to make recombinant DNA.

re·stric·tive (ri strik′tiv), *adj.* restricting; limiting. Some laws are prohibitive; some are only restrictive. —**re·stric′tive·ly,** *adv.*

rest·room (rest′rüm′) or **rest room,** lavatory in a public building.

re·sult (ri zult′), *n.* **1** that which happens because of something; what is caused: *the result of the fall was a broken leg.* **2** good or useful outcome: *we want results, not talk.* **3** quantity, value, etc., obtained by calculation. —*v.* **1** be a result; follow as a consequence: *sickness often results from getting too little sleep.* **2** have as a result; end: *too little sleep often results in sickness.* [< L *resultare* rebound, ult. < *re–* back + *salire* spring]

re·sult·ant (ri zul′tənt), *adj.* resulting. —*n.* result.

re·sume¹ (ri züm′), *v.,* **–sumed, –sum·ing. 1** begin again; go on: *resume reading where we left off.* **2** get or take again: *those standing may resume their seats.* [< L, < *re–* again + *sumere* take up] —**re·sum′a·ble,** *adj.* —**re·sum′er,** *n.*

res·u·me² or **rés·u·mé** (rez′ů mā′), *n.* summary, esp. of a person's education and work experience. [< F, orig. pp. of *résumer* resume]

re·sump·tion (ri zump′shən), *n.* a resuming: *the resumption of duties after absence.* —**re·sump′tive,** *adj.*

re·sur·gent (ri sèr′jənt), *adj.* rising or tending to rise again. —**re·sur′gence,** *n.*

res·ur·rect (rez′ə rekt′), *v.* **1** raise from the dead; bring back to life. **2** bring back to sight, use, etc.

res·ur·rec·tion (rez′ə rek′shən), *n.* **1** a coming to life again; rising from the dead. **2** a being alive again after death. **3** restoration from decay, disuse, etc.; revival.

the Resurrection, the rising of Christ after his death and burial. [< L *resurrectio,* ult. < *re–* again + *surgere* rise] —**res′ur·rec′tion·al,** *adj.*

re·sus·ci·tate (ri sus′ə tāt), *v.,* **–tat·ed, –tat·ing.** bring or come back to life or

consciousness; revive. [< L *resuscitatus,* ult. < *re–* again + *sub–* up + *citare* rouse] —**re·sus′ci·ta′tion,** *n.* —**re·sus′ci·ta′tive,** *adj.* —**re·sus′ci·ta′tor,** *n.*

re·tail (*n., adj., v.* **1** rē′tāl; *v.* **2** ri tāl′), *n.* sale of goods in small quantities at a time: *our grocer buys at wholesale and sells at retail.* —*adj.* of or engaged in selling in small quantities: *the retail trade, a retail merchant.* —*v.* **1** sell or be sold in small quantities. **2** tell over again: *retail gossip.* [< OF, scrap, ult. < *re–* back + *tailler* cut (see TALLY)] —**re′tail·er,** *n.*

re·tain (ri tān′), *v.* **1** continue to have or hold; keep: *china dishes retain heat longer than metal pans do.* **2** hold or keep in possession: *retain television rights.* **3** keep in mind; remember. **4** employ by payment of a fee: *he retained a lawyer.* [< OF < L, < *re–* back + *tenere* hold] —**re·tain′a·ble,** *adj.* —**re·tain′ment,** *n.*

re·tain·er¹ (ri tān′ər), *n.* person who serves a person of rank; vassal; attendant; follower.

re·tain·er² (ri tān′ər), *n.* fee paid to secure services. [< F *retenir,* n. use of inf., RETAIN]

re·take (*v.* ri tāk′; *n.* rē′tāk′), *v.,* **–took, –tak·en, –tak·ing,** —*v.* **1** take again. **2** take back. —*n.* a retaking of a scene in a film or of a photograph.

re·tal·i·ate (ri tal′i āt), *v.,* **–at·ed, –at·ing.** pay back wrong, injury, etc.; return like for like, usually to return evil for evil. [< L *retaliatus* < *re–* in return + *tal–* pay] —**re·tal′i·a′tion,** *n.* —**re·tal′i·a·to′ry, re·tal′i·a·tive,** *adj.*

re·tard (ri tärd′), *v.* make slow; delay the progress of; keep back; hinder: *bad roads retarded the car.* [< L, ult. < *re–* back + *tardus* slow] —**re′tar·da′tion,** *n.* —**re·tard′er,** *n.*

re·tard·ant (ri tär′dənt), *n.* something, esp. a chemical, that slows a process, action, etc.: *fabric treated with a flame retardant.* —*adj.* slowing; retarding.

re·tard·ed (ri tär′did), *adj.* slow in development; backward: *retarded in various ways.*

retch (rech), *v.* make efforts to vomit; make movements like those of vomiting. [OE *hrǣcan* clear the throat]

retd. or **ret′d., 1** retained. **2** returned.

re·ten·tion (ri ten′shən), *n.* **1** a retaining or being retained. **2** power to retain. **3** ability to remember.

re·ten·tive (ri ten′tiv), *adj.* **1** able to hold or keep. **2** able to remember. —**re·ten′tive·ly,** *adv.* —**re·ten′tive·ness, re′ten·tiv′i·ty,** *n.*

ret·i·cence (ret′ə səns), *n.* tendency to be silent or say little; reserve in speech. Also, **reticency.**

ret·i·cent (ret′ə sənt), *adj.* disposed to keep silent or say little; not speaking freely; reserved in speech. [< L *reticens* keeping silent < *re–* back + *tacere* be silent] —**ret′i·cent·ly,** *adv.*

re·tic·u·la·tion (ri tik′yə lā′shən), *n.* **1** a netlike formation, arrangement, or appearance; network. **2** one of the meshes of a network. [< L, ult. < *reticulum*, dim. of *rete* net]

re·tic·u·lum (ri tik'yə ləm), *n.*, *pl.* **-la** (-lə). **1** any system or structure like a network. **2** second stomach of a ruminant.

ret·i·na (ret'ə nə), *n.*, *pl.* **-nas, -nae** (-nē). layer of cells at the back of the eyeball that is sensitive to light and receives the images of things looked at. [< Med.L, < L *retinacula*, pl., band, reins] **—ret'i·nal,** *adj.*

ret·i·nue (ret'ə nü; -nū), *n.* group of attendants or retainers; following: *a king's retinue.* [< OF, orig. fem. pp. of *retenir* RETAIN]

re·tire (ri tīr'), *v.*, **-tired, -tir·ing. 1** give up an office, occupation, etc.: *our teachers retire at 65.* **2** remove from an office, occupation, etc.: *retire officers after a war.* **3** go away; retreat: *retire to the country, we retire early.* **4** withdraw (money) from circulation. **5** put out (a batter, side, etc.) in baseball. [< F, < *re-* back + *tirer* draw]

re·tired (ri tīrd'), *adj.* **1** withdrawn from one's occupation: *a retired sea captain.* **2** withdrawn in manner; shy. **3** secluded; shut off; hidden: *a retired location.*

re·tire·ment (ri tīr'mənt), *n.* **1** a retiring or being retired; withdrawal. **2** a quiet way or place of living: *she lives in retirement.*

re·tir·ing (ri tīr'ing), *adj.* shrinking from society or publicity; reserved; shy. **—re·tir'ing·ly,** *adv.* **—re·tir'ing·ness,** *n.*

re·tort[1] (ri tôrt'), *v.* **1** reply quickly or sharply. **2** return in kind; turn back on: *retort blow for blow.* **—n.** a sharp or witty reply. [< L *retortus* thrown back < *re-* back + *torquere* twist]

re·tort[2] (ri tôrt'; rē'tôrt), *n.* container used for distilling or decomposing substances by heat. [< Med.L *retorta*, orig. fem. pp. See RETORT[1].]

re·touch (rē tuch'), *v.* improve by new touches or slight changes.

re·trace (ri trās'), *v.*, **-traced, -trac·ing.** go back over: *we retraced our steps to where we started.* [< F, < *re-* back + *tracer* TRACE[1]] **—re·trace'a·ble,** *adj.*

re·trace (rē trās'), *v.*, **-traced, -trac·ing.** trace over again: *retrace these drawings.* **—re·trace'a·ble,** *adj.*

re·tract (ri trakt'), *v.* **1** draw back or in: *the dog snarled and retracted his lips.* **2** withdraw; take back: *retract an offer or an opinion.* [< L *retractare*, ult. < *re-* back + *trahere* draw] **—re·tract'a·ble,** *adj.* **—re·tract'a·bil'i·ty,** *n.* **—re·trac'tive,** *adj.* **—re·trac'tor,** *n.*

re·trac·ta·tion (rē'trak tā'shən), *n.* a retracting of a promise, statement, etc.

re·trac·tile (ri trak'təl), *adj.* capable of being drawn back or in. **—re'trac·til'i·ty,** *n.*

re·trac·tion (ri trak'shən), *n.* **1** a drawing or being drawn back or in. **2** withdrawal of a promise, statement, etc.

re·tread (*v.* rē tred'; *n.* rē'tred'), *v.*, **-tread·ed, -tread·ing,** *n.* **—v.** put a new tread on. **—n.** a retreaded tire.

re·treat (ri trēt'), *v.* **1** go or move back; withdraw. **2** make a forced withdrawal: *the enemy retreated before the advance of our soldiers.* **—n. 1** act of going back or withdrawing. **2** forced withdrawal, often in a hurried and disorderly manner. **3** signal for retreat: *the drums beat a retreat.* **4** signal on a bugle or drum, given in the army at sunset. **5** a safe, quiet place; place of rest or refuge. [< OF *retraite*, orig. pp. of *retraire* < L *retrahere* RETRACT]

re·trench (ri trench'), *v.* cut down or reduce (expenses, etc.): *we must retrench.* [< earlier F *retrencher.* See RE-, TRENCH.] **—re·trench'er,** *n.* **—re·trench'ment,** *n.*

ret·ri·bu·tion (ret'rə bū'shən), *n.* a deserved punishment; return for evil done, or sometimes for good done. [< L, ult. < *re-* back + *tribuere* assign] **—re·trib'u·tive, re·trib'u·to'ry,** *adj.* **—re·trib'u·tive·ly,** *adv.*

re·trieve (ri trēv'), *v.*, **-trieved, -triev·ing,** *n.* **—v. 1** get again; recover: *retrieve a lost pocketbook.* **2** bring back to a former or better condition; restore: *retrieve one's fortunes.* **3** make good; make amends for; repair: *retrieve a mistake.* **4** find and bring to a person: *a dog can be trained to retrieve game.* **—n.** act of retrieving; recovery; possibility of recovery. [< OF, < *re-* again + *trouver* find] **—re·triev'a·ble,** *adj.* **—re·triev'al,** *n.*

re·triev·er (ri trēv'ər), *n.* **1** one that retrieves. **2** dog trained to find killed or wounded game and bring it to a hunter.

ret·ro (ret'rō), *n.* revival of style, art, etc., from an earlier period: *the word for fashion is retro.* *adj.* of or characteristic of such a revival: *retro designs.*

retro-, *prefix.* backward; back; behind, as in *retrogress.* [< L, < *retro*, adv.]

ret·ro·ac·tive (ret'rō ak'tiv), *adj.* acting back; having an effect on what is past. A retroactive law applies to events that occurred before the law was passed. **—ret'ro·ac'tive·ly,** *adv.* **—ret'ro·ac·tiv'i·ty,** *n.*

ret·ro·fit (ret'rə fit'), *v.*, **-fit·ted, -fit·ting.** change by adding parts after something has already been made, esp. to bring to a higher standard. **—n.** a retrofitting of a machine or structure.

ret·ro·grade (ret'rə grād), *adv.*, *v.*, **-grad·ed, -grad·ing.** **—adj. 1** moving backward; retreating. **2** becoming worse. **—v. 1** move or go backward. **2** fall back toward a worse condition; grow worse; decline. [< L, ult. < *retro-* backward + *gradi* go]

ret·ro·gress (ret'rə gres; ret'rə gres'), *v.* **1** move backward; go back. **2** become worse. [< L *retrogressus*, pp. of *retrogradi.* See RETROGRADE.] **—ret'ro·gres'sion,** *n.* **—ret'ro·gres'sive,** *adj.* **—ret'ro·gres'sive·ly,** *adv.*

ret·ro·spect (ret'rə spekt), *n.* survey of past time, events, etc.; thinking about the past. **—v.** think of (something past).

in retrospect, when looking back. [ult. < L *retrospectus* < *retro-* back + *specere* to look] **—ret'ro·spec'tive·ly,** *adv.*

ret·ro·spec·tion (ret'rə spek'shən), *n.* a looking back on things, events, or experiences.

ret·ro·spec·tive (ret'rə spek'tiv), *adj.* **1** looking back on what is in the past. **2** applying to what is past; retroactive. **—n.** Also, **retrospective show.** exhibition of an artist's or a group of artists' works done over a long period of time.

ret·ro·vi·rus (ret'rō vī'rəs), *n.* any of a group of viruses that produce tumors and use RNA rather than DNA to carry genetic information. **—ret'ro·vi'ral,** *adj.*

re·turn (ri tèrn'), *v.* **1** go back; come back: *my brother will return this summer.* **2** bring, give, send, hit, put, or pay back: *return that book to the library.* **3** yield: *the concert returned about $50 over expenses.* **4** report or announce officially: *the jury returned a verdict of guilty.* **5** reply: *"No!" he returned crossly.* **6** elect to a lawmaking body. **—n. 1** a going or coming back; happening again. **2** thing returned. **3** a bringing, giving, sending, hitting, or putting back: *a poor return for kindness.* **4** Often, **returns.** profit; amount received. **5** report; account: *election returns.* **—adj. 1** of or pertaining to a return: *a return ticket.* **2** sent, given, done, etc., in return: *a return game.*

in return, as a return; to return something. [< OF *retourner.* See RE-, TURN.] **—re·turn'a·ble,** *adj.*

re·turn·ee (ri tèrn'ē'; ri tèrn'ē), *n.* person who has returned.

Reu·ben (rü'bən) or **Reuben sandwich,** sandwich made on rye bread with corned beef, melted Swiss cheese, sauerkraut, salad dressing, and served hot. [prob. < *Reuben's*, the name of a New York City sandwich shop]

re·un·ion (rē ūn'yən), *n.* **1** a coming together again. **2** a social gathering of persons who have been separated or who have interests in common.

re·u·nite (rē'ū nīt'), *v.*, **-nit·ed, -nit·ing.** bring or come together again. **—re'u·nit'a·ble,** *adj.* **—re'u·nit'er,** *n.*

re·up (rï up'), *v.*, **-upped, -up·ping.** reenlist in the armed services.

rev (rev), *n.*, *v.*, **revved, rev·ving. —n.** a revolution (of an engine or motor). **—v.** increase the speed of (an engine or motor).

rev., revised; revision.

Rev., 1 Revelation. **2** Reverend.

re·vamp (rē vamp'), *v.* patch up; repair.

re·veal (ri vēl'), *v.* **1** make known: *never reveal my secret.* **2** display; show. [< L, ult. < *re-* back + *velum* veil] **—re·veal'a·ble,** *adj.* **—re·veal'er,** *n.* **—re·veal'ment,** *n.*

rev·eil·le (rev'ə lē), *n.* a signal on a bugle or drum to waken soldiers or sailors in the morning. [< F *réveillez(-vous)* awaken!, ult. < L *re-* again + *ex-* up + *vigil* awake]

rev·el (rev'əl), *v.*, **-eled, -el·ing,** *n.* **—v. 1** take great pleasure (in): *the children revel in country life.* **2** make merry; take part in boisterous merrymaking. —*n.* a noisy good time; merrymaking: *the New Year's revels.* [< OF < L *rebellare.* Doublet of REBEL.] —**rev′el·er,** *n.*

rev·e·la·tion (rev′ə lā′shən), *n.* **1** act of making known. **2** the thing made known.

Revelation, often, **Revelations.** the last book of the New Testament.

rev·el·ry (rev′əl ri), *n., pl.* **-ries.** boisterous reveling or festivity; wild merrymaking.

re·venge (ri venj′), *n., v.,* **-venged, -venging.** —*n.* **1** harm done in return for a wrong; vengeance. **2** desire for vengeance. —*v.* do harm in return for.

be revenged or **revenge oneself,** get revenge. [< OF *revengier,* ult. < L *re-* back + *vindicare* avenge. See VINDICATE.] —**re·veng′er,** *n.*

re·venge·ful (ri venj′fəl), *adj.* feeling or showing a strong desire for revenge. —**re·venge′ful·ly,** *adv.* —**re·venge′ful·ness,** *n.*

rev·e·nue (rev′ə nü; -nū), *n.* **1** money coming in; income. **2** the income of a government from taxation, excise duties, customs, etc., appropriated to the payment of public expenses. [< F, orig. fem. pp. of *revenir* < L *re-* back + *venire* come]

rev·e·nu·er (rev′ə nü ər), *n.* revenue agent, esp. one who enforces the laws against smuggling or illegally making liquor.

re·ver·ber·ate (ri vèr′bər āt), *v.,* **-at·ed, -at·ing. 1** echo back. **2** cast or be cast back; reflect (light or heat). [< L *reverberatus* beaten back, ult. < *re-* back + *verber* a blow] —**re·ver′ber·a′tion,** *n.* —**re·ver′ber·a·to′ry,** *adj.*

re·vere (ri vir′), *v.,* **-vered, -ver·ing.** love and respect deeply; honor greatly; show reverence for. [< L, < *re-* back + *vereri* be awed]

rev·er·ence (rev′ər əns; rev′rəns), *n., v.,* **-enced, -enc·ing.** —*n.* **1** a feeling of deep respect, mixed with wonder, awe, and love. **2** a deep bow. —*v.* regard with reverence; revere.

rev·er·end (rev′ər ənd; rev′rənd), *adj.* worthy of great respect. —*n.* clergyman.

Reverend, title for clergymen. [< L *reverendus* to be respected. See REVERE[1].]

rev·er·ent (rev′ər ənt; rev′rənt), *adj.* feeling reverence; showing reverence. [< L *reverens* revering. See REVERE[1].] —**rev′er·ent·ly,** *adv.*

rev·er·en·tial (rev′ər en′shəl), *adj.* reverent. —**rev′er·en·tial·ly,** *adv.* —**rev′er·en′tial·ness,** *n.*

rev·er·ie (rev′ər i), *n.* dreamy thoughts; dreamy thinking of pleasant things: *indulge in reveries about the future.* Also, **revery.** [< F, < *rêver* to dream]

re·ver·sal (ri vèr′səl), *n.* change to the opposite; reversing or being reversed.

re·verse (ri vèrs′), *n., adj., v.,* **-versed, -vers·ing.** —*n.* **1** the opposite or contrary: *she did the reverse of what I*

ordered. **2** gear that reverses the movement of machinery. **3** a change to bad fortune; check; defeat: *unexpected reverses.* **4** the back: *the reverse of a medal.* —*adj.* **1** turned backward; opposite or contrary in position or direction: *the reverse side of a fabric.* **2** causing an opposite or backward movement. —*v.* **1** turn the other way; turn inside out; turn upside down: *reverse a piece to fit.* **2** change to the opposite: *reverse a vote.* **3** repeal; annul: *the court reversed its decree.* **4** cause to act in a backward or opposite direction: *reversed the car.* [< L *reversus,* pp. of *revertere* turn around. See REVERT.] —**re·verse′ly,** *adv.* —**re·vers′er,** *n.*

re·vers·i·ble (ri vèr′sə bəl), *adj.* **1** that can be reversed; that can reverse. **2** finished on both sides so that either can be used as the right side. —**re·vers′i·bil′i·ty, re·vers′i·ble·ness,** *n.* —**re·vers′i·bly,** *adv.*

re·ver·sion (ri vèr′zhən; -shən), *n.* **1** return to a former condition, practice, belief, etc.; return. **2** return of property to the grantor or his or her heirs. **3** right to possess a certain property under certain conditions. —**re·ver′sion·al,** *adj.* —**re·ver′sion·ar′y,** *adj.*

re·vert (ri vèrt′), *v.* **1** go back; return: *if a man dies without heirs, his property reverts to the state.* **2** go back to an earlier state of development. [< OF < L, < *re-* back + *vertere* turn] —**re·vert′i·ble,** *adj.*

rev·er·y (rev′ər i), *n., pl.* **-er·ies.** =reverie.

re·view (ri vū′), *v.* **1** study again; look at again: *he reviewed the scene of the crime.* **2** looked back on; examine again: *reviewed the day's events.* A superior court may review decisions of a lower court. **3** inspect formally: *the President reviewed the fleet.* **4** examine to give an account of: *Mr. Brown reviews books for a living.* —*n.* **1** a studying again. **2** a looking back on; survey. **3** reexamination of the decision or proceedings in a case. **4** an examination or inspection, esp. a formal inspection of military or naval forces. **5** account of a book, play, etc., giving its merits and faults. **6** magazine containing articles on subjects of current interest, including accounts of books, etc.: *a law review, a movie review.* **7** =revue. [< F *revue,* orig. pp., seen again, ult. < L *re-* again + *videre* see] —**re·view′a·ble,** *adj.*

re·view·er (ri vū′ər), *n.* **1** person who reviews. **2** person who writes articles discussing books, plays, etc.

re·vile (ri vīl′), *v.,* **-viled, -vil·ing.** heap reproaches on; abuse with words. [< OF *reviler* despise < *re-* again + *vil* VILE] —**re·vile′ment,** *n.* —**re·vil′er,** *n.* —**re·vil′ing·ly,** *adv.*

re·vise (ri vīz′), *v.,* **-vised, -vis·ing,** *n.* —*v.* **1** read carefully in order to correct; look over and change; examine and improve. **2** change; alter. —*n.* **1** process of revising. **2** a revised form or version. [< F

reviser, ult. < L *re-* again + *videre* see] —**re·vis′er,** *n.*

Revised Standard Version, American Protestant revision of the Bible, completed in 1952.

Revised Version, the revised form of the Authorized Version (King James) of the Bible (1881, 1885).

re·vi·sion (ri vizh′ən), *n.* **1** act or work of revising: *a revision of taxes.* **2** a revised form: *a revision of his book.* —**re·vi′sion·al,** *adj.* —**re·vi′sion·ism,** *n.*

re·vi·sion·ist (ri vizh′ə nist), *n.* one who favors or supports revision.

re·vi·tal·ize (rē vī′tə līz), *v.,* **-ized, -iz·ing.** bring new life or vitality to. —**re·vi′tal·i·za′tion,** *n.*

re·viv·al (ri vīv′əl), *n.* **1** a bringing or coming back to life or consciousness. **2** restoration to vigor or health. **3** a bringing or coming back to style, use, activity, etc. **4** an awakening or increase of interest in religion. **5** Also, **revival meeting.** special services or efforts made to awaken or increase interest in religion.

re·viv·al·ist (ri vīv′əl ist), *n.* person who holds special services to awaken interest in religion. —**re·viv′al·ism,** *n.*

re·vive (ri vīv′), *v.,* **-vived, -viv·ing. 1** bring back or come back to life or consciousness: *revive a half-drowned person.* **2** bring or come back to a fresh, lively condition: *flowers revive in water.* **3** make or become fresh; restore: *hot coffee revived the cold, tired man.* **4** bring back or come back to notice, use, fashion, memory, activity, etc.: *an old play is sometimes revived on the stage.* [< L, < *re-* again + *vivere* live] —**re·viv′er,** *n.*

re·viv·i·fy (rē viv′ə fī), *v.,* **-fied, -fy·ing.** restore to life; give new life to. —**re·viv′i·fi·ca′tion,** *n.* —**re·viv′i·fi′er,** *n.*

rev·o·ca·ble (rev′ə kə bəl), *adj.* that can be repealed, canceled, or withdrawn. —**rev′o·ca·bil′i·ty,** *n.* —**rev′o·ca·bly,** *adv.*

rev·o·ca·tion (rev′ə kā′shən), *n.* repeal; canceling; withdrawal.

rev·o·ca·to·ry (rev′ə kə tô′ri; -tō′-), *adj.* revoking; recalling; repealing.

re·voke (ri vōk′), *v.,* **-voked, -vok·ing.** *n.* —*v.* take back; repeal; cancel; withdraw: *the king revoked his decree.* [< L, < *re-* back + *vocare* call] —**re·vok′er,** *n.*

re·volt (ri vōlt′), *n.* act or state of rebelling: *the fleet was already in revolt.* —*v.* **1** turn away from and fight against a leader; rise against the government's authority: *the people revolted against the dictator.* **2** turn away with disgust: *revolt at a bad smell.* **3** cause to feel disgust. [< F < Ital. *rivolta,* ult. < L *revolvere* REVOLVE] —**re·volt′er,** *n.*

re·volt·ing (ri vōl′ting), *adj.* disgusting; repulsive. —**re·volt′ing·ly,** *adv.*

rev·o·lu·tion (rev′ə lü′shən), *n.* **1** a complete overthrow of an established government or political system. **2** a complete change: *the automobile caused a revolution in ways of traveling.* **3**

movement, real or apparent, in a circle or curve around some point: *one revolution of the earth around the sun takes a year.* **4** act or fact of turning round a center or axis; rotation: *the revolution of the earth causes day and night.* **5** time or distance of one revolution. **6** a complete cycle or series of events: *the revolution of the four seasons fills a year.* [< L *revolutio* < *revolvere* REVOLVE]

rev·o·lu·tion·ar·y (rev´ə lü′shən er´i), *adj., n., pl.* **-ar·ies.** —*adj.* **1** of or connected with a revolution. **2** bringing or causing great changes. —*n.* =revolutionist.

Revolutionary, of or having to do with the American Revolution, or those who fought in it.

Revolutionary War, =American Revolution.

rev·o·lu·tion·ist (rev´ə lü′shən ist), *n.* person who advocates, or takes part in, a revolution.

rev·o·lu·tion·ize (rev´ə lü′shən īz), *v.,* **-ized, -iz·ing. 1** cause a revolution in the government of. **2** change completely; produce a very great change in.

re·volve (ri volv′), *v.,* **-volved, -volv·ing. 1** move in a circle; move in a curve round a point: *the moon revolves around the earth.* **2** turn round a center or axis; rotate: *the wheels of a moving car revolve.* **3** turn over in the mind; consider from many points of view. [< L, < *re–* back + *volvere* roll] —**re·volv′a·ble,** *adj.* —**re·volv′ing,** *adj.*

re·volv·er (ri vol′vər), *n.* pistol that can be fired several times without loading it again.

re·vue (ri vū′), *n.* a theatrical entertainment with singing, dancing, parodies of recent plays, humorous treatments of happenings and fads of the year, etc. [< F. See REVIEW.]

re·vul·sion (ri vul′shən), *n.* a sudden, violent change or reaction. [< L *revulsio,* ult. < *re–* back + *vellere* tear away]

re·ward (ri wôrd′), *n.* **1** return made for something done. **2** a money payment given or offered for the detection or capture of offenders against the law, the return of lost property, etc. —*v.* **1** give a reward to: *reward a person for his services.* **2** give a reward for: *reward his past services liberally.* **3** be a reward for: *the good results rewarded him for his efforts.* [< var. of OF *regarder* REGARD] —**re·ward′a·ble,** *adj.* —**re·ward′er,** *n.*

Rey·kja·vík (rā′kyə vēk´), *n.* capital and seaport of Iceland, in the SW part.

R.F., r.f., radio frequency.

R.F.D., Rural Free Delivery.

Rh, rhodium.

rhap·sod·ic (rap sod′ik), **rhap·sod·i·cal** (–ə kəl), *adj.* of or characteristic of rhapsody; extravagantly enthusiastic; ecstatic.

rhap·so·dize (rap′sə dīz), *v.,* **-dized, -diz·ing.** talk or write with extravagant enthusiasm.

rhap·so·dy (rap′sə di), *n., pl.* **-dies. 1** utterance or writing marked by extravagant enthusiasm. **2** an instrumental composition irregular in form. [< L < Gk. *rhapsoidia* verse-composition, ult. < *rhaptein* to stitch] —**rhap′so·dist,** *n.*

rhe·a (rē′ə), *n.* any of several large birds of South America that are much like the ostrich, but are smaller and have three toes instead of two.

Rhen·ish (ren′ish), *adj.* of the river Rhine or the regions near it. —*n.* Rhine wine.

rhe·ni·um (rē′ni əm), *n.* a rare, hard, grayish metallic element, Re, that has chemical properties similar to those of manganese. [< L *Rhenus* Rhine]

rhe·o·stat (rē′ə stat), *n.* instrument for regulating the strength of an electric current by introducing different amounts of resistance into the circuit. [< Gk. *rheos* current + *statos* standing still] —**rhe′o·stat′ic,** *adj.*

rhe·sus (rē′səs), *n.* a small, yellowish-brown monkey with a short tail, found in India. [from a character in the *Iliad*]

Rhe·sus factor (rē′səs), Rh factor.

rhet·o·ric (ret′ə rik), *n.* **1** art of using words in speaking or writing. **2** book about this art. **3** mere display in language. [< L < Gk. *rhetorike (techne)* art of an orator]

rhe·tor·i·cal (ri tôr′ə kəl; –tor′–), *adj.* **1** of or pertaining to rhetoric. **2** using rhetoric. **3** intended especially for display; artificial. —**rhe·tor′i·cal·ly,** *adv.*

rhetorical question, question asked only for effect, not for information.

rhet·o·ri·cian (ret´ə rish′ən), *n.* person skilled in rhetoric.

rheum (rüm), *n.* a watery discharge, such as mucus, tears, or saliva. [< OF < L < Gk. *rheuma* a flowing < *rheein* to flow] —**rheum′y,** *adj.*

rheu·mat·ic (rü mat′ik), *adj.* **1** of rheumatism. **2** having rheumatism; liable to have rheumatism. —*n.* person who has rheumatism.

rheumatic fever, an acute disease that often has very harmful aftereffects.

rheu·ma·tism (rü′mə tiz əm), *n.* disease with inflammation, swelling, and stiffness of the joints. [< L < Gk., ult. < *rheuma* RHEUM]

Rh factor, antigen found in the red blood cells of most human beings and the higher mammals. Blood containing this substance (**Rh positive**) does not combine favorably with blood lacking it (**Rh negative**). [< *rh*esus monkey (it was first discovered in its blood)]

rhi·nal (rī′nəl), *adj.* of or pertaining to the nose; nasal.

rhine·stone (rīn′stōn´), *n.* an imitation diamond, made of glass. [trans. of F *caillou du Rhin*]

Rhine wine, wine, usually a white wine, produced in the valley of the Rhine.

rhi·ni·tis (rī nī′tis), *n.* inflammation of the nose or its mucous membrane. [< NL, < Gk. *rhis* nose]

rhi·no (rī′nō), *n., pl.* **-nos** or **-no.** *Informal.* rhinoceros.

rhi·noc·er·os (rī nos′ər əs), *n., pl.* **-os·es** or (*esp. collectively*) **-os.** a large, thick-skinned animal of Africa and Asia with one or two upright horns on the snout. [< L < Gk. *rhinokeros,* ult. < *rhis* nose + *keras* horn]

rhi·zome (rī′zōm), *n.* a rootlike stem lying along or under the ground, which usually produces roots below and shoots from the upper surface; rootstock. [< Gk., ult. < *rhiza* root]

rho (rō), *n.* the 17th letter of the Greek alphabet (P, ρ).

Rhode Island (rōd), a New England state of the United States. —**Rhode Islander.**

rho·di·um (rō′di əm), *n.* a grayish-white metallic element, Rh, forming salts that give rose-colored solutions. [< Gk. *rhodon* rose]

rho·do·den·dron (rō´də den′drən), *n.* an evergreen shrub somewhat like an azalea with beautiful pink, purple, or white flowers. [< NL < Gk., < *rhodon* rose + *dendron* tree]

rhom·boid (rom′boid), *n.* parallelogram with equal opposite sides that is not a rectangle. —*adj.* Also, **rhom·boi′dal.** shaped like a rhombus or rhomboid.

rhom·bus (rom′bəs), *n., pl.* **rhom·bus·es.** parallelogram with equal sides, having two obtuse angles and two acute angles; diamond. [< L < Gk. *rhombos*] —**rhom′bic,** *adj.*

rhu·barb (rü′bärb), *n.* **1** a garden plant with very large leaves, whose sour stalks are used for making sauce, pies, etc. **2** the stalks. **3** the sauce made of them. **4** a heated dispute, often of no importance and usually marked by derisive comment. [< OF]

rhyme (rīm), *v.,* **rhymed, rhym·ing,** *n.* —*v.* **1** sound alike in the last part. *Long* and *song* rhyme. *Go to bed* rhymes with *sleepy head.* **2** put or make into rhyme: *rhyme a translation.* **3** make rhymes. **4** use (a word) with another that rhymes with it: *rhyme "love" and "dove."* —*n.* **1** agreement in the final sounds of words or lines. **2** word or line having the same last sound as another. *Cat* is a rhyme for *mat.* **3** verses or poetry with a regular return of similar sounds

without rhyme or reason, having no system or sense. [< OF < L < Gk. *rhythmos* rhythm. Doublet of RHYTHM.] —**rhym′er,** *n.*

rhyme·ster (rīm′stər), *n.* maker of rather poor rhymes or verse.

rhythm (riṯẖ′əm), *n.* **1** movement with a regular repetition of a beat, accent, rise and fall, or the like: *the rhythm of dancing, the rhythm of the tides, the rhythm of one's heartbeats.* **2** repetition of an accent; arrangement of beats in a line of poetry. **3** grouping by accents or beats: *triple rhythm.* [< L < Gk. *rhythmos* < *rheein* to flow. Doublet of RHYME.]

rhythm and blues, popular music combining a strong beat with elements of the blues.

rhyth·mi·cal (riᵗʰ′mə kəl), **rhyth·mic** (–mik), *adj.* having rhythm; of or pertaining to rhythm. —**rhyth′mi·cal·ly,** *adv.*

RI, (*zip code*) Rhode Island.

R.I., Rhode Island.

ri·al (rī′əl), *n.* an Iranian silver coin and unit of money.

ri·al·to (ri al′tō), *n., pl.* **-tos.** marketplace or exchange. [< It.]

Ri·al·to (ri al′tō), *n.* **1** former business district of Venice. **2** famous bridge in Venice that crosses the Grand Canal. **3** a theater district, esp. on Broadway in New York City.

rib (rib), *n., v.,* **ribbed, rib·bing.** —*n.* **1** one of the curved bones extending from the backbone and enclosing the upper part of the body. **2** cut of meat containing a rib. **3** piece that forms a frame. An umbrella has ribs. **4** a thick vein of a leaf. **5** ridge in cloth, knitting, etc. —*v.* **1** furnish or strengthen with ribs. **2** mark with riblike ridges. **3** tease; mock. [OE *ribb*] —**ribbed,** *adj.*

rib·ald (rib′əld), *adj.* offensive in speech; coarsely mocking. —*n.* a ribald person. [< OF *ribauld,* ult. < MDu. *ribe* prostitute]

rib·ald·ry (rib′əld ri), *n.* ribald language.

rib·bon (rib′ən), *n.* **1** strip or band of silk, satin, velvet, etc. **2** a narrow strip of cloth: *torn to ribbons.* **3** band charged with ink for use in a typewriter. **4** a long, narrow strip of anything. —*v.* **1** adorn with ribbons. **2** separate into ribbons. [< OF *ruban* < Gmc.] —**rib′boned,** *adj.*

rib·cage (rib′kāj′), *n.* framework of the chest formed by the ribs.

ri·bo·fla·vin (rī′bō flā′vin), *n.* constituent of the vitamin B complex, $C_{17}H_{20}N_4O_6$, present in liver, eggs, milk, spinach, etc.; lactoflavin; vitamin B_2; vitamin G. [< *ribose* (ult. < *gum arabic*) + L *flavus* yellow]

ri·bo·nu·cle·ic acid (rī′bō nü klē′ik; –nyü–), chains of ribose, posphoric acid, and chemical bases, found in all living cells, important in making proteins and in the transmission of genetic information; RNA.

ri·bo·some (rī′bə sōm), *n.* granular particle made up of mostly ribonucleic acid and found in the cytoplasm of cells, responsible for the synthesis of proteins and enzymes. [< *ribo*nucleic acid + –*some* body]

rice (rīs), *n., v.,* **riced, ric·ing.** —*n.* **1** the starchy seeds or grain of a plant grown in warm climates. Rice is an important food in India, China, and Japan. **2** the plant itself. —*v.* reduce to a form like rice: *rice potatoes.* [< OF < Ital., ult. < Gk. *oryza* < Iranian]

rice paper, a thin paper made from the straw of rice.

ric·er (rīs′ər), *n.* utensil for ricing cooked potatoes, etc., by pressing them through small holes.

rich (rich), *adj.* **1** having much money or property: *a rich man.* **2** abundantly supplied with resources: *the United States is rich in oil and coal.* **3** abundant: *a rich harvest.* **4** producing or yielding abundantly; fertile: *rich soil, a rich mine.* **5** valuable; costly; elegant: *rich dress.* **6** having many desirable elements or qualities, esp. containing plenty of butter, eggs, flavoring, etc. **7** (of colors, sounds, smells, etc.) deep; full; vivid. **8** amusing; ridiculous; absurd. —*n.pl.* **the rich,** rich people.

strike it rich, *Informal. Fig.* have sudden, great success. [< OE *rīce* < Celtic] —**rich′ly,** *adv.* —**rich′ness,** *n.*

rich·es (rich′iz), *n.pl.* wealth; abundance of property; much money, land, goods, etc. [< OF *richesse* < *riche* rich < Gmc. See RICH.]

Rich·mond (rich′mənd), *n.* capital of Virginia.

Rich·ter scale (rik′tər), scale that indicates the size of earthquakes, for example, 1.5 measuring a minor earthquake and 8 to 8.9 measuring an earthquake of major destructiveness. [< Charles Francis *Richter,* 1900–85, American seismologist who developed it]

rick (rik), *n.* stack of hay, straw, etc., esp. one made so that the rain will run off it. —*v.* form into a rick or ricks. [OE *hrēac*]

rick·ets (rik′its), *n.* disease of childhood, caused by lack of vitamin D or calcium, that results in softening, and sometimes bending, of the bones; rachitis. [appar. alter. of *rachitis;* infl. by *wrick* wrench, strain]

rick·etts·ia (ri ket′sē ə), *n.* microorganisms found in the tissues of arthropods, and sometimes transmitted to humans, that cause diseases such as typhus. [< Howard T. *Ricketts,* 1871–1910, pathologist who studied them]

rick·et·y (rik′it i), *adj.* liable to fall or break down; shaky: *a rickety old chair.* **2** joints. —**rick′et·i·ness,** *n.*

rick·shaw (rik′shô), *n.* =jinrikisha.

ric·o·chet (rik′ə shā′), *n., v.,* **-cheted** (–shād′), **-chet·ing** (–shā′ing). —*n.* the skipping or jumping motion of an object as it goes along a flat surface. —*v.* move in this way. [< F]

rid (rid), *v.,* **rid** or **rid·ded, rid·ding.** make free (from): *what will rid a house of rats?*

be rid of, be freed from.

get rid of, a get free from. **b** do away with. [OE *(ge)ryddan* to clear land] —**rid′der,** *n.*

rid·dance (rid′əns), *n.* a clearing away or out; removal.

rid·dle¹ (rid′əl), *n., v.,* **-dled, -dling.** —*n.* **1** a puzzling question, statement, problem, etc. *Example:* When is a door not a door? *Answer:* When it is ajar. **2** person or thing that is hard to understand, explain, etc. —*v.* speak in riddles. [OE *rǣdels* < *rǣdan* guess, explain; ME *redels*

taken as pl.] —**rid′dler,** *n.* —**rid′dling·ly,** *adv.*

rid·dle² (rid′əl), *v.,* **-dled, -dling.** make many holes in: *the door of the fort was riddled with bullets.* [OE *hriddel* sieve]

ride (rīd), *v.,* **rode, rid·den** (rid′ən), **rid·ing,** *n.* —*v.* **1** sit on and manage a horse, camel, bicycle, etc.: *he rides every morning, ride a bicycle.* **2** admit of being ridden: *a horse that rides easily.* **3** be carried along in or by anything: *ride on a train.* **4** ride over, along, or through (a road, boundary, region, etc.). **5** be carried on; move on; float: *the eagle rides on the winds; the ship rides at anchor in the harbor.* **6** control, dominate, or tyrannize over: *be ridden by foolish fears.* —*n.* a trip on the back of a horse, in a carriage, car, train, boat, etc.

hitch a ride, get a free ride.

let ride, not meddle with; not disturb.

ride high, do well; enjoy success.

ride out, a withstand (a gale, etc.) without damage. **b** endure successfully: *ride out a crisis.*

ride up, move up from the proper position: *that coat rides up at the back.*

take for a ride, cheat. [OE *rīdan*] —**ride′a·ble,** *adj.*

rid·er (rīd′ər), *n.* **1** person who rides. **2** anything added to a record, document, legislative bill, or statement after it was supposed to be completed. —**rid′er·less,** *adj.*

ridge (rij), *n., v.,* **ridged, ridg·ing.** —*n.* **1** the long and narrow upper part of something: *the ridge of an animal's back.* **2** line where two sloping surfaces meet: *the ridge of a roof.* **3** a long, narrow chain of hills or mountains: *the Blue Ridge of the Appalachian Mountains.* **4** any raised narrow strip: *the ridges on corduroy cloth.* —*v.* **1** form or make into ridges. **2** cover or mark with ridges. [OE *hrycg*] —**ridg′y,** *adj.*

ridge·pole (rij′pōl′), *n.* the horizontal timber along the top of a roof or tent.

rid·i·cule (rid′ə kūl), *v.,* **-culed, -cul·ing,** *n.* —*v.* laugh at; make fun of. —*n.* laughter in mockery; words or actions that make fun of somebody or something. [< F < L *ridiculum,* neut. adj., RIDICULOUS] —**rid′i·cul′er,** *n.*

ri·dic·u·lous (ri dik′yə ləs), *adj.* deserving ridicule; absurd; laughable. [< L *ridiculus* < *ridere* to laugh] —**ri·dic′u·lous·ly,** *adv.* —**ri·dic′u·lous·ness,** *n.*

rife (rīf), *adj.* **1** happening often; numerous; widespread. **2** full; abounding: *the land was rife with rumors of war.* [OE *rīfe*] —**rife′ness,** *n.*

riff (rif), *n.* **1** improvisations on a melodic theme or phrase by individual musicians in a jazz performance. **2** a stage routine or bit of business. —*v.* perform riffs.

rif·fle (rif′əl), *n., v.,* **-fled, -fling.** —*n.* **1** a rapid. **2** a ripple. **3** act of shuffling cards. —*v.* shuffle (cards) by bending the edges slightly so that the two divisions of the deck slide into each other.

riff·raff (rif′raf′), *n.* **1** worthless people. **2** trash. —*adj.* worthless. [< OF *rif et raf* every scrap < *rifler* RIFLE² + *raffler* carry off (see RAFFLE)]

ri·fle¹ (rī′fəl), *n., v.,* **–fled, –fling.** —*n.* **1** gun with spiral grooves in its barrel to spin the bullet as it is fired. **2** such a gun that is fired from the shoulder. —*v.* cut spiral grooves in (a gun). [ult. < F *rifler* to scratch, groove, RIFLE²]

ri·fle² (rī′fəl), *v.,* **–fled, –fling. 1** search and rob; ransack and rob. **2** steal; take away. **3** strip bare. [< OF *rifler* < Gmc.] —**ri′fler,** *n.*

ri·fle·man (rī′fəl mən), *n., pl.* **–men. 1** soldier armed with a rifle. **2** man who uses a rifle.

ri·fle·ry (rī′fəl rī), *n.* **1** shooting a rifle esp. as an art or sport. **2** firing from rifles: *the occasional crack of riflery.*

ri·fling (rī′fling), *n.* **1** act or process of cutting spiral grooves in a gun barrel. **2** system of spiral grooves in a rifle.

rift (rift), *n., v.* split; break; crack. [< Scand. *ript*] —**rift′y,** *adj.*

rig (rig), *v.,* **rigged, rig·ging,** *n.* —*v.* **1** get ready for use. **2** put together in a hurry or by using odds and ends. **3** arrange dishonestly for one's own advantage. **4** equip; fit out. **5** equip (a ship) with masts, sails, ropes, etc. **6** move (a shroud, boom, stay, etc.) to its proper place. —*n.* **1** outfit; equipment: *an oil rig.* **2** arrangement of masts, sails, ropes, etc., on a ship. A schooner has a fore-and-aft rig. [< Scand. (Dan.) *rigge*] —**rigged,** *adj.* —**rig′ger,** *n.*

Ri·ga (rē′gə), *n.* capital of Latvia, on the Baltic Sea.

rig·ging (rig′ing), *n.* **1** ropes, chains, etc., used to support and work the masts, yards, sails, etc., on a ship. **2** tackle; equipment.

right (rīt), *adj.* **1** correct; true: *the right answer.* **2** proper; fitting: *say the right thing.* **3** good; just; lawful: *right conduct.* **4** healthy; normal: *be in one's right senses.* **5** meant to be seen; most important: *the right side of cloth.* **6** opposite of left; belonging or pertaining to the side of anything which is turned east when the main side is turned north: *one's right hand or right glove.* —*adv.* **1** correctly: *she guessed right.* **2** favorably; in good or suitable condition: *turn out right, put things right.* **3** in a way that is just or lawful: *it serves you right to lose if you cheat.* **4** to the right hand: *turn right.* **5** exactly; just; precisely: *put it right here.* **6** at once; immediately: *stop playing right away.* **7** in a straight line; directly: *look me right in the eye.* **8** completely: *his hat was knocked right off.* —*n.* **1** that which is right: *know the difference between right and wrong.* **2** a just claim, title, or privilege: *the right to vote.* **3** fair treatment; justice: *equal treatment is a matter of right.* **4** blow struck with the right hand. **5** the right side or what is on the right side. **6** Also **Right.** politcially

conservative or reactionary; not liberal. —*v.* **1** make correct: *right errors.* **2** put in order: *right a room.* **3** do justice to: *right the oppressed.* **4** get or put into proper position: *the ship righted as the wave passed.*

by right or **by rights,** justly; properly: *the payment is mine by rights.*

in the right, right: *which side is in the right?*

right along, a without stopping: *move right along.* **b** without difficulty: *her recovery moved right along.*

right and left, from all sides: *criticism right and left.*

right away or **off,** immediately.

right on, *Informal.* exactly right; correct.

rights, a civil rights. **b** share in a property.

the Right, often **the right,** part of a law-making body, made up of conservative or reactionary political groups, that sits on the right of the presiding officer.

to rights, in or into proper condition, order, etc.: *put a closet to rights.* [OE *riht*] —**right′a·ble,** *adj.* —**right′less,** *adj.* —**right′ly,** *adv.* —**right′ness,** *n.*

right angle, angle of 90 degrees.

right-an·gled (rīt′ang′gəld), *adj.* containing a right angle or right angles; rectangular.

right·eous (rī′chəs), *adj.* **1** doing right; virtuous; behaving justly. **2** morally right or justifiable: *righteous indignation.* —**right′eous·ly,** *adv.* —**right′eous·ness,** *n.*

right field, 1 the outfield beyond first base. **2** position of a baseball player in this part of the field.

right·ful (rīt′fəl), *adj.* **1** according to law; by rights: *the rightful owner of this dog.* **2** just and right; proper. *one's rightful position.* —**right′ful·ly,** *adv.* —**right′ful·ness,** *n.*

right-hand (rīt′hand′), *adj.* **1** on or to the right. **2** of, for, or with the right hand. **3** most helpful or useful.

right-hand·ed (rīt′han′did), *adj.* **1** using the right hand more easily and readily than the left. **2** done with the right hand. **3** made to be used with the right hand. **4** turning from left to right: *a right-handed screw.* —**right′-hand′ed·ness,** *n.*

right·ist (rīt′ist), *n.* person who has conservative or reactionary ideas in politics. —*adj.* having conservative or reactionary ideas in politics.

right-mind·ed (rīt′mīn′did), *adj.* having right opinions or principles.

right of way, 1 right to go first; precedence over all others. **2** right to pass over property belonging to someone else. **3** strip of land on which a railroad, power line, etc., is built.

right-to-die (rīt′tə dī′), *adj.* opposed to extreme measures to keep a person alive who cannot recover from an illness or injury.

right-to-life (rīt′tə līf′), *adj.* opposed to legal abortion.

right triangle, triangle one of whose angles is a right angle.

right·ward (rīt′wərd), *adv., adj.* to or toward the right. Also, **rightwards.**

right wing, the conservative or reactionary members, as of a political party. —**right′-wing′,** *adj.* —**right′-wing′er,** *n.*

rig·id (rij′id), *adj.* **1** stiff; firm; not bending: *a rigid support.* **2** inflexible; strict; not changing: *rigid rules.* **3** severely exact; rigorous: *a rigid examination.* [< L *rigidus* < *rigere* be stiff] —**ri·gid′i·ty, rig′id·ness,** *n.* —**rig′id·ly,** *adv.*

rig·ma·role (rig′mə rōl), *n.* foolish talk; words without meaning; nonsense. [earlier *ragman roll* < *ragman* list + *roll*]

rig·or (rig′ər), *n.* **1** strictness; severity; harshness: *the rigors of a long, cold winter.* **2** stiffness; rigidity. [< OF < L, < *rigere* be stiff]

rig·or mor·tis (rig′ər môr′tis), the stiffening of the muscles after death. [< L, stiffness of death]

rig·or·ous (rig′ər əs), *adj.* **1** very severe; harsh; strict: *the rigorous discipline in a prison.* **2** thoroughly logical and scientific; exact: *the rigorous methods of science.* —**rig′or·ous·ly,** *adv.* —**rig′or·ous·ness,** *n.*

rile (rīl), *v.,* **riled, ril·ing. 1** irritate; vex. **2** make (water) muddy. [var. of *roil*]

rill (ril), *n.* a tiny stream; little brook. [cf. Du *ril* groove, furrow]

rim (rim), *n., v.,* **rimmed, rim·ming.** —*n.* an edge, border, or margin on or around anything: *the rim of a wheel.* —*v.* form or put a rim around. [OE *rima*] —**rim′less,** *adj.* —**rimmed,** *adj.*

rime¹ (rīm), *v.,* **rimed, rim·ing,** *n.* =rhyme. —**rim′er,** *n.*

rime² (rīm), *n., v.,* **rimed, rim·ing.** —*n.* white frost; hoarfrost. —*v.* cover with rime. [OE *hrīm*] —**rim′y,** *adj.*

rime·ster (rīm′stər), *n.* =rhymester.

rind (rīnd), *n.* the firm outer covering (of fruits, plants, cheeses, etc.). [OE]

ring¹ (ring), *n., v.,* **ringed, ring·ing.** —*n.* **1** circle: *dance in a ring.* **2** a thin circle of metal or other material: *a napkin ring.* **3** the outer edge or border of a coin, plate, wheel, or layer of wood produced yearly in a tree trunk. **4** an enclosed space for races, games, circus performances, etc. The ring for a prize fight is square. **5** group of people combined for a selfish or bad purpose. —*v.* **1** put a ring around; enclose. **2** provide with or form a ring. **3** cut away the bark in a ring around a tree or branch. [OE *hring*] —**ringed,** *adj.* —**ring′er,** *n.*

ring² (ring), *v.,* **rang, rung, ring·ing,** *n.* —*v.* **1** give forth a clear sound: *ring the bell.* **2** make (a sound) by ringing: *the bells rang a joyous peal.* **3** announce or proclaim; repeat: *ring a person's praises.* **4** resound; sound: *the room rang with shouts of laughter, his words rang true.* **5** have a sensation as of sounds of bells:

my ears ring. **6** call on the telephone. —*n.* **1** act of ringing. **2** sound of a bell or like a bell. **3** a characteristic sound or quality, indicating genuineness or the reverse.

run rings around, easily beat; easily do much better than. [OE *hringan*] —**ring′er,** *n.*

ring·lead·er (ring′lēd′ər), *n.* person who leads others in opposition to authority or law.

ring·let (ring′lit), *n.* **1** a little ring. **2** curl: *wear hair in ringlets.* —**ring′let·ed,** *adj.*

ring·mas·ter (ring′mas′tər; –mäs′–), *n.* person in charge of the performances in the ring of a circus.

ring·side (ring′sīd′), *n.* **1** place just outside the ring at a circus, prize fight, etc. **2** place affording a close view.

ring·worm (ring′wėrm′), *n.* a contagious skin disease, caused by parasites and characterized by ring-shaped patches.

rink (ringk), *n.* **1** sheet of ice for skating. **2** a smooth floor for roller skating. [< Scotch < OF *renc* course, RANK[1]]

rink·y-dink (ring′ki dingk′), *adj.* cheap; out-of-date; commonplace.

rinse (rins), *v.,* **rinsed, rins·ing,** *n.* —*v.* **1** wash with clean water: *rinse the soap out of your hair.* **2** wash lightly: *rinse your mouth with salt water.* —*n.* a rinsing. [< OF *reincer,* ult. < L *recens* fresh] —**rins′er,** *n.*

ri·ot (rī′ət), *n.* **1** disturbance of the peace by an unlawful assembly of persons: *a march that became a riot.* **2** wild disorder; violent confusion. **3** loose living; wild reveling. **4** bright display: *the garden was a riot of color.* —*v.* **1** behave in a wild, disorderly way. **2** revel.

read the riot act, give orders for disturbance to cease.

run riot, a act without restraint. **b** grow wildly or luxuriantly. [< OF *riote* dispute, ult. < L *rugire* to roar] —**ri′ot·er,** *n.*

ri·ot·ous (rī′ət əs), *adj.* **1** taking part in a riot. **2** boisterous; disorderly: *riotous conduct, riotous glee.* —**ri′ot·ous·ly,** *adv.* —**ri′ot·ous·ness,** *n.*

rip[1] (rip), *v.,* **ripped, rip·ping,** *n.* —*v.* **1** cut roughly; tear apart; tear off: *rip the cover off this box.* **2** cut or pull out (the threads in the seams of a garment). **3** saw (wood) along the grain, not across the grain. **4** move fast or violently. —*n.* a torn place; seam burst in a garment. [ME *rippe(n)*] —**rip′per,** *n.*

rip[2] (rip), *n.* **1** stretch of rough water made by cross currents meeting. **2** a swift current made by the tide. [? special use of *rip*[1]]

R.I.P., may he or she (they) rest in peace. [< L < *Requiescat (requiescant) in pace*]

ri·par·i·an (ri pãr′i ən; rī–), *adj.* of or on the bank of a river, a lake, etc.: *riparian rights.* [< L, < *ripa* riverbank]

rip cord, cord that opens a parachute.

ripe (rīp), *adj.,* **rip·er, rip·est. 1** fullgrown and ready to be gathered and eaten: *ripe fruit.* **2** fully developed and fit

to use: *ripe knowledge.* **3** ready: *ripe for mischief.* **4** advanced in years. [OE *rīpe*] —**ripe′ly,** *adv.* —**ripe′ness,** *n.*

rip·en (rīp′ən), *v.* become or make ripe. —**rip′en·er,** *n.*

rip·ple (rip′əl), *n., v.,* **-pled, -pling.** —*n.* **1** a very little wave. **2** anything that seems like a tiny wave: *ripples in sand.* **3** sound that reminds one of little waves: *a ripple of laughter.* —*v.* **1** make a sound like rippling water. **2** form or have ripples. **3** make little ripples on. —**rip′pler,** *n.* —**rip′pling,** *adj.* —**rip′pling·ly,** *adv.* —**rip′ply,** *adj.*

rip-roar·ing (rip′rôr′ing; –rōr′–), *adj. Informal.* hilarious; uproarious.

rip·saw (rip′sô′), *n.* saw for cutting wood along the grain, not across the grain.

rise (rīz), *v.,* **rose, ris·en** (riz′ən), **ris·ing,** *n.* —*v.* **1** get up from sleep, rest, or a position of lying, sitting, or kneeling: *rise from a chair, rise at dawn.* **2** go, come, move, or extend up: *fog rises from a river, the tower rises 60 feet, hills rise in the distance, yeast makes dough rise.* **3** go higher; increase: *prices are rising.* **4** advance to a higher level of action, thought, feeling, expression, rank, position, etc.: *he rose from errand boy to president.* **5** become louder or of higher pitch. **6** come into being or action: *the wind rose; quarrels often rise from trifles.* **7** become more animated or more cheerful: *his spirits rose.* **8** revolt; rebel. —*n.* **1** an upward movement; ascent: *the rise of a balloon.* **2** an upward slope or high ground; hill. **3** increase. **4** advance in rank, power, etc. **5** origin; beginning: *rise of a stream in a mountain.*

give rise to, start; begin; cause; bring about.

rise to, be equal to; be able to deal with: *they rose to the occasion.* [OE *rīsan*]

ris·er (rīz′ər), *n.* **1** person or thing that rises: *an early riser.* **2** the vertical part of a step.

ris·ing (rīz′ing), *n.* **1** act of one that rises. **2** revolt. **3** something that rises; prominence. —*adj.* **1** that rises. **2** advancing to adult years: *the rising generation.*

risk (risk), *n.* **1** chance of harm or loss; danger. **2** person or thing with reference to the chance of loss from insuring him, her, or it. —*v.* **1** expose to the chance of harm or loss: *a soldier risks his life.* **2** take the risk of: *they risked getting wet.* [< F *risque* < Ital., *risicare* to dare] —**risk′er,** *n.*

risk·y (ris′ki), *adj.,* **risk·i·er, risk·i·est. 1** full of risk; dangerous. **2** somewhat improper; risqué. —**risk′i·ly,** *adv.* —**risk′i·ness,** *n.*

ri·sot·to (ri sōt′tō), *n.* Italian dish made of rice cooked with broth, cheese, poultry, or seafood. [< It.]

ris·qué (ris kā′), *adj.* suggestive of indecency; somewhat improper. [< F, pp. of *risquer* to RISK]

rit. or **ritard.,** ritardando.

ri·tar·dan·do (ri′tär dän′dō), *adv., adj.* gradually slower in tempo. —*n.* a gradually slowing tempo. [< It.]

rite (rīt), *n.* **1** a solemn ceremony. The church has rites for baptism, marriage, and burial. **2** any customary ceremony or observance. **3** a particular form or system of ceremonies. [< L *ritus*] —**rite′less,** *adj.*

rit·u·al (rich′ü əl), *n.* **1** form or system of rites. The rites of baptism, marriage, and burial are parts of the ritual of the church. **2** book containing rites or ceremonies. **3** the carrying out of rites. —*adj.* of rites; done as a rite: *ritual laws, a ritual dance.* [< L, < *ritus* rite] —**rit′u·al·ly,** *adv.*

rit·u·al·ism (rich′ü əl iz′əm), *n.* **1** fondness for ritual; insistence upon ritual. **2** study of ritual practices or religious rites. —**rit′u·al·ist,** *n.* —**rit′u·al·is′tic,** *adj.* —**rit′u·al·is′ti·cal·ly,** *adv.*

ri·val (rī′vəl), *n., adj., v.,* **-valed, -val·ing.** —*n.* **1** person who wants and tries to get the same thing as another; one who tries to equal or do better than another. **2** thing that will bear comparison with something else; equal; match. —*adj.* wanting the same thing as another; being a rival. —*v.* **1** try to equal or outdo. **2** engage in rivalry; compete. **3** equal; match. [< L *rivalis* using the same stream < *rivus* stream] —**ri′val·less,** *adj.*

ri·val·ry (rī′vəl ri), *n., pl.* **-ries.** action, position, or relation of a rival or rivals; competition.

riv·en (riv′ən), *adj.* torn apart; split. [< Scand. *rifa*]

riv·er (riv′ər), *n.* **1** a large natural stream of water. **2** any abundant stream or flow. [< OF *rivere* < L *riparius* of a riverbank < *ripa* bank] —**riv′ered,** *adj.* —**riv′er·less,** *adj.*

riv·er·head (riv′ər hed′), *n.* source of a river.

riv·er·side (riv′ər sīd′), *n.* bank of a river. —*adj.* on the bank of a river: *a riverside path.*

riv·et (riv′it), *n.* a metal bolt with each end hammered into a head. Rivets fasten heavy steel beams together. —*v.* **1** fasten with a rivet or rivets. **2** fasten firmly; fix firmly. [< OF, < *river* fix < VL *ripare* come to shore < L *ripa* bank] —**riv′et·er,** *n.*

riv·u·let (riv′yə lit), *n.* a very small stream. [< Ital. *rivoletto,* ult. < L *rivus* stream]

rm., *pl.* **rms. 1** ream. **2** room.

Rn, radon.

R.N., 1 registered nurse. **2** Royal Navy.

RNA or **rna,** ribonucleic acid.

roach[1] (rōch), *n.* =cockroach. [short for *cockroach*]

roach[2] (rōch), *n., pl.* **roach·es** or (*esp. collectively*) **roach. 1** a European freshwater fish related to the carp. **2** any of various similar fishes, such as the American sunfish. [< OF *roche*]

road (rōd), *n.* **1** highway between places; way made for trucks or automobiles to travel on. **2** way or course. **3** =railroad. **4** Also, **roadstead.** place near the shore where ships can ride at anchor.

on the road, a on tour, as a theater company or orchestra. **b** traveling, esp. as a salesperson. [OE *rād* a riding] **—road′less,** *adj.*

road·bed (rōd′bed′), *n.* foundation of a road or of a railroad.

road·block (rōd′blok), *n.* an obstacle.

road runner, a long-tailed bird of the deserts of the SW United States, related to the cuckoo.

road·side (rōd′sīd′), *n.* side of a road. **—adj.** beside a road.

road·way (rōd′wā′), *n.* road.

roam (rōm), *v.* go about with no special plan or aim; wander: *roam through the fields.* **—n.** a walk with no special aim; wandering. [ME *rome(n)*] **—roam′er,** *n.*

roam·ing (rōm′ing), *n.* the shift from one cell phone provider to another when a signal is weak or overwhelmed by the volume of calls.

roan (rōn), *adj.* yellowish- or reddish-brown sprinkled with gray or white. **—n.** a roan horse. [< F < Sp. *roano*]

roar (rôr; rōr), *v.* **1** make a loud, deep sound; make a loud noise: *a lion roars.* **2** utter loudly: *roar out a command.* **3** make or put by roaring: *the crowd roared itself hoarse.* **4** laugh loudly. **5** move with a roar: *the train roared past us.* **—n.** a loud, deep sound; loud noise. [OE *rārian*] **—roar′er,** *n.*

roast (rōst), *v.* **1** cook by dry heat; cook before a fire; bake. **2** prepare by heating: *roast coffee, roast a metal ore.* **3** make or become very hot. **4** be baked. **5** *Informal.* make fun of; ridicule. **—n.** piece of roasted meat; piece of meat to be roasted. **—adj.** roasted: *roast beef.* [< OF *rostir* < Gmc.]

roast·er (rōs′tər), *n.* **1** pan used in roasting. **2** chicken, young pig, etc., fit to be roasted. **3** person or thing that roasts.

rob (rob), *v.*, **robbed, rob·bing.** take away from by force or threats; steal from; steal. [< OF *robber* < Gmc.] **—rob′ber,** *n.*

robber baron, person who acquires great wealth and power by unscrupulous or ruthless business practices, esp. of the late 1800s.

rob·ber·y (rob′ər i; rob′ri), *n., pl.* **–ber·ies.** act of robbing.

robe (rōb), *n., v.,* **robed, rob·ing. —n. 1** a long, loose outer garment. **2** garment that shows rank, office, etc.: *a judge's robe.* **3** a covering or wrap. **—v.** put a robe on; dress. [< OF, orig., plunder, booty. Cf. ROB.] **—robed,** *adj.*

rob·in (rob′ən), *n.* **1** a large American thrush with a reddish breast. **2** a small European bird with a yellowish-red breast. [< OF, dim. of *Robert*]

rob·in's-egg blue (rob′ənz eg′), greenish blue.

ro·bot (rō′bət; rob′ət), *n.* **1** machine that imitates some human abilities; mechanical device that does work in response to commands. **2** *Fig.* person who acts or works in a dull, mechanical way. [invented by Karel Capek for his play, *R.U.R.*; suggested by Czech *robota* work, *robotnik* serf]

ro·bot·ics (rō bot′iks), *n.* science or technology of robots, esp. their design and use.

ro·bust (rō bust′; rō′bust), *adj.* **1** strong and healthy; sturdy; vigorous: *a robust person, a robust mind.* **2** suited to or requiring bodily strength: *robust exercises.* **3** rough; rude. [< L *robustus,* orig., oaken < *robur* oak] **—ro·bust′ly,** *adv.* **—ro·bust′ness,** *n.*

rock¹ (rok), *n.* **1** a large mass of stone. **2** any piece of stone; a stone. **3 a** the mass of mineral matter of which the earth's crust is made up. **b** a particular layer or kind of such matter. **4** *Fig.* something like a rock: *Mother was the rock of the family.* **—adj.** made of rock.

on the rocks, a wrecked; ruined. **b** bankrupt. [< OF *roque* < VL *rocca*]

rock² (rok), *v.* **1** move backward or forward, or from side to side; sway. **2** put (to sleep, rest, etc.) with swaying movements. **3** move or sway violently with emotion. **—n.** a rocking movement. [OE *roccian*]

rock·a·bil·ly (rok′əbil′i), *n.* rock'n'roll music with a hillbilly influence.

rock-and-roll (rok′ən rōl′), *n.* =rock'n' roll.

rock bottom, the very bottom; lowest level.

rock-bot·tom (rok′bot′əm), *adj.* down to the very bottom; very lowest.

rock-bound (rok′bound′), *adj.* surrounded by rocks; rocky.

rock candy, sugar in the form of large, hard crystals.

rock crystal, a colorless, transparent variety of quartz that is often used for jewelry, ornaments, etc.

rock·er (rok′ər), *n.* **1** one of the curved pieces on which a cradle, rocking chair, etc., rocks. **2** a rocking chair. **3** any of various devices that operate with a rocking motion. **4** rock'n'roll singer or musician.

rock·et (rok′it), *n.* a self-propelling device operating by means of gases escaping from a nozzle or jet at the rear of a combustion chamber. The rocket principle is used in some types of projectiles and the driving power in many aircraft.

rock·et·ry (rok′ət ri), *n.* **1** the science of designing and firing rockets or missiles. **2** rockets collectively: *long-range rocketry.*

rock garden, garden with flowers planted among rocks.

rocking chair, chair mounted on rockers, or on springs, so that it can rock back and forth.

rocking horse, toy horse on rockers for a child to ride.

rock'n'roll (rok′ən rōl′), *n.* popular music with a simple melody and strong bass and beat, derived from jazz, blues, and folk music.

rock-ribbed (rok′ribd′), *adj.* **1** having ridges of rock. **2** unyielding.

rock salt, salt in large crystals.

rock·y¹ (rok′i), *adj.,* **rock·i·er, rock·i·est. 1** full of rocks. **2** made of rock. **3** like rock; hard; firm.

rock·y² (rok′i), *adj.,* **rock·i·er, rock·i·est. 1** likely to rock; shaky. **2** unpleasantly uncertain. **3** sickish; weak; dizzy. **—rock′i·ness,** *n.*

Rocky Mountain goat, the white antelope of the Rocky Mountains.

ro·co·co (rō kō′kō; rō′kə kō′), *n.* style of architecture and decoration with elaborate ornamentation, combining shellwork, scrolls, foliage, etc., much used in the first half of the 18th century. **—adj.** of or pertaining to this style. [< F, ? < *rocaille* shellwork]

rod (rod), *n.* **1** a thin, straight bar of metal or wood. **2** anything like a rod in shape. **3** a stick used to beat or punish. **4** fishing rod. **5** a measure of length; 5½ yards or 16½ feet. A square rod is 30¼ square yards or 272¼ square feet. **6** *Slang.* pistol.

spare the rod, fail to punish. [OE *rodd*]

rode (rōd), *v.* pt. of **ride.**

ro·dent (rō′dənt), *n.* any of a group of mammals having teeth especially adapted for gnawing wood and similar material. Rats, mice, and squirrels are rodents. **—adj.** of or like a rodent. [< L *rodens* gnawing]

ro·de·o (rō′di ō; rō dā′ō), *n., pl.* **–de·os.** contest or exhibition of skill in roping cattle, riding horses, etc. [< Sp., < *rodear* go around]

roe¹ (rō), *n.* **1** fish eggs. **2** the spawn of various crustaceans. [ME *rowe*]

roe² (rō), *n., pl.* **roes** or (*esp. collectively*) **roe.** a small deer of Europe and Asia, with forked antlers. [OE *rā*]

roe·buck (rō′buk′), *n.* a male roe deer.

roent·gen (rent′gən), *n.* international unit for measuring the intensity of X rays and gamma rays. [see ROENTGEN RAYS]

Roent·gen rays (rent′gən), =X rays. [after W. K. *Roentgen,* physicist]

rog·er (roj′ər), *interj.* U.S. OK; message received and understood. [from the signaler's word for the letter *r,* for "received"]

rogue (rōg), *n.* **1** a tricky, dishonest, or worthless person; cheat; rascal. **2** a mischievous person. **3** animal with a savage nature that lives apart from the herd. [? short for earlier *roger* beggar]

ro·guer·y (rō′gər i), *n., pl.* **–guer·ies. 1** conduct of rogues; dishonest trickery. **2** playful mischief.

rogues' gallery, 1 collection of photographs of known criminals. **2** *Fig.* any collection of pictures of people, as of family members.

ro·guish (rō′gish), *adj.* **1** dishonest; rascally. **2** playfully mischievous. **—ro′guish·ly,** *adv.* **—ro′guish·ness,** *n.*

roil (roil), v. 1 make (water, etc.) muddy by stirring up sediment. 2 disturb; irritate; vex. [< earlier F *ruiler* mix mortar, ult. < L *regula* rule] —**roil'y,** *adj.*

role (rōl), n. 1 an actor's part in a play: *the leading role.* 2 part played in real life. [< F, the roll (of paper, etc.) on which a part is written]

roll (rōl), v. 1 move by turning over and over: *a ball rolls.* 2 wrap around on itself or on some other thing: *roll the string into a ball.* 3 move or be moved on wheels: *the car rolled along.* 4 move smoothly; sweep along: *the years roll on.* 5 move from side to side: *the ship rolled in the waves.* 6 rise and fall in gentle slopes: *rolling country.* 7 make flat or smooth with a roller; spread out with a rolling pin, etc. 8 make deep, loud sounds: *thunder rolls.* 9 beat (a drum) with rapid continuous strokes. 10 *Slang.* rob (a person). 11 utter with a trill: *roll one's r's.* 12 have more than enough: *be rolling in money.* —n. 1 something rolled up; cylinder formed by rolling: *a roll of carpet.* 2 continued motion up and down, or from side to side. 3 rapid continuous beating on a drum. 4 a deep, loud sound: *the roll of thunder.* 5 act of rolling. 6 motion like that of waves; undulation: *the roll of a prairie.* 7 record; list; list of names: *call the roll.* 8 kind of bread or cake.

on a roll, *Informal.* experiencing a period of great success or intense activity.

roll back, return prices, wages, etc., to an earlier, lower level.

roll up, increase; pile up or become piled up. [< OF *roller,* ult. < L *rota* wheel] —**roll'a·ble,** *adj.*

roll·bar (rōl'bär'), or **roll bar,** n. strong overhead bar to protect passengers or the driver of a vehicle if it rolls over.

roll call, the calling of a list of names, as of soldiers, pupils, etc., to find out who are present.

roll·er (rōl'ər), n. thing that rolls; cylinder on which something is rolled along or rolled up or used for smoothing, pressing, crushing, etc.

roll·er·blade (rō'lər blād'), v., **-blad·ed, -blad·ing.** skate on inline skates. —n. 1 =inline skate. 2 **Rollerblade.** trademark for this type of roller skate. —**roll'er·blad'er, Roll'er·blad'er,** n.

roller coaster, railway for amusement, consisting of inclined tracks along which small cars roll, bump, etc.

roller skate, a skate with small wheels instead of a runner, for use on a floor or sidewalk.

roll·er·skate (rōl'ər skāt'), v., **-skat·ed, -skat·ing.** move on roller skates.

rol·lick·ing (rol'ik ing), **rol·lick·some** (-səm), *adj.* frolicking; jolly; merry; lively.

roll·ing (rōl'ing), n. action, motion, or sound of anything that rolls or is being rolled: *the rolling of a ball, the rolling of*

thunder. —*adj.* 1 that rolls. 2 of land, rising and falling in gentle slopes.

rolling pin, cylinder of wood or glass for rolling out dough.

roll·o·ver (rōl'ō'vər), n. 1 an overturning of a vehicle. 2 extension of time for repayment of a loan.

ro·ly-po·ly (rō'li pō'li), *adj., n., pl.* **-lies.** —*adj.* short and plump. —n. a short, plump person or animal. [appar. < *roll*]

Rom., 1 Roman. 2 Romania; Romanian. 3 Romanic. 4 *Bible.* Romans. 5 Romany.

ROM (rom), n. read-only memory (in a computer, data that can be read but not manipulated).

Ro·ma·ic (rō mā'ik), n. the everyday speech of modern Greece. —*adj.* of or pertaining to this speech.

ro·maine (rō mān'), n. variety of lettuce having long green leaves with crinkly edges, which are joined loosely at the base, [< F, fem. adj., Roman]

Ro·man (rō'mən), *adj.* 1 of or pertaining to Rome or its people. 2 of or pertaining to the Roman Catholic Church. 3 **roman,** of or in roman type. —n. 1 native, inhabitant, or citizen of Rome. 2 a Roman Catholic. 3 **roman,** style of type most used in printing and typewriting.

Roman candle, kind of firework consisting of a tube that shoots out balls of fire, etc.

Roman Catholic, 1 of, pertaining to, or belonging to the Christian church that recognizes the Pope as the supreme head. 2 member of this church. —**Roman Catholicism.**

ro·mance (n. rō mans', rō'mans; v. rō mans'), n., v., **-manced, -manc·ing.** —n. 1 a love story. 2 story or poem telling of heroes, love, colorful adventures, or noble deeds: *the romances about King Arthur and his knights.* 3 romantic character, quality, or spirit. 4 a love affair. —v. 1 think or talk in a romantic way. 2 exaggerate; lie. [ult. < OF *romanz,* ult. < VL *romanice* in a Romance language < L *Romanus* Roman < *Roma* Rome] —**ro·manc'er,** n.

Romance languages, French, Italian, Spanish, Portuguese, Romanian, Provençal, and other languages that came from Latin, the language of the Romans.

Roman Empire, empire of ancient Rome that lasted from 27 B.C. to A.D. 395.

Ro·man·esque (rō'mən esk'), n. style of architecture using round arches and vaults, popular in Europe during the early Middle Ages, between the periods of Roman and Gothic architecture. —*adj.* of, in, or having to do with this style of architecture.

Ro·ma·ni·a (rō mā'niə; –mān'yə), n. country in S Europe.

Ro·ma·ni·an (rō mā'ni ən; –mān'yən), *adj.* of or having to do with Romania, its inhabitants, or language. —n. 1 native or inhabitant of Romania. 2 language of Romania.

Ro·man·ic (rō man'ik), *adj.* derived from Latin. French, Italian, and Spanish are Romanic languages; Romance languages. —n. a Romanic language.

Ro·man·ize (rō'mən īz), v., **-ized, -iz·ing.** 1 make or become Roman in character. 2 make or become Roman Catholic. —**Ro'man·i·za'tion,** n.

Roman numerals, numerals like XXIII, LVI, and MDCCLX, in which I = 1, V = 5, X = 10, L = 50, C = 100, D = 500, and M = 1000.

Ro·ma·no (rō mä'nō), Italian cheese that is hard and dry and has a sharp, salty taste. [< It.]

Ro·mans (rō'mənz), n. book of the New Testament, an epistle written by Saint Paul to the Christians of Rome.

ro·man·tic (rō man'tik), *adj.* 1 characteristic of romances or romance; appealing to fancy and the imagination: *romantic tales of love and war.* 2 having ideas or feelings suited to romance: *a romantic schoolgirl.* 3 romance. 4 fond of making up fanciful stories. —n. a romantic person. [< F *romantique* < earlier *romant* a ROMANCE] —**ro·man'ti·cal·ly,** *adv.*

ro·man·ti·cism (rō man'tə siz əm), n. 1 romantic spirit or tendency. 2 the romantic tendency in literature and art. —**ro·man'ti·cist,** n.

Rom·a·ny (rom'ə ni), n., pl. **-nies,** *adj.* —n. 1 a person belonging to a group of wandering people, originally from India and now living around the world; Gypsy. b the Romany as a group. 2 the Indic language of the Romany. —*adj.* belonging or pertaining to the Romany, their customs, or their language.

Rom. Cath., Roman Catholic.

Rome (rōm), n. capital of Italy, on the Tiber River.

romp (romp), v. play in a rough, boisterous way; rush, tumble, and punch in play. —n. a rough, lively play or frolic. [ult. var. of *ramp,* v.] —**romp'er,** n. —**romp'ish,** *adj.* —**romp'ish·ness,** n.

romp·ers (romp'ərz), n., pl. one-piece garment with short pants like bloomers, worn by infants and very young children.

ron·do (ron'dō; ron dō'), n., pl. **-dos.** a work or movement having one principal theme to which return is made after the introduction of each subordinate theme.

rood (rüd), n. 1 crucifix. 2 40 square rods; one fourth of an acre. [OE *rōd*]

roof (rüf; rüf), n. 1 the top covering of a building. 2 something like it: *the roof of a cave, of a car, of the mouth, etc.* —v. cover with a roof; form a roof over.

raise the roof, *Informal.* a cause an uproar or confusion. b complain noisily (about something). go through or hit the roof, *Informal.* become very angry. [OE *hrōf*] —**roof'er,** n. —**roof'less,** *adj.*

roof·ing (rüf'ing; rüf'–), n. 1 act of covering with a roof. 2 material used for roofs, as shingles.

rook[1] (rúk), *n.* a European crow that often nests in trees near buildings. [OE *hrōc*]

rook[2] (rúk), *n.* one of the pieces with which the game of chess is played; castle. [< OF, ult. < Pers. *rukh*]

rook·er·y (rúk′ər i), *n., pl.* **-er·ies.** a breeding place of rooks; colony of rooks.

rook·ie (rúk′i), *n.* **1** an inexperienced recruit. **2** beginner; novice.

room (rüm; rúm), *n.* **1** a part of a house, or other building, with walls separating it from the rest of the building of which it is a part. **2** space occupied by, or available for, something: *there is little room to move in a crowd.* **3** opportunity: *room for improvement.* —*v.* **1** occupy a room; lodge. **2** provide with a room.
rooms, lodgings. [OE *rūm*]

room·er (rüm′ər; rúm′–), *n.* person who lives in a rented room or rooms in another's house; lodger.

room·ful (rüm′fúl; rúm′–), *n., pl,* **-fuls.** enough to fill a room.

rooming house, house with rooms to rent.

room·mate (rüm′māt′; rúm′–), *n.* person who shares a room with another or others.

room·y (rüm′i; rúm′–), *adj.,* **room·i·er, room·i·est.** having plenty of room; large; spacious. —**room′i·ly,** *adv.* —**room′i·ness,** *n.*

Roo·se·velt (rō′zə velt), *n.* **1 Franklin Delano,** 1882–1945, the 32nd president of the United States, 1933–45. **2 Theodore,** 1858–1919, the 26th president of the United States, 1901–09.

roost (rüst), *n.* **1** bar, pole, or perch on which birds rest or sleep. **2** place for birds to roost in. —*v.* sit as birds do on a roost; settle for the night.
come home to roost, backfire; come back to bother or annoy the person originally responsible for an act or remark.
rule the roost, be master. [OE *hrōst*]

roost·er (rüs′tər), *n.* a male domestic fowl.

root[1] (rüt; rút), *n.* **1** part of a plant that grows downward, to hold the plant in place and absorb water and mineral foods from the soil. **2** any underground part of a plant. **3** something like a root in shape, position, use, etc.: *the root of a tooth, the roots of the hair.* **4** thing from which other things grow and develop; cause; source: *"The love of money is the root of all evil."* **5** quantity that produces another quantity when multiplied by itself a certain number of times. 2 is the square root of 4. —*v.* **1** send out roots and begin to grow; become fixed in the ground: *some plants root quickly.* **2** fix firmly: *rooted to the spot by surprise.* **3** pull, tear, or dig (up, out, etc.) by the roots; get completely rid of.
take root, a send out roots and begin to grow. **b** *Fig.* become firmly fixed or established. [< Scand. *rōt*] —**root′less,** *adj.* —**root′y,** *adj.*

root[2] (rüt; rút), *v.* **1** dig with the snout, as swine do. **2** poke; pry; search. [OE *wrōtan*] —**root′er,** *n.*

root[3] (rüt; rút), *v.* cheer or support a contestant, etc., enthusiastically. [prob. < earlier *rout* to shout, roar < Scand. *rauta*] —**root′er,** *n.*

root beer, a soft drink made from the juice of the roots of certain plants, such as sarsaparilla, sassafras, etc.

root canal, 1 narrow tube in the root of a tooth through which blood vessels and nerves pass to the pulp. **2** dental procedure to clean out infection or decayed material in a canal.

root·ed (rüt′id; rút′–), *adj.* **1** having roots. **2** *Fig.* having taken root; firmly implanted: *a rooted belief.* —**root′ed·ly,** *adv.* —**root′ed·ness,** *n.*

root hair, a hairlike outgrowth from a root that absorbs water and dissolved minerals from the soil.

root·less (rüt′lis; rút′–), *adj.* **1** having no roots. **2** *Fig.* not fixed or established; not having family ties.

root·stock (rüt′stok; rút′–), *n.* =rhizome.

rope (rōp), *n., v.,* **roped, rop·ing.** —*n.* **1** a strong, thick line or cord made by twisting smaller cords together. **2** *W.* lasso. **3** number of things twisted or strung together: *a rope of pearls.* **4** a sticky, stringy mass. —*v.* **1** tie, bind, or fasten with a rope. **2** catch (a horse, calf, etc.) with a lasso.
at the end of one's rope, at the end of one's resources; desperate.
know the ropes, a know about the various ropes of a ship. **b** know about a business or activity.
rope in, *Informal.* get or lead in by tricking. [OE *rāp*]

rop·y (rōp′i), *adj.,* **rop·i·er, rop·i·est. 1** forming sticky threads; stringy: *a ropy syrup.* **2** like a rope or ropes. —**rop′i·ly,** *adv.* —**rop′i·ness,** *n.*

Roque·fort (rōk′fərt), *n.* a strongly flavored French cheese made of goats' milk, veined with mold.

Ror·schach test (rôr′shäk), a psychological test based on the subject's interpretation of different ink blot designs.

ro·sa·ry (rō′zə ri), *n., pl.* **-ries. 1** string of beads for keeping count in saying a series of prayers. **2** a series of prayers. [< Med.L *rosarium* < L, rose garden, ult. < *rosa* rose[1]]

rose[1] (rōz), *n.* **1** flower that grows on a bush with thorny stems. Roses are red, pink, white, or yellow and usually smell very sweet. **2** the bush itself. **3** any of various related or similar plants or flowers. **4** a pinkish-red color. —*adj.* pinkish-red. [< L *rosa*]

rose[2] (rōz), *v.* pt. of **rise.**

rose beetle, beetle destructive to roses.

rose·bud (rōz′bud′), *n.* bud of a rose.

rose·bush (rōz′búsh′), *n.* shrub or vine bearing roses.

rose·col·ored (rōz′kul′ərd), *adj.* **1** pinkish-red. **2** optimistic.

rose·mar·y (rōz′mār′i), *n., pl.* **-mar·ies.** an evergreen shrub whose leaves yield a fragrant oil used in making perfume. [< L *ros maris,* lit., dew of the sea; assoc. with *rose* and *Mary*]

rose of Sharon, shrub with bright flowers; althea.

ro·se·o·la (rō zē′ə lə), *n.* **1** mild, childhood disease characterized by a rash and fever. **2** =German measles.

ro·sette (rō zet′), *n.* ornament, object, or arrangement shaped like a rose. Rosettes are often made of ribbon. Carved or molded rosettes are used in architecture. [< F, dim. of *rose* ROSE[1]]

rose water, water made fragrant with oil of roses.

rose window, an ornamental circular window, esp. one with a pattern of small sections that radiate from a center.

rose·wood (rōz′wúd′), *n.* **1** a beautiful reddish wood used in fine furniture. **2** the tropical tree that it comes from.

Rosh Ha·sha·na (rosh′ hə shä′nə; rōsh′), the Jewish New Year.

ros·in (roz′ən), *n.* a hard, yellow substance that remains when turpentine is evaporated from pine resin. Rosin is rubbed on violin bows and on the shoes of acrobats to keep them from slipping. —*v.* cover or rub with rosin. [var. of *resin*]

ros·ter (rōs′tər), *n.* **1** list giving each person's name and duties. **2** any list. [< Du. *rooster*]

ros·trum (ros′trəm), *n., pl.* **-trums, -tra** (–trə). platform for public speaking. [< L, beak, < *rodere* gnaw; with ref. to the speakers' platform in the Roman forum, which was decorated with the beaks of captured war galleys] —**ros′tral,** *adj.*

ros·y (rōz′i), *adj.,* **ros·i·er, ros·i·est. 1** like a rose; rose-red; pinkish-red. **2** made of roses. **3** bright; cheerful. —**ros′i·ly,** *adv.* —**ros′i·ness,** *n.*

rot (rot), *v.,* **rot·ted, rot·ting,** *n.* —*v.* decay; spoil. —*n.* **1** process of rotting; decay. **2** rotten matter. **3** a disease of plants and animals, esp. of sheep. **4** *Fig.* become corrupted; decay. [OE *rotian*]

ro·ta·ry (rō′tə ri), *adj.* **1** turning like a top or a wheel; rotating. **2** having parts that rotate. —*n.* **1** =traffic circle. **2** rotary engine or machine.

rotary engine, engine in which the pistons, armiture, etc., rotate, rather than moving in a straight line.

ro·tate (rō′tāt), *v.,* **-tat·ed, -tat·ing. 1** move around a center or axis; turn in a circle; revolve. Wheels, tops, and the earth rotate. **2** change in a regular order; take turns or cause to take turns: *farmers rotate crops.* [< L *rotatus < rota* wheel] —**ro′tat·a·ble,** *adj.* —**ro′tat·a·bly,** *adv.* —**ro′ta·tive,** *adj.* —**ro′ta·tor,** *n.*

ro·ta·tion (rō tā′shən), *n.* **1** act or process of moving around a center or axis; turning in a circle; revolving. **2** change in a regular order.

in rotation, in turn; in regular succession. —**ro·ta′tion·al, ro′ta·to′ry,** *adj.*

R.O.T.C., Reserve Officers' Training Corps.

rote (rōt), *n.* a set, mechanical way of doing things.

by rote, by memory without thought of the meaning.

ro·tor (rō′tər), *n.* the rotating part of a machine or apparatus, esp. the blades of a helicopter. [short for *rotator*]

ro·to·till·er (rō′tə til′ər), *n.* motorized rotary tiller or cultivator. [< E *rotary* + *tiller*] —**ro′to·till′,** *v.*

rot·ten (rot′ən), *adj.* **1** decayed; spoiled: *a rotten egg.* **2** foul; bad-smelling: *rotten air.* **3** not in good condition; unsound; weak: *rotten ice.* **4** corrupt; dishonest. **5** bad; nasty. [< Scand. *rotinn*] —**rot′ten·ly,** *adv.* —**rot′ten·ness,** *n.*

ro·tund (rō tund′), *adj.* **1** round; plump: *a rotund face.* **2** sounding rich and full; full-toned: *a rotund voice.* [< L *rotundus,* ult. < *rota* wheel. Doublet of ROUND.] —**ro·tun′di·ty, ro·tund′ness,** *n.* —**ro·tund′ly,** *adv.*

ro·tun·da (rō tun′də), *n.* a circular building or part of a building, esp. one with a dome. [< L, fem. adj. See ROTUND.]

rou·é (rü ā′; rü′ā), *n.* a dissipated man; rake. [< F, orig. pp. of *rouer* break on the wheel; first applied to 18th-century group of profligates]

rouge (rüzh), *n.* **1** a red powder, paste, or liquid for coloring the cheeks or lips. **2** a red powder, chiefly ferric oxide, used for polishing metal, jewels, etc. [< F, red]

rough (ruf), *adj.* **1** not smooth; not level; not even: *rough boards, rough bark.* **2** without polish or fine finish: *rough diamonds.* **3** without luxury and ease: *rough life in camp.* **4** not completed or perfected; done as a first try; without details: *a rough drawing, a rough idea.* **5** coarse and tangled: *a dog with a rough coat of hair.* **6** harsh; not gentle: *rough manners, a rough crowd.* **7** requiring strength rather than skill: *rough work.* **8** stormy: *rough weather, a rough sea.* **9** harsh to the ear or taste: *rough sounds.* —*n.* **1** a coarse, violent person. **2** rough ground. **3** a rough thing or condition. —*v.* **1** make or become rough; roughen. **2** treat roughly: *rough up somebody.* **3** shape or sketch roughly. —*adv.* in a rough manner.

in the rough, not polished or refined; coarse; crude.

rough it, live without comforts and conveniences. [OE *rūh*] —**rough′er,** *n.* —**rough′ish,** *adj.* —**rough′ly,** *adv.* —**rough′ness,** *n.*

rough·age (ruf′ij), *n.* **1** rough or coarse material. **2** the coarser parts or kinds of food, as bran, fruit skins, and straw.

rough-and-read·y (ruf′ənd red′i), *adj.* **1** good enough for the purpose; roughly effective. **2** showing rough vigor.

rough-and-tum·ble (ruf′ənd tum′bəl), *adj.* with little regard for rules; roughly vigorous; boisterous.

rough·en (ruf′ən), *v.* make or become rough.

rough-hew (ruf′hū′), *v.,* **-hewed, -hewed** or **-hewn, -hew·ing. 1** hew (timber, stone, etc.) roughly or without smoothing or finishing. **2** give crude form to.

rough·house (ruf′hous′), *n., v.,* **-housed, -hous·ing.** —*n.* rough play; rowdy conduct; disorderly behavior. —*v.* act in a rough or disorderly way.

rough·neck (ruf′nek′), *n.* a rough, coarse fellow.

rough·shod (ruf′shod′), *adj.* having horseshoes with sharp calks to prevent slipping.

ride roughshod over, show no consideration for; treat roughly.

rou·lette (rü let′), *n.* a gambling game in which the players bet on the turn of a wheel. [< F, ult. < *roue* < L *rota* wheel]

round (round), *adj.* **1** shaped like a ball, a ring, a cylinder, or the like; having a circular or curved outline or surface: *a round hoop.* **2** plump: *her figure was short and round.* **3** full; complete; large: *a good round sum of money.* **4** plainly expressed; plain-spoken; frank: *scold in good round terms.* **5** with a full tone: *a mellow, round voice.* —*n.* **1** anything shaped like a ball, circle, cylinder, or the like. The rungs of a ladder are sometimes called rounds. **2** a fixed course ending where it begins: *the watchman makes his rounds.* **3** a series (of duties, events, etc.); routine: *a round of parties at the holidays, a round in a fight.* **4** discharge of firearms by a group of soldiers at the same time. **5** bullets, powder, etc., for such a shot. **6** a single outburst of applause, cheers, etc. **7** a short song, sung by several persons or groups beginning one after the other. The "Three Blind Mice" is a round. —*v.* **1** make or become round: *round the corners of a table.* **2** go wholly or partly around: *the ship rounded Cape Horn.* **3** turn around; wheel about: *the bear rounded and faced the hunters.* —*adv.* **1** in a circle; with a whirling motion: *wheels go round.* **2** in circumference: *the pumpkin measures 50 inches round.* **3** by a longer road or way: *we went round by the candy store on our way home.* **4** from one to another: *a report is going round.* **5** through a round of time: *summer will soon come round again.* **6** here and there: *just looking round.* **7** for all: *there is just enough cake to go round.* —*prep.* **1** on all sides of; so as to encircle or surround: *build a fence round the yard.* **2** so as to make a turn to the other side of: *walk round the corner.* **3** in a circuit or course through; to all or various parts of: *we took our cousins round the town.*

get round (someone), a outwit (someone). **b** wheedle (someone).

go the round, be passed, told, shown, etc., by many people from one to another: *the rumor went the round of every office in the building.*

make or **go the rounds,** follow a fixed course from one place to the next, ending where it began: *made the rounds of every shoe store in town.*

round off or **out, a** make or become round. **b** *Fig.* finish; complete.

round up, collect; draw or drive together: *rounded up friends to help; round up cattle.* [< OF < L *rotundus.* Doublet of ROTUND.] —**round′ish,** *adj.* —**round′ish·ness,** *n.* —**round′ness,** *n.*

round·a·bout (round′ə bout′), *adj.* indirect: *a roundabout route, hear in a roundabout way.* —*n.* an indirect way, course, or speech.

roun·de·lay (roun′də lā), *n.* song in which a phrase or a line is repeated again and again. [< OF *rondelet,* dim. of *rondel* RONDEL; infl. by *lay*⁴]

round·ly (round′li), *adv.* **1** in a round manner. **2** *Fig.* bluntly; severely. **3** fully; completely.

round number, 1 a whole number without a fraction. **2** number in even tens, hundreds, thousands, etc. 3874 in round numbers would be 3900 or 4000.

round robin, petition, protest, etc., with the signatures written in a circle, so that it is impossible to tell who signed first.

round-shoul·dered (round′shōl′-dərd), *adj.* having the shoulders bent forward.

round table, group of persons assembled for an informal discussion, etc. —**round′-ta′ble,** *adj.*

round trip, trip to a place and back again.

round·up (round′up′), *n.* **1** *W.* **a** act of driving or bringing cattle together from long distances. **b** the men and horses that do this. **2** *Fig.* any similar gathering. **3** *Fig.* summary: *a roundup of today's news.*

round·worm (round′wèrm′), *n.* any of a group of unsegmented worms that have long, round bodies, as the hookworm and trichina.

rouse (rouz), *v.,* **roused, rous·ing.** arouse; wake up; stir up: *I was roused by the telephone, the dogs roused a deer from the bushes, he was roused to anger by the insult.* —**rous′er,** *n.* —**rous′ing,** *adj.* —**rous′ing·ly,** *adv.*

roust·a·bout (roust′ə bout′), *n.* an unskilled laborer on wharves, ships, ranches, etc.

rout¹ (rout), *n.* **1** flight of a defeated army in disorder. **2** a complete defeat. —*v.* **1** put to flight. **2** defeat completely. [< OF *route* detachment, ult. < L *rumpere* to break]

rout² (rout), *v.* **1** put (out); force (out): *rout the lazy boys out of bed.* **2** dig with the snout. [var. of *root*²]

route (rüt; rout), *n., v.,* **rout·ed, rout·ing.** —*n.* way to go; road: *go the northern route.* —*v.* **1** arrange the route for. **2** send by a certain route. [< OF < L *rupta (via)* (a way) opened up, (a passage) forced < *rumpere* break]

rout·er (rou′tər), *n.* tool for gouging and shaping wood, as to form mouldings, beveled edges, etc., esp. one with an electric motor.

rou·tine (rü tēn′), *n.* a fixed, regular method of doing things; habitual doing of the same things in the same way. —*adj.* using routine: *routine methods.* [< F, < *route* ROUTE] —**rou·tin′ism**, *n.*

rou·tin·ize (rü tē′nīz), *v.,* **–ized, –iz·ing.** make routine or habitual. —**rou·tin′i·za′tion**, *n.*

rove[1] (rōv), *v.,* **roved, rov·ing.** wander; wander about; roam: *rove over the fields and woods.* —**rov′er**, *n.*

rove[2] (rōv), *v.* pt. and pp. of **reeve**[2].

row[1] (rō), *n.* **1** line of people or things **2** line of seats, as in a theater. **3** street with a line of buildings on either side.
hard row to hoe, a difficult thing to do. [OE *rāw*]

row[2] (rō), *v.* **1** use oars to propel a boat. **2** convey in a rowboat: *we were rowed to the shore.* **3** perform (a race, etc.) by rowing. —*n.* **1** act of using oars. **2** trip in a rowboat. [OE *rōwan*] —**row′er**, *n.*

row[3] (rou), *n.* a noisy quarrel; disturbance; clamor; squabble. —*v.* quarrel noisily; make noise.

row·an (rō′ən; rou′–), *n.* **1** the mountain ash. **2** its red, berrylike fruit. [< Scand. (Norw.) *raun*]

row·boat (rō′bōt′), *n.* boat moved by oars.

row·dy (rou′di), *n., pl.* **–dies,** *adj.,* **–di·er, –di·est.** —*n.* a rough, disorderly, quarrelsome person. —*adj.* rough; disorderly; quarrelsome. —**row′di·ly,** *adv.* —**row′di·ness,** *n.* —**row′dy·ism**, *n.*

row·el (rou′əl), *n.* a small wheel with sharp points, attached to the end of a spur. [< OF *roel*, ult. < L *rota* wheel]

row house (rō), one of a row of attached houses, as on a city street.

row·lock (rō′lok), *n.* =oarlock.

roy·al (roi′əl), *adj.* **1** of kings and queens: *the royal family, royal power.* **2** favored or encouraged by a king or queen; serving a king or queen: *the Royal Academy.* **3** like a king; noble. **4** fine; excellent. **5** beyond the common or ordinary in size, quality, etc. —*n.* a small mast or sail set above the topgallant. [< OF < L *regalis*. Doublet of REGAL, REAL[2].] —**roy′al·ly**, *adv.*

roy·al·ist (roi′əl ist), *n.* supporter of a king or of a royal government.

royal palm, a tall palm tree that has a whitish trunk and is often planted for ornament.

roy·al·ty (roi′əl ti), *n., pl.* **–ties.** **1** a royal person; royal persons. Kings, queens, princes, and princesses are royalty. **2** rank or dignity of a king or queen; royal power. **3** kingliness; royal quality; nobility. **4** share of the receipts or profits paid to an owner of a patent or copyright; payment for the use of any of various rights.

rpm or **r.p.m.,** revolutions per minute.

R.R., 1 railroad. **2** Right Reverend.

R.S.V., Revised Standard Version (of the Bible).

R.S.V.P. or **r.s.v.p.,** please answer. [< F *répondez s'il vous plaît*]

Ru, ruthenium.

rub (rub), *v.,* **rubbed, rub·bing,** *n.* —*v.* **1** move (one thing) back and forth (against another); move (two things) together: *rub your hands to warm them.* **2** move one's hand or an object over the surface of; push and press along the surface of: *the nurse rubbed my lame back.* **3** press as it moves: *that door rubs on the floor.* **4** make or bring (to some condition) by sliding the hand or some object: *rub silver bright.* **5** irritate or make sore by rubbing. —*n.* **1** act of rubbing. **2** something that rubs or hurts the feelings. **3** difficulty.
rub down, rub (the body); massage.
rub off on, become part of; cling: *his good manners rubbed off on his friend.*
rub out, a erase. **b** *Informal.* kill; murder. [ME *rubbe(n)*]

rub·ber[1] (rub′ər), *n.* **1** an elastic substance obtained from the milky juice of various tropical plants, or by various chemical processes. Rubber will not let air or water through. **2** something made from this substance. We wear rubbers on our feet when it rains. **3** person or thing that rubs. —*adj.* made of rubber. —**rub′ber·y,** *adj.*

rub·ber[2] (rub′ər), *n.* **1** a series of games of an odd number, usually three, the last of which is played to decide the contest when each side has won the same number of games. **2** the deciding game in a series of this kind.

rub·ber·ize (rub′ər īz), *v.,* **–ized, –iz·ing.** cover or treat with rubber.

rub·ber·neck (rub′ər nek′), *v.* stretch the neck or turn the head to look at something; stare.

rubber plant, 1 any plant yielding rubber. **2** an ornamental house plant with oblong, shining, leathery leaves.

rubber stamp, person or group that approves or endorses something without thought.

rub·ber-stamp (rub′ər stamp′), *v.* approve or endorse (a policy, bill, etc.) without thought.

rub·bing (rub′ing), *n.* reproduction of engraving or carving made by pressing paper onto its surface and rubbing it with crayon, charcoal, etc.: *a rubbing from an old brass plaque.*

rub·bish (rub′ish), *n.* **1** waste stuff of no use; trash. **2** silly words and thoughts; nonsense. —**rub′bish·y,** *adj.*

rub·ble (rub′əl), *n.* **1** rough broken stones, bricks, etc. **2** masonry made of this. [ME *robel*] —**rub′bly,** *adj.*

rub·down (rub′doun′), *n.* a rubbing of the body; massage.

Ru·bi·con (rü′bə kon), *n.* **cross the Rubicon,** make an important decision from which one cannot turn back.

ru·bi·cund (rü′bə kund), *adj.* reddish; ruddy. [< L *rubicundus* < *rubere* be red] —**ru′bi·cun′di·ty,** *n.*

ru·bid·i·um (rü bid′i əm), *n.* a silver-white metallic element, Rb, resembling potassium. [< NL, < L *rubidus* red; its spectrum has red lines]

ru·ble (rü′bəl), *n.* a Russian monetary unit and silver coin or piece of paper money.

ru·bric (rü′brik), *n.* **1** title or heading of a chapter, a law, etc., written or printed in red or in special lettering. **2** any heading. **3** direction for the conducting of religious services inserted in a prayer book, ritual, etc. [< L *rubrica* red coloring matter < *ruber* red] —**ru′bri·cal,** *adj.* —**ru′bri·cal·ly,** *adv.*

ru·by (rü′bi), *n., pl.* **–bies,** *adj.* —*n.* **1** a clear, hard, red precious stone. **2** its color. —*adj.* deep, glowing red. [< OF *rubi*, ult. < L *rubeus* red]

ruck·us (ruk′əs), *n.* a noisy disturbance or uproar.

rud·der (rud′ər), *n.* **1** a hinged, flat piece of wood or metal at the rear end of a boat or ship, by which it is steered. **2** a similar piece in an airplane, dirigible, etc. [OE *rōthor*] —**rud′dered,** *adj.* —**rud′der·less,** *adj.*

rud·dy (rud′i), *adj.,* **–di·er, –di·est. 1** red. **2** healthy red: *ruddy cheeks.* [OE *rudig*] —**rud′di·ly,** *adv.* —**rud′di·ness,** *n.*

rude (rüd), *adj.,* **rud·er, rud·est. 1** impolite; not courteous: *it is rude to stare, a rude reply.* **2** roughly made or done; without finish or polish; coarse: *rude tools, a rude cabin.* **3** rough in manner or behavior; violent; harsh: *a rude shock.* **4** harsh to the ear; unmusical. [< L *rudis*] —**rude′ly,** *adv.* —**rude′ness,** *n.*

ru·di·ment (rü′də mənt), *n.* **1** part to be learned first; beginning: *the rudiments of grammar.* **2** something in an early stage; an organ or part incompletely developed in size or structure. [< L *rudimentum* < *rudis* rude] —**ru′di·men′tal,** *adj.*

ru·di·men·ta·ry (rü′də men′tə ri; –tri), *adj.* **1** to be learned or studied first; elementary. **2** in an early stage of development; undeveloped. —**ru′di·men′ta·ri·ly,** *adv.*

rue[1] (rü), *v.,* **rued, ru·ing.** be sorry for; regret. [OE *hrēowan*] —**ru′er,** *n.*

rue[2] (rü), *n.* a strong-smelling plant with yellow flowers and bitter leaves. [< OF < L *ruta*, ? < Gk. *rhyte*]

rue·ful (rü′fəl), *adj.* **1** sorrowful; unhappy; mournful: *a rueful expression.* **2** causing sorrow or pity: *a rueful sight.* —**rue′ful·ly,** *adv.* —**rue′ful·ness,** *n.*

ruff (ruf), *n.* **1** a deep frill stiff enough to stand out, worn around the neck by men and women in the 16th century. **2** collar of specially marked feathers or hairs on the neck of a bird or animal. [akin to *ruffle*[1]] —**ruffed,** *adj.*

ruffed grouse, a North American game bird with a tuft of feathers on each side of the neck. It is in some places called a partridge and in others a pheasant.

ruf·fi·an (ruf′i ən), *n.* a rough, brutal, or cruel person. —*adj.* rough, lawless, and brutal. [< early F] —**ruf′fi·an·ism,** *n.*

ruf·fle[1] (ruf′əl), *v.,* **–fled, –fling,** *n.* —*v.* **1** make rough or uneven; wrinkle: *a breeze ruffled the lake.* **2** gather into a ruffle. **3** trim with ruffles. **4** disturb; annoy. —*n.* **1** roughness or unevenness in some surface; wrinkling. **2** strip of cloth, ribbon, or lace gathered along one edge and used for trimming. **3** disturbance; annoyance. [cf. Scand. *hrufla* scratch] —**ruf′fler,** *n.*

ruf·fle[2] (ruf′əl), *n.,* *v.,* **–fled, –fling.** —*n.* a low, steady beating of a drum. —*v.* beat (a drum) in this way. [? imit.]

rug (rug), *n.* **1** a heavy floor covering. **2** a thick, warm cloth used as covering, like a blanket.

pull the rug (out) from under, upset the plans of.

sweep under the rug, hide something, esp. something embarrassing or scandalous. [< Scand. (Norw. dial.) *rugga* coarse covering]

rug·by or **Rug·by** (rug′bi) *n.* Also, **Rugby football.** one form of the game of football.

rug·ged (rug′id), *adj.* **1** covered with rough projections; rough and uneven: *rugged rocks, a rugged ascent.* **2** sturdy or strong rather than elegant; robust; vigorous. **3** roughly irregular; hard in outline and form: *rugged features.* **4** tempestuous; severe: *rugged weather, rugged times.* [< Scand. (Sw.) *rugga* roughen. Cf. RUG.] —**rug′ged·ly,** *adv.* —**rug′ged·ness,** *n.*

ru·in (rü′ən), *n.* **1** very great damage; destruction; overthrow; decay: *his enemies planned the duke's ruin.* **2** condition of destruction, decay, or downfall: *the house had gone to ruin and neglect.* **3** cause of destruction, decay, or downfall: *gambling brought his ruin.* **4** bankruptcy. —*v.* **1** bring to ruin; destroy; spoil: *the rain has ruined my new hat.* **2** come to ruin.

ruins, that which remains after destruction or decay, esp. a building, wall, etc., that has fallen to pieces. [< OF < L *ruina* a collapse] —**ru′in·a·ble,** *adj.* —**ru′in·er,** *n.*

ru·in·a·tion (rü′ə nā′shən), *n.* ruin; destruction; downfall.

ru·in·ous (rü′ə nəs), *adj.* **1** bringing ruin; causing destruction. **2** fallen into ruins; in ruins. —**ru′in·ous·ly,** *adv.* —**ru′in·ous·ness,** *n.*

rule (rül), *n.,* *v.,* **ruled, rul·ing.** —*n.* **1** statement of what to do and not to do; a law; principle governing conduct, action, arrangement, etc.: *obey the rules of the game.* **2** order by a law court referring to only one particular case. **3** control; government: *in a democracy the people have the rule.* **4** a regular method; thing that usually happens or is done;

what is usually true: *fair weather is the rule in Arizona.* **5** a straight strip used to measure or as a guide to drawing. —*v.* **1** make a rule; decide. **2** decide formally or authoritatively; decree: *the judge ruled the question out of order.* **3** control; govern; direct. **4** prevail; be current: *prices of wheat and corn ruled high all the year.* **5** mark with lines.

as a rule, usually; generally.

rule out, decide against; exclude. [< OF < L *regula* straight stick < *regere* to guide. Doublet of RAIL[1].] —**rul′a·ble,** *adj.*

rule of thumb, 1 rule based on experience or practice rather than on scientific knowledge. **2** a rough practical method of procedure.

rul·er (rül′ər), *n.* **1** person who governs. **2** a straight strip of wood, metal, etc., used in drawing lines or in measuring.

rul·ing (rül′ing), *n.* **1** a decision of a judge or court. **2** ruled lines. —*adj.* **1** that rules; governing. **2** controlling; predominating; prevalent. —**rul′ing·ly,** *adv.*

rum (rum), *n.* an alcoholic liquor made from sugar cane, molasses, etc.

Rum., Rumanian.

Ru·ma·ni·a (rü mā′ni ə; –mān′yə), *n.* = Romania. —**Ru·ma′ni·an,** *adj., n.*

rum·ba (rum′bə), *n.,* *v.,* **–baed, –ba·ing.** —*n.* **1** a Cuban dance. **2** music for such a dance. —*v.* dance the rumba. [< Sp., prob. < African lang.]

rum·ble (rum′bəl), *v.,* **–bled, –bling,** *n.* —*v.* **1** make a deep, heavy, continuous sound. **2** move with such a sound. **3** utter with such a sound. —*n.* **1** a deep, heavy, continuous sound: *the far-off rumble of thunder.* **2** *Informal.* a gang fight. [? ult. imit.] —**rum′bler,** *n.* —**rum′bling,** *adj.*

ru·men (rü′mən), *n.,* *pl.* **–mi·na, –mens.** **1** first stomach of a ruminant. **2** cud of a ruminant.

ru·mi·nant (rü′mə nənt), *n.* animal that chews the cud, as cows, sheep, camels, etc. —*adj.* **1** belonging to the group of ruminants. **2** *Fig.* meditative; reflective. [< L *ruminans* chewing a cud < *rumen* gullet] —**ru′mi·nant·ly,** *adv.*

ru·mi·nate (rü′mə nāt), *v.,* **–nat·ed, –nat·ing. 1** chew the cud. **2** chew again: *a cow ruminates its food.* **3** *Fig.* ponder; meditate. [< L *ruminatus < rumen* gullet] —**ru′mi·nat′ing,** *adj.* —**ru′mi·na′tion,** *n.* —**ru′mi·na′tive,** *adj.*

rum·mage (rum′ij), *v.,* **–maged, –maging,** *n.* —*v.* **1** search thoroughly by moving things about. **2** search in a disorderly way. **3** pull from among other things; bring to light. —*n.* **1** a rummaging search. **2** odds and ends. [< early F *arrumage < arrumer* stow cargo]

rum·my (rum′i), *n.* a kind of card game.

ru·mor (rü′mər), *n.* **1** a story or statement talked of as news without any proof that it is true. **2** vague, general talk: *rumor has it that Italy will quarrel with France.* —*v.* tell or spread by rumor. [< OF < L]

rump (rump), *n.* **1** the hind part of the body of an animal, where the legs join the back. **2** cut of beef from this part. [< Scand. (Dan.) *rumpe*]

rum·ple (rum′pəl), *v.,* **–pled, –pling,** *n.* —*v.* crumple; crush; wrinkle. —*n.* wrinkle; crease. [cf. MDu. *rompel*] —**rum′ply,** *adj.*

rum·pus (rum′pəs), *n.* **1** a noisy quarrel; disturbance. **2** noise; uproar.

run (run), *v.,* **ran, run, run·ning,** *n.* —*v.* **1** go faster than walking: *run to the house.* **2** go hurriedly; hasten: *run to a person's aid.* **3** go; move; keep going or doing: *run errands, this train runs to Buffalo.* **4** go on, along, or proceed: *prices of hats run as high as $50, vines run along the sides of the road, shelves run along the walls.* **5** trace; draw: *run that report back to its source.* **6** drive; force; thrust: *run a knife into a person.* **7** flow; flow with: *the streets ran blood, my nose runs.* **8** bring, come to, or have a certain condition: *the well ran dry, these potatoes run large.* **9** spread: *the color ran when the dress was washed.* **10** continue; last: *a lease to run two years.* **11** take part in a race, contest, or election. **12** expose oneself to: *run a risk.* **13** move easily, freely, or smoothly; keep operating: *a rope runs in a pulley, run a machine, run a business.* **14** be worded or expressed: *how does the first verse run?* **15** get past or through: *enemy ships tried to run the blockade.* **16** publish (an advertisement, story, etc.) in a newspaper: *he ran an ad in the evening paper.* **17** soften; become liquid; melt. —*n.* **1** act of running: *set out at a run.* **2** spell or period of causing (a machine, etc.) to operate; amount of anything produced in such a period: *during a run of eight hours the factory produced a run of 100 cars.* **3** spell of causing something liquid to run or flow, or the amount that runs: *the run of sap from maple trees.* **4** unit of score in baseball. **5** a continuous spell or course: *a run of bad luck, run of strange events.* **6** a rapid succession of tones in music. **7** kind or class: *the common run of mankind.* **8** freedom to go over or through, or to use: *the guests were given the run of the house.* **9** number of fish moving together: *a run of salmon.* **10** stretch or enclosed space for animals: *a chicken run.*

a run for one's money, a strong competition. **a** satisfaction for one's efforts.

in the long run, on the whole; in the end.

on the run, a hurrying. **b** in retreat or rout; fleeing.

run across, meet by chance.

run after, a chase; pursue. **b** take up with; follow eagerly.

run against, oppose.

run away with, a win easily. **b** slope with. **c** overrun; defeat: *allow greed to run away with good judgment.*

run down, a cease to go; stop working. **b** pursue until caught or killed;

hunt down. **c** knock down by running against. **d** speak evil against. **e** decline or reduce in vigor or health. **f** fall off, diminish, or decrease; deteriorate.

run for it, run for safety.

run in, arrest and put in jail.

run into, a meet by chance. **b** crash into; collide with.

run off, a cause to run or be played. **b** flee.

run out, come to an end; become exhausted.

run out of, use up; have no more.

run over, a ride or drive over. **b** overflow. **c** go through quickly.

run through, a consume or spend rapidly or recklessly. **b** pierce.

run up, a make quickly. **b** accumulate; mount: *run up a huge bill.* **c** raise (a flag).

run up against, encounter difficulty. [< pp. of OE *rinnan* run]

run·a·bout (run′ə bout′), *n.* a light carriage with a single seat.

run·a·round (run′ə round′), *n.* avoidance; evasion.

run·a·way (run′ə wā′), *n.* person, horse, etc., that runs away. —*adj.* **1** out of control. **2** easily won.

run·down (run′doun′), *adj.* **1** tired; sick. **2** falling to pieces; partly ruined. **3** that has stopped going or working. —*n.* a summary listing: *give me a quick rundown of the important facts in the case.*

rune (rün), *n.* **1** any letter of an ancient Teutonic alphabet. **2** mark that looks like a rune and has some mysterious, magic meaning. [< Scand. *rūn*]

rung[1] (rung), *v.* pp. of **ring**[2].

rung[2] (rung), *n.* **1** a round rod or bar used as a step of a ladder. **2** crosspiece set between the legs of a chair or as part of the back or arm of a chair. **3** spoke of a wheel. **4** bar of wood having a similar shape and use. [OE *hrung*]

ru·nic (rü′nik), *adj.* **1** consisting of runes; written in runes; marked with runes. **2** like a rune.

run·ner (run′ər), *n.* **1** person, animal, or thing that runs; racer. **2** person who runs or works a machine, etc. **3** something in or on which something else runs or moves. **4** either of the narrow pieces on which a sleigh or sled slides. **5** blade of a skate. **6** a long, narrow strip: *runners of linen and lace on bureaus.* **7** a slender stem that takes root along the ground, thus producing new plants.

run·ner-up (run′ər up′), *n.* player or team that takes second place in a contest.

run·ning (run′ing), *n.* **1** act of a person or thing that runs: *running a store, running a race.* **2** that which runs. —*adj.* **1** cursive: *a running hand.* **2** discharging matter: *a running sore.* **3** flowing. **4** going or carried on continuously: *a running comment.* **5** repeated continuously: *a running pattern.* **6** following in succession: *for three nights running.* **7** moving or proceeding easily or smoothly. **8** that

is measured in a straight line. **9** operating as a machine.

in the running, having a chance to win.

out of the running, having no chance to win.

running knot, knot so made as to slide along the rope.

running mate, candidate running on the same ticket with another, but for a subordinate office, as a candidate for Vice-President.

run·ny (run′i), *adj.,* **–ni·er, –ni·est.** that runs: *a runny faucet.*

run·off or **run-off** (run′ôf; –of′), *n.* **1** water that drains or runs off, esp. from rain or overflowing streams. **2** a final, deciding race or contest.

run-of-the-mill (run′əv tħə mil′), *adj.* without particular merit; ordinary.

runt (runt), *n.* **1** a stunted animal, person, or plant. **2** ox or cow of a small breed. [OE *hrunta* (in sword name) < *hrung* RUNG[2]] —**runt′y,** *adj.*

run-through (run′thrü′), *n.* **1** brief review or summary. **2** rehearsal.

run-up (run′up′), *n.* **1** an increase: *a huge run-up in the price of gas.* **2** period immediately before some event: *in the run-up to the election.*

run·way (run′wā′), *n.* **1** way, track, groove, trough, or the like, along which something moves, slides, etc. **2** the beaten track of deer or other animals. **3** strip having a hard surface on which aircraft land and take off. **4** walkway for models in a fashion show.

ru·pee (rü pē′), *n.* a unit of money of India, Pakistan, and other Asian countries. [< Hind. *rūpiyah* < Skt. *rūpya* silver]

ru·pi·ah (rü pē′ə), *n.* the unit of money of Indonesia.

rup·ture (rup′chər), *n., v.,* **–tured, –turing.** —*n.* **1** a break; breaking: *the rupture of a blood vessel.* **2** the sticking out of some tissue or organ of the body through the wall of the cavity that should hold it in; hernia. —*v.* **1** break; burst; break off. **2** affect with or suffer hernia. [< L *ruptura* < *rumpere* burst]

ru·ral (rùr′əl), *adj.* in, belonging to, or like that of the country. [< L *ruralis* < *rus* country] —**ru′ral·ly,** *adv.*

ruse (rüz; rüs), *n.* trick; stratagem. [< F, < *ruser* dodge, RUSH[1]]

rush[1] (rush), *v.* **1** move with speed or force: *we rushed along.* **2** come, go, pass, act, etc., with speed or haste: *tears rush to the eyes.* **3** send, push, force, etc., with speed or haste: *rush a message.* **4** attack with much speed and force: *they rushed the enemy.* —*n.* **1** act of rushing: *the rush of the flood.* **2** busy haste; hurry: *the rush of city life.* **3** effort of many people to go somewhere or get something: *the Christmas rush.* **4** eager demand; pressure: *a sudden rush of business.* **5** =rush hour. **6** attempt to carry the ball through the opposing line in football. —*adj.* requiring haste: *a rush order.*

rushes, in motion pictures, the first prints of recent shots projected for cutting, criticism, etc.

with a rush, suddenly; quickly. [orig., force out of place by violent impact; cf. OE *hrȳsc* a blow] —**rush′er,** *n.* —**rush′ing,** *adj.* —**rush′ing·ly,** *adv.*

rush[2] (rush), *n.* **1** plant with pithy or hollow stems, that grows in wet ground. **2** stem of such a plant, used for making chair seats, baskets, etc. [OE *rysc*]

rush hour, time when traffic is heaviest.

rusk (rusk), *n.* **1** piece of bread or cake toasted in the oven. **2** a kind of light, soft, sweet biscuit. [< Sp., Pg. *rosca* roll]

Russ., Russia; Russian.

rus·set (rus′it), *adj.* yellow-brown; reddish-brown. —*n.* **1** yellowish brown; reddish brown. **2** coarse, russet-colored cloth. The peasants used to wear russet. **3** kind of potato with a rough, brown skin. **4** kind of apple with a rough brownish skin. [< OF *rousset,* ult. < L *russus* red] —**rus′set·y,** *adj.*

Rus·sia (rush′ə), *n.* **1** country in E Europe and NW Asia. **2** formerly, the Soviet Union (United Soviet Socialist Republics). **3** a former empire in E Europe and NW Asia ruled by a czar, with its capital at St. Petersburg.

Rus·sian (rush′ən), *adj.* of or having to do with Russia, its people, or their language. —*n.* **1** native or inhabitant of Russia, esp. a member of the dominant Slavic race of Russia. **2** Slavic language of Russia.

Russian Federation, =Russia (def. 1).

Russian thistle, a large weed with spiny branches that develops into a tumbleweed.

rust (rust), *n.* **1** the reddish-brown or orange coating that forms on iron or steel when exposed to air or moisture. **2** any film or coating on any other metal due to oxidization, etc. **3** a plant disease that spots leaves and stems. **4** a reddish brown or orange. —*v.* **1** become covered with rust. **2** coat with rust. **3** have or cause to have the disease rust. —*adj.* reddish-brown of orange.

rust out, disintegrate from rust. [OE *rūst*] —**rust′less,** *adj.*

rus·tic (rus′tik), *adj.* **1** belonging to or suitable for the country; rural. **2** simple; plain: *his rustic speech and ways made him uncomfortable in the city school.* **3** rough; awkward. —*n.* a country person. [< L, < *rus* country] —**rus′ti·cal·ly,** *adv.*

rus·ti·cate (rus′tə kāt), *v.,,* **–cat·ed, –cating. 1** go to or stay in the country. **2** send to the country. [< L, < *rusticus* RUSTIC] —**rus′ti·ca′tion,** *n.* —**rus′ti·ca′tor,** *n.*

rus·tle (rus′əl), *n., v.,* **–tled, –tling.** —*n.* sound that leaves make when moved by the wind; sound like this. —*v.* **1** make such a sound. **2** move or stir (something) so that it makes such a sound: *rustle the papers.* **3** steal (cattle, etc.).

rustle up, a gather; find: *rustle up a suitable outfit.* **b** prepare; fix, esp. from the food on hand: *rustle up some dinner.*

[OE *hrūxlian* make noise] —**rus′tling,** *adj.* —**rus′tling·ly,** *adv.*

rus·tler (rus′lər), *n.* a cattle thief.

rust·proof (rust′prüf′), *adj.* resisting rust.

rust·y (rus′ti), *adj.,* **rust·i·er, rust·i·est. 1** covered with rust; rusted: *a rusty knife.* **2** made by rust. **3** colored like rust. **4** faded: *a rusty black.* **5** damaged by lack of use. **6** out of practice. —**rust′i·ly,** *adv.* —**rust′i·ness,** *n.*

rut[1] (rut), *n., v.,* **rut·ted, rut·ting.** —*n.* **1** track made in the ground by wheels. **2** a fixed or established way of acting. —*v.* make ruts in. [? var. of *route*]

rut[2] (rut), *n., v.,* **rut·ted, rut·ting.** —*n.* **1** sexual excitement of deer, goats, sheep, etc., occurring at regular intervals. **2** period during which it lasts. —*v.* be in rut. [< OF < L *rugitus* bellowing < *rugire* bellow]

ru·ta·ba·ga (rü′tə bā′gə; –beg′ə), *n.* kind of large yellow turnip. [< Swed. (dial.) *rotabagge*]

Ruth (rüth), *n.* book of the Old Testament.

ru·the·ni·um (rü thē′ni əm), *n.* a brittle gray metal, Ru. It is an element similar to platinum. [< NL, < Med.L *Ruthenia* Russia; because discovered in the Urals] —**ru·then′ic,** *adj.* —**ru·the′ni·ous,** *adj.*

ruth·less (rüth′lis), *adj.* having no pity; showing no mercy; cruel. —**ruth′less·ness,** *n.*

rut·ty (rut′i), *adj.,* **–ti·er, –ti·est.** full of ruts.

RV, recreational vehicle.

R.V., Revised Version (of the Bible).

Rx, prescription (for medication). [< L ℞ symbol for *recipe* take!]

Ry., railway.

-ry, *suffix.* **1** occupation or work of a ____, as in *dentistry, chemistry.* **2** act of a ____, as in *mimicry.* **3** quality, state, or condition of a ____, as in *rivalry.* **4** group of ____s, considered collectively, as in *jewelry, peasantry.* [short form of *-ery*]

rye (rī), *n.* **1** a hardy annual plant widely grown in cold regions. **2** its seeds or grain. **3 a** flour made from them. **b** bread made from rye flour; rye bread. **4** Also, **rye whiskey,** whiskey made from rye. [OE *ryge*]

Ryu·kyu Islands (rü′kū′), chain of 55 islands extending from Japan to Taiwan.

S, s (es), *n., pl.* **S's; s's,** *adj.* —*n.* **1** the 19th letter of the alphabet. **2** anything shaped like an S. —*adj.* shaped like an S.

S, 1 south; southern. **2** sulfur.

S., 1 *pl.* **SS.** Saint. **2** Saturday. **3** September. **4** South; south. **5** Southern; southern. **6** Sunday.

s., 1 second. **2** singular. **3** south; southern.

S.A., 1 Salvation Army. **2** South Africa. **3** South America. **4** South Australia.

Sab·bath (sab′əth), *n.* **1** day of the week used for rest and worship. Sunday is the Christian Sabbath; Saturday is the Jewish Sabbath. **2 sabbath,** period of rest, quiet, etc. —*adj.* of or belonging to the Sabbath. [< L < Gk. < Heb., < *shabath* rest]

sab·bat·i·cal (sə bat′ə kəl), *adj.* **1** of or suitable for the Sabbath. **2 a** of or for a rest from work. **b** denoting a time of absence from duty for purposes of study and travel given to teachers: *sabbatical leave.* [< Gk. *sabbatikos.* See SABBATH.] **sab·bat·i·cal·ly,** *adv.*

sa·ber (sā′bər), *n., v.,* **-bered, -bering.** —*n.* a heavy, curved sword with a sharp edge, used by cavalry. —*v.* strike, wound, or kill with a saber. [< F *sabre,* alter. of *sable,* ult. < Hung., < *szabni* cut] —**sa′bered,** *adj.* —**sa′ber·like′,** *adj.*

saber-toothed tiger or **cat,** extinct mammal somewhat like like a tiger, but having long, curved upper canine teeth.

sa·ble (sā′bəl), *n.* **1** a small flesh-eating mammal valued for its dark brown, glossy fur. **2** its fur. —*adj.* black; dark. [< OF, ult. < Slavic] —**sa′ble·ness,** *n.*

sab·ot (sab′ō; *Fr.* sä bō′), *n.* **1** shoe hollowed out of a single piece of wood, worn by peasants in France, Belgium, etc. **2** a coarse leather shoe with a thick wooden sole. [< F]

sab·o·tage (sab′ə täzh), *n., v.,* **-taged, -tag·ing.** —*n.* **1** damage done to work, tools, machinery, etc., by workers as an attack or threat against an employer. **2** such damage done by civilians of a conquered nation to injure the conquering forces. **3** damage done by enemy agents or sympathizers in an attempt to slow down a nation's war effort. —*v.* damage or destroy deliberately. [< F, < *saboter* bungle, walk noisily < *sabot* sabot]

sab·o·teur (sab′ə tèr′), *n.* person who practices sabotage. [< F]

sa·bra (sä′brə), *n., pl.* **sa·brot** (sä brôt′). *Hebrew.* person born in Israel.

sac (sak), *n.* a baglike part in an animal or plant, often one containing liquids, as the sac of a honeybee. [< L *saccus* SACK¹] —**sac′like′,** *adj.*

sac·cha·ride (sak′ə rīd), *n.* compound of one or more simple sugars; carbohydrate.

sac·cha·rin (sak′ə rin), *n.* a very sweet substance obtained from coal tar, used as a substitute for sugar in some diets.

sac·cha·rine (sak′ə rin), *adj.* sugary; very sweet: *a saccharine smile.* —*n.* =saccharin. [< Med.L *saccharum* sugar < Gk. *sakcharon*] —**sac′cha·rine·ly,** *adv.* —**sac′cha·rin′i·ty,** *n.*

sac·er·do·tal (sas′ər dō′təl), *adj.* of priests or the priesthood; priestly. [< L, < *sacerdos* priest < *sacer* holy] —**sac′er·do′tal·ly,** *adv.*

sa·chem (sā′chəm), *n.* chief of an American Indian tribe. [< Algonquian]

sa·chet (sa shā′), *n.* a small bag or pad containing perfumed powder. [< F, dim. of *sac* sack¹]

sack¹ (sak), *n.* **1** a large bag made of coarse cloth. **2** such a bag with what is in it: *two sacks of corn.* **3** *U.S.* any bag or what is in it: *a sack of candy.* **4** a discharge from employment. —*v.* **1** put into a sack or sacks. **2** discharge from employment; fire. [< L < Gk. < Heb. *saq*]

sack² (sak), *v.* plunder (a captured city). —*n.* a plundering of a captured city. [< F *sac* < Ital. *sacco*] —**sack′er,** *n.*

sack³ (sak), *n.* sherry or other strong, light-colored wine. [< F (*vin*) *sec* dry (wine) < L *siccus*]

sack·but (sak′but), *n.* a musical wind instrument of the Middle Ages, somewhat like the trombone. [< F *saquebute* < *saquer* pull + *bouter* push]

sack·cloth (sak′klôth′; -kloth′), *n.* **1** coarse cloth for making sacks. **2** coarse cloth worn as a sign of penitence.

sack·ful (sak′fûl), *n., pl.* **-fuls.** enough to fill a sack.

sack·ing (sak′ing), *n.* coarse cloth for making sacks, etc.

sac·ra·ment (sak′rə mənt), *n.* **1** a solemn religious ceremony of the Christian church. Baptism is a sacrament. **2** Often, **Sacrament.** the Eucharist, or Lord's Supper. **3** something especially sacred. [< L *sacramentum,* ult. < *sacer* holy] —**sac′ra·men′tal,** *adj.* —**sac′ra·men′tal·ly,** *adv.*

Sac·ra·men·to (sak′rə men′tō), *n.* capital of California, in the C part.

sa·cred (sā′krid), *adj.* **1** belonging to or dedicated to God or a god; holy: *the sacred altar, a sacred building.* **2** connected with religion; religious: *sacred music, sacred writings.* **3** worthy of reverence: *the sacred memory of a dead hero.* **4** that must not be violated or disregarded: *sacred oaths.* [orig. pp. of ME *sacre(n)* sanctify < L, < *sacer* holy] —**sa′cred·ly,** *adv.* —**sa′cred·ness,** *n.*

sacred cow, 1 the cow, believed to be sacred, esp. among Hindus. **2** *Fig.* something believed in so strongly that it cannot be questioned or criticized: *the free market is a sacred cow to some economists.*

sac·ri·fice (sak′rə fīs), *n., v.,* **-ficed, -ficing.** —*n.* **1** act of offering to a god; the thing offered: *the ancient Hebrews killed animals on the altars as sacrifices to God.* **2** a giving up one thing for another. **3** the thing given up or devoted. **4** loss: *sell a house at a sacrifice.* **5** Also, **sacrifice hit** or **fly,** bunt or fly in baseball that helps the runner to advance although the batter is put out. —*v.* **1** give or offer to a god. **2** permit injury or disadvantage to, for the sake of something else; give up: *a mother will sacrifice her life for her children.* **3** sell at a loss: *sacrifice a house.* **4** help a base runner in baseball to advance by a sacrifice. [< OF < L *sacrificium,* ult. < *sacra* rites + *facere* perform] —**sac′ri·fic′er,** *n.*

sac·ri·fi·cial (sak′rə fish′əl), *adj.* **1** having to do with sacrifice. **2** used in a sacrifice. —**sac′ri·fi′cial·ly,** *adv.*

sacrificial lamb, person or thing given up or otherwise sacrificed to gain an advantage.

sac·ri·lege (sak′rə lij), *n.* an intentional injury to anything sacred. [< OF < L *sacrilegium* temple robbery < *sacrum* sacred object + *legere* pick up]

sac·ri·le·gious (sak′rə lij′əs; -lē′jəs), *adj.* injurious or insulting to sacred persons or things. —**sac′ri·le′gious·ness,** *n.*

sac·ris·tan (sak′ris tən), *n.* person in charge of a sacristy. [< Med.L, ult. < L *sacer* holy. Doublet of SEXTON.]

sac·ris·ty (sak′ris ti), *n., pl.* **-ties.** place where the sacred vessels, robes, etc., of a church are kept. [< Med.L *sacristia,* ult. < L *sacer* holy]

sac·ro·sanct (sak′rō sangkt), *adj.* set apart as sacred; consecrated; very holy or sacred. [< L, ult. < *sacer* sacred + *sancire* consecrate] —**sac′ro·sanc′ti·ty,** *n.*

sa·crum (sā′krəm), *n., pl.* **-cra** (-krə), **-crums.** bone at the lower end of the spine, which is formed by the joining of several vertebrae and which makes the back of the pelvis. [< LL (*os*) *sacrum* sacred (bone); from its being offered as a dainty in sacrifices] —**sa′cral,** *adj.*

sad (sad), *adj.,* **sad·der, sad·dest. 1** not happy; full of sorrow; grieving: *sad looks, a sad disappointment.* **2** dull in color; dark. **3** extremely bad: *a sad mess.* [OE *sæd* sated] —**sad′ly,** *adv.* —**sad′ness,** *n.*

sad·den (sad′ən), *v.* make or become sad.

sad·dle (sad′əl), *n., v.,* **-dled, -dling.** —*n.* **1** seat for a rider on a horse's back, on a bicycle, etc. **2** part of a harness that holds the shafts, or to which a checkrein is attached. **3** thing shaped or placed like a saddle. **4** ridge between two mountain peaks. **5** piece of meat consisting of the upper back portion of an animal. —*v.* **1** put a saddle on. **2** *Fig.* put as a burden or responsibility on; burden: *saddle with too many responsibilities.*

in the saddle, in a position of control. [OE *sadol*]

sad·dle·bag (sad′əl bag′), *n.* one of a pair of bags laid over an animal's back behind the saddle.

saddle blanket, heavy cloth placed under a horse's saddle. Also, **saddle cloth.**

sad·dler (sad′lər), *n.* person who makes or sells saddles and harness.

sad·dler·y (sad′lər i), *n., pl.* **–dler·ies. 1** work or shop of a saddler. **2** saddles, harness, and other equipment for horses.

saddle soap, soap made for cleaning saddles and other leather goods.

sa·dism (sā′diz əm; sad′iz–), *n.* **1** perverse cruelty. **2** cruelty indulged in as a sexual perversion. [< F; from the Count de *Sade,* who wrote of it] **—sa′dist,** *n., adj.* **—sa·dis′tic** *adj.* **—sa·dis′ti·cal·ly,** *adv.*

sa·do·mas·och·ism (sā′dō mas′ə kiz əm; –maz′–), *n.* enjoyment of both giving and receiving pain; combination of sadism and masochism. **—sa′do·mas′-och·ist,** *n.* **2 sa′do·mas′och·is′tic,** *adj.*

sa·fa·ri (sə fä′ri), *n., pl.* **–ris. 1** journey or hunting expedition, esp. in E Africa. **2** a long trip. [< Ar.]

safe (sāf), *adj.,* **saf·er, saf·est,** *n.* **—adj. 1** free from harm or danger: *keep money in a safe place.* **2** not harmed: *return from war safe and sound.* **3** out of danger; secure: *we feel safe with the dog in the house.* **4** put beyond power of doing harm: *a tiger safe in its cage.* **5** careful: *a safe move.* **6** that can be depended on: *a safe guide.* **—n. 1** a steel or iron box for money, jewels, papers, etc. **2** place made to keep things safe: *a meat safe.* [< OF *sauf* < L *salvus*] **—safe′ly,** *adv.* **—safe′ness,** *n.*

safe-con·duct (sāf′kon′dukt), *n.* **1** privilege of passing safely through a region, esp. in time of war. **2** paper granting this privilege.

safe·crack·er (sāf′krak′ər), *n.* person skilled at opening locked safes, esp. a robber. **—safe′crack′ing,** *n.*

safe·guard (sāf′gärd′), *v.* keep safe; guard against hurt or danger; protect: *pure food laws safeguard our health.* **—n.** protection; defense.

safe house, place where someone can stay in secret and safety.

safe·keep·ing (sāf′kēp′ing), *n.* protection.

safe sex, sexual intercourse practiced with safeguards, esp. the condom, against the spread of sexually transmitted disease such as AIDS.

safe·ty (sāf′ti), *n., pl.* **–ties,** *adj.* **—n. 1** quality or state of being safe; freedom from harm or danger. **2** device to prevent injury. **—adj.** giving safety; making harm unlikely.

safety pin, pin bent back on itself to form a spring and having a guard that covers the point.

safety valve, 1 valve in a steam boiler or the like that opens and lets steam or fluid escape when the pressure becomes too great. **2** *Fig.* a harmless outlet for anger, stress, etc.

saf·flow·er (saf′lou′ər), *n.* herb whose seeds yield a cooking oil and whose red flower petals are used as a dye.

saf·fron (saf′rən), *n.* **1** an orange-yellow coloring matter obtained from a kind of crocus, used to color and flavor food, etc.

2 an autumn crocus with purple flowers having orange-yellow stigmas. **3** an orange yellow. **—adj.** orange-yellow. [< F *safran,* ult. < Ar. *za′farān*]

S. Afr., South Africa; South African.

sag (sag), *v.,* **sagged, sag·ging,** *n.* **—v. 1** sink under weight or pressure; bend down in the middle: *a sagging board.* **2** hang down unevenly: *a sagging door.* **3** become less firm or elastic; droop; sink: *sagging spirits.* **4** decline in value. **—n. 1** a sagging. **2** place where anything sags. [cf. Du. *zakken* sink]

sa·ga (sä′gə), *n.* **1** an old Norse story of heroic deeds. **2** any long story of heroic deeds or overcoming difficulties. [< Scand.]

sa·ga·cious (sə gā′shəs), *adj.* **1** wise in a keen, practical way; shrewd. **2** intelligent. [< L *sagax*] **—sa·ga′cious-ness,** *n.*

sa·gac·i·ty (sə gas′ə ti), *n., pl.* **–ties.** keen, sound judgment; mental acuteness; shrewdness.

sag·a·more (sag′ə môr; –mōr), *n.* in some American Indian tribes, a chief or great man.

sage[1] (sāj), *adj.,* **sag·er, sag·est,** *n.* **—adj. 1** wise. **2** showing wisdom or good judgment: *a sage reply.* **—n.** a profoundly wise man. [< OF, ult. < L *sapere* be wise] **—sage′ly,** *adv.*

sage[2] (sāj), *n.* **1** a plant whose leaves are used as seasoning and in medicine. **2** its dried leaves. **3** sagebrush. [< OF *sauge* < L *salvia.* Doublet of SALVIA.]

sage·brush (sāj′brush′), *n.* a grayish-green shrub, common on the dry plains of the W United States.

sage grouse, a very large grouse common on the plains of W North America.

sage hen, 1 sage grouse. **2** a female sage grouse.

Sag·it·tar·i·us (saj′ə tār′i əs), *n.* **1** a southern constellation that was thought of as arranged in the shape of a centaur drawing a bow. **2** the ninth sign of the zodiac; the Archer.

sa·hib (sä′ib), *n.* sir; master. [< Hind. < Ar. *çāhib* lord]

said (sed), *v.* pt. and pp. of **say. —adj.** named or mentioned before: *the said witness.*

sail (sāl), *n.* **1** piece of cloth spread to the wind to make a ship move through the water. **2** something like a sail, as the arm of a windmill. **3** trip on a boat with sails or on any vessel. **—v. 1** travel on water by the action of wind on sails. **2** travel on a steamboat, airship, etc. **3** move smoothly like a ship with sails: *the eagle sailed by.* **4** sail upon, over, or through: *sail the seas.* **5** manage a ship or boat: *learn to sail.* **6** begin a trip by water: *we sail at 2 p.m.*

sail into, *Informal.* **a** attack; beat. **b** criticize; scold.

set sail, begin a trip by water.

take in sail, a lower the sails or reduce the area of a ship's sails. **b** *Fig.* lessen or reduce one's hopes, ambitions, etc.

trim one's sails, change one's behavior or adjust one's opinions in order to get along.

under sail, with sails spread out. [OE *segl*] **—sail′ing,** *n.* **—sail′less,** *adj.*

sail·board (sāl′bôrd′; –bōrd′), *n.* surf board equipped with a mast and sail. **—sail′board′ing,** *n.*

sail·boat (sāl′bōt′), *n.* boat that is moved by a sail or sails.

sail·cloth (sāl′klôth′; –kloth′), *n.* canvas or other material used for making sails.

sail·er (sāl′ər), *n.* a ship with reference to its sailing power: *a fast sailer.*

sail·fish (sāl′fish′), *n., pl.* **–fish·es** or (*esp. collectively*) **–fish.** a large saltwater fish that has a long, high fin on its back.

sail·or (sāl′ər), *n.* **1** person whose work is sailing. **2** person who works on a ship. **3** member of a ship's crew, not an officer. **4** a flat-brimmed hat modeled after the kind of hat sailors used to wear years ago. **—adj.** like that of a sailor: *a sailor suit.* **—sail′or·ly,** *adj.*

sail·plane (sāl′plān′), *n.* lightweight glider esp. designed to catch air currents.

saint (sānt), *n.* **1** a very holy person. **2** person who has gone to heaven. **3** person declared a saint by the Roman Catholic Church. **4** person like a saint. **—v. 1** make a saint of; canonize. **2** call or consider a saint. **—adj.** holy; sacred. [< OF < L *sanctus* consecrated] **—saint′hood, saint′ship,** *n.* **—saint′like′,** *adj.*

Saint. For place names beginning with "Saint" look under the St. words.

Saint Ber·nard (bər närd′), a big, tan-and-white dog with a large head.

saint·ed (sān′tid), *adj.* **1** declared to be a saint. **2** thought of as a saint; gone to heaven. **3** sacred; very holy. **4** saintly.

saint·ly (sānt′li), *adj.,* **–li·er, –li·est. 1** like a saint; very holy. **2** very good. **—saint′li·ness,** *n.*

Saint Patrick's Day, March 17.

Saint Val·en·tine's Day (val′ən tīnz), February 14.

sake[1] (sāk), *n.* **1** cause; account; interest: *for appearances' sake.* **2** purpose; end.

for the sake of, a because of; on account of: *for the sake of appearances.* **b** to help; to please.

for your own sake, on your own account; to help yourself. [OE *sacu* cause at law]

sa·ke[2] (sä′kē), *n.* a Japanese fermented alcoholic beverage made from rice. [< Jap.]

sal (sal), *n.* salt, used esp. in druggists' terms, such as *sal ammoniac.* [< L]

sa·laam (sə läm′), *n.* a greeting in Arabic countries that means "Peace." **—v.** greet with a salaam. [< Ar. *salām* peace]

sal·a·ble (sāl′ə bəl), *adj.* that can be sold; fit to be sold; easily sold. Also, **saleable. —sal′a·bil′i·ty, sal′a·ble·ness,** *n.* **—sal′a·bly,** *adv.*

sa·la·cious (sə lā′shəs), *adj.* lustful; lewd; obscene; indecent. [< L *salax*] **—sa·la′-cious·ly,** *adv.*

sal·ad (sal′əd), *n.* **1** raw, green vegetables, such as lettuce, cabbage, and celery, served with a dressing. Often cold meat, fish, eggs, cooked vegetables, or fruits are used along with, or instead of, the raw green vegetables. **2** any green vegetable that can be eaten raw. [< OF < Pr. *salada,* ult. < L *sal* salt]

salad days, days of youthful inexperience.

sal·a·man·der (sal′ə man′dər), *n.* **1** any of various lizardlike amphibians with long tails and short limbs. **2** a mythical lizard or reptile supposed to live in fire. [< OF < L < Gk. *salamandra*]

sa·la·mi (sə lä′mi), *n.* a kind of sausage. [< Ital., pl. of *salame,* ult. < L *sal* salt]

sal ammoniac, ammonium chloride.

sal·a·ry (sal′ə ri; sal′ri), *n., pl.* **-ries.** fixed pay for regular work. [< AF < L *salarium* soldier's allowance for salt < *sal* salt] —**sal′a·ried,** *adj.* —**sal′a·ry·less,** *adj.*

sale (sāl), *n.* **1** act of selling; exchange of goods for money: *no sale yet this morning.* **2** amount sold: *today's sales were larger than yesterday's.* **3** chance to sell; demand; market: *there is almost no sale now for carriages.* **4** a selling at lower prices than usual: *a sale on suits.* **for** or **on sale,** to be sold. [OE *sala*]

sale·a·ble (sāl′ə bəl), *adj.* =salable. —**sale′a·bil′i·ty,** *n.* —**sale′a·bly,** *adv.*

Sa·lem (sā′ləm), *n.* capital of Oregon, in the NW part.

sales·girl (sālz′gėrl′), *n.* =saleswoman.

sales·la·dy (sālz′lā′di), *n., pl.* **-dies.** =saleswoman.

sales·man (sālz′mən), *n., pl.* **-men.** =salesperson.

sales·man·ship (sālz′mən ship), *n.* **1** work of a salesperson. **2** ability at selling.

sales·peo·ple (sālz′pē′pəl), *n.pl.* salespersons.

sales·per·son (sālz′pėr′sən), **sales·clerk** (-klėrk′), *n.* person whose work is selling in a store.

sales·room (sālz′rüm′; -rùm′), *n.* room where things are sold or shown for sale.

sales talk, 1 talk designed to sell something. **2** *Fig.* any talk intended to persuade.

sales tax, tax based on the amount received for articles sold.

sales·wom·an (sālz′wùm′ən), *n., pl.* **-wom·en.** woman whose work is selling in a store.

sal·i·cyl·ic acid (sal′ə sil′ik), a solid white substance, $C_7H_6O_3$, used as a mild antiseptic and medicine. Aspirin is a common preparation of salicylic acid.

sa·li·ent (sā′li ənt; sāl′yənt), *adj.* **1** standing out; easily seen or noticed; prominent; striking: *the salient features in a landscape, the salient points in a speech.* **2** pointing outward; projecting: *a salient angle.* —*n.* **1** a salient angle or part. **2** part of a fort or line of trenches that projects toward the enemy. [< L *saliens* leaping] —**sa′li·ence,** *n.* —**sa′li·ent·ly,** *adv.*

sa·line (sā′līn), *adj.* like salt; salty. [< L *sal* salt] —**sa·lin′i·ty,** *n.*

sa·li·va (sə lī′və), *n.* liquid that the salivary glands secrete into the mouth to keep it moist, aid in chewing, and start digestion. [< L]

sal·i·var·y gland (sal′ə ver′i), any of various glands that empty their secretions into the mouth. The salivary glands of human beings and most other vertebrates are digestive glands that secrete saliva containing enzymes, salts, etc.

sal·i·vate (sal′ə vāt), *v.,* **-vat·ed, -vat·ing.** produce a secretion of saliva. —**sal′i·va′tion,** *n.*

sal·low (sal′ō), *adj.* having a sickly, yellowish color or complexion. —*v.* make yellowish. [OE *salu*] —**sal′low·ish,** *adj.* —**sal′low·ness,** *n.*

sal·ly (sal′i), *n., pl.* **-lies,** *v.,* **-lied, -lying.** —*n.* **1** a sudden attack made from a defensive position; sortie. **2** a sudden rushing forth. **3** excursion. **4** a witty remark. —*v.* **1** go suddenly from a defensive position to attack an enemy. **2** set out briskly. **3** exchange clever remarks. [< F *saillie,* ult. < L *salire* to leap]

sal·ma·gun·di (sal′mə gun′di), *n.* any mixture, medley, or miscellany. [< F *salmigondis,* ult. < Ital. *salami conditi* pickled sausages]

salm·on (sam′ən), *n., pl.* **-ons** or (*esp. collectively*) **-on,** *adj.* —*n.* **1** a large marine and freshwater fish with silvery scales and yellowish-pink flesh, common in the N Atlantic near the mouths of large rivers which it ascends in order to spawn. **2** a variety of this species confined to lakes (**landlocked salmon**). **3** any of various fishes of the same family but different genera, which are common in the N Pacific and the rivers flowing into it. **4** a yellowish-pink color. —*adj.* yellowish-pink. [< OF < L *salmo*]

sal·mo·nel·la (sal′mə nel′ə), *n., pl.* **-nel·las, -nel·lae** (-nel′i). any one of various bacteria that causes food poisoning, typhoid fever, etc. [< NL *Salmonella,* genus name, < Daniel E. *Salmon,* 1850–1914, American pathologist]

salmon trout, kind of trout resembling a salmon.

sa·lon (sə lon′), *n., pl.* **-lons. 1** a large room for receiving or entertaining guests. **2** assembly of guests in such a room. **3** place used to exhibit works of art. [< F < Ital. *salone* < *sala* hall]

sa·loon (sə lün′), *n.* **1** place where alcoholic drinks are sold and drunk. **2** a large room for general or public use: *the dining saloon of a ship.* [< F *salon* SALON]

sa·loon·keep·er (sə lün′kēp′ər), *n.* man who keeps a saloon (def. 1).

sal·sa (säl′sä), *n.* **1** mild to hot spicy sauce served with Mexican or SW American food. **2 a** popular music from the Caribbean. **b** dance performed to this music. [< Sp., lit. sauce]

sal·si·fy (sal′sə fī), *n.* **1** a root with an oyster-like flavor, eaten as a vegetable. **2** the purple-flowered plant having this root. [< F < Ital. < L *saxifraga.* Doublet of SAXIFRAGE.]

salt (sôlt), *n.* **1** a white substance found in the earth and in sea water; sodium chloride. Salt is used to season and preserve food. **2** a compound derived from an acid by replacing the hydrogen wholly or partly by a metal or an electropositive radical. Baking soda is a salt. **3** that which gives liveliness, piquancy, or pungency to anything. **4** saltcellar. **5** sailor. **6** wit. —*adj.* **1** containing salt. **2** tasting like salt. **3** overflowed with or growing in salt water: *salt marshes.* **4** cured or preserved with salt. —*v.* **1** mix or sprinkle with salt: *salt an egg.* **2** cure or preserve with salt: *salt meat.* **3** make pungent; season: *talk salted with wit.*

rub salt in a wound, make a bad situation worse.

salt away or **down, a** pack with salt to preserve. **b** *Fig.* store away; save.

salt of the earth, the best, most good-hearted person.

salts, a medicine that acts as a laxative. **b** smelling salts.

with a grain of salt, with some reservation or allowance: *take that story with a grain of salt.*

worth one's salt, worth one's support, wages, etc. [OE *sealt*] —**salt′ed,** *adj.* —**salt′er,** *n.*

salt-and-pep·per (sôlt′ən pep′ər), *adj.* white and dark gray or black: *salt-and-pepper fabric, salt-and-pepper hair.* Also, **pepper-and-salt.**

salt·cel·lar (sôlt′sel′ər), *n.* shaker or dish for holding salt, used on the table.

Salt Lake City, capital of Utah, in the N part.

salt lick, 1 place where natural salt is found on the surface of the ground and where animals go to lick it up. **2** block of salt set out for livestock to lick.

salt·pe·ter (sôlt′pē′tər), *n.* **1** potassium nitrate; niter. **2** kind of fertilizer; sodium nitrate. [< Med.L *sal petrae* salt of rock]

salt·wa·ter (sôlt′wô′tər; -wot′ər), *adj.* **1** consisting of or containing salt water. **2** living in the sea or in water like sea water.

salt·y (sôl′ti), *adj.,* **salt·i·er, salt·i·est. 1** containing salt; tasting of salt. **2** to the point; witty and a bit improper: *a salty remark.* —**salt′i·ly,** *adv.* —**salt′i·ness,** *n.*

sa·lu·bri·ous (sə lü′bri əs), *adj.* healthful. [< L *salubris* < *salus* good health] —**sa·lu′bri·ous·ly,** *adv.* —**sa·lu′bri·ty,** *n.*

sal·u·tar·y (sal′yə ter′i), *adj.* **1** beneficial: *salutary advice.* **2** good for the health; wholesome: *salutary exercise.* [< L *salutaris* < *salus* good health] —**sal′u·tar′i·ness,** *n.*

sal·u·ta·tion (sal′yə tā′shən), *n.* **1** a greeting; saluting: *the man raised his hat in salutation.* **2** something uttered, written, or done to salute. You begin a letter with a salutation, such as "Dear Sir."

sa·lu·ta·to·ri·an (sə lü'tə tô'ri ən; –tō'–), *n.* in American colleges and schools, student who delivers the salutatory address.

sa·lu·ta·to·ry (sə lü'tə tô'ri; –tō'–), *adj., n., pl.* **–ries.** —*adj.* expressing greeting; welcoming. —*n.* an opening address welcoming guests at the graduation of a class.

sa·lute (sə lüt'), *v.,* **–lut·ed, –lut·ing,** *n.* —*v.* **1** honor in a formal manner by raising the hand to the head, by firing guns, or by dipping flags: *salute the flag.* **2** meet with kind words, a bow, a kiss, etc.; greet: *salute one's friends.* **3** come to; meet: *shouts of welcome saluted their ears.* —*n.* **1** act of saluting; sign of welcome, farewell, or honor. **2** position of the hand, gun, etc., in saluting. [< L *salutare* greet < *salus* good health] —**sa·lut'er,** *n.*

Sal·va·dor (sal'və dôr'), *n.* =El Salvador. —**Sal'va·do'ran, Sal'va·do'ri·an,** *adj., n.*

sal·vage (sal'vij), *n., v.,* **–vaged, –vag·ing.** —*n.* **1** act of saving a ship or its cargo from wreck, capture, etc. **2** payment for saving it. **3** rescue of property from fire, etc. **4** property salvaged: *the salvage from a shipwreck or a fire.* —*v.* save from fire, shipwreck, etc. [< F, or < Med.L *salvagium,* ult. < L *salvus* safe] —**sal'vage·a·ble,** *adj.* —**sal'vag·er,** *n.*

sal·va·tion (sal vā'shən), *n.* **1** a saving or being saved. **2** person or thing that saves. **3** a saving of the soul; deliverance from sin and from punishment for sin. [< LL, ult. < L *salvus* safe]

salve[1] (sav; säv), *n., v.,* **salved, salv·ing.** —*n.* **1** a soft, greasy substance put on wounds and sores; healing ointment. **2** *Fig.* something soothing: *kind words are a salve to hurt feelings.* —*v.* **1** put salve on. **2** *Fig.* soothe; smooth over: *he salved his conscience by the thought that his lie harmed no one.* [OE *sealf*]

salve[2] (salv), *v.,* **salved, salv·ing.** save from loss or destruction; salvage. [< SALVAGE] —**sal'va·ble,** *adj.*

sal·ver (sal'vər), *n.* tray. [< F < Sp. *salva,* orig., foretasting, ult. < L *salvus* safe]

sal·vi·a (sal'vi ə), *n.* **1** a garden plant with racemes of bright-red flowers; scarlet sage. **2** any plant of the same family. [< L, prob. < *salvus* healthy; with ref. to its supposed healing properties. Doublet of SAGE[2].]

sal·vo (sal'vō), *n., pl.* **–vos, –voes.** the discharge of several guns at the same time as a broadside or as a salute. [< Ital., ult. < L *salve* hail!, be in good health!]

Sam., Samuel, the name of two books of the Bible.

S. Am., South America; South American.

sam·a·ra (sam'ə rə; sə mār'ə), *n.* any dry fruit that has a winglike extension and does not split open when ripe. [< L, elm seed]

Sa·mar·i·tan (sə mar'ə tən), *n.* **1** the good Samaritan. **2** *Fig.* person who unselfishly helps another in distress.

sa·mar·i·um (sə mãr'i əm), *n.* a rare metal, Sm, an element of the cerium group.

sam·ba (sam'bə), *n.* an African dance adapted and modified in Brazil.

same (sām), *adj.* **1** not another; identical: *we came back the same way we went.* **2** just alike; not different: *her name and mine are the same.* **3** unchanged in character, condition, etc.: *he is the same kind old man.* **4** just spoken of; aforesaid. —*pron.* **1** the same person or thing. **2 the same,** in the same manner. *Sea* and *see* are pronounced the same.

all the same, notwithstanding; nevertheless.

just the same, a in the same manner. **b** nevertheless. [OE] —**same'ness,** *n.*

sam·ite (sam'īt; sā'mīt), *n.* a heavy, rich silk fabric, sometimes interwoven with gold, worn in the Middle Ages. [< OF < Med.Gk. *hexamiton* < Gk. *hex* six + *mitos* thread]

Sa·mo·a (sə mō'ə), *n.* group of independent islands in the S Pacific; Western Samoa. —**Sa·mo'an,** *adj., n.*

sam·o·var (sam'ə vär; sam'ə vär'), *n.* a metal urn used for heating water for tea. [< Russ., lit., self-boiler]

sam·pan (sam'pan), *n.* any of various small boats of China, etc. A sampan is sculled by one or more oars at the stern. [< Chinese < Pg.; orig. uncert.]

sam·ple (sam'pəl; säm'–), *n., adj., v.,* **–pled, –pling.** —*n.* part to show what the rest is like; one thing to show what the others are like: *shoving in line is one sample of bad manners.* —*adj.* serving as a sample: *a sample copy.* —*v.* take a part of; test a part of: *sample a cake.* [var. of *essample,* var. of *example*]

sam·pler (sam'plər; säm'–), *n.* **1** person who samples. **2** piece of cloth embroidered to show skill in needlework.

Sam·son (sam'sən), *n.* any very strong man.

Sam·u·el (sam'yü əl), *n.* either of two books in the Old Testament.

sam·u·rai (sam'ú rī), *n., pl.* **–rai. 1** the military class in feudal Japan. **2** member of this class. [< Jap.]

san·a·to·ri·um (san'ə tô'ri əm; –tō'–), *n., pl.* **–to·ri·ums, –to·ri·a** (–tô'ri ə; –tō'–). sanitarium; health resort. [< NL, neut. of LL *sanatorius* health-giving, ult. < L *sanus* healthy]

san·a·to·ry (san'ə tô'ri; –tō'–), *adj.* healing; having power to cure. [< LL, ult. < L *sanus* healthy]

sanc·ti·fied (sangk'tə fīd), *adj.* consecrated.

sanc·ti·fy (sangk'tə fī), *v.,* **–fied, –fy·ing. 1** make holy: *a life of sacrifice had sanctified her.* **2** set apart as sacred; observe as holy: *a service to sanctify the work of the missionaries.* **3** justify; make right. [< L, < *sanctus* holy + *facere* make] —**sanc'ti·fi·ca'tion,** *n.* —**sanc'ti·fi'er,** *n.*

sanc·ti·mo·ni·ous (sangk'tə mō'ni əs), *adj.* making a show of holiness; putting on airs of sanctity. —**sanc'ti·mo'ni·ous·ly,** *adv.* —**sanc'ti·mo'ni·ous·ness,** *n.*

sanc·ti·mo·ny (sangk'tə mō'ni), *n.* show of holiness; airs of sanctity.

sanc·tion (sangk'shən), *n.* **1** permission with authority; support; approval: *the sanction of the law.* **2** action by several nations toward another, intended to force it to obey international law, as a blockade, military force, etc. —*v.* authorize; approve; allow: *we do not sanction cheating.* [< L, < *sancire* ordain] —**sanc'tion·er,** *n.*

sanc·ti·ty (sangk'tə ti), *n., pl.* **–ties. 1** holiness; saintliness; godliness. **2** sacredness; holy character: *the sanctity of a church.* [< L, < *sanctus* holy]

sanc·tu·ar·y (sangk'chú er'i), *n., pl.* **–ar·ies. 1** a sacred place. A church is a sanctuary. **2** part of a church around the altar. **3** a sacred place of refuge or protection. **4** any asylum or place of refuge: *a bird sanctuary.* [< L, ult. < *sanctus* holy]

sanc·tum (sangk'təm), *n.* **1** a sacred place. **2** a private room or office where a person can be undisturbed. [< L, orig. neut. adj., holy]

Sanc·tus (sangk'təs, sängk'tús), *n.* **1** hymn that begins with the Latin "Sanctus, Sanctus, Sanctus" ("Holy, Holy, Holy"). **2** musical setting for this, esp. in a longer composition of a mass. [< L]

sand (sand), *n.* tiny grains of worn-down or disintegrated rocks. —*v.* **1** sprinkle with sand. **2** clean, smooth, or polish with sand, sandpaper, etc.

sands, tract or region composed mainly of sand. [OE]

san·dal (san'dəl), *n.* **1** kind of shoe made of a sole fastened to the foot by straps. **2** kind of cutout slipper. [< F < L, ult. < Gk. *sandalon*] —**san'daled,** *adj.*

san·dal·wood (san'dəl wüd'), *n.* **1** a fragrant wood used for making boxes, fans, etc., and burned as incense. **2** the tree that it comes from.

sand·bag (sand'bag'), *n., v.,* **–bagged, –bag·ging.** —*n.* bag filled with sand, used to build dikes, etc. —*v.* **1** furnish with sandbags. **2** hit or stun with a sandbag. —**sand'bag'ger,** *n.*

sand·bank (sand'bangk'), *n.* ridge of sand, esp. at the water's edge; sand bar.

sand bar, ridge of sand formed by the action of tides or currents.

sand·blast (sand'blast'; –bläst'), *n.* **1** blast of air or steam containing sand, used to clean, grind, cut, or decorate hard surfaces, such as glass, stone, or metal. **2** =sandblaster. —*v.* use a sandblaster.

sand·blast·er (sand'blas'tər), *n.* **1** machine used to sandblast. **2** person who sandblasts.

sand·box (sand'boks'), *n.* large, low box to hold sand, esp. for children to play in.

sand·hog (sand'hog'; –hôg'), *n.* person who works underground or underwater, esp. building a tunnel or setting piers for a bridge.

sand·man (sand′man′), *n.* the fabled man said to make children sleepy, by sprinkling sand on their eyes.

sand·pa·per (sand′pā′pər), *n.* a strong paper with a layer of sand glued on it, used for smoothing, cleaning, or polishing. —*v.* smooth, clean, or polish with this.

sand·pip·er (sand′pīp′ər), *n.* a small bird with a long bill, living on sandy shores.

sand·stone (sand′stōn′), *n.* kind of rock formed mostly of sand.

sand·storm (sand′stôrm′), *n.* storm of wind that bears along clouds of sand.

sand·wich (sand′wich), *n.* two or more slices of bread with meat, jelly, cheese, or some other filling between them. —*v.* put in (between): *he was sandwiched between two fat people.* [from the Earl of *Sandwich*]

sand·y (san′di), *adj.,* **sand·i·er, sand·i·est.** 1 containing or consisting of sand; covered with sand. 2 yellowish-red: *sandy hair.* 3 shifting like sand; not stable. —**sand′i·ness,** *n.*

sane (sān), *adj.,* **san·er, san·est.** 1 having a healthy mind; not crazy. 2 having or showing good sense; sensible. [< L *sanus* healthy] —**sane′ly,** *adv.* —**sane′ness,** *n.*

sang (sang), *v.* pt. of **sing.**

sang-froid (sän frwä′), *n.* coolness of mind; calmness; composure. [F, lit., cold blood]

san·gri·a (sang gri′ə), *n.* Spanish drink of red or white wine, fruit juice, sliced fruit, and soda water. [< Sp. *sangría* < *sangre* blood]

san·gui·nar·y (sang′gwə ner′i), *adj.* 1 with much blood or bloodshed; bloody: *a sanguinary battle.* 2 delighting in bloodshed; bloodthirsty. [< L *sanguinarius* < *sanguis* blood] —**san′gui·nar′i·ly,** *adv.* —**san′gui·nar′i·ness,** *n.*

san·guine (sang′gwin), *adj.* 1 naturally cheerful and hopeful: *a sanguine disposition.* 2 confident; hopeful: *sanguine of success.* 3 having a healthy red color; ruddy: *a sanguine complexion.* 4 =sanguinary. [< L *sanguineus.* See SANGUINARY.] —**san′guine·ly,** *adv.* —**san′guine·ness,** *n.*

san·i·tar·i·um (san′ə tãr′i əm), *n., pl.* **-tar·i·ums, -tar·i·a** (-tãr′i ə). establishment for treatment of the sick or convalescent; nursing home. [< L *sanitas* health < *sanus* healthy]

san·i·tar·y (san′ə ter′i), *adj.* 1 of or pertaining to health; favorable to health; preventing disease: *sanitary regulations.* 2 free from dirt and filth. [< F *sanitaire,* ult. < L *sanus* healthy] —**san′i·tar′i·ly,** *adv.* —**san′i·tar′i·ness,** *n.*

san·i·ta·tion (san′ə tā′shən), *n.* the working out and practical application of sanitary measures.

san·i·tize (san′ə tīz), *v.,* **-tized, -tiz·ing.** 1 clean; free of germs; disinfect. 2 *Fig.* make (something) appear more wholesome or acceptable; clean up.

san·i·ty (san′ə ti), *n.* 1 soundness of mind; mental health. 2 soundness of judgment; sensibleness; reasonableness. [< L, < *sanus* healthy]

San Jo·sé (san′ hō zā′), capital of Costa Rica.

San Juan (san hwän′), seaport and capital of Puerto Rico, in the NE part.

sank (sangk), *v.* pt. of **sink.**

San Ma·ri·no (sän′ mä rē′nō), an independent republic in the E part of the Italian peninsula.

sans (sanz; *Fr.* sän), *prep.* French. without. [< F < L *absentia* (abl.) in the absence (of), infl. by L *sine* without]

San Sal·va·dor (san sal′və dôr), capital of El Salvador.

San·sei or **san·sei** (sän′sā′), *n., pl.* **-sei** or **-seis.** person born in America or Canada whose grandparents were Japanese immigrants.

sans-ser·if (sanz′sèr′if), *n.* or **sans serif,** style of type without serifs. [< F *sans* without + E *serif*]

San·skrit, San·scrit (san′skrit), *n.* the ancient literary language of India, esp. important in the study of the development of European languages. —*adj.* of or having to do with Sanskrit.

San·ta (san′tə *for 1;* san′tə, sän′tä *for 2*), *n.* 1 Santa Claus. 2 a Spanish or an Italian word meaning *saint,* used in combinations.

San·ta Claus (san′tə klôz′), Saint Nicholas, the saint of Christmas-giving, according to modern conception.

San·ta Fe (san′tə fā′), capital of New Mexico, in the N part.

San·ti·a·go (san′ti ä′gō), *n.* capital of Chile, in the C part.

San·to Do·min·go (san′tō də ming′gō), capital of the Dominican Republic.

São To·mé (soun tü me′), capital of São Tomé e Principe on the island of São Tomé.

São To·mé e Prín·ci·pe (soun tü me′ e prin′si pə), country composed of several islands off the W coast of Africa.

sap¹ (sap), *n.* 1 liquid that circulates through a plant, carrying water, food, etc., as blood does in animals. Rising sap carries water and salt from the roots; sap traveling downward carries sugar, gums, resins, etc. 2 any life-giving liquid. 3 sapwood. 4 a silly, stupid person; fool. [OE *sæp*] —**sap′less,** *adj.*

sap² (sap), *v.,* **sapped, sap·ping.** 1 dig under or wear away the foundation of. 2 weaken; use up: *the extreme heat sapped our strength.* [< F or Ital. < LL *sappa* spade]

sa·pi·ent (sā′pi ənt), *adj.* wise; sage. [< L *sapiens* being wise] —**sa′pi·ence,** *n.* —**sa′pi·ent·ly,** *adv.*

sap·ling (sap′ling), *n.* 1 a young tree. 2 a young person.

sap·o·dil·la (sap′ə dil′ə), *n.* 1 a large evergreen tree of tropical America that yields chicle and bears large, edible berries that look and taste somewhat like pears. 2 its fruit.

sa·pon·i·fy (sə pon′ə fī), *v.,* **-fied, -fy·ing.** 1 make (a fat or oil) into soap by treating with an alkali. 2 become soap. [< NL, < L *sapo* soap + *facere* make]

sap·phire (saf′īr), *n.* 1 a bright-blue precious stone, that is hard and clear like a diamond. 2 a bright blue. 3 variety of corundum of gem quality and colors other than red. —*adj.* bright-blue. [< L < Gk. *sappheiros*]

sap·py (sap′i), *adj.,* **-pi·er, -pi·est.** 1 full of sap. 2 vigorous; energetic. 3 *Informal.* silly; foolish; overly sentimental. —**sap′pi·ly,** *adv.* —**sap′pi·ness,** *n.*

sap·ro·phyte (sap′rō fīt), *n.* a vegetable organism that lives on decaying organic matter. Certain fungi are saprophytes. [< Gk. *sapros* rotten + E *-phyte* < Gk. *phyton* plant] —**sap′ro·phyt′ic,** *adj.*

sap·suck·er (sap′suk′ər), *n.* a small American woodpecker that feeds on the sap and sapwood of trees.

sap·wood (sap′wŭd′), *n.* the soft, new, living wood between the bark and the hard, inner wood of most trees.

Sar·a·cen (sar′ə sən), *n.* a Muslim at the time of the Crusades. —*adj.* of or pertaining to the Saracens.

sa·ran wrap, (sə ran′) thin, clear plastic film, used esp. to wrap and preserve food. [< *Saran,* trademark of this film]

sar·casm (sär′kaz əm), *n.* 1 a sneering or cutting remark; ironical taunt. 2 act of making fun of a person to hurt his feelings; bitter irony. [< LL < Gk. *sarkasmos* < *sarkezein* sneer, strip off flesh < *sarx* flesh]

sar·cas·tic (sär kas′tik), *adj.* using sarcasm; sneering; cutting. —**sar·cas′ti·cal·ly,** *adv.*

sar·co·ma (sär kō′mə), *n., pl.* **-mas, -ma·ta** (-mə tə). any of various harmful tumors of connective tissue. [< NL < Gk., ult. < *sarx* flesh] —**sar·co′ma·tous,** *adj.*

sar·coph·a·gus (sär kof′ə gəs), *n., pl.* **-gi** (-jī), **-gus·es.** a stone coffin, esp. an ornamental one. [< L < Gk., orig., flesh-eating (stone) < *sarx* flesh + *phagein* eat]

sar·dine (sär dēn′), *n., pl.* **-dines** or (*esp. collectively*) **-dine.** kind of small fish preserved in oil for food. [< F < Ital. < L *sardina* < *sarda*]

sar·don·ic (sär don′ik), *adj.* bitter; sarcastic; scornful; mocking: *a fiend's sardonic laugh.* [< F < L < Gk. *Sardonios,* a supposed Sardinian plant that produced hysterical convulsions] —**sar·don′i·cal·ly,** *adv.*

sa·ri (sä′ri), *n., pl.* **-ris.** a long piece of cotton or silk, the outer garment of Hindu women, worn, wound around the body with one end thrown over the head or shoulder. [< Hind.]

sa·rong (sə rông′; -rong′), *n.* 1 a rectangular piece of cloth, usually a brightly colored printed material, worn as a skirt by men and women in the Malay

Archipelago, East Indies, etc. 2 woman's skirt made to resemble the sarong. [< Malay *sārung*]

sar·sa·pa·ril·la (sas′pə ril′ə; sär′sə pə–), *n.* 1 a tropical American plant of the smilax genus, or its root. 2 a cooling drink made from the root. [< Sp. *zarzaparilla* < *zarza* bramble + *parra* vine]

sar·to·ri·al (sär tô′ri əl; –tō′–), *adj.* of tailors or their work. [< L *sartorius* of a tailor, ult. < *sarcire* to patch]

sash[1] (sash), *n.* a long, broad strip of cloth or ribbon, worn as an ornament round the waist or over one shoulder, [ult. < Ar. *shāsh* turban]

sash[2] (sash), *n.* 1 frame for the glass of a window or door. 2 such frames. —*v.* furnish with sashes. [alter. of *chassis*, taken as pl.]

sa·shay (sa shā′), *v.*, glide, move, or go about. [< F, *alter.* of *chassé* gliding step]

Sas·katch·e·wan (sas kach′ə won), *n.* province in W Canada.

sas·sa·fras (sas′ə fras), *n.* 1 a slender American tree that has fragrant, yellow flowers and bluish-black fruit. 2 the aromatic dried bark of its root, used in medicine and to flavor candy, soft drinks, etc. 3 the flavor. [< Sp. *sasafras*]

sas·sy (sas′i), *adj.*, **–si·er**, **–si·est.** *U.S.* saucy.

sat (sat), *v.* pt. and pp. of **sit.**

Sat., Saturday.

Sa·tan (sā′tən), *n.* the evil spirit; the enemy of goodness; the Devil. [< L < Gk. < Heb. *sātān* adversary] —**sa·tan′ic,** *adj.* —**sa·tan′i·cal·ly,** *adv.*

sate (sāt), *v.*, **sat·ed, sat·ing.** 1 satisfy fully (any appetite or desire). 2 supply with more than enough, so as to disgust or weary. [alter. of *sade* (OE *sadian* glut; cf. SAD) under infl. of L *satiare* SATIATE]

sa·teen (sa tēn′), *n.* a cotton cloth made to imitate satin, often used for lining sleeves, [var. of *satin*]

sat·el·lite (sat′ə līt), *n.* 1 a small planet that revolves around a larger planet. 2 a sphere or other object launched into an orbit around the earth. 3 *Fig.* follower or attendant upon a person of importance. [< L *satelles* attendant]

sa·ti·a·ble (sā′shi ə bəl; sā′shə bəl), *adj.* that can be satiated. —**sa′ti·a·bil′i·ty, sa′ti·a·ble·ness,** *n.* —**sa′ti·a·bly,** *adv.*

sa·ti·ate (sā′shi āt), *v.*, **–at·ed, –at·ing.** 1 feed fully; satisfy fully. 2 supply with too much; weary or disgust with too much. [< L, < *satis* enough] —**sa′ti·a′tion,** *n.*

sa·ti·e·ty (sə tī′ə ti), *n.* the feeling of having had too much; satiated condition. [< L *satietas*. See SATIATE.]

sat·in (sat′ən), *n.* a silk or rayon cloth with one very smooth, glossy side. —*adj.* of or like satin; smooth and glossy. [< OF, ult. < VL *seta* silk] —**sat·in′like′,** *adj.* —**sat′in·y,** *adj.*

sat·in·wood (sat′ən wüd′), *n.* 1 the smooth wood of an East Indian tree, used to ornament furniture, etc. 2 the tree itself.

sat·ire (sat′īr), *n.* 1 use of sarcasm or irony to attack or ridicule a habit, idea, custom, etc. 2 poem, essay, story, etc., that attacks or ridicules in this way. [< L *satira,* var. of (*lanx*) *satura* full (dish)]

sa·tir·i·cal (sə tir′ə kəl), **sa·tir·ic** (–ik), *adj.* of satire; containing satire; fond of using satire. —**sa·tir′i·cal·ly,** *adv.* —**sa·tir′i·cal·ness,** *n.*

sat·i·rist (sat′ə rist), *n.* writer of satires; person who uses satire.

sat·i·rize (sat′ə rīz), *v.*, **–rized, –riz·ing.** attack with satire; criticize with mockery; seek to improve by ridicule. —**sat′i·riz′er,** *n.*

sat·is·fac·tion (sat′is fak′shən), *n.* 1 condition of being satisfied or pleased and contented. 2 anything that makes a person feel pleased or contented. 3 fulfillment; gratification. 4 payment of debt; discharge of obligation; making up for wrong or injury done.

give satisfaction, a satisfy. **b** fight a duel because of an insult.

sat·is·fac·to·ry (sat′is fak′tə ri; –tri), *adj.* satisfying; good enough to satisfy. —**sat′is·fac′to·ri·ly,** *adv.* —**sat′is·fac′to·ri·ness,** *n.*

sat·is·fy (sat′is fī), *v.*, **–fied, –fy·ing.** 1 give enough to; fulfill (desires, hopes, demands, etc.); put an end to (needs, wants, etc.): *satisfy one's appetite.* 2 make contented; please: *are you satisfied now?* 3 pay (a debt or creditor): *satisfy a bill.* 4 make right (a wrong); make reparation to (a person): *satisfy claims for damage.* 5 set free from doubt; convince: *he was satisfied that it was an accident.* [< OF < L, < *satis* enough + *facere* do] —**sat′is·fi′a·ble,** *adj.* —**sat′is·fi′er,** *n.* —**sat′is·fy′ing·ly,** *adv.*

sa·trap (sā′trap; sat′rap), *n.* 1 ruler, often a tyrant, who is subordinate to a higher ruler. 2 governor of a province under the ancient Persian monarchy. [< L < Gk. *satrapes* < OPers.]

sa·trap·y (sā′trə pi; sat′rə–), *n.*, pl. **–trap·ies.** province or authority of a satrap.

sat·u·ra·ble (sach′ə rə bəl), *adj.* that can be saturated. —**sat′u·ra·bil′i·ty,** *n.*

sat·u·rate (sach′ə rāt), *v.*, **–rat·ed, –rat·ing.** 1 soak thoroughly; fill full: *saturate the moss with water before planting the bulbs in it.* 2 cause (a substance) to unite with the greatest possible amount of another substance. A **saturated solution** (of sugar, salt, etc.) is one that cannot dissolve any more (sugar, salt, etc.). [< L *saturatus* glutted < *satur* full]

sat·u·ra·tion (sach′ə rā′shən), *n.* 1 act or process of saturating. 2 fact of being saturated; saturated condition.

saturation point, 1 point at which a substance will take up no more of another substance. 2 *Fig.* condition which a person can endure no more.

Sat·ur·day (sat′ər di; –dā), *n.* the seventh day of the week, following Friday.

Sat·urn (sat′ərn), *n.* large planet that has rings around it.

sauce (sôs), *n., v.*, **sauced, sauc·ing.** —*n.* 1 something, usually a liquid, served with food to make it taste better: *tomato sauce.* 2 stewed fruit: *applesauce.* 3 *Fig.* something that adds interest or relish: *a sauce of witty conversation.* —*v.* season. [< OF < L *salsa,* fem. adj., salted, ult. < *sal* salt]

sauce·pan (sôs′pan′), *n.* a metal pot with a handle, used for stewing, boiling, etc.

sau·cer (sô′sər), *n.* 1 a shallow dish to set a cup on. 2 something round and shallow like a saucer. [< OF *saucier* sauce dish < *sauce* SAUCE] —**sau′cer·less,** *adj.*

sau·cy (sô′si), *adj.*, **–ci·er, –ci·est.** 1 showing lack of respect; rude: *saucy remarks.* 2 pert; smart: *a saucy hat.* [< SAUCE] —**sau′ci·ly,** *adv.* —**sau′ci·ness,** *n.*

Sa·u·di Arabia (sä ü′di), country in C Arabia.

sau·er·bra·ten (sour′brä′tən), *n.* pot roast of beef marinated in vinegar and herbs before it is cooked. [< G *sauer* sour + *Braten* roast meat]

sauer·kraut (sour′krout′), *n.* cabbage cut fine, salted, and allowed to ferment. [< G, < *sauer* sour + *kraut* cabbage]

Sauk (sak, sôk), *n.,* pl. **Sauk, Sauks.** 1 member of a tribe of North American Indians of Algonkian descent, originally living in Michigan and Wisconsin. 2 their language. —*adj.* of or having to do with the Sauk. Also, **Sac.**

Saul (sôl), *n.* the original name of the apostle Paul. Acts 9:1–31.

sau·na (sô′nä; sou′–), *n.* 1 steam bath in which steam is produced by pouring water on hot stones. 2 room or small outbuilding for it.

saun·ter (sôn′tər; sän′–), *v.* walk along slowly and happily; stroll: *saunter through the park.* —*n.* 1 a leisurely or careless gait. 2 a stroll. —**saun′ter·ing·ly,** *adv.*

sau·ri·an (sô′ri ən), *adj.* of or belonging to the lizards, or to the lizards and certain other reptiles. [< NL, < Gk. *sauros* lizard]

sau·sage (sô′sij), *n.* chopped pork, beef, or other meats, seasoned and usually stuffed into a thin tube. [< OF < LL *salsicia,* ult. < L *sal* salt]

sau·té (sō tā′), *adj., n., v.*, **–téed, –té·ing.** —*adj.* cooked or browned in a little fat. —*n.* dish of food cooked in this way. —*v.* fry quickly in a little fat. [< F, pp., jumped]

sau·terne (sō tèrn′), *n.* a French white wine. [from *Sauterne,* in France, where the grapes are grown]

sav·age (sav′ij), *adj.* 1 fierce, ferocious, or cruel: *a savage dog.* 2 not civilized; barbarous: *savage customs.* 3 wild or rugged, as country or scenery. —*n.* 1 member of a people in the lowest stage of development or cultivation. 2 a fierce, brutal, or cruel person. [< OF *sauvage* < LL *salvaticus,* ult. < L *silva* forest] —**sav′age·ly,** *adv.* —**sav′age·ness,** *n.*

sav·age·ry (sav′ij ri), *n., pl.* **–ries. 1** an uncivilized condition: *live in savagery.* **2** fierceness; cruelty; brutality.

sa·van·na, sa·van·nah (sə van′ə), *n.* a treeless plain. [< earlier Sp. *zavana* < Carib]

sa·vant (sə vänt′; sav′ənt), *n., pl.* **sa·vants.** person of learning or science. [< earlier F ppr. of *savoir* know < L *sapere* be wise]

save[1] (sāv), *v.,* **saved, sav·ing. 1** make or keep safe from harm, danger, loss, etc.; rescue: *save a drowning man, save one's honor.* **2** lay aside; store up: *save pieces of string.* **3** keep from spending or wasting: *save your strength, save for a bicycle.* **4** prevent; make less: *save work, save trouble.* [< OF < LL *salvare* < L *salvus* safe] **—sav′a·ble, save′a·ble,** *adj.* **—sav′er,** *n.*

save[2] (sāv), *prep.* except; but: *work every day save Sundays.* [var. of *safe,* in sense of "not being involved"]

sav·ing (sāv′ing), *adj.* **1** that saves. **2** accustomed to save; economical. **3** making a reservation: *a saving clause.* —*n.* **1** act or way of saving money, time, etc.: *it will be a saving to take this short cut.* **2** that which is saved. —*prep.* **1** save; except. **2** with all due respect to or for: *saving your presence.* —*conj.* with the exception of.

savings, money saved. **—sav′ing·ly,** *adv.* **—sav′ing·ness,** *n.*

saving grace, a quality that redeems: *one saving grace is humor.*

savings bank, bank which pays interest even on small deposits.

sav·ior (sāv′yər), *n.* one who saves or rescues.

the Saviour, or **Savior,** Jesus Christ.

sa·voir-faire (sav′wär fãr′), *n.* knowledge of just what to do; tact. [< F, lit., knowing how to act]

sa·vor (sā′vər), *n.* **1** taste or smell; flavor: *the soup has a savor of onion.* **2** a pleasing flavor or distinctive quality. —*v.* **1** taste or smell (*of*): *a sauce that savors of lemon.* **2** taste with pleasure. **3** have the quality or nature (*of*): *a request that savors of a command.* [< OF < L *sapor*] **—sa′vor·er,** *n.* **—sa′vor·ous,** *adj.*

sa·vor·y[1] (sā′vər i), *adj.* **-vor·i·er, -vor·i·est,** *n., pl.* **-vor·ies.** *adj.* **1** pleasing in taste or smell. **2** morally pleasing; agreeable. —*n.* highly seasoned, appetizing dish served at the beginning or end of a dinner. [< OF *savoure,* ult. < L *sapor* taste] **—sa′vor·i·ly,** *adv.* **—sa′vor·i·ness,** *n.*

sa·vor·y[2] (sā′vər i), *n., pl.* **-vor·ies.** any of several fragrant herbs of the mint family used for seasoning food. [< L *satureia*]

sa·voy (sə voi′), *n.* kind of spinach or cabbage with wrinkled leaves. [after *Savoy,* a region in France]

sav·vy (sav′i), *v.,* **-vied, -vy·ing,** *n.* —*v.* know; understand. —*n.* understanding; intelligence; sense. —*adj.* intelligent; sensible. [partly < F *savez(-vous)?* do you know?, partly < Sp. *sabe* or *sabes* you know; both ult. < L *sapere* be wise]

saw[1] (sô), *n., v.,* **sawed, sawed** or **sawn, saw·ing.** —*n.* tool for cutting, made of a thin blade with sharp teeth on the edge. —*v.* **1** cut with a saw. **2** make or form with a saw. **3** use a saw. **4** be sawed: *wood that saws easily.* [OE *sagu*] **—saw′er,** *n.*

saw[2] (sô), *v.* pt. of **see**[1].

saw[3] (sô), *n.* wise saying; proverb. "A stitch in time saves nine" is a familiar saw. [OE *sagu;* akin to SAY]

saw·buck (sô′buk′), *n.* **1** =sawhorse. **2** *Informal.* a ten-dollar bill. [(def. 1) < Du. *zaagbok;* (def. 2) with ref. to the x-shaped ends of a sawyer's sawbuck, X being the Roman numeral for 10]

saw·dust (sô′dust′), *n.* particles of wood made by sawing.

saw·fish (sô′fish′), *n., pl.* **-fish·es** or (*esp. collectively*) **-fish.** fish like a shark, with a long, flat snout like a saw.

saw·horse (sô′hôrs′), *n.* frame for holding wood that is being sawed.

saw·mill (sô′mil′), *n.* a building where machines saw timber into planks, boards, etc.

sawn (sôn), *v.* pp. of **saw**[1].

saw·tooth (sô′tüth′), *n., pl.* **-teeth, -tooths.** *n.* **1** tooth on a sawblade. **2** notched tooth of an animal or machine. —*adj.* having sawteeth or like sawteeth. **—saw′toothed′,** *adj.*

saw·yer (sô′yər), *n.* person whose work is sawing timber.

sax·i·frage (sak′sə frij), *n.* a low, spreading plant with rosettes of thick leaves with silvery, toothed edges, often grown in rock gardens. [< L *saxifraga,* ult. < *saxum* rock + *frangere* break. Doublet of SALSIFY.]

Sax·on (sak′sən), *n.* **1** member of a German tribe dwelling in NW Germany in ancient times. With the Angles and Jutes, the Saxons conquered Britain in the fifth and sixth centuries A.D. **2** language of the Saxons. —*adj.* pertaining to the early Saxons or their language.

sax·o·phone (sak′sə fōn), *n.* a brass musical instrument with keys for the fingers and a reed mouthpiece. [after A. *Sax,* the inventor] **—sax′o·phon′ist,** *n.*

say (sā), *v.,* **said, say·ing,** *n.* —*v.* **1** speak: *what did you say?* **2** put into words; express; declare: *say what you think.* **3** recite; repeat: *say your prayers.* **4** suppose; take for granted: *you can learn in, say, ten lessons.* **5** express an opinion: *it is hard to say.* —*n.* **1** what a person says or has to say: *I have had my say.* **2** chance to say something.

that is to say, that is; in other words.

the (final) say, power; authority; final word: *the boss has the final say, of course.*

to say nothing of, without mentioning.

when all is said and done, in the end; ultimately. [OE *secgan*] **—say′a·ble,** *adj.* **—say′er,** *n.*

say·est (sā′ist), **sayst** (sāst), *v. Archaic.* say. "Thou sayest" means "you say."

say·ing (sā′ing), *n.* **1** something said; statement. **2** proverb.

go without saying, be too obvious to need mention.

say-so (sā′sō), *n.* **1** an unsupported statement. **2** authority; power.

Sb, antimony.

Sc, scandium.

Sc., Scotch; Scottish.

sc., 1 scene. **2** science.

SC, (*zip code*) South Carolina.

S.C., 1 Signal Corps. **2** South Carolina.

s.c., small capitals.

scab (skab), *n., v.,* **scabbed, scab·bing.** —*n.* **1** crust that forms over a sore during healing. **2** worker who will not join a labor union or who takes a striker's place. —*v.* **1** become covered with a scab. **2** act or work as a scab. [< Scand. (Dan.) *skab*]

scab·bard (skab′ərd), *n.* sheath or case for the blade of a sword, etc. [< AF *escaubers,* pl.]

scab·by (skab′i), *adj.,* **-bi·er, -bi·est. 1** covered with scabs. **2** consisting of scabs. **—scab′bi·ly,** *adv.* **—scab′bi·ness,** *n.*

sca·bies (skā′bēz; -bi ēz), *n.* disease of the skin caused by mites that live as parasites under the skin and cause itching. [< L, itch, < *scabere* to scratch]

sca·brous (skā′brəs), *adj.* **1** somewhat indelicate, salacious, or risqué. **2** full of difficulties; harsh. [< LL, < L *scaber* scaly] **—sca′brous·ly,** *adv.*

scad (skad), *n. Infomal.* Usually, **scads.** a large quantity. [< Scand. (Norw.) *skadd;* akin to SHAD]

scaf·fold (skaf′əld), *n.* **1** a temporary structure for holding workrs and materials during the erection, repair, or decoration of building. **2** a raised platform on which criminals are put to death. —*v.* furnish or support with a scaffold. [< var. of OF *eschaffaut,* from same source as *catafalque*]

scaf·fold·ing (skaf′əl ding), *n.* **1** scaffold. **2** materials for scaffolds.

scal·a·wag (skal′ə wag), *n.* a good-for-nothing person; scamp; rascal.

scald (skôld), *v.* **1** burn with hot liquid or steam. **2** pour boiling liquid over; use boiling liquid on. **3** heat or be heated almost to boiling, but not quite. —*n.* **1** burn caused by hot liquid or steam. **2** any of several parasitic plant diseases. [< dial. OF *escalder* < LL, < L *ex-* very + *calidus* hot]

scale[1] (skāl), *n., v.,* **scaled, scal·ing.** —*n.* **1** one of the thin, flat, hard plates forming the outer covering of some fishes, snakes, and lizards. **2** a thin layer like a scale: *scales of skin peel off after scarlet fever.* **3** one of the parts that unite to cover a bud in winter. **4** Also, **scale insect.** insect that has a shieldlike covering under which it hides and feeds. —*v.* **1** remove scales from. **2** come off in scales. **3** remove in thin layers. [< OF *escale* < Gmc.] **—scal′a·ble,** *adj.* **—scale′less,** *adj.* **—scale′like′,** *adj.*

scale² (skāl), *n., v.,* **scaled, scal·ing.** —*n.* **scales.** a balance; instrument for weighing. —*v.* **1** weigh: *he scales 180 pounds.* **2** weigh in scales; measure; compare. **Scales,** Libra (constellation).

tip the scales, a weigh: *tip the scales at 40 pounds.* **b** *Fig.* overbalance; unbalance: *having money tipped the scales in his favor.*

turn the scales, decide: *public scorn turned the scales against the first plan.* [< Scand. *skāl;* akin to SHALE, SHELL]

scale³ (skāl), *n., v.,* **scaled, scal·ing.** —*n.* **1** series of steps or degrees; scheme of graded amounts: *a scale of wages ranging from $50 to $150 a day.* **2** series of marks made along a line at regular distances to use in measuring. A thermometer has a scale. **3** instrument marked in this way, used for measuring, etc. **4** size of a plan, map, drawing, or model compared with what it represents: *a map drawn to the scale of one inch for each 100 miles.* **5** relative size or extent: *entertain on a large scale.* **6** series of tones ascending or descending in pitch. —*v.* **1** *U.S.* reduce by a certain proportion: *all prices were scaled down 10 percent.* **2** make according to a scale. **3** climb; climb over. [< L *scala* ladder] —**scal'er,** *n.*

sca·lene (skā lēn'; skā'lən), *adj.* of a triangle, having three unequal sides. [< LL < Gk. *skalenos,* orig., staggering]

scal·lion (skal'yən), *n.* **1** kind of onion. **2** =shallot. **3** =leek. [< OF < L (*caepa*) *Ascalonia* (onion) from Ascalon, in Palestine]

scal·lop (skol'əp; skal'-), *n.* **1** shellfish somewhat like a clam. In some species the large muscle that opens and closes the shell is edible. **2** one of the two parts of the shell. **3** one of a series of curves on an edge of a dress, etc. —*v.* **1** bake with sauce and bread crumbs in a dish; escallop: *scalloped oysters, scalloped tomatoes.* **2** make with a series of curves on: *she scallops the edge of the paper.* [< OF *escalope* shell < Gmc.] —**scal'lop·er,** *n.*

scal·lop·pi·ne or **scal·lop·pi·ni** (skal'ə pi'ni), *n., pl.* very thin slices of veal cooked in wine, mushrooms, cheese, and tomato paste. [< It. *scaloppine,* pl. of *scaloppina* small thin slice]

scalp (skalp), *n.* **1** skin and hair on the top and back of the head. **2** part of this skin and hair cut off as a token of victory. —*v.* **1** cut or tear the scalp from. **2** buy and sell to make small quick profits. **3** trade in (tickets to theaters, games, etc.). [< Scand. *skālpr* sheath] —**scalp'er,** *n.*

scal·pel (skal'pəl), *n.* a small, straight knife used by surgeons. [< L *scalpellum,* dim. of *scalprum* knife]

scal·y (skāl'i), *adj.,* **scal·i·er, scal·i·est.** **1** covered with scales; having scales like a fish. **2** suggesting scales. —**scal'i·ness,** *n.*

scam (skam), *n.* fraud; swindle.

scamp (skamp), *n.* rascal; rogue; worthless person. [< dial. *scamp* roam, prob.

< *scamper*] —**scamp'er,** *n.* —**scamp'ish,** *adj.*

scam·per (skam'pər), *v.* run quickly. —*n.* a quick run. [ult. < OF *escamper* run away, ult. < L *ex-* out of + *campus* field]

scam·pi (skäm'pi), *n.* shrimp cooked in butter and garlic. [< It. shrimps]

scan (skan), *v.,* **scanned, scan·ning,** *n.,* —*v.* **1** look at closely; examine with care. **2** glance at; look over hastily. **3** mark off (lines of poetry) into feet. *Example:* Sing' a song' of six'pence. **4** be according to the rules for marking off lines of poetry into feet. **5 a** expose bits of a surface in rapid succession to beams of electrons in order to transmit a television picture. **b** examine a part of the body by using electromagnetic beams or X rays. **6** convert a document into electronic form for use or storage in a computer. —*n.* act or fact of scanning. [< LL *scandere* < L, climb]

Scand., 1 Scandinavia. **2** Scandinavian.

scan·dal (skan'dəl), *n.* **1** a shameful action that brings disgrace or offends public opinion. **2** damage to reputation; disgrace. **3** public talk about a person that will hurt his reputation; evil gossip. [< L < Gk. *skandalon* trap. Doublet of SLANDER.]

scan·dal·ize (skan'dəl īz), *v.,* **-ized, -iz·ing.** offend by something wrong or improper; shock. —**scan'dal·iz'er,** *n.*

scan·dal·mon·ger (skan'dəl mung'gər; -mong'-), *n.* person who spreads scandal and evil gossip.

scan·dal·ous (skan'dəl əs), *adj.* **1** disgraceful to reputation; shameful; shocking. **2** spreading scandal or slander; slandering. —**scan'dal·ous·ly,** *adv.* —**scan'dal·ous·ness,** *n.*

Scan·di·na·vi·a (skan'də nā'vi ə; -nāv'yə), *n.* Norway, Sweden, and Denmark.

Scan·di·na·vi·an (skan'də nā'vi ən; -nāv'yən), *adj.* of Scandinavia, its people, or their languages. —*n.* **1** native or inhabitant of Scandinavia. **2** languages of Scandinavia and Iceland, both modern and historical.

scan·di·um (skan'di əm), *n.* a rare metallic element, Sc. [< NL, < L *Scandia* Scandinavia]

scan·ner (skan'ər), *n.* **1** device that converts images into electronic data. **2** machine that uses electromagnetic or X rays to examine the body. **3** radar antenna.

scan·sion (skan'shən), *n.* the marking off of lines of poetry into feet; scanning. [< L *scansio* < *scandere* scan]

scant (skant), *adj.* **1** not enough in size or quantity: *her coat was short and scant.* **2** barely enough; barely full; bare. —*v.* make scant; cut down; limit; stint.

scant of, having not enough: *scant of breath.* [< Scand. *skamt,* neut. adj., short] —**scant'ly,** *adv.* —**scant'ness,** *n.*

scant·y (skan'ti), *adj.,* **scant·i·er, scant·i·est.** **1** not enough: *his scanty clothing did not keep out the cold.* **2** barely enough;

meager: *a scanty harvest.* —**scant'i·ly,** *adv.* —**scant'i·ness,** *n.*

scape·goat (skāp'gōt'), *n.* person or thing made to bear the blame for the mistakes or sins of others. [< *scape,* var. of *escape* + *goat.* The ancient Jewish high priests used to lay the sins of the people upon a goat which was then driven out into the wilderness.]

scape·grace (skāp'grās'), *n.* a reckless, good-for-nothing person; scamp.

scap·u·la (skap'yə lə), *n., pl.* **-lae** (-lē), **-las.** shoulder blade. [< L]

scap·u·lar (skap'yə lər), *adj.* of the shoulder or shoulder blade. [< NL < LL, < L *scapula* shoulder]

scar (skär), *n., v.,* **scarred, scar·ring.** —*n.* **1** mark left by a healed cut, wound, burn, or sore. **2 a** any mark like this. **b** *Fig.* a healed wound on the mind: *scars from her military experience.* —*v.* **1** mark with a scar. **2** form a scar; heal. [< OF < L < Gk. *eschara* scab, hearth]

scar·ab (skar'əb), *n.* **1** beetle, esp. the sacred beetle of the ancient Egyptians. **2** image of this beetle, much used in ancient Egypt as a charm or ornament. [< F < L *scarabaeus*]

scar·a·mouch (skar'ə mouch'; -müsh'), *n.* **1** a cowardly braggart. **2** rascal. [< F < Ital. *scaramuccia* SKIRMISH]

scarce (skärs), *adj.,* **scarc·er, scarc·est,** *adv.* —*adj.* **1** hard to get; rare: *a scarce book.* **2** not abundant or plentiful: *some vegetables were scarce because of the drought.* —*adv.* scarcely.

make oneself scarce, a go away. **b** stay away. [< OF *escars,* ult. < L *ex-* out + *carpere* pluck] —**scarce'ness,** *n.*

scarce·ly (skärs'li), *adv.* **1** not quite; barely: *we could scarcely see through the thick fog.* **2** decidedly not: *he can scarcely have said that.* **3** very probably not: *I will scarcely pay that much.*

scar·ci·ty (skär'sə ti), *n., pl.* **-ties.** too small a supply; lack; rarity.

scare (skär), *v.,* **scared, scar·ing,** *n.* —*v.* frighten. —*n.* **1** fright. **2** frightened condition. **scare up,** *Informal.*

get; raise: *scare up some eggs.* [< Scand. *skirra* < *skjarr* timid] —**scar'er,** *n.* —**scar'ing·ly,** *adv.*

scare·crow (skär'krō'), *n.* figure of a man dressed in old clothes, set in a field to frighten birds away from crops.

scarf¹ (skärf), *n., pl.* **scarfs, scarves. 1** a long, broad strip of silk, wool, etc., worn about the neck, shoulders, head, or waist. **2** a long strip of cloth, etc., used as a cover for a bureau, table, piano, etc. [prob. < dial. OF *escarpe* < Gmc.]

scarf² (skärf), *n., pl.* **scarfs,** *v.* —*n.* joint in which the ends of beams are cut so that they lap over and join firmly. —*v.* join by a scarf. [< Scand. (Sw.) *skarva*]

scarf³ (skärf), *v.,* **scarfed, scarf·ing.** *Informal.* eat greedily, quickly: *scarfed down a huge breakfast.* [? < *scaff* eat heavily < Afrikaans]

scar·i·fy (skar′ə fī), v., **-fied, -fy·ing. 1** make scratches or cuts in the surface of (the skin, etc.). **2** criticize severely; hurt the feelings of. **3** loosen (soil) without turning it over. [< LL, < L *scarifare* < Gk., < *skariphos* stylus] —**scar′i·fi·ca′-tion,** n. —**scar′i·fi′er,** n.

scar·let (skär′lit), n. **1** a very bright red, much lighter than crimson. **2** cloth or clothing having this color. —adj. very bright red. [< OF *escarlate,* ? ult. < Pers. *saqalāt* rich cloth]

scarlet fever, a disease characterized by rash, sore throat, and fever.

scarlet runner, a tall bean vine of tropical America that has showy scarlet flowers, and long pods with large black seeds; kidney bean.

scarlet sage, =salvia.

scarlet tanager, the common tanager of North America. The male has black wings and tail and a scarlet body.

scarp (skärp), n. **1** a steep slope. **2** the inner slope or side of a ditch surrounding a fortification. —v. make into a steep slope; slope steeply. [< Ital. *scarpa* < Gmc.]

scarves (skärvz), n. pl. of scarf¹.

scar·y (skãr′i), adj., **scar·i·er, scar·i·est. 1** causing fright or alarm. **2** easily frightened.

scat¹ (skat), v., **scat·ted, scat·ting.** go off in a great hurry. —interj. exclamation used to scare away an animal.

scat² (skat), v., **scat·ted, scat·ting.** speak or sing nonsense, esp. to jazz. —n. nonsense spoken or sung to jazz music.

scathe (skāth), n., v., **scathed, scath·ing.** —v. hurt; harm. —v. criticize severely. [< Scand. *skathi* injury]

scath·ing (skāth′ing), adj. bitterly severe. —**scath′ing·ly,** adv.

scat·o·log·i·cal (skat′ə loj′ə kəl), adj. obscene. —**sca·tol′o·gy,** n.

scat·ter (skat′ər), v. **1** throw here and there; sprinkle: *scatter sand on the icy sidewalk.* **2** separate and drive off in different directions: *scatter the mob.* **3** separate and go in different directions: *the hens scattered.* —n. act or fact of scattering. [akin to *shatter*] —**scat′ter·er,** n.

scat·ter·brain (skat′ər brān′), n. a thoughtless, heedless person. —**scat′ter·brained′,** adj.

scav·enge (skav′inj), v., **-enged, -eng·ing. 1** cleanse. **2** act as scavenger. [< *scavenger*]

scav·en·ger (skav′in jər), n. **1** animal that feeds on decaying matter. [alter. of *scavager,* lit., inspector < *scavage* toll < OF, < *escauwer* inspect < Flemish *scauwen*]

sce·nar·i·o (si när′i ō; –nä′ri–), n., pl. **-nar·i·os. 1** outline giving the main facts about an event, film, or play; outline of any play, opera. etc. **2** *Fig.* the working out of an imaginary situation. [< Ital., ult. < L *scena* SCENE]

scene (sēn), n. **1** time, place, circumstances, etc., of a play or story: *the scene* of the novel is laid in Virginia during the Civil War. **2** the painted screens, hangings, etc., used in a theater to represent places: *the scene represents a city street.* **3** part of an act of a play: *the king comes to the castle in Act I, Scene 2.* **4** a particular incident of a play: *the trial scene in the "Merchant of Venice."* **5** action, incident, situation, etc., occurring in reality or represented in literature or art: *the scene of one's childhood.* **6** view; picture: *the boats make a pretty scene.* **7** show of strong feeling in front of others; exhibition; display: *make a scene.*

behind the scenes, a out of sight of the audience. **b** privately; secretly, not publicly. [< L < Gk. *skene,* orig., tent, where actors changed costumes]

scen·er·y (sēn′ər i; sēn′ri), n., pl. **-er·ies. 1** the painted hangings, fittings, etc., used in a theater to represent places. **2** the general appearance of a landscape: *mountain scenery.*

sce·nic (sē′nik; sen′ik), adj. **1** of or pertaining to natural scenery; having much fine scenery: *a scenic route.* **2** of or belonging to the stage of a theater; dramatic; theatrical: *scenic effects.* **3** representing an action, incident, situation, etc., in art. —**sce′ni·cal·ly,** adv.

scent (sent), n. **1** smell: *the scent of roses.* **2** sense of smell: *bloodhounds have a keen scent.* **3** smell left in passing: *dogs follow a fox by the scent.* **4** perfume. **5** means by which a thing or a person can be traced: *the police are on the scent of the thieves.* —v. **1** smell: *the dog scented a rabbit.* **2** hunt by using the sense of smell: *the dog scented about for the trail.* **3** perfume. **4** fill with scent: *roses scent the air.* **5** have a suspicion of; be aware of: *I scent trouble.* [< OF *sentir* smell < L *sentire* feel]

scep·ter (sep′tər), n., v., **-tered, -ter·ing.** —n. **1** the rod or staff carried by a ruler as a symbol of royal power or authority. **2** royal or imperial power or authority. —v. furnish with a scepter. [< OF < L < Gk. *skeptron* staff] —**scep′tered,** adj.

sched·ule (skej′ul), n., v., **-uled, -ul·ing.** —n. **1** a written or printed statement of details; list. A timetable is a schedule of the coming and going of trains. **2** a classified or tabular statement. —v. **1** make a schedule of; enter in a schedule. **2** plan or arrange to be, have, or do something at a definite future date: *schedule the convention for the fall.* [< OF < LL *schedula,* dim. of L *scheda* < Gk. *schede* sheet of papyrus] —**sched′u·lar,** adj.

sche·mat·ic (skē mat′ik), adj. pertaining to or having the nature of a diagram, plan, or scheme; diagrammatic. —n. schematic drawing or diagram. —**sche·mat′i·cal·ly,** adv.

scheme (skēm), n., v., **schemed, schem·ing.** —n. **1** program of action; plan: *a scheme for extracting gold from sea water.* **2** plan of action to attain some end, often one characterized by self-seeking or intriguing: *a scheme to cheat the government.* **3** system of connected things, parts, thoughts, etc.: *the color scheme of a room.* —v. plan; plot. [< Gk. *schema* figure, appearance] —**schem′er,** n.

schem·ing (skēm′ing), adj. making tricky schemes; crafty. —**schem′ing·ly,** adv.

scher·zo (sker′tsō), n., pl. **-zos, -zi** (–tsi). a light or playful part of a sonata or symphony. [< Ital. < G *scherz* joke]

schil·ling (shil′ing), n. unit of money used in Austria. [< G]

schism (siz′əm), n. **1** division because of some difference of opinion about religion. **2 a** a division into hostile groups. **b** division between two people. [< L < Gk. *schisma* < *schizein* to split]

schis·mat·ic (siz mat′ik), adj. **1** causing or likely to cause schism. **2** inclined toward, or guilty of, schism. —**schis·mat′i·cal·ly,** adv.

schist (shist), n. kind of crystalline rock that splits easily into layers. [< F < L < Gk. *schistos* cleft < *schizein* to split]

schiz·o (skit′sō; skiz′–), Informal. schizophrenic; unbalanced; hyper.

schiz·oid (skiz′oid; skits′–), adj. **1** having schizophrenia. **2** resembling schizophrenia.

schiz·o·phre·ni·a (skiz′ə frē′ni ə; skits′–; –frēn′yə), n. psychosis characterized by dissociation from environment and deterioration of personality. [< NL, < Gk. *schizein* to split + *phren* mind] —**schiz′o·phren′ic,** adj., n.

schmaltz or **schmalz** (shmälts), n. sickly sentimentality. —**schmaltz′y, schmalz′y,** adj.

schmuck (shmuk), n. Informal. stupid person; jerk. [< Yiddish *shmok*]

schnapps, schnaps (shnäps), n. beer or liquor. [< G]

schnau·zer (shnou′zər), n. a wire-haired German terrier with a long head and heavy eyebrows, mustache, and beard. [< G, lit., snarler < *schnauze* snout]

schol·ar (skol′ər), n. **1** a learned person; person having much knowledge. **2** student who is given money by some institution to help him or her continue studies. **3** pupil at school; learner. [< LL, < L *schola* SCHOOL¹]

schol·ar·ly (skol′ər li), adj. **1** of, befitting, or like that of a scholar: *scholarly habits.* **2** having much knowledge; learned. **3** fond of learning; studious. —**schol′ar·li·ness,** n.

schol·ar·ship (skol′ər ship), n. **1** possession of knowledge gained by study; quality of learning and knowledge. **2** grant of money to help a student continue his or her studies.

scho·las·tic (skə las′tik), adj. Also, **scho·las′ti·cal. 1** of schools, scholars, or education; academic: *scholastic achievements.* **2** of or like scholasticism. —n. theologian and philosopher in the Middle Ages. [< L < Gk., ult. < *schole* school] —**scho·las′ti·cal·ly,** adv.

scho·las·ti·cism (skə las′tə siz əm), *n.*
1 system of theological and philosophical teaching dominant in the Middle Ages, based chiefly on the authority of the church and of Aristotle. **2** adherence to traditional doctrines and methods.

school¹ (skül), *n.* **1** place for teaching and learning: *go to school.* **2** building where there is a school. **3** a regular course of meetings of teachers and pupils for instruction: *begin school as a young child.* **4** those who are taught and their teachers. **5** *Fig.* any place, situation, experience, etc., as a source of instruction or training: *the school of adversity.* **6** *Fig.* those who exhibit in practice the same general methods, principles, tastes, or intellectual bent: *the Dutch school of painting, a gentleman of the old school.* **7** a particular department or group in a university: *a dental school.* —*v.* **1** educate in a school; teach. **2** train; discipline: *school yourself to control your temper.* [< L < Gk. *schole,* orig., leisure] —**school′able,** *adj.*

school² (skül), *n.* a large group of the same kind of fish or water animals swimming together. [< Du. Cf. SHOAL².]

school·book (skül′bu̇k′), *n.* book for study in schools.

school·boy (skül′boi′), *n.* boy attending school.

school·girl (skül′gėrl′), *n.* girl attending school.

school·house (skül′hous′), *n.* a building used as a school.

school·ing (skül′ing), *n.* **1** instruction in school; education received at school. **2** cost of instruction. **3** the training of a horse and rider.

school·mas·ter (skül′mas′tər; –mäs′–), *n.* person, esp. a man, who teaches in or manages a school.

school·mate (skül′māt′), *n.* companion at school.

school·mis·tress (skül′mis′tris), *n.* woman who teaches in or manages a school.

school·room (skül′rüm′;–ru̇m′), *n.* room in which pupils are taught.

school·teach·er (skül′tēch′ər), *n.* person who teaches in a school.

school·work (skül′wėrk′), *n.* lessons, assignments of a student in school.

school year, time during a year when school is in session.

schoon·er (skün′ər), *n.* ship with two or more masts and fore-and-aft sails. [< *scoon,* skim, prob. < Scand.]

schot·tische (shot′ish), *n.* **1** a dance somewhat like the polka. **2** music for it. [< G, lit., Scottish]

schwa (shwä), *n.* an unstressed vowel sound such as *a* in *about* or *u* in *circus,* represented by the symbol ə; neutral vowel. [< G < Heb. *sh'wa*]

sci., science; scientific.

sci·at·ic (sī at′ik), *adj.* **1** of the hip. **2** affecting the sciatic nerves. [< LL < Gk. *ischiadikos* < *ischion* hip joint]

sci·at·i·ca (sī at′ə kə), *n.* pain in a sciatic nerve and its branches; neuralgia of the hips, thighs, and legs. —**sci·at′i·cal,** *adj.*

sciatic nerve, a large nerve along the back part of the thigh and leg.

sci·ence (sī′əns), *n.* **1** knowledge of facts and laws based upon observation and arranged in an orderly system. **2** branch of such knowledge. Biology, chemistry, physics, and astronomy are **natural sciences.** Economics and sociology are **social sciences.** Agriculture and engineering are **applied sciences. 3** skill; technique. [< OF < L *scientia* knowledge < *scire* know]

science fiction, a novel or short story based on some actual or fanciful elements of science.

sci·en·tif·ic (sī′ən tif′ik), *adj.* **1** trained in or using the facts and laws of science, or some branch of science: *a scientific farmer.* **2** of or pertaining to science or the sciences; used in science: *scientific instruments.* **3** based on or conforming to the principles of science: *the scientific method.* [< LL, < *scientia* knowledge + *facere* make] —**sci′en·tif′i·cal·ly,** *adv.*

sci·en·tist (sī′ən tist), *n.* person who is trained in, or is familiar with, science.

sci-fi (sī′fī′), *n. Informal.* science fiction.

scil·i·cet (sil′ə set), *adv.* to wit; namely. [< L, < *scire* to know + *licet* it is allowed]

scim·i·tar, scim·i·ter (sim′ə tər), *n.* a short, curved sword used by Turks, Persians, etc. [< Ital. *scimitarra*]

scin·til·la (sin til′ə), *n.* spark; particle; trace: *barely a scintilla of proof.* [< L, spark. Doublet of TINSEL.]

scin·til·late (sin′tə lāt), *v.,* –**lat·ed, –lat·ing.** sparkle; flash; twinkle: *the snow scintillates in the sun like diamonds.* [< L, < *scintilla* spark] —**scin′til·lat′ing,** *adj.* —**scin′til·la′tion,** *n.*

sci·o·list (sī′ə list), *n.* person who pretends to great knowledge. —**sci′o·lous,** *adj.*

sci·on (sī′ən), *n.* **1** bud or branch cut for grafting. **2** descendant. [< OF *cion*]

scis·sor (siz′ər), *v.* cut with scissors.

scis·sors (siz′ərz), *n. pl.* **1** tool or instrument for cutting that has two sharp blades so fastened that they will work toward each other. **2** a wrestling hold with the legs. [< OF *cisoires,* pl., < LL *cisorium,* sing., tool for cutting, ult. < L *caedere* cut; confused with L *scissor* cutter]

scler·a (sklir′ə), *n.* =sclerotic. [< NL < Gk. *sklērós* hard] —**scler′al,** *adj.*

scle·ro·sis (skli rō′sis), *n., pl.* –**ses** (–sēz). a hardening of a tissue or part of the body by an increase of connective tissue or the like. [< Med.L < Gk., < *sklērós* hard] —**scle·ro′sal,** *adj.*

scle·rot·ic (skli rot′ik), *n.* Also, **sclerotic coat.** the hard, white outer membrane of the eye. —*adj.* **1** of or pertaining to the sclerotic. **2** of, with, or having sclerosis.

scoff (skôf; skof), *v.* make fun to show one does not believe something; mock. —*n.*

mocking words or acts. [< Scand. (Dan.) *skuffe* deceive] —**scoff′er,** *n.*

scoff·law (skôf′lô′; skof′–), *n.* person who habitually disregards the law, esp. law dealing with operation of motor vehicles.

scold (skōld), *v.* find fault with; blame with angry words: *scold a naughty boy.* —*n.* person who scolds, esp. a noisy, scolding woman. [prob. < Scand. *skāld* poet, in sense of "lampooner"] —**scold′er,** *n.* —**scold′ing,** *adj., n.* —**scold′ing·ly,** *adv.*

sco·li·o·sis (skō′li ō′sis; skol′i–), *n.* a curving of the spine to the side. [< NL < Gk. *skoliōsis* curviture, crookedness]

sconce (skons), *n.* bracket projecting from a wall, used to hold a candle or other light. [< Med.L *sconsa,* ult. < L < *abscondere* hide]

scone (skōn; skon), *n.* a thick, flat, round cake cooked on a griddle; a similar cake baked in an oven. Some scones taste much like bread; some are like buns. [prob. < MDu. *schoon(brot)* fine (bread)]

scoop (sküp), *n.* **1** tool like a shovel. **2** part of a dredge, steam shovel, etc., that holds coal, sand, etc. **3** a kitchen utensil to take out flour, sugar, etc., from a container. **4** amount taken up at one time by a scoop. **5** act of taking up. **6** place hollowed out. **7 a** the publishing of a piece of news before a rival newspaper does. **b** the piece of news. —*v.* **1** take up or out with a scoop, or as a scoop does. **2** hollow out; dig out; make by scooping. **3** publish a piece of news before (a rival newspaper). [partly < MDu. *schoepe* bucket, partly < MDu. *schoppe* shovel]

scoop·ful (sküp′fu̇l), *n., pl.* –**fuls.** enough to fill a scoop.

scoot (sküt), —*v.* go quickly; dart. —*n.* act of scooting. [prob. < Scand.; akin to SHOOT]

scoot·er (sküt′ər), *n.* **1** a vehicle consisting of two wheels, one in front of the other, and a footboard between, steered by a handle bar and propelled by pushing against the ground with one foot. **2** a similar vehicle run by a motor.

scope¹ (skōp), *n.* **1** distance the mind can reach; extent of view: *very hard words are not within the scope of a child's understanding.* **2** space; opportunity: *football gives scope for courage and quick thinking.* [< Ital., ult. < Gk. *skopos* aim, object]

scope² (skōp), *n. Informal.* **1** instrument for looking at something, as a microscope, telescope, etc. **2** telescopic rifle sight.

scope out, look around; check out: *scope out the restaurants in town.* [< tele*scope,* micro*scope,* etc.]

scor·bu·tic (skôr bū′tik), *adj.* **1** pertaining to or of the nature of scurvy. **2** affected with scurvy. [< NL, < *scorbutus* scurvy < F *scorbut* < Gmc.]

scorch (skôrch), *v.* **1** burn slightly; burn on the outside: *scorch a shirt in ironing* it. 2 dry up; wither: *grass scorched by the sun.* 3 go or drive very fast. 4 *Fig.* criticize with burning words. —*n.* a slight burn. —**scorch′ing,** *adj.*

scorch·er (skôr′chər), *n.* 1 a very hot day. 2 *Fig.* burning remark or rebuke. 3 person known for great speed, as a driver or cyclist.

score (skôr; skōr), *n., v.,* **scored, scor·ing.** —*n.* 1 record of points made in a game, contest, test, etc.: *the score was 9 to 2 in our favor.* 2 reason; ground: *don't worry on that score.* 3 a written or printed piece of music arranged for different instruments or voices: *the score of a musical comedy.* 4 a group or set of twenty; twenty: *a score or more were present.* —*v.* 1 make, as points in a game, contest, test, etc. 2 keep a record of (the number of points in a game, contest, etc.). 3 gain or win: *he scored five runs for our team, score a success.* 4 arrange (a piece of music) for different instruments or voices. 5 cut; scratch; mark; line.

settle or **pay off a score,** get even for an injury or wrong.

scores, a great number: *scores died in the epidemic.* [< Scand. *skor* notch] —**scor′er,** *n.*

score·board (skôr′bôrd′; skōr′bōrd′), *n.* 1 board where scores are posted during a sporting event or game. 2 *Fig.* results; record: *the scoreboard for last year's sales.*

score·card (skôr′kärd′; skōr′–), *n.,* or **score card,** card on which the score of a game is kept, esp. while it is in progress. 2 *Fig.* performance, as of a business executive.

scorn (skôrn), *v.* 1 look down upon; think of as mean or low; despise: *scorn a traitor.* 2 reject or refuse as low or wrong: *the judge scorned to take a bribe.* —*n.* 1 a feeling that a person, animal, or act is mean or low; contempt. 2 person, animal, or thing that is scorned or despised. [< OF *escarn* < Gmc.] —**scorn′er,** *n.*

scorn·ful (skôrn′fəl), *adj.* showing contempt; mocking; full of scorn. —**scorn′ful·ly,** *adv.*

Scor·pi·o (skôr′pi ō), *n.* 1 a southern constellation that was thought of as arranged in the shape of a scorpion. 2 the eighth sign of the zodiac; the Scorpion.

scor·pi·on (skôr′pi ən), *n.* a small animal belonging to the same group as the spider and having a poisonous sting in its tail. [< L, ult. < Gk. *skorpios*]

Scot (skot), *n.* native or inhabitant of Scotland.

Scot., 1 Scotch; Scottish. 2 Scotland.

Scotch (skoch), *adj.* Scottish. —*n.* 1 the people of Scotland. 2 Scottish (def. 2). 3 whiskey made in Scotland.

scotch (skoch), *v.* 1 crush; render harmless: *scotch a rumor, scotch a snake without killing it.* 2 cut or gash.

Scotch-Gael·ic (skoch′gāl′ik), *n.* the Celtic language of the Scottish Highlanders; Erse.

Scotch·man (skoch′mən), **Scots·man** (skots′–), *n., pl.* **–men.** native or inhabitant of Scotland.

Scotch tape, 1 transparent tape with adhesive on one side, used for sealing, mending tears, etc. 2 trademark for this tape. —**scotch′–tape′,** *v.*

Scotch terrier, kind of short-legged terrier with rough, wiry hair and pointed ears.

scot-free (skot′frē′), *adj.* free from injury, punishment, etc.; unharmed.

Sco·tia (skō′shə), *n. Poetic.* Scotland.

Scot·land (skot′lənd), *n.* country N of England and a part of the United Kingdom of Great Britain and Northern Ireland.

Scotland Yard, 1 headquarters of the London police. 2 the London police, esp. the department that does detective work.

Scots (skots), *adj.* Scottish. —*n.* people of Scotland.

Scot·ti·cism (skot′ə siz əm), *n.* way of speaking peculiar to the Scottish dialect.

scot·tie (skot′i), *n.* =Scottish terrier.

Scot·tish (skot′ish), *adj.* of or pertaining to Scotland, its people, or their language. —*n.* 1 Scotch (def. 1). 2 dialect of English spoken by the people of Scotland.

scoun·drel (skoun′drəl), *n.* person without honor or good principles; villain; rascal. —**scoun′drel·ly,** *adj.*

scour¹ (skour), *v.* 1 clean or polish by vigorous rubbing. 2 remove dirt and grease from (anything) by rubbing. 3 make clear by flowing through or over: *the stream had scoured a channel.* 4 clean; cleanse. —*n.* act of scouring. [prob. < MDu. < OF *escurer,* ult. < L *ex–* completely + *cura* care] —**scour′er,** *n.*

scour² (skour), *v.* 1 move quickly over. 2 go swiftly in search or pursuit. [prob. < OF *escourre* run forth, ult. < L *ex–* out + *currere* run]

scourge (skėrj), *n., v.,* **scourged, scourg·ing.** —*n.* 1 a whip. 2 any means of punishment. 3 some thing or person that causes great trouble or misfortune. —*v.* 1 whip; punish. 2 trouble very much; afflict. [< OF *escorge,* ult. < L *ex–* out + *corium* a hide] —**scourg′er,** *n.*

scout (skout), *n.* 1 a person who is sent to get information about the enemy. 2 airplane, ship, etc., used to discover enemy positions. 3 person belonging to the Boy Scouts or Girl Scouts. 4 fellow; person: *he's a good scout.* —*v.* 1 act as a scout; hunt around to find something: *go out and scout for wood.* 2 observe or examine to get information. [< OF, < *escouter* listen < L *auscultare*] —**scout′er,** *n.* —**scout′ing·ly,** *adv.*

scout·mas·ter (skout′mas′tər; –mäs′–), *n.* man in charge of a troop or band of Boy Scouts.

scow (skou), *n.* a large, flat-bottomed boat used to carry freight, sand, etc. [< Du. *schouw*]

scowl (skoul), *v.* 1 look angry or sullen by lowering the eyebrows; frown. 2 express with a scowl. —*n.* an angry, sullen look; frown. [< Scand. (Dan.) *skule*] —**scowl′er,** *n.* —**scowl′ing·ly,** *adv.*

scrab·ble (skrab′əl), *v.,* **–bled, –bling,** *n.* —*v.* 1 scratch or scrape about with hands, claws, etc. 2 scrawl; scribble. —*n.* a scraping. [< Du. *schrabbelen,* frequentative of *schrabben* scratch]

scrag (skrag), *n.* 1 a lean, skinny person or animal. 2 a lean, bony part.

scrag·gly (skrag′li), *adj.,* **–gli·er, –gli·est.** rough; irregular; ragged.

scrag·gy (skrag′i), *adj.,* **–gi·er, –gi·est.** 1 lean; thin. 2 scraggly. —**scrag′gi·ness,** *n.*

scram (skram), *v.,* **scrammed, scram·ming.** *Informal.* go at once. [short for *scramble*]

scram·ble (skram′bəl), *v.,* **–bled, –bling,** *n.* —*v.* 1 make one's way by climbing, crawling, etc.: *scramble up a rocky hill.* 2 struggle with others for something: *scramble for the ball.* 3 cook (eggs) with the whites and yolks mixed together. —*n.* 1 a climb or walk over rough ground. 2 struggle to possess: *the scramble for wealth.* [var. of *scrabble*] —**scram′bler,** *n.* —**scram′bling·ly,** *adv.*

scrap¹ (skrap), *n., v.,* **scrapped, scrap·ping.** —*n.* 1 a small piece; little bit; small part left over. 2 bit of something written or printed. —*v.* 1 make into scraps; break up. 2 throw aside as useless or worn out. [< Scand. *skrap*]

scrap² (skrap), *n., v.,* **scrapped, scrap·ping.** fight; quarrel; struggle. [var. of *scrape*] —**scrap′per,** *n.*

scrap·book (skrap′búk′), *n.* book in which pictures or clippings are pasted and kept.

scrape (skrāp), *v.,* **scraped, scrap·ing,** *n.* —*v.* 1 rub with something sharp or rough; make smooth or clean thus: *scrape your muddy shoes with this old knife.* 2 remove by rubbing with something sharp or rough: *the man scraped some paint off the table.* 3 rub with a harsh sound; rub harshly: *the branch of the tree scraped against the window.* 4 collect by scraping or with difficulty: *scrape together enough money for one year at college.* 5 manage with difficulty: *that family can just scrape along.* —*n.* 1 act of scraping. 2 a scraped place. 3 a harsh, grating sound. 4 position hard to get out of; difficulty. [< Scand. *skrapa*] —**scrap′er,** *n.*

scrap·ple (skrap′əl), *n.* scraps of pork boiled with corn meal and seasoned with sage, etc., made into loaves, sliced, and fried. [< *scrap¹*]

scrap·py¹ (skrap′i), *adj.,* **–pi·er, –pi·est.** made up of odds and ends; fragmentary; disconnected. —**scrap′pi·ly,** *adv.* —**scrap′pi·ness,** *n.*

scrap·py² (skrap′i), *adj.,* **–pi·er, –pi·est.** fond of fighting. —**scrap′pi·ly,** *adv.* —**scrap′pi·ness,** *n.*

scratch (skrach), *v.* **1** break, mark, or cut slightly with something sharp or rough: *don't scratch the paint.* **2** tear or dig with the nails or claws: *the cat scratched him.* **3** rub or scrape to relieve itching; rub some part of one's body: *he scratched his head.* **4** rub with a harsh noise; rub: *this pen scratches.* **5** write in a hurry or carelessly. **6** scrape out; strike out; draw a line through. **7** withdraw (a horse, etc.) from a race or contest. —*n.* **1** mark made by scratching: *there are scratches on this new desk.* **2** a very slight cut. **3** sound of scratching: *the scratch of a pen.* **4** any act of scratching. —*adj.* collected or prepared hastily, and often of poor quality. **from scratch,** from nothing. **up to scratch,** up to standard. [alter. of earlier *scrat,* infl. by obs. *cratch;* ult. orig. uncert.] —**scratch′er,** *n.*

scratch pad, pad of paper for hurried writing.

scratch·y (skrach′i), *adj.,* **scratch·i·er, scratch·i·est. 1** that scratches, scrapes, or grates. **2** consisting of mere scratches. —**scratch′i·ly,** *adv.* —**scratch′i·ness,** *n.*

scrawl (skrôl), *v.* write or draw poorly or carelessly. —*n.* poor, careless handwriting. —**scrawl′er,** *n.* —**scrawl′y,** *adj.*

scraw·ny (skrô′ni), *adj.,* **-ni·er, -ni·est.** lean; thin; skinny. [< Scand. (dial. Norw.) *skran*] —**scraw′ni·ness,** *n.*

scream (skrēm), *v.* **1** make a loud, sharp, piercing cry. People scream in fright, in anger, and in sudden pain. **2** utter loudly. **3** laugh loudly. —*n.* **1** a loud, sharp, piercing cry. **2** something extremely funny. [< Scand. *skræma* scare] —**scream′er,** *n.* —**scream′ing,** *adj.*

screech (skrēch), *v.* make a loud, piercing cry. —*n.* a loud, piercing cry. [earlier *scritch,* imit.] —**screech′er,** *n.* —**screech′y,** *adj.*

screech owl, 1 any of various small owls having hornlike tufts of feathers. **2** owl that screeches, as distinguished from one that hoots.

screen (skrēn), *n.* **1** a covered frame that hides, protects, or separates. **2** wire woven together with small openings in between: *put the screens on the windows.* **3** an ornamental partition. **4** anything like a screen. **5** surface on which motion pictures, etc., are shown. **6** sieve for sifting sand, gravel, coal, seed, etc. —*v.* **1** shelter, protect, or hide with, or as with, a screen: *screen one's face from the fire with a fan.* **2** sift (sand, gravel, coal, etc.) with a sieve. [< OF *escren* < Gmc.] —**screen′a·ble,** *adj.* —**screen′er,** *n.*

screen·ing (skrē′ning), **1** fine wire mesh used to make window screens and doors. **2** showing of a film, esp. to a small group of people: *a private screening.*

screw (skrü), *n.* **1** kind of nail, with a ridge twisted evenly round its length: *turn the screw to the right to tighten it.* **2 a** cylinder with a ridge winding round it to raise and lower something, esp. something heavy. **b** the threaded part into

which this cylinder fits and advances. **c** threaded bolt used to separate parts. **3** propeller of a boat or any other thing that turns like a screw or looks like one. **4** a turn of a screw. **5** former instrument of torture for compressing the thumbs. —*v.* **1** turn as one turns a screw; twist: *screw the lid on the jar.* **2** wind; twist. **3** fasten or tighten with a screw or screws. **4** force, press, or stretch tight by using a screw or screws. **5** gather for an effort: *screw up one's courage.*

have a screw loose, a have something wrong or out of order. **b** *Fig.* be very eccentric; crazy.

put the screws on, use pressure or force to get something. [< OF *escroue* nut]

screw·ball (skrü′bôl′), *n.* an eccentric person. *adj.* eccentric; unpredictable: *screwball comedy.*

screw·driv·er (skrü′drīv′ər), **screw driver,** *n.* tool for putting in or taking out screws by turning them.

screw propeller, a revolving hub with radiating blades for propelling a ship, aircraft, etc.

screw·y (skrü′i), *adj. Informal.* odd; strange.

scrib·ble (skrib′əl), *v.,* **-bled, -bling,** *n.* —*v.* **1** write or draw carelessly or hastily: *scribble a note.* **2** make marks that do not mean anything. —*n.* something scribbled. [< Med.L *scribillare,* ult. < L *scribere* write]

scrib·bler (skrib′lər), *n.* **1** person who scribbles. **2** *Fig.* author of light or unimportant work.

scribe (skrīb), *n.* **1** person whose occupation is writing, esp. copying manuscripts. Before printing was invented, there were many scribes. **2** person who writes something for someone who does not know how to write. **3** writer; author. **4** teacher of Jewish law in ancient times. [< L *scriba* < *scribere* write] —**scrib′al,** *adj.*

scrim·mage (skrim′ij), *n., v.,* **-maged, -mag·ing.** —*n.* play in football that takes place when the two teams are lined up and the ball is snapped back. —*v.* in football, take part in a scrimmage. [ult. var. of *skirmish*]

scrimp (skrimp), *v.* **1** be sparing of; use too little of. **2** be very economical; stint; skimp: *many parents have to scrimp to keep their children in school.* **3** treat stingily or very economically.

scrimp·y (skrimp′i), *adj.,* **scrimp·i·er, scrimp·i·est.** scanty; meager. —**scrimp′i·ly,** *adv.*

scrim·shaw (skrim′shô′), *n.* **1** carving on whale teeth, walrus tusks, etc., originally done by sailors on long voyages. **2** such an engraved article.

scrip (skrip), *n.* **1** a writing. **2** receipt, certificate, or other document showing a right to something. **3** paper money issued by a government in an emergency or as an occupier of another country. [var. of *script*]

script (skript), *n.* **1** written letters, figures, signs, etc.; handwriting: *German script.* **2** style of type that looks like handwriting. **3** manuscript of a play or actor's part. **4** manuscript used in broadcasting. [< L *scriptum,* orig. neut. pp., written] —**script′writ′er,** *n.*

scrip·ture (skrip′chər), *n.* **1** any sacred writing. **2** Scripture. Also, **the Scriptures, the Holy Scripture.** the Bible. [< L *scriptura* a writing < *scribere* write] —**scrip′tur·al, Scrip′tur·al,** *adj.*

scriv·en·er (skriv′nər), *n. Archaic.* clerk; notary. [< obs. *scrivein* < OF *escrivein,* ult. < L *scribere* write]

scrod (skrod), *n.* a young cod, esp. one cut up for cooking. [< MDu. *schrode* piece cut off]

scrof·u·la (skrof′yə lə), *n.* form of tuberculosis characterized by the enlargement of the lymph glands, esp those in the neck. [< Med.L, sing. < L *scrofulae,* pl. < *scrofa* a sow] —**scrof′u·lous,** *adj.* —**scrof′u·lous·ly,** *adv.*

scroll (skrōl), *n.* **1** roll of parchment or paper, esp. one with writing on it. **2** ornament resembling a partly unrolled sheet of paper, or having a spiral or coiled form. [alter. of *scrow* (infl. by *roll*), ult. < OF *escroe* scrap < Gmc.]

scroll saw, a very narrow saw for cutting thin wood in curved or ornamental patterns.

scro·tum (skrō′təm), *n., pl.* **-ta** (-tə). pouch that contains the testicles. [< L] —**scro′tal,** *adj.*

scrounge (skrounj), *v.,* **scrounged, scroung·ing.** pilfer. —**scroung′er,** *n.*

scrub¹ (skrub), *v.,* **scrubbed, scrub·bing,** *n.* —*v.* **1** rub hard; wash or clean by rubbing. **2** wash. —*n.* a scrubbing. [? < MDu. *schrubben*]

scrub² (skrub), *n.* **1** low, stunted trees or shrubs. **2** anything small, or below the usual size. **3** player not on the regular team, etc. —*adj.* **1** small; poor; inferior: *a scrub ball team.* **2** of or for players not on the regular team. [var. of SHRUB] —**scrub′by,** *adj.*

scrub·ber (skrub′ər), *n.* **1** person who scrubs: *a good scrubber in the bath.* **2** brush for scrubbing. **3** apparatus that removes impurities from a gaseous mixture: *scrubbers clean the smoke.*

scruff (skruf), *n.* nape of the neck.

scruf·fy (skruf′i), *adj.,* **scruf·fi·er, scruf·fi·est.** dirty; shabby.

scrump·tious (skrump′shəs), *adj.* elegant; splendid; first-rate: *a scrumptious meal.*

scru·ple (skrü′pəl), *n., v.,* **-pled, -pling.** —*n.* **1** a feeling of doubt about what one ought to do. **2** a feeling of uneasiness that keeps a person from doing something. **3** a weight of 20 grains. Three scruples make 1 dram. **4** a very small amount. —*v.* **1** hesitate or be unwilling (to do something): *he does not scruple to deceive.* **2** have scruples. [< L *scrupulus,* orig. dim. of *scrupus* sharp stone]

scru·pu·lous (skrü′pyə ləs), *adj.* **1** having or showing a strict regard for what is right. **2** attending thoroughly to details; very careful: *pay scrupulous attention.* —**scru′pu·lous·ness,** *n.* —**scru′pu·lous·ly,** *adv.*

scru·ti·nize (skrü′tə nīz), *v.,* **-nized, -niz·ing.** examine closely; inspect carefully. —**scru′ti·niz′er,** *n.* —**scru′ti·niz′ing·ly,** *adv.*

scru·ti·ny (skrü′tə ni), *n., pl.* **-nies.** close examination; careful inspection. [< LL *scrutinium* < L *scrutari* ransack]

scu·ba (skü′bə), *n.* underwater breathing equipment used by skin divers. [< *s*(elf)-*c*(ontained) *u*(nderwater) *b*(reathing) *a*(pparatus)]

scud (skud), *v.,* **scud·ded, scud·ding,** *n.* —*v.* run or move swiftly: *clouds scudding across the sky.* —*n.* **1** a scudding. **2** clouds or spray driven by the wind. [? var. of *scut* a short tail, esp. of a rabbit or deer (< Scand. *skutr* stern); first applied to a running of a hare]

scuff (skuf), *v.* **1** walk without lifting the feet; shuffle. **2** wear or injure the surface of by hard use. —*n.* a scuffing. [var. of SCUFFLE]

scuf·fle (skuf′əl), *v.,* **-fled, -fling,** *n.* —*v.* **1** struggle or fight in a rough, confused manner. **2** shuffle. —*n.* **1** a confused, rough struggle or fight. **2** a shuffling. [< Scand. (Sw.) *skuffa* push] —**scuf′fler,** *n.*

scull (skul), *n.* **1** oar worked with a side twist over the end of a boat to make it go. **2** one of a pair of oars used, one on each side, by a single rower. **3** act of propelling by sculls. **4** a light racing boat for one or more rowers. —*v.* propel (a boat), by a scull or by sculls. —**scull′er,** *n.*

scul·ler·y (skul′ər i; skul′ri), *n., pl.* **-ler·ies.** a small room where the dirty, rough work of a kitchen is done. [< OF *escuelerie,* ult. < L *scutella* platter]

sculp·tor (skulp′tər), *n.* person who carves or models figures; artist in sculpture.

sculp·tress (skulp′tris), *n.* a woman sculptor.

sculp·ture (skulp′chər), *n., v.,* **-tured, -tur·ing.** —*n.* **1** art of carving or modeling figures. Sculpture includes the cutting of statues from blocks of marble or wood, casting in bronze, and modeling in clay or wax. **2** sculptured work; piece of such work. —*v.* **1** carve or model. **2** cover or ornament with sculpture. [< L, < *sculpere* carve] —**sculp′tur·al,** *adj.* —**sculp′tur·al·ly,** *adv.* —**sculp′tured,** *adj.*

scum (skum), *n., v.,* **scummed, scum·ming.** —*n.* **1** a thin layer that rises to the top of a liquid; *green scum floats on the pond.* **2** low, worthless people. —*v.* **1** form scum; become covered with scum. **2** skim. [? < MDu. *schuum*]

scum·my (skum′i), *adj.,* **-mi·er, -mi·est.** **1** of or containing scum. **2** low; worthless.

scup·per (skup′ər), *n.* an opening in the side of a ship to let water run off the deck.

scur·ri·lous (skėr′ə ləs), *adj.* **1** coarsely joking. **2** abusive and indecent. [< L, < *scurra* buffoon] —**scur′ri·lous·ly,** *adv.* —**scur′ri·lous·ness,** *n.*

scur·ry (skėr′i), *v.,* **-ried, -ry·ing,** *n., pl.* **-ries.** —*v.* run or cause to run quickly; hurry. —*n.* a hasty running; hurrying; flurry.

scur·vy (skėr′vi), *n.* disease characterized by swollen and bleeding gums, livid spots on the skin, and prostration, due to lack of vitamin C in the diet. Scurvy used to be common among sailors when they had little to eat except bread and salt meat. [< SCURF] —**scur′vi·ly,** *adv.* —**scur′vi·ness,** *n.*

scut·tle[1] (skut′əl), *n.* kind of bucket for holding or carrying coal. [< L *scutella* platter]

scut·tle[2] (skut′əl), *v.,* **-tled, -tling,** *n.* scamper; scurry. [var. of *scuddle* < *scud*] —**scut′tler,** *n.*

scut·tle[3] (skut′əl), *n., v.,* **-tled, -tling.** —*n.* an opening in the deck or side of a ship, with a lid or cover. —*v.* cut a hole or holes through the bottom or sides of (a ship) to sink it. [? < F < Sp. *escotilla* hatchway] —**scut′tler,** *n.*

scut·tle·butt (skut′əl but′), *n. Informal.* rumor and stories not based on fact.

Scyl·la (sil′ə), *n.* **between Scylla and Charybdis,** between two dangers, one of which must be met.

scythe (sīth), *n., v.,* **scythed, scyth·ing.** —*n.* a long, slightly curved blade on a long handle, for cutting grass, etc. —*v.* cut with a scythe. [OE *sīthe;* spelling infl. by L *scindere* to cut]

SD, *(zip code)* South Dakota.

S. Dak., S.D., South Dakota.

Se, selenium.

SE, S.E., or **s.e.,** southeast; southeastern.

sea (sē), *n.* **1** any large body of salt water, smaller than an ocean, partly or wholly enclosed by land: *the North Sea.* **2** the ocean. **3** a large, heavy wave. **4** the swell of the ocean. **5** an overwhelming amount or number.

at sea, a out on the sea. **b** *Fig.* puzzled; confused.

go to sea, a become a sailor. **b** begin a voyage on the sea.

put to sea, begin a voyage on the sea. [OE *sǣ*]

sea anemone, a flowerlike polyp with a fleshy, cylindrical body and a mouth surrounded by many tentacles.

sea bass, **1** a common food fish of the Atlantic coast with a peculiar tail fin. **2** any of various similar fishes.

sea·bee (sē′bē′), *n.* member of the construction battalion of the U.S. Navy. [from the initials *C.B.,* for Construction Battalion]

sea·board (sē′bôrd′; –bōrd′), *n.* land near the sea; seacoast; seashore: *the Atlantic seaboard.*

sea bream, any of certain fishes belonging to the family which includes scups, porgies, etc.

sea breeze, light wind blowing from the sea to land.

sea calf, the common seal, often called the harbor seal.

sea·coast (sē′kōst′), *n.* land along the sea.

sea cow, 1 manatee, dugong, or any similar mammal living in the sea. **2** =walrus.

sea cucumber, any of a group of small echinoderms, most of which have flexible bodies that look somewhat like cucumbers.

sea dog, a sailor, esp. one with long experience.

sea elephant, kind of very large seal, the male of which has a trunklike snout.

sea·far·er (sē′fãr′ər), *n.* **1** sailor. **2** traveler on the sea.

sea·far·ing (sē′fãr′ing), *adj.* traveling or working on the sea. —*n.* **1** a sailor's life. **2** act or fact of traveling by sea.

sea·food (sē′füd′), *n.* edible saltwater fish and shellfish.

sea·go·ing (sē′gō′ing), *adj.* **1** going by sea. **2** fit for going to sea.

sea green, light bluish green.

sea gull, =gull[1].

sea horse, a kind of small fish (2 to 10 inches long) with a prehensile tail and a head suggesting that of a horse.

seal[1] (sēl), *n.* **1** design stamped on a piece of wax, etc., to show ownership or authenticity; a paper, circle, mark, etc., representing it. The seal of the United States is attached to important government papers. **2** stamp for marking things with such a design: *a seal with one's initials on it.* **3** thing that fastens or closes something tightly. **4** pledge: *under seal of secrecy.* **5** mark; sign. —*v.* **1** mark (a document) with a seal as evidence of authenticity or confirmation. **2** ratify, certify, or make binding (an agreement, etc.). **3** mark with a seal as evidence of legal or standard exactness, measure, quality, etc. **4** fasten (a letter, etc.) with a seal, wax, etc. **5** close tightly; shut; fasten. **6** settle; determine.

seal off, completely close off; make inaccessible. [< OF, ult. < L *sigillum,* dim. of *signum* sign] —**seal′a·ble,** *adj.* —**seal′er,** *n.*

seal[2] (sēl), *n., pl.* **seals** or *(esp. collectively)* **seal** for 1, *v.* —*n.* **1** a marine carnivorous mammal with large flippers, living usually in cold regions. Some kinds are hunted for their valuable fur. **2** the fur. **3** leather made from the skin of a seal. —*v.* hunt seals. [OE *seolh*] —**seal′er,** *n.*

sea lane, course on the ocean commonly used by ships.

sea legs, get or **have one's,** become accustomed to walking or moving on steady surfaces or ground.

sea level, surface of the sea, esp. when halfway between mean high and low water. Heights of mountains are measured as so many feet above sea level.

sea lily, =crinoid.

sealing wax, a hard kind of wax made of resin and shellac, soft when heated, used for sealing letters, packages, etc.

sea lion, a large seal of the Pacific coast.

seal·skin (sēl'skin'), *n.* **1** skin of the fur seal, prepared for use. **2** garment made of this fur.

Sea·ly·ham (sē'li ham; –əm), *n.* one of a breed of white wire-haired terriers with short legs and square jaws.

seam (sēm), *n.* **1** line formed by sewing two pieces of cloth, canvas, leather, etc., together. **2** any line where edges join. **3** any mark or line like a seam. **4** layer; stratum. —*v.* **1** sew the seam of; join with a seam. **2** mark (the face, etc.) with wrinkles, scars, etc. [OE *sēam*] —**seam'less,** *adj.*

sea·man (sē'mən), *n,, pl.* **-men.** **1** =sailor. **2** sailor who is not an officer. —**sea'man·like',** **sea'man·ly,** *adj.*

sea·man·ship (sē'mən ship), *n.* skill in managing a ship.

seam·stress (sēm'stris), *n.* woman whose work is sewing.

seam·y (sēm'i), *adj.,* **seam·i·er, seam·i·est.** **1** having or showing seams. **2** worst; least pleasant: *the seamy side of life.* —**seam'i·ness,** *n.*

sé·ance (sā'äns), *n.* **1** a sitting; session. **2** a meeting of people trying to communicate with spirits of the dead by the help of a medium. [< F, < *seoir* sit < L *sedere*]

sea·plane (sē'plān'), *n.* hydroplane (def. 2).

sea·port (sē'pôrt'; –pōrt'), *n.* port or harbor on the seacoast; city or town with a harbor that ships can reach from the sea.

sear (sir), *v.* **1** burn or char the surface of. **2** make hard or unfeeling. **3** dry up; wither. —*n.* mark made by searing. —*adj.* Also, **sere.** dried up; withered. [OE *sēar;* v. < adj.]

search (sėrch), *v.* **1** try to find by looking; seek: *search for a lost cat.* **2** go through and examine carefully and in detail, esp. for something concealed: *search a ship.* **3** probe: *the doctor searched the wound.* —*n.* act of searching; examination.

in search of, trying to find; looking for.

search out, a look for. **b** find by searching. [< OF *cerchier,* ult. < L *circus* circle] —**search'a·ble,** *adj.* —**search'er,** *n.*

search·ing (sėr'ching), *adj.* **1** examining carefully. **2** piercing; sharp. —**search'ing·ly,** *adv.*

search·light (sėrch'līt'), *n.* **1** device that can throw a very bright beam of light in any direction desired. **2** the beam of light.

search warrant, a legal document authorizing the search of a house or building for stolen goods, criminals, etc.

sea·shore (sē'shôr'; –shōr'), *n.* land along the sea.

sea·sick (sē'sik'), *adj.* sick because of a ship's motion. —**sea'sick'ness,** *n.*

sea·side (sē'sīd'), *n.* seacoast; seashore.

sea·son (sē'zən), *n.* **1** one of the four periods of the year; spring, summer, autumn, or winter. **2** any period of time marked by something special: *the Christmas season.* **3** time when something is occurring, active, at its best, or in fashion: *the baseball season.* **4** a period of time: *a bad season.* **5** a suitable or fit time. —*v.* **1** improve the flavor of: *season soup with salt.* **2** give interest or character to: *season conversation with wit.* **3** make fit for use by a period of keeping or treatment: *wood is seasoned for building by drying and hardening it.* **4** become fit for use. **5** accustom; make used: *a doctor seasoned to gunshot wounds by years spent in a city emergency room.* **6** make less severe; soften: *season justice with mercy.*

for a season, for a time; for part of the year.

in season, a at the right or proper time. **b** in the time for eating, harvesting, etc.: *oysters in season.* **c** early enough.

out of season, not in season: *many vegetables are out of season in winter.* [< OF < L *satio* a sowing < *serere* to sow] —**sea'son·er,** *n.*

sea·son·a·ble (sē'zən ə bəl; sēz'nə bəl), *adj.* **1** suitable to the season: *seasonable weather.* **2** coming at the right or proper time: *seasonable aid.* —**sea'son·a·ble·ness,** *n.* —**sea'son·a·bly,** *adv.*

sea·son·al (sē'zən əl), *adj.* having to do with the seasons; depending on a season; happening at regular intervals. —**sea'son·al·ly,** *adv.*

sea·son·ing (sē'zən ing; sēz'ning), *n.* **1** something that gives a better flavor, as salt, pepper, or spices. **2** something that gives interest or character: *a speech with a seasoning of humor.*

seat[1] (sēt), *n.* **1** thing to sit on. **2** place to sit. **3** place in which one has the right to sit: *a seat in Congress.* **4** that part of a chair, bench, stool, etc., on which one sits. **5** that part of the body on which one sits, or the clothing covering it. **6** manner of sitting, as on horseback. **7** that on which anything rests; base. —*v.* **1** set or place on a seat: *seat a person on a chair.* **2** have seats for (a specified number). **3** provide with a seat or seats. **4** put a seat on.

be seated, a sit down. **b** be sitting. **c** be situated. [< Scand. *sæti*] —**seat'er,** *n.*

seat[2] (sēt), *n.* **1** an established place or center. **2** residence; home, esp. of an aristocrat. —*v.* fix in a particular or proper place; settle; locate: *seated in the west.* [OE *sǣte*]

sea trout, 1 species of trout that spends part of its life in salt water. **2** one of several kinds of weakfish.

sea urchin, a small sea animal with a spiny shell.

sea wall, wall or bank of earth constructed to keep water and waves from washing away a shoreline.

sea·ward (sē'wərd), *adv.* Also, **sea'wards.** toward the sea. —*adj.* lying, facing, or tending toward the sea. —*n.* direction toward the sea.

sea·way (sē'wā'), *n.* **1** a way over the sea. **2** progress of a ship through the waves. **3** an inland waterway that is deep enough to permit ocean shipping.

sea·weed (sē'wēd'), *n.* any plant or plants growing in the sea.

sea·wor·thy (sē'wėr'ᵺi), *adj.* fit for sailing on the sea; able to stand storms at sea. —**sea'wor'thi·ness,** *n.*

se·ba·ceous (si bā'shəs), *adj.* **1** pertaining to fat; fatty; greasy. **2** secreting a fatty matter, as certain glands. [< L, < *sebum* grease]

sec., 1 secant. **2** *pl.* **secs.** second. **3** secondary. **4** secretary. **5** *pl.* **secs.** section.

se·cant (sē'kənt; –kant), *n.* **1** line that intersects. **2 a** a straight line drawn from the center of a circle through one extremity of an arc to the tangent from the other extremity of the same arc. **b** ratio of the length of this line to the length of the radius of the circle. [< L *secans* cutting]

se·cede (si sēd'), *v.,* **–ced·ed, –ced·ing.** withdraw formally from an organization. [< L, < *se–* apart + *cedere* go] —**se·ced'er,** *n.*

se·ces·sion (si sesh'ən), *n.* **1** a formal withdrawing from an organization. **2** Often, **Secession,** the withdrawal of eleven Southern states in 1860–61, which brought on the Civil War. —**se·ces'sion·ist,** *n.*

se·clude (si klüd'), *v.,* **–clud·ed, –clud·ing.** keep apart from company; shut off from others. [< L *secludere* < *se–* apart + *claudere* shut]

se·clud·ed (si klüd'id), *adj.* shut off from others; undisturbed. —**se·clud'ed·ness,** *n.*

se·clu·sion (si klü'zhən), *n.* **1** a secluding or being secluded; retirement. **2** a secluded place. —**se·clu'sive,** *adj.* —**se·clu'sive·ly,** *adv.* —**se·clu'sive·ness,** *n.*

sec·ond[1] (sek'ənd), *adj.* **1** next after the first: *the second house on the block.* **2** below the first; inferior: *the second officer.* **3** another; other: *her second self.* —*adv.* in the second group, division, rank, etc.; secondly. —*n.* **1** person or thing that is second. **2** person who supports or aids another; backer: *the prize fighter had a second.* —*v.* **1** support; back up; assist: *second another person's idea.* **2** act as second to (a prize fighter, etc.).

seconds, articles below first quality. Seconds have some defect. [< F < L *secundus* < *sequi* follow] —**sec'ond·er,** *n.*

sec·ond[2] (sek'ənd), *n.* **1** $\frac{1}{60}$ of a minute; $\frac{1}{3600}$ of an hour. **2** a very short time. **3** $\frac{1}{3600}$ of a degree of an angle. 120° 10′ 30″ means 12 degrees, 10 minutes, 30 seconds. [< F < Med.L *secunda (minuta)* second (minute), i.e., the result of the second division of the hour into sixty parts]

sec·ond·ar·y (sek'ən der'i), *adj., n., pl.* **–ar·ies.** —*adj.* **1** next after the first in order, place, time, etc. **2** not main or chief; having less importance. **3** not original; derived. —*n.* person or thing that is secondary, second in importance, or subordinate. —**sec′ond·ar´i·ly,** *adv.*

secondary accent, 1 a stress accent that is weaker than the strongest stress in a word (primary accent), but stronger than no stress. The second syllable of *ab·bre´vi·a′tion* has a secondary accent. **2** mark (′) used to show this.

secondary school, =high school.

sec·ond-best (sek′ənd best′), *adj.* almost of first quality; next to best.

second childhood, enjoyment, felt by an adult, similar to that experienced as a child from pure pleasure.

sec·ond-class (sek′ənd klas′; –kläs′), *adj.* of inferior grade or quality; second-rate. —*adv.* on a second-class ship, train, etc.

sec·ond-guess (sek′ənd ges′), *v.* **1** guess or anticipate what will happen. **2** criticize after the fact, with the benefit of hindsight.

sec·ond-hand (sek′ənd hand′), *adj.* **1** not original; obtained from another: *second-hand information.* **2** not new; used already by someone else. **3** dealing in used goods: *a second-hand bookshop.*

second hand, hand on a clock or watch, pointing to the seconds, that moves around the dial once in a minute.

second lieutenant, an army officer who ranks next below a first lieutenant.

sec·ond·ly (sek′ənd lı), *adv.* in the second place; second.

second nature, habit, quality, knowledge, etc., that a person has acquired and had for so long that it seems to be almost a part of his or her nature.

second person, form of a pronoun or verb used to indicate the person spoken to.

sec·ond-rate (sek′ənd rāt′), *adj.* **1** rated as second-class. **2** inferior. —*adv.* in an inferior manner. —**sec′ond-rat′er,** *n.*

second sight, the supposed power of seeing distant objects or future events as if they were present.

sec·ond-string (sek′ənd string′), *adj.* **1** not on the regular or starting team in a sport. **2** =second-rate.

se·cre·cy (sē′krə si), *n., pl.* –**cies. 1** condition of being secret: *an affair conducted in strict secrecy.* **2** ability to keep things secret. **3** tendency to conceal; lack of frankness.

se·cret (sē′krit), *adj.* **1** done, made, or conducted without the knowledge of others: *a secret marriage.* **2** keeping to oneself what one knows: *be as secret as the grave.* **3** known only to a few: *a secret society.* **4** kept from sight; hidden: *a secret drawer.* —*n.* **1** something secret or hidden; thing known only to a few. **2** a hidden cause or reason.

in secret, secretly; in private; not openly. [< F < L *secretus* set apart < *se–* apart + *cernere* separate. Doublet of SECRETE.] —**se′cret·ly,** *adv.* —**se′cret·ness,** *n.*

secret agent, agent of the government secret service.

sec·re·tar·i·al (sek′rə tār′i əl), *adj.* of a secretary; having to do with a secretary.

sec·re·tar·i·at (sek′rə tār′i ət; -at), *n.* **1** office or position of secretary. **2** group of secretaries. **3** place where a secretary transacts business.

sec·re·tar·y (sek′rə ter´i), *n., pl.* –**tar·ies. 1** person who writes letters, keeps records, etc., for a person, company, club, etc. **2** person who has charge of a department of the government. The Secretary of the Treasury is the head of the Treasury Department. **3** a writing desk with a set of drawers and often with shelves for books. [< LL *secretarius* confidential officer < L *secretum,* n., SECRET] —**sec′re·tar´y·ship,** *n.*

secretary bird, a large, long-legged African bird of prey that feeds on reptiles, so called because its crest suggests pens stuck over the ear.

se·crete[1] (si krēt′), *v.,* –**cret·ed,** –**cret·ing. 1** keep secret; hide. **2** take in secret: *secrete funds from the general account.* [< L *secretus.* Doublet of SECRET.] —**se·cre′tor, se·cret′er,** *n.*

se·crete[2] (si krēt′), *v.* –**cret·ed,** –**cret·ing.** produce and discharge: *glands secrete enzymes.* [< *secretion*]

se·cre·tion (si krē′shən), *n.* **1** substance that is secreted by some part of an animal or plant. **2** process or function of discharging various substances, as bile. —**se·cre′tion·ar´y, se·cre′tion·al,** *adj.*

se·cre·tive (si krē′tiv), *adj.* **1** having the habit of secrecy; not frank and open. **2** causing or aiding secretion. —**se·cre′tive·ly,** *adv.* —**se·cre′tive·ness,** *n.*

se·cre·to·ry (si krē′tə ri), *adj., n., pl.* –**ries.** —*adj.* secreting; of or causing secretion. —*n.* organ of the body that secretes.

secret service, 1 branch of a government that makes secret investigations. **2** an official service that is secret. **3 Secret Service,** branch of the U.S. Treasury Department concerned with discovering and preventing counterfeiting, protecting the President, etc.

sect (sekt), *n.* **1** group of people having the same principles, beliefs, or opinions. **2** a religious group separated from an established church. [< L *secta* party, school < *sequi* follow]

sec·tar·i·an (sek tār′i ən), *adj.* **1** of or pertaining to a sect. **2** characteristic of one sect only. —*n.* **1** a devoted member of a sect, esp. a narrow-minded or strongly prejudiced member. **2** member of a sect. —**sec·tar′i·an·ism,** *n.*

sec·tion (sek′shən), *n.* **1** part cut off; part; division; slice: *divide the cake into sections.* **2** one of several parts that can be put together to form a whole: *the sections of a pipe, an orchestra's string section.* **3** division of a book: *Chapter X has seven sections.* **4** region; part of a country, city, etc.: *a town has a business section, residential sections, etc.* **5** act of

cutting. **6** a representation of a thing as it would appear if cut straight through. —*v.* cut into sections. [< L < *secare* cut]

sec·tion·al (sek′shən əl), *adj.* **1** pertaining to a particular section; local. **2** made of sections: *a sectional bookcase.* —**sec′tion·al·ist,** *n.* —**sec′tion·al·ly,** *adv.*

sec·tion·al·ism (sek′shə nə liz′əm), *n.* division based on local interests or concerns; sectional prejudice.

sec·tor (sek′tər), *n.* **1** a plane figure bounded by two radii and the included arc of a circle, ellipse, or the like. **2** a clearly defined area which a particular unit of a military force protects or covers with fire; part of a front held by a unit. [< LL, < L, cutter, < *secare* to cut] —**sec·to′ri·al,** *adj.*

sec·u·lar (sek′yə lər), *adj.* **1** worldly, not religious or sacred: *secular music.* **2** living in the world; not belonging to a religious order. [< L, < *saeculum* age, world] —**sec′u·lar·ism,** *n.* —**sec′u·lar·ist,** *n.* —**sec′u·lar·ly,** *adv.*

sec·u·lar·ize (sek′yə lər īz), *v.,* –**ized,** –**iz·ing.** make secular or worldly; separate from religious connection or influence: *secularize the schools.* —**sec′u·lar·i·za′tion,** *n.* —**sec′u·lar·iz´er,** *n.*

se·cure (si kyūr′), *adj., v.,* –**cured,** –**cur·ing.** —*adj.* **1** safe against loss, attack, escape, etc.: *a secure hiding place.* **2** sure; certain; that can be counted on: *our victory is secure.* **3** free from care or fear: *a secure old age.* **4** firmly fastened; not liable to give way: *the boards of this bridge do not look secure.* —*v.* **1** make safe; protect. **2** make (something) sure or certain. **3** make firm or fast: *secure the locks on the windows.* **4** get; obtain: *secure your tickets early.* [< L, < *se–* free from + *cura* care. Doublet of SURE.] —**se·cure′ly,** *adv.* —**se·cur′er,** *n.*

se·cu·ri·ty (si kyūr′ə ti), *n., pl.* –**ties. 1** freedom from danger, care, or fear; feeling or condition of being safe. **2** something that secures or makes safe: *a watchdog is a security against burglars.* **3** Usually, **securities.** bond or stock certificate: *these railroad securities can be sold for $5000.* **4** something given as a pledge that a person will fulfill some duty, promise, etc.: *a life-insurance policy may serve as security for a loan.* **5** person who agrees to be responsible for another.

securities, stocks or bonds or other financial instruments.

secy., sec′y., secretary.

se·dan (si dan′), *n.* **1** a closed automobile seating four or more persons. **2** sedan chair.

sedan chair, a covered chair carried on poles by two men.

se·date (si dāt′), *adj.* quiet; calm; serious. [< L *sedatus* calmed] —**se·date′ly,** *adv.* —**se·date′ness,** *n.*

sed·a·tive (sed′ə tiv), *n.* **1** medicine that lessens pain or excitement. **2** anything soothing or calming. —*adj.* **1** lessening pain or excitement. **2** soothing; calming.

sed·en·tar·y (sed'ən ter´ī), *adj.* **1** used to sitting still much of the time: *sedentary people.* **2** that keeps one sitting still much of the time: *a sedentary occupation.* **3** fixed to one spot; not migratory. [< L *sedentarius,* ult. < *sedere* sit] —**sed'en·tar´i·ly,** *adv.* —**sed'en·tar´i·ness,** *n.*

sedge (sej), *n.* a grasslike plant that grows in wet places. [OE *secg*] —**sedged, sedg'y,** *adj.*

sed·i·ment (sed'ə mənt), *n.* **1** matter that settles to the bottom of a liquid. **2** matter deposited, as by water. [< F < L, < *sedere* settle] —**sed´i·men·ta'tion,** *n.*

sed·i·men·ta·ry (sed´ə men'tə ri), *adj.* **1** of or having to do with sediment. **2** formed from sediment. —**sed´i·men'ta·ri·ly,** *adv.*

se·di·tion (si dish'ən), *n.* speech or action causing discontent or rebellion against the government; incitement to discontent or rebellion. [< L *seditio* < *se-* apart + *ire* go] —**se·di'tion·ar´y,** *adj.*

se·di·tious (si dish'əs), *adj.* **1** stirring up discontent or rebellion. **2** taking part in sedition; guilty of sedition. **3** pertaining to sedition. —**se·di'tious·ly,** *adv.* —**se·di'tious·ness,** *n.*

se·duce (si düs'; –dūs'), *v.,* **–duced, –duc·ing. 1** tempt to wrongdoing; persuade to do wrong. **2** lead away from virtue; lead astray; beguile. **3** entice (a woman) to a surrender of chastity. [< L, < *se-* aside + *ducere* lead] —**se·duc'er,** *n.* —**se·duc'i·ble,** *adj.* —**se·duc'ing·ly,** *adv.* —**se·duc'tion,** *n.*

se·duc·tive (si duk'tiv), *adj.* alluring; captivating; charming. —**se·duc'tive·ly,** *adv.* —**se·duc'tive·ness,** *n.*

sed·u·lous (sej'ə ləs), *adj.* hard-working; diligent; painstaking. [< L *sedulus* < *se dolo* without deception] —**se·du'li·ty,** *n.* —**sed'u·lous·ly,** *adv.*

see[1] (sē), *v.,* **saw, seen, see·ing. 1** perceive or examine with the eyes; look at; observe: *see that black cloud, see a tennis match.* **2** have the power of sight: *the blind do not see.* **3** take in with the mind; understand: *I see what you mean.* **4** find out; learn: *please see who it is.* **5** take care; make sure: *see that the work is properly done.* **6** have knowledge or experience of: *that coat has seen hard wear.* **7** attend; go with: *see a child home.* **8** meet; call on: *will you see him at his home?*
see (someone) off, go with someone to the place where he or she begins a trip.
see through, a understand the real character or hidden purpose of. **b** go through with; finish. **c** watch over or help through a difficulty.
see to (it), look after; make sure of (something). [OE *sēon*] —**see'a·ble,** *adj.*

see[2] (sē), *n.* **1** position or authority of a bishop. **2** diocese; bishopric. [< OF *sie* < L *sedes* abode]

seed (sēd), *n., pl.* **seeds, seed,** *v.* —*n.* **1** thing from which a flower, vegetable, or other plant grows; small grainlike fruit. **2** bulb, sprout, or any part of a plant

from which a new plant will grow. **3** *Fig.* beginning; source. **4** *Fig.* children; descendants. —*v.* **1** sow with seeds; scatter seeds over: *the farmer seeded his field with corn, dandelions seed themselves.* **2** remove the seeds from: *seed raisins.* **3** scatter or distribute (the names of players) so that the best players do not meet in the early part of a tournament. **4** scatter dry ice or other chemicals into (clouds) from an airplane in an effort to produce rain artificially.
go to seed, a come to the time of yielding seeds. **b** come to the end of vigor, usefulness, prosperity, etc. [OE *sǣd*] —**seed'er,** *n.* —**seed'less,** *adj.* —**seed'like´,** *adj.*

seed·case (sēd'kās´), *n.* any pod, capsule, or other dry, hollow fruit that contains seeds.

seed coat, outer covering of a seed.

seed·ing (sēd'ing), *n.* **1** act or fact of distributing seeds. **2** distribution of players in a tournament. **3** in rain making, the dropping of dry ice or other chemicals into clouds.

seed leaf, =cotyledon.

seed·ling (sēd'ling), *n.* **1** a young plant grown from a seed. **2** a small young tree less than three feet high.

seed·y (sēd'i), *adj.,* **seed·i·er, seed·i·est. 1** full of seed. **2** gone to seed. **3** shabby; no longer fresh or new: *seedy clothes.* —**seed'i·ly,** *adv.* —**seed'i·ness,** *n.*

see·ing (sē'ing), *n.* sight. —*adj.* that sees. —*conj.* in view of the fact; considering: *seeing that it is 10 o'clock, we will wait no longer.*

Seeing Eye, organization that breeds and trains dogs as guides for blind people.

seek (sēk), *v.,* **sought, seek·ing. 1** try to find; look for: *seek a new home, seek something lost.* **2** try to get: *friends sought his advice, he seeks to make peace.* **3** go to: *being sleepy, he sought his bed.*
sought after, in demand. [OE *sēcan*] —**seek'er,** *n.*

seem (sēm), *v.* **1** appear; appear to be: *he seemed a very old man, it seems likely to rain.* **2** appear to oneself: *I still seem to hear the music.* **3** appear to exist: *there seems no need to wait longer.* [< Scand. *sǣma* conform to]

seem·ing (sēm'ing), *adj.* apparent; that appears to be: *a seeming advantage.* —*n.* appearance; likeness. —**seem'ing·ly,** *adv.* —**seem'ing·ness,** *n.*

seem·ly (sēm'li), *adj.,* **–li·er, –li·est,** *adv.* —*adj.* **1** suitable; proper. **2** having a pleasing appearance. —*adv.* properly; becomingly. —**seem'li·ness,** *n.*

seen (sēn), *v.* pp. of **see**[1].

seep (sēp), *v.* ooze; trickle; leak: *water seeps through sand.* [? OE *sīpian*] —**seep'y,** *adj.*

seep·age (sēp'ij), *n.* **1** a seeping; leakage. **2** moisture or liquid that seeps.

seer (sir *for 1, 3;* sē'ər *for 2*), *n.* **1** person who foresees or foretells future events; prophet. **2** one that sees. **3** one who tells fortunes.

seer·suck·er (sir'suk´ər), *n.* cloth woven into alternating plain and crinkled stripes. [< Hind. < Pers. *shir o shakkar,* lit., milk and sugar]

see·saw (sē'sô´), *n.* **1** plank resting on a support near its middle so the ends can move up and down, esp. for children to ride on. **2** moving up and down on such a plank. **3** motion up and down or back and forth. —*v.* **1** move up and down on a balanced plank. **2** move up and down or back and forth. **3** *Fig.* go back and forth between two alternatives; be undecided. —*adj.* moving up and down or back and forth. [varied reduplication of *saw*[1]]

seethe (sēth), *v.,* **seethed, seeth·ing. 1** bubble and foam: *seething waters.* **2** be excited; be disturbed: *seething with discontent.* [OE *sēothan*] —**seeth'ing·ly,** *adv.*

seg·ment (seg'mənt), *n.* **1** part cut, marked, or broken off; division; section: *an orange is easily pulled apart into its segments.* **2** part of a circle, sphere, etc., cut off by a line or plane. —*v.* divide into segments. [< L *segmentum* < *secare* to cut] —**seg·men'tal, seg'men·tar´y,** *adj.* —**seg·men'tal·ly,** *adv.*

seg·men·ta·tion (seg´mən tā'shən), *n.* division into segments.

se·go lily (sē'gō), or **sego,** *n., pl.* **–gos.** plant that has trumpet-shaped flowers, common in the SW part of the United States. [< Am.Ind.]

seg·re·gate (*v.* seg'rə gāt; *adj.* seg'rə git, –gāt), *v.,* **–gat·ed, –gat·ing,** *adj.* —*v.* **1** separate from others; set apart; isolate. **2** separate from the rest and collect in one place, as in crystallization. —*adj.* segregated. [< L *segregatus* < *se-* apart from + *grex* herd] —**seg're·ga´tive,** *adj.* —**seg're·ga´tor,** *n.*

seg·re·ga·tion (seg´rə gā'shən), *n.* **1** a segregating or being segregated. **2** separation of blacks from other racial groups, esp. in schools and other public places. School segregation was ruled unconstitutional by the United States Supreme Court in 1954.

seg·re·ga·tion·ist (seg´rə gā'shən ist), *n.* person who believes in the separation of racial groups, esp. of blacks. —*adj.* of or having to do with segregation: *segregationist rhetoric.*

se·gue (sā'gwā), *v.,* **–gued, –gue·ing. 1** more from one thing to another without pause: *segued from death on the highway to news of a captive panda's birth.* **2** proceed from one section of a musical composition to the next, without pause. —*n.* an immediate transition, esp. to something entirely different. [< It., lit., it follows]

sei·gneur (sēn yèr'), *n.* a feudal lord or landowner. [< F. Doublet of SEIGNIOR and SIEUR.]

seign·ior (sēn'yər), *n.* **1** lord; lord of a manor; gentleman. **2** title of respect. **3** =seigneur. [< OF < acc. of L *senior* SENIOR. Doublet of SEIGNEUR and SIEUR.] —**seignêior'i·al,** *adj.*

seine (sān), *n., v.,* **seined, sein·ing.** —*n.* a fishing net that hangs straight down in the water. It has floats at the upper edge and sinkers at the lower. —*v.* **1** fish with a seine. **2** catch with a seine. [< L < Gk. *sagene*]

seis·mic (sīz′mik; sīs′–), *adj.* **1** of earthquakes or an earthquake. **2** caused by an earthquake. [< Gk. *seismos* earthquake < *seiein* to shake]

seis·mo·graph (sīz′mə graf; –gräf; sīs′–), *n.* instrument for recording the direction, intensity, and duration of earthquakes. [< *seismo–* (< Gk. *seismos* earthquake) + –GRAPH] —**seis·mog′ra·pher,** *n.* —**seis′mo·graph′ic,** *adj.* —**seis·mog′ra·phy,** *n.*

seis·mol·o·gy (sīz mol′ə ji; sīs–), *n.* study of earthquakes and other movements of the earth's crust. [< *seismo–* (< Gk. *seismos* earthquake) + –LOGY] —**seis′mo·log′i·cal, seis′mo·log′ic,** *adj.* —**seis′mo·log′i·cal·ly,** *adv.* —**seis·mol′o·gist,** *n.*

seize (sēz), *v.,* **seized, seiz·ing. 1** take hold of suddenly; clutch; grasp. **2** grasp with the mind. **3** grasp and use: *seize an opportunity.* **4** take possession of: *seize smuggled goods, a fever seized her.* **5** take into custody; capture: *men were seized for rioting.*

seize on or **upon, a** take hold of suddenly. **b** take possession of.

seize up, a become jammed, unable to move or turn, as of a joint or motor. **b** *Fig.* be unable to function: *the singer simply seized up and left the stage.* [< OF *seisir,* ult. < Gmc.] —**seiz′a·ble,** *adj.* —**seiz′er,** *n.*

sei·zure (sē′zhər), *n.* **1** act of seizing: *seizure of smuggled goods.* **2** condition of being seized: *after his seizure he was imprisoned.* **3** a sudden attack of disease.

sel·dom (sel′dəm), *adv.* rarely; not often: *he is seldom ill.* [OE *seldum*] —**sel′dom·ness,** *n.*

se·lect (si lekt′), *v.* choose; pick out: *select the book you want.* —*adj.* **1** picked as best; chosen specially: *a select crew.* **2** choice; superior. **3** careful in choosing; particular as to friends, company, etc.: *a very select club.*

select out, exclude; weed out. [< L *selectus* < *se–* apart + *legere* choose] —**se·lect′ly,** *adv.* —**se·lect′ness,** *n.* —**se·lec′tor,** *n.*

se·lec·tion (si lek′shən), *n.* **1** choice. **2** person, thing, or group chosen. **3** the selecting of animals or plants to survive. —**se·lec′tion·ist,** *n.*

se·lec·tive (si lek′tiv), *adj.* **1** selecting; having the power to select. **2** having to do with selection. —**se·lec′tive·ly,** *adv.* —**se·lec′tive·ness,** *n.*

se·lec·tiv·i·ty (si lek′tiv′ə ti), *n.* quality of being selective.

se·lect·man (si lekt′mən), *n., pl.* **-men.** one of a board of town officers in New England, chosen each year to manage certain public affairs.

se·le·ni·um (si lē′ni əm), *n.* a nonmetallic element, Se, resembling sulfur in chemical properties, used in photoelectric cells. [< NL, < Gk. *selene* moon]

self (self), *n., pl.* **selves.** *pron., pl.* **selves.** —*n.* **1** one's own person: *his very self.* **2** one's own welfare, interests, etc.: *a selfish person puts self first.* **3** nature, character, etc., of a person or thing: *one's former self.* —*pron.* myself; himself; herself; yourself: *a check made payable to self.* [OE]

self–, *prefix.* **1** of or over oneself, etc., as in *self-conscious, self-control.* **2** by or in oneself, etc., as in *self-inflicted, self-evident.* **3** to or for oneself, etc., as in *self-addressed, self-respect.* **4** automatic; automatically, as in *self-starter, self-closing.* [< *self*]

self-a·base·ment (self′ə bās′mənt), *n.* abasement of self.

self-ab·sorbed (self′ab sôrbd′; –zôrbd′), *adj.* absorbed in one's own thoughts, affairs, etc. —**self′-ab·sorp′tion,** *n.*

self-act·ing (self′ak′ting), *adj.* working of itself: *a self-acting machine.*

self-ad·dressed (self′ə drest′), *adj.* addressed to oneself.

self-as·ser·tion (self′ə sėr′shən), *n.* insistence on one's own wishes, opinions, claims, etc. —**self′-as·ser′tive,** *adj.* —**self′-as·ser′tive·ly,** *adv.*

self-as·sur·ance (self′ə shŭr′əns), *n.* self-confidence. —**self′-as·sured′,** *adj.*

self-cen·tered (self′sen′tərd), *adj.* **1** occupied with one's own interests and affairs. **2** selfish. **3** being a fixed point around which other things move. —**self′cen′tered·ness,** *n.*

self-com·mand (self′kə mand′; –mänd′), *n.* control of oneself.

self-con·ceit (self′kən sēt′), *n.* conceit; too much pride in oneself or one's ability. —**self′-con·ceit′ed,** *adj.* —**self′-conceit′ed·ness,** *n.*

self-con·fessed (self′kən fest′), *adj.* admitted to by oneself: *self-confessed gambler.*

self-con·fi·dence (self′kon′fə dəns), *n.* belief in one's own ability, power, judgment, etc.; confidence in oneself. —**self′-con′fi·dent,** *adj.*

self-con·scious (self′kon′shəs), *adj.* made conscious of how one is appearing to others; shy. —**self′-con′scious·ly,** *adv.* —**self′-con′scious·ness,** *n.*

self-con·tained (self′kən tānd′), *adj.* **1** saying little; reserved. **2** containing in oneself or itself all that is necessary; independent of what is external. —**self′-con·tain′ment,** *n.*

self-con·tra·dic·tion (self′kon′trə dik′-shən), *n.* statement containing elements that are contradictory. —**self′-con′tra·dic′to·ry,** *adj.*

self-con·trol (self′kən trōl′), *n.* control of one's actions, feelings, etc. —**self′-con·trolled′,** *adj.*

self-de·feat·ing (self′di fēt′ing), *adj.* **1** against one's own interest or purpose.

2 against a stated goal or purpose: *some taxes are self-defeating.*

self-de·fense (self′di fens′), *n.* defense of one's own person, property, reputation, etc. —**self′-de·fen′sive,** *adj.*

self-de·ni·al (self′di nī′əl), *n.* sacrifice of one's own desires and interests; going without things one wants. —**self′-de·ny′ing,** *adj.*

self-de·ter·mi·na·tion (self′di tėr′mə nā′-shən), *n.* **1** direction from within only, without influence or force from without. **2** the deciding by the people of a nation what form of government they shall have. —**self′-de·ter′mined,** *adj.* —**self′-de·ter′min·ing,** *adj.*

self-dis·ci·pline (self′dis′ə plin), *n.* careful control and training of oneself.

self-de·struct (self′di strukt′), *v.* destroy oneself or itself. —**self′des·truc′tion,** *n.*

self-ef·face·ment (self′i fās′mənt), *n.* act or habit of modestly keeping oneself in the background. —**self′-ef·fac′ing,** *adj.*

self-es·teem (self′es tēm′), *n.* **1** self-respect. **2** conceit.

self-ev·i·dent (self′ev′ə dənt), *adj.* evident by itself; needing no proof. —**self′-ev′i·dence,** *n.* —**self′-ev′i·dent·ly,** *adv.*

self-ex·am·i·na·tion (self′ig zam′ə nā′shən), *n.* examination into one's own state, conduct, motives, etc.

self-ex·plan·a·to·ry (self′iks plan′ə tô′ri; –tō′–), **self-ex·plain·ing** (–iks plān′ing), *adj.* explaining itself; obvious.

self-ex·pres·sion. (self′iks presh′ən), *n.* expression of one's personality.

self-gov·ern·ment (self′guv′ərn mənt), *n.* **1** government of a group by its own members. **2** self-control. —**self′-gov′erned,** *adj.* —**self′-gov′ern·ing,** *adj.*

self-help (self′help′), *n.* a helping oneself; getting along without assistance from others. —**self′-help′ful,** *adj.*

self-im·por·tant (self′im pôr′tənt), *adj.* having or showing too high an opinion of one's own importance. —**self′-im·por′tance,** *n.*

self-im·posed (self′im pōzd′), *adj.* imposed on oneself by oneself.

self-im·prove·ment (self′im prüv′mənt), *n.* improvement of one's character, mind, etc., by one's own efforts. —**self′-im·prov′ing,** *adj.*

self-in·duced (self′in düst′; –dūst′), *adj.* induced by itself; induced by oneself.

self-in·dul·gence (self′in dul′jəns), *n.* gratification of one's own desires, passions, etc., with too little regard for the welfare of others. —**self′-in·dul′gent,** *adj.*

self-in·flict·ed (self′in flik′tid), *adj.* inflicted on oneself by oneself.

self-in·ter·est (self′in′tər ist; –trist), *n.* **1** interest in one's own welfare with too little care for the welfare of others; selfishness. **2** personal advantage. —**self′-in′ter·est·ed,** *adj.*

self·ish (sel′fish), *adj.* **1** caring too much for oneself; caring too little for others. **2** characterized by or showing care solely

or chiefly for oneself: *selfish motives.*
—**self′ish·ly,** *adv.* —**self′ish·ness,** *n.*

self·less (self′lis), *adj.* having no regard or thought for self; unselfish. —**self′less·ly,** *adv.* —**self′less·ness,** *n.*

self-made (self′mād′), *adj.* **1** made by oneself. **2** successful through one's own efforts.

self-mail·er (self′mā′lər), *n.* folded card that can be mailed without an envelope.

self-pit·y (self′pit′i), *n.* pity for oneself. —**self′-pit′y·ing,** *adj.* —**self′-pit′y·ing·ly,** *adv.*

self-pos·sessed (self′pə zest′), *adj.* having or showing control of one's feelings and acts; calm. —**self′-pos·ses′sion,** *n.*

self-pres·er·va·tion (self′prez′ər vā′shən), *n.* preservation of oneself from harm or destruction.

self-pro·claimed (self′prə klāmd′), *adj.* claimed about oneself by oneself: *a self-proclaimed investment counselor.*

self-pro·tec·tion (self′prə tek′shən), *n.* protection of oneself.

self-re·gard·ing (self′ri gar′ding), *adj.* focusing on or overly concerned with oneself; self-serving. —**self′-re·gard′,** *n.*

self-reg·u·lat·ing (self′reg′yə lāt′ing), *adj.* regulating oneself or itself. —**self′-reg′u·la′tion,** *n.* —**self′-reg′u·la′tive,** *adj.*

self-re·li·ance (self′ri lī′əns), *n.* reliance on one's own acts, abilities, etc. —**self′-re·li′ant,** *adj.* —**self′-re·li′ant·ly,** *adv.*

self-re·proach (self′ri prōch′), *n.* blame by one's own conscience.

self-re·spect (self′ri spekt′), *n.* respect for oneself; proper pride. —**self′-re·spect′-ing,** *adj.*

self-re·straint (self′ri strānt′), *n.* self-control. —**self′-re·strained′,** *adj.*

self-right·eous (self′rī′chəs), *adj.* thinking that one is more moral than others; thinking that one is very good and pleasing. —**self′-right′eous·ly,** *adv.* —**self′-right′eous·ness,** *n.*

self-sac·ri·fice (self′sak′rə fīs), *n.* sacrifice of one's own interests and desires, as for one's duty or another's welfare. —**self′-sac′ri·fic′ing,** *adj.*

self-same (self′sām′), *adj.* very same. —**self′same′ness,** *n.*

self-sat·is·fied (self′sat′is fīd), *adj.* pleased with oneself. —**self′-sat′is·fac′tion,** *n.*

self-seek·ing (self′sēk′ing), *adj.* selfish. —*n.* selfishness. —**self′-seek′er,** *n.*

self-serv·ice (self′sèr′vis), *n.* act or process of serving oneself in a restaurant, store, etc.

self-serv·ing (self′sèr′ving), *adj.* useful or helpful to oneself; advancing one's own interests.

self-start·er (self′stär′tər), *n.* an electric motor or other device used to start an engine automatically. —**self′-start′ing,** *adj.*

self-styled (self′stīld′), *adj.* called by oneself; self-proclaimed.

self-suf·fi·cient (self′sə fish′ənt), *adj.* **1** asking no help; independent. **2** conceited. —**self′-suf·fi′cien·cy,** *n.*

self-suf·fic·ing (self′sə fīs′ing), *adj.* self-sufficient. —**self′-suf·fic′ing·ness,** *n.*

self-sup·port (self′sə pôrt′; -pōrt′), *n.* unaided support of oneself. —**self′-sup·port′ed,** *adj.*

self-sup·port·ing (self′sə pôr′ting; -pōr′-), *adj.* earning one's expenses; getting along without help.

self-sus·tain·ing (self′səs tān′ing), *adj.* **1** self-supporting. **2** continuing to operate or function once started or begun. —**self′-sus·tain′ing·ly,** *adv.*

self-taught (self′tôt′), *adj.* taught by oneself without aid from others.

self-wind·ing (self′wīn′ding), *adj.* that is wound automatically.

sell (sel), *v.,* **sold, sell·ing. 1** exchange for money or other payment: *sell a house.* **2** deal in; keep for sale: *jewelers sell watches.* **3** be on sale; be sold: *good cars sell at a high price.* **4** give up; betray, esp. for a price or to gain some advantage: *sell one's friend.* **5** *Fig.* cause to be accepted, approved, or adopted: *sell an idea to the public.*

sell off, get rid of by selling.

sell out, a sell all that one has of; get rid of by selling. **b** betray by a secret bargain. [OE *sellan*]

sell-by date (sel′bī′). **1** date printed on a product label or package showing the date by which it must be sold. **2** *Fig.* time when a person or thing is not considered productive or useful.

sell·er (sel′ər), *n.* **1** person who sells. **2** thing considered with reference to its sale: *this book is a best seller.*

sell·out or **sell-out** (sel′out′), *n.* **1** a selling out; betrayal. **2** performance of a play, etc., for which no unsold seats are left.

sel·vage, sel·vedge (sel′vij), *n.* edge of a fabric finished off to prevent raveling; border; edge. [< *self + edge*; because it serves itself as an edge]

selves (selvz), *n., pl.* of **self:** *he had two selves.*

se·man·tic (sə man′tik), *adj.* pertaining to signification or meaning.

se·man·tics (sə man′tiks), *n.* **1** the study of the meanings and the development of meanings of words. **2** the study of the relations between symbols or signs and what they denote. [< LL < Gk. *semantikos* having meaning, ult. < *sema* sign] —**se·man′ti·cist,** *n.*

sem·a·phore (sem′ə fôr; -fōr), *n., v.,* **-phored, -phor·ing.** —*n.* apparatus for signaling; upright post or structure with movable arms, an arrangement of lanterns, flags, etc., used in signaling. —*v.* signal by semaphore. [< Gk. *sema* signal + *-phoros* carrying]

sem·blance (sem′bləns), *n.* **1** likeness; copy. **2** the outward aspect; appearance. **3** an assumed or unreal appearance. [< OF, < *sembler* seem, ult. < L *similis* similar]

se·men (sē′mən), *n.* fluid containing the male reproductive cells. [< L, seed]

se·mes·ter (sə mes′tər), *n.* half of a school year. [< G < L *semestris* semiannual, ult. < *sex* six + *mensis* month]

sem·i (sem′i), *n.* =semitrailer.

semi-, *prefix.* **1** half, as in *semicircle.* **2** partly; incompletely, as in *semicivilized.* **3** twice. Semi___ly means in each half of a ___, or twice in a ___, as in *semimonthly.* [< L]

sem·i·an·nu·al (sem′i an′yü əl), *adj.* **1** occurring every half year. **2** lasting a half year. —**sem′i·an′nu·al·ly,** *adv.*

sem·i·ar·id (sem′i ar′id), *adj.* having very little rainfall.

sem·i·au·to·mat·ic (sem′i ô′tə mat′ik), *adj.* partly automatic in operation, as with a firearm which loads automatically but fires only when the trigger is pulled. —*n.* semiautomatic gun. —**sem′i·au′to·mat′i·cal·ly,** *adv.*

sem·i·breve (sem′i brēv′), *n.* whole note.

sem·i·cir·cle (sem′i sèr′kəl), *n.* half of a circle. —**sem′i·cir′cu·lar,** *adj.*

semicircular canal, any of three curved, tubelike canals in the inner part of the ear that help us keep our balance.

sem·i·co·lon (sem′i kō′lən), *n.* mark of punctuation (;) that shows a separation not so complete as that shown by a period.

sem·i·con·duc·tor (sem′i kən duk′tər), *n.* silicon or other mineral substance that is an effective conductor of electricity between metals and insulators, used in converters and transistors.

sem·i·con·scious (sem′i kon′shəs), *adj.* half-conscious; not fully conscious. —**sem′i·con′scious·ly,** *adv.* —**sem′i·con′scious·ness,** *n.*

sem·i·de·tached (sem′i di tacht′), *adj.* partly detached, used esp. of either of two houses joined by a common wall but separated from other buildings.

sem·i·fi·nal (sem′i fī′nəl), *n.* one of the two rounds, matches, etc., that immediately precede the final one. —*adj.* designating or pertaining to such a round, match, etc. —**sem′i·fi′nal·ist,** *n.*

sem·i·month·ly (sem′i munth′li), *adj., adv., n., pl.* **-lies.** —*adj.* occurring or appearing twice a month. —*adv.* twice a month. —*n.* something that occurs or appears twice a month; magazine or paper published twice a month.

sem·i·nal (sem′ə nəl), *adj.* **1** of or pertaining to semen or seed. **2** like seed; having the possibility of future development. —**sem′i·nal·ly,** *adv.*

sem·i·nar (sem′ə när), *n.* **1** group of college or university students doing research under direction. **2** course of study or work for such a group. [< G < L *seminarium* plant nursery, hotbed < *semen* seed. Doublet of SEMINARY.]

sem·i·nar·y (sem′ə ner′i), *n., pl.* **-nar·ies. 1** school, esp. one beyond high school. **2** school or college for training students to be priests, ministers, etc. [< L *seminarium.* Doublet of SEMINAR.] —**sem′i·nar′i·an,** *n.*

sem·i·na·tion (sem′ə nā′shən), *n.* a sowing; propagation; dissemination.

Sem·i·nole (sem′ə nōl), *n., pl.* **-nole, -noles,** *adj.* —*n.* member of a tribe of American Indians living in Florida and Oklahoma. —*adj.* of or having to do with this tribe.

se·mi·ot·ics (sē′mi ot′iks), *n.* science of signs or symbols. [< Gk. *semeion* sign] —**se′mi·ot′ic,** *adj.*

sem·i·per·me·a·ble (sem′i pėr′mi ə bəl), *adj.* permeable to some substances but not to others.

sem·i·pre·cious (sem′i presh′əs), *adj.* having value but not great value.

sem·i·qua·ver (sem′i kwā′vər), *n.* sixteenth note in music.

sem·i·skilled (sem′i skild′), *adj.* partly skilled.

sem·i·sweet (sem′i swēt′), *adj.* somewhat sweet; lightly sweetened: *semisweet chocolate.*

Sem·ite (sem′īt; sē′mīt), *n.* member of the linguistic family that includes the Hebrews, Arabs, Syrians, Phoenicians, Assyrians, etc.

Se·mit·ic (sə mit′ik), *adj.* of or pertaining to the Semites or their languages. —*n.* group of languages including Hebrew, Arabic, etc.

sem·i·tone (sem′i tōn′), *n.* half-tone on the musical scale. —**sem′i·ton′ic,** *adj.*

sem·i·trail·er (sem′i trā′lər), *n.* trailer for a truck that has wheels only on the back end and is supported at the front by the tractor that pulls it.

sem·i·trop·i·cal (sem′i trop′ə kəl), *adj.* half-way between tropical and temperate.

sem·i·week·ly (sem′i wēk′li), *adj., adv., n., pl.* **-lies.** —*adj.* occurring or appearing twice a week. —*adv.* twice a week. —*n.* something that occurs or appears twice a week; magazine or paper published twice a week.

sem·i·year·ly (sem′i yir′li), *adj., adv., n., pl.* **-lies.** —*adj.* occurring or appearing twice a year. —*adv.* twice a year. —*n.* something that occurs or appears twice a year.

sem·o·li·na (sem′ə lē′nə), *n.* the parts of hard wheat remaining after the flour has been sifted through, used in making puddings, macaroni, etc. [< Ital. *semolino,* ult. < L *simila* fine flour]

sen (sen), *n., pl.* **sen.** a Japanese copper or bronze coin, equal to $\frac{1}{100}$ of a yen.

Sen., sen., 1 Senate; Senator. 2 Senior.

sen·ate (sen′it), *n.* 1 a governing or law-making assembly. 2 **Senate,** the upper house of Congress or of a state legislature. 3 the upper house of the legislature of certain other countries, as Canada, Australia, etc. 4 a governing, advisory, or disciplinary body, as in certain universities. [< L *senatus* < *senex* old man]

sen·a·tor (sen′ə tər), *n.* member of a senate. —**sen′a·to′ri·al,** *adj.*

send (send), *v.,* **sent, send·ing.** 1 cause or force to go: *send ten men, send for*

the ambulance. 2 cause to be carried: *send a letter.* 3 cause to come, occur, be, etc.: *send relief to flood victims.* 4 drive; impel; throw: *send an arrow.*

send packing, send away hurriedly; dismiss. [OE *sendan*] —**send′er,** *n.*

send-off (send′ôf′; -of′), *n.* 1 a friendly demonstration in honor of a person setting out on a journey, course, career, etc. 2 a favorable or unfavorable start given to a person or thing.

send-up (send′up′), *n.* comic routine, esp. one that parodies or ridicules a famous person.

Sen·e·ca (sen′ə kə), *n.* 1 member of the largest tribe of the Iroquois Confederacy of American Indians living in W New York State. 2 their Iroquoian language. [< Du. *Sennaacas* Five Nations < Algonkian (Mohegan).]

Sen·e·gal (sen′ə gôl′), *n.* 1 republic in W Africa on the Atlantic. —**Sen′e·gal·ese′,** *adj., n.*

se·nes·cent (sə nes′ənt), *adj.* growing old; beginning to show old age. [< L *senescens* growing old, ult. < *senex* old] —**se·nes′cence,** *n.*

sen·es·chal (sen′ə shəl), *n.* steward in charge of a royal palace, nobleman's estate, etc., in the Middle Ages. [< OF; from a Gmc. compound meaning "old servant"]

se·nile (sē′nīl; -nil), *adj.* 1 of old age. 2 showing the weakness of old age. 3 caused by old age. [< L, < *senex* old] —**se·nil′i·ty,** *n.*

sen·ior (sēn′yər), *adj.* 1 older: *senior citizen.* 2 the older; designating a father whose son has the same given name: *John Parker, Senior.* 3 higher in rank or longer in service: *Mr. Jones is the senior member of the firm of Jones and Brown.* 4 of or pertaining to the graduating class. —*n.* 1 the older person: *Paul is his brother's senior by two years.* 2 an older, esp. retired, person. 3 person of higher rank or longer service. 4 member of the graduating class. [< L, compar. of *senex* old. Doublet of SIRE.]

senior citizen, an older person, esp. considered as part of a voting bloc and a recipient of special government benefits.

senior high school, school attended after junior high school. It usually has grades 10, 11, and 12.

sen·ior·i·ty (sēn yôr′ə ti; -yor′-), *n., pl.* **-ties.** superiority in age or standing; state or fact of being older.

se·ñor (sā nyôr′), *n., pl.* **-ño·res** (-nyō′rās). *Spanish.* 1 as a term of address, sir. 2 as a title, Mr. 3 gentleman.

se·ño·ra (sā nyō′rä), *n. Spanish.* 1 Mrs.; Madame. 2 lady.

se·ño·ri·ta (sā′nyō rē′tä), *n. Spanish.* 1 Miss. 2 a young lady.

sen·sa·tion (sen sā′shən), *n.* 1 action of the senses; power to see, hear, feel, taste, smell, etc.: *a dead body is without sensation.* 2 feeling: *he had a sad sensation.* 3

strong or excited feeling: *the announcement of war caused a sensation.* 4 cause of such feeling. [< LL *sensatio,* ult. < L *sensus* SENSE]

sen·sa·tion·al (sen sā′shən əl), *adj.* 1 arousing strong or excited feeling. 2 trying to arouse strong or excited feeling. 3 of the senses; having to do with sensation. —**sen·sa′tion·al·ist,** *n.* —**sen·sa′tion·al·ly,** *adv.*

sen·sa·tion·al·ism (sen sā′shən əl iz′əm), *n.* sensational methods; sensational writing, language, etc.

sense (sens), *n., v.,* **sensed, sens·ing.** —*n.* 1 power of the mind to know what happens outside itself. Sight, hearing, touch, taste, and smell are senses. 2 feeling: *a sense of well-being.* 3 understanding; appreciation: *a sense of humor.* 4 judgment; intelligence: *common sense.* 5 meaning: *in every sense of the word.* 6 general opinion: *the sense of the assembly was clear before the vote.* —*v.* 1 be aware; feel. 2 understand.

in a sense, in some respects; to some degree.

make or **talk sense,** be understandable; be reasonable.

senses, clear, sound condition of mind: *quickly come to her senses.* [< L *sensus* < *sentire* perceive]

sense·less (sens′lis), *adj.* 1 unconscious. 2 foolish; stupid. 3 meaningless, as words. —**sense′less·ly,** *adv.* —**sense′less·ness,** *n.*

sense organ, eye, ear, or other part of the body by which a person or an animal receives sensations of heat, colors, sounds, smells, etc.

sen·si·bil·i·ty (sen′sə bil′ə ti), *n., pl.* **-ties.** 1 ability to feel or perceive: *some drugs lessen a person's sensibilities.* 2 fineness of feeling: *she has an unusual sensibility for colors.* 3 tendency to feel hurt or offended too easily.

sensibilities, a sensitive feelings. **b** emotional capacities.

sen·si·ble (sen′sə bəl), *adj.* 1 having or showing good judgment; wise. 2 aware; conscious: *overly sensible to the cold.* [< LL *sensibilis,* ult. < L *sentire* feel] —**sen′si·ble·ness,** *n.* —**sen′si·bly,** *adv.*

sen·si·tive (sen′sə tiv), *adj.* 1 receiving impressions readily: *the eye is sensitive to light.* 2 easily affected or influenced: *a thermometer is sensitive to temperature.* 3 easily hurt or offended. [< Med.L *sensitivus* < L *sensus* SENSE] —**sen′si·tive·ly,** *adv.* —**sen′si·tiv′i·ty, sen′si·tive·ness,** *n.*

sen·si·tize (sen′sə tīz), *v.,* **-tized, -tiz·ing.** make sensitive. —**sen′si·ti·za′tion,** *n.* —**sen′si·tiz′er,** *n.*

sen·sor (sen′sər; -sôr), *n.* 1 device that reacts to change, as of light, temperature, motion, etc. 2 any sensing device, as a radar system or photoelectric cell.

sen·so·ry (sen′sə ri), **sen·so·ri·al** (sen sô′ri əl; -sō′-), *adj.* of or pertaining to sensation.

sen·su·al (sen′shŭ əl), *adj.* **1** pertaining to the bodily senses rather than to the mind or soul: *sensual pleasures.* **2** caring too much for the pleasures of the senses. **3** lustful; lewd. [< LL, < L *sensus* SENSE] —**sen′su·al·ism,** *n.*

sen·su·al·i·ty (sen′shŭ al′ə ti), *n., pl.* –**ties.** **1** sensual nature. **2** excessive indulgence in the pleasures of the senses. **3** lewdness.

sen·su·al·ize (sen′shŭ əl īz), *v.,* –**ized,** –**iz·ing.** make sensual. —**sen′su·al·i·za′tion,** *n.*

sen·su·ous (sen′shŭ əs), *adj.* **1** of or derived from the senses; having an effect on the senses; perceived by the senses: *the sensuous thrill of a warm bath, a sensuous love of color.* **2** enjoying the pleasures of the senses. —**sen′su·ous·ly,** *adv.* —**sen′su·ous·ness,** *n.*

sent (sent), *v.* pt. and pp. of **send.**

sen·tence (sen′təns), *n., v.,* –**tenced,** –**tenc·ing.** —*n.* **1** group of words that expresses a complete thought. **2 a** decision by a judge on the punishment of a criminal. **b** the punishment itself. —*v.* pronounce punishment on. [< F < L *sententia,* orig., opinion < *sentire* feel] —**sen′tenc·er,** *n.* —**sen·ten′tial,** *adj.*

sen·ten·tious (sen ten′shəs), *adj.* **1** full of meaning; saying much in few words. **2** speaking as if one were a judge settling a question. **3** inclined to make wise sayings; abounding in proverbs. [< L, < *sententia* SENTENCE] —**sen·ten′tious·ly,** *adv.* —**sen·ten′tious·ness,** *n.*

sen·tient (sen′shənt), *adj.* **1** that can feel; of or having feeling. **2** characterized by sensation or feeling. [< L *sentiens* feeling] —**sen′tience, sen′tien·cy,** *n.* —**sen′tient·ly,** *adv.*

sen·ti·ment (sen′tə mənt), *n.* **1** mixture of thought and feeling. Admiration, patriotism, and loyalty are sentiments. **2** feeling, esp. refined or tender feeling. **3** an attitude or personal opinion. [< LL, < L *sentire* feel]

sen·ti·men·tal (sen′tə men′təl), *adj.* **1** having or showing much tender feeling: *sentimental poetry.* **2** likely to act from feelings rather than from logical thinking. **3** having too much sentiment. —**sen′ti·men′tal·ly,** *adv.*

sen·ti·men·tal·ism (sen′tə men′təl iz əm), *n.* **1** tendency to be influenced by sentiment rather than reason. **2** excessive indulgence in sentiment. —**sen′ti·men′tal·ist,** *n.*

sen·ti·men·tal·i·ty (sen′tə men tal′ə ti), *n., pl.* –**ties.** sentimental quality, behavior, etc.

sen·ti·men·tal·ize (sen′tə men′təl īz), *v.,* –**ized,** –**iz·ing.** affect sentiment; make sentimental.

sen·ti·nel (sen′tə nəl), *n., v.,* –**neled,** –**nel·ing.** —*n.* =sentry (def. 1). —*v.* watch over as a sentry does. [< F < Ital. *sentinella*]

sen·try (sen′tri), *n., pl.* –**tries.** **1** one stationed to watch and guard against surprise. **2** *Fig.* anyone or thing that guards: *our dog, the family's sentry.*

stand sentry, watch; guard: *we stood sentry over the sleepers.* [? abbrev. of *centrinel,* var. of *sentinel*]

Seoul (sōl; sā ül′), *n.* capital of South Korea.

se·pal (sē′pəl), *n.* one of the leaflike divisions of the calyx, or outer covering, of a flower. [< NL *sepalum,* short for L *separatum petalum* separate petal] —**se′paled,** *adj.*

sep·a·ra·ble (sep′ə rə bəl; sep′rə bəl), *adj.* that can be separated. —**sep′a·ra·bil′i·ty, sep′a·ra·ble·ness,** *n.* —**sep′a·ra·bly,** *adv.*

sep·a·rate (*v.* sep′ə rāt; *adj., n.* sep′ə rit, sep′rit), *v.,* –**rat·ed,** –**rat·ing,** *adj., n.* —*v.* **1** put apart; take apart; divide: *separate fighting dogs, separate your tools from mine.* **2** become parted, go, come, or draw apart: *the rope separated under the strain.* **3** remove or withdraw from association or relations: *the partners have separated.* **4** keep apart: *the Atlantic separates Europe from America.* —*adj.* **1** disconnected; being or standing apart: *a row of separate houses.* **2** existing independently: *separate organizations.* **3** unconnected; distinct: *two separate questions, each separate item.* —*n.* something separate.

separates, separate items of women's clothing, as blouses, jackets, pants, etc., that can be worn in different combinations to make an outfit. [< L, < *se*– apart + *parare* get] —**sep′a·rate·ly,** *adv.* —**sep′a·rate·ness,** *n.* —**sep′a·ra′tive,** *adj.* —**sep′a·ra′tor,** *n.*

sep·a·ra·tion (sep′ə rā′shən), *n.* **1** a separating or being separated. **2** line or point of separating. **3 a** divorce. **b** the living apart of husband and wife by agreement.

sep·a·ra·tist (sep′ə rā′tist; sep′ə rə–; sep′rə–), *n.* member of a group that separates or withdraws from a larger group. —**sep′a·ra·tism′,** *n.*

se·pi·a (sē′pi ə), *n.* **1** a brown paint or ink prepared from the inky fluid of cuttlefish. **2** a dark-brown color. —*adj.* **1** dark-brown. **2** done in sepia: *a sepia print.* [< L < Gk.]

se·poy (sē′poi), *n.* formerly, a native of India who was a soldier in the British army. [< Pg. < Hind. < Pers. *sipāhī* soldier < *sipāh* army]

sep·sis (sep′sis), *n.* blood poisoning. [< NL < Gk., putrefaction, < *sepein* to rot]

Sept., September.

Sep·tem·ber (sep tem′bər), *n.* the ninth month, containing 30 days. [< L, < *septem* seven; from the order of the Roman calendar]

sep·ten·ni·al (sep ten′i əl), *adj.* **1** lasting seven years. **2** occurring every seven years. [< L *septennium* seven-year period < *septem* seven + *annus* year] —**sep·ten′ni·al·ly,** *adv.*

sep·tet, sep·tette (sep tet′), *n.* **1** a musical composition for seven voices or instruments. **2** seven singers or players. **3** any group of seven. [< G, < L *septem* seven; modeled after *duet*]

sep·tic (sep′tik), *adj.* **1** causing infection or putrefaction. **2** infected. [< L < Gk., < *sepein* to rot] —**sep·tic′i·ty,** *n.*

sep·ti·ce·mi·a (sep′tə sē′mi ə), *n.* blood poisoning, esp. a form in which microorganisms as well as their toxins are absorbed by the blood. [< NL < Gk. *septikos* septic (ult. < *sepein* to rot) + *haima* blood] —**sep′ti·ce′mic,** *adj.*

septic tank, tank in which sewage is acted on by bacteria.

sep·til·lion (sep til′yən), *n.* **1** in the United States and France, 1 followed by 24 zeros. **2** in Great Britain, 1 followed by 42 zeros. [< F (< L *septem* seven), modeled after *million* MILLION] —**sep·til′lionth,** *adj., n.*

sep·tu·a·ge·nar·i·an (sep′chŭ ə jə nār′iən; –tū–), **sep·tu·ag·e·nar·y** (–aj′ə ner′i), *adj., n., pl.* –**nar·i·ans;** –**nar·ies.** —*adj.* of the age of 70 years, or between 70 and 80 years old. —*n.* person who is 70, or between 70 and 80, years old. [<L, ult. < *septuaginta* seventy]

sep·tum (sep′təm), *n., pl.* –**ta** (–tə). a dividing wall of bone, cartilage, or tissue; partition, as in the nose or heart or in some vegetables. [< L, a fence, < *saepire* hedge in] —**sep′tal,** *adj.*

sep·tu·ple (sep′tŭ pəl; –tyŭ–; sep tü′pəl; –tū′–), *adj., v.,* –**pled,** –**pling.** *adj.* seven times as great; sevenfold. —*v.* make seven times as great. [< LL *septuplus* < L *septem* seven + –*plus* –fold]

sep·ul·cher (sep′əl kər), *n.* place of burial; tomb; grave. [< OF < L *sepulcrum* < *sepelire* bury]

se·pul·chral (sə pul′krəl), *adj.* quiet, dark, and gloomy, suggesting a tomb.

seq., the following. [< L *sequens*]

seqq., the following (items). [< L *sequentia*]

se·quel (sē′kwəl), *n.* **1** that which follows; continuation. **2** something that follows as a result of some earlier happening; result. **3** a complete story continuing an earlier one about the same people. [< L, < *sequi* follow]

se·quence (sē′kwəns), *n.* **1** the coming of one thing after another; succession; order of succession. **2** a connected series. **3** something that follows; result. [< LL, ult. < L *sequi* follow]

se·quen·tial (si kwen′shəl), *adj.* forming a sequence or connected series. —**se·quen′tial·ly,** *adv.*

se·ques·ter (si kwes′tər), *v.* **1** remove or withdraw from public use or from public view. **2** take away (property) for a time from an owner until a debt is paid or some claim is satisfied. **3** seize by authority; take and keep. [< L, < *sequester* trustee, mediator < *sequi* follow] —**se·ques′tered,** *adj.*

se·ques·trate (si kwes′trāt), *v.,* –**trat·ed,** –**trat·ing.** confiscate.

se·ques·tra·tion (sē′kwes trā′shən; si kwes′–), *n.* **1** the seizing and holding of property until legal claims are satisfied. **2** forcible or authorized seizure; confiscation. **3** separation or withdrawal from others; seclusion.

se·quin (sē′kwin), *n.* a small spangle used to ornament dresses, scarfs, etc. [< F < Ital. *zecchino* < *zecca* mint < Ar. *sikka* a stamp] —**se′quined,** *adj.*

se·quoi·a (si kwoi′ə), *n.* either of two species of very tall evergreen trees of California. [< NL, < *Sequoya* (Cherokee *Sikwayi*), an Indian who invented a system of Cherokee writing]

se·ragl·io (si ral′yō; –räl′–), *n., pl.* **–ragl·ios.** the women's quarters of a Muslim house or palace; harem. [< Ital. *serraglio,* ult. < L *serare* lock up; infl. by Turk. *serāi* palace]

se·ra·pe (sə rä′pē), *n.* shawl or blanket, often having bright colors, worn by Spanish American Indians. [< dial. Sp.]

ser·aph (ser′əf), *n., pl.* **–aphs, –a·phim** (–ə fim). one of the highest order of angels. [< *seraphim,* pl., < LL < Heb.] —**se·raph′ic,** *adj.* —**se·raph′i·cal·ly,** *adv.*

Serb (sėrb), *n.* **1** native or inhabitant of Serbia. **2** language of Serbia. —*adj.* of Serbia, its people, or their language.

Ser·bi·a (sėr′bi ə), *n.* a Balkan country in S Europe. —**Ser′bi·an,** *adj., n.*

sere (sir), *adj.* sear. [var. of *sear*]

ser·e·nade (ser′ə nād′), *n., v.,* **–nad·ed, –nad·ing.** —*n.* **1** music played or sung outdoors at night, esp. by a lover under his lady's window. **2** piece of music suitable for such a performance. —*v.* **1** sing or play to in this way. **2** sing or play a serenade. [< < Ital. *serenata,* ult. < L *serenus* serene] —**ser′e·nad′er,** *n.*

ser·en·dip·i·ty (ser′ən dip′ə ti), *n.* the facility to find, by accident, interesting or unexpected facts, proofs, etc. [a coined word] —**ser′en·dip′i·tous,** *adj.*

se·rene (sə rēn′), *adj.* **1** peaceful; calm: *a serene smile.* **2** clear; bright; not cloudy. [< L *serenus*] —**se·rene′ly,** *adv.* —**se·rene′ness,** *n.*

se·ren·i·ty (sə ren′ə ti), *n., pl.* **–ties. 1** quiet peace; calmness. **2** clearness; brightness.

serf (sėrf), *n.* **1** slave who cannot be sold off the land, but passes from one owner to another with the land. **2** person who is mistreated, underpaid, etc. [< F < L *servus* slave] —**serf′dom,** *n.*

serge (sėrj), *n.* a kind of cloth having slanting lines or ridges on its surface. [< F, ult. < L *serica* (*vestis*) silken (garment) < Gk., < *Seres* the Chinese]

ser·geant (sär′jənt), *n.* **1** an officer ranking next above a corporal. Sergeants and corporals are noncommissioned officers. **2** a police officer ranking next above an ordinary policeman and next below a captain or lieutenant. **3** sergeant at arms. [< OF < L *serviens,* ppr. of *servire* serve] —**ser′gean·cy, ser′geant·ship,** *n.*

sergeant at arms, ser·geant-at-arms (sär′jənt ət ärmz′), *n., pl.* **sergeants at arms; ser·geants-at-arms.** officer who keeps order in a legislature, law court, etc.

se·ri·al (sir′i əl), *n.* story published or broadcast one part at a time, once a week, every day, etc. —*adj.* **1** of or having to do with a serial. **2** published or broadcast one part at a time. **3** of, arranged in, or making a series. [< NL, < L *series* SERIES] —**se′ri·al′i·ty,** *n.* —**se′ri·al·ly,** *adv.*

se·ri·al·ize (sir′i ə līz), **–ized, –iz·ing.** publish or broadcast as a series; make a serial.

serial number, an individual number given to a person, article, etc.

se·ri·a·tim (sir′i ā′tim; ser′i–), *adv.* in a series; one after the other. [< Med.L]

se·ries (sir′iz), *n., pl.* **–ries. 1** number of similar things in a row: *a series of rooms opened off the long hall.* **2** number of things placed one after another. **3** number of things, events, etc., coming one after the other: *a series of rainy days, a television series about Columbus.* **4** arrangement of batteries, capacitors, etc., that are connected so that an electric current runs through each one in turn. **5 a** succession of terms related by some law, and consequently predictable. **b** their sum.
the Series, the World Series (of baseball). [< L, < *serere* join]

ser·if (ser′if), *n.* a thin or smaller line used to finish off a main stroke of a letter, as at the top and bottom of M.

se·ri·o-com·ic (sir′i ō kom′ik), **se·ri·o-com·i·cal** (–ə kəl), *adj.* partly serious and partly comic. —**se′ri·o-com′i·cal·ly,** *adv.*

se·ri·ous (sir′i əs), *adj.* **1** thoughtful; grave: *a serious mood.* **2** in earnest; not joking; sincere: *he was serious about the subject.* **3** needing thought; important: *racial prejudice is a serious problem.* **4** important because it may do much harm; dangerous: *serious trouble.* [< LL *seriosus* < L *serius* earnest] —**se′ri·ous·ly,** *adv.* —**se′ri·ous·ness,** *n.*

ser·mon (sėr′mən), *n.* **1** a public talk on religion or something connected with religion. **2** a serious talk about morals, conduct, duty, etc. **3** a long, tiresome speech. [< L *sermo* a talk]

ser·mon·ize (sėr′mən īz), *v.,* **–ized, –iz·ing. 1** give a sermon; preach. **2** preach or talk seriously to; lecture. —**ser′mon·iz′er,** *n.*

se·rol·o·gy (si rol′ə ji), *n.* science of serums. —**se′ro·log′i·cal,** *adj.* —**se·rol′o·gist,** *n.*

se·ro·to·nin (sir′ō tō′nən), *n.* substance in the blood, the brain, and smooth muscles, chemically related to adrenalin.

se·rous (sir′əs), *adj.* **1** of or having to do with serum. **2** like serum; watery. Tears are drops of a serous fluid. —**se·ros′i·ty,** *n.*

ser·pent (sėr′pənt), *n.* **1** snake; big snake. **2** *Fig.* a sly, treacherous person. [< L *serpens,* orig., creeping]

ser·pen·tine (sėr′pən tēn; –tīn), *adj.* **1** of or like a serpent. **2** winding; twisting. **3** cunning; sly; treacherous. [< LL, < L *serpens* serpent] —**ser′pen·ti′nous,** *adj.*

ser·rate (ser′āt; –it), **ser·rat·ed** (–āt id), *adj.* notched like the edge of a saw; toothed. [< L, < *serra* a saw] —**ser·ra′tion,** *n.*

ser·ried (ser′id), *adj.* crowded closely together. [< F *serré,* pp. of *serrer* press close]

se·rum (sir′əm), *n., pl.* **se·rums, se·ra** (sir′ə). **1** a clear, pale-yellow, watery part of the blood that separates from the clot when blood coagulates. **2** liquid used to prevent or cure a disease, usually obtained from the blood of an animal made immune to the disease. Diphtheria antitoxin is a serum, as is polio vaccine. **3** any watery animal liquid. Lymph is a serum. [< L, whey]

serv·ant (sėr′vənt), *n.* **1** person employed in a household. **2** person employed by another. Police officers and firefighters are public servants. **3** person devoted to any service. Ministers are called the servants of God. [< OF, ppr. of *servir* SERVE] —**ser′vant·less,** *adj.*

serve (sėrv), *v.,* **served, serv·ing,** *n.* —*v.* **1** be a servant of; give service; work for or in: *serve an employer, he served as butler.* **2** wait on at table; bring food or drink, the waiter served the first course. **3** go through a term of service as a soldier, etc.: *he served in the army.* **4** supply; furnish; help; aid: *let me know if I can serve you in any way.* **5** be useful; be what is needed: *a grasshopper will serve as bait.* **6** pass; spend: *the thief served a term in prison.* **7** deliver or present (with an order from a court, etc.): *serve with a notice to appear in court.* **8** put (the ball) in play by hitting it in tennis and similar games. —*n.* act or way of serving a tennis ball.

serve one right, be exactly what one deserves. [< OF < L, < *servus* slave]

serv·er (sėr′vər), *n.* **1** person who serves; waiter. **2** tray for dishes. **3** player who serves the ball in tennis. **4** central processing unit of a computer network.

serv·ice (sėr′vis), *n., v.,* **–iced, –ic·ing.** —*n.* **1** helpful act or acts; conduct that is useful to others: *he performed many services for his country.* **2** supply; arrangements for supplying: *the train service was good.* **3** work for others; performance of duties; work: *the services of a doctor, telephone service, emergency services.* **4** department of government or public employment: *the civil service.* **5** duty in the army or navy: *be on active service.* **6** a religious meeting, ritual, or ceremony. **7** manner of serving food; the food served. **8** set of dishes, etc.: *a solid silver tea service.* **9** the serving of a process or writ upon a person. **10** in tennis, etc., act or manner of putting the ball in play; the ball as put into play. —*v.* make fit for service; keep fit for service.

at one's service, ready to do what one wants.

break service, win a game from the server in tennis.

of service, helpful; useful. [< OF < L *servitium* < *servus* slave]

serv·ice·a·ble (sėr′vis ə bəl), *adj.* capable of giving good service; useful; able to stand much use. **—serv′ice·a·bil′i·ty, serv′ice·a·ble·ness,** *n.* **—serv′ice·a·bly,** *adv.*

serv·ice·man (sėr′vis man′), *n., pl.* **-men.** member of the armed forces.

service station, place for supplying automobiles with gasoline, oil, water, etc.

ser·vile (sėr′vəl), *adj.* **1** like that of slaves; mean; base: *servile flattery.* **2** of slaves; pertaining to slaves. [< L, < *servus* slave] **—ser′vile·ly,** *adv.* **—ser·vil′i·ty, ser′vile·ness,** *n.*

ser·vi·tude (sėr′və tüd; -tūd), *n.* **1** slavery; bondage. **2** forced labor as a punishment. [< L, < *servus* slave]

ses·a·me (ses′ə mē), *n.* **1** an East Indian plant. **2** its seeds, used for food and in medicine. [< Gk. < Semitic]

ses·qui·cen·ten·ni·al (ses′kwi sen ten′i əl), *n.* a 150th anniversary or its celebration. **—adj.** pertaining to, or marking the completion of, a period of a century and a half. [< L *sesqui–* one and a half + E *centennial*]

ses·sile (ses′əl), *adj.* attached by the base instead of by a stem. [< L *sessilis* sitting < *sedere* sit]

ses·sion (sesh′ən), *n.* **1** a sitting or meeting of a court, council, legislature, etc.: *Congress is now in session.* **2** a series of such sittings. **3** a single continuous term or period of such sittings. **4** period of lessons and study. [< L *sessio* < *sedere* sit] **—ses′sion·al,** *adj.*

set (set), *v.,* **set, set·ting,** *adj., n.* **—v. 1** put in some place; put; place: *set the plate on the table.* **2** put in the right place, position, or condition: *set a broken bone, set a clock.* **3** put in some condition or relation: *a spark set the woods on fire, set a person at ease.* **4** put as the measure of a person or thing: *set great store by a thing, set high value on friendship.* **5** provide for others to follow: *set a good example.* **6** put in a fixed, rigid, or settled state; become fixed or rigid: *set a limit, set one's teeth, jelly sets as it cools, set a diamond in gold.* **7** go down; sink below the horizon: *the sun sets.* **8** sit on eggs to hatch them; place (eggs) under a hen. **9** hang or fit in a particular manner: *that coat sets well.* **10** begin to apply; start: *have you set to work?* **11** adapt; fit: *set words to music.* **12** in printing, put (type) in the order required. **—adj. 1** fixed or appointed beforehand; established: *a set time, set rules.* **2** fixed; rigid: *a set smile, a man set in his ways.* **3** firm; hard. **—n. 1** number of things or persons belonging together; outfit: *a set of dishes.* **2** scenery of a play. **3** device for receiving by radio, telephone, television, etc. **4** way a thing is put or placed; form; shape: *his jaw had a*

stubborn set. **5** slip or shoot for planting. **6** group of six or more games in tennis.

all set, ready; prepared.

set about, start work upon; begin: *set about washing the dishes.*

set against, a make unfriendly or hostile toward. **b** balance; compare: *when the reasons for going are set against those for staying.*

set apart, reserve.

set aside, a put to one side. **b** put by for later use. **c** discard, dismiss, or leave out; reject; annul.

set back, stop; hinder; check.

set down, a deposit or let alight; put down. **b** put down in writing or printing. **c** consider; ascribe: *set down the remark to jealousy.*

set forth, a make known; express; declare. **b** start to go: *set forth on a journey.*

set in, begin: *winter set in with a fury.*

set loose, free; let go.

set off, a explode. **b** start to go: *set off toward home.* **c** increase by contrast: *a blue dress set off her fair skin.* **d** *Fig.* cause; touch off: *inflation set off this recession.*

set on or **upon,** attack.

set out, a start to go: *set out on vacation.* **b** spread out to show, sell, or use. **c** plant.

set right, restore; fix: *an apology set things right.*

set sail, a hoist and spread the sails. **b** start on a journey by ship.

set to, a begin. **b** begin fighting.

set up, a build. **b** begin; start. **c** put up; raise in place, position, power, pride, etc. **d** claim; pretend; trick: *set up by a clever crook.*

set upon, attack someone without warning. [OE *settan*]

set·back (set′bak′), *n.* **1** a check to progress; reverse. **2** a setting back, similar to steps, of the outside wall in a tall building.

set piece, scene in a novel, play, painting, etc., that is familiar and stylized: *a brilliant set piece of the family gathering.*

set·screw (set′skrü′), *n.* a machine screw used to fasten gears, pulleys, etc., to a shaft.

set·tee (se tē′), *n.* sofa or long bench with a back and, usually, arms. [< *set*]

set·ter (set′ər), *n.* **1** person or thing that sets. **2** a long-haired hunting dog, trained to stand motionless and point his nose toward the game that he scents.

set·ting (set′ing), *n.* **1** frame or other thing in which something is set. The mounting of a jewel is its setting. **2** scenery of a play. **3** place, time, etc., of a play or story. **4** surroundings; background. **5** music composed to go with certain words.

set·tle¹ (set′əl), *v.,* **-tled, -tling. 1** determine; decide; agree (upon): *have you settled on a time?* **2** put or be put in order; arrange: *settle one's affairs.* **3** pay;

arrange payment: *settle a bill.* **4** arrange, set, or be set in a position, place, or way of life: *settle in Utah, settled in a new home, settle in a comfortable chair.* **5** put or come to rest in a particular place; put in or come to a definite condition: *his cold settled in his lungs.* **6** make or become quiet: *hot milk will settle your nerves.* **7** go down; sink. **8** of liquid, make or become clear.

settle down, a live a more regular life. **b** direct steady effort or attention.

settle for, accept, often reluctantly; agree upon: *settle for the smaller apartment.* [OE *setlan* < *setl* settle²]

set·tle² (set′əl), *n.* a long bench. [OE *setl*]

set·tle·ment (set′əl mənt), *n.* **1** act of settling or state of being settled: *settlement on a date.* **2** arrangement: *settlement of a dispute.* **3** payment: *settlement of a debt.* **4** the settling of persons in a new country. **5** colony. **6** group of buildings and the people living in them. **7** the settling of property upon someone or the amount so given.

set·tler (set′lər), *n.* **1** person who settles. **2** person who settles in a new country.

set-to (set′tü′), *n., pl.* **-tos.** *Informal.* a fight; dispute.

set-up (set′up′), *n.* **1** arrangement of apparatus, machinery, etc. **2** arrangement of an organization. **3** *Slang.* a prize fight, game, etc., whose outcome has been fixed.

sev·en (sev′ən), *n.* **1** a cardinal number, one more than six. **2** symbol of this number; 7. **3** card with seven spots. **—adj.** one more than six. [OE *seofon*]

sev·en·fold (sev′ən fōld′), *adj.* **1** seven times as much or as many. **2** having seven parts. **—adv.** seven times as much or as many.

seven seas, all the oceans; the Arctic, Antarctic, North Atlantic, South Atlantic, North Pacific, South Pacific, and Indian Oceans.

sev·en·teen (sev′ən tēn′), *n.* **1** a cardinal number, seven more than ten. **2** symbol of this number; 17. **—adj.** seven more than ten. **—sev′en·teenth′,** *adj., n.*

sev·enth (sev′ənth), *adj.* **1** next after the sixth; last in a series of 7. **2** being one of 7 equal parts. **—n. 1** next after the sixth; last in a series of 7. **2** one of 7 equal parts. **3** *Music.* **a** interval between two tones that are seven degrees apart. **b** combination of two such tones. **—sev′enth·ly,** *adv.*

seventh heaven, 1 the highest part of heaven. **2** the highest place or condition of joy and happiness.

sev·en·ty (sev′ən ti), *n., pl.* **-ties,** *adj.* **—n. 1** a cardinal number, seven times ten. **2** symbol of this number; 70. **—adj.** seven times ten. **—sev′en·ti·eth,** *adj., n.*

sev·er (sev′ər), *v.* **1** part; separate; divide: *a church severed into two factions.* **2** cut off; break off: *sever the rope.* [< OF, ult. < L *separare* SEPARATE] **—sev′er·a·ble,** *adj.* **—sev′er·er,** *n.*

sev·er·al (sev′ər əl; sev′rəl), *adj.* **1** being more than two or three but not many: *gain several pounds.* **2** separate; individual; respective: *the boys went their several ways.* **3** various: *several steps in a process.* —*n.* more than two or three but not many; some; a few: *several have given their consent.* [< AF, ult. < L *separ* distinct < *separare* SEPARATE]

sev·er·al·ly (sev′ər əl i; sev′rəl i), *adv.* **1** separately; singly; individually. **2** respectively.

sev·er·ance (sev′ər əns; sev′rəns), *n.* **1** a severing or being severed; separation; division. **2** a breaking off: *the severance of diplomatic relations.*

severance pay, additional pay granted to departing employees, based on seniority.

se·vere (sə vir′), *adj.,* **–ver·er, –ver·est. 1** very strict; stern; harsh: *the judge imposed a severe penalty on the criminal.* **2** serious; grave: *a severe illness.* **3** very plain or simple; without ornament: *a severe style of architecture.* **4** sharp; violent: *a severe criticism.* **5** difficult: *a severe test.* [< L *severus*] —**se·vere′ly,** *adv.* —**se·vere′ness,** *n.*

se·ver·i·ty (sə ver′ə ti), *n.,* pl. **–ties. 1** strictness; sternness; harshness. **2** simplicity of style or taste; plainness. **3** violence; sharpness. **4** seriousness.

sew (sō), *v.,* **sewed, sewed** or **sewn, sewing. 1** work with needle and thread. **2** fasten with stitches. **3** close with stitches. [OE *seowian*] —**sew′a·ble,** *adj.* —**sew′er,** *n.*

sew·age (sü′ij), *n.* the waste matter that passes through sewers.

sew·er (sü′ər), *n.* an underground pipe or channel for carrying off waste water and refuse. [<OF *sewiere* sluice from a pond, ult. < L *ex* out + *aqua* water]

sew·er·age (sü′ər ij), *n.* **1** removal of waste matter by sewers. **2** system of sewers. **3** =sewage.

sew·ing (sō′ing), *n.* work done with a needle and thread; something to be sewed. —*adj.* for sewing; used in sewing.

sewn (sōn), *v.* pp. of **sew.**

sex (seks), *n.* **1** one of the two divisions of human beings, animals, etc. Men, bulls, and roosters are of the male sex; women, cows, and hens are of the female sex. **2** the character of being male or female: *people were admitted without regard to age or sex.* **3** attraction of one sex for the other. **4 a** behavior relating to sex. **b** sexual intercourse. —*v.* determine the sex of. —*adj.* of or having to do with sex.

have sex, engage in sexual activity; have sexual relations.

sex up, *Fig.* make more interesting or exciting. [< L *sexus*] —**sex′less,** *adj.* —**sex′less·ly,** *adv.* —**sex′less·ness,** *n.*

sex·a·ge·nar·i·an (sek′sə jə när′i ən), **sex·ag·e·nar·y** (seks aj′ə ner′i), *adj., n., pl.* **–nar·i·ans; –nar·ies.** —*adj.* of the age of 60 years, or between 60 and 70 years old. —*n.* person who is 60, or between

60 and 70, years old. [< L, ult. < *sexaginta* sixty]

sex·a·ges·i·mal (sek′ə jes′ə məl), *adj.* of or based on the number 60, as a fraction whose denominator is 60. [ult. < L *sexāgintā* sixty]

sex appeal, personal charm tending to draw together persons of the opposite sex.

sex chromosome, chromosome which, in combination with another, determines the sex and sex-linked characteristics of an offspring.

sex gland =gonad.

sex hormone, hormone that regulates the reproductive organs and sexual characteristics, as androgen and estrogen.

sex·ism, sexual discrimination or prejudice. —**sex′ist,** *adj., n.*

sex·tant (seks′tənt), *n.* instrument used by navigators, surveyors, etc., for measuring the angular distance between two objects. Sextants are used at sea to measure the altitude of the sun, a star, etc., in order to determine latitude and longitude. [< L *sextans* a sixth < *sex* six]

sex·tet, sex·tette (seks tet′), *n.* **1** piece of music for six voices or instruments. **2** six singers or players. [alter. of *sestet* after L *sex* six]

sex·til·lion (seks til′yən), *n.* **1** in the United States and France, 1 followed by 21 zeros. **2** in Great Britain, 1 followed by 36 zeros. [< F (< L *sextus* sixth), modeled after *million* MILLION] —**sex·til′lionth,** *adj., n.*

sex·ton (seks′tən), *n.* person who takes care of a church. [< OF < Med.L *sacristanus* sacristan. Doublet of SACRISTAN.]

sex·tu·ple (seks′tù pəl; –tyù–; seks tü′pəl; –tū′–), *adj., n., v.,* **–pled, –pling.** —*adj.* **1** consisting of six parts; sixfold. **2** six times as great. **3** characterized by six beats to the measure. —*n.* number or amount six times as great as another. —*v.* make or become six times as great. [< L *sextus* sixth; modeled after *quadruple*]

sex·tu·plet (seks′tù plit; –tyù–; seks tü′plit; –tū′–), *n.* one of six children, animals, etc., born of the same mother at the same time.

sex·u·al (sek′shù əl), *adj.* **1** of or pertaining to sex. **2** of or between the sexes. **3** having sex; separated into two sexes. —**sex′u·al′i·ty,** *n.* —**sex′u·al·ly,** *adv.*

sexual harassment, harassment of a person based on his or her sex.

sexual intercourse, the joining of sexual organs; coitus; copulation.

sexually transmitted disease, contagious disease spread mainly by sexual activity, as AIDS.

sex·y (sek′si), *adj.* **1** charming or attractive sexually. **2** sexually exciting. **3** preoccupied or concerned with sex.

sf., sforzando.

sfor·zan·do (sfôr tsän′dō), *n., pl.* **–dos, –di** (–di). chord, phrase, or passage of music given greater emphasis or played

suddenly louder. —*adj., adv.* with sudden emphasis; louder. [< It.]

Sgt., Sergeant.

shab·by (shab′i), *adj.,* **–bi·er, –bi·est. 1** much worn. **2** wearing old or much worn clothes. **3** not generous; mean; unfair. [< *shab* scab, OE *sceabb*] —**shab′bi·ly,** *adv.* —**shab′bi·ness,** *n.*

shack (shak), *n.* a roughly built hut or cabin; house in bad condition.

shack up with, *Informal.* cohabit with someone. [? ult. < *ramshackle*]

shack·le (shak′əl), *n., v.,* **–led, –ling.** —*n.* **1** a metal band fastened around the ankle or wrist of a prisoner, slave, etc. Shackles are usually fastened to each other, the wall, floor, etc., by chains. **2** link fastening together the two rings for the ankles and wrists of a prisoner. **3** *Fig.* anything that prevents freedom of action, thought, etc. **4** thing for fastening or coupling. —*v.* **1** put shackles on. **2** restrain; hamper. **3** fasten or couple with a shackle.

shackles, fetters; chains. [OE *sceacel*] —**shack′ler,** *n.*

shad (shad), *n., pl.* **shad** or (*for different kinds*) **shads.** any of several saltwater fishes related to the herrings that ascend rivers in the spring to spawn. [OE *sceadd*]

shad·bush (shad′bùsh′), *n.* a North American shrub or small tree with white flowers and berrylike fruit, which blossoms about the time when shad appear in the rivers.

shade (shād), *n., v.,* **shad·ed, shad·ing.** —*n.* **1** a partly dark place, not in the sunshine. **2** a slight darkness or coolness: *the shade of a tree.* **3** place or condition of obscurity. **4** something that shuts out light: *pull down the shades of the windows.* **5** lightness or darkness of color. **6** a very small difference, amount, or degree: *a shade too long, a shade of doubt troubled her.* **7** ghost; spirit. —*v.* **1** screen from light; keep light from; reduce light on. **2** make darker than the rest. **3** show small differences; change little by little.

in or **into the shade, a** out of the light. **b** *Fig.* in or into a condition of being unknown or unnoticed.

shades, *Informal.* sunglasses.

shades of, reminiscent of.

the shades, *Class. Myth.* Hades. [OE *sceadu*] —**shade′less,** *adj.* —**shad′er,** *n.*

shad·ing (shād′ing), *n.* **1** a covering from the light. **2** use of black or color to give the effect of shade in a picture. **3** a slight variation or difference of color, character, etc.

shad·ow (shad′ō), *n.* **1** shade made by some person, animal, or thing. **2** darkness; partial shade. **3** a little bit; small degree; slight suggestion. **4** ghost. **5** a faint image. **6** person who follows another closely and secretly, as a spy, detective, etc. **7** a constant companion; follower. **8** sadness; gloom. **9** obscurity. —*v.* **1** protect from light; shade. **2** cast a shadow on. 3 follow closely and secretly. 4 make sad or gloomy.

afraid of one's (own) shadow, extremely timid; frightened of the slightest thing.

cast a long shadow, have great influence.

in or **under the shadow of,** very near to.

the shadows, darkness after sunset. [from oblique case forms of OE *sceadu* shade] —**shad'ow·er,** *n.* —**shad'ow·less,** *adj.*

shad·ow·y (shad'ō i), *adj.* **1** having much shadow or shade; shady. **2** like a shadow; dim, faint, or slight. —**shad'ow·i·ly,** *adv.* —**shad'ow·i·ness,** *n.*

shad·y (shād'i), *adj.* **shad·i·er, shad·i·est.** **1** in the shade; shaded. **2** giving shade. **3** of doubtful honesty, character, etc. —**shad'i·ly,** *adv.* —**shad'i·ness,** *n.*

shaft (shaft; shäft), *n.* **1** bar to support parts of a machine that turn, or to help move parts. **2** a deep passage sunk in the earth. The entrance to a mine is called a shaft. **3** a well-like passage: *an elevator shaft.* **4** the long, slender stem of an arrow, spear, etc. **5** arrow; spear. **6** ray or beam of light. **7** one of the two wooden poles between which a horse is harnessed to a carriage, etc. **8** column or the main part of a column. —*v. Slang.* use (someone) unfairly; victimize. [OE *sceaft*] —**shaft'ed,** *adj.*

shag¹ (shag), *n.* **1** rough, matted hair, wool, etc. **2** the long, rough nap of some kinds of cloth. **3** cloth having such a nap. [OE *sceacga*]

shag² (shag), *v.,* **shagged, shag·ging.** throw and catch balls, for practice or amusement.

shag·bark (shag'bärk'), *n.* **1** a hickory tree with very rough bark. **2** nut of this tree.

shag·gy (shag'i), *adj.* **-gi·er, -gi·est. 1** covered with a thick, rough mass of hair, wool, etc. **2** long, thick, and rough: *shaggy eyebrows.* [< *shag*] —**shag'gi·ly,** *adv.* —**shag'gi·ness,** *n.*

shake (shāk), *v.,* **shook, shak·en, shak·ing** *n.* —*v.* **1** move quickly backwards and forwards, up and down, or from side to side: *shake a rug.* **2** bring, throw, force, rouse, scatter, etc., by or as if by movement: *shake snow off one's clothes.* **3** clasp (hands) in greeting, congratulating, etc., another: *shake hands.* **4** make tremble: *shake with cold, the explosion shook the town, shake the foundations of society.* **5** disturb; make less firm: *his lie shook my faith in his honesty.* **6** *Slang.* get rid of: *can't you shake him?* —*n.* **1** act or fact of shaking: *a shake of the head.* **2** drink made by shaking ingredients together: *a milk shake.* **3** *Informal.* a moment: *I'll be there in two shakes.*

no great shakes, not unusual, extraordinary, or important.

shake down, a bring or throw down by shaking: *shake down ripe apples from the tree.* **b** cause to settle down, as into

a routine. **c** bring into working order: *shake down the team.* **d** *Informal.* get money from dishonestly.

shake up, a shake hard. **b** stir up. **c** *Fig.* jar; rattle; disturb in body or nerves: *the accident really shook him up.* [OE *sceacan*] —**shak'ing,** *n.* —**shak'ing·ly,** *adv.*

shake·down or **shake-down** (shāk'-doun´), *n.* **1** *Slang.* an exaction of money, etc., by compulsion. **2** a bringing into working order by practice.

shake·out (shāk'out´), *n.* reorganization or change that involves the removal or omission of some persons, items, etc.

shak·er (shāk'ər), *n.* **1** person who shakes something. **2** container for pepper, salt, etc., having a perforated top.

Shaker, member of an American religious sect, so called from movements of the body that form part of their worship.

Shake·spear·i·an, Shake·spear·e·an, (shāk spir'i ən), *adj.* of or having to do with William Shakespeare, sixteenth-century English poet and dramatist, or his works.

shake-up (shāk'up´), *n.* a sudden and complete change.

shak·o (shak'ō), *n., pl.* **shak·os.** a high, stiff military hat with a plume or other ornament. [<Hung. *csákó* peaked (cap)]

shak·y (shāk'i), *adj.* **shak·i·er, shak·i·est. 1** shaking: *a shaky voice.* **2** liable to break down; weak: *a shaky porch.* **3** not to be depended on; not reliable. —**shak'i·ly,** *adv.* —**shak'i·ness,** *n.*

shale (shāl), *n.* a fine-grained rock, formed from clay or mud, that splits easily into thin layers. [OE *scealu* shell] —**shal'y,** *adj.*

shall (shal; *unstressed* shəl), *v., pres.* **shall,** *past* **should. 1** (used to denote future time): *we shall miss you.* **2** (used to denote promise or determination): *you shall hear from us, he shall not do it.* [OE *sceal* (inf., *sculan*)]

shal·lop (shal'əp), *n.* a small, light open boat with sail or oars. [< F *chaloupe* < Du. *sloepe.* Doublet of SLOOP.]

shal·lot (shə lot'), *n.* **1** a small plant much like an onion, but with a bulb composed of sections or cloves. **2** bulb or clove of this plant. **3** a small brown onion. [ult. < F *eschalotte,* alter. of OF *eschaloigne* SCALLION]

shal·low (shal'ō), *adj.* not deep: *shallow water, a shallow mind.* —*n.* a shallow place. —*v.* become or make less deep. [prob. ult. < OE *sceald*] —**shal'low·ness,** *n.*

shalt (shalt), *v. Archaic.* shall.

sham (sham), *n., adj., v.,* **shammed, sham·ming.** —*n.* pretense; fraud. —*adj.* pretended; feigned. —*v.* pretend; feign. [orig. dial. var. of *shame* —**sham'mer,** *n.*

sha·man (shä'mən), *n.* **1** priest with magical powers over diseases and evil spirits. **2** American Indian medicine man. —**sha'man·ism,** *n.*

sham·ble¹ (sham'bəl), *v.,* **-bled, -bling,** *n.* —*v.* walk awkwardly or unsteadily.

—*n.* a shambling walk. [prob. ult. special use of *shamble²*; with ref. to the straddling legs of a bench]

sham·ble² (sham'bəl), *n.* **1 shambles** (*often sing. in use*), slaughter house. **2 shambles** (*often sing. in use*). **a** place of butchery or of great destruction and confusion. **b** great disorder. [< L *scamellum,* dim. of *scamnum* bench; orig., a table on which meat was sold]

shame (shām), *n., v.,* **shamed, sham·ing.** —*n.* **1** a painful feeling of having done something wrong, improper, or silly: *blush with shame.* **2** a disgrace; dishonor: *bring shame on one's family.* **3** fact to be sorry about: *it is a shame to be so wasteful.* **4** person or thing to be ashamed of; cause of disgrace. —*v.* **1** cause to feel shame. **2** drive or force by shame. **3** bring disgrace upon.

for shame! shame on you!

put to shame, a disgrace; make ashamed. **b** surpass; make dim by comparison. [OE *sceamu*] —**sham'er,** *n.*

shame·faced (shām'fāst´), *adj.* **1** bashful; shy. **2** showing shame and embarrassment. —**shame´fac'ed·ly,** *adv.*

shame·ful (shām'fəl), *adj.* **1** causing shame; bringing disgrace. **2** scandalous. —**shame'ful·ly,** *adv.* —**shame'ful·ness,** *n.*

shame·less (shām'lis), *adj.* **1** without shame. **2** not modest. **3** insensible to disgrace. —**shame'less·ly,** *adv.* —**shame'less·ness,** *n.*

sham·poo (sham'pü'), *v.,* **-pooed, -poo·ing,** *n.* —*v.* wash (the hair or scalp). —*n.* **1** a washing of the hair or scalp. **2** preparation used for shampooing. [< Hind. *champo,* lit., press!] —**sham·poo'er,** *n.*

sham·rock (sham'rok), *n.* **1** a bright-green leaf composed of three parts. The shamrock is the national emblem of Ireland. **2** any of various plants that have leaves like this, such as white clover, wood sorrel, etc. [< Irish *seamróg,* dim. of *seamar* clover]

shang·hai (shang'hī; shang hī'), *v.,* **-haied, -hai·ing. 1** make unconscious by drugs, liquor, etc., and put on a ship to serve as a sailor. **2** bring by trickery or force. [with ref. to the practice of securing sailors by foul means for long voyages, often to *Shanghai*]

Shan·gri-la, Shan·gri-La (shang'gri lä'), *n.* an idyllic earthly paradise. [an inaccessible land in *Lost Horizon,* a novel by James Hilton]

shank (shangk), *n.* **1** the part of the leg between the knee and the ankle. **2** the corresponding part in animals. **3** the whole leg. **4** the latter end or part of anything: *the shank of the evening.* [OE *sceanca*] —**shanked,** *adj.*

shan't (shant; shänt), shall not.

shan·tung (shan'tung), *n.* kind of soft silk.

shan·ty¹ (shan'ti), *n., pl.* **-ties.** a roughly built hut or cabin. [< Irish *seantig* hut]

shan·ty² (shan'ti), *n., pl.* **-ties.** =chantey.

shape (shāp), *n.*, *v.*, **shaped, shap·ing.**
—*n.* **1** the outward contour or outline; form; figure: *the shape of a triangle, a gift in the shape of money.* **2** definite form; proper arrangement: *things are taking shape.* **3** condition: *his affairs are in bad shape.* [OE (*ge*)*sceap*] —*v.* **1** form: *the child shapes clay into balls.* **2** take shape; assume form: *his plan is shaping well.* **3** adapt in form: *shape a sleeve to a person's arm.* **4** direct; plan: *shape one's course in life.*

shape up, a take on a certain form or appearance; develop. **b** show a certain tendency. [OE *sceapen*, pp. of *scieppan* create] —**shap′er,** *n.*

shape·less (shāp′lis), *adj.* **1** without definite shape. **2** having an unattractive shape. —**shape′less·ly,** *adv.* —**shape′less·ness,** *n.*

shape·ly (shāp′li), *adj.*, **–li·er, –li·est.** having a pleasing shape; well-formed. —**shape′li·ness,** *n.*

shard (shärd), *n.* **1** a broken piece; fragment. **2** piece of broken earthenware or pottery. [OE *sceard*]

share¹ (shār), *n.*, *v.*, **shared, shar·ing.** —*n.* **1** part belonging to one individual; portion; part: *do your share of the work.* **2 a** a definite part of something owned in common with others. **b** each of the parts into which the ownership of a company or corporation is divided: *the ownership of this railroad is divided into several million shares.* —*v.* **1** use together; enjoy together; have in common. **2** divide into parts, each taking a part. **3** have a share; take part.

share and share alike, share equally. [OE *scearu* division] —**shar′er,** *n.*

share² (shār), *n.* plowshare. [OE *scear*]

share·crop (shār′krop′), *v.*, **–cropped, –crop·ping.** farm or raise (a crop) on land owned by someone else, with payment for the use of the land made in a part of the crop. —**share′crop′ping,** *n.*

share·crop·per (shār′krop′ər), *n.* person who farms land for the owner in return for part of the crops.

share·hold·er (shār′hōl′dər), *n.* person owning shares of stock.

shark¹ (shärk), *n.* any of a group of fishes, mostly marine, certain species of which are large and ferocious, and destructive to other fishes and sometimes dangerous to humans.

shark² (shärk), *n.* **1** a dishonest person who preys on others. **2** *Slang.* person unusually good at something; expert. [< G *schork,* var. of *schurke* scoundrel]

shark·skin (shärk′skin′), *n.* **1** cloth made from fine fibers of wool, rayon, or cotton, used in suits. **2 a** skin of a shark. **b** leather made from the skin of a shark.

sharp (shärp), *adj.* **1** having a thin cutting edge or a fine point: *a sharp knife, a sharp pencil.* **2** with a sudden change of direction: *a sharp turn.* **3** severe; biting: *a sharp wind, sharp words.* **4** feeling somewhat like a cut or prick: *a sharp pain.* **5** clear; distinct: *the sharp contrast between black and white.* **6** keen; eager: *a sharp appetite.* **7** being aware of things quickly: *a sharp eye, sharp ears.* **8** quick in mind; shrewd; clever: *sharp at a bargain.* **9** high in pitch; shrill. **10 a** above the true pitch; raised a half step in pitch: *F sharp.* **b** having sharps in the signature. —*adv.* **1** promptly; exactly: *one o'clock sharp.* **2** in a sharp manner; in an alert manner; keenly: *look sharp!* **3** suddenly: *pull a horse up sharp.* —*n.* **a** tone one half step above a given tone. **b** the sign (#) that shows this.

sharps, sewing needles. [OE *scearp*] —**sharp′ly,** *adv.* —**sharp′ness,** *n.*

sharp·en (shär′pən), *v.,* make or become sharp. —**sharp′en·er,** *n.*

sharp-eyed (shärp′īd′), *adj.* **1** having good eyesight. **2** watchful; observant.

sharp·shoot·er (shärp′shüt′ər), *n.* person who shoots very well. —**sharp′shoot′ing,** *n.*

sharp-tongued, (shärp′tungd′), *adj.* severely critical; given to biting criticism.

sharp-wit·ted (shärp′wit′id), *adj.* having or showing a quick, keen mind.

shat·ter (shat′ər), *v.* **1** break into pieces: *a stone shattered the window.* **2** disturb greatly; destroy: *a shattered mind.* **3** damage.

shave (shāv), *v.,* **shaved, shaved** or **shav·en, shav·ing,** *n.* —*v.* **1** remove hair with a razor; cut hair from (the face, chin, etc.) with a razor. **2** cut off (hair) with a razor. **3** cut off in thin slices; cut in thin slices. **4** cut very close. **5** *Fig.* come very close to; graze. —*n.* **1** the cutting off of hair with a razor. **2** tool for shaving, scraping, removing thin slices, etc. **3** a thin slice. **4** *Fig.* a narrow miss or escape. [OE *sceafan*]

shav·en (shāv′ən), *adj.* **1** shaved. **2** closely cut. **3** tonsured. —*v.* pp. of **shave.**

shav·er (shāv′ər), *n.* **1** person who shaves. **2** device for shaving. **3** *Informal.* youngster.

Sha·vi·an (shā′vi ən), *adj.* of, having to do with, or characteristic of George Bernard Shaw.

shav·ing (shāv′ing), *n.* Often, **shavings.** a very thin piece or slice.

shawl (shôl), *n.* a square or oblong piece of cloth to be worn about the shoulders or head. [<Pers. *shāl*]

Shaw·nee (shô nē′), *n.,* *pl.* **-nee, -nees.** **1** member of a tribe of American Indians formerly living in Tennessee and South Carolina, now in Oklahoma. **2** their Algonkian language. [< Algonkian (Shawnee) *Shawunogi* southerners]

shay (shā), *n.* light, two-wheeled carriage; chaise.

she (shē), *pron.,* *sing. nom.* **she,** *poss.* **her** or **hers,** *obj.* **her;** *pl. nom.* **they,** *poss.* **their** or **theirs,** *obj.* **them;** *n., pl.* **shes.** —*pron.* **1** girl, woman, or female animal spoken about or mentioned before. **2** anything thought of as female and spo- ken about or mentioned before. —*n.* girl; woman; female animal. [OE *hēo*]

sheaf (shēf), *n., pl.* **sheaves** (shēvz). bundle of things of the same sort bound together or so arranged that they can be bound together: *a sheaf of wheat, a sheaf of arrows.* [OE *scēaf*]

shear (shir), *v.,* **sheared** or (*Archaic*) **shore, sheared** or **shorn, shear·ing,** *n.* —*v.* **1** cut with shears or scissors. **2** cut the wool or fleece from. **3** cut close; cut off; cut. —*n.* **1** act or process of shearing. **2** that which is taken off by shearing. **3** one blade of a pair of shears. **4** pair of shears. [OE *sceran*] —**shear′er,** *n.*

shears (shirz), *n.pl.* **1** large scissors. **2** any cutting instrument resembling scissors. [OE *scēar*]

sheath (shēth), *n., pl.* **sheaths** (shēthz). **1** case or covering for the blade of a sword, knife, etc. **2** any similar covering, esp. on an animal or plant. [OE *scēath*] —**sheath′less,** *adj.*

sheathe (shēth), *v.,* **sheathed, sheath·ing.** **1** put (a sword, etc.) into a sheath. **2** enclose in a case or covering. —**sheath′er,** *n.*

sheath·ing (shēth′ing), *n.* **1** casing; covering as the plywood on the rafters or joists of a house. **2** material used to enclose or cover something.

She·ba (shē′bə), *n.* **1** an ancient country in S Arabia. **2 Queen of,** queen who visited Solomon to learn of his great wisdom. I Kings 10:1–13.

she·bang (shə bang′), *n. U.S. Slang.* **1** outfit; concern. **2** affair; event.

shed¹ (shed), *n.* a building used for shelter, storage, etc., usually having only one story: *a wagon shed, a sheep shed.* [OE *sced* shelter]

shed² (shed), *v.,* **shed, shed·ding.** **1** pour out; let fall: *the girl shed tears.* **2** throw off: *a snake sheds its skin.* **3** scatter abroad; give forth: *flowers shed perfume.* **shed blood,** destroy life; kill. [OE *scēadan*] —**shed′der,** *n.*

she'd (shēd), **1** she had. **2** she would.

sheen (shēn), *n.* brightness; luster. Satin and polished silver have a sheen. [OE *scēne* bright]

sheep (shēp), *n., pl.* **sheep.** **1** animal raised for wool and mutton. **2** a weak, timid, or stupid person. **3** leather made from the skin of sheep. [OE *scēap*]

sheep dog, collie or other dog trained to help a shepherd watch and tend sheep.

sheep·fold (shēp′fōld′), *n.* pen for sheep.

sheep·herd·er (shēp′hėr′dər), *n.* person who watches and tends large numbers of sheep while they are grazing on unfenced land.

sheep·ish (shēp′ish), *adj.* **1** awkwardly bashful or embarrassed. **2** like a sheep; timid; weak; stupid. —**sheep′ish·ly,** *adv.* —**sheep′ish·ness,** *n.*

sheep·man (shēp′man′), *n., pl.* **-men.** **1** person who owns and raises sheep. **2** =sheepherder.

sheep·skin (shēp′skin′), *n.* **1** skin of a sheep, esp. with the wool on it. **2** leather or parchment made from it. **3** diploma.

sheep sorrel, a kind of sorrel with reddish flowers.

sheer[1] (shir), *adj.* **1** very thin; almost transparent. **2** unmixed with anything else; complete: *sheer weariness.* **3** straight up and down; steep: *a sheer drop of 100 feet.* —*adv.* **1** completely; quite. **2** very steeply. —*n.* dress of transparent material worn over a slip. [OE *scīr* bright; vowel from Scand. *skǣrr* bright] —**sheer′ly,** *adv.* —**sheer′ness,** *n.*

sheer[2] (shir), *v.* turn from a course; turn aside; swerve. —*n.* **1** a turning of a ship from its course. **2** the upward curve of a ship's deck or lines from the middle toward each end. [var. of *shear, v.*]

sheet[1] (shēt), *n.* **1** a large piece of cloth esp. cotton, used to sleep on or under. **2** a broad, thin piece of anything. **3** a single piece of paper. **4** a broad, flat surface: *covered by a sheet of water.* —*v.* furnish or cover with a sheet. [OE *scēte*]

sheet[2] (shēt), *n.* rope that controls the angle at which a sail is set. [OE *scēata*]

sheet·ing (shēt′ing), *n.* **1** cloth for bed sheets. **2** a lining or covering of timber or metal, used to protect a surface.

sheet metal, metal in thin pieces or flat plates.

sheet music, music printed on unbound sheets of paper.

sheikh or **sheik,** (shēk), *n.* **1** an Arab chief or head of a family, village, or tribe. **2** a Muslim religious leader. [<Ar. *shaikh,* orig., old man]

shek·el (shek′əl), *n.* an ancient silver coin of the Hebrews that weighed about half an ounce. [<Heb. *sheqel*]

shel·drake (shel′drāk′), *n., pl.* **-drakes** or (*esp. collectively*) **-drake. 1** any of various large ducks of Europe and Asia, many of which have variegated plumage. **2** any merganser. [< obs. *sheld* variegated + *drake*]

shelf (shelf), *n., pl.* **shelves. 1** a thin, flat piece of wood, metal, stone, etc., fastened to a wall or frame to hold things, such as books, dishes, etc. **2** anything like a shelf.

off the shelf, as is; without any adjustment or modification.

on the shelf, put aside as no longer useful or desirable. [prob. <LG *schelf*]

shelf life, 1 length of time an item can be kept without being spoiled or useless. **2** *Fig.* length of time a person's talents, abilities, experience, etc., are considered useful.

shell (shel), *n.* **1** a hard outside covering of an animal, as of a mollusk, turtle, etc. **2** the hard outside covering of a nut, seed, fruit, egg, etc. **3** a casing of pastry, used for pies, tarts, etc. **4** a hollow projectile for a cannon, etc., filled with an explosive charge; cartridge. **5** something like a shell, as the framework of a house. **6** a shy, reserved attitude. —*v.*

1 take out of a shell. **2** separate (grains of corn) from the cob. **3** bombard by cannon fire.

come out of one's shell, become more sociable, less reserved.

shell out, *Informal.* hand over (money); pay up. [OE *sciell*] —**shell′er,** *n.* —**shell′-less,** *adj.* —**shell′-like′,** *adj.* —**shell′y,** *adj.*

she'll (shēl), **1** she shall. **2** she will.

shel·lac (shə lak′), *n., v.,* **-lacked, -lacking.** —*n.* **1** liquid that gives a smooth, shiny appearance to wood, metal, etc. Shellac is made from a resinous substance dissolved in alcohol. **2** the resinous substance used. —*v.* **1** put shellac on; cover or fasten with shellac. **2** *Informal.* completely defeat. [*shell + lac*[1]; trans. of F *laque en écailles* lac in thin plates] —**shel·lack′er,** *n.*

shel·lack·ing (shə lak′ing), *n.* an absolute, thorough defeat.

shell·fire (shel′fīr′), *n.* the firing of explosive shells or projectiles.

shell·fish (shel′fish′), *n., pl.* **-fish·es** or (*esp. collectively*) **-fish.** a water animal (not a fish in the ordinary sense) having a shell. Oysters, clams, crabs, and lobsters are shellfish.

shell shock, any of the many types of nervous or mental disorder resulting from the strain of war; post-traumatic stress disorder. —**shell′-shocked′,** *adj.*

shel·ter (shel′tər), *n.* **1** something that covers or protects from weather, danger, or attack. **2** protection; refuge. —*v.* **1** protect; shield; hide. **2** find shelter. —**shel′ter·er,** *n.* —**shel′ter·ing·ly,** *adv.* —**shel′ter·less,** *adj.*

shel·ty, shel·tie (shel′ti), *n., pl.* **-ties. 1** Shetland pony. **2** Shetland sheep dog.

shelve[1] (shelv), *v.,* **shelved, shelv·ing. 1** put on a shelf. **2** lay aside. **3** furnish with shelves. [ult. < *shelf*]

shelve[2] (shelv), *v.,* **shelved, shelv·ing.** slope gradually.

shelves (shelvz), *n.* pl. of **shelf.**

shelv·ing (shel′ving), *n.* **1** wood, metal, etc., for shelves. **2** shelves.

she·nan·i·gan (shə nan′ə gən), *n. Informal.* Usually, **shenanigans.** mischief or trickery.

shep·herd (shep′ərd), *n.* **1** person who takes care of sheep. **2** person who cares for and protects. **3** a spiritual guide; pastor. —*v.* **1** take care of. **2** guide; direct. [OE *scēaphierde < scēap* sheep + *hierde < heord* herd]

shepherd dog, =sheep dog.

shep·herd·ess (shep′ər dis), *n.* woman who takes care of sheep.

sher·bet (shėr′bət), *n.* a frozen dessert made of fruit juice, sugar, and water, milk, or whites of eggs. [<Turk., Pers. <Ar. *sharbah* drink]

sher·iff (sher′if), *n.* the most important law-enforcing officer of a county. A sheriff appoints deputies to help him keep order in the county. [OE *scīrgerēfa < scīr* shire + *gerēfa* reeve[1]]

sher·ry (sher′i), *n., pl.* **-ries.** a strong wine made in S Spain, or a wine like it made elsewhere. It varies in color from pale yellow to brown. [earlier *sherris* (taken as pl.) wine from *Xeres,* Spanish town]

she's (shēz), **1** she is. **2** she has.

Shetland pony, a small, sturdy, rough-coated pony, originally from the Shetland Islands.

Shetland sheep, primitive breed of small sheep with long, fine wool, originally from the Shetland Islands, NE of Scotland.

Shetland sheep dog, long-haired working dog, somewhat like a collie, originally from the Shetland Islands.

Shetland wool, fine wool from Shetland sheep, used to make sweaters, shawls, etc.

Shi·ah or **Shia** (shē′ə), *n.* one of two main sects of Islam [< Ar. *shi'ah* sect]

shew (shō), *v.,* **shewed, shewn, shew·ing,** *n. Esp. Brit. or Archaic.* show.

shib·bo·leth (shib′ə lith), *n.* any test word, watchword, or pet phrase of a political party, a class, sect, etc. [<Heb., stream; used as a password by the Gileadites to distinguish the fleeing Ephramities, because they could not pronounce *sh.* Judges 12:4–6]

shied (shīd), *v.* pt. and pp. of **shy.**

shield (shēld), *n.* **1** piece of armor carried on the arm to protect the body in battle. **2** a covering for moving parts of machinery. **3** anything used to protect. —*v.* **1** be a shield to; protect; defend. **2** serve as a shield. [OE *sceld*] —**shield′er,** *n.*

shift (shift), *v.* **1** change from one place, position, person, sound, etc., to another; change: *shift blame or responsibility, the scene shifts.* **2** manage to get along; contrive: *when his parents died, Tom had to shift for himself.* **3** change the position of (the gears of an automobile). —*n.* **1** a substituting in the place of another person or thing; change: *there are two shifts of work at the factory.* **2** group of workers; group: *this man is on the night shift.* **3** time during which such a group works. [OE *sciftan* arrange] —**shift′er,** *n.*

shift·less (shift′lis), *adj.* lazy; inefficient. —**shift′less·ly,** *adv.* —**shift′less·ness,** *n.*

shift·y (shif′ti), *adj.,* **shift·i·er, shift·i·est.** not straightforward; tricky. —**shift′i·ly,** *adv.* —**shift′i·ness,** *n.*

Shi·ite (shē′īt), *n.* member of the Shiah sect of islam. —*adj.* of or having to do with the Shiites or their faith. [see SHIAH]

shil·le·lagh, shil·la·lah, shil·le·lah (shə lā′li; -lə), *n. Irish.* a stick to hit with; cudgel [from *Shillelagh,* Irish village]

shil·ling (shil′ing), *n.* **1** a British money of account and silver coin. **2** formerly, a corresponding piece of money of one of the thirteen American colonies. [OE *scilling*]

shil·ly-shal·ly (shil′i shal′i), *adj., adv., v.,* **-lied, -ly·ing,** *n.* —*adj.* vacillating;

wavering; hesitating; undecided. —*adv.* in a vacillating or hesitating manner. —*v.* be undecided; vacillate; hesitate. —*n.* inability to decide; hesitation. [reduplication of *shall I?*]

shim (shim), *n., v.* **shimmed, shimming.** —*n.* thin wedge or piece of wood, metal, etc., used to raise a part, make a part fit against another, or fill a gap. —*v.* use a shim or shims on. [Am. E. orig. uncert.]

shim·mer (shim′ər), *v.* gleam faintly. —*n.* a faint gleam or shine. [OE *scimerian*] —**shim′mer·y,** *adj.*

shim·my (shim′i), *n., pl.* **–mies,** *v.,* **–mied, –my·ing.** —*n.* an unusual shaking or vibration. —*v.* shake; vibrate. [var. of *chemise* (taken as pl.)]

shin (shin), *n., v.,* **shinned, shin·ning.** —*n.* **1** the front part of the leg from the knee to the ankle. **2** the lower part of the foreleg in beef cattle. —*v.* climb. [OE *scinu*]

shin·bone (shin′bōn′), *n.* =tibia.

shin·dig (shin′dig), *n. Informal.* a merry or noisy dance, party, etc. [? < *shin* + *dig,* a blow on the shin]

shine (shīn), *v.,* **shone** or **shined, shin·ing,** *n.* —*v.* **1** send out light; be bright with light; reflect light; glow: *the sun shines.* **2** do very well; be brilliant; excel: *a shining athlete.* **3** make bright; polish: *shine shoes.* **4** cause to shine: *shine a light.* —*n.* **1** light; brightness. **2** luster; polish; gloss, as of silk. **3** polish put on shoes. **4** *Slang.* trick; prank.

take a shine to, *Informal.* become fond of; like.

take the shine out of or **off** or **from,** spoil; take some of the brightness or cheer from. [OE *scīnan*]

shin·er (shīn′ər), *n.* **1** person or thing that shines. **2** a small American freshwater fish with glistening scales. **3** *Informal.* a black eye.

shin·gle¹ (shing′gəl), *n., v.,* **–gled, –gling.** —*n.* **1** a thin piece of wood, etc., used to cover roofs, etc. Shingles are laid in overlapping rows with the thicker ends exposed. **2** a small signboard, esp. for a doctor's or lawyer's office. —*v.* cover with shingles: *shingle a roof.* [var. of earlier *shindle* <L *scindula*] —**shin′gler,** *n.*

shin·gle² (shing′gəl), *n. Esp. Brit.* **1** coarse gravel. **2** beach or other place covered with this. —**shin′gly,** *adj.*

shin·gles (shing′gəlz), *n. sing.* or *pl.* a virus disease that causes painful irritation of a group of nerves and an outbreak of itching spots or blisters. [< Med.L *cingulus,* var. of L *cingulum* girdle; trans. of Gk. *zoster* girdle, shingles]

shin·ing (shīn′ing), *adj.* **1** that shines; bright. **2** brilliant; outstanding. —**shin′ing·ly,** *adv.*

Shin·to (shin′tō), *n.* **1** Also, **Shin′to·ism.** the native religion of Japan, primarily a system of nature worship and ancestor worship. **2** adherent of this religion. —*adj.* of or pertaining to Shinto. —**Shin′to·ist,** *n., adj.*

shin·y (shīn′i), *adj.,* **shin·i·er, shin·i·est.** **1** shining; bright. **2** worn to a glossy smoothness: *a coat shiny from hard wear.* —**shin′i·ness,** *n.*

ship (ship), *n., v.,* **shipped, ship·ping.** —*n.* **1** a large seagoing vessel, as a steamship, a battleship, an airship, etc. **2** officers and crew of a vessel. —*v.* **1** put, take, or receive on board a ship. **2** send or carry from one place to another by a ship, plane, truck, etc. **3** take a job on a ship. **4** take in (water) over the side, as a vessel does when the waves break over it.

jump ship, a desert a ship. **b** leave (a job, place, etc.) suddenly and without notice.

when one's ship comes in, when one's fortunes change; when money is plentiful. [OE *scip*]

–ship, *suffix.* **1** office, status, or rank of ____, as in *clerkship, governorship.* **2** quality, state, or condition of ____, as in *kinship.* **3** act, acts, power, or skill of ____, as in *horsemanship, dictatorship.* **4** relation between ____s, as in *comradeship.* [OE *–scipe*]

ship·board (ship′bôrd′; –bōrd′), *n.* ship. **on shipboard,** on or inside a ship.

ship·build·er (ship′bil′dər), *n.* person who designs or constructs ships. —**ship′build′ing,** *n., adj.*

ship·load (ship′lōd′), *n.* a full load for a ship.

ship·mas·ter (ship′mas′tər; –mäs′–), *n.* master, commander, or captain of a ship.

ship·mate (ship′māt′), *n.* a fellow sailor on a ship.

ship·ment (ship′mənt), *n.* **1** act of shipping goods. **2** goods sent at one time to a person, firm, etc.

ship·own·er (ship′ōn′ər), *n.* person who owns a ship or ships.

ship·per (ship′ər), *n.* person who ships goods.

ship·ping (ship′ing), *n.* **1** act or business of sending goods by water, air, etc. **2** a body of ships. **3** the ships of a nation, city, or business.

ship·shape (ship′shāp′), *adj.* in good order; trim. —*adv.* in a trim, neat manner.

ship·wreck (ship′rek′), *n.* **1** destruction or loss of a ship. **2** a wrecked ship. **3** destruction; ruin. —*v.* **1** wreck; ruin; destroy. **2** suffer shipwreck.

ship·wright (ship′rīt′), *n.* person who builds ships.

ship·yard (ship′yärd′), *n.* place near the water where ships are built or repaired.

shire (shīr), *n.* one of the countries into which Great Britain is divided. [OE *scīr*]

shirk (shėrk), *v.* avoid or get out of doing (work, a duty, etc.). —*n.* person who shirks or does not do his or her share. [? < G *schurke* rascal] —**shirk′er,** *n.*

shirr (shėr), —*v.* **1** draw up or gather (cloth) on parallel threads. **2** bake (eggs) in a shallow dish with butter, etc. —*n.* a shirred arrangement of cloth, etc.

shirt (shėrt), *n.* **1** garment for the upper part of the body. **2** undergarment for the upper part of the body. [OE *scyrte.* Cf. SKIRT.]

shirt dress, dress made like a long shirt, usually with a belt or sash at the waist.

shirt·ing (shėr′ting), *n.* cloth for shirts.

shirt-sleeve (shėrt′slēv′), *adj. informal.*

shirt·waist (shėrt′wāst′), *n.* a woman's loose blouse, worn with a separate skirt.

shish·ke·bab (shish′kə bob′), *n.* pieces of meat, usually beef or lamb, on a skewer, often with tomatoes, onions, etc., and broiled or roasted. [< Armenian *shish kabab*]

Shi·va (shē′və), *n.* =Siva.

shiv·a·ree (shiv′ə ri′), *n.* mocking serenade to a newly married couple, performed by beating on kettles and pots. [respelling, based on pronunciation, of *chari-vari* < OF *chalivali* discordant noise]

shiv·er¹ (shiv′ər), *v.* shake with cold, fear, etc. —*n.* a shaking from cold, fear, etc. [ME *schivere(n)*] —**shiv′er·y,** *adj.*

shiv·er² (shiv′ər), *v.* break into small pieces. —*n.* a small piece; splinter.

shoal¹ (shōl), *adj.* shallow. —*n.* **1** place where the water is shallow. **2** sandbank or sand bar that makes the water shallow: *wrecked on the shoals.* —*v.* become shallow. [OE *sceald* shallow]

shoal² (shōl), *n.* a large number; crowd: *a shoal of fish.* —*v.* form into a shoal. [OE *scolu*]

shoat (shōt), *n.* a young pig able to feed itself. Also, **shote.**

shock¹ (shok), *n.* **1** a sudden, violent shake, blow, or crash. **2** a sudden, violent, or upsetting disturbance. **3** a collapsing or weakening of the body or mind caused by some violent impression on the nerves: *suffer from shock.* **4** disturbance produced by an electric current passing through the body. —*v.* **1** strike together violently. **2** cause to feel surprise, horror, or disgust. **3** give an electric shock to. [prob. < F *choc,* n., *choquer,* v.] —**shock′er,** *n.*

shock² (shok), *n.* group of cornstalks or bundles of grain set up on end together. —*v.* make into shocks. [? <LG or MDu. *schok*] —**shock′er,** *n.*

shock³ (shok), *n.* a thick, bushy mass.

shock absorber, anything that absorbs or lessens shocks, as for a car.

shock·ing (shok′ing), *adj.* **1** causing intense and painful surprise. **2** offensive; disgusting; revolting. **3** very bad. —**shock′ing·ly,** *adv.* —**shock′ing·ness,** *n.*

shock wave, disturbance of the atmosphere created by the movement of an aircraft, rocket, etc. at velocities greater than that of sound.

shod (shod), *v.* pt. and pp. of shoe.

shod·dy (shod′i), *n., pl.* **–dies,** *adj.,* **–di·er, –di·est.** —*n.* **1** an inferior kind of wool made of woolen waste, old rags, yarn, etc. **2** anything inferior made to look like what is better. —*adj.* **1** made of woolen waste. **2** falsely claiming superiority. **3** making vulgar pretensions. —**shod′di·ly,** *adv.* —**shod′di·ness,** *n.*

shoe (shü), *n., pl.* **shoes,** *v.,* **shod, shoe·ing.** –*n.* **1** an outer covering, often of leather, for a person's foot. **2** thing like a shoe in shape or use. **3** a horseshoe. **4** the part of a brake that presses on a wheel; wheel drag. **5** a sliding plate or contact by which an electric current passes from the third rail. —*v.* furnish with a shoe or shoes.

drop the other shoe, have the rest, usually of something unwanted, happen or occur.

fill one's shoes, take one's place.

if the shoe fits, provided something, esp. an unflattering description, is right or accurate.

in another's shoes, in another's place, situation, etc.

the shoe is on the other foot, the situation is reversed. [OE *scōh*]

shoe·horn (shü′hôrn′), *n.* piece of metal, horn, etc., inserted at the heel of a shoe to make it slip on easily.

shoe·lace (shü′lās′), *n.* cord, braid, or leather strip for fastening a shoe.

shoe·mak·er (shü′māk′ər), *n.* person who makes or mends shoes. —**shoe′mak′ing,** *n.*

shoe·string (shü′string′), *n.* **1** =shoelace. **2** *Informal. Fig.* a very small amount of money used to start or carry on a business, investment, etc.: *done on a shoestring.*

shoe tree, form for keeping a shoe in shape or for stretching it.

sho·gun (shō′gun; –gün), *n.* a hereditary commander in chief of the Japanese army. The shoguns were the real rulers of Japan for hundreds of years until 1867. [< Jap. < Chinese *chiang chun* army leader]

shone (shōn), *v.* pt. and pp. of **shine.**

shoo (shü), *v.,* **shooed, shoo·ing.** scare or send away; drive off. —*n.* exclamation used to scare off an animal.

shoo-in (shü′in′), *n. Informal.* **1** a definite, certain winner. **2** something easy to win. [< *shoo* + *in*]

shook (shúk), *v.* pt. of **shake.**

shoot (shüt), *v.,* **shot, shoot·ing,** *n.* —*v.* **1** hit, wound, or kill with a bullet, arrow, etc.: *shoot a rabbit.* **2** send swiftly: *he shot question after question at us.* **3** fire or use (a gun, etc.): *this gun shoots straight.* **4** move suddenly and swiftly: *a car shot by us.* **5** grow; grow rapidly. **6** take (a picture) with a camera; photograph. **7** measure the altitude of: *shoot the sun.* **8** send (a ball, etc.) toward the goal, pocket, etc. —*n.* **1** shooting practice. **2** trip, party, or contest for shooting. **3** a new part growing out; young bud or stem.

shoot at or **for,** try for; aim for.

shoot down, a cause to fall out of the air by shooting. **b** *Fig.* kill off or dismiss an idea or proposal.

shoot up, a grow quickly. **b** rise quickly: *shot up the stairs, the building shot up overnight, it seemed.* **c** *Slang.* inject into a vein. [OE *scēotan*] —**shoot′er,** *n.*

shooting gallery, 1 place especially designed to practice shooting a firearm. **2** *Slang.* place where addicts take drugs.

shooting star, star seen falling or darting through the sky; meteor.

shop (shop), *n., v.,* **shopped, shop·ping.** —*n.* **1** place where things are sold; store. **2** place where things are made or repaired. **3** place where a certain kind of work is done: *a barber shop.* —*v.* visit stores to look at or to buy things.

talk shop, talk about one's work. [OE *sceoppa*] —**shop′per,** *n.*

shop·keep·er (shop′kēp′ər), *n.* person who carries on business in a shop or store.

shop·lift·er (shop′lif′tər), *n.* person who steals goods from a shop or store while pretending to be a customer. —**shop′lift′,** *v.* —**shop′lift′ing,** *n.*

shop·talk (shop′tôk), *n.* the colloquial vocabulary of an occupation.

shop·worn (shop′wôrn′; –worn′), *adj.* soiled by being displayed or handled in a store.

shore¹ (shôr; shōr), *n.* **1** land at the edge of a sea, lake, etc. **2** land near a sea. **3** land.

in shore, in or on the water, near to the shore or nearer to the shore.

off shore, in or on the water, not far from the shore. [? < LG or MDu. *schore*] —**shore′less,** *adj.*

shore² (shôr; shōr), *n., v.,* **shored, shor·ing.** —*n.* prop placed against or beneath something to support it. —*v.* **1** prop up or support with shores. **2** *Fig.* strengthen with support or help: *shore up a failing enterprise.* [? < MDu. *schore* prop]

shore³ (shôr; shōr), *v. Archaic.* pt. of **shear.**

shore·line (shôr′līn′; shōr′–), *n.* line where shore and water meet.

shore·ward (shôr′wərd; shōr′–), *adv., adj.* toward the shore.

shor·ing (shôr′ing; shōr′-), *n.* shore or props for supporting a building, ship, etc.

shorn (shôrn: shōrn), *v.* pp. of **shear.**

short (shôrt), *adj.* **1** of less than usual height or expected length; not long or tall; of small extent: *a short distance, a short tail, a short man, short grass.* **2** extending or reaching but a little way: *a short memory.* **3** less than the right amount, measure, standard, etc.: *short weighted.* **4** not reaching a mark or the like: *a short throw.* **5** concise; brief: *a short essay.* **6** so brief as to be rude: *a short answer.* **7** of vowels or syllables, occupying a relatively short time in utterance. The vowels are short in *fat, net.* **8** breaking or crumbling easily, as pastry. —*adv.* **1** so as to be or make short: *cut a thing short.* **2** abruptly; suddenly: *the horse stopped short.* **3** briefly.

4 on the near side of an intended or particular point: *the throw fell short.* **5** without going the full length (*of*): *stop short of actual crime.* —*n.* **1** something short, esp. a short sound or syllable. **2** a short circuit.

in short, briefly; in a word: *in short, he's crazy!*

fall short, a fail to reach. **b** be insufficient.

run short, a not have enough. **b** not be enough.

short for, shortened form of: *Bea, short for Beatrice.*

short of, a not up to; less than: *nothing short of your best work will satisfy me.* **b** not having enough of: *short of ready cash.*

short on, having little of; lacking: *short on help.*

short out, a short-circuit. **b** *Fig.* become irrational (over something).

shorts, a short trousers that reach just above the knee. **b** man's underwear: *boxer shorts.* [OE *sceort*] —**short′ish,** *adj.* —**short′ness,** *n.*

short·age (shor′tij), *n.* **1** too small an amount; lack. **2** amount by which something is deficient.

short·bread (shôrt′bred′), *n.* a rich cake or cooky that crumbles easily.

short·cake (shôrt′kāk′), *n.* **1** cake made of rich biscuit dough and shortening, covered or filled with berries or other fruit. **2** a sweet cake filled with fruit.

short-change (shôrt′chānj′), *v.,* **–changed, –chang·ing. 1** give less than the right change to. **2** cheat. —**short′-chang′er,** *n.*

short circuit, a side circuit of electricity of relatively low resistance, connecting two points of a larger electric current so as to carry most of the current.

short-cir·cuit (shôrt′sėr′kit), *v.* **1** make a short circuit in. **2** make a short circuit. **3** *Informal. Fig.* go around; by-pass.

short·com·ing (shôrt′kum′ing), *n.* fault; defect.

short cut, a less distant or quicker way.

short·en (shôr′tən), *v.* **1** make shorter; cut off. **2** make rich with butter, lard, etc. **4** take in (sail). —**short′en·er,** *n.*

short·en·ing (shôr′tən ing; shôrt′ning), *n.* butter, lard, or other fat, used to make pastry, cake, etc., crisp or crumbly.

short·fall (shôrt′fôl′), *n.* an amount less than expected; decrease: *a shortfall in sales.*

short·hand (shôrt′hand′), *n.* method of rapid writing that uses symbols in place of letters, syllables, words, and phrases; stenography. —*adj.* **1** using shorthand. **2** written in shorthand.

short-hand·ed (shôrt′han′did), *adj.* not having enough workers or helpers. —**short′-hand′ed·ness,** *n.*

short·horn (shôrt′hôrn′), *n.* any of a breed of cattle with short horns, raised for beef.

short-lived (shôrt′līvd′; –livd′), *adj.* living only a short time; lasting only a short time.

short-order (shôrt′ôr′dər), *adj.* quickly prepared and served: *a short-order cook.* **in short order,** quickly: *get an apology in short order.*

short·ly (shôrt′li), *adv.* 1 in a short time; before long; soon. 2 in a few words; briefly. 3 briefly and rudely.

short shrift, little mercy, respite, or delay.

short-sight·ed (shôrt′sīt′id), *adj.* 1 near-sighted; not able to see far. 2 lacking in foresight; not prudent. —**short′-sight′ed·ly,** *adv.* —**short′-sight′ed·ness,** *n.*

short·stop (shôrt′stop′), *n.* a baseball player stationed between second base and third base.

short story, a prose story with a full plot, but much shorter than a novel.

short-tem·pered (shôrt′tem′pərd), *adj.* easily made angry; quick-tempered.

short-term (shôrt′tèrm′), *adj.* falling due in a short time.

short ton, 2000 pounds avoirdupois.

short wave, a radio wave having a wave length of 60 meters or less. —**short′-wave′,** *adj.*

short-wave (shôrt′wāv′), *v.,* **-waved, -wav·ing.** transmit by short waves.

short-wind·ed (shôrt′win′did), *adj.* getting out of breath too quickly; having difficulty in breathing. —**short′-wind′ed·ness,** *n.*

Sho·sho·ne (shō shō′ni), *n.* 1 member of a tribe of North American Indians who once occupied an area from Wyoming to California, now living in Wyoming, Nevada, and Idaho. 2 the language of this tribe. —*adj.* of or having to do with this tribe or their language.

Sho·sho·ne·an (shō shō′nē ən), *adj.* of or belonging to North American Indian tribes of the W U.S. whose languages have common roots, including the Hopi, Shoshone, Comanche, and others.

shot¹ (shot), *n., pl.* **shots** or (for defs. 2, 3) **shot** or **shots,** *v.* **shot·ted, shot·ting.** —*n.* 1 act of shooting. 2 ball or balls for a gun or cannon. 3 discharge of a gun or cannon. 4 person who shoots: *he is a good shot.* 5 an aimed stroke in a game. 6 remark aimed at some person or thing: *she made a parting shot.* 7 an attempt; try: *take a shot at the job.* 8 picture taken with a camera; photograph: *he took a shot of the beautiful scene.* 9 drink: *a shot of whiskey.* —*v.* load or weight with shot.
a long shot, an attempt at something difficult.
call the shots, control; manage.
like a shot, very fast; immediately.
shot in the arm, a stimulant; incentive. **b** something that revives.
shot in the dark, wild guess; something based on little or no evidence. [OE *sceot*]

shot² (shot), *v.* pt. and pp. of **shoot.** —*adj.* woven so as to show a play of colors: *blue silk shot with gold.*

shote (shōt), *n.* shoat.

shot·gun (shot′gun′), *n.* a smoothbore gun for firing cartridges filled with small shot.

should (shood; *unstressed* shəd), *v.* 1 pt. of **shall.** See **shall** for ordinary uses. 2 *Should* has special uses: **a** to express duty: *you should try to make fewer mistakes.* **b** to make statements less direct or blunt: *I should not call her beautiful.* **c** to express uncertainty: *if John should win the prize, how happy he would be.* **d** to make statements about something that might have happened but did not: *I should have gone if you had asked me.* **e** to express a condition or reason for something: *he was pardoned on the condition that he should leave the country.* [OE *sceolde*]

shoul·der (shōl′dər), *n.* 1 the part of the body to which an arm or foreleg or wing is attached. 2 part of a garment covering this. 3 foreleg and adjoining parts of a slaughtered animal. 4 a shoulderlike part or projection. —*v.* 1 take upon or support with the shoulder or shoulders: *shoulder a tray.* 2 bear (a burden, blame, etc.); assume (responsibility, expense, etc.). 3 push with the shoulders: *he shouldered his way through the crowd.*
shoulders, a the two shoulders and upper part of the back. **b** *Fig.* strength to support or sustain: *a huge responsibility on her shoulders.*
shoulder to shoulder, a side by side; together. **b** with united effort. **straight from the shoulder,** *Fig.* frankly. [OE *sculdor*]

shoulder blade, the flat bone of the shoulder; scapula.

should·n't (shood′ənt), should not.

shouldst (shoodst), **should·est** (shood′ist), *v. Archaic.* 2nd pers. sing of **should.**

shout (shout), *v.* 1 call or cry loudly and vigorously. 2 talk or laugh very loudly. 3 express by a shout or shouts. —*n.* 1 a loud, vigorous call or cry. 2 a loud outburst of laughter. [? ult. var. of *scout²*] —**shout′er,** *n.*

shove (shuv), *v.,* **shoved, shov·ing,** *n.* —*v.* push. —*n.* a push.
shove off, a push away from the shore; row away. **b** leave; start. [OE *scūfan*] —**shov′er,** *n.*

shov·el (shuv′əl), *n., v.,* **-eled, -el·ing.** —*n.* 1 tool with a broad scoop, used to lift and throw loose matter: *a coal shovel, a steam shovel.* 2 a shovelful. —*v.* 1 lift and throw with a shovel. 2 make with a shovel: *shovel a path.* 3 throw in large quantities: *shovel the food into one's mouth.* [OE *scofl*] —**shov′el·er,** *n.*

shov·el·ful (shuv′əl ful), *n., pl.* **-fuls.** as much as a shovel can hold.

show (shō), *v.,* **showed, shown** or **showed, show·ing,** *n.* —*v.* 1 let be seen; put or be in sight; reveal; appear: *anger showed in his face, she showed us her new car.* 2 point out; direct; guide: *show him the way.* 3 make clear; explain to: *show us how to do the problem.* 4 grant; give:

show mercy, show favor. —*n.* 1 display: *the jewels made a fine show, a house furnished for show, not comfort.* 2 any kind of public exhibition or display: *a horse show.* 3 a showing: *the club voted by a show of hands.* 4 appearance: *a sorry show.* 5 false appearance: *a show of sincerity.* 6 entertainment: *a Broadway show.*
for show, for effect; to attract attention.
run the show, take complete change of something.
show off, a make a show of; display one's good points, etc. **b** attract attention: *talked too much and generally showed off.*
show up, a expose. **b** stand out. **c** put in an appearance.
steal the show, attract the most attention; be liked the most. [OE *scēawian* look at] —**show′er,** *n.*

show·boat (shō′bōt′), *n.* steamboat with a theater for plays.

show·case (shō′kās′), *n.* a glass case to display and protect articles in stores, museums, etc.

show·down (shō′doun′), *n.* decisive confrontation, esp. involving facts, purposes, etc.

show·er (shou′ər), *n.* 1 a short fall of rain or snow. 2 anything like a fall of rain: *a shower of tears or sparks.* 3 party for giving presents to a woman about to be married or have a baby. 4 bath in which water pours down on the body from above in small jets. —*v.* 1 rain or snow for a short time. 2 come in a shower. 3 send in a shower; pour down. [OE *scūr*] —**show′er·y,** *adj.*

show·ing (shō′ing), *n.* 1 exhibition; show. 2 appearance; performance: *a good showing, a poor showing in sales.*

show·man (shō′mən), *n., pl.* **-men.** 1 man who manages a show. 2 person skilled in showmanship or publicity. —**show′man·ship,** *n.*

shown (shōn), *v.* pp of **show.**

show-off (shō′ôf′; -of′), *n.* 1 a showing off. 2 person who shows off.

show piece, something displayed as the best of its kind, of a collection, etc.; centerpiece.

show·room (shō′rüm′; -rum′), *n.* room used for the display of goods or merchandise.

show·y (shō′i), *adj.,* **show·i·er, show·i·est.** 1 making a display; striking; conspicuous. A peony is a showy flower. 2 gaudy; garish. —**show′i·ly,** *adv.* —**show′i·ness,** *n.*

shrank (shrangk), *v.* pt. of **shrink.**

shrap·nel (shrap′nəl), *n.* fragments scattered by a shell on explosion. [after the inventor, H. *Shrapnel,* British officer]

shred (shred), *n., v.,* **shred·ded** or **shred, shred·ding.** —*n.* 1 a very small piece torn off or cut off; very narrow strip; scrap. 2 fragment; particle; bit. —*v.* tear or cut into small pieces. [OE *scrēade*] —**shred′der,** *n.*

shrew (shrü), *n.* **1** a bad-tempered, quarrelsome woman. **2** a mouselike animal with a long snout and brownish fur, that eats insects and worms. [OE *scrēawa*] —**shrew'ish**, *adj.* —**shrew'ish·ly**, *adv.* —**shrew'ish·ness**, *n.*

shrewd (shrüd), *adj.* **1** having a sharp mind; showing a keen wit; clever. **2** keen; sharp. [earlier *shrewed*, < *shrew*, v., in sense of "scold"] —**shrewd'ly**, *adv.* —**shrewd'ness**, *n.*

shriek (shrēk), *n.* **1** a loud, sharp, shrill sound. **2** a loud, shrill laugh. —*v.* **1** make such a sound. **2** utter loudly and shrilly. [akin to Scand. *skrækja*] —**shriek'er**, *n.*

shrike (shrīk), *n.* bird with a strong, hooked beak that feeds on large insects, frogs, and sometimes on other birds. [OE *scrīc*]

shrill (shril), *adj.* **1** having a high pitch; high and sharp in sound; piercing. Crickets, locusts, and katydids make shrill noises. **2** full of shrill sounds. —*v.* **1** make a shrill sound. **2** sound sharply. —*n.* a shrill sound. —*adv.* with a shrill sound. [ME *shrille*] —**shrill'ness**, *n.* —**shril'ly**, *adv.*

shrimp (shrimp), *n., pl.* **shrimps** or for 1 (*esp. collectively*) **shrimp.** **1** a small, long-tailed shellfish, used for food. **2** a small or insignificant person.

shrine (shrīn), *n., v.,* **shrined, shrin·ing.** —*n.* place or object considered as sacred because of its memories, history, etc. —*v.* enclose in a shrine or something like a shrine. [< L *scrinium* case]

shrink (shringk), *v.,* **shrank** or **shrunk, shrunk** or **shrunk·en, shrink·ing,** *n.* —*v.* **1** draw back. **2** make or become smaller; cause to contract. —*n.* a shrinking. [OE *scrincan*] —**shrink'a·ble**, *adj.* —**shrink'er**, *n.* —**shrink'ing·ly**, *adv.*

shrink·age (shringk'ij), *n.* **1** fact or process of shrinking. **2** amount or degree of shrinking.

shrinking violet, timid person.

shriv·el (shriv'əl), *v.,* **-eled, -el·ing.** dry up; wither; shrink and wrinkle.

shroud (shroud), *n.* **1** cloth or garment in which a dead person is wrapped for burial. **2** something that covers, conceals, or veils. **3** Usually, **shrouds.** rope from a mast to the side of a ship. Shrouds help support the mast. —*v.* **1** wrap for burial. **2** cover; conceal; veil. [OE *scrūd*] —**shroud'less**, *adj.*

shrove (shrōv), *v.* pt. of **shrive.**

shrub (shrub), *n.* a woody plant smaller than a tree, usually with many separate stems starting from or near the ground; bush. [OE *scrybb* brush] —**shrub'by**, *adj.* —**shrub'bi·ness**, *n.* —**shrub'like'**, *adj.*

shrub·ber·y (shrub'ər i; shrub'ri), *n., pl.* **-ber·ies.** shrubs.

shrug (shrug), *v.,* **shrugged, shrug·ging,** *n.* —*v.* raise (the shoulders), as an expression of dislike, doubt, indifference, impatience, etc. —*n.* a raising of the shoulders in this way.

shrug off, dismiss as unimportant.

shrunk (shrungk), *v.* pp. and pt. of **shrink.**

shrunk·en (shrungk'ən), *adj.* grown smaller; shriveled. —*v.* pp. of **shrink.**

shuck (shuk), *n.* husk; pod. —*v.* remove the shucks from.

shuck off, remove; get rid of: *shuck off a coat and toss it on a chair.* —**shuck'er**, *n.*

shucks (shuks), *interj. Informal.* exclamation of disgust, regret, impatience, etc.

shud·der (shud'ər), *v.* tremble with horror, fear, cold, etc. —*n.* a trembling; quivering. [ME *shodder(en)*, frequentative of OE *scūdan* shake]

shuf·fle (shuf'əl), *v.,* **-fled, -fling,** *n.* —*v.* **1** walk without lifting the feet: *the old man shuffles feebly along.* **2** dance with a shuffle. **3** mix (cards, etc.) so as to change the order. —*n.* **1** a scraping or dragging movement of the feet. **2** dance with a shuffle. **3** a shuffling of cards. **4** right or turn to shuffle (cards). [? < LG *schuffeln;* akin to SHOVE]

shuf·fle·board (shuf'əl bôrd'; -bōrd'), *n.* a game played by pushing large disks along a surface to certain spots.

shun (shun), *v.,* **shunned, shun·ning.** keep away from; avoid. [OE *scunian*] —**shun'ner**, *n.*

shunt (shunt), *v.* **1** move out of the way; turn aside; sidetrack. **2** carry part of an electric current by means of a shunt. —*n.* **1** a turning aside; shift. **2** wire or other conductor joining two points in a circuit and forming a path through which a part of the electric current will pass. [? < *shun*]

shut (shut), *v.,* **shut, shut·ting,** *adj.* —*v.* **1** close (a receptacle or opening) by pushing or pulling a lid, door, some part, etc., into a place: *shut a box.* **2** close (eyes, a knife, a book, etc.) by bringing parts together. **3** close tight; close securely: *shut a house for the summer.* **4** confine: *shut in prison.* —*adj.* closed; fastened up; enclosed.

shut down, a close by lowering. **b** close (a factory or the like), for a time; stop work. **c** put a stop or check on.

shut in, keep from going out.

shut off, close; obstruct; check; bar.

shut out, a keep from coming in. **b** defeat (a team) without allowing it to score.

shut up, a shut the doors and windows of. **b** *Informal.* stop talking. **c** keep from going out. [OE *scyttan* bolt up]

shut-down (shut'doun'), *n.* a closing of a factory, or the like, for a time; shutting down.

shut-eye (shut'ī'), *n. Informal.* sleep.

shut-in (shut'in'), *adj.* confined. —*n.* person who is kept from going out by sickness, weakness, etc.

shut-out (shut'out'), *n.* **1** defeat of a team without allowing it to score. **2** =lockout.

shut·ter (shut'ər), *n.* **1** a movable cover for a window. **2** a movable cover, slide, etc., for closing an opening. The device that opens and closes in front of the lens of a camera is the shutter. **3** person or thing that shuts. —*v.* put a shutter or shutters on or over. [< *shut*]

shut·tle (shut'əl), *n., v.,* **-tled, -tling.** —*n.* **1** train, bus, or plane that carries passengers between two points. **2** instrument that carries the thread from one side of the web to the other in weaving. **3** the sliding container that carries the lower thread in a sewing machine. —*v.* move quickly to and fro. [OE *scutel* a dart < *scēotan* to shoot]

shut·tle·cock (shut'əl kok'), *n.* a weighted cork with feathers stuck in one end, hit back and forth in the game of badminton.

shy (shī), *adj.* **shy·er, shy·est** or **shi·er, shi·est,** *v.,* **shied, shy·ing,** *n., pl.* **shies.** —*adj.* **1** uncomfortable in company; bashful. **2** easily frightened away; timid. **3** cautious; wary. **4** short in amount, degree, etc., to a certain extent. —*v.* **1** start back or aside suddenly. **2** shrink. —*n.* a sudden start to one side. [OE *scēoh*] —**shy'er**, *n.* —**shy'ly**, *adv.* —**shy'ness**, *n.*

Shy·lock (shī'lok), *n.* **1** the relentless and revengeful moneylender in Shakespeare's play *The Merchant of Venice.* **2** a greedy moneylender.

shy·ster (shī'stər), *n.* lawyer or other person who uses improper or questionable methods in his or her business or profession.

si (sē), *n.* the seventh tone of the musical scale. [see GAMUT]

Si, silicon.

S.I., Staten Island.

Si·am (sī am'; sī'am), *n.* Thailand.

Si·a·mese (sī'ə mēz'; -mēs'), *adj., n., pl.* **-mese.** —*adj.* of or pertaining to Thailand, its people, or their language. —*n.* **1** native of Thailand. **2** language of Thailand.

sib·i·lant (sib'ə lənt), *adj.* **1** hissing. **2** making, having, or representing a hissing sound. —*n.* a hissing sound, letter, or symbol. S and sh are sibilants. [< L *sibilans* hissing]

sib·ling (sib'ling), *n.* one of two or more children of a family. —*adj.* of or pertaining to a brother or sister.

sib·yl (sib'əl), *n.* prophetess; fortuneteller; witch. [< L < Gk. *sibylla*] —**sib'yl·line**, *adj.*

sic[1] (sik), *adv. Latin.* so; thus, as copied from an original.

sic[2] (sik), *v.,* **sicked, sick·ing.** **1** set upon or attack. **2** incite to set upon or attack. [var. of *seek*]

sick (sik), *adj.* **1** in poor health; having some disease; ill. **2** feeling nausea. **3** for a sick person; connected with sickness. **4** weary; tired. **5** affected with sorrow or longing: *sick at heart.* —*n.* sick people. [OE *sēoc*] —**sick'ish**, *adj.* —**sick'ish·ly**, *adv.* —**sick'ish·ness**, *n.*

sick bay, place on a ship used as a hospital.

sick·bed (sik'bed'), *n.* bed of a sick person.

sick·en (sik'ən), *v.* make or become sick. —**sick'en·er,** *n.* —**sick'en·ing,** *adj.* —**sick'en·ing·ly,** *adv.*

sick headache, =migraine.

sick·le (sik'əl), *n.* tool consisting of a short, curved blade on a short handle, used for cutting grass, etc. [< L *secula*] —**sick'le-shaped',** *adj.*

sickle cell anemia, hereditary anemia characterized by sickle-shaped red blood cells which are inefficient in carrying oxygen and easily destroyed.

sick·ly (sik'li), *adj.* **–li·er, –li·est,** *adv., v.,* **–lied, –ly·ing.** —*adj.* **1** often sick; not strong; not healthy. **2** of or pertaining to sickness. **3** causing sickness. **4** faint; weak; pale. —*adv.* in a sick manner. —*v.* make sickly, esp. in appearance. —**sick'li·ness,** *n.*

sick·ness (sik'nis), *n.* **1** condition of being sick; illness; disease. **2** nausea; vomiting.

side (sīd), *n., adj., v.,* **sid·ed, sid·ing.** —*n.* **1** surface or line bounding a thing: *the sides of a square.* **2** one of the two surfaces of an object that is not the front, back, top, or bottom: *there is a door at the side of the house.* **3** either of the two surfaces of paper, cloth, etc.: *write only on one side of the paper.* **4** aspect; phase: *all sides of a question.* **5** either the right or the left part of a person or thing; either part or beyond a central line: *the east side of a city, a pain in one's side.* **6** slope of a hill or bank of a river. **7** position, course, attitude, or part of one person or party: *be on the winning side of a dispute, the man is English on his mother's side.* —*adj.* **1** at one side; on one side: *the side aisles of a theater.* **2** from one side: *a side view.* **3** toward one side: *a side glance.* **4** less important: *a side issue.* —*v.* put siding on, as a building.

by one's side, a with or near one. **b** *Fig.* in support of one.

on the side, in addition to one's ordinary duties.

side against, oppose.

side by side, beside one another.

side with, take the part of; favor (one among opposing or different groups or persons).

take sides, place oneself with one person or group against another. [OE *sīde*]

side arms, sword, revolver, bayonet, etc., carried at the side or in the belt.

side·bar (sīd'bär'), *n.* additional information that supplements what is in a news story, article, etc., often placed to the side of the primary story or article.

side·board (sīd'bôrd'; -bōrd'), *n.* piece of dining room furniture. A sideboard has drawers and shelves for holding silver and linen, and space on top for dishes.

side·burns (sīd'bėrnz'), *n.pl. Am.* short whiskers just below the hairline on both cheeks. [alter. of *burnsides,* from A.E. *Burnside,* American general]

side effect, secondary effect or reaction to something, esp. a drug.

side-kick (sīd'kik'), *n. Informal.* partner or very close friend.

side light, 1 light coming from the side. **2** incidental information about a subject.

side·line (sīd'līn'), *n., v.,* **–lined, –lin·ing.** —— *n.* **1** line at the side of something. **2** line that marks the limit of play on the side of the field in football, etc. **3** *Fig.* an additional line of goods or of business. force or be forced out of participation.

sidelines, a area just beyond the marked boundaries of a playing field. **b** not actively playing on a team or as part of a venture: *sit on the sidelines.*

side·long (sīd'lông'; -long'), *adj., adv.* to one side; toward the side.

side·piece (sīd'pēs'), *n.* piece forming a side or part of a side, or fixed by the side, of something.

si·de·re·al (sī dir'i əl), *adj.* **1** of or pertaining to the stars. **2** measured by the apparent daily motion of the stars. A **sidereal day** is about four minutes shorter than a mean solar day. [< L *sidereus* astral < *sidus* star]

side·sad·dle (sīd'sad'əl), *n.* a woman's saddle so made that both of the rider's legs are on the same side of the horse.

side show, 1 a small show in connection with a principal one. **2** any minor proceeding or affair connected with a more important one.

side·slip (sīd'slip'), *n., v.,* **–slipped, –slip·ping.** —*n.* a slip to one side. —*v.* slip to one side.

side step, a step or stepping to one side.

side-step (sīd'step'), *v.,* **–stepped, –step·ping. 1** step aside. **2** avoid by stepping aside; evade: *side-step a responsibility.* —**side'-step'per,** *n.*

side·stroke (sīd'strōk'), *n.* swimming stroke done with the swimmer on his or her side propelled forward by downward arm strokes and scissor movements of the legs.

side·swipe (sīd'swīp'), *v.,* **–swiped, –swip·ing,** *n.* —*v.* hit with a sweeping blow along the side. —*n.* a sweeping blow along the side.

side·track (sīd'trak'), *n.* a short railroad track to which a train may be switched from a main track. —*v.* **1** switch (a train, etc.) to a sidetrack. **2** put aside; turn aside.

side·walk (sīd'wôk'), *n.* place to walk at the side of a street, usually paved.

side·ward (sīd'wərd), *adj.* directed toward one side. —*adv.* Also, **side'wards.** toward one side

side·way (sīd'wā'), *adv., adj.* sideways.

side·ways (sīd'wāz'), **side·wise** (–wīz'), *adv., adj.* **1** toward one side. **2** from one side. **3** with one side toward the front.

side-wheel (sīd'hwēl'), *adj.* having a paddle wheel on each side. —**side'-wheel'er,** *n.*

side whisker, hair growing long on the side of the face. —**side'-whis'kered,** *adj.*

sid·ing (sīd'ing), *n.* **1** boards forming the sides of a wooden building. **2** a short railroad track to which cars can be switched from a main track.

si·dle (sī'dəl), *v.,* **–dled, –dling,** *n.* —*v.* **1** move sideways. **2** move sideways slowly so as not to attract attention. —*n.* movement sideways.

SIDS, sudden infant death syndrome.

siege (sēj), *n., v.,* **sieged, sieg·ing.** —*n.* **1** the surrounding of a fortified place by an army trying to capture it, mainly by shutting off its supplies; besieging or being besieged. **2** any long or persistent effort to overcome resistance; any long-continued attack: *siege of illness.* —*v.* besiege.

lay siege to, a besiege. **b** attempt to win or get by long and persistent effort. [< OF, ult. < L *sedere* sit]

si·en·na (si en'ə), *n.* **1** a yellowish-brown coloring matter (**raw sienna**) made from earth containing iron. **2** a reddish-brown coloring matter (**burnt sienna**) made by roasting earth containing iron. **3** a yellowish brown or reddish brown. [short for Ital. *terra di Sien(n)a* earth of Siena, a city in Italy]

si·er·ra (si er'ə), *n.* chain of hills or mountains with jagged peaks. [< Sp., lit., a saw < L *serra*]

si·es·ta (si es'tə), *n.* a nap or rest taken at noon or in the afternoon. [< Sp.]

sieve (siv), *n., v.,* **sieved, siev·ing.** —*n.* utensil having holes that let liquids and smaller pieces pass through, but not the larger pieces. Shaking flour through a sieve removes lumps. —*v.* put through a sieve. [OE *sife*]

sift (sift), *v.* **1** separate large pieces of from small by shaking in a sieve. **2** put through a sieve. **3** use a sieve. **4** fall through, or as if through, a sieve: *the snow sifted softly down.* **5** examine very carefully: *sift the evidence.* [OE *siftan* < *sife* sieve] —**sift'er,** *n.*

sigh (sī), *v.* **1** let out a very long, deep breath because one is sad, tired, relieved, etc. **2** make a sound like a sigh. **3** wish very much; long: *sigh for home.* **4** lament with sighing: *sigh over one's unhappy fate.* —*n.* **1** act or sound of sighing. [ME *sighe(n),* ult. < OE *sīcan*] —**sigh'er,** *n.* —**sigh'ing·ly,** *adv.*

sight (sīt), *n.* **1** power of seeing; vision: *birds have better sight than dogs.* **2** act of seeing; look; glance; gaze: *love at first sight.* **3** limit or range of seeing: *land was in sight.* **4** glimpse: *I caught a sight of him.* **5** something worth seeing: *see the sights of the city.* **6** something that looks queer: *her clothes were a sight.* **7** device on a gun, surveying instrument, etc., to assist in taking aim or observing. **8** observation taken with a telescope or other instrument; aim with a gun, etc. —*v.* **1** see: *at last Columbus sighted land.*

2 take a sight or observation of. **3** aim by means of sights. **4** adjust the sight (of a gun, etc.). **5** provide with sights.
at first sight, immediately upon being seen.
at or **on sight,** as soon as seen.
catch sight of, see; glimpse.
in sight, within view.
lose sight of, forget.
out of sight, *Informal.* unbelievable; extraordinary.
out of sight of, a where one cannot see. **b** where one cannot be seen. [OE (ge)*siht*]
sight·ed (sī′tid), *adj.* **1** able to see. **2** having sights, as on a gun. —*n.* person who can see.
sight·less (sīt′lis), *adj.* **1** blind. **2** not in sight; invisible.
sight·ly (sīt′li), *adj.,* **–li·er, –li·est. 1** pleasing to the sight. **2** affording a fine view. —**sight′li·ness,** *n.*
sight-read (sīt′rēd′), *v.,* **–read, –read·ing.** read a passage on first seeing it, esp. a piece of music.
sight·see·ing (sīt′sē′ing), *n., adj.* going around to see objects or places of interest. —**sight′se′er,** *n.*
sig·ma (sig′mə), *n.* the 18th letter of the Greek alphabet (Σ).
sign (sīn), *n.* **1** any mark or thing used to mean, represent, or point out something. +, –, and ÷ are mathematical signs: *most streets are marked with a street sign and many have a stop sign.* **2** motion or gesture intended to express or convey an idea: *applause is a sign of approval.* **3** indication: *no signs of life, signs of a storm, the hunter found signs of deer.* —*v.* **1** attach one's name to; write: *sign your initials here.* **2** hire; accept employment: *they signed for three years.* **3** communicate by gesture: *sign assent.*
sign away, give by signing one's name; assign.
sign in, register one's presence or arrival by signing.
sign off, a stop broadcasting. **b** quit.
sign on or **up,** join; enlist.
sign out, note one's leaving by signing.
sign over, hand over by signing one's name. [< OF < L *signum*]
sig·nal (sig′nəl), *n., v.,* **–naled, –nal·ing.** *adj.* —*n.* **1** sign giving notice of something. **2** any impulse, sound, etc., transmitted or received. —*v.* **1** make a signal or signals (to). **2** make known by a signal or signals. —*adj.* **1** used as a signal or in signaling. **2** remarkable; striking; notable. [< F, ult. < L *signum* sign] —**sig′nal·er,** *n.*
Signal Corps, part of the United States Army in charge of signaling and communication.
sig·nal·ize (sig′nəl īz), *v.,* **–ized, –iz·ing.** make stand out; make notable.
sig·nal·ly (sig′nəl i), *adv.* remarkably; strikingly; notably.

sig·nal·man (sig′nəl mən; –man′), *n., pl.* **–men.** person in charge of the signals on a railroad, in the army or navy, etc.
sig·na·to·ry (sig′nə tô′ri; –tō′–), *n., pl.* **–ries,** *adj.* —*n.* a signer of a document. —*adj.* signing.
sig·na·ture (sig′nə chər), *n.* **1** a person's name written by himself. **2** a writing of one's name. **3** signs printed at the beginning of a staff to show the pitch, key, and time of a piece. [< LL *signatura,* ult. < L *signum* sign]
sign·board (sīn′bôrd′; –bōrd′), *n.* board having a sign, notice, advertisement, etc., on it.
sig·net (sig′nit), *n.* a small seal: *the order was sealed with the king's signet.* [< OF, ult. < L *signum* seal]
sig·nif·i·cance (sig nif′ə kəns), **sig·nif·i·can·cy** (–kən si), *n.* **1** importance; consequence. **2** meaning. **3** expressiveness; significant quality.
sig·nif·i·cant (sig nif′ə kənt), *adj.* **1** full of meaning; important; of consequence. **2** having a meaning; expressive. **3** having or expressing a hidden meaning. [< L, ppr. of *significare* SIGNIFY] —**sig·nif′i·cant·ly,** *adv.*
significant other, person one lives with but is not married to; partner.
sig·ni·fi·ca·tion (sig′nə fə kā′shən), *n.* **1** meaning; sense. **2** act or process of signifying. Signification relies largely upon words and gestures. —**sig·nif′i·ca′tive,** *adj.*
sig·ni·fy (sig′nə fī), *v.,* **–fied, –fy·ing. 1** be a sign of; mean. **2** make known by signs, words, or actions. **3** have importance; be of consequence; matter: *what a fool says does not signify.* [< L, < *signum* sign + *facere* make] —**sig′ni·fi′er,** *n.*
sign language, communication by means of gestures or specific motions of the hands, esp. as developed for deaf people. American Indians also used sign language.
sign of the zodiac, any of the twelve divisions of the zodiac. Each of them is named after a group of stars.
si·gnor (sē nyôr′), *n. Italian.* **1** Mr.; sir. **2** gentleman.
si·gno·ra (sē nyō′rä), *n., pl.* **–re** (–rā). *Italian.* **1** Mrs. **2** lady.
si·gno·re (sē nyō′rā), *n., pl.* **–ri** (–rē). *Italian.* **1** gentleman. **2** sir.
si·gno·ri·na (sē′nyo re′nä), *n., pl.* **–ne** (–nä). *Italian.* **1** Miss. **2** a young lady.
sign·post (sīn′pōst′), *n.* =guidepost.
Sikh (sēk), *n.* member of a religious sect of N India, famous as fighters.
si·lage (sī′lij), *n.* green food for farm animals, preserved in a silo.
si·lence (sī′ləns), *n., v.,* **–lenced, –lenc·ing,** *interj.* —*n.* **1** absence of sound or noise; stillness. **2** a keeping still; not talking. **3** omission of mention. **4** secrecy. —*v.* stop the speech or noise of; make silent; quiet. —*interj.* be silent! [< OF < L, ult. < *silere* be silent]

si·lenc·er (sī′lən sər), *n.* **1** person or thing that silences. **2** device for deadening the sound of a gun.
si·lent (sī′lənt), *adj.* **1** quiet; still; noiseless: *the silent hills.* **2** not speaking; saying little or nothing: *a silent person.* **3** not spoken; not said out loud: *a silent prayer.* The *e* in *time* is a silent letter. **4** not active; taking no open or active part: *a silent partner.* [< L *silens* being silent] —**si′lent·ly,** *adv.* —**si′lent·ness,** *n.*
sil·hou·ette (sil′ú et′), *n., v.,* **–et·ted, –et·ting.** —*n.* **1** an outline portrait cut out of a black paper or filled in with some single color. **2** a dark image outlined against a lighter background. —*v.* show in outline. [after E. de *Silhouette,* French politician]
sil·i·ca (sil′ə kə), *n.* a hard, white or colorless substance, silicon dioxide, SiO_2. Flint, quartz, and sand are forms of silica. [< NL, < L *silex* flint]
sil·i·cate (sil′ə kit; –kāt), *n.* compound containing silicon with oxygen and an alkali. Mica, soapstone, asbestos, and feldspar are silicates.
sil·i·con (sil′ə kən), *n.* a nonmetallic element, Si, found only combined with other substances. [< *silica*]
sil·i·cone (sil′ə kōn), *n.* organic compound containing silicon, used in lubricants, varnishes, etc.
sil·i·co·sis (sil′ə kō′sis), *n.* disease of the lungs caused by continually breathing air filled with dust from quartz or silicates.
silk (silk), *n.* **1** a fine, soft thread spun by silkworms. **2** cloth made from it. **3** garment of such material. **4** anything like silk: *corn silk.* —*adj.* of, like, or pertaining to silk. [OE *sioloc* < Slavic < Gk. *serikos* < *Seres* the Chinese]
silk·en (sil′kən), *adj.* **1** made of silk: *a silken dress.* **2** like silk; smooth, soft, and glossy: *silken hair.*
silk-stock·ing (silk′stok′ing), —*adj.* elegant; aristocratic: *a silk-stocking affair.* —*n.* an elegant, aristocratic person.
silk·worm (silk′wèrm′), *n.* caterpillar that spins silk to form a cocoon.
silk·y (sil′ki), *adj.,* **silk·i·er, silk·i·est. 1** like silk; smooth, soft, and glossy. **2** of silk. —**silk′i·ly,** *adv.* —**silk′i·ness,** *n.*
sill (sil), *n.* **1** piece of wood or stone across the bottom of a door, window, or house frame. **2** a large, wooden beam on which the wall of a house, etc., rests. [OE, *syll*]
sil·ly (sil′i), *adj.,* **–li·er, –li·est,** *n., pl.* **–lies.** —*adj.* **1** without sense or reason; foolish. **2** stunned; dazed. —*n.* a silly person. [OE *sǣlig* happy < *sǣl* happiness] —**sil′li·ly,** *adv.* —**sil′li·ness,** *n.*
si·lo (sī′lō), *n., pl.* **–los,** *v.,* **–loed, –lo·ing.** —*n.* an airtight building or pit in which green food for farm animals is stored. —*v.* preserve in a silo. [< Sp. < L < Gk. *siros* graincellar]
silt (silt), *n.* very fine earth, sand, etc., carried by moving water and deposited as

sediment. —*v.* fill or choke up with silt. [prob. akin to SALT] —**silt′y,** *adj.*

sil·van (sil′vən), *adj.* =sylvan.

sil·ver (sil′vər), *n.* **1** a shining white, precious metallic element, Ag, used for coins, jewelry, spoons, dishes, etc. **2** coins made from this metal. **3** utensils or dishes made from it: *table silver.* **4** something like silver. **5** the color of silver. —*adj.* **1** made of or plated with silver. **2** of or pertaining to silver. **3** having the color of silver. **4** eloquent: *a silver tongue.* **5** indicating the 25th anniversary. —*v.* cover or coat with silver or something like silver: *silver a mirror.* [OE *siolfor*] —**sil′ver·er,** *n.* —**sil′ver·like′,** *adj.*

sil·ver·fish (sil′vər fish′), *n., pl.* **-fish·es** or (*esp. collectively*) **-fish.** any of various silver-colored insects which damage books and things made of paper.

silver fox, 1 fox whose fur is composed of black hairs with white bands near the tips. **2** this fur.

silver lining, the brighter side of a sad or unfortunate situation.

sil·ver·plat·ed (sil′vər plāt′id), *adj.* covered with a thin layer of silver or similar material.

silver screen, a film or the screen on which motion pictures are shown, esp in a theater: *saw it on the silver screen.*

sil·ver·smith (sil′vər smith′), *n.* person who makes articles of silver.

sil·ver·ware (sil′vər wãr′), *n.* articles made of silver; utensils or dishes made from silver.

sil·ver·y (sil′vər i), *adj.* **1** like silver; like that of silver. **2** containing silver; covered with silver. —**sil′ver·i·ness,** *n.*

sim·i·an (sim′i ən), *adj.* like or characteristic of an ape or monkey. —*n.* ape; monkey. [< L *simia* ape]

sim·i·lar (sim′ə lər), *adj.* **1** much the same; alike; like. **2** of figures, having the same shape. [< F *similaire* < L *similis* like] —**sim′i·lar·ly,** *adv.*

sim·i·lar·i·ty (sim′ə lar′ə ti), *n., pl.* **-ties. 1** being similar; likeness; resemblance. **2** point of resemblance.

sim·i·le (sim′ə lē), *n.* an expressed comparison of two different things or ideas. *Examples:* a face like marble, as brave as a lion. [< L, neut. adj., like]

si·mil·i·tude (sə mil′ə tüd; -tūd), *n.* **1** similarity; likeness; resemblance. **2** comparison. **3** copy; image. [< L, < *similis* like]

sim·i·tar (sim′ə tər), *n.* =scimitar.

sim·mer (sim′ər), *v.* **1** make a murmuring sound while boiling gently. **2** keep at or just below the boiling point; boil gently. **3** be on the point of breaking out: *tensions simmer, anger has simmered for weeks.* —*n.* **1** process of cooking at or just below the boiling point. **2** state of simmering.

simmer down, cool off; calm down.

si·mo·ny (sī′mə ni; sim′ə–), *n.* the making of money out of sacred things. **2** sin

of buying or selling positions, promotions, etc., in the church. [< LL *simonia,* from *Simon* Magus, who tried to buy the power of conferring the Holy Spirit. Acts 8:9–24.] —**si′mon·ist,** *n.*

simp (simp), *n. Informal.* simpleton; fool.

sim·per (sim′pər), *v.* **1** smile in a silly, affected way. **2** express by a simper; say with a simper. —*n.* a silly, affected smile. —**sim′per·er,** *n.* —**sim′per·ing·ly,** *adv.*

sim·ple (sim′pəl), *adj.,* **-pler, -plest,** *n.* —*adj.* **1** easy to do or understand: *simple language.* **2** having few parts; not complex; not involved; elementary: *simple arithmetic.* **3** with nothing added; plain; mere: *the simple truth, simple clothes.* **4** natural; honest; sincere: *a simple manner, a simple heart.* **5** common; ordinary: *a simple soldier, his parents were simple people.* **6** dull; stupid; weak in mind. **7** not divided into parts: *a simple leaf.* **8** not compound; elementary: *a simple, one-celled organism.* **9** composed of only one element. —*n.* **1** a foolish, stupid person. **2** something simple. [< OF < L *simplex*] —**sim′ple·ness,** *n.*

sim·ple-heart·ed (sim′pəl här′tid), *adj.* **1** having or showing a simple, unaffected nature. **2** guileless; sincere. —**sim′ple-heart′ed·ness,** *n.*

simple machine, any of the elementary devices that magnify mechanical force on which other machines are based. The lever, wedge, pulley, wheel and axle, inclined plane, and screw are often called the six simple machines.

sim·ple-mind·ed (sim′pəl mīn′did), *adj.* **1** artless; inexperienced. **2** ignorant; foolish; stupid. **3** feeble-minded. —**sim′ple-mind′ed·ly,** *adv.* —**sim′ple-mind′ed·ness,** *n.*

simple sentence, sentence made up of only one clause, as in, "The dog ran fast."

simple sugar, =monosaccharide.

sim·ple·ton (sim′pəl tən), *n.* a silly person; fool. [< *simple*]

sim·plic·i·ty (sim plis′ə ti), *n., pl.* **-ties. 1** a being simple. **2** freedom from difficulty; clearness. **3** plainness; sincerity. **4** lack of shrewdness; dullness. [< L, < *simplex* simple]

sim·pli·fy (sim′plə fī), *v.,* **-fied, -fy·ing.** make simpler; make plainer or easier. —**sim′pli·fi·ca′tion,** *n.* —**sim′pli·fi′er,** *n.*

sim·plis·tic (sim plis′tik), *adj.* attempting to explain something complex by a single principle; too simple; naive.

sim·ply (sim′pli), *adv.* **1** in a simple manner. **2** without much ornament; without pretense or affectation; plainly: *simply dressed.* **3** merely; only: *he did not simply cry, he yelled.*

sim·u·late (sim′yə lāt), *v.,* **-lat·ed, -lat·ing,** *adj.* —*v.* **1** pretend; feign. **2** act like; look like; imitate: *certain insects simulate leaves.* [< L *simulatus* < *similis* like] —**sim′u·la′tion,** *n.* —**sim′u·la′tive,**

adj. —**sim′u·la′tive·ly,** *adv.* —**sim′u·la′tor,** *n.*

sim·u·lat·ed (sim′yə lat əd), *adj.* fake; pretend; imitative.

si·mul·cast (sī′məl kast′; -käst′), *v.,* **-cast** or **-cast·ed, -cast·ing.** transmit a program over radio and television simultaneously. [< *simul-*(*taneous*) + (*broad*)*cast*]

si·mul·ta·ne·ous (sī′məl tā′ni əs; sim′əl–), *adj.* existing, done, or happening at the same time. [< Med.L *simultaneus* simulated; confused in sense with L *simul* at the same time] —**si′mul·ta′ne·ous·ly,** *adv.* —**si′mul·ta′ne·ous·ness,** *n.*

sin (sin), *n., v.,* **sinned, sin·ning.** —*n.* **1** a breaking of the law of God deliberately. **2** an immoral act; wrongdoing. **3** offense: *sins against good taste.* —*v.* **1** break the law of God. **2** do wrong. **3** offend. [OE *synn*]

since (sins), *prep.* **1** from a past time continuously till now: *the package has been ready since noon.* **2** at any time between (some past time or event and the present): *we have not seen him since Saturday.* —*conj.* **1** in the course of the period following the time when: *he has not written since he left us.* **2** continuously from or counting from the time when: *he has been busy ever since he came.* **3** because: *since you ask, I will tell you.* —*adv.* **1** from then till now: *he got sick last Saturday and has been in bed ever since.* **2** at some time between a particular past time and the present: *at first he refused but since has accepted.* **3** before now; ago: *I heard that old joke long since.* [ME *sinnes, sithenes* < OE *siththan* then, later < *sīth* late]

sin·cere (sin sir′), *adj.,* **-cer·er, -cer·est.** free from pretense or deceit; genuine; real. [< L *sincerus*] —**sin·cere′ly,** *adv.* —**sin·cere′ness,** *n.*

sin·cer·i·ty (sin ser′ə ti), *n., pl.* **-ties.** freedom from pretense or deceit; honesty.

sine (sīn), *n.* in a right triangle, the ratio of the length of the side opposite an acute angle to the length of the hypotenuse. [< L *sinus* bend, bosom, trans. of Ar. *jaib* sine, bosom]

si·ne·cure (sī′nə kyür; sin′ə–), *n.* an extremely easy job; position requiring little or no work and usually paying well. [< Med.L (*beneficium*) *sine cura* (benefice) without cure (of souls)]

si·ne di·e (sī′nē dī′ē), without a day fixed for future action: *the committee adjourned sine die.* [< L, without a day]

si·ne qua non (sī′nē kwā non′), something essential; indispensable condition. [< L, lit., without which not]

sin·ew (sin′ū), *n.* **1** a tough, strong band or cord that joins muscle to bone; tendon. **2** strength; energy. **3** means of strength; source of power. —*v.* furnish with sinews; strengthen as by sinews. [OE *sionu*] —**sin′ew·less,** *adj.*

sin·ew·y (sin′ū i), *adj.* **1** having strong sinews; strong; powerful. **2** vigorous;

forcible. **3** like sinews; tough; stringy. —**sin′ew·i·ness,** *n.*

sin·ful (sin′fəl), *adj.* full of sin; wicked; wrong. —**sin′ful·ly,** *adv.* —**sin′ful·ness,** *n.*

sing (sing), *v.,* **sang** or **sung, sung, sing·ing,** *n.* —*v.* **1** make music with the voice: *he sings on the concert stage.* **2** make pleasant musical sounds: *birds sing.* **3** bring, send, put, etc., with or by singing, or as if by singing: *sing the baby to sleep, he sang the deeds of heroes, sing a person's praises.* **4** make a ringing, whistling, humming, or buzzing sound. —*n.* a singing, esp. in a group.

sing out, call loudly; shout. [OE *singan*]

sing., singular.

singe (sinj), *v.,* **singed, singe·ing,** *n.* —*v.* **1** burn a little, esp. on the ends or edges. **2** remove by a slight burning. —*n.* a minor burn. [OE *sengan*]

sing·er (sing′ər), *n.* person who sings.

Sin·gha·lese (sing′gə lēz′; -lēs′), *n., pl.* **-lese. 1** member of the principal native people of Sri Lanka. **2** their language. —*adj.* of or having to do with these people or their language.

sing·ing (sing′ing), *n.* **1** sound made by one that sings. **2** a ringing in the ears. —*adj.* that sings.

sin·gle (sing′gəl), *adj., n., v.,* **-gled, -gling.** —*adj.* **1** one and no more; only one: *a single piece of paper.* **2** for only one; individual: *a single bed.* **3** not married: *a single man.* **4** having only one on each side: *the knights engaged in single combat.* **5** sincere; honest; genuine: *single devotion to a cause.* —*n.* **1** a single thing or person. **2** hit that allows the batter to reach first base only. —*v.* **1** pick from among others: *the teacher singled Harry out for praise.* **2** make a hit in baseball that allows the batter to reach first base.

singles, game played with only one person on each side. [< OF < L *singulus*] —**sin′gle·ness,** *n.*

sin·gle-breast·ed (sing′gəl bres′tid), *adj.* overlapping across the breast just enough to fasten with only one row of buttons.

single file, line of persons or things arranged one behind another.

sin·gle-hand·ed (sing′gəl han′did), *adj.* without help from others; working alone. —**sin′gle-hand′ed·ly,** *adv.*

sin·gle-mind·ed (sing′gəl mīn′did), *adj.* **1** having only one purpose in mind; determined. **2** sincere; straightforward. —**sin′gle-mind′ed·ly,** *adv.* —**sin′gle-mind′ed·ness,** *n.*

sin·gle·ton (sing′gəl tən), *n.* something occurring singly or apart from others.

sin·gle-track (sing′gəl trak′), *adj.* able to go or act in only one way.

sin·gle·tree (sing′gəl trē′), *n.* =whiffletree.

sin·gly (sing′gli), *adv.* **1** by itself; individually; separately: *consider each point singly.* **2** one by one; one at a time: *misfortunes never come singly.* **3** by one's own efforts; without help.

sing·song (sing′sông′; -song′), *n.* a monotonous tone or rhythm. —*adj.* monotonous in rhythm.

sin·gu·lar (sing′gyə lər), *adj.* **1** extraordinary; unusual: *a scene of singular beauty, singular nocturnal happenings.* **2** being the only one of its kind: *an event singular in history.* **3** one in number. *Boy* is singular; *boys* is plural. **4** separate; individual; private: *a singular matter.* —*n.* **1** the singular number. **2** a word in the singular number. [< L, < *singulus* single] —**sin′gu·lar′i·ty, sin′gu·lar·ness,** *n.* —**sin′gu·lar·ly,** *adv.*

sin·is·ter (sin′is tər), *adj.* **1** showing ill will; threatening: *a sinister rumor, a sinister look.* **2** bad; evil; dishonest. [< L, left; the left side being considered unlucky] —**sin′is·ter·ly,** *adv.* —**sin′is·ter·ness,** *n.*

sink (singk), *v.,* **sank** or **sunk, sunk** or **sunk·en, sink·ing,** *n.* —*v.* **1** go down; go lower and lower: *the sun is sinking, the ship sank with all its crew.* **2** become lower or weaker; reduce: *her voice sank to a whisper.* **3** enter; penetrate: *let the lesson sink into your mind.* **4** make go deep; dig: *the men are sinking a well.* **5** become worse: *sink into poverty, his spirits sank.* —*n.* **1** a shallow basin or tub with a drainpipe. **2** a low-lying area in land where water collects.

sink in, be understood.

sink or swim, fail or try hard to succeed. [OE *sincan*] —**sink′a·ble,** *adj.*

sink·er (singk′ər), *n.* **1** person or thing that sinks. **2** a lead weight for sinking a fishing line or net.

sink·hole (singk′hōl′), *n.* **1 a** hole that drains off surface water. **b** hole where water collects. **c** hole in the ground caused by water underground washing away the dirt, rocks, etc., which supported the surface. **2** drain in a sink. **3** *Fig.* corrupt, wicked place: *a rundown sinkhole at the edge of town.*

sin·ner (sin′ər), *n.* person who sins or does wrong.

sin·u·ous (sin′yü əs), *adj.* **1** having many curves or turns; winding. **2** indirect; morally crooked. [< L, < *sinus* curve] —**sin′u·ous·ly,** *adv.* —**sin′u·ous·ness, sin′u·os′i·ty** *n.*

si·nus (sī′nəs), *n.* **1** cavity in a bone of the skull. **2** a long, narrow abscess with a small opening. **3** a curved hollow; cavity. [< L]

si·nus·i·tis (sī′nəs ī′tis), *n.* inflammation of a sinus, esp. a nasal sinus.

Si·on (sī′ən), *n.* =Zion.

Sioux (sü), *n., pl.* **Sioux** (sü; süz), *adj.* —*n.* **1** member of a group of tribes of American Indians of the Midwestern U.S. **2** the language of the Sioux. —*adj.* of these tribes or their language. —**Siou′an,** *adj.*

sip (sip), *v.,* **sipped, sip·ping,** *n.* —*v.* drink little by little. —*n.* **1** act of sipping. **2** a very small drink. [OE *sypian* take in moisture] —**sip′per,** *n.*

si·phon (sī′fən), *n.* a bent tube through which liquid can be drawn over the

edge of one container into another at a lower level by air pressure. —*v.* draw off by means of a siphon or pass through a siphon. [< L < Gk., pipe]

sir (sèr; *unstressed* sər), *n.* **1** a respectful or formal term of address used to a man. **2 Sir,** title of a knight or baronet: *Sir Walter Scott.* [var. of *sire*]

sire (sīr), *n., v.,* **sired, sir·ing.** —*n.* **1** a male ancestor. **2** the male parent. **3** title of respect used formerly to a great noble and now to a king. —*v.* be the father of. [< OF < VL *seior* < L *senior,* nom., older. Doublet of SENIOR.]

si·ren (sī′rən), *n.* **1** in Greek mythology, nymph who, by her sweet singing, lured sailors to destruction upon the rocks. **2** *Fig.* an alluring, beautiful woman. **3** very loud, wailing horn: *fire sirens.* [< L < Gk. *seiren.*]

Sir·i·us (sir′i əs), *n.* the brightest (fixed) star in the sky; the Dog Star. —**Sir′i·an,** *adj.*

sir·loin (sèr′loin), *n.* cut of beef from the part of the loin in front of the rump. [< var. of OF *surlonge* < *sur* over (< L *super*) + *longe* LOIN]

si·roc·co (sə rok′ō), *n., pl.* **-cos. 1** a hot, dry, dust-laden wind blowing from N Africa across the Mediterranean and S Europe. **2** a moist, warm, south or southeast wind in these same regions. **3** any hot, unpleasant wind. [< F < Ital < Ar. *shoruq* < *sharq* east]

sir·up (sir′əp; sèr′-), *n.* =syrup. —**sir′up·y,** *adj.*

sis (sis), *n.* sister.

sis·al (sis′əl; sī′səl), or **sisal hemp,** *n.* **1** a strong, white fiber, used for making rope, twine, etc. **2** plant that it comes from. [from *Sisal,* town in Yucatán]

sis·sy (sis′i), *n., pl.* **-sies. 1** fearful, timid person. **2** boy or man who acts in a girlish way. **3** sister. [dim. of *sis,* < *sister*] —**sis′sy·ish,** *adj.*

sis·ter (sis′tər), *n.* **1** daughter of the same parents or parent. **2** person or thing resembling or closely associated with another. **3** a female fellow member of a society, church, etc. **4** member of a religious order of women; nun: *Sisters of Charity.* —*adj.* being a sister; related as if by sisterhood. [< Scand. *systir*] —**sis′ter·ly,** *adj.* —**sis′ter·li·ness,** *n.*

sis·ter·hood (sis′tər hùd), *n.* **1** bond between sisters; feeling of sister for sister. **2** association of women with some common aim, characteristic, belief, experience, etc.

sis·ter-in-law (sis′tər in lô′), *n., pl.* **sis·ters-in-law. 1** sister of one's husband or wife. **2** wife of one's brother. **3** wife of the brother of one's husband or wife.

sit (sit), *v.,* **sat, sit·ting. 1** rest on the lower part of the body, with the weight off the feet: *she sat in a chair.* **2** have place or position: *the clock has sat on that shelf for years.* **3** have a seat in an assembly, etc.; be a member of a council: *sit in Congress.* **4** hold a session: *the court* *sits next month.* **5** perch: *a bird sat on the fence.* **6** cover eggs so that they will hatch; brood. **7** fit: *the coat sits well.*

sit down, take a seat; put oneself in a sitting position.

sit in, take part (in a game, conference, etc.): *sometimes sat in with a jazz group.*

sit in on, be present as an observer.

sit on or **upon, a** sit in judgment or council on. **b** have a seat on a jury, commission, etc.

sit through, be present throughout; endure: *sit through a boring film.*

sit tight, wait and not intervene in something.

sit up, a raise the body to a sitting position. **b** keep such a position. **c** stay up instead of going to bed. [OE *sittan*]

sit·com (sit′kom′), *n.* situation comedy.

sit-down strike (sit′doun′), or **sit-down,** *n.* strike in which the workers stay in the factory, store, etc., without working until their demands are met or an agreement is reached.

site (sīt), *n.* position or place (of anything). [< L *situs*]

sit-in (sit′in′), demonstration where protesters sit down and refuse to move, usually to protest against some administrative or government policy, etc.

sit·ter (sit′ər), *n.* **1** person who sits. **2** =baby sitter.

sit·ting (sit′ing), *n.* **1** act of one that sits. **2** a meeting or session of a legislature, court, etc. **3** time of remaining seated.

sitting duck, an easy target or mark.

sit·u·ate (sich′ů āt), *v.,* **–at·ed, –at·ing.** place; locate. [< LL, < L *situs* location]

sit·u·at·ed (sich′ů āt′id), *adj.* **1** placed; located. **2** of persons, being in certain circumstances.

sit·u·a·tion (sich′ů ā′shən), *n.* **1** position; location; place. **2** circumstances; case; condition: *act reasonably in all situations.* **3** place to work; job.

situation comedy, comedy that depends on a contrived or ridiculous situation for its humor.

sit-up (sit′up′), *n.* exercise in which a person lies on the floor and comes to a sitting position without using the hands, arms, or legs to help.

six (siks), *n.* **1** a cardinal number, one more than five. **2** symbol of this number; 6. **3** card or die with six spots. —*adj.* one more than five.

at sixes and sevens, in confusion. [OE *siex*]

six·fold (siks′fōld′), *adj.* **1** six times as much or as many. **2** having six parts. —*adv.* six times as much or as many.

Six Nations, a federation of the Iroquois.

six·pence (siks′pəns), *n.* a British coin, worth about 6 cents.

six·pen·ny (siks′pen′i; –pən i), *adj.* **1** worth or costing sixpence. **2** of little worth; cheap.

six-shoot·er (siks′shüt′ər), *n.* revolver that can fire six shots without being reloaded.

six·teen (siks′tēn′), *n.* **1** a cardinal number, six more than ten. **2** symbol of this number; 16. —*adj.* six more than ten. —**six′teenth,** *adj., n.*

sixteenth note, a musical note having one sixteenth of the time value of a whole note; semiquaver.

sixth (siksth), *adj.* **1** next after the fifth; last in a series of 6. **2** being one of 6 equal parts. —*n.* **1** next after the fifth; last in a series of 6. **2** one of six equal parts. —**sixth′ly,** *adv.*

sixth sense, an unusual power of perception; intuition.

six·ty (siks′ti), *n., pl.* **–ties,** *adj.* —*n.* **1** a cardinal number, six times ten. **2** symbol of this number; 60. —*adj.* six times ten. —**six′ti·eth,** *adj., n.*

six·ty-fourth note (siks′ti fôrth′; –fōrth′), a musical note having the time value of one sixty-fourth of a whole note.

siz·a·ble, size·a·ble (sīz′ə bəl), *adj.* fairly large. —**siz′a·ble·ness, size′a·ble·ness,** *n.* —**siz′a·bly, size′a·bly,** *adv.*

size¹ (sīz), *n., v.,* **sized, siz·ing,** *adj.* —*n.* **1** amount of surface or space a thing takes up: *the size of a city.* **2** extent; amount; magnitude: *size of an industry, undertaking, etc.* **3** a great extent or magnitude: *seek size rather than quality.* **4** one of a series of measures: *his shoes are size 10.* **5** *Informal. Fig.* the actual condition; true description: *that's the size of things here.* —*v.* **1** arrange according to size or in sizes. **2** make of certain size. —*adj.* having size.

cut down to size, reduce the size, self-importance, self-satisfaction, etc., of.

of a size, of the same size.

size up, a form an opinion of; estimate. **b** come up to some size or grade. [ult. var. of *assize,* in sense of "to set standard of weights and measures"]

size² (sīz), *n., v.,* **sized, siz·ing.** —*n.* Also, **siz·ing** (sīz′ing). a sticky substance made from glue, starch, etc., used to glaze paper, cover plaster, stiffen cloth, etc. —*v.* coat or treat with size. [? special use of *size¹*]

siz·zle (siz′əl), *v.,* **–zled, –zling,** *n.* —*v.* make a hissing sound, as fat does when frying. —*n.* a hissing sound.

skate¹ (skāt), *n., v.,* **skat·ed, skat·ing.** —*n.* **1** frame with a blade fastened to a shoe so that a person can glide over ice. **2** a shoe with such a blade fastened to it. **3** a roller skate. —*v.* glide or move along on skates. [< Du. *schaats* < OF *escache* stilt < Gmc.] —**skat′er,** *n.*

skate² (skāt), *n., pl.* **skates** or (*esp. collectively*) **skate.** a kind of broad, flat fish. [< Scand. *skata*]

skate·board (skāt′bôrd′; –bōrd′), *n.* narrow board resembling a surfboard, with roller-skate wheels attached to each end, used for skating. —**skate′board′,** *v.* —**skate′board′er, skate′board′ing,** *n.*

skein (skān), *n.* **1** a small, coiled bundle of yarn or thread. There are 120 yards in a

skein of cotton yarn. **2** a confused tangle. [< OF *escaigne*]

skel·e·ton (skel′ə tən), *n.* **1** the bones of a body, fitted together in their natural places. The skeleton is a frame that supports the muscles, organs, etc. **2** a very thin person or animal. **3** frame: *the steel skeleton of a building.* **4** outline. —*adj.* **1** of, like, or consisting of a skeleton. **2** greatly reduced in numbers; fractional: *a skeleton crew.*

skeleton in the closet, something kept hidden that is embarrassing or shameful. [< NL ≲ Gk., neut. adj., dried up] —**skel′e·tal,** *adj.* —**skel′e·ton·less,** *adj.*

skeleton key, key made to open most locks.

skep·tic (skep′tik), *n.* **1** person who questions the truth of theories or apparent facts; doubter. **2** person who doubts or questions the possibility or certainty of our knowledge of anything. **3** person who doubts the truth of religious doctrines. —*adj.* doubting; skeptical. [< L < Gk. *skeptikos* reflective]

skep·ti·cal (skep′tə kəl), *adj.* **1** of or like a skeptic; inclined to doubt; not believing easily. **2** questioning the truth of theories or apparent facts. —**skep′ti·cal·ly,** *adv.* —**skep′ti·cal·ness,** *n.*

skep·ti·cism (skep′tə siz əm), *n.* **1** a skeptical attitude; doubt; unbelief. **2** doubt or unbelief with regard to religion. **3** doctrine that nothing can be proved absolutely.

sketch (skech), *n.* **1** a rough, quickly done drawing, painting, or design. **2** outline; plan. **3** a short description, story, play, etc. —*v.* **1** make a sketch of; draw roughly. **2** make sketches. [< Du. *schets* < Ital. *schizzo,* ult. < L < Gk. *schedios* impromptu] —**sketch′a·ble,** *adj.* —**sketch′er,** *n.*

sketch·book (skech′bůk′), *n.* **1** book to draw or paint sketches in. **2** book of short descriptions, stories, plays, etc.

sketch·y (skech′i), *adj.,* **sketch·i·er, sketch·i·est. 1** like a sketch; having or giving only outlines or main features. **2** incomplete; done very roughly. —**sketch′i·ly,** *adv.* —**sketch′i·ness,** *n.*

skew (skū), *adj.* **1** twisted to one side; slanting. **2** having a part that deviates from a straight line, right angle, etc. **3** unsymmetrical. —*n.* a twisting or slanting position. —*v.* **1** slant; twist. **2** give a slanting form, position, direction, etc., to. **3** turn aside; swerve. **4** *Fig.* represent unfairly; distort. [< dial. OF *eskiuer* shy away from, eschew < Gmc.]

skew·er (skū′ər), *n.* a long pin of wood or metal stuck through meat to hold it together while it is cooking. —*v.* fasten with or as if with a skewer or skewers.

ski (skē; *Norw.* shē), *n., pl.* **skis, ski,** *v.,* **skied, ski·ing.** —*n.* one of a pair of long, slender pieces of hard wood, fiberglass, etc. that are fastened on to special boots to enable a person to glide over snow. —*v.* glide over the snow on skis. [< Norw.] —**ski′er,** *n.*

skid (skid), *n., v.,* **skid·ded, skid·ding.** —*n.* **1** a slip or slide sideways. **2** a timber, frame, etc., on which something rests, or on which something heavy may slide. —*v.* **1** slip or slide sideways while moving: *the car skidded.* **2** slide along on a skid or skids.

on the skids, *Informal.* headed for dismissal, failure, or other disaster. [cf. OFris, *skid* stick of wood] —**skid′der,** *n.*

skiff (skif), *n.* **1** a light rowboat. **2** a small, light boat. [< F < Ital. *schifo* < Gmc.]

ski lift, means of transporting skiers to the top of a ski slope, often a cable with seats that moves above the ground.

skill (skil), *n.* **1** ability gained by practice, knowledge, etc.; expertness. **2** ability to do things well with one's body or with tools. [< Scand. *skil* distinction] —**skilled,** *adj.* —**skill′less,** *adj.*

skil·let (skil′it), *n.* a shallow pan with a long handle, used for frying.

skill·ful, skil·ful (skil′fəl), *adj.* **1** having skill; expert: *a skillful surgeon.* **2** showing skill: *a skillful production.* —**skill′ful·ly, skil′ful·ly,** *adv.* —**skill′ful·ness, skil′ful·ness,** *n.*

skim (skim), *v.,* **skimmed, skim·ming,** *n.* —*v.* **1** remove from the top: *the cook skims the cream from the milk.* **2** *Fig.* take from; steal, esp. profits, general accounts, etc. **3** move lightly over; glide along: *the swallows were skimming by.* **4** send skimming: *skim a flat stone over the water.* **5** read hastily or carelessly. **6** cover with a thin layer of ice, scum, etc. —*n.* **1** that which is skimmed off. **2** act of skimming. [prob. < OF *escumer* < *escume* scum < Gmc.] —**skim′mer,** *n.*

skim milk, milk from which the butterfat has been removed: *skim milk, also called "fat-free."*

skimp (skimp), *v.* **1** supply in too small an amount. **2** be very saving or economical. **3** do imperfectly. —**skimp′ing·ly,** *adv.*

skimp·y (skimp′i), *adj.,* **skimp·i·er, skimp·i·est. 1** scanty; not enough. **2** too saving or economical. —**skimp′i·ly,** *adv.* —**skimp′i·ness,** *n.*

skin (skin), *n., v.,* **skinned, skin·ning.** —*n.* **1** the covering of the body in persons, animals, fruits, etc., esp. when soft and flexible. **2** hide; pelt. **3** any outer covering. —*v.* **1** take the skin off. **2** shed skin. **3** *Informal.* swindle of money, etc.; cheat. [< Scand. *skinn*] —**skin′less,** *adj.* —**skin′ner,** *n.*

skin-deep (skin′dēp′), *adj.* shallow; slight.

skin diver, swimmer equipped to go skin diving.

skin diving, swimming about under water for long periods of time equipped with oxygen tanks and other gear, esp. as a sport.

skin·flint (skin′flint′), *n.* a stingy person.

skin·ny (skin′i), *adj.,* **-ni·er, -ni·est. 1** very thin; very lean. **2** like skin. **3** infor-

mation, esp. gossip or rumor. —**skin′ni·ness,** *n.*

skip (skip), *v.,* **skipped, skip·ping,** *n.* —*v.* **1** leap lightly; spring; jump: *skip rope.* **2** send or go bounding along a surface: *skip stones on a lake.* **3** pass over; fail to notice; omit: *skip a page.* **4** advance in school, bypassing one or more grades. **5** leave in a hurry. —*n.* **1** a light spring or leap. **2** a passing over. [cf. Scand. (MSw.) *skuppa*] —**skip′per,** *n.*

skip·per (skip′ər), *n.* **1** captain of a ship, esp. of a small trading or fishing boat. **2** any captain or leader. —*v.* act as leader of. [< MDu. *schipper* < *schip* ship]

skirl (skėrl), *v. Scot.* of bagpipes, sound loudly and shrilly. —*n.* sound of a bagpipe. [< Scand. (dial. Norw.) *skrylla*]

skir·mish (skėr′mish), *n.* **1** a slight fight between small groups of soldiers. **2** a slight conflict, argument, contest, etc. —*v.* take part in a skirmish. [< OF *eskirmiss–,* orig., ward off < Gmc.] —**skir′mish·er,** *n.*

skirt (skėrt), *n.* **1** the part of a dress that hangs from the waist. **2** a woman's or girl's garment that hangs from the waist. **3** something like a skirt. **4** border; edge. **5** Usually, **skirts.** outskirts. —*v.* **1** border or edge. **2** pass along the border or edge: *skirt a town to avoid traffic.* **3** be, lie, live, etc., along the border of: *many suburban areas skirt New York City.* [< Scand. *skyrta* shirt] —**skirt′er,** *n.*

skit (skit), *n.* a short sketch that contains humor or satire. [cf. Scand. *skyti* shooter]

ski tow, rope that pulls skiers to the top of a slope.

skit·tish (skit′ish), *adj.* **1** apt to start, jump, or run; easily frightened. **2** fickle; changeable. **3** coy. [prob. < Scand. root akin to *skjōta* shoot] —**skit′tish·ly,** *adv.* —**skit′tish·ness,** *n.*

skit·tles (skit′əlz), *n.* game in which the players try to knock down nine wooden pins by rolling or throwing wooden disks or balls at them. [< Scand. (Dan.) *skyttel* shuttle]

skoal (skōl), *n., interj.* a Scandinavian word used in drinking a health. —*v.* drink the health of. [< Dan., Norw. *skaal* < ONorse *skāl* bowl]

Skt., Sanskrit.

sku·a (skū′ə), or **skua gull,** *n.* any of several large brown sea birds that are related to the gulls; jaeger. [cf. Scand. *skūfr*]

skul·dug·ger·y (skul dug′ər i; –dug′ri), *n.* trickery; dishonesty.

skulk (skulk), *v.* **1** keep out of sight to avoid danger, work, duty, etc.; hide or lurk in a cowardly way. **2** move in a stealthy, sneaking way. —*n.* person who skulks. [< Scand. (Dan.) *skulke*] —**skulk′er,** *n.* —**skulk′ing·ly,** *adv.*

skull (skul), *n.* **1** the bones of the head; the group of bones around the brain. **2** head; brain. [< Scand. (dial. Norw.) *skul* shell] —**skulled,** *adj.* —**skull′-less,** *adj.*

skull·cap (skul′kap′), *n.* a close-fitting cap without a brim.

skunk (skungk), *n.* **1** a black, bushy-tailed animal, usually with white stripes along its back. It is about the size of a cat and gives off a very strong, unpleasant smell when frightened or attacked. **2** fur of this animal, used on coats, etc. **3** *Informal. Fig.* a mean, contemptible person. —*v.* defeat utterly. [< Algonkian]

skunk cabbage, a low, ill-smelling, broad-leaved plant, growing commonly in moist ground.

sky (skī), *n., pl.* **skies,** *v.,* **skied** or **skyed, sky·ing.** —*n.* **1** Often, **skies.** the covering over the world; the region of the clouds or the upper air. **2** Often, **skies.** the heavens or firmament. **3** the celestial heaven. —*v.* hit, throw, or raise high into the air.

out of a clear (blue) sky, suddenly; unexpectedly: *then, out of a clear sky, this letter arrived.*

to the skies, very highly: *praised her to the skies.* [< Scand. *skȳ* cloud]

sky-box (skī′boks′), *n., pl.* **sky·box·es.** place high up in a stadium from which a game can be viewed in comfort. [< *sky* + *box* seat]

sky diving or **sky·div·ing** (skī′dī′ving), *n.* sport of diving from an airplane and opening a parachute only after having fallen a certain distance. —**sky′dive′,** *v.* —**sky diver.**

sky·jack (skī′jak′), *v.* commandeer an aircraft in flight and force it to fly to a different destination. [< *sky* + hi*jack*] —**sky′jack′er,** *n.*

sky·lark (skī′lärk′), *n.* the common European lark, a small bird that sings very sweetly as it flies toward the sky. —*v.* play pranks; frolic. —**sky′lark′er,** *n.*

sky·light (skī′līt′), *n.* window in a roof or ceiling.

sky·line (skī′līn′), *n.* **1** horizon. **2** outline of buildings, mountains, trees, etc., as seen against the sky.

sky marshal, law-enforcement officer assigned to protect passengers and aircraft while in flight.

sky·rock·et (skī′rok′it), *n.* fireworks rocket. —*v.* rise much and quickly, as prices, etc.

sky·scrap·er (skī′skrāp′ər), *n.* a very tall building.

sky·ward (skī′wərd), *adj.* directed toward the sky. —*adv.* Also, **sky′wards.** toward the sky.

sky·writ·ing (skī′rīt′ing), *n.* the tracing of words, etc., against the sky from an airplane, using smoke or some similar substance.

slab (slab), *n.* **1** a broad, flat, thick piece (of stone, wood, meat, etc.). **2** a rough outside piece cut from a log. [ME *slabbe*]

slack (slak), *adj.* **1** not tight or firm; loose: *the rope was slack.* **2** careless: *she is a slack housekeeper.* **3** slow: *a slack pace.* **4** not active; not brisk; dull: *business is slack at this season.* —*n.* **1** part that hangs loose: *the slack of a rope.* **2** a dull season; quiet period: *a slack in business.* **3** a stopping of a strong flow of the tide or a current of water. —*v.* **1** make slack; let up on: *they did not slack their pace.* **2** slake (lime). —*adv.* in a slack manner.

cut (one) some slack, *Slang.* give (one) some time; be patient.

slack off, a loosen. **b** lessen one's efforts.

slack up, slow down; go more slowly. [OE *slæc*] —**slack′ly,** *adv.* —**slack′ness,** *n.*

slack·en (slak′ən), *v.* **1** make or become slower. **2** become less active, vigorous, brisk, etc. **3** make looser: *slacken the rope.* —**slack′en·er,** *n.*

slack·er (slak′ər), *n. Informal.* person who shirks work or evades responsibilities.

slacks (slaks), *n.pl.* loose trousers.

slag (slag), *n., v.,* **slagged, slag·ging.** —*n.* **1** the rough, hard waste left after metal is separated from ore by melting. **2** a light, spongy lava. —*v.* form slag; change into slag. [< MLG *slagge*] —**slag′gy,** *adj.*

slain (slān), *v.* pp. of **slay.**

slake (slāk), *v.,* **slaked, slak·ing. 1** satisfy (thirst, revenge, wrath, etc.); cause to be less active, intense, etc. **2** put out (a fire). **3** change (lime) from CaO to Ca(OH)$_2$ (**slaked lime**) by leaving it in the moist air or putting water on it. **4** become less active, vigorous, intense, etc. [OE *slacian* < *slæc* slack]

sla·lom (slä′lom; slä′ləm), *n.* in skiing, a race over a downhill, twisting course. [< Norw.]

slam (slam), *v.,* **slammed, slam·ming,** *n.* —*v.* **1** shut with force and noise; close with a bang. **2** throw, push, hit, or move hard with force. **3** criticize harshly. —*n.* **1** a violent and noisy closing, striking, etc.; bang. **2** harsh criticism.

slam-bang (slam′bang′), *adj.* forceful.

slam dunk, 1 basketball shot in which the player jumps high enough to place the ball in the hoop. **2** an easy win or success. **3** *Fig.* an absolute uncertainty.

slam·mer (slam′ər), *n. Slang.* Usually, **the slammer.** jail.

slan·der (slan′dər; slän′–), *n.* **1** a false statement meant to do harm. **2** the spreading of false reports. —*v.* **1** talk falsely about. **2** speak or spread slander. [< OF *esclandre* scandal < L *scandalum.* Doublet of SCANDAL.] —**slan′der·er,** *n.*

slan·der·ous (slan′dər əs; –drəs; slän′–), *adj.* **1** containing a slander. **2** speaking or spreading slanders. —**slan′der·ous·ly,** *adv.* —**slan′der·ous·ness,** *n.*

slang (slang), *n.* **1** words, phrases, etc., usually characterized by a special vividness or coloring, and not generally used in formal English. *Nut* and *slammer* are slang. **2** the specialized language of a particular class of people. —**slang′y,** *adj.* —**slang′i·ly,** *adv.* —**slang′i·ness,** *n.*

slant (slant; slänt), *v.* slope. —*n.* **1** slope. **2** mental attitude; way of regarding something. —*adj.* sloping. [? < Scand. (Norw.), *slent* stratum] —**slant′ing,** *adj.* —**slant′ing·ly,** *adv.* —**slant′ly,** *adv.*

slant·wise (slant′wīz′; slänt′–), *adv.* Also, **slant·ways** (slant′wāz′; slänt′–), in a slanting manner; obliquely. —*adj.* slanting; oblique.

slap (slap), *n., v.,* **slapped, slap·ping,** *adv.* —*n.* **1** a blow with the open hand or with something flat. **2** a direct insult or rebuff. —*v.* **1** strike with the open hand or with something flat. **2** put, dash, or cast with force. —*adv.* **1** straight; directly. **2** suddenly. [< LG *slappe*] —**slap′per,** *n.*

slap·dash (slap′dash′), *adv.* hastily and carelessly. —*adj.* hasty and careless. —*n.* hasty, careless action, methods, or work.

slap-hap·py (slap′hap′i), *adj. U.S.* groggy; witless.

slap·stick (slap′stik′), *n.* **1** comedy full of rough play. **2** device made of two long, narrow sticks fastened so as to slap together loudly when a clown, actor, etc., hits somebody with it. —*adj.* full of rough play. In slapstick comedy, the actors knock each other around to make people laugh.

slash (slash), *v.* **1** cut with a sweeping stroke of a sword, knife, etc.; gash: *he slashed the bark off the tree with his knife.* **2** make a slashing stroke. **3** *Fig.* criticize sharply, severely, or unkindly. **4** cut down severely; reduce a great deal. —*n.* **1** a sweeping, slashing stroke. **2** a cut or wound made by such a stroke. [ME *slaschen*] —**slash′er,** *n.* —**slash′ing,** *adj., n.*

slat (slat), *n., v.,* **slat·ted, slat·ting.** —*n.* a long, thin, narrow piece of wood or metal. —*v.* furnish with slats. [ult. < OF *esclat* split piece]

slate (slāt), *n., v.,* **slat·ed, slat·ing,** *adj.* —*n.* **1** a bluish-gray rock that splits easily into thin, smooth layers. Slate is used to cover roofs and for blackboards. **2** a thin piece of this rock. **3** a dark, bluish gray. **4** list of candidates, officers, etc., to be considered for appointment, nomination, etc. —*v.* cover with slate. —*adj.* dark bluish-gray. [< OF *esclate,* var. of *esclat* slat] —**slat′er,** *n.* —**slat′y,** *adj.*

slat·tern (slat′ərn), *n.* woman who is dirty, careless, or untidy in her dress, her ways, her housekeeping, etc. [< *slatter* slop; orig. uncert.] —**slat′tern·ly,** *adj.* —**slat′tern·li·ness,** *n.*

slaugh·ter (slô′tər), *n.* **1** a killing; butchering for food. **2** a massacre. —*v.* **1** kill; butcher. **2** massacre. [< Scand. *slátr* butcher-meat] —**slaugh′ter·er,** *n.*

slaughter house, place where animals are killed for food.

Slav (släv; slav), *n.* member of a group of peoples in E Europe whose languages are related. Russians, Poles, Czechs, Slovaks, Bulgarians, and Yugoslavs are Slavs. —*adj.* of or having to do with the Slavs.

slave (slāv), *n., v.,* **slaved, slav·ing.** —*n.* **1** person who is the property of another. Slaves were bought and sold like horses. **2** *Fig.* person who is controlled or ruled by some desire, habit, or influence: *a slave of drugs.* **3** person who works like a slave. **4** ant that is captured and forced to work for other ants. —*v.* work extremely hard and for long hours. [< OF < Med.L *Sclavus* Slav < LGk. *Sklabos*] —**slave′less,** *adj.*

slave driver, 1 oversee of slaves. **2** an exacting taskmaster.

slave·hold·ing (slāv′hōl′ding), *adj.* owning slaves. —*n.* the owning of slaves. —**slave′hold′er,** *n.*

slav·er[1] (slā′vər), *n.* **1** dealer in slaves. **2** ship used in the slave trade

slav·er[2] (slav′ər), *v.* **1** let saliva run from the mouth. **2** wet with saliva. —*n.* saliva running from the mouth. [< Scand. *slafra*] —**slav′er·er,** *n.*

slav·er·y (slāv′ər i; slāv′ri), *n.* **1** condition of being a slave, the property of another. Many African Americans are the descendants of native Africans who were captured and sold into slavery. **2** custom of owning slaves. **3** *Fig.* condition like that of a slave. **4** hard work like that of a slave.

Slav·ic (släv′ik; slav′–), *adj.* of or pertaining to the Slavs or their languages. —*n.* language or group of languages spoken by the Slavs.

slav·ish (slāv′ish), *adj.* **1** of or pertaining to a slave or slaves. **2** like a slave; mean; base. **3** *Fig.* weakly submitting. **4** like that of slaves; fit for slaves. **5** *Fig.* lacking originality and independence. —**slav′ish·ly,** *adv.* —**slav′ish·ness,** *n.*

Sla·vo·ni·an (slə vō′ni ən), *n.* =Slavic.

slaw (slô), *n.* =coleslaw. [< Du. *sla,* contraction of *salade* SALAD]

slay (slā), *v.,* **slew, slain, slay·ing.** kill with violence. [OE *slēan*] —**slay′er,** *n.*

slea·zy (slē′zi), *adj.,* **–zi·er, –zi·est. 1** flimsy and poor: *sleazy cloth.* **2** cheap; disreputable: *a sleazy bar.* —**slea′zi·ly,** *adv.* —**slea′zi·ness,** *n.*

sled (sled), *n., v.,* **sled·ded, sled·ding.** —*n.* a wooden framework mounted on runners for use on snow or ice. —*v.* **1** ride on a sled. **2** carry on a sled. [< MDu. *sledde*] —**sled′der,** *n.*

sled·ding (sled′ing), *n.* a riding on a sled. **hard** or **tough sledding,** unfavorable conditions; difficulties.

sledge[1] (slej), *n., v.,* **sledged, sledg·ing.** —*n.* sled; sleigh. —*v.* **1** carry on a sledge. **2** ride in a sledge. [< MDu. *sledse*]

sledge[2] (slej), *n., v.,* **sledged, sledg·ing.** —*n.* a sledge hammer (def. 1). —*v.* pound or strike with a sledge. [OE *slecg*]

sledge hammer, 1 a large, heavy hammer. **2** anything powerful and crushing.

sleek (slēk), *adj.* **1** soft and glossy; smooth: *sleek hair.* **2** having smooth, soft skin, hair, fur, etc.: *a sleek cat.* **3** *Fig.* smooth of speech, manners, etc.: *a sleek salesman.* —*v.* **1** smooth. **2** make smooth and glossy; make tidy. [var. of *slick*] —**sleek′er,** *n.* —**sleek′ly,** *adv.* —**sleek′ness,** *n.* —**sleek′y,** *adj.*

sleep (slēp), v., **slept, sleep·ing,** n. —v. **1** rest body and mind; be without ordinary consciousness. **2** pass in sleeping: *sleep away the morning.* **3** be asleep in a particular state or condition: *sleep through winter in hibernation, he slept the sleep of exhaustion.* —n. **1** a condition in which body and mind are very inactive, occurring naturally and regularly in animals. **2** *Fig.* state or condition like sleep: *put those concerns to sleep.*

last sleep, death.

lose sleep over, be unable to sleep because of worry.

sleep off, get rid of by sleeping.

sleep over, spend the night at someone else's house. [OE *slǣpan*] —**sleep′ing,** *adj., n.* —**sleep′less,** *adj.* —**sleep′less·ly,** *adv.* —**sleep′less·ness,** *n.*

sleep·er (slēp′ər), n. **1** person or thing that sleeps. **2** a horizontal beam. **3** a tie to support a railroad track. **4** *Fig.* someone or something that is much better or is more successful than was anticipated.

sleeping bag, a waterproof bag, usually warmly lined, to sleep in out of doors.

sleeping sickness, disease causing fever, inflammation of the brain, sleepiness, and usually death.

sleep·walk·ing (slēp′wôk′ing), n. act of walking while asleep. —*adj.* that walks about while asleep. —**sleep′walk′er,** n.

sleep·wear (slēp′wār′), n. pajamas, nightgowns, etc.; clothing worn in bed.

sleep·y (slēp′ē), *adj.,* **sleep·i·er, sleep·i·est. 1** ready to go to sleep; inclined to sleep. **2** *Fig.* not active; quiet. —**sleep′i·ly,** *adv.* —**sleep′i·ness,** *n.*

sleet (slēt), n. **1** half-frozen rain. **2** the coating of thin ice that coats trees, houses, etc., during winter rains. —v. come down in sleet. [ME] —**sleet′y,** *adj.* —**sleet′i·ness,** *n.*

sleeve (slēv), *n., v.,* **sleeved, sleev·ing.** —n. **1** the part of a garment that covers the arm. **2** tube into which a rod or another tube fits. **3** envelope for a book or disk. —v. furnish with sleeves.

laugh in (or **up**) **one's sleeve,** be amused but not show it.

roll up one's sleeves, get to work, esp. on something difficult.

up one's sleeve, in reserve; ready for use when needed. [OE *slīefe*] —**sleeved,** *adj.* —**sleeve′less,** *adj.*

sleigh (slā), n. carriage or cart mounted on runners for use on ice or snow. —v. travel or ride in a sleigh. [< Du. *slee,* var. of *slede* sled] —**sleigh′er,** n. —**sleigh′ing,** n.

sleight (slīt), n. **1** skill; dexterity. **2** a clever trick. [< Scand. *slǣgth* < *slǣgr* sly]

sleight of hand, 1 skill and quickness in moving the hands. **2** tricks or skill of a modern magician; juggling.

slen·der (slen′dər), *adj.* **1** long and thin; not big around: *a slender girl, a slender pen.* **2** slight; small; scanty: *a slender meal, a slender hope.* [ME *slendre*]

sclendre] —**slen′der·ly,** *adv.* —**slen′der·ness,** *n.*

slen·der·ize (slen′dər īz), v. **–ized, –iz·ing. 1** make slender. **2** cause to look slender.

slept (slept), v. pt. and pp. of **sleep.**

sleuth (slüth), n. **1** bloodhound. **2** detective. —v. be or act like a detective. [< Scand. *slōth* trail]

slew[1] (slü), v. pt. of **slay.**

slew[2] (slü), *v., n.* turn; swing; twist. Also, **slue.**

slew[3] (slü), n. a swampy place; marshy inlet. Also, **slough, slue.** [var. of *slough*[1]]

slew[4] (slü), n. *Informal.* a lot; large number or amount: *a slew of guests.* Also, **slue.** [? < Irish *sluagh* host, crowd]

slice (slīs), *n., v.,* **sliced, slic·ing.** —n. **1** a thin, flat, broad piece cut from something. **2** a slicing hit, in golf. —v. **1** cut into slices. **2** cut (off) as a slice. **3** hit (a golf ball) so that it curves to one's right, if right-handed. [< OF *esclice* thin chip < Gmc.] —**slic′er,** n.

slick (slik), *adj.* **1** sleek; smooth: *slick hair.* **2** slippery; greasy. **3** *Fig.* sly; tricky. [ME *slike;* akin to OE *slician* make smooth] —v. **1** make sleek or smooth. **2** make smart or pretentious. —n. a smooth place or spot. —*adv.* smoothly; slyly; cleverly. [OE *slician*] —**slick′ly,** *adv.* —**slick′ness,** *n.*

slick·er (slik′ər), n. a long, loose waterproof coat.

slide (slīd), *v.,* **slid** (slid), **slid** or **slidden** (slid′ən), **slid·ing,** n. —v. **1** move smoothly along a surface: *slide on ice.* **2** move easily or quietly or secretly: *the thief slid in the window.* **3** pass without heeding or being heeded: *let things slide.* **4** pass by degrees; slip: *slide into bad habits, time slid by.* —n. **1** act of sliding. **2** a smooth surface for sliding on. **3** mass of earth, snow, etc., sliding down. **4** the sliding down of such a mass. **5** a small, thin sheet of glass on which objects are put for microscopic examination. **6** shoe without a back. [OE *slīdan*] —**slid′er,** n. —**slid′ing,** *adj.*

sliding scale, scale of wages, prices, taxes, etc., that can be adjusted according to certain conditions.

slight (slīt), *adj.* **1** not much; not important; small: *the event had slight consequence.* **2** not big around; slender: *a slight person.* **3** frail; flimsy: *a slight excuse.* —v. treat as of little value; pay too little attention to; neglect: *slight work, feel slighted.* —n. a slighting treatment; act of neglect. [OE *–sliht* level, as in *eorthslihtes* level with the ground] —**slight′er,** n. —**slight′ing,** *adj.* —**slight′ing·ly,** *adv.* —**slight′ly,** *adv.*

sli·ly (slī′li), *adv.* =slyly.

slim (slim), *adj.,* **slim·mer, slim·mest,** *v.,* **slimmed, slim·ming.** —*adj.* **1** slender; thin. **2** small; slight; weak: *a slim answer.* —v. **1** make slim. **2** become slim. [< Du., bad] —**slim′ly,** *adv.* —**slim′mish,** *adj.* —**slim′ness,** *n.*

slime (slīm), *n., v.,* **slimed, slim·ing.** —n. **1** soft, sticky mud or something like it. **2** a sticky substance given off by snails, slugs, fish, etc. **3** disgusting filth. —v. **1** cover or smear with or as with slime. **2** remove slime from. [OE *slīm*]

slim·y (slīm′i), *adj.,* **slim·i·er, slim·i·est. 1** covered with slime. **2** of or like slime. **3** disgusting; filthy. —**slim′i·ly,** *adv.* —**slim′i·ness,** *n.*

sling (sling), *n., v.,* **slung, sling·ing.** —n. **1** strip of leather with a string fastened to each end, for throwing stones. **2** a throw; hurling. **3** a hanging loop of cloth fastened around the neck to support a hurt arm. **4** loop of rope, band, chain, etc., by which heavy objects are lifted, carried, or held. [< v.] —v. **1** throw with a sling. **2** throw; cast; hurl; fling. **3** raise, lower, etc., with a sling. **4** hang in a sling; hang so as to swing loosely. [< Scand. *slyngva*] —**sling′er,** n.

sling·back (sling′bak′), n. women's shoe that has a strap around the heel rather than a closed back.

sling·shot (sling′shot′), n. a Y-shaped stick with a rubber band fastened to its prongs, used to shoot pebbles, etc.

slink (slingk), *v.,* **slunk** or (*Archaic*) **slank, slunk, slink·ing.** move in a sneaking, guilty manner; sneak [OE *slincan*] —**slink′ing·ly,** *adv.*

slink·y (sling′ki), *adj.* **slink·i·er, slink·i·est. 1** stealthy; sneaky. **2** close fitting: *long, slinky dress.*

slip[1] (slip), *v.,* **slipped** or (*Archaic*) **slipt, slipped, slip·ping,** n. —v. **1** go or move smoothly, quietly, easily, or quickly: *she slipped out of the room, time slips by, the ship slips through the waves.* **2** slide; move out of place: *the knife slipped and cut him.* **3** slide suddenly without wanting to: *he slipped on the icy sidewalk.* **4** put, pass, or draw smoothly, quietly, or secretly: *slip one's shoes off, slip the note into Mary's hand.* **5** get away from; escape from: *your name has slipped my mind.* **6** make a mistake or error. —n. **1** act or fact of slipping. **2** thing that can be slipped on or off; covering: *pillows are covered by slips.* **3** a sleeveless garment worn under a dress. **4** mistake; error: *he makes slips in grammar.* **5** space for ships between wharves or in a dock.

let slip, tell without meaning to.

slip one over on, get the advantage of, esp. by trickery.

slip up, make a mistake or error. [prob. < MLG *slippen*]

slip[2] (slip), *v.,* **slipped** or (*Archaic*) **slipt, slipped, slip·ping.** —v. cut branches from (a plant) to grow new plants; take (a part) from a plant. —n. **1** a narrow strip of paper, wood, etc. **2** a young, slender person. **3** a small branch or twig cut from a plant, used to grow a new plant. [prob. MDu., MLG *slippe* a cut]

slip case, cardboard boxlike cover for a book, several disks, etc.

slip cover, a removable cloth cover for upholstered furniture.

slip knot, 1 knot made to slip along the rope or cord around which it is made. **2** knot that can be undone by a pull.

slip-on (slip'on; –ôn´), *adj.* **1** that can be put on or taken off easily or quickly: *slip-on shoes.* **2** that must be put on or taken off over the head. —*n.* a slip-on blouse, sweater, etc.

slip·page (slip'ij), *n.* **1** a slipping; slide. **2** amount or extent of slipping: *an annual rate of slippage that is too great.*

slip·per (slip'ər), *n.* **1** a kind of light, low shoe. **2** person or thing that slips. —**slip'pered,** *adj.*

slip·per·y (slip'ər i; slip'ri), *adj.,* **–per·i·er, –per·i·est, 1** causing or likely to cause slipping. **2** slipping away easily. **3** shifty; tricky. [ME alter. of OE *slipor* slippery] —**slip'per·i·ness,** *n.*

slippery elm, 1 an elm tree of E North America having an inner bark which becomes slippery when moistened. **2** the inner bark.

slip·shod (slip'shod´), *adj.* careless in dress, habits, speech, etc.; untidy; slovenly. —**slip'shod'ness,** *n.*

slip·stream (slip'strēm´), *n.* **1** current of air produced by a propeller or jet engine. **2** current of air left behind a moving vehicle.

slipt (slipt), *v. Archaic.* pt. of **slip.**

slip-up (slip'up´), *n.* mistake; error.

slit (slit), *v.,* **slit, slit·ting,** *n.* —*v.* cut or tear in a straight line; make a long, straight cut or tear in. —*n.* a straight, narrow cut, tear, or opening. [OE *slitc*] —**slit'ter,** *n.*

slith·er (slith'ər), *v.* slide down or along a surface, esp. unsteadily; go with a sliding motion. —*n.* such a movement; a slide. [OE *slidrian*]

slith·er·y (slith'ər i), *adj.* slippery; crawly; creepy.

sliv·er (sliv'ər), *n.* **1** a long, thin piece that has been split off, broken off, or cut off; splinter. **2** a loose fiber of wool, cotton, etc. —*v.* split or break into slivers. [ult. < OE *slifan* split] —**sliv'er·er,** *n.*

slob (slob), *n.* a lazy, careless, or untidy person. [prob. < Irish *slab* mud < Gmc.]

slob·ber (slob'ər), *v.* **1** let liquid run out from the mouth; drool. **2** wet or smear with saliva, etc. **3** *Fig.* speak in a silly, sentimental way. —*n.* **1** saliva or other liquid running out from the mouth. **2** *Fig.* silly, sentimental talk or emotion; drivel. [prob. ult. < Du. *slabberen*] —**slob'ber·er,** *n.* —**slob'ber·ing,** *adj.* —**slob'ber·ing·ly,** *adv.* —**slob'ber·y,** *adj.* —**slob'ber·i·ness,** *n.*

sloe (slō), *n.* **1** a dark-purple, plumlike fruit. **2** a thorny shrub that it grows on; blackthorn. [OE *slāh*]

sloe-eyed (slō'īd´), *adj.* having dark or slanted eyes.

slog (slog), *v.,* **slogged, slog·ging,** *n.* —*v.* **1** hit hard. **2** plod heavily. —*n.* a hard blow. [var. of *slug²*] —**slog'ger,** *n.*

slo·gan (slō'gən), *n.* **1** word or phrase used by a business, club, political party, etc., to advertise its purpose; motto. **2** a war cry; battle cry. [< Scotch Gaelic, < *sluagh* army + *gairm* cry]

sloop (slüp), *n.* sailboat having one mast, a mainsail, a jib, and sometimes other sails. [< Du. *sloep,* earlier *sloepe.* Doublet of SHALLOP.]

slop (slop), *v.,* **slopped, slop·ping,** *n.* —*v.* **1** spill liquid upon; spill; splash. **2** splash through mud, slush, or water. —*n.* **1** liquid carelessly spilled or splashed about. **2** a thin liquid mud or slush.

slop over, a spill or slosh liquid over. **b** *Fig.* show too much feeling, enthusiasm, etc.

slops, a dirty water; liquid garbage; swill. **b** liquid or semiliquid food; a bland, unappetizing food. [cf. OE *cūsloppe* cow slobber]

slope (slōp), *v.,* **sloped, slop·ing,** *n.* —*v.* go up or down at an angle: *the land slopes toward the sea.* —*n.* **1** any line, surface, land, etc., that goes up or down at an angle. **2** amount of slope. [< OE *slopen,* pp. of *–slūpan* slip] —**slop'er,** *n.* —**slop'ing,** *adj.* —**slop'ing·ly,** *adv.* —**slop'ing·ness,** *n.*

slop·py (slop'i), *adj.,* **–pi·er, –pi·est. 1** very wet; slushy. **2** splashed or soiled with liquid. **3** careless; slovenly. —**slop'pi·ly,** *adv.* —**slop'pi·ness,** *n.*

slosh (slosh), *v.* **1** splash in slush, mud, or water. **2** dump or pour water or other liquid: *sloshed the coffee.* **3** swirl water or liquid in a bucket.

slot (slot), *n.,* *v.,* **slot·ted, slot·ting.** —*n.* a small, narrow opening or depression. —*v.* make a slot or slots in. [< OF *esclot* the hollow between breasts]

sloth (slōth; slôth), *n.* **1** unwillingness to work or exert oneself; laziness; idleness. **2** a very slow-moving animal of South and Central America that lives in trees. Sloths hang upside down from tree branches. [< *slow*]

sloth·ful (slōth'fəl; slôth'–), *adj.* unwilling to work or exert oneself; lazy; idle. —**sloth'ful·ly,** *adv.* —**sloth'ful·ness,** *n.*

slot machine, machine, esp. for gambling or for dispensing snacks and drinks, that is worked by dropping a coin into a slot.

slouch (slouch), *v.* **1** stand, sit, walk, or move in an awkward, drooping manner: *the weary man slouched along.* **2** droop or bend downward. —*n.* **1** a bending forward of head and shoulders; awkward, drooping way of standing, sitting, or walking. **2** *Esp. U.S.* an awkward, slovenly, or inefficient person. —**slouch'ing,** *adj.* —**slouch'y,** *adj.* —**slouch'i·ly,** *adv.* —**slouch'i·ness,** *n.*

slough¹ (slou *for 1 and 3;* slü *for 2*), *n.* **1** a soft, deep muddy place; mud hole. **2** =slew³. **3** hopeless despair; discouragement. [OE *slōh*] —**slough'y,** *adj.*

slough² (sluf), *n.* the old skin shed or cast off by a snake. —*v.* drop off; throw off; shed. [ME *slugh(e),* *slouh*] —**slough'y,** *adj.*

Slo·vak (slō'vak), *n.* **1** member of a Slavic people living in Slovakia. The Slovaks are closely related to the Bohemians and the Moravians. **2** their language. —*adj.* of or having to do with Slovakia, its people, or their language.

Slo·va·ki·a (slō vä'ki ə; –vak'i ə), *n.* country in C Europe. —**Slo·va'ki·an,** *adj., n.*

slov·en (sluv'ən), *n.* person who is untidy, dirty, or careless in dress, appearance, habits, work, etc. —*adj.* untidy; dirty; careless. [? ult. < Flem. *sloef* dirty, Du. *slof* careless]

Slo·vene (slō'vēn), *n.* **1** member of a Slavic group of people living in Slovenia. The Slovenes are closely related to the Croats, Serbians, and other S Slavs. **2** their language. —*adj.* of or having to do with Slovenia, its people, or their language. Also **Slovenian.**

Slo·ve·ni·a (slō vē'ni ə; –vēn'yə), *n.* country in SE Europe. —**Slo·ve'ni·an,** *adj., n.*

slov·en·ly (sluv'ən li), *adj.,* **–li·er, –li·est,** *adv.* —*adj.* untidy, dirty, or careless in dress, appearance, habits, work, etc. —*adv.* in a slovenly manner. —**slov'en·li·ness,** *n.*

slow (slō), *adj.* **1** taking a long time; taking longer than usual; not fast or quick: *a slow journey.* **2** behind time; running at less than proper speed: *a slow runner, a slow clock.* **3** causing a lower rate of speed: *a slow track.* **4** burning or heating gently: *a slow flame.* **5** sluggish; dull: *a slow pupil, this book is very slow.* —*v.* make slow or slower; reduce the speed of: *slow down a car, slow up when you go through a town.* —*adv.* in a slow manner. [OE *slāw*] —**slow'ly,** *adv.* —**slow'ness,** *n.*

slow mo·tion (slō'mō'shən), *adj.* **1** moving at less than normal speed. **2** showing action at much less than its actual speed.

slow·poke (slō'pōk´), *n. Informal.* someone or something that moves very slowly.

sludge (sluj), *n.* **1** soft mud; mire; slush. **2** small broken pieces of floating ice.

slue¹ (slü), *v.,* **slued, slu·ing,** *n.* slew².

slue² (slü), *n.* slew³.

slue³ (slü), *n.* slew⁴.

slug¹ (slug), *n.* **1** a slow-moving animal like a snail, without a shell or with only a very small shell. **2** caterpillar or larva that looks like a slug. **3** any slow-moving person, animal, wagon, etc. **4** bullet for firing from a gun. [? < Scand. (dial. Sw.) *slogga* be sluggish]

slug² (slug), *v.,* **slugged, slug·ging,** *n.* —*v.* **1** hit hard with the fist. **2** strike violently. —*n.* a hard blow with the fist. —**slug'ger,** *n.* —**slug'ging,** *n.*

slug·gard (slug'ərd), *n.* a lazy, idle person. —*adj.* lazy; idle [ult. < *slug¹*] —**slug'gard·ly,** *adj.*

slug·gish (slug'ish), *adj.* **1** slow-moving; not active; lacking energy or vigor. **2**

lazy; idle. [< slug[1]] —slug′gish·ly, adv. —slug′gish·ness, n.

sluice (slüs), n., v., sluiced, sluic·ing. —n. 1 structure with a gate for holding back or controlling the water of a canal, river, or lake. 2 Also, sluice gate. gate that holds back or controls the flow of water. 3 a long, sloping trough through which water flows, used to wash gold from sand, dirt, or gravel. 4 channel for carrying off water. —v. 1 flow or pour in a stream; rush. 2 flush or cleanse with a rush of water; pour or throw water over. 3 send (logs, etc.) along a channel of water. [< OF escluse, ult. < L ex- out + claudere shut]

slum (slum), n., v., slummed, slum·ming. —n. street, alley, etc., in a crowded, dirty part of a city or town. —v. 1 go into or visits slums. 2 Fig. go to a place thought of as inferior to what one is accustomed to, as a bar or dance hall.

the slums, a crowded, dirty part of a city or town, where the poorest people live. —slum′ming, n.

slum·ber (slum′bər), v. 1 sleep. 2 be inactive: the volcano had slumbered for years. —n. 1 a light sleep. 2 an inactive state or condition. [ult. < OE slūma, n.] —slum′ber·er, n. —slum′ber·less, adj.

slum·ber·ous (slum′bər əs), slum·brous (-brəs), adj. 1 sleepy. 2 causing sleep. 3 inactive; sluggish; calm.

slump (slump), v., drop heavily; fall suddenly. —n. a heavy or sudden fall.

slung (slung), v. pt. and pp. of sling.

slunk (slungk), v. pt. and pp. of slink.

slur (slėr), v., slurred, slur·ring, n. —v. 1 pass lightly over; go through hurriedly or in a careless way: slur over a person's faults. 2 pronounce indistinctly: many persons slur "how do you do." 3 speak or write sounds, letters, etc., so indistinctly that they run into each other. 4 a sing or play (two or more tones of different pitch) without a break; run together in a smooth, connected manner. b mark with a slur. 5 harm the reputation of; insult; slight. —n. 1 a slurred pronunciation, sound, etc. 2 a a slurring of tones. b a curved mark (⌢) (⌣) indicating this. 3 blot or stain (upon reputation); insulting or slighting remark: slur on a person's good name. [ME slor mud] —slur′ring·ly, adv.

slurp (slėrp), v. Informal. eat or drink with a sloppy, gurgling noise. —n. sloppy, gurgling noise.

slush (slush), n. 1 partly melted snow; snow and water mixed. 2 soft mud. 3 silly, sentimental talk, writing, etc. —slush′y, adj. —slush′i·ness, n.

slush fund, money siphoned off from general funds and put aside for usually illegal purposes.

slut (slut), n. 1 a dirty, untidy woman. 2 woman of loose morals. —slut′tish, adj. —slut′tish·ly, adv. —slut′tish·ness, n.

sly (slī), adj., sly·er, sly·est, or sli·er, sli·est, n. —adj. 1 able to do things without letting others know; acting secretly: a sly thief. 2 cunning; crafty; tricky; wily: a sly plot, sly questions. 3 playfully mischievous or knowing: a sly wink.

on the sly, in a sly way; secretly. [< Scand. slœgr] —sly′ish, adj. —sly′ly, adv. —sly′ness, n.

Sm, samarium.

smack[1] (smak), n. 1 a slight taste or flavor. 2 trace; suggestion. —v. have a smack. [OE smœcc]

smack[2] (smak), v. 1 open (the lips) quickly so as to make a sharp sound. 2 kiss loudly. 3 slap. —n. 1 a smacking movement of the lips. 2 the sharp sound made in this way. 3 a loud kiss, slap, or crack. —adv. 1 directly; squarely. 2 suddenly and sharply; with or as if with a smack. [ult. imit.]

smack[3] (smak), n. a small sailboat with one mast. [prob. <Du. smak]

smack[4] (smak), n. Slang. heroin.

smack·ing (smak′ing), adj. lively, brisk, or strong.

small (smôl), adj. 1 not large; little; not great in amount, degree, extent, duration, value, strength, etc.: a small house, a small dose, small hope of success. 2 not important: a small matter. 3 not prominent; of low social position; humble; poor: both the great and the small mourned Lincoln's death. 4 having little land, capital, etc.: a small farmer. 5 mean; not generous: a small nature. 6 of letters, not capital. —adv. 1 into small pieces. 2 in low tones. 3 in a small manner. —n. 1 that which is small. 2 the small, narrow, or scanty part.

feel small, be ashamed or humiliated. [OE smœl] —small′ish, adj. —small′ness, n.

small arms, weapons easily carried by a person, such as rifles or revolvers.

small change, 1 coins of small value, as nickels or dimes. 2 Fig. anything unimportant or of small worth.

small fry, 1 babies or children; small or young creatures. 2 small fish. 3 unimportant people or things.

small hours, the early hours of the morning.

small intestine, part of the intestines, from the stomach to the large intestine.

small potatoes, Informal. an unimportant person or thing; unimportant persons or things.

small·pox (smôl′poks′), n. a very contagious disease characterized by fever and blisterlike eruptions on the skin that often leave permanent scars shaped like little pits.

small talk, conversation about unimportant matters; chat.

small-time (smôl′tīm′), adj. second-rate; inconsequential.

smart (smärt), v. 1 cause or feel sharp pain: his eyes smarted. 2 feel or suffer distress or irritation: he smarted from

the scolding. [OE smeortan] —n. a sharp pain: the smart of a cut. —adj. 1 sharp; severe: a smart blow. 2 keen; active; lively: a smart pace. 3 clever; bright; shrewd: a smart child. 4 fresh and neat; in good order: smart in his uniform. 5 stylish; fashionable: smart restaurants. —adv. in a smart manner.

smarts, Informal. intelligence. [OE smeart] —smart′ly, adv. —smart′ness, n.

smart al·eck (al′ik), a conceited, obnoxious person. —smart′-al′eck·y, adj.

smart·en (smär′tən), v. 1 improve in appearance; brighten. 2 make or become brisker.

smart·y (smär′ti), n. brash, self-confident person; smart aleck.

smash (smash), v. 1 break into pieces with violence and noise: smash a window. 2 destroy; shatter; ruin: smash an argument. 3 be broken to pieces: the dishes smashed on the floor. 4 become ruined. 5 rush violently; crash: the car smashed into a tree. 6 crush; defeat: smash an attack. 7 hit (a tennis ball) with a hard, fast overhand stroke. 8 hit a hard blow. —n. 1 a violent breaking; shattering; crash: smash of two automobiles. 2 sound of a smash or crash: the smash of broken glass. 3 a crushing defeat; disaster. 4 a hard, fast overhand stroke in tennis. 5 a hard blow. [blend of SMACK[2] and MASH] —smash′er, n.

smash-up (smash′up′), n. a bad collision; wreck.

smat·ter·ing (smat′ər ing), n. slight or superficial knowledge. —smat′ter·ing·ly, adv.

smear (smir), v. 1 cover or stain with anything sticky, greasy, or dirty. 2 rub or spread (oil, grease, paint, etc.). 3 Fig. harm; soil; spoil: smear a person's reputation. —n. 1 mark or stain left by smearing. 2 Fig. a malicious attack. [OE smeoru grease]

smell (smel), v., smelled or smelt (smelt), smell·ing, n. —v. 1 perceive with the nose: smell smoke. 2 use the sense of smelling. 3 give out a smell. 4 give out a bad smell; have a bad smell. 5 Fig. find a trace or suggestion of, esp. through shrewdness: smell trouble brewing. 6 Fig. have the trace (of): the plan smells of trickery. 7 hunt or find by smelling or as if by smelling: smell out a fugitive, smell out a theft. —n. 1 act of smelling. 2 sense of smelling. 3 quality in a thing that affects the sense of smell: the smell of smoke. 4 Fig. trace; suggestion: the distinctive smell of corruption. [ME smelle(n)] —smell′a·ble, adj. —smell′er, n. —smell′y, adj.

smelling salts, a form of ammonia inhaled to relieve faintness, headaches, etc.

smelt[1] (smelt), v. melt (ore) in order to get the metal out of it. [< MDu., MLG smelten]

smelt[2] (smelt), n., pl. smelts or (esp. collectively) smelt. a small, edible sea fish with silvery scales. [OE]

smelt·er (smel′tər), *n.* **1** place where ores or metals are smelted. **2** furnace for smelting ores.

smi·lax (smī′laks), *n.* **1** a twining, trailing plant or vine, much used by florists in decoration. **2** any of a large group of woody vines with prickly stems, umbrella-shaped clusters of flowers, and blackish or red berries. [< L < Gk.]

smile (smīl), *v.,* **smiled, smil·ing,** *n.* —*v.* **1** look pleased or amused; show pleasure, favor, kindness, amusement, etc., by an upward curve of the mouth. **2** *Fig.* look pleasant or agreeable; look with favor: *fortune smiled upon the enterprise.* **3** bring, put, drive, etc., by smiling: *smile one's tears away, smile consent.* —*n.* **1** act of smiling. **2** *Fig.* a favoring look or regard; pleasant look or aspect. [ME *smile(n)*] —**smile′less,** *adj.* —**smil′er,** *n.* —**smil′ing·ly,** *adv.* —**smil′ing·ness,** *n.*

smirch (smėrch), *v.* soil with soot, dirt, dust, dishonor, disgrace, etc. —*n.* a dirty mark; blot. [? < OF *esmorcher* torture] —**smirch′er,** *n.*

smirk (smėrk), *v.* smile in an affected, silly, self-satisfied way. —*n.* an affected, silly, self-satisfied smile. [OE *smearcian* to smile] —**smirk′er,** *n.* —**smirk′ing·ly,** *adv.*

smite (smīt), *v.,* **smote, smit·ten** or **smit** (smit), **smit·ing. 1** strike; strike or hit hard. **2** affect with sudden pain, disease, etc. [OE *smītan*]

smith (smith), *n.* **1** person who makes or shapes things out of metal. **2** =blacksmith. [OE]

smith·er·eens (smith′ər ēnz′), *n.pl.* small pieces; bits.

smith·y (smith′i; smith′i), *n.,* pl. **smith·ies.** workshop of a smith, esp. a blacksmith. [< *smith*]

smit·ten (smit′ən), *adj.* **1** hard hit; struck. **2** suddenly and strongly affected. **3** very much in love. —*v.* pp. of **smite.**

smock (smok), *n.* a loose outer garment worn to protect clothing. —*v.* ornament (a dress etc.) with a honeycomb pattern made of lines of stitches crossing each other diagonally. [OE *smocc*] —**smock′ing,** *n.*

smog (smog), *n.* a combination of smoke and fog in the air. [blend of *smoke* and *fog*]

smoke (smōk), *n.,* *v.,* **smoked, smok·ing.** —*n.* **1** a visible mixture of gases and particles of carbon which rises when anything burns; cloud caused by anything burning. **2** something resembling this. **3** that which is smoked; cigar, cigarette, pipe, etc. **4** act of smoking tobacco. —*v.* **1** give off smoke or steam, or something like it. **2** cure (meat, fish, etc.) by smoking. **3** draw into the mouth and puff out the smoke of burning tobacco or the like.

go up in smoke, disappear; vanish: *plans went up in smoke.*

smoke out, a drive out with smoke. **b** find out and make known. [OE *smoca*]

smoke·house (smōk′hous′), *n.* a building or place in which meat, fish, etc., are treated with smoke to keep them from spoiling.

smoke·less (smōk′lis), *adj.* **1** making or giving off little or no smoke: *smokeless powder.* **2** having little or no smoke.

smok·er (smōk′ər), *n.* **1** person who smokes tobacco. **2** device that produces smoke, as for smoking out bees.

smoke screen, mass of thick smoke used to hide a ship, airplane, etc., from the enemy.

smoke·stack (smōk′stak′), *n.* **1** a tall chimney. **2** pipe that discharges smoke, etc. —*adj.* of or having to do with heavy industry, esp. those factories that pollute.

smok·y (smōk′i), *adj.,* **smok·i·er, smok·i·est. 1** giving off much smoke. **2** full of smoke. **3** darkened or stained with smoke. **4** like smoke or suggesting smoke: *a smoky taste.* —**smok′i·ly,** *adv.* —**smok′i·ness,** *n.*

smol·der (smōl′dər), *v.* **1** burn and smoke without flame. **2** exist inwardly with little or no outward sign. **3** show suppressed feeling: *the angry man's eyes smoldered.* —*n.* a slow, smoky burning without flame; smoldering fire. Also, **smoulder.** [var. of ME *smorther* SMOTHER] —**smol′der·ing·ly,** *adv.*

smooth (smüth), *adj.* **1** having an even surface, like glass, silk, or still water; flat; level: *smooth stones.* **2** free from unevenness or roughness: *smooth sailing.* **3** without lumps: *smooth sauce.* **4** without hair: *a smooth face.* **5** without trouble or difficulty; easy: *a smooth course of affairs.* **6** polished; pleasant; polite: *a smooth talker.* **7** not harsh in sound or taste: *smooth wine.* —*v.* **1** make smooth or smoother. **2** *Fig.* make calmer. **3** *Fig.* make easy: *smooth away obstacles.* **4** remove (projections, etc.). —*adv.* in a smooth manner.

smooth over, make (something) seem less wrong or unpleasant: *smooth over a disagreement.* [OE *smōth*] —**smooth′er,** *n.* —**smooth′ly,** *adv.* —**smooth′ness,** *n.*

smooth·bore (smüth′bôr′; -bōr′), *adj.* not rifled.

smooth·ie (smü′thē), *n.* **1** urbane, pleasant person. **2** cold drink made with fruit, yogurt, and crushed ice blended together. Also, **smoothy.**

smooth muscle, muscle contracted involuntarily, as of the intestines.

smooth-tongued (smüth′tungd′), *adj.* speaking smoothly; agreeable; suave; plausible.

smor·gas·bord, smör·gås·bord (smôr′-gəs bôrd), *n.* an elaborate Scandinavian meal, featuring a large variety of hors d'oeuvres. [< Sw., lit., bread-and-butter table]

smote (smōt), *v.* pt. of **smite.**

smoth·er (smuth′ər), *v.* **1** make unable to get air; kill by depriving of air. **2** be unable to breathe freely; suffocate. **3** cover thickly. **4** deaden or put out by covering thickly: *smother a fire.* **5** *Fig.* keep back; check; suppress: *he smothered a sharp reply.* **6** cook in a covered pot or baking dish: *smothered chicken.* [ME *smorther,* n. < OE *smorian* suffocate] —**smoth′er·er,** *n.*

smoul·der (smōl′dər), *v., n.* =smolder.

smudge (smuj), *n., v.,* **smudged, smudging.** —*n.* **1** a dirty mark; smear. **2** a smoky fire made to drive away insects or to protect fruit from frost. —*v.* mark with dirty streaks; smear. —**smudg′y,** *adj.* —**smudg′i·ly,** *adv.* —**smudg′i·ness,** *n.*

smug (smug), *adj.,* **smug·ger, smug·gest,** too pleased with one's own goodness, cleverness, respectability, etc.; self-satisfied; complacent. [prob. < Du., LG *smuk* spruce, adj.] —**smug′ly,** *adv.* —**smug′ness,** *n.*

smug·gle (smug′əl), *v.,* **-gled, -gling. 1** bring into or take out of a country secretly and against the law. **2** bring, take, put, etc., secretly. [< LG *smuggeln*] —**smug′gler,** *n.*

smut (smut), *n., v.,* **smut·ted, smut·ting.** —*n.* **1** soot, dirt, etc. **2** indecent, obscene talk or writing; obscenity. **3** a plant disease in which the ears of grain are changed to a black dust. —*v.* **1** soil or be soiled with smut. **2** become affected with smut. [OE *smitte;* infl. by *smudge, smutch*]

smut·ty (smut′i), *adj.,* **-ti·er, -ti·est. 1** soiled with smut, soot, etc.; dirty. **2** indecent; obscene. **3** having the plant disease called smut. —**smut′ti·ly,** *adv.* —**smut′ti·ness,** *n.*

Sn, tin. [< L *stannum*]

snack (snak), *n.* **1** a light meal. **2** share; portion. [< MLG *snakken*]

snack bar, place where light meals and snacks are served.

snaf·fle (snaf′əl), *n., v.,* **-fled, -fling.** —*n.* a slender, jointed bit used on a bridle. —*v.* **1** put a snaffle on (a horse, etc.). **2** control or manage by a snaffle. [cf. Du. *snavel* beak]

sna·fu (sna fü′), *adj., v.,* **-fued, -fu·ing.** *Informal.* —*adj.* being in great disorder; snarled; confused. —*v.* **1** put in disorder or in a chaotic state. **2** mishandle.

snag (snag), *n., v.,* **snagged, snag·ging.** —*n.* **1** tree or branch held fast in a river or lake. **2** any sharp or rough projecting point, such as the broken end of a branch. **3** a hidden or unexpected obstacle. —*v.* **1** run or catch on a snag. **2** hinder. [? < Scand. (dial. Norw.) *snage* point of land] —**snagged,** *adj.* —**snag′gy,** *adj.*

snag·gle·tooth (snag′əl tüth′), *n.,* pl. **-teeth.** tooth that grows apart from or beyond the others. —**snag′gle-toothed′,** *adj.*

snail (snāl), *n.* **1** a small, soft-bodied mollusk that crawls very slowly. Most snails have spirally coiled shells on their backs into which they can withdraw for protection. **2** *Fig.* a lazy, slow-moving person. [OE *snegel*]

snake (snāk), *n., v.,* **snaked, snak·ing.**
—*n.* **1** a long, slender, crawling reptile without limbs. Some snakes are venomous. **2** *Fig.* a sly, treacherous person. **3** long, flexible wire used by plumbers to clear pipes, drains, etc. —*v.* move, wind, or curve like a snake. [OE *snaca*] —**snake′like′,** *adj.*

snake oil, 1 medicine that is supposed to cure most ailments but is completely ineffective. **2** *Fig.* any ineffective remedy.

snak·y (snāk′i), *adj.,* **snak·i·er, snak·i·est. 1** of a snake or snakes. **2** like a snake; like the curving and turning of a snake; twisting; winding. —**snak′i·ly,** *adv.* —**snak′i·ness,** *n.*

snap (snap), *v.,* **snapped, snap·ping,** *n., adj., adv.* —*v.* **1** make or cause to make a sudden, sharp sound: *this wood snaps as it burns.* **2** move, shut, catch, etc., with a snap: *the latch snapped.* **3** break suddenly or sharply: *the violin string snapped.* **4** *Fig.* become suddenly unable to endure a strain: *his nerves snapped.* **5** seize suddenly: *the dog snapped up the meat, she snapped at the chance.* **6** speak quickly and sharply: *"Silence!" snapped the teacher.* **7** *Fig.* move quickly and sharply: *snap to attention.* —*n.* **1** a quick, sharp sound. **2** a sudden, sharp breaking or the sound of breaking. **3** a quick, sudden bite or snatch. **4** liveliness; dash; vim. **5** a short spell of weather: *a cold snap.* **6** fastener; clasp. **7** a thin, crisp cooky. **8** an easy job, piece of work, etc. —*adj.* **1** made or done suddenly; offhand: *snap judgment.* **2** that moves, shuts, catches, etc., with a snap. —*adv.* in a brisk or sharp manner.

snap back, a recover quickly. **b** reply sharply and quickly.

snap to it, move quickly; hurry.

snap up, seize or purchase immediately, esp. a bargain. [< MDu., MLG *snappen*]

snap·drag·on (snap′drag′ən), *n.* a garden plant with showy flowers of crimson, purple, white, yellow, etc.

snap·per (snap′ər), *n.* **1** person or thing that snaps. **2** a snapping turtle. **3** a red fish of tropical seas used for food.

snapping turtle, a large turtle of American rivers that has powerful jaws with which it snaps at its prey.

snap·pish (snap′ish), *adj.* **1** apt to snap. **2** quick and sharp in speech or manner; impatient. —**snap′pish·ly,** *adv.* —**snap′pish·ness,** *n.*

snap·py (snap′i), *adj.,* **-pi·er, -pi·est. 1** snappish; sharp. **2** quick or sudden. **3** having snap, crispness, smartness, liveliness, etc.: *snappy clothes, snappy conversation.* —**snap′pi·ly,** *adv.* —**snap′pi·ness,** *n.*

snap·shot (snap′shot′), *n.* photograph taken in an instant.

snare (snār), *n., v.,* **snared, snar·ing.** —*n.* **1** noose for catching small animals and birds. **2** trap. **3** one of the strings of gut or rawhide stretched across the bottom of a snare drum. **3** *Fig.* anything that traps or beguiles: *the snare of flattery.* —*v.* **1** catch with a snare. **2** trap: *snared by a lie.* [< Scand. *snara*] —**snar′er,** *n.*

snare drum, a small drum with strings of gut or wire stretched across the bottom to make a rattling sound.

snarl¹ (snärl), *v.* **1** growl sharply and show one's teeth. **2** speak harshly in a sharp, angry tone. **3** say or express with a snarl. —*n.* **1** act of snarling. **2** a sharp, angry growl. **3** sharp, angry words. [earlier *snar;* cf. MDu., MLG *snarren* rattle; akin to SNORE] —**snarl′er,** *n.* —**snarl′ing,** *adj.* —**snarl′ing·ly,** *adv.*

snarl² (snärl), *n.* **1** tangle: *she combed the snarls out of her hair.* **2** *Fig.* confusion: *his legal affairs were in a snarl.* —*v.* **1** tangle or become tangled. **2** *Fig.* confuse. [ult. < *snare* or its source] —**snarl′y,** *adj.*

snatch (snach), *v.* **1** seize suddenly; grasp hastily. **2** save or attain by quick action: *snatch victory from defeat.* —*n.* **1** act of snatching. **2** a short time. **3** a small amount; bit; scrap.

snatch at, a try to seize or grasp; seize; grasp. **b** eagerly take advantage of. [cf. MDu. *snakken*] —**snatch′er,** *n.*

sneak (snēk), *v.* **sneaked** or **snuck, sneaking. 1** move in a stealthy, sly way. **2** get, put, pass, etc., in a stealthy, sly way. **3** act in a mean, contemptible, cowardly way —*n.* **1** act of sneaking. **2** person who sneaks; cowardly, contemptible person.

sneak out of, avoid by slyness: *sneak out of an invitation with a slight untruth.* [cf. OE *snīcan*] —**sneak′ing,** *adj.* —**sneak′ing·ly,** *adv.* —**sneak′y,** *adj.* —**sneak′i·ly,** *adv.* —**sneak′i·ness,** *n.*

sneak·er (snēk′ər), *n.* **1** a light canvas shoe with a soft rubber sole; tennis shoe. **2** a sneak.

sneakers, pair of such shoes.

sneer (snir), *v.* **1** show scorn or contempt by looks or words. **2** utter with scorn or contempt. —*n.* look or words expressing scorn or contempt. [ME *snere(n);* akin to SNORE, SNARL¹] —**sneer′er,** *n.* —**sneer′ing,** *adj.* —**sneer′ing·ly,** *adv.*

sneeze (snēz), *v.,* **sneezed, sneez·ing,** *n.* —*v.* expel air suddenly and violently through the nose and mouth by an involuntary spasm. —*n.* a sudden, violent expelling of air through the nose and mouth.

sneeze at, treat with contempt; despise. [var. of earlier *fnese(n),* OE *fnēosan*] —**sneez′er,** *n.* —**sneez′ing,** *n.*

snick·er (snik′ər), **snig·ger** (snig′ər), *n.* a half-suppressed and usually disrespectful laugh; sly or silly laugh; giggle. —*v.* laugh in this way. [imit.] —**snick′er·er,** *n.* —**snick′er·ing·ly,** *adv.*

snide (snīd), *adj.* slyly insinuating.

sniff (snif), *v.* **1** draw air through the nose in short, quick breaths that can be heard. **2** clear one's nasal passages thus. **3** smell with sniffs. **4** try the smell of. **5** draw in through the nose with the breath: *he sniffed the medicine.* **6** suspect; detect. —*n.* **1** act or sound of sniffing. **2** a single breathing in of something; breath. [akin to *snivel*] —**sniff′er,** *n.* —**sniff′ing·ly,** *adv.* —**sniff′y,** *adj.*

snif·fle (snif′əl), *v.,* **-fled, -fling,** *n.* —*v.* **1** breathe audibly through a partly clogged nose. **2** sniff again and again. —*n.* a sniffling.

the sniffles, a fit of sniffling; tendency to sniffle. **b** a slight cold in the head. —**snif′fler,** *n.*

snip (snip), *v.,* **snipped, snip·ping,** *n.* —*v.* cut with a small, quick stroke or series of strokes with scissors. —*n.* **1** act of snipping. **2** a small piece cut off. [< Du., LG *snippen*]

snipe (snīp), *n., pl.* **snipes** or (*esp. collectively*) **snipe,** *v.,* **sniped, snip·ing.** —*n.* any of various marsh birds with long bills. —*v.* **1** hunt snipe. **2** shoot, as at soldiers one at a time as a sportsman shots at game; shoot from a concealed place. [< Scand. *snīpa*] —**snip′er,** *n.*

snip·pet (snip′it), *n.* **1** a small piece snipped off. **2** a small or unimportant person.

snip·py (snip′i), *adj.,* **-pi·er, -pi·est. 1** sharp; curt. **2** haughty; disdainful. [< *snip*] —**snip′pi·ness,** *n.*

snitch¹ (snich), *v.* snatch; steal. —**snitch′er,** *n.*

snitch² (snich), *v.* be an informer; tell tales. —*n.* informer. —**snitch′er,** *n.*

sniv·el (sniv′əl), *v.,* **-eled, -el·ing,** *n.* —*v.* **1** cry with sniffling. **2** put on a show of grief; whine. **3** run at the nose; sniffle. —*n.* **1** whining. **2** sniffling. [akin to OE *snofl* mucus] —**sniv′el·er,** *n.*

snob (snob), *n.* person who cares too much for rank, wealth, position, etc., and too little for real merit. —**snob′ber·y,** *n.* —**snob′bish,** *adj.* —**snob′bish·ly,** *adv.* —**snob′bish·ness,** *n.*

snook·er (snù′kər), *n.* version of billiards. —*v.* **1** block (a snooker player) from making a straight shot. **2** *Informal.* cheat (someone). [orig. uncert.]

snoop (snüp), —*v.* go about in a sneaking, prying way; prowl; pry. —*n.* **1** person who snoops. **2** act of snooping. [< Du. *snoepen* eat in a secret] —**snoop′er,** *n.* —**snoop′y,** *adj.*

snoot·y (snüt′i), *adj.,* **snoot·i·er, snoot·i·est.** *U.S.* snobbish; conceited.

snooze (snüz), *v.,* **snoozed, snooz·ing,** *n.* —*v.* take a nap; sleep; doze. —*n.* nap; doze.

snore (snôr; snōr), *v.,* **snored, snor·ing,** *n.* —*v.* breathe during sleep with a harsh, rough sound. —*n.* the sound so made. [ME *snore(n)*]

snor·kel (snôr′kəl), *n.* **1** a periscopelike intake and exhaust shaft which allows submarines to remain submerged for a very long period of time. **2** tube, curved at one end with a mouthpiece at the other, that allows swimmers to breathe while submerged. [< LG, slang for nose < unrecorded MLG *snorkeln,* frequentative of *snorken* snore because it is the nose of the submarine]

snort (snôrt), *v.* **1** force the breath violently through the nose with a loud, harsh sound: *the horse snorted.* **2** make a sound like this. **3** show contempt, defiance, anger, etc., by snorting. **4** say or express with a snort. —*n.* act of snorting; the sound made. [< *snore*] —**snort′er**, *n.*

snout (snout), *n.* **1** the projecting part of an animal's head that contains the nose, mouth, and jaws. Pigs, dogs, and crocodiles have snouts. **2** anything like an animal's snout. **3** a large or ugly nose. [ME *snoute*]

snout beetle, a small, snouted beetle that eats grain, nuts, and fruit.

snow (snō), *n.* **1** water vapor frozen into crystals that fall to earth in soft, white flakes and spread upon it as a white layer. **2** a fall of snow. **3** cocaine or heroin. —*v.* **1** fall as snow: *snow all day.* **2** let fall or scatter as snow. **3** cover, block up, etc., with snow or as if with snow. **4** deceive or persuade with flattery.

snow in, shut in by snow.

snow under, a cover with snow. **b** overwhelm. [OE *snāw*]

snow·ball (snō′bôl′), *n.* **1** ball made of snow pressed together. **2** shrub with white flowers in large clusters like balls. —*v.* **1** throw balls of snow at. **2** increase rapidly by additions like a snowball. —**snow′ball·ing,** *n.*

snow·bank (snō′bangk′), *n.* a large mass or drift of snow.

snow·ber·ry (snō′ber′i), *n., pl.* **ries. 1** a North American shrub that bears clusters of white berries in the fall. **2** the berry.

snow·bird (snō′bėrd′), *n.* **1** a small American bird that has a slate-gray back and a white breast, and is often seen in flocks during the winter. **2** the snow bunting. **3** *Informal.* person who goes to a warm climate for the winter, esp. to Florida.

snow-blind (snō′blīnd′), *adj.* temporarily or partly blind from exposure of the eyes to the glare of snow. —**snow blindness.**

snow·board (snō′bôrd′; –bōrd′), *n.* broad, short ski with bindings for the feet, used for downhill skiing. Also, **skiboard. —snow′board′er, snow′board′-ing,** *n.*

snow-bound (snō′bound′), *adj.* shut in by snow.

snow bunting, a small, white finch with black and brownish markings that inhabits cold regions.

snow-capped (snō′kapt′), *adj.* having its top covered with snow.

snow·drift (snō′drift′), *n.* **1** mass or bank of snow piled up by the wind. **2** snow driven before the wind.

snow·drop (snō′drop′), *n.* a small plant with white flowers that blooms early in the spring.

snow·fall (snō′fôl′), *n.* **1** a fall of snow. **2** amount of snow falling in a certain time and area.

snow·flake (snō′flāk′), *n.* a small, feathery piece of snow.

snow job, *Informal.* something used to overwhelm, as a flow of fast, persuasive talk.

snow·plow (snō′plou′), *n.* machine for clearing away snow from streets, railroad tracks, etc.

snow·shoe (snō′shü′), *n.* a light, wooden frame with strips of leather stretched across it, worn to keep from sinking in deep, soft snow.

snow·slide (snō′slīd′), *n.* **1** the sliding down of a mass of snow on a steep slope. **2** the mass of snow that slides.

snow·storm (snō′stôrm′), *n.* storm with much snow.

snow-white (snō′hwīt′), *adj.* white as snow.

snow·y (snō′i), *adj.,* **snow·i·er, snow·i·est. 1** having snow. **2** covered with snow. **3** like snow; white as snow. —**snow′i·ly,** *adv.* —**snow′i·ness,** *n.*

snub (snub), *v.,* **snubbed, snub·bing,** *n., adj.* —*v.* **1** treat coldly, scornfully, or with contempt. **2** check or stop (a boat, horse, etc.) suddenly. —*n.* **1** cold, scornful, or disdainful treatment. **2** a sudden check or stop. **3** a sharp rebuke. —*adj.* short and turned up at the tip: *a snub nose.* [< Scand. *snubba* reprove] —**snub′ber,** *n.*

snub-nosed (snub′nōzd′), *adj.* having a snub nose.

snuff¹ (snuf), *v.* **1** draw in through the nose; draw up into the nose. **2** examine by smelling; sniff; smell. **3** take powdered tobacco into the nose by snuffing; use snuff. —*n.* **1** powdered tobacco taken into the nose. **2** act of snuffing. **3** amount snuffed.

up to snuff, up to the usual standards. [< MDu. *snuffen* sniff] —**snuff′y,** *adj.* —**snuff′i·ness,** *n.*

snuff² *v.* **1** cut or pinch off the burned wick of. **2** put out (a candle); extinguish. —*n.* the burned part of a candlewick.

snuff out, a put out; extinguish. **b** put an end to suddenly and completely. **c** kill. —**snuff′er,** *n.*

snuff·ers (snuf′ərz), *n.pl.* small tongs for taking off burned wick or putting out the light of a candle.

snuf·fle (snuf′əl), *v.,* **–fled, –fling,** *n.* —*v.* **1** breathe noisily through a partly clogged nose. **2** smell; sniff. **3** speak, sing, etc., through the nose or with a nasal tone. —*n.* act or sound of snuffling.

the snuffles, fit of snuffling; stuffed-up condition of the nose, caused by a cold, hay fever, etc. [ult. < *snuff¹* or its source] —**snuf′fler,** *n.* —**snuf′fling·ly,** *adv.*

snug (snug), *adj.,* **snug·ger, snug·gest,** *v.,* **snugged, snug·ging,** *adv.* —*adj.* **1** comfortable; warm; sheltered: *a snug corner.* **2** neat; trim; compact: *a snug cabin.* **3** fitting closely. —*v.* make snug. —*adv.* in

a snug manner. [cf. Sw. *snygg* neat, trim] —**snug′ly,** *adv.* —**snug′ness,** *n.*

snug·gle (snug′əl), *v.,* **–gled, –gling. 1** lie or press closely for warmth or comfort or from affection; nestle. **2** draw closely [< *snug*]

so¹ (sō; *unstressed before consonants* sə), *adv.* **1** in that way; in the same way or degree: *is that really so?, do not walk so fast, he was not so cold as she was.* **2** very or very much: *you are so kind, my head aches so.* **3** for this reason; therefore: *the dog was hungry, so we fed it.* —*conj.* with the result that; in order that: *go away so I can rest, I did the work so he would not need to.* —*interj.* well! all right! —*pron.* more or less: *a pound or so.*

and so, a likewise; also: *she left and so did I.* **b** accordingly: *the car broke down and so we never got there.*

and so on, et cetera.

so as, with the result or purpose: *get up early so as to be ready in time.*

so far, up to this point.

so that, with the result or purpose that.

so what?, *Informal.* what difference does it make?; who cares? [OE *swā*]

so² (sō), *n.* sol.

so³ (sō), fifth tone in a musical scale. [see GAMUT]

So., South; south; southern.

soak (sōk), *v.* **1** make very wet; wet through; saturate. **2** let remain in water or other liquid until wet clear through. **3** make its way; enter; go: *water will soak through the earth.* **4** *Slang.* make pay too much; charge or tax heavily. —*n.* act or process of soaking.

soak up, a absorb. **b** take into the mind. [OE *socian*] —**soak′er,** *n.* —**soak′ing·ly,** *adv.*

so-and-so (sō′ənd sō′), *n., pl.* **-sos.** some person or thing not named.

soap (sōp), *n.* **1** substance used for washing, usually made of a fat and caustic soda or potash. **2** any metallic salt of an acid derived from a fat. —*v.* rub or treat with soap. [OE *sāpe*]

soap·ber·ry (sōp′ber′i; –bər i), *n., pl.* **-ries. 1** the fruit of any of certain tropical trees, used as a substitute for soap. **2** any of the trees bearing such fruit.

soap·box (sōp′boks′), *n.* an empty box used as a temporary platform by agitators or other speakers addressing gatherings on the streets.

soap opera, a daytime television drama presented in serial form, usually featuring emotional domestic situations.

soap·stone (sōp′stōn′), *n.* stone that feels somewhat like soap.

soap·suds (sōp′sudz′), *n.pl.* bubbles and foam made with soap and water.

soap·y (sōp′i), *adj.,* **soap·i·er, soap·i·est. 1** covered with soap or soapsuds. **2** containing soap. **3** like soap; smooth; greasy. —**soap′i·ly,** *adv.* —**soap′i·ness,** *n.*

soar (sôr; sōr), *v.* **1** fly at a great height; fly upward: *an eagle soars.* **2** rise beyond what is common and ordinary; aspire:

his ambition soared to the throne. **3** fly or move through the air by means of rising air currents. —*n.* **1** act of soaring. **2** height attained in soaring. [< OF *essorer*, ult. < L *ex*– out + *aura* breeze] —**soar′er,** *n.* —**soar′ing·ly,** *adv.*

sob (sob), *v.,* **sobbed, sob·bing,** *n., adj.* —*v.* **1** cry or sigh with short, quick breaths. **2** put, send, etc., by sobbing: *she sobbed herself to sleep.* **3** make a sound like a sob. **4** utter with sobs. —*n.* a catching of short, quick breaths because of grief, etc. —*adj. Informal.* intended to arouse feelings of pity, sadness, etc.: *sob stories.* [prob. ult. imit.] —**sob′bing,** *n.* —**sob′bing·ly,** *adv.*

so·ber (sō′bər), *adj.* **1** not drunk. **2** temperate; moderate: *a sober, hard-working life.* **3** quiet; serious; solemn: *a sober expression.* **4** quiet in color: *dressed in sober gray.* —*v.* make or become sober. **sober up,** recover from too much alcoholic drink. [< OF < L *sobrius*] —**so′ber·ly,** *adv.* —**so′ber·ness,** *n.*

so·ber-mind·ed (sō′bər mīn′did), *adj.* self-controlled; sensible. —**so′ber-mind′ed·ness,** *n.*

so·bri·e·ty (sə brī′ə ti), *n., pl.* **-ties. 1** soberness. **2** temperance in the use of strong drink. **3** moderation. **4** quietness; seriousness.

so·bri·quet (sō′brə kā), *n.* nickname. [< F]

so-called (sō′kôld′), *adj.* **1** called thus improperly or incorrectly. **2** called thus.

soc·cer (sok′ər), *n.* game played between two teams of eleven people each, using a round ball; association football. The ball may be struck with any part of the body except the hands and arms. [< assoc., abbrev. of *association*]

so·cia·ble (sō′shə bəl), *adj.* **1** liking company; friendly. **2** marked by conversation and companionship: *we had a sociable afternoon together.* —**so′cia·bil′i·ty, so′-cia·ble·ness,** *n.* —**so′cia·bly,** *adv.*

so·cial (sō′shəl), *adj.* **1** concerned with human beings in their relations to each other: *social problems, man is a social creature.* **2** for companionship or friendliness: *social club.* **3** liking company: *she has a social nature.* **4** living together in organized communities: *ants and bees are social insects.* —*n.* a social gathering or party. [< L, < *socius* companion, orig. adj., sharing in] —**so′cial·ly,** *adv.* —**so′cial·ness,** *n.*

social climber, person who associates with others who, because of their wealth or status, will improve his or her standing in society. —**social climbing.**

so·cial·ism (sō′shəl iz əm), *n.* **1** system of social organization by which the means of production and distribution are owned collectively and controlled through the government. **2** a political movement associated with this system. —**so′cial·ist,** *n., adj.* —**so′cial·is′tic,** *adj.*

Socialist Party, political party that favors and supports socialism.

so·cial·ite (sō′shəl īt), *n.* a prominent person in society.

so·cial·ize (sō′shəl īz), *v.,* **-ized, -iz·ing. 1** make social. **2** make fit for living with others. **3** adapt to community needs. **4** establish or regulate in accordance with socialism. —**so′cial·i·za′tion,** *n.*

socialized medicine, medical care and hospital services for a whole society, esp. through government administration.

social science, study of people, their activities, and their customs in relationship to others. History, sociology, economics, and civics are social sciences. —**social scientist.**

social security, system of federal pensions for employed persons. The government pays part of the pension, part is deducted from the employee's salary, and part is paid by his or her employer.

social studies, course of studies in elementary, middle, and high school that includes history, civics, geography, etc.

social work, social service, work directed toward the betterment of social conditions in a community. Child welfare departments, district nursing organizations, etc., are forms of social work. —**social worker.**

so·ci·e·ty (sə sī′ə ti), *n., pl.* **-ties. 1** group of persons joined together for a common purpose or by a common interest. A club, a fraternity, a lodge, or an association may be called a society. **2** all the people; the people of any particular time or place: *the good of society demands that wrongdoing be punished.* **3** company; companionship. **4** fashionable people; their doings. [< L *societas* < *socius* sharing in]

Society of Friends. the Quakers. See **friend** (def. 4).

Society of Jesus. the Jesuit religious order.

so·ci·o·bi·ol·o·gy (sō′si ō bī ol′ə ji; –shi–), *n.* study of the role of biology in the social behavior of all animals.

so·ci·o·lin·guis·tics (sō′si o ling gwis′-tiks; –shi–), *n.* branch of linguistics concerned with social influences on language and speech.

so·ci·ol·o·gy (sō′si ol′ə ji; –shi–), *n.* study of the nature, origin, and development of human society and community life; science of society. Sociology deals with the facts of crime, poverty, marriage, divorce, the church, the school, etc. [< L *socius* companion + –LOGY] —**so′ci·o·log′i·cal,** *adj.* —**so′ci·o·log′i·cal·ly,** *adv.* —**so′ci·ol′o·gist,** *n.*

so·ci·o·path (sō′si ə path; –shi–), *n.* completely antisocial person. —**so′ci·o·path′ic,** *adj.*

sock[1] (sok), *n.* a short stocking, esp. one that reaches about halfway to the knee. [< L *soccus* a light shoe worn by actors in comedy]

sock[2] (sok), *v.* strike or hit hard. —*n.* a hard blow.

sock·et (sok′it), *n.* **1** a hollow part or piece for receiving and holding something. Eyes are set in sockets. **2** a connecting place for electric wires and plugs. [< AF *soket* < *soc* plowshare < Celtic]

sod (sod), *n., v.,* **sod·ded, sod·ding.** —*n.* **1** ground covered with grass. **2** piece or layer of this containing the grass and its roots. —*v.* cover with sods. [< MDu., MLG *sode*]

so·da (sō′də), *n.* **1** sodium carbonate; washing soda. **2** sodium bicarbonate; baking soda. **3** sodium hydroxide; caustic soda. **4** soda water. **5** soda water flavored with fruit juice or syrup, and often containing ice cream. [< Med.L]

soda ash, partly purified sodium carbonate.

so·dal·i·ty (sō dal′ə ti), *n., pl.* **-ties. 1** fellowship; friendship. **2** an association, society, or fraternity. [< L, < *sodalis* sociable]

soda water, water charged with carbon dioxide to make it bubble and fizz, often served with the addition of syrup, ice cream, etc.

sod·den (sod′ən), *adj.* **1** soaked through. **2** heavy and moist. **3** dull-looking; stupid. [old pp. of *seethe*] —**sod′den·ness,** *n.*

so·di·um (sō′di əm), *n.* a soft, silver-white metallic element, Na, occurring in nature only in compounds. Salt and soda contain sodium. [< *soda*]

sodium bicarbonate, a powdery white substance, $NaHCO_3$, used in cooking, medicine, etc.: baking soda.

sodium borate, =borax.

sodium carbonate, a salt, Na_2CO_3, that occurs in a powdery white form and in a hydrated crystalline form; washing soda. It is used for softening water, making soap and glass, etc.

sodium chloride, common salt, NaCl.

sodium hydroxide, a white solid, NaOH, that is a strong, corrosive alkali; caustic soda.

sodium nitrate, colorless crystals, $NaNO_3$, used in making fertilizers, explosives, etc.; Chile saltpeter.

sod·om·y (sod′əm i), *n.* unnatural sexual intercourse. [< OF *sodomie* < *Sodome* Sodom]

so·ev·er (sō ev′ər), *adv.* **1** in any case; in any way; in any degree: *no matter how long soever the work may take.* **2** of any kind; at all.

so·fa (sō′fə), *n.* a long, upholstered seat or couch having a back and arms. [< F < Ar. *soffah*]

sofa bed, sofa that can be converted into a bed; convertible sofa.

So·fi·a (sō′fi ə; sō fē′ə), *n.* capital of Bulgaria.

soft (sôft; soft), *adj.* **1** not hard; yielding readily to touch or pressure: *a soft pillow.* **2** not hard compared with other things of the same kind: *lead is a soft metal.* **3** fine in texture; not rough or coarse; smooth: *soft skin.* **4** pleasant; mild; not sharp or harsh: *a soft voice, soft light.* **5** gentle; kind; tender: *a soft heart.* **6** containing no mineral salts which interfere with the action of soap: *soft water.* **7** weak: *soft from lack of exercise, soft in the head.* **8** pronounced as a fricative or an affricate, rather than as an explosive sound. The *c* and *g* in *city* and *gem* are "soft"; in *corn* and *get* they are "hard." —*adv.* softly; quietly; gentle. —*n.* that which is soft; soft part. [OE *softe*] —**soft′ish,** *adj.* —**soft′ly,** *adv.* —**soft′ness,** *n.*

soft·ball (sôft′bôl′; soft′–), *n.* a modified kind of baseball employing a larger, softer ball.

soft-boiled (sôft′boild′; soft′–), *adj.* boiled only a little so as to keep (egg yolks, etc.) soft.

soft coal =bituminous coal.

soft drink, drink that contains no alcohol.

soft·en (sôf′ən; sof′–), *v.* make or become softer. —**soft′en·er,** *n.* —**soft′en·ing,** *n.*

soft goods, textiles, groceries, etc. —**soft′goods,** *adj.*

soft-heart·ed (sôft′här′tid; soft′–), *adj.* gentle; kind; tender. —**soft′-heart′ed·ness,** *n.*

soft landing, 1 the landing of a spacecraft on a celestial object that is slow enough to prevent jarring or damage to the craft. **2** *Fig.* descent from an economic boom that is not damaging to the general economy.

soft lens, contact lens that is made of plastic and is not rigid.

soft palate. See **palate** (def. 1).

soft-ped·al (sôft′ped′əl; soft′–), *v.* –**aled,** –**al·ing. 1** soften sound on a piano with a pedal. **2** *Fig.* make less important; tone down. —**soft pedal,** *n.*

soft sell, selling by persuasion rather than by aggressive tactics or pressure.

soft shoe, tap dance performed with shoes that do not have metal taps. —**soft′-shoe′** *v.*

soft-spo·ken (sôft′ spō′kən; soft′–), *adj.* **1** spoken in a low, soft voice. **2** *Fig.* persuasive; mild: *a soft-spoken critic.*

soft·ware (sôft′wãr′; soft′–). *n.* **1** programs for a computer that allow it to perform different tasks. **2** *Fig.* anything peripheral to a task, system, etc.: *buckles are military software, bullets are not.*

soft soap, 1 a liquid or semiliquid soap. **2** flattery.

soft-soap (sôft′sōp′; soft′–), *v.* flatter.

soft·wood (sôft′wùd′; soft′–), *n.* **1** in forestry, tree that has needles or does not have broad leaves. **2** wood of such a tree.

soft·y (sôf′ti; sof′–), *n., pl.* **soft·ies.** a person who is easily imposed upon.

sog·gy (sog′i), *adj.,* –**gi·er,** –**gi·est. 1** thoroughly wet; soaked: *a soggy washcloth.* **2** damp and heavy: *soggy bread.* —**sog′gi·ness,** *n.*

soil¹ (soil), *n.* **1** ground; earth; dirt: *sandy soil.* **2** land; country. [< AF < L *solium* seat, infl. by L *solum* soil] —**soiled,** *adj.*

soil² (soil), *v.* **1** make or become dirty: *he soiled his clean clothes.* **2** spot; stain: *the splashing paint soiled the wall.* **3** *Fig.* disgrace; dishonor: *soil the family name.* —*n.* a spot; stain. [< OF *soillier,* ult. < L *suile* pigsty < *sus* pig]

soi·ree (swä rā′), *n.* an evening party or social gathering. [< F, < *soir* evening]

so·journ (*v.* sō jėrn′, sō′jėrn; *n.* sō′jėrn), *v.* stay for a time. —*n.* a brief stay. [< OF *sojorner,* ult. < L *sub* under + *diurnus* of the day] —**so·journ′er,** *n.* —**so·journ′ment,** *n.*

Sol (sol), *n.* sun.

sol (sōl), *n.* the fifth tone of the scale. Also, **so.** [see GAMUT.]

sol·ace (sol′is), *n., v.,* –**aced,** –**ac·ing.** —*n.* comfort; relief. —*v.* comfort; relieve. [< OF < L *solacium* < *solari* console] —**sol′ace·ment,** *n.* —**sol′ac·er,** *n.*

so·lar (sō′lər), *adj.* **1** of the sun: *a solar eclipse.* **2** having to do with the sun: *solar phenomena.* **3** coming from the sun: *solar energy.* **4** measured or determined by the earth's motion in relation to the sun: *a solar year.* **5** working by means of the sun's light or heat: *a solar battery.* [< L, < *sol* sun]

solar battery, a device to trap sunlight and convert it into electrical energy.

solar cell, device to convert solar radiation into electrical energy.

so·lar·i·um (sə lãr′i əm), *n., pl.* –**lar·i·a** (–lãr′i ə). room, porch, etc., where people can lie or sit in the sun. [< L, < *sol* sun]

solar plexus, network of nerves situated at the upper part of the abdomen, behind the stomach and in front of the aorta.

solar system, sun and all the planets, satellites, comets, etc., that revolve around it.

solar wind, changed particles sent from the sun in a continuous stream through space.

solar year, =astronomical year.

sold (sōld), *v.* pt. and pp. of **sell.**

sol·der (sod′ər), *n.* **1** metal or alloy that can be melted and used for joining or mending metal surfaces, parts, etc. **2** anything that unites firmly or joins closely. —*v.* **1** fasten, mend, or join with solder. **2** unite firmly; join closely. **3** mend; repair; patch. [< OF *soldure,* ult. < L *solidus* solid] —**sol′der·er,** *n.*

sol·dier (sōl′jər), *n.* **1** person who serves in an army. **2** an enlisted person in the army, not a commissioned officer. **3** person having skill or experience in war. **4** person who serves in any cause. —*v.* **1** act or serve as a soldier. **2** pretend to work but do very little. [< OF, < *soulde* pay < L *solidus,* a Roman coin] —**sol′dier·ly,** *adj.* —**sol′dier·li·ness,** *n.*

soldier of fortune, person serving or ready to serve as a soldier under any government for money, adventure, or pleasure.

sol·dier·y (sōl′jər i), *n.* **1** soldiers. **2** military training of knowledge.

sole¹ (sōl), *adj.* **1** one and only; single: *the sole survivor, sole heir.* **2** only: *the sole grounds for action were based on hearsay.* **3** of or for only one person or group and not others; exclusive: *the sole right of use.* **4** without help; alone: *a sole undertaking.* [< L *solus*] —**sole′ness,** *n.*

sole² (sōl), *n., v.,* **soled, sol·ing.** —*n.* **1** the bottom or under surface of the foot. **2** bottom of a shoe, slipper, boot, etc. **3** the under surface; under part; bottom. —*v.* put a sole on. [< L *solea* < *solum* bottom, ground] —**soled,** *adj.*

sole³ (sōl), *n., pl.* **soles** or (*esp. collectively*) **sole.** a kind of flatfish. European sole is valued highly as food. [< F < L *solea,* orig., *sole²*]

sol·e·cism (sol′ə siz əm), *n.* **1** violation of the grammatical or other accepted usages of a language; mistake in using words. "I done it" is a solecism. **2** mistake in social behavior; breach of good manners or etiquette. **3** any error. [< L < Gk. *soloikismos,* supposedly < *Soloi,* Greek colony in Cilicia] —**sol′e·cist,** *n.* —**sol′e·cis′tic,** *adj.* —**sol′e·cis′ti·cal·ly,** *adv.*

sole·ly (sōl′li), *adv.* **1** as the only one or ones; alone: *solely responsible for the accident.* **2** only: *the plant can be found solely in the United States.* **3** wholly: *a solely fictitious story.*

sol·emn (sol′əm), *adj.* **1** serious; grave; earnest: *a solemn face.* **2** causing serious or grave thoughts. **3** done with form and ceremony. **4** connected with religion; sacred. **5** legally correct. [< L *sollemnis*] —**sol′emn·ly,** *adv.* —**sol′emn·ness,** *n.*

so·lem·ni·ty (sə lem′nə ti), *n., pl.* –**ties. 1** solemn feeling; seriousness; impressiveness. **2** Often, **solemnities.** a solemn, formal ceremony.

sol·em·nize (sol′əm nīz), *v.,* –**nized,** –**niz·ing. 1** observe with ceremonies. **2** hold or perform (a ceremony or service). **3** make serious or grave. —**sol′em·ni·za′tion,** *n.*

so·le·noid (sō′lə noid), *n.* coil of wire that acts like a magnet when electricity passes through it, used in automobile directional signal lights, starters, etc. [< F *solénoide* < Gk. *sōlēn* channel + *eídos* form]

sol-fa (sōl′fä′), *n.* system of singing the syllables *do, re, mi, fa, sol, la, ti, do* to tones of the scale. [< Ital., < *sol* + *fa.* See GAMUT.]

so·lic·it (sə lis′it), *v.* **1** try to obtain orders or business: *solicit for a business firm.* **2** ask earnestly for: *solicit advice.* **3** make appeals or requests: *solicit for contributions.* **4** accost with immoral offers. **5** influence to do wrong; tempt; entice. [< L *sol(l)icitare* < *sol(l)icitus* wholly moved] —**so·lic′i·ta′tion,** *n.*

so·lic·i·tor (sə lis′ə tər), *n.* **1** person who entreats or requests. **2** person who seeks trade, business, donations, etc. **3** in England, a lawyer. A solicitor prepares a case, and a barrister pleads it. —**so·lic′i·tor·ship′**, *n.*

solicitor general, *pl.* **solicitors general. 1** a law officer who assists the attorney general and ranks next below him. **2** the chief law officer in a state having no attorney general.

so·lic·it·ous (sə lis′ə təs), *adj.* **1** showing care or concern; anxious; concerned: *parents are solicitous for their children's progress.* **2** desirous; eager. [< L *sol(l)icitus.* See SOLICIT.] —**so·lic′it·ous·ly**, *adv.* —**so·lic′it·ous·ness**, *n.*

so·lic·i·tude (sə lis′ə tüd; –tūd), *n.* anxious care; anxiety; concern. —**so·lic′i·tu′di·nous**, *adj.*

sol·id (sol′id), *adj.* **1** not a liquid or a gas: *solid particles floating in water.* **2** not hollow: *a solid ball of matter.* **3** dense; thick; heavy: *solid masses of smoke.* **4** strongly put together; hard; firm: *solid construction.* **5** alike throughout: *the cloth is a solid blue.* **6** firmly united: *the country was solid for peace.* **7** real; serious: *chemistry and physics are solid subjects.* **8** genuine: *solid comfort.* **9** that can be depended on; having good judgment; sensible: *a solid citizen, a solid thinker.* **10** financially sound or strong: *a solid business.* **11** whole; undivided; continuous: *three solid hours, a solid row of houses.* **12** written without a hyphen. *Earthworm* is a solid word. —*n.* **1** substance or body that is not a liquid or a gas. **2** body that has length, breadth, and thickness. [< L *solidus*] —**sol′id·ly**, *adv.* —**sol′id·ness**, *n.*

sol·i·dar·i·ty (sol′ə dar′ə ti), *n., pl.* –**ties.** unity or fellowship arising from common responsibilities and interests.

solid geometry, mathematics that deals with three dimensions, length, breadth, and thickness.

so·lid·i·fy (sə lid′ə fī), *v.,* –**fied**, –**fy·ing. 1** make or become solid; harden. **2** unite firmly. —**so·lid′i·fi′a·ble**, *adj.* —**so·lid′i·fi·ca′tion**, *n.*

so·lid·i·ty (sə lid′ə ti), *n., pl.* –**ties.** a being solid; firmness; hardness; density.

so·lil·o·quize (sə lil′ə kwīz), *v.,* –**quized**, –**quiz·ing. 1** talk to oneself. **2** speak a soliloquy. —**so·lil′o·quist, so·lil′o·quiz′er**, *n.* —**so·lil′o·quiz′ing·ly**, *adv.*

so·lil·o·quy (sə lil′ə kwi), *n., pl.* –**quies. 1** a talking to oneself. **2** speech made by an actor to him or herself when alone on the stage. It reveals his or her thoughts and feelings to the audience, but not to the other characters in the play. [< LL, < L *solus* alone + *loqui* speak]

sol·i·taire (sol′ə tār), *n.* **1** a card game played by one person. **2** diamond or other gem set by itself. [< F < L *solitarius.* Doublet of SOLITARY.]

sol·i·tar·y (sol′ə ter′i), *adj., n., pl.* –**tar·ies.** —*adj.* **1** alone; single; only: *a solitary*

passenger. **2** without companions; away from people; lonely: *a solitary kind of life.* —*n.* person living alone, away from people. [< L *solitarius,* ult. < *solus* alone. Doublet of SOLITAIRE.] —**sol′i·tar′i·ly**, *adv.* —**sol′i·tar′i·ness**, *n.*

sol·i·tude (sol′ə tüd; –tūd), *n.* **1** a being alone. **2** a lonely place. **3** loneliness. [< L, < *solus* alone]

sol·mi·za·tion (sol′mə zā′shən), *n.* system of singing the syllables, esp. the sol-fa syllables, to the tones of the scale. [< F *solmisation,* ult. < *sol* + *mi.* See GAMUT.]

so·lo (sō′lō), *n., pl.* –**los**, –**li** (–lē), *adj., v.* —*n.* **1** piece of music for one voice or instrument. **2** anything done without a partner, companion, instructor, etc. —*adj.* **1** arranged for and performed by one voice or instrument. **2** playing the solo part. **3** without a partner, companion, instructor, etc.; alone. —*v.* fly alone. [< Ital., alone, < L *solus*]

so·lo·ist (sō′lō ist), *n.* person who performs a solo or solos.

Sol·o·mon (sol′ə mən), *n.* man of great wisdom.

Sol·o·mon's-seal (sol′ə mənz sēl′), *n.* a kind of plant that has small flowers hanging from the bases of the leaves and a rootstock with seallike scars.

So·lon (sō′lən; –lon), *n.* a wise man; sage. [< the name of the Athenian lawgiver, 633?–558? B.C.] —**So·lon′ic**, *adj.*

so long, good-by; farewell.

sol·stice (sol′stis), *n.* either of the two times in the year, when the sun is at its greatest distance from the celestial equator. In the Northern Hemisphere, June 21 or 22, the **summer solstice,** is the longest day of the year, and December 21 or 22, the **winter solstice,** is the shortest. [< OF < L *solstitium,* ult. < *sol* sun + *sistere* stand still] —**sol·sti′tial**, *adj.*

sol·u·ble (sol′yə bəl), *adj.* **1** that can be dissolved or made into liquid. **2** that can be solved. [< L *solubilis* < *solvere* dissolve] —**sol′u·bil′i·ty, sol′u·ble·ness**, *n.* —**sol′u·bly**, *adv.*

so·lu·tion (sə lü′shən), *n.* **1** the solving of a problem. **2** explanation. **3** process of dissolving; changing of a solid or gas to a liquid by treatment with a liquid. **4** liquid or mixture formed by dissolving. **5** a separating into parts. **6** condition of being dissolved. Sugar and salt can be held in solution in water. [< L *solutio* < *solvere* loosen] —**so·lu′tion·al**, *adj.*

solution set, set which contains all of the solutions to an open sentence in mathematics.

solve (solv), *v.,* **solved**, **solv·ing.** find the answer to; clear up; explain. [< L *solvere* loosen] —**solv′a·ble**, *adj.* —**solv′a·bil′i·ty, solv′a·ble·ness**, *n.* —**solv′er**, *n.*

sol·vent (sol′vənt), *adj.* **1** able to pay all that one owes. **2** able to dissolve. —*n.* **1** substance, usually a liquid, that can dissolve other substances. **2** thing that

solves. [< L *solvens* loosening, paying] —**sol′ven·cy**, *n.*

So·ma·li (sə mä′li), *n., pl.* –**li, –lis.** member of a people living in E Africa or their language.

So·ma·lia (sə mä′lyə), *n.* country in E Africa.

so·mat·ic (sō mat′ik), *adj.* **1** of or pertaining to the body. **2** pertaining to the cavity of the body, or its walls. [< Gk., < *sôma* body] —**so·mat′i·cal·ly**, *adv.*

so·mat·o·plasm (sō′mə tə plaz′əm), *n.* protoplasm of all cells of the body except germ cells. [< Gk. *sôma* body + *plásma* something molded]

som·ber (som′bər), *adj.* **1** dark; gloomy. **2** melancholy; dismal. [< F *sombre*] —**som′ber·ly**, *adv.* —**som′ber·ness**, *n.*

som·bre·ro (som brār′ō), *n., pl.* –**brer·os.** a broad-brimmed hat worn in the SW United States, Mexico, etc. [< Sp., ult. < L *umbra* shade]

some (sum; *unstressed* səm), *adj.* **1** certain, but not known or named: *some people sleep more than others.* **2** a number of: *he was here some weeks ago.* **3** a quantity of: *have some water.* **4** a; any: *ask some girl to come here.* **5** about: *some twenty people saw it.* **6** notable; big; good: *that was some storm!* —*pron.* **1** certain unnamed persons or things: *some think so.* **2** a certain number or quantity: *may I have some of that?* —*adv.* **1** to some degree or extent; somewhat: *he is some better today.* **2** to a great degree or extent: *that's going some!*

and then some, *Informal.* with a good deal more. [OE *sum*]

–some¹, *suffix.* **1** tending to, as in *frolicsome.* **2** causing, as in *awesome, troublesome.* **3** to a considerable degree, as in *lonesome.* [OE *–sume*]

–some², *suffix.* group of, as in *twosome, foursome.* [< *some*]

some·bod·y (sum′bod′i; –bə di), *pron., n., pl.* –**bod·ies.** —*pron.* person not known or named; some person; someone. —*n.* person of importance.

some·how (sum′hou), *adv.* in a way not known or not stated; in one way or another.

somehow or other, in one way or another.

some·one (sum′wun; –wən), *pron., n.* some person; somebody.

som·er·sault (sum′ər sôlt), *n.* a roll or jump, turning the heels over the head. —*v.* perform a somersault.

turn a somersault, somersault: *turned somersaults on the mat.* [< earlier F *sombresault* < Pr., ult. < L *supra* over + *saltus* jump]

some·thing (sum′thing), *n.* **1** some thing; particular thing not named or known: *he has something on his mind.* **2** a certain amount or quantity; part; little: *something yet of doubt remains.* **3** thing or person of some value or importance: *he thinks he's something.* **4** thing or person that is to a certain extent an example of what is named: *Einstein was something of a violinist.* —*adv.* somewhat; to some extent or degree: *he is something like his father.*

something else, *Informal.* something special or remarkable.

some·time (sum′tīm), *adv.* **1** at an indefinite time in the future: *come over sometime.* **2** at an indefinite point of time: *sometime last March.* —*adj.* former: *a sometime pupil.*

some·times (sum′tīmz), *adv.* now and then; at times: *he comes to visit sometimes.*

some·what (sum′hwot), *adv.* to some extent or degree; slightly: *somewhat round.* —*n.* some part; some amount: *somewhat of a musician.*

some·where (sum′hwär), *adv.* **1** in or to some place; in or to one place or another: *he lives somewhere in the neighborhood.* **2** at some time: *it happened somewhere in the last century.* —*n.* an undetermined or unspecified place.

som·nam·bu·late (som nam′byə lāt), *v.*, **-lat·ed, -lat·ing.** walk in one's sleep.

som·nam·bu·lism (som nam′byə liz əm), *n.* sleepwalking. [< L *somnus* sleep + *ambulare* to walk] —**som·nam′bu·list,** *n.* —**som·nam′bu·lis′tic,** *adj.* —**som·nam′bu·lis′ti·cal·ly,** *adv.*

som·nif·er·ous (som nif′ər əs), *adj.* **1** causing sleep. **2** sleepy. [< L, < *somnus* sleep + *ferre* bring] —**som·nif′er·ous·ly,** *adv.*

som·no·lent (som′nə lənt), *adj.* sleepy; drowsy. [< L, < *somnus* sleep] —**som′no·lence, som′no·len·cy,** *n.* —**som′no·lent·ly,** *adv.*

son (sun), *n.* **1** a male child. **2** a male descendant. **3** boy or man attached to country, etc., as a child is to its parents. **4** anything thought of as a son in relation to its origin. **5** term of address to a boy or man from an older person, priest, etc.

the Son, Jesus Christ. [OE *sunu*]

so·nant (sō′nənt), *adj.* of sound; having sound; sounding. [< L *sonans* sounding < *sonus,* n., sound] —**so′nance,** *n.*

so·na·ta (sə nä′tə), *n.* piece of music, usually for the piano and sometimes another instrument, having three or four movements in contrasted rhythms but related keys. [< Ital., lit., sounded (on an instrument, as distinguished from sung), ult. < L *sonus* sound]

son·a·ti·na (son′ə tī′nə), *n.*, *pl.* **-nas, -ni** (-nā). short sonata. [< Ital., dim. of *sonata*]

song (sông; song), *n.* **1** something to sing; short poem set to music. **2** poetry that has a musical sound. **3** piece of music for, or as if for, a poem that is to be sung. **4** act or practice of singing. **5** any sound like singing: *the song of the brook.* **6** a mere trifle; low price: *buy things for a song.*

for a song, cheaply.

song and dance, *Informal,* explanation or account, not necessarily true, and often intended to impress or deceive. [OE *sang*]

song·bird (sông′bėrd′; song′-), *n.* **1** bird that sings. **2** a woman singer.

song·less (sông′lis; song′-), *adj.* without song; not able to sing, esp. of a bird.

Song of Solomon, The, a book of the Old Testament.

song sparrow, a small North American songbird with black, brown, and white feathers.

song·ster (sông′stər; song′-), *n.* **1** singer. **2** writer of songs or poems. **3** songbird.

song·stress (sông′stris; song′-), *n.* **1** a woman singer. **2** a woman writer of songs or poems; poetess. **3** a female songbird.

song thrush, 1 the wood thrush. **2** a European bird noted for its song; the mavis.

son·ic (son′ik), *adj.* **1** of, having to do with, or using sound waves. **2** having to do with the rate at which sound travels in air (1087 feet per second).

sonic barrier, point at which an aircraft or projectile attains the same rate of speed as sound; sound barrier. Air disturbances are encountered at this point.

sonic boom, loud noise produced by shock waves caused when an aircraft's speed is greater than the speed of sound.

son-in-law (sun′in lô′), *n.*, *pl.* **sons-in-law.** the husband of one's daughter.

son·net (son′it) *n.* poem having 14 lines, usually in iambic pentameter, and a certain arrangement of rhymes. [< F < Ital. < Pr. *sonet,* ult. < L *sonus* sound]

son·net·eer (son′ə tir′), *n.* writer of sonnets. —*v.* write sonnets.

son·ny (sun′i), *n.*, *pl.* **-nies.** little son.

so·no·rous (sə nô′rəs; -nō′-), *adj.* **1** giving out or having a deep, loud sound. **2** full and rich in sound. **3** having an impressive sound; high-sounding. [< L *sonorus,* ult. < *sonus* sound] —**so·nor′i·ty, so·no′rous·ness,** *n.* —**so·no′rous·ly,** *adv.*

soon (sün), *adv.* **1** in a short time; before long: *I will see you again soon.* **2** before the usual or expected time; early: *why have you come so soon?* **3** readily; willingly: *I would as soon ride as walk.* [OE *sōna* at once] —**soon′ness,** *n.*

soot (sut; süt), *n.* a black substance in the smoke from burning coal, wood, oil, etc. —*v.* cover or blacken with soot. [OE *sōt*]

sooth (süth), *Archaic.* —*n.* truth. —*adj.* true. —*adv.* in truth. [OE *sōth*] —**sooth′ly,** *adv.*

soothe (süth), *v.,* **soothed, sooth·ing. 1** quiet; calm; comfort. **2** make less painful; relieve; ease. [OE *sōthian*] —**sooth′er,** *n.* —**sooth′ing,** *adj.* —**sooth′ing·ly,** *adv.* —**sooth′ing·ness,** *n.*

sooth·say·er (süth′sā′ər), *n.* person who claims to tell what will happen; person who makes predictions. —**sooth′say′ing,** *n.*

soot·y (sut′i; süt′i), *adj.,* **soot·i·er, soot·i·est. 1** covered or blackened with soot. **2** dark-brown or black; dark-colored. —**soot′i·ly,** *adv.* —**soot′i·ness,** *n.*

sop (sop), *n.*, *v.*, **sopped, sop·ping.** —*n.* **1** piece of food dipped or soaked in milk, broth, etc. **2** *Fig.* something given to soothe or quiet; bribe. —*v.* **1** dip or soak. **2** take up (water, etc.); wipe; mop. **3** drench. [OE *sopp*]

soph·ism (sof′iz əm), *n.* **1** a clever but misleading argument; argument based on false or unsound reasoning. **2** fallacy. [< L < Gk., ult. < *sophos* clever]

soph·ist (sof′ist), *n.* **1** a clever but misleading reasoner. **2** Often, **Sophist. a** one of a class of teachers of rhetoric, philosophy, ethics, etc., in ancient Greece. **b** any member of this class at a later date who was concerned with clever, rather than sound, argument. **3** man of learning. —**so·phis′ti·cal, so·phis′tic,** *adj.* —**so·phis′ti·cal·ly,** *adv.* —**so·phis′ti·cal·ness,** *n.*

so·phis·ti·cate (*v.* sə·fis′tə·kāt; *adj., n.* sə·fis′tə·kāt, -kit), *v.,* **-cat·ed, -cat·ing,** *adj., n.* —*v.* make experienced in worldly ways. —*adj.* sophisticated. —*n.* a sophisticated person. [< Med.L *sophisticatus.* See SOPHISM.]

so·phis·ti·cat·ed (sə fis′tə kāt′id), *adj.* **1** experienced in worldly ways. **2** appealing to the tastes of sophisticated people.

so·phis·ti·ca·tion (sə fis′tə kā′shən), *n.* worldly experience or ideas.

soph·ist·ry (sof′is tri), *n.*, *pl.* **-ries. 1** unsound reasoning. **2** a clever but misleading argument. **3** art, practice, or learning of the ancient Greek sophists, esp. of their type of argument.

soph·o·more (sof′ə môr; sof′môr; -mōr), *n.* student in the second year of high school or college. —*adj.* of or pertaining to second-year students. [< *sophom,* var. of *sophism*]

soph·o·mor·ic (sof′ə môr′ik; sof môr′ik; -mor′-), *adj.* **1 a** of, pertaining to, or like a sophomore or sophomores. **b** *Fig.* intellectually immature. **2** conceited and pretentious but crude and ignorant. —**soph′o·mor′i·cal·ly,** *adv.*

so·po·rif·ic (sō′pə rif′ik; sop′ə-), *adj.* **1** causing or tending to cause sleep. **2** sleepy; drowsy. —*n.* drug that causes sleep. [< L *sopor* deep sleep + *facere* make]

sop·ping (sop′ing), *adj.* soaked; drenched.

sop·py (sop′i), *adj.,* **-pi·er, -pi·est. 1** soaked; very wet. **2** *Fig.* annoyingly or too sentimental.

so·pran·o (sə pran′ō; -prä′nō), *n.*, *pl.* **-pran·os, -pra·ni** (-prä′nē), *adj.* —*n.* **1** the highest singing voice in women and boys. **2** singer with such a voice. **3** a soprano part. —*adj.* of, sung by, or composed for a soprano. [< Ital., < *sopra* above < L *supra*]

sor·cer·er (sôr′sər ər), *n*. person who practices magic with the aid of evil spirits; magician.

sor·cer·ess (sôr′sər is), *n*. woman who practices magic with the aid of evil spirits; witch.

sor·cer·y (sôr′sər i), *n., pl.* **-cer·ies.** magic performed with the aid of evil spirits; witchcraft. [< OF *sorcerie,* ult. < L *sors* lot] **—sor′cer·ous,** *adj.* **—sor′cer·ous·ly,** *adv.*

sor·did (sôr′did), *adj.* **1** dirty; filthy. **2** caring too much for money; meanly selfish; mean; low; base. [< L *sordidus* dirty < *sordere* be dirty] **—sor′did·ly,** *adv.* **—sor′did·ness,** *n.*

sore (sôr; sōr), *adj.,* **sor·er, sor·est,** *n.* —*adj.* **1** painful; aching; tender; smarting: *a sore throat, a sore finger.* **2** suffering bodily pain from wounds, etc.: *his body was very sore.* **3** sad; distressed: *the suffering of the poor makes her heart sore.* **4** offended; angered; vexed. **5** *Fig.* causing pain, misery, anger, or offense; vexing: *a sore subject.* —*n.* **1** a painful place on the body where the skin or flesh is broken or bruised. **2** cause of pain, sorrow, sadness, anger, offense, etc. [OE *sār*] **—sore′ly,** *adv.* **—sore′ness,** *n.*

sore·head (sôr′hed′; sōr′-), *n. Informal.* person who is angry or offended. **—sore′head′ed,** *adj.*

sor·ghum (sôr′gəm), *n.* **1** a tall cereal plant resembling corn. One variety has a sweet juice used for making molasses, others provide food for livestock, and furnish material for brushes or brooms. **2** molasses or syrup made from a sorghum plant. [< NL < Ital. < Med.L *surgum*]

so·ror·i·ty (sə rôr′ə ti; -ror′-), *n., pl.* **-ties. 1** a sisterhood. **2** club or society of women or girls. [prob. < Med.L *sororitas* < L *soror* sister]

sor·rel[1] (sôr′əl; sor′-), *adj.* reddish-brown. —*n.* **1** a reddish-brown color. **2** a reddish-brown horse. [< OF *sorel* < *sor* yellowish-brown]

sor·rel[2] (sôr′əl; sor′-), *n.* any of several plants with sour leaves. [< OF *surele* < *sur* sour < Gmc.]

sor·row (sor′ō; sôr′ō), *n.* **1** grief; sadness; regret: *his sorrow was caused by the death of his brother.* **2** cause of grief, sadness, or regret; trouble; suffering; misfortune: *her sorrows have aged her.* —*v.* **1** feel or show grief, sadness, or regret. **2** be sad; feel sorry; grieve. [OE *sorg*] **—sor′row·er,** *n.* **—sor′row·ing·ly,** *adv.*

sor·row·ful (sor′ə fəl; sôr′-), *adj.* full of sorrow; feeling sorrow; sad. **—sor′row·ful·ly,** *adv.* **—sor′row·ful·ness,** *n.*

sor·ry (sor′i; sôr′-), *adj.,* **-ri·er, -ri·est. 1** feeling pity, regret, sympathy, etc.; sad: *be sorry for a loss.* **2** wretched; poor; pitiful: *a sorry sight.* **3** melancholy; dismal; gloomy. [OE *sārig* < *sār* sore] **—sor′ri·ly,** *adv.* **—sor′ri·ness,** *n.*

sort (sôrt), *n.* kind; class: *what sort of work does he do? art of a certain sort, he is a good sort.* —*v.* **1** arrange by kinds or classes. **2** separate from others; put.

of sorts, a of one kind or another. **b** of a poor or mediocre quality.

out of sorts, ill, cross, or uncomfortable.

sort of (*used adverbially*), somewhat; rather. [< OF, ult. < L *sors,* orig., lot] **—sort′a·ble,** *adj.* **—sort′er,** *n.*

sor·tie (sôr′tē), *n.* **1** a sudden attack by troops from a defensive position. **2** a single round trip of an aircraft on a tactical mission. [< F, < *sortir* go out]

SOS (es′ō′es′), **1** signal of distress consisting of the letters *s o s* of the international Morse alphabet (... — — — ...), originally used in wireless telegraphy. **2** any urgent call for help. **3** shoot on sight.

so·so, so·so (sō′sō′), or **so so,** *adj.* neither very good nor very bad. —*adv.* passably; indifferently; tolerably.

sos·te·nu·to (sos′tə nü′tō), *adj., adv.* **1** held longer; sustained, of a musical note or passage of music. **2** becoming slower in tempo. [< Ital. sustained]

sot (sot), *n.* person made stupid and foolish by drinking too much alcohol; drunkard. [< Med.L *sottus*] **—sot′tish,** *adj.* **—sot′tish·ly,** *adv.* **—sot′tish·ness,** *n.*

So·tho (sō′thō), *n., pl.* **-tho, -thos. 1** member of a people of S Africa. **2** Bantu language of the Sotho.

sot·to vo·ce (sot′ō vō′chē), **1** in an undertone. **2** aside; privately. [< Ital., lit., below (normal) voice]

sou (sü), *n.* **1** a former French coin. **2** anything of little value. [F, ult. < L *solidus,* a Roman coin]

sou·brette (sü bret′), *n.* **1** maidservant in a play or opera, displaying coquetry, pertness, and a spirit of intrigue. **2** person taking such a part. [< F < Pr. *soubreto* coy < *soubra* set aside]

sou·bri·quet (sü′brə kā), *n.* =sobriquet.

souf·flé (sü flā′; sü′flā), *n.* a frothy baked dish, usually made light by beaten eggs. —*adj.* puffed up. [< F, orig. pp. of *souffler* puff up]

sough (suf; sou), *v.* make a rustling or murmuring sound. —*n.* such a sound. [OE *swōgan*]

sought (sôt), *v.* pt. and pp. of **seek.**

soul (sōl), *n.* **1** the part of the human being that thinks, feels, and makes the body act; the spiritual part of a person. **2** energy of mind or feelings; spirit: *his writing has no soul.* **3** the essential part: *brevity is the soul of wit, the soul of honor.* **4** person: *don't tell a soul.* **5** =soul music.

upon my soul! as I hope to be saved! indeed! [OE *sāwol*]

soul food, 1 food typical of the S United States, esp. among blacks. **2** any food associated with home, comfort, etc.

soul·ful (sōl′fəl), *adj.* **1** full of feeling; deeply emotional. **2** expressing or suggesting a deep feeling. **—soul′ful·ly,** *adv.* **—soul′ful·ness,** *n.*

soul·less (sōl′lis), *adj.* having no soul; without spirit or noble feelings. **—soul′less·ly,** *adv.*

soul music, music influenced by jazz, rhythm and blues, and gospel, esp. as developed and performed by black musicians.

sound[1] (sound), *n.* **1** what can be heard; noise, note, tone, etc.: *the sound of music.* **2** one of the vocal elements in the oral communication of a language: *a vowel sound.* **3** effect produced on the mind by what is heard: *a warning sound.* —*v.* **1** make a sound or noise: *the horn sounded.* **2** be heard: *the bells sounded in his ears.* **4** order or direct by a sound: *sound a retreat.* **5** seem: *that excuse sounds queer.* **6** be filled with sound. [< OF *son* < L *sonus*]

sound[2] (sound), *adj.* **1** free from injury, disease or defect: *sound fruit, a sound body and mind.* **2** strong; safe; secure: *a sound business firm.* **3** correct; right; reasonable; reliable: *sound advice.* **4** having conventional ideas: *politically sound.* **5** thorough; hearty: *a sound sleep.* —*adv.* deeply; thoroughly. [OE (*ge*)*sund*] **—sound′ly,** *adv.* **—sound′ness,** *n.*

sound[3] (sound), *v.* **1** measure the depth of (water) by letting down a weight fastened to the end of a line. **2** examine or test by a line arranged to bring up a sample. **3** inquire into the feelings, inclination, etc., of (a person); examine; investigate: *sound him out on the idea.* **4** go toward the bottom; dive: *the whale sounded.* [< OF *sonder,* prob. < Gmc. source of *sound*[4]] **—sound′a·ble,** *adj.* **—sound′er,** *n.*

sound[4] (sound), *n.* **1** a narrow passage of water joining two seas, or between the mainland and an island: *Long Island Sound.* **2** arm of the sea: *Puget Sound.* **3** a sac in fishes containing air or gas that helps them in floating. [OE *sund* swimming; partly < Scand. *sund* strait]

sound barrier, point approximating the speed of sound at which an aircraft creates a shock wave as it reaches the speed of sound; sonic barrier.

sound·ing (soun′ding), *adj.* **1** that sounds. **2** resounding.

sound·ings (soun′dingz), *n.pl.* **1** Often, **sounding.** meaning the depth of water by letting down a weight fastened to the end of a line. **2** depths of water found by measuring in this way. **3** water not more than 600 feet deep.

sound·less (sound′lis), *adj.* without sound; making no sound. **—sound′less·ly,** *adv.*

sound·proof (sound′prüf′), *adj.* not letting sound pass through. —*v.* make soundproof.

sound track, recording of words, music, etc., made along one edge of a motion-picture film.

soup[1] (süp), *n.* a liquid food made by boiling meat, vegetables, fish, etc. [< F *soupe* < Gmc.]

soup² (süp), v. **soup up,** increase the horsepower of (a motor, etc.); add additional power to. [< supe(rcharge)]

soup·çon (süp sôn; süp′sôn), n. a slight trace or flavor. [< F]

soup·y (süp′i), adj., **soup·i·er, soup·i·est,** like soup.

sour (sour), adj. **1** having a taste like vinegar or lemon juice: *most green fruit is sour.* **2** fermented; spoiled: *sour milk.* **3** having a sour or rank smell. **4** *Fig.* disagreeable; bad-tempered; peevish: *a sour remark.* —v. **1** make or become sour; turn sour. **2** make or become peevish, bad-tempered, or disagreeable. —n. **1** something sour. **2** an acid beverage containing alcohol. —adv. in a sour manner. [OE *sūr*] —**sour′ish,** adj. —**sour′ly,** adv. —**sour′ness,** n.

sour·ball (sour′bôl′), n. round, hard candy, usually fruit-flavored, with a slightly sour taste.

source (sôrs; sōrs), n. **1** beginning of a brook or river; fountain; spring. **2** place from which anything comes or is obtained. **3** person, book, statement, etc., that supplies information. [< OF, ult. < L *surgere* rise, surge]

sour cream, thick cream made sour by a culturing process, used in cooking, baking, etc.

sour·dough (sour′dō′), n. prospector or pioneer in Alaska or Canada. [so called from their practice of saving a lump of sour dough from each breadmaking to start fermentation in subsequent baking]

sour grapes, something that a person pretends not to like or want because it is unattainable.

sour gum, the tupelo.

souse (sous), v., **soused, sous·ing,** n. —v. **1** plunge into liquid; drench; soak in a liquid. **2** soak in vinegar, brine, etc.: pickle. **3** *Slang.* make or become intoxicated. —n. **1** a plunging into a liquid. **2** liquid used for pickling. **3** something soaked or kept in pickle, esp. the head, ears, and feet of a pig. **4** *Slang.* drunkard. [ult. < OF *sous* pickled pork < Gmc.]

south (south), n. **1** direction to the right as one faces the rising sun; direction just opposite north. **2** Also, **South.** part of any country toward the south. **3 the South.** the part of the United States lying south of the Mason-Dixon Line, the Ohio River, Missouri, and Kansas. —adj. **1** lying toward or situated in the south. **2** originating in or coming from the south: *a south wind.* **3** South, in the southern part; southern: *South China.* —adv. **1** toward the south. **2** in the south. [OE *sūth*]

South Africa, Republic of, country in S Africa. —**South African.**

South African Dutch, =Afrikaans.

South America, continent in the Western Hemisphere, SE of North America. —**South American.**

South Carolina, a S state of the United States. —**South Carolinian.**

South Da·ko·ta (də kō tə), a Middle Western state of the United States. —**South Dakotan.**

South·down (south′doun′), n. any of an English breed of small, hornless sheep.

south·east (south′ēst′), adj. **1** halfway between south and east. **2** lying toward or situated in the southeast. **3** originating in or coming from the southeast. **4** directed toward the southeast. —n. **1** a southeast direction. **2** place that is in the southeast part or direction. —adv. **1** toward the southeast. **2** from the southeast. **3** in the southeast.

south·east·er (south′ēs′tər; sou′–), n. wind or storm from the southeast.

south·east·er·ly (south′ēs′tər li), adj., adv. **1** toward the southeast. **2** from the southeast.

south·east·ern (south′ēs′tərn), adj. **1** toward the southeast. **2** from the southeast. **3** of or pertaining to the southeast.

south·east·ward (south′ēst′wərd), adv. Also, **south′east′wards.** toward the southeast. —adj. **1** toward the southeast. **2** southeast. —n. =southeast.

south·east·ward·ly (south′ēst′wərd li), adj., adv. **1** toward the southeast. **2** of winds, from the southeast.

south·er (south′ər), n. wind or storm from the south.

south·er·ly (suth′ər li), adj., adv. **1** toward the south. **2** from the south. —**south′er·li·ness,** n.

south·ern (suth′ərn), adj. **1** toward the south. **2** from the south. **3** of or in the south. **4 Southern,** of or in the S part of the United States. —**south′ern·most,** adj.

Southern Cross, four bright stars in the form of a cross, used in finding the direction south.

south·ern·er (suth′ər nər), n. **1** native or inhabitant of the south. **2 Southerner,** native or inhabitant of the South of the U.S.

Southern Hemisphere, the half of the earth that is south of the equator.

South Island, largest island of New Zealand.

South Korea, country in the southern part of the Korean peninsula.

south·land (south′lənd; –land′), n. land in the south; southern part of a country.

south·paw (south′pô′), n. a left-handed baseball pitcher. —adj. -left-handed.

South Pole, the southern end of the earth's axis.

south·ward (south′wərd), adv. Also, **south′wards.** toward the south. —adj. **1** toward the south. **2** =south. —n. =south.

south·ward·ly (south′wərd li), adj., adv. **1** toward the south. **2** of winds, coming from the south.

south·west (south′west′), adj. **1** halfway between south and west. **2** lying toward or situated in the southwest. **3** originat-

ing in or coming from the southwest: *a southwest wind.* **4** directed toward the southwest. —n. **1** a southwest direction. **2** place that is in the southwest part or direction. **3** —adv. **1** toward the southwest. **2** from the southwest. **3** in the southwest.

the Southwest, New Mexico, Arizona, and S California.

south·west·er (south′west′tər for 1; sou′– for 2), n. **1** wind or storm from the southwest. **2** =sou′wester.

south·west·er·ly (south′wes′tər li), adj., adv. **1** toward the southwest. **2** from the southwest.

south·west·ern (south′wes′tərn), adj. **1** toward the southwest. **2** from the southwest. **3** of southwest; having to do with the southwest. **4 southwestern,** of, having to do with, or in New Mexico, Arizona, or S California.

south·west·ward (south′west′wərd; sou′–), adv. Also, **south′west′wards.** toward the southwest. —adj. **1** toward the southwest. **2** =southwest. —n. =southwest.

south·west·ward·ly (south′west′wərd li), adj., adv. **1** toward the southwest. **2** of winds, from the southwest.

sou·ve·nir (sü′və nir′; sü′və nir), n. **1** something to remind one of a place, person, or occasion; keepsake. **2** a memory. [< F, orig. inf., < L *subvenire* come to mind < *sub–* up + *venire* come]

sou'west·er (sou′wes′tər), n. a waterproof hat having a broader brim behind to protect the neck, worn esp. by seamen.

sov·er·eign (sov′rən), n. **1** king or queen; supreme ruler; monarch. **2** a former British gold coin, worth 20 shillings. —adj. **1** having the rank or power of a sovereign. **2** greatest in rank or power. **3** independent of the control of other governments. **4** above all others; supreme; greatest. **5** very excellent or powerful. [< OF *soverain,* ult. < L *super* over] —**sov′er·eign·ly,** adv.

sov·er·eign·ty (sov′rən ti), n., pl. **–ties. 1** supreme power or authority; exercise of power without outside control or interference. **2** rank, power, or jurisdiction of a sovereign.

so·vi·et (sō′vi et; –it; sov′i–), n. council; assembly, esp. in the former Soviet Union. —adj. **1** of or pertaining to soviets. **2 Soviet,** of or pertaining to the former Soviet Union. [< Russ., council]

Soviet Russia, =Soviet Union.

Soviet Union former union of fifteen Soviet republics in E Europe and W and N Asia.

sow¹ (sō), v., **sowed, sown** (sōn) or **sowed, sowing. 1** scatter (seed) on the ground; plant (seed); plant seed in. **2** scatter (anything). [OE *sāwan*] —**sow′er,** n.

sow² (sou), n. fully grown female pig. [OE *sū*]

sox (soks), n. pl. *Informal.* socks (short stockings).

soy (soi), **soy·a** (soi′ə), n. **1** a Chinese and Japanese sauce for fish, meat, etc., made from fermented soybeans. 2 =soybean. [< Jap. < Chinese, < *shi* condiment + *yu* oil]

soy·bean (soi′bēn′), *n.* 1 a bean widely grown in China, Japan, and the United States. 2 plant that it grows on.

Sp., 1 Spain. 2 Spaniard. 3 Spanish.

sp., 1 special. 2 species. 3 specific. 4 specimen. 5 spelling.

spa (spä), *n.* 1 a mineral spring. 2 place where there is a mineral spring. 3 place that offers diet, exercise, beauty treatments, etc. [after *Spa,* Belgian resort city]

space (spās), *n., v.,* **spaced, spac·ing.** —*n.* 1 a unlimited room or place extending in all directions: *the earth moves through space.* b =outer space. 2 limited place or room: *a space 2½ by 4 by 8 inches.* 3 distance: *a space of ten miles.* 4 length of time: *a space of two hours.* 5 *Music.* one of the intervals between the lines of a staff. 6 accommodations on an airplane, etc. —*v.* 1 fix the space or spaces of; separate by spaces. 2 divide into spaces. **space out,** *Informal.* be inattentive; preoccupied: *a bad idea to space out in class.* [< OF < L *spatium*] —**spac′er,** *n.*

space age, period characterized by development of various spacecraft and exploration of outer space.

space cadet, *Informal.* person who is inattentive or preoccupied.

space·craft (spās′kraft′; –kräft′), *n.* any vehicle used for spaceflight.

space·flight (spās′flīt′) or **space flight,** flight into outer space.

space shuttle, vehicle that is capable of making repeated trips from earth to space and back.

space station, a structure consisting of a satellite in orbit around the earth, used as an observatory or a launching site for travel in outer space.

space ship, =spacecraft.

space suit, an airtight suit designed to protect travelers in outer space from radiation, heat, and lack of oxygen.

space·walk (spās′wôk′), *n.* moving and working outside a spacecraft in space, esp. to make repairs, launch a satellite, etc.

spa·cious (spā′shəs), *adj.* containing much space; with plenty of room; vast. —**spa′cious·ly,** *adv.* —**spa′cious·ness,** *n.*

spac·y (spā′si), *adj.,* **spac·i·er, spac·i·est.** *Informal.* inattentive; preoccupied. Also, **spacey.**

spade¹ (spād), *n., v.,* **spad·ed, spad·ing.** —*n.* tool for digging; a kind of shovel. —*v.* dig with a spade. **call a spade a spade,** call a thing by its real name; speak plainly and frankly. [OE *spadu*] —**spad′er,** *n.*

spade² (spād), *n.* 1 a black figure (♠) used on playing cards. 2 a playing card bearing such figures. **spades,** suit of playing cards bearing such figures, usually the highest rank-ing suit. [< Ital. < L < Gk. *spathe* sword, broad blade]

spade·work (spād′wėrk′), *n.* 1 digging with a spade. 2 *Fig.* research; preparation for doing something.

spa·dix (spā′diks), *n., pl.* **spa·dix·es, spa·di·ces** (spā dī′sēz). spike composed of minute flowers on a fleshy stem. A spadix is usually enclosed in a petallike leaf called a spathe, as in the jack-in-the-pulpit and the calla lily. [< L < Gk., palm branch]

spa·ghet·ti (spə get′i), *n.* long, slender sticks made of a mixture of flour and water, soft when cooked. [< Ital., pl. dim. of *spago* cord]

Spain (spān), *n.* country in SW Europe.

spake (spāk), *v. Archaic.* pt. of **speak.**

span¹ (span), *n., v.,* **spanned, span·ning.** —*n.* 1 distance between two supports: *the arch had a fifty-foot span.* 2 part between two supports: *the bridge crossed the river in three spans.* 3 the distance between the tip of a person's thumb and the tip of the little finger when the hand is spread out; about 9 inches. 4 the full extent: *the span of life, the span of memory.* 5 a short length of time: "*A life's but a span.*" —*v.* 1 extend over: *a bridge spanned the river.* 2 measure by the hand spread out. [OE *spann*]

span² (span), *n.* pair of horses or other animals harnessed and driven together. [< Du., LG, < *spannen* stretch, yoke]

span³ (span), *v. Archaic.* pt. of **spin.**

span·gle (spang′gəl), *n., v.,* **–gled, –gling.** —*n.* 1 a small piece of glittering metal used for decoration. 2 any small bright bit: *this rock shows spangles of gold.* —*v.* 1 decorate with spangles. 2 sprinkle with small bright bits: *the sky is spangled with stars.* 3 glitter. [dim. of earlier *spang,* prob. < MDu. *spange* brooch] —**span′gler,** *n.* —**span′gly,** *adj.*

Span·iard (span′yərd), *n.* native or inhabitant of Spain.

span·iel (span′yəl), *n.* any of various breeds of dogs, usually of small or medium size with long, silky hair and drooping ears. [< OF *espagneul,* orig., Spanish < L *Hispania* Spain]

Span·ish (span′ish), *adj.* of Spain; pertaining to Spain, its people, or their language. —*n.* 1 the people of Spain. 2 the language of Spain.

Spanish America, countries and islands S of the United States, in which the principal language is Spanish; Latin America. —**Spanish American.**

Spanish Main, 1 originally, the mainland of America adjacent to the Caribbean Sea, esp. between the mouth of the Orinoco River and the Isthmus of Panama. 2 in later use, the Caribbean Sea.

Spanish moss, plant growing on the branches of certain trees, from which it hangs in gray streamers, found in the S United States.

spank (spangk) *v.* strike, esp. with the open hand, on the buttocks. —*n.* a blow with the open hand; slap. [imit.]

spank·er (spangk′ər), *n.* a fore-and-aft sail on the mast nearest the stern.

spank·ing (spangk′ing), *adj.* 1 blowing briskly. 2 quick and vigorous. 3 *Informal.* unusually fine, great, large, etc. [cf. Dan. *spanke* strut]

span·ner (span′ər), *n.* 1 one that spans. 2 =wrench.

spar¹ (spär), *n., v.,* **sparred, spar·ring.** —*n.* 1 a stout pole used to support or extend the sails of a ship; mast, yard, gaff, boom, etc., of a ship. 2 the main beam of an airplane wing. —*v.* provide (a ship) with spars. [ME *sparre.* Cf. Scand. *sparri,* MDu. *sparre.*]

spar² (spär), *v.,* **sparred, spar·ring,** *n.* —*v.* 1 make motions of attack and defense with the arms and fists; box. 2 *Fig.* dispute. —*n.* 1 a boxing match. 2 *Fig.* a dispute.

spar³ (spär), *n.* a shiny mineral that splits into flakes easily. [OE *spœr–*] —**spar′ry,** *adj.*

spare (spār), *v.,* **spared, spar·ing,** *adj.,* **spar·er, spar·est,** *n.* —*v.* 1 show mercy to; refrain from harming or destroying: *he spared his enemy.* 2 save from labor, pain, etc.: *spare a person's feelings, spare you the trouble.* 3 use in small quantities or not at all; be saving of: *spare gas.* 4 get along without; do without: *can you spare a dime?* —*adj.* 1 free for other use: *spare time.* 2 extra: *a spare tire.* 3 thin; lean: *a spare person.* 4 small in quantity; meager; scanty. —*n.* a spare thing, part, tire, etc. [OE *sparian*] —**spare′ly,** —*adv.* —**spare′ness,** *n.* —**spar′er,** *n.*

spare·rib (spār′rib′), *n* rib of pork having less meat than the ribs near the loins.

spar·ing (spār′ing), *adj.* 1 that spares. 2 economical; frugal. —**spar′ing·ly,** *adv.* —**spar′ing·ness,** *n.*

spark (spärk), *n.* 1 a small bit of fire: *a spark from his match caused the fire.* 2 flash given off when electricity jumps across an open space. 3 flash; gleam: *a spark of light.* 4 *Fig.* a small amount: *a spark of interest.* —*v.* 1 flash; gleam. 2 send out small bits of fire; produce sparks. 3 fire (one's associates, etc.) with enthusiasm; enliven. [OE *spearca*]

spar·kle (spär′kəl), *v.,* **–kled, –kling,** *n.* —*v.* 1 send out little sparks, esp. as fire. 2 shine; glitter; flash; gleam. 3 be brilliant; be lively. 4 bubble: *a sparkling drink.* —*n.* 1 a little spark. 2 shine; glitter; flash; gleam. 3 brilliance; liveliness. [< *spark¹*] —**spar′kling,** *adj.* —**spar′kling·ly,** *adv.*

spar·kler (spär′klər), *n.* firework that sends out little sparks.

spark plug, device in the cylinder of a gasoline engine by which the mixture of gasoline and air is exploded by an electric spark.

spar·row (spar′ō), *n.* any of many small finches, such as the song sparrow, the

English sparrow, and the chipping sparrow. [OE *spearwa*]

sparrow hawk 1 small falcon of N America that feeds on insects, mice, etc. **2** hawk of Europe and Asia.

sparse (spärs), *adj.,* **spars·er, spars·est.** thinly scattered; occurring here and there: *a sparse population.* [< L *sparsus,* pp. of *spargere* scatter] —**sparse′ly,** *adv.* —**sparse′ness, spar′si·ty,** *n.*

Spar·tan (spär′tən), *adj.* like the Spartans; simple, frugal, severe, and sternly disciplined. —*n.* person who is like the Spartans —**Spar′tan·ism,** *n.*

spasm (spaz′əm), *n.* **1** a sudden, abnormal, involuntary contraction of a muscle or muscles. **2** any sudden, brief fit of activity. [< L < Gk. *spasmos* < *spaein* draw up, tear away]

spas·mod·ic (spaz mod′ik), **spas·mod·i·cal** (–ə kəl), *adj.* **1** pertaining to spasms; resembling a spasm. **2** sudden and violent, but brief; occurring very irregularly. **3** having or showing bursts of excitement. —**spas·mod′i·cal·ly,** *adv.*

spas·tic (spas′tik), *adj.* **1** caused by a spasm or spasms. **2** of, having to do with, or characterized by spasms. —*n.* person suffering from a paralysis of a muscle or muscles. —**spas′ti·cal·ly,** *adv.*

spat¹ (spat), *n., v.,* **spat·ted, spat·ting.** —*n.* a slight quarrel. —*v.* quarrel slightly. [? imit.]

spat² (spat), *v.* pt. and pp. of **spit¹.**

spate (spāt), *n.* **1** a sudden outburst: *a spate of muggings.* **2** large number: *a spate of reality TV shows.* **3** flood; freshet. [ME; akin to OE *spātan* to spit]

spathe (spāth), *n.* a large bract or pair of bracts that enclose a flower cluster. The calla lily has a white spathe around a yellow flower cluster. [< Gk., palm branch. oar blade] —**spathed,** *adj.*

spa·tial (spā′shəl), *adj.* **1** of or pertaining to space. **2** existing in space. —**spa′ti·al′i·ty,** *n.* —**spa′tial·ly,** *adv.*

spat·ter (spat′ər), *v.* **1** scatter or dash in drops or particles. **2** fall in drops or particles: *rain spatters on the sidewalk.* **3** strike in a shower; strike in a number of places: *a rain of bullets spattered the building.* **4** splash or spot with mud, slander, disgrace, etc. —*n.* **1** a spattering: *a spatter of mud.* **2** sound of spattering. **3** a splash or spot. [cf. Du., LG *spatten* spout] —**spat′ter·ing·ly,** *adv.*

spat·u·la (spach′ə lə), *n.* tool with a broad, flat, flexible blade, used for mixing drugs, spreading paints, frostings, etc. [< L, dim. of *spatha* flat blade < Gk. *spathe*] —**spat′u·lar,** *adj.*

spav·in (spav′ən), *n.* disease of horses in which a bony swelling forms at the hock, causing lameness. [< OF *espavain*] —**spav′ined,** *adj.*

spawn (spôn), *n.* **1** eggs of fish, frogs, shellfish, and the like. **2** young newly hatched from such eggs. **3** a swarming brood; offspring. **4** product; result. [< v.] —*v.* bring forth; give birth to.

[< OF < L *expandere* spread out. Doublet of EXPAND.]

spay (spā), *v.* remove the ovaries of. [< AF *espeier,* ult. < OF *espee* sword < L *spatha.* See SPADE².]

speak (spēk), *v.,* **spoke** or (*Archaic*) **spake, spo·ken** or (*Archaic*) **spoke, speak·ing. 1** say words; talk: *do not speak to me.* **2** make a speech: *who is going to speak at the forum?* **3** tell; express; make known: *speak the truth.* **4** use (a language): *do you speak French?*

so to speak, to speak in such a manner.

speak for, a speak in the interest of; represent. **b** ask or apply for.

speak of, mention; refer to.

speak out or **up,** speak loudly, clearly, or freely.

speak out (or **up**) **for,** speak in defense or support of: *speak out for angry homeowners.* [OE *specan*] —**speak′a·ble,** *adj.*

speak·eas·y (spēk′ēz′ī), *n., pl.* **-eas·ies.** place where alcoholic liquors are sold contrary to law.

speak·er (spēk′ər), *n.* **1** person who speaks. **2** a presiding officer. —**speak′er·ship,** *n.*

Speaker of the House, the presiding officer of the House of Representatives.

speak·ing (spēk′ing), *n.* act, utterance, or discourse of a person who speaks. —*adj.* **1** used in, suited to, or involving speech: *within speaking distance.* **2** permitting conversation: *a speaking acquaintance with a person.* **3** that speaks: *a speaking dummy.* —**speak′ing·ly,** *adv.*

spear¹ (spir), *n.* weapon with a long shaft and a sharp-pointed head. —*v.* pierce with a spear. [OE *spere*] —**spear′er, spear′man,** *n.*

spear² (spir), *n.* sprout or shoot of a plant: *a spear of grass.* —*v.* sprout or shoot into a long stem. [var. of *spire;* infl. by *spear¹*]

spear·head (spir′hed′), *n.* **1** the sharp-pointed striking end of a spear. **2** *Fig.* part that comes first in an attack, undertaking, etc. —*v.* go first; head.

spear·mint (spir′mint′), *n.* common mint, a fragrant herb much used for flavoring.

spec., special.

spe·cial (spesh′əl), *adj.* **1** of a particular kind; distinct from others; not general: *a special key, the special features of a plan.* **2** different from what is ordinary or usual; exceptional: *a special occasion, special importance.* —*n.* **1** any special person or thing. **2** featured product, esp. one with a reduced price: *this week's specials.* [< L, < *species* appearance] —**spe′cial·ly,** *adv.* —**spe′cial·ness,** *n.*

spe·cial·ist (spesh′əl ist), *n.* person who devotes or restricts himself or herself to one particular branch of study, business, etc. —**spe′cial·ism,** *n.* —**spe′cial·is′tic,** *adj.*

spe·ci·al·i·ty (spesh′i al′ə ti), *n., pl.* **-ties. 1** a special or distinctive quality or char-

acteristic. **2** a special point; particular; detail. **3** specialty.

spe·cial·ize (spesh′əl īz), *v.,* **-ized, -iz·ing. 1** pursue some special branch of study, work, etc.: *many students specialize in engineering.* **2** adapt to special conditions; give special form, use, duty, etc., to; limit. **3** develop in a special way; take on a special form, use, etc. —**spe′cial·i·za′tion,** *n.* —**spe′cial·iz′er,** *n.*

spe·cial·ty (spesh′əl ti), *n., pl.* **-ties. 1** a special study; special line of work, profession, trade, etc. **2** product, article, etc., to which special attention is given: *a specialty of good service and reliable products.*

spe·ci·a·tion (spē′shi ā′shən), *n.* evolutionary formation of a new species. —**spe′ci·ate,** *v.*

spe·cie (spē′shi), *n.* money in the form of coins; metal money. [< L (*in*) *specie* (in) kind, abl. of *species* kind]

spe·cies (spē′shiz), *n., pl.* **-cies. 1** group of animals or plants that have certain permanent characteristics in common. **2** kind; sort; distinct kind or sort. [< L, orig., appearance. Doublet of SPICE.]

specif., specific; specifically.

spe·cif·ic (spi sif′ik), *adj.* definite; precise; particular: *a specific rule, a scaly skin is a specific feature of snakes.* —*n.* any specific statement, quality, etc. [< LL, < L *species* sort + *facere* make] —**spe·cif′i·cal·ly,** *adv.* —**spec′i·fic′i·ty, spe·cif′ic·ness.** *n.*

spec·i·fi·ca·tion (spes′ə fə kā′shən), *n.* **1** act of specifying; definite mention; detailed statement of particulars. **2** Often, **specifications.** a detailed description of the dimensions, materials, etc., for a building, road, dam, boat, etc. **3** something specified; particular item, article, etc.

specific gravity, ratio of the weight of a given volume of any substance to that of the same volume of some other substance taken as a standard, water being used for solids and liquids, and hydrogen or air for gases.

specific heat, 1 number of calories of heat required to raise the temperature of one gram of a substance one degree centigrade. **2** the ratio of the amount of heat required to raise the temperature of a substance one degree as compared with another substance.

spec·i·fy (spes′ə fī), *v.,* **-fied, -fy·ing. 1** mention or name definitely; state or describe in detail: *specify what you want.* **2** include in the specifications. [< LL, < *specificus* SPECIFIC] —**spec′i·fi·a·ble,** *adj.* —**spec′i·fi′er,** *n.*

spec·i·men (spes′ə mən), *n.* one of a group or class taken to show what the others are like; single part, thing, etc., regarded as an example of its kind. [< L, < *specere* to view]

spe·cious (spē′shəs), *adj.* making a good appearance; seeming desirable, reasonable, or probable, but not really so.

[< L, < *species* appearance] —**spe′cious·ly,** *adv.* —**spe′cious·ness,** *n.*

speck (spek), *n.* **1** a small spot; stain. **2** a tiny bit; particle. —*v.* mark with specks. [OE *specca*]

speck·le (spek′əl), *n., v.,* **-led, -ling.** —*n.* a small spot or mark. —*v.* mark with speckles.

specs (speks), *n. pl.* **1** spectacles.

spec·ta·cle (spek′tə kəl), *n.* **1** thing to look at; sight.

make a spectacle of oneself, draw attention to oneself in public, esp. by embarrassing or unsuitable behavior.

spectacles, pair of glasses to help a person's sight or to protect his eyes. [< L *spectaculum,* ult. < *specere* to view] —**spec′ta·cled,** *adj.*

spec·tac·u·lar (spek tak′yə lər), *adj.* **1** making a great display. **2** pertaining to a spectacle or show. —*n.* spectacular show or event. —**spec·tac′u·lar′i·ty,** *n.* —**spec·tac′u·lar·ly,** *adv.*

spec·ta·tor (spek′tā tər; spek tā′–), *n.* person who watches without taking part. [< L, < *spectare* to watch < *specere* to view]

spec·ter (spek′tər), *n.* ghost. [< L *spectrum* appearance. See SPECTRUM.]

spec·tral (spek′trəl), *adj.* **1** of or like a specter; ghostly. **2** of or produced by the spectrum: *spectral colors.* —**spec′tral·ness,** *n.* —**spec′tral·ly,** *adv.*

spec·trom·e·ter (spek trom′ə tər), *n.* spectroscope that has a scale for measuring spectra were lengths. —**spec·trom′e·try,** *n.*

spec·tro·scope (spek′trə skōp), *n.* instrument for obtaining and examining the spectrum of a ray from any source. —**spec′tro·scop′ic, spec′tro·scop′i·cal,** *adj.* —**spec′tro·scop′i·cal·ly,** *adv.*

spec·tros·co·py (spek tros′kə pi; spek′trə skō′pi), *n.* **1** science having to do with the examination and analysis of spectra. **2** use of the spectroscope. —**spec·tros′co·pist,** *n.*

spec·trum (spek′trəm), *n., pl.* **-tra** (-trə), **-trums. 1** the band of colors formed when a beam of light is broken up by being passed through a prism or by some other means. A rainbow has all the colors of the spectrum: red, orange, yellow, green, blue, indigo, and violet. **2** band of colors formed when any radiant energy is broken up. The ends of such a band are not visible to the eye, but are studied by photography, heat effects, etc. **3** the wave-length range between 30,000 meters and 3 centimeters. **4** *Fig.* range; breadth; scope: *the spectrum of her knowledge.* [< L, appearance, < *specere* to view]

spec·u·late (spek′yə lāt), *v.,* **-lat·ed, -lat·ing. 1** reflect; meditate; consider; conjecture. **2** buy or sell when there is a large risk, with the hope of making a profit from future price changes. [< L, < *specula* watchtower]

spec·u·la·tion (spek′yə lā′shən), *n.* **1** thought; reflection; conjecture. **2** a buy-ing or selling when there is a large risk, with the hope of making a profit from future price changes.

spec·u·la·tive (spek′yə lā′tiv; –lə tiv), *adj.* **1** thoughtful; reflective. **2** theoretical rather than practical. **3** risky. **4** of or involving speculation in land, stocks, etc. —**spec′u·la′tive·ly,** *adv.*

spec·u·la·tor (spek′yə lā′tər), *n.* person who speculates.

speech (spēch), *n.* **1** act of speaking; talk: *express anger in speech.* **2** power of speaking: *the gift of speech.* **3** manner of speaking: *slurred speech.* **4** what is said; the words spoken. **5** a public talk: *an after-dinner speech.* **6** language: *native speech.* [OE *spǣc*] —**speech′ful,** *adj.*

speech·i·fy (spēch′ə fī), *v.,* **-fied, -fy·ing.** *Informal.* make a speech or speeches. —**speech′i·fi′er,** *n.*

speech·less (spēch′lis), *adj.* **1** not able to speak. **2** silent. —**speech′less·ly,** *adv.* —**speech′less·ness.** *n.*

speed (spēd), *n., v.,* **sped** (sped) or **speed·ed, speed·ing.** —*n.* **1** a swift or rapid movement: *the speed of a rocket.* **2** rate of movement: *at full speed.* —*v.* **1** go fast: *the boat sped over the water.* **2** make go faster: *speed production, speed an undertaking.* **3** *Slang.* =methamphetamine.

speed up, go or cause to go faster; increase in speed. [OE *spēd*] —**speed′ster,** *n.*

speed·boat (spēd′bōt), *n.* motorboat built to go fast.

speed·er (spēd′ər), *n.* person or thing that speeds, esp. a person who drives an automobile at a higher speed than is legal or safe.

speed limit, restriction on the speed a vehicle can lawfully travel on a highway or road.

speed·om·e·ter (spēd om′ə tər), *n.* instrument to indicate speed.

speed trap, place where drivers exceeding the lawful speed are often caught by police.

speed·up (spēd′up′), *n.* a speeding up; increase in speed.

speed·well (spēd′wel), *n.* any of various low plants with blue, purple, pink, or white flowers; veronica.

speed·y (spēd′i), *adj.,* **speed·i·er, speed·i·est. 1** moving, going, or acting with speed: *speedy workers, speedy progress, a speedy change.* **2** prompt: *a speedy decision.* —**speed′i·ly,** *adv.* —**speed′i·ness,** *n.*

spe·le·ol·o·gy (spē′li ol′ə ji), *n.* branch of science dealing with caves. —**spe′le·ol′o·gist,** *n.*

spell[1] (spel), *v.,* **spelled** or **spelt, spell·ing. 1** write or say the letters of (a word) in order: *spell a word.* **2** mean; imply: *delay spells danger.*

spell out, a explain simply and lucidly. **b** read with difficulty. [< OF *espeller* < Gmc.]

spell[2] (spel), *n.* **1** word or set of words having magic power. **2** fascination; charm.

cast a spell on, fascinate.

under a spell, fascinated. [OE, story]

spell[3] (spel), *n., v.,* **spelled, spell·ing.** —*n.* **1** period of work or duty: *the sailor's spell at the wheel was four hours.* **2** period or time of anything. [ME; akin to v.] —*v.* work in place of (another) for a while. [OE *spelian,* v.]

spell·bind (spel′bīnd′), *v.,* **-bound, -bind·ing.** make spellbound; enchant. —**spell′bind′er,** *n.*

spell·bound (spel′bound′), *adj.* too interested to move; fascinated; enchanted.

spell·er (spel′ər), *n.* **1** person who spells words. **2** book for teaching spelling.

spell·ing (spel′ing), *n.* **1** the writing or saying of the letters of a word in order. **2** way that a word is spelled.

spelling bee, a spelling contest.

spend (spend), *v.,* **spent, spend·ing. 1** pay out: *how much money did you spend?* **2** pay out money: *earn before you spend.* **3** use (labor, words, time, etc.) on some object, etc.: *don't spend any more time on that job.* **4** pass (time) in a particular manner: *spend a day at the beach.* **5** wear out; exhaust: *the storm has spent its force.* [OE *spendan* < L *expendere.* Doublet of EXPEND.] —**spend′a·ble,** *adj.* —**spend′er,** *n.*

spend·thrift (spend′thrift′), *n.* person who wastes money. —*adj.* extravagant with money.

spent (spent), *v.* pt. and pp. of **spend.** —*adj.* **1** used up. **2** worn out; tired: *a spent swimmer.*

sperm[1] (spėrm), *n.* **1** the fluid of a male animal that fertilizes the eggs of the female. **2** one of the male germ cells in it; spermatozoon. [< L < Gk. *sperma* seed < *speirein* sow]

sperm[2] (spėrm), *n.* **1** spermaceti. **2** a sperm whale. **3** sperm oil. [short for *spermaceti*]

sper·ma·cet·i (spėr′mə set′i; –sē′ti), *n.* a whitish, waxy substance obtained from the oil in the head of the sperm whale and used in making fine candles, ointments, cosmetics, etc. [< Med.L *sperma ceti* sperm of a whale]

sper·mat·ic (spėr mat′ik), *adj.* **1** of or pertaining to sperm; seminal; generative. **2** pertaining to a sperm gland.

sper·ma·tid (spėr′mə tid), *n.* cell that develops into a sperm.

sper·ma·to·phyte (spėr′mə tə fīt′), *n.* plant that produces seeds. The spermatophytes form the largest division of the plant kingdom. [< *spermato–* (< Gk. *sperma* seed) + *–phyte* (< Gk. *phyton* plant)] —**sper′ma·to·phyt′ic,** *adj.*

sper·ma·to·zo·on (spėr′mə tə zō′ ən), *n., pl.* **-zo·a** (-zō′ə). the male reproductive cell; sperm cell. A spermatozoon unites with an ovum to fertilize it. [< *spermato–* (< Gk. *sperma* seed) + *–zoon* (< Gk. *zoion* animal)] —**sper′ma·to·zo′al, sper′ma·to·zo′an, sper′ma·to·zo′ic,** *adj.*

sperm oil, a light-yellow oil from the sperm whale, used for lubricating.

sperm whale, a large, square-headed, toothed whale that has a large cavity in its head filled with sperm oil and spermaceti.

spew (spū), *v.* throw out; cast forth; vomit. [OE *spīwan*] —**spew′er,** *n.*

sp. gr., specific gravity.

sphag·num (sfag′nəm), *n.* any of various soft mosses, found chiefly on the surface of bogs. **2** a mass or quantity of this moss used by gardeners in potting and packing plants, etc. [< NL < Gk. *sphagnos,* kind of moss]

sphere (sfir), *n., v.,* **sphered, spher·ing.** —*n.* **1** a round body whose surface is at all points equally distant from the center; globe; ball. **2** place or surroundings in which a person or thing exists, acts, works, etc.: *woman's sphere.* **3** range; extent; region: *sphere of influence.* **4** any of the stars or planets. —*v.* **1** enclose in or as if in a sphere. **2** form into a sphere. [< L < Gk. *sphaira*]

spher·i·cal (sfer′ə kəl), *adj.* **1** shaped like a sphere. **2** of or pertaining to a sphere or spheres. —**spher′i·cal·ness,** *n.*

sphe·roid (sfir′oid), *n.* a body shaped somewhat like a sphere. **2** a solid generated by the revolution of an ellipse about one of its axes. —*adj.* almost spherical. —**sphe·roi′dal,** *adj.* —**sphe·roi′dal·ly,** *adv.*

sphinc·ter (sfingk′tər), *n.* a ringlike muscle that surrounds an opening or passage of the body, and can contract to close it. [< LL < Gk. *sphinkter < sphingein* squeeze] —**sphinc′ter·al,** *adj.*

sphinx (sfingks), *n., pl.* **sphinx·es, sphin·ges** (sfin′jēz). **1** statue of a lion's body with the head of a man, ram, or hawk. **2** **Sphinx,** a huge statue with a man's head and a lion's body, near Cairo, Egypt. **3** a puzzling or mysterious person. [< L < Gk.]

sphyg·mo·ma·nom·e·ter (sfig′mō mə nom′ə tər), *n.* device that measures blood pressure. [< Gk. *sphygmós* throbbing, heartbeat + *manós* at intervals + E *-meter*]

spi·cate (spī′kāt), *adj.* **1** of a plant, having or arranged in spikes. **2** of an animal, having the form of a spike; pointed. [< L *spīcātus* furnished with spikes]

spice (spīs), *n., v.,* **spiced, spic·ing.** —*n.* **1** seasoning. Pepper, cinnamon, cloves, ginger, and nutmeg are common spices. **2** a spicy, fragrant odor. **3** something that adds flavor or interest. —*v.* **1** put spice in; season: *spiced pickles.* **2** add flavor or interest to. [< OF, ult. < L *species* sort. Doublet of SPECIES.] —**spiced,** *adj.* —**spic′er,** *n.*

spick-and-span (spik′ən span′), *adj.* neat and clean; spruce or smart; fresh; new: *a spick-and-span uniform.* [short for *spick-and-span-new; spick,* var. of *spike;*

span-new < Scand. *spān-nȳr < spānn* chip + *nȳr* new]

spic·ule (spik′ūl), *n.* **1** a small, slender, sharp-pointed piece, usually bony or crystalline. **2** such a piece, as the skeletal element of sponges, etc. **3** a small spike of flowers. [< L *spiculum,* dim. of *spicum,* var. of *spica* ear of grain]

spic·y (spīs′i), *adj.,* **spic·i·er, spic·i·est. 1** flavored with spice. **2** like spice. **3** lively; keen. —**spic′i·ly,** *adv.* —**spic′i·ness,** *n.*

spi·der (spī′dər), *n.* **1** any of the eight-legged, wingless arachnids, many of which spin webs to catch insects for food. **2** something like or suggesting a spider. **3** frame with three legs to support a pot or pan over a fire. [OE *spīthra < spinnan* spin] —**spi′der·y,** *adj.*

spider monkey, monkey of Central and South America that has a long, slim body and long tail.

spi·der·wort (spī′dər wėrt′), *n.* a trailing plant that takes root at the knots of its stems and has clusters of flowers.

spiel (spēl), *n.* *Informal.* talk; speech; harangue, esp. one of a cheap, noisy nature. [< dial. G, play]

spiff·y (spif′i), *adj.,* **spiff·i·er, spiff·i·est.** *Informal.* smart; neat; trim.

spig·ot (spig′ət), *n.* **1** *U.S.* faucet. **2** peg or plug used to stop the small hole of a cask, barrel, etc.

spike[1] (spīk), *n., v.,* **spiked, spik·ing.** —*n.* **1** a large, strong nail. **2** a sharp-pointed piece or part. —*v.* **1** fasten with spikes. **2** provide with spikes. **3** pierce or injure with a spike. **4** put an end or stop to; make useless; block. **5** add liquor to (a drink, etc.).

spikes, a shoes with spikes on the sole, used in track, baseball, etc. **b** women's shoes with very high heels. [< Scand. *spīk*] —**spike′like′,** *adj.* —**spik′er,** *n.*

spike[2] (spīk), *n.* **1** ear of grain. **2** a long, pointed flower cluster. [< L *spica*]

spike heel, high, narrow heel on a woman's shoe.

spike·let (spīk′lit), *n.* a small spike or flower cluster.

spike·nard (spīk′nərd; -närd), *n.* **1** a sweet-smelling ointment used by the ancients. **2** the fragrant East Indian plant from which it was probably obtained. [< Med.L *spica nardi* ear of nard]

spill (spil), *v.,* **spilled** or **spilt, spill·ing,** *n.* —*v.* **1** let (liquid or any matter in loose pieces) run or fall: *spill milk or salt.* **2** cause to fall from a horse, car, boat, etc. **3** make known; tell. —*n.* **1** a spilling. **2** quantity spilled. **3** a fall. [OE *spillan*] —**spill′er,** *n.*

spill·way (spil′wā′), *n.* channel or passage for the escape of surplus water from a dam, river, etc.

spin (spin), *v.,* **spun** or (*Archaic*) **span, spun, spin·ning,** *n.* —*v.* **1** draw out and twist (cotton, flax, wool. etc.) into thread. **2** make (a thread, web, cocoon, etc.) by giving out from the body sticky material that hardens into thread: *spiders*

spin webs. **3** turn or make turn rapidly: *the boy spins his top.* **4** feel dizzy: *my head spun after the rough boat ride.* **5** fabricate; produce; tell: *spin yarns about adventures at sea.* —*n.* **1** a spinning. **2** a rapid run, ride, drive, etc. **3** a flight maneuver in which an airplane descends in a vertical spiral path.

spin off, a shed; sell: *spin off a subsidiary company.* **b** create from something already done: *spin off a TV series from a film.*

spin out, a skid and turn rapidly in a vehicle. **b** make long and slow; draw out; prolong. [OE *spinnan*]

spin·ach (spin′ich; -ij), *n.* **1** a plant whose green leaves are boiled and eaten. **2** the leaves. [< OF (*e*)*spinache* < Med.L < Sp. *espinaca* < Ar. *isbānakh*]

spi·nal (spī′nəl), *adj.* of the spine or backbone; pertaining to the backbone. —**spi′nal·ly,** *adv.*

spinal column, the spine; the backbone.

spinal cord, a thick, whitish cord of nerve tissue in the backbone or spine.

spin·dle (spin′dəl), *n., v.,* **-dled, -dling.** —*n.* **1** the rod or pin used in spinning to twist, wind, and hold thread. **2** any rod or pin that turns around, or on which something turns, such as an axle, axis, shaft. **3** arrangement of fibrous cells in a line at the center of a dividing cell and along which chromosomes line up during the metaphase, or second stage, of mitosis. —*v.* grow tall and slender; grow too tall and slender. [OE *spinel < spinnan* spin]

spin·dle·legs (spin′dəl legz′), **spin·dle·shanks** (-shangks′), *n. pl.* **1** long, thin legs. **2** (*sing. in use*) person with long, thin legs.

spin·dling (spin′dling), *adj.* very long and slender; too tall and thin.

spin·dly (spin′dli), *adj.,* **-dli·er, -dli·est.** spindling.

spine (spīn), *n.* **1** series of small bones down the middle of the back; backbone. **2** anything like a backbone; long, narrow ridge or support. **3** a stiff, sharp-pointed outgrowth on a plant or animal; thorn or something like it. A cactus has spines; so has a porcupine. **4** the supporting back portion of a book cover. [< L *spina,* orig., thorn] —**spined,** *adj.* —**spine′like′,** *adj.*

spine·less (spīn′lis), *adj.* **1** without spines. **2** having no backbone. **3** *Fig.* without character, resolution, or courage; weak-willed; feeble. —**spine′less·ly,** *adv.* —**spine′less·ness,** *n.*

spin·et (spin′it; spi net′), *n.* **1** a compact upright piano. **2** an old-fashioned musical instrument like a small harpsichord. [< F < Ital. *spinetta,* prob. after G. Spinetti, Italian inventor]

spin·na·ker (spin′ə kər), *n.* a large, triangular sail carried by yachts on the side opposite the mainsail when running before the wind. [supposedly from *Sphinx,* a yacht on which first used]

spin·ner (spin′ər), *n.* person, animal, or thing that spins.

spin·ner·et (spin′ər et), *n.* organ by which spiders, silkworms, etc., spin their threads.

spin·ning (spin′ing), *adj.* that spins. —*n.* act or procedure of one that spins.

spinning jenny, an early type of spinning machine having more than one spindle, whereby one person could spin a number of threads at the same time.

spinning wheel, a large wheel and a spindle arranged for spinning cotton, flax, wool, etc., into thread or yarn.

spin-off or **spin·off** (spin′ôf; –of), *n.* 1 part of a company or a subsidiary that becomes an independent business. 2 by-product of a film, book, etc.

spin·ster (spin′stər), *n.* 1 an unmarried woman. 2 an elderly woman who has not married; old maid. —**spin′ster·hood,** *n.* —**spin′ster·ish,** *adj.*

spin·y (spīn′i), *adj.,* **spin·i·er, spin·i·est.** 1 covered with spines; having spines; thorny: *a spiny cactus, a spiny porcupine.* 2 spinelike. 3 *Fig.* difficult; thorny. —**spin′i·ness,** *n.*

spi·ra·cle (spī′rə kəl; spir′ə–), *n.* an opening for breathing. Insects take in air through tiny spiracles. A whale breathes through a spiracle in the top of its head. [< L *spiraculum* < *spirare* breathe]

spi·rae·a, spi·re·a (spī rē′ə), *n.* any of various shrubs that have clusters of small white, pink, or red flowers with five petals. [< L < Gk. *speiraia*]

spi·ral (spī′rəl), *n., adj., v.,* **–raled, –raling.** —*n.* 1 a winding and gradually widening coil; the shape of a watch spring; the shape of the thread of a screw. 2 a single turn of a spiral. —*adj.* coiled, as a snail's shell: *spiral stairs.* —*v.* 1 a move in a spiral. b *Fig.* move like a spiral: *spiral out of control.* 2 form into a spiral. [< Med.L, < L *spira* a coil < Gk. *speira*] —**spi′ral·ly,** *adv.*

spi·rant (spī′rənt), *n.* =fricative. [< L *spirans* breathing]

spire (spīr), *n.* 1 the top part of a tower or steeple that narrows to a point. 2 anything tapering and pointed. [OE *spīr*] —**spired,** *adj.* —**spire′like′,** *adj.* —**spir′y,** *adj.*

spir·it (spir′it), *n.* 1 soul: *he is present in spirit, though absent in body.* 2 humans' moral, religious, or emotional nature. 3 a supernatural being. 4 influence that stirs up and rouses: *a spirit of reform.* 5 person; personality: *a noble spirit.* 6 courage; vigor; liveliness: *a race horse must have spirit.* 7 the real meaning or intent: *the spirit of a law.* —*v.* 1 stir up; encourage; cheer. 2 carry (away or off) secretly: *the child has been spirited away.* 3 conjure (up).

spirits, a state of mind; disposition; temper: *in good spirits.* b vigor; cheerfulness: *an animal full of spirits.* c strong alcoholic liquor. [< L *spiritus,* orig., breath < *spirare* breathe. Doublet of SPRITE.]

—**spir′it·less,** *adj.* —**spir′it·less·ly,** *adv.* —**spir′it·less·ness,** *n.*

spir·it·ed (spir′it id), *adj.* lively; dashing. —**spir′it·ed·ly,** *adv.* —**spir′it·ed·ness,** *n.*

spir·it·u·al (spir′i chù əl), *adj.* 1 of the spirit or soul. 2 caring much for things of the spirit or soul. 3 sacred; religious. —*n.* 1 a matter of religion or the church. 2 a sacred song or hymn that originally came from blacks of the S United States. —**spir′it·u·al·ly,** *adv.* —**spir′it·u·al·ness, spir′it·u·al′i·ty,** *n.*

spir·it·u·al·ism (spir′i chù əl iz′əm), *n.* 1 belief that spirits of the dead communicate with the living, esp. through persons called mediums. 2 insistence on the spiritual; doctrine that spirit alone is real. —**spir′it·u·al·ist,** *n.* —**spir′it·u·al·is′tic,** *adj.*

spir·it·u·al·ize (spir′i chù əl īz′), *v.,* **–ized, –iz·ing.** make spiritual. —**spir′it·u·al·i·za′tion,** *n.*

spi·ro·chete (spī′rə kēt), *n.* any of the bacteria that have a spiral shape. [< NL, < Gk. *speira* coil + *chaite* hair] —**spi′ro·che′tal, spi′ro·chae′tal,** *adj.*

spi·ro·gy·ra (spī′rə ji′rə), *n.* green algae that form scum on freshwater ponds.

spit¹ (spit), *v.,* **spat** or **spit, spit·ting,** *n.* —*v.* 1 throw out saliva from the mouth: *a cat spits when angry.* 2 throw out: *the gun spits fire.* —*n.* 1 the liquid produced in the mouth; saliva. 2 noise or act of spitting. 3 a frothy or spitlike secretion given off by some insects. [OE *spittan*] —**spit′ter,** *n.*

spit² (spit), *n.* 1 a sharp-pointed, slender rod or bar on which meat is roasted. 2 a narrow point of land running into the water. [OE *spitu*]

spit·ball (spit′bôl′), *n.* 1 a small ball of chewed-up paper, used as a missile. 2 variety of curve pitched by moistening one side of the ball with saliva.

spite (spīt), *n., v.* **spit·ed, spit·ing.** —*n.* ill will; grudge. —*v.* show ill will toward; annoy.

in spite of, not prevented by; notwithstanding. [ult. < *despite*] —**spite′ful,** *adj.* —**spite′ful·ly,** *adv.* —**spite′ful·ness,** *n.*

spit·fire (spit′fīr′), *n.* 1 person, esp. a woman or girl, who has a quick and fiery temper. 2 something that sends forth fire, such as a cannon or some kinds of fireworks. —*adj.* of or like a spitfire.

spitting image, *Informal.* an exact likeness of another: *the spitting image of his father.*

spit·tle (spit′əl), *n.* saliva; spit. [< *spit*]

spit·toon (spi tün′), *n.* =cuspidor.

spitz (spits), *n.* =Pomeranian. [< G, pointed]

splash (splash), *v.* 1 cause (water, mud, etc.) to fly about: *the baby splashes in his tub, the waves splashed on the beach.* 2 wet, spatter, or soil. —*n.* 1 sound of splashing; splashing. 2 spot of liquid splashed upon a thing.

make a splash, attract attention; cause excitement. [alter. of *plash, n.,* < OE *plœsc* puddle] —**splash′er,** *n.* —**splash′y,** *adj.*

splat (splat), *n.* sound like a splash or splatter: *the splat of fat raindrops.* [< *splatter*]

splat·ter (splat′ər), *v., n.* splash; spatter. [blend of *spatter* and *splash*]

splay (splā), *v.* spread out; flare. —*adj.* 1 spread out. 2 wide and flat. —*n.* spread; flare. [< *display*]

splay-foot (splā′füt′), *n., pl.* **–feet.** a broad, flat foot, esp. one turned outward. —**splay′foot′ed,** *adj.*

spleen (splēn), *n.* 1 ductless glandlike organ at the left of the stomach in humans, and near the stomach or intestine in other vertebrates that stores and filters the blood. People used to think that the spleen caused low spirits, bad temper, and spite. 2 bad temper; spite; anger. 3 low spirits. [< L < Gk. *splen*] —**spleen′ful,** *adj.* —**spleen′ish, spleen′y,** *adj.*

splen·did (splen′did), *adj.* 1 brilliant; magnificent: *splendid jewels, a splendid name in history.* 2 very good; fine; excellent: *a splendid chance.* [< L *splendidus* < *splendere* be bright] —**splen′did·ly,** *adv.* —**splen′did·ness,** *n.*

splen·dor (splen′dər), *n.* 1 great brightness; brilliant light. 2 magnificent show; pomp; glory. [< L, < *splendere* be bright] —**splen′dor·ous,** *adj.*

sple·net·ic (spli net′ik), *adj.* 1 pertaining to the spleen. 2 bad-tempered; irritable; peevish. [< LL, < *splen* SPLEEN] —**sple·net′i·cal·ly,** *adv.*

splice (splīs), *v.,* **spliced, splic·ing,** *n.* —*v.* 1 join together (ropes, wires, etc.) by weaving together ends that have been untwisted. 2 join two pieces of something together by overlapping, esp. of film or timber. 3 join together ends of genetic material. —*n.* a joining of ropes or timbers by splicing. [< MDu. *splissen*] —**splic′er,** *n.*

splint (splint), *n.* 1 arrangement of wood, metal, plaster, etc., to hold a broken or dislocated bone in place. 2 a thin strip of wood, such as is used in making baskets. [< MDu., MLG *splinte*]

splin·ter (splin′tər), *n.* a thin, sharp piece of wood, bone, glass, etc. —*adj.* pertaining to dissenting groups that break away from regular political groups, religious organizations, etc.: *a splinter party.* —*v.* split or break into splinters. [< MDu.] —**splin′ter·y,** *adj.*

split (split), *v.,* **split, split·ting,** *n., adj.* —*v.* 1 break or cut from end to end, or in layers. 2 separate into parts; divide. 3 a divide (a molecule) into two or more individual atoms. b divide (an atomic nucleus) into two portions of approximately equal mass by forcing the absorption of a neutron. 5 *Informal.* leave suddenly; clear out. —*v.* 1 division in a group, party, etc.: *there was a split in* *the Republican Party.* **2** a splitting; break; crack. **3** share; portion. **4** Often, **splits.** an acrobatic trick of sinking to the floor with the legs spread far apart in opposite directions. **5** bottle of a drink half the usual size. **6** a sweet dish made of sliced fruit, ice cream, etc. —*adj.* broken or cut from end to end; divided.

split hairs, make too fine distinctions.

split one's vote or **ticket,** vote for candidates of different political parties. [< MDu. *splitten*] —**split'ter,** *n.*

split infinitive, infinitive having an adverb between to and the verb. *Example:* He wants to never work, but to always play.

split-lev·el (split'lev'əl), *adj.* (of a house) having certain rooms on a level less than a full story higher than others.

split personality, 1 =schizophrenia. **2** personality that appears to have contradictory traits.

split second, very brief time; instant. —**split-second,** *adj.*

split·ting (split'ing), *adj.* **1** that splits. **2** very severe; extreme; violent.

splotch (sploch), *n.* a large, irregular spot; splash. —*v.* make splotches on. [? blend of *spot* and *blotch*] —**splotch'y,** *adj.*

splurge (splėrj), *n., v.,* **splurged, splurg·ing.** —*n.* a showing off; showy display; outburst: *a splurge of color.* —*v.* spend extravagantly.

splut·ter (splut'ər), *v.* **1** talk in a hasty, confused, or incoherent way. **2** make spitting or popping noises; sputter. —*n.* a spluttering. —**splut'ter·er,** *n.*

spoil (spoil), *v.,* **spoiled** or **spoilt** (spoilt), **spoil·ing,** *n.* —*v.* **1** damage; injure; destroy: *rain spoiled the picnic.* **2** be damaged; become bad or unfit for use: *fruit spoils if kept too long.* **3** injure the character or disposition of, esp. by excessive indulgence: *spoil a child.* **4** take by force; steal; rob. —*n.* **1** Often, **spoils.** things taken by force; things won: *the soldiers carried the spoils back to their own land.* **2** an object of plundering; prey. **3** Usually, **spoils.** government offices and positions filled by the successful political party.

spoil for, want a fight or dispute. [< OF *espoillier,* ult. < L *spolium,* n.] —**spoil'a·ble,** *adj.* —**spoil'er,** *n.*

spoil·age (spoil'ij), *n.* **1** act of spoiling. **2** that which is spoiled.

spoil·sport (spoil'spôrt'; –spōrt'), *n.* person who behaves in a manner that spoils others' pleasure or disrupts plans, etc.

spoils system, the system or practice in which public offices with their salaries and advantages are at the disposal of the victorious political party for its own purposes and in its own interest.

spoke[1] (spōk), *v.* **1** pt. of **speak. 2** *Archaic.* pp. of **speak.**

spoke[2] (spōk), *n.* one of the bars from the center of a wheel to the rim. [OE *spāca*]

spo·ken (spō'kən), *v.* pp. of **speak.** —*adj.* **1** expressed with the mouth; uttered;

told: *the spoken word.* **2** speaking in a certain way: *a soft-spoken man.*

spokes·man (spōks'mən), *n., pl.* **-men.** person who speaks for another or others.

spokes·per·son (spōks'pėr´sən), *n., pl.* **-peo·ple, -per·sons.** person who speaks for another or others.

spokes·wom·an (spōks'wùm´ən), *n., pl.* **-wom·en** woman who speaks for another or others.

spo·li·a·tion (spō´li ā'shən), *n.* a plundering or despoiling; robbery. [< L, ult. < *spolium* booty]

spon·dee (spon'dē), *n.* a foot or measure in poetry consisting of two long or accented syllables. The spondee is used to vary other meters. [< L < Gk., < *sponde* libation; orig. used in songs accompanying libations] —**spon·da'ic,** *adj.*

sponge (spunj), *n., v.,* **sponged, spong·ing.** —*n.* **1** a kind of sea animal having a tough, fiberlike skeleton or framework. **2** its light framework used for soaking up water in bathing, cleaning, etc. **3** a sponging. **4** something like a sponge, such as bread dough, a kind of cake, a kind of pudding, etc. **5** *Fig.* person who continually lives at the expense of others; parasite. —*v.* **1** wipe or rub with a wet sponge; make clean or damp in this way. **2** live or profit at the expense of another.

throw in the sponge, give up; admit defeat. [< L < Gk. *spongia*] —**sponge'like',** *adj.* —**spong'er,** *n.* —**spon'gy,** *adj.* —**spon'gi·ness,** *n.*

sponge cake, a light, spongy cake made with eggs, sugar, flour, etc., but no butter.

spon·son (spon'sən), *n.* part projecting from the side of a ship or boat, used for support or protection.

spon·sor (spon'sər), *n.* **1** person who is responsible for a person or thing: *the sponsor of a law.* **2** person who takes vows for an infant at baptism; godfather or godmother. **3** company, store, or other business firm that pays the costs of a radio or television program advertising its products. —*v.* act as sponsor for. [< L, < *spondere* give assurance] —**spon·so'ri·al,** *adj.* —**spon'sor·ship,** *n.*

spon·ta·ne·i·ty (spon´tə nē'ə ti), *n., pl.* **-ties, 1** a state, quality, or fact of being spontaneous. **2** a spontaneous action, movement, etc.

spon·ta·ne·ous (spon tā'ni əs), *adj.* **1** caused by natural impulse or desire; not forced or compelled; not planned beforehand: *a spontaneous cheer.* **2** taking place without external cause or help; caused entirely by inner forces. **3** growing or produced naturally; not planted, cultivated, etc. [< LL, < L *sponte* of one's own accord] —**spon·ta'ne·ous·ly,** *adv.* —**spon·ta'ne·ous·ness,** *n.*

spontaneous combustion, the bursting into flame of a substance without any-

one's having set it on fire. In spontaneous combustion, the heat produced by chemical action within the substance itself causes it to catch on fire.

spoof (spüf), *v., n.* trick; hoax; joke. [coined by A. Roberts, British comedian]

spook (spük), *n.* ghost; specter. [< Du.] —**spook'ish,** *adj.* —**spook'y,** *adj.*

spool (spül), *n.* **1** a cylinder of plastic, wood, or metal on which thread, wire, etc., is wound. **2** something like a spool in shape or use. —*v.* wind on a spool. [< MDu. *spoele*] —**spool'er,** *n.*

spoon (spün), *n.* **1** utensil consisting of a small, shallow bowl at the end of a handle and used to take up or stir food or drink. **2** something shaped like a spoon, as a lure used in casting or trolling for fish. **3** a kind of golf club with a wooden head that has more loft than a brassie. —*v.* **1** take up in a spoon. **2** make love by cuddling, carressing, etc. [OE *spōn* chip, shaving]

spoon·bill (spün'bil´), *n.* **1** a long-legged wading bird that has a long, flat bill with a spoon-shaped tip. **2** any of various birds that have a similar bill. —**spoon'-billed',** *adj.*

spoon·ful (spün'fùl), *n., pl.* **-fuls.** as much as a spoon can hold.

spoor (spùr), *n.* trail of a wild animal; track. —*v.* track by or follow a spoor. [< Du.]

spo·rad·ic (spə rad'ik), **spo·rad·i·cal** (–ə kəl), *adj.* appearing or happening at intervals in time or in scattered instances: *sporadic cases of scarlet fever.* [< Med.L < Gk. *sporadikos* scattered, ult. < *spora* a sowing] — **spo·rad'i·cal·ly,** *adv.*

spo·ran·gi·um (spə ran'ji əm), *n., pl.* **-gi·a** (–ji ə). receptacle containing spores; spore case. The little brown spots sometimes seen on the under side of ferns are sporangia. [< NL, < Gk. *spora* seed + *angeion* vessel]

spore (spôr; spōr), *n., v.,* **-spored, spor·ing.** —*n.* **1** a single cell capable of growing into a new plant or animal. Ferns produce spores. **2** germ; seed. —*v.* produce spores. [< NL < Gk. *spora* seed]

spo·ro·phyte (spô'rə fīt; spō'–), *n.* any plant or generation of a plant that produces asexual spores.

spo·ro·zo·an (spôr´ə zō'ən; spōr'–), *n.* very small protozoan that lives as a parasite and causes diseases in humans and animals.

spor·ran (spôr'ən; spor'–), *n.* in a Scottish Highland costume, a large purse, commonly of fur, hanging from the belt in front. [< Scotch Gaelic *sporan*]

sport (spôrt; spōrt), *n.* **1** form of amusement or play; game; contest. Baseball, football, golf, tennis, fishing, hunting, and racing are outdoor sports. **2** playful joking: *say a thing in sport.* **3** person of sportsmanlike or admirable qualities. **4** one who is willing to take a chance;

good fellow: *be a sport.* **5** animal or plant that varies suddenly or in a marked manner from the normal type. —*v.* **1** amuse oneself with some pleasant pastime. **2** display: *sport a new hat.* —*adj.* of sports; suitable for sports.

make sport of, make fun of; laugh at; ridicule. [ult. short for *disport*] —**sport′er,** *n.* —**sport′ful,** *adj.*

sport·ing (spôr′ting; spōr′–), *adj.* **1** of, interested in, or engaging in sports. **2** playing fair. **3** willing to take a chance; uncertain. —**sport′ing·ly,** *adv.*

spor·tive (spôr′tiv; spōr′–), *adj.* playful; jocose; merry. —**spor′tive·ly,** *adv.*

sports (spôrts; spōrts), *adj.* **1** of sports; suitable for sports: *a sports dress.* **2** sporty: *a sports car.*

sports·cast (spôrts′kast′; spōrts′–), *n.* broadcast of a sports event.

sports·cast·er (spôrts′kas′tər; spōrts′–), *n.* person who describes the action or comments on it during a sportscast.

sports·man (spôrts′mən; spōrts′–), *n.,* *pl.* **-men.** **1** person who takes part in sports, esp. hunting, fishing, or racing. **2** person who likes sports. **3** person who plays fair. —**sports′man·like′, sports′·man·ly,** *adj.* —**sports′man·ship,** *n.*

sports·wear (spôrts′wãr′; spōrts′–), *n.* informal clothing suitable for outdoor activity or athletics.

sports·wom·an (spôrts′wum′ən; spōrts′–), *n.* a female sportsman.

sport·y (spôr′ti; spōr′–), *adj.,* **sport·i·er, sport·i·est.** smart in dress, appearance, manners, etc. —**sport′i·ness,** *n.*

spot (spot), *n.,* *v.,* **spot·ted, spot·ting,** *adj.* —*n.* **1** mark, stain, or speck, as on a surface: *a spot of ink on the paper.* **2** a moral stain or flaw: *his character is without spot.* **3** a small part unlike the rest: *his tie is blue with white spots.* **4** a small amount; little bit: *a spot of lunch.* —*v.* **1** make spots on: *spots a dress.* **2** place in a certain spot; scatter in various spots: *lookouts were spotted all along the coast.* **3** pick out; find out; recognize: *spot a friend in the crowd.* **4** blemish; stain: *he spotted his reputation.* —*adj.* **1** on hand; ready: *a spot answer.* **2** pertaining to or involving immediate cash payment: *a spot transaction.*

hit the spot, be just right; be satisfactory.

in a spot, in difficulty or trouble.

in spots, a here and there. **b** now and then.

on the spot, a at the very place. **b** at once. **c** in trouble or difficulty. [ME] —**spot′less,** *adj.* —**spot′less·ly,** *adv.* —**spot′less·ness,** *n.* —**spot′ta·ble,** *adj.*

spot check, an inspection made without warning.

spot·light (spot′līt′), *n.,* *v.,* **-light·ed,** or **-lit, -light·ing.** *n.* **1** a strong light thrown upon a particular place or person. **2** the lamp that gives the light: *a spotlight in a theater.* **3** conspicuous attention; public notice. —*v.* **1** light with

a spotlight; train a spotlight on. **2** *Fig.* call attention to.

spot·ted (spot′id), *adj.* **1** stained with spots: *a spotted reputation.* **2** marked with spots: *a spotted dog.* —**spot′ted·ness,** *n.*

spot·ter (spot′ər), *n.* person or thing that spots, esp. one that locates enemy positions.

spot·ty (spot′i), *adj.,* **-ti·er, -ti·est. 1** having spots; spotted. **2** *Fig.* not of uniform quality. —**spot′ti·ly,** *adv.* —**spot′ti·ness,** *n.*

spous·al (spouz′əl), *adj.* of or pertaining to marriage.

spouse (spous; spouz), *n.* husband or wife. [< OF < L *sponsus, sponsa,* pp. of *spondere* bind oneself] —**spouse′less,** *adj.*

spout (spout), *v.* **1** throw out (a liquid) in a stream or spray: *the fountain spouted water, water spouted from a break in the pipe.* **2** *Fig.* speak, as if from memory, or without much thought. —*n.* **1** stream; jet. **2** pipe for carrying off water. **3** tube or lip by which liquid is poured. A teakettle, a coffee pot, and a syrup jug have spouts. [cf. MDu. *spouten*] —**spout′er,** *n.* —**spout′less,** *adj.*

sprain (sprān), *v.* injure (a joint or muscle) by a sudden twist or wrench: *sprain your ankle.* —*n.* injury caused in this way.

sprang (sprang), *v.* pt. of **spring.**

sprat (sprat), *n.* a small food fish related to the herring, found along the Atlantic coast of Europe. [OE *sprott*]

sprawl (sprôl), *v.* **1** lie or sit with the limbs spread out, esp. ungracefully. **2** spread out in an irregular or awkward manner: *a sprawling vine.* —*n.* **1** act or position of sprawling. **2** *Fig.* a spreading: *urban sprawl.* [OE *sprēawlian*] —**sprawl′er,** *n.* —**sprawl′y,** *adj.*

spray¹ (sprā), *n.* **1** liquid going through the air in small drops. **2** something like this: *a spray of bullets.* **3** instrument that sends a liquid out as spray. —*v.* **1** scatter spray on; sprinkle. **2** direct numerous small missiles. etc., upon. [? < MDu. *sprayen*] —**spray′er,** *n.*

spray² (sprā), *n.* **1** a small branch or piece of some plant with its leaves, flowers, or fruit. **2** an ornament like this.

spread (spred), *v.,* **spread, spread·ing,** *n.,* —*v.* **1** cover or cause to cover a large or larger area; stretch out; unfold; open: *spread rugs on the floor, fields of corn spread out before us.* **2** move further apart: *spread out your fingers.* **3** scatter; distribute: *he spread the news.* **4** cover with a thin layer: *spread bread with butter, spread paint evenly.* **5** set (a table) for a meal. —*n.* **1** extent; amount of spreading: *the spread of a deer's antlers.* **2** capacity for spreading: *the spread of an elastic material.* **3** food put on the table; feast. **4** a cloth covering for a bed, table, etc. **5** something spread. Butter and jam are spreads. [OE *sprǣdan*] —**spread′er,** *n.*

spread-ea·gle (spred′ē′gəl), *adj., v.,* **-gled, -gling.** —*adj.* **1** having the form of an eagle with wings spread out. —*v.* stretch out flat and sprawling; tie with arms and legs outstretched.

spread·sheet (spred′shēt′), *n.* arrangement of data in rows and columns for computation and analysis, esp. as produced on a computer.

spree (sprē), *n.* a lively frolic.

sprig (sprig), *n.* shoot, twig, or small branch. —**sprig′gy,** *adj.*

spright·ly (sprīt′li), *adj.,* **-li·er, -li·est,** *adv.* —*adj.* lively. —*adv.* in a lively manner. [< *spright,* var. of *sprite*] —**spright′li·ness,** *n.*

spring (spring), *v.,* **sprang** or **sprung, sprung, spring·ing,** *n., adj.* —*v.* **1** move rapidly or suddenly; leap; jump: *spring into the air.* **2** fly back or away as if by elastic force: *spring a trap.* **4** come from some source; arise; grow: *great industries sprang up.* **5** begin to move, act, grow, etc., suddenly; burst forth: *sparks sprang from the fire.* **6** bring out, produce, or make suddenly: *spring a surprise on someone.* **7** cause game to fly or jump from cover. **8** *Slang.* release (a person) from jail, as by bail. —*n.* **1** leap or jump: *a spring over the fence.* **2** an elastic device that returns to its original shape after being pulled or held out of shape: *beds have wire springs.* **3** a flying back from a forced position. **4** season (in North America, March, April, May) when plants begin to grow. **5** a small stream of water coming from the earth. —*adj.* **1** having a spring or springs: *a spring mechanism.* **2** of, pertaining to, characteristic of, or suitable for the season of spring: *spring hats.* **3** from a spring: *spring water.*

spring a leak, crack and begin to let water through. [OE *springan*] —**spring′er,** *n.*

spring·board (spring′bôrd′; -bōrd′), *n.* **1** a projecting board from which persons dive. **2** an elastic board used in vaulting, etc.

spring·bok (spring′bok′), *n., pl.* **-boks** or (*esp. collectively*) **-bok.** a gazelle or small antelope of South Africa. [< Du., springing buck]

spring chicken, 1 young chicken with tender meat. **2** *Informal. Fig.* young person: *Katy's just a spring chicken.*

spring-clean·ing (spring′klē′ning), *n.* thorough cleaning of a house, office, etc., in mild weather. —**spring′-clean′,** *v.*

spring fever, a listless, lazy feeling felt by some people, caused by the first sudden warm weather of spring.

Spring·field (spring′fēld), *n.* capital of Illinois, in the C part.

spring peeper, small brown tree frog characterized by its peeping call in the spring. Also, **peeper.**

spring tide, 1 the high tide at its highest level, coming at the time of the new moon or the full moon. **2** any great flood, swell, or rush.

spring·time (spring′tīm′), **spring·tide** (–tīd′), *n.* the season of spring.

spring·y (spring′i), *adj.*, **spring·i·er, spring·i·est. 1** that springs; elastic. **2** having many springs of water. —**spring′i·ly,** *adv.* —**spring′i·ness,** *n.*

sprin·kle (spring′kəl), *v.*, –kled, –kling. *n.*—*v.* **1** scatter in drops or tiny bits: *sprinkle sand on an icy sidewalk.* **2** spray or cover with small drops: *sprinkle flowers with water.* **3** dot or vary with something scattered here and there. **4** rain a little. —*n.* **1** a sprinkling; small quantity. **2** a light rain. [cf. Du. *sprenkelen*] —**sprin′kler,** *n.* —**sprin′kling,** *n.*

sprint (sprint), *v.* **1** run at full speed, esp. for a short distance. **2** *Fig.* work quickly to finish a task or job. —*n.* **1** a short race at full speed. **2** *Fig.* a fast pace at the end of a job: *a sprint to the end of the book.* [ME *sprente(n)*] —**sprint′er,** *n.*

sprit (sprit), *n.* a small pole that supports and stretches up a sail. [OE *sprēot*]

sprite (sprīt), *n.* elf; fairy; goblin. [< OF *esprit* spirit < L *spiritus.* Doublet of SPIRIT.]

spritz (sprits), *v.* spray or sprinkle water on. —*n.* a fine spray or sprinkle: *a spritz is enough.* [< G *spritzen* to splash, squirt]

spritz·er (sprit′sər), *n.* cold drink made with wine or juice and carbonated water.

sprock·et (sprok′it), *n.* **1** one of a set of projections on the rim of a wheel, arranged so as to fit into the links of a chain. The sprockets keep the chain from slipping. **2** wheel made with sprockets.

sprout (sprout), *v.* **1** begin to grow: *buds sprout, seeds sprout, rain has sprouted the corn.* —*n.* a shoot of a plant.

sprouts, Brussels sprouts. [OE, as in *āsprūtan*]

spruce[1] (sprüs), *n.* **1** a coniferous evergreen tree with needle-shaped leaves. **2** its wood. [ult. var. of *Pruce* Prussia]

spruce[2] (sprüs), *adj.*, **spruc·er, spruc·est,** *v.*, **spruced, spruc·ing.** —*adj.* neat; trim. —*v.* make or become spruce: *John spruced himself up for dinner.* [? special use of earlier *Spruce* Prussia (i.e., made in Prussia, therefore smart-looking)] —**spruce′ly,** *adv.* —**spruce′ness,** *n.*

sprung (sprung), *v.* pp. of **spring.** —*adj.* warped; bent: *a sprung gate.*

spry (sprī), *adj.*, **spry·er, spry·est,** or **spri·er, spri·est.** active; lively; nimble: *a mouse is a spry animal.* —**spry′ly,** *adv.* —**spry′ness,** *n.*

spud (spud), *n.* potato. [cf. Dan. *spyd* spear]

spue (spū), *v.*, **spued, spu·ing.** spew.

spume (spūm), *n.*, *v.*, **spumed, spum·ing.** foam; froth. [< L *spuma*] —**spu′mous, spum′y,** *adj.*

spu·mo·ni or **spu·mo·ne** (spə mō′nē), *n.* a type of Italian ice cream, usually containing fruit, nuts, etc. [< Ital.]

spun (spun), *v.* pt. and pp. of **spin.**

spunk (spungk), *n.* courage; pluck; spirit; mettle. [< Irish or Scotch Gaelic < L *spongia* SPONGE]

spunk·y (spungk′i), *adj.*, **spunk·i·er, spunk·i·est.** courageous; plucky; spirited. —**spunk′i·ly,** *adv.* —**spunk′i·ness,** *n.*

spur (spėr), *n.*, *v.*, **spurred, spur·ring.** —*n.* **1** a pricking instrument worn on a horseman's heel for urging a horse on. **2** anything that urges on: *ambition is a spur.* **3** something like a spur; point sticking out: *a spur of rock.* **4** ridge projecting from the main body of a mountain or mountain range. **5** any short branch: *a spur of a railroad.* —*v.* **1** prick with spurs. **2** urge on: *pride spurred the boy to fight.*

on the spur of the moment, on a sudden impulse.

win one's spurs, attain distinction. [OE *spura*] —**spur′less,** *adj.* —**spur′like′,** *adj.*

spurge (sperj), *n.* =euphorbia. [< OF *espurge,* ult. < L *ex* out + *purgare* purge]

spu·ri·ous (spyùr′i əs), *adj.* not coming from the right source; not genuine; false; sham: *a spurious document.* [< L *spurius*] —**spu′ri·ous·ly,** *adv.* —**spu′ri·ous·ness,** *n.*

spurn (spėrn), *v.* refuse with scorn; scorn: *spurn an apology.* —*n.* disdainful rejection; contemptuous treatment. [OE *spurnan*] —**spurn′er,** *n.*

spurt (spėrt), *v.* **1** flow suddenly in a stream or jet; gush out; squirt. **2** put forth great energy for a short time; show great activity for a short time: *the runners spurted near the end of the race.* —*n.* **1** a sudden rushing forth; jet: *spurts of flame.* **2** a great increase of effort or activity for a short time. Also, **spirt.** [var. of *sprit,* OE *spryttan*]

sput·ter (sput′ər), *v.* **1** make spitting or popping noises: *the motor sputtered and died.* **2** throw out (drops of saliva, bits of food, etc.) in excitement or in talking too fast. **3** say (words or sounds) in haste and confusion. —*n.* **1** confused talk. **2** a sputtering; sputtering noise. [< SPOUT] —**sput′ter·er,** *n.* —**sput′ter·ing·ly,** *adv.*

spu·tum (spū′təm), *n.*, pl. **–ta** (–tə), **1** saliva; spit. **2** what is coughed up from the lungs and spat out. [< L, < *spuere* spit]

spy (spī), *n.*, pl. **spies,** *v.*, **spied, spy·ing.** —*n.* **1** person who keeps secret watch on the action of others. **2** person who, in time of war, tries to get information about the enemy, usually by visiting the enemy's territory in disguise or under false pretenses. —*v.* **1** find out or try to find out by careful observation; search. **2** keep secret watch: *spy on the neighbors; spy out what's happening.* **3** catch sight of; see: *he spied a plane overhead.* [< OF *espier* < Gmc.]

spy·glass (spī′glas′; –gläs′), *n.* a small telescope.

sq., 1 square. **2** the following.

squab (skwob), *n.* a very young bird, esp. a young pigeon.

squab·ble (skwob′əl), *n.*, *v.*, –bled, –bling. —*n.* a petty, noisy quarrel. —*v.* take part in a petty, noisy quarrel. —**squab′bler,** *n.*

squad (skwod), *n.*, *v.*, **squad·ded, squad·ding.** —*n.* **1** a number of soldiers grouped for drill, inspection, or work. A squad is the smallest tactical unit in an army. **2** any small group of persons working together. —*v.* **1** form into squads. **2** assign to a squad. [< F < Ital. *squadra* SQUARE]

squad·ron (skwod′rən), *n.* **1** a part of a naval fleet used for special service. **2** a formation of airplanes, usually two or three flights, that fly or fight together. [< Ital. *squadrone* < *squadra* SQUARE]

squal·id (skwol′id), *adj.* filthy; degraded; wretched. [< L *squalidus* < *squalere* be filthy] — **squal′id·ly,** *adv.* —**squal′id·ness, squa·lid′i·ty,** *n.*

squall[1] (skwôl), *n.* a sudden, violent gust of wind, often with rain, snow, or sleet. —*v.* blow in a squall. [cf. Sw. *skval-regn*] —**squall′y,** *adj.*

squall[2] (skwôl), *v.* cry out loudly; scream violently: *the baby squalled.* —*n.* a loud, harsh cry. [< Scand. *skvala* cry out] —**squall′er,** *n.*

squal·or (skwol′ər), *n.* misery and dirt; filth. [< L, < *squalere* be filthy]

squan·der (skwon′dər), *v.* spend foolishly; waste. —**squan′der·er,** *n.* —**squan′der·ing·ly,** *adv.*

square (skwãr), *n.*, *adj.*, **squar·er, squar·est,** *v.*, **squared, squar·ing,** *adv.* —*n.* **1** a plane figure with four equal sides and four equal angles (□). **2** anything of or near this shape. **3** space in a city or town bounded by streets on four sides. **4** distance along one side of such a space; block. **5** an open space in a city or town bounded by streets on four sides, often planted with grass, trees, etc. **6** an L-shaped or T-shaped instrument used for making or testing right angles. **7** Also, **square number,** product obtained when a number in multiplied by itself. 16 is the square of 4. **8** *Informal.* person who is conventional or old-fashioned. —*adj.* **1** having four equal sides and four right angles. **2** of a specified length on each side of a square: *a room ten feet square, a square inch.* **3** having breadth more nearly equal to length or height than is usual: *a square jaw.* **4** *Fig.* leaving no balance; even: *make accounts square.* **5** just; fair; honest: *a square deal.* **6** *Informal.* conventional; old-fashioned: *he is so square.* **7** multiplied by itself. —*v.* **1** make square; make rectangular; make cubical. **2** bring to the form of a right angle: *square a picture on the wall.* **3** make straight, level, or even: *square the corners of a board.* **4** adjust; settle: *square accounts.* **5** agree; conform: *his acts do not square with his promises.* **6 a** find the equivalent of in square measure. **b** multiply by itself. —*adv.* **1** fairly or honestly: *fair and square.* **2** so as to be square; in square or rectangular form; at right angles.

all square, even; with nothing owed.

at or **to square one,** the beginning; where one or something began: *had to go back to square one.*

on the square, a at right angles. **b** justly; fairly; honestly.

square off, put oneself in a position of defense or attack.

square oneself, a make up for something one has said or done. **b** get even. [< OF *esquar(r)e,* ult.< L *ex* out + *quadrus* square] —**square′ly,** *adv.* —**square′ness,** *n.* —**squar′er,** *n.* —**squar′ish,** *adj.*

square dance, dance performed by a set of couples arranged in some set form. The quadrille and Virginia reel are square dances. —**square′-dance′,** *v.* —**square dancer.** —**square dancing.**

square deal, fair and honest treatment.

square foot, unit of measure of an area equal to 1 foot by 1 foot.

square inch, unit of measure of an area equal to 1 inch by 1 inch.

square knot, knot whose free ends come out alongside of the other parts. It will not slip and is easily untied.

square meal, a substantial or satisfying meal.

square measure, system of measurement of volume in square units: *144 square inches = 1 square foot.*

square-rigged (skwär′rigd′), *adj.* having the principal sails set at right angles across the masts. —**square′-rig′ger,** *n.*

square root, number that produces a given number when multiplied by itself. The square root of 16 is 4.

square sail, a four-sided sail.

squash¹ (skwosh), *v.* **1** press until soft or flat; crush. **2** make a squashing sound; move with a squashing sound. **3** put an end to; stop by force. **4** crowd; squeeze. —*n.* **1** something squashed; a crushed mass. **2** a squashing. **3** a squashing sound. **4** game somewhat like handball and tennis. [< OF *esquasser,* ult. < L *ex* out + *quassare* shake] —**squash′er,** *n.*

squash² (skwosh), *n.* **1** fruit of any of various vinelike plants, often eaten as a vegetable or made into a pie. **2** plant it grows on. [< Algonquian]

squash·y (skwosh′i), *adj.,* **squash·i·er, squash·i·est. 1** easily squashed. **2** soft and wet. —**squash′i·ly,** *adv.* —**squash′i·ness.** *n.*

squat (skwot), *v.,* **squat·ted,** or **squat, squat·ing,** *adj., n.* —*v.* **1** crouch on the heels. **2** sit on the ground or floor with the legs drawn up closely beneath or in front of the body. **3 a** settle on another's land without title or right. **b** occupy an abandoned building illegally. —*adj.* **1** crouching: *a squat figure sat in front of the fire.* **2** short and thick; low and broad. —*n.* **1** act of squatting; squatting posture. **2** a building illegally occupied. [< OF *esquatir* crush, ult. < L *ex-* out +

coactus forced < *co-* together + *agere* drive] —**squat′ter,** *n.*

squat·ty (skwot′i), *adj.,* **-ti·er, -tie·est.** short and thick; low and broad.

squaw (skwô), *n.* an American Indian woman or wife. [< Algonquian]

squawk (skwôk), *v.* **1** make a loud, harsh sound; *hens and ducks squawk when frightened.* **2** utter harshly and loudly. **3** *Informal.* complain loudly. —*n.* **1** a loud, harsh sound. **2** *Informal.* a loud complaint. —**squawk′er,** *n.*

squeak (skwēk), *v.* make a short, sharp, shrill sound: *a mouse squeaks.* —*n.* a short, sharp, shrill sound.

narrow squeak, a narrow escape. [cf. Sw. *sqväka* croak] —**squeak′er,** *n.* —**squeak′y,** *adj.* —**squeak′i·ly, squeak′ing·ly,** *adv.* —**squeak′i·ness,** *n.*

squeal (skwēl), *v.* **1** make a long, sharp, shrill cry: *a pig squeals when it is hurt.* **2** *Slang.* turn informer. —*n.* a long, sharp, shrill cry. [imit.] —**squeal′er,** *n.*

squeam·ish (skwēm′ish), *adj.* **1** too proper, modest, etc.; easily shocked. **2** too particular; too scrupulous. **3** slightly sick at one's stomach. **4** easily turned sick. **5** dainty; delicate; fastidious. [var. of earlier *squeamous* < AF *escoymous*] —**squeam′ish·ly,** *adv.* —**squeam′ish·ness,** *n.*

squig·gle (skwig′əl), *n., v.,* **-gled, -gling. 1** make twisting, curling lines. **2** wiggle; squirm. —*n.* wiggly, twisty curve. [? blend of *squirm* + *wriggle*]

squint (skwint), *v.* **1** look with the eyes partly closed: *squint in the sun.* **2** look sideways. —*n.* **1** act of squinting. **2** a sidelong look; hasty look; look. **3** tendency to look sideways. [< *asquint*] —**squint′er,** *n.* —**squint′ing·ly,** *adv.* —**squint′y,** *adj.*

squire (skwīr), *n., v.,* **squired, squir·ing.** —*n.* **1** in England, a country gentleman, esp. the chief landowner in a district. **2** a young man of noble family who attended a knight till he himself was made a knight. —*v.* **1** attend as a squire. **2 a** escort a woman. **b** show the sights to. [ult. var. of *esquire*]

squirm (skwėrm), *v.* **1** wriggle; writhe; twist. **2** show great embarrassment, annoyance, confusion, etc. —*n.* a wriggle; writhe; twist. [? imit.] —**squirm′y,** *adj.*

squir·rel (skwėr′əl; skwėrl), *n.* **1** a small, bushy-tailed animal that lives in trees. **2** its gray, reddish, or dark-brown fur. [< AF *esquirel* < L *sciurus* < Gk., < *skia* shadow + *oura* tail]

squirt (skwėrt), *v.* **1** force out (liquid) through a narrow opening. **2** come out in a jet or stream. —*n.* **1** act of squirting. **2** jet of liquid, etc. **3** an insignificant person. —**squirt′er,** *n.* —**squirt′ing,** *adj.*

Sr, strontium.

Sr., **1** senior. **2** Sir.

SRO, S.R.O., 1 standing room only.: *available tickets to the show are SRO.* **2** single-room occupancy: *an SRO hotel.*

S.S., 1 Secretary of State. **2** Secret Service. **3** steamship.

SSE, S.S.E., direction halfway between south and southeast.

SSW, S.S.W., direction halfway between south and southwest.

St., 1 Saint. **2** Strait. **3** Street.

st., 1 stanza. **2** stet. **3** street.

stab (stab), *v.,* **stabbed, stab·bing,** *n.* —*v.* **1** pierce or wound with a pointed weapon. **2** thrust with or as with a pointed weapon: *stab at an adversary.* **3** penetrate suddenly and sharply; pierce. **4** *Fig.* deeply wound or injure the feelings. —*n.* **1** thrust or blow made with a pointed weapon; any thrust. **2** wound made by stabbing. **3** an injury to the feelings. **4** an attempt.

have or **make a stab at,** try: *you may fail, but make a stab at it anyway.*

stab in the back, attempt to injure in a sly, treacherous manner; slander. [ult. akin to *stub*] —**stab′ber,** *n.*

sta·bil·i·ty (stə bil′ə ti), *n., pl.* **-ties. 1** being fixed in position; firmness. **2** permanence. **3** steadfastness of character, purpose, etc.

sta·bi·lize (stā′bə līz), *v.,* **-lized, -liz·ing. 1** make stable or firm. **2** prevent changes in; hold steady: *stabilize prices.* **3** keep (an airplane, etc.) steady by special construction or automatic devices. —**sta′bi·li·za′tion,** *n.*

sta·bi·liz·er (stā′bə līz′ər), *n.* **1** person or thing that makes something stable. **2** device for keeping an aircraft, ship, etc., steady.

sta·ble¹ (stā′bəl), *n., v.,* **-bled, -bling.** —*n.* **1** a building where horses or cattle are kept and fed. **2** group of animals housed in such a building. **3** Often, **stables.** buildings and grounds where race horses are quartered and trained. **4** *Fig.* groups of people able to do something in particular: *a large stable of writers.* —*v.* put, keep, or live in a stable. [< OF < *stabulum*] —**sta′bler,** *n.* —**sta′bling,** *n.*

sta·ble² (stā′bəl), *adj.* **1** not likely to move or change; steadfast; firm; steady. **2** lasting without change; permanent. **3** able to return to its original position. **4 a** in a balanced condition; not readily destroyed or decomposed, as a compound. **b** resisting molecular change. [< F < L *stabilis*] —**sta′ble·ness,** *n.* —**sta′bly,** *adv.*

sta·ble·boy (stā′bəl boi′), *n.* boy who works in a stable.

stac·ca·to (stə kä′tō), *adj.* **1** with breaks between the successive tones; not held for the full time of a note. **2** disconnected; abrupt: *staccato speech.* —*adv.* in a staccato manner. [< Ital., lit., detached]

stack (stak), *n.* **1** a large pile of hay, straw, etc. Haystacks are often made round and arranged to shed water. **2** pile of anything, usually in orderly arrangement: *a stack of wood.* **3** a large quantity. **4** chimney. —*v.* **1** pile or arrange in a stack: *stack hay, firewood, etc.* **2** arrange (playing cards) unfairly.

blow one's stack, get angry; lose one's temper.

have the cards stacked against one, be at a great disadvantage.

stacks, a rack with shelves for books, CD's, etc. **b** part of a library in which the main collection of books is shelved. [< Scand. *stakkr*] **—stack'er,** *n.*

sta·di·um (stā'di əm), *n., pl.* **-di·ums, -di·a** (–di ə). an oval or U-shaped structure with rows of seats around a large open space for athletic games. [< L < Gk. *stadion*]

staff (staf; stäf), *n., pl.* **staves** or **staffs** for 1 and 2, **staffs** for 3 and 4, *v.* **—n. 1** stick; pole; rod: *the flag hangs on a staff.* **2** something that supports or sustains: *bread is called the staff of life.* **3** group assisting a chief; group of employees. **4** the five lines and the four spaces between them on which music is written. **—v.** provide with a staff. [OE *stæf*]

stag (stag), *n.* **1** a full-grown male deer. **2** the male of various other animals. esp. one castrated when full grown. **3** man who goes to a dance, party, etc., alone or with other men. **—adj.** attended by, or for men only. [OE *stagga*]

stage (stāj), *n., v.,* **staged, stag·ing. —n. 1** the raised platform in a theater on which the actors perform. **2** the theater; the drama; actor's profession: *Shakespeare wrote for the stage.* **3** scene of action: *the stage of politics.* **4** a section of a rocket or missile having its own motor and fuel. A three-stage rocket has three motors, one in each stage, which separate one after another from the rocket after use. **5** place of rest on a journey; regular stopping place. **6** distance between stops. **7** stagecoach; bus. **8** one step or degree in a process; period of development: *the first stage of a disease.* **—v. 1** put on a stage; arrange: *the play was excellently staged.* **2** arrange to have an effect: *the angry people staged a riot.*

by easy stages, a little at a time; slowly; often stopping.

on the stage, being an actor.

set the stage, *Fig.* prepare ahead; create the right conditions. [< OF *estage,* ult. < L *stare* stand]

stage·coach (stāj'kōch´), *n.* coach carrying passengers and parcels over a regular route.

stage·craft (stāj'kraft´; –kräft´), *n.* the art of writing, adapting, or presenting plays.

stage fright, fear of performing in front of an audience.

stage·hand (stāj'hand´), *n.* person whose work is moving scenery, arranging lights, etc., in a theater.

stage-struck (stāj'struk´), *adj.* wanting very much to become an actor or actress.

stage whisper, a loud whisper on a stage meant for the audience to hear.

stag·ger (stag'ər), *v.* **1** sway or reel (from weakness, a heavy load, or drunkenness). **2** become unsteady; waver. **3** *Fig.* cause to hesitate or become confused. **4** *Fig.* confuse or astonish greatly. **5** arrange in a zigzag order or in overlapping intervals, to relieve traffic, increase the efficiency etc. **—n.** a swaying; reeling.

staggers (*sing. in use*), a nervous disease of horses, cattle, etc., that makes them stagger or fall suddenly. [ult. < Scand. *stakra*] **—stag'ger·er,** *n.* **—stag'ger·ing·ly,** *adv.*

stag·ger·ing (stag'ər ing), *adj.* **1** causing to reel or waver: *a staggering revelation.* **2** tremendous; enormous: *a staggering number of casualties.*

stag·ing (stāj'ing), *n.* **1** a temporary platform or structure of posts and boards for support, as in building; scaffolding. **2** act or process of putting a play on the stage.

stag·nant (stag'nənt), *adj.* **1** not running or flowing. **2** foul from standing still. **3** *Fig.* not active; sluggish; dull: *a stagnant economy.* [< L *stagnans* stagnating. See STAGNATE.] **—stag'nan·cy,** *n.* **—stag'nant·ly,** *adv.*

stag·nate (stag'nāt), *v.,* **-nat·ed, -nat·ing.** be stagnant; become or make stagnant. [< L, < *stagnum* standing water] **—stag·na'tion,** *n.*

stag·y (stāj'i), *adj.,* **stag·i·er, stag·i·est. 1** of or pertaining to the stage. **2** suggestive of the stage; theatrical. **3** artificial; pompous; affected. **—stag'i·ly,** *adv.* **—stag'i·ness,** *n.*

staid (stād), *adj.* having a settled, quiet character; sober; sedate. **—v.** *Archaic.* pt. and pp. of **stay¹.** [orig. pp. of *stay¹* in sense of "restrain"] **—staid'ly,** *adv.* **—staid'ness,** *n.*

stain (stān), *n.* **1** discoloration; spot. **2** patch of different color. **3** *Fig.* cause of reproach; blemish. **—v. 1** discolor with spots; soil. **2** *Fig.* bring reproach upon; blemish. **3** color in a particular way. **4** produce a stain. [earlier *distain* < OF *desteindre* take out the color, ult. < L *dis-* off + *tingere* dye] **—stain'a·ble,** *adj.* **—stain'er,** *n.* **—stain'less,** *adj.* **—stain'less·ly,** *adv.*

stained glass, 1 pieces of colored glass used to create images or designs, as for church windows. **2** any colored, pointed, or enameled glass.

stainless steel, steel containing chromium, nickel, or some other metal that prevents rusting or staining.

stair (stār), *n.* **1** one of series of steps for going from one level or floor to another. **2** set of such steps.

stairs, series of steps for going from one level or floor to another. [OE *stæger*]

stair·case (stār'kās´), *n.* flight of stairs with its framework; stairs.

stair·step (stār'step´), *n.* a step in a stairway. **—adj. 1** arranged like steps. **2** *Fig.* rising or falling like steps; changing one step at a time. **3** *Fig.* like stairsteps in order, size, etc.

stair·way (stār'wā´), *n.* a way up and down by stairs; stairs.

stair·well (stār'wel´) *n.* or **stair well,** open space surrounding a flight of stairs in a building.

stake¹ stāk), *n., v.,* **staked, stak·ing. —n. 1** stick or post pointed at one end for driving into the ground. **2** stick or post to which a person is bound and burned alive. **—v. 1** fasten to a stake or with a stake. **2** mark, protect, etc. (a claim) with stakes; mark the boundaries of a claim.

pull up stakes, move away.

stake out, a claim; reserve for oneself or a special purpose. **b** watch secretly (a building, person, etc.).

the stake, execution by burning: *a barbaric death at the stake.* [OE *staca*] **—stak'er,** *n.*

stake² (stāk), *v.* **staked, stak·ing,** *n.* **—v. 1** risk (money or something valuable) on the result of a game or on any chance. **2** grubstake. **3** furnish with money or materials. **—n. 1** money risked; what is staked. **2** Often, **stakes.** the prize in a race or contest. **3** something to gain or lose; interest; share in a property.

at stake, to be won or lost; risked. **—stak'er,** *n.*

stake·hold·er (stāk'hōl´dər), *n.* person who takes care of what is bet and pays it to the winner.

sta·lac·tite (stə lak'tīt; stal'ək–), *n.* a formation of lime, shaped like an icicle, hanging from the roof of a cave. Stalactites and stalagmites are formed by dripping water that contains lime. [< NL, < Gk. *stalaktos* dripping < *stalassein* trickle]

sta·lag·mite (stəlag'mīt; stal'əg–), *n.* a formation of lime, shaped like a cone, built up on the floor of a cave. [< NL, < Gk. *stalagmos* a drop < *stalassein* trickle]

stale (stāl), *adj.,* **stal·er, stal·est,** *v.,* **staled, stal·ing. —adj. 1** not fresh; hard and dry: *stale bread.* **2** no longer new or interesting: *a stale joke.* **3** out of condition: *go stale from too much sitting.* **—v.** make or become stale. [ME] **—stale'ly,** *adv.* **—stale'ness,** *n.*

stale·mate (stāl'māt´), *n., v.,* **-mat·ed, -mat·ing. —n. 1** position of the pieces in chess when no move can be made by a player in his or her turn without putting the king in check, thus forcing a drawn game. **2** *Fig.* any position in which no action can be taken; complete standstill: *reach a stalemate in negotiations.* **—v.** put in such a position; bring to a complete standstill. [< ME *stale* stalemate (prob. < AF *estale* standstill) + MATE²]

stalk¹ (stok), *n.* **1** stem or main axis of a plant. **2** any slender, supporting or connecting part of a plant. A flower or leaf blade may have a stalk. **3** any similar part of an animal. The eyes of a crawfish are on stalks. [ME *stalke*] —**stalk′less,** *adj.* —**stalk′like′**, *adj.* —**stalk′y,** *adj.*

stalk² (stôk), *v.* **1** approach (wild animals) without being seen or heard by them. **2** pursue (an animal or a person) without being seen or heard. **3** *Fig.* spread silently and steadily: *disease stalked through the land.* **4** walk with slow, stiff, or haughty strides. —*n.* **1** haughty gait. **2** a stalking. [OE, as in *bestealcian* steal along] —**stalk′er,** *n.*

stalk·ing-horse (stôk′ing hôrs′), *n.* **1** horse or figure of a horse, behind which a hunter conceals himself in stalking game. **2** *Fig.* anything used to hide plans or acts; pretext.

stall¹ (stôl), *n.* **1** place in a stable for one animal. **2** a small place for selling things. **3** seat in the choir of a church. **4** of an airplane, condition of stalling. —*v.* **1** live in a stall, stable, kennel, etc. **2** stop or bring to a standstill, usually contrary to one's wish. **3** stick fast in mud, snow, etc.; come to a standstill. **4** of an airplane, lose so much speed that it cannot be controlled. [OE *steall*] —**stalled,** *adj.*

stall² (stôl), *n.* pretext, esp. as a means of delay. —*v.* **1** pretend; evade; deceive. **2** delay. [< AF *estal* decoy < Gmc.]

stal·lion (stal′yən), *n.* an uncastrated male horse, esp. one kept for breeding purposes. [< OF *estalon* < Gmc.]

stal·wart (stôl′wərt), *adj.* **1** strongly built: *a stalwart body.* **2** strong and brave: *a stalwart knight.* **3** firm; steadfast: *a stalwart supporter.* —*n.* **1** a stalwart person. **2** a loyal supporter of a political party. [OE *stælwierthe* serviceable < *stathol* position + *wierthe* worthy] —**stal′wart·ly,** *adv.* —**stal′wart·ness,** *n.*

sta·men (stā′mən), *n., pl.* **sta·mens, stam·i·na** (stam′ə nə). part of a flower that contains the pollen, consisting of a slender, threadlike stem or filament and an anther. [< L, warp, thread] —**sta′mened,** *adj.*

stam·i·na (stam′ə nə), *n.* strength; endurance. [< L, threads (of life, spun by the Fates)]

stam·mer (stam′ər), *v.* **1** repeat the same sound, esp. involuntarily, in an effort to speak; hesitate in speaking. **2** utter thus: *stammer an excuse.* —*n.* a stammering; stuttering. [OE *stamerian*] —**stam′mer·er,** *n.* —**stam′mer·ing·ly,** *adv.*

stamp (stamp), *v.* **1** bring down (one's foot) with force. **2** walk in this way: *she stamped out of the room.* **3** fix firmly or deeply: *the scene was stamped in her memory.* **4** impress, cut, etc. (a design). **5** show to be of a certain quality or character; indicate: *his speech stamps him as an educated man.* **6** put postage on. —*n.* **1** act of stamping. **2** instrument that cuts, shapes, or impresses a design on (paper, wax, metal, etc.); thing that puts a mark on. **3** the mark made with it. **4** an official mark or seal. **5** impression; marks: *her face bore the stamp of suffering.* **6** *Fig.* kind; type: *men of his stamp are rare.* **7** a

small piece of paper with a sticky back, put on letters, papers, parcels, etc., to show that a charge has been paid.

stamp out, a put out by stamping: *stamp out flames.* **b** put an end to by force. [ME *stampe(n)*] —**stamped,** *adj.* —**stamp′er,** *n.*

stam·pede (stam pēd′), *n., v.,* **-ped·ed, -ped·ing.** —*n.* **1** a sudden scattering or headlong flight of a frightened herd of cattle or horses. **2** *Fig.* any headlong flight of a large group. **3** *Fig.* a general rush. —*v.* **1** scatter or flee in a stampede. **2** *Fig.* make a general rush. [< Mex.Sp. *estampida* (in Sp., uproar) < *estampar* stamp, ult. < Gmc.] —**stam·ped′er,** *n.*

stance (stans), *n.* position of the feet of a player when making a stroke in golf or other games. [< F, ult. < L *stare* stand]

stanch¹ (stänch; stanch), *v.* **1** stop or check the flow of (blood, etc.). **2** cease flowing. [< OF *estanchier*] —**stanch′er,** *n.* —**stanch′less,** *adj.*

stanch² (stänch; stanch), *adj.* **1** firm; strong; substantial: *stanch walls, a stanch defense.* **2** loyal; steadfast. **3** watertight: *a stanch boat.* [< OF *estanche,* fem.] —**stanch′ly,** *adv.* —**stanch′ness.** *n.*

stan·chion (stan′shən), *n.* an upright bar, post, or support (in a window, in a stall for cattle, on a ship, etc.). [< OF *estanchon,* ult. < L *stare* stand]

stand (stand), *v.,* **stood, stand·ing,** *n.* —*v.* **1** be upright on one's feet: *he stands six feet in his socks.* **2** be set upright; place; be located: *the box stands over there, stand the box here.* **3** *Fig.* be in a certain rank, scale, etc.: *he stood first in his class.* **4** take or keep a certain position: *"Stand back!", stand firm for justice.* **5** *Fig.* be in a special condition: *he stands innocent of any wrong.* **6** *Fig.* be unchanged; hold good; remain the same: *the rule against lateness will stand.* **7** stay in place; last: *the old house has stood for many years.* **8** undergo; bear; endure: *stand trial.* **9** withstand without being hurt or giving way: *cloth that will stand wear.* —*n.* **1** a halt; stop. **2** stop for defense, resistance, etc.: *make a last stand.* **3** place where a person stands; position: *a stand for free speech, make a stand against a bully.* **4** a raised place where people can sit or stand. **5** something to put things on or in. **6** place or fixtures for a small business: *stand that sells newspapers.* **7** group of growing trees or plants.

stand a chance, have a chance.

stand by, a be near. **b** stand with; help; support. **c** keep; maintain. **d** be or get ready for use, action, etc.

stand down, a withdraw, as a military force. **b** leave the stand, as a witness in a trial.

stand for, a represent; mean. **b** be on the side of; take the part of; uphold. **c** be a candidate for. **d** put up with: *I will not stand for rudeness.*

stand in, substitute for another.

stand out, a project. **b** be noticeable or prominent.

stand pat, hold to things as they are and refuse to change.

stand up, a get to one's feet. **b** endure; last. **c** fail to meet, as an appointment or engagement.

stand up for, take the past of; defend; support.

stand up to, meet or face boldly. [OE *standan*] —**stand′er,** *n.*

stand·ard (stan′dərd), *n.* **1** anything taken as a basis of comparison; model; rule: *good standards of living, your work is not up to standard.* **2** an authorized measure. **3** flag, emblem, or symbol. —*adj.* **1** used as a standard; according to rule. **2** having recognized excellence or authority. **3** indicating a specified manner of speaking and writing which is approved by a particular society: *standard English.* [< OF *estandart* < Gmc.]

stand·ard·bear·er (stan′dərd bār′ər), *n.* **1** person who carries a banner in a procession. **2** a conspicuous leader of a movement, political party, etc.

stand·ard·ize (stan′dər dīz), *v.,* **-ized, -iz·ing. 1** make standard in size, shape, weight, quality, strength, etc.: *the parts of an automobile are standardized.* **2** regulate by a standard. —**stand′ard·i·za′tion,** *n.* —**stand′ard·iz′er,** *n.*

standard of living, way of living that a person or community considers necessary to provide enough material things for comfort, happiness, etc.

standard time, time officially adopted for a region or country.

stand·by or **stand·by** (stand′bī′), *n., pl.* **-bys.** person or thing that can be relied upon; chief support; ready resource.

on stand-by, prepared and ready.

stand·ee (stan dē′), *n.* person who has to stand in a theater, etc.

stand-in (stand′in′), *n.* person whose work is standing in the place of another, as for a motion-picture actor or actress while the lights, camera, etc., are being arranged.

stand·ing (stan′ding), *n.* **1** position; reputation: *men of good standing.* **2** *Fig.* duration: *a habit of long standing.* **3** act of standing; place of standing. —*adj.* **1** straight up; erect. **2** done from an erect position: *a standing jump.* **3** established; permanent: *a standing army.* **4** not flowing; stagnant.

standing room, 1 space to stand in. **2** space to stand in after all the seats are taken.

stand-off (stand′ôf′; -of′), *n.* **1** a standing off or apart; reserve; aloofness. **2** situation involving a balance between opposing elements; a tie or draw, as in a game. —*adj.* standing off or apart; reserved; holding aloof. —**stand′-off′ish,** *adj.* —**stand′-off′ish·ness,** *n.*

stand-out or **standout** (stand′out′), *n.* person or thing that is outstanding or excellent of its kind. —*adj.* outstanding; excellent.

stand·pat (stand′pat′), *adj.* standing firm for things as they are; opposing any change.

stand·pipe (stand′pīp′), *n.* a large vertical pipe or tower to hold water.

stand·point (stand′point′), *n.* point at which one stands to view something; point of view; mental attitude.

stand·still (stand′stil′), *n.* a complete stop; halt; pause: *during the strike, production came to a standstill.*

stand-up (stand′up′), *adj.* **1** standing upright. **2** performed while standing: *stand-up comedy.* **3** taken while standing: *stand-up lunch.*

stang (stang), *v. Archaic or Obs.* pt. of **sting.**

stank (stangk), *v.* pt. of **stink.**

stan·nic (stan′ik), *adj.* containing tin with a valence of four.

stan·nous (stan′əs), *adj.* containing tin with a valence of two.

stan·num (stan′əm), *n.* tin. [< LL]

stan·za (stan′zə), *n.* group of lines of poetry, commonly four or more, arranged according to a fixed plan; verse of a poem. [< Ital., orig., stopping place, ult. < L *stare* stand]

sta·pes (stā′pēz), *n.* the innermost of the three small bones in the middle ear; the stirrup bone.

staph (staf), *n. Informal.* staphylococcus or staphylococci. —*adj.* staphylococcal.

staph·y·lo·coc·cus, (staf′ə lə kok′əs), *n., pl.* **-coc·ci** (-kok′sī). round, parasitic bacteria that can cause serious infections in humans. —**staph′y·lo·coc′cal,** *adj.*

sta·ple¹ (stā′pəl), *n., v.,* **-pled, -pling.** —*n.* **1** a U-shaped piece of metal with pointed ends. Staples are driven into doors, etc., to hold hooks, pins, or bolts. **2** a bent piece or wire used to hold together papers, parts of a book, etc. —*v.* fasten with a staple or staples. [OE *stapol* post] —**sta′pler,** *n.*

sta·ple² (stā′pəl), *n.,* **1** the most important or principal article grown or manufactured in a place. Cotton is the staple in many S states. **2** a chief element or material. **3** a raw material. **4** fiber of cotton, wool. etc. —*adj.* **1** most important; principal. **2** established in commerce: *a staple trade.* **3** regularly produced in large quantities for the market. [< OF *estaple* mart < Gmc.] —**sta′pler,** *n.*

star (stär), *n., v.,* **starred, star·ring,** *adj.* —*n.* **1** any of the celestial bodies appearing as bright points in the sky at night. **2** a plane figure having five points, or sometimes six, like these: ☆ ✳. **3** thing having or suggesting this shape. **4** asterisk (*). **5** person who is celebrated as an actor, singer, etc., esp. one who plays the lead in a performance: *a movie star.* **6** fate; fortune. —*v.* **1** set with stars; ornament with stars. **2** mark with a star or an asterisk. **3** be prominent; be a leading

performer: *star in many movies.* **4** present as a star. —*adj.* chief; best; leading; excellent. [OE *steorra*] —**star′less,** *adj.* —**star′like′,** *adj.*

star·board (stär′bərd; –bôrd; –bōrd), *n.* the right side of a ship, when facing forward. —*adj.* on the right side of a ship. —*adv.* toward the right side. [OE *stēorbord.* See STEER¹, BOARD.]

starch (stärch), *n.* **1** a white, tasteless food substance. Potatoes, wheat, rice, and corn contain much starch. **2** preparation of it used to stiffen clothes, curtains, etc. **3** a stiff, formal manner; stiffness. —*v.* stiffen (clothes, curtains, etc.) with starch.

starches, foods containing much starch.

take the starch out of, weary; fatigue. [OE *stercan* (in *stercedferhth* stouthearted) < *stearc* stiff, strong] —**starch′y,** *adj.* —**starch′i·ness,** *n.*

Star Chamber, 1 in English history, a court that used arbitrary, secret, and unfair methods of trial. **2** any court, committee, or group like this.

star-crossed (stär′krôst′; –krost′), *adj.* ill-fated; unfortunate.

star·dom (stär′dəm), *n.* **1** condition of being a star actor or performer. **2** star actors or performers as a group.

stare (stär), *v.,* **stared, star·ing,** *n.* —*v.* **1** look long and directly with the eyes wide open. A person stares in wonder, surprise, rudeness. **2** bring to a named condition by staring: *stare one down.* **3** gaze at. —*n.* a long and direct look with the eyes wide open.

stare one in the face, be very evident; seem very likely. [OE *starian*] —**star′er,** *n.* —**star′ing,** *adj.* —**star′ing·ly,** *adv.*

star·fish (stär′fish′), *n., pl.* **-fish·es** or (*esp. collectively*) **-fish.** a star-shaped sea animal.

stark (stärk), *adj.* **1** downright; complete: *stark nonsense.* **2** stiff: *the dog lay stark in death.* **3** harsh; stern. —*adv.* **1** entirely; completely. **2** in a stark manner. [OE *stearc* stiff, strong] —**stark′ly,** *adv.*

star·let (stär′lit), *n.* **1** a young actress or singer who is being coached for leading roles in motion pictures. **2** a little star.

star·light (stär′līt′), *n.* light from the stars.

star·ling (stär′ling), *n.* **1** a common European bird which nests about buildings and is easily tamed. **2** a kind of American blackbird. [OE *stærling*]

star·lit (stär′lit′), *adj.* lighted by the stars.

star-of-Beth·le·hem (stär′əv beth′li əm; –lə hem), *n.* plant of the lily family that grows from a small bulb and has a tall cluster of white, star-shaped flowers.

star·ry (stär′i), *adj.,* **-ri·er, -ri·est. 1** lighted by stars; containing many stars: *a starry sky.* **2** shining like stars: *starry eyes.* **3** like a star in shape. **4** of or having to do with stars. —**star′ri·ly,** *adv.* —**star′ri·ness,** *n.*

Stars and Stripes, the flag of the United States.

Star-Span·gled Banner (stär′spang′gəld), the American national anthem.

start (stärt), *v.* **1** get in motion; set out; begin a journey: *the train started on time.* **2** begin: *start a book, start a race.* **3** set moving, going, acting, etc.; cause to set out; cause to begin: *start an automobile, start a person in business.* **4** move, come, rise, or spring suddenly: *start in surprise, tears started from her eyes.* **5** rouse: *start a rabbit.* —*n.* **1** the beginning of a movement, act, journey, race, etc. **2** a setting in motion: *his father gave him his start.* **3** a sudden movement; jerk. **4** spurt of activity: *work by fits and starts.* **5** place, where a race begins.

start in, out, or **up,** start. [< var. of OE *styrtan* leap up] —**start′er,** *n.*

star·tle (stär′təl), *v.,* **-tled, -tling,** *n.* —*v.* **1** frighten suddenly; surprise. **2** move suddenly in fear or surprise. —*n.* a sudden shock of surprise or fright. [OE *steartlian* struggle] —**star′tler,** *n.* —**star′tling,** *adj.* —**star′tling·ly,** *adv.* —*v.*

star·va·tion (stär vā′shən), *n.* **1** a starving. **2** suffering from extreme hunger; being starved.

starve (stärv), *v.,* **starved, starv·ing. 1** die because of hunger. **2** suffer severely because of hunger or a need. **3** force by lack of food: *they starved the enemy into surrendering.* **4** feel hungry; have a craving. [OE *steorfan* die] —**starv′er,** *n.*

stash (stash), *v.* hide or put away for safekeeping or future use. —*n.* what is hidden or put away.

state (stāt), *n., v.,* **stat·ed, stat·ing,** *adj.* —*n.* **1** condition of a person or thing: *in an excited state, ice is water in a solid state.* **2** a person's position in life; rank; station: *humble state.* **3** high style of living; dignity; pomp: *a coach of state.* **4** Also, **State. a** a nation. **b** one of several organized political groups of people that together form a nation. The State of Texas is one of the United States. **5** the civil government; highest civil authority: *affairs of state.* —*v.* **1** tell in speech or writing; express; says: *state one's views.* **2** set forth in proper or definite form: *state a problem.* —*adj.* **1** used on or reserved for very formal and special occasions; ceremonious; formal: *state robes.* **2** of or having to do with civil government or authority: *state control.*

lie in state, lie in a coffin where it can be viewed by the public in a formal setting before being buried: *the king lay in state for three days.*

State or **state,** maintained, controlled, or established by a state: *a State road.*

the States, the United States: *returned to the States after three years abroad.* [< L *status* condition, position < *stare* stand; common in L phrase *status rei publicae* condition of the republic] —**stat′a·ble,** *adj.* —**state′hood,** *n.*

state·craft (stāt′kraft′; –kräft′), *n.* **1** statesmanship. **2** crafty statesmanship.

stat·ed (stāt'id), *adj.* **1** said; told. **2** fixed; settled. —**stat'ed·ly,** *adv.*

state·house (stāt'hous´), *n.* U.S. building in which the legislature of a state meets.

state·ly (stāt'li), *adj.,* **–li·er, –li·est.** dignified; imposing; grand; majestic. —**state'li·ness,** *n.*

state·ment (stāt'mənt), *n.* **1** act or manner of stating something. **2** something stated; report: *a written statement.* **3** summary of an account, showing the amount owed or due.

state of affairs, conditions; the way things are going.

state-of-the-art (stāt'əv t͡hi ört'), *adj.* best; most highly developed: *a state-of-the-art computer.*

state·room (stāt'rüm´; –rùm´), *n.* a private room on a ship.

state's evidence, testimony given in court by a criminal against his associates in a crime.

turn state's evidence, testify in court against one's associates in a crime.

state·side (stāt'sīd´), **states·side** (stāts'-sīd´), *adj.* of or in the United States. —*adv.* in or in the direction of the United States.

states·man (stāts'mən), *n., pl.* **-men.** person skilled in the management of public or national affairs. —**states'man·like´, states'man·ly,** *adj.*

states·man·ship (stāts'mən ship), *n.* the qualities of a statesman; skill in the management of public affairs.

states' rights, powers belonging to the separate states of the United States, under the Constitution.

states·wom·an (stāts'wùm´ən), *n., pl.* **-wom·en.** a female statesman.

stat·ic (stat'ik), *adj.* **1** at rest; standing still: *civilization does not remain static, but changes constantly.* **2** characterized by stability and lack of change: *a static society.* **3** having to do with stationary electrical charges that balance each other. Static electricity can be produced by rubbing a glass rod with a silk cloth. **4** of or pertaining to atmospheric electricity that interferes with radio reception. —*n.* **1** atmospheric electricity. **2** interference due to such electricity. [< Gk. *statikos* causing to stand] —**stat'i·cal·ly,** *adv.*

stat·ics (stat'iks), *n. pl. (sing. in use).* branch of mechanics that deals with objects at rest or forces that balance each other.

sta·tion (stā'shən), *n.* **1** place in which anything stands; place which a person is appointed to occupy in the performance of some duty; assigned post: *the policeman took his station at the corner.* **2** a regular stopping place, as on a railroad or bus line. **3** building or buildings at such a stopping place; depot. **4** a building or place equipped for some particular kind of work, research, etc.: *a postal station.* **5** place or equipment for sending out or receiving programs, messages, etc., by radio or television. **6** *Fig.* social position; rank. —*v.* assign a station to; place. [< L, < *stare* stand]

sta·tion·ar·y (stā'shən er´i), *adj.* **1** having a fixed station or place; not movable. **2** standing still; not moving. **3** not changing in size, number, activity, etc. [< L, < *statio* STATION]

sta·tion·er (stā'shən ər), *n.* person who sells paper, pens, pencils, etc. [< Med. L *stationarius* shopkeeper, orig., stationary, as distinct from a roving peddler]

sta·tion·er·y (stā'shən er´i), *n.* writing materials; paper, cards, and envelopes.

station wagon, closed automobile that can be used as a light truck, with a wide door at the back for easy loading.

stat·ism (stāt'iz əm), *n.* highly centralized governmental control of the economy newspapers, etc., of a state or nation.

sta·tis·tic (stə tis'tik), *adj.* =statistical. —*n.* a numerical fact.

sta·tis·ti·cal (stə tis'tə kəl), *adj.* of or pertaining to statistics; consisting of or based on statistics. —**sta·tis'ti·cal·ly,** *adv.*

stat·is·ti·cian (stat´is tish'ən), *n.* expert in statistics.

sta·tis·tics (stə tis'tiks), *n.* **1** (*pl. in use*) numerical facts about people, the weather, business conditions, etc. Statistics are collected and classified systematically. **2** (*sing. in use*) science of collecting, classifying, and interpreting such facts. [ult. < G < NL *statisticus* political, ult. < L *status* STATE]

stat·u·ar·y (stach'ü er´i), *n., pl.* **-ar·ies,** *adj.* —*n.* statues. —*adj.* of or for statues.

stat·ue (stach'ü), *n.* image of a person or animal carved in stone or wood, cast in bronze, or modeled in clay or wax. [< F < L *status,* ult. < *stare* stand]

stat·u·esque (stach´ü esk'), *adj.* like a statue in dignity, formal grace, or classic beauty. —**stat´u·esque'ly,** *adv.* —**stat´u·esque'ness,** *n.*

stat·u·ette (stach´ü et'), *n.* a small statue.

stat·ure (stach'ər), *n.* **1** height. **2** *Fig.* development; physical, mental, or moral growth. [< OF < L *statura* < *stare* stand]

sta·tus (stā'təs; stat'əs), *n.* **1** condition; state. **2** social or professional standing; position; rank: *his status as a doctor.* **3** legal position. [< L < *stare* stand]

status quo (kwō), the way things are; the existing state of affairs. [< L, the state in which]

stat·ute (stach'üt), *n.* **1** law enacted by a legislative body. **2** a law; decree. [< F *statut,* ult. < L *statuere* establish, ult. < *stare* stand]

statute law, written law; law established by statutes or legislative enactments.

statute of limitations, law restricting the time allowed to file legal claims or prosecute certain crimes.

stat·u·to·ry (stach'ü tô´ri; –tō´–), *adj.* **1** pertaining to a statute. **2** fixed by statute. **3** punishable by statute. —**stat'u·to´ri·ly,** *adv.*

staunch¹ (stônch; stänch), *v., adj.* =stanch. —**staunch'ly,** *adv.* —**staunch'ness,** *n.*

staunch² (stônch, stänch), *adj.* **1** firm; steadfast. **2** loyal. Also, **stanch.**

stave (stāv), *n., v.,* **staved** or **stove, stav·ing.** —*n.* **1** one of the curved pieces of wood that form the sides of a barrel, tub, etc. **2** rung of a ladder. **3** verse or stanza of a poem or song. **4** the musical staff. —*v.* **1** become smashed or broken in. **2** furnish with staves.

stave off, put off; keep back; delay or prevent. [< *staves,* pl. of *staff*]

staves (stāvz), *n.* **1** pl. of **staff.** **2** pl. of **stave.**

stay¹ (stā), *v.,* **stayed** or **staid, stay·ing,** *n.* —*v.* **1** continue to be as indicated; remain: *stay clean.* **2** live for a while; dwell: *stay at a hotel.* **3** stop; pause; remain for: *stay to dinner.* **4** delay; restrain; check: *stay the spread of disease.* **5** endure: *unable to stay to the end of a race.* —*n.* **1** a staying; a stop; time spent: *a pleasant stay in the country.* **2** check; restrain: *a stay on his activity, the judge granted the condemned man a stay for an appeal.* **3** endurance.

stay put, remain in place. [< OF *ester* stand < L *stare*] —**stay'er,** *n.*

stay² (stā), *n., v.,* **stayed, stay·ing.** —*n.* a support; prop; brace. —*v.* support; prop; hold up.

stays, corset. [prob. ult. < OF *estayer* < Gmc.] —**stay'er,** *n.*

stay³ (stā), *n., v.,* **stayed, stay·ing,** —*n.* **1** a strong rope, often of wire, which supports a mast of a ship. **2** any rope or chain similarly used. —*v.* **1** support or secure with stays. **2** of a ship, change to the other tack. [OE *stæg*]

staying power, endurance; determination to see something through to a conclusion.

stay·sail (stā'sāl´; –səl), *n.* a sail fastened on a stay or rope.

STD, sexually transmitted disease.

stead (sted), *n.* the place of a person or thing as occupied by a successor or substitute.

stand in good stead, be of advantage or service to. [OE *stede*]

stead·fast (sted'fast; –fäst; –fəst), *adj.* firmly fixed; constant; not moving or changing. —**stead'fast·ly,** *adv.* —**stead'fast·ness,** *n.*

stead·y (sted'i), *adj.,* **stead·i·er, stead·i·est,** *v.,* **stead·ied, stead·y·ing,** *n., pl.* **stead·ies.** —*adj.* **1** firmly fixed; firm; not swaying or shaking: *hold a ladder steady.* **2** changing little; uniform; regular: *steady progress.* **3** not easily excited; calm: *steady nerves.* **4** reliable; having good habits: *a steady young man.* **5** keeping nearly upright in a heavy sea. —*v.* **1** make or keep steady. **2** become steady. —*n.* a person's regular companion or sweetheart. [< *stead*] —**stead'i·er,** *n.* —**stead'i·ly,** *adv.* —**stead'i·ness,** *n.*

steady state, in physics, a system in equilibrium.

steak (stāk), *n.* slice of meat or fish for broiling or frying. *Steak* often means *beefsteak.* [< Scand. *steik*]

steal (stēl), *v.,* **stole, sto·len, steal·ing,** *n.* —*v.* **1** take (something) that does not belong to one; take dishonestly: *steal money.* **2** take, get, or do secretly: *steal a look at someone.* **3** take, get, or win by art, charm, or gradual means: *she steals all hearts.* **4** move secretly or quietly: *she stole out of the house.* **5** run to (a base) without being helped by a hit or error. —*n.* **1** act of stealing. **2** the thing stolen. [OE *stelan*] —**steal′er,** *n.* —**steal′ing·ly,** *adv.*

stealth (stelth), *n.* secret or sly action. [< *steal*]

stealth·y (stel′thi), *adj.,* **stealth·i·er, stealth·i·est.** done in a secret manner; secret; sly. —**stealth′i·ly,** *adv.* —**stealth′i·ness,** *n.*

steam (stēm), *n.* **1** water in the form of vapor or gas. Steam is used to heat houses, run engines, etc. **2** any vapor. **3** *Fig.* power; energy; force. —*v.* **1** give off steam: *a cup of steaming coffee.* **2** rise in steam. **3** move by steam: *the ship steamed off.* **4** cook, soften, or freshen by steam. **5** become covered with condensed steam, as a mirror. —*adj.* **1** moved by steam. **2** operated by steam. **3** carrying steam.

blow off steam, a relieve pent-up feelings or emotion. **b** work off pent-up energy.

get up a head of steam, gather the energy necessary. [OE *stēam*] —**steam′i·ly,** *adv.* —**steam′i·ness,** *n.*

steam bath, 1 bath taken in a room filled with steam, as in a sauna or Turkish bath. **2** the room where such a bath is taken.

steam·boat (stēm′bōt′), *n.* boat moved by steam.

steam engine, engine operated by steam, typically one in which a sliding piston in a cylinder is moved by the expansive action of steam generated in a boiler.

steam·er (stēm′ər), *n.* **1** steamboat; steamship. **2** container in which something is steamed.

steam fitter, person who installs and repairs steam pipes, radiators, boilers, etc. —**steam fitting.**

steam roller, 1 a heavy roller used to crush and level materials in making roads. **2** *Fig.* means of crushing opposition.

steam-roll (stəm′rōl′) or **steam-roll·er** (stēm′rōl′ər), *v.* **1** smooth; flatten. **2** *Fig.* crush, as opposition.

steamship (stēm′ship′), *n.* ship moved by steam.

steam·y (stēm′i), *adj.* **1** of, like, or having to do with steam. **2** full of steam. **3** *Informal. Fig.* full of passion: *a steamy film.*

ste·ap·sin (sti ap′sin), *n.* a digestive enzyme secreted in the pancreatic juice, which changes fats into glycerol and fatty acids. [blend of *stea(rin)* and *(pe)psin*]

ste·a·rin (stē′ə rin; stir′in), *n.* **1** a colorless, odorless substance, $C_3H_5O_3$ $(C_{17}H_{35}CO)_3$, that is the chief constituent of many animal and vegetable fats. **2** a mixture of fatty acids used for making candles, solid alcohol, etc. [< F *stéarine* < Gk. *stear* fat] —**ste·ar′ic,** *adj.*

sted·fast (sted′fast; –fäst; –fəst), *adj.* =steadfast.

steed (stēd), *n.* **1** horse, esp. a riding horse. **2** a high-spirited horse. [OE *stēda*]

steel (stēl), *n.* **1** iron mixed with carbon so that it is very hard, strong, and tough. Most tools are made from steel. **2** something made from steel. **3** sword. **4** *Fig.* steellike hardness, strength, or color: *nerves of steel.* —*adj.* **1** made of steel. **2** like steel in hardness, strength, or color: *steel nerves.* —*v.* **1** point, edge, or cover with steel. **2** *Fig.* make hard or strong like steel. [OE *stēle*] —**steel′y,** *adj.* —**steel′i·ness,** *n.*

steel·work·er (stēl′wėr′kər), *n.* person who works in a place where steel is made.

steel·works (stēl′wėrks′), *n. pl. or sing.* place where steel is made.

steel·yard (stēl′yärd; stil′yərd), *n.* a scale for weighing. A steelyard has unequal arms, the longer one having a movable weight and the shorter a hook for holding the object to be weighed.

steen·bok (stēn′bok′; stān′–), *n.* any of various small African antelopes frequenting rocky places. [< Du., < *steen* stone + *bok* buck]

steep¹ (stēp), *adj.* **1** having a sharp slope; almost straight up and down. **2** *Fig.* unduly high; extravagant; unreasonable: *a steep price.* —*v.* a steep slope. [OE *stēap*] —**steep′ly,** *adv.* —**steep′ness,** *n.*

steep² (stēp), *v.* **1** soak: *let the tea steep in boiling water for five minutes.* **2** *Fig.* immerse; imbue: *ruins steeped in gloom.* —*n.* **1** a soaking. **2** liquid in which something is soaked. [prob. < OE *stēap* bowl] —**steep′er,** *n.*

steep·en (stē′pən), *v.* make or become steep or steeper: *the slope steepened higher up.*

stee·ple (stē′pəl), *n.* a high tower on a church, usually with a spire. [OE *stēpel* < *stēap* steep] —**stee′pled,** *adj.*

stee·ple·chase (stē′pəl chās′), *n.* **1** a horse race over a course having ditches, hedges, and other obstacles. **2** a horse race across country. —**stee′ple·chas′er,** *n.*

stee·ple·jack (stē′pəl jak′), *n.* person who climbs steeples, tall chimneys, or the like, to make repairs, etc.

steer¹ (stir), *v.* **1** guide the course of (anything in motion): *steer a ship, an automobile, an airplane, etc.* **2** guide a ship, automobile, airship, etc.: *the pilot steered for the harbor.* **3** direct one's way or course: *steer between extremes.*

give (or **get**) **a bum steer,** give or receive bad advice or wrong information.

steer clear of, keep away from; avoid. [OE *stēoran*] —**steer′a·ble,** *adj.* —**steer′er,** *n.*

steer² (stir), *n.* **1** a young ox, usually two to four years old. **2** any male of beef cattle. [OE *stēor*]

steer·age (stir′ij), *n.* part of a passenger ship occupied by passengers traveling at the cheapest rate.

steers·man (stirz′mən), *n., pl.* **–men.** person who steers a ship. —**steers′man·ship,** *n.*

stein (stīn), *n.* a beer mug. [< G, stone]

stein·bock (stīn′bok′), *n.* =steenbok.

stel·lar (stel′ər), *adj.* **1** of or pertaining to the stars; of or like a star. **2** chief: *a stellar role.* [< L. < *stella* star]

stel·late (stel′āt; –it), *adj.* spreading out like the points of a star; star-shaped. [< L, < *stella* star] —**stel′late·ly,** *adv.*

stem¹ (stem), *n., v.,* **stemmed, stem·ming.** —*n.* **1** the main part of a plant above the ground. The stem supports the branches, etc. **2** the part of a flower, a fruit, or a leaf that joins it to the plant or tree. **3** anything like or suggesting the stem of a plant: *the stem of a goblet, the stem of a pipe, watch, etc.* **4** the unchanged part in a series of inflectional forms. **5** the bow or front end of a boat. —*v.* remove the stem from (a leaf, fruit, etc.).

from stem to stern, from one end to the other; thoroughly; completely: *search the house from stem to stern.*

stem from, originate or spring from. [OE *stemn*] —**stem′less,** *adj.* —**stemmed,** *adj.* —**stem′mer,** *n.*

stem² (stem), *v.,* **stemmed, stem·ming. 1** stop; check; dam up. **2** make progress against: *stem the swift current.* [< Scand. *stemma*]

stench (stench), *n.* a very bad smell; stink. [OE *stenc* < *stincan* smell] —**stench′y,** *adj.*

sten·cil (sten′səl), *n., v.,* **–ciled, –cil·ing.** —*n.* **1** a thin sheet of metal, paper, etc., having letters or designs cut through it. When it is laid on a surface and ink or color is spread on, these letters or designs are made on the surface. **2** the letters or designs so made. —*v.* mark or paint with a stencil. [ult. < OF *estanceler* ornament with colors, ult. < L *scintilla* spark] —**sten′cil·er,** *n.*

ste·nog·ra·pher (stə nog′rə fər), *n.* person whose work is stenography, as a court stenographer.

ste·nog·ra·phy (stə nog′rə fi), *n.* **1** method of rapid writing that uses symbols in place of letters, sounds, and words. **2** act of writing in such symbols or using a stenographic machine. [< Gk. *stenos* narrow + E *-graphy* (< Gk. *graphein* write)] —**sten′o·graph′ic,** *adj.* —**sten′o·graph′i·cal·ly,** *adv.*

sten·to·ri·an (sten tô′ri ən; –tō′–), *adj.* very loud or powerful in sound. [from *Stentor,* a Greek herald in the Trojan War, whose voice was as loud as the voices of fifty men] —**sten·to′ri·an·ly,** *adv.*

step (step), *n., v.,* **stepped, step·ping.** —*n.* **1** a movement made by lifting the foot and putting it down again in a new position, as in walking, running, dancing, etc. **2** distance covered by one such movement: *she was three steps away when he called her back.* **3** a short distance; little way: *the school is only a step away.* **4** place for the foot in going up or coming down: *a rung of a ladder is a step.* **5** sound made by putting the foot down: *hear steps.* **6** footprint: *see steps in the mud.* **7** an action, as toward a result: *the college took steps to prevent epidemics.* **8 a** a degree in a scale, as a ranking. **b** the musical staff or scale. [< v.] —*v.* **1** move by stepping: *step forward.* **2** walk a short distance: *step this way.* **3** measure (a distance, ground, etc.) by steps: *step off the distance.* **4** put the foot down: *step on a worm.* **5** come as if by a step: *step into a good job.*

in step, a stepping in time with music or with the pace or steps of another or others. **b** *Fig.* in agreement with, esp. of an opinion or belief.

out of step, a not stepping in time with music or with the pace or steps of another or others. **b** *Fig.* not in agreement with, esp. of an opinion or belief.

step aside, a step out of the way. **b** *Fig.* withdraw.

step back, a take a step backward. **b** *Fig.* withdraw.

step by step, little by little; slowly.

step down, a come down. **b** resign. **c** *Fig.* decrease.

step in, come in; intervene; take part.

step on it, *Informal.* go faster; hurry up.

step out, go out for entertainment.

step up, a go up. **b** move forward. **c** *Fig.* increase.

watch one's step, be careful. [OE *steppan*]

step-, *prefix.* related by the remarriage of a parent, not by blood, as in *stepmother, stepsister.* [OE *steop-*]

step-and-fetch-it (step′ən fech′it), *n.* person who runs errands for another, goes and gets things, etc.; gofer.

step·broth·er (step′bruth′ər), *n.* a stepfather's or stepmother's son by a former marriage.

step·child (step′chīld′), *n., pl.* **-chil·dren.** child of one's husband or wife by a former marriage.

step·daugh·ter (step′dô′tər), *n.* daughter of one's husband or wife by a former marriage.

step·father (step′fä′ᵺər), *n.* man who has married one's mother after the death or divorce of one's real father. —**step′fa′ther·ly,** *adj.*

step·lad·der (step′lad′ər), *n.* ladder with flat steps instead of rungs.

step·moth·er (step′muᵺ′ər), *n.* woman who has married one's father after the death or divorce of one's real mother.

steppe (step), *n.* a vast treeless plain. [< Russ. *step*]

stepped-up (stept′up′), *adj.* speeded up or intensified; increased.

step·per (step′ər), *n.* person, etc., that steps.

stepping stone, anything serving as a means of advancing or rising.

step·sis·ter (step′sis′tər), *n.* a stepfather's or stepmother's daughter by a former marriage.

step·son (step′sun′), *n.* son of one's husband or wife by a former marriage.

stept (stept), *v. Poetic.* pt. and pp. of **step.**

step-up (step′up′), *n.* an increase: *a step-up in activity.*

-ster, *suffix.* **1** one that ___s, as in *fibster.* **2** one that makes ___, as in *maltster, rhymester.* **3** one that is ___, as in *youngster.* **4** special meanings, as in *gangster, teamster.* [OE *-estre, -istre*]

stere (stir), *n.* a cubic meter. [< F < Gk. *stereos* solid]

ster·e·o (ster′i ō; stir′-), *adj., n., pl.* **-e·os.** —*adj.* **1** in photography, optics, etc., reproducing or simulating binocular vision. **2** in acoustics, stereophonic. —*n.* a stereophonic system of sound reproduction.

ster·e·o·phon·ic (ster′i ə fon′ik; stir′-), *adj.* reproducing or simulating the acoustic effect of a sound as it would be heard with both ears. —**ster′e·o·phon′i·cal·ly,** *adv.*

ster·e·op·ti·con (ster′i op′tə kən; stir′-), *n.* form of magic lantern, having a powerful light. [< NL, < Gk. *stereos* solid + *optikos* relating to vision]

ster·e·o·scope (ster′i ə skōp′; stir′-), *n.* instrument through which two pictures of the same object or scene are viewed, one by each eye. —**ster′e·o·scop′ic, ster′e·o·scop′i·cal,** *adj.* —**ster′e·o·scop′i·cal·ly,** *adv.*

ster·e·o·type (ster′i ə tīp′; stir′-), *n., v.,* **-typed, -typ·ing.** —*n.* a fixed form; something that never changes; convention. —*v.* **1** make a stereotype of. **2** *Fig.* give a fixed or settled form to. —**ster′e·o·typ′i·cal,** *adj.*

ster·e·o·typed (ster′i ə tīpt′; stir′-), *adj.* conventional; of a type.

ster·ile (ster′əl), *adj.* **1** free from living germs: *a doctor's instruments must be kept sterile.* **2** barren: *sterile land.* **3** not producing offspring: *a sterile cow.* **4** not producing results: *sterile hopes.* [< L *sterilis*] —**ster′ile·ly,** *adv.* —**ste·ril′i·ty,** *n.*

ster·i·lize (ster′ə līz), *v.,* **-lized, -liz·ing.** **1** free from living germs: *the water had to be sterilized by boiling to make it fit to drink.* **2** deprive of fertility. —**ster′i·li·za′tion,** *n.* —**ster′i·liz′er,** *n.*

ster·ling (stėr′ling), *n.* **1** sterling silver or things made of it. **2** British money. —*adj.* **1** of standard quality; containing 92.5 percent pure silver. **2** made of sterling silver. **3** of British money; payable in British money. **4** *Fig.* genuine; excellent;

dependable. [prob. ult. < OE *steorra* star (as on certain early coins)]

stern¹ (stėrn), *adj.* **1** severe; strict; harsh: *a stern master, a stern frown.* **2.** hard; not yielding; firm: *stern necessity.* **3** grim: *stern mountains.* [OE *stirne*] —**stern′ly,** *adv.* —**stern′ness,** *n.*

stern² (stėrn), *n.* the hind part of a ship or boat. [prob. < Scand. *stjörn* steering] —**stern′most,** *adj.*

ster·num (stėr′nəm), *n., pl.* **-na** (-nə), **-nums.** the breastbone. [< NL < Gk.]

stet (stet), *n., v.,* **stet·ted, stet·ting.** —*n.* "let it stand," a direction on printer's proof, a manuscript, or the like, to retain canceled matter (usually accompanied by a row of dots under or beside the matter). —*v.* mark for retention [< L, let it stand]

steth·o·scope (steth′ə skōp), *n.* instrument used by doctors when listening to sounds in the lungs, heart, etc. [< Gk. *stethos* chest + E *-scope* < Gk. *skopeein* watch] —**steth′o·scop′ic,** *adj.*

ste·ve·dore (stē′və dôr; -dōr), *n.* person who loads and unloads ships. [< Sp. *estivador,* ult. < L *stipare* pack down]

stew (stü; stū), *v.* **1** cook by slow boiling. **2** worry; fret. —*n.* **1** food cooked by slow boiling: *beef stew.* **2** state of worry; fret. [< OF *estuver* < VL *extufare* < L *ex-* out + Gk. *typhos* vapor] —**stewed,** *adj.*

stew·ard (stü′ərd; stū′-), *n.* **1** person who takes charge of the food and table service for a club, ship, railroad train, etc. **2** person on a ship who waits on table, attends to staterooms, etc. **3** person who manages another's property or financial affairs. [OE *stigweard* < *stig* hall, sty + *weard* keeper, ward]

stew·ard·ess (stü′ər dis; stū′-), *n.* **1** a woman steward. **2** woman employed on shipboard, an airplane, etc., to wait upon passengers.

stick¹ (stik), *n.* **1** branch or shoot of a tree or shrub cut or broken off. **2** a long, thin piece of wood. **3** such a piece of wood shaped for a special use: *a walking stick.* **4** something like a stick in shape: *a stick of candy.* **5** the bat or thin, curved wand used in hockey, lacrosse, etc.

the sticks, the outlying districts; backwoods. [OE *sticca*]

stick² (stik), *v.,* **stuck, stick·ing,** *n.* —*v.* **1** pierce with a pointed instrument; thrust into; stab: *stick a potato on a fork.* **2** fasten by thrusting the point or end into or through something: *he stuck a flower in his buttonhole.* **3** put into a position: *don't stick your head out of the window, his arms stick out of his coat sleeves.* **4** fasten by causing to adhere; attach: *stick a stamp on a letter.* **5** keep close: *the boy stuck to his mother's heels.* **6** bring to a stop; become fixed; be at a standstill: *our car stuck in the mud.* **7** keep on; hold fast: *stick to a task.* **8** puzzle. **9** charge exorbitantly; cheat. —*n.* a thrust.

stick around, *Informal.* stay or wait nearby

stick at, hesitate or stop for: *stick at nothing once he gets started.*

stick it out, stay or endure despite unpleasant conditions.

stick out, a stand out; be obvious. **b** put up with to the end.

stick together, stay together.

stick up, hold up; rob.

stick up for, support; defend. [OE *stician*]

stick·er (stik′ər), *n.* **1** person or thing that sticks. **2** a gummed label. **3** bur; thorn.

stick·le·back (stik′əl bak´), *n., pl.* **-backs** or (*esp. collectively*) **-back.** a small scaleless fish with a row of sharp spines on the back. The male builds an elaborate nest for the eggs.

stick·ler (stik′lər), *n.* person who insists on or is willing to argue for even unimportant things he or she believes are important.

stick·shift (stik′shift´), *n.* **1** lever for shifting gears fastened to the floor of an automobile. **2** automobile having this kind of gear shift.

stick·up (stik′up´), *n.* holdup; robbery.

stick·y (stik′i), *adj.*, **stick·i·er, stick·i·est.** **1** that sticks; adhesive: *sticky glue.* **2** covered or smeared with adhesive material: *transparent tape is sticky.* **3** of weather, humid. **—stick′i·ness,** *n.*

stiff (stif), *adj.* **1** not easily bent: *a stiff collar.* **2** hard to move; not able to move easily: *he was stiff and sore.* **3** not easy or natural in manner; formal: *a stiff bow, a stiff style of writing.* **4** strong and steady in motion: *a stiff breeze.* **5** hard to deal with; hard: *a stiff examination.* **6** strong: *a stiff drink.* **7** more than seems suitable: *a stiff price.* —*n.* corpse [OE *stif*] **—stiff′ish,** *adj.* **—stiff′ly,** *adv.* **—stiff′ness,** *n.*

stiff-backed (stif′bakt′), *adj.* **1** having a straight back; erect posture. **2** *Fig.* rigid; unbending; distant.

stiff·en (stif′ən), *v.* make or become stiff. **—stiff′en·er,** *n.* **—stiff′en·ing,** *n., adj.*

stiff-necked (stif′nekt′), *adj.* **1** having a stiff neck. **2** *Fig.* stubborn; obstinate.

sti·fle (stī′fəl), *v.*, **-fled, -fling. 1** stop the breath of; smother: *the smoke stifled the firefighters.* **2** be unable to breathe freely: *I am stifling in this close room.* **3** keep back; suppress; stop: *stifle a yawn, stifle a rebellion.* [< Scand. *stīfla* dam up] **—sti′fler,** *n.* **—sti′fling,** *adj.* **—sti′fling·ly,** *adv.*

stig·ma (stig′mə), *n., pl.* **stig·mas, stig·ma·ta** (stig′mə tə), **1** mark of disgrace; stain or reproach on one's reputation. **2** a distinguishing mark or sign. **3** a small mark, spot, pore, or the like on an animal. **4** a spot on the skin, esp. one that bleeds or turns red. **5** the part of the pistil of a plant that receives the pollen. [< L < Gk.] **—stig·mat′ic** *adj., n.*

stig·ma·tize (stig′mə tīz), *v.*, **-tized, -tizing.** set some mark of disgrace upon; reproach. **—stig′ma·ti·za′tion,** *n.* **—stig′ma·tiz´er,** *n.*

stile (stīl), *n.* step or steps for getting over a fence or wall. [OE *stigel* < *stīgan* climb]

sti·let·to (stə let′ō), *n., pl.* **-tos, -toes. 1** a dagger with a narrow blade. **2** woman's shoe with a very high heel. [< Ital., ult. < L *stilus* pointed instrument]

stiletto heel, high, tapered heel on a woman's shoe.

still¹ (stil), *adj.* **1** without motion; without noise; quiet; tranquil: *a still scene.* **2** soft; low; subdued: *a still small voice.* **3** without waves: *still water.* **4** not bubbling: *still wine.* **5** not showing motion: *still feet.* —*v.* **1** make quiet: *still a crying child.* **2** calm; relieve. —*n.* photograph of a person or other subject at rest. —*adv.* **1** at this or that time: *he came yesterday and he is still here.* **2** up to this or that time: *the matter is still unsettled.* **3** in the future as in the past: *it will still be here.* **4** even; yet: *still more, still worse, he still tries.* **5** without moving; quietly. —*conj.* yet; nevertheless: *I can see your point of view; still I don't agree with you.* [OE *stille*] **—still′ness,** *n.*

still² (stil), *n.* **1** apparatus for distilling liquids, esp. one used in making alcohol. **2** distillery. [n. use of *still,* short form of *distill*]

still·born (stil′bôrn′), *adj.* dead when born.

still life, 1 inanimate objects, as flowers, pottery, etc., shown in a picture. **2** picture containing such things. **—still′-life´,** *adj.*

still·ly (stil′li), *adv.* calmly, quietly.

stilt (stilt), *n.* one of a pair of poles, each with a support for the foot at some distance above the ground on which one walks. [ME *stilte*]

stilt·ed (stil′tid), *adj.* uncomfortably dignified or formal: *stilted conversation.* **—stilt′ed·ly,** *adv.* **—stilt′ed·ness,** *n.*

stim·u·lant (stim′yə lənt), *n.* **1** food, drug, medicine, etc., that temporarily increases the activity of some part of the body. Tea, coffee, and alcoholic drinks are stimulants. **2** motive, influence, etc., that rouses one to action. —*adj.* stimulating.

stim·u·late (stim′yə lāt), *v.*, **-lat·ed, -lating. 1** spur on; stir up; rouse to action. **2** increase temporarily the functional activity of (a part of the body, etc.) **3** act as a stimulant or a stimulus. [< L, < *stimulus* goad] **—stim′u·lat´er, stim′u·la´tor,** *n.* **—stim´u·la´tion,** *n.*

stim·u·la·tive (stim′yə lā´tiv; -lə tiv), *adj.* tending to stimulate; stimulating. —*n.* =stimulus.

stim·u·lus (stim′yə ləs), *n., pl.* **-li** (-lī). **1** something that stirs to action or effort. **2** something that excites some part of the body to activity. [< L, orig., goad]

sting (sting), *v.*, **-stung** or (*Archaic or Obs.*) **stang, stung, sting·ing,** *n.* —*v.* **1** prick with a small point; wound. *be stung by a bee.* **2** *Fig.* pain sharply: *stung by ridicule.* **3** have a sting: *my arm stings.* **4** cause a feeling like that of a sting:

mustard stings. **5** *Fig.* drive or stir up as if by a sting: *their ridicule stung him into making a sharp reply.* **6** *Informal. Fig.* impose upon; charge exorbitantly. —*n.* **1** act of stinging. **2** prick; wound: *put mud on the sting to take away the pain.* **3** the sharp-pointed part of an insect, animal, or plant that pricks or wounds and often poisons. **4** *Fig.* sharp pain: *the sting of defeat.* **5** thing that causes a sharp pain. **6** *Fig.* thing that drives or urges sharply. [OE *stingan*] **—sting′er,** *n.* **—sting′ing·ly,** *adv.* **—sting′ing·ness,** *n.* **—sting′less,** *adj.*

sting ray, a broad, flat fish that can inflict a severe wound with sharp spines on its tail.

stin·gy (stin′ji), *adj.*, **-gi·er, -gi·est. 1** reluctant to spend or give money; close-fisted; not generous: *he saved money without being stingy.* **2** scanty; meager. [akin to STING] **—stin′gi·ly,** *adv.* **—stin′gi·ness,** *n.*

stink (stingk), *n., v.*, **stank** or **stunk, stunk, stink·ing.** —*n.* a very bad smell. —*v.* **1** have a bad smell. **2** cause to have a very bad smell. **3** *Fig.* have a very bad reputation; be in great disfavor. [OE *stincan* to smell] **—stink′er,** *n.* **—stink′ing,** *adj.* **—stink′ing·ly,** *adv.*

stink·bug (stingk′bug´), *n.* any bad smelling bug.

stink·weed (stingk′wēd´), *n.* any of various ill-smelling plants, as the jimson weed.

stint (stint), *v.* **1** keep on short allowance; be saving or careful in using or spending; limit: *the parents stinted themselves of food to give it to their children.* **2** be saving; get along on very little. —*n.* **1** limit; limitation: *give without stint.* **2** amount or share set aside. **3** task assigned: *a daily stint.* [OE *styntan* blunt] **—stint′er,** *n.* **—stint′ing·ly,** *adv.* **—stint′less,** *adj.*

stipe (stīp), *n.* stalk; stem. [< F < L *stipes* trunk]

sti·pend (stī′pend), *n.* **1** fixed or regular pay; salary. **2** any periodic payment. [< L *stipendium* < *stips* wages, orig., coin + *pendere* weigh out]

stip·ple (stip′əl), *v.*, **-pled, -pling,** *n.* —*v.* **1** paint, draw, or engrave by dots. **2** produce this effect on. **3** apply (paint) by this method. —*n.* **1** Also, **stip′pling,** this method of painting, drawing, or engraving. **2** effect produced by this method. **3** stippled work. [< Du. *stippelen*] **—stip′pler,** *n.*

stip·u·late (stip′yə lāt), *v.*, **-lat·ed, -lating.** arrange definitely; demand as a condition of agreement. [< L *stipulatus,* pp. of *stipulari* stipulate] **—stip′u·la´tor,** *n.*

stip·u·la·tion (stip´yə lā′shən), *n.* **1** act of stipulating. **2** a definite arrangement; agreement. **3** a condition in an agreement or bargain.

stip·ule (stip′ūl), *n.* one of the pair of little leaflike parts at the base of a leaf stem.

[< L *stipula,* akin to *stipes* trunk. Doublet of STUBBLE.] **—stip′uled,** *adj.*

stir (stėr), *v.,* **stirred, stir·ring,** *n.* —*v.* **1** move: *the wind stirs the leaves.* **2** move about: *no one was stirring in the house.* **3** mix by moving around with a spoon, fork, stick, etc.: *stir sugar into one's coffee.* **4** set going; affect strongly; excite: *John stirs the other children to mischief, the countryside was stirring with new life.* —*n.* **1** movement. **2** excitement. **3** act of stirring.

stir oneself, move briskly; act decisively.

stir up, stimulate; excite: *stir up the dog by throwing a ball.* [OE *styrian*] **—stir′rer,** *n.*

stir·cra·zy (stėr′krā′zi), *adj.* irritable or excitable from being confined, as by bad weather or nonstop work.

stir-fry (stėr′frī′), *v.,* **-fried, -fry·ing.** stir while frying in a small amount of oil. —*n.* food, esp. Chinese food, prepared this way.

stir·ring (stėr′ing), *adj.* **1** moving; active; lively: *stirring times.* **2** rousing; exciting: *a stirring speech.* **—stir′ring·ly,** *adv.*

stir·rup (stėr′əp; stir′–), *n.* **1** a support for the rider's foot, hung from a saddle. **2** piece somewhat like a stirrup used as a support. [OE *stigrāp* < *stige* climbing + *rāp* rope]

stirrup bone, the stapes.

stitch (stich), *n.* **1** one complete movement of a threaded needle through cloth in sewing. **2** one complete movement in knitting, crocheting, embroidering, etc. **3** a particular method of taking stitches: *buttonhole stitch.* **4** loop of thread, etc., made by a stitch. **5** piece of cloth or clothing. **6** a sudden, sharp pain: *a stitch in my side.* —*v.* **1** make stitches in; fasten with stitches. **2** sew. [OE *stice* puncture] **—stitch′er,** *n.* **—stitch′ing,** *n.*

sti·ver (sti′vər), *n.* Dutch coin, one twentieth of a guilder. [< Du. *stuiver*]

St. John's, capital of Newfoundland.

St.-John's-wort (sānt jonz′wėrt′), *n.* shrub or plant that has many clusters of showy yellow flowers.

stoat (stōt), *n.* **1** the ermine, esp. in its summer coat of brown. **2** weasel.

stock (stok), *n.* **1** things for use or for sale; supply used as it is needed: *this store keeps a large stock of toys.* **2** cattle or other farm animals; livestock. **3** the capital of a company or corporation, divided into shares of uniform amount; shares in a company. **4** *Fig.* **a** a related group of people, animals, or plants; race; family: *she is of old New England stock.* **b** group of related languages. **5** part used as a support or handle; part to which other parts are attached: *the wooden stock of a rifle.* **6** raw material: *rags are used as a stock for making paper.* **7** broth in which meat or fish has been cooked, used as a base for soups, sauces, etc. **8** various plays produced by a company

at a single theater. —*v.* **1** lay in a supply of; supply: *stock fodder for the winter months.* **2** keep regularly for use or for sale: *a toy store stocks toys.* **3** provide with wild life: *stock a lake with fish.* —*adj.* **1** kept on hand regularly: *stock sizes.* **2** in common use; commonplace; everyday: *a stock topic of conversation, give stock answers.* **3** of or pertaining to stock or stocks.

in stock, ready for use or sale; on hand.

out of stock, lacking, either temporarily or permanently; no longer on hand.

take or **put stock in,** take an interest in; consider important; trust: *don't take much stock in what they say.*

take stock, make an estimate or examination.

take stock of, look at; evaluate.

the stocks, wooden frame with holes to hold a person's feet, and sometimes hands, once used as punishment. [OE *stocc*]

stock·ade (stok ād′), *n.* **1** defense made of large, strong posts set upright in the ground. **2** pen or other enclosed space made with upright posts, stakes, etc. [< F *estacade,* ult. < Pr. *estaca* stake < Gmc.]

stock·bro·ker (stok′brō′kər), *n.* person who buys and sells stocks and bonds for others for a commission. **—stock′bro′ker·age,** *n.*

stock car, ordinary passenger automobile modified for racing.

stock company, 1 company whose capital is divided into shares. **2** a theatrical company at a theater that performs many different plays.

stock exchange, 1 place where stocks and bonds are bought and sold. **2** association of brokers and dealers in stocks and bonds.

stock·hold·er (stok′hōl′dər), *n.* owner of stocks or shares in a company. **—stock′hold′ing,** *n., adj.*

Stock·holm (stok′hōm; –hōlm), *n.* seaport and capital of Sweden, in the SE part.

stock·ing (stok′ing), *n.* **1** a close-fitting, knitted covering of wool, cotton, synthetic fibers, etc., for the foot and leg. **2** something like a stocking. [< *stock* stocking]

stock·man (stok′mən), *n., pl.* **-men. 1** person who raises livestock. **2** person in charge of a stock of materials or goods.

stock market, 1 a stock exchange. **2** the buying and selling in such a place. **3** prices of stocks and bonds.

stock·pile (stok′pīl′), *n., v.,* **-piled, -pil·ing.** —*n.* a supply of raw materials, essential items, etc. built up and held in reserve for use during time of emergency or shortage. —*v.* collect or bring together a stockpile.

stock raising, the raising of livestock. **—stock raiser.**

stock-still (stok′stil′), *adj.* motionless.

stock·y (stok′i), *adj.,* **stock·i·er, stock·i·est.** having a solid or sturdy form or

build; thick for its height. **—stock′i·ly,** *adv.* **—stock′i·ness,** *n.*

stock·yard (stok′yärd′), *n.* place with pens and sheds for cattle, sheep, hogs, and horses, where they are kept before being sent to market or slaughtered.

stodg·y (stoj′i), *adj.,* **stodg·i·er, stodg·i·est.** dull or uninteresting; tediously commonplace: *a stodgy book.* **—stodg′i·ly,** *adv.* **—stodg′i·ness,** *n.*

Sto·ic (stō′ik), *n.* **1** member of a school of ancient Greek philosophy which taught that men should be free from passion, unmoved by life's happenings, and should submit without complaint to unavoidable necessity. **2 stoic,** person who remains calm, represses his or her feelings, and is indifferent to pleasure and pain. —*adj.* **1** pertaining to this philosophy, or to its followers. **2 stoic,** stoical. [< L < Gk. *stoikos,* lit., pertaining to a *stoa* portico (esp. the portico in Athens where Zeno taught)]

sto·i·cal (stō′əkəl), *adj.* calm or austere; impassive. **—sto′i·cal·ly,** *adv.* **—sto′i·cal·ness,** *n.*

Sto·i·cism (stō′ə siz əm), *n.* **1** philosophy of the Stoics. **2 stoicism,** patient endurance; indifference to pleasure and pain.

stoke (stōk), *v.,* **stoked, stok·ing. 1** poke, stir up, and feed (a fire); tend the fire of (a furnace). **2** tend a fire.

stoke up, a provide with fuel: *take up a wood fire.* **b** *Fig.* get ready; be prepared: *stoke up with a good breakfast.* [< *stoker*]

stok·er (stōk′ər), *n.* person who tends the fires of a furnace or boiler. [< Du., < *stoken* stoke]

stole[1] (stōl), *v.* pt. of **steal.**

stole[2] (stōl), *n.* **1** a narrow strip of silk or other material worn around the neck by a member of the clergy during certain church functions. **2** a woman's scarf of fur or cloth worn across the back with ends hanging down in front. [< L < Gk. *stole* robe]

sto·len (stō′lən), *v.* pp. of **steal.**

stol·id (stol′id), *adj.* hard to arouse; not easily excited; showing no emotion; seeming dull. [< L *stolidus*] **—stol·id·i·ty, stol′id·ness,** *n.* **—stol′id·ly,** *adv.*

sto·ma (stō′mə), *n., pl.* **sto·ma·ta** (stō′mə tə; stom′ə–), a small opening; mouth; pore. [< NL < Gk., mouth]

stom·ach (stum′ək), *n.* **1** the bag of tissue in the body that receives food and partially digests it before the food passes into the intestines. **2** the part of the body containing the stomach; abdomen; belly. **3** appetite. **4** *Fig.* desire; liking: *I have no stomach for that kind of writing.* —*v.* **1** be able to eat or keep in one's stomach. **2** *Fig.* put up with; bear; endure: *he could not stomach such insults.* [< OF < L < Gk., < *stoma* mouth]

stom·ach·er (stum′ək ər), *n.* a part of a woman's dress covering the stomach and chest, a style esp. of the 1500's and 1600's.

stone (stōn), *n., adj., v.,* **stoned, ston·ing.**
—*n.* **1** hard mineral matter that is not metal; rock: *a wall of stone.* **2** piece of rock: *some boys throw stones.* **3** piece of rock used for a particular purpose, as a gravestone, or grindstone. **4** something hard, which forms in the kidneys or gall bladder. **5** gem; jewel. **6** a hard seed: *peach stones, plum stones.* —*adj.* **1** made of stone. **2** pertaining to stone. **3** made of stoneware or coarse clay. —*v.* **1** throw stones at: *Saint Stephen was stoned.* **2** take stones or seeds out of: *stone cherries or plums.*

cast the first stone, be the first to criticize.

leave no stone unturned, do everything necessary or possible. [OE *stān*]
—**stone'less,** *adj.* —**stone'er,** *n.*

Stone Age a prehistoric period when people used tools and weapons made from stone.

stone·cut·ter (stōn'kut´ər), *n.* one that cuts or carves stones. —**stone'cut´ting,** *n.*

stoned (stōnd), *adj.* **1** having the pits or stones removed: *stoned peaches.* **2** under the influence of a drug. **3** drunk.

stone·ma·son (stōn'mā´sən), *n.* person who cuts stone or builds walls, etc., of stone. —**stone'ma´son·ry,** *n.*

stone's throw, short distance: *just a stone's throw from here.*

stone·ware (stōn'wār´), *n.* a coarse, hard, glazed pottery.

stone·work (stōn'wėrk´), *n.* **1** work in stone. **2** the part of a building made of stone. —**stone'work´er,** *n.*

ston·y (stōn'i), *adj.,* **ston·i·er, ston·i·est. 1** having many stones: *the beach is stony.* **2** pertaining to or characteristic of stone. **3** resembling stone: *a stony mass.* **4** *Fig.* without expression or feeling: *a stony stare.* —**ston'i·ly,** *adv.* —**ston'i·ness,** *n.*

stood (stůd), *v.* pt. and pp. of **stand.**

stooge (stüj), *n.* **1** person on the stage who asks questions of a comedian and is the butt of the comedian's jokes. **2** person who plays a compliant, subordinate role.

stool (stül), *n.* **1** seat without back or arms. **2** a similar article used to rest the feet on, or to kneel on. **3** movement of the bowels; waste matter from the bowels. [OE *stōl*]

stool pigeon, a spy for the police; informer.

stoop[1] (stüp), *v.* **1** carry head and shoulders bent forward: *stoop from old age.* **2** *Fig.* lower oneself; descend: *stoop to retaliate.* —*n.* **1** a forward bend of the head and shoulders. **2** *Fig.* condescension. [OE *stūpian*] —**stoop'er,** *n.* —**stoop'ing·ly,** *adv.*

stoop[2] (stüp), *n.* porch or platform at the entrance of a house. [< Du. *stoep*]

stop (stop), *v.,* **stopped** or (*Poetic*) **stopt, stop·ping,** *n.* —*v.* **1** keep from moving, acting, doing, being, etc.; interrupt; check: *stop a clock, stop supplies, his clever reply stopped the derogatory*

remarks. **2** stay; halt: *stop at a hotel.* **3** close by filling; fill in; close: *stop a hole, a leak, a wound, a bottle.* **4** block; obstruct: *a fallen tree stopped traffic.* —*n.* **1** a stopping or being stopped; ending of movement or action; check. **2** thing that stops; obstacle. **3** place where a stop is made: *a bus stop.* **4** any piece or device that serves to check or control movement or action in a mechanism. **5 a** a thing that controls pitch of a musical instrument. **b** in organs, a graduated set of pipes of the same kind, or the knob or handle that controls them. **6** a sudden, complete stopping of the breath stream, followed by its sudden release. *P, t, k, b, d, g* are stops.

pull out all the stops, a do the maximum. **b** make a grand display; spare no expense.

put a stop to, stop; end.

stop by or **in** or **off,** stop for a short visit or stay.

stop over, a make a short stay. **b** stop in the course of a trip. [ult. < L *stuppa* tow < Gk. *styppe*] —**stopped,** *adj.*

stop·cock (stop'kok´), *n.* faucet; valve.

stop·gap (stop'gap´), *n.* a temporary substitute. —*adj.* serving as a stopgap.

stop·o·ver (stop'ō´vər), *n.* a stopping over in the course of a journey.

stop·page (stop'ij), *n.* **1** a stopping or being stopped. **2** block; obstruction.

stop·per (stop'ər), *n.* **1** plug or cork for closing a bottle, tube, etc. **2** person or thing that stops. —*v.* close or fit with a stopper.

stop sign, traffic sign at an intersection directing drivers to stop before proceeding.

stop street, street with a stop sign at an intersection.

stop watch, a watch having a hand that can be stopped or started at any instant. A stop watch indicates fractions of a second and is used for timing races and contests.

stor·age (stôr'ij; stōr'–), *n.* **1** act or fact of storing goods. **2** condition of being stored. **Cold storage** is used to keep eggs and meat from spoiling. **3** place for storing: *she has put her furniture in storage.* **4** price for storing.

storage battery, a battery of cells which transform electrical energy into chemical changes when a current flows through them in one direction, and yield electrical energy by the reversal of these changes.

store (stôr; stōr), *n., v.,* **stored, stor·ing.** —*n.* **1** place where goods are kept for sale. **2** thing or things laid up for use; supply; stock. **3** place where supplies are kept for future use. —*v.* **1** supply or stock. **2** put away for future use; lay up.

in store, on hand; in reserve; saved for the future.

set store by, value; esteem. [< OF *estorer*, orig., restore < L *instaurare*] —**stor'a·ble,** *adj.* —**stor'er,** *n.*

store·house (stôr'hous´; stōr'–), *n.* place where things are stored: *this factory has many storehouses for its products, a library is a storehouse of information.*

store·keep·er (stôr'kēp´ər; stōr'–), *n.* person who has charge of a store or stores.

store·room (stôr'rüm´; –rùm´; stōr'–), *n.* room where things are stored.

sto·rey (stō'ri; stō'–), *n., pl.* **–reys.** story[2].

sto·ried[1] (stō'rid; stō'–), *adj.* celebrated in story or history.

sto·ried[2] (stō'rid; stō'–), *adj.* having stories or floors: *a two-storied house.*

stork (stôrk), *n.* a large, long-legged wading bird with a long neck and a long bill. [OE *storc*]

storm (stôrm), *n.* **1** a strong wind with rain, snow, hail, or thunder and lightning. In deserts, there are storms of sand. **2** a heavy fall of rain, snow or hail; violent outbreak of thunder and lightning. **3** anything like a storm: *a storm of arrows.* **4** *Fig.* a violent outburst or disturbance: *a storm of angry words.* **5** *Fig.* a violent attack: *the castle was taken by storm.* —*v.* **1** blow hard; rain; snow; hail. **2** *Fig.* be violent; rage: *she storms when something goes wrong.* **3** rush violently: *storm out of the room.* **4** attack violently: *the troops stormed the city.* [OE] —**storm'er,** *n.* —**storm'less,** *adj.*

storm cellar, cellar for shelter during cyclones, tornadoes, etc.

storm center, 1 center of a violent storm, as a hurricane, where the winds are relatively calm. **2** *Fig.* source or center of trouble.

storm surge, huge mass of tidal water blown on shore by extremely strong winds, as in a hurricane.

storm warning, 1 prediction of a strong storm that could cause great damage. **2** *Fig.* sign of trouble approaching.

storm·y (stôr'mi), *adj.,* **storm·i·er, storm·i·est. 1** having storms; likely to have storms; troubled by storms. **2** *Fig.* rough and disturbed; violent. —**storm'i·ly,** *adv.* —**storm'i·ness,** *n.*

stormy petrel, any of several small black-and-white sea birds called petrels, whose presence is supposed to give warning of a storm.

sto·ry[1] (stō'ri; stō'–), *n., pl.* **–ries,** *v.,* **–ried, –ry·ing.** —*n.* **1** account of some happening or group of happenings. **2** such an account, either true or made-up, intended to interest the reader or hearer; tale. **3** falsehood. **4** stories as a branch of literature: *a character famous in story.* **5** plot of a play, novel, etc. **6** a newspaper article, or material for such an article. —*v.* ornament with stories or pictures: *storied tapestries.* [< AF *estorie* < L *historia* history. Doublet of HISTORY.]

sto·ry[2] (stō'ri; stō'–), *n., pl.* **–ries, 1** set of rooms on the same floor forming a complete horizontal section of a building; one of the structural divisions in the height of a building: *a house of two stories.* **2** each of a series of divisions or stages of anything placed horizontally one above the other. [? ult. special use of *story*[1] in sense of "row of historical statues across a building front"]

story board, drawings arranged in a sequence that outline the various scenes to be filmed, as for a movie, cartoon, commercial, etc.

stor·y·book (stô′ri buk′), *adj.* of or like a story in a book, esp. a fairy tale. —*n.* a book containing stories for children.

sto·ry·tell·er (stô′ri tel′ər; stō′–), *n.* **1** person who tells stories. **2** person who tells falsehoods; liar. —**sto′ry·tell′ing,** *n., adj.*

stout (stout), *adj.* **1** fat and large: *a stout body.* **2** strongly built; firm; strong: *a stout wall.* **3** brave; bold: *a stout heart.* **4** not yielding; stubborn: *stout resistance.* —*n.* a strong, dark-brown beer. [< OF *estout* strong < Gmc. root *stolt*- proud < L *stultus* foolish] —**stout′ly,** *adv.* —**stout′ness,** *n.*

stout-heart·ed (stout′här′tid), *adj.* brave; bold; courageous. —**stout′-heart′ed·ly,** *adv.* —**stout′-heart′ed·ness,** *n.*

stove[1] (stōv), *n.* apparatus for cooking and heating. There are wood, coal, gas, oil, and electric stoves. [OE *stofa* warm bathing room]

stove[2] (stōv), *v.* pt. and pp. of **stave.**

stove·pipe (stōv′pīp′), *n.* pipe of sheet metal serving as the chimney of a stove, or to connect a stove with the chimney flue.

stow (stō), *v.* **1** pack: *the cargo was stowed in the ship's hold.* **2** pack things closely in, as for storage or reserve; fill by packing.
stow away, hide on a ship, plane, etc., to get a free ride. [ult. < OE *stōw* place] —**stow′er,** *n.*

stow·age (stō′ij), *n.* **1** act of stowing. **2** room or place for stowing. **3** what is stowed. **4** a charge for stowing something.

stow·a·way (stō′ə wā′), *n.* person who hides on a ship, train, etc., to get a free passage or to escape secretly.

St. Paul, capital of Minnesota, in the SE part.

stra·bis·mus (strə biz′məs), *n.* a disorder of vision due to the turning of one eye or both eyes from the normal position so that both cannot be directed at the same point or object at the same time. [< NL < Gk., ult. < *strabos* squint-eyed] —**stra·bis′mal, stra·bis′mic,** *adj.*

strad·dle (strad′əl), *v.,* **-dled, -dling,** *n.* —*v.* **1** walk, stand, or sit with the legs wide apart. **2** have a leg on each side of (a horse, bicycle, chair, ditch, etc.). **3 a** avoid taking sides. **b** attempt to favor both sides of (a question, etc.). —*n.* **1** a straddling. **2** distance straddled. [< var. of *stride*] —**strad′dler,** *n.* —**strad′dling·ly,** *adv.*

strafe (strāf; sträf), *v.,* **strafed, straf·ing. 1** machine-gun enemy ground positions from an aircraft. **2** shell or bombard heavily. [from the German slogan *Gott*

strafe England God punish England] —**straf′er,** *n.*

strag·gle (strag′əl), *v.,* **-gled, -gling. 1** wander about in a scattered fashion: *cows straggled along the lane.* **2** stray from the rest; wander away. **3** spread in an irregular, rambling manner. —**strag′gler,** *n.* —**strag′gling·ly,** *adv.* —**strag′gly,** *adj.*

straight (strāt), *adj.* **1** without a bend or curve; direct: *hold the shoulders straight, a straight path.* **2** frank; honest; upright: *straight conduct.* **3** in proper order or condition; right; correct: *keep your accounts straight.* **4** not modified: *a straight Republican, straight whiskey.* **5** *Fig.* **a** conventional; orthodox. **b** heterosexual. **6** in poker, made up of a sequence of five cards: *a straight flush.* —*adv.* **1** in a line: *walk straight.* **2** in a straight form or position: *sit straight.* **3** directly: *he went straight home.* **4** frankly; honestly; uprightly: *live straight.* **5** continuously: *drive straight on.* —*n.* **1** straight form, position, or line. **2** a straight part, as of a race course. **3** in poker, a sequence of five cards.
go straight, *Informal. Fig.* **a** give up a life of crime. **b** give up drugs, alcohol, etc.
straight away or **off,** at once; immediately. [OE *streht,* pp. of *streccan* stretch] —**straight′ly,** *adv.* —**straight′ness,** *n.*

straight·a·way (strāt′ə wā′), *n.* a straight course. —*adj.* in a straight course.

straight-arm (strāt′ärm′), *v.* **1 a** hold or fend off someone by extending the arm straight out. **b** such a move in football. **2** *Fig.* deflect unwanted attention, criticism, etc.

straight·en (strāt′ən), *v.* **1** make or become straight. **2** put in the proper order or condition. —**straight′en·er,** *n.*

straight face, an expressionless face; a face that shows no particular reaction, emotion, etc.: *hard to keep a straight face.* —**straight′-faced′,** *adj.*

straight·for·ward (strāt′fôr′wərd), *adj.* **1** honest; frank. **2** going straight ahead; direct. —*adv.* Also, **straight′for′wards.** directly or continuously ahead. —**straight′for′ward·ly,** *adv.* —**straight′for′ward·ness,** *n.*

straight-out (strāt′out′), *adj.* out-and-out; complete; thorough.

strain[1] (strān), *v.* **1** draw tight; stretch: *the dog strained at his leash.* **2** stretch as much as possible: *strain every nerve.* **3** use to the utmost: *she strained her eyes to see.* **4** injure or harm by too much effort or by stretching: *strain a muscle, strain the truth.* **5** press or pour through a strainer. —*n.* **1** force or weight that stretches. **2** a great or excessive effort: *the strain of lifting a heavy weight.* **3** injury caused by too much effort or by stretching. **4** any severe, trying, or wearing pressure: *the strain of worry.*

strains, part of a piece of music; melody; song. [< OF < L *stringere* draw tight] —**strained,** *adj.*

strain[2] (strān), *n.* **1** line of descent; race; stock; breed. **2** *Fig.* an inherited quality; hereditary character or disposition. **3** trace or streak. [var. of OE *strēon* gain, begetting]

strain·er (strān′ər), *n.* thing that strains, as a filter, a sieve, or a colander.

strait (strāt), *n.* **1** Often, **straits** (*sing. in use*). a narrow channel connecting two larger bodies of water. **2** Often, **straits.** difficulty; need; distress. [< OF < L *strictus* drawn tight. Doublet of STRICT.] —**strait′ly,** *adv.* —**strait′ness,** *n.*

strait·en (strāt′ən), *v.* **1** limit by the lack of something, esp. money; restrict: *in straitened circumstances.* **2** restrict in range, extent, amount, etc.

strait jacket, a strong coat that holds the arms close to the sides, used to keep a violent person from harming himself, herself, or others.

strait-laced (strāt′lāst′), *adj.* very strict in matters of conduct; prudish.

strand[1] (strand), *v.* **1** run aground; drive on the shore. **2** bring or come into a helpless position. [OE]

strand[2] (strand), *n.* **1** one of the threads, strings, or wires that are twisted together to make a rope. **2** thread or string: *a strand of pearls, a strand of hair.*

strange (strānj), *adj.,* **strang·er, strang·est,** *adv.* —*adj.* **1** unusual; queer; peculiar: *a strange accident.* **2** not known, seen, or heard of before; unfamiliar: *strange faces, strange language.* **3** unaccustomed (to); inexperienced (at): *strange to a job.* **4** out of place; not at home: *the farmer felt strange in the city.* —*adv.* in a strange manner: *act strange.* [< OF < L *extraneus* foreign. Doublet of EXTRANEOUS.] —**strange′ly,** *adv.* —**strange′ness,** *n.*

stran·ger (strān′jər), *n.* **1** person not known, seen, or heard of before: *he was a stranger to us.* **2** person or thing new to a place: *a stranger in town.* **3** person who is out of place or not at home in something: *he is a stranger to your method of working.* **4** person from another country.

stran·gle (strang′gəl), *v.,* **-gled, -gling. 1** kill by squeezing the throat to stop the breath. **2** suffocate; choke. [< OF < L < Gk. *strangalaein,* ult. < *strangos* twisted] —**stran′gler,** *n.*

stran·gu·late (strang′gyə lāt), *v.,* **-lat·ed, -lat·ing. 1** compress or constrict so as to stop the circulation in, or hinder the action of. **2** strangle; choke. [< L *strangulatus.* See STRANGLE.] —**stran′gu·la′tion,** *n.*

strap (strap), *n., v.,* **strapped, strap·ping.** —*n.* a narrow strip of leather or cloth for fastening things, holding things together, etc. —*v.* **1** fasten with a strap. **2** beat with a strap. [var. of *strop*] —**strap′like′,** *adj.* —**strap′per,** *n.*

strap·hang·er (strap′hang′ər), *n.* passenger in a train, etc., who cannot get a seat and stands holding on to a strap, handrail, etc.

strap·less (strap′lis), *adj.* having no straps: *a strapless dress.*

strap·ping (strap′ing), *adj.* tall, strong, and healthy.

stra·ta (strā′tə; strat′ə), *n. pl.* of **stratum.**

strat·a·gem (strat′ə jəm), *n.* scheme or trick for deceiving the enemy; trick; trickery. [< F < L < Gk. *strategema,* ult. < *strategos* general. See STRATEGY.]

stra·te·gic (strə tē′jik), **stra·te·gi·cal** (–jə kəl), *adj.* of strategy; based on strategy; useful in strategy. —**stra·te′gi·cal·ly,** *adv.*

strat·e·gist (strat′ə jist), *n.* person trained or skilled in strategy.

strat·e·gy (strat′ə ji), *n., pl.* **–gies. 1** Also, **strategics.** science or art of war; planning and directing of military movements and operations. **2** plan based on this. **3** the skillful planning and management of anything. [< Gk. *strategia* < *strategos* general < *stratos* army + *agein* lead]

strat·i·fy (strat′ə fī), *v.,* **–fied, –fy·ing.** arrange in layers or strata; form into layers or strata. —**strat′i·fi·ca′tion,** *n.*

stra·to·cu·mu·lus or **stra·to·cu·mu·lus** (strā′to kyü′myə ləs), *n., pl.* **–li** (–lī). formation of dark, round clouds above a layer of clouds that are flat, esp. seen in winter.

strat·o·sphere (strat′ə sfir; strā′tə–), *n.* the upper region of the atmosphere, which begins about seven miles above the earth. In the stratosphere, temperature varies little with changes in altitude, and the winds are chiefly horizontal. [< L *stratus* a spreading out + E *sphere*]

strat·o·spher·ic (strat′ə sfer′ik), *adj.* **1** of or having to do with the stratosphere. **2** *Fig.* extremely high; very great, as of costs or prices.

stra·tum (strā′təm; strat′əm), *n., pl.* **strata, stra·tums. 1** layer of material, esp. one of several parallel layers placed one upon another. **2** social level; group having about the same education, culture, development, etc. **3** layer of one kind of sedimentary rock. [< NL < L, neut. pp. of *sternere* spread]

straw (strô), *n.* **1** the stalks or stems of grain after drying and threshing. Straw is used for bedding for horses and cows, for making hats, and for many other purposes. **2** stem or stalk, as of wheat, rye, etc. **3** a hollow tube for sucking up beverages, etc. —*adj.* **1** made of straw. **2** sham; fictitious.

grab or **clutch at straws,** try anything in desperation. [OE *strēaw*] —**straw′y,** *adj.*

straw·ber·ry (strô′ber′i; –bər i), *n., pl.* **–ries. 1** a small, juicy, red fruit. **2** plant that it grows on.

straw man, 1 imagined opponent or opposition. **2** person who acts as a front for others in a deceitful enterprise.

stray (strā), *v.* **1** lose one's way; wander; roam. **2** turn from the right course; go wrong. —*adj.* **1** wandering; lost. **2** scattered. **3** isolated: *a stray copy of a book.* —*n.* wanderer; lost animal. [< OF *estraier,* ult. < L *extra vagari* roam outside] —**stray′er,** *n.*

streak (strēk), *n.* **1** a long, thin mark or line: *a streak of lightning.* **2** layer: *bacon has streaks of fat and streaks of lean.* **3** strain; element: *a streak of humor.* **4** *Fig.* a brief period; spell: *a streak of luck.* —*v.* **1** put long, thin marks or lines on; cause to have streaks. **2** become streaked. **3 a** move very fast; go at full speed. **b** run very fast in public with no clothes on. **like a streak,** very fast; at full speed. [OE *strica*] —**streak′y,** *adj.* —**streak′i·ly,** *adv.* —**streak′i·ness,** *n.*

stream (strēm), *n.* **1** flow of liquid; running water, as a river or a brook. **2** any steady flow: *a stream of words, a stream of light.* —*v.* **1** flow. **2** *Fig.* move steadily; move swiftly: *soldiers streamed out of the fort.* **3** pour out: *the wound streamed blood.* **4** be so wet as to drip in a stream: *streaming eyes.* **5** float or wave: *flags streamed in the wind.* [OE *strēam*]

stream·er (strēm′ər), *n.* **1** any long, narrow, flowing thing: *streamers of ribbon hung from her hat.* **2** a long, narrow flag. **3** stream of light, esp. one appearing in some forms of the aurora borealis.

stream·line (strēm′līn), *adj., n., v.,* **–lined, –lin·ing.** —*adj.* having a shape that offers the least possible resistance in passing through air or water. —*n.* a streamline shape. —*v.* **1** give a streamline shape to, as an airplane or automobile. **2** *Fig.* bring up to date.

stream·lined (strēm′līnd′), *adj.* **1** streamline. **2** *Fig.* brought up to date; made more efficient.

street (strēt), *n.* **1** road in a city or town, usually with buildings on both sides. **2 a** people who live in the buildings on a street. **b** *Informal.* neighborhood people on a street: *the street thinks it's gang warfare.*

on easy street, financially comfortable and secure.

on the street, homeless.

the Street, a Wall Street; the financial district and stock market. **b** financial businesses and the people who work in them. [< LL (*via*) *strata* paved (road), pp. of L *sternere* lay out]

street·car (strēt′kär′), *n.* car that runs in the streets, usually by electricity and on rails, and carries passengers.

street·walk·er (strēt′wôk′ər), *n.* prostitute who walks the streets soliciting business.

strength (strengkth; strength), *n.* **1** quality of being strong; power; force; vigor: *Samson was a man of great strength.* **2** power to resist or endure: *strength of a wire, strength of a fort.* **3** effective force: *the strength of an argument.* **4** intensity, as of light, color, sound, flavor, or odor. **5** something that makes strong; support: *Justice is our strength.*

on the strength of, relying or depending on; with the support or help of. [OE, < *strang* strong] —**strength′less,** *adj.*

strength·en (strengk′thən; streng′-), *v.* make or grow stronger. —**strength′en·er,** *n.*

stren·u·ous (stren′yü əs), *adj.* very active; full of energy. [< L *strenuus*] —**stren′u·ous·ly,** *adv.* —**stren′u·ous·ness,** *n.*

strep·to·coc·cus (strep′tə kok′əs), *n., pl.* **–coc·ci** (–kok′sī). any of a group of spherical bacteria that multiply by dividing in only one direction, usually forming chains, and cause serious infections. [< NL, < Gk. *streptos* curved + *kokkos* grain] —**strep′to·coc′cal,** *adj.*

strep·to·my·cin (strep′tō mī′sin), *n.* a powerful substance similar to penicillin, effective against tuberculosis, typhoid fever, and certain other bacterial infections. [< Gk. *streptos* curved + *mykes* fungus]

stress (stres), *n.* **1** distressing, painful, or adverse force or influence: *the stress of hunger, do something under stress.* **2** physical pressure, pull, or other force exerted on one thing by another: *the stress of a load or weight.* **3** emphasis; importance: *lay stress upon promptness.* **4** the relative loudness in the pronunciation of syllables, words in a sentence, etc.; accent. —*v.* **1** put pressure upon. **2** treat as important; emphasize. **3** pronounce with stress. [partly < *distress,* partly < OF *estrecier,* ult. < L *strictus* drawn tight]

stretch (strech), *v.* **1** draw out; extend (oneself, body, limbs, wings, etc.) to full length: *stretch out on the couch.* **2** continue over a distance; extend from one place to another; fill space; spread: *the highway stretches from coast to coast.* **3** reach out; hold out: *he stretched out his hand for the money.* **4** become longer or wider without breaking: *rubber stretches.* **5** *Fig.* extend beyond proper limits: *he stretched the law to suit his purpose.* —*n.* **1** an unbroken length; extent: *a stretch of water.* **2** period; term: *for hours at a stretch.* **3** course, direction. **4** stretching or being stretched. [OE *streccan*] —**stretch′a·ble,** *adj.*

stretch·er (strech′ər), *n.* **1** one that stretches: *a glove stretcher.* **2** canvas stretched on a frame for carrying the sick, wounded, or dead.

strew (strü), *v.,* **strewed, strewed** or **strewn, strew·ing. 1** scatter; sprinkle. **2** cover with something scattered or sprinkled. **3** be scattered over; be sprinkled over. [OE *strēowian*]

stri·at·ed (strī′āt id), **stri·ate** (strī′it; –āt), *adj.* striped; streaked; furrowed. [< L *striatus*] —**stri·a′tion,** *n.*

striated muscle, muscles with fibrous cross bands, esp. those that move the arms, legs, neck, etc., by voluntary action.

strick·en (strik′ən), *adj.* **1** affected, as by wounds, diseases, trouble, sorrows, etc.:

a stricken deer. **2** deeply affected: *stricken with grief.* —*v.* pp. of **strike.**

strict (strikt), *adj.* **1** very careful in following a rule: *strict observance of a law.* **2** harsh; severe: *a strict parent.* **3** rigorously enforced or maintained: *strict discipline.* **4** exact; precise; accurate: *he told the strict truth.* **5** perfect; complete; absolute: *in strict confidence.* [< L *strictus* bound tight. Doublet of STRAIT.] —**strict′ly,** *adv.* —**strict′ness,** *n.*

stric·ture (strik′chər), *n.* **1** an unfavorable criticism; critical remark. **2** an unhealthy narrowing of some duct or tube of the body. [< L *strictura* < *stringere* bind tight]

stride (strīd), *v.,* **strode, strid·den** (strid′ən), **strid·ing,** *n.* —*v.* **1** walk with long steps. **2** pass with one long step: *he strode over the brook.* **3** straddle: *stride a fence.* —*n.* **1** a long step. **2** distance covered by a stride.

hit one's stride, reach one's regular speed or normal activity.

make great or **rapid strides,** make great progress; advance rapidly.

take in one's stride, do or take without difficulty, hesitation, or special effort. [OE *strīdan*] —**strid′er,** *n.*

stri·dent (strī′dənt), *adj.* harsh-sounding; creaking; shrill. [< L *stridens* sounding harshly] —**stri′dence, stri′den·cy,** *n.* —**stri′dent·ly,** *adv.*

strid·u·late (strij′ə lāt), *v.,* –**lat·ed,** –**lat·ing.** produce a shrill, grating sound, esp. to do so as a cricket or katydid does, by rubbing together certain parts of the body. —**strid′u·la′tion,** *n.* —**strid′u·la′tor,** *n.* —**strid′u·la·to′ry,** *adj.*

strife (strīf), *n.* **1** quarreling; fighting; discord. **2** a quarrel; fight. [< OE *estrif* < Gmc. Cf. STRIVE.]

strike (strīk), *v.,* **struck, struck** or **strick·en, strik·ing,** *n.* —*v.* **1** hit: *strike a person, the ship struck a rock, a car struck the stop sign.* **2** make by stamping, printing, etc.: *strike a coin.* **3** set or be set on fire by hitting or rubbing: *strike a match.* **4** *Fig.* fall upon: *sunlight struck the hillside, bird calls strike the ear.* **5** sound: *the clock struck midnight.* **6** affect; afflict suddenly; overcome: *they were struck with terror, the news struck them dumb.* **7** *Fig.* impress: *the plan strikes me as silly.* **8** attack: *the enemy will strike at dawn.* **9** *Fig.* occur to: *suddenly struck with a great idea.* **10** find or come upon (ore, oil, water, etc.). **11** stop work to get better pay, shorter hours, etc.: *the coal miners struck.* **12** go quickly or suddenly; go: *we struck out across the fields.* **13** get by figuring: *strike an average.* **14** make; decide; enter upon: *the employer and the workers have struck an agreement.* **15** lower or take down (a sail, flag, tent, etc.). —*n.* **1** act of striking. **2** a general quitting of work in order to force an employer or employers to agree to the workers' demands, as for higher wages. **3** failure of the batter to hit a pitched

ball, or any act ruled equivalent to this. **4** an upsetting of all the pins with the first ball bowled. **5** act or fact of finding rich ore in mining, oil in boring, etc.

on strike, stopping work to get more pay, shorter hours, etc.

strike a balance, a find the difference between the two sides of an account. **b** *Fig.* find a moderate course: *struck a balance between work and play.*

strike down, *Fig.* overturn: *strike down a law.*

strike it rich, have a sudden or unexpected great success.

strike off, take off: *strike off in a new direction.*

strike out, a cross out; rub out. **b** fail to hit a pitched ball three times: *the batter struck out.* **c** *Informal. Fig.* fail: *strike out on an exam.*

strike up, begin: *strike up a friendship.* [OE *strīcan* rub, stroke]

strike·break·er (strīk′brāk′ər), *n.* person who helps to break up a strike of workers by taking a striker's job or by furnishing persons who will do so.

strike·break·ing (strīk′brāk′ing), *n.* forceful measures taken to halt a strike.

strik·er (strīk′ər), *n.* **1** person or thing that strikes. **2** worker who is on strike.

strik·ing (strīk′ing), *adj.* **1** that strikes. **2** engaged in a strike. **3** attracting attention; very noticeable. —**strik′ing·ly,** *adv.* —**strik′ing·ness,** *n.*

string (string), *n.,* *v.,* **strung, strung** or (*Rare*) **stringed, string·ing.** —*n.* **1** a thick thread, small cord or wire, or very thin rope, used for tying packages, etc. **2** such a thread with things on it: *she wore a string of beads around her neck.* **3** a special cord for musical instruments, bows, etc.: *the strings of a violin.* **4** anything used for tying: *apron strings.* **5** a number of things that can form in a line or row: *a string of cars, a string of horses.* **6** *Fig.* condition: *an offer with a string attached to it.* —*v.* **1 a** put on a string: *string beads.* **b** *Fig.* put together: *string words into paragraphs.* **2** furnish with strings: *he had his tennis racket strung.* **3** tie with string; hang with a string or rope. **4** *Fig.* make tense or excited: *her nerves were strung to a high pitch.* **5** move in a line or series: *the cars kept stringing along.*

on a string, under control: *she's got him on a string.*

pull strings, a direct the actions of others secretly. **b** use secret influence.

string along, a keep (someone) waiting; stall. **b** fool; trick.

string out, prolong; stretch; extend: *the program was strung out too long.*

strings, violins, cellos, and other stringed instruments.

string up, hang: *string up Christmas tree lights.* [OE *streng*] —**string′er,** *n.* —**string′less,** *adj.* —**string′like′,** *adj.*

string bean, 1 any of various bean plants, the unripe pod of which is used as a

vegetable. **2** pod of any of these plants. **3** very tall, thin person.

stringed instrument, a musical instrument having strings.

strin·gent (strin′jənt), *adj.* **1** strict; severe: *stringent laws.* **2** lacking ready money; tight: *a stringent market for loans.* **3** convincing; forcible: *stringent arguments.* [< L *stringens* binding tight] —**strin′gen·cy, strin′gent·ness,** *n.* —**strin′gent·ly,** *adv.*

string·y (string′i), *adj.,* **string·i·er, string·i·est.** **1** of or like a string or strings. **2** forming strings: *a stringy syrup.* **3** having tough fibers: *stringy roots.* **4** sinewy or wiry: *a stringy man.* —**string′i·ness,** *n.*

strip[1] (strip), *v.,* **stripped** or (*Rare*) **stript, strip·ping.** **1** make bare or naked; undress (a person, thing, etc.). **2** undress (oneself). **3** take off the covering of. **4** dismantle (guns, ships, etc.). **5** take away: *the boys stripped the fruit from the trees, robbers stripped the house.* **6** tear off the teeth of (a gear, etc.). **7** break the thread of (a bolt, nut, etc.).

strip of, a take away from; deprive of: *stripped of honor and respect.* **b** rob of (money, possessions, etc.). [OE, as in *bestrīepan* to plunder] —**strip′per,** *n.*

strip[2] (strip), *n.,* *v.,* **stripped, strip·ping.** —*n.* **1** a long, narrow, flat piece (of cloth, paper, bark, etc.) **2** a comic strip. —*v.* cut into strips. [prob. < MLG *strippe* strap]

strip[3] (strip), *n.* a long, narrow runway for aircraft to take off from and land on.

stripe[1] (strīp), *n.,* *v.,* **striped, strip·ing.** —*n.* **1** a long, narrow band different from the rest of a surface or thing: *a tiger has stripes.* **2** a particular style or pattern of such bands. **3** a striped fabric. **4** sort; type: *a man of quite a different stripe.* —*v.* mark with stripes.

stripes, a number or combination of strips of braid on the sleeve of a uniform to show rank, length of service, etc. [< MDu.] —**striped,** *adj.*

stripe[2] (strīp), *n.* a stroke or lash with a whip. [? special use of *stripe*[1]]

strip·ling (strip′ling), *n.* boy just coming into manhood; youth; lad.

strip mine, a mine on the surface of the ground from which ore is removed from the top in layers. —**strip′-mine′,** *v.*

stripped-down (stript′down′), *adj.* with anything unnecessary removed: *stripped-down cars, a stripped-down proposal.*

strip·per (strip′ər), *n.* **1a** a substance that removes paint. **b** tool used to remove roofing, etc. **2** stripteaser.

strip·tease (strip′tēz′), *n.* an act, esp. in a nightclub, in which a woman removes her clothing to a musical accompaniment. —**strip′-tease′,** *adj.* —**strip′teas′er,** *n.*

strive (strīv), *v.,* **strove, striv·en** (striv′ən), **striv·ing.** **1** try hard; work hard: *strive for self-control.* **2** struggle vigorously, as in opposition or resistance: *strive against the stream.* **3** fight. [< OF *estriver* < Gmc.] —**striv′er,** *n.* —**striv′ing·ly,** *adv.*

strode (strōd), *v.* pt. of **stride.**

stroke¹ (strōk), *n.* **1** act of striking; blow: *a stroke of lightning.* **2** sound made by striking: *we arrived at the stroke of three.* **3** piece of luck, fortune, etc., befalling one: *a stroke of bad luck.* **4** a single complete movement to be made again and again: *he swims a fast stroke.* **5** movement or mark made by a pen, pencil, brush, etc. **6** *Fig.* a single vigorous effort; very successful effort: *a bold stroke for liberty.* **7** an act, piece, or amount of work, etc. **8** attack of paralysis; apoplexy. [prob. ult. < *strike* or its source]

stroke² (strōk), *v.,* **stroked, strok·ing,** *n.* —*v.* move the hand gently over: *stroke a kitten.* —*n.* such a movement. [OE *strācian*]

stroll (strōl), *v.* **1** take a quiet walk for pleasure; walk. **2** go from place to place: *strolling musicians.* **3** stroll along or through. —*n.* a leisurely walk.

stroll·er (strōl′ər), *n.* **1** wanderer. **2** a strolling player or actor. **3** lightweight baby carriage in which the child sits up.

strong (strông; strong), *adj.* **1** having much force or power: *a strong wind, a strong pull, strong muscles or rope.* **2** able to last, endure, resist, etc.: *a strong fort, a strong wall.* **3** not easily influenced, changed, etc.; firm: *a strong will, strong arguments, a strong prejudice.* **4** having a certain number: *a group that is 100 strong.* **5** having a concentrated or intense quality: *a strong acid, a strong voice, a strong light.* **6** containing much alcohol: *a strong drink.* **7** having much flavor or odor: *strong seasoning, strong coffee.* **8** inflecting by a vowel change within the stem of the word rather than by adding endings. *Examples:* find, found; give, gave. **9** characterized by steady or advancing prices: *a strong market for rubber.* —*adv.* with force; powerfully; vigorously; in a strong manner. [OE *strang*] —**strong′ly,** *adv.* —**strong′ness,** *n.*

strong-arm (strông′ärm′; strong′-), *adj.* using or involving the use of force or violence. —*v.* use force or violence on.

strong·box (strông′boks′; strong′-), *n.* a small safe for valuables.

strong force, force which causes particles to hold together in the nucleus of an atom and is the strongest known force. Also, **strong interaction.**

strong·hold (strông′hōld′; strong′-), *n.* a strong place; safe place; fort; fortress.

strong-mind·ed (strông′mīn′did; strong′-), *adj.* **1** having a strong mind; mentally vigorous. **2** independent. —**strong′-mind′ed·ly,** *adv.* —**strong′-mind′ed·ness,** *n.*

stron·ti·um (stron′shi əm; –ti əm), *n.* a hard, yellowish metallic element, Sr, resembling calcium. [< NL, < *Strontian,* a parish in Scotland]

stro·phe (strō′fē), *n.* **1** the part of an ancient Greek ode sung by the chorus when moving from right to left. **2** group of lines of poetry; stanza. [< Gk., orig., a

turning (i.e., section sung by the chorus while turning)] —**stroph′ic,** *adj.*

strove (strōv), *v.* pt. of **strive.**

struck (struk), *v.* pt. and pp. of **strike.** —*adj.* closed or affected in some way by a strike of workers.

struc·tur·al (struk′chər əl), *adj.* **1** used in building. **Structural steel** is steel made into beams, girders, etc. **2** of or having to do with structure or structures. —**struc′tur·al·ly,** *adv.*

structural gene, gene that controls the sequence of amino acids and the structure of proteins in DNA.

structure (struk′chər), *n.* **1** a building; something built. **2** anything composed of parts arranged together. **3** manner of building; way parts are put together; construction. **4** arrangement of parts, elements, etc.: *the structure of a molecule or a novel.* [< L *structura* < *struere* arrange]

stru·del (strü′dəl; *Ger.* shtrü′dəl), *n.* a pastry, usually filled with fruit or cheese. [< G]

strug·gle (strug′əl), *v.,* **-gled, -gling,** *n.* —*v.* **1** make great efforts with the body; try hard; work hard against difficulties: *struggle for existence.* **2** get, move, or make one's way with great effort: *the old man struggled to his feet.* —*n.* **1** great effort; hard work. **2** fighting; conflict. —**strug′gler,** *n.* —**strug′gling,** *adj.* —**strug′gling·ly,** *adv.*

strum (strum), *v.,* **strummed, strumming,** *n.* —*v.* play on (a stringed musical instrument) unskillfully or carelessly. —*n.* **1** act of strumming. **2** sound of strumming. —**strum′mer,** *n.*

strum·pet (strum′pit), *n.* prostitute.

strung (strung), *v.* pt. and pp. of **string.**

strut¹ (strut), *v.,* **strut·ted, strut·ting,** *n.* —*v.* walk in a vain, important manner. —*n.* a strutting walk. [OE *–strūtian*] —**strut′ter,** *n.* —**strut′ting·ly,** *adv.*

strut² (strut), *n.* a supporting piece; brace. [ult. akin to *strut¹*]

strych·nine (strik′nin; –nēn; –nīn), *n.* a poisonous drug consisting of colorless crystals obtained from nux vomica and related plants. It is used in medicine in small doses as a tonic. [< F, < L < Gk. *strychnos* nightshade]

stub (stub), *n., adj., v.,* **stubbed, stubbing.** —*n.* **1** a short piece that is left: *the stub of a pencil.* **2** the short piece of each leaf in a checkbook, etc., kept as a record. **3** something unusually short and blunt. —*v.* strike (one's toe) against something. [OE] —**stub′ber,** *n.*

stub·ble (stub′əl), *n.* **1** Usually, **stubbles.** the lower ends of stalks of grain left in the ground after the grain is cut. **2** any short, rough growth, as of a beard. [< OF < LL *stupula,* var. of L *stipula* stem. Doublet of STIPULE.] —**stub′bled,** *adj.* —**stub′bly,** *adj.*

stub·born (stub′ərn), *adj.* **1** fixed in purpose or opinion; not giving in to argument or requests: *a stubborn child.* **2**

hard to deal with or manage; refractory: *facts are stubborn things.* [prob. ult. < *stub*] —**stub′born·ly,** *adv.* —**stub′born·ness,** *n.*

stub·by (stub′i), *adj.,* **-bi·er, -bi·est. 1** short and thick. **2** short, thick, and stiff. **3** having many stubs or stumps. —**stub′bi·ness,** *n.*

stuc·co (stuk′ō), *n., pl.* **-coes, -cos,** *v.,* **-coed, -co·ing.** —*n.* plaster for covering exterior walls of buildings. —*v.* cover with stucco. [< Ital. < Gmc.] —**stuc′co·er,** *n.* —**stuc′co·work′,** *n.*

stuck (stuk), *v.* pt. and pp. of **stick²**.

stuck-up (stuk′up′), *adj.* too proud; conceited; vain; haughty.

stud¹ (stud), *n., v.,* **stud·ded, stud·ding.** —*n.* **1** nailhead, knob, etc., sticking out from a surface, as on the soles of shoes, tire treads, etc.: *the belt was ornamented with silver studs.* **2** a kind of small detachable button used in men's shirts. **3** post to which boards are nailed in making walls in houses. —*v.* **1** set with studs or something like studs. **2** be set or scattered over. [OE *studu*]

stud² (stud), *n.* **1** collection of horses kept for breeding, hunting, etc. **2** stallion. **3** *Slang.* an attractive man. [OE *stod*]

stud·ded (stud′id), *adj.* provided with or having studs: *studded golf shoes.*

stu·dent (stü′dənt; stū′–), *n.* **1** person who studies. **2** person who is studying in a school, college, or university. [< L *studens,* orig., being eager] —**stu′dent·ship,** *n.*

stud·horse (stud′hôrs′), *n.* =stallion.

stud·ied (stud′id), *adj.* **1** resulting from study; carefully considered. **2** done on purpose; resulting from deliberate effort. —**stud′ied·ly,** *adv.* —**stud′ied·ness,** *n.*

stu·di·o (stuü′di ō; stū′–), *n., pl.* **-di·os,** *adj.* —*n.* **1** workroom of a painter, sculptor, photographer, etc. **2** place where motion pictures are made. **3** place where a radio or television program is produced. **4** =studio apartment. —*adj.* of, pertaining to, or suitable for a studio. [< Ital. < L *studium* study, enthusiasm. Doublet of STUDY.]

studio apartment, one-room apartment.

stu·di·ous (stü′di əs; stū′–), *adj.* **1** fond of study. **2** showing careful consideration; careful; thoughtful; zealous: *studious of the comfort of others.* —**stu′di·ous·ly,** *adv.* —**stu′di·ous·ness,** *n.*

stud·y (stud′i), *n., pl.* **stud·ies,** *v.,* **stud·ied, stud·y·ing.** —*n.* **1** effort to learn by reading or thinking. **2** a careful examination; investigation: *make a study of plants.* **3** branch of learning: *the study of chemistry, sociological studies.* **4** a room for study, reading, writing, etc. **5** sketch for a picture, story, etc. **6** deep thought; reverie. —*v.* **1** try to learn. **2** examine carefully: *we studied the map.* **3** consider with care; think (out); plan: *the prisoner studied ways to escape.*

quick study, person who learns something quickly. [< L *studium,* orig., eagerness. Doublet of STUDIO.] —**stud′-er,** *n.*

stuff (stuf), *n.* **1** what a thing is made of; material. **2** thing or things; substance. **3** goods; belongings. **4** worthless material; useless things: *old, worn-out stuff in boxes.* **5** *Fig.* inward qualities; character. —*v.* **1** pack full; fill. **2** fill (a ballot box) with fraudulent votes. **3** stop (up); block; choke (up). **4** fill the skin of (a dead animal) to make it look as it did when alive. **5** fill (a chicken, turkey, etc.) with seasoned bread crumbs, etc. **6** force; push; thrust. **7** eat too much. [< OF *estoffe,* ult. < Gk. *styphein* pull together] —**stuff′er,** *n.*

stuffed shirt, person of insignificant abilities but of pompous or imposing manners.

stuff·ing (stuf′ing), *n.* **1** act of one that stuffs. **2** material used to fill or pack something. **3** seasoned bread crumbs, etc., used to stuff a chicken, turkey, etc., before cooking. **3** *Fig.* inner qualities; character: *have the right stuffing.*

stuff·y (stuf′i), *adj.,* **stuff·i·er, stuff·i·est. 1** lacking fresh air: *a stuffy room.* **2** lacking freshness or interest; dull: *a stuffy conversation.* **3** stopped up: *a cold makes one's head feel stuffy.* —**stuff′i·ly,** *adv.* —**stuff′i·ness,** *n.*

stul·ti·fy (stul′tə fī), *v.,* **-fied, -fy·ing. 1** frustrate: *indifference stultifies change.* **2** cause to appear foolish or absurd; reduce to foolishness or absurdity. [< LL, < L *stultus* foolish + *facere* make] —**stul′ti·fi·ca′tion,** *n.* —**stul′ti·fi′er,** *n.*

stum·ble (stum′bəl), *v.,* **-bled, -bling,** *n.* —*v.* **1** trip by striking the foot against something. **2** walk unsteadily. **3** speak, act, etc., in a clumsy or hesitating way: *stumble through a speech.* **4** make a mistake; do wrong. **5** come by accident or chance: *stumble across an old friend.* —*n.* **1** a wrong act; mistake. **2** a stumbling. [cf. Norw. *stumla*] —**stum′bler,** *n.* —**stum′bling·ly,** *adv.*

stumbling block, obstacle; hindrance.

stump (stump), *n.* **1** the lower end of a tree or plant, left after the main part is cut off. **2** part of an arm, leg, tooth, etc., left after part is removed. **3** stub: *the stump of a pencil, etc.* **4** *Informal.* leg. **5** place where a political speech is made. **6** a heavy step. **7** sound made by stiff walking or heavy steps. —*v.* **1** make political speeches in: *the candidates for governor will stump the state.* **2** walk in a stiff, clumsy way. **3** make unable to answer, do, etc.; embarrass. [cf. MLG *stump*] —**stump′y,** *adj.* —**stump′i·ly,** *adv.* —**stump′i·ness,** *n.*

stun (stun), *v.,* **stunned, stun·ning,** *n.* —*v.* **1** make senseless; knock unconscious. **2** daze; bewilder; shock; overwhelm. —*n.* a stunning; being stunned. [OE *stunian* crash, resound; infl. by OF *estoner* resound, stun]

stung (stung), *v.* pt. and pp. of **sting.**

stun gun, =taser.

stunk (stungk), *v.* pt. and pp. of **stink.**

stun·ner (stun′ər), *n.* **1** person, thing, or blow that stuns. **2** *Informal.* a very striking or attractive person or thing.

stun·ning (stun′ing), *adj.* **1** having striking excellence, beauty, etc. **2** that stuns or dazes; bewildering. —**stun′ning·ly,** *adv.*

stunt¹ (stunt), *v.* check in growth or development: *lack of proper food stunts a child.* —*n.* **1** a stunting. **2** a stunted creature. [OE, foolish]

stunt² (stunt), *n.* feat to attract attention; act showing boldness or skill. —*v.* perform stunts.

stunt·man (stunt′man′), *n., pl.* **-men.** person who performs dangerous stunts in place of an actor, esp. in films.

stu·pe·fac·tion (stüü′pə fak′shən; stü′-), *n.* **1** dazed or senseless condition; stupor. **2** overwhelming amazement.

stu·pe·fy (stü′pə fī; stü′-), *v.,* **-fied, -fy·ing. 1** make stupid, dull, or senseless. **2** overwhelm with amazement; astound. [< L, < *stupere* be amazed + *facere* make] —**stu′pe·fi′er,** *n.* —**stu′pe·fy′ing·ly,** *adv.*

stu·pen·dous (stü pen′dəs; stü-), *adj.* amazing; marvelous; immense: *Niagara Falls is a stupendous sight.* [< L *stupendus* < *stupere* be amazed] —**stu·pen′dous·ly,** *adv.*

stu·pid (stü′pid; stü′-), *adj.* **1** not intelligent; dull: *a stupid person.* **2** not interesting: *a stupid book.* **3** dazed; senseless. —*n.* a stupid person. [< L *stupidus*] —**stu·pid′i·ty,** *n.* —**stu′pid·ly,** *adv.*

stu·por (stü′pər; stü′-), *n.* a dazed condition; loss or lessening of the power to feel. [< L] —**stu′por·ous,** *adj.*

stur·dy (stėr′di), *adj.,* **-di·er, -di·est. 1** strong; stout: *sturdy legs.* **2** not yielding; firm: *sturdy resistance, sturdy defenders.* [< OF *esturdi* violent, orig., dazed] —**stur′di·ly,** *adv.* —**stur′di·ness,** *n.*

stur·geon (stėr′jən), *n., pl.* **-geons** or (*esp. collectively*) **-geon.** a large food fish whose long body has a tough skin with rows of bony plates. Caviar is obtained from sturgeons. [< AF, ult. < Gmc.]

stut·ter (stut′ər), *v.* repeat (the same sound) involuntarily or spasmodically in an effort to speak. —*n.* act or habit of stuttering. [< dial. *stut.* Cf. Du. *stotteren.*] —**stut′ter·er,** *n.* —**stut′ter·ing·ly,** *adv.*

St. Vi·tus's dance (vī′təs iz), **St. Vitus dance,** =chorea.

sty¹ (stī), *n., pl.* **sties. 1** pen for pigs. **2** *Fig.* any filthy or disorderly place. [OE *stig*]

sty², **stye** (stī), *n., pl.* **sties; styes.** a small inflamed swelling on the edge of the eyelid. A sty is like a small boil. [prob. <ME *styanye* (taken to mean "sty on eye"), ult. < OE *stīgend* rising + *ēage* eye]

Styg·i·an (stij′i ən), *adj.* **1** pertaining to the river Styx or the lower world; infernal. **2** dark; gloomy.

style (stīl), *n., v.,* **styled, styl·ing.** —*n.* **1** fashion: *dress in the latest styles.* **2** manner; method; way: *the Gothic style of architecture.* **3** way of writing or speak-

ing: *a pedantic style.* **4** good style: *she dresses in style, his painting lacks style.* **5** a pointed instrument for writing, drawing, etching, etc. **6** the stemlike part of the pistil of a flower containing the stigma at its top. —*v.* **1** name; call: *Joan of Arc was styled "the Maid of Orleans."* **2** make fashionable and attractive. [< OF < L *stilus,* orig., pointed writing instrument; infl. in modern spelling by Gk. *stylos* column] —**style′less,** *adj.*

style·book (stīl′bůk′), *n.* **1** book containing rules of punctuation, capitalization, etc., used by printers, writers, etc. **2** book showing fashions.

styl·ish (stīl′ish), *adj.* having style; fashionable. —**styl′ish·ly,** *adv.* —**styl′ish·ness,** *n.*

styl·ist (stīl′ist), *n.* person who designs or advises concerning interior decorations, clothes, etc. —**sty·lis′tic,** *adj.* —**sty·lis′ti·cal·ly,** *adv.*

styl·ize (stīl′īz), *v.,* **-ized, -iz·ing.** make or design to conform to a particular or to a conventional style. —**styl′i·za′tion,** *n.*

sty·lus (stī′ləs), *n.* a pointed instrument for writing on wax. [< L *stilus.* See STYLE.]

sty·mie (stī′mi), *v.,* **-mied, -mie·ing.** block completely.

styp·tic (stip′tik), *adj.* able to stop or check bleeding; astringent. —*n.* something that stops or checks bleeding by contracting the tissue. [< L < Gk. *styptikos* < *styphein* constrict] —**styp·tic′i·ty,** *n.*

sty·ro·foam (stī′rə fōm′), *n.* **1** waterproof, light-weight plastic foam, used to make esp. cups and other containers. **2 Styrofoam.** trademark for this foam. —*adj.* of styrofoam: *styrofoam cups.*

sua·sion (swā′zhən), *n.* an advising or urging; persuasion. [< L *suasio* < *suadere* persuade] —**sua′sive,** *adj.* —**sua′sive·ly,** *adv.* —**sua′sive·ness,** *n.*

suave (swäv), *adj.* smoothly agreeable or polite. [< F < L *suavis* agreeable] —**suave′ly,** *adv.* —**sua′vi·ty,** *n.*

sub (sub), *n., adj., v.,* **subbed, sub·bing.** —*n., adj.* **1** substitute. **2** submarine. **3** subordinate. —*v.* act as a substitute.

sub-, prefix. **1** under; below, as in *submarine.* **2** down; further; again, as in *subclassify, sublease.* **3** near; nearly, as in *subarctic.* **4 a** lower; subordinate; assistant, as in *subaltern.* **b** of less importance, as in *subhead.* [< L *sub,* prep.; also (by assimilation to the following consonant), *su–, suc–, suf–, sug–, sum–, sup–*]

sub., **1** subscription. **2** substitute. **3** suburban.

sub·al·tern (sə bôl′tərn; sub′əl tèrn), *n.* **1** *Esp. Brit.* a commissioned officer in the army, ranking below a captain. **2** one who has a subordinate position. —*adj.* **1** *Esp. Brit.* ranking below a captain. **2** having lower rank; subordinate. [< LL, < L *sub–* under + *alternus* alternate]

sub·arc·tic (sub ärk′tik; -är′tik), *adj.* near, or just below, the arctic region; pertaining to or occurring in regions just S of the arctic circle.

sub·com·mit·tee (sub′kə mit′i), *n.* a small committee chosen from a larger general committee for some special duty.

sub·con·scious (sub kon′shəs), *adj.* **1** existing or operating in one's mind, but not felt: *subconscious worries, subconscious thoughts.* **2** not wholly conscious. —*n.* subconscious thoughts, feelings, impulses, etc. —**sub·con′scious·ly,** *adv.* —**sub·con′scious·ness,** *n.*

sub·con·tract (*n.* sub kon′trakt; *v.* sub - kon′trakt, sub′kən trakt′), *n.* contract for carrying out a previous contract or a part of it. —*v.* make a subcontract; make a subcontract for. —**sub·con′trac·tor,** *n.*

sub·cu·ta·ne·ous (sub′kū tā′ni əs), *adj.* **1** under the skin. **2** placed or performed under the skin. —**sub′cu·ta′ne·ous·ly,** *adv.*

sub·di·vide (sub′də vīd′; sub′də vīd′), *v.,* **–vid·ed, –vid·ing.** divide again; divide into smaller parts.

sub·di·vi·sion (sub′də vizh′ən; sub′də - vizh′ən), *n.* **1** division into smaller parts. **2** part of a part. **3** tract of land divided into building lots.

sub·dom·i·nant (sub dom′ə nənt), *n.* note or tone next below the dominant, or fifth note or tone, in the scale. —*adj.* of or having to do with this note or tone.

sub·duc·tion (sub duk′shən), *n.* a sinking movement of one geological plate under another where the edges of each plate meet.

sub·due (səb dü′; -dū′), *v.,* **–dued, –du·ing. 1** conquer and bring into subjection. *the Spaniards subdued the Indian tribes in Mexico.* **2** repress (feelings, impulses, etc.): *we subdued a desire to laugh.* **3** tone down; soften: *a subdued light.* [ult. < L *subducere* draw away < *sub–* from under + *ducere* lead; infl. in meaning by L *subdere* subdue] —**sub·du′a·ble,** *adj.* —**sub·dued′,** *adj.* —**sub·dued′ly,** *adv.* —**sub·dued′ness,** *n.* —**sub·du′er,** *n.*

sub·head (sub′hed′), **sub·head·ing** (–ing), *n.* **1** a subordinate head or title. **2** subordinate division of a head or title.

sub·hu·man (sub hyü′mən), *adj.* less than human; not quite human. —*n.* a subhuman creature.

subj., 1 subject. **2** subjunctive.

sub·ject (*n., adj.* sub′jikt; *v.* səb jekt′), *n.* **1** something thought about, discussed, studied, etc.: *a subject of conversation.* **2** person who owes allegiance to a government and lives under its protection. **3** person or thing that undergoes or experiences something: *the dog was the subject of their experiment.* **4** word or words referring to the person or thing that performs or, when the verb is passive, receives the action of the verb. **5** theme or melody on which a musical work is based. **6** object, scene, etc., represented in art. —*adj.* **1** under some power or influence: *we are subject to our country's laws.* **2** exposed: *subject*

to ridicule. **3** likely to have: *subject to headaches.* **4** being dependent or conditional: *subject to your approval.* —*v.* **1** bring under some power or influence: *Rome subjected all Italy to its rule.* **2** cause to undergo or experience something: *subject a person to ridicule.* [< L *subjectus* placed under < *sub* under + *jacere* throw]

sub·jec·tion (səb jek′shən), *n.* **1** a bringing under some power or influence; conquering: *the subjection of the rebels took years.* **2** condition of being under some power or influence: *women used to live in subjection to men.*

sub·jec·tive (səb jek′tiv), *adj.* **1** existing in the mind; belonging to the person thinking rather than to the object thought of: *base your subjective opinions on objective facts.* **2** about the thoughts and feelings of the speaker, writer, painter, etc.; personal: *a subjective poem.* **3** pertaining to or constituting the subject of a sentence. —**sub·jec′tive·ly,** *adv.* —**sub·jec′tive·ness,** *n.*

sub·jec·tiv·i·ty (sub′jek tiv′ə ti), *n.* subjective quality; existence in the mind only.

subject matter, 1 something considered, talked or written about. **2** substance of a creative work, such as a film or novel, as opposed to its form or style.

sub·ju·gate (sub′jə gāt), *v.,* **–gat·ed, –gat·ing.** subdue; conquer. [< L, < *sub–* under + *jugum* yoke] —**sub′ju·ga′tion,** *n.* —**sub′ju·ga′tor,** *n.*

sub·junc·tive (səb jungk′tiv), *n.* **1** the mood of a verb which expresses a state, act, or event as possible, conditional, or dependent, rather than as actual. **2** verb in this mood, as in, "if we were to go", *were* being in the subjunctive. —*adj.* noting or pertaining to this mood. [< LL *subjunctivus,* ult. < L *sub–* under + *jungere* join] —**sub·junc′tive·ly,** *adv.*

sub·king·dom (sub king′dəm; sub′king′–), *n.* any primary division of the animal kingdom, usually called a phylum.

sub·lease (*n.* sub′lēs′; *v.* sub lēs′, sub′-lēs′), *n., v.,* **–leased, –leas·ing.** —*n.* lease granted by a person who rents the property him or herself. —*v.* grant or take a sublease of. —**sub′les·see′,** *n.* —**sub-les′sor,** *n.*

sub·let (sub let′; sub′let′), *v.,* **–let, –letting.** rent to another (something which has been rented to oneself). —*n.* house, apartment, etc. that has been sublet.

sub·li·mate (*v.* sub′lə māt; *adj., n.* sub′-lə mit, –māt), *v.,* **–mat·ed, –mat·ing.** *adj., n.* —*v.* **1** purify; refine. **2** sublime (a solid substance). **3** modify less acceptable impulses or traits into more acceptable behavior. —*adj.* sublimated. —*n.* material obtained when a substance is sublimed. [< L *sublimatus,* orig., raised < *sublimis* lofty] —**sub′li·ma′tion,** *n.*

sub·lime (səb līm′), *adj., n., v.,* **–limed, –lim·ing.** —*adj.* **1** elevated in thought, sentiment, language, deed, etc.; lofty;

noble: *sublime courage.* **2** inspiring awe or veneration; majestic. —*n.* that which is lofty, noble, exalted, etc. —*v.* **1 a** convert (a solid substance) by heat into a vapor, which on cooling condenses again to solid form, without apparent liquefaction. **b** cause to be given off by this or some analogous process. **2** make lofty or sublime. [< L *sublimis*] —**sub·lime′ly,** *adv.* —**sub·lime′ness,** *n.*

sub·lim·i·nal (sub lim′ə nəl; –lī′mə–), *adj.* **1** subconscious; below the threshold of consciousness: *subliminal perception.* **2** too weak or small to be felt or noticed.

sub·lim·i·ty (səb lim′ə ti), *n., pl.* **–ties. 1** lofty excellence; grandeur; majesty; exalted state. **2** a sublime person or thing.

sub·ma·chine gun (sub′mə shēn′), a lightweight automatic or semiautomatic gun, designed to be fired from the shoulder or hip.

sub·ma·rine (*n.* sub′mə rēn′; *adj.* sub′-mə rēn′), *n.* boat that can operate under water, used in warfare for discharging torpedoes, etc. —*adj.* **1** placed, growing, or used below the surface of the sea. **2** of, pertaining to, or carried on by submarine boats. —**sub′ma·rine′ly,** *adv.*

sub·max·il·lar·y (sub mak′sə ler′i), *adj.* of or pertaining to the lower jaw or lower jawbone.

sub·men·u or **sub-men·u** (sub men′yü), *n.* options in a computer program that are available under a larger category or function: *addresses are available in a submenu.*

sub·merge (səb mèrj′), *v.,* **–merged, –merg·ing. 1** put under water; cover with water. **2** *Fig.* cover; bury: *his talent was submerged by his shyness.* **3** sink under water; go below the surfaces. [< L, < *sub–* under + *mergere* plunge] —**sub·mer′gence,** *n.* —**sub·mer′gi·ble,** *adj.*

sub·merse (səb mèrs′), *v.,* **–mersed, –mers·ing.** =submerge. [< L *submersus,* pp. of *submergere* SUBMERGE] —**sub·mers′i·ble,** *adj., n.* —**sub·mer′sion,** *n.*

sub·mis·sion (səb mish′ən), *n.* **1** a submitting; yielding to the power, control, or authority of another. **2** obedience; humbleness. **3** a referring or being referred to the consideration or judgment of another or others.

sub·mis·sive (səb mis′iv), *adj.* yielding to the power, control, or authority of another. —**sub·mis′sive·ly,** *adv.* —**sub-mis′sive·ness,** *n.*

sub·mit (səb mit′), *v.,* **–mit·ted, –mit·ting. 1** yield to the power, control, or authority of another or others; surrender; yield: *submit to arrest.* **2** refer to the consideration or judgment of another or others: *submit a report.* **3** represent or urge in a respectful manner. [< L, < *sub–* under + *mittere* let go] —**sub·mit′tal,** *n.* —**sub·mit′ter,** *n.*

sub·nor·mal (sub nôr′məl), *adj.* below normal; inferior to the normal. —**sub′nor·mal′i·ty,** *n.*

sub·or·bit·al (sub ôr′bə təl), *adj.* of less than a full orbit: *suborbital rockets.*

sub·or·der (sub′ôr′dər; sub ôr′–), *n.* group of plants or animals ranking above a family and below an order.

sub·or·di·nate (*adj., n.* sə bôr′də nit; *v.* sə bôr′də nāt), *adj., n., v.,* **–nat·ed, –nat·ing.** —*adj.* **1** inferior in rank. **2** inferior in importance; secondary. **3** under the control or influence of something else; dependent. A complex sentence has one main clause and one or more subordinate clauses. **4** subordinating. *Because, since, if, as,* and *whether* are subordinate conjunctions. —*n.* a subordinate person or thing. —*v.* make subordinate. [< Med.L, ult. < L *sub–* under + *ordo* order] —**sub·or′di·nate·ly,** *adv.* —**sub·or′di·nate·ness,** *n.* —**sub·or′di·na′tive,** *adj.*

sub·or·di·na·tion (sə bôr′də nā′shən), *n.* **1** a subordinating or being subordinated. **2** subordinate position or importance. **3** submission to authority; willingness to obey; obedience.

sub·orn (sə bôrn′), *v.* **1** persuade or cause (a witness) to give false testimony in court. **2** persuade or cause (a person) to do an evil deed. [< L, < *sub–* secretly + *ornare* equip] —**sub·or′na′tion,** *n.* —**sub·orn′er,** *n.*

sub·poe·na (sə pē′nə), *n., v.,* **–naed, –na·ing.** —*n.* an official written order commanding a person to appear in law court. —*v.* summon with such an order. Also, **subpena.** [< NL *sub poena* under penalty]

sub·plot (sub′plot′), *n.* secondary or subordinate plot in a novel, play, etc.

sub·pro·gram (sub′prō′gram; –grəm), *n.* **1** a part of a computer program. **2** a program that directs the operation of another program in a computer.

sub·ro·ga·tion (sub′rō gā′shən), *n.* act of substituting for another, esp. the substitution of one person for another as a creditor.

sub ro·sa (sub rō′zə), in strict confidence; privately. [< L, under the rose]

sub·scribe (səb skrīb′), *v.,* **–scribed, –scrib·ing. 1** promise to give or pay (a sum of money): *he subscribed $20 to the hospital fund.* **2** write one's name at the end of a document, etc.; sign one's name: *John Hancock was the first man to subscribe to the Declaration of Independence.* **3** show one's consent or approval by signing: *thousands of citizens subscribed the petition.* **4** give one's consent or approval; agree: *he will not subscribe to anything unfair.*

subscribe to or **for,** promise to take and pay for, as a magazine, newspaper, etc. [< L, < *sub–* under + *scribere* write] —**sub·scrib′er,** *n.*

sub·script (sub′skript), *adj.* written underneath or low on the line. —*n.* number, letter, etc., written underneath and to one side of a symbol. In H_2SO_4 the *2* and *4* are subscripts. [< L *subscriptus.* See SUBSCRIBE.]

sub·scrip·tion (səb skrip′shən), *n.* **1** a subscribing. **2** money subscribed; contribution. **3** the right obtained for the money: *his subscription to the newspaper expires next week.* **4** sum of money raised by a number of persons: *we are raising a subscription for a new hospital.* **5** assent or agreement expressed by signing one's name. —**sub·scrip′tive,** *adj.*

sub·sec·tion (sub′sek′shən; sub sek′shən), *n.* part of a section.

sub·se·quent (sub′sə kwənt), *adj.* coming after; following; later: *subsequent events.*

subsequent to, after; following; later than: *on the day subsequent to your call.* [< L, < *sub–* up + *sequi* follow] —**sub′se·quence,** *n.* —**sub′se·quen′tial,** *adj.* —**sub′se·quent·ly,** *adv.* —**sub′se·quent·ness,** *n.*

sub·serve (səb sėrv′), *v.,* **–served, –serv·ing.** be of use or service in helping along (a purpose, action, etc.).

sub·ser·vi·ent (səb sėr′vi ənt), *adj.* **1** tamely submissive; slavishly polite and obedient; servile. **2** useful as a means to help a purpose or end; serviceable. [< L, < *sub–* under + *servire* serve] —**sub·ser′vi·ence, sub·ser′vi·en·cy,** *n.* —**sub·ser′vi·ent·ly,** *adv.*

sub·set (sub′set′), *n.* a set whose members are each a member of another set.

sub·side (səb sīd′), *v.,* **–sid·ed, –sid·ing. 1** sink to a lower level: *after the rain stopped the flood waters subsided.* **2** grow less; die down; become less active: *the storm finally subsided.* **3** fall to the bottom; settle. [< L, < *sub–* down + *sidere* settle] —**sub·sid′ence,** *n.*

sub·sid·i·ar·y (səb sid′i er′i), *adj., n., pl.* **–ar·ies.** —*adj.* **1** useful to assist or supplement; auxiliary; supplementary. **2** subordinate; secondary. —*n.* **1** thing or person that assists or supplements. **2** company having over half of its stock owned or controlled by another company. [< L, < *subsidium* reserve troops] —**sub·sid′i·ar′i·ly,** *adv.*

sub·si·dize (sub′sə dīz), *v.,* **–dized, –diz·ing. 1** aid or assist with a grant of money. **2** buy the aid or assistance of with a grant of money. —**sub′si·di·za′tion,** *n.* —**sub′si·diz′er,** *n.*

sub·si·dy (sub′sə di), *n., pl.* **–dies.** grant or contribution of money, esp. one made by a government: *subsidies to farmers encourage certain practices.* [< L *subsidium* aid, reserve troops]

sub·sist (səb sist′), *v.* **1** keep alive; live: *people in the far north subsist on fish and meat.* **2** continue to be; exist: *many superstitions still subsist.* [< L, < *sub–* up to + *sistere* stand]

sub·sist·ence (səb sis′təns), *n.* **1** state or fact of keeping alive; living. **2** existence; continuance. **3** means of keeping alive; livelihood. —**sub·sist′ent,** *adj.*

sub·soil (sub′soil′), *n.* layer of earth that lies just under the surface soil: *clay subsoil.*

sub·son·ic (sub son′ik), *adj.* having to do with or designed for use at a speed less than that of sound.

sub·stance (sub′stəns), *n.* **1** what a thing consists of; matter; material: *ice and water are the same substance.* **2** the real, main, or important part of anything. **3** the real meaning: *give the substance of the speech in your own words.* **4** solid quality: *claims lacking substance.* **5** body: *a soup with substance.* **6** wealth; property. **7** a particular kind of matter: *the little pond is covered with a green substance.*

in substance, a essentially; mainly. **b** really; actually. [< OF < L, < *substare* stand firm < *sub–* up to + *stare* stand] —**sub′stance·less,** *adj.*

sub·stand·ard (sub stan′dərd; sub′stan′-dərd), *adj.* below standard.

sub·stan·tial (səb stan′shəl), *adj.* **1** real; actual: *not a ghost or a dream, but a substantial person.* **2** large; important; ample: *a substantial improvement.* **3** strong; firm; solid: *a substantial building.* **4** in the main; in essentials: *the two stories were in substantial agreement.* **5** well-to-do; wealthy. [< L, < *substantia* SUBSTANCE] —**sub·stan′ti·al′i·ty,** *n.* —**sub·stan′tial·ly,** *adv.* —**sub·stan′tial-ness,** *n.*

sub·stan·ti·ate (səb stan′shi āt), *v.,* **–at·ed, -at·ing. 1** establish by evidence; prove: *substantiate a claim.* **2** give concrete or substantial form to; make real. —**sub·stan′ti·a′tion,** *n.* —**sub·stan′ti·a′tive,** *adj.* —**sub·stan′ti·a′tor,** *n.*

sub·stan·tive (sub′stən tiv), *n.* noun or pronoun; any adjective, phrase, or clause used as a noun. —*adj.* **1** independent. **2** real; actual. **3** essential. **4 a** used as a noun; of the nature of a noun. **b** showing or expressing existence. The verb *to be* is the substantive verb. [< LL *substantivus,* ult. < *substare.* See SUBSTANCE.] —**sub′stan·ti′val,** *adj.* —**sub′stan·ti′val·ly,** *adv.* —**sub′stan·tive·ly,** *adv.* —**sub′stan·tive·ness,** *n.*

sub·sta·tion (sub′stā′shən), *n.* a branch station.

sub·sti·tute (sub′stə tüt; –tūt), *n., v.,* **–tut-ed, –tut·ing,** *adj.* —*n.* thing used instead of another; person taking the place of another. —*v.* **1** put in the place of another. **2** take the place of another. —*adj.* put in or taking the place of another. [< L *substitutus* < *sub–* instead + *statuere* establish] —**sub′sti·tut′er,** *n.* —**sub′sti·tu′tion·ar′y,** *adj.*

sub·sti·tu·tion (sub′stə tü′shən; –tū′–), *n.* use of one thing for another; putting (one person or thing) in the place of another; taking the place of another. —**sub′sti·tu′tion·al,** *adj.* —**sub′sti·tu′-tion·al·ly,** *adv.*

sub·stra·tum (sub strā′təm; –strat′əm), *n., pl.* **–stra·ta** (–strā′tə; –strat′ə), **–stra-tums. 1** layer lying under another. **2** subsoil. **3** basis. —**sub·stra′tal,** *adj.* —**sub·stra′tive,** *adj.*

sub·struc·ture (sub'struk´chər; sub - struk'-), *n.* structure forming a foundation. —**sub·struc'tur·al,** *adj.*

sub·ten·ant (sub ten'ənt; sub'ten´-), *n.* a tenant of a tenant; one who rents land, a house, or the like, from a tenant. —**sub·ten'an·cy,** *n.*

sub·tend (səb tend'), *v.* extend under or be opposite to; stretch across. [< L, < *sub*- under + *tendere* stretch]

sub·ter·fuge (sub'tər fūj), *n.* trick, excuse, or expedient used to escape something unpleasant. [< LL, ult. < L *subter*- from under + *fugere* flee]

sub·ter·ra·ne·an (sub´tə rā'ni ən), *adj.* **1** underground. **2** *Fig.* carried on secretly; hidden. [< L, < *sub*- under + *terra* earth] —**sub´ter·ra'ne·an·ly,** *adv.*

sub·text (sub'tekst´), *n.* **1** meaning that is implied or that underlies a literary or other creative work. **2** *Fig.* anything not openly stated but indirectly a part of something: *the subtext of the president's speech is his unpopularity.*

sub·ti·tle (sub'ti´təl), *n.* an additional or subordinate title of a book or article.

sub·tle (sut'əl), *adj.* **1** delicate and elusive; thin; fine: *a subtle odor of perfume.* **2** faint; mysterious: *a subtle smile.* **3** having a keen, quick mind; discerning; acute: *a subtle understanding.* **4** sly; crafty; tricky: *subtle schemers.* [< OF < L *subtilis,* orig., woven underneath] —**sub'tle·ness,** *n.* —**sub'tly,** *adv.*

sub·tle·ty (sut'əl ti), *n., pl.* **-ties. 1** a subtle quality. **2** something subtle.

sub·tonic (sub ton'ik), *n.* note or tone next below the upper dominant, or eighth, note or tone in the scale.

sub·tract (səb trakt'), *v.* **1** take away (one number from another). **2** take away (something) from a whole. [< L *subtractus* < *sub*- from under + *trahere* draw] —**sub·tract'er,** *n.* —**sub·trac'tion,** *n.* —**sub·trac'tive,** *adj.*

sub·tra·hend (sub'trə hend), *n.* number or quantity to be subtracted from another. In 10 − 2 = 8, the subtrahend is 2. [< L, < *subtrahere* SUBTRACT]

sub·treas·ur·y (sub'trezh´ər i; -trezh´ri; sub trezh'-), *n., pl.* **-ur·ies. 1** a branch treasury. **2** any branch of the United States treasury. —**sub'treas´ur·er,** *n.*

sub·trop·i·cal (sub trop'ə kəl), *adj.* **1** bordering on the tropics; nearly tropical. **2** pertaining to or occurring in a region between tropical and temperate. —**sub'trop´ics,** *n.pl.*

sub·urb (sub'ėrb), *n.* **1** district, town, or village just outside the boundaries of a city. **2** Usually, **suburbs.** outlying parts.

the suburbs, residential sections near the boundary of a city. [< L *suburbium* < *sub*- below + *urbs* city]

sub·ur·ban (sə bėr'bən), *adj.* **1** pertaining to a suburb; in a suburb. **2** characteristic of a suburb or its inhabitants. —**sub·ur'ban·ite,** *n.*

sub·ur·bi·a (sə bėr'bi ə), *n.* the suburbs.

sub·ven·tion (səb ven'shən), *n.* money granted, esp. by a government or some other authority, to aid or support some cause, institution, or undertaking; subsidy. —**sub·ven'tion·ar´y,** *adj.*

sub·ver·sion (səb vėr'zhən; -shən), *n.* **1** overthrow; destruction; ruin. **2** anything that tends to overthrow or destroy; cause of ruin. —**sub·ver'sion·a·ry,** *adj.*

sub·ver·sive (səb vėr'siv), *adj.* tending to overthrow; destructive; causing ruin. —*n.* person who seeks to overthrow or undermine (a government, etc.)

sub·vert (səb vėrt'), *v.* **1** ruin (something established or existing); overthrow; destroy; cause the downfall, ruin, or destruction of. **2** undermine the principles of; corrupt. [< L, < *sub*- up from under + *vertere* turn] —**sub·vert'er,** *n.* —**sub·vert'i·ble,** *adj.*

sub·way (sub'wā´), *n.* **1** an underground passage. **2** an electric railroad beneath the surface of the streets in a city.

suc·ceed (sək sēd'), *v.* **1** turn out well; do well; have success: *he finally succeeded.* **2** accomplish what is attempted or intended: *the attack succeeded beyond all expectations.* **3** come next after; follow; take the place of: *week succeeds week.* **4** come next after another; follow another; take the place of another: *when Edward VIII abdicated, George VI succeeded to the throne.* [< L, < *sub*- up (to) + *cedere* go] —**suc·ceed'er,** *n.*

suc·cess (sək ses'), *n.* **1** a favorable result; wished-for ending; good fortune: *efforts crowned with success.* **2** the gaining of wealth, position, etc.: *he has had little success in life.* **3** person or thing that succeeds: *he was a success in business.* **4** result; outcome; fortune: *what success did you have?* [< L *successus* < *succedere* SUCCEED]

suc·cess·ful (sək ses'fəl), *adj.* having success; ending in success; prosperous; fortunate. —**suc·cess'ful·ly,** *adv.* —**suc·cess'ful·ness,** *n.*

suc·ces·sion (sək sesh'ən), *n.* **1** group of things happening one after another; series: *a succession of events.* **2** the coming of one person or thing after another: *a succession of kings.* **3** the right or process by which one person takes the office, rank, estate, or other rights or liabilities of another person. **4** set or arrangement of persons having such a right of succeeding.

in succession, one after another. —**suc·ces'sion·al,** *adj.* —**suc·ces'sion·al·ly,** *adv.*

suc·ces·sive (sək ses'iv), *adj.* coming one after another; following in order: *it rained for three successive days.* —**suc·ces'sive·ness,** *n.*

suc·ces·sive·ly (sək ses'iv li), *adv.* one after another; in order.

suc·ces·sor (sək ses'ər), *n.* **1** person who succeeds another in office, position, or ownership or property. **2** one that follows in a series. —**suc·ces'sor·ship,** *n.*

suc·cinct (sək singkt'), *adj.* expressed briefly and clearly; expressing much in few words; concise. [< L *succinctus,* pp. of *succingere* tuck up clothes for action < *sub*- up + *cingere* gird] —**suc·cinct'ly,** *adv.* —**suc·cinct'ness,** *n.*

suc·cor (suk'ər), *n.* help; relief; aid. —*v.* help or aid, esp. in difficulty, want, or distress. [< OF *sucurs,* ult. < L *succurrere* run to help < *sub*- up (to) + *currere* run]

suc·co·tash (suk'ə tash), *n.* corn and beans cooked together. [< Algonkian]

suc·cu·lent (suk'yə lənt), *adj.* **1** juicy: *a succulent fruit.* **2** interesting; not dull. **3** having thick, fleshy leaves and stems. [< L, < *succus* juice] —**suc'cu·lence, suc'cu·len·cy,** *n.* —**suc'cu·lent·ly,** *adv.*

suc·cumb (sə kum'), *v.* **1** give way; yield: *he succumbed to temptation.* **2** die.

succumb to, die of. [< L, < *sub*- down + *-cumbere* lie]

such (such), *adj.* **1** of that kind; of the same kind or degree: *I never have seen such a sight, the food, such as it was, was plentiful.* **2** of the kind already spoken of or suggested: *tea, coffee, and such commodities.* **3** so great, so bad, so good, etc.: *he is such a liar.* **4** some; certain: *in such and such a town.* —*pron.* such a person or thing: *take from the blankets such as you need.*

as such, as being what is indicated or implied: *a leader, as such, deserves obedience.*

such as, a for example. **b** of the same stature: *few politicians such as Lincoln.* **c** of a particular kind: *behavior such as expected of a guest.* [OE *swylc, swelc* < *swa* so + *lic* like]

such·like (such'līk´), *adj.* of such kind; of a like kind. —*pron.* things of such kind: *"deceptions, disguises, and suchlike."*

suck (suk), *v.* **1** draw into the mouth: *lemonade can be sucked through a straw.* **2** draw something from with the mouth: *suck an orange.* **3** drink; take; absorb: *a sponge sucks in water.* **4** hold in the mouth and lick: *the child sucked a lollipop.* —*n.* act of sucking.

suck in, a pull in; flatten, esp. the stomach. **b** cheat; swindle: *get sucked in with promises of a lot of money.* [OE *sūcan*]

suck·er (suk'ər), *n.* **1** animal or thing that sucks. **2** any of various freshwater fishes that suck in food or have mouths that suggest sucking. **3** a shoot growing from an underground stem or root. **4** *Fig. Informal.* person easily deceived. **5** lollipop. —*v.* **1** take suckers from (corn, etc.). **2** *Fig. Informal.* treat as a fool or sucker.

suck·le (suk'əl), *v.,* **-led, -ling. 1** feed with milk from the breast, udder, etc. **2** *Fig.* nourish; bring up. [< *suck*] —**suck'ler,** *n.*

suck·ling (suk'ling), *n.* a very young animal or child, esp. one not yet weaned. —*adj.* very young, esp. not yet weaned; sucking.

Su·cre (sü′krə), *n.* one of the two capitals (La Paz is the other) of Bolivia, in the S part.

su·crose (sü′krōs), *n.* ordinary sugar, $C_{12}H_{22}O_{11}$, obtained from sugar cane, sugar beets, etc. [< F *sucre* SUGAR]

suc·tion (suk′shən), *n.* 1 the drawing of a liquid, gas, etc., into a space by sucking out or removing part of the air. 2 the force caused by sucking out or removing part of the air in a space. —*adj.* causing a suction; working by suction. [< L *suctio* < *sugere* suck]

Su·dan (sü dan′), *n.* country in NE Africa.

Su·da·nese (sü′də nēz′), *n.,* *pl.* **-nese.** native or inhabitant of Sudan. —*adj.* of or having to do with Sudan or its people.

sud·den (sud′ən), *adj.* 1 happening unexpectedly: *a sudden storm.* 2 made or done unexpectedly: *a sudden decision, act, etc.* 3 appearing unexpectedly: *a sudden turn in the road.* —*n.* **all of a sudden,** in a sudden manner. [< OF < L *subitaneus* < *subitus* sudden] —**sud′den·ly,** *adv.* —**sud′den·ness,** *n.*

sudden infant death syndrome, condition that causes the death of a healthy infant while sleeping, from an unknown cause; SIDS.

suds (sudz), *n.pl.* 1 soapy water. 2 bubbles and foam on soapy water. 3 any froth or foam. [? < MDu. *sudse* bog] —**suds′y,** *adj.*

sue (sü), *v.,* **sued, su·ing.** 1 start a lawsuit against. 2 take action in law: *sue for damages.* 3 beg or ask; make petition; plead: *messengers came suing for peace.* [< AF *suer,* ult. < L *sequi* follow] —**su′er,** *n.*

suede (swād), *n.* 1 a soft leather that has a velvety nap on one or both sides. 2 a kind of cloth that has a similar appearance. —*adj.* made of suede. [< F, lit., Sweden]

su·et (sü′it), *n.* the hard fat about the kidneys and loins of cattle or sheep. Beef suet is used in cooking and for making tallow. [dim. of AF *sue* tallow < L *sebum*] —**su′et·y,** *adj.*

suf. or **suff.,** suffix.

suf·fer (suf′ər), *v.* 1 undergo, experience, or be subjected to (pain, grief, injury, etc.): *his health suffered from overwork.* 2 undergo any action, process, etc.: *suffer change.* 3 allow; permit: *"Suffer the little children to come unto me."* 4 bear with patiently; tolerate; endure: *I will not suffer such insults.* [< L, < *sub-* up + *ferre* bear] —**suf′fer·a·ble,** *adj.* —**suf′fer·a·ble·ness,** *n.* —**suf′fer·a·bly,** *adv.* —**suf′fer·er,** *n.*

suf·fer·ance (suf′ər əns; suf′rəns), *n.* 1 permission given only by a failure to object or prevent. 2 power to bear or endure; patient endurance.

on sufferance, allowed or tolerated, but not really wanted.

suf·fer·ing (suf′ər ing; suf′ring), *n.* pain; the enduring of pain. —**suf′fer·ing·ly,**

suf·fice (sə·fīs′), *v.,* **-ficed, -fic·ing.** 1 be enough or adequate: *the money will suffice for one year.* 2 satisfy; content: *a small amount sufficed him.* [< L *sufficere* < *sub-* up (to) + *facere* make] —**suf·fic′er,** *n.* —**suf·fic′ing·ly,** *adv.* —**suf·fic′ing·ness,** *n.*

suf·fi·cien·cy (sə fish′ən si), *n.,* *pl.* **-cies.** 1 a sufficient amount; large enough supply. 2 state or fact of being sufficient; adequacy.

suf·fi·cient (sə fish′ənt), *adj.* as much as is needed; enough: *sufficient proof.* —**suf·fi′cient·ly,** *adv.*

suf·fix (*n.* suf′iks; *v.* sə fiks′, suf′iks), *n.* an addition made at the end of a word to change the meaning or form a new word. *-er, -ment, -less, -ic, -able,* and *-ible* are suffixes. —*v.* add at the end; put after. [< NL < L *suffixum,* neut. pp. < *sub-* upon + *figere* fasten] —**suf′fix·al,** *adj.* —**suf·fix′ion,** *n.*

suf·fix·a·tion (suf′ik sā′shən), *n.* 1 the attaching of a suffix at the end of a word. 2 formation of suffixes.

suf·fo·cate (suf′ə kāt), *v.,* **-cat·ed, -cat·ing.** 1 kill by stopping the breath. 2 keep from breathing; hinder in breathing. 3 die for lack of air. 4 *Fig.* smother; suppress: *suffocated by too much attention.* [< L *suffocatus* < *sub-* up + *fauces* throat] —**suf′fo·cat′ing·ly,** *adv.* —**suf′fo·ca′tion,** *n.* —**suf′fo·ca′tive,** *adj.*

suf·fra·gan (suf′rə gən), *n.* 1 bishop consecrated to assist another bishop. 2 any bishop considered in relation to his archbishop. —*adj.* assisting. [< OF, ult. < L *suffragium* suffrage]

suf·frage (suf′rij), *n.* 1 a vote; a vote for some person or thing. 2 the right to vote. [< L *suffragium*]

suf·fra·gette (suf′rə jet′), *n.* woman who advocated suffrage for women.

suf·fra·gist (suf′rə jist), *n.* a person who favors giving suffrage to more people, esp. to women. —**suf′fra·gism,** *n.*

suf·fuse (sə fūz′), *v.,* **-fused, -fus·ing.** overspread (with a liquid, dye, etc.): *eyes suffused with tears.* [< L *suffusus* < *sub-* (up from) under + *fundere* pour] —**suf·fu′sion,** *n.* —**suf·fu′sive,** *adj.*

Su·fi (sü′fī), *n.* 1 Muslim sect that originated early in the history of Islam in Persia (Iran). 2 a member of this sect. [< Ar. *ṣūfī,* lit., man of wool, in reference to their clothing] —**su′fism,** *n.*

sug·ar (shug′ər), *n.* 1 sweet substance, $C_{12}H_{22}O_{11}$, obtained chiefly from sugar cane or beets and used extensively in food products. 2 any of the class of carbohydrates to which this substance belongs: *grape sugar, milk sugar.* —*v.* 1 put sugar in; sweeten with sugar. 2 cover with sugar; sprinkle with sugar. 3 form sugar: *honey sugars if kept too long.* 4 make maple sugar. 5 *Fig.* cause to seem pleasant or agreeable.

sugar off, complete the boiling down of maple syrup. [< OF, ult. < Ar. *sukkar* < Pers. *shakar* < Skt. *ṡarkarā,* orig., grit] —**sug′ar·less,** *adj.* —**sug′ar·y,** *adj.* —**sug′ar·i·ness,** *n.*

sugar beet, a large beet with a white root that yields sugar.

sugar bowl, bowl, usually with two handles and a cover, for sugar used at the table.

sugar cane, a very tall grass with a strong, jointed stem and flat leaves, growing in warm regions. Sugar cane is the main source of sugar.

sug·ar-coat (shug′ər kōt′), *v.* 1 cover with sugar. 2 *Fig.* cause to seem more pleasant or agreeable. —**sug′ar-coat′ing,** *n.*

sugar maple, maple tree common in E North America, that yields a valuable hard wood and sweet sap from which maple syrup and maple sugar are made.

sug·ar·plum (shug′ər plum′), *n.* piece of candy; bonbon.

sug·gest (səg jest′; sə jest′), *v.* 1 bring to mind; call up the thought of: *the thought of summer suggests swimming.* 2 propose: *John suggested having a party.* 3 show in an indirect way; hint: *his yawns suggested that he would like to go to bed.* [< L *suggestus* < *sub-* up + *gerere* bring] —**sug·gest′er,** *n.*

sug·gest·i·ble (səg jes′tə bəl; sə jes′–), *adj.* 1 capable of being influenced by suggestion. 2 that can be suggested. —**sug·gest′i·bil′i·ty,** *n.*

sug·ges·tion (səg jes′chən; sə jes′–), *n.* 1 a suggesting: *the trip was made at his suggestion.* 2 thing suggested: *the picnic was an excellent suggestion.* 3 a very small amount; slight trace: *speak with a suggestion of a foreign accent.*

sug·ges·tive (səg jes′tiv; sə jes′–), *adj.* 1 tending to suggest ideas, acts, or feelings. 2 tending to suggest something improper or indecent. —**sug·ges′tive·ly,** *adv.* —**sug·ges′tive·ness,** *n.*

su·i·cide[1] (sü′ə sīd), *n.* 1 the killing of oneself on purpose. 2 destruction of one's own interests or prospects.

commit suicide, kill oneself on purpose. [< NL, < L *sui* of oneself + *–cidium* act of killing] —**su′i·cid′al,** *adj.* —**su′i·cid′al·ly,** *adv.*

su·i·cide[2] (sü′ə sīd), *n.* person who kills himself on purpose. [< NL, < L *sui* of oneself + *–cida* killer]

suit (süt), *n.* 1 set of clothes to be worn together, esp. a man's matching jacket and trousers or jacket and skirt for a woman. 2 case in a law court; application to a court for justice: *he started a suit to collect damages for his injuries.* 3 one of the four sets of cards (spades, hearts, diamonds, and clubs). 4 request; asking; wooing: *his suit was successful and she married him.* 5 set or series of like things; suite. —*v.* 1 make suitable; make fit: *suit the punishment to the offense.* 2 be suitable for; agree with: *a cold climate suits apples, which date suits* *best?* **3** be becoming to: *her blue hat suits her complexion.* **4** please; satisfy: *it is hard to suit everyone.*

follow suit, a play a card of the same suit as that first played. **b** *Fig.* follow the example of another.

suit oneself, do as one pleases.

suit up, put on a special uniform or outfit: *the astronauts suited up.* [< AF *suite,* ult. < L *sequi* follow. Doublet of SUITE.]

suit·a·ble (süt′ə bəl), *adj.* right for the occasion; fitting; proper. —**suit′a·bil′i·ty, suit′a·ble·ness,** *n.* —**suit′a·bly,** *adv.*

suit·case (süt′kās′), *n.* a flat, rectangular traveling bag.

suite (swēt; *also* süt *for 3*), *n.* **1** a connected series of rooms to be used by one person or family. **2** set or series of like things. **3** set of furniture that matches. **4** series of connected instrumental movements. [< F. Doublet of SUIT.]

suit·or (süt′ər), *n.* **1** man who is courting a woman. **2** person bringing suit in a law court. **3** anyone who sues or petitions. —**suit′or·ship,** *n.*

su·ki·ya·ki (sü′ki yä′ki), *n.* a Japanese dish of thin strips of beef and diced vegetables, cooked briefly in sauce. [< Jap.]

sul·fa (sul′fə), *adj.* of or pertaining to a family of drugs containing sulfurous anhydride (SO_2) and derived from sulfanilamide, used in treating various bacterial infections. —*n.* a sulfa drug.

sul·fa·nil·a·mide (sul′fə nil′ə mīd; –mid), *n.* a white, crystalline substance, derived from coal tar and used in treating various infections.

sul·fate (sul′fāt), *n., v.,* –**fat·ed,** –**fat·ing.** —*n.* any salt of sulfuric acid. —*v.* **1** combine, treat, or impregnate with sulfuric acid or with a sulfate or sulfates. **2** convert into a sulfate.

sul·fide (sul′fīd), *n.* any compound of sulfur with another element or radical.

sul·fite (sul′fīt), *n.* any salt of sulfurous acid.

sul·fur (sul′fər), *n.* **1** a light-yellow substance, S, that burns with a blue flame and a stifling odor. It is a nonmetallic chemical element. **2** a greenish yellow. —*adj.* greenish-yellow. [< L *sulfur, sulpur*] —**sul·fu′re·ous,** *adj.*

sul·fu·rate (sul′fə rāt; –fyə–), *v.,* –**rat·ed,** –**rat·ing.** combine, treat, or impregnate with sulfur, the fumes of burning sulfur, or the like.

sulfur dioxide, a heavy, colorless gas, SO_2, that has a sharp odor, used as a bleach, disinfectant, preservative, and refrigerant.

sul·fu·ric (sul fyur′ik), *adj.* pertaining to or containing sulfur with a valence of six.

sulfuric acid, oil of vitriol, a heavy colorless, oily, very strong acid, H_2SO_4, a dibasic acid of sulfur. Sulfuric acid is used in making explosives and fertilizers, in refining petroleum, etc.

sul·fur·ous (sul′fər əs; –fyər–; sul fyur′əs), *adj.* **1** of or having to do with sulfur. **2**

containing sulfur. **3 a** like sulfur; like burning sulfur. **b** extremely critical or angry, esp. comment.

sulk (sulk), *v.* hold aloof in a sullen manner; be sulky. —*n.* **1** a sulking. **2** a fit of sulking. [< *sulky*] —**sulk′er,** *n.*

sulk·y (sul′ki), *adj.,* **sulk·i·er, sulk·i·est,** *n., pl.* **sulk·ies,** —*adj.* silent and bad-humored because of resentment; sullen. —*n.* a light carriage with two wheels, for one person. [cf OE *āsolcen* lazy] —**sulk′i·ly,** *adv.* —**sulk′i·ness,** *n.*

sul·len (sul′ən), *adj.* **1** silent because of bad humor or anger: *the sullen child refused to answer my question.* **2** showing bad humor or anger: *a sullen act.* **3** gloomy; morose; dismal: *the sullen skies threatened rain.* [< OF *solain,* ult. < L *solus* alone] —**sul′len·ly,** *adv.*

sul·ly (sul′i), *v.,* –**lied,** –**ly·ing.** *n., pl.* –**lies.** soil; stain; tarnish. [OE *sōlian* < *sōl* dirty]

sul·pha (sul′fə), *adj., n.* =sulfa.

sul·phur (sul′fər), *n.* **1** =sulfur. **2** an orange or yellow butterfly, as the common sulphur of the E and Midwestern United States. **3** a greenish yellow; sulfur. —*adj.* greenish yellow; sulfur.

sul·tan (sul′tən), *n.* ruler of a Muslim country. Turkey was ruled by a sultan until 1922. [ult. < Ar. *sulṭān*] —**sul·tan′ic,** *adj.* —**sul·tan·ship,** *n.*

sul·tan·a (sul tan′ə; –tä′nə), *n.* **1** wife of a sultan. **2** mother, sister, or daughter of a sultan. **3** a small seedless raisin.

sul·tan·ate (sul′tən āt), *n.* **1** position, authority, or period of rule of a sultan. **2** territory ruled over by a sultan

sul·try (sul′tri), *adj.,* –**tri·er,** –**tri·est. 1** oppressively hot, close and moist: *we expect sultry weather during July.* **2** hot. [ult. < *swelter*] —**sul′tri·ly,** *adv.* —**sul′tri·ness,** *n.*

sum (sum), *n., v.,* **summed, sum·ming.** —*n.* **1** total of two or more numbers or things taken together. **2** the whole amount; total amount: *it represents the sum of my work.* **3** substance or gist of a matter: *the sum of his speech was this.* **4** the amount of money: *he paid a large sum for the house.* —*v.* **1** find the total of.

in sum, briefly; in conclusion: *in sum, it was a bad decision.*

sum up, a collect into a whole. **b** express briefly. **c** review the chief points (of). **d** *Fig.* form an opinion of; evaluate. [< L *summa,* orig. fem. adj., highest]

su·mac (sü′mak; shü′–), *n.* **1** a shrub or small tree which has divided leaves that turn scarlet in the autumn and cone-shaped clusters of red fruit. **2** its dried leaves, used in tanning and dyeing. [< OF < Ar. *summāq*]

sum·ma cum lau·de (súm′ə kúm lou′də; sum′ə kum lô′dē), *Latin.* with the highest honor.

sum·ma·rize (sum′ə rīz), *v.,* –**rized,** –**riz·ing.** make or represent a summary of; give only the main points of;

express briefly. —**sum′ma·ri·za′tion,** *n.* —**sum′ma·riz′er,** *n.*

sum·ma·ry (sum′ə ri), *n., pl.* –**ries,** *adj.* —*n.* a brief statement giving the main points: *a summary of a book.* —*adj.* **1** concise and comprehensive; brief. **2** direct and prompt; without delay or formality: *summary jurisdiction.* [< L, < *summa* sum] —**sum′ma·ri·ly,** *adv.*

sum·ma·tion (sum ā′shən), *n.* **1** process of finding the sum or total; addition. **2** the total. **3** the final presentation of facts and arguments by the opposing counsel.

sum·mer (sum′ər), *n.* **1** season of the year between spring and autumn. **2** the warmest season. —*adj.* of summer; coming in summer. —*v.* pass the summer: *summer at the seashore.* [OE *sumor*] —**sum′mer·y,** *adj.*

sum·mer·house (sum′ər hous′), *n.* an open building in a park or garden in which to sit in warm weather.

sum·mer·sault (sum′ər sôlt), *n., v.* =somersault.

summer solstice. See solstice.

summer squash, any of various squashes used as a summer vegetable.

sum·mer·time (sum′ər tīm′), *n.* summer.

sum·mit (sum′it), *n.* **1** the highest point; top. **2** the highest level of authority, esp. the leaders of individual governments, as dealing in international affairs. [< F *sommet,* ult. < L *summus* highest]

sum·mon (sum′ən), *v.* **1** call with authority, esp. to some particular duty; order to come; send for: *summon men to defend their country, summon an assembly.* **2** stir to action; rouse: *the fire alarm summoned the people.* [< L *summonere* hint to < *sub–* secretly + *monere* warn]

sum·mon·er (sum′ən ər), *n.* person who summons.

sum·mons (sum′ənz), *n., pl.* –**mons·es,** *v.* —*n.* **1** an order to appear at a certain place, esp. in a law court. **2** a command; message; signal. —*v.* summon to court. [< OF *somonse* < *somondre* SUMMON]

su·mo (sü′mō), *n.* Japanese wrestling. [< Jap.]

sump (sump), *n.* pit or reservoir for collecting water, oil, etc. [< MDu. *somp* or MLG *sump* swamp]

sump·tu·ous (sump′chù əs), *adj.* luxuriously fine or elegant. [< L, < *sumptus* expense < *sumere* spend]

sun (sun), *n., v.,* **sunned, sun·ning.** —*n.* **1** the brightest object in the sky; the celestial body around which the earth and planets revolve. **2** the light and warmth of the sun: *sit in the sun.* **3** something like the sun in brightness or splendor. —*v.* **1** expose to the sun's rays: *she suns herself each day.* **2** warm or dry in the sunshine: *she suns the clothes after washing them.*

from sun to sun, from sunrise to sunset.

in the sun, in an advantageous or comfortable position.

under the sun, on earth; in the world. [OE *sunne*] **—sun'less,** *adj.*

Sun., Sunday.

sun·beam (sun'bēm'), *n.* ray of sunlight.

Sun·belt or **sun·belt** (sun'belt'), *n.* the S United States that has a warm, sunny climate.

sun block lotion or cream to prevent sunburn by blocking harmful rays.

sun·bon·net (sun'bon'it), *n.* a large bonnet that shades the face and neck.

sun·burn (sun'bėrn'), *n., v.,* **-burned** or **-burnt, -burn·ing, —***n.* 1 a burning of the skin by the sun's rays. A sunburn is often red and painful. 2 the color of red or tan resulting from sunburn. —*v.* 1 burn the skin by the sun's rays; burn the skin of. 2 become burned by the sun.

sun·burst (sun'bėrst'), *n.* 1 sudden appearance of brilliant sunlight through a break in the clouds. 2 *Fig.* anything resembling this: *a sunburst design.*

sun·dae (sun'di), *n.* ice cream served with syrup, crushed fruits, nuts, etc., over it.

Sun·day (sun'di; –dā), *n.* the first day of the week. —*adj.* 1 of, on, or having to do with Sunday. 2 not regular; occasional: *Sunday drivers.*

Sunday school, 1 school held on Sunday for teaching religion. 2 its members.

sun·der (sun'dər), *v.* separate; part; sever; split. [OE *sundrian* < *sundor* apart]

sun·di·al (sun'dī'əl), *n.* instrument for telling the time of day by the position of a shadow cast by the sun.

sun·down (sun'doun'), *n.* sunset; the time of sunset.

sun·dried (sun'drīd'), *adj.* dried by the sun.

sun·dries (sun'driz), *n.pl.* sundry things; items not named; odds and ends.

sun·dry (sun'dri), *adj.* several; various. —*n.* **all and sundry,** all, both collectively and individually. [OE *syndrig* separate < *sundor* apart]

sun·fish (sun'fish'), *n., pl.* **-fish·es** or (*esp. collectively*) **-fish.** 1 a large fish with tough flesh that lives in tropical or temperate seas. 2 a small freshwater fish of North America, used for food.

sun·flow·er (sun'flou'ər), *n.* 1 a tall plant having large yellow flowers with brown centers and edible seeds. 2 any of various similar plants.

sung (sung), *v.* pt. and pp. of **sing.**

sun·glass·es (sun'glas'iz; –gläs'–), *n.pl.* spectacles to protect the eyes from the glare of the sun, usually made with colored glass.

sunk (sungk), *v.* pt. and pp. of **sink.**

sunk·en (sungk'ən), *adj.* 1 sunk: *a sunken ship.* 2 submerged: *a sunken rock.* 3 situated below the general level: *a sunken garden.* 4 fallen in; hollow: *sunken eyes.* —*v.* pp. of **sink.**

sun·light (sun'līt'), *n.* the light of the sun.

sun·lit (sun'lit'), *adj.* lighted by the sun.

Sun·ni (su'ni), *n., pl.* **-ni** or **-nis.** orthodox Muslim, member of one of two main sects of Islam. —*adj.* of or having to do with the Sunni or their faith. [< Ar. *sunna, lit.,* form, course, rule]

sun·ny (sun'i), *adj.,* **-ni·er, -ni·est.** 1 having much sunshine: *a sunny day.* 2 exposed to, lighted by, or warmed by the direct rays of the sun: *a sunny room.* 3 like the sun; like sunshine. 4 *Fig.* bright; cheerful; happy. —**sun'ni·ly,** *adv.* —**sun'ni·ness,** *n.*

sun·rise (sun'rīz'), **sun·up** (sun'up'), *n.* 1 the rising of the sun. 2 the first appearance of the sun in the morning. 3 the time when the top of the sun rises above the horizon.

sun·screen (sun'skrēn'), *n.* lotion to prevent sunburn.

sun·set (sun'set'), *n.* 1 the setting of the sun. 2 the last appearance of the sun in the evening. 3 the time when the top of the sun goes below the horizon. 4 *Fig.* period of decline. —*adj.* of or having to do with an ending: *a sunset provision in the law.*

sun·shine (sun'shīn'), *n.* 1 the shining of the sun; light or rays of the sun. 2 *Fig.* brightness; cheerfulness; happiness. —*adj.* open; transparent: *sunshine laws.* —**sun'shin'y,** *adj.*

sun·spot (sun'spot'), *n.* one of the dark spots that appear at regular intervals of time on the sun.

sun·stroke (sun'strōk'), *n.* a sudden illness caused by the sun's rays or by too much heat.

sun·suit (sun'süt'), *n.* short pants with a bib and shoulder straps, worn by young children in hot weather.

sun·tan (sun'tan'), *n.* darkening of the skin from exposure to sun. —**sun'tanned',** *adj.*

sun·ward (sun'wərd), *adj.* toward or facing the sun. —*adv.* Also, **sun'wards.** toward the sun.

sup[1] (sup), *v.,* **supped, sup·ping.** 1 eat the evening meal; take supper. 2 give a supper to or for. [< OF *soper* < Gmc.]

sup[2] (sup), *v.,* **supped, sup·ping.** *n.* =sip. [OE *sūpan*]

sup., 1 superior. 2 superlative. 3 supplement; supplementary. 4 supra.

su·per (sü'pər), *n.* 1 supernumerary. 2 superintendent. —*adj.* superfine; excellent.

super–, *prefix.* 1 over; above, as in *superimpose, superstructure.* 2 besides, as in *superadd, supertax.* 3 in high proportion; to excess; exceedingly, as in *superabundant, supersensitive.* 4 surpassing, as in *superman, supernatural.* [< L *super* over, above]

su·per·a·ble (sü'pər ə bəl), *adj.* capable of being overcome; surmountable. —**su'per·a·bil'i·ty,** *n.*

su·per·a·bun·dant (sü'pər ə bun'dənt), *adj.* 1 very abundant. 2 more than enough. —**su'per·a·bun'dance,** *n.*

su·per·an·nu·ate (sü'pər an'yù āt), *v.,* **-at·ed, -at·ing.** 1 retire on a pension because of age or infirmity. 2 make

old-fashioned or out-of-date. [< Med.L *superannatus* more than a year old < L *super annum* beyond a year; infl. in spelling by *annuus* annual]

su·per·an·nu·at·ed (sü'pər an'yù āt'id), *adj.* 1 retired on a pension. 2 too old for work, service, etc. 3 old-fashioned; out-of-date.

su·perb (su pėrb'), *adj.* 1 stately; majestic; magnificent; splendid: *superb jewels, superb beauty.* 2 rich; elegant; sumptuous. 3 very fine; first-rate; excellent: *a superb book.* [< L *superbus*] —**su·perb'ly,** *adv.* —**su·perb'ness,** *n.*

su·per·charge (sü'pər chärj'), *v.,* **-charged, -charg·ing.** 1 increase the power of an engine. 2 charge to excess, as with excitement, tension, etc.

su·per·cil·i·ous (sü'pər sil'i əs), *adj.* haughty, proud, and contemptuous; disdainful. [< L, < *supercilium* eyebrow < *super*–above+*cel*–cover] —**su'per·cil'i·ous·ly,** *adv.*

su·per·con·duc·tor (sü'pər kən duk'tər), *n.* metal or ceramic material that conducts an electric current with no resistance.

su·per·cool (sü'pər kül'), *v.* cool a liquid below the freezing point without causing it to become a solid.

su·per·e·rog·a·to·ry (sü'pər ə rog'ə tô'ri; –tō'–), *adj.* 1 doing more than duty requires. 2 unnecessary; superfluous.

su·per·fi·cial (sü'pər fish'əl), *adj.* 1 of or pertaining to the surface: *superficial measurement.* 2 on or at the surface: *a superficial wound.* 3 concerned with or understanding only what is on the surface; not thorough; shallow: *a superficial education.* 4 without profound effects or significance: *superficial changes.* [< L, < *superficies* surface < *super*– above + *facies* form] —**su'per·fi'ci·al'i·ty,** *n.* —**su'per·fi'cial·ly,** *adv.*

su·per·fine (sü'pər fīn'), *adj.* 1 very fine; extra fine. 2 too refined; too nice.

su·per·flu·i·ty (sü'pər flü'ə ti), *n., pl.* **-ties.** 1 a greater amount than is needed; excess. 2 something not needed.

su·per·flu·ous (su pėr'flü əs), *adj.* 1 more than is needed. 2 needless. [< L, ult. < *super*– over + *fluere* flow] —**su·per'flu·ous·ly,** *adv.* —**su·per'flu·ous·ness,** *n.*

su·per·gi·ant (sü'pər jī'ənt), *n.* an extremely large, bright star, some more than 10,000 times brighter than the sun.

su·per·heat (sü'pər hēt'), *v.* 1 heat very hot; heat too hot; heat hotter than usual. 2 heat (a liquid) above its boiling point without producing vaporization. 3 heat (steam) until it resembles a dry gas. —**su'per·heat'er,** *n.*

su·per·high·way (sü'pər hī'wā), *n.* highway for fast travel, as a thruway or interstate highway.

su·per·hu·man (sü'pər hü'mən), *adj.* 1 above or beyond what is human. 2 above or beyond ordinary human power, experience, etc.

su·per·im·pose (sü´pər im pōz´), *v.*, **-posed, -pos·ing. 1** put on top of something else. **2** put or join as an addition. —**su´per·im´po·si´tion**, *n.*

su·per·in·tend(sü´prin tend´;sü´pər in–), *v.* oversee and direct (work or workers); manage (a place, institution, etc.) —**su´per·in·tend´ence**, *n.*

su·per·in·tend·ent (sü´prin ten´dənt; sü´-pər in–), *n.* person who oversees, directs, or manages. —*adj.* superintending.

su·pe·ri·or (sə pir´i ər; sü–), *adj.* **1** above the average; very good; excellent: *superior work in school.* **2** higher in quality or quantity; better; greater: *superior numbers of soldiers.* **3** higher in position, rank, importance, etc.: *superior officer.* **4** showing a feeling of being above others; proud: *superior airs, superior manners.* —*n.* **1** person who is superior: *a captain is a lieutenant's superior.* **2** head of a monastery or convent.

superior to, a higher than; above. **b** better than; greater than. **c** not giving in to; above yielding to. [< L, compar. of *superus,* adj., above < *super,* prep., above]

su·pe·ri·or·i·ty (sə pir´i ôr´ə ti;–or´–;sü–), *n.* superior quality or condition: *the superiority of DVDs over tapes.*

superl., superlative.

su·per·la·tive (sə pėr´lə tiv; sü–), *adj.* **1** of the highest kind; above all others; supreme: *King Solomon had superlative wisdom.* **2** expressing the highest degree of comparison of an adjective or adverb. *Fairest, best,* and *most slowly* are the superlative forms of *fair, good,* and *slowly.* —*n.* **1** person or thing above all others; supreme example. **2 a** the superlative degree. **b** form or combination of words that shows this degree.

talk or **speak in superlatives,** exaggerate. [< LL *superlativus,* ult. < *super–* beyond + *latus,* pp. to *ferre* carry] —**su·per´la·tive·ly,** *adv.*

su·per·ma·jor·i·ty (sü´pər mə jôr´ə ti, –jôr´–), *n., pl.* **-ties.** majority of three-fifths of the votes cast, used for ratification of treaties and Constitutional amendments.

su·per·man (sü´pər man´), *n., pl.* **-men. 1** man having more than human powers. **2** man so able as to seem superhuman. [< G *Übermensch,* lit., above man]

super·mar·ket (sü´pər mär´kit), *n.* a large grocery store in which customers select their purchases from open shelves and pay for them on a cash-and-carry basis.

su·per·nat·u·ral (sü´pər nach´ə rəl; –nach´rəl), *adj.* above or beyond what is natural. —*n.* **the supernatural,** supernatural agencies, influences, or phenomena. —**su´per·nat´u·ral·ism,** *n.* —**su´per·nat´u·ral·ist,** *n., adj.* —**su´per·nat´u·ral·is´tic,** *adj.* —**su´per·nat´u·ral·ly,** *adv.*

su·per·no·va (sü´pər nō´və), *n., pl.* **-vas, -vae** (–vi). an exceptionally bright nova, as much as 100 million times brighter than the sun.

su·per·nu·mer·ar·y (sü´pər nü´mər er´i; –nü´–), *adj., n., pl.* **-ar·ies.** —*adj.* more than the usual or necessary number; extra. —*n.* an extra person or thing.

su·per·pow·er (sü´pər pou´ər), *n.* **1** country with power great enough to affect policies and actions of other, less powerful, countries. **2** extraordinary power.

su·per·scribe (sü´pər skrīb´), *v.,* **-scribed, -scrib·ing.** write (words, letters, one's name, etc.) above, on, or outside of something. [< LL, < L, < *super–* above + *scribere* write]

su·per·script (sü´pər skript), *adj.* written above. —*n.* number, letter, etc., written above and to one side of a symbol. In $a^3 \times b^n$ the 3 and the *n* are superscripts. —**su´per·scrip´tion,** *n.*

su·per·sede (sü´pər sēd´), *v.,* **-sed·ed, -sed·ing. 1** take the place of; cause to be set aside; displace. **2** fill the place of; replace. [< L *supersedere* be superior to, refrain from < *super–* above + *sedere* sit] —**su´per·sed´ence,** *n.* —**su´per·sed´er,** *n.*

su·per·sen·si·tive (sü´pər sen´sə tiv), *adj.* extremely or morbidly sensitive. —**su´per·sen´si·tive·ly,** *adv.* —**su´per·sen´si·tive·ness,** *n.*

su·per·son·ic (sü´pər son´ik), *adj.* **1** of or pertaining to sound waves beyond the limit of human audibility (above frequencies of 20,000 cycles per second). **2** greater than the speed of sound in air (1087 feet per second). **3** capable of moving at a speed greater than the speed of sound.

su·per·star (sü´pər stär´), *n.* **1** extraordinarily successful actor, athlete, etc., far more successful than others in his or her field. **2** exceedingly large star or celestial body.

su·per·sti·tion (sü´pər stish´ən), *n.* **1** an unreasoning fear of what is unknown or mysterious; unreasoning expectation. **2** belief or practice founded on ignorant fear or mistaken reverence. **3** any blindly accepted and unreasonable belief. [< L *superstitio* < *super* above + *stare* stand]

su·per·sti·tious (sü´pər stish´əs), *adj.* full of superstition; likely to believe superstitions; caused by or pertaining to superstition. —**su´per·sti´tious·ness,** *n.*

su·per·struc·ture (sü´pər struk´chər), *n.* **1** structure built on something else. **2** all of a building above the foundation. **3** parts of a ship above the main deck. —**su´per·struc´tur·al,** *adj.*

su·per·tax (sü´pər taks´), *n.* tax in addition to a normal tax.

su·per·vene (sü´pər vēn´), *v.,* **-vened, -ven·ing.** come as something additional or interrupting. [< L, < *super–* upon + *venire* come] —**su´per·ven´tion** *n.*

su·per·vise (sü´pər vīz), *v.,* **-vised, -vis·ing.** look after and direct (work or workers, a process, etc.); oversee; superintend. [< Med.L *supervisus* < L *super–* over + *videre* see] —**su´per·vi´sor,** *n.* —**su´per·vi´so·ry,** *adj.*

su·per·vi·sion (sü´pər vizh´ən), *n.* management; direction; oversight.

su·pine (sü pīn´), *adj.* **1** lying flat on the back. **2** lazily inactive; listless. [< L *supinus*] —**su·pine´ly,** *adv.* —**su·pine´ness,** *n.*

supp., suppl., supplement.

sup·per (sup´ər), *n.* the evening meal; meal eaten early in the evening if dinner is near noon, or late in the evening if dinner is at six or later. [< OF *soper,* orig. inf., SUP¹] —**sup´per·less,** *adj.*

sup·plant (sə plant´; –plänt´), *v.* **1** take the place of; displace or set aside. **2** take the place of by unfair methods or by treacherous means. [< L *supplantare* trip up < *sub–* under + *planta* sole of the foot] —**sup´plan·ta´tion,** *n.* —**sup·plant´er,** *n.*

sup·ple (sup´əl), *adj.,* **-pler, -plest. 1** bending easily: *supple leather.* **2** readily adaptable to different ideas, circumstances, people, etc.; yielding: *a supple mind.* **3** limber; lithe: *supple movements.* [< OF < L *supplex* submissive] —**sup´ple·ly,** *adv.*

sup·ple·ment (*n.* sup´lə mənt; *v.* sup´-lə ment), *n.* something added to complete a thing, or to make it larger or better. —*v.* supply what is lacking in; add to; complete. [< L *supplementum,* ult. < *sub–* up + *-plere* fill] —**sup´ple·ment´er,** *n.*

sup·ple·men·ta·tion (sup´lə men tā´-shən), *n.* **1** act of supplementing. **2** something supplementary; addition.

sup·ple·men·ta·ry (sup´lə men´tə ri; –tri), **sup·ple·men·tal** (–men´təl), *adj.* **1** additional. **2** added to supply what is lacking. **3** of or pertaining to the relationship of two angles whose sum is 180 degrees. —**sup´ple·men´ta·ri·ly,** *adv.*

sup·pli·ant (sup´li ənt), *adj.* asking humbly and earnestly: *a suppliant prayer for help.* —*n.* person who asks humbly and earnestly. [< F, ppr. of *supplier* SUPPLI-CATE] —**sup´pli·ant·ly,** *adv.*

sup·pli·cant (sup´lə kənt), *n., adj.* suppliant. [< L *supplicans,* ppr. of *supplicare* SUPPLICATE]

sup·pli·cate (sup´lə kāt), *v.,* **-cat·ed, -cat·ing. 1** beg humbly and earnestly. **2** pray humbly. [< L *supplicatus* < *sub–* down + *plicare* bend] —**sup´pli·cat´ing·ly,** *adv.* —**sup´pli·ca´tion,** *n.* —**sup´pli·ca´tor,** *n.*

sup·ply (sə plī´), *v.,* **-plied, -ply·ing,** *n., pl.* **-plies.** —*v.* **1** furnish; provide: *supply a person with money, clothing, etc.* **2** make up for; satisfy, fill: *a stump supplied the place of a chair.* —*n.* **1** quantity ready for use; stock; store: *a supply of pencils and erasers, a supply of coffee.*

supplies, any necessary material things. Supplies for an army include food, clothing, medicines, etc. [< OF < L, *sub–* up + *-plere* fill] —**sup·pli´er,** *n.*

sup·ply-side economics (sə plī´sīd´), economic theory based on the premise that by lowering taxes on individuals and businesses, economic activity will be stimulated and prosperity will increase. —**sup·ply′-sid′er**, *n.*

sup·port (sə pôrt′; –pōrt′), *v.* **1** keep from falling; hold up: *walls support the roof.* **2** give strength or courage to; keep up; help: *support one's endeavors.* **3** provide shelter, clothing, etc. for: *parents support their family.* **4** be in favor of; back; second: *he supports the President.* **5** advocate or uphold (a theory, etc.): *support socialism.* **6** help prove; bear out: *the facts support his claim.* **7** act with (a leading actor); assist; attend. —*n.* **1** act of supporting; condition of being supported; help; aid: *he needs our support.* **2** maintenance: *support of a family.* **3** person or thing that supports; prop. [< OF < L *supportare* bring up < *sub–* up + *portare* carry] —**sup·port′er**, *n.* —**sup·port′ing·ly**, *adv.*

sup·port·a·ble (sə pôr′tə bəl; –pōr′–), *adj.* capable of being supported; bearable or endurable; sustainable; maintainable. —**sup·port′a·bil′i·ty**, *n.* —**sup·port′a·bly**, *adv.*

sup·pose (sə pōz′), *v.,* –**posed, –pos·ing. 1** assume (something); consider as a possibility: *suppose we wait until tomorrow.* **2** believe; think; presume: *what do you suppose he'll do?, I supposed that you had gone, an invention supposes an inventor.* [< OF, < *sub–* under + *poser* POSE] —**sup·pos′a·ble**, *adj.* —**sup·pos′a·bly**, *adv.* —**sup·pos′er**, *n.*

sup·posed (sə pōzd′), *adj.* accepted as true; considered as possible or probable; assumed. —**sup·pos′ed·ly**, *adv.*

sup·pos·ing (sə pōz′ing), *conj.* in the event that; if: *supposing it rains, shall we go?*

sup·po·si·tion (sup′ə zish′ən), *n.* **1** act of supposing. **2** thing supposed; belief; opinion. —**sup′po·si′tion·al**, *adj.* —**sup′po·si′tion·al·ly**, *adv.*

sup·press (sə pres′), *v.* **1** put an end to; stop by force; put down: *suppress a revolution.* **2** keep in; hold back; keep from appearing: *suppress a yawn, each nation suppressed news not favorable to it.* **3** check the flow of; stop: *suppress bleeding.* [< L *suppressus* < *sub–* down + *premere* press] —**sup·press′er, sup·pres′sor**, *n.* —**sup·press′i·ble**, *adj.* —**sup·press′ive**, *adj.*

sup·pres·sion (sə presh′ən), *n.* **1** a putting down by force or authority; putting an end to: *the suppression of the revolt.* **2** a keeping in; holding back: *suppression of a fear.*

sup·pu·rate (sup′yə rāt), *v.,* –**rat·ed, –rat·ing.** form pus; discharge pus; fester. [< L *suppuratus* < *sub–* under + *pus* pus] —**sup′pu·ra′tion**, *n.* —**sup′pu·ra′tive**, *adj.*

su·pra·re·nal (sü′prə rē′nəl), *adj.* **1** =adrenal. **2** pertaining to or connected with a suprarenal. —*n.* a ductless gland, situated on or near the kidney, that secretes adrenalin and other hormones. [< *supra–* above (< L) + L *renes* kidneys]

su·prem·a·cy (sə prem′ə si; sù–), *n.* **1** state of being supreme. **2** supreme authority or power.

su·preme (sə prēm′; sù–), *adj.* **1** highest in rank or authority: *the supreme commander.* **2** highest in degree; greatest; utmost: *supreme disgust.* **3** highest in quality: *supreme courage.* **4** last: *the supreme moment.* [< L *supremus,* ult. < *super* above] —**su·preme′ly**, *adv.* —**su·preme′ness**, *n.*

Supreme Being, God.

Supreme Court, 1 a the highest court in the United States. It consists of a chief justice and eight associate justices. **b** the highest court in some states. **2** a similar court in other countries.

Supt., supt., superintendent.

sur·charge (*n.* sèr′chärj′; *v.* sèr chärj′), *n., v.,* –**charged, –charg·ing.** —*n.* an extra charge. —*v.* **1** charge extra. **2** overcharge. [< OF, < *sur–* over (< L *super–*) + *charg(i)er* CHARGE] —**sur·charg′er**, *n.*

sur·cin·gle (sèr′sing gəl), *n.* a strap or belt around a horse's body to keep a saddle, blanket, or pack in place. [< OF, < *sur–* over (< L *super–*) + *cengle* girdle < L *cingula*]

sur·coat (sèr′kōt′), *n.* an outer coat, esp. a garment worn by knights over their armor. [< OF, < *sur–* over (< L *super–*) + *cote* COAT]

surd (sèrd), *n.* quantity that cannot be expressed in whole numbers. *Example:* $\sqrt{2}$. —*adj.* that cannot be expressed in whole numbers. [< L *surdus* unheard]

sure (shùr), *adj.,* **sur·er, sur·est,** *adv.* —*adj.* **1** free from doubt; certain; convinced: *sure of a person's guilt, he is sure to come.* **2** to be trusted; reliable; unfailing; unerring: *sure aim, a sure messenger.* **3** firm or stable: *stand on sure ground.* —*adv.* surely; certainly.

be sure, be careful; do not fail.

for sure, surely; certainly.

make sure, a act so as to make something certain. **b** get sure knowledge.

to be sure, surely; certainly. [< OF < L *securus.* Doublet of SECURE.] —**sure′ness**, *n.*

sure·foot·ed (shür′füt′id), *adj.* not liable to stumble, slip, or fall. —**sure′-foot′ed·ness**, *n.*

sure·ly (shùr′li), *adv.* **1** undoubtedly; certainly: *half a loaf is surely better than none.* **2** without mistake; without missing, slipping, etc.; firmly: *the goat leaped surely from rock to rock.* **3** without fail: *slowly but surely.*

sure·ty (shùr′ə ti), *n., pl.* –**ties. 1** security against loss, damage, or failure to do something: *an insurance company gives surety.* **2** person who agrees to be responsible for another. —**sur′e·ty·ship**, *n.*

surf (sèrf), *n.* waves or swell of the sea breaking on the shore or upon shoals, reefs, etc. —*v.* **1** ride the waves on a surfboard. **2 a** switch from channel to channel on television to see what

programs are available. **b** search the Internet without looking for anything in particular.

sur·face (sèr′fis), *n., adj., v.,* –**faced, –fac·ing.** —*n.* **1** the outside of anything: *the surface of a golf ball, the surface of a mountain.* **2** any face or side of a thing: *a cube has six surfaces.* **3** that which has length and breadth but no thickness: *a plane surface in geometry.* **4** extent or area of outer face. **5** the outward appearance, esp. as distinguished from the inner nature: *he is very kind below the surface.* —*adj.* **1** of or on the surface; pertaining to the surface. **2** apparent rather than real; superficial: *surface manners.* —*v.* put a surface on; make smooth: *surface a road.* [< MF, < *sur–* above (< L *super–*) + *face* FACE] —**sur′fac·er**, *n.*

sur·face-to-air (sèr′fis tü ār′), *adj.* **1** launched from the ground or a ship to intercept and destroy a flying aircraft or missile. **2** of a rescue, lifted from the ground, water, or a ship to a waiting aircraft.

sur·face-to-sur·face (sèr′fis tü sèr′fis), *adj.* launched from the ground or a ship to destroy a target on the ground.

surface tension, tension of the surface film of a liquid that reduces the area of the film.

surf·board (sèrf′bôrd′; –bōrd′), *n.* a long, narrow board for riding the surf. —**surf′board′er, surf′board′ing**, *n.*

surf·boat (sèrf′bōt′), *n.* a strong boat specially made for use in heavy surf. —**surf′boat′man**, *n.*

sur·feit (sèr′fit), *n.* **1** too much; excess, esp. in eating or drinking. **2** disgust caused by excess or satiety. —*v.* overfeed; satiate. [< OF *surfait,* orig. pp., overdone < *sur–* above (< L *super–*) + *faire* do < L *facere*]

surg., surgery; surgical.

surge (sèrj), *v.,* **surged, surg·ing**, *n.* —*v.* **1** rise and fall; move like waves: *the crowd surged through the streets.* **2** increase suddenly; rush: *blood surged to his face.* —*n.* **1** a swelling wave; sweep or rush of waves; something like a wave: *a surge of anger.* **2** the swelling and rolling of the sea. **3** a sudden rush of electrical current; violent oscillation. [ult. (prob. through OF) < L *surgere* rise] —**surg′y**, *adj.*

sur·geon (sèr′jən), *n.* doctor who performs operations. [< AF *surgien,* OF *cirurgien* < *cirurgie* SURGERY]

sur·ger·y (sèr′jər i), *n., pl.* –**ger·ies. 1** the art and science of treating diseases, injuries, etc., by operations and instruments. Malaria can be cured by medicine, but a ruptured appendix requires surgery. **2** office, laboratory, or operating room of a surgeon. [< OF *surgerie, cirurgerie,* < *cirurgie* < L < Gk. *cheirourgia,* ult. < *cheir* hand + *ergon* work]

sur·gi·cal (sèr′jə kəl), *adj.* **1** of or having to do with surgery. **2** used in surgery. **3** performed by a surgeon. **4** *Fig.* done with great precision: *surgical strike.* —**sur′gi·cal·ly,** *adv.*

Su·ri·name (sŭr′ə nam), *n.* country in the N part of South America.

Su·ri·nam·ese (sŭr′ə nam′ēz), *n.* Also, **Surinamer.** person born or living in Suriname. —*adj.* of Suriname or its people.

sur·ly (sėr′li,), *adj.,* **-li·er, -li·est.** bad-tempered and unfriendly; rude; gruff. [ult. < *sir,* in sense of "lord"] —**sur′li·ly,** *adv.* —**sur′li·ness,** *n.*

sur·mise (*v.* sər mīz′; *n.* sər mīz′, sėr′mīz), *v.,* **-mised, -mis·ing,** *n.* —*v.* form a conjecture (regarding); guess. —*n.* **1** a mental conception; conjecture. **2** a matter of conjecture. [< OF, accusation, ult. < *sur-* upon (< L *super-*) + *mettre* put < L *mittere* send] —**sur·mis′er,** *n.*

sur·mount (sər mount′), *v.* **1** rise above. **2** be above or on top of: *the peak surmounts the valley.* **3** go up and across: *surmount a hill.* **4** overcome: *he surmounted many difficulties.* [< OF, < *sur-* over (< L *super-*) + *monter* MOUNT¹] —**sur·mount′a·ble,** *adj.*

sur·name (sėr′nām′), *n., v.,* **-named, -nam·ing.** —*n.* **1** a last name; family name. **2** name added to a person's real name. William I of England had the surname "the Conqueror." —*v.* give an added name to; call by a surname. [< F, < *sur-* over (< L *super-*) + *nom* name < L *nomen;* infl. by E *name*]

sur·pass (sər pas′; -päs′), *v.* **1** do better than; be greater than; excel: *his work surpassed expectations.* **2** be too much or too great for; go beyond; exceed: *the horrors of the battlefield surpassed description.* [< F, < *sur-* beyond + *passer* pass] —**sur·pass′a·ble,** *adj.* —**sur·pass′er,** *n.* —**sur·pass′ing·ly,** *adv.*

sur·plice (sėr′plis), *n.* a broad-sleeved, white gown worn by clergymen and choir singers over their other clothes. [< OF, < *sur-* over (< L *super-*) + *pelice* fur garment, ult. < L *pellis* hide]

sur·plus (sėr′pləs; -plus), *n.* amount over and above what is needed; extra quantity left over; excess. —*adj.* more than is needed; excess: *surplus wheat and cotton are shipped abroad.* [< OF, < *sur-* over (< L *super-*) + *plus* PLUS]

sur·prise (sər prīz′; sə-), *n., v.,* **-prised, -pris·ing,** *adj.* —*n.* **1** a feeling caused by something unexpected. **2** something unexpected. **3** a catching unprepared; coming upon suddenly. —*v.* **1** cause to feel surprised; astonish: *the magician's trick surprised me.* **2** catch unprepared; come upon suddenly: *the enemy surprised the fort.* **3** lead or bring (a person, etc.) unawares: *the news surprised her into tears.* —*adj.* that is not expected; surprising: *a surprise party, a surprise visit.*

take by surprise, a catch unprepared; come on suddenly and unexpectedly. **b** astonish. [< OF, < *sur-* over (< L *super-*) + *prendre* take < L *prehendere*] —**sur·pris′al,** *n.* —**sur·pris′ed·ly,** *adv.* —**sur·pris′er,** *n.*

sur·pris·ing (sər prīz′ing; sə-), *adj.* causing surprise. —**sur·pris′ing·ly,** *adv.*

sur·re·al (sə rē′əl), *adj.* outside the bounds of reality; odd in the extreme.

sur·re·al·ism (sə rē′əl iz əm), *n.* a modern movement in painting, sculpture, literature, etc., that tries to show what takes place in dreams or the subconscious mind. —**sur·re′al·ist,** *n., adj.* —**sur·re′al·is′tic,** *adj.* —**sur·re′al·is′ti·cal·ly,** *adv.*

sur·ren·der (sə ren′dər), *v.* give up; give (oneself or itself) up; yield: *the captain had to surrender to the enemy, surrender oneself to grief.* —*n.* act of surrendering. [< OF *sur-* over (< L *super-*) + *rendre* RENDER] —**sur·ren′der·er,** *n.*

sur·rep·ti·tious (sėr′əp tish′əs), *adj.* **1** stealthy; secret. **2** secret and unauthorized. [< L *surrepticius,* ult. < *sub-* secretly + *rapere* snatch] —**sur′rep·ti′tious·ly,** *adv.* —**sur′rep·ti′tious·ness,** *n.*

sur·rey (sėr′i) , *n., pl.* **-reys.** a light, four-wheeled carriage having two seats. [after *Surrey,* England]

sur·ro·gate (*n.* sėr′ə gāt, -git; *v.* sėr′ə gāt), *n., v.,* **-gat·ed, gat·ing.** —*n.* **1** a substitute; deputy, esp. the deputy of a bishop. **2** Also **surrogate mother.** woman who carries in her womb another woman's embryo. **3** in certain states, a judge having charge of the probate of wills, the administration of estates, etc. —*v.* put into the place of another; substitute for another. [< L *surrogatus* substituted < *sub-* instead + *rogare* ask for] —**sur′ro·gate·ship′,** *n.*

sur·round (sə round′), *v.* **1** shut in on all sides; extend around: *a high fence surrounds the field.* **2** encircle: *they surrounded the invalid with every comfort.* —*n.* something that surrounds, as a border or frame. [< AF *surounder* surpass < LL *superundare* overflow < L *super-* over + *unda* wave; infl. in meaning by *round*] —**sur·round′er,** *n.*

sur·round·ing (sə roun′ding), *n.* that which surrounds. —*adj.* enclosing; surrounding; enveloping.

surroundings, surrounding things, conditions, etc.

sur·tax (sėr′taks′), *n.* an additional or extra tax. [< F *surtaxe* < *sur-* over + *taxe* tax]

sur·veil·lance (sər vāl′əns; -yəns), *n.* **1** watch kept over a person: *the police kept the criminal under strict surveillance.* **2** supervision.

sur·veille (sər vāl′), *v.,* **-veilled, -veil·ling.** keep under surveillance; watch: *surveille a crowd.* [< F, < *sur-* over (< L *super-*) + *veiller* watch < L *vigilare*] —**sur·veil′lant,** *adj.*

sur·vey (*v.* sər vā′; *n.* sėr′vā, sər vā′), *v., n., pl.* **-veys.** —*v.* **1** look over; view; examine: *survey a field of study.* **2** measure for size, shape, position, boundaries, etc.: *men are surveying the land before it is divided into house lots.* —*n.* **1** a general look; view. **2** a formal examination or inspection. **3** a written statement or description of this. **4** map, plan, or description of land measurement. [< AF *surveier,* ult. < L *super-* over + *videre* see] —**sur·vey′a·ble,** *adj.*

sur·vey·ing (sər vā′ing), *n.* **1** business or act of making surveys of land. **2** mathematical instruction in the principles and art of making surveys.

sur·vey·or (sər vā′ər), *n.* person who surveys, esp. land.

surveyor's measure, system of measuring used by surveyors. The unit is usually a chain 66 ft. long with links 7.92 in. long. 100,000 square links = 1 square acre.

sur·viv·al (sər vīv′əl), *n.* **1** act or fact of surviving; continuance of life; living or lasting longer than others. **2** person, thing, custom, belief, etc., that has lasted from an earlier time.

sur·vive (sər vīv′), *v.,* **-vived, -viv·ing. 1** live longer than; remain alive after: *he survived his wife by three years; survive an accident.* **2** exist longer than: *the crops survived the drought.* **3** continue to exist; remain: *books have survived from the time of the Egyptians.* [< AF, < *sur-* over (< L *super-*) + *vivre* live < L *vivere*] —**sur·viv′ing,** *adj.* —**sur·vi′vor,** *n.*

sus·cep·ti·bil·i·ty (sə sep′tə bil′ə ti), *n., pl.* **-ties.** quality or state of being susceptible; readiness to receive impressions; sensitiveness.

susceptibilities, sensitive feelings.

sus·cep·ti·ble (sə sep′tə bəl), *adj.* **1** easily influenced by feelings or emotions; very sensitive: *a susceptible heart.*

susceptible of, a capable of receiving or undergoing: *oak is susceptible of a high polish.* **b** sensitive to.

susceptible to, easily affected by; liable to; open to: *vain people are susceptible to flattery.* [< LL *susceptibilis,* ult. < L *sub-* up + *capere* take] —**sus·cep′ti·ble·ness,** *n.* —**sus·cep′ti·bly,** *adv.*

su·shi (sü′ shi), *n.* Japanese and Hawaiian dish of raw fish and rice, formed into decorative rolls or balls. [< Jap.]

sus·pect (*v.* səs pekt′; *n.* sus′pekt; *adj.* sus′pekt, səs pekt′), *v.* **1** imagine to be so; think likely: *the old fox suspected danger.* **2** believe guilty, false, bad, etc., without proof: *the policeman suspected the thief of lying.* **3** feel no confidence in; doubt: *the judge suspected the truth of the thief's excuse.* —*n.* person suspected. —*adj.* open to suspicion; suspected. [< L, < *sub-* under + *specere* look] —**sus·pect′a·ble,** *adj.* —**sus·pect′er,** *n.*

sus·pend (səs pend′), *v.* **1** hang down by attaching to something above: *the lamp was suspended from the ceiling.* **2** hold in place as if by hanging: *smoke suspended in still air.* **3** stop for a while: *suspend work.* **4** remove or exclude for a while from some privilege or job: *he was suspended for bad conduct.* **5** refrain from concluding definitely; keep undecided; put off: *the court suspended judgment till next Monday.* [< L, < *sub–* up + *pendere* hang]

sus·pend·ers (səs pen′dərz), *n. pl.* straps worn over the shoulders to hold up trousers.

sus·pense (səs pens′), *n.* **1** condition of being uncertain: *the detective story kept me in suspense until the last chapter.* **2** anxious uncertainty; anxiety: *mothers feel suspense when their children are very sick.* **3** condition of being undecided: *the matter hung in suspense for a few days.* [< OF (*en*) *suspens* (in) abeyance, ult. < L *suspendere* SUSPEND] —**sus·pense′ful,** *adj.*

sus·pen·sion (səs pen′shən), *n.* **1** a suspending or being suspended. **2** support on which something is suspended. **3** a temporary abolishment or setting aside of a law, rule, etc. **4** arrangement of springs for supporting the body of an automobile, railroad car, etc. **5 a** mixture in which very small particles of a solid remain suspended without dissolving. **b** the condition of the solid in such a mixture. **c** a solid in such condition.

suspension bridge, bridge hung on cables or chains between towers.

sus·pen·so·ry (səs pen′sə ri), *adj.* **1** holding up; supporting: *a suspensory muscle.* **2** stopping for a while; leaving undecided.

sus·pi·cion (səs pish′ən), *n.* **1** state of mind of a person who suspects; suspecting: *the real thief tried to turn suspicion toward others.* **2** condition of being suspected: *they are above suspicion.* **3** a very small amount; notion; suggestion: *a suspicion it was true, she spoke with a suspicion of spite.*

on suspicion, because of being suspected.

under suspicion, suspected. [< L. See SUSPECT.]

sus·pi·cious (səs pish′əs), *adj.* **1** causing one to suspect: *a man was hanging about the house in a suspicious manner.* **2** feeling suspicion; suspecting: *our dog is suspicious of strangers.* **3** showing suspicion: *the dog gave a suspicious sniff at my leg.* —**sus·pi′cious·ly,** *adv.* —**sus·pi′cious·ness,** *n.*

suss (sus), *v.,* **sussed, sus·sing.** *Informal.* Usually, **suss out.** deduce; figure out; understand. [? < *suspect*]

sus·tain (səs tān′), *v.* **1** keep up; keep going: *hope sustains him in his misery.* **2** supply with food, provisions, etc.: *sustain an army.* **3** hold up; support: *arches sustain the weight of the roof.* **4** bear; endure: *the sea wall sustains the shock of the waves, sustain a great loss.* **5** allow; admit; favor: *the court sustained his suit.* [< OF < L, < *sub–* up + *tenere* hold] —**sus·tain′a·ble,** *adj.* —**sus·tain′ed·ly,** *adv.* —**sus·tain′er,** *n.* —**sus·tain′ment,** *n.*

sus·te·nance (sus′tə nəns), *n.* **1** food. **2** means of living; support.

sut·ler (sut′lər), *n.* person who follows an army and sells provisions, etc., to the soldiers. [< earlier Du. *soeteler* < *soetelen* ply a low trade]

sut·tee (su tē′; sut′ē), *n.* Hindu widow who throws herself on the burning funeral pile of her husband. [< Hind. < Skt. *satī* faithful wife]

su·ture (sü′chər), *n., v.,* **-tured, -tur·ing.** —*n.* **1** seam formed in sewing up a wound or joining two parts, as of a nerve or vein. **2** method of doing this. **3 a** one of the stitches or fastenings used. **b** material used as sutures. **4** a sewing together or a joining as if by sewing. —*v.* unite by suture or as if by a suture. [< L, < *suere* sew] —**su′tur·al,** *adj.*

SUV, sports utility vehicle (truck designed as a family car).

su·ze·rain (sü′zə rin; –rān), *n.* **1** a feudal lord. **2** state or government exercising political control over a dependent state. [< F, < *sus* above (< L *sursum* upward), modeled on *souverain* sovereign]

su·ze·rain·ty (sü′zə rin ti; –rān′–), *n., pl.* **-ties.** position or authority or a suzerain.

s.v., under the word or heading. [< L *sub verbo* or *sub voce*]

svelte (svelt), *adj.* slender; lithe. [< F]

SW, S.W., s.w., southwest; southwestern.

Sw., **1** Sweden. **2** Swedish.

swab (swob), *n., v.,* **swabbed, swab·bing.** —*n.* **1** a mop for cleaning decks, floors, etc. **2** a bit of sponge, cloth, or cotton for cleansing some part of the body or for applying medicine to it. —*v.* clean with a swab; apply a swab to: *swab a person's throat.* [< *swabber,* < Du. *zwabber* < *zwabben* swab] —**swab′ber,** *n.*

swad·dle (swod′əl), *v.,* **-dled, -dling.** *n.* —*v.* bind (a baby) with long, narrow strips of cloth; wrap tightly with clothes, bandages, etc. —*n.* cloth used for swaddling. [OE *swæthel* band(age); akin to SWATHE]

swaddling clothes, long, narrow strips of cloth for wrapping a newborn infant.

swag (swag), *n.* **1** *Informal.* things stolen; loot; plunder. **2** *Australian.* bundle of personal belongings. [prob. < Scand. (dial. Norw.) *svagga* sway]

swag·ger (swag′ər), *v.* **1** walk with a bold, rude, or superior air; strut about or show off in a vain or insolent way. **2** bluster; affect by bluster; bluff. —*n.* a swaggering way of walking or acting. [< *swag*] —**swag′ger·er,** *n.* —**swag′ger·ing·ly,** *adv.*

swain (swān), *n. Archaic or Poetic.* **1** lover. **2** a young man who lives in the country. [< Scand. *sveinn* boy]

swal·low¹ (swol′ō), *v.* **1** take into the stomach through the throat: *swallow food.* **2** *Fig.* take in; absorb: *the waves swallowed up the boat.* **3** *Fig.* believe too easily; accept without question or suspicion: *he will swallow any story.* **4** *Fig.*

take meekly; accept without resisting: *swallow the insult.* **5** *Fig.* take or keep back: *swallow words said in anger, she swallowed her displeasure and smiled.* —*n.* **1** a swallowing: *he took the medicine at one swallowing.* **2** amount swallowed at one time. [< OE *swelgan*] —**swal′low·a·ble,** *adj.* —**swal′low·er,** *n.*

swal·low² (swol′ō), *n.* **1** a small, swift-flying bird with a deeply forked tail, noted for the extent and regularity of its migratory movements. **2** a martin or other bird of the same family as the swallow. **3** any of certain swifts that resemble swallows. [OE *swealwe*] —**swal′low·like′,** *adj.*

swal·low·tail (swol′ō tāl′), *n.* **1** thing shaped like or suggesting the deeply forked tail of a swallow. **2** =swallow-tailed coat. —**swal′low·tailed′,** *adj.*

swallow-tailed coat, a man's coat with tails, worn at formal occasions.

swam (swam), *v.* pt. of swim.

swa·mi (swä′mi), *n., pl.* **-mis.** title of a Hindu religious teacher. [< Hind., master, < Skt. *svāmin*]

swamp (swomp; swômp), *n.* wet, soft land. —*v.* **1** plunge or sink in a swamp or in water. **2** fill with water and sink: *their boat swamped, the wave swamped the boat.* **3** overwhelm or be overwhelmed as by a flood; make or become helpless. [akin to SUMP] —**swamp′ish,** *adj.* —**swamp′less,** *adj.* —**swamp′y,** *adj.*

swamp·land (swomp′land′; swômp′–), *n.* tract of land covered by swamps.

swan (swon; swôn), *n.* a large, graceful water bird with a long, slender, curving neck, and in most species a pure white plumage in the adult. [OE] —**swan′like′,** *adj.*

swan dive, a graceful dive in which the legs are held straight from the toes to the hips, the back is curved, and the arms are spread like the wings of a gliding bird.

swang (swang), *v. Archaic and Dial.* pt. of swing.

swank·y (swang′ki), stylish; smart; dashing. [cf. OE *swancor* lithe] —**swank′i·ly,** *adv.* —**swank′i·ness,** *n.*

swan's-down, swans·down (swonz′-doun′; swônz′–), *n.* the soft down of a swan, used for trimming, powder puffs, etc.

swan song, 1 song which a dying swan is supposed to sing. **2** a person's last piece of work.

swap (swop), *v.,* **swapped, swap·ping,** exchange; barter; trade. —*n.* an exchange or trade. —**swap′per,** *n.*

sward (swôrd), *n.* a grassy surface; turf. [OE *sweard* skin] —**sward′y,** *adj.*

swarm (swôrm), *n.* **1** group of bees that leave a hive and fly off together to start a new colony. **2** group of bees settled together in a hive. **3** a large group of insects flying or moving about together. **4** *Fig.* group of persons or things moving about in a confused mass; crowd.

—v. 1 of bees, fly off together to start a new colony. 2 fly or move about in great numbers; be in very great numbers. 3 be crowded: *the swamp swarms with mosquitoes.* [OE *swearm*] —**swarm′er**, *n.*

swarth·y (swôr′thi; –thi), *adj.*, **swarth·i·er**, **swarth·i·est.** dark-colored or having a dark skin. [earlier *swarfy* < *swarf* grit, OE *geswearf*] —**swarth′i·ly**, *adv.* —**swarth′i·ness**, *n.*

swash (swosh), *v.* dash (water, etc.) about; splash. —*n.* such action or sound. [prob. imit.] —**swash′er**, *n.* —**swash′ing·ly**, *adv.*

swash·buck·le (swosh′buk′əl), *v.*, **–led**, **–ling.** swagger; bully. —**swash′buck′-ling**, *n.*, *adj.*

swash·buck·ler (swosh′buk′lər), *n.* a swaggering swordsman, bully, or boaster. [< *swash* + *buckler*]

swas·ti·ka (swos′tə kə), *n.* an ancient symbol or ornament consisting of a cross with arms of equal length, each arm having a continuation at right angles, and all four continuations turning the same way. [< Skt., < *svasti* luck < *su* well + *as* be]

swat (swot), *v.*, **swat·ted**, **swat·ting**, —*v.* hit with a smart or violent blow. —*n.* a smart or violent blow. —**swat′ter**, *n.*

swatch (swoch), *n.* sample of cloth or other material.

swath (swoth; swôth), *n.* 1 the space covered by a single cut of a scythe or by one cut of a mowing machine. 2 row of grass, grain, etc., cut by a scythe or mowing machine. 3 a strip. **cut a wide swath**, make a showy display; splurge. [OE *swæth* track, trace]

swathe¹ (swāth), *v.*, **swathed**, **swath·ing**, *n.* —*v.* 1 wrap up closely or fully. 2 bind; wrap; bandage. 3 envelop or surround like a wrapping. —*n.* a wrapping; bandage. [OE *swathian*]

swathe² (swāth), *n.* =swath.

sway (swā), *v.* 1 swing back and forth; swing from side to side, or to one side: *the tree sways in the wind.* 2 move to one side; turn aside; change in opinion, feeling, etc.: *nothing could sway his political beliefs.* 3 incline to one side; lean. 4 influence; control; rule. —*n.* 1 a swaying. 2 influence; control; rule. [< Scand. *sveigja*] —**sway′er**, *n.* —**sway′ingly**, *adv.*

sway·back (swā′bak′), *n.* hollow or sag of the back. —*adj.* sway-backed.

sway-backed (swā′bakt′), *adj.* 1 of horses, etc., strained in the back by overwork or the like. 2 having the back sagged or hollowed to an unusual degree.

Swa·zi·land (swä′zē land′), *n.* country in SE Africa. —**Swa′zi**, *adj.*, *n.*

swear (swār), *v.*, **swore** or (*Archaic*) **sware**, **sworn**, **swear·ing**. 1 make a solemn statement, appealing to God or some other sacred being or object for confirmation; take oath. 2 bind by an oath; require to promise: *members of the club were sworn to secrecy.* 3 promise

solemnly; vow. 4 use profane language; curse.

swear by, a name as one's witness in taking an oath. **b** have great confidence in.

swear in, admit to office or service by giving an oath: *swear in a witness.*

swear off, promise to give up. [OE *swerian*] —**swear′er**, *n.*

sweat (swet), *n.*, *v.*, **sweat** or **sweat·ed**, **sweat·ing.** —*n.* 1 moisture coming through the pores of the skin. 2 fit or condition of sweating: *he was in a cold sweat from fear.* 3 moisture given out by something or gathered on its surface. —*v.* 1 give out moisture through the pores of the skin. 2 give out moisture; collect moisture from the air: *a pitcher of ice water sweats on a hot day.* 3 suffer from anxiety, impatience, etc. 4 cause to work hard and under bad conditions: *that employer sweats his workers.* 5 *Slang.* subject (a person) to a brutal or unfair questioning, etc., in order to extract information. 6 heat (solder) till it melts; joint (metal parts) by heating.

no sweat, *Informal.* not difficult; not troublesome.

sweat it out, *Informal. Fig.* await anxiously the outcome of something. [OE *swætan*] —**sweat′less**, *adj.* —**sweat′y**, *adj.* —**sweat′i·ly**, *adv.* —**sweat′i·ness**, *n.*

sweat·er (swet′ər), *n.* a knitted outer garment, usually of wool.

sweat gland, a small gland, just under the skin, that secretes sweat.

sweat pants, loose pants made of soft, absorbent fabric, gathered at the ankle, worn by athletes and as casual clothing.

sweats (swets), *n. Informal.* sweat pants or sweat shirt.

sweat shirt, loose shirt that is pulled on over the head, made of soft, absorbent fabric, and worn by athletes and as casual clothing.

sweat·shop (swet′shop′), *n.* place where workers are employed at low pay for long hours under bad conditions.

sweat suit, sweat shirt and sweat pants worn together for athletics or as casual wear.

Swede (swēd), *n.* native or inhabitant of Sweden.

Swe·den (swē′dən), *n.* country in N Europe, E and S of Norway.

Swed·ish (swēd′ish), *adj.*, of or pertaining to Sweden, its people, or their language. —*n.* 1 people of Sweden. 2 language of Sweden.

sweep (swēp), *v.*, **swept**, **sweep·ing**, *n.* —*v.* 1 clean or clear (a floor, etc.) with a broom, brush, etc.; use a broom or something like one to remove dirt; brush: *sweep the steps.* 2 *Fig.* move, drive, or take away with or as with a broom, brush, etc.: *the wind sweeps the snow into drifts.* 3 remove with a sweeping motion; carry along: *a flood swept away the bridge.* 4 trail upon: *her dress sweeps the ground.* 5 move swiftly; pass swiftly: *guerrillas swept down on the*

town. 6 move with dignity: *she swept out of the room.* 7 *Fig.* move or extend in a long course or curve: *the shore sweeps to the south for miles.* —*n.* 1 act of sweeping; clearing away; removing: *he made a clean sweep of all his debts.* 2 a steady, driving motion or swift onward course of something: *the sweep of the wind.* 3 a curve; bend: *the sweep of a road.* 4 *Fig.* a continuous extent; stretch: *a wide sweep of farming country, the mountain is beyond the sweep of your eye.* 5 person who sweeps chimneys, streets, etc. [OE (*ge*)*swēpa* sweepings] —**sweep′er**, *n.*

sweep·ing (swēp′ing), *adj.* 1 passing over a wide space: *a sweeping glance.* 2 having wide range: *a sweeping victory, a sweeping statement.* —*n.* **sweepings**, dust, rubbish, scraps, etc., swept out or up. —**sweep′ing·ly**, *adv.* —**sweep′ingness**, *n.*

sweep·stakes (swēp′stāks′), **sweep·stake** (–stāk′), *n.* 1 scheme for gambling on horse races, etc. People buy tickets, and the money they pay goes to the drawer or drawers of winning tickets. 2 the race or contest. 3 prize in such a race or contest.

sweet (swēt), *adj.* 1 having a taste like sugar or honey: *this pie is too sweet.* 2 having a pleasant taste or smell: *sweet flowers.* 3 pleasant; attractive; charming: *a sweet smile.* 4 fresh; not sour, salty, bitter, or spoiled: *sweet butter.* 5 of soil, good for farming. 6 dear; darling. —*n.* 1 something sweet. 2 a sweet dessert. 3 sweetheart. —*adv.* in a sweet manner.

be sweet on, be in love with.

sweets, a candy or other sweet things. **b** *Fig.* pleasant or agreeable things. [OE *swēte*] —**sweet′ish**, *adj.* —**sweet′ly**, *adv.* —**sweet′ness**, *n.*

sweet alyssum, a common low-growing plant with clusters of small white flowers.

sweet·bread (swēt′bred′), *n.* the pancreas or thymus of a calf, lamb, etc., used as meat.

sweet·bri·er, sweet·bri·ar (swēt′brī′ər), *n.* =eglantine.

sweet corn, a kind of corn that is eaten when it is soft. Sweet corn is sometimes called green corn.

sweet·en (swēt′ən), *v.* 1 make or become sweet. 2 make more rewarding or acceptable, as a contract or loan. —**sweet′en·er**, *n.*

sweet·en·ing (swēt′ən ing; swēt′ning), *n.* something that sweetens.

sweet flag, a water plant with long sword-shaped leaves and a pungent, aromatic rootstock.

sweet gum, 1 a North American tree with star-shaped leaves that turn scarlet in the fall. 2 balsam from this tree.

sweet·heart (swēt′härt′), *n.* a loved one; beloved; lover.

sweet·meats (swēt′mēts′), *n. pl.* 1 candy; candied fruits; sugar-covered nuts; bonbons. 2 preserves.

sweet pea, 1 an annual climbing plant with delicate, fragrant flowers of various colors. **2** the flower.

sweet pepper, 1 a mild-flavored species of pepper plant. **2** its fruit.

sweet potato, 1 a sweet, thick yellow or reddish root of a vine, used as a vegetable. **2** the vine that it grows on. **3** =ocarina.

sweet-tem·pered (swēt′tem′pərd), *adj.* having a gentle or pleasant nature.

sweet william or **William,** plant with dense, rounded clusters of small flowers, that belongs to the same family as the pink.

swell (swel), *v.,* **swelled, swelled** or **swollen, swell·ing,** *n., adj.* —*v.* **1** grow or make bigger: *bread dough swells as it rises, his head swelled where he bumped it.* **2** be larger or thicker in a particular place; stick out; cause to stick out: *a barrel swells in the middle.* **3** increase in amount, degree, force, etc.: *savings may swell into a fortune.* **4** rise in waves: *the waters swelled in the ocean.* **5** grow or make louder: *swell the chorus.* **6** *Fig.* become filled with an emotion: *swell with pride.* —*n.* **1** act of swelling; increase in amount, degree, force, etc. **2** condition of being swollen. **3** a long, unbroken wave or waves. **4** a swelling tone or sound. **5** device in an organ to control the volume of sound. —*adj.* excellent; first-rate. [OE *swellan*]

swelled head, self-importance; arrogant: *suffer from a swelled head.*

swell·ing (swel′ing), *n.* an increase in size; swollen part. —*adj.* that swells; increasing.

swel·ter (swel′tər), *v.* **1** suffer from heat. **2** perspire freely; sweat. —*n.* a sweltering condition. [ult. < OE *sweltan* die] —**swel′ter·ing,** *adj.* —**swel′ter·ing·ly,** *adv.*

swept (swept), *v.* pt. and pp. of **sweep.**

swept-back (swept′bak′), *adj.* (of the wings of an airplane) extending outward and sharply backward from the fuselage.

swerve (swėrv), *v.,* **swerved, swerv·ing,** *n.* —*v.* sharply turn aside. —*n.* a turning aside: *the swerve of the ball made it hard to hit.* [OE *sweorfan* rub, file] —**swerv′er,** *n.*

swift (swift), *adj.* **1** moving very fast: *a swift horse.* **2** coming or happening quickly: *a swift response.* **3** quick, rapid, or prompt to act, etc.: *swift to suspect.* —*adv.* in a swift manner. —*n.* a small bird with long wings, somewhat like a swallow. [OE] —**swift′ly,** *adv.*

swig (swig), *n., v.,* **swigged, swig·ging.** *Informal.* —*n.* a big drink. —*v.* drink heartily or greedily.

swill (swil), *n.* **1** kitchen refuse, esp. when partly liquid; garbage; slops. **2** a deep drink. **3** any liquid matter. [< v.] —*v.* drink greedily; drink too much. [OE *swilian*] —**swill′er,** *n.*

swim (swim), *v.,* **swam** or (*Archaic*) **swum, swum, swim·ming,** *n.* —*v.* **1** move along on or in the water by using arms, legs, fins, etc.: *fish swim.* **2** make swim: *he swam his horse across the stream.* **3** float: *swimming in gravy.* **4** be overflowed or flooded with: *her eyes were swimming with tears.* **5** be dizzy; whirl: *my head swims!* —*n.* act, time, motion, or distance of swimming.

the swim, the current of affairs, activities, etc. [OE *swimman*] —**swim′mer,** *n.*

swim·ming·ly (swim′ing li), *adv.* with great ease or success.

swin·dle (swin′dəl), *v.,* **-dled, -dling,** *n.* —*v.* **1** cheat; defraud: *honest merchants do not swindle their customers.* **2** get by fraud. —*n.* an act of swindling; cheat or fraud. [< *swindler*]

swin·dler (swin′dlər), *n.* person who cheats or defrauds. [< G *schwindler* < *schwindeln* be dizzy, act thoughtlessly, cheat]

swine (swīn), *n., pl.* **swine. 1** hogs; pigs. **2** a hog. **3** a coarse or beastly person. [OE *swīn*] —**swin′ish,** *adj.*

swine·herd (swīn′hėrd′), *n.* person who tends pigs or hogs.

swing (swing), *v.,* **swung** or (*Archaic and Dial.*) **swang, swung, swing·ing,** *n., adj.* —*v.* **1** move back and forth, esp. with a regular motion: *the hammock swings.* **2** turn on a hinge or as if on a hinge: *the door swings smoothly.* **3** move in a curve: *he swung the automobile around the corner, swing a bat.* **4** move with a free, swaying motion: *the soldiers came swinging down the street.* **5** hang: *swing a hammock between two trees.* **6** manage or influence successfully: *swing a business deal.* —*n.* **1** act or manner of swinging. **2** amount of swinging. **3** seat hung from ropes in which one may sit and swing. **4** shift or period of work. **5** a swinging blow. **6** freedom of movement. **7** Often, **swing music.** jazz dance music in which the players improvise freely on the original melody. —*adj.* of or pertaining to swing (def. 7) or its style.

in full swing, going on actively and completely; without restraint: *a summer vacation in full swing.* [OE *swingan* beat] —**swing′er,** *n.* —**swing′ing·ly,** *adv.*

swin·gle·tree (swing′gəl trē′), *n.* =whiffletree.

swipe (swīp), *n., v.,* **swiped, swip·ing.** —*n.* a sweeping stroke; hard blow. —*v.* **1** strike with a sweeping blow. **2** steal.

take a swipe at, a try to hit. **b** attempt to do something. [cf. OE *swipu* scourge] —**swip′er,** *n.*

swirl (swėrl), *v.* **1** move or drive along with a twisting motion; whirl: *dust swirling in the air.* **2** twist; curl. —*n.* **1** a swirling movement; whirl; eddy. **2** a twist; curl. [cf. Du. *zwirrelen* whirl]

swish (swish), *v.* move with a thin, light, hissing or brushing sound; make such a sound: *the whip swished through the air.* —*n.* a swishing movement or sound. [? imit.]

Swiss (swis), *adj.* **1** of or having to do with Switzerland or its people. **2** characteristic of Switzerland or its people. —*n.* **1** native or inhabitant of Switzerland. **2** people of Switzerland.

Swiss chard (chärd), any of several varieties of beets whose leaves are often eaten as a vegetable. [< F *carde*]

Swiss cheese, a firm, pale-yellow or whitish cheese with many large holes.

switch (swich), *n.* **1** a slender stick used in whipping. **2** a stroke; lash: *a switch of a whip.* **3** device for shifting a train from one track to another. **4** device for turning an electric current off or on. **5** a turn; change; shift: *a switch of votes to another candidate.* —*v.* **1** whip; strike. **2** move or swing like a switch. **3** change, turn, or shift (a car, train, etc.) onto another track. **4** turn (an electric current, etc.) off or on. [prob. < var. of LG *swutsche*] —**switch′er,** *n.* —**switch′like′,** *adj.*

switch·back (swich′bak′), *n.* a road climbing a steep grade in a zigzag course.

switch·blade (swich′blād′), *n.* knife with a blade that springs out from the handle at the touch of a button on the handle.

switch·board (swich′bôrd′; -bōrd′), *n.* panel containing the necessary switches, meters, etc., for opening, closing, combining, or controlling electric circuits.

Switz·er·land (swit′sər lənd), *n.* a small country in C Europe, N of Italy.

swiv·el (swiv′əl), *n., v.,* **-eled, -el·ing.** —*n.* **1** a fastening that allows the thing fastened to turn round freely upon it. **2** support allowing free motion of an attached part on a horizontal plane. **3** support on which a chair can revolve. —*v.* **1** turn on a swivel. **2** fasten or support by a swivel. **3** swing round; rotate; turn. [ult. < OE *swīfan* move] —**swiv′el·like′,** *adj.*

swivel chair, chair having a seat that turns on a swivel.

swol·len (swōl′ən), *adj.* **1** swelled; bulging. **2** filled to bursting; overfull, as a stream or river. **3** bombastic. —*v.* pp. of **swell.**

swoon (swün), *v.* **1** faint: *she swoons at the sight of blood.* **2** fade or die away gradually. **3** be thrilled or enchanted: *swoon over the new baby.* —*n.* a faint. [ult. < OE *geswōgen* in a swoon] —**swoon′ing·ly,** *adv.*

swoop (swüp), *v.* **1** come down with a rush; descend in a sudden, swift attack: *the soldiers swooped upon the enemy.* **2** take at one stroke; snatch. —*n.* a rapid downward rush; sudden, swift descent or attack.

in one fell swoop, in a single blow, act, etc. [ult. < OE *swāpan* sweep] —**swoop′er,** *n.*

sword (sôrd; sōrd), *n.* weapon, usually metal, with a long, sharp blade fixed in a handle or hilt.

at swords' points, very unfriendly.

cross swords, a fight. **b** quarrel; dispute.
put to the sword, kill with a sword; slaughter in war.
the sword, military power. [OE *sweord*] —**sword′less,** *adj.* —**sword′like′,** *adj.*

sword·fish (sôrd′fish′; sōrd′–), *n., pl.* **–fish·es** or (*esp. collectively*) **–fish.** a very large saltwater food fish with a long swordlike projection from its upper jaw.

sword·play (sôrd′plā′; sōrd′–), *n.* action, practice, or art of wielding a sword; fencing.

swords·man (sôrdz′mən; sōrdz′–), *n., pl.* **–men. 1** person skilled in using a sword. **2** fencer. —**swords′man·ship,** *n.*

swore (swôr; swōr), *v.* pt. of **swear.**

sworn (swôrn; swōrn), *v.* pp. of **swear.** —*adj.* **1** having taken an oath; bound by an oath. **2** declared, promised, etc., with an oath.

swum (swum), *v.* **1** pp. of **swim. 2** *Archaic.* pt. of **swim.**

swung (swung), *v.* pt. and pp. of **swing.**

syc·a·more (sik′ə môr; –mōr), *n.* **1** a shade tree, the buttonwood. **2** in England, a kind of maple. [< L < Gk. *sykomoros*]

syc·o·phant (sik′ə fənt), *n.* a servile or self-seeking flatterer. [< L < Gk. *sykophantes* informer, slanderer] —**syc′o·phan·cy,** *n.* —**syc′o·phan′tic,** *adj.* —**syc′o·phan′ti·cal·ly,** *adv.*

syl·lab·ic (sə lab′ik), *adj.* **1** of or pertaining to syllables; consisting of syllables. **2** forming a separate syllable. The second *l* in *little* is syllabic. **3** representing a syllable. **4** pronounced syllable by syllable. —*n.* a syllabic sound. —**syl·lab′i·cal·ly,** *adv*

syl·lab·i·cate (sə lab′ə kāt), *v.,* **–cat·ed, –cat·ing.** form or divide into syllables. —**syl·lab′i·ca′tion,** *n.*

syl·lab·i·fy (sə lab′ə fī), *v.,* **–fied, –fy·ing.** divide into syllables. —**syl·lab′i·fi·ca′tion,** *n.*

syl·la·ble (sil′ə bəl), *n., v.,* **–bled, –bling.** —*n.* **1** part of a word pronounced as a unit, consisting of a vowel alone or with one or more consonants. *American* is a word of four syllables. *This* is a word of one syllable. **2** letter or group of letters representing a syllable in writing and printing. **3** the slightest bit; word: *do not breathe a syllable of this.* —*v.* pronounce in syllables; utter distinctly; utter. [< OF < L < Gk. *syllabe,* orig., a taking together < *syn*– together + *labein* take]

syl·la·bus (sil′ə bəs), *n., pl.* **–bus·es, –bi** (–bī). a brief statement of the main points of a speech, a book, a course of study, etc. [< NL, erroneous reading of L, Gk. *sittyba* parchment label]

syl·lo·gism (sil′ə jiz əm), *n.* **1** a form of argument or reasoning, consisting of two statements and a conclusion drawn from them. *Example:* All trees have roots; an oak is a tree; therefore, an oak has roots. **2** reasoning in this form; deduction. [< L < Gk., ult. < *syn*– together + *logos* a reckoning] —**syl′lo·gis′tic,** *adj.* —**syl′lo·gis′ti·cal·ly,** *adv.*

sylph (silf), *n.* **1** a slender, graceful girl or woman. **2** a slender, graceful spirit of the air. [< NL *sylphes,* pl.; a coinage of Paracelsus] —**sylph′like′,** **sylph′ish,** *adj.*

syl·van (sil′vən), *adj.* of or pertaining to the woods; in the woods; consisting of woods; having woods. [< L, < *silva* forest]

sym., 1 symbol. **2** symphony. **3** symptom.

sym·bol (sim′bəl), *n.* something that stands for or represents something else; emblem; sign: *the lion is the symbol of courage, the marks +, −, ×, and ÷ are symbols for add, subtract, multiply, and divide.* [< L < Gk. *symbolon* token, ult. < *syn*– together + *ballein* throw]

sym·bol·ic (sim bol′ik), *adj.* **1** used as a symbol: *a lily is symbolic of purity.* **2** of, pertaining to, or expressed by a symbol; using symbols. —**sym·bol′i·cal·ly,** *adv.*

sym·bol·ism (sim′bəl iz əm), *n.* **1** use of symbols; representation by symbols. **2** system of symbols.

sym·bol·ist (sim′bəl ist), *n.* person who uses or studies symbols or symbolism.

sym·bol·is·tic (sim′bəl is′tik), *adj.* of symbolism or symbolists. —**sym′bol·is′ti·cal·ly,** *adv.*

sym·bol·ize (sim′bəl īz), *v.,* **–ized, –iz·ing. 1** be a symbol of; stand for; represent. **2** represent by a symbol or symbols. **3** use symbols. —**sym′bol·i·za′tion,** *n.* —**sym′bol·iz′er,** *n.*

sym·me·try (sim′ə tri), *n., pl.* **–tries. 1** a regular, balanced arrangement on opposite sides of a line or plane, or around a center or axis. **2** pleasing proportions between the parts of a whole; well-balanced arrangement of parts; harmony. [< L < Gk., < *syn*– together + *metron* measure] —**sym·met′ri·cal, sym·met′ric,** *adj.* —**sym·met′ri·cal·ly,** *adv.* —**sym·met′ri·cal·ness,** *n.* —**sym′me·trist,** *n.*

sym·pa·thet·ic (sim′pə thet′ik), *adj.* **1** having or showing kind feelings toward others; sympathizing: *a sympathetic friend.* **2** approving; agreeing: *sympathetic to another's dreams.* **3** enjoying the same things and getting along well together. —**sym′pa·thet′i·cal·ly,** *adv.*

sympathetic nervous system, part of the autonomic nervous system that produces involuntary reactions such as increased heartbeat.

sym·pa·thize (sim′pə thīz), *v.,* **–thized, –thiz·ing. 1** feel or show sympathy. **2** share in or agree with a feeling or opinion; have sympathy. —**sym′pa·thiz′er,** *n.* —**sym′pa·thiz′ing·ly,** *adv.*

sym·pa·thy (sim′pə thi), *n., pl.* **–thies. 1** having the same feeling: *the twins were in complete sympathy.* **2** a sharing of another's sorrow or trouble: *sympathy for a sick person.* **3** agreement; approval; favor: *enlist the sympathy of the public.* [< L < Gk., < *syn*– together + *pathos* feeling]

sympathy strike, strike by workers in support of other workers on strike.

sym·pho·ny (sim′fə ni), *n., pl.* **–nies. 1** an elaborate musical composition for an orchestra. It usually has three or more movements in different rhythms but related keys. **2** harmony of sounds. **3** harmony of colors: *in autumn the woods are a symphony in red, brown, and yellow.* [< L < Gk. *symphonia* harmony, concert, band < *syn*– together + *phone* voice, sound] —**sym·phon′ic,** *adj.*

sym·po·si·um (sim pō′zi əm), *n., pl.* **–si·ums, –si·a** (–zi·ə). **1** a collection of the opinions of several persons on some subject. **2** a meeting for the discussion of some subject. [< L < Gk., < *syn*– together + *posis* drinking] —**sym·po′si·ac,** *adj.*

symp·tom (simp′təm), *n.* **1** sign; indication: *quaking knees and paleness are symptoms of fear.* **2** a noticeable change in the normal working of the body that indicates or accompanies disease, sickness, etc. [< LL < Gk. *symptoma* a happening, ult. < *syn*– together + *piptein* fall] —**symp′tom·less,** *adj.*

symp·to·mat·ic (simp′tə mat′ik), *adj.* signifying; indicative: *riots are symptomatic of social unrest, the vaccine can cause a symptomatic fever.* —**symp′to·mat′i·cal·ly,** *adv.*

syn–, *prefix.* with; together; jointly; at the same time, as in *synchronous, synopsis,* and *synthesis.* [< Gk. *syn* with, together; also (by assimilation to the following consonant), *sy–, syl–, sym–, sys–*]

syn., synonym.

syn·a·gogue (sin′ə gôg; –gog), *n.* **1** assembly of Jews for religious instruction and worship. **2** a building used by Jews for religious instruction and worship. [< L < Gk. *synagoge,* lit., assembly, ult. < *syn*– together + *agein* bring]

syn·apse (si naps′; sin′aps) *n.* place where a nerve impulse passes from one nerve cell to another. [< Gk. *synapsis* conjunction < *syn*– together + *haptein* fasten]

syn·chro·nism (sing′krə niz əm), *n.* occurrence at the same time; agreement in time.

syn·chro·nize (sing′krə nīz), *v.,* **–nized, –niz·ing. 1** occur at the same time; agree in time. **2** move or take place at the same rate and exactly together. **3** make agree in time: *synchronize all the clocks in a building.* [< Gk., < *synchronos* SYNCHRONOUS] —**syn′chro·ni·za′tion,** *n.* —**syn′chro·niz′er,** *n.*

syn·chro·nous (sing′krə nəs), *adj.* **1** occurring at the same time; simultaneous. **2** moving or taking place at the same rate and exactly together. **3** having the same frequency, or the same frequency and phase. [< LL < Gk., < *syn*–together + *chronos* time] —**syn′chro·nous·ly,** *adv.*

syn·co·pate (sing′kə pāt; sin′–), *v.,* **–pat·ed, –pat·ing. 1** shorten (a word) by omitting sounds from the middle, as in syncopating *Gloucester* to *Gloster*. **2 a** begin (a tone) on an unaccented beat and hold it into an accented one. **b** use such rhythms in a passage or piece of music. [< LL, < *syncope* SYNCOPE] —**syn′co·pa′tor, syn′co·pat′er,** *n.*

syn·co·pa·tion (sing′kə pā′shən; sin′-), *n.* **1** a syncopating or being syncopated. **2** music characterized by syncopation, as jazz and ragtime.

syn·co·pe (sing′kə pē; sin′-), *n.* contraction of a word by omitting sounds from the middle, as in *ne'er* for never. [< LL < Gk. *synkope,* orig., a cutting off, ult. < *syn-* together + *koptein* cut] —**syn·cop′ic, syn·cop′tic,** *adj.*

syn·dic (sin′dik), *n.* person who manages the business affairs of a university or other corporation. [< LL < Gk. *syndikos* advocate < *syn-* together + *dike* justice]

syn·di·cate (*n.* sin′də kit; *v.* sin′də kāt), *n., v.,* **-cat·ed, -cat·ing.** —*n.* **1** combination of persons or companies to carry out some undertaking. **2** association for purchasing articles, stories, etc., and publishing them simultaneously in a number of newspapers or periodicals. —*v.* **1** combine into a syndicate. **2** manage by a syndicate. **3** publish through a syndicate. [< F *syndicat* < *syndic* SYNDIC] —**syn′di·ca′tion,** *n.* —**syn′di·ca′tor,** *n.*

syn·ec·do·che (si nek′də kē), *n.* a figure of speech by which a part is put for the whole, or the whole for a part, the special for the general, or the general for the special, or the like. *Example:* a factory employing 500 *hands* (persons). [< LL < Gk. *synekdoche,* ult. < *syn-* with + *ex-* out + *dechesthai* receive] —**syn′ec·doch′ic,** *adj.*

syn·drome (sin′drōm), *n.* **1** group of symptoms which are indicative of a particular disease or condition. **2** any group of signs considered to be indicators of particular types of behavior: *the collector's syndrome means a house full of stuff.*

syn·er·gy (sin′ər ji), *n.* the working together of separate parts which, in combination, have greater effect than they would if working separately: *the synergy of expertise in both companies, a synergy from the combination of drugs prescribed.* [< NL *synergia* < Gk. *synergía* working together] —**syn′er·gis′tic,** *adj.* —**syn′er·gize,** *v.*

syn·fuel (sin′fyü′əl), synthetic fuel. [blend of *syn*thetic + *fuel*]

syn·gas (sin′gas′), *n.* synthetic gas, esp. that made from coal. [*syn*thetic + *gas*]

syn·od (sin′əd), *n.* **1** assembly called together under authority to discuss and decide church affairs; church council. **2** assembly; convention; council. [< LL

< Gk., < *syn-* together + *hodos* a going] —**syn′od·al,** *adj.*

syn·od·ic (si nod′ik), **syn·od·i·cal** (-ə kəl), *adj.* **1** having to do with the conjunctions of the celestial bodies. The synodic period of the moon is the time between one new moon and the next. **2** of or having to do with a synod. —**syn·od′i·cal·ly,** *adv.*

syn·o·nym (sin′ə nim), *n.* **1** word having a meaning that is the same or nearly the same as another in a language. *Fleet* is a synonym of *swift.* **2** word or expression accepted as another name for something. *Reds* became a synonym for *communists.* [< LL < Gk. *synonymon,* orig. neut. adj., SYNONYMOUS] —**syn′o·nym′i·cal,** *adj.* —**syn′o·nym′i·ty,** *n.*

syn·on·y·mous (si non′ə məs), *adj.* having the same or nearly the same meaning. [< Med.L < Gk., < *syn-* together + (dial.) *onyma* name] —**syn·on′y·mous·ly,** *adv.*

syn·on·y·my (si non′ə mi), *n., pl.* **-mies. 1** character of being synonymous; equivalence in meaning. **2** study of synonyms. **3** set, list, or system of synonyms.

syn·op·sis (si nop′sis), *n., pl.* **-ses** (-sēz). a brief statement giving a general view of some subject, book, play, etc.; summary. [< LL < Gk., < *syn-* together + *opsis* a view]

syn·op·tic (si nop′tik), **syn·op·ti·cal** (-tə kəl), *adj.* **1** giving a general view. **2** Often, **Synoptic.** taking a common view. *Matthew, Mark,* and *Luke* are called the **Synoptic Gospels** because they are much alike in contents, order, and statement. —**syn·op′ti·cal·ly,** *adv.* —**syn·op′tist,** *n.* —**syn′op·tis′ti·cal·ly,** *adv.*

syn·tac·ti·cal (sin tak′tə kəl), **syn·tac·tic** (-tik), *adj.* of or having to do with syntax; in accordance with the rules of syntax. —**syn·tac′ti·cal·ly,** *adv.*

syn·tax (sin′taks), *n.* **1** construction or use of a word, phrase, or clause in a sentence. **2** sentence structure; arrangement of the words of a language into phrases, clauses, and sentences. **3** part of grammar dealing with this. [< LL < Gk. *syntaxis,* ult. < *syn-* together + *tassein* arrange]

syn·the·sis (sin′thə sis), *n., pl.* **-ses** (-sēz). **1** combination of parts or elements into a whole. **2** a complex whole made up of parts or elements combined. [< L < Gk. < *syn-* together + *theinai* put] —**syn′the·sist,** *n.*

syn·the·size (sin′thə sīz), *v.,* **-sized, -siz·ing. 1** combine into a complex whole. **2** make up by combining parts or elements.

syn·the·siz·er (sin′thə sī′zər), *n.* **1** someone or something that synthesizes: *a good synthesizer of facts that seem unrelated.* **2** electronic device that simulates sounds and blends them: *using a synthesizer instead of live musicians.*

syn·thet·ic (sin thet′ik), **syn·thet·i·cal** (-ə kəl), *adj.* **1** of or having to do with

synthesis. **2** proceeding by or involving synthesis: *synthetic chemistry.* **3** made artificially: *synthetic rubies.* **4** using many compound words; tending to combine words: *German is a more synthetic language than French.* —**syn·thet′i·cal·ly,** *adv.*

syph·i·lis (sif′ə lis), *n.* a contagious sexually transmitted disease contracted congenitally or by sexual contact. [< NL, < *Syphilus,* hero of Fracastoro's poem describing the disease, 1530] —**syph′i·lit′ic,** *adj., n.*

Syr·i·a (sir′i ə), *n.* country in W Asia, along the E end of the Mediterranean. —**Syr′i·an,** *adj., n.*

Syr·i·ac (sir′i ak), *adj.* of or having to do with Syria or its language. —*n.* the ancient language of Syria.

sy·rin·ga (sə ring′gə), *n.* a shrub with fragrant white flowers blooming in early summer; mock orange. [< NL, < Gk. *syrinx* shepherd's pipe]

sy·ringe (sə rinj′; sir′inj), *n., v.,* **-ringed, -ring·ing.** —*n.* **1** device fitted with a piston or rubber bulb for drawing in a quantity of fluid and then forcing it out in a stream. Syringes are used for cleaning wounds, injecting fluids into the body, etc. **2** =hypodermic syringe. —*v.* clean, wash, inject, etc., by means of a syringe. [< Gk. *syrinx* pipe]

syr·inx (sir′ingks), *n., pl.* **sy·rin·ges** (sə rin′jēz), **syr·inx·es. 1** the vocal organ of birds, situated where the trachea divides into the right and left bronchi. **2** the Eustachian tube. [< L < Gk., shepherd's pipe]

syr·up (sir′əp; sėr′-), *n.* a sweet, thick liquid. Sugar boiled with water or fruit juices makes a syrup. [< OF *sirop* < Ar. *sharāb* drink] —**syr′up·like′,** *adj.*

syr·up·y (sir′ə pi; sėr′-), *adj.* **1** sweet, sticky; thick; like syrup. **2** *Fig.* cloyingly sweet or sentimental.

sys·tem (sis′təm), *n.* **1** set of things or parts forming a whole: *a mountain system, the digestive system.* **2** an ordered group of facts, principles, beliefs, etc.: *a system of government, education, etc.* **3** plan; scheme; method: *a system for betting.* **4** an orderly way of getting things done: *work that shows system.* [< LL < Gk. *systema* < *syn-* together + *stesai* cause to stand] —**sys′tem·less,** *adj.*

sys·tem·at·ic (sis′təm at′ik), *adj.* **1** according to a system; having a system, method, or plan. **2** arranged in or comprising an ordered system. **3** orderly in arranging things or in getting things done. —**sys′tem·at′i·cal·ly,** *adv.*

sys·tem·a·tize (sis′təm ə tīz), *v.,* **-tized, -tiz·ing.** arrange according to a system; make into a system; make more systematic. —**sys′tem·a·ti·za′tion,** *n.* —**sys′tem·a·tiz′er,** *n.*

sys·tem·ic (sis tem′ik), *adj.* **1** of or pertaining to a system. **2** pertaining to a particular system of parts or organs of the body. —**sys·tem′i·cal·ly,** *adv.*

sys·tem·ize (sis′təm īz), *v.,* **–ized, –iz·ing.** =systematize. —**sys′tem·i·za′tion,** *n.* —**sys′tem·iz′er,** *n.*

systems analysis, scientific analysis of how systems work, esp. to improve their efficiency, safety, accuracy, etc. —**systems analyst.**

sys·to·le (sis′tə lē), *n.* the normal rhyth-- mical contraction of the heart, esp. that of the ventricles, which drives the blood into the aorta and the pulmonary artery. [< NL < Gk., contraction, < *syn-* together + *stellein* wrap] —**sys·tol′ic,** *adj.*

T, t (tē), *n., pl.* **T's; t's.** the 20th letter of the alphabet. **to a T,** exactly; perfectly.

T., **1** Territory. **2** Testament. **3** Tuesday.

t., **1** teaspoon. **2** temperature. **3** tenor. **4** tense. **5** time. **6** ton; tons.

Ta, tantalum.

tab (tab), *n., v.,* **tabbed, tab·bing.** —*n.* **1** a small flap, strap, loop, or piece. **2** tag; label. —*v.* furnish or ornament with a tab or tabs

keep tab or **tabs on,** keep track of; keep a check on.

tab·ard (tab'ərd), *n.* **1** a short, loose coat worn by heralds. **2** mantle worn over armor by knights. [< OF *tabart*]

Ta·bas·co (tə bas'kō), *n. Trademark.* a kind of pungent sauce, used on fish, meat, etc., prepared from the fruit of a variety of capsicum. [< the name of a state in Mexico]

tab·by (tab'i), *n., pl.* **–bies,** *adj.* —*n.* **1** a brown or gray cat with dark stripes. **2** a female cat. —*adj.* brown or gray with dark stripes. [< F < Ar. *'attābi*]

tab·er·nac·le (tab'ər nak'əl), *n.* **1** a Jewish temple. **2** place of worship for a large audience. **3** the human body as the temporary dwelling of the soul. [< L *tabernaculum* < *taberna* cabin]

ta·ble (tā'bəl), *n., v.,* **–bled, –bling.** —*n.* **1** piece of furniture having a smooth, flat top on legs. **2** food put on a table to be eaten. **3** the persons seated at a table: *the whole table laughed at his joke.* **4** very condensed tabulated information; list. **5** a thin, flat piece of wood, stone, metal, etc.; tablet. —*v.* **1** put on a table. **2** put off discussing (a bill, motion, etc.).

lay or **set the table,** make the table ready for a meal by setting out dishes, silverware, etc.

tables, multiplication tables.

turn the tables, reverse conditions or circumstances completely.

under the table, hidden; in secret: *a gift under the table.* [< L *tabula* plank, tablet]

tab·leau (tab'lō), *n., pl.* **–leaux** (–lōz), **–leaus. 1** a striking scene; picture. **2** representation of a scene, etc., by a person or group posing in appropriate costume. [< F, dim. of *table* TABLE]

ta·ble·cloth (tā'bəl klôth'; –kloth'), *n.* cloth for covering a table.

ta·ble d'hôte (tä'bəl dōt'; tab'əl), a meal served at a fixed time and price. [< F, lit., host's table]

ta·ble·land (tā'bəl land'), *n.* a high plain; plateau.

table linen, tablecloths, napkins, place mats, etc., for the table.

ta·ble·spoon (tā'bəl spün'), *n.* **1** a spoon larger than a teaspoon or dessert spoon, used to serve vegetables, etc.; a standard unit of measure in cookery. **2** =tablespoonful.

ta·ble·spoon·ful (tā'bəl spün'ful), *n., pl.* **–fuls.** as much as a tablespoon holds. **3** teaspoonfuls = 1 tablespoonful. 1 tablespoonful = ½ fluid ounce.

tab·let (tab'lit), *n.* **1** number of sheets of writing paper fastened together at the edge. **2** a small, flat surface with an inscription. **3** a small, flat piece of medicine, candy, etc.: *aspirin tablets.* [< F, < *table* TABLE]

table talk, conversation at meals; conversation suitable for mealtime.

table tennis, =ping pong.

ta·ble·ware (tā'bəl wār'), *n.* dishes, knives, forks, spoons, etc., used at meals.

tab·loid (tab'loid), *n.* a newspaper, usually having half the ordinary size newspaper page, that has short articles. —*adj.* condensed. [< *tablet*]

ta·boo, ta·bu (tə bü'), *adj., v.,* **–booed, –boo·ing; –bued, –bu·ing,** *n., pl.* **–boos; –bus.** —*adj.* **1** forbidden; prohibited; banned: *a taboo word.* **2** set apart as sacred or cursed. Among the Polynesians certain things, places, and persons are taboo. —*v.* forbid; prohibit; ban. —*n.* **1** a prohibition; a ban: *place a taboo on gambling.* **2** system or act of setting things apart as sacred or cursed. [< Tongan (lang. of the Tonga Islands in the S Pacific) *tabu*]

ta·bor, ta·bour (tā'bər), *n.* a small drum, used to accompany a pipe or fife. [< OF *tabur;* of Oriental orig.]

tab·u·lar (tab'yə lər), *adj.* **1** of or arranged in tables or lists; written or printed in columns. **2** computed by the use of tables. **3** flat like a table: *a tabular rock.* —*tab'u·lar·ly, adv.*

tab·u·late (*v.* tab'yə lāt; *adj.* tab'yə lit, –lāt), *v.,* **–lat·ed, –lat·ing,** *adj.* —*v.* arrange (facts, figures, etc.) in tables or lists. —*adj.* shaped like a table; tabular. —*tab'u·la'tion, n.* **tab'u·la'tor, n.**

ta·chom·e·ter (tə kom'ə tər), *n.* any of various instruments for measuring or indicating the speed of a machine, a river, etc. [< Gk. *tachos* speed + –METER] —*ta·chom'e·try, n.*

tac·it (tas'it), *adj.* **1** unspoken; silent: *a tacit prayer.* **2** implied or understood without being openly expressed: *tacit reproach.* [< L *tacitus,* pp. of *tacere* be silent] —*tac'it·ly, adv.*

tac·i·turn (tas'ə tèrn), *adj.* speaking very little; not fond of talking. [< L, < *tacitus* TACIT] —*tac'i·tur'ni·ty, n.* —*tac'i·turn'ly, adv.*

tack (tak), *n.* **1** a short, sharp-pointed nail or pin having a broad, flat head: *carpet tacks.* **2** stitch used as a temporary fastening. **3** direction in which a ship moves in regard to the position of her sails. **4** a zigzag movement; one of the movements in a zigzag course. **5** *Fig.* course of action or conduct: *he took the wrong tack to get what he wanted.* —*v.* **1** fasten with tacks. **2** *Fig.* attach; add: *he tacked a postscript to the end of the letter.* **3 a** sail in a zigzag course against the wind. **b** change from one tack to another. [< dial. OF *taque* nail < Gmc.] —*tack'er, n.*

tack·le (tak'əl), *n., v.,* **–led, –ling.** —*n.* **1** equipment; apparatus; gear: *fishing tackle.* **2** ropes and pulleys for lifting, lowering, or moving. **3** act of tackling. **4** football player between the guard and the end on either side of the line. —*v.* **1** try to deal with: *everyone has his own problems to tackle.* **2** lay hold of; seize: *tackle a thief.* **3** seize and stop (an opponent having the football) by bringing to the ground. **4** harness. [< Mdu., MLG *takel*] —*tack'ler, n.*

tack·y (tak'i), *adj.,* **tack·i·er, tack·i·est. 1** shabby; dowdy. **2** sticky; gummy.

tac·o (tä'kō), *n.* tortilla filled with meat, beans, etc., rolled up and served hot. [< Mexican Sp.]

tac·o·nite (tak'ə nīt), *n.* kind of rock consisting of about 30 percent iron ore. [< *Taconic* system of strata < *Taconic* Mts. (Mass. and Vt.)]

tact (takt), *n.* ability to say and do the right things; skill in dealing with people or handling difficult situations without causing offense. [< L *tactus* sense of feeling < *tangere* touch]

tact·ful (takt'fəl), *adj.* **1** having tact. **2** showing tact. —*tact'ful·ly, adv.* —*tact'ful·ness, n.*

tac·tic (tak'tik), *n.* **1** a small part or maneuver of military tactics. **2** *Fig.* skillful move or maneuver.

tac·ti·cal (tak'tə kəl), *adj.* **1** of or concerning tactics. **2** pertaining to the disposal of military or naval forces in supporting action against an enemy. **3** *Fig.* characterized by adroit procedure and skillful expedients. —*tac'ti·cal·ly, adv.*

tac·ti·cian (tak tish'ən), *n.* person skilled or trained in tactics: *a brilliant legal tactician, a military tactician.*

tac·tics (tak'tiks), *n.* **1** (*sing. in use*) art or science of disposing military or naval forces in action. **2** (*pl. in use*) the operations themselves. **3** *Fig.* (*pl. in use*) procedures to gain advantage or success; methods. [< NL < Gk. *taktike* (*techne*) the art of arranging < *tassein* arrange]

tac·tile (tak'təl), *adj.* **1** of or pertaining to touch. **2** that can be felt by touch. [< L *tactilis* < *tangere* touch] —*tac·til'i·ty, n.*

tact·less (takt'lis), *adj.* **1** without tact: *a tactless person.* **2** showing no tact: *a tactless reply.* —*tact'less·ly, adv.* —*tact'less·ness, n.*

tad (tad), *n. Informal.* a little bit: *just a tad of jam.* —*adj.* very little: *a tad foolish.* [? < *tadpole*]

tad·pole (tad'pōl'), *n.* a very young frog or toad at the stage when it has a tail and lives in water. [< ME *tad* toad + *pol* poll (head); appar. "a toad that is all head"]

tael (tāl), *n.* a weight of E Asia equal to 1⅓ ounces avoirdupois. [< Pg. < Malay *tahil*]

ta·en (tān), *Poetic.* taken.

taf·fe·ta (taf'ə tə), *n.* **1** a rather stiff silk cloth with a smooth, glossy surface. **2** a similar cloth of linen, rayon, etc. [< OF < Pers. *tāftah* silk or linen]

taff·rail (taf′rāl′), *n.* a rail around a ship's stern. [< Du. *tafereel* panel, dim. of *tafel* TABLE]

taf·fy (taf′i), *n.* a kind of chewy candy made of brown sugar or molasses boiled down, often with butter.

Taft (taft), *n.* **William Howard,** 1857–1930, the 27th president of the United States, 1909–13; chief justice of the Supreme Court, 1921–30.

tag[1] (tag), *n., v.,* **tagged, tag·ging.** —*n.* **1** piece of card, paper, etc., to be tied or fastened to something: *a price tag, a name tag.* **2** a small, hanging piece; loose end; tatter. **3** the last line or lines of a song, play, actor's speech, etc. —*v.* **1** furnish with a tag or tags. **2** follow closely.

tag[2] (tag), *n., v.,* **tagged, tag·ging.** —*n.* a children's game in which the player who is "it" chases the others until he or she touches one. The one touched is then "it" and must chase the others. —*v.* touch or tap with the hand, as in tag.

tag end, last bit; scrap.

tag sale, private sale of household goods usually with each item having a price indicated on a tag.

tail (tāl), *n.* **1** the hinder part of an animal's body, esp. that which extends beyond the main part. **2** something like an animal's tail: *the tail of a kite.* **3** the after portion of an airplane. **4** the luminous train extending from the head of a comet. **5** the hind part of anything; back; rear; conclusion. **6** =coattail. **7** *Informal.* person who follows another. —*v.* **1** form a tail. **2** *Informal.* follow close behind and secretly. —*adj.* **1** at the tail, back, or rear. **2** coming from behind: *a tail wind.*

on one's tail, close behind; at one's heels.

tail off, end gradually; fade away.

tails, a reverse side of a coin. **b** coat with long tails, worn on formal occasions. **c** full-dress uniform or outfit.

turn tail, run away from danger, trouble, etc. [< OE *tægel*] —**tail′less,** *adj.* —**tail′like′,** *adj.*

tail·board (tāl′bôrd′; –bōrd′), *n.* =tailgate.

tail·gate (tāl′gāt′), *n., v.,* –gat·ed, –gat·ing. —*n.* rear door on a vehicle, or a board at the back of a wagon, that can be let down for loading or unloading. —*v.* follow too closely behind another vehicle.

tail light, light, usually red, at the back end of a vehicle.

tai·lor (tā′lər), *n.* person whose business is making or repairing clothes. —*v.* **1** make by tailor's work. **2** fit or furnish with clothes made by a tailor. [< AF *taillour,* ult. < LL *taliare* cut < L *talea* rod, cutting] —**tai′lor·ing,** *n.*

tai·lor·bird (tā′lər bėrd′), *n.* a small bird of Asia and Africa that stitches leaves together to form and hide its nest.

tai·lor-made (tā′lər mād′), *adj.* **1** made by, or as if by, a tailor; simple and fitting well. **2** *Fig.* exactly suitable for a person, situation, purpose, etc.

tail·piece (tāl′pēs′), *n.* piece forming the end or added at the end.

tail spin, 1 a downward, spinning movement of an airplane, with the nose first. **2** *Fig.* emotional distress or confusion.

taint (tānt), *n.* stain or spot; trace of decay, corruption, or disgrace. —*v.* give a taint to; spoil; decay. [partly var. of *attaint;* partly < OF *teint,* pp. of *teindre* dye < L *tingere*]

Tai·pei (tī′pe′), *n.* capital of Taiwan.

Tai·wan (tī won′), *n.* island off the SE coast of mainland China and seat of the Republic of China.

Ta·jik·i·stan (tä ji′kə stän), *n.* country in SC Asia, between China and Afghanistan.

take (tāk), *v.,* **took, tak·en, tak·ing,** *n.* —*v.* **1** lay hold of; seize; grasp: *he took the child by the hand, take an animal in a trap.* **2** accept: *take my advice, won't take a penny less.* **3** receive: *she takes boarders, take news calmly, took first prize.* **4** make use of; use: *take a train, took a seat, take the opportunity, take a vacation.* **5** submit to; put up with: *take hard punishment.* **6** need; require: *it will take courage, it will take all day.* **7** choose; select: *take the shortest way home.* **8** take away: *her paleness takes from her beauty, take 3 from 7 and you have 4.* **9** lead: *where will this road take me? take her home.* **10** carry: *take your lunch along.* **11** do; make; obtain: *take a photograph, take pride in one's work, take my temperature.* **12** understand; suppose: *do you take my meaning? I take it the train was late, let us take an example.* **13** assume (responsibility, blame, etc.): *she took charge of the household.* **14** engage; hire; lease: *take a house, take a newspaper.* **15** write down; record: *take minutes of a meeting.* **16** please; attract; charm: *it took her fancy, the scene took his eye.* **17** go: *take to the woods.* **18** become affected by: *he took sick, marble takes a polish.* —*n.* **1** amount taken: *a great take of fish.* **2** act of taking. **3** a that which is taken. **b** *Informal.* receipts; profits. **4** act or process of making a scene in a motion picture. **5** *Informal. Fig.* **a** opinion: *my take on this.* **b** imitation; impression: *does a great take of the president.*

on the take, receiving illegal payments or bribes.

take a break, stop and rest for a short time; do something different for a short time.

take after, be like; resemble.

take amiss, a misinterpret. **b** be offended by.

take apart, a dismantle. **b** *Fig.* analyze critically; criticize.

take back, a withdraw; retract. **b** *Fig.* remind of the past.

take down, a write down. **b** *Fig.* lower the pride or confidence of. **c** remove: *take down pictures before painting the wall.* **d** *Informal.* eliminate.

take five, *Informal.* take a short rest; stop for a moment.

take for, suppose to be: *taken for a nincompoop.*

take in, a receive; admit. **b** make smaller. **c** understand. **d** deceive; trick; cheat.

take in vain, use (esp. a name) carelessly or irreverently.

take it out on, relieve one's anger or annoyance by scolding or hurting.

take kindly to, be accepting of; be friendly to: *not take kindly to criticism.*

take lying down, *Informal.* accept passively, without protest.

take off, a go into the air: *the rocket took off successfully, hundreds of birds took off all at once.* **b** give an amusing imitation of.

take on, a engage; hire. **b** undertake to deal with. **c** *Informal.* show great excitement, grief, etc.

take one up on, *Informal.* accept: *take them up on the invitation.*

take (one's) time, not hurry.

take out, a remove: *take out a spot in the rug.* **b** get: *take out a book, took out a permit for the farm.* **c** go with; escort: *take out to lunch.* **d** destroy: *take out the enemy's radar.* **e** *Informal.* murder: *took out a rival.*

take over, assume ownership or control of: *take over a company.*

take the floor, rise to speak, as in a legislature, club, meeting, etc.

take to, form a liking for; become fond of.

take up, a soak up; absorb. **b** begin; undertake. **c** make shorter or smaller.

take up with, become friendly with; associate with. [< Scand. *taka*] —**tak′er,** *n.*

take-off or **take·off** (tāk′ôf′; –of′), *n.* **1** an amusing imitation; mimicking. **2** the leaving of the ground in a leap or in the start of a flight, as of birds or an aircraft; taking off. **3** a leap: *the broadjumper's take-off.* **4** successful launch of something; a start, as of a business.

tak·est (tāk′ist), *v. Archaic.* take.

tak·eth (tāk′ith), *v. Archaic.* takes.

tak·ing (tāk′ing), —*n.* seizure.

takings, money taken in; receipts.

talc (talk), *n.* a soft, smooth mineral, used in making talcum powder, tailors' chalk, etc. [< Med.L *talcum* < Ar. *talq* < Pers. *talk*]

tal·cum (tal′kəm), *n.* **1** =talcum powder. **2** =talc.

talcum powder, powder made of purified white talc, for use on the face and body.

tale (tāl), *n.* **1** narrative; story: *he told us tales of his boyhood.* **2** falsehood; lie. **3** piece of gossip or scandal.

tell tales, spread gossip or scandal. [OE *talu*]

tale·bear·er (tāl′bār′ər), *n.* person who spreads gossip or scandal; telltale. —**tale′bear′ing,** *n., adj.*

tal·ent (tal′ənt), *n.* **1** a special natural ability; ability: *a talent for music.* **2** people who have talent. **3** an ancient unit of weight or money. [< L < Gk. *talanton*] —**tal′ent·ed,** *adj.* —**tal′ent·less,** *adj.*

tal·ent·ed (tal′ən tid), *adj.* having natural ability.

ta·ler (tä′lər), *n., pl.* **–ler.** =thaler.

tales·man (tālz′mən; tā′lēz–), *n., pl.* **–men.** person chosen from among the bystanders or those present in court to serve on a jury when too few of those originally summoned are qualified to be on a jury. [< Med.L *tales* (*de circumstantibus*) such (of the bystanders) + *man*]

tale·tell·er (tāl′tel′ər), *n.* talebearer. —**tale′tell′ing,** *n., adj.*

Tal·i·ban (tal′ə ban), *n.* Muslim Islamist Sunni sect, composed mainly of Pashtun from Afghanistan and NW Pakistan, which ruled Afghanistan from 1996–2001. [< Ar., *lit.* those who study the book (Koran)]

tal·is·man (tal′is mən; –iz–), *n., pl.* **–mans.** 1 a stone, ring, etc., engraved with figures or characters supposed to have magic power; charm. 2 anything that acts as a charm. [< Ar. < LGk. *telesma* < Gk., initiation into the mysteries, < *teleein* perform]

talk (tôk), *v.* 1 use words; speak: *a child learns to talk, talk about the weather, talk sense, talk French.* 2 bring, put, drive, influence, etc., by talk: *talk a person to sleep.* 3 discuss; confer: *talk politics, talk with one's doctor.* 4 spread ideas by other means than speech: *talk by signs.* —*n.* 1 the use of words; spoken words; speech; conversation. 2 a way of talking: *baby talk.* 3 gossip; report: *she is the talk of the town.*

talk back, answer rudely or disrespectfully.

talk big, *Informal.* boast.

talk down, silence by talking louder or longer.

talk down to, speak condescendingly to.

talk out, discuss thoroughly, esp. to resolve a difference.

talk over, a discuss; consider together. **b** persuade or convince by argument.

talk up, talk about, esp. to convince. [ME *talke(n)*, ult. akin to *tell*]

talk·a·tive (tôk′ə tiv), *adj.* having the habit of talking a great deal; fond of talking. —**talk′a·tive·ly,** *adv.* —**talk′a·tive·ness,** *n.*

talk·er (tôk′ər), *n.* 1 person who talks. 2 a talkative person.

talk·ie (tôk′i), *n.* a motion picture with sound.

talking book, recording of a book.

talking heads, television program that features people talking about something.

talking point, something to be discussed.

talk·ing-to (tôk′ing tü′), *n., pl.* **-tos.** a scolding.

talk radio, radio broadcasting that features only talk.

talk show, radio or television program that consists of interviews or, sometimes, conversations with guests.

tall (tôl), *adj.* 1 higher than the average: *a tall building.* 2 of the specified height: *six feet tall.* 3 exaggerated: *a tall tale.* [OE (ge)*tæl* prompt, active] —**tall′ness,** *n.*

Tal·la·has·see (tal′ə has′i), *n.* capital of Florida, in the N part.

tall·boy (tôl′boi′), *n.* =highboy.

Tal·linn (tal′in), *n.* capital of Estonia.

tal·low (tal′ō), *n.* the hard fat from sheep, cows, etc., used for making candles and soap. [ME *talgh*] —**tal′low·y,** *adj.*

tall ship, sailing vessel with tall masts, as a square-rigger.

tall tale, fantastic story, often invented; fish story.

tal·ly (tal′i), *n., pl.* **-lies,** *v.,* **-lied, -ly·ing.** —*n.* 1 stick of wood in which notches are cut to represent numbers, formerly used to show the amount of a debt or payment. 2 anything on which a score or account is kept. 3 account; reckoning; score: *a tally of a game.* 4 correspondence; agreement. —*v.* 1 mark on a tally; count up: *tally a score.* 2 agree; correspond: *your account tallies with mine.* [< OF, ult. < L *talea* rod] —**tal′li·er,** *n.*

tal·ly·ho (*n.* tal′i hō′; *interj.* tal′i hō′), *n., pl.* **-hos,** *interj.* —*n.* 1 a coach drawn by four horses. 2 a sounding of "tallyho" by a hunter. —*interj.* a hunter's cry on catching sight of the fox.

tally sheet, a sheet on which a record or score is kept, esp. a record of votes.

Tal·mud (tal′mud), *n.* the sixty-three volumes containing the Jewish civil and canonical law. —**Tal·mud′ic,** *adj.* —**Tal′mud·ist,** *n.* —**Tal′mud·is′tic,** *adj.*

tal·on (tal′ən), *n.* claw of a bird of prey; claw.

talons, clawlike fingers; grasping hands. [< OF, heel, ult. < L *talus* ankle] —**tal′oned,** *adj.*

ta·lus¹ (tā′ləs), *n., pl.* **-li** (–lī). the uppermost bone of the tarsus; anklebone; astragalus. [< L]

ta·lus² (tā′ləs), *n.* 1 a slope. 2 a sloping side or face of a wall, rampart, parapet, or other fortification. 3 a sloping mass of rocky fragments lying at the base of a cliff or the like. [< F < L]

tam (tam), *n.* =tam-o'-shanter.

ta·ma·le (tə mä′lē), *n.* a Mexican food made of corn meal and meat, cheese, chilis, etc., wrapped in cornhusks, and roasted or steamed. [< Am.Sp. < Mex. *tamalli*]

tam·a·rack (tam′ə rak), *n.* an American larch tree. [< Algonkian]

tam·a·rind (tam′ə rind), *n.* 1 a tropical tree grown for its wood and fruit. 2 its fruit, used in foods, drinks, and medicine. [ult. < Ar. *tamrhindī*, *lit.*, date of India]

tam·bou·rine (tam′bə rēn′), *n.* a small drum with metal disks, played by striking it with the knuckles or by shaking it. [< F *tambourin*, dim. of *tambour* drum]

tame (tām), *adj.,* **tam·er, tam·est,** *v.,* **tamed, tam·ing.** —*adj.* 1 taken from the wild state and made obedient: *a tame bear.* 2 without fear; gentle: *the squirrels are very tame.* 3 *Fig.* without spirit; dull: *a tame story.* —*v.* 1 make tame; break in. 2 become tame. 3 deprive of courage; tone down; subdue. [OE *tam*] —**tame′a·ble, tam′a·ble,** *adj.* —**tame′ly,** *adv.* —**tame′ness,** *n.* —**tam′er,** *n.*

tame·less (tām′lis), *adj.* that has never been tamed; that cannot be tamed. —**tame′less·ness,** *n.*

Tam·il (tam′əl), *n.* 1 one of the Dravidian people of S India, Sri Lanka, Singapore, and Malaysia. 2 their language. —*adj.* of or having to do with the Tamils or their language.

tam-o'-shan·ter (tam′ə shan′tər), *n.* a Scotch cap. [from the name of the hero in a poem by Burns]

tamp (tamp), *v.* 1 pack down: *tamp the earth about a newly planted tree.* 2 in blasting, to fill (the hole containing explosive) with dirt, etc. —**tamp′er,** *n.*

tam·per (tam′pər), *v.* meddle; meddle improperly.

tamper with, a bribe; corrupt. **b** change so as to damage or falsify. [ult. var. of *temper*] —**tam′per·er,** *n.*

tam·pi·on (tam′pi ən), *n.* 1 a wooden plug placed in the muzzle of a gun to keep out dampness and dust. 2 plug for the top of an organ pipe.

tam·pon (tam′pon), *n.* plug of cotton or the like inserted in a wound, etc., to stop bleeding or absorb secretions. —*v.* fill or plug with a tampon. [< F]

tan (tan), *v.,* **tanned, tan·ning,** *n., adj.* —*v.* 1 make (a hide) into leather by soaking in a special liquid containing tannin. 2 make brown from exposure to sun and air. —*n.* 1 the brown color of a person's skin resulting from being in the sun and air. 2 a yellowish brown. 3 bark used in tanning hides. 4 tannin. —*adj.* yellowish-brown. [< Med.L *tannare*] —**tan′ning,** *n.*

tan·a·ger (tan′ə jər), *n.* any of various small American oscine birds. The males are usually brilliantly colored. [< NL < Tupi *tangara*]

tan·bark (tan′bärk′), *n.* crushed bark used in tanning hides.

tan·dem (tan′dəm), *adv.* one behind the other: *drive horses tandem.* —*adj.* having animals, seats, parts, etc., arranged tandem. —*n.* 1 two horses so harnessed. 2 a carriage drawn by two horses so harnessed. 3 a bicycle with two seats, one behind the other.

in tandem, a one behind another: *travel in tandem.* **b** in cooperation: *work in tandem.* [< L, at length, < *tam* so]

tang (tang), *n.* 1 a strong taste or flavor: *the tang of mustard, the salt tang of sea air.* 2 a distinctive flavor or quality. 3 *Fig.* a smack, touch, or suggestion of something. [< Scand. *tangi* point] —**tang′y,** *adj.*

tan·gent (tan′jənt), *adj.* 1 touching. 2 touching at one point only and not intersecting. These circles are tangent

∞. —*n.* **1** a tangent line, curve, or surface. **2** in a right triangle, the ratio of the length of the side opposite to an (acute) angle to the length of the side (not the hypotenuse) adjacent to the angle.

fly off or **go off at a tangent,** change suddenly from one course of action or thought to another. [< L *tangens* touching] —**tan·gen·cy,** *n.* —**tan·gen′tial,** *adj.* —**tan·gen′tial·ly,** *adv.*

tan·ge·rine (tan′jə rēn′), *n.* a small, deep-colored orange with a very loose peel. [< *Tangier*]

tan·gi·ble (tan′jə bəl), *adj.* **1** capable of being touched or felt by touch: *ghosts are visible but not tangible.* **2** real; definite: *a tangible reason.* —*n.* **tangibles,** things whose value is easily appraised; material assets. [< LL *tangibilis* < *tangere* touch] —**tan′gi·bil′i·ty, tan′gi·ble·ness,** *n.* —**tan′gi·bly,** *adv.*

tan·gle (tang′gəl), *v.,* –**gled,** –**gling,** *n.* —*v.* **1** twist and twine together in a confused mass. **2** catch and hold in or as in a net. **3** involve in something that hampers or obstructs. —*n.* **1** a confused mass; snarl. **2** a tangled condition. **3** perplexity. [prob. var. of *tagle* entangle < Scand. (dial. Sw.) *taggla* disorder] —**tan′gle·ment,** *n.* —**tan′gler,** *n.* —**tan′gly,** *adj.*

tan·go (tang′gō), *n., pl.* –**gos,** *v.,* –**goed,** –**go·ing.** —*n.* **1** a Latin-American dance with special music and gliding steps, figures, and poses. **2** music for it. —*v.* dance the tango. [< Sp.]

tank (tangk), *n.* **1** a large container for liquid or gas. **2** an armored combat vehicle carrying machine guns and cannons and moving on an endless tract on each side. —*v.* **1** put or store in a tank. **2** *Informal. Fig.* fail: *the company tanked.* [ult. < OF *estanc* pool]

tank·ard (tangk′ərd), *n.* a large drinking mug with a handle and a hinged cover.

tank car, a railroad car with a tank for carrying liquids or gases.

tank·er (tangk′ər), *n.* ship with tanks for carrying oil or other liquid freight.

tank top, sleeveless shirt with wide shoulder straps, often of knit fabric.

tan·ner (tan′ər), *n.* person whose work is tanning hides.

tan·ner·y (tan′ər i), *n., pl.* –**ner·ies.** place where hides are tanned.

tan·nic (tan′ik), *adj.* of or obtained from tanbark or tannin.

tan·nin (tan′ən), **tannic acid,** *n.* acid obtained from the bark or galls of oaks, etc., and from certain other plants. It is used in tanning, dyeing, making ink, and in medicine.

tan·sy (tan′zi), *n., pl.* –**sies.** a coarse, strong-smelling plant with large, toothed leaves and clusters of small yellow flowers. Tansy was formerly much used in cooking and medicine. [< OF < LL < Gk. *athanasia,* orig., immortality]

tan·ta·lize (tan′tə līz), *v.,* –**lized,** –**liz·ing.** torment or tease by keeping something desired in sight but out of reach, or by

holding out hopes that are repeatedly disappointed. [< *Tantalus,* in Greek legend, a king who had to stand in water up to his chin while over his head were fruit-laden branches he could not reach] —**tan′ta·liz′ing·ly,** *adv.*

tan·ta·lum (tan′tə ləm), *n.* a rare, grayish metallic element, Ta, that is very resistant to acids. [< *Tantalus;* because it will not absorb acid]

tan·ta·mount (tan′tə mount), *adj.* equivalent. [prob. < AF *tant amunter* amount to as much. See AMOUNT.]

tan·trum (tan′trəm), *n.* fit of bad temper or ill humor.

Tan·za·ni·a (tan zə nē′ə), *n.* country in E Africa.

Tao·ism (tou′iz əm), *n.* one of the three main religions of China, founded on the doctrines of the ancient philosopher, Lao-tse. —**Tao′ist,** *n., adj.* —**Tao·is′tic,** *adj.*

tap[1] (tap), *v.,* **tapped, tap·ping,** *n.* —*v.* **1** strike lightly: *tap on a window, she tapped her foot on the floor.* **2** make, put, etc., by light blows: *tap a rhythm.* **3** =tap-dance. —*n.* **1** a light blow: *there was a tap at the door.* **2** sound of a light blow. **3** =tap-dancing. [< OF *taper*]

tap[2] (tap), *n., v.,* **tapped, tap·ping.** —*n.* **1** a stopper or plug to close a hole in a cask containing liquid. **2** a means of turning on or off a flow of liquid; faucet. **3** room in which liquor is sold and drunk. **4** =a wiretap. **5** tool for cutting threads of internal screws. —*v.* **1** make a hole in to let out liquid: *tap a cask.* **2** open up: *this highway taps a large district.* **3** make a connection on, esp. secretly; wiretap: *tap a phone line.* **4** make internal screw threads in.

on tap, a ready to be let out of a keg or barrel and served. **b** ready for use; on hand: *huge store of supplies on tap.* **c** ready for work or to help: *numerous volunteers on tap.* [OE *tœppa*]

ta·pa (tä′pə), *n.* **1** an unwoven cloth of the Pacific islands, made by steeping and beating the inner bark of a mulberry tree. **2** the bark. [< Polynesian]

tap dance, dance in which the steps are accented by loud, rapid taps of the foot, toe, or heel.

tap-dance (tap′dans′; –däns′), *v.,* –**danced, –danc·ing.** do a tap dance.

tap-danc·ing (tap′dan′sing; –dän′–), *n.* art or act of doing a tap dance. —*adj.* of or having to do with or like a tap dance. —**tap′-dan′cer,** *n.*

tape (tāp), *n., v.,* **taped, tap·ing.** —*n.* **1** a long, narrow woven strip of cotton, linen, etc. **2** a long, narrow strip of other material: *steel tape.* **3** strip, string, etc., stretched across a race track at the finish line. **4 a** thin magnetic strip to record sound. **b** a recording on such a strip. **5** adhesive. —*v.* **1** furnish with tape or tapes. **2** fasten or wrap with tape. **3** record on magnetic tape. [OE *tœppe*]

tape measure, a long narrow strip of cloth or steel marked in inches, feet, etc., for measuring.

ta·per (tā′pər), *v.* **1** make or become gradually smaller toward one end: *a church spire tapers off to a point.* **2** grow less gradually; diminish. [< *n.*] —*adj.* becoming smaller toward one end. —*n.* **1** a slender candle. **2** long wick coated with wax, used to light a lamp or candle with its flame. **3** a gradual decrease of force, capacity, etc. [OE *tapor*] —**ta′per·ing·ly,** *adv.*

tape recording, 1 the recording of sound on a tape. **2** the sound thus recorded. —**tape′-re·cord′,** *v.*

tap·es·try (tap′is tri), *n., pl.* –**tries,** *v.,* –**tried, –try·ing.** —*n.* **1** fabric with pictures or designs woven in it, used to hang on walls, cover furniture, etc. **2** a picture in tapestry. —*v.* **1** picture in tapestry. **2** cover with tapestry; cover with a pattern like that of tapestry. [< F *tapisserie,* ult. < *tapis* < Gk. *tapetion,* dim of *tapes* carpet]

tape·worm (tāp′wėrm′), *n.* a long, flat worm that lives during its adult stage as a parasite in the intestine of humans and other vertebrates.

tap·i·o·ca (tap′i ō′kə), *n.* a starchy food obtained from the root of the cassava plant. [ult. < Tupi-Guarani *tipioca*]

ta·pir (tā′pər), *n.* a large piglike animal of tropical America that has a flexible snout. [< Tupi *tapira*]

tap·room (tap′rüm′; –rùm′), *n.* =barroom.

tap·root (tap′rüt′; –rùt′), *n.* a main root growing downward.

taps (taps), *n.pl.* signal, esp. on a bugle, to put lights out, and played at the burial of a person in the military. [< OF; see **tap**[1]]

tar[1] (tär), *n., v.,* **tarred, tar·ring,** *adj.* —*n.* a black, sticky substance obtained by the distillation of wood or coal. —*v.* cover or smear with tar. —*adj.* of, like, or covered with tar.

tar and feather, pour heated tar on and cover with feathers as a punishment. [OE *teoru*]

tar[2] (tär), *n.* =sailor. [special use of *tar*[1]]

tar·an·tel·la (tar′ən tel′ə), *n.* **1** a whirling southern Italian dance in very quick rhythm. **2** music for this dance. [< Ital.]

ta·ran·tu·la (tə ran′chə lə), *n., pl.* –**las,** –**lae** (-lē), a large, hairy spider whose bite is painful. People used to think that its bite caused an insane desire to dance.[< Med.L. ult. < L *Tarentum* Taranto, city in Italy]

tar·dy (tär′di), *adj.,* –**di·er,** –**di·est. 1** behind time; late. **2** slow. [< F, ult. < L *tardus*] —**tar′di·ly,** *adv.* —**tar′di·ness,** *n.*

tare[1] (tär), *n.* **1** vetch. **2** any of various injurious weeds in the Bible. [cf. Mdu. *tarwe* wheat]

tare[2] (tär), *n.* **1** the difference between the gross weight and the net weight of an article being shipped. It is usually the weight of the materials in which the article is wrapped or packed. **2** a deduction made from the gross weight to allow for this. [< F, ult. < Ar. *ṭarḥah* < *ṭaraḥah* reject]

tar·get (tär′git), *n.* **1 a** paper with circles on it or a circular object filled with sawdust, hay, etc. to be aimed at in shooting practice or contests. **b** anything aimed at. **2** *Fig.* goal; objective. **3** *Fig.* object of abuse, scorn, criticism, etc.: *he was the target for their caustic remarks.* [< F *targuete*, ult. < Gmc.]

tar·iff (tar′if), *n.* **1** list of duties or taxes on imports or exports. **2** system of duties or taxes on imports or exports. **3** any duty or tax in such a list or system: *a tariff on jewelry.* [< Ital. < Ar. *tarīf* information]

tar·mac (tär′mak′), *n.* road or runway surface of blacktop: *planes waited on the tarmac.* [< trademark for *tarmacadam* < *tar¹* + *macadam*]

tar·nish (tär′nish), *v.* **1** dull the luster or brightness of. **2** *Fig.* cast a stain upon; sully: *his actions tarnished his reputation.* —*n.* **1** loss of luster or brightness. **2** a tarnished surface, esp. of silver. [< F *terniss–* < *terne* dark, ? < Gmc.] —**tar′nish·a·ble,** *adj.*

ta·ro (tä′rō), *n., pl.* –**ros.** **1** a starchy root grown for food in the Pacific islands and other tropical regions. **2** the plant, grown for ornament also. [< Polynesian]

tar·ot (tar′ət), *n.* a card with a picture on it, one of a set of such cards, used in fortunetelling. [< F < It. *tarocchi*, name of a card game]

tarp (tärp), *n.* =tarpaulin.

tar·pau·lin (tär pô′lən), *n.* strong, waterproof canvas, plastic, etc., esp. a sheet of this used as a covering. [< *tar¹* + *pall* in sense of "covering"]

tar·pon (tär′pon), *n., pl.* –**pons** or (*esp. collectively*) –**pon.** a large, silver-colored fish found in the warmer parts of the Atlantic Ocean.

tar·ra·gon (tar′ə gon), *n.* **1** wormwood of E Europe and Asia. **2** its leaves, used as an herb.

tar·ry¹ (tar′i), *v.,* –**ried,** –**ry·ing.** **1** remain; stay. **2** wait; delay. —**tar′ri·er,** *n.*

tar·ry² (tär′i), *adj.,* –**ri·er,** –**ri·est.** **1** of tar; like tar. **2** covered with tar.

tar·sal (tär′səl), *adj.* of or pertaining to the tarsus. —*n.* bone or cartilage in the ankle.

tar·sus (tär′səs), *n., pl.* –**si** (–sī). **1 a** the ankle. **b** the group of small bones composing it. **2 a** shank of a bird's leg. **b** the last segment of an insect's leg. [< NL < Gk. *tarsos* sole of the foot, orig., crate]

tart¹ (tärt), *adj.* **1** having a sharp taste; sour. **2** sharp: *a tart reply.* [OE *teart*] —**tart′ly,** *adv.* —**tart′ness,** *n.*

tart² (tärt), *n.* **1** pastry filled with cooked fruit, jam, etc. In the United States, a tart is small and the fruit shows; in England, any fruit pie is a tart. **2** *Infor-*

mal. **a** woman who dresses in a sexually suggestive way. **b** prostitute. [< OF *tarte*; def. 2 orig. a term of endearment]

tar·tan (tôr′tən), *n.* **1** a plaid woolen cloth. Each Scottish Highland clan has its own pattern of tartan. **2** the pattern or design itself. —*adj.* **1** made of tartan. **2** of, like, or having to do with tartan.

Tar·tar (tär′tər), *n.* **1** member of a mixed horde of Mongols and Turks who overran Asia and E Europe during the Middle Ages. Tartars now live in C and W Asia. **2 tartar,** person who has a bad temper. —*adj.* of or pertaining to a Tartar or Tartars. Also, **Tatar.**

tar·tar (tär′tər). *n.* **1** an acid substance deposited on the inside of wine casks. After it is purified, this substance is called cream of tartar and is used with baking soda to make baking powder. **2** a hard substance deposited on the teeth. [< F *tartre*, ? < Ar.] —**tar·tar′e·ous, tar′-tar·ous,** *adj.*

tar·tar·ic (tär tar′ik; -tär′-), *adj.* of or pertaining to tartar; containing tartar; derived from tartar.

tartaric acid, a colorless crystalline compound, $C_4H_6O_6$, obtained from grapes, etc.

tas·er (tā′zər), *n.* small weapon that delivers an electric shock, used to control rioters, prisoners, etc. —*v.* attack with a taser; use a taser. [< trademark *Tele-Active Shock Electronic Repulsion*]

task (task; täsk), *n.* work to be done; piece of work; duty. —*v.* **1** put a task on; force to work. **2** burden; strain.

call or **take to task,** blame; scold; reprove. [< dial. OF *tasque*, var. of *taxa* < L *taxare* tax] —**task′er,** *n.*

task force, a temporary group of units, esp. naval units, assigned to one commander for carrying out a specific operation.

task·mas·ter (task′mas′tər; täsk′mäs′–), *n.* person who sets tasks for others to do, esp. a demanding or exacting person.

tas·sel (tas′əl), *n., v.,* –**seled,** –**sel·ing.** —*n.* **1** a hanging bunch of threads, small cords, beads, etc., fastened together at one end, used as decorative trim. **2** something like this: *corn has tassels.* —*v.* **1** put tassels on. **2** grow tassels. [< OF, mantle fastener]

taste (tāst), *n., v.,* **tast·ed, tast·ing.** —*n.* **1** flavor: *a sweet, sour, salty, or bitter taste.* **2** the sense by which the flavor of things is perceived. **3** a little bit; sample: *take a taste of a cake, a taste of independence.* **4** a liking: *suit your own taste.* **5** ability to enjoy what is appropriate or excellent: *a man of taste.* **6** a style that shows such ability: *her house is furnished in excellent taste.* —*v.* **1** try the flavor of (something). **2** get the flavor of: *she tasted almond in the cake, the soup tastes of onion.* **3** experience; have: *taste freedom.* [< OF *taster*, orig., feel] —**tast′a·ble,** *adj.*

taste bud, any of certain small groups of cells in the lining of the tongue or mouth that are sense organs of taste.

taste·ful (tāst′fəl), *adj.* **1** having good taste. **2** showing or done in good taste. —**taste′ful·ly,** *adv.* —**taste′ful·ness,** *n.*

taste·less (tāst′lis), *adj.* **1** without taste. **2** without good taste; in poor taste. —**taste′less·ly,** *adv.* —**taste′less·ness,** *n.*

tast·er (tās′tər), *n.* person who tastes, esp. one whose work is judging the quality of wine, tea, coffee, etc., by the taste.

tast·y (tās′ti), *adj.,* **tast·i·er, tast·i·est.** tasting good; pleasing to the taste. —**tast′i·ly,** *adv.* —**tast′i·ness,** *n.*

tat (tat), *v.,* **tat·ted, tat·ting.** make a kind of lace by looping and knotting (threads) with a shuttle.

Ta·tar (tä′tər), *n., adj.* =Tartar. —**Ta·tar′i·an, Ta·tar′ic,** *adj.*

tat·ter (tat′ər), *n.* a torn piece; rag. —*v.* tear or wear to pieces; make or become worn or ragged.

tatters, torn or ragged clothing. [ult. < Scand., var. of *tötturr* rag] —**tat′tered,** *adj.*

tat·ting (tat′ing), *n.* **1** process or work of making a kind of lace by looping and knotting cotton or linen thread with a shuttle. **2** lace made in this way.

tat·tle (tat′əl), *v.,* –**tled,** –**tling,** *n.* —*v.* **1** tell tales or secrets. **2** talk foolishly; gossip. —*n.* idle or foolish talk; gossip; telling tales or secrets. [cf. Mdu. *tatelen* stutter] —**tat′tler,** *n.* —**tat′tling,** *adj.* —**tat′tling·ly,** *adv.*

tat·tle·tale (tat′əl tāl′), *n., adj.* telltale.

tat·too¹ (ta tü′), *n., pl.* –**toos.** **1** a signal on a bugle, drum, etc., calling soldiers or sailors to their quarters at night. **2** series of raps, taps, etc.: *the hail beat a loud tattoo on the windowpane.* [< Du. *taptoe* < *tap* taproom + *toe* to, shut] —**tat·too′er,** *n.*

tat·too² (ta tü′), *v.,* –**tooed, –too·ing,** *n., pl.* –**toos.** —*v.* mark (the skin) with designs or patterns by pricking it and putting in colors: *the sailor had a ship tattooed on his arm.* —*n.* mark or design made by tattooing. [< Polynesian *tatau*] —**tat·too′er,** *n.*

tat·ty (tat′i), *adj.,* –**ti·er, –ti·est.** ragged; worn-out.

tau (tô; tou), *n.* the 19th letter (T, τ) of the Greek alphabet.

taught (tôt), *v.* pt. and pp. of **teach.**

taunt (tônt; tänt), *v.* **1** subject to mockery; jeer at; reproach. **2** get or drive by taunts: *they taunted him into taking the dare.* —*n.* a bitter or insulting remark. —**taunt′er,** *n.* —**taunt′ing·ly,** *adv.*

taupe (tōp), *n., adj.* dark, brownish gray. [< F, orig., mole, < L *talpa*]

Tau·rus (tô′rəs), *n., gen.* –**ri** (–rī). **1** the Bull, a zodiacal constellation. **2** the second sign of the zodiac. [< L, bull]

taut (tôt), *adj.* **1** tightly drawn: *a taut rope.* **2** tense: *taut nerves.* [earlier *taught*, appar. var. of TIGHT] —**taut′ly,** *adv.* —**taut′ness,** *n.*

tau·tog (tô tog′; –tôg′), *n.* a food fish common on the Atlantic coast of the United States. [< Algonquian]

tau·tol·o·gy (tä tol′ə ji), *n., pl.* **–gies.** saying a thing over again in other words without adding clearness or force; useless repetition. *Example:* the *modern* college student of *today.* [< LL < Gk. *tautologia,* ult. < *to auto* the same (thing) + *legein* say] —**tau′to·log′i·cal,** *adj.* —**tau′to·log′i·cal·ly,** *adv.*

tav·ern (tav′ərn), *n.* **1** place where alcoholic drinks are sold and drunk; saloon. **2** inn. [< OF < L *taberna,* orig., rude dwelling]

taw·dry (tô′dri), *adj.,* **–dri·er, –dri·est.** showy and cheap; gaudy. [ult. alter. of *St. Audrey,* from cheap laces sold at St. Audrey's fair in Ely, England] —**taw′dri·ly,** *adj.* —**taw′dri·ness,** *n.*

taw·ny (tô′ni), *adj.,* **–ni·er, –ni·est,** *n.* —*adj.* brownish-yellow: *a lion has tawny fur.* —*n.* a brownish yellow. [< OF *tane,* pp. of *taner* TAN] —**taw′ni·ness,** *n.*

tax (taks), *n.* **1** money paid by people for the support of the government. **2** *Fig.* a burden, duty, or demand that oppresses; strain. —*v.* **1** put a tax on: *tax imports, tax cigarettes.* **2** *Fig.* lay a heavy burden on; be hard for: *the job taxed his strength.* **3** reprove; accuse: *they taxed him with rudeness.* [< L *taxare,* orig., censure] —**tax′er,** *n.*

tax·a·ble (tak′sə bəl), *adj.* liable to be taxed; subject to taxation. —**tax′a·bil′i·ty, tax′a·ble·ness,** *n.* —**tax′a·bly,** *adv.*

tax·a·tion (taks ā′shən), *n.* **1** a taxing: *taxation is necessary to provide roads, schools, and police.* **2** a tax imposed. **3** amount people pay for the support of the government; taxes.

tax haven, country or place with low or no taxation where a person can deposit or invest funds and avoid paying taxes in his or her own country.

tax·i (tak′si), *n., pl.* **tax·is,** *v.,* **tax·ied, tax·i·ing** or **tax·y·ing.** —*n.* =taxicab. —*v.* **1** ride in a taxi. **2** of an airplane, move slowly on the surface of the ground or water under its own power.

tax·i·cab (tak′si kab′), *n.* automobile for hire, with a meter (**taximeter**) to record the amount to be paid. [contraction of *taximeter cab; taximeter* < F, < *taxe* fare, TAX + *mètre* METER]

tax·i·der·my (tak′sə dėr′mi), *n.* art of preparing the skins of animals and stuffing and mounting them in lifelike form. [< Gk. *taxis* arrangement (< *tassein* arrange) + *derma* skin] **tax′i·der′mic,** *adj.* —**tax′i·der′mist,** *n.*

tax·on·o·my (taks on′ə mi), *n.* **1** classification, esp. in relation to its principles or laws. **2** branch of science dealing with classification. [< F, < Gk. *taxis* arrangement (< *tassein* arrange) + *–nomos* assigning] —**tax′o·nom′ic,** *adj.* —**tax′o·nom′i·cal·ly,** *adv.* —**tax·on′o·mist,** *n.*

tax·pay·er (taks′pā′ər), *n.* person who pays a tax or is required by law to do so.

tax shelter, financial arrangement, as certain kinds of investment funds, etc., that protects a person or company from having to pay taxes.

Tay·lor (tā′lər), *n.* **Zachary,** 1784–1850, the 12th president of the United States, 1849–50.

Tb, terbium.

t.b., 1 trial balance. **2** Also **T.B.** or **TB.** tuberculosis.

tbs., tbsp., tablespoon; tablespoons.

Tc, technetium.

T cell or **T-cell** (tē′sel′), *n.* lymphocyte produced by the thymus, that destroys foreign bodies. [< *t*hymus-derived *cell*]

te (tē), *n.* seventh tone in a musical scale. [see GAMUT]

Te, tellurium.

tea (tē), *n.* **1** the dried and prepared leaves of a certain shrub, from which a drink is made by infusion with hot water. **2** the shrub itself. **3** the drink so made. **4** a meal in the late afternoon or early evening, at which tea is commonly served. **5** an afternoon reception at which tea is served. **6** something to drink prepared from some other thing: *beef tea.* [< dial. Chinese *t'e*]

tea·cart (tē′kärt′), *n.* =tea wagon.

teach (tēch), *v.,* **taught, teach·ing. 1** show how to do; make understand: *teach a dog tricks.* **2** give lessons in: *he teaches mathematics.* **3** act as teacher: *she teaches for a living.* [OE *tǣcan* show] —**teach′a·ble,** *adj.* —**teach′a·bil′i·ty, teach′a·ble·ness,** *n.* —**teach′a·bly,** *adv.*

teach·er (tēch′ər), *n.* person who teaches, esp. one who teaches in a school. —**teach′er·ship,** *n.*

teach·ing (tēch′ing), *n.* **1** work or profession of a teacher. **2** act of one who teaches. **3** instruction; precept; doctrine.

tea·cup (tē′kup′), *n.* **1** cup for drinking tea. **2** the quantity that such a cup may hold.

tea·cup·ful (tē′kup ful), *n., pl.* **–fuls.** as much as a teacup holds, usually four fluid ounces.

teak (tēk), *n.* **1** a large tree of the East Indies with a hard, durable, yellowish-brown wood. **2** this wood, used for shipbuilding, making fine furniture, etc. [< Pg. < Malayalam *tēkka*]

tea·ket·tle (tē′ket′əl), *n.* kettle for heating water to make tea, etc.

teal (tēl), *n., pl.* **teals** or (*esp. collectively*) **teal.** any of several varieties of small freshwater duck.

team (tēm), *n.* **1** number of people working or acting together, esp. one of the sides in a match: *a football team, a debating team.* **2** two or more horses or other animals harnessed together to work. —*v.* **1** join together in a team. **2** drive a team. **3** work, carry, etc., with a team. [OE *tēam*]

team·mate (tēm′māt′), *n.* a fellow member of a team.

team·ster (tēm′stər), *n.* person whose work is hauling things with a truck, originally, someone who drove a team of horses.

team·work (tēm′wėrk′), *n.* the acting together of a number of people to make

the work of the group successful and effective.

tea·pot (tē′pot′), *n.* a covered container with a handle and a spout for making and serving tea.

tear¹ (tir), *n.* Also, **tear′drop′. a** drop of salty fluid flowing from the eye. **b** something like or suggesting a tear. **in tears,** shedding tears; crying. [OE *tēar*] —**tear′less,** *adj.* —**tear′y,** *adj.*

tear² (tār), *v.,* **tore, torn, tear·ing,** *n.* —*v.* **1** pull apart by force: *tear a box open, the jagged stone tore his skin.* **2** make by pulling apart: *she tore a hole in her dress.* **3** pull hard or violently: *he tore at the hindering ropes.* **4** rend; divide: *the political party was torn by two factions.* **5** remove by effort: *he could not tear himself from that spot.* **6** make miserable; distress: *she was torn by anguish.* **7** move with great haste: *an automobile came tearing along.* —*n.* **1** a torn place. **2** act or process of tearing. **3** a rushing movement; dash. **4** a violent rage; tantrum. [OE *teran*] —**tear′er,** *n.*

tear·ful (tir′fəl), *adj.* **1** full of tears; weeping. **2** causing tears; sad. —**tear′ful·ly,** *adv.* —**tear′ful·ness,** *n.*

tear gas (tir), gas that irritates the eyes, causing tears and temporary blindness, used esp. in breaking up riots. —**tear′gas′,** *v.*

tea·room (tē′rüm′; –rum′), *n.* a room or shop where tea, coffee, and light meals are served.

tease (tēz), *v.,* **teased, teas·ing,** *n.* —*v.* **1** vex or worry by jokes, questions, requests, etc.; annoy. **2** beg: *the child teases for everything he sees.* **3** comb out; shred (wool, etc.). **4** raise nap on (cloth). —*n.* **1** person who teases. **2** act of teasing or state of being teased. [OE *tǣsan*] —**teas′er,** *n.* —**teas′ing·ly,** *adv.*

tea·sel (tē′zəl), *n., v.,* **–seled, –sel·ing.** —*n.* **1** a plant with stiff, prickly flower heads. **2** one of these used for raising nap on cloth. **3** a mechanical device used for the same purpose. —*v.* raise a nap on (cloth) with teasels. Also, **teazel, teazle.** [OE *tǣsel*] —**tea′sel·er,** *n.*

tea·spoon (tē′spün′), *n.* **1** a spoon smaller than a tablespoon, commonly used to stir tea or coffee; a standard of measure in cookery. **2** teaspoonful.

tea·spoon·ful (tē′spün ful′), *n., pl.* **–fuls.** as much as a teaspoon holds. 1 teaspoonful = ⅓ tablespoon. 1 teaspoonful = 1½ fluid drams.

teat (tēt; tit), *n.* protuberance on the breast or udder in female mammals, where the milk ducts discharge; nipple. [< OF *tete* < Gmc.]

tea wagon, small table on wheels, used for serving drinks, food, etc.

tea·zel (tē′zəl), *n., v.,* **–zeled, –zel·ing.** =teasel.

tea·zle (tē′zəl), *n., v.,* **–zled, –zling.** =teasel.

tech., 1 technical. **2** technology.

tech·ne·ti·um (tek nē′shi əm), *n.* an artificially produced metallic element, Tc.

tech·nic (tek′nik), *n.* =technique. —*adj.* =technical. [< Gk., < *techne* art, skill, craft]

tech·ni·cal (tek′nə kəl), *adj.* **1** of or having to do with a mechanical or industrial art or applied science: *a technical school.* **2** of or having to do with the special facts of a science or art: *electrolysis, tarsus, and proteid are technical words.* **3** of or having to do with any art or science: *technical skill in singing.* **4** strictly by the rules, as in art, game, etc. [< *technic*] —**tech′ni·cal·ly,** *adv.* —**tech′ni·cal·ness,** *n.*

tech·ni·cal·i·ty (tek′nə kal′ə ti), *n., pl.* **–ties. 1** a technical matter, point, detail, term, expression, etc. **2** technical quality or character.

tech·ni·cian (tek nish′ən), *n.* **1** person experienced in the technicalities of a subject. **2** person skilled in the technique of an art.

tech·nics (tek′niks), *n.* **1** study or science of an art or of arts in general, esp. of the mechanical or industrial arts. **2** technic or technique.

tech·nique (tek nēk′), *n.* **1** method or way of performing the mechanical details of an art; technical skill. **2** a special method or system used to accomplish something. [< F]

tech·noc·ra·cy (tek nok′rə si), *n.* government by technical experts. [< Gk. *techne* craft + E *–cracy* < Gk. *kratos* rule, strength] —**tech′no·crat,** *n.* —**tech′no·crat′ic,** *adj.*

tech·nol·o·gy, (tek nol′ə ji), *n.* **1** the science of the industrial arts: *engineering is studied at a school of technology.* **2** technical words, terms, or expressions used in an art, science, etc. [< Gk. *technologia* systematic treatment < *techne* art + *–logos* treating of] —**tech′no·log′i·cal,** *adj.* —**tech′no·log′i·cal·ly,** *adv.* —**tech·nol′o·gist,** *n.*

tec·ton·ic (tek ton′ik), *adj.* **1** of or having to do with tectonics: *tectonic plates.* **2** *Fig.* basic; fundamental: *tectonic shift of opinion.*

tec·ton·ics (tek ton′iks), *n.* branch of geology that deals with the structure of the earth's crust.

ted·der (ted′ər), *n.* machine that spreads out hay for drying. [cf. Scand. *tethja* spread manure]

ted·dy (ted′i) or **ted·dy bear, 1** child's soft, furry toy bear. **2** person who is a comforting friend, like the toy. [< *Teddy,* nickname for President Theodore Roosevelt, who appeared in a cartoon with a little bear]

Te De·um (tē dē′əm), **1** a hymn of praise and thanksgiving sung at morning service, and also on special ocasions. **2** music for this hymn. [< L, the first words of the hymn]

te·di·ous (tē′di əs; tē′jəs), *adj.* long and tiring. [< LL, < L *taedium* TEDIUM] —**te′di·ous·ly,** *adv.* —**te′di·ous·ness,** *n.*

te·di·um (tē′di əm), *n.* state of being wearisome; tediousness. [< L, < *taedet* it is wearisome]

tee (tē), *n., v.,* **teed, tee·ing.** —*n.* place from which a player starts in playing each hole in golf. —*v.* put (a golf ball) on a tee.

tee off, drive (a golf ball) from a tee.

teem (tēm), *v.* be full (of); abound; swarm: *the swamp teemed with mosquitoes.* [OE *tēman* < *tēam* progeny] **teem′ing·ly,** *adv.*

teen (tēn), *n.* a teenager. —*adj.* of or having to do with the teenage years.

teen·age (tēn′āj′), *n.* period of the teen years. —**teen′āj′er,** *n.*

teens (tēnz), *n.pl.* the years of life from 13 to 19 inclusive. [OE *–tīene*]

tee·pee (tē′pē), *n.* =tepee.

tee·ter (tē′tər), *n.* a seesaw. —*v.* move unsteadily; waver; seesaw. [var. of *titter* < Scand. *titra* shake]

tee·ter totter, =seesaw.

teeth (tēth), *n.* pl. of **tooth.**

cut one's teeth, a have teeth show through the gum: *the baby has begun to cut her teeth.* **b** *Fig.* get experience in something new: *cut her teeth in journalism as an intern at the newspaper.*

in the teeth of, a straight into: *in the teeth of the storm.* **b** in defiance of: *in the teeth of his parents' opposition.*

kick in the teeth, a severe disappointment or setback.

put teeth in or **into,** give some force to.

sink or **get one's teeth into,** get a grip on; begin to deal with effectively.

teethe (tēth), *v.,* **teethed, teeth·ing.** grow teeth; have teeth grow through the gums.

tee·to·tal (tē tō′təl), *adj.* of, pertaining to, advocating, or pledged to total abstinence from alcoholic liquor. [< *total,* with initial letter repeated] —**tee·to′tal·er,** *n.*

Te·gu·ci·gal·pa (tä gü′sē gäl′pä), *n.* capital of Honduras, in the S part.

teg·u·ment (teg′yə mənt), *n.* a natural covering of an animal body, or of any part of it, as a turtle's shell. [< L *tegumentum* < *tegere* cover]

Te·hran (te′ə rän′; –ran′; –hə–), *n.* capital of Iran, in the N part.

tele-, tel-, *combining form.* **1** over a distance; far. **2** television, as in *telecast.* [< Gk. *tele* far]

tel·e·cast (tel′ə kast′; -käst′), *v.,* **–cast** or **–cast·ed, –cast·ing,** *n.* —*v.* broadcast by television. —*n.* a television program. [< *tele*(*vision*) + (*broad*)*cast*] —**tel′e·cast′er,** *n.*

tel·e·com·mu·ni·ca·tion (tel′ə kə myü′nə kā′shən), *n.* communication by electronic devices, radio, etc.

telecommunications, study of such communication.

tel·e·con·fer·ence (tel′ə kon′fer əns), *n.* conference of people in different places linked by telephone or an electronic hookup.

tel·e·gen·ic (tel′ə jen′ik), *adj.* attractive or suitable for telecasting.

tel·e·gram (tel′ə gram), *n.* message sent by telegraph.

tel·e·graph (tel′ə graf; –gräf), *n.* apparatus, system, or process which sent messages by electricity. —*v.* **1** send (a message) by telegraph. **2** *Fig.* communicate by facial expression, gesture, etc. —**te·leg′ra·pher,** *n.* —**tel′e·graph′ic,** *adj.* —**tel′e·graph′i·cal·ly,** *adv.*

te·leg·ra·phy (tə leg′rə fi), *n.* the making or operating of telegraphs.

tel·e·mar·ket·ing (tel′ə mär′ki ting), *n.* process of obtaining sales by telephone. —**tel′e·mar′ket,** *v.* —**tel′e·mar′ket·er,** *n.*

te·lep·a·thy (tə lep′ə thi), *n.* communication of one mind with another by means beyond what is ordinary or normal. —**tel′e·path′ic,** *adj.* —**tel′e·path′i·cal·ly,** *adv.* —**te·lep′a·thist,** *n.*

tel·e·phone (tel′ə fōn), *n., v.,* **–phoned, –phon·ing.** —*n.* apparatus, system, or process for transmitting sound or speech by electricity. —*v.* talk through a telephone; send (a message) by telephone. [< *tele-* far + *–phone* < Gk. *phone* sound, voice] —**tel′e·phon′ic,** *adj.* —**tel′e·phon′i·cal·ly,** *adv.*

te·leph·o·ny (tə lef′ə ni), *n.* the making or operating of telephones.

tel·e·pho·to (tel′ə fō′tō), *adj.* of or having to do with telephotography.

tel·e·pho·to·graph (tel′ə fō′tə graf; –gräf), *n.* picture taken with a camera having a telephoto lens. —*v.* take a picture with a camera having a telephoto lens.

tel·e·pho·tog·ra·phy (tel′ə fə tog′rə fi), *n.* method or process of photographing distant objects by using a camera with a telephoto lens. —**tel′e·pho′to·graph′ic,** *adj.*

telephoto lens, lens used in a camera for producing an enlarged image of a distant object.

tel·e·scope (tel′ə skōp), *n., v.,* **–scoped, –scop·ing,** *adj.* —*n.* an instrument for making distant objects appear nearer and larger. The stars are studied by means of telescopes. —*v.* **1** force or be forced together one inside another like the sliding tubes of some telescopes: *when two railroad trains crash into each other, the cars are sometimes telescoped.* **2** shorten; condense. —*adj.* telescopic. [< NL, ult. < Gk. *tele* far + *–skopion* instrument for observing < *skopeein* watch]

tel·e·scop·ic (tel′ə skop′ik), *adj.* **1** of or having to do with a telescope. **2** obtained or seen by means of a telescope: *a telescopic view of the moon.* **3** consisting of parts that slide one inside another like the tubes of some telescopes. —**tel′e·scop′i·cal·ly,** *adv.*

tel·e·vise (tel′ə vīz), *v.,* **–vised, –vis·ing. 1** send by television. **2** receive by television.

tel·e·vi·sion (tel′ə vizh′ən), *n.* **1** process of transmitting the image of an object, scene, or event by radio or wire so that a person in some other place can see it at once. **2** apparatus on which these images may be seen.

tell (tel), *v.*, **told, tell·ing. 1** put in words; say: *tell the truth, tell us about it.* **2** make known: *don't tell where the money is.* **3** give evidence (of): *the smashed automobile told a sad story.* **4** recognize; know; distinguish: *he couldn't tell which house it was.* **5** say to; order; command: *tell him to stop!* **6** have effect or force: *every blow told.*

tell off, a count off; count off and detach for some special duty. **b** strike back sharply in words; castigate.

tell on, inform on; tell tales about.

tell time, know what time it is by the clock. [OE *tellan* < *talu* tale]

tell-all (tel'ôl´), *adj.* revealing everything; withholding or hiding nothing: *a tell-all biography.*

tell·er (tel'ər), *n.* **1** person who tells. **2** person in a bank who takes in, gives out, and counts money.

tell·ing (tel'ing), *adj.* having effect or force; striking: *a telling blow.* —**tell'ing·ly,** *adv.*

tell·tale (tel'tāl´), *n.* **1** person who tells tales on others; person who reveals private or secret matters from malice. **2** thing that informs or warns. —*adj.* telling what is not supposed to be told; revealing.

tel·lu·ri·um (te lùr'i əm), *n.* a rare silver-white element, Te, resembling sulfur in its chemical properties and usually occurring in nature combined with gold, silver, or other metals. [< NL, < L *tellus* earth]

tel·o·phase (tel´əfāz), *n.* final stage of mitosis, just before the cell divides into two cells.

tem·blor (tem blôr´), *n.* earthquake. [< Sp., < *temblar* tremble]

te·mer·i·ty (tə mer'ə ti), *n.* reckless boldness; rashness. [< L, < *temere* heedlessly]

temp., 1 temperature. **2** temporary.

tem·per (tem'pər), *n.* **1** state of mind; disposition; condition: *she was in a good temper.* **2** angry state of mind: *in her temper she broke a vase.* **3** calm state of mind: *he became angry and lost his temper.* **4** the hardness, toughness, etc., of a mixture: *the temper of the clay was right for shaping.* —*v.* **1** tone down; moderate; soften: *temper justice with mercy.* **2** bring or be brought to a proper or desired condition by mixing or preparing. Steel is tempered by heating it and working it till it has the proper degree of hardness. [< L *temperare,* orig., observe due measure < *tempus* time, interval]

tem·per·a (tem'pər ə), *n.* a method of painting in which colors are mixed with white of egg or other substances instead of oil. [< Ital.]

tem·per·a·ment (tem'pər ə mənt; –prə-mənt), *n.* **1** a person's nature or disposition: *she has a nervous temperament.* **2** an unusual nature or disposition that is not inclined to submit to ordinary rules or restraints: *an actress often has temperament.* [< L, < *temperare* TEMPER]

tem·per·a·men·tal (tem´pər ə men'təl; –prə men´–), *adj.* **1** due to temperament; constitutional: *cats have a temperamental dislike for water.* **2** showing a strongly marked individual temperament. **3** subject to moods and whims; easily irritated; sensitive. —**tem´per·a·men'tal·ly,** *adv.*

tem·per·ance (tem'pər əns; –prəns), *n.* **1** moderation in action, speech, habits, etc. **2** moderation in the use of alcoholic drinks. **3** the principle and practice of not using alcoholic drinks at all.

tem·per·ate (tem'pər it; –prit), *adj.* **1** not very hot and not very cold: *a temperate climate.* **2** self-restrained; moderate in behavior: *he spoke in a temperate manner.* [< L, pp. of *temperare* TEMPER] —**tem'per·ate·ly,** *adv.*

Temperate Zone, temperate zone, either of the two parts of the earth between the tropics and the polar circles.

tem·per·a·ture (tem'pər ə chər; –prə chər), *n.* **1** degree of heat or cold. The temperature of freezing water is 32 degrees Fahrenheit and 0 degrees Celsius. **2** degree of heat of a living body. **3** the excess of this above the normal (98.6 degrees Fahrenheit in adult humans); fever: *the sick man had 3 degrees of temperature.* [< L *temperatura,* ult. < *tempus* time, season]

tem·pered (tem'pərd), *adj.* **1** softened, moderated. **2** having a (specified) quality of disposition: *a good-tempered person.* **3** treated so as to become hard but not too brittle: *tempered steel.*

tem·pest (tem'pist), *n.* **1** a violent storm with much wind. **2** a violent disturbance. —*v.* disturb violently. [< OF *tempest(e)* < var. of L *tempestas* < *tempus* time, season]

tem·pes·tu·ous (tem pes'chù əs), *adj.* **1** stormy: *a tempestuous night.* **2** violent: *a tempestuous argument.* —**tem·pes'tu·ous·ly,** *adv.* —**tem·pes'tu·ous'ness,** *n.*

tem·plate (tem'plit; –plāt), *n.* **1** pattern or form used in shaping something. **2** *Fig.* any pattern used as a model: *their experience was our template for action.*

tem·ple¹ (tem'pəl), *n., v.,* –**pled,** –**pling.** —*n.* **1** a building used for the service or worship of a god or gods. **2** Also, **Temple.** any of three temples in ancient Jerusalem built at different times by the Jews. —*v.* provide with a church or temple. [< L *templum*] —**tem'pled,** *adj.*

tem·ple² (tem'pəl), *n.* the flattened part of the skull on either side of the forehead. [< OF, ult. < L *tempus*]

tem·po (tem'pō), *n., pl.* –**pos,** –**pi** (–pē). **1** time or rate of movement; proper or characteristic speed of movement in music. **2** rhythm; characteristic rhythm,

as of work, activity, etc. [< Ital., time, < L *tempus.* Doublet of TENSE².]

tem·po·ral¹ (tem'pə rəl; –prəl), *adj.* **1** of time. **2** lasting for a time only. **3** of this life only. **4** not religious or sacred; worldly. [< L, < *tempus* time] —**tem'po·ral·ly,** *adv.*

tem·po·ral² (tem'pə rəl; –prəl), *adj.* of the temples or sides of the forehead. [< L, < *tempus* temple²]

tem·po·rar·y (tem'pə rer'i), *adj.* lasting for a short time only; used for the time being; not permanent. [< L, < *tempus* time] —**tem'po·rar´i·ly,** *adv.* —**tem'po·rar´i·ness,** *n.*

tem·po·rize (tem'pə rīz), *v.,* –**rized,** –**riz·ing. 1** evade immediate action or decision in order to gain time, avoid trouble, etc. **2** fit one's acts to the time or occasion. **3** come to terms; effect a compromise. [< MF *temporiser,* ult. < L *tempus* time] —**tem'po·riz´er,** *n.* —**tem'po·riz´ing·ly,** *adv.*

tempt (tempt), *v.* **1** make or try to make (a person) do something: *the sight of food tempted the hungry man to steal, his offer tempted me.* **2** act presumptuous toward; provoke: *it is tempting fate to go in that old boat.* [< L *temptare* try] —**tempt'a·ble,** *adj.* —**tempt'er,** *n.*

temp·ta·tion (temp tā'shən), *n.* **1** a tempting. **2** fact or state of being tempted. **3** instance of this. **4** thing that tempts.

tempt·ing (temp'ting), *adj.* that tempts; alluring; inviting. —**tempt'ing·ly,** *adv.* —**tempt'ing·ness,** *n.*

tempt·ress (temp'tris), *n.* woman who tempts.

tem·pur·a (tem pùr´ə), *n.* dish of seafood, vegetables, etc., dipped in batter and deep-fried. [< Jap.]

tem·pus fu·git (tem'pəs fū'jit), *Latin.* time flies.

ten (ten), *n.* **1** a cardinal number, one more than nine. **2** symbol of this number; 10. —*adj.* one more than nine; 10. [OE *tēn*]

ten·a·ble (ten'ə bəl), *adj.* capable of being held or defended: *a tenable position, a tenable theory.* [< F, < *tenir* hold < L *tenere*] **ten´a·bil'i·ty, ten'a·ble·ness,** *n.* —**ten'a·bly,** *adv.*

te·na·cious (ti nā'shəs), *adj.* **1** holding fast: *the tenacious jaws of a bulldog.* **2** persistent: *a tenacious salesman.* **3** able to remember: *a tenacious memory.* [< L *tenax* < *tenere* hold] —**te·na'cious·ly,** *adv.* —**te·na'cious'ness,** *n.*

te·nac·i·ty (ti nas'ə ti), *n.* **1** firmness in holding fast. **2** stubbornness; persistence. **3** ability to remember.

ten·an·cy (ten'ən si), *n., pl.* –**cies. 1** state of being a tenant; occupying and paying rent for land or buildings. **2** property so held. **3** length of time a tenant occupies a property.

ten·ant (ten'ənt), *n.* **1** person paying rent for the temporary use of the land or buildings of another person. **2** person or thing that occupies: *birds are tenants of* *the trees.* —*v.* hold or occupy as a tenant; inhabit. [< F, orig. ppr. of *tenir* hold < L *tenere*] —**ten′ant·a·ble,** *adj.* —**ten′ant-ship,** *n.*

Ten Commandments, the ten rules for living and for worship that God revealed to Moses on Mount Sinai, according to the Bible. Exod. 20:2–17; Deut. 5:6–22.

tend[1] (tend), *v.* **1** be apt; incline (to): *fruit tends to decay.* **2** move (toward); be directed: *the coastline tends to the south here.* [< OF < L *tendere* stretch, aim. Doublet of TENOR[2].]

tend[2] (tend), *v.* **1** attend to by work, services, care, etc.: *he tends shop for his father.* **2** watch over and care for: *a nurse tends her patient.* [< *attend*]

tend·en·cy (ten′dən si), *n.,* *pl.* **–cies. 1** inclination; leaning: *he has a tendency to get angry easily.* **2** a natural disposition to move, proceed, or act in some direction or toward some point, end, or result: *the tendency of falling bodies toward the earth.* **3** trend or drift, as of a book, discourse, etc. [< Med.L *tendentia* < L *tendere* tend[1]] —**ten·den′tial,** *adj.*

ten·der[1] (ten′dər), *adj.* **1** not hard or tough; soft: *tender meat.* **2** not strong and hardy; delicate: *tender young grass.* **3** kind; affectionate; gentle: *tender words, pat the dog in a tender manner.* **4** young; immature: *a tender age.* **5** sensitive; painful; sore: *a tender wound.* [< OF < L *tener*] —**ten′der-ly,** *adv.* —**ten′der·ness,** *n.*

ten·der[2] (ten′dər), *v.* **1** offer formally: *he tendered his thanks.* **2** offer (money, goods, etc.) in payment of a debt or other obligation, esp. in exact accordance with provided terms. —*n.* **1** a formal offer: *she refused the tender of purchase of the farm.* **2** thing offered. Money that must be accepted as payment for a debt is called legal tender. [< F *tendre* < L *tendere* extend. Doublet of TEND[1].] —**ten′der·a·ble,** *adj.* —**ten′der-er,** *n.*

tend·er[3] (ten′dər), *n.* **1** person or thing that tends another. **2** a small boat used for carrying supplies and passengers to and from larger ships. [< *tend*[2]]

ten·der·foot (ten′dər fut′), *n.,* *pl.* **–foots, –feet. 1** newcomer to pioneer life. **2** person not used to rough living and hardships. **3** *Fig.* an inexperienced person; beginner.

ten·der-heart·ed (ten′dər här′tid), *adj.* kindly; sympathetic. —**ten′der-heart′ed-ness,** *n.*

ten·der·loin (ten′dər loin′), *n.* a tender part of the loin of beef or pork.

ten·don (ten′dən), *n.* a tough, strong band or cord of tissue that joins a muscle to a bone or some other part; sinew. [< Med.L *tendo* < Gk. *tenon*; infl. by L *tendere* stretch]

ten·dril (ten′drəl), *n.* **1** a threadlike part of a climbing plant that attaches itself to something and helps support the plant. **2** something similar: *tendrils of hair.* [< F *tendrillon,* ult. < L *tener* tender]

ten·e·ment (ten′ə mənt), *n.* a building divided into sets of rooms occupied by separate families, esp. such a building in the poorer sections of large cities. [< OF, ult. < L *tenere* hold]

ten·et (ten′it), *n.* doctrine, principle, belief, or opinion held as true. [< L, he holds]

ten·fold (ten′fōld′), *adj.* **1** ten times as much or as many. **2** having ten parts. —*adv.* ten times as much or as many.

Tenn., Tennessee.

Ten·nes·see (ten′ə sē′), *n.* a S state of the United States. —**Ten′nes·se′an,** *n., adj.*

ten·nis (ten′is), *n.* a game played by two or four players on a specially marked, oblong court (**tennis court**), in which a ball is knocked back and forth over a net with a racket (**tennis racket**). [< AF *tenetz* hold!, ult. < L *tenere*]

tennis shoe, =sneaker.

ten·on (ten′ən), *n.* the end of a piece of wood cut so as to fit into a hole (the mortise) in another piece and so form a joint. —*v.* **1** cut so as to form a tenon. **2** fit together with tenon and mortise. [< OF, ult. < L *tenere* hold]

ten·or (ten′ər), *n.* **1** the general tendency; course: *the tenor of his life has been calm.* **2** the general meaning or drift: *the tenor of a speech.* **3 a** the adult male voice ranging between the baritone and alto voices. **b** part sung by, or written for, such a voice. **c** singer or instrument with such a voice or compass. —*adj.* of or for the tenor voice. [< L, orig., a holding on, < *tenere* hold]

tenor clef, C clef when on the fourth line of the staff.

ten·pins (ten′pinz′), *n.* **1** (*sing. in use*) game played with ten wooden pins at which a ball is bowled to knock them down. **2** (*pl. in use*) the pins used.

tense[1] (tens), *adj.,* **tens·er, tens·est,** *v.,* **tensed, tens·ing.** —*adj.* **1** stretched tight; strained to stiffness: *a tense rope.* **2** in a state of mental or nervous strain: *a tense person.* **3** *Fig.* stressful; anxious: *a tense moment.* —*v.* stretch tight; stiffen: *he tensed his muscles for the leap.* [< L *tensus* stretched] —**tense′ly,** *adv.* —**ten′si-ty, tense′ness,** *n.*

tense[2] (tens), *n.* **1** a form of a verb showing the time of the action or state shown. **2** set of such forms for the various persons. [< OF *tens* time < L *tempus.* Doublet of TEMPO.]

ten·sile (ten′səl), *adj.* **1** of or having to do with tension: *steel has great tensile strength.* **2** capable of being stretched; ductile. —**ten·sil′i·ty,** *n.*

ten·sion (ten′shən), *n.* **1** a stretching. **2** a stretched condition: *the tension of the spring is caused by the weight.* **3** mental strain: *a mother feels tension when her baby is sick.* **4** strained condition of relations: *political tension.* [< LL *tensio* < L *tendere* stretch] —**ten′sion·al,** *adj.*

ten·sor (ten′sər; –sôr), *n.* muscle that stretches or tightens some part of the body. [< NL]

tent (tent), *n.* a portable shelter, usually made of canvas, supported by a pole or poles. —*v.* **1** live in a tent. **2** cover with a tent. [< OF *tente,* ult. < L *tendere* stretch] —**tent′like′,** *adj.*

ten·ta·cle (ten′tə kəl), *n.* **1** a long, slender, flexible growth on the head or around the mouth of an animal, used to touch, hold, or move; feeler. **2** a sensitive, hairlike growth on a plant. [< NL *tentaculum* < L *tentare* feel out] —**ten·tac′u-lar,** *adj.*

ten·ta·tive (ten′tə tiv), *adj.* done as a trial or experiment; experimental: *a tentative plan.* [< Med.L, < L *tentare* try out] —**ten′ta·tive·ly,** *adv.* —**ten′ta·tive-ness,** *n.*

tent caterpillar, a caterpillar that lives in tentlike silken webs attached to a tree branch.

ten·ter·hook (ten′tər hùk′), *n.* **on tenterhooks,** in painful suspense; anxious.

tenth (tenth), *adj.* **1** next after the 9th; last in a series of 10. **2** being one of 10 equal parts. —*n.* **1** next after the 9th; last in a series of 10. **2** one of 10 equal parts. —**tenth′ly,** *adv.*

ten·u·i·ty (ten ū′ə ti; ti nü′–), *n.* lacking density; thinness; slightness.

ten·u·ous (ten′yù əs), *adj.* **1** thin; slender: *tenuous filaments.* **2** not dense; rarefied: *air ten miles above the earth is very tenuous.* **3** having slight importance; not substantial. [< L *tenuis* thin] —**ten′u-ous·ly,** *adv.* —**ten′u·ous·ness,** *n.*

ten·ure (ten′yər), *n.* **1** length of time of holding or possessing: *the President's tenure of office is four years.* **2** a holding of property, esp. real property; possessing. [< OF, ult. < L *tenere* hold] —**ten-u′ri·al,** *adj.* —**ten·u′ri·al·ly,** *adv.*

te·pee (tē′pē), *n.* tent of the American Indians; wigwam. [< Am.Ind. (Dakota) *tipi*]

tep·id (tep′id), *adj.* slightly warm; lukewarm. [< L *tepidus*] —**te·pid′i·ty, tep′id-ness,** *n.* —**tep′id·ly,** *adv.*

ter·bi·um (tèr′bi əm), *n.* a rare metallic element, Tb, of the yttrium group. [< *terb*–, abstracted from *Ytterby,* Swedish town]

ter·cen·te·nar·y (tèr sen′tə ner′i; tèr′-sen ten′ə ri), *adj., n., pl.* **–nar·ies.** —*adj.* having to do with a period of 300 years. —*n.* **1** a period of 300 years. **2** a 300th anniversary. [< L *ter* three times + E *centenary*]

term (tèrm), *n.* **1** word or phrase used in a recognized and definite sense in some particular subject, science, art, business, etc.: *medical terms.* **2** a set period of time; length of time that a thing lasts: *term of office.* **3** one of the long periods into which the school year is divided: *the fall term.* **4 a** one of the members in a proportion or ratio. **b** one of the parts of a compound algebraic expression. In $13ax^2 - 2bxy + y$, $13ax^2$, $2bxy$, and y are the terms. —*v.* name, call: *he might be termed handsome.*

bring to terms, compel to agree, consent, or submit: *bring to terms through arbitration.*

come to terms, reach an agreement.

terms, a conditions: *the terms of a treaty.* **b** way of speaking: *in flattering terms.* **c** personal relations: *on good terms, on speaking terms.* [< OF *terme* < L *terminus* end, boundary line. Doublet of TERMINUS.] —**term′less,** *adj.*

ter·ma·gant (tèr′mə gənt), *n.* a violent, quarreling, scolding woman. —*adj.* violent; quarreling; scolding. [ult. < OF *Tervagan,* fictitious Muslim deity] —**ter′ma·gan·cy,** *n.*

ter·mi·na·ble (tèr′mə nə bəl), *adj.* **1** that can be ended, as an agreement, contract, etc. **2** coming to an end after a certain time: *a loan terminable in 10 years.*

ter·mi·nal (tèr′mə nəl), *adj.* **1** at the end; forming the end part: *a terminal bud.* **2** coming at the end: *terminal leave.* **3** having to do with the end of life; resulting in death: *a terminal illness.* —*n.* **1** the end; end part. **2** station, sheds, tracks, etc., at either end of a railroad line. **3** device attached to an apparatus, by means of which an electrical connection is established. —**ter′mi·nal·ly,** *adv.*

ter·mi·nate (tèr′mə nāt), *v.,* –**nat·ed,** –**nat·ing.** **1** bring or come to an end; put an end to: *terminate a partnership, his contract terminates soon.* **2** occur at or form the end of; bound; limit. [< L, < *terminus* end] —**ter′mi·na′tive,** *adj.* —**ter′mi·na′tive·ly,** *adv.* —**ter′mi·na′tor,** *n.*

ter·mi·na·tion (tèr′mə nā′shən), *n.* **1** an ending or being ended. **2** an end part. —**ter′mi·na′tion·al,** *adj.*

ter·mi·nol·o·gy (tèr′mə nol′ə ji), *n., pl.* –**gies.** the special words or terms used in a science, art, business, etc.: *medical terminology.* —**ter′mi·no·log′i·cal,** *adj.*

ter·mi·nus (tèr′mə nəs), *n., pl.* –**ni** (–nī), –**nus·es.** **1** either end of a railroad line, bus line, etc. **2** city or station at the end of a railroad line, bus line, etc. **3** an ending place; final point; goal; end. [< L. Doublet of TERM.]

ter·mite (tèr′mīt), *n.* any of the various soft-bodied insects that look like pale-colored ants and are often called white ants. Termites are very destructive to buildings, furniture, provisions, etc. [< NL *termes,* special use of L, woodworm]

term paper, essay for a course, often due at the end of a school term.

tern (tèrn), *n.* a sea bird like a gull but with a more slender body and bill and a long, forked tail. [< Scand. (Dan.) *terne*]

ter·race (ter′is), *n., v.,* –**raced,** –**rac·ing.** —*n.* **1** a flat, raised piece of land; raised level. **2** street along the side or top of a slope. **3** a paved outdoor space adjoining a house, used for relaxing, dining, etc. —*v.* form into a terrace or terraces; furnish with terraces. [< OF, ult. < L *terra* earth]

ter·ra cot·ta (ter′ə kot′ə), **1** a kind of hard, brownish-red earthenware, used for vases, statuettes, etc. **2** a dull brownish red. [< Ital., < *terra* earth + *cotta* baked] —**ter′ra-cot′ta,** *adj.*

ter·ra fir·ma (ter′ə fèr′mə), solid earth. [< L]

ter·rain (te rān′; ter′ān), *n.* land; tract of land, esp. considered as to its extent and natural features. [< F, ult. < L *terra* land]

ter·ra·my·cin (ter′ə mī′sin), *n.* an antibiotic derived from a soil microorganism, used in the treatment of certain bacterial infections, etc. [< L *terra* earth + Gk. *mykes* fungus]

ter·ra·pin (ter′ə pin), *n.* a freshwater or tidewater North American turtle used for food. [< Algonquian]

ter·rar·i·um (tə rār′i əm), *n., pl.* –**i·ums,** –**i·a** (–i ə). **1** glass or plastic container in which plants grow in a soil mixture. **2** a similar container for small land animals. [< NL, < L *terra* land]

ter·res·tri·al (tə res′tri əl), *adj.* **1** of or having to do with the earth: *terrestrial matters.* **2** of land, not water: *islands and continents make up the terrestrial parts of the earth.* **3** living on the ground; not in the air or water or in trees: *a terrestrial plant.* [< L *terrestris* < *terra* earth] —**ter·res′tri·al·ly,** *adv.*

ter·ri·ble (ter′ə bəl), *adj.* causing great fear; dreadful; awful: *a terrible storm, a terrible temper.* [< L, < *terrere* terrify] —**ter′ri·ble·ness,** *n.* —**ter′ri·bly,** *adv.*

ter·ri·er (ter′i ər), *n.* a kind of small, active dog, formerly used to pursue prey into its burrow, occurring in numerous breeds, as the fox terrier, Airedale, Scotch terrier, etc. [< F, ult. < L *terra* earth]

ter·rif·ic (tə rif′ik), *adj.* **1** causing great fear; terrifying. **2** very great, severe, etc. [< L, < *terrere* terrify + –*ficus* making] —**ter·rif′i·cal·ly,** *adv.*

ter·ri·fy (ter′ə fī), *v.,* –**fied,** –**fy·ing.** fill with great fear; frighten very much. [< L, < *terrere* terrify + *facere* make] —**ter′ri·fied′ly,** *adv.* —**ter′ri·fi′er,** *n.* —**ter′ri·fy′ing·ly,** *adv.*

ter·ri·to·ri·al (ter′ə tô′ri əl; –tō′–), *adj.* **1** of or having to do with territory. **2** protective of an area an animal claims as its own. **3 Territorial,** of or having to do with a U.S. Territory. —**ter′ri·to′ri·al·ist,** *n.* —**ter′ri·to′ri·al·ly,** *adv.*

ter·ri·to·ry (ter′ə tô′ri; –tō′–), *n., pl.* –**ries.** **1** land; region: *much territory in Africa is desert.* **2** land belonging to a government; land under the rule of a distant government. Gibraltar is British territory. **3 Territory,** district not admitted as a state but having its own law-making body. The Virgin Islands is a territory. **4** region assigned to a salesperson or agent. **5** an area in which an animal lives and defends as its own. [< L *territorium* < *terra* land]

ter·ror (ter′ər), *n.* **1** great fear. **2** a cause of great fear. [< L] —**ter′ror·less,** *adj.*

ter·ror·ism (ter′ər iz əm), *n.* **1** a terrorizing; use of terror. **2** condition of fear and submission produced by frightening people. **3** method of opposing a government internally through the use of terror. —**ter′ror·ist,** *n.* —**ter′ror·is′tic,** *adj.*

ter·ror·ize (ter′ər īz), *v.,* –**ized,** –**iz·ing.** **1** fill with terror. **2** rule or subdue by causing terror. —**ter′ror·i·za′tion,** *n.* —**ter′ror·iz′er,** *n.*

ter·ry (ter′i), or **terry cloth,** *n., pl.* –**ries.** a rough, absorbent cloth made of uncut looped yarn.

terse (tèrs), *adj.,* **ters·er, ters·est.** brief and to the point (said of writing, speaking, writers, or speakers). [< L *tersus,* pp. of *tergere* rub, polish] —**terse′ly,** *adv.* —**terse′ness,** *n.*

ter·ti·ar·y (tèr′shi er′i; tèr′shə ri), *adj., n., pl.* –**ar·ies.** —*adj.* of the third degree, order, rank, formation, etc.; third. —*n.* **1** one of a bird's flight feathers. **2 Tertiary.** earlier geological period of the Cenozoic era when mountain systems formed and animals developed rapidly. [< L, < *tertius* third]

test (test), *n.* **1** a determining of quality or genuineness; examination; trial. **2** means of trial: *trouble is a test of character.* **3** examination of a substance to see what it is or what it contains. —*v.* examine by a test; try out. [< OF, vessel used in assaying, < L *testum* earthen vessel] —**test′a·ble,** *adj.* —**test′er,** *n.*

Test., Testament.

tes·ta·ment (tes′tə mənt), *n.* **1** written instructions telling what to do with a person's property after his death; will. **2 Testament, a** a main division of the Bible; the Old Testament or the New Testament. **b** the New Testament. [< L, ult. < *testis* witness]

tes·ta·men·ta·ry (tes′tə men′tə ri; –tri), *adj.* **1** of or having to do with a testament or will. **2** given, done, or appointed by a testament or will. —**tes′ta·men′ta·ri·ly,** *adv.*

tes·tate (tes′tāt), *adj.* having made and left a valid will.

tes·ta·tor (tes′tā tər; tes tā′tər), *n.* person who makes a will, esp. one who has died leaving a valid will.

tes·ta·trix (tes tā′triks), *n., pl.* –**tri·ces** (–trə sēz). woman who makes a will; woman who has died leaving a valid will.

test ban, prohibition on testing, esp. of nuclear weapons.

test case, legal case that may determine whether or not a law is constitutional or creates a legal precedent.

tes·ti·cle (tes′tə kəl), *n.* one of the two sex glands in the male which secrete the spermatozoa. [< L *testiculus,* dim. of *testis* TESTIS] —**tes·tic′u·lar,** *adj.*

tes·ti·fy (tes′tə fī), *v.,* –**fied,** –**fy·ing.** **1** give evidence; bear witness: *the excellence of Shakespeare's plays testifies to his genius.* **2** declare or give evidence under oath in a law court. [< L, < *testis* witness + *facere* make] —**tes′ti·fi′er,** *n.*

tes·ti·mo·ni·al (tes´tə mō´ni əl), *n.* **1** certificate of character, conduct, qualifications, value, etc.; recommendation. **2** something given or done to show esteem, admiration, gratitude, etc. —*adj.* given or done as a testimonial.

tes·ti·mo·ny (tes´tə mō´ni), *n., pl.* **-nies. 1** statement of a witness under oath, used for evidence or proof: *a witness gave testimony that Mr. Doe was at home at 9 p.m.* **2** evidence: *the pupils presented their teacher with a watch in testimony of their respect and affection.* [< L, < *testis* witness]

tes·tis (tes´tis), *n., pl.* **-tes** (-tēz). =testicle. [< L, witness (of virility)]

tes·tos·ter·one (tes tos´tər ōn), *n.* a hormone, $C_{19}H_{28}O_2$, usually obtained from bulls' testicles.

test pilot, a pilot employed to test new or experimental airplanes.

test tube, a thin glass tube closed at one end, used in making chemical tests.

test-tube (test´tüb´; -tyüb´), *adj.* **1** of or having to do with a test tube: *a test-tube culture.* **2** *Fig.* chemically produced; synthetic. **3** *Fig.* not conceived naturally: *test-tube sheep; a test-tube baby.*

tes·ty (tes´ti), *adj.,* **-ti·er, -ti·est.** easily irritated; impatient. [< AF *testif* headstrong < *teste* head < L *testa* pot] —**tes´ti·ness,** *n.*

tet·a·nus (tet´ə nəs), *n.* a disease caused by bacilli entering the body through wounds, characterized by violent spasms, stiffness of many muscles, and even death. Tetanus of the lower jaw is called lockjaw. [< L < Gk. *tetanos* < *teinein* stretch]

tête-à-tête (tāt´ə tāt´), *adv.* two together in private: *they dined tête-à-tête.* —*adj.* of or for two people in private. —*n.* a private conversation between two people. [< F, head to head]

teth·er (teth´ər), *n.* rope or chain for fastening an animal so that it can graze or move only within certain limits. —*v.* fasten with a tether.

at the end of one's tether, at the end of one's resources or endurance. [prob. < Scand. *tjōthr*]

tet·ra·he·dron (tet´rə hē´drən), *n., pl.* **-drons, -dra** (-drə). a solid bounded by four plane sides. The most common tetrahedron is a pyramid whose base and three sides are equilateral triangles. [< LGk., < *tettares* four + *hedra* seat, base] —**tet´ra·he´dral,** *adj.*

te·tral·o·gy (te tral´ə ji), *n., pl.* **-gies.** series of four connected dramas, operas, etc. [< Gk., < *tettares* four + *logos* discourse]

te·tram·e·ter (te tram´ə tər), *n.* line of verse having four measures or feet. —*adj.* consisting of four measures or feet. [< L < Gk., < *tettares* four + *metron* measure]

tet·ra·va·lent (tet´rə vā´lənt; te trav´ə-), *adj.* having a valence of four.

te·trox·ide (te trok´sīd; -sid), *n.* any oxide having four atoms of oxygen in each molecule.

tet·ter (tet´ər), *n.* an itching skin disease. Eczema is a tetter. [OE *teter*]

Teu·ton (tü´tən; tū´-), *n.* **1** German. **2** member of a group of N Europeans that includes Germans, Dutch, and Scandinavians. —*adj.* German.

Teu·ton·ic (tü ton´ik; tū-), *adj.* **1** of or pertaining to the ancient Germanic tribes. **2** German. **3** of or having to do with the Teutons or their languages. —*n.* Germanic.

Tex., Texas.

Tex·as (tek´səs), *n.* a S state of the United States. —**Tex´an,** *adj., n.*

Tex-Mex (teks´meks´), *adj.* combining both Texan and Mexican elements: *Tex-Mex food.*

text (tekst), *n.* **1** the main body of reading matter in a book: *this history contains 300 pages of text.* **2** the original words of a writer. A text is often changed here and there when it is copied. **3** a short passage in the Bible, used as the subject of a sermon. **4** topic; subject. **5** textbook. [ult. < L *textus,* orig., texture < *texere* weave]

text·book (tekst´bůk´), *n.* book for regular study by pupils. Most arithmetics and geographies are textbooks.

tex·tile (teks´til; -tīl), *adj.* **1** woven. Cloth is a textile fabric. **2** suitable for weaving. Cotton and wool are common textile materials. **3** of or having to do with weaving: *the textile art.* —*n.* **1** a woven fabric; cloth. **2** material suitable for weaving. [< L, < *texere* weave]

tex·tu·al (teks´chů əl), *adj.* of a text; pertaining to a text. A misprint is a textual error. —**tex´tu·al·ly,** *adv.*

tex·ture (teks´chər), *n.* **1** arrangement of threads in a woven fabric. Burlap has a much coarser texture than a linen handkerchief. **2** arrangement of the parts of anything; structure; constitution; make-up. Sandstone and granite have different textures. [< L, < *texere* weave] —**tex´tur·al,** *adj.* —**tex´tur·al·ly,** *adv.* —**tex´tured,** *adj.*

Th, thorium.

Thai·land (tī´land), *n.* country in SE Asia bordered by Myanmar and Laos and Cambodia.

thal·a·mus (thal´ə məs), *n., pl.* **-mi** (-mī). **1** a part of the brain where a nerve emerges or appears to emerge. The **optic thalami** are two large, oblong masses of gray matter forming a part of the midbrain. **2** a receptacle of a flower [< L, inside room, < Gk. *thalamos*] —**tha·lam´ic,** *adj.*

tha·ler (tä´lər), *n., pl.* **-ler.** a former German coin, replaced by the mark.

thal·li·um (thal´i əm), *n.* a soft, malleable, rare metallic element, Tl. [< NL, < Gk. *thallos* green shoot (from green band of spectrum)]

thal·lo·phyte (thal´ə fīt), *n.* any of a large group of plants that have no leaves, stems, or roots. Bacteria, algae, fungi, and lichens are thallophytes. [< Gk.

thallos green shoot + *phyton* plant] —**thal´lo·phyt´ic,** *adj.*

thal·lus (thal´əs), *n., pl.* **-li** (-ī), **-lus·es.** a plant not divided into leaves, stem, and root. Mushrooms, toadstools, and lichens are thalli. [< NL < Gk. *thallos* green shoot]

than (ŦHan; *unstressed* ŦHən), *conj.* **1** in comparison with; compared to that which: *this train is faster than that one.* **2** except; besides: *how else can we come than on foot?*

than whom, compared to whom. [OE]

thane (thān), *n.* **1** man who ranked between an earl and an ordinary freeman in early England. Thanes held lands of the king or lord and gave military service in return. **2** a Scottish baron or lord. [OE *thegn*] —**thane´ship,** *n.*

thank (thangk), *v.* say that one is pleased and grateful for something given or done; express gratitude to. —*n.* **thanks, a** I thank you. **b** pleasure for something given or done; feeling of kindness; gratitude: *my thanks for what you did.*

have oneself to thank, be to blame: *you have only yourself to thank for missing the train.*

thanks to, owing to; because of: *thanks to your help, we got the job done.* [OE *thanc,* orig., thought] —**thank´er,** *n.*

thank·ful (thangk´fəl), *adj.* feeling or expressing thanks; grateful. —**thank´ful·ly,** *adv.* —**thank´ful·ness,** *n.*

thank·less (thangk´lis), *adj.* **1** not feeling or expressing thanks; not grateful. **2** not likely to be rewarded with thanks; not appreciated. **3** unrewarding: *a thankless task.* —**thank´less·ly,** *adv.* —**thank´less·ness,** *n.*

thanks·giv·ing (thangks giv´ing), *n.* **1** a giving of thanks. **2** expression of thanks. **Thanksgiving,** =Thanksgiving Day.

Thanksgiving Day, a day set apart every year to acknowledge past blessings and God's favor, the last Thursday in November.

that (ŦHat; *unstressed* ŦHət), *adj.* **1** indicating some person, thing, idea, etc., already mentioned, or emphasized: *do you know that boy?* **2** indicating the farther of two or more things: *shall I buy this dress or that?* **3** showing contrast: *this hat is prettier but that one costs less.* —*pron.* **1** some person, thing, idea, etc, already mentioned or emphasized: *that is the right way.* **2** the farther of two or more things: *I like that better.* **3** something contrasted: *which hat do you want, this or that?* **4** who; whom; which: *the boy that I know, the year that we went abroad.* —*conj.* **1** to introduce a noun clause: *that he will be here on time is not certain.* **2** to show purpose or result: *he ran so fast that he was five minutes early.* —*adv.* to such an extent or degree; so: *he cannot stay up that late.*

at that, a with no more talk, work, etc. **b** considering everything.

in that, because.

that's that, that is settled or decided. [OE *thœt*]

thatch (thach), *n.* **1** straw, rushes, palm leaves, etc., used as material for a roof or covering. **2** roof or covering of thatch. —*v.* roof or cover with thatch. [OE *thœc*] —**thatch′er,** *n.* —**thatch′y,** *adj.*

that'll (thạt′əl), that will or shall.

that's (thạts), that is or has.

thaw (thô), *v.* **1** melt: *the pond thaws in April.* **2** become warm enough to melt ice, snow, etc.: *if the sun stays out, it will probably thaw today.* **3** make or become less stiff and formal in manner; soften: *his shyness thawed under her kindness.* —*n.* **1** a thawing. **2** weather above the freezing point (32 degrees Farenheit, 0 degrees Celsius); time of melting. **3** a becoming less stiff and formal in manner; softening. [OE *thawian*] —**thaw′er,** *n.* —**thaw′less,** *adj.*

the[1] (*unstressed before a consonant* thə; *unstressed before a vowel* thi; *stressed* thē), *definite article.* The word *the* shows that a certain one (or ones) is meant: *the Alps, the dog is a quadruped, visit the sick.* [OE *thē, the*]

the[2] (thə; thi), *adv.* The word *the* is used to modify an adjective or adverb in the comparative degree: *if you start now, you will be back the sooner, the more the merrier, the sooner the better.* [OE *thȳ, thē, thon*]

the·a·ter (thē′ə tər), *n.* **1** place where plays are acted or motion pictures are shown. **2** place of action: *theatre of a war.* **3** plays; writing and producing plays; the drama. [< L < Gk. *theatron*]

the·a·ter·go·er (thē′ə tər gō′ər), *n.* person who goes to the theater, esp. often. —**the′a·ter·go′ing,** *adj., n.*

the·at·ri·cal (thi at′rə kəl), *adj.* Also, **the·at′·ric. 1** of or pertaining to the theater or actors. **2** suggesting a theater or acting; for display or effect; artificial. —*n.* **theatricals,** dramatic performances. —**the·at′ri·cal·ism,** *n.* —**the·at′ri·cal′i·ty,** *n.* —**the·at′ri·cal·ly,** *adv.*

thee (thē), *pron.* the objective case of **thou.** [OE *thē*]

theft (theft), *n.* **1** act of stealing. **2** an instance of stealing. [OE *thēoft < thēof* thief]

their (thãr), *pron.* the possessive case of **they,** used before a noun. [< Scand *their(r) a*]

theirs (thãrz), *pron.* **1** of them; belonging to them: *those books are theirs, not mine.* **2** the one or ones belonging to them: *our house is white; theirs is brown.*

the·ism (thē′iz əm), *n.* belief in one God, the creator and ruler of the universe. [< Gk. *theos* god] —**the′ist,** *n.* —**the·is′tic,** *adj.* —**the·is′ti·cal·ly,** *adv.*

them (thẹm; *unstressed* thəm), *pron.* the objective case of **they.** [< Scand. *theim*]

theme (thēm), *n.* **1** topic, as of a speech, discussion, book, etc.; subject. **2** a short written composition. **3 a** the principal melody in a piece of music. **b** a short melody repeated in different forms in an elaborate musical composition. [< L < Gk. *thema,* lit., something set down] —**the·mat′ic,** *adj.* —**the·mat′i·cal·ly,** *adv.*

them·selves (thẹm selvz′; thəm–), *pron.* **1** the emphatic form of **they** or **them:** *they did it themselves.* **2** the reflexive form of **them:** *they injured themselves.*

then (thẹn), *adv.* **1** at that time: *prices were then lower.* **2** soon afterwards: *the noise stopped, and then began again, first comes spring, then summer, now one boy does best and then another.* **3** also; besides: *the dress seems too good to discard, and then it is so becoming.* **4** in that case; therefore: *if you didn't know, then you should have said so.* —*n.* that time: *by then we shall know the result.*

but then, at the same time: *could have gone, but then she had much to do.*

then and there, at that time and place: *should have stopped then and there.*

what then?, what happens next, or in that case?: *if that's true, what then?* [OE *thœnne*]

thence (thẹns), *adv.* **1** from that place; from there: *a few miles thence is a river.* **2** for that reason; therefore: *you didn't work, thence no pay.* **3** from that time; from then: *a few years thence.* [ME *thennes* < OE *thanan(e)*]

thence·forth (thẹns′fôrth′; –fōrth′), **thence·for·ward** (–fôr′wərd), **thence·for·wards** (–wərdz), *adv.* from then on; from that time forward.

the·oc·ra·cy (thi ok′rə si), *n., pl.* **–cies. 1** government in which God is recognized as the supreme civil ruler and his laws are taken as the laws of the state. **2** government by religious leaders. **3** country or nation governed by a theocracy. [< Gk., < *theos* god + *kratos* rule] —**the′o·crat′ic,** *adj.* —**the′o·crat′i·cal·ly,** *adv.*

the·od·o·lite (thi od′ə līt), *n.* a surveying instrument for measuring horizontal and vertical angles.

theol., theology.

the·o·lo·gian (thē′ə lō′jən; –ji ən), *n.* person skilled or trained in theology.

the·o·log·i·cal (thē′ə loj′ə kəl), *adj.* **1** of or pertaining to theology. **2** referring to the nature and will of God. —**the′o·log′i·cal·ly,** *adv.*

the·ol·o·gy (thi ol′ə ji), *n., pl.* **–gies. 1** study of the nature of God and his relations to man and the universe. **2** study of religion and religious beliefs. **3** system of religious beliefs. [< L < Gk., < *theos* god + *–logos* treating of] —**the·ol′o·gist,** *n.*

the·o·rem (thē′ə rəm), *n.* **1** statement in mathematics to be proved. **2** statement of mathematical relations that can be expressed by an equation or formula. **3** statement or rule that can be proved to be true. [< L < Gk. *theorema < theoreein* consider]

the·o·ret·i·cal (thē′ə ret′ə kəl), **the·o·ret·ic** (–ik), *adj.* **1** planned or worked out in the mind, not from experience; based on theory, not on fact; limited to theory. **2** dealing with theory only; not practical. —**the′o·ret′i·cal·ly,** *adv.*

the·o·re·ti·cian (thē′ə rə tish′ən), *n.* person who knows much about the theory of an art, science, etc.

the·o·rist (thē′ə rist), *n.* person who forms theories.

the·o·rize (thē′ə rīz), *v.,* **–rized, –riz·ing.** form a theory or theories; speculate. —**the′o·ri·za′tion,** *n.* —**the′o·riz′er,** *n.*

the·o·ry (thē′ər ē; thir′ē), *n., pl.* **–ries. 1** explanation; explanation based on thought; explanation based on observation and reasoning. **2** the principles or methods of a science or art rather than its practice: *the theory of music.* **3** abstract knowledge. **4** thought or fancy as opposed to fact or practice. [< LL < Gk., < *theoreein* consider]

the·os·o·phy (thi os′ə fi), *n.* a philosophy or religion that claims to have a special insight into the divine nature through spiritual self-development. [< Med.L < LGk., ult. < Gk. *theos* god + *sophos* wise] —**the′o·soph′ic, the′o·soph′i·cal,** *adj.* —**the·os′o·phist,** *n.*

ther·a·peu·tic (ther′ə pū′tik), *adj.* having to do with the treatment or curing of disease; curative. [< NL, ult. < Gk. *therapeuein* cure, treat < *theraps* attendant] —**ther′a·peu′ti·cal·ly,** *adv.*

ther·a·peu·tics (ther′ə pū′tiks), *n.* branch of medicine that deals with the remedial treatment of disease; therapy.

ther·a·py (ther′ə pi), *n., pl.* **–pies.** treatment of physical and mental disorders. —**ther′a·pist,** *n.*

there (thãr; *unstressed* thər), *adv.* **1** in, to, or at that place: *sit there, go there at once.* **2** at that point; in that matter: *you may stop there, you are mistaken there.* **3** *There* is used when the verb comes before its subject: *is there a drugstore near here?* and to call attention to some person or thing: *there goes the bell.* —*n.* that place: *from there go on to New York.* —*interj. There* is used to express dismay, comfort, etc.: *there, there! don't cry.* —*adj.* **all there,** *Informal.* **a** wide-awake; alert. **b** sane; not crazy. [OE *thœr*]

there·a·bouts (thãr′ə bouts′), **there·a·bout** (-bout′), *adv.* near that place; time, or amount.

there·af·ter (thãr af′tər; –äf′–), *adv.* **1** after that; afterward. **2** accordingly.

there·at (thãr at′), *adv.* at that time or place; because of that.

there·by (thãr bī′; thãr′bī), *adv.* in that way or connection: *thereby hangs a tale.*

there'd (thãrd), there had or would.

there·for (thãr fôr′), *adv.* for that; for this; for it.

there·fore (thãr′fôr′; –fōr), *adv.* for that reason; as a result of that; consequently.

there·from (thãr from′; –frum′), *adv.* from that; from this; from it.

there·in (thãr in′), *adv.* in that place or matter.

there·in·to (thãr in′tü; thãr´in tü′), *adv.* into that place or matter.

there'll (thãrl), there will or shall.

there·of (thãr ov′; –uv′), *adv.* of that or from it.

there·on (thãr on′; –ôn′), *adv.* on that; immediately after that.

there's (thãrz), there is or has.

there·to (thãr tü′), *adv.* to that; also.

there·to·fore (thãr´tə fôr′; –fōr′), *adv.* before that time; until then.

there·un·der (thãr un′dər), *adv.* under that; according to that.

there·un·to (thãr un′tü; thãr´un tü′), *adv.* to that; to it.

there·up·on (thãr′ə pon′; –pôn′), *adv.* 1 immediately after that. 2 on that; on it.

there·with (thãr with′; –with′), *adv.* 1 with that; also. 2 immediately after that; then.

ther·mal (thèr′məl), *adj.* 1 of or pertaining to heat. 2 warm; hot. —*n.* in aeronautics and aerodynamics, a current of rising warm air. [< Gk. *therme* heat] —**ther′mal·ly, ther′mi·cal·ly,** *adv.*

thermal barrier, heat barrier.

thermal pollution, discharge of heat into water or air causing a damaging rise in temperature of an environment.

thermo-, therm-, *combining form.* heat. [< Gk. *therme*]

ther·mo·dy·nam·ic (thèr′mō dī nam′ik; –di–), *adj.* 1 of or having to do with thermodynamic. 2 using force due to heat or to the conversion of heat into mechanical energy.

ther·mo·dy·nam·ics (thèr′mō dī nam′iks; –di–), *n.* branch of physics that deals with the relations between heat and mechanical energy.

ther·mom·e·ter (thər mom′ə tər), *n.* instrument for measuring temperature, as by means of the expansion and contraction of mercury or alcohol in a capillary tube and bulb. —**ther′mo·met′ric,** *adj.*

ther·mo·nu·cle·ar (thèr′mō nü′kli ər; –nū′–), *adj.* of or designating the fusion of atoms through very high temperature: *a thermonuclear reaction.*

ther·mo·plas·tic (thèr′mō plas′tik), *adj.* becoming soft and capable of being molded when heated. —*n.* such a material, esp. a plastic.

ther·mos (thèr′məs), *n.* 1 bottle, flask, or jug having a case or jacket that heat cannot pass through easily. It will keep its contents at about their original temperature for hours. 2 trademarked name of this bottle or jug. [< Gk. *thermos* hot]

ther·mo·sphere (thèr′mə sfir), *n.* farthest part of the atmosphere where the temperature increases with height.

ther·mo·stat (thèr′mə stat), *n.* an automatic device that responds to conditions of temperature by turning heat on or off, opening a valve, sounding an alarm, etc. [< THERMO- + Gk. *-states* that stands] —**ther′mo·stat′ic,** *adj.* —**ther′mo·stat′i·cal·ly,** *adv.*

the·sau·rus (thi sô′rəs), *n., pl.* **-ri** (–rī). 1 dictionary in which words are organized according to their relationship to each other or to certain subjects. 2 a dictionary, encyclopedia, or other book that is a storehouse of information. [< L < Gk. *thesaurus.* Doublet of TREASURE.]

these (thēz), *adj., pron.* pl. of **this.**

the·sis (thē′sis), *n., pl.* **-ses** (–sēz). 1 proposition or statement to be debated or to be maintained against objections. 2 subject for a composition. 3 essay; essay presented by a candidate for a diploma or degree: *a senior thesis.* [< L < Gk., orig., a setting down]

thes·pi·an or **Thes·pi·an** (thes′pi ən), *adj.* of or having to do with the drama or tragedy; dramatic; tragic. —*n.* actor or actress. [< *Thespis,* Greek poet]

Thes·sa·lo·ni·ans (thes′ə lō′ni ənz), *n.* either of two books of the New Testament written by Saint Paul.

the·ta (thā′tə; thē′tə), *n.* the eighth letter (Θ, θ) of the Greek alphabet.

they (thā), *pron., nom.,* **they;** *poss.,* **their, theirs, of them, of theirs;** *obj.,* **them.** 1 nom. pl. of **he, she,** or **it:** *they are related.* 2 some people; any people; persons: *they say he's in trouble.* [< Scand. *their*]

they'd (thād), they had or would.

they'll (thāl), they will or shall.

they're (thãr), they are.

they've (thāv), they have.

thi·a·mine (thī′ə min; –mēn), *n.* a complex organic compound, $C_{12}H_{17}CIN_4OS$, found in cereals, yeast, etc., or prepared synthetically. Its chloride, vitamin B_1, aids in preventing beriberi, etc.

thick (thik), *adj.* 1 with much space from one side to the opposite side; not thin: *a thick wall.* 2 measuring between two opposite sides: *two inches thick.* 3 set close together; dense: *thick hair.* 4 many; abundant: *bullets thick as hail, thick with flies.* 5 dense; not clear: *thick soup, thick air, a thick voice.* 6 stupid; dull: *thick as a plank.* —*adv.* in a thick manner. —*n.* 1 that which is thick. 2 the thickest part: *in the thick of the fight.*

thick and fast, in numbers and rapidly: *words flew thick and fast.*

thick and thin, good times and bad; easy situations and hard. [OE *thicce*] —**thick′ly,** *adv.* —**thick′ness,** *n.*

thick·en (thik′ən), *v.* 1 make or become thick or thicker. 2 make or become more dense, foggy, hoarse, obscure, or complicated. —**thick′en·er,** *n.*

thick·en·ing (thik′ən ing; thik′ning), *n.* 1 material or ingredient used to thicken something. 2 a thickened part.

thick·et (thik′it), *n.* shrubs, bushes, or small trees growing close together. [OE *thiccet < thicce* thick] —**thick′et·ed,** *adj.*

thick·head·ed (thik′hed′id), *adj.* stupid; dull. —**thick′-head′ed·ness,** *n.*

thick·set (thik′set′), *adj.* thickly set: *a thick-set hedge, a thick-set man.*

thick·skinned (thik′skind′), *adj.* 1 having a thick skin. 2 not sensitive to

criticism, reproach, rebuff, or the like. —**thick′skin′,** *n.*

thief (thēf), *n., pl.* **thieves** (thēvz). person who steals, esp. one who steals secretly and without using force. [OE *thēof*]

thieve (thēv), *v.,* **thieved, thiev·ing.** steal. [OE *thēofian < thēof* thief] —**thiev′ish,** *adj.* —**thiev′ish·ly,** *adv.* —**thiev′ish·ness,** *n.*

thiev·er·y (thēv′ər i; thēv′ri), *n., pl.* **-er·ies.** act of stealing; theft.

thigh (thī), *n.* 1 in humans, the part of the leg between the hip and the knee. 2 a corresponding part of the hind limbs of other animals. [OE *thēoh*]

thigh·bone (thī′bōn′), *n.* bone of the leg between the hip and the knee; femur.

thim·ble (thim′bəl), *n.* a small metal or plastic cap worn on the finger to protect it when pushing the needle in sewing. [OE *thymel < thūma* thumb]

thim·ble·ful (thim′bəl fúl), *n., pl.* **-fuls.** amount a thimble can hold; a very little bit.

thin (thin), *adj.,* **thin·ner, thin·nest,** *adv., v.,* **thinned, thin·ning.** —*adj.* 1 with little space from one side to the opposite side; not thick: *thin paper, thin wire.* 2 having little flesh; slender; lean: *a thin person.* 3 scanty; not abundant: *a thin audience, thin hair.* 4 not dense: *thin mountain air, thin milk.* 5 having little depth, fullness, or intensity: *a thin color, a shrill, thin voice.* 6 easily seen through; flimsy: *a thin excuse, a thin fabric.* —*adv.* in a thin manner. —*v.* make or become thin. [OE *thynne*] —**thin′ly,** *adv.* —**thin′ner,** *n.* —**thin′ness,** *n.* —**thin′nish,** *adj.*

thine (thīn), *Archaic or Poetic.* —*pron.* 1 belonging to thee; yours. 2 the one or ones belonging to thee; yours. —*adj.* thy; your. [OE *thīn*]

thing[1] (thing), *n.* 1 any object: *what are those things in the field?, what sort of thing is it?* 2 whatever is spoken or thought of; fact, event, idea, etc.: *a strange thing happened.* 3 a matter; affair; business: *how are things going?*

do one's (own) thing, *Informal.* do what one enjoys most or does best.

for one thing, first of all.

know a thing or two, *Informal.* be experienced or wise.

make a good thing of, *Informal.* profit from.

see things, a have hallucinations. **b** imagine too much.

the thing, a the fashion or style. **b** the important fact or idea.

things, a belongings; possessions. **b** clothes. [OE]

things[2] (thing; ting), *n.* in Scandinavian countries, a legislative assembly, court of law, or other public meeting. [< Icelandic]

think (thingk), *v.,* **thought, think·ing.** 1 have an idea; form in the mind; use the mind: *think clearly, he thought that he would go.* 2 have an opinion; believe; consider: *think of others first, think* *before answering.* **3** imagine: *you can't think how surprised I was.* **4** remember: *I can't think of his name.*

think aloud, say what one is thinking.

think better of, a think more favorably of. **b** change one's mind concerning.

think out, plan, solve, or understand by thinking.

think over or **through,** think about esp. until one reaches conclusion.

think twice, hesitate.

think up, plan. [OE *thencan*] —**think′a·ble,** *adj.* —**think′er,** *n.*

think·ing (thingk′ing), *adj.* **1** that thinks; reasoning. **2** thoughtful. —*n.* thought. —**think′ing·ly,** *adv.*

think tank, institute or center dedicated to research in social and political issues, foreign policy, etc.

thin-skinned (thin′skind′), *adj.* **1** having a thin skin. **2** sensitive to criticism, rebuff; touchy. —**thin′-skinned′-ness,** *n.*

third (thėrd), *adj.* **1** next after the second; last in a series of three. **2** being one of three equal parts. —*n.* **1** next after the second; last in a series of three. **2** one of three equal parts. **3 a** tone three degrees from another tone. **b** interval between such tones. **c** combination of such tones. **4** =third basc. [OE *thirda*, var. of *thridda* < *thrēo* three] —**third′ly,** *adv.*

third base, 1 base next after second that a runner in baseball must touch. **2** position covering third base.

third-class (thėrd′klas′; –kläs′), *adj.* of or belonging to a third class; inferior. —*adv.* on a third-class ship, train, etc.

third degree, abusive questioning in an attempt to get information or a confession.

third estate, persons not in the nobility or clergy; common people.

third party, 1 person or entity not directly involved in something, as in a lawsuit. **2** political party that is an alternative to the two major parties in the United States.

third person, form of a pronoun or verb used to refer to the person spoken of. *He, she, it,* and *they* are pronouns of the third person.

third rail, rail paralleling the ordinary rails of a railroad and carrying a powerful electric current.

third-rate (thėrd′rāt′), *adj.* **1** of a third class. **2** distinctly inferior.

third world or **Third World,** the underdeveloped nations of the world.

thirst (thėrst), *n.* **1** a dry feeling caused by having nothing to drink; desire or need for something to drink. **2** *Fig.* a strong desire: *a thirst for excitement.* —*v.* **1** feel thirst; be thirsty. **2** *Fig.* have a strong desire. [OE *thurst*]

thirst·y (thėrs′ti), *adj.,* **thirst·i·er, thirst·i·est. 1** feeling thirst; having thirst. **2** without water or moisture; dry. **3** *Fig.* having a strong desire; eager. —**thirst′i·ly,** *adv.* —**thirst′i·ness,** *n.*

thir·teen (thėr′tēn′), *n.* **1** a cardinal number, three more than ten. **2** symbol of this number; 13. —*adj.* three more than ten; 13. —**thir′teenth′,** *adj., n.*

thir·ty (thėr′ti), *n., pl.* **-ties,** *adj.* —*n.* **1** a cardinal number, three times ten. **2** symbol of this number; 30. —*adj.* three times ten; 30. —**thir′ti·eth,** *adj., n.*

thir·ty-sec·ond note (thėr′ti sek′ənd), musical note ¹⁄₃₂ of a whole note.

this (this), *pron., pl.* **these,** *adj., adv.* —*pron.* **1** the person, thing, event, quality, condition, idea, etc., that is present, mentioned, or referred to now: *this is the best, after this you must go home.* **2** the one emphasized or contrasted with another called "that": *this is newer than that.* —*adj.* present; near; spoken of; referred to: *this minute, this child, this idea.* —*adv.* to this extent or degree; so: *you can have this much.* [OE]

this·tle (this′əl), *n.* plant with a prickly stalk and leaves. The purple thistle is the national flower of Scotland. [OE *thistel*] —**this′tly,** *adj.*

this·tle·down (this′əl doun′), *n.* the down or fluff of a ripened thistle.

thith·er (thith′ər; thith′ər), *adv.* to that place; toward that place; there. —*adj.* on that side; farther. [OE *thider*]

tho, tho' (thō), *conj., adv.* =though.

thole (thōl), or **thole·pin** (thōl′pin′), *n.* a peg on the side of a boat to hold an oar in rowing. [OE *tholl*]

Thom·as (tom′əs), *n.* one of the twelve disciples chosen by Jesus as apostles. He at first doubted the resurrection. John 20:24–29.

thong (thông; thong), *n.* **1** a narrow strip of leather, etc., esp. used as a fastening. **2** lash of a whip. **3** sandal held on the foot with a narrow strap that fits between the large and second toes. **4** scanty underpants. [OE *thwang*]

tho·rac·ic (thô ras′ik; thō–), *adj.* of or having to do with the thorax, esp. the organs within the cavity, as the heart and lungs: *a thoracic surgeon.*

tho·rax (thô′raks; thō′–), *n., pl.* **–rax·es, –ra·ces** (–rə sēz). **1** the part of the body between the neck and the abdomen; chest. **2** the second division of an insect's body, between the head and the abdomen. [< L < Gk.]

tho·ri·um (thô′ri əm; thō′–), *n.* a radioactive metallic element, Th, present in certain rare minerals. [< NL, < *Thor*] —**thor′ic,** *adj.*

thorn (thôrn), *n.* **1** a sharp-pointed growth on a stem or branch of a tree or plant. **2** tree or plant that has thorns on it. **3** something that annoys or causes discomfort. [OE] —**thorn′like′,** *adj.*

thorn apple, 1 fruit of the hawthorn; haw. **2** hawthorn. **3** jimson weed.

thorn·y (thôr′ni), *adj.,* **thorn·i·er, thorn·i·est. 1** full of thorns. **2** *Fig.* troublesome; annoying: *a thorny problem.* —**thorn′i·ly,** *adv.* —**thorn′i·ness,** *n.*

tho·ron (thô′ron; thō′–), *n.* a rare element, Tn or Th Em, a radioactive gas.

thor·ough (thėr′ō), *adj.* **1** being all that is needed; complete. **2** doing all that should be done and slighting nothing. [OE *thuruh*, var. of *thurh* through] —**thor′ough·ly,** *adv.* —**thor′ough·ness,** *n.*

thor·ough·bred (thėr′ō bred′), *adj.* of pure breed or stock. —*n.* a thoroughbred horse or other animal.

thor·ough·fare (thėr′ō fãr′), *n.* **1** a passage, road, or street open at both ends. **2** a main road; highway.

thor·ough·go·ing (thėr′ō gō′ing), *adj.* thorough; complete.

those (thōz), *adj., pron.* pl. of **that.**

thou (thou), *pron.* you; the one spoken to. —*v.* address familiarly as thou. [OE *thū*]

though (thō), *conj.* **1** in spite of the fact that; notwithstanding the fact that: *though it was pouring, they went out.* **2** even if; supposing that: *though I fail, I shall try again.* —*adv.* however: *I am sorry about our quarrel; you began it, though.*

as though, as if; as it would be if. [ME *thoh*]

thought (thôt), *n.* **1** what one thinks; idea; notion: *do you understand my thought?* **2** power or process of thinking; mental activity; reasoning: *thought helps solve problems.* **3** consideration; attention; regard: *give some thought to others.* **4** intention: *we had thoughts of going.* **5** expectation: *I had no thought of seeing you here.* **6** a little bit; trifle: *be a thought more polite.* —*v.* pt. and pp. of **think.** [OE *thōht*]

thought·ful (thôt′fəl), *adj.* **1** full of thought; thinking. **2** careful; considerate. —**thought′ful·ly,** *adv.* —**thought′ful·ness,** *n.*

thought·less (thôt′lis), *adj.* **1** without thought. **2** careless; not considerate. —**thought′less·ly,** *adv.* —**thought′less·ness,** *n.*

thou·sand (thou′zənd), *n.* **1** a cardinal number, ten times one hundred. **2** symbol of this number; 1000. —*adj.* ten times one hundred; 1000. [OE *thūsend*] —**thou′sandth,** *adj., n.*

thou·sand·fold (thou′zənd fōld′), *adj.* **1** 1000 times as much or as many. **2** having 1000 parts. —*adv.* 1000 times as much or as many.

thrall (thrôl), *n.* **1** person in bondage; slave. **2** thralldom. **3** *Fig.* person who is a slave to something, as a habit or addiction. [< Scand. *thrēll*]

thrall·dom, thrall·dom (thrôl′dəm), *n.* bondage; slavery.

thrash (thrash), *v.* **1** beat: *the man thrashed the burglar.* **2** move violently; toss: *the patient thrashed about in his bed.* **3** thresh (wheat, etc.). —*n.* act of thrashing; beating.

thrash out, settle by thorough discussion.

thrash over, go over again and again. [var. of *thresh*]

thrash·er (thrash′ər), *n.* **1** person or thing that thrashes. **2** Also, **thrasher shark.** thresher (def. 3). **3** any of several American birds related to the mockingbird.

thread (thred), *n.* **1** cotton, silk, flax, etc., spun out into a fine cord. **2** something long and slender like a thread: *threads of a spider's web.* **3** the main thought that connects the parts of a story, speech, etc. **4** the winding, sloping ridge of a screw, etc. —*v.* **1** pass a thread through: *thread a needle.* **2** form into a thread: *cook the syrup until it threads.* **3** make one's way through: *he threaded his way through the crowd.* **4** form a thread on (a screw, etc.).

hang by a thread, be in an insecure or risky condition: *their survival hung by a thread.*

threads, *Informal.* clothes: *like my threads?* [OE *thrēd*] —**thread′er,** *n.* —**thread′like**′, *adj.*

thread·bare (thred′bār′), *adj.* **1** having the nap worn off; worn so much that the threads show. **2** wearing clothes worn to the threads; shabby. **3** old and worn; stale: *a threadbare excuse.* —**thread′bare′ness,** *n.*

threat (thret), *n.* **1** statement of what will be done to hurt or punish someone. **2** sign or cause of possible evil or harm. [OE *thrēat*]

threat·en (thret′ən), *v.* **1** make a threat against; say what will be done to hurt or punish: *threaten with imprisonment.* **2** utter threats: *do you mean to threaten?* **3** be a sign of (possible evil or harm, etc.): *black clouds threaten rain.* **4** be a cause of possible evil or harm to: *a flood threatened the city.* [OE *thrēatnian*] —**threat′en·er,** *n.* —**threat′en·ing·ly,** *adv.*

three (thrē), *n.* **1** a cardinal number, one more than two. **2** symbol of this number; 3. **3** set of three persons or things. —*adj.* one more than two; 3. [OE *thrēo*]

3-D or **three-D** (thrē′dē′), *n.* three dimensional: *a three-D person.*

three-di·men·sion·al (thrē′də men′-shən əl), *adj.* **1** having height, width, and depth, or appearing to. **2** *Fig.* real; substantial: *a three-dimensional story.*

three·fold (thrē′fōld′), *adj.* **1** three times as much or as many. **2** having three parts. —*adv.* three times as much or as many.

three·pence (thrip′əns; threp′əns), *n.* **1** three British pennies; three pence. **2** coin of this value. Also, **thrip·pence.**

three-ply (thrē′plī′), *adj.* having three thicknesses, layers, folds, or strands.

three-ring circus (thrē′ring′), **1** circus that has three different acts proceeding at the same time. **2** *Fig.* any very busy or confusing situation.

three R's, reading, writing, and arithmetic.

three·score (thrē′skôr′; –skōr′), *adj.* three times twenty; 60.

three·some (thrē′səm), *n.* group of three people.

thren·o·dy (thren′ə di), *n., pl.* **–dies.** song of lamentation, esp. at a person's death. [< Gk., < *threnos* lament + *oide* song]

thresh (thresh), *v.* **1** separate the grain or seeds from (wheat, etc.), as by beating with a flail. **2** toss about; move violently; thrash.

thresh out, settle by thorough discussion.

thresh over, go over again and again. [OE *threscan*]

thresh·er (thresh′ər), *n.* **1** person or thing that threshes. **2** machine used for separating the grain or seeds from wheat, etc. **3** Also, **thresher shark.** a large shark with a very long tail.

thresh·old (thresh′ōld; thresh′hōld), *n.* **1** piece of wood or stone under a door. **2** doorway. **3** *Fig.* point of entering; beginning point: *the scientist was on the threshold of an important discovery.* [OE *thresc(w)old*]

threw (thrü), *v.* pt. of **throw.**

thrice (thrīs), *adv.* **1** three times. **2** very; extremely. [ME *thries* < OE *thriga* thrice]

thrift (thrift), *n.* absence of waste; saving; economical management; habit of saving. [< *thrive*] —**thrift′less,** *adj.* —**thrift′less-ly,** *adv.* —**thrift′less·ness,** *n.*

thrift shop, shop that sells second-hand items at low prices.

thrift·y (thrif′ti), *adj.,* **thrift·i·er, thrift·i-est. 1** careful in spending; economical; saving. **2** thriving; flourishing; prosperous: *a thrifty plant.* —**thrift′i·ly,** *adv.* —**thrift′i·ness,** *n.*

thrill (thril), *n.* **1** a shivering, exciting feeling. **2** a thrilling quality, as of a play or story. **3** a quivering; vibration. —*v.* **1** give a shivering, exciting feeling to. **2** have such a feeling. **3** quiver; tremble. [var. of *thirl,* OE *thyrlian* pierce < *thurh* through] —**thrill′ing,** *adj.* —**thrill′ing-ly,** *adv.* —**thrill′ing·ness,** *n.*

thrill·er (thril′ər), *n.* **1** person or thing that thrills. **2** a sensational play or story, esp. one involving a murder.

thrip·pence (thrip′əns), *n.* =threepence.

thrive (thrīv), *v.,* **throve** or **thrived, thrived** or **thriv·en** (thriv′ən), **thriv·ing.** be successful; grow rich; grow strong; prosper. [< Scand. *thrīfa(sk)*] —**thriv′er,** *n.* —**thriv′ing,** *adj.* —**thriv′ing·ly,** *adv.*

thro′, thro (thrü), *prep., adv., adj.* =through.

throat (thrōt), *n.* **1** the front of the neck. **2** the passage from the mouth to the stomach or the lungs. **3** any narrow passage: *the throat of a mine.*

at each other's throat or **throats,** violent quarrelling.

have by the throat, have at one's mercy; have in complete control.

jump down one's throat, attack or criticize someone suddenly and violently.

lump in the throat, feeling unable to swallow, esp. from feeling sad.

stick in one's throat, be hard or unpleasant to say. [OE *throte*]

throat·y (thrōt′i), *adj.,* **throat·i·er, throat-i·est. 1** produced or modified in the throat, as sounds: *a throaty sound.* **2** of a woman's voice, low-pitched and resonant. —**throat′i·ly,** *adv.* —**throat′i·ness,** *n.*

throb (throb), *v.,* **throbbed, throb·bing,** *n.* —*v.* **1** beat rapidly or strongly: *the long climb made her heart throb.* **2** beat steadily. —*n.* **1** a rapid or strong beat: *a throb of pain shot through his head.* **2** a steady beat: *the throb of a pulse.* —**throb′ber,** *n.* —**throb′bing·ly,** *adv.* —**throb′less,** *adj.*

throe (thrō), *n.* a violent pang; great pain.

throes, a anguish; agony. **b** *Fig.* a desperate struggle; violent disturbance. [earlier throwe; see THROW]

throm·bo·sis (throm bō′sis), *n.* formation of a blood clot in a blood vessel or in the heart causing a blockage. [< NL < Gk., ult. < *thrombos* clot] —**throm-bot′ic,** *adj.*

throne (thrōn), *n., v.,* **throned, thron·ing.** —*n.* **1** chair on which a king, queen, bishop, or other person of high rank sits during ceremonies. **2** power or authority of a king, queen, etc. —*v.* =enthrone. [< L < Gk. *thronos*] —**throne′less,** *adj.*

throng (thrông; throng), *n.* a crowd; multitude. —*v.* **1** crowd; fill with a crowd. **2** come together in a crowd; go or press in large numbers. [OE *(ge)thrang*]

throt·tle (throt′əl), *n., v.,* **–tled, –tling.** —*n.* **1** valve regulating the flow of steam, gasoline vapor, etc., to an engine. **2** lever, pedal, etc., working such a valve. **3** throat. —*v.* **1** stop the breath of by pressure on the throat; strangle. **2** *Fig.* check or stop the flow of; suppress: *regulations throttle innovation.* **3** lessen the speed of (an engine) by closing a throttle. [< *throat*] —**throt′tler,** *n.*

through (thrü), *prep.* **1** from side to side or beginning to end of: *pass through a door, a tunnel through a mountain.* **2** here and there in; over; around: *travel through a country.* **3** because of; by means of: *they ran through fear, we found out through him.* **4** finished with: *be through one's work.* —*adv.* **1** from beginning to end: *read a letter through.* **2** completely; thoroughly: *chilled through.* **3** all the way: *the train goes through to Boston.* —*adj.* **1** going all the way: *a through street.* **2** finished: *I am almost through.*

through and through, completely; thoroughly. [earlier *thourgh,* OE *thurh*]

through·out (thrü out′), *prep.* all the way through; through all; in every part of. —*adv.* in every part.

throve (thrōv), *v.* pt. of **thrive.**

throw (thrō), *v.,* **threw, thrown, throw·ing,** *n.* —*v.* **1** cast; toss; hurl: *throw a ball.* **2** bring to the ground: *his horse threw him.* **3** put, send, build, etc., hastily: *throw a bridge across a river, she threw us a glance.* **4** move (a lever, etc.) that connects or disconnects parts of a switch, clutch, or other mechanism. **5** shed. **6** let an opponent win (a race, game, etc.), as for money or other ulterior motives. —*n.* **1** a cast, toss, etc. **2** distance a thing is or may be thrown. **3** scarf; light covering.

throw away, a get rid of; discard. **b** fail to use.

throw back, revert to an ancestral type.

throw cold water on, discourage by being indifferent or unwilling.

throw in, add as a gift.

throw off, get rid of.

throw oneself at, try very hard to get the love, friendship, or favor of.

throw open, a open suddenly or widely. **b** remove all obstacles or restrictions from.

throw out, a get rid of; discard. **b** reject.

throw over, give up; discard; abandon.

throw together, a put together hastily: *throw a meal together.* **b** come into contact by chance: *thrown together at the office and became good friends.*

throw up, a vomit. **b** give up; abandon. **c** build rapidly. [OE *thrāwan* twist] —**throw′er,** *n.*

throw·back (thrō′bak′), *n.* **1** a throwing back. **2** setback or check. **3** reversion to an ancestral type.

thru (thrü), *prep., adv., adj.* =through.

thrum (thrum), *v.,* **thrummed, thrum·ming,** *n.* —*v.* **1** play on a stringed instrument by plucking the strings: *thrum a guitar.* **2** drum or tap idly with the fingers. —*n.* the sound made by such playing or tapping. [imit.] —**thrum′mer,** *n.*

thrush (thrush), *n.* **1** any of a large group of migratory songbirds that includes the robin, the bluebird, the wood thrush, etc. **2** a brown bird with a spotted white breast, that has a very sweet song. [OE *thrȳsce*]

thrust (thrust), *v.,* **thrust, thrust·ing,** *n.* —*v.* **1** push with force. **2** stab: *thrust a knife into an apple.* **3** put forcibly into some position, condition, etc.: *thrust oneself into danger.* —*n.* **1** a forcible push; drive. **2** a stab. **3** *Fig.* sudden attack: *a sarcastic thrust from her opponent.* **4** in mechanics, architecture, etc., the force of one thing pushing on another. [< Scand. *thrȳsta*] —**thrust′er,** *n.*

thru·way (thrü′wā′), *n.* an express highway.

thud (thud), *n., v.,* **thud·ded, thud·ding.** —*n.* **1** a dull sound. **2** a blow or thump. —*v.* hit, move, or strike with a thud. [OE *thyddan* strike]

thug (thug), *n.* **1** ruffian; cutthroat. **2** member of a former religious organization of robbers and murderers in India. [< Hind. *ṭhag* < Skt. *sthaga* rogue]

thu·li·um (thü′li əm), *n.* a rare element, Tm, of the yttrium group.

thumb (thum) *n.* **1** the short, thick finger of the human hand, next to the forefinger. **2** part of a glove or mit-

ten that covers the thumb. —*v.* **1** soil or wear by handling with the thumbs: *the books were badly thumbed.* **2** turn pages of (a book, etc.) rapidly, reading only portions. **3** handle awkwardly: *all thumbs today, dropping everything.* **4** get a free ride by signaling with the thumb: *thumbed his way from coast to coast.*

thumb a ride, get a free ride by signaling with the thumb.

thumbs down, sign of disapproval or rejection: *got a thumbs down on that idea.*

thumbs up, sign of approval or acceptance: *a thumbs up on an application.*

under the thumb of, under the power or influence of. [OE *thūma*] —**thumb′like′,** *adj.*

thumb·nail (thum′nāl′), *n.* **1** nail of the thumb. **2** *Fig.* something very small or short. —*adj.* very small or short.

thumb·screw (thum′skrü′), *n.* **1** a screw made so that its head can be easily turned with the thumb and a finger. **2** instrument of torture that squeezed the thumbs.

thumb·tack (thum′tak′), *n.* tack with a broad, flat head, that can be pressed into a wall, board, etc., with the thumb.

thump (thump), *v.* **1** strike against with something: *he thumped the table with his fist, the shutters thumped the wall.* **2** make a dull sound; pound: *the hammer thumped against the wood.* **3** beat violently: *his heart thumped.* —*n.* **1** a blow with something thick and heavy; heavy knock. **2** the dull sound made by a blow, knock, or fall. [imit.] —**thump′er,** *n.*

thun·der (thun′dər), *n.* **1** the loud noise that often follows a flash of lightning, caused by a disturbance of the air resulting from the discharge of electricity. **2** any noise like thunder. **3** *Fig.* threat; denunciation. —*v.* **1** give forth thunder. **2** utter very loudly; roar: *thunder a reply.*

steal one's thunder, a use another's idea, plan, etc., as one's own without asking permission or giving credit. **b** draws recognition away from the person who should have it. [OE *thunor*] —**thun′der·er,** *n.*

thun·der·bird (thun′dər bėrd′), *n.* giant bird in North American Indian folklore that makes thunder by flapping its wings and lightning by blinking its eyes.

thun·der·bolt (thun′dər bōlt′), *n.* **1** a flash of lightning and the thunder that follows it. **2** *Fig.* something sudden, startling, and terrible: *the news of his death came as a thunderbolt.*

thun·der·clap (thun′dər klap′), *n.* **1** a loud crash of thunder. **2** *Fig.* something sudden or startling.

thun·der·cloud (thun′dər kloud′), *n.* a dark, electrically charged cloud that brings thunder and lightning.

thun·der·head (thun′dər hed′), *n.* one of the round, swelling masses of cumulus clouds often appearing before thunder-

storms and frequently developing into thunderclouds.

thun·der·ous (thun′dər əs; –drəs), *adj.* **1** producing thunder. **2** making a noise like thunder. —**thun′der·ous·ly,** *adv.*

thun·der·show·er (thun′dər shou′ər), *n.* a shower with thunder and lightning.

thun·der·storm (thun′dər stôrm′), *n.* storm with thunder and lightning.

thun·der·struck (thun′dər struk′), *adj.* overcome, as if hit by a thunderbolt; astonished; amazed.

Thurs., Thur., Thursday.

Thurs·day (thėrz′di; –dā), *n.* the fifth day of the week, following Wednesday.

thus (ᴛhus), *adv.* **1** in this way; in the way just stated, indicated, etc.; in the following manner: *he spoke thus.* **2** accordingly; consequently; therefore: *thus we decided that he was wrong.* **3** to this extent or degree; so: *thus far.* [OE]

thwack (thwak), *v.* strike vigorously with a stick or something flat. —*n.* a sharp blow with a stick or something flat. —**thwack′er,** *n.*

thwart (thwôrt), *v.* oppose and defeat; keep from doing something. —*n.* **1** a seat across a boat, on which a rower sits. **2** a brace in a canoe. —*adj.* lying across. —*adv.* across; crosswise. [< Scand. *thvert,* neut., transverse] —**thwart′er,** *n.*

thy (ᴛhī), *pron., adj.* Mainly Archaic or Poetic. your. [OE *thīn*]

thyme (tīm), *n.* a small plant that has a mint-like fragrance. The leaves of the common **garden thyme** are used for seasoning. The common **wild thyme** is a creeping evergreen. [< L < Gk. *thymon*]

thy·mine (thī′min; –mēn), *n.* substance found in nucleic acid in cells and one of the bases of DNA.

thy·mus (thī′məs), *adj.* of or having to do with the thymus gland. —*n.* the thymus gland. [< NL < Gk. *thymos*]

thymus gland, a small ductless gland near the base of the neck. The thymus of calves is used for food and called sweetbread.

thy·roid (thī′roid), *n.* **1** the thyroid gland. **2** medicine made from the thyroid glands of animals, used in the treatment of goiter, obesity, etc. **3** the thyroid cartilage. —*adj.* of or having to do with the thyroid gland or thyroid cartilage. [ult. < Gk. *thyreoeides* shieldlike < *thyreos* oblong shield]

thyroid cartilage, the principal cartilage of the larynx; Adam's apple.

thyroid gland or **body,** an important ductless gland in the neck of vertebrates that affects growth and metabolism.

thy·rox·in (thī rok′sin), *n.* the principal secretion of the thyroid gland.

thy·self (ᴛhī self′), *pron.* Archaic yourself.

ti (tē), *n.* the seventh tone of the scale. [see GAMUT]

Ti, titanium.

ti·ar·a (tī ãr′ə; tī ä′rə), *n.* a band of gold, jewels, or flowers worn around the head as an ornament. [< L < Gk.]

Ti·bet (ti bet′), *n.* former country on a lofty plateau in S Asia, now a province of China. —**Ti·bet′an,** *adj., n.*

tib·i·a (tib′i ə), *n., pl.* **–i·ae** (–i ē), **–i·as.** the inner and thicker of the two bones of the leg from the knee to the ankle; shinbone. [< L] —**tib′i·al,** *adj.*

tic (tik), *n.* a habitual, involuntary twitching of the muscles, esp. those of the face. [< F]

tick¹ (tik), *n.* **1.** a sound made by a clock or watch. **2** a sound like it. **3** a small mark. We use ✓ or/as a tick. —*v.* **1** make a tick, as a clock. **2** mark off: *the clock ticked away the minutes.* **3** mark with a tick; check: *he ticked off the items one by one.* [prob. ult. imit.]

tick² (tik), *n.* a tiny insect that attaches itself to the skin of humans and animals and sucks their blood. [OE *ticia*]

tick³ (tik), *n.* the cloth covering of a mattress or pillow. [prob. ult. < L *theca* case < Gk. *theke*]

tick·er (tik′ər), *n.* **1** person or thing that ticks. **2** *Informal.* the heart.

tick·et (tik′it), *n.* **1** a card or piece of paper that gives its holder a right or privilege: *a theater ticket.* **2** summons given to an offender to appear in court, usually with reference to traffic violations: *a ticket for speeding.* **3** a card or piece of paper attached to something to show its price, etc. **4** the list of candidates to be voted on that belong to one political party. —*v.* **1** put a ticket on; mark with a ticket. **2** give a traffic summons to. [< F *étiquette* ticket, ETIQUETTE]

tick·ing (tik′ing), *n.* a strong cotton or linen cloth, used to cover mattresses and pillows and to make tents and awnings.

tick·le (tik′əl), *v.,* **–led, –ling,** *n.* —*v.* **1** touch lightly causing little thrills, shivers, or wriggles. **2** have a feeling like this; cause to have such a feeling: *my nose tickles.* **3** *Fig.* excite pleasantly; amuse: *the story tickled him.* **4** play, stir, get, etc., with light touches or strokes. —*n.* **1** a tingling or itching feeling. **2** a tickling. —**tick′ler,** *n.*

tick·lish (tik′lish), *adj.* **1** sensitive to tickling: *a ticklish person.* **2** *Fig.* requiring careful handling; delicate; risky: *a ticklish situation.* **3** easily upset; unstable: *a canoe is a ticklish craft.* —**tick′lishness,** *n.*

tick-tack-toe (tik′tak tō′), *n.* game of nine boxes played on paper in which each of two players tries to mark three boxes in a row with an X or O.

tid·al (tīd′əl), *adj.* **1** of tides; having tides; caused by tides. **2** depending on the tide.

tidal wave, 1 a large, destructive ocean wave produced by an earthquake, hurricane, etc. **2** either of two great swellings of the ocean surface (due to the attraction of the moon and sun) that move around the globe on opposite sides and cause the tides. **3** *Fig.* any great movement or manifestation of feeling, opinion, or the like.

tid·bit (tid′bit′), *n.* a very pleasing bit of food, news, etc. Also, **titbit.** [< *tid* nice + *bit* morsel]

tide (tīd), *n., v.,* **tid·ed, tid·ing.** —*n.* **1** the rise and fall of the ocean about every twelve hours, caused by the attraction of the moon and the sun. **2** anything that rises and falls like the tide: *the tide of popular opinion.* **3** stream; current; flood. **4** season; time. —*v.* carry as the tide does.

tide over, help along for a time.

turn the tide, change from one condition to the opposite. [OE *tīd,* orig., time]

tide·land (tīd′land′), *n.* submerged coastal land within the historical boundaries of a state and belonging to that state.

tide·wa·ter (tīd′wô′tər; –wot′ər), *n.* **1** water having tides. **2** low-lying land along the coast; seacoast. —*adj.* of or along tidewater.

ti·dings (tī′dingz), *n.pl.* news; information. [OE *tīdung* < *tīdan* happen]

ti·dy (tī′di), *adj.,* **–di·er, –di·est,** *v.,* **–died, –dy·ing.** —*adj.* **1** neat and in order: *a tidy room.* **2** inclined to keep things neat and in order: *a tidy person.* **3** considerable; fairly large: *a tidy sum of money.* —*v.* put in order; make tidy. [ult. < OE *tīd* time] —**ti′di·er,** *n.* —**ti′di·ly,** *adv.* —**ti′di·ness,** *n.*

tie (tī), *v.,* **tied, ty·ing,** *n.* —*v.* **1** fasten with string or the like; bind: *tie a package.* **2** tighten and fasten the string or strings of: *tie one's shoes.* **3** restrain; restrict; limit: *he did not want to be tied to a steady job.* **4** make the same score; be equal in points: *the two teams tied.* —*n.* **1** anything connecting or holding together two or more things or parts. **2** necktie. **3** thing that unites; bond; obligation: *family ties.* **4** beam, rod, or the like that connects or holds together two or more parts, such as rails of a railroad. **5** equality in points, votes, or a contest in which this occurs. **6** a curved line set above or below notes that are to be played or sung continuously.

tie down, limit; confine; restrict.

tie in, connect: *ties in with the rest of the story.*

tie into, attack.

tie up, a tie firmly or tightly. **b** wrap up: *tie up a box, (Fig.) tie up a contract.* **c** stop; delay: *tie up the commuter lines.* **d** make unavailable: *tie up in a meeting.* [OE *tīgan* < *tēag* rope] —**ti′er,** *n.*

tie-dye (tī′dī′), *v.,* **–dyed, –dy·ing.** tie fabric into knots before dying it, creating abstract patterns from the uneven exposure to dye.

tie-in (tī′in′), *n.* connection; relationship.

tier (tir), *n.* one of a series of rows arranged one above another: *tiers of seats at a baseball game.* —*v.* arrange in tiers. [< F, orig., order] —**tiered,** *adj.*

tie-up (tī′up′), *n.* a stopping of work or operations on account of a strike, storm, accident, etc.

tiff (tif), *n.* a little quarrel. —*v.* have a little quarrel.

ti·ger (tī′gər), *n.* **1** a large, fierce Asiatic animal of the cat family that has dull-yellow fur striped with black **2** =tiger cat (def. 1). [< L < Gk. *tigris*] —**ti′gerish, ti′grish, ti′ger·like′,** *adj.*

tiger cat, 1 domestic cat with markings somewhat like the tiger. **2** small wildcat resembling a tiger.

tiger lily, a lily that has dull-orange flowers spotted with black.

tiger shark, large shark found in the Atlantic and Pacific Oceans that has yellow stripes on its back.

tight (tīt), *adj.* **1** firm; held firmly; packed or put together firmly: *a tight knot, a tight canvas.* **2** close; fitting closely; fitting too closely: *tight clothing.* **3** not letting water, air, or gas in or out. **4** hard to deal with or manage; difficult: *his lies got him in a tight place.* **5** almost even; close: *it was a tight race.* **6** hard to get; scarce: *money is tight just now.* **7** stingy. **8** drunk. —*adv.* firmly.

sit tight, keep the same position, opinion, etc. [OE *getyht,* pp. of *tyhtan* stretch] —**tight′ly,** *adv.* —**tight′ness,** *n.*

tight·en (tīt′ən), *v.* make tight or become tight. —**tight′en·er,** *n.*

tight-fist·ed (tīt′fis′tid), *adj.* stingy.

tight-lipped (tīt′lipt′), *adj.* **1** keeping the lips firmly together. **2** saying little or nothing.

tight·rope (tīt′rōp′), *n.* **1** rope stretched tight on which acrobats perform. **2** *Fig.* difficult, potentially dangerous situation. —*adj.* of or pertaining to a tight-rope.

tights (tīts), *n.pl.* a close-fitting covering for the legs and lower body, worn by acrobats, dancers, etc.

tight·wad (tīt′wod′), *n. Informal.* a stingy person.

ti·gress (tī′gris), *n.* a female tiger.

til·de (til′də), *n.* **1** a diacritical mark (~) used over *n* in Spanish when it is pronounced *ny,* as in *cañon* (kä nyōn′). **2** in the pronunciations in this book, a mark used over *a* to show that it is pronounced as in *fare* (fãr). [< Sp. < L *titulus* title]

tile (tīl), *n., v.,* **tiled, til·ing.** —*n.* **1 a** a thin piece of baked clay, stone, etc. Tiles are used for covering roofs, paving floors, and ornamenting. **b** thin piece of plastic, rubber, etc., used in similar ways. **2** pipe for draining land. **3** tiles collectively. —*v.* put tiles on or in. [< L *tegula*] —**til′er,** *n.*

til·ing (tīl′ing), *n.* **1** tiles collectively. **2** the work of covering with tiles. **3** work consisting of tiles.

till¹ (til), *prep., conj.* until; up to the time of; up to the time when. [OE *til*]

till² (til), *v.* cultivate (land); plow. [OE *tilian*] —**till′a·ble,** *adj.* —**till′er,** *n.*

till³ (til), *n.* a small drawer for money under or behind a counter. [ult. < OE *–tyllan* draw, as in *betyllan* lure]

till·age (til′ij), *n.* **1** cultivation of land. **2** fact or condition of being tilled. **3** tilled land. **4** crops growing on tilled land.

till·er (til′ər), *n.* bar or handle used to turn the rudder in steering a boat. [< OF *telier* weaver's beam, ult. < L *tela* web, loom] **—till′er·less,** *adj.*

tilt (tilt), *v.* **1** slope; slant; lean; tip: *this table tilts.* **2** rush, charge, or fight with lances. **—n. 1** a slope; sloping position. **2** act or fact of tilting; state of being tilted. **3** a fight on horseback with lances.

full tilt, at full speed; with full force: *his car ran full tilt against the tree.*

tilt at windmills, attack imaginary enemies. [ult. < OE *tealt* shaky] **—tilt′er,** *n.*

tim·ber (tim′bər), *n.* **1** *U.S.* wood used for building and making things. **2** a large piece of wood used in building. Beams and rafters are timbers. **3** a curved piece forming a rib of a ship. **4** growing trees; forests. **—v.** cover, support, or furnish with timber. [OE] **—tim′bered,** *adj.* **—tim′ber·ing,** *n.* **—tim′ber·land′,** *n.*

timber line, line beyond which trees will not grow on mountains and in the polar regions because of the cold.

timber wolf, a large gray or brindled wolf of North America.

tim·bre (tim′bər; tam′–), *n.* the quality in sounds that distinguishes a certain voice, instrument, etc., from other voices, instruments, etc. [< OF, ult. < Gk. *tympanon* kettledrum. Doublet of TYMPANUM.]

time (tīm), *n., v.,* **timed, tim·ing,** *adj.* **—n. 1** all the days there have been or ever will be; the past, present, and future: *space and time are two fundamental conceptions.* **2** a part of time: *a long time, for the time being.* **3** a particular point in time: *what time is it? dinner time, this time we will succeed.* **4** the right part or point of time: *it is time to eat.* **5** way of reckoning time: *daylight-saving time.* **6** condition or experience during life: *hard times, a good time.* **7** a rate of movement in music; rhythm: *waltz time.* **b** length of a note or rest in music. **8 a** amount of time that one has worked. **b** pay for this: *give me my time.* **9** free time; leisure: *have time to read.* **—v. 1** measure the time of: *time a race.* **2** do at regular times; do in rhythm with; set the time of: *the dancers time their steps to the music.* **3** choose the moment or occasion for. **—adj. 1** of or pertaining to time. **2** provided with a clocklike mechanism so that it will explode or ignite at a given moment: *a time bomb.* **3** pertaining to purchases to be paid for at a future date.

about time, near the proper time: *about time to go.*

against time, trying to finish before a certain time: *hard to work against time.*

at the same time, however; nevertheless.

at times, now and then; once in a while.

behind the times, out-of-date.

buy time, stall; delay.

do time, *Informal.* serve time in prison.

for the time being, for now.

from time to time, now and then; once in a while.

in no time, soon.

in time, a after a while. **b** soon enough. **c** in the right tempo, in music, marching, dancing, etc.

keep time, a measure time correctly: *the clock keeps perfect time.* **b** record time or the rate of speed: *kept time for the race.* **c** move at the right pace: *keep time to the music.*

kill time, spend time doing unprotective or uninteresting things; pass time.

on time, a at the right time; not late. **b** with time in which to pay: *buy on time.*

take one's time, move slowly, deliberately; not hurry.

tell time, read the time.

time after time or **time and again,** again and again.

times, multiplied by; x. [OE *tīma*]

time·card (tīm′kärd′), *n.* card for recording the amount of time that a person works.

time clock, clock with a device to record the time when workers arrive and leave.

time-hon·ored (tīm′on′ərd), *adj.* honored because old and established.

time·keep·er (tīm′kēp′ər), *n.* person or thing that keeps time.

time-lapse (tīm′laps′), *adj.* of or having to do with a photographic technique that makes a very slow process appear to be fast, as in the opening of a flower.

time·less (tīm′lis), *adj.* **1** never ending; eternal. **2** referring to no special time.

time line, 1 time when events occurred, pictured on a chart in a long line: *a time line of the Revolution.* **2** =timetable.

time·ly (tīm′li), *adj.,* **-li·er, -li·est.** at the right time. **—time′li·ness,** *n.*

time·piece (tīm′pēs′), *n.* clock or watch.

tim·er (tīm′ər), *n.* **1** person or thing that times. **2** =timepiece. **3** in an internal-combustion engine, an automatic device that causes the spark for igniting the charge to occur just at the time required.

time slot, position in a schedule, esp. of radio or television programs.

time·ta·ble (tīm′tā′bəl), *n.* schedule showing the times when trains, boats, buses, airplanes, etc., arrive and depart.

time·worn (tīm′wôrn′; –wōrn′), *adj.* worn by long existence or use.

time zone, geographical region where the same standard time is used. The world is divided into 24 time zones, the United States has four.

tim·id (tim′id), *adj.* easily frightened; shy. [< L *timidus*] **—tim′id·ly,** *adv.* **—tim′id·ness,** *n.*

ti·mid·i·ty (ti mid′ə ti), *n.* state or character of being timid; shyness.

tim·ing (tīm′ing), *n.* regulation of the speed of motions, musical tempo, etc., to secure the greatest possible effect.

tim·or·ous (tim′ər əs), *adj.* easily frightened; timid. [< Med.L, < L *timor* fear] **—tim′or·ous·ly,** *adv.* **—tim′or·ous·ness,** *n.*

tim·o·thy (tim′ə thi), *n.* a kind of coarse grass with long, cylindrical spikes, often grown for hay. [after *Timothy* Hanson, early American cultivator]

Tim·o·thy (tim′ə thi), *n.* **1** a disciple of the Apostle Paul. **2** either of the two books of the New Testament written as letters by Paul to Timothy.

tim·pa·ni (tim′pə ni), *n. pl., sing.* **–no** (–nō). kettledrums. [< Ital., pl. of *timpano* TYMPANUM] **—tim′pa·nist,** *n.*

tin (tin), *n., adj., v.,* **tinned, tin·ning. —n. 1** a metallic element, Sn, resembling silver in color and luster but softer and cheaper. **2** tin plate. **3** any can, box, pan, or other container made of tin: *a pie tin.* **—adj.** made of tin. **—v.** cover with tin. [OE] **—tinned, tin′like′,** *adj.*

tinc·ture (tingk′chər), *n., v.,* **–tured, –turing. —n. 1** solution of medicine in alcohol: *tincture of iodine.* **2** trace; tinge. **3** color; tint. **—v. 1** give a trace or tinge to. **2** color; tint. [< L *tinctura* < *tingere* tinge]

tin·der (tin′dər), *n.* anything that catches fire easily. [OE *tynder*] **—tin′der·like′,** *adj.*

tin·der·box (tin′dər boks′), *n.* **1** box for holding tinder, flint, and steel for making a fire. **2** *Fig.* a very inflammable thing or person.

tine (tīn), *n.* a sharp projecting point or prong: *the tines of a fork.* [OE *tind*] **—tined,** *adj.*

ting (ting), *v.* make or cause to make a clear ringing sound. **—n.** such a sound. [imit.]

tinge (tinj), *v.,* **tinged, tinge·ing** or **ting·ing,** *n.* **—v. 1** color slightly: *a drop of ink will tinge a glass of water.* **2** add a trace of some quality to; change slightly: *sad memories tinged their present joy.* **—n. 1** a slight coloring or tint. **2** a very small amount; trace. [< L *tingere*] **—tin′ger,** *n.* **—tin′gi·ble,** *adj.*

tin·gle (ting′gəl), *v.,* **–gled, –gling,** *n.* **—v. 1** have a feeling of thrills or a pricking, stinging feeling. **2** cause this feeling in; be thrilling: *the newspaper story tingled with excitement.* **—n.** a pricking, stinging feeling. [prob. var. of *tinkle*] **—tin′gler,** *n.* **—tin′gling·ly,** *adv.*

tink·er (tingk′ər), *n.* **1** person who mends pots, pans, etc. **2** unskilled work; activity that is rather unproductive. **3** person who does such work. **—v. 1** mend; patch. **2** work or repair in an unskilled or amateur way. **3** work or keep busy in a rather unproductive way. [ult. < *tin*] **—tink′er·er,** *n.*

tin·kle (ting′kəl), *v.,* **–kled, –kling,** *n.* **—v. 1** make short, light, ringing sounds: *little bells tinkle.* **2** move with a tinkle; call, make known, etc., by tinkling: *the* *little clock tinkled out the hours.* —*n.* series of short, light, ringing sounds. [ult. imit.] —**tin′kler,** *n.* —**tin′kling,** *n., adj.* —**tink′ly,** *adj.*

tin·ner (tin′ər), *n.* person who works with tin.

tin·ny (tin′i), *adj.,* **-ni·er, -ni·est. 1** of tin; containing tin. **2** like tin in looks or sound. —**tin′ni·ly,** *adv.* —**tin′ni·ness,** *n.*

tin plate, thin sheets of iron or steel coated with tin. Ordinary tin cans are made of tin plate.

tin·sel (tin′səl), *n., adj.* —*n.* **1** glittering thin strips, threads, etc., esp. used to trim Christmas trees. **2** *Fig.* anything showy but having little value. —*adj.* of or like tinsel; showy but not worth much. [< F *étincelle* spark < L *scintilla* spark. Doublet of SCINTILLA.] —**tin′sel·ly,** *adj.*

tin·smith (tin′smith′), *n.* person who works with tin; maker of tinware.

tint (tint), *n.* **1** variety of a color: *several tints of blue.* **2** a delicate or pale color. **3** variety of a color produced by mixing it with white. —*v.* put a tint on; color slightly. [earlier *tinct* < L *tinctus* a dyeing < *tingere* to dye] —**tint′er,** *n.*

tin·type (tin′tīp′), *n.* photograph taken on a sheet of enameled tin or iron.

tin·ware (tin′wār′), *n.* articles made of tin.

ti·ny (tī′ni), *adj.,* **-ni·er, -ni·est.** very small; wee.

–tion, *suffix.* **1** act or state of ____ing, as in *addition, opposition.* **2** condition or state of being ____ed, as in *exhaustion.* **3** result of ____ing, as in *apparition.* [< L *-tio*]

tip¹ (tip), *n., v.,* **tipped, tip·ping.** —*n.* **1** the terminal portion; end; point: *the tips of the fingers.* **2** the uppermost portion; summit; top: *the tip of a steeple.* **3** a small piece put on the end of something. —*v.* put a tip on; furnish with a tip. [ME *tippe*]

tip² (tip), *v.,* **tipped, tip·ping,** *n.* —*v.* **1** slope; slant: *she tipped the table toward her.* **2** upset; overturn. **3** take off (a hat) in salutation. —*n.* a slope; slant. —**tip′per,** *n.*

tip³ (tip), *n., v.,* **tipped, tip·ping,** —*n.* **1** a small present of money. **2** piece of secret information: *a tip on a race horse.* **3** a useful hint, suggestion, etc.: *household tips.* **4** a light, sharp blow; tap. —*v.* **1** give a small present of money to. **2** give secret information to. **3** give a tip. **4** hit lightly and sharply; tap.

tip off, a give secret information to. **b** warn. —**tip′per,** *n.*

tip-off (tip′ôf′; -of′), *n. Informal.* **1** piece of secret information. **2** a warning.

tip·pet (tip′it), *n.* **1** scarf for the neck and shoulders with ends hanging down in front, esp. a long black scarf worn by clergy in choir. **2** a long, narrow, hanging part of a hood, sleeve, or scarf. [prob. < *tip¹*]

tip·ple (tip′əl), *v.,* **-pled, -pling,** *n.* —*v.* drink (alcoholic liquor) often. —*n.* an alcoholic liquor. —**tip′pler,** *n.*

tip·ster (tip′stər), *n.* person who makes a business of furnishing private or secret information for use in betting, speculation, etc.

tip·sy (tip′si), *adj.,* **-si·er, -si·est.** somewhat intoxicated but not thoroughly drunk. [prob. < *tip²*] —**tip′si·ly,** *adv.* —**tip′si·ness,** *n.*

tip·toe (tip′tō′), *n., v.,* **-toed, -toe·ing,** *adj., adv.* —*n.* the tips of the toes. —*v.* walk on the tips of the toes. —*adj.* **1** standing or walking on tiptoe. **2** eagerly expectant. **3** cautious; stealthy. —*adv.* on tiptoe.

on tiptoe, a walking on one's toes. **b** eager. **c** in a secret.

tip-top (tip′top′), *n.* the very top; highest point. —*adj.* **1** at the very top or highest point. **2** first-rate; excellent. —**tip′top′per,** *n.*

ti·rade (tī′rād; tə rād′), *n.* **1** a long, vehement speech. **2** a long, scolding speech. [< F < Ital. *tirata* < *tirare* shoot]

Ti·ra·na or **Ti·ra·ne** (ti rä′nə), *n.* capital of Albania, in the C part.

tire¹ (tīr), *v.,* **tired, tir·ing.** make or become weary: *the work tired him.*

tire out, make very weary. [OE *tȳrian*]

tire² (tīr), *n., v.,* **tired, tir·ing.** —*n.* a band of rubber or metal around a wheel. —*v.* furnish with a tire. [< *attire,* in sense of "covering"]

tired (tīrd), *adj.* weary; wearied; exhausted. —**tired′ly,** *adv.* —**tired′ness,** *n.*

tire·less (tīr′lis), *adj.* **1** never becoming tired; requiring little rest: *a tireless worker.* **2** never stopping: *tireless efforts.* —**tire′less·ly,** *adv.*

tire·some (tīr′səm), *adj.* tiring; boring: *a tiresome speech.* —**tire′some·ly,** *adv.*

'tis (tiz), it is.

tis·sue (tish′ü), *n.* **1** substance forming the parts of animals and plants; a mass of cells: *brain tissue, skin tissue.* **2** web; network: *her whole story was a tissue of lies.* **3** tissue paper. [< OF *tissu,* orig. pp. of *tistre* weave < L *texere*]

tissue paper, a very thin, soft paper.

tissue typing, procedure used to determine if tissues from a donor are compatible with tissues of the recipient of a transplant.

tit¹ (tit), *n.* **1** =titmouse. **2** any of various other small birds. [cf. Scand. *tittr* titmouse]

tit² (tit), *n.* nipple; teat. [OE *titt*]

ti·tan (tī′tən), *n.* person or thing having enormous size, strength, power, etc.; giant.

ti·tan·ic (tī tan′ik), *adj.* having great size, strength, or power; gigantic; huge.

ti·ta·ni·um (tī tā′ni əm; ti-), *n.* metallic element, Ti, occurring in various minerals. [< *Titan* family of giants in Greek mythology] —**ti·tan′ic,** *adj.*

tit for tat, blow for blow; like for like.

tithe (tīŧħ), *n., v.,* **tithed, tith·ing.** —*n.* **1** one tenth. **2** Often, **tithes.** tax of one tenth of the yearly produce of land, animals, and personal work, paid for the support of the church and the clergy. **3** a very small part. **4** any small tax, levy, etc. —*v.* **1** put a tax of a tenth on. **2** pay a tithe on. **3** give one tenth of one's income to the church or to charity. [OE *teogotha* tenth] —**tith′er,** *n.*

ti·tian (tish′ən), *n.* an auburn or golden red used extensively by Titian, Italian painter. —*adj.* auburn; golden-red.

tit·il·late (tit′ə lāt), *v.,* **-lat·ed, -lat·ing.** excite pleasantly; stimulate agreeably. [< L] —**tit′il·la′tion,** *n.* —**tit′il·la′tor,** *n.*

tit·lark (tit′lärk′), *n.* a small bird like a lark; pipit.

ti·tle (tī′təl), *n., v.,* **-tled, -tling.** —*n.* **1** the name of a book, poem, picture, song, etc. **2** name showing rank, occupation, or condition in life. King, captain, professor, Madame are titles. **3** any descriptive name. **4** a fist-place position; championship: *the tennis title.* **5 a** a legal right to the possession of property. **b** document giving such a right. —*v.* call by a title; name. [< OF < L *titulus.* Doublet of TITTLE.] —**ti′tled,** *adj.*

title page, the page at the beginning of a book that contains the title, the author's name, etc.

title role, the part or character for which a play is named. Hamlet is a title role.

tit·mouse (tit′mous′), *n., pl.* **-mice.** any of certain small birds with short bills and dull-colored feathers, as the chickadee. [ME *titmose* < *tit* titmouse + OE *māse* titmouse]

ti·trate (tī′trāt; tit′rāt), *v.,* **-trat·ed, -trat·ing,** *n.* —*v.* analyze (a solution) by titration. —*n.* solution to be analyzed in this way. [< F, < *titre* quality, TITLE]

ti·tra·tion (tī trā′shən; ti–), *n.* process of determining the amount of some substance present in a solution by measuring the amount of a different substance that must be added to cause a chemical change.

tit·ter (tit′ər), *v.* laugh in a half-restrained manner; giggle. —*n.* such a laugh. —**tit′ter·er,** *n.* —**tit′ter·ing·ly,** *adv.*

tit·tle (tit′əl), *n.* **1** a very little bit; particle; whit. **2** a small stroke or mark over a letter in writing or printing. The dot over an *i* is a tittle. [< Med.L *titulus* diacritical mark < L, title. Doublet of TITLE.]

tit·tle-tat·tle (tit′əl tat′əl), *n., v.,* **-tled, -tling.** gossip. —**tit′tle-tat′tler,** *n.*

tit·u·lar (tich′ə lər; tit′yə–), *adj.* **1** in title or name only: *he is a titular prince without any power.* **2** having a title. **3** pertaining to a title. [< L *titulus* title] —**tit′u·lar·ly,** *adv.*

Ti·tus (tī′təs), *n.* **1** convert and companion of Saint Paul. **2** epistle of the New Testament written to Titus by Saint Paul.

tiz·zy (tiz′i), *n., pl.* **-zies.** a very excited state; dither.

Tl, thallium.

Tm, thulium.

Tn., thoron.

tn., ton.

TN, (*zip code*) Tennessee.

TNT, trinitrotoluene, a colorless solid used as an explosive.

to (tü; *unstressed* tŭ, tə), *prep.* **1** in the direction of: *go to the right.* **2** as far as; until: *rotten to the core, faithful to the end.* **3** into: *she tore the letter to pieces.* **4** along with; with: *we danced to the music, it is not to my liking.* **5** compared with: *the score was 9 to 5.* **6** belonging with; of: *the key to my room.* **7** on; against: *fasten it to the wall.* **8** about; concerning: *what did he say to that?* **9** *To* is used to show action toward: *give the book to me, speak to her, come to the rescue.* **10** *To* is used with the infinitive form of verbs: *he likes to read, he went to sleep, the birds began to sing.* —*adv.* **1** toward a person, thing, or point implied or understood; forward: *he wore his cap wrong side to.* **2** together; touching; closed: *the door slammed to.* **3** to action or work: *we turned to gladly.* **4** to consciousness: *she came to.*

to and fro, first one way and then back again; back and forth. [OE *tō*]

toad (tōd), *n.* **1** a small animal somewhat like a frog, living most of the time on land rather than in water. **2** any tailless amphibian; any frog. **3** *Fig.* contemptible person. [OE *tāde*] —**toad′like′,** *adj.*

toad·fish (tōd′fish′), *n.* fish with a thick head, a wide mouth, and slimy skin without scales.

toad·stool (tōd′stül′), *n.* **1** =mushroom. **2** a poisonous mushroom.

toad·y (tōd′i), *n., pl.* **toad·ies,** *v.,* **toad·ied, toad·y·ing.** —*n.* a fawning flatterer. —*v.* **1** act like a toady. **2** fawn upon; flatter. —**toad′y·ish,** *adj.* —**toad′y·ism,** *n.*

to-and-fro (tü′ənd frō′), *adj.* back-and-forth.

toast¹ (tōst), *n.* bread browned by heat. [< v.] —*v.* **1** brown by heat. **2** heat thoroughly. [< OF *toster,* ult. < L *torrere* parch] —**toast′er,** *n.*

toast² (tōst), *n.* **1** person or thing whose health is proposed and drunk: *"the King" was the first toast drunk by the officers.* **2** a call on another or others to drink to some person or thing. **3** act of drinking to the health of a person or thing. —*v.* **1** propose as a toast; drink to the health of. **2** drink toasts. [from the custom of putting toast into drinks]

toast·mas·ter (tōst′mas′tər; –mäs′–), *n.* **1** person who presides at a dinner and introduces the speakers. **2** person who proposes toasts.

to·bac·co (tə bak′ō), *n., pl.* **-cos, -coes. 1** the prepared leaves of certain plants of the nightshade family, used for smoking or chewing or as snuff. **2** one of these plants. [< Sp. *tabaco* < Carib]

to·bac·co·nist (tə bak′ə nist), *n.* dealer in tobacco.

to·bog·gan (tə bog′ən), —*n.* a long, narrow, flat sled that curves up in the front and has no runners. —*v.* **1** slide downhill on such a sled. **2** *Informal. Fig.* decline sharply and rapidly in value. [< F (Canadian) *tabagane* < Algonquian] —**to·bog′gan·er, to·bog′gan·ist,** *n.*

toc·ca·ta (tə kä′tə), *n.* composition for the piano or organ intended to exhibit the player's technique. [< Ital., orig. pp. of *toccare* touch]

toc·sin (tok′sən), *n.* **1** alarm sounded on a bell; warning signal. **2** bell used to sound an alarm. [< F < Pr. *tocasenh* < *tocar* strike + *senh* bell]

to·day (tə dā′), *n.* this day; the present time. —*adv.* **1** on this day. **2** at the present time; now. [OE *tō dæge*]

tod·dle (tod′əl), *v.,* **-dled, -dling,** *n.* —*v.* walk with short, unsteady steps, as a baby does. —*n.* **1** act of toddling. **2** such a way of walking.

tod·dler (tod′lər), *n.* child just learning to walk.

tod·dy (tod′i) *n., pl.* **-dies. 1** fermented palm sap. **2** drink made of whiskey, brandy, etc., with hot water and sugar. [< Hind. *tāyī* palm sap < *tāy* palm]

to-do (tə dü′), *n., pl.* **-dos.** fuss; bustle; commotion.

toe (tō), *n., v.,* **toed, toe·ing.** —*n.* **1** one of the five end parts of the foot. **2** the part of a stocking, shoe, etc., that covers the toes. **3** the fore part of a foot or hoof. **4** anything like a toe: *the toe and heel of a golf club.* —*v.* **1** touch or reach with the toes: *toe a line.* **2** turn the toes in walking, standing, etc.: *toe in, toe out.* **3** furnish with a toe or toes. **4** drive (a nail) slantwise. **5** fasten by nails driven slantwise.

on one's toes, ready for action; alert.

step on one's toes, offend or annoy one.

toe to toe, facing one another; confronting directly. [OE *tā*] —**toe′less,** *adj.* —**toe′like′,** *adj.*

toe dance, dancing on the tips of the toes, as in ballet. —**toe′-dance′,** *v.* —**toe dancer.**

toe·hold (tō′hōld′), *n.* **1** crack, edge, etc., large enough for the toes in rock climbing. **2** *Fig.* any way of getting a start or expanding, as in a job.

toe·nail (tō′nāl′), *n.* **1** the nail growing on a toe of the human foot. **2** in carpentry, a nail driven obliquely.

tof·fee (tôf′i; tof′i), *n., pl.* **-fees.** =taffy.

to·fu (tō′fü), *n.* semi-soft food made from soybeans.

tog (tog), *n.* garment.

togs, clothes. [prob. ult. < F *toge* cloak or L *toga*]

to·ga (tō′gə), *n., pl.* **-gas, -gae** (-jē). a loose outer garment worn by men of ancient Rome. [< L] —**to′gaed,** *adj.*

to·geth·er (tə geth′ər), *adv.* with each other; in company; in or into one mass body: *call people together, consider several cases together, this one cost more than all the others together.* **2** into or in union, contact, collision, etc.: *sew things together, the cars came together with a crash, squeeze a thing together.* **3** at the same time: *you cannot have both together.*

together with, along with. [OE *tōgædere* < *to* to + *gædere* together] —**to·geth′er·ness,** *n.*

tog·gle (tog′əl), *n., v.,* **-gled, -gling.** —*n.* **1** pin, bolt, or rod put through the eye of a rope or the link of a chain to keep it in place, to hold two ropes together, to serve as a hold for the fingers, etc. **2** a toggle joint, or a device furnished with one. —*v.* furnish with a toggle; fasten with a toggle.

toggle joint, a kneelike joint that transmits pressure at right angles.

toggle switch, electric switch that opens and closes an electric circuit by means of a projecting lever, as in a light switch.

To·go (tō′gō), *n.* republic in W Africa on the Gulf of Guinea.

toil¹ (toil), *n.* hard work; labor. —*v.* **1** work hard. **2** move with difficulty, pain, or weariness. [< AF, ? ult. < L *tudicula* olive press] —**toil′er,** *n.*

toil² (toil), *n.* Often, **toils.** net; snare: *the thief was caught in the toils of the law.* [< F *toile,* lit., cloth < L *tela* web]

toi·let (toi′lit), *n.* **1** =bathroom. **2** a water closet. **3** process of dressing, including bathing, combing the hair, etc. **4** Also, **toi·lette** (toi let′), a person's dress; costume. —*adj.* of or for the toilet. [< F *toilette,* dim. of *toile.* See TOIL².]

toi·let·ry (toi′lit ri), *n., pl.* **-ries.** soap, face powder, perfumery, etc., used for the toilet.

toilet water, a fragrant liquid not so strong as perfume.

toil·some (toil′səm), *adj.* requiring hard work; laborious; wearisome. —**toil′some·ly,** *adv.* —**toil′some·ness,** *n.*

toil·worn (toil′wôrn′; –wōrn′), *adj.* worn by toil; showing the effects of toil.

To·kay (tō kā′), *n.* **1** a rich, sweet wine made near Tokay, a town in Hungary. **2** the large, firm, reddish, sweet grape from which it is made.

to·ken (tō′kən), *n.* **1** something serving to indicate some fact, feeling, event, etc.; mark or sign: *wear black as a token of mourning.* **2** sign of friendship; keepsake. **3** piece of metal stamped for a higher value than the metal is worth. Tokens are used for some purposes instead of money. **4** piece of metal indicating a right or privilege. —*adj.* having only the semblance of; serving as a symbol; nominal; partial: *a token payment, token resistance.*

by the same token, moreover.

in token of, as a token of; to show. [OE *tācen*]

to·ken·ism (tō′kə niz əm), *n.* the making of token signs of dealing with social issues, esp. discrimination.

To·ky·o (tō′ki ō), *n.* capital of Japan, in the SE part.

told (tōld), *v.* **1** pt. and pp. of **tell. 2** all told, including all.

tol·er·a·ble (tol′ər ə bəl), *adj.* **1** able to be borne or endured. **2** fairly good: *in tolerable health.* [< L, < *tolerare* tolerate] —**tol′er·a·ble·ness,** *n.* —**tol′er·a·bly,** *adv.*

tol·er·ance (tol′ər əns), *n.* **1** a willingness to be tolerant and patient toward people whose opinions or ways differ from one's own. **2** the power of enduring or resisting the action of a drug, poison, etc. **3** action of tolerating. **4** an allowed amount of variation from a standard, as in the weight of coins or the size of a wire, bolt, shaft, or other product.

tol·er·ant (tol′ər ənt), *adj.* **1** willing to let other people do as they think best; willing to endure beliefs and actions of which one does not approve. **2** able to endure or resist the action of a drug, poison, etc. —**tol′er·ant·ly,** *adv.*

tol·er·ate (tol′ər āt), *v.,* **-at·ed, -at·ing. 1** allow; permit. **2** bear; endure. **3** endure or resist the action of (a drug, poison, etc.). [< L *toleratus*] —**tol′er·a′tive,** *adj.* —**tol′er·a′tor,** *n.*

tol·er·a·tion (tol′ər ā′shən), *n.* **1** willingness to put up with beliefs and actions of which one does not approve; tolerance. **2** recognition of a person's right to worship as he or she thinks best without loss of civil rights or social privileges; freedom of worship. **3** recognition and acceptance by a society of people of other races and their right to benefit from the same privileges and responsibilities.

toll[1] (tōl), *v.* **1** sound with single strokes slowly and regularly repeated: *bells were tolled all over the country at the President's death.* **2** call, announce, etc., by tolling. —*n.* **1** a stroke or sound of a bell. **2** act or fact of tolling. [akin to OE *-tyllan* draw. See TILL[3].] —**toll′er,** *n.*

toll[2] (tōl), *n.* **1** tax or fee paid for some right or privilege: *we pay a toll when we use the bridge.* **2** charge for a certain service: *there is a toll on long-distance telephone calls.* **3** something paid, lost, suffered, etc.: *automobile accidents take a heavy toll of human lives.* —*v.* collect tolls from; take as toll. [< L < Gk. *telonion* toll house, ult. < *telos* tax] —**toll′a·ble,** *adj.* —**toll′er,** *n.*

toll call, a long-distance telephone call, for which there is a specific charge.

toll·gate (tōl′gāt′), *n.* gate where toll is collected.

toll·keep·er (tōl′kēp′ər), *n.* person who collects the toll at a tollgate.

Tol·tec (tol′tek), *n.* one of an ancient people that ruled Mexico before the Aztecs and greatly influenced their culture. —*adj.* Also, **Tol′tec·an.** of or having to do with this people.

tol·u·ene (tol′yü ēn), *n.* a colorless liquid, $C_6H_5CH_3$, somewhat like benzene, obtained from coal tar and coal gas and used as a solvent and for making explosives, dyes, etc.

tom, Tom (tom), *n.* the male of various animals; male. [< *Tom,* proper name, short for *Thomas*]

tom·a·hawk (tom′ə hôk), *n.* a light ax used by North American Indians as a weapon and a tool. —*v.* strike or kill with a tomahawk. [< Algonquian]

to·ma·to (tə mā′tō; -mä′-), *n., pl.* **-toes. 1** a juicy fruit used as a vegetable. Most tomatoes are red, but some kinds are yellow. **2** the plant it grows on. [< Sp. < Mex. *tomatl*]

tomb (tüm), *n.* grave, vault, mausoleum, etc., for a dead body. —*v.* put in a tomb; shut up as if in a tomb. [< OF < LL < Gk. *tymbos*] —**tomb′less,** *adj.* —**tomb′like′,** *adj.*

tom·boy (tom′boi′), *n.* girl who likes to play boys' games; boisterous, romping girl. —**tom′boy·ish,** *adj.*

tomb·stone (tüm′stōn′), *n.* stone that marks a tomb or grave.

tom·cat (tom′kat′), *n.* a male cat.

tome (tōm), *n.* book, esp. a large, heavy book. [< F < L < Gk. *tomos,* orig., piece cut off]

tom·fool (tom′fül′), *n.* a silly fool; stupid person.

tom·fool·er·y (tom′fül′ər i), *n., pl.* **-er·ies.** silly behavior; nonsense.

Tommy gun, tommy gun, a Thompson submachine gun. —**Tommy gunner, tommy gunner.**

tom·my·rot (tom′i rot′), *n. Informal.* nonsense; rubbish; foolishness.

to·mor·row (tə môr′ō; -mor′ō), *n.* the day after today. —*adv.* on the day after today.

Tom Thumb, 1 a diminutive hero of folk tales. **2** anyone or anything that is very small.

tom·tit (tom′tit′), *n.* a small bird, esp. a tit-mouse.

tom-tom (tom′tom′), *n.* a native drum, usually beaten with the hands. [< Hind. *tam-tam*] —**tom′-tom′mer,** *n.*

ton (tun), *n.* **1** measure of weight; 2000 pounds in the United States and Canada, 2,240 pounds in England. **2** measure of volume that varies with the thing measured, as the unit of internal capacity of a ship is 100 cubic feet, unit of carrying capacity of a ship is 40 cubic feet, or unit of water a ship will displace is 35 cubic feet.

long ton, 2,240 pounds.

metric ton, 1,000 kilograms.

short ton, 2,000 pounds. [var. of *tun*]

ton·al (tōn′əl), *adj.* of or pertaining to tones or tone. —**ton′al·ly,** *adv.*

to·nal·i·ty (tō nal′ə ti), *n., pl.* **-ties. 1 a** sum of relations, melodic and harmonic, existing between the tones of a scale or musical system. **b** a key or system of musical tones. **2** the color scheme of a painting, etc.

tone (tōn), *n., v.,* **toned, ton·ing.** —*n.* **1** any sound considered with reference to its quality, pitch, strength, source, etc.: *sweet, shrill, or loud tones.* **2 a** a musical sound; musical sound of definite pitch and character. **b** the difference in pitch between two notes. C and D are

one tone apart. **3** manner of speaking or writing: *a moral tone, a vulgar tone.* **4** spirit; character; style: *a tone of quiet elegance prevails in her home.* **5** normal healthy condition; vigor. **6** effect of color and of light in a picture. **7** shade of color. —*v.* **1** harmonize: *this rug tones in well with the wallpaper.* **2** give a tone to.

tone down, soften: *tone down your words.* [< L < Gk. *tonos,* orig., a stretching, taut string] —**tone′less,** *adj.* —**tone′less·ly,** *adv.* —**tone′less·ness,** *n.* —**ton′er,** *n.*

tone-deaf (tōn′def′), *adj.* **1** unable to hear the difference between musical tones. **2** *Fig.* insensitive to the effects of how what one says affects another; obtuse.

tone language, language that uses tones to distinguish between words that have different meanings but are pronounced the same, as in Chinese.

tong (tông; tong), *n.* a secret Chinese organization or club in the United States. [< Chinese *t'ang, t'ong,* orig., meeting hall]

tongs (tôngz; tongz), *n. pl.* (*sometimes sing. in use*) tool with two hinged or pivoted arms for seizing, holding, or lifting. [OE *tang*]

tongue (tung), *n., v.,* **tongued, tongu·ing.** —*n.* **1** the movable piece of flesh in the mouth, used in tasting and, by people, for talking. **2** an animal's tongue used as food. **3** power of speech. **4** way of speaking; speech; talk: *a flattering tongue.* **5** the language of a people: *the English tongue.* **6** something shaped or used like a tongue: *tongues of flame.* **7** the strip of leather under the laces of a shoe. **8** a movable piece inside a bell that swings and rings. —*v.* modify tones of (a flute, cornet, etc.) with the tongue.

hold one's tongue, keep still.

on the tip of one's tongue, almost spoken.

with tongue in cheek, with intent to mislead, esp. in jest. [OE *tunge*] —**tongue′less,** *adj.*

tongue-lashing (tung′lash′ing), *n.* a severe scolding or reprimand.

tongue-tied (tung′tīd′), *adj.* **1** unable to speak because of shyness, embarrassment, etc. **2** having the motion of the tongue hindered.

tongue twister, phrase or sentence difficult to say without error: *unique New York is one tongue twister.*

ton·ic (ton′ik), *n.* **1** anything that gives strength; medicine to give strength. **2** the first note of a scale; keynote. [< Gk. *tonikos* < *tonos* TONE] —**ton′i·cal·ly,** *adv.*

to·nic·i·ty (tō nis′ə ti), *n.* **1** a tonic quality or condition. **2** the property of possessing bodily tone.

to·night (tə nīt′), *n.* the night of this day; this night. —*adv.* on or during this night.

ton·nage (tun′ij), *n.* **1** the carrying capacity of a ship expressed in tons of 100 cubic feet. **2** the freight-carrying capacity of a ship. **3** the total amount of shipping in tons. **4** duty or tax on ships at so much a ton. **5** weight in tons.

ton·sil (ton′səl), *n.* either of the two oval masses of glandular tissue on the sides of the throat, just back of the mouth. [< L *tonsillae,* pl.] —**ton′sil·lar, ton′sil·ar,** *adj.*

ton·sil·lec·to·my (ton′sə lek′tə mi), *n., pl.* -**mies.** removal of the tonsils.

ton·sil·li·tis (ton′sə lī′tis), *n.* inflammation of the tonsils.

ton·sure (ton′shər), *n., v.,* -**sured, -sur·ing.** —*n.* **1** a clipping of the hair or shaving of a part or the whole of the head of a person entering the priesthood or an order of monks. **2** the shaved part of the head of a priest or monk. —*v.* shave the head of. [< L *tonsura < tondere* shear, shave] —**ton′sured,** *adj.*

too (tü), *adv.* **1** also; besides: *young, clever, and rich too.* **2** beyond what is desirable, proper, or right; more than enough: *too long, too much.* **3** very; exceedingly: *I am only too glad to help.* [var. of *to*]

took (tůk), *v.* pt. of **take.**

tool (tül), *n.* **1** a knife, hammer, saw, shovel, or any instrument used in doing work. **2** *Fig.* person used by another like a tool: *he is a tool of the party boss.* —*v.* **1** use a tool on. **2** work with a tool. **3** ornament with a tool. [OE *tōl*] —**tool′er,** *n.*

tool·ing (tül′ing), *n.* **1** work done with a tool. **2** ornamentation made with a tool.

toot (tüt), *n.* sound of a horn, whistle, etc. —*v.* give forth a short blast. [prob. ult. imit.] —**toot′er,** *n.*

tooth (tüth), *n., pl.* **teeth,** *v.* —*n.* **1** one of the hard bonelike parts in the mouth, used for biting and chewing. **2** something like a tooth, as one of the projecting parts of a comb, rake, or saw. **3** taste, relish, or liking (for): *a sweet tooth.* —*v.* **1** furnish with teeth; put teeth on. **2** indent; cut teeth on the edge of.

fight tooth and nail, fight fiercely, with all one's force. [OE *tōth*] —**toothed,** *adj.* —**tooth′less,** *adj.*

tooth·ache (tüth′āk′), *n.* pain in a tooth or the teeth.

tooth·brush (tüth′brush′), *n.* a small brush for cleaning the teeth.

tooth·paste (tüth′pāst′), *n.* paste used in cleaning the teeth.

tooth·pick (tüth′pik′), *n.* a small, pointed piece of wood or a sharpened quill for removing bits of food from between the teeth.

tooth·some (tüth′səm), *adj.* **1** pleasing to the taste; tasting good. **2** *Fig.* pleasing to look at; pretty. —**tooth′some·ly,** *adv.* —**tooth′some·ness,** *n.*

top[1] (top), *n., adj., v.,* **topped, top·ping.** —*n.* **1** the highest point or part: *the top of a mountain, he is at the top of his class, the top of one's voice.* **2** the upper part or surface: *the top of a shoe or table.* **3** one that occupies the highest or leading position: *he is top in his profession.* **4** cover of an automobile, can, etc. —*adj.*

1 pertaining to, situated at, or forming the top: *the top shelf.* **2** highest in degree; greatest: *at top speed.* **3** chief; foremost: *top honors.* —*v.* **1** put a top on: *top a box.* **2** be on top of; be the top of: *a church tops the hill.* **3** rise high; rise above: *the sun topped the horizon.* **4** exceed in height, amount, number, etc.: *the expense topped $100,000.* **5** do better than; outdo; excel: *his story topped all the rest.*

blow one's top, *Informal.* lose one's temper.

from the top, from the beginning.

off the top of one's head, *Informal.* without considering; spontaneously.

on top, with success; with victory: *the team came out on top.*

over the top, too much: *decorations over the top.*

top off, a complete; finish; end: *a beautiful cake topped off the meal.* **b** refill to the top, esp. a gas tank. [OE *topp*]

top[2] (top), *n.* toy that spins on a point. **sleep like a top,** sleep soundly. [OE *topp*]

to·paz (tō′paz), *n.* **1** a crystalline mineral that occurs in various forms and colors. Transparent yellow topaz is used as a gem. **2** any of various other minerals, as a yellow variety of sapphire (**oriental topaz**) or a yellow variety of quartz (**false topaz**). [< L < Gk. *topazos*]

top·coat (top′kōt′), *n.* **1** overcoat; loose overcoat; lightweight overcoat. **2** final coat of paint, varnish, etc.

To·pe·ka (tə pē′kə), *n.* capital of Kansas, in the NE part.

top·flight (top′flīt′), *adj.* of highest rank or quality.

top·gal·lant (top′gal′ənt), *n.* the mast or sail above the topmast; the third section of a mast above the deck. —*adj.* next above the topmast.

top hat, a tall, black silk hat worn by men in formal clothes.

top·heav·y (top′hev′i), *adj.* too heavy at the top. —**top′-heav′i·ness,** *n.*

to·pi·ar·y (tō′pi er′i), *adj.* **1** of plants, clipped and trimmed to look like animals, pyramids, etc. **2** of or having to do with such shaping of plants: *a topiary garden.* [< L *topiārius* ornamental gardening < Gk. *tópia* a field]

top·ic (top′ik), *n.* subject that people think, write, or talk about: *the topics of the day.* [sing. of *topics* < L *topica* < Gk. (*ta*) *topika,* a study of logical and rhetorical commonplaces (by Aristotle) < *topos* place]

top·i·cal (top′ə kəl), *adj.* **1** having to do with topics of the day; of current interest. **2** of or using topics; having to do with the topics of a speech, writing, etc. **3** limited to a certain spot or part of the body; local. —**top′i·cal·ly,** *adv.*

top·knot (top′not′), *n.* a knot of hair or a tuft of feathers on the top of the head. —**top′knot′ted,** *adj.*

top·lev·el (top′lev′əl), *adj.* of or having the highest authority or rank.

top·mast (top′mast′; -mäst′), *n.* the second section of a mast above the deck.

top·most (top′mōst), *adj.* highest.

top·notch (top′noch′), *adj. Informal.* first-rate; best possible.

to·pog·ra·pher (tə pog′rə fər), *n.* person who describes the surface features of a place or region.

to·pog·ra·phy (tə pog′rə fi), *n., pl.* -**phies.** **1** the detailed description or drawing of places or their surface features. **2** the surface features of a place or region. The topography of a region includes hills, valleys, streams, lakes, bridges, tunnels, roads, etc. [< LL < Gk. < *topos* place + *graphein* write] —**top′o·graph′ic, top′o·graph′i·cal,** *adj.* —**top′o·graph′i·cal·ly,** *adv.*

top·ping (top′ing), *n.* something, as a sauce or whipped cream, put on top of a food as a garnish or finishing touch.

top·ple (top′əl), *v.,* -**pled, -pling. 1** fall forward; tumble down: *the chimney toppled onto the roof.* **2** throw over or down; overturn: *the wrestler toppled his opponent.*

tops (tops), *adj.* of the highest degree in quality, excellence, etc.

top·sail (top′sāl′), *n.* the second sail above the deck on a mast.

top secret, a most important and highly guarded secret.

top·se·cret (top′sē′krit), *adj.* of utmost secrecy; extremely confidential.

top sergeant, the first sergeant of a military company.

top·side (top′sīd′), *n.* the upper part of a ship's side, esp. the part above the water line.

top·soil (top′soil′), *n.* the upper part of the soil; soil above the subsoil.

top·sy·tur·vy (top′si tėr′vi), *adv., adj., n., pl.* -**vies.** —*adv.* **1** upside down. **2** in confusion or disorder. —*adj.* **1** turned upside down; inverted. **2** confused; disordered. —*n.* **1** inversion of the natural order or state. **2** confusion; disorder. [prob. ult < *top*[1] + *tirve* overturn, akin to OE *tearflian* roll over] —**top′sy·tur′vi·ly,** *adv.* —**top′sy·tur′vi·ness,** *n.*

toque (tōk), *n.* hat without a brim; small hat with very little brim. [< F]

To·rah (tô′rə; tō′-), *n.* Mosaic law; the Pentateuch. [< Heb.]

torch (tôrch), *n.* **1** light to be carried around or stuck in a holder on a wall. A piece of pine wood or anything that burns easily makes a good torch. **2** device for producing a very hot flame, used esp. to burn off paint, to solder metal, and to melt metal. **3** *Fig.* something thought of as a source of enlightenment: *the torch of civilization.* [< OF *torche,* prob. ult. < L *torquere* twist]

torch·bear·er (tôrch′bār′ər), *n.* one who carries a torch.

torch·light (tôrch′līt′), *n.* light of a torch or torches.

tore (tôr; tōr), *v.* pt. of **tear**[2].

tor·e·a·dor (tôr′i ə dôr′), *n.* a Spanish bullfighter. [< Sp., ult. < *toro* bull < L *taurus*]

to·ri·i (tô′ri ē; tō′–), *n., pl.* **–ri·i.** gateway at the entrance to a Japanese temple, built of two uprights and two crosspieces. [< Jap.]

tor·ment (*v.* tôr ment′; *n.* tôr′ment), *v.* 1 cause very great pain to. 2 worry or annoy very much. —*n.* 1 cause of very great pain. 2 very great pain. 3 cause of very much worry or annoyance. [< OF *tormenter*, ult. < L *tormentum*, orig., twisted sling < *torquere* twist] **—tor·ment′ing,** *adj.* **—tor·ment′ing·ly,** *adv.* **—tor·ment′ing·ness,** *n.* **—tor·men′tor, tor·ment′er,** *n.*

torn (tôrn; tōrn), *v.* pp. of **tear**²

tor·na·do (tôr nā′dō), *n., pl.* **–does, –dos.** 1 an extremely violent and destructive whirlwind, moving forward as a whirling funnel extending down from a mass of dark clouds. 2 any extremely violent windstorm. 3 *Fig.* violent outburst. [alter. of Sp. *tronada* < *tronar* thunder] **—tor·nad′ic,** *adj.*

tor·pe·do (tôr pē′dō), *n., pl.* **–does,** *v.,* **–doed,, –do·ing.** —*n.* 1 a large, cigarshaped shell that contains explosives and travels by its own power under water to blow up enemy ships. 2 an explosive put on a railroad track which makes a loud noise when a wheel of the engine runs over it. —*v.* 1 attack or destroy with a torpedo. 2 *Fig.* wreck; destroy: *torpedo someone's plans.* [< L, the electric ray (a fish), orig., numbness]

tor·pid (tôr′pid), *adj.* 1 dull in nature; inactive; sluggish. 2 not moving or feeling. Snakes are torpid all winter in cold climates. [< L *torpidus*] **—tor·pid′i·ty, tor′pid·ness,** *n.* **—tor′pid·ly,** *adv.*

tor·por (tôr′pər), *n.* a torpid condition. [< L] **—tor·por′if·ic,** *adj.*

torque (tôrk), *n.* 1 force causing rotation. 2 the amount of turning power exerted by a shaft. [< L *torques*]

tor·rent (tôr′ənt; tor′–), *n.* 1 a violent, rushing stream of water. 2 a heavy downpour. 3 *Fig.* any violent, rushing stream; flood: *a torrent of abuse.* [< L *torrens* boiling, parching]

tor·ren·tial (tô ren′shəl; to–), *adj.* of, caused by, or like a torrent. **—tor·ren′tial·ly,** *adv.*

tor·rid (tôr′id; tor′–), *adj.* 1 very hot. Brazil is in the Torrid Zone. July is a torrid month. 2 *Fig.* hotly ardent; passionate. [< L *torridus*] **—tor·rid′i·ty, tor′rid·ness,** *n.* **—tor′rid·ly,** *adv.*

Torrid Zone, the very warm region between the tropic of Cancer and the tropic of Capricorn. The equator divides the Torrid Zone.

tor·sion (tôr′shən), *n.* 1 act or process of twisting. 2 state of being twisted. 3 *Mechanics.* **a** the twisting of a body by two equal and opposite forces. **b** the internal tendency of a twisted object to return to its previous condition. [< LL

torsio < L *torquere* twist] **—tor′sion·al,** *adj.* **—tor′sion·al·ly,** *adv.* **—tor′sion·less,** *adj.*

tor·so (tôr′sō), *n., pl.* **–sos, –si** (–sē). 1 the trunk of the human body. 2 the trunk or body of a statue without any head, arms, or legs. [< Ital., orig., stalk < L < Gk. *thyrsos* wand]

tort (tôrt), *n.* a civil wrong for which the law requires damages (except a breach of contract). [< OF < Med.L *tortum* injustice < L *torquere* turn awry, twist]

tor·tel·li·ni (tôr′tə li′ni), *n. pl.* small round pieces of noodle dough filled with finely chopped meat, cheese, etc., cooked in boiling water and often served in a sauce.

tor·til·la (tôr tē′yə), *n.* a thin, flat, round bread made of corn meal or flour. [< Sp.]

tor·toise (tôr′təs), *n., pl.* **–tois·es, –toise.** 1 turtle, esp. one living on land. 2 *Fig.* a slow-moving person or thing. [< Med.L *tortuca,* ult. < L *torquere* twist]

tortoise shell, the mottled yellow-and-brown shell of a turtle or tortoise. Tortoise shell is much used for combs and ornaments. 2 butterfly having brown and yellow spots. 3 domestic cat marked like tortoise shell. **—tor′toise-shell′,** *adj.*

tor·tu·ous (tôr′chù əs), *adj.* 1 full of twists, turns, or bends; twisting; winding; crooked. 2 mentally or morally crooked; not straightforward. [< L *tortuosus,* ult. < *torquere* twist] **—tor′tu·ous·ly,** *adv.* **—tor′tu·ous·ness,** *n.*

tor·ture (tôr′chər), *n., v.,* **–tured, –turing.** —*n.* 1 act or fact of inflicting very severe pain. Torture is officially banned, but is still used to make people give evidence about crimes or provide information about an enemy. 2 very severe pain. —*v.* 1 cause very severe pain to. 2 twist the meaning of. 3 *Fig.* twist or force out of its natural form: *winds tortured the trees.* [< L *tortura* < *torquere* twist] **—tor′tur·er,** *n.* **—tor′tur·ing·ly,** *adv.*

To·ry (tô′ri; tō′–), *n., pl.* **–ries,** *adj.* —*n.* 1 in British politics, originally a member of the party that favored the greatest possible amount of royal power, etc. In modern England, members of the Conservative Party are often called Tories. 2 an American who favored England at the time of the American Revolution. —*adj.* 1 of or having to do with Tories. 2 Also, **tory.** opposed to change; conservative. **—To′ry·ism,** *n.*

toss (tôs; tos), *v.,* **tossed** or (*Poetic*) **tost, tossing,** *n.* —*v.* 1 throw lightly with the palm upward; cast; fling: *toss a ball.* 2 throw about; pitch about: *the ship is tossed by the waves; to toss restlessly in bed.* 3 lift quickly; throw upward: *she tossed her head, he was tossed by the bull.* 4 throw a coin to decide something by the side that falls upward. —*n.* 1 distance to which something is or can be tossed. 2 a throw; tossing.

toss off, do or make quickly and easily. [? < Scand. (dial. Norw.) *tossa* strew] **—toss′er,** *n.*

toss-up or **toss-up** (tôs′up′; tos′–), *n.* 1 a tossing of a coin to decide something. 2 an even chance.

tot (tot), *n.* a little child.

to·tal (tō′təl), *adj., n., v.,* **–taled, –tal·ing.** —*adj.* 1 whole; entire: *the total amount expended.* 2 complete: *a total failure, total indifference.* —*n.* the whole amount; sum. —*v.* 1 find the sum of; add. 2 reach an amount of; amount to. [< Med.L, < L *totus* all] **—to′tal·ly,** *adv.*

total eclipse, eclipse in which the sun or moon is completely obscured.

to·tal·i·tar·i·an (tō′tal ə tãr′i ən), *adj.* of or having to do with a government controlled by one political group that permits no other political groups. —*n.* person in favor of totalitarianism. **—to·tal′i·tar′i·an·ism,** *n.*

to·tal·i·ty (tō tal′ə ti), *n., pl.* **–ties.** 1 entirety. 2 the total amount.

tote (tōt), *v.,* **tot·ed, tot·ing,** *n.* —*v.* carry; haul. —*n.* 1 act or course of toting. 2 thing toted. 3 =tote bag. **—tot′er,** *n.*

tote bag, large bag made of canvas, plastic, etc., with handles, for carrying things.

to·tem (tō′təm), *n.* 1 among American Indians, a natural object, often an animal, taken as the emblem of a tribe, clan, family, etc. 2 image of a totem. 3 *Fig.* any revered object; charm. [< Algonkian] **—to′tem·ism,** *n.*

totem pole, pole carved and painted with representations of totems, erected by the Indians of the NW coast of America, esp. in front of their houses.

tot·ter (tot′ər), *v.* 1 stand or walk with shaky, unsteady steps. 2 be unsteady; shake as if about to fall. 3 shake; tremble. —*n.* a tottering. **—tot′ter·er,** *n.* **—tot′ter·ing·ly,** *adv.* **—tot′ter·y,** *adj.*

tou·can (tü′kan; tü kän′) *n.* a bright-colored bird of tropical America, with an enormous beak. [< Carib]

touch (tuch), *v.* 1 put the hand or some other part of the body on or against: *he touched my hand.* 2 be against; come against: *your sleeve is touching the butter, a part of the road touched the river.* 3 strike lightly or gently: *touch the strings of a harp.* 4 injure slightly: *the flowers were touched by the frost.* 5 affect with some feeling: *the story touched us.* 6 have to do with; concern: *the matter touches your interests; our conversation did not touch on that.* 7 handle; use: *he won't touch tobacco.* 8 *Informal.* borrow from: *touch a man for a quarter.* —*n.* 1 a touching or being touched: *a bubble bursts at a touch.* 2 the sense by which a person perceives things by feeling, handling, or coming against them: *the blind have a keen touch.* 3 sensation so caused: *an object with a slimy touch, the touch of their hands.* 4 a close relation of communication, sympathy, etc.: *a news-*

paper keeps one in touch with the world. **5** act or manner of playing a musical instrument: *a pianist with an excellent touch.* **6** a distinctive manner or quality: *the work showed an expert's touch.* **7** a slight amount; little bit: *a touch of salt, a touch of fever.*

in touch, in contact: *keep in touch with friends.*

out of touch, unable to be in sympathy, feel interest or concern because of lack of contact: *he was distant because he was out of touch with us.*

touch off, cause to go off; fire.

touch on or **upon,** mention; treat lightly.

touch up, change a little; improve: *touch up a photograph, touch up makeup.* [< OF *touchier*] —**touch′a·ble,** *adj.* —**touch′er,** *n.*

touch and go, an uncertain or risky situation. —**touch′-and-go′,** *adj.*

touch·back (tuch′bak′), *n.* act of touching the football to the ground by a player behind his own goal line when driven there by the other side.

touch dancing, dancing in which partners hold each other and move with complementary steps.

touch·down (tuch′doun′), *n.* **1** act of a player in putting the football on the ground behind the opponents' goal line. **2** the score made in this way. **3** landing of an aircraft or spacecraft.

touched (tucht), *adj.* **1** *Informal.* odd; slightly crazed. **2** *Fig.* stirred emotionally.

touch football, game like football, but played informally, without equipment and tackling.

touch·hole (tuch′hōl′), *n.* a small opening in an old-time gun through which the gunpowder inside was set on fire.

touch·ing (tuch′ing), *adj.* arousing tender feeling. —*prep.* concerning; about. —**touch′ing·ly,** *adv.*

touch-me-not (tuch′mi not′), *n.* plant whose ripe seed pods burst open when touched.

touch·stone (tuch′stōn′), *n.* **1** a black stone used to test the purity of gold or silver by the color of the streak made on the stone by rubbing it with the metal. **2** any means of testing; a test.

touch·y (tuch′i), *adj.,* **touch·i·er, touch·i·est.** **1** apt to take offense at trifles; too sensitive. **2** requiring skill in handling; ticklish; precarious: *loading bombs is a touchy job.* —**touch′i·ly,** *adv.* —**touch′i·ness,** *n.*

tough (tuf), *adj.* **1** bending without breaking: *leather is tough.* **2** hard to cut, tear, or chew: *tough meat.* **3** strong; hardy: *a tough plant, a tough beard.* **4** hard; difficult: *tough work, a tough experience, a tough struggle.* **5** rough; disorderly: *a tough neighborhood.* —*n.* U.S. a rough person; rowdy. [OE *tōh*] —**tough′ly,** *adv.* —**tough′ness,** *n.*

tough·en (tuf′ən), *v.* make or become tough or tougher. —**tough′en·er,** *n.*

tou·pee (tü pā′), *n.* a wig or patch of false hair worn to cover a bald spot. [< F *toupet* < OF *toupe* tuft]

tour (tùr), *v.* **1** travel from place to place; travel through: *last year they toured Europe.* **2** walk around in: *tour the museum.* [< n.] —*n.* **1** a long journey. **2** walk around: *a tour of the boat.* **3** a turn to do something; a shift of work or duty.

on tour, touring, said esp. of theatrical companies, symphony orchestras, etc. [< F < L *tornus* turner's wheel, lathe < Gk. *tornos.* Cf. TURN.]

tour de force (tür də fôrs′), *French.* a notable feat of strength or ingenuity.

tour·ist (tùr′ist), *n.* person traveling for pleasure.

tour·ma·line (tùr′mə lin; –lēn), *n.* semiprecious colored mineral, the transparent varieties of which are used in jewelry. [< F < Singhalese *tòramalli* a carnelian]

tour·na·ment (tėr′nə mənt; tùr′–), *n.* **1** a meeting for sports; the activities at such a meeting. **2** contest of many persons in some sport: *a golf tournament.* **3** contest between two groups of knights on horseback who fought for a prize. [< OF *torneiement* < *torneier* TOURNEY]

tour·ni·quet (tùr′nə ket; –kā; tėr′–), *n.* device for stopping bleeding by compressing a blood vessel, such as a bandage tightened by twisting with a stick. [< F, < *tourner* to turn]

tou·sle (tou′zəl), *v.,* **–sled, –sling,** *n.* —*v.* put into disorder; make untidy; muss: *tousled hair.* —*n.* a disordered mass, esp. of hair. [< ME *touse(n)*]

tout (tout), *v.* praise highly and insistently. [< var. of OE *tȳtan* peep out] —**tout′er,** *n.*

tow (tō), *v.* pull by a rope, chain, etc. —*n.* **1** that which is towed. **2** the rope, chain, etc., used.

in tow, a condition of being towed: *the sailboat was in tow.* **b** under one's care or influence. [OE *togian* drag] —**tow′er,** *n.*

tow·age (tō′ij), *n.* **1** a towing. **2** act or state of being towed. **3** charge for towing.

to·ward (*prep.* tôrd, tōrd, tə wôrd′; *adj.* tôrd, tōrd), *prep.* Also, **towards.** **1** in the direction of: *walk toward the north.* **2** with respect to; regarding; about; concerning: *he was friendly toward the idea.* **3** near: *toward two o'clock.* **4** for: *give money toward a person's expenses.* —*adj.* about to happen; impending. [OE *tōweard* < *tō* to + –*weard* –ward]

tow·boat (tō′bōt′), *n.* flat-bottomed tugboat, used esp. on rivers.

tow·el (tou′əl), *n., v.,* **–eled, –el·ing.** —*n.* piece of cloth or paper for wiping and drying something wet. —*v.* dry with a towel.

throw in the towel, give up; admit defeat. [< OF *toaille* < Gmc.]

tow·el·ing (tou′əl ing), *n.* material used for towels, esp. cotton.

tow·er (tou′ər), *n.* **1** a high structure. It stands alone or forms part of a church, castle, or other building. **2** means of defense; protection. **3** *Fig.* person or thing that is like a tower, above the ordinary: *a tower of strength.* —*v.* rise high up. [< OF < L *turris*] —**tow′er·y,** *adj.*

tow·er·ing (tou′ər ing), *adj.* **1** very high. **2** *Fig.* very great. **3** *Fig.* very violent. —**tow′er·ing·ly,** *adv.*

tow·head (tō′hed′), *n.* **1** a head of very light, pale-yellow hair. **2** person having such hair. —**tow′head′ed,** *adj.*

tow·line (tō′līn′), *n.* rope, chain, etc., for towing.

town (toun), *n.* **1** a large group of houses and buildings, smaller than a city. **2** any large place with many people living in it. **3** the people of a town. **4** the part of a town or city where the stores and office buildings are. —*adj.* **1** of a town or towns. **2** characteristic of towns.

go to town, *Informal.* **a** accomplish a great deal: *went to town raising money.* **b** do or participate with enthusiasm: *go to town on the dessert.*

on the town, visiting or going about a city: *a night on the town.* [OE *tūn*]

town clerk, official who keeps the records of a town.

town crier, a public crier in a city or town.

town hall, a buiding used for a town's business.

town house, house in town, esp. one of a row of similar houses.

town meeting, a general meeting of the inhabitants of the town.

town·ship (toun′ship), *n.* **1** in the U.S. and Canada, an administrative division of a county, with varying corporate powers. **2** in U.S. surveys of public land, a region or district of 6 miles square.

towns·man (tounz′mən), *n., pl.* **–men.** **1** person who lives in a town. **2** selectman.

towns·peo·ple (tounz′pē′pəl), **towns·folk** (–fōk′), *n. pl.* the people of a town.

tow·path (tō′path′; –päth′), *n.* a path along the bank of a canal or river for use in towing boats.

tow·rope (tō′rōp′), *n.* rope used for towing.

tow truck, specially equipped truck that is able to tow disabled vehicles.

tox·e·mi·a (toks ē′mi ə), *n.* a form of blood poisoning, esp. one in which the toxins produced by certain microorganisms enter the blood. [< NL, < L *toxicum* poison (see TOXIC) + Gk. *haima* blood] —**tox·e′mic,** *adj.*

tox·ic (tok′sik), *adj.* poisonous; of poison: caused by poison. [< Med.L. *toxicus,* ult. < Gk. *toxikon (pharmakon)* (poison) for shooting arrows < *toxon* bow] —**tox·ic′i·ty,** *n.*

tox·i·col·o·gy (tok′sə kol′ə ji), *n.* science that deals with poisons, their effects, antidotes, detection, etc. [< Gk. *toxikon* poison (see TOXIC) + –LOGY] —**tox′i-**

co·log′i·cal, *adj.* **—tox′i·co·log′i·cal·ly,** *adv.* **—tox′i·col′o·gist,** *n.*

toxic shock or **toxic shock syndrome,** serious bacterial infection that causes fever, vomiting, diarrhea, a sudden drop in blood pressure, and, sometimes, death.

tox·in (tok′sən), *n.* any poisonous product of animal or vegetable metabolism, esp. one of those produced by bacteria and constituting the causative agents in such diseases as tetanus, diphtheria, etc. [< *toxic*]

tox·oid (tok′soid), *n.* a toxin treated to eliminate its ability to poison but able to stimulate the production of antitoxins when injected into the body.

toy (toi), *n.* **1** something for a child to play with; plaything. **2** thing that has little value or importance. **3** something small or diminutive like a plaything. *—adj.* of, made as, or like a toy. *—v.* amuse oneself; play; trifle.

tp., township.

Tr, terbium.

tr., 1 transitive. **2** translation; translator. **3** transpose. **4** treasurer.

trace¹ (trās), *n., v.,* **traced, trac·ing.** *—n.* **1** footprint or other mark left; track; trail: *traces of rabbits on the snow.* **2** mark, token, or evidence of the former existence, presence, or action of something; vestige: *the explorer found traces of an ancient city.* **3** a very small amount; little bit: *there wasn't a trace of gray in her hair.* **4** thing marked out or drawn. [< *v.*] *—v.* **1** follow by means of marks, tracks, or signs: *trace deer.* **2** follow the course of: *trace one's family back.* **3** mark out; draw: *the spy traced a plan of the fort.* **4** copy by following the lines of. [< OF *tracer,* ult. < L *trahere* drag] **—trace′a·ble,** *adj.* **—trace′a·bly,** *adv.* **—trace′less,** *adj.* **—trace′less·ly,** *adv.*

trace² (trās), *n.* either of the two straps, ropes, or chains by which an animal pulls a wagon, carriage, etc.

kick over the traces, throw off control; become unruly. [< OF *traiz,* pl., ult. < L *trahere* drag]

trac·er (trās′ər), *n.* **1** person or thing that traces. **2** inquiry sent from place to place to trace a missing person, letter, parcel, etc. **3** firework attached to a bullet to show its course. **4** an element (**tracer element**) or atom (**tracer atom**), usually radioactive, which can be traced and observed in a biological process or used to detect small quantities of its isotope in analysis.

trac·er·y (trās′ər i; trās′ri), *n., pl.* **-er·ies. 1** ornamental work consisting of intersecting or ramified ribs, bars, or the like, as in the upper part of a Gothic window. **2** any delicate interlacing work of lines, threads, etc., as in carving and embroidery.

tra·che·a (trā′ki ə; trə kē′ə), *n., pl.* **-che·ae** (-ki ē; -kē′ē). **1** the windpipe. **2** in insects and other arthropods, the

air-conveying tube of the respiratory system. [< LL, ult. < Gk. *tracheia (arteria),* lit., rough (windpipe)] **—tra′che·al,** *adj.*

tra·che·ot·o·my (trā′ki ot′ə mi), *n., pl.* **-mies.** surgical incision into the trachea, as for insertion of a breathing tube.

tra·cho·ma (trə kō′mə), *n.* **1** a contagious inflammation of the eyelids that can cause blindness. **2** granular eyelids, a much less serious condition. [< NL < Gk., roughness, < *trachys* rough]

trac·ing (trās′ing), *n.* **1** copy of something made by marking or drawing over it. **2** line made by marking or drawing.

track (trak), *n.* **1** footprint or other mark left, as by a wheel: *the tracks of a rabbit, the tracks of a truck.* **2** line of travel or motion; path; trail; road: *a track in the woods.* **3** line of metal rails for rail cars to go on. **4** a course for running or racing: *a race track.* **5** the sport made up of contests in running, jumping, throwing, etc. **6** linked steel treads of a bulldozer, tractor, etc., that move it forward or in reverse. *—v.* **1** make footprints or other marks on (a floor, etc.): *don't track the floor.* **2** bring (snow or mud) into a place on one's feet: *track mud into the house.* **3** follow by means of footprints, marks, smell, etc.: *track a bear.* **4** trace in any way: *track down a criminal.*

in one's tracks, right where one is.

keep track of, keep within one's sight, knowledge, or attention.

lose track of, fail to keep track of.

make tracks, go very fast; run away.

off the track, off the subject; wrong.

on the track, on the subject; right. [OF *trac*] **—track′er,** *n.* **—track′less,** *adj.* **—track′less·ly,** *adv.*

track·age (trak′ij), *n.* all the tracks of a railroad.

track meet, series of contests in running, jumping, throwing, etc.

tract¹ (trakt), *n.* **1** stretch of land, water, etc.; extent; region; area. **2** system of related parts or organs in the body: *the digestive tract.* **3** period of time. [< L *tractus,* orig., hauling < *trahere* drag. Doublet of TRAIT.]

tract² (trakt), *n.* a little book or pamphlet. [appar. < L *tractatus,* a handling, ult. < *trahere* drag]

trac·ta·ble (trak′tə bəl), *adj.* **1** easily managed or controlled; easy to deal with; docile. **2** easily worked, as copper or gold. [< L, < *tractare.* See TREAT.] **—trac′ta·bil′i·ty, tract′a·ble·ness,** *n.* **—tract′a·bly,** *adv.*

trac·tile (trak′təl), *adj.* capable of being drawn out to a greater length. **—trac·til′i·ty,** *n.*

trac·tion (trak′shən), *n.* **1** a drawing or pulling; a being drawn: *laid up with broken bones and in traction.* **2** kind of power used to draw or pull along a road or track. Electric traction is used on some railroads. **3** friction: *wheels slip on ice because there is too little trac-*

tion. [< Med.L *tractio* < L *trahere* drag] **—trac′tive** *adj.*

trac·tor (trak′tər), *n.* **1** engine for a large truck or trailer, able to haul long distances. **2** engine on wheels, used for pulling wagons, plows, etc., along roads or over fields. [< Med.L, < L *trahere* drag]

trade (trād), *n., v.,* **trad·ed, trad·ing.** *—n.* **1** a buying and selling; exchange of goods; commerce: *foreign trade.* **2** a bargain; business deal: *he made a good trade.* **3** kind of work; business, esp. one requiring skilled mechanical work: *a carpenter or plumber learns his trade.* **4** people in the same kind of work or business; *the building trade.* **5** customers: *that store has a lot of trade.* *—v.* **1** buy and sell; exchange goods; be in commerce: *trade with England.* **2** exchange: *trade seats.* **3** bargain; deal.

the trades, a the trade winds. **b** *Informal.* trade journals or newspapers.

trade in, give an automobile, etc., as part payment for something.

trade off, get rid of by trading.

trade on, take advantage of.

trade up, trade in, esp. a car, for something better and more expensive. [< MDu., MLG, track]

trade-in (trād′in′), *n.* thing given or accepted as payment or part payment for something.

trade·mark (trād′märk′), *n.* mark, picture, name, or letters owned and used by a manufacturer or merchant to distinguish goods from the goods of others. *—v.* **1** distinguish by means of a trademark. **2** register the trademark of.

trade name, 1 name used by a manufacturer or merchant for some article that he or she sells. **2** a name under which a company does business.

trad·er (trād′ər), *n.* person who trades.

trade school, school where trades are taught.

trades·man (trādz′mən), *n., pl.* **-men.** storekeeper; shopkeeper.

trades·peo·ple (trādz′pē′pəl) *n. pl.* storekeepers; shopkeepers.

trade union, 1 association of workers in any trade or craft to protect and promote their interests. **2** a labor union. **—trade unionism. —trade unionist.**

trade wind, a wind blowing steadily toward the equator from about 30° north latitude to about 30° south latitude. North of the equator, it blows from the northeast; south of the equator, from the southeast.

trading post, a store or station of a trader, esp. in remote places.

tra·di·tion (trə dish′ən), *n.* **1** the handing down of beliefs, opinions, customs, stories, etc., from parents to children. **2** what is handed down in this way. [< L *traditio < tradere* hand down < *trans-* over + *dare* give. Doublet of TREASON.] **—tra·di′tion·ist,** *n.*

tra·di·tion·al (trə dish′ən əl; -dish′nəl), *adj.* **1** of or according to tradition. **2**

handed down by tradition. **3** customary. —**tra·di'tion·al·ly,** *adv.*

tra·duce (trə düs'; -dūs'), *v.,* **-duced, -duc·ing.** speak evil of (a person) falsely; slander. [< L *traducere* parade in disgrace < *trans-* across + *ducere* lead]

traf·fic (traf'ik), *n., v.,* **-ficked, -fick·ing.** —*n.* **1** people, automobiles, wagons, ships, etc., coming and going along a way of travel. **2** their movement along such a way. **3** a buying and selling; commerce; trade. **4** business done by a railroad line, airline, etc.; number of passengers or amount of freight carried. **5** *Fig.* contact; dealings. —*v.* carry on trade; buy; sell; exchange: *the men trafficked with local producers.* [< OF < Ital., < *trafficare* < *tras-* across (< L *trans-*) + *ficcare* shove, poke, ult. < L *figere* fix] —**traf'fick·er,** *n.*

tra·ge·di·an (trə jē'di ən), *n.* **1** actor in tragedies. **2** writer of tragedies.

tra·ge·di·enne (trə jē'di en'), *n.* actress in tragedies

trag·e·dy (traj'ə di), *n., pl.* **-dies. 1** a serious play having an unhappy ending. *Hamlet* is a tragedy. **2** the writing of such plays. **3** *Fig.* a very sad or terrible happening. [< L < Gk. *tragoidia* < *tragos* goat (connection obscure) + *oide* song]

trag·ic (traj'ik), *adj.* **1** of or having to do with tragedy: *a tragic actor.* **2** *Fig.* very sad; dreadful: *a tragic death.* [< L < Gk. *tragikos*] —**trag'i·cal·ly,** *adv.*

trag·i·com·e·dy (traj'i kom'ə di), *n., pl.* **-dies. 1** play having both tragic and comic elements. *The Merchant of Venice* is a tragicomedy. **2** incident or situation in which serious and comic elements are blended. —**trag'i·com'ic, trag'i·com'i·cal,** *adj.* —**trag'i·com'i·cal·ly,** *adv.*

trail (trāl), *v.* **1** pull or drag along behind: *her dress trails on the ground.* **2** grow along: *poison ivy trailed by the road.* **3** follow along behind; follow: *the dog trailed him constantly.* **4** form a track or trail: *smoke trailed from the engine.* **5** go along slowly: *the snake trailed through the long grass.* **6** pass little by little: *her voice trailed off into silence.* —*n.* **1** anything that follows along behind: *the car left a trail of dust behind it.* **2** track or smell: *the trail of the rabbit.* **3** path across a wild or unsettled region. [< OF *trailler* tow, ult. < L *tragula* dragnet] —**trail'ing·ly,** *adv.*

trail·blaz·er (trāl'blā'zər), *n.* person or thing that prepares the way for something new: *a trailblazer in AIDS research.*

trail·er (trāl'ər), *n.* **1** a vehicle, often large, pulled along the highway by a truck lacking a body of its own. **2** a mobile furnished house pulled by an automobile. **3** a few scenes shown to advertise a forthcoming motion picture; preview. **4** a trailing plant; vine that grows along the ground. **5** person or animal that follows a trail.

trailer park, the grounds, equipped with utilities and other facilities, for accommodating trailers and recreational vehicles.

train (trān), *n.* **1** a connected line of railroad cars moving along together. **2** line of people, animals, vehicles, etc., moving along together: *a train of covered wagons.* **3** series or succession of proceedings, events, circumstances, etc.: *a long train of misfortunes.* **4** *Fig.* series of connected ideas, etc.: *one's train of thought.* **5** something that is drawn along behind; trailing part: *the train of a dress.* **6** group of followers. [< v.] —*v.* **1** bring up; rear; teach: *train a child.* **2** make skillful by teaching and practice: *train women as nurses.* **3** make or become fit by exercise and diet: *runners train for races.* **4** point; aim: *train cannon upon a fort.* **5** bring into a particular position: *train the vine around this post.* [< OF *trainer* < L *trahere* drag] —**train'a·ble,** *adj.* —**train'er,** *n.*

train·ee (trān ē'), *n.* person who is receiving training.

train·ing (trān'ing), *n.* **1** practical education in some art, profession, etc.: *training for teachers.* **2** development of strength and endurance. **3** good condition maintained by exercise, diet, etc.

train·load (trān'lōd'), *n.* as much as a train can hold or carry.

train·man (trān'mən), *n., pl.* **-men. 1** person who works on a railroad train. **2** brakeman.

traipse (trāps), *v.,* **traipsed, traips·ing. 1** walk about aimlessly. **2** tramp over or through: *traipsed through the flower bed.*

trait (trāt), *n.* a distinguishing feature or quality; characteristic. [< F, ult. < L *trahere* drag. Doublet of TRACT[1].]

trai·tor (trā'tər), *n.* **1** person who betrays his or her country or ruler. **2** person who betrays a trust, duty, friend, etc. [< OF, ult. < L *traditor,* ult. < *trans-* over + *dare* give]

trai·tor·ous (trā'tər əs), *adj.* like a traitor; treacherous; faithless. —**trai'tor·ous·ly,** *adv.*

tra·jec·to·ry (trə jek'tə ri; -tri), *n., pl.* **-ries.** the curved path of a projectile, comet, or planet. [< Med.L *trajectories* throwing across, ult. < L *trans-* across + *jacere* throw]

tram (tram), *n.* =streetcar. [< MDu., MLG *trame* beam]

tram·mel (tram'əl), *v.,* **-meled, -mel·ing.** hinder; restrain. [< OF < L *tremaculum* < *tres* three + *macula* mesh]

tramp (tramp), *v.* **1** walk heavily: *he tramped across the room in his heavy boots, he tramped on the flowers.* **2** go on foot; walk: *we tramped through the streets.* **3** travel through on foot. **4** go or wander as a tramp. —*n.* **1** sound of a heavy step. **2** a long, steady walk; hike. **3** man who wanders about and begs. **4** a freight ship that takes a cargo when and where it can. [? < LG *trampen*] —**tramp'er,** *n.*

tram·ple (tram'pəl), *v.,* **-pled, -pling,** *n.* —*v.* **1** tread heavily on; crush. **2** treat cruelly, harshly, or scornfully. —*n.* act or sound of trampling.

trample under foot, trample on or upon, treat cruelly, harshly, or scornfully. [< *tramp*]

tram·po·line (tram'pə lēn'), *n.* canvas or other strong fabric stretched across a metal frame and held in place by springs to make a resilient surface, used for acrobatics, jumping, etc.

trance (trans; trans), *n., v.,* **tranced, tranc·ing.** —*n.* **1** state or condition of unconsciousness somewhat like sleep. **2** a dreamy, absorbed, or hypnotic condition. —*v.* hold in a trance; enchant. [< OF *transe,* ult. < L *trans-* across + *ire* go]

tran·quil (trang'kwil; tran'-), *adj.,* **-quil·er, -quil·est.** calm; peaceful; quiet. [< L *tranquillus*] —**tran'quil·ly,** *adv.*

tran·quil·ize (trang'kwil īz; tran'-), *v.,* **-ized, -iz·ing.** make or become calm, peaceful, or quiet.

tran·quil·iz·er (trang'kwil īz'ər), *n.* any of various drugs that reduce tension, nervous strain, etc.

tran·quil·li·ty (trang kwil'ə ti; tran-), *n.* calmness; peacefulness; quiet.

trans-, *prefix.* **1** across; over; through, as in *transfluent, transflux.* **2** beyond; on the other side of, as in *transcend.* **3** across, etc.; and also beyond, on the other side of, as in *transoceanic, transpolar,* and other geographical terms, such as *trans-African.* [< L *trans,* prep.]

trans., **1** transactions. **2** transitive. **3** translation. **4** transportation.

trans·act (tran zakt'; trans akt'), *v.* **1** attend to; manage; do. **2** carry on business; deal. [< L *transactus* accomplished < *trans-* through + *agere* drive] —**trans·ac'tor,** *n.*

trans·ac·tion (tran zak'shən; trans ak'-), *n.* **1** the carrying on (of business). **2** fact of being transacted. **3** piece of business.

transactions, records, reports, etc., of a learned society or the like.

trans·al·pine (tranz al'pīn; trans-), *adj.* across the Alps, esp. as viewed from Italy. [< L *trānsalpīnus* < *trāns* across + *alpīnus* Alpine]

trans·at·lan·tic (trans'ət lan'tik; tranz'-), *adj.* **1** crossing the Atlantic. **2** on the other side of the Atlantic.

trans·scend (tran send'), *v.* **1** go beyond the limits or powers of; exceed; be above. **2** be higher or greater than; excel. [< L *transcendere* < *trans-* beyond + *scandere* climb]

tran·scend·ent (tran sen'dənt), *adj.* surpassing ordinary limits; excelling; superior; extraordinary. —**tran·scend'ence, tran·scend'en·cy,** *n.*

tran·scen·den·tal (tran'sen den'təl), *adj.* **1** transcendent. **2** supernatural. **3** obscure; incomprehensible; fantastic. —**tran'scen·den'tal·ly,** *adv.*

tran·scen·den·tal·ism (tran´sen den´-tal iz əm), *n.* **1** transcendental quality, thought, language, or philosophy. **2** any philosophy based upon the doctrine that the principles of reality are to be discovered by a study of the processes of thought, not from experience. **3** the religious and philosophical doctrines of Emerson and others in New England about 1840, which had an important influence on American thought and literature. —**tran´scen·den´tal·ist,** *n.*

trans·con·ti·nen·tal (trans´kon tə nen´-tal), *adj.* **1** crossing a continent. **2** on the other side of a continent.

tran·scribe (tran skrīb´), *v.,* **-scribed, -scrib·ing. 1** copy in writing. **2** set down in writing or print. **3** arrange (a piece of music) for a different instrument or voice. **4** process of duplicating genetic information in RNA molecules by using DNA as a template. [< L, < *trans-* over + *scribere* write] —**tran·scrib´er,** *n.*

tran·script (tran´script), *n.* **1** a written or printed copy. **2** a copy or reproduction of anything. —**tran·scrip´tive,** *adj.*

tran·scrip·tion (tran skrip´shən), *n.* **1** a transcribing; copying. **2** transcript; copy. **3** arrangement of a piece of music for a different instrument or voice.

tran·sept (tran´sept), *n.* **1** the shorter part of a cross-shaped church. **2** either end of this part. [< Med.L, ult. < L *trans-* across + *saeptum* fence]

trans·fer (*v.* trans fėr´; trans´fėr; *n.* trans´-fėr), *v.,* **-ferred, -fer·ring,** *n.* —*v.* **1** convey or remove from one person or place to another; hand over: *transfer a title to land.* **2** convey (a drawing, design, pattern) from one surface to another. **3** change from one bus, train, etc., to another. —*n.* **1** a transferring or being transferred. **2** thing transferred, as a drawing, pattern, etc., printed from one surface onto another. **3** ticket allowing a passenger to continue journey on another bus, train, etc. [< L, < *trans-* across + *ferre* bear] —**trans·fer´a·ble,** *adj.* —**trans´fer·a·bil´i·ty,** *n.*

trans·fer·ence (trans fėr´əns), *n.* **1** a transferring. **2** in psychology, the transferring of emotions and feelings, formerly attached to one person, to another; displacement.

transfer RNA, ribonucleic acid that delivers amino acids to the ribosomes during protein synthesis.

trans·fig·u·ra·tion (trans fig´yə rā´shən), *n.* a change in form or appearance; transformation.

the Transfiguration, a the change in appearance of Christ on the mountain. Matt. 17; Mark 9 **b** the church festival on August 6 in honor of this.

trans·fig·ure (trans fig´yər), *v.,* **-ured, -ur·ing. 1** change in form or appearance; transform: *new paint had transfigured the old house.* **2** change so as to glorify; exalt. [< L, < *trans-* across + *figura* figure] —**trans·fig´ure·ment,** *n.*

trans·fix (trans fiks´), *v.* make motionless (with amazement, terror, etc.). [< L *transfixus* < *trans-* through + *figere* fix]

trans·form (trans fôrm´), *v.* **1** change in form, appearance, condition, nature, or character. **2** change (one form of energy) into another. A dynamo transforms mechanical energy into electricity. **3** change (an electric current) into one of higher or lower voltage. [< L, < *trans-* across + *forma* form] —**trans·form´a·ble, trans·form´a·tive,** *adj.*

trans·for·ma·tion (trans´fər mā´shən), *n.* a transforming.

trans·form·er (trans fôr´mər), *n.* **1** person or thing that transforms. **2** device for changing an alternating current into one of higher or lower voltage.

trans·fuse (trans fūz´), *v.,* **-fused, -fus·ing. 1** pour from one container into another. **2** transfer (blood) from one person or animal to another. **3** inject (a solution) into a blood vessel. **4** *Fig.* infuse; instill: *the speaker transfused his enthusiasm into the audience.* [< L *transfusus* < *trans-* across + *fundere* pour] —**trans·fus´er,** *n.* —**trans·fus´i·ble,** *adj.*

trans·fu·sion (trans fū´zhən), *n.* act or fact of transfusing.

trans·gress (trans gres´; tranz–), *v.* **1** break a law, command, etc.; sin. **2** go beyond (a limit or bound): *her manners transgressed the bounds of good taste.* [< L *transgressus* having gone beyond < *trans-* across + *gradi* to step] —**trans·gres´sor,** *n.*

trans·gres·sion (trans´gresh´ən; tranz–), *n.* a transgressing; breaking a law, command, etc.; sin.

tran·ship (trans ship´), *v.,* **-shipped, -ship·ping.** = transship. —**tran·ship´ment,** *n.*

tran·sient (tran´shənt), *adj.* **1** passing soon; fleeting; not lasting. **2** passing through and not staying long: *a transient guest.* **3** introduced casually and not necessary to the harmony. —*n.* a visitor or boarder who stays for a short time. [< L *transiens* passing through < *trans-* through + *ire* go] —**tran´sience, tran´sien·cy,** *n.* —**tran´sient·ly,** *adv.*

tran·sis·tor (tran zis´tər), *n.* a small crystal device consisting of germanium or silicon which controls the flow of electricity in electronic devices. [< *trans-* + L *sistere* send, convey]

trans·it (tran´sit; –zit), *n., v.,* **-it·ed, -it·ing.** —*n.* **1** a passing across or through. **2** a carrying or being carried across or through: *the goods were damaged in transit.* **3** instrument used in surveying to measure angles. **4** passage of a small celestial body across the disk of a larger one. —*v.* pass; pass across; pass through. [< L *transitus* < *transire.* See TRANSIENT.] —**trans´it·a·ble,** *adj.*

tran·si·tion (tran zish´ən), *n.* **1** a change or passing from one condition, place, thing, activity, topic, etc., to another. **2** a change of key. [< L *transitio* < *transire.*

See TRANSIENT.] —**tran·si´tion·al,** *adj.* —**tran·si´tion·al·ly,** *adv.*

tran·si·tive (tran´sə tiv), *adj.* **1** of verbs, taking a direct object. *Bring* and *raise* are transitive verbs. **2** involving transition. —*n.* a transitive verb. —**tran´si·tive·ly,** *adv.*

tran·si·to·ry (tran´sə tô´ri; –tō´–; –zə–), *adj.* passing soon or quickly; lasting only a short time. —**tran´si·to´ri·ly,** *adv.* —**tran´si·to´ri·ness,** *n.*

trans·late (trans lāt´; tranz–; trans´lāt; tranz´–), *v.,* **-lat·ed, -lat·ing. 1** change from one language into another. **2** change into other words. **3** *Fig.* explain the meaning of. **4** use genetic information in messenger RNA to direct protein synthesis. [< L *translatus,* pp. to *transferre.* See TRANSFER.] —**trans·lat´a·ble,** *adj.* —**trans·la´tor,** *n.*

trans·la·tion (trans lā´shən; tranz–), *n.* **1** act of translating. **2** result of translating; version. **3** formation of amino acids from genetic information carried in messenger RNA.

trans·lit·er·ate (trans lit´ər āt; tranz–), *v.,* **-at·ed, -at·ing.** change (letters, words, etc.) into corresponding characters of another alphabet or language, as to transliterate the Greek X as *ch* and ø as *ph,* or transliterate Arabic words into English letters. [< TRANS- + L *litera* letter] —**trans·lit´er·a´tion,** *n.* —**trans·lit´er·a´tor,** *n.*

trans·lu·cent (trans lü´sənt; tranz–), *adj.* letting light through without being transparent. Frosted glass is translucent. [< L, < *trans-* through + *lucere* shine] —**trans·lu´cence, trans·lu´cen·cy,** *n.* —**trans·lu´cent·ly,** *adv.*

trans·mi·grate (trans mī´grāt; tranz–), *v.,* **-grat·ed, -grat·ing. 1** move from one place or country to another; migrate. **2** pass at death into another body. —**trans´mi·gra´tion,** *n.* —**trans´mi·gra·tor,** *n.* —**trans´mi·gra·to´ry** *adj.*

trans·mis·si·ble (trans mis´ə bəl; tranz–), *adj.* capable of being transmitted: *a transmissible disease.* —**trans·mis´si·bil´i·ty,** *n.*

trans·mis·sion (trans mish´ən; tranz–), *n.* **1** a sending over; passing on; passing along; letting through: *mosquitoes are the only means of transmission of malaria.* **2** fact of being transmitted. **3** something transmitted. **4** the part of an automobile that transmits power from the engine to the front or rear axle. **5** passage through space of radio waves from the transmitting station to the receiving station. —**trans·mis´sive,** *adj.*

trans·mit (trans mit´; tranz–), *v.,* **-mit·ted, -mit·ting. 1** send over; pass on; pass along; let through. **2** communicate, as information, news, etc. **3** pass on to successors or posterity. **4** send out (signals, voice, music, pictures, etc.) by radio or television. [< L, < *trans-* across + *mittere* send] —**trans·mit´tal, trans·mit´tance,** *n.* —**trans·mit´ti·ble,** *adj.*

trans·mit·ter (trans mit′ər; tranz–), *n.* **1** person or thing that transmits something. **2** that part of a telegraph or telephone by which messages are sent. **3** apparatus for sending out signals, voice, music, pictures, etc., by radio or television.

trans·mute (trans mūt′; tranz–), *v.,* **–mut·ed, –mut·ing.** change from one nature, substance, or form into another. We can transmute water power into electrical power. [< L, < *trans–* thoroughly + *mutare* change] —**trans·mut′a·ble,** *adj.* —**trans·mu′a·bil′i·ty, trans·mut′a·ble·ness,** *n.* —**trans′mu·ta′tion,** *n.* —**trans·mut′er,** *n.*

trans·o·ce·an·ic (trans′ō shi an′ik; tranz′–), *adj.* **1** crossing the ocean. **2** on the other side of the ocean.

tran·som (tran′səm), *n.* **1** window over a door or other window, usually hinged for opening. **2** cross-bar separating a door from the window over it. [< L *transtrum,* orig., crossbeam]

tran·son·ic (tran son′ik), *adj.* moving at speeds just below or above the speed of sound, or between 600 and 800 miles per hour.

trans·pa·cif·ic (trans′pə sif′ik), *adj.* **1** crossing the Pacific. **2** on the other side of the Pacific.

trans·par·en·cy (trans pãr′ən si; –par′–), *n., pl.* **–cies. 1** Also, **trans·par′ence.** transparent quality or condition. **2** something transparent. **3** picture, design, or the like, made visible by light shining through from behind.

trans·par·ent (trans pãr′ənt; –par′–), *adj.* **1** transmitting light so that bodies beyond or behind can be distinctly seen. Window glass is transparent. **2** frank: *a boy of transparent honesty.* **3** *Fig.* easily seen through or detected: *transparent excuses.* [< Med.L *transparens* showing light through < L *trans–* through + *parere* appear] —**trans·par′ent·ly,** *adv.*

tran·spire (tran spīr′), *v.,* **–spired, –spir·ing. 1** take place; happen. **2** leak out; become known. **3** pass off or send off in the form of vapor through a wall or surface, as from the human body or from leaves. [< Med.L, < L *trans–* through + *spirare* breathe] —**tran′spi·ra′tion,** *n.*

trans·plant (trans plant′; –plänt′), *v.* **1** plant again in a different place. **2** remove from one place to another. **3** transfer (skin, an organ, etc.) from one person, animal, or part of the body to another. —**trans·plant′a·ble,** *adj.* —**trans′plan·ta′tion,** *n.* —**trans·plant′er,** *n.*

trans·port (*v.* trans pôrt′, –pôrt′; *n.* trans′-pôrt; –pôrt), *v.* **1** carry from one place to another: *wheat is transported from farms to mills.* **2** *Fig.* carry away by strong feeling: *transported with joy.* —*n.* **1** a carrying from one place to another: *trucks are much used for transport.* **2** ship used to carry men and supplies. **3** a strong feeling. [< L, < *trans–* across + *portare* carry]

—**trans·port′a·ble,** *adj.* —**trans·port′a·bil′i·ty,** *n.* —**trans·port′er,** *n.*

trans·por·ta·tion (trans′pər tā′shən), *n.* **1** a transporting. **2** state of being transported. **3** means of transport. **4** cost of transport; ticket for transport.

trans·pose (trans pōz′), *v.* **–posed, –pos·ing. 1** change the position or order of; interchange. **2** change the usual order of (letters or words). **3** change the key of. **4** in algebra, transfer (a term) to the other side of an equation, changing plus to minus or minus to plus. [< F *transposer.* See TRANS–, POSE.] —**trans·pos′a·ble,** *adj.* —**trans·pos′a·bil′i·ty,** *n.* —**trans·pos′er,** *n.* —**trans′po·si′tion,** *n.* —**trans′po·si′tion·al,** *adj.*

trans·ship (trans ship′), *v.,* **–shipped, –ship·ping.** transfer from one ship, train, car, etc., to another. —**trans·ship′-ment,** *n.*

trans·son·ic (trans son′ik), *adj.* =transonic.

tran·sub·stan·ti·a·tion (tran′səb stan′shi-ā′shən), *n.* **1** a changing of one substance into another. **2** the changing of the substance of the bread and wine of the Eucharist into the substance of the body and blood of Christ.

trans·ver·sal (trans vėr′səl; tranz–), *adj.* transverse. —*n.* a line intersecting two or more other lines. —**trans·ver′sal-ly,** *adv.*

trans·verse (trans vėrs′; tranz–; trans′-vėrs; tranz′–), *adj.* lying across, placed crosswise; crossing from side to side: *transverse beams.* —*n.* **1** something transverse. **2** the longer axis of an ellipse. [< L *transversus* < *trans–* across + *vertere* turn] —**trans·verse′ly,** *adv.*

trans·ves·tite (trans ves′tīt), *n.* person who chooses to dress in the clothing of the opposite sex.

trap (trap), *n., v.,* **trapped, trap·ping.** —*n.* **1** thing or means for catching animals; snare. **2** trick or other means for catching someone off guard. **3** a device in a pipe to prevent the escape of air, water, gas, etc. **4** a device to throw clay pigeons, etc., into the air to be shot at. —*v.* **1** catch in a trap. **2** set traps for animals.

traps, drums, cymbals, bells, gongs, etc.; percussion instruments. [OE *træppe*]

trap door, door in a floor or roof.

tra·peze (trə pēz′; tra–), *n.* a short horizontal bar hung by ropes like a swing, used in gymnasiums and circuses. [< F < LL < Gk. *trapezion,* dim. of *trapeza* table]

tra·pe·zi·um (trə pē′zi əm) *n., pl.* **–zi·ums, –zi·a** (–zi ə). **1** a four-sided plane figure having no sides parallel. **2** bone in the wrist, at the base of the thumb. [< LL < Gk. *trapezion,* orig., little table. See TRAPEZE.]

trap·e·zoid (trap′ə zoid), *n.* **1** four-sided plane figure having two sides parallel and two sides not parallel. **2** bone in the wrist at the base of the forefinger.

[< NL < Gk., < *trapeza* table + *eidos* form] —**trap′e·zoi′dal,** *adj.*

trap·per (trap′ər), *n.* person who traps, esp. a person who traps wild animals for their furs.

trap·pings (trap′ingz), *n. pl.* **1** ornamental coverings for a horse. **2** things worn; ornaments: *trappings of a king and his court.*

Trap·pist (trap′ist), *n.* monk belonging to an extremely austere branch of the Cistercian order established in 1664. —*adj.* of or pertaining to the Trappists. [< F *trappiste,* from the monastery of *La Trappe*]

trap·shoot·ing (trap′shüt′ing), *n.* shooting at clay pigeons, etc., thrown into the air. —**trap′shoot′er,** *n.*

trash (trash), *n.* **1** worthless stuff; rubbish. **2** foolish notions, talk, or writing; nonsense. **3** a disreputable or worthless person. [cf. Scand. (dial. Norw.) *trask*]

trash·y (trash′i), *adj.,* **trash·i·er, trash·i·est.** like or containing trash; worthless. —**trash′i·ly,** *adv.* —**trash′i·ness,** *n.*

trau·ma (trô′mə; trou′–), *n., pl.* **–mas. 1** a physical or psychic wound; injury. **2** the condition (neurosis, etc.) produced by it. [< Gk., wound]

trau·mat·ic (trô mat′ik; trou–), *adj.* **1** of, having to do with, or produced by a wound, injury, or shock. **2** for or dealing with the treatment of wounds, injuries, or shock.

trav·ail (trav′āl; trə vāl′), *n.* **1** toil; labor. **2** trouble; hardship. —*v.* toil; labor. [< OF, ult. < LL *trepalium* torture device, prob. < L *tres* three + *palus* stake]

trav·el (trav′əl), *v.,* **–eled, –el·ing.** *n.* —*v.* **1** go from one place to another; journey: *travel across the country.* **2** move in a fixed course, as a moving part in a machine does. **3** move; proceed; pass: *light and sound travel in waves.* **4** pass through or over: *travel a road.* —*n.* **1** movement in general. **2** going in trains, in planes, cars, etc., from one place to another; journeying. [var. of *travail*] —**trav′el·er,** *n.*

trav·eled (trav′əld), *adj.* **1** having journeyed widely. **2** much used by travelers.

trav·e·logue, trav·e·log (trav′ə lôg; –log), *n.* lecture describing travel or a motion picture depicting travel.

trav·erse (*v., adv.* trav′ərs, trə vėrs′; *n., adj.* trav′ərs), *v.,* **–ersed, –ers·ing, *n., adj., adv.* —*v.* pass across, over, or through: *traverse a plain.* —*n.* **1** act of crossing. **2** something put or lying across. —*adj.* lying across; being across. —*adv.* across; crosswise. [< OF *traverser* < *travers* TRANSVERSE] —**trav′ers·a·ble,** *adj.* —**trav′ers·er,** *n.*

trav·es·ty (trav′is ti), *n., pl.* **–ties.** any treatment or imitation that makes a serious thing seem ridiculous. [< F *travesti* disguised, ult. < L *trans–* over + *vestire* dress]

tra·vois (trə voi′), *n., pl.* **–vois.** device for carrying things used by the North

American Plains Indians, which consisted of two poles with a crosspiece on which goods were stacked, and dragged behind a horse.

trawl (trôl), *n.* a strong net dragged along the bottom of the sea. —*v.* fish with a net by dragging it along the bottom of the sea. [< MDu. *traghel* < L *tragula* dragnet. Cf. TRAIL.]

trawl·er (trôl′ər), *n.* boat used in trawling.

tray (trā), *n.* **1** a flat, shallow holder or container with a low rim around it. **2** tray with dishes of food on it. **3** a shallow box that fits into a trunk, cabinet, etc. [OE *trēg*]

treach·er·ous (trech′ər əs), *adj.* **1** not to be trusted; not faithful; disloyal: *the treacherous soldier carried reports to the enemy.* **2** having a false appearance of strength, security, etc.; not reliable; deceiving: *thin ice is treacherous.* —**treach′er·ous·ly,** *adv.* —**treach′er·ous·ness,** *n.*

treach·er·y (trech′ər i), *n., pl.* -**er·ies.** a breaking of faith; treacherous behavior; deceit. [< OF *trecherie* < *trechier* cheat]

trea·cle (trē′kəl), *n.* molasses, esp. that produced during the refining of sugar. [< OF *treacle* antidote < L < Gk. *theriake,* ult. < *ther* wild beast] —**trea′cly,** *adj.*

tread (tred), *v.,* **trod** or (*Archaic*) **trode, trodden** or **trod, tread·ing,** *n.* —*v.* **1** set the feet on; walk on or through; step across: *tread the streets.* **2** press under the feet; trample; crush: *tread grapes.* **3** dominate harshly; repress. **4** make, form, or do by walking: *tread a path.* —*n.* **1** act or sound of treading; step: *the tread of marching feet.* **2** way of walking: *he walks with a heavy tread.* **3** the part of stairs or a ladder that a person steps on. **4** the part of a wheel or tire that touches the ground. **5** distance between opposite wheels of an automobile. **6** sole of the foot or of a shoe.

tread on one's toes, offend or annoy one.

tread water, a keep oneself from sinking by moving the feet and legs up and down in movements similar to running. **b** *Fig.* stay in the same place or condition; fail to make progress. [OE *tredan*] —**tread′er,** *n.*

trea·dle (tred′əl), *n., v.,* -**dled, -dling.** —*n.* lever worked by the foot to operate a machine: *the treadle of a sewing machine.* —*v.* work a treadle. [OE *tredel* < *tredan* tread]

tread·mill (tred′mil′), *n.* **1** apparatus to turn something by having a person or animal walk on the moving steps of a wheel or of a sloping, endless belt. **2** any wearisome or monotonous round of work or life.

treas., treasurer; treasury.

trea·son (trē′zən), *n.* betrayal of one's country or ruler. [< AF *treson* < L *traditio.* Doublet of TRADITION.]

trea·son·a·ble (trē′zən ə bəl; trēz′nə bəl), **trea·son·ous** (-əs), *adj.* of treason; involv-

ing treason; traitorous. —**trea′son·a·ble·ness,** *n.* —**trea′son·a·bly,** *adv.*

treas·ure (trezh′ər; trā′zhər), *n., v.,* -**ured, -ur·ing.** —*n.* **1** wealth or riches stored up; valuable things. **2** any thing or person that is much loved or valued. —*v.* **1** value highly. **2** put away for future use; store up. [< OF *tresor* < L < Gk. *thesauros.* Doublet of THESAURUS.]

treas·ur·er (trezh′ər ər; trezh′rər; trā′zhər ər; trāzh′rər), *n.* person in charge of money. —**treas′ur·er·ship′,** *n.*

treas·ure-trove (trezh′ər trōv′; trā′zhər-) *n.* **1** money, jewels, or other treasure that a person finds, esp. if the owner of it is not known. **2** any valuable discovery: *a treasure-trove of ancient artifacts.* [< AF *tresor trové* treasure found]

treas·ur·y (trezh′ər i; trezh′ri; trā′zhər i; trāzh′ri), *n., pl.* **ur·ies. 1** place where money is kept. **2** money owned; funds. **3** department that has charge of the income and expenses of a country. **4** place where treasure is kept. **5** *Fig.* book or person thought of as a valued source.

treat (trēt), *v.* **1** act toward in some specified manner: *the farmer treats his cows well.* **2** think of; consider; regard: *treat a matter as unimportant.* **3** deal with: *the dentist is treating my tooth, treat a metal plate with acid in engraving, this magazine treats the progress of medicine, treat a theme realistically.* **4** entertain with food, drink, or amusement: *treat guests to tea.* **5** discuss terms; arrange terms: *messengers came to treat for peace.* —*n.* **1** act of treating. **2** gift of food, drink, or amusement. **3** anything that gives pleasure. [< OF *tretier* < L *tractare,* orig., drag violently, handle, frequentative of *trahere* drag] —**treat′a·ble,** *adj.* —**treat′er,** *n.*

trea·tise (trē′tis), *n.* book or writing dealing with some subject. A treatise is more formal and systematic than most books or writings. [< AF *tretiz,* ult. < L *tractare* TREAT]

treat·ment (trēt′mənt), *n.* **1** act or process of treating. **2** way of treating. **3** thing done or used to treat a disease, condition, etc.

trea·ty (trē′ti), *n., pl.* -**ties.** agreement, esp. one between nations, signed and approved by each nation. [< OF *traite,* orig. pp. of *traiter* TREAT]

tre·ble (treb′əl), *adj., v.,* -**bled, -bling.** —*adj.* **1** three times; threefold; triple. **2** of or for the treble. —*v.* make or become three times as much: *treble one's money.* —*n.* **a** the highest part in music; soprano. **b** voice, singer, or instrument that takes this part. [< OF < L *triplus* triple. Doublet of TRIPLE.] —**tre′bly,** *adv.*

treble clef, symbol indicating that the pitch of the notes on a staff is above middle C.

tree (trē), *n., v.,* **treed, tree·ing.** —*n.* **1** a large perennial plant with a woody trunk, branches, and leaves. **2** piece of structure of wood for some special pur-

pose: *clothes tree, shoe tree.* **3** diagram with branches showing how the members of a family are related. —*v.* chase up a tree: *the cat was treed by a dog.*

bark up the wrong tree, pursue the wrong thing or use the wrong means to obtain something: *if he wants to find the answers, he's barking up the wrong tree.*

up a tree, a chased up a tree. **b** *Informal. Fig.* in a difficult position. [OE *trēo*] —**tree′less,** *adj.* —**tree′less·ness,** *n.* —**tree′like′,** *adj.*

tree frog, 1 a small frog that lives in trees. **2** a tree toad.

tree surgeon, expert in the care and treatment of trees, esp. damaged or diseased trees. —**tree surgery.**

tree toad, a small toad living in trees, that has adhesive disks or suckers on its toes.

tre·foil (trē′foil), *n.* **1** plant having threefold leaves, as the common clovers. **2** ornament like a threefold leaf. [< OF < L, < *tri-* three + *folium* leaf]

trek (trek), *v.,* **trekked, trek·king,** *n.* —*v.* travel slowly by any means; travel. —*n.* **1** act of trekking. **2** journey. [< Du. *trekken,* orig., draw, pull] —**trek′ker,** *n.*

trel·lis (trel′is), *n.* frame of light strips of wood or metal crossing one another with open spaces in between; lattice, esp. one supporting growing vines. —*v.* **1** furnish with a trellis. **2** support on a trellis. [< OF *trelis,* ult. < L *trilix* triple-twilled]

trem·a·tode (trem′ə tōd; trē′mə-), *n.* flatworm that lives as a parasite in or on other animals. —*adj.* belonging to the group of trematodes. [< NL, < Gk. *trematodes* holed < *trema* hole]

trem·ble (trem′bəl), *v.,* -**bled, -bling,** *n.* —*v.* **1** shake because of fear, excitement, weakness, cold, etc. **2** feel fear, anxiety, etc. —*n.* a trembling. [< OF *trembler,* ult. < L *tremulus* TREMULOUS] —**trem′bler,** *n.* —**trem′bling,** *adj.* —**trem′bling·ly,** *adv.*

trem·bly (trem′bli), *adj.* trembling; tremulous.

tre·men·dous (tri men′dəs), *adj.* **1** dreadful; awful. **2** very great; enormous: *a tremendous house.* **3** extraordinary: *have a tremendous time.* [< L *tremendus,* lit., to be trembled at < *tremere* tremble] —**tre·men′dous·ly,** *adv.* —**tre·men′dous·ness,** *n.*

trem·o·lo (trem′ə lō), *n., pl.* -**los. 1** a trembling or vibrating quality in tones. The tremolo is used to express emotion. **2** device in an organ used to produce this quality. [< Ital. Doublet of TREMULOUS.]

trem·or (trem′ər), *n.* **1** an involuntary shaking or trembling: *a nervous tremor in the voice.* **2** vibration: *an earthquake followed by tremors.* **3** *Fig.* thrill of emotion or excitement. [< L] —**trem′or·less,** *adj.*

trem·u·lous (trem′yə ləs), *adj.* **1** trembling; quivering. **2** timid; fearful. [< L *tremulus* < *tremere* tremble. Doublet of TREMOLO.] —**trem′u·lous·ly,** *adv.* —**trem′u·lous·ness,** *n.*

trench (trench), *n.* **1** a long, narrow ditch with earth thrown up in front to protect soldiers. **2** a deep furrow; ditch; cut. —*v.* **1** surround with a trench; fortify with trenches. **2** dig a trench in. **3** dig ditches. [< OF *trenchier,* cut, appar. ult. < L *truncare* lop off < *truncus* mutilated]

trench·ant (tren′chənt), *adj.* **1** sharp; keen; cutting: *trenchant wit.* **2** vigorous; effective: *a trenchant policy.* [< OF, cutting. See TRENCH.] —**trench′an·cy, trench′ant·ness,** *n.* —**trench′ant·ly,** *adv.*

trench·er (tren′chər), *n.* a wood platter on which meat was formerly served and carved. Originally, a trencher was a slice of bread used instead of a wooden or metal plate. [< AF *trenchour* knife, ult. < *trenchier* to cut. See TRENCH.]

trench mouth, 1 a contagious inflammation of the mouth and gums. **2** any inflammation of the mouth and gums.

trend (trend), *n.* a general direction; course; tendency. —*v.* have a general direction; tend; run. [OE *trendan*]

Tren·ton (tren′tən), *n.* capital of New Jersey, in the W part.

tre·pan (tri pan′), *n., v.,* **-panned, -pan·ning.** —*n.* **1** a cylindrical saw for cutting out part of the skull. **2** a boring tool. —*v.* bore through with a trepan. [< Med.L < Gk. *trypanon* < *trypaein* bore]

trep·i·da·tion (trep′ə dā′shən), *n.* **1** nervous dread; fear; fright. **2** a trembling. [< L, ult. < *trepidus* alarmed]

tres·pass (tres′pəs), *v.* **1** go on somebody's property without any right. **2** go beyond the limits of what is right, proper, or polite: *I won't trespass on your time any longer.* **3** do wrong; sin. —*n.* **1** act or fact of trespassing. **2** a wrong; a sin. **3** an unlawful act done by force against the person, property, or rights of another. [< OF *trespasser* < *tres-* across (< L *trans-*) + *passer* PASS] —**tres′pass·er,** *n.*

tress (tres), *n.* a lock, curl, or braid of hair. [< F *tresse*] —**tressed,** *adj.*

tres·tle (tres′əl), *n.* **1** frame used as a support, consisting usually of a horizontal beam fixed at each end to a pair of spreading legs. **2** a supporting framework, as for carrying railroad tracks across a gap. [< OF *trestel* crossbeam, ult. < L *transtrum*]

trey (trā), *n.* card, die, or domino with three spots. [< OF *trei* < L *tres* three]

tri-, *combining form.* **1** three; having three; having three parts, as in *triangle.* **2** three times; into three parts, as in *trisect.* **3** containing three atoms, etc., of the substance specified, as in *trioxide.* **4** once in three; every third, as in *trimonthly.* [< L or Gk.]

tri·a·ble (trī′ə bəl), *adj.* **1** that can be tested or tried. **2** that can be tested in a law court.

tri·ad (trī′ad; -əd), *n.* **1** group of three, esp. of three closely related persons or things. **2** musical chord of three tones. **3** element, atom, or radical having a valence of three. [< L < Gk. *trias* < *treis* three]

tri·al (trī′əl), *n.* **1** the examining and deciding of a case in court. **2** process of trying or testing. **3** condition of being tried or tested: *he is employed on trial.* **4** trouble; hardship: *lack of money causes many trials.* **5** attempt; effort. —*adj.* **1** of or pertaining to trial. **2** done or used by way of trial, test, proof, or experiment. [< AF, < *trier* TRY]

trial and error, learning about or testing something by trying it out to eliminate errors.

trial balance, comparison of debit and credit totals in a ledger. If they are not equal, there is an error.

trial balloon, 1 small weather balloon sent aloft to measure temperature, wind, etc. **2** *Fig.* launch or announce something, as a plan or project, to test public reaction to it.

trial jury, group of 6 or 12 persons chosen to decide a case in court.

tri·an·gle (trī′ang′gəl), *n.* **1** a plane figure having three sides and three angles. **2** something shaped like a triangle. **3** a musical instrument consisting of a triangle of steel that is struck with a steel rod. **4** two men in love with the same woman; two women in love with the same man. [< L, < *tri-* three + *angulus* corner]

tri·an·gu·lar (trī ang′gyə lər), *adj.* **1** shaped like a triangle; three-cornered. **2** concerned with three persons, groups, etc. —**tri·an′gu·lar′i·ty,** *n.* —**tri·an′gu·lar·ly,** *adv.*

tri·an·gu·late (*v.* trī ang′gyə lāt; *adj.* trī ang′gyə lit; -lāt), *v.,* **-lat·ed, -lat·ing,** *adj.* —*v.* **1** divide into triangles. **2** survey (a region) by dividing (it) into triangles and measuring their angles. **3** find by trigonometry: *triangulate the height of a mountain.* **4** make triangular. —*adj.* triangular. —**tri·an′gu·la′tion,** *n.* —**tri·an′gu·la′tor,** *n.*

Tri·as·sic (trī as′ik), *n.* earliest geological period of the Mesozoic era, characterized by the appearance of dinosaurs and great volcanic activity.

tri·ath·lon (trī ath′lon), *n.* athletic event that combines swimming, bicycling, and running. [< *tri-* three + Gk. *áthlon* contest] —**tri·ath′lete,** *n.*

tribe (trīb), *n.* **1** group of people united by race and customs under the same leaders. **2** class or set of people. **3** class, kind, or sort of animals, plants, or other things. **4** one of the twelve divisions of the ancient Hebrews. **5** in ancient Rome, one of the three divisions of the Roman people. [< L *tribus*] —**trib′al,** *adj.* —**trib′al·ism,** *n.* —**trib′al·ly,** *adv.* —**tribe′ship,** *n.*

tribes·man (trībz′mən), *n., pl.* **-men.** member of a tribe.

trib·u·la·tion (trib′yə lā′shən), *n.* great trouble; severe trial; affliction. [< LL *tribulatio,* ult. < L *tribulum* threshing sledge]

tri·bu·nal (tri bū′nəl; trī-), *n.* **1** court of justice; place of judgment. **2** place where judges sit in a law court. [< L, < *tribunus* TRIBUNE[1]]

trib·une[1] (trib′ūn), *n.* **1** official in ancient Rome chosen by the plebeians to protect their rights and interests. **2** defender of the people. [< L *tribunus* < *tribus* tribe] —**trib′une·ship,** *n.*

trib·une[2] (trib′ūn), *n.* a raised platform; rostrum. [< Ital. *tribuna* tribunal]

trib·u·tar·y (trib′yə ter′i), *n., pl.* **-tar·ies,** *adj.* —*n.* **1** stream that flows into a larger stream or body of water. The Ohio River is a tributary of the Mississippi River. **2** one that pays tribute. —*adj.* **1** flowing into a larger stream or body of water. **2** paying tribute; required to pay tribute. **3** *Fig.* contributing; helping. —**trib′u·tar′i·ly,** *adv.*

trib·ute (trib′ūt), *n.* **1** money paid by one nation to another for peace or protection or because of some agreement. **2** any forced payment, as a tax, etc. **3** an acknowledgment of thanks or respect; compliment. Memorial Day is a tribute to our dead soldiers. [< L, < *tribuere* allot < *tribus* tribe]

trice (trīs), *n.* a very short time; moment; instant. [abstracted from phrase *at a trice* at a pull]

tri·ceps (trī′seps), *n.* the large muscle at the back of the upper arm. It extends or straightens the arm. [< NL < L, three-headed, < *tri-* three + *caput* head]

tri·cer·a·tops (trī ser′ə tops), *n.* dinosaur having a very large skull, horns above the eyes, one horn on the nose, and a large bony collar extending behind the neck. [< NL < Gk *trikératos* three-horned]

tri·chi·na (tri kī′nə), *n., pl.* **-nae** (-nē). a small, slender worm that lives in the intestines and muscles of humans and some animals. [< NL < Gk., fem. adj., of hair < *thrix* hair]

trich·i·no·sis (trik′ə nō′sis), *n.* disease due to the presence of trichinae in the intestines and muscular tissues.

trick (trik), *n.* **1** something done to deceive or cheat: *the false message was a trick to get him to leave town.* **2** a clever act; feat of skill: *we enjoyed the tricks of the trained animals.* **3** the best way of doing or dealing with something: *the trick of making pies.* **4** piece of mischief; prank: *play a trick on a person.* **5** a peculiar habit or way of acting: *he has a trick of pulling at his collar.* **6** the cards played in one round. —*v.* **1** deceive; cheat. **2** play tricks. —*adj.* **1** of or having the nature of a trick or tricks. **2** made for or used in tricks.

do or **turn the trick,** do what one wants done.

trick out, dress up; ornament. [< OF *trique*] —**trick′er,** *n.*

trick·er·y (trik′ər i; trik′ri), *n.*, *pl.* **-er·ies.** use of tricks; deception; cheating.

trick·le (trik′əl), *v.*, **-led, -ling,** *n.* —*v.* 1 flow or fall in drops or in a small stream: *tears trickled down her cheeks.* 2 come, go, pass, etc., slowly and unevenly: *people began to trickle into the theater.* —*n.* 1 a small flow or stream. 2 a trickling. [? earlier *strickle,* ult. < *strike*]

trick·ster (trik′stər), *n.* cheat.

trick·y (trik′i) *adj.,* **trick·i·er, trick·i·est.** 1 full of tricks; deceiving; cheating. 2 not doing what is expected; dangerous or difficult to handle. —**trick′i·ly,** *adv.* —**trick′i·ness,** *n.*

tri·col·or (trī′kul′ər), *adj.* having three colors. —*n.* 1 flag having three colors. 2 the flag of France.

tri·cot (trē′kō), *n.* 1 a knitted fabric made by hand or machine. 2 a kind of woolen cloth.

tri·cus·pid (trī kus′pid), *adj.* having three points or flaps. —*n.* a tricuspid tooth. [< L *tricuspis* three-pointed < *tri-* three + *cuspis* tip]

tri·cy·cle (trī′sə kəl; -sik′əl), *n.* a three-wheeled vehicle worked by pedals or handles. [< F. See TRI-, CYCLE.]

tri·dent (trī′dənt), *n.* a three-pronged spear. —*adj.* three-pronged. [< L, < *tri-* three + *dens* tooth]

tried (trīd), *adj.* tested; proved. —*v.* pt. and pp. of **try.**

tri·en·ni·al (trī en′i əl), *adj.* 1 lasting three years. 2 occurring every three years. —*n.* 1 period of three years. 2 event that occurs every three years. 3 the third anniversary of an event. [< L *triennium* three-year period < *tri-* three + *annus* year] —**tri·en′ni·al·ly,** *adv.*

tri·fle (trī′fəl), *n.,* *v.,* **-fled, -fling.** —*n.* 1 thing having little value or importance. 2 a small amount; little bit: *a trifle of sugar, he sold the picture for a mere trifle.* 3 a rich dessert made of sponge cake, whipped cream, custard, fruit, wine, etc. —*v.* 1 talk, act, or treat lightly, not seriously. 2 spend (time, effort, money, etc.) on things having little value: *she had trifled away the whole morning.* [< OF *trufle*] —**tri′fler,** *n.*

tri·fling (trī′fling), *adj.* 1 having little value; not important; small. 2 frivolous; shallow. —*n.* trifling behavior; worthless activity.

tri·fo·li·ate (trī fō′li it; -āt), *adj.* having three leaves, or three parts like leaves. Clover is trifoliate.

tri·fo·ri·um (trī fô′ri əm; -fō′-), *n., pl.* **-ri·a** (-ri ə). gallery in a church above a side aisle or transept. [< Med.L, appar. < L *tri-* three + *foris* door]

trig., trigonometric; trigonometry.

trig·ger (trig′ər), *n., v.,* **-gered, -ger·ing.** —*n.* 1 the small lever pulled back by the finger in firing a gun. 2 lever pulled or pressed to release a spring, catch, etc. —*v.* 1 set off (an explosion). 2 initiate; start: *trigger an outburst of violence.*

quick on the trigger, a quick to shoot. **b** *Informal. Fig.* quick to act or respond; alert. [ult. < Du. *trekker* < *trekken* pull]

trigger-happy (trig′ər hap′i), *adj.* aggressive; too quick to respond by shooting.

trig·o·nom·e·try (trig′ə nom′ə tri), *n.* branch of mathematics that deals with the relations between the sides and angles of triangles (plane or spherical) and the calculations based on these. [< NL, ult. < Gk. *tri-* three + *gonia* angle + *metron* measure] —**trig′o·no·met′ric, trig′o·no·met′ri·cal,** *adj.* —**trig′o·no·met′ri·cal·ly,** *adv.*

tri·he·dron (trī hē′drən), *n., pl.* **-drons, -dra** (-drə). figure formed by three planes meeting at a point. —**tri·he′dral,** *adj.*

tri·lat·er·al (trī lat′ər əl), *adj.* having three sides. —**tri·lat′er·al·ly,** *adv.*

trill (tril), *v.* 1 sing, play, sound, or speak with a tremulous, vibrating sound. 2 of birds, sing or warble. —*n.* 1 act or sound of trilling. 2 a quick alternation of two notes either a tone or a half tone apart. [< Ital. *trillare* < Gmc.]

tril·lion (tril′yən), *n.* 1 in the United States and France, 1 followed by 12 zeros. 2 in Great Britain, 1 followed by 18 zeros. —*adj.* one trillion in amount. [< F, < *tri-* three, modeled on *million* million] —**tril′lionth,** *adj., n.*

tril·li·um (tril′i əm), *n.* plant of the same family as the lily, with three leaves around a single flower. [< NL, < L *tri-* three]

tri·lo·bite (trī′lə bīt), *n.* an extinct arthropod, with three divisions of the body and jointed limbs. [< NL, < Gk. *tri-* three + *lobos* lobe]

tril·o·gy (tril′ə ji), *n., pl.* **-gies.** three plays, operas, novels, etc., that, while each is complete in itself, fit together to make a related series. [< Gk., < *tri-* three + *logos* story]

trim (trim), *v.,* **trimmed, trim·ming,** *adj.,* **trim·mer, trim·mest,** *n., adv.* —*v.* 1 put in good order; make neat by cutting away parts: *trim a hedge, trim dead leaves off plants.* 2 decorate: *trim a Christmas tree.* 3 balance (a boat, airplane, etc.) by arranging the load carried. 4 change (opinions, etc.) to suit circumstances. 5 arrange (the sails) to fit wind and direction. 6 *Informal.* defeat; beat. —*adj.* in good condition or order; neat: *a trim appearance.* —*n.* 1 good condition or order: *get in trim for a race.* 2 condition; order: *that ship is in poor trim for a voyage.* 3 trimming: *the trim on a dress.* 4 equipment; outfit. 5 a set of a ship in the water. b adjustment of sails with reference to the wind and direction. 6 the visible woodwork inside a building. —*adv.* in a trim manner. [OE *trymman* strengthen, make ready] —**trim′ly,** *adv.* —**trim′ness,** *n.*

tri·mes·ter (trī mes′tər), *n.* 1 period of three months. 2 division of a school year into three terms. [< L *trimestris* of

three months' duration < Gk. *tri-* three + *mēnsis* month]

trim·e·ter (trim′ə tər), *n.* poetry having three feet or measures in each line. —*adj.* consisting of three feet or measures. [< L < Gk., < *tri-* three + *metron* measure]

trim·mer (trim′ər), *n.* 1 a person or thing that trims. b machine that trims edges, as of grass or lumber. 2 *Fig.* person who changes opinions according to circumstances.

trim·ming (trim′ing), *n.* 1 decoration; ornament. 2 a defeat; beating. 3 a scolding. 4 **trimmings, a** parts cut away in trimming. b additions to simple food: *turkey with all the trimmings.*

Trin·i·dad and To·ba·go (trin′ə dad ənd tə bā′gō), country in the West Indies, near Venezuela.

Trin·i·tar·i·an (trin′ə tãr′i ən), *adj.* 1 believing in the Trinity. 2 pertaining to the Trinity. —*n.* person who believes in the Trinity. —**Trin′i·tar′i·an·ism,** *n.*

tri·ni·tro·tol·u·ene (trī nī′trō tol′ yü ēn), *n.* –TNT (a powerful explosive, $CH_3C_6H_2(NO_2)_3$).

trin·i·ty (trin′ə ti), *n., pl.* **-ties.** 1 group of three; triad. 2 **the Trinity.** the union of Father, Son, and Holy Ghost in one divine nature. [< OF < L, < *trinus* triple]

trin·ket (tring′kit), *n.* 1 any small fancy article, bit of jewelry, or the like. 2 trifle.

tri·no·mi·al (trī nō′mi əl), *n.* expression or name consisting of three terms. $a + bx^2 - 2$ is a trinomial. —*adj.* consisting of three terms. [< *tri-* + *nomial* from *binomial*]

tri·o (trē′ō), *n., pl.* **tri·os.** 1 piece of music for three voices or instruments. 2 three singers or players. 3 any group of three. [< Ital., ult. < L *tres* three]

tri·ox·ide (trī ok′sīd; -sid), *n.* any oxide having three atoms of oxygen in each molecule.

trip (trip), *n., v.,* **tripped, trip·ping.** —*n.* 1 a traveling about; journey; voyage. 2 a loss of footing; stumble; slip. 3 mistake; blunder. 4 a light, quick tread; stepping lightly. 5 a projecting part, catch, or the like for starting or checking some movement. [< v.] —*v.* 1 lose footing; stagger and fall; stumble: *trip on the stairs.* 2 make a mistake; do something wrong: *he tripped on that difficult question.* 3 take light, quick steps: *she tripped across the floor.* 4 release or operate suddenly (a catch, clutch, etc.); operate, start, or set free (a mechanism, weight, etc.). [< OF *tripper* < Gmc.]

tri·par·tite (trī pär′tīt), *adj.* 1 divided into three parts. 2 having three corresponding parts or copies. 3 made or shared by three parties: *a tripartite agreement.* —**tri·par′tite·ly,** *adv.*

tripe (trīp), *n.* 1 the walls of the first and second stomachs of an ox, etc., used as food. 2 *Informal. Fig.* something foolish, worthless, offensive, etc. [< OF, entrails, < Ar. *tharb*]

trip·ham·mer (trip′ham′ər), *n.* a heavy hammer raised and then let fall by machinery.

tri·ple (trip′əl), *adj., n., v.,* **-pled, -pling.** —*adj.* **1** having three parts. **2** three times as much or as many. —*n.* **1** number, amount, etc., that is three times as much or as many. **2** hit by which a batter gets to third base. —*v.* **1** make or become three times as much or as many. **2** hit a triple. [< L, < *tres* three + *-plus* fold. Doublet of TREBLE.] —**tri′ply,** *adv.*

triple play, play in baseball that puts three men out.

tri·plet (trip′lit), *n.* **1** one of three offspring born at the same time from the same mother. **2** group of three. **3** group of three notes to be performed in the time of two.

triplets, a set of three children born at the same time to the same mother. [< *triple*]

triple threat 1 football player who can pass, kick, and run especially well. **2** person who has three, or multiple, well-developed skills.

triple time, time or rhythm in music having three beats to the measure.

trip·li·cate (*v.* trip′lə kāt; *adj., n.* trip′-lə kit), *v.,* **-cat·ed, -cat·ing,** *adj., n.* —*v.* make threefold; triple. —*adj.* triple; threefold. —*n.* one of three things exactly alike.

in triplicate, with three copies exactly alike. [< L *triplicatus* < *triplex* threefold]

tri·pod (trī′pod), *n.* a stool, frame, or stand with three legs, as one for supporting a camera. [< L < Gk., < *tri-* three + *pous* foot]

trip·per (trip′ər), *n.* **1** person or thing that trips. **2** device in a machine that releases a catch, etc. **3** person who takes trips, esp. short ones: *a dedicated tripper.*

trip·ping (trip′ing), *adj.* **1** that trips. **2** light and quick. —**trip′ping·ly,** *adv.*

trip·tych (trip′tik), *n.* a set of three panels side by side, having pictures, carvings, or the like, on them. [< Gk. *triptychos* three-layered < *tri-* three + *ptyx* fold]

tri·reme (trī′rēm), *n.* an ancient ship with three rows of oars, one above the other, on each side. [< L, < *tri-* three + *remus* oar]

tri·sac·cha·ride (trī sak′ə rīd; -ə rid), *n.* carbohydrate that yields three molecules of simple sugar.

tri·sect (trī sekt′), *v.* **1** divide into three parts. **2** divide into three equal parts. [< TRI- + L *sectus,* pp. of *secare* cut] —**tri·sec′tion,** *n.* —**tri·sec′tor,** *n.*

tri·syl·la·ble (tri sil′ə bəl; trī-), *n.* word of three syllables, as *educate.* —**tri′syl·lab′ic,** *adj.*

trite (trīt), *adj.,* **trit·er, trit·est.** worn out by use; no longer new or interesting; common-place. [< L *tritus* rubbed away] —**trite′ly,** *adv.* —**trite′ness,** *n.*

trit·i·um (trit′i əm; trish′i əm), *n.* an isotope of hydrogen, T or H³, the explosive used in a hydrogen bomb.

tri·ton (trī′tən), *n.* nucleus of a tritium atom.

tri·umph (trī′umf), *n.* **1** victory; success: *the triumphs of science.* **2** joy because of victory or success: *bring home the prize in triumph.* **3** something that is successful: *the new dress was a triumph.* —*v.* **1** gain victory; win success: *our team triumphed over theirs.* **2** gain the mastery; prevail: *his sense of duty triumphed.* **3** rejoice because of victory or success.

in triumph, triumphant; triumphantly. [< L *triumphus*] —**tri·um′phal,** *adj.* —**tri·um′phal·ly,** *adv.* —**tri·umph′er,** *n.*

tri·um·phant (trī um′fənt), *adj.* **1** victorious; successful. **2** prevailing. **3** rejoicing because of victory or success. —**tri·um′-phant·ly,** *adv.*

tri·um·vi·rate (trī um′və rit; -rāt), *n.* **1** government by three people together. **2** any association of three in office or authority. **3** any group of three.

tri·va·lent (trī vā′lənt; triv′ə-), *adj.* having a valence of three. —**tri·va′-lence,** *n.*

triv·et (triv′it), *n.* a stand or support with three legs or feet. Trivets are used over fires and under platters. [< L *tri-* three + OE *-fēte* footed]

triv·i·a (triv′i ə), *n. pl.* trifles; trivialities.

triv·i·al (triv′i əl), *adj.* not important; trifling; insignificant. [< L *trivialis* vulgar, orig., of the crossroads, ult. < *tri-* three + *via* road] —**triv′i·al·ly,** *adv.* —**triv′i-al·ness,** *n.*

triv·i·al·i·ty (triv′i al′ə ti), *n., pl.* **-ties. 1** trivial quality. **2** a trivial thing, remark, affair, etc.; trifle.

tRNA, transfer RNA.

tro·che (trō′kē), *n.* a small medicinal tablet or lozenge, usually round. [< obs. *trochisk* < F < LL < Gk. *trochiskos,* dim. of *trochos* wheel]

tro·chee (trō′kē), *n.* a foot or measure in poetry consisting of two syllables, the first accented and the second unaccented or the first long and the second short. [< L < Gk. *trochaios,* orig., running] —**tro·cha′ic,** *adj., n.*

trod (trod), *v.* pt. and pp. of TREAD.

trod·den (trod′ən), *v.* pp. of TREAD.

trog·lo·dyte (trog′lə dīt), *n.* **1** a cave man. **2** *Fig.* person living in seclusion; hermit. **3** *Fig.* person unacquainted with affairs of the world. **4** an anthropoid ape, as the gorilla. [< L < Gk., < *trogle* cave + *dyein* go in]

Tro·jan (trō′jən), *adj.* of or pertaining to Troy or its people. —*n.* **1** native or inhabitant of Troy. **2** person who shows courage or energy: *they all worked like Trojans.*

Trojan horse, 1 *Gk. Legend.* a huge wooden horse in which the Greeks concealed soldiers and brought them into Troy during the Trojan War. **2** *Fig.* anyone or anything positioned or capable of causing destruction from within: *a Trojan horse computer virus, fear is a powerful Trojan horse.*

Trojan War, *Gk. Legend.* a ten years' war carried on by the Greeks against Troy to get back Helen of Troy, who was carried off by Paris, son of King Priam.

troll¹ (trōl), *v.* **1** sing in a full, rolling voice. **2** sing in the manner of a round. **3** fish with a moving line. —*n.* **1** song whose parts are sung in succession. **2** reel of a fishing rod. [< OF *troller* wander < Gmc.] —**troll′er,** *n.*

troll² (trōl), *n.* in Scandinavian folklore, an ugly dwarf or giant living underground in caves, etc. [< Scand.]

trol·ley (trol′i), *n., pl.* **-leys. 1** pulley moving against a wire to carry electricity to a streetcar, electric engine, etc. **2** a trolley car. **3** pulley running on an overhead track, used to support and move a load. [prob. < *troll*¹ in sense of "roll"]

trolley car, streetcar propelled electrically, the current often taken from an overhead wire by a trolley.

trol·lop (trol′əp), *n.* **1** an untidy or slovenly woman. **2** prostitute.

trom·bone (trom′bōn; trom bōn′), *n.* a large brass musical instrument, usually with a sliding piece for varying the length of the tube. [< Ital., < *tromba* trumpet < Gmc.] —**trom′bon·ist,** *n.*

troop (trüp), *n.* **1** group or band of persons. **2** herd, flock, or swarm of birds or animals. **3** a cavalry unit. **4** unit of boy scouts. **5 troops,** soldiers. —*v.* **1** gather in troops or bands; move together. **2** come or go; walk, sometimes in great numbers: *children trooped across the street.* [< F, ult. < LL *troppus* herd < Gmc.]

troop·er (trüp′ər), *n.* **1** soldier in a troop of cavalry. **2** a mounted police officer. **3** person who remains good-humored and works hard throughout a difficult period.

troop·ship (trüp′ship′), *n.* ship used to carry soldiers; transport.

trope (trōp), *n.* **1** the use of a word or phrase in a sense different from its ordinary meaning. **2** word or phrase so used. [< L < Gk. *tropos* turn] —**trop′ist,** *n.*

tro·phy (trō′fi), *n., pl.* **-phies. 1** a memorial of victory: *a golf trophy.* **2** a prize. [< F < L < Gk. *tropaion* < *trope* rout, orig., turn] —**tro′phied,** *adj.*

trop·ic (trop′ik), *n.* **1** either of the two circles around the earth, one 23.45 degrees north and one 23.45 degrees south of the equator. The **tropic of Cancer** is the northern circle, and the **tropic of Capricorn** is the southern circle. **2** either of two circles in the celestial sphere, the limits reached by the sun in its apparent journey north and south. **3 tropics, Tropics,** zone between latitudes 23½ degrees north and south or between 30 degrees north and south, the hottest part of the earth. —*adj.* of the tropics; belonging to the Torrid Zone. [< L < Gk. *tropikos* pertaining to a turn < *trope* turn]

trop·i·cal (trop′ə kəl), *adj.* **1** of or having to do with the tropics; inhabiting the tropics: *tropical fruit.* **2** very hot; burning or fervent. —**trop′i·cal·ly,** *adv.*

tro·pism (trō′piz əm), *n.* tendency of an animal or plant to turn or move in response to a stimulus. [< Gk. *trope* a turning] —**tro·pis′tic,** *adj.*

trop·o·sphere (trop′ə sfir), *n.* layer of the atmosphere between the earth and the stratosphere, within which there is a steady fall of temperature with increasing altitude. Most cloud formations occur in the troposphere.

trot (trot), *v.,* **trot·ted, trot·ting,** *n.* —*v.* **1** of horses, etc., go at a gait between a walk and a run by lifting the right forefoot and the left hind foot at about the same time. **2** ride a horse at a trot. **3** make (a horse, etc.) trot. **4** run, but not fast. —*n.* **1** the motion or gait of a trotting horse. **2** a brisk, steady movement. **3** *Informal.* translation of a book, used by a pupil instead of doing the translating.
trot out, *Informal.* bring out for others to see. [< OF *trotter* < Gmc.]

troth (trôth; trōth), *n.* **1** faithfulness; fidelity; loyalty. **2** promise. —*v.* promise; betroth.
plight one's troth, a promise to marry. **b** promise to be faithful. [OE *trēowth* faith]

trot·ter (trot′ər), *n.* **1** horse that trots. **2** a horse bred and trained to trot. **3** the foot of a sheep or a pig used for food.

trou·ba·dour (trü′bə dôr; –dōr; –dúr), *n.* one of the lyric poets of S France, E Spain, and N Italy from the 11th to the 13th centuries. The troubadours wrote mainly about love and chivalry. [< F < Pr. *trobador,* ult. < LL *tropus* song < L, TROPE]

trou·ble (trub′əl), *v.,* **–bled, –bling,** *n.* —*v.* **1** cause distress or worry to: *the lack of business troubled him.* **2** cause bodily pain or inconvenience to: *his shoulder troubled him.* **3** stir up; make turbid; disturb: *troubled waters.* **4** cause oneself extra work, effort, or inconvenience: *don't trouble to come to the door.* —*n.* **1** distress; worry; difficulty: *financial trouble.* **2** disturbance; agitation: *political troubles.* **3** a physical disorder; ailment; disease. **4** extra work; bother; effort: *take the trouble.* [< OF *troubler,* ult. < L *turba* turmoil] —**trou′bler,** *n.* —**trou′bling·ly,** *adv.*

trou·ble·mak·er (trub′əl māk′ər), *n.* person who is always causing trouble for others.

trou·ble-shoot·er (trub′əl shüt′ər), *n.* person who discovers and eliminates causes of trouble.

trou·ble·some (trub′əl səm), *adj.* **1** causing trouble; annoying. **2** laborious; difficult. —**trou′ble·some·ly,** *adv.* —**trou′ble·some·ness,** *n.*

trou·blous (trub′ləs), *adj.* **1** disturbed; restless. **2** =troublesome.

trough (trôf, trof; *dial.* trôth, troth), *n.* **1** a long, narrow container for holding food or water. **2** something shaped like this: *a trough for kneading dough.* **3** channel for carrying water; gutter. **4** a long hollow between two ridges, etc.: *trough between waves.* **5** *Fig.* a low point: *an economic trough.* [OE *trōh*]

trounce (trouns), *v.,* **trounced, trouncing.** **1** beat; thrash. **2** defeat, as in a contest.

troupe (trüp), *n.* troop; band; company, esp. a group of actors, singers, or acrobats. [< F]

troup·er (trüp′ər), *n.* **1** member of a theatrical troupe. **2** an old, experienced actor.

trou·sers (trou′zərz), *n. pl.* a two-legged outer garment reaching from the waist to the ankles or knees; pants. [< *trouse* < Irish *triubhas*]

trous·seau (trü sō′; trü′sō), *n., pl.* **–seaux** (–sōz′; –sōz), **–seaus.** a bride's outfit of clothes, linen, etc. [< F, orig., bundle]

trout (trout), *n., pl.* **trouts** or (*esp. collectively*) **trout.** any of certain freshwater food and game fishes of the salmon family. [< L < Gk. *troktes,* lit., gnawer < *trogein* gnaw]

trove (trōv), *n.* something found, esp. something valuable.

trow·el (trou′əl), *n., v.,* **–eled, –el·ing.** —*n.* **1** tool for spreading or smoothing plaster or mortar. **2** tool for taking up plants, loosening dirt, etc. —*v.* **1** apply or smooth with a trowel. **2** dig up or loosen with a trowel. [< OF, ult. < L *trulla* ladle < *trua* skimmer] —**trow′el·er,** *n.*

troy weight, a standard system of weights used for gems and precious metals. One pound troy equals a little over four-fifths of an ordinary pound. [after *Troyes,* France]

tru·ant (trü′ənt), *n.* **1** child who stays away from school without permission. **2** person who neglects duty. —*adj.* **1** staying away from school without permission. **2** neglecting duty. **3** lazy. **4** wandering. [< OF, prob. < Celtic] —**tru′an·cy,** *n.* —**tru′ant·ly,** *adv.*

truce (trüs), *n.* **1** a stop in fighting; peace for a short time. **2** a rest from trouble or pain; respite.

truck¹ (truk), *n.* **1 a** motor vehicle for carrying loads. **b** strongly built wagon, cart, etc., to more heavy loads. **2** frame on small wheels or a flat platform with wheels to move heavy objects. **3** frame with wheels that supports the front of a locomotive or a railroad car. —*v.* **1** carry on a truck. **2** drive a truck. —*adj.* of or for a truck; used on trucks. [? < L *trochus* iron hoop < Gk. *trochos* wheel] —**truck′age,** *n.*

truck² (truk), *n.* **1** vegetables raised for market. **2** rubbish; trash. **3** dealings. [< v.] —*v.* exchange; barter. —*adj.* of or having to do with truck. [< OF *troquer*]

truck·er (truk′ər), *n.* **1** person who drives a truck. **2** person whose business is carrying goods, etc., by trucks.

truck farm, vegetable farm.

truck·le (truk′əl), *v.,* **–led, –ling,** *n.* —*v.* move on rollers. —*n.* a small wheel. [< L *trochlea* < Gk. *trochilea* sheaf of a pulley]

truckle bed, a low bed moving on small wheels or casters, pushed under a regular bed when not in use. [< *truckle²* + *bed*]

truc·u·lent (truk′yə lənt), *adj.* fierce, savage, and cruel. [< L *truculentus* < *trux* fierce] —**truc′u·lence,** *n.* —**truc′u·lently,** *adv.*

trudge (truj), *v.,* **trudged, trudg·ing,** *n.* —*v.* walk, esp. wearily or with effort. —*n.* a hard or weary walk. —**trudg′er,** *n.*

true (trü), *adj.,* **tru·er, tru·est,** *n., v.,* **trued, tru·ing,** *adv.* —*adj.* **1** agreeing with fact; not false: *a true account of the events of the war.* **2** real; genuine: *true gold, have a true interest in a person's welfare.* **3** faithful; loyal: *a true patriot, true to one's friends.* **4** agreeing with a standard; right; proper; correct; exact; accurate: *a true copy, a sweet potato is not a true potato.* **5** rightful; lawful: *the true heir.* —*n.* exact or accurate formation, position, or adjustment: *a slanting door is out of true.* —*v.* make true; shape, place, or make in the exact position, form, etc., required: *true up the doorway.* —*adv.* in a true manner; truly; exactly: *ring true.* [OE *trēowe*] —**true′ness,** *n.*

true bill, bill of indictment found by a grand jury to be supported by enough evidence to justify hearing the case.

true-blue (trü′blü′), *adj.* **1** unchanging. **2** stanch; loyal.

true·love (trü′luv′), *n.* a faithful lover; sweetheart.

truf·fle (truf′əl; trü′fəl), *n.* a fungus that grows underground, valued as a food. [prob. ult. < F *truffe*]

tru·ism (trü′iz əm), *n.* statement that almost everybody knows is true.

tru·ly (trü′li), *adv.* **1** in a true manner; exactly; rightly; faithfully. **2** in fact; really.

Tru·man (trü′mən), *n.* **Harry S.,** 1884–1972, the 33rd president of the United States 1945–53.

trump (trump), *n.* **1** any playing card of a suit that for the time ranks higher than the other suits. **2** the suit itself. —*v.* **1** take (a trick, card, etc.) with a trump. **2** play a card of this suit. **3** be better than; surpass; beat. **4** make (up) to deceive. [alter. of *triumph*]

trump·er·y (trump′ər i; trump′ri), *n., pl.* **–er·ies,** *adj.* —*n.* something showy but without value; useless stuff; nonsense. —*adj.* showy but without value; trifling; worthless. [< F, *tromper* deceive]

trum·pet (trum′pit), *n.* **1** a musical wind instrument that has a powerful tone, commonly a curved tube of brass with a flaring bell at one end. **2** thing shaped like a trumpet, as an ear trumpet, once used to aid hearing. **3** a sound like that of a trumpet. —*v.* **1** blow a trumpet. **2** make a sound like a trumpet, as an elephant. **3** *Fig.* proclaim loudly or widely. [< OF *trompette,* ult. < Gmc.]

trum·pet·er (trum′pit ər), *n.* **1** person who blows a trumpet. **2** one who proclaims or announces something. **3** a large North American wild swan. **4** a large South American bird with long legs and neck, related to the cranes.

trun·cate (trung′kāt), *v.,* **-cat·ed, -cat·ing,** *adj.* —*v.* cut off a part of. —*adj.* cut off; blunt, as if cut off: *the truncate leaf of the tulip tree.* [< L, < *truncus* maimed] —**trun′cate·ly,** *adv.* —**trun·ca′tion,** *n.*

trun·cheon (trun′chən), *n.* stick; club: *a policeman's truncheon.* [< OF *tronchon,* ult. < L *truncus* TRUNK]

trun·dle (trun′dəl), *v.,* **-dled, -dling,** *n.* —*v.* roll along; push along. —*n.* **1** a rolling; rolling along. **2** a small wheel; caster. **3** bed, truck, etc., on small wheels or casters. [OE *-tryndel,* as in *sintryndel* round] —**trun′dler,** *n.*

trunk (trungk), *n.* **1** the main stem of a tree. **2** a big box for holding clothes, etc., when traveling. **3** a body without the head, arms, and legs. **4** enclosed compartment at the rear of automobile for storing luggage, spare tire, tools, etc. **5** the main part of anything: *the trunk of a column.* **6** line between telephone exchanges. **7** the main line of a railroad, canal, etc. **8** an elephant's snout. —*adj.* main; chief: *the trunk line of a railroad.*

trunks, short pants worn for swimming or other athletic activities. [< L *truncus,* maimed]

trun·nion (trun′yən), *n.* either of the two round projections of a cannon, one on each side, which support it on its carriage. [< F *trognon* trunk, ult. < L *truncus;* infl. by F *moignon* stump of an amputated limb]

truss (trus), *v.* **1** tie; fasten. **2** support (a roof, bridge, etc.) with trusses. —*n.* **1** beams or other supports connected to support a roof, bridge. etc. **2** bandage, pad, etc. that provides support. [< OF *trusser,* ult. < L *torquere* twist] —**truss′er,** *n.*

trust (trust), *n.* **1** firm belief in the honesty, truthfulness, justice, or power of a person or thing; faith. **2** person or thing trusted: *God is our trust.* **3** confident expectation or hope: *our trust is that she will soon be well.* **4** something managed for the benefit of another; something committed to one's care. **5** obligation or responsibility imposed on one in whom confidence or authority is placed: *breach of trust, a position of trust.* **6** illegal combination of companies that is able to eliminate competition by controlling production and prices. —*v.* **1** believe firmly in the honesty, truth, justice, or power of; have faith in: *he is a man to be trusted.* **2** rely on; depend on: *a forgetful*

man should not trust his memory. **3** commit to the care of; leave without fear: *can I trust the keys to him?* **4** hope; believe: *I trust you can come.* —*adj.* managing for an owner. A **trust company** undertakes to manage property for others.

in trust, as a thing taken charge of for another: *funds left in trust for the children.*
on trust, a on credit, with payment later. **b** without investigation: *took her statement on trust.*
trust to, rely on; depend on: trust to luck. [< Scand. *traust*] —**trust′a·ble,** *adj.* —**trust′er,** *n.*

trus·tee (trus tē′), *n.* person responsible for the property or affairs of another person, or of a company, institution, etc. —**trus·tee′ship,** *n.*

trust·ful (trust′fəl), *adj.* ready to confide; ready to have faith in; trusting; believing. —**trust′ful·ly,** *adv.* —**trust′ful·ness,** *n.*

trust·ing (trus′ting), *adj.* that trusts; trustful. —**trust′ing·ly,** *adv.* —**trust′ing·ness,** *n.*

trust·wor·thy (trust′wėr ′thī), *adj.* that can be depended on; reliable. —**trust′wor′thi·ly,** *adv.* —**trust′wor′thi·ness,** *n.*

trust·y (trus′ti), *adj.,* **trust·i·er, trust·i·est.** *n., pl.* that can be depended on; reliable. —**trust′i·ly,** *adv.* —**trust′i·ness,** *n.*

truth (trüth), *n., pl.* **truths** (trü⁴hz; trüths). **1** that which is true. **2** conformity with fact or reality. **3** a true, exact, honest, sincere, or loyal quality or nature. **4** principle, law, etc., that is established or fixed: *basic scientific truth.*

in truth, truly; really; in fact. [OE *trīewth < trīewe* truc]

truth·ful (trüth′fəl), *adj.* **1** telling the truth. **2** conforming to truth. —**truth′ful·ly,** *adv.* —**truth′ful·ness,** *n.*

try (trī), *v.,* **tried, try·ing,** *n., pl.* **tries.** —*v.* **1** attempt; attempt to do or accomplish; strive: *he tried to do the work; it seems easy until you try it.* **2** experiment on or with; make trial of: *try a new invention.* **3** find out about; test: *try one's luck.* **4** investigate in a law court: *the man was tried and found guilty.* **5** put to severe test; strain: *her mistakes try my patience.* **6** make pure by melting or boiling. —*n.* an attempt; test; experiment.

try on, put on to test the fit, looks, etc.
try out, a test the effect or result of. **b** enter as a test or trial of fitness for: *try out for the dance company.* [< OF *trier* cull]

try·ing (trī′ing), *adj.* hard to endure; annoying; distressing. —**try′ing·ly,** *adv.* —**try′ing·ness,** *n.*

try·out (trī′out′), *n.* test made to ascertain fitness for a specific purpose.

tryp·sin (trip′sin), *n.* an enzyme in the digestive juice secreted by the pancreas. Trypsin changes proteins into peptones. [irreg. < Gk. *tripsis* rubbing < *tribein* rub]

try·sail (trī′sāl′; -səl), *n.* a small fore-and-aft sail used in stormy weather.

try square, instrument for drawing right angles and testing the squareness of anything.

tryst (trist), *n.* **1** appointment to meet at a certain time and place. **2** a meeting thus prearranged. **3** place of meeting. [< OF *triste*]

tsar (zär; tsär), *n.* =czar.

tsar·e·vitch (zär′ə vich; tsär′–), *n.* =czarevitch.

tsa·ri·na (zä rē′nə; tsä-), *n.* =czarina.

tset·se fly (tset′sē), any of the bloodsucking flies of Africa, some of which spread sleeping sickness. [*tsetse* < Bantu]

T-shirt (tē′shėrt′), *n.* tee shirt.

tsp., teaspoon.

T square, a T-shaped ruler used for making parallel lines, etc. The shorter arm slides along the edge of the drawing board, which serves as a guide.

tsu·na·mi (tsü nä′mi), *n.* **1** oceanic tidal wave caused by an earthquake under the ocean. **2** *Fig.* anything like a tsunami, as a sudden and over powering event.

Tu, thulium.

Tu., Tuesday.

tub (tub), *n., v.,* **tubbed, tub·bing.** —*n.* **1** a large, open container for washing or bathing. **2** =bathtub. **3** a round wooden container for holding butter, lard, etc. **4** as much as a tub can hold. **5** a clumsy, slow boat or ship. —*v.* place or put in a tub. [cf. MDu., MLG *tubbe*] —**tub′ba·ble,** *adj.* —**tub′like′,** *adj.*

tu·ba (tü′bə; tü′-), *n.* a very large brass instrument of the trumpet class, of low pitch. [< L, war trumpet]

tub·by (tub′i), *adj.,* **-bi·er, -bi·est.** tub-shaped; short and fat. —**tub′bi·ness,** *n.*

tube (tüb; tūb), *n.* **1** a long pipe of metal, glass, rubber, etc., used to hold or carry liquids or gases. **2** a small cylinder of thin, easily bent metal with a cap that screws on the open end, used for holding toothpaste, paint, etc. **3** anything like a tube. **4** any hollow, cylindrical vessel or organ. [< L *tubus*] —**tubed,** *adj.* —**tube′like′,** *adj.*

tu·ber (tü′bər; tü′-), *n.* **1** the thick part of an underground stem. A potato is a tuber. **2** =tubercle. [< L, lump]

tu·ber·cle (tü′bər kəl; tü′-), *n.* **1** a small, rounded swelling or knob on an animal or plant. [< L *tuberculum,* dim. of *tuber* lump]

tu·ber·cu·lar (tə bėr′kyə lər; tü–; tū–), *adj.* **1** having tuberculosis. **2** of or having to do with tuberculosis. —**tu·ber′cu·lar·ly,** *adv.*

tu·ber·cu·lo·sis (tə bėr′kyə lō′sis; tü–; tū–), *n.* an infectious disease affecting various tissues of the body, but most often the lungs, caused by the tubercle bacillus. [< NL, < L *tuberculum* TUBERCLE] —**tu·ber′cu·lous,** *adj.*

tube·rose (tüb′rōz′; tüb′–; tü′bə rōs; tü′–), *n.* a bulbous plant with a spike of fragrant white flowers.

tu·ber·ous (tü′bər əs; tü–), *adj.* **1** bearing tubers. **2** of or like tubers. **3** covered with rounded knobs or swellings.

tub·ing (tüb′ing; tüb′–), *n.* **1** material in the form of a tube: *rubber tubing.* **2** tubes collectively. **3** a piece of tube.

tu·bu·lar (tü′byə lər; tü′–), *adj.* **1** shaped like a tube; round and hollow. **2** of or having to do with a tube or tubes. —**tu′bu·lar·ly,** *adv.*

tu·bule (tü′byül; tyü′–), *n.* very small, fine tube in an animal or plant body. [< F < L *tubulus* small tube, pipe]

tuck (tuk), *v.* **1** thrust into some narrow space or into some retired place: *he tucked the letter into his pocket.* **2** thrust the edge or end of (a garment, covering, etc.) closely into place: *tuck your shirt in.* **3** cover snugly: *tuck the children in bed.* **4** draw close together; fold. **5** sew a fold in (a garment) for trimming or to make it shorter or tighter. —*n.* **1** a fold sewed in a garment. **2** any tucked piece or part.

tuck away or **into,** eat or drink with gusto. [ME *tuken* stretch, OE *tūcian* torment]

tuck·er¹ (tuk′ər), *n.* **1** piece of muslin, lace, etc., worn around the neck or over the chest. **2** person or thing that tucks.

tuck·er² (tuk′ər), *v. Informal.* tire; weary.

Tues., Tuesday.

Tues·day (tüz′di; –dā; tūz′–), *n.* the third day of the week, following Monday.

tuft (tuft), *n.* **1** bunch of feathers, hair, grass, etc., held together at one end. **2** clump of bushes, trees, etc. —*v.* **1** put tufts on; furnish with tufts; divide into tufts. **2** grow in tufts. [? < OF *touffe* < LL *tufa* helmet crest] —**tuft′ed,** *adj.* —**tuft′er,** *n.*

tug (tug), *v.,* **tugged, tug·ging,** *n.* —*v.* **1** pull with force or effort; pull hard. **2** tow by a tugboat. —*n.* **1** a hard pull. **2** a hard strain, struggle, effort, or contest. **3** tugboat. [akin to *tow*] —**tug′ger,** *n.* —**tug′ging·ly,** *adv.*

tug·boat (tug′bōt′), *n.* a small, powerful boat used to tow other boats, barges, etc.

tug of war, 1 contest between two teams pulling at the ends of a rope, each trying to drag the other over a line marked between them. **2** *Fig.* any hard struggle.

tu·i·tion (tü ish′ən; tū–), *n.* **1** money paid for instruction. **2** instruction. [< L *tuitio* protection < *tueri* watch over]

tu·la·re·mi·a (tü′lə rē′mi ə), *n.* an infectious disease of rabbits and other rodents that is sometimes transmitted to people; rabbit fever. [< (*bacterium*) *tular(ense),* the organism that causes the disease + –*emia* < Gk. *haima* blood]

tu·lip (tü′lip; tū′–), *n.* **1** any of certain plants of the same family as the lily, that grow from bulbs and have large cup-shaped flowers. Most tulips are brilliantly colored and bloom in the spring. **2** the flower. **3** the bulb. [ult. < Turk. *tülbend* < Pers. *dulband* turban. Doublet of TURBAN.]

tulip tree, a large North American tree with greenish-yellow flowers shaped like tulips.

tu·lip·wood (tü′lip wud′; tyü′–), *n.* wood of the tulip tree, used in fine cabinetry.

tulle (tül), *n.* a thin, fine net made of silk or synthetic fiber. [after *Tulle,* French town]

tum·ble (tum′bəl), *v.,* **–bled, –bling,** *n.* —*v.* **1** fall: *tumble down the stairs.* **2** fall rapidly in value or price. **3** move in a hurried or awkward way. **4** perform leaps, springs, somersaults, etc. —*n.* **1** a fall. **2** confusion; disorder. [ult. < OE *tumbian* dance about]

tum·ble-down (tum′bəl doun′), *adj.* ready to fall down; dilapidated.

tum·bler (tum′blər), *n.* **1** person who performs leaps, springs, etc.; acrobat. **2** a drinking glass; the contents of a glass. **3** part in the lock that must be moved from a certain position in order to release the bolt.

tum·ble·weed (tum′bəl wēd′), *n.* plant growing in the W United States, that breaks off from its roots and is blown about by the wind.

tum·brel (tum′brəl), *n.* a two-wheeled farmer's cart. [prob. < OF *tombere* cart < *tomber* fall]

tum·my (tum′i), *n., pl.* **–mies.** *Informal.* abdomen; stomach: *everyone wants to have a flat tummy.* [< child's pronunciation of *stomach*]

tu·mor (tü′mər; tū′–), *n.* **1** a swelling. **2** abnormal growth in the body caused by disease. [< L] —**tu′mor·ous,** *adj.*

tumult (tü′mult; tū′–), *n.* **1** noise; uproar. **2** a violent disturbance or disorder. [< L *tumultus*]

tu·mul·tu·ous (tə mul′chù əs; tü–; tū–), *adj.* **1** characterized by tumult; very noisy or disorderly; violent. **2** greatly disturbed. **3** rough; stormy. —**tu·mul′tu·ous·ly,** *adv.* —**tu·mul′tu·ous·ness,** *n.*

tu·mu·lus (tü′myə ləs; tyü′–), *n., pl.* **–lus·es, –li** (–lī). **1** mound of earth marking an ancient gravesite. **2** low, rounded hill. [< L to swell]

tun (tun), *n.* a large cask for holding liquids. [OE *tunne,* prob. < Celtic]

tu·na (tü′nə), or **tuna fish,** *n.* **1** a large sea fish closely related to the tunny, used for food. It sometimes grows to a length of ten feet or more. **2** =the tunny. [< Amer. Sp., ult. < L *tunnus* TUNNY]

tun·dra (tun′drə; tùn′–), *n.* a vast, level, treeless plain in the arctic regions. [< Russ.]

tune (tün; tūn), *n., v.,* **tuned, tun·ing.** —*n.* **1** a pleasing, rhythmical succession of musical sounds forming a melody; air. **2** the proper pitch: *he can't sing in tune.* **3** mood; manner; tone: *he'll soon change his tune.* **4** agreement; harmony: *a person out of tune with his surroundings is unhappy.* **5** due agreement: **a** of pitch with two or more musical instruments. **b** of frequency of television or radio broadcasts. —*v.* **1** be in tune; be in harmony. **2** put in tune: *a man is tuning the piano.* **3** adjust (a radio) to a transmitted signal; adjust a radio to hear (what is wanted); adjust a radio to get rid of (a signal or interference that is unwanted). **4 a** bring (musical instruments) to the same. **b** begin to play, or sing, cry, etc. **c** get into the best working order.

call the tune, make decisions; dictate.

change one's tune, =sing a different tune.

sing a different tune, talk or behave differently.

to the tune of, to the amount or sum of.

tune in, a adjust (a radio) to a transmitted signal. **b** *Fig.* be alert or sensitive to.

tune out, a turn off a television or radio. **b** *Fig.* ignore: *finally simply tune out the complaints.*

tune up, a bring (musical instruments) to the same pitch. **b** begin to play, sing, cry, etc. **c** get into the best working order. [var. of *tone*] —**tun′a·ble, tune′a·ble,** *adj.* —**tun′a·ble·ness,** *n.* —**tun′a·bly,** *adv.*

tune·ful (tün′fəl; tūn′–), *adj.* musical; melodious. —**tune′ful·ly,** *adv.* —**tune′ful·ness,** *n.*

tune·less (tün′lis; tūn′–), *adj.* without tune; not musical. —**tune′less·ly,** *adv.*

tun·er (tü′nər; tyü′–), *n.* **1** person who tunes pianos, organs, or other musical instruments. **2** device for adjusting a radio to accept one frequency and reject others: *a sensitive tuner will tune out interference.*

tung·sten (tung′stən), *n.* former name of **wolfram,** a metallic element, W, used in making steel and for electric lamp filaments. [< Swed., < *tung* heavy + *sten* stone]

tu·nic (tü′nik; tū′–), *n.* **1** garment like a shirt or gown, worn by the ancient Greeks and Romans. **2** any garment like this. **3** a woman's garment extending below the waist and worn over a skirt or pants. **4** a short, close-fitting coat worn by soldiers, police officers, etc. [< L *tunica*]

tuning fork, a small, two pronged steel instrument that, when struck, vibrates at a fixed, constant, known rate and so makes a musical tone of a certain pitch.

Tu·nis (tü′nis; tū′–), *n.* capital of Tunisia, in the NE part.

Tu·ni·sia (tü nish′ə; tū–), *n.* country in N Africa. —**Tu·ni′sian,** *adj., n.*

tun·nel (tun′əl), *n., v.,* **–neled, –nel·ing.** —*n.* an underground passage, esp. an underground roadway for a railroad, a passage in a mine, or an animal's burrow. —*v.* **1** make as or like a tunnel: *tunnel a passage.* **2** make a tunnel through or under. [< OF *tonel* cask < *tonne* tun] —**tun′nel·er,** *n.*

tunnel vision, 1 visual disorder which causes a narrowing of vision to only objects directly in the line of sight. **2** *Fig.* narrow-mindedness; single-mindedness.

tun·ny (tun′i), *n., pl.* **–nies** or (*esp. collectively*) **–ny.** a large sea fish of the mackerel family, used for food. [< F, ult. < Gk. *thynnos*]

tu·pe·lo (tü′pə lō; tū′–), *n., pl.* **–los.** 1 a large North American tree of the dogwood family; sour gum. 2 its strong, tough wood. [< Am. Ind.]

Tu·pi (tü pē′), *n., pl.* **–pi** or **–pis.** 1 member of a group of native tribes of Brazil, Paraguay, and Uraguay. 2 their language, of the Tupi-Guarani linguistic stock.

Tu·pi-Gua·ra·ni (tü pē′gwä′rä nē′), *n.* a native linguistic stock of C South America, occurring particularly along the lower Amazon.

tup·pence (tup′əns), *n.* =two pence.

tur·ban (tėr′bən), *n.* 1 a scarf wound around the head or around a cap, worn by men in Eastern countries. 2 hat or headdress like this. [< Turk. < Ar. < Pers. *dulband*. Doublet of TULIP.] —**tur′baned,** *adj.*

tur·bid (tėr′bid), *adj.* 1 muddy; thick; not clear: *a turbid river.* 2 *Fig.* confused; disordered: *a turbid imagination.* [< L, < *turba* turmoil] —**tur′bid·ness,** *n.*

tur·bine (tėr′bən; –bīn), *n.* an engine or motor in which a wheel with vanes is made to revolve by the force of water, steam, or air. [< F < L *turbo* whirling object or motion]

tur·bo·jet (tėr′bō jet′), *n.* a jet-propulsion engine having a turbine-driven air compressor.

tur·bot (tėr′bət), *n., pl.* **–bots** or (*esp. collectively*) **–bot.** 1 a large European flatfish, much valued as food. 2 any of various similar fishes, such as certain flounders. [< OF *tourbout*]

tur·bu·lent (tėr′byə lənt), *adj.* 1 disorderly; unruly; violent. 2 greatly disturbed: *turbulent water.* [< L *turbulentus* < *turba* turmoil] —**tur′bu·lence, tur′bu·len·cy,** *n.* —**tur′bu·lent·ly,** *adv.*

tu·reen (tə rēn′; tü–), *n.* a deep, covered dish for serving soup, etc. [< F *terrine* earthen vessel, ult. < L *terra* earth]

turf (tėrf), *n., pl.* **turfs,** *v.* —*n.* 1 grass with its matted roots; sod. 2 piece of this. 3 peat. —*v.* cover with turf.

the turf, *Informal.* **a** the racetrack. **b** horse racing. [OE]

tur·gid (tėr′jid), *adj.* 1 swollen; bloated. 2 *Fig.* using big words and elaborate comparisons; bombastic: *turgid prose.* [< L *turgidus*] —**tur·gid′i·ty, tur′gid·ness,** *n.* —**tur′gid·ly,** *adv.*

Turk (tėrk), *n.* native or inhabitant of Turkey.

Turk., 1 Turkey. 2 Turkish.

Tur·ke·stan, Tur·ki·stan (tėr′kə stan′; –stän′), *n.* region in W and C Asia, now a part of Turkmenistan, Uzbekistan, Tajikistan, Kyrgyzstan, Kazakhstan, China, and Afghanistan.

tur·key (tėr′ki), *n., pl.* **–keys.** 1 a large wild bird of E North America, having a bare head and neck and brown feathers, that lives mainly on the ground, flying only short distances. A variety of turkey is found also in Mexico and C America.

b a large domesticated American bird. 2 its flesh, used for food. 3 *Informal.* play or motion picture that is a failure.

talk turkey, *Informal.* talk frankly and bluntly. [ult. < *Turkey*]

Tur·key (tėr′ki), *n.* country in W Asia and SE Europe.

turkey buzzard, vulture of South and Central America and S United States, having a bare, reddish head and dark plumage. Also, **turkey vulture.**

Turk·ic (tėr′kik), *adj.* 1 of or having to do with a branch of the Ural-Altaic language family spoken in Turkey and SC Asia. 2 =Turkish.

Turk·ish (tėr′kish), *adj.* of Turkey or the Turks. —*n.* the language of the Turks.

Turkish bath, a kind of bath in which the bather is kept in a heated room until he or she sweats freely and then is bathed and massaged.

turkish towel, a thick cotton towel with a long nap made of uncut loops.

Turk·men·i·stan (tėrk men′ə stän), *n.* country in W Asia, E of the Caspian Sea.

Tur·ko·man (tėr′kə mən for def. 1, tėrk′-mən for def. 2), *n., pl.* **–mans.** 1 member of any of various nomadic Turkic tribes living in parts of Afghanistan and Iran. 2 their Turkic language.

tur·mer·ic (tėr′mər ik), *n.* 1 a yellow powder prepared from the root of an East Indian plant, used as a seasoning, as a yellow dye, in medicine, etc. 2 the plant itself. 3 its root. [< Med.L *terra merita,* lit., worthy earth < L *terra* earth + *merere* deserve]

tur·moil (tėr′moil), *n.* commotion; tumult.

turn (tėrn), *v.* 1 move round as a wheel does; rotate: *the merry-go-round turned, turn a crank, turn over on your back.* 2 do by turning; open, close, make lower, higher, tighter, looser, etc., by moving around: *turn a key in the lock.* 5 take a new direction: *the road turns to the north here.* 3 change: *turn a page, turn water into ice, she turned pale.* 4 change for or to a worse condition; sour; spoil: *warm weather turns milk.* 5 put out of order; unsettle: *praise turns his head, bad food turned her stomach.* 6 depend: *it all turns on the result of the election.* 7 cause to go, send, etc.: *turn a person from one's door.* 8 put or apply to some purpose, use, etc.: *turn money to good use.* 9 direct (eyes, thoughts, etc.): *he turned his thoughts toward home, she turned her face away.* 10 pass (a certain age, time, etc.): *he has turned forty.* 11 make in a lathe. 12 of leaves, change color. —*n.* 1 motion like that of a wheel. 2 change of direction: *a turn to the left, a turn in the road.* 3 a change: *a turn for the better.* 4 a twist: *a turn of rope.* 5 time for action which comes in due rotation or order to each of a number of persons, etc.: *it's your turn now.* 6 time or spell of action: *have a turn at a thing.* 7 deed;

act: *a good turn.* 8 a walk, drive, or ride: *a turn in the park.* 9 form; style: *a happy turn of expression.*

at every turn, every time; without exception.

by turns, one after another.

in turn, in proper order.

out of turn, not in proper order.

take turns, play, act, etc., one after another, in proper order.

to a turn, to just the right degree.

turn about or **turn and turn about,** one after another in proper order.

turn down, a bend downward: *turn down a hat brim.* **b** fold down: *turn down the quilt.* **c** place face downward: *turn a letter down on the desk.* **d** refuse: *turn down a plan.* **e** lower by turning something: *turn down the flame under a pot.*

turn in, a turn and go in: *turn in the drive.* **b** go to bed. **c** give back: *turn in library books.* **d** exchange: *turn in a car.* **e** hand over; deliver: *turn in the week's work.* **f** inform on: *turn in someone to the police.*

turn off, a shut off: *turn off the gas.* **b** put out: *turn off the light.* **c** *Informal.* lose interest.

turn on, a start the flow of; put on: *turn on water, turn on the lights.* **b** attack; resist; oppose. **c** *Fig.* depend on. **d** *Informal. Fig.* stimulate interest, enthusiasm: *mysteries turn me on.*

turn out, a put out; shut off. **b** let go out: *turn out the cat, will you?* **c** drive out: *turn out of the driveway.* **d** come or go out: *everyone turned out for the circus.* **e** make; produce. **f** *Fig.* result or become: *turn out a good actor.* **g** equip; fit out: *turned out in a smart suit.*

turn over, a give; hand over: *turn over the keys to the car.* **b** think carefully about; consider in different ways: *turn over a problem in your mind.* **c** buy and then sell; use in business: *frequently turns over his stock holdings.* **d** convert to different use: *the old house has been turned over to a business.*

turn to, a refer to: *turn to the phone book.* **b** go to for help: *turned to my mother for advice.* **c** get busy; set to work: *turned to and cleaned the barn.*

turn up, a fold up or over: *turn up a collar.* **b** make a lamp burn brighter: *turn up the lantern.* **c** make a radio, television, etc., louder. **d** be directed upwards: *turns up her face for a kiss.* **e** appear: *guess who turned up?* [< L *tornare* turn on a lathe < *tornus* lathe < Gk. *tornos.* Cf. TOUR.] —**turn′er,** *n.*

turn·buck·le (tėrn′buk′əl), *n.* a short, hollow piece turning on a screw at each end, used to unite and tighten two parts.

turn·coat (tėrn′kōt′), *n.* person who changes party or principles; renegade.

turn·down (tėrn′doun′), *adj.* that is or can be turned down: *a turndown collar.*

—*n.* **1** rejection. **2** decline, esp. in economic activity.

turning point, point at which a notable change takes place.

tur·nip (tèr′nəp), *n.* **1** any of certain plants of the same family as the cabbage, with large, roundish roots that are used as vegetables. **2** the root of any of these plants. [prob. ult. < *turn* (from its rounded shape) + ME *nepe* turnip < L *napus*]

turn·key (tèrn′kē′), *n., pl.* **-keys.** person in charge of the keys of a prison; keeper of a prison.

turn·off (tèrn′ôf′; -of′), *n.* **1** place to exit from a road. **2** *Informal.* something that causes rejection or dislike: *his manner was a complete turnoff for me.*

turn·on or **turn-on** (tèrn′on′; -ôn), *n.* *Informal.* something that causes interest or excitement.

turn·out (tèrn′out′), *n.* **1** a gathering of people. **2** output. **3** act of turning out. **4** way in which somebody or something is equipped; equipment.

turn·o·ver (tèrn′ō′vər), *n.* **1** a turning over; upset. **2** the amount of changing from one job to another: *employers wish to reduce labor turnover.* **3** the paying out and getting back of the money in a business transaction: *the store reduced prices to make a quick turnover.* **4** the total amount of business done in a given time: *he made a profit of $6000 on a turnover of $90,000.* **5** a small pie made by folding half the crust over the filling and upon the other half. —*adj.* having a part that turns over: *a turnover collar.*

turn·pike (tèrn′pīk′), *n.* road that has, or used to have, a toll.

turn·stile (tèrn′stīl′), *n.* post with two crossed bars that turn, set in an entrance.

turn·stone (tèrn′stōn′), *n.* a small migratory shore bird that turns over stones in search of food.

turn·ta·ble (tèrn′tā′bəl), *n.* **1** a revolving circular platform used for turning things around. **2** the rotating disk on a phonograph upon which records are placed.

tur·pen·tine (tèr′pən tīn), *n.* **1** an oil obtained from various cone-bearing trees. Turpentine is used in mixing paints and varnishes, etc. **2** the mixture of oil and resin from which the prepared oil is made. [< L < Gk., < *terebinthos* turpentine tree]

tur·pi·tude (tèr′pə tüd; -tūd), *n.* shameful wickedness; baseness. [< L, < *turpis* vile]

tur·quoise (tèr′koiz; -kwoiz), *n.* **1** a sky-blue or greenish-blue precious stone. **2** a sky blue; greenish blue. —*adj.* sky-blue; greenish-blue. [< F, orig. fem. adj., Turkish]

tur·ret (tèr′it), *n.* **1** a small tower, often on the corner of a building. **2** a low armored structure which revolves, armored tanks. **3** a small enclosure protruding from the fuselage of a military aircraft containing movable machine guns. [< OF *touret,* ult. < L *turris* tower] —**tur′ret·ed,** *adj.*

tur·tle (tèr′təl), *n.* any of certain marine reptiles having the body enclosed in a hard shell from which the head, tail, and four legs protrude.

turn turtle, turn bottom side up. [< Sp. *tortuga* tortoise; infl. by E *turtle* turtledove]

tur·tle·dove (tèr′təl duv′), *n.* a kind of small, slender dove, noted for the affection that the mates have for each other. [*turtle* < L *turtur*]

turtle neck or **tur·tle·neck** (tèr′təl nek′), *n.* **1** high collar, attached to the neck of a sweater or other knitted shirt, that covers much of the wearer's neck. **2** sweater or shirt with such a neck.

tusk (tusk), *n.* **1** a very long, pointed, projecting tooth. Elephants have tusks. **2** any tusklike tooth or part. —*v.* gore with a tusk; dig or tear with tusks. [ME *tuske,* var. of OE *tux,* var. of *tusc*] —**tusked** *adj.* —**tusk′er,** *n.* —**tusk′less,** *adj.*

tus·sle (tus′əl), *v.,* **-sled, -sling,** *n.* struggle; wrestle; scuffle. [var. of *tousle*]

tu·te·lage (tü′tə lij; tū′-), *n.* **1** guardianship; protection. **2** instruction.

tu·te·lar·y (tü′tə ler′i; tū′-), *adj., n., pl.* **-lar·ies** —*adj.* Also, **tu·te·lar** (-lər). **1** protecting; guardian: *a tutelary saint.* **2** of a guardian; used as a guardian. —*n.* a tutelary saint, spirit, divinity, etc. [< L, < *tutela* protection]

tu·tor (tü′tər; tū′-), *n.* a private teacher. —*v.* **1** teach; instruct, esp. individually or privately. **2** train; discipline. **3** act as tutor. [< L, guardian, < *tueri* watch over] —**tu·to′ri·al,** *adj.*

tut·ti-frut·ti (tü′ti frü′ti), *n.* **1** preserve of mixed fruits. **2** ice cream containing a variety of fruits or fruit flavorings. —*adj.* flavored by mixed fruits. [< Ital., all fruits]

tu·tu (tü′tü), *n.* short, full skirt worn by a ballerina.

Tu·va·lu (tü vä′lü), *n.* small island country in the W Pacific, N of Fiji.

tux (tuks), *n.* *Informal.* tuxedo.

tux·e·do, (tuk sē′dō), *n., pl.* **-dos, -does.** a man's coat for evening wear, made without tails. [after *Tuxedo* Park, N.Y.]

TV, television.

twad·dle (twod′əl), *n.* tiresome, inconsequential talk or writing.

twain (twān), *n., adj. Archaic* or *Poetic.* two. [OE *twēgen*]

Twain (twān), *n.* **Mark,** 1835–1910, American author and humorist. His real name was Samuel Langhorne Clemens.

twang (twang), *n.* **1** a sharp ringing or vibrating sound. **2** a sharp nasal tone. —*v.* **1** make or cause to make a sharp, ringing sound: *the banjos twanged.* **2** speak with a sharp nasal tone.

tweak (twēk), *v.* seize and pull with a sharp jerk and twist. —*n.* a sharp pull and twist. [< var of OE *twiccian* pluck]

tweed (twēd), *n.* a woolen cloth with a rough surface, usually woven of yarns of two or more colors.

tweeds, clothes made of tweed. [said to be misreading of *tweel,* var. of *twill*]

tweet (twēt), *n., interj.* the note of a young bird. —*v.* utter such a sound.

tweet·er (twēt′ər), *n.* a small loud-speaker designed esp. to reproduce high treble sounds.

tweez·ers (twēz′ərz), *n. pl.* small pincers for pulling out hairs, picking up small objects, etc. [< *tweeze* instrument case, ult. < F *étui* < OF *estuier* keep < LL *studiare* be zealous] —**tweeze,** *v.*

twelfth (twelfth), *adj.* **1** next after the 11th; last in a series of 12. **2** being one of 12 equal parts. —*n.* **1** next after the 11th; last in a series of 12. **2** one of 12 equal parts.

twelve (twelv), *n.* **1** a cardinal number, one more than 11. **2** symbol of this number; 12. **3** set of twelve persons or things. —*adj.* one more than 11; 12. [OE *twelf*]

twelve·fold (twelv′fōld′), *adj.* **1** twelve times as much or as many. **2** having 12 parts. —*adv.* twelve times as much or as many.

twelve·month (twelv′munth′), *n.* twelve months; a year.

twelve-tone (twelv′tōn′), *adj.* of or having to do with a musical scale of twelve semitones having no tone center; atonal.

twen·ty (twen′ti), *n., pl.* **-ties,** *adj.* —*n.* **1** a cardinal number, two times ten. **2** symbol of this number: 20. —*adj.* two times ten. —**twen′ti·eth,** *adj., n.*

24/7 or **twenty-four-seven** (twen′ti fôr′-sev′ən), all the time; all day and all night. [< *twenty-four* hours a day, *seven* days a week]

twerp (twèrp), *n.* dull, inconsequential person. Also, **twirp.**

twice (twīs), *adv.* **1** two times. **2** doubly. [ME *twies* < OE *twiga* twice]

twid·dle (twid′əl), *v.,* **-dled, -dling. 1** twirl: *twiddle one's pencil.* **2** play with idly.

twiddle one's thumbs, a keep turning one's thumbs idly about each other. **b** do nothing; be idle. —**twid′dler,** *n.*

twig (twig), *n.* a slender shoot of a tree or other plant; very small branch. [OE *twigge*] —**twigged,** *adj.* —**twig′less,** *adj.*

twi·light (twī′līt′), *n.* **1** the faint light reflected from the sky before the sun rises and after it sets. **2** time when this light prevails. **3** any faint light. **4** condition or period after or before full development, glory, etc. —*adj.* of twilight; like that of twilight: *the twilight hour.* [ME, < *twi-* two + *light*[1]]

twill (twil), *n.* **1** cloth woven in raised diagonal lines. **2** a diagonal line or pattern formed by such weaving. —*v.* weave (cloth) in this way. [OE *twilic* < L *bilix* with a double thread < *bi-* two + *licium* thread] —**twilled,** *adj.*

twin (twin), *n.*, *adj.*, *v.*, **twinned, twin‐ning.** —*n.* **1** one of two children or animals born at the same time from the same mother. **2** one of two persons or things exactly alike. —*adj.* **1** being a twin: *twin sisters.* **2** being one of two things very much alike: *twin beds.* **3** having two like parts. —*v.* **1** give birth to twins. **2** join closely; pair. **Twins,** Gemini. [OE *twinn*]

twine (twīn), *n.*, *v.*, **twined, twin‐ing.** —*n.* **1** a strong thread or string made of two or more strands twisted together. **2** a twisting; twisting together. **3** a twist; twisted thing. —*v.* **1** twist together. **2** encircle; enfold; wreathe. **3** wind. [OE *twīn*] —**twin′er,** *n.*

twinge (twinj), *n.*, *v.*, **twinged, twing‐ing.** —*n.* a sudden sharp pain: *a twinge of rheumatism, a twinge of remorse.* —*v.* feel such pain [OE *twengan* pinch]

twin‐kle (twing′kəl), *v.*, **‐kled, ‐kling,** *n.* —*v.* **1** shine with quick little gleams. **2** move quickly: *the dancer's feet twinkled.* **3** wink; blink. —*n.* **1** a twinkling; sparkle; gleam. **2** a quick motion. **3** a quick motion of the eye; wink; blink. **4** time required for a wink. [OE *twinclian*] —**twin′kler,** *n.*

twin‐kling (twing′kling), *n.* **1** a little, quick gleam. **2** an instant. —**twin′kling‐ly,** *adv.*

twirl (twėrl), *v.* **1** revolve rapidly; spin; whirl. **2** twist; curl; flourish. —*n.* **1** a twirling; spin; whirl; turn. **2** a twist; curl; flourish. [blend of *twist* and *whirl*] —**twirl′er,** *n.*

twist (twist), *v.* **1** turn, wind. *she twisted her ring on her finger.* **2** wind together: *twist flowers into a wreath.* **3** have a winding shape; curve or bend in any way: *the path twists in and out among the rocks.* **4** force out of shape or place: *his face was twisted with pain.* **5** give a wrong meaning to: *twist a person's words.* [< n.] —*n.* **1** a curve; crook; bend. **2** a twisting; being twisted. **3** anything made by twisting: *a twist of bread.* **4** a peculiar bias or inclination: *his answer showed a mental twist.* **5** torsional strain or stress. [OE *‐twist,* as in *mæsttwist* mast rope, stay] —**twist′a‐ble,** *adj.* —**twist′ed‐ly,** *adv.* —**twist′ing‐ly,** *adv.*

twist‐er (twis′tər), *n.* **1** person or thing that twists. **2** whirlwind: tornado; cyclone.

twit (twit), *v.*, **twit‐ted, twit‐ting,** *n.* —*v.* jeer at; reproach; taunt; tease. —*n.* a stupid, irritating person; nitwit. [OE *ætwītan* < *æt* at + *wītan* blame]

twitch (twich), *v.* move with a quick jerk. —*n.* **1** a quick jerky movement of some part of the body. **2** a short, sud‐den pull or jerk. [akin to OE *twiccian* pluck] —**twitch′er,** *n.* —**twitch′ing,** *adj.* —**twitch′ing‐ly** *adv.*

twit‐ter (twit′ər), *n.* **1** sound made by birds; chirping. **2** a titter; giggle. —*v.* make a twittering sound. [imit.] —**twit′ter‐er,** *n.*

'twixt (twikst), *prep. Poetic or Dial.* betwixt.

two (tü), *n.*, *pl.* **twos,** *adj.* —*n.* **1** a cardinal number, one more than one. **2** symbol of this number; 2. **3** a playing card, die face, etc., with two spots. —*adj.* one more than one; 2.

in two, in two parts or pieces.

put two and two together, form an obvious conclusion from the facts. [OE *twā*]

two‐by‐four (tü′bī fôr′; ‐fōr′), *adj.* mea‐suring two inches, feet, etc., by four inches, feet, etc. —*n.* piece of lumber about 4 inches wide and 2 inches thick.

two‐edged (tü′ejd′), *adj.* **1** having two edges; cutting both ways. **2** effective either way.

two‐faced (tü′fāst′), *adj.* **1** having two faces. **2** deceitful; hypocritical. —**two′fac′ed‐ly,** *adv.* —**two′‐fac′ed‐ness,** *n.*

two‐fold (tü′fōld′), *adj.* **1** two times as much or as many; double. **2** having two parts. —*adv.* two times as much or as many; doubly.

two‐hand‐ed (tü′han′did), *adj.* **1** having two hands. **2** using both hands equally well. **3** involving the use of both hands; requiring both hands to wield or man‐age: *a two‐handed sword.* **4** requiring two persons to operate: *a two‐handed saw.* **5** engaged in by two persons: *a two‐handed game.*

two‐pence (tup′əns), *n.* **1** two British pennies; two pence. **2** coin of this value.

two‐pen‐ny (tup′ən i), *adj.* **1** worth two‐pence. **2** trifling, worthless.

two‐ply (tü′plī′), *adj.* having two thick‐nesses, folds, layers, or strands.

two‐some (tü′səm), *n.* **1** group of two people. **2** game played by two people. **3** the players.

two‐step (tü′step′), *n.*, *v.*, **‐stepped, ‐stepping.** —*n.* **1** a dance in march time. **2** music for it. —*v.* dance the two‐step.

two‐way (tü′wā′), *adj.* **1** allowing move‐ment in two directions. **2** *Fig.* coop‐erative; mutually supportive: *two‐way friendship.* **3** involving two people: *a two‐way political race.* **4** used for two purposes.

TX, (*zip code*) Texas.

‐ty[1], *suffix.* tens, as in *sixty, seventy, eighty.* [OE *‐tig*]

‐ty[2], *suffix.* fact, quality, state, condition, etc., of being ____, as in *safety, sover‐eignty, surety.* *‐ity* is often used instead of *‐ty,* as in *artificiality, complexity, humidity.* [< OF, < L *‐tas*]

ty‐coon (tī kün′), *n.* **1** an important busi‐nessperson. **2** title given by foreigners to the Japanese shogun. [< Jap. *taikun* < Chinese *tai* great + *kiun* lord]

ty‐ing (tī′ing), *v.* ppr. of **tie.**

tyke (tīk), *n.* a mischievous or trouble‐some child. [< Scand. *tik* bitch]

Ty‐ler (tī′lər), *n.* **John,** 1790–1862, tenth president of the United States, 1841–45.

tym‐pa‐ni (tim′pə ni), *n. pl.* percussion section of an orchestra.

tym‐pan‐ic membrane (tim pan′ik), =eardrum.

tym‐pa‐nist (tim′pə nist), *n.* member of an orchestra who plays a drum, cymbals, and other percussion instruments.

tym‐pa‐num (tim′pə nəm), *n.*, *pl.* **‐nums, ‐na** (‐nə), **1 a** the eardrum. **b** the middle ear, comprising that part of the ear situ‐ated in the recess behind the eardrum. **2** a drum. [< L, drum, < Gk. *tympanon.* Doublet of TIMBRE.] —**tym‐pan′ic,** *adj.*

type (tīp), *n.*, *v.*, **typed, typ‐ing.** —*n.* **1** a kind, class, or group having common characteristics; general form, style, or character of some kind, class, or group: *she is above the ordinary type.* **2** piece of metal having on its upper surface a raised letter in reverse for use in printing. **3** collection of such pieces. **4** a blood type. —*v.* **1** be a type of. **2** find out the type of: *type a person's blood.* **3** =typewrite. [< L < Gk. *typos* dent, impression]

type‐cast (tīp′kast′; ‐käst′), *v.*, **‐cast, ‐cast‐ing. 1** assign a role to an actor suited to his or her looks, personality, etc. **2** *Fig.* arbitrarily assign a role or character to someone.

type‐set‐ter (tīp′set′ər), *n.* person or machine that sets type for printing. —**type′set′ting,** *n. adj.*

type‐write (tīp′rīt′), *v.*, **‐wrote, ‐writ‐ten, ‐writ‐ing.** write with a typewriter. —**type′writ′ing,** *n.* —**type′writ′ten,** *adj.*

type‐writ‐er (tīp′rīt′ər), *n.* machine for making letters on paper.

ty‐phoid (tī′foid), *adj.* **1** of or pertain‐ing to typhoid fever. **2** like typhus. —*n.* typhoid fever. [< *typhus*]

typhoid fever, an infectious, often fatal, fever with intestinal inflammation, caused by a germ taken into the body with food or drink.

ty‐phoon (tī fün′), *n.* in the W Pacific, a violent storm; hurricane. [< Chinese *tai fung* big wind; infl. by Gk. *typhon* whirl‐wind] —**ty‐phon′ic,** *adj.*

ty‐phus (tī′fəs), *n.* an acute infectious disease caused by germs carried by fleas, lice, etc. [< NL < Gk. *typhos* stupor, orig., smoke] —**ty′phous,** *adj.*

typ‐i‐cal (tip′ə kəl), *adj.* **1** being a type; representative: *a typical tourist.* **2** char‐acteristic; distinctive: *a typical summer cabin.* —**typ′i‐cal‐ly,** *adv.* —**typ′i‐cal‐ness,** *n.*

typ‐i‐fy (tip′ə fī), *v.*, **‐fied, ‐fy‐ing. 1** be a symbol of. **2** have the common char‐acteristics of. Daniel Boone typifies the pioneer. —**typ′i‐fi′er,** *n.*

typ‐ist (tīp′ist), *n.* person operating a keyboard or typewriter, esp. as a regular occupation.

ty‐po (tī′pō′), *n.* typographical error.

ty‐pog‐ra‐pher (tī pog′rə fər), *n.* a printer.

ty‐po‐graph‐i‐cal (tī′pə graf′ə kəl), **ty‐po‐graph‐ic** (‐ik), *adj.* of or having to do with printing. Catt *and* hoRse *contain typographical errors.* —**ty′po·graph′i·cal·ly,** *adv.*

ty·pog·ra·phy (tī pog′rə fi), *n.* **1** printing with types. **2** arrangement, appearance, or style of printed matter.

ty·ran·ni·cal (ti ran′ə kəl; tī–), *adj.* of or like a tyrant; arbitrary; cruel; unjust. [< *tyrannic* < L < Gk. *tyrannikos* < *tyrannos* tyrant] —**ty·ran′ni·cal·ly,** *adv.*

tyr·an·nize (tir′ə nīz), *v.,* –**nized,** –**niz·ing. 1** use power cruelly or unjustly. **2** rule cruelly; oppress. —**tyr′an·niz′er,** *n.* —**tyr′an·niz′ing·ly,** *adv.*

ty·ran·no·saur·us (ti ran′ə sôr′əs; tī–), *n.* enormous dinosaur that walked on its two hind legs and lived in North America.

tyr·an·nous (tir′ə nəs), *adj.* acting like a tyrant; cruel or unjust; arbitrary.

tyr·an·ny (tir′ə ni), *n., pl.* –**nies. 1** cruel or unjust use of power. **2** a tyrannical act. **3** government by an absolute ruler. **4** state with such a government.

ty·rant (tī′rənt), *n.* **1** person who uses his or her power cruelly or unjustly. **2** a cruel or unjust ruler; cruel master. **3** an absolute ruler. Some tyrants of Greek cities were mild and just rulers. [< OF < L < Gk. *tyrannos* (def. 3)]

ty·ro (tī′rō), *n., pl.* –**ros.** beginner in learning anything; novice. [< L *tiro* recruit]

tzar (zär; tsär), *n.* =czar.

tzar·e·vitch (zär′ə vich; tsär′–), *n.* =czarevitch.

tza·ri·na (zä rē′nə; tsä–), *n.* =czarina.

tzet·ze fly (tset′sē), or **tzetze,** *n.* =tsetse fly.

U, u (ū), *n., pl.* **U's; u's.**
1 the 21st letter of the alphabet. **2** anything shaped like a U.
U, 1 uranium. **2** Also **U.** university.

UAW, U.A.W., United Automobile Workers.

u·biq·ui·tous (ū bik′wə təs), *adj.* being everywhere at the same time; present everywhere. [< *ubiquity*] **—u·biq′ui·tous·ly,** *adv.*

u·biq·ui·ty (ū bik′wə ti), *n.* **1** being everywhere at the same time. **2** ability to be everywhere at once. [< NL, < L *ubique* everywhere]

U-boat (ū′bōt′), *n.* a German submarine. [half-trans. of G *U-boot,* short for *unterseeboot* undersea boat]

u.c., upper case (capital letter[s]).

ud·der (ud′ər), *n.* the milk gland, esp. when baggy and with more than one teat, as in cows, goats, etc. [OE *ūder*] **—ud′dered,** *adj.*

UFO (yü ef′ō′), *n., pl.* **UFO's, UFOs.** unidentified flying object; flying saucer.

U·gan·da (ū gan′də; ü gän′dä), *n.* country in E Africa.

ug·ly (ug′li), *adj.,* **-li·er, ·li·est. 1** very unpleasant to look at: *an ugly design, ugly furniture.* **2** bad; disagreeable; offensive: *an ugly task.* **3** likely to cause trouble; threatening; dangerous: *an ugly wound, ugly clouds.* [< Scand. *uggligr* dreadful] **—ug′li·ly,** *adv.* **—ug′li·ness,** *n.*

U.K., United Kingdom.

u·kase (ū kās′; ū′kās), *n.* **1** formerly, an order of the ruler or government of Russia. **2** any official proclamation or order. [< Russ. *ukaz*]

U·kraine (ū krān′; ū′krān; ū krīn′; ū′krīn), *n.* a republic, SW of Russia. **—U·krain′i·an,** *adj., n.*

u·ku·le·le (ū′kə lā′lē), *n.* a small guitar having four strings. [< Hawaiian, orig., flea]

ul·cer (ul′sər), *n.* **1** an open sore that discharges pus. **2** a moral sore spot. [< L *ulcus*]

ul·cer·ate (ul′sər āt), *v.,* **-at·ed, -at·ing.** affect or be affected with an ulcer; form an ulcer. **—ul′cer·a′tion,** *n.* **—ul′cer·a′tive,** *adj.*

ul·cer·ous (ul′sər əs), *adj.* **1** having an ulcer or ulcers. **2** of an ulcer or ulcers.

ul·na (ul′nə), *n., pl.* **-nae** (-nē), **-nas. 1** the bone of the forearm on the side opposite the thumb. **2** a corresponding bone in the foreleg of an animal. [< NL <L, elbow] **—ul′nar,** *adj.*

ult., ultimately.

ul·te·ri·or (ul tir′i ər), *adj.* **1** beyond what is seen or expressed; concealed; hidden. **2** more distant; on the farther side. **3** further; later. [< L, compar. of root of *ultra, ultro,* adv., beyond] **—ul·te′ri·or·ly,** *adv.*

ul·ti·mate (ul′tə mit), *adj.* **1** coming at the end; last possible; final: *the ultimate effect of speeding.* **2** fundamental; basic. **3**

greatest possible. **—n.** an ultimate point, result, fact, etc. [< Med.L, pp. of *ultimare* < Ital., bring to an end < L, come to an end < *ultimus* last] **—ul′ti·mate·ly,** *adv.* **—ul′ti·mate·ness,** *n.*

ul·ti·ma·tum (ul′tə mā′təm), *n., pl.* **-tums, -ta** (-tə). a final proposal or statement of conditions. [< NL, orig. neut. of Med.L *ultimatus* ULTIMATE]

ul·tra (ul′trə), *adj.* beyond what is usual; very; excessive; extreme. [< L, beyond]

ultra– *prefix.* **1** beyond, as in *ultraviolet.* **2** beyond what is usual; very; excessively, as in *ul′tra·con·serv′a·tive, ul′tra·fash′ion·a·ble, ul′tra·lib′er·al, ul′tra·mod′ern, ul′tra·re·li′gious, ul′tra·zeal′ous.*

ul·tra·light (ul′trə līt′), *adj.* extremely light in weight. **—n.** small airplane for one person, made of aluminum tubing and cloth.

ul·tra·ma·rine (ul′trə mə rēn′), *n.* **1** a deep blue. **2** a blue paint made from powdered lapis lazuli. **3** an imitation of this. **—adj.** deep-blue.

ul·tra·son·ic (ul′trə son′ik), *adj.* of or pertaining to sound waves beyond the limit of human audibility; supersonic.

ul·tra·vi·o·let (ul′trə vī′ə lit), *adj.* of or having to do with the invisible part of the spectrum just beyond the violet. **Ultraviolet rays** are present in sunlight.

ul·u·late (ūl′yə lāt ; ul′-), *v.,* **-lat·ed, -lat·ing.** howl, as a dog or wolf. [< L *ululat-,* pp. stem of *ululare* howl] **—ul′u·la′tion,** *n.*

um·bel (um′bəl), *n.* a flower cluster in which stalks nearly equal in length spring from a common center and form a flat or slightly curved surface, as in parsley. [< L *umbella* parasol, dim. of *umbra* shade] **—um′bel·lar,** *adj.*

um·ber (um′bər), *n.* **1** an earth used in its natural state (**raw umber**) as a brown pigment, or after heating (**burnt umber**) as a reddish-brown pigment. **2** a brown or reddish brown. **—adj.** brown or reddish-brown. [< Ital. (*terra di*) *ombra* (earth of) shade, but ? orig. < Ital. province *Umbria*]

um·bil·i·cal (um bil′ə kəl), *adj.* of or having to do with the umbilical cord or navel. **—n. 1** umbilical cord. **2** hoselike connection between an astronaut and spacecraft that provides oxygen, etc.

umbilical cord, cord connecting the fetus of a mammal with the placenta.

um·bra (um′brə), *n., pl.* **-brae** (-brē). **1** a shadow of the earth or moon that completely hides the sun. **2** shade; shadow. [< L]

um·brage (um′brij), *n.* suspicion that one has been slighted or injured; feeling offended; resentment. [< F *ombrage,* ult. < L *umbra* shade]

um·brel·la (um brel′ə), *n.* a light, folding frame covered with cloth, used as a protection against rain or sun. **—adj.** covering, like an umbrella: *an umbrella term, umbrella organization.* [< Ital. *ombrella,* ult. < L *umbra* shade]

u·mi·ak (ü′mi ak), *n.* an open Eskimo boat. [< Eskimo]

um·laut (üm′lout), *n.* **1** change in vowel sound in the Germanic languages because of the influence of another vowel. **2** the sign (¨) used to indicate such a vowel, as in German *süss.* [< G, < *um* about + *laut* sound]

um·pire (um′pīr), *n., v.,* **-pired, -pir·ing. —n. 1** person who rules on the plays in a game. **2** person chosen to settle a dispute. **—v.** act as umpire. [earlier *a numpire* (taken as *an umpire*) < OF *nonper* not even, odd < *non* not (< L) + *per* equal < L *par*] **—um′pire·ship,** *n.*

ump·teenth (um′tēnth′), *adj.* uncountable; too many to be counted: *for the umpteenth time.*

UMW, U.M.W., United Mine Workers.

un–¹, *prefix.* not; the opposite of, as in *unfair, unjust, unequal.* [OE]
In the following list are examples of the use of *un–* meaning "not."
un′ac·cept′a·ble
un′a·fraid′
un·cared′-for′
un′com·pli·men′ta·ry
un′dem·o·crat′ic
un′dis·put′ed
un·dreamed′
un′ec·o·nom′i·cal
un′ex·pressed′
un·fash′ion·a·ble
un′for·got′ten
un·gen′er·ous
un·help′ful
un′in·ter·est·ing
un·lit′
un·man′age·a·ble
un·mus′i·cal
un′ob·jec′tion·a·ble
un′pa·tri·ot′ic
un′pre·pared′
un′re·ceived′
un′re·flec′tive
un′re·ward′ing
un·said′
un′sat·is·fac′to·ry
un·shak′en
un·shown′
un·smil′ing
un·sold′
un·spent′
un·sports′man·like′
un·sprung′
un′suc·cess′ful
un·sure′
un·swept′
un·tech′ni·cal
un·thought′
un·torn′
un·trust′wor′thy
un·var′y·ing
un·wel′come
un·want′ed
un·world′li·ness

un–², *prefix.* do the opposite of; do what will reverse the act, as in *undress, unlock, untie.* [OE *un–, on–*]

In the following list are examples of the use of un– **meaning** "do the reverse of."

un·chain′
un·fix′
un′·in·vite′
un·learn′
un·make′
un·reel′
un·strap′
un·thread′
un·twine′
un·wrin′kle

UN, U.N., United Nations.

un·a·ble (un ā′bəl), *adj.* not able; lacking ability or power (*to*).

un·ac·count·a·ble (un′ə koun′tə bəl), *adj.* 1 that cannot be accounted for or explained. 2 not responsible. —**un′ac·count′a·bly,** *adv.*

un·ac·cus·tomed (un′ə kus′təmd), *adj.* 1 not accustomed. 2 not familiar; unusual; strange.

un·ad·vised (un′əd vīzd′), *adj.* 1 not advised; without advice. 2 not prudent or discreet; rash. —**un′ad·vis′ed·ly** *adv.*

un·af·fect·ed¹ (un′ə fek′tid), *adj.* not influenced.

un·af·fect·ed² (un′ə fek′tid), *adj.* simple and natural; sincere. —**un′af·fect′ed·ness,** *n.*

un·A·mer·i·can (un′ə mer′ə kən), *adj.* not American; not characteristic of or proper to America; foreign or opposed to the American character, usages, standards, etc.

u·na·nim·i·ty (ū′nə nim′ə ti), *n.* complete accord or agreement.

u·nan·i·mous (ū nan′ə məs), *adj.* 1 in complete accord or agreement; agreed. 2 characterized by or showing complete accord: *a unanimous vote.* [< L *unanimus* < *unus* one + *animus* mind] —**u·nan′i·mous·ly,** *adv.*

un·an·swer·a·ble (un an′sər ə bəl; –än′–), *adj.* 1 that cannot be answered. 2 that cannot be disproved. —**un·an′swer·a·bly,** *adv.*

un·an·swered (un an′sərd; –än′–), *adj.* 1 not replied to. 2 not refuted: *an unanswered argument.* 3 not returned: *unanswered love.*

un·ap·proach·a·ble (un′ə prōch′ə bəl), *adj.* 1 very hard to approach; distant. 2 unrivaled; without an equal. —**un′ap·proach′a·bly,** *adv.*

un·armed (un armd′), *adj.* having no weapons: *an unarmed civilian.*

un·as·sum·ing (un′ə süm′ing), *adj.* modest.

un·at·tached (un′ə tacht′), *adj.* 1 not attached; independent. 2 *Fig.* not engaged or married.

un·a·vail·ing (un′ə vāl′ing), *adj.* not successful; useless. —**un′a·vail′ing·ly,** *adv.*

un·a·void·a·ble (un′ə void′ə bəl), *adj.* that cannot be avoided. —**un′a·void′a·bly,** *adv.*

un·a·ware (un′ə wãr′), *adj.* not aware; unconscious. —*adv.* without thought; unawares.

un·a·wares (un′ə wãrz′), *adv.* 1 without knowing. 2 without being expected; by surprise.

un·bal·ance (un bal′əns), *n., v.,* –**anced, –anc·ing.** —*n.* lack of balance. —*v.* throw out of balance.

un·bal·anced (un bal′ənst), *adj.* 1 not balanced. 2 not entirely sane.

un·bar (un bär′), *v.,* –**barred, –bar·ring.** remove the bars from; unlock.

un·bear·a·ble (un bãr′ə bəl), *adj.* beyond endurance. —**un·bear′a·ble·ness,** *n.* —**un·bear′a·bly,** *adv.*

un·be·com·ing (un′bi kum′ing), *adj.* 1 not becoming; not appropriate: *unbecoming clothes.* 2 not fitting; not proper: *unbecoming behavior.* —**un′be·com′ing·ly,** *adv.*

un·be·known (un′bi nōn′), *adj.* not known. Also, **unbeknownst.**

un·be·liev·a·ble (un′bi lē′və bəl), *adj.* not to be believed; incredible.

un·be·liev·ing (un′bi lēv′ing), *adj.* not believing; doubting. —**un′be·liev′ing·ly,** *adv.*

un·bend (un bend′), *v.,* –**bent** or –**bend·ed, –bend·ing.** 1 straighten. 2 release from strain. 3 relax.

un·bend·ing (un ben′ding), *adj.* 1 not bending or curving; rigid. 2 not yielding; firm: *an unbending attitude.* —*n.* relaxation. —**un·bend′ing·ly,** *adv.*

un·bi·ased (un bī′əst), *adj.* not prejudiced; impartial; fair.

un·bid·den (un bid′ən), *adj.* 1 not bidden; not invited. 2 not commanded.

un·bind (un bīnd′), *v.,* –**bound, –bind·ing.** release from bonds or restraint; untie; unfasten.

un·blessed, (un blest′), *adj.* 1 not blessed. 2 not holy. 3 unhappy.

un·blush·ing (un blush′ing), *adj.* not blushing; shameless. —**un·blush′ing·ly,** *adv.*

un·bolt (un bōlt′), *v.* draw back the bolts of (a door, etc.).

un·bolt·ed¹ (un bōl′tid), *adj.* not fastened.

un·bolt·ed² (un bōl′tid), *adj.* not sifted.

un·born (un bôrn′), *adj.* not yet born; still to come; of the future: *unborn generations.* —*n.* =fetus.

un·bos·om (un bùz′əm; –bü′zəm), *v.* reveal; disclose.

un·bound·ed (un boun′did), *adj.* 1 not limited; very great; boundless. 2 not kept within limits; not controlled. —**un·bound′ed·ly,** *adv.*

un·bowed (un boud′), *adj.* 1 not bowed or bent. 2 not forced to yield or submit.

un·bri·dled (un brī′dəld), *adj.* 1 not having a bridle on. 2 not controlled; not restrained.

un·bro·ken (un brō′kən), *adj.* 1 not broken; whole. 2 not interrupted; continuous. 3 not tamed. —**un·bro′ken·ly,** *adv.*

un·buck·le (un buk′əl), *v.,* –**led, –ling.** 1 unfasten the buckle or buckles of. 2 unfasten.

un·bur·den (un bėr′dən), *v.* 1 free from a burden. 2 relieve (one's mind or heart) by talking.

un·but·ton (un but′ən), *v.* unfasten the button or buttons of.

un·but·toned (un but′ənd), *adj.* 1 not fastened; not done up. 2 *Fig.* relaxed.

un·cage (un kāj′), *v.,* –**caged, –cag·ing.** 1 release from a cage. 2 release.

un·called-for (un kôld′fôr′), *adj.* 1 not called for. 2 unnecessary and improper.

un·can·ny (un kan′i), *adj.* strange and mysterious; weird. —**un·can′ni·ness,** *n.*

un·cer·e·mo·ni·ous (un′ser ə mō′ni əs), *adj.* not as courteous as would be expected; informal. —**un′cer·e·mo′ni·ous·ly,** *adv.*

un·cer·tain (un sėr′tən), *adj.* 1 not sure; doubtful: *the election results were still uncertain.* 2 not fixed: *the date was left uncertain.* 3 not decided: *be uncertain of one's facts.* 4 likely to change; not reliable: *uncertain prospects.* 5 not constant; varying: *an uncertain flicker of light.* 6 vague; indefinite: *an uncertain shape.* —**un·cer′tain·ly,** *adv.*

un·change·a·ble (un chān′jə bəl), *adj.* that cannot be changed. —**un·change′a·ble·ness ,** *n.*

un·char·i·ta·ble (un char′ə tə bəl), *adj.* not generous; severe; harsh. —**un·char′i·ta·bly,** *adv.*

un·chaste (un chāst′), *adj.* not chaste.

un·chris·tian (un kris′chən), *adj.* 1 not Christian. 2 unworthy of Christians. —**un·chris′tian·like′,** *adj.*

un·church (un chėrch′), *v.* expel from a church; deprive of church rights and privileges.

un·ci·al (un′shi əl; un′shəl), *n.* a kind of letter used in old manuscripts. —*adj.* pertaining to such letters. [< L, < *uncia* inch]

un·civ·il (un siv′əl), *adj.* 1 not civil; rude; impolite. 2 not civilized. —**un·civ′il·ly,** *adv.*

un·civ·i·lized (un siv′ə līzd), *adj.* not civilized; barbarous; savage.

un·clad (un klad′), *adj.* not dressed; unclothed.

un·clasp (un klasp′; –kläsp′), *v.* 1 unfasten. 2 release or be released from a clasp or grasp.

un·cle (ung′kəl), *n.* 1 brother of one's father or mother. 2 husband of one's aunt. 3 an elderly man. [< OF < L *avunculus* one's mother's brother]

un·clean (un klēn′), *adj.* 1 not clean; dirty; filthy. 2 not pure morally; not chaste; evil.

un·clean·ly¹ (un klen′li), *adj.* not cleanly; unclean. —**un·clean′li·ness,** *n.*

un·clean·ly² (un klēn′li), *adv.* in an unclean manner.

Uncle Sam, the government or people of the United States. [from the initials *U.S.*]

un·cloak (un klōk′), *v.* 1 remove the coat from. 2 *Fig.* reveal; expose.

un·coil (un koil′), *v.* unwind.

un·com·fort·a·ble (un kumf′tə bəl; –kum′fər tə bəl), *adj.* 1 not comfortable. 2 uneasy. 3 disagreeable; causing discomfort. —**un·com′fort·a·bly,** *adv.*

un·com·mon (un kom′ən), *adj.* 1 rare; unusual. 2 unusual in amount or degree.

3 remarkable. —**un·com′mon·ly**, *adv.* —**un·com′mon·ness**, *n.*

un·com·mu·ni·ca·tive (un′kə mū′nə kā′-tiv; –kə tiv), *adj.* not giving out any information, opinions, etc.; talking little; silent. —**un′com·mu′ni·ca′tive·ly**, *adv.*

un·com·pro·mis·ing (un kom′prə mīz′-ing), *adj.* unyielding; firm. —**un·com′-pro·mis′ing·ly**, *adv.*

un·con·cerned (un′kən sėrnd′), *adj.* not concerned; not interested; free from care or anxiety; indifferent. —**un′con·cern′ed·ly**, *adv.*

un·con·di·tion·al (un′kən dish′ən əl; –dish′nəl), *adj.* without conditions; absolute. —**un′con·di′tion·al·ly**, *adv.*

un·con·quer·a·ble (un kong′kər ə bəl), *adj.* that cannot be conquered. —**un·con′quer·a·bly**, *adv.*

un·con·scion·a·ble (un kon′shən ə bəl), *adj.* 1 not influenced or guided by conscience. 2 unreasonable; very great. —**un·con′scion·a·bly**, *adv.*

un·con·scious (un kon′shəs), *adj.* 1 not conscious. 2 not aware. 3 not meant; not intended: *unconscious neglect.* —*n.* **the unconscious**, one's unconscious thoughts, desires, fears, etc. —**un·con′-scious·ly**. *adv.* —**un·con′scious·ness**, *n.*

un·con·sti·tu·tion·al (un′kon stə tü′-shən əl; –tū′–), *adj.* contrary to the constitution. —**un′con·sti·tu′tion·al′i·ty**, *n.* —**un′con·sti·tu′tion·al·ly**, *adv.*

un·con·ven·tion·al (un′kən ven′shən əl; –vensh′nəl), *adj.* not bound by or conforming to convention, rule, or precedent.

un·cork (un kôrk′), *v.* pull the cork from.

un·count·ed (un koun′tid), *adj.* 1 not counted; not reckoned. 2 very many; innumerable.

un·couth (un küth′), *adj.* 1 awkward; clumsy; crude. 2 strange and unpleasant. 3 uncanny. [OE *uncūth* < *un-*[1] + *cūth*, pp. of *cunnan* know]

un·cov·er (un kuv′ər), *v.* 1 remove the cover from. 2 make known; reveal; expose. 3 remove the hat, cap, etc., of.

unc·tion (ungk′shən), *n.* 1 an anointing with oil, ointment, or the like, as a religious rite. 2 the oil, ointment, or the like, used for anointing. 3 something soothing or comforting: *the unction of flattery.* 4 a soothing, sympathetic, and persuasive quality in speaking. [< L *unctio* < *unguere* anoint]

unc·tu·ous (ungk′chù əs), *adj.* 1 like an oil or ointment; oily; greasy. 2 soothing, sympathetic, and persuasive. 3 too smooth and oily: *the salesman's unctuous manner.* [< Med.L *unctuosus*, ult. < L *unguere* anoint] —**unc′tu·ous·ness**, *n.*

un·curl (un kėrl′), *v.* straighten out.

un·daunt·ed (un dôn′tid; –dän′–), *adj.* not afraid; not discouraged; fearless.

un·de·cid·ed (un′di sīd′id), *adj.* 1 not decided or settled. 2 not having one's mind made up. —**un′de·cid′ed·ness**, *n.*

un·de·ni·a·ble (un′di nī′ə bəl), *adj.* 1 not to be denied. 2 unquestionably good; excellent. —**un′de·ni′a·bly**, *adv.*

un·der (un′dər), *prep.* 1 below; beneath: *under the table, under the ground, hit under the belt.* 2 less than: *it will cost under ten dollars.* 3 lower in rank, dignity, etc.: *a corporal is under a sergeant.* 4 during the time, influence, etc., of: *England under the four Georges, work under a famous scientist.* 5 affected by: *under the new rules.* 6 with the favor or aid of: *under protection.* 7 because of or according to: *under the law.* 8 represented by: *under a new name.* 9 required or bound by: *under obligation.* 10 in the class of: *that book belongs under "Fiction."* —*adv.* 1 below or beneath something. 2 in or to a lower place or condition. —*adj.* lower in position, rank, degree, amount, price, etc.: *the under layer.* [OE]

under–, *prefix.* 1 on the underside; to a lower position; from a lower position; below; beneath, as in *underarch, underarm, underlay, undermentioned, underspecified, underwash.* 2 being beneath, worn beneath, as in *undercrust, underfeathers, underflooring, underseam.* 3 lower, as in: *underbelly, underfloor. underregion, undersurface.* 4 lower in rank; subordinate, as in *underagent, underplan.* 5 not enough; insufficiently, as in *underarmed, undercooked, underdeveloped, underdone, underdressed, underpaid, underrate, undersupply.* 6 below normal, as in *underadjustment, underdevelopment.*

un·der·a·chiev·er (un′dər ə chēv′ər), *n.* person, esp. a student, who fails to do something as well as he or she could.

un·der·age (un′dər āj′), *adj.* not of full age; of less than the usual age.

un·der·bid (un′dər bid′), *v.,* **–bid, –bid·ding.** make a lower bid than. —**un′der·bid′der**, *n.*

un·der·brush (un′dər brush′), *n.* bushes, small trees, etc., growing under large trees in woods or forests.

un·der·class (un′dər klas′), *n.* the group having the lowest economic and social standing in a society.

un·der·class·man (un′dər klas′mən; –kläs′–), *n., pl.* **–men.** freshman or sophomore.

un·der·clothes (un′dər klōz′; –klōŧҺz′), *n. pl.* clothes worn under a suit or dress.

un·der·cov·er (un′dər kuv′ər), *adj.* working or done in secret; secret.

un·der·cur·rent (un′dər kėr′ənt), *n.* 1 current below the upper currents, or below the surface, of a body of water, air, etc. 2 an underlying tendency.

un·der·cut (un′dər kut′), *v.,* **–cut, –cut·ting.** 1 cut under or beneath; cut away material from so as to leave a portion overhanging. 2 sell or work for less than (some other person).

un·der·de·vel·oped (un′dər di vel′əpt), *adj.* 1 not normally or fully developed, as an unusually small animal or plant. 2 not fully developed economically: *the underdeveloped countries need investment.*

un·der·dog (un′dər dôg′; –dog′), *n.* dog or person having the worst of an encounter.

un·der·es·ti·mate (*v.* un′dər es′tə māt; *n.* un′dər es′tə mit, –māt), *v.,* **–mat·ed, –mat·ing.** *n.* —*v.* estimate at too low a value, amount, rate, or the like. —*n.* an estimate that is too low. —**un′der·es′ti·ma′tion**, *n.*

un·der·foot (un′dər fůt′), *adv.* 1 under one's foot or feet; underneath. 2 in the way.

un·der·go (un′dər gō′), *v.,* **–went, –gone, –going.** 1 go through; pass through; be subjected to. 2 endure; suffer.

un·der·grad·u·ate (un′dər graj′ù it), *n.* a student in a school, college, or university who has not received a degree for a course of study.

un·der·ground (*adv., adj.* un′dər ground′; *n.* un′dər ground′), *adv.* 1 beneath the surface of the ground. 2 in or into secrecy or concealment. —*adj.* 1 being, working, or used beneath the surface of the ground. 2 secret. 3 resisting (tyrannical government, etc.) secretly. —*n.* 1 place or space beneath the surface of the ground. 2 a secret organization, or grouping of such organizations, working to free a country from foreign domination or an autocratic regime.

underground railroad, a secret method of assisting the escape of fugitives.

un·der·growth (un′dər grōth′), *n.* underbrush.

un·der·hand (un′dər hand′), *adj.* Also, **un′der·hand′ed.** 1 not open or honest; secret; sly. 2 with the hand below the shoulder. —*adv.* 1 secretly; slyly. 2 with the hand below the shoulder: *pitch underhand.* —**un′der·hand′ed·ly**, *adv.* —**un′der·hand′ed·ness**, *n.*

un·der·lie (un′dər lī′), *v.,* **–lay, –lain, –ly·ing.** 1 lie under; be beneath. 2 be at the basis of; form the foundation of.

un·der·line (un′dər līn′; un′dər līn′), *v.,* **–lined, –lin·ing.** draw a line or lines under.

un·der·ling (un′dər ling), *n.* usually disparagingly, a person of lower rank or position.

un·der·ly·ing (un′dər lī′ing), *adj.* 1 lying under or beneath. 2 *Fig.* fundamental; basic; essential. —*v.* ppr. of **underlie.**

un·der·mine (un′dər mīn′; un′dər mīn′), *v.,* **–minded, –min·ing.** 1 make a passage or hole under; dig under. 2 wear away the foundations of. 3 weaken or destroy gradually.

un·der·neath (un′dər nēth′), *prep.* beneath; below: *sit underneath a tree, a cellar underneath a house.* —*adv.* beneath or below something: *someone was pushing underneath.* —*n.* the lower part or surface.

un·der·nour·ished (un′dər nėr′isht), *adj.* not sufficiently nourished.

un·der·pants (un′dər pants′), *n.* pants worn as an undergarment.

un·der·pass (un′dər pas′; -päs′), *n.* path underneath; road under railroad tracks or under another road.

un·der·pin·ning (un′dər pin′ing), *n.* 1 the supports under a building. 2 a new foundation beneath a wall. 3 a support: *one underpinning of democracy being a free press.*

un·der·priv·i·leged (un′dər priv′ə lijd), *adj.* having fewer advantages than most people have, esp. because of poor economic or social status.

un·der·score (*v.* un′dər skôr′, -skōr′; *n.* un′dər skôr′, -skōr′), *v.*, **-scored, -scor·ing,** *n.* —*v.* underline. —*n.* an underscored line.

un·der·sea (*adj.* un′dər sē′; *adv.* un′dər sē′), *adj.* being, working, or used beneath the surface of the sea. —*adv.* Also, **underseas.** beneath the surface of the sea.

un·der·sec·re·tar·y (un′dər sek′rə ter′i), *n., pl.* **-tar·ies.** an assistant secretary, esp. of a government department.

un·der·sell (un′dər sel′), *v.*, **-sold, -sell·ing.** sell things at a lower price than is usual.

un·der·shirt (un′dər shèrt′), *n.* shirt worn next to the skin under other clothing.

un·der·shot (un′dər shot′), *adj.* 1 having the lower jaw projecting beyond the upper. 2 driven by water passing beneath: *an undershot wheel.*

un·der·side (un′dər sīd′), *n.* 1 the bottom side. 2 *Fig.* the unseen or illicit side; the gloomy or seamy side, as of society.

un·der·sign (un′dər sīn′; un′dər sīn′), *v.* sign one's name at the end of (a letter or document).

un·der·signed (un′dər sīnd′), *n.* **the undersigned,** the person or persons signing a letter or document.

un·der·slung (un′dər slung′; un′dər slung′), *adj.* of vehicles, having the frame below the axles.

un·der·stand (un′dər stand′), *v.*, **-stood, -stand·ing.** 1 get the meaning; comprehend; realize: *now I understand the teacher's words, understand the nature of electricity.* 2 know how to deal with; know well; know: *a good teacher should understand children.* 3 be informed; learn: *I understand that he is leaving town.* 4 take as a fact; believe: *it is understood that you will come, what are we to understand from his words?*

understand each other, a know each other's meaning and wishes. **b** agree.

un·der·stand·a·ble (un′dər stan′də bəl), *adj.* able to be understood. —**un′der·stand′a·bil′i·ty,** *n.* —**un′der·stand′a·bly,** *adv.*

un·der·stand·ing (un′dər stan′ding), *n.* 1 act of one that understands; comprehension; knowledge. 2 ability to learn and know; intelligence. 3 knowledge of each other's meaning and wishes: *come to an understanding.* —*adj.* that understands; intelligent. —**un′der·stand′ing·ly,** *adv.*

un·der·state (un′dər stāt′), *v.*, **-stat·ed, -stat·ing.** 1 state too weakly. 2 say less than the full truth about. —**un′der·state′ment,** *n.*

un·der·stud·y (un′dər stud′i), *v.*, **-stud·ied, -stud·y·ing,** *n., pl.* **-stud·ies.** —*v.* learn (a part) in order to replace the regular performer when necessary. —*n.* person who can act as a substitute for an actor or actress.

un·der·take (un′dər tāk′), *v.*, **-took, -tak·en, -tak·ing.** 1 set about; try; attempt. 2 agree to do; take upon oneself. 3 promise; guarantee.

un·der·tak·er (un′dər tāk′ər *for 1*; un′dər tāk′ər *for 2*), *n.* 1 person who undertakes something. 2 person whose business is preparing the dead for burial and taking charge of funerals.

un·der·tak·ing (un′dər tāk′ing *for 1 and 2*; un′dər tāk′ing *for 3*), *n.* 1 something undertaken; task; enterprise. 2 promise; guarantee. 3 business of preparing the dead for burial and taking charge of funerals.

un·der-the-count·er (un′dər tħə koun′tər), *adj.* done stealthily; hidden from view; secret.

un·der-the-ta·ble (un′dər tħə tā′bəl), *adj.* =under-the-counter.

un·der·tone (un′dər tōn′), *n.* 1 a low or very quiet tone: *talk in undertones.* 2 a subdued color; color seen through other colors. 3 an underlying quality, condition, or element.

un·der·tow (un′dər tō′), *n.* 1 any strong current below the surface, moving in a direction different from that of the surface current. 2 the backward flow from waves breaking on a beach.

un·der·val·ue (un′dər val′ū), *v.*, **-ued, -u·ing.** put too low a value on. —**un′der·val′u·a′tion,** *n.*

un·der·wa·ter (un′dər wô′tər; -wot′ər), *adj.* 1 below the surface of the water. 2 made for use under the water.

un·der·wear (un′dər wâr′), *n.* clothing worn next to the skin, under one's outer clothes.

un·der·weight (*adj.* un′dər wāt′; *n.* un′dər wāt′), *adj.* having too little weight. —*n.* weight that is not up to standard.

un·der·went (un′dər went′), *v.* pt. of **undergo.**

un·der·world (un′dər wèrld′), *n.* 1 the lower, degraded, or criminal part of human society. 2 the lower world; Hades.

un·der·write (un′dər rīt′; un′dər rīt′), *v.*, **-wrote, -writ·ten, -writ·ing.** 1 insure (property) against loss. 2 agree to meet the expense of. —**un′der·writ′er,** *n.*

un·de·sir·a·ble (un′di zīr′ə bəl), *adj.* objectionable; disagreeable. —*n.* an undesirable person or thing.

un·dis·ci·plined (un dis′ə plind), *adj.* not disciplined; without proper control; untrained.

un·do (un dü′), *v.*, **-did, -done, -do·ing.** 1 unfasten; untie. 2 do away with; cause to be as if never done; spoil; destroy. 3 bring to ruin. 4 explain; solve. —**un·do′er,** *n.*

un·dock (un dok′), *v.* 1 move a ship from a dock. 2 separate a spacecraft from another one it was attached to while in space.

un·doc·u·ment·ed (un dok′yə men′tid), *adj.* 1 lacking the necessary official documents: *undocumented workers.* 2 not proven: *undocumented allegations.*

un·do·ing (un dü′ing), *n.* 1 a doing away with; spoiling; destroying. 2 cause of destruction or ruin.

un·doubt·ed (un dout′id), *adj.* not doubted; accepted as true. —**un·doubt′ed·ly,** *adv.*

un·dress (*v.* un dres′; *n., adj.* un′dres′), *v.* take the clothes off; strip. —*n.* ordinary clothes. —*adj.* of or having to do with ordinary clothes or work clothes.

un·due (un dü′; -dū′), *adj.* 1 not fitting; not right; improper. 2 too great; too much.

un·du·lant (un′dyə lənt), *adj.* waving; wavy.

un·du·late (*v.* un′dyə lāt; *adj.* un′dyə lit, -lāt), *v.*, **-lat·ed, -lat·ing,** *adj.* —*v.* 1 move in waves. 2 have a wavy form or surface. —*adj.* having a waved form, surface, or margin; wavy. [< L *undulatus* diversified as with waves < *unda* wave] —**un′du·lat′ing·ly,** *adv.* —**un′du·la′tion,** *n.* —**un′du·la·to′ry,** *adj.*

un·du·ly (un dü′li; -dū′-), *adv.* 1 improperly. 2 excessively.

un·dy·ing (un dī′ing), *adj.* deathless; immortal; eternal. —**un·dy′ing·ly,** *adv.*

un·earth (un èrth′), *v.* 1 dig up. 2 find out; discover: *unearth a plot.*

un·earth·ly (un èrth′li), *adj.* 1 supernatural. 2 strange; weird. —**un·earth′li·ness,** *n.*

un·ease (un ēz′), *n.* 1 restlessness; anxiety. 2 discomfort. 3 awkwardness.

un·eas·y (un ēz′i), *adj.*, **-eas·i·er, -eas·i·est.** 1 restless; disturbed; anxious. 2 not comfortable. 3 not easy in manner; awkward. —**un·eas′i·ly,** *adv.* —**un·eas′i·ness,** *n.*

un·em·ploy·a·ble (un′em ploi′ə bəl), *adj.* 1 that cannot be employed. 2 not fit to work.

un·em·ployed (un′em ploid′), *adj.* not employed; not in use; having no work. —*n.* **the unemployed,** people out of work.

un·em·ploy·ment (un′em ploi′mənt), *n.* lack of employment; being out of work.

un·e·qual (un ē′kwəl), *adj.* 1 not the same in amount, size, number, value, merit, rank, etc. 2 not balanced; not well matched. 3 not fair; one-sided: *an unequal contest.* 4 not enough; not adequate: *unequal to the task.* 5 not regular; not even; variable. —**un·e′qual·ly,** *adv.* —**un·e′qual·ness,** *n.*

un·e·qualed (un ē′kwəld), *adj.* not equaled; matchless.

un·e·quiv·o·cal (un´i kwiv´ə kəl), *adj.* clear; plain. **—un´e·quiv´o·cal·ly,** *adv.*

un·err·ing (un ėr´ing; –er´–), *adj.* making no mistakes; exactly right. **—un·err´ing·ly,** *adv.*

U·NES·CO, U·nes·co (ü nes´kō), *n.* the United Nations Educational, Scientific, and Cultural Organization.

un·e·ven (un ē´vən), *adj.* 1 not level: *uneven ground.* 2 not equal: *an uneven contest.* 3 of a number, that cannot be divided by 2 without a remainder. **—un·e´ven·ly,** *adv.*

un·e·vent·ful (un´i vent´fəl), *adj.* without important or striking occurrences. **—un´e·vent´ful·ly,** *adv.* **—un´e·vent´ful·ness,** *n.*

un·ex·am·pled (un´ig zam´pəld; –zäm´–), *adj.* having no equal or like; without precedent or parallel; without anything like it.

un·ex·cep·tion·al (un´ik sep´shən əl), *adj.* 1 ordinary. 2 admitting of no exception. **—un´ex·cep´tion·al·ly,** *adv.*

un·ex·pect·ed (un´iks pek´tid), *adj.* not expected. **—un´ex·pect´ed·ly,** *adv.*

un·fail·ing (un fāl´ing), *adj.* 1 never failing; tireless; loyal. 2 never running short; endless. 3 sure; certain. **—un·fail´ing·ly,** *adv.*

un·fair (un fãr´), *adj.* not honest; unjust. **—un·fair´ly,** *adv.* **—un·fair´ness,** *n.*

un·faith·ful (un fāth´fəl), *adj.* 1 not faithful; not true to duty or one's promises; faithless. 2 not accurate; not exact. 3 guilty of adultery. **—un·faith´ful·ly,** *adv.* **—un·faith´ful·ness,** *n.*

un·fa·mil·iar (un´fə mil´yər), *adj.* 1 not well known; unusual; strange. 2 not acquainted. **—un´fa·mil´i·ar´i·ty,** *n.*

un·fas·ten (un fas´ən; –fäs´–), *v.* undo; loose; open.

un·fa·vor·a·ble (un fā´vər ə bəl; –fāv´rə–), *adj.* not favorable; adverse; harmful. **—un·fa´vor·a·bly,** *adv.*

un·fazed (un fāzd´), *adj.* not worried or disturbed.

un·feel·ing (un fēl´ing), *adj.* 1 hardhearted; cruel. 2 not able to feel. **—un·feel´ing·ly,** *adv.*

un·feigned (un fānd´), *adj.* sincere; real. **—un·feign´ed·ly,** *adv.* **—un·feign´ed·ness,** *n.*

un·fin·ished (un fin´isht), *adj.* 1 not finished; not complete. 2 without some special finish; not polished; rough.

un·fit (un fit´), *adj., v.,* **–fit·ted, –fit·ting.** *—adj.* 1 not fit; not suitable. 2 not good enough; unqualified. 3 not adapted. *—v.* make unfit; spoil.

un·flag·ging (un flag´ing), *adj.* not drooping or failing. **—un·flag´ging·ly,** *adv.*

un·flap·pable (un flap´ə bəl), *adj. Informal.* not easily disturbed or excited; calm.

un·flinch·ing (un flin´ching), *adj.* not drawing back from difficulty, danger, or pain; firm; resolute. **—un·flinch´ing·ly,** *adv.*

un·fold (un fōld´), *v.* 1 open the folds of; spread out. 2 reveal; show; explain. 3 open; develop. **—un·fold´er,** *n.*

un·fore·seen (un´fôr sēn´; –fōr–), *adj.* not known beforehand; unexpected.

un·for·get·ta·ble (un´fər get´ə bəl), *adj.* that can never be forgotten. **—un´for·get´ta·bly,** *adv.*

un·for·tu·nate (un fôr´chə nit), *adj.* 1 not lucky; having bad luck. 2 not suitable; not fitting. *—n.* an unfortunate person. **—un·for´tu·nate·ly,** *adv.*

un·found·ed (un foun´did), *adj.* without foundation; baseless.

un·fre·quent·ed (un´fri kwen´tid), *adj.* not frequented; seldom visited; rarely used.

un·friend·ly (un frend´li), *adj.* 1 not friendly; hostile. 2 not favorable. *—adv.* in an unfriendly manner. **—un·friend´li·ness,** *n.*

un·frock (un frok´), *v.* deprive (a priest or minister) of his office.

un·furl (un fėrl´), *v.* spread out; shake out; unfold: *unfurl a sail.*

un·gain·ly (un gān´li), *adj.* awkward; clumsy. *—adv.* awkwardly; clumsily. **—un·gain´li·ness,** *n.*

un·glue (un glü´), *v.* **–glued, –glu·ing.** separate or open (something glued or stuck together).
   come unglued, *Informal. Fig.* fall apart; go to pieces: *he simply came unglued on hearing the news.*

un·god·ly (un god´li), *adj.* 1 not religious; wicked; sinful. 2 very annoying; shocking. **—un·god´li·ness,** *n.*

un·gov·ern·a·ble (un guv´ər nə bəl), *adj.* impossible to control; very hard to control or rule; unruly. **—un·gov´ern·a·ble·ness,** *n.*

un·grace·ful (un grās´fəl), *adj.* not graceful; clumsy; awkward. **—un·grace´ful·ly,** *adv.*

un·gra·cious (un grā´shəs), *adj.* 1 not polite; rude. 2 unpleasant; disagreeable. **—un·gra´cious·ly,** *adv.* **—un·gra´cious·ness,** *n.*

un·grate·ful (un grāt´fəl), *adj.* 1 not grateful; not thankful. 2 unpleasant; disagreeable. **—un·grate´ful·ly,** *adv.* **—un·grate´ful·ness,** *n.*

un·ground·ed (un groun´did), *adj.* without foundation; without reasons.

un·guard·ed (un gär´did), *adj.* 1 not protected. 2 careless. **—un·guard´ed·ness,** *n.*

un·guent (ung´gwənt), *n.* ointment for sores, burns, etc.: salve. [< L *unguentum* < *unguere* anoint]

un·gu·late (ung´gyə lit; –lāt), *adj.* having hoofs; belonging to the group of animals having hoofs. *—n.* animal that has hoofs.

un·hand (un hand´), *v.* let go; take the hands from.

un·hand·y (un han´di), *adj.* 1 not easy to handle or manage. 2 not skillful in using the hands. **—un·hand´i·ly,** *adv.*

un·hap·py (un hap´i), *adj.,* **–pi·er, –pi·est.** 1 sad; sorrowful. 2 unlucky. 3 not suitable. **—un·hap´pi·ly,** *adv.* **—un·hap´pi·ness,** *n.*

un·har·ness (un här´nis), *v.* 1 remove harness from (a horse, etc.); free from harness or gear. 2 remove harness or gear.

un·health·y (un hel´thi), *adj.* 1 not possessing good health; not well: *an unhealthy child.* 2 characteristic of or resulting from poor health: *an unhealthy paleness.* 3 hurtful to health; unwholesome: *an unhealthy climate.* **—un·health´i·ness,** *n.*

un·heard (un hėrd´), *adj.* 1 not perceived by the ear. 2 not given a hearing. 3 not heard of; unknown.

un·heard-of (un hėrd´ov´; –uv´), *adj.* 1 that was never heard of; unknown. 2 such as was never known before; unprecedented.

un·hinge (un hinj´), *v.,* **–hinged, –hing·ing.** 1 take (a door, etc.) off its hinges. 2 remove the hinges from. 3 separate from something; detach. 4 *Fig.* unsettle; disorganize; upset: *an unhinged mind.*

un·ho·ly (un hō´li), *adj.,* **–li·er, –li·est.** 1 not holy; wicked; sinful. 2 not seemly; fearful. **—un·ho´li·ness,** *n.*

un·hook (un húk´), *v.* 1 loosen from a hook. 2 undo by loosening a hook or hooks.

un·horse (un hôrs´), *v.,* **–horsed, –hors·ing.** throw from a horse's back; cause to fall from a horse.

uni–, *combining form.* one. [< L *unus* one]

u·ni·cam·er·al (ü´nə kam´ər əl), *adj.* of a lawmaking body, composed of only one group.

U·NI·CEF, U·ni·cef (yü´nə sef), *n.* United Nations Children's Fund.

u·ni·cel·lu·lar (ü´nə sel´yə lər), *adj.* having one cell only. The amoeba is a unicellular animal.

u·ni·corn (ü´nə kôrn), *n.* a mythical animal like a horse, but having a single long horn in the middle of its forehead. [< L, < *unus* one + *cornu* horn]

u·ni·cy·cle (ü´nə sī´kəl), *n.* a one-wheeled cycle, propelled by pedals, used esp. in circuses. [< *uni–* + *–cycle,* as in bicycle]

u·ni·fi·ca·tion (ü´nə fə kā´shən), *n.* 1 formation into one unit; union. 2 a making or being made more alike.

unified field theory, a theory that attempts to encompass different physical theories or laws within a single, unifying theoretical framework.

u·ni·form (ü´nə fôrm), *adj.* 1 always the same; not changing: *uniform temperature.* 2 all alike; not varying: *bricks of uniform size, a uniform pace. —n.* the distinctive clothes worn by the members of a group when on duty, by which they may be recognized as belonging to that group. Soldiers, policemen, and nurses wear uniforms. *—v.* clothe or furnish with a uniform. [< L, < *unus* one + *forma* form] **—u´ni·form´ly,** *adv.* **—u´ni·form´ness,** *n.*

u·ni·form·i·ty (ü´nə fôr´mə ti), *n., pl.* **–ties.** uniform condition or character; sameness throughout.

u·ni·fy (ü´nə fī), *v.,* **–fied, –fy·ing.** make or form into one; unite. [< LL, < L *unus* one + *facere* make] **—u´ni·fi´er,** *n.*

u·ni·lat·er·al (ū′nə lat′ər əl), *adj.* **1** of, on, or affecting one side only. **2** having all the parts arranged on one side of an axis; one-sided. **3** affecting one party or person only. **4** concerned with or considering only one side of a matter. —**u′ni·lat′er·al·ly,** *adv.*

un·im·peach·a·ble (un′im pēch′ə bəl), *adj.* free from fault; blameless. —**un′im·peach′a·bly,** *adv.*

un·im·por·tant (un′im pôr′tənt), *adj.* insignificant; trifling. —**un′im·por′tance,** *n.*

un·in·tel·li·gi·ble (un′in tel′jə bəl), *adj.* that cannot be understood. —**un′in·tel′li·gi·bil′i·ty,** *n.* —**un′in·tel′li·gi·bly,** *adv.*

un·in·ter·rupt·ed (un′in tə rup′tid), *adj.* without interruption; continuous. —**un′in·ter·rupt′ed·ly,** *adv.*

un·ion (ūn′yən), *n.* **1** a uniting or being united: *the United States was formed by the union of thirteen states.* **2** group of people, states, etc., united for some special purpose: *the American colonies formed a union.* **3** a labor union; trade union. **4** marriage. **5** any of various devices for connecting parts of machinery or apparatus.

the Union, the United States of America. [< L, < *unus* one]

un·ion·ism (ūn′yən iz əm), *n.* **1** the principle of union. **2** system, principles, or methods of labor unions. —**un′ion·ist,** *n., adj.*

un·ion·ize (ūn′yən īz), *v.,* **-ized, -iz·ing.** form into a labor union. —**un′ion·i·za′tion,** *n.*

Union Jack, the British national flag.

union shop, a factory or business in which most of the employees belong to a recognized labor union.

u·nique (ū nēk′), *adj.* **1** having no like or equal; being the only one of its kind. **2** rare; unusual. [< F < L *unicus*] —**u·nique′ly,** *adv.* —**u·nique′ness,** *n.*

u·ni·sex (ū′nə seks′), *adj.* **1** suitable for either sex. **2** catering to either sex: *a unisex hair salon.*

u·ni·son (ū′nə zən; -sən), *n.* **1** agreement. **2** agreement in pitch of two or more tones, voices, etc. [< Med.L *unisonus* sounding the same < L *unus* one + *sonus* sound]

u·nit (ū′nit), *n.* **1** a single thing or person. **2** any group of things or persons considered as one. **3** one of the individuals or groups into which a whole can be analyzed. **4** a standard quantity or amount. A foot is a unit of length. **5** the smallest whole number; 1. [prob. < *unity*]

U·ni·tar·i·an (ū′nə tār′i ən), *n.* person who maintains that God exists as one being. Unitarians accept the moral teachings of Jesus, but do not believe that he was divine. —*adj.* of or pertaining to Unitarians. —**U′ni·tar′i·an·ism,** *n.*

u·ni·tar·y (ū′nə tār′i), *adj.* **1** of or having to do with the unit. **2** concerned with

or based on unity: *a unitary policy.* **3** unified; centralized: *a unitary structure of government.*

u·nite (ū nīt′), *v.,* **u·nit·ed, u·nit·ing.** join together; make one; join in action, interest, opinion, feeling, etc.; combine. [< L, < *unus* one] —**u·nit′er,** *n.*

u·nit·ed (ū nīt′id), *adj.* **1** made one; joined; combined. **2** pertaining to or produced by two or more. —**u·nit′ed·ly,** *adv.* —**u·nit′ed·ness,** *n.*

United Kingdom, country in NW Europe in the British Isles, including England, Scotland, Wales, and Northern Ireland.

United Nations, worldwide organization devoted to establishing and maintaining world peace and supporting social and economic improvement.

United States, or **United States of America,** country in North America, extending from the Atlantic to the Pacific Oceans and from the Gulf of Mexico to Canada, with Alaska lying W and NW of Canada, Hawaii lying W in the Pacific, the District of Columbia, the territory of Puerto Rico and other possessions.

u·ni·ty (ū′nə ti), *n., pl.* **-ties. 1** oneness; being united. A circle has more unity than a row of dots. **2** union of parts forming a complex whole. **3** harmony. **4** the number one (1). [< L, < *unus* one]

univ., 1 universal. **2** university.

u·ni·va·lent (ū′nə vā′lənt; ū niv′ə-), *adj.* having a valence of one. —**u′ni·va′lence,** *n.*

u·ni·ver·sal (ū′nə vėr′səl), *adj.* **1** of or for all; done, used, held, etc., by everybody. **2** existing everywhere. **3** covering a whole group of persons, things, cases, etc.: general. **4** adaptable to different sizes, angles, kinds of work, etc. —**u′ni·ver·sal′i·ty, u′ni·ver′sal·ness,** *n.*

U·ni·ver·sal·ist (ū′nə vėr′səl ist), *n.* a member of a Protestant church holding the belief that all people will finally be saved. —**U′ni·ver′sal·ism,** *n.*

u·ni·ver·sal·i·ty (ū′nə vėr sal′ə ti), *n., pl.* **-ties.** a being universal; universal character or range of knowledge.

u·ni·ver·sal·ly (ū′nə vėr′səl i), *adv.* **1** in every instance; without exception. **2** everywhere.

Universal Product Code, =bar code.

u·ni·verse (ū′nə vėrs), *n.* all things; everything there is: *our world is but a small part of the universe.* [< L *universum,* orig. neut. adj., whole, turned into one < *unus* one + *vertere* turn]

u·ni·ver·si·ty (ū′nə vėr′sə ti), *n., pl.* **-ties.** institution of learning of the highest grade. A university usually has schools, as of law, medicine, teaching, business, etc., and in the United States, colleges for general instruction. [< AF < Med.L *universitas* corporation < L aggregate, whole < *universus.* See UNIVERSE.]

un·just (un just′), *adj.* not just; not fair. —**un·just′ly,** *adv.* —**un·just′ness,** *n.*

un·kempt (un kempt′), *adj.* **1** not combed. **2** neglected; untidy. [< UN-[1] + OE *cem-*

bed combed, pp. of *cemban* < *camb* comb] —**un·kempt′ness,** *n.*

un·kind (un kīnd′), *adj.* harsh; cruel. —**un·kind′ly,** *adv.* —**un·kind′li·ness,** *n.* —**un·kind′ness,** *n.*

un·known (un nōn′), *adj.* **1** not known. **2** not familiar; strange.

un·lace (un lās′), *v.,* **-laced, -lac·ing.** undo the laces of.

un·latch (un lach′), *v.* unfasten or open by lifting a latch.

un·law·ful (un lô′fəl), *adj.* **1** contrary to the law; against the law; forbidden; illegal. **2** illegitimate. —**un·law′ful·ly,** *adv.* **un·law′ful·ness,** *n.*

un·learn·ed (un lėr′nid *for 1;* un lėrnd′ *for 2*), *adj.* **1** not educated; ignorant. **2** not learned; known without being learned.

un·leash (un lēsh′), *v.* **1** release from a leash. **2** let loose: *unleash one's temper.*

un·leav·ened (un lev′ənd), *adj.* not leavened. Unleavened bread is made without yeast.

un·less (ən les′; un–), *conj.* if it were not that; if not: *we shall go unless it rains.* —*prep.* except. [< *on* + *less,* i.e., on a less condition (than)]

un·let·tered (un let′ərd), *adj.* **1** not educated. **2** not able to read or write.

un·like (un līk′), *adj.* not like; different: *the two problems are quite unlike.* —*prep.* different from: *act unlike others.* —**un·like′ness.** *n.*

un·like·li·hood (un līk′li hùd), *n.* improbability.

un·like·ly (un līk′li), *adj.* **1** not likely; not probable: *unlikely to succeed.* **2** not likely to succeed: *an unlikely adventure.* —**un·like′li·ness.** *n.*

un·lim·it·ed (un lim′it id), *adj.* **1** without limits; boundless. **2** not restricted. **3** not definite. —**un·lim′it·ed·ness,** *n.*

un·list·ed (un lis′tid), *adj.* **1** not available from a usual list: *an unlisted organization, an unlisted phone number.* **2** not traded on a stock exchange.

un·load (un lōd′), *v.* **1** remove (a load). **2** get rid of. **3** remove powder, shot, etc., from (a gun). **4** discharge a cargo: *the ship is unloading.* —**un·load′er,** *n.*

un·lock (un lok′), *v.* **1** open the lock of; open (anything firmly closed). **2** disclose; reveal.

un·looked-for (un lùkt′fôr′), *adj.* unexpected; unforeseen.

un·loose (un lüs′), **un·loos·en** (–lüs′ən), *v.,* **-loosed, -loos·ing; -loos·ened, -loos·en·ing.** let loose; set free; release.

un·luck·y (un luk′i), *adj.* not lucky; unfortunate; bringing bad luck. —**un·luck′i·ly,** *adv.*

un·man (un man′), *v.,* **-manned, -man·ning. 1** deprive of the qualities of a man. **2** weaken or break down the spirit of.

un·man·ly (un man′li), *adj.* not manly; weak; cowardly. —**un·man′li·ness,** *n.*

un·man·ner·ly (un man′ər li), *adj.* having bad manners; discourteous. —*adv.* with bad manners; rudely. —**un·man′ner·li·ness,** *n.*

un·mask (un mask′; –mäsk′), *v.* **1** remove a mask or disguise. **2** expose the true character of.

un·men·tion·a·ble (un men′shən ə bəl; –mensh′nə bəl), *adj.* that cannot be mentioned; not fit to be spoken about.

un·mer·ci·ful (un mèr′si fəl), *adj.* having no mercy; showing no mercy. —**un·mer′ci·ful·ly,** *adv.* —**un·mer′ci·ful·ness,** *n.*

un·mis·tak·a·ble (un′mis tāk′ə bəl), *adj.* that cannot be mistaken or misunderstood; clear; plain; evident. —**un′mis·tak′a·bly,** *adv.*

un·muz·zle (un muz′əl), *v.,* –**zled, –zling.** **1** remove a muzzle from (a dog, etc.). **2** free from restraint.

un·nat·u·ral (un nach′ə rəl; –nach′rəl), *adj.* not natural; not normal. —**un·nat′u·ral·ly,** *adv.*

un·nec·es·sar·y (un nes′ə ser′i), *adj.* not necessary; needless. —**un·nec′es·sar′i·ly,** *adv.*

un·nerve (un nèrv′), *v.,* –**nerved, –nerv·ing.** deprive of nerve, firmness, or self-control.

un·num·bered (un num′bərd), *adj.* **1** not numbered; not counted. **2** too many to count.

un·oc·cu·pied (un ok′yə pīd), *adj.* **1** without an occupant; vacant. **2** not employed; idle.

un·or·gan·ized (un ôr′gən īzd), *adj.* **1** not formed into an organized or systematized whole. **2** not organized into labor unions. **3** not being a living organism.

un·pack (un pak′), *v.* take out (things packed in a box, trunk, etc.).

un·pal·at·a·ble (un pal′it ə bəl), *adj.* not agreeable to the taste; distasteful; unpleasant. —**un·pal′at·a·bly,** *adv.*

un·par·al·leled (un par′ə leld), *adj.* having no parallel; unequaled; matchless.

un·peo·ple (un pē′pəl), *v.,* –**pled, –pling.** deprive of people. —**un·peo′pled,** *adj.*

un·pin (un pin′), *v.,* –**pinned, –pin·ning.** take out a pin or pins from; unfasten.

un·pleas·ant (un plez′ənt), *adj.* not pleasant; disagreeable. —**un·pleas′ant·ly,** *adv.* —**un·pleas′ant·ness,** *n.*

un·plumbed (un plumd′), *adj.* **1** not measured; of unknown depth. **2** having no plumbing.

un·pop·u·lar (un pop′yə lər), *adj.* not generally liked; disliked. —**un′pop·u·lar′i·ty,** *n.* —**un·pop′u·lar·ly,** *adv.*

un·prac·ti·cal (un prak′tə kəl), *adj.* =impractical. *n.*

un·prac·ticed, (un prak′tist) *adj.* **1** not skilled. **2** not used.

un·prec·e·dent·ed (un pres′ə den′tid), *adj.* having no precedent; never done before; never known before. **un·prec′e·dent′ed·ly,** *adv.*

un·prej·u·diced (un prej′ə dist), *adj.* **1** without prejudice; impartial. **2** not impaired.

un·pre·tend·ing (un′pri ten′ding), *adj.* unassuming; modest. —**un′pre·tend′ing·ly,** *adv.*

un·pre·ten·tious (un′pri ten′shəs), *adj.* modest. —**un′pre·ten′tious·ly,** *adv.* —**un′pre·ten′tious·ness** , *n.*

un·prin·ci·pled (un prin′sə pəld), *adj.* lacking good moral principles; bad.

un·print·a·ble (un prin′tə bəl), *adj.* not fit to be printed.

un·pro·fes·sion·al (un′prə fesh′ən əl; –fesh′nəl), *adj.* **1** contrary to professional etiquette; unbecoming in members of a profession. **2** not pertaining to or connected with a profession. **3** not belonging to a profession. —**un′pro·fes′sion·al·ly,** *adv.*

un·pro·voked (un′prə vōkt′), *adj.* without provocation.

un·qual·i·fied (un kwol′ə fīd), *adj.* **1** not qualified; not fitted. **2** not modified, limited, or restricted in any way: *unqualified praise, an unqualified failure.*

un·ques·tion·a·ble (un kwes′chən ə bəl), *adj.* beyond dispute or doubt; certain. —**un·ques′tion·a·bly,** *adv.*

un·quote (un kwōt′), *v.,* –**quot·ed, –quot·ing,** *n.* —*v.* end a quotation. —*n.* end of a quotation.

un·rav·el (un rav′əl), *v.,* –**eled, –el·ing.** **1** separate the threads of; pull or come apart. **2** bring or come out of a tangled state: *unravel a mystery.*

un·read (un red′), *adj.* **1** not read: *an unread book.* **2** not having read much: *an unread person.*

un·read·y (un red′i), *adj.* **1** not ready; not prepared. **2** not prompt or quick. —**un·read′i·ness,** *n.*

un·re·al (un rē′əl), *adj.* imaginary; not real; not substantial; fanciful. —**un′re·al′i·ty,** *n.*

un·rea·son·a·ble (un rē′zən ə bəl), *adj.* **1** not reasonable. **2** not moderate; excessive. —**un·rea′son·a·bly,**

un·rea·son·ing (un rē′zən ing; –rēz′ning), *adj.* not using reason; reasonless.

un·re·lent·ing (un′ri len′ting), *adj.* **1** hard-hearted; merciless. **2** not slackening or relaxing. —**un′re·lent′ing·ly** *adv.*

un·re·li·a·ble (un′ri lī′ə bəl), *adj.* not reliable; not to be depended on. —**un′re·li′a·bil′i·ty,** *n.* —**un′re·li′a·bly,** *adv.*

un·re·mit·ting (un′ri mit′ing), *adj.* never stopping; not slackening; maintained steadily. —**un′re·mit′ting·ly,** *adv.*

un·re·served (un′ri zèrvd′), *adj.* **1** frank; open. **2** not restricted; without reservation. —**un′re·serv′ed·ly,** *adv.* —**un′re·serv′ed·ness,** *n.*

un·rest (un rest′), *n.* **1** lack of ease and quiet; restlessness. **2** agitation or disturbance amounting almost to rebellion.

un·right·eous (un rī′chəs), *adj.* wicked; sinful; unjust. —**un·right′eous·ly,** *adv.* —**un·right′eous·ness,** *n.*

un·ripe (un rīp′), *adj.* not ripe; green. —**un·ripe′ness,** *n.*

un·ri·valed (un rī′vəld), *adj.* having no rival; without an equal.

un·roll (un rōl′), *v.* **1** open or spread out (something rolled). **2** lay open; display.

un·ruf·fled (un ruf′əld), *adj.* **1** not ruffled; smooth. **2** not disturbed; calm.

un·ru·ly (un rü′li), *adj.* hard to rule or control; lawless. —**un·ru′li·ness,** *n.*

un·sad·dle (un sad′əl), *v.,* –**dled, –dling.** take the saddle off (a horse).

un·safe (un sāf′), *adj.* dangerous. —**un·safe′ly,** *adv.* —**un·safe′ness,** *n.* —**un·safe′ty,** *n.*

un·san·i·tar·y (un san′ə ter′i), *adj.* not healthful. —**un·san′i·tar′i·ness.** *n.*

un·sa·vor·y (un sā′vər i; –sāv′ri), *adj.* **1** tasteless. **2** unpleasant in taste or smell. **3** morally unpleasant; offensive. —**un·sa′vor·i·ness,** *n.*

un·scathed (un skāᵗʰd′), *adj.* not harmed; uninjured.

un·sci·en·tif·ic (un′sī ən tif′ik), *adj.* **1** not in accordance with the facts or principles of science. **2** not acting in accordance with such facts or principles. —**un′sci·en·tif′i·cal·ly,** *adv.*

un·scram·ble (un skram′bəl), *v.,* –**bled, –bling.** reduce from confusion to order; bring out of a scrambled condition.

un·screw (un skrü′), *v.* **1** take out the screw or screws from. **2** loosen or take off by turning; untwist: *unscrew a cap.*

un·scru·pu·lous (un skrü′pyə ləs), *adj.* not careful about right or wrong; without principles or conscience. —**un·scru′pu·lous·ly,** *adv.* —**un·scru′pu·lous·ness** , *n.*

un·seal (un sēl′), *v.* **1** break or remove the seal of: *unseal a box of cookies.* **2** open: *the threat unsealed her lips.*

un·search·a·ble (un sèr′chə bəl), *adj.* not to be searched into; mysterious.

un·sea·son·a·ble (un sē′zən ə bəl; –sēz′nə bəl), *adj.* **1** not suitable to the season. **2** coming at the wrong time. —**un·sea′son·a·ble·ness,** *n.* —**un·sea′son·a·bly,** *adv.*

un·seat (un sēt′), *v.* **1** displace from a seat. **2** throw (a rider) from a saddle. **3** remove from office.

un·seem·ly (un sēm′li), *adj.* not seemly; not suitable; improper. —*adv.* improperly; unsuitably.

un·seen (un sēn′), *adj.* **1** not seen: *enter a building unseen.* **2** not visible: *unseen forces at work.*

un·self·ish (un sel′fish), *adj.* considerate of others; generous. —**un·self′ish·ly,** *adv.* —**un·self′ish·ness,** *n.*

un·set·tle (un set′əl), *v.,* –**tled, –tling.** make or become unstable; disturb; shake; weaken. —**un·set′tled,** *adj.* —**un·set′tled·ness,** *n.*

un·sex (un seks′), *v.* deprive of the attributes of one's sex.

un·shack·le (un shak′əl), *v.,* –**led, –ling.** remove shackles from; set free.

un·sheathe (un shēᵗʰ′), *v.,* –**sheathed, –sheath·ing.** draw (a sword, knife, or the like) from a sheath.

un·ship (un ship′), *v.,* –**shipped, –ship·ping.** put off or take off from a ship.

un·shod (un shod′), *adj.* without shoes: *an unshod horse, an unshod beggar.*

un·sight·ly (un sīt′li), *adj.* ugly or unpleasant to look at. —**un·sight′li·ness,** *n.*

un·skilled (un skild′), *adj.* **1** not skilled; not trained. **2** not using skill.

un·skill·ful, un·skil·ful (un skil′fəl), *adj.* awkward; clumsy. —**un·skill′ful·ly, un·skil′ful·ly,** *adv.*

un·snap (un snap′), *v.,* **–snapped, –snapping.** unfasten the snap or snaps of.

un·snarl (un snärl′), *v.* untangle.

un·so·cia·ble (un sō′shə bəl), *adj.* not sociable; not associating easily with others. —**un′so·cia·bil′i·ty, un·so′cia·ble·ness,** *n.* —**un·so′cia·bly,** *adv.*

un·so·phis·ti·cat·ed (un′sə fis′tə kāt′id), *adj.* simple; natural; artless. —**un′so·phis′ti·cat′ed·ness, un′so·phis′ti·ca′tion,** *n.*

un·sound (un sound′), *adj.* **1** not in good condition; not sound. **2** not based on truth or fact. **3** not deep; not restful; disturbed: *an unsound sleep.* —**un·sound′ly,** *adv.*

un·spar·ing (un spār′ing), *adj.* **1** very generous; liberal. **2** not merciful; severe. —**un·spar′ing·ly,** *adv.*

un·speak·a·ble (un spēk′ə bəl), *adj.* **1** that cannot be expressed in words. **2** extremely bad; so bad that it is not spoken of. —**un·speak′a·bly,** *adv.*

un·sta·ble (un stā′bəl), *adj.* **1** not firmly fixed; easily moved, shaken, or overthrown: *an unstable chair, an unstable mind.* **2** not constant; variable: *unstable weather.* **3** *Chem.* easily decomposed; readily changing into other compounds. —**un·sta′ble·ness,** *n.* —**un·sta′bly,** *adv.*

un·stead·y (un sted′i), *adj.* **1** not steady; shaky. **2** likely to change; not reliable. **3** not regular in habits. —**un·stead′i·ly,** *adv.* —**un·stead′i·ness,** *n.*

un·stop (un stop′), *v.,* **–stopped, –stopping.** **1** remove the stopper from (a bottle, etc.). **2** free from any obstruction; open.

un·string (un string′), *v.,* **–strung, –string·ing.** **1** take off or loosen the string or strings of. **2** take from a string. **3** *Fig.* weaken the nerves of; make nervous.

un·strung (un strung′), *adj.* nervous. —*v.* pt. and pp. of **unstring.**

un·stud·ied (un stud′id), *adj.* not planned ahead; natural.

un·sub·stan·tial (un′səb stan′shəl), *adj.* flimsy; slight; unreal.

un·suit·a·ble (un süt′ə bəl), *adj.* not suitable; unfit. —**un′suit·a·bil′i·ty, un·suit′a·ble·ness,** *n.* —**un·suit′a·bly,** *adv.*

un·suit·ed (un süt′id), *adj.* unfit.

un·sung (un sung′), *adj.* **1** not sung. **2** not honored.

un·tan·gle (un tang′gəl), *v.,* **–gled, –gling.** **1** take the tangles out of; disentangle. **2** *Fig.* straighten out or clear up (anything confused or perplexing).

un·taught (un tôt′), *adj.* **1** not educated. **2** learned naturally.

un·think·ing (un thingk′ing), *adj.* thoughtless; heedless; careless. —**un·think′ing·ly,** *adv.*

un·thought-of (un thôt′ov′; –uv′), *adj.* not imagine or considered.

un·ti·dy (un tī′di), *adj.* not in order; not neat. —**un·ti′di·ly** *adv.* —**un·ti′di·ness,** *n.*

un·tie (un tī′), *v.,* **–tied, –ty·ing.** loosen; unfasten.

un·til (ən til′; un–), *prep.* **1** up to the time of: *wait until tomorrow.* **2** before: *he did not go until night.* —*conj.* **1** up to the time when: *he worked until the job was completed.* **2** before: *he did not come until the meeting was half over.* **3** to the degree or place that: *he worked until he was tired.* [ME, < Scand. *und* up to + *till*[1]]

un·time·ly (un tīm′li), *adj.* at a wrong time or season: *snow in May is untimely.* —*adv.* too early; too soon. —**un·time′li·ness,** *n.*

un·tir·ing (un tīr′ing), *adj.* tireless; unwearying. —**un·tir′ing·ly,** *adv.*

un·to (un′tü; un′tù), *prep. Archaic or Poetic.* **1** to. **2** until. [ME, < *un–* (see UNTIL) + *to*]

un·told (un tōld′), *adj.* **1** not told; not revealed. **2** too many to be counted or numbered; very great: *untold numbers.*

un·touch·a·ble (un tuch′ə bəl), *adj.* **1** that cannot be touched; out of reach. **2** that must not be touched. —*n.* Hindu of the lowest caste in India, whose touch was at one time thought to defile members of higher castes. In modern India, discrimination against this caste is forbidden by the constitution.

un·to·ward (un tôrd′; –tōrd′), *adj.* **1** unfavorable; unfortunate. **2** perverse; stubborn; willful.

un·tram·meled (un tram′əld), *adj.* not hindered or restrained; free.

un·trod (un trod′), *adj.* not trodden.

un·true (un trü′), *adj.* **1** false; incorrect. **2** not faithful. **3** not true to a standard or rule. —**un·true′ness,** *n.* —**un·tru′ly,** *adv.*

un·truth (un trüth′), *n.* **1** lack of truth; falsity. **2** a lie; falsehood.

un·truth·ful (un trüth′fəl), *adj.* not truthful; contrary to the truth. —**un·truth′ful·ly,** *adv.* —**un·truth′ful·ness,** *n.*

un·tu·tored (un tü′tərd; –tū′–), *adj.* untaught.

un·twist (un twist′), *v.* **1** undo or loosen something twisted; unravel. **2** become untwisted.

un·used (un ūzd′), *adj.* **1** not used: *an unused room.* **2** not accustomed: *hands unused to labor.* **3** never having been used: *unused drinking cups.*

un·u·su·al (un ū′zhù əl), *adj.* beyond the ordinary; not common; rare. —**un·u′su·al·ly,** *adv.*

un·ut·ter·a·ble (un ut′ər ə bəl), *adj.* that cannot be expressed; unspeakable. —**un·ut′ter·a·bly,** *adv.*

un·var·nished (un vär′nisht), *adj.* **1** not varnished. **2** plain; unadorned: *the unvarnished truth.*

un·veil (un vāl′), *v.* **1** remove a veil from. **2** remove a veil; reveal oneself; become unveiled. **3** *Fig.* disclose; reveal.

un·war·rant·a·ble (un wôr′ən tə bəl; –wor′–), *adj.* not justifiable; illegal; improper. —**un·war′rant·a·bly,** *adv.*

un·war·y (un wār′i), *adj.* not cautious; not careful; unguarded. —**un·war′i·ly,** *adv.* —**un·war′i·ness,** *n.*

un·well (un wel′), *adj.* ill; sick.

un·wept (un wept′), *adj.* **1** not wept for. **2** not shed: *unwept tears.*

un·whole·some (un hōl′səm), *adj.* bad for the body or the mind; unhealthy. —**un·whole′some·ness,** *n.*

un·wield·y (un wēl′di), *adj.* not easily handled or managed because of size, shape, or weight; bulky and clumsy: *the unwieldy armor of knights.* —**un·wield′i·ness,** *n.*

un·will·ing (un wil′ing), *adj.* not willing; not consenting. —**un·will′ing·ly,** *adv.* —**un·will′ing·ness,** *n.*

un·wind (un wīnd′), *v.,* **–wound, –wind·ing.** **1** wind off; take from a spool, ball, etc. **2** become unwound. **3** disentangle.

un·wise (un wīz′), *adj.* not wise; not showing good judgment; foolish. —**un·wise′ly,** *adv.*

un·wit·ting (un wit′ing), *adj.* not knowing; unaware; unconscious; unintentional. —**un·wit′ting·ly,** *adv.*

un·wont·ed (un wun′tid; –wōn′–), *adj.* **1** not customary; not usual. **2** not accustomed; not used. —**un·wont′ed·ly,** *adv.* —**un·wont′ed·ness,** *n.*

un·wor·thy (un wėr′ŧħi), *adj.* **1** not worthy; not deserving. **2** base; shameful. —**un·wor′thi·ly,** *adv.* —**un·wor′thi·ness,** *n.*

un·wrap (un rap′), *v.,* **–wrapped, –wrap·ing.** **1** remove a wrapping from; open. **2** become opened.

un·writ·ten (un rit′ən), *adj.* **1** not written. **2** understood or customary, but not actually expressed in writing. **3** not written on; blank.

unwritten law, the common law.

un·yoke (un yōk′), *v.* **–yoked, –yok·ing.** **1** free from a yoke. **2** disconnect; separate.

up (up), *adv., prep., adj., n., v.,* **upped, up·ping.** —*adv.* **1** to a higher place or condition; to, toward, or near the top: *up in a tree.* **2** to or at any point, place, or condition that is considered higher: *prices have gone up, up north, the sun is up.* **3** in or into an erect position; not lying or sitting down: *stand up, get up.* **4** thoroughly; completely; entirely: *the house burned up.* **5** at an end; over: *his time is up.* **6** in or into being or action; happening: *don't stir up trouble, what's up over there?* **7** together: *add those up.* **8** to or in an even position; not behind: *catch up in a race, keep up with the times, be up on computers.* **9** in or into view, notice, or consideration: *bring up a new topic.* **10** into safe-keeping, storage, etc.: *lay up supplies.* **11** at bat in baseball. —*prep.* **1** to or at a higher place on or in: *up a tree, up the hill.* **2** along; through: *she walked* *up the street.* **3** toward or in the inner or upper part of: *we sailed up the river, he lives up county.* —*adj.* **1** advanced; forward. **2** moving upward; directed upward: *an up trend in the economy.* **3** above the ground: *the wheat is up.* **4** near; close. **5** at bat in baseball. —*n.* **1** an upward movement, course, or slope. **2** piece of good luck. —*v.* put or get up.

on the up and up, honest; real: *his offer was on the up and up.*

up against, facing as a thing to be dealt with: *up against real competition.*

up and doing, busy; active.

up to, a doing; about to do: *up to mischief.* **b** equal to; capable of doing: *up to a task.* **c** plotting; scheming: *what are you up to?* **d** as far as; as much as: *up to my neck in work.* **e** till; until: *worked up to the deadline.* [< OE *upp(e)*]

up·braid (up brād′), *v.* find fault with; blame; reprove. [OE *upbregdan* < *upp* up + *bregdan* weave, braid]

up·braid·ing (up brād′ing), *n.* a severe reproof; scolding. —*adj.* full of reproach.

up·bring·ing (up′bring′ing), *n.* care and training given to a child while growing up.

up·coun·try (up′kun′tri), —*n.* the interior of a country. —*adv.* toward or in the interior of a country. —*adj.* remote from the coast or border; interior.

up·date (up′dāt), *v.,* **-dat·ed, -dat·ing.** make current: *update figures.* —*n.* new information, esp. that changes how something is done or what is done: *the weather update caused school closings and workers to hurry home.*

up·end (up end′), *v.* set on end; stand on end. —**up·end′ed,** *adj.*

up·grade (*n.* up′grād′; *adv., adj.* up′grād′), —*n.* **1** an upward slope or incline. **2** a change from one class to a better class ticket: *an upgrade from business class to first class.* **3** improvement in position, responsibility, pay, etc. —*adv., adj.* uphill. —*v.* move someone or something to a higher, or better status.

up·heav·al (up hēv′əl), *n.* a heaving up; being heaved up.

up·heave (up hēv′), *v.,* **-heaved** or **-hove, -heav·ing.** **1** heave up; lift up. **2** rise.

up·hill (up′hil′), *adj.* **1** going or pointing up the slope of a hill; upward. **2** *Fig.* difficult: *an uphill flight.* —*adv.* up the slope of a hill.

up·hold (up hōld′), *v.,* **-held, -hold·ing. 1** keep from falling; support. **2** give moral support to. **3** sustain; approve; confirm: *the higher court upheld the lower court's decision.* —**up·hold′er,** *n.*

up·hol·ster (up hōl′stər), *v.* provide (furniture) with coverings, cushions, springs, stuffing, etc. [ult. < *uphold*] —**up·hol′-stered,** *adj.* —**up·hol′ster·er,** *n.*

up·hol·ster·y (up hōl′stər i; -stri), *n., pl.* **-ster·ies. 1** coverings for furniture. **2** curtains cushions, carpets, and hangings. **3** business of upholstering.

up·keep (up′kēp′), *n.* **1** maintenance. **2** cost of operating and repair.

up·land (up′lənd; -land′), *n.* high land. —*adj.* of high land; living or growing on high land.

up·lift (*v.* up lift′; *n.* up′lift′), *v.* **1** lift up; raise. **2** exalt emotionally or spiritually. —*n.* **1** act of lifting up; elevation. **2** emotional or spiritual exaltation. **3** a forcing upward of the earth's crust: *hills formed by uplift.*

up·link (up′lingk′), *n.* relay transmission of electromagnetic signals by satellite, esp. from one transmission station to another, distant receiver: *uplinks provide television images from around the world.*

up·most (up′mōst), *adj.* uppermost.

up·on (ə pon′; ə pôn′), *prep.* on. [ME, < *up + on*]

up·per (up′ər), *adj.* **1** higher: *the upper lip, the upper rows.* **2** higher in rank, office, etc.; superior. **3** more recent. —*n.* **1** part of a shoe or boot above the sole. **2** *Informal.* antidepressant drug; stimulant.

on one's uppers, a with the soles of one's shoes worn out. **b** *Fig.* very shabby or poor.

upper case, capital letters. —**up′per-case′,** *adj.*

up·per-class (up′ər klas′; -kläs′), *adj.* **1** of or pertaining to a superior class. **2** in universities, schools, etc., of or pertaining to the junior and senior classes.

up·per·class·man (up′ər klas′mən; -kläs′-), *n., pl.* **-men.** junior or senior.

up·per·cut (up′ər kut′), *n., v.,* **-cut, -cut·ting.** —*n.* a swinging blow directed upwards. —*v.* strike with an uppercut.

upper hand, the, control; advantage.

Upper House, Often **upper house.** the higher and more exclusive house, usually having fewer members, in a legislature, deliberative body, etc.

up·per·most (up′ər mōst), *adj.* Also, **up′-most. 1** highest; topmost. **2** having the most force or influence; most prominent. —*adv.* **1** in the highest place. **2** first.

up·pish (up′ish), *adj.* somewhat arrogant, self-assertive, or conceited. —**up′pish·ly,** *adv.* —**up′pish·ness,** *n.*

up·pi·ty (up′ə ti), *adj.* =uppish.

up·right (up′rīt′; up rīt′), *adj.* **1** standing up straight; erect. **2** good; honest; righteous. —*adv.* straight up; in a vertical position. —*n.* **1** a vertical part of piece. **2** something upright, as a goal post or an upright piano. —**up′right′ly,** *adv.* —**up′right′ness,** *n.*

up·ris·ing (up′rīz′ing; up rīz′-), *n.* **1** revolt. **2** an upward slope; ascent.

up·roar (up′rôr′; -rōr′), *n.* **1** a noisy or violent disturbance. **2** a loud or confused noise. [< Du. *oproer* insurrection, tumult; infl. by assoc. with *roar*]

up·roar·i·ous (up rôr′i əs; -rōr′-), *adj.* **1** noisy and disorderly: *an uproarious crowd.* **2** loud and confused: *uproarious laughter.* —**up·roar′i·ous·ly,** *adv.* —**up·roar′i·ous·ness,** *n.*

up·root (up rüt′; -rüt′), *v.* **1** tear up by the roots. **2** *Fig.* remove completely.

up·set (*v., adj.* up set′; *n.* up′set′), *v.,* **-set, -set·ting,** *n., adj.* —*v.* **1** tip over; overturn: *upset a boat.* **2** disturb greatly; disorder: *rain upset our plans for a picnic, the shock upset her nerves.* **3** overthrow; defeat: *upset a government.* —*n.* **1** a tipping over; overturn. **2** a great disturbance; disorder. **3** an overthrowing; defeat. —*adj.* **1** tipped over; overturned. **2** greatly disturbed; disordered. —**up·set′ter,** *n.*

up·shot (up′shot′), *n.* conclusion; climax; result.

up·side (up′sīd′), *n.* the upper side.

upside down, 1 having what should be on top at the bottom. **2** in complete disorder: *the room was upside down.* —**up′side′-down′,** *adj.*

up·si·lon (ūp′sə lon), *n.* the 20th letter (Υ υ) of the Greek alphabet.

up·stage (up′stāj′), *adv.* toward or at the back of the stage. —*adj.* **1** toward or at the back of the stage. —*adj.* **1** toward or at the back of the stage. **2** haughty; aloof; supercilious.

up·stairs (up′stãrz′), *adv.* **1** up the stairs. **2** on an upper floor. —*adj.* on an upper floor. —*n.* the upper story.

up·stand·ing (up stan′ding), *adj.* **1** standing up; erect. **2** honorable.

up·start (up′stärt′), *n.* **1** person who has suddenly risen from a humble position to wealth, power, or importance. **2** an unpleasant, conceited, and self-assertive person.

up·state (up′stāt′), *adj.* of the more inland or northern part of a state. —*n.* the more inland or northern part of a state: *upstate New York.* —**up′stat′er,** *n.*

up·stream (up′strem′), *adv., adj.* against the current of a stream; up a stream.

up·swing (up′swing′), *n.* **1** an upward swing; movement upward. **2** marked improvement.

up·take (up′tāk′), *n.* **1** shaft or flue that carries upward foul air or fumes. **2** absorption, as of a mineral in the body.

up-to-date (up′tə dāt′), *adj.* **1** extending to the present time. **2** keeping up with the times in style, ideas, etc.; modern. —**up′-to-date′ness,** *n.*

up·town (up′toun′), *adv.* to or in the upper part of a town. —*adj.* **1** in the upper part of a town. **2** of or pertaining to the fashionable or residential area of a city, town, etc. —*n.* the fashionable or residential area of a city, town, etc.

up·turn (*v.* up tėrn′; *n.* up′tėrn′), *v.* turn up. —*n.* an upward turn. —**up·turned′,** *adj.*

up·ward (up′wərd), *adv.* Also, **up′wards. 1** toward a higher place. **2** toward a higher or greater rank, amount, age, etc. **3** above; more. —*adj.* directed or moving toward a higher place; in a higher position.

upward or **upwards of,** more than. —**up′ward·ly,** *adv.*

U·ral-Al·ta·ic (yùr′əl al tā′ik), *adj.* of or having to do with a large group of languages spoken in E Europe and N Asia.

u·ra·ni·um (yù rā′ni əm), *n.* a heavy, white, radioactive metallic elements, U or Ur. [< NL, < *Uranus*, the planet]

U·ra·nus (yù′rā nəs; yùr′ə-), *n.* one of the larger planets, seventh in order from the sun.

ur·ban (ėr′bən), *adj.* 1 of or having to do with cities or towns. 2 living in cities. 3 characteristic of cities. [< L *urbanus* < *urbs* city]

ur·bane (ėr bān′), *adj.* 1 courteous; refined; elegant. 2 smoothly polite. [< L *urbanus*, orig., URBAN] —**ur·bane′ly,** *adv.* —**ur·bane′ness,** *n.*

ur·ban·i·ty (ėr ban′ə ti), *n., pl.* -ties. 1 courtesy; refinement; elegance. 2 smooth politeness.

ur·ban·ize (ėr′bən īz), *v.,* -ized, -iz·ing. render urban: *urbanize a district or its people.* —**ur′ban·i·za′tion,** *n.*

ur·chin (ėr′chən), *n.* 1 a mischievous child. 2 a poor, ragged child. [< OF *irechon* < L *ericius* < *er* hedgehog]

-ure, *suffix.* 1 act or fact of ___ing, as in *failure.* 2 state of being ___ed, as in *pleasure.* 3 result of ___ing, as in *enclosure.* 4 thing that ___s, as in *legislature.* 5 thing that is ___ed, as in *disclosure.* 6 other special meanings, as in *procedure, sculpture, denture.* [< F *-ure* < L *-ura*]

u·re·a (yù rē′ə; yùr′i ə), *n.* a soluble crystalline solid, $CO(NH_2)_2$, present in the urine of mammals. [< NL, ult. < Gk. *ouron* urine] —**u·re′al,** *adj.*

u·re·mi·a (yù rē′mi ə), *n.* a poisoned condition resulting from the accumulation in the blood of waste products that should normally be eliminated in the urine. [< NL, < Gk. *ouron* urine + *haima* blood] —**u·re′mic,** *adj.*

u·re·ter (yù rē′tər; yùr′ə tər), *n.* duct that carries urine from a kidney to the bladder. [< NL < Gk. *oureter*, ult. < *ouron* urine]

u·re·thra (yù rē′thrə), *n., pl.* -thrae (-thrē), -thras. duct by which urine is discharged from the bladder. [< LL < Gk. *ourethra*, ult. < *ouron* urine] —**u·re′thral,** *adj.*

urge (ėrj), *v.,* urged, urg·ing, *n.* —*v.* 1 drive with force, threats, etc.; push forward with effort: *he urged his horse along.* 2 try to persuade with arguments; ask earnestly: *they urged him to stay.* 3 plead or argue earnestly for; recommend strongly: *motorists urged better roads.* 4 press upon the attention; refer to often and with emphasis: *urge a claim.* —*n.* 1 a driving force or impulse. 2 act of urging. [< L *urgere*]

ur·gen·cy (ėr′jən si), *n., pl.* -cies. 1 urgent character; need for immediate action or attention: *a matter of great urgency.* 2 insistence.

ur·gent (ėr′jənt), *adj.* 1 demanding immediate action or attention; pressing; important. 2 insistent. —**ur′gent·ly,** *adv.*

u·ric (yùr′ik), *adj.* of or pertaining to urine or urea.

uric acid, a solid white substance, $C_5H_4N_4O_3$, only slightly soluble in water, that is formed in the body as a waste product from proteins.

u·ri·nal (yùr′ə nəl), *n.* 1 container for urine. 2 place for urinating.

u·ri·nal·y·sis (yùr′ə nal′ə sis), *n., pl.* -ses (-sēz). analysis of a sample of urine.

u·ri·nar·y (yùr′ə ner′i), *adj.* 1 of or having to do with urine. 2 of or having to do with the organs that secrete and discharge urine.

u·ri·nate (yùr′ə nāt), *v.,* -nat·ed, -nat·ing. discharge urine from the body. —**u′ri·na′tion,** *n.* —**u′ri·na′tive,** *adj.*

u·rine (yùr′ən), *n.* the fluid that is secreted by the kidneys, passes into the bladder, and is then discharged from the body. [< L *urina*]

URL, universal or uniform resource locator (for searching Internet addresses).

urn (ėrn), *n.* 1 covered vase with a foot or pedestal, esp. one used to hold the ashes of the dead. 2 place of burial; grave; tomb. 3 a coffee pot or teapot with a faucet, used for making or serving coffee or tea at the table. [< L *urna*]

u·ro·gen·i·tal (yùr′ō jen′ə təl), *adj.* noting or pertaining to the urinary and genital organs. [< *uro-* (< Gk. *ouron* urine) + *genital*]

u·rol·o·gy (yù rol′ə ji), *n.* branch of medicine that deals with diseases and conditions of the urogenital and urinary tracts. —**u·rol′o·gist,** *n.* —**u′ro·log′i·cal,** *adj.*

u·ros·co·py (yù ros′kə pi), *n.* examination of the urine as a means of diagnosis, etc.

Ur·sa Ma·jor (ėr′sə mā′jər), *gen.* **Ur·sae Ma·jo·ris** (ėr′sē mə jô′ris; -jō′-), the northern constellation that includes the stars of the Big Dipper; the Great Bear. [< L]

Ur·sa Mi·nor (ėr′sə mī′nər), *gen.* **Ur·sae Mi·no·ris** (ėr′sē mi nô′ris; -nō′-), the northern constellation that includes the stars of the Little Dipper; the Little Bear. [< L]

ur·sine (ėr′sīn; -sin), *adj.* of or pertaining to bears; bearlike. [< L, < *ursus* bear]

U·ru·guay (yùr′ə gwā; -gwī), *n.* country in the SE part of South America. —**U′ru·guay′an,** *adj., n.*

us (us; *unstressed* əs), *pron.* the objective case of we: *Mother went with us.* [OE *ūs*]

U.S. or **US,** the United States.

U.S.A. or **USA,** 1 the United States of America. 2 the United States Army.

us·a·ble (ūz′ə bəl), *adj.* that can be used; fit for use. Also, **useable.** —**us′a·bil′i·ty, us′a·ble·ness,** *n.*

USAF, U.S.A.F., United States Air Force.

us·age (ūs′ij; ūz′-), *n.* 1 way or manner of using; treatment: *the car has had rough usage.* 2 a long-continued practice; customary use; habit; custom: *travelers*

should learn many of the usages of the countries they visit. 3 the customary way of using words: *usage determines what is good English.*

USCG, U.S.C.G., United States Coast Guard.

use (*v.* ūz; *n.* ūs), *v.,* used, us·ing, *n.* —*v.* 1 put into action or service: *use a knife, may I use your cellphone?* 2 consume or expend: *we have used most of the amount.* —*n.* 1 action or service: *the use of tools, methods long out of use, a thing of no practical use.* 2 purpose: *find a new use for something.* 3 way of treating; treatment: *poor use of material.* 4 help, profit, or resulting good: *what's the use of talking?*

have no use for, a not need or want: *I have no further use for it.* **b** dislike.

in use, being used.

used to, a accustomed to: *used to hardship.* **b** was or were accustomed to: *he used to come every day.*

use up, consume or expend entirely. [< OF *user* < VL *usare*, intensive of L *uti* use] —**us′er,** *n.*

use·a·ble (ūz′ə bəl), *adj.* usable. —**use′a·bil′i·ty, use′a·ble·ness,** *n.*

used (ūzd; ūst), *adj.* 1 not new; secondhand: *a used car.* 2 not clean or fresh: *stale, used air.* 3 in use: *the space is used.*

use·ful (ūs′fəl), *adj.* of use; giving service; helpful. —**use′ful·ly,** *adv.* —**use′ful·ness,** *n.*

use·less (ūs′lis), *adj.* of no use; worthless. —**use′less·ly,** *adv.* —**use′less·ness,** *n.*

us·er-friend·ly (ū′zər frend′li), *adj.* easy to use or made to be easy to use: *a surprisingly user-friendly computer.*

U-shaped (ū′shāpt′), *adj.* having the shape of the letter U.

ush·er (ush′ər), *n.* person who shows people to their seats in a church, theater, etc. —*v.* conduct; escort; show: *he ushered the visitors to the door.* [< AF < VL *ustiarius* doorkeeper < *ustium,* var. of L *ostium* door]

USMC, U.S.M.C., United States Marine Corps.

USN, U.S.N., United States Navy.

USNG, U.S.N.G., United States National Guard.

USPS, United States Postal Service.

U.S.S., Also, **USS.** United States Ship, Steamer, or Steamship.

u·su·al (ū′zhù əl), *adj.* in common use; ordinary; customary.

as usual, in the usual manner. [< LL *usualis*, ult. < *uti* use] —**u′su·al·ly,** *adv.* —**u′su·al·ness,** *n.*

u·su·rer (ū′zhə rər), *n.* person who lends money at an extremely high or unlawful rate of interest. [< OF < LL *usurarius* < *usuria* USURY]

u·su·ri·ous (ū zhùr′i əs), *adj.* 1 taking extremely high or unlawful interest for the use of money. 2 of or having to do with usury. —**u·su′ri·ous·ly,** *adv.* —**u·su′ri·ous·ness,** *n.*

u·surp (ū zėrp′; ū sėrp′), *v.* seize and hold (power, position, authority, etc.) by force or without right. [< L *usurpare,* ult. < *usus* use + *rapere* seize] —**u·surp′er,** *n.*

u·sur·pa·tion (ū′zər pā′shən; ū′sər–), *n.* a usurping; the seizing and holding of the place or power of another by force or without right.

u·su·ry (ū′zhə ri), *n., pl.* **-ries. 1** the lending of money at an extremely high or unlawful rate of interest. **2** an extremely high or unlawful interest. [< Med.L *usuria,* ult. < *uti* use]

UT, (*zip code*) Utah.

Ut., Utah.

U·tah (ū′tô; ū′tä), *n.* a W state of the United States. —**U′tah·an,** *adj., n.*

Ute (ūt), *n., pl.* **Ute, Utes. 1** member of a group of American Indian tribes now living in New Mexico, Colorado, and Utah. **2** their Shoshonean language. [< Shoshonean (Ute), meaning person, people]

u·ten·sil (ū ten′səl), *n.* **1** container or implement used for practical purposes. Pots, pans, kettles, and mops are kitchen utensils. **2** instrument or tool used for some special purpose. Pens and pencils are writing utensils. [< Med.L, < L *utensilis* useful < *uti* use]

u·ter·ine (ū′tər in; -īn), *adj.* of or pertaining to the uterus.

u·ter·us (ū′tər əs), *n., pl.* **-ter·i** (-tər ī). the part of the body in mammals that holds and nourishes the young till birth; womb. [< L]

u·til·i·tar·i·an (ū til′ə tār′i ən), *adj.* **1** having to do with utility. **2** aiming at usefulness rather than beauty, style, etc. —*n.* adherent of utilitarianism.

u·til·i·tar·i·an·ism (ū til′ə tār′i ən iz′əm), *n.* **1** the doctrine or belief that the greatest good of the greatest number should be the purpose of human conduct. **2** the doctrine or belief that actions are good if they are useful.

u·til·i·ty (ū til′ə ti), *n., pl.* **-ties. 1** usefulness; power to satisfy people's needs. **2** company that performs a public service. Railroads, bus lines, gas and electric companies are utilities. [< L *utilitas,* ult. < *uti* use]

u·ti·lize (ū′tə līz), *v.,* **-lized, -liz·ing.** make use of; put to some practical use. —**u′ti·li·za′tion,** *n.* —**u′ti·liz′er,** *n.*

ut·most (ut′mōst), *adj.* **1** greatest possible; extreme: *the utmost effort.* **2** most distant; farthest: *the utmost part of the country.* —*n.* the most that is possible; extreme limit. [OE *ūtemest* < *ūte* outside + *-mest* –MOST]

u·to·pi·a (ū tō′pi ə), *n.* **1 Utopia.** an ideal commonwealth described in *Utopia* by Sir Thomas More. **2** an ideal place or state with perfect laws. **3** a visionary, impractical system of political or social perfection. [< NL, < Gk. *ou* not + *topos* place]

u·to·pi·an (ū tō′pi ən), *adj.* **1 Utopian.** of, having to do with, or resembling Utopia. **2** visionary; impractical. —*n.* Also, **Utopian.** an ardent but impractical reformer; idealist. —**u·to′pi·an·ism,** *n.*

ut·ter[1] (ut′ər), *adj.* complete; total; absolute. [OE *ūtera* outer] —**ut′ter·ly,** *adv.*

ut·ter[2] (ut′ər), *v.* **1** pronounce; speak: *the last words he uttered.* **2** make known; express: *utter one's thoughts.* **3** give; give out: *he uttered a cry of pain.* [ult. < OE *ūt* out] —**ut′ter·a·ble,** *adj.* —**ut′ter·er,** *n.*

ut·ter·ance (ut′ər əns). *n.* **1** an uttering; expression in words or sounds: *the child gave utterance to his grief.* **2** way of speaking. **3** something uttered; a spoken word or words.

ut·ter·most (ut′ər mōst), *adj., n.* =utmost.

u·vu·la (ū′vyə lə), *n., pl.* **-las, -lae** (-lē). the small piece of flesh hanging down from the soft palate in the back of the mouth. [< LL, dim. of L *uva,* orig., grape)

u·vu·lar (ū′vyə lər), *adj.* of or having to do with the uvula.

Uz·bek (uz′bek), *n.* **1** member of a people of Turkestan. **2** their Turkic language.

Uz·bek·i·stan (uzbek′ə stän), *n.* country in W Asia, N of Afghanistan.

V, v (vē), *n., pl.* **V's; v's.**
1 the 22nd letter of the
alphabet. **2** anything
shaped like a V. **3** the
Roman numeral for 5.

V, 1 vanadium. **2** Victory. **3** volt.

v., 1 see. [< L *vide*] **2** verb. **3** versus. **4** volt;
voltage; volts. **5** volume. **6** von.

VA, 1 Also, **V.A.,** Veterans' Administration. **2** (*zip code*) Virginia.

Va., Virginia.

va·can·cy (vā′kən si), *n., pl.* **-cies. 1** state
of being vacant; emptiness. **2** an unoccupied position: *a vacancy in a business.*
3 state of being or becoming unoccupied. **4** a room, space, or apartment for
rent; empty space.

va·cant (vā′kənt), *adj.* **1** not occupied:
a vacant house. **2** not filled; empty:
vacant space. **3** without thought or intelligence: *a vacant smile.* **4** not being used:
vacant time. [< L *vacans* being empty]
—va′cant·ly, *adv.*

va·cate (vā′kāt), *v.,* **-cat·ed, -cat·ing. 1** go
away from and leave empty or unoccupied; make vacant. **2** leave. **3** make void;
annul; cancel. [< L *vacatus* emptied]

va·ca·tion (vā kā′shən), *n.* time of rest
and freedom from work. *—v.* take a
vacation. **—va·ca′tion·er,** *n.*

vac·ci·nate (vak′sə nāt), *v.,* **-nat·ed, -nat·ing.** inoculate with vaccine as a protection against disease. **—vac′ci·na′tion,** *n.*
—vac′ci·na′tor, *n.*

vac·cine (vak′sēn; -sin), *n.* **1** the virus
causing cowpox, used for the protection of people against smallpox. **2** any
preparation of disease germs, or the like,
that is used for preventive inoculation.
—adj. of or having to do with a vaccine
or vaccination. [< L *vaccinus* pertaining
to cows < *vacca* cow]

vac·il·late (vas′ə lāt), *v.,* **-lat·ed, -lat·ing.**
1 move first one way and then another;
waver. **2** waver in mind or opinion.
[< L, pp. of *vacillare*] **—vac′il·lat′ing,**
adj. **—vac′il·lat′ing·ly,** *adv.* **—vac′il·la′·
tion,** *n.*

va·cu·i·ty (va kū′ə ti), *n., pl.* **-ties. 1** emptiness. **2** an empty space; vacuum. **3** lack
of thought or intelligence. **4** something
foolish or stupid.

vac·u·ole (vak′yū ōl), *n.* a tiny cavity in
a living cell, containing fluid. [< F, < L
vacuus empty]

vac·u·ous (vak′yū əs), *adj.* **1** showing no
thought or intelligence; foolish; stupid. **2**
empty. [< L *vacuus*] **—vac′u·ous·ly,** *adv.*
—vac′u·ous·ness, *n.*

vac·u·um (vak′yùm; -yù əm), *n., pl.* **vac·
u·ums, vac·u·a** (vak′yū ə), *v. —n.* **1** an
empty space without even air in it. **2**
space from which almost all air, gas, etc.,
has been removed. **3** an empty space;
void. **4** a vacuum cleaner. *—v.* clean
with a vacuum cleaner. [< L, neut. adj.,
empty]

vacuum cleaner, apparatus for cleaning
carpets, curtains, floors, etc., by suction.

vacuum pump, pump or device by which
a partial vacuum can be produced.

vag·a·bond (vag′ə bond), *n.* **1** an idle
wanderer; tramp. **2** a good-for-nothing person; rascal. *—adj.* **1** wandering.
2 good-for-nothing; worthless. **3** moving hither and thither; drifting. [< OF
< L *vagabundus,* ult. < *vagus* rambling]
—vag′a·bond·ism, *n.*

va·gar·y (və gãr′i; vā′gə ri), *n., pl.* **-gar·
ies. 1** an odd fancy; extravagant notion:
the vagaries of a dream. **2** odd action;
caprice; freak: *the vagaries of fashion.*
[prob. < L *vagari* wander < *vagus* roving]
—va·gar′i·ous, *adj.*

va·gi·na (və jī′nə), *n., pl.* **-nas, -nae** (-nē).
1 in female mammals, passage from the
uterus to the vulva or external opening.
2 sheath; sheathlike part. [< L, orig.,
sheath] **—vag′i·nal,** *adj.*

va·gran·cy (vā′grən si), *n., pl.* **-cies. 1**
a wandering idly from place to place
without proper means, or ability to earn
a living. **2** a wandering. **3** a vagrant act
or idea.

va·grant (vā′grənt), *n.* an idle wanderer;
tramp. *—adj.* **1** moving in no definite
direction or course; wandering. **2** wandering without proper means of earning
a living. **3** of or pertaining to a vagrant.
[? alter. of AF *wakerant,* infl. by L *vagari*
wander] **—va′grant·ly. —va′grant·
ness,** *n.*

vague (vāg), *adj.,* **va·guer, va·guest. 1** not
definite: *vague promises.* **2** not clear; not
distinct: *vague forms.* [< OF < L *vagus*
wandering] **—vague′ly,** *adv.*

vain (vān), *adj.* **1** having too much pride
in one's looks, ability, etc. **2** of no use;
without effect or success; producing no
good result: *vain attempts.* **3** of no value
or importance; worthless; empty: *a vain
boast.*

in vain, without effect; unsuccessfully.
[< OF < L *vanus*] **—vain′ly,** *adv.*

vain·glo·ri·ous (vān′glô′ri əs; -glō′-),
adj. excessively proud or boastful;
extremely vain. **—vain′glo′ri·ous·ly,**
adv. **—vain′glo′ri·ous·ness,** *n.*

vain·glo·ry (vān′glô′ri; -glō′-), *n.* **1** an
extreme pride in oneself; boastful vanity.
2 worthless pomp or show.

val·ance (val′əns), *n.* a drapery for the top
of a window. [? < derivative of OF *valer*
to lower] **—val′anced,** *adj.*

vale (vāl), *n.* valley. [< OF < L *vallis*]

val·e·dic·to·ri·an (val′ə dik tô′ri ən; -tō′-),
n. the student who gives the farewell
address at the graduating exercises, often
the student ranked highest in the class.

val·e·dic·to·ry (val′ə dik′tə ri; -dik′tri), *n.,
pl.* **-ries,** *adj.* *—n.* a farewell address, esp.
at the graduating exercises of a school
or college. *—adj.* bidding farewell. [< L
valedictum, pp of *valedicere* bid farewell
(< *vale* be well! + *dīcere* say) + E *-ory*]

va·lence (vā′ləns), **va·len·cy** (-lən si), *n.,
pl.* **-len·ces; -cies.** combining capacity of an atom measured by a unit of
hydrogen. The valence of hydrogen or

chlorine is 1, of oxygen is 2, of aluminum is 3. [< L *valentia* strength < *valere*
be strong]

val·en·tine (val′ən tīn), *n.* **1** a greeting
card or small gift sent on Valentine's
Day, February 14. **2** a sweetheart chosen
on this day.

va·le·ri·an (və lir′i ən), *n.* **1** a strong-
smelling drug used to quiet the nerves. **2**
group of plants grown for their medicinal root. [< OF *valeriane* or Med.L *vale-
riana* < L *Valerius,* Roman gens name]

val·et (val′it; val′ā), *n., v.,* **-et·ed, -et·ing.**
—n. **1** servant who takes care of a man's
clothes, helps him dress, etc. **2** a similar
servant in a hotel who cleans or presses
clothes. *—v.* serve as a valet. [< F, var. of
OF *vaslet* VARLET] **—val′et·less,** *adj.*

val·e·tu·di·nar·i·an (val′ə tü′də nãr′i ən;
-tū′-), *n.* **1** an invalid. **2** person who
thinks he or she is ill when they are
not. *—adj.* **1** sickly. **2** thinking too much
about health. [< L *valetudinarius* sickly
< *valetudo* (good or bad) health < *valere*
be strong]

val·iant (val′yənt), *adj.* brave; courageous.
[< OF *vaillant,* ppr. of *valoir* be strong
< L *valere*] **—val′iant·ly,** *adv.* **—val′iant·
ness,** *n.*

val·id (val′id), *adj.* **1** supported by facts or
authority; sound; true: *a valid argument.*
2 having legal force; legally binding. [< L
validus strong] **—val′id·ly,** *adv.* **—val′id·
ness,** *n.*

val·i·date (val′ə dāt), *v.,* **-dat·ed, -dat·
ing. 1** make or declare legally binding;
give legal force to. **2** support by facts or
authority; confirm. **—val′i·da′tion,** *n.*

va·lid·i·ty (və lid′ə ti), *n., pl.* **-ties. 1** truth;
soundness: *the validity of an argument.* **2**
legal soundness or force. **3** effectiveness.

val·ley (val′i), *n., pl.* **-leys. 1** a low land
between hills or mountains. **2** a wide
region drained by a great river system:
the Mississippi valley. **3** any hollow or
structure like a valley. [< OF *valee < val*
vale < L *vallis*]

val·or (val′ər), *n.* bravery; courage. [< LL,
< L *valere* be strong] **—val′or·ous,** *adj.*

val·u·a·ble (val′yù ə bəl), *adj.* **1** having
value; being worth something. **2** having
great value. **3** that can have its value
measured. *—n.* Usually, **valuables.** an
article of value. **—val′u·a·ble·ness,** *n.*
—val′u·a·bly, *adv.*

val·u·a·tion (val′yù ā′shən), *n.* **1** value
estimated or determined: *the jeweler's
valuation of the necklace was $10,000.*
2 an estimating or determining of the
value of something. **—val′u·a′tion·al,**
adj.

val·ue (val′ū), *n., v.,* **-ued, -u·ing.** *—n.*
1 worth; excellence; usefulness; importance: *the value of education.* **2** the real
worth; proper price: *he bought the house
for less than its value.* **3** power to buy:
the value of the dollar has varied greatly.
4 estimated worth: *he placed a value
on his furniture.* **5** an excellent buy;
bargain. **6** meaning; effect; force: *the*

value of a symbol. **7** number or amount represented by a symbol: *the value of XIV is fourteen.* —*v.* **1** rate at a certain value or price; estimate the value of. **2** think highly of; regard highly: *value one's judgment.*

values, the established ideals of life as accepted by a group or culture. [< OF, < pp. of *valoir* be worth < L *valere*] —**val′u·er,** *n.*

val·ued (val′ūd), *adj.* **1** having its value estimated or determined. **2** regarded highly. **3** having the value specified.

value judgment, subjective judgment of someone or something; judgment based on personal values.

val·ue·less (val′yù lis), *adj.* without value; worthless.

valve (valv), *n., v.,* **valved, valv·ing.** —*n.* **1** a movable part that controls the flow of a liquid, gas, etc., through a pipe by opening and closing the passage. A faucet is one kind of valve. **2** a membrane that works similarly. The valves of the heart control the flow of blood. **3** one of the parts of hinged shells like those of oysters and clams. **4** device in wind instruments for changing the pitch of the tone by changing the direction and length of the column of air. Cornets and French horns have valves. —*v.* control the flow of (a liquid, gas, etc.) by a valve. [< L *valva* one of a pair of folding doors] —**valve′less,** *adj.* —**valve′like′,** *adj.*

val·vu·lar (val′vyə lər), *adj.* **1** having to do with valves, esp. with the valves of the heart. **2** having the form of a valve. **3** furnished with valves; working by valves.

va·moose (va müs′), **va·mose** (–mōs′), *v.,* **–moosed, –moos·ing; –mosed, –mos·ing.** *Informal.* go away quickly. [< Sp. *vamos* let us go]

vamp[1] (vamp), *n.* the upper front part of a shoe or boot. [< OF *avanpie* < *avant* before (< L *ab* from + *ante* before) + *pie* foot < L *pes*]

vamp[2] (vamp), *n.* an unscrupulous flirt. —*v.* flirt with. [< *vampire*] —**vamp′er,** *n.*

vam·pire (vam′pīr), *n.* **1** a corpse supposed to come to life at night and suck the blood of people while they sleep. **2** person who preys ruthlessly on others. **3** woman who flirts with men to get money or to please her vanity. **4** Also, **vampire bat.** any of various South and Central American bats, including a species which actually sucks the blood of animals and humans. [< F < Hung. *vampir,* ? ult. < Turk. *uber* witch]

van[1] (van), *n.* the front part of an army, fleet, or other advancing group. [< *vanguard*]

van[2] (van), *n.* a covered truck or wagon for moving furniture, etc. [< *caravan*]

va·na·di·um (və nā′di əm), *n.* a rare metallic element, V, used in making **vanadium steel,** a tough and durable steel.

Van Bu·ren (van byùr′ən), **Martin,** 1782–1862, the eighth president of the United States, 1837–41.

van·dal (van′dəl), *n.* **1** person who willfully or ignorantly destroys or damages beautiful or valuable things. —*adj.* destructive. —**van′dal·ism,** *n.* —**van′dal·ize,** *v.*

van·dyke (van dīk′), *n.* a short, pointed beard.

vane (vān), *n.* **1** a movable device that shows which way the wind is blowing. **2** blade of a windmill, a ship's propeller, etc. **3** the flat, soft part of a feather. [OE *fana* banner] —**vaned,** *adj.* —**vane′less,** *adj.*

van·guard (van′gärd′), *n.* **1** soldiers marching ahead of the main part of an army to clear the way and guard against surprise. **2** *Fig.* the foremost or leading position, as of social reform or politics. **3** *Fig.* leaders of a movement. [< OF *avangarde* < *avant* before (< L *ab* from + *ante* before) + *garde* GUARD]

va·nil·la (və nil′ə), *n.* **1** a flavoring extract used in candy, ice cream, perfume, etc. **2** the tropical plant that yields the beans used in making this flavoring. **3** Also, **vanilla bean.** the long, slender pod itself. [< NL < Sp. *vainilla,* lit., little pod, ult. < L *vagina* sheath]

van·ish (van′ish), *v.* **1** disappear; disappear suddenly. **2** pass away; cease to be. [< OF *evaniss–,* ult. < L *evanescere* < *ex–* out + *vanus* empty] —**van′ish·er,** *n.* —**van′ish·ing·ly,** *adv.*

van·i·ty (van′ə ti), *n., pl.* **–ties. 1** too much pride in one's looks, ability, etc.: *girlish vanity.* **2** lack of real value; worthlessness: *the vanity of wealth.* **3** a useless or worthless thing. **4** worthless pleasure or display. **5** a dressing table and mirror. [< OF < L, < *vanus* empty]

van·quish (vang′kwish; van′–), *v.* conquer; defeat; overcome. [< OF *vencus,* pp. of *veintre* or < OF *vainquiss–,* both < L *vincere* conquer] —**van′quish·a·ble,** *adj.* —**van′quish·er,** *n.*

van·tage (van′tij; vän′–), *n.* a better position or condition; advantage. [ult. < *advantage*]

vap·id (vap′id), *adj.* without much life or flavor; tasteless; dull. [< L *vapidus*] —**va·pid′i·ty, vap′id·ness,** *n.* —**vap′id·ly,** *adv.*

va·por (vā′pər), *n.* **1** steam from boiling water; moisture in the air that can be seen; fog; mist. **2** a gas formed from a substance that is usually a liquid or a solid. **3** *Fig.* something without substance; empty fancy. —*v.* **1** pass off as vapor. **2** sent out in vapor. **3** boast; swagger; brag. [< L] —**va′por·ing·ly,** *adv.* —**va′por·ish,** *adj.* —**va′por·less,** *adj.*

va·por·ize (vā′pər īz), *v.,* **–ized, –iz·ing.** change into vapor. —**va′por·iz′a·ble,** *adj.* —**va′por·i·za′tion,** *n.* —**va′por·iz′er,** *n.*

va·por·ous (vā′pər əs), *adj.* **1** full of vapor; misty. **2** like vapor. **3** soon passing; worthless. —**va′por·ous·ly,** *adv.* —**va′por·ous·ness,** *n.*

vapor trail, visible stream of moisture left by the engines of a jet plane flying at high altitude; contrail.

va·que·ro (vä kär′ō), *n., pl.* **–ros.** *SW* cowboy; herdsman; cattle driver. [< Sp., ult. < L *vacca* cow]

var., **1** variant. **2** variety. **3** various.

var·i·a·ble (vãr′i ə bəl), *adj.* **1** apt to change; changeable; uncertain: *variable winds.* **2** that can be varied: *these curtain rods are of variable length.* **3** deviating from the strict biological type. —*n.* **1** a thing or quantity that varies. **2** in science, a quantity whose varying amounts are related to known facts or possibilities. **3** a shifting wind. —**var′i·a·bil′i·ty, var′i·a·ble·ness,** *n.* —**var′i·a·bly,** *adv.*

var·i·ance (vãr′i əns), *n.* **1** difference; discrepancy; deviation. **2** discord; dissension; quarrel. **3** a varying; change.

var·i·ant (vãr′i ənt), *adj.* **1** varying; different: *"rime" is a variant spelling of "rhyme."* **2** variable; changing. —*n.* **1** a different form. **2** a different pronunciation or spelling of the same word.

var·i·a·tion (vãr′i ā′shən), *n.* **1** a varying in condition, degree, etc.; change. **2** amount of change. **3** a varied or changed form. **4** tune or theme repeated with changes. **5** deviation of an animal or plant from type. —**var′i·a′tion·al,** *adj.*

var·i·col·ored (vãr′i kul′ərd), *adj.* **1** having various colors. **2** divergent; varied.

var·i·cose (var′ə kōs; vãr′–), *adj.* swollen or enlarged: *varicose veins.* [< L *varicosus* < *varix* dilated vein] —**var′i·cos′i·ty, var′i·cose·ness,** *n.*

var·ied (vãr′id), *adj.* **1** of or characterized by different kinds; having variety. **2** changed; altered. —**var′ied·ness,** *n.*

var·i·e·gate (vãr′i ə gāt; –i gāt), *v.,* **–gat·ed, –gat·ing. 1** vary in appearance; mark, spot, or streak with different colors. **2** give variety to. [< L, pp. of *variegare*] —**var′i·e·ga′tion,** *n.* —**var′i·e·ga′tor,** *n.*

var·i·e·gat·ed (vãr′i ə gāt′id; –i gāt′id), *adj.* **1** varied in appearance; marked with different colors, Pansies are usually variegated. **2** having variety.

va·ri·e·ty (və rī′ə ti), *n., pl.* **–ties. 1** lack of sameness; difference; variation. **2** number of different kinds: *the store has a great variety of toys.* **3** kind; sort: *all varieties of fortune.* **4** a different form, phase, etc., of something. **5** a division of a species.

variety show, entertainment with different kinds of acts and many performers.

var·i·form (vãr′ə fôrm), *adj.* having various forms. [< L *varius* various + E –*form*]

va·ri·o·la (və rī′ə lə), *n.* =smallpox. [< Med.L, < L *varius* various, spotted] —**va·ri′o·lar,** *adj.*

var·i·o·rum (vãr′i ô′rəm; –ō′rəm), *n.* edition of a book that has the comments and notes of several editors, critics, etc. [< L (*cum notis*) *variorum* (with notes) of various people]

var·i·ous (vãr′i əs), *adj.* **1** differing from one another; different. **2** several; many. **3** varied; many-sided: *lives made various by learning.* **4** varying; changeable.

[< L *varius*] —**var′i·ous·ly,** *adv.* —**var′i·ous·ness,** *n.*

var·let (vär′lit), *n. Archaic.* 1 rascal. 2 attendant [< OF, var. of *vaslet,* orig., young man < Celtic]

var·mint (vär′mənt), *n. Dial.* 1 vermin. 2 an objectionable animal or person.

var·nish (vär′nish), *n.* 1 a liquid that gives a smooth, glossy appearance to wood, metal, etc., made from resinous substances dissolved in oil or turpentine. 2 the smooth, hard surface made by this liquid when dry. 3 a glossy appearance. 4 *Fig.* a false or deceiving appearance; pretense: *a varnish of amiability.* —*v.* 1 put varnish on. 2 give a false or deceiving appearance to: *varnish the facts.* [< OF *vernisser,* v., < *vernis,* n., ult. < Gk. *Berenice,* ancient city in Libya] —**var′nish·er,** *n.*

var·si·ty (vär′sə ti), *n., pl.* **-ties.** the most important team in a given sport in a university, college, or school. [< (*uni*)*versity*]

var·y (vār′i), *v.,* **var·ied, var·y·ing.** 1 make or become different, as in form, degree, etc.; change: *the weather varies.* 2 repeat (a tune or theme) with changes and ornament. 3 be different; differ: *the stars vary in brightness.* 4 give variety to: *vary one's style of writing.* [< L, < *varius* various] —**var′i·er,** *n.* —**var′y·ing·ly,** *adv.*

vas (vas), *n., pl.* **va·sa** (vā′sə). duct; vessel. [< L, vessel]

vas·cu·lar (vas′kyə lər), *adj.* pertaining to, made of, or provided with vessels that carry blood, sap, etc. [< NL *vascularis,* ult. < L *vas* vessel] —**vas′cu·lar′i·ty,** *n.* —**vas′cu·lar·ly,** *adv.*

vascular bundle, strand of vascular tissue in plants, containing xylem and phloem.

vascular tissue, tissue in a vascular plant, consisting mainly of xylem and phloem.

vas de·fe·rens (vas def′ə renz), *pl.* **va·sa de·fe·ren·ti·a** (vā′sə def′ə ren′shē ə). duct that carries semen from the testicle to the urethra. [< NL < L *vās* vessel + *dēferēns* carrying down]

vase (vās; vāz), *n.* a holder or container used for ornament or for holding flowers. [< F < L *vas* vessel] —**vase′like′,** *adj.*

Vas·e·line (vas′ə lēn), *n. Trademark.* name for various products derived from petroleum, esp. an ointment.

vas·o·mo·tor (vas′ō mō′tər), *adj.* regulating the tension and size of blood vessels, as certain nerves. [< L *vas* vessel + E *motor,* adj.]

vas·sal (vas′əl), *n.* 1 person who held land from a lord or superior, to whom in return he gave help in war or some other service. A great noble could be a vassal of the king and have many other men as his vassals. 2 servant, follower, or slave. —*adj.* like a vassal; like that of a vassal. [< OF < Med.L *vassallus* < LL *vassus* < Celtic] —**vas′sal·less,** *adj.*

vas·sal·age (vas′əl ij), *n.* 1 the condition of being a vassal. 2 the homage or service due from a vassal to his lord or superior. 3 dependence; servitude. 4 land held by a vassal.

vast (vast; väst), *adj.* very great; immense: *a billion dollars is a vast amount of money.* [< L *vastus*] —**vast′ly,** *adv.* —**vast′ness,** *n.*

vat (vat), *n.* a large container for liquids; tank: *a vat of dye.* [OE *fæt*]

Vat·i·can (vat′ə kən), *n.* 1 collection of buildings grouped about the palace of the Pope, next to Saint Peter's Church in Rome. 2 the government, office, or authority of the Pope.

vau·de·ville (vo′də vil; vod′vil), *n.* theatrical entertainment consisting of a variety of acts, including songs, dances, acrobatic feats, short plays, trained animals, etc. [< F, < *Vau de Vire,* valley in Normandy] —**vau′de·vil′lian,** *n.*

vault¹ (vôlt), *n.* 1 an arched roof or ceiling; series of arches. 2 an arched space or passage. 3 something like an arched roof. 4 an underground cellar or storehouse. 5 place for storing valuable things and keeping them safe. Vaults are often made of steel. 6 place for burial. —*v.* 1 make in the form of a vault. 2 cover with a vault. [< OF *vaulte,* ult. < L *volvere* roll] —**vault′ed,** *adj.* —**vault′like′,** *adj.*

vault² (vôlt), *v.* 1 jump or leap over by using a pole or the hands. 2 jump or leap. —*n.* such a jump. [< OF *volter,* ult. < L *volvere* roll] —**vault′er,** *n.*

vault·ing¹ (vôl′ting), *n.* 1 a vaulted structure. 2 vaults collectively.

vault·ing² (vôl′ting), *adj.* 1 that vaults. 2 overly aggressive; exaggerated: *vaulting ambition.*

vaunt (vônt; vänt), *v., n.* boast. [< F < LL *vanitare* < *vanus* vain] —**vaunt′er,** *n.* —**vaunt′ing,** *adj.* —**vaunt′ing·ly,** *adv.*

vb., verb; verbal.

V.C., 1 Vice-Chairman. 2 Vice-Chancellor. 3 Victoria Cross.

VCR, videocassette recording.

VCR player (vē′sē är′), device that plays videocassettes.

veal (vēl), *n.* meat from a calf. [< OF *veel,* ult. < L *vitellus,* dim. of *vitulus* calf]

vec·tor (vek′tər), *n.* 1 quantity involving direction as well as magnitude. 2 line representing both the direction and the magnitude of some force, etc. 3 insect or other organism that transmits disease germs. [< L, carrier, < *vehere* carry] —**vec′to·ri·al,** *adj.*

V-E Day, date of the Allied victory in Europe in World War II.

veer (vir), *v.* change in direction; shift; turn: *the wind veered to the south.* —*n.* a shift; turn. [< F *virer*] —**veer′ing·ly,** *adv.*

Ve·ga (vē′gə), *n.* a bluish-white star of the first magnitude, in the northern skies.

veg·an (ve′gən), *n.* very strict vegetarian. [< *vegetarian*]

veg·e·ta·ble (vej′tə bəl; vej′ə tə-), *n.* 1 plant grown for food, as the cabbage, carrot, bean, etc. 2 the part of such a plant that is eaten. 3 any plant. 4 *Fig.* person who perceives or can respond to very little and seems to be completely unaware of his or her surroundings. —*adj.* 1 of or pertaining to plants; like plants: *the vegetable kingdom.* 2 consisting of or made from vegetables. [< OF, or < LL *vegetabilis* vivifying, refreshing < *vegetus* vigorous]

veg·e·tal (vej′ə təl), *adj.* 1 of or like plants. 2 *Fig.* insensible; unaware. —**veg′e·tal′i·ty,** *n.*

veg·e·tar·i·an (vej′ə tār′i ən), *n.* person who eats vegetables but no meat. —*adj.* 1 devoted to or advocating vegetarianism. 2 eating vegetables but no meat. 3 containing no meat.

veg·e·tar·i·an·ism (vej′ə tār′i ən iz′əm), *n.* practice or principle of eating vegetables but no meat.

veg·e·tate (vej′ə tāt), *v.,* **-tat·ed, -tat·ing.** 1 grow as plants do. 2 *Fig.* live with very little action, thought, or feeling. [< L *vegetatus* enlivened < *vegetus* lively]

veg·e·ta·tion (vej′ə tā′shən), *n.* 1 plant life; growing plants. 2 a vegetating; the growth of plants. 3 *Fig.* existing, like a vegetable. —**veg′e·ta′tion·al,** *adj.*

veg·e·ta·tive (vej′ə tā′tiv), *adj.* 1 growing as plants do. 2 of plants or plant life. 3 helping growth in plants: *vegetative mold.* 4 *Fig.* having very little action, thought, or feeling; vegetating. —**veg′e·ta′tive·ly,** *adv.*

ve·he·ment (vē′ə mənt), *adj.* 1 having or showing strong feeling; caused by strong feeling; eager; passionate. 2 forceful; violent. [< L *vehemens*] —**ve′he·mence, ve′he·men·cy,** *n.* —**ve′he·ment·ly,** *adv.*

ve·hi·cle (vē′ə kəl), *n.* 1 a carriage, cart, wagon, automobile, sled, or any other conveyance used on land. 2 *Fig.* a means of carrying or conveying. Language is the vehicle of thought. 3 in painting, a liquid in which a pigment is applied to a surface. Linseed oil is a vehicle for paint. [< L *vehiculum* < *vehere* carry] —**ve·hic′u·lar,** *adj.*

veil (vāl), *n.* 1 piece of very thin material worn to protect or hide the face, or as an ornament. 2 piece of material worn so as to fall over the head and shoulders, as the headdress of a nun. 3 *Fig.* anything that covers or hides: *a veil of silence.* 4 disguise; pretense. —*v.* 1 cover with a veil. 2 *Fig.* cover; hide.

take the veil, become a nun. [< OF < L *velum* covering. Doublet of VOILE.] —**veiled,** *adj.* —**veil′less,** *adj.* —**veil′like′,** *adj.*

veil·ing (vāl′ing), *n.* 1 a veil. 2 material for veils.

vein (vān), *n.* 1 one of the blood vessels or tubes that carry blood to the heart from all parts of the body. 2 one of the strands or bundles of vascular tissue forming the principal framework of a leaf. 3 rib of an insect's wing. 4 a crack or seam in rock filled with a different mineral: *a* vein of copper. **5** *Fig.* a special character or disposition; state of mind; mood: *a vein of cruelty, in a joking vein.* —*v.* cover with veins; mark with veins. [< OF < L *vena*] —**veined,** *adj.* —**vein′less,** *adj.* —**vein′like′,** *adj.* —**vein′ous,** *adj.*

vein·ing (vān′ing), *n.* arrangement of veins.

ve·lar (vē′lər), *adj.* **1** of or pertaining to a velum. **2** pronounced by the aid of the soft palate. *C* in *coo* has a velar sound, *c* in *cat* does not. —*n.* a velar sound.

vel·cro (vel′krō), *n.* **1** fastener made of two strips of tape, one with minute hooks and the other with loops, that adhere when pressed together, used on clothing, bags, etc. **2 Velcro.** trademark for this type of fastener. [< *velvet* + *crochet*]

veld (velt; felt), *n.* open country in South Africa, having grass or bushes but few trees. [< Du., field]

vel·lum (vel′əm), *n.* **1** the finest kind of parchment, used for writing, binding books, diplomas, etc. **2** paper or cloth imitating such parchment. [< OF *velin* < *veel* calf, VEAL]

ve·loc·i·pede (və los′ə pēd), *n.* **1** a child's tricycle. **2** an early kind of bicycle or tricycle. [< F, < L *velox* swift + *pes* foot]

ve·loc·i·ty (və los′ə ti), *n.,* pl. **–ties. 1** rapidity of motion; swiftness; quickness: *fly with the velocity of a bird.* **2** rate of motion; the change of position of a point per unit of time: *the velocity of light is about 186,000 miles per second.* [< L, < *velox* swift]

ve·lour (və lür′), *n.* a fabric like velvet, made of silk, wool, or cotton, used for clothing, draperies, upholstery, etc. [< F, velvet, earlier *velous* < Pr., ult. < L *villus* shaggy hair]

ve·lum (vē′ləm), *n.,* pl. **–la** (–lə). **1** a veil-like membranous covering or partition. **2** the soft palate. [< L, covering]

ve·lure (və lür′), *n.* a soft material like velvet. [var. of *velour* VELOURS]

vel·vet (vel′vit), *n.* **1** cloth with a thick, soft pile, made of silk, rayon, cotton, etc., or some combination of these. **2** something like velvet. —*adj.* **1** made of velvet. **2** like velvet. [< Med.L *velvetum,* ult. < L *villus* tuft or hair] —**vel′vet·ed,** *adj.* —**vel′vet·y, vel′vet·like′,** *adj.*

vel·vet·een (vel′və tēn′), *n.* velvet made of synthetic fiber, cotton, or silk and cotton.

ve·na ca·va (vē′nə kā′və), pl. **ve·nae ca·vae** (vē′ni kā′vi). either of the two large veins that carry blood from the upper and lower halves of the body to the heart. [< L empty vein]

ve·nal (vē′nəl), *adj.* **1** willing to sell one's services or influence basely; open to bribes; corrupt. **2** influenced or obtained by bribery: *venal conduct.* [< L, *venum* sale] —**ve·nal′i·ty,** *n.* —**ve′nal·ly,** *adv.*

ve·na·tion (vē nā′shən), *n.* **1** arrangement of veins in a leaf or in an insect's wing. **2** these veins. —**ve·na′tion·al,** *adj.*

vend (vend), *v.* sell; peddle. [< L *vendere* < *venum dare* offer for sale]

vend·er, ven·dor (ven′dər), *n.* **1** seller, esp. a peddler. **2 vending machine.** machine from which one obtains candy, stamps, etc., when a coin is dropped in.

ven·det·ta (ven det′ə), *n.* **1** feud in which a murdered person's relatives try to kill the slayer or his or her relatives. **2** any bitter dispute that lasts a long time. [< Ital. < L *vindicta* revenge] —**ven·det′tist,** *n.*

vend·i·ble (ven′də bəl), *adj.* salable.

ve·neer (və nir′), *v.* **1** cover (wood) with a thin layer of finer wood or other material: *veneer a pine desk with mahogany.* **2** *Fig.* cover (anything) with a layer of something else to give an appearance of superior quality. —*n.* **1** a thin layer of wood or other material used in veneering. **2** *Fig.* surface appearance or show. [earlier *fineer* < G *furnir* < F *fournir* FURNISH] —**ve·neer′er,** *n.*

ven·er·a·ble (ven′ər ə bəl), *adj.* worthy of reverence; deserving respect because of age, character, or associations. —**ven′er·a·bil′i·ty, ven′er·a·ble·ness,** *n.* —**ven′er·a·bly,** *adv.*

ven·er·ate (ven′ər āt), *v.,* **-at·ed, -at·ing.** regard with deep respect; revere. [< L *veneratus*]

ven·er·a·tion (ven′ər ā′shən), *n.* deep respect; reverence. —**ven′er·a′tive,** *adj.*

ve·ne·re·al (və nir′i əl), *adj.* **1** of or having to do with sexual intercourse. **2** caused or transmitted by sexual intercourse: *venereal bacteria.* [< L *venereus* < *Venus* Venus]

Ve·ne·tian (və nē′shən), *adj* of Venice or its people. —*n.* native or inhabitant of Venice.

Venetian blind, a window blind made of horizontal wooden, plastic, or metal slats that can be opened or closed and raised or lowered to regulate the light.

Ven·e·zue·la (ven′ə zwē′lə; –zwā′–), *n.* country in the N part of South America. —**Ven′e·zue′lan,** *adj., n.*

venge·ance (ven′jəns), *n.* punishment in return for a wrong; revenge.

with a vengeance, a with great force or violence. **b** extremely. **c** much more than expected. [< OF, ult. < L *vindex* avenger]

venge·ful (venj′fəl), *adj.* feeling or showing a strong desire for vengeance. —**venge′ful·ly,** *adv.* —**venge′ful·ness,** *n.*

ve·ni·al (vē′ni əl; vēn′yəl), *adj.* that can be forgiven; not very wrong; pardonable. [< L, < *venia* forgiveness] —**ve′ni·al′i·ty, ve′ni·al·ness,** *n.* —**ve′ni·al·ly,** *adv.*

ve·ni·re (və nī′rē), *n.* writ by a sheriff summoning a person to serve on a jury. [< L, you may cause (him) to come]

ven·i·son (ven′ə zən; –sən), *n.* the flesh of a deer, used for food; deer meat. [< OF < L *venatio* hunting < *venari* hunt]

ven·om (ven′əm), *n.* **1** the poison of snakes, spiders, etc. **2** *Fig.* spite; malice. [< OF *venin* < L *venenum* poison] —**ven′om·less,** *adj.*

ven·om·ous (ven′əm əs), *adj.* **1** poisonous. Rattlesnakes are venomous. **2** *Fig.* spiteful; malicious: *venomous words.* —**ven′om·ous·ly,** *adv.*

ve·nous (vē′nəs), *adj.* **1** of, in, or having to do with veins. **2** having veins. —**ve′nous·ly,** *adv.* —**ve′nous·ness,** *n.*

vent (vent), *n.* **1** hole; opening, esp. one serving as an outlet. **2** slit in a garment. **3** *Fig.* a way out of something; outlet; expression: *her grief found vent in tears.* —*v.* **1** relieve (oneself) by expressing something freely; give utterance to. **2** make public. **3** make a vent in. [< OF *fente* slit, ult. < L *findere*; infl. by F *vent* wind < L *ventus* and F *évent* < L *ex–* out + *ventus* wind] —**vent′er,** *n.* —**vent′less,** *adj.*

ven·ti·late (ven′tə lāt), *v.,* **-lat·ed, -lat·ing. 1** change the air in: *we ventilate a room by opening windows.* **2** purify by fresh air: *the lungs ventilate the blood.* **3** *Fig.* make known publicly; discuss openly. **4** furnish with a vent or opening for the escape of air, gas, etc. [< L *ventilatus* fanned < *ventus* wind] —**ven′ti·la′tion,** *n.*

ven·ti·la·tor (ven′tə lā′tər), *n.* **1** something that ventilates. **2** any apparatus or means for changing or improving the air. **3** medical device that assists breathing.

ven·tral (ven′trəl), *adj.* **1** of or pertaining to the belly; abdominal. **2** of, pertaining to, or on the surface or part opposite the back. [< LL, < L *venter* belly] —**ven′tral·ly,** *adv.*

ven·tri·cle (ven′trə kəl), *n.* either of the two lower chambers of the heart that receive blood and force it into the arteries. [< L *ventriculus,* dim. of *venter* belly] —**ven·tric′u·lar,** *adj.*

ven·tril·o·quism (ven tril′ə kwiz əm), **ven·tril·o·quy** (–kwi), *n.* art or practice of speaking or uttering sounds with the lips nearly shut so that the voice may seem to come from some other source than the speaker. [< L *ventriloquus* ventriloquist < *venter* belly + *loqui* speak] —**ven·til′o·quist,** *n.*

ven·ture (ven′chər), *n., v.,* **-tured, -tur·ing.** —*n.* **1** a risky or daring undertaking. **2** speculation to make money. **3** thing risked; stake. —*v.* **1** expose to risk or danger: *he ventured his money in the new business.* **2** run a risk; dare: *venture to say what one thinks.* **3** dare to say or make: *venture an objection.* **4** dare to come, go, or proceed: *venture from a hiding place.* [< earlier *aventure* ADVENTURE] —**ven′tur·er,** *n.*

venture capital, capital invested in a new and risky venture in return for a larger than usual share of earnings. —**venture capitalist.**

ven·ture·some (ven′chər səm), *adj.* **1** inclined to take risks; rash; daring. **2** hazardous: *a venturesome project.* —**ven′ture·some·ly,** *adv.*

ven·tur·ous (ven′chər əs), *adj.* **1** rash; daring; adventurous. **2** risky; dangerous. —**ven′tur·ous·ly,** *adv.* —**ven′tur·ous·ness,** *n.*

ven·ue (ven′ū), *n.* **1** the place or neighborhood of a crime or cause of action. **2** the place where the jury is gathered and the case tried. **3** scene or location of a novel, film, etc. [< OF, coming, ult. < L *venire* come]

Ve·nus (vē′nəs), *n.* **1** a very beautiful woman. **2** the most brilliant planet, second in order from the sun.

Ve·nus's-fly·trap (vē′nəs iz flī′trap′), *n.* a plant whose hairy leaves have two lobes at the end that fold together to trap and digest insects.

ve·ra·cious (və rā′shəs), *adj.* **1** truthful. **2** true. [< L *verax* < *verus* true] —**ve·ra′cious·ly,** *adv.* —**ve·ra′cious·ness,** *n.*

ve·rac·i·ty (və ras′ə ti), *n., pl.* **-ties. 1** truthfulness. **2** truth. **3** correctness; accuracy. [< Med.L, < L *verax* VERACIOUS]

ve·ran·da (və ran′də), *n.* a large porch along one or more sides of a house. [< Hind. and other Indian langs. < Pg. *varanda* railing]

verb (vėrb), *n.* word that tells what is or what is done; the part of speech that expresses action or being. *Do, go, come, be, sit, think, know,* and *eat* are verbs. [< L *verbum,* orig., word] —**verb′less,** *adj.*

ver·bal (vėr′bəl), *adj.* **1** in words; of words. **2** expressed in spoken words; oral: *a verbal promise.* **3** word for word; literal: *a verbal translation.* **4** pertaining to or concerned with words only, rather than ideas, etc.: *make verbal changes in a manuscript.* **5 a** pertaining to a verb. Two common verbal endings are *-ed* and *-ing.* **b** derived from a verb: *a verbal noun.* —*n.* a noun, adjective, or other word derived from a verb. [< L, < *verbum* word, verb] —**ver′bal·ly,** *adv.*

ver·bal·ism (vėr′bəl iz əm), *n.* **1** a verbal expression; word, phrase, etc. **2** a stock phrase or formula in words with little meaning. **3** too much attention to mere words. **4** wordiness.

ver·bal·ize (vėr′bəl īz), *v.,* **-ized, -iz·ing. 1** express in words. **2** use too many words; be wordy. **3** change (a noun, etc.) into a verb. —**ver′bal·i·za′tion,** *n.* —**ver′bal·iz′er,** *n.*

verbal noun, 1 noun derived from a verb. **2** gerund or an infinitive that functions as a noun in a sentence.

ver·ba·tim (vėr bā′tim), *adv., adj.* word for word; in exactly the same words. [< Med.L, < L *verbum* word]

ver·be·na (vər bē′nə), *n.* any of certain low-growing garden plants with elongated or flattened spikes of flowers having various colors. [< L, leafy branch]

ver·bi·age (vėr′bi ij), *n.* use of too many words; abundance of useless words.

ver·bose (vėr bōs′), *adj.* using too many words; wordy. [< L, < *verbum* word] —**ver·bose′ly,** *adv.* —**ver·bose′ness, ver·bos′i·ty,** *n.*

ver·bo·ten (fer bō′tən), *adj.* forbidden by authority; prohibited. [< G]

ver·dan·cy (vėr′dən si), *n.* **1** greenness. **2** *Fig.* inexperience.

ver·dant (vėr′dənt), *adj.* **1** green. **2** *Fig.* inexperienced. [< *verdure*] —**ver′dant·ly,** *adv.*

ver·dict (vėr′dikt), *n.* **1** the decision of a jury. **2** decision; judgment. [< AF *verdit* < *ver* true (< L *verus*) + *dit,* pp. of *dire* speak < L *dicere*]

ver·di·gris (vėr′də grēs; -gris), *n.* a green or bluish coating that forms on brass, copper, or bronze when exposed to the air for long periods of time. [< OF *vert de grice,* lit., green of Greece]

ver·dure (vėr′jər), *n.* **1** a fresh greenness. **2** a fresh growth of green grass, plants, or leaves. [< OF, ult. < L *viridis* green] —**ver′dured,** *adj.* —**ver′dur·ous,** *adj.*

verge¹ (vėrj), *n., v.,* **verged, verg·ing.** —*n.* **1** edge; rim; brink: *his business is on the verge of ruin.* **2** a limiting belt, strip, or border of something. —*v.* be on the verge; border. [< OF < L *virga* staff]

verge² (vėrj), *v.,* **verged, verg·ing.** tend; incline: *she was plump, verging toward obese.* [< L *vergere*]

ver·i·fi·a·ble (ver′ə fī′ə bəl), *adj.* that can be checked or tested and proved to be true. —**ver′i·fi·a·bil′i·ty, ver′i·fi′a·ble·ness,** *n.*

ver·i·fi·ca·tion (ver′ə fə kā′shən), *n.* proof by evidence or testimony; confirmation. —**ver′i·fi·ca′tive,** *adj.*

ver·i·fy (ver′ə fī), *v.,* **-fied, -fy·ing. 1** prove (something) to be true; confirm: *the driver's report of the accident was verified by eyewitnesses.* **2** state to be true, esp. under oath. **3** test the correctness of; check for accuracy. [< OF < Med.L, < L *verus* true + *facere* make] —**ver′i·fi′er,** *n.*

ver·i·ly (ver′ə li), *adv.* in truth; truly; really.

ver·i·sim·i·lar (ver′ə sim′ə lər), *adj.* appearing true or real; probable.

ver·i·si·mil·i·tude (ver′ə sə mil′ə tüd; -tūd), *n.* **1** appearance of truth or reality; probability. **2** apparent truth. [< L, < *verus* true + *similis* like]

ver·i·ta·ble (ver′ə tə bəl), *adj.* true; real; actual. [< F, < *verité* VERITY] —**ver′i·ta·bly,** *adv.*

ver·i·ty (ver′ə ti), *n., pl.* **-ties. 1** truth. **2** a true statement or fact. **3** reality. [< L, < *verus* true]

ver·meil (vėr′məl; -māl), *n.* **1** silver, copper, or bronze with a gilt coating. **2** the color vermilion. —*adj.* **1** of or resembling vermeil. **2** vermilion.

ver·mi·cel·li (vėr′mə sel′i; -chel′i), *n.* a mixture of flour and water, like macaroni and spaghetti, but made in long, slender, solid threads. [< Ital., lit., little worms, ult. < L *vermis* worm]

ver·mi·cide (vėr′mə sīd), *n.* any agent that kills worms, esp. a drug used to kill parasitic intestinal worms. —**ver′mi·cid′al,** *adj.*

ver·mi·form (vėr′mə fôrm), *adj.* shaped like a worm. [< Med.L, < L *vermis* worm + *forma* form]

vermiform appendix, a slender tube, closed at one end, growing out of the large intestine in the lower right-hand part of the abdomen. Appendicitis is inflammation of the vermiform appendix.

ver·mi·fuge (vėr′mə fūj), *n.* medicine to expel worms from the intestines. [< F, < L *vermis* worm + *fugare* cause to flee]

ver·mil·ion (vər mil′yən), *n.* **1** a bright red. **2** a bright-red coloring matter. —*adj.* bright-red. [< OF *vermillion,* ult. < L *vermis* worm]

ver·min (vėr′mən), *n. pl. or sing.* **1** small animals that are troublesome or destructive. Fleas, lice, bedbugs, rats, and mice are vermin. **2** *Fig.* a nasty, vile person or persons. [< OF, ult. < L *vermis* worm] —**ver′min·ous,** *adj.* —**ver′min·ous·ly,** *adv.*

Ver·mont (vər mont′), *n.* a state forming the NW part of New England. —**Ver·mont′er,** *n.*

ver·mouth (vər müth′; vėr′müth), *n.* a white wine flavored with wormwood or other herbs and used as a liqueur or in cocktails. [< F < G *wermut(h)*]

ver·nac·u·lar (vər nak′yə lər), *n.* **1** a native language; language used by the people of a certain country or place. **2** everyday language; informal speech. **3** *Fig.* language of a profession, trade, etc.: *the vernacular of the lawyers.* —*adj.* **1** used by the people of a certain country, place, etc.; native: *English is our vernacular tongue.* **2** of or in the native language, rather than a literary or learned language. [< L *vernaculus* domestic, native < *verna* home-born slave] —**ver·nac′u·lar·ly,** *adv.*

ver·nal (vėr′nəl), *adj.* **1** of spring; pertaining to spring: *vernal green, vernal flowers.* **2** like spring; suggesting spring. **3** *Fig.* youthful. [< L *vernalis* < *ver* spring] —**ver′nal·ly,** *adv.*

vernal equinox. See **equinox.**

ver·ni·er (vėr′ni ər), or **vernier scale,** *n.* a small, movable scale for measuring a fractional part of one of the divisions of a fixed scale. [after P. *Vernier,* French mathematician]

ve·ron·i·ca (və ron′ə kə), *n.* a kind of plant or shrub with blue, purple, pink, or white flowers.

ver·sa·tile (vėr′sə təl), *adj.* able to do many things well. [< L *versatilis* turning, ult. < *vertere* turn] —**ver′sa·tile·ly,** *adv.* —**ver′sa·til′i·ty, ver′sa·tile·ness,** *n.*

verse (vėrs), *n.* **1** poetry. **2** a single line of poetry. **3** a group of lines or short portion in poetry. **4** poem. **5** type of poetry; meter: *blank verse, iambic verse.* **6** a short division of a chapter in the Bible. [< L *versus,* orig., row, furrow < *vertere* turn around]

versed (vėrst), *adj.* experienced; practiced; skilled: *a doctor should be well versed in medical theory.*

ver·si·cle (vėr′sə kəl), *n.* one of a series of short sentences said or sung by the minister during services, to which the people make response. [< L *versiculus,* dim. of *versus* VERSE]

ver·si·fi·ca·tion (vėr´sə fə kā´shən), *n.* **1** the making of verses. **2** art or theory of making verses. **3** form or style of poetry; metrical structure.

ver·si·fy (vėr´sə fī), *v.,* **–fied, –fy·ing. 1** write verses. **2** tell in verse. **3** turn (prose) into poetry. **—ver'si·fi´er,** *n.*

ver·sion (vėr´zhən; –shən), *n.* **1** a translation from one language to another. **2** one particular statement, account, or description: *this is my version of the quarrel.* [< L *versio,* orig., a turning < *vertere* turn]

ver·sus (vėr´səs), *prep.* **1** against. **2** compared against: *conservative versus liberal political philosophy.* [< L, turned toward, pp. of *vertere* turn]

ver·te·bra (vėr´tə brə), *n., pl.* **–brae** (–brē) **–bras.** one of the bones of the backbone. [< L, < *vertere* turn] **—ver'te·bral,** *adj.*

ver·te·brate (vėr´tə brāt; -brit), *n.* animal that has a backbone. Fishes, Amphibia, reptiles, birds, and mammals are vertebrates. **—adj.** having a backbone.

ver·tex (vėr´teks), *n., pl.* **–tex·es, –ti·ces** (–tə sēz). **1** the highest point; top. **2** point opposite the base of a triangle, pyramid, etc. [< L, orig., whirl, < *vertere* turn]

ver·ti·cal (vėr´tə kəl), *adj.* **1** straight up and down; perpendicular to a level surface. A person standing up straight is in a vertical position. **2** of or at the highest point; of the vertex. **3** directly overhead; at the zenith. **4** so organized as to include many or all stages in the production of some manufactured product: *a vertical union, vertical trusts.* **5** of or having to do with a vertex; opposite to the base: *a vertical angle.* **—n.** a vertical line, plane, circle, position, part, etc. **—ver´ti·cal´i·ty, ver'ti·cal·ness,** *n.* **—ver'ti·cal·ly,** *adv.*

ver·tig·i·nous (vėr tij´ə nəs), *adj.* **1** whirling; rotary. **2** affected with vertigo; dizzy. **—ver·tig'i·nous·ly,** *adv.*

ver·ti·go (vėr´tə gō), *n., pl.* **ver·ti·goes.** dizziness; giddiness. [< L, < *vertere* turn]

verve (vėrv), *n.* vigorous spirit; enthusiasm; energy; liveliness. [< F]

ver·y (ver´i), *adv., adj.,* **ver·i·er, ver·i·est. —adv. 1** much; greatly; extremely: *the sun is very hot.* **2** absolutely; exactly: *he stood in the very same place for an hour.* **—adj. 1** same; identical: *the very people who used to love her hate her now.* **2** even; mere; sheer: *the very thought of blood makes her sick.* **3** real; true; genuine: *she seemed a very queen.* **4** actual: *he was caught in the very act of stealing.* [< OF *verai,* ult. < L *verus* true]

ves·i·cant (ves´ə kənt), *adj.* producing a blister or blisters. **—n.** a vesicant agent or substance.

ves·i·cate (ves´ə kāt), *v.,* **–cat·ed, –cat·ing.** cause blisters on; blister. **—ves´i·ca'tion,** *n.*

ves·i·ca·to·ry (ves´ə kə tô´ri; –tō´–; və sik´ə tô´ri; –tō´–), *adj., n., pl.* **–ries.** vesicant.

ves·i·cle (ves´ə kəl), *n.* a small bladder, cavity, sac, or cyst. A blister is a vesicle

in the skin. [< L *vesicula,* dim. of *vesica* bladder, blister] **—ve·sic'u·lar, ve·sic'u·late,** *adj.* **—ve·sic'u·lar·ly,** *adv.*

ves·per (ves´pər), *n.* **1** evening. **2** an evening prayer, hymn, or service; evening bell. **—adj. 1** of evening. **2** Sometimes, **Vesper.** of or having to do with a vesper service.

Vesper, the evening star. [< L]

ves·pers, Ves·pers (ves´pərz), *n.pl.* a church service held in the late afternoon or in the evening.

ves·sel (ves´əl), *n.* **1** a large boat; ship. **2** a hollow holder or container, as a cup, bowl, pitcher, bottle, barrel, tub, etc. **3** tube carrying blood or other fluid. Veins and arteries are blood vessels. [< OF < L *vascellum,* double dim. of *vas* vessel]

vest (vest), *n.* **1** a short, sleeveless garment worn by men under the coat. **2** garment like this worn by women; the facing in a waist or coat made to look like a vest. **3** =undershirt. **—v. 1** clothe; robe; dress in vestments: *the vested priest stood before the altar.* **2** furnish with powers, authority, rights, etc.: *Congress is vested with the power to declare war.* **3** put in the possession or control of a person or persons: *the management of the hospital is vested in a board of trustees.* [< OF, ult. < L *vestis* garment] **—vest'less,** *adj.*

ves·tal (ves´təl), *adj.* pure; chaste.

vest·ed (ves´tid), *adj.* **1** placed in the possession or control of a person or persons; fixed; settled: *vested rights.* **2** clothed or robed, esp. in church garments: *a vested choir.*

ves·ti·bule (ves´tə būl), *n.* **1** passage or hall between the outer door and the inside of a building; antechamber. **2** cavity of the body that leads to another cavity: *the vestibule of the ear.* [< L *vestibulum*] **—ves·tib'u·lar,** *adj.*

ves·tige (ves´tij), *n.* **1** a slight remnant; trace. **2** part, organ, etc., that is no longer fully developed or useful. [< F < L *vestigium* footprint]

ves·tig·i·al (ves tij´i əl), *adj.* **1** remaining as a vestige of something that has disappeared. **2** no longer fully developed or useful. **—ves·tig'i·al·ly,** *adv.*

vest·ment (vest´mənt), *n.* garment worn by a clergyman in performing sacred duties. [< OF *vestement,* ult. < L *vestis* garment] **—vest'ment·al,** *adj.*

vest-pock·et (vest´pok´it), *adj.* able to fit into a vest pocket; very small.

ves·try (ves´tri), *n., pl.* **–tries. 1** room in a church, where vestments are kept. **2** a committee that helps manage church business.

ves·try·man (ves´tri mən), *n., pl.* **–men.** member of a committee that helps manage church business.

ves·ture (ves´chər), *n.* **1** clothing; garments. **2** covering. [< OF, ult. < L *vestis* garment] **—ves'tur·al,** *adj.*

vet¹ (vet), *n.* veterinarian.

vet² (vet), *n.* veteran.

vet., 1 veteran. **2** veterinarian; veterinary.

vetch (vech), *n.* vine or plant of the same family as the pea, grown as food for cattle and sheep. [< dial. OF < L *vicia*] **—vetch'like´,** *adj.*

vet·er·an (vet´ər ən; vet´rən), *n.* **1** person who has served in the armed forces. **2** person who has had much experience in some position, occupation, etc. **—adj. 1** having had experience in war. **2** grown old in service; having had much experience. **3** of, pertaining to, or characteristic of veterans. [< L *veteranus* < *vetus* old]

Veterans Day, Nov. 11, formerly Armistice Day.

vet·er·i·nar·i·an (vet´ər ə nãr´i ən; vet´-ə nãr´–), *n.* doctor or surgeon who treats animals.

vet·er·i·nar·y (vet´ər ə ner´i; vet´ə ner´i), *adj., n., pl.* **–nar·ies. —adj.** pertaining to the medical or surgical treatment of animals. **—n.** =veterinarian. [< L, < *veterinus* pertaining to domestic animals]

ve·to (vē´tō), *n., pl.* **–toes,** *adj., v.,* **–toed, –to·ing. —n. 1** the right of a president, governor, etc., to reject bills passed by a lawmaking body. **2** the use of this right: *the governor's veto kept the bill from becoming a law.* **3** statement of the reasons for disapproval of a bill passed by the legislature. **4** power or right to prevent action. **5** refusal of consent. **—adj.** having to do with a veto: *veto power.* **—v. 1** reject by a veto. **2** refuse to consent to. [< L, I forbid] **—ve'to·er,** *n.* **—ve'to·less,** *adj.*

vex (veks), *v.* **1** anger by trifles; annoy; provoke. **2** disturb; trouble: *Florida has been vexed by many hurricanes.* [< L *vexare*] **—vexed,** *adj.* **—vex'ed·ness,** *n.*

vex·a·tion (veks ā´shən), *n.* **1** a vexing or being vexed. **2** thing that vexes.

vex·a·tious (veks ā´shəs), *adj.* vexing; annoying. **—vex·a'tious·ly,** *adv.* **—vex·a'tious·ness,** *n.*

Vi, virginium.

V.I., Virgin Islands.

v.i., intransitive verb.

vi·a (vī´ə; vē´ə), *prep.* by way of; by a route that passes through. [< L, abl. of *via* way]

vi·a·ble (vī´ə bəl), *adj.* able to keep alive. [< F, < *vie* life < L *vita*] **—vi´a·bil'i·ty,** *n.*

vi·a·duct (vī´ə dukt), *n.* bridge for carrying a road or railroad over a valley, a part of a city, etc. [< L *via* road + *ductus* a leading; patterned on *aqueduct*]

vi·al (vī´əl), *n.* a small glass bottle for holding medicines or the like; bottle. [var. of *phial*]

vi·and (vī´ənd), *n.* article of food.

viands, articles of choice food. [< OF *viande* < LL *vivenda* things for living < L, pl., to be lived]

vi·brant (vī´brənt), *adj.* **1** vibrating. **2** resounding; resonant. **3** full of energy; vigorous. [< L *vibrans* vibrating] **—vi'bran·cy,** *n.* **—vi'brant·ly,** *adv.*

vi·bra·phone (vī´brə fōn), *n.* musical instrument like a xylophone, but with metal bars and electric resonators that enrich the sound. Also, **vibraharp.** [< *vibrate* + –*phone* sound] —**vi′bra·phon′ist,** *n.*

vi·brate (vī′brāt), *v.,* –**brat·ed, –brat·ing. 1** move rapidly to and fro. **2** cause to swing to and fro; set in motion. **3** measure by moving to and fro: *a pendulum vibrates seconds.* **4** be moved; quiver. **5** resound: *the clanging vibrated in his ears.* [< L *vibratus* shaken]

vi·bra·tion (vī brā′shən), *n.* **1** a rapid movement to and fro; quivering motion; tremor. **2** a rapid or slow movement to and fro. **3** motion back and forth across a position of equilibrium; one complete movement of this sort. **4** the vibrating motion of a string or other sonorous body, producing musical sound. —**vi·bra′tion·al,** *adj.* —**vi·bra′tion·less,** *adj.*

vi·bra·to·ry (vī′brə tô′ri; –tō′–), *adj.* **1** vibrating. **2** pertaining to vibration. **3** causing vibration. **4** capable of vibration. **5** consisting of vibration.

vi·bur·num (vī bėr′nəm), *n.* **1** any of several shrubs or small trees of the same family as the honeysuckle. **2** the dried bark of certain species, used in medicine. [< L]

vic·ar (vik′ər), *n.* **1** clergyman who has charge of one chapel in a parish. **2** a Roman Catholic clergyman who represents the Pope or a bishop. [< OF < L *vicarius.* Doublet of VICARIOUS.]

vic·ar·age (vik′ər ij), *n.* **1** residence of a vicar. **2** position or duties of a vicar. **3** salary paid to a vicar.

vi·car·i·ous (vī kãr′i əs; vi–), *adj.* **1** done or suffered for others: *vicarious work.* **2** felt by sharing in others' experience: *her son's successes gave her vicarious joy.* **3** taking the place of another: *a vicarious agent.* **4** delegated: *vicarious authority.* [< L *vicarius* < *vicis* (gen.) turn, substitution. Doublet of VICAR.] —**vi·car′i·ous·ly,** *adv.*

vice (vīs), *n.* **1** an evil habit or tendency. **2** evil; wickedness. **3** an undesirable habit; fault; defect, as in a horse. [< OF < L *vitium*] —**vice′less,** *adj.*

vice–, *prefix.* substitute; deputy; subordinate, as in *vice-president, vice-admiral, vice-chairman, vice-chancellor.* [< LL < L *abl.* of *vicis* turn, change]

vice-ad·mi·ral (vīs′ad′mə rəl), *n.* a naval officer ranking next below an admiral and next above a rear admiral. —**vice′-ad′mi·ral·ty,** *n.*

vice-con·sul (vīs′kon′səl), *n.* person next in rank below a consul, who substitutes for the regular consul or acts as his or her assistant. —**vice′-con′sul·ship,** *n.*

vice-pres·i·dent (vīs′prez′ə dənt; –prez′-dənt), **vice president,** *n.* officer next in rank to the president, who takes the president's place when necessary. —**vice′-pres′i·den·cy,** *n.* —**vice′-pres·i·den′tial,** *adj.*

vice-re·gal (vīs rē′gəl), *adj.* of or pertaining to a viceroy. —**vice·re′gal·ly,** *adv.*

vice-re·gent (vīs′rē′jənt), *n.* person who takes the place of the regular regent whenever necessary. —**vice′-re′gen·cy,** *n.*

vice·roy (vīs′roi), *n.* person ruling a country or province as the deputy of the sovereign. [< F, < *vice* VICE³ + *roi* king < L *rex*] —**vice·roy′al,** *adj.* —**vice·roy′al·ty, vice′roy·ship,** *n.*

vice squad, local police squad responsible for enforcement of laws against vices, as gambling or prostitution.

vi·ce ver·sa (vī′sə vėr′sə; vīs), the other way round; conversely. [< L]

vi·cin·i·ty (və sin′ə ti), *n., pl.* –**ties. 1** region near or about a place; neighborhood; surrounding district. **2** nearness in place; being close. [< L, < *vicinus* neighboring < *vicus* quarter, village]

vi·cious (vish′əs), *adj.* **1** disposed to evil; wicked. **2** characterized by vice or immorality; depraved. **3** having bad habits or a bad disposition: *a vicious horse.* **4** not correct; having faults: *vicious reasoning.* **5** spiteful; malicious: *vicious words.* **6** unpleasantly severe: *a vicious headache.* —**vi′cious·ly,** *adv.* —**vi′cious·ness,** *n.*

vicious circle, 1 two or more undesirable things each of which keeps causing the other. **2** false reasoning that uses one statement to prove a second statement when the first statement really depends on the second for proof.

vi·cis·si·tude (və sis′ə tüd; –tūd), *n.* **1** change in circumstances, fortune, etc.: *the vicissitudes of life may suddenly make a rich man very poor.* **2** change; variation. [< L *vicissitudo* < *vicis* (gen.) change]

vic·tim (vik′təm), *n.* **1** person or animal sacrificed, injured, or destroyed: *victims of war, victims of an accident.* **2** Fig. dupe: *the victim of a swindler.* **3** a person or animal killed as a sacrifice to a god. [< L *victima*]

vic·tim·ize (vik′təm īz), *v.,* –**ized, –iz·ing. 1** make a victim of; cause to suffer. **2** cheat; swindle. —**vic′tim·i·za′tion,** *n.* —**vic′tim·iz′er,** *n.*

vic·tor (vik′tər), *n.* winner; conqueror. —*adj.* victorious. [< L, < *vincere* conquer]

Vic·to·ri·an (vik tô′ri ən; –tō′–), *adj.* **1** of or pertaining to the time of Queen Victoria. **2** possessing characteristics attributed to Victorians, as prudishness, bigotry, etc. —*n.* **1** person, esp. an author, who lived during the reign of Queen Victoria. **2** the style of the time of Queen Victoria: *an entire room of high Victorian.* —**Vic·to′ri·an·ism,** *n.*

vic·to·ri·ous (vik tô′ri əs; –tō′–), *adj.* **1** having won a victory; conquering. **2** having to do with victory. —**vic·to′ri·ous·ly,** *adv.*

vic·to·ry (vik′tə ri; –tri), *n., pl.* –**ries.** defeat of an enemy or opponent; success in a contest. [< L *victoria,* ult. < *vincere* conquer]

vict·ual (vit′əl), *n., v.,* –**ualed, –ual·ing.** —*n.* Usually, **victuals.** food. —*v.* **1** sup-

ply with food. **2** take on a supply of food: *the ship will victual before sailing.* [< OF *vitaille* < L *victualia,* pl. *ult.* < *vivere* live] —**vict′ual·less,** *adj.*

vi·cu·ña (vi kün′yə; –kū′nə), *n.* **1** a South American animal somewhat like a camel, having a soft, delicate wool. **2** Also, **vicuña cloth.** cloth made from this wool, or from some substitute. [< Sp. < Quechua (a South American Indian lang.)]

vid., see (Latin *vide*).

vi·de·li·cet (və del′ə set), *adv.* that is to say; to wit; namely. *Viz.* is the abbreviation of videlicet. [< L, for *videre licet* it is permissible to see]

vid·e·o (vid′i ō), *adj.* **1** of or used in the transmission or reception of images, as in television. **2** using a television or computer screen, as a video game. —*n.* **1** =television. **2** =videotape. [< L, I see]

vid·e·o·cas·sette (vid′i ō kə set′), *n.* video tape recording packaged in a cassette.

vid·e·o·disc or **vid·e·o·disk** (vid′i ō disk′), *n.* disk on which images and sound are digitally recorded.

video game, electronic game played on a computer, a television set, or a hand-held device.

vid·e·o·phone (vid′i ō fōn′), *n.* telephone equipped with a very small television camera and screen.

vid·e·o·tape (vid′i ō tāp′), *n.* magnetic tape on which sounds and images are recorded. —*v.* record on videotape, as a television program.

vie (vī), *v.,* **vied, vy·ing.** strive for superiority; contend in rivalry; compete. [< F *envier* challenge < L *invitare* invite]

Vi·en·na (vi en′ə), *n.* capital of Austria, on the Danube River. —**Vi′en·nese′,** *adj., n.*

Vien·tiane (vyen tyän′), *n.* capital of Laos, in the C part.

Vi·et·nam (vē et′näm′; vē′et–), *n.* country in SE Asia. —**Vi·et′nam·ese′,** *adj., n.*

view (vū), *n.* **1** power of seeing; range of the eye; sight: *a ship came into view.* **2** thing seen; scene: *the view from the mountain.* **3** picture of some scene: *various views of the desert hung on the walls.* **4** a mental picture; way of looking at a matter; opinion: *what are your views on the subject?* —*v.* **1** see; look at: *they viewed the scene with pleasure.* **2** consider; regard: *the plan was viewed favorably.*

in view, as a purpose, intention, or hope; as an expectation: *the end of our worries is in view.*

in view of, considering; because.

on view, to be seen; open for people to see: *old manuscripts on view.*

take a dim view (of), look with disfavor, doubt, etc.: *he takes a dim view generally, take a dim view of reformers.*

with a view to, with the purpose, intention, or hope of; expecting. [< AF, < OF *veoir* see < L *videre*] —**view′er,** *n.*

view·find·er (vū′fīn′dər), *n.* device on a camera that shows how much of a scene will be photographed.

view·less (vū'lis), *adj.* **1** that cannot be seen. **2** without views or opinions. —**view'less·ly,** *adv.*

view·point (vū'point'), *n.* **1** place from which one looks at something. **2** attitude of mind; point of view.

vig·il (vij'əl), *n.* **1** a staying awake for some purpose; a watching; watch: *all night the mother kept vigil over the sick child.* **2** a night spent in prayer. [< OF < L *vigilia* < *vigil* watchful]

vig·i·lance (vij'ə ləns), *n.* **1** watchfulness; alertness; caution: *vigilance will avoid accidents in driving.* **2** sleeplessness.

vig·i·lant (vij'ə lənt), *adj.* **1** watchful; alert. **2** keenly attentive to detect danger; wary. [< L *vigilans* watching < *vigil* watchful] —**vig'i·lant·ly,** *adv.*

vig·i·lan·te (vij'ə lan'tē), *n.* member of a committee to maintain order and punish criminals. [< Sp., VIGILANT] —**vig'i·lan'tism,** *n.*

vi·gnette (vin yet'), *n., v.,* **-gnet·ted, -gnet·ting.** —*n.* **1** a decorative design on a page of a book, esp. on the title page. **2** a literary sketch; short verbal description. —*v.* make a vignette of. [< F, dim. of *vigne* VINE]

vig·or (vig'ər), *n.* **1** active strength or force. **2** healthy energy or power. **3** legal force; validity. [< OF < L]

vig·or·ous (vig'ər əs), *adj.* full of vigor; strong and active; energetic; forceful. —**vig'or·ous·ly,** *adv.* —**vig'or·ous·ness,** *n.*

Vi·king (vī'king), *n.* one of the daring Scandinavian seafarers and raiders who harried the coasts and rivers of Europe during the eighth, ninth, and tenth centuries A.D., sometimes establishing settlements.

vile (vīl), *adj.,* **vil·er, vil·est. 1** very bad: *vile weather.* **2** highly objectionable; disgusting; obnoxious: *a vile smell.* **3** evil; low; immoral: *vile language.* **4** poor; mean; lowly: *a vile tenement.* [< OF < L *vilis* cheap] —**vile'ly,** *adv.* —**vile'ness,** *n.*

vil·i·fy (vil'ə fī), *v.,* **-fied, -fy·ing.** make vile; speak evil of; revile; slander. [< LL, < *vilis* vile + *facere* make] —**vil'i·fi·ca'tion,** *n.* —**vil'i·fi'er,** *n.*

vil·la (vil'ə), *n.* a house in the country or suburbs, sometimes at the seashore. A villa is usually a large or elegant residence. [< Ital. < L] —**vil'la·like',** *adj.*

vil·lage (vil'ij), *n.* **1** group of houses, usually smaller than a town. **2** the people of a village. [< OF, ult. < L *villa* country house]

vil·lag·er (vil'ij ər), *n.* person who lives in a village.

vil·lain (vil'ən), *n.* a very wicked person; dangerous scoundrel. [< OF < Med. L *villanus* farmhand < L *villa* country house] —**vil'lain·ess,** *n. fem.*

vil·lain·ous (vil'ən əs), *adj.* **1** very wicked. **2** extremely bad; vile. —**vil'lain·ous·ly,** *adv.*

vil·lain·y (vil'ən i), *n., pl.* **-lain·ies. 1** great wickedness. **2** a very wicked act; crime.

vil·lein (vil'ən), *n.* one of a class of half-free peasants in the Middle Ages. A villein was under the control of his lord, but in his relations with other men had the rights of a freeman. [var. of *villain*]

vim (vim), *n.* force; energy; vigor. [< L, accus. of *vis* force]

vin·ai·grette (vin'ə gret'), *n.* sauce of oil, vinegar, and herbs, used esp. on salad; vinaigrette dressing. [< F, < *vinaigre* VINEGAR]

vin·ci·ble (vin'sə bəl), *adj.* conquerable. [< L, < *vincere* conquer] —**vin'ci·bil'i·ty, vin'ci·ble·ness,** *n.*

vin·di·cate (vin'də kāt), *v.,* **-cat·ed, -cat·ing. 1** clear from suspicion, dishonor, hint, or charge of wrongdoing, etc.: *the verdict of "Not guilty" vindicated him.* **2** defend successfully against opposition; uphold; justify: *vindicate a claim to a fortune.* [< L *vindicatus* < *vindex* defender] —**vin'di·ca·ble,** *adj.* —**vin'di·ca'tion,** *n.* —**vin·dic'a·tive,** *adj.* —**vin'di·ca'tor,** *n.*

vin·dic·tive (vin dik'tiv), *adj.* feeling or showing a strong tendency toward revenge; bearing a grudge. —**vin·dic'tive·ly,** *adv.* —**vin·dic'tive·ness,** *n.*

vine (vīn), *n.* **1** plant with a long, slender stem, that grows along the ground or that climbs by attaching itself to a wall, tree, or other support. **2** =grapevine. [< OF < L *vinea* < *vinum* wine] —**vine'less,** *adj.* —**vine'like',** *adj.*

vin·e·gar (vin'ə gər), *n.* **1** a sour liquid produced by the fermentation of cider, wine, etc., consisting largely of dilute, impure acetic acid. Vinegar is used in flavoring and preserving food. **2** *Fig.* sour disposition or speech. [< OF, < *vin* wine (< *vinum*) + *egre* sour] < L *acer*] —**vin'e·gar·ish, vin'e·gar·y,** *adj.*

vine·yard (vin'yərd), *n.* place planted with grapevines.

vin·i·cul·ture (vin'ə kul'chər), *n.* cultivation of grapes for making wine.

vi·no (vē'nō), *n.* =wine. [< Sp. and It.]

vi·nous (vī'nəs), *adj.* **1** of, like, or having to do with wine. **2** caused by drinking wine. [< L, < *vinum* wine]

vin·tage (vin'tij), *n.* **1** the wine from a certain crop of grapes. **2** a year's crop of grapes. **3** the gathering of grapes for making wine. **4** *Fig.* anything produced or fashionable at a particular time: *a hat of 1930 vintage.* —*adj.* popular or fashionable in a previous time: *vintage cars, vintage clothes.* [< AF, alter. of OF *vendange* < L *vindemia* < *vinum* wine + *demere* take off; infl. by *vintner*]

vint·ner (vint'nər), *n.* dealer in wine. [earlier *vinter* < AF, ult. < L *vinum* wine]

vi·nyl (vī'nil; vin'il), *n.* **1** the univalent radical CH_2: CH derived from ethylene. Thermoplastic resins are formed by polymerization of some vinyl compounds. **2** long-playing record.

vi·ol (vī'əl), *n.* a stringed musical instrument played with a bow and held on the lap or between the knees while being played. [< F *viole*]

vi·o·la (vi ōlə; vī–), *n.* a musical instrument like a violin, but somewhat larger; a tenor or alto violin. [< Ital.]

vi·o·la·ble (vī'ə lə bəl), *adj.* that can be violated. —**vi·o·la·bil'i·ty,** *n.* —**vi·o·la·bly,** *adv.*

vi·o·late (vī'ə lāt), *v.,* **-lat·ed, -lat·ing. 1** break (a law, rule, agreement, promise, etc.); act contrary to; fail to perform: *violate a law.* **2** treat with disrespect or contempt: *he violated their beliefs, violate the right of free speech.* **3** break in upon; disturb: *violate one's privacy.* **4** use force against (a woman or girl); rape. [< L *violatus* < *vis* violence] —**vi'o·la'tor,** *n.*

vi·o·la·tion (vī'ə lā'shən), *n.* **1** use of force; violence. **2** a breaking (of a law, rule, agreement, promise, etc.). **3** treatment (of a holy thing) with contempt. **4** ravishment; rape.

vi·o·lence (vī'ə ləns), *n.* **1** rough force in action: *he slammed the door with violence.* **2** rough or harmful action or treatment. **3** harm; injury: *it would do violence to her principles to join the military.* **4** unlawful use of force. **5** strength of action, feeling, etc.

vi·o·lent (vī'ə lənt), *adj.* **1** acting or done with strong, rough force: *a violent blow.* **2** caused by strong, rough force: *a violent death.* **3** showing or caused by very strong feeling, action, etc.: *violent language.* **4** severe; extreme; very great: *violent pain.* [< L *violentus* < *vis* force] —**vi'o·lent·ly,** *adv.*

vi·o·let (vī'ə lit), *n.* **1** any of various stemless or leafy-stemmed plants with purple, blue, yellow, or white flowers. **2** the flower. **3** a bluish purple. —*adj.* **1** bluish-purple. **2** having the scent of fragrant violets. [< OF *violete,* ult. < L *viola*] —**vi'o·let·like',** *adj.*

vi·o·lin (vī'ə lin'), *n.* **1** musical instrument with four strings, held horizontally against the shoulder and played with a bow. **2** any modern instrument of the same general class, as a viola or violoncello. **3** in an orchestra, a violinist. [< Ital. *violino,* dim. of *viola* viol]

vi·o·lin·ist (vī'ə lin'ist), *n.* person who plays the violin.

vi·ol·ist (vī'əl ist), *n.* person who plays the viol.

vi·o·lon·cel·lo (vī'ə lən chel'ō; vē'ə–), *n., pl.* **-los.** cello. [< Ital., ult. < *viola* viol] —**vi'o·lon·cel'list,** *n.*

VIP, very important person.

vi·per (vī'pər), *n.* **1** a thick-bodied poisonous snake with a pair of large perforated fangs. **2** a spiteful, treacherous person. [< L *vipera* < *vivus* alive + *parere* bring forth] —**vi'per·ish, vi'per·like',** *adj.*

vi·per·ous (vī'pər əs), *adj.* **1** of or pertaining to a viper or vipers. **2** like a viper. **3** spiteful; treacherous. —**vi'per·ous·ly,** *adv.*

vi·ral (vī'rəl), *adj.* **1** of, having to do with, or caused by a virus. **2** of, having to do with, or caused by a computer virus.

vir·e·o (vir′ĭ ō), *n.*, *pl.* **-e·os. 1** a small, olive-green, insect-eating American songbird. **2** any bird of the same family. [< L, kind of bird]

vi·res·cent (vī res′ənt), *adj.* turning green; tending to a green color; greenish. [< L *virescens* turning green] **—vi·res′cence,** *n.*

vir·gin (vėr′jən), *n.* **1** a maiden; unmarried woman. **2** person who has not had sexual intercourse. *—adj.* **1** of or pertaining to a virgin; suitable for a virgin: *virgin modesty.* **2** pure; spotless: *virgin snow.* **3** not yet used: *virgin wool, a virgin forest.*

the Virgin, the Virgin Mary. [< OF < L *virgo*]

vir·gin·al (vėr′jən əl), *adj.* of or suitable for a virgin; maidenly; pure. *—n.* a musical instrument like a small piano, but set in a box without legs. It was much used in the 16th and 17th centuries. [< L *virginalis* < *virgo* maiden]

Vir·gin·ia (vər jin′yə), *n.* a state in the E United States. **—Vir·gin′ian,** *adj.*, *n.*

Virginia creeper, a climbing plant having leaves with five leaflets and bluish-black berries; woodbine; American ivy.

Virginia reel, a dance in which the partners form two lines facing each other and perform a number of dance steps.

vir·gin·i·ty (vər jin′ə ti), *n.* virgin condition; maidenhood.

vir·gin·i·um (vər jin′i əm), *n.* a rare metallic element, Vi. [< NL, after the state of *Virginia*]

Virgin Mary, the mother of Jesus.

Vir·go (vėr′gō), *n.*, *gen.* **Vir·gi·nis** (vėr′jə nis). **1** a zodiacal constellation. **2** the sixth sign of the zodiac.

vir·gule (vėr′gūl), *n.* a slanting stroke (/) between two words indicating that the meaning of either word pertains, as in *and/or.* [< L *virgula* little rod]

vir·i·des·cent (vir′ə des′ənt), *adj.* greenish. [< LL *viridescens* turning green < L *viridis* green] **—vir′i·des′cence,** *n.*

vir·ile (vir′əl), *adj.* **1** manly; masculine. **2** full of manly strength of masculine vigor. **3** *Fig.* vigorous; forceful. [< L, < *vir* man] **—vir′ile·ly,** *adv.*

vi·ril·i·ty (və ril′ə ti), *n.*, *pl.* **-ties. 1** manly strength; masculine vigor. **2** power of procreation. **3** *Fig.* vigor; forcefulness.

vi·rol·o·gy (vī rol′ə ji), *n.* medical science that deals with viruses and the diseases caused by them. **—vi′ro·log′i·cal,** *adj.* **—vi·rol′o·gist,** *n.*

vir·tu·al (vėr′chù əl), *adj.* being something in effect, though not so in name; actual; real. **—vir′tu·al′i·ty,** *n.*

vir·tu·al·ly (vėr′chù əl i), *adv.* in effect, though not in name; actually; really.

virtual reality, 1 reality, as created on a computer; cyberspace. **2** *Fig.* fake or counterfeit reality: *the backwards world of virtual reality.*

vir·tue (vėr′chü), *n.* **1** moral excellence; goodness. **2** a particular moral excellence: *kindness is a virtue.* **3** a good quality: *he praised the virtues of the car.* **4** chastity; purity. **5** power to produce effects: *there is little virtue in that medicine.*

by virtue of, relying on; because of; on account of. [< L *virtus* manliness < *vir* man. Doublet of VIRTU.] **—vir′tue·less,** *adj.*

vir·tu·os·i·ty (vėr′chù os′ə ti), *n.*, *pl.* **-ties.** character or skill of a virtuoso.

vir·tu·o·so (vėr′chù ō′sō), *n.*, *pl.* **-sos,** **-si** (-sē). **1** person especially skilled in the method of an art, esp. in playing a musical instrument. **2** person who has a cultivated appreciation of artistic excellence. [< Ital., learned]

vir·tu·ous (vėr′chù əs), *adj.* **1** good; moral; righteous. **2** chaste; pure. **—vir′tu·ous·ly,** *adv.* **—vir′tu·ous·ness,** *n.*

vir·u·lent (vir′yə lənt; vir′ə–), *adj.* **1** very poisonous or harmful; deadly. **2** intensely bitter or spiteful; violently hostile. [< L, < *virus* poison] **—vir′u·lence,** *n.* **—vir′u·lent·ly,** *adv.*

vi·rus (vī′rəs), *n.* **1** any of a group of disease-producing agents smaller than any known bacteria and dependent upon the living tissue of hosts for their reproduction and growth. **2** =computer virus. **3** *Fig.* corrupting influence. [< L, poison]

vi·sa (vē′zə), *n.*, *v.*, **-saed, -sa·ing.** *—n.* an official signature or endorsement by a representative of another country on a passport, granting permission for the bearer to travel in that country. *—v.* examine and sign a passport. [< F, ult. < L *videre* see]

vis·age (viz′ij), *n.* **1** face. **2** appearance. [< OF, < *vis* face < L *visus* a look < *videre* see] **—vis′aged,** *adj.*

vis-à-vis (vē′zə vē′), *adv.*, *adj.* face to face; opposite: *we sat vis-à-vis.* [< F]

vis·cer·a (vis′ər ə), *n. pl.*, *sing.* **vis·cus** (vis′kəs). the most inside parts of the body. The heart, stomach, liver, intestines, kidneys, etc., are viscera. [< L, pl. of *viscus*] **—vis′cer·al,** *adj.*

vis·cid (vis′id), *adj.* thick and sticky like heavy syrup or glue. [< LL, < L *viscum* bird lime] **—vis·cid′i·ty,** *n.* **—vis′cid·ly,** *adv.*

vis·cose (vis′kōs), *n.* a plastic material prepared by treating cellulose with caustic soda and carbon bisulfide. Viscose is used in manufacturing artificial silk, in making a product resembling celluloid, for sizing, and for other purposes. [< L *viscosus* VISCOUS]

vis·cos·i·ty (vis kos′ə ti), *n.*, *pl.* **-ties. 1** viscous quality. **2** resistance of a fluid to the motion of its molecules among themselves.

vis·count (vī′kount), *n.* a nobleman ranking next below an earl or count and next above a baron. [< AF < OF, < *vis–* vice– + *conte* COUNT²]

vis·count·ess (vī′koun tis), *n.* **1** wife or widow of a viscount. **2** woman holding in her own right a rank equivalent to that of a viscount.

vis·cous (vis′kəs), *adj.* **1** of a liquid, sticky; thick like syrup or glue. **2** of a solid, able to change its shape gradually under stress. [< L, < *viscum* bird lime] **—vis′cous·ness,** *n.*

vise (vīs), *n.* tool having two jaws moved by a screw, used to hold an object firmly while work is being done on it. [< OF *vis* screw < VL *vitium* < L *vitis* vine] **—vise′like′,** *adj.*

Vish·nu (vish′nü), *n.* in Hindu religion, one of the three chief divinities, called "the Preserver."

vis·i·bil·i·ty (viz′ə bil′ə ti), *n.*, *pl.* **-ties. 1** condition or quality of being visible. **2** condition of light, atmosphere, etc., with reference to the distance at which things can be clearly seen.

vis·i·ble (viz′ə bəl), *adj.* that can be seen: *the shore was barely visible through the fog, visible means of support.* [< L *visibilis* < *videre* see] **—vis′i·ble·ness,** *n.* **—vis′i·bly,** *adv.*

Vis·i·goth (viz′i goth), *n.* member of the western division of the Goths that plundered Rome in A.D. 410 and formed a monarchy in France and northern Spain about A.D. 418. **—Vis′i·goth′ic,** *adj.*

vi·sion (vizh′ən), *n.* **1** power of seeing; sense of sight. **2** a seeing; sight. **3** power of perceiving by the imagination or by clear thinking: *a prophet of great vision.* **4** something seen in the imagination, in a dream, in one's thoughts, etc. *—v.* see in, or as if in, a vision. [< L *visio* < *videre* see] **—vi′sion·al,** *adj.* **—vi′sion·al·ly,** *adv.* **—vi′sion·less,** *adj.*

vi·sion·ar·y (vizh′ən er′i), *adj.*, *n.*, *pl.* **-aries.** *—adj.* **1** not practical; dreamy: *visionary plans.* **2** not actual; imaginary. *—n.* person who is not practical; dreamer. **—vi′sion·ar′i·ness,** *n.*

vis·it (viz′it), *v.* **1** go or come to see: *visit New York, visit one's aunt.* **2** pay a call; make a stay; be a guest: *visit in the country.* **3** go or come to inspect or examine officially: *the inspector visited the factory.* **4** come upon; afflict: *he was visited by many troubles.* **5** send upon; inflict: *visit one's anger on someone.* *—n.* **1** a visiting; a call from friendship, for purpose of inspection, for medical treatment, etc. **2** a stay or sojourn as a guest. [< L *visitare*, ult. < *videre* see] **—vis′it·a·ble,** *adj.*

vis·it·a·tion (viz′ə tā′shən), *n.* **1** act of visiting. **2** a visit for the purpose of making an official inspection or examination.

visiting card, a calling card.

vis·i·tor (viz′ə tər), *n.* person who visits or is visiting; guest.

vi·sor (vī′zər), *n.* **1** the movable front part of a helmet, covering the face. **2** the projecting brim of a cap. [< AF *viser* < *vis* face, ult. < L *videre* see] **—vi′sored,** *adj.* **—vi′sor·less,** *adj.*

vis·ta (vis′tə), *n.* **1** view. **2** *Fig.* a mental view. [< Ital., ult. < L *videre* see]

vis·u·al (vizh′ù əl), *adj.* **1** of sight; having to do with sight. **2** of or perceived by vision; having vision; done by vision. **3** that can be seen; visible.

visuals, pictures or film without sound. [< LL,< L *visus* sight < *videre* see] —**vis′u·al·ly,** *adv.*

vis·u·al·ize (vizh′ü əl īz), *v.,* **-ized, -iz·ing. 1** form a mental picture of. **2** make visible. —**vis′u·al·i·za′tion,** *n.* —**vis′u·al·iz′er,** *n.*

vi·tal (vī′təl), *adj.* **1** of life; having to do with life: *vital statistics.* **2** having life; living. **3** necessary to life: *vital organs.* **4** *Fig.* very necessary; very important; essential. **5** full of life and spirit; lively. —*n.* **vitals, a** parts or organs necessary to life, as the heart, brain, or lungs. **b** essential parts or features. [< L, < *vita* life] —**vi′tal·ly,** *adv.* —**vi′tal·ness,** *n.*

vi·tal·i·ty (vī tal′ə ti), *n., pl.* **-ties. 1** a vital force; power to live. **2** power to endure and be active. **3** strength or vigor of mind or body.

vi·tal·ize (vī′təl īz), *v.,* **-ized, -iz·ing. 1** give life to. **2** put vitality into. —**vi′tal·i·za′tion,** *n.* —**vi′tal·iz′er,** *n.*

vi·ta·min, (vī′tə min), *n.* any of certain special substances present in variable quantities in natural foodstuffs, required for the normal growth and nourishment of the body. Lack of vitamins in food causes such diseases as rickets and scurvy. —*adj.* of or having to do with vitamins. [< L *vita* life + E *amine* (< *ammonia*)]

vitamin A, the fat-soluble vitamin in milk, egg yolk, liver, leafy green vegetables, etc., that increases resistance to infection and prevents night blindness.

vitamin B₁, =thiamine.

vitamin B₁₂, a liver extract.

vitamin B complex, group of different vitamins including vitamin B₁, B₂, etc., in yeast and liver.

vitamin C, the antiscorbutic vitamin, in citrus fruits; ascorbic acid.

vitamin D, the vitamin in milk and egg yolk, necessary for the growth and health of bones and teeth.

vitamin E, vitamin in wheat, lettuce, milk, etc., necessary for reproductive processes.

vitamin K, the fat-soluble vitamin in green leafy vegetables, tomatoes, egg yolk, etc., that promotes blood clotting.

vi·ti·ate (vish′i āt), *v.,* **-at·ed, -at·ing. 1** impair the quality of; spoil. **2** destroy the legal force or authority of. [< L, < *vitium* fault] —**vi′ti·at′ed,** *adj.* —**vi′ti·a′tion,** *n.* —**vi′ti·a′tor,** *n.*

vit·i·cul·ture (vit′ə kul′chər; vī′tə–), *n.* the cultivation of grapes. [< L *vitis* vine + E *culture*] —**vit′i·cul′tur·al,** *adj.* —**vit′i·cul′tur·ist,** *n.*

vit·re·ous (vit′ri əs), *adj.* **1** glassy; like glass. **2** pertaining to glass. [< L, < *vitrum* glass] —**vit′re·ous·ly,** *adv.* —**vit′re·ous·ness,** *n.*

vitreous humor, the transparent, jellylike substance that fills the eyeball in back of the lens.

vit·ri·form (vit′rə fôrm), *adj.* having the structure or appearance of glass.

vit·ri·fy (vit′rə fī), *v.,* **-fied, -fy·ing.** change into glass or something like glass. [< F, < L *vitrum* glass + *facere* make] —**vit′ri·fi′a·ble,** *adj.* —**vit′ri·fi·a·bil′i·ty,** *n.* —**vit′ri·fi·ca′tion, vit′ri·fac′tion,** *n.*

vit·ri·ol (vit′ri əl), *n.* **1 a** any of certain sulfates. **b** sulfuric acid. **2** *Fig.* very sharp speech or severe criticism. [< Med.L *vitriolum,* ult. < L *vitrum* glass]

vit·ri·ol·ic (vit′ri ol′ik), *adj.* **1** of, containing, or obtained from vitriol. **2** like vitriol. **3** *Fig.* bitterly severe; biting; sharp.

vi·tu·per·ate (vī tü′pər āt; –tū′–; vi–), *v.,* **-at·ed, -at·ing.** find fault with in abusive words; revile. [< L *vituperatus* < *vitium* fault + *parare* prepare] —**vi·tu′per·a′tion,** *n.* —**vi·tu′per·a′tive,** *adj.*

vi·va (vē′və), *interj.* (long) live (the person or thing named). [< Ital.]

vi·va·ce (vē vä′chä), *adj.* in tempo, lively; brisk. —*adv.* in a lively or brisk manner. [< It.]

vi·va·cious (vī vā′shəs; vi–), *adj.* lively; sprightly; animated. [< L *vivax*] —**vi·va′cious·ly,** *adv.* —**vi·va′cious·ness,** *n.*

vi·vac·i·ty (vī vas′ə ti; vi–), *n., pl.* **-ties** liveliness; sprightliness; animation. [< L, < *vivax* lively]

vi·var·i·um (vī vār′i əm), *n., pl.* **-i·ums, -i·a** (–i ə), place where animals or plants are kept in, or under circumstances simulating, their natural state. [< L]

vive (vēv), *interj. French.* (long) live (the person or thing named).

viv·id (viv′id), *adj.* **1** brilliant; strikingly bright: *dandelions are a vivid yellow.* **2** full of life; lively: *a vivid description.* **3** strong and distinct: *a vivid memory.* [< L *vividus*] —**viv′id·ly,** *adv.* —**viv′id·ness,** *n.*

viv·i·fy (viv′ə fī), *v.,* **-fied, -fy·ing. 1** give life or vigor to. **2** enliven; make vivid. [< L, < *vivus* alive + *facere* make] —**viv′i·fi·ca′tion,** *n.* —**viv′i·fi′er,** *n.*

vi·vip·a·rous (vī vip′ə rəs), *adj.* bringing forth living young, rather than eggs. Dogs, cats, cows, and human beings are viviparous. [< L, < *vivus* alive + *parere* bring forth] —**vi·vip′a·rous·ly,** *adv.*

viv·i·sect (viv′ə sekt; viv′ə sekt′), *v.* practice vivisection.

viv·i·sec·tion (viv′ə sek′shən), *n.* cutting into or experimenting on living animals for scientific study. [< L *vivus* alive + E *section*] —**viv′i·sec′tion·al,** *adj.* —**viv′i·sec′tion·ist,** *n.*

vix·en (vik′sən), *n.* **1** a female fox. **2** *Fig.* a bad-tempered or quarrelsome woman. [OE *fyxen* < *fox* fox] —**vix′en·ish, vix′en·like′,** *adj.*

viz., namely.

vi·zir (vi zir′), *n.* a high official in Muslim countries; minister of state. [< Turk. < Ar. *wazīr,* orig., porter] —**vi·zir′ate, vi·zir′ship,** *n.* —**vi·zir′i·al,** *adj.*

V-J Day, date of the Allied victory over Japan in World War II.

VL, Vulgar Latin.

V-neck (vē′nek′), *n.* neck of a sweater, dress, etc., shaped like a V. —**V′-necked,** *adj.*

voc. vocative.

vocab., vocabulary.

vo·cab·u·lar·y (vō kab′yə ler′i), *n., pl.* **-lar·ies. 1** stock of words used by a person, class of people, profession, etc. Reading will increase your vocabulary. **2** a collection or list of words, usually in alphabetical order and defined. [< Med.L *vocabularius* < L *vocabulum* VOCABLE]

vo·cal (vō′kəl), *adj.* **1** of, by, for, with, or pertaining to the voice: *vocal organs, vocal power.* **2** having a voice; giving forth sound. Humans are vocal beings. **3** rendered by or intended for singing: *vocal music.* **4** *Fig.* aroused to speech; inclined to talk freely: *he became vocal with indignation.* [< L *vocalis* < *vox* voice. Doublet of VOWEL.] —**vo·cal′i·ty, vo′cal·ness,** *n.*

vocal cords, two pairs of membranes in the throat. The lower pair can be pulled tight and the passage of breath between them then causes them to vibrate, which produces the sound of voice.

vo·cal·ic (vō kal′ik), *adj.* **1** of or like a vowel sound. **2** having many vowel sounds.

vo·cal·ist (vō′kəl ist), *n.* =singer.

vo·cal·ize (vō′kəl īz), *v.,* **-ized, -iz·ing. 1** speak, sing, shout, etc. **2** make vocal; utter. **3 a** change into a vowel; use as a vowel. Some people vocalize the *r* in *four.* **b** utter with the voice, and not just with the breath. —**vo′cal·i·za′tion,** *n.* —**vo′cal·iz′er,** *n.* —**vo′cal·ly,** *adv.*

vo·ca·tion (vō kā′shən), *n.* occupation; business; profession; trade. [< L *vocatio,* lit., a calling < *vocare* call]

vo·ca·tion·al (vō kā′shən əl; –kāsh′nəl), *adj.* **1** having to do with some occupation, trade, etc. **2** guiding or preparing for a vocation: *a vocational school.* —**vo·ca′tion·al·ly,** *adv.*

vo·cif·er·ate (vō sif′ər āt), *v.,* **-at·ed, -at·ing.** cry out loudly or noisily; shout. [< L *vociferatus* < *vox* voice + *ferre* bear] —**vo·cif′er·a′tion,** *n.* —**vo·cif′er·a′tor,** *n.*

vo·cif·er·ous (vō sif′ər əs), *adj.* loud and noisy; shouting; clamoring: *a vociferous person, vociferous cheers.* [< L *vociferari* VOCIFERATE] —**vo·cif′er·ous·ly,** *adv.* —**vo·cif′er·ous·ness,** *n.*

vod·ka (vod′kə), *n.* a Russian liquor distilled from potatoes, or from grain. [< Russ., dim. of *voda* water]

vogue (vōg), *n.* **1** the fashion: *hoop skirts were in vogue many years ago.* **2** popularity; acceptance: *that song had a great vogue at one time.* [< F, a rowing, course, success < *voguer* float < Ital. *vogare*]

voice (vois), *n., v.,* **voiced, voic·ing.** —*n.* **1** sound made through the mouth, esp. by people in speaking, singing, shouting, etc. **2** power to make sounds through the mouth. **3** anything like speech or song: *the voice of the wind.* **4** ability as a singer. **5** expression: *they gave voice to their joy.* **6** opinion, choice, wish, etc.: *his voice was for compromise, we have no voice in the matter.* **7** a form of the verb that shows whether the subject is active or passive. —*v.* **1** express; utter. **2** utter with a sound made by vibration of the vocal cords. *Z* and *v* are voiced; *s* and *f* are not.

in voice, in condition to sing or speak well.

lift up one's voice, a shout; yell. **b** protest; complain.

with one voice, unanimously. [< OF < L *vox*] —**voiced,** *adj.* —**voic′er,** *n.*

voice box, =larynx.

voice·less (vois′lis), *adj.* **1** having no voice; dumb; silent. **2** spoken without vibration of the vocal cords. The consonants *p, t,* and *k* are voiceless. —**voice′less·ly,** *adv.* —**voice′less·ness,** *n.*

voice mail, computer system that stores telephone messages to be retrieved later.

voice·o·ver or **voice-o·ver** (vois′ō′vər), *n.* voice of someone off-camera who narrates a film or television show.

voice print, record of the sound patterns of a person's voice, used for identification.

void (void), *adj.* **1** without legal force or effect; not binding in law. **2** empty; vacant: *a void space.* **3** without effect; useless. —*v.* **1** make of no force or effect in law. **2** empty out. —*n.* an empty space.

void of, devoid of; without; lacking. [< OF *voide* < VL *vocitus,* ult. < var. of L *vacuus* empty] —**void′a·ble,** *adj.* —**void′a·ble·ness,** *n.* —**void′er,** *n.*

voile (voil), *n.* a very thin cloth with an open weave. [< F, orig., *veil.* Doublet of VEIL.]

voir dire (vwär dir′), **1** oath to answer questions truthfully, given to a prospective witness or juror during a preliminary hearing. **2** such a hearing. [< OF *voir* truth + *dire* say < L *vera* truth + *dire* say]

vol., *pl.* **vols.** volume.

vol·a·tile (vol′ə təl), *adj.* **1** evaporating rapidly; changing into vapor easily: *gasoline is volatile.* **2** changing rapidly from one mood or interest; fickle; frivolous. **3** *Fig.* fleeting; transient. [< L *volatilis* flying < *volare* fly] —**vol′a·til′i·ty, vol′a·tile·ness,** *n.*

vol·a·til·ize (vol′ə təl īz), *v.,* –ized, –iz·ing. change into vapor; evaporate. —**vol′a·til·iz′a·ble,** *adj.* —**vol′a·til·i·za′tion,** *n.*

vol·can·ic (vol kan′ik), *adj.* **1** of or caused by a volcano; having to do with volcanoes: *a volcanic eruption.* **2** characterized by the presence of volcanoes: *volcanic country.* **3** *Fig.* like a volcano; liable to break out violently: *a volcanic temper.* —**vol·can′i·cal·ly,** *adv.* —**vol′can·ic′i·ty,** *n.*

vol·can·ism (vol′kən iz əm), *n.* phenomena connected with volcanoes and volcanic activity.

vol·ca·no (vol kā′nō), *n., pl.* –**noes,** –**nos.** **1** an opening in the surface of the earth through which steam, ashes, and lava are expelled. **2** a cone-shaped hill or mountain around this opening, built up of material thus expelled. [< Ital. < L *Vulcanus* Vulcan]

vol·can·ol·o·gy (vol′kə nol′ə ji), *n.* scientific study of volcanoes and volcanic activity. —**vol′can·ol′o·gist,** *n.*

vo·li·tion (vō lish′ən), *n.* **1** act of willing: *the man went away by his own volition.* **2** power of willing: *the use of drugs has weakened his volition.* [< Med.L *volitio* < L *volo* I wish] —**vo·li′tion·al, vo·li′tion·ar′y,** *adj.* —**vo·li′tion·al·ly,** *adv.*

vol·ley (vol′i), *n., pl.* –**leys,** *v.,* –**leyed,** –**ley·ing.** —*n.* **1** shower of stones, bullets, arrows, words, oaths, etc. **2** the discharge of a number of guns at once. **3 a** flight of a tennis ball in play before touching the ground. **b** the hitting or return of a tennis ball before it touches the ground. —*v.* **1** discharge or be discharged in a volley. **2** hit or return (a tennis ball, etc.) before it touches the ground. [< F *volée* flight < *voler* fly < L *volare*] —**vol′ley·er,** *n.*

vol·ley·ball (vol′i bôl′), *n.* **1** game played with a large ball and a high net. The ball is hit with the hands back and forth over the net without letting it touch the ground. **2** the ball.

volt (vōlt), *n.* the unit of electromotive force. One volt causes a current of one ampere to flow through a resistance of one ohm. [after A. *Volta,* physicist]

volt·age (vōl′tij), *n.* electromotive force expressed in volts. A current of high voltage is used in transmitting electric power over long distances.

vol·ta·ic (vol tā′ik), *adj.* **1** producing an electric current by chemical action. **2** of or pertaining to electric currents produced by chemical action; galvanic.

volt·am·e·ter (vol tam′ə tər), *n.* device for measuring the quantity of electricity passing through a conductor or for measuring the strength of a current.

volt·am·pere (vōlt′am′pir), *n.* unit of electric measurement equal to the product of one volt and one ampere.

volte·face (vôl′tə fäs′; volt fäs′), *n.* complete reverse in judgment, belief, policy, etc.; about face. [< F < It. *volta* or turn + *faccia* face]

volt·me·ter (vōlt′mē′tər), *n.* instrument for measuring voltage.

vol·u·ble (vol′yə bəl), *adj.* **1** tending to talk much; fond of talking. **2** having a smooth, rapid flow of words. [< L *volubilis,* orig., rolling < *volvere* roll] —**vol′u·bil′i·ty, vol′u·ble·ness,** *n.* —**vol′u·bly,** *adv.*

vol·ume (vol′yəm), *n.* **1** collection of printed or written sheets bound together to form a book. **2** book forming part of a set or series. **3** space occupied: *the storeroom has a volume of 400 cubic feet.*

4 amount; quantity: *volumes of smoke poured from the chimneys of the factory.* **5** amount of sound; fullness of tone.

speak volumes, express much; be full of meaning. [< OF < L *volumen* book roll, scroll < *volvere* roll]

vol·u·met·ric (vol′yə met′rik), *adj.* of or having to do with measurement by volume. —**vol′u·met′ri·cal·ly,** *adv.*

vo·lu·mi·nous (və lü′mə nəs), *adj.* **1** forming, filling, or writing a large book or many books. **2** of great size; very bulky; large. —**vo·lu′mi·nous·ly,** *adv.* —**vo·lu′mi·nous·ness,** *n.*

vol·un·tar·y (vol′ən ter′i), *adj., n., pl.* –**tar·ies.** —*adj.* **1** done, made, given, etc., of one's own free will; not forced or compelled: *a voluntary contribution.* **2** acting of one's own free will or choice: *a voluntary substitute.* **3** able to act of one's own free will: *a voluntary agent.* **4** deliberately intended; done on purpose: *voluntary manslaughter.* **5** controlled by the will. Talking is voluntary; breathing is only partly so. —*n.* **1** anything done, made, given, etc., of one's own free will. **2** an organ solo played before, during, or after a church service. [< L, < *voluntas* will] —**vol′un·tar′i·ly,** *adv.* —**vol′un·tar′i·ness,** *n.*

vol·un·teer (vol′ən tir′), *n.* person who enters any service of his or her own free will, as social, public, or military service. —*v.* **1** offer one's services: *as soon as war was declared, many men volunteered.* **2** offer of one's own free will: *volunteer to do the job.* **3** tell or say voluntarily: *she volunteered the information.* —*adj.* **1** of or made up of volunteers: *a volunteer fire company.* **2** serving as a volunteer: *a volunteer fireman.* **3** voluntary. [< F *volontaire,* orig., adj., VOLUNTARY]

vo·lup·tu·ar·y (və lup′chu er′i), *n., pl.* –**ar·ies.** person who cares much for luxurious or sensual pleasures. [< L, < *voluptas* pleasure]

vo·lup·tu·ous (və lup′chu əs), *adj.* **1** caring much for the pleasures of the senses. **2** giving pleasure to the senses. [< L, < *voluptas* pleasure] —**vo·lup′tu·ous·ly,** *adv.* —**vo·lup′tu·ous·ness,** *n.*

vom·it (vom′it), *v.* **1** throw up what has been eaten. **2** *Fig.* throw up; throw out with force: *the chimneys vomited smoke.* **3** *Fig.* come out with force or violence. —*n.* the substance thrown up from the stomach. [< AF, or < L *vomitus* spewed forth] —**vom′it·er,** *n.*

von (fôn; *English* von), *prep.* German. from; of.

voo·doo (vü′dü), *n., pl.* –**doos,** *adj.* —*n.* **1** mysterious rites, including magic and conjuration, originally African and still prevalent in the West Indies and in a few parts of the United States. Also vodou, Vodun. **2** person who practices such rites. —*adj.* of or pertaining to such rites. [of African origin] —**voo′doo·ism,** *n.* —**voo′doo·ist,** *n.* —**voo′doo·is′tic,** *adj.*

vo·ra·cious (və rā′shəs), *adj.* **1** eating much; greedy in eating; ravenous. **2** very eager; unable to be satisfied. [< L *vorax* greedy] —**vo·ra′cious·ly**, *adv.* —**vo·rac′i·ty**, *n.*

vor·tex (vôr′teks), *n., pl.* **-tex·es, -ti·ces** (-tə sēz). **1** a whirling mass of water, air, etc., that sucks in everything near it; whirlpool; whirlwind. **2** *Fig.* whirl of activity or other situation from which it is hard to escape: *the vortex of war.* [< L, var. of *vertex* VERTEX] —**vor′ti·cal**, *adj.* —**vor′ti·cal·ly**, *adv.*

vo·ta·ress (vō′tə ris), *n.* a woman votary.

vo·ta·ry (vō′tə ri), **vo·ta·rist** (-rist), *n., pl.* **-ries; -rists. 1** person devoted to something; devotee. **2** person bound by vows to a religious life. [< L *votum* vow]

vote (vōt), *n., v.,* **vot·ed, vot·ing.** —*n.* **1** a formal expression of a wish or choice: *the person receiving the most votes is elected.* **2** the right to give such an expression: *not everybody has a vote.* **3** what is expressed or granted by a majority of voters. **4** votes considered together: *the labor vote, the vote of the people.* **5** voter. **6** ticket; ballot. —*v.* **1** give or cast a vote: *he voted for the Democrats.* **2** support by one's vote: *vote the Republican ticket.* **3** pass, determine, or grant by a vote. **4** declare, esp. by general consent. [< L *votum* vow] —**vot′a·ble**, *adj.* —**vote′less**, *adj.*

vote of confidence, 1 vote by a majority of members of a parliament that supports the action or policy of the government in power. **2** any expression of approval or support.

vot·er (vōt′ər), *n.* **1** person who votes. **2** person who has the right to vote.

voting machine, an electronic or mechanical device for registering and counting votes.

vo·tive (vō′tiv), *adj.* promised by a vow; done, given, etc., because of a vow. [< L, < *votum* vow]

vouch (vouch), *v.* be responsible; give a guarantee; answer for. [< AF *voucher* < L *vocare* call]

vouch·er (vouch′ər), *n.* **1** person or thing that vouches for something. **2** a written evidence of payment; receipt. **3** written evidence of school taxes paid which entitles the bearer to a credit toward tuition at a school in another district or at a nonpublic school.

vouch·safe (vouch sāf′), *v.,* **-safed, -saf·ing.** be willing to grant or give; deign (to do or give). [orig. meaning "guarantee," to *vouch* for as *safe*]

vow (vou), *n.* **1** a solemn promise: *a vow of secrecy.* **2** promise made to God: *a nun's vows.* —*v.* **1** make a vow. **2** declare earnestly or emphatically. [< OF *vou* < L *votum* < *vovere* to vow]

vow·el (vou′əl), *n.* **1** a voiced sound in the production of which the breath stream is relatively unimpeded. A vowel can form a syllable by itself, as the first syllable of *awful* (ô′fəl). **2** a letter representing such a sound. *A, e, i, o,* and *u* are vowels. —*adj.* of or having to do with or like a vowel. [< OF < L (*littera*) *vocalis* sounding (letter) < *vox* voice. Doublet of VOCAL.]

voy·age (voi′ij), *n., v.,* **-aged, -ag·ing.** —*n.* journey, esp. a long journey; passage or travel: *a voyage around the world by ship, a space voyage.* —*v.* make or take a voyage. [< F < L *viaticum.* Doublet of VIATICUM.] —**voy′ag·er**, *n.*

vo·ya·geur (vwä yä zhœr′), *n., pl.* **-geurs** (-zhœr′). a French Canadian or half-breed accustomed to travel on foot or by canoe through unsettled regions. [< F, ult. < *voyage* VOYAGE]

vo·yeur (vwä′yœr′), *n.* person who derives pleasure from watching in secret the private acts of others. [< F < *voir* to see < L *vidēre*] —**vo·yeur′ism**, *n.* —**vo·yeur·is′tic**, *adj.*

V.P., VP, or **V. Pres.,** Vice-President.

vs., 1 verse. **2** versus.

V-shaped (vē′shäpt′), *adj.* shaped like the letter V.

VT, (*zip code*) Vermont.

Vt., Vermont.

v.t., transitive verb.

vul·can·ize (vul′kən īz), *v.,* **-ized, -iz·ing.** treat (rubber) with sulfur and heat to make it more elastic and durable. [< *Vulcan* Roman god of fire] —**vul′can·i·za′tion**, *n.* —**vul′can·iz′er**, *n.*

vul·gar (vul′gər), *adj.* **1** showing a lack of good breeding, manners, taste, etc.; not refined; coarse; low. **2** common; in common use; ordinary. **3** of the common people. [< L *vulgaris* < *vulgus* common people] —**vul′gar·ly**, *adv.* —**vul′gar·ness**, *n.*

vul·gar·i·an (vul gār′i ən), *n.* **1** a vulgar person. **2** a rich person who lacks good breeding, manners, taste, etc.

vul·gar·ism (vul′gər iz əm), *n.* **1** word, phrase, or expression used only in ignorant or coarse speech. In "I disremember his name," *disremember* is a vulgarism. **2** vulgar character or action; vulgarity. **3** a vulgar expression.

vul·gar·i·ty (vul gar′ə ti), *n., pl.* **-ties. 1** lack of refinement; lack of good breeding, manners, taste, etc.; coarseness. **2** action, habit, speech, etc., showing vulgarity.

vul·gar·ize (vul′gər īz), *v.,* **-ized, -iz·ing.** make vulgar. —**vul′gar·i·za′tion**, *n.*

Vulgar Latin, a popular form of Latin, the main source of French, Spanish, Italian, and Portuguese.

Vul·gate (vul′gāt), *n.* the Latin translation of the Bible, made in the fourth century A.D.

vul·ner·a·bil·i·ty (vul′nər ə bil′ə ti), *n.* vulnerable quality or condition.

vul·ner·a·ble (vul′nər ə bəl), *adj.* **1** capable of being wounded or injured; open to attack: *Achilles was vulnerable only in his heel.* **2** sensitive to criticism, temptations, influences, etc.: *most people are vulnerable to ridicule.* [< LL *vulnerabilis* wounding, ult. < *vulnus* wound] —**vul′ner·a·ble·ness**, *n.* —**vul′ner·a·bly**, *adv.*

vul·pine (vul′pīn; -pin), *adj.* of or like a fox; clever; sly. [< L, < *vulpus* fox]

vul·ture (vul′chər), *n.* **1** a large bird of prey related to eagles, hawks, etc., that eats the flesh of dead animals. **2** a greedy, ruthless person. [< L *vultur*] —**vul′ture·like′**, *adj.* —**vul′tur·ous**, *adj.*

vul·va (vul′və), *n., pl.* **-vae** (-vē), **-vas.** the external genital organs of the female. [< L, womb] —**vul′val, vul′var**, *adj.*

vy·ing (vī′ing), *v.* ppr. of **vie.** —*adj.* that vies. —**vy′ing·ly**, *adv.*

W, w (dub′əl yū), *n., pl.*
W's; w's. the 23rd letter of
the alphabet.
W, 1 tungsten. 2 watt. 3
west; western.
W., 1 Wednesday. 2 west; western.
w., 1 watt. 2 west; western. 3 wide.
WA, *(zip code)* Washington.
wab·ble (wob′əl), *v.,* **–bled, –bling,** *n.*
=wobble.
wack·y (wak′i), *adj.* unconventional in
behavior; eccentric; crazy.
wad (wod), *n., v.,* **wad·ded, wad·ding.**
—*n.* 1 a small, soft mass: *a wad of cotton.*
2 a tight roll; compact bundle or mass. 3
a roll of paper money. 4 *Informal.* stock
of money. —*v.* 1 make into a wad; press
into a wad. 2 stuff with a wad: *wad cloth
to fill a hole.* 3 pad. [< Med.L *wadda,* ?
< Ar. *bāṭin* lining] —**wad′der,** *n.*
wad·ding (wod′ing), *n.* a soft material
for padding, stuffing, packing, etc., esp.
carded cotton in sheets.
wad·dle (wod′əl), *v.,* **–dled, –dling,** *n.*
—*v.* walk with short steps and an awkward swaying motion, as a duck does.
—*n.* 1 act of waddling. 2 an awkward,
swaying gait. [< *wade*] —**wad′dler,** *n.*
—**wad′dling·ly,** *adv.*
wade (wād), *v.,* **wad·ed, wad·ing,** *n.* —*v.*
1 walk through water, snow, sand, mud,
or anything that hinders free motion.
2 make one's way with difficulty: *wade
through an uninteresting book.* 3 cross
or pass through by wading. —*n.* act of
wading.
wade in, *Informal.* thrust oneself into
the middle of something and become
thoroughly involved.
wade into, *Informal.* attack or go to
work on vigorously. [OE *wadan* pro-
ceed] —**wad′er,** *n.*
wad·er (wā′dər), *n.* 1 person or thing that
wades. 2 long-legged bird, as a crane or
sandpiper, that wades in shallow water
looking for food.
waders, high rubber boots used by fishermen and others who stand in water.
wa·di (wä′di), *n., pl.* **–dis; –dies.** 1 valley or ravine in Arabia, N Africa, etc.,
through which a stream flows during the rainy season. 2 stream or torrent running through such as ravine.
[< Ar.]
wa·fer (wā′fər), *n.* 1 a very thin cake or
biscuit, sometimes flavored or sweetened. 2 the thin, round piece of unleavened bread used in Holy Communion.
[< AF *wafre* < Gmc.] —**wa′fer·like′,**
adj.
wa·fer·y (wā′fər i), *adj.* like a wafer.
waf·fle[1] (wof′əl), *n.* a batter cake cooked
in a special griddle (**waffle iron**) that
makes the cakes very thin in places.
[< Du. *wafel*]
waf·fle[2] (wof′əl), *v.,* **–fled, –fling.** *Informal.* act indecisively; mislead. [< E
dial.]
waft (waft; wäft), *v.* 1 carry over water or
through air. 2 float. —*n.* 1 act of waft-

ing. 2 a waving movement. 3 a breath
or puff of air, wind, etc. [< earlier *wafter*
convoy ship < Du., LG *wachter* guard]
—**waft′er,** *n.*
wag (wag), *v.,* **wagged, wag·ging,** *n.* —*v.*
move from side to side or up and down,
esp. rapidly and repeatedly. —*n.* 1 act of
wagging; a wagging motion. 2 person
who is fond of making jokes.
wag the tongue, talk, talk much; gossip.
[< Scand. *vagga* rock] —**wag′ger,** *n.*
wage (wāj), *n., v.,* **waged, wag·ing.** —*n.*
Usually, **wages** (*sometimes sing. in use*).
a amount paid for work: *his wages
are $600 a week.* **b** something given
in return: *the wages of sin.* —*v.* carry
on: *doctors wage war against disease.*
[< OF *wagier* < Gmc. Doublet of GAGE[1].]
—**wage′less,** *adj.*
wa·ger (wā′jər), *n.* 1 something staked on
an uncertain event. 2 act of betting; bet.
—*v.* bet; gamble. [< AF *wageure* < OF
wage pledge < Gmc.] —**wa′ger·er,** *n.*
wag·gish (wag′ish), *adj.* 1 fond of
making jokes. 2 characteristic of a
wag. —**wag′gish·ly,** *adv.* —**wag′gish-
ness,** *n.*
wag·gle (wag′əl), *v.,* **–gled, –gling,** *n.* —*v.*
move quickly and repeatedly from side
to side; wag. —*n.* a waggling motion.
—**wag′gling·ly,** *adv.*
wag·on, (wag′ən), *n.* a four-wheeled vehicle, esp. one for carrying loads: *a milk
wagon, a station wagon.* 2 child's toy cart.
—*v.* convey by wagon.
off the wagon, returning to drinking
alcohol.
on the wagon, not drinking alcoholic
liquors. [< Du. *wagen*] —**wag′on·less,**
adj.
wag·on·er (wag′ən ər), *n.* person who
drives a wagon.
wag·on·load (wag′ən lōd′), *n.* amount a
wagon carries.
wagon train, group of wagons moving
along in a line one after another.
Wa·ha·bi or **Wah·ha·bi** (wä hä′bi), *n.*
member of a Muslim sect, prominent
in Saudi Arabia, which strictly follows
the Koran and rejects all writings except
those of Muhammad's followers. [< Ar.
'Abd al-Wahhāb, Muslim reformer]
waif (wāf), *n.* 1 person without home or
friends; homeless or neglected child. 2
anything without an owner; stray thing,
animal, etc. [< AF, prob. < Scand.]
wail (wāl), *v.* 1 cry loud and long because
of grief or pain. 2 lament; mourn. —*n.* 1
a long cry of grief or pain. 2 a sound like
such a cry. [< Scand. *vœla*] —**wail′er,**
n. —**wail′ful,** *adj.* —**wail′ful·ly,** *adv.*
—**wail′ing·ly,** *adv.*
wain·scot (wān′skət; –skot), *n., v.,* **–scot-
ed, –scot·ing.** —*n.* 1 a lining of wood,
usually in panels, on the walls of a room.
2 the lower part of the wall of a room
when it is decorated differently from
the upper part. —*v.* line with wood.
[< MLG *wagenschot* < *wagen* wagon +
schot partition]

wain·scot·ing (wān′skət ing; –skot–), *n.*
1 =wainscot. 2 material used for wain-
scots.
wain·wright (wān′rīt′), *n.* =wagonmaker.
waist (wāst), *n.* 1 the part of the human
body between the ribs and the hips. 2
=waistline. 3 a garment or part of a garment covering the body from the neck
or shoulders to the waistline. 4 the middle part. [< root of *wax*[2]] —**waist′less,**
adj.
waist·band (wāst′band′), *n.* a band
around the waist of a pair of trousers
or a skirt.
waist·coat (wāst′kōt′; wes′kət), *n.* a man's
vest.
waist·line (wāst′līn′), *n.* an imaginary
line around the body at the smallest part
of the waist.
wait (wāt), *v.* 1 stay or be inactive until
someone comes or something happens:
*let's wait in the shade, wait for a bus, that
matter can wait until tomorrow.* 2 delay
or put off: *wait dinner for him, wait for
a train.* 3 act as a servant; change plates,
pass food, etc., at table. —*n.* act or time
of waiting.
lie in wait, stay hidden, ready to attack.
wait on or upon, a be a servant to; serve,
esp. at the table. **b** call on (someone) to
pay a respectful visit.
wait out, wait until the end of; endure.
wait up, stay up (waiting for someone or
something). [< OF *waitier,* orig., watch
< Gmc.]
wait·er (wāt′ər), *n.* 1 person who waits. 2
person who waits on table in a hotel or
restaurant.
wait·ing (wāt′ing), *adj.* 1 that waits. 2 used
to wait in. —*n.* time that one waits.
in waiting, in attendance on a king,
queen, prince, princess, etc.
waiting room, room at a railroad station,
doctor's office, etc., for people to wait in.
wait·ress (wāt′ris), *n.* woman who waits
on table in a dining room, hotel, or
restaurant.
waive (wāv), *v.,* **waived, waiv·ing.** 1 give
up (a right, claim, etc.); refrain from
claiming or pressing; do without; relinquish. 2 put aside; defer. [< AF *weyver*
abandon, prob. < Scand.]
waiv·er (wāv′ər), *n.* 1 a giving up of a
right, claim, etc. 2 a written statement
of this.
Wa·kash·an (wä kash′ən), *adj.* of or having to do with the American Indian
linguistic stock of the NW United States
and W Canada. —*n.* this linguistic
stock.
wake[1] (wāk), *v.,* **waked** or **woke, waked**
or (*Archaic and Dial.*) **wo·ken, wak·ing,**
n. —*v.* 1 stop sleeping: *wake up early in
the morning, wake at seven every morning.* 2 cause to stop sleeping: *the noise
of the traffic always wakes him.* 3 be
awake; stay awake: *all his waking hours.*
4 become alive or active: *the flowers
wake in the spring, he needs some interest
to wake him up.* —*n.* 1 a watching, esp.

for some solemn purpose. 2 watch kept beside the body of a dead person. [OE *wacian*] —**wak′er,** *n.*

wake[2] (wāk), *n.* track left behind a moving thing.

in the wake of, following; behind; after. [< MDu.]

wake·ful (wāk′fəl), *adj.* 1 not able to sleep. 2 without sleep. 3 watchful. —**wake′fully,** *adv.* —**wake′ful·ness,** *n.*

wak·en (wāk′ən), *v.* =wake. [OE *wœcnan*] —**wak′en·er,** *n.*

wake-rob·in (wāk′rob′ən), *n.* 1 =trillium. 2 =jack-in-the-pulpit.

wale (wāl), *n., v.,* **waled, wal·ing.** —*n.* 1 a streak or ridge made on the skin by a stick or whip; welt. 2 a ridge in the weave of cloth, as in corduroy. 3 texture of a cloth. —*v.* 1 mark with wales; raise wales on. 2 weave with ridges. [OE *walu*]

walk (wôk), *v.* 1 go on foot. In walking, a person always has one foot on the ground. 2 roam: *the ghost will walk tonight.* 3 go over, on, or through: *the captain walked the deck.* 4 make, put, drive, etc., by walking: *walk off a headache.* 5 **a** go to first base after the pitcher has thrown four balls. **b** of a pitcher, give (a batter) a base on balls. —*n.* 1 act of walking, esp. walking for pleasure or exercise: *a walk in the country.* 2 distance to walk: *it is a long walk from here.* 3 place for walking; path; sidewalk; promenade. 4 way of living: *different walks of life.* 5 permitting a batter to reach first base on balls; pass. 6 *Informal.* an easy win or success.

take a walk, get out; depart.

walk all over, trample on; disregard.

walk away from, a progress much faster than. **b** not be injured by: *walk away from an accident.*

walk off with, a take; get; win. **b** steal.

walk out, a go on strike. **b** leave suddenly.

walk out on, desert. [OE *wealcan* roll]

walk·a·way (wôk′ə wā′), *n.* an easy victory.

walk·er (wôk′ər), *n.* 1 person who walks. 2 lightweight framework of four legs and cross pieces that provides support to someone who has difficulty walking.

walk·ie-talk·ie (wôk′i tôk′i), *n.* a small, portable receiving and transmitting set.

walk-in (wôk′in′), *adj.* 1 large enough to walk into. 2 entered from the street: *a walk-in apartment.* 3 that can be entered without an appointment: *a walk-in clinic.* —*n. Informal.* 1 a patient or client who comes in from the street, without an appointment. 2 an apartment entered directly from the street. 3 an easy victory: *the election was a walk-in.*

walking papers, dismissal from a position, etc.

walking stick, 1 cane. 2 any of various insects having a body like a stick.

walk-on (wôk′on′), *n.* 1 part in a play or film in which the performer merely appears but does not speak. 2 performer having such a part.

walk-out (wôk′out′), *n.* strike of workers.

walk-o·ver (wôk′ō′vər), *n.* an easy victory.

walk-up (wôk′up′), *n.* an apartment house or building having no elevator. —*adj.* not having an elevator.

wall (wôl), *n.* 1 side of a house, room, or other hollow thing. 2 structure of stone, brick, or other material built up to enclose, divide, support, or protect. 3 Often, **walls.** rampart. 4 something like a wall in looks or use. —*v.* enclose, divide, protect, or fill with a wall, or as if with a wall.

drive one up the wall, *Informal.* annoy one a great deal; drive one crazy: *rainy days drive any mother up the wall.*

drive or **push to the wall,** make desperate or helpless.

go to the wall, give way; be defeated.

off the wall, *Informal.* a little crazy; odd; unusual.

up against a (blank, stone, etc.) wall, unable to overcome an obstacle.

wall off or **out,** *Fig.* become unapproachable; withdraw. [< L *vallum*] —**walled,** *adj.* —**wall′-less,** *adj.* —**wall′-like′,** *adj.*

wal·la·by (wol′ə bi), *n., pl.* **-bies** or (*esp. collectively*) **-by.** a kangaroo of the smaller sorts. Some wallabies are no larger than rabbits. [from native Australian name]

wall·board (wôl′bôrd′; -bōrd′), *n.* board made of paper and plaster used instead of wooden boards or plaster to make or cover walls.

wal·let (wol′it; wôl′it), *n.* a small, flat leather case for carrying paper money, cards, etc., in one's pocket; folding pocketbook.

wall·eye (wôl′ī′), *n.* any of various fishes with large staring eyes.

wall·eyed (wôl′īd′), *adj.* 1 having eyes that show much white and little color. 2 having both eyes turned away from the nose. 3 having large staring eyes. The pike is a walleyed fish. [< Scand. *vagl-eygr* < *vagl,* prob., beam in the eye + *auga* eye]

wall·flow·er (wôl′flou′ər), *n.* 1 person who sits by the wall at a dance instead of dancing. 2 a perennial plant with sweet-smelling yellow, orange, or red flowers, found growing on walls, cliffs, etc.

Wal·loon (wo lün′), *n.* 1 one of a group of people inhabiting chiefly the S and SE parts of Belgium and adjacent regions in France. 2 their language, the French dialect of Belgium. —*adj.* of or having to do with the Walloons or their language.

wal·lop (wol′əp), —*v.* 1 beat soundly; thrash. 2 hit very hard. —*n.* a very hard blow. [< OF *waloper* GALLOP] —**wal′lop·er,** *n.* —**wal′lop·ing,** *n., adj.*

wal·low (wol′ō), *v.* 1 roll about; flounder: *the pigs wallowed in the mud.* 2 *Fig.* indulge oneself in an emotion, pleasure, attitude, etc.: *wallow in self-pity.* —*n.* 1 act of wallowing. 2 place where animals wallow. [OE *wealwian* roll] —**wal′lower,** *n.*

wall·pa·per (wôl′pā′pər), *n.* paper for covering walls. —*v.* put wallpaper on.

Wall Street, the money market or the financiers of the United States, esp. those located on Wall Street in New York City.

wal·nut (wôl′nut; -nət), *n.* 1 a large, round, edible nut with a plain division between its two halves. 2 the tree that it grows on. 3 its wood. 4 the brown color of polished walnut wood. [OE *wealhhnutu* < *wealh* foreign + *hnutu* nut]

Wal·pur·gis (väl pur′gis) **night,** the night of April 30, when witches were supposed to hold revels with the devil.

wal·rus (wôl′rəs; wol′-), *n., pl.* **-rus·es** or (*esp. collectively*) **-rus.** a large sea animal of the arctic regions, resembling a seal but having long tusks. [< Du. *walrus, walros* < *wal-* (*visch*) whale + *ros* horse]

waltz (wôlts), *n.* 1 a smooth, even, gliding dance to music having three beats to the measure. 2 music for it. —*v.* 1 dance a waltz. 2 move nimbly or quickly. [< G *walzer* < *walzen* roll] —**waltz′er,** *n.* —**waltz′like′,** *adj.*

wam·pum (wom′pəm; wôm′-), *n.* 1 beads made from shells, formerly used by American Indians as money and ornament. [< Algonkian]

wan (won), *adj.,* **wan·ner, wan·nest.** 1 pale in color or hue; pallid. 2 looking worn or tired; faint; weak: *the sick boy's wan smile.* [OE *wann* dark] —**wan′ly,** *adv.* —**wan′ness,** *n.*

wand (wond), *n.* 1 a slender stick or rod: *the magician waved his wand.* 2 rod borne as a sign of office or authority; scepter. 3 baton. [< Scand. *vöndr*] —**wand′like′,** *adj.*

wan·der (won′dər), *v.* 1 move here and there without any special purpose: *wander about the world.* 2 go aimlessly over or through. 3 go from the right way; stray: *wander off and become lost.* 4 *Fig.* be delirious; be incoherent: *he wandered during his illness.* [OE *wandrian*] —**wan′der·er,** *n.* —**wan′der·ing·ly,** *adv.*

wan·der·lust (won′dər lust′), *n.* a strong desire to wander. [< G, < *wandern* wander + *lust* desire]

wane (wān), *v.,* **waned, wan·ing,** *n.* —*v.* become smaller; become smaller gradually: *the moon wanes after it has become full.* 2 decline in power, influence, importance, etc. 3 decline in strength, intensity, etc.: *the light of day wanes in the evening.* 4 draw to a close: *summer wanes as autumn approaches.* —*n.* a waning. [OE *wanian*]

wan·gle (wang′gəl), *v.,* **-gled, -gling.** 1 manage to get by schemes, tricks, persuasion, etc. 2 make one's way through difficulties. —**wan′gler,** *n.*

wan·na·be (won′nə bē′), *n.* 1 person who strives to be like someone else, esp. someone successful and famous. 2

company or organization that imitates the success of another.

wan·nish (won′ish), *adj.* somewhat wan.

want (wont; wônt), *v.* **1** wish for; wish: *he wants to become an engineer, he wants a new car.* **2** be without; lack; need: *plants want water, want judgment.* **3** need food, clothing, and shelter; be very poor. —*n.* **1** thing desired or needed; desire: *his wants are few.* **2** a lack; need: *supply a long felt want, want of rain.* **3** a lack of food, clothing, or shelter; great poverty.

for want of, because of the lack or absence of.

want for, lack.

want out, *Informal.* desire to leave, quit, have no part in. [< Scand. *vanta*] —**want′er,** *n.* —**want′less,** *adj.*

want ad, a small notice in a newspaper stating that something is wanted, as an employee, an apartment, etc.: classified ad.

want·ing (won′ting; wôn′–), *adj.* **1** lacking; missing: *one volume of the set is wanting.* **2** not coming up to a standard or need: *weighed and found wanting.* —*prep.* without; less; minus: *a year wanting three days.*

wan·ton (won′tən), *adj.* **1** reckless or disregardful of right, justice, humanity, etc.: *wanton cruelty.* **2** done, shown, used, etc., maliciously or unjustifiably: *a wanton attack.* **3** not moral; not chaste: *a wanton person.* **4** frolicsome; playful: *a wanton kitten.* —*v.* act in a wanton manner. [ME *wantowen* < OE *wan–* not (cf. WANE) + *togen* brought up, pp. of *tēon* bring] —**wan′ton·ly,** *adv.* —**wan′ton·ness,** *n.*

wap·i·ti (wop′ə ti), *n., pl.* **-tis** or (*esp. collectively*) **-ti.** a North American deer with long, slender antlers; the American elk. [< Algonkian]

war (wôr), *n., v.,* **warred, war·ring,** *adj.* —*n.* **1** a fight carried on by armed force between nations or parts of a nation. **2** *Fig.* any fighting; strife; conflict: *war against poverty.* **3** the occupation or art of fighting with weapons; military science. —*v.* fight; make war: *a country ready to war.* —*adj.* used in war; having to do with war; caused by war.

at war, taking part in a war.

go to war, a start a war. **b** go as a soldier. [< OF *werre* < Gmc.] —**war′less,** *adj.*

war·ble (wôr′bəl), *v.,* **-bled, -bling,** *n.* —*v.* **1** sing with trills, quavers, or melodious turns: *birds warbled in the trees.* **2** make a sound like that of a bird warbling. —*n.* a warbling. [< OF *werbler* < Gmc.]

war·bler (wôr′blər), *n.* **1** person, bird, etc., that warbles. **2** any of a great variety of small songbirds, often brightly colored.

war bonnet, ceremonial headdress of North American Indians, distinguished by its luxuriant feathers, esp. a tail of feathers extending down the back.

war crime, violation of the international rules of war, esp. any cruel or inhuman

act against civilians or prisoners of war. —**war criminal.**

war cry, word or phrase shouted in fighting; battle cry.

ward (wôrd), *n.* **1** person under the care of a guardian or of a court. **2** a district of a city or town. **3** a division of a hospital or prison. **4** custody; prison. —*v. Archaic.* keep watch over; protect.

ward off, keep away; turn aside. [OE *weardian* guard. Doublet of GUARD.]

-ward, *suffix.* in the direction of; that is, moves, or faces toward; toward, as in *backward, heavenward, onward, seaward.* See also **-wards.** [OE *-weard*]

war dance, dance of esp. Indian tribes before going to war or to celebrate a victory.

ward·en (wôr′dən), *n.* **1** keeper; guard: *a game warden.* **2** the administrative head of a prison. **3** the head of certain colleges, schools, etc. **4** =churchwarden. [< OF *wardein,* ult. < Gmc.] —**ward′en·ship,** *n.*

ward·er (wôr′dər), *n.* **1** guard; watchman. **2** warden; jailer. —**ward′er·ship,** *n.*

ward heeler, follower of a political boss, who goes around asking for votes, etc.

ward·robe (wôrd′rōb′), *n.* **1** stock of clothes: *a spring wardrobe.* **2** room, closet, or piece of furniture for holding clothes.

ward·room (wôrd′rüm′; –rum′), *n.* the living and eating quarters for commissioned officers on a warship.

-wards, *suffix.* in the direction of, as in *backwards, upwards.* See also **-ward.**

ward·ship (wôrd′ship), *n.* **1** guardianship, esp. over a minor or ward; custody. **2** condition of being a ward.

ware (wār), *n.* **1** Usually, **wares.** a manufactured thing; article for sale: *street peddlers spread their wares on the sidewalks.* **2** pottery. Delft is a blue-and-white ware. [OE *waru*]

ware·house (wār′hous′), *n., v.,* **-housed, -hous·ing.** —*n.* place where goods are kept; storehouse. —*v.* store or put in a warehouse. —**ware′hous·er,** *n.*

war·fare (wôr′fār′), *n.* war; fighting.

war game a training exercise that imitates war. It may be a virtual, or electronic exercise, an exercise on a map, or maneuvers with actual troops, weapons, and equipment.

war·head (wôr′hed), *n.* the forward part of a torpedo, missile, etc., that contains the explosive.

war horse, 1 horse used in war. **2** person who has taken part in many battles, struggles, etc. **3** *Fig.* **a** seasoned actor, public figure, etc. **b** any too well-known work or activity.

war·i·ly (wār′ə li), *adv.* cautiously; carefully.

war·i·ness (wār′i nis), *n.* caution; care.

war·like (wôr′līk′), *adj.* **1** fit for war; ready for war; fond of war. **2** threatening war: *a warlike speech.* **3** of or having to do with war. —**war′like′ness,** *n.*

war·lord (wôr′lôrd′) or **war lord,** *n.* commander, esp. of a private army or militia, who completely controls a region. —**war′lord′ism,** *n.*

warm (wôrm), *adj.* **1** more hot than cold; having heat; giving forth heat: *a warm fire, a warm climate, be warm from running.* **2** that makes or keeps warm: *a warm coat.* **3** having or showing affection, enthusiasm, or zeal: *a warm welcome, warm friends.* **4** easily excited; lively; brisk: *a warm temper or dispute.* **5** fresh and strong: *a warm scent.* **6** near what one is searching for. **7** suggesting heat. Red, orange, and yellow are called warm colors. **8** uncomfortable; unpleasant: *make things warm for a person.* —*v.* **1** make or become warm: *warm a room.* **2** make or become cheered, interested, friendly, or sympathetic: *warm one's heart.*

warm over, reheat: *warm over last night's dinner.*

warm up, practice or exercise for a few minutes before entering a game, contest, etc. [OE *wearm*] —**warm′er,** *n.* —**warm′ly,** *adv.* —**warm′ness,** *n.*

warm-blood·ed (wôrm′blud′id), *adj.* **1** pertaining to animals, as mammals and birds, having warm blood and a body temperature from 98 degrees to 112 degrees. **2** with much feeling; eager; ardent.

warm-heart·ed (wôrm′här′tid), *adj.* kind; sympathetic; friendly. —**warm′-heart′ed·ly,** *adv.* —**warm′-heart′ed·ness,** *n.*

warming pan, a covered pan with a long handle, formerly filled with hot coals and used to warm beds.

war·mon·ger (wôr′mung′gər; –mong′–), *n.* one who is in favor of war or attempts to bring it about. —**war′mon′ger·ing,** *n., adj.*

warmth (wôrmth), *n.* **1** being warm: *the warmth of the open fire.* **2** moderate or gentle heat. **3** *Fig.* friendliness. **4** *Fig.* liveliness of feeling or emotions; fervor.

warn (wôrn), *v.* **1** give notice to in advance; put on guard (against danger, evil, harm, etc.): *the clouds warned us of a storm.* **2** give notice to; inform: *warn trespassers off.* [OE *warnian*] —**warn′er,** *n.*

warn·ing (wôr′ning), *n.* something that warns; notice given in advance. —*adj.* that warns. —**warn′ing·ly,** *adv.*

warp (wôrp), *v.* **1** bend or twist out of shape. **2** mislead; pervert: *prejudice warps our judgment.* —*n.* **1** a bend or twist; distortion. **2** the threads running lengthwise in a fabric: *in weaving, the warp is crossed by the woof.* [OE *weorpan* to throw]

war paint, 1 paint put on the face or body, esp. by native people, before going to war. **2** *Fig.* full dress; fancy ornaments.

war·path (wôr′path′; –päth′), *n.* way taken by a fighting expedition of American Indians.

on the warpath, a ready for war. **b** looking for a fight; angry.

war·plane (wôr′plān′), *n.* airplane used in war.

war·rant (wôr′ənt; wor′–), *n.* **1** that which gives a right; authority: *he had no warrant for his action.* **2** a written order giving authority for something: *a warrant to search the house.* **3** a good and sufficient reason; promise; guarantee: *he had no warrant for his hopes.* **4** a document certifying something, esp. to a purchaser. **5** official certificate of appointment issued to a noncommissioned officer in the army or navy. —*v.* **1** authorize: *the law warrants his arrest.* **2** justify: *nothing can warrant such rudeness.* **3** give one's word for; guarantee; promise: *the storekeeper warranted the quality of the coffee.* **4** declare positively; certify. [< OF *warant* < Gmc.] —**war′rant·a·ble,** *adj.* —**war′rant·a·ble·ness,** *n.* —**war′rant·a·bly,** *adv.*

war·ran·tee (wôr′ən tē′; wor′–), *n.* person to whom a warranty is made.

war·rant·er (wôr′ən tər; wor′–), *n.* person who warrants.

war·rant·less (wôr′ənt lis; wor′–), *adj.* **1** without a warrant; unauthorized: *warrantless wiretaps.* **2** not justified: *warrantless behavior.*

warrant officer, an army or navy officer who has received a certificate of appointment, but not a commission, ranking between commissioned officers and enlisted men and women.

war·ran·ty (wôr′ən ti; wor′–), *n., pl.* **–ties.** **1** warrant; authority; justification. **2** promise or pledge that something is what it is claimed to be; guarantee. [< OF *warantie.* See WARRANT. Doublet of GUARANTY.]

war·ren (wôr′ən; wor′–), *n.* piece of ground filled with burrows, where rabbits live or are raised. [< AF *warenne* < Celtic]

war·ri·or (wôr′i ər; wor′–), *n.* a fighting person; experienced soldier. —**war′ri·or·like′,** *adj.*

War·saw (wôr′sô), *n.* capital and largest city of Poland, in the E part.

war·ship (wôr′ship′), *n.* ship used in war.

wart (wôrt), *n.* **1** a small, hard lump on the skin. **2** a similar lump on a plant. [OE *wearte*]

wart hog, a wild hog of Africa that has two large tusks and two large wartlike growths on each side of its face.

war·time (wôr′tīm′), *n.* a time of war.

war whoop, a war cry of American Indians.

war·y (wār′i), *adj.,* **war·i·er, war·i·est. 1** on one's guard against danger, deception, etc. **2** cautious; careful.

wary of, cautious about; careful about. [< *ware* watchful (OE *wær*)]

was (woz; wuz; *unstressed* wəz), *v.* the 1st and 3rd pers. sing., past indicative of **be:** *I was late.* [OE *wæs*]

wash (wosh; wôsh), *v.* **1** clean with water or other liquid: *wash clothes, wash one's face, wash a spot out.* **2** wash oneself:

wash for supper. **3** wash clothes. **4** be carried along or away by water or other liquid: *the road washed out during the storm, washed ashore by the waves, the cliffs are being washed away by the waves.* **5** flow or beat with a lapping sound: *the waves washed upon the rocks.* **6** sift (earth, ore, etc.) by action of water to separate valuable material. **7** *Informal. Fig.* stand being put to the proof: *patriotism that won't wash.* —*n.* **1** a washing or being washed. **2** quantity of clothes washed or to be washed. **3** material carried and then dropped by water. **4** motion, rush, or sound of water: *wash of the waves.* **5** tract of land sometimes overflowed with water; fen, marsh, or bog. **6** liquid for a special use: *a hair wash.* **7** a thin coating of color or metal. **8** the rough or broken water left behind a moving ship. **9** disturbance in air made by an airplane. —*adj.* that can be washed without damage.

wash one's hands of, renounce all interest in or responsibility for.

wash out, a *Fig.* ruin; destroy: *washed out all hope of returning.* **b** cancel because of rain. **c** fail and be dismissed, esp. from a school.

wash up, wash hands, dishes, etc.; clean up. [OE *wascan*]

Wash., the state of Washington.

wash·a·ble (wosh′ə bəl; wôsh′–), *adj.* that can be washed without damage: *washable silk.*

wash·bowl (wosh′bōl′; wôsh′–), **wash·ba·sin** (-bā′sən), *n.* bowl for holding water to wash one's hands and face.

wash·cloth (wosh′klôth′; –kloth′; wôsh′–), *n.* a small cloth for washing oneself.

wash·day (wosh′dā′; wôsh′–), *n.* day when clothes are washed.

washed-out (wosht′out′; wôsht′–), *adj.* **1** lacking color; faded. **2** lacking life, spirit, etc.

washed-up (wosht′up′; wôsht′–), *adj.* **1** done with; through, esp. after having failed. **2** fatigued.

wash·er (wosh′ər; wôsh′–), *n.* **1** person who washes. **2** machine that washes. **3** a flat ring of metal, rubber, leather, etc., used with bolts or nuts, or to make joints tight.

wash·ing (wosh′ing; wôsh′–), *n.* **1** a cleaning with water. **2** clothes, etc., washed or to be washed.

washing machine, machine that washes clothes, etc.

Wash·ing·ton (wosh′ing tən; wôsh′–), *n.* **1** capital of the United States, coextensive with the District of Columbia. **2** a NW state of the United States, on the Pacific Coast. **3** George, 1732–99, commander in chief of the American army in the Revolutionary War and the first president of the United States, 1789–97.

Wash·ing·to·ni·an (wosh′ing tō′ni ən; wôsh′–), *n.* native or inhabitant of Washington. —*adj.* of or having to do with Washington, D.C., or the state of Washington.

wash·out (wosh′out′; wôsh′–), *n.* **1** a washing away of earth, a road, etc., by water. **2** the hole or break made by it. **3** failure; disappointment.

wash·rag (wosh′rag′; wôsh′–), *n.* =washcloth.

wash·room (wosh′rüm′; –rùm′; wôsh′–), *n.* room where people can wash themselves; lavatory.

wash·stand (wosh′stand′; wôsh′–), *n.* **1** bowl with pipes and faucets for running water to wash one's hands and face. **2** stand for holding a basin, pitcher, etc., for washing.

wash·tub (wosh′tub′; wôsh′–), *n.* tub used to wash or soak clothes in.

wash·y (wosh′i; wôsh′i), *adj.,* **wash·i·er, wash·i·est.** too much diluted; weak; watery.

was·n't (woz′ənt, wuz′–), was not.

wasp (wosp; wôsp), *n.* a kind of insect that has a slender body and a powerful sting. [OE *wæsp*] —**wasp′like′, wasp′y,** *adj.*

Wasp or **WASP,** White Anglo-Saxon Protestant, middle- and upper-class Americans of British and European descent.

wasp·ish (wos′pish; wôs′–), *adj.* **1** like a wasp; like that of a wasp. **2** bad-tempered; irritable. **3** like a Wasp; upper-class. —**wasp′ish·ly,** *adv.* —**wasp′ish·ness,** *n.*

was·sail (wos′əl; was′–), *n.* **1** a drinking party; revel with drinking of healths. **2** spiced ale or other liquor drunk at a wassail. **3** a salutation meaning "Your health!" —*v.* **1** take part in a wassail; revel. **2** drink to the health ot. —*interj.* "Your health!" [< Scand. *ves heill* be healthy!] —**was′sail·er,** *n.*

Was·ser·mann test (wos′ər mən), test for syphilis, made on a sample of a person's blood or spinal fluid.

wast·age (wās′tij), *n.* **1** loss by use, wear, decay, leakage, etc.: waste. **2** amount wasted.

waste (wāst), *v.,* **wast·ed, wast·ing,** *n.,* *adj.* —*v.* **1** make poor use of; spend uselessly; fail to get value from: *waste money, waste an opportunity.* **2** wear down little by little; destroy or lose gradually: *wasted by disease.* **3** damage greatly; destroy: *the soldiers wasted the enemy's fields.* —*n.* **1** poor use; useless spending; failure to get the most out of something: *waste of money, time, etc., waste of opportunity.* **3** gradual destruction or decay: *waste of bodily tissue.* **4** useless or worthless material; stuff to be thrown away: *garbage is waste.* **5** bare or wild land; desert; wilderness. —*adj.* **1** thrown away as useless or worthless. **2** left over; not used. **3** cultivated; that is a desert or wilderness; bare; wild. **4** in a state of desolation or ruin.

go to waste, be wasted.

lay waste, damage greatly; destroy; ravage. [< OF, ult. < L *vastus,* vast, waste, infl. by cognate Gmc. word] —**wast′er,** *n.*

waste·bas·ket (wāst′bas′kit; –bäs′–), *n.* basket or other container for wastepaper or trash.

waste·ful (wāst′fəl), *adj.* using or spending too much. —**waste′ful·ly,** *adv.* —**waste′ful·ness,** *n.*

waste·pa·per (wāst′pā′pər), **waste paper,** *n.* paper thrown away or to be thrown away as trash.

waste pipe, pipe for carrying off waste water, etc.

wast·ing (wās′ting), *adj.* **1** laying waste; devastating. **2** gradually destructive to the body.

wast·rel (wās′trəl), *n.* **1** waster. **2** idler.

watch (woch; wôch), *v.* **1** look at; observe: *watch a play.* **2** look or wait with care and attention; be very careful: *watch for the approach of an enemy, the dog watched the little boy.* **3** stay awake for some purpose: *the nurse watches with the sick.* —*n.* **1** a careful looking; attitude of attention: *be on the watch for automobiles when you cross the street.* **2** a protecting; guarding: *a man keeps watch over the bank at night.* **3** person or persons kept to guard. **4** period of time for guarding. **5** wakefulness, esp. a staying awake for some purpose. **6** device for telling time, small enough to be carried in a pocket or worn on the wrist. **7 a** the time of duty of one part of a ship's crew. A watch usually lasts four hours. **b** the part of a crew on duty at the same time.

watch out, be careful; be on guard.

watch over, guard; protect. [OE *wæccan*] —**watch′er,** *n.*

watch·dog (woch′dôg′; –dog′; wôch′–), *n.* **1** dog kept to guard property. **2** a watchful guardian.

watch fire, fire kept burning at night in camps, etc.

watch·ful (woch′fəl; wôch′–), *adj.* watching carefully; on the lookout; wide-awake. —**watch′ful·ly,** *adv.* —**watch′ful·ness,** *n.*

watch·mak·er (woch′māk′ər; wôch′–), *n.* person who makes and repairs watches. —**watch′mak′ing,** *n.*

watch·man (woch′mən; wôch′–), *n., pl.* –**men.** person who keeps watch; guard.

watch·tow·er (woch′tou′ər; wôch′–), *n.* tower from which a lookout is kept for enemies, fires, ships, etc.

watch·word (woch′wėrd′; wôch′–), *n.* **1** a secret word that allows a person to pass a guard; password. **2** motto; slogan.

wa·ter (wô′tər; wot′ər), *n.* **1** liquid that constitutes rain, oceans, rivers, lakes, and ponds, compound of hydrogen and oxygen, H_2O. **2** liquid from the body, as tears, sweat, saliva, urine, serum, etc. **3** any liquid preparation that suggests water: *rose water.* **4** body of water; sea, lake, river, etc., esp. with reference to its relative height, etc.: *high or low water.* **5** a wavy marking on silk, metal, etc. —*v.* **1** sprinkle or wet with water. **2** supply with water. **3** fill with water; discharge water:

her eyes watered. **4** weaken by adding water. **5** make a wavy marking on.

above water, *Fig.* out of trouble or difficulty.

back water, make a boat go backward.

blow out of the water, *Informal. Fig.* thoroughly destroy; expose, esp. as a fraud.

by water, on a ship or boat.

hold water, *Fig.* stand the test; be true, dependable, effective, etc.

like water, very freely: *spend money like water.*

of the first water, of the highest degree.

pour, throw, or **dash cold water on,** discourage; be unwilling or indifferent.

water down, reduce in strength or effect.

waters, a flowing water. **b** water moving in waves; the sea; the high sea. **c** spring water; mineral water. [OE *wæter*] —**wa′ter·er,** *n.* —**wa′ter·less,** *adj.*

water bird, bird that swims or wades in water.

wa·ter·borne (wô′tər bôrn′; –bōrn′; wot′ər–), *adj.* **1** supported by water; floating. **2** conveyed by a boat or the like.

water buffalo, the buffalo of Asia and the Philippines.

water bug, an insect that lives in, on, or near water.

water closet, toilet flushed by water.

water color, 1 paint mixed with water instead of oil. **2** a painting with water colors. **3** picture made with water colors. —**wa′ter·col′or,** *adj.* —**wa′ter·col′or·ist,** *n.*

wa·ter·cool (wô′tər kül′; wot′ər–), *v.* cool by means of water circulating in a jacket or pipes. —**wa′ter·cooled′,** *adj.*

water cooler, any device for cooling water, or for cooling something by means of water, esp. one that dispenses cold drinking water.

wa·ter·course (wô′tər kôrs′; –kōrs′; wot′ər–), *n.* **1** stream of water; river; brook. **2** channel for water.

water cress, a plant that grows in water, used for salad and as a garnish. —**wa′ter·cress′,** *adj.*

water cycle, natural cycle of evaporation of water from lakes, oceans, etc., with the resulting formation of clouds that return the water to earth as rain and snow.

wa·ter·fall (wô′tər fôl′; wot′ər–), *n.* fall of water from a high place.

wa·ter·fowl (wô′tər foul′; wot′ər–), *n., pl.* –**fowls** or (*esp. collectively*) –**fowl. 1** a water bird. **2** water birds, esp. birds that swim.

water front, 1 land at the water's edge. **2** the part of a city beside a river, lake, or harbor.

water gap, gap in a mountain ridge through which a stream flows.

water glass, wa·ter·glass (wô′tər glas′; –gläs′; wot′ər–), *n.* **1** glass to hold water; tumbler. **2** gauge which indicates the level of water.

water hole, hole in the ground that collects water.

watering can, container with a long spout for giving water to plants.

watering hole, 1 =water hole. **2** *Informal. Fig.* =watering place. **3** *Informal. Fig.* popular restaurant or, esp., a bar.

watering place, 1 resort with springs containing mineral water or where there is bathing, boating, etc. **2** place where water may be obtained.

water level, 1 the surface level of a body of water. **2** water line.

water lily, a water plant having flat, floating leaves and showy, fragrant flowers. The flowers of the common American water lily are white, or sometimes pink.

water line, wa·ter·line (wô′ter līn′; wot′ər–), *n.* **1** line where the surface of the water touches the side of a ship or boat. **2** pipe to carry water.

wa·ter·logged (wô′tər lôgd′; –logd′; wot′ər–), *adj.* **1** so full of water that it will barely float. **2** thoroughly soaked with water.

water main, a large pipe for carrying water.

wa·ter·man (wô′tər mən; wot′ər–), *n., pl.* –**men. 1** =boatman. **2** =oarsman. —**wa′ter·man·ship′,** *n.*

wa·ter·mark (wô′tər märk′; wot′ər–), *n.* **1** a mark showing how high water has risen or how low it has fallen. **2** a faint design made in some kinds of paper during manufacture. —*v.* put a watermark in.

wa·ter·mel·on (wô′tər mel′ən; wot′ər–), *n.* **1** a large, juicy melon with red or pink pulp and a hard green rind. **2** vine bearing these melons.

water moccasin, 1 a poisonous snake of the S United States that lives in swamps and along streams; the cottonmouth. **2** any of various similar but harmless snakes.

water ouzel, any of various small birds related to the thrushes, that wade and dive in deep water for food.

water power, the power from flowing or falling water. It can be used to drive machinery and make electricity.

wa·ter·proof (wô′tər prüf′; wot′ər–), *adj.* that will not let water through; resistant to water. —*v.* make waterproof.

water rat, 1 any type of ratlike rodent that lives on the banks of streams or lakes. **2** =muskrat.

wa·ter·shed (wô′tər shed′; wot′ər–), *n.* **1** ridge between the regions drained by two different river systems. **2** the region drained by one river system.

wa·ter·side (wô′tər sīd′; wot′ər–), *n.* land along the sea, a lake, a river, etc.

wa·ter·ski·ing (wô′tər skē′ing; wot′ər–), *n.* sport of gliding on the water on a pair of skis or a special board, pulled by a motorboat. —**water ski.** —**wa·ter·ski,** *v.*

wa·ter·soak (wô′tər sōk′; wot′ər–), *v.* soak thoroughly with water.

water spaniel, a curly-haired dog that is often trained to swim out for wild ducks, geese, etc., that have been shot down by hunters.

wa·ter·spout (wô′tər spout′; wot′ər–), *n.* **1** pipe which takes away or spouts water. **2** whirlwind over the ocean or a large lake. It looks like a column of water reaching upward to the clouds.

water sprite, sprite supposed to live in water.

water strider, insect with long, thin legs that moves along the surface of ponds, streams, etc.

water table, the level below which the ground is saturated with water.

wa·ter·tight (wô′tər tīt′; wot′ər–), *adj.* **1** so tight that no water can get in or out: *the watertight compartments of a ship.* **2** leaving no opening for misunderstanding, criticism, etc.; perfect. **—wa′ter·tight′ness,** *n.*

water tower, 1 a big tower to hold water. **2** a fire-extinguishing apparatus used to throw water on the upper parts of tall buildings.

water vapor, water in a gaseous state, esp. when below the boiling point and fairly diffused, as distinguished from steam.

wa·ter·way (wô′tər wā′; wot′ər–), *n.* **1** river, canal, or other body of water that ships can go on. **2** channel for water.

water wheel, 1 wheel turned by water and used to do work. **2** wheel for raising water.

wa·ter·works (wô′tər wėrks′; wot′ər–), *n. pl. (often sing. in use)* **1** system of pipes, reservoirs, water towers, pumps, etc., for supplying a city or town with water. **2** pumping station. **3** *Informal. Fig.* dramatic flow of tears.

wa·ter·worn (wô′tər wôrn′; –wōrn′; wot′ər–), *adj.* worn or smoothed by the action of water.

wa·ter·y (wô′tər i; wot′ər–), *adj.* **1** of water; connected with water. **2** full of water; wet: *a watery sky.* **3** like water. **4** weak; thin; poor; pale: *a watery blue.* **5** in or under water: *a watery grave.* **—wa′ter·i·ness,** *n.*

watt (wot), *n.* a unit of electric power, equivalent to one joule per second. [after J. Watt]

watt·age (wot′ij), *n.* electric power expressed in watts. A flatiron that uses 5 amperes of current on a 110-volt circuit has a wattage of 550.

wat·tle (wot′əl), *n., v.,* **-tled, -tling.** —*n.* **1** Also, **wattles.** sticks interwoven with twigs or branches; framework of wicker. **2** the red flesh hanging down from the throat of a chicken, turkey, etc. —*v.* twist or weave together (twigs, branches, etc.). [OE *watul*] **—wat′tled,** *adj.*

wave (wāv), *n., v.,* **waved, wav·ing.** —*n.* **1** a moving ridge or swell of water. **2** a movement of particles to and fro; vibration. **3** a swell, surge, or rush; increase of some emotion, influence, condition, etc.; outburst: *a wave of enthusiasm.* **4** a waving, esp. of something, as a signal. **5** a curve or series of curves. —*v.* **1** move as waves do; move up and down or back and forth; sway. **2** have a wavelike form: *her hair waves naturally.* **3** signal or direct by waving: *she waved him away.*

make waves, *Informal.* disturb or upset esp. the normal state of things. [OE *wafian*] **—wav′a·ble,** *adj.* **—wave′less,** *adj.* **—wave′like′,** *adj.* **—wav′er,** *n.*

wave length, the distance between any particle of a medium through which waves are passing and the next particle that is in the same phase with it.

wave·let (wāv′lit), *n.* a little wave.

wa·ver (wā′vər), *v.* **1** move to and fro; flutter. **2** vary in intensity; flicker. **3** be undecided; hesitate. **4** become unsteady; begin to give way. —*n.* a wavering. [ult. < *wave*] **—wa′ver·er,** *n.* **—wa′ver·ing·ly,** *adv.* **—wa′ver·y,** *adj.*

wav·y (wā′vi), *adj.,* **wav·i·er, wav·i·est.** having waves; having many waves: *wavy hair, a wavy line.* **—wav′i·ly,** *adv.* **—wav′i·ness,** *n.*

wax¹ (waks), *n.* **1** a yellowish substance made by bees for constructing their honeycomb. **2** any substance like this. —*v.* rub, stiffen, polish, etc., with wax. —*adj.* of wax. [OE *weax*] **—wax′er,** *n.* **—wax′like′,** *adj.*

wax² (waks), *v.,* **waxed, waxed** or (*Poetic*) **wax·en, wax·ing. 1** grow bigger or greater; increase. **2** become: *the party waxed merry.* [OE *weaxan*]

wax bean, a yellow string bean.

wax·en (wak′sən), *adj.* **1** made of wax. **2** like wax; smooth, soft, and pale.

wax myrtle, any of various shrubs or trees whose small berries are coated with wax. The bayberry is a wax myrtle.

wax paper, paper coated with paraffin, used to wrap food.

wax·wing (waks′wing′), *n.* any of several small birds with a showy crest and red markings at the tips of the wings, as the cedarbird.

wax·work (waks′wėrk′), *n.* figure or figures made of wax.

waxworks (*sing. in use*), exhibition of figures made of wax. **—wax′work′er,** *n.*

wax·y (wak′si), *adj.,* **wax·i·er, wax·i·est. 1** made of or covered with wax; containing wax. **2** like wax. **3** smooth and pliable; yielding. **—wax′i·ness,** *n.*

way (wā), *n.* **1** manner; style: *reply in a polite way, that is only his way.* **2** method; means: *new ways to prevent disease.* **3** point; feature; respect; detail: *a plan defective in several ways.* **4** direction: *look this way.* **5** motion along a course: *the guide led the way, the ship slowly gathered way.* **6** distance: *the sun is a long way off.* **7** road; path; street; course: *find one's way.* **8** one's wish; will: *he wants his own way.* **9** condition; state: *that sick man is in a bad way.* —*adv.* away.

all the way, without reservation; thoroughly: *she was behind me all the way.*

by the way, a while coming or going: *had a snack by the way.* **b** in that connection; incidentally: *by the way, when will you finish this book?*

by way of, a by the route of; through. **b** as; for: *by way of introduction.*

come a long way, accomplish a great deal.

come one's way, happen to one: *luck came my way.*

give way, a make way; yield; retreat. **b** break down; fall. **c** abandon oneself to emotion.

go a long way (toward), help very much.

go out of the way, make a special effort.

have a way with (one), be persuasive: *have a way with animals.*

in a way, to some extent.

in the way, being an obstacle, hindrance, etc.

know one's way around, be familiar with; know the ropes.

make one's way, a go. **b** get ahead; succeed.

make way, a give space for passing or going ahead; make room. **b** move forward.

no way, *Informal.* no; never.

on the way, getting nearer; coming closer.

out of the way, a so as not to be an obstacle, hindrance, etc. **b** far from where most people live or go. **c** unusual; strange.

pave the way, prepare.

pick one's way, move carefully.

under way, going on; in motion; in progress.

ways, timbers on which a ship is built and launched. [OE *weg*]

way·far·er (wā′fãr′ər), *n.* traveler.

way·far·ing (wā′fãr′ing), *adj.* traveling.

way·lay (wā′lā′; wā′lā′), *v.,* **-laid, -lay·ing.** lie in wait for; attack on the way: *Robin Hood waylaid travelers and robbed them.* **—way′lay′er,** *n.*

-ways, *suffix* forming adverbs showing direction or position, as in *edgeways, sideways,* or adverbs showing manner, as in *anyways, noways.* [< *way*]

ways and means, methods and techniques for getting something, esp. raising funds.

way·side (wā′sīd′), *n.* edge of a road or path. —*adj.* along the edge of a road or path.

way·ward (wā′wərd), *adj.* **1** turning from the right way; disobedient; willful. **2** irregular; unsteady. **—way′ward·ly,** *adv.* **—way′ward·ness,** *n.*

we (wē; *unstressed* wi), *pron., pl. nom.; poss.,* **our** or **ours;** *obj.,* **us.** the 1st pers. nom. pl. of **I.** [OE *wē*]

weak (wēk), *adj.* **1** that can easily be broken, crushed, overcome, torn, etc.: not strong: *a weak foundation, weak defenses.* **2** lacking bodily strength or health: *a weak constitution.* **3** lacking power, authority, force, etc.: *a weak* *government.* **4** lacking mental power: *a weak mind.* **5** lacking moral strength or firmness; vacillating: *a weak character.* **6** lacking or poor in amount, volume, loudness, taste, intensity, etc.: *a weak voice, weak arguments.* **7** lacking or poor in something specified: *a composition weak in spelling.* **8** (of Germanic verbs) inflected by additions of consonants to the stem, not by vowel change. English weak verbs form the past tense and past participle by adding *–ed, –d,* or *–t.* [< Scand. *veikr*] —**weak′ness,** *n.*

weak·en (wēk′ən), *v.* make or become weak or weaker. —**weak′en·er,** *n.* —**weak′en·ing·ly,** *adv.*

weak·fish (wēk′fish′), *n., pl.* **-fish·es** or (*esp. collectively*) **-fish.** a spiny-finned saltwater food fish with a tender mouth.

weak interaction, interaction between elementary particles that causes radioactive decay and no measurable release of energy. Also, **weak force.**

weak-kneed (wēk′nēd′), *adj.* yielding easily to opposition, intimidation, etc.

weak·ling (wēk′ling), *n.* a weak person or animal.

weak·ly (wēk′li), *adv., adj.,* **-li·er, -li·est.** —*adv.* in a weak manner. —*adj.* weak; feeble; sickly. —**weak′li·ness,** *n.*

weak-mind·ed (wēk′mīn′did), *adj.* **1** having or showing little intelligence; feeble-minded. **2** lacking firmness of mind. —**weak′-mind′ed·ness,** *n.*

weal (wēl), *n.* streak or ridge on the skin made by a stick or whip; welt.

wealth (welth), *n.* **1** much money or property; riches. **2** all things that have value. **3** *Fig.* a large quantity; abundance: *a wealth of words.* [< *well¹* or *weal*]

wealth·y (wel′thi), *adj.,* **wealth·i·er, wealth·i·est. 1** having wealth; rich. **2** abundant; ample. —**wealth′i·ly,** *adv.* —**wealth′i·ness,** *n.*

wean (wēn), *v.* **1** accustom (a child or young animal) to food other than its mother's milk. **2** accustom (a person) to do without something; cause to turn away; detach. [OE *wenian*] —**wean′er,** *n.*

weap·on (wep′ən), *n.* any instrument used in fighting; means of attack or defense. Swords, arrows, guns, and claws are weapons. [OE *wæpen*] —**weap′oned,** *adj.* —**weap′on·less,** *adj.*

weap·on·ry (wep′ən ri), *n.* weapons collectively: *nuclear weaponry.*

wear (wãr), *v.,* **wore, worn, wear·ing,** *n.* —*v.* **1** have on the body: *we wear clothes.* **2** cause or suffer loss or damage to by using: *these shoes are worn out.* **3** make by rubbing, scraping, washing away, etc.: *walking wore a hole in my shoe.* **4** tire; weary: *running wears him out.* **5** last long; give good service: *this coat has worn well.* **6** have; show: *the house wore an air of sadness.* **7** pass or go gradually: *it became hotter as the day wore on.* —*n.* **1** a wearing; a being worn: *clothing for summer wear.* **2** clothing: *the store sells*

children's wear. **3** gradual loss or damage caused by use: *the rug shows wear.* **4** lasting quality; good service: *there is still wear in these shoes.*

wear and tear, loss or damage caused by use.

wear away, scrape, rub, or wash away.

wear down, a tire; weary. **b** overcome by persistent effort. **c** reduce in height.

wear off, become less.

wear thin, a weaken; wear out. **b** become uninteresting or dull. [OE *werian*] —**wear′a·ble,** *adj.* —**wear′a·bil′i·ty, wear′a·ble·ness,** *n.* —**wear′er,** *n.*

wear·ing (wãr′ing), *adj.* wearisome.

wearing apparel, clothes.

wea·ri·some (wir′i səm), *adj.* wearying; tiring; tiresome. —**wea′ri·some·ly,** *adv.* —**wea′ri·some·ness,** *n.*

wea·ry (wir′i), *adj.,* **-ri·er, -ri·est,** *v.,* **-ried, -ry·ing.** —*adj.* **1** tired: *weary feet, a weary brain.* **2** causing fatigue; tiring: *a weary wait.* **3** having one's patience, tolerance, or liking exhausted. —*v.* make or become weary; tire. [OE *wērig*] —**wea′ri·less,** *adj.* —**wea′ri·ly,** *adv.* —**wea′ri·ness,** *n.* —**wea′ry·ing·ly,** *adv.*

wea·sel (wē′zəl), *n.* **1** a small, quick, sly animal with a long, slender body and short legs. Weasels feed on rats, birds, eggs, etc. **2** a cunning, sneaking person. [OE *weosule*]

weath·er (weth′ər), *n.* **1** condition of the atmosphere with respect to temperature, moisture, or other meteorological phenomena. **2** windy or stormy weather. —*v.* **1** expose to the weather. **2** become discolored or worn by air, rain, sun, frost, etc. **3** go or come through safely: *the ship weathered the storm.* —*adj.* **1** toward the wind; windward. **2** of the side exposed to the wind.

keep one's weather eye open, be on the lookout for possible danger or trouble.

under the weather, sick; ailing. [OE *weder*] —**weath′ered,** *adj.*

weath·er-beat·en (weth′ər bēt′ən), *adj.* worn or hardened by the wind, rain, and other forces of the weather.

weath·er-bound (weth′ər bound′), *adj.* delayed by bad weather: *a weather-bound ship.*

weath·er·cock (weth′ər kok′), *n.* a weather vane, esp. one in the shape of a cock.

weath·er·ing (weth′ər ing), *n.* process by which rocks are decomposed by air, water, frost, etc.

weath·er·ize (weth′ə rīz), *v.,* **-ized, -iz·ing.** insulate and otherwise prepare a building to withstand cold weather and to conserve heat. —**weath′er·i·za′tion,** *n.*

weath·er·man (weth′ər man′), *n., pl.* **-men.** person who forecasts the weather.

weath·er·proof (weth′ər prüf′), *adj.* protected against rain, snow, or wind; able to stand exposure to all kinds of weather. —*v.* make weatherproof.

weather station, installation where meteorological observations are made.

weath·er-strip (weth′ər strip′), *v.,* **-stripped, -strip·ping.** fit with weather stripping.

weather stripping, a roll of narrow stripping to cover space between a window and its casing or a door and its frame.

weather vane, device to show which way the wind is blowing.

weath·er-wise (weth′ər wīz′), *adj.* **1** skillful in forecasting the changes of the weather. **2** skillful in forecasting changes in opinion, etc.

weave (wēv), *v.,* **wove** or (*Rare*) **weaved, wo·ven** or **wove, weav·ing,** *n.* —*v.* **1** form (threads or strips) into a thing or fabric: *weave thread into cloth.* **2** make out of thread, etc.: *she is weaving a rug.* **3** combine into a whole: *the author wove the incident into a story.* —*n.* method or pattern of weaving: *a cloth of coarse weave.*

weave one's way, make one's way by twisting and turning. [OE *wefan*]

weav·er (wēv′ər), *n.* **1** person who weaves. **2** person whose work is weaving. **3** weaverbird.

weav·er·bird (wēv′ər bėrd′), *n.* a bird of Asia and Africa, that builds an elaborately woven nest.

web¹ (web), *n.* **1** something woven. **2** fabric of delicate, silken threads spun by a spider or by the larvae of certain insects. **3** anything like a web: *a web of lies, the web of life.* **4** the skin joining the toes of ducks, geese, and other swimming birds. [OE *webb*] —**webbed,** *adj.* —**web′less,** *adj.* —**web′like′,** *adj.*

web² or **Web** (wəb), *n.* World Wide Web

web·bing (web′ing), *n.* **1** cloth woven into strong strips for belts. **2** the plain foundation fabric woven at the edge of some rugs, etc., to prevent raveling. **3** skin joining the toes, as in a duck's feet.

web-foot (web′fút′), *n., pl.* **-feet.** foot in which the toes are joined by a web. —**web′foot′ed,** *adj.*

wed (wed), *v.,* **wed·ded, wed·ded** or **wed, wed·ding. 1** marry. **2** *Fig.* unite. [OE *weddian*]

we'd (wēd), **1** we had. **2** we would; we should.

Wed., Wednesday.

wed·ded (wed′id), *adj.* **1** married. **2** united. **3** devoted.

wed·ding (wed′ing), *n.* **1** the marriage ceremony. **2** an anniversary of it.

wedge (wej), *n., v.,* **wedged, wedg·ing.** —*n.* **1** piece of wood or metal with a tapering thin edge, used in splitting, separating, etc. **2** something shaped like a wedge or used like a wedge: *an entering wedge into society.* —*v.* **1** split or separate with a wedge. **2** fasten or tighten with a wedge. **3** thrust or pack in tightly; squeeze: *he wedged himself through the narrow window.* [OE *wecg*] —**wedge′like′, wedg′y,** *adj.*

wed·lock (wed'lok), *n.* married life; marriage. [OE *wedlāc* pledge < *wedd* pledge + *–lāc,* noun suffix]

Wednes·day (wenz'di; –dā), *n.* the fourth day of the week, following Tuesday.

wee (wē), *adj.,* **we·er, we·est.** very small; tiny. [from the phrase *a little wee* a little bit < OE *wǣg* weight]

weed (wēd), *n.* **1** a useless or troublesome plant; plant occurring in cultivated ground to the exclusion or injury of the desired crop. **2** *Informal.* **a** marijuana **b** tobacco or cigarette. **3** a thin, ungainly person or animal. —*v.* take weeds out of.

weed out, a free from what is useless or worthless. **b** remove as useless or worthless. [OE *wēod*] —**weed'er,** *n.* —**weed'less,** *adj.* —**weed'like',** *adj.*

weed·kill·er (wēd'kil'ər), *n.* =herbicide.

weed·y (wēd'i), *adj.,* **weed·i·er, weed·i·est. 1** full of weeds. **2** of or like weeds. **3** thin and lanky; weak. —**weed'i·ly,** *adv.* —**weed'i·ness,** *n.*

week (wēk), *n.* **1** seven days, one after another. **2** the time from Sunday through Saturday. **3** the working days of a seven-day period.

week in, week out, week after week. [OE *wice*]

week·day (wēk'dā'), *n.* any day except Sunday. —*adj.* of or on a weekday.

week·end (wēk'end'), *n.* Saturday and Sunday as a time for recreation, visiting, etc. —*adj.* of or on a weekend. —*v.* spend a weekend. —**week'end'er,** *n.*

week·ly (wēk'li), *adj., adv., n., pl.* **–lies.** —*adj.* **1** of a week; for a week; lasting a week. **2** done or happening once a week. —*adv.* once each week; every week. —*n.* a newspaper or magazine published once a week.

weep (wēp), *v.,* **wept, weep·ing,** *n.* —*v.* **1** shed tears; cry: *wept bitter tears.* **2** mourn. **3** be very damp; drip; exude. —*n.* act or fact of weeping. [OE *wepan*] —**weep'er,** *n.* —**weep'y,** *adj.*

weep·ing (wēp'ing), *adj.* **1** that weeps. **2** having thin, drooping branches: *a weeping willow.* —**weep'ing·ly,** *adv.*

weeping willow, large willow tree, native to Asia but cultivated widely, that has long, slender, drooping branches.

wee·vil (wē'vəl), *n.* **1** a small beetle whose larvae destroy grain, nuts, cotton, fruit, etc. **2** any of various small insects that destroy stored grain. [OE *wifel*] —**wee'viled, wee'villed,** *adj.* —**wee'vil·y, wee'vil·ly,** *adj.*

weft (weft), *n.* woof. [OE, < *wefan* weave]

weigh (wā), *v.* **1** find the weight of; have as a measure by weight: *I weighed 110 pounds.* **2** bend or bear down by weight; burden: *the mistake weighed heavily.* **3** balance in the mind; consider carefully: *he weighed the idea before speaking.* **4** have importance or influence. **5** lift up (an anchor).

weigh down, oppress; overburden.

weigh in, find out one's weight before a contest.

weigh on, be a burden to.

weigh one's words, think carefully before speaking and choose each word with care. [OE *wegan*] —**weigh'a·ble,** *adj.* —**weigh'er,** *n.*

weight (wāt), *n.* **1** how heavy a thing is; the amount a thing weighs: *the dog's weight is 50 pounds.* **2** quality that makes all things tend toward the center of the earth; heaviness: *gas has hardly any weight.* **3** system of units for expressing weight: *avoirdupois weight, troy weight.* **4** piece of metal having a specific weight, used in weighing things: *a pound weight.* **5** a heavy thing or mass: *a weight keeps the papers in place.* **6** load; burden: *the weight of responsibility.* **7** influence; importance; value: *an opinion of great weight.* —*v.* **1** load down; burden. **2** add weight to; put weight on.

by weight, measure by weighing.

pull one's weight, do one's part or share.

throw one's weight around, *Informal.* use one's position, importance, etc., to influence others. [OE *wiht* < *wegan* weigh] —**weight'less,** *adj.*

weight·y (wāt'i), *adj.,* **weight·i·er, weight·i·est. 1** heavy. **2** *Fig.* burdensome: *weighty cares of state.* **3** important: *weighty negotiations.* **4** influential: *a weighty speaker.* **5** convincing: *weighty arguments.* —**weight'i·ly,** *adv.* —**weight'i·ness,** *n.*

weir (wir), *n.* **1** dam in a river. **2** fence of stakes or broken branches put in a stream or channel to catch fish. [OE *wer*]

weird (wird), *adj.* **1** unearthly; mysterious. **2** odd; fantastic; queer. [OE *wyrd* fate] —**weird'ly,** *adv.* —**weird'ness,** *n.*

wel·come (wel'kəm), *interj., n., v.,* **-comed, -com·ing,** *adj.* —*interj.* word of kindly greeting: *welcome home!* —*n.* **1** a kindly greeting. **2** a kind reception: *you will always have a welcome here.* —*v.* **1** greet kindly. **2** receive gladly. —*adj.* **1** gladly received; agreeable: *a welcome letter.* **2** gladly or freely permitted: *you are welcome to pick the flowers.* **3** free to enjoy courtesies, etc., without obligation (used in conventional response to thanks): *you are quite welcome.*

wear out one's welcome, stay too long visiting someone; become tiresome. [orig. meaning "agreeable guest," OE *wilcuma* < *wil–* (cf. *will* pleasure) + *cuma* comer] —**wel'come·less,** *adj.* —**wel'come·ly,** *adv.* —**wel'come·ness,** *n.* —**wel'com·er,** *n.*

weld (weld), *v.* **1** join together (metal, plastic, etc.) by hammering or pressing while soft and hot. **2** unite closely. **3** be welded or be capable of being welded. —*n.* **1** a welded joint. **2** a welding. [< *well²,* *v.*] —**weld'a·ble,** *adj.* —**weld'er,** *n.*

wel·fare (wel'fãr'), *n.* **1** health, happiness, and prosperity; being or doing well. **2** government assistance for needy people.

welfare state, state whose government provides for the welfare of its citizens, as

through social security, unemployment insurance, etc.

welfare work, work done to improve the conditions of people who need help, as in a community, business, etc. —**welfare worker.**

well¹ (wel), *adv.,* **bet·ter, best,** *adj., interj.* —*adv.* **1** in a satisfactory, favorable, or advantageous manner; all right: *the job was well done, he writes well.* **2** to a considerable degree; much: *shake well before using, well over a hundred dollars, know the subject well.* **3** fairly; reasonably; properly: *I couldn't very well refuse.* **4** sufficiently; adequately: *think well before you act.* —*adj.* **1** satisfactory; good; right: *all is well with us, I am very well.* **2** proper; advisable: *is it well to act so hastily?* **3** in a satisfactory position, condition, etc. —*interj.* expression used to show mild surprise, agreement, etc., or merely to fill in.

as well, a also; besides. **b** equally.

as well as, a in addition to; besides. **b** as much as. [OE *wel*] —**well'ness,** *n.*

well² (wel), *n.* **1** hole dug or bored in the ground to get water, oil, gas, etc. **2** spring; fountain; source: *a well of information.* **3** something like a well in shape or use. **4** shaft for stairs or elevator, extending vertically through the floors of a building. —*v.* spring; rise; gush. [OE *wella,* n., *weillan,* v.]

we'll (wēl; *unstressed* wil), we shall; we will.

well-ad·vised (wel'ad vīzd'), *adj.* **1** wise; careful. **2** given good or wise advice.

well-ap·point·ed (wel'ə poin'tid), *adj.* having good furnishings or equipment.

well-bal·anced (wel'bal'ənst), *adj.* **1** rightly balanced, adjusted, or regulated. **2** sensible; sane.

well-be·haved (wel'bi hāvd'), *adj.* showing good manners or conduct.

well-be·ing (wel'bē'ing), *n.* health and happiness; welfare.

well-born (wel'bôrn'), *adj.* belonging to a good family.

well-bred (wel'bred'), *adj.* well brought up; having or showing good manners.

well-con·tent (wel'kən tent'), *adj.* highly pleased or satisfied.

well-de·fined (wel'di fīnd'), *adj.* definite; clear.

well-dis·posed (wel'dis pōzd'), *adj.* **1** rightly or properly disposed. **2** well-meaning. **3** favorably or kindly disposed.

well-fed (wel'fed'), *adj.* showing the result of good feeding; fat; plump.

well-fixed (wel'fixt'), *adj.* well-to-do.

well-found·ed (wel'foun'did), *adj.* rightly or justly founded: *a well-founded faith in schools.*

well-groomed (wel'grümd'), *adj.* well cared for; neat and trim.

well-ground·ed (wel'ground'did), *adj.* **1** based on good reasons. **2** thoroughly instructed in the fundamental principles of a subject.

well-heeled (wel′hēld′), *adj.* wealthy.

well-in·formed (wel′in fôrmd′), *adj.* 1 having reliable or full information on a subject. 2 having information on a wide variety of subjects.

Wel·ling·ton (wel′ing tən), *n.* capital of New Zealand, on North Island.

well-kept (wel′kept′), *adj.* well cared for; carefully tended.

well-known (wel′nōn′), *adj.* 1 clearly or fully known. 2 generally or widely known; familiar.

well-man·nered (wel′man′ərd), *adj.* having or showing good manners; polite; courteous.

well-mean·ing (wel′mēn′ing), *adj.* 1 having good intentions. 2 Also, **well-meant** (wel′ment′). proceeding from good intentions.

well-nigh (wel′nī′), *adv.* very nearly; almost.

well-off (wel′ôf′; -of′), *adj.* 1 in a good condition or position. 2 fairly rich.

well-pre·served (wel′pri zėrvd′), *adj.* showing few signs of age.

well-read (wel′red′), *adj.* having read much; knowing a great deal about books and literature.

well-round·ed (wel′roun′did), *adj.* 1 well filled out. 2 *Fig.* complete; full: *a well-rounded education.*

well-spo·ken (wel′spō′kən), *adj.* 1 speaking well, fittingly, or pleasingly; polite in speech. 2 spoken well.

well·spring (wel′spring′), *n.* 1 fountainhead. 2 source, esp. of a supply that never fails.

well-suit·ed (wel′süt′id), *adj.* suitable; convenient.

well sweep, a tapering or weighted pole swung on a pivot and having a bucket hung on the smaller or lighter end.

well-thought-of (wel′thôt′ov′; -uv′), *adj.* having a very good reputation.

well-timed (wel′tīmd′), *adj.* timely.

well-to-do (wel′tə dü′), *adj.* having enough money to live well; prosperous.

well-wish·er (wel′wish′ər), *n.* person who wishes well to a person, cause, etc.

well-worn (wel′wôrn′; -wōrn′), *adj.* 1 much worn by use. 2 used too much; trite; stale.

Welsh (welsh; welch), *adj.* of or pertaining to Wales, its people, or their Celtic language. —*n.* 1 the people of Wales. 2 their language.

welsh (welsh; welch), *v. Informal.* evade paying a bet or fulfilling an obligation. —**welsh′er,** *n.*

Welsh·man (welsh′mən; welch′-), *n., pl.* **-men.** native of Wales.

Welsh rabbit, sauce containing cheese, beer, eggs, etc., cooked and poured over toast.

Welsh rarebit, =Welsh rabbit.

welt (welt), *n.* 1 a strip of leather between the upper part and the sole of a shoe. 2 the narrow border, trimming, etc., on the edge of a garment or upholstery. 3 a streak or ridge made on the skin by a stick or whip. —*v.* put a welt on. [ME *welte, walte*]

wel·ter (wel′tər), *v.* roll or toss about; wallow. —*n.* 1 a rolling and tossing. 2 confusion; commotion. [< MDu., MLG *welteren*]

wel·ter·weight (wel′tər wāt′), *n.* boxer or wrestler weighing between 135 and 147 pounds. [earlier *welter* (< *welt,* def. 2) + *weight*]

wen (wen), *n.* a harmless tumor of the skin. [OE *wenn*]

wench (wench), *n.* 1 girl or young woman. 2 a woman servant. [< *wenchel* child, OE *wencel*]

wend (wend), *v.,* **wend·ed** or (*Archaic*) **went, wend·ing.** 1 direct (one's way): *we wended our way home.* 2 go. [OE *wendan*]

went (went), *v.* pt. of **go:** *I went home.*

wept (wept), *v.* pt. and pp. of **weep.**

were (wėr; *unstressed* wər), *v.* 1 pl. and 2nd pers. sing. past indicative of **be:** *we were delayed.* 2 past subjunctive of **be:** *if I were rich, I would travel.*

as it were, as if it were; so to speak; in some way. [OE *wæron*]

were·wolf, wer·wolf (wir′wulf′), *n., pl.* **-wolves** (-wulvz′). in folklore, a person who has been changed into a wolf; person who can change himself into a wolf. [OE *werwulf* < *wer* man + *wulf* wolf]

Wes·ley·an (wes′li ən; *esp. Brit.* wez′li ən), *n.* member of the church founded by John Wesley; Methodist. —*adj.* of or having to do with John Wesley or the Methodist Church.

west (west), *n.* 1 the direction of the sunset; the point of the compass to the left as one faces north. 2 Also, **West.** the part of any country toward the west. 3 West, western part of the United States. —*adj.* 1 lying toward or situated in the west. 2 originating in or coming from the west: *a west wind.* —*adv.* 1 toward the west. 2 in the west, countries in Europe and America as distinguished from those in Asia, esp. SE Asia. [OE]

west·er·ly (wes′tər li), *adj., adv.* 1 toward the west. 2 from the west. —**west′er·li·ness,** *n.*

west·ern (wes′tərn), *adj.* 1 toward the west. 2 from the west. 3 of or in the west. —*n.* story or motion picture dealing with life in the West, esp. cowboy life.

Western, a of or in the W part of the United States. **b** of or in Europe and the Americas. **c** of or in the Western Hemisphere. —**west′ern·most,** *adj.*

Western Church, the part of the Catholic Church that acknowledges the Pope as its spiritual leader and follows the Latin Rite.

Western civilization, European and American civilization as contrasted with Eastern civilization.

West·ern·er (wes′tər nər), *n.* 1 person born or living in the W part of the United States. 2 westerner, native or inhabitant of the west.

Western Hemisphere, the half of the world that includes North and South America.

West Indies, islands between Florida and South America; Greater Antilles, Lesser Antilles, and the Bahamas. —**West Indian.**

West Virginia, an E state of the United States. —**West Virginian.**

west·ward (west′wərd), *adv.* Also, **west′wards.** toward the west. —*adj.* 1 toward the west. 2 west. —*n.* west.

west·ward·ly (west′wərd li), *adj., adv.* 1 toward the west. 2 of winds, from the west.

wet (wet), *adj.,* **wet·ter, wet·test,** *v.,* **wet** or **wet·ted, wet·ting,** *n.* —*adj.* 1 covered or soaked with water or other liquid: *wet hands.* 2 watery; liquid: *wet paint.* 3 rainy: *a wet day.* 4 having or favoring laws that permit making and selling of alcoholic drinks. —*v.* make or become wet. —*n.* 1 water or other liquid. 2 wetness; rain. 3 person who favors laws that permit making and selling of alcoholic drinks.

all wet, *Informal.* mistaken; all wrong. [ME *wett,* pp. of *wete(n),* OE *wœtan*] —**wet′ness,** *n.* —**wet′tish,** *adj.*

wet·back (wet′bak′), *n.* a Latin American who enters the U.S. illegally, esp. by swimming or wading across the Rio Grande. [< *wet* + *back*]

wet blanket, person or thing that has a discouraging or depressing effect.

weth·er (weth′ər), *n.* a castrated male sheep. [OE]

wet·land (wet′land′), *n.* Often, **wetlands.** marshy area; swamp.

wet nurse, woman employed to suckle the infant of another.

w.f., wf, wrong font.

whack (hwak), *n.* 1 a sharp, resounding blow. 2 *Informal.* trial or attempt. —*v.* strike with a sharp, resounding blow. [? imit.] —**whack′er,** *n.*

whack·y (hwak′i), *adj.* =wacky.

whale[1] (hwāl), *n., pl.* **whales** or (*esp. collectively*) **whale,** *v.,* **whaled, whal·ing.** —*n.* 1 any of various fishlike mammals that are air-breathing and suckle their young. 2 *Informal. Fig.* something very big, great, impressive, etc. —*v.* hunt and catch whales. [OE *hwœl*]

whale[2] (hwāl), *v.,* **whaled, whal·ing.** beat; hit hard. [appar. var. of *wale*]

whale·boat (hwāl′bōt′), *n.* a long, narrow rowboat, sharp at both ends.

whale·bone (hwāl′bōn′), *n.* an elastic, horny substance growing in place of teeth in the upper jaw of certain whales and forming a series of thin, parallel plates.

whal·er (hwāl′ər), *n.* 1 person who hunts whales. 2 ship used for whaling.

whal·ing (hwāl′ing), *n.* the hunting and killing of whales.

wham (hwam), *v.,* **whammed, whamming,** *n. interj.* —*v.* hit or strike hard: *whammed into the closed door.* —*n. interj.*

exclamation or sound made by hitting something hard: *and wham went the wind against the house.* —**wham'my,** *n.*

wharf (hwôrf), *n., pl.* **wharves** (hwôrvz), **wharfs.** platform built on the shore or out from the shore, beside which ships can load and unload. [OE *hwearf*] —**wharf'less,** *adj.*

wharf·age (hwôr'fij), *n.* **1** the use of a wharf for mooring a ship, storing and handling goods, etc. **2** the charge made for this. **3** wharves.

what (hwot; hwut), *pron., pl.* **what,** *adj., adv.* —*pron.* **1** word used in asking questions about persons or things: *what is your name?, what if I did?* **2 a** that or those which; anything that: *I know what you mean, do what you please, not what it was.* —*adj.* **1** word used in asking questions about persons or things: *what time is it?* **2** that or those which; any that: *take what supplies you will need.* **3** word used to show surprise, doubt, etc., or emphasis: *what foolishness!* —*adv.* **1** how much; how: *what does it matter?* **2** partly: *what with the wind and rain, our walk was spoiled.* **3** word used to show surprise, etc., or emphasis: *what happy times!*

and what not, and all kinds of other things.

what for?, why.

what have you, *Informal.* and anything else.

what if, what would happen if.

what of it?, what does it matter.

what's what, *Informal.* the true state of affairs.

what then?, what would happen (in that case).

what with, in consideration of: *what with so much to do, we won't be able to go.* [OE *hwæt*]

what·ev·er (hwot ev'ər; hwət–), *pron.* **1** anything that: *do whatever you like.* **2** any amount that: *he will give whatever you may need.* **3** no matter what: *whatever happens, he is safe.* **4** what, used emphatically in questions: *whatever do you mean?* —*adj.* **1** any that: *take whatever books you like.* **2** no matter what: *whatever excuse he makes will not be believed.* **3** at all: *I see nothing whatever.*

what's (hwots), what is; what has.

what·so·ev·er (hwot'sō ev'ər; hwut'–), *pron., adj.* whatever.

wheal (hwēl), *n.* a small burning or itching swelling on the skin. [cf. OE *hwelian* suppurate]

wheat (hwēt), *n.* **1** the grain of a widely distributed cereal grass, used to make flour. **2** the plant that it grows on. [OE *hwǣte*] —**wheat'en,** *adj.* —**wheat'less,** *adj.*

whee·dle (hwē'dəl), *v.,* –**dled,** –**dling.** **1** persuade by flattery, smooth words, caresses, etc.; coax. **2** get by wheedling. [OE *wǣdlian* beg] —**whee'dler,** *n.* —**whee'dling,** *adj.* —**whee'dling·ly,** *adv.*

wheel (hwēl), *n.* **1** a round frame turning on a pin or shaft in the center. **2** any instrument, machine, apparatus, etc., shaped or moving like a wheel: *a spinning wheel, steering wheel.* **3** anything resembling or suggesting a wheel in shape or movement: *the wheel of fortune.* **4** *Fig.* any force thought of as moving or propelling: *the wheels of the government.* —*v.* **1** turn: *he wheeled around suddenly.* **2** move or perform in a curved or circular direction. **3** move on wheels: *the workman was wheeling a load of bricks.* —*adj.* of, pertaining to, next to, or containing a wheel.

at the wheel, a driving a car. **b** *Informal. Fig.* in control.

wheels, a machinery. **b** *Informal.* an automobile.

wheels within wheels, complicated circumstances, motives, influences, etc. [OE *hwēol*] —**wheeled,** *adj.* —**wheel'less,** *adj.*

wheel·bar·row (hwēl'bar'ō), *n.* frame with a wheel at one end and two handles at the other, used for carrying loads.

wheel·base (hwēl'bās'), **wheel base,** *n.* in automobiles, etc., the distance in inches between the centers of the front and rear axles.

wheel·chair (hwēl'chār'), *n.* chair mounted on wheels, used esp. by invalids.

wheel·er (hwēl'ər), *n.* **1** person or thing that wheels. **2** thing that has a wheel or wheels.

wheel·er-deal·er (hwēl'ər dēl'ər), *n.* person who delights in bold financial undertakings.

wheel horse, person who works effectively.

wheel·wright (hwēl'rīt'), *n.* person whose work is making or repairing wheels, carriages, and wagons.

wheeze (hwēz), *v.,* **wheezed, wheez·ing,** *n.* —*v.* **1** breathe with difficulty and a whistling sound. **2** make a sound like this: *the old engine wheezed.* **3** say with a wheeze. —*n.* a whistling sound caused by difficult breathing. [? < Scand. *hvæsa* hiss] —**wheez'er,** *n.* —**wheez'ing·ly,** *adv.* —**wheez'y,** *adj.* —**wheez'i·ly,** *adv.* —**wheez'i·ness,** *n.*

whelk (hwelk), *n.* a mollusk with a spiral shell, used for food in Europe. [OE *weoloc*]

whelm (hwelm), *v.* **1** overwhelm. **2** submerge. [akin to OE *–hwelfan,* as in *āhwelfan* cover over]

whelp (hwelp), *n.* **1** puppy or cub; young dog, wolf, bear, lion, tiger, etc. **2** a brash, rude boy or young man. —*v.* give birth to (whelps). [OE *hwelp*]

when (hwen; *unstressed* hwən), *adv.* at what time: *when will you come?* —*conj.* **1** at the time that: *rise when one's name is called, you play when you should work.* **2** at any time that: *he is impatient when he is kept waiting.* **3** at which time; and then: *the dog growled till his mas-*

ter spoke, when he gave a joyful bark. —*pron.* what time; which time: *since when have you known?* —*n.* the time or occasion: *the when and where of an act.* [OE *hwænne*]

whence (hwens), *adv.* **1** from what place; from where: *whence do you come?* **2** from what source or cause; from what: *whence has he so much wisdom?* —*conj.* from what place, source, cause, etc.: *the country whence he came.* [ME *whennes* < OE *hwanone*]

when·e'er (hwen ãr'; hwən–), *conj., adv. Poetic.* whenever.

when·ev·er (hwen ev'ər; hwən–), *conj., adv.* when; at whatever time; at any time that.

when·so·ev·er (hwen'sō ev'ər), *conj., adv.* whenever; at whatever time.

where (hwãr), *adv.* **1** in, to, at, or from what place: *where is he? where are you going? where did you get that story?* **2** in, at, or to which: *the house where he was born.* **3** in what way; in what respect: *where is the harm in trying?* **4** in what position, direction, circumstances, etc.: *where does he stand on health care?* —*n.* **1** what place: *where does he come from?* **2** place; scene. —*conj.* **1** in the place in which; at the place at which: *the book is where you left it, I will go where you go, the town where they stayed the night.* **2** in any place in which; at any place at which: *use the ointment where the pain is felt.* **3** in the case, circumstances, respect, etc., in which: *some people worry where it does no good.* [OE *hwǣr*]

where·a·bouts (hwar'ə bouts'), *adv., conj.* where; near what place: *whereabouts can I find a doctor?* —*n.* place where a person or thing is: *do you know the whereabouts of the cottage?*

where·as (hwãr az'), *conj.* **1** on the contrary; but; while: *some children like school, whereas others do not.* **2** considering that; since: *"Whereas the people of the colonies have been grieved and burdened with taxes," etc.* —*n.* document or statement beginning with "Whereas."

where·at (hwãr at'), *adv., conj.* at what; at which.

where·by (hwãr bī'), *adv., conj.* by what; by which.

wher·e'er (hwãr ãr'), *conj., adv. Poetic.* wherever.

where·fore (hwãr'fôr; –fōr), *adv.* **1** for what reason; why. **2** for which reason; therefore; so. —*conj.* for what reason; why. —*n.* reason.

where·in (hwãr in'), *adv., conj.* in what; in which; how.

where·of (hwãr ov'; –uv'), *adv., conj.* of what; of which; of whom.

where·on (hwãr on'; –ôn'), *adv., conj.* on which; on what.

where·so·ev·er (hwãr'sō ev'ər), *conj., adv.* wherever.

where·to (hwãr tü'), *adv., conj.* **1** to what; to which; where. **2** for what purpose; why.

where·up·on (hwãr′ə pon′; –pon′), *adv., conj.* **1** upon what; upon which. **2** at which; after which.

wher·ev·er (hwãr ev′ər), *conj., adv.* where; to whatever place; in whatever place: *wherever are you going?, sit wherever you like, he will be happy wherever he lives.*

where·with (hwãr witħ′; –witħ′), *adv., conj.* with what; with which. —*n.* wherewithal.

where·with·al (*n.* hwãr′witħ ōl; *adv.* hwãr′witħ ôl′), *n.* means, supplies, or money needed: *has she the wherewithal to pay for the trip? —adv.* wherewith.

whet (hwet), *v.,* **whet·ted, whet·ting,** *n.* —*v.* **1** sharpen by rubbing: *whet a knife.* **2** *Fig.* make keen or eager; stimulate: *the smell of food whetted my appetite.* —*n.* act of whetting. [OE *hwettan*] —**whet′ter,** *n.*

wheth·er (hwetħ′ər), *conj.* **1** expressing a choice: *it matters little whether we go or stay, he does not know whether to work or play.* **2** either: *whether sick or well, she is always cheerful.* **3** if: *he asked whether he should finish the work.*
whether or not, in any case; no matter what happens. [OE *hwether*]

whet·stone (hwet′stōn′), *n.* a stone for sharpening knives or tools.

whew (hwū), *interj., n.* exclamation of surprise, dismay, etc.

whey (hwā), *n.* the watery part of milk that separates from the curd when milk sours and becomes coagulated or when cheese is made. [OE *hwæg*] —**whey′ey, whey′ish, whey′like′,** *adj.*

which (hwich), *pron.* **1** word used in asking questions about persons or things: *which seems the best plan?* **2** word used in connecting a group of words with some word in the sentence: *read the book which you have.* **3** the one that; any that: *choose which you like.* **4** a thing that: *and, which is worse, you were late.* —*adj.* **1** word used in asking questions about persons or things: *which boy won the prize?, which books are yours?* **2** word used in connecting a group of words with some word in the sentence: *be careful which way you turn.*
which is which?, which is one and which is the other. [OE *hwilc*]

which·ev·er (hwich ev′ər), *pron., adj.* **1** any one that; any that: *take whichever you want.* **2** no matter which: *whichever side wins, I shall be satisfied.*

whiff (hwif), *n.* **1** a slight gust; puff; breath. **2** a slight smell; puff of air having an odor. **3** puff of tobacco smoke. —*v.* **1** blow; puff. **2** puff tobacco smoke from (a pipe, etc.); smoke. —**whiff′er,** *n.*

whif·fle (hwif′əl), *v.,* **–fled, –fling. 1** blow in puffs or gusts. **2** veer; shift. **3** blow lightly; scatter. —**whiff′ler,** *n.*

whif·fle·ball (hwif′əl bôl′), *n.* **1** light, hollow, plastic ball with holes in it to catch the air and slow it down. **2** game like baseball played with this ball and a plastic bat.

whif·fle·tree (hwif′əl trē′), *n.* the swinging bar of a carriage or wagon, to which the traces of a harness are fastened.

Whig (hwig), *n.* **1** member of a former political party in Great Britain that favored reforms and progress. **2** political party in the United States that became the Republican Party in the mid-1850s. **3** an American who favored the Revolution against England. —*adj.* **1** composed of Whigs; having to do with Whigs; like Whigs. **2** being a Whig. —**Whig′gish,** *adj.* —**Whig′gish·ly,** *adv.* —**Whig′gish·ness,** *n.* —**Whig′gism,** *n.*

while (hwīl), *n., conj., v.,* **whiled, whil·ing.** —*n.* time; space of time: *the postman came a while ago.* —*conj.* **1** during the time that; in the time that; as long as: *while I was speaking he said nothing, while the condition exists, it is a menace to everyone.* **2** in contrast with the fact that; although: *while I like the color of the hat, I do not like its shape.* —*v.* pass or spend in some easy, pleasant manner: *the children while away many afternoons on the beach.*
once in a while, now and then.
the while, during the time: *ate and talked the while.*
worth one's while, worth time, attention, or effort. [OE *hwīl*]

whilst (hwīlst), *conj.* =while.

whim (hwim), *n.* a sudden fancy or notion; freakish or capricious idea or desire.

whim·per (hwim′pər), *v.* **1** cry with low, broken, mournful sounds: *the sick child whimpered.* **2** complain in a weak way; whine. —*n.* a whimpering cry or sound. —**whim′per·er,** *n.* —**whim′per·ing,** *adj.* —**whim′per·ing·ly,** *adv.*

whim·si·cal (hwim′zə kəl), *adj.* **1** having many odd notions or fancies; fanciful; odd. **2** full of whims. —**whim′si·cal′i·ty, whim′si·cal·ness,** *n.* —**whim′si·cal·ly,** *adv.*

whim·sy (hwim′zi), *n., pl.* **–sies; –seys. 1** an odd or fanciful notion; quaintness. **2** something showing this. **3** =whim.

whine (hwīn), *v.,* **whined, whin·ing,** *n.* —*v.* **1** make a low, complaining cry or sound. **2** complain in a peevish, childish way. —*n.* **1** a low, complaining cry or sound. **2** a peevish, childish complaint. [OE *hwīnan*] —**whin′er,** *n.* —**whin′ing, *adj.* —whin′ing·ly,** *adv.* —**whin′y,** *adj.*

whin·ny (hwin′i), *n., pl.* **–nies,** *v.,* **–nied, –ny·ing.** —*n.* the sound that a horse makes. —*v.* make such a sound. [akin to *whine*]

whip (hwip), *n., v.,* **whipped** or **whipt, whipping.** —*n.* **1** thing to whip with, usually a stick with a lash at the end. **2** a whipping motion. **3** dessert made by beating cream, eggs, etc., into a froth. **4** member of a political party who controls and directs the other members in a lawmaking body. —*v.* **1** strike; beat; lash: *he whipped the horse.* **2** move, put, or pull quickly and suddenly: *he*

whipped off his coat. **3** defeat. **4** beat (cream, eggs, etc.) to a froth. **5** sew with stitches passing over and over an edge. **6** wind closely with thread or string; wind (cord, twine, or thread) around something. [cf. MDu., MLG *wippe* swing] —**whip′like′,** *adj.* —**whip′per,** *n.*

whip hand, 1 the hand that holds the whip in driving. **2** *Fig.* position of control; advantage.

whip·lash (hwip′lash′), *n.* **1** lash of a whip. **2** injury esp. to the neck caused by a sudden jolt that makes the head jerk backward and forward, as when a car is hit from behind.

whip·per·snap·per (hwip′ər snap′ər), *n.* an insignificant or young person who thinks he or she is smart or important.

whip·pet (hwip′it), *n.* very swift dog that looks somewhat like a small greyhound, often used in racing. [< *whip* in sense of "move quickly"]

whip·ping (hwip′ing), *n.* **1** a beating; flogging. **2** arrangement of cord, twine, or the like, wound about a thing.

whipping boy, scapegoat.

whipping post, post to which lawbreakers are tied to be whipped.

whip·ple·tree (hwip′əl trē′), *n.* =whiffletree.

whip·poor·will (hwip′ər wil′; hwip′-ər wil), *n.* an American bird whose call sounds somewhat like its name. It is active at night or twilight. [imit.]

whip·saw (hwip′sô′), *n.* a long, narrow saw with its ends held in a frame. —*v.* **1** cut with such a saw. **2** get the better of (a person) no matter what he does.

whip·stitch (hwip′stich′), *v.* sew with stitches passing over and over an edge. —*n.* stitch so made.

whir (hwėr), *n., v.,* **whirred, whirring.** —*n.* a noise that sounds like whir-r-r. —*v.* move quickly or work with such a noise: *the motor whirs.* [cf. Dan. *hvirre* whirl]

whirl (hwėrl), *v.* **1** turn or swing round and round; spin: *whirl a lasso.* **2** move round and round: *the merry-go-round whirled.* **3** turn about or aside quickly: *he whirled from the path.* **4** move or carry quickly: *we were whirled away in a helicopter.* **5** feel dizzy or confused. —*n.* **1** a whirling movement. **2** something that whirls. **3** dizzy or confused condition. **4** a short drive, run, walk, or the like. **5** a rapid round of happenings, parties, etc. [< Scand. *hvirfla* < *hverfa* turn] —**whirl′er,** *n.*

whirl·i·gig (hwėr′li gig′), *n.* **1** toy that whirls; pinwheel. **2** merry-go-round. **3** *Fig.* anything that whirls round and round: *a whirligig of parties.* [< *whirl* + *gig*]

whirl·pool (hwėrl′pül′), *n.* **1** water whirling round and round rapidly and violently. **2** anything like a whirlpool.

whirl·wind (hwėrl′wind′), *n.* **1** current of air whirling violently round and round; whirling windstorm. **2** anything like a whirlwind.

whish (hwish), *n.* a soft rushing sound; whiz; swish. —*v.* make this sound.

whisk[1] (hwisk), *v.* **1** sweep or brush (dust, crumbs, etc.) from a surface. **2** move quickly. **3** draw or snatch lightly and rapidly. —*n.* **1** a quick sweep. **2** a light, quick movement. [< Scand. (Sw.) *viska*]

whisk[2] (hwisk), *v.* beat or whip to a froth. [< n.] —*n.* **1** a whisk broom. **2** a wire beater for eggs, cream, etc. [< Scand. *visk* wisp]

whisk broom, a small broom for brushing clothes, etc.

whisk·er (hwis′kər), *n.* **1** Usually, **whiskers.** hair growing on a man's cheeks. **2** a single hair of a man's beard. **3** a long, stiff hair growing near the mouth of a cat, rat, etc. [< *whisk*[2]] —**whisk′ered,** *adj.* —**whisk′er·less,** *adj.*

whis·key (hwis′ki), *n., pl.* **–keys.** a strong alcoholic drink made from grain, as barley, rye, etc. Whiskey is about half alcohol. [ult. < Gaelic *uisgebeatha,* lit., water of life]

whis·per (hwis′pər), *v.* **1** speak very softly and low. **2** speak to in a whisper. **3** tell secretly or privately. **4** *Fig.* make a soft, rustling sound. **5** speak without vibration of the vocal cords. —*n.* **1** a very soft, low spoken sound. **2** something told secretly or privately. **3** *Fig.* a soft, rustling sound. **4** speech without vibration of the vocal cords. [OE *hwisprian*] —**whis′per·er,** *n.* —**whis′per·ing,** *n., adj.* —**whis′per·ing·ly,** *adv.*

whist (hwist), *n.* a card game somewhat like bridge for two pairs of players. [alter. of *whisk*[1] infl. by *whist*[2]]

whis·tle (hwis′əl), *v.,* **–tled, –tling,** *n.* —*v.* **1** make a clear, shrill sound by forcible blowing the breath through a small opening contracting the lips. **2** blow or sound a whistle. **3** produce or utter by whistling: *whistle a tune.* **4** move with a shrill sound: *the wind whistled around the house.* —*n.* **1** the sound made by whistling. **2** an instrument for making whistling sounds.

blow the whistle on, a declare illegal or dishonest. **b** expose: *blow the whistle on cheaters.*

clean as a whistle, a without fault or error: *a record as clean as a whistle.* **b** completely clean.

whistle for, go without; fail to get.

wet one's whistle, take a drink. [OE *hwistlian*] —**whis′tler,** *n.* —**whis′tling,** *n., adj.* **whis′tling·ly,** *adv.*

whit (hwit), *n.* a very small bit: *the sick man is not a whit better.* [var. of OE *wiht* thing, wight]

white (hwīt), *n., adj.,* **whit·er, whit·est,** —*n.* **1** the color of snow or salt, opposite to black. **2** a white coloring matter. **3** something white; white or colorless part: *the white of an egg, the whites of the eyes.* **4** a white person. —*adj.* **1** having the color of snow or salt; reflecting light without absorbing any of the rays composing it. **2** approaching this color; pale; light-col-

ored: *white wines, white meat.* **3** having a light-colored skin; noting or pertaining to the Caucasian race. **4** silvery; gray: *white hair.* **5** blank: *white space.*

bleed white, use up or take away all of one's money, strength, etc. [OE *hwīt*]

white ant, a pale-white insect; termite.

white blood cell or **corpuscle,** colorless blood cell that destroys disease germs; leucocyte.

white·cap (hwīt′kap′), *n.* wave with a foaming white crest.

white clover, a kind of clover with white flowers, common in fields and lawns.

white-col·lar (hwīt′kol′ər), *adj.* of or pertaining to clerical, professional, or business work or workers.

white elephant, 1 whitish Indian elephant, regarded as holy in some Asian countries. **2** anything that is expensive and troublesome to keep and take care of. **3** any troublesome possession.

white feather, symbol of cowardice.

white·fish (hwīt′fish′), *n., pl.* **–fish·es** or (*esp. collectively*) **–fish. 1** a food fish with white or silvery sides, found in lakes and streams. **2** any of various other whitish fish.

white flag, a plain white flag used as a sign of truce or surrender.

white gold, alloy of gold that looks much like platinum and is used for jewelry, commonly containing gold, nickel, copper, and zinc.

White·hall (hwīt′hôl′), *n.* the British government or its policies.

white heat, 1 extremely great heat at which things give off a dazzling white light. **2** *Fig.* state of extremely great activity, excitement, or feeling.

white-hot (hwīt′hot′), *adj.* **1** white with heat; extremely hot. **2** very enthusiastic; excited; violent.

White House, the, office, authority, opinion, etc., of the President of the United States.

white lead, a compound of lead used in making paint; basic carbonate of lead.

white lie, lie about some small matter; polite or harmless, lie.

white-liv·ered (hwīt′liv′ərd), *adj.* **1** cowardly. **2** pale; unhealthy looking.

white matter, tissue of the brain, spinal cord, etc., that consists chiefly of nerve fibers.

whit·en (hwīt′ən), *v.* make or become white. —**whit′en·er,** *n.*

white noise, sound used to cover noises that distract or disturb.

white oak, 1 oak of E North America having a light-gray or whitish bark and a hard, durable wood. **2** any similar species of oak. **3** the wood of any of these trees.

white pepper, spice made from husked dried pepper berries.

white pine, 1 a tall pine tree of E North America, valued for its soft, light wood. **2** this wood, much used for building. **3** any of various similar pines.

white poplar, a poplar tree whose leaves have silvery-white down on the under surface.

white potato, a very common variety of potato with a whitish inside; Irish potato.

white sauce, sauce made of milk, butter, and flour cooked together.

white slave, 1 a woman forced to be a prostitute. **2** a white person held as a slave. —**white slavery.**

white·wash (hwī′wosh′; –wôsh′), *n.* **1** liquid for whitening walls, woodwork, etc., usually made of lime and water. **2** *Fig.* the covering up of faults or mistakes. **3** *Fig.* anything that covers up faults or mistakes. —*v.* **1** whiten with whitewash. **2** *Fig.* cover up the faults or mistakes of. —**white′wash′er,** *n.*

white water, rushing, roiling water that creates foam, as at rapids on a river.

whith·er (hwitth′ər), *adv., conj.* to what place; to which place; where. [OE *hwider*]

whit·ing (hwīt′ing), *n., pl.* **–ings** or (*esp. collectively*) **–ing. 1** a European fish like the cod. **2** the silver hake. **3** any of several other food fishes. [var. of OE *hwītling*]

whit·ish (hwīt′ish), *adj.* somewhat white. —**whit′ish·ness,** *n.*

whit·low (hwit′lō), *n.* abscess on a finger or toe, usually near the nail. [earlier *whitflaw,* prob. < *white* + *flaw*]

Whit·sun (hwit′sən), *adj.* of or pertaining to Whitsunday or Whitsuntide.

Whit·sun·day (hwit′sun′di; –dā; hwit′-sən dā′), *n.* the seventh Sunday after Easter; Pentecost. [< *white* + *Sunday*]

Whit·sun·tide (hwit′sən tīd′), **Whitsun Tide,** *n.* the week beginning with Whitsunday, esp. the first three days.

whit·tle (hwit′əl), *v.,* **–tled, –tling. 1** cut shavings or chips from (wood, etc.) with a knife. **2** shape by whittling; carve.

whittle down or **away,** cut down little by little. [earlier *thwittle,* ult. < OE *thwītan* cut] —**whit′tler,** *n.*

whiz, whizz (hwiz), *n., v.,* **whizzed, whizzing.** —*n.* **1** a humming or hissing sound. **2** *Informal.* a very clever person; expert. —*v.* make a humming or hissing sound; move or rush with such a sound: *an arrow whizzed past his head.* [imit.] —**whiz′zer,** *n.* —**whiz′zing·ly,** *adv.*

who (hü; *unstressed relative* ü), *pron., poss.* **whose,** *obj.* **whom. 1** what person or persons: *who is your friend?, who told you?, who is the man in uniform?* **2** the person that; any person that; one that: *the girl who spoke is my best friend.*

who's who, a which is one person and which is the other. **b** which people are important. [OE *hwā*]

whoa (hwō; wō), *interj.* stop!

who·dun·it (hü dun′it), *n.* story or motion picture dealing with crime and its detection. [< spelling alter. of *who done it*]

who·ev·er (hü ev′ər), *pron.* **1** who; any person that: *whoever wants the book may* have it. **2** no matter who: *whoever else goes hungry, he won't.*

whole (hōl), *adj.* **1** having all its parts or elements; complete: *a whole set of dishes.* **2** entire: *a whole melon, a whole year.* **3** not injured, broken, or defective: *get out of a fight with a whole skin.* **4** in one piece; undivided: *swallow a thing whole.* —*n.* **1** all of a thing; the total: *four quarters make a whole.* **2** thing complete in itself.

as a whole, as one complete thing; altogether.

made out of whole cloth, entirely false or imaginary.

on the whole, a considering everything. **b** for the most part. [OE *hāl*] —**whole′ness,** *n.*

whole-heart-ed (hōl′här′tid), *adj.* earnest; sincere; hearty; cordial. —**whole′-heart′ed·ly,** *adv.* —**whole′-heart′ed·ness,** *n.*

whole milk, milk that has all of its natural constituents, as butter fat.

whole note, note indicating a tone to be given as much time as four quarter notes; semibreve.

whole number, integer, such as 2, 5, 15, 106, etc.

whole·sale (hōl′sāl′), *n., adj., adv., v.,* **-saled, -sal·ing.** —*n.* sale of goods in large quantities at a time, usually to retailers rather than to consumers directly. —*adj.* in large lots or quantities: *the wholesale price.* **2** selling in large quantities: *the wholesale meat business.* **3** broad and general; extensive and indiscriminate: *wholesale rioting.* —*adv.* in a wholesale manner. —*v.* sell in large quantities. —**whole′sal′er,** *n.*

whole·some (hōl′səm), *adj.* **1** good for the health; healthful: *a wholesome food.* **2** healthy-looking; suggesting health: *a wholesome face.* **3** good for the mind or morals; beneficial: *a wholesome book.* —**whole′some·ly,** *adv.*

whole step, whole tone, an interval equal to one sixth of an octave, such as D to E.

whole-wheat (hōl′hwēt′), *adj.* made of the entire wheat kernel.

who'll (hül), who will; who shall.

whol·ly (hōl′i), *adv.* to the whole amount or extent; completely; entirely; totally.

whom (hüm), *pron.* the objective case of **who:** *we know whom to blame.*

whoop (hüp; hwüp), *n.* **1** a loud cry or shout. **2** cry of an owl, crane, etc.; hoot. —*v.* **1** shout loudly. **2** hoot.

whoop it up, *Informal.* make a noisy disturbance. [imit.]

whoop·ee (hwüp′ē; hwúp′ē), *interj.* a cry expressing merriment or excitement.

whoop·ing cough (hüp′ing; húp′-), an infectious disease of children, characterized by fits of coughing that end with a loud, gasping sound.

whooping crane, a large white crane having a loud raucous cry.

whoosh (hwüsh), *n.* a muffled roar; rushing sound. —*v.* go with such a sound; rush.

whop·per (hwop′ər), *n.* **1** something very large. **2** a big lie.

whop·ping (hwop′ing), *adj.* very large of its kind; huge.

whore (hôr; hōr), *n., v.,* **whored, whor-ing.** —*n.* =prostitute. —*v.* **1** act as a whore. **2** have intercourse with whores. [OE *hōre*]

whorl (hwėrl; hwôrl), *n.* **1** circle of leaves or flowers round a stem of a plant. **2** one of the turns of a spiral shell. **3** one of the turns in the cochlea of the ear. **4** anything that circles or turns on or around something else. A person can be identified by the whorls of his or her fingerprints. [prob. var. of *whirl*] —**whorled,** *adj.*

whor·tle·ber·ry (hwėr′təl ber′i), *n., pl.* **-ries. 1** a small blackish berry much like the huckleberry. **2** the shrub that it grows on. [< *whortle* (ult. < OE *horte* whortleberry) + *berry*]

whose (hüz), *pron.* the possessive case of **who** and of **which.**

who·so·ev·er (hü′sō ev′ər), *pron.* whoever; anybody who.

why (hwī), *adv., n., pl.* **whys,** *interj.* —*adv.* **1** for what cause, reason, or purpose: *why did you do it?, I don't know why I did it.* **2** for which; because of which: *that is the reason why he failed.* **3** the reason for which: *that is why he raised the question.* —*n.* cause; reason; purpose: *she tried to find out the whys and wherefores of his behavior.* —*interj.* expression used to show surprise, doubt, etc., or just to fill in. [OE *hwȳ,* instrumental case of *hwā* who and *hwæt* what]

WI, (*zip code*) Wisconsin.

W.I., West Indies; West Indian.

wick (wik), *n.* the part of an oil lamp or candle that is lighted. The oil or melted wax is drawn up the wick and burned. —*v.* take up moisture: *a fabric that wicks sweat away.* [OE *wēoce*] —**wick′less,** *adj.*

wick·ed (wik′id), *adj.* **1** bad; evil; sinful: *a wicked person.* **2** mischievous; playfully sly: *a wicked smile.* **3** unpleasant; severe: *a wicked task.* [< *wick* wicked, prob. ult. < OE *wicca* wizard] —**wick′ed·ly,** *adv.* —**wick′ed·ness,** *n.*

wick·er (wik′ər), *n.* **1** a slender, easily bent branch or twig. **2** twigs or branches woven together. Wicker is used in making baskets and furniture. —*adj.* made a wicker. [< Scand. (dial. Sw.) *vikker* willow] —**wick′ered,** *adj.*

wick·er·work (wik′ər wėrk′), *n.* **1** twigs or branches woven together; wicker. **2** objects made of wicker.

wick·et (wik′it), *n.* **1** a small door or gate. **2** a small window or opening. **3** gate by which a flow of water is regulated. **4** a wire arch stuck in the ground to knock a croquet ball through. [< AF, ult. < Scand.]

wick·ing (wik′ing), *n.* material for wicks.

wick·i·up (wik′i up′), *n.* W and SW American Indian hut made of brush-

wood or matting. [< Algonkian (Sauk or Fox) *wikiyapi* lodge, dwelling]

wide (wīd), *adj.,* **wid·er, wid·est,** *adv., n.* —*adj.* **1** filling space from side to side; not narrow; broad: *a wide street.* **2** extending a certain distance from side to side: *a door three feet wide.* **3** of great range: *wide reading.* **4** far or fully open; distended: *stare with wide eyes.* **5** far from a named point, object, target, etc.: *wide of the truth, hit the ball wide and high.* —*adv.* **1** to a great or relatively great extent from side to side: *wide apart.* **2** over an extensive space or region: *far and wide.* **3** to the full extent; fully: *open your mouth wide.* **4** aside; astray: *the shot went wide.* —*n.* a wide space or expanse. [OE *wīd*] —**wide′ly,** *adv.* —**wide′ness,** *n.* —**wid′ish,** *adj.*

wide-an·gle (wīd′ang′gəl), *adj.* having a short-focus lens whose field extends through a wide angle.

wide-a·wake (wīd′ə wāk′), *adj.* **1** with the eyes wide open; fully awake. **2** alert; keen; knowing. —**wide′-a·wake′ness,** *n.*

wide-eyed (wīd′īd′), *adj.* with the eyes wide open.

wid·en (wīd′ən), *v.* make or become wide or wider. —**wid′en·er,** *n.*

wide-o·pen (wīd′ō′pən), *adj.* opened as much as possible.

wide-ranging (wīd′rān′jing), *adj.* extensive far-reaching: *wide-ranging interests.*

wide·spread (wīd′spred′), **wide·spread-ing** (–ing), *adj.* **1** spread widely. **2** spread over a wide space. **3** occurring in many places or among many persons far apart: *widespread revolt.*

widg·eon (wij′ən), *n., pl.* **-eons** or (*esp. collectively*) **-eon.** any of several kinds of freshwater ducks, slightly larger than a teal; scaup duck.

wid·ow (wid′ō), *n.* woman whose husband is dead and who has not married again. —*v.* make a widow or widower of. [OE *widuwe*] —**wid′ow·hood,** *n.*

wid·ow·er (wid′ō ər), *n.* man whose wife is dead and who has not married again.

width (width; witth), *n.* **1** how wide a thing is; distance across; breadth: *the room is 12 feet in width.* **2** piece of a certain width: *a width of cloth.*

width′ways (width′wāz′; witth′-), **width-wise** (–wīz′), *adv.* in the direction of the width.

wield (wēld), *v.* **1** hold and use; manage; control: *wield a sword, a pen, power, authority, etc.* **2** exercise authority; govern; rule. [OE *wieldan*] —**wield′a·ble,** *adj.* —**wield′er,** *n.* —**wield′y,** *adj.*

wie·ner (wē′nər), *n.* =frankfurter. [< G, Viennese sausage]

wife (wīf), *n., pl.* **wives.** a married woman. [OE *wīf*] —**wife′hood, wife′dom,** *n.* —**wife′less,** *adj.*

wife·ly (wīf′li), *adj.,* **-li·er, -li·est.** of or like a wife; suitable for a wife.

wi-fi or Wi-Fi (wī′fi), *n.* wireless Internet access. [< Trademark]

wig (wig), *n.*, *v.*, **wigged, wig·ging.** —*n.* an artificial covering of hair for the head. —*v.* furnish with a wig or wigs. [< *periwig*] —**wigged,** *adj.* —**wig′less,** *adj.* —**wig′like′,** *n.*

wig·eon (wij′ən), *n.* =widgeon.

wig·gle (wig′əl), *v.*, **-gled, -gling.** —*v.* move with short, quick movements from side to side; wriggle. —*n.* such a movement. [cf. Du. *wiggelen*] —**wig′gly,** *adj.*

wig·gler (wig′lər), *n.* **1** person or thing that wiggles. **2** the larva of a mosquito.

wig·wag (wig′wag′), *v.*, **-wagged, -wagging,** *n.* —*v.* **1** move to and fro. **2** signal by movements of arms, flags, lights, etc., according to a code. —*n.* such signaling. —**wig′wag′ger,** *n.*

wig·wam (wig′wom; -wôm), *n.* a hut of poles covered with bark, mats, or skins, made by American Indians. [< Algonkian]

wild (wīld), *adj.* **1** living or growing in the forests or fields; not tamed; not cultivated: *a wild animal, a wild flower.* **2** with no people living in it: *wild land.* **3** not civilized; savage: *wild tribes.* **4** not checked; not restrained: *a wild rush for the ball, wild boys.* **5** violent: *wild rage, a wild storm.* **6** rash; crazy: *wild schemes, wild notions.* —*n.* an uncultivated or desolate region or tract; waste; desert. —*adv.* in a wild manner; to a wild degree.

run wild, live or grow without restraint: *children run wild, a garden run wild.*

wilds, wild country: *live in the wilds of Minnesota.* [OE *wilde*] —**wild′ish,** *adj.* —**wild′ly,** *adv.* —**wild′ness,** *n.*

wild boar, a wild hog of Europe, S Asia, and N Africa.

wild·cat (wīld′kat′), *n.*, *adj.*, *v.*, **-cat·ted, -cat·ting.** —*n.* **1** a lynx or other wild animal like a cat, but larger. **2** well drilled for oil or gas in a region where none has hitherto been found. —*adj.* **1** speculative; reckless: *wildcat schemes.* **2** not authorized by proper union officials; precipitated by small groups or local unions: *a wildcat strike.* —*v.* drill wells in regions not known to contain oil. —**wild′cat′ter,** *n.* —**wild′cat′ing,** *n.*, *adj.*

wil·de·beest (wil′də bēst′), *n.* =gnu. [< Du., wild beast]

wil·der·ness (wil′dər nis), **1** a wild place; region with no people living in it. **2** a bewildering mass or collection: *a wilderness of streets.* [< ME *wilderne* wild, OE *wildēorn,* ult. < *wilde* wild + *dēor* animal]

wild-eyed (wīld′īd′), *adj.* having wild eyes; staring wildly or angrily.

wild·fire (wīld′fīr′), *n.* fire hard to put out.

like wildfire, very rapidly.

wild·flower (wīld′flou′ər), *n.* **1** any flowering plant that grows in the woods, fields, etc.; uncultivated plant. **2** flower of such a plant.

wild fowl, birds, ordinarily hunted, such as wild ducks or geese, partridges, quail, etc.

wild-goose chase, useless search or attempt.

wild·life (wīld′līf′), *n.* wild animals and plants collectively, usually those native to an area.

wild oat, an oatlike grass growing as a weed in meadows, etc.

wild oats, youthful dissipation.

sow one's wild oats, indulge in youthful dissipation before settling down in life.

wild West, Wild West, the western United States during pioneer days.

wild·wood (wīld′wùd′), *n.* =forest.

wile (wīl), *n.*, *v.*, **wiled, wil·ing.** —*n.* **1** a trick to deceive; cunning way. **2** subtle trickery; slyness; craftiness. —*v.* coax; lure; entice: *the sunshine wiled me from work.*

wile away, while away; pass easily or pleasantly. [OE *wīgle* magic]

will[1] (wil; *unstressed* wəl), *auxiliary v.*, *pres. indic. sing., 1st and 3rd pers.* **will,** *2nd* **will** or (*Archaic*) **wilt,** *3rd* **will,** *pl.* **will;** *pt. 1st* **would,** *2nd* **would** or (*Archaic*) **wouldst,** *3rd* **would,** *pl.* **would;** *pp.* **would** or (*Obs.*) **wold;** imperative and infinitive lacking. **1** am going to; is going to; are going to: *he will come tomorrow.* **2** am willing to; is willing to; are willing to: *I will go if you do.* **3** wish; desire: *we cannot always do as we will.* **4** be able to; can: *the pail will hold four gallons.* **5** must: *you will do it at once!* **6** do often or usually: *she will read for hours at a time.* [OE *willan*]

will[2] (wil), *n.*, *v.*, **willed, will·ing.** —*n.* **1** the power of the mind to decide and do; deliberate control over thought and action: *strength of will.* **2** purpose; determination: *the will to live.* **3** wish; desire: *what is your will?* **4 a** a legal statement of a person's wishes about what shall be done with property after he or she is dead. **b** document containing such a statement. **5** feeling toward another: *good will, ill will.* —*v.* **1** decide by using power of the mind; try to influence by thought and action: *she willed the person in front of her to turn around.* **2** determine; decide: *fate has willed it otherwise.* **3** give by a will: *will a house to someone.*

against one's will, in opposition to one's desire; unwilling.

at will, whenever one wishes.

do the will of, obey.

with a will, with energy and determination. [OE] —**will′a·ble,** *adj.* —**will′er,** *n.* —**will′less,** *adj.*

willed (wild), *adj.* having a certain kind of will: *strong-willed.*

will·ful (wil′fəl), *adj.* **1** wanting or taking one's own way; stubborn. **2** done on purpose; intended: *willful murder, willful waste.* —**will′ful·ly,** *adv.* —**will′fulness,** *n.*

wil·lies (wil′iz), *n. Informal.* spell of nervousness.

will·ing (wil′ing), *adj.* **1** ready; consenting. **2** cheerfully ready. —**will′ing·ly,** *adv.* —**will′ing·ness,** *n.*

will-o'-the-wisp (wil′ə tẖə wisp′), *n.* **1** a moving light appearing at night over marshy places, caused by combustion of marsh gas. **2** thing that deceives or misleads by luring on.

wil·low (wil′ō), *n.* **1** tree or shrub with tough, slender branches and narrow leaves. **2** its wood. The branches of most willows bend easily and are used to make furniture. —*adj.* made of willow. [ult. < OE *welig*] —**wil′low·like′,** *adj.*

wil·low·y (wil′ō i), *adj.* **1** like a willow; slender; supple; graceful. **2** having many willows.

wil·ly-nil·ly (wil′i nil′i), *adv.* willingly or not; with or against one's wishes. —*adj.* undecided. [< *will I* (*he, ye*), *nill I* (*he, ye*); *nill* not will, OE *nyllan* < *ne* not + *willan* will]

Wil·son (wil′sən), *n.* **(Thomas) Woodrow,** 1856–1924, 28th president of the United States, 1913–21.

wilt[1] (wilt), *v.* **1** become limp and drooping; wither. **2** lose strength, vigor, assurance, etc. **3** cause to wilt. —*n.* a wilting. [? alter. of *welk;* cf. MDu., MLG *welken*]

wilt[2] (wilt), *v. Archaic.* will.

wil·y (wil′i), *adj.*, **wil·i·er, wil·i·est.** using subtle tricks to deceive; crafty; cunning; sly. —**wil′i·ly,** *adv.* —**wil′i·ness,** *n.*

wimp (wimp), *n. Informal.* unassertive, weak person. —**wimp′y,** *adj.*

wim·ple (wim′pəl), *n.*, *v.*, **-pled, -pling.** —*n.* cloth for the head arranged in folds about the head, cheeks, chin, and neck, worn by nuns and formerly by other women. —*v.* cover or muffle with a wimple. [OE *wimpel*]

win (win), *v.*, **won** or (*Archaic*) **wan, won, winning,** *n.* —*v.* **1** get victory or success, esp. by striving or effort: *the tortoise won in the end, he won the race, win a bet.* **2** get by effort; gain: *win fame.* **3** gain the favor of; persuade: *the speaker won his audience.* **4** get to; reach, often by effort: *win the summit of a mountain.* —*n.* act or fact of winning; success; victory. [OE *winnan*]

wince (wins), *v.*, **winced, winc·ing,** *n.* —*v.* draw back suddenly; flinch slightly. —*n.* act of wincing. [< var. of OF *guencir* < Gmc.] —**winc′er,** *n.*

winch (winch), *n.* a machine for lifting or pulling, turned by a crank. [OE *wince*] —**winch′er,** *n.*

wind[1] (*n.* wind, *Archaic and Poetic* wīnd; *v.* wind), *n.*, *v.*, **wind·ed, wind·ing.** —*n.* **1** air in motion. The wind varies in force from a slight breeze to a strong gale. **2** power of breathing; breath: *a runner needs good wind.* **3** empty, useless talk. —*v.* **1** expose to wind or air. **2** put out of breath; cause difficulty in breathing.

get wind of, a find out about; get a hint of. **b** smell: *get wind of the garbage dump.*

in the wind, happening; about to happen; impending: *political change is in the wind.*

take the wind out of one's sails, take away one's advantage, argument, etc., suddenly or unexpectedly.

twist in the wind, suffer uncertainty or suspense: *waiting to hear, just twisting in the wind.*

winds, wind instruments. [OE] —**wind′less,** *adj.*

wind² (wīnd), *v.,* **wound** or (*Rare*) **wind-ed, wind·ing,** *n.* —*v.* **1** move this way and that; move in a crooked way; change direction; turn: *a stream winding through the woods, we wound our way through the streets.* **2** make (one's way) by indirect or insidious procedure: *wind one's way into another's confidence.* **3** fold, wrap, or place about something: *the mother wound her arms about the child.* **4** roll into a ball or on a spool: *wind yarn.* **5** twist or turn around something: *the vine winds round a pole.* **6** make (some machine) go by turning some part of it: *wind a clock.* —*n.* a bend; turn; twist.

wind down, diminish activity; relax.

wind up, a end; settle; conclude. **b** make the movements that a baseball pitcher does just before pitching the ball. **c** roll or coil; wind completely. [OE *windan*] —**wind′a·ble,** *adj.* —**wind′er,** *n.* —**wind′ing·ly,** *adv.*

wind·bag (wind′bag′), *n.* person who talks a great deal but does not say much.

wind-blown (wind′blōn′), *adj.* blown by the wind.

wind-borne (wind′bôrn′; –bōrn′), *adj.* carried by the wind, as pollen or seed.

wind·break (wind′brāk′), *n.* shelter from the wind.

wind·ed (win′did), *adj.* **1** out of breath. **2** having wind or breath (as specified: *shortwinded.* —**wind′ed·ness,** *n.*

wind·fall (wind′fôl′), *n.* **1** fruit blown down by the wind. **2** *Fig.* an unexpected piece of good luck or advantage: *a windfall of profits.*

wind·ing (wīn′ding), *n.* **1** act of one that winds. **2** bend; turn. **3** something that is wound or coiled. —*adj.* bending; turning. —**wind′ing·ly,** *adv.*

winding sheet, =shroud.

wind instrument, instrument sounded by blowing air into it. Horns, flutes, and trombones are wind instruments.

wind·jam·mer (wind′jam′ər), *n.* a sailing ship.

wind·lass (wind′ləs), *n.* machine for pulling or lifting things; winch. [< ME *windel* (< *wind²*) + Scand. *āss* pole]

wind·mill (wind′mil′), *n.* a mill or machine operated by the wind. Windmills are used to pump water and generate electricity.

tilt at windmills, fight against an imaginary opponent; be a quixotic reformer.

win·dow (win′dō), *n.* **1** an opening in the wall or roof of a building, boat, car, etc., to let in light or air. **2** such an opening with the frame, panes of glass, etc., that fill it. **3** any opening that suggests a window. —*v.* furnish with windows.

[< Scand. *vindauga* < *vindr* wind + *auga* eye] —**win′dowed,** *adj.* —**win′dow·less,** *adj.*

window box, container fastened outside under a window to hold flowering plants.

window dressing, 1 arrangement of goods in a store window to attract shoppers. **2** *Fig.* false display to create a good impression.

win·dow·pane (win′dō pān′), *n.* piece of glass in a window.

window sash, frame for the glass in a window.

window seat, bench built into the wall of a room, under a window.

win·dow-shop (win′dō shop′), *v.,* –**shopped,** –**shop·ping.** examine or gaze at merchandise in store windows without buying. —**win′dow-shop′per,** *n.* —**win′dow-shop′ping,** *adj., n.*

window sill, piece of wood or stone across the bottom of a window.

wind·pipe (wind′pīp′), *n.* the passage from the throat to the lungs; trachea.

wind·row (wind′rō′), *n.* **1** row of hay raked together to dry before being made into heaps. **2** any similar row, as of sheaves of grain, made for the purpose of drying; row of dry leaves, dust, etc., swept together by wind or the like. —*v.* arrange in a windrow or windrows. —**wind′row′er,** *n.*

wind shear, sudden strong shift in wind speed and direction: *wind shear caused the plane to crash.*

wind·shield (wind′shēld′), *n.* in an automobile, a sheet of glass above the dashboard to keep off the wind.

wind sleeve or **sock,** a cone-shaped sleeve mounted on a pole or the like, showing the direction of the wind.

Windsor chair, a kind of comfortable wooden chair, with a spindle back and slanting legs.

wind·storm (wind′stôrm′), *n.* storm with much wind but little or no rain.

wind·surf·ing (wind′sėr′fing), *n.* sport of sailboarding. —**wind′surf′er,** *n.*

wind-up (wīnd′up′), *n.* **1** a winding up. **2** end; close; conclusion. **3** series of movements made by a pitcher just before pitching the ball.

wind·ward (wind′wərd), *adv.* toward the wind. —*adj.* **1** on the side toward the wind. **2** in the direction from which the wind is blowing. —*n.* **1** the side toward the wind. **2** direction from which the wind is blowing.

wind·y (win′di), *adj.,* **wind·i·er, wind·i·est. 1** having much wind. **2** *Fig.* made of wind; unsubstantial; empty: *windy talk.* **3** *Fig.* talking a great deal; voluble. **4** like wind. **5** exposed to the wind. —**wind′i·ly,** *adv.* —**wind′i·ness,** *n.*

wine (wīn), *n., v.,* **wined, win·ing.** —*n.* **1** the juice of grapes after it has fermented and contains alcohol. **2** the fermented juice of other fruits or plants: *currant wine, dandelion wine.* **3** dark red; the

color of red wine. —*v.* entertain with wine. [ult. < L *vinum*] —**wine′less,** *adj.*

wine cellar, 1 cellar where wine is stored. **2** wine stored there.

wine-col·ored (wīn′kul′ərd), *adj.* dark purplish-red.

wine·glass (wīn′glas′; –gläs′), *n.* a small drinking glass for wine.

wine-grow·er (wīn′grō′ər), *n.* person who raises grapes and makes wine. —**wine′grow′ing,** *n., adj.*

wine press or **presser, 1** machine for pressing the juice from grapes. **2** vat in which grapes are trodden in the process of making wine.

win·er·y (wīn′ər i), *n., pl.* –**er·ies.** place where wine is made.

Wine·sap, wine·sap (wīn′sap′), *n.* a variety of red winter apple of the United States.

wine·skin (wīn′skin′), *n.* container made of the nearly complete skin of a goat, hog, etc., used in some countries for holding wine.

wing (wing), *n.* **1** the part of a bird, insect, etc., by which it flies; corresponding part in a bird, insect, etc., that does not fly. **2** anything like a wing in shape or use. **3** one of the major lifting and supporting surfaces, or airfoils, of an airplane. **4** part of a building that sticks out sidewise from the main part. **5** either of the spaces to the right or left of the stage in a theater. **6** that part of a military force to the right or left of the main body. **7** part of an organization; faction: *the radicals of a political group are called the left wing.* **8** flying; winged flight. **9** player whose position is on either side of the center in certain games. —*v.* **1** give speed to: *terror winged his steps.* **2** wound in the wing or arm.

clip one's wings, restrict one's activities or independence.

in the wings, behind the scenes; out of sight.

on the wing, moving; active; busy.

take wing, a fly away. **b** *Fig.* depart.

under the wing of, under the sponsorship or protection of.

wing its way, fly: *wing its way south for the winter.*

wings, insignia given to qualified pilots, navigators, etc. [< Scand. *væNgr*] —**wing′less,** *adj.* —**wing′like′,** *adj.*

wing case, either of the hardened front wings of certain insects.

wing chair, a comfortable upholstered chair with side pieces as high as the back.

winged (wingd, *esp. Poetic* wing′id *for 1 and 2;* wingd *for 3 and 4), adj.* **1** having wings. **2** moving as if on wings; swift; rapid. **3** of birds, disabled in a wing. **4** of persons, wounded in the arm or some other nonvital part.

wing·span (wing′span′), *n.* =wing spread.

wing·spread (wing′spred′), *n.* **1** distance between the tips of a bird's wings when they are spread. **2** distance the wings extend on an aircraft.

wink (wingk), v. **1** close the eyes and open them again quickly. **2** close one eye and open it again as a hint or signal. **3** move or affect by winking: *wink back tears*. **4** flicker; twinkle: *the stars winked*. —n. **1** a winking. **2** a hint or signal given by winking. **3** a flickering; twinkle. **4** a very short time: *I didn't sleep a wink*.

forty winks, a short sleep; nap.

wink at, pretend not to see. [OE *wincian*]

wink·er (wingk'ər), n. person or thing that winks.

win·kle (wing'kəl), n. a sea snail used for food. [OE *wincle*, as in *pinewincle periwinkle*]

win·ner (win'ər), n. person or thing that wins.

win·ning (win'ing), adj. **1** that wins. **2** charming; attractive. —n. **1** act of one that wins. **2** Usually, **winnings.** what is won; money won. —**win'ning·ly,** adv.

win·now (win'ō), v. **1** blow off the chaff from (grain); drive or blow away (chaff). **2** Fig. sort out; separate; sift: *winnow truth from half-truths*. **3** fan (with wings); flap (wings). —n. **1** a winnowing. **2** device for winnowing grains, etc. [OE *windwian < wind* wind[1]] —**win'now·er,** n.

win·some (win'səm), adj. charming; attractive; pleasing. [OE *wynsum < wynn* joy] —**win'some·ly,** adv. —**win'some·ness,** n

win·ter (win'tər), n. **1** the coldest of the four seasons; last season of the year. **2** Fig. the last period of life; period of decline, dreariness, or adversity. —adj. of, pertaining to, or characteristic of winter. —v. **1** pass the winter. **2** keep, feed, or manage during winter. [OE —**win'ter·er,** n. —**win'ter·less,** adj.

win·ter·green (win'tər grēn'), n. **1** a small evergreen plant of North America with bright-red berries and aromatic leaves. An oil made from its leaves (**oil of wintergreen** or **wintergreen oil**) is used in medicine and candy. **2** this oil. **3** its flavor.

win·ter·ize (win'tər īz), v., **–ized, –iz·ing.** make (an automobile, etc.) ready for cold winter weather.

win·ter·kill (win'tər kil'), v. kill by or die from exposure to cold weather. —**win'ter·kill'ing,** adj., n.

winter solstice See **solstice.**

win·ter·time (win'tər tīm'), **win·ter·tide** (–tīd'), n. =winter.

winter wheat, wheat planted in the autumn and ripening in the following spring or summer.

win·try (win'trī), **win·ter·y** (win'tər i), adj., **–tri·er, –tri·est; –ter·i·er, –ter·i·est.** of or pertaining to winter; like winter: *a wintry sky, a wintry manner.* —**win'tri·ly,** adv. —**win'tri·ness,** n.

win·y (wīn'i), adj. **1** of, pertaining to, or characteristic of wine. **2** tasting, smelling, or looking like wine. **3** affected by wine.

wipe (wīp), v., **wiped, wip·ing,** n. —v. **1** rub with paper, cloth, etc., in order to clean or dry: *wipe the table.* **2** take (away, off, or out) by rubbing: *wipe away your tears.* **3** rub or draw something over a surface. —n. act of wiping.

wipe out, a remove; as by death; destroy completely: *a town wiped out by the earthquake.* **b** remove: *the rain wiped out all the footprints.* [OE *wīpian*] —**wip'er,** n.

wire (wīr), n., adj., v., **wired, wir·ing.** —n. **1** metal drawn out into a thread. **2** such metal as a material. **3** a long piece of such metal used for electrical transmission, as in electric lighting, telephones, etc. **4** telegraph: *he sent a message by wire.* **5** telegram. —adj. made of or consisting of wire. —v. **1** furnish with wire: *wire a house for electricity.* **2** fasten with wire. **3** transfer funds electronically. **4** send by telegraph.

down to the wire, to the very last minute: *work down to the wire.*

under the wire, just before it is too late: *got to the airport just under the wire.*

wear a wire, wear a hidden recording device. [OE *wīr*] —**wir'a·ble,** adj. —**wired,** adj. —**wire'like',** adj. —**wir'er,** n.

wired (wīrd), adj. **1** having the appropriate electrical wires, cable or telephone system, etc., installed. **2** Informal. Fig. over-stimulated; over-excited.

wire gauge, device for measuring the diameter of wire, the thickness of metal sheets, etc., usually a disk with different-sized notches in it.

wire-haired (wīr'hārd'), adj. having coarse, stiff hair: *a wire-haired fox terrier.*

wire·less (wīr'lis), adj. **1** having no wire; operated without wire or wires: *wireless Internet access.* **2** Esp. Brit., radio.

wire puller, person who uses secret influence to accomplish his or her purposes.

wire·tap (wīr'tap'), v., **–tapped, –tapping.** attach a listening device to a telephone or telephone line to listen secretly to conversations. —n. instance or use of wiretapping.

wire tapping, the making of a secret connection with telephone wires to monitor their use. —**wire tapper.**

wir·ing (wīr'ing), n. system of wires to carry an electric current.

wir·y (wīr'i), adj., **wir·i·er, wir·i·est. 1** made of wire. **2** like wire. **3** lean, strong, and tough. —**wir'i·ly,** adv. —**wir'i·ness,** n.

Wis., Wisc., Wisconsin.

Wis·con·sin (wis kon'sən), n. a Middle Western state of the United States.

wis·dom (wiz'dəm), n. **1** knowledge and good judgment based on experience; being wise. **2** something wise; wise act or saying. [OE *wīsdōm < wīs* wise] —**wis'dom·less,** adj.

wisdom tooth, the back tooth on either side of each jaw, ordinarily appearing between the ages of 17 and 25.

wise[1] (wīz), adj., **wis·er, wis·est. 1** having or showing knowledge and good judg-

ment: *a wise judge, wise plans.* **2** having knowledge or information: *we are none the wiser for his explanations.* **3** learned; erudite. **4** cognizant; aware. [OE *wīs*] —**wise'ly,** adv. —**wise'ness,** n.

wise[2] (wīz), n. **1** way of proceeding; manner. **2** respect; degree: *in no wise.* [OE *wise*]

-wise, suffix. **1** in ____ manner, as in *anywise* and *likewise.* **2** in a ____ing manner, as in *slantwise.* **3** in the characteristic way of a ____. *Clockwise* means in the way the hands of a clock go. **4** in the direction of the ____, as in *lengthwise.* **5** special meanings, as in *sidewise.* [< *wise*[2]]

wise·crack (wīz'krak'), n., v. a snappy comeback; smart remark. —**wise'crack'er,** n.

wish (wish), v. **1** have a desire for; be glad to have, do, etc.; want: *he wished for a new house.* **2** desire that (someone) shall be or have; have a hope for; express a hope for: *we wish all men health, I wish you a Happy New Year.* —n. **1** a turning of the mind toward the doing, having, getting, etc., of something; desire or longing. **2** expression of a wish. **3** thing wished for: *the girl got her wish.*

wish (something) on, Informal. pass (something) on to; foist (something) on: *no one should wish that job on anyone.* [OE *wȳscan*] —**wish'er,** n. —**wish'less,** adj.

wish·bone (wish'bōn'), n. the forked bone in the front of the breastbone in poultry and other birds.

wish·ful (wish'fəl), adj. having or expressing a wish; desiring; desirous. —**wish'ful·ly,** adv. —**wish'ful·ness,** n.

wishful thinking, believing something to be true that one wishes or wants to be true. —**wishful thinker.**

wish·y-wash·y (wish'i wosh'i; –wôsh'i), adj. **1** thin and weak; watery. **2** lacking in substantial qualities; feeble; inferior.

wisp (wisp), n. **1** a small bundle; small bunch: *a wisp of hay.* **2** a small tuft, lock, or portion of anything: *a wisp of smoke.* **3** a little thing: *a wisp of a girl.* [cf. W Frisian *wisp*] —**wisp'y, wisp'ish, wisp'like',** adj.

wis·te·ri·a (wis tir'i ə), **wis·tar·i·a** (–tār'-i ə), n. a climbing shrub with large clusters of purple, yellow, or white flowers. [after C. *Wistar*, scientist]

wist·ful (wist'fəl), adj. **1** longing; yearning. **2** pensive; melancholy. —**wist'ful·ly,** adv. —**wist'ful·ness,** n.

wit[1] (wit), n. **1** the power to perceive quickly and express cleverly ideas that are unusual, striking, and amusing. **2** person with such power. **3** understanding; mind; sense: *have wit enough to earn a living.*

at one's wit's end, not knowing what to do or say.

keep one's wits about one, be alert.

live by one's wits, manage by clever devices and schemes rather than by a regular job.

wits, mental faculties or senses: *out of one's wits with fright.* [OE *witt*]

wit[2] (wit), *v., pres. 1st pers.* **wot,** *2nd pers.* **wost,** *3rd pers.* **wot,** *pl.* **wit;** *pt. and pp.* **wist;** *ppr.* **wit·ting.** *Archaic.* know.

to wit, that is to say; namely. [OE *witan*]

witch (wich), *n.* **1** woman supposed to be under the influence of evil spirits and to have magic power. **2** an ugly old woman. —*v.* **1** use the power of a witch on. **2** charm; fascinate; bewitch. —*adj.* of a witch. [OE *wicce*] —**witch′like′,** *adj.*

witch·craft (wich′kraft′; –kräft′), *n.* what a witch does or can do; magic power or influence.

witch doctor, medicine man, esp. among African peoples.

witch·er·y (wich′ər i; wich′ri), *n., pl.* **-er·ies. 1** witchcraft; magic. **2** charm; fascination.

witch hazel, 1 shrub of E North America that has yellow flowers in the fall or winter after the leaves have fallen. **2** lotion for cooling and soothing the skin, made from the bark and leaves of this shrub.

witch hunt, persecuting or defaming (a person) to gain a political advantage.

witch·ing (wich′ing), *adj.* bewitching; magical; enchanting. —**witch′ing·ly,** *adv.*

with (with; with), *prep.* **1** in the company of: *come with me, leave the dog with me.* **2** among: *they will mix with the crowd.* **3** having, wearing, carrying, etc.: *a man with brains, a telegram with bad news.* **4** by means of; by using: *cut meat with a knife, work with care.* **5** added to: *do you want sugar with your tea?* **6** in regard or relation to: *friendly with us, pleased with the house, power increased with their number.* **7** because of: *shake with cold, with this battle the war ended, shadows move with the sun.* **8** for: *I am with you on that question.* **9** from: *part with a thing.* **10** against: *the English fought with the Germans.*

with it, *Informal.* up-to-date; informed. [OE, against]

with·draw (with drô′; with–), *v.,* **-drew, -drawn, -draw·ing. 1** draw back or away: *withdraw one's hand from a hot stove.* **2** take back; remove: *worn-out paper money is withdrawn from use by the government.* **3** go away: *she withdrew from the room.* —**with·draw′al, with·draw′ment,** *n.*

withe (with; with; with), *n.* a willow twig. [OE *withthe*]

with·er (with′ər), *v.* **1** lose or cause to lose freshness, vigor, etc.; dry up; shrivel. **2** cause to feel ashamed or confused. [< *weather*] —**with′er·ing·ly,** *adv.*

with·ers (with′ərz), *n. pl.* the highest part of a horse's or other animal's back, behind the neck.

with·hold (with hōld′; with–), *v.,* **-held, -hold·ing. 1** refuse to give: *withhold one's consent.* **2** hold or keep back: *withhold soldiers from attack.* —**with·hold′er,** *n.* —**with·hold′ment,** *n.*

with·in (with in′; with–), *prep.* **1** inside or inside of: *within the city, within the body, within a house.* **2** at or to some amount or degree not exceeding: *come within a dollar of.* **3** in the course or period of: *within one's lifetime.* **4** not transgressing: *within reason, within the law.* —*adv.* **1** in or into the inner part; inside: *they went within.* **2** in the mind; inwardly: *keep one's thoughts within.*

with·out (with out′; with–), *prep.* **1** with no; not having; free from; lacking: *without a home, without food, without exception.* **2** so as to omit, avoid, or neglect: *she walked past without noticing us.* **3** outside of; beyond: *without the city.* —*adv.* **1** in or into a space outside: *stand without, they were waiting without.* **2** lacking (something implied): *eat what is here or go without (food).*

from without, from the outside (of someone or something): *dangers from without.*

with·stand (with stand′; with–), *v.,* **-stood, -stand·ing.** stand against; hold out against; oppose, esp. successfully.

wit·less (wit′lis), *adj.* lacking sense; stupid; foolish. —**wit′less·ly,** *adv.*

wit·ness (wit′nis), *n.* **1** person or thing able to give evidence; person who saw something happen. **2** evidence; testimony. **3** person writing his or her name on a document to show that he or she saw the maker sign it. —*v.* **1** see; perceive: *he witnessed the accident.* **2** give evidence; testify. **3** sign (a document) as a witness.

bear witness, be evidence; give evidence; testify. [OE *witnes* knowledge < *wit*[1]] —**wit′ness·er,** *n.*

witness stand, place where a witness stands or sits to give evidence in a law court.

wit·ti·cism (wit′ə siz əm), *n.* a witty remark. [< *witty*, on model of *criticism*]

wit·ting·ly (wit′ing li), *adv.* knowingly.

wit·ty (wit′i), *adj.,* **-ti·er, -ti·est.** full of wit; clever and amusing. [OE *wittig*] —**wit′ti·ly,** *adv.* —**wit′ti·ness,** *n.*

wive (wīv), *v.,* **wived, wiv·ing.** marry a woman. [OE *wīfian*]

wives (wīvz), *n. pl. of* **wife.**

wiz·ard (wiz′ərd), *n.* **1** person supposed to have magic power; sorcerer. **2** a very clever person; expert. [ult. < *wise*[1]] —**wiz′ard·like′,** *adj.* —**wiz′ard·ly,** *adj.*

wiz·ard·ry (wiz′ərd ri), *n.* magic; magic skill.

wiz·ened (wiz′ənd), *adj.* dried up; withered; shriveled. [pp. of *wizen*, OE *wisnian*]

wk., 1 *pl.* **wks.** week. **2** work.

WMD, weapons of mass destruction, as nuclear or biological weapons.

WNW, W.N.W., between west and northwest.

wob·ble (wob′əl), *v.,* **-bled, -bling,** *n.* —*v.* **1** move unsteadily from side to side; shake; tremble. **2** *Fig.* be uncertain, unsteady, or inconstant; waver.

—*n.* a wobbling motion. [cf. LG *wabbeln*] —**wob′bler,** *n.* —**wob′bling,** *adj.* —**wob′bling·ly,** *adv.* —**wob′bly,** *adj.*

woe, (wō) *n.* great grief, trouble, or distress. —*interj.* an exclamation of grief, trouble, or distress. [OE *wā,* interj.]

woe·be·gone (wō′bi gôn′; –gon′), *adj.* looking sad, sorrowful, or wretched.

woe·ful (wō′fəl), *adj.* **1** full of woe; sad; sorrowful; wretched. **2** pitiful. **3** of wretched quality. —**woe′ful·ly,** *adv.* —**woe′ful·ness,** *n.*

wok (wok), *n.* metal pan with a rounded bottom, used in Chinese cookery. [< Cantonese]

woke (wōk), *v.* pt. and pp. of **wake**[1].

wold (wōld), *n.* high, rolling country, bare of woods. [OE *weald* a wood]

wolf (wulf), *n., pl.* **wolves,** *v.* —*n.* **1** a carnivorous wild animal somewhat like a dog, and belonging to the same family. **2** *Fig.* a cruel, greedy person. **3** man who possesses a special talent for and interest in enticing women. —*v.* eat greedily. [OE *wulf*] —**wolf′ish,** *adj.* —**wolf′ish·ly,** *adv.* —**wolf′ish·ness,** *n.* —**wolf′like′,** *adj.*

wolf·hound (wulf′hound′), *n.* a large dog of any of various breeds once used in hunting wolves.

wol·fram (wul′frəm), *n.* **1** a metallic element, W, used in making steel and for electric lamp filaments; formerly called tungsten. It has stable and radioactive isotopes. **2** wolframite. [< G]

wol·fram·ite (wul′frəm īt), *n.* an ore consisting of compounds of wolfram with iron and manganese.

wolfs·bane (wulfs′bān′), *n.* a poisonous plant with yellow flowers, a kind of aconite.

wol·ver·ine, wol·ver·ene (wul′vər ēn′), *n.* **1** a clumsy, heavily built, meat-eating animal of northern regions, related to the weasel and badger. **2** its fur. [earlier *wolvering* < *wolf*]

wolves (wulvz), *n. pl. of* **wolf.**

wom·an (wum′ən), *n., pl.* **wom·en,** *adj.* —*n.* **1** the adult human female. **2** women as a group; the average woman. **3** a female servant. —*adj.* of, pertaining to, or characteristic of women. [OE *wīfman* < *wīf* woman + *man* human being] —**wom′an·less,** *adj.*

wom·an·hood (wum′ən hud), *n.* **1** condition or time of being a woman: *matured into womanhood.* **2** character or qualities of a woman. **3** women as a group.

wom·an·ish (wum′ən ish), *adj.* **1** characteristic of a woman. **2** imitating a woman. —**wom′an·ish·ly,** *adv.* —**wom′an·ish·ness,** *n.*

wom·an·ize (wum′ə nīz), *v.,* **-ized, -iz·ing. 1** pursue women, esp. to use them. **2** make effeminate, weak. —**wom′an·iz′er,** *n.*

wom·an·kind (wum′ən kīnd′), *n.* the female sex; women.

wom·an·like (wum′ən līk′), *adj.* **1** like a woman; womanly. **2** suitable for a woman.

wom·an·ly (wùm′ənli), *adj.* **1** like a woman. **2** as a woman should be. **3** suitable for a woman. —**wom′an·li·ness,** *n.*

woman suffrage, 1 the political right of women to vote. **2** women's votes. —**wom′an·suf′frage,** *adj.* —**wom′an·suf′fra·gist,** *n.*

womb (wüm), *n.* **1** the organ of the body that holds and nourishes the young till birth; uterus. **2** place containing or producing anything. [OE *wamb*]

wom·bat (wom′bat), *n.* an Australian animal that looks like a small bear. A female wombat has a pouch for carrying her young. [< Australian lang.]

wom·en (wim′ən), *n., pl.* of **woman.**

wom·en·folk (wim′ən fōk′), **wom·en·folks** (–fōks′), *n.pl.* =women.

women's rights, social, political, and legal rights for women, equal to those of men.

won (wun), *v.* pt. and pp. of **win.**

won·der (wun′dər), *n.* **1** a strange and surprising thing or event: *see the wonders of a city, it is a wonder he turned down the offer.* **2** the feeling caused by what is strange and surprising: *stare in open-mouthed wonder.* —*v.* **1** feel wonder: *wonder at a thing.* **2** be surprised or astonished: *I shouldn't wonder if he wins the prize.* **3** be curious; be curious about; think about; wish to know: *I wonder what happened.*

do or work wonders, get or achieve extraordinary results.

no or small wonder, it is not surprising. [OE *wundor*] —**won′der·er,** *n.* —**won′der·ing,** *adj.* —**won′der·ing·ly,** *adv.*

won·der·ful (wun′dər fəl), *adj.* causing wonder; marvelous; remarkable. —**won′der·ful·ly,** *adv.* —**won′der·ful·ness,** *n.*

won·der·land (wun′dər land′), *n.* a land full of wonders.

won·der·ment (wun′dər mənt), *n.* wonder; surprise.

won·drous (wun′drəs), *adj.* wonderful. —*adv.* wonderfully. —**won′drous·ly,** *adv.* —**won′drous·ness,** *n.*

wonk (wongk), *n. Informal.* studious, bookish person.

wont (wunt; wōnt), *adj.* accustomed. —*n.* custom; habit. [orig. pp., ult. < OE *wunian* be accustomed]

won't (wōnt; wunt), will not.

wont·ed (wun′tid; wōn′–), *adj.* accustomed; customary; usual. —**wont′ed·ly,** *adv.* —**wont′ed·ness,** *n.*

won·ton (won′ton′), *n.* **1** Chinese dumpling filled with vegetables, shrimp, etc. **2** soup made with these dumplings. [< Chinese]

woo (wu), *v.* **1** court; seek to marry. **2** seek to win; try to get: *woo fame.* **3** try to persuade; urge. [OE *wōgian*] —**woo′er,** *n.* —**woo′ing·ly,** *adv.*

wood (wùd), *n.* **1** the hard substance beneath the bark of trees and shrubs. **2** trees cut up for use. —*adj.* made of wood. —*v.* plant with trees; reforest.

out of the woods, no longer in danger or difficulty.

woods, a large number of trees; forest. [OE *wudu*] —**wood′ed,** *adj.* —**wood′less,** *adj.*

wood alcohol, a poisonous, inflammable liquid often made by distilling wood; methyl alcohol. It is used as a solvent, fuel, etc.

wood·bine (wùd′bīn′), *n.* **1** =honeysuckle. **2** the Virginia creeper, a climbing vine with bluish-black berries. [OE *wudubind(e)* < *wudu* wood + *binde* wreathe]

wood·chuck (wùd′chuk′), *n.* a North American marmot; the ground hog. Woodchucks grow fat in summer and sleep in their holes in the ground all winter. [< Algonkian; infl. by *wood*]

wood·cock (wùd′kok′), *n., pl.* –**cocks** or (*esp. collectively*) –**cock.** a small game bird with a long bill and short legs.

wood·craft (wùd′kraft′; –kräft′), *n.* art of making things from wood. —**wood′crafts′man,** *n.*

wood·cut (wùd′kut′), **wood block,** *n.* **1** an engraved block of wood to print from. **2** a print from such a block.

wood·cut·ter (wùd′kut′ər), *n.* person who cuts down trees or chops wood. —**wood′cut′ting,** *n.*

wood·en (wùd′ən), *adj.* **1** made of wood. **2** *Fig.* stiff; awkward. **3** *Fig.* dull; stupid. —**wood′en·ly,** *adv.* —**wood′en·ness,** *n.*

wood·en·head·ed (wùd′ən hed′id), *adj.* dull; stupid. —**wood′en·head′ed·ness,** *n.*

wood·en·ware (wùd′ən war′), *n.* containers, utensils, etc., made of wood. Pails, tubs, and rolling pins are woodenware.

wood·land (*n.* wùd′land′, –lənd; *adj.* wùd′lənd), *n.* land covered with trees. —*adj.* of or in the woods; pertaining to woods.

wood·land·er (wùd′lən dər), *n.* person who lives in the woods.

wood·lark (wùd′lärk′), *n.* a European lark closely related to the skylark.

wood lot or **wood·lot** (wùd′lot′), *n.* plot of land with trees grown for firewood, timber, etc.

wood·man (wùd′mən), *n., pl.* –**men. 1** man who cuts down trees. **2** person who lives in the woods.

wood nymph, 1 =dryad. **2** brown butterfly with yellow spots.

wood·peck·er (wùd′pek′ər), *n.* a bird with a hard, pointed bill for pecking holes in trees to get insects.

wood·pile (wùd′pīl′), *n.* pile of wood, esp. wood for fuel.

wood pulp, wood made into pulp for making paper.

wood·shed (wùd′shed′), *n.* shed for storing wood.

woods·man (wùdz′mən), *n., pl.* –**men. 1** person used to life in the woods and skilled in hunting, fishing, trapping, etc. **2** lumberman.

wood sorrel, plant with sour juice and with leaves composed of three heart-shaped leaflets.

woods·y (wùd′zi), *adj.* of or like the woods.

wood thrush, thrush common in the thickets and woods of E North America.

wood wind (wind), any one of the wood wind instruments.

wood winds, the wooden wind instruments of an orchestra, as clarinets, bassoons, etc. —**wood′-wind′,** *adj.*

wood·work (wùd′wėrk′), *n.* things made of wood; wooden parts inside of a house, such as doors, stairs, moldings, and the like. —**wood′work′er,** *n.* —**wood′work′ing,** *n., adj.*

wood·worm (wùd′wėrm′), *n.* worm or larva that is bred in wood or bores in wood.

wood·y (wùd′i), *adj.,* **wood·i·er, wood·i·est. 1** having many trees; covered with trees. **2** consisting of wood. **3** like wood; like that of wood. —**wood′i·ness,** *n.*

woof (wüf), *n.* **1** the threads running from side to side across a woven fabric. **2** fabric; cloth; texture. [OE *ōwef*]

woof·er (wüf′ər), *n.* a loud-speaker designed esp. to reproduce low bass sounds.

wool (wùl), *n.* **1** the soft, curly hair or fur of sheep and some other animals. **2** short, thick, curly hair. **3** something like wool. **4** yarn, cloth, or garments made of wool. —*adj.* made of wool.

pull the wool over one's eyes, deceive or trick one. [OE *wull*]

wool·en (wùl′ən), *adj.* **1** made of wool. **2** of or having to do with wool or cloth made of wool. —*n.* **woolens,** cloth or clothing made of wool.

wool·gath·er·ing (wùl′gath′ər ing; –gath′ring), *n.* absorption in thinking or daydreaming; absent-mindedness. —*adj.* inattentive; absent-minded; dreamy. —**wool′gath′er·er,** *n.*

wool·grow·er (wùl′grō′ər), *n.* person who raises sheep for their wool. —**wool′grow′ing,** *n.*

wool·ly (wùl′i), *adj.,* –**li·er, –li·est,** *n., pl.* –**lies.** —*adj.* Also, **wooly. 1** consisting of wool. **2** like wool. **3** covered with wool or something like it. —*n.* article of clothing made from wool. —**wool′li·ness,** *n.*

wool·sack (wùl′sak′), *n.* bag of wool.

wool·y (wùl′i), *adj.,* **wool·i·er, wool·i·est.** woolly. —**wool′i·ness,** *n.*

wooz·y (wüz′i; wùz′i), *adj.* muddled; dizzy.

word (wėrd), *n.* **1** a sound or a group of sounds that has meaning and is an independent unit of speech. We speak words when we talk. **2** the writing or printing that stands for a word. *Bat, bet, bit, bot,* and *but* are words. **3** a short talk; speech: *may I have a word with you? honest in word and deed, a word of praise.* **4** command; order: *his word was law.* **5** promise: *the boy kept his word.* **6** news: *no word has come from home.* **7** **words,**

the text of a song as distinguished from the notes. —*v.* put into words: *word a question.*

by word of mouth, by spoken words; orally.

eat one's words, take back or regret what one has said: *I wish I could eat my words.*

from the word go, *Informal.* at the outset; from the start.

in a word, briefly.

in so many words, literally.

the Word or **the Word of God,** the Bible.

word for word, in the exact words.

words, angry talk; quarrel; dispute: *we had words.* [OE] —**word′less,** *adj.*

word·age (wėrd′ij), *n.* words collectively.

word·book (wėrd′bůk′), *n.* list of words for some special purpose; dictionary; vocabulary.

word·ing (wėr′ding), *n.* way of saying a thing; choice and use of words.

word of honor, a solemn promise.

word·y (wėr′di), *adj.*, **word·i·er, word·i·est.** using too many words. —**word′i·ly,** *adv.* —**word′i·ness,** *n.*

wore (wôr; wōr), *v.* pt. of **wear.**

work (wėrk), *n., v.,* **worked** or **wrought, working,** *adj.* —*n.* **1** effort in doing or making something: *hard work.* **2** something to do; occupation; employment: *he is out of work.* **3** something made or done; result of effort; task: *a work of art, she did her work at a desk.* **4 a** transference of energy from one body or system to another. **b** that which is accomplished by a force when it acts through a distance. **5** an engineering structure; fortification. —*v.* **1** do work; labor: *most people must work for a living, he works at an airplane factory.* **2** put effort on; operate: *he worked his farm with success, this pump will not work, the plan worked, work a scheme.* **3** cause to do work: *he works his men long hours.* **4** treat or handle in making; knead; mix: *work dough.* **5** come or become (up, round, loose, etc.): *the clay has worked up through the crushed stone, the catch has worked loose.* **6** move; stir; excite: *don't work yourself into a temper.* **7** solve: *work all the problems on the page.* —*adj.* of, for, or pertaining to work: *a work horse.*

at work, working.

make short work of, do or get rid of quickly.

work off, get rid of.

work on or **upon,** try to persuade or influence.

work out, a plan; develop. **b** solve; find out; accomplish; result. **c** give exercise to; practice.

work over, *Informal.* rough up; beat up.

work up, a plan; develop. **b** excite; stir up.

works, a (often sing. in use) place for doing some kind of work; factory. **b** the moving parts of a machine or device: *the*

---

works of a watch. **c** righteous deeds. [OE *weorc*] —**work′a·ble,** *adj.* —**work′a·bil′i·ty, work′a·ble·ness,** *n.* —**work′less,** *adj.*

work·a·day (wėr′kə dā′), *adj.* of working days; practical; commonplace; ordinary.

work·bench (wėrk′bench′), *n.* table at which a mechanic or artisan works.

work·book (wėrk′bůk′), *n.* **1** book containing outlines for the study of some subject, questions to be answered, etc. **2** book containing rules for doing certain work. **3** book for notes of work planned or work done.

work·day (wėrk′dā′), **working day,** *n.* **1** day for work; day that is not Sunday or a holiday. **2** part of a day during which work is done. —*adj.* =workaday.

work·er (wėr′kər), *n.* **1** person or thing that works. **2** bee, ant, wasp, or other insect that works for its community. —**work′er·less,** *adj.*

work·fare (wėrk′fãr′), *n.* program requiring that people who receive public assistance work at a job or get job training. [< *work* + wel*fare*]

work·ing (wėr′king), *n.* **1** method or manner of work; operation; action. **2** act or process of working. —*adj.* **1** that works. **2** used in working. **3** operating successfully. **4** used to operate with or by: *a working majority.*

workings, parts of a mine, quarry, tunnel, etc., where work is being done.

work·man (wėrk′mən), **work·ing·man** (wėr′king man′), *n., pl.* **-men. 1** =worker. **2** person who works with his or her hands or with machines. —**work′man·ly,** *adj., adv.*

work·man·like (wėrk′mən līk′), *adj.* skillful; well-done. —*adv.* skillfully.

work·man·ship (wėrk′mən ship′), *n.* **1** the art or skill in a worker or his or her work. **2** quality or manner of work. **3** the work done.

work·out (wėrk′out′), *n.* **1** exercise; practice. **2** trial; test.

work·room (wėrk′rüm′; –rům′), *n.* room where work is done.

work·shop (wėrk′shop′), *n.* **1** shop where work is done. **2** course of study, discussion, etc., in a particular field: *a writers' workshop.*

work·ta·ble (wėrk′tā′bəl), *n.* **1** table at which one works. **2** table holding utensils and materials for work, such as one holding sewing materials.

world (wėrld), *n.* **1** the earth. **2** a particular division of the earth: *the New World.* **3** the earth, with its inhabitants, affairs, etc., during a particular period: *the ancient world.* **4** any sphere, realm, or domain, with all that pertains to it: *the insect world.* **5** a particular class of humankind, with common interests, aims, etc.: *the world of fashion.* **6** all people; the human race; the public: *the whole world knows it.* **7** the things of this life and the people devoted to them: *man of the world.* **8** a great deal; very

---

much; large amount: *the rest did her a world of good.*

come into the world, be born.

for all the world, a for any reason, no matter how great. **b** in every respect; exactly.

out of this world, *Informal.* without equal; marvelous. [OE *weorold*]

world·ling (wėrld′ling), *n.* a worldly person.

world·ly (wėrld′li), *adj.,* **-li·er, -li·est,** *adv.* —*adj.* **1** of or pertaining to this world; not of heaven. **2** caring much for the interests and pleasures of this world. —*adv.* in a worldly manner. —**world′li·ness,** *n.*

world·ly-wise (wėrld′li wīz′), *adj.* wise about the ways and affairs of this world.

world series, series of baseball games played each fall between the winners of the two major league championships, to decide the professional championship of the United States.

World War, 1 Also, **World War I.** war in Europe, Asia, Africa, and elsewhere, from July 28, 1914 to Nov. 11, 1918. **2** Also, **World War II.** war from September 1, 1939 to August 14, 1945 between Great Britain, the United States, and Russia on one side and Germany, Italy, and Japan on the other.

world·wide (wėrld′wīd′), *adj.* spread throughout the world.

World Wide Web, Internet link between servers worldwide that support HTML.

worm (wėrm), *n.* **1** any of numerous small, slender, crawling or creeping animals, usually soft-bodied and legless. **2** something like a worm in shape or movement, such as the thread of a screw. —*v.* **1** move like a worm; crawl or creep like a worm. **2** work or get by persistent and secret means. **3** remove worms from.

worms, disease caused by worms in the body. [OE *wyrm*] —**worm′er,** *n.* —**worm′less,** *adj.* —**worm′like′,** *adj.* —**worm′y,** *adj.* —**worm′i·ness,** *n.*

worm-eat·en (wėrm′ēt′ən), *adj.* **1** eaten into by worms. **2** worn-out; worthless; out-of-date.

worm gear, 1 a worm wheel. **2** a worm wheel and an endless screw together. By a worm gear the rotary motion of one shaft can be transmitted to another shaft at right angles to it.

worm·hole (wėrm′hōl′), *n.* hole made by a worm. —**worm′holed′,** *adj.*

worm wheel, wheel with teeth that fit into a revolving screw.

worm·wood (wėrm′wůd′), *n.* **1** a bitter plant used in medicine, absinthe, etc. **2** something bitter or extremely unpleasant. [< OE *wermōd,* infl. by *worm, wood*]

worn (wôrn; wōrn), *v.* pp. of **wear.** —*adj.* **1** damaged by use: *worn rugs.* **2** *Fig.* tired; wearied: *a worn face.*

worn-out (wôrn′out′; wōrn′–), *adj.* **1** used until no longer fit for use. **2** fatigued.

wor·ri·some (wėr′i səm), *adj.* **1** causing worry. **2** inclined to worry. —**wor′ri·some·ly,** *adv.*

wor·ry (wėr′i), *v.,* -**ried,** -**ry·ing,** *n., pl.* -**ries.** —*v.* **1** feel anxious or uneasy: *worry about one's job.* **2** annoy; bother: *don't worry me with questions.* **3** seize and shake with the teeth; bite at; snap at. —*n.* **1** a worrying. **2** anxiety; uneasiness; trouble; care: *worry kept her awake.* **3** cause of trouble or care: *a mother of sick children has many worries.*

worry along, manage somehow. [OE *wyrgan* strangle] —**wor′ri·er,** *n.* —**wor′ri·less,** *adj.* —**wor′ry·ing·ly,** *adv.*

wor·ry·wart (wėr′i wôrt′), *n.* person who worries too much.

worse (wėrs), *adj.* (*comparative of* **bad**). **1** less well; more ill: *the patient is worse.* **2** less good; more evil. **3** more unfavorable. —*adv.* in a more severe or evil manner or degree: *it is raining worse than ever.* —*n.* that which is worse. [OE *wyrsa*]

wors·en (wėr′sən), *v.* make or become worse.

wor·ship (wėr′ship), *n., v.,* -**shiped, -ship·ing.** —*n.* **1** great honor and respect: *the worship of God, hero worship.* **2** ceremonies or services in honor of God. **3** great love and admiration; adoration. —*v.* **1** pay great honor and respect to. **2** take part in a religious service. **3** consider extremely precious; hold very dear; adore: *a miser worships money.* [OE *weorthscipe* < *weorth* worth + *-scipe* -ship] —**wor′ship·er,** *n.*

wor·ship·ful (wėr′ship fəl), *adj.* **1** honorable. **2** worshiping. —**wor′ship·ful·ly,** *adv.* —**wor′ship·ful·ness,** *n.*

worst (wėrst), *adj.* (*superlative of* **bad**). **1** least well; most ill. **2** least good; most evil. **3** most unfavorable. —*adv.* to an extreme degree of badness or evil. —*n.* that which is worst. —*v.* beat; defeat: *the hero worsted his enemies.*

at worst, under the least favorable circumstances.

if worst comes to worst, if the very worst thing happens. [OE *wyrresta*]

wor·sted (wùs′tid), *n.* **1** a firmly twisted woolen thread or yarn. **2** cloth made from such thread or yarn. **3** a woolen yarn for knitting, crocheting, and needlework. —*adj.* made of worsted. [after *Worsted,* England (now Worstead)]

worth (wėrth), *adj.* **1** good or important enough for; deserving of: *the book is worth reading.* **2** equal in value to: *not worth a cent.* **3** having property that amounts to: *that man is worth millions.* —*n.* **1** merit; usefulness; importance: *show one's worth in a crisis, a man of worth.* **2** value: *you got your money's worth.* **3** a quantity of something of specified value: *a dollar's worth of sugar.* **4** property; wealth. [OE *weorth*]

worth·less (wėrth′lis), *adj.* without worth; good-for-nothing; useless. —**worth′less·ly,** *adv.* —**worth′less·ness,** *n.*

worth·while (wėrth′hwīl′), *adj.* worth time, attention, or effort. —**worth′while′ness,** *n.*

wor·thy (wėr′ᵺi), *adj.,* -**thi·er, -thi·est,** *n., pl.* -**thies.** —*adj.* **1** having worth or merit. **2** deserving; meriting. —*n.* person of great merit; admirable person.

worthy of, a deserving. **b** having enough worth for. —**wor′thi·ly,** *adv.* —**wor′thi·ness,** *n.*

would (wùd; *unstressed* wəd), *v.* **1** pt. of **will. 2** *Would* has special uses: **a** to express action done again and again: *the children would play for hours on the beach.* **b** to express a wish: *would I were dead!* **c** to make a statement or question less direct or blunt: *would that be fair?* **d** to express conditions: *if he would only try, he could do it.* [OE *wolde*]

would-be (wùd′bē′), *adj.* **1** wishing or pretending to be. **2** intended to be.

would·n't (wùd′ ənt), would not.

wouldst (wùdst), *v. Archaic and Poetic.* would.

wound[1] (wünd), *n.* **1** a hurt or injury caused by cutting, stabbing, shooting, etc. **2** any hurt or injury to feelings, reputation, etc. —*v.* **1** injure by cutting, stabbing, shooting, etc.; hurt. **2** injure in feelings, reputation, etc. [OE *wund*] —**wound′er,** *n.* —**wound′less,** *adj.*

wound[2] (wound), *v.* pt. and pp. of **wind**[2].

wove (wōv), *v.* pt. and pp. of **weave.**

wo·ven (wō′vən), *v.* pp. of **weave.**

wow (wou), *n.* **1** unqualified success; hit. **2** Interj. great! wonderful! —*v. Informal.* overwhelm with something wonderful or special.

wrack (rak), *n.* **1** =wreckage. **2** ruin; destruction. [< MDu., MLG *wrak* wreck]

wraith (rāth), *n.* specter; ghost. [? < Scand. *vörthr* guardian] —**wraith′like′,** *adj.*

wran·gle (rang′gəl), *v.,* -**gled, -gling,** *n.* —*v.* **1** dispute noisily; quarrel angrily. **2** argue. **3** W. herd or tend (horses, etc.) on the range. —*n.* a noisy dispute; angry quarrel. [? < LG *wrangeln*]

wran·gler (rang′glər), *n.* **1** person who wrangles. **2** herder in charge of horses.

wrap (rap), *v.,* **wrapped** or **wrapt, wrap·ping,** *n.* —*v.* **1** cover by winding or folding something around: *wrap oneself in a shawl.* **2** cover with paper and tie up or fasten. **3** *Fig.* cover; envelop; hide. —*n.* Often, **wraps.** outer covering. Shawls, scarfs, coats, and furs are wraps.

under wraps, kept secret.

wrapped up in, a devoted to; thinking mainly of. **b** involved in; associated with.

wrap up, put on warm outer clothes.

wrap·per (rap′ər), *n.* **1** person or thing that wraps. **2** thing in which something is wrapped; covering; cover. **3** a long, loose garment; bathrobe.

wrap·ping (rap′ing), *n.* Usually, **wrappings.** paper, cloth, etc., in which something is wrapped.

wrap-up (rap′up′), *n.* summary, as of the news or a discussion.

wrath (rath; räth), *n.* **1** a very great anger; rage. **2** vengeance; punishment. [OE *wrǣththu*] —**wrath′less,** *adj.*

wrath·ful (rath′fəl; räth′-), *adj.* feeling or showing wrath; very angry. —**wrath′ful·ly,** *adv.* —**wrath′ful·ness,** *n.*

wreak (rēk), *v.* **1** give expression to; work off (feelings, desires, etc.). **2** inflict (vengeance, punishment, etc.). [OE *wrecan*] —**wreak′er,** *n.*

wreath (rēth), *n., pl.* **wreaths** (rēᵺz). **1** a ring of flowers or leaves twisted together. **2** something suggesting a wreath. [OE *wrǣth*] —**wreath′less,** *adj.* —**wreath′like′,** *adj.*

wreathe (rēᵺ), *v.,* **wreathed, wreathed, wreath·ing. 1** make into a wreath; twist. **2** decorate or adorn with wreaths. **3** make a ring around; encircle; envelop. **4** move in rings: *the smoke wreathed upward.* —**wreath′er,** *n.*

wreck (rek), *n.* **1** partial or total destruction of a ship, building, train, automobile, or aircraft. **2** destruction or serious injury. **3** what is left of anything that has been destroyed or much injured. **4** person who has lost health or money. —*v.* **1** cause the wreck of; destroy; ruin. **2** be wrecked; suffer serious injury. **3** cause to lose health or money. [< Scand.]

wreck·age (rek′ij), *n.* **1** what is left of a thing that has been wrecked. **2** a wrecking or being wrecked.

wreck·er (rek′ər), *n.* **1** person who causes wrecks. **2** person whose work is tearing down buildings. **3** person, car, train, or machine that removes wrecks. **4** person or ship that recovers wrecked or disabled ships or their cargoes.

wren (ren), *n.* any of a number of small songbirds with slender bills and short tails. [OE *wrenna*]

wrench (rench), *n.* **1** a violent twist or twisting pull. **2** injury caused by twisting. **3** grief; pain. **4** tool for turning nuts, bolts, etc. —*v.* **1** twist or pull violently. **2** injure by twisting: *he wrenched his back in falling from the horse.* **3** affect distressingly. [OE *wrencan* twist]

wrest (rest), *v.* **1** twist, pull, or tear away with force; wrench away. **2** take by force. **3** twist or turn from the proper meaning, use, etc. —*n.* a wresting; forcible twist. [OE *wrǣstan*] —**wrest′er,** *n.*

wres·tle (res′əl), *v.,* -**tled, -tling,** *n.* —*v.* **1** try to throw or force (an opponent) to the ground. **2** contend with as if in wrestling; struggle. —*n.* **1** a wrestling match. **2** struggle. [ult. < *wrest*] —**wres′tler,** *n.*

wres·tling (res′ling), *n.* sport or contest in which each of two opponents tries to throw or force the other to the ground.

wretch (rech), *n.* **1** a very unfortunate or unhappy person. **2** a very bad person. [OE *wrecca* exile]

wretch·ed (rech′id), *adj.* **1** very unfortunate or unhappy. **2** very unsatisfactory;

miserable; very bad. —**wretch′ed·ly,** *adv.* —**wretch′ed·ness,** *n.*

wrig·gle (rig′əl), *v.,* **-gled, -gling,** *n.* —*v.* 1 twist and turn. 2 move by twisting and turning. 3 make one's way by shifts and tricks: *wriggle out of a difficulty.* —*n.* a wriggling. [cf. Du. *wriggelen*] —**wrig′gly,** *adj.*

wrig·gler (rig′lər), *n.* 1 person who wriggles. 2 larva of a mosquito.

wright (rīt), *n.* (now usually in combinations) a maker of something, as in *wheelwright, playwright.* [OE *wryhta,* var. of *wyrhta* < *weorc* work]

wring (ring), *v.,* **wrung, wring·ing,** *n.* —*v.* 1 twist with force; squeeze hard: *wring clothes.* 2 force by twisting or squeezing: *wring water out of clothes.* 3 clasp tightly: *wring another's hand in greeting.* 4 get by force, effort, or persuasion: *the old beggar could wring money from anyone by his sad story.* 5 cause pain, pity, etc., in: *their poverty wrung his heart.* —*n.* a twist; squeeze.

wring out, force (water, etc.) from by twisting or squeezing. [OE *wringan*]

wring·er (ring′ər), *n.* one who wrings.

wrin·kle¹ (ring′kəl), *n., v.,* **-kled, -kling.** —*n.* ridge; fold. —*v.* 1 make a wrinkle or wrinkles in: *he wrinkled his forehead.* 2 have wrinkles; acquire wrinkles: *these sleeves wrinkle.* [cf. OE *gewrinclod,* pp. winding] —**wrin′kle·less,** *adj.* —**wrin′kly,** *adj.*

wrin·kle² (ring′kəl), *n.* a useful hint or idea; clever trick. [? special use of *wrinkle¹*]

wrist (rist), *n.* 1 the joint connecting hand and arm; carpus. 2 a corresponding joint or part of the forelimb of an animal. 3 part of the arm between forearm and hand. [OE]

wrist·band (rist′band′; riz′bənd), *n.* the band of a sleeve fitting around the wrist.

writ (rit), *n.* 1 something written; piece of writing. The Bible is Holy Writ. 2 a formal order directing a person to do or not to do something. —*v. Archaic.* pt. and pp. of **write.** [OE, < *wrītan* write]

write (rīt), *v.,* **wrote** or (*Archaic*) **writ, writ·ten** (rit′ən) or (*Archaic*) **writ, writ·ing.** 1 make letters, words, etc., with pen, pencil, chalk, etc. 2 mark with letters, words, etc.: *write a check.* 3 put down the letters, words, etc., of: *write a sentence.* 4 make (books, stories, articles, poems, letters, etc.) by using written letters, words, etc.; compose: *her ambition was to write.* 5 write a letter. 6 show plainly: *honesty is written on his face.*

write down, a put into writing. **b** put a lower value on.

write in, a insert in a piece of writing. **b** send a letter to a company, person in charge, etc. **c** vote by inserting the name of an unlisted candidate on a ballot.

write off, cancel.

write out, a put into writing. **b** write in full.

write up, a write a description or account of. **b** write in detail. [OE *wrītan,* orig., scratch]

write-in (rīt′in′), *n.* 1 the casting of a vote for someone whose name is not on the official ballot by writing his or her name in. 2 the name written in.

write-off (rīt′ôf′), *n.* deduction or cancellation, as of a tax.

writ·er (rīt′ər), *n.* 1 person who writes. 2 person whose profession or business is writing; author.

write-up (rīt′up′), *n.* a written description or account.

writhe (rīth), *v.,* **writhed, writhed** or (*Obs. except Poetic*) **writh·en, writh·ing,** *n.* —*v.* 1 twist and turn. 2 suffer mentally; be very uncomfortable. —*n.* a writhing movement. [OE *wrīthan*] —**writh′er,** *n.* —**writh′ing·ly,** *adv.*

writ·ing (rīt′ing), *n.* 1 act of making letters, words, etc., with pen, pencil, etc. 2 written form: *put your ideas in writing.* 3 handwriting. 4 something written; letter, document, etc. 5 book, story, article, poem, etc. —*adj.* used to write with; used to write on.

wrong (rông; rong), *adj.* 1 not right; bad; unjust; unlawful: *it is wrong to tell lies.* 2 incorrect: *the wrong answer.* 3 unsuitable; improper: *the wrong clothes for the occasion.* 4 in a bad state or condition; out of order; amiss: *is something wrong with you?* 5 not meant to be seen; less or least important: *cloth often has a wrong side and a right side.* —*adv.* in a wrong manner; in the wrong direction; badly. —*n.* 1 what is wrong; wrong thing or things: *two wrongs do not make a right.* 2 injustice; injury. —*v.* do wrong to; treat unjustly; injure.

go wrong, a turn out badly. **b** stop being good and become bad.

in the wrong, wrong. [< Scand. (OSw.) *vranger* crooked] —**wrong′er,** *n.* —**wrong′ful,** *adj.* —**wrong′ful·ly,** *adv.* —**wrong′ly,** *adv.*

wrong·do·er (rông′dü′ər; rong′-), *n.* person who does wrong. —**wrong′do′ing,** *n.*

wrong-head·ed (rông′hed′id; rong′-), *adj.* 1 wrong in judgment or opinion. 2 stubborn even when wrong. —**wrong′-head′ed·ly,** *adv.* —**wrong′-head′ed·ness,** *n.*

wrote (rōt), *v.* pt. of **write.**

wroth (rôth; roth), *adj.* angry. [OE *wrāth*]

wrought (rôt), *v.* pt. and pp. of **work.** —*adj.* 1 fashioned; made: *a well-wrought statue.* 2 manufactured or treated; not in a raw state. 3 formed with care; not rough or crude; ornamented. 4 of metals, formed by hammering.

wrought iron, a tough form of iron with little carbon in it. Wrought iron will not break as easily as cast iron.

wrought-up (rôt′up′), *adj.* stirred up; excited.

wrung (rung), *v.* pt. and pp. of **wring.**

wry (rī), *adj.,* **wri·er, wri·est.** turned to one side; twisted: *she made a wry face to show her disgust.* [ult. < OE *wrīgian* turn] —**wry′ly,** *adv.* —**wry′ness,** *n.*

WSW, W.S.W., between west and southwest.

wt., weight.

WV, (*zip code*) West Virginia.

W. Va., West Virginia.

www or **WWW,** World Wide Web.

WY, (*zip code*) Wyoming.

Wy., Wyoming.

Wy·an·dot (wī′ən dot), *n.* 1 Iroquoian American Indian of the Huron Confederacy. 2 their Iroquoian language.

Wy·an·dotte (wī′ən dot), *n.* any of an American breed of medium-sized, hardy domestic fowls.

Wyo., Wyoming.

Wy·o·ming (wī ō′ming), *n.* a W state of the United States. —**Wy·o′ming·ite,** *n.*

X, x (eks), *n., pl.* **X's; x's.**
1 the 24th letter of the alphabet. **2** a term often used to designate a person, thing, agency, factor, or the like whose true name is unknown or withheld. **3** anything shaped like an X. **4** the Roman numeral for 10. **5** an unknown quantity.

X (eks), *v.,* **x-ed** or **x'd, x-ing** or **x'ing. 1** cross out: *x out a mistake.* **2** mark with an x.

xan·thous (zan′thəs), *adj.* yellow. [< Gk. *xanthos*]

X chromosome, chromosome related to femaleness. An egg containing two X chromosomes, one from each parent, develops into a female.

Xe, xenon.

xe·non (zē′non; zen′on), *n.* a heavy, colorless gas, Xe, that is chemically inactive. It is a rare element that occurs in the air in very small quantities. [< Gk., neut. adj., strange]

xen·o·pho·bi·a (zen′ə fō′bi ə), *n.* hatred or fear of foreigners. [< NL, < Gk. *xenos* stranger + *phobos* fear] —**xen′o·phobe,** *n.* —**xen′o·pho′bic,** *adj.*

xe·rog·ra·phy (zi rog′rə fi), *n.* **1** dry printing process for making copies of letters, documents, etc. **2 Xerography.** trademark for the process.

xe·ro·phyte (zir′ə fīt), *n.* plant that loses very little water and can grow in deserts or very dry ground, as cacti, sagebrush, etc. [< Gk. *xeros* dry + *phyton* plant]

xe·rox (zir′oks), *v.,* **-roxed, -rox·ing.** make copies by xerography. —*n.* **1** a copy made this way. **2** copying machine. [< *Xerography,* trademark]

xi (sī; zī; ksē), *n.* the 14th letter (Ξ, ξ) of the Greek alphabet.

Xmas (kris′məs, eks′məs) *n.* Christmas.

X-rated (eks′rā′tid), *adj.* **1** appropriate for adult audiences only. **2** *Informal.* pornographic.

X ray or **x-ray, 1** a ray with an extremely short wave length formed when cathode rays impinge upon a solid body (as the wall of a vacuum tube) that can penetrate opaque substances; a Roentgen ray. **2** a picture made by means of X rays.

X-ray (eks′rā′), *v.* examine, photograph, or treat with X rays. —*adj.* of, by, or pertaining to X rays.

X-ray star, a stellar body that emits X rays.

xy·lem (zī′lem), *n.* the woody part of plants. [< G < Gk. *xylon* wood]

xy·lo·phone (zī′lə fōn; zil′ə–), *n.* a musical instrument consisting of a row of wooden bars, sounded by striking them with small wooden hammers. [< Gk. *xylon* wood + *phone* sound] —**xy′lo·phon′ist,** *n.*

Y, y (wī), *n., pl.* **Y's; y's.**
1 the 25th letter of the alphabet. **2** something resembling the letter Y in shape. **3** an unknown quantity.

Y, yttrium.

–y¹, *suffix.* **1** full of, composed of, containing, having, or characterized by, as in *airy, cloudy, dewy, icy, juicy, watery.* **2** somewhat, as in *chilly, salty, whity.* **3** inclined to, as in *chatty, fidgety.* **4** resembling; suggesing, as in *messy, sloppy, sugary, willowy.* **5** In certain words, such as *paly, steepy, stilly, vasty,* the addition of *y* does not change the meaning. [OE *–ig*]

–y², *suffix.* small, as in *dolly;* used also to show kind feeling or intimacy, as in *aunty, Dicky.* [ME]

–y³, *suffix.* **1** state or quality, as in *jealousy, victory.* **2** activity, as in *delivery, entreaty.* [< L *ia,* Gk. *–ia,* F *–ie*]

yacht (yot), *n.* boat for pleasure trips or racing. —*v.* sail or race on a yacht. [< earlier Du. *jaght* < *jaghtschip* chasing ship] —**yacht′er,** *n.* —**yacht′ing,** *n., adj.*

yachts·man (yots′mən), *n., pl.* **–men.** person who owns or sails a yacht. —**yachts′man·ship,** *n.*

yah (yä), *interj.* noise made to express derision, disgust, or impatience.

ya·hoo (yä′hü; yä hü′), *n.* a rough, coarse, or uncouth person.

Yah·weh (yä′wā), *n.* a name of God in the Hebrew text of the Old Testament, often used by writers on the religion of the Hebrews.

yak (yak), *n.* the long-haired ox of Tibet and C Asia. [< Tibetan *gyag*]

yam (yam), *n.* **1** the starchy root of a vine grown for food in warm countries. **2** the vine itself. **3** a kind of sweet potato. [< Sp. *iñame,* ult. < Senegalese *nyami* eat]

yam·mer (yam′ər), *v.* **1** whine; whimper. **2** howl; yell. —*n.* act of yammering. [< OE]

yank (yangk), *v., n.* jerk.

Yank (yangk), *n., adj.* Yankee.

Yan·kee (yang′ki), *n.* **1** native of New England. **2** native of any of the N states. **3** *U.S.* a Northerner (usually in a contemptuous or hostile sense). **4** native or inhabitant of the United States. —*adj.* of or having to do with Yankees: *Yankee shrewdness.* [prob. ult. < Du. *Jan Kees* John Cheese (nickname), the *–s* being taken for pl. ending]

Yan·kee·ism (yang′ki iz əm), *n.* Yankee character or characteristics.

yap (yap) *n., v.,* **yapped, yap·ping.** —*n.* **1** a snappish bark; yelp. **2** snappish, noisy, or foolish talk. —*v.* **1** bark snappishly; yelp. **2** talk snappishly, noisily, or foolishly. [imit.]

yard¹ (yärd), *n.* **1** piece of ground near or around a house, barn, school, etc. **2** piece of enclosed ground for some special purpose or business: *a chicken yard.* **3** space with tracks where railroad cars are stored, shifted around, etc. —*v.* put into or enclose in a yard. [OE *geard*]

yard² (yärd), *n.* **1** measure of length; 36 inches; 3 feet. **2** a long, slender beam or pole fastened across a mast, used to support a sail. [OE *gierd* rod]

yard·age (yär′dij), *n.* **1** length in yards. **2** amount measured in yards.

yard·arm (yärd′ärm′), *n.* either end of a long, slender beam or pole used to support a square sail.

yard sale, private sale of household goods held outdoors, in the yard of a person's house.

yard·stick (yärd′stik′), *n.* **1** a stick one yard long, used for measuring. **2** any standard of judgment or comparison.

yar·mul·ka (yär′məl kə), *n.* skullcap worn by Jewish men and boys. [< Yiddish < Pol.]

yarn (yärn), *n.* **1** any spun thread, esp. that prepared for weaving or knitting. **2** tale; story. —*v.* tell stories. [OE *gearn*]

yar·row (yar′ō), *n.* a common plant with finely divided leaves and flat clusters of white or pink flowers. [OE *gearwe*]

yaw (yô), *v.* **1** turn from a straight course; go unsteadily. **2** of an aircraft, turn from a straight course by a motion about its vertical axis. —*n.* such a movement.

yawl (yôl), *n.* **1** boat like a sloop with a second short mast set near the stern. **2** a ship's boat rowed by four or six oars. [< Du. *jol*]

yawn (yôn), *v.* **1** open the mouth wide because one is sleepy, tired, or bored. **2** open wide. —*n.* **1** a yawning. **2** an open space; opening; chasm. [OE *geonian*] —**yawn′er,** *n.* —**yawn′ing·ly,** *adv.* —**yawn′y,** *adj.*

yaws (yôz), *n.pl.* a contagious disease of the tropics, characterized by sores on the skin. [< Carib]

Yb, ytterbium.

Y chromosome, chromosome related to maleness. An egg containing a Y chromosome develops into a male.

y·clept, y·cleped (i klept′), *adj. Archaic.* called; named; styled. [OE *geclipod* named]

yd., *pl.* **yds.** yard.

ye¹ (yē; *unstressed* yi), *pron. pl. Archaic.* you. [OE *gē*]

ye² (thē; *incorrectly* yē), *definite article. Archaic.* the.

yea (yā), *adv.* **1** yes. **2** indeed; truly. —*n.* an affirmative vote or voter. [OE *gēa*]

year (yir), *n.* **1** 12 months or 365 days (366 every fourth year); January 1 to December 31; calendar year. **2** 12 months reckoned from any point. A **fiscal year** is a period of 12 months. **3** the part of a year spent in a certain activity. A school year is from 8–10 months. **4** period of the earth's revolution around the sun; 365 days. **5** the time it takes the sun to travel from a given fixed star back to it again; 20 minutes longer than the earth year.

years, a age. **b** a very long time.

year by year, with each succeeding year; as years go by.

year in, year out, always; continuously. [OE *gēar*]

year·book (yir′bùk′), *n.* a book or report published every year.

year·ling (yir′ling; yėr′–), *n.* an animal one year old. —*adj.* **1** one year old: *a yearling colt.* **2** of a year's duration.

year·long (yir′lông′; –long′), *adj.* **1** lasting for a year. **2** lasting for years.

year·ly (yir′li), *adj.* **1** once a year; in every year. **2** lasting a year. —*adv.* once a year; in every year.

yearn (yėrn), *v.* **1** feel a longing or desire; desire earnestly. **2** feel pity; have tender feelings. [OE *giernan*] —**yearn′ful,** *adj.* —**yearn′ful·ly,** *adv.*

yearn·ing (yėr′ning), *adj.* that yearns. —*n.* earnest or strong desire; longing. —**yearn′ing·ly,** *adv.*

year-round (yir′round′), *adj.* during the entire year.

yeast (yēst), *n.* **1** the substance used in raising bread, making beer, etc. Yeast consists of very small plants or cells that grow quickly in a liquid containing sugar. **2** a yeast plant or yeast cell. **3** =yeast cake. **4** influence, element, etc., that acts as a leaven. [OE *gist*]

yeast cake, small square containing yeast, used in baking.

yeast·y (yēs′ti), *adj.* of, containing, or resembling yeast.

yell (yel), *v.* **1** cry out with a strong, loud sound. **2** say with a yell. —*n.* a strong, loud cry. [OE *giellan*] —**yell′er,** *n.*

yel·low (yel′ō), *n.* **1** the color of gold, butter, or ripe lemons. **2** a yellow pigment or dye. **3** yolk of an egg. —*adj.* **1** having a yellow color. **2** having a yellowish skin. **3** jaundiced. **4** jealous; envious. **5** cowardly. **6** sensational: *a yellow journal.* —*v.* turn yellow. [OE *geolu*] —**yel′low·ish,** *adj.* —**yel′low·ly,** *adv.* —**yel′low·ness,** *n.*

yel·low·bird (yel′ō bėrd′), *n.* **1** the goldfinch of America. **2** the yellow warbler of America. **3** any of various other yellow birds, such as an oriole of Europe.

yellow fever, an infectious tropical disease transmitted by the bite of a mosquito.

yel·low·ham·mer (yel′ō ham′ər), *n.* **1** a European bird with a yellow head, neck, and breast. **2** the flicker or golden-winged woodpecker of E North America.

yellow jack, =yellow fever.

yellow jacket, wasp or hornet marked with bright yellow.

yellow metal, gold.

yellow pine, 1 a pine tree with yellowish wood. **2** its wood.

yellow warbler, a small American warbler. The male has yellow plumage streaked with brown.

yelp (yelp), *n.* the quick, sharp bark or cry of a dog, fox, etc. —*v.* make such a bark or cry. [OE *gielpan* boast] —**yelp′er,** *n.*

Yem·en (yem′ən), *n.* country in SW Arabia.

yen[1] (yen), *n., pl.* **yen.** unit of money of Japan. [< Jap. < Chinese *yüan* round object]

yen[2] (yen), *n., v.,* **yenned, yen·ning.** —*n.* a fanciful desire. —*v.* desire.

have a yen for, desire.

yeo·man (yō′mən), *n., pl.* **–men. 1** a petty officer who performs clerical duties. **2** formerly in Britain, a person who owned some land and, often, farmed it. **3** *Archaic.* a servant or attendant of a lord or king.

yeo·man·ly (yō′mən li), *adj.* of or suitable for a yeoman; sturdy; honest. —*adv.* like a yeoman; bravely.

yeo·man·ry (yō′mən ri), *n.* yeomen.

yeoman's service, good, useful service; faithful support or assistance.

yes (yes), *adv., n., pl.* **yes·es,** *v.,* **yessed, yes·sing.** —*adv.* **1** word used to express agreement, consent, or affirmation: *Will you go? Yes.* **2** and what is more; in addition to that: *it is good, yes, very good.* —*n.* an answer that agrees, consents, or affirms. —*v.* say yes. [OE *gēse* < *gēa* yea + *sī* be it]

yes man, *Informal.* person who habitually agrees with his or her employer, superior officer, party, etc., without criticism.

yes·ter·day (yes′tər di; –dā), *n.* **1** the day before today. **2** the recent past. —*adv.* **1** on the day before today. **2** recently. [OE *geostrandæg* < *geostran* yesterday + *dæg* day]

yes·ter·year (yes′tər yir′), *n., adv.* last year; the year before this.

yet (yet), *adv.* **1** up to the present time; now: *the work is not yet finished, don't go yet, it was not yet dark, she is talking yet.* **2** sometime: *the thief will be caught yet.* **3** also; again: *yet once more I forbid you to go.* **4** moreover; even: *he won't do it for you nor yet for me, the king spoke yet more harshly, strange and yet true.* —*conj.* nevertheless; however: *the work is good, yet it could be better.*

as yet, up to now. [OE *gīet(a)*]

yew (ū), *n.* **1** an evergreen tree native to Europe and Asia. **2** the wood of this tree. [OE *īw*]

Yid·dish (yid′ish), *n.* a language which developed from a dialect of Middle High German. —*adj.* in or pertaining to Yiddish.

yield (yēld), *v.* **1** produce: *land yields crops, fruit yields seeds.* **2** give; grant: *yield consent.* **3** give up; surrender: *yield a position to the enemy.* **4** give way: *the surface yielded under the weight.* **5** give place: *we yield to nobody in love of freedom.* —*n.* amount yielded; product. [OE *gieldan* pay] —**yield′a·ble,** *adj.* —**yield′er,** *n.*

yield·ing (yēl′ding), *adj.* not resisting; submissive. —**yield′ing·ly,** *adv.*

yip (yip), *v.,* **yipped, yip·ping,** *n.* —*v.* esp. of dogs, bark or yelp briskly. —*n.* a sharp barking sound. [imit.]

Y.M.C.A., Young Men's Christian Association.

Y.M.H.A., Young Men's Hebrew Association.

yo·del (yo′dəl), *v.,* **-deled, -del·ing.** *n.* —*v.* sing with frequent changes from the ordinary voice to a forced shrill voice. —*n.* act or sound of yodeling. [< G *jodeln*] —**yo′del·er,** *n.*

yo·ga (yō′gə), *n.* system of Hindu religious philosophy that requires intense concentration and deep meditation upon the universal spirit. [< Hind. < Skt., union]

yo·gi (yō′gi), *n., pl.* **-gis.** person who practices or follows yoga. —**yo′gism,** *n.*

yo·gurt (yō′gərt), *n.* food made from whole or partly skimmed milk, curdled by means of bacteriological cultures, often eaten with fruit.

yo-heave-ho (yō′hēv′hō′), *interj.* exclamation used by sailors in pulling or lifting together.

yoke (yōk), *n., v.,* **yoked, yok·ing.** —*n.* **1** a wooden frame to fasten two work animals together, usually consisting of a crosspiece with two bow-shaped pieces beneath. **2** pair fastened together by a yoke. **3** anything resembling a yoke in shape or use. **4** *Fig.* something that joins or unites; bond; tie. **5** something that holds people in slavery or submission. —*v.* **1** fasten by a yoke or harness: *yoke the horses.* **2** fasten to by a yoke or harness: *yoke the chariot.* **3** *Fig.* join; unite. [OE *geoc*]

yo·kel (yō′kəl), *n.* country fellow.

yolk (yōk; yōlk), *n.* the yellow part of an egg. [OE *geolca* < *geolu* yellow] —**yolked,** *adj.* —**yolk′less,** *adj.* —**yolk′y,** *adj.*

yolk sac, sac filled with yolk and attached to the embryo, providing food to it.

yon (yon), **yond** (yond), *adj., adv. Archaic or Dial.* yonder. [OE *geon*]

yon·der (yon′dər), *adv.* within sight, but not near; over there: *away off yonder.* —*adj.* **1** situated over there; being within sight, but not near: *he lives in yonder cottage.* **2** farther; more distant: *the yonder side.* [ME]

yore (yôr; yōr), *n.* **of yore,** of long ago; in the past; formerly. [OE *geāra,* gen. pl. of *gēar* year]

Yorkshire pudding, unsweetened batter cake often served with roast beef.

Yorkshire terrier, any of an English breed of small, shaggy dogs.

you (ū; *unstressed* yu̇, yə), *pron. pl. or sing.* **1** the person or persons spoken to: *are you ready?* **2** one; anybody: *you push this button to get a light.* [OE *ēow,* dative and accus. of *gē* ye[1]]

you'd (üd), you would; you had.

you'll (ül), you will; you shall.

young (yung), *adj.* **1** in the early part of life or growth; not old: *a young child, she looks young for her age.* **2** of youth; early: *one's young days.* **3** not so old as another: *young Mr. Jones worked for his father.* **4** in an early stage; not far advanced: *night was still young when they left.* **5** without much experience or practice: *I was too young in the trade to be successful.* —*n.* young ones.

the young, young people.

with young, pregnant. [OE *geong*] —**young′ish,** *adj.* —**young′ly,** *adv.* —**young′ness,** *n.*

young·ber·ry (yung′ber′i), *n., pl.* **-ries.** hybrid between a blackberry and dewberry, grown largely in SW United States.

young blood, youthful people; youthful energy, ideas, etc.

young·ling (yung′ling), *n.* **1** a young person, animal, or plant. **2** novice; beginner. —*adj.* young; youthful.

young·ster (yung′stər), *n.* **1** child. **2** a young person.

your (yu̇r; *unstressed* yər), *pron. pl. or sing., possessive form of* **you. 1** belonging to you: *your book.* **2** having to do with you: *your enemies.* **3** that you know, esp. as a type; well-known; that you speak of; that is spoken of: *your real lover of music, your modern girl.* [OE *ēower,* gen. of *gē* ye[1]]

you're (yu̇r), you are.

yours (yu̇rz), *pron. sing. and pl., possessive form of* **you. 1** belonging to or having to do with you: *this pencil is yours.* **2** the one or ones belonging to or having to do with you: *where are yours?* **3** at your service: *yours truly.* **4 of yours,** belonging to you.

your·self (yu̇r self′; yər–), *pron., pl.* **-selves** (–selvz′). **1** the emphatic form of **you:** *you yourself know the story is not true.* **2** the reflexive form of **you:** *you will hurt yourself.* **3** your real self: *you aren't yourself today.*

youth (ūth), *n., pl.* **youths** (ūths; ū*th*s) or *(collectively)* **youth. 1** fact or quality of being young: *she keeps her youth well.* **2** the time between childhood and adulthood. **3** a young person or young people. **4** the first or early stage of anything; early period of growth or development: *during the youth of this country.* [OE *geoguth*] —**youth′hood,** *n.*

youth·ful (ūth′fəl), *adj.* **1** young. **2** of youth; suitable for young people. **3** having the looks or qualities of youth. —**youth′ful·ly,** *adv.* —**youth′ful·ness,** *n.*

you've (ūv), you have.

yo-yo (yō′yō), *n., pl.* **-yos.** a small disk-shaped toy, which is spun out and reeled in by an attached string.

yowl (youl), *n.* a long, distressful, or dismal cry; howl. —*v.* howl. [imit.]

yr., **1** year; years. **2** your.

yrs., **1** years. **2** yours.

Yt, yttrium.

yt·ter·bi·um (i tér′bi əm), *n.* a rare metallic element, Yb, belonging to the yttrium group. [< NL, ult. < *Ytterby,* Sweden] —**yt·ter′bic,** *adj.*

yt·tri·um (it′ri əm), *n.* a rare metallic element, Y or Yt. Compounds of yttrium are used for incandescent gas mantles. [< NL, ult. < *Ytterby,* Sweden] —**yt′tric,** *adj.*

yuc·ca (yuk′ə), *n.* plant that has sword-shaped evergreen leaves and a cluster of large, white, lilylike flowers on a tall stalk. [< NL < Sp. *yuca*]

yuck (yuk), *interj. Informal.* exclamation expressing disgust, distaste. —**yuck′y,** *adj.*

Yu·go·sla·vi·a (ū′gō slä′vi ə), *n.* former country in SE Europe. —**Yu′go·sla′vi·an,** *adj., n.*

Yule (ūl), *n.* **1** =Christmas. **2** the Christmas season. [OE *gēol*]

Yule log, a large log burned at Christmas.

Yule·tide (ūl′tīd′), *n.* Christmas time; the Christmas season.

yum·my (yum′i), *adj.,* **-mi·er, -mi·est.** delicious; tasty.

Y.W.C.A., Young Women's Christian Association.

Y.W.H.A., Young Women's Hebrew Association.

Z, z (zē), *n., pl.* **Z's; z's.** the 26th and last letter of the alphabet.

Z, 1 atomic number. **2** zenith.

z., zone.

Zam·bi·a (zam′bē ə), *n.* country in SE Africa.

za·ny (zā′ni), *n., pl.* **–nies.** fool. *—adj.* foolish. [< F < dial. Ital. *zanni,* orig. var. of *Giovanni* John]

Zan·zi·bar (zan′zə bär), *n.* **1** island near the E coast of Africa, part of the country of Tanzania.

zap (zap), *v.,* **zapped, zap·ping. 1** turn off a television commercial or program with a remote control. **2** *Informal.* kill.

zeal (zēl), *n.* eager desire; earnest enthusiasm. [< L < Gk. *zelos*]

zeal·ot (zel′ət), *n.* person who shows too much zeal; fanatic.

zeal·ot·ry (zel′ət ri), *n.* too great zeal; fanaticism.

zeal·ous (zel′əs), *adj.* full of zeal; eager; earnest; enthusiastic. **—zeal′ous·ly,** *adv.* **—zeal′ous·ness,** *n.*

ze·bra (zē′brə), *n.* a wild animal like a horse but striped with dark bands on white. [< African lang.]

ze·bu (zē′bū), *n.* an animal resembling an ox but with a large hump. The zebu is a domestic animal in Asia and E Africa. [< F]

Zech·a·ri·ah (zek′ə rī′ə), *n.* **1** prophet of Israel, in the sixth century B.C. **2** book of the Old Testament written by him.

zee (zē), *n. Esp. U.S.* the letter Z, z.

Zen Buddhism (zen), Japanese form of Buddhism emphasizing meditation, introspection, etc., to achieve spiritual enlightenment.

ze·nith (zē′nith), *n.* **1** the point in the heavens directly overhead. **2** the highest point; culmination. [< OF or Med. L *senit* < Ar. *samt* (*ar-rās*) the way (over the head)] **—ze′nith·al,** *adj.*

Zeph·a·ni·ah (zef′ə nī′ə), *n.* **1** a Hebrew prophet. **2** a book of the Old Testament containing his prophecies.

zeph·yr (zef′ər), *n.* **1** the west wind. **2** any soft, gentle wind; mild breeze. [< L < Gk. *zephyros*]

ze·ro (zir′ō), *n., pl.* **–ros, –roes,** *adj. —n.* **1** naught; 0. **2** point marked with a zero on the scale of a thermometer, etc. **3** temperature that corresponds to zero on the scale of a thermometer; complete absence of quantity; nothing. **4** the lowest point: *his courage was at zero. —adj.* **1** of or at zero. **2** not any; none at all. [< Ital. < Ar. *ṣifr* empty. Doublet of CIPHER.]

zero hour, time set for beginning an attack, etc.

zer·o-sum (zir′ō-sum′) *adj.* having losses and gains that are exactly equal.

zest (zest), *n.* **1** keen enjoyment; relish: *a hungry man eats with zest.* **2** a pleasant or exciting quality, flavor, etc.: *wit gives zest to conversation. —v.* give a zest to. [< F *zeste* orange or lemon peel]

—zest′ful, *adj.* **—zest′ful·ly,** *adv.* **—zest′ful·ness,** *n.* **—zest′less,** *adj.*

ze·ta (zā′tə; zē′tə), *n.* the sixth letter (Z, ζ) of the Greek alphabet.

zig·zag (zig′zag′), *adj., adv., v.,* **-zagged, -zag·ging,** *n. —adj., adv.* with short, sharp turns from one side to the other. *—v.* move in a zigzag way. *—n.* **1** a zigzag line or course. **2** one of the short, sharp turns of a zigzag. [< F]

zinc (zingk), *n., v.,* **zincked** (zingkt), **zinck·ing** (zingk′ing); **zinced, zinc·ing.** *—n.* a bluish-white metal, Zn, very little affected by air and moisture. *—v.* coat or cover with zinc. [< G *zink*] **—zinc′ic, zinc′ous,** *adj.*

zinc ointment, salve containing zinc oxide, used esp. in treating skin disorders.

zinc oxide, an insoluble white powder, ZnO, used in making paint, rubber, glass, cosmetics, ointments, etc.

zing (zing), *n., interj.* a sharp humming sound. *—v.* make such a sound, esp. in going rapidly. [imit.]

zing·er (zing′ər), *n. Informal.* **1** a spirited remark that is very effective. **2** something that has great effect.

zin·ni·a (zin′i ə), *n.* a garden plant grown for its showy flowers of many colors. [< NL; named after J. G. *Zinn,* botanist]

zip (zip), *n., v.,* **zipped, zip·ping.** *—n.* **1** a sudden, brief hissing sound, as of a flying bullet. **2** energy or vim. *—v.* **1** make a sudden, brief hissing sound. **2** proceed with energy. **3** fasten or close with a zipper. [imit.]

zip code or **ZIP code** (zip), a U.S. Postal Service code which assigns an identifying numeral to each zone of mail delivery. [< Z(one) I(mprovement) P(lan)]

zip·per (zip′ər), *n.* a sliding fastener for clothing, shoes, etc.

zip·py (zip′i), *adj.,* **-pi·er, -pi·est.** full of energy; lively; gay.

zir·con (zèr′kon), *n.* a crystalline mineral, ZrSiO$_4$, that occurs in various forms and colors. Transparent zircon is used as a gem. [prob. < F < Ar. *zarqūn*]

zir·co·ni·um (zər kō′ni əm), *n.* a rare metallic element, Zr, used in alloys for wires, filaments, etc. **—zir·con′ic,** *adj.*

zit (zit), *n. Informal.* pimple; blemish.

zith·er (zith′ər), *n.* a musical instrument having 30 to 40 strings, played with a plectrum and the fingers. [< G < L < Gk. *kithara.* Doublet of CITHARA and GUITAR.] **—zith′er·ist,** *n.*

zlo·ty (zlô′ti), *n., pl.* **-tys** or (*collectively*) **-ty. 1** a monetary unit of Poland. **2** a Polish nickel coin.

Zn, zinc.

zo·di·ac (zō′di ak), *n.* **1** a belt of the heavens extending on both sides of the apparent yearly path of the sun. The zodiac is divided into 12 equal parts, called signs, named after 12 groups of stars. **2** diagram representing the zodiac, used in astrology. [< L < Gk. *zoidiakos* (*kyklos*), lit., (circle) of animals, ult. < *zoion* animal] **—zo·di′a·cal,** *adj.*

zom·bie (zom′bi), *n., pl.* **–bis; –bies.** *Am.* **1** a corpse brought back to life by supernatural agency. **2** *Fig.* a very unintelligent and morbid appearing person. Also **zombi.** [< Haitian Creole *zôbi* < African (Congo) *nsumbi* devil]

zon·al (zōn′əl), *adj.* **1** of a zone; having to do with zones. **2** divided into zones. **3** of soils, manifesting influences of vegetation and climate as a result of the maturation of parent materials. **—zon′al·ly,** *adv.*

zone (zōn), *n., v.,* **zoned, zon·ing.** *—n.* **1** any of the five great divisions of the earth's surface, bounded by lines parallel to the equator. **2** any region or area especially considered or set off: *a war zone.* **3** area or district in a city or town under special restrictions as to building. **4** in the U.S. parcel-post system, an area to all points within which the same rate of postage prevails for parcel-post shipments from a particular place. *—v.* **1** divide into zones. **2** be formed into zones.

zone out, daydream. [< L *zona* < Gk. *zone,* orig., girdle] **—zoned,** *adj.* **—zone′less,** *adj.*

zon·ing (zōn′ing), *n.* building restrictions in an area of a city or town.

zoo (zü), *n.* place where wild animals are kept and shown; zoological garden.

zoo–, *combining form.* living being; animal, as in *zoology.* [< Gk., < *zoion* animal]

zo·o·ge·og·ra·phy (zō′ə ji og′rə fi), *n.* study of the distribution of animals over the surface of the earth. **—zo′o·ge·og′ra·pher,** *n.* **—zo′o·ge′o·graph′ic, zo′o·ge′o·graph′i·cal,** *adj.* **—zo′o·ge′o·graph′i·cal·ly,** *adv.*

zo·og·ra·phy (zō og′rə fi), *n.* a complete description of animals and their habits; descriptive zoology. **—zo·og′ra·pher,** *n.* **—zo′o·graph′ic, zo′o·graph′i·cal,** *adj.*

zo·oid (zō′oid), *n.* **1** free-moving cell or other organism, such as a sperm. **2** independent organism produced asexually. **3** each distinct individual that makes up a compound or colonial organism.

zool., zoology.

zoological garden, =zoo.

zo·ol·o·gy (zō ol′ə ji), *n.* **1** the science of animals; the study of animals and animal life. Zoology deals with the form, structure, physiology, development, and classification of animals. **2** the collective animal life of a particular region. **—zo′o·log′i·cal,** *adj.* **—zo′o·log′i·cal·ly,** *adv.* **—zo·ol′o·gist,** *n.*

zoom (züm), *v.* **1** make a loud humming sound. **2** move suddenly upward: *the airplane zoomed.* **3** change focus quickly when filming: *zoom in for a close-up.* *—n.* a sudden upward flight. [imit.]

zoom lens, camera lens that can adjust quickly from wide-angle to close up pictures.

zo·o·phyte (zō′ə fīt), *n.* animal that looks somewhat like a plant, such as a coral, sea anemone, etc. [< zoo– + Gk. *phyton* plant] —**zo′o·phyt′ic, zo′o·phyt′i·cal,** *adj.*

Zou·ave (zü äv′; zwäv), *n.* **1** soldier wearing an Eastern style of uniform. **2** member of certain regiments in the French army, formerly stationed in French territory in N Africa.

zounds (zoundz), *interj. Archaic.* an oath expressing surprise or anger. [< *God's wounds!*]

zow·ie (zou′i), *interj.* exclamation of wonder, delight, surprise.

Zr, zirconium.

zuc·chi·ni (zü kē′ni), *n.* **1** dark-green squash that resembles a cucumber, eaten as a vegetable. **2** the plant it grows on. [< It.]

Zu·lu (zü′lü), *n., pl.* **–lus, –lu,** *adj.* —*n.* **1** member of a people in SE Africa. **2** their language. —*adj.* of this tribe.

Zu·ñi (zün′yi; sün′-), *n., pl.* **–ñis, –ñi,** *adj.* —*n.* member of a tribe of American Pueblo Indians living in W New Mexico. —*adj.* of this tribe.

zwie·back (tswē′bäk′; swē′–; swī′–; zwī′–), *n.* a kind of bread cut into slices and toasted brown and crisp in an oven. [< G, < *zwie–* two + *backen* bake]

zy·go·spore (zī′gə spôr′), *n.* spore formed by the union of two similar gametes, as in algae.

zy·gote (zī′gōt; zig′ōt), *n.* any cell formed by the union of two gametes (i.e., reproductive cells). A fertilized egg is a zygote. [< Gk. *zygotos* yoked < *zygon* yoke]

zy·mase (zī′mās), *n.* **1** an enzyme in yeast that changes sugar into alcohol and carbon dioxide. **2** any of a group of enzymes that change certain carbohydrates into CO_2 and H_2O when oxygen is present, or into CO_2 and alcohol or into lactic acid when no oxygen is present. [< F, < Gk. *zyme* leaven]

zy·mur·gy (zī′mėr ji), *n.* branch of chemistry dealing with the processes of fermentation, as in brewing, etc. [< Gk. *zyme* leaven + *–ourgia* working]